Mexico

John Noble

Kate Armstrong, Ray Bartlett, Greg Benchwick, Tim Bewer, Beth Kohn, Tom
Masters, Kevin Raub, Michael Read, Josephine Quinterao, Daniel C Schecter,
Adam Skolnick, César G Soriano, Ellee Thalheimer

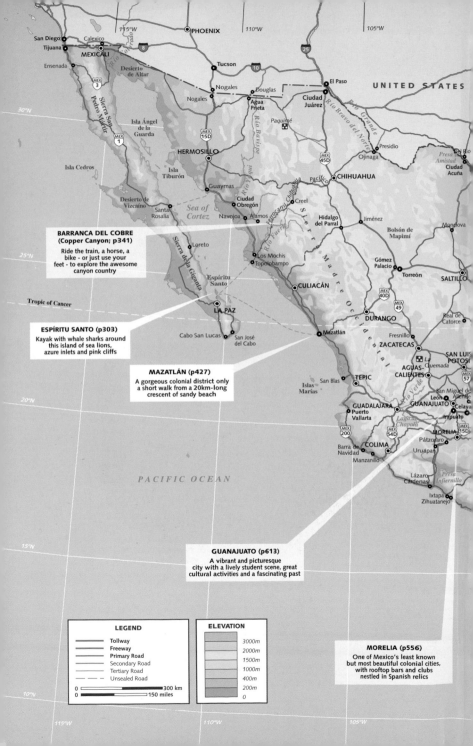

BARRANCA DEL COBRE
(Copper Canyon; p341)
Ride the train, a horse, a bike - or just use your feet - to explore the awesome canyon country

ESPÍRITU SANTO (p303)
Kayak with whale sharks around this island of sea lions, azure inlets and pink cliffs

MAZATLÁN (p427)
A gorgeous colonial district only a short walk from a 20km-long crescent of sandy beach

GUANAJUATO (p613)
A vibrant and picturesque city with a lively student scene, great cultural activities and a fascinating past

MORELIA (p556)
One of Mexico's least known but most beautiful colonial cities, with rooftop bars and clubs nestled in Spanish relics

LEGEND
- Tollway
- Freeway
- Primary Road
- Secondary Road
- Tertiary Road
- Unsealed Road

0 ——— 300 km
0 ——— 150 miles

ELEVATION
3000m
2000m
1500m
1000m
400m
200m
0

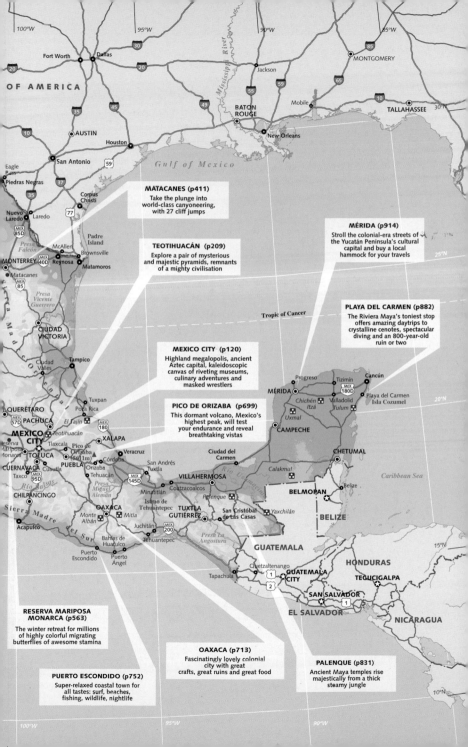

MATACANES (p411)
Take the plunge into world-class canyoneering, with 27 cliff jumps

MÉRIDA (p914)
Stroll the colonial-era streets of the Yucatán Peninsula's cultural capital and buy a local hammock for your travels

TEOTIHUACÁN (p209)
Explore a pair of mysterious and majestic pyramids, remnants of a mighty civilisation

PLAYA DEL CARMEN (p882)
The Riviera Maya's toniest stop offers amazing daytrips to crystalline cenotes, spectacular diving and an 800-year-old ruin or two

MEXICO CITY (p120)
Highland megalopolis, ancient Aztec capital, kaleidoscopic canvas of riveting museums, culinary adventures and masked wrestlers

PICO DE ORIZABA (p699)
This dormant volcano, Mexico's highest peak, will test your endurance and reveal breathtaking vistas

RESERVA MARIPOSA MONARCA (p563)
The winter retreat for millions of highly colorful migrating butterflies of awesome stamina

OAXACA (p713)
Fascinatingly lovely colonial city with great crafts, great ruins and great food

PALENQUE (p831)
Ancient Maya temples rise majestically from a thick steamy jungle

PUERTO ESCONDIDO (p752)
Super-relaxed coastal town for all tastes: surf, beaches, fishing, wildlife, nightlife

THE TREASURES OF MEXICO

Mexico is a big country with space for a vast variety of wonders. From the northern deserts to the southern jungles, from massive urban conurbations to dusty one-street pueblos, this is a country where you can find most kinds of landscape and environment – and an infinite range of experiences. Shop for colorful crafts, lie on a beach, climb a pyramid, snorkel a coral reef, party at a fiesta or a nightclub, bargain at a market, hike a cloud forest, surf a Pacific swell... For best results, combine classic sights and experiences with some of the many lesser-known, unheralded places and opportunities that we highlight in this book – and even some that we don't cover!

Celebrations & Markets

Mexico's many fiestas are explosions of color, music and crowds. Mexicans also love to gather to buy, sell, barter and mingle at their countless fascinating markets, which range from large city markets selling everything to small affairs that may specialize in crafts, art or even organic food.

Author Tip

Accommodations and transportation fill up fast for Mexico's big fiestas, so try to reserve your room and your bus ticket ahead of time. At markets, unlike shops, a spot of bargaining is the norm.

❶ Carnaval in Veracruz

This nine-day party (p689) will put you through the spin cycle. Veracruz's annual pre-Lent bacchanalia features flamboyant parades, fireworks, folklore, salsa and samba. You'll come out wearing feathers and smelling of rum.

❷ The Cervantino

Colonial Guanajuato plays host to music, drama and dance groups from around the world every October in one of Latin America's foremost arts extravaganzas (p619). It's the opportunity for a huge party for the city's big student population and their many thousands of visitors.

❸ Las Jornadas Villistas

The unassuming northern town of Hidalgo del Parral goes crazy for one debauched week in July (p377), as hundreds of horse riders and thousands of bikers descend on it to mark the anniversary of the assassination of legendary revolutionary Pancho Villa.

❹ Mercado San Juan de Dios

One of Mexico's great urban markets and meeting places, Guadalajara's cavernous San Juan de Dios (p540) stretches three stories high over two city blocks and sells everything from cowboy boots to DVDs, plus some of the tastiest and cheapest eats in town.

❺ Tianguis Cultural del Chopo

Mingle with Mexico City's urban tribes at this alternative street market (p189) on Saturdays. Hundreds of stalls hawk music CDs, kids bring crates of them to swap, and young and hungry alternative, metal and punk bands play for their futures.

❻ San Juan Chamula

Thousands of colorfully attired Tzotzil Maya stream over the hills into the highland Chiapas village of Chamula (p825) every Sunday to trade, shop and visit the Templo de San Juan, where Catholicism commingles with pre-Hispanic ceremonial.

Creative Genius

Mexicans have been excited by color forever and have always shown a high talent
for artistic representation. From the awesome sculptures and frescos of the ancients
through the great muralists of the 20th
century to the cutting-edge experimenta-
tion of today, Mexican art is one of the
country's greatest gifts to the world.

Author Tip
Almost every Mexican city has a good art museum. For contemporary work, look for commercial galleries, open studios, art markets or artists' homes.

❶ Frida Kahlo & Diego Rivera
Explore Kahlo's both Rivera's world views at Mexico City's Museo Dolores Olmedo Patiño (p155). Other good places to find Kahlo's work are the Museo de Arte Moderno (p153), and the Museo Frida Kahlo (p158), where she was born, lived and died. See Rivera's ambitious murals of Mexican history and identity at Secretaría de Educación Pública (p145) and Palacio Nacional (142; pictured).

❷ The Art of Death
Aguascalientes' fabulous Museo de los Muertos (p598) addresses Mexico's fascination with death through everything from toys to skeleton figures and canvases, both historical and contemporary. It's colorful, humorous and almost turns dying into an art form.

❸ Rock Art of Baja
Even before they had houses, Mexicans were artists of genius. The petroglyphs of land and sea creatures, warfare and rituals in Baja California's Sierra de San Francisco (p295), preserved by the dry climate, are among the world's finest collections of rock paintings.

❹ Oaxaca, Crucible of Talent
The city of Oaxaca is one of Mexico's creative melting pots. Get a taste of the best of contemporary art at Oaxaca's many galleries (p719) and be amazed by the inspiration of ancient artisans at the Museo Rufino Tamayo (p719).

❺ Capula
Artist Juan Torres' property (p575) in this small foothill town in Michoacán is decked out with his magical and hugely varied art, from sculptures and canvases to hundreds of clay *Catrina* skeletons.

Urban & Urbane

Cities in Mexico span the spectrum from jewels of colonial architecture to glittering coastal resorts and bustling modern business hubs. They're packed with street life, markets and green parks, and most have ample cultural attractions, plenty of good restaurants and an array of spots to whoop it up after dark. There's no excuse for being bored in urban Mexico.

5

Author Tip
Give a little thought to which neighborhood you're going to stay in. Downtown options are generally most convenient for access to sights, restaurants and nightlife, but the bigger cities in particular have accommodations in a number of areas, some preferable for a more tranquil stay, a special neighborhood ambience or particular attractions.

❶ The Center of Everything
Soak up the atmosphere of El Zócalo (p141), Mexico City's vast central plaza, surrounded by government palaces, the Metropolitan Cathedral and the remains of the Aztecs' most important temple. It's Km 0 of all roads leading out of the city and in Aztec belief their temple was the center of the universe.

❷ Xalapa
University city Xalapa (p677) deviates from the traditional: you can eat falafel and wash it down with a soy milk shake after spending the day checking out the top-notch Museo de Antropología, strolling in the fine parks and checking out the bohemian boutiques.

❸ Monterrey
Mexico's richest and third-biggest city (p396) boasts iconic modern architecture, slick restaurants and top-class museums. And it's a great place to party, with flashy techno clubs, lovely lounges and a dynamic live-music scene. Nearby mountains and canyons are perfect for outdoor adventures.

❹ Zacatecas
Feel part of Mexico's colonial history in this spectacularly sited city (p585) on the edge of the northern deserts, with its incredible architecture and dramatic silver mines. Zacatecas has contemporary museums, great restaurants and an excellent tourist infrastructure too.

❺ Campeche
Toddle along the ramparts of the walled Gulf of Mexico city of Campeche (p947), imagining the waves of terror brought down by marauding pirates. The city's bastions were constructed after a pirate attack in 1663 left the city in ruins..

Adventures on Land

Mexico's dramatic, highly varied terrain invites adventurers to get going. Whether you prefer to be climbing a cliff or striding along a forest path, the infrastructure and outfitters to help you do it are in place and well enough established to make Mexico an adventurer's joy.

4

Author Tip

Some Mexican adventures can be done on your own, but in many cases you'll need equipment, logistical support or guides from local operators. Good outfitters and tour firms, many of which are recommended throughout this book, know local conditions and have experienced, qualified and knowledgeable guides to help you get the most out of the experience.

❶ Hike the Cloud Forests

The Pueblos Mancomunados (p747) of Oaxaca's northern mountains are remote, co-operatively organized villages linked by trails through the cloud forests. A community tourism operation provides comfortable, inexpensive accommodations and meals for overnight stops, and will rent you horses or bikes if you prefer those to walking.

❷ Thrilling Descent

Mountain-bike the back roads through the wild Sierra Madre del Sur from the colonial city of Oaxaca to Puerto Escondido on the gorgeous Pacific coast, with Bicicletas Pedro Martínez (p723), run by an amiable Mexican Olympic cyclist.

❸ Scaling Walls & Jumping Cliffs

Those who like their terrain vertical should head to the mountains around Monterrey (p409), where there's canyoneering (27 cliff jumps) at Matacanes (pictured), world-class climbing at Potrero Chico (600-plus routes), and a six- to eight-hour fixed climbing route with zip-lines, overhanging ladders and rappels in the Cañón de la Huasteca.

❹ Copper Canyon Trek

Enjoy a close-up encounter with the canyons, ravines, rock towers and multiple ecosystems of the spectacular Barranca del Cobre (Copper Canyon; p341) on the two- to three-day hike between the canyon-bottom towns of Urique (p347) and Batopilas (p354).

Adventures on Water

Mexico's thousands of miles of coastline bring out a traveler's adventurous side. Get off the beach towel, strap on a tank and dive into this country's warm, clear seas, surf its waves and crests, or snorkel among its reefs, or kayak past the craggy shores and inlets of its coasts.

Author Tip
Before embarking on a diving or snorkeling trip, be aware of local laws, regulations and etiquette about the marine environment, and be sure to use good common sense. Engage the services of qualified and knowledgeable local guides and operators, who can keep you and the marine life you encounter safe from harm.

❶ Dive Cozumel
There are great dives to be enjoyed all along the Caribbean coast of the Yucatán Peninsula, but Isla Cozumel (p886), with its 65 surrounding reefs, remains peerless for its fantastic year-round visibility and jaw-dropping variety of marine life, from spotted eagle rays and barracudas to turtles and brain coral.

❷ Kayak the Sea of Cortez
The Sea of Cortez, with pristine beaches and rocky islands, is a paradise for water-based activities. One fabulous adventure is to kayak the 200km along the coast from the mangrove-lined delta of the Río Mulegé to Loreto (p299), home to the 2065-sq-km Bahía de Loreto Marine National Park.

❸ Learn to Surf in San Blas
Almost the entire length of Mexico's Pacific coast is a surfer's paradise, but the beaches and point breaks of San Blas (p442) make it the town of choice for beginner and intermediate surfers eager to hone their skills. Waves range from mellow swells to long crests that curl into Mantanchén Bay.

❹ Snorkel with Whale Sharks off Isla Holbox
Watch the massive whale sharks dine up close between July and September, when they congregate off the shores of Isla Holbox to feed on plankton. Swim with, but don't touch, these awesome, gentle giants (see boxed text, p880).

5

Beaches for Everyone

When people think Mexico, many see golden sand, blue water and green palms. Hundreds of beaches fit this bill: some near-empty with a few palm-thatched eateries and cabañas; others busy urban beaches. Most of the best are on the Pacific or the Caribbean coasts.

4

5

2

3 6

1

1

Author Tip
Mexican beach spots cater to many interests beyond sunbathing and swimming. At many you can go snorkeling, diving, surfing, dolphin-watching, kayaking, fishing, banana-riding or whatever else grabs you.

❶ Playa del Carmen
The hippest town on the Yucatán Peninsula. Playa's sands (p882) aren't quite as powder-perfect as at some other Mexican Caribbean spots, and the waters aren't quite so azure, but the beaches are jammed with the bronzed, blond and beautiful (and often – unusually for Mexico – topless).

❷ Playa Maruata
A beautiful deserted Michoacán beach for those who need nothing more than a stretch of sand, clear water and a cold drink. Maruata (p482) is a tranquil, friendly Nahua fishing village, and the favorite Mexican beach of the black sea turtle, which lays eggs here from June to December.

❸ Puerto Escondido
The Mexican Pipeline's surf, a string of gentler beaches, coastal wildlife and Puerto's traditional incarnations as fishing port and market town add up to a place that suits just about everyone (p752). The accommodations and food are getting even better, too.

❹ Los Cerritos
This beach at Todos Santos (p316) has some of Baja California's nicest surfing swells – powerful but great for beginners too. Or you can just hang out at sunset and watch the sun dip into the Pacific. Sea turtles lay here as well. Go soon before development changes things too much.

❺ Playa de los Muertos
A Puerto Vallarta beach (p454) that's a quintessential people-watching spot: mariachis stroll about looking for business, kids catch a free ride on the river as it enters the sea and drummer circles coalesce in the sweaty heat of the afternoon. Settle down with a *coca fría* and scan the horizon for whales.

❻ Zipolite
A 2km strip of pale sand crashing Pacific breakers, Zipo (p768) is a legendary travelers' hideout with a cosmic vibe, and an ever better selection of places to stay and eat. Caution: the riptides and undertow are deadly.

The Green Places

Many of Mexico's most beautiful fauna- and flora-rich areas are under official, though not always effective, protection. In some areas locals are also getting together to look after their own ecosystems, often through ecotourism schemes designed to replace ecologically damaging activities.

Author Tip

If you visit wild places with local community tourism or ecotourism programs, you not only help them sustain their environment – you gain the benefit of your guides' and hosts' voluminous local knowledge, and may get unexpected insights into local human as well as animal and plant life.

❶ Monarchs in their Millions

Millions of monarch butterflies winter in mountains west of Mexico City as part of a complex annual migratory pattern from the Great Lakes of Canada to Mexico and back via the southeastern USA. The Reserva Mariposa Monarca (Monarch Butterfly Reserve; p563) has the best viewing experience.

❷ Watch the Whales

Guerrero Negro (p292; pictured) is the best base for watching Baja California's spectacular gray whales, which migrate here from Siberian and Alaskan waters from mid-December to mid-April. In nearby Laguna Ojo de Liebre (p293), calves draw their first breaths already weighing 700kg.

❸ Macaw Refuge

Chiapas' Lacandón Jungle may be the final Mexican refuge of the scarlet macaw, a spectacular member of the parrot family. Reforma Agraria has a beautiful ecolodge, Las Guacamayas (p847). Local guides will lead you to the macaws and other wildlife.

❹ Turtle Sanctuary

Seven of the world's eight species of sea turtle nest along Mexico's beaches. All are endangered, and there are many turtle sanctuaries on Mexico's beaches. El Tortuguero (p479), near the small town of Cuyutlán, has released more than 500,000 turtle hatchlings into the ocean since it was founded in 1993.

❺ Cactus Forest

The Zapotitlán Salinas zone (p241) of the Tehuacán–Cuicatlán Biosphere Reserve is an unexpected high-level desert near Tehuacán that is the setting for a unique and otherworldly forest of towering cacti, home to a rich population of bird life.

❻ Tufted Jay Preserve

In the Sierra Madre Occidental canyons, this nature preserve (p441) was once the domain of logging interests. Thanks to a forward-thinking development plan, nature lovers come for hiking, bird-watching, horseback riding and pleasant rustic accommodations.

4

Cities of the Ancestors

Mexico is peppered with ruins from the Aztecs, Maya, Toltecs, Zapotecs and count-less other ancient cultures. Besides the famous, spectacular ancient cities, more are still being discovered. Some smaller ruins are surprisingly beautiful, and many have spectacular hilltop or forest settings.

5

Author Tip

Remote and still-being-explored archaeological sites may unleash your inner Lara Croft just as effectively as the much-visited, better-known ones. Getting to them may be an adventure in itself, and sites that are only partly excavated and developed can leave more for the imagination to work with.

❶ Palenque

Exquisite Maya architecture and carving are visible on palaces, temples and tombs, all with a backdrop of emerald-green, jungle-covered hills. Palenque (p831) has become a lifelong obsession for some archaeologists. Don't miss it..

❷ Teotihuacán

Two giant pyramids, the Avenue of the Dead, the Temple of Quetzalcóatl – Teotihuacán (p209), 50km from Mexico City, is the grandest of Mexico's ancient cities. A millennium before anyone had heard of the Aztecs, it was the center an empire that may have stretched as far south as El Salvador.

❸ Chichén Itzá

Stroll through the massive ball court and unravel the secrets of the amazing time temple, El Castillo, at Chichén Itzá (p937) on the Yucatán Peninsula, to discover why this site was voted one of the 'seven modern wonders of the world.'

❹ Yaxchilán

Buzz down the jungle-lined Río Usumacinta in a motor launch to this superb Maya site (p845) echoing with the roars of howler monkeys. Climb Building 41 to look across the top of the jungle to the distant mountains of Guatemala.

❺ Cobá

Battle your way to the top of the Nohoch Mul, the towering great pyramid of Cobá (p901) – the highest Maya building on the Yucatán Peninsula. The jungle views are worth the effort.

❻ Cantona

Remote and almost unknown, but incredibly well preserved, Cantona (p238) has no pyramids but at least 24 ball courts, and it may be the biggest ancient city in Mexico or Central America. It's spread over 12 sq km on an ethereal lava-bed landscape dotted with cacti and yucca.

6

Hands that Work Wonders

Mexicans are wonderfully skilled artisans with wood, cloth, clay, iron, leather, silver, tin – any material with a practical or decorative use. The many appealing *artesanías* (crafts) exhibit a combination of pre-Hispanic, Spanish colonial and contemporary influences.

3
4 5 6 1 2

1

Author Tip
If you're buying crafts, doing so direct from artisans or from craft cooperatives ensures that the money you pay for the artifacts – some of which take months to make – goes straight to the creators.

① Oaxaca

With many indigenous artisans, Oaxaca state has a thriving crafts scene. Oaxaca city (713) sells beautiful locally made crafts (pictured). To buy direct from artisans, head to villages like San Antonio Arrazola (p745), Teotitlán del Valle (p741), San Bartolo Coyotepec (p744) or Atzompa (p746).

② Sna Jolobil

This cooperative of 800 women weavers fosters the skilled indigenous art of backstrap-loom weaving and produces magnificently colorful and elaborate *huipiles* (women's tunics), blouses, skirts and rugs. Sna Jolobil products are on sale in its San Cristóbal de Las Casas store (p821).

③ Huichol Art

Jalisco's Huichol people make colorful yarn pictures and beadwork bowls and masks, often representing unique myths or sacred peyote cactus–induced visions. Places you can see and buy their work include Real de Catorce (p608) and Zacatecas' Museo Zacatecano (p588).

④ Tlaquepaque & Tonalá

Some of Mexico's finest ceramics and wooden furniture come from these two Guadalajara suburbs (p529). As well as workshops and stores, Tlaquepaque and Tonalá have craft museums and markets. Slicker Tlaquepaque has some fine restaurants and hotels. Both places are great for a day of browsing.

⑤ Tócuaro

Traditional masks, made of anything from wood or papier-mâché to feathers or hair, are among Mexico's most original creations. Some of the finest mask makers live in the Michoacán town of Tócuaro (p575). There are no shops here – just family compounds with workshops and showrooms.

⑥ The Silversmiths of Taxco

The colonial silver-mining town of Taxco (p258) turned to crafting the metal as its own veins ran short in the 20th century. Today its hundreds of silver artisans turn out much of the silverware, both inspired and humdrum, that you see around Mexico.

3

Contents

Regional Map Contents

Northwest Mexico p319

Baja California p275

Central North Mexico p358

Northeast Mexico p387

Northern Central Highlands p584

Central Pacific Coast p428

Western Central Highlands p519

Around Mexico City pp204–5

Mexico City pp126–27

Central Gulf Coast p656

Yucatán Peninsula p865

Tabasco & Chiapas p788

Oaxaca State p712

Destination Mexico

Climbing a 1300-year-old Maya pyramid as parrots screech and howler monkeys growl in the sweaty emerald jungle around you. This is Mexico. Sliding from a palm-fringed sandy beach into the warm, turquoise waves of the Pacific. This, too, is Mexico. Dining on salmon enchiladas and chrysanthemum salad at a Mexico City fusion restaurant, dancing through the night at a high-energy Guadalajara nightclub, kayaking at dawn past a colony of Baja California sea lions – all these are unique Mexican experiences. Every visitor goes home with their own unforgettable images. Such a large country, straddling temperate and tropical zones, reaching 5km into the sky and stretching 10,000km along its coasts, with a city of 19 million people at its center and countless tiny pueblos everywhere, can hardly fail to provide a huge variety of options for human adventure.

Mexico is what you make of it. Its multi-billion-dollar tourism industry is adept at satisfying those who like their travel easy. But adventure is what you'll undoubtedly have if you take a just a few steps off the pre-packaged path. Activity-based tourism, community tourism and genuine ecotourism – the type that actually helps conserve local environments – are developing fast in rural areas. The opportunities for getting out to Mexico's spectacular wild places and interacting with local communities are greater than ever – from world-class canyoneering near Monterrey or cooking lessons in the Veracruz countryside to hiking the Oaxaca cloud forests and snorkeling the coral reefs of the Yucatán.

Mexico's cities still juxtapose manicured poodles and begging grandmothers, but are increasingly sophisticated places with slick restaurants and coffee houses, ever-better cultural and entertainment offerings, and parks and pedestrian areas where you can escape the grinding, polluting traffic. A hip, bohemian, student-based, artsy scene reveling in Mexico's thriving music and art currents has emerged in most cities. This creative country is enjoying a deserved resurgence of international acclaim and interest in its art, its movies, its design, its music and its cuisine. Even Mexico's hotels and inns have jumped aboard the ship of style and design. The country's lodgings are charming, tasteful and appealing, often designed using combinations of contemporary and traditional styles, and always with that bold use of color in which Mexico has long specialized.

Whether this burgeoning of creativity has anything to do with the political changes the country has seen since the dying years of the 20th century may be debated for a long time. Mexico at last threw off eight decades of 'one-party democracy' under the PRI (Institutional Revolutionary Party) in 2000, when it voted Vicente Fox of the right-of-center PAN (National Action Party) into the presidency, in the first presidential vote held since the PRI itself had finally reformed the corrupt electoral system.

The Fox presidency disappointed most people on most scores. There are no easy panaceas for the deep-seated economic inequalities between one Mexican and another, and between Mexico and the US, nor to other problems such as the growing might of Mexico's ruthlessly violent drug gangs. Nevertheless, the Fox era did see an increasing opening and confidence in Mexican society, encouraged by the new regulations on electoral and governmental transparency.

FAST FACTS

Population: 107 million

Annual population growth: 1.15%

Area: 1.9 million sq km

GDP per person: US$7800

US share of Mexican exports: 85%

Adult literacy: 91%

Remittances to Mexico by Mexicans living in the US: US$24 billion (2006)

Cost of being smuggled across Mexico-US Border: US$1000-5000

Routine bribe to traffic police: M$50

Number of languages spoken: 50

Vicente Fox was succeeded in 2006 by a second PAN president, Felipe Calderón. Whether or not Calderón finds any answers that Fox and the PRI didn't, one certainty is that Mexicans' longer-term enduring qualities that contribute so much to the pleasure of visiting their country – their creativity, their warmth, their strong family and community bonds, their refreshingly relaxed pace of life – will outlive his six-year term of office.

Getting Started

Mexico is a great country for making plans as you go. You can just pick a spot on the map (or in this guidebook), hop on a plane or bus or get in the car, and enjoy choosing what to do when you get there. Accommodations for all budgets are easy to find, and transportation is plentiful and inexpensive. If you have limited time and specific goals, you can work out a detailed itinerary and reserve accommodations in advance. But be ready to change plans once you get there: Mexico offers so many wonderful things to see and do that you're guaranteed to want to fit more in. There'll always be that colorful local festival happening, or that beautiful unknown beach you hear about, or that great new horseback ride/boat trip/waterfall hike/crafts village. These are times to put the guidebook down and do you own exploring.

If this is your first trip to Mexico, especially if it's your first trip outside the developed world, be ready for more crowds, noise, bustle and poverty than you're accustomed to. But don't worry – most Mexicans will be only too happy to help you feel at home in their country. Invest a little time before your trip in learning even just a few phrases of Spanish – every word you know will make your trip that little bit easier and more enjoyable.

See Climate Charts (p966), Festivals & Events (p970) and Holidays (p971) for information to help you decide when to go.

WHEN TO GO

No time is a bad time to visit Mexico, though the coastal and low-lying regions, especially in the southern half of the country, are fairly hot and humid from May to September (these are the months of highest rainfall and highest temperatures almost everywhere). The interior of the country has a more temperate climate than the coasts. In fact, it's sometimes decidedly chilly in the north and the center from November to February.

July and August are peak holiday months for both Mexicans and foreigners. Other big holiday seasons are mid-December to early January (for foreigners and Mexicans) and a week either side of Easter (for Mexicans). At these times the coastal resorts attract big tourist crowds, room prices go up in popular places, and accommodations and public transportation can be heavily booked, so advance reservations are advisable.

DON'T LEAVE HOME WITHOUT...

- an adventurous palate (p91)
- all the necessary paperwork if you're driving (p986)
- any necessary immunizations or medications (p999)
- adequate insurance (p972)
- checking your foreign ministry's Mexico travel information (p968)
- clothes for Mexico's climatic variations and air-conditioned buses
- a flashlight (torch) for some of those not-so-well-lit Mexican streets and stairways, and for power outages
- a small padlock
- a mosquito net if you plan to sleep outdoors
- as much Spanish as you can muster
- a love of the unpredictable.

COSTS & MONEY

HOW MUCH?

One-person hammock
M$200

Silver ring from M$100

Local small-car rental per
day M$500-600

2km city taxi ride
M$30-40

Major museum or
archaeological site
M$30-35

See also the Lonely
Planet Index on the Quick
Reference page inside the
front cover.

Your dollar, euro or pound will go a long way in Mexico. Assuming the peso's exchange rate against the US dollar remains fairly stable, you'll find this is an affordable country to travel in. Midrange travelers can live pretty well in most parts of the country on US$75 to US$125 per person per day. Between US$40 and US$70 will get you a pleasant, clean and comfortable room for two people, with private bathroom and fan or air-conditioning, and you have the rest to pay for food (a full lunch or dinner in a decent restaurant typically costs US$15 to US$25), admission fees, transport, snacks, drinks and incidentals. Budget travelers staying in hostels can easily cover the cost of accommodation and two restaurant meals a day with US$40. Add in other costs and you'll spend US$60 to US$80.

The main exceptions to this are the Caribbean coast, parts of Baja California and some Pacific resort towns, where rooms can easily cost 50% more than elsewhere.

Extra expenses such as internal airfares, car rentals and shopping push your expenses up, but if you have someone to share expenses with, basic costs per person drop considerably. Double rooms often cost only a few dollars more than singles, and triple or family rooms only a few dollars more than doubles. Rental cars start at around US$50 to US$60 per day, plus fuel, and cost no more for four people than for one.

At the top end of the scale are a few hotels and resorts that charge over US$200 for a room, and restaurants where you can pay US$50 per person. But you can also stay in smaller classy hotels for US$80 to US$120 a double and eat extremely well for US$40 to US$50 per person per day.

TRAVELING RESPONSIBLY

Since our inception in 1973, Lonely Planet has encouraged our readers to tread lightly, travel responsibly and enjoy the magic independent travel affords. International travel is growing at a jaw-dropping rate, and we still firmly believe in the benefits it can bring – but, as always, we encourage you to consider the impact your visit will have on both the global environment and the local economies, cultures and ecosystems.

Environment

Mexico's fabulously varied environment is home to countless biological riches. Yet its forests are shrinking and many of its cities and rivers are terribly polluted. Large-scale tourism development can destroy coastal wetlands, strain water resources and overwhelm sewage systems. But as a traveler your interaction *can* be beneficial. Ask questions about the local environmental situation, and give your business to hotels, guides and tour operators with avowedly sustainable practices. Instead of ripping up the terrain and scaring every living creature on an ATV convoy, take a birding or kayaking trip with a guide who wants to show you nature without disturbing it.

Our GreenDex (p1052) is a quick-reference tool to listings and reviews in this book of tourism businesses, programs and sites with particularly sustainable credentials.

Culture

Mexico's diverse regional cultures, with their folklore, traditional dress, fiestas, sense of community and beautiful handicrafts, are strong and resilient, yet communities can stand only so much emigration by their men forced to look for work in Mexico City or the US, and only so much homogenizing outside influence. Travelers can help fortify Mexican culture by visiting community museums, buying local crafts, demonstrating that they value local customs and traditions, or supporting community tourism programs.

Getting There & Around

Many tourists have no option but to fly to Mexico, with an inevitable contribution to greenhouse gases. Carbon offset schemes can at least help to neutralize that effect – see the boxed text on p984. Getting around Mexico you'll inevitably use motor vehicles unless you're a very committed cyclist. The country's passenger rail system died in the 1990s. But once you're based in a place for a few days, you can get out on your own feet or maybe horseback or a bike, or ride the metro systems in the three big cities. The more you focus your explorations on specific areas, the less carbon dioxide you'll emit.

See Accommodations (p959) and Getting Around (p989) for tips on places to stay and how to travel around in Mexico.

Tourism in Mexico

International tourism brings more than US$1 billion per month into Mexico, and without it even more Mexicans would be heading north to the US to look for work. But profits from many big businesses don't stay in Mexico and social balances can be disrupted as villagers flock to work in resorts.

If you give your business to smaller-scale local enterprises – family-run hotels or restaurants, individual artisans, community tourism schemes – more of your money will end up with the local people who need it most, and you won't exacerbate the alienating 'them and us' effect that mass tourism can have.

Interaction

Looking for small-group or individual activities, and ways to do things *with* Mexicans rather than simply pay them money, enables more meaningful interchange. In any case, truly local guides will always have that much more interesting knowledge to impart.

Going beyond the well-trodden path is another way to spread the benefit. More and more small Mexican communities are now welcoming tourists, and you'll experience more of real, unpredictable Mexican life if you get away from pre-packaged experiences.

See the Language chapter (p1007) for some basic Spanish words and phrases.

As you go, you can let people know that the outside world values and respects things many Mexicans have and many others don't, such as strong family and community bonds, age-old traditions and closeness to nature.

Volunteer work can be another great way of interacting. Through this book we try to highlight volunteer opportunities, and you'll find an overview of possibilities on p980.

For More Information

Ecotravel.com (www.ecotravel.com) Has a sizable directory of ecologically responsible accommodations and operators in Mexico.

International Ecotourism Society (www.ecotourism.org)

Mexican Adventure and Ecotourism Association (www.amtave.org) Sixty member organizations and companies around the country.

Mexiconservación (www.mexiconservacion.org) Has an online Green Guide to the Mexican Caribbean.

Planeta.com (www.planeta.com) Multifarious ecotravel and sustainable tourism resource, with a strong Mexico emphasis.

responsibletravel.com (www.responsibletravel.com) Promotes tourism for the benefit of local people and the environment as well as for tourists, and lists sustainable holidays in Mexico.

Transitions Abroad.com (www.transitionsabroad.com) Magazine and web portal helping people meet and interact with people from other countries, designed as an 'antidote to tourism.'

TOP 10

MEXICO

Mexico City •

GREEN MEXICO

These ecotourism and community tourism programs and sites will be thrilled to be on your itinerary. See our GreenDex (p1052) for businesses and projects that put sustainability first.

1 Expediciones Sierra Norte (p723)

2 Servicios Ecoturísticos La Ventanilla (p774)

3 Área de Protección de Flora y Fauna Cuatrociénegas (p389)

4 The forests of southern Veracruz – sites like Ruíz Cortines (p704), Las Margaritas (p708), Miguel Hidalgo (p708) and Mateo López (p708)

5 Sierra Madre Oriental – Reservas da la Biosfera El Cielo (p423) and Sierra Gorda (boxed text, p651)

6 Turtle conservation centers – La Pesca (boxed text, p421), Grupo Ecologista Vida Milenaria (p674), El Tortuguero (p479), Campamento Tortuguero (p855) and Isla Mujeres Turtle Farm (boxed text, p877).

7 Las Guacamayas (p847)

8 Reserva de la Biosfera Sian Ka'an (p904)

9 Reserva de la Biosfera Ría Celestún (p934)

10 Reserva de la Biosfera Calakmul – ecotourism among the jungles and Maya ruins of the biosphere reserve (p955)

FIESTAS

If you build one or more of these events into your trip, you'll really get a special taste of Mexico. See p970 for further information.

1 Carnaval, Feb/Mar, best in Veracruz (p689), Mazatlán (p434), La Paz (p303)

2 Semana Santa, Mar/Apr, best in San Miguel de Allende (p635), Pátzcuaro (p569)

3 Noche de los Rábanos, December 23, Oaxaca (p725)

4 La Morisma, late Aug, Zacatecas (p589)

5 Festival Internacional Cervantino, Oct, Guanajuato (p619)

6 Fiestas de Octubre, Oct, Guadalajara (p531)

7 Día de Todos los Santos and Día de Muertos, Nov 1 and 2, nationwide (p71)

8 Día de Nuestra Señora de Guadalupe, Dec 12, Mexico City (p166), Monterrey (p404)

9 Vernal and autumnal equinoxes, late Mar and Sep, Chichén Itzá (p937)

10 Las Jornadas Villistas, July 20, Hidalgo del Parral (p377)

MOVIES

Prepare your imagination for Mexico with some of these Mexican and non-Mexican movies set in the country – and see p83 for more on Mexican cinema.

1 *Traffic* – directed by Steven Soderbergh (2000)

2 *Amores Perros* (Love's a Bitch) – directed by Alejandro González Iñárritu (2000)

4 *Y Tu Mamá También* (And Your Mother Too) – directed by Alfonso Cuarón (2002)

5 *El Crimen del Padre Amaro* (The Crime of Father Amaro) – directed by Carlos Carrera (2002)

6 *Frida* – directed by Julie Taymor (2002)

3 *El Violín* (The Violin) – directed by Francisco Vargas (2007)

7 *7 Días* (7 Days) – directed by Fernando Kalife (2005)

8 *Los Olvidados* (The Forgotten Ones) – directed by Luis Buñuel (1950)

9 *El Mariachi* – directed by Robert Rodriguez and spawning two major quasi-sequels (1992)

10 *Apocalypto* – directed by Mel Gibson (2006)

TRAVEL LITERATURE

In the Sierra Madre Ben Biggers chronicles a year among the Rarámuri of the Copper Canyon in this amusing and well-informed book.

Into a Desert Place Self-confessed couch potato Graham Mackintosh takes a 3000-mile walk round the coast of Baja California.

The Lawless Roads Graham Greene wandered through Mexico to Chiapas in the 1930s, a time of conflict between Catholics and an atheistic state.

Narcocorrido Elijah Wald's fascinating book is both travel narrative and an investigation of a popular song genre built around the travails of ordinary folk involved in drug-running on Mexico's northern border.

Sliced Iguana: Travels in Unknown Mexico British writer Isabella Tree takes peyote with the Huicholes and meets the matriarchs of Juchitán in this warm, perceptive account of Mexico and its indigenous cultures.

Time Among the Maya Ronald Wright investigates the Maya concept of time and their tragic modern history

A Visit to Don Otavio Sybille Bedford's witty and lyrical tale of travels in the now-vanished Mexico of the 1950s is still surprisingly relevant.

INTERNET RESOURCES

Many websites listed in this guidebook are in Spanish, though there are many websites in English that will equip you with plenty of up-to-the-minute info.

Lanic (http://lanic.utexas.edu/la/mexico) Best broad collection of Mexico links, from the University of Texas.

Lonely Planet (www.lonelyplanet.com) Succinct summaries on travel in Mexico; the popular Thorn Tree bulletin board; travel news; and great links to the best travel resources elsewhere on the web.

Mexico Connect (www.mexconnect.com) Goldmine of articles, forums and information on everything under the Mexican sun.

Mexico Online (www.mexonline.com) News, bulletin boards and lots more.

Mexperience (www.mexperience.com) Wide-ranging practical guide to Mexican travel.

Planeta.com (www.planeta.com) Great articles and listings for anyone interested in Mexican travel or the Mexican environment.

Itineraries
CLASSIC ROUTES

BAJA ROAD TRIP
One to Four Weeks

The Transpeninsular Highway from the Mexico–US border to Los Cabos forms the route of an all-time classic Mexican road trip. Start off by getting a feel for the famous border buzz of **Tijuana** (p276). Next, head down to sample the surf and wines of **Ensenada** (p283) before moving south to watch the whales from close quarters on **Laguna Ojo de Liebre** (p292). Cross the Vizcaíno desert to the leafy oasis of **San Ignacio** (p294) and check out the ancient rock art of the **Sierra de San Francisco** (p295). Follow this up by hitting the Sea of Cortez for diving or kayaking in the waters off either **Mulegé** (p297) or **Loreto** (p299). Further south, cosmopolitan **La Paz** (p302) provides access to brilliant beaches and the spectacular marine life of **La Ventana** (p307). Try snorkeling or diving the coral reef of uncrowded **Cabo Pulmo** (p307) before hitting the towns of Los Cabos at the foot of the peninsula – the tranquil **San José del Cabo** (p308) and the frenetic party scene of **Cabo San Lucas** (p311). Slip away to artsy **Todos Santos** (p315) for a change of pace, not to mention some of Baja California's best surf.

This 1800km trip along the world's second longest peninsula takes you from surf beaches to colonial missions, across cactus-strewn deserts and into waters teeming with spectacular marine life. In a hurry you can do it a week; to savor it, find a month.

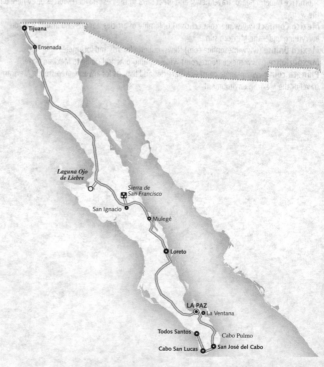

LANDS OF THE MAYA   Three Weeks

From the pre-packaged attractions of **Cancún** (p867) slip over to beach-fringed **Isla Mujeres** (p874) for some fine snorkeling or diving. Then head up to **Isla Holbox** (p879), where you can lie back in a hammock or snorkel with whale sharks. Moving west, stop at the relaxed colonial town of **Valladolid** (p941) en route to the world-renowned Maya and Toltec pyramids of **Chichén Itzá** (p937). Next stop: **Mérida** (p914), with colonial architecture, classy museums, fine food and great shopping. Mérida makes a good base for trips to magnificent **Uxmal** (p925) and other Maya sites along the **Ruta Puuc** (p930). Move to the Gulf coast to chill out and watch flamingos at the sleepy fishing village of **Celestún** (p934). Continue to historic **Campeche** (p947), and then southwestward to the state of Chiapas for the fabulous ancient Maya sites of **Palenque** (p831) and **Yaxchilán** (p845), and the soulful mountain town of **San Cristóbal de Las Casas** (p811), surrounded by highly traditional modern Maya villages. Return across the south of the Yucatán Peninsula and visit some of the region's most fascinating, remote ruins such as sprawling **Calakmul** (p955) and secluded **Río Bec** (p958). Back on the Caribbean coast, take kayaking, fishing or mangrove trips through the remote **Reserva de la Biosfera Sian Ka'an** (p904) before you reach **Tulum** (p895), which has one of Mexico's most perfect beaches and most spectacularly sited Maya ruins. From Tulum you can visit the major Maya ceremonial center of **Cobá** (p901) and take a guided snorkel or dive tour of the amazing underwater caverns of **Cenote dos Ojos** (p894). Wind up your trip with a stop at chic **Playa del Carmen** (p882), a great base camp for the superlative diving and snorkeling on the island of **Cozumel** (p886).

The lands of the ancient and modern Maya extend over Mexico, Guatemala and Belize. In Mexico alone they encompass countless natural marvels, fabulous beaches and busy cities and resorts, as well as timeless temples. Allow three weeks to do justice to this 3200km circuit.

BEACHES, CITIES & TEMPLES   One Month

This magnificent classic journey leads travelers south from Mexico's colonial heartland to its glorious Caribbean beaches. Start by exploring fascinating **Mexico City** (p120), including a visit to the awesome pyramids of **Teotihuacán** (p209). Then head east to colonial **Puebla** (p216) before crossing the mountains southward to **Oaxaca** (p713), a lovely colonial city with Mexico's finest handicrafts at the heart of a beautiful region with a large indigenous population, and the ancient Zapotec capital, **Monte Albán** (p737).

Cross the Sierra Madre del Sur to one of the sun-baked beach spots on the Oaxaca coast, such as **Puerto Escondido** (p752), **Mazunte** (p773) or **Zipolite** (p768). Then move east to **San Cristóbal de Las Casas** (p811), a beautiful highland town surrounded by intriguing indigenous villages, the lovely jungle lake **Laguna Miramar** (p829) and **Palenque** (p831), perhaps the most stunning of all Maya cities, with a backdrop of emerald-green jungle.

Head northeast to colonial **Mérida** (p914), the Yucatán Peninsula's cultural capital and the base for visiting the fine Maya ruins of **Uxmal** (p925) and those along the **Ruta Puuc** (p930). Next stop is **Chichén Itzá** (p937), the Yucatán's most awesome ancient Maya site. From there, head directly to **Tulum** (p895) on the Caribbean coast, a Maya site with a glorious beachside setting, and then make your way northward along the Riviera Maya toward Mexico's glitziest resort, **Cancún** (p867). On the way, halt at hip **Playa del Carmen** (p882) and take a side trip to **Cozumel** (p886) for world-class snorkeling and diving.

This 2800km, one-month adventure takes you from the center of Mexico through Oaxaca and Chiapas states – with their colorful indigenous populations, pre-Hispanic ruins and dramatic scenery – to the ancient Mayan cities and Caribbean beaches of the Yucatán Peninsula.

PACIFIC DREAMS   Four to Six Weeks

Mexico's Pacific coast is a glittering sequence of busy resorts, pristine jungle-lined beaches and every grade of coastal dream in between. A great approach to the coast is from **Chihuahua** (p367) via the awesome **Barranca del Cobre** (Copper Canyon; p341), with its dramatic railroad and spectacular hiking.

Spend an evening sipping margaritas on the lively plaza in **Mazatlán** (p427) before venturing to the ancient island of **Mexcaltitán** (p442) and the wildlife rich lagoons of laid back **San Blas** (p442). Then it's on to nightclubs, gourmet food, whale-watching and shopping in **Puerto Vallarta** (p453).

Isolated beaches abound on the Costalegre, home to some of the world's most luxurious resorts. Spend a day snorkeling here at **Playa Tenacatita** (p468), and don't miss the street tacos in **San Patricio-Melaque** (p468). Hang out at tranquil **Playa Maruata** (p482), the most beautiful beach in Michoacán, or rent a beach-bum bungalow at the quaint surfer haven of **Barra de Nexpa** (p482). Surf, snorkel and take romantic sunset walks in **Troncones** (p485) before hiring a fishing boat in **Zihuatanejo** (p489).

Pick up the pace to hit the discos, see the cliff divers and learn a little Mexican history in **Acapulco** (p501). **Puerto Escondido** (p752) has A-grade surf and a lively little after-dark scene. To end your trip, lie back in a hammock at the low-budget paradise beaches of **Mazunte** (p773) or **Zipolite** (p768), or relax at the resort of **Bahías de Huatulco** (p776), set along a string of beautiful, sheltered bays.

The entire trip from Chihuahua to Huatulco involves 3200km of travel, including 670km by rail at the outset, and can take up to six weeks if you stop in every recommended place. Some travelers approach the coast through Nogales and Hermosillo instead of Chihuahua. Several cities along the way have airports, so it's easy to shorten the route if you wish.

ROADS LESS TRAVELED

GULF COAST MEANDER   Two Weeks

Inland from industrial Tampico, the Huasteca region harbors an astonishing 376m-deep sinkhole, the **Sótano de las Golondrinas** (p664), and **Las Pozas** (p665), a surreal fantasy land created by an English eccentric. Near Papantla are the spectacular pyramids of **El Tajín** (p672), the greatest monument of the Classic Veracruz – witness the spectacular *voladores* rite of the indigenous Totonac people, with four men 'flying' from the top of a single vertical pole.

Beaches on the **Costa Esmeralda** (p674) are mostly empty outside holiday times. Nearby **Tlapacoyan** (p675) is a center for white-water rafting on rivers rushing down from the Sierra Madre Oriental. Inland, **Xalapa** (p677) is an urbane university city with one of Mexico's best archaeological museums. The 5611m dormant volcano **Pico de Orizaba** (p699) is the country's highest peak – a steep, though not technically difficult, challenge for mountaineers.

The most vibrant city on the Gulf coast is **Veracruz** (p684), the historic maritime gateway to Mexico and a fun-loving city with a wild pre-Lent carnival. Southeast from here is **Los Tuxtlas** (p708), an area of green hills, beaches, scattered rainforest, lakes and incipient community ecotourism. The southern hinterland of the Gulf of Mexico was also the heartland of the ancient Olmec culture, whose heritage is best seen at the **Parque-Museo La Venta** (p792) in Villahermosa, capital of steamy Tabasco state. Tabasco has some little-known Gulf beaches, such in and around **Paraíso** (p798), and is also home to the vast wetlands of the **Reserva de la Biosfera Pantanos de Centla** (p802).

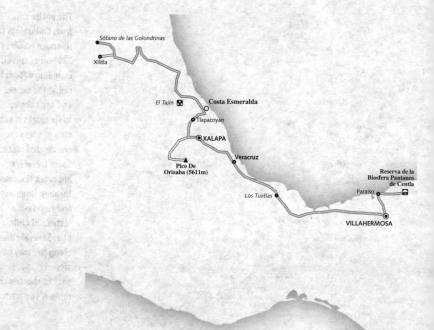

NORTHERN ESCAPE   Three Weeks

Awesome natural configurations, adrenalin-charging adventures and bizarre discoveries await intrepid travelers in the remoter reaches of Mexico's north. Make the pre-Hispanic desert trading settlement **Paquimé** (p363) your first port of call. From here, visit the renowned potters' village **Mata Ortiz** (p365). Then head south to the pre-Hispanic cliff dwellings amid the forests of the Sierra Madre Occidental at **Cuarenta Casas** (p366) and the **Cañón de Huápoca** (p367).

Move southeast to **Cuauhtémoc** (p374), where you can board the **Ferrocarril Chihuahua Pacífico** (p341) to explore the spectacular **Barranca del Cobre** (Copper Canyon; p341). Next, follow the footsteps of legendary revolutionary Pancho Villa through **Chihuahua** (p367), **Hidalgo del Parral** (p375), **Canutillo** (p378) and **Torreón** (p378).

En route to Torreón, visit **Mapimí** (p379) and the ghost town of **Ojuela** (p379), the heart of a once-booming mining area. Head northeast across the deserts from Torreón for (what else?) a spot of swimming and snorkeling at the bizarrely beautiful oasis of the **Cuatrociénegas reserve** (p389), then go south to quaff a *copa* of desert wine at **Parras** (p395). Move on to laid-back **Saltillo** (p390), with its Churrigueresque cathedral and first-class desert museum. Drop into **Monterrey** (p396) if by now you're missing a little urban sophistication, and head to the nearby **Cañón de la Huasteca** (p410) and **Potrero Chico** (p411) for some top-class climbing, canyoneering, rappelling and zip-lining. Then turn south to magical **Real de Catorce** (p608), a former silver-mining center coming back to creative life. For one more natural marvel, head east for some hiking and bird-watching in the cloud forests of the **Reserva de la Biosfera El Cielo** (p423).

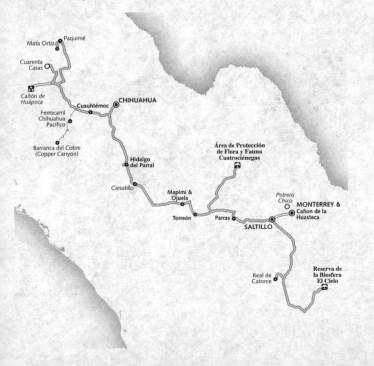

INHERITORS OF ANCIENT TRADITIONS   Three Weeks

Mexico possesses some of the American continent's most colorful and distinctive traditional cultures, directly descended from people who were here long before Europeans arrived. A good place to make contact with the Nahua people, related to the ancient Aztecs, is the hill village of **Cuetzalan** (p238), north of Puebla. The largest indigenous populations are concentrated in southern Mexico. The Zapotecs and Mixtecs of Oaxaca state are wonderful artisans in ceramics, textiles, wood and much more – see their wares at bustling markets and in city stores. The city of **Oaxaca** (p713) stages the country's most exciting celebration of indigenous dance, the annual Guelaguetza festival in July. In the remote highlands of **Chiapas** (p803), Maya groups such as the Tzotziles and Tzeltales cling to mysterious, age-old religious, social and medical practices, and their colorful traditional costumes, still worn daily, are complex works of art and symbolism.

In Veracruz state, the Totonac people regularly re-enact ancient rituals with their spectacular *voladores* rite, 'flying' from a tall pole at places like **El Tajín** (p672). The Huicholes from the borders of Jalisco, Nayarit and Zacatecas in western Mexico make an annual pilgrimage across the mountains and deserts to seek the cactus that bears the powerful hallucinogen peyote, essential to their religion and their highly colorful art, near the remote town of **Real de Catorce** (p608).

In the northwest the Rarámuri, who dwell in the rugged canyons of the **Barranca del Cobre** (Copper Canyon; p341), are famed for their amazing long-distance running feats, while the Seris of Sonora, found in places like **Bahía de Kino** (p327), are celebrated for their beautiful ironwood carvings.

TAILORED TRIPS

WORLD HERITAGE

Mexico's 27 Unesco World Heritage listings feature three natural sites, including **El Vizcaíno** (p292) and **Sian Ka'an biosphere reserve** (p904). The rest are cultural listings, with pre-Hispanic sites being prominent: the towering pyramids of **Teotihuacán** (p209); the exquisite Maya architecture of **Palenque** (p831), **Uxmal** (p925), **Chichén Itzá** (p937) and deep-in-the-jungle **Calakmul** (p955), as well as the maze-like northern trading center **Paquimé** (p363); the old Zapotec capital **Monte Albán** (p737); the outstanding rock art of Baja California's **Sierra de San Francisco** (p295); and the curious niched pyramids of **El Tajín** (p672) near the Gulf coast. The magnificent stone architecture of colonial Mexico is represented by the historic centers of **Mexico City** (p120), **Oaxaca** (p713), **Puebla** (p216), **Guanajuato** (p613), **Morelia** (p556), **Zacatecas** (p585), **Querétaro** (p643) and **Campeche** (p947), while the historic and architectural heritage of early Christian missionaries in Mexico is recognized in the Unesco listing of **Jalpan** (p653) and the other **Franciscan missions** (p653) in the Sierra Gorda. Mexico's contribution to 20th-century art and architecture is marked by the **UNAM university campus** (p157) in Mexico City, Guadalajara's **Instituto Cultural de Cabañas** (p526), which contains the mural masterpieces of José Clemente Orozco.

BIOSPHERE RESERVES

Biosphere reserves are protected natural areas that aim to combine conservation with sustainable human economic activity. Sustainable tourism schemes in these reserves provide opportunities to get out into some of the most pristine, spectacular and remote areas of Mexico. The country has some 40 biosphere reserves (reservas de la biosfera) totaling well over 100,000 sq km and encompassing huge ecological variety, from the northern deserts of **Bolsón de Mapimí** (p380) to the southern forests of **Montes Azules** (p829) and **Calakmul** (p955). The coastal wetland reserves of **Sian Ka'an** (p904) on the Caribbean, **La Encrucijada** (p856) on the Pacific, and **Ría Celestún** (p934) and **Ría Lagartos** (p945) on the Gulf of Mexico all harbor bountiful wildlife and developed infrastructure for visitors. Not far from Sian Ka'an is the large coral atoll reserve of **Banco Chinchorro** (p906). **El Vizcaíno** (p292) in Baja California encompasses both deserts and lagoons where gray whales calve, while the **Volcán Tacaná reserve** (p860) protects a towering, forest-clad volcano on Mexico's border with Guatemala. **El Triunfo** (p854), high in the mountains of Chiapas, has spectacular birdlife including the iconic resplendent quetzal. The **Mariposa Monarca reserve** (p563) in central Mexico protects the breeding grounds of millions of magnificent monarch butterflies. The **Sierra Gorda reserve** (boxed text, p651) and **El Cielo** (p423) reserves are transition zones between Gulf lowlands and the heights of the Sierra Madre Oriental, with great diversity of birds, plants and other wildlife.

ON THE BEACH

Mexico has peerless *playas* for every taste. Baja offers prime surf at **San Miguel** (p284), **Los Cerritos** (p316) and **Costa Azul** (p311), great kayaking at **Mulegé** (p297) and **Espíritu Santo** (p303), or just party time at **Cabo San Lucas** (p311).

Over on the mainland Pacific coast, you can make a beeline for the lagoon-backed beaches of **San Blas** (p442) before hitting **Puerto Vallarta** (p453), with its beach parties and marine wildlife. Slow down on the nearly empty beaches of the **Costalegre** (p468) or soak in the rolling waves of **San Patricio-Melaque** (p468).

There more's top surf at **Barra de Nexpa** (p482), **Boca de Pascuales** (p480) and **Troncones** (p485). Revive on the soothing bay at **Zihuatanejo** (p489) before you take on high-energy **Acapulco** (p501).

On the Oaxaca coast, the 'Mexican Pipeline' has spawned a fun surfer–traveler scene at **Puerto Escondido** (p752), or you can simply stroll the sands and lie back in a hammock at the backpacker haven of **Zipolite** (p768).

On the Yucatán Peninsula's Caribbean coast it's always party time at **Cancún** (p867) while **Playa del Carmen** (p882) is the hip beach town to hang out in. Offshore, **Isla Mujeres** (p874) provides relaxation and some good snorkeling, or head to **Cozumel** (p886) for world-class diving. **Tulum** (p895), with beachside Maya ruins, has one of Mexico's most beautiful beaches, with palm-fringed white sand. Or slip over to 30km-long **Isla Holbox** (p879), where you can snorkel with whale sharks, explore endless beaches or simply lie back in a hammock.

FOOD TRIP

Mexico City neighborhoods such as **Condesa** (p174) and **Roma** (p176) are the country's capital of *nuevo mexicano* (new Mexican) and fusion cuisine, but the city is also home to some incredible **market food** (p176).

Anywhere along the Pacific coast you are guaranteed to get fabulous fresh seafood. Bigger resorts like **Ensenada** (p283), **Mazatlán** (p427), **Puerto Vallarta** (p453), **Zihuatanejo** (p489) and **Acapulco** (p501) have a greater assortment of restaurants where you can enjoy finely prepared dishes. The humble fish tacos of **Baja California** (boxed text, p311) can be just as divine, and seafood snacks can even reign supreme inland, as at Guadalajara's legendary **Mariscos El Social** (p536). For delicious *pescado a la veracruzana* (fish in a tomato, onion and chili-based sauce) head over to the **Gulf coast** (p691).

Meat lovers will be happy in most of Mexico but especially the ranching country of the north, with the big steaks of **Chihuahua** (p367), the *cabrito al pastor* (roast kid) of **Monterrey** (p396), the *carne asada* (marinated grilled beef) of **Sonora** (p331), and flavorsome *tacos al carbón* (with char-grilled meats or seafood) everywhere.

The colonial city of **Puebla** (p216) is home to Mexico's most famous *mole* (sauce) for meat, the chocolate-based *mole poblano*, but *mole* lovers have many further destinations to head for. The southern city of **Oaxaca** (p713) is famed for its seven varieties of *mole* (see boxed text, p726) and it will teach visitors how to make them – and other Mexican dishes – at its many cooking schools.

History

Mexico's story is always extraordinary and at times barely credible. How could a 2700-year-long tradition of ancient civilization, involving the Olmecs, the Maya and the Aztecs – all intellectually sophisticated and aesthetically gifted, yet at times astoundingly bloodthirsty – crumble in two short years at the hands of a few hundred adventurers from Spain? How could Mexico's 11-year War for Independence from Spain lead to three decades of dictatorship by Porfirio Díaz? How could the people's Revolution that ended that dictatorship yield 80 years of one-party rule? And how was it that, after so many years of turbulent upheavals, one-party rule just laid down and died in Mexico's first-ever peaceful regime change in 2000?

Travel in Mexico is a fascinating encounter with this unique story and the modern country that it has produced. From the awesome ancient cities to the gorgeous colonial palaces, through the superb museums and the deep-rooted traditions and beliefs of the Mexicans themselves, Mexico's ever-present past will never fail to enrich your journey.

Historian Alan Knight has written one of the most recent comprehensive histories of Mexico, in three volumes: *Mexico – From the Beginning to the Spanish Conquest; Mexico – The Colonial Era;* and *Mexico – The Nineteenth & Twentieth Centuries.*

THE ANCIENT CIVILIZATIONS

From nomadic hunter-gatherer beginnings, early Mexicans first developed agriculture, then villages, then cities with advanced civilizations, then great empires. The political map shifted constantly as one city or state sought domination over another, and a sequence of powerful states rose and fell through invasion, internal dissension or environmental disasters. But the diverse cultures of ancient Mexico had much in common, as religion, forms of social organization and economic basics were transmitted from lords to masters and from one generation to the next. Human sacrifice, to appease ferocious gods, was practiced by many societies; observation of the heavens was developed to predict the future and determine propitious times for important events like harvests; society was heavily stratified and dominated by priestly ruling classes; women were restricted to domestic and child-bearing roles; versions of a ritual ball game (p73) were played almost everywhere on specially built courts.

Most Mexicans today are, at least in part, descended from the country's original inhabitants, and varied aspects of modern Mexico – from spirituality and artistry to the country's continued domination by elites – owe a great deal to the pre-Hispanic heritage.

For concise but pretty complete accounts of the ancient cultures of Mexico and Guatemala, read *Mexico: From the Olmecs to the Aztecs* and *The Maya*, both by Michael D Coe.

TIMELINE

7000–3000 BC	1200–900 BC	800–400 BC
Agriculture develops in the Tehuacán valley. First, chili seeds and squashes are planted; later, corn and beans are cultivated, enabling people to live semi-permanently in villages.	The first great Olmec center, San Lorenzo, flourishes. Objects found there from Guatemala and the Mexican highlands indicate that San Lorenzo was involved in trade over a large region.	The second great Olmec center, at La Venta in Tabasco, flourishes before being violently destroyed. Jade, a favorite pre-Hispanic ornamental material, makes its appearance in a tomb here.

There are many ways of analyzing the pre-Hispanic eras, but one common (if oversimplified) framework divides into three main periods: Preclassic, before AD 250; Classic, AD 250–900; and Postclassic, AD 900–1521. The Classic period saw the flourishing of some of the most advanced cultures, including the Maya and the empire of Teotihuacán.

BEGINNINGS

It's accepted that, barring a few Vikings in the north and some possible direct transpacific contact with Southeast Asia, the pre-Hispanic inhabitants of the Americas arrived from Siberia. They came in several migrations during the last ice age, between perhaps 60,000 and 8000 BC, crossing land now submerged beneath the Bering Strait. The first Mexicans hunted big animal herds in the grasslands of the highland valleys. When temperatures rose at the end of the Ice Age, the valleys became drier, ceasing to support such animal life and forcing the people to derive more food from plants. In central Mexico's Tehuacán Valley (p240), archaeologists have traced the slow beginnings of agriculture between 7000 and 3000 BC, leading to a sufficiently dependable supply of food for people to be able to settle in fixed villages. Pottery appeared by 2000 BC.

Hundreds of museums around Mexico display marvelous artifacts from the country's ancient cultures. The best single place to get an overview of everything is Mexico City's Museo Nacional de Antropología. You can make a preliminary visit there at www.mna.inah.gob.mx.

THE OLMECS

Mexico's 'mother culture' was the mysterious Olmec civilization, which appeared near the Gulf coast in the humid lowlands of southern Veracruz and neighboring Tabasco. The name Olmec – 'People from the Region of Rubber' – was coined by archaeologists in the 1920s. The evidence of the masterly stone sculptures they left behind indicates that Olmec civilization was well organized and able to support talented artisans, but lived in thrall to fearsome deities. Its best-known artifacts are the awesome 'Olmec heads,' stone sculptures up to 3m high with grim, pug-nosed faces and wearing curious helmets.

Xalapa's Museo de Antropología and Villahermosa's Parque-Museo La Venta have top-class collections of Olmec heads and other Olmec artifacts.

Ten Olmec heads were found at the first great Olmec center, San Lorenzo (p709), and at least seven at the second great site, La Venta (p799). The Olmecs were obviously capable of a high degree of social organization, as the stone from which the heads and many other stone monuments were carved was probably dragged, rolled or rafted to San Lorenzo and La Venta from hills 60km to 100km away. They were also involved in trade over large regions. Olmec sites found in central and western Mexico, far from the Gulf coast, may well have been trading posts or garrisons to ensure the supply of jade, obsidian and other luxuries for the Olmec elite.

In the end, both San Lorenzo and La Venta were destroyed violently, but Olmec art, religion and society had a profound influence on later Mexican civilizations. Olmec gods, such as the feathered serpent and their fire and corn deities, persisted right through the pre-Hispanic era.

AD 0–150	250–600	250–900
A huge planned city is laid out in a grid arrangement at Teotihuacán in central Mexico, and the 70m-high Pirámide del Sol (Pyramid of the Sun) is constructed there.	Teotihuacán grows into a city of an estimated 125,000 people, the Pirámide de la Luna (Pyramid of the Moon) is built, and Teotihuacán comes to control the biggest of Mexico's pre-Hispanic empires.	The brilliant Classic Maya civilization flowers in southeast Mexico, Guatemala, Belize and parts of Honduras and El Salvador.

TEOTIHUACÁN

The first great civilization in central Mexico arose in a valley about 50km northeast of the middle of modern Mexico City. The grid plan of the magnificent city of Teotihuacán (p209) was laid out in the 1st century AD. It was a basis for the famous Pyramids of the Sun and Moon as well as avenues, palaces and temples that were added during the next 600 years. At its peak, the city had a population of about 125,000, and it was the center of probably the biggest pre-Hispanic Mexican empire. Developed after around AD 400, this domain extended all the way south to parts of modern Honduras and El Salvador. It was an empire seemingly geared toward tribute-gathering rather than full-scale occupation, and it helped to spread Teotihuacán's advanced civilization – including writing and books, a numbering system based on bar-and-dot numerals and a calendar system that included the 260-day 'sacred year' composed of 13 periods of 20 days – far from its original heartland.

Within Teotihuacán's cultural sphere was Cholula (p227), with a pyramid even bigger than the Pyramid of the Sun. Teotihuacán may also have had hegemony over the Zapotecs of Oaxaca, whose capital, Monte Albán (p737), grew into a magnificent city in its own right between AD 300 and 600.

Like all other ancient Mexican civilizations and empires, Teotihuacán's time in the sun had to end. Probably already weakened by the rise of rival powers in central Mexico, Teotihuacán was burned, plundered and abandoned in the 8th century. But its legacy for Mexico's later cultures was huge. Many of Teotihuacán's gods, such as the feathered serpent Quetzalcóatl (an all-important symbol of fertility and life, itself inherited from the Olmecs) and Tláloc (the rain and water deity) were still being worshipped by the Aztecs a millennium later. Aztec royalty made pilgrimages to the great pyramids and believed Teotihuacán was the place where the gods had sacrificed themselves to set the sun in motion and inaugurate the world that the Aztecs inhabited. Today, New Age devotees converge on Teotihuacán to imbibe mystical energies at the vernal equinox.

Teotihuacán – The City of the Gods (http://archae ology.la.asu.edu/TEO) is a welcome website on this grand city.

Teotihuacán's Pirámide del Sol (Pyramid of the Sun) is the third-biggest pyramid in the world. The biggest is Egypt's Pyramid of Cheops, and the second biggest is Mexico's little-known Pirámide Tepanapa, or the Great Pyramid of Cholula.

THE CLASSIC MAYA

The Classic Maya, in many experts' view the most brilliant civilization of pre-Hispanic America, flowered in three areas:

- North – Mexico's low-lying Yucatán Peninsula
- Central – the Petén forest of present-day northern Guatemala, and the adjacent lowlands in Chiapas and Tabasco in Mexico (to the west) and Belize (to the east)
- South – the highlands Guatemala and a small section of Honduras.

It was in the northern and central areas that the Maya blossomed most brilliantly, attaining heights of artistic and architectural expression, and of

600–900	695	700–900
El Tajín, the major center of the Classic Veracruz civilization, a group of small states with a shared culture near the Gulf coast, is at its peak.	The great Maya city of Tikal (in modern-day Guatemala) conquers Maya rival Calakmul (in Mexico), but is unable to exert unified control over Calakmul's former Maya subjects.	Maya civilization in the central Maya heartland – Chiapas, El Petén, Belize – collapses, probably because of prolonged severe droughts.

learning in fields like astronomy, mathematics and astrology, which were not to be surpassed by any other pre-Hispanic civilization.

The Classic Maya were divided among many independent city-states – often at war with each other – but in the first part of the Classic period most of these appear to have been grouped into two loose military alliances, centered on Tikal (Guatemala) and Calakmul (p955) in the south of the Yucatán Peninsula.

Maya Cities

A typical Maya city functioned as the religious, political and market hub for surrounding farming hamlets. Its ceremonial center focused on plazas surrounded by tall temple pyramids (usually the tombs of deified rulers) and lower buildings – so-called palaces, with warrens of small rooms. Steles (tall standing stones) and altars were carved with dates, histories and elaborate human and divine figures. Stone causeways called *sacbeob,* probably for ceremonial use, led out from the plazas.

Within Mexico there were four main zones of Classic Maya concentration: one in lowland Chiapas and three on the Yucatán Peninsula.

The chief Chiapas sites are Yaxchilán (p845), Bonampak (p842), Toniná (p828) and Palenque (p833). For many people the most beautiful of all Maya sites, Palenque rose to prominence under the 7th-century ruler Pakal, whose treasure-loaded tomb deep inside the fine Templo de las Inscripciones was discovered in 1952.

In the southern Yucatán, the Río Bec and Chenes zones, noted for the lavish monster and serpent carvings on their buildings, are in wild areas where archaeological investigations are relatively unadvanced. The sites here, which include Calakmul, Becán (p956), Xpuhil (p957) and Río Bec itself (boxed text, p958), draw relatively few visitors.

The third concentration of Classic Maya culture on the Yucatán Peninsula was the Puuc zone, the most important city of which was Uxmal (p925), south of Mérida. Puuc ornamentation, which reached its peak on the Governor's Palace at Uxmal, featured intricate stone mosaics, often incorporating faces of the hook-nosed rain god, Chac. The amazing Codz Poop (Palace of Masks) at Kabah (p930) is covered with nearly 300 Chac faces. Chichén Itzá (p937), east of Mérida, is another Puuc site, though it owes more to the later Toltec era.

Calendar & Religion

The Maya developed a complex writing system – partly pictorial, partly phonetic – with 300 to 500 symbols. The deciphering of this system in the 1980s enabled huge advances in the understanding of this culture. The Maya also refined a calendar used by other pre-Hispanic peoples into a tool for the exact recording and forecasting of earthly and heavenly events. Every

Sidebar notes

Chronicle of the Maya Kings & Queens (2000) by Simon Martin and Nikolai Grube tells in superbly illustrated detail the histories of 11 of the most important Maya city-states and their rulers.

Handbook to Life in the Ancient Maya World by Lynn V Foster is a readable introduction to all the important aspects of the Maya, incorporating recent discoveries.

Joyce Kelly's *Archaeological Guide to Central & Southern Mexico* gives visitors practical and background information on 70 sites.

Timeline

900–1150	c 1000	1325
The Toltec empire, based at Tula, dominates central Mexico with a militaristic culture based on warrior orders dedicated to different animal gods: the coyote, jaguar and eagle knights.	The city of Chichén Itzá, on the Yucatán Peninsula, is taken over by a Toltec-type culture and is developed into one of Mexico's most magnificent ancient cities, in a fusion of Toltec and Maya styles.	The Aztecs settle at Tenochtitlán, on the site of present-day Mexico City. Within a century they become the most powerful tribe in the Valle de México, going on to rule an empire extending over nearly all of central Mexico.

major work of Maya architecture had a celestial plan. Temples were aligned so as to enhance observation of the sun, moon and certain stars or planets, especially Venus, helping the Maya predict eclipses of the sun and the movements of the moon and Venus. They measured time in various interlocking cycles, ranging from 13-day 'weeks' to the 1,872,000-day 'Great Cycle'. They believed the current world to be just one of a succession of worlds destined to end in cataclysm and be succeeded by another. This cyclical nature of things enabled the future to be predicted by looking at the past.

Religion permeated every facet of Maya life. The Maya believed in predestination and followed a complex astrology. To win the gods' favors they carried out elaborate rituals involving dances, feasts, sacrifices, consumption of the alcoholic drink *balche*, and bloodletting from ears, tongues or penises. The Classic Maya seem to have practiced human sacrifice on a small scale, the later Postclassic Maya on a larger scale. Beheading was probably the most common method. At Chichén Itzá, victims were thrown into a deep cenote (well) to bring rain.

The Maya inhabited a universe with a center and four directions, each with a color: east was red; north, white; west, black; south, yellow; the center, green. The heavens had 13 layers, and Xibalbá, the underworld to which the dead descended, had nine. The earth was the back of a giant reptile floating on a pond. (It's not *too* hard to imagine yourself as a flea on this creature's back as you look across a lowland Maya landscape!)

Important Maya gods included: Itzamná, the fire deity and creator; Chac, the rain god; Yum Kaax, the corn and vegetation god; and Ah Puch, the death god. The feathered serpent, known to the Maya as Kukulcán, was introduced from central Mexico in the Postclassic period. Also worshiped were dead ancestors, particularly rulers, who were believed to be descended from the gods.

Maya people – direct descendants of the ancient Maya – still inhabit the Yucatán Peninsula, Chiapas, Guatemala and Belize today. The more traditional of them, mostly in the highlands of Chiapas and Guatemala, still wear clothes with pre-Hispanic designs and practice animistic rites alongside Christianity.

THE TOLTECS

After the fall of Teotihuacán, control over central Mexico was disputed between a number of cities. One of the most important was Xochicalco (p258), a hilltop site near Cuernavaca, with Maya influences and impressive evidence of a feathered-serpent cult. But it was the Toltec empire, based at Tula (p207), 65km north of Mexico City, that came to exert most influence over the course of Mexican history. The name Toltec (Artificers) was coined by the Aztecs, who looked back to them with awe and considered them as royal ancestors.

The first Maya Great Cycle (period of 1,872,000 days) ends on December 23, 2012 (or December 25, depending whose calculation you trust). The ends of time cycles are highly significant – even cataclysmic – moments in Maya cosmology. Stay tuned around Christmas 2012.

Mesoweb (www.mesoweb.com), Maya Exploration Center (www.mayaexploration.org) and goMaya (www.gomaya.com) are all fabulous resources on the Maya, past and present.

Mundo Maya Online (www.mayadiscovery.com) features articles on Maya cosmology, navigation and agriculture, among other aspects of this incredible ancient civilization.

1487	1492	1517–18
Twenty thousand human captives are sacrificed for the dedication of Tenochtitlan's Great Temple.	Christopher Columbus, searching for a new trade route from Spain to the Orient, comes across the Bahamas, Cuba and Hispaniola. In the following years further Spanish expeditions explore the Caribbean and found settlements there.	The Spanish send expeditions from Cuba to explore the large land mass to the west. Expeditions led by Francisco Hernández de Córdoba and Juan de Grijalva are driven back from Mexico's Gulf Coast by hostile locals.

WHY DID THE MAYA COLLAPSE?

In the second half of the 8th century, trade between the Maya city-states started to shrink and conflict began to grow. By the early 10th century, the several million inhabitants of the flourishing central Maya heartland in Chiapas, El Petén and Belize had virtually disappeared, and the Classic era was at an end – a cataclysm known as the Classic Maya Collapse.

Expert and amateur Mayanists have expended much effort trying to explain this mysterious occurrence. Overpopulation and consequent ecological and political crises rank high among the theories. The Maya heartland underwent a big population explosion between AD 600 and 800. This seems to have led to greater competition and conflict for resources between the city-states. At the same time, deforestation followed by a sequence of erosion, higher temperatures and scarce water may have been disastrous for a people who depended on water stored in pools and reservoirs for their survival.

In 2003 scientists analyzing seabed sediments off Venezuela came up with new data that made the jigsaw a lot more complete. The sediments were composed of light and dark layers, each about 1mm thick, the dark layers containing titanium which was washed into the sea during rainy seasons. Unusually thin dark layers therefore indicated unusually dry rainy seasons. The investigators worked out that the weather in the region in the 9th and 10th centuries was unusually dry, and that there had been three or four particularly intense droughts, each lasting several years, during the period that saw the collapse of Classic Maya civilization. It was this exceptional dryness that probably drove the Maya out of their heartland.

The people of these areas did not just vanish in a puff of dust – many of them probably migrated to the northern Maya area (the Yucatán Peninsula) or the highlands of Chiapas, where their descendants live on today. The jungle grew back up around the ancient lowland cities, and only today is it being cut down again.

It's hard to disentangle myth from history in the Toltec story, but a widely accepted version is that the Toltecs were one of many semicivilized tribes from the north who moved into central Mexico after the fall of Teotihuacán. Tula became their capital, probably in the 10th century, and grew into a city of about 35,000. Tula's ceremonial center is dedicated to the feathered serpent god Quetzalcóatl, but annals relate that Quetzalcóatl was displaced by Tezcatlipoca (Smoking Mirror), a newcomer god of warriors and sorcery who demanded a regular diet of the hearts of sacrificed warriors. A king identified with Quetzalcóatl, Topiltzin, fled to the Gulf coast and set sail eastward on a raft of snakes, promising one day to return – a legend that was to have extremely fateful consequences centuries later when the Spanish arrived.

Tula seems to have become the capital of a militaristic kingdom that dominated central Mexico. Mass human sacrifice may have started here. Toltec influence spread to the Gulf coast and as far north as Paquimé (p363), and is even suspected in temple mounds and artifacts found in Tennessee and Illinois. But it was in the Yucatán Peninsula that they left their most cel-

1519–20	1521	1524
A new Spanish expedition, under Hernán Cortés, gets a friendlier reception and makes its way to the Aztec capital, Tenochtitlán. Initially well-received, the Spaniards are attacked and driven out on the 'Noche Triste' (Sad Night), June 30, 1520.	The Spanish, with 100,000 native Mexican allies, take three months to finally capture Tenochtitlán, razing it building by building. They then rename it 'México' and rebuild it as capital of Nueva España (New Spain).	Virtually all the Aztec empire, plus other Mexican regions such as Colima, the Huasteca and the Isthmus of Tehuantepec, have been brought under Spanish control.

ebrated imprint. Maya scripts relate that around the end of the 10th century much of the northern Yucatán Peninsula was conquered by one Kukulcán, who bears many similarities to Tula's banished Quetzalcóatl. The Yucatán site of Chichén Itzá (p937) contains many Tula-like features, including gruesome Chac-Mools (reclining stone figures holding dishes for sacrificial human hearts). Tiers of grinning skulls engraved on a massive stone platform suggest sacrifice on a massive scale. And there's a resemblance that can hardly be coincidental between Tula's Pyramid B and Chichén Itzá's Temple of the Warriors. Many writers therefore believe that Toltec exiles invaded the Yucatán and created a new, even grander version of Tula at Chichén Itzá.

Tula itself was abandoned around the start of the 13th century, seemingly destroyed by one of the hordes of barbarian raiders from the north known as Chichimecs. But later Mexican peoples revered the Toltec era as a golden age.

> The website of the Foundation for the Advancement of Mesoamerican Studies (www.famsi .org) contains numerous resources for broadening your understanding of early Mexican history.

THE AZTECS

The Aztecs' legends related that they were the chosen people of their tribal god, the hummingbird deity Huizilopochtli. Originally nomads from somewhere to the west or north, they were led by their priests to the Valle de México where they settled on islands in the valley's lakes. By the 15th century the Aztecs (also known as the Mexica) had fought their way up to become the most powerful group in the valley, with their capital at Tenochtitlán (on the site of present-day downtown Mexico City). Legend tells that the site was chosen because there the Aztecs witnessed an eagle standing on a cactus and devouring a snake, a sign that they should stop wandering and build a city. The eagle-snake-cactus emblem sits in the middle of the Mexican flag.

The Aztecs formed the Triple Alliance with two other valley states, Texcoco and Tlacopan, to wage war against Tlaxcala and Huejotzingo, east of the valley. The prisoners they took formed the diet of sacrificed warriors that voracious Huizilopochtli demanded to keep the sun rising every day.

The Triple Alliance brought most of central Mexico – from the Gulf coast to the Pacific, though not Tlaxcala – under its control. This was an empire of 38 provinces and about five million people, ruled by fear and geared to exacting tribute of resources absent from the heartland. Jade, turquoise, cotton, paper, tobacco, rubber, cacao and precious feathers were needed for the glorification of the Aztec elite, and to support the many nonproductive servants of its war-oriented state.

> For a wealth of information about the Aztecs and their modern descendants, and other indigenous Mexicans, see the US-based Azteca Web Page (www.mexica.net). The website includes a Náhuatl dictionary and lessons in the language.

Economy & Society

Tenochtitlán and the adjoining Aztec city of Tlatelolco (p161) grew to house more than 200,000 inhabitants. The Valle de México as a whole had more than a million people. They were supported by a variety of intensive farming

1534–92	1540s	1605
The Spanish find huge lodes of silver at Pachuca, Zacatecas, Guanajuato and San Luis Potosí, north of Mexico City.	The Yucatán Peninsula is brought under Spanish control by three related conquistadors all named Francisco de Montejo. Nueva España's northern border runs roughly from modern Tampico to Guadalajara; beyond it dwell fierce semi-nomads.	Mexico's indigenous population has declined from an estimated 25 million at the time of the Spanish conquest to little over a million, mainly because of new diseases.

methods that used only stone and wooden tools, and involved irrigation, terracing and swamp reclamation.

The basic unit of Aztec society was the *calpulli*, consisting of a few dozen to a few hundred extended families, who owned land communally. The king held absolute power but delegated important roles, such as priestly duties or tax collecting, to members of the *pilli* (nobility). Military leaders were usually *tecuhtli*, elite professional soldiers. Another special group was the *pochteca*, militarized merchants who helped extend the empire, brought goods to the capital and organized the large markets that were held daily in big towns. At the bottom of society were pawns (paupers who could sell themselves for a specified period), serfs and slaves.

Richard F Townsend's The Aztecs is the best introduction to this enigmatic empire.

Culture & Religion

Tenochtitlán–Tlatelolco had hundreds of temple complexes. The greatest of these, Templo Mayor (p143), set on and around modern Mexico City's Zócalo, was, to the Aztecs, the center of the universe. Its main temple was dedicated to Huizilopochtli and the rain god, Tláloc.

Much of Aztec culture was drawn from earlier Mexican civilizations. They had writings, bark-paper books and the Calendar Round (the dating system used by the Maya, Olmecs and Zapotecs). They observed the heavens for astrological purposes. Celibate priests performed cycles of great ceremonies, typically including sacrifices and masked dances or processions enacting myths.

The Aztecs believed they lived in the 'fifth world,' whose four predecessors had each been destroyed by the death of the sun and of humanity. Aztec human sacrifices were designed to keep the sun alive. Like the Maya, the Aztecs saw the world as having four directions, 13 heavens and nine hells. Those who died by drowning, leprosy, lightning, gout, dropsy or lung disease went to the paradisiacal gardens of Tláloc, the god who had killed them. Warriors who were sacrificed or died in battle, merchants killed while traveling far away, and women who died giving birth to their first child all went to heaven as companions of the sun. Everyone else traveled for four years under the northern deserts in the abode of the death god Mictlantecuhtli, before reaching the ninth hell, where they vanished altogether.

You can pay a virtual visit to the Aztecs' main temple at www.conaculta .gob.mx/templomayor

OTHER POSTCLASSIC CIVILIZATIONS

On the eve of the Spanish conquest, most Mexican civilizations shared deep similarities. Each was politically centralized and divided into classes, with many people occupied in specialist tasks, including professional priests. Agriculture was productive, despite the lack of draft animals, metal tools and the wheel. Corn tortillas, *pozol* (corn gruel) and beans were staple foods, and many other crops, such as squash, to-

1767	September, 1810	Oct–Nov, 1810
Jesuits are expelled from all Spanish dominions, fomenting discontent among the criollos in Mexico.	Priest Miguel Hidalgo y Costilla launches Mexico's War of Independence with his Grito de Dolores (Cry of Dolores), a call to rebellion in the town of Dolores. A mob massacres *peninsulares* in Guanajuato.	The rebels capture Zacatecas, San Luis Potosí and Morelia, and defeat loyalist forces at Las Cruces outside Mexico City, but do not attack the capital. They occupy Guadalajara, but are then pushed northward.

matoes, chilies, avocados, peanuts, papayas and pineapples, were grown in various regions. Luxuries for the elite included turkey, domesticated hairless dog, game and chocolate drinks. War between different cities and empires was widespread, and often connected with the need for prisoners to sacrifice to a variety of gods.

Apart from the Toltecs and Aztecs, several important regional cultures arose in the Postclassic period:

Yucatán Peninsula The city of Mayapán (p932) dominated most of the Yucatán after the Toltec phase at Chichén Itzá ended around 1200. Mayapán's hold dissolved from about 1440, and the Yucatán became a quarreling ground for numerous city-states, with a culture much decayed from Classic Maya glories.

Oaxaca After 1200 the Zapotec settlements, such as Mitla (p743) and Yagul (p742), were increasingly dominated by the Mixtecs, who were metalsmiths and potters from the uplands around the Oaxaca–Puebla border. Much of Oaxaca fell to the Aztecs in the 15th and 16th centuries.

Michoacán The Tarascos, skilled artisans and jewelers, ruled Michoacán with their capital at Tzintzuntzan (p574), about 200km west of Mexico City. They were one group which managed to avoid conquest by the Aztecs.

THE SPANISH ARRIVE

Ancient Mexican civilization, nearly 3000 years old, was shattered in two short years by a tiny group of invaders who destroyed the Aztec empire, brought in a new religion and reduced the native people to second-class citizens and slaves. Rarely in world history has a thriving society undergone such a total transformation so fast. Why the Spanish embarked on this conquest, how they were able to subdue Mexico so easily, and why their arrival had such a devastating effect, are questions whose answers lie partly in the characters of the two societies involved, but also in some pure happenstance and luck. The characters of the leading protagonists – the ruthless, Machiavellian genius of the ambitious Spanish leader, Hernán Cortés, and the superstitious hesitancy of the Aztec emperor, Moctezuma II Xocoyotzin – were of supreme importance to the outcome.

So alien to each other were the newcomers and the indigenous Mexicans that each doubted whether the other was human (Pope Paul III declared indigenous Mexicans to be human in 1537). Yet from their traumatic encounter arose modern Mexico. Most Mexicans are *mestizo*, of mixed indigenous and European blood, and thus descendants of both cultures. But while Cuauhtémoc, the last Aztec emperor, is now an official Mexican hero, Cortés, the leader of the Spanish conquerors, is today considered a villain and his indigenous allies as traitors.

Mexico Online (www.mexonline.com) has good history links, among much other information.

Bernal Díaz del Castillo gives a detailed first-hand account of the conquest of Mexico in *History of the Conquest of New Spain*, while *The Broken Spears: Aztec Account of the Conquest of Mexico*, edited by Miguel Leon-Portilla, is a rare piece of history from the losers' point of view.

1811	1813	1815
Rebel numbers shrink and their leaders, including Hidalgo, are captured and executed in Chihuahua. José María Morelos y Pavón, another priest and a former student of Hidalgo, assumes the rebel leadership.	Morelos' forces blockade Mexico City for several months. He holds a congress at Chilpancingo that adopts principles for the independence movement, including universal male suffrage, popular sovereignty and the abolition of slavery.	Morelos is captured and executed. His forces then split into several guerrilla bands, the most successful of which is led by Vicente Guerrero in the state of Oaxaca.

THE SPANISH BACKGROUND

In 1492, with the capture of the city of Granada, Spain's Christian armies finally completed the 700-year Reconquista (Reconquest), in which they had gradually recovered territories on the Spanish mainland from Islamic rule. Under its Catholic monarchs, Fernando and Isabel, Spain was an aggressively expanding state to which it came naturally to seek new avenues of commerce and conquest. With their odd mix of brutality, bravery, gold lust and piety, the Spanish *conquistadores* of the Americas were the natural successors to the crusading knights of the Reconquista.

The notion that the world was round was already widespread in Europe, and Spain's Atlantic location placed it perfectly to lead the search for new westward trade routes to the spice-rich Orient. Its explorers, soldiers and colonists landed first in the Caribbean, establishing bases on the islands of Hispaniola and Cuba where they quickly put the local populations to work mining gold and raising crops and livestock. Realizing that they had not reached the East Indies, the Spanish began seeking a passage through the land mass to their west, and soon became distracted by tales of gold, silver and a rich empire there.

After the first Spanish expeditions sent west from Cuba had been driven back from Mexico's Gulf coast, Spain's governor on the island, Diego Velázquez, asked Hernán Cortés, a colonist there, to lead a new expedition westward. As Cortés gathered ships and men, Velázquez became uneasy about the costs and Cortés' loyalty, and tried to cancel the expedition. But Cortés, sensing a once-in-history opportunity, ignored him and set sail on February 15, 1519, with 11 ships, 550 men and 16 horses. This tension between Cortés' individual ambition and the authorities' efforts to bring him to heel persisted until his death in Spain in 1547.

THE CONQUEST

The Cortés expedition landed first at Cozumel island, then sailed around the coast to Tabasco, defeating inhospitable locals in the Battle of Centla in modern-day Frontera (p801), where the enemy fled in terror from Spanish horsemen, thinking horse and rider to be a single fearsome beast. Afterwards Cortés delivered the first of many lectures to Mexicans on the importance of Christianity and King Carlos I of Spain – a constant theme of the conquest – and the locals gave him 20 maidens, among them Doña Marina (La Malinche), who became his indispensable interpreter, aide and lover.

The Spaniards were greatly assisted by the hostility felt toward the Aztecs by other Mexican peoples. Resentful Aztec subject towns on the Gulf coast, such as Zempoala (p676), welcomed them. And as they moved inland toward Tenochtitlán, they made allies of the Aztecs' long-time enemies, the Tlaxcalans.

Pay a virtual visit to Monterrey's excellent Museum of Mexican History at www.museo historiamexicana.org.mx.

Neil Young's 1975 album *Zuma* featured a track called 'Cortez the Killer,' inspired by the Mexican exploits of the conquistador.

1821	1821–22	1824
Royalist general Agustín de Iturbide defects and, with Guerrero, establishes guarantees for an independent Mexico: religious dominance by the Catholic Church, a constitutional monarchy and equal rights for criollos and *peninsulares*.	The Plan de Iguala wins over all influential sections of society, and the incoming Spanish viceroy agrees to Mexican independence. Iturbide, who has command of the army, takes the new Mexican throne as Emperor Agustín I.	A new constitution establishes a federal Mexican republic of 19 states and four territories. Guadalupe Victoria, a former independence fighter, becomes its first president.

Aztec legends and superstitions and the indecisive character of Emperor Moctezuma also worked to the Spaniards' advantage. As soon as the Spanish ships arrived along the coast, news of 'towers floating on water,' bearing fair-skinned beings, was carried to Moctezuma. According to the Aztec calendar, 1519 would see the legendary Toltec god-king Quetzalcóatl return from the east. Was Cortés actually Quetzalcóatl? Moctezuma could only play a waiting game to find out. Omens proliferated: lightning struck a temple, a comet sailed through the night skies and a bird 'with a mirror in its head' was brought to Moctezuma, who saw warriors in it.

The Spaniards, with 6000 indigenous allies, were invited to enter Tenochtitlán, a city bigger than any in Spain, on November 8, 1519. Moctezuma was carried out to meet Cortés on a litter with a canopy of feathers and gold borne by some of his nobles, and the Spaniards were lodged, as befitted gods, in the palace of Moctezuma's father, Axayácatl.

Though entertained in luxury, the Spaniards were trapped. Unsure of Moctezuma's intentions, they took him hostage. Believing Cortés a god, Moctezuma told his people he went willingly, but tensions rose in the city, aggravated by the Spaniards' destruction of Aztec idols. Eventually, after some six or seven months and apparently fearing an attack, some of the Spaniards killed about 200 Aztec nobles in an intended pre-emptive strike. Cortés persuaded Moctezuma to try to pacify his people. According to one version of events, the emperor tried to address the crowds from the roof of Axayácatl's palace, but was killed by missiles; other versions say the Spaniards killed him.

The Spaniards fled, losing several hundred of their own and thousands of indigenous allies, on what's known as the Noche Triste (Sad Night). The survivors retreated to Tlaxcala, where they built boats in sections, then carried them across the mountains for a waterborne assault on Tenochtitlán. When the 900 Spaniards re-entered the Valle de México in May, 1521, they were accompanied by some 100,000 native allies. For the first time, the odds were in their favor. The defenders resisted fiercely, but after three months the city had been razed to the ground and the new emperor, Cuauhtémoc, was captured.

At 17 years of age, Moctezuma's heir, Tecuichpo, bore Cortés' illegitimate daughter, Doña Leonor Cortés y Moctezuma.

MEXICO AS A COLONY

Spain's policy toward conquered Mexico, as for all its conquests in the Americas, can be summed up in one word: exploitation. The Spanish crown saw the New World as a silver cow to be milked to finance its endless wars in Europe, a life of luxury for its nobility and a deluge of churches, palaces and monasteries that were erected around Spain in the 16th and 17th centuries. The crown was entitled to a fifth (the *quinto real*, or royal fifth) of all bullion

The most readable and useful tellings of the whole story include The Course of Mexican History by Michael C Meyer and William L Sherman, Lynn V Foster's A Brief History of Mexico, Kenneth Pearce's Traveller's History of Mexico and Brian R Hamnett's A Concise History of Mexico.

1836	**1838–42**	**1845–48**
US settlers in the Mexican territory of Texas, initially welcomed by the authorities, grow restless and declare Texas independent. President Santa Anna's army wipes out the defenders of the Alamo mission, but is routed on the San Jacinto River.	Santa Anna's left leg is amputated at Veracruz during the 'Pastry War' with France. Four years later, he has it disinterred and paraded triumphantly through Mexico City.	US Congress votes to annex Texas, sparking the Mexican–American War (1846–48), in which US troops capture Mexico City. Mexico cedes Texas, California, Utah, Colorado and most of New Mexico and Arizona to the US.

SOME WE LOVE, SOME WE LOVE TO HATE

Mexicans have strong opinions about some of their historical characters. Some are held up as shining examples for every Mexican to be proud of, with statues in every city and streets named for them all over the country. Others, just as influential, are considered objects of shame and ridicule.

Mexico's Top Six Heroes

- **Cuauhtémoc** – Aztec leader who resisted the Spanish invaders
- **Benito Juárez** – reforming, liberal, indigenous president who fought off French occupiers
- **Miguel Hidalgo** – the priest who launched the War for Independence
- **José María Morelos** – the priest who took up the sword of the independence movement after Hidalgo's death
- **Pancho Villa** – larger-than-life revolutionary
- **Emiliano Zapata** – Land and Liberty!

Mexico's Top Six Villains

- **Hernán Cortés** – the original evil Spanish conqueror
- **Carlos Salinas de Gortari** – president from 1988 to 1994, blamed for peso crisis, drugs trade, corruption, Nafta, you name it…
- **Santa Anna** – he won at the Alamo, but lost Texas, California, Arizona, Utah, Colorado and New Mexico
- **Porfirio Díaz** – 19th-century dictator
- **Nuño de Guzmán** – conquistador of legendary cruelty
- **La Malinche** – Doña Marina, Hernán Cortés' indigenous translator and lover

sent back from the New World. Individual conquistadors and colonists saw the American empire as a chance to get rich, and by the 18th century some of them had amassed huge fortunes in Mexico from mining, commerce or agriculture, and possessed enormous estates (haciendas).

The populations of the conquered peoples of Nueva España (New Spain), as the Spanish named their Mexican colony, declined disastrously, mainly from epidemics of new diseases introduced by the invaders. The indigenous peoples' only real allies were some of the monks who started arriving in 1523. The monks' missionary work helped extend Spanish control over Mexico – by 1560 they had converted millions of people and built more than 100 monasteries – but many of them were compassionate and brave men, who protected local people from the colonists' worst

1847–48	1858–61	1861–63
The Maya people of the Yucatán Peninsula rise up against their criollo overlords in the 'War of the Castes' and narrowly fail to drive them off the peninsula.	Liberal government laws requiring the church to sell much of its property precipitate the War of the Reform: Mexico's liberals (with their 'capital' at Veracruz) defeat the conservatives (based in Mexico City).	Benito Juárez becomes Mexico's first indigenous president, but Mexico suffers the French Intervention: France invades Mexico, taking Mexico City in 1863 despite a defeat at Puebla on May 5, 1862.

excesses. Indigenous slavery was abolished in the 1550s, but partly replaced by black slavery.

Cortés granted his soldiers *encomiendas,* which were rights to the labor or tribute of groups of indigenous people. Spain began to exert control by setting up Nueva España's first *audiencia,* a high court with government functions, in 1527. Later, authority was vested in viceroys, the Spanish crown's personal representatives in Mexico.

Northern Mexico remained beyond Spanish control until big finds of silver at Zacatecas, Guanajuato and elsewhere spurred Spanish attempts to subdue it. The northern borders were slowly extended by missionaries and a few settlers, and by the early 19th century Nueva España included (albeit loosely) most of the modern US states of Texas, New Mexico, Arizona, California, Utah and Colorado.

As the decades passed, many Spaniards put down roots in Mexico, and those born and bred in the colony began to develop their own identity and a growing alienation from the mother country. When Mexico came to its next big turning point – the throwing off of the colonial yoke – it was these criollos, people born of Spanish parents in Nueva España, who engineered the separation.

A person's place in colonial Mexican society was determined by skin color, parentage and birthplace. At the top of the tree, however humble their origins in Spain, were Spanish-born colonists. Known as *peninsulares,* they were a minuscule part of the population, but were considered nobility in Nueva España.

Next on the ladder were the criollos, some of whom were enormously rich. Not surprisingly, criollos sought political power commensurate with their wealth and grew to resent Spanish authority over the colony.

Below the criollos were the *mestizos* (people of mixed ancestry), and at the bottom of the pile were the indigenous people and African slaves. Though the poor were paid for their labor by the 18th century, they were paid very little. Many were *peones* (bonded laborers tied by debt to their employers) and indigenous people still had to pay tribute to the crown.

Social stratification follows similar patterns in Mexico today with, broadly speaking, the 'pure-blood' descendants of Spaniards at the top of the tree, the *mestizos* in the middle, and the indigenous people at the bottom.

Criollo discontent with Spanish rule really began to stir following the expulsion of the Jesuits (many of whom were criollos) from the Spanish empire in 1767. When the crown confiscated church assets in 1804, the church had to call in many debts, which hit criollos hard. The catalyst for rebellion came in 1808 when Napoleon Bonaparte occupied Spain, and direct Spanish control over Nueva España evaporated. Rivalry between *peninsulares* and criollos intensified.

Mexico Connect (www .mexicoconnect.com) has plenty of informative but not-too-heavy stuff on Mexican history.

Anna Lanyon's *The New World of Martín Cortés* tells the fascinating and poignant story of the first *mestizo,* the son of Hernán Cortés and La Malinche.

1864–67	1876–1911	1910–11
Napoleon III sends Maximilian of Hapsburg over as emperor in 1864, but starts to withdraw his troops in 1866. Maximilian is executed by Juárez's forces in 1867.	The Porfiriato: Mexico is ruled by conservative Porfirio Díaz, who brings stability and some economic progress but curbs civil liberties and democratic rights, and concentrates wealth in the hands of a small minority.	Mexico rises in revolution against the Díaz regime on November 20, 1910. When revolutionaries under Pancho Villa take Ciudad Juárez in May, 1911, Díaz resigns. Reformist Francisco Madero is elected president in November, 1911.

THE YOUNG REPUBLIC

The city of Querétaro (p643), north of Mexico City, became a hotbed of intrigue among disaffected criollos plotting rebellion against Spanish rule. The rebellion was finally launched in 1810 by Padre Miguel Hidalgo (see boxed text, p629) in his parish of Dolores on September 16 – a date that is still celebrated as a Mexican national holiday. The path to independence was a hard one, involving almost 11 years of fighting between rebels and loyalist forces, and the deaths of Hidalgo and several other rebel leaders. But eventually rebel general Agustín de Iturbide sat down with incoming Spanish viceroy Juan O'Donojú in Córdoba (see Ex-Hotel Zevallos, p694) in 1821 and agreed the terms for Mexico's independence.

As a warning to other rebels, Miguel Hidalgo's head was put on public display for 10 years in Guanajuato. His skull is now inside Mexico City's Monumento a la Independencia.

The country's first nine decades as a free nation started with a period of chronic political instability and wound up with a period of stability so repressive that it triggered a social revolution. A consistent theme throughout was the opposition between liberals, who favored a measure of social reform, and conservatives, who didn't. Of the era's three major figures, one, Benito Juárez, was a liberal. The other two, Antonio López de Santa Anna and Porfirio Díaz, started out as liberals but ended up as conservatives – a fairly common transition for those who acquire power and one that Mexico's entire governing party, the PRI, underwent in the 20th century.

Between 1821 and the mid-1860s, the young Mexican nation was invaded by three different countries, lost large chunks of its territory to the US and underwent nearly 50 changes of head of state. No one did much to stir the economy, and corruption became entrenched. The dominant figures were almost all men of Spanish origin, and another consistent theme was the repeated intervention in politics by ambitious soldiers. The paragon of these military opportunists was Santa Anna, who first hit the limelight by deposing independent Mexico's first head of state, Emperor Agustín I, in 1823. He defeated a small Spanish invasion force at Tampico in 1829 and two years later overthrew the conservative president Anastasio Bustamante. Santa Anna himself was elected president in 1833, the first of his 11 terms in 22 years, during which the presidency changed hands 36 times.

Visit Morelia, the home town of independence fighter, José Morelos, to see a host of sites associated with him.

But Santa Anna is most remembered for helping to lose large chunks of Mexican territory to the US. After his 1836 defeat in Texas and his disastrous territorial losses in the Mexican–American War in 1848 (the US has had the upper hand in American–Mexican relations ever since), a Santa Anna government sold Mexico's last remaining areas of New Mexico and Arizona to the US for US$10 million in the Gadsden Purchase of 1853. This precipitated the Revolution of Ayutla that ousted him for good in 1855.

1913–14	1917	1920–24
Madero is deposed and executed by conservative rebel Victoriano Huerta. Northern revolutionary leaders unite against Huerta. His troops terrorize the countryside, but he is forced to resign in July 1914.	Reformists emerge victorious over radicals in the revolutionary conflict and a new reformist constitution, still largely in force today, is enacted at Querétaro.	President Álvaro Obregón turns to national reconstruction after the devastation of the Revolution. More than a thousand rural schools are built, and some land is redistributed from big landowners to peasants.

Amazingly, it was an indigenous Zapotec from Oaxaca who played the lead role in Mexican affairs for almost two tumultuous decades thereafter. Lawyer Benito Juárez was a key member of the new liberal government in 1855, which ushered in the era known as the Reform, in which it set about dismantling the conservative state that had developed in Mexico. Juárez became president in 1861. Come the French Intervention almost immediately afterwards, his government was forced into exile, eventually to regain control in 1866. Juárez immediately set an agenda of economic and educational reform. Schooling was made mandatory, a railway was built between Mexico City and Veracruz, and a rural police force, the *rurales*, was organized to secure the transportation of cargo through Mexico. Juárez is one of the few Mexican historical figures with a completely unsullied reputation, and his sage maxim, '*El respeto al derecho ajeno es la paz*' (Respect for the rights of others is peace), is widely quoted.

Juárez was succeeded at Mexico's helm by Porfirio Díaz, who ruled as president for 31 of the 35 years from 1876 to 1911, a period known as the Porfiriato. Díaz brought Mexico into the industrial age, stringing telephone, telegraph and railway lines and launching public works projects throughout the country. He kept Mexico free of the civil wars that had plagued it for more than 60 years – but at a cost. Political opposition, free elections and a free press were banned. Peasants were cheated out of their land by new laws, workers suffered appalling conditions and the country was kept quiet by a ruthless army and the now-feared *rurales*. Land and wealth became concentrated in the hands of a small minority. All this led, in 1910, to the Mexican Revolution.

The Caste War of Yucatán, by Nelson Reed, is a page-turning account of the modern Maya's insurrection against the criollo elite and establishment of an independent state.

THE MEXICAN REVOLUTION

The revolution was no clear-cut struggle between good and evil, left and right or any other pair of simple opposites. It was a 10-year period of shifting allegiances between forces and leaders of all political stripes. The conservatives were pushed aside fairly early on, but the reformers and revolutionaries who had lined up against them could never agree among themselves. Successive attempts to create stable governments were wrecked by new outbreaks of devastating fighting. The overall outcome was that one in eight Mexicans lost their lives and the country swapped the right-wing dictatorship of Porfirio Díaz for a radical government that later lost its revolutionary verve but kept a grip on power right through the 20th century.

Francisco Madero, a wealthy liberal from Coahuila, would probably have won the presidential election in 1910 if Porfirio Díaz hadn't jailed him. On his release, Madero called successfully for the nation to revolt,

The best movie of the Mexican Revolution is Elia Kazan's Viva Zapata! *(1952), starring Marlon Brando. John Steinbeck's script is historically sound for the first phase of the revolution, up to the meeting between Pancho Villa and Emiliano Zapata in Mexico City. Beyond that point it flounders until Zapata is assassinated.*

1924–36	1934–40	1938
President Plutarco Elías Calles closes monasteries and church schools and prohibits religious processions, precipitating the Cristero Rebellion (until 1929). Calles founds the Partido Nacional Revolucionario, a precursor to today's PRI, in 1929.	President Lázaro Cárdenas redistributes almost 200,000 sq km of land, establishes the Confederación de Trabajadores Mexicanos (Confederation of Mexican Workers), and reorganizes the PNR as the Partido de la Revolución Mexicana.	President Cárdenas boldly expropriates foreign oil-company operations in Mexico, forming Petróleos Mexicanos (Pemex, the Mexican Petroleum Company). After the oil expropriation, foreign investors avoid Mexico, slowing the economy.

which spread quickly across the country. Díaz resigned in May, 1911, and Madero was elected president six months later. But Madero could not contain the diverse factions that were now fighting for power throughout the country. The basic divide was between liberal reformers like Madero and more radical leaders such as Emiliano Zapata (see boxed text, p249), who was fighting for the transfer of hacienda land to the peasants, with the cry '¡Tierra y libertad!' (Land and freedom!). Madero sent federal troops to disband Zapata's forces, and the Zapatista movement was born.

When Madero's government was brought down in 1913, it was by one of his own top generals, Victoriano Huerta, who defected to conservative rebels. Madero was executed and Huerta became president – which succeeded only in (temporarily) uniting the revolutionary forces in opposition to him. Three main leaders in the north banded together under the Plan de Guadalupe: Venustiano Carranza, a Madero supporter, in Coahuila; Francisco 'Pancho' Villa (see boxed text, p376) in Chihuahua; and Álvaro Obregón in Sonora. Zapata also fought against Huerta.

But fighting then broke out again between the victorious factions, with Carranza and Obregón (the 'Constitutionalists,' with their capital at Veracruz) pitted against the radical Zapata and the populist Villa. The latter pair, despite a famous meeting in Mexico City in 1915, never formed a serious alliance, and it was Carranza who emerged the victor. The Zapatistas continued to demand reforms in the state of Morelos, south of Mexico City, but Carranza had Zapata assassinated in 1919. The following year Carranza himself was in turn assassinated on the orders of his former ally Obregón. Pancho Villa was killed in 1923.

The 10 years of violent fighting and upheaval had cost up to two million lives and shattered the economy.

MEXICO AS A ONE-PARTY DEMOCRACY

From 1920 to 2000, Mexico was ruled by the reformists who emerged victorious from the Revolution and their successors in the political party they set up, which since the 1940s has borne the self-contradictory name Partido Revolucionario Institucional, or PRI as it's universally known. Starting out with some genuinely radical social policies, these governments became steadily more conservative, more corrupt, more repressive and more self-interested as the 20th century wore on. Mexico rode many economic ups and downs, and ended the century with a bigger middle class but still a great wealth disparity between the prosperous few and many poor. Rampant population growth became a critical problem in the mid-20th century but by the end of the century growth rates had slowed sharply.

Get the Economist's country profile on Mexico at www.economist .com/countries/Mexico.

In the 1920s, outstanding Mexican artists such as Diego Rivera were commissioned to decorate important public buildings with large, vivid murals on social and historical themes. Many of these can be seen in Mexico City.

1940s & '50s	1958–64	1964–70
The Mexican economy expands, helped by industry and exports growth during WWII, major infrastructure projects and the development of tourism. The population almost doubles in two decades, and millions migrate to urban areas.	Popular President Adolfo López Mateos nationalizes foreign utility concessions, implements new social welfare and rural education programs, and redistributes 120,000 sq km of land to small farmers.	President Gustavo Díaz Ordaz resists democratizing the PRI. Demonstrations against one-party rule reach a crescendo just before the 1968 Mexico City Olympics. An estimated 400 protestors are massacred at Tlatelolco, Mexico City.

One of Mexico's longest-standing and most bitterly resented inequities – land ownership – was addressed by the redistribution of more than 400,000 sq km from large estates to peasants and small farmers between the 1920s and '60s. This included most of the country's arable land, and nearly half the population received land, mainly in the form of *ejidos* (communal landholdings). However, by the end of the century, small-scale agriculture came under severe pressure from the effects of the 1994 North American Free Trade Agreement (Nafta), which permitted cheaper imports from the US and Canada with which traditional Mexican growers found it hard to compete.

At the other end of the economic spectrum, Mexico developed a worrying dependence on its huge oil reserves in the Gulf of Mexico. The 1970s and '80s saw the country veer from oil-engendered boom to oil-engendered slump as world oil prices swung rapidly up then just as suddenly down. Today, Mexico has managed to significantly reduce its reliance on oil for both government tax revenue and exports by developing other industries.

The huge government-owned oil company, Pemex, was just one face of a massive state-controlled economic behemoth that developed as the PRI sought control over all important facets of Mexican life. The PRI was born as an institution for bringing together the most important influence sectors in Mexican society and politics – labor, the military, farmers and political groupings. It became effectively a monolithic state party that, while governing in the name, and ostensibly the interests, of the people, inevitably bred corruption, inefficiency and violent intolerance of political opposition.

The PRI's antipathy to civil liberties first attracted opposition in the 1960s, especially in the 1968 student-led protests in Mexico City, which resulted in the Tlatelolco Massacre, where an estimated 400 protesters were shot dead (see boxed text p123). Though it has never been revealed who was really responsible, Tlatelolco discredited the PRI forever in the minds of many Mexicans. The party came to depend increasingly on strong-arm tactics and fraud to win elections, especially as rival parties, such as the business-oriented Partido Acción Nacional (PAN) and the left-of-center Partido de la Revolución Democrática (PRD; Party of the Democratic Revolution), gained growing support in the following decades.

Mexicans' cynicism about their leaders reached a crescendo with the 1988–94 presidency of Carlos Salinas de Gortari, who won the presidential election only after a mysterious computer failure had halted vote-tallying at a crucial stage. During Salinas' term, drug trafficking grew into a huge business in Mexico (many believe he and other PRI high-ups were themselves deeply involved in it), and mysterious assassinations proliferated. Salinas did take steps to liberalize the monolithic state-dominated economy. The apex of his program, Nafta, undoubtedly helped to boost exports and industry, but it was unpopular with farmers and small businesses threatened by inexpensive imports from the US. Shortly before Salinas left office he

A contingent of 250,000 Mexican and Mexican-American men fought in WWII. One thousand were killed in action, 1500 received purple hearts and 17 received the Congressional Medal of Honor.

Universidad Nacional Autónoma de México, one of the major Mexican projects of the 1950s, has the world's largest mosaic mural. Created by Juan O'Gorman, the 4000-sq-meter mural on the library depicts scenes of Mexican history.

1970s	**1980s**	**1985**
Mexico enjoys an economic boom thanks to a jump in world oil prices. On the strength of the country's vast oil reserves, international institutions begin lending Mexico billions of dollars.	Oil prices plunge and Mexico suffers its worst recession in decades. Amid economic helplessness and rampant corruption, dissent and protests increase, even inside the PRI.	On September 19 a massive earthquake, with a magnitude of 8.1 on the Richter scale, strikes Mexico City. At least 10,000 people are killed.

MEXICO'S DEADLY DRUG GANGS

Mexico has long been a marijuana and heroin producer, but it was a 1980s US crackdown on drug shipments from Colombia through the Caribbean that gave a huge leg-up to Mexican drug gangs, as drugs being transported from South America to the US went through Mexico instead.

Three main Mexican cartels emerged, each controlling different sectors of the Mexico–US border: the Pacific (or Tijuana) cartel, the (Ciudad) Juárez cartel and the Matamoros-based Gulf cartel. In recent years a fourth mob, the Sinaloa cartel, has muscled in on the scene. These cartels buy up politicians, antidrug officials and whole police forces. Many Mexicans believe organized crime in the early 1990s was actually controlled by the PRI.

By 1997 most illegal drugs entering the US were going through Mexico. In 2007, more than 90% of cocaine reaching the US went through Mexico, and Mexican labs were stepping up methamphetamine production to make up for a crackdown in the US.

Presidents Zedillo (1994–2000), Fox (2000–06) and Calderón (since 2006) all brought the armed forces into the fight against the drug mobs. Calderón deployed 25,000 federal troops to cities and states where the drug gangs are most powerful. But despite some high-profile arrests, business goes on for the gangs, as does their killing of police, soldiers, judges and journalists – and of each other in their vicious turf wars. An estimated 1500 people died in drug gang–related violence in 2005, 2100 people in 2006, and 2500 in 2007. Border cities such as Tijuana and Nuevo Laredo have usually seen the worst of this, but since 2006 places such as Monterrey, Michoacán and Acapulco have suffered shootouts and killings. The mobs are just too powerful and dangerous to be easily defeated.

A decline in tourism to Mexico's northern border areas in 2007 was blamed on fear of drug violence. In reality travelers need not be unduly concerned, as they are not targets of this violence and it normally takes place well away from touristed areas.

---

spent nearly all of Mexico's foreign-exchange reserves in a futile attempt to support the peso, engendering a slump that he left his successor, Ernesto Zedillo, to deal with.

It was also left to Zedillo to respond to the now almost irresistible clamor for democratic change in Mexico. He established a new, independently supervised electoral system that saw growing numbers of non-PRI mayors and state governors elected during his term, and opened the way for the country's first-ever peaceful change of regime at the end of his term in 2000.

A major problem for Mexico in the middle of the 20th century was that of population growth. Mexico's population grew from 20 million in 1940 to 35 million in 1960 and to 67 million in 1980 – more than trebling in 40 years. Many people migrated from the villages to urban areas in search of work, often living in desperate conditions in shanty towns around the edges of cities. Mexico City's population multiplied 10-fold between the 1940s and 1980s. However, publicity campaigns, education

1988–94	1994	1994–2000
The PRI's Carlos Salinas de Gortari narrowly defeats left-of-center Cuauhtémoc Cárdenas in a disputed presidential election, and reforms Mexico's state-dominated economy into one of private enterprise and free trade.	Nafta takes effect. The left-wing Zapatista uprising in Chiapas state begins. Luis Donaldo Colosio, Salinas' chosen successor as PRI presidential candidate, is assassinated. Days after Salinas leaves office, Mexico's currency, the peso, collapses.	Under President Ernesto Zedillo, Mexico slowly emerges from a deep recession triggered by the peso collapse. Crime and emigration to the US increase. Zedillo sets up a more independent and transparent electoral system.

and family planning clinics all helped to slow things down. In 1970, the average Mexican woman gave birth seven times in her lifetime. Today the figure is just 2.4 – and the overall population growth rate has sunk from 3.4% a year to 1.15%. A major safety valve is emigration to the US, something very large numbers of Mexicans, especially men from rural areas, do for at least part of their lives. By some estimates, 15 million Mexicans are now (legally or illegally) in the US, where average wages are six times higher than in Mexico.

MEXICO UNDER THE PAN

The independently run electoral system installed by President Zedillo in the 1990s duly unseated his own party, the PRI, when Vicente Fox of the right-of-center PAN, a son of Basque and German-American immigrants and former chief of Coca-Cola's operations in Mexico, won the 2000 presidential election.

Fox's election itself, after 80 years of one-party rule, was really the biggest news about his six-year term. A charismatic, 6ft 5in (nearly 2m) rancher, he entered office with the goodwill of a wide range of Mexicans, who hoped a change of ruling party would bring real change in the country. In the end, his presidency was considered a disappointment by most. He had no magic solutions to the same economic and social problems that previous governments had struggled with. Without the full support of Mexico's Congress, where the PAN did not enjoy a majority, Fox was unable to push through the reforms that he believed were key to stirring Mexico's slumbering economy. His government consequently lacked money to improve education, social welfare or roads. At least government had become more transparent, honest and accountable, and Mexicans less cynical about their political system.

Fox was succeeded in late 2006 by another PAN president, the less charismatic but potentially more effective Vicente Calderón. Again, it was the manner of his election that signified most. His victory over the PRD candidate, Andrés Manuel López Obrador, was by the narrowest of margins. López Obrador, who had led all the way in the opinion polls, cried 'fraud' and his supporters staged several weeks of large protests in Mexico City. But the protestors could find no convincing evidence of foul play by the PAN. The fact that the electoral apparatus had come unscathed through a second election and survived a severe cross-examination was at least as significant for Mexico's future as the name or party of the winning candidate. It had taken a decade of independence war for Mexico to throw off Spanish rule, and a decade of revolution to throw off the post-colonial elite that entrenched itself after independence. The elite party that entrenched itself after the Revolution had, in the end, given way with barely a shot fired.

You'll certainly get a feel for the scary brutality and corruption of the cross-border narco world from Steven Soderbergh's 2000 movie *Traffic*.

See the Mexican presidency's angle on things at www.presidencia .gob.mx.

2000	2000–06	2006
The PRI finally loses power as Vicente Fox of the right-of-center PAN (Partido Acción Nacional) wins the presidential election – the first ever peaceful change of regime in Mexican history.	The Fox presidency sees reasonable economic progress but fails to enact reforms to really spark growth, rein in the violent drug mobs, or to reach an accord with the Zapatistas. Society becomes more open and a little less corrupt.	The PAN's Felipe Calderón narrowly defeats Andrés Manuel López Obrador of the left-of-center PRD in the presidential election. López Obrador supporters stage massive protests alleging electoral fraud.

The Culture

LIFE, DEATH & THE FAMILY

The last thing you can do with Mexicans is encapsulate them in simple formulae. They adore fun, music and a fiesta, yet in many ways are deeply serious. They work hard but relax and enjoy life to the full in their time off. They're hospitable and warm to guests, yet are most truly themselves only within their family group. They will laugh at death, but have a profound vein of spirituality. You may read about anti-gringo sentiment in the media, but Mexicans will treat you, as a visitor to their country, with refreshing warmth and courtesy.

Mexico is the home of machismo, that exaggeration of masculinity whose manifestations range from a certain way of trimming a moustache to aggressive driving, heavy drinking or the carrying of weapons. The other side of the machismo coin is the exaggeratedly feminine female. But gender equalization has come a long way: today you'll find most Mexicans, especially among the increasingly educated and worldly younger generations, ready to relate simply as one person to another.

Mexico's 'patron saint' – not actually a saint but a manifestation of the Virgin Mary – is the dark-skinned Virgin of Guadalupe, who made her appearance before an Aztec potter in 1531 on a hill near Mexico City. Universally revered, she's both the archetypal mother and the pre-eminent focus of Mexicans' inborn spirituality, which has its roots both in Spanish Catholicism and in the complex belief systems of Mexico's pre-Hispanic civilizations. Elements of ancient religions survive alongside Catholicism among the country's many indigenous peoples, and most Mexicans still inhabit a world in which omens, portents, coincidences and curious resemblances take on great importance. The ancient belief in the cyclical, repetitive nature of time persists too, somewhere in most Mexicans' subconscious.

On a more mundane level, you'll find most Mexicans are chiefly concerned with earning a crust for themselves and their strongly knit families – and also with enjoying the leisurely side of life, whether partying at clubs, bars or fiestas, or relaxing over a long, extended-family Sunday lunch at a country or beachside restaurant.

On a political level, the country has become fairer and more pluralistic, but most Mexicans still have little faith that it will ever be governed well. They mock their country's failings, but at the same time are a proud people: proud of their families, their villages and towns, proud of Mexico. So close to the US, where millions of them spend years of their lives, many Mexicans take on board a certain amount of US culture and consciousness, but they also strongly value the positives they see in Mexican life – a more human pace, a strong sense of community and family, their own very distinctive cuisine, their unique *mestizo* (mixed indigenous and Spanish) heritage and their thriving, multifaceted national culture.

LIFESTYLE

Around three-quarters of Mexicans now live in cities and towns, and the proportion grows as rural folk are sucked into cities in search of work. Most urban dwellers inhabit crowded, multigenerational family homes on tightly packed streets in crowded neighborhoods, with few parks or open spaces. Fly into Mexico City and you'll get a bird's-eye view of just how little space is not occupied by housing or roads. Around the edges of the city, new streets climb the steep slopes of extinct volcanoes, while the poorest arrivals inhabit

Nobel Prize–winning Mexican writer Octavio Paz argues in *The Labyrinth of Solitude* that Mexicans' love of noise, music and crowds is just a temporary escape from personal isolation and gloom. Make your own judgment!

A UN development program study in 2004 reported that while the wealthiest zones of Mexico City and Monterrey could be compared to rich European cities, other parts of the capital and rural areas in the south of Mexico were more like parts of Africa.

Mexico City's Universidad Nacional Autónoma de México (UNAM) was one of only three Latin American universities included in Britain's *Times Higher Education* 2007 list of Top 200 World Universities. UNAM was placed 192nd, lower than two Brazilian universities.

MANNERS FOR MEXICO

Locals in much of Mexico are accustomed to foreign visitors and tolerant of their strange ways. But dressing conservatively is still recommended in small towns, churches and in places off the beaten track.

Mexicans love to hear that you're enjoying their country, and will appreciate it if you start any conversation with a few words of Spanish. As a rule, Mexicans are slow to criticize or argue, expressing disagreement more by nuance than by blunt contradiction. An invitation to a Mexican home is an honor for an outsider; as a guest you will be treated hospitably and will enter a part of the real Mexico to which few outsiders are admitted. Take a small gift if you can.

Some indigenous people adopt a somewhat cold attitude toward visitors: they have come to mistrust outsiders after five centuries of rough treatment. They don't like being gawked at by tourists and can be very sensitive about cameras. If in any doubt about whether it's OK to take a photo, ask first.

shacks on the city's fringes made from a few concrete blocks, wooden boards or sheets of tin. Many of these people barely scrape a living as street hawkers, buskers or home workers in the 'informal economy,' rarely earning more than M$50 a day.

More affluent city neighborhoods often have blocks of relatively spacious apartments. In the wealthiest quarters, imposing detached houses with well-tended gardens and satellite dishes sit behind high walls with strong security gates. Domestic staff can be seen walking dogs or babies.

Out in the villages and small towns, people work the land and often live in yards with a few separate small buildings for members of an extended family – buildings of adobe, wood or concrete, often with earth floors, and with roofs sometimes of tile but more commonly of cheaper tin. Inside these homes are few possessions – beds, a cooking area, a table with a few chairs and a few aging photos of departed relatives. Villages may or may not be reached by paved roads, but are nearly always accessible by decrepit buses, pickups or some other public transport, as few of their inhabitants own cars.

Some 35 million adult Mexicans have not completed the basic nine years of primary and secondary schooling.

While rich kids go clubbing in flashy cars and attend private universities (or go to school in the US), poor villagers may dance only at local fiestas and often leave school before they reach 15. Millions of kids from poorer families are likely to complete the basic nine-year education only because of government cash handouts that are conditional upon school attendance. Mexican state schooling remains old-fashioned, emphasizing rote learning more than creativity and original thought. In comparisons of educational levels, Mexico does poorly against other major Latin American countries.

Mexicans' family and hometown ties remain strong. Even if they are not actually living together, large family groups take holidays or spend Sunday lunches together, while Mexicans in the US send money back to their families or to fund schools or clinics in their hometowns.

When sick, many Mexicans prefer to visit a traditional curandero *– a kind of cross between a naturopath and a witch doctor – rather than resort to a modern* médico.

Mexico is more broad-minded about sexuality than you might expect. Gays and lesbians rarely attract open discrimination or violence, and there are large, growing and confident gay communities in Mexico City (which recently legalized gay unions), Guadalajara, Monterrey and Puerto Vallarta.

Tradition remains powerful. Holidays for saints' days, patriotic anniversaries and festivals such as Semana Santa (Holy Week), Día de Muertos (Day of the Dead, November 2), the Día de la Virgen de Guadalupe (Day of the Virgin of Guadalupe, December 12) and Christmas are essential to the rhythm of Mexican life, ensuring that people get a break from work every few weeks and bringing them together for the same processions and rituals year after year.

GIVING SOMETHING BACK

Travelers who find themselves visiting some of the more impoverished places in Mexico often wish they could do something to help. Spending money there is, of course, one way to contribute. Stop for something to eat or drink; see what the shops and markets are selling; stay the night if there is suitable accommodation. Buying crafts and commodities direct from villages or from the artisans themselves ensures that your cash goes to those who deserve it most. In some areas there are local community organizations working in tourism – ecotourism initiatives, crafts cooperatives, guide associations and the like. Using their services, you'll be helping to develop a potentially long-term source of income that could save local people from having to migrate to cities for work.

If you would really like to get involved, you can do some volunteer work – see p980 for some pointers.

ECONOMY

Since the North American Free Trade Agreement (Nafta) came into force in 1994, trade with the US has replaced oil as the most important element in Mexico's economy. Nafta has steadily eliminated restrictions on commerce and investment between the US, Mexico and Canada, with the result that Mexican trade with the US has more than doubled. The US now receives 85% of Mexican exports and supplies more than half of Mexican imports.

Nafta is unpopular in rural areas and among Mexico's poor in general, especially in the southern half of the country, for its effect on Mexican small-scale agriculture, which struggles to compete with subsidized imports from the US and Canada. There is now no tariff on imports of corn (maize) to Mexico from the US, where corn growers are heavily subsidized by the government.

The 20th century saw Mexico transform from a backward agricultural economy to one of Latin America's most industrialized nations. Motor vehicles, processed food, steel, chemicals, paper and textiles joined more traditional industries such as sugar, coffee and mining. Most of Mexico's exports today are manufactured goods, and over half of these come from the *maquiladoras* (factories, usually foreign-owned) that import materials and parts for processing or assembly by inexpensive Mexican labor, then export the products, usually to the US.

Since most *maquiladoras*, and most industry in general, are concentrated in the north of the country and Mexico City, Nafta had the effect of widening the wealth gap between Mexico's north and its mainly agricultural and underdeveloped south. Draw a line across the middle of Mexico from about Tampico to Colima and you divide very neatly – with the exceptions of the Yucatán Peninsula and Mexico City – those states whose production is near or above the national average from those that are well below it.

Service industries contribute about 70% of Mexico's Gross Domestic Product and employ about 30% of the workforce. Tourism is one of the most important service industries. Some 20 million foreign visitors a year – more than half of them cross-border day-trippers – bring in more than US$12 billion of foreign exchange, and the domestic tourism business is three times as big. Agriculture employs nearly a quarter of Mexico's workers but produces only 4% of the national product.

Under the 2000–06 presidency of Vicente Fox, Mexico had achieved a degree of economic stability rare in its turbulent past, which had suffered periodic debt crises and bursts of rapid inflation. By 2006 job creation was almost keeping pace with the growth in the workforce engendered by the rising population. Fox's successor, Felipe Calderón, also from the business-

Since 1994 economic growth in most of northern Mexico has been running at more than 4% a year; in most of the center and south of Mexico it has been under 2%.

friendly National Action Party (PAN) nevertheless faced numerous stiff challenges if he was to keep the momentum going and really unlock Mexico's economic potential.

The country's nationalized oil industry, provider of 40% of federal government revenue, faced falling production and falling reserves, having failed to invest enough in new exploration and refineries.

Around half of Mexicans still work in the 'informal economy' (street vendors, home workers, traffic signal fire-eaters, criminals – anybody whose work is not officially registered). Few of these people scrape together much more than M$50 a day. They don't pay taxes and they don't contribute to the country's social security system, which provides health care and pensions. The Mexican government's non–oil tax revenue is equivalent to only 11% of GDP, well below levels in the developed world and even below the average for Latin America.

Early tax and pensions reforms by the Calderón government were aimed at boosting the government's income in order to reduce oil dependency and strengthen social security programs. Greater spending on infrastructure projects and more competition are two of Calderón's main priorities. As well as oil, the telecommunications, electricity, cement and beer industries are all dominated by a very small number of companies, state-owned or private, with prices for these products generally higher than they could be. Mexico also faces serious competition from the rapidly growing economies of India and especially China, with much lower wage levels than Mexico's, meaning that their products are often cheaper and that they can more easily attract foreign investment.

POPULATION

In 2008 Mexico's population was estimated at 107 million. About 75% of these people live in towns or cities, and a third are aged under 15. The biggest cities are Mexico City (with around 23 million people), Guadalajara (with a conurbation estimated at four million) and Monterrey (conurbation estimated at 3.6 million). Tijuana, Puebla, Ciudad Juárez, León and the Torreón, and San Luis Potosí conurbations all have populations above one million. The most populous state is the state of México, which includes the rapidly growing outer areas of Mexico City, though not the Distrito Federal (the city core), and has more than 15 million people.

MULTICULTURALISM

Mexicans are a far from uniform people, and their ethnic diversity is one of the most fascinating aspects of traveling around the country. The major distinction is between *mestizos* and *indígenas*. *Mestizos* are people of mixed ancestry – usually a compound of Spanish and indigenous, although African slaves and other Europeans are significant elements. *Indígenas* (indigenous people; less respectfully called *índios,* meaning 'Indians') are descendants of Mexico's pre-Hispanic inhabitants – the Maya, the Zapotecs, the Nahua, the Mixtecs and other peoples here before the Spanish arrived – who have retained a distinct ethnic identity. *Mestizos* make up the great majority of the population and, together with the few people of supposedly pure Spanish ancestry, they hold most positions of power and influence in Mexican society.

Other groups in Mexico – chiefly the result of immigration in the 20th century and mostly resident in the bigger cities – include small numbers of South Americans, Jews, Germans, Italians, Chinese, Lebanese, Koreans and Cubans, and uncounted numbers of (often illegal) migrant workers from Central America. There are also numerous US and Canadian expatriates,

Mexico is still the world's sixth biggest oil producer, but now imports 40% of its gasoline from the USA.

Anthropologist Guillermo Bonfil Batalla argues in *México Profundo: Reclaiming a Civilization* that Mexico's urban and rural poor, *mestizo* and indigenous, constitute a uniquely Mesoamerican civilization quite distinct from Mexico's European- and American-influenced middle class.

Mary Jane Gagnier's *Oaxaca Celebration* is beautifully photographed and written portrait of life in a Mexican village, Teotitlán del Valle, Oaxaca, by a long-time resident.

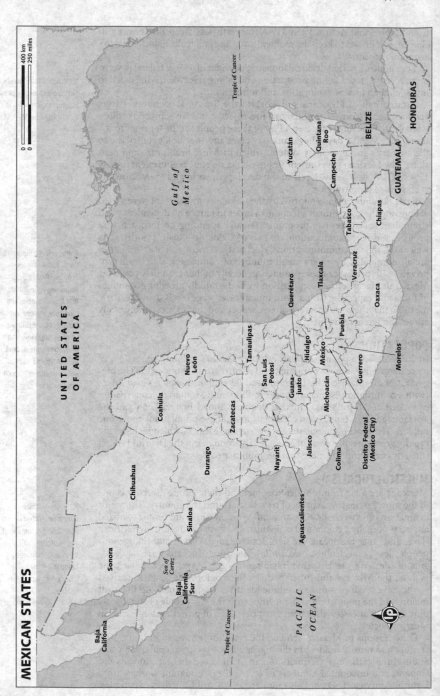

especially near the Lago de Chapala (south of Guadalajara) and at San Miguel de Allende.

Indigenous Peoples

Researchers have listed at least 139 vanished indigenous languages (and therefore 139 vanished indigenous cultures). The 60 or so that remain have survived primarily because of their rural isolation. Each group has its own language and traditions and, often, its own unique costumes, though the distinct identity of smaller and less resilient groups continues to be nibbled away by the forces of homogenization. Indigenous people generally remain second-class citizens, often restricted to the worst land or forced to migrate to city slums or the US in search of work. Their main wealth is traditional and spiritual, and their way of life is imbued with communal customs, beliefs and rituals bound up with nature.

In the 1990s, the Zapatista rebels in Chiapas spearheaded a campaign for indigenous rights. The San Andrés Accords of 1996, agreed between Zapatista and government negotiators, promised a degree of autonomy to Mexico's indigenous peoples, but were never made law.

At least the cause of indigenous languages took a step forward with the passing of a Law of Linguistic Rights in 2002. This recognizes indigenous tongues as 'national' languages and aims to develop Mexico's linguistic plurality through teaching. But while 1.2 million primary school kids now receive bilingual teaching (in 54 different languages), truly bilingual teachers are in short supply.

In the most recent national census (in 2000), just 7% of Mexicans listed themselves as speakers of indigenous languages, but people of predominantly indigenous ancestry may actually total two or three times that figure. The biggest indigenous group is the Nahua, descendants of the ancient Aztecs. More than two million Nahua are spread around central Mexico. Southeastern Mexico has a particularly high indigenous population. The approximately 1.5 million Yucatec Maya on the Yucatán Peninsula are direct descendants of the ancient Maya, and the Tzotziles and Tzeltales of Chiapas (400,000 to 500,000 of each) are probably descendants of Maya who migrated there at the time of the Classic Maya downfall.

Also directly descended from well-known pre-Hispanic peoples are the estimated 800,000 Zapotecs, mainly in Oaxaca; the 700,000-plus Mixtecs, mainly in Oaxaca, Guerrero and Puebla; the 400,000 Totonacs in Veracruz and Puebla; and the 200,000 Purépecha in Michoacán (descendants of the pre-Hispanic Tarascos). There are 50 or so other indigenous peoples, some now comprising only a few hundred people.

RELIGION
Roman Catholicism

Nearly 90% of Mexicans profess Roman Catholicism, making this the world's second-biggest Catholic country, after Brazil. Almost half of Mexican Catholics attend church weekly, and few of them do not have at least some underlying religious sentiment. Most Mexican fiestas are built around local saints' days, usually involving processions with sacred images as well as other celebrations, and pilgrimages to important shrines such as those at Chalma (p272), Plateros (p593), Zapopan (p528), San Juan de los Lagos (p543) and Real de Catorce (p608) are a big feature of the Mexican calendar. Prayers to the Virgin, Christ and saints offer many Mexicans at least hope for escape from all manner of problems.

The church's most binding symbol is Nuestra Señora de Guadalupe, the dark-skinned manifestation of the Virgin Mary who appeared to an Aztec

The word 'gringo' isn't exactly a compliment, nor is it necessarily an insult: the term is often simply a neutral synonym for 'American'.

The successful 2002 Mexican film *El Crimen del Padre Amaro* (The Crime of Father Amaro), starring Gael García Bernal, paints an ugly picture of church corruption in a small Mexican town.

potter, Juan Diego, near Mexico City in 1531. A crucial link between Catholic and indigenous spirituality, the Virgin of Guadalupe is now the whole country's religious patron, her blue-cloaked image is ubiquitous and her name is invoked in religious ceremonies, political speeches and literature. December 12, the Día de Nuestra Señora de Guadalupe, sees large-scale celebrations and pilgrimages all over the country, biggest of all in Mexico City (p166) and Monterrey (p404).

For more on Nuestra Señora de Guadalupe, check out www.interlupe .com.mx.

The Mexican Catholic Church is one of Latin America's more conservative. Only in the south of the country have its leaders become involved in current political issues such as human rights and poverty, most notably Samuel Ruiz, long-time bishop of San Cristóbal de Las Casas, who retired in 1999.

Indigenous Religion

The missionaries of the 16th and 17th centuries won the indigenous people over to Catholicism by grafting it onto pre-Hispanic religions. Old gods were renamed as Christian saints, and old festivals continued to be celebrated much as they had been in pre-Hispanic times, but on the nearest saint's day. Acceptance of the new religion was greatly helped by the 1531 appearance of the Virgin of Guadalupe.

Indigenous Christianity is still fused with ancient beliefs today. In some remote regions Christianity is only a veneer at most. Jalisco's Huichol people (see boxed text, p613) have two Christs, but neither is a major deity. More important is Nakawé, the fertility goddess. The hallucinogen peyote is a crucial source of wisdom in the Huichol world. Elsewhere, among peoples such as the Rarámuri of the Barranca del Cobre (Copper Canyon) and many Tzotzil people in highland Chiapas, intoxication is an almost sacred element at festival times. In a visit to the church at the Tzotzil village of San Juan Chamula (p825), you may see chanting *curanderos* (healers) carrying out shamanic rites.

The secrets of physical and spiritual health of a Nahua *curandera* are revealed in *Woman Who Glows in the Dark* by Elena Ávila.

The Totonac people's famous flying *voladores* performance (see p673) is very likely a version of an ancient fertility ritual.

In the traditional indigenous world almost everything has a spiritual dimension – trees, rivers, plants, wind, rain, sun, animals and hills have their own gods or spirits. Witchcraft, magic and traditional medicine survive. Illness may be seen as a 'loss of soul' resulting from the sufferer's wrongdoing or from the malign influence of someone with magical powers. A soul can be 'regained' if the appropriate ritual is performed by a *brujo* (witch doctor) or *curandero*.

Other Christian Faiths

Around 7% of Mexicans practice other varieties of Christianity. Some are members of the Methodist, Baptist, Presbyterian or Anglican churches set up by US missionaries in the 19th century. Others have been converted since the 1970s by a wave of American Pentecostal, Evangelical, Mormon, Seventh-Day Adventist and Jehovah's Witness missionaries. These churches have gained millions of converts, particularly among the rural and indigenous poor of southeast Mexico, some of whom have come to view Catholicism as just another part of a political apparatus that has subjugated them for centuries. This has led to some strife with Catholics.

LaNeta (www.laneta .apc.org), the internet portal for Mexican civil society, has links to many Mexican women's organizations.

WOMEN IN MEXICO

Machismo is no longer the norm among the more educated younger generation. Education and jobs are more accessible for young women, with enrolment rates at all levels of education similar to those for men, and women holding 42% of the country's professional and technical jobs and 29% of

COMMUNING WITH DEPARTED SOULS

Mexico's most characteristic and perhaps oddest fiesta, Día de Muertos (Day of the Dead), has its origins in the belief of the pre-Hispanic Tarasco people of Michoacán that the dead could return to their homes on one day each year.

The underlying philosophy is that death does not represent the end of a life but the continuation of life in a parallel world. The day when the dead could return was a month after the autumn equinox. The occasion required preparations to help the spirits find their way home and make them welcome. An arch made of bright yellow marigold flowers was put up in each home, as a symbolic doorway from the underworld. *Tamales*, fruits, corn and salt were placed in front of the arch on an altar, along with containers of water (because spirits always arrived thirsty after their journey). Traditionally, the spirits of departed children visited on the first night and dead adults came on the following night, when they joined their living relatives to eat, drink, talk and sing.

Come the Spanish conquest, the Catholic celebrations of All Saints' Day (November 1) and All Souls' Day (November 2) were easily superimposed on the old 'day of the dead' traditions, which shared much of the same symbolism – flowers, candles and offerings of food and drink. All Souls' Day is the Catholic day of prayers for those in purgatory; All Saints' Day was understood as a visit by the spirits of children who immediately became *angelitos* (little angels) when they died. The growing *mestizo* community evolved a new tradition of visiting graveyards and decorating graves of family members.

Día de Muertos persisted in the guise of Catholic celebration throughout the colonial period, when the idea of death as a great leveler and release from earthly suffering must have provided comfort for the overwhelmingly poor populace. After Mexican independence, poets used the occasion to publish verses ridiculing members of the social elite by portraying them as dead, with all their wealth and pretensions rendered futile. The great Mexican engraver José Guadalupe Posada (1852–1913) expressed similar sentiments in his famous *calaveras* – skeletal figures of Death cheerfully engaging in everyday life, working, dancing, courting, drinking and riding horses into battle. One of his most enduring characters is La Calavera Catrina, a female skeleton in an elaborate low-cut dress and flamboyant flower-covered hat, suggestively revealing a bony leg and an ample bust that is all ribs and no cleavage.

Among indigenous communities, most notably the Purépecha of Michoacán (descendants of the pre-Hispanic Tarascos), Muertos is still very much a religious and spiritual event. For them, the observance is more appropriately called Noche de Muertos (Night of the Dead), because families actually spend whole nights at the graveyard – the night of October 31/November 1 with the sprits of dead children, the following night with the spirits of dead adults.

For Mexico's *mestizo* majority, Muertos is more of a popular folk festival and family occasion. People may visit a graveyard to clean and decorate family graves, but they do not usually maintain an all-night vigil. And though they may pray for the souls of the departed and build altars in their homes to welcome them back, the Catholic belief is that those souls are in heaven or in purgatory, not actually back on a visit to Earth. Sugar skulls, chocolate coffins and toy skeletons are sold in markets everywhere as gifts for children as well as graveyard decorations; they derive as much from Posada's work as from the ancient death cults.

legislative, senior official and management posts. But women's wages overall still average less than half of men's. Among the poor majority, women still tend to play out traditional domestic and mothering roles – something that goes back in part to pre-Hispanic cultures and has also been fostered by the Catholic faith – though they often also have part time jobs or sell produce at market.

Women's organizations in Mexico are growing in size and number, but campaigns against violence and for better health care and wages have had few successes – although when abortion on demand in the first 12 weeks of pregnancy was legalized in Mexico City in 2007, it was seen as a landmark for women's rights in Latin America. Some radical groups such as the Zapatistas

Hollywood turned its attention to the Ciudad Juárez feminicides with *Bordertown*, filmed in 2005, in which Jennifer Lopez plays a US reporter sent to investigate the killings.

actively promote gender equality and women's empowerment, but they are in a minority, as are women in leadership positions in society. In politics, the most high-profile women are Patricia Espinosa (foreign minister and one of only three women in President Calderón's cabinet as of 2008) and Beatriz Paredes, leader of the opposition PRI party.

Violence against women, especially among the poor and the socially dislocated, remains a national problem. It may be most widespread, though less reported, in impoverished rural areas. Women are often fearful of reporting violence, and in rape cases the victim bears the burden of proof. One hopeful sign is that women's confidence about reporting domestic violence may be on the increase. The southern state of Chiapas, one of Mexico's poorest areas, registered a huge increase in domestic violence denouncements, from 4000 in 2006 to 16,000 in 2007.

Women have had the vote since 1947 and currently hold 21% of seats in the national Congress.

SPORTS
Football (Soccer)

No sport ignites Mexicans' passions as much as *fútbol*. Games in the 18-team national Primera División (First Division) are watched by large crowds and followed by millions on TV. Mexico City's Estadio Azteca (Aztec Stadium) hosted the 1970 and 1986 World Cup finals. Attending a game is fun, and rivalry between opposing fans is generally good-humored. Tickets are sold at the entrance for anything from M$50 to M$250, depending on the seat.

The Spanish-language Femexfut (www.femex fut.org.mx) and FutMex (www.futmex.com) give Mexican soccer scores, standings, upcoming games, news and links to club websites.

The two most popular teams in the country are América, of Mexico City, known as the Águilas (Eagles), and Guadalajara (Chivas – the Goats). They have large followings wherever they play, and matches between the two, known as 'Los Clásicos,' are the biggest games of the year. Other leading clubs are: Cruz Azul (known as La Máquina – the Machine) and UNAM (Universidad Autónoma de Mexico, known as Pumas), both from Mexico City; Universidad Autónoma de Guadalajara (Los Tecos) and Atlas, both from Guadalajara; Monterrey and Universidad Autónoma de Nuevo León (Los Tigres – the Tigers), both from Monterrey; Toluca, Pachuca, Necaxa (of Aguascalientes), Atlante (of Cancún) and Santos of Torreón. It was at Pachuca that soccer was introduced to Mexico by miners from Cornwall, England, in the 19th century.

Crowds at Primera División games normally range from a few thousand to 70,000. Games are spaced over the weekend from Friday to Sunday, with details printed in the newspapers. The Primera División's season is divided into the Torneo de Apertura (Opening Tournament, August to December) and the Torneo de Clausura (Closing Tournament, January to June), each ending in eight-team play-offs (La Liguilla) and eventually a two-leg final to decide the champion.

Something very similar to the Pelota Purépecha is depicted on the murals of the Palaciop de Tepantitla at Teotihuacán (p211).

Mexico's national team, known as El Tri (short for Tricolor, the name for the national flag), reached the last 16 of the World Cup in 1994, 1998 and 2002 – though it will take Mexicans a long time to get over the disappointment of being eliminated by the US in Korea in 2002!

Women's soccer is a growing sport; there's even a national league, the Super Liga Femenil, though as yet the national women's team has done worse than the men's.

Bullfighting

Bullfighting is another Mexican passion, though less widespread than soccer. Fights take place chiefly in the larger cities, usually on Sunday afternoons and often during local festivals.

GREAT BALLS OF FIRE!

Probably all ancient Mexican cultures played some version of the Mesoamerican ritual ball game, the world's first-ever team sport. More than 500 ball courts have survived at archaeological sites around Mexico and Central America. The game varied with time and place, but seems always to have involved two teams, with the object being to keep a rubber ball off the ground by flicking it with various parts of the body. The game had (at least sometimes) deep religious significance, serving as an oracle with the result indicating which of two courses of action should be taken. Games could be followed by the sacrifice of one or more of the players.

The ancient ball game survives in Mexico today, somewhat modified (and without human sacrifice), in at least three areas and several different forms. All are team sports of around five a side, generally played on narrow courts from about 50m to 200m long on open ground or occasionally in village streets. The Pelota Mixteca (Mixtec Ball Game) is played regularly in numerous towns and villages in Oaxaca state, including Ejutla, Nochixtlán and Bajos de Chila near Puerto Escondido. Participants hit the ball back and forth on a long, narrow court, using thick, heavy gloves and with a scoring system not unlike tennis. Oaxacan migrants have exported the game to other parts of Mexico and even to California.

In Sinaloa the game is known as *ulama* and has some resemblance to volleyball, with a highly complicated scoring system. There are two main variants, both requiring high skill: in *ulama de cadera*, played only in Mazatlán and Escuinapa, players hit the ball with their hips, which are protected with leather and deerskin belts and wrappings. In *ulama de antebrazo*, played in Culiacán, Angostura and a few other towns, the ball is hit with the forearm.

The Pelota Purépecha (Purépecha Ball Game) is played in the state of Michoacán, including in Uruapan, Paracho, Angahuan and villages around the Lago de Pátzcuaro. This game, played by women as well as men, resembles field hockey. The amazing Pelota Purépecha Encendida (Burning Purépecha Ball Game) version is played with a burning rubber-and-cloth ball, making it resemble the sun or a comet.

The website of the **Federación Mexicana de Juegos y Deportes Autóctonos y Tradicionales** (www.codeme.org.mx/autoctonoytradicional) tells in Spanish where all these games are played, with some pictures and even their official rules.

To many gringo eyes, the *corrida de toros* (literally, running of the bulls) hardly seems to be sport. To Mexicans it's as much a ritualistic dance as a fight, and it's said that Mexicans arrive on time for only two events – funerals and bullfights.

Usually six bulls are fought in an afternoon, and each is fought in three *suertes* (acts) or *tercios* (thirds). In the first, the cape-waving *toreros* spend a few minutes tiring the bull by luring him around the ring, then two *picadores*, on heavily padded horses, jab long *picas* (lances) into the bull's shoulders to weaken him. Next is the *suerte de banderillas*, when the *toreros* stab three pairs of elongated darts into the bull's shoulders. Finally comes the *suerte de muleta*, in which the matador has exactly 16 minutes to kill the bull. After some fancy cape work to tire the animal, the matador takes sword in hand to deliver the fatal *estocada* (lunge). This must be done into the neck from a position directly in front of the animal.

In northern Mexico the bullfighting season generally runs from March or April to August or September. In Mexico City's Monumental Plaza México, one of the world's biggest bullrings, and other rings in central and southern Mexico, the main season is from October or November to March. The veteran Eloy Cavasos, from Monterrey, is often acclaimed as Mexico's top matador. Eulalio 'Zotoluco' López is another major established name. Ignacio Garibay and José Luis Angelino are younger stars in their twenties and early thirties. Bullfights featuring star matadors from Spain have extra spice.

For details of upcoming fights, biographies of matadors and plenty more on bullfighting, visit Portal Taurino (www .portaltaurino.com), in Spanish and (sort of) English.

Baseball

Professional *béisbol* has a strong following. The winner of the October-to-January Liga Mexicana del Pacífico, with teams from northwest Mexico, represents Mexico in the February Serie del Caribe (the biggest event in Latin American baseball) against the champions of Venezuela, Puerto Rico and the Dominican Republic. Traditionally the two strongest clubs are the Tomateros of Culiacán and the Naranjeros of Hermosillo. Younger American players on the way up often play in the Pacific league. The Liga Mexicana de Béisbol, with 16 teams spread down the center and east of the country from Monclova to Cancún, plays from March to September.

The Mesoamerican Ballgame (www.ballgame .org) is an interesting educational website about the indigenous ball game, with video of a contest in action.

Other Sports

Charreadas (rodeos) are held, mainly in the northern half of Mexico, during fiestas and at regular venues often called *lienzos charros*.

The highly popular *lucha libre* (wrestling) is more showbiz than sport. Participants in this pantomime-like activity give themselves names like Shocker, Tarzan Boy, Virus and Heavy Metal, then clown around in Day-Glo tights and lurid masks. For the audience it provides a welcome change from real life because the good guys win. Most bouts pit *técnicos* (craftsmen) against *rudos* (rule-breakers). The *rudos,* who generally wear black, usually get the upper hand early on, only to be pounded by the *técnicos* in a stunning reversal of fortune.

Mexico has produced many world champions in boxing. The legendary Julio César Chávez won five world titles at three different weights, and achieved an amazing 90 consecutive wins after turning pro in 1980. Chávez was a classic Mexican boxer – tactically astute but also able to take punishment and hand out even more.

Decharros (www.dechar ros.com) has a calendar of events and much more on *charreadas*, all in Spanish.

Mexico also has a popular professional men's basketball league, the Liga Nacional de Baloncesto Profesional, with teams mainly from the north and center of the country. In 2008–09, teams from Monterrey, Tijuana and Gómez Palacio played in the American Basketball Association.

Golfer Lorena Ochoa, from Guadalajara, is enjoying a fantastically successful career in women's golf, and gained the world number one ranking of the Ladies Professional Golf Association in 2007 – a year in which she won more than US$4 million in prize money.

MEDIA

Mexican network TV is still dominated by the Televisa group, the biggest TV company in the Spanish-speaking world, which runs four national networks and has many local affiliates, and is strongly linked with the PRI, the political party that ran Mexico as a virtual one-party state for 70 years until 2000. Since the PRI's grip was loosened, the rival Azteca group (two networks) has started to undermine Televisa's dominance. Network programming continues to comprise mainly soap operas *(telenovelas)*, ads, game shows, comedy, soccer and a bit of reality TV. However, many hotel rooms now have multichannel cable or satellite systems giving access to international TV. Many home viewers have cable systems too, but still switch to Televisa for news and *telenovelas*. Two good noncommercial Mexican channels, with plenty of arts and documentaries, are Once TV (11 TV), run by Mexico City's Instituto Politécnico Nacional, and Canal 22, run by Conaculta, the National Culture and Arts Council.

For the online editions of about 300 Mexican newspapers and magazines, and links to hundreds of Mexican radio and TV stations and other media sites, visit www .zonalatina.com.

Mexico has around 1400 regional and local radio stations offering a good quota of local news and perky talk, as well as music.

Print media reflect Mexico's political and regional variety, with a spectrum of national and local daily newspapers, and some serious magazine journalism. But the most popular press still lives on a diet of crime and road accidents, with gory photos of the victims. In many cases journalists are constrained by their publishers' commercial requirements, and they can be subject to political pressures and the threat of violence if they make unwelcome revelations. The international watchdog group Reporters Without Borders has declared Mexico to be Latin America's most dangerous country for journalists, with at least 20 journalists murdered between 2005 and 2007. Intimidation by drug gangs is largely to blame, and some local media have stopped covering the gangs' activities.

New media such as online news sites and blogs are less easily influenced or intimidated. You'll find good links to Mexico news providers, including new media, on the **Latin America Network Information Center** (LANIC; http://lanic .utexas.edu/la/mexico/) and on **Planeta** (www.planeta.com).

The Narco News Bulletin (www.narconews.com) provides an alternative left-wing perspective on the drug trade and Mexican human rights issues.

The Arts

Wherever you go in Mexico you'll be amazed by the marvelous creativity on display. Colorful art and beautiful crafts are everywhere; Aztec dancers vibrate in the very heart of Mexico City; musicians strike up on the streets and in the bars and buses; and so many of the country's buildings are works of fine art in themselves. This is a country that has given the world some of its finest painting, music, movies and writing. As you see for yourself how the arts form an essential part of everyday life in this country, you'll start to understand why.

Mexico Connect (www .mexconnect.com) and Mexico Online (www .mexonline.com) feature a wealth of articles and links on Mexican arts.

PAINTING & SCULPTURE

Since pre-Hispanic times, Mexicans have had a love of color and form, and an exciting talent for painting and sculpture. The wealth of modern and historic art in mural form and in the country's many galleries are highlights of the country. Contemporary artists, galleries and patrons have made Mexico City one of the hotspots of today's international art scene.

PRE-HISPANIC

Mexico's first civilization, the Olmecs of the Gulf coast, produced remarkable stone sculptures depicting deities, animals and wonderfully lifelike human forms. Most awesome are the huge Olmec heads, which combine the features of human babies and jaguars.

The Classic Maya of southeast Mexico, at their cultural height from about AD 250 to 800, were perhaps ancient Mexico's most artistically gifted people. They left countless beautiful stone sculptures, complicated in design but possessing great delicacy of touch. Subjects are typically rulers, deities and ceremonies. The art of the later Aztecs reflects their harsh worldview, with many carvings of skulls and complicated symbolic representations of gods.

COLONIAL PERIOD

Mexican art during Spanish rule was heavily Spanish-influenced and chiefly religious in subject, though portraiture grew in popularity under wealthy patrons. The influence of indigenous artisans is seen in the elaborate altar-pieces and sculpted walls and ceilings, overflowing with tiny detail, in churches and monasteries, as well as in fine frescoes. Miguel Cabrera (1695–1768), from Oaxaca, was arguably the most talented painter of the era. His scenes and figures have a sureness of touch lacking in the more labored efforts of others. Cabrera's work can be seen in churches and museums all over Mexico.

MEXICO'S TOP THREE ANCIENT MURAL SITES

- Teotihuacán's **Palacio de Tepantitla** (p211)
- **Cacaxtla** (p236)
- **Bonampak** (p842)

INDEPENDENT MEXICO

The landscapes of José María Velasco (1840–1912) capture the magical qualities of the countryside around Mexico City and areas farther afield, such as Oaxaca.

The years before the 1910 Revolution saw a break from European traditions and the beginnings of socially conscious art. Slums, brothels and indigenous poverty began to appear on canvases. The engravings and cartoons of José Guadalupe Posada (1852–1913), with their characteristic *calavera* (skull) motif, satirized the injustices of the Porfiriato period, launching a long tradition of political and social subversiveness in Mexican art. Gerardo Murillo (1875–1964), also known as Dr Atl, displayed some scandalously orgiastic paintings at a 1910 show marking the centenary of the independence movement.

You can see good collections of José María Velasco's art at Mexico City's Museo Nacional de Arte (p146) and Toluca's Velasco museum (p268).

THE MURALISTS

In the 1920s, immediately following the Mexican Revolution, education minister José Vasconcelos commissioned leading young artists to paint series of public murals to spread a sense of Mexican history and culture and the need for social and technological change. The trio of great muralists – all great painters in smaller scales too – were Diego Rivera (1886–1957), José Clemente Orozco (1883–1949) and David Alfaro Siqueiros (1896–1974).

Rivera's work carried a clear left-wing message, emphasizing past oppression of indigenous people and peasants. His art pulled the country's indigenous and Spanish roots together in colorful, crowded tableaux depicting historical people and events, or symbolic scenes of Mexican life, with a simple moral message. Rivera's works are found in many locations in and around Mexico City.

For the best view of José Guadalupe Posada's creations, head to the Museo José Guadalupe Posada (p598) in his home town of Aguascalientes.

Siqueiros, who fought on the Constitutionalist side in the Revolution (while Rivera was in Europe), remained a political activist afterward. His murals lack Rivera's realism but convey a more clearly Marxist message through dramatic, symbolic depictions of the oppressed and grotesque caricatures of the oppressors. Some of his best works are at the Palacio de Bellas Artes (p147), Castillo de Chapultepec (p153) and Ciudad Universitaria (p157), all in Mexico City.

Orozco, from Jalisco, focused more on the universal human condition than on historical specifics. He conveyed emotion, character and atmosphere. By the 1930s Orozco had grown disillusioned with the Revolution. His work was at its peak in Guadalajara between 1936 and 1939, particularly in the 50-odd frescoes in the Instituto Cultural de Cabañas (p526).

The best books on Diego Rivera include his autobiography *My Art, My Life*, and Patrick Marnham's biography, *Dreaming with His Eyes Open*.

Chief among their successors, Rufino Tamayo (1899–1991) from Oaxaca (also represented in Mexico City's Palacio de Bellas Artes) was absorbed by abstract and mythological scenes and effects of color. Many of his works are easily identified by his trademark watermelon motif (his father was a fruit seller). Juan O'Gorman (1905–82), a Mexican of Irish ancestry, was even more realistic and detailed than Rivera. His multicolored mosaic interpretation of Mexican culture on the Biblioteca Central at Mexico City's Ciudad Universitaria (p157) is his best-known work.

OTHER 20TH-CENTURY ARTISTS

Frida Kahlo (1907–54), physically crippled by a road accident and mentally tormented in her tempestuous marriage to Diego Rivera, painted anguished self-portraits and grotesque, surreal images that expressed her left-wing views and externalized her inner tumult. Kahlo's work suddenly seemed to strike an international chord in the 1980s, becoming as renowned as Rivera's almost overnight. Thanks to the 2002 Hollywood biopic *Frida*, she's now better known worldwide than any other Mexican artist. Her Mexico City home (Museo Frida Kahlo, p158) is a don't-miss for any art lover.

After WWII, the young Mexican artists of La Ruptura (the Rupture) reacted against the muralist movement, which they saw as too didactic and too obsessed with *mexicanidad* (Mexicanness). They explored their urban selves and opened Mexico up to world trends such as abstract expressionism and pop art. The leader of La Ruptura was José Luis Cuevas (b 1934), some of whose work you can see at the Mexico City art museum he founded (p144).

Mexican Muralists by Desmond Rochfort covers the whole muralist movement.

Other fine artists to look for include Juan Soriano (1920–2006), with his iconoclastic, often fantasy-inclined paintings and sculptures; María Izquierdo (1902–55) whose paintings have a dreamlike quality for which many later artists strove; and Oaxacans Francisco Toledo (b 1940) and Rodolfo Morales (1925–2001), who informed their contemporary vision with an exploration of pre-Hispanic roots.

Among the most internationally renowned Mexican artists who emerged in the later 20th century is sculptor Sebastián (b 1947) from Chihuahua, famed for his large, mathematics-inspired sculptures that adorn cities around the world.

CONTEMPORARY ART

The unease and irony of postmodernism found fertile ground among Mexico's ever-questioning intelligentsia from the late 1980s onward. Contemporary art displays a vast diversity of attempts to interpret the urban and global uncertainties of the 21st century. Frida Kahlo, with her unsettling, disturbing images from which many postmodernists drew inspiration, stands as a kind of mother figure amid the maelstrom.

Frida fans should read Hayden Herrera's *Frida: A Biography of Frida Kahlo* and Malka Drucker's *Frida Kahlo*.

Mexico is experiencing a bout of art fever as, thanks to the activities of dynamic independent galleries and patrons, and the globalization of the world's art scenes, the works of Mexican artists are reaching galleries the world over, and art from around the globe is being seen in Mexico. Installations are in vogue, and new cultural centers and art spaces, both publicly and privately run, are springing up all over the country. Even some of the more sedate art museums are staging more temporary exhibits, often showcasing video and other non-mainstream art.

The abstract painting of Francisco Castro Leñero (b 1954) is an extension of La Ruptura; his works have been likened to musical compositions. In general, though, the pendulum has swung away from abstraction to hyper-representation, photo-realism and innovative forms like installations and video. Rocío Maldonado (b 1951), Rafael Cauduro (b 1950) and Roberto Cortázar (b 1962) all paint classically depicted figures against amorphous, bleak backgrounds. Check out Cauduro's hyper-realist murals on state-sponsored crime in Mexico City's Supreme Court building (p145).

The leading lights of Mexico City's contemporary scene, such as Miguel Calderón (b 1971) and Gabriel Orozco (b 1962), spread their talents across many media from sculpture, photography and painting to video and installations, always setting out to challenge preconceptions in one way or another. Another major protagonist of the scene is not an artist but a patron: Eugenio López, heir to the Grupo Jumex fruit-juice empire, has the biggest collection of contemporary Mexican art and, with galleries in Mexico City and Los Angeles, is a major force in its globalization.

Mexico City's new Museo de Arte Popular (p149) showcases the country's folk arts. You can pay a virtual visit at www.map.org.mx.

Fashionable Mexico City suburbs such as Roma and Polanco are full of contemporary galleries, and the youthful cutting edge of the art scene has recolonized streets such as San Jerónimo in the oldest part of the city, the Centro Histórico, with alternative galleries and cafés. Many other cities such as Monterrey (with its Museo de Arte Contemporáneo, p398), Oaxaca,

Tijuana, Hermosillo, Mazatlán, Chihuahua, Cuernavaca, Guadalajara and Morelia all have thriving art scenes. Top international artists are themselves attracted to Mexico: Britain's Damien Hirst, for example, lives part of his life at Troncones on the Pacific coast.

A good way to hook into the art scene is to check some contemporary art sites on the internet (see boxed text, below) then visit some of the galleries and shows. *La Jornada* newspaper has a very good cultural section with daily listings of exhibitions and culture of all kinds.

ARCHITECTURE

Mexico's beautiful and awe-inspiring architectural heritage is one of its top attractions.

PRE-HISPANIC

The ancient civilizations produced some of the most spectacular, eye-pleasing architecture ever built. You can still see fairly intact pre-Hispanic cities at Teotihuacán (p209), Monte Albán (p737), Chichén Itzá (p937) and Uxmal (p925). Their spectacular ceremonial centers were designed to awe, with great stone pyramids, palaces and ball courts. Pyramids usually functioned as the bases for small shrines on their summits. Mexico's three biggest pyramids are the Pirámide del Sol (p211) and Pirámide de la Luna (p211), both at Teotihuacán, and the Pirámide Tepanapa (p228) at Cholula, near Puebla.

The Art of Mesoamerica by Mary Ellen Miller is an excellent survey of pre-Hispanic art and architecture.

There were many differences in architectural styles between the pre-Hispanic civilizations: while Teotihuacán, Monte Albán and Aztec buildings were relatively simple in design, intended to impress with their grand scale, Maya architecture paid more attention to aesthetics, with intricately patterned facades, delicate 'combs' (grid-like arrangements of stone with multiple gaps) on temple roofs, and sinuous carvings. Buildings at such Maya sites as Uxmal, Chichén Itzá and Palenque (p833) are among the most beautiful human creations in the Americas. Maya buildings are characterized by the corbeled vault, their version of the arch: two stone walls leaning toward one another, nearly meeting at the top and surmounted by a capstone.

COLONIAL PERIOD

Many of the fine mansions, churches, monasteries and plazas that today contribute so much to Mexico's beauty were created during the 300 years of Spanish rule. Most were in Spanish styles, but with unique local variations.

Gothic and renaissance styles dominated building in Mexico in the 16th and early 17th centuries. Gothic is typified by soaring buttresses,

---

TOP WEBSITES FOR CONTEMPORARY & MODERN MEXICAN ART

Arte de Oaxaca (www.artedeoaxaca.com) Window on the Oaxacan scene.

Arte México (www.arte-mexico.com) Extensive guide to art in Mexico City.

Artes Visuales (www.artesvisuales.com.mx) Covers Mexico City galleries and museums.

Galería Nina Menocal (www.ninamenocal.com) Mexico City gallery highlighting emerging Latin American artists.

Galería OMR (www.galeriaomr.com) Leading Mexico City gallery with a strong international presence.

Kurimanzutto (www.kurimanzutto.com) Trendy Mexico City gallery with a specialty in installations.

Museo Andrés Blaisten (www.museoblaisten.com) Comprehensive online gallery of 19th- and 20th-century Mexican art.

pointed arches, clusters of round columns and ribbed ceiling vaults. The renaissance saw a return to the disciplined ancient Greek and Roman ideals of harmony and proportion, dominated by shapes like the square and the circle. In Mexico, renaissance architecture usually took the form of plateresque (from *platero,* meaning 'silversmith,' because its decoration resembled ornamented silverwork). Plateresque commonly appears on the facades of buildings, particularly church doorways, which have round arches bordered by classical columns and stone sculpture. A later, more austere renaissance style was called Herreresque, after the Spanish architect Juan de Herrera. Mérida's Catedral de San Ildefonso (p915) and Casa de Montejo (p917) are outstanding renaissance buildings. The cathedrals of Mexico City (p142) and Puebla (p218) mingle renaissance and baroque styles.

Baroque style, which reached Mexico from Spain in the early 17th century, combined renaissance influences with other elements aimed at a dramatic effect – curves, color, contrasts of light and dark, and increasingly elaborate decoration. Painting and sculpture were integrated with architecture, most notably in ornate, often enormous *retablos* (altarpieces – see p90). The finest baroque architecture in Mexico includes the marvelous facade of Zacatecas' cathedral (p586). Mexican baroque reached its final form, Churrigueresque, between 1730 and 1780. This was characterized by spectacularly out-of-control ornamentation – check out the Sagrario Metropolitano (p143) in Mexico City, the Ocotlán sanctuary (p234) at Tlaxcala and Santa Prisca church (p259) in Taxco.

Indigenous artisans added profuse sculpture in stone and colored stucco to many baroque buildings, such as the Capilla del Rosario in Puebla's Templo de Santo Domingo (p220) and the nearby village church of Tonantzintla (p230).

Neoclassical style, dominant in Mexico from about 1780 to 1830, was another return to sober Greek and Roman ideals. An outstanding example is Guanajuato's Alhóndiga de Granaditas (p616).

19TH TO 21ST CENTURIES

Independent Mexico in the 19th and early 20th centuries saw revivals of Gothic and colonial styles and imitations of contemporary French or Italian styles. Mexico City's semi–art nouveau Palacio de Bellas Artes (p147) is one of the finest buildings from this era.

After the Revolution, art deco made an appearance, but more important was the attempt to return to pre-Hispanic roots in the search for a national identity. This trend was known as Toltecism, and many public buildings exhibit the heaviness of Aztec or Toltec monuments. Toltecism culminated in the 1950s with the UNAM campus (p157) in Mexico City, where many buildings are covered with colorful murals.

Modern architects have provided some cities with some eye-catching and adventurous buildings as well as a large quota of dull concrete blocks. Modernist Pedro Ramírez Vásquez (b 1919) designed three vast public buildings in Mexico City: the 1960s Estadio Azteca (p187) and Museo Nacional de Antropología (p153) and the 1970s Basílica de Guadalupe (p162). His work more or less ignores Mexican traditions. The biggest name in contemporary architecture is Ricardo Legorreta (b 1931), who has designed a slew of large buildings in bold concrete shapes and 'colonial' orangey-brown hues. Legorreta is responsible for Mexico City's Centro Nacional de las Artes (p184), Monterrey's Museo de Arte Contemporáneo (p398) and the towers of Mexico City's Plaza Juárez (p148).

Bacaanda (www .bacaanda.org.mx) is a group of pioneering creative folk promoting creativity in many media from visual and plastic arts to design, writing and multimedia.

Pay a virtual visit to Monterrey's excellent Museo de Arte Contemporáneo at www.marco .org.mx.

MUSIC

Music is everywhere in Mexico. It comes booming out of sound systems in markets, shopping streets and passing automobiles, and live musicians may start up at any time, on plazas, in buses or on the Mexico City metro. These performers are playing for a living and range from marimba (wooden xylophone) teams and mariachi bands (trumpeters, violinists, guitarists and a singer, all dressed in smart Wild West–style costumes) to ragged lone buskers with out-of-tune guitars. Mariachi music, perhaps the most 'typical' Mexican music, originated in the Guadalajara area (see p538) but is played nationwide. Marimbas are particularly popular in the southeast and on the Gulf coast.

These performers are among the most visible actors in a huge and vibrant popular music scene that encompasses great stylistic and regional variety. Its outpourings can be heard live at fiestas, nightspots and concerts, or bought from music shops.

ROCK & HIP-HOP

So close to the big US Spanish-speaking market, Mexico can claim to be the most important hub of *rock en español*. Talented Mexico City bands such as Café Tacuba and Maldita Vecindad emerged in the early 1990s and took Mexican rock to new heights and new audiences (well beyond Mexico), mixing a huge range of influences – from rock, hip-hop and ska to traditional Mexican *son* (folk music), bolero or mariachi. Café Tacuba's exciting ability to handle so many styles yet retain their own strong musical identity keeps them at the forefront of Mexican rock today. The albums *Re* (1994), *Avalancha de Éxitos* (1996), *Tiempo Transcurrido* (2001) and *Sino* (2007) are all full of great songs.

The city of Monterrey took the helm in the late 1990s and early 2000s, producing twosome Plastilina Mosh (a kind of Mexican Beastie Boys), hip-hoppers Control Machete, controversial rap-metal band Molotov (who have upset just about everyone with their expletive-laced lyrics), the Britpop-like Zurdok and ragamuffin band El Gran Silencio, most of whom are still active and popular today. Monterrey is also home to Mexico's best-known indie band, Niña, who meld punk, metal, folk and glam influences, and the city continues to throw up creative combinations, although a lot of the most creative and experimental rock is now coming from the indie bands of Guadalajara, with a heavy punk and electronic influence. Look out for bands No+Mas, Buró and Pito Pérez.

Still one of the country's most popular bands is Jaguares, mystical Def Leppard–type rockers who spearheaded the coming of age of Mexican rock in the 1980s under the earlier name Caifanes.

The Mexican band most famous outside its home country is probably Guadalajara's Maná, an unashamedly commercial band with British and Caribbean influences, reminiscent of the Police. And not to be forgotten are El Tri, the grandfathers of Mexican rock, who are still pumping out energetic rock 'n roll after four decades.

POP

Skinny Paulina Rubio is Mexico's answer to Shakira. She has also starred in several Mexican films and TV series. The new generation of Mexicans topping the charts throughout the Hispanic world is headed up by singer Belinda and boy-girl group RBD, all of whom started out as TV soap stars. Balladeer Luis Miguel (born in Veracruz in 1970), meanwhile, is Mexico's Julio Iglesias

Find out what's coming up at Guanajuato's Cervantino festival, Mexico's foremost arts extravaganza, at www.festivalcervantino.gob.mx.

Foreign rock acts were not allowed to play in Mexico until the late 1980s.

and incredibly popular, as is Juan Gabriel, who has sold millions of his own albums and written dozens of hit songs for other singers.

ELECTRONIC MUSIC

Mexico has a big *punchis-punchis* (as Mexicans accurately call it) scene. Almost every weekend there's a big event in or around one of the big cities, where you can enjoy sessions by the country's top DJs and international guests. Top Mexican DJs include Vazik (psychedelic/progressive), Shove (trance) and Forza (trance).

Though they went separate ways (at least temporarily) in 2008, the Tijuana-based Nortec Collective, centered on DJ Bostich and chemical engineer Pepe Mogt, spent several years melding traditional Mexican music with electronica into a unique, fun genre known as Nortec. Look for *The Nortec Sampler* (2000), *Tijuana Sessions Vol 1* (2001) or *Tijuana Sessions Vol 3* (2005). (There's no Volume 2.)

Kinky, from Monterrey, is a group that successfully fuses Latin rock with electronics and gives great live shows. Their most recent album is *Reina* (2006).

Kinetik.tv (www.kinetik.tv) has details of upcoming raves and parties.

REGIONAL & FOLK MUSIC

The deepest-rooted Mexican folk music is *son* (literally, 'sound'), a broad term covering a range of country styles that grew out of the fusion of indigenous, Spanish and African musical cultures. *Son* is essentially guitars plus harp or violin, often played for a foot-stamping dance audience with witty, frequently improvised lyrics.

The most celebrated brands of Mexican *son* come from four areas. From the Huasteca area, inland from Tampico, *son huasteco* features a solo violinist and two guitarists singing falsetto between soaring violin passages. Keep an eye open for *son* festivals or performances by top group Camperos de Valles. In Jalisco, the *sones jaliscenses* originally formed the repertoire of many mariachi bands. The baking-hot Río Balsas basin, southwest of Mexico City, produced perhaps the greatest *son* musician of recent decades, violinist Juan Reynoso. Around Veracruz, the exciting local *son jarocho* is particularly African-influenced; its principal instruments are harp, guitars and the *jarana*, a small guitar-shaped instrument. Harpist La Negra Graciana is one of the greats; Grupo Mono Blanco lead a revival of the genre with contemporary lyrics. The universally known *La Bamba* is a *son jarocho*!

Modern Mexican regional music is rooted in a strong rhythm from several guitars, with voice, accordion, violin or brass providing the melody. *Ranchera* is Mexico's urban 'country music.' This is mostly melodramatic stuff with a nostalgia for rural roots – vocalist-and-combo music, maybe with a mariachi backing. The hugely popular Vicente Fernández, Ana Bárbara, Juan Gabriel and Alejandro Fernández (Vicente's son) are among the leading *ranchera* artists now that past generations of beloved stars like Lola Beltrán, Lucha Reyes, Chavela Vargas and Pedro Infante have died or retired.

Mexico City's annual contemporary art fair, MACO (www.femaco.com), pulls in cognoscenti from the world over.

Norteño is country ballad and dance music, originating in northern Mexico but nationwide in popularity. Its roots are in *corridos*, heroic ballads with the rhythms of European dances such as the polka or waltz, which were brought to southern Texas by 19th-century German and Czech immigrants. Originally the songs were tales of Latino–Anglo strife in the borderlands or themes from the Mexican Revolution. The gritty modern ballads known as *narco-corridos* deal with drug-runners, coyotes and other small-time crooks trying to survive amid big-time corruption and crime, and with the injustices and problems faced by Mexican immigrants in the US. The superstars of *norteño* are Los Tigres del Norte, originally from Sinaloa but now based in California. They play to huge audiences on both sides of the frontier. *Norteño* groups *(conjuntos)* go for 10-gallon hats, with backing centered on the accordion and the *bajo sexto* (a 12-string guitar), along with bass and drums. Los Tigres del Norte added saxophone and absorbed popular *cumbia* rhythms from Colombia. Other leading *norteño* exponents include groups Los Tucanes de Tijuana and Los Huracanes del Norte, and accordionists Ramón Ayala and Flaco Jiménez.

Banda is Mexican big-band music, with large brass sections replacing *norteño's* guitars and accordion. Popular since the 1970s in the hands of Sinaloa's Banda el Recodo, it exploded in popularity nationwide and among US Hispanics in the 1990s.

An exciting talent is Oaxaca-born Lila Downs, who has an American father and Mexican Mixtec mother. Lila has emerged as a passionate and original reinterpreter of Mexican folk songs, often with a jazz influence. Her major albums include *La Sandunga* (1997), *Border* (2001) and *La Cantina* (2006). She sang several songs on the soundtrack of the 2002 movie *Frida*.

Fearful of *narco-corridos'* tendency to glorify the activities of drug runners, several Mexican state governments have encouraged radio stations to ban them.

MÚSICA TROPICAL

Though its origins lie in the Caribbean and South America, several brands of *música tropical* or *música afroantillana* have become integral parts of the Mexican musical scene. Two types of dance music – *danzón,* originally from Cuba, and *cumbia,* from Colombia – both took deeper root in Mexico than in their original homelands (see p87). Some *banda* and *norteño* groups throw in a lot of *cumbia. Cumbia sonidera* is *cumbia* as played by some DJs in central Mexico and the US, with their own mixes, speeds, intros and outros.

TROVA

This genre of troubadour-type folk music has roots in 1960s and '70s songs. Typically performed by singer–songwriters *(cantautores)* with a solitary guitar, it's still popular. Fernando Delgadillo and Nicho Hinojosa are leading artists.

Many *trova* singers are strongly inspired by Cuban political musician Silvio Rodríguez. Powerful and popular singers like Eugenia León, Tania Libertad and the satirical cabaret artist Astrid Hadad are sometimes categorized under *trova,* but they actually range widely over Mexican song forms and are all well worth hearing.

CINEMA

A clutch of fine, gritty movies by young directors has thrust modern Mexican cinema into the limelight, garnering commercial success as well as critical acclaim after decades in the doldrums. These films confronted the ugly and the absurd in Mexican life as well as the beautiful, comical and sad. Alfonso Arau's *Como Agua para Chocolate* (Like Water for Chocolate; 1992) and Guillermo del Toro's 1993 horror movie *Cronos* set the ball rolling, then in 1999 Mexicans flocked to see Antonio Serrano's *Sexo, Pudor y Lágrimas* (Sex, Shame and Tears), a comic but sad tale of young couples' relationships.

But the first to really catch the world's eye was the 2000 film *Amores Perros* (Love's a Bitch), directed by Alejandro González Iñárritu and starring Gael García Bernal. Set in contemporary Mexico City, with three plots connected by one traffic accident, it's a raw, honest movie with its quota of graphic blood, violence and sex.

Arguably the most famous of all Mexican film actors was Zorba the Greek – Anthony Quinn (1915-2001), born Antonio Quiñones in Chihuahua. His family moved to the US when he was four months old.

MEXICO GOES TO HOLLYWOOD – OR NOT?

It might seem at first glance that the brightest talents of new Mexican cinema are turning their backs on their home country for the glamour and big dollars of Hollywood. In reality, these top directors and actors retain strong Mexican links not only in their themes and settings but also in their production companies. While Alejandro González Iñárritu followed his Mexican-made *Amores Perros* with two Hollywood productions in *21 Grams* and *Babel*, he kept in touch with Mexico by setting one of the plots of *Babel* astride the US–Mexico border and casting Gael García Bernal in it. Screenwriter for all three of these successful movies was Mexican Guillermo Arriaga, although unfortunately the pair reportedly fell out after *Babel*.

Alfonso Cuarón had already made Hollywood movies (including *A Little Princess* and *Great Expectations*) before coming home to Mexico for *Y Tu Mamá También*, then returning to Hollywood for *Harry Potter and the Prisoner of Azkaban* and *Children of Men*. Cuarón looks set to return to Mexico in every way with the eagerly awaited *Mexico 68*, a film about the 1968 Tlatelolco Massacre, due out in 2009.

Guillermo del Toro made his 1993 success, *Cronos*, in Mexico, but moved to California in 1998 after his father was kidnapped in Mexico. He set up his own production company, the Tequila Gang, to make films such as *the Devil's Backbone* (2001) and *Pan's Labyrinth* (2006), both set in Spain, but looks likely to turn to Hollywood backing if, as is mooted, he directs *The Hobbit*.

Actor Gael García Bernal starred in three of the biggest Mexican-made successes – *Amores Perros*, *Y Tu Mamá También* and *El Crimen del Padre Amaro* – and starred in the Mexican leg of González Iñárritu's *Babel*. García Bernal at least kept a Latin American focus in his biggest non-Mexican role, playing Che Guevara in *The Motorcycle Diaries*, directed by Brazil's Walter Salles for the British production company FilmFour. He is set to star in a film of the greatest Mexican novel, Juan Rulfo's *Pedro Páramo*, with top Spanish director Mateo Gil.

Y Tu Mamá También (And Your Mother Too), Alfonso Cuarón's 2002 'growing up' road movie of two teenagers (Gael García Bernal and Diego Luna) from privileged Mexico City circles, was at the time the biggest grossing Mexican film ever, netting more than US$25 million.

Another 2002 success, *El Crimen del Padre Amaro* (The Crime of Father Amaro), directed by Carlos Carrera and again starring Gael García Bernal, painted an ugly picture of corruption in the Catholic church in a small Mexican town.

After *Amores Perros*, Alejandro González Iñárritu moved to Hollywood to direct two more great movies with interconnected multiple plots. *21 Grams* (2003), with Sean Penn, Benicio del Toro and Naomi Watts, had nothing to do with Mexico, but the global *Babel* (2006), with Brad Pitt, Cate Blanchett and (yet again) Gael García Bernal, weaves a sad US–Mexico cross-border tale in with its other Moroccan and Japanese threads. *Babel* received seven Oscar nominations.

Alfonso Cuarón stepped from *Y Tu Mamá También* to *Harry Potter and the Prisoner of Azkaban* (2004), then directed *Children of Men* (2006), a grim but highly acclaimed science fiction tale set in a future England featuring Clive Owen, Julianne Moore and Michael Caine, which received three Oscar nominations. Guillermo del Toro's *Pan's Labyrinth* was one of the most internationally successful films of 2006, winning three Academy Awards with a dual plot in which a young girl lives out fairy-tale adventures in a fantasy world, against a background of the harsh realities of post–Civil War 1940s Spain.

Mexican-made films also continued to flourish. Carlos Reygadas' *Batalla en el Cielo* (Battle in Heaven; 2005) was a graphic tale of kidnapping, prostitution and brutal Mexico City realities, but the country's big hit of that year was Fernando Kalife's *7 Días* (7 Days), the story of a lowly music promoter's miraculous coup of getting U2 to play in his home town,

Monterrey. The big success of 2007 was *El Violín* (The Violin), directed by Francisco Vargas, with a great performance by Ángel Tavira in a story set amid the country's rural guerrilla struggles of the 1970s.

The historical golden age of Mexican movie-making was WWII, when the country was turning out up to 200 films a year, typically epic, melodramatic productions. Hollywood reasserted itself after the war and Mexican filmmakers have struggled for funds ever since. But Mexico has the world's seventh-biggest cinema audience, and locally made films attract around 10% of that group. Mexico still has a high-class movie-making infrastructure, with plenty of technical expertise and up-to-the-minute equipment. The country now produces more than 50 films a year, a big increase on a decade ago. Several cities hold annual film festivals, including Morelia (p560), Mexico City (p183) and Monterrey (p404).

LITERATURE

Mexicans such as Carlos Fuentes, Juan Rulfo and Octavio Paz produced some of the great Spanish-language writing of the 20th century, and the contemporary literary scene is throwing up some bold talents.

Internationally, the prolific novelist and commentator Carlos Fuentes (b 1928) is probably Mexico's best-known writer. His first and one of his best novels, *Where the Air is Clear* (1958), traces the lives of various Mexico City dwellers through Mexico's post-revolutionary decades in a critique of the Revolution's failure. *The Death of Artemio Cruz* (1962) takes another critical look at the post-revolutionary era through the eyes of a dying, corrupted press baron and landowner. Fuentes' *Aura* (1962) is a magical book with one of the most stunning endings of any novel. *La Silla del Águila* (The Eagle Throne; 2003) again deals with political corruption and cynicism. It's set in 2020 when an all-powerful US has cut Mexico's access to telecommunications and computers, Condoleezza Rice is US president, and a vicious struggle is being played out for the lifetime presidency of Mexico.

In Mexico, Juan Rulfo (1918–86) is widely regarded as the supreme novelist. His *Pedro Páramo* (1955), about a young man's search for his lost father among ghostlike villages in western Mexico, is a scary, desolate work with confusing shifts of time – a kind of Mexican *Wuthering Heights* with a spooky, magical-realist twist. Some regard it as the ultimate expression of Latin American existence, and Rulfo certainly never felt the need to write anything else afterward.

Octavio Paz (1914–98), poet, essayist and winner of the 1990 Nobel Prize in Literature, wrote a probing, intellectually acrobatic analysis of Mexico's myths and the Mexican character in *The Labyrinth of Solitude*

Despite faint critical praise, *Frida,* Julie Taymor's 2002 factually informative movie biography, shouldn't be missed for its strong Mexican period atmosphere and a fine performance by Salma Hayek as Ms Kahlo.

THREE FILMS YOU PROBABLY DIDN'T KNOW WERE SHOT IN MEXICO

Titanic Twentieth Century Fox built an entire 184,000 sq meter studio near Playas de Rosarito, Baja California, for the 1997 multi-Oscar epic. The facility has since been used for *Pearl Harbor, Jackass* and *Master and Commander: The Far Side of the World.*

Romeo & Juliet Baz Luhrmann transplanted his 1996 version of Shakespeare's Italian tragedy, with Leonardo di Caprio and Claire Danes, to a fictional Florida city called Verona Beach – really a combination of Mexico City and Veracruz.

Missing Costa-Gavras' chilling 1982 political thriller about the coup that overthrew Salvador Allende in Chile used Mexico City as a substitute for Santiago. Jack Lemmon and Sissy Spacek starred.

(1950). Decide for yourself whether you agree with his pessimistic assessments of his fellow Mexicans. Paz's *Sor Juana* (1982) reconstructed the life of Mexico's earliest literary giant, Sister Juana Inés de la Cruz, a 17th-century courtesan-turned-nun (and proto-feminist) whose love poems, plays, romances and essays were aeons ahead of their time.

The 1960s-born novelists who form the *movimiento crack* have nothing to do with drugs – they take their name from the sound of a limb falling off a tree, an image that represents these writers' desire to break with Mexico's literary past. Their work tends to adopt global themes and international settings. Best known is Jorge Volpi, whose *In Search of Klingsor* (1999) has been an international best-seller. With an exciting plot around post-WWII efforts to unmask the scientist in charge of Nazi Germany's atomic weapons program, it also weaves in a good deal of scientific theory to make sure your brain cells don't rest. Ignacio Padilla also took Nazism as a theme in his sophisticated *Shadow Without a Name* (2000).

The relationship between Diego and Frida and the cultural upheaval they lived through are explored in the well-illustrated *Frida Kahlo and Diego Rivera* by Isabel Alcantara and Sandra Egnolff.

Northern Mexican writers, mostly born in the 1960s and focusing on themes like violence, corruption, drug trafficking, the border and conflicts of identity, have produced some of the most immediate and gritty new Mexican writing. Juan José Rodríguez (*Mi Nombre es Casablanca,* 2003), Raúl Manríquez (*La Vida a Tientas,* 2003) and Élmer Mendoza (*Un Asesino Solitario,* 1999) tell of explosive violence provoked by drug conflicts.

The Mexican Revolution yielded a school of novels: the classic is *The Underdogs,* the story of a peasant who becomes a general, by Mariano Azuela (1873–1952). Modern writers have also been inspired by the Revolution and its aftermath: Laura Esquivel (b 1950) made her name with *Like Water for Chocolate* (1989), a rural love story interwoven with both fantasy and cooking recipes set during the Revolution, while *Tear This Heart Out* (1985), by Ángeles Mastretta (b 1949), is amusingly written as the memoir of the wife of a ruthless political boss. Two more fine books by Mastretta are *Lovesick* (1996), about a woman torn between two very different lovers, and *Women with Big Eyes* (2004), a set of tales of women who played important roles in her own life.

Rosario Castellanos (1925–74), from Chiapas, an early champion of women's and indigenous rights, wrote of the injustices that provoked the 1994 Zapatista rebellion decades before it happened. *The Book of Lamentations* (1962) draws on earlier historical events for its story of an indigenous uprising in the 1930s.

In poetry, the great figures are Octavio Paz and a reclusive figure from Chiapas, Jaime Sabines (1925–99), who both treated themes of love and death with stark, vivid imagery.

DANCE

INDIGENOUS DANCE

Traditional indigenous dances are among the most colorful ingredients of many Mexican fiestas. There are hundreds of them, some popular in several parts of the country, others danced only in a single town or village. Many bear traces of pre-Hispanic ritual, having evolved from old fertility rites and other ancient practices. Other dances tell stories of Spanish or colonial origin – Oaxaca's Danza de las Plumas (Feather Dance) represents the Spanish conquest of Mexico, while the fairly widespread Moros y Cristianos re-enacts the victory of Christians over Muslims in 15th-century Spain.

MEXICO IN OTHERS' WORDS

Mexico has inspired much fine writing from non-Mexicans. Graham Greene's *The Power and the Glory* dramatizes the state–church conflict that followed the Mexican Revolution. *Under the Volcano* (1938) by Malcolm Lowry follows a dipsomaniac British diplomat in Mexico who drinks himself to death on the Day of the Dead.

B Traven is best known as the author of the 1935 adventure story of gold and greed in northwest Mexico, *The Treasure of the Sierra Madre*. But he wrote many other novels set in the country, chiefly the six of the Jungle series – among them *The Rebellion of the Hanged*, *General from the Jungle* and *Trozas* – focusing on pre-revolutionary oppression in Chiapas. The identity of Traven himself is one of literature's great mysteries. Was he really a Bavarian anarchist called Ret Marut, or a Norwegian American living reclusively in Acapulco called Traven Torsvan? Quite likely he was both.

The beat generation spent plenty of time in Mexico, too: William Burroughs' early novel *Queer* chronicles the guilt, lust and drug excesses of an American in Mexico City in the 1940s. The city was also the scene of parts of Burroughs' *Junky* and Jack Kerouac's *On the Road* and *Tristessa*, and was where Kerouac wrote his long work of jazz poetry *Mexico City Blues*, as well as two other novels.

Recent decades have brought some fine new English-language novels set in Mexico. Cormac McCarthy's marvelous *All the Pretty Horses* is the laconic, tense, poetic tale of three young latter-day cowboys riding south of the border. *The Crossing* and *Cities of the Plain* completed McCarthy's Border Trilogy. James Maw's *Year of the Jaguar* (1996) catches the feel of Mexican travel superbly, taking its youthful English protagonist from the US border to Chiapas in an exciting search for a father he has never met. Australian Meaghan Delahunt's *In the Casa Azul* (2002) revolves around a Mexico City fling between Frida Kahlo and Russian Leon Trotsky, against the canvas of Trotsky's mortal struggle with his Soviet rival Stalin.

For nonfiction travel writing set in Mexico, see p34.

Nearly all traditional dances require special colorful costumes, sometimes including masks. The Danza de las Plumas and the Danza de los Quetzales (Quetzal Dance), from Puebla state, both feature enormous feathered headdresses or shields.

Today some of these dances are performed outside their sacred context, as simple spectacles. The Ballet Folklórico (p184) in Mexico City brings together traditional dances from all over the country in a spectacular stage show. Other folkloric dance performances can be seen in several cities and at festivals such as the Oaxaca's July Guelaguetza (p727).

LATIN DANCE

Caribbean and South American dances are highly popular in Mexico. This is tropical ballroom dancing to percussion-heavy, infectiously rhythmic music. The capital city has numerous clubs and large dance halls devoted to this scene (see p185), often hosting bands from the Caribbean or South America. One of the more formal, old-fashioned varieties of Latin dance is the elegant *danzón*, originally from Cuba and associated mostly with the port city of Veracruz. *Cumbia*, from Colombia but now with its adopted home in Mexico City, is livelier, more flirtatious and less structured. It rests on thumping bass lines with brass, guitars, mandolins and sometimes marimbas.

Salsa developed in New York when jazz met *son*, and cha-cha and rumba came from Cuba and Puerto Rico. Musically it boils down to brass (with trumpet solos), piano, percussion, singer and chorus – the dance is a hot one with a lot of exciting turns. Merengue, mainly from the Dominican Republic, is a *cumbia*–salsa blend with a hopping step; the rhythm catches the shoulders, the arms go up and down. The music is strong on maracas, and the musicians go for puffed-up sleeves.

FOLK ART

Popularte (www.uv.mx /popularte) provides an online introduction to Mexican *artesanías*, albeit with slightly confusing navigation.

Mexicans' skill with their hands and their love of color, beauty, fun and tradition are expressed everywhere in their myriad appealing *artesanías* (handicrafts). The decorative crafts that catch the eye in shops and markets today are counterparts to the splendid costumes, beautiful ceramics and elaborate jewelry used by the ancient Aztec and Maya nobility, and many modern craft techniques, designs and materials are easily traced to pre-Hispanic origins. Selling folk art to tourists and collectors has been an ever-growing business for Mexican artisans since before WWII.

TEXTILES

If you get out to some of Mexico's indigenous villages you'll be stunned by the variety of intensely colorful, intricately decorated everyday attire, differing from area to area and often village to village. Traditional costume – more widely worn by women than men – serves as a mark of the community to which a person belongs. Some garments are woven or embroidered with webs of animal, human, plant and mythical shapes that can take months to complete.

Diamond shapes on some *huipiles* from San Andrés Larrainzar, in Chiapas, represent the universe of the villagers' Maya ancestors, who believed that the earth was a cube and the sky had four corners.

Four main types of women's garments have been in use since long before the Spanish conquest. A long, sleeveless tunic *(huipil)* is found mainly in the southern half of the country. The *enredo* is a wraparound skirt, almost invisible if worn beneath a long *huipil*. The *enredo* is held in place by a *faja* (waist sash). The *quechquémitl* is a shoulder cape with an opening for the head, found mainly in the center and north of Mexico.

Spanish missionaries introduced blouses, which are now often embroidered with just as much care and detail as the more traditional garments. Also dating from Spanish times is the *rebozo*, a long shawl that may cover the shoulders or head or be used for carrying. The male equivalent of the *rebozo* is the sarape, a blanket with an opening for the head.

The basic materials of indigenous weaving are cotton and wool, though synthetic fibers are now common too. Dye, too, is often synthetic today, but natural dyes are still in use or are being revived – deep blues from the indigo plant; reds and browns from various woods; reds, pinks and purples from the cochineal insect (chiefly used in Oaxaca state).

The Crafts of Mexico is a gorgeously illustrated coffee-table volume by Margarita de Orel-lana and Albertio Ruy Sánchez, editors of the superb magazine *Artes de México*, focusing on ceramics and textiles.

The basic indigenous weavers' tool – used only by women – is the *telar de cintura* (back-strap loom) on which the warp (long) threads are stretched between two horizontal bars, one of which is fixed to a post or tree, while the other is attached to a strap that goes around the weaver's lower back; the weft (cross) threads are then woven in. A variety of sophisticated techniques is used to weave amazing patterns into the cloth. *Huipiles* in the southern states of Oaxaca and Chiapas are among Mexico's most intricate and eye-catching garments.

One textile art that's practised by men is weaving on a treadle loom, which is operated by foot pedals. The treadle loom can weave wider cloth than the back-strap loom and tends to be used for blankets, rugs, *rebozos*, sarapes and skirt material. It allows for great intricacy in design. Mexico's most famous rug-weaving village is Teotitlán del Valle, Oaxaca.

The 'yarn paintings' of the Huichol people – created by pressing strands of wool or acrylic yarn onto a wax-covered board – depict scenes resembling visions experienced under the influence of the drug peyote, which is central to Huichol culture.

CERAMICS

Because of its durability, pottery tells us much of what we know about Mexico's ancient cultures. Today the country still has many small-scale potters' workshops turning out everything from plain cooking pots to elaborate decorative pieces that are true works of art.

One highly attractive variety of Mexican pottery is Talavera, made chiefly in Puebla and Dolores Hidalgo and characterized by bright colors (blue and yellow are prominent) and floral designs. The Guadalajara suburbs of Tonalá and Tlaquepaque are the country's most renowned pottery centers, producing a wide variety of ceramics. In northern Mexico the villagers of Mata Ortiz make a range of beautiful earthenware, drawing on the techniques and designs of pre-Hispanic Paquimé, similar to some of the native American pottery of the US southwest. Another distinctive Mexican ceramic form is the *árbol de la vida* (tree of life). These large, elaborate, candelabra-like objects are molded by hand and decorated with numerous tiny figures of people, animals, plants and so on. The Garden of Eden is one common subject. Some of the best are made in the towns of Acatlán de Osorio and Izúcar de Matamoros, in Puebla state, and Metepec, in the state of México. Metepec is also the source of colorful clay suns.

The areas producing the most exciting *artesanías* are mostly those with prominent indigenous populations, in states such as Chiapas, Guerrero, México, Michoacán, Oaxaca, Puebla and Sonora.

MASKS

For millennia Mexicans have worn masks for magical purposes in dances, ceremonies and shamanistic rites: the wearer temporarily becomes the creature, person or deity represented by the mask. Today, these dances often have a curious mixture of pre-Hispanic and Christian or Spanish themes. A huge range of masks exists, and you can admire their artistry at museums in cities such as San Luis Potosí, Zacatecas, Morelia and Colima, and at shops and markets around the country. The southern state of Guerrero has probably the broadest range of fine masks.

Wood is the basic material of most masks, but papier-mâché, clay, wax and leather are also used. Mask-makers often paint or embellish their masks with real teeth, hair, feathers or other adornments. 'Tigers,' often looking more like jaguars, are common, as are other animals and birds, and also Christ, devils and Europeans with comically pale, wide-eyed, mustachioed features.

Today, masks are also made for hanging on walls.

LACQUERWARE & WOODWORK

Gourds, the hard shells of certain squash-type fruits, have been used in Mexico since antiquity as bowls, cups and small storage vessels. Today they also serve as children's rattles, maracas and even hats. The most eye-catching decoration technique is lacquering, in which the gourd is coated with layers of paste or paint, each left to harden before the next is applied. The final layer is painted with the artisan's chosen design, then coated with oil varnish. All this makes the gourd nonporous and, to some extent, heat resistant.

Most lacquerware you'll see in Mexico today is pine or a sweetly scented wood from remote Olinalá in Guerrero. Olinalá boxes, trays, chests and furniture are lacquered by the *rayado* method, in which designs are created by scraping off part of the top coat of paint to expose a different-colored layer below.

Among Mexico's finest wooden crafts are the polished ironwood carvings of the Seri people of Sonora, who work the hard wood into dramatic human, animal and sea-creature shapes (see boxed text, p329). Also attractive are

Chronicle Books publishes beautiful photo essays on Mexican style and crafts, including *Mexicolor* by Melba Levick, Tony Cohan and Masako Takahashi (on Mexican design) and *In a Mexican Garden* by Melba Levick and Gina Hyams.

the brightly painted copal dragons and other imaginary beasts, known as *alebrijes,* produced by villagers around Oaxaca city.

JEWELRY & METALWORK

Some ancient Mexicans were expert metalsmiths and jewelers, but the Spanish banned indigenous people from working gold and silver for a time during the colonial period. Indigenous artisanship was revived in the 20th century, most famously in Taxco, by the American William Spratling, who initiated a silver-craft industry that now supplies more than 300 shops in the town. Silver is much more widely available than gold in Mexico, and is fashioned in all manner of styles and designs, with artistry ranging from the dully imitative to the superb.

Precious stones are less common than precious metals. True jade, beloved of ancient Mexicans, is now a rarity – most 'jade' jewelry is actually jadeite, serpentine or calcite.

Oaxaca city is the center of a thriving craft in tinplate, stamped into low relief and painted in hundreds of colorful designs.

RETABLOS

An engaging Mexican custom is to adorn the sanctuaries of saints or holy images with *retablos* (also called *exvotos*), small paintings giving thanks to a saint for answered prayers. Typically done on small sheets of tin, but sometimes on glass, wood or cardboard, they depict these miracles in touchingly literal images painted by their beneficiaries. They may show a cyclist's hair's-breadth escape from a hurtling bus, or an immigrant worker's safe return home from the US, beside a representation of the saint and a brief message along the lines of 'Thanks to San Miguel for taking care of me – José Suárez, June 6, 2006.' The Basílica de Guadalupe (p162) in Mexico City, the Santuario de Plateros (p593) near Fresnillo in Zacatecas, and the church at Real de Catorce (p609) in San Luis Potosí state all have fascinating collections of *retablos.*

Chloe Sayer's fascinating *Arts and Crafts of Mexico* traces the evolution of crafts from pre-Hispanic times to the present, with many fine photos.

See a great collection of modern *retablos* and *exvotos* in *Contemporary Mexican Votive Painting* by Alfredo Vilchis Roque.

Food & Drink Mauricio Velázquez de León

In Mexico we love food, especially our own. When visiting the country you will soon get a sense of how important food is in our lives. Ask a group of Mexicans where to find, say, the best *carnitas* (braised pork) in Mexico City or the best *mole* in Oaxaca and you are up for a passionate, lengthy and well-informed debate that will fill a notebook with names of places that you *must* go to and specialties that you *must* try. Interestingly, if you ask who is the best cook they know, they all will be in agreement: *mi madre* (my mother). Another point most Mexicans agree with is that Mexican cuisine has little to do with what is served as Mexican fare in restaurants outside the country. For many visitors their first experience with real Mexican food will be a surprise. There will be no big hats and piñatas hanging from the ceiling, no flavored margaritas, oversized burritos, or cheese nachos on the menu. The food will be fresh, simple and, frequently, locally grown – and, most likely, somebody's mom will be running the kitchen.

During your visit you'll find that the ingredients and methods are far-reaching and varied, and closely connected with the history of each of the country's regions and the character of its peoples. Take a look at the history of the Mayas and you'll see that corn plays a main role. Should you read about the gargantuan markets in Aztec cities you will share the amazement of the Spanish conquistadores. In Diego Rivera's murals you will discover the vast range of Mexican produce. Not surprisingly, one of Mexico's best-known contemporary films, *Like Water for Chocolate*, is based on the power of food. So, if you want to know Mexico and its people, to understand its history and its regions, you ought to try the food.

When the Spanish arrived in Mexico in 1519 they found that the Aztec, Maya, Mixtec and other Mesoamerican civilizations had built a horticultural system that produced different strains of beans, squashes, chilies, sweet potatoes, tomatoes and the small-husked green tomatoes known as tomatillos. Avocados, papayas and pineapples were plentiful, and so was an incredible variety of fish. Turkey, duck, quail and venison were slowly simmered in sauces using seeds, nuts and chilies. Moreover, the conquistadores found that a wild maize had been domesticated into corn, creating the building blocks of an entire civilization's cuisine that lives to this day. The Spaniards, in turn, brought spices like cinnamon, black pepper and clove, old-world staples like wheat, rice, onions and grapes, and introduced hogs, cattle and chickens to the new continent. For the next 500 years, the Mexican cuisine evolved into what we know today. Dishes such as *pipián*, a sauce thickened with pumpkin seeds, chilies and tomatoes, stayed the same, while others, such as *Huachinango a la veracruzana,* a dish of red snapper cooked in a sauce with tomatoes, jalapeño chilies, cinnamon, capers, olives and white

Mauricio was born in Mexico City, where he was given boiled chicken feet and toasted corn tortillas to sooth his teething pains. Mauricio has worked for a variety of newspapers and magazines, and his food writing has been widely published. He currently works in New York City as an editor, writer and father of twin toddlers, whose teething pains were soothed with toasted corn tortillas.

THE LADIES BEHIND THE COMAL (GRIDDLE)

The Mexican kitchen is very much a matriarchal place where woman have run the show for centuries. Currently, the most visible women cooks are cookbook author and owner of Izote restaurant (p177) Patricia Quintana, chef and owner of El Bajío restaurant (p177) Carmen 'Titita' Ramirez, author and restaurateur Alicia Gironella and British-born bestselling author Diana Kennedy, but it is in the hands and memories of ordinary Mexican women that the food of this country is practiced and preserved every day.

wine, became classic Mexican dishes by blending indigenous and Spanish ingredients and techniques.

By 1864, Mexico's culinary map was again redefined, this time by the invasion of French troops. The French army's goal was to collect part of the debt Mexico owed in the aftermath of the Mexican Revolution, and Napoleon III sent Maximilian of Hapsburg to rule as emperor. Maximilian and his wife, Carlota, brought to Mexico many customs of French society – architecture, fashion and food – and while privileged Mexicans quickly embraced this chic cultural influx, the majority of the population received the invaders violently. Within four years they had killed Maximilian, forced Carlota back to Europe (where she went insane) and regained control of the country. But what Mexican patriots revolted against, Mexican cooks embraced – when the French left, their cooking techniques stayed. Today it is natural to see a cook in a Mexican kitchen preparing a number of dishes using a *baño maría* (bainmarie) or filling puff pastry shells to make savory *bolovanes* (vol-au-vent). The famous Mexican *tortas* are made with a type of bread that in Mexico City we call *bolillo* and in Guadalajara it is called *birote*, but any foodie outside Mexico will call French Roll.

STAPLES & SPECIALTIES

The staples of Mexican food are corn, an array of dry and fresh chilies and beans. Corn's main manifestation is in the tortilla but, according to historian Eusebio Dávalos Hurtado there are more than 700 dishes that use corn as a base in Mexico.

Contrary to popular belief, not all food in Mexico is spicy, at least not for the regular palate. Chilies are used as flavoring ingredients and to provide intensity in sauces, *moles* and *pipiáns,* and many appreciate their depth over their piquancy. But beware. Many dishes indeed have a kick, reaching daredevil levels in some cases. The *habanero* chili in the Yucatan is the most spicy pepper in the world, and the *chile de árbol* used in the famous *tortas ahogadas* (drowned *tortas*) in Guadalajara can be terribly fierce. A good rule of thumb is that when chilies are cooked and incorporated into the dishes as sauces they tend to be on the mild side, but when they are prepared for salsas or relishes, intended for use as condiments over tacos and other foods, they can be really hot.

There are other Mexican food staples that give this food its classic flavoring. Among them are spices like cinnamon, clove and cumin, and herbs such as thyme, oregano and, most importantly, cilantro and *epazote. Epazote* may be the unsung hero of Mexican cooking. This pungent-smelling herb (called pigweed or Jerusalem oak in the US) is used for flavoring beans, soups, stews and certain *moles.* You may never see it in your dish, as it is removed when the cooking is finished.

Specialties vary dramatically from region to region, but there is no doubt that *mole* (see the boxed text, p94) and *antojitos* are in the center of what represents Mexican cooking. The problem with the word *antojitos* is that it can encompass everything, as the word *antojo* translates as 'a whim, a sudden craving.' Hence an *antojito* is a little whim but, as any Mexican will quickly point out, it is not just a snack. In my view, *antojitos* are more like the Spanish tapas. You can have an entire meal of *antojitos,* or have a couple as appetizers, or yes, eat one as a *tentempíe* (quick bite), before hopping in the subway or while standing outside a bar. The American award-wining chef and author Rick Bayless has a great way to define *antojitos* by grouping them according to the one component present in all: corn masa (dough). Using this criterion we can say that there are eight types of *antojitos*: tacos, quesadillas, enchiladas, tostadas, *sopes, gorditas, chilaquiles* and *tamales.*

Tacos The quintessential culinary fare in Mexico can be made of any cooked meat, fish or vegetable wrapped in a tortilla, with a dash of salsa and garnished with onion and cilantro. Soft corn tortillas are used to wrap grilled meats in *tacos al carbón*, an array of stews in *tacos de guisado* or with griddle-cooked meats and vegetables in *tacos a la plancha*. When tacos are filled with chicken, barbacoa, potatoes or cheese and lightly fried they are called *tacos dorados*. If you are in northern Mexico, chances are you will find tacos with flour tortilla (*tortilla de harina*) and the fillings will be more meat-based than vegetarian.

Quesadillas Fold a tortilla with cheese, heat it on a griddle and you have a quesadilla. (*Queso* means cheese, hence the name.) But real quesadillas are much more than that. In restaurants and street stalls quesadillas are stuffed pockets made with raw corn masa that is lightly fried or griddled until crisp. They can be stuffed with *chorizo* and cheese, squash blossoms, mushrooms with garlic, *chicharrón*, beans, stewed chicken or meat.

Enchiladas In Spanish *enchilar* means to put chili over something; therefore enchiladas are a group of three or four lightly fried tortillas filled with chicken, cheese or eggs and covered with a cooked salsa, such as tomatillo (*enchiladas verdes*), tomato (*enchiladas rojas*) or enchiladas with *mole*. Enchiladas are usually a main dish, and can also be baked, like the famous *enchiladas suizas* (Swiss-style enchiladas).

Tostadas Tortillas that have been baked or fried until they get crisp and and are then cooled. The idea is that in this state they can hold a variety of toppings. *Tostadas de pollo* are a beautiful layering of beans, chicken, cream, shredded lettuce, onion, avocado and *queso fresco* (a fresh cheese).

Sopes Small masa shells, 2 or 3 inches in diameter, that are shaped by hand and cooked on a griddle with a thin layer of beans, salsa and cheese. *Chorizo* is also a common topping for *sopes*.

Gorditas Round masa cakes that are baked until they puff. Sometimes *gorditas* are filled with a thin layer of fried black or pinto beans, or even fava beans. In some regions, *gorditas* have an oval shape and are known as *tlacoyos*.

Chilaquiles Started as a way to utilize leftover tortillas and typically served as breakfast. Corn tortillas are cut in triangles and fried until crispy. At this point they are indeed tortilla chips, or *totopos*, as they are known in Mexico. When cooked in a tomatillo (*chilaquiles verdes*) or tomato salsa (*chilaquiles rojos*) they become soft and are then topped with shredded cheese, sliced onions and sour cream. If you want a hearty breakfast, order them topped with shredded chicken (*chilaquiles con pollo*) or topped with two fried eggs (*chilaquiles con huevo*).

Tamales Made with masa mixed with lard, stuffed with stewed meat, fish or vegetables, wrapped and steamed. The word comes from the Náhuatl word *tamalli* and refers to anything wrapped up. Every region in the country has its own special *tamal*, the most famous being the Oaxacan-style tamales with *mole* and wrapped in banana leaves, the Mexico City *tamales* with chicken and green tomatillo sauce wrapped in corn husks, and the Yucatecan style, made with chicken marinated in *achiote* (annatto paste) and wrapped in banana leaves.

MARKETS

Markets are perfect places to experiment the Mexican way of life and munch on some really good *antojitos*. You can find a *mercado* in any city, but the food offerings will vary from region to region. Markets tend to have a specific section for prepared foods where you can sit around a small counter or at large communal tables. In the gargantuan Mercado de la Merced in Mexico City (p189; covering 113 acres, it's the largest market in Latin America) the best *antojito* may be the *huarache*, a foot-long tortilla shaped like the shoe for which it is named, grilled and topped with salsa, onions, cheese and a choice of *chorizo*, steak, squash blossoms and more. The *huarache* competitor can be found in the markets of Oaxaca City where large flat tortillas called *tlayudas* are spread with refried beans and topped with Oaxacan string cheese, salsa and pork strips. In the street that separates the Mercado Juárez and Mercado 20 de Noviembre in Oaxaca you may want to try the *chapulines*, or grasshoppers, fried with garlic, two types of chili and lime. The Mercado San Juan de Dios (p540) in Guadalajara covers 500,000 sq ft and has three levels, more than 70 entrances, and one of the most diverse food sections of any Mexican

Josefina Velázquez de León is considered the mother of Mexican cuisine. Born in Aguascalientes in 1899, Doña Josefina ran a successful culinary school in Mexico City and wrote more than 140 cookbooks. Her most ambitious project was her landmark book *Platillos Regionales de la Republica Mexicana* (Regional Dishes of the Mexican Republic), which is widely considered to be the first book to collect Mexico's enormously regional cuisine in a single volume. You can check Josefina's work at www.josefina-food.com and http://josefina-food.blogspot.com/.

MULLI (MOLE)

Zarela Martinez, the Mexican chef, author and owner of the eponymous restaurant in New York once told me that in *mole* the sauce is the dish. What she meant was that when we eat *mole* we eat it because we want the sauce. The meat – whether it be chicken, turkey or pork – plays a secondary role. The word *mole* comes from the Náhuatl word *molli* or *mulli*. A complex sauce made with nuts, chilies and spices, *mole* defines Mexican cuisine. Although *mole* is often called chocolate sauce, this is not accurate as only a very small percentage of *moles* include this ingredient. The confusion is somewhat understandable since the recipe for *mole poblano*, *mole* from the state of Puebla, the most widely known *mole* in the country (and around the world), includes a small amount of chocolate. But most Mexicans would agree that when it comes to *mole*, Oaxaca is the place to go. It's known as the 'Land of Seven *Moles*': they include *mole negro* (black *mole*), which uses a chili called *chilhuacate negro*; *almendrado* (thickened with almonds and *chile ancho*, dried peppers); *mancha manteles* (tablecloth-stainer) with *chile ancho*, pineapples and bananas; and *mole verde* (green *mole*), a delicacy thickened with corn masa and made with white beans, tomatillos, *epazote* and *hoja santa*, an indigenous herb from Mexico that adds a beautiful anise flavor to it.

Eating good *mole* is a fantastic experience. The nuts, seeds and dry chilies used in *moles* are toasted and ground to release their aroma. Fresh chilies, tomatoes, tomatillos and garlic are also slow-roasted, giving the sauce a great smoky flavor. Fresh herbs are quickly fried and mixed with the rest of the ingredients, which have been pureed. Then the *mole* is left to simmer until it thickens. This long process gives *moles* a great depth and many layers of flavor. *Moles* can be spicy or sweet, or they can be spicy and sweet at the same time.

market. Stands selling an array of tacos and *tortas* abound, but there are also many stalls selling Chinese food and incredible and delicious seafood. Nothing shouts out to you in this *mercado* as loud as the *birria* stands serving the goat stew that is quintessential Guadalajara. Try a taco, or two!

DRINKS
Tequila

In Mexico we love tequila. We drink it on large and small national holidays, at funerals and anniversaries, at casual lunches and at dinner with friends. Legally, tequila is our champagne. All tequila has to come from the state of Jalisco and is protected with a DO (Designation of Origin) by the Consejo Regulador del Tequila (Tequila Regulate Council). This organization ensures that all tequila sold throughout the world comes from this state in central south Mexico. This arid area with highland soil creates the perfect conditions for the blue agave, the plant from which tequila is distilled, to grow. No tequila made in China (or elsewhere), *por favor*. We drink it because we are proud of its Mexican provenance, and because we really like its taste.

Taste is a key word when it comes to tequila. Visitors interested in discovering its real taste should stay away from the image of big testosterone-driven machos gulping shot after shot of tequila and throw away its reputation as an quick intoxicator. Tequila has become more and more sophisticated and today is considered a refined drink that rivals an imported single-malt whiskey or a quality cognac, and not only in price but also in its smooth, warm taste. Today's finest tequilas are meant to be enjoyed in a small glass, with pleasure, in tiny sips.

The process of making tequila starts by removing the *piña* (heart) of the blue agave plant. This *piña* is then steamed for up to 36 hours, a process that softens the fibers and releases the *aguamiel*, or honey water. This liquid is funneled into large tanks where it is fermented. Fermentation determines whether the final product will be 100% agave or *mixto* (mixed). The highest-quality tequila is made from fermenting and then distilling only *aguamiel* mixed with some water. In tequilas *mixtos* the *aguamiel* is mixed with other sugars, usually cane sugar with water. When tequila is 100% agave it will say so on the label. If it doesn't say 100% it is a *mixto*.

The next step in the tequila making process is to distill the *aguamiel* and store it in barrels for aging. The aging is important, especially for today's fancier tequilas, because it determines the color, taste, quality and price. Silver or *blanco* (white) is clear and is aged for no more than 60 days. Tequila *blanco* is used primarily for mixing and blends particularly well into fruit-based drinks. Tequila *reposado* (rested) is aged from two to nine months. It has a smooth taste and light gold color. Tequila *añejo* (old) is aged in wooden barrels for a minimum of 12 months. The best quality *añejos* are aged up to four years. Tequila *añejo* has a velvety flavor and a deep dark color. These three kinds of tequila are equally popular in Mexico, and it is entirely a matter of personal taste that determines which one to drink.

Drinking tequila straight from a small glass is still the most traditional way, and although the old technique of using lime and salt is still popular there are other options. In many places tequila is served alongside a small glass of *sangrita*. *Sangrita* (not to be confused with Spanish sangria, made with wine) is a bright-red chaser made with tomato juice, orange or grapefruit juice, a dash or Worchester and Tabasco, a bit of grenadine or sugar, and salt. *Sangrita* has a sharp tart flavor that blends well with the smokiness of tequila. If you want to go one step further order a *bandera* (flag), and you will be served one small glass with lime, one with tequila, and another one with *sangrita*. The presentation resembles the colors of the Mexican flag (green, white and red) and the experience of drinking one sip of each at a time is like no other. The practice of serving chilled tequila is becoming more and more popular in Mexico. Bars and restaurants keep bottles in the freezer and serve it directly to your glass on the table. Straight cold tequila is creamy and smooth, and it is a great refreshment when eating outdoors in warm weather.

The margarita, of course, has done more for the popularity of tequila than any other cocktail, and you will find this sweet-and-sour beverage in every tourist place in the country. But the margaritas are far from being the only tequila cocktail in Mexico. A *paloma* (dove) mixes tequila, lime juice, and grapefruit soda, while a Bloody María uses tequila to create a version of a spicy Bloody Mary. In trendy bars you will find an array of martinis using tequila in lieu of vodka or gin.

Mezcal

Mezcal is tequila's brother. Like tequila, it is distilled from the agave plant, but *mezcal* doesn't have to come from blue agave, or from the tequila-producing areas of Jalisco. In other words, all tequila is *mezcal*, but not all *mezcal* is tequila. Since *mezcal* can be made with any type of agave plant, it can also be produced throughout the country, where sometimes it is known by other names, such as *bacanora* in Sonora State or *sotol* in Chihuahua. But unlike tequila, the *piña* from the agave is roasted (not steamed) in fire pits, giving it a great smoky flavor.

In Oaxaca, the 'Mezcal Capital of the World,' the spirit is traditionally served in small earthenware cups with lime wedges and *sal de gusano*, an orange-colored salt that has been spiced with smoked agave worms. These are the same legendary worms that you find in some bottles of *mezcal*, and they are actually the larvae of moths that live on the plant. There are many legends about why the worm is added to the bottle, but all of them are too vague to single one out. What is irrefutable is the fact that consuming the worm is completely harmless. Another fact is that high-end *mezcals* don't include a worm in their bottles.

Although it is commonly referred as a cactus, the agave is classified in its own family, *agavaceae*, which consists of more than 120 species. In Mexico the agave plant is known as *maquey*.

American-born Cristina Potters is a writer and blogger living in Morelia, Michoacán. Her blog (www.mexicocooks .typepad.com) is the most compelling and well-informed blog about Mexican food and culture to be found on the web. Cristina writes weekly about food and drink, art, culture and travel.

Pulque

If tequila and *mezcal* are brothers, then pulque would be the father of Mexican spirits. Two thousand years ago the Aztecs started to extract the juice of the agave plant to produce a milky, slightly alcoholic drink that they called *octli poliqhui*. *Octli* had religious significance, and consumption was limited to specific holidays and rituals when large tubs were set up in public squares. When the Spanish arrived in Mexico they started to call the drink pulque. Early attempts to distill pulque were unsuccessful, and the resulting spirit was harsh and unpleasant. It was soon discovered, however, that cooking the agave produced a sweet sap. After fermentation and distillation this juice became what we know today as *mezcal*.

Although pulque has lower alcohol content than tequila or *mezcal* it is much harder on the palate. Because it is not distilled, it retains an earthy, vegetal taste and has a thick, foamy consistency that some people find unpleasant. In some places it is mixed with fruit juices such as mango or strawberry to make it more palatable. When pulque is mixed with juices it is called *curado*.

Pulque flavor changes dramatically over short periods, and therefore is a not easy to store and preserve. Some attempts at preserving and canning pulque have been developed with very little success. This is why pulque is usually sold today as it has been for hundreds of years: directly in bulk from the *tinacal* (a large vat) or in bars called *pulquerías*.

English sailors coined the term 'cocktail' upon discovering that their drinks in the Yucatán port of Campeche were stirred with the thin, dried roots of a plant called *cola de gallo*, which translates as 'cock's tail'.

Beer

For many visitors, 'Una cerveza por favor' is among the first the phrases they learn in Spanish. For some, it is their most commonly used phrase while in Mexico. This makes sense. Mexican cerveza is big, and although you don't need to travel to the country to try it (Mexican beers are among the best-selling brands all over the world), drinking beer here makes a big difference because Mexican beer is a great match with, well, Mexican food! Most Mexican brands are light and quench beautifully the spiciness of a plate of enchiladas. They are also great companion for the thousands of *fútbol* (soccer) matches that we follow in this country with religious zeal.

Cantina El Nivel holds Mexico City liquor license number 1, dating back to 1855. It has remained an unofficial requirement for Mexico's president-elect to get drunk there prior to taking office.

Two major breweries dominate the Mexican market. Grupo Modelo, based in Mexico City and Guadalajara, makes twelve brands, among them Corona, Victoria, Modelo Especial, Pacifico, Montejo and Negra Modelo. Although Corona is the fifth best-selling beer in the world, beer aficionados regard Negra Modelo, a darker beer, as the brewery's jewel. In the north of the country, in the industrial city of Monterrey, Cervecería Cuauhtémoc Moctezuma produces Sol, Carta Blanca, Dos Equis, Superior, Tecate and Bohemia, among others. With its gold foil wrapping, Bohemia is marketed as the premium Mexican beer. It competes head-to-head with Negra Modelo and is also popular among experts. But the array of Mexican beer allows for drinking them in many different environments. A day on the beach calls for a Corona, a Superior or a Pacifico. Victoria and Montejo are good matches for seafood, and meat goes really well with Modelo Especial and Carta Blanca. A night in a bar feels very Dos Equis to me, and a Bohemia or Negra Modelo would pair perfectly with a very good, decadent dinner.

The practice of a beer served with a wedge of lime in its mouth is not as common in Mexico as it is in foreign bars, and you will find that establishments that serve lime with your beer would most likely do it on a small plate. There are many legends around the origin of the practice. Some say that it began as a way of keeping the flies away from the bottles, others maintain that it appeared as a way to clean the rustiness on the mouth of the bottle caused by the old metal caps. In any case some lighter Mexican brands can benefit from the addition of a squeeze of lime, but most Mexican beers don't need anything.

Wine

Now may be the right time to expand your Spanish vocabulary to include 'Una copa de vino por favor.' Although the wine industry is still much smaller than that of tequila or beer, Mexican wines are leaping forward at a great rate.

Mexico became the first wine-producing region in the Americas after the Spaniards brought the first grapes in 1524. But by the mid-1600s Spain started controlling wine production in order to protect its home industry, and in 1699 winemaking was forbidden in Mexico. An exception was made for the Catholic Church, which continued using wine for the communion, and was allowed to make homegrown wine for it. Mexican wineries began using their grapes for brandy. Since the 1990s, challenged in part by the success of Californian, Chilean and Argentinean wines, Mexican producers began yielding good wines in nine regions, from Queretaro to Sonora, with the best coming from the north of Baja California. The two larger wineries in Mexico, Pedro Domeq and LA Cetto, offer solid table wines and some premium labels like Chateu Domecq and Limited Reserve Nebbiolo. Many 'boutique wineries' with names like Monte Xanic, Casa de Piedra and Casa Valmar are also producing great wine in smaller quantities.

Be aware that wine consumption in Mexico is still pretty much restricted to upper-class establishments, especially outside the larger cities and wine-producing regions. Because most waiters are not much help in recommending wines, the best way to discover new Mexican wines is by conducting your own tasting. Ask for a small taste before ordering a glass or committing to the full bottle. Most establishments will try to help you decide.

Nonalcoholic Drinks

The great variety of fruits, plants and herbs that grow in this country are a perfect fit for the kind of nonalcoholic drinks Mexicans love. All over the country you will find classic *juguerías,* street stalls or small establishments selling all kinds of fresh-squeezed orange, tangerine, strawberry, papaya or carrot juices. These places also sell *licuados,* a Mexican version of a milk-shake that normally includes banana, milk, honey and fruit. Many of these places serve incredibly creative combinations, such as *nopal* (cactus leaves), pineapple, lemon and orange, or vanilla, banana and avocado.

In *taquerías* and *fondas* you will find *aguas frescas,* or fresh waters. Some of them resemble iced teas. In *agua de tamarindo* the tamarind pods are boiled and then mixed with sugar before being chilled, while *agua de jamaica* is made with dried hibiscus leaves. Others like *horchata* are made with melon seeds and/or rice. *Agua de chia* (a plant from the salvia family) is typical during holy week celebrations in Chiapas, and in the Yucatan Peninsula the

---

MY COLD BEER

In Mexico we frequently call our beer *chela,* and by all accounts this moniker is the origin of the famous *micheladas* (*mi chela helada,* meaning 'my cold beer'). *Micheladas* are prepared chilled beers, and they range from really simple drinks to complex cocktails. The basic *michelada* will be a mix of the juice of one or two Key limes on a previously chilled mug, a few ice cubes, a dash of salt and a Mexican cold beer. In many places they are served with a few drops of hot sauce, Worcestershire sauce and Maggi seasoning. Don't be surprised if you see *micheladas* with Clamato or tomato juice, or even with a couple of ounces of tequila or rum in addition to the beer: *micheladas* are a blank canvas.

leaves from the native shrub *chaya* (also known as tree spinach) are mixed with lime, honey and pineapple to create *agua de chaya*.

CELEBRATIONS

Food and fiestas go hand-to-hand in Mexico. They can be national holidays, religious festivals, local fiestas or personal celebrations, but chances are you will get caught in one of them during your visit. During national holidays food is always present, but toasting with tequila is a prerequisite, especially during Día de la Independencia (September 16), which celebrates independence from Spain. The largest religious festivity is the Día de la Virgen de Guadalupe (December 12), where *tamales*, *mole* and an array of *antojitos* are traditional fare. During Lent, meatless dishes such as *romeritos* (a wild plant that resembles rosemary served with dried shrimp, potatoes and *mole*) show up on most menus. On Día de los Santos Reyes (January 6), the day when the Three Wise Men arrived bearing their treasured gifts for the Baby Jesus, we celebrate by eating *rosca de reyes*, a large oval sweetbread decorated with candied fruit. The *rosca* is served with corn *tamales* and hot chocolate. During Christmas, a traditional Mexican menu includes turkey, *bacalao* (dry codfish cooked with olives, capers, onions and tomatoes) and *romeritos*. Family and personal celebrations such as *bodas* (weddings), *cumpleaños* (birthdays) and La Fiesta de Quince Años (a girl's 15th birthday) are celebrated in a big way in Mexico. Plenty of food and drinks are served, and in some occasions the fiesta goes on for an entire weekend. But there is no celebration in Mexico with more mystique than El Día de Muertos (Day of the Dead), held on the second day of November. Its origins date back to the Aztecs, and it celebrates the passing of relatives and loved ones. By celebrating death we salute life, and we do it the way we celebrate everything else, with food, drinks and music. An altar to death is set up in a house or, as some families prefer, in the graveyard. It is decorated with bright *cempasuchil* (marigold) flowers, plates of *tamales*, sugar-shaped skulls and *pan de muerto* (bread of the dead; a loaf made with egg yolks, *mezcal* and dry fruits), and the favorite foods of the deceased are laid out so that they feel welcome upon their return.

Under the Jaguar Sun by Italian writer Italo Calvino is a compelling account of a husband and wife discovering Mexico and its cuisine. The couple in the story becomes so enamored of the cuisine that their passion is transferred from the bedroom to the dining table.

WHERE TO EAT & DRINK

It's easy to find a place to eat in Mexico. From an early snack at a small *puesto* (street or market stall) to a lavish late dinner at a fine restaurant, food seems to always be available. One thing you should know, though, is that mealtimes in Mexico are different from what you might be used to. *Desayuno* (breakfast) is usually served in restaurants and *cafeterías* from 8:30am to 11am, and it tends to be on the heavy side. Those who have a light breakfast or skipped it altogether can have an *almuerzo* (a type of brunch) or an *antojito* or other quick bite. *Taquerías* (places specializing in tacos), *torterías* (small establishments selling *tortas*) and *loncherías* (places that serve light meals) are good options for an *almuerzo*. In Mexico the main meal is the *comida*. It is usually served from 2pm to 4:30pm in homes, restaurants and cafés. Places called *fondas* are small, family-run eateries that serve *comida corrida*, an inexpensive prix-fix menu that includes a soup, rice, a main dish, beverage and dessert. In some small towns people will have a *merienda*, a light snack between the *comida* and *la cena* (supper), but in most large cities people are too busy working or commuting and don't eat again until dinner time. Frequently dinner is not served until 9pm, and it is usually light when eaten at home. In restaurants dinner can be a complete meal that lasts until midnight.

When we go out to a bar, a club or a late movie, we often stop off for a quick taco before returning home. Many famous *taquerías* cater to these hungry insomniacs and don't close until the wee hours. On Fridays and

---

TIPPING AND TAXES

A mandatory 15% of IVA (or value-added tax) is added to restaurant checks in Mexico, but the *propina* (gratuity) is not. The average tip is 15% to 20%, and although some people argue that the tip should be calculated before IVA, It Is Just easier to tip the same amount, or a bit more, than the amount marked for the IVA. For instance, in a check that marks IVA 82 pesos, a tip between 80 and 100 pesos would be appropriate.

Saturdays so many customers visit these places that sometimes you have to wait for a table at 3am!

Cantinas are the traditional Mexican watering holes. Until not long ago, women, military personnel and children were not allowed in cantinas, and some cantinas still have a rusted sign stating this rule. Today everybody is allowed, although the more traditional establishments retain a macho edge. Beer, tequila and *cubas* (rum and coke) are served at square tables where patrons play dominos and watch soccer games on large TV screens. Cantinas are famous for serving *botanas* (appetizers) like *quesadillas de papa con guacamole* (potato quesadillas with guacamole) or escargots in *chipotle* sauce.

VEGETARIANS & VEGANS

In Guadalajara's market there is large sign for an eatery named *Restaurant Vegetariano* (Vegetarian Restaurant) listing some menu items underneath. It has salads, rice, beans, grilled chicken and fish in garlic sauce. This sign shows one of the problems for vegetarians and vegan in Mexico: the concept is not always fully understood. Many Mexicans think of a vegetarian as a person who doesn't eat meat, and by 'meat' they mean red meat. Many more have never heard the word *veganista*, the Spanish term for vegan. The good news is that almost every city, large or small, has real vegetarian restaurants, and their popularity is increasing. Also, many traditional Mexican dishes are vegetarian: *ensalada de nopales* (cactus leaves salad); quesadillas made with mushrooms, cheeses and even flowers like zucchini flowers; *chiles rellenos de queso* (cheese-stuffed poblano chilies); and *arroz a la mexicana* (Mexican-style rice). Be warned, however, that many dishes are prepared using chicken or beef broth, or some kind of animal fat, such as *manteca* (lard). Most waiters will be happy to help you in choosing vegetarian or vegan dishes, but you have to make your requirements clear.

EATING WITH KIDS

In most restaurants in Mexico you will see entire families and their kids eating together, especially at weekends. Waiters are used to accommodating children and will promptly help you with high chairs (*silla para niños* or *silla periquera*), and in some places they will bring crayons or toys to keep them entertained. Across Mexico it is common to see children having dinner in restaurants after 8 or 9pm.

COOKING COURSES

Cooking schools in Mexico can differ greatly depending on their location. A school in Oaxaca would focus on different ingredients and techniques from a school in Monterrey or Sonora.

Mexican-born chef Rose Marie Plaschinski runs **Xilonen** (www.cookinginmexico .com.mx), the school of traditional cuisine, in Guadalajara. Xilonen has full-day and weeklong classes. It also has private lessons for individual and groups, and special classes for culinary professionals.

Cookbook author Susana Trilling operates **Seasons of My Heart** (www.seasons ofmyheart.com) in Rancho Aurora Oaxaca. Susana offers day and long-weekend classes, weeklong courses and culinary tours of the state of Oaxaca and other regions of Mexico.

Closer to Mexico City, in the small village of Tepotztlán, New York native Magda Bogin runs **Cocinar Mexicano** (www.cocinarmexicano.com). The program includes weeklong classes and weekend courses specially designed for travelers.

EAT YOUR WORDS

Knowing at least a few words in Spanish indicates a respect for the locals and their culture, not to mention a willingness to risk embarrassment, and that can make a huge difference.

Useful Phrases

Are you open?
   e·*sta* a·*byer*·to   *¿Está abierto?*
When are you open?
   kwan·do e·*sta* a·*byer*·to   *¿Cuando está abierto?*
Are you now serving breakfast/lunch/dinner?
   a·*o*·ra e·*sta* ser·*vyen*·do de·sa·*yoo*·no/   *¿Ahora, está sirviendo desayuno/*
   la ko·*mee*·da/la *se*·na   *la comida/la cena?*
I'd like to see a menu.
   kee·*sye*·ra ver la *kar*·ta/el me·*noo*   *Quisiera ver la carta/el menu.*
Do you have a menu in English?
   tye·nen oon me·*noo* en een·*gles*   *¿Tienen un menú en inglés?*
Can you recommend something?
   pwe·de re·ko·men·*dar* al·*go*   *¿Puede recomendar algo?*
I'm a vegetarian.
   soy ve·khe·te·*rya*·no/a   *Soy vegetariano/a.* (m/f)
I can't eat anything with meat or poultry products, including broth.
   no *pwe*·do ko·*mer* al·*go* de *kar*·ne o *a*·ves   *No puedo comer algo de carne o aves,*
   een·kloo·*yen*·do *kal*·do   *incluyendo caldo.*
I'd like mineral water/natural bottled water.
   kee·*ye*·ro *a*·gwa mee·ne·*ral*/*a*·gwa poo·ree·fee·*ka*·da   *Quiero agua mineral/agua purificada.*
Is it (chili) hot?
   es pee·*ko*·so   *¿Es picoso?*
The check, please.
   la *kwen*·ta por fa·*vor*   *La cuenta, por favor.*

Food Glossary

a la parilla	a la pa·*ree*·ya	grilled
a la plancha	a la *plan*·cha	pan-broiled
adobada	a·do·*ba*·da	marinated with *adobo* (chili sauce)
agua mineral	*a*·gwa mee·ne·*ral*	mineral water or club soda
agua purificado	*a*·gwa poo·ree·fee·*ka*·do	bottled, uncarbonated water
al albañil	al al·ba·*nyeel*	'bricklayer style' – served with a hot chili sauce
al carbón	al kar·*bon*	char-broiled
al mojo de ajo	al *mo*·kho de *a*·kho	with garlic sauce
al pastor	al *pas*·tor	cooked on a pit, shepherd's style
albóndigas	al·*bon*·dee·gas	meatballs
antojitos	an·to·*khee*·tos	'little mexican whims,' and tortilla-based snacks like tacos and *gorditas*
arroz mexicana	*a*·ros me·khee·*ka*·na	pilaf-style rice with a tomato base
ate	*a*·te	jam, preserves
atole	a·*to*·le	gruel made with ground corn

avena	a·*ve*·na	oatmeal
aves	*a*·ves	poultry
azucar	a·soo·*kar*	sugar
barbacoa	bar·ba·*ko*·a	pit-smoked barbecue
biftec	beef·*tek*	steak
bolillo	bo·*lee*·yo	French-style roll
brocheta	bro·*che*·ta	shishkabob
buñuelos	boo·*nywe*·los	tortilla-size fritters with a sweet, anise sauce
burrito	boo·*ree*·to	a filling in a large flour tortilla
cabra	*ka*·bra	goat
cabrito	ka·*bree*·to	kid goat
café con crema/leche	ka·*fe* kon *kre*·ma/*le*·che	coffee with cream/milk
cajeta	ka·*khe*·ta	goat's milk and sugar boiled to a paste
calabacita	ka·la·ba·*see*·ta	squash
calamar	ka·la·*mar*	squid
caldo	*kal*·do	broth or soup
camarones	ka·ma·*ro*·nes	shrimp
cangrejo	kan·*gre*·kho	crab
carne	*kar*·ne	meat
carne de puerco	*kar*·ne de *pwer*·ko	pork
carne de res	*kar*·ne de res	beef
carnero	kar·*ne*·ro	mutton
carnitas	kar·*nee*·tas	pork simmered in lard
cebolla	se·*bo*·ya	onion
cecina	se·*see*·na	thin cut of meat flavored with chili and sautéed or grilled
cerdo	*ser*·do	pork
chalupas	cha·*loo*·pas	open-faced, canoe-shaped cooked corn dough, topped with meat and chilies
chicharrones	chee·cha·*ro*·nes	fried pork skins
chilaquiles	chee·la·*kee*·les	fried tortilla strips cooked with a red or green chili sauce, and sometimes meat and eggs
chile relleno	chee·le re·*ye*·no	chili stuffed with meat or cheese, usually fried with egg batter
chiles en nogada	chee·les en no·*ga*·da	mild green chilies stuffed with meat and fruit, fried in batter and served with a sauce of cream, ground walnuts and cheese
chorizo	cho·*ree*·so	Mexican-style bulk sausage made with chili and vinegar
chuleta de puerco	choo·*le*·ta de *pwer*·ko	pork chop
churros	choo·ros	doughnut-like fritters
cochinita pibil	ko·chee·*nee*·ta pee·*beel*	pork, marinated in chilies, wrapped in banana leaves, and pit-cooked or baked
coco	*ko*·ko	coconut
coctel de frutas	kok·*tel* de *froo*·tas	fruit cocktail
cordero	kor·*de*·ro	lamb
costillas de res	kos·*tee* yas de res	beef ribs
crema	*kre*·ma	cream
crepas	*kre*·pas	crepes or thin pancakes
elote	e·*lo*·te	fresh corn
empanada	em·pa·*na*·da	pastry turnover filled with meat, cheese or fruits

empanizado	em·pa·nee·sa·do	sautéed
enchilada	en·chee·la·da	corn tortilla dipped in chili sauce, wrapped around meat or poultry, and garnished with cheese
ensalada	en·sa·la·da	salad
filete	fee·le·te	filet
filete al la tampiqueña	fee·le·te al la tam·pee·ke·nya	steak, tampico style, a thin tenderloin, grilled and served with chili strips and onion, a quesadilla and enchilada
flor de calabaza	flor de ka·la·ba·sa	squash blossom
fresa	fre·sa	strawberry
frijoles a la charra	free·kho·les a la cha·ra	beans cooked with tomatoes, chilies and onions (also called frijoles rancheros)
frijoles negros	free·kho·les ne·gros	black beans
frijoles refritos	free·kho·les re·free·tos	refried beans
frito	free·to	fried
galleta	ga·ye·ta	cookie
gelatina	khe·la·tee·na	gelatin; also Jello (English jelly)
gorditas	gor·dee·tas	small circles of tortilla dough, fried and topped with meat and/or cheese
guacamole	gwa·ka·mo·le	mashed avocado, often with lime juice, onion, tomato and chili
helado	e·la·do	ice cream
hígado	ee·ga·do	liver
horchata	hor·cha·ta	a soft drink made with melon
huachinango veracruzana	wa·chee·nan·go ve·ra·kroo·sa·na	Veracruz-style red snapper with a sauce of tomatoes, olives, vinegar and capers
huevos fritos	hwe·vos free·tos	fried eggs
huevos motuleños	hwe·vos mo·too·le·nyos	fried eggs sandwiched between corn tortillas, and topped with peas, tomato, ham and cheese
huevos rancheros	hwe·vos ran·che·ros	fried eggs served on a corn tortilla, topped with a sauce of tomato, chilies, and onions, and served with refried beans
huevos revueltos	hwe·vos re·vwel·tos	scrambled eggs
huitlacoche	weet·la·ko·che	corn mushrooms — a much-esteemed fungus that grows on corn
jaiba	khay·ba	crab
jamón	kha·mon	ham
jitomate	khee·to·ma·te	red tomato
jugo de manzano	khoo·go de man·sa·na	apple juice
jugo de naranja	khoo·go de na·ran·kha	orange juice
jugo de piña	khoo·go de pee·nya	pineapple juice
langosta	lan·gos·ta	lobster
leche	le·che	milk
lengua	len·gwa	tongue
licuado	lee·kea·do	smoothie
limón	lee·mon	lime (lemons are rarely found in Mexico)
lomo de cerdo	lo·mo de ser·do	pork loin
machacado	ma·cha·ka·do	pulverized jerky, often scrambled with eggs

mantequilla	man·te·*kee*·ya	butter
mariscos	ma·*rees*·kos	seafood
menudo	me·*noo*·do	stew of tripe
milanesa	mee·la·*ne*·sa	thin slices of beef or pork, breaded and fried
mixiote	mee·*shyo*·te	chili-seasoned lamb steamed in agave membranes or parchment
mole negro	mo·le *ne*·gro	chicken or pork prepared in a very dark sauce containing chilies, fruits, nuts, spices and chocolate
mole poblano	mo·le po·*bla*·no	chicken or turkey in a sauce of chilies, fruits, nuts, spices and chocolate
mole	*mo*·le	a traditional stew
mollejas	mo·*ye*·khas	sweetbreads (thymus or pancreas)
nieve	*nye*·ve	sorbet
nopalitos	no·pa·*lee*·tos	sautéed or grilled, sliced cactus paddles
ostras/ostiones	*os*·tras/os·*tyo*·nes	oysters
pan	pan	bread
papas fritas	*pa*·pas *free*·tas	French fries
papas	*pa*·pas	potatoes
pastel	pas·*tel*	cake
pato	*pa*·to	duck
pay	*pa*·ee	pie
pechuga	pe·*choo*·ga	breast
picadillo	pee·ka·*dee*·yo	a ground beef filling that often includes fruit and nuts
piña	*pee*·nya	pineapple
pipian verde	pee·*pyan ver*·de	a stew of chicken, with ground squash seeds, chilies and *tomatillos*
platano	*pla*·ta·no	banana
platano macho	*pla*·ta·no *ma*·cho	plantain
pollo	*po*·yo	chicken
postre	*pos*·tre	dessert
pozole	pa·*so*·le	a soup or thin stew of hominy, meat, vegetables and chilies
pulpo	*pool*·po	octopus
quesadilla	ke·sa·*dee*·ya	cheese folded between a tortilla and fried or grilled
queso fundido	*ke*·so foon·*dee*·do	cheese melted, often with *chorizo* or mushrooms, and served as an appetizer with tortillas
rajas	*ra*·khas	strips of mild green chili fried with onions
sábana	*sa*·ba·na	filet mignons pounded paper thin and seared
sopa	*so*·pa	soup, either 'wet' or 'dry' – as in rice and pasta
sopa de ajo	*so*·pa de *a*·kho	garlic soup
sopa de cebolla	*so*·pa de se·*bo*·ya	onion soup
sopa de pollo	*so*·pa de *po*·yo	chicken soup
sope	*so*·pe	a type of *gordita*

taco	*ta·*ko	filling of meat, poultry or vegetables wrapped in a tortilla
té de manzanillo	te de man·sa·*nee·*ya	chamomile tea
té negro	te *ne·*gro	black tea
tinga poblana	*teen·*ga po·*bla·*na	a stew of pork, vegetables and chilies
tocino	to·*see·*no	bacon
tomates verdes	to·*ma·*tes *vair·*des	tomatillos
toronja	to·*ron·*kha	grapefruit
tuna	*too·*na	cactus fruit
venado	ve·*na·*do	venison
verduras	ver·*doo·*ras	vegetables

Regional Cuisines of Mexico

Mauricio Velázquez de León

Want to try all the different kinds of Mexican *tamales?* Good luck. The *Diccionario Enciclopédico de Gastronomía Mexicana* documents 170 different styles prepared throughout the country. It's a similar story with *moles* or any kind of *antojito*. Mexican food is extremely regionalized. What you'll find on your plate is dictated by the national staples (corn, beans and chilies) and the geography, climate and history of the particular region.

THE NORTHERN STATES: BAJA CALIFORNIA, BAJA CALIFORNIA SUR, SONORA, CHIHUAHUA, DURANGO, COAHUILA, NUEVO LEÓN & TAMAULIPAS

Fish tacos, beach, beer – perfect
JOHN ELK III / ALAMY

Beef, flour (as opposed to corn) and seafood are the staples of the big northern region. Five of the eight states share a border with territories that once belonged to Mexico and are now part of the US, so it is not surprising that some of the regional specialties are counterparts of what California, Texas and Arizona consider their own regional food, such as burritos, fajitas and nachos. But the northern Mexican region is home to an authentic cuisine that can only be found on this side of the border.

The north is extremely dry, especially in its center, where Mexico's two largest deserts, the Sonora and Chihuahua, define the environment. This is beef territory. Think *mochomos,* for example, a Sonora and Chihuahua specialty of dry beef cooked with onions and garlic and used as a filling for tacos in *tortillas de harina* (flour tortillas).

The mainstay of the rich, industrial state of Nuevo León and its capital, Monterrey, is *cabrito asado* (roasted kid goat), cooked on big metal skewers in an open fire and served in large pieces to order. *Frijoles borrachos* (drunken beans), made with beans, tomato, garlic, cilantro, bacon and beer, is the perfect pal to a good *cabrito.*

Baja California cuisine relies on its surrounding oceans. *Mariscos* (shellfish) and

top five
THE NORTHERN STATES

Antojitos
Tacos de pescado in Baja California and *mochomos* in Sonora and Chihuahua.

Dishes
Cabrito asado in Monterrey and *jaiba rellena* in Tamaulipas

Beverages
Baja California wines

Product
Tortillas de harina

Restaurants
Fonda de la Tía Chona (p383) in Durango

pescado (fish) are prepared *al ajillo* (in garlic and *guajilllo* chili sauce), *a la plancha* (grilled) or *a la diabla* (with garlic, tomato and *cascabel* chili). *Tacos de pescado* (fish tacos), including lobster and black bean tacos, are a favorite and are consumed for breakfast, lunch and dinner. Seafood continues its rule on the long and narrow state of Tamaulipas where *jaibas rellenas* (blue crabs stuffed with crabmeat, tomato, chili, capers, olives and raisins) or *al chilpachole* (crab soup with *epazote* – pigweed – *chile chipotle* and tomatoes) are strong favorites.

CENTRAL PACIFIC COAST: SINALOA, NAYARIT, JALISCO & COLIMA

Wedged between the Sierra Madre Oriental range and the Pacific Ocean are these four states, well known for the resort areas in Puerto Vallarta, Manzanillo and Mazatlán.

With a moderate climate and short but intense rain seasons, Sinaloa, Nayarit and Colima shape an area with a rich agricultural tradition and an even richer coastline. *Tamales de camarón* are a specialty in Sinaloa, and *pescado zarandeado* (fish grilled on the beach inside a *zaranda* or wooden grill) is a classic preparation in Nayarit. Colima also enjoys an array of seafood dishes, but it is the *tatemado de puerco* (a *mole*-type stew of chilies, ginger and spices over a loin of pork) that better represents the state.

top five
CENTRAL PACIFIC COAST

Antojitos
Tortas ahogadas in Guadalajara and *tamales de camarón* in Sinaloa

Dishes
Tatemado de puerco in Colima and *birria* in Guadalajara

Beverages
Tequila

Culinary Spots
Mercado Libertad in Guadalajara

Restaurants
Los Xitomates (p463) in Puerto Vallarta

A bit of lime with your *birria*?

GREG ELMS

Jalisco is the state responsible for many traditions regarded as Mexican symbols (mariachis, tequila, etc), and it is in its capital, Guadalajara, where food is best represented. *Tapatios,* as people from the city are known, boast an unmatched regional pride when it comes to where to find the best *birria* (goat stew cooked wrapped in agave leaves and spiced with *chile de árbol*) or most authentic *tortas ahogadas* (drowned tortas), a sandwich stuffed with *carnitas* (fried pork) and beans then drowned in a very spicy salsa.

SOUTHERN PACIFIC COAST: OAXACA, GUERRERO & CHIAPAS

This is an area where indigenous cultures and the bounty of ingredients in a sub-tropical climate have produced some of the most interesting culinary traditions in the country.

Oaxaca is known as the 'Land of Seven *Moles*' and also the '*Mezcal* Capital of the World.' The seven *moles* include the world-famous *mole negro* (black *mole*), *almendrado* (thickened with almonds and *chile ancho*) and *mole verde* (green *mole*), made with beans, *tomatillos, epazote* and *hoja santa,* an indigenous herb. An array of *tamales* and soups such as *tamales oaxaqueños* (with *mole negro*) or *caldillo de nopales con camarón* (shrimp and cactus leaf soup) are also popular in the state. Oaxaca is also the place to eat bugs. Fried or roasted *chapulines* (grasshoppers) with lime and salt are commonly served as *botanas* (snacks).

From the tourist resorts of Acapulco and Ixtapa Zihuatanejo to the state's small fishing settlements and mountain towns, Guerrero has a great assortment of seafood dishes. *Ceviches* made with sierra fish, *pescado a la talla* (fish marinated in *chile ancho* and

top five
SOUTHERN PACIFIC COAST

Antojitos
Chapulines and maguey worms in salsa in Oaxaca

Dishes
Guerrero-style green *pozole* and *mole negro,* one of Oaxaca's seven *moles*

Beverages
Margaritas in Acapulco and *mezcal* in Oaxaca

Culinary Spots
Mercado 20 de Noviembre (p729) in Oaxaca

Restaurants
La Biznaga (p730) in Oaxaca and Casas Viejas (p859) in Chiapas

Chapulines at an Oaxaca market

CHARLOTTE HINDLE

spices and cooked on an open flame) and *camarones Barra Vieja* (shrimp cooked with *chile guajillo* and *chipotle,* spices and fish broth) are served in beach shacks and fancy restaurants. Although the state's average temperature is 32°C (90°F), a hot, hearty bowl of *pozole* is the local favorite, traditionally eaten on Thursdays. The *pozole* in Guerrero is made with *epazote,* ground pumpkinseeds and *tomatillos,* served with an assortment of condiments.

Chiapas' large indigenous population preserves old culinary traditions. Dishes like *armadillo en adobo* (armadillo in a thick chili sauce) or *en escabeche* (pickled), *bazo relleno* (beef stuffed with plantains, potatoes, hard-boiled egg, raisins and olives) and *bosto de sardina* (grilled sardines wrapped in banana leaves) are centuries-old popular foods in the state.

THE YUCATÁN PENINSULA: YUCATÁN, CAMPECHE & QUINTANA ROO

The regional staple is the *chile habanero,* the spiciest pepper in the world, but don't let this keep you away from the wonderful cuisine of the Yucatán Peninsula. Cancún, Playa del Carmen and other tourist towns are here, but it is in old cities and towns like Mérida, Valladolid, Motul and Chetumal where you discover the dynamic culinary marriage of Maya and Caribbean traditions. *Recado* is the generic name for local marinades combining dry chilis, spices, herbs and vinegar that are rubbed into meats and poultry. A common one is *recado rojo,* containing the *achiote* (annatto) seeds that infuse an intense red color and flavor to *cochinita pibil* (pork pibil style), the region's most famous dish. *Pib* means a hole in the ground, and cooking *'al pibil'* is a cooking technique that has been used for centuries in this region. Despite the fierce reputation of the *chile habanero,* food in this region is not spicy. The *habanero* is most commonly found in table salsas, so it's up to you how much to add. Try a little on top of papaadzules (tacos stuffed with hard-boiled eggs and pumpkinsee sauce) or *panuchos,* small corn tortillas that puff when heated. Filled with beans and hard-boild egg, they are lightly fried, they are topped with meat or shredded *cochinita pibil* and pickled red onions.

top five
THE YUCATÁN PENINSULA

Antojitos
Papadzules and *panuchos*

Dishes
Cochinita pibil and *sopa de lima*

Beverages
Xtabentún, the so-called liqueur of the gods

Produce
Habanero chili

Restaurants
Checándole (p872) in Cancún and Príncipe de Tutul-Xiu in Maní

Cochinita pibil

GREG ELMS

MEXICO CITY

When it comes to food, Mexico City has no match. It has always been the recipient of an overwhelming migration of people and their foods. Surfing a chaotic transportation system, the *capitalinos* (as people in the city are called) are always on the move, creating one of the most vibrant street-food cultures on the planet and an endless series of eateries, from humble *loncherías* (lunch stalls) to superb restaurants. It is said that you can eat breakfast, lunch and dinner in a different place here for a year without repeating a venue.

Mexico City is the *antojito* capital. They're found almost anywhere: in a basket attached to a bicycle; in plaza *puestos* (street stalls); in market eateries; and in the thousands of *taquerias* and *torterías. Huaraches* (foot-long tortillas) are classic fare at Mercado de la Merced and other markets, where squash flowers and *huitlacoche* quesadillas also abound. In plazas,

Squash flower at a local market

GREG ELMS

esquites (warm braised corn seasoned with epazote, lime juice and powdered chili) are traditional treats.

Cuisine from all of Mexico is represented in the city's eateries and fondas, and places focusing on one region or cuisine are plentiful. Vegetarians can enjoy ensalada de nopales (cactus leaves salad), and carnitas (braised pork) is a standard. More formal restaurants like Los Danzantes (p178) serve brilliant Oaxacan cuisine. Others, like El Bajío (p177), have terrific multiregional traditional fare. Many restaurants are epicenters of nueva cocina mexicana, where chefs bring haute-cuisine techniques and sophistication to traditional Mexican recipes. Patricia Quintana prepares dishes like lobster enchiladas with pumpkinseed sauce in her restaurant, Izote (p177), while chef Enrique Olvera of Pujol (p177) is acclaimed for dishes like ravioles de aguacate, camarón y mayonesa picante (avocado ravioli with shrimp and spicy mayonnaise).

GULF COAST: VERACRUZ & TABASCO

La Villa Rica de la Vera Cruz (now called Veracruz) was the first town to be founded in the American continent by the Spanish conquistadors, and it became the main point of contact with the Caribbean and Europe. This mélange of cultures explains the area's rich and varied cuisine: antojitos like tostadas de jaiba (blue crab tostadas), gorditas infladas (puffed masa cakes) and tamales de frijol con polvo de aguacate (bean tamales with avocado dust) are definitively pre-Hispanic, while huachinango a la veracruzana (red snapper in tomato, olives, capers and onion) has strokes of Mediterranean. Dishes like mondongo (tripe soup), molotes (battered plantains) and the use of crops like sugarcane and yucca exemplify the influence that the transit of slaves from the Caribbean and Africa has had in the state.

Sugarcane and coffee fields dominate a great deal of the Veracruz landscape. From sugarcane, Veracruz residents make aguardiente (literally fiery water), an unrefined alcoholic drink that is definitely not suitable for the faint of heart. Mexico's first coffee beans were cultivated in Acayucan, Veracruz, in 1800. The high terrain, constant clouds and mist found in many areas throughout the state became fertile ground for the high-quality coffea Arabica strain. Today, towns like Coatepec, Huatusco and Coscomatepec produce some of the best coffee in the world. A good place to try some is Gran Café de la Parroquia (p691) in Veracruz city, which has been serving café con leche and other java treats since 1809.

top five
GULF COAST

Antojitos
Tostadas de jaiba and *gorditas infladas*

Dishes
Huachinango a la veracruzana

Beverages
Aguardiente and local coffee

Produce
Cacao and vanilla

Restaurants
La Fonda (p681) in Xalapa and Gran Café de la Parroquia (p691) in Veracruz

Coffee served Veracruz style

GREG ELMS

EL BAJÍO: QUERÉTARO, GUANAJUATO, MICHOACÁN, SAN LUIS POTOSÍ, AGUASCALIENTES & ZACATECAS

El Bajío is an area of temperate climate and fertile land where the northern cattle-rich states meet the produce-plentiful states in the south. The Purépecha populated most of today's Michoacán, and their cuisine has a large influence in the area. *Ichúscutas* and *yururichustasas* are regional *gorditas* (masa cakes) and the *uchepos* (sweet corn *tamales*) are among other *purépecha antojitos*. *Churípo,* a stew made with beef, cabbage, potatoes, chickpeas, carrots and *chile guajillo,* is a traditional Michoacán dish. In Uruapan it's *carnitas* with avocado.

Avocado, a staple produce of El Bajío

GREG ELMS

top five
EL BAJÍO

Antojitos
Corundas and *uchepos (tamales)* in Michoacán

Dishes
Enchiladas queretanas in Queretaro, *churípo* and *carnitas* in Michoacán

Beverages
Pulque and *atoles*

Produce
Avocado

Restaurants
Los Dorados de Villa (p591) in Zacatvecas

In San Luis Potosí *cabuches* (the edible flowers of the barrel cactus) and *el asado de la boda* (pork cooked with *chile ancho*) compete only with the famous *enchiladas potosinas* as the local favorites. The ancient drink *atole* is popular in the region. It is made by boiling corn with water or milk and is usually sweetened with sugar or *piloncillo* and flavored with local fruits. Not all *atoles* are sweet: the *chileatole* includes chili and in the old days it was given to new mothers right after labor.

top five
CENTRAL MEXICO

Antojitos
Tacos de cecina de Yecapixtla in Morelos and *gusanos de maguey con salsa borracha* in Tlaxcala

Dishes
Mole poblano and *chiles en nogada* in Puebla

Beverages
Pulque

Produce
Nopales

Restaurants
Fonda Santa Clara in Puebla

Puebla's delicious *mole poblano*

GREG ELMS

CENTRAL MEXICO: PUEBLA, TLAXCALA, HIDALGO & MORELOS

Mole poblano was created by nuns working in one of Puebla's many convents. It is the perfect marriage between indigenous and Spanish ingredients and techniques. A good vegetarian option is nopales (edible cactus leaves). *Chiles en nogada* are another Puebla specialty, and one with patriotic undertones. This delicacy is made with a green pepper stuffed with ground beef and dried fruits, topped with a white *nogada* (walnut cream sauce) and sprinkled with red pomegranate seeds. Green, red and white: the colors of the Mexican flag. The story is that it was first served in 1821 when Agustin de Iturbide, one of the New Republic's leaders, visited Puebla after the signing of Mexican independence from Spain. Puebla city held a lavish banquet, but Iturbide refused to eat, fearing enemies may have poisoned the food. However, when he was presented with a plate of *chiles en nogada* he was so seduced by the dish's beauty that he threw caution to the wind and started munching.

Environment

One of the unfailing thrills of travel in Mexico is the incredible, never-ending spectacle of its environment. From the snow-capped volcanoes and cactus-strewn deserts to the lush tropical forests and the coastal lagoons teeming with aquatic life, there's never a dull moment for the eye. Nature lovers will revel in this country which, thanks to its location straddling temperate and tropical regions, is home to the fourth greatest biological diversity on the planet. With little over 1% of the world's land, Mexico cradles more than 10% of the earth's bird, mammal, reptile, fish and plant species, and many of them exist nowhere else – including more than 150 types of mammal.

THE LAND

Nearly two million sq km in area, with a coast 10,000km long and half its land above the 1000m mark, Mexico has a spectacularly rugged and diverse topography.

High Plains & Sierras

Northern Mexico is dominated by continuations of the mountains and uplands of the western half of the US. A string of broad plateaus down the middle of the country, the Altiplano Central, is fringed by two long mountain chains – Sierra Madre Occidental on the west and Sierra Madre Oriental on the east. Most of the northern altiplano is occupied by the sparsely vegetated Desierto Chihuahuense (Chihuahuan Desert), which extends north into Texas and New Mexico. The southern altiplano is mostly rolling hills and broad valleys, and includes some of best Mexican farming and ranching land.

The two *sierras madre* meet where they run into the Cordillera Neovolcánica. This spectacular volcanic chain, strung east to west across the middle of Mexico, includes the active volcanoes Popocatépetl (5452m) and Volcán de Fuego (3820m), as well as the nation's other highest peaks – Pico de Orizaba (5611m) and Iztaccíhuatl (5220m).

Coastal Plains

Narrow coastal plains lie between the *sierras madre* and the seas. The Gulf coast plain is crossed by many rivers flowing down from the Sierra Madre Oriental. On the west side of Mexico, a relatively dry coastal plain stretches south from the US border almost to Tepic, in Nayarit state. Its northern end is part of a second great desert straddling the Mexico–US border, the Desierto Sonorense (Sonoran Desert).

South of the resort destination of Puerto Vallarta, the Pacific plain narrows. Another mountain chain, the Sierra Madre del Sur, stretches across the states of Guerrero and Oaxaca, ending at the Isthmus of Tehuantepec, the narrowest part of Mexico at just 220km wide. The north side of the isthmus is a wide, marshy plain, strewn with meandering rivers.

The Far South

East of the Isthmus of Tehuantepec, Chiapas, Mexico's southernmost state, rises sharply from a fertile Pacific plain, El Soconusco, to highlands almost 3000m high, then falls away to lowland jungles that stretch into northern Guatemala. The jungle melts into a region of tropical savanna on the Yucatán Peninsula, a flat, low limestone platform that separates the Gulf of Mexico from the Caribbean Sea.

Only two transportation routes make it right across the wide, rugged Sierra Madre Occidental: the Ferrocarril Chihuahua Pacífico (Chihuahua Pacific Railway) through the Copper Canyon, and the dramatic Hwy 40 from Durango to Mazatlán.

RJ Secor's *Mexico's Volcanoes: A Climbing Guide* is invaluable for those planning to pit themselves against Mexico's central volcanic belt.

Mexico's youngest volcano, Paricutín (2800m), in Michoacán, arose only in 1943.

WILDLIFE

From the whales, sea lions and giant cacti of Baja California to the big cats, howler monkeys, quetzal birds and cloud forests of the southeast, Mexico's fauna and flora are exotic and fascinating. A growing number of ecotourism and active tourism firms are ready to take you out to Mexico's most exciting natural sites.

Animals

In the north, urban growth, ranching and agriculture have pushed the puma (mountain lion), bobcat, bighorn sheep, wolf, deer and coyote into isolated, often mountainous, pockets.

Tropical Mexico – The Ecotravellers' Wildlife Guide by Les Beletsky is a well-illustrated, informative guide to the land, air and sea life of southeastern Mexico.

Baja California is famous for whale-watching in the early months of the year. Gray whales swim 10,000km from the Arctic to breed in its coastal waters (see boxed text, p293). Between Baja and the mainland, the Sea of Cortez (Golfo de California) hosts more than a third of all the world's marine mammals, including sea lions, fur and elephant seals, and four species of whale.

Mexico's coasts, from Baja to Chiapas and from the northeast to the Yucatán Peninsula, are among the world's chief breeding grounds for sea turtles. Seven of the world's eight species are found in Mexican waters, with some female turtles swimming unbelievable distances (right across the Pacific Ocean in the case of some loggerhead turtles) to lay eggs on the beaches where they were born. Killing sea turtles or taking their eggs is illegal in Mexico, and there are more than 100 protected nesting beaches.

Dolphins play along the Pacific and Gulf coasts, while many coastal wetlands, especially in the south of the country, harbor crocodiles. Underwater life is richest of all on the coral reefs off the Yucatán Peninsula's Caribbean coast, where there's world-class diving and snorkeling.

For the state of the world's sea turtles, check SWOT (www.seaturtle status.org).

Back on land, the surviving tropical forests of the southeast still harbor five species of large cat (jaguar, puma, ocelot, jaguarundi and margay), plus spider and howler monkeys, tapirs, anteaters and some mean tropical reptiles, including a few boa constrictors. The cats are reduced to isolated pockets mainly in eastern Chiapas, Tabasco and parts of the Yucatán Peninsula.

Coastal Mexico is a fantastic bird habitat, especially its estuaries, lagoons and islands. An estimated three billion migrating birds pass by or over the Yucatán Peninsula each year, and the state of Veracruz is a migration corridor for huge numbers of birds of prey. Even in the drier inland areas, surprising numbers of birds abound. Tropical species such as trogons, hummingbirds, parrots and tanagers start to appear south of Tampico in the east of the country and from around Mazatlán in the west. The southeastern jungles and cloud forests are home to colorful macaws, toucans, guans and quetzals. Yucatán has spectacular flamingo colonies at Celestún and Río Lagartos.

Mexico's most unforgettable insect marvel is Michoacán's Reserva Mariposa Monarca (p563), where the trees and earth turn orange when millions of monarch butterflies arrive every winter.

ENDANGERED SPECIES

The World Conservation Union (www.iucn.org) provides information on threatened species.

The Mexican government has a different classification system for endangered species from the World Conservation Union (WCU), which publishes the widely recognized Red List of endangered and threatened species. Either way, the numbers are large. On one or other or both lists you'll find such wonderful creatures as the jaguar, ocelot, golden anteater, Central American tapir, spider and howler monkeys, sea otter, seven sea turtle species, boa constrictor, resplendent quetzal, keel-billed toucan and northern elephant seal. The Margarita Island kangaroo rat and Oaxacan pocket gopher may be less glamorous, but their disappearance will still forever affect the other

---

GIVING THE EARTH A VOICE

American Ron Mader founded **Planeta** (www.planeta.com), a 'global journal of practical ecotourism,' back in 1994. The first-ever website dedicated to ecotourism, Planeta has grown into an influential, much-visited resource and debating chamber. Its span is global, but it has always had a strong emphasis on Mexico, where Ron has lived since 1997.

What made you decide to launch a website on ecotourism? Living in Austin, Texas, I had access to innovative and inexpensive technology. I focused on ecotourism as that has always been the focal point of my travels. Could we use the brand-new web to showcase local environmental and cultural conservation? I called the site Planeta as part of a meditation – if the world could speak, would we listen?

How would you characterize responsible tourism? It's treating others the way they wish to be treated. Tourism campaigns have long touted 'destinations' – in fact, we are simply entering a place that is someone else's home. A growing number of travelers want their journeys to be less invasive and more beneficial to the local community. They want to better understand the culture of the places they visit. Travelers and locals are seeking ways of building constituencies with the shared goal of making tourism more responsible.

How much of this is going on in Mexico? Mexico is a leader in the responsible tourism movement, but you have to look beyond the glitzy brochures. Tour companies have built their fame and profitability on the fact that they can create local jobs while educating and entertaining visitors. I am a big fan of the small mom-and-pop operators such as Pedro Martínez (p723) who runs a biking outfit in Oaxaca. What he offers to locals and travelers is mutually beneficial tours that respect people and place.

Is everything peaches and cream or are there setbacks in Mexico? At the national tourism level Mexico still does not share the wisdom of 'small is beautiful.' Preferential investment and promotion favors the large resorts rather than community endeavors. Golf courses in the desert and marinas by the sea are developed with an eye toward the jet-setting crowd. Oddly enough, the greatest threat to Mexico's responsible and sustainable tourism are the bureaucrats who promote Mexico.

What's your number one piece of advice for travelers who care about the Mexican environment? Think smart, travel slow. There's no better way to respect the environment than by making trips longer. Weekend getaways come at a high environmental cost in terms of carbon emissions. Longer trips – one to six months – allow an opportunity to experience Mexico in a deeper, more satisfying manner, particularly if travelers do some research ahead of time, make a few contacts and network in the online forums such as Planeta and **Thorn Tree** (www.lonelyplanet.com/thorntree). Finally, and key in the 'slow travel' code, is to reflect after the journey on the lessons learned and to share some recommendations and tips with others.

---

plants and animals around them. Additionally, they're endemic to Mexico. Once gone from here, they're gone from the universe.

By WCU figures for 2007, 141 of Mexico's 2945 animal species are critically endangered, a further 215 are endangered, and another 223 vulnerable. The percentages in these three most serious categories are higher in Mexico than any country on the American mainland except the USA.

Of endangered Mexican endemics, the most iconic is the vaquita – or harbor porpoise – the world's smallest marine mammal, found only in the northern Sea of Cortez and now numbering less than 600.

Plants

Northern Mexico's deserts are the world's most biologically diverse deserts. More than 400 cactus species can be found in the Desierto Chihuahuense. Isolated Baja California has a rather specialized and diverse flora, from the 20m-high cardón, the world's tallest cactus, to the bizarre boojum tree, which looks like an inverted carrot.

Birders should carry *Mexican Birds* by Roger Tory Peterson and Edward L Chalif or *Birds of Mexico & Adjacent Areas* by Ernest Preston Edwards.

Mexico's great mountain chains still have big stretches of pine forest and (at lower elevations) oak forest. Half the world's pine species and 135 types of oak are found here, and the mountain chains host a quarter of the country's plant species. In the southern half of the country, high-altitude pine forests are often covered in clouds, turning them into cloud forests with lush, damp vegetation, an enormous variety of colorful wildflowers, and epiphytes growing on tree branches.

The natural vegetation of the low-lying areas of southeast Mexico is predominantly evergreen tropical forest (rainforest in parts). This forest is dense and diverse, with ferns, epiphytes, palms, tropical hardwoods such as mahogany, and fruit trees such as the mamey and sapodilla. Despite ongoing destruction, the Selva Lacandona (Lacandón Jungle) in Chiapas is the largest remaining tropical-forest area in the country, containing a large number of Chiapas' 10,000 plant species. It's part of the 24,000-sq-km Maya tropical forest stretching into Guatemala, Belize and the southern Yucatán Peninsula. The northern Yucatán is dry forest, with thorny bushes and small trees (including many acacias), resembling the drier parts of the Pacific coastal plain. Mexico has the northern hemisphere's largest tropical dry forests.

ENDANGERED SPECIES

By WCU figures, 40 Mexican plant species are critically endangered, 75 endangered and 146 vulnerable.

PARKS & RESERVES

Mexico has spectacular national parks and other protected areas – about 11% (more than 200,000 sq km) of its territory is under some kind of federal, state or local protection. Governments have never had enough money for effective protection of these areas against unlawful hunting, logging, farming, grazing and species collection, but help from Mexican and international conservation organizations is turning increasing numbers of protected areas from 'paper parks' into real ones.

National Parks

Mexico's 68 *parques nacionales* (national parks) total 15,050 sq km. Many are tiny (smaller than 10 sq km) and around half of them were created in the 1930s, often for their archaeological, historical or recreational value rather than for ecological reasons. Most of the more recently created national parks, such as Baja California's Bahía de Loreto (created in 1996) and Archipiélago Espíritu Santo (2007), or the Yucatán Peninsula's Arrecifes de Xcalak (2000), protect coastal areas, offshore islands or coral reefs. Despite illegal logging, hunting and grazing, national parks have succeeded in protecting big tracts of forest, especially the high, coniferous forests of central Mexico.

Biosphere Reserves

Reservas de la biosfera (biosphere reserves) are based on the recognition that it is impracticable to put a complete stop to economic exploitation of many ecologically important areas. Instead, these reserves encourage sustainable local economic activities within their territory, except in strictly protected core areas *(zonas núcleo)*. Today, Mexico recognizes 37 biosphere reserves, covering 115,813 sq km, most of which are also included in Unesco's world biosphere reserves network. They protect some of Mexico's most beautiful and biologically fascinating areas, and all focus on whole ecosystems with genuine biodiversity. Sustainable, community-based tourism is an important source of support for several of them, and successful visitor programs are in

---

You may well see howler monkeys, or hear their eerie growls, near the Maya ruins at Palenque (p833) and Yaxchilán (p845).

The World Wildlife Fund's Wildfinder (www.world wildlife.org/wildfinder) is a database of over 26,000 animal species, searchable by species or place. For each of 60 Mexican ecoregions it'll give a list of hundreds of species with their names in English and Latin, their threatened status, and often pictures.

For information on Unesco biosphere reserves, visit www .unesco.org/mab.

Park/Reserve	Features	Activities	Best Time to Visit
Área de Protección de Flora y Fauna Cuatrociénegas (p389)	beautiful desert oasis with hundreds of clear pools and unique turtles and fish	swimming, snorkeling	year-round
Parque Marino Nacional Bahía de Loreto (p300)	islands, shores & waters of the Sea of Cortez	snorkeling, kayaking, diving	year-round
Parque Nacional Cumbres de Monterrey (p411)	mountains outside Mexico's third-biggest city	canyoneering, climbing, hiking, mountain biking, rappelling	Apr-Sep (canyoneering), Oct-Apr (climbing)
Parque Nacional Iztaccíhuatl-Popocatépetl (p231)	live & extinct volcanic giants on rim of Valle de México	hiking, climbing	Nov-Feb
Parque Nacional Pico de Orizaba (p699)	Mexico's highest peak (5611m)	volcano hiking & climbing	Oct-Mar
Parque Nacional Volcán Nevado de Colima (p555)	live & extinct volcanoes; pumas, coyotes, pine forests	volcano hiking	Dec-May
Reserva de la Biosfera Calakmul (p955)	rainforest with major Maya ruins	visiting ruins, wildlife spotting	year-round
Reserva de la Biosfera El Cielo (p423)	mountainous transition zone btwn tropical & temperate ecosystems; birds, bats, orchids	hiking, birding, fishing, 4WD trips	year-round
Reserva de la Biosfera El Triunfo (p854)	cloud forests; many rare birds including quetzals	guided hiking, birding, wildlife-spotting	Jan-May
Reserva de la Biosfera El Vizcaíno (p292)	deserts & coastal lagoons where gray whales calve	whale-watching, hikes to ancient rock art	Dec-Apr
Reserva Mariposa Monarca (p563)	forests festooned with millions of monarch butterflies	butterfly observation, hiking	Dec-Feb
Reserva de la Biosfera Montes Azules (p829)	tropical jungle, lakes, rivers	jungle hikes, birding, canoeing, rafting, boat trips, wildlife-watching	year-round
Reserva de la Biosfera Ría Celestún (p934)	estuary with petrified forest & plentiful bird life including flamingos	bird-watching, boat trips	Mar-Sep
Reserva de la Biosfera Sian Ka'an (p904)	Caribbean coastal jungle, wetlands & islands with incredibly diverse wildlife	birding, snorkeling & nature tours, mostly by boat	year-round

place in reserves like Calakmul, El Cielo, El Triunfo, El Vizcaíno, Mariposa Monarca and Sian Ka'an.

ENVIRONMENTAL ISSUES

Mexico faces many serious environmental problems, which it is only just beginning to come to grips with. For most of the 20th century, its governments saw urban industrial growth, chemical-based agriculture, and the destruction of forests for logging and development as the way to prosperity. Today, Mexico is among the world's 15 major producers of carbon dioxide. The Calderón government's national development plan, released in 2007, pledges to reverse deforestation, promote cleaner, more efficient technologies, and develop a plan for reducing greenhouse-gas emissions – the first time a Mexican government has planned concerted action on global warming.

Mexico City

The capital is a high-altitude metropolis that is now spreading over the mountainous rim of the Valle de México and threatening to fuse with the cities of Puebla and Toluca. The ring of mountains traps polluted air in the city, causing health problems for residents. In an effort to limit pollution levels, many vehicles are banned from the roads one day a week (see p200). Mexico City consumes two-thirds of Mexico's electricity and, despite extracting groundwater at a rate that causes the earth to sink all over the city, it still has to pump up about a quarter of its water needs from outside the Valle de México.

Mexico's Comisón Nacional de Áreas Naturales Protegidas (www.conanp .gob.mx) lists protected areas (in Spanish) in its 'Lo Que Hacemos' section.

Water

Mexico faces challenges both in getting its water and in getting rid of it. While the south has 70% of the water, the north and center of the country have 75% of the people. Overall, about 11 million Mexicans – 10% of the population – have no domestic water supply, and 15 million live without drainage systems. Surface and underground aquifers in the north and center are under increasing pressure, for both city and industrial use, as well as agricultural use. The north has suffered several droughts in the past two decades, affecting agricultural production. The situation is predicted to get worse with global warming, and not only in the north.

Much of the available water is wasted. Leakages soak up about half the water supply to cities. Half of the 75% of Mexico's water supply that goes to agriculture is not productively utilized.

About four-fifths of waste water goes untreated, which, along with agrochemical run-off and the large amounts of garbage emptied into rivers and lakes, means that three-quarters of Mexico's surface waters suffer some degree of pollution. Much of Mexico City's sewage ends up in the Río Pánuco, which enters the Gulf of Mexico at Tampico. The Río Lerma, which also supplies water to Mexico City, receives sewage and industrial effluent from many other towns on its way into poor Lago de Chapala – Mexico's biggest natural lake.

Forests

Forest conservation is crucial not only to combat global warming but also because forests are often the source of water supplies. Today, only around

---

HOW TO HELP

Travelers can help protect Mexico's fragile environment by following guidelines such as these:

- Don't buy turtle, iguana, crocodile or black-coral products.

- Don't disturb coral or nesting turtles.

- Don't collect wild cacti, their seeds or wild orchids.

- Support projects that promote sustainable development and value wildlife and natural environments rather than destroying them. Check our GreenDex (p1052) for listings.

- Try to observe wildlife in its natural environment, and hire local guides to take you. This helps provide local communities with a non-harmful source of income, and also attaches value to nature and wildlife.

- Don't hesitate to ask about your ecotourism operator's policy on disturbing wildlife and on observing rules of parks and reserves. Genuine operators can rarely promise sightings of wild animals.

- Keep water use down, especially in areas that have signs requesting you to do so.

15% of the country (300,000 sq km) is forested, and this is being reduced by around 7000 sq km a year for grazing, logging and farming. The southern states of Chiapas and Tabasco have probably lost more than half their tropical jungles since 1980. Deforestation followed by cattle grazing or intensive agriculture on unsuitable terrain often leads to erosion, with consequent silting of rivers and wetlands and loss of fertile land.

The Calderón government, in office since 2006, has made reforestation a priority and pledged zero tolerance of illegal logging. Official forest protection has often not been enough to stop the loggers, and the logging industry can be extremely ruthless in dealing with its opponents. Activist Aldo Zamora was shot dead in 2007 as he gathered information on illegal logging for Greenpeace in México state — one of a string of such incidents in recent years.

Development & Expansion

Most of Mexico's faster growing cities face difficulties of water supply, sewage treatment, overcrowding and traffic pollution.

Large-scale tourism development brings its own set of problems and is threatening fragile ecosystems, especially in Baja California and on the Caribbean coast. In Baja, the Los Cabos corridor is already a disaster of unplanned urban development, and further large-scale developments, often with US or Canadian investment, are underway or planned at places like Loreto and Todos Santos, and at Puerto Peñasco on the mainland side of the Sea of Cortez. New hotels, golf courses, marinas and villas all threaten to deplete water supplies, increase pollution, destroy wetlands and attract larger permanent populations.

Rampant development along the Caribbean coast has fragmented wildlife habitats and encroached on turtle-nesting beaches. As the Riviera Maya pushes south, conservationists are worried that the Sian Ka'an Biosphere Reserve may be affected by water pollution or altered hydrology.

Environmental Movement

Environmental awareness is increasingly strong among individual Mexicans as they cope with daily problems like traffic pollution. There is no large-scale environmental movement but rather a number of smaller organizations working on local issues. Some successful campaigns in recent years have benefited from broader-based support, even from outside Mexico. One was the defeat in 2000 of the plan for a giant saltworks at Laguna San Ignacio in Baja California, a gray-whale breeding ground. Probably the most influential Mexican environmental group is **Pronatura** (www.pronatura.org .mx), which deploys around M$100 million a year chiefly on climate change projects, priority species and the conservation of lands and watersheds.

The Nature Conservancy (www.nature.org), Conservation International (www.conservation.org) and World Wildlife Fund (www.panda.org) all provide lots of information on the Mexican environment, including on their programs in the country.

Certification schemes for sustainable forestry are in operation but as yet have very limited reach, covering only 5000 sq km.

Mexico City

Vibrant, cosmopolitan capital or smog-choked, crime-plagued urban stain that's best avoided? Is Mexico City closer to the magical realism of *Frida* or the asphalt jungle of *Amores Perros*?

Well, yes. Mexico City is a place of multifaceted offerings.

This is a city of serene parks and European-style plazas, teeming street life and bustling markets, boisterous bullrings and civilized cantinas, gleaming office towers and centuries-old monasteries, old-fashioned dance halls and minimalist electronica clubs. Over a hundred museums display pre-Hispanic, colonial and modern art or cover the city's long history. For culinary travelers, it's an endless banquet, from soulful taco stalls to world-class restaurants. Music is everywhere: emerging from the opera house, you're greeted by an organ-grinder. Over 2km high, Mexico City enjoys a springlike climate year-round. And the Chilangos, or *defeños*, or *capitalinos*, or whatever you name the locals, are a remarkably patient and helpful bunch.

Yet it's impossible to overlook the city's very real problems. Express kidnappings and taxi holdups, often dangerous levels of ozone and airborne particulates, intolerable traffic jams, overcrowded public transportation, practically unlimited urban sprawl: name your poison, it's here. But the polluted air improved considerably after the introduction of strict emission controls, and downtown streets have been made unquestionably safer than in previous decades.

Remember that Mexico City is, and has ever been, the sun in the Mexican solar system. To truly understand the country, you've got to come to grips with El Gran Tenochtitlán.

HIGHLIGHTS

- Study Diego Rivera's tableau of Mexican history at the **Palacio Nacional** (p142)
- Sip some smooth and smoky *mezcals* at the **tasting salons** (boxed text, p183) of Roma and Condesa
- Cheer on the 'good guys' at the *lucha libre* bouts of **Arena Coliseo** (p188)
- Gaze upon the Aztec sun stone and other superb relics from Mexico's pre-Hispanic past at the **Museo Nacional de Antropología** (p153)
- Share Frida's pain at her blue birthplace, the Casa Azul, now home to the **Museo Frida Kahlo** (p158), in Coyoacán

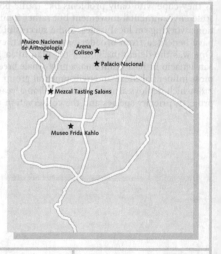

Museo Nacional de Antropología ★   Arena Coliseo ★
★ Palacio Nacional
★ Mezcal Tasting Salons
★ Museo Frida Kahlo

| ■ TELEPHONE CODE: 55 | ■ ELEVATION: 2240M | ■ POPULATION: 19.2 MILLION |

HISTORY

Driving over the sea of asphalt that now overlays this highland basin, you'd be hard pressed to imagine that, a mere five centuries ago, it was filled by a chain of lakes. It would further stretch your powers to think that today's downtown was on an islet crisscrossed by canals, or that the communities who inhabited this island and the banks of the lake spoke a patchwork of languages that had as little to do with Spanish as Malay or Urdu. As their chronicles related, the Spaniards who arrived at the shores of that lake in the early 1500s were just as amazed to witness such a scene.

That lake covered much of the floor of the Valle de México when humans began moving in as early as 30,000 BC. Eventually the lake started shrinking and hunting became tougher, so the inhabitants turned to agriculture. A loose federation of farming villages had evolved around Lago de Texcoco by approximately 200 BC. The biggest, Cuicuilco, was destroyed by a volcanic eruption three centuries later.

Breakthroughs in irrigation techniques and the development of a maize-based economy contributed to the rise of a civilization at Teotihuacán, 40km northeast of the lake. For centuries Teotihuacán was the capital of an empire whose influence extended as far as Guatemala. However, it was unable to sustain its burgeoning population, and fell in the 8th century. The Toltecs, possibly descended from the nomadic tribes who invaded Teotihuacán, arose as the next great civilization, building their capital at Tula, 65km north of modern-day Mexico City. By the 12th century the Tula empire had collapsed as well, leaving a number of statelets to compete for control of the Valle de México. It was the Aztecs who emerged supreme.

Aztec Mexico City

The Aztecs, or Mexica (meh-*shee*-kah), arrived a century after the Toltecs' demise. A wandering tribe that claimed to have come from Aztlán, a mythical region in northwest Mexico, they acted as mercenary fighters for the Tepanecas, who resided on the lake's southern shore, and they were allowed to settle upon the inhospitable terrain of Chapultepec. After being captured by the warriors of rival Culhuacán, the Aztecs played the same role for their new masters. Cocoxtli, Culhuacán's ruler, sent them into battle against nearby

Xochimilco, and the Aztecs delivered over 8000 human ears as proof of their victory. They later sought a marriage alliance with Culhuacán, and Cocoxtli offered his own daughter's hand to the Aztec chieftain. But at the wedding banquet, his pride turned to horror: a dancer was garbed in the flayed skin of his daughter, who had been sacrificed to Huizilopochtli, the hummingbird god.

Fleeing from the wrath of Culhuacán, the tribe wandered the swampy fringes of the lake, finally reaching an island near the western shore around 1325. There, according to legend, they witnessed an eagle standing atop a cactus and devouring a snake, which they interpreted as a sign to stop and build a city, Tenochtitlán.

Tenochtitlán rapidly became a sophisticated city-state whose empire would, by the early 16th century, span most of modern-day central Mexico from the Pacific to the Gulf of Mexico and into far southern Mexico. The Aztecs built their city on a grid plan, with canals as thoroughfares and causeways to the lakeshore. At the city's heart stood the main *teocalli* (sacred precinct), with its temple dedicated to Huizilopochtli and the water god, Tláloc. In the marshier parts, they created raised gardens by piling up vegetation and mud, and planting willows. These *chinampas* (versions of which still exist at Xochimilco in southern Mexico City) gave three or four harvests yearly but were still not enough to feed the growing population.

To supplement their resources, the Aztecs extracted tribute from conquered tribes. In the mid-15th century they formed an alliance with the lakeshore states of Texcoco and Tlacopan to conduct wars against Tlaxcala and Huejotzingo, which lay east of the valley. The purpose was to gain a steady supply of sacrificial victims to sate Huizilopochtli's vast hunger, so that the sun would rise each day.

When the Spanish arrived in 1519, Tenochtitlán's population was 200,000 to 300,000, while the entire Valle de México had perhaps 1.5 million inhabitants, making it one of the world's densest urban areas. For an account of the Spanish conquest of Tenochtitlán, see p53.

Capital of Nueva España

So assiduously did the Spanish raze Tenochtitlán that only a handful of structures from the Aztec period remain today. Having wrecked the Aztec capital, they set about re-building it as their own. The conquistador Hernán Cortés hoped to preserve the arrangement whereby Tenochtitlán siphoned off the bounty of its vassal states.

Ravaged by disease, the Valle de México's population shrank drastically – from 1.5 million to under 100,000 within a century of the conquest. But the city emerged as the prosperous, elegant capital of Nueva España. Broad, straight streets were laid over the Aztec causeways and canals. Indigenous labor built hospitals, palaces and a university according to Spanish designs with local materials such as *tezontle,* a red volcanic rock that the Aztecs had used for their temples. The various Catholic orders had massive monastic complexes erected.

Building continued through the 17th century but problems arose as the weighty colonial structures began sinking into the soft, squishy lakebed. Furthermore, lacking natural drainage, the city suffered floods caused by the partial destruction in the 1520s of the Aztecs' canals. Lago de Texcoco often overflowed, damaging buildings, bringing disease and forcing thousands to relocate. One torrential rain in 1629 left the city submerged for five years!

Urban conditions improved in the 1700s as new plazas and avenues were installed, along with sewage and garbage collection systems. This was Mexico City's gilded age. But the shiny capital was largely the domain of a Spanish and Creole elite who had prospered through silver mining. The masses of Indian and mixed-race peasants who served them were confined to the outskirts.

Independence

On October 30, 1810, some 80,000 independence rebels, fresh from victory at Guanajuato, overpowered Spanish loyalist forces west of the capital. Unfortunately, they were ill equipped to capitalize on this triumph, and their leader, Miguel Hidalgo, chose not to advance on the city – a decision that cost Mexico 11 more years of fighting before independence was achieved.

Under the reform laws instituted by President Benito Juárez, the monasteries and churches were appropriated by the government then sold off, subdivided and put to other uses. During his brief reign, Emperor Maximilian laid out the Calzada del Emperador (today's Paseo de la Reforma) to connect Bosque de Chapultepec with the center.

Mexico City entered the modern age under the despotic Porfirio Díaz, who ruled Mexico for most of the years from 1876 to 1911 and attracted much foreign investment. Díaz ushered in a construction boom, building Parisian-style mansions and theaters, while the city's wealthier residents escaped the center for newly minted neighborhoods toward the west. Some 150km of electric tramways threaded the streets, industry grew, and by 1910 the city had more than half a million inhabitants. A drainage canal and tunnel finally succeeded in drying up much of Lago de Texcoco, allowing further expansion.

Modern Megalopolis

After Díaz fell in 1911, the Mexican Revolution (see p59) brought war, hunger and disease to the streets of Mexico City. Following the Great Depression, a drive to industrialize attracted more money and people, and by 1940 the population had reached 1.7 million. Factories and skyscrapers sprang up in the following decades, but the supply of housing, jobs and services could not keep pace. Economic growth continued in the 1960s, but political and social reform lagged behind, as was made painfully evident by the massacre of hundreds of students in the lead-up to the 1968 Olympic Games (see boxed text, opposite).

Mexico City continued to mushroom in the 1970s, as the rural poor sought economic refuge in its thriving industries, and the population surged from 8.7 to 14.5 million. Unable to contain the masses of new arrivals, the Distrito Federal (DF) spread into the adjacent state of México. The result of such unbridled growth was some of the world's worst traffic and pollution, only partly alleviated by the metro system (opened in 1969) and by attempts in the 1990s to limit traffic. On September 19, 1985, an earthquake measuring over eight on the Richter scale hit Mexico City, killing at least 10,000 and displacing thousands more. Still, people kept pouring in.

Today the metropolitan area counts 22 million inhabitants by some estimates, around a fifth of the country's population. Though growth has slowed in the last decade, there are still some 100,000 newcomers and 150,000 births annually. Mexico City is the industrial, financial and communica-

ECHOES OF TLATELOLCO

The year 1968 marked a pivotal moment for Mexican democracy. Perhaps due to the subversive mood of the era, unrest was rife and students took to the streets to denounce political corruption and authoritarianism. Mexico had been chosen that year to host the Olympics, and President Gustavo Díaz Ordaz was anxious to present an image of stability to the world. Known for his authoritarian style, Díaz Ordaz employed heavy-handed tactics to stop the protests, in turn generating further unrest, with the mantle now being taken up by a broader coalition of middle-class *capitalinos*.

On the afternoon of October 2, a week before the Olympics were to begin, a demonstration was held on Tlatelolco's Plaza de las Tres Culturas. Helicopters hovered overhead and a massive police contingent cordoned off the zone. Suddenly a flare dropped from one of the choppers and shots rang out, apparently from the balcony that served as a speakers platform. Police then opened fire on the demonstrators and mayhem ensued. Later, government-authorized accounts blamed student snipers for igniting the incident and reported 20 protesters killed, although the real number is acknowledged to be closer to 400. News of the massacre was swept under the rug and the Olympic games went on without a hitch.

There are numerous theories as to what actually occurred that October day. But the generally accepted version is that the government staged the massacre, planting snipers on the balcony to make it seem as if the students had provoked the violence. Many Mexicans viewed the killings as a premeditated tactic to suppress dissent, and the massacre permanently discredited the post-revolutionary regime.

Almost four decades later, the Tlatelolco massacre was still recalled bitterly by a generation of Mexicans after an investigation – authorized by President Vicente Fox, the country's first opposition party president in modern history – failed to yield any new revelations. Meanwhile, a new museum, the Centro Culturas Universitario Tlatelolco (p162), was inaugurated beside the scene of the carnage to commemorate and document the epochal incident.

tions center of the country; its industries generate a quarter of Mexico's wealth, and its people consume two-thirds of the country's energy. Its cost of living is the highest in the nation.

For seven decades, the federal government ruled the DF directly, with presidents appointing 'regents' to head notoriously corrupt administrations. Finally, in 1997, the DF gained political autonomy. In 2000 Andrés Manuel López Obrador, a member of the left-leaning PRD (Party of the Democratic Revolution), was elected. *Capitalinos* overwhelmingly approved of 'Amlo.' His initiatives included an ambitious makeover of the Centro Histórico (financed in part by Carlos Slim Helú, the world's richest man as of 2007) and the construction of an overpass for the city's ring road.

While López Obrador was narrowly defeated in the presidential election of 2006 (an outcome he fiercely contested), his former police chief Marcelo Ebrard won a sweeping victory in Mexico City, consolidating the PRD's grip on the city government. Also registering an overwhelming takeover of the Federal

District's legislative assembly, the PRD passed a flood of progressive initiatives, including the sanctioning of gay unions and the legalization of abortion and euthanasia. Though Ebrard doesn't inspire the sort of fervor demonstrated by Amlo's followers, his progressive initiatives may have longer-lasting effects.

ORIENTATION

The Distrito Federal (DF) is comprised of 16 *delegaciones* (boroughs), which are in turn subdivided into some 1800 *colonias* (neighborhoods, more of which are added each year as the city expands). Though this vast urban expanse appears daunting, the main areas of interest to visitors are fairly well defined and easy to traverse.

Note that some major streets, such as Av Insurgentes, keep the same name for many kilometers, but the names (and numbering) of many lesser streets switch every few blocks.

Full addresses normally include the *colonia*. Often the easiest way to find an address is by asking for the nearest metro station.

Besides their regular names, many major streets are termed Eje (axis). The Eje system establishes a grid of priority roads across the city. The north–south Eje Central Lázaro Cárdenas, running from Coyoacán in the south to Tenayuca in the north, passes just east of the Alameda Central. Major north–south roads west of the Eje Central are termed Eje 1 Poniente, Eje 2 Poniente etc, while roads to the east of Eje Central are labeled Oriente. The same goes for major east–west roads to the north and south of the Alameda Central and Zócalo – Rayón is Eje 1 Norte, Fray Servando Teresa de Mier is Eje 1 Sur.

Maps

Mexico City tourist modules hand out color maps with enlargements of the Centro Histórico, Coyoacán and San Ángel. Those needing more detail should pick up a Guía Roji foldout map of Mexico City (M$80), or a Guía Roji Ciudad de México street atlas (M$215), updated annually, with a comprehensive index. Find them at Sanborns stores and at larger newsstands.

Inegi (Map pp128-9; ☎ 5512-1873; www.inegi.gob.mx; Balderas 71, Centro; ☿ 9am-4pm Mon-Fri; Ⓜ Juárez), Mexico's national geographical institute, publishes topographical maps covering the whole country (subject to availability). Another outlet is at the **airport** (☎ 5786-0212; Sala C; ☿ 8am-8pm), and Inegi headquarters are in **Colonia Mixcoac** (Map pp126-7; ☎ 5278-1000, ext 1207; Patriotismo 711; ☿ 8:30am-9pm Mon-Fri; Ⓜ Mixcoac).

Centro Histórico & Alameda Central

The historic heart of the city is the wide plaza known as the Zócalo, surrounded by the presidential palace, the metropolitan cathedral and the excavated site of the main temple of Aztec Tenochtitlán. The 34-block area surrounding the Zócalo is known as the Centro Histórico (Historic Center), and is crammed with notable old buildings and interesting museums, as well as a number of reasonably priced hotels.

Av Madero and Av 5 de Mayo (or Cinco de Mayo) link the Zócalo with the Alameda Central park, eight blocks to the west. On the east side of the Alameda stands the magnificent Palacio de Bellas Artes. The landmark Torre Latinoamericana (Latin American Tower) stands a block south of Bellas Artes, beside one of the city's main north–south arterial roads, the Eje Central Lázaro Cárdenas.

Plaza de la República

Some 750m west of the Alameda is the Plaza de la República, marked by the somber Monumento a la Revolución. This residential area has many budget and midrange hotels. The San Rafael and Juárez are west and south of here, respectively.

Paseo de la Reforma

Mexico City's grandest boulevard runs through the city's heart, connecting the Alameda to the Bosque de Chapultepec. Along the way, the Monumento a la Independencia (aka 'El Ángel') marks the northern side of the Zona Rosa, a glitzy shopping, hotel and nightlife district, while the Torre Mayor, the city's tallest building, stands at the gateway to Chapultepec Park.

Bosque de Chapultepec

Known to gringos as Chapultepec Park, this expanse of greenery and lakes spreads west of the Zona Rosa. It holds many major museums, including the renowned Museo Nacional de Antropología. North of the park is the swanky Polanco district, filled with embassies and upscale shopping and dining establishments.

North of the Centro

Six kilometers north is the Basílica de Guadalupe, Mexico's most revered shrine, about 1km beyond the Terminal Norte, the largest of the four bus terminals.

South of the Centro

Av Insurgentes Sur connects Paseo de la Reforma to most points of interest in the south. Just south of the Zona Rosa is Colonia Roma (the Roma neighborhood), a quaint area of Porfiriato-era architecture, art galleries and plazas. West of Roma is Colonia Condesa, a trendy neighborhood with pleasant parks and plentiful restaurants and cafés. About 10km further south are the former villages of San Ángel and Coyoacán and the campus of the national university. In the southeast of the city are the canals and gardens of Xochimilco.

INFORMATION

Drop into the **Instituto Nacional de Migración** (Map pp136-7; ☎ 2581-0100; Av Ejército Nacional 862, Polanco; ☿ 9am-1:30pm Mon-Fri) to get your tourist card stamped or check what other documents are needed.

Bookstores

Books in English and some other common languages can be found in top-end hotels and major museums, as well as most of the following bookstores.

CENTRO HISTÓRICO

American Bookstore (Map pp128-9; ☎ 5512-0306; Bolívar 23; ✆ 10am-7pm Mon-Sat; Ⓜ Allende) Has novels and books on Mexico in English.

Gandhi (✆ 10am-9pm Mon-Fri, 11am-8pm Sat & Sun) Bellas Artes (Map pp128-9; ☎ 5512-4360; Juárez 4; Ⓜ Bellas Artes); Madero (Map pp128-9; ☎ 2625-0606; Madero 32; Ⓜ Zócalo) Citywide chain with a voluminous range of texts on Mexico and Mexico City, plus a worthwhile music section.

Librería Alemana (Map pp128-9; ☎ 5578-3074; Eje Central Lázaro Cárdenas 61, Piso 3; ✆ 10am-4pm & 5-7pm Mon-Sat; Ⓜ Doctores) German pop fiction and literature.

Librería Madero (Map pp128-9; ☎ 5510-2068; Madero 12; ✆ 10am-6:30pm Mon-Fri, 10am-2pm Sat; Ⓜ Allende) Mexican history, art and architecture, including many secondhand titles.

Palacio de Bellas Artes (Map pp128-9; ☎ 5512-2593; Av Hidalgo & Eje Central Lázaro Cárdenas; ✆ 10am-9pm Mon-Sat, 9am-2pm Sun; Ⓜ Bellas Artes) Branch of government-sponsored Conaculta bookstore, with ample selection of posters, cards and art books.

OTHER AREAS

Rare-book aficionados can dig up some gems in the used bookstores along Av Álvaro Obregón in Colonia Roma.

Cenca (Map pp136-7; ☎ 5280-1666; Temístocles 73B, Polanco; ✆ 7:30am-9pm Mon-Fri, 9am-9pm Sat & Sun; Ⓜ Polanco) Wide variety of foreign magazines, plus bestsellers in English.

Gandhi (Map p139; ☎ 5661-0911; Av Miguel Ángel de Quevedo 121; ✆ 9am-10pm Mon-Fri, 10am-10pm Sat & Sun; Ⓜ Miguel Ángel de Quevedo) The large San Ángel branch has outlets on both sides of Quevedo.

Librería Pegaso (Map pp132-3; ☎ 5208-0174; Álvaro Obregón 99; ✆ 11am-8pm Mon-Sat, 10am-7pm Sun; Ⓜ Insurgentes) Inside the Casa Lamm; carries Spanish-language titles with a small English literature section, plus some Lonely Planet guides.

Emergency

The Policía Turística, recognizable by their neat blue-and-gray uniforms with white belts across their chests, patrol Paseo de la Reforma and the Centro Histórico, some zipping around on Segways. They are supposed to be able to speak English. Mobile units of the GJDF (Federal District Attorney General's Office) can assist crime victims on the spot; call ☎ 061.

Agencias del Ministerio Público (✆ 9am-5pm) Centro Histórico (Map pp128-9; ☎ 5346-8720, ext 16520; Victoria 76; Ⓜ Juárez); Plaza de la República (Map pp128-9; ☎ 5592-2677, ext 1114; Paseo de la Reforma 42; Ⓜ Hidalgo); Zona Rosa (Map pp132-3; ☎ 5345-5382; Amberes 54; Ⓜ Insurgentes) Report crimes and get legal assistance. All offices have English-speaking personnel. They will help you complete forms to report an incident and give you a number to follow it up online.

Cruz Roja (Red Cross; ☎ 065, 5395-1111)

Fire (☎ 068)

Hospital ABC (Map pp126-7; ☎ emergency 5230-8161; Sur 136 No 116, Colonia Las Américas; Ⓜ Observatorio)

Hospital Ángeles Clínica Londres (Map pp132-3; ☎ emergency 5229-8445; Durango 64, Roma; Ⓜ Cuauhtémoc)

Internet Access

Public internet services are easily located. Rates range from M$10 to M$30 per hour. In addition, many cafés (including Starbucks) offer wireless internet.

CENTRO HISTÓRICO

Café Internet 105 (Map pp128-9; Hidalgo 105; ✆ 8am-9pm; Ⓜ Hidalgo)

Esperanto (Map pp128-9; ☎ 5512-4123; Independencia 66; ✆ 8am-10pm Mon-Sat, noon-6pm Sun; Ⓜ Juárez)

Keep in Touch (✆ 10am-7pm Mon-Fri, 10am-2pm Sat) Gante (Map pp128-9; ☎ 5512-4186; Gante 6, Pasaje Iturbide; Ⓜ Allende); Pasaje América (Map pp128-9; Pasaje América; Ⓜ Allende)

ZONA ROSA

Plenty of cybercafés occupy the Insurgentes roundabout.

Conecte Café (Map pp132-3; Génova 71, cnr Londres; ✆ 10am-11pm Mon-Sat, 10am-9pm Sun; Ⓜ Insurgentes)

CONDESA & ROMA

Cafenauta (Map pp132-3; ☎ 5553-1517; Ensenada 6, Colonia Condesa; ✆ 10am-10pm Mon-Sat, noon-8pm Sun; Ⓜ Patriotismo)

Ciber City (Map pp132-3; ☎ 5207-2586; Jalapa 51, Colonia Roma; ✆ 10:30am-9pm Mon-Fri; Ⓜ Insurgentes)

COYOACÁN

Papelería Dabo (Map p140; ☎ 5659-5547; Allende 45, cnr Cuauhtémoc & Coyoacán; ✆ 9am-8pm Mon-Sat, 10am-7pm Sun; Ⓜ Viveros)

MEXICO CITY

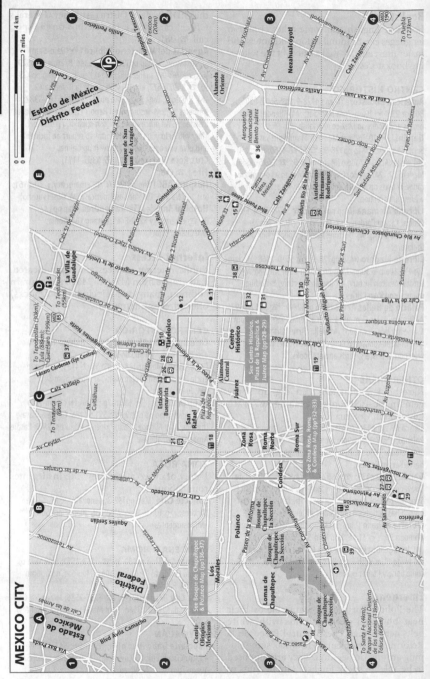

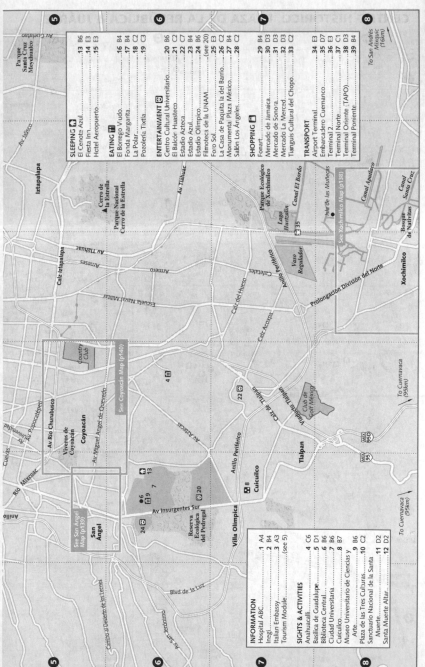

INFORMATION
Hospital ABC	1 A4
Inegi	2 B4
Italian Embassy	3 A3
Tourism Module	(see 5)

SIGHTS & ACTIVITIES
Anahuacalli	4 C6
Basílica de Guadalupe	5 D1
Biblioteca Central	6 B6
Ciudad Universitaria	7 B6
Cuicuilco	8 B7
Museo Universitario de Ciencias y Arte	9 B6
Plaza de las Tres Culturas	10 C2
Sanctuario Nacional de la Santa Muerte	11 D2
Santa Muerte Altar	12 D2

SLEEPING
El Cenote Azul	13 B6
Fiesta Inn	14 E3
Hotel Aeropuerto	15 E3

EATING
El Borrego V'udo	16 B4
Fonda Margarita	17 B4
La Polar	18 C2
Pozolería Tixtla	19 C3

ENTERTAINMENT
Centro Cultural Universitario	20 B6
El Balcón Huasteco	21 C7
Estadio Azteca	22 C7
Estadio Olímpico	23 B4
Filmoteca de la UNAM	24 B6
Foro Sol	(see 20)
La Casa de Paquita la del Barrio	25 E3
Monumental Plaza México	26 C2
Salón Los Ángeles	27 B4
	28 C2

SHOPPING
Fonart	29 B4
Mercado de Jamaica	30 D3
Mercado de Sonora	31 D3
Mercado La Merced	32 D3
Tianguis Cultural del Chopo	33 C2

TRANSPORT
Airport Terminal	34 E3
Embarcadero Cuemanco	35 D7
Terminal 2	36 E3
Terminal Norte	37 C1
Terminal Oriente (TAPO)	38 D3
Terminal Poniente	39 B4

CENTRO HISTÓRICO, PLAZA DE LA REPÚBLICA & JUÁREZ

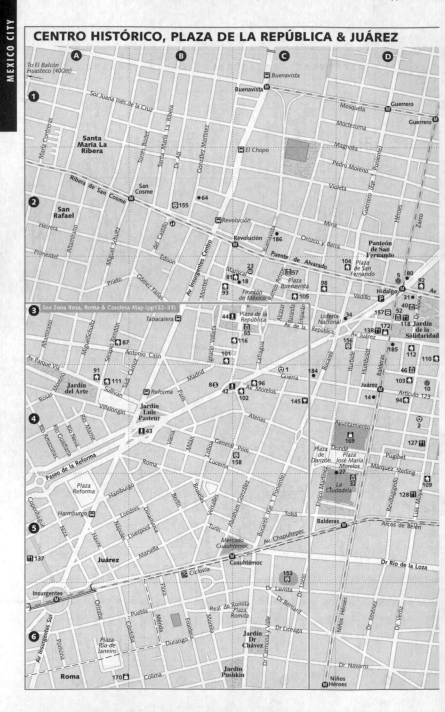

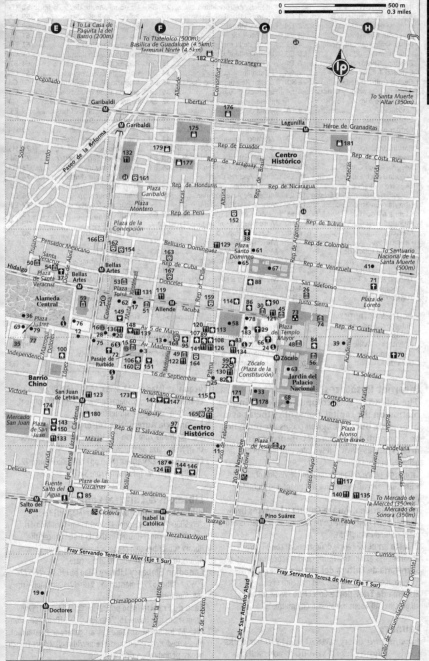

MEXICO CITY

Internet Resources

The following sites compile oodles of information on the capital. Some offer their pages in English, but the English pages are often not as thorough or are barely comprehensible.

Artes Visuales (www.artesvisuales.com.mx) Covers DF galleries and museums.

Chilango (www.chilango.com) Online version of glossy what's-on mag with extensive restaurant and nightlife listings.

Consejo Nacional Para la Cultura y las Artes (www .cnca.gob.mx) Up-to-date guide to museums, theaters and other cultural institutions.

DFiesta en el DF (www.defiestaeneldf.com) Tourism department's exhaustive listings and practical information.

Secretaría de Cultura del Distrito Federal (www .cultura.df.gob.mx) Festivals and museum events.

Sistema de Transporte Colectivo (www.metro .df.gob.mx) All about the Mexico City metro.

Laundry

Lavanderías charge M$50 to M$90 for a 3kg load – slightly less if you do it yourself.

Acqualav (Map pp132-3; ☎ 5514-7348; Orizaba 42, Colonia Roma; ☽ 8:30am-7pm Mon-Fri, 9am-5pm Sat, 9am-3pm Sun; Ⓜ Insurgentes)

Lavandería Automática Édison (Map pp128-9; Édison 91; ☽ 10am-7pm Mon-Fri, 10am-6pm Sat; Ⓜ Revolución) Near Plaza de la República.

Lavandería Lavamex (Map pp132-3; Río Pánuco 122; ☽ 9am-7pm Mon-Fri, 9am-3pm Sat)

Libraries & Cultural Centers

Biblioteca Benjamín Franklin (Map pp132-3; ☎ 5080-2733; Liverpool 31; ☽ 11am-7pm Mon-Fri; Ⓜ Cuauhtémoc) Housed in the US Trade Center, the library subscribes to a range of periodicals, from *Foreign Affairs* to *Mad*. Leave your ID at the gate.

Canadian Embassy Library (Map pp136-7; ☎ 5724-7960; Schiller 529, Polanco; ☽ 9am-12:30pm Mon-Fri; Ⓜ Auditorio)

Casa de Francia (Map pp132-3; ☎ 5511-3151; www .francia.org.mx; Havre 15, Zona Rosa; ☽ 10am-8pm Mon-Sat; Ⓜ Insurgentes) There's an art gallery and restaurant, plus a *mediateca* (multimedia center/library). Offers French books, periodicals, videos and CDs.

Hotel Édison.....93 B3
Hotel Fleming.....94 D4
Hotel Gillow.....95 F4
Hotel Imperial.....96 C4
Hotel Isabel.....97 F4
Hotel Jena.....98 C3
Hotel Majestic.....99 G4
Hotel Marlowe.....100 E4
Hotel Mayaland.....101 B3
Hotel Missión Reforma.....102 C4
Hotel Monte Real.....103 D4
Hotel Mónaco.....104 D3
Hotel New York.....105 C3
Hotel Principal.....106 F4
Hotel Rioja.....107 F4
Hotel San Antonio.....108 F4
Hotel San Diego.....109 D5
Hotel San Francisco.....110 D3
Hotel Sevilla.....111 A4
Hotel Sheraton Centro Histórico.....112 D3
Hotel Washington.....113 F3
Mexico City Hostel.....114 G3
NH Centro Histórico.....115 F4
Palace Hotel.....116 C3

EATING
Al Andalus.....117 H5
Café Colón.....118 D3
Café de Tacuba.....119 F3
Café El Popular.....120 F3
Casa de las Sirenas.....121 G3
Casino Español.....122 F4
Churrería El Moro.....123 E4
Cloister Café.....(see 50)
Coox Hanal.....124 F5
Costillas del Sitio.....125 F4
El Cardenal.....126 F4
El Cuadrilátero.....127 D4
El Regiomontano.....128 D5
Hostería de Santo Domingo.....129 G3
La Terraza del Zócalo.....130 G4
Los Girasoles.....131 F3
Mercado San Camilito.....132 F2
Mi Fonda.....133 E4
Puro Corazón.....134 G4
Restaurante Chon.....135 H5
Restaurante Vegetariano.....136 F3
Sanborns.....137 A5
Sanborns.....138 D3
Tacos de Canasta Chucho.....139 F3
Taquería Los Paisás.....140 H5
Vegetariano Madero.....141 F4

DRINKING
Bar Mancera.....142 F4
Café Cordobés.....143 E4
Café Jakemir.....144 F5
Café La Habana.....145 C4
Hostería La Bota.....146 F5
La Faena.....147 F4
La Gioconda.....148 F3
La Selva Café.....(see 160)
La Ópera Bar.....149 F3
Las Duelistas.....150 E4
Salón Corona.....151 F4

ENTERTAINMENT
Arena Coliseo.....152 G2
Arena de México.....153 C5
Bar Oasis.....154 F3
Cinematógrafo del Chopo.....155 B2
Cinemex Palacio.....156 D3
Cinemex Real.....157 D3
Cream.....158 C4
Cultural Roots.....159 F3
Dada X.....160 F4
El Tenampa.....161 F2
El Viena.....162 F3
La Perla.....163 F3
Mixup.....(see 49)
Palacio de Bellas Artes.....(see 59)
Pasagüero.....164 F4
Pervert Lounge.....165 F4
Salon Cinematográfico Fósforo.....(see 26)
Teatro Blanquita.....166 E3
Teatro de la Ciudad.....167 F3
Zinco Jazz Club.....168 F4

SHOPPING
Centro de Artesanías La Ciudadela.....169 D4
Dulcería de Celaya.....170 A6
El Palacio de Hierro.....171 G4
Fonart.....172 D3
La Bodeguita del Habano.....173 F4
La Europea.....174 E4
La Lagunilla Building 1.....175 F2
La Lagunilla Building 2.....176 G1
La Lagunilla Building 3.....177 F2
Liverpool.....178 G4
Palacio de las Máscaras.....179 F2
Plaza de la Computación y Electrónica.....180 E4
Tepito.....181 H2
Tianguis Dominical de la Lagunilla.....182 F1

TRANSPORT
Bicycle Loans.....183 G3
Magnicharters.....184 C4
Mexicana.....185 D3
Ticketbus Buenavista.....186 C2
Ticketbus Centro.....187 F5
Ticketbus Zócalo.....(see 25)

Centro Cultural de España (Spanish Cultural Center; Map pp128-9; ☎ 5521-1925; www.ccemx.org; República de Guatemala 18; admission free; 10am-8pm Tue & Wed, 10am-11pm Thu-Sat, 10am-4pm Sun; M Zócalo) See p144 for more details.

Instituto Goethe (Map pp132-3; ☎ 5207-0487; www.goethe.de/mex; Liverpool 89, Colonia Juárez; 9am-1:30pm & 4-7:30pm Tue-Thu, 10am-1:45pm Sat; M Insurgentes) Subscribes to *Die Zeit* and other German periodicals.

Media

After a five-year hiatus, the *News* is back. Sold at Sanborns stores and Zona Rosa newsstands, the English-language daily has news plus some local cultural coverage. *Inside México* (www.insidemex.com) is a free monthly in English that covers expat life in Mexico; pick up a copy at cafés and hotels around town.

Tiempo Libre, the city's Spanish-language what's-on weekly, comes out Thursdays and is sold at newsstands everywhere.

Recommended Spanish-language newspapers include *La Jornada,* with excellent cultural coverage, *El Universal* and *Reforma,* the latter available at convenience stores and some metro stations.

English-language newspapers and magazines are sold at Sanborns stores and at **La Torre de Papel** (Map pp128-9; ☎ 5512-9703; Filomena Mata 6A; 8am-7pm Mon-Fri, 8:30am-2:30pm Sat; M Allende), which also stocks newspapers from around Mexico.

Medical Services

For recommendation of a doctor, dentist or hospital, call your embassy or **Sectur** (☎ 800-987-82-24), the tourism ministry. A list of area hospitals and English-speaking physicians (with their credentials) is on the US embassy website (www.usembassy-mexico.gov/medical_lists.html). A private doctor's consultation generally costs between M$500 and M$1000.

Hospital ABC (American British Cowdray Hospital; Map pp126-7; ☎ 5230-8000, emergency 5230-8161; www.abchospital.com; Sur 136 No 116, Colonia Las Américas; M Observatorio) English-speaking staff, great hospital.

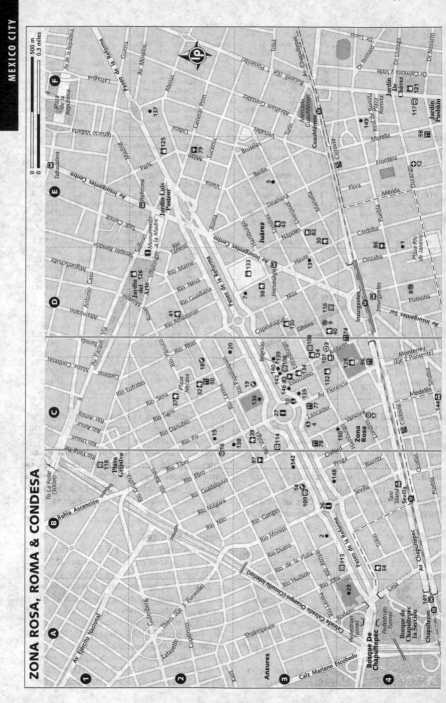

ZONA ROSA, ROMA & CONDESA

MEXICO CITY

Hospital Ángeles Clínica Londres (Map pp132–3; ☎ 5229-8400, emergency 5229-8445; www.hospital angelesclinicalondres.com; Durango 64, Roma; Ⓜ Cuauhtémoc)

The pharmacies in Sanborns stores are among the most reliable, as are the following.

Farmacia de Ahorros (Map pp132–3; ☎ 5264-3128; Yucatán 40; ⏱ 24hr; 🚍 Álvaro Obregón)
Farmacia París (Map pp128–9; ☎ 5709-5349; República de El Salvador 97, Centro; ⏱ 8am-10:30pm Mon-Sat, 10am-9pm Sun; Ⓜ Isabel la Católica)
Médicor (Map pp128–9; ☎ 5512-0431; Independencia 66; ⏱ 10am-8pm Mon-Fri, 10am-6:30pm Sat; Ⓜ Juárez)

Money

Most banks and *casas de cambio* (exchange offices) change cash and traveler's checks, but some handle only Euros and US or Canadian dollars. Rates vary, so check a few places. The greatest concentration of ATMs, banks and *casas de cambio* is on Paseo de la Reforma between the Monumento a Cristóbal Colón and the Monumento a la Independencia.

American Express (Map pp132-3; ☎ 5207-7049; Paseo de la Reforma 350; ⊙ 9am-6pm Mon-Fri, 9am-1pm Sat) Take a 'La Villa' or 'Metro Chapultepec' pesero.

Cambios Centro Histórico (Map pp128-9; ☎ 5512-9536; Madero 13; ⊙ 9:30am-6:30pm Mon-Sat, 10am-6pm Sun; Ⓜ Bellas Artes)

Centro de Cambios y Divisas (Map pp128-9; ☎ 5705-5656; Paseo de la Reforma 87F; ⊙ 8:30am-7:30pm Mon-Fri, 9am-5pm Sat, 9am-2:30pm Sun; 🚇) Take a 'La Villa' or 'Metro Chapultepec' pesero.

Post

The stamp windows, marked *estampillas*, at **Palacio Postal** (Map pp128-9; ☎ 5521-1408; Tacuba 1; Ⓜ Bellas Artes) stay open beyond normal post-office hours (until 8pm Monday to Friday, and on Sunday). Even if you don't need stamps, check out the sumptuous interior (see p148).

Other branches, scattered around town, are open 9am to 3pm Monday to Friday and 9am to 1pm Saturday unless otherwise noted.

Cuauhtémoc (Map pp132-3; ☎ 5207-7666; Río Tiber 87; Ⓜ Insurgentes)

Plaza de la República (Map pp128-9; ☎ 5592-1783; Arriaga 11; Ⓜ Revolución)

Zócalo (Map pp128-9; ☎ 5512-3661; Plaza de la Constitución 7; Ⓜ Zócalo) On the west side of the square, inside an arcade of jewelry shops.

Zona Rosa (Map pp132-3; ☎ 5514-3029; Londres 208; ⊙ 9am-5pm Mon-Fri, 9am-1pm Sat; Ⓜ Sevilla)

Telephone & Fax

There are thousands of Telmex card phones scattered around town. Pick up cards at shops or newsstands bearing the blue-and-yellow 'Ladatel' sign.

Some *papelerías* (stationery stores), copy shops and internet cafés offer fax service; look for *fax público* signs. Sending one page to the US or Canada costs about M$10; receiving a fax costs M$5.

Toilets

Use of the bathroom is free at Sanborns stores. Most market buildings have public toilets; look for the 'WC' signs. Hygiene standards vary at these latter facilities, and a fee of M$3 to M$5 is usually charged. Toilet paper is dispensed by an attendant on request, or may be taken from a common roll outside the stalls.

Tourist Information

The Mexico City Ministry of Tourism has modules in key areas, including at the airport and bus stations. They can answer your queries and distribute a map and practical guide, free of charge. At least one staff member should speak English.

These offices are open from 9am to 6pm daily, unless otherwise noted.

Antropología (Map pp136-7; ☎ 5286-3850; Paseo de la Reforma; Ⓜ Auditorio) At the entry to the Museo Nacional de Antropología.

Basílica de Guadalupe (Map pp126-7; ☎ 5748-2085; Plaza de las Américas 1; Ⓜ La Villa-Basílica)

Bellas Artes (Map pp128-9; ☎ 5518-2799; cnr Juárez & Peralta; Ⓜ Bellas Artes)

Catedral (Map pp128-9; ☎ 5518-1003; Monte de Piedad; Ⓜ Zócalo) West of the Catedral Metropolitana.

Del Ángel (Map pp132-3; ☎ 5208-1030; Paseo de la Reforma & Florencia; Ⓜ Insurgentes) On the Zona Rosa side of Monumento a la Independencia.

San Ángel (Map p139; Plaza San Jacinto; ⊙ 10am-6pm Sat & Sun; Ⓜ Miguel Ángel de Quevedo)

Templo Mayor (Map pp128-9; ☎ 5512-8977; Seminario; Ⓜ Zócalo) East side of Catedral Metropolitana.

Xochimilco (Map p138; ☎ 5653-5209; Mercado) At the Nativitas boat landing. Additional tourism modules are at other landings, open Saturday and Sunday only.

Additionally, these city *delegaciones* (urban governmental subdivisions) operate tourist information offices:

Coyoacán (Map p140; ☎ 5658-0221; Jardín Hidalgo 1; ⊙ 9am-8pm Mon-Fri, 8am-8pm Sat & Sun; Ⓜ Viveros) Inside the Casa de Cortés.

Xochimilco (Map p138; ☎ 5676-0810; Pino 36; ⊙ 9am-9pm Mon-Fri, 8am-8pm Sat & Sun) Just off the Jardín Juárez.

The office of **Corazón de México** (Map pp128-9; ☎ 5518-1869; www.elcorazondemexico.com.mx; Gante 15; ⊙ 10am-6pm; Ⓜ San Juan de Letrán) provides information on Hidalgo, Morelos, Michoacán, Guerrero and Estado de México.

The national tourism ministry, **Sectur** (Map pp136-7; ☎ 3002-6300, toll-free 078; Av Presidente Masaryk 172; ⊙ 8am-6pm Mon-Fri, 10am-3pm Sat; Ⓜ Polanco), hands out brochures on the entire country, though you're better off at the tourism modules for up-to-date information about the capital.

BOSQUE DE CHAPULTEPEC & POLANCO

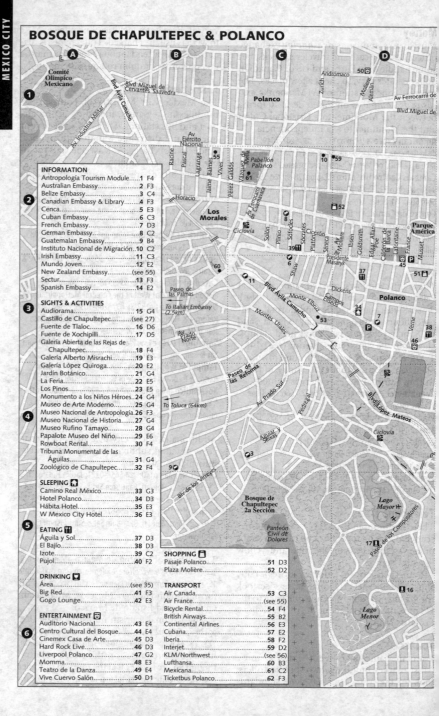

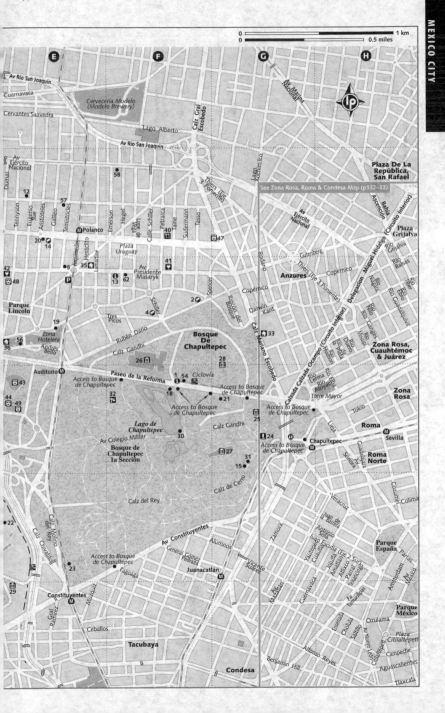

MEXICO CITY

XOCHIMILCO

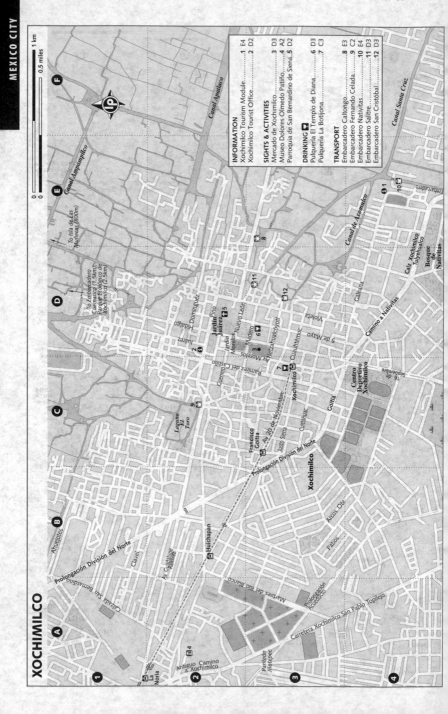

INFORMATION
Xochimilco Tourism Module.......1 E4
Xochimilco Tourist Office..........2 D2

SIGHTS & ACTIVITIES
Mercado de Xochimilco............3 D3
Museo Dolores Olmedo Patiño....4 A2
Parroquia de San Bernardino de Siena..5 D2

DRINKING 🍺
Pulquería El Templo de Diana.....6 D3
Pulquería La Botijona.............7 C3

TRANSPORT
Embarcadero Caltongo............8 E3
Embarcadero Fernando Celada....9 C2
Embarcadero Nativitas...........10 E4
Embarcadero Salitre.............11 D3
Embarcadero San Cristóbal......12 D3

SAN ÁNGEL

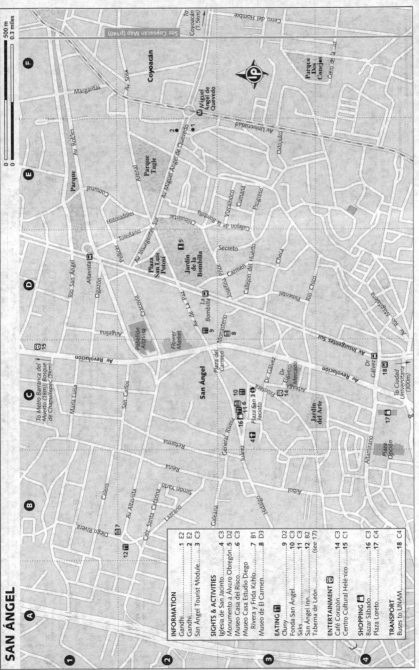

INFORMATION	
Gandhi	1 E2
Gandhi	2 E2
San Ángel Tourist Module	3 C3

SIGHTS & ACTIVITIES	
Iglesia de San Jacinto	4 C3
Monumento a Álvaro Obregón	5 D2
Museo Casa del Risco	6 C3
Museo Casa Estudio Diego Rivera y Frida Kahlo	7 B1
Museo de El Carmen	8 D3

EATING 🍴	
Cluny	9 D2
Fonda San Ángel	10 C3
Saks	11 C3
San Ángel Inn	12 B2
Taberna de León	(see 17)

ENTERTAINMENT 🎭	
Café Corazón	14 C3
Centro Cultural Helénico	15 C1

SHOPPING 🛍	
Bazar Sábado	16 C3
Plaza Loreto	17 C4

TRANSPORT	
Buses to UNAM	18 C4

COYOACÁN

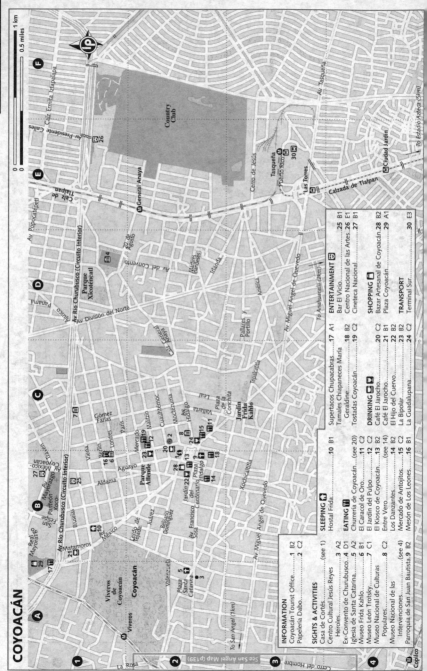

0   0.5 miles
0   1 km

Travel Agencies

A number of midrange and top-end hotels have an *agencia de viajes* on-site or can recommend one nearby.

Mundo Joven (www.mundojoven.com; 9am-8pm Mon-Fri, 10am-5pm Sat) Airport (Map pp126-7; 2599-0155; Sala E3, international arrivals); Polanco (Map pp136-7; 5250-7191; Eugenio Sue 342, cnr Homero; Polanco); Zócalo (Map pp128-9; 5518-1755; República de Guatemala 4; Zócalo) Specializes in travel for students and teachers, with reasonable airfares from Mexico City. Issues ISIC, ITIC, IYTC and HI cards. Airport branch also open 10a, to 2pm Sunday.

Turismo Zócalo (Map pp128-9; 8596-9649; www .turismozocalo.com; Palma 34, Centro; Zócalo) Inside the Gran Plaza Ciudad de México mall; also functions as a Ticketbus outlet.

DANGERS & ANNOYANCES

Mexico City is generally portrayed as an extremely crime-ridden city, so first-time visitors are often surprised at how safe and human it feels. While the incidence of street crime remains too significant to downplay – four kidnappings, 70 car thefts and 55 muggings a day in 2006 – there is no need to walk in fear. A few precautions greatly reduce any dangers. See p968 for some general hints.

Robberies happen most often in areas frequented by foreigners, including the Bosque de Chapultepec, around the Museo Nacional de Antropología and the Zona Rosa. Be on your guard at the airport and bus stations. Avoid pedestrian underpasses that are empty or nearly so. Crowded metro cars and buses are favorite haunts of pickpockets. Stay alert and keep your hand on your wallet and you'll be fine.

Unless absolutely necessary, avoid carrying ATM cards or large amounts of cash. If you become a robbery victim, don't resist. Give the perpetrator your valuables rather than risking injury or death.

A more immediate danger is traffic, which statistically takes more lives in the capital than street crime (though things have improved slightly with the installation of timed crossing signals at major intersections). Obvious as it sounds, always look both ways when crossing streets. Some one-way streets have bus lanes running counter to the traffic flow, and traffic on some divided streets runs in just one direction. Never assume that a green light means it's safe to cross, as cars may turn into your path. Take the 'safety in numbers' approach, crossing with other pedestrians.

Taxi Crime

Although they're not as prevalent a danger as in the 1990s, taxi assaults still do occur. Many victims have hailed a cab on the street and been robbed by armed accomplices of the driver. In particular, taxis parked in front of nightclubs or restaurants should be avoided, unless specifically authorized by the management. Rather than taking the risk of hailing cruising cabs, phone a radio *sitio* (taxi service). See p200 for more information on taxis and a list of recommended companies.

SIGHTS

One could spend months exploring all the museums, monuments, plazas, colonial buildings, monasteries, murals, galleries, archaeological finds, statuary, shrines and religious relics this encyclopedia of a city has to offer.

Centro Histórico

Packed with magnificent buildings and absorbing museums, the 34-block area defined as the Centro Histórico is the obvious place to start your explorations. More than 1500 of its buildings are classified as historic or artistic monuments and it is on the Unesco World Heritage list. It also vibrates with modern-day street life and nightlife, and is a convenient area to stay, with hotels in all price categories.

Since 2000, money has been poured into upgrading the image and infrastructure of the Centro. Streets have been repaved, buildings refurbished, lighting and traffic flow improved and security bolstered. New museums, restaurants and clubs have moved into the renovated structures, and festivals and cultural events are staged in the plazas, spurring a real renaissance.

ZÓCALO

The heart of Mexico City is the Plaza de la Constitución, though residents began calling it the Zócalo (Map pp128–9), meaning 'base,' in the 19th century, when plans for a major monument to independence went unrealized, leaving only the pedestal. Measuring 220m from north to south, 240m from east to west, it's one of the world's largest city squares.

The ceremonial center of Aztec Tenochtitlán, known as the Teocalli, lay immediately northeast of the Zócalo. In the 1520s

Cortés paved the plaza with stones from the ruins of the complex. In the 18th century, the Zócalo was given over to a maze of market stalls until it was dismantled by Santa Anna, who placed the unfinished monument in its center.

Today, the Zócalo is home to the powers that be. On its east side is the Palacio Nacional (the presidential palace), on the north the Catedral Metropolitana, and on the south the offices of the city government. Jewelry shops and extravagant hotels line the arcade known as the Portal de Mercaderes on the plaza's west side.

It is the very emptiness of the square that allows it to be adapted and rearranged for multiple uses. It has variously served as a forum for mass protests, a free concert venue, a human chessboard, a gallery of spooky Day of the Dead altars and a great ice-skating rink. It's even been a canvas for photo artist Spencer Tunick, who filled the square with 18,000 nude Mexicans in May 2007 (a record for Tunick, who has staged similar photo shoots in cities around the world).

The huge Mexican flag flying in the middle of the Zócalo is ceremonially raised at 8am by soldiers of the Mexican army, then lowered at 6pm.

PALACIO NACIONAL

Home to the offices of the president of Mexico, the Federal Treasury and dramatic murals by Diego Rivera, this **palace** (National Palace; Map pp128-9; ☎ 9158-1252; Plaza de la Constitución; admission free, ID required; ⏱ 9am-5pm; Ⓜ Zócalo) fills the entire east side of the Zócalo.

The first palace on this spot was built by Aztec emperor Moctezuma II in the early 16th century. Cortés destroyed the palace in 1521, rebuilding it as a fortress with three interior courtyards. In 1562 the crown purchased the building from Cortés' family to house the viceroys of Nueva España, a function it served until Mexican independence.

As you face the palace you'll see three portals. On the right (south) is the guarded entrance for the president. High above the center door hangs the **Campana de Dolores**, the bell rung in the town of Dolores Hidalgo by Padre Miguel Hidalgo in 1810 at the start of the War of Independence. From the balcony underneath it, the president delivers the *grito* (shout) – *¡Viva México!* – on September 15 to commemorate independence.

Enter the palace through the center door. The **Diego Rivera murals** along the main staircase, painted between 1929 and 1935, depict Mexican civilization from the arrival of Quetzalcóatl (the Aztec plumed serpent god) to the postrevolutionary period. The nine murals covering the north and east walls of the first level above the patio depict indigenous life before the Spanish Conquest.

CATEDRAL METROPOLITANA

Mexico City's most iconic structure, this **cathedral** (Metropolitan Cathedral; Map pp128-9; ☎ 5510-0440; admission free; ⏱ 7:30am-8pm; Ⓜ Zócalo) is a monumental edifice, measuring 109m long, 59m wide and 65m high. Started in 1573, it remained a work in progress during the entire colonial period, and thus displays a catalogue of architectural styles, with successive generations of builders striving to incorporate the innovations of the day.

Original architect Claudio Arciniega modeled the building after Seville's seven-nave cathedral, but after running into difficulties with the spongy subsoil he scaled it down to a five-nave design of vaults on semi-circular arches. The baroque portals facing the Zócalo, built in the 17th century, have two levels of columns and marble panels with bas-reliefs. The central panel shows the Assumption of the Virgin Mary, to whom the cathedral is dedicated. The upper levels of the towers, with unique bell-shaped tops, were added in the late 18th century. The exterior was completed in 1813, when architect Manuel Tolsá added the clock tower – topped by statues of Faith, Hope and Charity – and a great central dome.

The first thing you notice upon entering is the elaborately carved and gilded Altar de Perdón (Altar of Forgiveness). There's invariably a line of worshippers at the foot of the Señor del Veneno (Lord of the Poison), the dusky Christ figure on the right. Legend has it that the figure attained its color when it miraculously absorbed a dose of poison through its feet from the lips of a clergyman, to whom an enemy had administered the lethal substance.

The cathedral's chief artistic treasure is the gilded 18th-century **Altar de los Reyes** (Altar of the Kings), behind the main altar. Fourteen richly decorated chapels line the two sides of the building, while intricately carved late-17th-century wooden choir stalls by Juan de Rojas occupy the central nave. Enormous

THAT SINKING FEELING

Strolling around the Centro Histórico, you can't help but notice a rather worrisome issue – Mexico City is sinking into the ground. The metropolitan cathedral, which appears to be tilting westward, is just the most obvious example. But notice how the facade of the Iglesia de la Santa Veracruz, near the Alameda Central, slouches toward the north. The Palacio de Bellas Artes, an early-20th-century structure, has sunk so far on its right side that you have to go downstairs to pass through what used to be a street-level entrance.

All told, the historic center has dropped some 10m over the past 100 years. But the phenomenon is not exclusive to the center. The entire city has been sinking since colonial times, when the Spaniards got the bright idea of draining the lake that filled the highland basin. The spongy subsoil that remained was hardly the best place to erect churches and palaces, the formidable weight of which was more than the lakebed could handle. The problem has greatly intensified in recent decades, as an increasingly thirsty city sucks water from its underground aquifers faster than they're replenished, thus removing a crucially buoyant counterbalance to the settling subsoil.

To make matters worse, some of the historic buildings are sinking unevenly, causing structural cracks and, in some cases, total collapse. That's because their Aztec predecessors had compacted the earth beneath them. A good example is the Sagrario Metropolitano, next door to the cathedral, which was built upon the site of the Aztec Temple of the Sun.

New technology has addressed the problem to some extent. An ambitious project to prevent the deterioration of the cathedral entails the excavation of underground shafts to remove the subsoil at certain key points. Rather than stopping the sinking process entirely, the higher parts are allowed to sink to the same level as the lower ones, thus ensuring the building's structural integrity. And newly built behemoths like the Torre Mayor are anchored by pilots drilled deep beneath the subsoil to the underlying bedrock.

painted panels by colonial masters Juan Correa and Cristóbal de Villalpando cover the walls of the sacristy, the first component of the cathedral to be built.

Visitors may wander freely, though they're asked not to do so during mass. A M$10 donation is requested to enter the **sacristy** or **choir**, where docents provide commentary, and you can climb the **bell tower** (admission M$12; 10:30am-12:30pm & 3:30-6pm). Mexico's archbishop conducts mass at noon on Sundays.

Adjoining the east side of the cathedral is the 18th-century **Sagrario Metropolitano** (7:30am-7:30pm). Originally built to house the archives and vestments of the archbishop, it is now the city's main parish church. Its front entrance and mirror-image eastern portal are superb examples of the ultra-decorative Churrigueresque style.

TEMPLO MAYOR

Before the Spaniards demolished it, the Teocalli of Tenochtitlán covered the site where the cathedral now stands and the blocks to its north and east. It wasn't until 1978, after electricity workers happened on an eight-ton stone-disc carving of the Aztec goddess Coyolxauhqui, that the decision was taken to demolish colonial buildings and excavate the **Templo Mayor** (Map pp128-9; 5542-4943; www.con aculta.gob.mx/templomayor; Seminario 8; admission M$45, free Sun; 9am-5pm Tue-Sun; Zócalo). The temple is thought to be on the exact spot where the Aztecs saw their symbolic eagle, perching on a cactus with a snake in its beak – the symbol of Mexico today. In Aztec belief this was, literally, the center of the universe.

Like other sacred buildings in Tenochtitlán, the temple was enlarged several times, with each rebuilding accompanied by the sacrifice of captured warriors. What we see today are sections of the temple's different phases. At the center is a platform dating from about 1400; on its southern half, a sacrificial stone stands in front of a shrine to Huizilopochtli, the Aztec war god. On the northern half is a *chac-mool* (a Maya reclining figure) before a shrine to the water god, Tláloc. By the time the Spanish arrived, a 40m-high double pyramid towered above this spot, with steep twin stairways climbing to shrines to the two gods.

The entrance to the temple site and museum is east of the cathedral, across the hectic **Plaza del Templo Mayor**, with a model of Tenochtitlán. Authorized tour guides (with Sectur ID) offer their services by the entrance. Alternatively, rent a recorded audio guide available in English (M$60) inside the museum.

The **Museo del Templo Mayor** houses artifacts from the site and gives a good overview of Aztec civilization. Pride of place is given to the great wheel-like stone of Coyolxauhqui (She of Bells on her Cheek), best viewed from the top-floor vantage point. She is shown decapitated, the result of her murder by Huizilopochtli, her brother, who also killed her 400 brothers en route to becoming top god.

Ongoing excavation continues to turn up major pieces. Just west of the temple, a monolithic stone carved with the image of Tlaltecuhtli, the goddess of earth fertility, was unearthed in October 2006. Archaeologists believe it marks the tomb of Ahuízotl, the Aztec emperor who immediately preceded Moctezuma II and whose military conquests greatly expanded Aztec domains. Excavation of the tomb was proceeding at the time of research.

AROUND THE CATHEDRAL

Facing the cathedral's west side is Mexico's national pawnshop, the **Nacional Monte de Piedad** (Map pp128-9; Monte de Piedad 7; 8:30am-6pm Mon-Fri, 8:30am-1pm Sat; Zócalo), founded in 1774 by silver magnate Pedro Romero de Terreros. People pawn their jewelry and other possessions in the central hall for loans at 12% interest; unclaimed items are sold in shops off the central passageway.

Around the back of the cathedral, the **Centro Cultural de España** (Spanish Cultural Center; Map pp128-9; 5521-1925; www.ccemx.org; República de Guatemala 18; admission free; 10am-8pm Tue & Wed, 10am-11pm Thu-Sat, 10am-4pm Sun; Zócalo) has a variety of cutting-edge exhibitions going on. The splendidly restored building, which conquistador Hernán Cortés once awarded to his butler, has a rooftop terrace for tapas-munching and, on weekends, late-night DJ sessions.

The recently opened **Museo Archivo de la Fotografía** (Photographic Archive Museum; Map pp128-9; 2616-7057; www.maf.df.gob.mx; República de Guatemala 34; admission free; 10am-6pm Tue-Sun; Zócalo) draws from a century's worth of images taken for the *Gaceta Oficial del Distrito Federal* – the DF public record – to preserve the memory of its streets, plazas, buildings and people.

CALLE MONEDA

Flanked by magnificent *tezontle* (red, volcanic rock) buildings, Calle Moneda, north of the Palacio Nacional, is an unlikely stage for the never-ending cat-and-mouse antics between *ambulantes* (mobile street vendors) and the city's shock troops. The **Museo de la Secretaría de Hacienda y Crédito Público** (Museum of the Finance Secretariat; Map pp128-9; 9158-1245; Moneda 4; admission M$8, free Sun; 10am-6pm Tue-Sun; Zócalo) shows off its vast collection of Mexican art, much of it contributed by painters and sculptors in lieu of paying taxes. The former colonial archbishop's palace also hosts a full program of cultural events (many free), from puppet shows to chamber-music recitals.

Constructed in 1567 as the colonial mint, the **Museo Nacional de las Culturas** (National Museum of Cultures; Map pp128-9; 5512-7452; Moneda 13; admission free; 9:30am-6pm Tue-Sat, 10am-5pm Sun; Zócalo) exhibits art, dress and handicrafts of the world's cultures. A block further east, then a few steps north, a former convent houses the **Museo José Luis Cuevas** (Map pp128-9; 5522-0156; www.museojoseluiscuevas.com.mx; Academia 13; admission M$20, free Sun; 10am-5:30pm Tue-Sun; Zócalo). The museum showcases the works of artist Cuevas, a leader of the 1950s Ruptura movement which broke with the politicized art of the post-revolutionary regime. Cuevas' **La Giganta**, an 8m-tall bronze female figure with some male features, dominates the central patio.

Two blocks further east, the **Templo de la Santísima Trinidad** (Map pp128-9) sports a hyper-baroque facade with cherubs and apostles set into the finely filigreed stonework.

PLAZA SANTO DOMINGO

Two blocks north of the Zócalo is this smaller, less formal plaza. The printers who work beneath the **Portal de Evangelistas**, along its west side, are descendants of the scribes who did the paperwork for merchants using the customs building (now the Education Ministry) across the square. To the north stands the maroon stone **Iglesia de Santo Domingo** (Map pp128-9), a beautiful baroque church dating from 1736. The three-tiered facade merits a close look: statues of St Francis and St Augustine stand in the niches alongside the doorway. The middle panel shows Saint Dominic de Guzmán receiving a staff and the Epistles from St Peter and St Paul, respectively. At the top is a bas-relief of the Assumption of the Virgin Mary.

Opposite the church, the 18th-century **Palacio de la Inquisición** (Map pp128-9) was headquarters of the Holy Inquisition in Mexico until Spain decreed its closure in 1812. Its official shield shows up at the top of the facade.

MODERN DANCE

As you emerge from Metro Zócalo onto the vast central plaza, you'll invariably hear the booming of drums from the direction of the cathedral – the Aztec dancers are doing their thing. Wearing snakeskin loincloths, elaborately feathered headdresses and shell ankle bracelets, they move in a circle and chant in Náhuatl in what appears to be a display of pre-Hispanic aerobics. At the center, engulfed in a cloud of fragrant copal smoke, drummers bang on the conga-like *huehuetl* (indigenous drum) and the barrel-shaped, slitted *teponaztli*.

Variously known as Danzantes Aztecas, Danza Chichimeca or Concheros, the ritual is performed daily near the Templo Mayor, often throbbing on for hours without pause. It is meant to evoke the Aztec *mitote*, a frenzied ceremony performed by pre-Conquest Mexicans at harvest times. Yet scant evidence exists that their moves bear any resemblance to those of their forebears. Prohibited by the Spanish colonists from performing their dances or using the *huehuetl*, indigenous Mexicans fused elements of Christian worship into their rituals, dancing in the atriums of churches and playing mandolin-like instruments backed by an armadillo shell, or *concha* (from which the name Concheros derives).

Today's Zócalo dancers, however, reject any association with Christianity, seeking instead a purer connection to their pre-Hispanic roots. Critics mock their representation of a sacred but unknowable past as a pastiche of New Age nonsense. Yet this celebration of Mexica heritage appears to be developing into a movement, as it's embraced by more and more young Mexicans seeking a continuity with their past, many of whom you'll see gyrating along in their street clothes. Stranger still, the dance craze is being taken up by the descendants of the conquistadors, as roots-minded youth in Madrid go Aztec.

MURALS

In the 1920s the post-revolution Minister of Education, José Vasconcelos, commissioned talented young artists – among them Diego Rivera, David Alfaro Siqueiros and José Clemente Orozco – to decorate numerous public buildings with dramatic, large-scale murals conveying a new sense of Mexico's past and future.

One such building was the former monastery that housed the newly established **Secretaría de Educación Pública** (Secretariat of Education; Map pp128-9; ☎ 3003-1000; República de Brasil 31; admission free; ⏱ 9am-6pm Mon-Fri; Ⓜ Zócalo). The two front courtyards (on the opposite side of the building from the entrance off Plaza Santo Domingo) are lined with 120 fresco panels painted by Diego Rivera in the 1920s. Together they form a tableau of 'the very life of the people,' in the artist's words. Each courtyard is thematically distinct: the one on the east end deals with labor, industry and agriculture, while the interior one depicts traditions and festivals. On the latter's top level is a series on proletarian and agrarian revolution, underneath a continuous red banner emblazoned with a Mexican *corrido* (folk song). The likeness of Frida Kahlo appears in the first panel as an arsenal worker.

A block back toward the Zócalo, then east, is the **Antiguo Colegio de San Ildefonso** (Map pp128-9; ☎ 5702-6378; www.sanildefonso.org.mx; Justo Sierra 16; admission M$45, free Tue; ⏱ 10am-5:30pm Tue-Sun; Ⓜ Zócalo). Built in the 16th century as a Jeher training institute. In the 1920s, Rivera, Orozco, Siqueiros and others were brought in to do murals. Most of the work on the main patio is by Orozco; look for his portrait of Cortés and La Malinche underneath the staircase. The amphitheater, off the lobby, holds Rivera's first mural, *La Creación*, undertaken upon his return from Europe in 1923. Mural tours (in Spanish) are given at noon and 4pm. Nowadays, the San Ildefonso hosts outstanding temporary exhibitions, as well as the Filmoteca of the national university (p183).

More Orozco murals are inside the **Suprema Corte de Justicia** (Supreme Court; Map pp128-9; Pino Suárez 2; admission free, ID required; ⏱ 9am-5pm Mon-Fri; Ⓜ Zócalo), south of the Zócalo. In 1940, the artist painted four panels around the first level of the central stairway, two of which deal with the theme of justice. A more contemporary take on the same subject, *Los Siete Crímenes Mayores* (The Seven Worst Crimes), by Rafael Cauduro, unfolds over the three levels of the building's southwest stairwell. Executed in his hyperrealist style, the series catalogues the horrors of state-sponsored crimes against the

MEXICO CITY

populace, including the ever-relevant torture-induced confession. Cauduro's mural is one of four justice-related works recently commissioned by the Supreme Court for each of the building's corner stairwells.

The **Mercado Abelardo Rodríguez** (Map pp128–9; República de Venezuela, cnr Rodríguez Puebla; ☽ 8am-5pm; Ⓜ Zócalo), east of the Zócalo, became a canvas for a group of young international artists under the tutelage of Diego Rivera in the 1930s. Some of the most exuberant (and best-preserved) works, created by the American Greenwood sisters, cover the stairwell leading up to the community center, at the market's northeast corner. On the 1st floor, *Historia de México*, by the Japanese artist Isama Noguchi, is a dynamic three-dimensional mural sculpted of cement and plaster that symbolizes the struggle against fascism. Other murals inside the market's entry corridors are paeans to rural laborers and their traditions, though sadly, some are fading from neglect.

A block south, the **Templo de Nuestra Señora de Loreto** (Map pp128–9) has a remarkable dome. Ringed at the base by stained-glass images, it crowns an unusual four-lobed cross with semicircular chapels in the lobes. After the 1985 earthquake the building was raided of its treasures, and the murals that covered the underside of the cupola were allowed to deteriorate.

PLAZA TOLSÁ
Several blocks west of the Zócalo is this handsome square, named after the illustrious late-18th-century sculptor and architect who completed the Catedral Metropolitana.

Manuel Tolsá also created the bronze equestrian statue of the Spanish king Carlos IV (who reigned from 1788 to 1808) that is the plaza's centerpiece. It originally stood in the Zócalo, then on Paseo de la Reforma, before being moved here in 1979 ('as a work of art,' a chiseled plaque emphasizes).

King Carlos rides in front of the **Museo Nacional de Arte** (National Art Museum; Map pp128–9; ☎ 5130-3400; www.munal.com.mx; Tacuba 8; admission M$30, free Sun; ☽ 10:30am-5:30pm Tue-Sun; Ⓜ Bellas Artes). Built around 1900 in the style of an Italian renaissance palace, it holds collections representing every school of Mexican art until the early 20th century. A highlight is the work of José María Velasco, depicting the Valle de México in the late 19th century.

Opposite is the **Palacio de Minería** (Palace of Mining; Map pp128–9; ☎ 5623-2982; Tacuba 5; admission

M$25; ☽ tours 10am-3pm Sat & Sun; Ⓜ Bellas Artes), where mining engineers were trained in the 19th century. Today it houses a branch of the national university's engineering department. A neoclassical masterpiece, the palace was designed by Tolsá and built between 1797 and 1813. Visits are by guided tour only. The palace contains a small **museum** (admission M$10; ☽ 10am-6pm Wed-Sun) on Tolsá's life and work.

One block east of the plaza, the former hospital of the Bethlehemites (the only religious order to be established in the Americas), has since 2006 been the home of the **Museo Interactivo de la Economía** (Interactive Museum of Economics; Map pp128–9; ☎ 5130-4600; www.mide.org.mx; Tacuba 17; adult/child M$45/35; ☽ 9am-6pm Tue-Sun; Ⓜ Allende). A slew of hands-on exhibits are aimed at breaking down economic concepts. For coin connoisseurs, the highlight is the Banco de México's numismatic collection. Only a few of the exhibits provide English text.

AVENIDA MADERO
This stately avenue west of the Zócalo boasts a veritable catalogue of architectural styles interspersed with opticians and jewelers. Housed in a gorgeous neoclassical building two blocks from the square, the **Museo del Estanquillo** (Map pp128–9; ☎ 5521-3052; www.museodelestanquillo.com.mx; Isabel La Católica 26; admission free; ☽ 10am-6pm Wed-Mon; Ⓜ Allende) contains the vast pop-culture collection amassed over the decades by DF essayist and pack rat Carlos Monsivais. The recently inaugurated museum illustrates various phases in the capital's development by means of the numerous photos, paintings, board games, movie posters, comic strips and so on from the collection.

A few blocks westward you'll encounter the baroque facade of the late-18th-century **Palacio de Iturbide** (Map pp128–9; ☎ 1226-0011; Madero 17; admission free; ☽ 10am-7pm Wed-Mon; Ⓜ Allende). Built for colonial nobility, in 1821 it became the residence of General Agustín Iturbide, a hero of the struggle for independence who was proclaimed emperor here in 1822. (He abdicated less than a year later, after General Santa Anna announced the birth of a republic.) Now known as the Palacio de Cultura Banamex, it hosts exhibits drawn from the bank's vast Mexican art collection, as well as contemporary Mexican handicrafts. Some of the original salons are displayed on the upper level.

Half a block past the pedestrian corridor Gante stands the amazing **Casa de Azulejos** (House of Tiles; Map pp128-9; ☎ 5512-9820; Madero 4; ☯ 7am-1am; Ⓜ Allende). Dating from 1596, it was built for the Condes (Counts) del Valle de Orizaba. Most of the tiles that adorn the outside walls were produced in China and shipped to Mexico on the Manila *naos* (Spanish galleons used up to the early 19th century). The building now houses a Sanborns restaurant in a covered courtyard around a Moorish fountain. The staircase has a 1925 mural by Orozco.

Across the way, the **Templo de San Francisco** (Map pp128-9; Madero 7) is a remnant of the vast Franciscan monastery erected in the early 16th century over the site of Moctezuma's private zoo. In its heyday it extended two blocks south and east. The monastic complex was divvied up under the post-independence reform laws; in 1949, it was returned to the Franciscan order in a deplorable state and subsequently restored. The entrance is reached through a broad atrium where art exhibitions are held. The elaborately carved doorway is a shining example of 18th-century baroque.

Rising alongside the monastery, the **Torre Latinoamericana** (Latin American Tower; Map pp128-9; ☎ 5518-7423; Eje Central Lázaro Cárdenas 2; adult/child M$50/40; ☯ 9am-10pm; Ⓜ Bellas Artes) was Latin America's tallest building when constructed in 1956. (It's Mexico City's fifth-tallest tower today.) Thanks to the deep-seated pylons that anchor the building, it has withstood several major earthquakes. Views from the 44th-floor observation deck are spectacular, smog permitting.

MUSEO DE LA CIUDAD DE MÉXICO
For a good overview of the megalopolis, visit this **museum** (Museum of Mexico City; Map pp128-9; ☎ 5542-0083; Pino Suárez 30; admission M$20, Wed free; ☯ 10am-6pm Tue-Sun; Ⓜ Pino Suárez). The innovative permanent exhibit, 'It All Fits in a Basin,' presents a concise history of the city with models and maps; one room is devoted exclusively to the Zócalo and its role as a stage for social movements. Upstairs is the former studio of Joaquín Clausell, considered Mexico's foremost impressionist. The artist used the four walls of the windowless room as an ongoing sketchbook during the three decades he worked there until his death in 1935.

Alameda Central & Around
Emblematic of the downtown renaissance, the green rectangle immediately northwest of the Centro Histórico holds a vital place in Mexico City's cultural life. Surrounded by historically significant buildings, the Alameda Central has been the focus of ambitious redevelopment over the past decade. In particular, the high-rise towers on the Plaza Juárez have transformed the zone south of the park, much of which was destroyed in the 1985 earthquake. Metro stations Bellas Artes and Hidalgo are located on the Alameda's east and west sides, respectively.

ALAMEDA CENTRAL
Created in the late 1500s by mandate of then-viceroy Luis de Velasco, the Alameda (Map pp128–9) took its name from the *álamos* (poplars) planted over its rectangular expanse. By the late 19th century, the park was graced with European-style statuary and lit by gas lamps. It became the place to be seen for the city's elite. Today the Alameda is a popular refuge, particularly on Sunday when families stroll its broad pathways and gather for open-air concerts.

PALACIO DE BELLAS ARTES
Dominating the east end of the Alameda is this splendid white-marble **palace** (Palace of Fine Arts; Map pp128-9; ☎ 5130-0900; Av Juárez & Eje Central Lázaro Cárdenas; admission M$35, free Sun; ☯ 10am-6pm Tue-Sun; Ⓜ Bellas Artes), a concert hall and arts center commissioned by President Porfirio Díaz. Construction began in 1905 under Italian architect Adamo Boari, who favored neoclassical and art nouveau styles. Complications arose as the heavy marble shell sank into the spongy subsoil, and then the Mexican Revolution intervened. Architect Federico Mariscal eventually finished the interior in the 1930s, utilizing the more modern art deco style.

Immense murals dominate the upper floors. On the 2nd floor are two early-1950s works by Rufino Tamayo: *México de Hoy* (Mexico Today) and *Nacimiento de la Nacionalidad* (Birth of Nationality), a symbolic depiction of the creation of the mestizo identity.

At the west end of the 3rd floor is Diego Rivera's famous *El Hombre En El Cruce de Caminos* (Man at the Crossroads), originally commissioned for New York's Rockefeller Center. The Rockefellers had the original destroyed because of its anti-capitalist themes, but Rivera re-created it here in 1934.

On the north side are David Alfaro Siqueiros' three-part *La Nueva Democracía*

(New Democracy) and Rivera's four-part *Carnaval de la Vida Mexicana* (Carnival of Mexican Life); to the east is José Clemente Orozco's *La Katharsis* (Catharsis), depicting the conflict between humankind's 'social' and 'natural' aspects.

The 4th-floor **Museo Nacional de Arquitectura** (☎ 5512-2593; admission M$30, free Sun; ☺ 10am-6pm Tue-Sun) features changing exhibits on contemporary architecture.

The Bellas Artes theater (only available for viewing at performances) is itself a masterpiece, with a stained-glass curtain depicting the Valle de México. Based on a design by Mexican painter Gerardo Murillo (aka Dr Atl), it was assembled by New York jeweler Tiffany & Co from almost a million pieces of colored glass.

In addition, the palace stages outstanding temporary art exhibitions and the Ballet Folclórico de México (see p184). A worthwhile bookstore and elegant café are on the premises too.

PALACIO POSTAL

More than just Mexico City's central post office, this early-20th-century **palace** (Map pp128-9; ☎ 5521-1408; Tacuba 1; Ⓜ Bellas Artes) is an Italianate confection designed by the Palacio de Bellas Artes' original architect, Adamo Boari. The beige stone facade features baroque columns and carved filigree around the windows; inside, the bronze railings on the monumental staircase were cast in Florence. Philatelists can ogle the first stamp ever issued in Mexico in the 1st-floor **postal museum** (admission free; ☺ 10am-5:30pm Mon-Fri, 10am-1:30pm Sat).

PLAZA DE SANTA VERACRUZ

The sunken square north of the Alameda across Av Hidalgo is named for the slanting structure on the right, the **Iglesia de la Santa Veracruz**. Elaborately carved pillars flank the doorway of the 18th-century church.

On the opposite side of the plaza, the **Museo Franz Mayer** (Map pp128-9; ☎ 5518-2266; www .franzmayer.org.mx; Hidalgo 45; admission M$35, Tue free; ☺ 10am-5pm Tue & Thu-Sun, 10am-7pm Wed; Ⓜ Bellas Artes) is housed in the old hospice of the San Juan de Dios order, which under the brief reign of Maximilian became a halfway house for prostitutes. The museum is the fruit of the efforts of Franz Mayer, born in Mannheim, Germany, in 1882. Prospering as a financier in his adopted Mexico, Mayer amassed the collection of Mexican silver, textiles, ceramics and furniture that is now on display. The exhibit halls open off a sumptuous colonial patio with the excellent Cloister Café.

Adjacent to the museum across an alley, the **Museo Nacional de la Estampa** (Map pp128-9; ☎ 5521-2244; Av Hidalgo 39; admission M$10, free Sun; ☺ 10am-5:45pm Tue-Sun) is devoted to the graphic arts, with thematic exhibits from its collection of more than 10,000 prints.

MUSEO MURAL DIEGO RIVERA

Among Diego Rivera's most famous works is *Sueño de una Tarde Dominical en la Alameda* (Dream of a Sunday Afternoon in the Alameda), painted in 1947. In the 15m-long mural, the artist imagined many of the figures who walked in the city from colonial times onward, among them Cortés, Juárez, Porfirio Díaz and Francisco Madero. All are grouped around a *Catrina* (skeleton in prerevolutionary women's garb). Rivera himself, as a pug-faced child, and Frida Kahlo stand beside the skeleton. Charts identify all the characters.

Just west of the Alameda, the **Museo Mural Diego Rivera** (Diego Rivera Mural Museum; Map pp128-9; ☎ 5510-2329; cnr Balderas & Colón; admission M$15, free Sun; ☺ 10am-6pm Tue-Sun; Ⓜ Hidalgo) was built in 1986 to house the mural, after its original location, the Hotel del Prado, was wrecked by the 1985 earthquake.

LABORATORIO DE ARTE ALAMEDA

As is often the case with museums in the Centro Histórico, the building that contains the **Laboratorio de Arte Alameda** (Alameda Art Laboratory; Map pp128-9; ☎ 5510-2793; www.artealameda .inba.gob.mx; Dr Mora 7; admission M$15, free Sun; ☺ 9am-5pm Tue-Sun; Ⓜ Hidalgo) is at least as interesting as its contents. The former church is just a fragment of the 17th-century Convento de San Diego that was dismantled under the post-independence reform laws. As the museum's name suggests, it hosts installations by leading experimental artists from Mexico and abroad, with an emphasis on current electronic, virtual and interactive media.

PLAZA JUÁREZ

Representing the new face of the zone, this modern plaza is opposite the Alameda's **Hemiciclo a Juárez**, a marble monument to post-independence president Benito Juárez, and behind the fully restored **Templo de Corpus Christi**, which now holds the DF's archives. The plaza's centerpiece is a pair of Tetris-block towers by leading Mexican architect Ricardo Legorreta: the 24-story **Foreign Relations Secretariat** and the 23-story **Tribunales** (courts) building. Fronting these monoliths is some interesting art, including a bronze aviary by sculptor Juan Soriano and, near the west entrance, a David Siqueiros mosaic originally designed for a Chrysler factory. Perhaps the most arresting piece is a set of 1034 reddish pyramids in a broad pool, a collaboration between Legorreta and Spanish artist Vicente Rojo. The plaza also hosts excellent photo exhibits.

MUSEO DE ARTE POPULAR

Opened recently (in 2006), this **museum** (Museum of Popular Art; Map pp128-9; ☎ 5510-2201; www.map .org.mx; Revillagigedo 11; admission free; ☉ 10am-5pm Tue-Sun, 10am-9pm Thu; Ⓜ Juárez) is a major showcase for Mexico's folk arts and traditions. Contemporary crafts from all over Mexico are thematically displayed on the museum's three levels, including pottery from Michoacán, carnival masks from Chiapas, *alebrijes* (fanciful animal figures) from Oaxaca and trees of life from Puebla. The museum occupies the former fire department headquarters, itself an outstanding example of 1920s art deco by architect Vicente Mendiola. Not surprisingly, the ground-level shop is an excellent place to look for quality handicrafts.

LA CIUDADELA

The formidable compound now known as 'The Citadel' started off as a tobacco factory in the late 18th century, though it's best known as the scene of the Decena Trágica (Tragic Ten Days), the coup that brought down the Madero government in 1913. Today it is home to the **Biblioteca de México José Vasconcelos** (National Library; Map pp128-9; ☎ 9172-4730; Plaza de la Ciudadela 4; ☉ 8:30am-7:30pm; Ⓜ Balderas), with holdings of over 260,000 volumes and an extensive maps collection. The central halls are given over to art exhibits.

At the Calle Balderas entrance is the **Centro de la Imagen** (Map pp128-9; ☎ 9172-4724; www.con aculta.gob.mx/cimagen; admission free; ☉ 11am-6pm Tue-Sun; Ⓜ Balderas), the city's photography museum. This innovatively designed space stages compelling exhibitions, often focusing on documentary views of Mexican life by some of the country's sharpest observers.

Plaza de la República & Around

This plaza, west of the Alameda Central, is dominated by the vaguely Stalinist domed Monumento a la Revolución. The grand

---

MEXICO CITY IN...

Two Days

Day one dawns and you're overlooking the Zócalo from one of the rooftop restaurants on the west side of the grand plaza. Descend into the capital's Aztec underpinnings at the **Templo Mayor** (p143), then admire Diego Rivera's ambitiouscinematic murals at the **Palacio Nacional** (p142). Take the **Turibús** (p165) for a survey of the city's neighborhoods, getting off in **Polanco** (p155) or the **Zona Rosa** (p151) for lunch and shopping. Spend the evening relaxing at a café near your hotel, or if you're up for it, tequila-tasting with the mariachis at Plaza Garibaldi. Day two, delve into Mexico's past at the **Museo Nacional de Antropología** (p153) and **Castillo de Chapultepec** (p153).

Four Days

With a couple more days, head out to the pyramids at **Teotihuacán** (p209). Spend a morning roaming around the **Alameda Central** (p147), making time to acquaint yourself with the **Palacio de Bellas Artes** (p147) and newly minted **Plaza Juárez** (opposite). Have the quintessential Mexican *comida* (lunch) at **El Cardenal** (p173), then do some *artesanías* (crafts) shopping at **La Ciudadela** (above). In the evening plug into the lively nightlife scene in **Condesa** (p186).

One Week

Get to know the southern districts: visit the **Museo Frida Kahlo** (p158) in Coyoacán; hire a *trajinera* (gondola) for a cruise along the ancient canals of **Xochimilco** (p155); shop for quality crafts at San Ángel's **Bazar Sábado market** (p189). Reserve Wednesday or Sunday evening for the **Ballet Folclórico** (p184) at the Palacio de Bellas Artes.

art deco building northeast of the plaza is the Frontón de México, a now-defunct jai-alai arena.

MONUMENTO A LA REVOLUCIÓN

Begun in the 1900s under Porfirio Díaz, this monument (Map pp128-9) was originally meant to be a legislative chamber. But construction (not to mention Díaz' presidency) was interrupted by the Revolution. Though they considered demolishing it, the new regime chose instead to modify the structure and give it a new role. Unveiled in 1938, it contained the tombs of the revolutionary and post-revolutionary heroes Pancho Villa, Francisco Madero, Venustiano Carranza, Plutarco Elías Calles and Lázaro Cárdenas.

Underlying the plaza, the **Museo Nacional de la Revolución** (National Museum of the Revolution; Map pp128-9; ☎ 5546-2115; Plaza de la República; admission M$15, free Sun; ⏰ 9am-5pm Tue-Sun; Ⓜ Revolución) covers a 63-year period, from the implementation of the constitution guaranteeing human rights in 1857 to the installation of the post-revolutionary government in 1920. Despite the compelling subject matter, explanatory text remains untranslated.

MUSEO NACIONAL DE SAN CARLOS

This **museum** (Map pp128-9; ☎ 5566-8342; Puente de Alvarado 50; admission M$25, Mon free; ⏰ 10am-6pm Wed-Mon; Ⓜ Revolución) exhibits a formidable collection of European art from the 16th to the early 20th century, including works by Rubens, Van Dyck and Goya. Occupying the former mansion of the Conde de Buenavista, the unusual rotunda structure was designed by Manuel Tolsá in the late 18th century.

Paseo de la Reforma

Mexico City's grandest thoroughfare traces a bold southwestern path from Tlatelolco to Bosque de Chapultepec, skirting the Alameda Central and Zona Rosa before heading due west through Bosque de Chapultepec. Emperor Maximilian of Hapsburg laid out the boulevard to connect his castle on Chapultepec Hill with the old city center. After his execution, it was given its current name to commemorate the reform laws instituted by President Benito Juárez. Under the López Obrador administration, the avenue was smartly refurbished and its broad, statue-studded medians became a stage for book fairs and art exhibits. It is currently undergoing aggressive development,

with office towers and new hotels springing up along its length.

Paseo de la Reforma links a series of monumental *glorietas* (traffic circles). A couple of blocks west of the Alameda Central is **El Caballito** (Map pp128-9), a bright-yellow representation of a horse's head by the sculptor Sebastián. It commemorates another equestrian sculpture that stood here for 127 years and today fronts the Museo Nacional de Arte (p146). A few blocks southwest is the **Monumento a Cristóbal Colón** (Map pp128-9), an 1877 statue of Columbus gesturing toward the horizon.

Reforma's busy intersection with Av Insurgentes is marked by the **Monumento a Cuauhtémoc** (Map pp128-9), memorializing the last Aztec emperor. Two blocks northwest is the **Jardín del Arte**, site of a lively Sunday art market (p189).

The **Centro Bursátil** (Map pp132-3), an angular tower and mirror-ball ensemble housing the nation's stock exchange (Bolsa), marks the northeast corner of the Zona Rosa. Continuing west past the US embassy, you reach the symbol of Mexico City, the **Monumento a la Independencia** (Map pp132-3; admission free; ⏰ 10am-6pm; Ⓜ Insurgentes). Known as 'El Ángel,' this gilded Winged Victory on a 45m pillar was sculpted for the independence centennial of 1910. Inside the monument are the remains of Miguel Hidalgo, José María Morelos, Ignacio Allende and nine other notables.

At Reforma's intersection with Sevilla is the monument commonly known as **La Diana Cazadora** (Diana the Huntress; Map pp132-3), a 1942 bronze sculpture actually meant to represent the Archer of the North Star. The League of Decency under the Ávila Camacho administration had the sculptor add a loincloth to the buxom babe, which wasn't removed until 1966.

A 2003 addition to the Mexico City skyline, the **Torre Mayor** (Map pp132-3; Paseo de la Reforma 505) stands like a sentinel before the gate to Bosque de Chapultepec. The green-glass tower soars 225m above the capital, making it Latin America's tallest building. The earthquake-resistant structure is anchored below by 98 seismic shock absorbers. Unfortunately, the building's top tower observation deck was shut in 2006.

Metro Hidalgo accesses Paseo de la Reforma on the Alameda end, while the Insurgentes and Sevilla stations provide the best approach to

DEATH'S NEW FACE

Garbed in a sequined white gown, wearing a wig of dark tresses and clutching a scythe in her bony hand, the skeletal figure bears an eerie resemblance to Mrs Bates from the film *Psycho*. Santa Muerte (Saint Death), as she is known, is the object of a fast-growing cult in Mexico, particularly in the rough Barrio Tepito, where the principal **altar** (Map pp126-7; Ⓜ Tepito) stands on Alfarería north of Mineros. Possibly rooted in pre-Hispanic ritual, Santa Muerte has been linked to Mictlantecuhtli, the Mexican god of death.

On the first day of each month, as many as 5000 followers line up at the Tepito altar to express their devotion and leave candles, bottles of tequila and other tokens of their affection. The proceedings are overseen by the cheerful Enriqueta 'Doña Queta' Romero, who built the shrine herself back in 2001.

At the saint's official home 1km south of the shrine, however, Doña Queta is nowhere to be seen. Instead, the **Santuario Nacional de la Santa Muerte** (National Sanctuary of Saint Death; Map pp126-7; ☎ 5702-8607; Bravo 35; 🕑 10am-6pm Tue-Fri, 11am-6pm Sun; Ⓜ Morelos) has a new figure of worship, a tall, winged woman with a ghostly pale complexion (though like her predecessor, she bears a scythe). In August 2007, the church substituted this ethereal Angel of Saint Death because, as its bishop explained, Santa Muerte had become associated with drug runners, Satanists and other bad elements, an image, he claimed, that runs counter to her nature.

Some attribute the image change to other factors. The saint's popularity, especially among the lower echelons of society, is feared to be rivaling that of the Virgin of Guadalupe, and the Roman Catholic Church has harshly denounced the cult. The Traditional Catholic Mex-USA Church, the cross-border sect's official title, had recently lost its recognition (and associated tax benefits) by Mexico's Board of Religious Associations and is petitioning to regain its former status. But if the new version of Santa Muerte is in fact the church's attempt to demonstrate a more wholesome mission, it runs the risk of losing its more fervent devotees to keepers of the flame like Doña Queta.

While the altar and sanctuary are open to the public, travelers should be aware that the Tepito neighborhood is notorious among Mexicans as a scene of criminal activity and that church members may not welcome the scrutiny of curious onlookers.

the Zona Rosa. From the Insurgentes metrobus, take the 'Reforma' or 'Hamburgo' stops north and south of the avenue, respectively. Along Reforma itself, any westbound 'Metro Auditorio' bus goes through the Bosque de Chapultepec, while 'Metro Chapultepec' buses terminate at the east end of the park. In the opposite direction, 'Metro Hidalgo' and 'La Villa' buses head up Reforma to the Alameda Central and beyond.

Zona Rosa

Wedged between Paseo de la Reforma and Av Chapultepec, the 'Pink Zone' was developed as an international playground and shopping district during the 1950s, when it enjoyed a cosmopolitan panache. It's been in decline since the installation of Metro Insurgentes on its southern edge, arriving at its current condition as a hodgepodge of touristy boutiques, strip clubs, discos and fast-food franchises. People-watching from its sidewalk cafés reveals a higher degree of diversity than elsewhere: it's the city's principal gay and lesbian district and an expat haven, with a significant Korean population. Recently, the Ebrard administration has been busy face-lifting the Calle Génova pedestrian mall in attempts to put the zone back in the pink.

Condesa

Colonia Condesa's architecture, palm-lined esplanades and parks echo its origins as a haven for a newly emerging elite in the early 20th century. Only recently has 'La Condesa' earned its reputation as a trendy area of informal restaurants, hip boutiques and hot nightspots. Fortunately, much of the neighborhood's old flavor remains, especially for those willing to wander outside the valet-parking zones. Stroll the pedestrian medians along Ámsterdam, Tamaulipas or Mazatlán to admire art-deco and California colonial-style buildings. A focus is the peaceful **Parque México** (Map pp132–3), with an oval shape that reflects its earlier use as a horse-racing track. It makes for a delightful ramble, especially in spring when lavender jacaranda blossoms carpet the paths. Two blocks northwest is **Parque España** (Map pp132–3), with a children's fun fair.

Immediately northeast of Parque México, the **Edificio Basurto** (México 187), an aerodynamically streamlined structure from the mid-1940s, is a paragon of the deco style. Ask the doorman to let you peek inside at the amazing snail-shell staircase. Across the way, the **Edificio Tehuacán** (México 188), recently converted into the upscale Hippodrome Hotel (p171), features a typical deco marquee, as well as a Maya-influenced arch around the entryway.

Roma

Northeast of Condesa, Roma is a bohemian enclave inhabited by artists and writers. This is where beat writers William S Burroughs and Jack Kerouac naturally gravitated during their 1950s sojourn to Mexico City. Built at the turn of the 20th century, the neighborhood is a showcase for the Parisian-influenced architecture favored by the Porfirio Díaz regime. Some of the most outstanding examples stand along Calles Colima and Tabasco. When in Roma, browse the secondhand-book stores, linger in the cafés and check out a few art galleries. A stroll down Calle Orizaba passes two lovely plazas – Río de Janeiro, with a statue of David, and Luis Cabrera, which has dancing fountains. On weekends inspect the **antique market** along Av Álvaro Obregón, the main thoroughfare.

GALLERIES

Small, independent art galleries are scattered around Roma – see www.arte-mexico.com (in Spanish) for a map.

Centro de Cultura Casa Lamm (Map pp132-3; ☎ 5511-0899; www.galeriascasalamm.com.mx; Álvaro Obregón 99; admission free; ☒ 10am-6pm Tue-Sun; Ⓜ Insurgentes) This cultural complex contains a gallery for contemporary Mexican painting and photography as well as an excellent art library.

Galería Nina Menocal (Map pp132-3; ☎ 5564-7209; www.ninamenocal.com; Zacatecas 93; ☒ 9am-7pm Mon-Fri, 10am-1pm Sat; ▣ Álvaro Obregón) Highlights emerging Cuban and Latin American artists.

MUCA Roma (Map pp132-3; ☎ 5511-0925; Tonalá 51; ☒ 10am-6pm; ▣ Durango) Roma branch of the university museum (p157).

Bosque de Chapultepec

Chapultepec – Náhuatl for 'Hill of Grasshoppers' – served as a refuge for the wandering Aztecs before becoming a summer residence for their noble class. It was the nearest freshwater supply for Tenochtitlán; in the 15th century Nezahualcóyotl, ruler of nearby Texcoco, oversaw the construction of an aqueduct to channel its waters over Lago de Texcoco to the pre-Hispanic capital.

Today Mexico City's largest park, the Bosque de Chapultepec covers more than 4 sq km, with lakes, a zoo and several excellent museums. It also remains an abode of Mexico's high and mighty, containing the current presidential residence, **Los Pinos** (Map pp136–7), and a former imperial palace, the Castillo de Chapultepec.

Sunday is the park's big day as vendors line the main paths and throngs of families come to picnic, navigate the big lake on rowboats and crowd into the museums. Most of the major attractions are in or near the eastern **1a Sección** (1st Section; Map pp136-7; ☒ 5am-5pm Tue-Sun), while a large amusement park and children's museum dominate the **2a Sección** (2nd Section; Map pp136-7; ☒ 24hr).

A pair of bronze lions overlook the main gate at Paseo de la Reforma and Lieja, across from the Torre Mayor building. Other access points are opposite the Museo Nacional de Antropología and by Metro Chapultepec. The fence along Paseo de la Reforma serves as the **Galería Abierta de las Rejas de Chapultepec**, an outdoor photo gallery extending from the zoo entrance to the Rufino Tamayo museum.

Chapultepec metro station is at the east end of the Bosque de Chapultepec, near the Monumento a los Niños Héroes and Castillo de Chapultepec. Auditorio metro station is on the north side of the park, 500m west of the Museo Nacional de Antropología. See p150 for information on Reforma bus routes.

To get to the 2a Sección and La Feria, from metro Chapultepec take the 'Paradero' exit and catch a 'Feria' bus at the top of the stairs. These depart continuously and travel nonstop to the 2a Sección, dropping off riders at the Papalote Museo del Niño, Museo Tecnológico and La Feria.

MONUMENTO A LOS NIÑOS HÉROES

The six marble columns marking the eastern entrance to the park (Map pp136–7), near Chapultepec metro, commemorate the 'boy heroes,' six brave cadets who perished in battle. On September 13, 1847, more than 8000 American troops stormed Chapultepec Castle, which then housed the national military academy. Mexican General Santa Anna retreated before the onslaught, excusing the cadets from fighting, but the youths, aged 13 to 20, chose to defend the castle. Legend has it that one of them, Juan Escutia, wrapped himself in a Mexican flag and leapt to his death rather than surrender.

CASTILLO DE CHAPULTEPEC

A visible reminder of Mexico's bygone aristocracy, the 'castle' that stands atop Chapultepec Hill was begun in 1785 but not completed until after independence, when it became the national military academy. When Emperor Maximilian and Empress Carlota arrived in 1864, they refurbished it as their residence. It then sheltered Mexico's presidents until 1939 when President Lázaro Cárdenas converted it into the **Museo Nacional de Historia** (National History Museum; Map pp136-7; ☎ 5061-9200; www.castillo dechapultepec.inah.gob.mx; adult/under 13yr M$45/free, free Sun; ☒ 9am-5pm Tue-Sun; Ⓜ Chapultepec).

Historical exhibits chronicle the period from the rise of colonial Nueva España to the Mexican Revolution. In addition to displaying such iconic objects as the sword wielded by José María Morelos in the Siege of Cuautla and the Virgin of Guadalupe banner borne by Miguel Hidalgo in his march for independence, the museum features a number of dramatic interpretations of Mexican history by leading muralists including Juan O'Gorman's panoramic *Retablo de la Independencia* (Panel of Independence) in room 6. Explanatory text is untranslated.

The east end of the castle preserves the palace occupied by Maximilian and Carlota, with sumptuously furnished salons opening onto an exterior deck that affords sweeping city views. On the upper floor, Porfirio Díaz' opulent rooms surround a patio where a tower marks the top of Chapultepec Hill, 45m above street level.

To reach the castle, follow the road that curves up the hill behind the Monumento a los Niños Héroes. Alternatively, a train-like vehicle (M$10 round trip) runs up every 15 minutes while the castle is open.

Back at ground level, follow the south side of the hill's base to find the formidable **Tribuna Monumental de las Águilas** (Map pp136-7) dedicated to Mexico's WWII veterans. On the left side of the monument, enter the **Audiorama** (Map pp136-7), a pebbly garden with body-contoured benches where you can enjoy opera or classical music.

JARDÍN BOTÁNICO

Gardening is an ancient pastime in Mexico – Nezahualcóyotl was planting cypresses here six centuries ago for their sheer aesthetic value – and the recently opened **Jardín Botánico** (Botanical Garden; Map pp136-7; ☎ 5553-8114; admission free; ☒ 10am-4pm), 300m east of the anthropology museum, carries the tradition forward. Highlighting Mexico's plant diversity, the 4-hectare complex is divided in sections that reflect the country's varied climate zones, with a special emphasis on the plants and trees of central Mexico. Still in a nascent stage, it features a desert-like patch of diminutive cactuses and a greenhouse full of rare orchids.

MUSEO DE ARTE MODERNO

This **museum** (Museum of Modern Art; Map pp136-7; ☎ 5211-8331; cnr Paseo de la Reforma & Gandhi; admission M$2, free Sun; ☒ 10am-6pm Tue-Sun; Ⓜ Chapultepec) exhibits work by noteworthy 20th-century Mexican artists. The main building consists of four skylit rotundas, housing canvasses by Dr Atl, Rivera, Siqueiros, Orozco, Kahlo, Tamayo and O'Gorman, among others. *Las Dos Fridas*, possibly Frida Kahlo's most well-known painting, is in the Sala Xavier Villarrutia. Just northwest of the Monumento a los Niños Héroes (access is via Paseo de la Reforma), the museum has a pleasant café beside a sculpture garden.

ZOOLÓGICO DE CHAPULTEPEC

Home to a wide range of the world's creatures in large open-air enclosures, the **Chapultepec Zoo** (Map pp136-7; ☎ 5553-6263; www.chapultepec.df.gob .mx; admission free; ☒ 9am-4:30pm Tue-Sun; Ⓜ Auditorio) was the first place outside China where pandas were born in captivity. The zoo has three of these rare bears, descendants of the original pair donated by the People's Republic in 1975. Endangered Mexican species include the Mexican grey wolf and the hairless xoloitzcuintle, the only surviving dog species from pre-Hispanic times. Parrots, macaws, toucans, flamingos and other Mexican species swoop around the Aviario Moctezuma (only 20 visitors allowed in at a time).

MUSEO NACIONAL DE ANTROPOLOGÍA

This **museum** (National Museum of Anthropology; Map pp136-7; ☎ 5553-6381; www.mna.inah.gob.mx; cnr Paseo de la Reforma & Gandhi; admission M$48; 🕑 9am-7pm Tue-Sun; Ⓜ Auditorio) stands in an extension of the Bosque de Chapultepec. The spacious complex, constructed in the 1960s, is the work of Mexican architect Pedro Ramírez Vázquez. An immense umbrella-like stone fountain rises up from the center of the courtyard.

Its long, rectangular courtyard is surrounded on three sides by two-level display halls. The 12 ground-floor *salas* (halls) are dedicated to pre-Hispanic Mexico, while upper-level *salas* show how Mexico's indigenous descendants live today, with the contemporary cultures located directly above their ancestral civilizations. The ground-floor exhibits spill out to the surrounding gardens, where replicas of temples stand. Everything is superbly displayed, with much explanatory text translated into English. Audio-guide devices, in English, are available at the entrance (M$60).

The vast museum offers more than most people can absorb in a single visit. Concentrate on the regions you plan to visit or have visited, with a quick look at some of the other eye-catching exhibits. Here's a brief guide to the ground-floor halls, proceeding counterclockwise around the courtyard.

Culturas Indígenas de México Currently serves as a space for temporary exhibitions.

Introducción a la Antropología Introduces visitors to the field of anthropology.

Poblamiento de América Demonstrates how the hemisphere's earliest settlers got here and survived in their new environment.

Preclásico en el Altiplano Central Focuses on the pre-classic period, approximately 2300 BC to AD 100, and the transition from a nomadic hunting life to a more settled farming life in Mexico's Central Highlands.

Teotihuacán Displays models and objects from the Americas' first great and powerful state.

Los Toltecas y Su Época Covers cultures of central Mexico between about AD 650 and 1250; on display is one of the four basalt warrior columns from Tula's Temple of Tlahuizcalpantecuhtli.

Mexica Devoted to the Mexicas, aka Aztecs. Come here to see the famous sun stone, unearthed beneath the Zócalo in 1790, and other magnificent sculptures from the pantheon of Aztec deities.

Culturas de Oaxaca Displays the legacy of Oaxaca's Zapotec and Mixtec civilizations.

Culturas de la Costa del Golfo Spotlights the important civilizations along the Gulf of Mexico including the Olmec, Totonac and Huastec. Stone carvings include two Olmec heads weighing in at almost 20 tons.

Maya Exhibits findings from southeast Mexico, Guatemala, Belize and Honduras. A full-scale replica of the tomb of King Pakal, discovered deep in the Templo de las Inscripciones at Palenque, is breathtaking.

Culturas del Occidente Profiles cultures of western Mexico.

Culturas del Norte Covers the Casas Grandes (Paquimé) site and other cultures from northern Mexico, and traces their links with indigenous groups of the US southwest.

In a clearing about 100m in front of the museum's entrance, indigenous Totonac people perform their spectacular *voladores* rite – 'flying' from a 20m-high pole – several times a day.

MUSEO RUFINO TAMAYO

A multilevel concrete-and-glass structure east of the Museo Nacional de Antropología, the **Tamayo Museum** (Map pp136–7; ☎ 5286-6519; www .museotamayo.org; admission M$15, free Sun; 🕑 10am-6pm Tue-Sun; Ⓜ Auditorio) was built to house international modern art donated by Oaxaca-born Rufino Tamayo and his wife, Olga, to the people of Mexico. Exhibitions of cutting-edge modern art from around the globe alternate with thematically arranged shows from the Tamayo collection.

SEGUNDA (2A) SECCIÓN

The second section of the Bosque de Chapultepec lies west of the Periférico. In addition to family attractions, there is a pair of upscale lake-view restaurants on the Lago Mayor and Lago Menor.

Kids will enjoy **La Feria** (Map pp136–7; ☎ 5230-2121; passes from M$50; 🕑 10am-6pm Tue-Fri, 10am-7pm Sat, 10am-8pm Sun; Ⓜ Constituyentes), an old-fashioned amusement park with some hair-raising rides. A 'Super Ecolín' passport (M$80) is good for everything but the rollercoaster.

Your children won't want to leave **Papalote Museo del Niño** (Map pp136–7; ☎ 5237-1773; www .papalote.org.mx; adult/2-11yr & seniors M$85/80; 🕑 9am-6pm Mon-Wed & Fri, 9am-11pm Thu, 10am-7pm Sat & Sun; Ⓜ Constituyentes). At this innovative, hands-on museum, kids can put together a radio program, lie on a bed of nails, join an archaeological dig and try out all manner of technological gadget-games. The museum also features a 3D IMAX movie theater.

About 200m west of the Papalote, turn right to reach the **Fuente de Tláloc** (Map pp136–7), an oval pool inhabited by a huge mosaic-skinned sculpture of the rain god by Diego Rivera.

There's more Rivera art inside the Chapultepec water works, behind the fountain. The artist painted a series of murals entitled **El Agua, El Origen de la Vida** (Water, Origin of Life; admission M$10; 🕙 10am-6pm Sat) for the inauguration of the project, constructed in the 1940s to channel the waters of the Río Lerma into giant cisterns to supply the city. Experimenting with waterproof paints, Rivera covered the collection tank and part of the pipeline with images of amphibious beings. Though technically only open Saturdays, the guard can be persuaded to let you in for a tip.

To the north is the beautiful **Fuente de Xochipilli** (Map pp136–7), dedicated to the Aztec 'flower prince,' with terraced fountains around a pyramid in the style of a *talud tablero* (a building style typical of Teotihuacán).

Polanco

The affluent neighborhood of Polanco, north of Bosque de Chapultepec, arose in the 1940s as a residential alternative for a burgeoning middle class anxious to escape the overcrowded Centro. Looking northward for architectural inspiration, builders erected many homes in the California Colonial style, a Hollywood take on Andalucian splendor. Polanco is known as a Jewish enclave though the community has largely migrated further west to Lomas de Chapultepec.

Today the area is known for its exclusive hotels, fine restaurants, nightlife and designer stores, with much of the retail activity along Av Presidente Masaryk. Some of the city's most prestigious art galleries are here, including the **Galería López Quiroga** (Map pp136-7; ☎ 5280-1710; Aristóteles 169) and the **Galería Alberto Misrachi** (Map pp136-7; ☎ 5281-7456; Campos Elíseos 215), inside the Hotel Nikko. Metro Polanco accesses the center of the neighborhood while Metro Auditorio is on its southern edge.

Xochimilco & Around

Almost at the southern edge of the Distrito Federal, a network of canals flanked by gardens is a vivid reminder of the city's pre-Hispanic legacy. Remnants of the *chinampas* where the indigenous inhabitants grew their food, these 'floating gardens' are still in use today. Gliding along the canals in a fancifully decorated *trajinera* (gondola) is an alternately tranquil and festive experience that should seduce even the most jaded traveler. As if that weren't reason enough for an ex-

cursion, Xochimilco also boasts an endlessly explorable public market, a handful of visitor-friendly *pulquerías*, and one of the city's best art museums.

To reach Xochimilco, take the metro to Tasqueña station, then continue on the Tren Ligero (M$2) to its last stop. Upon exiting the station, turn left (north) and follow Av Morelos to the market, plaza and church. If you don't feel like walking, bicycle taxis (M$30 to M$50) will shuttle you to the *embarcaderos* (boat landings).

MUSEO DOLORES OLMEDO PATIÑO

Possibly the most important Diego Rivera collection of all belongs to this **museum** (Map p138; ☎ 5555-1221; Av México 5843; admission M$40, free Tue; 🕙 10am-6pm Tue-Sun), ensconced in a peaceful 17th-century hacienda 2km west of central Xochimilco.

Dolores Olmedo Patiño, who resided here until her death in 2002, was a socialite and a patron of Rivera. The museum's 144 Rivera works – including oils, watercolors and lithographs from various periods – are displayed alongside pre-Hispanic figurines and folk art. Another room is reserved for Frida Kahlo's paintings. Outside the exhibit halls, you'll see xoloitzcuintles, a pre-Hispanic hairless canine breed, roaming the estate's extensive gardens.

To get there take the Tren Ligero from metro Tasqueña and get off at La Noria. Leaving the station, turn left at the top of the steps and descend to the street. Upon reaching an intersection with a footbridge, take a sharp left, almost doubling back on your path, onto Antiguo Camino a Xochimilco. The museum is 300m down this street.

CANALS

Xochimilco, Náhuatl for 'Place where Flowers Grow,' was an early target of Aztec hegemony, probably due to its inhabitants' farming skills. The Xochimilcas piled up vegetation and mud in the shallow waters of Lake Xochimilco, a southern offshoot of Lago de Texcoco, to make fertile gardens called *chinampas*, which later became an economic base of the Aztec empire. As the *chinampas* proliferated, much of the lake was transformed into a series of canals. Approximately 180km of these waterways remain today and provide a favorite weekend destination for Chilangos. The *chinampas* are still under cultivation, mainly for garden

MEXICO CITY

plants and flowers such as poinsettias and marigolds. Owing to its cultural and historical significance, Xochimilco was designated a Unesco World Heritage Site in 1987.

On weekends a fiesta atmosphere takes over as the waterways become jammed with boats carrying groups of families and friends. Local vendors and musicians hover alongside the partygoers serving food and drink, playing marimbas and taking photos with old box cameras. (Midweek, the mood is far mellower.)

Hundreds of colorful *trajineras* await passengers at the village's nine *embarcaderos*. Nearest to the center are Salitre and San Cristóbal, both 400m east of the plaza, and Fernando Celada, 400m west on Guadalupe Ramírez. Boats seat 14 to 20 persons; official cruise prices (M$140 to M$160 per hour) are posted. On Saturday, Sunday and holidays, 60-person *lanchas colectivos* (boat taxis) run between the Salitre, Caltongo and Nativitas *embarcaderos*, charging M$20 per passenger round trip.

You can get a taste of Xochimilco in an hour, but it's worth going for longer; you'll see more and get a proper chance to relax. You can arrange for your *trajinera* to stop at Nativitas *embarcadero* for some shopping at its *artesanías* market.

Though the canals are definitely the main attraction, Xochimilco village has plenty to see. East of Jardín Juárez is the 16th-century **Parroquia de San Bernardino de Siena** (Map p138), with elaborate gold-painted *retablos* (altarpieces) and a tree-studded atrium. South of the plaza, the bustling **Mercado de Xochimilco** (Map p138) covers two vast buildings: the one nearer the Jardín Juárez has colorful flower displays and an eating 'annex' for tamales and other prepared foods; the one nearer the train station sells mostly produce and household goods, with a few pottery stalls.

San Ángel

Settled by the Dominican order soon after the Spanish conquest, San Ángel, 12km southwest of the center, maintains its colonial splendor despite being engulfed by the metropolis. It's often associated with the big Saturday crafts market held alongside the Plaza San Jacinto. Though the main approach via Av Insurgentes is typically chaotic, wander westward to experience the old village's cobblestoned soul; it's a tranquil enclave of colonial mansions with

massive wooden doors, potted geraniums behind window grills and bougainvillea spilling over stone walls.

The La Bombilla station of the Av Insurgentes metrobus is about 500m east of the Plaza San Jacinto. Otherwise, catch a pesero from Metro Miguel Ángel de Quevedo, 1km east, or Metro Barranca del Muerto, 1.5km north along Av Revolución.

PLAZA SAN JACINTO
Every Saturday the Bazar Sábado (p189) brings masses of color and crowds of people to this square, half a kilometer west of Av Insurgentes. Midway along the plaza's north side, look for the elaborate fountain inside the courtyard **Museo Casa del Risco** (Map p139; ☎ 5616-2711; Plaza San Jacinto 15; admission free; ☺ 10am-5pm Tue-Sun; Ⓜ Miguel Ángel de Quevedo), a mad mosaic of Talavera tile and Chinese porcelain. Upstairs is a treasure trove of Mexican baroque and medieval European paintings.

About 50m west of the plaza is the 16th-century **Iglesia de San Jacinto** (Map p139) and its peaceful gardens.

MUSEO CASA ESTUDIO DIEGO RIVERA Y FRIDA KAHLO
If you saw the movie *Frida*, you'll recognize this **museum** (Diego Rivera & Frida Kahlo Studio Museum; Map p139; ☎ 5550-1518; Diego Rivera 2, Av Altavista; admission M$10, free Sun; ☺ 10am-6pm Tue-Sun), 1km northwest of Plaza San Jacinto. Designed by their friend, the architect and painter Juan O'Gorman, the innovative abode was the home of the artistic couple from 1934 to 1940, with a separate house for each of them. Rivera's house preserves his upstairs studio, while Frida's (the blue one) has changing exhibits from the memorabilia archives.

Across the street is the San Ángel Inn (p177). Now housing a prestige restaurant, the former pulque hacienda is historically significant as the place where Pancho Villa and Emiliano Zapata agreed to divide control of the country in 1914.

MUSEO DE EL CARMEN
A storehouse of magnificent sacred art, this **museum** (Map p139; ☎ 5616-2816; Av Revolución 4; admission M$39, free Sun; ☺ 10am-5pm Tue-Sun) occupies a former school run by the Carmelite order, adjacent to its 17th-century Templo de El Carmen. (The village was named for the Carmelite's patron saint, San Ángelo Mártir.)

The collection includes eight oils by Mexican master Cristóbal Villalpando; equally splendid are the polychrome and gilt designs on the ceilings. The big draw, however, is the collection of a dozen mummies in the crypt. Thought to be the bodies of 17th-century benefactors of the order, they were uncovered during the revolution by Zapatistas looking for buried treasure.

JARDÍN DE LA BOMBILLA

In this tropically abundant park spreading east of Av Insurgentes, paths encircle the **Monumento a Álvaro Obregón** (Map p139), a monolithic shrine to the post-revolutionary Mexican president. The monument was built to house the revolutionary general's arm, lost in the 1915 Battle of Celaya, but the limb was cremated in 1989. 'La Bombilla' was the name of the restaurant where Obregón was assassinated during a banquet in 1928. The killer, José de León Toral, was involved in the Cristero rebellion against the government's anti-Church policies.

In July, the park explodes with color as the main venue for Feria de las Flores, a major flower festival.

Ciudad Universitaria

Two kilometers south of San Ángel, the **Ciudad Universitaria** (University City; Map pp126-7; www.unam .mx) is the main campus of the Universidad Nacional Autónoma de México (UNAM). With over 280,000 students and 31,000 teachers, it is Latin America's largest university. Five former Mexican presidents are among its alumni, as is Carlos Slim Helú, ranked the world's richest man in 2007.

Founded in 1551 as the Royal and Papal University of Mexico, UNAM is the second-oldest university in the Americas. It occupied various buildings in the center of town until the campus was transferred to its current location in the 1950s. Although it is a public university open to all, UNAM remains 'autonomous,' meaning the government may not interfere in its academic policies. It has often been a center of political dissent, most notably prior to the 1968 Mexico City Olympics (see boxed text, p123).

An architectural showpiece, UNAM was placed on Unesco's list of World Heritage sites in 2007. Most of the faculty buildings are scattered at the north end. As you enter from Av Insurgentes, it's easy to spot the **Biblioteca Central** (Central Library; Map pp126-7), 10 stories high and covered with mosaics by Juan O'Gorman. The south wall, with two prominent zodiac wheels, covers colonial times, while the north wall deals with Aztec culture. **La Rectoría**, the administration building at the west end of the vast central lawn, has a vivid, three-dimensional Siqueiros mosaic on its south wall, showing students urged on by the people.

South of the Rectoría, the **Museo Universitario de Ciencias y Arte** (Map pp126-7; ☎ 5622-0305; www .muca.unam.mx; admission free, ID required; ✆ 10am-6pm Tue-Sun) hosts eclectic exhibitions from the university collection.

Across Av Insurgentes stands the Estadio Olímpico (p187), built of volcanic stone for the 1968 Olympics. With seating for over 72,000, it is now home to UNAM's Pumas soccer club, which competes in the national league's Primera División. Over the main entrance is Diego Rivera's dramatic sculpted mural on the theme of sports in Mexican history.

East of the university's main esplanade, the **Facultad de Medicina** (medical school) features an intriguing mosaic mural by Francisco Eppens on the theme of Mexico's *mestizaje* (blending of indigenous and European races).

A second section of the campus, about 2km south, contains the **Centro Cultural Universitario** (see p184), with five theaters and two cinemas, and the **Museo Universitario de Ciencias** (Universum; ☎ 5622-7287; www.universum.unam.mx; adult/child M$40/35; ✆ 9am-6pm Mon-Fri, 10am-6pm Sat & Sun), a science museum with kids' activities. Also found here is the university sculpture garden, with a trail leading through volcanic fields past a dozen or so innovative pieces. The most formidable work, an enormous ring of concrete blocks by sculptor Mathias Goeritz, is found just north of the cultural complex.

Student cafés, open to everyone during academic sessions, are in both the architecture and philosophy buildings at the Jardín Central's west end, and in the Centro Cultural Universitario.

To get to the University City, take the metrobus to its southern terminus, where you can catch a 'Villa Coapa' pesero to the west side of the university. For the northern part of the campus, get off at the first yellow footbridge, just before the Estadio Olímpico. For the southern section, get off at the second yellow footbridge after the stadium. Returning, catch any pesero marked

'San Ángel-Revolución,' getting off just after it turns left to catch the metrobus.

Coyoacán

Coyoacán ('Place of Coyotes' in the Náhuatl language), 10km south of downtown, was Cortés' base after the fall of Tenochtitlán. Only in recent decades has urban sprawl overtaken the outlying village, and Coyoacán retains its restful identity, with narrow colonial-era streets, cafés and a lively atmosphere. Once home to Leon Trotsky and Frida Kahlo (whose houses are now fascinating museums), it has a decidedly countercultural vibe, most evident on weekends, when assorted musicians, mimes and crafts markets draw large but relaxed crowds from all walks of life to Coyoacán's central plazas.

The nearest metro stations to central Coyoacán, 1.5km to 2km away, are Viveros, Coyoacán and General Anaya. If you don't fancy a walk, get off at Viveros station, walk south to Av Progreso and catch an eastbound 'M(etro) Gral Anaya' pesero to the market. Returning, 'Metro Viveros' peseros go west on Malitzin; 'Metro Coyoacán' and 'Metro Gral Anaya' peseros depart from the west side of Plaza Hidalgo.

San Ángel–bound peseros and buses head west on Av Miguel Ángel de Quevedo, five blocks south of Plaza Hidalgo.

VIVEROS DE COYOACÁN

A pleasant approach is via the **Viveros de Coyoacán** (Map p140; ☎ 5554-1851; admission free; ☥ 6am-6pm; Ⓜ Viveros), the principal nurseries for Mexico City's parks and gardens. The 390,000-sq-meter swath of greenery, 1km west of central Coyoacán, is popular with joggers and great for a stroll, but watch out for belligerent squirrels! From metro Viveros, walk south (right, as you face the fence) along Av Universidad and take the first left, Av Progreso.

A block south of Viveros is the quaint **Plaza Santa Catarina,** with the modest, mustard-colored church that gives the square its name. Across the street, the **Centro Cultural Jesús Reyes Heroles** (Map p140; ☎ 5658-5281; Francisco Sosa 202; 8am-8pm; Ⓜ Viveros) is a colonial estate hosting book presentations, dance classes and so on. Take a wander round the grounds, with yuccas and jacarandas springing from carefully tended gardens, The 700m walk east along Av Francisco Sosa to Jardín del Centenario

passes some fine colonial buildings, several of which house cafés.

PLAZA HIDALGO & JARDÍN DEL CENTENARIO

The focus of Coyoacán life, and scene of most of the weekend fun, is its central plaza – actually two adjacent plazas: the **Jardín del Centenario**, with the village's iconic coyotes frolicking in its central fountain; and the larger, cobblestoned **Plaza Hidalgo**, with a statue of the eponymous independence hero.

The **Casa de Cortés** (Map p140; ☎ 5484-4500; Jardín Centenario 16; admission free; ☥ 8am-8pm; Ⓜ Viveros), on the north side of Plaza Hidalgo, is where conquistador Cortés established Mexico's first municipal seat during the siege of Tenochtitlán, and later had the defeated emperor Cuauhtémoc tortured to make him divulge the location of Aztec treasure (the scene is depicted on a mural inside the chapel). Cortés resided here until 1523 when the colonial government was transferred to Mexico City. The building now houses Coyoacán's delegation offices.

The **Parroquia de San Juan Bautista** (Map p140) and its adjacent ex-monastery dominate the east side of Plaza Hidalgo. First erected in 1592 by the Franciscans, the single-nave church has a lavishly ornamented interior, with painted scenes all over the vaulted ceiling. Be sure to inspect the cloister, featuring Tuscan columns and a checkerboard of carved relief panels on the corner ceilings.

Half a block east, the **Museo Nacional de Culturas Populares** (Map p140; ☎ 9172-8840; www.culturaspopulareseindigenas.gob.mx; Hidalgo 289; admission free; ☥ 10am-6pm Tue-Thu, 10am-8pm Fri-Sun; Ⓜ Viveros) stages innovative exhibitions on folk traditions, indigenous crafts and celebrations in its various courtyards and galleries.

MUSEO FRIDA KAHLO

Renowned Mexican artist Frida Kahlo was born in, and lived and died in, the 'Blue House,' now a **museum** (Map p140; ☎ 5554-5999; www.museofridakahlo.org; Londres 247; admission M$45; ☥ 10am-6pm Tue-Sun; Ⓜ Coyoacán), six blocks north of Plaza Hidalgo. Almost every visitor to Mexico City makes a pilgrimage there to gain a deeper understanding of the painter (and maybe to pick up a Frida handbag).

Built by her father Guillermo three years before Frida's birth, the house is littered with mementos and personal belongings that evoke her long, often tempestuous relationship with husband Diego Rivera and the leftist intellectual circle they often entertained there. Kitchen implements, jewelry, outfits, photos and other objects from the artist's everyday life are interspersed with art, as well as a variety of pre-Hispanic pieces and Mexican crafts. The collection was greatly expanded in 2007 upon the discovery of a cache of previously unseen items that had been stashed in the attic.

The Kahlo art expresses the anguish of her existence as well as her flirtation with socialist icons: portraits of Lenin and Mao hang around her bed, and in the upstairs studio an unfinished portrait of Stalin stands before a poignantly positioned wheelchair. In another painting, *Retrato de la Familia* (Family Portrait), the artist's Hungarian-Oaxacan roots are fancifully entangled.

MUSEO LÉON TROTSKY
Having come second to Stalin in the power struggle in the Soviet Union, Trotsky was expelled in 1929 and condemned to death in absentia. In 1937 he found refuge in Mexico. At first Trotsky and his wife, Natalia, lived in Frida Kahlo's Blue House, but after falling out with Kahlo and Rivera they moved a few streets northeast, to Viena 45.

The Trotsky home, now a **museum** (Map p140; ☎ 5658-8732; Río Churubusco 410; admission M$30; ☾ 10am-5pm Tue-Sun; Ⓜ Coyoacán) remains much as it was on the day when a Stalin agent, a Catalan named Ramón Mercader, finally caught up with the revolutionary and smashed an ice pick into his skull. Memorabilia and biographical notes are displayed in buildings off the patio, where a tomb engraved with a hammer and sickle contains the Trotskys' ashes.

The main entrance is at the rear of the old residence, facing the Circuito Interior.

EX-CONVENTO DE CHURUBUSCO
Scene of a historic military defeat, the 17th-century former Monastery of Churubusco stands within peaceful wooded grounds, 1.5km east of Plaza Hidalgo. On August 20, 1847, Mexican troops defended the monastery against US forces advancing from Veracruz in a dispute over the US annexation of Texas. The Mexicans fought until they ran out of ammunition and were beaten only after hand-to-hand fighting.

The US invasion was but one example in a long history of foreign intervention, as com-

pellingly demonstrated by the **Museo Nacional de las Intervenciones** (National Interventions Museum; Map p140; ☎ 5604-0699; cnr Calle 20 de Agosto & General Anaya; admission M$39, free Sun; ☾ 9am-6pm Tue-Sun; Ⓜ General Anaya), inside the former *convento*. Displays include an American map showing operations in 1847, material on the French occupation of the 1860s and the plot by US ambassador Henry Lane Wilson to bring down the Madero government in 1913. (None of the explanatory text is translated.)

The superbly restored exhibit rooms, bordered by original frescoes, surround a small cloister where numbered stations provided instructions for meditating monks. Leaving the museum, you may wander amid the monastery's old orchard which now holds wonderful gardens.

To reach Churubusco, catch an eastbound 'M(etro) Gral Anaya' pesero or bus from Xicoténcatl, a few blocks north of Plaza Hidalgo. Otherwise, walk 500m from the General Anaya metro station.

ANAHUACALLI
Designed by Diego Rivera to house his collection of pre-Hispanic art, this **museum** (Map pp126-7; ☎ 5617-4310; www.anahuacallimuseo.org; Calle del Museo 150; admission M$45; ☾ 10am-6pm Tue-Sun), 3.5km south of Coyoacán, is a temple-like structure of dark volcanic stone. The 'House of Anáhuac' (Aztec name for the Valle de México) also contains one of Rivera's studios and some of his work, including a study for 'Man at the Crossroads,' the mural that was commissioned for the Rockefeller Center in 1934. In November, elaborate Day of the Dead offerings pay homage to the painter.

The entry fee includes admission to the Museo Frida Kahlo (see opposite).

To get to Anahuacalli, take the Tren Ligero (from metro Tasqueña) to the Xotepingo station. Exit on the west side and walk 200m to División del Norte; cross and continue 600m along Calle del Museo.

Cuicuilco
One of the oldest significant remnants of pre-Hispanic settlement within the DF, **Cuicuilco** (Map pp126-7; ☎ 5606-9758; Insurgentes Sur; admission free; ☾ 9am-5pm) echoes a civilization that stood on the shores of Lago de Xochimilco as far back as 800 BC. In its heyday in the 2nd century BC, the 'place of singing and dancing' counted as many as 40,000 inhabitants and rivaled

FRIDA & DIEGO

A century after Frida Kahlo's birth, and 50 years after Diego Rivera's death, the pair's fame and recognition are stronger than ever. In 2007, a retrospective of Kahlo's work at the Palacio de Bellas Artes attracted more than 440,000 visitors. Though attendance at the Rivera survey that followed was not so phenomenal, the show reminded visitors that the prolific muralist had been an international star in his own lifetime. Their memory is inseparably linked, and both artists were frequent subjects in each other's work.

Diego Rivera first met Frida Kahlo, 21 years his junior, while painting at the Escuela Nacional Preparatoria, where she was a student in the early 1920s. Rivera was already at the forefront of Mexican art; his commission at the school was the first of many semi-propaganda murals on public buildings that he was to execute over three decades. He had already fathered children by two Russian women in Europe and in 1922 he married Lupe Marín in Mexico. She bore him two more children before their marriage broke up in 1928.

Kahlo was born in Coyoacán in 1907 to a Hungarian-Jewish father and Oaxacan mother. She contracted polio at age six, leaving her right leg permanently thinner than her left. In 1925 she was horribly injured in a trolley accident that broke her right leg, collarbone, pelvis and ribs. She made a miraculous recovery but suffered much pain thereafter and underwent many operations to try to alleviate it. It was during convalescence that she began painting. Pain – physical and emotional – was to be a dominating theme of her art.

Kahlo and Rivera both moved in left-wing artistic circles, and they met again in 1928; they married the following year. The liaison, described as 'a union between an elephant and a dove,' was always a passionate love-hate affair. Rivera wrote: 'If I ever loved a woman, the more I loved her, the more I wanted to hurt her. Frida was only the most obvious victim of this disgusting trait.'

In 1934, after a spell in the US, the pair moved into a new home in San Ángel, now the Museo Casa Estudio Diego Revera Y Frida Kahlo (p156), with separate houses linked by an aerial walkway. After Kahlo discovered that Rivera had had an affair with her sister Cristina, she divorced him in 1939, but they remarried the following year. She moved back into her childhood home, the Casa Azul, in Coyoacán and he stayed at San Ángel – a state of affairs that endured for the rest of their lives, though their relationship endured too. Kahlo remained Rivera's most trusted critic, and Rivera was Kahlo's biggest fan.

Despite the worldwide wave of Fridamania that followed the hit biopic *Frida* in 2002, Kahlo had only one exhibition in Mexico in her lifetime, in 1953. She arrived at the opening on a stretcher. Rivera said of the exhibition, 'Anyone who attended it could not but marvel at her great talent.' She died at the Blue House the following year. Rivera called it 'the most tragic day of my life... Too late I realized that the most wonderful part of my life had been my love for Frida.'

Teotihuacán in stature. The site was abandoned a couple of centuries later, however, after an eruption of the nearby Xitle volcano covered most of the community in lava.

The principal structure is a huge circular platform of four levels, faced with volcanic stone blocks, that probably functioned as a ceremonial center. Set amid a park studded with cactus and shade trees, the platform can be easily scaled for sweeping views of the southern districts including the formidable Xitle. The site includes a small museum.

To reach Cuicuilco, take the Insurgentes metrobus to the end of the line, cross Dr Gálvez and catch a 'Villa Coapa' pesero south. You'll see the entrance to the archaeological park just south of the Periférico freeway.

Tlalpan

Tlalpan today is 'what Coyoacán used to be' – an outlying village with a bohemian atmosphere coupled with some impressive colonial architecture. The municipal seat of Mexico City's largest *delegación*, Tlalpan sits at the foot of the southern Ajusco range and enjoys a cooler, more moist climate. There are some fine restaurants along the arcades of the cute plaza and a boisterous cantina nearby called **La Jalisciense** (☎ 5573-5586; Plaza de la Constitución 6).

Half a block from the plaza, the **Museo de Historia de Tlalpán** (☎ 5485-9048; Plaza de la Constitución 10; admission free; ☉ 10am-7pm Tue-Sun) hosts compelling historical exhibits in naturally lit galleries off the courtyard.

There's a sublime simplicity about the **Capilla de las Capuchinas Sacramentarias** (☎ 5573-2395; Hidalgo 43; admission M$50; ✆ 10am-noon & 4-6pm Mon-Thu), the chapel of a convent for Capuchin nuns designed by modernist architect Luis Barragán in 1952. The austere altar, free of the usual iconography, consists only of a trio of gold panels. Visit in the morning to appreciate how light streams through the stained-glass window by Mathias Goeritz.

To get here, take the Insurgentes metrobus to the end of the line, cross Dr Gálvez and catch a 'Villa Coapa' pesero south. Beyond Cuicuilco, this bus turns left on San Fernando. Get off at Calle Juárez, and walk three blocks south to Tlalpan's main square.

Parque Nacional Desierto de los Leones

Cool, fragrant pine and oak forests dominate this 20-sq-km **national park** (off Map pp126-7; ✆ 6am-5pm) in the hills surrounding the Valle de México. Some 23km southwest of Mexico City and 800m higher, it makes a fine escape from the carbon monoxide and concrete.

The name derives from the **Ex-Convento del Santo Desierto de Nuestra Señora del Carmen** (Camino al Desierto de los Leones; ☎ 5814-1171; admission M$10; ✆ 10am-5pm Tue-Sun), the 17th-century former Carmelite monastery within the park. The Carmelites called their isolated monasteries 'deserts' to commemorate Elijah, who lived as a recluse in the desert near Mt Carmel. The 'Leones' in the name may stem from the presence of wild cats in the area, but more likely refers to José and Manuel de León, who once administered the monastery's finances.

The restored monastery has exhibition halls and a restaurant. Tours in Spanish (weekends only) are run by guides garbed in cassock and sandals who lead you through the patios within and expansive gardens around the buildings, as well as some underground passageways.

The rest of the park has extensive walking trails. (Robberies have been reported, so stick to the main paths.)

On Saturdays and Sundays, buses depart from Metro Viveros for the former *convento*. During the week, there's no transportation directly to the monastery, but you can take one of Flecha Roja's frequent 'Toluca Intermedio' buses from the Terminal Poniente bus station and get off at the La Venta toll booth. From there, take the footbridge over the highway and follow signs for the Desierto de Leones road.

Tlatelolco & Guadalupe
PLAZA DE LAS TRES CULTURAS

So named because it symbolizes the fusion of pre-Hispanic and Spanish roots into the Mexican *mestizo* identity, this **plaza** (Plaza of the Three Cultures; Map pp126-7; ☎ 5583-0295; Eje Central Lázaro Cárdenas, cnr Flores Magón; admission free; ✆ 8am-5:30pm) displays the architectural legacy of three cultural facets: the Aztec pyramids of **Tlatelolco**, the 17th-century Spanish **Templo de Santiago** and the modern tower that now houses the **Centro Cultural Universitario**. A calm oasis north of the city center, the plaza is nonetheless haunted by echoes of its turbulent history.

Recent archaeological finds have altered long-held views about Tlatelolco's history. According to the conventional version, Tlatelolco was founded by an Aztec faction in the 14th century on a separate island in Lago de Texcoco and later conquered by the Aztecs of Tenochtitlán. But a pyramid excavated on the site in late 2007 actually predates the establishment of Tenochtitlán by as much as 200 years. All agree, however, that Tlatelolco was the scene of the largest public market in the Valle de México, connected by causeway to Tenochtitlán's ceremonial center.

During the siege of the Aztec capital, Cortés defeated Tlatelolco's defenders, led by Cuauhtémoc. An inscription about that battle in the plaza translates: 'This was neither victory nor defeat. It was the sad birth of the mestizo people that is Mexico today.'

Tlatelolco is also a symbol of modern troubles. On October 2, 1968, hundreds of student protesters were massacred by government troops on the eve of the Mexico City Olympic Games (see boxed text, p123). The area subsequently suffered some of the worst damage of the 1985 earthquake when apartment blocks collapsed, killing hundreds.

You can view the remains of Tlatelolco's main pyramid-temple and other Aztec buildings from a walkway around them. Like the Templo Mayor of Tenochtitlán, Tlatelolco's main temple was constructed in stages, with each of seven temples superimposed atop its predecessors. The double pyramid on view, one of the earliest stages, has twin staircases which supposedly ascended to temples dedicated to Tláloc and Huitzilopochtli. Numerous calendar glyphs are carved into the outer walls.

Recognizing the significance of the site, the Spanish erected the **Templo de Santiago** here in

1609, using stones from the Aztec structures as building materials. Just inside the main (west) doors of this church is the **baptismal font of Juan Diego** (see below).

Inaugurated in 2007, the **Centro Cultural Universitario Tlatelolco** (☎ 5597-4061; www.tlatelolco.unam.mx; Flores Magón 1; admission M$20; 🕑 10am-6pm Tue-Sun) occupies the former Foreign Relations Secretariat building. A component of the UNAM, it contains two interesting permanent exhibits. The **Colección Andrés Blaisten**, on the 1st floor, comprises the largest privately owned collection of Mexican 20th-century art, with paintings, prints and sculptures by both obscure and famed artists such as María Izquierdo and Juan Soriano. Downstairs, the **Memorial del 68** both chronicles and memorializes the 1968 student massacre at Tlatelolco (see boxed text, p123). Through film clips, newspaper articles, photos, posters and numerous taped interviews with leading intellectuals (in Spanish), the exhibit evokes the mood of the times and follows the sequence of events leading up to the government-sponsored slaughter of student protesters on October 2.

Along Eje Central Lázaro Cárdenas, northbound 'Central Autobuses del Norte' trolleybuses pass right by the Plaza de las Tres Culturas.

BASÍLICA DE GUADALUPE

In December 1531, the story goes, an indigenous Christian convert named Juan Diego stood on Cerro del Tepeyac (Tepeyac Hill), site of an old Aztec shrine, and beheld a beautiful lady dressed in a blue mantle trimmed with gold. She sent him to tell the bishop, Juan de Zumárraga, that he had seen the Virgin Mary, and that she wanted a shrine built in her honor. But the bishop didn't believe him. Returning to the hill, Juan Diego had the vision several more times. After her fourth appearance, the lady's image was miraculously emblazoned on his cloak, causing the church to finally accept his story, and a cult developed around the site.

Over the centuries Nuestra Señora de Guadalupe came to receive credit for all manner of miracles, hugely aiding the acceptance of Catholicism by Mexicans. Despite the protests of some clergy, who saw the cult as a form of idolatry with the Virgin as a Christianized version of the Aztec goddess Tonantzin, in 1737 the Virgin was officially declared the patron of Mexico. Two centuries later she was named celestial patron of Latin America and empress of the Americas, and in 2002 Juan Diego was canonized by Pope John Paul II. Today the Virgin's image is seen throughout the country, and her shrines around the Cerro del Tepeyac are the most revered in Mexico, attracting thousands of pilgrims daily and hundreds of thousands on the days leading up to her feast day, December 12 (see Día de Nuestra Señora de Guadalupe, p166). Some pilgrims travel the last meters to the shrine on their knees.

Around 1700, the four-towered Basilica de Guadalupe was erected at the site of an earlier shrine to accommodate the faithful flock. But by the 1970s, the old yellow-domed building proved inadequate to the task, so the new **Basílica de Nuestra Señora de Guadalupe** (Map pp126-7; Ⓜ La Villa-Basilica) was built next door. Designed by Pedro Ramírez Vázquez, it's a vast, round, open-plan structure with a capacity for over 40,000 people. The image of the Virgin hangs above and behind the main altar, with moving walkways to bring visitors as close as possible.

The rear of the Antigua Basílica is now the **Museo de la Basílica de Guadalupe** (☎ 5577-6022; admission M$5; 🕑 10am-6pm Tue-Sun), with a fine collection of colonial art interpreting the miraculous vision.

Stairs behind the Antigua Basílica climb about 100m to the hilltop **Capilla del Cerrito** (Hill Chapel), where Juan Diego had his vision, then lead down the east side of the hill to the Parque de la Ofrenda with gardens and waterfalls around a sculpted scene of the apparition. Continue on down to the baroque **Templo del Pocito**, a circular structure with a trio of tiled cupolas, built in 1787 to commemorate the miraculous appearance of a spring where the Virgen de Guadalupe had stood. From there the route leads back to the main plaza, re-entering it beside the 17th-century **Capilla de Indios** (Chapel of Indians).

An easy way to reach the Basílica de Guadalupe is to take the metro to La Villa-Basílica station, then walk two blocks north along Calz de Guadalupe. You can reach the same point on any 'Metro Hidalgo–La Villa' bus heading northeast on Paseo de la Reforma. To return downtown, walk to Calz de los Misterios, a block west of Calz de Guadalupe, and catch a southbound 'Metro Hidalgo' or 'Metro Chapultepec' pesero.

ACTIVITIES

Bicycling

Sunday mornings Paseo de la Reforma is closed to auto traffic from Bosque de Chapultepec down to the Alameda Central, and you can join the legions of Chilangos who happily skate or cycle down the avenue each week.

For a more ambitious trek, the urban cycling group **Bicitekas** (www.bicitekas.org) organizes rides starting from the Monumento a la Independencia at 9pm every Wednesday. Groups of up to 100 cyclists ride to destinations like Coyoacán and Ciudad Satélite. Participants must be sufficiently robust to handle treks of up to 40km. Helmets and rear lights are required.

For information on renting bicycles and around-town routes, see p197.

Gyms

Some top-end hotels, especially those with spas, have day rates available for nonguests. Otherwise there are several city gyms where you can use the equipment and take classes inexpensively.

Centro Caba (Map pp132-3; ☎ 5574-1976; Álvaro Obregón 160, Roma; per day M$45; ☼ 7am-10pm Mon-Fri, 8am-10pm Sat, 9am-4pm Sun; ᵬ Álvaro Obregón)
Centro Qi (Map pp132-3; ☎ 5584-4880; www.qi.com .mx; Amsterdam 317, Condesa; per day M$185; ☼ 6am-11pm Mon-Thu, 8am-6pm Sat, 9am-4pm Sun; ᵬ Sonora) Stylish Condesa gym with climbing wall, tanning beds and yoga classes.

Ice Skating

As part of Mayor Marcelo Ebrard's campaign to bring fun recreational activities to the city's poorer inhabitants, a huge ice-skating rink is installed in the Zócalo during the Christmas holiday season. Loans of ice skates are provided free of charge, if you don't mind waiting as much as two hours to get them.

Jogging

One popular place for a morning run is the path that skirts the oval Parque México (p151). Runners also use the broad and narrow paths that crisscross Viveros de Coyoacán (p158), the city's botanical gardens. Bosque de Chapultepec (see p152), of course, offers many kilometers of tree-shaded trails; those on the south (Condesa) side tend to be less crowded.

WALKING TOUR

The historical hub of all Mexico, the Centro Histórico is best explored on foot. After getting a bell-tower overview from the **Catedral Metropolitana** (1; p142), pop into the **Nacional Monte de Piedad** (2; p144), the national pawn shop, across the way – you might find a bargain. Take República de Brasil north two blocks to the **Plaza Santo Domingo** (3; p144). On your left, printers ply their trade beneath the Portal de Evangelistas. On the right, the **Secretaría de Educación Pública** (4; p145) houses Diego Rivera's dramatic murals on Mexican life and culture. Exiting on the far side of the building, go left, then right at the corner into República de Venezuela. A block east, the building on your right is the ancient **Templo de San Pedro y San Pablo (5)**, which today houses the interactive Museo de Luz (Museum of Light; entrance one block south). Just beyond, the tall arcade on the left fronts the **Teatro del Pueblo (6)** – inside, the theater is decorated with art deco and indigenous motifs. Enter the adjacent **Mercado Abelardo Rodríguez** (7; p146) to admire numerous murals painted by Rivera's students in the 1920s. Turn right at the corner (Rodríguez Puebla). A block south, the **Templo de Nuestra Señora de Loreto** (8; p146) has a magnificent cupola, best viewed from inside. Across the eponymous plaza on Justo Sierra stands Mexico City's first **synagogue** (9), built by the Syrian Jews who formerly populated this zone. Follow Calle Loreto one block south, turn left, then go right on Santísima. The below-street-level walkway follows the course of an earlier waterway for produce from the southern community of Xochimilco. On the next corner is the hyper-baroque **Templo de la Santísima Trinidad** (10; p144).

Now head west on Calle Zapata, which becomes Moneda. Two blocks along, on your left, stands the **Academia de San Carlos (11)**, where Mexico's 19th-century painters learned their skills. Strike half a block north on Academia to stand face-to-ankle with José Luis Cuevas' **La Giganta** (12; p144), an 8m-tall figure.

WALK FACTS

Start Catedral Metropolitana
Finish Plaza del Templo Mayor
Distance 2.2km
Duration 2½ hours

MEXICO CITY

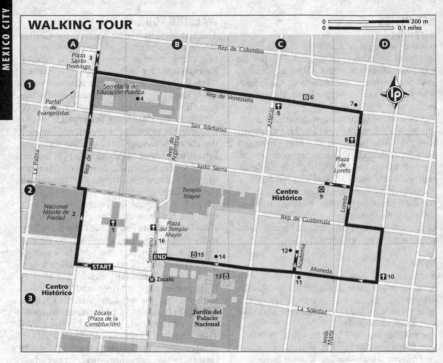

WALKING TOUR

Return to Moneda and continue west. Just past Correo Mayor on your left is the building that Calle Moneda was named for, the old colonial mint, now the **Museo Nacional de las Culturas** (13; p144). A bit further west, the building at the corner of Licenciado Primo Verdad housed the Americas' **first printing press** (14). Across the way is the former archbishop's palace, now the **Museo de la Secretaría de Hacienda y Crédito Público** (15; p144), now the Museo de la Secretaría de Hacienda y Crédito Público, a showcase for the tax bureau's vast art collection. Celebrate the conclusion of the tour by joining the Aztec dancers at the **Plaza del Templo Mayor** (16; p143).

COURSES

Centro Cultural Tepeticpac Tlahtolcalli (Map pp128-9; ☎ 5518-2020; www.tepeticpac.com; Dr Mora 5; Ⓜ Hidalgo) If you'd like to brush up on your Náhuatl – or Mixtec or Otomí – this cultural center offers courses in indigenous languages. On Saturdays you can join workshops on Aztec dance, codex reading or *huehuetl* (indigenous drum) playing.

Centro de Enseñanza Para Extranjeros (Foreigners Teaching Center; ☎ 5622-2467; www.cepe.unam.mx; Uni-

versidad 3002, Ciudad Universitaria) The national university (p157) offers six-week intensive classes meeting three hours daily (US$340). Students who already speak Spanish may take courses on Mexican art and culture, which are taught in Spanish and run concurrently with the UNAM semester.

MEXICO CITY FOR CHILDREN

As elsewhere in Mexico, kids take center stage in the capital. Many theaters stage children's plays and puppet shows on weekends and during school holidays, including the **Centro Cultural del Bosque** (p184). Cartoons are a staple at cinemas around town, with weekend matinees at the **Cineteca Nacional** (p183) and the hotel **Condesa df** (p171), though keep in mind that children's films are often dubbed in Spanish. Consult the Niños sections of *Tiempo Libre* and *Donde Ir* magazines for current programs.

Museums often organize hands-on activities for kids. Both the **Museo Nacional de Arte** (p146) and **Museo Nacional de Culturas Populares** (p158) offer children's art workshops Saturday and Sunday.

Mexico City's numerous parks and plazas are usually buzzing with kids' voices. Bosque de Chapultepec is the obvious destination, with the **Papalote Museo del Niño** (p154), **La Feria** (p154) and the **Chapultepec zoo** (p153), not to mention several lakes with rowboat rentals. But also consider Condesa's **Parque México** (p151), where Sunday is family activities day. **Plaza Hidalgo** (p158) in Coyoacán is another fun-filled spot with balloons, street mimes and cotton candy.

In **Xochimilco** (p155), kids find the sensation of riding the gondolas through the canals as magical as any theme park. Also in this part of town is the **Museo Dolores Olmedo Patiño** (p155), where a pack of pre-Hispanic dogs roam the gardens, and children's shows are performed in the patio on Saturday and Sunday at 1pm.

QUIRKY MEXICO CITY

Anyone who's spent time in Mexico will understand why French poet André Breton called it 'the surrealist country par excellence.' Something strange lurks beneath the surface of everyday life.

Isla de las Muñecas (Map pp126-7) For a truly surreal experience, head for Xochimilco (p155) and hire a *trajinera* to the Island of the Dolls, where thousands of dolls, many partially decomposed or missing limbs, hang from trees and rafters. The installation was created by an island resident who fished the playthings from the canals to mollify the spirit of a girl who had drowned nearby. The best departure point for the four-hour round trip is the Cuemanco landing, near the Parque Ecológico de Xochimilco (pp126–7).

La Faena (Map pp128-9; ☎ 5520-4427; Venustiano Carranza Tacuba 49B; ☑ 11am-midnight; Ⓜ San Juan de Letrán) This forgotten relic of a bar doubles as a bullfighting museum, with matadors in sequined outfits glaring intently from dusty cases and bucolic canvasses of grazing bulls.

Mercado de Sonora (Map pp126-7; cnr Fray Servando & Rosales; Ⓜ Merced) Has all the ingredients for Mexican witchcraft. Aisles are crammed with stalls hawking potions, amulets, voodoo dolls and other esoterica. Located south of Mercado de la Merced, this is also the place for a *limpia* (spiritual cleansing), a ritual that involves clouds of incense and a herbal brushing.

Pemex Kid (Map pp128-9; González Martínez, cnr Orozco y Berra; Ⓜ San Cosme) Opposite the Museo Universitario del Chopo (closed for renovations at time of research), a sneaker-wearing youth sits upon the roof staring dejectedly down at the adjacent Pemex station. Even after you realize it's just a dummy, perhaps placed there as an artistic statement, his brooding presence makes an eerie and unforgettable impression.

Virgen del Metro (Map pp128-9; cnr Paseo de la Reforma & Zarco; Ⓜ Hidalgo) Housed in a tiled shrine is this evidence of a recent miracle. Metro riders in June 1997 noticed that a water leak in Hidalgo station had formed a stain in the likeness of the Virgin of Guadalupe. Following the discovery, thousands flocked to witness the miraculous image. The stone section was removed and encased in glass at the Zarco entrance to metro Hidalgo.

TOURS

Journeys Beyond the Surface (☎ 5922-0123; www .travelmexicocity.com.mx) Offers personalized walking tours on aspects of the DF experience, with an off-the-beaten-track attitude.

Mexico Soul and Essence (☎ 5564-8457; www .mexicosoulandessence.com) Culinary/cultural excursions by articulate bicultural guides with a passionate interest in their subject. Tours combine browsing markets for ingredients, kitchen instruction with well-regarded chefs and dining in some of the city's finest restaurants.

Tranvía (Map pp128-9; ☎ 5491-1615; adult/child M$35/25; ☑ 10am-5pm) Motorized version of a vintage streetcar runs a 45-minute circuit of the Centro Histórico, with guides relating fascinating bits of lore (in Spanish) along the way. On Thursday night there's a special cantina tour (M$100 including wine, reservation required). Tours depart from Av Juárez by Bellas Artes. A similar tour operates in Coyoacán, departing from in front of the Museo Nacional de Culturas Populares.

Turibús Circuito Turístico (Map pp128-9; ☎ 5133-2488; www.turibus.com.mx; adult/4-12yr M$100/50, 2-day pass M$140/70; ☑ 9am-9pm) Provides tourist-eye view of the key areas. The total *recorrido* (route) lasts about three hours, but you can get off and back on the red double-decker bus at any designated stop along the way. Buses pass every 30 minutes or so, stopping at the west side of the cathedral among other places. The fare includes headphones for recorded explanations in six languages.

FESTIVALS & EVENTS

Mexico City celebrates some unique local events in addition to all the major nationwide festivals (see p970), which often take on a special flavor in the capital.

Festival de México en el Centro Histórico (www .fchmexico.com) In late March the Centro Histórico's plazas, temples and theaters become venues for a slew of international artists and performers.

Semana Santa The most evocative events of Holy Week (late March or early April) are in the Iztapalapa district, 9km southeast of the Zócalo, where a gruesomely realistic Passion Play is enacted. The most evocative scenes are performed on Good Friday.

Foundation of Tenochtitlán Held on August 13, this is a major summit for *conchero* dancers on Plaza de las Tres Culturas (p161) in Tlatelolco to celebrate the foundation of the Mexica capital.

MEXICO CITY

Grito de la Independencia Thousands gather in the Zócalo for this September 15 (the eve of Independence Day) celebration to hear the Mexican president's version of the Grito de Dolores (Cry of Dolores), Hidalgo's famous call to rebellion against the Spanish in 1810, from the central balcony of the Palacio Nacional at 11pm. Afterwards, there's a spectacular fireworks display over the cathedral.

Día de Muertos In the lead-up to the Day of the Dead (November 2), elaborate *ofrendas* (altars) show up everywhere from public markets to metro stations. Some of the best are at the Anahuacalli (p159) and the Museo Dolores Olmedo Patiño (p155), while a contest for the most creative *ofrenda* is held at the Zócalo. Major vigils take place in the Panteón Civil de Dolores cemetery, in the Bosque de Chapultepec's 2a Sección, and at San Andres Mixquic, in the extreme southeast of the Distrito Federal.

Fiesta de Santa Cecilia The patron saint of musicians is honored with special fervor at Plaza Garibaldi (Map pp128–9) on November 22.

Día de Nuestra Señora de Guadalupe At the Basílica de Guadalupe (p162), the Day of Our Lady of Guadalupe caps 10 days of festivities honoring Mexico's religious patron. The numbers of pilgrims reach the millions by December 12, when groups of indigenous dancers perform nonstop on the basilica's broad plaza and religious services go on almost round the clock.

SLEEPING

As a frequent destination for both Mexican and foreign visitors, the DF overflows with lodging options – everything from no-frills guesthouses to top-flight hotels. Some of the most reasonable places are in the Centro Histórico, while more luxurious accommodations, including branches of some major international chains, are concentrated in Polanco and the Zona Rosa. Midrange lodgings, most featuring restaurants and bars, abound in the Alameda and Plaza de la República areas; they tend to trade character for neutral modern comfort. (Note that places with the word *garage* on the sign generally cater to short-term trysting guests.) Those on a tight budget will find an increasing number of low-cost hostels, particularly in the center of town.

Centro Histórico

For non-business travelers, the historic center is the obvious place to stay. Ongoing renovations of its infrastructure and preservation of its numerous historic edifices have boosted the zone's appeal, but it remains one of the more affordable areas.

BUDGET

our pick **Mexico City Hostel** (Map pp128-9; ☎ 5512-3666; www.mexicocityhostel.com; República de Brasil 8; dm incl breakfast from M$100, s/d M$200/300; Ⓜ Zócalo; 🖳) Steps from the Zócalo, this colonial structure has been artfully restored, with original wood beams and stone walls as a backdrop for modern, energy-efficient facilities. For instance, the halls and bathrooms are equipped with movement-activated sensor lights. Spacious dorms have three or four sturdy bunk beds on terracotta floors. Immaculate bathrooms trimmed with *azulejo* tiles amply serve around 100 occupants.

Hostal Virreyes (Map pp128-9; ☎ 5521-4180; www.hostalvirreyes.com.mx; Izazaga 8; dm M$120, s/d M$320/370; Ⓜ Salto del Agua; 🖳) Once a prestigious hotel, the Virreyes has naturally morphed into a hostel-student residence. Dorms are spacious if bare bones and the retro lobby lounge hosts hip events.

Hostal Moneda (Map pp128-9; ☎ 5522-5803; www.hostalmoneda.com.mx; Moneda 8; dm incl breakfast & dinner M$120-155, d M$355; Ⓜ Zócalo; 🖳) An altogether more modest affair than the nearby Hostel Catedral, the Moneda remains a favored stop on the international backpackers circuit. Chief among its assets are a well-informed, bilingual staff and a terrific multipurpose rooftop.

Hostel Mundo Joven Catedral (Map pp128-9; ☎ 5518-1726; www.hostelcatedral.com; República de Guatemala 4; dm incl breakfast M$140, d with shared bathroom M$380; Ⓜ Zócalo; 🖳) Backpacker central, the capital's only HI affiliate is abuzz with a global rainbow of young travelers. Every facility you might need is here, the location couldn't be more central and the place is cordially managed. Off the guest kitchen, a delightful deck overlooks the cathedral.

Hotel Isabel (Map pp128-9; ☎ 5518-1213; www.hotel-isabel.com.mx; Isabel la Católica 63; s/d with shared bathroom M$150/220, s/d/tr with private bathroom M$220/320/460; Ⓜ Isabel la Católica; 🖳) Just a few blocks from the Zócalo, the Isabel is a long-time budget-traveler's favorite, offering large, well-scrubbed rooms with old but sturdy furniture, high ceilings and great balconies, plus a hostel-like social scene.

Hotel San Antonio (Map pp128-9; ☎ 5518-1625; fax 5512-9906; 2a Callejón 5 de Mayo 29; d with shared/private bathroom M$200/220, tr M$320; Ⓜ Allende) Inside an L-shaped passage linking Av 5 de Mayo to Palma, the San Antonio remains slightly aloof from the bustle. Smallish rooms face either the little-used alley or whitewashed interior court.

Hotel Principal (Map pp128-9; ☎ 5521-1333; www .hotelprincipal.com.mx; Bolívar 29; s/d/tr M$225/315/410; Ⓜ Allende) A longtime favorite with frugal travelers, the Principal boasts enormous rooms with high ceilings surrounding a plant-draped central hall. Cafés and clubs dot this revitalized section of the Centro.

Hotel Azores (Map pp128-9; ☎ 5521-5220; www .hotelazores.com; República de Brasil 25; s/d from M$300/360; Ⓜ Zócalo; Ⓟ) Just off the fascinating Plaza Santo Domingo, the modern Azores boasts a cheerily designed and scrupulously maintained interior. Of the 65 rooms, eight overlook the street through picture windows.

The following bargains are in the thick of it all:

Hotel Rioja (Map pp128-9; ☎ 5521-8333; Av 5 de Mayo 45; s/d from M$220/250; Ⓜ Allende) Front rooms (slightly pricier) have balconies overlooking 5 de Mayo.

Hotel Washington (Map pp128-9; ☎ 5512-3502; Av 5 de Mayo 54; s/d/tr M$240/300/340; Ⓜ Allende) Try to snag a balcony room; airless interior units are best avoided.

MIDRANGE

Hotel Canadá (Map pp128-9; ☎ 5518-2106; www.hotel canada.com.mx; Av 5 de Mayo 47; s/d M$420/500; Ⓜ Allende; Ⓟ) This longstanding local has redone its smallish rooms, adding new carpets, peach-toned headboards and sepia photos of old Mexico. Affable staff cater to a primarily business clientele who may unwind in the TV amphitheater downstairs or quaff fresh-squeezed juices next door.

Hotel Gillow (Map pp128-9; ☎ 5518-1440; www .hotelgillow.com; Isabel la Católica 17; s/d M$468/600; Ⓜ Allende; Ⓟ Ⓛ) A historic building with standard midrange facilities, the Gillow boasts old-fashioned service and spacious carpeted rooms around a sunlit central courtyard. For views, request an Av 5 de Mayo or Isabel la Católica unit.

Hotel Catedral (Map pp128-9; ☎ 5518-5232; www .hotelcatedral.com.mx; Donceles 95; s/d M$475/660; Ⓜ Zócalo; Ⓟ Ⓛ) Though short on colonial charm, this comfortable lodging has clearly considered its location, directly behind the cathedral. Even if you get an interior room, you can lounge on the rooftop terraces with impressive cityscape views.

TOP END

Holiday Inn Zócalo (Map pp128-9; ☎ 5130-5130, 800-5521-2122; www.hotelescortes.com; Av 5 de Mayo 61; r from M$1264; Ⓜ Zócalo; Ⓟ Ⓧ Ⓧ Ⓛ) The northernmost of three upper-echelon hotels facing the

Zócalo, this seems the least pretentious, eschewing colonial trimmings for contemporary comfort. And its rooftop-terrace restaurant ranks with those of its neighbors.

NH Centro Histórico (Map pp128-9; ☎ 5130-1850; www.nh-hotels.com; Palma 42; r/ste incl breakfast M$1551/1693; Ⓜ Zócalo; Ⓟ Ⓧ Ⓛ) Riding the downtown development wave, Spanish chain NH planted a branch in the center. Lounges and rooms get a Euro-minimal treatment normally associated with pricier digs. Spacious suites occupy the curved corners of the aerodynamically designed 1940s structure.

Gran Hotel Ciudad de México (Map pp128-9; ☎ 1083-7700; www.granhotelciudaddemexico.com.mx; Av 16 de Septiembre 82; r/ste M$1636/2691; Ⓜ Zócalo; Ⓟ Ⓧ Ⓛ) The Gran Hotel flaunts the French art-nouveau style of the pre-revolutionary era. Crowned by a stained-glass canopy crafted by Tiffany in 1908, the atrium is a fin de siècle fantasy of curved balconies, wrought-iron elevators and chirping birds in giant cages. Rooms do not disappoint in comparison.

Hotel Majestic (Map pp128-9; ☎ 5521-8600; www .hotelmajestic.com.mx; Madero 73; r US$135, ste from US$172; Ⓜ Zócalo; Ⓟ Ⓧ Ⓛ) This Best Western franchise has an attractive colonial interior, an unbeatable location and perhaps the most panoramic terrace restaurant on the Zócalo. Rooms, however, are less fabulous than you'd expect at these prices.

Alameda Central & Around

Like the Centro Histórico, this section is undergoing major renovations, though pockets of neglect are reminders of the 1985 earthquake that devastated the zone. Though by day the neighborhood bustles with shoppers, after dark it quiets down considerably and, apart from its small Chinatown district, offers little incentive to wander.

BUDGET

Hotel San Diego (Map pp128-9; ☎ 5510-3523; Luis Moya 98; s/d M$250/400; Ⓜ Balderas) This generic option two blocks east of La Ciudadela should appeal to peso-pinchers. Above the lobby's imitation leather sofas and plastic plants are bright, decent-sized rooms with furniture of recent vintage and newly tiled bathrooms.

MIDRANGE

Hotel Marlowe (Map pp128-9; ☎ 5521-9540; www.hotelmarlowe.com.mx; Independencia 17; s/d/tr M$480/600/740; Ⓜ San Juan de Letrán; Ⓟ Ⓧ Ⓛ) The peach-concrete Marlowe stands across from Chinatown's pagoda gate. Above a bright, airy lobby are spacious rooms with good carpet, colorful bedspreads, soothing art and inset lighting. Fitness freaks will appreciate the gym-with-a-view.

Hotel Mónaco (Map pp128-9; ☎ 5566-8333; www.hotel-monaco.com.mx; Guerrero 12; s/d M$485/520; Ⓜ Hidalgo; Ⓟ ✖) Steps from the metro and opposite cute Plaza de San Fernando, this refurbished older hotel is poised between run-down Colonia Guerrero and the Reforma business corridor. Bellboys in blue suits proudly escort you down marble-floored hallways with piped-in muzak to your neatly furnished, color-coordinated room.

Hotel San Francisco (Map pp128-9; ☎ 5533-1032; sanfrancisco@hotelesdelangel.com; Luis Moya 11; s/d/tr M$700/760/818; Ⓜ Juárez; Ⓟ) Popular with European groups, this 14-story stepped tower boasts big rooms with old-fashioned furniture and dated lobby decor. The best Alameda views are from the north-facing units above the 11th floor.

Similarly unremarkable but perfectly comfortable places with decent restaurants abound in this zone.

Hotel Fleming (Map pp128-9; ☎ 5510-4530; www.hotelfleming.com.mx; Revillagigedo 35; s/d/tr M$360/430/490; Ⓜ Juárez; Ⓟ 🖥)

Hotel Monte Real (Map pp128-9; ☎ 5518-1150; www.hotelmontereal.com.mx; Revillagigedo 23; s/d/tr M$650/700/800; Ⓜ Juárez; Ⓟ ✖ 🖥) Opposite the new Museo de Artes Populares.

TOP END

Hotel Sheraton Centro Histórico (Map pp128-9; ☎ 5130-5300; www.sheraton.com.mx; Juárez 70; r from US$220; Ⓜ Hidalgo; Ⓟ ✖ ✖ 🖥 🐕) A cornerstone in the downtown redevelopment, the sleek Sheraton towers above quaint Alameda Central. Most guests are here on business, but anyone desiring a dose of comfort and sublime cityscapes should be satisfied. The 6th-floor terrace features an open-air leisure complex, with saunas, massage clinic and 'comfort food' restaurant.

Hotel de Cortés (Map pp128-9; ☎ 5518-2181; www.hotel decortes.com.mx; Hidalgo 85; r M$1385-2398, ste M$1962-2992; Ⓜ Hidalgo; ✖ 🖥) Once a hospice for Augustinian pilgrims, this World Hotels property has a long history of sheltering travelers, with rooms encircling a lovely 18th-century patio. If you don't mind the price tag, staying here will give you a genuine taste of colonial Mexico.

Plaza de la República & Around

Further from the Zócalo, the area around the Monument to the Revolution is awash with hotels, with a number of dives interspersed amid the business-class establishments. Unaffected by the wave of development sweeping the Centro and Reforma corridor, the semi-residential zone offers glimpses of neighborhood life.

BUDGET

Casa de los Amigos (Map pp128-9; ☎ 5705-0521; www.casadelosamigos.org; Mariscal 132; dm M$100, r with shared bathroom M$290; Ⓜ Revolución; ✖ 🖥) The Quaker-run Casa is primarily a residence for NGOs, researchers and others seeking social change, but welcomes walk-in travelers. Meditation sessions, discussions with community members and Spanish conversation are available to guests, who may volunteer to help run the Casa for a reduced rate. A hearty breakfast (M$15) is served Monday to Friday in the ground-floor dining room. There's a two-night minimum stay.

Hotel Édison (Map pp128-9; ☎ 5566-0933; Édison 106; s/d/tr M$219/299/359; Ⓜ Revolución; 🖥) Beyond the bunker-like exterior, accommodations face a rectangular garden surrounded by pre-Hispanic motifs. Despite faded wallpaper and dated fixtures, rooms are enormous with massive marble washbasins and closets. There's a bakery and laundry across the street.

MIDRANGE

All of the following places have on-site restaurants serving 'international' cuisine.

Hotel Sevilla (Map pp128-9; ☎ 5566-1866; www.sevilla.com.mx; Serapio Rendón 124; s M$276-495, d M$445-573; 🚌 Reforma; Ⓟ ✖ 🖥) Opposite the Jardín del Arte this oft-recommended business hotel is divided into 'traditional' and 'new' sections. Those in the latter are more slickly appointed with air-conditioning and hair dryers.

Hotel New York (Map pp128-9; ☎ 5566-9700; Édison 45; s/d M$310/520; Ⓜ Revolución; Ⓟ) A few blocks northeast of Plaza de la República, this is a stylish option in a zone crammed with cut-rate hotels. Rates include breakfast and wireless internet.

Palace Hotel (Map pp128-9; ☎ 5566-2400; fax 5535-7520; Ignacio Ramírez 7; s/d M$351/409; 🚌 Revolución; Ⓟ) Run by gregarious Asturians, the Palace has large, neatly maintained rooms in an appealing range of blues. Broad balconies give terrific views down palm-lined Ramírez to the domed monument. Cash-paying guests get substantial discounts.

Hotel Mayaland (Map pp128-9; ☎ 5566-6066; www .hotelmayaland.com.mx; Antonio Caso 23; s/d M$430/560; Ⓜ Juárez; Ⓟ ⌨) A business-oriented hotel on a sterile street, this has well-maintained facilities with a Maya motif. Typically neutral-modern rooms feature textured pink walls, flowery canvasses and inset lighting.

Hotel Jena (Map pp128-9; ☎ 5097-0277; www .hoteljena.com.mx; Jesús Terán 12; s/d/ste M$667/761/1287; Ⓜ Hidalgo; Ⓟ ✖ ⌨ ⏷) Not as tall as it looks (the black tower is strictly for show), but the giant rooms are among the most luxurious in this range. Just 1½ blocks from Reforma.

The following two lodgings are just above the Jardín del Arte. What they lack in character they make up for in convenience and comfort.

Hotel Compostela (Map pp128-9; ☎ 5566-0733; Sullivan 35; s M$299-410, d M$320-475; Ⓑ Reforma; Ⓟ) 'Modern' rooms are more luxurious.

Hotel Astor (Map pp128-9; ☎ 5148-2644; hotel .astor@mexico.com; Antonio Caso 83; s/d M$440/580; Ⓑ Reforma; Ⓟ ✖ ⌨) Sleek and sterile, with discreet reception; near classic Café Gran Premio.

TOP END

Hotel Misión Reforma (Map pp128-9; ☎ 5141-0442; www.hotelesmision.com.mx; Morelos 110; r/ste M$1300/2303; Ⓑ Reforma; Ⓟ ✖ ⌨) One of several business hotels around the Columbus circle, this terracotta monolith is a branch of a Mexican chain. Spacious rooms get liberal doses of color and comfort and afford fine views of the grand boulevard below.

Hotel Imperial (Map pp128-9; ☎ 5705-4911; www.hotel imperial.com.mx; Paseo de la Reforma 64; r/ste M$1521/2457; Ⓑ Reforma; ✖ ⌨) Dictator Díaz unwrapped this cake wedge of a building in 1904. Spacious suites occupy the upper levels, while 50 standard rooms line the Paseo de la Reforma and Av Morelos sides. Unfortunately, room decor fails to match the building's Porfiriato splendor.

Zona Rosa & Around

Foreign businesspeople and tourists check in at the glitzy hotels in this international commerce and nightlife area. Less expensive establishments dot the quieter streets of Colonia Cuauhtémoc, north of Reforma, and Juárez, east of Insurgentes.

MIDRANGE

our pick **Casa González** (Map pp132-3; ☎ 5514-3302; casa .gonzalez@prodigy.net.mx; Río Sena 69; s/d from M$428/588; Ⓜ Insurgentes; ⌨) A family-run operation for nearly a century, the Casa is a perennial hit with mature travelers. Set around several flower-filled patios and semi-private terraces, it's extraordinarily *tranquilo*. Original portraits and landscapes decorate the rooms, apparently done by a guest in lieu of payment. Guests meet over breakfast, which is served on old china in the dining room.

Hotel Del Principado (Map pp132-3; ☎ 5233-2944; www.hoteldelprincipado.com.mx; Londres 42; s/d/tr incl breakfast M$500/650/750; Ⓜ Insurgentes; Ⓟ ⌨ ♿) Conveniently poised between the Zona Rosa and Colonia Roma, this friendly little place makes a nice cocoon. Its carpet was recently replaced with faux wood floors, installed light stained furniture and they keys have been updated to cards. A breakfast buffet includes fruit, *chilaquiles* and much more. Look for weekend discounts.

Hotel Bristol (Map pp132-3; ☎ 5533-6060; www .hotelbristol.com.mx; Plaza Necaxa 17; s/d M$563/656; Ⓟ ✖ ✖ ⌨) A good-value option in the pleasant but central Cuauhtémoc neighborhood, the Bristol caters primarily to business travelers, offering quality carpet, soothing colors and an above-average restaurant. Take a 'La Villa' or 'Metro Chapultepec' pesero.

6M9 Guest House (Map pp132-3; ☎ 5208-8347; www .purpleroofs.com/6m9-mx.html; Marsella 69; s/d M$640/950; Ⓜ Insurgentes; ⌨) Oriented toward a gay male clientele, the 6M9 occupies a Porfiriato-era building within walking distance of Pink Zone bars. The fun-filled facilities include a small pool, sun deck, tiled steam room and complimentary bar. There are nine spacious, well-maintained rooms (reservations online only).

Hotel María Cristina (Map pp132-3; ☎ 5703-1212; www.hotelmariacristina.com.mx; Río Lerma 31; s/d from M$695/775; Ⓜ Insurgentes; Ⓟ ✖ ⌨) Dating from the 1930s, this facsimile of an Andalucian estate makes an appealing retreat, particularly the adjacent bar with patio seating. Though lacking the lobby's colonial splendor, rooms are generally bright and comfortable.

Hotel Del Ángel (Map pp132-3; ☎ 5533-1032; www .hotelesdelangel.mexicohoteles.com; Río Lerma 154; s/d/tr M$761/878/995; Ⓟ ✖ ⌨) Nearby construction has blocked views of the iconic monument it's named after, but rather than brood, the hotel is jazzing up its facilities from the top down, adding postmodern furniture and fixtures to the uppermost units. Take a 'La Villa' or 'Metro Chapultepec' pesero.

Hotel Cityexpress (Map pp132-3; ☎ 5208-1717; www.cityexpress.com.mx; Havre 21; r incl breakfast M$807; 🚭 Hamburgo; P ✕ ✕) The new Cityexpress emphasizes comfort and functionality – a place to crash between deals. But decor outshines the neutral-modern favored by most hotels in this price category, with captivating views of the nearby towers springing up in this transitional zone.

TOP END

Hotel Geneve (Map pp132-3; ☎ 5080-0800; www.hotel geneve.com.mx; Londres 130; r from M$1355; M Insurgentes; P ✕ ✕ 🖳) Celebrating its centennial, this Zona Rosa institution strives to maintain a belle époque ambience despite the globalized mishmash around it. Rooms get the colonial treatment, with handsome carved wood headboards and colonial dressers and nightstands. The classy lobby connects to a skylit Sanborns café.

Four Seasons Hotel (Map pp132-3; ☎ 5230-1818; www.fourseasons.com/mexico; Paseo de la Reforma 500; r US$370; M Sevilla; P ✕ ✕ 🖳 🖳 🖳) One of the city's most elegant lodgings, the Four Seasons was designed to resemble a French-Mexican late-19th-century structure, with aristocratically furnished rooms facing a beautifully landscaped central courtyard.

Roma
BUDGET

Versalles 104 (Map pp132-3; ☎ 5705-3247; www .versalles104.com; Versalles 104; dm/d from M$115/240; M Cuauhtémoc; 🖳) Managed by a friendly binational couple, this 'boutique hostel' is a hit with young, mostly European travelers. Two rooms facing a small patio are outfitted as mixed-gender dorms sharing a tiny bathroom. Much of the interaction takes place in the front-end café/theater.

Hostel Home (Map pp132-3; ☎ 5511-1683; www .hostelhome.com.mx; Tabasco 303; dm M$120; 🚭 Ávaro Obregón; 🖳) Housed in a fine Porfiriato-era building, this 20-bed hostel is on narrow tree-lined Calle Tabasco, a gateway to the Roma neighborhood. Managed by easygoing staff, the Home is a good place to meet other travelers and find out what's happening.

MIDRANGE

Hotel Milán (Map pp132-3; ☎ 5584-0222; www.hotelmilan .com.mx; Álvaro Obregón 94; s/d M$390/500; M Insurgentes; P 🖳) The Milán makes a good place to land in Mexico City. Though lacking in character,

it's comfortable and well maintained and sits on the main corridor of bohemian Roma.

Hotel Stanza (Map pp132-3; ☎ 5208-0052; www.stanza hotel.com; Álvaro Obregón 13; r M$564-702; M Cuauhtémoc; P ✕ 🖳) A business travelers' block on the east end of Álvaro Obregón, the Stanza makes a cushy, relatively inexpensive landing pad or reentry chamber. The recently renovated hotel offers two categories of accommodations: 'executive' (with air-con) and 'standard' (cheaper furniture and smaller bathrooms).

Casa de la Condesa (Map pp132-3; ☎ 5574-3186; www.extendedstaymexico.com; Plaza Luis Cabrera 16; ste from M$643; M Insurgentes) Right on the delightful Plaza Luis Cabrera, the Casa makes a tranquil base for visitors on an extended stay, offering 'suites' that are essentially studio apartments with kitchens.

TOP END

Quality Inn (Map pp132-3; ☎ 1085-9500; www.choice hotelsmexico.com; Álvaro Obregón 38; r M$1222; M Cuauhtémoc; P ✕ 🖳) Facing Álvaro Obregón's leafy median, Roma's newest hotel resembles its pricier downtown counterparts. Equipped with iPod hookups and softly illuminated desk nooks, its 91 ultra-comfortable units surround a skylight-capped central atrium.

La Casona (Map pp132-3; ☎ 5286-3001; www.hotel lacasona.com.mx; Durango 280; r incl breakfast US$217; M Sevilla; ✕) This stately mansion was restored to its early-20th-century splendor to become one of the capital's most distinctive boutique hotels. Each of the 29 rooms is uniquely appointed to bring out its original charm.

Condesa

Thanks to the recent appearance of several attractive lodgings, this neighborhood south of Bosque de Chapultepec can make an excellent base, with plenty of after-hours restaurants and cafés.

Hotel Roosevelt (Map pp132-3; ☎ 5208-6813; www .hotelroosevelt.com.mx; Insurgentes Sur 287, cnr Yucatán; s/d M$450/630; 🚭 Álvaro Obregón; P 🖳) On the eastern edge of Condesa and within easy reach of the Cuban club district, this friendly if functional hotel should appeal to nocturnally inclined travelers.

our pick **Red Tree House** (Map pp132-3; ☎ 5584-3829; www.theredtreehouse.com; Culiacán 6, cnr Ámsterdam; s with shared/private bathroom US$50/70, plus per additional person US$15, penthouse US$150; M Chilpancingo; 🖳) Just off the delightful Plaza Citlaltépetl, the area's first B&B has all the comforts of home, if your home happens to be decorated with exquisite taste. Each of the three bedrooms on the middle level is uniquely furnished, and the top-floor apartment has its own terrace. Downstairs, guests have the run of a cozy living room with fireplace and lovely rear garden, the domain of friendly pooch Abril.

Condesa df (Map pp132-3; ☎ 5241-2600; www.con desadf.com; Veracruz 102; r from US$182; Ⓜ Chapultepec; ⊠ ▣ ♿) Setting Condesa hipness standards since its 2005 opening, this is where Paris Hilton and U2 stayed during recent visits. The 1920s structure opposite Parque España has been quirkily made over and furnished with an array of specially designed objects. Rooms encircle an atrium/bar that draws scenemakers nightly.

Hippodrome Hotel (Map pp132-3; ☎ 5512-2110; www.thehippodromehotel.com; Av Mexico 188; r from US$230; Ⓜ Chilpancingo; Ⓟ ▣) North of Parque México, this new boutique hotel occupies one of the neighborhood's art deco gems, with the interior restored to a contemporary Mexican aesthetic. Original modern art complements stylish furniture, all designed in-house. With just 16 rooms, it's a smaller, more businesslike affair than Condesa df and features a similarly subdued restaurant, Hip Kitchen (see p175).

Polanco

North of Bosque de Chapultepec, Polanco has some of the best business accommodations and one excellent boutique hotel.

Hotel Polanco (Map pp136-7; ☎ 5280-8082; www.hotel polanco.com; Edgar Allan Poe 8; s/d M$1395/1455; Ⓜ Auditorio; ⊠ ⊠ ▣) This resembles a European guesthouse of the sort Basil Fawlty runs, complete with Italian bistro and snippy desk manager. The 71 rooms eschew hipness for a sober ambience. It's in a quiet, leafy quarter with easy access to the National Auditorium.

Camino Real México (Map pp136-7; ☎ 5263-8888; www.caminoreal.com; Calz Mariano Escobedo 700; r/ste US$135/340; Ⓜ Chapultepec; Ⓟ ⊠ ⊠ ▣ ⊠ ♿) With over 700 rooms and covering 33,000 sq meters, the Camino Real is a monumental endeavor. It's also a national architectural landmark, boldly designed by Mexican Ricardo Legorreta, whose trademark geometric solids and great swathes of color lend it a refreshing simplicity. Off the broad arc of the reception desk lie the main garden and pool, surrounded by honeycombed structures that house the guest rooms. Accommodations are

certainly luxurious, though other than a bold color scheme the Camino has fairly standard business-class design and amenities.

Hábita Hotel (Map pp136-7; ☎ 5282-3100, www .hotelhabita.com; Av Presidente Masaryk 201; s/d US$228/310; Ⓜ Polanco; Ⓟ ⊠ ⊠ ▣ ⊠) Architect Enrique Norten turned a functional apartment building into a smart boutique hotel. Decor in the 36 rooms is boldly minimal, and the rooftop bar, Área (p182), is a hot nightspot.

W Mexico City Hotel (Map pp136-7; ☎ 9138-1800; www.whotels.com; Campos Elíseos 252; r US$445; Ⓜ Auditorio; Ⓟ ⊠ ⊠ ▣ ⊠ ♿) One of the four sentinels opposite the Auditorio Nacional, Latin America's first W is a 25-floor business hotel that's determined to break away from the stodginess of its neighbors.

Coyoacán & Ciudad Universitaria

Despite Coyoacán's appeal, the southern community has only one central place to stay. Check with the Coyoacán tourist office (p135) about short-term home stays.

El Cenote Azul (Map pp126-7; ☎ 5554-8730; www .elcenoteazul.com; Alfonso Pruneda 24; dm M$100; Ⓜ Copilco) This laid-back hostel near the UNAM campus has just four neatly kept four- or two-bed rooms sharing two Talavera-tiled bathrooms. The downstairs café is a hangout for university students.

Hostal Frida (Map p140; ☎ 5659-7005; www.hostal fridabyb.com.mx; Mina 54; d M$500; Ⓜ Viveros) Run by an English-speaking couple whose kids have moved on, this 'empty nest' is being refilled with international travelers. Each of the five wood-floored doubles occupies its own level in adjacent towers, and most include kitchens. It's four blocks west of Frida's place and around the corner from a branch of Café El Jarocho.

Airport

Besides the two upscale hotels linked to the terminal, these more economical lodgings are across the street. Turn left outside the domestic terminal; beyond the metro, take a left onto Blvd Puerto Aéreo and cross via the pedestrian bridge.

Hotel Aeropuerto (Map pp126-7; ☎ 5785-5851; fax 5784-1329; Blvd Puerto Aéreo 380; s/d M$500/600; Ⓜ Terminal Aérea; Ⓟ) Not as bleakly functional as the aluminum facade portends, the only non-chain in the zone has helpful reception staff and neutral modern rooms, some overlooking the airport runway through soundproof windows.

Fiesta Inn (Map pp126-7; ☎ 5133-6600; www.fiestainn .com; Blvd Puerto Aéreo 502; r M$1538; Ⓜ Terminal Aérea; Ⓟ ⊗ ⊗ ▢ ⊡ ▥) This securely enclosed branch of the business chain offers rooms with balconies around a pool. Transportation to or from your flight is included, and rates are about 20% cheaper on weekends.

EATING

The capital offers eateries for all tastes and budgets, from taco stalls to exclusive restaurants. In recent years, the city has emerged as a major destination for culinary travelers, as Mexican chefs win the sort of praise formerly reserved for their counterparts in New York and Paris. Most of the hottest venues for contemporary cuisine show up in Polanco and Condesa.

Budget eaters will find literally thousands of restaurants and holes in the wall serving *comida corrida* (set lunch) for as little as M$25. Market buildings are good places to look for these while *tianguis* (weekly street markets) customarily have an eating section offering tacos, *barbacoa* (roasted mutton) and quesadillas (cheese folded between tortillas and fried or grilled). See also the boxed text on p176.

Certain items can be found all over town. In the evening *tamales* are delivered by bicycle, their arrival heralded by an eerie moan through a cheap speaker. You'll know the *camote* (sweet potato) man is coming by the shrill steam whistle emitting from his cart, heard for blocks around.

The city is also peppered with modern chain restaurants, the predictable menus of which make a sound, if unexciting, fallback. Branches of VIPS, Sanborns, Wings and California restaurants serve US-style coffeeshop fare and Mexican standards. International chains, from KFC to Starbucks, are well represented, too.

Centro Histórico

The historic center is a great place to enjoy traditional Mexican dishes in elegant surroundings at places like El Cardenal and Café de Tacuba. In general, though, it's more of a daytime place than an evening destination, with many places only open for breakfast and lunch. Restaurant options tend to be sparse after dark.

QUICK EATS

Tacos de Canasta Chucho (Map pp128-9; ☎ 5521-0280; Av 5 de Mayo 17A; tacos M$5; ☼ 9am-6pm Mon-Fri, 8am-5pm Sat; Ⓜ Allende) These bite-sized tacos are filled with things like refried beans, *chicharrón* and *mole* (just the sauce), and arranged in a big basket. A couple of pails contain the garnishes: spicy guacamole and marinated carrot chunks and chilies.

Taquería Los Paisás (Map pp128-9; ☎ 5542-8139; Jesús María 131; tacos M$10; ☼ 8am-midnight; Ⓜ Pino Suárez) Run by three goateed brothers, this corner taco stand east of the Zócalo offers overstuffed steak, sausage and *pastor* tacos – or *campechano*, all mixed up. Help yourself from the heaping trays of garnishes: mashed potatoes, *pico de gallo*, cactus paddles and *habanero*-spiked onions, among others.

BUDGET

Café El Popular (Map pp128-9; ☎ 5518-6081; Av 5 de Mayo 52; dishes M$40-60; ☼ 24hr; Ⓜ Allende) So popular was this tiny round-the-clock café that they opened another more amply proportioned branch next door to catch the considerable overflow. Fresh pastries and good combination breakfasts (fruit, eggs, frijoles – beans – and coffee) are the main attractions. *Café con leche* (coffee with milk) is served *chino* style (ie you specify the strength).

Costillas El Sitio (Map pp128-9; ☎ 5521-1545; República de Uruguay 82D; ribs M$55; ☼ 9am-7:30pm; Ⓜ Zócalo) Lunchtime crowds squeeze into booths or share tiny red tables at this volume-oriented steak place. Grilled and brushed with salsa verde, the cuts are tasty if not the most tender in town. Add black beans, grilled green onions and sopes, and you've got a gut-stuffing meal. For dessert there's homemade flan.

Vegetariano Madero (Map pp128-9; ☎ 5521-6880; Madero 56; set lunch from M$63; ☼ 8am-7pm; Ⓜ Allende; Ⓥ) Despite the austere entrance, there's a lively restaurant upstairs where a pianist plinks out old favorites. The meatless menu includes a range of tasty variations on Mexican standards. Balcony seating lets you observe the street activity. A nearby street-level branch, the Restaurante Vegetariano (Filomena Mata 13), displays the day's offerings out front.

MIDRANGE

Hostería de Santo Domingo (Map pp128-9; ☎ 5526-5276; Domínguez 72; dishes M$70-180; ☼ 9am-10pm; Ⓜ Allende; Ⓟ) Whipping up classic Mexican fare since 1860, this hugely popular (though not touristy) restaurant has a festive atmosphere, enhanced by chamber music. It's famous for its enormous *chiles en nogada* (M$180), an Independence Day favorite, served here year-round.

Café de Tacuba (Map pp128-9; ☎ 5518-4950; Tacuba 28; mains M$70-150, 5-course lunch M$180; Ⓜ Allende) Before the band there was the restaurant. Way before. A fantasy of colored tiles, brass lamps and oil paintings, this mainstay has served *antojitos* (tortilla-based snacks like tacos and gorditas) since 1912. Never mind the tourists, the atmosphere is just right for a plate of *pambazos* (filled rolls fried in chili sauce) or *tamales* with hot chocolate.

Al Andalus (Map pp128-9; ☎ 5522-2528; Mesones 171; dishes M$90-125; Ⓨ 8am-6pm; Ⓜ Pino Suárez) Al Andalus caters to the capital's substantial Lebanese community, serving shawarma, kebabs, kibbe (spiced lamb fritters), felafel and so on in a superb colonial mansion in the Merced market district.

Casino Español (Map pp128-9; ☎ 5510-2967; Isabel la Católica 29; 4-course lunch M$93; Ⓨ lunch Mon-Fri; Ⓜ Allende) The old Spanish social center, housed in a fabulous Porfiriato-era building, has a popular cantina-style eatery downstairs and an elegant restaurant upstairs. Stolid execs loosen their ties here for a long leisurely lunch, and the courses keep coming. Spanish fare, naturally, highlights the menu though *tacos dorados* (chicken tacos, rolled and deep fried) and *chiles en nogada* are equally well prepared.

TOP END

our pick El Cardenal (Map pp128-9; ☎ 5521-8815; La Palma 23; dishes M$90-280; Ⓨ 8am-7pm Mon-Sat, 9am-7pm Sun; Ⓜ Zócalo; Ⓟ) Possibly the finest place in town for a traditional meal, El Cardenal occupies three floors of a Parisian-style mansion with a pianist sweetly playing in the background. Breakfast is a must, served with a tray of just-baked sweet rolls and a pitcher of frothy, semi-sweet chocolate. For lunch, go for the oven-roasted veal breast, Oaxaca-style *chiles rellenos*, or in summer, *escamoles* (ant larvae, a much coveted specialty).

Los Girasoles (Map pp128-9; ☎ 5510-0630; Plaza Manuel Tolsá; mains M$120-150; Ⓨ 1pm-midnight Tue-Sat, 1-9pm Sun & Mon; Ⓜ Allende; Ⓟ) This fine restaurant boasts an encyclopedic range of Mexican fare, from pre-Hispanic (ant larvae), to colonial (turkey in tamarind *mole*), to innovative (snapper fillet in rosehip salsa). Try to get a table overlooking the grand Plaza Tolsá, or on the terrace adjacent to it.

Restaurante Chon (Map pp128-9; ☎ 5542-0873; Regina 160; mains M$180; Ⓨ lunch Mon-Sat; Ⓜ Pino Suárez) Pre-Hispanic fare is the specialty of this cantina-style restaurant. Sample maguey worms (in season), grasshoppers, wild boar and other delicacies.

Alameda Central & Around

Though places on the immediate perimeter of the Alameda cater to an upscale clientele, head down Luis Moya or along Ayuntamiento, south of the Alameda, for pockets of the neighborhood's rustic heritage in the form of *torta* stands and chicken-soup vendors. Mexico City's modest Chinatown covers a single paper-lantern-strung block of Calle Dolores, a couple of blocks south of the park.

Both the Cloister Café at the Museo Franz Mayer (p148) and the more upscale Café del Palacio at Bellas Artes (p147) offer sandwiches, salads and pastries between exhibits.

Churrería El Moro (Map pp128-9; ☎ 5512-0896; Eje Central Lázaro Cardenas 42; hot chocolate with 4 churros M$25; Ⓨ 24hr; Ⓜ San Juan de Letrán) A fine respite from the Eje Central crowds, El Moro manufactures long, slender deep-fried *churros* (doughnut-like fritters), just made to be dipped in thick hot chocolate. It's a popular late-night spot, perfect for winding down after hours.

Café Colón (Map pp128-9; ☎ 5521-6343; Colón 1; breakfast combos M$30-49, 4-course lunch M$40; Ⓜ Hidalgo) Dishing out traditional fare from this location for almost half a century, Café Colón remains popular with local office workers who pour in mid-morning for coffee or mid-afternoon for the filling *comida*.

Mi Fonda (Map pp128-9; ☎ 5521-0002; López 101; paella M$35; Ⓨ lunch; Ⓜ San Juan de Letrán) Working-class Chilangos line up for their share of *paella valenciana*, made fresh daily and patiently ladled out by women in white bonnets. Jesús from Cantabria oversees the proceedings. Space is limited but you can share a table.

El Cuadrilátero (Map pp128-9; ☎ 5521-3060; Luis Moya 73; tortas M$35-70; Ⓨ 7am-8pm Mon-Sat; Ⓜ Juárez) Owned by *luchador* (wrestler) Super Astro, this shrine to *lucha libre* features a wall of wrestlers' masks. Not just wrestlers, but also ordinary denizens of the Centro frequent the joint for its gigantic tortas, versions of which are displayed at the entrance. If you manage to consume a 1.3kg cholesterol-packed Torta Gladiador in 15 minutes, it's free.

MEXICO CITY

SQUARE MEALS

Perhaps the quintessential Mexico City experience is dining or sipping cocktails overlooking the vast Zócalo with the Mexican *tricolor* waving proudly over the scene. The three upscale hotels on the plaza's west side offer abundant buffet breakfasts, although the food isn't as spectacular as the vista. (If it's not too busy you can enjoy the view for the price of a drink.) Two recently inaugurated restaurants on the same side and one longtime establishment north of the cathedral promise more enticing culinary experiences.

Puro Corazón (Map pp128-9; ☎ 5518-0300; Monte de Piedad 11; breakfast combos M$65-95; ⏰ 8am-9pm) On the plaza's northwest corner, offering heart-thumping views of the cathedral from its 6th-floor perch, along with exciting contemporary Mexican dishes that incorporate native ingredients like pulque (a fermented maguey beverage) and *flor de calabaza* (squash blossoms).

La Terraza del Zócalo (Map pp128-9; ☎ 5521-7934; Plaza de la Constitución 13, 6th fl; dishes M$110-150; ⏰ 1-8pm Sun-Thu, 1pm-midnight Fri & Sat) Has a broad balcony opposite the National Palace with tables built into the railing or on a raised platform behind them. Oaxaca-style enchiladas and *cecina de Yecapixtla* (thinly sliced salted meat) highlight a menu of regional classics. Enter at ground level through the jewelry arcade and look for the elevator.

Casa de las Sirenas (Map pp128-9; ☎ 5704-3345; República de Guatemala 32; mains M$160; ⏰ 8am-11pm Mon-Thu, 8am-2am Fri & Sat, 8am-7pm Sun) Housed in a 17th-century relic, Sirenas has a top-floor terrace that looks toward the Zócalo via the Plaza del Templo Mayor. It's an ideal perch to nibble on stuffed chilies laced with walnut sauce or other Oaxaca-influenced fare — along with a shot of tequila from the downstairs cantina's extensive selection.

Zona Rosa & Around

While the Zona Rosa is packed with places to eat and drink, it's dominated by uninspiring 'international' fare and fast-food franchises. Notably outside this stream are the numerous restaurants catering to the neighborhood's growing Korean community.

BUDGET
Café Mangia (Map pp132-3; ☎ 5533-4503; Río Sena 85; paninis M$65, salads M$65; ⏰ 8am-8pm Mon-Fri; Ⓜ Insurgentes) This bohemian, white-brick space has an uncomplicated menu of paninis stuffed with pesto and smoked cheese, roast beef and herbs, or smoked salmon with cream cheese.

MIDRANGE
Yug Vegetariano (Map pp132-3; ☎ 5533-3872; Varsovia 3; buffet lunch M$75, dishes M$60-75; ⏰ 7am-9pm Mon-Fri, 8:30am-8pm Sat & Sun; Ⓜ Insurgentes; Ⓥ) The menu is gastro-heaven for vegetarians and vast enough for most carnivore folk to find something they fancy – even if it is a soy-substitute burger. Choose from specialties like squash-flower crepes and chop suey with brown rice, or go the buffet route.

our pick **Young Bin Kwan** (Map pp132-3; ☎ 5208-9399; Av Florencia 15; soups M$80, mains M$120-150; ⏰ 9:30am-11pm; Ⓜ Insurgentes; Ⓟ) This two-level dining hall is straight out of Seoul with large-screen TVs providing continuous Asian programming. Enormous portions of *bulgogi* (marinated beef grilled at your table) are complemented by a fabulous array of side dishes (sesame leaves, bean sprouts, kimchi, etc).

Fonda El Refugio (Map pp132-3; ☎ 5525-8128; Liverpool 166; dishes M$110; ⏰ 1-11pm Mon-Sat, 1-10pm Sun; Ⓜ Insurgentes; Ⓟ) Amid a collection of colorful pots, paintings and whimsical ceramic ornaments, the family-run *fonda* serves regional dishes like *mole poblano* (breast of chicken drenched in a rich chocolate-based sauce) and *albondigas chipotle* (meatballs laced with spicy chili).

TOP END
Tezka (Map pp132-3; ☎ 5228-9918; Amberes 78; dishes M$195-275; Ⓜ Insurgentes; Ⓟ) Contemporary Basque cuisine is the specialty: try sea bass and red snapper in a green chili sauce or codfish in a garlic and red pepper marinade.

Condesa

La Condesa has become the hub of the eating-out scene, and dozens of informal bistros and cafés, many with sidewalk tables, compete for space along several key streets. The neighborhood's culinary heart is at the convergence of Calles Michoacán, Vicente Suárez and Tamaulipas; other good restaurants and cafés ring Parque México. After 8pm the following places are often filled to capacity and getting a table means waiting around for a while.

QUICK EATS

El Tizoncito (Map pp132-3; ☎ 5286-7321; Tamaulipas 122, cnr Campeche; tacos from M$8; ⏱ noon-3:30am Sun-Thu, noon-4:30am Fri & Sat; Ⓜ Patriotismo) The original branch of the citywide chain has been going for nearly 40 years. It claims to have invented tacos *al pastor* (ie cooked on a spit, shepherd style), and half the fun is watching the grill-men deftly put them together. If there are no seats, try the bigger location two blocks east on Campeche.

ourpick **Taquería Hola** (Map pp132-3; ☎ 5286-4495; Ámsterdam 135, cnr Michoacán; tacos M$11; ⏱ 9am-5:30pm Mon-Fri, 9am-2pm Sat) Mid-morning, local snack-ers crowd this friendly hole in the wall for a stand-up chomp. Choose from a remarkable array of taco fillings, all temptingly displayed in clay dishes. Tacos are served on two tortil-las, the second to catch the overflow, and gar-nished on request with guacamole or crumbly white cheese.

Nevería Roxy (Map pp132-3; ☎ 5286-1258; Mazatlán 81, cnr Montes de Oca; scoop M$12, banana split M$45; ⏱ 11am-8:30pm; Ⓜ Chapultepec) The old-fashioned Roxy makes its own ice cream and sherbet on-site, including such tropical flavors as *zapote* (sapodilla) and guava. Another branch is at Tamaulipas 161 at Alfonso Reyes, close to metro Patriotismo.

El Califa (Map pp132-3; ☎ 5271-7666; Altata 22, cnr Alfonso Reyes; tacos M$30; ⏱ 1:30pm-3:30am; Ⓜ Chilpanc-ingo; Ⓟ) This popular *taquería* on Condesa's southern edge puts its own spin on the classic snack, grilling slices of beef and tossing them on handmade tortillas. Tables are set with a palette of savory salsas in sturdy clay bowls.

BUDGET

Orígenes Orgánicos (Map pp132-3; ☎ 5208-6678; Plaza Popocatépetl 41A; salads M$40-85, 3-course lunch M$120; ⏱ 8am-10pm Mon-Fri, 9am-7pm Sat, 10am-6pm Sun Ⓥ) More than just a place to buy soy milk and certified organic produce, this store/café facing one of Condesa's loveliest plazas prepares tasty meals with an emphasis on fresh, seasonal, organic ingredients.

La Rauxa (Map pp132-3; ☎ 5211-2927; Parras 15; 4-course lunch M$70; ⏱ 1-6pm Mon-Sat; Ⓢ Sonora; Ⓥ) Here's an interesting twist on the *comida corrida* concept, featuring uniquely created Catalan-influenced fare by chef/owner Quim Jardí. Instead of a printed menu, Quim de-

scribes what's being served, with at least one vegetarian main-course option daily. Pleasant terrace seating under a big tree is usually filled by 2:30pm.

MIDRANGE

El Diez (Map pp132-3; ☎ 5276-2616; Benjamín Hill 187; steaks M$88, pizzas from M$60; ⏱ 1pm-midnight Sun-Thu, 1pm-1am Fri & Sat; Ⓜ Patriotismo; Ⓟ) The popular-ity of this unpretentious steak place might be attributed to its prices. Quality Argentine cuts, served on a cutting board with zesty dressed salad alongside, average under M$100, and Malbec wines are similarly reasonable. Those with less carnivorous appetites can order pizza by the square meter.

Café La Gloria (Map pp132-3; ☎ 5211-4180; Vicente Suárez 41; dishes M$85-100; ⏱ 1pm-midnight Mon-Sat, 1-11pm Sun; Ⓜ Patriotismo; Ⓟ) A hip bistro in the heart of the zone, La Gloria remains a popular meeting place for both Chilangos and foreign-ers, thanks to the generous salads, zesty pastas and surprising blackboard specials, not to mention the quirky art on display.

Fonda Garufa (Map pp132-3; ☎ 5286-8295; Av Michoacán 93; pasta M$85, steaks M$140-200; ⏱ 8am-mid-night Tue & Wed, 8am-1am Thu-Sat, 8am-11pm Sun; Ⓜ Patri-otismo; Ⓟ) One of the first in the zone to put tables on the sidewalk and fire up a grill, La Garufa owes its longevity to the quality of its Argentine cuts and better-than-average pastas, as well as a romantic candlelit ambience.

Rojo Bistrot (Map pp132-3; ☎ 5211-3705; Ámsterdam 71; mains M$90-150; ⏱ 2pm-midnight Mon-Sat, 2-6pm Sun; Ⓢ Sonora) On a leafy corner near Parque México, this eatery is popular as much for its vibrant social scene as for the French-inspired cuisine. Regulars recommend the duck in pas-sion fruit sauce and octopus risotto.

TOP END

Hip Kitchen (Map pp132-3; ☎ 5212-2110; Av México 188; starters M$85-120, mains M$165-270; ⏱ 1pm-midnight Mon-Sat; Ⓢ Sonora; Ⓟ) At the stylish bistro of Condesa's Hippodrome Hotel (p171), star chefs fuse Mexican and Asian ingredients in exciting ways: miso-glazed salmon gets brushed with *chipotle*, and *pico de gallo* is served alongside your saku tuna. Dining is in a narrow, romantic space with a wall-length sofa and art deco fixtures. Reservations are highly recommended.

Lampuga (Map pp132-3; ☎ 5286-1525; Ometusco 1, cnr Av Nuevo León; mains M$135-160; ⏱ 2pm-midnight Mon-Sat, 2-6pm Sun; Ⓜ Chilpancingo) Fresh seafood is the

MEXICO CITY

MEXICO CITY'S TOP MARKET FARE

Some of the best eating in Mexico City is not found in any restaurant but in the covered *mercados* and the *tianguis* (weekly street markets).

- **Mercado San Camilito** (Map pp128-9; Plaza Garibaldi; pozole M$44; 🕐 24hr; Ⓜ Garibaldi) The block-long building contains over 70 kitchens serving Jalisco-style *pozole,* a broth brimming with hominy kernels and pork, served with garnishes like radishes and oregano. (Specify *maciza* if pig noses and ears fail to excite you.)

- **Mercado Medellín** (Map pp132-3; Coahuila, btwn Medellín & Monterrey; 🚌 Campeche) Features an extensive eating area with cheap and filling *comidas corridas,* as well as several excellent seafood restaurants.

- **Parrillada Bariloche** (Map pp132-3; Bazar de Oro; 🕐 Wed, Sat & Sun; 🚌 Durango) This stall along the southern aisle of an upscale street market grills some of the least-expensive Uruguayan-style steaks and sausages in town, along with excellent side salads.

- **Tianguis de Pachuca** (Map pp132-3; Melgar; 🕐 10am-4pm Tue; Ⓜ Chapultepec) The food section at the north end of the weekly Condesa street market offers many tempting options, but none so mouthwatering as the *mixiotes,* steamed packets of seasoned mutton, whose contents may be rolled into thick tortillas and garnished with fiery *chiles de manzana* (very hot, yellow chili peppers).

- **Mercado de Antojitos** (Map p140; Higuera, cnr Plaza Hidalgo & Caballo Calco; Ⓜ Coyoacán) Near Coyoacán's main plaza, this busy spot has all kinds of snacks, including deep-fried quesadillas, *pozole, esquites* (boiled corn kernels served with a dollop of mayo) and *flautas* (chicken tacos, rolled long and thin then deep-fried).

- **Tostadas Coyoacán** (Map p140; ☎ 5659-8774; Allende btwn Malitzin & Xicoténcatl; tostadas M$20-30; 🕐 noon-6pm Ⓜ Viveros) Inside Coyoacán's main market, these tostadas are piled high with things like ceviche, marinated octopus and pig's feet, mushrooms and shredded chicken.

---

focus of this French-bistro style restaurant where a blackboard over the bar announces the daily specials. Tuna tostadas make great starters, as does the Greek-style octopus; for a main course, have the catch of the day grilled over coals. It may be hard to find a table at lunchtime.

Roma

QUICK EATS

An unassuming street stall labeled **hamburguesas** (Map pp132-3; cnr Morelia & Colima; burgers M$20; 🕐 10am-midnight Mon-Thu, 10am-1:30am Fri-Sun; Ⓜ Cuauhtémoc) does a roaring trade in hamburgers *al carbón* (charcoal-broiled), garnished with lettuce, tomatoes and chilies. Look for superb *tamales oaxaqueños* at the corner of Álvaro Obregón and Tonalá in the morning.

BUDGET

Taquitos Frontera (Map pp132-3; ☎ 5207-4546; Frontera 120; tacos M$19; 🕐 1:30pm-4am Mon-Thu, 1:30pm-6am Fri & Sat; Ⓜ Insurgentes) One of several late-night *taquerías* along Roma's main drag, this humble alternative has cheerful staff, a smoky open

grill and leather tables and chairs. In addition to the main attraction, there are great sides like *frijoles charros* (cowboy beans) and *cebollitas* (grilled green onions).

Los Bisquets Obregón (Map pp132-3; ☎ 5584-2802; Álvaro Obregón 60; breakfast M$45, antojitos M$50; Ⓜ Insurgentes; 🅿 🛇) The flagship branch of this nationwide chain overflows most mornings; fortunately there are a couple more nearby. Chilangos flock here for the *pan chino* (Chinese pastries) and *café con leche,* dispensed from two pitchers, Veracruz style.

Non Solo Panino (Map pp132-3; ☎ 3096-5128; Plaza Luis Cabrera 10; sandwiches M$50-70; 🕐 1pm-midnight Mon-Sat; Ⓜ Insurgentes; 🅿) The dancing fountains make a lovely backdrop for Italian sandwiches with things like mozzarella, pesto and smoked salmon stuffed into fresh-baked baguettes.

MIDRANGE & TOP END

Contramar (Map pp132-3; ☎ 5514-9217; Durango 200; starters M$60-100, mains M$130-150; 🕐 1:30-6:30pm; 🚌 Durango; 🅿) Fresh seafood is the star attraction at this stylish dining hall with a seaside ambience. The specialty is tuna fillet

Contramar style – split, swabbed with red chili and parsley sauces, and grilled to perfection.

Il Postino (Map pp132-3; ☎ 5208-3644; Plaza de la Villa de Madrid 6; dishes M$100-165; 🚇 Durango; **P**) Run by a pair of chefs from Rome and Milan, this superior Italian restaurant features terrace dining along an arc of the Plaza Cibeles (aka Plaza Villa de Madrid). You might start off with an octopus carpaccio, followed by sea bass wrapped in calzone. Otherwise, ask chef Claudio for his inspiration of the day.

Tierra de Vinos (Map pp132-3; ☎ 5208-5133; Durango 197; dishes M$120-240; 🕑 1-8pm Mon & Tue, 1pm-midnight Wed-Sat; 🚇 Durango; **P**) The focus is on the wine, with hundreds of vintages lining the cellar-like walls, but there's also fine Spanish cuisine to complement your chosen tipple. Sit at the front bar and nosh on tapas while sampling the month's featured vintage or take a table in the lively rear dining room. Waiters gladly suggest what to have with, say, a plate of paprika-laced *patatas bravas* (florals such as a shiraz), or sea bream over black rice (go with a barrel-aged *tempranillo*).

Polanco & Bosque de Chapultepec

Polanco is home to the signature restaurants of several of Mexico City's internationally hot chefs. These places present some of Mexico's best local ingredients in unique combinations to create meals that are well worth the price.

El Bajío (Map pp136-7; ☎ 5281-8246; Alejandro Dumas 7; dishes M$70-120; **M** Auditorio) Owner Carmen 'Titita' Ramirez has built a reputation on producing down-home Veracruz-style food, though sumptuous regional dishes from all over Mexico are served in this folksy setting. Meaty meals like *barbacoa* (mutton cooked in maguey leaves) are El Bajío's signature fare, but the sea bass in banana leaves is equally satisfying.

Izote (Map pp136-7; ☎ 5280-1671; Av Presidente Masaryk 513; dishes M$230-300; 🕑 1-11pm Mon-Sat **M** Polanco; **P**) Patricia Quintana is the celebrated owner of this fashionable upbeat restaurant with an innovative menu. Simple yet superbly presented dishes include *tamales* filled with *huitlacoche* (corn fungus) or squash blossoms. For a main course, the shrimp in spicy *adobo* sauce get a top rating.

Pujol (Map pp136-7; ☎ 5545-4111; Petrarca 254; dishes M$250-350; 🕑 1-11pm Mon-Sat **M** Polanco; **P**) Classic Mexican recipes with a soupçon of Europe and Asia are served in this smartly minimalist room. Delectable seasonal offerings include

cactus salad garnished with oregano sherbet and rack of lamb with a rich *mole* sauce from the Veracruz mountain village of Xico. Indecisive eaters can sample seven of chef Enrique Olvera's signature dishes by ordering the *menu degustación*.

Águila y Sol (Map pp136-7; ☎ 5281-8354; Castelar 127; dishes M$250-375; 🕑 1-11pm Mon-Sat; **M** Polanco; **P**) A culinary goddess in these parts, owner Martha Ortiz takes truly traditional dishes and ingredients to a new level. Start off with a tropical fruit margarita, then slide into the dynamic taste of pork loin in yellow *mole* accompanied by gingered mango, or try cornmeal-encrusted salmon.

San Ángel
MIDRANGE

Cluny (Map p139; ☎ 5550-7350; Av de la Paz 57; dishes M$75; 🕑 12:30pm-midnight Mon-Sat, 12:30pm-11pm Sun; 🚇 La Bombilla; **P**) For unpretentious French cuisine, this bistro in a shopping arcade hits the spot. Quiche, salads, crepes, decadently delicious desserts and generous portions are the order of the day.

Saks (Map p139; ☎ 5616-1601; Plaza San Jacinto 9; dishes M$75-120; 🕑 7:30am-6pm Sun-Thu, 7:30am-midnight Fri & Sat; 🚇 La Bombilla; **P** **V**) Hang out on Saks' sunbathed terrace, with live music, and choose from meatless specialties like *poblano* chilies stuffed with truffle-like corn fungus, Camembert soufflé, huge salads and squash-blossom crepes.

Fonda San Ángel (Map p139; ☎ 5550-1641; Plaza San Jacinto 3; dishes M$90; 🚇 La Bombilla; **P**) On weekends, this attractive restaurant by the plaza does an abundant brunch buffet (M$120), with all kinds of egg dishes, pastries and fresh-squeezed juices, plus great quesadillas.

TOP END

Taberna de León (Map p139; ☎ 5616-2110; Plaza Loreto 173; dishes M$155-270; 🕑 2-11pm Mon-Thu, 2pm-midnight Sat, noon-6pm Sun; 🚇 Doctor Gálvez; **P**) Chef Monica Patiño is one of the new breed of female stars who are stirring up traditional cuisine in innovative ways. This is her original, and most popular, restaurant. Seafood is the specialty with the likes of Baja California stone crab and corn blinis with Norwegian salmon and caviar.

San Ángel Inn (Map p139; ☎ 5616-1402; Diego Rivera 50; mains M$200-350; 🕑 1pm-1am Mon-Sat, 1-10pm Sun; **P**) Classic Mexican meals are served in the various elegant dining rooms of this historic

MEXICO CITY

estate next to the Museo Casa Estudio Diego Rivera y Frida Kahlo (see p156). Even if you don't splurge for dinner, have one of their renowned margaritas in the garden. Walk or take a taxi 1km northwest from Plaza San Jacinto.

Coyoacán
QUICK EATS
Supertacos Chupacabras (Map p140; Av Río Churubusco, cnr Av México; tacos M$8; ⏰ 7am-3am; Ⓜ Coyoacán) Named after the mythical 'goat sucker' (something like the Loch Ness monster), this mega taco stall stands beneath a freeway overpass, but true mavens should not be deterred. The beef and sausage tacos (with 'a secret ingredient of 127 spices') can be enhanced by availing yourself of the fried onions, *nopales* and other tasty toppings that fill half a dozen huge clay casseroles in front.

Churrería de Coyoacán (Map p140; Allende 38; bag of 4 churros M$8; Ⓜ Viveros) Coyoacán's best deep-fried snacks. Get in line for a bag – cream-filled or straight up – then stroll over to Café El Jarocho (p182) for coffee.

El Kiosko de Coyoacán (Map p140; Plaza Hidalgo 6; 1 scoop M$15; 11am-11pm Sun-Wed, 1pm-1am Thu-Sat; Ⓜ Viveros) This obligatory weekend stop has homemade ice cream and popsicles in flavors ranging from mango with chili to *tuna* (cactus fruit).

BUDGET
Mesón de Los Leones (Map p140; ☎ 5554-5916; Allende 161; dishes M$60; ⏰ 11am-6pm Sun-Fri; Ⓜ Viveros) This longtime family-run restaurant satisfies diners with its unwaveringly authentic menu and genial atmosphere. Dig into specialties like *carne asada estilo de Léon* – roasted meat with *mole* sauce accompanied by guacamole and beans.

MIDRANGE
El Caracol de Oro (Map p140; ☎ 5658-9489; Higuera B16; dishes M$65-80; Ⓜ Viveros) Coyoacán's alternative set occupy the jazzily painted tables here, munching on nouveau natural fare like apple curry with chicken, and goat's cheese and mango-stuffed chilies.

El Jardín del Pulpo (Map p140; cnr Allende & Malitzin; fish dishes M$75; ⏰ 11am-5pm; Ⓜ Viveros) Weekends, visitors descend on the communal tables at this market-corner locale to devour shrimp tacos, fried whole fish, shrimp and oyster cocktails, *caldos* (broths) and the namesake *pulpo en su tinta* (octopus cooked in its own ink).

Los Danzantes (Map p140; Jardín del Centenario 12; dishes M$75-150; Ⓜ Viveros) Los Danzantes puts a contemporary spin on Mexican cuisine with dishes like salmon enchiladas and chrysanthemum salad. You'll also find *mezcal* from its own distillery (see boxed text, p183) and cigars from San Andrés in Veracruz.

Entre Vero (Map p140; ☎ 5659-0066; Jardín Centenario 14C; pizza M$80, dishes M$80-150; Ⓜ Viveros) Here's another nice plaza-side spot where the grilled meats from the Southern Cone are well regarded. Non-meat options include tuna steaks, a grilled vegetable platter and thin-crust pizzas.

Other Neighborhoods
El Borrego Viudo (Map pp126-7; Revolución 241, Tacubaya; tacos M$5-8; ⏰ noon-3am) At this busy neighborhood *taquería* just below the Viaducto freeway (take a 'San Ángel-M Barranca del Muerto' pesero), the menu announces the taco variations in sparkly type: *suadero* (beef), *longaniza* (sausage), tender tongue and their specialty, *pastor*, sliced off a huge cone by the entrance. The tacos are small but substantial, bathed in a potent salsa verde, and are best washed down with a mug of *tepache*, a pineapple drink fermented in a wood barrel.

Fonda Margarita (Map pp126-7; Adolfo Prieto 1364; mains half/full portion M$21/32; ⏰ 5:30-11:30am Mon-Sat; 🚇 Parque Hundido) Possibly the capital's premier hangover-recovery spot – witness the line down the street on Saturday mornings – the humble eatery under a tin roof whips up batches of comfort food for the day ahead. Soulful fare like pork back in *chile guajillo* sauce is doled out of giant clay dishes. The *fonda* is beside Plaza Tlacoquemécatl, six blocks east of Av Insurgentes.

DRINKING
Cafés, bars and cantinas are all key social venues on the capital's landscape. The traditional watering holes are, of course, cantinas, no-nonsense places with simple tables, long polished bars and serious waiters in formal white jackets. A humbler kind of drinking establishment rooted in ancient Mexican tradition, *pulquerías* serve pulque, a slightly alcoholic pre-Hispanic beverage. These places are lately experiencing a resurgence, with young Chilangos rediscovering the joys of sharing a pitcher of the milky quaff. Another drink that is being 'taken back' by Mexican youth is *mezcal*, the rustic mother of tequila.

AROUND MEXICO IN A DAY

The capital has long attracted opportunity-seekers from all over the republic. Fortunately these ex-Oaxacans, Yucatecans and Sinaloans strive to keep their traditions alive, first and foremost in the kitchen. This means Mexico City is the perfect place to try out authentic regional cuisines just as they're prepared back home.

Coox Hanal (Map pp128-9; ☎ 5709-3613; Isabel La Católica 83, 2nd fl; dishes M$40-60; ⊗ 10:30am-7pm; Ⓜ Isabel la Católica) Started in 1953 by boxer Raúl Salazar from Mérida, this establishment over a billiard hall prepares Yucatecan fare just as it's done in Don Raúl's hometown. The *poc chuc* (grilled pork marinated in sour orange juice), *papadzules* (tacos stuffed with chopped hard-boiled egg and laced with pumpkin-seed sauce) and *cochinita pibil* (pit-cooked pork) are of a high standard. Tables are set with the obligatory four-alarm *habanero* salsa.

El Regiomontano (Map pp128-9; ☎ 5518-0196; Luis Moya 115; grilled goat M$187; ⊗ 11am-10pm; Ⓜ Balderas) Lettered on the window is the message, BABY GOATS VERY YOUNG KIDS, and there they are, splayed on stakes and grilling over a circle of coals, just as they're done in Monterrey or Saltillo. A single platter serves two.

La Polar (Map pp126-7; ☎ 5546-5066; Guillermo Prieto 129, San Rafael; birria M$85; ⊗ 8am-1am; Ⓜ San Cosme; Ⓟ) Run by a family from Ocotlán, Jalisco, this boisterous beer hall has essentially one item on the menu: *birria*, a soulfully spiced goat stew. Their version of this Guadalajara favorite is considered the best in town. Spirits are raised further by mariachis and *norteña* combos who work the half-dozen salons here.

La Sabia Virtud (Map pp132-3; ☎ 5286-6480; Iamaulipas 134B, Condesa; mains M$100; ⊗ 11am-11pm Mon-Sat, 9am-6pm Sun; Ⓜ Patriotismo; Ⓟ) Nouvelle cuisine from Puebla is lovingly presented at this cozy Condesa spot. *Mole* is prepared in the classic Santa Clara convent style or the restaurant's own *verde* version.

María del Alma (Map pp132-3; ☎ 5553-0403; Cuernavaca 68, Condesa; starters M$60, mains M$100-165; ⊗ 1:30-11pm Mon-Fri, until 1:30am Sat, until 6pm Sun; Ⓜ Patriotismo; Ⓟ) A culinary escape to the state of Tabascodine in a leafy patio among tweeting birds and a romantically inclined pianist. Enjoy a guanabana margarita before digging into regional favorites like *tamales de chipilín* and *uliche*, a chicken stew thickened with cornmeal and seasoned with fiery *mashita* chilies.

Pozolería Tixtla (Map pp126-7; ☎ 5233-2081; Hernández y Dávalos 35; pozole M$50; ⊗ 11am-9pm; Ⓜ Lázaro Cárdenas) East of Roma, in working-class Colonia Algarín, this old-fashioned dining hall specializes in Guerrero-style green *pozole*, a soulful variation on the classic pork and hominy broth, garnished with crackling *chicharrón* and creamy avocado slices.

Tamales Chiapanecos María Geraldine (Map p140; ☎ 5608-8993; Plaza Hidalgo; tamales M$24; ⊗ noon-9pm Sat, 8am-9pm Sun) At the passageway next to the arched wing of San Juan Bautista church, look for these incredible *tamales* by Chiapas native Doña María Geraldine. Wrapped in banana leaves, stuffed with ingredients like olives, prunes and almonds, and laced with sublime salsas, they're a meal in themselves.

Beer is generally cheap, with bottles of Corona or Victoria going for around M$20 (M$30 in Condesa or Polanco). Expect to pay M$70 or M$80 for a shot of top-shelf whiskey or tequila.

Centro Histórico

CAFÉS

Café Jakemir (Map pp128-9; ☎ 5709-7038; Isabel la Católica 88; ⊗ 9am-8pm Mon-Sat; Ⓜ Isabel la Católica) Run by a family of Lebanese coffee traders from Orizaba, this old distribution outlet, now transformed into a popular café, has excellent and inexpensive cappuccinos.

Café La Habana (Map pp128-9; ☎ 5546-2555; Av Morelos 62; Ⓜ Juárez) This grand coffee house is a traditional haunt for writers and journalists, who linger for hours over a *café americano*. Legend has it that Fidel and Che plotted strategy here prior to the Cuban revolution.

La Selva Café (Map pp128-9; ☎ 5521-4111; Bolívar 31; Ⓜ Allende) Branch of the Chiapas coffee distributor in the stunning patio of a colonial building.

Café Cordobés (Map pp128-9; ☎ 5512-5545; Ayuntamiento 18; ⊗ 8am-8pm Mon-Sat, 10am-6pm Sun; Ⓜ San Juan de Letrán) Good spot for a stand-up *cortado* (espresso with a little foamed milk) amid a busy shopping district; bulk coffee from Veracruz at reasonable prices.

BARS & CANTINAS

Bar Mancera (Map pp128-9; ☎ 5521-9755; Venustiano Carranza Tacuba 49; cover Fri & Sat night M$50; ⊗ noon-10pm Mon-Thu, noon-2am Fri & Sat; Ⓜ San Juan de Letrán) This atmospheric gentlemen's salon seems preserved in amber, with ornate carved paneling, flowery upholstered armchairs and well-used domino tables. Lately it's been adopted by young clubbers, who set up turntables Friday night from around 9pm.

Hostería La Bota (Map pp128-9; ☎ 5709-1117; www .casavecina.com; Callejón de Mesones 7; ☒ 11am-8pm Tue, 11am-1:30am Wed-Sat; Ⓜ Isabel la Católica) This fun and funky bar is one component of the Casa Vecina community arts center, a cultural beachhead in the Centro's rough southern fringe. Tapas and tequilas are served amid a profusion of warped bullfighting bric-a-brac and mismatched furniture.

La Gioconda (Map pp128-9; ☎ 5518-7823; Filomena Mata 18; ☒ 4-11pm Mon-Thu, 4pm-2am Fri & Sat; Ⓜ Allende) Dark and light draft beer are poured in this happening little pub off a pedestrian thoroughfare.

La Ópera Bar (Map pp128-9; ☎ 5512-8959; Av 5 de Mayo 10; ☒ 1pm-midnight Mon-Sat, 1-6pm Sun; Ⓜ Allende) With booths of dark walnut and an ornate tin ceiling (said to have been punctured by Pancho Villa's bullet), this late-19th-century watering hole remains a bastion of tradition.

Las Duelistas (Map pp128-9; Aranda 30; ☒ 9am-9pm; Ⓜ Salto del Agua) Now graffitied with pre-Hispanic psychedelia, this classic *pulquería* alongside the Mercado San Juan has been rediscovered by young Chilangos. Despite the new look, the pulque is still dispensed straight from the barrel in a variety of flavors like mango and coconut.

Salón Corona (Map pp128-9; ☎ 5512-5725; Bolívar 24; ☒ 8am-midnight Sun-Wed, 8am-2am Thu-Sat; Ⓜ Allende) Punks and suits crowd this boisterous, no-nonsense beer hall, running since 1928. Amiable staff serve up *tarros* (mugs) of light or dark *cerveza de barril* (draft beer) and bottles of almost every known Mexican beer.

Zona Rosa & Around
The Pink Zone, the capital's international party center, boasts the highest concentration of bars and clubs in town, and prices at the numerous venues along Londres and Florencia reflect its tourist orientation. Calle Amberes has become the hub of the gay- and lesbian-oriented bar scene.

CAFÉS
Sanborns Café (Map pp132-3; ☎ 5207-9760; Londres 149; ☒ 24hr; Ⓜ Insurgentes) By day a popular business breakfast locale, after hours this round-the-clock coffeeshop makes a convenient port of call between clubs.

Cafetería Gabi's (Map pp132-3; ☎ 5511-7637; Nápoles 55, cnr Liverpool; ☒ Mon-Sat; Ⓜ Insurgentes) Cluttered with caffeine-related paraphernalia, this family-run coffeehouse buzzes with conversation midmornings and early evenings, when the occupants of neighboring offices pour in for a rich *café con leche* and a crispy *banderilla* (stick-like glazed pastry).

BARS
Bar Milán (Map pp132-3; ☎ 5592-0031; Milán 18; ☒ 9pm-midnight Tue & Wed, 9pm-3am Thu-Sat; Ⓜ Cuauhtémoc) Tucked away on a quiet backstreet, this cave-like hangout overflows most weekends with a youthful mixed-nationality crowd. Purchase beer tickets *(milagros)*, then make your way over to the cactus-trimmed bar. The soundtrack ranges from classic rock to Café Tacuba.

Papa Bill's Saloon (Map pp132-3; ☎ 5207-6669; Río Guadalquivir 88; ☒ 1pm-midnight or 1am Mon-Sat, 1-8pm Sun; Ⓜ Insurgentes) For those who need their sports fix, this sprawling gringo-style parlor has plenty of flat-screen TVs showing the big game. Happy hours (two-for-one drinks) are from 2pm to 9pm.

Condesa
CAFÉS
Café Bola de Oro (Map pp132-3; ☎ 5286-5659; Av Nuevo León 192-B; ☒ 7am-10pm Mon-Fri, 9am-7pm Sat; Ⓜ Chilpancingo) An outlying branch of the Xalapa coffee purveyor, this is a good place to score a bag of Coatepec beans or simply enjoy a cup of Veracruz' fine, full-bodied blends.

Pastelería Maque (Map pp132-3; ☎ 2454-4662; Ozulama 4; ☒ Campeche) Condesa sophisticates gather in the mornings and evenings at this Parisian-style café-bakery near the south end of Parque México. Waiters bring around trays of fresh-baked croissants and *conchas* (round pastries sprinkled with sugar) – point to your preference.

BARS
Condesa's bar scene continues to thrive, and new places are popping up (and shutting down) all the time. The following are relatively well established and filled beyond capacity Thursday through Saturday evenings. The confluence of Tamaulipas and Nuevo León has emerged as a major bar zone, earning a reputation as a haven for *fresas* (literally 'strawberries,' a derogatory term for upper-class youth).

Black Horse (Map pp132-3; ☎ 5211-8740; Mexicali 85, cnr Tamaulipas; ☾ 6pm-2am Tue-Sat; Ⓜ Patriotismo) Besides preparing bangers and mash and screening the soccer match, this authentic British pub boasts an international social scene and has excellent bands playing the back room mid-week.

El Centenario (Map pp132-3; ☎ 5553-5451; Vicente Suárez 42; ☾ noon-midnight Mon-Sat; Ⓜ Patriotismo) Laden with bullfighting memorabilia, this cantina is an enclave of tradition amid the modish restaurant zone.

Malafama (Map pp132-3; ☎ 5553-5138; Av Michoacán 78; tables per hr M$80; Ⓜ Patriotismo) As trendy as its bars and cafés, Condesa's sleek billiard hall doubles as a gallery of photo art. The well-maintained tables are frequented by both pool sharks and novices.

Hookah Lounge (Map pp132-3; ☎ 5264-6275; Campeche 284; ☾ 1pm-12:30am Mon-Wed, 1pm-2am Thu-Sat; Ⓜ Chilpancingo) The fun revolves around the water pipes (from M$100), available in a bewildering array of flavors. Wednesday to Saturday nights, DJs produce an eclectic mix of electronica and Arabic rhythms, with no fewer than four turntables.

Pata Negra (Map pp132-3; ☎ 5211-5563; Av Tamaulipas 30; ☾ 1:30pm-2am; Ⓜ Patriotismo) Nominally a tapas bar, this oblong salon draws a friendly, clean-cut crowd of 20-something Chilangos and expats. There's live music on both levels, with the upper Salón Pata Negra striking a more bohemian tone.

T-Gallery (Map pp132-3; ☎ 5211-1222; www.tgallery design.com; Saltillo 39; ☾ 5pm-2am Mon-Sat; Ⓜ Patriotismo) A low-key, conversant crowd kicks back with cocktails in the various salons of this lovely old Condesa home, each appointed with a splendid array of kitschy sofas, coffee tables and mirrors. Jazz, blues and bossa nova combos jam downstairs nightly.

Rexo (Map pp132-3; ☎ 5553-5337; Saltillo 1; ☾ 1:30pm-1am Sun-Tue, 1:30pm-2am Wed-Sat; Ⓜ Patriotismo) A minimalist, triple-deck supper club, the perennially popular Rexo really packs them in toward the weekend. There's dining on the upper levels but the revelry converges on the bar at the bottom, which serves *mezcaltinis* and other unusual cocktails.

The bar of the fashionable Condesa df (p171) has become an essential stop on the Condesa circuit. Action focuses on the triangular atrium and wackily decorated alcoves around it. Up on the roof, guests lounge on big-wheel wicker sofas, nibble on sushi and enjoy views of verdant Parque España across the way.

Roma

CAFÉS

Enanos de Tapanco (Map pp132-3; ☎ 5564-2274; Orizaba 161, cnr Querétaro; ☾ 8am-11:30pm Mon-Fri, 9am-11:30pm Sat, 3:30-10:30pm Sun; Ⓜ Centro Médico) Possibly Mexico City's coolest café, the 'Dwarves of the Loft' also functions as an art gallery and story-telling den (Tuesday evening). Cappuccinos and quiches are served along with an eclectic music selection.

Maison de Thé Caravanserai (Map pp132-3; ☎ 5511-2877; Orizaba 101; ☾ 10am-9:30pm Mon-Fri, 12:30pm-9:30pm Sat, 3:30-9:30pm Sun; Ⓜ Insurgentes) This French-managed tea room has over 100 blends. They are categorized by their intended use or effects (Tokyo Springtime is 'a subtle tea for the afternoon'). Visitors relax on comfortable sofas to enjoy their chosen brews, which are ceremoniously served on silver trays.

Café Villa de Madrid (Map pp132-3; Plaza Villa de Madrid; ☾ 8:15am-6:30pm Mon-Sat; 🚇 Durango) With just a few sidewalk tables at the top of Plaza Villa de Madrid (aka Plaza Cibeles), this long-time storefront operation roasts beans from the family *finca* (farm) in Chiapas (they also roll their own cigars).

BARS

La Bodeguita del Medio (Map pp132-3; ☎ 5553-0246; Cozumel 37; ☾ 2pm-2am Tue-Sat, 2pm-midnight Sun & Mon; Ⓜ Sevilla) The walls are scribbled with verses and messages at this animated branch of the famous Havana joint. Have a *mojito*, a Cuban concoction of rum and mint leaves, and enjoy the excellent *son cubano* combos that perform here.

Cantina Covadonga (Map pp132-3; ☎ 5533-2922; Puebla 121; ☾ 1pm-3am Mon-Fri; Ⓜ Insurgentes) Echoing with the sounds of clacking dominoes, the old Asturian social hall is a traditionally male enclave, though hipsters of both sexes have increasingly moved in on this hallowed ground.

Travazares Taberna (Map pp132-3; ☎ 5264-1142; Orizaba 127; ☾ 1pm-2am; 🚇 Ávaro Obregón) The downstairs adjunct of a cultural center, this popular Roma hangout strikes a suitably bohemian tone. Recycled objects furnish a series of cozy, candlelit salons where artistically inclined youth sip wine or Cerveza Cosaco (a Mexican microbrew).

Tiki Bar (Map pp132-3; ☎ 5584-2668; Querétaro 227; ✹ 6pm-3am Wed-Sat; 🚇 Sonora) Amid the salsa dance clubs, this South Pacific spree spreads on the kitsch with bamboo-fringed walls and teak floors. The wacky cocktails are the real draw: not just mai tais but *chocotikis*, *mojotikis* and various other rum creations thrill a celebrity-studded crowd.

Bengala (Map pp132-3; ☎ 5211-4690; Sonora 34A; ✹ 9pm-4am Thu-Sat; Ⓜ Chapultepec) This low-lit concept bar evokes a desert trek, with decor influenced by *Casablanca* and *The Sheltering Sky*. Its slightly out-of-the-way location only adds to the conspiratorial air. Have a 'Module' (a green cocktail of cucumber, Pernod and *mezcal*) and mingle with the film and TV personalities who customarily pop up here.

Polanco

Though not as cutting-edge as Condesa, this well-heeled neighborhood gets quite lively after dark.

Área (Map pp136-7; ☎ 5282-3100; Av Presidente Masaryk 201; ✹ 7-11pm Mon-Wed, 7pm-2am Thu-Sat; Ⓜ Polanco) Atop the Hábita Hotel, this open-air roof lounge does a brisk trade in exotic martinis, with sweeping city views as a backdrop and videos projected on the wall of a nearby building.

Big Red (Map pp136-7; ☎ 5255-5277; Av Presidente Masaryk 101; ✹ 8:30am-2am Mon-Sat; Ⓜ Polanco) A volume dealer, with drinks priced by the ounce (M$14 for Bacardi, M$16 for Centenario tequila), plus whatever mixer you choose. Thus the place attracts a broader cross-section of the populace than the usual Polanco *antro* (bar). And rather than the icy electronica favored by such places, Big Red dares to blare banda.

Xochimilco

Pulquería El Templo de Diana (Map p138; ☎ 5653-4657; Madero 17, cnr Calle 5 de Mayo; ✹ 9am-9:30pm; Ⓜ Xochimilco) This classic *pulquería*, a block east of the main market, has a cheerful sawdust-on-the-floor vibe, with a mixed-age crowd enjoying giant mugs of the maguey-based beverage behind the swinging doors. Even a few females may pop in. Pulque is delivered fresh daily from Hidalgo state, and expertly blended with flavorings like mango, tomato and pine nut.

Pulquería La Botijona (Map p138; Morelos 109; ✹ 9am-9:30pm; Ⓜ Xochimilco) Possibly the cleanest pulque dispenser in town, this institutional-green hall near the train station is a friendly family-run establishment, with big plastic pails of the traditional quaff lining the shelves.

Coyoacán

Café El Jarocho (Map p140; ☎ 5658-5029; Cuauhtémoc 134, cnr Allende; ✹ 6am-1am; Ⓜ Coyoacán) This immensely popular joint churns out M$8 cappuccinos for long lines of java hounds. As there's no seating inside, people have their coffee standing in the street or sitting on curbside benches. Another branch (Map p140; ☎ 5659-9107; Av México 25-C) is convenient to Viveros park.

La Guadalupana (Map p140; ☎ 5554-6253; Higuera 2; ✹ noon-12:30am Mon-Sat; Ⓜ Viveros) Serving drinks for over seven decades, this rustic tavern breathes tradition down to the blasé waiters in white coats. There are *botanas* and *tortas* as well as heartier fare.

El Hijo del Cuervo (Map p140; ☎ 5658-7824; www .elhijodelcuervo.com.mx; Jardín Centenario 17, Coyoacán; ✹ 4pm-midnight Mon-Wed, 1pm-1:30am Thu, 1pm-2:30am Fri & Sat, 1-11:30pm Sun; Ⓜ Viveros) A Coyoacán institution, this enormous stone-walled hall on the Jardín Centenario is a thinking man's drinking man's habitat. Assorted musical ensembles perform Wednesday and Thursday nights in a small theater toward the back.

La Bipolar (Map p140; ☎ 5484-8230; Malintzin 155; ✹ 1pm-2am; Ⓜ Viveros) Owned by Mexican heartthrob Diego Luna of *Y Tu Mamá También* movie fame, this popular new cantina plays up the kitschier elements of Mexican popular culture, with wall panels fashioned from plastic crates and sliced tin buckets as light shades. Besides the Coronas and *mezcal* shots, it has revamped versions of classic Mexican snacks.

ENTERTAINMENT

There's so much going on in Mexico City on any given evening, it's hard to keep track. *Tiempo Libre*, the city's comprehensive what's-on magazine, helps you sort it all out. Published Thursday, it covers live music, theater, movies, dance, art and nightlife. Other useful guides include the comprehensive monthlies *Donde Ir* and *Chilango*, the latter with a *Time Out* supplement. *Primera Fila*, a Friday section of the *Reforma* newspaper, has lots of entertainment listings, too.

Ticketmaster (☎ 5325-9000; www.ticketmaster .mx) sells tickets for all the major venues via internet, phone or at any of these outlets:

MEZCAL RENAISSANCE

Mezcal, known erroneously as 'that drink with the worm in it,' is finally getting the respect it deserves. (The worm was a marketing gimmick for gullible American consumers.) Many think of It as a rustic relative to the more refined tequila, when in fact tequila is just one form of *mezcal* derived from a particular plant that grows in the state of Jalisco, the blue agave. But *mezcals* are produced from many varieties of agave (or maguey) throughout Mexico, including the states of Durango, Zacatecas, Michoacán, Guerrero and, most famously, Oaxaca. It is estimated there are some 136 varieties of the succulent plant, and each one produces a different version. New laws now require *mezcals* from the various regions to be labeled with an appellation of origin, as wines from regions of Spain and France are denominated. Many small-scale *mezcal* makers still produce the drink in limited, handcrafted batches.

Straight up, *mezcal* is typically served with slices of orange and an orangey salt blended with chili and – old myths die hard – a powder made from maguey worms, and chased by a Victorita mini bottle of beer. And like a fine single-malt scotch, it's meant to be savored slowly rather than knocked back.

A number of venues around Mexico City now serve *mezcal* to the new breed of discerning aficionados

Mestizo Lounge (Map pp132-3; ☎ 2454-1662; Chihuahua 121, Roma; ☾ 6pm-2am Tue-Sat; Ⓜ Insurgentes) This highly social hole in the wall is at the heart of the *mezcal* renaissance. Taste a smoky *cenizo* (a Zacatecas variety) or have a *mezcal* martini. They make excellent sandwiches, too.

La Botica (Map pp132-3; ☎ 5212-1167; Alfonso Reyes 120; ☾ 5pm-midnight Mon & Tue, 5pm-1:30am Wed-Sat; Ⓜ Patriotismo) Like an old apothecary, La Botica dispenses its elixirs from squat bottles lined up on the shelf. Available varieties are suitably scribbled on pieces of cardboard – try the *cuesh*, distilled from a wild maguey in Oaxaca. La Botica has been such a roaring success, it's opened other branches with similar hours at Campeche 396 in Condesa and Orizaba 161 in Colonia Roma.

Taberna Red Fly (Map pp132-3; ☎ 1054-3616; Orizaba 143; ☾ 6pm-midnight Mon-Wed, 6pm-2am Thu-Sat; 🚌 Álvaro Obregón) An elegantly furnished space in a typical Porfiriato-era residence, the Red Fly organizes monthly tastings, where *mezcal* fans can appreciate the subtle gradations in flavor based on where the beverage is distilled.

Los Danzantes (Map p140; ☎ 5658-6054; Jardín del Centenario 12; Ⓜ Viveros) This contemporary Mexican restaurant on Coyoacán's main square serves *tobalá*, a white *mezcal* extracted from a rare mountain agave and produced at its own distillery in Santiago Matatlán, Oaxaca.

Auditorio Nacional (Map pp136-7; Paseo de la Reforma 50; ☾ 11am-6pm; Ⓜ Auditorio)

Liverpool Centro (p190); Polanco (Map pp136-7; Mariano Escobedo 425; ☾ 11am-8pm; Ⓜ Polanco)

Mixup Centro (Map pp128-9; Madero 51; ☾ 10am-9pm Mon-Sat, 11am-8pm Sun; Ⓜ Zócalo); Zona Rosa (Map pp132-3; Génova 76; ☾ 9am-9pm; Ⓜ Insurgentes)

Cinemas

Mexico City is a banquet for moviegoers. Almost everything is screened here and ticket prices are around M$40, with many places offering discounts on Wednesday. Except for children's fare, movies are in original languages, with Spanish subtitles. *El Universal* and *La Jornada* have daily listings.

Multiplexes showing mostly Hollywood fare, with the odd Mexican hit, include **Cine Diana** (Map pp132-3; ☎ 5511-3236; Paseo de la Reforma 423; Ⓜ Sevilla), **Cinemex Palacio** (Map pp128-9; ☎ 5512-0348; www.cinemex.com; Iturbide 25; Ⓜ Juárez)

and **Cinemex Real** (Map pp128-9; ☎ 5512-7718; www .cinemex.com.mx; Colón 17; Ⓜ Hidalgo).

There are other theaters offering a more eclectic program, such as **Cinemex Casa de Arte** (Map pp136-7; ☎ 5280-9156; www.cinemex.com; France 120; Ⓜ Polanco) and **Lumiere Reforma** (Map pp132-3; ☎ 5514-0000; Río Guadalquivir 104; Ⓜ Sevilla).

In addition, several repertory cinemas cater to film buffs:

Filmoteca de la UNAM (Map pp126-7; ☎ 5665-0709; Insurgentes Sur 3000; tickets M$30) The two cinemas at the Centro Cultural Universitario screen films from a collection of over 35,000 titles. Programming for this and other UNAM-system cinemas can be found at www.filmoteca .unam.mx. See p157 for directions.

Cinematógrafo del Chopo (Map pp128-9; ☎ 5702-3494; Dr Atl 37, Colonia Santa María La Ribera; tickets M$30; Ⓜ San Cosme)

Cineteca Nacional (Map p140; ☎ 1253-9390; www .cinetecanacional.net; Av México-Coyoacán 389; tickets M$40; Ⓜ Coyoacán) Thematically focused film series are shown on six screens, with at least one for Mexican cinema. There are cafés and bookstores at the center of the complex, 700m east of metro Coyoacán. In November the Cineteca hosts the Muestra Internacional de Cine, Mexico City's international film festival.

Contempo Cinema (Map pp132-3; ☎ 5208-4044; Londres 161; www.contempocinema.com; M Insurgentes) Emphasis on gay and erotic themes; inside the Zona Rosa's Plaza Ángel shopping center.

Salon Cinematográfico Fósforo (Map pp128-9; ☎ 5702-3494; San Ildefonso 43; tickets M$30; M Zócalo) Inside the Antiguo Colegio de San Ildefonso (p145).

Dance, Classical Music & Theater

Orchestral music, opera, ballet, contemporary dance and theater are all abundantly represented in the capital's numerous theaters. Museums, too, serve as (often free) performance venues, including the **Museo de la Secretaría de Hacienda y Crédito Público** (p144) and the **Museo de la Ciudad de México** (p147). The national arts council (Conaculta) provides a rundown on its Spanish-language website (www.cnca.gob .mx) and in Friday's *La Jornada*.

Palacio de Bellas Artes (Map pp128-9; ☎ 5512-2593; www.bellasartes.gob.mx; Av Hidalgo 1; box office ⊙ 11am-7pm; M Bellas Artes) The Orquesta Sinfónica Nacional and prestigious opera and dance companies perform in the palace's ornate theater, while chamber groups appear in the recital halls. It's most famous, though, for the **Ballet Folclórico de México** (tickets M$360-600; ⊙ 8:30pm Wed, 9:30am & 8:30pm Sun), a two-hour festive blur of costumes, music and dance from all over Mexico. Tickets are usually available the day of the show at the Palacio or from Ticketmaster (p182).

Centro Cultural Universitario (Map pp126-7; ☎ 5665-0709; www.difusion.cultural.unam.mx; Av Insurgentes Sur 3000) Ensconced in the woodsy southern section of the national university campus, the complex comprises five theaters, including the Sala Nezahualcóyotl, home of the UNAM Philharmonic; the Teatro Alarcón, a dramatic stage; and the Sala Miguel Covarrubias, a contemporary dance venue. See p157 for directions.

Centro Nacional de las Artes (CNA; Map p140; ☎ 4155-0000; www.cenart.gob.mx; Río Churubusco 79; M General Anaya) This sprawling art institute near Coyoacán has events across the artistic spectrum, many of them free. Exit metro General Anaya (Línea 2) on the east side of Calz de Tlalpan, walk north to the corner and turn right.

Centro Cultural del Bosque (Map pp136-7; ☎ 5280-6228; cnr Paseo de la Reforma & Campo Marte; ⊙ box office noon-3pm & 5-7pm Mon-Fri & prior to events; M Auditorio) This complex behind the Auditorio Nacional features six theaters, including the Teatro de la Danza, dedicated to modern dance. On weekend afternoons, children's plays and puppet shows are staged.

If your Spanish is up to it, you might sample Mexico City's lively theater scene. The Spanish-language website **MegorTeatro** (www .mejorteatro.com.mx) covers the major venues. Performances are generally Thursday to Sunday evenings with weekend matinees.

Other cultural options:

Centro Cultural Helénico (Map p139; ☎ 4155-0919; www.helenico.gob.mx; Av Revolución 1500, Guadalupe Inn; tickets M$250; ⊙ Altavista) Complex includes 450-seat Teatro Helénico for major productions and cabaret-style La Gruta theater.

Foro Shakespeare (Map pp132-3; ☎ 5553-4642; Zamora 7, Condesa; tickets M$120-250; M Chapultepec) Small independent theater with eclectic program.

Teatro Blanquita (Map pp128-9; ☎ 5512-8264; Eje Central Lázaro Cardenas 16, Centro; tickets M$100-175; M Bellas Artes) Classic variety theater across from Plaza Garibaldi.

Live Music

The variety of music here is impressive, with traditional Mexican, Cuban, folk, jazz, rock and other styles being played in concert halls, clubs, bars, museums, on public transportation and on the street. The 'Conciertos' and 'Noche' sections in *Tiempo Libre* cover events.

Free concerts take place most weekends on the Zócalo. Coyoacán is another good bet most evenings and all day Saturday and Sunday: musicians, comedians and mimes turn its two central plazas into a big open-air party.

Additionally, a number of Roma and Condesa bars and restaurants turn into live-music venues after dark (see p180).

CONCERTS

Auditorio Nacional (Map pp136-7; ☎ 5280-9250; www .auditorio.com.mx; Paseo de la Reforma 50; M Auditorio) Major gigs by Mexican and visiting rock and pop artists take the stage at the 10,000-seat Auditorio Nacional (National Auditorium). The adjoining **Lunario del Auditorio** (www.lunario .com.mx) is a large club for jazz and folk acts.

Vive Cuervo Salón (Map pp136-7; ☎ 5255-5322; Andrómaco 17, cnr Moliere) A warehouse-sized venue for touring rock, world and salsa stars. With excellent sound, wall-length bar and dance floor for thousands, this is one of Mexico's most cutting-edge clubs. The cover price varies.

Teatro de la Ciudad (Map pp128-9; ☎ 5510-2942; Donceles 36; Ⓜ Allende) Built in 1918, this lavishly restored 1300-seat hall gets some of the more interesting touring groups.

MARIACHIS
Five blocks north of the Palacio de Bellas Artes, Plaza Garibaldi (Map pp128-9) is where the city's mariachi bands gather. Outfitted in fancy costumes, they toot their trumpets, tune their guitars and stand around with a drink until approached by someone who'll pay for a song (about M$100) or whisk them away to entertain at a party.

Plaza Garibaldi gets going by about 8pm and stays busy until around midnight. For food, try the Mercado San Camilito north of the plaza.

El Tenampa (Map pp128-9; ☎ 5526-6176; ⊙ 1pm-3am; Ⓜ Garibaldi), graced with murals of the giants of Mexican song and enlivened by its own songsters, is a festive cantina on the north side of the plaza; a visit here is obligatory.

ROCK
The street market Tianguis Cultural del Chopo (p189) has a stage at its north end every Saturday afternoon for young and hungry alternative, metal and punk bands.

Dada X (Map pp128-9; ☎ 2454-4310; www.recia.org/dadax; Bolívar 31, cnr Calle 16 de Septiembre; admission free-M$200; ⊙ from 9pm Thu-Sat; Ⓜ San Juan de Letrán) Black-clad youth gravitate toward this space on the upper floor of a magnificent colonial building. The varied program includes cult films, poetry readings and live music, which might be anything from ska to electronica.

Multiforo Alicia (Map pp132-3; ☎ 5511-2100; www.myspace.com/foroalicia; Av Cuauhtémoc 91; cover M$70; ⊙ 9pm-2am Fri & Sat; Ⓜ Cuauhtémoc) Behind the graffiti-scrawled facade is Mexico City's premier rock club. A suitably smoky, seatless space, the Alicia stages up-and-coming punk, surf and ska bands, who hawk their music at the store downstairs.

Pasagüero (Map pp128-9; ☎ 5512-6624; www.pasaguero.com; Motolinia 33; cover M$100; ⊙ 10pm-2:30am Thu-Sat; Ⓜ Allende) Some visionary developers took a historic building and transformed its stonewalled ground level into a space for various cultural happenings, especially rock and electronica gigs.

Hard Rock Live (Map pp136-7; ☎ 5327-7101; cover from M$220; Campos Elíseos 290; Ⓜ Auditorio) Occupying a superb old Polanco mansion near the Auditorio Nacional, this branch of the international club hosts the cream of *rock en español*, with groups like La Cuca, the Nortec Collective, La Gusana Ciega, Zoe and Molotov on stage.

Cultural Roots (Map pp128-9; ☎ 5521-6622; Tacuba 81; cover M$25; ⊙ 4-11pm Fri & Sun, 9pm-2am Sat; Ⓜ Allende) Portraits of Marcus Garvey, Haile Selassie and Emiliano Zapata glare down over the throngs of skanking youth who fill this warehouse-sized room where DJs pump out a heady blend of contemporary reggae.

JAZZ & BLUES
Papa Beto (Map pp132-3; ☎ 5592-1638; www.papabeto.com; Villalongín 196, Colonia Cuauhtémoc; cover M$80-100; ⊙ 1st/2nd set 9:30pm/11pm Tue-Sat; Ⓜ Insurgentes) Run by a Japanese expatriate to highlight the impressive wealth of local talent, this club remains the city's top jazz venue. Tuesday night is reserved for jam sessions with surprise guests.

Zinco Jazz Club (Map pp128-9; ☎ 5512-3369; www.zincojazz.com; Motolinía 20; cover M$100-200; ⊙ 9pm-2am Wed-Sat; Ⓜ Allende) A vital component in the Centro's rebirth, Zinco is a subterranean supper club featuring local jazz and funk outfits and occasional big-name touring artists. The intimate room fills up fast, so reserve ahead.

Ruta 61 (Map pp132-3; ☎ 5511-7602; Baja California 281; cover M$60-200; ⊙ music from 10pm Thu-Sat; Ⓜ Chilpancingo) Catering to the denim-clad blues cult, this split-level venue stages electric blues artists in the Buddy Guy/Howlin' Wolf mold. About once a month there's a direct-from-Chicago act, though you're more likely to see one of the many local cover bands.

LATIN DANCE
The city's many aficionados have a circuit of clubs and *salones de baile* (dance halls) to choose from. At the clubs listed here, it's customary to go in a group and share a bottle of rum or tequila (from around M$600, including mixers).

You might learn a few steps at the Plaza de Danzón (Map pp128-9), northwest of La Ciudadela near metro Balderas. Couples crowd the plaza every Saturday afternoon to do the *danzón*, an elegant and complicated

Cuban step that infiltrated Mexico in the 19th century. Lessons in *danzón* and other steps are given from around 3:30pm to 5:30pm.

Cuban dance clubs abound in Roma, particularly near the intersection of Insurgentes and Medellín.

El Gran León (Map pp132-3; ☎ 5564-7110; Querétaro 225, Roma; cover M$60; ⌚ 9pm-3:30am Thu-Sat; ☐ Sonora) Two or three top-notch Cuban *son* ensembles take the tropical stage nightly at this old-school club. Unescorted (and escorted) women should expect to be invited up onto the tightly packed dance floor.

Mamá Rumba (Map pp132-3 ☎ 5564-6920; Querétaro 230, cnr Medellín, Roma; cover M$70-80; ⌚ 9pm-3:30am Wed-Sat; ☐ Sonora) Managed by a Havana native, Mamá Rumba features contemporary salsa, with music by the house big band. Instructors will get you started Wednesday and Thursday evenings. On alternate Saturday nights the invariably packed club hosts reggaeton DJs and cabaret acts.

Salón Los Ángeles (Map pp126-7; ☎ 5597-5181; Lerdo 206; cover M$40; ⌚ 6-11pm Tue & Sun; ☐ Tlatelolco) Cuban-music fans shouldn't miss the outstanding orchestras, nor the graceful dancers who fill the vast floor of this atmospheric ballroom. Particularly on Tuesday evening, when an older crowd comes for *danzón*, it's like the set of a period film. It's in the rough Colonia Guerrero so take a taxi.

CABARET

La Casa de Paquita la del Barrio (Map pp126-7; ☎ 5583-8131; Zarco 202; cover M$150; ⌚ 8:30pm Fri & Sat; ☐ Guerrero) Located in the rough-and-tumble Guerrero district, this bastion of popular culture is the frequent venue for TV and recording star Paquita la del Barrio. The corpulent chanteuse customarily performs a sublime set of plaintive ballads, almost all of which express disdain for her suitors – her asides are deliciously bitter. Phone ahead to see if Paquita is performing.

El Bataclán (Map pp132-3; ☎ 5511-7390; www.labodega.com.mx; Popocatépetl 25, cnr Amsterdam; cover M$100-200; ⌚ 9pm Tue-Sat; ☐ Álvaro Obregón) A theater within a club (La Bodega), this intimate cabaret showcases some of Mexico's more offbeat performers, with frequent appearances by the wonderfully surreal Astrid Haddad. Afterwards, catch top-notch Cuban *son* combos in La Bodega's various salons.

Bar El Vicio (Map p140; ☎ 5659-1139; www.lasreinaschulas.com; Madrid 13; cover M$100-200; ☐ Coyoacán) With

liberal doses of politically and sexually irreverent comedy and a genre-bending musical program, this alternative cabaret is appropriately located in Frida Kahlo's old neighborhood.

TROVA & TRADITIONAL

Cafebrería El Péndulo (Map pp132-3; www.pendulo.com; cover varies; ⌚ shows at 9pm) Condesa (☎ 5286-9493; Av Nuevo León 115; Ⓜ Chilpancingo); Zona Rosa (☎ 5208-2327; Hamburgo 126; Ⓜ Insurgentes) Leading Mexican singer-songwriters play both branches of this café-bookstore.

El Balcón Huasteco (Map pp126-7; ☎ 5341-6762; www.elbalconhuasteco.com; Sor Juana Inés de la Cruz 248, Colonia Agricultura; cover M$40; ⌚ from 6pm Thu-Sat; Ⓜ Normal) This center for the preservation of the Huastec culture of Hidalgo and Veracruz stages performances by fiery trios. There are wooden platforms for traditional *zapateando* dancing and snacks from the area.

Cafe Corazón (Map p139; ☎ 5550-8854; Frontera 4; cover M$60-80; ⌚ 9:30pm Fri & Sat; ☐ La Bombilla) Folk singers in the Silvio Rodríguez mold take the stage at this temple of *trova* near San Ángel's Plaza San Jacinto.

Nightclubs

The capital's thriving club scene has become an obligatory stop on the international DJ circuit. To find out what's going on, pick up flyers at Condesa's Malafama billiard hall (p181).

Cibeles (Map pp132-3; ☎ 5208-2029; Plaza Villa de Madrid 17; ⌚ 7pm-2am Tue-Sat; ☐ Durango) This fashionable new *antro* is a low-ceilinged, L-shaped living room with a perversely eclectic array of mismatched sofas, armchairs and coffee tables. The mood swings throughout the week from quiet and conversational (Tuesday) to loud and raucous (Friday, when DJs mix '80s hits with loungey beats). Reservations are a must on weekends.

Cream (Map pp128-9; ☎ 5292-6114; Versalles 52; cover M$120; ⌚ from 10pm Thu-Sat; Ⓜ Cuauhtémoc) The longstanding El Colmillo club has been spruced up and reborn as one of the city's premier electronica venues. Beyond the ghoulishly red narrow front room, steps lead down to a hallucinatory party lounge where internationally renowned DJs work from a catwalk above a laser-lashed dance floor.

Gogo Lounge (Map pp136-7; ☎ 5281-8974; Dumas 105; cover M$100; ⌚ 10pm-5am Thu-Sat; Ⓜ Polanco) The honeycombed decor in this Polanco *antro* over a sushi bar seems lifted from the movie *Kill Bill*, with what is supposedly the largest mirror ball in Latin America. Merengue, reggaeton and pop keep a just post-pubescent crowd bouncing in a series of packed salons.

Momma (Map pp136–7; ☎ 5281-1537; Tennyson 102; ☷ 10pm-2am Mon-Sat; Ⓜ Polanco) Currently Polanco's hottest *antro*, Momma attracts hordes of party people. Beyond a chic, minimalist restaurant, the brightly lit hall of mirrors resounds with pop *en español* and hits from past decades. As elsewhere in Polanco, expect a discretionary admission policy. Cover prices vary.

Pervert Lounge (Map pp128–9; ☎ 5510-4457; República de Uruguay 70; cover M$100; ☷ 10:30pm-5am Thu-Sat; Ⓜ Isabel la Católica) A pioneering electronica venue in the heart of the center, the narrow stonewalled Pervert routinely hosts DJs of the stature of Luca Ricci and Satoshi Tomiie.

Young hipsters pack the roof terrace of the Centro Cultural de España (p144) each weekend (free admission, open 10pm till 2am Thursday to Saturday) for its excellent DJ sessions. Located directly behind the cathedral, the rebuilt colonial structure is usually quaking by midnight.

Sports

Most of the daily newspapers, including the *News*, have a generous sports section where you can find out who is kicking which ball where. True enthusiasts should look for *La Afición* (www.laaficion.com), a Spanish-language daily devoted to sports.

SOCCER

The capital stages two or three *fútbol* (soccer) matches in the national Primera División almost every weekend of the year. Mexico City has three teams: América, nicknamed Las Águilas (the Eagles), Las Pumas of UNAM, and Cruz Azul. The newspaper *Esto* has the best coverage. There are two seasons: January to June and August to December, each ending in eight-team playoffs and eventually a two-leg final to decide the champion.

The biggest match of all is El Clásico, between América and Guadalajara, filling the Estadio Azteca with 100,000 flag-waving fans. This is about the only game of the year when you should get tickets in advance.

The newspapers *La Afición* and *Esto* have good soccer coverage and there are plenty of websites related to Mexican soccer, including the comprehensive www.futmex.com and www.femexfut.org.mx. Tickets (M$80 to M$450 for regular season games) are usually available at the gate right up to game time, or from Ticketmaster (see p182). There are several stadiums that host games:

Estadio Azteca (Map pp126–7; ☎ 5617-8080; www .esmas.com/estadioazteca; Calz de Tlalpan 3665) The country's biggest stadium (capacity 114,000) is home to the América club. Games are played on weekend afternoons; check the website for kickoff times. Take the Tren Ligero from metro Tasqueña to Estadio Azteca station.

Estadio Azul (Map pp126–7; ☎ 5563-9040; www.cruz -azul.com.mx; Indiana 260, Colonia Nápoles; Ⓜ Ciudad de los Deportes) The stadium is next door to the Plaza México bullring. Cruz Azul home games kick off at 5pm on Saturday.

Estadio Olímpico (Map pp126–7; ☎ 5522-0491; www.pumasunam.com.mx; Insurgentes Sur 3000, Ciudad Universitaria) Home of the Pumas; games start at noon on Sunday. See p157 for directions.

BASEBALL

Mexico City has one team in the Liga Mexicana de Béisbol, the Diablos Rojos (www .diablos.com.mx). During the regular season (March to July) they play every other week at the **Foro Sol** (Map pp126–7; ☎ 5639-8722; cnr Av Río Churubusco & Viaducto Río de la Piedad; tickets M$25-90; ☷ 7pm Mon-Fri, 4pm Sat, noon Sun; Ⓜ Ciudad Deportiva). From the metro, it's a five-minute walk to the ballpark.

BULLFIGHTS

If you're not put off by the very concept, a *corrida de toros* is quite a spectacle, from the milling throngs and hawkers outside the arena to the pageantry and drama in the ring itself.

One of the largest bullrings in the world, **Monumental Plaza México** (Map pp126–7; ☎ 5563-3961; Rodin 241, Colonia Nápoles; Ⓜ Ciudad de los Deportes) is a deep concrete bowl holding 48,000 spectators. It's a few blocks west of Av Insurgentes.

From November to March, professional fights are held on Sunday from 4pm. From June to October, junior matadors fight young bulls. Six bulls are fought in an afternoon, two each by three matadors.

The cheapest seats are in the Sol General section – the top tiers on the sunny side of the arena. Seats in the Sombra General section, on the shaded side, cost slightly more. The best seats are in the Barreras, the seven front rows, and cost M$175 to M$300. Between the Barreras and General sections are the Primer (1er) Tendido and Segundo (2o) Tendido.

GAY & LESBIAN MEXICO CITY

Now that the DF assembly has passed an initiative sanctioning same-sex partnerships, Mexico City is perceived as a bastion of tolerance in an otherwise conservative country, and this new openness has created a special energy in the capital. The long-time heart of gay life is the Zona Rosa – in particular, Calle Amberes has seen a recent explosion of bars, discos, nightclubs, restaurants and cafés – but pockets of activity also exist in Roma and the Centro Histórico. *Homópolis* magazine, available free in some clubs, and www.zonagayonline.com.mx (in Spanish) have useful information.

BGay BProud Café México (Map pp132-3; ☎ 5208-2547; www.bgaybproud.com; Amberes 12B; 🕙 11am-11pm; Ⓜ Insurgentes) A good place to start your explorations, this casual café functions as a sort of nerve center for DF gay life, particularly among a younger crowd.

Black Out (Map pp132-3; ☎ 5511-9973; www.black-out.com.mx; Amberes 11; 🕙 5pm-2am; Ⓜ Insurgentes) The new hotspot on the Zona Rosa's hottest street is mostly male but frequented by buff clubbers of every persuasion. Designed by *Frida* art director Felipe Fernández del Paso to evoke the cosmopolitan New York theater world, the narrow space is draped in black velvet, with a sky-high bar of status liquors.

Bar Oasis (Map pp128-9; ☎ 5521-9740; República de Cuba 2G; 🕙 3pm-1am Sun-Thu, 3pm-3am Fri & Sat; Ⓜ Bellas Artes) Next door to El Viena, this packed disco cuts across class lines, with both cowboys and businessmen dancing against a Day-Glo cityscape. Stick around past midnight for shows featuring lip-synching trannies.

El Viena (Map pp128-9; ☎ 5512-0929; República de Cuba 2E; 🕙 1pm-3am; Ⓜ Bellas Artes) The city's only gay cantina is a friendly if nondescript place, attracting a varied male crowd, from truck drivers to journalists. And the jukebox is terrific.

Living (Map pp132-3; ☎ 5286-0671; www.living.com.mx; Paseo de la Reforma 483, Cuauhtémoc; cover M$150-170; 🕙 10pm-4am Fri & Sat; Ⓜ Sevilla) Housed in a magnificent Italianate mansion near the Torre Mayor, Living is a temple of ecstatic nightlife for the 20-something set, both gay and straight. On the enormous main dance floor, world-class DJs cook up high-volume house sessions as sculpted performance artists/exotic dancers gyrate on an overhead catwalk. Other scenes unfold in other lounges.

La Perla (Map pp128-9; ☎ 1997-7695; República de Cuba 44; cover M$120; 🕙 shows 11:30pm & 1:30am Fri & Sat; Ⓜ Bellas Artes) Once a red-light venue, this cabaret has been reborn in the age of irony as a cradle of kitsch, with hilarious drag shows featuring traditional Mexican songstresses. It attracts a mixed crowd, perhaps more straight than gay, in the mood to slum it. Be sure to arrive by 10:30pm to get in.

Tom's Leather Bar (Map pp132-3; ☎ 5564-0728; www.toms-mexico.com; Insurgentes 357; cover M$120; 🕙 9pm-4am Tue-Sun; 🚇 Sonora) For those who dare to get medieval, Tom's provides the props, with heraldic shields, crossed swords and candelabras highlighting a decidedly decadent decor. When the fat lady sings, the show's about to begin.

Except for the biggest *corridas,* tickets are available up to the killing of the third bull, though the best seats may sell out early. You can buy advance tickets from 9:30am to 1pm and 3:30pm to 7pm Saturday, and from 9:30am onward Sunday.

For more on bullfights, see p72.

LUCHA LIBRE (MEXICAN WRESTLING)

Mexico City's two wrestling venues, the 17,000-seat **Arena de México** (Map pp128-9; ☎ 5588-0266; www.arenamexico.com.mx; Dr Lavista 197, Colonia Doctores; tickets M$45-200; 🕙 8:30pm Fri; Ⓜ Cuauhtémoc) and the smaller **Arena Coliseo** (Map pp128-9; ☎ 5526-1687; República de Perú 77; 🕙 7:30pm Tue, 5pm Sun; Ⓜ Lagunilla) are taken over by a circus atmosphere each week, with flamboyant *luchadores* (wrestlers) like Shocker and Tarzan Boy

going at each other in teams or one-on-one. There are three or four bouts, building up to the most formidable match-ups.

SHOPPING

Shopping can be a real joy here, with *artesanía* vendors, quirky shops and street markets competing for your disposable income.

Markets

Mexico City's markets are worth visiting not just for their varied contents but also for a glimpse of the frenetic business conducted within. Besides the major ones listed here, neighborhood markets (indicated by 'Mi Mercado' signs) also make for an interesting wander.

Mercado Insurgentes (Map pp132-3; Londres, cnr Florencia, Zona Rosa; 🕙 9:30am-7:30pm Mon-Sat, 10am-4pm

Sun; **M** Insurgentes) Packed with crafts – silver, pottery, leather, carved wooden figures – but you'll need to bargain to get sensible prices.

Centro de Artesanías La Ciudadela (Map pp128-9; Balderas, cnr Dondé; ⏰ 10am-6pm; **M** Balderas) A favorite destination for good stuff from all over Mexico. Worth seeking out are Oaxaca *alebrijes*, whimsical painted animals (local 6, northernmost aisle, near Balderas entrance); guitars from Paracho (local 61 along Pasillo 4); and Huichol beadwork (local 163, off Dondé at parking entrance). Prices are generally fair even before you bargain.

La Lagunilla (Map pp128-9; cnr Rayón & Allende; ⏰ 9am-8pm Mon-Sat, 10am-7pm Sun; **M** Garibaldi) This enormous complex comprises three buildings: building No 1 contains clothes and fabrics, No 2 has food, and No 3 sells furniture.

Mercado de La Merced (Map pp126-7; Anillo de Circunvalación, cnr General Anaya; ⏰ 8am-7pm; **M** Merced) This occupies four whole blocks dedicated to the buying and selling of daily needs, with photogenic food displays.

Mercado de Jamaica (Map pp126-7; cnr Guillermo Prieto & Congreso de la Union, Colonia Jamaica; ⏰ 8am-7pm; **M** Jamaica) Huge, colorful flower market, featuring both baroque floral arrangements and exotic blooms.

Tianguis Dominical de la Lagunilla (Map pp128-9; cnr Gónzalez Bocanegra & Paseo de la Reforma; ⏰ Sun; **M** Garibaldi) Hunt for antiques, old souvenirs and bric-a-brac; books and magazines are alongside La Lagunilla building.

STREET MARKETS

In most neighborhoods, you'll find a *tianguis* (from the Nahua *tianquiztli*) at least once a week selling the freshest fruits and vegetables, with vendors shouting out '¿Que le damos?' (What can we give you?). *Tianguis* generally set up by 10am and break down around 5pm.

Bazar Artesanal de Coyoacán (Map p140; Plaza Hidalgo, Coyoacán; ⏰ Sat & Sun; **M** Viveros) Has handmade hippie jewelry and indigenous crafts, jugglers, fortune-tellers and incense.

Bazar de la Roma (Map pp132-3; Jardín Dr Chávez & Álvaro Obregón, Roma; ⏰ Sat & Sun; **M** Cuauhtémoc) East of Av Cuauhtémoc, this market has used and antique items, large and small: books, beer trays, posters and furniture. A similar antiques and art market runs along Álvaro Obregón on the same days.

Bazar del Oro (Map pp132-3; Calle de Oro, Roma; ⏰ Wed, Sat & Sun; **R** Durango) This upscale street market between Insurgentes and Plaza Cibeles

has clothing, gifts and an excellent eating section (see boxed text, p176).

Jardín del Arte (Map pp132-3; btwn Sullivan & Villalongín; ⏰ Sun; **R** Reforma) Paintings by local artists, plus art supplies, and some food.

Plaza del Ángel (Map pp132-3; Londres btwn Amberes & Florencia, Zona Rosa; ⏰ Sat & Sun; **M** Insurgentes) Flea market within a mall of high-end antique shops selling silver jewelry, paintings, ornaments and furniture.

Tepito (Map pp128-9; Héroe de Granaditas; ⏰ Wed-Mon; **M** Lagunilla) The mother of all street markets: maze of semipermanent stalls spreading east and north from La Lagunilla, with miles of clothes, pirated CDs and DVDs and electronics. Also known as the Thieves Market for its black-market goods and pickpockets.

Tianguis Cultural del Chopo (Map pp126-7; Calle Juan Nepomuceno; ⏰ 10am-4pm Sat; **M** Buenavista) Gathering place for the city's various youth subcultures, with most of the hundreds of vendor stalls devoted to music CDs. At the far end is a concert stage for young-and-hungry bands, plus a trading post where people bring crates of CDs to swap.

Shops

Chilangos increasingly shop in modern malls with designer-clothing stores, cosmeticians and Starbucks franchises, and more of these shrines to consumerism are popping up all the time. Among the more accessible are **Plaza Loreto** (Map p139) in San Ángel; the futuristic **Plaza Molière** (Map pp136-7), at Molière and Horacio in Polanco; and the spanking new **Plaza Reforma 222** (Map pp132-3), on Insurgentes at the east end of the Zona Rosa.

Fonart Alameda (Map pp128-9; ☎ 5521-0171; Av Juárez 89; ⏰ 10am-7pm; **M** Hidalgo); Mixcoac (Map pp126-7; ☎ 5093-6000; Patriotismo 691; ⏰ 9am-8pm Mon-Sat, 10am-7pm Sun; **M** Mixcoac); Reforma (Map pp132-3; ☎ 5328-5000; Paseo de la Reforma 116; ⏰ 10am-7pm Mon-Fri, 10am-6pm Sat; **M** Cuauhtémoc) The government-run handicrafts store sells quality wares from around Mexico, from Olinalá lacquered boxes to Teotitlán del Valle blankets, as well as pottery and glassware; the Mixcoac branch has the largest selection. Prices are fixed and fair.

Bazar Sábado (Map p139; Plaza San Jacinto 11, San Ángel; ⏰ 11am-6pm Sat; **R** La Bombilla) The Saturday bazaar showcases some of Mexico's best handcrafted jewelry, woodwork, ceramics and textiles. Artists and artisans also display work in Plaza San Jacinto itself and adjacent Plaza Tenanitla.

CENTRO HISTÓRICO

Mexico City's smartest department store chains, **El Palacio de Hierro** (Map pp128-9; ☎ 5728-9905; Av 20 de Noviembre 3; Ⓜ Zócalo) and **Liverpool** (Map pp128-9; ☎ 5133-2800; Venustiano Carranza 92) both maintain their original 1930s stores downtown.

The streets around the Zócalo are lined with stores that specialize in everyday goods; you'll find plenty of shops selling similar items along the same street. To the west, photography supplies and used books show up on Donceles, sports gear on Venustiano Carranza, and perfumes along Tacuba. Jewelry and gold outlets, as well as numismatists shops, are found along La Palma, while opticians are along Madero. To the south, shoes are available on Pino Suárez and Av 20 de Noviembre, and electric guitars along Bolívar. To the north, there's costume jewelry on Repúblicas de Colombia and Venezuela and beauty products along Calle del Carmen. Going east, there are tons of tools along Corregidora. Look for bicycles on San Pablo west of Mercado La Merced.

Hundreds of computer stores huddle in the **Plaza de la Computación y Electrónica** (Map pp128-9; Eje Central Lázaro Cárdenas; Ⓜ San Juan de Letrán), south of Uruguay.

Tucked away in the backstreets are some special items.

Dulcería de Celaya (Map pp128-9; ☎ 5521-1787; Av 5 de Mayo 39; ⏱ 10:30am-7pm; Ⓜ Allende) Candy store operating since 1874 with candied fruits and coconut-stuffed lemons; worth a look just for the ornate building.

La Bodeguita del Habano (Map pp128-9; ☎ 5510-1750; Bolívar 43; Ⓜ San Juan de Letrán) Cigar shop featuring Cuban brands like Montecristo and Quintero; one *habano* will cost you M$70, a box of 25 is around M$500.

La Europea (Map pp128-9; ☎ 5512-6005; Ayuntamiento 21; Ⓜ San Juan de Letrán) Reasonably priced tequilas and wines.

Palacio de las Máscaras (Map pp128-9; ☎ 5529-2849; Allende 84; ⏱ 11am-6pm Mon-Sat; Ⓜ Garibaldi) More than 5000 masks from all over the country; Lagunilla market area.

CONDESA & ROMA

Condesa presents an enticing array of trendy boutiques and quirky shops scattered around the neighborhood. In Roma, by contrast, much of the retail activity is along central Álvaro Obregón, with several voluminous secondhand bookstores.

Milagro (Map pp132-3; ☎ 5286-5764; www.collection-milagro.com; Atlixco 38; Ⓜ Patriotismo) Designer Sandra Gutierrez works with local artisans to create a natty line of tightly woven raffia and embroidered bags in brilliant colors and designs and all shapes and sizes.

NaCo Miscelánea (Map pp132-3; ☎ 5255-5286; Yautepec 126B; Ⓜ Patriotismo) This cheeky little streetwear store in the heart of Condesa carries the NaCo line of T-shirts, emblazoned with edgy or graphic messages relating to Mexican pop culture.

Chic by Accident (Map pp132-3; ☎ 5514-5723; Colima 180; ⏱ 10am-8pm Mon-Fri, 10am-5pm Sat; Ⓜ Insurgentes) French owner Emmanuel Picault has a fascinating collection of 20th-century furniture and objects here. The adjacent Sex By Accident concentrates on the erotica in art and sculpture.

Lemur (Map pp132-3; ☎ 3547-2182; Jalapa 85; Ⓜ Insurgentes) This funky store sells original toys, clothes and accessories, plus a streetwise range of slogan T-shirts, shiny bags and made-to-stand-out shoes and boots.

POLANCO

Polanco's Av Presidente Masaryk, lined with designer shops, has a global anonymity, especially when compared to the street-market bustle of the center. Pop into the **Pasaje Polanco** (Map pp136–7), just west of Dumas, a classy courtyard complex flanked by sophisticated boutiques as well as a handicrafts store.

ZONA ROSA

The Zona Rosa and surrounding neighborhoods are home to a potpourri of tacky, expensive and quality shops. The tree-lined streets west of Génova are a good place to start your shopoholic strolling.

Dione (Map pp132-3; ☎ 5514-5907; Hamburgo 124; Ⓜ Insurgentes) This designer from Guadalajara creates classic shoes for women in the softest of leather. Bags and wallets are also top notch.

Miniaturas Felguérez (Map pp132-3; ☎ 5525-8145; Hamburgo 85; Ⓜ Insurgentes) This is one souvenir you can fit in your luggage: tiny figurines in amusing scenes ranging from a group of mariachis to a cheerful family of naturists!

Somos Plata (Map pp132-3; ☎ 5511-8281; Amberes 24; Ⓜ Insurgentes) All the silver jewelry on display here is by Mexican designers, including a good choice of earring and necklace sets.

GETTING THERE & AWAY
Air

Aeropuerto Internacional Benito Juárez (Map pp126-7; ☎ 2482-2424; www.aicm.com.mx), 6km east of the

Zócalo, is Mexico City's only passenger airport, and Latin America's largest, with a capacity for about 24 million annual passengers.

A new terminal is expected to expand the airport's capacity. Located 3km away from the main terminal, Terminal 2 is connected by monorail, supposedly a five-minute ride. By the time it is fully operational in 2008, Delta, Aeroméxico, Continental, Lan Chile, Aeromar and Copa Airlines are expected to use the terminal, which will include a hotel, parking garage and shops.

See p983 for information on international flights and airlines serving Mexico. See the boxed text on p990 for information on domestic flights.

Terminal 1 is divided into eight *salas* (halls). Below is what each is for:

Sala A Domestic arrivals.
Sala B Check-in for Mexicana and Aero California; Hotel Camino Real access.
Sala C Check-in for Aviacsa.
Sala D Check-in for Magnicharters.
Sala E International arrivals.
Sala F & J Check-in for international flights.
Sala G International departures.

The terminal's shops and facilities include dozens of *casas de cambio*; **Tamibe** (☎ 5726-0578) in Sala E2 stays open 24 hours. Peso-dispensing ATMs on the Cirrus and Plus networks are easily found.

Card phones and internet terminals abound; cards are available from shops and machines. Car-rental agencies and luggage lockers are in Salas A and E2.

Direct buses to Cuernavaca, Querétaro, Toluca, Puebla and Córdoba depart from platforms adjacent to Sala E (see the table on p194). Ticket counters are on the upper level, off the food court.

AIRLINE OFFICES

Aero California (Map pp132-3; ☎ 5785-1162; Paseo de la Reforma 332, Zona Rosa; **M** Insurgentes)
Aeromar (Map pp132-3; ☎ 5133-1111, 800-237-66-27; Torre Mayor, Paseo de la Reforma 505; **M** Chapultepec)
Aeroméxico (☎ 5133-4010) Juárez (Map pp128-9; Paseo de la Reforma 80; **M** Reforma); Zona Rosa (Map pp132-3; Paseo de la Reforma 445; **M** Sevilla)
Air Canada (Map pp136-7; ☎ 9138-0280, ext 2228, 800-719-28-27; 13th fl, Blvd Ávila Camacho 1, Colonia Lomas de Chapultepec)
Air France (Map pp136-7; ☎ 5571-6150, 800-123-46-60; 8th fl, Jaime Balmes 8, Colonia Los Morales; **M** Polanco)

Alitalia (Map pp132-3; ☎ 5533-1240, 800-012-59-00; 6th fl, Río Tíber 103, Colonia Cuauhtémoc; **M** Insurgentes)
American Airlines (Map pp132-3; ☎ 5209-1400; Paseo de la Reforma 300, Zona Rosa; **M** Insurgentes)
Aviacsa (☎ 5716-9006, 800-011-43-57; Airport)
British Airways (Map pp136-7; ☎ 5387-0300; 14th fl, Jaime Balmes 8, Colonia Los Morales; **M** Polanco)
Continental Airlines (Map pp136-7; ☎ 5283-5500, 800-900-50-00; Andrés Bello 45, Polanco; **M** Auditorio)
Cubana (Map pp136-7; ☎ 5250-6355; Sol y Son Viajes, Homero 613, Polanco; **M** Polanco)
Delta Airlines (Map pp132-3; ☎ 5279-0909, 800-123-47-10; Paseo de la Reforma 381; **M** Sevilla)
Iberia (Map pp136-7; ☎ 1101-1515; Av Ejército Nacional 436, 9th fl, Colonia Chapultepec Morales; **M** Polanco)
Interjet (Map pp136-7; ☎ 1102-5555, 800-011-23-45; Centro Comercial Antara, Av Ejército Nacional 843-B)
Japan Air Lines (Map pp132-3; ☎ 5242-0150; 36th fl, Torre Mayor, Paseo de la Reforma 505; **M** Chapultepec)
KLM/Northwest (Map pp136-7; ☎ 5279-5390; 11th fl, Andrés Bello 45, Polanco; **M** Auditorio)
Lufthansa (Map pp136-7; 5230-0000; Paseo de las Palmas 239, Colonia Lomas de Chapultepec)
Magnicharters (Map pp128-9; ☎ 5679-1212; Donato Guerra 9, cnr Bucareli; **M** Juárez)
Mexicana (☎ 5448-0990, 800-502-20-00) Juárez (Map pp128-9; Av Juárez 82, cnr Balderas; **M** Juárez); Polanco (Map pp136-7; ☎ 5395-1211; Ejército Nacional 980, Centro Comercial Pabellón Polanco; **M** Polanco); Zona Rosa (Map pp132-3; Paseo de la Reforma 312; **M** Insurgentes)
United Airlines (Map pp132-3; ☎ 5627-0222; Hamburgo 213, 10th fl, Zona Rosa; **M** Sevilla)
Volaris (☎ 1102-8000)

Bus
Mexico City has four long-distance bus terminals serving the four compass points: Terminal Norte (north), Terminal Oriente (called TAPO, east), Terminal Poniente (west) and Terminal Sur (south). All terminals have baggage-check services or lockers (M$5 to M$12 per hr), as well as tourist information modules, newsstands, card phones, internet, ATMs and snack bars. For directions to the bus stations, see p196.

There are also buses to nearby cities from the airport (see the table, p193).

For trips of up to five hours, it usually suffices to go to the bus station, buy your ticket and go. For longer trips, many buses leave in the evening and may well sell out, so buy your ticket beforehand.

You can purchase advance tickets at **Ticketbus** (☎ 5133-2424, 800-702-80-00; www.ticketbus .com.mx), a booking agency for over a dozen bus lines out of all four stations. (A 10% surcharge is added to the cost of the ticket up to a maximum of M$50.) In addition to the Ticketbus locations listed here, a couple more are inside the international arrivals terminal at the airport. Outlets are generally open 9am or 10am to 7pm or 8pm Monday to Friday with an hour lunch break, mornings only on Saturday. Ticketbus also offers purchase by phone with Visa or Mastercard.

Buenavista (Map pp128-9; Buenavista 9; Ⓜ Revolución)
Centro Histórico (Map pp128-9; Isabel la Católica 83E; Ⓜ Isabel la Católica)
Condesa (Map pp132-3; Iztaccíhuatl 6, cnr Insurgentes; Ⓜ Chilpancingo)
Polanco (Map pp136-7; Av Presidente Masaryk, cnr Hegel; Ⓜ Polanco)
Reforma (Map pp132-3; Paseo de la Reforma 412; Ⓜ Sevilla) Across from La Diana Cazadora.
Roma Norte (Map pp132-3; Mérida 156; Ⓜ Hospital General)
Zócalo (Map pp128-9; Turismo Zócalo, Palma 34; Ⓜ Zócalo)

See the table on p194 for a list of daily services from Mexico City. More information can be found in other town and city sections of this book. It's all subject to change, of course.

Check schedules by phoning the bus lines or by visiting their websites.

ADO Group (☎ 5133-2424, 800-702-80-00; www.ticket bus.com.mx) Includes ADO, ADO GL, UNO, OCC and AU.
Autovías, Herradura de Plata (☎ 5567-4550)
Estrella Blanca Group (☎ 5729-0707; www.estrella blanca.com.mx) Includes Futura, Elite and Turistar.
Estrella de Oro (☎ 5649-8520; www.autobus.com.mx)
Estrella Roja (☎ 5130-1800, 800-712-22-84; www .estrellaroja.com.mx)
ETN (☎ 5089-9200, 800-800-0386; www.etn.com.mx)
Omnibus de México (☎ 800-765-66-36; www.odm .com.mx)
Primera Plus, Flecha Amarilla (☎ 800-375-7587; www.flecha-amarilla.com.mx)
Pullman de Morelos (www.pullman.com.mx)

TERMINAL NORTE
Largest of the four terminals, the **Terminal de Autobuses del Norte** (Map pp126-7; ☎ 5587-1552; www.centraldelnorte.com.mx; Av Cien Metros 4907, Colonia Magdalena de las Salinas) serves points north, including cities on the US border, plus some points west (Guadalajara, Puerto Vallarta),

east (Puebla, Veracruz) and south (Acapulco Oaxaca). Deluxe and 1st-class counters are mostly in the southern half of the terminal Luggage-storage services are at the far south end and in the central passageway; the latter section contains a hotel-booking agency.

TERMINAL ORIENTE
Terminal de Autobuses de Pasajeros de Oriente (Map pp126-7; ☎ 5762-5894; Calz Ignacio Zaragoza 200 Colonia Diez de Mayo), usually called TAPO, serves points east and southeast, including Puebla Veracruz, Yucatán, Oaxaca and Chiapas. Bus line counters are arranged around a rotunda with a restaurant and internet terminals at the center. There's an ATM outside the AU counters and left-luggage service in Tunnel 3 beside Estrella Roja.

TERMINAL PONIENTE
Central de Autobuses del Poniente (Map pp126-7 ☎ 5271-0149; Sur 122, Colonia Real del Monte) is the point for buses heading to Michoacán and shuttle services running to nearby Toluca. In addition, ETN offers service to Guadalajara.

TERMINAL SUR
Terminal Central del Sur (Map p140; ☎ 5689-9745 Av Taxqueña 1320, Colonia Campestre Churubusco) serves Tepoztlán, Cuernavaca, Taxco, Acapulco and other southern destinations, as well as Oaxaca Huatulco and Ixtapa-Zihuatanejo. Estrella de Oro (Acapulco, Taxco) and Pullman de Morelos (Cuernavaca) counters are on the right side of the terminal, while OCC and Estrella Roja (Tepoztlán) are on the left. In Sala 1, you'll find a left-luggage service, agents booking Acapulco hotels and an ATM.

Car & Motorcycle
RENTAL
Car-rental companies have offices at the airport at bus stations and in the Zona Rosa. Rates generally start at about M$500 per day, but you can often do better by booking online. For a list of rental agencies, check www.mexicocity.gob.mx then click 'Transporte' and 'Renta de Autos.'
Avis (Map pp132-3; ☎ 5511-2228; Paseo de la Reforma 308; Ⓜ Insurgentes)
Thrifty (Map pp132-3; ☎ 5207-1100; Paseo de la Reforma 322; Ⓜ Insurgentes)

ROADSIDE ASSISTANCE
The *Ángeles Verdes* (Green Angels) can provide assistance from 8am to 8pm. Phone

☎ 078 and tell them your location. For more information, see the boxed text on p994.

ROUTES IN & OUT OF THE CITY

Whichever way you come in, once you're past the last *caseta* (toll booth) you enter a no-man's-land of poorly marked lanes and chaotic traffic. These *casetas* are also the points from which 'Hoy No Circula' rules take effect (see p200).

East

From Puebla, the highway eventually feeds traffic left into Ignacio Zaragoza. Stay on Zaragoza for about 10km, then move left and follow signs for Río de la Piedad (aka Viaducto Miguel Alemán), exiting left after the metro crosses the highway. From the Viaducto, exits access all the key areas. Get off at Viaducto Tlalpan to reach the Zócalo, and Av Monterrey to Roma and the Zona Rosa.

Coming out of the airport, keep left to head south along Blvd Puerto Aéreo. After you cross Zaragoza, watch for signs to Río de la Piedad and Viaducto Alemán.

Heading for Puebla, Oaxaca or Veracruz, take the Viaducto Alemán east. This is most conveniently accessed off Av Cuauhtémoc (Eje 1 Poniente). Immediately after crossing over the Viaducto – by the Liverpool department store – turn left for the access ramp. Take the Viaducto to Av Zaragoza, then follow the signs for Oaxaca until you join the Puebla highway.

North

From Querétaro, the last toll booth as you approach the city is at Tepotzotlán. Continue south, following signs for Cd Satélite and Toreo. Move into the lateral at the first signs indicating the 'Río San Joaquín' exit, which appears just north of the giant dome of the Toreo arena. Take this exit; the ramp curves left over the Periférico. Keep right as you go over, then follow signs for 'Circuito Interior.' After passing the Corona factory, take the Thiers exit. Keep left, following signs for Reforma, and you'll end up on Río Misisipi, which intersects Reforma at the Diana roundabout. Turn left on Reforma to get to the Centro Histórico, or continue straight ahead for Roma.

Leaving the city, the simplest option is to take Reforma to the west end of Bosque de Chapultepec, then a right exit to pick up the Periférico northbound.

Coming from Pachuca, Hidalgo and northern Veracruz, the highway feeds into Av Insurgentes. Follow the signs for the Centro Histórico and Zona Rosa. Leaving the city, take Insurgentes north (also the route to Teotihuacán).

South

After the last *caseta* on the autopista from Cuernavaca, continue straight, taking a right exit for Calz Tlalpan (some signs are hidden behind trees). Calz Tlalpan eventually feeds into Av 20 de Noviembre, which ends at the Zócalo. Leaving town, turn right (south) at the Zócalo onto Pino Suárez, which becomes Calz Tlalpan. About 20km south, signs indicate a left exit for the *cuota* (toll highway) to Cuernavaca.

West

Coming from Toluca, about 4km past the high-rises of Santa Fe, keep left and follow signs for Paseo de la Reforma. Go straight down Reforma, past the Fuente de Petróleos and Bosque de Chapultepec to reach downtown. Heading west out of the city, take Paseo de la Reforma, which feeds right into the *cuota* to Toluca.

GETTING AROUND

Mexico City has an inexpensive, easy-to-use metro and an equally cheap and practical bus system plying all the main routes. Taxis are plentiful, but some are potentially hazardous (see p141).

To/From the Airport

The metro is convenient to the airport, though hauling luggage amid rush-hour crowds can be a Herculean task. Authorized taxis provide a painless, relatively inexpensive alternative.

METRO

The airport metro station is Terminal Aérea, on Línea 5 (yellow). It's 200m from the terminal: leave by the exit at the end of Sala A (domestic arrivals) and continue past the taxi stand to the station.

To the city center, follow signs for 'Dirección Politécnico'; at La Raza (seven stops away) change for Línea 3 (green) toward 'Dirección Universidad.' Metro Hidalgo, at the west end of the Alameda, is three stops south; it's also a transfer point for Línea 2 (blue) to the Zócalo.

BUSES FROM MEXICO CITY

Destination	Fare	Duration	Terminal in Mexico City	Bus company	Departures
Acapulco	executive M$475	5hr	Sur	Estrella de Oro	7 daily
	deluxe M$315	5hr	Sur	Estrella de Oro	every 30 min
	1st-class M$315	5hr	Sur	Futura	every 30 min 5am-8pm
	1st-class M$315	5hr	Norte	Futura	hourly
Bahías de Huatulco	deluxe M$678	14-15hr	Oriente (TAPO)	ADO GL	1 daily
	1st-class M$598	14-15hr	Norte	OCC	1 daily
	1st-class M$525	14-15hr	Sur	Futura	2 daily
Campeche	deluxe M$1016	17hr	Oriente (TAPO)	ADO GL	1 daily
	1st-class M$892	17hr	Oriente (TAPO)	ADO	5 daily
	1st-class M$892	17hr	Norte	ADO	5 daily
Cancún	deluxe M$1350	24hr	Oriente (TAPO)	ADO GL	1 daily
	1st-class M$1186	24hr	Oriente (TAPO)	ADO	5 daily
	1st-class M$1186	24hr	Norte	ADO	5 daily
Chetumal	1st-class M$916	19hr	Oriente (TAPO)	ADO	4 daily
Chihuahua	1st-class M$1052	20hr	Norte	Ómnibus de México	8 daily
Ciudad Juárez	1st-class M$1319	24hr	Norte	Ómnibus de México	10 daily
Cuernavaca	executive M$72	1¼hr	Sur	Pullman de Morelos	every 30 min to 9:30pm
	deluxe M$63	1¼hr	Sur	Pullman de Morelos	every 15 min to midnight
	1st-class M$125	1¼hr	Airport	Pullman de Morelos	every 30 or 40 min to 12:30am
Guadalajara	deluxe M$570	7hr	Norte	ETN	20 daily
	deluxe M$570	7hr	Poniente	ETN	7 daily
	1st-class M$470	7hr	Norte	Primera Plus	28 daily
Guanajuato	deluxe M$371	5hr	Norte	ETN	10 daily
	1st-class M$305	5hr	Norte	Primera Plus	11 daily
Matamoros	1st-class M$710	14hr	Norte	Futura	5 daily
	executive M$968	14hr	Norte	Turistar	2 daily
Mazatlán	1st-class M$808	15½hr	Norte	Elite	hourly
Mérida	deluxe M$1194	20hr	Oriente (TAPO)	ADO GL	1 daily
	1st-class M$1006	20hr	Oriente (TAPO)	ADO	6 daily
	1st-class M$1006	20hr	Norte	ADO	5 daily
Monterrey	deluxe M$828	11½hr	Norte	Turistar	7 daily
	1st-class M$687	11½hr	Norte	Futura	13 daily
Morelia	deluxe M$290	4-5hr	Poniente	ETN	every 30 min
	1st-class M$255	4-5hr	Norte	Primera Plus	hourly
Nuevo Laredo	deluxe M$1060	16hr	Norte	Turistar	5 daily
	1st-class M$815	16hr	Norte	Futura	10 daily
Oaxaca	deluxe M$614	6½hr	Oriente (TAPO)	UNO	3+ daily
	deluxe M$432	6½hr	Oriente (TAPO)	ADO GL	4+ daily
	deluxe M$432	6½hr	Norte	ADO GL	1 daily
	deluxe M$432	6½hr	Sur	ADO GL	1 daily
	1st-class M$362	6½hr	Oriente (TAPO)	ADO	17+ daily
	1st-class M$362	6½hr	Norte	ADO	5+ daily
Palenque	1st-class M$706	13½hr	Oriente (TAPO)	ADO	2 daily
	1st-class M$706	13½hr	Norte	ADO	1 daily

BUSES FROM MEXICO CITY (CONTINUED)

Destination	Fare	Duration	Terminal in Mexico City	Bus company	Departures
Papantla	1st-class M$220	5hr	Norte	ADO	4 daily
Pátzcuaro	1st-class M$286	5hr	Norte	Primera Plus	2 daily
	1st-class M$270	5hr	Norte	Autovías	5 daily
	1st-class M$270	5hr	Poniente	Autovías	13 daily
Puebla	deluxe M$170	2hr	Airport	Estrella Roja	hourly
	deluxe M$112	2hr	Oriente (TAPO)	Estrella Roja	every 40 min
	1st-class M$120	2hr	Norte	ADO GL	every 30 min
	1st-class M$96	2hr	Oriente (TAPO)	Estrella Roja	every 20 min
Puerto Escondido	1st-class M$604	14hr	Norte	OCC	1 daily
	1st-class M$568	14hr	Sur	OCC	2 daily
	1st-class M$514	14hr	Sur	Futura	3 daily
Puerto Vallarta	1st-class M$772	12½hr	Norte	Futura	4 daily
Querétaro	deluxe M$225	3hr	Norte	ETN	every 20 or 30 min
	1st-class M$235	3hr	Airport	Primera Plus	hourly
	1st-class M$173	3hr	Poniente	Primera Plus	5 daily
	1st-class M$138	3hr	Norte	Primera Plus	every 20 min
San Cristóbal de Las Casas	deluxe M$896	13hr	Oriente (TAPO)	ADO GL	2 daily
	deluxe M$896	13hr	Norte	ADO GL	1 daily
	1st-class M$770	13hr	Norte	OCC	4 daily
San Luis Potosí	deluxe M$410	5hr	Norte	ETN	hourly
	1st-class M$300	5hr	Norte	Primera Plus	hourly
San Miguel de Allende	deluxe M$276	4hr	Norte	ETN	4 daily
	deluxe M$225	4hr	Norte	Primera Plus	3 daily
Tapachula	deluxe M$1144	16-18hr	Oriente (TAPO)	UNO	1 daily
	deluxe M$916	16-18hr	Oriente (TAPO)	ADO GL	1 daily
	1st-class M$782	16-18hr	Oriente (TAPO)	OCC	6 daily
Taxco	deluxe M$105	2½hr	Sur	Estrella de Oro	8 daily
	1st-class M$105	2½hr	Sur	Estrella Blanca	hourly
Teotihuacán	2nd-class M$28	1hr	Norte	Autobuses Teotihuacán	every 15 min 6am-6pm
Tepoztlán	1st-class M$64	1¼hr	Sur	OCC	every 40 min
	1st-class M$63	1¼hr	Sur	Estrella Roja (to Caseta)	every 20 min 7:20am-10pm
Tijuana	1st-class M$1400	41hr	Norte	Elite	hourly
Toluca	deluxe M$100	1hr	Airport	TMT Caminante	hourly
	deluxe M$49	1hr	Poniente	ETN	every 20 or 30 min
	2nd M$34	1hr	Poniente	Flecha Roja	every 10 min to 11:30pm
Tuxtla Gutiérrez	deluxe M$1090	12hr	Oriente (TAPO)	UNO	1 daily
	deluxe M$876	12hr	Oriente (TAPO)	ADO GL	2 daily
	1st-class M$760	12hr	Oriente (TAPO)	OCC	6 daily
	1st-class M$760	12hr	Norte	OCC	4 daily
Uruapan	deluxe M$430	6hr	Poniente	ETN	7 daily
	1st-class M$360	6hr	Norte	Primera Plus	5 daily
	1st-class M$335	6hr	Poniente	Autovías	11 daily
Veracruz	deluxe M$526	5½hr	Oriente (TAPO)	UNO	4+ daily
	deluxe M$372	5½hr	Oriente (TAPO)	ADO GL	8 daily
	deluxe M$348	5½hr	Sur	ADO GL	3+ daily
	1st-class M$314	5½hr	Sur	ADO	hourly
	1st-class M$314	5½hr	Norte	ADO	6+ daily
	2nd-class M$244	7hr	Sur	AU	hourly

BUSES FROM MEXICO CITY (CONTINUED)

Destination	Fare	Duration	Terminal in Mexico City	Bus company	Departures
Villahermosa	executive M$998	10½hr	Oriente (TAPO)	UNO	1 daily
	deluxe M$698	10½hr	Oriente (TAPO)	ADO GL	3 daily
	deluxe M$698	10½hr	Norte	ADO GL	1 daily
	deluxe M$698	10½hr	Sur	ADO GL	1+ daily
	1st-class M$618	10½hr	Oriente (TAPO)	ADO	6 daily
	1st-class M$618	10½hr	Norte	ADO	4 daily
Xalapa	deluxe M$380	5hr	Oriente (TAPO)	UNO	5+ daily
	deluxe M$264	5hr	Oriente (TAPO)	ADO GL	6+ daily
	1st-class M$222	5hr	Norte	ADO	4 daily
Zacatecas	1st-class M$491	8hr	Norte	Ómnibus de México	14 daily
Zihuatanejo	executive M$550	9hr	Sur	Estrella de Oro	1 daily
	deluxe M$440	9hr	Sur	Estrella de Oro	3 daily
	1st-class M$440	9hr	Sur	Futura	5 daily
	1st-class M$420	9hr	Poniente	Autovías	6 daily

Note: + indicates additional departures on weekends

To get to the Zona Rosa from the airport, take Línea 5 to 'Pantitlán' the end of the line. Change for Línea 1 (pink) and get off at metro Insurgentes.

At the time of writing, there was no convenient metro link to Terminal 2, for Delta, Aeroméxico and Continental flights. You'll need to go to the main terminal and take the monorail, departing every five minutes from above Puerta 5, in the domestic arrivals area.

TAXI

Safe and reliable 'Transporte Terrestre' taxis, recognizable by their yellow doors and airplane logos, are controlled by a fixed-price ticket system.

Purchase taxi tickets from booths labeled 'Sitio 300,' located in Sala E1 (international arrivals), on your left as you exit customs, and by the Sala A (domestic arrivals) exit. Fares are determined by zones (shown on a map next to the booth). A ride to the Zócalo or Alameda Central is M$127, to the Zona Rosa or Plaza de la República, M$152. One ticket is valid for up to four passengers and luggage that will fit in the trunk.

Taxi stands for the Sitio 300 taxis are outside Salas A and at the far end of the international terminal. Porters may offer to take your ticket and luggage the few steps to the taxi, but hold on to the ticket and hand it to the driver. Drivers won't expect a tip for the ride, but will of course welcome one.

To reserve a Transporte Terrestre taxi to the airport call ☎ 5571-9344; fares are slightly higher in this direction.

To/From the Bus Terminals

The metro is the fastest and cheapest way to any bus terminal, but it's tricky to maneuver through crowded stations and cars. Taxis are an easier option: all terminals have ticket booths for secure *taxis autorizados*, with fares set by zone (M$20 surcharge from 10pm to 6am). An agent at the exit will assign you a cab.

TERMINAL NORTE

Metro Línea 5 (yellow) stops at Autobuses del Norte, just outside the terminal. To the center, follow signs for 'Dirección Pantitlán,' then change at La Raza for Línea 3 (green) toward 'Dirección Universidad.' (The La Raza connection is a six-minute hike through a 'Tunnel of Science.')

The taxi kiosk is in the central passageway; a cab for up to four people to the Alameda or Zócalo costs M$85.

TERMINAL ORIENTE (TAPO)

This bus terminal is next door to metro station San Lázaro. To the center or Zona Rosa, take Línea 1 (pink) toward 'Dirección Observatorio.'

The authorized taxi booth is at the top (metro) end of the main passageway from the rotunda. The fare to the Zócalo is M$60; to the Zona Rosa, M$70.

TERMINAL PONIENTE

Observatorio metro station, the eastern terminus of Línea 1 (pink), is a couple of minutes' walk across a busy street (the pedestrian bridge has been closed until further notice). A taxi ticket to Colonia Roma costs M$70; to the Zócalo it's M$98.

TERMINAL SUR

Terminal Sur is a two-minute walk from metro Tasqueña, the southern terminus of Línea 2 which stops at the Zócalo. For the Zona Rosa, transfer at Pino Suárez and take Línea 1 to Insurgentes (Dirección Observatorio). Going to the terminal, take the 'Autobuses del Sur' exit, which leads upstairs to a footbridge. Descend the last staircase on the left, then walk through a street market, to reach the building.

Authorized taxis from Terminal Sur cost M$95 to the Zona Rosa or Centro Histórico. Ticket booths are by the main exit and in Sala 3.

Bicycle

Bicycles can be a viable way to get around town and are often preferable to overcrowded, recklessly driven buses. Although careless drivers and potholes can make DF cycling an extreme sport, if you stay alert and keep off the major thoroughfares, it's manageable. Mexico City's Mayor Marcelo Ebrard has encouraged bicycle use, and though it still isn't a common mode of transportation in the capital (except by delivery boys), cycling does seem to be catching on slowly.

Bikes are loaned free from a module on the west side of the Catedral Metropolitana daily from 9am to 6pm. Leave a passport or driver's license for two hours of riding time. Otherwise, you can rent a bicycle from a **module** (Map pp128-9; ☾ 8am-6pm; per hr/day M$50/150) on Paseo de la Reforma, just outside the Museo de la Antropología.

The *ciclovía* is an extensive bike trail that follows the old bed of the Cuernavaca railroad as far as the Morelos border. It extends from Av Ejército Nacional in Polanco through the Bosque de Chapultepec, skirting the Periférico freeway from La Feria to Av San Antonio, with several steep bridges passing over the freeways.

Another path follows Av Chapultepec along a protected median from Bosque de Chapultepec to the Centro Histórico, though a detour through the streets of Colonia Roma is ignored by motorists – they drive or even park on it. A third route runs along Paseo de la Reforma from the Auditorio Nacional to the Museo Rufino Tamayo. Follow the red stripe.

Bus, Pesero & Trolleybus

Mexico City's thousands of buses and peseros (also called microbuses or combis) operate from around 5am till 8pm or 9pm daily; electric trolleybuses until 11:30pm. Only a few routes run all night, notably those along Paseo de la Reforma and the metrobus along Av Insurgentes. This means you'll get anywhere by bus and/or metro during the day but will probably have to take a few taxis after hours.

Peseros are generally gray-and-green minibuses operated by private firms. They follow fixed routes, often starting or ending at metro stations, and will stop at virtually any street corner. Route information is randomly displayed on cards attached to the windshield. Fares are M$2.50 for trips of up to 5km, M$3 for 5km to 12km. Add 20% to all fares between 11pm and 6am. Municipally operated full-size orange buses (labeled 'RTP') and trolleybuses only pick up at bus stops; fares are M$2 regardless of distance traveled.

A recently installed alternative to peseros, the metrobus plies a dedicated lane along Av Insurgentes from Metro Indios Verdes in the northern DF down to the southern end of San Ángel, near the national university (at the time of research, construction was under way to extend the line 8.5km further south to Tlalpan). These 18m-long wheelchair-accessible Volvo vehicles stop at metro-style stations in the middle of the street, spaced at three- to four-block intervals. Access is by prepaid card, issued by machines at the entrance to the platforms, and rides cost M$3.50. Rechargeable cards (M$8) are placed on a sensor device for entry. The metrobus runs round the clock, though frequency is reduced to every 20 minutes between midnight and 5am, when the fare increases to M$5.

Pesero routes ply practically every street that crisscrosses the Centro Histórico grid, while trolleybuses follow a number of the key *ejes* (priority roads) throughout the rest of the city.

MEXICO METRO

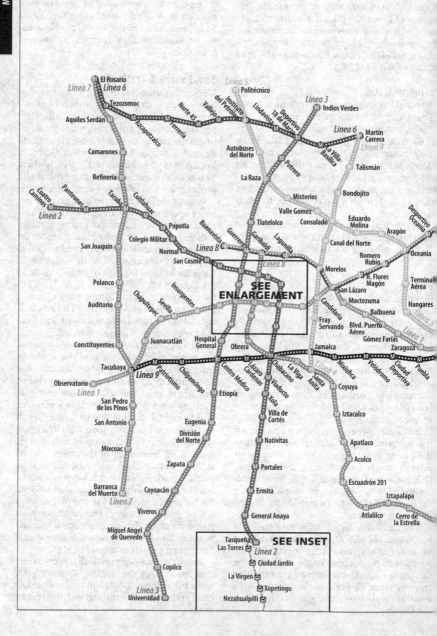

MEXICO METRO

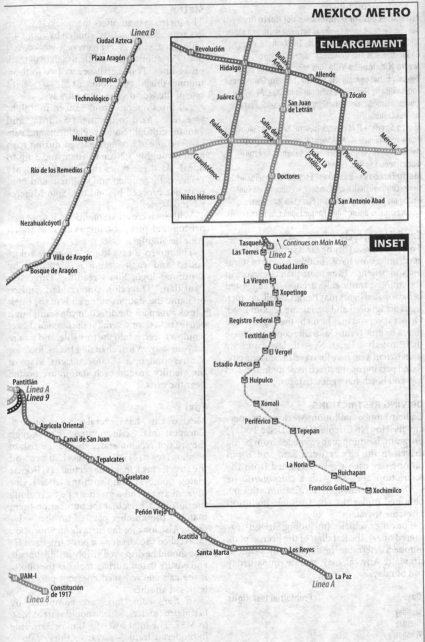

Linea B
- Ciudad Azteca
- Plaza Aragón
- Olímpica
- Technológico
- Muzquiz
- Río de los Remedios
- Nezahualcóyotl
- Villa de Aragón
- Bosque de Aragón

ENLARGEMENT
- Revolución
- Hidalgo
- Bellas Artes
- Allende
- Juárez
- San Juan de Letrán
- Zócalo
- Balderas
- Salto del Agua
- Merced
- Cuauhtémoc
- Isabel La Católica
- Pino Suárez
- Doctores
- Niños Héroes
- San Antonio Abad

INSET
- Tasqueña — Continues on Main Map
- Las Torres
- **Linea 2**
- Ciudad Jardín
- La Virgen
- Xopetingo
- Nezahualpilli
- Registro Federal
- Textitlán
- El Vergel
- Estadio Azteca
- Huipulco
- Xomali
- Periférico
- Tepepan
- La Noria
- Huichapan
- Francisco Goitia
- Xochimilco

Pantitlán
- **Linea A**
- **Linea 9**
- Agrícola Oriental
- Canal de San Juan
- Tepalcates
- Guelatao
- Peñón Viejo
- Acatitla
- Santa Marta
- Los Reyes
- La Paz
- **Linea A**

- UAM-I
- Constitución de 1917
- **Linea 8**

Some useful routes:

Autobuses del Sur & Autobuses del Norte (trolleybus) Eje Central Lázaro Cardenas between north and south bus terminals (stops at Plaza de las Tres Culturas; Plaza Garibaldi; Bellas Artes/Alameda; metro Hidalgo).

Metro Hidalgo–La Villa (bus or pesero) Paseo de la Reforma between Auditorio Nacional or metro Chapultepec and Basílica de Guadalupe (stops at Zona Rosa; Av Insurgentes; Alameda/metro Hidalgo; Plaza Garibaldi; Plaza de las Tres Culturas).

Metro Sevilla–P Masaryk (pesero) Between Colonia Roma and Polanco via Av Álvaro Obregón and Av Presidente Masaryk (stops at metro Niños Héroes; Av Insurgentes; metro Sevilla; Leibnitz).

Metro Tacubaya–Balderas–Escandón (pesero) Between Centro Histórico and Condesa, westbound via Puebla, eastbound via Durango (stops at Plaza San Juan; metro Balderas; metro Insurgentes; Parque España; Av Michoacán).

Car & Motorcycle

Touring Mexico City by car is strongly discouraged, unless you have a healthy reserve of stamina and patience. Even more than elsewhere in the country, traffic rules are seen as suggested behavior. Red lights may be run at will, no-turn signs are ignored and signals are seldom used. On occasion you may be hit by the bogus traffic fine, a routine means for traffic cops to increase their miserly salaries. Nevertheless, you may want to rent a car here for travel outside the city. Avoid parking on the street; most midrange and top-end hotels have guest garages.

DRIVING RESTRICTIONS

To help combat pollution, Mexico City operates its 'Hoy No Circula' (Don't Drive Today) program, banning many vehicles from being driven in the city between 5am and 10pm on one day each week. Exempted from the restriction are cars with a *calcomanía de verificación* (emissions verification sticker), obtained under the city's vehicle-pollution assessment system.

For other vehicles (including foreign-registered ones), the last digit of the license plate numbers determine the day when they cannot circulate. Any car may operate on Saturday and Sunday.

Day	Prohibited last digits
Monday	5, 6
Tuesday	7, 8
Wednesday	3, 4
Thursday	1, 2
Friday	9, 0

Metro

The metro system offers the quickest way to get around Mexico City. Ridden by about 4.6 million passengers on an average weekday, it has 175 stations and more than 200km of track on 11 lines. Trains arrive every two to three minutes during rush hours. At M$2 a ride, it's one of the world's cheapest subways.

All lines operate from 5am to midnight weekdays, 6am to midnight Saturday and 7am to midnight Sunday. Platforms and cars can become alarmingly packed during rush hours (roughly 7:30am to 10am and 3pm to 8pm). At these times the forward cars are reserved for women and children, and men may not proceed beyond the 'Solo Mujeres y Niños' gate.

With such crowded conditions, it's not surprising that pickpocketing occurs, so watch your belongings.

The metro is easy to use. Lines are color-coded and each station is identified by a unique logo. Signs reading 'Dirección Pantitlán,' 'Dirección Universidad' and so on name the stations at the ends of the lines. Check a map for the direction you want. Buy a *boleto* (ticket), or several, at the *taquilla* (ticket window), feed it into the turnstile, and you're on your way. When changing trains, look for 'Correspondencia' (Transfer) signs. Maps of the vicinity around each station are posted near the exits.

Taxi

Mexico City has several classes of taxi. Cheapest are the cruising street cabs, though they're not recommended due to the risk of assaults (see p141). If you must hail a cab off the street, check that it has actual taxi license plates: numbers begin with the letter L (for *libre*, or free), and a green stripe runs along the bottom. Check that the number on them matches the number painted on the bodywork. Also look for the *carta de identificación* (also called the *tarjetón*), a postcard-sized ID that should be displayed visibly inside the cab, and ensure that the driver matches the photo. If the cab you've hailed does not pass these tests, get another.

In *libre* cabs, fares are computed by *taxímetro* (meter), which should start at M$6 to M$7. The total cost of a 2km or 3km ride in moderate traffic – say, from the Zócalo to the Zona Rosa – should be M$40 to M$45. Between 11pm and 6am, add 20%.

A radio taxi costs about two or three times as much as the others, but this extra cost adds an immeasurable degree of security, which may not be such a bad thing. Their plates begin with S – for *sitio* (taxi stand) – and bear an orange stripe. When you phone, the dispatcher will tell you the cab number and the type of car.

Some reliable radio-taxi firms, available 24 hours, are listed below. Maps in this chapter show the locations of some key *sitios*.

Radio Maxi Seguridad (☎ 5768-8557, 5552-1376)
RET (☎ 8590-6720, 8590-6721)
Sitio Parque México (☎ 5286-7129, 5286-7164)
Taxi-Mex (☎ 9171-8888, 5634-9912)
Taxis Radio Unión (☎ 5514-8124)

Around Mexico City

With its daunting size and seemingly endless urban sprawl, the megalopolis of Mexico City may seem a challenging place to escape from, yet thousands of Chilangos (Mexico City residents) do so every weekend. Fast toll roads fan out in all directions to the cities, towns and the so-called *pueblos mágicos* (magical villages) that surround the Distrito Federal, taking you surprisingly easily into a world of ancient ruins, well-preserved colonial towns and beautiful mountain scenery.

Even if you're in Mexico City for a only week, make a point of taking a day trip out of the city to experience something of the 'other' Mexico, as Mexico City – like so many capitals – has little in common with even its neighboring provinces. Indeed, the area around Mexico City offers copious rewards for people who make time to explore places often overlooked by travelers eager to get to the coast.

While nearly all visitors day-trip from the capital to the stunning complex at Teotihuacán, this is just one of many extraordinary sights in the area. The gorgeous colonial towns of Taxco, Puebla and Cuernavaca shouldn't be missed, nor should the scenery of Valle de Bravo and Tepoztlán, the peaks of Popocatépetl and Iztaccíhuatl or the ruins of Xochicalco and Tula (to name just a few). Outside the weekends, you'll be able to enjoy many of these places without the tourist hordes. So give yourself a welcome change of pace, leave the hustle and bustle of the city and relax into the groove of life just outside the capital.

HIGHLIGHTS

- Take in the astonishing views of **Popocatépetl** (p231) and **Iztaccíhuatl** (p231), and descend to the beautiful volcanic lakes at **Nevado de Toluca** (p269)
- Be blown away by the sheer scale of the two huge pyramids at **Teotihuacán** (p209)
- Enjoy a sunset drink on the charming *zócalo* of tiny **Cuetzalan** (p238) amid the dramatic scenery of the Sierra Madre Oriental
- Discover some of the lesser-known ancient sites of central Mexico, often entirely free of other visitors, at **Xochicalco** (p258), **Yohualichán** (p240) and **Cantona** (p238)
- Wander cobbled side streets in magical villages such as easy-going **Malinalco** (p270), artsy **Tepoztlán** (p242) and beautiful **Valle de Bravo** (p269)

- PUEBLA JANUARY DAILY HIGH 24°C | 75°F
- PUEBLA JULY DAILY HIGH 27°C | 80°F

History

Long a cultural and economic crossroads, the region around present-day Mexico City played host to a succession of important indigenous civilizations (notably the Teotihuacán, Toltec and Aztec). By the late 15th century, the Aztecs had managed to dominate all but one of central Mexico's states. Many archaeological sites and museums preserve remnants of pre-Hispanic history; Puebla's Museo Amparo provides an excellent overview of the region's history and cultures.

Post-conquest, the Spanish transformed central Mexico, establishing ceramic industries at Puebla, mines at Taxco and Pachuca, and haciendas producing wheat, sugar and cattle. The Catholic church used the region as a base for its missionary activities, and left a series of imposing churches and fortified monasteries. Today, most towns retain a central plaza surrounded by colonial buildings.

Climate

The extra altitude outside Mexico City makes for a very agreeable climate – cooler and less humid than the lowlands, with most rain falling in brief summer downpours. Snow tops the highest peaks (*nevados*) for several months a year (October through March), but the populated areas in the foothills continue to enjoy a mild climate while cross-country skiers glide about up in the clouds.

Parks & Reserves

Several national parks within a day's drive of Mexico City are delightfully crowd-free and, with a bit of effort, are accessible via public transportation. Grutas de Cacahuamilpa (p265), the region's most popular park, preserves a staggering network of gaping caverns in a beautiful setting straddling a raging river. Rock formations attract climbers, and pine forests make for cool day hiking at diminutive, mountainous El Chico (p215) outside Pachuca.

Iztaccíhuatl-Popocatépetl (p231), in the foothills around Amecameca, offer some fine hiking. Popo remains off limits due to volcanic activity, while only experienced climbers should attempt to summit Izta. Near Puebla, the towering peak La Malinche, accessed via La Malintzi (p237), is a challenging nontechnical goal for day hikers. You can also drive right up to, or cross-country ski around, the extinct crater of Nevado de Toluca (p269).

Getting There & Around

The cities, towns and – to a lesser extent – even the villages around Mexico City enjoy excellent bus links to both the capital and each other. Even the very smallest backwaters have daily services to Mexico City and to the closest transportation hub. While airports also serve Puebla, Toluca, Cuernavaca and Pachuca in the region, it's nearly always cheaper and easier to fly to Mexico City and travel onward from there. Roads in the region, though they're busy, are some of the best-maintained and safest in the country, so hiring a car to explore is also a highly recommended option. However, for all but the most obscure sights, it's no problem to get almost anywhere by bus.

NORTH OF MEXICO CITY

The two big attractions north of Mexico City are both ancient sites: the extraordinary complex at Teotihucán, once the largest metropolis in the Americas and one of Mexico's most spectacular pre-Hispanic sights; and the lesser-known Tula, the Toltec capital northwest of Teotihuacán, far smaller but home to some truly extraordinary stone statues that have been almost perfectly preserved in a small central plaza.

Far more obscure but equally impressive is the Parque Nacional El Chico and the charming village of Mineral del Chico – the perfect escape from the big city, with stunning views, wide open spaces and friendly locals.

Pachuca, the fast-growing capital of dynamic Hidalgo state, has little to recommend it overall, although it does look charming from a distance, with its brightly painted houses, and it has a pretty colonial center and a great line in Cornish pasties. From Pachuca, well-paved routes snake east and north to the Gulf coast, traversing some spectacular country as the fringes of the Sierra Madre Oriental tumble to the coastal plain.

TEPOTZOTLÁN

☎ 55 / pop 45,000 / elevation 2300m

This little charmer is the easiest single-day trip from Mexico City, but it's hard to imagine anywhere less like the chaotic streets of the capital, despite the fact that urban sprawl gets closer and closer to Tepotzotlán's colonial streets every year.

AROUND MEXICO CITY

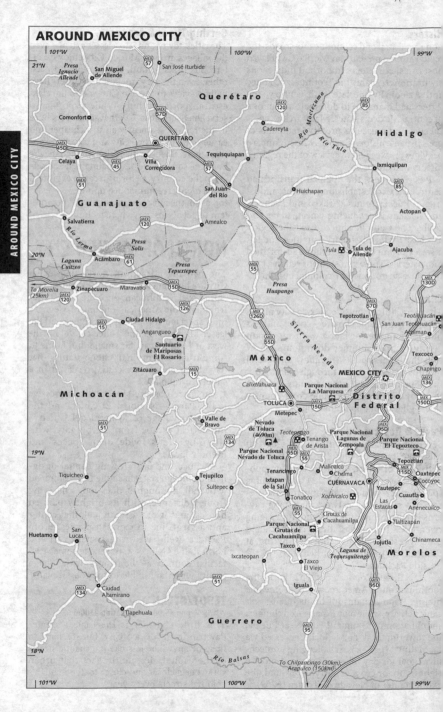

Sights

There's a very simple reason to visit: the wonderful **Museo Nacional del Virreinato** (National Museum of the Viceregal Period; ☎ 5876-2771; Plaza Hidalgo 99; admission M$43; ☺ 9am-6pm Tue-Sun), comprising the restored Jesuit **Iglesia de San Francisco Javier** and an adjacent **monastery**. Audioguides (M$40) are in Spanish only.

Once occupied by a Jesuit college of Indian languages, the complex dates from 1606, although various additions were made over the following 150 years, creating a fascinating showcase of the developing architectural styles of New Spain. Much of what is on display comes from Mexico City Cathedral's large collection, and the standard is very high. Among the folk art and fine art on display are silver chalices, pictures created from inlaid wood, porcelain, furniture and fine religious paintings and statues.

Don't miss the **Capilla Doméstica**, with a Churrigueresque main altarpiece that boasts more mirrors than a carnival fun house. The biggest crowds arrive on Sunday, when a crafts market convenes out front. The church was originally built between 1670 and 1682; additions carried out in the 18th century made it one of Mexico's most lavish places of worship. The facade is a phantasmagoric array of carved saints, angels, plants and people, while the interior walls and the Camarín del Virgen adjacent to the altar are swathed with a circus of gilded ornamentation.

Festivals

Tepotzotlán's highly regarded Christmas *pastorelas* (nativity plays) are performed inside the former monastery in the weeks leading up to December 25. Tickets, which include Christmas dinner and piñata smashing, can be purchased at La Hostería de Tepotzotlán (see right) or via Spanish-language **Ticketmaster** (☎ 5325-9000; www.ticketmaster.com.mx).

Sleeping

Tepotzotlán is geared toward day-trippers, but there are a few good-value hotels.

Hotel Posada San José (☎ /fax 5876-0340; Plaza Virreinal 13; r without/with view M$185/250) Within a gorgeous old colonial building on the south side of the *zócalo*, this well-run hotel has a great atmosphere, charming tiled bathrooms and decent rooms, although the furniture is not always as evocative of the colonial area complex as it could be. Avoid rooms 8 and 9,

which are directly below the building's noisy water pump.

Hotel Posada del Virrey (☎ /fax 5876-1864; Av Insurgentes 13; r M$250; ℗) This place, popular with weekenders, is set around a large, fairly charmless courtyard. The rooms are all fine with bathrooms and TV, but some can be a little dark, although the better ones have Jacuzzis in them.

Posada Castro (☎ 5876-0964; Av Insurgentes 11; r M$300-500; ℗) This friendly, family-run place has 17 smart and comfy rooms a short walk from the *zócalo*, all with bathroom and TV. The Virgin Mary adorns almost every wall, and a selection of religious icons and crucifixes completes the décor of each room.

Eating

La Hostería de Tepotzotlán (☎ 5876-0243; Plaza Virreinal 1; mains M$60-150; ℗ 12:30-5:30pm Tue-Sun) The town's most atmospheric place for lunch is this restaurant, housed within the monastery in a delightful little courtyard. It serves hearty soups along with original main courses like *huitlacoche* (earthy corn mushroom) crepes for brunch and lunch.

Restaurant-Bar Pepe (☎ 5876-0520; Plaza Virreinal; mains M$80-140; ℗ 8am-11pm) A charming place facing the Iglesia de San Francisco Javier across the *zócalo*, with a great terrace and an intimate, gently buzzing interior. Specialties include *camarones empanizados* (breaded shrimp), and there are good breakfasts for around M$65.

It's best to avoid the other almost indistinguishable restaurants aimed squarely at tourists elsewhere on the *zócalo* – the food is mediocre and prices high. A much better option is to join the locals at the *taquerías* (taco stalls) west of the plaza, or in the market behind the Palacio Municipal, where food stalls serve rich *pozole* (a thin stew of hominy, pork or chicken), *gorditas* (fried stuffed tacos in fat, handmade blue corn tortillas), and fresh-squeezed juices all day long. One particularly good option for tacos *al pastor* in a pleasant setting is **Taquería la Dueña** (tacos from M$16), just behind the Posada San José in the same colonial arcade. This beautifully decorated spot serves up a delicious range of tacos and other tasty snacks.

Getting There & Away

Tepotzotlán is en route from Mexico City to Querétaro, 1.5km west of the first tollbooth on Hwy 57D.

From Mexico City's Terminal Norte, Autotransportes Valle del Mezquital (AVM) buses stop at the tollbooth every 15 minutes en route to Tula. From there, catch a local bus (M$4) or taxi (M$30), or walk west for about 20 minutes along Av Insurgentes. You can also catch a *colectivo* to Tepotzotlán from Mexico City's Rosario metro station (M$15). In Tepotzotlán, returning 'Rosario' buses depart from Av Insurgentes opposite Posada San José.

TULA

☎ 773 / pop 27,000 / elevation 2060m

The probable capital of the ancient Toltec civilization is best known for its fearsome 4.5m-high stone warrior figures. Though less spectacular and far smaller than Teotihuacán, Tula is still an fascinating site and well worth the effort of a day trip. The modern town of Tula de Allende is surrounded by a Pemex refinery and an odoriferous petrochemical plant, but the center is pleasant enough for an overnight stay.

History

Tula was an important city from about AD 900 to 1150, reaching a peak population of 35,000. Aztec annals tell of a king called Topiltzin – fair-skinned, black-bearded and long-haired – who founded a Toltec capital in the 10th century. There's debate, however, about whether Tula was this capital.

The Toltecs were empire-builders upon whom the Aztecs looked with awe, going so far as to claim them as royal ancestors. Topiltzin was supposedly a priest-king, dedicated to peaceful worship (which only included sacrifices of animals) of the feathered serpent god Quetzalcóatl. Tula is known to have housed followers of the less likable Tezcatlipoca (Smoking Mirror), god of warriors, witchcraft, life and death; worshiping Tezcatlipoca required human sacrifices. The story goes that Tezcatlipoca appeared in various guises in order to provoke Topiltzin. As a naked chili-seller, he aroused the lust of Topiltzin's daughter and eventually married her. As an old man, he persuaded the teetotaling Topiltzin to get drunk.

Eventually, the humiliated leader left for the Gulf coast, where he set sail eastward on a raft of snakes, promising one day to return and reclaim his throne. (This caused the Aztec emperor Moctezuma much consternation when Hernán Cortés appeared on the Gulf coast in 1519.) The conventional wisdom is that Topiltzin set up a new Toltec state at Chichén Itzá in Yucatán, while the Tula Toltecs built a brutal, militaristic empire that dominated central Mexico.

Tula was a place of some splendor – the legends speak of palaces of gold, turquoise, jade and quetzal feathers, of enormous corn cobs and colored cotton that grew naturally. Possibly its treasures were looted by the Aztecs or Chichimecs.

In the mid-12th century, the ruler Huémac apparently moved the Toltec capital to Chapultepec after factional fighting at Tula, then committed suicide. Tula was abandoned in the early 13th century, seemingly after a violent destruction by the Chichimecs.

Orientation & Information

The Zona Arqueológica (Archaeological Zone) is 2km north of the center. Tula's principal avenue, Av Zaragoza, links the *zócalo* with the outskirts. Av Hidalgo, the other main drag, has essential services like internet access and ATMs.

Sights

ZONA ARQUEOLÓGICA

The **ruins** (admission M$37; ☉ 9am-5pm) of the main ceremonial center of Tula are perched on a hilltop, with good views over rolling countryside. These make up just a small part of the 16-sq-km site, but are home to the most interesting remnants. It costs M$35 to use a video.

From the main road and now disused guard boxes, it's a 300m walk to the ticket office and the excellent **site museum** (admission included in site ticket) displaying ceramics, metalwork, jewelry and large sculptures.

From here, walk around to the left another 800m through several souvenir markets and you'll reach the center of the ancient city. Explanatory signs at the site are in English, Spanish and Náhuatl.

From the museum, the first large structure you'll reach is the **Juego de Pelota No 1** (Ball Court No 1). Archaeologists believe its walls were decorated with sculpted panels that were removed under Aztec rule.

Also known as the Temple of Quetzalcóatl or Tlahuizcalpantecuhtli (the Morning Star), **Pirámide B** can be scaled via steps on its south side. At the top of the stairway, the remains of

AROUND MEXICO CITY

three columnar roof supports – which once depicted feathered serpents with their heads on the ground and their tails in the air – remain standing. The four basalt warrior telamones at the top and the four pillars behind supported the temple's roof. Wearing headdresses, breastplates shaped like butterflies and short skirts held in place by sun disks, the warriors hold spear-throwers in their right hands and knives and incense bags in their left. The telamon on the left side is a replica of the original, now in Mexico City's Museo Nacional de Antropología (p153). The columns behind the telamones depict crocodile heads (which symbolize the Earth), warriors, symbols of warrior orders, weapons and Quetzalcóatl's head.

On the pyramid's north wall are some of the carvings that once surrounded the structure. These show the symbols of the warrior orders: jaguars, coyotes, eagles eating hearts, and what may be a human head in Quetzalcóatl's mouth.

Now roofless, the **Gran Vestíbulo** (Great Vestibule) extends along the front of the pyramid, facing the plaza. The stone bench carved with warriors originally ran the length of the hall, possibly to seat priests and nobles observing ceremonies in the plaza.

Near the north side of Pirámide B is the **Coatepantli** (Serpent Wall), 40m long, 2.25m high and carved with rows of geometric patterns and a row of snakes devouring human skeletons. Traces remain of the original bright colors with which most of Tula's structures were painted.

Immediately west of Pirámide B, the **Palacio Quemado** (Burnt Palace) is a series of halls and courtyards with more low benches and relief carvings, one depicting a procession of nobles. It was probably used for ceremonies or reunion meetings.

The plaza in front of Pirámide B would have been the scene of religious and military displays. At its center is the *adoratorio* (ceremonial platform). On the east side of the plaza, **Pirámide C** is Tula's biggest structure, and was in the early stages of excavation at the time of writing. To the west is **Juego de Pelota No 2**, central Mexico's largest ball court at more than 100m in length.

On the far side of the plaza is a path leading to the **Sala de Orientación Guadalupe Mastache** (admission free), a small museum named after one of the archaeologists who pioneered excavations here. It includes large items taken from the site, including some huge caryatid feet, and a visual representation of how the site would have looked at its prime.

TOWN CENTER

On Av Zaragoza, Tula's fortress-like **cathedral** was part of the 16th-century monastery of San José. Inside, its vault ribs are picked out in gold. On the library wall opposite the *zócalo* is a colorful **mural** of Tula's history.

Sleeping & Eating

Hotel Casa Blanca (☎ 732-11-86; www.casablancatula .com; Pasaje Hidalgo 11; r from M$330; P 🖳) This pleasant option right in the heart of Tula is actually, contrary to what its name suggests, a pinkish color, and is located at the end of a narrow pedestrian street opposite the restaurant of the same name. The 36 comfortable rooms all have TV, bathroom and free wi-fi. Parking access is around back, via Zaragoza.

Hotel Lizbeth (☎ 732-00-45; www.tulaonline .com/hotellizbeth; Ocampo 200; s/d M$450/495; P 🖳) The Lizbeth is friendly and relaxed, with a motel feel and just moments from the bus station (turn right when you leave). The clean and comfortable rooms, with shared balconies and free wi-fi, are fine, although those with tiled floors smell much better than the carpeted ones.

our pick **Hotel Real Catedral** (☎ 732-08-13; www.tulaonline.com/hotelcatedral; Zaragoza 106; s/d/ste incl breakfast M$550/650/950; P 🖳) Another upmarket addition to Tula's accommodation scene, the Real Catedral is tasteful, central and comfortable. Many of the inside rooms lack natural daylight, though, so it's far more preferable to splash out on one of the lovely suites with small balconies and views onto the street below. There's a great selection of black-and-white photos of Tula in the lobby.

Best Western Tula (☎ 732-45-75; www.bestwestern tula.com; Zaragoza s/n; r M$822; P ✕ 🖳) Opened in 2006, the business-friendly Best Western has 18 stylish, comfortable rooms in the historic center. While it's still a rather bland place, it's small and friendly enough not to feel like an anonymous chain hotel.

Restaurant Casablanca (☎ 732-22-74; Hidalgo 114; mains M$40-110; ⏱ 10am-10pm; 🖳) The best place to eat in town is the friendly, though admittedly rather sterile, restaurant, which has a full traditional Mexican menu as well as a good buffet. It's about the only good option in town, and is just by the cathedral off the *zócalo*.

Getting There & Away

Tula's bus depot is on Xicoténcatl, three blocks downhill from the cathedral. To get to the town center from the main entrance, turn right, then immediately left on Rojo del Río and look for the church steeple atop the hill. First-class Ovnibus buses go to/from Mexico City's Terminal Norte (M$52, 1¾ hours, every 30 to 40 minutes) and to/from Pachuca (M$52, 1¾ hours, hourly). AVM runs 2nd-class buses (M$40) to the same destinations every 15 minutes. Buses to Mexico City can drop you at Caseta Tepotzotlán (M$25) for the town center.

Getting Around

If you arrive in Tula by bus, the easiest way to get to the Zona Arqueológica is to catch a taxi (M$25) outside the depot. From the center, 'Actopan' microbuses (M$6) depart from the corner of Calle 5 de Mayo and Zaragoza, and pass within 100m of the site entrance. Alternatively, all Pachuca-bound buses will also stop outside the site on request.

TEOTIHUACÁN

☎ 594 / elevation 2300m

This complex of awesome pyramids set amid what was once Mesoamerica's greatest city is just 50km northeast of Mexico City and is the region's number-one draw. It's a huge site that compares in significance to the ruins of the Yucatán and Chiapas. Anyone lucky enough to come here will be inspired by the astonishing technological might of the Teotihuacán (teh-oh-tee-wah-*kahn*) civilization.

Set in a mountain-ringed offshoot of the Valle de México, Teotihuacán is known for its two vast pyramids, Pirámide del Sol and Pirámide de la Luna, which dominate the remains of the metropolis. Teotihuacán was Mexico's biggest ancient city and the capital of what was probably Mexico's largest pre-Hispanic empire. (See p47 for an outline of its importance.) Exploring the site is fascinating, although rebutting the indefatigable hawkers can be exhausting and crowds can be huge, especially in the middle of the day. As usual, going early pays off, especially as the midday sun can be unbearable when trying to cover the huge site.

The city's grid plan was plotted in the early part of the 1st century AD, and the Pirámide del Sol was completed – over an earlier cave shrine – by AD 150. The rest of the city was developed between about AD 250 and 600. Social, environmental and economic factors hastened its decline and eventual collapse in the 8th century.

The city was divided into quarters by two great avenues that met near La Ciudadela (the Citadel). One, running roughly north–south, is the famous Calzada de los Muertos (Avenue of the Dead) so called because the later Aztecs believed the great buildings lining it were vast tombs, built by giants for Teotihuacán's first rulers. The major structures are typified by a *talud-tablero* style, in which the rising portions of stepped, pyramid-like buildings consist of both sloping *(talud)* and upright *(tablero)* sections. They were often covered in lime and colorfully painted. Most of the city was made up of residential compounds, some of which contained elegant frescoes.

Centuries after its fall, Teotihuacán remained a pilgrimage site for Aztec royalty, who believed that all of the gods had sacrificed themselves here to start the sun moving at the beginning of the 'fifth world,' inhabited by the Aztecs. It remains an important pilgrimage site: thousands of New Age devotees flock here each year to celebrate the vernal equinox and soak up the mystical energies believed to converge here.

Orientation

Though ancient Teotihuacán covered more than 20 sq km, most of what there is to see today lies along nearly 2km of the Calzada de los Muertos. Buses arrive at a traffic circle by the southwest entrance (Gate 1); four other entrances are reached by the ring road around the site. There are parking lots and ticket booths at each entrance. Your ticket allows you to re-enter via any of them on the same day. The site museum is just inside the main east entrance (Gate 5).

Information

There's an **information booth** (☎ 956-02-76; ✆ 9am-4pm) near the southwest entrance (Gate 1). Free site tours by authorized guides (in Spanish only) may be available here if a sizable group forms.

Crowds at the **ruins** (admission M$45; ✆ 7am-6pm) are thickest from 10am to 2pm, and it is busiest on Sunday, holidays and around the vernal equinox (between March 19 and March 21). Due to the heat and altitude, it's best to take it easy while exploring the expansive ruins. Bring a hat and water – most

AROUND MEXICO CITY

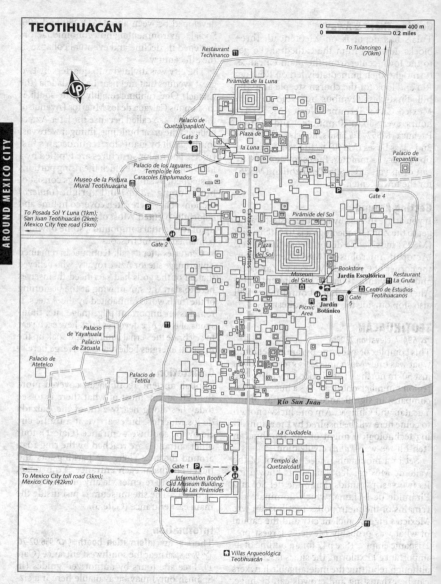

TEOTIHUACÁN

AROUND MEXICO CITY

visitors walk several kilometers, and the midday sun can be brutal. Afternoon rain showers are common from June to September.

Sights

CALZADA DE LOS MUERTOS

Centuries ago, the Avenue of the Dead must have seemed absolutely incomparable to its inhabitants, who were able to see its buildings at their best. Gate 1 brings you to the avenue in front of La Ciudadela. For 2km to the north, the avenue is flanked by former palaces of Teotihuacán's elite and other major structures, such as the Pirámide del Sol. The Pirámide de la Luna looms large at the northern end.

LA CIUDADELA

The expansive, square complex called the Citadel is believed to have been the residence of the city's supreme ruler. Four wide walls, each 390m long and topped by 15 pyramids, enclose a huge open space, of which the main feature, to the east, is a pyramid called the **Templo de Quetzalcóatl**. The temple is flanked by two large complexes of rooms and patios, which may have been the city's administrative center.

The temple's most fascinating feature is the facade of an earlier structure (from around AD 250 to 300 – the temple was built some time in the following century), which was revealed by excavating the more recent pyramid that had been built on the same site. The four surviving steps of this facade (there were originally seven) are adorned with striking carvings. In the *tablero* panels, the sharp-fanged feathered serpent deity, its head emerging from a necklace of 11 petals, alternates with a four-eyed, two-fanged creature often identified as the rain god Tláloc, but perhaps more authoritatively considered to be the fire serpent, bearer of the sun on its daily journey across the sky. On the *talud* panels are side views of the plumed serpent.

MUSEO DEL SITIO

Continuing north along Calzada de los Muertos across the river toward the pyramids, a path to the right leads to the **site museum** (☎ 958-20-81; admission incl with site ticket; 🕒 7am-6pm), just south of the Pirámide del Sol. It's a refreshing stop midway through a site visit. Nearby are the **Jardín Escultórica** (a lovely sculpture garden with Teotihuacán artifacts), the **Jardín Botánico** (Botanic Garden), public toilets, a snack bar, picnic tables and a bookstore.

The museum is divided thematically, with explanations in English and Spanish. There are excellent displays of artifacts, fresco panels and an impressive large-scale model of the city set under a transparent walkway, from where the real Pirámide del Sol can be viewed through a wall-size window.

CENTRO DE ESTUDIOS TEOTIHUACANOS

Situated just outside Gate 5, this research center is home to the interesting **Museo Manuel Gamio** (☎ 965-15-99; admission free; 🕒 7am-4pm Mon-Fri, 9am-4pm Sat & Sun), sponsored by the Instituto de Antropología e Historia (INAH), which presents bimonthly cultural exhibitions, and has a permanent exhibition exploring the history of pulque, complete with a full-scale replica of a traditional *pulquería*, an elite establishment where nobles would ritually drink pulque, an alcoholic extract of the maguey plant.

PIRÁMIDE DEL SOL

The world's third-largest pyramid, surpassed in size only by Egypt's Cheops and the pyramid of Cholula (p227), overshadows the east side of Calzada de los Muertos. The base is 222m long on each side, and it's now just over 70m high. The pyramid was cobbled together around AD 100, from three million tons of stone, without the use of metal tools, pack animals or the wheel.

The Aztec belief that the structure was dedicated to the sun god was validated in 1971, when archaeologists uncovered a 100m-long underground tunnel leading from the pyramid's west flank to a cave directly beneath its center, where they found religious artifacts. It's thought that the sun was worshiped here before the pyramid was built and that the city's ancient inhabitants traced the origins of life to this grotto.

At Teotihuacán's height, the pyramid's plaster was painted bright red, which must have been a radiant sight at sunset. Clamber up the pyramid's 248 steps – yes, we counted – for an inspiring overview of the ancient city.

PALACIO DE TEPANTITLA

This priest's residence, 500m northeast of Pirámide del Sol, is home to Teotihuacán's most famous fresco, the worn **Paradise of Tláloc**. The mural flanks a doorway in a covered patio, in the building's northeast corner. The rain god Tláloc, attended by priests, is shown on both sides. To the right of the door appears his paradise, a garden-like Eden with people, animals and fish swimming in a mountain-fed river. To the left of the door, tiny human figures are engaged in a unique ball game. Frescoes in other rooms show priests with feather headdresses.

PIRÁMIDE DE LA LUNA

The Pyramid of the Moon, at the north end of Calzada de los Muertos, is smaller than Pirámide del Sol, but it's more gracefully proportioned – far more aesthetically pleasing and not nearly as hulkish. Completed around

AD 300, its summit is nearly the same height, because it's built on higher ground.

The Plaza de la Luna, located just in front of the pyramid, is a handsome arrangement of 12 temple platforms. Some experts attribute astronomical symbolism to the total number of 13 (made up of the 12 platforms plus the pyramid), a key number in the day-counting system of the Mesoamerican ritual calendar. The altar in the plaza's center is thought to have played host to religious dancing.

PALACIO DE QUETZALPAPÁLOTL

Off the Plaza de la Luna's southwest corner is the Palace of the Quetzal Butterfly, reckoned to be the home of a high priest. A flight of steps leads up to a roofed portico with an abstract mural, and nearby a well-restored patio has columns carved with images of the quetzal bird or a hybrid quetzal butterfly.

The **Palacio de los Jaguares** (Jaguar Palace) and **Templo de los Caracoles Emplumados** (Temple of the Plumed Conch Shells) are behind and below the Palacio de Quetzalpapálotl. The lower walls of several chambers off the patio of the Jaguar Palace display parts of murals showing the jaguar god in feathered headdresses, blowing conch shells and apparently praying to the rain god Tláloc.

The Temple of the Plumed Conch Shells, entered from the Palacio de los Jaguares' patio, is a now-subterranean structure of the 2nd or 3rd century AD. Carvings on what was its facade show large shells – possibly used as musical instruments – decorated with feathers and four-petal flowers. The base on which the facade stands has a rainbow-colored mural of birds with water streaming from their beaks.

MUSEO DE LA PINTURA MURAL TEOTIHUACANA

On the ring road between Gates 2 and 3, this impressive **museum** (☎ 958-20-81; admission incl with site ticket; ☺ 9am-6pm) showcases murals from Teotihuacán, as well as reconstructions of murals you'll see at the ruins. Explanations of the exhibits are in Spanish only, but it's definitely worth a stop. Parking costs M$2.

PALACIO DE TETITLA & PALACIO DE ATETELCO

Another group of palaces lies west of the site's main area, several hundred meters northwest of Gate 1. Many of the murals, discovered in the 1940s, are well preserved

or restored, and perfectly intelligible. Inside the sprawling Tetitla Palace, no fewer than 120 walls are graced by murals, with Tláloc, jaguars, serpents and eagles among the easiest figures to make out. Some 400m west is the Atetelco Palace, whose vivid jaguar or coyote murals – a mixture of originals and restorations – are in the Patio Blanco (White Patio) in the northwest corner. Processions of these creatures in shades of red perhaps symbolize warrior orders.

About 100m further northeast are Zacuala and Yayahuala, a pair of enormous walled compounds that probably served as communal living quarters. Separated by the original alleyways, the two structures are made up of numerous rooms and patios, but few entranceways.

Sleeping

The uninteresting town of San Juan Teotihuacán, 2km south of the archaeological zone, has a few good overnight options, which make sense if you want to start early at the site before the crowds arrive. However, if you're looking for a romantic weekend away, head for the pricier accommodation at the site itself.

Teotihuacán Trailer Park (☎ 956-03-13; teotipark@ prodigy.net.mx; López Mateos 17, San Juan Teotihuacán; campsites per person M$60, campers per person M$75; ⓟ ▣) Pitch a tent in town, on a peaceful street behind the 16th-century Jesuit church, a couple of blocks southwest of the plaza and bus depot. The large park has 24/7 hot showers and helpful, English-speaking owners.

Hotel Posada Teotihuacán (☎ 956-04-60; Canteroco 5, San Juan Teotihuacán; s/d/t M$142/213/282; ⓟ) Despite looking like a bomb has hit it from the outside, the rooms at this centrally located posada are fine, smallish but clean. All rooms have TV and bathroom, and it's the cheapest hotel option around.

Hotel Posada Sol y Luna (☎ 956-23-68/71; www .posadasolyluna.com; Cantú 13, San Juan Teotihuacán; r/ste from M$330/450; ⓟ) This well-run place has 16 fine though unexciting and rather sterile rooms, all with TV and ensuite bathroom. Junior suites have rather ancient Jacuzzis in them – not worth paying extra for unless you have rheumatism. It's at the east end of town, en route to the pyramids. Also a good place to get breakfast (from M$60) for guests and non-guests alike.

Hotel & Motel Quinto Sol (☎ 956-18-81; www.hotel quintosol.com.mx; Av Hidalgo 26, San Juan Teotihuacán; s/d/t from M$670/815/949; ℗ 💻 🐾) Admittedly this is where most tourist groups stay and it's not exactly a boutique place, but the Quinto Sol is still the most comfortable option in town, with its excellent facilities including a decent-size pool and large, well-appointed rooms.

Villa Arqueológica Teotihuacán (☎ 55-5836-9020; www.teotihuacaninfo.com; r Sun-Thu/Fri & Sat M$875/1000; 💻 ℗ 🐾) By far the best option in the area is this Club Med–run complex just outside the site grounds. While it's not cheap, the place has plenty of charm and the rooms are all cozy, clean and well furnished. Amenities include a heated outdoor pool, a lit tennis court, a playground, a billiards table, nice gardens and a refined French–Mexican bar-restaurant. A couple of one-bedroom suites have in-room whirlpools.

Eating

If you're going to eat on the site, it's usually a pricey and not particularly enjoyable experience. You're far better off bringing a picnic, although there are a few okay options to look out for. The most convenient place is on the 3rd floor of the old museum building near Gate 1, where the busy Bar–Cafetería Las Pirámides provides panoramic views of La Ciudadela.

Restaurant Techinanco (☎ 958-23-06; Teotihuacán ring road; mains M$30-70; ☼ 10am-5pm) The interior won't blow you away and it's a fair walk from Gate 3 behind the Pirámide de la Luna, but this offers up excellent home cooking at reasonable prices. The small menu takes in local favorites from *tacos fritos* to enchiladas, authentic homemade *moles* and other flavorful traditional dishes. Ask the ebullient owner, Emma (nicknamed Maya), about her curative massage (from M$30); call 24 hours in advance to arrange a temascal (indigenous Mexican steam bath) for up to 15 people (around M$300 to M$500).

Restaurant La Gruta (☎ 956-01- 04/27; mains M$200; ☼ 11am-6pm) This deeply odd restaurant has quite the strangest setting of any in Mexico: a vast, subterranean, dank cave just a short distance from Gate 5 (don't be put off by the sign on the path that says it's 500m away; it's a misprint). It's aimed squarely at tourist parties, and while the food is very good, it's pricey too – and served in a subterranean, dank cave. On Saturday and Sunday after-

noons, there's live music and folkloric ballet (cover M$30). As you'd expect, all major credit cards are accepted.

Getting There & Away

During daylight hours, Autobuses México-San Juan Teotihuacán runs buses from Mexico City's Terminal Norte to the ruins (M$28, one hour) every 15 minutes from 7am to 6pm. When entering the Terminal Norte, turn left and walk to the second-last desk on the concourse. Make sure your bus is headed for 'Los Pirámides,' not the nearby town of San Juan Teotihuacán.

Buses arrive and depart from near Gate 1, also making stops at Gates 2 and 3. Return buses are more frequent after 1pm. The last bus back to Mexico City leaves at 6pm; some terminate at Indios Verdes metro station, but most continue to Terminal Norte.

Getting Around

To reach the pyramids from San Juan Teotihuacán, take a taxi (M$1.50) or any combi (M$6) labeled 'San Martín' departing from Av Hidalgo, beside the central plaza. Combis returning to San Juan stop at Gates 1, 2 and 3.

PACHUCA

☎ 771 / pop 320,000 / elevation 2425m

Scattered over a collection of steep, wide hills and crowned with a vast Mexican flag and an even higher statue of Christ, Pachuca is the unassuming capital of Hidalgo state. The charming, brightly painted town center is visible for miles around, although growth in recent years has sadly led to far-from-lovely urban sprawl developing beyond the candy-box houses of the old town.

Useful as a staging post for trips north and east into the dramatic Sierra Madre Oriental, Pachuca is a pleasant enough place to while away a few hours. Silver was unearthed nearby as early as 1534, and Real del Monte's mines still produce quite a respectable amount of ore. Pachuca was also the gateway through which *fútbol* (soccer) entered Mexico, introduced in the 19th century by miners from Cornwall, England. The Cornish population also gave the town its signature dish, meat pastries known as *pastes* (and recognizable to any Brit as a Cornish pastie, albeit with some typically Mexican fillings).

Orientation

The 40m-high Reloj Monumental (Clock Tower), built between 1904 and 1910 to commemorate the independence centennial, overshadows the north end of Pachuca's *zócalo*, Plaza de la Independencia, which is flanked by Av Matamoros on the east and Av Allende on the west. Guerrero runs parallel to Av Allende, 100m to the west. Some 700m to the south, Guerrero and Av Matamoros converge at the modern Plaza Juárez.

Information

ATMs are numerous around Plaza de la Independencia.

Internet (409 Matamoros; per hr M$10; ☉ 9am-10pm) Facing the revolutionary monument in the small park 100m south of the *zócalo*.

Tourist Module (☎ 715-14-11; www.pachuca.gob.mx; Plaza de la Independencia; ☉ 10am-6pm) Inside the clock tower; may have free city maps.

Sights

CENTRO CULTURAL DE HIDALGO

This handsome, sprawling **cultural center** (cnr Hidalgo & Arista; admission free; ☉ 10am-6pm Tue-Sun) is an oasis of calm at Pachuca's bustling heart. Formerly the Convento de San Francisco, the complex incudes two museums and a gallery, a theater, a library and several lovely plazas. It's worth looking into the impressive (and still functioning) Parroquia de San Francisco as well. It's two blocks east and four long blocks south of Plaza Juárez. The highlight of the complex is the excellent **Museo Nacional de la Fotografía** (admission free; ☉ 10am-6pm Tue-Sun), which displays early imaging technology and selections from the 1.5 million photos in the INAH archives. The images – some by Europeans and Americans, many more by pioneer Mexican photojournalist Agustín Victor Casasola – provide fascinating glimpses of Mexico from 1873 to the present.

MUSEO DE MINERÍA

Two blocks south and half a block east of the *zócalo*, Pachuca's **mining museum** (Mina 110; adult/student M$15/10; ☉ 10am-2pm & 3-6pm Wed-Sun) provides a good overview of the industry that shaped the region. Headlamps, miners' shrines and old mining maps are on display, and photos depict conditions in the shafts from the early years to the present. There's a 20-minute English-language video program, and engaging ex-miners give tours hourly in Spanish.

LOOKOUT POINTS

For jaw-dropping vistas, catch a 'Mirador' bus (M$6) from Plaza de la Constitución, a few blocks northeast of the *zócalo*, to the **mirador** on the road to Real del Monte. Even better panoramas can be seen from north of town, at the **Cristo Rey monument** on Cerro de Santa Apolonia. A cab (M$30) from town is the best way to get here, or it's a steep 30-minute walk.

Tours

Trolley tours run by **Tranvía Turistico** (☎ 718-71-20; per person M$45) depart hourly between 3pm and 6pm from the plaza's west side from Wednesday to Sunday. Guided 4½-hour trips to Real de Monte leave at noon on Saturday and Sunday.

Sleeping

Hotel Noriega (☎ 715-15-55; Av Matamoros 305; s/d M$200/245; P) The Noriega feels like it's a set for a spy movie; its large courtyard lobby oozes atmosphere. Rooms are total potluck, though, so have a look at a few rooms before checking in. Some are tiny and claustrophobic, while others are large and airy. TV is M$20 extra, or you can watch *lucha libre* (wrestling) in the courtyard with the staff.

Hotel de los Baños (☎ 713-07-00, fax 715-14-41; Av Matamoros 205; s/d M$235/295; P) With its beautifully tiled old-world lobby stuffed with antiques, the Baños is certainly one of Pachuca's most striking places to put up. The 56 rooms are fairly crummy, with old fittings and a lack of natural light, although some are much better than others and all have cable TV, phones and clean bathrooms. Parking is an extra M$30. It's a block southeast of the *zócalo*.

Hotel America (☎ 715-00-55; Victoria 203; r M$250) The best budget deal in town, the America is in a charming, quiet courtyard stuffed with plants and flowers and painted orange. Rooms are spacious and clean with small ensuite bathroom and TV.

Gran Hotel Independencia (☎ 715-05-15, www.granhotelindpendencia.com; Plaza Independencia 116; s/d M$420/460; P) Set around a charming yellow-painted courtyard, its railings bedecked with plants and flowerpots, the Gran Independencia is central but surprisingly quiet. Rooms overlooking the square are louder but have good views. All rooms are large and fitted out with ensuite bathroom and TV.

Hotel Emily (☎ 715-08-28, 800-501-63-39; www.hotelemily.com.mx; Plaza Independencia; s/d/ste M$500/550/720;

P X 🖳) This is the town's smartest hotel, stylishly set out (albeit with some horrendous lobby furniture) on the south side of the *zócalo*. Rooms are very decent, with TVs, temperamental wi-fi and balconies. There's also a good restaurant, room service and English-speaking staff.

Eating

Pastes are available all over town, including at the bus station. Baked in pizza ovens, they contain a variety of fillings probably never imagined by Cornish miners, such as beans, pineapple and rice pudding. Especially popular is Pastes Kiko's, with its main branch next to Gran Hotel Independencia and several others throughout the town.

Mi Antiguo Café (Matamoros 115; breakfasts M$45-80) A friendly place to drink coffee with the locals, this busy café on the eastern side of the *zócalo* serves crepes, good espresso, breakfasts and a decent set lunch (M$60).

Reforma (Matamoros 111; mains M$70-110) Despite looking like a grand old-world place from the street, inside Reforma is as relaxed as can be and does a mean *huevos rancheros* at breakfast time. Just avoid the dreadful coffee.

Mina La Blanca Restaurant Bar (☎ 715-19-64; Av Matamoros 201; mains M$45-125) Pachuca's most famous eatery, this pastie specialist is the most atmospheric and friendly in town. *Pastes* here come with a variety of delicious fillings, but set breakfasts, salads and seasonal regional *antojitos* are also on the menu. This is also the best place to come for a drink in the evening.

Getting There & Away

There's a 1st-class bus service to/from Terminal Norte in Mexico City (M$56, 1¼ hours, every 15 minutes), Poza Rica (M$112, five hours, six daily) and Tampico (M$264, eight hours, two daily).

Three scenic roads (Hwys 85, 105 and 130/132D) climb into the forested, often foggy, Sierra Madre Oriental. Buses serving nearby destinations, nearly all of which are 2nd-class, go frequently to and from Tula, Tulancingo and Tamazunchale, while several also go daily to and from Querétaro and Huejutla de Reyes.

Getting Around

Pachuca's bus station is 5km southwest of downtown, on the road to Mexico City. Green-striped *colectivos* marked 'Centro'

pass by Plaza de la Constitución (M$6), a short walk from the *zócalo*; in the reverse direction, hop on along Av Allende. The trip by taxi costs around M$30.

AROUND PACHUCA
Parque Nacional El Chico
☎ 771

An easy and very lovely day trip from Pachuca takes you to the charming old mining village **Mineral del Chico**, located inside El Chico National Park – a reserve since 1898. The views here are wonderful, the air is fresh and the mountains have some great hiking, spectacular rock formations and beautiful waterfalls, making this a popular weekend retreat. Ask at the local hotels or the park's visitor centers for details about possible guided outdoor activities.

SLEEPING & EATING

Mineral del Chico is very much a weekender place and can feel like a ghost town during the week. However, rates are lower at hotels that are open and you'll have the surrounding woods almost entirely to yourself.

Hospedaje El Chico (☎ 715-47-41; Corona del Rosal 1; r M$350) Located just up the hill from the bus stop, this small, 10-room homestay is the best budget option, with clean if unexciting rooms all with ensuite facilities. Larger master bedrooms cost an extra M$200.

Hotel Posada del Amanecer (☎ 715-01-90; www .hotelesecoturisticos.com.mx; Morelos 3; r Sun-Thu M$450, Fri & Sat M$600) This 11-room adobe complex has spacious rooms on two levels beside a lovely patio. With no phones or TVs, it's a peaceful getaway. Rooms with fireplaces cost M$100 extra, and full Mexican meal plans are available. Children under 12 stay free. Low-season rates are 25% less, and all rates include guided hiking and cycling tours. Massage, spa treatments and adventure activities like rock climbing are offered for an extra fee.

Hotel El Paraíso (☎ 715-56-56; www.hotelesecoturist icos.com.mx; r Sun-Thu from M$800, Fri & Sat from M$950; P 🖳) Nestled inside large, well-maintained grounds at the base of the mountain, with a fast-flowing stream running nearby, El Paraíso certainly has a location worthy of its name. The large, modern rooms lack individuality or any great charm, but they're very comfortable and the hotel is the best in town.

There are several **campgrounds** (per car/campsite M$30) with rudimentary facilities en route to Mineral del Chico between Km 7 and Km 10, plus a **trailer park** (RV hookups M$100) just inside the park's main entrance gate.

GETTING THERE & AWAY

From Pachuca, blue-and-white *colectivos* to Minerl del Chico (M$10) depart every 20 minutes from 8am to 6pm from Calle Hidalgo outside the Mercado Juárez (not to be confused with the market on Guerro) on the corner of Avenida de la Raza.

Mineral del Monte

Two kilometers past the Hwy 105 turnoff for Parque Nacional El Chico, **Real del Monte** (officially known as Mineral del Monte) was the scene of a miners' strike in 1776 – commemorated as the first strike in the Americas. Most of the town was settled in the 19th century, after a British company commandeered the mines. Cornish-style cottages line many of the steep cobbled streets.

Mine tours (☎ 771-715-27-63; adult/child M$140/100) descend 250m into some abandoned workings at weekends. The field opposite the Dolores mine was the site of Mexico's first soccer match; there's an English cemetery nearby.

The best place to stay is the charming and traditional 15-room **Hotel Real del Monte** (☎ 717-797-12-02/03; www.hotelesecoturisticos.com.mx; r Sun-Thu from M$450, Fri & Sat from M$600; P 🖵), run by the same high-standard company as the two main hotels in Mineral del Chico.

Second-class buses depart Pachuca's terminal for Mineral del Monte (M$9, 30 minutes, hourly) as well as *colectivos* (M$7, 30 minutes, every 30 minutes) from the northwest corner of Plaza de la Constitutión, north of the *zócalo*.

EAST OF MEXICO CITY

The views get seriously dramatic as you head east from the capital, the landscape peppered with the incredible peaks of Popocatépetl, Iztaccíhuatl and La Malinche rising up to create perfect snow-capped volcanoes visible for miles around. The rugged Sierra Nevada offers scope for anything from invigorating alpine strolls to demanding technical climbs. Unpredictable Popocatépetl, however, remains off limits due to volcanic activity.

The gorgeous colonial city of Puebla, Mexico's fifth largest, is the dominant regional center, a local transportation hub and a big tourist draw for its cathedral, culinary attractions and well-preserved history. The surrounding state of Puebla is predominantly rural, and home to approximately half a million indigenous people. This enduring presence lends Puebla a rich handicraft legacy, with products including pottery, carved onyx and fine handwoven and embroidered textiles.

Other towns in the region include Tlaxcala, the charming capital of the tiny state of same name, similarly famed for its rich pre-Hispanic and colonial history, and far-flung Cuetzalan, a real treat for anyone with their own transportation wanting to explore a charming, time-forgotten village amid beautiful and dramatic scenery.

PUEBLA

☎ 222 / pop 1.5 million / elevation 2160m

A bastion of conservatism, Catholicism and tradition, Puebla can sometimes feel as if the colonial era in Mexico never quite ended. For the most part this is a positive thing, giving Puebla its fantastic colonial center, a stunning cathedral and a wealth of beautiful churches, although it also contributes to the (quite unfair) Mexican stereotype of the criollo *poblanos* being snobbish and aloof.

The city is well worth a visit, with 70 churches in the historic center alone, more than a thousand colonial buildings adorned with the *azulejos* (painted ceramic tiles) for which the city is famous, and a long culinary history that can be explored in any restaurant or food stall.

A great deal of conservation and restoration has taken place in the Centro Histórico in the wake of the 1999 earthquake, which measured 6.9 on the Richter scale. For a city of its size, Puebla is far more relaxed and less gridlocked than you might expect. Its charming architecture and well-preserved colonial imprint in no way make the city feel like a museum piece, and part of its attraction is that it's so clearly a thriving city yet it still takes great pride in its past.

History

Founded by Spanish settlers in 1531, as Ciudad de los Ángeles, with the aim of sur-

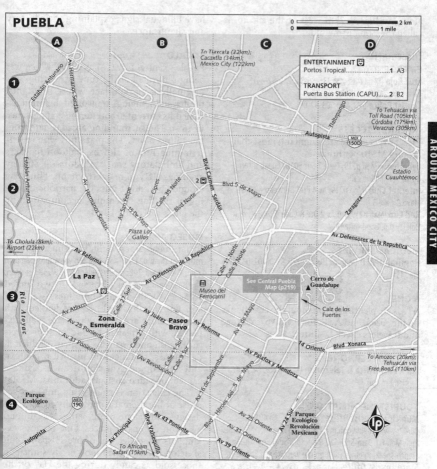

PUEBLA

ENTERTAINMENT 🎭
Portos Tropical......................1 A3

TRANSPORT
Puerta Bus Station (CAPU).....2 B2

See Central Puebla Map (p219)

AROUND MEXICO CITY

passing the nearby pre-Hispanic religious center of Cholula, the city became known as Puebla de los Ángeles ('La Angelópolis') eight years later, and quickly grew into an important Catholic center. Fine pottery had long been crafted from the local clay, and after the colonists introduced new materials and techniques, Puebla pottery evolved as both an art and an industry. By the late 18th century, the city emerged a major producer of glass and textiles. With 50,000 residents by 1811, Puebla remained Mexico's second-biggest city until Guadalajara overtook it in the late 19th century.

General Ignacio de Zaragoza fortified the Cerro de Guadalupe against the French invaders, and on May 5, 1862, his 2000 men defeated a frontal attack by 6000, many handicapped by diarrhea. This rare Mexican military success is the excuse for annual (and increasingly corporate-sponsored and drunken) national celebrations and hundreds of streets named 5 de Mayo. Few seem to remember that the following year the reinforced French took Puebla and occupied the city until 1867. *Touché!*

Orientation

Modern Puebla is still centered on the old town, the center of which is the large, leafy *zócalo,* with the cathedral flanking its south side. Most attractions, hotels and restaurants are within a few blocks of here. The upscale area of smart shops and refined restaurants along Av Juárez, 2km west of the *zócalo*, is called the Zona Esmeralda.

Information

EMERGENCY

Cruz Roja (Red Cross; ☎ 235-86-31, 235-82-44)
Fire (☎ 245-73-92/77-99)
Tourist Police (☎ 800-903-92-00)

INTERNET ACCESS

Places to get online are abundant; most charge around M$10 per hour.
Cyberbyte (Map p219; Calle 2 Sur 505B) Cheap international VoIP phone calls.
Internet Club (Map p219; Av 4 Pte) Between Av 5 de Mayo & Calle 3 Nte.
Red Cup (Map p219; cnr Av 2 Ote & Calle 4 Nte) Next to Holiday Inn. Good coffee.

MEDICAL SERVICES

Hospital UPAEP (Map p219; ☎ 229-81-00/02/03; Av 5 Pte 715)

MONEY

ATMs are plentiful throughout the city. Banks on the *zócalo* and Av Reforma have exchange and travelers check facilities.

POST & TELEPHONE

Main Post Office & Telecomm (Map p219; Av 16 de Septiembre s/n)

TOURIST INFORMATION

Municipal Tourist Office (Map p219; ☎ 404-50-08/47; www.puebla.gob.mx; Portal Hidalgo 14; ☻ 9am-8pm Mon-Fri, 9am-5pm Sat, 9am-3pm Sun) English- and French-speaking office (though the website's in Spanish).
State Tourist Office (Map p219; ☎ 246-20-44; Av 5 Ote 3; ☻ 8am-8pm Mon-Sat, 8am-2pm Sun) Faces the cathedral yard. English-speaking staff.

Sights

CATEDRAL

Puebla's superbly impressive **cathedral** (Map p219; cnr Avs 3 Ote & 16 de Septiembre; ☻ 10.30-12:30pm & 4-6pm Mon-Sat), which appears on Mexico's M$500 bill, occupies the entire block south of the *zócalo*. Its architecture is a blend of severe Herreresque-renaissance and early baroque styles. Construction began in 1550 but most of it took place under Bishop Juan de Palafox in the 1640s. At 69m, the towers are Mexico's highest. The dazzling interior, the frescoes and the elaborately decorated side chapels are all awesome, and most

have bilingual signs explaining their history and significance.

ZÓCALO

Puebla's central plaza (Map p219), which was being renovated at the time of writing, was originally a marketplace where bullfights, theater and hangings transpired, before it assumed its current arboretum-like appearance in 1854. The surrounding arcades date from the 16th century. The plaza fills with an entertaining mix of clowns, balloon hawkers and ambulatory snack vendors on Sunday evenings. If you're in town on Thursday around 6pm, don't miss the patriotic changing of the flag ceremony, accompanied by the city's marching band.

MUSEO AMPARO

By far Puebla's best sight, this superb private **museum** (Map p219; ☎ 229-38-50; www.museoamparo.com; Calle 2 Sur 708; adult/student M$35/25, free Mon; ☻ 10am-6pm Wed-Mon), housed in two linked 16th- and 17th-colonial buildings, is a must-see. The first has eight rooms loaded with pre-Hispanic artifacts, which are well displayed, with explanatory information sheets (in English and Spanish) of their production techniques, regional and historical context, and anthropological significance. Using a camera or video costs an additional M$50.

The collection is staggering, not least because of the thematic continuity in Mexican design – the same motifs appear again and again on dozens of pieces. One obvious example is the collection of pre-Hispanic cult skeleton heads, which look eerily similar to those sold as candy during the Day of the Dead celebrations.

Crossing to the second building, you enter a series of rooms rich with the finest colonial art and furnishings from all over Mexico. This building contains many religious artifacts important to everyday colonial life and a fascinating colonial-era kitchen.

An audioguide (rental M$10 plus a M$10 deposit) delivers details about the pre-Hispanic area in Spanish, English, French, German and Japanese. Two-hour guided group tours are offered in English (M$180) by request, and free two-hour tours in Spanish are given at noon on Sunday. The complex also houses a library, good bookstore, café with set lunches (M$45) and an upmarket Talavera gift shop.

CENTRAL PUEBLA

INFORMATION
Banamex (ATM)	1 C3
Banamex (ATM)	2 C3
Bancomer (ATM)	(see 2)
Banorte (ATM)	(see 6)
Cyberbyte	3 C4
Hospital UPAEP	4 B3
HSBC (ATM)	5 D4
HSBC (ATM)	6 D4
Internet Club	7 D3
Main Post Office & Telecomm	8 C4
Municipal Tourist Office	9 D3
Red Cup	10 D3
Scotiabank Inverlat (ATM)	11 C3
State Tourist Office	12 C4

SIGHTS & ACTIVITIES
Biblioteca Palafoxiana	(see 13)
Casa de la Cultura	13 D4
Catedral	14 D3
Iglesia de la Compañía	15 D4
Museo Amparo	16 D4
Museo Bello	17 C3
Museo Casa del Alfeñique	18 E3
Museo de Arte Popular Poblano	19 D2
Museo de la Revolución	20 D2
Museo del Ferrocarril	21 B1
Museo Poblano de Arte Virreinal	22 D3
Templo de San Francisco	23 E3
Templo de Santo Domingo	24 D3
Zócalo	25 D3

SLEEPING
Casa de la Palma	26 D4
Casona de la China Poblana	27 D3
El Sueño Hotel & Spa	(see 41)
Gilfer Hotel	28 D3
Gran Hotel San Agustín	29 B3
Holiday Inn Puebla Centro Histórico	30 D4
Hostal Santa María	31 D4
Hostal Santo Domingo	32 C2
Hotel Colonial	33 D4
Hotel Imperial	34 D3
Hotel Mesón de San Sebastián	(see 41)
Hotel Palace	35 D3
Hotel Posada San Pedro	36 D3
Hotel Provincia Express	37 C3
Hotel Puebla Plaza	38 B2
Hotel Reforma 2000	39 B2
Hotel Royalty	40 D3
Mesón Sacristía de Capuchinas	41 C4
Mesón Sacristía de la Compañía	42 D4
NH Puebla	43 D4
Posada de los Ángeles	44 C3

EATING 🍴
All Day Cafe	45 D4
Amalfi Pizza	46 D4
Fonda de Santa Clara	47 C3
Fonda de Santa Clara Main Branch	48 B2
Fonda La Mexicana	49 C4
La Poblana	50 C3
La Matraca	51 C4
La Zanahoria	52 D4
Las Brujas	53 D4
Restaurant Royalty	(see 40)
Restaurant Sacristía	(see 42)
Tacos Tony	54 C3
Vittorio's	55 D3

DRINKING 🍸
| La Bella | 56 D4 |

ENTERTAINMENT 🎭
La Batalla	57 D4
La Bella Época/La Proaadita	58 D4
La Boveda	(see 56)
Librería Cafetería Teorema	59 C2

SHOPPING 🛍
Barrio de Analco	60 E4
El Parián Crafts Market	61 E3
Plazuela de los Sapos (Antiques Market)	62 D4
Talavera Uriarte	63 B2

TRANSPORT
Buses to Africam Safari	64 D3
CAPU to Cerro de Guadalupe & CAPU	65 E4
Colectivos to CAPU	66 B2
Colectivos to Cholula	67 B1
Ticketbus	68 E4

500 m
0.3 miles

TEMPLO DE SANTO DOMINGO
This fine Dominican **church** (Map p219; cnr Av 5 de Mayo & Av 4 Pte; admission free; ☿ closed 1-4pm Mon-Sat) features a stunning **Capilla del Rosario** (Rosary Chapel), south of the main altar, which is the main reason to come here. Built between 1650 and 1690, it has a sumptuous baroque proliferation of gilded plaster and carved stone, with angels and cherubim seemingly materializing from behind every leaf. See if you can spot the heavenly orchestra.

MUSEO POBLANO DE ARTE VIRREINAL
Opened in 1999, this top-notch **museum** (Map p219; ☎ 246-58-58; Calle 4 Nte 203; adult/student M$15/10, free Tue; ☿ 10am-5pm Tue-Sun) is housed in the 16th-century Hospital de San Pedro. One gallery displays temporary exhibits on the art of the viceregal period (16th to 19th centuries); another has temporary exhibits of contemporary Mexican art; and the last houses a fascinating permanent exhibit on the hospital's history, including a fine model of the building. The excellent library and bookstore have many art and architecture books in English.

CASA DE LA CULTURA
Occupying the entire block facing the south side of the cathedral, the former bishop's palace is a classic 17th-century brick-and-tile edifice, which now houses government offices, the **Casa de la Cultura** (Map p219; ☎ 232-12-27; Av 5 Ote 5; ☿ 10am-8pm) and the State Tourist Office (p218). Inside are art galleries, a bookstore and cinema, and a congenial café out back in the courtyard.

Upstairs is the **Biblioteca Palafoxiana** (☎ 246-56-13; www.bpm.gob.mx; adult/child M$10/5, Tue free; ☿ 10am-5pm Tue-Fri, 10am-4pm Sat & Sun), housing thousands of rare books, including the 1493 *Nuremberg Chronicle*, with more than 2000 engravings.

IGLESIA DE LA COMPAÑÍA
This **Jesuit church** (Map p219; cnr Av Palafox y Mendoza & Calle 4 Sur) with a 1767 Churrigueresque facade is also called Espíritu Santo. Beneath the altar is a tomb said to be that of a 17th-century Asian princess, who was sold into slavery in Mexico and later freed. She was supposedly responsible for the colorful *china poblana* costume – a shawl, frilled blouse, embroidered skirt, and gold and silver adornments. This costume became a kind of 'peasant chic' in the 19th century. But *china* (*chee*-nah) also meant 'maidservant,' and the style may have evolved from Spanish peasant costumes.

Next door is the 16th-century **Edificio Carolino**, now the main building of Universidad Autónoma de Puebla.

MUSEO DEL FERROCARRIL
This excellent **railway museum** (Map p219; 11 Norte 1005; admission free; ☿ 10am-6pm Tue-Sun) is housed in what was once Puebla's train station and the spacious grounds surrounding it. While the station building itself was being refurbished at the time of writing, the grounds are crammed full of defunct Mexican rolling stock, from ancient steam-powered monsters to relatively recent passenger carriages. You can go inside many of them, and one carriage contains an excellent collection of photos of various derailments and other disasters that occurred during the 1920s and '30s.

TEMPLO DE SAN FRANCISCO
The north doorway of this **church** (Map p219; Av 14 Ote; ☿ 8am-8pm) is a good example of 16th-century plateresque; the tower and fine brick-and-tile facade were added in the 18th century. In the north chapel is the mummified body of San Sebastián de Aparicio, a Spaniard who migrated to Mexico in 1533, and planned many of the country's roads before becoming a monk. Since he's now the patron saint of drivers, merchants and farm workers, his canonized corpse attracts a dutiful stream of thankful worshipers.

MUSEO DE LA REVOLUCIÓN
This pockmarked 19th-century **house** (Map p219; ☎ 242-10-76; Av 6 Ote 206; adult/student M$15/10, free Tue; ☿ 10am-4:30pm Tue-Sun) was the scene of the first battle of the 1910 Revolution. Betrayed only two days before a planned uprising against the dictatorship of Porfirio Díaz, the Serdán family (Aquiles, Máximo, Carmen and Natalia) and 17 others fought 500 soldiers until only Aquiles, their leader, and Carmen were left alive. Aquiles, hidden under the floorboards, might have survived if the damp hadn't provoked a cough that gave him away. Both were subsequently killed. The house retains its bullet holes and some revolutionary memorabilia, including a room dedicated to female insurgents. Tours are available in English, German and Spanish.

AROUND MEXICO CITY

MUSEO DE ARTE POPULAR POBLANO

Housed in the 17th-century Ex-Convento de Santa Rosa, this **museum** (Map p219; ☎ 232-77-92; enter at Calle 3 Norte 1203; adult/child M$15/10, free Tue; ☻ 10am-5pm Tue-Sun) is home to an extensive collection of Puebla state handicrafts. You must join one of the hourly guided tours (last one at 4pm) to see the fine displays of traditional indigenous costumes, pottery, onyx, glass and metal work. Tours are in Spanish, but there are occasionally English-speaking guides available. *Mole poblano* is said to have originated in the nunnery's kitchen.

MUSEO CASA DEL ALFEÑIQUE

This colonial **house** (Map p219; ☎ 232-42-96; Av 4 Ote 416; adult/student M$15/10, free Tue; ☻ 10am-5pm Tue-Sun) is an outstanding example of the over-the-top 18th-century decorative style *alfeñique*, characterized by elaborate stucco ornamentation and named after a candy made from sugar and egg whites. The 1st floor details the Spanish conquest, including indigenous accounts in the form of drawings and murals. The 2nd floor houses a large collection of historic and religious paintings, local furniture and household paraphernalia, although sadly all labeling is in Spanish only.

MUSEO BELLO

This **house** (Map p219; ☎ 232-94-75; Av 3 Pte 302; adult/student M$15/10, free Tue; ☻ 10am-5pm Tue-Sun) is filled with the diverse art and crafts collection of the Bello 19th-century industrialist family. There is exquisite French, English, Japanese and Chinese porcelain and a large collection of Puebla Talavera. Optional tours are available in English and Spanish for no charge.

Tours

Ángel (☎ 273-83-00, 800-712-22-84) has 'tramway' tours (adult/child M$75/35 for a day pass, M$40/30 for one ride) carried out in a unningly disguised bus that loops around Puebla's Centro Histórico hourly between 10am and 6pm every day, with separate trips to Cholula (adult/child M$75/45) departing daily from the southeast corner of the *zócalo* around 11am. The ticket kiosk is opposite the cathedral on the south side of the plaza. Another full-day bus trip departs from Puebla's CAPU bus station for Teotihuacán (M$250/150) at 7.15am, taking in the Exconvento San Agustín in Acolman before arriving back in Puebla at 8pm.

Ninety-minute double-decker Turibus tours (adult/child M$100/50 for a day ticket, M$75/35 for one tour) of Puebla's Centro Histórico depart every 40 mins daily between 9am and 7pm from in front of the State Tourist Office (p218). Multilingual commentary (English, French, German, Italian, Japanese and Spanish) is delivered via audio headphones. You can hop on and off all day long with the full-price tickets.

Festivals & Events

Starting in late April and ending in late May, the **Feria de Puebla** honors the state's cultural and economic achievements with cultural and music events. In early June, the **Festival del Mole Poblano** celebrates culinary triumphs at several of the city's storied eateries. Leaving no culinary stone unturned, the city's savvy restaurateurs promote a **Festival del Chile en Nogada** in late August. Puebla has also jumped on the **Día de Muertos** bandwagon, with a four-day citywide cultural program starting in late October.

Sleeping

Puebla's hotel scene is crowded and competitive, with a huge range of accommodation options and new arrivals constantly stirring things up. In recent years a slew of boutique three- and four-star hotels aimed at discerning travelers have entered the market, and for the most part standards are high.

Most hotels in the city can be spotted some way off with illuminated red 'H' signs over their entrance, although some of the newer generation are clearly seeking discretion and don't advertise quite so directly. It's worth searching online for special last-minute, seasonal and weekend package rates.

Most colonial buildings have two types of room, interior and exterior, with the former often lacking windows and the latter often having balconies exposed to a noisy street. Nearly all of Puebla's hotels that lack on-site parking have an arrangement with nearby garages.

BUDGET

Gran Hotel San Agustín (Map p219; ☎ 232-50-89, 800-849-27-93; Av 3 Pte 531; r without/with TV M$170/210; ☻) This fairly dingy place has perfectly fine rooms, but they're not the kind of place you'll want to do anything but sleep in.

Most are lacking natural light and creature comforts, and staff seem pretty indifferent.

Hotel Reforma 2000 (Map p219; ☎ 242-33-63; Av 4 Pte 916; s/d/t M$200/250/350; (P)) This good-value option has comfortable rooms with TV, phone and ensuite facilities, but it's a little way from the heart of the old town. Built around a pleasant colonial-style courtyard, it has a relaxed and calm feel, although some of the rooms are very dark. Upstairs, exterior rooms with balconies are less dark but noisy.

Posada de los Ángeles (Map p219; ☎ 232-50-06; Av 3 Pte 301; s/d/q M$200/250/350) This prettily painted colonial house has just six rooms and, while plumbing can be a little rudimentary, this is a great deal for this great location. Go for one of the two rooms that face the street and have charming balconies. The friendly family who run the hotel also run a restaurant at the front that serves food all day.

Hostal Santo Domingo (Map p219; ☎ 232-16-71; hostalstodomingo@yahoo.com.mx; Av 4 Pte 312; dm/s/d/t/q M$100/250/290/350/445; (P) (X) (🖳)) This is Puebla's only real hostel, offering clean and safe mixed-sex dorms as well as a large range of private rooms. Those at the front of the building enjoy balconies and lots of daylight, and all have high ceilings. Noise from both the bar downstairs and the street can be a problem, but this is definitely a great place to meet other travelers and have fun. There's internet access for M$8 per hour in the courtyard.

Hotel Provincia Express (Map p219; ☎ 246-35-57; Av Reforma 141; s/d M$260/350; (P) (🖳)) Tile fetishists on a budget, look no further! This wonderful place has one of the most stunning traditional interiors in Puebla, and all at knock-down prices. Refitted in 2007, the rooms themselves are simple but modern and spotlessly clean, while the corridors and facade are superb.

MIDRANGE

Hotel Imperial (Map p219; ☎ 242-49-80, 800-874-49-80; www.hotelimperialpuebla.com; Av 4 Ote 212; s/d incl breakfast M$380/480; (P) (🖳)) The Imperial is in quite a shabby state, but it's friendly and generally good value. Lonely Planet readers get a discount, making a double cost M$400. Rooms are unexciting and a bit on the old side and the internet access is via an antique PC in the lobby, but the location is good and prices include breakfast.

Hotel Puebla Plaza (Map p219; ☎ 246-31-75, 800-926-27-03; www.hotelpueblaplaza.com.mx; Av 5 Pte 111; s/d M$382/499; (P) (🖳)) This charming place enjoys a great location and has very comfortable rooms and good service. As with many colonial-style hotels, the rooms at the back are depressing with little or no natural light, and it's worth paying extra for rooms on the street with little balconies. All rooms have TV, phone, private bathroom and free wi-fi.

Hotel Palace (Map p219; ☎ 232-24-30; hotel_palace _puebla@hotmail.com; Av 2 Ote 13; s/d/t M$430/580/720; (P) (🖳)) The serviceable, if somewhat optimistically named, Palace largely caters to business travelers with comfortable rooms (if sometimes short on natural light), free parking and wi-fi in the lobby. The lively El Ranchito restaurant in the lobby is also good.

Hostal Santa María (Map p219; ☎ 405-98-90; www .suhostalsantamaria.com; Av 3 Ote 603; s/d incl breakfast M$450/650; (P)) Built around a small, pink-painted courtyard, the Santa María has just five spacious rooms, all of which have some charm, even if some of the choices – such a the garish duvet covers or the cheap shower units – leave something to be desired. All the well-kept rooms have phone, cable TV, tiled bathroom and rustic furnishings, and all but one have balconies facing the street below (very loud on Friday and Saturday nights).

Gilfer Hotel (Map p219; ☎ 309-98-00; www.gilfer hotel.com.mx; Av 2 Ote 11; s/d/ste M$456/561/838; (P) (🖳)) Somewhat marooned in 1986, the Gilfer nevertheless continues to attract a loyal stream of customers, who come for the great location, large rooms and the excellent views you get from higher floors here. There are 92 simple yet comfortable rooms with safe, phone and satellite TV.

Hotel Royalty (Map p219; ☎ 242-02-02, 800-638-99-99; www.hotelr.com; Portal Hidalgo 8; s/d/t M$465/566/643, ste M$670-840; (P) (🖳)) Located on the *zócalo* 's north side, with an entrance off the arcade, the 45-room Royalty is a friendly, well-kept colonial-style place. The price hike here is for the superb location, and rooms are nothing special, but they're generally spotlessly clean and comfortable enough, although with the familiar natural daylight problems that haunt the city. The junior suites with cathedral views merit the extra peso. Downstairs, the sidewalk restaurant–café is perfect for people-watching.

our pick Hotel Colonial (Map p219; ☎ 246-46-12, 800-013-00-00; www.colonial.com.mx; Calle 4 Sur 105; s/d/tr M$590/690/790/890; (🖳)) This utter charmer is hard not to love, even though its size and good value has made it a magnet for tour groups

Once part of a 17th-century Jesuit monastery and existing as a hotel in various forms since the mid-19th century, the place oozes heritage from its many gorgeously furnished rooms (half of the 67 rooms have retained colonial décor, and half are modern). There's a good restaurant, lobby wi-fi and a fantastic gilt-clad elevator complete with liveried porters. Noise from live music and the street can be a problem, but otherwise this is an excellent choice with an unbeatable vibe and location. Book ahead.

Casa de la Palma (Map p217; ☎ 246-14-37; www.casa delapalmapuebla.com; Av 3 Ote 217; r/ste from M$825/1062; P ⬚) This sumptuous conversion of a colonial town house to a boutique hotel is a winner. If you want to pretend you're a 18th-century *poblano* aristocrat, look no further than the Porfiriana suite, stunning for its sheer size and over-the-top rococo flourishes. Opened in 2007, this hotel was still in its early days when we visited. Small qualms such as patchy wi-fi coverage and a lack of breakfast options will no doubt soon be resolved.

TOP END

Hotel Mesón de San Sebastián (Map p219; ☎ 242-65-23; www.mesonsansebastian.com; Av 9 Ote 6; r M$950, ste M$1300-1500; ⬚ ⬚) This boutique hotel gets top marks for being family oriented (a rarity in the world of designer bed sheets and ruthlessly selected *objets d'art*). Each of the 18 rooms is individually decorated with simplicity and named for a saint. The master suites are particularly stunning, yet all rooms have TV, phone, minibar and antique furnishings.

NH Puebla (Map p217; ☎ 309-19-19, 800-726-05-28; www.nh-hotels.com; Calle 5 Sur 105; r from M$990; P ⬚ ⬚ ⬚) This excellent and surprisingly affordable hotel is a new arrival on the scene, and very welcome it is too. Aiming itself equally at business travelers and pleasure seekers, there's a good mix of style and service while never becoming too stuffy. The rooms are large, sleek and almost boutique, with extremely comfortable beds, good views and access to the great rooftop bar and pool.

Hotel Posada San Pedro (Map p219; ☎ 891-57-00; Av 2 Ote 202; www.hotelposadasanpedro.com.mx; r/ste M$1200/1500; P ⬚ ⬚ ⬚) This classy old timer has been a reliable and comfortable base in Puebla for three decades. Although some of the rooms are not large and in some cases could do with some modernizing, there's a great vibe here, a charming courtyard and

pool, plus a good restaurant. Regular special offers see the room rates slashed by up to 50%.

El Sueño Hotel & Spa (Map p219; ☎ 232-64-23/89, 800-690-84-66; www.elsueno hotel.com; Av 9 Ote 12; s/d M$1400/1520, ste incl breakfast M$1875-2340; P ⬚ ⬚) This impressive boutique place is an oasis of minimalist chic amid the colonial bustle of Puebla's old town. Its pride and joy is the fact that the 11 suites are thematically decorated, each after a different female Mexican artist (though the sleek, high-ceilinged, contemporary rooms have little to do with the artists themselves and seem to owe more to *Wallpaper Magazine*). Huge shower rooms, plasma screen TVs, wi-fi and full entertainment systems make this a very stylish and fun place to kick back.

Mesón Sacristía de Capuchinas (Map p219; ☎ 232-80-88, 800-712-40-28, in the US 800-728-9098; www.mesones-sacristia.com; Av 9 Ote 16; r incl breakfast M$1600; P ⬚) This wonderful boutique antique hotel has just six beautifully presented rooms all featuring luxurious four-poster beds and various carefully selected *objets d'art* scattered around. The romantic El Santuario Restaurant is open on guests' request and crafts inspired contemporary takes on traditional Mexican cuisine. Breakfast in bed is simply divine. Perfect for romance, this is one of Puebla's very best options.

Mesón Sacristía de la Compañía (Map p219; ☎ 242-35-54, 800-712-40-28, in the US 800-728-9098; www.mesones-sacristia.com; Calle 6 Sur 304; r/ste incl breakfast M$1600/2000; P) The eight rooms in Mesón Sacristía's other Puebla property are set around a bright pink, somewhat eclectically decorated courtyard. The junior suites are actually just rooms, while the two master suites are bigger and worthy of the title. Admittedly some of the décor is an acquired taste, but the restaurant gets universally positive reviews and serves aromatic American breakfasts and refined *poblano* cuisine. The service is extremely good.

Holiday Inn Puebla Centro Histórico (Map p217; ☎ 223-66-00; www.holiday-inn.com/pueblacentro; Av 2 Ote 2; r/ste from M$1750/2300; P ⬚ ⬚ ⬚ ⬚) In terms of individuality this has to be one of the least-typical Holiday Inns in the world – think gorgeous neocolonial lobby, sleek bar and minimalist rooms. Excellently located and professionally run, this is a very good choice for anyone looking for an upmarket, modern hotel.

Casona de la China Poblana (Map p219; ☎ 242-56-21; www.casonadelachinapoblana.com; cnr Calle 4 Nt & Palafox de Mendoza; ste M$2225-4000; **P**) Puebla's latest boutique hotel has spared no expense – it's stunning and knows it. Shamelessly dubbing itself Puebla's 'most exclusive hotel,' China Poblana is certainly the priciest, with gorgeous suites decorated in a mixture of styles, a lovely courtyard and its Ekos restaurant with its super-stylish El Aposentillo bar.

Eating

Puebla's culinary heritage, of which *poblanos* are rightly proud, can be explored in a range of eateries throughout the city, from humble streetside food stalls to elegant colonial-style restaurants, although given the city's renown as a culinary center, it's surprising how few truly excellent restaurants there are. For something really special your best bet is the restaurants of the top Puebla hotels.

RESTAURANTS

Las Brujas (Map p219; ☎ 242-76-53; Av 3 Ote 407; mains M$40-80) Near Callejón de los Sapos, this fantastic hipster café is popular with local students and serves up a mean plate of *tacos al pastor* and an endless stream of ice-cold beers. A great hangout with good live music in the evenings.

Casa Puebla (Map p219; ☎ 403-32-22; Portal Morelos 2; mains M$40-90) This eccentric café features effigies of such luminaries as Fidel Castro, Marilyn Monroe, Gandhi and Napoleon sitting around drinking and smoking together on the walls. It's another popular place on the *zócalo* and does excellent breakfasts for around M$60.

All Day Cafe (Map p219; ☎ 242-44-54; Ave 7 Ote; sandwiches M$45) This great little joint just off the Plazuela de los Sapos serves up a great range of sandwiches, salads, pastries, coffees and cocktails all day long (as the name would suggest). It's housed in a bright little courtyard and makes a great pit stop when shopping for antiques and crafts.

Fonda La Mexicana (Map p219; ☎ 232-67-47; Av 16 de Septiembre 706; mains M$45-100; ✆ 11am-8pm) This unassuming eatery serves a great *mole poblano*, plus a set lunch (M$47) with a few options and other good-value Puebla and Oaxaca specialties.

Restaurant Royalty (Map p219; ☎ 242-47-40; Portal Hidalgo 8; mains M$50-150) The smart café-eatery at Hotel Royalty (p222) has a breakfast buffet and popular outdoor tables where you can watch the world go by for the price of a cappuccino. It also does well-prepared meat and fish dishes, and seasonal *poblano* treats such as *gusanos de maguey* (maguey worms).

our pick Amalfi Pizzeria (Map p219; ☎ 403-77-97; Av 3 Ote 207B; pizzas M$60-120) A new addition to the Puebla dining scene is this excellent pizzeria, a world away from the touristy feel of the *zócalo* and popular with local students. This pizza is undoubtedly the best in town, there's a good selection of wine, and there are other traditional Italian dishes available. There's also takeaway service.

Vittorio's (Map p219; ☎ 232-79-00; Morelos 106; mains M$70-180) Despite being somewhat pricey, this Italian bar–restaurant on the *zócalo* is always busy with locals and visitors alike. The pizzas are good, and there's a great atmosphere and sidewalk seating, not to mention live music on Friday and Saturday.

Fonda de Santa Clara (Map p219; ☎ 246-19-19; www.fondadesantaclara.com; Av 3 Pte 920; mains M$75-130) This classic *poblano* restaurant, founded in the 1960s by Alicia Torres de Araujo, focuses on local seasonal specialties, from maguey worms to grasshoppers. If you don't happen to be of the bug-eating persuasion, there's plenty of more standard *comida poblana* on offer, including enchiladas and chicken *mole*. This main branch, in a well-restored colonial mansion, is very festive since it attracts locals celebrating special occasions. It also has a gift shop full of Talavera items and typical sweets. There is a smaller branch at Av 3 Pte 307.

Restaurant Sacristía (Map p219; ☎ 242-45-13; Calle 6 Sur 304; mains M$85-110; ✆ 8am-11:30pm Mon-Sat, 8am-6pm Sun) This award-winning restaurant, in the delightful colonial patio of the Mesón Sacristía de la Compañía (p223), is an elegant place for a meal of authentic *mole* and creative twists on rich *poblano* cuisine, or a cocktail or coffee and dessert in the intimate Confesionario bar. Live piano and violin soloists lend a romantic ambience most nights from around 9pm. If you like what you taste, inquire about their small-group cooking classes.

CHEAP EATS

Tacos Tony (Map p219; ☎ 240-94-31; Av 3 Pte 149; tacos M$10-20) Follow your nose – or ring for delivery – for a torta or *pan árabe* taco (made with pita bread instead of tortillas), stuffed with seasoned pork sliced from a trio of enormous grilling cones.

PUEBLA'S UNFORGETTABLE SEASONAL TREATS

Puebla is rightly famous for its gastronomy (and especially for *mole poblano,* the classic spicy sauce you must seek out at a top restaurant while you're in the city to have really experienced Puebla). However, the city also has a range of unusual delicacies not likely to make it to your local Mexican restaurant any time soon. These are all seasonal, but any serious foodie should be brave and try whatever's cooking!

- **Escamoles** (March–June) Ant larvae, a delicacy that looks like rice, usually sautéed in butter. Delicious!
- **Gusanos de maguey** (April–May) Worms that inhabit maguey agave plants, fried in a drunken chili-and-pulque sauce.
- **Huitlacoche** (June–October) Corn mushrooms are an inky black fungus delicacy with an enchanting, earthy flavor. Sometimes spelt *cuitlacoche.*
- **Chiles en nogada** (July–September) Large green chilies stuffed with dried fruit and meat, covered with a creamy walnut sauce and sprinkled with red pomegranate seeds.
- **Chapulines** (October–November) Grasshoppers purged of digestive matter, then dried, smoked or fried in lime and chili powder.

La Poblana (Map p219; ☎ 246-09-93; Av 7 Ote 17; mains M$15-30; 🕑 10am-6pm) Around the corner from the Museo Amparo, this small, friendly place whips up (and delivers) a dozen styles of authentic Puebla *cemitas* (a type of sandwich with meat and cheese).

Super Tortas Puebla (Map p219; ☎ 298-25-05; Av 3 Pte 311; tortas M$14-55) Marinated chilies, carrots and onions spice up the basic breakfasts and super sandwiches at this cozy nook. Feeling lazy? Call for delivery.

La Zanahoria (Map p219; ☎ 232-48-13; Av 5 Ote 206; mains M$20-40; ⊠ Ⓥ) This entirely meat-free godsend for vegetarians is a great place for lunch, moments from the *zócalo* and the Museo Amparo. The restaurant is split into two – the express service area (including a juice bar and a health food shop) in the front and the more relaxed service of the spacious interior colonial courtyard where everything from veggie *hamburguesas* to *nopales rellenos* (stuffed cactus paddles) are served up. Set meals are available for M$50.

La Matraca (Map p219; ☎ 242-60-89; Av 5 Pte 105; mains M$20-50) This cheap and pleasant place in an attractive colonial mansion's courtyard with live salsa music is a good place for a big breakfast (the all you-can-eat buffet is M$43) or a filling lunch or dinner of traditional *poblana* classics.

Drinking

By day, students pack the sidewalk tables near the university, along the pedestrian-only block of Av 3 Ote. At night, macho mariachis lurk around Callejón de los Sapos – Calle 6 Sur between Avs 3 and 7 Ote – but they're being crowded out by the bars on nearby Plazuela de los Sapos. These rowdy watering holes, especially **La Bella** (Plazuela de los Sapos s/n), are packed pretty much every night of the week. After dark, many of these places become live-music venues.

Entertainment

Check the Spanish-language online monthly **A dónde Puebla** (www.adondepuebla.com) for the lowdown on cultural events. Or pick up the free biweekly *Andanzas* cultural guide at a tourist office. The weekly *Los Subterráneos,* a free tabloid supplement to the newspaper *Síntesis,* reviews alternative music in Puebla, Tlaxcala and Hidalgo.

our pick **Librería Cafetería Teorema** (Map p219; ☎ 242-10-14; Av Reforma 540; cover M$15; 🕑 10am-2:30pm & 4:30pm-3am) One of our very favorite places in the city is this wonderful old-world bookstore–café that fills up in the evenings with a mixed arty–student–professor crowd. This is where to catch up with the local bohemian scene. There are different genres of live music each night from 9:30pm to 1am.

La Bella Epoca/La Probadita (Map p219; Av 5 Ote 209; cover M$20-30) This eclectic hangout attracts a diverse crowd with live music most nights, ranging from dub, reggae and drum 'n bass to gothic and heavy metal.

Other nightspots:
La Batalla (Map p219; Calle 6 Sur 506) Favors karaoke and thumping dance music.
La Boveda (Map p219; Calle 6 Sur 503) Features rock and rock en español.

Puebla's student population has long made the clubs in Cholula its destination on Friday and Saturday night, meaning Puebla itself is quiet. Dancing hot spots include the disco **Portos Tropical** (Map p217; ☎ 284-06-11; Av Juárez 2923; ◷ 10pm-5am Wed-Sat), which features salsa and merengue.

Shopping
West of the Museo De Arte Popular Poblano, several shops along Av 18 Pte sell the colorful, handpainted ceramics known as Talavera. Designs reveal Asian, Spanish–Arabic and Mexican indigenous influences. Bigger pieces are expensive, delicate and difficult to transport. Smaller tiles fetch up to M$50, quality plates upwards of M$100. The finest Puebla pottery of all is the white ceramic dishware called *majolica*.

A number of shops along Av 6 Ote, east of Av 5 de Mayo, sell traditional handmade Puebla sweets, such as *camotes* (candied sweet potato sticks) and *jamoncillos* (bars of pumpkin seed paste). Stay away if you're allergic to bees!

A wonderful array of quirky antique shops dominates Callejón de los Sapos, around the corner of Av 5 Ote and Calle 6 Sur. Most shops open from 10am to 7pm. On Sunday, the **Plazuela de los Sapos** (Map p219) is the site of a lively outdoor antiques market. It's great for browsing, with a wonderful variety of old books, furniture and bric-a-brac.

Talavera Uriarte (Map p219; ☎ 232-15-98; Av 4 Pte 911; www.uriartetalavera.com.mx; ◷ 9am-7pm Mon-Fri, 10:30am-5:30pm Sat, 11:30am-4:30pm Sun) Unlike most of Puebla's Talavera shops, Uriarte still makes pottery onsite, and it has a factory and showroom. Factory tours (M$60) are offered Monday to Friday until 1pm in English and French, and later in Spanish as groups arrive.

El Parián crafts market (Map p219; Plaza Parián) Browse local Talavera, onyx and trees of life, as well as the sorts of leather, jewelry and textiles that you find in other cities. Some of the work is shoddy, but there's also some quality handiwork, and prices are reasonable.

Barrio de Analco market (Map p219) Held on Sunday between Avs 3 Ote and 5 Ote, this major market across town is where flowers, sweets, paintings and other items are sold.

Getting There & Away

AIR
Aeropuerto Hermanos Serdán (PBC; ☎ 232-00-32; www.aeropuerto.puebla.com), 22km west of Puebla off Hwy 190, has daily flights to/from Guadalajara and Tijuana by Aero California, to/from Mexico City (except Sunday) and Monterrey (except Saturday) with Aeromar, and to/from Houston with Continental. It also has regular connections to Acapulco and Tijuana with Avolar.

BUS
Puebla's full-service **Central de Autobuses de Puebla** (Map p217; CAPU; ☎ 249-72-11; Blvd Norte 4222) is 4km north of the *zócalo* and 1.5km off the autopista. Tickets for most routes can also be purchased downtown via **Ticketbus** (Map p219; ☎ 232-19-52; www.ticketbus.com.mx; Av Palafox y Mendoza 604; ◷ 9:30am-5pm) inside the Multipack office.

Most buses to and from Puebla use Mexico City's TAPO, with additional half-hourly services to Terminal Norte. The trip takes about two hours. Three bus lines have frequent services: the deluxe line **ADO GL** (☎ 800-702-80-00; www.ado.com.mx) runs buses every 40 minutes (M$104); **Estrella Roja** (ER; ☎ 800-712-22-84; www.estrellaroja.com.mx) runs 1st-class buses (M$104) every 20 minutes and 2nd-class buses (M$96) every 10 minutes; and **AU** (☎ 800-702-80-00; www.ticketbus.com.mx) offers 2nd-class trips (M$96) every 12 minutes. **Estrella de Oro** (EDO; ☎ 55-5689-3955; www.estrelladeoro.com.mx) and **UNO** (☎ 800-702-80-00; www.ado.com.mx) also service this area.

From Puebla's CAPU, there's daily service to most everywhere to the south and east:

Destination	Fare	Duration	Frequency
Cuernavaca	executive M$180	3½hr	hourly (EDO)
	1st-class M$140	3hr	hourly (EDO)
Huamantla	M$20	1hr	hourly
Oaxaca	deluxe M$212	4hr	4 daily (AU)
	1st-class M$256	4¼hr	4 daily (ADO)
Cuautla	M$100	2¼hr	hourly
Tlaxcala	M$16	30min	every 10 min
Cuetzalan	M$118	4hrs	hourly
Tehuacán	M$70	2hrs	hourly
Veracruz	M$184	3½hr	hourly

Frequent 'Cholula' *colectivos* (M$6, 30 minutes) stop at the corner of Av 6 Pte and Calle 13 Nte in Puebla.

AROUND MEXICO CITY

CAR & MOTORCYCLE

Puebla is 123km east of Mexico City by Hwy 150D (tolls total about M$100). East of Puebla, 150D continues to Orizaba (negotiating a cloudy, winding 22km descent from the 2385m-high Cumbres de Maltrata en route), Córdoba and Veracruz.

Getting Around

Most hotels and places of interest are within walking distance of Puebla's *zócalo*. From the CAPU bus station, take a taxi to the city center (flat rate M$50) – buy a ticket from the kiosk but beware of overpriced touts and take an official cab from the dispatch office. Alternatively, exit the station at the 'Autobuses Urbanos' sign and go up a ramp leading to the bridge over Blvd Norte. Once across the bridge, walk west (toward VIPS coffee shop) and stop in front of the Chedraui supermarket. From there, catch combi 40 to Av 16 de Septiembre, four blocks south of the *zócalo*. The ride takes 15 to 20 minutes.

From the city center to the bus station, catch any northbound 'CAPU' *colectivo* from Blvd 5 de Mayo at Av Palafox y Mendoza, three blocks east of the *zócalo*, or from the corner of Calle 9 Sur and Av Reforma. All city buses and *colectivos* cost M$5.

AFRICAM SAFARI

One of Mexico's best places to see both native and exotic wildlife is this drive-through **safari park** (☎ 222-281-70-00, in Mexico City 55-5575-2731; www.africamsafari.com.mx; Km 16.5 on road to Presa Valsequillo; adult/child M$150/140; ☷ 10am-5pm; ☖). More than 3000 animals – among them rhinoceroses, bears and tigers – live in spacious 'natural' settings, and you can view them up close from within your car, a taxi or an Africam bus. It's best to visit first thing in the morning, when the animals are most active. **Estrella Roja** (☎ 222-273-83-00) runs daily round-trip buses from CAPU to Africam (adult/child M$185/175, including admission and a four-hour park tour). Similarly priced Estrella Roja tours also depart from Puebla's *zócalo* daily at 11:30am.

CHOLULA

☎ 222 / pop 152,000 / elevation 2170m

Almost a suburb of Puebla these days, but far different in history and feel, the town of Cholula is home to the widest pyramid ever built, the Pirámide Tepanapa. Despite this claim to fame, it's a surprisingly ignored place, largely because, unlike its contemporaries Teotihuacán or Tula, the pyramid has been so neglected over the centuries as to be virtually unrecognizable as a manmade structure. Indeed, the pyramid was so overgrown even when the Spanish arrived that they built a church on the top, not realizing that their 'hill' was actually a native religious site.

Cholula itself is dominated by the pyramid and its famous church, but it has a buzzing nightlife thanks to its big student population and plenty of good eating and accommodation options centered on the huge *zócalo*.

History

Between around AD 1 and 600, Cholula grew into an important religious center, while powerful Teotihuacán flourished 100km to the northwest. The Great Pyramid was added several times. Around AD 600, Cholula fell to the Olmeca-Xicallanca, who built nearby Cacaxtla. Sometime between AD 900 and 1300, Toltecs and/or Chichimecs took over, and it later fell under Aztec dominance. There was also artistic influence from the Mixtecs to the south.

By 1519, Cholula's population had reached 100,000, and the Great Pyramid was already overgrown. Cortés, having befriended the neighboring Tlaxcalans, traveled here at the request of the Aztec ruler Moctezuma. Aztec warriors set an ambush, but the Tlaxcalans tipped off Cortés about the plot and the Spanish struck first. Within a day, they killed 6000 Cholulans before the city was looted by the Tlaxcalans. Cortés vowed to build a church here for each day of the year, or one on top of every pagan temple, depending on which legend you prefer. Today there are 39 churches – far from 365, but still plenty for a small town.

The Spanish developed nearby Puebla to overshadow the old pagan center, and Cholula never regained its importance, especially after a severe plague in the 1540s decimated its indigenous population.

Orientation & Information

Buses and *colectivos* stop two or three blocks north of the *zócalo*. Two blocks to the southeast, the pyramid, with its domed church on top, is tough to miss. Banks are on the *zócalo's* south side, and all change cash and have ATMs.

AROUND MEXICO CITY

CHOLULA

Gioconda Internet (Calle 3 Ote; per hr M$15) West of the *zócalo*.

El Globo Lavandería (Calle 5 Ote 9) per kilo M$10 – minimum 3kg – for machine wash-and-dry service.

Tourist Office (☎ 261-23-93; Portal Guerrero s/n; ☽ 9am-7pm Mon-Fri, 9am-2pm Sat & Sun)

Sights

ZONA ARQUEOLÓGICA

The incredible **Pirámide Tepanapa** looks more like a hill than a pyramid, but it's still the town's big draw, and, with miles of tunnels veining the inside of the structure, it's no let-down. The **Zona Arqueológica** (☎ 235-94-24, 235-97-20; admission M$37, Spanish/English guide M$90/120; ☽ 9am-6pm Tue-Sun) comprises the excavated areas around the pyramid and the tunnels

underneath. You enter via the tunnel on the north side, which takes you on a spooky route through the center of the pyramid. Several pyramids were built on top of each other during various reconstructions, and over 8km of tunnels have been dug beneath the pyramid by archaeologists to penetrate each stage. From the access tunnel, a few hundred meters long, you can see earlier layers of the building. You don't need a guide to follow the tunnel through to the structures on the pyramid's south and west sides, but since nothing is labeled, they can be helpful in pointing out and explaining various features.

The access tunnel emerges on the east side of the pyramid, from where you can follow a path around to the **Patio de los Altares** on the south side. Ringed by platforms and unique diagonal stairways, this plaza was the main approach to the pyramid. Three large stone slabs on its east, north and west sides are carved in the Veracruz interlocking scroll design. At its south end is an Aztec-style altar in a pit, dating from shortly before the Spanish conquest. On the mound's west side is a reconstructed section of the latest pyramid, with two earlier exposed layers.

The Pirámide Tepanapa is topped by the brightly decorated **Santuario de Nuestra Señora de los Remedios**. It's a classic symbol of conquest, but possibly an inadvertent one, as the church may have been built before the Spanish realized the mound contained a pagan temple. You can climb to the church for free via a path starting near the northwest corner of the pyramid.

The small **Museo de Sitio de Cholula** (Calz San Andrés; admission incl with site ticket), across the road from the ticket office and down some steps, provides the best introduction to the site: a cutaway model of the pyramid mound showing the various superimposed structures.

ZÓCALO

The **Ex-Convento de San Gabriel** (also known as Plaza de la Concordia), facing the east side of Cholula's huge zócalo, includes a tiny but interesting **Franciscan library** and three fine churches, all of which will appeal to travelers interested in antique books and early religious and Franciscan history. On the left, as you face the ex-convent from the zócalo, is the Arabic-style **Capilla Real**, which has 49 domes and dates from 1540. In the middle is the 19th-century **Capilla de la Tercera Orden**, and on the right is the **Templo de San Gabriel**, founded in 1530 on the site of a pyramid.

The excellent **Museo de la Ciudad de Cholula** (☎ 261-90-53; cnr Av 5 de Mayo & Calle 4 Pte; M$20/10 adult/child; �洪 9am-3pm Thu-Tue) is housed in a fantastically restored colonial building on the zócalo. The small but strong collection includes ceramics and jewelry from the Pirámide Tepanapa, as well as later colonial paintings and sculptures. Most interestingly, you can watch through a glass wall as museum employees painstakingly restore smashed ceramics and repair jewelry.

Festivals & Events

Of Cholula's many festivals, perhaps the most important is the **Festival de la Virgen de los Remedios**, celebrated the week of September 1, with daily traditional dances atop the Great Pyramid. Cholula's regional **feria** is held during the following weeks. On both the spring and fall equinoxes, a **Quetzalcóatl ritual** is re-enacted, with poetry, sacrificial dances, firework displays and music performed on pre-Hispanic instruments at the pyramids. On **Shrove Tuesday**, masked Carnaval dancers re-enact a battle between French and Mexican forces in Huejotzingo, 14km northwest of Cholula off Hwy 190.

Sleeping

With a clutch of good-value hotels and one real boutique favorite, Cholula makes a good alternative to staying in Puebla for those who prefer a laid-back pace. The town is also an increasingly popular base camp for climbing and trekking the east side of the Sierra Madre Oriental.

Hotel Reforma (☎ 247-01-49; Calle 4 Sur 101; s/d M$180/200; P) If you're not completely put off by the crumbling exterior, you'll see that the interior fares much better – a charming pink-and-white painted courtyard divided into 11 simple but clean rooms, all with their own bathrooms and plenty of character. Overnight parking costs M$20.

Plaza Santa Rosa Hotel (☎ 247-03-41, 247-77-19; psrosa_reserv@yahoo.com.mx; Portal Guerrero 5; s & d M$400, t & q M$500; P 🖳) Unusually located inside a shopping arcade just on the side of the zócalo, the Plaza Santa Rosa has 27 rather dark rooms, but they're spacious and comfortable with phone and TV. Parking and wi-fi are included in the price.

Casa Calli (☎ 261-5607; www.hotelcasacalli.com; Portal Guerrero 11; s/d M$450/500; P 🖳 🖳) If you fancy a boutique feel on a budget, this excellent hotel is a great option. Right on the zócalo, the hotel contains 40 stripped-down, stylishly minimalist rooms, a good pool, free wi-fi, friendly staff and an Italian restaurant.

Villa Arqueológica Cholula (☎ 273-79-00, 800-514-82-44; Calle 2 Pte 601; r Sun-Wed M$850, Thu-Sat M$950, ste from M$1200; P 🖳) This boutique 44-room Club Med property is within walking distance of the pyramid, across a large field of flowers. Rooms (most with one double bed and one single bed) are well furnished, and there are lush gardens, tennis courts, cozy fireplace-lit common areas and a good international restaurant.

our pick **Hotel La Quinta Luna** (☎ 247-89-15; www.laquintaluna.com; Calle 3 Sur 702; r incl breakfast M$1650, ste incl breakfast M$1900-3200; (P) (💻)) This rarefied hotel oozes colonial style and is popular with a wealthy weekender crowd. The six rooms occupy a thick-walled 17th-century mansion set around a charming garden and are a gorgeous mix of colonial antiques, contemporary art, plush bedding and wired amenities such as flat-screen TVs, DVD players and in-room wi-fi. There's a great library, and meetings with the featured artists are happily arranged. The excellent restaurant is open to non-guests who reserve.

Eating

Café Enamorada (mains M$30-60; 🕙 9am-11pm) Facing the *zócalo*, this café is one of the most popular places in town, at least on weeknights and for its Sunday brunch buffet. There's live music most nights and decent doses of the usual sandwiches, tacos and quesadillas.

Güero's (☎ 247-21-88; Av Hidalgo 101; mains M$35-80; 🕙 9am-11pm; 🚼) Decorated with antique photos of Cholula, this is a lively, family-friendly hangout. Besides pizza, pasta and burgers, hearty Mexican choices include *pozole, cemitas* and quesadillas, all served with a delicious *salsa roja*.

Jazzatlán (☎ 304-26-43; Morelos 419; mains M$40-60; 🕙 6pm-2am Wed-Sat) Welcome to the home of jazz in Cholula. This fantastic restaurant has a small performing space where there's jazz four nights a week. Food ranges from tasty pizza to salmon muffins and a delicious garlic mushroom *cazuelita*.

Los Jarrones (☎ 247-10-98; Portal Guerrero 7; mains M$45-90) Underneath the plaza's attractive arcade, this casual indoor/outdoor eatery serves set breakfasts and a wide menu of good-value regional dishes. There's a great terrace overlooking the plaza that is a favorite meeting point for young Cholulans.

El Rincón de Rivadavia (☎ 247-79-63; Calzada San Andres 10; mains M$45-120; 🕙 11am-10pm Tue-Sun) This friendly, classy restaurant is set in a sweet courtyard near the Pyramid. The menu is classic *poblano* cuisine – try their *mole*, which they claim is the best in Cholula.

Comedor el Portón (☎ 247-02-73; Av Hidalgo 302; mains M$60; 🕙 9.30am-midday & 1-6pm) The Portal is popular for its daily set menu (M$55), which includes a choice of three soups, a main course (chicken, beef or vegetables), coffee and dessert. It's set in a pleasant courtyard with a skylight and attracts locals as much as tourists.

Drinking & Entertainment

La Lunita (cnr Calzada San Andrés & 6 Nte) is a fantastic family-run bar (with good food too), decorated with an incredible collection of old advertising posters and other knick-knacks. It makes for a great drinking spot in the shadow of the Pyramid.

Bar Reforma (cnr Av 4 Nte & Calzada San Andrés) Attached to Hotel Reforma, Cholula's oldest drinking spot is a classic, smoky corner abode with swinging doors, specializing in iceless margaritas and freshly prepared sangrias. After 9pm, it's popular with the university pre-clubbing crowd.

Tacos Robert (cnr 14 Oriente & Av 5 de Mayo) Across the street, this place, where the beer is cold and *fútbol* is always on the *tele*, is also popular with the pre-clubbing university crowd.

East of the pyramid on Calle 14 Pte, around the Av 5 de Mayo intersection, bars and discos compete for the short attention span of the university students (many of whom live across the street in a gated complex) after 10pm Thursday to Saturday. The most consistently popular club on this stretch is **Mandrágora** (cnr Calzada San Andrés & Calle 3 Sur; no cover), a cavernous dance hall with different music each night. Much of Cholula's nightlife is now to be found in warehouse-like *antros* and discos (where cover averages M$50 to M$150), a couple of kilometers east, near the university exit of the 'Recta,' as the Cholula–Puebla highway is known. Your best bet is to quiz students or ask a cab driver where the current hot spots are. Wherever you end up, dress to impress and come prepared to wait to get in.

Getting There & Away

Frequent *colectivos* to Puebla (M$7, 20 to 30 minutes) leave from the corner of Calle 5 Pte and Calle 3 Sur. Estrella Roja runs hourly buses between Mexico City's TAPO and Puebla that stop in Cholula (M$61) on Calle 12 Pte. There are also hourly buses from here to Mexico City's Benito Juárez airport (M$155).

TONANTZINTLA & ACATEPEC

Tonantzintla is a few kilometers south of Cholula, off Hwy 190. The interior of Tonantzintla's **Templo de Santa María** (🕙 7am-2pm & 4-8pm) is among Mexico's most exuberant. Under the dome, the surface is plastered with colorful stucco saints, devils, flowers, fruit, birds and more – a great example of indigenous artisanship applied to Christian themes. Tonantzintla celebrates the **Festival de la Asunción** (Festival of the Assumption) on August 15 with a procession and traditional dances.

Acatepec, 1.5km southeast of Tonantzintla, is home to the **Templo de San Francisco** (7am-2pm & 4-8pm), which dates from the 1730s. The brilliant exterior is beautifully decorated with blue, green and yellow Talavera tiles set in red brick on an ornate Churrigueresque facade.

Autobuses Puebla–Cholula runs 'Chipilo' buses (M$10) from Puebla's CAPU bus terminal to Tonantzintla and Acatepec. In Cholula, pick them up on the corner of Calle 7 Pte and Blvd Miguel Alemán. Between the two villages, you can either walk or wait for the next bus.

POPOCATÉPETL & IZTACCÍHUATL

Mexico's second- and third-highest peaks, Popocatépetl (po-po-ka-*teh*-pet-l, Náhuatl for 'Smoking Mountain'; 5452m), also known as Don Goyo and Popo), and Iztaccíhuatl (iss-ta-*see*-wat-l; 5220m), form the eastern rim of the Valle de México, which is 43km west of Puebla and 72km southeast of Mexico City. While the craterless Iztaccíhuatl is dormant, Popo is very much active; a December 2005 explosion catapulted ash 5km into the sky. Between 1994 and 2001, Popo's major bursts of activity triggered evacuations of 16 villages and warnings to the 30 million people who live within striking distance of the crater.

Mexico's **Centro Nacional de Prevención de Desastres** (National Disaster Prevention Center; 24hr hotline 55-5205-1036; www.cenapred.unam.mx) monitors volcanic activity via variations in gas emissions and seismic intensity. Though almost entirely in Spanish, the website posts daily webcam photo captures and updates on conditions in English.

Historically, Popo has been relatively tranquil, with most activity occurring in the cooler winter months when ice expands and cracks the solidified lava around the crater rim. It's had 20 eruptive periods during the past 600 years, but none have caused a major loss of life or property. The last really big blast occurred over a thousand years ago, and volcanologists estimate that there's a 10% chance of one in the near future. At the time of writing, a crack team of scientists were continuing to observe Popo's increasingly predictable outbursts with great interest. The good news is that fetching Iztaccíhuatl (White Woman), 20km north of

Popo from summit to summit, remains open to climbers.

Amecameca

 597 / pop 32,000 / elevation 2480m

The sleepy town of Amecameca, 60km east of Mexico City, is the key staging point for an Izta climb. With volcanoes and 16th-century churches as a backdrop, it makes an appealing destination in itself. A lively market convenes daily next to the church, and there are ATMs and internet cafés around the plaza.

The 450,000-sq-meter **Parque Nacional Sacromonte**, 90m above Amecameca to the west, protects an important pilgrimage site built over a cave that was the retreat of the Dominican friar Martín de Valencia in the early 16th century. It makes a delightful acclimatization walk, with awesome views of the town spread out beneath the volcanoes. From the southwest side of the plaza, head out through the arch and walk down Av Fray Martín for two blocks until you see the stairs ascending the hill on your right. After hailing Mary, follow the stations of the cross uphill to the sanctuary.

Most climbers sack out at the unassuming **Hotel San Carlos** (978-07-46; Plaza de la Constitución 10; r M$100), facing the plaza's southwest corner, where the rooms are clean and spartan, but comfortable, and cost M$50 more with TV.

From Mexico City's TAPO, Volcanes and Sur run 2nd-class buses to/from Amecameca (M$28, 1½ hours, every 15 minutes). To reach the plaza from Amecameca's bus station, turn right and walk two blocks.

Hiking & Climbing

Izta's highest peak is **El Pecho** (5220m). All routes require a night on the mountain, and there's a shelter hut between the staging point at La Joya and Las Rodillas that can be used during an ascent of El Pecho. On average, it takes at least five hours to reach the hut from La Joya, another six hours from the hut to El Pecho, and six hours back to the base.

Before making the ascent, all climbers should contact the **Parque Nacional Iztaccíhuatl-Popocatépetl** (/fax 597-978-38-29/30; http://iztapopo .conanp.gob.mx; Plaza de la Constitución 9B; entry fee M$10; 9am-6pm Mon-Fri, 9am-3pm Sat), on the southeast side of Amecameca's *zócalo*. To arrange permission, call the office or submit a form that's available online. All visitors must pay the M$10 per day park entrance fee in advance at the national park office in Amecameca, or on Sunday at Paso Cortés. Technically, you do not need permission to climb Izta, but if you're starting from Amecameca, you'll need the permit to pass the military checkpoint near Paso de Cortés (3650m), in the saddle approximately halfway between Popo and Izta. Alternatively, you can depart from the village of San Rafael, 8km north of Amecameca, a longer and more rigorous climb.

There are plenty of lower-altitude trails through pine forests and grassy meadows near Paso de Cortés, some offering breathtaking glimpses of nearby peaks. Trails begin at the La Joya parking lot 4km from Paso de Cortés. Again, you need to arrange a permit, which may be available on Sundays at the checkpoint when the in-town office is closed. *Colectivos* departing from Amecameca's plaza for Paso de Cortés cost M$35. From the national park office, taxis will take groups to La Joya (40 minutes) for a negotiable M$250 to M$350.

Basic shelter is available at the **Altzomoni Lodge** (beds per person M$25), by a microwave station roughly halfway between Paso de Cortés and La Joya. Request the keys at Paso de Cortés before hiking up, and bring bedding, warm clothes and drinking water.

CLIMATE & CONDITIONS
It can be windy and well below freezing any time of year on Izta's upper slopes, and it's nearly always below freezing near the summit at night. Ice and snow are fixtures here; the average snow line is 4200m. The ideal months for ascents are November to February, when there is hard snowpack for crampons. The rainy season (April to October) brings with it the threat of whiteouts, thunderstorms and avalanches.

Anyone can be affected by altitude problems, including life-threatening altitude sickness. Even Paso de Cortés is at a level where you should know the symptoms (see p1004).

GUIDES
Iztaccíhuatl should be attempted *only* by experienced climbers. Because of hidden crevices on the ice-covered upper slopes, a guide is advisable. Besides the following reader recommendations, the national park office may have other suggestions.

Amecameca-based **José Luis Ariza** (☎ cell phone 597-9781335), a rescue-squad member who has scaled peaks throughout Latin America, leads climbers up Izta year-round. He charges

M$1200 for one person and M$600 for each additional person (transportation and equipment rental cost extra).

Mexico City–based **Mario Andrade** (☎ 55-1038-4008, 55-1826-2146; mountainup@hotmail.com), an authorized, English-speaking guide, has led many Izta ascents. His fee is M$3800 for one person, less per person for groups. The cost includes round-trip transportation from Mexico City, lodging, mountain meals and rope usage.

TLAXCALA
☎ 246 / pop 85,000 / elevation 2250m

The capital of Mexico's smallest state is a delightful Mexican anomaly – despite being less than two hours from Mexico City, Tlaxcala is a delightfully calm and traffic-free place, especially at the weekend. It's charming and friendly, with a few sights worth seeing if you're passing through, though there's nothing that warrants a special detour here. Despite this, many people really fall for the town for its atmosphere and lack of tourists. As such, it's one of the capital's least discovered satellite towns.

History
In the last centuries before the Spanish conquest, numerous small warrior kingdoms (*señoríos*) arose in and around Tlaxcala. Some of them formed a loose federation that remained independent of the Aztec empire as it spread from the Valle de México in the 15th century. The most important kingdom seems to have been Tizatlán, now on the northeast edge of Tlaxcala city.

When the Spanish arrived in 1519, the Tlaxcalans fought fiercely at first, but ultimately became Cortés' staunchest allies against the Aztecs (with the exception of one chief, Xicoténcatl the Younger, who tried to rouse his people against the Spanish and is now a Mexican hero). The Spanish rewarded the Tlaxcalans with privileges and used them to help pacify and settle Chichimec areas to the north. In 1527, Tlaxcala became the seat of the first bishopric in Nueva España, but a plague in the 1540s devastated the population and the town has played only a supporting role ever since.

Orientation
Two large central plazas converge at the corner of Independencia and Muñoz. The northern one, surrounded by colonial buildings, is

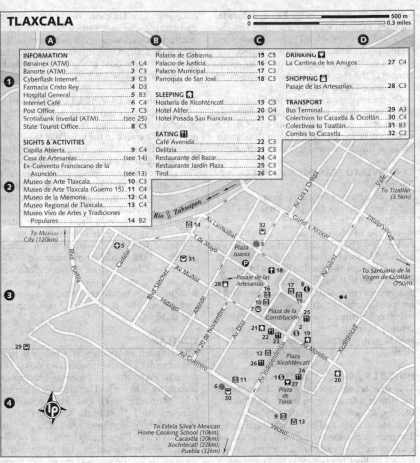

TLAXCALA

0 — 500 m
0 — 0.3 miles

INFORMATION
Banamex (ATM).................................1 C4
Banorte (ATM)...................................2 C3
Cyberflash Internet..........................3 C3
Farmacia Cristo Rey..........................4 D3
Hospital General...............................5 B3
Internet Café....................................6 C4
Post Office.......................................7 C3
Scotiabank Inverlat (ATM)............(see 25)
State Tourist Office..........................8 C3

SIGHTS & ACTIVITIES
Capilla Abierta..................................9 C4
Casa de Artesanías......................(see 14)
Ex-Convento Franciscano de la
Asunción....................................(see 13)
Museo de Arte Tlaxcala...................10 C3
Museo de Arte Tlaxcala (Guerro 15)..11 C4
Museo de la Memoria.......................12 C4
Museo Regional de Tlaxcala.............13 C4
Museo Vivo de Artes y Tradiciones
Populares......................................14 B2

Palacio de Gobierno........................15 C3
Palacio de Justicia...........................16 C3
Palacio Municipal............................17 C3
Parroquia de San José......................18 C3

SLEEPING
Hostería de Xicohténcatl.................19 C3
Hotel Alifer....................................20 D4
Hotel Posada San Francisco.............21 C3

EATING
Café Avenida..................................22 C4
Delitzia...23 C3
Restaurante del Bazar......................24 C4
Restaurante Jardín Plaza.................25 C3
Tirol..26 C4

DRINKING
La Cantina de los Amigos................27 C4

SHOPPING
Pasaje de las Artesanías..................28 C3

TRANSPORT
Bus Terminal..................................29 A3
Colectivos a Cacaxtla & Ocotlán......30 C4
Colectivos a Tizatlán.......................31 B3
Combis a Cacaxtla..........................32 C2

To Tizatlán
(3.5km)

Río Zahuapan

To Mexico
City (120km)

To Santuario de la
Virgen de Ocotlán
(750m)

To Estela Silva's Mexican
Home Cooking School (10km);
Cacaxtla (20km);
Xochitécatl (22km);
Puebla (32km)

the *zócalo*, called Plaza de la Constitución. Coming by bus you'll arrive a ten-minute walk from the town center at the town's hilltop bus station.

Information

Several banks around the *zócalo* exchange dollars and have ATMs.

Cyberflash Internet (Av 20 Noviembre; per hr M$15) Between Lardizabal & Guridi y Alcocer.

Farmacia Cristo Rey (Lardizabal 15; 24hr) Local pharmacy.

Hospital General (462-00-30/34-00; Corregidora s/n)

Internet Café (Av Guerro; per hr M$7) Between Díaz & Independencia.

Police (464-52-56/57)

Post Office (cnr Avs Muñoz & Díaz)

State Tourist Office (465-09-60 ext 1519, 800-509-65-57; www.tlaxcala.gob.mx/turismo; cnr Avs Juárez & Lardizabal; 9am-6pm Mon-Fri, 10am-6pm Sat & Sun) English-speaking staff are keen to sell you tickets to bullfights, as well as to give out a good free map of the town and book you on tram tours of the town (M$20, Friday to Sunday).

Sights

PLAZA DE LA CONSTITUCIÓN

Tlaxcala's shady, spacious *zócalo* is one of Mexico's most fetching. The 16th-century **Palacio Municipal**, a former grain storehouse, and the **Palacio de Gobierno** occupy most of its north side. Inside the latter there are vivid murals of Tlaxcala's history by Desiderio Hernández Xochitiotzin. The 16th-century building on the plaza's northwest side is the **Palacio de Justicia**, the former Capilla Real de Indios, built for the use of indigenous nobles. The handsome mortar bas-reliefs around its doorway include the seal of Castilla y León and a two-headed eagle, symbol of the Hapsburg monarchs who ruled Spain in the 16th and 17th centuries.

Off the northwest corner of the *zócalo* is the pretty-in-pink tile, brick and stucco **Parroquia de San José**. As elsewhere in the Centro Histórico, bilingual signs explain the significance of the church and its many fountains.

EX-CONVENTO FRANCISCANO DE LA ASUNCIÓN

This former monastery is up along a shaded path from the southeast corner of Plaza Xicohténcatl. Built between 1537 and 1540, it was one of Mexico's earliest monasteries, and its church – the city's cathedral – has a beautiful Moorish-style wooden ceiling. Next door is the **Museo Regional de Tlaxcala** (☎ 462-02-62; adult/student M$37/free; ☒ 10am-6pm Tue-Sun), with a large collection of religious paintings and a few pre-Columbian artifacts.

Just below the monastery, beside the 19th-century Plaza de Toros (bullring), is a **capilla abierta** with three unique Moorish-style arches.

MUSEO DE ARTE DE TLAXCALA

This new **art museum** (☎ 466-03-52; www.mat.org .mx; Plaza de la Constitución 21; adults/under 12/students M$20/free/10, free on Sunday; ☒ 10am-6pm Tue-Sun) is a fantastic addition to Tlaxcala's cultural scene. The main collection on the *zócalo* contains an excellent cache of early Frida Kahlo paintings, holds excellent temporary exhibits and has a good permanent collection of modern Mexican art. The smaller branch at Guerro 15 (admission free) is interactive and aimed at children.

MUSEO DE LA MEMORIA

This modern **history museum** (☎ 466-07-91; Av Independencia 3; admission M$10/5 adults/students, free on Tuesday; ☒ 10am-5pm Tue-Sun) looks at folklore through a multimedia lens, and has well-presented exhibits on indigenous government, agriculture and contemporary festivals. Explanations are only in Spanish.

MUSEO VIVO DE ARTES Y TRADICIONES POPULARES

This popular **arts museum** (☎ 462-23-37; Blvd Sánchez 1; adult/student M$6/4; ☒ 10am-6pm Tue-Sun)

has displays on Tlaxcalan village life, weaving and pulque-making, sometimes with demonstrations. Artisans serve as guides to the over 3000 artifacts on display. The café and handicrafts next door at the **Casa de Artesanías** are also worth a look.

SANTUARIO DE LA VIRGEN DE OCOTLÁN

One of Mexico's most spectacular **churches** (admission free; ☒ 9am-6pm) is an important pilgrimage site owing to the belief that the Virgin appeared here in 1541 – her image stands on the main altar in memory of the apparition. The classic Churrigueresque facade features white stucco 'wedding cake' decorations, contrasting with plain red tiles. During the 18th century, indigenous Mexican Francisco Miguel spent 25 years decorating the altarpieces and the chapel beside the main altar.

Visible from most of town, the hilltop church is 1km northeast of the *zócalo*. Walk north from the *zócalo* on Av Juárez for three blocks, then turn right onto Zitlalpopocatl. Alternatively, catch an 'Ocotlán' *colectivo* from near the corner of Avs Guerrero and Independencia.

TIZATLÁN

All that's left of Xicoténcatl's palace is preserved under a humble shelter: two altars with some faded frescoes of the gods Tezcatlipoca (Smoking Mirror), Tlahuizcalpantecuhtli (the Morning Star) and Mictlantecuhtli (Underworld). Next to the **ruins** (☎ 412-41-69; admission free; ☒ 10am-5pm Tue-Sun), Templo San Esteban has a 16th-century Franciscan *capilla abierta* and frescoes of angels playing instruments. The hilltop site is 4km north of town; take a 'Tizatlán Parroquia' *colectivo* from the corner of Blvd Sánchez and Av Muñoz.

Courses

Estela Silva's Mexican Home Cooking School (☎ /fax 468-09-78; www.mexicanhomecooking.com; courses incl accommodation US$1200) offers an intimate five-day gastronomic course, with hands-on instruction in the preparation of classic Mexican dishes. Tuition includes all meals, drinks, live music, transfers from Puebla and a trip to local markets, plus six nights of B&B lodging in comfortable private rooms with fireplaces. Students' guests not partaking in the course can stay for US$600. The bilingual lessons focus on the preservation of traditional French-inflected Puebla cuisine, and take place in the Talavera-tiled kitchen of fun-loving Estela's quaint hacienda-style country home in Tlacochcalco, a village 10km south of Tlaxcala.

Festivals & Events

On the third Monday in May, the figure of the **Virgen de Ocotlán** is carried from its hilltop perch (see opposite) to neighboring churches, attracting equal numbers of onlookers and believers. Throughout the month, processions commemorating the miracle attract pilgrims from around the country.

The neighboring town of Santa Ana Chiautempan sponsors the **Feria Nacional del Sarape** (National Sarape Fair) for two weeks on either side of July 26, to correspond with the celebration of its patron saint's day.

Tlaxcala's Teatro Xicohténcatl hosts dancers from around the country every September during the vibrant month-long **Nacional de Danza Folklórica** celebration.

Tlaxcala's **feria** (fair) draws participants from around the state between late October and mid-November, when *charrería* (horsemanship), bullfights and other rodeo-inspired pageantry take center stage. The festival kicks off with a *pamplonada* (running of the bulls) and includes Día de Muertos activities.

Sleeping

Hotel Alifer (☎ 462-56-78; www.hotelalifer.com; Av Morelos 11; s/d M$350/450; P 💻) One of the best budget options is the reasonable Hotel Alifer, up a small hill just a minute from the *zócalo*. Some rooms can be a bit dingy and dark (avoid bottom-floor rooms that face the echoing hallways and lack exterior windows), but they are clean and spacious with TV, phone and free wi-fi.

Hostería de Xicohténcatl (☎ 466-47-16; Portal Hildalgo 10; s/d M$350/450, ste M$600-1100; P) Half of the 16 rooms at this relative newcomer on Plaza Xicohténcatl are suites. All rooms are clean and quite large, if a little sterile, although the staff are friendly enough and location is excellent, just off the *zócalo*. Check out the collection of crosses in the lobby!

Hotel Posada San Francisco (☎ 462-56-22; www.posadasanfrancisco.com; Plaza de la Constitución 17; s/d/ste M$980/1155/1700; P 💻 🐾) The Posada San Francisco is the kind of place you'd expect to find a famous author getting plastered – check out the stained glass lobby roof, the beautiful bullfighter-themed bar, the large pool and the

airy restaurant. While it's definitely the best place to stay in town, the rooms are something of a letdown. They're absolutely fine, but could be anywhere in the world, and have none of the charm of the rest of the hotel.

Eating & Drinking

Tlaxcala has plenty of decent eating opportunities. The eastern side of the *zócalo* is full of eateries, although there are better options on the south side and on the nearby Plaza Xicohténcatl.

Delitzia (☎ 466-38-88; Plaza de la Constitución 14; sandwiches M$40-60; ⏰ midday-midnight Tue-Sun) This great lunch option serves up good baguettes, crepes, salads and *mole*, in a funky space with outdoor tables overlooking the *zócalo*. It's also a good bet for a post-sightseeing cocktail.

our pick **Café Avenida** (☎ 466-36-69; Plaza de la Constitución 16; mains M$48-110) A breath of fresh air away from the all-day brunches on the square's eastern flank. The pretty wooden interior is painted green and patronized by a friendly local crowd. The home-cooked three course lunch (M$56) is a great deal, and on top of that there's a huge choice of Mexican specialties as well as a full cocktail bar.

Restaurante Jardín Plaza (☎ 462-48-91; Av Independencia s/n; mains M$55-90) The best of the mediocre bar–restaurants competing for attention on the eastern side of the *zócalo*. It specializes in regional cookery such as anise-flavored *tamales*. There's also an espresso machine.

Tirol (☎ 462-37-54; Av Independencia 7A; set menu M$65-90) This sleek place overlooking Plaza Xicohténcatl is all white tablecloths and attentive service, and the gourmet Mexican food is excellent. If you don't fancy an elaborate set meal, just get takeout from the gourmet taco stand out front.

Restaurante del Bazar (Plaza Xicohténcatl 7B; mains M$80-90) A new addition to Tlaxcala's eating scene, this very upmarket restaurant offers dining in a gorgeous setting with stylish décor and excellent service. The menu is a large and frequently changing role-call of Mexican favorites with a modern twist.

The liveliest drinking establishment in town is **La Cantina de los Amigos** in the corner of Plaza Xicohténcatl, a friendly, attractive place where there's always a crowd.

Shopping

Watch out for the **craft market** (⏰ Sat & Sun) on Plaza Xicohténcatl. Some of the things on sale are horribly touristy, but some can also be great value. Embroidered *huipiles* (sleeveless tunics) from Santa Ana Chiautempan, carved canes from Tizatlán, and amaranth candies from San Miguel del Milagro are sold along the pedestrian-only **Pasaje de las Artesanías** alley, which forms an arc northeast of the Muñoz/Allende intersection.

Getting There & Away
Tlaxcala's sprawling **bus terminal** (☎ 462-03-62) is just under 1km west of the central plazas. For Mexico City's TAPO terminal, ATAH runs 1st-class 'expresso' buses (M$90, two hours) every 20 minutes in both directions until 9pm. Frequent 2nd-class Flecha Azul buses rumble to Puebla (M$15) and Pachuca (M$79).

Getting Around
Most *colectivos* (M$4) passing the bus terminal are heading into town, although it takes no time to walk. To reach the terminal from the center, catch a blue-and-white *colectivo* on the east side of Blvd Sánchez.

CACAXTLA & XOCHITÉCATL
Cacaxtla (ca-*casht*-la) is one of Mexico's most impressive ancient sites for the simple reason that there are so many high-quality, vividly painted depictions of daily life on display within the site itself, rather than being relegated to a museum collection. The frescoes include a nearly life-size jaguar and eagle warriors engaged in battle. Located on top of a scrubby hill, the ruins were discovered only in 1975, when men from the nearby village of San Miguel del Milagro, looking for a reputedly valuable cache of relics, dug a tunnel and uncovered a mural.

The much older ruins at Xochitécatl (so-chi-*teh*-catl), 2km away and accessible from Cacaxtla on foot, include an exceptionally wide pyramid as well as a circular one. A German archaeologist led the first systematic exploration of the site in 1969, but it wasn't until 1994 that the pyramids were opened to the public.

The two sites, about 20km southwest of Tlaxcala and 32km northwest of Puebla, are among Mexico's most intriguing. Both can be toured without a guide, but the bilingual explanatory signs tend to be either sketchy or overly technical. A good, if rushed, alternative is the guided Sunday tour conducted by Tlaxcala state tourist office (p233). It may be possible to hire a guide at the sites from Thursday to Sunday.

History
Cacaxtla was the capital of a group of Olmeca-Xicallanca, or Putún Maya, who arrived in central Mexico as early as AD 450. After the decline of Cholula (which they probably helped bring about) in around AD 600, they became the chief power in southern Tlaxcala and the Puebla valley. Cacaxtla peaked from AD 650 to 950, and was abandoned by AD 1000 in the face of possibly Chichimec newcomers.

Two kilometers west of Cacaxtla, atop a higher hill, the ruins of Xochitécatl predate Christ by a millennium. Just who first occupied the spot is a matter of dispute, but experts agree that whereas Cacaxtla primarily served as living quarters for the ruling class, Xochitécatl was chiefly used for gory Quecholli ceremonies honoring Mixcoatl, god of the hunt. That isn't to say Cacaxtla didn't hold similar ceremonies – the discovery of the skeletal remains of hundreds of mutilated children attest to Cacaxtla's bloody past.

Sights
CACAXTLA
From the parking lot opposite the site entrance it's a 200m walk to the **ticket office** (☎ 246-416-00-00; admission incl Xochitécatl M$46; ⏰ 10am-5pm Tue-Sun), museum and restaurant.

From the ticket office, it's another 600m downhill to the main attraction – a natural platform, 200m long and 25m high, called the **Gran Basamento** (Great Base), now sheltered under an expansive metal roof. Here stood Cacaxtla's main civic and religious buildings and the residences of its ruling priestly classes. At the top of the entry stairs is the **Plaza Norte**. From here, the path winds clockwise around the ruins until you reach the **murals**.

Archaeologists have yet to determine the muralists' identity; many of the symbols are clearly from the Mexican highlands, and yet a Mayan influence from southeastern Mexico appears in all of them. This combination of styles in a mural is unique to Cacaxtla, and the subject of much speculation.

Before reaching the first mural you come to a small patio, of which the main feature is an **altar** fronted by a small square pit, in which numerous human remains were discovered. Just beyond the altar, you'll find the **Templo de Venus**, which contains two anthropomorphic sculptures – a man and a woman – in blue wearing jaguar-skin skirts. The temple's name is attributed to the appearance of numerous half-stars around the female figure, which are associated with the Earth's sister planet, Venus.

On the opposite side of the path away from the Plaza Norte, the **Templo Rojo** contains four murals, only one of which is currently visible. Its vivid imagery is dominated by a row of corn and cacao crops, whose husks contain human heads.

Facing the north side of Plaza Norte is the long **Mural de la Batalla** (Battle Mural), dating from before AD 700. It shows two warrior groups, one wearing jaguar skins and the other bird feathers, engaged in ferocious battle. The Olmeca-Xicallanca (the jaguar warriors with round shields) are clearly repelling invading Huastecs (the bird warriors with jade ornaments and deformed skulls).

Beyond the Mural de la Batalla, turn left and climb the steps to see the second major **mural group**, behind a fence to your right. The two main murals (c AD 750) show a figure in a jaguar costume and a black-painted figure in a bird costume (believed to be the Olmeca-Xicallanca priest–governor) standing atop a plumed serpent.

XOCHITÉCATL

From the parking lot at the **site entrance** (☎ 246-462-41-69; admission incl Cacaxtla M$46; ☽ 10am-5pm Tue-Sun), follow a path to the circular **Pirámide de la Espiral**. Because of its outline and the materials used, archaeologists believe the pyramid was built between 1000 and 800 BC. Its form and hilltop location suggest it may have been used as an astronomical observation post or as a temple to Ehécatl, the wind god. From here, the path passes three other pyramids.

The **Basamento de los Volcanes**, all that remains of the first pyramid, is the base of the Pirámide de los Volcanoes, and it's made of materials from two periods. Cut square stones were placed over the original stones, visible in some areas, and then stuccoed over. In an interesting twist, the colored stones used to build Tlaxcala's municipal palace appear to have come from this site.

The **Pirámide de la Serpiente** gets its name from a large piece of carved stone with a snake head at one end. Its most impressive feature is the huge pot found at its center, carved from a single boulder, which was hauled from

another region. Researchers surmise it was used to hold water.

Experts speculate that rituals honoring the fertility god were held at the **Pirámide de las Flores**, due to the discovery of several sculptures and the remains of 30 sacrificed infants. Near the pyramid's base – Latin America's fourth widest – is a pool carved from a massive rock, where the infants were believed to have been washed before being killed.

Getting There & Away

Cacaxtla is 1.5km uphill from a back road between San Martín Texmelucan (near Hwy 150D) and Hwy 119, the secondary road between Tlaxcala and Puebla. Driving from Tlaxcala, turn west off Hwy 119 just south of town and watch for a sign pointing toward Cacaxtla, 1.5km west of the village of Nativitas.

By public transportation from Tlaxcala, catch a 'San Miguel del Milagro' *colectivo* near the northwest corner of Av 20 de Noviembre and Av Lardizabal, which will drop you off about 500m from Cacaxtla. Alternatively, a 'Nativitas–Texoloc–Tlaxcala' *colectivo*, which departs from the same corner, goes to the town of Nativitas, 3km east of Cacaxtla; from there, catch a 'Zona Arqueológica' *colectivo* directly to the site. Flecha Azul buses go direct from Puebla's CAPU terminal to Nativitas. Between Cacaxtla and Xochitécatl, take a taxi (M$40), or walk the 2km.

LA MALINCHE

The long, sweeping slopes of this dormant 4460m volcano, named after Cortés' indigenous interpreter and lover, dominate the skyline northeast of Puebla.

The main route to the volcano is via Hwy 136; turn southwest at the 'Centro Vacacional Malintzi' sign. Before you reach the center, you must register at the entrance of the **Parque Nacional La Malintzi**. La Malinche, Mexico's fifth tallest peak, is snowcapped only a few weeks each year, typically in May.

Run by the Mexican Social Security Institute, the **Centro Vacacional IMSS Malintzi** (☎ 246-462-40-98, in Mexico City 55-5627-6900, 800-001-09-00; Ⓟ ♿) has a handful of rustic cabins at a frosty 3333m. This family-oriented resort has woodsy grounds and fine views of the peak. The recently remodeled cabins are basic but include TV, fireplace, hot water and kitchen with refrigerator. It gets crowded from Friday to Sunday but is quiet midweek. Those not staying overnight can park here for a small fee. Camping is also a possibility.

Beyond the vacation center, the road becomes impassable by car. It's 1km by foot-path to a ridge, from where it's an arduous five-hour round-trip hike to the top. Hikers should take precautions against altitude sickness (see p1004).

Buses to the Centro Vacacional (M$12, 8am, noon and 4pm daily) make the 26km run from downtown Apizaco (served by frequent buses from Puebla and Tlaxcala), departing from the corner of Av Hidalgo and Aquiles Serdán.

HUAMANTLA
☎ 247 / pop 46,000 / elevation 2500m

With its lovely old *zócalo* and a charming colonial center, Huamantla is a pleasant enough base for exploring La Malinche once you get past its sprawling new town, which isn't particularly attractive.

Besides La Malinche looming over the town, the most notable attractions are the 16th-century **Ex-Convento de San Francisco** and the 17th-century baroque **Parroquia de San Luis Obispo de Tolosa**. Opposite the church, the **Museo de Títere** (National Puppet Museum; ☎ 472-10-33; Parque Juárez 15; adult/child M$10/5; ⏰ 10am-2pm & 4-6pm Tue-Sat, 10am-3pm Sun; ♿)), displaying dolls and marionettes from all around the world, is a fun stop for the young and young at heart.

During August, Huamantla sees a few sleepless nights during its annual **feria**. The day before the Feast of the Assumption (August 15), locals blanket the town's streets with beautiful carpets crafted from flowers and colored sawdust. The Saturday following this event, there's a Pamplona-esque running of the bulls, similar to that in Spain – but more dangerous since the uncastrated males charge from two directions!

During the feria, rates double and rooms are reserved well in advance. If everything is full, you can always find a room in Puebla or Tlaxcala.

Hotel Mesón del Portal (☎ 472-26-26; Parque Juárez 9; r from M$180; ℗)Overlooking the central plaza, this place has been the standard choice for years, but its rooms are very shabby and stink of air freshener, which must be disguising something! With places like the Centenario popping up, this is definitely a last resort,

although its more expensive rooms at M$260 are much better.

Hotel Centenario (☎ 472-05-87; Juárez Norte 209; s/d M$200/250) This is much the best option in town – just a short walk from the *zócalo*, all 33 rooms are spacious with brand new bathrooms and wi-fi access. Staff are helpful, and there's a good coffee shop downstairs.

Oro and Suriano have frequent services from Puebla. ATAH runs frequent buses from Tlaxcala.

CANTONA

Given its isolation, a good distance from any town of significance, the vast and incredibly well preserved Mesoamerican city of **Cantona** (admission M$24; ⏰ 10am-5pm) is almost totally unknown to travelers. With 24 ball courts discovered, this is now believed to be the biggest single urban center in Mesoamerica, stretched over 12 sq km in an ethereal lava-bed landscape dotted with cacti and yucca and enjoying incredible views of Pico de Orizba to the south.

The site was inhabited from AD 600 to 1000 and is of interest for two main reasons: unlike most other Mesoamerican cities, no mortar was used to build it, meaning all the stones are simply held in place by their weight; it's also unique in its design sophistication – all parts of the city are linked by an extensive network of raised roads connecting some 3000 residences. There are several small pyramids and an elaborate acropolis at the city's center. With good information panels in English and a newly completed access road, Cantona is now being promoted as a tourist attraction, although it's likely you'll be completely alone when you visit.

There's no public transportation here, but from Oriental, the nearest town, it's a 30-minute, well-signposted drive northeast. Count on paying M$150 for a round trip in a taxi. If you have your own transportation, visiting Cantona makes for a good side trip en route to Cuetzalan. Bring your own food and water – it's a big site and there's nothing on sale here.

CUETZALAN
☎ 233 / pop 6000 / elevation 980m

One of the most exhilarating trips to take in this region is the gorgeous drive to Cuetzalan. Beyond Zaragoza turnoff, the road becomes dramatic, snaking up hills, around sudden hairpin bends and often giving superb views. At the end of it all is the remote town of Cuetzalan ('Place of the Quetzals'), one of the most charming and unspoilt towns in all of Mexico. Built on a precipitous slope, Cuetzalan is famed for its vibrant festivals and Sunday *tianguis*, which attract scores of indigenous people in traditional dress. The humidity hovers around 90%, and on the clearest days, you can see all the way from the hilltops to the Gulf coast, 70km away, as the quetzal flies.

Orientation & Information

From the south, the main road into town passes the bus depot before hitting the *zócalo*. The center is on a hillside, and from the *zócalo* most hotels and restaurants are uphill. None-too-shy kids will offer to guide you around the slick, marble-cobbled streets for a small fee.

No English is spoken at the **tourist office** (☎ 331-05-27/62, 800-000-11-22; ✆ 9am-4pm), at the Palacio Municipal on the east side of the *zócalo*, but it's got much-needed (although very unclear) town maps. The **information kiosk** (✆ Thu-Tue) at the entrance to town keeps slightly longer, if irregular, hours. Just west of the *zócalo*, **Banamex** (Alvarado) has an ATM. There's a cyber-lair called **Internet** (per hr M$10) on the west side of the *zócalo*, and several others nearby.

Sights & Activities

Three structures rise above Cuetzalan's skyline: the plaza's free-standing **clock tower**, the Gothic spire of the **Parroquia de San Francisco** and, to the west, the tower of the French-Gothic **Santuario de Guadalupe**, with its highly unusual decorative rows of clay vases *(los jarritos)*. Between Banamex and the bus depot, the **Casa de Cultura** (Alvarado) houses a free regional **museum** (✆ 10am-5pm).

Two lovely waterfalls, collectively called **Las Brisas**, are 4km and 5km northeast of town. Hail a *colectivo* behind the Parroquia de San Francisco heading for the village of San Andrés Tziculan, or walk west along the dirt road from the bus depot, keeping to the right when it forks, until you reach San Andrés. Kids will offer to guide you to the falls for a few pesos – probably a good idea to accept, as there are no signs and many trails in the forest. The natural swimming pools beneath the falls are enticing – bring your bathing kit. Parts of a 32km network of caves can be

explored at **Atepolihui**, accessible from the village of San Miguel, a half-hour walk from the end of Hidalgo.

Festivals & Events

For several lively days around October 4, Cuetzalan celebrates both its patron saint, St Francis of Assisi, and the start of the coffee harvest with the **Feria del Café y del Huipil** (Festival of Coffee and Huipiles), featuring hearty drinking, traditional quetzal dancing and airborne *voladores* (literally 'fliers'), the Totonac ritual in which men, suspended by their ankles, whirl around a tall pole.

Sleeping

Posada Jaqueline (☎ 331-03-54; Calle 2 de Abril 2; s/d M$100/150) Jaqueline's 20 basic but clean rooms, overlooking the uphill side of the *zócalo*, are Cuetzalan's best in-town value. Some upstairs rooms share a balcony and have views over town.

Taselotzin (☎ /fax 331-04-80; www.laneta.apc.org/maseualsiua/hotel1.htm; Yoloxóchitl, Barrio Zacatipan; dm/s/d M$104/230/378; Ⓟ ♿) Just outside Cuetzalan, this hostel is run by an association of Nahua craftswomen who campaign for fair trade between locals and the outside world. It's an excellent initiative, and the hotel offers traditional massages, fair-traded handicrafts and herbal medicines. It has five fusty but cozy private rooms, with good views amid peaceful gardens, plus a surplus of dormitory-style cabins. The restaurant serves traditional local dishes, and horseback rides to waterfalls, caves and the pyramids can be arranged. Follow the right-hand fork past Cuetzalan's info kiosk off the Puebla road; watch for an inconspicuous sign on the right-hand side, about 300m downhill.

Posada Quinto Palermo (☎ 331-04-52; Calle 2 de Abril 2; s/d M$350/450) Right next to Posada Jaqueline, the Quinto Palermo has the very best location in town, with a superb terrace giving sumptuous views over the *zócalo* toward the Caribbean Sea. With a bit of hard work this could be one of the best places in town, but at the moment it's sadly not – the 15 basic, stuffy rooms are being held hostage by bad color patterns and horrendous taste in art.

Hotel Posada Cuetzalan (☎ 331-01-54; www.posadacuetzalan.com; Zaragoza 12; s/d M$380/510; Ⓟ ✆) At the top of the town, this friendly, well-run place has three large courtyards and was completing an extension at the time of writing.

AROUND MEXICO CITY

It has a swimming pool, a good restaurant featuring local fruit wines and liqueurs, two lovely courtyards full of chirping birds, and 35 well-kept rooms with tropical colors, tiled floors, lots of lightly stained wood and cable TV. It's 100m uphill from the zócalo.

Hotel La Casa de la Piedra (☎ 331-00-30, in Puebla 222-249-40-89; www.lacasadepiedra.com; García 11; s/d/ste M$480/530/580; P) Two blocks below the zócalo, the 'House of the Stone' is hands down Cuetzalan's most atmospheric hostelry. All 16 rooms in the renovated yet rustic former coffee-processing warehouse have large picture windows and refinished wood floors. Upstairs, the two-level suites accommodate up to four people and boast expansive views of the valley; downstairs rooms are equally well decorated, with tiled bathrooms, rough stone walls, and one or two beds.

Gran Hotel (☎ 331-00-19; www.granhotelcuetzalan .com; García 1; r/t/q M$350/510/560) Almost opposite the Casa de la Piedra, the Gran is its functional and rather sterile distant cousin. With 33 modern rooms, some with good views, the place is pleasant enough and well located, just off the zócalo, but otherwise totally unremarkable.

Eating & Drinking

Regional specialties, sold at many roadside stands, include fruit wines, smoked meats and herbal liqueurs.

Restaurant Yoloxochitl (☎ 331-03-55; Calle 2 de Abril; mains M$30-40) This fantastic place is great value. The space is beautifully decorated and features two ancient jukeboxes playing an incongruous selection of 45s from the 1950s, with views over the cathedral. Besides salads, antojitos and meat dishes, it offers wild mushrooms pickled in chile de chipotle.

La Terraza (☎ 331-02-62; Hidalgo 33; mains M$30-80) With its bright decorations and exotic indigenous theme, this extremely popular restaurant, housed in charming old colonial home, is a great place to sample the best of local produce. There's a large selection of breakfasts, mariscos, quesadillas and platillos de la región, and crawfish are the house specialty.

El Portal (☎ 331-00-48; Calle 2 de Abril; mains M$35) You can't beat a cold beer and plate of antojitos here, Cuetzalan's best-located restaurant. With views over the zócalo, a loyal clientele and friendly family service, this is a winner. The menu of home cooking takes in lots of simple but tasty local specialties. Try the excellent platillo especial El Portal as a sampler.

El Zarzo (☎ 331-01-61; Morelos 3; mains M$70-135; 5-10pm Tue-Sun) This quality pizza restaurant is located on the 1st floor of a steep, narrow side street a block from the zócalo. It's staffed by a friendly family and offers a good range of other Italian and local dishes in addition to its huge pizza menu.

Bar El Calate (☎ 331-05-66; Morelos 9B; shots from M$5) On the west side of the zócalo, this is the place to sup homemade hooch – flavored with coffee, limes, berries, you name it – orange wine, and the all-curing yolixpán, a medicinal herbal brew consisting of aguardiente (fire water) tempered by honey.

Getting There & Away

Vía buses (M$110, four hours) travel between Puebla and Cuetzalan hourly from 5am to 7:30pm, with extra services on Sunday and the last bus to Puebla at 5:30pm. It pays to double-check road conditions and buy your return bus tickets in advance during the rainy season. There are six buses a day between Cuetzalan and Mexico City's TAPO bus station (M$218, six hours).

YOHUALICHÁN

About 8km northeast of Cuetzalan, the last 2km via a steep cobblestone road, this ceremonial **pre-Hispanic site** (admission M$27; 10am-5pm Tue-Sun) has niche pyramids similar to El Tajín, which are in varying states of ruin. The site is impressive and well worth a visit, not least for the great views toward the coast and back to Cuetzalan from this side of the valley. The entrance is adjacent to Yohualichán's church and town plaza. To get here, board any colectivo (M$6) out of Cuetzalan and walk 20 minutes down from the stop where there's a blue sign with a pyramid on it. Alternatively, ask around the bus depot for a camión (truck) passing by the pyramids.

TEHUACÁN

☎ 238 / pop 265,000 / elevation 1640m

This bustling and somewhat remote city, 120km southeast of the Puebla capital, has little to draw visitors to it, but if you happen to be passing through then an overnight stop or even just a break for lunch on its lovely shady zócalo is a fine idea. It's also a good place to shop for handicrafts at the zócalo's Saturday market, and even as a possible weekend destination for some pampering at its upmarket Casas Cantarranas resort.

AROUND MEXICO CITY

UNIQUE HOTEL ROOMS AROUND MEXICO CITY

- **Mesón Sacristía de Capuchinas** (Puebla; p223) Antique-stuffed, highly individual rooms make this Puebla's premier spot to bed down in style.
- **Hotel La Quinta Luna** (Cholula; p229) This colonial mansion-cum-boutique hotel is inspirationally designed, providing a super-glamorous hideaway.
- **Posada del Tepozteco** (Tepoztlán; p244) This fabulous classic 1930s hillside hotel's best room is 18, with its own Jacuzzi and fantastic private balcony.
- **Las Mañanitas** (Cuernavaca; p255) Treat yourself to one of the enormous suites at this establishment favorite – all have large private verandas overlooking the extraordinary gardens.
- **Hotel Casanueva** (Valle de Bravo; p270) This affordable hotel has cleverly designed rooms with well-chosen art and local crafts on display; the suite overlooking the *zócalo* has the very best views.

Orientation & Information

Coming from Puebla, the main road into town, Av Independencia, passes by the ADO bus station before reaching the north side of the *zócalo*, Parque Juárez. The main north–south road is Av Reforma.

Essential services surround the *zócalo*. On its northwest corner, the sleepy **tourist information kiosk** (10am-2pm & 4-7pm) has city maps.

Sights

Tehuacán is best known for its mineral water, which is sold in bottles all over Mexico; there are free tours of the Cadbury-Schweppes–owned **Peñafiel plant** (Av José Garci-Crespo; 9am-noon & 4-6pm Sat-Thu), 100m north of the Casas Cantarranas (p242).

The arid Tehuacán Valley was the site of some of Mexico's earliest agriculture. By 7000 to 5000 BC, people were harvesting avocados, chilies, corn and cotton. Pottery, the sign of a truly settled existence, appeared around 2000 BC.

The **Museo del Valle de Tehuacán** (admission M$35; 10am-4:30pm Tue-Sun), three blocks northwest of the *zócalo* and inside the imposing Ex-Convento del Carmen, explains in Spanish some of the archaeological discoveries, and exhibits tiny preserved corn cobs thought to be among the first ever cultivated. There's also **Museo de Mineralogía** (adult/child M$10/5; 10am-5pm Tue-Sun), a well-maintained geological museum, in the same complex.

Easily reachable from Tehucán, the **Zapotitlán Salinas** zone of the **Reserva de la Biosfera de Tehuacán-Cuicatlán**, near the town of Zapotitlán Salinas, makes for a fascinating trip to another world. This small and highly unusual stretch of desert divided between Puebla and Oaxaca state is a biological eccentricity caused by the Eastern Sierra Madres blocking moisture-carrying winds coming from the Gulf of Mexico. The cactus forest here is unique for its large number of endemic cactuses and for its rich bird life. Towering cactuses can be seen in some of Mexico's most ethereal landscape at 1480m of altitude. To get here, take a bus to Zapotitlán Salinas (M$12, 30 minutes, every 20 minutes) from Tehuacán's bus station, and then take a taxi from Zapotitlán Salinas to the 'la zona de reserva' (M$50). You'll need to organize the taxi to come and pick you up again later.

Festivals & Events

The Sunday closest to October 15 marks the start of the two-week **La Matanza** festival, when goats are slaughtered en masse. *Mole de caderas* (goat stew) is the regional specialty that results from the carnage.

Sleeping & Eating

Hotel Iberia (383-15-00/11; Independencia Ote 211; s/d/t M$200/255/310; P 🖥 🖎) Just beyond the *zócalo* as you drive into town from the main road, this atmospheric place has a great lobby with a large courtyard bar and restaurants. The rooms are slightly less exciting – perfectly fine but lacking much natural daylight or charm.

Hotel Moniett (382-84-62; 2 Poniente 129; s/d/tw M$260/290/330; P 🖥 🖎) This place has the feel of a motel, but it's central and good value for money, with clean and comfortable (if rather sterile) rooms. Service is friendly, although the deposit for the TV remote control really clarifies the type of hotel this is.

Hotel México (☎ 382-00-19; cnr Reforma Nte & Independencia Pte; s/d M$500/560; P ⬛ ⬛) The best option in the center of town, the México has lots of charm, with 86 large, comfortable rooms and suites several courtyards, mineral water–fed pools and a good restaurant. It's a block northwest of the *zócalo*.

Casas Cantarranas (☎ 383-49-22; www.cantarranas .com.mx; Av José Garci-Crespo 2215; s/d/ste M$714/795/983; P ⬛ ⬛ ⬛) By far the town's grandest hotel, Casas Cantarranas is a way from the town center, so is really only a good idea for those with their own transportation. The resort is set in large gardens with 55 very good, spacious, modern rooms in a self-enclosed complex with a huge pool plus a spa, gym, restaurant and bar. Staff are charming and speak English. Coming into town on Independencia, turn left onto Calle 1 Nte, continue until you reach Calle 18 Pte (after the third set of traffic lights) where you turn left and then turn right onto José Garci-Crespo.

The lively *zócalo* is the place to head for a meal, and the best of the restaurants is **Plaza del Portal** (☎ 382-96-63; Calle 1 Sur 106; mains M$30-60) where, as well as admirable breakfasts and full meals any time of the day, there's always seasonal local specialties to try. It's very popular with a local crowd who vie for the best seats on the terrace.

Getting There & Away

ADO (☎ 800-702-80-00; www.ado.com.mx; Av Independencia 137) has 1st-class buses to/from Puebla (M$70, two hours, every 30 minutes), hourly services to/from Mexico City (M$140, four hours), a daily 6:30pm bus to Veracruz (M$128, four hours) and two daily buses to Oaxaca (M$135, three hours).

SOUTH OF MEXICO CITY

A host of great destinations sit south of the Mexican capital, including mystical Tepoztlán, breathtaking Taxco and the superb complex of caves at Grutas de Cacahuamilpa. The main road south from Mexico City, Hwy 95, climbs from the smog-choked Valle de México into refreshing pine forests above 3000m and then descends to Cuernavaca, 'the city of eternal spring', a long-time popular escape from Mexico City and a home-away-from-home for many Americans and Chilangos who own second houses here.

The state of Morelos, which encompasses Cuernavaca and Tepoztlán, is one of Mexico's smallest and most densely populated. Valleys at different elevations have a variety of microclimates, and many fruits, grains and vegetables have been cultivated here since pre-Hispanic times. The archaeological sites at Tepoztlán and Xochicalco show signs of the agricultural Tlahuica civilization and the Aztecs who subjugated them. During the colonial era, most of the region was controlled by a few families, including descendants of Cortés. You can visit their palaces and haciendas, along with 16th-century churches and monasteries. Unsurprisingly, the campesinos of Morelos were fervent supporters of the Mexican Revolution, and local lad Emiliano Zapata (see boxed text, p249) is the state's hero. Those with an interest should head to Cuautla for everything Emiliano.

Mountainous Guerrero state boasts such utter gems as silver mine-cum-tourist mecca Taxco, one of the best-preserved colonial towns in Mexico, and the unforgettable caves at Grutas de Cacahuamilpa, which extend well over a kilometer into the hillside and contain chambers of almost unbelievable size and beauty.

TEPOZTLÁN

☎ 739 / pop 15,000 / elevation 1700m

One weekend trip from the capital that rarely disappoints is that to gorgeous Tepoztlán, a wonderfully situated small town with a well-preserved historic center surrounded by soaring jagged cliffs just 80km south of Mexico City. As the birthplace of Quetzalcóatl, the omnipotent serpent god of the Aztecs, over 1200 years ago according to Mesoamerican legend, Tepoztlán is a major Náhuatl center and something of a Mecca for new-agers who believe the place has a creative energy. What is indubitable is that this *pueblo mágico* boasts an impressive pyramid, a great crafts market and a host of charming restaurants and hotels. It also retains indigenous traditions, with some elders still speaking Náhuatl and younger generations learning it in school, making it quite unlike most of the other towns ringing the Mexican capital.

Orientation & Information

Everything in Tepoztlán is easily accessible on foot, except the cliff-top Pirámide de

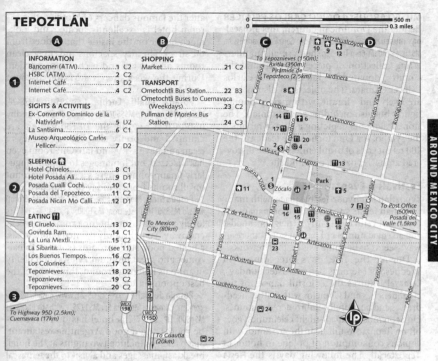

TEPOZTLÁN

INFORMATION
Bancomer (ATM)...............................1 C2
HSBC (ATM)......................................2 C2
Internet Café...................................3 D2
Internet Café...................................4 C2

SIGHTS & ACTIVITIES
Ex-Convento Domínico de la
   Natividad.....................................5 D2
La Santísima....................................6 C1
Museo Arqueológico Carlos
   Pellicer......................................7 D2

SLEEPING
Hotel Chinelos................................8 C1
Hotel Posada Ali.............................9 D1
Posada Cualli Cochi......................10 C1
Posada del Tepozteco...................11 C2
Posada Nican Mo Calli..................12 D1

EATING
El Ciruelo.......................................13 D2
Govinda Ram..................................14 C1
La Luna Mextli...............................15 C2
La Sibarita..................................(see 11)
Los Buenos Tiempos......................16 C2
Los Colorines.................................17 C1
Tepoznieves...................................18 D2
Tepoznieves...................................19 C2
Tepoznieves...................................20 C2

SHOPPING
Market..21 C2

TRANSPORT
Ometochtli Bus Station................22 B3
Ometochtli Buses to Cuernavaca
   (Weekdays).................................23 C2
Pullman de Morelos Bus
   Station.......................................24 C3

AROUND MEXICO CITY

Tepozteco, a 2.5km strenuous hike away. Street names change in the center of town, eg Av 5 de Mayo becomes Av Tepozteco north of the *zócalo*. On the west side of the plaza, Bancomer and HSBC have ATMs. There are several internet cafés scattered around town.

Sights

PIRÁMIDE DE TEPOZTECO

The uncontested main sight in town is this 10m-high **pyramid** (admission M$34, free on Sun; 9am-5:30pm), although it's actually some 400m *above* the town perched atop a sheer cliff at the end of a very steep path that begins at the end of Av Tepozteco. Built in honor of Tepoztécatl, the Aztec god of the harvest, fertility and pulque, the pyramid is more impressive for its location than for its actual size. Be warned that the path is exhausting. Heading off early is recommended to beat the heat (although on our last visit the ticket seller didn't turn up until 10am), and the 2km walk is not recommended to anyone not physically fit. At the top, depending on haze levels, you may be rewarded with a panorama of the val-

ley. Bring your own water, and good shoes are highly recommended. Video camera use is M$35.

EX-CONVENTO DOMÍNICO DE LA NATIVIDAD

This **monastery** (admission free; 10am-5pm Tue-Sun) and the attached church were built by Dominican priests between 1560 and 1588. The plateresque church facade has Dominican seals interspersed with indigenous symbols, floral designs and various figures, including the sun, moon and stars, animals, angels and the Virgin Mary.

The monastery's arched entryway is adorned with an elaborate **seed mural** of pre-Hispanic history and symbolism. Every year, during the first week of September, local artists sow a new mural from 60 varieties of seeds.

The 400-year-old complex was undergoing a major restoration at the time of writing; many murals from the 16th and 17th centuries have been meticulously restored. Upstairs, various cells house a bookstore, galleries and a **regional history museum**.

MUSEO ARQUEOLÓGICO CARLOS PELLICER
Behind the Dominican church, this **archaeology museum** (☎ 395-10-98; Pablo González 2; admission M$10; ⏰ 10am-6pm Tue-Sun) has a small but interesting collection of pieces from around the country, donated by Tabascan poet Carlos Pellicer Cámara. The objects on display here are lively and vibrant, with mainly human figures but also including some animals. The stone fragments depicting a pair of rabbits – the symbol for Ometochtli, the leader of the 400 rabbit gods of drunkenness – were discovered at the Tepozteco pyramid site.

Festivals & Events

Tepoztlán is a hyper-festive place, with many Christian feasts superimposed on pagan celebrations. With eight *barrios* (neighborhoods) and an equal number of patron saints, there always seems to be some excuse for fireworks.

During the five days preceding Ash Wednesday (46 days before Easter Sunday), **Carnaval** features the colorful dances of the Huehuenches and Chinelos with feather headdresses and beautifully embroidered costumes. On September 7, an all-night celebration goes off on Tepozteco hill near the pyramid, with copious consumption of pulque in honor of Tepoztécatl. The following day is the **Fiesta del Templo**, a Catholic celebration featuring theater performances in Náhuatl. The holiday was first intended to coincide with – and perhaps supplant – the pagan festival, but the pulque-drinkers get a jump on it by starting the night before.

Sleeping

Tepoztlán has a range of good accommodation options, but as a small town with lots of visitors, it can sometimes be hard to find a room during festivals and at weekends. If possible book ahead, although if you can't get a room, look out for weekend 'hospedaje económico' signs around town. Typically hotels and guesthouses discount rates by up to 30% from Sunday through to Thursday.

Hotel Posada Ali (☎ 395-19-71; Netzahualcóyotl 2C; s/d M$400/600; P ♨) The best-value option in town, this is a friendly, family-run set-up with 13 good rooms, all with some element of attractive design, most with double bed and cable TV. There's a communal sitting room, *frontón* (jai alai) court and a small pool.

Hotel Chinelos (☎ 395-36-53, www.hotelchinelos .com; Av del Tepozteco 25; r M$500; P 🖵 ♨) Named

after the famous dancers of Morelos, this 15-room hotel is excellently located and looks much better on the inside than it does from the street. The airy, spacious and super-clean rooms are set around a charming garden. During the week there's a M$100 discount on the room cost.

Posada Cualli Cochi (☎ 395-03-93/78-28; Netzahualcóyotl 2; s/d M$550/750; P 🖵 ♨) A standby option if Ali is full, the 10 rooms here are cramped and pretty charmless, but they're clean and have a TV and fan. One room even has a Jacuzzi, but it manages to remain singularly unappealing. There's a M$100 discount on all rooms from Sunday to Thursday.

Posada Nican Mo Calli (☎ 395-31-52; Netzahualcóyotl 4A; s/d M$850/1050, ste from M$1000; P 🖵 ♨) This lovely place is just right for a romantic weekend away. With brightly painted public areas, a heated pool, stylish rooms (some with balconies and great mountain views) and plenty of animals hanging around, this is one of the best options in town.

Posada del Valle (☎ 395-05-21; www.posadadelvalle .com.mx; Camino a Mextitla 5; r M$1725, r with spa packages M$4800; P ♨) This hotel has quiet, romantic rooms and a good Argentine restaurant. Spa packages include two nights at the hotel, breakfast, massages and a visit to the temascal (indigenous Mexican steam bath). Children under 16 are not allowed. It's 2km east of town – take Av Revolución 1910 east and follow the signs for the final 100m to the hotel.

our pick **Posada del Tepozteco** (☎ 395-00-10; www .posadadeltepozteco.com; Paraíso 3; r from M$1890, ste M$2640-3900; P 🖵 ♨) This gorgeous hotel was built as a hillside hacienda in the 1930s and is the society hotel of choice for Tepoztlán. The 20 rooms are airy and individually decorated in a pared-down way, and most have great views over the town. In the age of boutique luxury, some of the rooms may be underwhelming, but the focus of this old-world place is its refined atmosphere, wonderful garden and pool. Angelina Jolie stayed in room 5 when she dropped by, and unsurprisingly the guest book contains many other famous names. Service is top-notch, and rates are discounted up to 20% from Sunday to Thursday – even more if you stay several nights.

Eating

Tepoznieves (Av Revolución 1910 s/n; scoops M$10-20) This homegrown ice-cream emporium scoops out some 200 heavenly flavors, including exotics like cactus and pineapple-chili. It's an obligatory stop and has a couple more branches on the road to the pyramid, plus many imitators around town.

Los Buenos Tiempos (☎ 395-05-19; Av Revolución 1910 No 10; pastries M$10-30) Head here for the best pastries in the state – the smell drifting over the *zócalo* alone will probably bring you on autopilot. There's also good coffee and a lively social scene, and it's a great place to buy a pastry breakfast to take up to the pyramid with you.

Govinda Ram (cnr Av Tepozteco & La Cumbre; snacks & set meals M$30-55; **V**) As if you needed it, here's proof that Tepoztlán is well and truly central Mexico's biggest hippie haunt. A Hindu-inspired vegetarian café, Govinda Ram does a range of snacks and full meals, including an excellent Ayurveda buffet, good coffee and warming evening meals.

Los Colorines (☎ 395-01-98; Av Tepozteco 13; mains M$60-90; �9.30am-9pm) Specializing in *la comida sabrosa* (simply put, 'tasty food'), this recent addition to the scene here is a big two-storey place, vibrantly painted and with a large menu of great Mexican home cooking.

Axitla (☎ 395-05-19; Av Tepozteco; mains M$60-100; � 10am-7pm Wed-Sun) This place is definitely the oddest in town, a Swiss Family Robinson–style sprawling tree house venue just off the pathway up the archaeological site amid the thick forest. There's a good selection of breakfasts available (M$50) and a comprehensive Mexican and international menu. Avoid the coffee.

our pick **La Luna Mextli** (☎ 395-11-14; Av Revolución 1910 No 16; mains M$50-190) Yet another beautifully decorated and adorned space, La Luna Mextli is stuffed with local art, including its own in-house gallery. The food here is also excellent and good value, from Mexican standards to an entire list of different Argentinean steaks and Argentine-style *parrillada* (mixed grill).

La Sibarita (☎ 395-00-10; Posada del Tepozteco; mains M$90-150; � breakfast, lunch & dinner daily) Tepoztlán's finest dining is to be had at the restaurant of its top hotel, the Posada del Tepozteco. Given the prestigious 'H' certification by the Mexican Tourist Board for its high standards, you're in for an excellent meal here, with a menu taking in mussels au gratin, chicken in wine and thyme, and beef filet in tamarind sauce – not to mention a superb wine list. Another favorite is the weekend brunch. It's best to reserve a table.

El Ciruelo (☎ 395-12-03; www.elciruelo.com.mx; Zaragoza 17; mains M$115-196; ☙ 1-6pm Mon-Thu, 1-11pm Fri & Sat, 1-7pm Sun) Beautifully set out in a courtyard, this long-standing super-smart favorite serves an impressive upscale menu of dishes from *camarones al curry* and *salmón chileno a la mantequilla* to good pizzas, salads and international dishes. Reservations are recommended – ask for a table with views of the pyramid.

Shopping

Tepoz has a fantastic, atmospheric daily **market** that convenes on the *zócalo*, although it's at its fullest on Wednesday and Sunday. As well as the daily fruit, vegetable, clothing and crafts on sale, Saturday and Sunday sees stalls around the *zócalo* sell a huge range of handicrafts, including sarapes (blanket-like shawls), carvings, weavings, baskets and pottery. Shops lining adjacent streets also have interesting wares (some from Bali and India) at more upmarket prices. Popular local craft products are miniature villages carved from the cork-like spines of the pochote tree.

Getting There & Away

Pullman de Morelos/OCC (☎ 395-05-20; www.pullman .com.mx; Av 5 de Mayo 35) runs 1st-class buses to/from Mexico City's Terminal Sur (M$63, 1½ hours, hourly 5am to 8pm). Frequent buses to Cuautla (M$14, 15 minutes) depart from the Hwy 115D tollbooth just outside town. Pullman de Morelos runs free combis between the Av 5 de Mayo terminal and the gas station near the autopista entrance; from there, walk down the left (exit) ramp to the tollbooth.

Ometochtli direct (M$18, 45 minutes) and 'ordinario' (M$12, one hour) buses run to Cuernavaca every 10 minutes, 5am to 9pm. On Monday to Friday mornings, you can catch the bus downtown.

If driving north from Cuernavaca on Hwy 95D, don't get off at the Tepoztlán exit, which will dump you on the slow federal highway. Instead, take the subsequent Cuautla/Oaxtepec exit and follow the signs.

CUAUTLA

☎ 735 / pop 147,000 / elevation 1300m

Cuautla (*kwout*-la) can inspire or bemuse depending on your interests. It's got none of Tepoztlán's scenic beauty or the architectural merit of Cuernavaca, but it does have sulphur springs that have attracted people for centuries, as well as serious revolutionary credentials. Cuautla was a base for one of Mexico's first leaders in the independence struggle, José María Morelos y Pavón, until he was forced to leave when the royalist army besieged the town in 1812. A century later it became a center of support for Emiliano Zapata's revolutionary army. However, if modern Mexican history and *balnearios* aren't your thing, there's absolutely nothing for you here – modern Cuautla is a perfectly pleasant town, but there's little to see and do save the above.

Orientation

Cuautla spreads north to south roughly parallel to the Río Cuautla. The two main plazas – Plaza Fuerte de Galeana, better known as the Alameda (a favorite haunt of mariachis-for-hire at weekends), and the *zócalo* – are along the main north–south avenue, the name of which changes from Av Insurgentes to Batalla 19 de Febrero, then to Galeana, Los Bravos, Guerrero and Ordiera, on its way south through town.

Information

Banks ATMs are plentiful around the plazas.
Cyber Foster (next to Tony's Pizzas on the *zócalo*; per hr M$8)
Tourist office (☎ 352-52-21; ☽ 9am-8pm) On the platform of the old train station along Batalla 19 de Febrero. Upstairs, the Casa de Cultura runs a museum and hosts a full calendar of cultural events.

Sights

In 1911, presidential candidate Francisco Madero embraced Emiliano Zapata at Cuautla's old **railroad station** (in the Ex-Convento de San Diego). Steam enthusiasts will want to come on Saturdays, when Mexico's only steam-powered train fires up for short rides from 4pm to 9pm.

The former residence of José María Morelos houses the **Museo Histórico del Oriente** (☎ 352-83-31; Callejón del Castigo 3; admission M$27, free Sun; ☽ 9am-5pm Tue-Sun). Each room covers a different historical period with displays of pre-Hispanic pottery, good maps and early photos of Cuautla and Zapata.

The iconic rebel's remains lie beneath the imposing **Zapata monument** in the middle of Plazuela Revolución del Sur.

Cuautla's best-known *balneario* is the riverside **Agua Hedionda** (Stinky Water; ☎ 352-00-44; end of Av Progreso; adult/child M$45/35; ☽ 6:30am-5:30pm;

☽). Waterfalls replenish two lake-sized pools with sulfur-scented 27°C waters. Take an 'Agua Hedionda' bus (M$4) from Plazuela Revolución del Sur.

Other *balnearios* worth visiting include **El Almeal** (Hernández; adult/child M$60/40; ☽ 10am-6pm; ☽) and the nicer **Los Limones** (Gabriel Teppa s/n; adult/child M$40/30; ☽ 9am-6pm; ☽). Both places are served by the same spring (no sulfur) and have extensive shaded picnic grounds.

Sleeping

Hotel España (☎ 352-21-86; Calle 2 de Mayo 22; s/d/t M$130/170/230; P) Despite having a deeply unimpressive exterior, the Hotel España is far nicer inside than you might expect, with a pretty orange-and-white painted courtyard and 30 spacious remodeled rooms with hot water, fan and TV. Prices go up at the weekend.

Hotel Colón (☎ 352-29-90; Portal Guerrero 48; s/d/t M$140/180/260) The most central option in Cuautla is this 1970s timewarp on the *zócalo*. It's absolutely fine, but nothing more. The 20 simple, small rooms all have TV and hot water, but many of them lack daylight and charm.

Hotel Defensa del Agua (☎ 352-16-79; Defensa del Agua 34; s/d/t/q M$150/220/290/360; P ☽) Cuautla's most appealing option is this modern, clean hotel set out in a motel style with a pool and spacious rooms with TV, phone and fan. There's a very handy Italian Coffee Company branch in the building for breakfast. Avoid rooms with windows facing the noisy street. Weekend specials lower rates by up to M$100.

Hotel & Spa Villasor (☎ 352-65-21/61; www.hotel villasor.com.mx; Av Progreso; s/d M$390/510, ste M$618-990; P ☽ ☽) Out of town and located opposite the Agua Hedionda baths, this modern place has a large pool and comfortable rooms equipped with phone, fan and cable TV. With its own spa treatments, Villasor is the best option for relaxation, but it's not convenient for those without transportation.

Eating & Drinking

Tepoznieves (Av Insurgentes; scoops M$10-20; ☽ 10am-6pm) This heavenly ice creamery has oodles of delicious tastes (some acquired) – sample one of the flavors with chili or alcohol.

Tony's Pizzas (☎ 352-67-30; Portal Matamoros 6 pizzas M$60-200; ☽ 8am-midnight daily) This long-established place on the *zócalo* is a good bet for lunch. The pizzas are decent and there's a huge range available, while burritos and

CUAUTLA

| 0 | | | 500 m |
| 0 | | | 0.3 miles |

INFORMATION
Banamex (ATM)........................1 C2
Bancomer (ATM)......................2 C2
Banorte (ATM)......................(see 1)
Cyber Foster......................(see 17)
Post Office..............................3 C2
Telecomm Office......................4 C2
Tourist Office......................(see 6)

SIGHTS & ACTIVITIES
El Almeal...............................5 D1
Ex-Convento de San Diego........6 C2
Los Limones............................7 D2
Museo Histórico del Oriente......8 B3
Palacio Municipal......................9 B2
Zapata Monument....................10 B3

SLEEPING
Hotel Colón............................11 B3
Hotel Defensa del Agua............12 C2
Hotel España..........................13 C3

EATING
Las Golondrinas......................14 B2
Mikasa..................................15 C1
Tepoznieves...........................16 C1
Tony's Pizzas..........................17 B3

TRANSPORT
Bus to Agua Hedionda............18 B3
Combis to Anenecuilco &
    Chinameca......................19 B3

Estrella Roja Bus Station..........20 C3
OCC, Volcanes & Sur Bus
    Station...........................21 C3
Oro Bus Terminal.....................22 C3
Pullman de Morelos Bus
    Station...........................23 C3

To Hospital (3km);
Oaxtepec (10km);
Cocoyoc (10km);
Tetela del Volcán (26km);
Tepoztlán (25km);
Cuernavaca (41km);
Mexico City (70km)

AROUND MEXICO CITY

To Anenecuilco
(6km)

To Hotel & Spa Villasor (3km);
Agua Hedionda (3km);
Oaxaca (410km)

Río Cuautla

burgers are even cheaper. In the evening this is a popular drinking spot, too.

Mikasa (☎ 352-51-02; Av Insurgentes; sushi M$60) Cuautla is probably one of the last places you'd expect to find sushi, but you'll be pleasantly surprised by Mikasa, which serves a variety of Japanese dishes, including sushi, udon and teriyaki. Inspect the raw fish display before ordering – it's far from fine cuisine, but it's not bad for a small inland Mexican town.

Las Golondrinas (☎ 354-13-50, www.lasgolondrinas.com.mx; Catalán 19A; mains M$80) This place could do with a little more money and effort from its owners, but it's still got the best setting in town, in a 17th-century building filled with water features and greenery. The house specialty is the range of *molcajetes* (various spicy stews cooked in a large stone mortar) as well as its excellent *platos fuertes* such as *lomo al mango* (pork loin cooked in mango). The place can be a little hard to find – walk down a passageway next to a yellow photo shop.

Getting There & Away

OCC (☎ 800-702-80-00; www.ado.com.mx), a 1st-class line, and Sur and Volcanes, both 2nd class, share a bus depot at the eastern end of Calle 2 de Mayo. **Pullman de Morelos** (PDM; ☎ 352-73-71/81; www.pullman.com.mx) is across the street, with 1st-class service to Tepoztlán (M$20, every 20 minutes 9am to 9:30pm). **Estrella Roja** (ER; ☎ 800-712-22-84; www.estrellaroja.com.mx), a 2nd-class line, is a block west, and 1st-class **Estrella de Oro** (EDO; ☎ 55-5689-3955; www.estrelladeoro.com.mx) is a block south from there.

Destination	Fare	Duration	Frequency
Cuernavaca	M$40	1¼hr	every 20 min 5am-7:30pm (ER)
Mexico City	M$74	2½hr	every 20 min (ER)
Mexico City (Terminal Sur)	M$74	2hr	every 10 min (OCC)
Puebla	M$100	2½hr	hourly 5am-7pm (ER, EDO)
Tepoztlán	M$19	15 min	every 15 min (PDM)

CUERNAVACA

☎ 777 / pop 349,000 / elevation 1480m
There's always been a formidable glamour surrounding Cuernavaca (kwehr-nah-*vah*-kah), the high-society capital of Morelos state. With its vast gated haciendas and sprawling

estates, it has in the past attracted everyone from the Shah of Iran to Charlie Mingus with its year-round warmth, clean air and attractive architecture.

Today this tradition continues, even though urban sprawl has put a decisive end to the clean air, and you're less likely to meet international royalty and great artists in the street and far more likely to see vacationing Americans and college students studying Spanish on month-long courses.

While Cuernavaca has lots going for it, including some fantastic boutique hotels, good nightlife and fascinating nearby pre-Hispanic sites, it's fair to say that it's not the most accessible destination for those just passing through. Many of its most beautiful buildings are hidden behind high walls in private estates, so unless you're well connected in Mexico City high society or able to spend several weeks getting to know the town, then you may come away underwhelmed. However, the city has a great atmosphere, and definitely merits a stop on your way through.

History
Around AD 1200, the first settlers in the valleys of modern Morelos developed a highly productive agricultural society based at Cuauhnáhuac ('Place at the Edge of the Forest'). Later, the dominant Mexica (Aztecs) called them 'Tlahuica,' which means 'people who work the land.' In 1379 a Mexica warlord conquered Cuauhnáhuac, subdued the Tlahuica and exacted an annual tribute that included 16,000 pieces of *amate* (bark paper) and 20,000 bushels of corn. The tributes payable by the subject states were set out in a register the Spanish later called the Códice Mendocino, in which Cuauhnáhuac was represented by a three-branch tree; this symbol now graces Cuernavaca's coat of arms.

The Mexican lord's successor married the daughter of the Cuauhnáhuac leader, and from this marriage was born Moctezuma I Ilhuicamina, the 15th-century Aztec king, a predecessor to Moctezuma II Xocoyotzin encountered by Cortés. Under the Aztecs, the Tlahuica traded extensively and prospered. Their city was a learning and religious center, and archaeological remains suggest they had a considerable knowledge of astronomy.

When the Spanish arrived, the Tlahuica were fiercely loyal to the Aztecs. In April 1521 they were finally overcome, and Cortés

torched the city. Soon the city became known as Cuernavaca, a more Spanish-friendly version of its original appellation.

In 1529, Cortés received his somewhat belated reward from the Spanish crown when he was named Marqués del Valle de Oaxaca, with an estate that covered 22 towns, including Cuernavaca, and 23,000 indigenous Mexicans. After he introduced sugar cane and new farming methods, Cuernavaca became a Spanish agricultural center, as it had been for the Aztecs. Cortés' descendants dominated the area for nearly 300 years.

With its salubrious climate, rural surroundings and colonial elite, Cuernavaca became a refuge for the rich and powerful, including José de la Borda, the 18th-century Taxco silver magnate. Borda's lavish home was later a retreat for Emperor Maximilian and Empress Carlota. Cuernavaca also attracted many artists and achieved literary fame as the setting for Malcolm Lowry's 1947 novel, *Under the Volcano*.

Orientation
Most important sites, bus terminals and budget-conscious hotels are near Cuernavaca's Plaza de Armas. Hwy 95D, the Mexico City–Acapulco toll road, skirts the city's east side. If driving from the north, take the Cuernavaca exit and cross to Hwy 95 (where you'll see a statue of Zapata on horseback). Hwy 95 becomes Blvd Zapata, then Av Morelos as you descend south into town; south of Av Matamoros, Morelos is one-way, northbound only. To reach the center, veer left and go down Matamoros.

Information
BOOKSTORES
Sanborns (cnr Juárez & Abasolo) Upscale department store with a bilingual newsstand, popular bar and coffeeshop.

EMERGENCY
Ambulance (☎ 318-38-82)
Cruz Roja (Red Cross; ☎ 315-35-05/55)
Fire (☎ 317-14-89)
Tourist Police (☎ 800-903-92-00)

INTERNET ACCESS
There's also internet access at the Futura & Estrella Blanca bus station.
Copy@net (Av Morelos 178; per hr M$12; ☺ 8am-9pm Mon-Sat, 11am-5pm Sun; ☒)
Cyber Gasso (per hr M$7; ☺ 8am-10pm; ☒) Hidalgo (Hidalgo 40); Guternberg (Guternberg 198)

¡QUE VIVA ZAPATA!

A peasant leader from Morelos state, Emiliano Zapata (1879–1919) was the most radical of Mexico's revolutionaries, fighting for the return of hacienda land to the peasants with the cry '¡Tierra y libertad!' (Land and freedom!). The Zapatista movement was at odds with both the conservative supporters of the old regime and their liberal opponents. In November 1911, Zapata disseminated his Plan de Ayala, calling for restoration of all land to the peasants. After winning numerous battles against government troops in central Mexico (some in association with Pancho Villa), he was ambushed and killed in 1919. The following route traces some of Zapata's defining moments.

Ruta de Zapata

In Anenecuilco, 6km south of Cuautla, what's left of the adobe cottage where Zapata was born (on August 8, 1879), is now the **Museo de la Lucha para la Tierra** (Av Zapata; donation requested; 8am-9pm), which features photographs of the rebel leader. Outside is a mural by Roberto Rodríguez Navarro that depicts Zapata exploding with the force of a volcano into the center of Mexican history, sundering the chains that bound his compatriots.

About 20km south of Anenecuilco is the Ex-Hacienda de San Juan Chinameca (in a town of the same name), where in 1919 Zapata was lured into a fatal trap by Colonel Jesús Guajardo, following the orders of President Venustiano Carranza, who was eager to dispose of the rebel leader and consolidate the post-revolutionary government. Pretending to defect to the revolutionary forces, Guajardo set up a meeting with Zapata, who arrived at Chinameca accompanied by a guerrilla escort. Guajardo's men gunned down the general before he crossed the abandoned hacienda's threshold.

The hacienda, with a small **museum** (Cárdenas; donation requested; 9:30am-5pm), is on the left at the end of the town's main street, where there's a statue of Zapata astride a rearing horse. The exhibits (photos and newspaper reproductions) are pretty meager, but you can still see the bullet holes in the walls.

From Chinameca, Hwy 9 heads 20km northwest to Tlaltizapán, site of the **Cuartel General de Zapata** (Guerrero 67; donation requested; 9am-5pm Tue-Sun), the main barracks of the revolutionary forces. It contains relics from General Zapata's time, including the bed where he slept, his rifle (the trigger retains his fingerprints) and the outfit he was wearing at the time of his death (riddled with bullet holes and stained with blood).

From Cuautla, yellow 'Chinameca' combis traveling to Anenecuilco and Chinameca (M$6) leave from the corner of Garduño and Matamoros every 10 minutes.

LAUNDRY
Nueva Tintorería Francesa (Juárez 2; 9am-7pm Mon-Fri, 9am-2:30pm Sat) Per kg M$10.

MEDICAL SERVICES
Hospital INOVAMED (311-24-82/83/84; Cuauhtémoc 305) In Colonia Lomas de la Selva, 1km north of town.

POST
Main post office (Plaza de Armas; 8am-6pm Mon-Fri, 9am-1pm Sat)

TELEPHONE
Telecomm (Plaza de Armas; 8am-6pm Mon-Fri, 9am-1pm Sat)

TOURIST INFORMATION
There's an information booth in the cathedral and other kiosks around town, including at most bus stations. Ask at these places for maps.

Municipal tourist office (318-75-61; http://mac .cuernavaca.gob.mx/turismo; Av Morelos 278; 9am-5pm) Also has a tourist police office.

State Tourist Office (www.morelostravel.com; 8am-5pm Mon-Fri, Sat 10am-1pm) Main branch (/fax 314-38-72/81, 800-987-82-24; Av Morelos Sur 187); City Center (314-39-20; Calle Hidalgo)

Sights & Activities
PLAZA DE ARMAS & JARDÍN JUÁREZ
Cuernavaca's zócalo, Plaza de Armas, is flanked on the east by the Palacio de Cortés, on the west by the **Palacio de Gobierno** and on the northeast and south by restaurants and roving bands of mariachis. Although you can't enter the Palacio de Gobierno, it is a nice spot to contemplate some attractive architecture

AROUND MEXICO CITY

CUERNAVACA

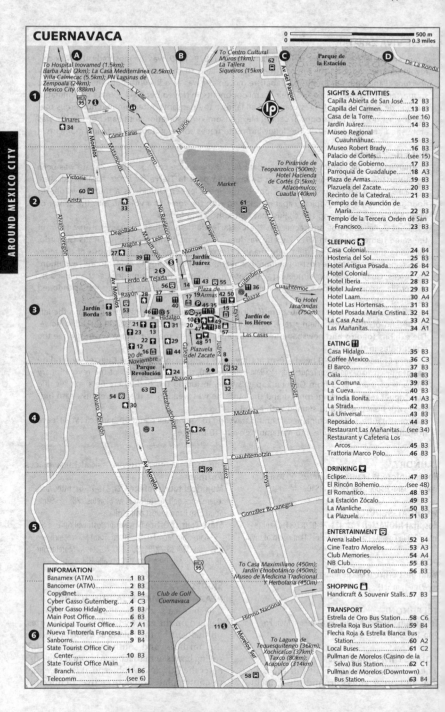

0   500 m
0   0.3 miles

To Hospital Inovamed (1.5km);
Barba Azul (2km); La Casa Mediterránea (2.5km);
Villa Calmecac (5.5km); PN Lagunas de
Zempoala (24km);
Mexico City (88km)

To Centro Cultural
Muros (1km);
La Tallera
Siqueiros (15km)

Parque de
la Estación

To Pirámide de
Teopanzolco (500m);
Hotel Hacienda
de Cortés (3.5km);
Atlacomulco;
Cuautla (40km)

Market

To Hotel
Jacarandas
(750m)

To Casa Maximiliano (450m);
Jardín Etnobotánico (450m);
Museo de Medicina Tradicional
Y Herbolaria (450m)

Club de Golf
Cuernavaca

To Laguna de
Tequesquitengo (36km);
Xochicalco (37km); Taxco (80km);
Acapulco (314km)

INFORMATION
Banamex (ATM)	1	B3
Bancomer (ATM)	2	B3
Copy@net	3	B4
Cyber Gasso Guternberg	4	C3
Cyber Gasso Hidalgo	5	B3
Main Post Office	6	B3
Municipal Tourist Office	7	A1
Nueva Tintorería Francesa	8	B3
Sanborns	9	B4
State Tourist Office City Center	10	B3
State Tourist Office Main Branch	11	B6
Telecomm	(see 6)	

SIGHTS & ACTIVITIES
Capilla Abierta de San José	12	B3
Capilla del Carmen	13	B3
Casa de la Torre	(see 16)	
Jardín Juárez	14	B3
Museo Regional Cuauhnáhuac	15	B3
Museo Robert Brady	16	B3
Palacio de Cortés	(see 15)	
Palacio de Gobierno	17	B3
Parroquia de Guadalupe	18	A3
Plaza de Armas	19	B3
Plazuela del Zacate	20	B3
Recinto de la Catedral	21	B3
Templo de la Asunción de María	22	B3
Templo de la Tercera Orden de San Francisco	23	B3

SLEEPING
Casa Colonial	24	B4
Hostería del Sol	25	B3
Hotel Antigua Posada	26	B4
Hotel Colonial	27	A2
Hotel Iberia	28	B3
Hotel Juárez	29	B3
Hotel Laam	30	A4
Hotel Las Hortensas	31	B3
Hotel Posada María Cristina	32	B3
La Casa Azul	33	A2
Las Mañanitas	34	A1

EATING
Casa Hidalgo	35	B3
Coffee Mexico	36	C3
El Barco	37	B3
Gaia	38	B3
La Comuna	39	B3
La Cueva	40	B3
La India Bonita	41	A3
La Strada	42	B3
La Universal	43	B3
Reposado	44	B3
Restaurant Las Mañanitas	(see 34)	
Restaurant y Cafetería Los Arcos	45	B3
Trattoria Marco Polo	46	B3

DRINKING
Eclipse	47	B3
El Rincón Bohemio	(see 48)	
El Romantico	48	B3
La Estación Zócalo	49	B3
La Manliche	50	B3
La Plazuela	51	B3

ENTERTAINMENT
Arena Isabel	52	B4
Cine Teatro Morelos	53	A3
Club Memories	54	A4
NB Club	55	B3
Teatro Ocampo	56	B3

SHOPPING
Handicraft & Souvenir Stalls	57	B3

TRANSPORT
Estrella de Oro Bus Station	58	C6
Estrella Roja Bus Station	59	B4
Flecha Roja & Estrella Blanca Bus Station	60	A2
Local Buses	61	C2
Pullman de Morelos (Casino de la Selva) Bus Station	62	C1
Pullman de Morelos (Downtown) Bus Station	63	B4

and enjoy the music. It's the only main plaza in Mexico without a church, chapel, convent or cathedral overlooking it.

Adjoining the northwest corner is the smaller **Jardín Juárez**, where the central gazebo (designed by tower specialist Gustave Eiffel) houses juice and sandwich stands, and hosts live band concerts on Thursday and Sunday evenings from 6pm. Roving vendors sell balloons, ice cream and corn on the cob under the trees, which fill up with legions of cacophonous grackles at dusk. Even more entertaining are the guitar trios who warm up their voices and instruments before heading to the cafés across the street to serenade willing patrons. You can request a ballad or two for around M$75.

PALACIO DE CORTÉS

Cortés' imposing medieval-style fortress stands opposite the southeast end of the Plaza de Armas. Construction of this two-storey stone fortress-style palace was accomplished between 1522 and 1532, and was done on the base of the city pyramid that Cortés destroyed after taking Cuauhnáhuac, still visible from various points on the ground floor. Cortés resided here until he turned tail for Spain in 1541. The palace remained with Cortés' family for most of the next century, but by the 18th century it was being used as a prison. During the Porfirio Díaz era it became government offices.

Today the palace houses the excellent **Museo Regional Cuauhnáhuac** (admission M$37; ⏱ 9am-6pm Tue-Sun, last ticket 5.30pm), which has two floors of exhibits highlighting Mexican cultures and history. On the ground floor, exhibits focus on pre-Hispanic cultures, including the local Tlahuica and their relationship with the Aztec empire. Most labeling is in Spanish only, with a few well-translated exceptions.

Upstairs covers events from the Spanish conquest to the present. On the balcony is a fascinating mural by Diego Rivera, commissioned in the mid-1920s by Dwight Morrow, the US ambassador to Mexico. From right to left, scenes from the conquest up to the 1910 Revolution emphasize the cruelty, oppression and violence that have characterized Mexican history.

RECINTO DE LA CATEDRAL

Cuernavaca's cathedral stands in a large highwalled *recinto* (compound) – the entrance gate is on Hidalgo. Like the Palacio de Cortés, the cathedral was built in a grand fortresslike style, in an effort to impress, intimidate and defend against the natives. Franciscans started work on what was one of Mexico's earliest Christian missions in 1526, using indigenous labor and stones from the rubble of Cuauhnáhuac. The first structure was the **Capilla Abierta de San José**, an open chapel on the cathedral's west side.

The cathedral itself, the **Templo de la Asunción de María**, is plain and solid, with an unembellished facade. The side door, which faces north to the compound's entrance, shows a mixture of indigenous and European features – the skull and crossbones above it is a symbol of the Franciscan order. Inside are frescoes rediscovered early in the 20th century. Cuernavaca was a center for Franciscan missionary activities in Asia, and the frescoes – said to show the persecution of Christian missionaries in Japan – were supposedly painted in the 17th century by a Japanese convert to Christianity.

The cathedral compound also holds two smaller churches. On the right as you enter is the **Templo de la Tercera Orden de San Francisco**. Its exterior was carved in 18th-century baroque style by indigenous artisans, and its interior has ornate, gilded decorations. On the left as you enter is the 19th-century **Capilla del Carmen**, where believers seek cures for illness.

MUSEO ROBERT BRADY

Let's face it, who wouldn't want to be independently wealthy and spend their life traveling around the world collecting gorgeous little things for their lavish Mexican mansion? If that option isn't open to you, visit this museum – easily Cuernavaca's best – and live vicariously. The one-time home of American artist and collector Robert Brady (1928–86), this **museum** (☎ 316-85-54; www.brady museum.org; Netzahualcóyotl 4; admission M$30; ⏱ 10am-6pm Tue-Sun), housed in the Casa de la Torre, is a wonderful place to spend time appreciating the exquisite taste of one man. Brady lived in Cuernavaca for 24 years after a spell in Venice, but his collections range from Papua New Guinea and India to Haiti and South America.

Originally part of the monastery within the Recinto de la Catedral, the house is a stunning testament to a man who knew what he liked. Every room, including the two gorgeous bathrooms and kitchen, is bedecked in paintings, carvings, textiles, antiques and folk arts from all corners of the earth. Among the treasures are works by well-known Mexican artists including Rivera, Tamayo, Kahlo and Covarrubias, as well as Brady's own paintings (check out his spot-on portrait of his friend Peggy Guggenheim). The gardens are lovely too, with a very tempting (but off-limits) swimming pool in one of them and a little café in the other.

JARDÍN BORDA

Beside the 1784 **Parroquia de Guadalupe**, this extravagant **property** (☎ 318-82-50; Av Morelos 271; adult/child M$30/15, free Sun; ⏰ 10am-5:30pm Tue-Sun), inspired by Versailles, was designed in 1783 for Manuel de la Borda as an addition to the stately residence built by his father, José de la Borda. From 1866, Emperor Maximilian and Empress Carlota entertained their courtiers here, and used the house as a summer residence.

From the entrance, you can tour the house and gardens to get an idea of how Mexico's 19th-century aristocracy lived. In typical colonial style, the buildings are arranged around courtyards. In one wing, the **Museo de Sitio** has exhibits on daily life during the empire period and original documents with the signatures of Morelos, Juárez and Maximilian.

Several romantic paintings in the **Sala Manuel M Ponce**, a recital hall near the entrance, show scenes of the garden in Maximilian's time. One of the most famous paintings depicts Maximilian in the garden with La India Bonita, the 'pretty Indian' who later became his lover.

The gardens are formally laid out on a series of terraces, with paths, steps and fountains, and they originally featured a botanical collection with hundreds of varieties of ornamental plants and fruit trees. The vegetation is still exuberant, with large trees and semitropical shrubs, though there is no longer a wide range of species. Because of a water shortage, the baroque-style fountains operate only on weekends. You can hire a rowboat for M$30 an hour, or take tea at the restaurant (mains M$50 to M$95) inside the entrance without purchasing a ticket.

CENTRO CULTURAL MUROS

Contemporary Mexican art and culture is celebrated at the city's best **art gallery** (☎ 310-38-48; www.muros.org.mx; Guerrero 205, Colonia Lomas de la Selva; admission M$30, free Tue & Sun; ⏰ 10am-6pm Tue-Sun), home to restored murals from Cuernavaca's Hotel Casino de la Selva and to a private collection of more than 320 paintings, sculptures, videos and photographs. Highlights include Frida Kahlo's *Diego en mi Pensamiento* and works by Rivera, Siquerios, Orozco, Tamayo and emerging modern artists.

PIRÁMIDE DE TEOPANZOLCO

This small **archaeological site** (☎ 314-40-46/48; cnr Río Balsas & Ixcateopan, Colonia Vista Hermosa; admission M$34; ⏰ 9am-5:30pm) is 1km northeast of the center. There are actually two pyramids, one inside the other. You can climb on the outer base and see the older pyramid within, with a double staircase leading up to the remains of a pair of temples. Tlahuicas built the older pyramid over 800 years ago; the outside one was being constructed by the Aztecs when Cortés arrived, and was never completed. The name Teopanzolco means 'Place of the Old Temple,' and may relate to an ancient construction to the west of the current pyramid, where artifacts dating from around 7000 BC have been found, as well as others with an Olmec influence.

Several other smaller platform structures surround the double pyramid. Near the rectangular platform to the west, a tomb containing the remains of 92 men, women and children mixed with ceramic pieces was discovered. They are believed to be victims of a type of human sacrifice in which decapitation and dismemberment were practised.

Catch a Ruta 4 'Barona' bus at the corner of Degollado and Guerrero, get off at Río Balsas, turn right and walk four blocks; or take a taxi to the site.

VOLUNTEERING

Por Un Mejor Hoy (www.hoycommunity.org) An excellent US-run non-profit organization based in Cuernavaca. Their aim is to mobilize the travel community to build bridges and assist local development through participatory trips. See their website to get involved.

Courses

Cuernavaca is a well-established center for studying Spanish at all levels, and has dozens of language schools. As such, standards are high, teaching is usually very thorough and prices very competitive. The best offer small-group or individual instruction, at all levels, with four to five hours per day of intensive instruction plus a couple of hours' conversation practice. Classes begin each Monday, and most schools recommend a minimum enrollment of four weeks.

With so many teaching styles and options, prospective students should research the choices carefully. Contact the tourist office (p249) for an extensive list of schools. The following are among the most frequently and highly recommended:

Cemanahuac (☎ 318-64-07; www.cemanahuac.com) Established in the 1970s, this place has an emphasis on language acquisition and social awareness, with many courses available taking in political and social issues in modern Mexico.

Center for Bilingual Multicultural Studies (☎ 317-10-87, in the US 1800-932-2068, 1800-574-1583; www.bilingual-center.com) Part of the Universidad Internacional, the CBMS is accredited by the Universidad Autónoma del Estado de Morelos and affiliated with many foreign universities.

Cetlalic (☎ /fax 313-26-37; www.cetlalic.org.mx) Emphasizes language learning, cultural awareness and social responsibility. Offers a large range of social justice programs including specially tailored gay and lesbian programs.

Cuauhnáhuac Spanish Language Institute (☎ 312-36-73; www.cuauhnahuac.edu.mx) The oldest language school in Cuernavaca helps students earn university language credits and members of the business and medical communities to develop language interests.

Encuentros (☎ 312-50-88; www.learnspanishinmexico .com) Offers personalized programs to professionals and travelers wanting to learn Spanish.

Ideal Latinoamerica (☎ 311-75-51; www.ideal -school.com) Program immerses students in Spanish language and Mexican culture, while respecting the individual's pace and style of learning.

Spanish Language Institute (SLI; ☎ 311-00-63; www.asli.com.mx) All levels catered for, aimed largely at professionals. Offers vocational courses such as Spanish for airline personnel, Spanish for medicine, and Spanish and golf.

TLALOC (☎ 317-52-78; www.tlaloc.com.mx) Run by teacher Alfredo Martínez, TLALOC was set up to provide a better deal for teachers and other Mexican employees who, according to Alfredo, get a bad deal from many of the other local language schools. Wages are higher here, teachers get paid sick leave and medical care, and there's a strong volunteering aspect to courses here. Nevertheless, it's cheaper than many of the bigger schools, making it a great place to give something back as well as to learn Spanish.

Universal Centro de Lengua y Comunicación (☎ 318-29-04; www.universal-spanish.com) Wide-ranging courses for all levels, aiming for quick learning in all fields. Study is combined with field trips and practical use in real-life situations.

Festivals & Events

Over the five days leading up to Ash Wednesday (falling late February or early March), Cuernavaca's colorful **Carnaval** celebrations feature parades and art exhibits, plus street performances by Tepoztlán's Chinelo dancers. From late March to early April, the city's **Feria de la Primavera** (Spring Fair) includes cultural and artistic events, plus concerts and a beautiful exhibit of the city's spring flowers.

Sleeping

There are some real gems among Cuerna's scores of hotels, although they tend to be the pricier options – a steady stream of upmarket boutique hotels have opened in recent years, and some of the best in the country are here, aimed squarely at weekend refugees from the capital. Budget hotels tend to be of poor quality (with some notable exceptions), while midrange places are thin on the ground. The town fills up with visitors from Mexico City at weekends and holidays, so it's best to arrive with prior reservations.

BUDGET

Hotel Juárez (☎ 314-02-19; Netzahualcóyotl 19; s/d without bathroom M$200/250, s/d M$300/350; P ☎) This is unlikely to be anyone's first choice, but it's a cheap fallback. The rooms are basic and old, many lacking natural light, so it's deeply uncharming, yet it's very well located and has a great pool in its garden.

Hotel Colonial (☎ 318-64-14; Aragón y León 19; s/d/t M$220/250/350) Another basic backpacker place that, while fine, is hard to recommend enthusiastically. Two people sharing one bed works out slightly cheaper than the prices listed, and upstairs rooms with balconies and tall ceilings are best.

Hotel Las Hortensas (☎ 318-52-65; Hidalgo 13; s/d M$250/290) It's cheap and central, but beyond that there's little to recommend Las Hortensas, although there is an incongruously charming garden at its center. The rooms are very basic, small and charmless, although the rooms upstairs are better, with more light and fresh air.

Hotel Iberia (☎ 312-60-40; www.hoteliberia.com.mx; Rayón 7; s/d M$290/370; P) Rooms may be a little small at this good-value student favorite. With iron bedsteads and matching fittings, the rooms have a modicum of style. Staff within the Talavera-tiled reception area are pretty indifferent, however.

our pick Hosteria del Sol (☎ 318-32-41; Callejón de la Bolsa del Diablo; r without/with bathroom M$300/400; 🖳) The moment you enter this perfectly located little charmer it's clear what's wrong with most of Cuernavaca's other budget accommodation. Prices here are rock bottom, but everything is spotless and beautifully decorated in traditional blue and yellow tones. With just six rooms (half of which share facilities), it's best to ring ahead, although staff don't speak a word of English.

MIDRANGE
La Casa Mediterránea (☎ 317-11-53; www.lacasamediterranea.com; Acacias 207, Colonia La Pradera; s/d incl breakfast M$350/500; P 🖳) Excellent value for money – you'd being paying twice as much were it in the town center – and a gorgeous place in its own right. Popular with language students, the seven-room family home is 3km out of town but features large, well-maintained rooms and a friendly welcome.

Villa Calmecac (☎ 313-29-18; www.villacalmecac.com; Zacatecas 114, Colonia Buenavista; dm/d incl breakfast M$450/650; P 🖳) Crafted from adobe and surrounded by organic gardens, this eco-friendly hostel is 7km from Cuernavaca's center. Yoga classes are offered, breakfast is an all-natural buffet and the bunks are in rustic-style rooms. It's 800m west of Hwy 95, a 20-minute ride from the corner of Av Morelos and Degollado on a Ruta 1, 2 or 3 bus (M$7). Zacatecas is two blocks past the Zapata monument on the left. Visitors must check in before 9pm.

Hotel Antigua Posada (☎ 310-21-79; www.hotelantiguaposada.com; Galeana 69; r/ste incl breakfast M$800/950-1100; P 🖳) This exclusive little hideaway boasts just 11 rooms behind its unpromising exterior, a short walk from the center of town. However, once inside there's a lovely courtyard and great service, and all the rooms are of very high standard, complete with wooden beams, rustic touches and full facilities including free wi-fi and valet parking.

Hotel Laam (☎ 314-44-11; www.laamhotel.com; Av Morelos 239; r M$850; P 🖳) This new addition to the Cuernavaca hotel scene has the feel of a motel, but its rooms are comfortable, if a little sterile, and some have huge terraces. It's set back from the main road so noise isn't a big problem, although the setting isn't exactly charming either. A small pool and delightful staff compensate for these shortcomings.

TOP END
La Casa Azul (☎ 314-21-41, 314-36-34; www.hotelcasaazul.com.mx; Arista 17; r/ste M$850/1880; P 🖳) This 24-room boutique hotel is a short walk from the town center and has lots of charm, although the suites are a big price jump from the rooms and they aren't that much bigger. Originally part of the Guadalupe Convent, the hotel has soothing fountains, two pools, free wi-fi and a great selection of local arts and crafts throughout. The staff are delightful, the setting is tranquil and the decor is classic Mexican.

Casa Colonial (☎ 312-70-33, 800-623-08-43; www.casacolonial.com; Netzahualcóyotl 37; r/ste from M$985/1215; P 🖳) One of the best places in town, the 16-room Casa Colonial oozes thought and style. Set in a charming garden around a large pool, this 19th-century mansion has been lovingly restored and cleverly updated, with beautifully furnished rooms, some of which feature saunas and fireplaces. The cheaper bungalows at the back are still of excellent standard.

Hotel Jacarandas (☎ 315-77-77/76, in Mexico City 55-5544-3098; www.jacarandas.com.mx; Cuauhtémoc 133, Colonia Chapultepec; r from M$1400, ste M$2600-4400; P 🖳) This large five-star place is designed for a true getaway from city life. Set in rambling grounds graced with lots of trees, exuberant gardens, a good restaurant and three pools of varying temperatures, this is a great – if pricey – weekend option. It's 2km east of the center.

Hotel Posada María Cristina (☎ 318-57-67, 800-713-74-07; reservaciones@maria-cristina.com; Juárez 300; r/ste from M$1887/2900; P 🖳) This centrally located 16th-century estate is one of Cuernavaca's long-time favorites. Highlights include 20 tastefully appointed rooms in a nicely restored colonial building, the charming *nueva cocina mexicana* restaurant and bar Calandria, with its popular Sunday champagne buffet, and an inviting pool and Jacuzzi amidst lovely hillside gardens.

Hotel Hacienda de Cortés (☎ 316-08-67, 800-220-76-97; www.hotelhaciendadecortes.com; Plaza Kennedy 90; r/ste from M$2350/3525; P 🖳) Built in the 16th century by Martín Cortés, who succeeded Hernán Cortés as Marqués del Valle de Oaxaca, this former sugar mill was renovated in 1980. It boasts 23 rooms of various levels of luxury, each with its own private garden and terrace. There's a swimming pool built around old stone columns. Sadly though, we've heard from several guests that the rooms weren't in the best state when they visited. However, this is still an incredible place for a memorable night or two.

Las Mañanitas (☎ 362-00-00, in Mexico City 800-221-52-99, in the US 888-413-9199; www.lasmananitas.com .mx; Linares 107; ste incl breakfast Sun-Thu M$2260-4642, Fri & Sat M$2623-5061; P ⊗ ☐ ☑) This utterly stunning place is where to head if you plan to impress someone. It's very much a destination hotel – you may not leave it for the whole weekend, after all – and so the fact that it's not in the exact center of town is irrelevant. The rooms are large, beautifully decorated yet understated, and many have large terraces overlooking the sumptuous private gardens, stuffed full of peacocks and featuring a heated pool. As you'd expect, it's home-away-from-home to Mexico's upper crust.

Eating

Cuernavaca has some great eating options, although, in a familiar pattern, it tends to be the upmarket options that really stand out.

BUDGET

La Comuna (☎ 318-27-57; Morrow 6; mains M$20-30; ☻ 8am-9pm Mon-Sat) One of the friendliest places in town, La Comuna is decorated with handicrafts and serves up excellent organic coffee, as well as cheap beer, cocktails, pies, *tamales* and fruit salads with granola. Drop by for the daily buffet breakfast, a generous set midday meal, or to browse its small gift shop.

La Cueva (no phone; Galeana; mains M$20-75; ☻ 8am-11pm) This sloped bar, which opens onto the bustling crowds of Galeana, serves up superb *pozole* (shredded meat and hominy in a delicious pork-based broth) and a range of other delicious snacks and light meals. This is a great place to come and eat with the locals at local prices. It's also an excellent place for breakfast, with a range on offer for just M$25.

Coffee Mexico (Gutenberg 206; ☻ 8am-9pm) This independent little coffee shop is a great spot to recharge or get breakfast. There are delicious pastries on sale, and it's popular with language students and local students alike.

El Barco (☎ 313-21-31; Rayón 5F; mains M$30-90; ☻ 11am-midnight) This popular, no-nonsense joint specializes in Guerrero-style *pozole*, the all-curing Mexican version of matzo-ball soup. Small or heaping clay bowls are accompanied by fine oregano, mildly hot red chili, shredded lettuce, limes and chopped onions. Specify *pollo* (chicken) *maciza* unless you'd like your soup to include bits of fat, and *especial* if you enjoy avocado. For refreshment, there's ice-cold beer, pitchers of *agua de jamaica* (hibiscus water) and top-shelf tequilas.

MIDRANGE

Restaurant y Cafetería Los Arcos (☎ 312-44-86; Jardín de los Héroes 4; mains M$40-120) Right in the thick of things just off the Plaza de Armas, Los Arcos is a European-style café that makes for a great meeting place, with huge terrace that's nearly always packed. Whether you come for early-morning coffee, late-night cocktails or a meal in between, you'll find friendly and efficient service. There's also a *gelatería* serving up great ice cream. Happy hours run from 2pm until 4pm and again from 8pm to 10pm.

Trattoria Marco Polo (☎ 318-40-32; Hidalgo 30; mains M$60-120, pizza M$45-200; ☻ 1-10:30pm Sun-Thu, 1pm-midnight Fri & Sat) This handy little place does decent Italian dishes in an attractive setting just across from the cathedral. The pizza list alone is huge, and there's friendly service and a decent choice of wine as well. Try for a table by the balcony.

La Universal (☎ 318-59-70; cnr Gutenberg & Guerrero; mains M$100) The Universal enjoys a strategic position on the corner of the two central plazas, with tables under an awning facing the Plaza de Armas. The people-watching is great, but you can find better eats elsewhere.

La Strada (☎ 318-60-85; Salazar 38; mains M$70-150) On the corner of Salazar and the walking street also known as Callejón del Cubo, this inviting slice of Rome presents authentic Italian–Mediterranean cuisine in a covered interior courtyard. The napkins are linen, the wine cellar well stocked, the lettuce organic and the service attentive. Considering its location near the Palacio de Cortés, it's not too touristy. Romance fills the air Friday and Saturday nights, when there's live violin music and opera singing.

TOP END

Restaurant Las Mañanitas (☎ 314-14-66; Linares 107; breakfast M$60-160, mains M$400; ☻ 1-5pm & 7-11pm) The restaurant and bar of the town's most famous hotel (left) is open to all, and it shouldn't be missed if you want a memorable, romantic dinner in ultra-smart surroundings. The menu has a heavy French accent, with dishes such as Entrecote Bourguignon and Royal Magret (duck breast), not to mention sumptuous deserts. Choose between tables inside the mansion or on the terrace, from where you can watch the wildlife wander around the emerald-green garden among fine modern sculptures. Reservations are recommended.

La India Bonita (☎ 318-69-67; Morrow 115; mains M$75-150; ❧ 8am-11pm Tue-Sat, 9am-5pm Sun & Mon) Cuernavaca's oldest restaurant is also undoubtedly one of its most charming, set in a lovely courtyard, but with the option of indoor dining available. The staff are friendly, and the traditional Mexican menu with a twist is enticing – from *brocheta al mezcal* to *chile en nogada* (*poblano* pepper in walnut sauce). There's an elaborate Sunday buffet brunch, a full bar and live folkloric ballet Saturdays from 7pm.

Reposado (☎ 169-72-32; www.reposado.com.mx; Netzahualcóyotl 33; mains M$80-165; ❧ 7pm-1am Tue-Sat, 4-11pm Sun) Synonymous with its celebrity chef Ana García, a local girl who has made a name for herself both in Mexico and the US with her promotion of Mexican *nouvelle cuisine*. Don't miss a chance to come to her charming, intimate restaurant and try her exciting, ever-changing menu of traditional Mexican cooking with innovations. The romantically candlelit tables are scattered throughout the colonial complex. There's a stylish cocktail lounge full of sofas in a loft overlooking the pool. Those really interested can arrange to stay in the small onsite hotel here and take cookery courses with Chef García – see the website for details.

our pick **Casa Hidalgo** (☎ 312-27-49, www.casa hidalgo.com; Hidalgo 6; mains M$160) Directly opposite the Palacio de Cortés with a great terrace and an even better upstairs balcony, this is one of Cuernavaca's most popular eateries and attracts a well-heeled crowd of local socialites and wealthy visitors. The menu is eclectic (try shrimp tacos with beans wrapped in banana skin, or braided red snapper and salmon in an orange-and-parsley sauce, for example). Super-friendly staff, a strong wine list and great views make this one of the best places in town for a meal.

Gaia (☎ 312-36-56, www.gaiarest.com.mx; Juárez 102; mains M$190; ❧ 2pm-midnight Mon-Sat, 1-6pm Sun) This gorgeous, stylish place, located in a delightful colonial building that was once the mansion of the 'Mexican Charlie Chaplin,' actor Mario Morenohas, has a very impressive international menu, with such dishes as linguini with shrimp in cilantro sauce and 'fish trilogy' served with tamarind and chili. Reserve a table with a view of the Diego Rivera mosaic that adorns the bottom of the swimming pool. Delivery and takeout are also available.

Drinking

There's buzzing nightlife in Cuernavaca, supported by a year-round student population that keeps places busy every night of the week. The most accessible bars are around Plazuela del Zacate and the adjacent alley Las Casas, where there's a selection of fun joints, most of which offer live music or karaoke, not making them great for a quiet beer. These places all open around sunset and typically don't shut their doors until around sunrise. There are no cover charges.

El Rincón Bohemio (Plazuela del Zacate) Popular with travelers and local students, there's live music every night, usually of the one-man-and-guitar variety, but this changes. Cheap beer deals keep people coming.

El Romántico (Plazuela del Zacate) Next door to El Rincón Bohemio, and with a very similar vibe.

Eclipse (Plazuela del Zacate) Across the road from El Rincón Bohemio and El Romántico, Eclipse has performers on two levels, folk on the bottom and rock on top.

La Plazuela (Las Casas) For those not into the guitar scene, this is the home of booming house and techno. Around the corner from the bars above.

La Estación Zócalo (cnr Blvd Juárez & Hidalgo) Opposite the Palacio de Cortés, this place attracts an even younger crowd with blaring rock music and two brightly colored but dimly lit dance floors.

Entertainment

Hanging around the central plazas is a popular activity, especially on Sundays from 6pm, when open-air concerts are often staged. Jardín Borda (p252) hosts recitals most Thursdays at 7pm.

NIGHTCLUBS

Better discos impose a cover charge of at least M$50, but women will often be allowed in for free. Some discos enforce dress codes, and trendier places post style police at the door. Things really get going after 11pm. Some recommended venues:

Barba Azul (☎ 311-55-11/55; Prado 10, Colonia San Jerónimo; ☽ 10pm-late Fri & Sat) Fab indoor gardens.

NB Club (☎ 318-89-29; Plaza de Armas) Large and centrally located.

Club Memories (☎ 318-43-80; Av Morelos 241; ☽ 10pm-late Wed, Fri & Sat) An upscale option.

THEATER

If your *español* is up to it, sample Cuernavaca's theater scene.

Cine Teatro Morelos (☎ 318-10-50; Av Morelos 188; tickets from M$20) Morelos' state theater hosts quality film series, plays and dance performances. There's a full schedule posted out front and a bookstore and café inside.

Teatro Ocampo (☎ 318-63-85; Jardín Juárez 2) Near Jardín Juárez, this theater stages contemporary plays. A calendar of cultural events is posted at its entrance.

LUCHA LIBRE

Arena Isabel (☎ 318-59-16; cnr Juárez & Abasolo; adult/child M$60/35; ♿) Are you ready to rumble, *amigo?* Less highbrow diversions, namely *lucha libre* (a form of wrestling), go down here in the squared ring. Check out the good-versus-evil lineups on posters pasted up around town. *Lucha libre* is very popular with kids.

Shopping

Cuernavaca lacks distinctive handicrafts, but if you crave an onyx ashtray, a leather belt or some second-rate silver, peruse the souvenir stalls adjacent to Palacio de Cortés or around the Plaza de Armas at weekends.

Getting There & Away

BUS

Cuernavaca's main-line bus companies operate the following separate long-distance terminals:

Estrella de Oro (EDO; ☎ 312-30-55; www.estrellade oro.com.mx; Av Morelos Sur 900)

Estrella Roja (ER; ☎ 318-59-34; www.estrellaroja.com .mx; cnr Galeana & Cuauhtemotzin)

Flecha Roja & Estrella Blanca (FR & EB; ☎ 312-26-26; www.estrellablanca.com.mx; Av Morelos 503, btwn Arista & Victoria) Futura services leave from here as well.

Pullman de Morelos (PDM; ☎ 318-69-85; www .pullman.com.mx) Casino de la Selva (☎ 318-92-05; Av del Parque s/n); Downtown (cnr Abasolo & Netzahualcóyotl)

Daily 1st-class and deluxe services from Cuernavaca include the following:

Destination	Fare	Duration	Frequency
Acapulco	M$265	4hr	every 2 hours (Futura)
Cuautla	M$40	1¼hr	every 15min 6am-8pm (ER)
Grutas de Cacahuamilpa	M$38	2hr	6 daily (ER)
Mexico City	executive M$75	1¼hr	every 10 min (from Casino de la Selva)
	M$65	4hr	every 1-2 hours (EB)
	deluxe M$63	1¼hr	every 15 min 5am-11:15pm (PDM from Casino de la Selva)
Mexico City Airport	M$125	2hr	every 10 min (PDM from Casino de la Selva)
Puebla	M$140	2¾hr	hourly (ER & EDO via Autopista Siglo XXI)
Taxco	M$52	1½hr	hourly (EB)
Tepoztlán	M$18	30min	every 15min 6am-8pm (ER); also departs a bit later from the local bus terminal at the city market.

CAR & MOTORCYCLE

Cuernavaca is 89km south of Mexico City, a 1½-hour drive on Hwy 95 or a one-hour trip via Hwy 95D. Both roads continue south to Acapulco – Hwy 95 detours through Taxco, Hwy 95D is more direct and much faster.

Getting Around

You can walk to most places of interest in central Cuernavaca. Local buses (M$6) advertise their destinations on their windshields. Many local buses, and those to nearby towns, leave from the southern corner of the city's labyrinthine market. Taxis serve most places in town for around M$30.

To get to the Estrella de Oro bus terminal, 1km south (downhill) of the center, hop on a Ruta 20 bus down Galeana; in the other direction, catch any bus heading up Av Morelos. Ruta 17 buses head up Av Morelos and stop within one block of the Pullman de Morelos terminal at Casino de la Selva. All other depots are within walking distance of the *zócalo*.

AROUND MEXICO CITY

XOCHICALCO

Atop a desolate plateau with views for miles around, Xochicalco (☎ 777-379-74-16; admission M$45; ⏲ 9am-5pm) is an impressive and relatively easy day trip from Cuernavaca that shouldn't be missed. It's large enough to make the journey worthwhile but not so well known as to be overrun with tourists. Note that a video permit costs M$35.

A Unesco World Heritage Site and one of central Mexico's most important archaeological sites, Xochicalco (so-chee-*cal*-co) is Náhuatl for 'place of the house of flowers.'

The collection of white stone ruins, many still to be excavated, covers approximately 10 sq km. They represent the various cultures – Toltec, Olmec, Zapotec, Mixtec and Aztec – for which Xochicalco was a commercial, cultural or religious center. When Teotihuacán began to weaken around AD 650 to 700, Xochicalco began to rise in importance, achieving its maximum splendor between AD 650 and 900, with far-reaching cultural and commercial relations. Around AD 650, Zapotec, Mayan and Gulf coast spiritual leaders convened here to correlate their respective calendars. Xochicalco remained an important center until around 1200, when its excessive growth precipitated a demise similar to that of Teotihuacán.

The site's most famous monument is the **Pirámide de Quetzalcóatl**. Archaeologists have surmised from its well-preserved bas-reliefs that astronomer–priests met here at the beginning and end of each 52-year cycle of the pre-Hispanic calendar. Another sight not to be missed is the **Observatory** (ask the guard to turn on the lights), which takes you deep into an eerie and dank room through which a beam of sunlight falls.

Site signs are in English and Spanish, but information at the excellent, ecologically sensitive **museum**, 200m from the ruins, is in Spanish only.

Getting There & Away

From Cuernavaca's market, 'Cuautepec' buses (M$12) depart every 30 minutes for the site entrance. The last return bus leaves around 6pm. Alternatively, Pullman de Morelos runs hourly buses (M$25) that will drop you off within 4km of the site, and Flecha Roja runs buses by the same intersection every two hours. From there it's a long, dull, uphill walk, or you can catch a shared taxi (M$5) to

the site. Just try to flag down anything you can. On arrival, you'll need to walk round to the museum to buy tickets – you can't get them at the site itself.

TAXCO

☎ 762 / pop 90,000 / elevation 1800m

The first sight of Taxco (*tahss*-ko) across the steep valley as you approach it on the curvy road from Mexico City is enough to take your breath away. Scattered down a precipitous hillside surrounded by dramatic mountains and cliffs, its perfectly preserved colonial architecture and the twin belfries of its baroque masterpiece, Parroquia Santa Prisca, make for one of the most beguiling views anywhere in the central highlands.

Taxco, 160km southwest of Mexico City, has ridden waves of boom and bust associated with the fantastically wealthy silver deposits discovered here in the 16th century and then repeatedly until the early 20th century. With its silver now almost all gone, the town has fallen back on tourism to sustain it. On the one hand Taxco is a rare example of development being carried out in close association with preservation. On the other, the town can sometimes feel like it's given itself over to the tour groups a little bit too much. Any day of the week you'll find visitors wandering the narrow cobblestone streets, peering into the endless rows of silver shops, while at the weekends Taxco is often flooded with weekenders from Mexico City. The sheer noise of the countless Beetle taxis that serve the entire population of this steepest of towns can also be a problem. You'll need to chose your accommodation carefully if you want a quiet night.

Despite these reservations, Taxco is a fabulous destination and one of the best weekend trips you can do from Mexico City. Unlike many colonial-era towns, Taxco has not become engulfed by industrial suburbs, and its status as a national historical monument means that even new buildings must conform to the old in scale, style and materials.

History

Taxco was called Tlachco (Ball-Playing Place) by the Aztecs, who dominated the region from 1440 until the Spanish arrived. The colonial city was founded by Rodrigo de Castañeda in 1529, with a mandate from Hernán Cortés. Among the town's first Spanish residents were three miners – Juan de Cabra, Juan Salcedo and Diego de Nava – and the carpenter Pedro Muriel. In 1531, they established the first Spanish mine in North America.

The Spaniards came searching for tin, which they found in small quantities, but by 1534 they had discovered tremendous lodes of silver. That year the Hacienda El Chorrillo was built, complete with water wheel, smelter and aqueduct – the remains of which form the old arches (Los Arcos) over Hwy 95 at the north end of town.

The prospectors quickly depleted the first silver veins and fled Taxco. Further quantities of ore were not discovered until 1743. Don José de la Borda, who had arrived in 1716 from France at the age of 16 to work with his miner brother, accidentally unearthed one of the region's richest veins. According to legend, Borda was riding near where the Templo de Santa Prisca now stands, when his horse stumbled, dislodged a stone and exposed the precious metal.

Borda went on to make three fortunes and lose two. He introduced new techniques of draining and repairing mines, and he reportedly treated his indigenous workers better than most colonial mines. The Templo de Santa Prisca was the devout Borda's gift to Taxco. His success attracted more prospectors, and new silver veins were found and played out. With most of the silver gone, Taxco became a quiet town with a dwindling population and economy.

In 1929, an American architect and professor named William (Guillermo) Spratling arrived and, at the suggestion of then US ambassador Dwight Morrow, set up a silver workshop as a way to rejuvenate the town. (Another version has it that Spratling was writing a book and resorted to the silver business because his publisher went bust. A third has it that Spratling had a notion to create jewelry that synthesized pre-Hispanic motifs with art deco modernism.) The workshop evolved into a factory, and Spratling's apprentices began establishing their own shops. Today, Taxco is home to hundreds of silver shops, many producing for export.

Orientation

While one of the joys of Taxco is getting lost while aimlessly wandering the pretty streets, it's actually a very easy place to find your way around. The twin belfries of Santa Prisca make the best landmark, situated as they are on the *zócalo*, Plaza Borda. Nearly all of the town's streets one-way, with the main road, Av de los Plateros, being the only major two-way street. This is where both bus stations are located, and is the road for entering and leaving the town. The basic minibus route is a counterclockwise loop going north on Av de los Plateros and south through the center of town.

Information

Several banks around the main plazas and bus stations have ATMs. There are card phones near Plaza Borda, and quieter ones in nicer hotel lobbies. The tourist info stand at the Futura bus station has free city maps, and there are a huge number of internet cafés in Taxco.

Cruz Roja (Red Cross; ☎ 622-32-32)

Net X Internet (Ruíz de Alarcón 11; per hr M$10) One of the better internet cafés.

Police (☎ 622-00-77)

Post office (Palacio Municipal, Benito Juarez 10)

Secretaría de Fomento Turístico (☎ 622-50-73; Av de los Plateros; ⏱ 9am-3pm & 4-6pm) At north end of town. English- and French-speaking staff arrange guided tours of Taxco.

Sights & Activities
TEMPLO DE SANTA PRISCA

The icon of Taxco, **Santa Prisca** (⏱ 9am-6pm) was a labor of love for town hero José de la Borda. The local Catholic hierarchy allowed the silver magnate to donate this church to Taxco on the condition that he mortgage his mansion and other assets to guarantee its completion. The project nearly bankrupted him, but the risk was well worth it – the resulting building is one of Mexico's most beautiful and striking pieces of baroque architecture. It was designed by Spanish architects Juan Caballero and Diego Durán, and was constructed between 1751 and 1758.

Perhaps Santa Prisca's most striking feature, best viewed side-on, is the contrast between its belfries, with their elaborate Churrigueresque facade overlooking the Plaza Borda, and the far more simple, constrained and elegant nave. The rose-colored stone used on the facade is extraordinarily beautiful in the sunlight – look out for the oval bas-relief depiction of Christ's baptism above the doorway. Inside, the intricately sculpted, gold-covered altarpieces are equally fine Churrigueresque specimens.

TAXCO

0		200 m
0		0.1 miles

INFORMATION
Banamex (ATM)...................................**1** B4	
Banamex ATM......................................**2** A5	
Bancomer (ATM)..................................**3** A5	
IMSS Hospital......................................**4** C6	
Net X Internet.....................................**5** B4	
Post Office....................................(see 10)	

SIGHTS & ACTIVITIES
Casa Borda (Centro Cultural Taxco)....**6** B4	
Centro de Enseñanza Para Extranjeros.**7** C3	
Museo de Arte Virreinal (Casa	
Humboldt)..**8** B4	
Museo Guillermo Spratling.................**9** B4	
Palacio Municipal...............................**10** B4	
Templo de Santa Prisca......................**11** B4	

SLEEPING
Casa de Huéspedes Arellano...............**12** B5	
Hotel Agua Escondida.........................**13** A4	
Hotel Best Western Taxco **14** A5	
Hotel Casa Grande..............................**15** A5	
Hotel Emilia Castillo...........................**16** B4	
Hotel Los Arcos..................................**17** B4	
Hotel Meléndez...................................**18** B4	
Hotel Mi Casita...................................**19** B4	
Hotel Posada San Javier.....................**20** B4	
Hotel Posada Santa Anita...................**21** C5	
Hotel Real de San Deigo.....................**22** C3	
Hotel Santa Prisca..............................**23** A5	
Posada de la Misión............................**24** D3	
Posada Los Balcones...........................**25** A4	

EATING
Acerto...**26** A5	
Café Borda..**27** A5	
Café Sacha..**28** B4	
Del Ángel Inn......................................**29** B4	
Del Convento......................................**30** B4	
Hostería Bar El Adobe.........................**31** A5	
La Casona......................................(see 29)	
La Concha Nostra...........................(see 15)	
La Hamburguesa.................................**32** B5	
Pozolería Tía Calla.............................**33** B4	
Restaurant Santa Fe...........................**34** A5	
Sotavento..**35** B4	

DRINKING
Bar Berta...**36** A5	

SHOPPING
Emilia Castillo................................(see 16)	
Handicrafts Stalls................................**37** B5	
Joyería Elena de los Ballesteros..........**38** B4	
Mercado de Artesanías Plata..............**39** B5	
Patio de las Artesanías ....(see 33)	
Pineda's...(see 38)	

TRANSPORT
Combis to Las Grutas de	
Cacahuamilpa....................................**40** C5	
Estrella de Oro Bus Station.................**41** A6	
Futura/Estrella Blanca Bus Station....**42** C5	

To Instituto de Artes Plásticas (750m);
Secretaría de Fomento Turístico (750m);
Los Arcos (800m); Teleférico to
Hotel Monte Taxco (800m);
Las Grutas de Cacahuamilpa (29km);
Cuernavaca (80km);
Mexico City (160km)

López Mateos

Av de los Plateros

Cerro de la Misión

La Garita

Reforma

Estacadas

Altos de
Redondo

Plazuela
de Bernal

Plaza
Taxco

Ex-Rastro

Plaza Taxco

Juárez

Juan Ruiz del Alarcón

Fundiciones

To Hotel Loma
Linda (100m)

Muñoz

Plaza
Borda
(Zócalo)

Delgado

Calle del Arco

Veracruz

Beccara Y Tanco

To Hotel
Victoria
(250m)

Cuauhtémoc

Los Pajaritos

El Fresno

Av de los Plateros

Plazuela
de San Juan

Market

Luis Montes de Oca

Hidalgo

Cena Obscuras

Tetitlán

Santa Ana

Cena Obscuras

Parque
Vicente
Guerrero

Morelos

Calle del Consuelo

To Pemex (500m);
Taxco El Viejo (14km);
Acapulco (266km)

Colegio Militar

MUSEO GUILLERMO SPRATLING

This very well laid-out three-storey **history and archaeology museum** (☎ 622-16-70; Delgado 1; admission M$27; ☉ 9am 6pm Tue-Sat, 9am-3pm Sun) is off an alley behind Templo de Santa Prisca. It contains a small but excellent collection of pre-Hispanic jewelry, art, pottery and sculpture from American silversmith William Spratling's private collection. The phallic cult pieces are a particular eye-opener. On the basement floor there are examples of Spratling's designs using pre-Hispanic motifs. The top floor hosts occasional temporary exhibits. Sadly for such a well-run museum, all the labeling is in Spanish only.

MUSEO DE ARTE VIRREINAL

This charming, rather rag-tag **religious art museum** (☎ 622-55-01; Ruiz de Alarcón 12; adult/student M$20/15; ☉ 10am-5.45pm Tue-Sat, 10am-3.45pm Sun) is housed in a wonderful old house that is often referred to as Casa Humboldt, even though the famous German explorer and naturalist Friedrich Heinrich Alexander von Humboldt slept here for only one night in 1803! The museum hosts a small but well-displayed collection, labeled in English and Spanish. The most interesting exhibit describes restoration work on Santa Prisca, during which some fabulous material (including tapestries, woodwork altar pieces and rich decorative fabrics) was discovered in the basement, and there's also an interesting display on the Manila Galleons, which pioneered trade between the Americas and the Far East.

CASA BORDA (CENTRO CULTURAL TAXCO)

Built by José de la Borda in 1759, the **Casa Borda** (☎ 622-66-34; Plaza Borda; admission free; ☉ 10am-5pm Tue-Sun) serves as a cultural center hosting experimental theater and exhibiting contemporary sculpture, painting and photography by Guerrero artists. The building, however, is the main attraction. Due to the unevenness of the terrain, the rear window looks out on a precipitous four-storey drop, even though the entrance is on the ground floor.

TELEFÉRICO

From the north end of Taxco, near Los Arcos, a Swiss-made **aerial cable car** (one-way/round-trip M$20/30; ☉ 7:45am-7pm) ascends 173m to the Hotel Monte Taxco resort (p263), af-fording fantastic views of Taxco and the surrounding mountains. To find the entrance, walk uphill from the south side of Los Arcos and turn right through the Instituto de Artes Plásticas gate.

Courses

Taxco is a popular place for foreigners to come and study.

Centro de Enseñanza Para Extranjeros (CEPE; ☎ 622-34-10; www.cepe.unam.mx; courses from M$4500) This branch of Mexico City's Universidad Nacional Autónoma de México offers intensive Spanish-language courses in the atmospheric Ex-Hacienda El Chorrillo. Advanced students may take additional courses in Mexican art history, geography and literature. CEPE can arrange lodging with local host families for M$1400 to M$2400 per month.

Escuela Nacional de Artes Plásticas (☎ 622-36-90; www.enap.unam.mx) Next door, this school offers arts workshops from M$1500 per month or M$8500 per semester.

Festivals & Events

Be sure to reserve your hotel in advance if your visit coincides with one of Taxco's annual festivals. Double-check exact dates of moveable feasts with the tourist office.

Fiestas de Santa Prisca & San Sebastián Taxco's patron saints are honored on January 18 (Santa Prisca) and January 20 (San Sebastián), when locals parade by the Templo de Santa Prisca for an annual blessing, their pets and farm animals in tow.

Jueves Santo The Thursday before Easter, the Eucharist is commemorated with street processions of hooded penitents who flagellate themselves with thorns as the procession winds through town.

Jornadas Alarconianas During this summertime cultural festival, which honors Taxco-born playwright Juan Ruiz de Alarcón, Taxco's plazas and churches host concerts and dance performances by internationally renowned performing artists.

Día del Jumil The Monday after Day of the Dead (November 2), the *jumil* – the edible beetle said to represent the giving of life and energy to Taxco residents for another year – is celebrated. Many families camp on the Cerro de Huixteco over the preceding weekend, and townsfolk climb the hill to collect *jumiles* and share food and camaraderie.

Feria de la Plata The week-long national silver fair convenes in late November or early December. Competitions are held in various categories (such as jewelry and statuary), and some of Mexico's best silverwork is on display. Other festivities include rodeos, concerts, dances and burro races.

Las Posadas From December 16 to 24, nightly candlelit processions fill Taxco's streets with door-to-door singing. Children are dressed up to resemble biblical characters. At the end of the night, they attack piñatas.

Sleeping

Taxco has a wealth of hotels, from large four- and five-star hotels to charming family-run posadas. It's always best to reserve ahead, and often essential at the weekend when the hordes arrive from Mexico City.

BUDGET

Casa de Huéspedes Arellano (☎ 622-0365; Los Pajaritos 23; dm per person M$100, s without/with bathroom M$140/160, d M$180/220) There's a large variety of basic but clean rooms in this, Taxco's most backpackery option. The ground floor rooms are the very cheapest (s/d M$100/150) as they have no balcony. Other rooms can sleep up to six people (M$600), and most others have balconies. It's well tended, with lots of flowers, caged birds, a variety of rooms and ample terraces for relaxing.

Hotel Casa Grande (☎ 622-09-69; Plazuela de San Juan 7; s without/with bathroom M$155/230, d M$230/355; 🖵) The basic rooms at the Casa Grande are very clean, and it's almost worth staying here just for the superb terrace overlooking the square. However, it's an extremely noisy place due to both the traffic and the music for La Concha Nostra (p264) downstairs. The apartments around the back are quieter, but also a bit run down. The one with three bedrooms (M$530) is recommended.

Hotel Posada Santa Anita (☎ 622-07-52; hpsta54@ hotmail.com; Av de los Plateros 320; s/d/t M$250/350/400; 🅿) Only two of the 25 rooms here have views; the others are rather dark, although the ones at the back are much quieter. Moments from the Futura bus station, Santa Anita is lacking in charm but makes up for it with value for money. All rooms have an en suite bathroom and most have TV.

MIDRANGE

Posada Los Balcones (☎ 622-02-50; posada_balcones@ hotmail.com; Plazuela de los Gallos 5; s/d/t M$300/450/550) This good-value, centrally located place has some surprisingly charming rooms, and – as the names suggests – many of these have balconies, which overlook the boisterous street below, just moments from Santa Prisca. All 15 rooms have TV and bathroom.

Hotel Santa Prisca (☎ 622-00-80; htl_staprisca@ yahoo.com; Cena Obscuras 1; s/d/t M$350/500/550; 🅿) The 31-room Santa Prisca has very sweet, traditionally Mexican décor within the walls of a gorgeous old hacienda complete with courtyard garden. It has a great location too, right in the thick of things. Rooms are smallish, but most have breezy private balconies with good views. All have two beds, and newer, sunnier ones fetch a bit more. The parking lot is reached via a tunnel at the hotel's uphill end.

Hotel Meléndez (☎ 622-00-06; Cuauhtémoc 6; s/d M$395/480) Street noise penetrates the exterior rooms at this reliable, family-run favorite. Upsides include its attractively tiled public areas, a sunny terrace, great views from the larger upper-level rooms and an unbeatable central location.

Hotel Emilia Castillo (☎ /fax 622-67-17; www.hotel emiliacastillo.com; Juan Ruiz de Alarcón 7; s/d/t M$400/450/500) The 14 rooms here all have beautiful tiled bathrooms and are spotlessly clean. Owned by a famous family of silver workers, this intimate place offers colonial charm at reasonable rates. Sadly, it's in a noisy location – ask for a room at the back, but don't miss the views from the rooftop terrace.

Hotel Los Arcos (☎ 622-18-36; www.hotellosarcos .net; Juan Ruiz de Alarcón 4; s/d/ste M$425/475/550; 🖵) This rustic hotel is furnished in a traditional style and housed in a gorgeous 17th-century former monastery, full of character. All 26 rooms are charming, if not much more than basic, and the location is excellent.

Hotel Real de San Diego (☎ 627-23-30; realde sandiego@hotmail.com; Ave de los Plateros 169; s/d/t M$440/500/560; 🅿 🕭) Go for the rooms on the 2nd floor if you stay here – they're bigger and some have balconies. This place is on the main road into Taxco a short walk from the town center. There's a small pool, newly installed bathrooms in the rooms and cable TV.

Hotel Posada San Javier (☎ 622-31-77; posada sanjavier@hotmail.com; Estacadas 32; s/d from M$460/490, ste M$605-1405; 🅿 🖵 🕭) This huge place is a combination of hotel and holiday apartments built around a very pleasant garden and pool. There are 22 rooms and numerous apartments in different corners of the complex. Rooms are comfortable but nothing special – the real attraction is the excellent location and pool.

Hotel Loma Linda (☎ 622-02-06; www.hotelloma linda.com; Av de los Plateros 52; s/d M$410/480, Fri & Sat r M$650; 🅿 🕭) The rooms here are larger than most, but it's not entirely conveniently located, perched as it is on the edge of a vast chasm, 1km north of town. At least the back rooms at this well-run motel have some good valley views. There's a restaurant, a heated pool, easy parking and cable TV in the 71 rooms, some of which have terraces.

our pick **Hotel Mi Casita** (☎ 627-17-77; www.hotelmi casita.com; Altos de Redondo 1; s/d/ste/apt incl breakfast from M$550/650/700/750; ✗) This absolute gem has 12 beautifully and individually decorated rooms just moments from the *zócalo* and with great views over the cathedral. A colonial home run by a family of jewelry designers, this is one of the best bets in town, but bring your earplugs. The comfortable rooms feature original hand-painted bathroom tiles, and some have private terraces. Three rooms have rustic Talavera bathtubs, and all have fans and cable TV.

Hotel Agua Escondida (☎ 622-07-26, 800-504-03-11; www.aguaescondida.com; Plaza Borda 4; s/d M$614/760; P ☐ ☒) Facing the *zócalo*, the 'Hidden Water' has a couple of pools and a café–bar on a high terrace with unmatchable views of Santa Prisca. The 60 comfy, if sterile, rooms (some remodeled, some not) have Mexican furnishings, cable TV and phone. Rooms with balconies overlooking the street suffer bad traffic noise – try for a room at the back. Prices rise at the weekend.

Hotel Victoria (☎ 622-00-04; www.victoriataxco.com; Nibbi 5-7; r/ste from M$550/850; P ☐) This odd place was totally deserted on our last visit, staffed only by a receptionist who seemed surprised to see us. Its 50 rooms are scattered along the hillside amid a dank, overgrown garden that feels more like a primordial forest. Rooms are large and of good quality, however, especially the suites with their huge balconies, although the bathrooms are a bit the worse for wear.

TOP END
Hotel Best Western Taxco (☎ 627-61-94, 800-561-26-63; www.bestwesterntaxco.com; Nibbi 2; s/d M$999/1100, ste M$1315-1515; P ☒ ☐) If you're not looking for a particularly colonial vibe, this rather stylish and well-run Best Western is a good option. Large rooms with small bathrooms but the odd boutique flounce make for a comfortable stay right in the center of town. Upstairs rooms are larger but lack balconies. No matter; everyone enjoys access to the rooftop sun deck with 360-degree city views.

Posada de la Misión (☎ 622-00-63, 800-008-29-20; www.posadamision.com; Cerro de la Misión 32; s/d incl breakfast M$1500/1650; P ☐ ☒) A short way from the town center on the top of a steep hillock, the large, rambling grounds of Posada de la Misión are an ideal weekend escape. The charming rooms (some of which have great balconies with breathtaking views of the town) are large, airy and bright. There's also a large pool and Jacuzzi under a beautiful mosaic of Cuauhtémoc, and an excellent restaurant with more stunning views. The hotel can be overrun with tour groups, although given the space available it's likely you could escape them.

Hotel Monte Taxco (☎ 622-13-00, 800-980-0000; www.montetaxco.com.mx; Lomas de Taxco; s/d from M$1638/1735; P ☒ ☒) This improbably located country club, accessible via a cable car (p261) from the edge of Taxco, is where to come and find the golfing classes. It's hard to see what all the fuss is about, though – the hotel is nothing special, and while good for views and a relaxed weekend away, the rooms are plain and somewhat neglected. Taxco itself is too much of an effort to get to – it'd be much better just drinking by the poolside. Use of the nine-hole golf course is extra.

Eating & Drinking
Many of the best spots in town to grab a bite are also a good place to down a drink.

Café Sacha (☎ 628-51-50; Juan Ruiz de Alarcón 1A; mains M$40-80; V) This wonderfully decorated hangout enjoys low lighting, little balcony tables and free wi-fi as well as a collection of antique Lonely Planet guides to most of Central America. It's a good place to come any time of day – it can get lively in the evenings – while the good vegetarian selection and Thai and Indian specialties grab diners at other times.

La Hamburguesa (☎ 622-09-41; Plazuela de San Juan 5; burgers from M$15; ✆ closed Wed) For a light meal or a quick lunch, try this popular place on the west side of Plazuela San Juan. It serves burger-and-fries combos and excellent enchiladas.

Pozolería Tia Calla (☎ 622-56-02; Plaza Borda 1; mains M$20-40; ✆ 1:30-11pm Wed-Mon) There are no fine vistas or breezy *terrazas* here – just authentic, no-nonsense *pozole*, served up in Auntie Calla's basement. Pick your poison: chicken or pork. Pork comes loaded with *chicharrón* (fried pork skin), avocado and all the fixings. No matter your meat choice, the broth is always pork-based. The beer steins are chilled, and there's *fútbol* on the *tele*. What more could you ask for?

AROUND MEXICO CITY

Café Borda (☎ 627-20-73; Plaza Borda 6; mains M$40) This tiny place has the single best view of Santa Prisca going, and if you're lucky you can get the one balcony table and own it temporarily. Good breakfasts, strong coffee, sandwiches and Mexican *antojitos* are served here by the friendly family owners.

Del Convento (☎ 622-32-72; Estacadas 32; mains M$40-105) For one of the best views in town, the restaurant of the Posada San Javier, with its vast roof terrace setting, is hard to beat. Come by for elaborate breakfasts, evening meals or cocktails.

Hostería Bar El Adobe (☎ 622-14-16; Plazuela de San Juan 13; mains M$45-110) Views here are less captivating than at neighboring touristy eateries, but the interior décor is lovely and there's a bar full of cocktails. Specialties include Taxco-style *cecina* (salted strip steak) and shrimp-spiked garlic soup.

Sotavento (☎ 627-12-17; Juárez 12; mains M$50-145) Next door to the Palacio Municipal, the Sotavento has a great terrace and a peaceful interior garden, as well as a good in-house art gallery. From breakfasts to cocktails, from *enchiladas de mole* to prime rib, it's all served up here.

Restaurant Santa Fe (☎ 622-11-70; Hidalgo 2; mains M$55-90) In business for more than 50 years, Santa Fe is a favorite with locals, serving fairly priced traditional Mexican fare such as *conejo en chile ajo* (rabbit in garlic chili) and fresh shrimp. It offers four different set breakfasts, a hearty four-course *comida corrida* (set menu; M$60) and three styles of *pozole* daily after 6pm. The walls are bedecked with photos of local patrons and some excellent black-and-white photos of ye olde Taxco.

La Casona (☎ 622-10-71; Muñoz 4; mains M$60; ☯ 8am-8pm) Cheaper than its neighbor Del Ángel, La Casona is also less touristy, more relaxed and more traditional in its menu choices. There are equally superb views from the tables at the back, although our favorite table is the one you share with the skeleton smoking a cigar! The excellent *menu del día* is a winner for M$80.

La Concha Nostra (☎ 622-79-44; Plazuela de San Juan 5; pizzas M$90) On the second floor of the Casa Grande (p262), this popular pizza-and-pasta restaurant serves food and drink until 1am. You can watch the action on Plazuela San Juan from the balcony. Live rock music shakes the house every Saturday night.

Acerto (☎ 622-00-64; Plaza Borda 7; mains M$90-190) This strikingly modern, sleek (and rather orange) conversion of a long-standing local favorite now functions as a restaurant, cocktail bar and internet café. The main attraction is the fantastic view across the Plaza Borda to Santa Prisca, although its delicious menu of salads, soups, *antojitos* and *moles*, and the superior cocktails are also good reasons to drop by.

Del Ángel Inn (☎ 622-55-25; Muñoz 4; mains M$130-150) Expect tour groups and mariachi bands here, one of Taxco's most enduringly popular restaurants. Despite this, the superb views over the town from the 2nd-floor roof terrace are hard to beat, and food quality is good, with a range of Mexican and international cuisine on offer.

Bar Berta (Cuauhtémoc; ☯ 11am-8pm) By rights Berta should be flooded with lost-looking tourists, but remarkably there's a clientele of tough-looking locals knocking back stiff drinks and watching *fútbol* instead. There's a tiny upstairs terrace for people watching over the *zócalo* should you not fancy the charming green-painted downstairs bar. Try a *Berta* (tequila, honey, lime and mineral water), the house specialty.

Shopping

SILVER

There are several shops in the **Patio de las Artesanías** (Plaza Borda) building. **Pineda's** (☎ 622-32-33; Muñoz 1) is justly famous; next door, **Joyería Elena de los Ballesteros** (☎ 622-37-67; Muñoz 4) is another worthwhile shop.

Inside Hotel Emilia Castillo, the tableware in the showroom of **Emilia Castillo** (☎ 622-34-71; Ruiz de Alarcón 7) is a unique blend of silver and porcelain. For quantity rather than quality, trawl the vast, poorly displayed masses of rings, chains and pendants at the **Mercado de Artesanías Plata** (☯ 11am-8pm).

HANDICRAFTS

It's easy to overlook them among the silver, but there are other things to buy in Taxco. Finely painted wood and papier-mâché trays, platters and boxes are sold along Calle del Arco, on the south side of Santa Prisca, as well as wood carvings and bark paintings. Quite a few shops sell semiprecious stones, fossils and mineral crystals, and some have a good selection of ceremonial masks, puppets and semi-antique carvings.

Getting There & Away

The shared 1st-class Futura/Estrella Blanca and 2nd-class terminal, downhill from the main market, offers luggage storage. Turista services leave from this terminal as well. The 1st-class Estrella de Oro (EDO) terminal is at the south end of town.

Directo 1st-class departures include the following:

Destination	Fare	Duration	Frequency
Acapulco	M$168	4-5hr	7 daily (Futura)
Chilpancingo	M$105	2-3hr	7 daily (EDO)
	M$105	2-3hr	6 daily (Futura)
Cuernavaca	M$50	1½hr	8 daily (EDO)
	M$52	1½hr	hourly (Futura)
Mexico City (Terminal Sur)	M$105	3hr	hourly (EDO)
	M$105	3hr	5 (Turistar)
	M$105	3hr	10 (Futura)

Getting Around

Apart from walking, combis (white Volkswagen minibuses) and taxis are the best way to navigate Taxco's steep and narrow cobbled streets.

Combis (M$4) are frequent and operate from 7am to 8pm. 'Zócalo' combis depart from Plaza Borda, go down Cuauhtémoc to Plazuela de San Juan, then head down the hill on Hidalgo. They turn right at Morelos, left at Av de los Plateros, and go north until La Garita, where they turn left and return to the *zócalo*. 'Arcos/Zócalo' combis follow the same route except that they continue past La Garita to Los Arcos, where they do a U-turn and head back to La Garita. Combis marked 'PM' (for Pedro Martín) go to the south end of town from Plaza Borda, past the Estrella de Oro bus station. Taxis cost M$15 to M$30 for trips around town.

Plaza Taxco shopping center has a large parking garage (M$15 an hour, with cheaper 24-hour rates via most hotels). Access is off Av de los Plateros, via Estacadas. An elevator takes you up to the shopping center, on Ruiz de Alarcón next door to the Casa Humboldt.

PARQUE NACIONAL GRUTAS DE CACAHUAMILPA

One of central Mexico's most stunning natural phenomena is the **Cacahuamilpa caverns** (☎ 104-01-55; www.cacahuamilpa.conanp.gob.mx; tours adult/child M$60/50; ☷ 10am-7pm, last ticket sold at 5pm), a must-

see for anyone visiting Taxco or Cuernavaca. The sheer scale of the caves is hard to conceive, with vast chambers up to 82m high leading 1.2km beneath the mountainside and containing stalactites and stalagmites that will blow your mind.

Sadly, though, the current visitor experience on offer is rather ho-hum – individual access is not allowed to the (perfectly safe) pathway, so visitors have to indulge the guides who lead each group (departures each hour on the hour) stopping off to point out various funny shapes (Santa Claus, a kneeling child, a gorilla) in the rock. Speleologists prepare to be appalled, and non-Spanish speakers might just be bemused, as the guides do not generally speak English. Thankfully, after the one hour tour, you can wander back to the entrance at your own pace, although you're often virtually in the dark.

From the cave exit it's possible to hike down a path to the fast-flowing **Río Dos Bocas**, which runs through the mountainside. There are some tranquil pools to swim in, and the views alone are spectacular. Bring some bug spray.

Saturday and Sunday can be very crowded. There are restaurants, snacks and souvenir shops near the entrance.

Getting There & Away

The most comfortable way to get to the caves is to take any Toluca or Ixtapan bus from the Futura terminal in Taxco (M$21, 45 minutes). Simply ask for a ticket to 'las grutas' – this is what the driver will call out at the crossroads where the road splits off to Cuernavaca. Get out here and walk the 350m downhill on the Cuernavaca road and the visitors center will appear on your right.

There are also direct Grutas combis (M$15, 45 minutes) that depart every hour or two from the Futura bus terminal and stop at the visitor center. The combis are pretty cramped compared to the comfy Futura buses. The last combis leave the site around 5pm midweek, and 6pm on Saturday and Sunday; afterwards you may be able to catch a bus to Taxco at the crossroads or take a M$50 taxi ride back to Taxco. **Estrella Blanca/Futura** (☎ 800-507-55-00; www.estrellablanca.com.mx) 1st-class buses arrive and depart the national park six times daily to and from Cuernavaca.

AROUND MEXICO CITY

WEST OF MEXICO CITY

The area to the west of Mexico City is dominated by the large industrial and administrative city of Toluca, the capital of the state of México. While pleasant, Toluca is a place that overall has very little to recommend it to travelers, although there's enough to pass the time on an overnight stop if you're passing through.

The area's biggest draws are two wonderful but surprisingly different colonial gems: Malinalco, a sleepy and remote village with some fascinating pre-Hispanic ruins perched above it in one of the most picturesque settings imaginable, and Valle de Bravo, a cosmopolitan getaway favored by Mexico's elite and located on the shores of a large artificial reservoir a dramatic two-hour drive west of Toluca. The countryside surrounding Toluca itself is scenic, with pine forests, rivers and a huge extinct volcano, Nevado de Toluca, which shouldn't be missed for its two dramatic crater lakes.

TOLUCA

☎ 722 / pop 505,000 / elevation 2660m

Like many once-charming colonial Mexican cities, Toluca's development has created a huge ring of urban sprawl around what remains a very picturesque old town. The traffic problems alone can be enough to dampen the old town's charm, but those who make time to come here will find a pleasant, if rather busy, place in which you can easily spend a day exploring attractive plazas, lively shopping arcades and a number of art galleries and museums.

Toluca was an indigenous settlement from at least the 13th century. The Spanish founded the modern city in the 16th century, after defeating the resident Aztecs and Matlazincas, and it became part of Hernán Cortés' expansive domain, the Marquesado del Valle de Oaxaca. Since 1830, it's been capital of México state, which surrounds the Distrito Federal on three sides, like an upside-down U.

Orientation

The main road from Mexico City becomes Paseo Tollocan on Toluca's eastern edge, before bearing southwest and becoming a ring road around the city center's southern edge. Toluca's bus station and the huge Mercado Juárez are 2km southeast of the center, off Paseo Tollocan.

The vast Plaza de los Mártires, with the cathedral and Palacio de Gobierno, marks the town center. Most of the action, however, is concentrated a block south in the pedestrian precinct. Shady Parque Alameda is three blocks west along Hidalgo.

Information

The free Spanish-language monthly *Agenda Cultural* publishes a schedule of art, music and theater events.

Banks There are many with ATMs near Portal Madero.

Cruz Roja (Red Cross; ☎ 217-33-33)

Internet Café (Hidalgo 406; per hr M$8)

Red Internet (Galeana 209; per hr M$10)

State Tourist Office (☎ 212-59-98; http://turismo.edomex.gob.mx; cnr Urawa & Paseo Tollocan) Inconveniently 2km southeast of the center, but with English-speaking staff and good maps.

Tourist Information Kiosk (Palacio Municipal) Helpful kiosk with free city map.

Sights

CITY CENTER

The 19th-century **Portal Madero**, running 250m along Av Hidalgo, is lively, as is the commercial arcade along the pedestrian street to the east, which attracts mariachis after 9pm. A block north, the large, open expanse of **Plaza de los Mártires** is surrounded by fine old government buildings; the 19th-century **cathedral** and the 18th-century **Templo de la Santa Veracruz** are on its south side.

Just northeast of Plaza de los Mártires is **Plaza Garibay**. At its east end stands the unique **Cosmo Vitral Jardín Botánico** (Cosmic Stained-Glass Window Botanical Garden; ☎ 214-67-85; cnr Juárez & Lerdo de Tejada; admission M$10; 🕑 10am-6pm Tue-Sun). Built in 1909 as a market, the building now houses 3500 sq meter of lovely gardens, lit through 48 stained-glass panels by the Tolucan artist Leopoldo Flores. On Plaza Garibay's north side is the 18th-century **Templo del Carmen**.

MERCADO JUÁREZ & CASART

The gigantic daily **Mercado Juárez** (cnr Fabela & Calle 5 de Mayo) is behind the bus station. On Friday, villagers swarm in to exchange fruit, flowers, pots, clothes and plastic goods. The market may be colorful, but it's also chaotic and not a great place to buy local handicrafts.

Nearby, you'll find quality arts and crafts in more peaceful surroundings at the state crafts store, **Casart** (Casa de Artesanía; 🕑 10am-7pm). There's a big range, and the crafts are often top-end pieces

from the villages where the craft styles originated. Prices are fixed, and higher than you can get with some haggling in markets; gauge prices and quality here before going elsewhere to buy. Craftspeople, such as basket weavers from San Pedro Actopan, often work in the store.

CENTRO CULTURAL MEXIQUENSE

This large **cultural center** (State of México Cultural Center ☎ 274-1200; Blvd Reyes Heroles 302; admission M$10, free Sun; ☼ 10am-6pm Mon-Sat, 10am-3pm Sun), 4.5km west of the city center, houses three good museums (which all keep the same hours). It's no must-see, but still a worthwhile diversion for visitors interested in local arts and crafts, local archaeology and modern art. To get here it's easiest to take one of the plentiful local buses (M$5) from outside the Mercado Juárez – just look for Centro Cultural on its destination board. The bus ride is a circuitous 20-min one. Get off by the large grass roundabout near the Monterrey University Toluca Campus, cross to the opposite side and the museum complex is through the gate and down the road.

The **Museo de Culturas Populares** has a wonderfully varied collection of México's traditional arts and crafts, with some astounding 'trees of life' from Metepec, whimsical Day of the Dead figures and a fine display of *charro* gear. There are also mosaics, traditional rugs, a loft and a gift shop.

The **Museo de Arte Moderno** is the least exciting museum of the three. It traces the development of Mexican art from the late-19th-century Academia de San Carlos to the Nueva Plástica and includes paintings by Tamayo, Orozco and many others, but frankly there's little to be excited about beyond the impressive spherical mural of people fighting against slavery, which makes up part of the building itself.

The **Museo de Antropología e História** is the stand-out museum, and presents exhibits on the state's history from prehistoric times to the 20th century, with a good collection of pre-Hispanic artifacts. It also traces pre Hispanic cultural influences to the modern day in tools, clothing, textiles and religion. Sadly, nearly all the labels are only in Spanish.

OTHER MUSEUMS

The ex-convent buildings adjacent to the Templo del Carmen, on the north side of Plaza

Garibay, house Toluca's **Museo de Bellas Artes**
(☎ 215-53-29; Degollado 102; admission M$10; ☑ 10am-
6pm Tue-Sat, 10am-3pm Sun), which exhibits paintings from the colonial period to the early 20th
century. On Bravo, opposite the Palacio de
Gobierno, are three museums: one dedicated
to landscape painter **José María Velasco** (☎ 213-
28-14; Lerdo de Tejada 400; admission M$10; ☑ 10am-6pm
Tue-Sat, 10am-1pm Sun), another to painter **Felipe
Santiago Gutiérrez** (☎ 213-26-47; Bravo Nte 303; admission M$4, free Sun & Wed; ☑ 10am-6pm Tue-Sun) and the
last to multifaceted Mexican–Japanese artist
Luis Nishizawa (☎ 215-74-65; Bravo Nte 305; adult/stu-
dent M$10/5; ☑ 10am-6pm Tue-Sat, 10am-3pm Sun).

Sleeping

Hotel San Carlos (☎ 21494-19, 214-43-36; www.hotel
sancarlostoluca.com; Portal Madero 210; s/d M$300/400; **P**)
There's a real attack of the 1970s when you
enter the lobby of this hotel, located right in
the thick of things within the Portal Madero.
The equally time-warped rooms are spacious,
clean and comfortable, with cable TV and
private bathrooms.

Hotel Colonial (☎ 215-97-00; Hidalgo Ote 103; s/d
M$350/400; **P**) The rooms overlooking the busy
main road are the best, but also the loudest,
at this well-run and excellent-value hotel. The
impressive lobby and friendly staff are other
good reasons to come here. Rates include free
parking nearby in a lot on Juárez.

El Gran Hotel (☎ 213-98-89; Allende 124; s/d
M$570/640; **P** 💻) By far the best place in town,
the modern, sleek Gran Hotel is a much-
needed addition to Toluca's lackluster hotel
scene. The smart rooms are airy and comfortable. Free wi-fi and a small gym complete
the picture.

Hotel San Francisco (☎ 213-44-15; Rayón 104; s/d
M$700/900; **P** 💻) While it might look like a
classy business hotel in the lobby, the rooms
at the San Francisco are rather neglected and
feel a bit old and, as such, they seem pretty
overpriced. All the 75 bedrooms here have
two double beds in them, as well as TV, phone
and bathroom.

Eating & Drinking

Toluqueños take snacking and sweets very seriously; join them in the arcades around Plaza
Fray Andrés de Castro. Stalls selling *tacos de
Obispo* (a sausage from Tenancingo) are easily found by following the crowds that flock
around them. The contents of the arm-width
sausages – barbecued chopped beef spiced

with *epazote* (wormseed, a pungent herb
similar to cilantro), almonds and raisins – are
stuffed into tortillas. Other stalls sell candied
fruit and *jamoncillos*, and *mostachones* (sweets
made of burned milk). Most eateries in the
center are open from around 8am to 9pm.

La Gloria Chocolatería y Pan 1876 (Quintana Roo;
snacks M$10-50; ☑ 10am-11:30pm Mon-Sat, 10am-10:30pm
Sun) You feel lucky just to be here, and you'll almost certainly be the only foreign visitor when
you are. This wonderful, friendly, family-run
snack spot and café serves up a tempting,
changing menu of local cuisine, from *tacos
al pastor* (spicy pork tacos) and *tortas* stuffed
with oven-baked pork or shredded chicken
bathed in red or green *mole poblano*.

La Vaquita Negra del Portal (sandwiches M$15-
35) On the northwest corner of the arcades,
smoked hams and huge green-and-red sausages hanging over the deli counter signal
first-rate *tortas*. Try a messy *toluqueña* (red
pork chorizo sausage, white cheese, cream,
tomato and *salsa verde*), and don't forget to
garnish your heaping sandwich with spicy
pickled peppers and onions.

Hostería Las Ramblas (☎ 215-54-88; Calle 20 de
Noviembre 107D; mains M$35-110) On a pedestrian
mall, one of Toluca's best and most atmospheric places to eat and drink (there's a full
bar) serves full breakfasts and a variety of
ambrosial *antojitos*, including *sopes* (soup),
mole verde and *conejo al ajillo* (liberally
garlicked rabbit).

Getting There & Away

Toluca's Aeropuerto Adolfo López Mateos
(☎ 213-15-44; www.aeropuertointernacionaldetoluca
.com) is conveniently located off Hwy 15, near
downtown, adjacent to the industrial zone
and a group of business-friendly chain hotels.
Domestic airline **Interjet** (www.interjet.com.mx) has
Toluca as its hub, offering flights from all over
Mexico for those wishing to travel cheaply to
the capital.

Continental Express (☎ 800-900-50-00, in the US 800-
523-3273; www.continental.com) shuttles to Houston,
and a couple of other Mexican airlines have
scheduled flights from here. There are frequent
buses from the airport to both Mexico City
and the capital's Aeropuerto Internacional,
which take an hour or two, depending on
traffic. A taxi from the airport to downtown
Toluca runs around M$12.

Toluca's **bus station** (Berriozábal 101) is 2km
southeast of the center. Ticket offices for many

destinations are on the platforms or at the gate entrances, and it's fair to say it can be a confusing place.

There are frequent departures to Morelia (M$200, every hour from gate 5), Valle de Bravo (M$48, every 20 minutes from gate 6), Chalma (M$28, every 5 minutes from gate 1), Cuernavaca (M$64, every hour from gate 12), Taxco (M$76, every hour from gate 12) and Ixtapan de la Sal (M$36, every 20 minutes from gate 12). Shuttle buses to Tenango (where you can change for the *colectivo* to Malinalco) leave every 5 minutes (M$8, from gate 9).

For Mexico City there are a range of services to Terminal Poniente. The 1st-class **TMT Caminante** (☎ 219-50-07; www.tmt-caminante.com.mx) line links the two cities (M$38, one hour) every five minutes from 5:30am to 10:30pm, while the even plusher deluxe ETN services (M$49, one hour) leave every half hour. From Toluca, TMT runs hourly direct service to the Mexico City airport from 4am to 10pm (M$100, 11½ hours).

Getting Around
'Centro' buses go from outside Toluca's bus station to the town center along Lerdo de Tejada. From Juárez in the center, 'Terminal' buses go to the bus station (M$5). Taxis from the bus station to the city center cost around M$50; fares around town are considerably cheaper.

NEVADO DE TOLUCA
The long-extinct volcano Nevado de Toluca (also known as Xinantécatl), Mexico's fourth tallest peak at 4690m, lies across the horizon south of Toluca. A road runs 48km up to its crater, which contains two lakes, El Sol and La Luna. The earlier you reach the summit, the better the chance of clear views. The summit area can be snowy from November to March, and is sometimes good for off-piste cross-country skiing, but **Parque Nacional Nevado de Toluca** is closed during the heaviest snowfalls.

From the park entrance, a road winds 3.5km up to the main gate at an area called **Parque de los Venados** (entrance per vehicle M$20; ☺ 8am-5pm, last entrance at 3pm). From there it's a 17km drive along an unsurfaced road up to the crater. Six kilometers from the crater, there's a gate, café and basic *refugio* (rustic shelter). From that point, the crater can also be reached by

a 2km hike via **Paso del Quetzal** (fee M$2), a very scenic walking track. Dress warmly – it gets chilly up top.

Sleeping & Eating
Albergue Ejidal (campsite/dm M$50/80) Two kilometers beyond Parque de los Venados, this community-run hostel has 64 bunk beds (sleeping bag required), hot water, a huge fireplace and a generator that runs on Saturday night. Ask an attendant at Parque de los Venados to open it up for you.

Posada Familiar (campsite/dm M$50/100) Just beyond the Parque de los Venados gate, this basic, heavily used refuge has shared hot showers, a kitchen (without utensils) and a common area with a fireplace. Bring extra blankets.

Just below the summit (at 4050m), the basic **state-run shelter** (dm M$60) has foam mattresses but no bathrooms.

On Saturday and Sunday, food is served at stalls around Parque de los Venados and at the gate near the summit. Midweek, bring your own food and water.

Getting There & Away
Buses on Hwy 134, the Toluca–Tejupilco road, will stop at the turnoff for Hwy 10 to Sultepec, which passes the park entrance 7km to the south. On Saturday and Sunday you should be able to hitch a ride for the 28km from the junction of Hwys 134 and 10 to the crater. From Toluca, taxis will take you to the top for upwards of M$200, or there and back (including time for a look around) for a negotiable M$400. Be sure to hire a newer taxi; the road up is very rough and dusty.

VALLE DE BRAVO
☎ 726 / pop 28,000 / elevation 1800m
With one of the loveliest colonial centers in Central Mexico, the *pueblo mágico* of Valle de Bravo is an utter charmer and a wonderful spot for an escape from Mexico City. A long, winding and occasionally stunning mountain road runs the 85km west from Toluca, taking you to shores of (artificial) Lake Avandaro, the result of the construction of a hydroelectric station.

The setting here is reminiscent of the northern Italian lakes, with thickly wooded, mist-clad hills and red terracotta roofing used throughout the town. Valle, as it's known, is famous for being the weekend retreat of choice for the capital's well-connected upper classes.

AROUND MEXICO CITY

The views at the lakeside are stunning, but the beguiling and largely intact colonial center is arguably the real draw here. Boating on the lake is very popular as well, as are hiking and camping in the hills around the town. Valle is set up well for visitors. There's a tourist info kiosk on the wharf, and essential services, including ATMs and internet cafés, are found around the main plaza, a 10-minute walk uphill from the waterfront.

In late October or early November, the weeklong **Festival de las Almas** international arts and culture extravaganza brings in music and dance troupes from all over Europe and Latin America.

Sleeping

Valle's accommodation options are generally very good value, and there's a large choice of budget and midrange options.

Posada Anthurios (☎ 262-04-90; jugj39@hotmail .com; Calle 16 de Septiembre 419; s/d M$250/350; **P**) An excellent budget option is this new family-run hotel just a short walk from the bus station. The bright, spotless rooms feature brand new bathrooms and overlook a small courtyard set back from the road.

Posada Los Girasoles (☎ 262-29-67; losgirasoles@ valledebravo.com.mx; Plaza Independencia 1; s/d M$400/500) The nine-room Girasoles overlooks the charming *zócalo* and offers spacious, clean and modern rooms complete with rustic touches such as exposed beams. The location is enviable and the staff charming.

our pick **Hotel Casanueva** (☎ 262-17-66; Villgrán 100; s/d/ste M$680/880/2300) Hands down the best place in town, the Casanueva is on the *zócalo* next to several other hotels, but it's very different from them, with individually designed rooms decorated with tasteful arts and crafts. While calling it a boutique hotel is a slight exaggeration, this is definitely the most stylish in town. The suite sleeps four and is lovely. Many of the rooms have private balconies over the square.

Eating & Drinking

There are scores of restaurants and cafés along the wharf and around the *zócalo*; most upscale places open only Friday to Sunday.

El Lobo (Salitre s/n; mains M$35-120; ☯ 10am-8pm) This friendly outdoor terrace across from the wharf is a popular local hangout. Try their delicious shrimp empanadas. Choose from three sizes and 10 degrees of hot sauce, and mix

several ingredients: shrimp, octopus, oyster, crab and sea snail. The beer is cold, and they also fry up fresh fish fillets a dozen ways.

Restaurante Paraiso (☎ 262-47-31; Fray Gregorio Jiménez de la Cuenca s/n; mains M$75-160; ☯ 8am-11pm) With fantastic lake views and a huge menu full of seafood specialties and including a large selection of imaginatively cooked trout, this is definitely one of Valle's better upmarket choices. Reserve a table on the upper terrace to get the best views.

For a nice, breezy, equilibrium-challenging ambience, try a drink or a meal at either of the following:

Los Pericos (☎ 262-05-58; mains M$65-150; ☯ 8am-11pm Thu-Tue)

La Balsa (☎ 262-25-53; mains M$75-160; ☯ 8am-10pm Wed-Mon) A floating lakefront bar–restaurant.

Getting There & Away

Valle's remodeled bus terminal is on Calle 16 de Septiembre. Autobuses Zinacantepec run hourly 2nd-class *directos* until 5:30pm to Mexico City's Terminal Poniente (M$100, three hours), all of which make a stop near Toluca's terminal. There is also a twice-daily service to Zitácuaro (M$56). If driving between Toluca and Valle de Bravo, the southern route via Hwy 134 is quicker and more scenic than Hwy 1.

MALINALCO

☎ 714 / pop 7500 / elevation 1740m

The word has slowly got out about this *pueblo mágico*, but come soon and you'll still get to enjoy it without the weekend crowds that descend on its more easily accessible cousins. True, there are already a clutch of hippie stores with names like Gandhi and a couple of boutique hotels here, but for the most part life in Malinalco is a far cry from that in Tepoztlán.

The drive to Malinalco is one of the most enjoyable to be had in the area, with dramatic scenery south of Toluca lining the road. The village itself has a charming colonial core set around a well-preserved convent and two central plazas. There's an ATM on Hidalgo, on the convent's north side, and **Internet Quetzal** is on Progresso, to one side of the Palacio Municipal.

A short but bracing hike up the mountainside above Malinalco takes you to one of the country's few reasonably well-preserved **Aztec temples** (admission M$37; ☯ 9am-6pm Tue-Sun, last ticket sold at 5pm), from where there are stunning views of the valley and beyond. From the main square follow signs to the *zona arqueológica*, which takes you up the hillside on a well-maintained footpath with signs in Spanish, English and Náhuatl. The site itself is fascinating, and includes *El Paraíso de los Guerros*, a mural that once covered an entire wall, depicting fallen warriors becoming deities and living in paradise.

The Aztecs conquered the region in 1476 and were busy building a ritual center here when they were conquered by the Spanish. **El Cuauhcalli**, thought to be the Temple of Eagle and Jaguar Warriors – where sons of Aztec nobles were initiated into warrior orders – survived because it was hewn from the mountainside itself. The entrance is carved in the form of a fanged serpent.

Temple IV, on the far side of the site, continues to baffle archaeologists. As the room is located in order to allow the first rays of the sun to hit it at dawn, there has been speculation that it was part of a Mexica sun cult, although other interpretations claim the temple was a solar calendar or a meeting place for nobles.

Near the site entrance, the **Museo Universitario Dr Luis Mario Schneider** (☎ 147-12-88; admission M$10; ☺ 10am-6pm Tue-Sun) explores the region's history and archaeology in a beautifully set out modern space. The highlight is a mock-up of the full *El Paraíso de los Guerros* mural from the site and a replica of the Cuauhcalli chamber you aren't able to enter in the temple proper.

A well-restored 16th-century **Augustinian convent** (admission free), fronted by a tranquil tree-lined yard, faces the central plaza. Impressive frescoes fashioned from herb- and flower-based paint adorn its cloister. Just uphill from the plaza, the **tourist office** (☎ 147-13-63; www .malinalco.net; ☺ 8:30am-6pm Mon-Sat) is inside the Palacio Municipal on the 2nd floor.

Sleeping

Like other destinations near Mexico City, Malinalco is geared toward weekend visitors, which means you'll have no trouble finding a room Sunday to Thursday nights, but your dining options may be limited. Hotel reservations are recommended for Friday and Saturday.

The best of the bunch are two very stylish boutique hotels, the Mora and the Limón, both of which can be fiendish to find in the poorly signposted backstreets of Malinalco.

Neither is very conveniently located, and both are squarely aimed at drivers. Both make for a sublime weekend retreat, but neither is for children.

El Asoleadero (☎ 147-01-84; cnr Aldama & Comercio; s/d/q from M$300/350/450; P ☎) This old-timer offers excellent value for money if you're not looking for a boutique place to stay. The spacious and airy rooms, some with balconies, look over the quiet street, while views from the courtyard overlooking the pool are spectacular.

Villa Hotel (☎ 147-00-01; Guerrero 101; s/d M$300/600) Hardly romantic, the friendly Villa has six rooms: some have cliff views while others (some with better beds) face the plaza. Some rooms were suffering from damp on our last visit. You get a M$50 reduction if you don't have a TV in your room.

Hotel Santa Mónica (☎ 147-00-31; Hidalgo 109; r M$350) Moments from the *zócalo* toward the archaeological zone, this is one of the better budget options, with clean rooms – all with private bathroom and TV – scattered around a pretty garden courtyard.

Casa Mora (☎ 147-05-72; www.casamora.net; Calle de la Cruz 18; ste M$1800-2000; P ☎) This beautifully appointed oasis is a hotel where you feel more like a house guest than a tourist. It's the pet project of a local artist, who maintains five beautiful rooms all of which enjoy an intimate and romantic atmosphere.

our pick Casa Limón (☎ 147-02-56; www.casalimon .com; Río Lerma 103; r/ste incl breakfast from M$2100/2500; P ☐ ☎) Malinalco's most famous hotel features beautifully styled, modern, minimalist rooms, enhanced with individually selected pieces of art and the odd antique. A slate swimming pool, classy bar and excellent restaurant complete the scene.

Eating & Drinking

For such a small place, Malinalco has some excellent dining, although some of the better restaurants open only for the *fin de semana* (Thursday to Sunday), when the out-of-towners come to visit. During the week there are plenty of eateries around the *zócalo* for a cheap meal.

Café La Fé (☎ 147-01-77; Guerro; ☺ 11am-8pm Fri-Sun) Between the museum and *zócalo*, this coffee shop and juice bar is a great place for a drink after having scaled the cliffside to visit the Aztec ruins. Everything sold on site is 100% organic, including locally grown coffee beans.

Restaurant El Puente (☎ 147-17-43; Hidalgo 104; mains M$40-90; ⊗ 9am-10pm Mon-Fri, 9am-midnight Fri & Sat, 9am-7pm Sun) Just after the tiny bridge as you leave the *zócalo* for the ruins, this atmospheric colonial house has two smart dining rooms as well as a great back garden where you can try a selection of *antojitos*, pastas, soups and steaks.

Beto's (☎ 147-03-11; Morelos 8; mains M$50-95; ⊗ noon-8pm Tue-Sun) At Beto's you'll get the best seafood in town by a long way (the fresh trout is superb), as well as ice-cold beer served with salt on the rim. The friendly owner–chef couple will fuss over you until you're stuffed and then bring you a *beso de ángel* (coffee liqueur and condensed milk on ice, dusted with cinnamon) with the check.

Ehécatl (Hidalgo 10; mains M$55-70; ⊗ 9am-6pm; Ⓥ) A beautiful space with a gorgeously verdant courtyard, Ehécatl is named after the Aztec god of the wind and rain and is one of Malinalco's best choices. As well as good breakfasts (M$40 to M$50) and a large range of fresh fish, it also offers a complete list of traditional Mexican cooking.

Koi (☎ 147-16-21; Morelos 18; mains M$140-170; ⊗ 11am-10pm Fri-Sun) Fusion cookery has arrived in Malinalco via this very trendy (and not particularly cheap) restaurant. The exciting menu runs from *camarones al coco* to Pad Thai and fish tempura, all served within a minimalist space you'd frankly not normally expect to find in a Mexican village.

Casa Limón (☎ 147-02-56; Rio Lerma 103; mains M$140-180; ⊗ midday-10pm Thu-Sun) The restaurant of Malinalco's smartest hotel is also superb – a classy indoor/outdoor space with white tablecloths and silver service but a friendly atmosphere. Mains are classic international, from *coq au vin* to almond trout, and the wine list is superb.

Getting There & Away

Most public transportation to Malinalco goes via Tenancingo. There are three buses a day from Mexico City's Observatorio Terminal Poniente (M$52, two hours). From Toluca there's a direct service to Malinalco on Saturday and Sunday (M$26, 90 minutes, three per day) or, the rest of the time, take a bus to Tenancingo and ask the driver to let you off for the *colectivo* to Malinalco (M$15, one hour, every 20 minutes). If driving from Mexico City, turn south at La Marquesa and follow the signs to Malinalco.

CHALMA

One of Mexico's most important shrines is in the village of Chalma, 10km east of Malinalco. In 1533 an image of Christ, El Señor de Chalma, miraculously appeared in a cave to replace one of the local gods, Oxtéotl, and proceeded to stamp out dangerous beasts and do other wondrous things. The Señor now resides in Chalma's 17th-century church. The biggest of many annual pilgrimages here is for **Pentecost** (the seventh Sunday after Easter), when thousands of people camp out and perform traditional dances.

Tres Estrellas del Centro runs hourly 2nd-class buses (M$34) from Toluca to Chalma. Several companies run 2nd-class buses from Mexico City's Terminal Poniente. There's also frequent bus service from Malinalco.

IXTAPAN DE LA SAL

☎ 721 / pop 20,000 / elevation 1880m

Ixtapan is known throughout Mexico for its curative waters, which have attracted visitors since the town was founded centuries ago by indigenous travelers from the Pacific coast who were amazed to discover salt water inland on their way to Tenochtitlan. Despite its long history, there's not much to see here, and the only reason to stop is to visit the **Spa y Parque Acuático** (☎ 143-30-00; adult/child M$150/80; ⊗ spa 8am-7pm, aquatic park 9am-6pm; ♿), a sprawling water park mixing curative thermal water pools with waterfalls, water slides, a wave pool and a miniature railway. Most foreign visitors stay adjacent to the *balneario* at the recently renovated **Ixtapan Spa Hotel & Golf Resort** (☎ 143-24-40, 800-904-7200, in Mexico City 55-5264-2613, in the US 800-638-7950; www.spamexico.com; s/d with meals from M$1200/1500), popular with expat retirees and Mexican families from the Distrito Federal.

Baja California

Baja is the earth's second longest peninsula – more than 1200km of the mystical, ethereal, majestic and untamed. Some people sip something special while the sun plunges into the Pacific. Some feel the rush of adrenalin as they surf that perfect wave. Others hike in awestruck wonder through sherbet-colored canyons…then sleep beneath scattered-diamond stars. Still others head for the beaches, or the all-night parties that are like spring break year-round. More people each year arrive in Baja and never get around to going home, and even *they* realize there's always more to see and do here.

Don't be afraid to hit the road: Baja's one place where it pays to rent a car. Roads are less trafficked and you generally won't need a 4WD, so get out and discover things for yourself. The Transpeninsular (Hwy 1) runs from Tijuana all the way to the Cabos, with stunning vistas at every turn. You'll find the middle of nowhere is more beautiful than you ever imagined. Side roads pass through tiny villages or wind drunkenly along the sides of mountains. A condor carves circles into unblemished blue sky. Even a quick day trip will leave you breathless, wanting more.

Unfortunately, the clock is ticking: the unchecked development is turning deserts into golf courses, hillsides into hotels, majestic cardón cacti into condos…and there's little reason to think this trend will stop. It remains to be seen whether visitors to Baja in a decade will enjoy it…or think of Joni Mitchell's immortal lyric, 'They paved Paradise and put up a parking lot.' Either way, come see Baja *now*, while it lasts.

HIGHLIGHTS

- Kayak with whale sharks at **Espíritu Santo** (p303) as the big Baja sun drops into the bay

- Ride the perfect Pacific swell at **San Miguel** (p284) as Jim Morrison's ghost looks on

- Dive or snorkel at mystical **Las Sirenitas** (p308), in Cabo Pulmo National Marine Park, home to the Sea of Cortez's only living coral reef

- Hike through majestic cardón cacti and maybe glimpse a cougar in the **Sierra de la Laguna** (p308)

- Slip across the world's most crossed border in **Tijuana** (p276) to gawk, shop or party to your heart's content

★ Tijuana
San Miguel ★

★ Espíritu Santo
Sierra de la Laguna ★
Las Sirenita ★

■ TIJUANA JANUARY DAILY HIGH: 20°C | 68°F
■ TIJUANA JULY DAILY HIGH: 29°C | 84°F

History

Before Europeans arrived, an estimated 48,000 mobile hunter-gatherers were living in today's Baja; their mysterious murals grace caves and canyon walls. European settlement failed to reach Baja until the Jesuit missions of the 17th and 18th centuries, and the missions soon collapsed as European-introduced diseases ravaged the indigenous people. Ranchers, miners and fishermen were the next inheritors. During the US prohibition era of the 1920s, Baja became a popular south-of-the-border destination for gamblers, drinkers and other 'sinners,' and the border towns remain popular for those same reasons. Baja continues to grow in economic power, population and popularity, with problematic ecological and environmental consequences.

Climate

Baja makes people think 'warm,' but temperatures range from the suffocatingly hot to the downright frigid. The Pacific cools air temperatures along the west coast, making the cape region humid but comfortable all year. Elsewhere, it's a different story: locals will confirm that you don't know the meaning of the word 'hot' until you've been to Mexicali in August.

Parks & Reserves

Baja's parks and reserves are some of Mexico's most varied and most beautiful – ranging from the surreal desertscape of the grand Reserva de la Biosfera El Vizcaíno (p292) to the underwater reef wonderland of Cabo Pulmo (p307). Parque Nacional Constitución de 1857 (p288) and Parque Nacional Sierra San Pedro Mártir (p288) offer highland pine forests and glimpses of bobcats and bighorn sheep. The Sierra de San Francisco (p295), part of the Vizcaíno reserve, holds over 60 cave painting sites. At Baja's southern tip, Reserva de la Biosfera Sierra de la Laguna (p308) is great for trekking through cardón and palo verde forests, with jewel-like springs or even waterfalls along the way. These places harbor fragile creatures and plants that exist nowhere else on the planet; now development of surrounding land and pressure from tourism is causing serious problems – do your part by asking your guide what steps they take to protect these resources, stay on marked paths and adhere to conservation regulations. Many reserves require an entry fee of M$20 to M$40.

Dangers & Annoyances

Basic caution and awareness, such as making an effort to keep valuables (including surfboards) out of sight and doors locked, will minimize risk, but most crime is not tourist-related.

Sanitation standards in Baja are generally higher than in other parts of Mexico, and water – even tap water – is usually safe to drink. As in mainland Mexico, toilet paper is usually discarded in the trash can, not flushed.

Getting There & Around

There are six official border crossings from the US state of California to Baja. At any crossing, Mexican authorities will issue and stamp tourist cards and process car permits. US and Canadian citizens can cross without a tourist card, but only if they are staying north of Ensenada or San Felipe, and only for 72 hours, or they can get a free tourist card with a seven-day limit and the same restrictions on movement. Any longer stay (up to 180 days) requires the standard tourist card (M$237).

Mexican mainland, US and international flights leave from and arrive at La Paz, Loreto and San José del Cabo. Ferries from Santa Rosalía and La Paz connect Baja California to the mainland by sea. A vehicle permit is not required for taking a car into Baja, however, it is necessary to have one if you are shipping a car to mainland Mexico. These can be obtained at La Paz but not at Santa Rosalía. If you intend to take a vehicle by boat from Santa Rosalía, you need to get the permit beforehand.

Air-conditioned, nonsmoking and reasonably priced buses operate daily between towns all along the peninsula; however, car travel is often the only way to reach isolated villages, mountains and beaches. Rent cars in larger cities and major tourist destinations, such as Los Cabos, La Paz, Loreto and the border towns.

Highways are good and there are few toll roads. Drivers using the 'Scenic' (Cuota) route to Ensenada will need M$81; the Tijuana–Mexicali route costs M$163. Denominations larger than US$20 or M$200 are not accepted.

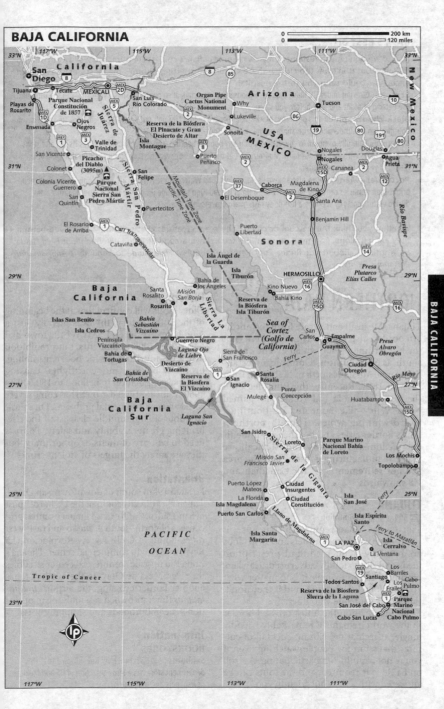

BAJA CALIFORNIA

BAJA'S BEST BITES...

(...and we don't mean restaurant reviews.) Some of Baja's coolest creatures are well worth getting to know, but don't get too close – these critters are sporting nature's meanest defenses and an encounter could send you to the hospital.

Scorpion Glowing under UV light, Baja's scorpions sting, especially if stepped on. Shake your shoes in the morning, use netting at night and look before you sleep.

Black Widow Spider This pea-sized black spider packs a potent (though rarely fatal) punch. Look for the crimson hourglass on the underside of the abdomen for positive ID.

Stingrays Painfully common in the shallows of many popular beaches, the stingray usually flicks its tail and stabs heels or ankles with a poisonous barb. Minimize risk at the beaches by wearing surf booties and/or dragging your feet until you're in deeper water.

Portuguese Man O' War Also known as *Agua Mala* (Bad Water), these jellyfish are stunningly pretty, but their bright-blue tentacles can sting long after the animal is dead. Don't pick one up on the beach, and minimize risk during water sports by wearing a full-body rash guard or wetsuit.

Whether you think they're cool or creepy, these are creatures that will rarely cause you harm if they are left alone. For more information, track down a copy of *Baja California Plant Field Guide* by Norman C Roberts or Roger Tory Peterson's book *A Field Guide to Venomous Animals and Poisonous Plants.*

NORTHERN BAJA

Tijuana, Mexicali and Tecate form the northern border, also known as La Frontera (not the border line itself), which extends as far south as San Quintín. Dominicans established nine missions north of El Rosario from 1773 to 1821. Recently, the Ruta del Vino (between Ensenada and Tecate) has gained Napa Valley–like fame for its boutique, award-winning wines. Though northern Baja's border cities and beaches are undeniably hedonistic, Tijuana and Mexicali are major manufacturing centers, and the area is a hot retirement spot for Canadian and US snowbirds.

TIJUANA
☎ 664 / pop 1.28 million

Tijuana has a bad reputation that, sure, it partly deserves. Bars, brothels and strip clubs are brazenly frequented, and prescription meds and drugs loudly advertised. Hawkers brashly proclaim to 'have it' (no matter what you might be looking for), and if they don't, they know someone who does.

Yet the town on the 'most crossed border in the world' remains a remarkably friendly jungle, a fascinating, vibrant cocktail of cultures that's fun for people-watching even if you're not planning on participating. A stroll on La Revo is required, and the touts can be answered with a firm but friendly 'no.'

History

Older locals will confirm that at the beginning of the 20th century, this was literally 'just a mud hole.' At the end of WWI the town had fewer than 1000 inhabitants, but prohibition drove US tourists here for booze, gambling, brothels, boxing and cockfights, causing Tijuana's population to balloon to 180,000 by 1960. With continued growth has come severe social and environmental problems. On a positive note, a large middle class is on the rise, bringing greater stability and safety. Tourists need to be wary of thefts of opportunity, but they are rarely the targets of violent crime.

Orientation

Located 19km south of downtown San Diego, Tijuana lies directly south of the US border post of San Ysidro, California. Tijuana's central grid consists of north–south *avenidas* and east–west *calles*. South of Calle 1A, Av Revolución (La Revo) is the main commercial center. Tijuana's Zona Río upscale commercial center straddles the river. Mesa de Otay, to the northeast, has another border crossing, the airport, *maquiladoras* (foreign-owned assembly-plant operations), neighborhoods and shopping areas.

Information
BOOKSTORES

Sanborns (☎ 688-14-62; Av Revolución 1102) This department store has a large selection of US and Mexican newspapers and magazines.

EMERGENCY
Tourist Assistance hotline (☎ 078)

INTERNET ACCESS
Internet access is available in many places along Av Revolución and its side streets.
World Net (☎ 685-65-14; Calle 2a No 8174; per hr M$15; ☺ 7am-11pm) Cheap, with lots of computers and English-speaking staff. Free bread with coffee purchase.

INTERNET RESOURCES
See Tijuana (www.seetijuana.com) A Tijuana tourism site.
Tijuana Online (www.tijuanaonline.org) Run by Cotuco.

LAUNDRY
Lavamaticas 'Danny' (☎ 638-50-69; Av Constitución 1021; ☺ 7am 10pm) Self-service and wash-and-fold service.

MEDICAL SERVICES
Hospital General (☎ 684-00-78; Av Padre Kino, Zona Río) Northwest of the junction with Av Rodríguez.

MONEY
Use caution when changing money, especially at night. Everyone accepts US dollars. Travelers heading south or east by bus can use the *casa de cambio* at the Central Camionera. Most banks have ATMs, which is often the quickest and easiest way to get cash. Banks in town include Banamex, Banorte and HSBC.
Banjercito (☎ 683-62-44; www.banjercito.com.mx; Calle José María Larroque s/n) The only bank in town to process vehicle permit payments.

POST
Central post office (☎ 684-00-78; cnr Av Negrete & Calle 11a)

TOURIST INFORMATION
Cotuco (Comité de Turismo y Convenciones, Committee on Tourism & Conventions); airport visitors center (☎ 683-82-44; airport baggage claim; ☺ 9am-6pm Mon-Sat); Av Revolución visitors center (☎ 685-31-17; Av Revolución btwn Calle 3a & Calle 4a; ☺ 10am-4pm Mon-Thu, 10am-7pm Fri-Sun); head office (☎ 684-05-37; Suite 201, Paseo de los Héroes 9365; ☺ 9am-6pm Mon-Fri); pedestrian border-entrance visitors center (☎ 607-30-97; ☺ 9am-6pm Mon-Thu, 9am-7pm Fri & Sat, 9am-3pm Sun)
State Tourism Office (Secretaría de Turismo del Estado; ☎ 682-33-67; Clle Juan Ruiz de Alarcón No 1572, Zona Río; ☺ 8am-8pm Mon-Fri, 9am-1pm Sat & Sun)

Dangers & Annoyances
If you're not looking for trouble (and it's there, no question), you'll probably be fine. 'Almost free,' 'Cheaper than Wal-Mart!' and other invitations are best answered with '*no necesito*' (I don't need it).

Don't drink on the streets or carry drugs without a doctor's prescription.

Coyotes and *polleros* (both mean 'people smugglers') congregate along the river west of the San Ysidro crossing. After dark, avoid this area and Colonia Libertad, east of the crossing.

Sights & Activities
South of Calle 1a, **La Revo** (Av Revolución) is the heart of Tijuana's tourist area. A brief stroll and you'll see crowded discos, restaurants, bars, loud hawkers, brash taxi drivers and souvenir shops.

Tijuana's funky **Centro Cultural Tijuana** (Cecut; ☎ 687-96-50; www.cecut.gob.mx; cnr Paseo de los Héroes & Av Independencia; ☺ 9am-7pm Mon-Fri, 10am-7pm Sat & Sun) is a cultural center of which any comparably sized city north of the border would be proud. It houses an art gallery, the **Museo de las Californias** (admission M$20; ☺ 10am-6:30pm Tue-Sun), a theater and the globular **Cine Omnimax** (tickets from M$45; ☺ 1-9pm Tue-Sun). Until 1998 *frontón* (jai alai, a type of handball) tournaments were held at the **Frontón Palacio Jai Alai**. The oddly attractive building, built over two decades from 1926 to 1947, remains a landmark and centerpiece for La Revo.

Vinícola LA Cetto (LA Cetto Winery; ☎ 685-30-31; Cañón Johnson 2108; ☺ 10am-6:30pm Mon-Fri, 10am-5pm Sat), southwest of Av Constitución, offers tours and tasting (M$20, M$50 with souvenir glass). LA Cetto produces a range of tasty varietals, as well as sparkling wines and a decent brandy.

Most of the motley crew at the **Museo de Cera** (Wax Museum; ☎ 688-24-78; Calle 1A No 8281; admission M$15; ☺ 10am-6pm) look mildly constipated, but it's fun anyway. Madonna appears to have had open-heart surgery, Michael Jackson looks creepy and John Lennon, yep, appears appropriately stoned.

Scattered all over town are monuments to everyone from Abraham Lincoln to Migueal Hidalgo.

Festivals & Events
As Tijuana's reputation as a cultural center continues to grow, so does its annual calendar of cultural events.

BAJA CALIFORNIA

lonelyplanet.com

BAJA CALIFORNIA

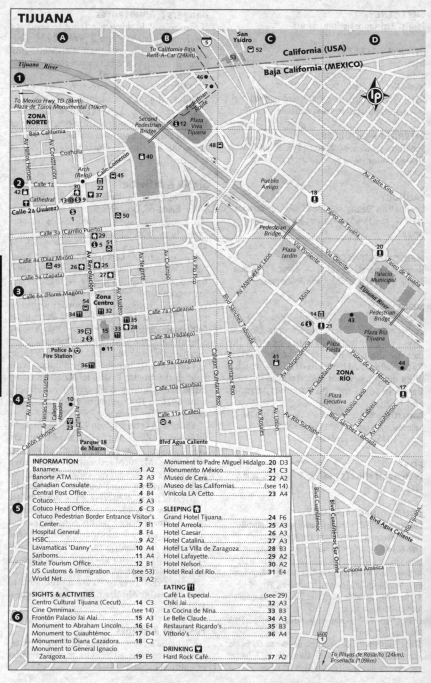

TIJUANA

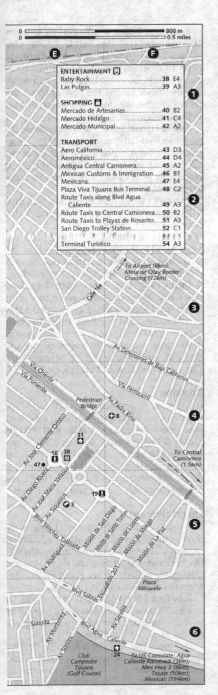

ENTERTAINMENT ☑
Baby Rock...................................38 E4
Las Pulgas..................................39 A3

SHOPPING ☐
Mercado de Artesanías................40 B2
Mercado Hidalgo.......................41 C4
Mercado Municipal....................42 A2

TRANSPORT
Aero California...........................43 D3
Aeroméxico................................44 D4
Antigua Central Camionera.........45 A2
Mexican Customs & Immigration..46 B1
Mexicana...................................47 E4
Plaza Viva Tijuana Bus Terminal...48 C2
Route Taxis along Blvd Agua
    Caliente................................49 A3
Route Taxis to Central Camionera..50 B2
Route Taxis to Playas de Rosarito..51 A3
San Diego Trolley Station............52 C1
Terminal Turístico......................54 A3

To Airport (8km);
Mesa de Otay Border
Crossing (12km)

To Central
Camionera
(1.5km)

To US Consulate; Agua
Caliente Racetrack (3km);
Mex Hwy 2 (8km);
Tecate (50km);
Mexicali (194km)

Muestra Internacional de Danza (International Dance Festival) Held in April. Local and international groups compete to celebrate and demonstrate contemporary dance.

Feria Del Platillo Mexicano (Mexican Food Festival) Held in September. Plates are piled high with goodies – and gobbled down.

Festival del Tequila (Tequila Festival) Held in October. Mmm...tequila!

Festival Hispano-Americano de Guitarra (Hispanic-American Guitar Festival) Held in November. National guitar graduates and professional players from around the world demonstrate the richness and beauty of the guitar. Rock bands do their best to remind people that the instrument can also just make a lot of noise, too.

Día de Muertos (Day of the Dead) This nationwide November festival mixes traditional celebration with US-style Halloween festivities.

International Craft Beer Festival (www.tjbeerfest .com) First week in November, so you can hit Oktoberfest in Germany and then stumble over here. Some of the best beers, both new and old, can be chugged down here. Mix with Clamato for the true Mexican experience.

Sleeping

The cheapest rooms in Tijuana are often shared with, ahem, hourly-rate clientele and are often shabbier than most folks are ready for. La Revo can be noisy, so try the side streets if you're keen on getting your Zs.

BUDGET

Hotel Catalina (☎ 685-97-48; cnr Calle 5a & Madero 2039; s M$220, d M$260-320) This inexpensive, clean and secure hotel, a block away from Av Revolución, is comparable to the Lafayette but quieter.

Hotel Arreola (☎ 685-90-81; cnr Av Revolución & Calle 5A 1080; s/d M$270/330) A cheap place that's anything but fancy, but has clean tile floors with plastic over the furniture. Rooms are over-chlorined but have TV. The lobby is fancier than the rooms due to recent remodeling, with interesting pics of the Tijuana of yesteryear.

Hotel Lafayette (☎ 685-39-40; Av Revolución 926; r M$295) Downtown's most popular budget hotel is the Lafayette, above Café La Especial. The rooms overlooking the cacophonous Av Revolución are not tranquil havens; request one in the back.

MIDRANGE

Hotel Caesar (☎ 685-16-06; Av Revolución & Calle 5a No 1079; s/d M$390/450) The lobby is spotless...actually empty, due to a recent remodeling.

BAJA CALIFORNIA

The snazzy white tile looks nice though, and rooms are small and clean, with TV and orange bedspreads. Bottled water is included when you check in.

Hotel Nelson (☎ 685-43-02; Av Revolución 721; r M$398 Mon-Thu, s/d M$499/560 Fri-Sun) The friendly Nelson is a longtime favorite with high ceilings and 1950s-era touches such as a real live barbershop of old. Tidy, carpeted rooms come with color TV. Rooms can be musky, but some have a view of the (less-than-soothing!) Av Revo.

Hotel La Villa de Zaragoza (☎ 685-18-32; www.hotel lavilla.biz; Av Madero 1120; s/d M$490/580; 🅿 ⊠ 🖳 🖵) Rooms at this modern hotel, directly behind the Frontón, include TV and telephone, with attractive arched columns outside. There's laundry, wi-fi, a restaurant, a leafy courtyard and room service.

TOP END

Hotel Real del Río (☎ 634-31-00; www.realdelrio.com /index_english.html; Av Velazco 1409A; r/ste M$945/2595; 🅿 ⊠ 🖳 🖵) The modern, characterless and efficient Real del Río provides excellent service and well-appointed, comfortable rooms. It's a high-end option that's reasonably priced, but you'll need to use a taxi to get to Av Revo. Prices jump for US holidays.

Grand Hotel Tijuana (☎ 681-70-00; www.grand hoteltij.com.mx; Blvd Agua Caliente 4500; r/ste from M$1674/2272; 🅿 ⊠ 🖳 🖵) Classical music wafts through the lobby and makes for a soothing check-in, though the hallways are a bit dark. The two 23-story buildings also have a shopping mall, offices, restaurants and convention facilities, and there's even an adjacent golf course.

Eating

Avoid the 'free' drink offers from hawkers on the street and head to the real deals listed below for some great cheap eats or fun surprises.

La Belle Claude (☎ 685-07-44; Calle 7a 8186A; ⏱ 7am-10:30pm Mon-Thu, 7am-11pm Fri-Sun; pastries M$10-35) Get mouthwatering pastries and creamy lattes perfect for a morning stroll or a late-night snack. The jars of pickled goods are homemade.

La Cocina de Nina (cnr Av Madero & Hidalgo; tacos M$10, mains M$30-50; ⏱ 8am-4pm Mon-Sat) In addition to tacos and quesadillas served with all the accoutrements, this family-run place also serves platters of fish, beef or pork, with the usual sides of rice and beans.

Restaurant Ricardo's (☎ 685-31-46; Av Madero 1410; breakfast M$41-67, tortas M$34-55; ⏱ 24hr) One of Tijuana's best-value places is this bright and cheerful diner-style joint, with two hours of free parking. Excellent breakfasts and *tortas* (sandwiches), among the best in town, are served around the clock. The waterfall adds to the ambience.

Café La Especial (☎ 685-66-54; Av Revolución 325; dinner mains M$41-121) A mainstay since 1952, this restaurant (look down at the bottom of the alley stairs) offers decent Mexican food at reasonable prices and is far quieter than the average eatery on La Revo.

Vittorio's (☎ 685-17-29; Av Revolución 1691; pizzas M$95, pastas M$120; ⏱ 10am-1am) For years this cozy Italian restaurant has been serving generous portions of reasonably priced pizza and pasta. Head to the back and you'll feel like the Godfather in the plush leather booths with dim lighting. Daily specials cost only M$66.

Chiki Jai (☎ 685-49-55; Av Revolución 1388; dinner mains M$150; ⏱ 11:30am-9pm) Gorgeous tiled walls and a spectacular painted ceiling make this small eatery stand out from other La Revo options. Try the salmon or the paella if you're in a seafood mood, or the tongue or *menudo* (tripe stew) if you're feeling adventurous. Three hours of free parking is included.

Drinking

If you want to get plastered you'll feel like a dog that's found too many fire hydrants. Start your well-deserved bender at the **Hard Rock Café** (☎ 685-02-06; Av Revolución 520), then ask around. Head to Plaza Fiesta at Zona Río for the local club scene, where you'll also encounter a dozen or so restaurants and bars – the names change frequently but the party never ends.

Entertainment

If you get sick of stumbling down La Revo, try some of the city's diverse sporting and cultural offerings. The tourist information booths will have current suggestions, and entertainment listings are available at www.seetijuana.com. Most fancier discos are in the Zona Río.

Baby Rock (☎ 634-24-04; Av Diego Rivera 1482; Sat cover M$100) Zona Río's old standard nightclub: look for the giant fake rock and fake petroglyphs. Way tacky, but fun.

Las Pulgas (☎ 685-95-94; Av Revolución 1127) Av Revo's fave spot to hang, dance and drink. Offers three floors of fun with a nice mix of locals and tourists. The cover charge varies.

Centro Cultural Tijuana (☎ 687-96-00; www.cecut .gob.mx; cnr Paseo de los Héroes & Av Independencia; films M$44) The theater here is the city's apex of drama, dance and musical performance, with several events scheduled each month. It sports one of the world's largest 3D movie screens.

Shopping
If you can't find a souvenir in Tijuana you're either hopeless or dead, but be cautious when buying gold and silver – much of it is fake (at those prices it would *have* to be, right?). Jewelry, blankets, furniture, baskets, silver, pottery and leather goods are available in stores on Av Revolución and Av Constitución, at the **Mercado Municipal** (Av Niños Héroes; ☽ 8am-6pm) and the sprawling **Mercado de Artesanías** (Av Ocampo) just south of Comercio (Calle 1a).

Mercado Hidalgo (Blvd Taboada & Av Independencia) is where locals come to buy spices, dried chilies, exotic produce, fresh tortillas and seasonal specialties made from Aztec grains. Be sure to check with Customs before taking fruits or vegetables over the border. Dried hibiscus flowers make excellent tea.

Getting There & Away
Mexican tourist cards are available 24 hours a day at the San Ysidro–Tijuana border in the Mexican **immigration office** (☎ 682-64-39). They are also available – although less dependably – at a small office in the main bus terminal (Central Camionera, below). You are required to have one as you cross the border, but this is rarely enforced north of Ensenada.

AIR
The **Aeropuerto Internacional Abelardo L Rodríguez** (☎ 683-24-18) is in Mesa de Otay, east of downtown.

Aero California (☎ 684-21-00; Plaza Río Tijuana) Flies to La Paz and serves many mainland destinations from Mexico City northward.

Aeroméxico (☎ 683-84-44, 684-92-68; Local A 12-1, Plaza Río Tijuana) Serves many mainland Mexican destinations, and has nonstop flights to La Paz and flights to Tucson and Phoenix, both via Hermosillo.

Mexicana & Click Mexicana (☎ 634-65-66; Av Diego Rivera 1511, Zona Río) Flies daily to Los Angeles (but not from Los Angeles) and also serves many mainland Mexican cities.

BUS
About 5km southeast of downtown, the main bus terminal is the **Central Camionera** (☎ 621-29-

82), where **Elite** (☎ 621-29-58; www.estrellablanca.com .mx) and **Estrella** (☎ 621-29-55; www.estrellablanca.com .mx) offer 1st-class buses with air-con and toilets. Destinations in mainland Mexico include Guadalajara (M$1000, 36 hours) and Mexico City (M$1400, 42 hours). All lines stop at major mainland destinations. Autotransportes del Pacífico, Norte de Sonora and ABC also leave from the Central Camionera and operate mostly 2nd-class buses to mainland Mexico's Pacific coast and around Baja California. **ABC** (☎ 621-24-24 ext 7472) offers buses to the following destinations:

Destination	Fare	Duration
Ensenada	1st-class M$121	1½hr
	2nd-class M$111	1½hr
Guerrero Negro	M$723	12hr
La Paz	M$1510	24hr
Loreto	M$1147	16hr
Mexicali	deluxe M$236	3hr
	1st-class M$206	3hr
	2nd-class M$187	3hr
San Felipe	M$362	5-6hr
Tecate	M$60	45min-1hr

Suburbaja (☎ 688-00-45; ☽ 6am-9pm) uses the handy downtown **Antigua Central Camionera** (☎ 686-06-95; Av Madero & Calle 1A), with buses leaving for Tecate (M$45, 1½ hours, every 15 minutes) and Rosarito (M$14, one hour); these are local buses that make many stops.

For border crossings by bus, **Mexicoach** (www .mexicoach.com) runs frequent buses (US$5) from its **San Ysidro terminal** (☎ 619-428-95-17; 4570 Cam de la Plaza) to the **Terminal Turístico** (☎ 685-14-70; Av Revolución 1025) between 8am and 9pm. It also runs to Rosarito (M$90, one hour, between 9am and 7pm).

Between 5am and 11pm, buses leave from the **San Diego Greyhound terminal** (☎ 619-239-32-66, in the US 800-231-2222; 120 West Broadway, San Diego) and stop at **San Ysidro** (☎ in the US 619-428-1194; 799 East San Ysidro Blvd), en route to Tijuana's Central Camionera bus terminal or the airport. Fares to both locations are US$15 one way, US$29 round trip.

TROLLEY
San Diego's popular **trolley** (☎ 619-233-30-04) runs from downtown San Diego through to San Ysidro (US$2.50) every 15 minutes from about 5am to midnight. From San Diego's Lindbergh Field airport, city bus 992 (US$2.25) goes to the Plaza America trolley

BAJA CALIFORNIA

stop in downtown San Diego, across from the Amtrak depot.

CAR & MOTORCYCLE

The San Ysidro border crossing, which is a 10-minute walk from downtown Tijuana, is open 24 hours, but motorists may find the Mesa de Otay crossing (also open 24 hours) less congested; it's 8km to the east of San Ysidro.

Rental agencies in San Diego are the cheapest option, but most of them only allow journeys as far as Ensenada. **California Baja Rent-A-Car** (☎ 619-470-7368; www.cabaja.com), in Spring Valley, California, 32km from downtown San Diego and 24km from San Ysidro, is a pricey option but allows you to continue driving beyond Ensenada.

Getting Around
BUS & TAXI

For about M$8, local buses go everywhere, but the slightly pricier route taxis are much quicker. To get to the Central Camionera take any 'Buena Vista,' 'Centro' or 'Central Camionera' bus from Calle 2a, east of Av Constitución. Alternately, take a gold-and-white 'Mesa de Otay' route taxi from Av Madero between Calles 2a and 3a (M$10). Regular taxis will charge about M$100.

To get to the airport, take any 'Aeropuerto' blue-and-white bus (M$5) from the street just south of the San Ysidro border taxi stand; from downtown, catch it on Calle 5a between Avs Constitución and Niños Héroes. Sharing can reduce the cost of a taxi (about M$150, if hailed on the street).

Tijuana taxis often lack meters, but most rides cost about M$60 or less. However, beware of the occasional unscrupulous taxi driver and make sure to agree to a fare beforehand to avoid misunderstandings.

AROUND TIJUANA
Playas de Rosarito
☎ 661 / pop 56,887

Once a deserted, sandy beach that marked the original border between California and Mexico, then a Hollywood film location, Playas de Rosarito is finally coming into its own. Developments and condos are everywhere, but despite the construction clamor, Rosarito is a quieter place to party and is an easy day trip (or overnight) from Tijuana or San Diego. Hotel Rosarito (now the landmark Rosarito Beach Hotel) and its long, sandy beach pioneered local tourism in the late 1920s. Fox Studios Baja, built in 1996 for the filming of *Titanic*, has since served as a primary filming location for *Pearl Harbor* and, recently, *Master and Commander: The Far Side of the World* and the greatly esteemed *Jackass*.

Despite the studio's influence, in many ways Playas de Rosarito remains a one-horse, one-street town. The amphitheater at the beachfront **Parque Municipal Abelardo L Rodríguez** contains Juan Zuñiga Padilla's impressive 1987 mural *Tierra y Libertad* (Land and Liberty).

Blvd Juárez, Rosarito's only major street (and part of the Carretera Transpenínsular, Hwy 1) has many restaurants, clubs and accommodations where the prices balloon to the outrageous during spring break.

SLEEPING

Motel Sonia (☎ 612-12-60; Juárez 781; s/d M$300/600; P) Rooms are basic to the point of grungy, with no TV, but there's no cheaper place to stay so close to beaches or clubs, and there's off-street parking. A deposit (M$300) is requested on top of the room fee.

Hotel del Sol Inn (☎ 612-25-52; Juárez 32; s/d M$440/550; P ✕) A definite step up from the Sonia, Sol has clean, carpeted rooms with TV, bottled water and simple furniture. Some rooms are reserved for non-smokers. Note that prices double during the spring-break holiday.

Festival Plaza Hotel (☎ 612-29-50; www.hotel festivalplaza.com; Juárez 1207; r Sun-Thu M$850, Fri & Sat M$1096; P ☃) Small, bland rooms with colorful names like 'Rock & Roll Taco.' The vibe is the college party crowd. And in case you didn't notice, there's a ferris wheel.

EATING & DRINKING

Panadería La Espiga (☎ 612-14-59; Juárez 298; ⏲ 6:30am-9pm Mon-Sun) The scent of fresh-baked rolls, sweets and breads will have your mouth watering long before you enter Panadería La Espiga. Some items are naturally sweetened with Baja honey from La Paz.

Tacos Manuel (⏲ 8am-2pm; tacos M$11) Well-regarded place near Rosarito's north entrance. Serves mainly beef.

Tacos El Yaqui (cnr Palma & Mar del Norte; tacos M$23; ⏲ 10am-4:30pm Mon, Tue & Thu, 8am-9:30pm Fri-Sun) This delicious taco stand is so popular that they often close early when the ingredients run out.

Capuchino's (☎ 612 29-79; Juárez 890; pastries M$35; ❤ 8am-9:30pm) If you're tired of partying or it's the morning after, head here for a hot cuppa joe and a homemade pastry.

Los Arcos (☎ 612-04-91; Juárez 29; mains M$55; ❤ 8am-7pm Thu-Tue, later on weekends) For shrimp or fish tacos try this family-owned place, which has tacos and various *antojitos*, excellent salsa and friendly staff.

Papas & Beer (❤ 11am-3am) Foam dances, a mechanical bull and drunken reveling.

GETTING THERE & AROUND

From downtown Tijuana, *colectivos* for Playas de Rosarito (M$15) leave from Av Madero between Calles 3a and 4a. Look for a yellow station wagon with a triangular white patch on the door. You can catch a Mexicoach shuttle (M$90) to Tijuana from the parking lot of the Rosarito Beach Hotel every two hours between 10am and 8pm.

Tecate

☎ 665 / pop 59,124

Tecate isn't just a great beer, it's a fun town too. Of all the Frontera towns, Tecate is the closest to a mainland Mexican village, and it's pretty laid back. The December 2007 assassination of the city's police chief and discovery of a drug tunnel into the US have brought Tecate into the headlines for unfortunate reasons, but tourist-related crime is uncommon.

Its landmark **Cuauhtémoc Moctezuma Brewery** (☎ 654-94-78; Hidalgo & Obregón; free tours ❤ 11am-4pm Mon-Fri, 10am-2pm Sat) produces two of Mexico's best-known beers, Tecate and Carta Blanca, but *maquiladoras* drive the local economy.

For lodging, the best value in town is offered by **Motel La Hacienda** (☎ 654-12-50; Av Juárez 861; s/d M$400/500; P ❤), which has clean, carpeted rooms with TV and pretty orange trees in the courtyard. A nice outdoor **market** at the corner of Juárez and Hidalgo has fresh fruit, shoes, clothes, pottery and *aguas* (watery juice drinks) of all varieties.

Tecate is 55km east of Tijuana by Hwy 2, the east–west route linking Tijuana and Mexicali. The **border crossing** (❤ 6am-10pm) is less congested than either Tijuana or Mesa de Otay.

ENSENADA

☎ 646 / pop 260,075

Ensenada, 108km south of the border, is hedonistic Tijuana's cosmopolitan sister. The city has a quirky mix of just-off-the-boat cruise shippers, drive-by tourists from Cali, tourists from mainland Mexico and seen-it-all locals. In case you've forgotten you're in Mexico (what with all those US dollars and the English menus) just look up: a Mexican flag so large it's probably visible from space flutters proudly over the tourist zone. Wander here and you'll find almost anything: ceramics, hammocks, textiles, jewelry…side by side with tasteless T-shirts, raunchy gifts and a host of items you definitely wouldn't give grandma for the holidays. Some of Mexico's best wines come from this region; if you're an oenophile, don't miss the Ruta del Vino and its vineyards and museums – lately this region has come to the attention of vintners world-wide.

Av López Mateos (Calle 1a), a landscaped, pedestrian-oriented artery, is lined with interesting shops, cafés, restaurants, sidewalk seating and many hotels, but outside the tourist zone the prices drop, food gets authentic and hotels become cheap. Singer Jim Morrison, of Doors fame, used to sip tequila and watch surfers just north at San Miguel (p284).

Ensenada's first permanent settlement was established in 1804. The discovery of gold in 1870 at Real del Castillo, 35km inland, brought a short-lived boom. Ensenada was the capital of Baja territory from 1882 to 1915, but the capital shifted to Mexicali during the revolution. After the revolution the city catered to 'sin' industries until the federal government outlawed gambling in the 1930s…but judging from the strip clubs, peep shows and bars, sin still goes on as big here today as it did in days of old.

Orientation

Coming south from Tijuana keep to the water to enter the tourist zone – where you could easily never leave. Hotels and restaurants line Blvd Costero (aka Blvd Cárdenas). Av López Mateos (Calle 1a) lies parallel to Blvd Costero a short distance inland (north). The official tourist district is between Av Ryerson and Av Castillo – the further away you get, the cheaper, dicier and more authentic your Ensenada experience will be. Hwy 3 heads northeast to Tecate; at the southeast edge of town it leads east toward Ojos Negros and Parque Nacional Constitución de 1857 (Laguna Hanson) before continuing south to Valle de Trinidad and San Felipe. The Ruta del Vino is north, just before San Miguel. Hwy 1 continues southward all the way to Los Cabos

Information

BOOKSTORES
Librerías de Cristal (☎ 178-84-48; Av López Mateos 690; ☼ 10am-8pm Mon-Sat, 10am-6pm Sun) Good selection of books in Spanish and English.

EMERGENCY
Municipal Police (☎ 066, 176-45-96)
State Police (☎ 066, 177-05-51)
Tourist Assistance (☎ 078)

INTERNET ACCESS
Internet cafés are sprinkled throughout the tourist zone; most charge M$15 to M$25 per hour.
equinoxio c@fé (☎ 174-04-55; Av Cardeñas 267; per hr M$20; ☼ 8am-10pm Mon-Sat, noon-10pm Sun)

INTERNET RESOURCES
Discover Baja California (www.discoverbajacalifornia .com) The state's tourism site.
Enjoy Ensenada (www.enjoyensenada.com) Ensenada's tourism site.

LAUNDRY
Lavematica Blanco (☎ 176-25-48; Plaza Bahía Shopping Center, cnr Calz Cortez & Av Reforma)

MEDICAL SERVICES
Hospital Del Carmen (☎ 178-34-77; cnr Av Obregón & Calle 11)

MONEY
Most banks and *casas de cambio* are near the intersection of Av Ruiz and Av Juárez. There are numerous ATMs throughout Ensenada, and banks can change money or perform the usual transactions during business hours.

POST
Main post office (cnr Avs López Mateos & Riviera)

TOURIST INFORMATION
Proturismo tourist office (☎ 178-24-11, 078; cotu coe@telnor.net; Blvd Costero 540; ☼ 8am-8pm Mon-Fri, 9am-1pm Sat & Sun) Dispenses maps, brochures and current hotel information. There's another booth in the Plaza Cívica.

State tourist office (☎ 172-54-44; Blvd Costero 1477; ☼ 8am-8pm Mon-Fri, 9am-1pm Sat & Sun) Carries similar information to the Proturismo office.

Sights
Opened in the early 1930s as Hotel Playa Ensenada, the extravagant **Riviera del Pacífico**, a Spanish-style former casino on Blvd Costero, is rumored to have been a regular haunt of Al Capone. It now houses the small **Museo de Historia de Ensenada** (☎ 177-05-94; admission M$20; ☼ 9am-5pm) and Bar Andaluz (p287), and the Casa de Cultura offers classes, retrospective film screenings and art exhibitions.

For an informative introduction to Baja's wine industry, **Bodegas de Santo Tomás** (☎ 178-33-33; Av Miramar 666; tours M$50; ☼ 10am-5pm Mon-Sat) holds tours of its cellars and wine tastings hourly from 10am to 1pm and at 3pm. Sample its signature big red, the award-winning 2000 Cabernet. Alternatively, tipple your way along the Ruta del Vino (p286) and discover things for yourself.

Built in 1886 by the US-owned International Company of Mexico, Ensenada's oldest public building, formerly the Aduana Marítima de Ensenada, houses the **Museo del Instituto Nacional de Antropología e Historia** (Museo del INAH; ☎ 178-25-31; Av Ryerson 99; admission free; ☼ 9am-4pm Mon-Fri), a historical and cultural museum. It has a relatively small but comprehensive collection of artifacts, and discusses (mainly in Spanish) the area's history from prehistoric times up to now.

Atop the Colinas de Chapultepec, **El Mirador** offers panoramic views of the city and Bahía de Todos Santos. Climb or drive to this highest point in town, up Av Alemán from the western end of Calle 2a in central Ensenada.

Activities
The beach at **San Miguel**, 11km to the north of town, has a wonderful point break and often hosts surfing contests and was once a hangout for Doors legend Jim Morrison. Camping (M$120 per car, M$180 per RV, parking M$30) is available. When the waves are big it's an awesome ride. For something a little less predictable, head west of Ensenada by boat to the **Isla de Todos Santos** (an island off Ensenada's coast, not to be confused with the town near Los Cabos), where you'll find a legendary spot called **El Martillo** (The Hammer) with swells rising 4m to 5m. Boats run out to the breaks every day; check at the harbor.

ENSENADA

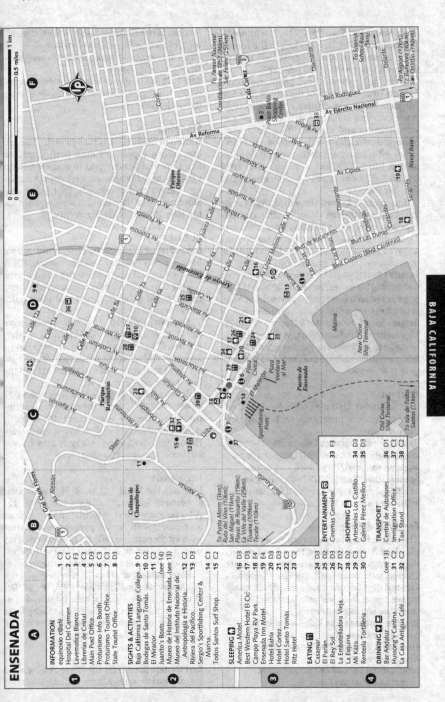

BAJA CALIFORNIA

INFORMATION
equinoxio c@afe	1 C3
Hospital Del Carmen	2 C1
Lavemática Blanco	3 F3
Librerías de Cristal	4 C3
Main Post Office	5 D3
Proturismo Info Booth	6 C3
Proturismo Tourist Office	7 C3
State Tourist Office	8 D3

SIGHTS & ACTIVITIES
Baja California Language College	9 D1
Bodegas de Santo Tomás	10 D2
El Mirador	11 C2
Juanito's Boats	(see 14)
Museo de Historia de Ensenada	(see 13)
Museo del Instituto Nacional de Antropología e Historia	12 C2
Riviera del Pacífico	13 D3
Sergio's Sportfishing Center & Marina	14 C3
Todos Santos Surf Shop	15 C2

SLEEPING
America Motel	16 D3
Best Western Hotel El Cid	17 D3
Campo Playa RV Park	18 E4
Ensenada Inn Motel	19 E4
Hotel Bahía	20 D3
Hotel Cortez	21 D3
Hotel Santo Tomás	22 C3
Ritz Hotel	23 C2

EATING
Casamar	24 D3
El Parián	25 D2
El Rey Sol	26 D3
La Embotelladora Vieja	27 D2
La Esquina	28 C3
Mi Kaza	29 C3
Rentería Tortillería	30 C2

DRINKING
Bar Andaluz	(see 13)
Hussong's Cantina	31 C2
La Casa Antigua Café	32 C2

ENTERTAINMENT
Cinemas Gemelos	33 F3

SHOPPING
Artesanías Los Castillo	34 D3
Galería Pérez Meillon	35 D3

TRANSPORT
Central de Autobuses	36 D1
Immigration Office	37 C3
Taxi Stand	38 C2

BAJA CALIFORNIA

Todos Santos Surf Shop (☎ 175-71-79; Av Ryerson 59; ☽ 10am-8pm Mon-Sat, 11am-6pm Sun), in the tourist zone downtown, rents boards (M$330 per day) and wetsuits (M$150 per day).

Oenophiles should head posthaste to the **Ruta del Vino**, just north of the city before San Miguel. Maps are available at the tourist info desks and at many hotels, but it's fun to just meander and discover it on your own. Vineyards stretch for miles through rust and ochre hills; many are dotted with dolomites and at times look like a moonscape. **Jatay** (☎ 109-97-31; www.jataytours.com) offers half- and full-day tours.

Ensenada is known the world over for its excellent **sportfishing**. Most charter companies also offer **whale-watching tours** from late December to March. The following options are well regarded and can be found on the sportfishing pier off El Malecón.

Juanito's Boats (☎ 174-09-53; www.sailorschoice .com/juanitos) Day-trip rates start at M$2700 for up to four people, not including fishing tackle or park admission. Juanito's also does diving and Todos Santos surfing charters.

Sergio's Sportfishing Center & Marina (☎ 178-21-85; www.sergios-sportfishing.com) Expect to pay M$660 per person for day fishing trips, including gear and Mexican fishing license. Private charter boats start at M$3300 and go up to 10 times that.

Courses

The following language schools offer similar immersion programs with homestay opportunities.

Baja California Language College (☎ 174-17-21; www.bajacal.com; Av Riveroll 1287) Courses cost from M$250 per hour or M$2790 per week.

Spanish School Baja (☎ 178-76-00; www.spanish schoolbaja.com; Calle Felipe Angeles 15) Costs start at M$2800 for a week plus M$300 materials fee.

Festivals & Events

The events listed below constitute a tiny sample of the 70-plus sporting, tourist and cultural happenings that take place each year. Dates change, so contact tourist offices for details.

Carnaval Mardi Gras celebration in mid-February, though the date depends on Ash Wednesday and Easter. The streets flood with floats and dancers.

Rosarito-Ensenada Bike Ride Twice-yearly bicycle race in April and September.

Fiesta de la Vendimia Wine harvest, held throughout August. Cheers!

International Seafood Fair Sample September's scrumptious seafood surprises.

Mexican Surf Fiesta Grand finals of local surf competition in mid-October. Everyone just hangs loose.

Fiesta del Tequila Last week in October. Punish that liver to your heart's content.

Baja 1000 Baja's biggest off-road race, held mid-November. See 'truggies' (truck-buggies) tear up the desert to the cheers of just about everyone.

Sleeping

Although Ensenada has many hotels, demand can exceed supply at times, particularly on Saturday and Sunday and in summer. Rates vary substantially between weekdays (Monday to Friday) and weekends (Saturday and Sunday)…and they jump up even more for the Baja 1000 or other big events.

BUDGET

Campo Playa RV Park (☎ 176-29-18; cnr Blvd Las Dunas & Sanginés; car or camp site M$198, motor home M$275) A bit spartan and dusty when the wind blows, but the Campo Playa offers secure, well-maintained facilities, a restaurant and some palm trees for shade.

Ritz Hotel (☎ 174-05-01; explotur@prodigy.net.mx; Calle 4a 379; s/d/tr M$295/320/460; ▓) Not at all ritzy, but friendly and inexpensive. Carpeted rooms are small and dark, but friendly staff and easy access to the tourist zone, restaurants and the bus station make up for it.

America Motel (☎ 176-13-33; Av López Mateos 1309; s/d M$320/400; Ⓟ) One of the finest budget options, the friendly America motor lodge is quiet, clean and yet only a five-minute walk from the tourist zone. Many rooms have a kitchenette at no extra charge.

MIDRANGE

Ensenada Inn Motel (☎ 182-98-91; www.sdro.com /ensenadainn/; Sanginés 237; s/d M$650/850; Ⓟ ▓ ▓) A bit far away from the tourist zone, but clean and quiet, with secure parking and rooms with kitchenette. Excellent choice for drivers planning to get an early start for a southward journey. Prices are lower during the week.

Hotel Bahía (☎ 178-21-01; www.hotelbahia .mx; Av López Mateos 850; s/d M$699/935; Ⓟ ▓ ▓) Welcome margaritas, a nice pool and balconies that look out at the port are why folks keep coming here. Psychedelic tiles in the lobby add to the fun.

TOP END

Best Western Hotel El Cid (☎ 178-24-01; www.mexon line.com/elcid.htm; Av López Mateos 993; s/d M$1062/1540;

P ⊠ ⬚ ⬚) This four-star hotel has unique rooms, an outstanding restaurant and a lively bar. Prices include continental breakfast with fresh juice. Beds are firm and the bilingual staff are friendly.

Hotel Santo Tomás (☎ 178-15-03; hst@bajainn.com; Blvd Costero 609; r up to 3 persons M$1072; P) Slick and snazzy, with satellite TV in each room. The lobby elevator, on a raised platform with mirrors, will make you feel like you're stepping into a Star Trek teleportation device. Rates increase on Friday and Saturday. Beam me up, Scottie.

Hotel Cortez (☎ 178-23-07; fax 178-39-04; Av López Mateos 1089; r M$1078; P ⊠ ⬚) This large, family-friendly hotel has a gym, a basketball court and a popular bar and restaurant.

Punta Morro (☎ 178-35-07; www.punta-morro.com; Transpenínsular Km 106; s/d M$1550/2850; P ⊠ ⬚ ⬚) One of Ensenada's newest and fanciest resorts, the Punta Morro – located slightly north of town – has an unbeatable location overlooking the Pacific, posh suites with all the services one expects from a top-end place, and a restaurant that's worth visiting even if you're staying in town.

La Ville del Valle (☎ 183-92-49; www.lavilledelvalle.com; d M$1750; P ⊠ ⬚) A beautiful B&B overlooking the rolling vineyards and fields in the Ruta del Vino. The owners grow their own lavender, make their own personal care products and have fantastic meals. No pets or children.

Eating

Ensenada has eateries ranging from corner taco stands to places serving the best of Mexican and international cuisine. Seafood lovers, in particular, will leave sated and smiling.

Rentería Tortillería (☎ 178-35-79; Calle 2a No 558; ⏰ 5am-4pm) Tiny little grocery store with freshly made flour tortillas for M$10 per kg. Enjoy both smells and smiles as you watch them being made.

Mi Kaza (☎ 178-82-11; Av Riveroll 87-2; breakfasts M$35-70, dinner mains M$59-129; ⏰ 6:30am-10pm) Enjoy inexpensive Mexican or American dishes at this not-so-greasy greasy spoon. Princess Diana lovers will enjoy the tribute wall of photos at the back.

El Parián (☎ 178-82-32; Calle 4a & Castillo 401; dinner mains M$40-85; ⏰ noon-midnight Thu-Tue) Great enchiladas, quesadillas, burritos, *agua de jamaica* (hibiscus water) and friendly service make this perfect for anyone watching their pesos. Flat-screen televisions at every corner mean you (or the wait staff) never have to miss a moment of that cheesy Mexican soap.

La Esquina (☎ 178-35-57; Av Miramar & Calle 6a 666; mains M$80-140) Tucked away at the back of the old distillery, La Esquina lets you dine in quiet elegance…and escape from the tourist zone. Be sure to look up at the copper piping and old distilling tanks.

Casamar (☎ 174-04-17; Blvd Costero 987; dinner mains M$114-455, lobster dishes M$210-370) This family-owned restaurant features elegant seafood dining and a full bar that offers great views of the port. Try the Abalone Casamar with crabmeat. Yum.

La Embotelladora Vieja (☎ 178-16-60; cnr Av Miramar & Calle 7a; dinner mains M$145-205) This elegant establishment was once a wine-aging warehouse. Beautiful brick arches, wax-dripped candelabras and an outstanding wine selection make this a spot to seek for that special celebration. The delicious tuna *Embotelladora* is a treat.

El Rey Sol (☎ 178-17-33; Av López Mateos 1000; dinner mains M$150-235) This venerable Franco-Mexican institution has elegant French food with unusual fusion delicacies, but the treats like tableside Caesar salad or the Bananas Foster are what set this place apart.

Drinking

Ensenada is a perfect place to start (or continue) that long-awaited vacation bender. On weekends, most bars and cantinas along Av Ruiz are packed from noon to early morning. If that's not your scene, head for one of the many quality hotels and fine restaurants where you're likely to find a laid-back spot to sip a top-shelf tequila.

Hussong's Cantina (☎ 178-32-10; Av Ruiz 113; ⏰ 10am-2am) The oldest and perhaps liveliest cantina in the Californias has been serving tequila since 1892. It's one of the few bars filled with people who aren't just 20-somethings trying to get plastered.

Bar Andaluz (☎ 177-17-30; Blvd Costero; ⏰ 11am-11pm) For a complete change in ambience, visit the cultured bar inside the Riviera del Pacífico, where having a drink is an exercise in nostalgia. It's quiet, perfect for a nightcap with friends.

La Casa Antigua Café (☎ 175-73-20; lacasaantiguacafe@hotmail.com; Av Obregón 110; coffee M$35, sandwiches M$30-60; ⏰ 8am-11pm) Vintage photos and clapboards separate this place from the coffee megachains. Delicate pastries, good bagels and sandwiches and rich coffee are all worth ducking away from the strip for.

BAJA CALIFORNIA

Entertainment

Entertainment opportunities in Ensenada are primarily of the drinking, eating, shopping and sinning varieties. **Cinemas Gemelos** (☎ 176-36-16; cnr Avs López Mateos & Balboa; tickets M$44) has recent Hollywood fare, often dubbed into Spanish.

Shopping

Galería Pérez Meillon (☎ 171-61-27; Blvd Costero 1094; ☼ 9-5pm) In the Centro Artesanal de Ensenada, this gallery sells authenticated pottery from the Paipai (one of Baja California's indigenous peoples known for fine craftwork, particularly pottery and baskets) and Mata Ortiz (a major pottery center in central north Mexico) and Kumai weaving. Opening time can vary.

Artesanías Los Castillo (☎ 178-29-62; Av López Mateos 815; ☼ 10am-7pm) Taxco silver is available here, at cruise-ship prices that let you know it's genuine.

Getting There & Away

The **immigration office** (☎ 174-01-64; Blvd Azueta 101; document delivery ☼ 8am-6pm Mon-Fri, document pickup 1-3pm) sells tourist cards.

AIR

Primarily a military airport, **Aeropuerto El Ciprés** (☎ 177-45-03; Carretera Transpeninsular Km 114.5) is just south of town off the Transpeninsular. The only regularly scheduled flights serving Ensenada are run by **Aerocedros** (☎ 177-35-34), which flies to Guerrero Negro and Isla Cedros.

BUS

Ensenada's **Central de Autobuses** (☎ 178-66-80; Av Riveroll 1075) is 10 blocks north of Av López Mateos. **Elite** (☎ 178-67-70) serves mainland Mexican destinations as far as Guadalajara (M$1100, 38 hours) and Mexico City (M$1553, 48 hours). **ABC** (☎ 178-66-80) is the main peninsular carrier, and offers buses to the following destinations.

Destination	Fare	Duration
Guerrero Negro	M$614	9hr
La Paz	M$1401	20hr
Mexicali	1st-class M$301	4hr
	2nd-class M$278	4hr
Rosarito	M$76	1hr
San Felipe	M$248	4hr
Tecate	M$97	2hr
Tijuana	M$111	1½hr

Getting Around

The main taxi stand is at the corner of Avs López Mateos and Miramar; taxis also congregate along Av Juárez. Most fares within the city cost from M$50 to M$80.

The asking price for a taxi trip to the airport is M$150 for one to four passengers. Surfers can get a trip out to San Miguel and a pick-up later in the day for M$100 each way.

Ensenada's main avenues are well served by buses and vans; most routes are designated by street name and charge M$7 for the first 5km.

AROUND ENSENADA

La Bufadora is a popular tidewater blowhole 40km south of Ensenada. Technically just a notched rock, it sends a jet of water up to 30m into the sky, drenching cheering onlookers. Catch a taxi (M$100 per person round trip) or a shuttle tour (M$150), or drive south on the Transpeninsular to the 'Bufadora' sign, then follow the road all the way around to the Pacific side. Parking is M$20.

PARQUE NACIONAL CONSTITUCIÓN DE 1857

At the end of a fun 43km dirt road out of Ojos Negros (east of Ensenada at Km 39 on Hwy 3), Parque Nacional Constitución de 1857 has beauiful conifers, fields of wildflowers and a sometimes-dry lake, **Laguna Hanson** (also known as Laguna Juárez) at an altitude of 1200m. **Cabañas** (M$700) or campsites are available, but livestock contaminate the water so bring your own.

It's a sublime spot for mountain biking, hiking or just getting away from it all, as long as everyone else isn't getting away at the same time – in peak holiday times it can be busy, but it's a beautiful spot any time of year. The park is also accessible by a steeper road east of Km 55.2, 16km southeast of the Ojos Negros junction. The **Restauran y Hotel Ojos Negros** (☎ 646-153-30-06; Entrada principal; r M$250), which has basic rooms and a great restaurant, is a very convenient stop for anyone wanting to get to the park early the next morning. Some rooms open onto the sunny courtyard; others face a wall.

PARQUE NACIONAL SIERRA SAN PEDRO MÁRTIR

Bobcats, deer, bighorn sheep and condors await visitors to San Pedro Mártir national

---

NOTHING LIKE TAKING A GOOD PISMO...

Tiny San Quintín is the pismo clam capital, but these mouthwatering, meaty morsels are well worth stopping for anywhere along this northerly part of the Transpeninsular. Look for 'Almeja Ahumada' signs as you drive southwards...or if time and itinerary permits, stop in at **Palapas de Mariscos El Paraíso** (☎ 616-165-29-06) and bring your appetite – it serves big, juicy smoked clams with garlic, tomato and a side of broth. If you're really a do-it-yourselfer, sharpen your clam rake, get a license (M$250 per week) from the Oficina de Pesca (Fisheries Office) and dig them on your own. Yum!

---

park, east of San Telmo de Abajo and west of San Felipe. Conifers scrape the sky, the air is pine-scented and clean, and the (tortuously winding) drive passes through boulder-studded, ethereal landscapes that seem otherworldly.

The **Observatorio Astronómico Nacional** (☎ 646-174-45-80; ☾ 10am-1pm) is the country's national observatory, from where it's possible to observe both the Pacific Ocean and the Sea of Cortez. On clear days one can see all the way to the Mexican mainland. To reach the park, turn left at the sign at approx Km 140 on the Transpeninsular, south of Colonet. A paved road climbs 80km to the east through an ever-changing desert landscape, affording satisfying vistas all along the way. Climbers should contact **Baja Vertical** (☎ 646-178-23-83; bajax_treme@hotmail.com) for this and other local climbing adventures. Camping is possible (no toilets, bring water) in designated areas, but there are no cabañas or other facilities.

MEXICALI
☎ 686 / pop 653,046

Mexicali is what Tijuana must have been before the tourist boom – gritty and authentic, even scary – but the city offers some decent restaurants and outdoor activities. Be particularly careful around the border areas after dark. The Zona Hotelera, far safer at night than the border, is on the east side, along Calz Juárez from Plaza Azteca to Independencia and beyond.

Information

Plentiful *casas de cambio* keep long hours, while banks (including Banamex) offer exchange services Monday to Friday mornings only. Most banks in Mexicali and Calexico have ATMs. On Av Reforma and Av Obregón, near the US border, are many health-care providers offering quality services at a fraction of the cost north of the border.

Bancomer (cnr Azueta & Av Madero)

Hospital Hispano-Americano (☎ 552-23-00; fax 552-29-42; Av Reforma 1000)

Librería Packy (☎ 165-39-23; Av Madero 400; ☾ 10am-5pm Mon-Sat) Good maps, not much else.

Main post office (☎ 552-25-08; Av Madero; ☾ 8am-5pm Mon-Fri, 8am-noon Sat)

Mexican Tourism and Convention Bureau (☎ 551-98-00; cnr Calz López Mateos & Camelias; ☾ 8am-6pm Mon-Fri) Similar offerings to the state office; it's in front of Muséo Sol de Niño.

State tourist office (☎ 566-12-77; Calz Juárez 1; ☾ 8am-8pm Mon-Fri, 9am-1pm Sat) Patient, bilingual staff and plenty of information about regional attractions and events.

Tourist Assistance (☎ 078)

Sights & Activities

Plaza Constitución is a good place to hear *banda* groups rehearse in the late afternoon (hence its nickname: Plaza del Mariachi).

Most of Mexicali's historic buildings are northeast of Calz López Mateos. The **Catedral de la Virgen de Guadalupe** (cnr Av Reforma & Morelos) is the city's major religious landmark. Now the rectory of the **Universidad Autónoma de Baja California**, the former Palacio de Gobierno, built between 1919 and 1922, interrupts Av Obregón just east of Calle E.

Sleeping

If you don't fancy sleeping in a hotel that has iron bars on the reception windows and hourly-rate customers, you're better off in the pricier Zona Hotelera.

Hotel Cosmos Posada (☎ 568-97-44; Juárez 4257; s/d incl breakfast M$450/550; [P] [X]) Rooms here are dark but clean, with decorative columns outside and deep-green tiles. It's nicely located for anyone going south.

Hotel del Norte (☎ 552-81-01; hoteldelnorte@hotmail.com; Av Madero 205; s M$500-600, d M$600-700; [P] [X] [□]) The most pleasant of the border options, the landmark Hotel del Norte has carpeted rooms, some with color TV, and friendly, English-speaking staff.

BAJA CALIFORNIA

MEXICALI

Araiza (☎ 564-11-00; www.araizahoteles.com; Calz Juárez 2220; d M$1560; P ⊠ ⊠ ⊠) This family-friendly deluxe hotel has well-appointed rooms, two excellent restaurants, bar, tennis courts, a fountain and a convention center. There are lobby computers for guests who need them.

Eating

Mexicali's strongest draw is the variety of its restaurants. Almost any kind of food can be found here and it's all good.

Baguette (☎ 568-32-73; Calz Juárez 1799-13; bread M$5-10, coffee M$23; ☼ 7am-9pm) Coffee, ice cream and wi-fi mix well in this sunny, spotless café. Cheap breads are great for the road.

Tacos Yubby (cnr Juárez & Churubusco; tacos M$12; ☼ 8am-midnight Mon-Sat) Clean and quick and served with flair, Yubby's pork, chicken or beef tacos are as good as cheap food gets. If you're lucky, there'll be a drunken mariachi or two blaring out a tune.

Petunia 2 (☎ 552-69-51; Av Madero 436; breakfast M$59, lunch M$60) Huge *jugo natural* (fresh squeezed juice) and delicious quesadillas are a great way to start the day at this cheap eat close to the border.

El Sarape (☎ 554-22-87; Bravo 140; dinner mains M$75-140; ☼ 10am-3am) Mariachi band at the ready, this traditional Mexican restaurant has a menu that will delight carnivores, as well as margaritas that, though small, pack a cool, refreshing ice-cream headache.

Los Arcos (☎ 556-09-03; Av Calafia 454; dinner mains M$123-230) Mexicali's most popular seafood restaurant. The *shrimp culichi* (shrimp in a creamy green chili sauce) is spectacular. Live music brightens the night Thursday and Friday.

Getting There & Away

AIR

Aeropuerto Internacional General Rodolfo Sánchez Taboada (☎ 553-67-42) is 18km east of town. **Aeroméxico** (☎ 557-25-51; Pasaje Alamos 1008D, Centro Cívico-Comercial) Flies to La Paz, Mexico City, Mazatlán and other mainland points.

Mexicana & Click Mexicana (☎ 553-59-20; Obregón 1170) Flies daily to Guadalajara, Mexico City and intermediate points.

BUS

Long-distance bus companies leave from the **Central de Autobuses** (☎ 557-24-15; Calz Independencia), near Calz López Mateos. Autotransportes del Pacífico, Norte de Sonora and Elite serve mainland Mexican destinations, while ABC serves the Baja peninsula. Destinations and sample fares include the following.

Destination	Fare	Duration
Ensenada	M$278	3½hr
Guadalajara	1st-class M$1030	30hr
	2nd-class M$870	30hr
Guerrero Negro	M$837	14hr
La Paz	M$1556	24hr
Loreto	M$1229	18hr
Mazatlán	M$745	18hr
Mexico City	M$1323	48hr
San Felipe	M$171	2½hr
Tijuana	1st-class M$236	2½hr
	2nd-class M$163	2½hr

Greyhound (☎ Mexicali 558-79-95, Calexico 760-357-18-95; www.greyhound.com) has offices in Mexicali and directly across the border in Calexico. Several departures daily go to Los Angeles (one way/round trip M$380/713) and four to San Diego (M$299/598) as well as anywhere else in the US.

CAR & MOTORCYCLE

The main Calexico–Mexicali border crossing is open 24 hours. Vehicle permits are available at the border, as are tourist cards for those traveling beyond Ensenada or San Felipe. US and Mexican authorities have opened a second border complex east of downtown to ease congestion. It's open 6am to 10pm.

Getting Around

Cabs to the airport cost M$160 but may be shared.

Most city buses start from Av Reforma, just west of Calz López Mateos; check the placard for the destination. Local fares are about M$10.

A taxi to the Centro Cívico-Comercial or Zona Hotelera from the border averages about M$50, but agree on the fare first.

SAN FELIPE

☎ 686 / pop 14,831

Once a fishing community on the Sea of Cortez (Golfo de California), San Felipe, 200km due south of Mexicali, has become a kind of US suburb: quiet and peaceful, but increasingly less Mexican. Its charm lies in its beaches: the long expanses of tide flats make beachcombing fun, and the views are nice, especially on the route north to Mexicali.

BAJA CALIFORNIA

Bancomer (Av Mar de Cortez 160; 8:30am-4pm Mon-Fri, 10am-2pm Sat) exchanges traveler's checks and has an ATM. Check email at **La Taza** (577-05-72; Av Mar de Cortez 238; per hr M$20; 7am-10pm).

Posada del Sol – Baja (577-17-27; www.posadadelsolbaja.com; Av Mar de Cortez 238; s/d M$500/800; P X X) has small, clean rooms with terra cotta tiles, fridge and microwave. Guests can use the café computers next door for free.

Costa Azul Hotel (577-15-48; cnr Av Mar de Cortez & Ensenada; r M$770-1100; P X) is a midrange family option – two children can stay for free. It has a cheery pastel blue and white theme and the beach doesn't get any closer. Prices change according to the day of the week and whether there's a holiday.

Good seafood and drinks are on offer at **La Hacienda de la Langosta Roja** (577-04-83; www.sanfelipelodging.com; Chetumal 125; dinner M$136-260, lobster M$420; 7am-11pm), which is also a hotel. Fishing photos add flair to the large, well-polished bar.

Doña Chuy (577-02-58; cnr Mananillo & Mar Negro; tortas M$25-35) has great cheap eats, such as *tortas* and quesadillas, near the bus station.

Shoppers need go no further than the crammed *malecón* (waterfront boulevard) for deals and steals on fabrics, clothes, hats, trinkets and glassware.

By Hwy 5, San Felipe is 2½ hours from the Mexicali border crossing. At the **bus terminal** (577-15-16; Av Mar Caribe), **ABC** (www.abc.com.mx) operates to the following destinations:

Ensenada (M$248, four hours, departs 1am and 8am)
Mexicali (M$171, 2½ hours, five daily)
Tijuana (M$362, 5½ hours, four daily)

AROUND SAN FELIPE

The 85km road from San Felipe to the scenic, quiet village of **Puertecitos** is passable but go slow to avoid potholes. Beyond that, 4WDs can continue all the way to Hwy 1 – a slower but beautiful ride.

MISIÓN SAN BORJA

This well-restored mission is roughly between El Rosarito and Bahía de los Angeles in pristine, spectacular Boojum-tree and cardón desert. A family descended from the original pre-conquest inhabitants is restoring it by hand and will proudly show you the mission, freshwater spring, a secret tunnel (now walled up, shucks!) and the old Jesuit ruins. Heading west from Bahía de los Angeles, turn left about 21km after leaving the coast.

SOUTHERN BAJA

Parts of southern Baja look more like pages of a Dr Seuss illustration than real life and no plant exemplifies this more than the funky Boojum tree (Cirio), which looks like a giant inverted carrot with some yellow fluff at the top. You can't help but smile. Cardón cacti, ocotillo, cholla and other desert marvels thrive in areas that sometimes don't see any rain for a decade. Crumbling missions, leafy date palms, coconuts and mangrove swamps are all items to look for as you meander southward.

Remember that mountain time (to the south) is an hour ahead of Pacific time (to the north). Here you also enter the 25,000-sq-km **Reserva de la Biosfera El Vizcaíno**, one of Latin America's largest single protected areas. It sprawls from the Península Vizcaíno across to the Sea of Cortez and includes the major gray-whale calving areas of Laguna San Ignacio and Laguna Ojo de Liebre, and the Sierra de San Francisco with its stunning pre-Hispanic rock art – over 60 sites, many of which can be viewed only by archaeologists.

The vast, desolate, yet starkly beautiful Desierto de Vizcaíno is punctuated by the oasis of San Ignacio. Paralleling the gulf, the Sierra de la Giganta divides the region into an eastern subtropical zone and a western zone of elevated plateaus and dry lowlands. Mulegé, Santa Rosalía and Loreto each have slightly different charms.

The southernmost part of the peninsula contains La Paz, small seaside towns and villages, and the popular resorts of San José del Cabo and Cabo San Lucas, aka 'Los Cabos.' After the quiet isolation of the north, Los Cabos will either be a jarring shock or a welcome relief.

GUERRERO NEGRO

615 / pop 11,894

After the snazziness of the touristy border towns, unassuming Guerrero Negro – a town that sprang up to service the lone salt factory – is a welcome relief. People actually speak Spanish here and nobody's barking out invitations to titty bars. Though the main tourist draw is the proximity to whales in whale season, there's excellent birding in the shallow marshes, friendly hotels and restaurants, and the salt factory's odd white crystalline plains are quite beautiful. The nearby Laguna Ojo

CALIFORNIA GRAY WHALES

The migration of gray whales from Siberian and Alaskan waters to the lagoons of Baja is one amazing animal event. In calving grounds such as **Laguna Ojo de Liebre** (Scammon's Lagoon; below), southwest of Guerrero Negro, and Laguna San Ignacio, southwest of San Ignacio, 700kg calves will draw their first breath and begin learning the lessons of the sea from their ever-watchful mothers.

Peak months to see mothers and calves in the lagoons are February to early April, but the official whale-watching season begins December 15 and lasts until April 15. After two to three months in these sheltered waters and nearly doubling their birth weight, the calves with their mothers head back to the open sea to begin the three-month glide home to their rich feeding grounds in the frozen north. The following year, they will return.

If you've got *ballena* (whale) fever, one of these destinations will provide a cure:

- Laguna Ojo de Liebre (Scammon's Lagoon; below)
- Laguna San Ignacio (p295)
- Puerto López Mateos (p301)
- Puerto San Carlos (p302)

de Liebre (known in English as Scammon's Lagoon), which annually becomes the mating and breeding ground of California gray whales, is the prime attraction.

Orientation & Information

The town comprises two sectors: a strip along Blvd Zapata, west of the Transpeninsular, and an orderly company town further west, run by Exportadora de Sal (ESSA). Nearly all accommodations, restaurants and other services are along Blvd Zapata; places in Guerrero Negro do not have street numbers.

There's a Banamex with an ATM at the far end of the commercial district on Blvd Zapata, just at the start of the company town. Get money here if you'll need it in San Ignacio, as that town has no bank.

Ciber@migos (☎ 157-26-51; internet access per hr M$25; ✆ 10am-9pm), off Zapata, is just a few streets away from Motel Las Ballenas.

Guerrero Negro's main medical facility is the **Clínica Hospital IMSS** (☎ 157-04-33; Blvd Zapata), located where the road curves southwest.

Whale-Watching

Agencies arrange whale-watching trips on the shallow waters of **Laguna Ojo de Liebre**, where visitors are guaranteed a view of whales in their natural habitat. **Malarrimo Eco Tours** (☎ 157-01-00; www.malarrimo.com; Blvd Zapata), at the beginning of the strip, offers four-hour tours (adult/child M$450/350). A bit further south *pangueros* (boatmen) from Ejido Benito Juárez take visitors for whale-watching excur-

sions (adult/child M$300/250). Baja Outpost (p300) also offers whale-watching tours out of Loreto. If whales aren't around, try bird-watching, cave-painting viewing or touring the salt factory (one to two hours, M$200 per person). Head to the Old Pier if you're a bird-watcher, as there are 11km of prime territory for ducks, coots, eagles, curlews, terns, herons and other birds.

Sleeping

The whale-watching season can strain local accommodations; reservations are advisable from January through March.

Malarrimo Trailer Park (☎ 157-01-00; www.malarrimo.com; cnr Blvd Zapata & Guerrero; tents M$140, RV sites M$140-200; P) This park, at the eastern entrance to town, has 45 camp sites with full hookups, plenty of hot water and clean toilets.

Motel Las Ballenas (☎ 157-01-16; Victoria Sánchez 10; r M$250; P) Fourteen clean and comfortable rooms with color TV. Not fancy, but they still take the time to twist the towels into the shape of kissing swans.

Hotel El Morro (☎ 157-04-14; Blvd Zapata; s/d M$290/340; P) Convenient to the bus station on the north side of Blvd Zapata, this hotel has 34 comfortable, basic rooms.

Cabañas Malarrimo (☎ 157-01-00; www.malarrimo .com; cnr Blvd Zapata & Guerrero; d M$400-450; P) Hot, strong showers and a lot more ambience than the other options in town. Same ownership as the Malarrimo Trailer Park. Whale headboards and a general whale theme make it impossible to forget why you've come here.

BAJA CALIFORNIA

Eating

Cafetería del Motel El Morro (☎ 157-04-14; Blvd Zapata; dinner mains M$50-80, lobster M$200) Adjacent to the Hotel El Morro, this place serves up inexpensive Mexican fare and seafood, including great breakfasts and a near-perfect *chile relleno* (chili stuffed with meat or cheese).

Los Faroles (☎ 157-15-10; Blvd Zapata; dinner mains M$50-80) *Sopes* hit the spot at this friendly café, with Mexican music and white tablecloths.

About 8km south of Guerrero Negro, a good graded road leads 25km west to the **Campo de Ballenas** (Whale-watching Camp) on the edge of the lagoon. Here a M$50 parking fee includes the right to camp, and the *ejido* (communal landholding) runs a simple restaurant (open in the whale season only).

Getting There & Away

Guerrero Negro's airport is 2km north of the state border, west of the Transpeninsular.

The Aeroméxico subsidiary **Aeroméxico Connect** (☎ 157-17-45; Blvd Zapata), on the north side of Blvd Zapata, flies Tuesday, Thursday and Saturday to Hermosillo, connecting to mainland Mexican cities.

Aerocedros (☎ 157-16-26; Blvd Zapata) flies to Isla Cedros and Ensenada Monday, Wednesday and Friday.

The **bus station** (☎ 157-06-11; Blvd Marcello Rubio; 24hr) is served by **ABC** (www.abc.com.mx) and Autotransportes Águila, one of its subsidiaries. Destinations include the following:

Destination	Fare (Águila/ABC)	Duration
Ensenada	M$569/614	9hr
La Paz	M$729/785	12hr
Loreto	M$392/423	5-6hr
Mulegé	M$262/285	4hr
Tijuana	M$671/723	12hr

SAN IGNACIO
☎ 615 / pop 719

Sleepy San Ignacio seems out of place after the endless Desierto de Vizcaíno – the town's lush, leafy date palms and quiet lake are almost shocking. Lazy mornings, hikes in the mountains along El Camino Real, whale-watching day trips and excursions to the spectacular pre-Hispanic rock-art sites in the Sierra de San Francisco (opposite) make this a great place to stay.

Jesuits located the **Misión San Ignacio de Kadakaamán** here, but Dominicans supervised construction of the striking church (finished in 1786) that still dominates the cool, laurel-shaded plaza. With lava-block walls nearly 1.2m thick and surrounded by bougainvillea, this is one of Baja's most beautiful churches. A small self-guiding **museum** (⏱ 8am-5pm Mon-Sat) offers a glimpse of the area's natural history.

Most services are around the plaza, including public telephones, but there is no bank. International calls can be made from the Hotel La Pinta. Internet access is available at **Fischer Internet** (☎ 154-04-49; per hr M$25; ⏱ 9am-10pm), which can also arrange tours.

Sleeping & Eating

San Ignacio has excellent accommodations choices tucked away beneath its swaying palms. Many can arrange tours to area attractions.

our pick **Casa Lereé** (☎ 154-01-58; www.murietawebdesign.com/test/leree/index.html; Morelos s/n; with private/shared bathroom M$750/400) Part guest house, part museum, this beautiful old building sits around a verdant garden with all kinds of tropical trees. Rooms are small but very tastefully decorated, there's wi-fi and the owner is a wealth of information about all aspects of San Ignacio, especially hiking and history.

Ricardo's Hotel & RV Park (☎ 154-02-83; d/r M$750/1250, RV sites M$250; P X Q) A squeaky clean hotel offering satellite TV and two queen-sized beds per room. There's a nice restaurant onsite and staff use fresh lime juice in the margaritas. RV sites are spartan but adequate.

Hotel La Pinta (☎ 154-03-00; r M$871; P X Q) This service-oriented hotel about 1.6km south of Hwy 1 on the paved road to San Ignacio offers luxurious, spacious rooms with large mirrors. The restaurant serves local beef, good *antojitos* and seafood (M$120). A beautiful pool and hummingbirds buzzing in the courtyard make this a relaxing escape.

El Padrino Restaurant & Bar (Flojos; mains M$50-130) An unassuming greasy spoon and RV park (camping with/without electricity M$140/80) with a pool table, TV and friendly staff. Try the fish in *mojo de ajo* (garlic sauce). Everything is good.

La Misión Kadakaaman (mains M$80-120) Dine beneath the shadow of the gorgeous plaza church on entrées such as fish filet in peanut or cilantro sauce, along with the usual Mexican suspects.

Buy a bag of dates, available everywhere in season, for M$10 to M$20 if you want a quick snack or energy for the road.

Getting There & Away

Buses pick up passengers at the bus station near the San Lino junction outside of town, arriving about every two hours from 5am to 11pm.

AROUND SAN IGNACIO
Sierra de San Francisco

The sheer quantity of beautiful petroglyphs in this region is impressive, but the ochre, red, black and white paintings remain shrouded in mystery. Some researchers believe they depict what may be religious rites, hunting rituals or warfare; others suggest they are warnings for neighboring tribes or possibly messages. The fact that some of the sites depict fish and whales indicates that the peoples had contact with oceans despite living far from them. In recognition of its cultural importance, the Sierra de San Francisco has been declared a Unesco World Heritage Site. It is also part of the Reserva de la Biosfera El Vizcaíno.

Cueva del Ratón, named for an image of what inhabitants once thought was a rat (or mouse) but is more likely a deer, is the most easily accessible site. Drivers can get there on their own after registering and paying the park entry (M$34) and guide fee (M$70) at the **Instituto Nacional de Antropología e Historia** (INAH; ☎ 154-02-22; ⏲ 8am-3pm Mon-Sat) office, adjacent to the Misión San Ignacio on the plaza in San Ignacio, then picking up their guide in the pueblo closest to the ruins. Bringing a camera costs M$35. Tours start at M$1300.

The dramatic **Cañón San Pablo** has sites that are better preserved. At **Cueva Pintada**, Cochimí painters and their predecessors decorated 150m of high rock overhangs with vivid red-and-black representations of human figures, bighorn sheep, pumas and deer, as well as with more abstract designs. **Cueva de las Flechas**, across Cañón San Pablo, has similar paintings, but curiously, some of the figures have arrows through them.

The beautiful muleback descent of Cañón San Pablo requires at least two days, preferably three. Excursions to Cañón San Pablo are best done through a tour operator; Kuyimá (see right) can arrange the three-day/six-day trips for M$4686/10197 per person (four per-

son minimum). Fischer Internet (opposite) is another option.

Laguna San Ignacio

Along with Laguna Ojo de Liebre and Bahía Magdalena, Laguna San Ignacio is one of the Pacific coast's major winter whale-watching sites, with three-hour excursions costing around M$440 per person. **Kuyimá** (☎ 154-00-70; www.kuyima.com; Morelos 23), a cooperative based at the east end of the plaza in San Ignacio, can arrange transportation and accommodations. The 65km drive to the camping ground (where cabins are also available) takes about two hours over rough roads.

SANTA ROSALÍA
☎ 615 / pop 9768

Come here to see cool crumbling buildings in honorable disrepair. Brightly painted clapboard-sided houses, the prefab church, a port and *malecón*, black-sand beaches, lazy pelicans and great views from the surrounding hills are all attractions of Santa Rosalía. For southbound travelers, Santa Rosalía offers the first glimpse of the Sea of Cortez after a long, dry crossing of the Desierto de Vizcaíno.

Orientation & Information

Central Santa Rosalía is a cluster of densely packed houses, restaurants, inns and stores. Plaza Benito Juárez, four blocks west of the highway, is the town center.

The post office is on Av Constitución at Calle 2. Hotel del Real, on the exit road from town, has long-distance *cabinas* (call centers). Check your email at **Cafe Internet PC Vision** (☎ 152-28-75; cnr 6th & Obregón; per hr M$20; ⏲ 10am-10pm).

Sights

Built in 1885 by the French to house the offices of the Boleo Company, the **Museo Histórico Minero de Santa Rosalía** (admission M$20; ⏲ 8am-2pm Mon-Fri) watches over the town and the rusting copperworks from its perch on the hill near the Hotel Francés, surrounded by cool abandoned locomotives and other machinery.

Designed and erected for Paris' 1889 World's Fair, disassembled and stored in Brussels, intended for West Africa, Gustave Eiffel's (Yes, of Eiffel Tower fame) prefabricated **Iglesia Santa Bárbara** was shipped here when a Boleo Company director signed for its delivery to the town in 1895. Many travelers agree that the church is interesting more as an example of early prefabricated architecture than for its beauty.

Sleeping & Eating

Of all the towns in central Baja, Santa Rosalía has perhaps the best variety of well-priced accommodations choices, from the historic to the picturesque.

Motel San Victor (☎ 152-01-16; cnr Progreso 36 & Calle 9a; r M$150; P 🅿️) Rooms are dark and simple but the quiet, shaded courtyard and off-street parking are nice, and the owner speaks English.

Hotel del Real (☎ 152-00-68; Av Montoya 7; r M$300-350; 🅿️) Has a new wing of tidy rooms with two beds and an older and mustier wing. All rooms have cable TV.

Hotel Francés (☎ 152-20-52; Cousteau 15; r M$600; P ❌ 🅿️) Overlooking the Sea of Cortez and curious rusting hulks of mine machinery, the Hotel Francés is charming and historic. Built in 1886 and originally the dormitory for 'working girls' of a brothel near the mine, the hotel features beautiful rooms with high ceilings, cloth-covered walls and charming stained-wood details. Onsite is a restaurant open Monday to Saturday, for breakfast. Tours cost M$10.

Panadería El Boleo (☎ 152-03-10; Obregón 30; breads M$8-25) Since 1901, this has been an obligatory stop for the rare find of good French bread in Baja. The pastries are good too. Find it between Calles 3 and 4.

Restaurant Don Pedro (Calle 5 No 3; antojitos M$30-45) This restaurant, just north of Obregón, serves reasonably priced tacos, *antojitos* and a delicious *machaca* (shredded beef).

Playas Negras (☎ 152-06-85; breakfast M$45, dinner mains M$85-130) South of downtown and with a gorgeous view and a funky map of Baja done in abalone shell, this waterfront restaurant serves sumptuous seafood as well as steak, chicken and pizza.

El Muelle (☎ 152-09-31; cnr Constitución & Calle Plaza; mains M$65-110; 🕐 8am-11pm) The dock theme fits well with seaside Santa Rosalía. Locals come here for everything from egg breakfasts to the popular Red Enchiladas.

For cheap eats or fruit for the road, check out the small **fruit market** (🕐 6am-6pm) on Montoya between Hotel del Real and the highway, or hit one of the many taco stands of high quality along Av Obregón. Most charge M$8 for a fish taco.

Getting There & Around

AIR

Aéreo Servicio Guerrero (☎ 615-152-31-81; 🕐 8am-1pm, 3-6pm Mon-Sat) offers flights to Guaymas (M$870, daily) and Hermosillo (M$1500, Monday to Saturday) on the Mexican mainland. The ticket office is located in the ferry terminal.

BOAT

The passenger/auto ferry *Santa Rosalía*, operated by Operadora Rotuaria del Noroeste, sails to Guaymas at 9am Tuesday, Wednesday, Friday and Sunday, arriving at 7am the next morning; the return ferry from Guaymas sails at 8pm Monday, Thursday and Saturday, arriving at 6am. Strong winter winds may cause delays, and the Monday and Tuesday trips are often cancelled due to lack of demand. It's best to check the day before whether the ferry will run. Also note that Sonora doesn't use daylight savings, so at certain times of the year Guaymas will be ahead by one hour.

The ticket office is at the **ferry terminal** (☎ 152-12-46; www.ferrysantarosalia.com; 🕐 10am-7pm Mon-Sat), on the highway. Passenger fares are M$650 in general seating, M$750 additional for shared cabins (children's tickets are half-price, and there is a general Sunday discount). Advance reservations are recommended. Vehicle rates vary with vehicle length. See the accompanying chart for vehicle fares. The office opens at 7am or 8am on the day of a departure.

Vehicle	Fare
car or pickup up to 5m	M$2480, plus M$990 per extra meter
trailer truck up to 15m	M$9500
motorhome	M$3500
motorcycle	M$1350

Before shipping vehicles to the mainland, officials require a vehicle permit (see p987). These can be obtained at **Banjercito** (www.banjercito.com .mx), the only bank that processes vehicle permit payments, at its Tijuana, Mexicali or La Paz branches. Alternatively, you can organize one on its Spanish website.

BUS

At least five buses daily in each direction stop at the **bus terminal** (☎ 152-14-08; 🕐 24hr), which is in the same building as the ferry

ON A MISSION FROM GOD...

Baja's missions have a dubious history – built by Jesuits and Dominicans intent on bringing salvation, they instead brought death through introduced European diseases. Many missions were abandoned as populations dropped below sustainable levels. Today however, these beautiful buildings, whether in use or out in the middle of nowhere, make for great photos and fun day trips, and they're an undeniable part of Baja's checkered past. You should not need a 4WD to visit any of the ones listed here, though the roads can be impressively bad (or impassable) at times.

Misión San Francisco Javier de Viggé-Biaundó (p301) Remote and beautifully preserved; it feels like stepping back in time. The drive there offers awesome vistas and even some cave paintings along the way.

Misión Santa Rosalía de Mulegé (below) Extremely photogenic. Don't miss the view from behind looking out over the palm-edged river.

Misión San Borja (p292) Out in the middle of nowhere but well worth the drive. Its treasures include a hot spring and a secret tunnel (now walled up). One family, descended from the original pre-conquest inhabitants, is restoring the building rock by rock, by hand.

Misión Nuestra Señora de Loreto (p300) The oldest, an impressive monument still in use today.

Resources for further reading include *Las Misiones Antiguas,* by Edward W Vernon, and www.vivabaja.com/bajamissions; both feature beautiful photos of these interesting ruins.

---

terminal on the highway just south of the entrance to town. Destinations include the following:

Destination	Fare (ABC/Aguila)	Duration
Ensenada	M$835/774	12hr
Guerrero Negro	M$220/204	3hr
La Paz	M$566/524	8hr
Loreto	M$202/168	3hr
Mexicali	M$1097/1041	16hr
Mulegé	M$63/59	1hr
San Ignacio	M$75/70	1hr
San José del Cabo	M$717/679	12hr
Tijuana	M$944/875	14hr

MULEGÉ

☎ 615 / pop 3317

The palm- and mangrove-lined Río Mulegé, with its delta, birds, wildlife, snorkeling and diving, makes Mulegé a great stop for the outdoorsy or for those with kids. The ancient mission and town square give the town a quiet charm that's fast disappearing in other parts of Baja. Despite the new eyesore at the entrance to town and the fact that it finally has a bank/ATM, Mulegé still feels like part of yesteryear.

Most services are on or near Jardín Corona, the town plaza. Bancomer and the ATM are on Zaragoza between Martinez and Madero. To get online try **Carlos' Place** (per hr M$30; ⏰ 9am-1pm & 4-8pm Mon-Sat), across from Los Equipales (p298). Hotel Mulegé (p298) is another option.

Sights & Activities

Come to the hilltop **Misión Santa Rosalía de Mulegé** (founded in 1705, completed in 1766 and abandoned in 1828) for great photos of the mission and river valley.

The former territorial prison is now the **Museo Mulegé** (Barrio Canenea; donation M$10; ⏰ 9am-2pm Mon-Sat). Its eclectic holdings include objects from the Mission de Santa Rosalía and prehistoric artifacts.

DIVING

Mulegé's best diving spots can be found around the Santa Inés Islands (north of town) and just north of Punta Concepción (south of town). **Cortez Explorers** (☎ 153-05-00; www.cortez-explorers.com; Moctezuma 75A; ⏰ 8:30am-6pm), under new English ownership, offers all levels of diving instruction from zero to instructor level, squid-diving excursions, snorkeling gear and kayak or bicycle rental. One- or two-tank dives cost M$990 per person, snorkeling M$550.

KAYAKING

The beautiful river, the estuary delta and the southern beaches make Mulegé one of the prime spots for kayaking. Baja Outpost (p300) in Loreto is one of the few places for long-term rentals or for those wanting to follow the coastline south over a few days. **NOLS Mexico** (☎ in the US 800-710-6657, 307-332-5300; www.nols.edu/courses/locations/mexico/about_mexico.shtml) has sea-kayaking courses out of its sustainable,

BAJA CALIFORNIA

eco-friendly facility on Coyote Bay, south of Mulegé.

Sleeping

Casa de Huéspedes Manuelita (☎ 153-01-75; Moctezuma; r M$250) Rooms are behind a beautiful grape arbor and, while basic, they are clean and have hot showers. The parakeets are a nice touch.

Hotel Las Casitas (☎ 153-00-19; www.historicolascasitas.com.mx; Madero 50; s/d M$341/393; P ✷) Beloved Mexican poet Alán Gorosave once inhabited this well-run hotel near Martínez, perhaps inspired by its beautiful courtyard shaded by a well-tended garden of tropical plants. The restaurant serves excellent breakfasts and has an open-fire grill. Drew Barrymore is rumored to have stayed here.

Hotel Hacienda (☎ 153-00-21; hotelhacienda_mulege@hotmail.com; Madero 3; r M$350; ✷ ✺) The oldest hotel in town, the green-and-white atmospheric Hacienda offers rooms with twin beds and a fridge. It even has its own old well that, though unused, still contains water.

Hotel Mulegé (☎ 153-04-16; Moctezuma s/n; s/d M$380/400; P ✷ ▯) Mulegé's only busines hotel has spotless doubles with carpeted floors, bottled water and cable TV. Internet (M$25 per hour) in the lobby is another plus.

Hotel Cuesta Real (☎ 153-03-21; http://cuestarealhotel.tripod.com; Transpenínsular Km 132; s/d M$390/490, RV hookups M$200; P ✷ ▯ ✺) This hotel offers large, spotless rooms and easy access to Río Mulegé as it empties into the sea (very convenient for kayakers). The grounds also boast a pleasant restaurant. Take in scenic mangrove swamps and pelicans on the way into town. Internet costs M$25 per hour.

Eating & Drinking

The sidewalks are rolled up pretty early in Mulegé, so dine earlier than usual and rest up for that big day tomorrow.

Restaurante Doney (☎ 153-00-95; mulegedoney@hotmail.com; Moctezuma s/n; tacos & snacks M$13-110) There's counter or table seating here, with colorful tablecloths and good *antojitos* and tacos.

Scott's El Candil (Zaragoza s/n; mains M$60-120; ☽ 11am-11pm Mon-Sat, 11am-7pm Sun) Nice brick building with open courtyard in the back and arched windows onto Zaragoza for those who want to watch the world (or at least Mulegé's portion of it!) pass by.

Los Equipales (☎ 153-03-30; Moctezuma; mains M$130-220) Just west of Zaragoza, this restau-

rant and bar has gargantuan meals and a breezy balcony seating that's perfect for an afternoon margarita or an evening chat with friends. Shrimp are snapped up as soon as they are served.

Getting There & Away

Mulegé's **bus terminal** (☽ 7am-11pm) is inconveniently located north of town, at Km 136.5 on the Transpeninsular. ABC/Águila northbound buses to Santa Rosalía (M$63/59, one hour) stop about every two hours. Southbound buses pass daily to destinations including Loreto (M$139/129, 2½ hours) and La Paz (M$503/466, seven hours).

AROUND MULEGÉ
Cañón La Trinidad

Trinity Canyon is great for bird-watchers, with the chance to see Vermillion Flycatchers, Gila woodpeckers and a host of raptors and buteos. The narrow, sherbet-colored canyon walls and shimmering pools of water are stunning, as are the pre-Hispanic cave paintings. Rendered in shades of ochre and rust, the paintings feature shamans, manta rays, whales and the famous Trinity Deer, leaping gracefully from the walls of the cave as arrows pass harmlessly over its head. Dams and climate change have kept the canyon dry for over a decade. You're not allowed to enter by yourself, but Mulegé native Salvador Castro of **Mulegé Tours** (☎ 615-153-02-32; day excursions per person M$400) knows just about everything about the site you could want to know – plants, animals, even how to avoid the two nasty beehives that 'guard' the paintings.

Beaches

As you wind your way south you'll pass some of Baja's most pristine *playas* (beaches). You can string up a hammock, pop the top on something frosty and watch the pelicans dive-bomb the fish. Some beaches have bars, restaurants or *cabañas*. Bahía Concepción, with its pelican colonies, funky rock formations and milky blue-green water, remains a top stop for kayakers, many of whom camp in makeshift RV colonies. **Playa Escondido** (Km 112), **Playa Santispac** (Km 113.5) and **Playa Perla** (Km 91) are just a few of the possible stops along Hwy 1 on the way. Be extremely cautious about weather alerts – the glassy water here and in Loreto can quickly become dangerous in high winds.

LORETO

SIGHTS & ACTIVITIES
Misión Nuestra Señora de Loreto	7 C2
Museo de las Misiones	8 C2

INFORMATION
.com	1 D2
Bancomer	2 C2
Centro de Salud	3 B3
Municipal Department of Tourism	4 D2
Parque Nacional Bahía de Loreto	5 D1
Post Office	6 A3

SLEEPING 🏠
Baja Outpost	9 D3
Hotel Junípero	10 C3
Hotel Posada San Martín	11 C2
Iguana Inn	12 C2
Motel Salvatierra	13 B3

EATING 🍴
Antojitos Mexicanos	14 C3
Café Olé	15 D2
La Fuente de Loreto	16 B3
México Lindo Y Que Rico	17 C3
Tacos & Beer César	18 C3

SHOPPING 🛍
El Alacrán	19 C2
Silver Desert	20 C2

TRANSPORT
Budget	21 D2
Bus Station	22 A3

BAJA CALIFORNIA

LORETO
☎ 613 / pop 10,283

The Loreto area is considered by anthropologists to be the oldest human settlement on the Baja Peninsula. Indigenous cultures thrived here due to plentiful water and food. In 1697 Jesuit Juan María Salvatierra established the peninsula's first permanent mission at this modest port some 135km south of Mulegé. These days, Loreto has the reputation as Baja's water sports paradise. It's home to the Parque Marino Nacional Bahía de Loreto, with shoreline, ocean and offshore islands protected from pollution and uncontrolled fishing, though massive development of the shoreline is already causing irreparable changes.

Orientation
Most hotels and services are near the landmark mission church on Salvatierra, while the attractive *malecón* is ideal for evening strolls. The Plaza Cívica is just north of Salvatierra, between Madero and Davis.

Information
Bancomer (cnr Salvatierra & Madero) Has an ATM and changes US cash and traveler's checks Monday to Friday.
Centro de Salud (☎ 133-00-39; Salvatierra 68; ⊗ 24hr) A local health center.
.com (☎ 135-18-46; Madero s/n; per hr M$20; ⊗ 8am-4pm Mon-Sat) Next to Café Olé and convenient to the town center.
Municipal Department of Tourism (☎ 135-04-11; turismoloreto@hotmail.com; ⊗ 8am-3pm Mon-Fri) On

the west side of the Plaza Cívica, has a good selection of brochures and flyers.

Parque Nacional Bahía de Loreto (☎ 135-04-77; ✆ 8:30am-2pm Mon-Fri) Pay the M$21 entrance fee to the park here in the marina. Staff are a good source of information for all water activities in the area.

Post office (☎ 135-06-47; Deportiva; ✆ 8am-2:30pm Mon-Fri)

Sights & Activities

Including the 2065 sq km **Parque Marino Nacional Bahía de Loreto**, Loreto is a world-class destination for all types of outdoor activities; a number of outfitters offer everything from kayaking and diving along the reefs around Isla del Carmen and Coronado to horseback riding, hiking and mountain biking in the Sierra de la Giganta.

Baja Outpost (see right) offers diving, snorkeling, biking and kayaking expeditions in addition to accommodations. Note that its whale-watching tours (M$2035 per person) run a full seven hours, unlike many others (some are as short as 1½ hours), and the owner can offer both blue and gray whale viewing tours to a variety of locations.

The **Misión Nuestra Señora de Loreto**, dating from 1697, was the first permanent mission in the Californias and the base for the expansion of Jesuit missions up and down the Baja peninsula. Alongside the church, INAH's revamped **Museo de las Misiones** (☎ 135-04-41; cnr Salvatierra & Misioneros; admission M$30; ✆ 9am-1pm & 1:45-6pm Tue-Fri) chronicles the settlement of Baja California.

Sleeping

Most of Loreto's accommodations choices are on or near the picturesque *malecón*.

BUDGET

Hotel Posada San Martín (☎ 135-11-07; Juárez 4; r M$200-350; ✖) The best value in town and probably the cleanest M$200 place in all of Baja, this hotel has large rooms (some with cable TV) and a great location near the plaza.

Motel Salvatierra (☎ 135-00-21; Salvatierra 123; s/d/tr/q M$270/300/350/420) Near the bus station, this bright ochre motel offers clean, basic rooms that are some of Loreto's least expensive.

MIDRANGE & TOP END

Hotel Junípero (☎ 135-01-22; Av Hidalgo; s/d/tr M$350/400/450; ✖) Overlooking the mission and the town plaza, this family-run hotel has

seen better days but rooms in the back have excellent views of the mission. Golf-ball key rings are out of place, but fun.

Iguana Inn (☎ 135-16-27; www.iguanainn.com; Juarez s/n; bungalows M$550-660; ✆ Oct-Aug; **P** ✖ ✖) Kitchenettes, a video library and clean, comfortable beds make this a great option. Very close to the town center and still within easy walking distance of the *malecón*. A new casita sleeps up to five people for M$935.

our pick **Baja Outpost** (☎ 135-11-34; www.bajaoutpost.com; Blvd López Mateos; r incl breakfast M$760, palapa M$935; **P** ✖) This posh, tastefully finished B&B offers regular rooms, beautiful *palapas*, great breakfasts made to order and multilingual staff (Leon, the owner, speaks six languages). Located off the busy *malecón*, convenient to the town center and the beach. A testament to Leon's sainthood, or his faith in guestkind, is the well-stocked, honor-system bar. All manner of tours can be done from here as well.

Eating & Drinking

Loreto has a good selection of restaurants preparing the regional standards: excellent seafood with plenty of lime and cilantro, potent margaritas and fruity *aguas frescas* (ice drinks). Unfortunately, of late mistakes in the bill have become common; don't be afraid to do the arithmetic after the tab arrives.

Tacos & Beer César (☎ 135-17-45; cnr Hidalgo & Colegio; mains M$10-66) Look for the charcoal grill (often in use). Great tacos and other Mexican specialties in a festive outdoor patio. Passing mariachis can be flagged down if you're in the mood for some *música romántica*.

Antojitos Mexicanos (Hidalgo s/n; mains M$12-50; ✆ closed Wed) This tiny new hole in the wall is family run – get *comida económica* (cheap food) and great shrimp tacos and ceviche, served with pride and a smile. On weekends, try the *birria* – simmered goat meat.

Café Olé (☎ 135-04-96; Madero 14; dinner mains M$24-66) The inexpensive Café Olé has good, basic fare: great Mexican breakfasts, lunches and dinners. Leave a business card in the wicker wall to stake your claim to fame.

México Lindo Y Que Rico (☎ 135-11-75; Hidalgo s/n; dinner mains M$37-120, lobster dishes M$230; ✆ closed Mon) The fountain and wrought-iron furniture are nice touches, and the food is great: try the chicken in pipian sauce and follow with creamy flan. Live music adds flair on weekends. There's also a popular Sunday breakfast buffet.

La Fuente de Loreto (Salvatierra 88; mains M$55-140; ☼ 7am-5pm Mon-Sat) Great *antojitos* and Mexican dishes as well as a variety of Western options. Chicken *chilaquiles* (corn tortillas and spicy chili paste) are fantastic.

Shopping

The pedestrian mall between Madero and Independencia has many shops selling jewelry and souvenirs.

El Alacrán (☎/fax 135-00-29; Salvatierra 47; ☼ 9:30am-1pm & 2:30-7pm Mon-Sat) is the place to try for varied handicrafts, while **Silver Desert** (☎ 135-06-84; Salvatierra 36; ☼ 9am-2pm & 3-8:30pm Mon-Sat, 9am-2pm Sun) has Taxco sterling-silver jewelry of good quality.

Getting There & Away

Aeropuerto Internacional de Loreto (☎ 135-04-54) is now served by several international airlines. **Aero California** (☎ 135-05-00) has daily nonstop flights to La Paz, San José del Cabo and Los Angeles. **AeroCalafia** (☎ 135-09-99), also with an office at the airport, flies daily to and from La Paz and Los Angeles.

Loreto's **bus station** (☎ 135-07-67; ☼ 24hr) is near the convergence of Salvatierra, Paseo de Ugarte and Paseo Tamaral. There are services to the following destinations (note there are only two daily to Santa Rosalía).

Destination	Fare	Duration
Guerrero Negro	M$392	6hr
La Paz	M$337	5hr
Mexicali	M$1229	20hr
San José del Cabo	M$540	8hr
Santa Rosalía	M$188	3hr
Tijuana	M$1063	17hr

The car-rental agency **Budget** (☎ 135-10-90; Av Hidalgo) has economy models starting at about M$550 per day, including appropriate insurance.

Getting Around

Taxis from the airport, 4km south of Loreto, cost M$160 if you step outside the door, or M$100 if you walk to the edge of the airport grounds. Groups are M$70 per person.

AROUND LORETO

Whale-watching tours are the biggest tourist draw between Loreto and La Paz, but the wonderful **Misión San Francisco Javier de Viggé-Biaundó** (and the drive to get there!) is well worth a daytime detour. The windy road passes minor cliff paintings and some beautiful arroyos before arriving at the mission. Be sure to wander in back to see the 300-year-old olive tree with ropelike bark that looks like something out of a Tolkien fantasy. The mission itself is almost unchanged from its look of three centuries ago. Head south on Hwy 1 and look for the sign shortly after you leave Loreto, leading you to the right, up into the mountains. It's about a one-hour drive, usually accessible to any car, though 4WDs are sometimes needed.

Puerto López Mateos
☎ 613 / pop 2171

Shielded by the offshore barrier of Isla Magdalena, Puerto López Mateos is one of Baja's best whale-watching sites. During the season, the narrow waterway that passes by town becomes a veritable *ballena* cruising strip. Curva del Diablo (The Devil's Bend), 27km south of town, is reported to be the best viewing spot. Three-hour *panga* (skiff) excursions from Puerto López Mateos (M$650 per hour for up to six people, from 8am to 5pm in season) are easy to arrange.

Free camping (bring water), with pit toilets only, is possible at tidy Playa Boca de la Soledad, which is near Playa El Faro, 1.6km east of town (turn left at the water tower). The only other accommodations in Puerto López Mateos are at the small but serviceable **El Camarón Feliz** (☎ 131-50-32; r M$300). It also has a nice restaurant, replete with a 'Big Mouth Billy Bass' singing rubber fish on the wall. **Baja Mar** (☎ 131-51-96; mains M$35-120) offers family-style Mexican dishes.

Puerto López Mateos is 34km west of Ciudad Insurgentes. The bus service to Ciudad Constitución leaves inconveniently at 6:30am and 2:30pm.

Ciudad Constitución
☎ 613 / pop 37,221

Primarily a farming and industrial city, Ciudad Constitución offers little for tourists other than hotels for whale-watching day trips. Transportation to the port cities of López Mateos and San Carlos is infrequent – it's best to have your own set of wheels. Loreto (p299) or La Paz (p302) have the closest rental agencies.

Ciudad Constitución's lodgings are limited; none of them are fancy and prices rise at the peak of the season.

Hotel Conchita (☎ 132-02-66; Olachea 180 at Hidalgo; r M$270; ✻) offers basic rooms with yellow bedspreads, TV and privacy glass that blocks any possible view. Watch your step on that uneven staircase.

Rooms at the Hotel Maribel (☎ 132-01-55; Guadalupe Victoria 156; s M$250-270, d M$320-330; ✻) are spartan, but small balconies brighten them a bit, and there's a convenient restaurant downstairs. More expensive rooms have phones.

Spotless and peach pink all over, Posadas del Ryal (☎ 132-48-00; Victoria s/n; r M$360; P ✻), just off Olachea, has dark rooms with cable TV and a cheery fountain in the courtyard.

At the bus terminal (☎ 132-03-76; cnr Zapata & Pino Suárez) you have two daily departures for Puerto López Mateos (M$64, 12:30pm and 7:30pm) and Puerto San Carlos (M$52, 11am and 6pm). Other destinations include La Paz (M$153, frequent) and Tijuana (M$1203, five daily from 10am to 11pm).

Taxis, just outside the bus station, charge M$800 for a round-trip ride to Puerto López Mateos and M$600 for a round trip to Puerto San Carlos.

Puerto San Carlos
☎ 613 / pop 4716
On Bahía Magdalena, 56km west of Ciudad Constitución, Puerto San Carlos is a deepwater port and fishing town. The *ballenas* arrive in January to calve in the warm lagoon and the town turns its attention to both whales and travelers. From January through March, *pangueros* take up to six passengers for whale-watching excursions (M$650 per hour for one to six people).

With several hotels and restaurants to choose from, San Carlos is a good choice for whale-watching adventures. Accommodations can be tougher to find during the high season, but free camping is possible north of town on the public beach (no toilets). The Motel Las Brisas (Puerto Madero; s/d M$150/180; P) has dark, basic rooms that are inexpensive.

The green-trimmed Hotel Brennan (☎ 136-02-88; www.hotelbrennan.com.mx; Puerto La Paz; s/d M$550/650) has smallish but intimate rooms and plentiful patio space. With similar amenities, the Hotel Alcatraz (☎ 136-00-17; Puerto Acapulco; s/d M$450/600; P ✻) offers 25 rooms with satellite TV, parking and laundry service.

At the Hotel Alcatraz, Restaurant Bar El Patio (☎ 136-00-17; buffet M$120) is the town's best eatery, with – you guessed it – a buffet. Not to be outdone, Mariscos Los Arcos (☎ 136-03-47; Puerto La Paz 170; tacos M$30, dinner mains M$45-280) has tremendous shrimp tacos and seafood soup, a full breakfast menu and a small bar.

From a small house (☎ 136-04-53) on Calle Puerto Morelos, Autotransportes Águilar runs buses at 7:30am and 1:45pm daily to Ciudad Constitución (M$52). This is the only public transportation from Puerto San Carlos.

A network of dirt roads also connects Puerto San Carlos with Puerto López Mateos. Drive through the dust and marvel at the majestic monotony of this parched desert – cholla and old-man cactus predominate. To reach La Florida, at the marshy coast, you will need a 4WD or risk sinking in the soft, blowing sand. Bring extra water and check the spare tire, just in case.

LA PAZ
☎ 612 / pop 189,176
Cosmopolitan La Paz is a mix of laid-back, old-world beauty and chi-chi upscale trend. It's surprisingly international – you're as likely to hear French, Portuguese or Italian here as English or Spanish. Its quirky history includes American occupation and even being temporarily declared its own republic. Hernán Cortés established Baja's first European outpost near La Paz, but permanent settlement waited until 1811. Its rich pearl industry disappeared during the revolution of 1910–20.

The beachside *malecón,* unique restaurants and funky stores make it a great place to meander, and you can shop uninterrupted by touts' invitations. The city is a great hub for day trips to Cabo Pulmo (p307) or even Todos Santos (p315).

The port of Pichilingue receives ferries from the mainland ports of Topolobampo and Mazatlán, and the airport is served by several US carriers.

Orientation
La Paz' grid makes basic orientation easy, but the center's crooked streets and alleys change names almost every block. The city's heart is Jardín Velasco (Plaza Constitución), three blocks southeast of the tourist pier.

Information
BOOKSTORES
Museo Regional de Antropología e Historia
(☎ 122-01-62; cnr Calle 5 de Mayo & Altamirano; ⊙ 9am-6pm) Museum store with good selection of Spanish-language books on Baja California and mainland Mexico.

EMERGENCY
Tourist Police (☎ 122-59-39, 078; ☯ 8am-10pm) Small booth on Obregón.

INTERNET ACCESS
Cafe El Callejón (☎ 125-40-06; Callejón La Paz 51; per hr M\$15) Also a restaurant, the Callejón has several computers. It has live music and is open late.
Hotel Perla (Paseo Obregón 1570) Two machines in the lobby that members of the public are welcome to use.

INTERNET RESOURCES
Viva La Paz (www.vivalapaz.com) La Paz' official tourism site.

LAUNDRY
La Paz Lava (☎ 122-31-12; cnr Ocampo & Mutualismo) Self-service machines and delivery service to hotels or homes.

MEDICAL SERVICES
Hospital Salvatierra (☎ 122-14-96; Bravo; ☯ 24hr) English-speaking staff.

MONEY
Most banks (most with ATMs) and *casas de cambio* are on or around Calle 16 de Septiembre.

POST
Main post office (cnr Constitución & Revolución; ☯ 8am-3pm Mon-Fri, 9am-1pm Sat)

TOURIST INFORMATION
State tourist information booth (☎ 124-01-03; Obregón; ☯ 8am-3pm Mon-Sat) Brochures and pamphlets are available in English. Some of the staff speak English too.

Sights
The **Museo Regional de Antropología e Historia** (☎ 122-01-62; cnr Calle 5 de Mayo & Altamirano; admission free; ☯ 9am-6pm) is a large, well-organized museum chronicling the peninsula's history from prehistory to the revolution of 1910 and its aftermath.

Across from the Jardín Velasco, La Paz' former Casa de Gobierno is now the **Biblioteca de la Historia de las Californias** (cnr Madero & Av Independencia; ☯ 8am-3pm Mon-Fri), a history library.

A sprawling concrete edifice, the **Teatro de la Ciudad** is the most conspicuous element of the **Unidad Cultural Profesor Jesús Castro Agúndez** (☎ 125-02-07; ☯ 8am-3pm Mon-Fri), a cultural center that takes up most of the area

bounded by Altamirano, Navarro, Héroes de la Independencia and Legaspi. At the periphery of the grounds is the small **Museo Comunitario de la Ballena** (Community Whale Museum; cnr Navarro & Altamirano; admission free; ☯ 9am-1pm Tue-Sat). A few blocks west, the **Santuario de la Virgen de Guadalupe** (☎ 122-15-18; cnr Calle 5 de Febrero & Aquiles Serdán) is La Paz' biggest religious monument. Its 12m-tall altar is impressive.

Activities
La Paz makes a great hub for almost any outdoor activity. The nearby island of **Espíritu Santo** is a treasure of shallow azure inlets and sorbet-pink cliffs, and there's even a sea-lion colony. Hiking in the desert, swimming, diving and snorkeling with whale sharks are all possible. Renting a *panga* for trips to look at whale sharks will cost about M\$600 for two hours. Bargain at the beach along the *malecón*. To ensure success you will need to pay for a Cessna spotting plane.

For tours and rentals, try the following:
Baja Paradise (☎ 128-60-97; www.bajaparadiseoutdoors.com; Madero 23) Offers guided camping tours on Espíritu Santo, plus all other activities. Hostel-type accommodations are possible and the owner is a professor in the local university's ecological tourism program who takes care to make the trips as 'green' and low-impact as possible.
Carey.com (☎ 128-40-48; www.carey.com.mx; cnr Topete & Legaspi 3040) A family-run establishment that offers diving and snorkeling day trips to Espíritu Santo, along with other trips and tours.
Mar y Aventuras (☎ 122-70-39; www.kayakbaja.com; cnr Calle 5 de Febrero & Topete) Book a kayak expedition or outfit a self-guided trip.

Courses
Centro de Idiomas, Cultura y Comunicación
(☎ 125-75-54; www.cicclapaz.com; Madero 2460) Offers intensive Spanish classes and 'Xmas on the beach' classes, and will help coordinate homestay lodging.
Se Habla…La Paz (☎ 122-7763; www.sehablalapaz.com; Madero 540) Courses cost M\$2750 per week plus M\$700 registration. All levels of Spanish classes including a medical and legal specialty.

Festivals & Events
Festivals and other seasonal events often take place at the Plaza Constitución, between Revolución and Madero at Calle 5 de Mayo.

La Paz' pre-Lent **Carnaval** is among the country's best. In early May, *paceños* (people from La Paz) celebrate the **Fundación de la Ciudad** (Hernán Cortés' 1535 landing).

BAJA CALIFORNIA

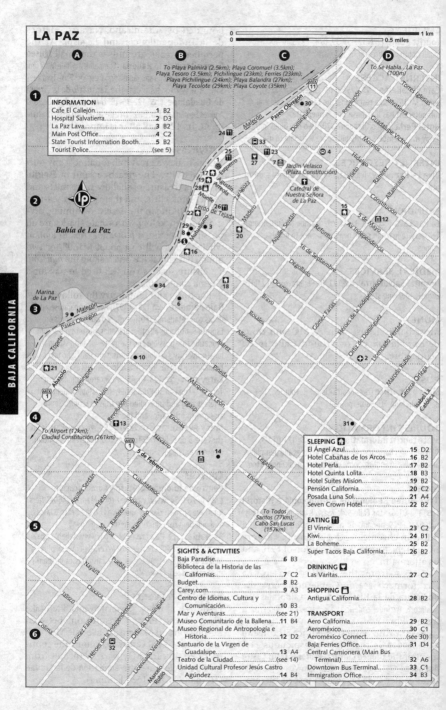

LA PAZ

0 _____ 1 km
0 _____ 0.5 miles

To Playa Palmira (2.5km); Playa Coromuel (3.5km);
Playa Tesoro (3.5km); Pichilingue (23km); Ferries (23km);
Playa Pichilingue (24km); Playa Balandra (27km);
Playa Tecolote (29km); Playa Coyote (35km)

To Se Habla...La Paz (100m)

INFORMATION
Cafe El Callejón......................................1 B2
Hospital Salvatierra...............................2 D3
La Paz Lava...3 B2
Main Post Office.....................................4 C2
State Tourist Information Booth.............5 B2
Tourist Police.................................(see 5)

Bahía de La Paz

Marina de La Paz

To Airport (12km);
Ciudad Constitución (261km)

To Todos Santos (77km);
Cabo San Lucas (157km)

SIGHTS & ACTIVITIES
Baja Paradise..6 B3
Biblioteca de la Historia de las
  Californias..7 C2
Budget...8 B2
Carey.com...9 A3
Centro de Idiomas, Cultura y
  Comunicación.....................................10 B3
Mar y Aventuras.............................(see 21)
Museo Comunitario de la Ballena....11 B4
Museo Regional de Antropología e
  Historia..12 D2
Santuario de la Virgen de
  Guadalupe...13 A4
Teatro de la Ciudad......................(see 14)
Unidad Cultural Profesor Jesús Castro
  Agúndez...14 B4

SLEEPING 🏠
El Ángel Azul...15 D2
Hotel Cabañas de los Arcos................16 B2
Hotel Perla...17 B2
Hotel Quinta Lolita...............................18 B3
Hotel Suites Mision..............................19 B2
Pensión California.................................20 C2
Posada Luna Sol...................................21 A4
Seven Crown Hotel...............................22 B2

EATING 🍴
El Vinnic..23 C2
Kiwi...24 B1
La Boheme...25 B2
Super Tacos Baja California.................26 B2

DRINKING 🍷
Las Varitas...27 C2

SHOPPING 🛍
Antigua California................................28 B2

TRANSPORT
Aero California......................................29 B2
Aeroméxico...30 C1
Aeroméxico Connect...................(see 30)
Baja Ferries Office................................31 D4
Central Camionera (Main Bus
  Terminal)...32 A6
Downtown Bus Terminal.....................33 C1
Immigration Office...............................34 B3

Sleeping

Accommodations in La Paz run the gamut from budget digs to big swanky hotels. Midrange accommodations here are varied and of good quality.

BUDGET

Pensión California (☎ 122-28-96; pensioncalifornia@ prodigy.net.mx; Degollado 209; s/d M$170/200) Primary blue and bright yellow, this quirky pension is popular and often full. Cement furniture, icy showers and padlocks give it a meat-locker feel, but the youth hostel-like ambience is fun and the plant-filled courtyard and plastic furniture lend themselves to good conversations.

Hotel Quinta Lolita (☎ 125-30-31; Revolución 1501; d M$300; 🔀) Simple, small, clean – a nice alternative if Pensión California is full. Bring a peso or two and join a cutthroat game of Dominos on the front steps.

MIDRANGE

Posada Luna Sol (☎ 120-70-39; cnr Calle 5 de Febrero & Topete; r M$650; 🅿 🔀 🖳) Excellent hotel run by the folks at Mar y Aventuras (p303), with well-decorated rooms and an excellent rooftop terrace with bay views.

Hotel Suites Misión (☎ 128-77-67; Obregón 220; r M$750-900) Funky multi-level suites done in 1970s pastels right on the *malecón*. All have kitchenettes.

Hotel Perla (☎ 122-07-77; www.hotelperlabaja.com; Obregón 1570; r incl breakfast M$926; 🅿 🔀 🔀 🖳) Supposedly La Paz' first hotel, this standby offers clean rooms and a popular restaurant and nightclub. Some rooms have nice balconies, so ask. Includes late coffee for night owls.

Hotel Cabañas de los Arcos (☎ 122-27-44; fax 125-43-13; Obregón 487; d/cabaña M$967/1209; 🅿 🔀) Rooms set around a lush garden have fireplaces, thatched roofs, tiled floors, TV, air-con and minibars. If you feel like splurging, this is not a bad way to go.

TOP END

Seven Crown Hotel (☎ 128-77-88; www.seven crownhotels.com; Obregón 1710; r/ste M$1040/1465; 🅿 🔀 🖳 🔀) Some of the standard rooms here feel like suites – the place is done in sage fabric and faux-marble, and many rooms have balconies. When you're done strolling the *malecón* you can soak away your troubles in the 5th-floor Jacuzzi. Mmm.

El Ángel Azul (☎ 125-51-30; cnr Av Independencia & Prieto; d incl breakfast M$1100-1870; 🔀) Possibly the loveliest of La Paz' lodging options, El Ángel Azul offers elegantly appointed rooms and beautifully landscaped grounds in a historic building.

Eating

La Paz' restaurant scene has become increasingly sophisticated over the past 10 years and now offers much more than the typical *antojitos* and seafood.

Super Tacos Baja California (Hermanos Gonsales; Lerdo de Tejada; tacos M$15-20) The delicious fish, shrimp and manta ray tacos at this popular stand, between Constitución and Zaragoza, are served with freshly made salsas. As with potato chips, it's hard to eat just one. Also has a stand conveniently located outside the Pensión California.

El Vinnic (☎ 122-88-85; cnr Calle 5 de Mayo & Dominguez; set meals M$40) Offers casual Yucatecan fare that include soup, main and dessert. The *agua de melón* (cantaloupe water) is also fantastic.

Kiwi (☎ 123-32-82; dinner mains M$69-148; 🕑 8am-midnight Mon-Fri, 8am-3am Sat & Sun) The only restaurant on the ocean side of the *malecón*, between Calle 5 de Mayo and Constitución, Kiwi offers great views you can enjoy while eating decent Mexican and American fare.

La Boheme (☎ 125-60-80; Esquerro 10; dinner mains M$90-340; 🕑 11am-11:30pm) One of the nicest restaurants in La Paz, reasonably priced La Boheme offers friendly service and excellent meals, set in a candlelit courtyard in a historic building. The cream of asparagus soup, simple though it sounds, is exquisite. Whiskey-flavored shrimps are mouth-watering.

Drinking & Entertainment

The following watering holes are within stumbling distance of the *malecón*, where many travelers have been known to practice their drunken-sailor routine. La Boheme (above) is a good place for unwinding with a glass of red or a hand-crushed mojito.

Las Varitas (☎ 125-20-25; Av Independencia 111; cover M$50) Bring your earplugs and your dancing shoes to this popular club, where live music often plays to a packed house.

Shopping

Local stores that cater to tourists have plenty of junk and a smattering of good stuff. **Antigua California** (☎ 125-52-30; Obregón 220) features a wide selection of crafts from throughout the country.

Getting There & Away

AIR

The airport, **Manuel Márquez de León** (☎ 124-63-36; Transpeninsular Km 9) is about 9km southwest of the city. It has an **immigration office** (☎ 124-63-49; ◷ 7am-11pm).

Aeroméxico (☎ 124-63-66; Obregón) has flights every day but Sunday between La Paz and Los Angeles, and daily flights to Tijuana and mainland Mexican cities. Aeroméxico Connect, at the same address and phone number, flies daily to Loreto and Tucson.

Aero California (☎ 125-43-53; Obregón 55; ◷ 9am-9pm Mon-Fri, 9am-5pm Sat) operates daily nonstop flights to Los Angeles and Tijuana and to mainland Mexican destinations, including Los Mochis (for the Copper Canyon Railway), Mazatlán and Mexico City. It also has a branch at the airport.

The airport is also served by Delta, Alaska and Alma airlines.

BOAT

Ferries to Mazatlán and Topolobampo leave from the ferry terminal at Pichilingue, 23km north of La Paz. **Baja Ferries** (☎ 123-66-00; www .bajaferries.com; ◷ 8am-6pm Mon-Fri, 8am-3pm Sat) has a small office at the port and an imposing new office in town. Mazatlán ferries depart at 3pm Monday, Wednesday and Friday, arriving the following morning; return ferries leave Mazatlán at 3pm Tuesday, Thursday and Saturday. Passenger fares are M$835 (M$435 for children) in *salón* (numbered seats); cabins with four beds cost M$250 extra, cabins with two beds and a bath are M$400 extra. Topolobampo services departs at 3pm daily. The return ferry from Topolobampo to La Paz leaves at 11:30pm daily, arriving in Pichilingue at 5am. Passenger fares are M$750 in *salón;* cabins for up to four people cost M$760 extra.

Make sure that you arrive at the pier a full two hours before departure in order to ensure passage. Vehicle rates, which are paid in addition to passenger fares, vary with vehicle length (see the table below).

Route	Vehicle	Fare
La Paz-Mazatlán	car 5m or less	M$2150
La Paz-Mazatlán	motor home	M$13100
La Paz-Mazatlán	motorcycle	M$1600
La Paz-Topolobampo	car 5m or less	M$1040
La Paz-Topolobampo	motor home	M$6600
La Paz-Topolobampo	motorcycle	M$760

Before shipping any vehicle to the mainland, officials require a vehicle permit if you plan to travel further south than Sonora. You can obtain a permit at **Banjército** (www.banjercito.com .mx; ◷ 9am-1:30pm Mon-Sat, 9am-noon Sun), at the ferry terminal, or from the bank's website and branches in Mexicali and Tijuana.

There's an **immigration office** (☎ 122-04-29; Obregón; ◷ 8am-8pm Mon-Fri, 9am-3pm Sat) near the center.

BUS

ABC (☎ 122-78-98) and **Autotransportes Águila** (☎ 122-78-98) both leave from the **downtown bus terminal** (☎ 122-78-98; cnr Malecón & Av Independencia) along the *malecón*. Buses leave for the following destinations hourly between 5am and 9pm:

Destination	Fare	Duration
Cabo San Lucas	M$144	3hr
Ciudad Constitución	M$196-246	2hr
Ensenada	M$1401/1298	18hr
Guerrero Negro	M$724-786	11hr
Loreto	M$337-363	5hr
Mulegé	M$466-501	6hr
San Ignacio	M$596-642	9hr
San José del Cabo	M$170	3hr
Tijuana	M$1399-1510	22hr
Todos Santos	M$77	2hr

Autotransportes Águila also operates five daily buses to Playa Tecolote (M$20, 30 minutes) and six to Playa Pichilingue (M$20, 20 minutes) between 10am and 5pm.

Getting Around

The government-regulated minivan service **Transporte Terrestre** (☎ 125-11-56) charges M$150 per person to or from the airport. Private taxis cost approximately M$250, but they may be shared.

Car-rental rates start around M$500 per day. **Budget** (☎ 125-47-47; cnr Obregón & Bravo) is one of several agencies. All have locations both at the airport and along the *malecón*.

AROUND LA PAZ

Beaches

On Península Pichilingue, the beaches nearest to La Paz are **Playa Palmira** (with the Hotel Palmira and a marina), **Playa Coromuel** and **Playa Caimancito** (both with restaurant-bars, toilets and *palapas*). **Playa Tesoro**, the next beach north, has a restaurant. Some 100m north of the ferry terminal is **Playa Pichilingue**,

---

FOR THE LOVE OF THE LAND

'I could have gone to Yucatán, where my ancestors are from,' says 21-year-old Mariana Ledesma, a university student majoring in ecotourism. 'Or here to La Paz. Those are the only two places in all of Mexico where universities offer a degree specifically in ecotourism and environmental protection. I was worried when I arrived, because La Paz seemed so different from Mexico City, but now that I've been here I feel like this is my real home. I went hiking in the Desierto de la Laguna with my boyfriend recently. It was just amazing. The stars were so bright I felt like I could touch them. But it was a little scary too – we lost the trail at one point and then realized that there was a mountain lion very close by. So we returned after only two days. But it was one of my best experiences. For my birthday I'm going to camp in Espíritu Santo with my class. I can't wait.'

---

with camping, restaurants, bar, toilets and shade. **Playa Balandra** is a beautiful enclosed cove with shallow azure water, great for snorkeling. The surrounding hillsides are soon to be developed, alas. **Playa Tecolote** has plenty of car camping spots and launches leave from here for Espíritu Santo (p303). Often called the 'best' beach, but car break-ins are common, so leave valuables at home.

LA VENTANA
☎ 612 / pop 183

Come to this unspoiled strip of seaside to watch whale sharks, sea lions, whales, sea turtles and a myriad of fish – without the crowds. Diving is best in the summer when the water visibility reaches 25m or 30m (80ft or 100ft). The same winds that made Los Barriles (below) a windsurfing mecca also blow here.

Quiet, *palapa*-style *cabañas* at **Palapas Ventana** (☎ 114-01-98; www.palapasventana.com; cabañas M$123-174; P X X □) include hearty, home-style breakfasts that hit the spot. They outfit for diving, snorkeling, windsurfing, kitesurfing, sportfishing, petroglyph hikes and just about anything else available.

Rafa's Tacos (☎ 114-01-82; 9am-9:30pm Nov-Mar) is a casual roadside taco stand that has plastic chairs and serves up great *antojitos*.

LOS BARRILES
☎ 624 / pop 1056

South of La Paz, the Transpeninsular brushes the gulf at Los Barriles, where brisk winter westerlies, averaging 20 to 25 knots, make this Baja's windsurfing capital. The lack of breaking waves is what makes the entire coastline so spectacular. From April to August the winds die down, making windsurfing impossible.

Get online at the **Office** (☎ 141-01-42; theoffice@ prodigy.net.mx; 10am-8pm Mon-Sat, 10am-6pm Sun) for

a wallet-busting M$45 per hour. **Vela Windsurf** (www.velawindsurf.com) is one of many beachside places that rent gear and offer lessons.

Hotel Los Barriles (☎ 141-00-24; www.losbarriles hotel.com; s/d M$663/800) is a laid-back place offering clean, comfortable rooms. Prices rise during the Christmas/New Year holiday. It also rents out scuba, snorkeling and windsurfing gear. Get your morning latte fix at **Caleb's Cafe** (☎ 141-03-30; Barriles s/n; mains M$60-120; 7am-2pm Tue-Sun). Some travelers say Caleb's gooey, buttery sticky buns are the only thing worth stopping for in Barriles.

Tio's Tienda (☎ 141-03-30; Calle 20 de Noviembre; 7:30am-10pm) has a great collection of Baja-related books and souvenirs.

Fairly good dirt roads follow the coast south to San José del Cabo. Beyond Cabo Pulmo and Bahía Los Frailes, they are sandy but passable for most vehicles, but are impassable for RVs and may be difficult for any vehicles after rainstorms. This road offers awesome glimpses of the coast, Shipwreck Point, and the 'green' desertscape. It too is slated for development, so see it now before the condos, villas and time-shares block the view.

CABO PULMO
☎ 624 / pop 58

If you're looking for snorkeling or diving without the crowds, slip away from the rowdier southern neighbors and come to Cabo Pulmo, a National Marine Park that's home to the only Pacific coral reef in the Sea of Cortez. You don't need a 4WD to enjoy the drive out here along the spectacular East Cape (from the south) coastal road or through the Sierra de la Laguna (to the north). Unfortunately, much of the surrounding land is slated for development pronto, which will lead to sedimentary erosion that will likely kill or permanently

BAJA CALIFORNIA

BAJA'S BEST UNBEATEN ROUTES

You're on your own with these. Routes have numerous turn offs to ranches or dead ends. Plan on getting lost...and loving it. Bring extra water and check that spare tire (and bring GPS!) in case of an emergency and remember that even if you're in a 4WD, this is not the Baja 1000. Treat these roads, and the people and animals living here, with respect. Times are only basic one-way estimates.

Playa El Tecolote toward La Ventana (one hour) Jackrabbits, secluded beaches and awesome snorkeling. It ends up just turning into rock-strewn ravines...you can't go all the way.

Los Frailes to Las Casitas (two hours) A 4WD-only road offers canyon vistas and desert wash, chances to spot a silver fox and commune with majestic cardón cacti. Los Frailes is just south of Cabo Pulmo. This and the Los Naranjos route cut an east–west route from one side of the East Cape to the other.

Los Naranjos to Pescadero (five hours) High clearance 4WD trail with hair-raising turns, river fording (in season) and views of the Pacific from flower-festooned desertscape. Pescadero is just south of Todos Santos

San José del Cabo to Cabo Pulmo (three hours) Sandy coastal track that offers awesome views of the Sea of Cortez the whole way. Bring your surfboard...or just a picnic lunch.

Puerto López Mateos to La Florida (three hours) 4WD your way through majestic monotony of cholla and acacia all the way to the estuary. Vultures, rodents and cows.

Non-4WDs may want to try Hwy 3 between San Felipe and Ensenada, the Ruta del Vino (p286) toward Tecate or head toward Punta Abreojos past the Laguna de San Ignacio. The 'boulderscape' of Cataviña is well worth stopping for on the Transpeninsular.

---

alter the reef. Contact **Pulmo Amigos** (www.pulmo amigos.org) to help protect this fragile area. *Pronto*...there's little time to waste.

Cabo Pulmo refers to both the park and the tiny village where the following establishments are located.

Snorkel right from the beach at **Los Arbolitos**, or follow the shoreline hiking trail to **Las Sirenitas**, where wind and wave erosion has made the rocks look like melting wax sculptures. Eerie and beautiful, they're accessible by boat as well.

Offshore snorkeling, diving and sea-lion colony trips can be booked through **Pepe's Dive Center** (9am-5pm, tours leave at 10am; 2 tank dives M$850, snorkeling M$150), which also offers internet access.

Nancy's B&B (in the US 617-524-4440; cabañas with private/shared bathroom M$50/40; P) is simply furnished, quiet and has great mattresses.

El Caballero, when its open, has fantastic Mexican meals at very reasonable prices. Hours vary – it's usually open for lunch and sometimes for dinner.

RESERVA DE LA BIOSFERA SIERRA DE LA LAGUNA

Hardcore backpackers can strap on their hiking boots, fill their water bottles and head into the uninterrupted wilds of the lush and rugged Sierra de la Laguna biosphere reserve, at the intersection of the Transpeninsular and Hwy 19. This is not a place for inexperienced hikers, or for anyone unfamiliar with the unique challenges presented by desert trails. **Baja Sierra Adventures** (612-161-45-01; http://bajasierradventures .com), in a tiny ranch called El Chorro, offers day and overnight trips, biking and trekking through this unique region.

SAN JOSÉ DEL CABO

624 / pop 48,518

San José del Cabo is quiet and peaceful, the 'mild' sister of 'wild' Cabo San Lucas. San José offers quiet shopping, an attractive plaza, a beautiful church and excellent dining opportunites.

Orientation

San José del Cabo consists of San José proper, about 1.5km inland, and a Zona Hotelera with large beachfront hotels, condos and eyesores...er, time-shares. Linking the two areas, just south of shady Plaza Mijares, Blvd Mijares is a *gringolandia* of restaurants and souvenir shops.

Information

Several *casas de cambio* here keep long hours. Banks pay better rates but keep shorter hours.

Bancomer (cnr Zaragoza & Morelos) Cashes traveler's checks and has an ATM.

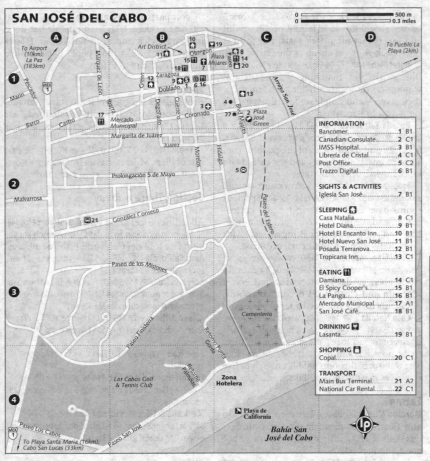

SAN JOSÉ DEL CABO

INFORMATION

Bancomer	1 B1
Canadian Consulate	2 C1
IMSS Hospital	3 B1
Librería de Cristal	4 B1
Post Office	5 C2
Trazzo Digital	6 B1

SIGHTS & ACTIVITIES

Iglesia San José	7 B1

SLEEPING

Casa Natalia	8 C1
Hotel Diana	9 B1
Hotel El Encanto Inn	10 B1
Hotel Nuevo San José	11 B1
Posada Terranova	12 B1
Tropicana Inn	13 C1

EATING

Damiana	14 C1
El Spicy Cooper's	15 B1
La Panga	16 B1
Mercado Municipal	17 A1
San José Café	18 B1

DRINKING

Lasanta	19 B1

SHOPPING

Copal	20 C1

TRANSPORT

Main Bus Terminal	21 A2
National Car Rental	22 C1

IMSS Hospital (☎ non-emergency 142-00-76, emergency 142-01-80; cnr Hidalgo & Coronado)

Librería de Cristal (☎ 142-44-33; Blvd Mijares 41) A small bookstore with items in English and Spanish.

Post office (Blvd Mijares 1924; ☺ 8am-6pm Mon-Fri)

Secretaria Municipal de Turismo (☎ 142-29-60 ext 150; Transpeninsular; ☺ 8am-5pm Mon-Sat) Has a stock of brochures and maps on hand.

Tourist Aid (☎ 078)

Trazzo Digital (☎ 142-03-03; www.trazzo-digital.com; Zaragoza; per hr M$43; ☺ Mon-Sat) Internet access. Has fast connections and large monitors.

Sights & Activities

The colonial-style **Iglesia San José**, built on the site of the 1730 Misión San José Del Cabo, faces the spacious Plaza Mijares.

Between raids on Spanish galleons, 18th-century pirates took refuge at the **Arroyo San José**, now a protected wildlife area replenished by a subterranean spring. A riverside **Paseo del Estero** (Marshland Trail) runs parallel to Blvd Mijares all the way to the Zona Hotelera. The best beaches for swimming are along the road to Cabo San Lucas. **Playa Santa María** at Km 13 is one of the nicest beaches in Los Cabos.

The **Fiesta de San José**, on March 19, celebrates the town's patron saint.

Sleeping

During the peak winter months, it's a good idea to make reservations. Free camping is possible at Pueblo La Playa, east of the center.

BAJA CALIFORNIA

Hotel Nuevo San José (☎ 142-17-05; cnr Obregón & Guerrero; r M$220-380; ☒) Despite peeling paint and toilets that often lack seats, this joint is often packed. It's as cheap as the Cabos get.

Hotel Diana (☎ 142-04-90; Zaragoza 30; d M$350; ☒) Blue swirly tiles, matching bedspreads and windowless rooms are anything but fancy, but they have TV and simple wooden dressers. It's right next to Bancomer.

Posada Terranova (☎ 142-05-34; Degollado s/n; d M$700; P ☒ ☒ ▯) There's art on the walls, it's clean and it has views of the pueblo from some rooms. It also has a good restaurant and kind, English-speaking staff.

Tropicana Inn (☎ 142-15-80; www.tropicanacabo .com; Blvd Mijares 30; d/ste M$1166/1254; ☒ ☒) Spacious rooms have satellite TV, fridge and coffee-maker, and the bucolic courtyard has a huge pool and real live parrots. Bring a cracker for Polly. Rates include continental breakfast.

Hotel El Encanto Inn (☎ 142-03-88; www.elencantoinn .com; Morelos 133; d/ste M$1254/1636; ☒ ☒) Beautiful landscaped gardens, interesting pottery, a fountain and clean, well-decorated rooms. Also rents cars, if you need a set of wheels.

Casa Natalia (☎ 146-71-00; www.casanatalia.com; ste from M$3894; P ☒ ☒ ▯) The posh Natalia opens onto San José's plaza and, in addition to the pool, has shuttles to its beachside club. The walk-in bathrooms are big enough to live in. Prices rise during holidays.

Eating

Mercado Municipal (Ibarra) Between Coronado and Castro, this clean market has numer-ous stalls offering simple and inexpensive but good, filling meals.

San José Café (☎ 142-61-91; cnr Zaragoza & Morelos; breakfast from M$40; ☻ 8am-10pm Mon-Sat) A quintes-sential coffee shop with nice touches – get a bagel and coffee and head to the rooftop terrace for a relaxing meal.

Damiana (☎ 142-04-99, www.damiana.com.mx; Plaza Mijares 8; dinner mains M$190-360) A romantic seafood restaurant in a restored 18th-century house. Abalone in garlic sauce is superb.

La Panga (☎ 142-40-41; www.lapanga.com; Zaragoza 20; dinner mains M$230-465) Dim lighting and a mul-tilevel courtyard make it romantic; however, you pay premium for the ambience, as the food is only so-so.

Drinking

Head to Cabo San Lucas if you're looking for nightlife. San José del Cabo is almost mousy in comparison. **Lasanta** (☎ 142-67-67; www.las anta.com.mx; Obregón 1732) is an upscale bar done in wood, brick and deep red velour. **El Spicy Cooper's** (☎ 156-87-17) has pool tables and live music Thursday to Friday.

Shopping

Blvd Mijares is a good place to start. Obregón to Degollado is the self-proclaimed 'Art District' with numerous galleries, studios and stores.

Copal (☎ 142-30-70; Plaza Mijares 10), on the east side of Plaza Mijares, has an interesting assort-ment of crafts, jewelry, rugs and masks.

Getting There & Away

AIR

All airline offices are at **Los Cabos airport** (☎ 146-50-13), north of San José del Cabo, which serves both San José del Cabo and Cabo San Lucas.

Aero California (☎ 146-52-52) Flies daily to and from Los Angeles and Guadalajara.

Aeroméxico (☎ 146-50-97) Flies daily to and from San Diego and to many mainland Mexican destinations, with international connections via Mexico City.

Alaska Airlines (☎ 146-51-06) Flies to and from Los Angeles, Phoenix, San Diego, San Francisco and San Jose, California.

American (☎ 146-53-00) Flies daily to Los Angeles and Dallas.

Continental Airlines (☎ 146-50-50, in the US 800-900-5000) Flies to and from Houston and, during the high season, Newark.

Mexicana & Click Mexicana (☎ 143-53-53) Flies daily to Los Angeles and to mainland destinations such as Mexico City, Guadalajara and Mazatlán.

BUS

From the main **bus terminal** (☎ 130-73-39; González Conseco), east of the Transpeninsular, buses depart for the following destinations:

Destination	Fare	Duration	Frequency
Barriles	M$72	1½hr	frequent
Cabo San Lucas	M$30	1hr	hourly
La Paz	M$175	3hr	hourly
La Paz airport	M$250	3hr	3 daily
Ensenada	M$1581	22hr	frequent
Tijuana	M$1574-1690	24hr	frequent

CAR & MOTORCYCLE

The usual agencies rent from the airport – rates start at about M$600 per day, cheaper with an internet reservation. Also try **National Car Rental** (☎ 142-24-24; Blvd Mijares).

TOP SPOTS FOR FANTASTIC FISH TACOS

Simple, versatile, the humble fish taco is Baja's comfort food. Done right they're magical. These spots are all worth seeking out for a taste of this drool-creating classic:

Super Tacos Baja California (La Paz; p305) Loads of salsas and crispy golden batter made this joint a La Paz institution.

Venado (Cabo San Lucas; p314) Flaky, moist morsels on corn or flour. Shrimp tacos are just as good.

Los Arcos (Playas de Rosarito; p283) Casual family-run place with guacamole, sour cream and *pico de gallo* (fresh chopped salsa).

Restaurante Doney (Mulegé; p298) Right by the roadside, tacos here are small, but you can grab a few for the road before catching the next bus. Yum!

El Caballero (Cabo Pulmo; p308) These come with a homemade salsa that's picante without being smolderingly hot. Great for snacking after a long, invigorating snorkel.

Getting Around

Taxi drivers are required by law to display a sanctioned price list. The official, government-run company runs bright yellow taxis and minibuses to the airport for about M$150. Local buses from the main bus terminal to the airport junction cost less than M$25, but taking one means a half-hour walk to the air terminal. The toll road costs M$27.

LOS CABOS CORRIDOR

Nowhere in Baja is the desert disappearing faster than in the Los Cabos 'Corridor,' the strip of coast between San José del Cabo and Cabo San Lucas – in its place, cookie-cutter resorts, aquifer-depleting golf courses and all-inclusive hotels line the once-spectacular coastline.

Experienced surfers claim that summer reef and point breaks at **Costa Azul** (aka Zippers) match Hawaii's best. The reefs off **Playa Chileno** are excellent for diving. **Playa Santa María**, at Km 13, is one of the nicest for swimming.

CABO SAN LUCAS

☎ 624 / pop 56,811

Come to Cabo expecting to toss your inhibitions to the wind – everyone else is. Certain clubs round up conga lines so that waiters can pour tequila down dancers' throats, but that notwithstanding, Cabo San Lucas has a curious charm. The beaches are protected by beautiful Land's End, and the activities are endless: jet-skis, banana boats, parasailing, snorkeling, kite sailing, diving and horseback riding can all be done just by walking down to the beach. If you rent a car and get outside the city limits you'll be surrounded by majestic cardón cacti, caracara birds and mystical arroyos that will impress you just as much as that crazy club ('I did *what* last night?!') you partied at the night before.

Orientation

Northwest of Cárdenas, tourist Cabo has a fairly regular grid; southeast of Cárdenas, Blvd Marina curves along the Harbor Cabo San Lucas toward Land's End (Finisterra), the tip of the peninsula where the Pacific Ocean and the Sea of Cortez meet.

Information

It's an indication of who calls the shots here that Cabo has no government-sanctioned tourist offices. The 'info' booths you'll see are owned by time-shares, condos and hotels. The staff are friendly and can offer maps and info, but their only pay comes from commissions off selling time-share visits: expect an aggressive, sometimes desperate, pitch for you to visit model homes. Be warned – the promised freebies are rarely worth wasting precious vacation time.

Internet cafés with DSL or broadband now abound and many hotels, such as the Siesta Suites, have lobby computers the public can use. Rates are, not surprisingly, cheaper as you go further away from the water. Banks will cash traveler's checks and have ATMs.

All About Cabo (www.allaboutcabo.com) A useful site for visitors.

American Express (☎ 143-57-88; Plaza Bonita; ☯ 9am-6pm Mon-Fri, 9am-1pm Sat)

AmeriMed American Hospital (☎ 143-96-70; Blvd Cárdenas) Near Paseo de la Marina.

Bancomer (cnr Blvd Cárdenas & Paseo San José)

InternetPuntoCom (☎ 144-41-90; cnr Leona Vicaría & Calle 20 de Noviembre; per hr M$25)

Librerías de Cristal (☎ 143-31-73; Plaza de la Danza, Blvd Marina) Books in English and Spanish.

Post office (Blvd Cárdenas; ☯ 8am-4pm Mon-Fri) Near Calle 20 de Noviembre.

Tourist Assistance (☎ 078)

BAJA CALIFORNIA

BAJA CALIFORNIA

Sights

Land's End is by far the most impressive attraction Cabo has to offer. Get on a *panga* (M$10) and head to **El Arco** (the Arch), a jagged natural feature which partially fills with the tide. Pelicans, sea lions, sea, sky – this is what brought people to Cabo in the first place and it's still magical, despite the mammoth cruise ships towering behind it.

For sunbathing and calm waters **Playa Médano**, in front of what once was the Hacienda Beach Resort on the Bahía de Cabo San Lucas, is ideal. **Playa Solmar**, on the Pacific, is pretty but has a reputation for dangerous breakers and rip tides. Nearly unspoiled **Playa del Amor** (Lover's Beach) shouldn't be missed; near Land's End, it is accessible by boat. Appropriately, **Playa del Divorcio** (Divorce Beach) is nearby, across the point on the Pacific side.

Activities

The best **diving** areas are Roca Pelícano, the sea-lion colony off Land's End, and the reef off Playa Chileno, at Bahía Chileno east of town. Two-tank dives cost around M$700 and full-certification courses M$3750 to M$4500. **Cabo Acuadeportes** (☎ 143-01-17), at the beach, is the largest water-sports outfitter, but there are numerous alternatives. Surprisingly good **snorkeling** can be done right from Playa del Amor, swimming left, toward the marina. A mask, snorkel and fins should run about M$150 per day. *Panga* rides cost about M$120 round trip

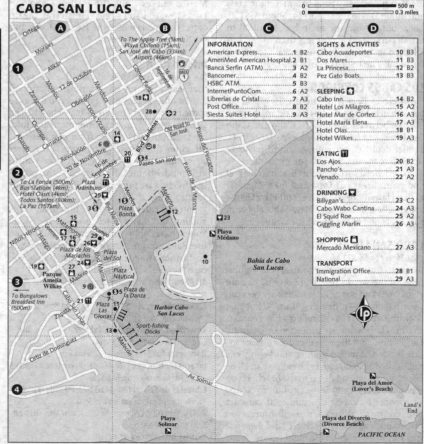

CABO SAN LUCAS

0 _____ 500 m
0 _____ 0.3 miles

INFORMATION	
American Express.................1	B2
AmeriMed American Hospital.2	B1
Banca Serfin (ATM)............3	A2
Bancomer.........................4	B2
HSBC ATM........................5	B3
InternetPuntoCom..............6	A2
Librerías de Cristal.............7	A3
Post Office.......................8	B2
Siesta Suites Hotel.............9	A3

SIGHTS & ACTIVITIES	
Cabo Acuadeportes...........10	B3
Dos Mares......................11	B3
La Princesa.....................12	B2
Pez Gato Boats................13	B3

SLEEPING	
Cabo Inn........................14	B2
Hotel Los Milagros............15	A2
Hotel Mar de Cortez..........16	A3
Hotel María Elena.............17	A3
Hotel Olas......................18	B1
Hotel Wilkes...................19	A3

EATING	
Los Ajos.........................20	B2
Pancho's.........................21	A3
Venado..........................22	A2

DRINKING	
Billygan's........................23	C2
Cabo Wabo Cantina...........24	A3
El Squid Roe....................25	A2
Giggling Marlin................26	A3

SHOPPING	
Mercado Mexicano............27	A3

TRANSPORT	
Immigration Office............28	B1
National.........................29	A3

CABO IN...

Two Days

Take a *panga* to **Playa del Amor** (opposite) and see **El Arco** (opposite) at the same time. Laze for a while or snorkel, then head back for grub or a margarita. Get tipsy on a gorgeous sunset **tour** (below) and then finish the job at **El Squid Roe** (p315). Then choose between quiet shopping at **San José del Cabo** (p308) or something active: surfing at **Los Cerritos** (p316) or diving at **Cabo Pulmo** (p307).

Four Days

Four days gives you all of the above. Or you could rent yourself some wheels and do a loop of the Southern Cape. Start heading east, through **San José del Cabo** (p308) and take in the awesome scenery of the East Cape, one of Baja's best unbeaten paths (see boxed text, p308). Stay in **Cabo Pulmo** (p307) for snorkeling and diving, then cruise north for Day 2 to **La Paz** (p302). Hikers will want to see the **Sierra de la Laguna** (p308). Spend Day 3 in the chi-chi galleries and great restaurants of **Todos Santos** (p315) or **surfing** (p315). Head back to Cabo San Lucas on Day 4 and end with a fancy meal at **La Fonda** (p314) or a relaxing sunset **tour** (below).

---

if you bargain directly with a captain. Tipping M$10 to M$30 is appropriate.

Courses

Apple Tree (☎ 174-28-47; www.theappletree.com.mx) offers immersion Spanish classes at a variety of levels.

Tours

Dos Mares (☎ 143-89-71; Plaza Las Glorias) Runs three-hour, glass-bottomed boat tours (M$100) to Playa del Amor, near Land's End. Departures take place every hour from 9am to 5pm. It also offers snorkeling tours to Santa María (M$350).

La Princesa (☎ 143-76-76; info@cabosports.com; dock M–O; tours M$390) Found behind Hotel Costa Real, this outfit offers sunset booze trips along with other daytime packages.

Pez Gato I & Pez Gato II (☎ 143-37-97; www.pez gatocabo.com) Offers two-hour sunset sailings on catamarans (adult M$35) and segregates its clientele into 'booze cruises' and 'romantic cruises.' Children are half price and, despite the labels, either should be okay for kids.

Festivals & Events

Cabo San Lucas is a popular staging ground for fishing tournaments in October and November. The main events are the **Gold Cup**, **Bisbee's Black & Blue Marlin Jackpot** and the **Cabo Tuna Jackpot**.

Sammy Hagar's birthday party, in early October, is a major Cabo event. Invitations (free) are required – try concierges at the bigger hotels or look out for giveaways. Bring your liver and prepare to punish it.

Día de San Lucas (October 18) is a local celebration honoring the town's patron saint, with fireworks, food stalls, dancing and partying.

Sleeping

Cabo has plenty of accommodations in all price categories – if you start at pricey and end with 'It costs WHAT per night?!' If you want something on a true backpacker budget you'll need to sleep in an unlocked car.

MIDRANGE

Hotel Oasis (☎ 143-20-98; Carretera a Todos Santos; s/d M$380/480; P ⊠ ⓡ) Only a stone's throw from the bus station, the shockingly peach Oasis offers clean singles or doubles at rates that are hard to ignore. You can even swim with a killer whale in the oversize pool.

Hotel María Elena (☎ 143-32-89; Matamoros s/n btwn Niños Heroes & Cardenas; s/d M$480/650) Accessed via a narrow staircase above a laundromat, the María Elena has spick-and-span rooms with art on the walls and kitchenettes.

Hotel Olas (☎ 143-17-80; cnr Revolución & Gómez Farias; r M$550; P ⊠) The Olas has clean, simple rooms. The grandfatherly owner has a wealth of information about Baja and speaks some English. Giant clam shells and other maritime items add to the courtyard décor.

Hotel Wilkes (☎ 105-07-11; cnr Cabo San Lucas & Calle 5 de Mayo; s/d M$550/700) The cute and cozy Wilkes has white wrought-iron railings and rooms that are so spacious they feel empty. Verdant potted plants and proximity to Cabo's excesses are additional pluses.

BAJA CALIFORNIA

SURF'S UP

Baja is a prime surfer's paradise with swells coming in off the Pacific that, even on bad days, are challenging and fun. Boards can be rented from surf shops. If you're looking for waves, check out the following:

San Miguel (p284) Rocky point break which offers awesome rides when the waves are big. Todos Santos island is another option for the serious.

Los Cerritos (p316) Beautiful sand, nice waves, mellow vibe – this is a great beginner beach with powerful Pacific swell...and eagle rays below.

San Pedrito (p316) Locals say 'She's a fin stealer' – this is a mid- to expert-level break with barrels that rival Hawaii's. Sea-urchin spines, coral and rocks await those who time things wrong.

Costa Azul (p311) Needs southerly swell, but this intermediate break is a whole lot of fun and it's close to either of the Cabos.

For more info on surfing, check out the no-nonsense, brown-and-black covered *Surfer's Guide to Baja* by Mike Parise.

Hotel Mar de Cortez (☎ 143-00-32; www.mardecortez.com; cnr Blvd Cárdenas & Guerrero; r M$610-670, ste M$790; 🅿 🕸) This quiet, colonial-style hotel has an outdoor restaurant-bar and a large family-friendly pool area. Rooms are ample, clean and quiet.

Cabo Inn (☎ 143-08-19; cnr Calle 20 de Noviembre & Leona Vicario; r M$649-1320; 🕸) This former brothel retains an aura of sensual languor and has a lush, tropical feel. They've recently added a new, modern Jacuzzi.

Hotel Los Milagros (☎ 143-45-66; www.losmilagros.com.mx; Matamoros 116; d M$880-1400; 🅿 🕸 🖥 🕸) The tranquil courtyard and 11 unique rooms provide a perfect escape from Cabo's excesses. A desert garden (complete with resident iguanas), a beautiful deep blue pool, friendly and courteous service and no TVs make this stay unforgettable. The place can also be rented in its entirety for groups, such as weddings or birthday parties.

TOP END

our pick Bungalows Breakfast Inn (☎ 143-50-35; www.cabobungalows.com; cnr Libertad & Herrera; bungalows incl breakfast from US$153, ste from US$186; 🅿 🕸 🕸 🖥) Extremely attentive service, delicious breakfasts, tastefully furnished rooms, fragrant palm-thatched *palapas*, hammocks and a noncaustic, salt-cleansed swimming pool set this B&B apart. Fresh-fruit smoothies, fruit juices, excellent coffee and warm, welcoming bilingual staff make the Bungalows feel like home. Beautiful handmade soaps are one of the many tiny details that makes this *the* place to splurge. Note that US dollars are used here.

Eating

Cabo's culinary scene features a great variety of eateries, from humble taco stands to gourmet restaurants.

Venado (☎ 147-69-21; Niños Heroes btwn Zaragoza & Morelos; dinner mains M$20-80; 🕒 noon-6am) Open all night and packed from 3am until dawn, Venado has delicious fish tacos, fresh salsas and other *antojitos*. If it's slow, the friendly waitresses might drop a coin in the jukebox and invite you to dance.

Los Ajos (☎ 143-77-06; Blvd Cárdenas btwn Vicario & Mendoza; breakfasts M$30-140, buffet M$90) This casual, clean, family-run place has great breakfasts and an inexpensive lunch and dinner buffet. Look for the large ceramic chef outside the door.

La Fonda (☎ 143-69-26; lafonda@solmar.com.mx; cnr Hidalgo & 12 de Octubre; M$140-230) Superb Mexican cuisine that's worlds away from the typical *antojitos* – try the cream of poblano soup with pumpkin flowers or the *huitlacoche* (corn mushroom) stuffed chicken. The 'Don Julio' margarita vies for the best in Baja.

Pancho's (☎ 143-28-91; www.panchos.com; cnr Hidalgo & Zapata; dinner mains M$190-250, with tequila tasting M$700) Offers 'all you want to know about tequila' in a festive atmosphere. Aromas from the open grill mix with the mariachi band's tunes. The tequila tasting is like an intensive tequila class, but offers inebriation in place of graduation.

Drinking

Cabo is a proud party town, and alcoholic revelry is encouraged all day long. The following places are all open well past midnight.

Giggling Marlin (☎ 143-11-82; cnr Matamoros & Blvd Marina) Wildly popular bar in the center.

El Squid Roe (☎ 143-12-69; cnr Blvd Cárdenas & Zaragoza) Crazy. Just crazy.

Cabo Wabo Cantina (☎ 143-11-88; cnr Guerrero & Madero) Much like a college frat party, only everyone's older. And drunker.

Billygan's (☎ 143-04-02; Playa Médano) Great for people-watchers and a sunset margarita.

Shopping

Mercado Mexicano (cnr Madero & Hidalgo) Cabo's most comprehensive shopping area is this sprawling market that contains dozens of stalls with crafts from all around the country.

Getting There & Away

There's an **immigration office** (☎ 143-01-35; cnr Cárdenas & Gómez Farías; ⏱ 9am-1pm Mon-Sat) near the center.

AIR

The closest airport is Los Cabos (p310), north of San José del Cabo. Airport shuttle vans (M$150) can drop you off at your hotel. A taxi to or from the airport costs M$600.

BUS & CAR

Bus service to and from Cabo is provided by **Águila** (☎ 143-78-80; Hwy 19), located at the Todos Santos crossroad, north of downtown.

Destination	Fare	Duration
La Paz	M$144	2½-4hr
Loreto	M$481	8hr
San José del Cabo	M$30	1hr
Tijuana	M$1554	24hr
Todos Santos	M$67	1hr

From a terminal near Águila station, **Auto-transportes de La Paz** (cnr Calle 5 de Febrero & Hidalgo) has eight daily La Paz buses (M$100, 2½ hours).

Numerous car-rental agencies have booths along Blvd Marina and elsewhere in town. **National** (☎ 143-14-14; cnr Blvd Marina & Matamoros) offers rentals starting at M$60 per day.

Getting Around

The **airport shuttle bus** (☎ 146-53-93; per person M$150) leaves every two hours (10am to 4pm) from Plaza Las Glorias. Cab fares within town range from M$50 to M$70.

TODOS SANTOS

☎ 612 / pop 4078

This quiet dusty town, well, ain't what she used to be. Todos Santos has witnessed an invasion from the north as well-heeled New Mexico artists, organic farmers and even some Hollywood types have snapped up property and put down roots. Locals and tourists alike all say, 'I'm lucky I got to see this place two years ago.' Change is happening that fast, and environmental protection laws mean little when so much money can change hands. The sea turtle and surfing beach Los Cerritos has been slated for development: hotels, houses, condos and bars are already going up and it's unlikely anyone will turn off the lights each spring during egg-laying season.

Todos Santos' newfound prosperity does not reflect its history. Founded in 1723, but nearly destroyed by the Pericú rebellion in 1734, Misión Santa Rosa de Todos los Santos limped along until its abandonment in 1840. In the late 19th century Todos Santos became a prosperous sugar town with several brick *trapiches* (mills), but depleted aquifers have nearly eliminated this thirsty industry.

Orientation & Information

Todos Santos has a regular grid, but residents rely more on landmarks than street names for directions. The plaza is surrounded by Márquez de León, Legaspi, Av Hidalgo and Centenario.

Todos Santos lacks an official tourist office, but **El Tecolote** (☎ 145-02-95; cnr Juárez & Av Hidalgo), an English-language bookstore, has magazines with town maps and a sketch map of nearby beach areas. Save pesos by going to **Multiservicios Miro** (☎ 145-07-02; cnr Rangel & Márquez de León; ⏱ 9am-9pm Mon-Sat; per hr M$25) for internet instead of to the pricey machines inside the real estate offices.

Banorte (cnr Juárez & Obregón) Exchanges cash and traveler's checks and has an ATM.

Post office (Heróico Colegio Militar) Between Av Hidalgo and Márquez de León.

Sights & Activities

Scattered around town are several former *trapiches*, including **Molino El Progreso**, the ruin of what was formerly El Molino restaurant, and **Molino de los Santana** on Juárcz, opposite the hospital. The restored **Teatro Cine General Manuel Márquez de León** is on Legaspi, facing the plaza.

Housed in a former schoolhouse, the **Centro Cultural** (☎ 145-00-41; Juárez; admission free; ⏱ 8am-7pm Mon-Fri, 10am-3pm Sat & Sun), near Topete, is home to some interesting nationalist and revolutionary murals dating from 1933. Also on display is an uneven collection of artifacts evoking the history of the region, lots of old photos and a replica ranch house.

Surfers come here for some of the nicest swells in all of Baja. **San Pedrito** offers Hawaii-like tubes (and Hawaii-like sea urchins if you wipe out). Catch that perfect wave as eagle rays glide below you, or just hang out with the mellow crowd on **Los Cerritos** and watch the coral sun plunge into the Pacific. Boards can be rented for M$150 per day at Pescadero Surf Camp (below), near the beaches. Just down the road from Pescadero Surf Camp is a competition-grade skateboard park.

Festivals & Events

Todos Santos' two-day **Festival de Artes** (Arts Festival) is held in early February. At other times it's possible to visit local artists in their home studios, and there are galleries galore.

Sleeping

Pescadero Surf Camp (☎ 134-04-80; www.pescadero surf.com; casitas M$300-400, camp sites per person M$100) Friendly and helpful, Pescadero Surf Camp has everything a surfer could need – rentals, lessons, advice, a community kitchen and even a BYOB swim-up bar.

Motel Guluarte (☎ 145-00-06; cnr Juárez & Morelos; s/d M$350/450; P 🐾) This breezy, whitewashed budget option with laundromat has small rooms with refrigerators and a common balcony. No pets, please.

Hotel Ziranda (☎ 122-58-06; Pescadero s/n; r M$400; P 💻) Kitchenettes here are anything but fancy; however, this place is well located for surfers or beachgoers on a budget. It has a restaurant and internet café as well.

Todos Santos Inn (☎ 145-00-40; todossantosinn@ yahoo.com; Legaspi 33; d M$2085-2843, ste M$4106) This 19th-century building has been converted into a swanky hotel with gorgeous interiors and an excellent restaurant. Rates include a simple breakfast.

ourpick **Posada La Posa** (☎ 145-04-00; www.lapoza .com; ste US$195-480; P ❌ 🐾 💻 🐾) Boasting 'Mexican hospitality combined with Swiss quality,' this beautiful boutique retreat is right on the Pacific. A saltwater swimming pool, freshwater lagoon, lush garden and superb restaurant with excellent Mexican wines set it apart. A Mexican sweat lodge and Jacuzzi offer alternate ways to let stress slip away. There are no TVs or phones in the rooms, but you will

find a pair of binoculars and even a bird book. Kayak use, bikes and fishing gear are always included. This establishment works with US dollars, though they may accept pesos.

Eating

Taco stands, along Heróico Colegio Militar between Márquez de León and Degollado, offer cheap eats.

Caffé Todos Santos (☎ 145-03-00; Centenario 33; breakfast M$55-90, dinner mains M$90-170) Coffee-conscious travelers can consume cappuccinos with savory pastries, mammoth muffins or great main dishes.

Il Giardino (☎ 151-98-74; Degollado s/n; mains M$90-280, pizzas M$190) Brown paper tablecloths belie the awesome pizzas and sumptuous entrées at this casual Italian eatery. Pears in red wine sauce is a perfect finish to a great meal.

ourpick **Café Santa Fe** (☎ 145-03-40; Centenario 4; dinner mains M$180-440; 🕙 Wed-Mon) The *insalata Mediterranea* (steamed seafood drizzled in lemon juice and oil) will make even seafood haters change their evil ways. The open-air kitchen, designed by the owner himself, allows you to see the food as it's being prepped for your table. Anything on the menu will delight, surprise, tantalize, but if you need suggestions go for the mussels in wine or any one of the various handmade raviolis: lobster, *carne* (meat) or just spinach and ricotta cheese. This is surely one of the best restaurants in Baja and is well worth the splurge.

El Gusto! (☎ 145-45-00; Posada La Poza; mains M$190-340; 🕙 Fri-Wed) This beautiful restaurant was recently voted a top place to watch a Pacific sunset – sip a margarita on the terrace or in the beautifully decorated dining area. In season, whales head by as you eat. The extensive wine list is made up of Mexico's finest – selected with care by the owner himself.

Shopping

There are numerous galleries to wander through, especially around the plaza. Do it yourself on this one. **El Tecolote** (☎ 145-02-95; cnr Juárez & Av Hidalgo) has beautiful postcards, books and souvenirs.

Getting There & Away

Hourly between 6:30am and 10:30pm, buses head to La Paz (M$77, two hours) and to Cabo San Lucas (M$67, one hour) from the **bus stop** (☎ 148-02-89) at Heróico Colegio Militar between Zaragoza and Morelos.

Northwest Mexico

A battle of blues characterizes northwest Mexico, a diverse region notable for the striking lucidity of the azure Sea of Cortez waters and the crystal-clear cobalt skies of the Sierra Madre. In between is a region of deep canyons, dusty deserts and colonial villages with cobblestone streets.

Most visitors to this dusty delight are bound for one of two surreal landscapes: the Barranca del Cobre – spectacular gorges and mountain cliffs that comprise a system of canyons that surpasses the Grand Canyon in mass, depth and accessibility – and the thrilling railway that runs through it; or the postcard-perfect beaches of the Sea of Cortez, so easily accessed from the southwestern US that many towns here – Puerto Peñasco and San Carlos among them are beginning to offer more vacation condos and burger joints than beach shacks and burritos.

While these folks lend a conspicuously American feel to many communities, there is no shortage of indigenous wonders. The area around Bahía de Kino is known for its alive-and-well Seri culture, while the Barranca del Cobre thrives with the vibrantly clad cave-dwelling Rarámuri, who offset the warm earth tones of the canyons with kaleidoscopic bursts of color in the chasms.

The area has a couple of major cities, including laid-back Hermosillo, plus charming villages like Álamos and El Fuerte. And you're never too far from the 12,950-sq-km Desierto Sonorense, an ecological treasure of biological riches. No matter where you go, keep your eyes on the horizon: the entire northwest erupts with dreamlike vistas, whether it be the glow of a desert sunset or the penetrating cerulean skies across the dramatic Barranca del Cobre.

NORTHWEST MEXICO

HIGHLIGHTS

- Lose yourself for a few days in the mellow village of **Bahía de Kino** (p327)
- Lazily walk off a belly full of Doña Lola's incredible enchiladas *suizas* through the sleepy colonial streets of **Álamos** (p333)
- Suck in the brisk canyon air between cars as you ride the **Ferrocarril Chihuahua Pacífico** (p341) through the spectacular Barranca del Cobre
- Manage your adrenaline on the breathtaking descents to the wonderful canyon-bottom towns of **Urique** (p347) and **Batopilas** (p354)
- Cool off in the spray at the bottom of the mighty **Cascada de Basaseachi** (p354), Mexico's highest full-time waterfall

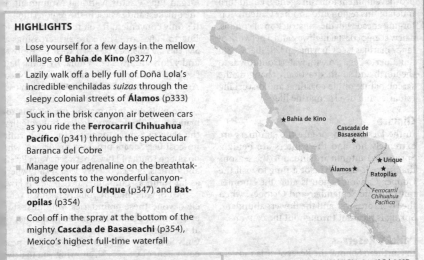

- HERMOSILLO JANUARY DAILY HIGH: 15.5°C | 60°F
- HERMOSILLO JULY DAILY HIGH: 31.6°C | 89°F

History

The lands that stretch south from Nogales have served as a gateway to Mexico since the first explorers passed this way some 30,000 years ago. The Pima – direct descendants of those early visitors – established an elaborate system of irrigation that transformed the desert into agricultural lands. The region's colonial history dates from 1687, when the Italian Jesuit missionary Father Eusebio Francisco Kino began establishing missions and making inroads with the indigenous peoples, ultimately tying their destinies to the rest of Nueva España.

In the 19th century, the coastal waters of the Sea of Cortez (Golfo de California) were witness to many naval battles, with most of the action centered on the port jewel of Guaymas, as various world powers challenged Mexico's fledgling independence and coveted its mineral wealth. Between Guaymas and Ciudad Obregón is the ancestral home of the fiercely independent Yaqui tribe, which aggressively resisted the forces of colonialism up until its last rebellion in 1901. The nomadic Seris of the central Sonoran coastal and desert lands fought a losing battle for their way of life, though their population is now steadily increasing.

In recent years, the northwest region of Mexico has seen an influx of tourism, causing an economic boom and raising eyebrows with environmentalists and culture conservationists who worry that Fonatur (Mexico's gung-ho, pro-development tourism agency) could turn much of this region into another Cancún. It is forging ahead with the construction of condos, a new scenic coastal highway and a network of fancy marinas (see Guaymas, p329) that would link Puerto Peñasco with waterfront towns to the north and south, drastically changing the serene nature of the coastline and disturbing estuaries and diverse marine life.

Climate

In the Desierto Sonorense the summers are extremely hot and the winters are benign. Spring and autumn are similar to the seasons that precede them. The best time to visit the Copper Canyon region is after the summer rains, in late September and October, when the rivers are swift and the flowers abundant. Spring is pleasant throughout the canyons.

Parks & Reserves

In Northern Sonora, the Reserva de la Biosfera El Pinacate y Gran Desierto de Altar (see boxed text, p324) stretches its volcanic landscape across a 714,556-hectare area full of moon-like craters and massive dunes.

Off the coast of Bahía de Kino, Mexico's largest island, Isla del Tiburón (p328) is a Seri-controlled migratory bird refuge and nature-lovers paradise.

The wonderful Parque Nacional Cascada de Basaseachi (p354) is home to Mexico's majestic Basaseachi waterfall, the country's highest full-time falls.

Getting There & Around

Hwy 15, Mexico's principal northern Pacific coast highway, begins at the border town of Nogales, Sonora, about 1½ hours (108km) south of Tucson. This is one of the most convenient border crossings between western Mexico and the US. From Nogales, Hwy 15/15D heads south through the Desierto Sonorense for about four hours (260km) to Hermosillo and then cuts over to the coast at Guaymas. From Guaymas the highway parallels the beautiful Pacific coast for about 1000km finally turning inland at Tepic (see p446) and heading on to Guadalajara and Mexico City. There are regular tollbooths along Hwy 15 (including two between Nogales and Hermosillo that charge around M$78 in total).

The **Lukeville–Sonoyta crossing** (⊙ 6am-midnight), 357km west of Nogales opposite Lukeville, Arizona, immediately south of Organ Pipe Cactus National Monument, is the quickest and easiest in the region (though it's only convenient if you're heading west to Puerto Peñasco). There are also crossings at **San Luis Río Colorado** (⊙ 24hr) west of Sonoyta and 42km southwest of Yuma, Arizona; **Naco** (⊙ 24hr), 90km east of Nogales, opposite Naco, Arizona; and **Agua Prieta** (⊙ 24hr), 130km east of Nogales opposite Douglas, Arizona.

See p986 for information on permits for bringing a vehicle into Mexico, but note that the state of Sonora operates the no-permit no-cost **Only Sonora** program for drivers who do not go south of Hwy 2 between Agua Prieta and Imuris, or east of Hwy 15/15D anywhere as far south as Empalme, at Km 98 on Hwy 15 east of Guaymas. If you are taking a vehicle beyond these boundaries, you must stop at a vehicle permit station at Empalme, or at Cananea on Hwy 2, and obtain either an Only Sonora vehicle permit, costing the peso equivalent of US$25.30, allowing you to drive in the rest of Sonora state (for example to

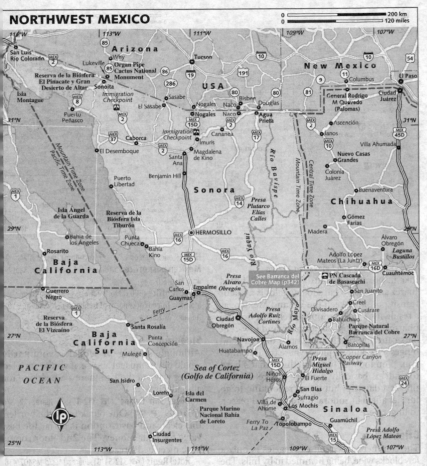

NORTHWEST MEXICO

Álamos), or an all-Mexico permit (US$29.70) if you want to go beyond Sonora state.

Vehicle and passenger ferries link Guaymas with Santa Rosalía (Baja California) three times a week, and Topolobampo (near Los Mochis) with La Paz (Baja California) daily.

Nogales, Hermosillo and Los Mochis are the primary hubs for bus travel. Buses of all classes ply the cities and towns along Hwy 15 with great frequency, making it possible to travel from northwest Mexico to destinations throughout the mainland or to the US with ease. Many travelers begin their journey through the Copper Canyon at Los Mochis, traveling northeast by train on the Ferrocarril Chihuahua Pacífico. Others do the trip in reverse, beginning in Chihuahua.

The major airports for the region are at Hermosillo, which has several flights to and from the US, and Los Mochis, which serves several mainland destinations.

SONORA

Chock-full of pristine beaches, sleepy colonial villages, colorful indigenous peoples and surreal desert landscapes, Sonora, Mexico's second-largest state (bordering Chihuahua is first) borders the US to the north but shows remarkable cultural diversity within its 180,000 sq km. The state is like a piñata full of the country's best offerings, on its way to being pummeled into tourism oblivion.

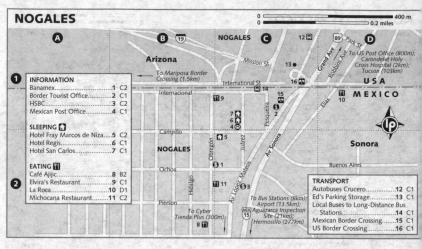

NOGALES

INFORMATION
Banamex	1 C2
Border Tourist Office	2 C1
HSBC	3 C1
Mexican Post Office	4 C1

SLEEPING
Hotel Fray Marcos de Niza	5 C2
Hotel Regis	6 C1
Hotel San Carlos	7 C1

EATING
Café Ajijic	8 B2
Elvira's Restaurant	9 C1
La Roca	10 D1
Michocana Restaurant	11 C2

TRANSPORT
Autobuses Crucero	12 C1
Ed's Parking Storage	13 C1
Local Buses to Long-Distance Bus Stations	14 C1
Mexican Border Crossing	15 C1
US Border Crossing	16 C1

NOGALES

☎ 631 / pop 189,760 / elevation 1170m

Like its border-city cousins Tijuana, Ciudad Juárez and Nuevo Laredo, Nogales is a major transit point between the US and Mexico; as a result, it's a zoo of money-exchange houses, pharmacies, cheesy curio shops and low-rent bars catering mostly to gringos on weekend binges – the kind of place where trouble finds you. 'You looking for something that's hard to find?' is basically a greeting here. It suits fine as a day trip, but if you're looking to go further afield in Sonora, there's no real reason to linger here.

Orientation

The commercial section of Nogales is only a few blocks wide, being hemmed in by hills. The main commercial street is Obregón, two blocks west of the border crossing, which eventually runs south into Mexico's Hwy 15.

Information

Almost everything you'll need is within walking distance of the border crossing.

Border tourist office (☎ 312-06-66; 9am-1pm & 2-6pm Wed-Mon) Beside the border customs office.

Banamex (cnr Obregón & Ochoa; 9am-4pm Mon-Fri) Has an ATM.

Carondelet Holy Cross Hospital (☎ 520-285-3000; 1171 W Target Range Rd, Nogales, Arizona) On the US side of the border, this small regional hospital offers emergency and walk-in care.

Cyber Tienda Plus (López Mateos 291; internet access per hr M$12; 9am-8pm Mon-Sat)

HSBC (López Mateos 171; 9am-4pm) Has an ATM.

Mexican post office (cnr Juárez & Campillo; 8am-4pm Mon-Fri)

US post office (300 N Morley Ave; 8:30am-5pm Mon-Fri) Three blocks north of the border crossing in Nogales, Arizona.

Sleeping

Although staying in Nogales voluntarily would be an unusual choice, if you've traveled a long way via the US, there's a bed here for all budgets.

Hotel San Carlos (☎ 312-15-57; Juárez 22; s/d M$357/429; P) One block from the border, this clean and basic option is by far the best value for your money. The 2nd-floor rooms have nicer bedspreads.

Hotel Regis (☎ 312-51-81; Juárez 34; s/d M$407/438,) Located just next door, it's a colorful alternative to the San Carlos – check those multi-hued bedspreads and highlighter-green walls. There's a historic saloon attached as well.

Hotel Fray Marcos de Niza (☎ 312-16-51; Campillo 91; s/d M$560/622; P) The nicest digs in town, though a bit dark. The chilly hallways offer a welcomed respite from the heat.

Eating

Michocana Restaurant (☎ 311-25-89; Obregón 123; mains M$12-60; 7am-7pm) A great little find serving *comida corrida* (set meals), fresh juices and killer *chilaquiles verdes* (fried tortillas with cheese and green salsa) for breakfast.

Café Ajijic (☎ 312-50-74; Obregón 182; mains M$35-135; 8am-midnight Sun-Wed, 8am-3am Thu-Sat) Serves an extensive Mexican menu to day-tripping gringos on a colorful outdoor patio with a lovely fountain. Ignore the constant barrage of hawkers and mariachi.

Elvira's Restaurant (☎ 312-47-73; Obregón 1; mains M$87 220; ☿ 11am-10pm) Mexican folk art meets *2001: A Space Odyssey* at this longstanding institution serving excellent Mexican classics (nine types of *mole*) with a free shot of tequila.

La Roca (☎ 312-07-60; Elías 91; mains M$137-330; ☿ 11am-midnight) The upscale La Roca serves a diverse menu of Sonoran and regional Mexican in a low-light romantic setting under colonial archways and cavernous stone walls.

Getting There & Away

If you are heading further south into Mexico, pick up a Mexican tourist permit at the immigration office in the large modern building at the border crossing. The tourist permit is also available at the vehicle checkpoint 21km south of the border. If you're driving your own vehicle (buses don't stop there), it is more convenient to get it at this checkpoint at the same time as your vehicle permit (see p987). Both offices are open 24 hours a day.

AIR

The Nogales International Airport is located 13.5km southeast of the city center but it closed due to lack of funds in 2007. The nearest working airport is in Tucson, Arizona, about 100km (1½ hours) north.

BUS

From Nogales' **main bus station** (Hwy 15), 8km south of the city center, **Elite** (☎ 313-16-03) travels to Guadalajara (M$1043, 25 hours), Mexico City (M$1440, 32 hours), Chihuahua (M$590, 12 hours) and Hermosillo (M$140, three hours). **Autobuses Crucero** (☎ 319-42-65) buses also leave from the main bus station, stopping at the station on the Arizona side and going to Tucson (M$143, two hours), Phoenix (M$341, four hours), Las Vegas (M$902, 12 hours) and Los Angeles (M$847, 13 hours). From Nogales, Arizona, **Autobuses Crucero** (☎ in the US 520-287-5628; www.crucero-usa .com; 35 N Terrace Ave) a block from the border crossing, has frequent buses to Tucson (US$9, one hour), Phoenix (US$26, 3½ hours) and Hermosillo (US$19, four hours).

Transportes y Autobuses del Pacífico (TAP; ☎ 319-41-54; www.tap.com.mx) has shiny new offices three blocks north of the bus station. From there, 1st-class air-conditioned buses head south along Hwy 15 to Guadalajara (M$1045, 28 hours) and on to Mexico City (M$1440, 35 hours). Other destinations include Guaymas (M$210, 5½ hours), Tijuana (M$455, 25 hours) and Los Mochis (M$400, 13 hours).

Transportes Baldomero Corral (☎ 313-28-80) serves the major cities along Hwy 15, with a 1st-class bus departing from its station two blocks north of the main station every two hours from 7:30am; stops include Hermosillo (M$167, 3½ hours) and Álamos (M$362, nine hours). Next door, **Tufesa** (☎ 313-38-62; www.tufesa.com.mx) operates hourly 1st-class buses that go south as far as Culiacán (M$588), as well as north to Phoenix (M$330) and Los Angeles (M$653).

To get to the main bus station from the border crossing (8km away), you can take a taxi or hop onto one of the frequent local buses marked 'Central Camionera,' from a corner of Av López Mateos, just a couple of blocks from the border (M$4).

CAR & MOTORCYCLE

Approaching Nogales, Arizona, from Tucson, the left lanes go to central Nogales. The right lanes, which go to the **Mariposa border crossing** (☿ 6am- midnight) outside the city, are the quickest way to enter Mexico, though only the Deconcini crossing is open 24/7. As you approach Nogales, you'll see plenty of signs for Mexican auto insurance, which you'll need if you're bringing a vehicle into Mexico.

Temporary vehicle-import procedures for those who are driving beyond Sonora state into the rest of Mexico are dealt with at the Aguazarca inspection site at the 21km point on the highway south of Nogales. See p318 for information on the simplified Only Sonora program for drivers who are not going beyond Sonora state limits.

Day-trippers should note that several attended lots near the border crossing offer parking on the US side for US$8 per day. **Ed's Parking Storage** (☎ in the US 520-287-2025; cnr N Terrace & W Crawford; ☿ 8am-8pm Mon-Sat, 8am-6pm Sun) is the most secure (it's located behind McDonald's).

With more than 11,000 vehicles crossing into the US at Nogales each day, getting through the border quickly when heading north requires luck, or perhaps some foresight. The **US Department of Homeland Security** (http://apps. cbp.gov/bwt) posts estimated wait times online.

NORTHWEST MEXICO

DETOUR: ASADERO LEO'S

As you breech the hill around Km 210 along Hwy 15 an hour and a half out of Nogales, the smoke rising from the grill can be seen a good 200m away. *Carne asada!* **Asadero Leo's** (Carretera Internacional No 189, Ímuris), nothing but a streetside stall and a few seats indoors, looks like it is going up in flames. Do yourself a favor and pull over immediately. First comes the most colorful, fragrant tray of fresh condiments you've ever seen: guacamole, three types of salsa, pickled carrots, radishes, onions, limes, *pico de gallo* (finely choppsed sals) and cucumbers. This is followed by as many *carne asada* (marinated grilled beef) tacos you can get down for M$12 each. Unforgettable.

PUERTO PEÑASCO

☎ 638 / pop 44,875 / elevation 48m

On the northeast coast of the Sea of Cortez (Golfo de California), this town has for years been a popular destination for the beach-craving residents of Arizona's desert cities. But Rocky Point, as the US visitors call it, is not the quaint little seaside town it used to be. It has become a gringo free-for-all and is now home to so many non-natives that it has basically become the seaside retirement community Arizona never had. Its main stretch of waterfront, Sandy Beach (also known as Sandy Point), is home to a dozen massive condo-hotel resorts, which offer luxury rooms with views, sports bars, expensive restaurants and not a hint of Mexican culture. Fans like to call it 'the new Cancún'; haters might opt for Puerto Condo.

Over US$300 million was pumped into this area in 2007 alone, with another US$1.2 billion on its way. As a result, Peñasco is Mexico's fastest-growing town, with a leg up on similar resort cities like Acapulco, Cancún and Puerta Vallarta due to its accessibility by car from the US. When the new international airport opens in 2009, all hell should break loose.

Orientation

Just an hour south of the Arizona border (from the no-fuss Lukeville–Sonoyta crossing), Puerto Peñasco sits at the end of Mexico's Hwy 8. After driving through the general downtown and residential blocks, you'll reach the Old Port district to the west and, west of

that, the resort-filled stretch of Sandy Beach. Las Conchas and CEDO are to the east.

Information

Santander, Bancomer, Banamex and Banorte, all on Blvd Juárez, have ATMs.

CEDO (Freemont Blvd; ☼ 9am-5pm Mon-Sat, 10am-2pm Sun) This nature center (below) has a small gift shop with some good books about the region in both English and Spanish.

Max's Café (La Marina Center; ☼ 8am-10pm) Free internet on one computer.

Post office (1285 Av Chiapas; ☼ 8am-2pm Mon-Fri, 8am-3pm Sat, 8am-11am Sun)

Rocky Point Convention & Visitors Bureau (☎ 388-04-44, in the US 877-843-3717; www.cometorockypoint .com; Blvd Juárez & Calle 11) In the Circle K parking lot.

Santa Fe Clinic (☎ 383-24-47; Av Morua; ☼ 24hr)

Sights & Activities

The **Acuario Cet-Mar** (☎ 382-00-10; Av Freeman, Las Conchas; admission M$30; ☼ 10am-5pm Mon-Fri) is an aquarium a little worse for wear, but it's worth a peek in to check out the varieties of green sea turtles and the very friendly sea lion, Arthur.

Just down the road, **CEDO** (Intercultural Center for the Study of Desert & Oceans; ☎ 382-01-13; www.cedo intercultural.org; Freemont Blvd, Las Conchas; admission free; ☼ 9am-5pm Mon-Sat, 10am-2pm Sat) is a wonderful source of information about the fascinating desert-meets-the-sea ecosystem of Rocky Point. It has a museum, library, whale-skeleton exhibit, history displays and free natural-history talks (in English) on Tuesday at 2pm and Saturday at 4pm. The place also offers guided tours of the local ecosystems if you arrange in advance (check website for availability), from a two-hour **Tidepool Tour** (adult/child M$165/110) to a six-hour **Kayak Caper** (M$935, adults only).

Festivals & Events

Spring Break March is probably a good time to stay away, as this is when the town is overtaken by margarita-chugging college students from the US.

Bathtub Races This odd event has expats racing down the street in bathtubs-on-wheels in October.

Rocky Point Rally In early November, 10,000 Harley-Davidsons descend on the town.

Sleeping

While the most visible of accommodations these days are the new resorts – just stand at the edge of the Old Port and look toward Sandy Beach for the big picture – there are some great down-to-earth options too (though it's slim pickings for those on tight budgets).

BUDGET & MIDRANGE

Posada La Roca Hotel (☎ 383-31-99; Av Primero de Junio 2; s/d M$440/490; P ❄) This 1927 inn in the Old Port was the first building in town and supposedly a hideout for Al Capone during the US prohibition. It's a stately old stone building with 20 basic rooms (all with renovated bathrooms) off a beautiful stained glass–lit stone hallway.

Hotel Viña Del Mar (☎ 383-01-00; www.vinadelmarhotel.com; Av Primero de Junio y Malecón Kino; s/d/ste M$670/770/1120; P ❄ 🏊 ♿) A decent motel-style option in the Old Port. The basic rooms have nice wood-beam ceilings; the best rooms surround the colorful, mosaic pool area.

Hacienda Del Mar Bed & Breakfast (☎ 383-08 00; www.haciendabnb.com; Freemont Blvd, Las Conchas; r M$825-990, ste M$1210-1265; P ✕ ❄ 🏊) Water pressure here could stand a dose of shower Viagra, but this is otherwise a wonderful five-room respite from the resorts, tucked away down a sandy residential development just a block from the ocean. All guests have use of a common kitchen, a peaceful backyard barbecue and wet-bar area, and prices include a fab breakfast.

TOP END

Playa Bonita Hotel (☎ 383-25-86, in the US 888-232-8142; www.playabonitaresort.com; Paseo Balboa; r M$990-1210, ste M$2090-3300; P ✕ ❄ 🖥 🍴 ♿) This large cement-block complex laid out in traditional Mexican style features 124 perfectly decent rooms, a private beach and connecting Mexican restaurant offering spectacular patio sunsets. It's one of the few beachfront properties with no condos, though they're on the way.

Las Palomas Beach & Golf Resort (☎ 108-10-00, in the US 866-360-2324; www.laspalomasresort.net; Sandy Beach; condos M$1925-5500; P ✕ ❄ 🖥 🍴 ♿) Love it or hate it, this is the new face of Rocky Point. This gargantuan resort and 18-hole golf course is a flashy conglomerate of modern towers, several pools and a lazy river, and sleek one- to three-bedroom condos, 320 of which are in the rental pool. It's sophisticated across the board, from the excellent La Maria Bistro right down to the Gilchrist and Soames of London amenities.

Eating & Drinking

It takes a little work to find authentic Mexican cuisine here between all the sports bars and barbecue joints, but there is some surprisingly good grub between the cracks as well as a few great upscale options. For killer tacos, get yourself to the Mexican side of town.

Tacos el Grillo (☎ 383-40-44; Av Ruiz Cortínez & Blvd Juárez; mains M$12-36; ☉ 8am-3pm Thu-Tue) Perfect Sonoran *carne asada* tacos (without a gringo in sight) are the star attraction at this taco joint, just behind La Buena dairy.

El Rey del Taco (Av Prieto & Juan Aldama; mains M$12-36; ☉ 8:30am-1pm Mon-Fri, 8:30am-2pm Sat) Hidden behind the Burger King on Blvd Juárez, Rey del Taco doesn't look like much inside or out, but the tacos doused in house-made green and red salsa are addictive. *Carnitas* (braised pork) and *papas y carne* (steamed beef with potatoes) tacos are the highlights here.

Coffee's Haus (☎ 388-10-65; www.coffeeshaus.com; Blvd Juárez 216B; mains M$55-70; ☉ 7:30am-4pm Tue-Sat, 7:30am-2pm Sun; 🅥) This newly renovated German-Mexican co-owned café is famous about town for its apple strudel, excellent coffee and numerous salad selections.

El Rincón de Regina (☎ 383-89-66; Av Alcantar 20; mains M$95-155; ☉ 8am-10pm Mon-Sat) A festively decorated hideaway on a quiet street in the Old Port serving tasty Mexican specialties at affordable prices. Try the *molcajete* (traditional stone mortar and pestle) specialty.

La Maria Bistro (☎ 108-10-00; Blvd Costero 150, Las Palomas Resort, Sandy Beach; mains M$105-280; ☉ breakfast 7-11am, lunch noon-4pm, dinner 5-10:30pm) The most sophisticated meal in town, fit for a special-occasion blowout on the new face of Mexican cooking. The French chef morphs a taste of home into his Franco-Sonoran fusions; what emerges, such as the grilled shrimp over plantain and sweet potato mash with sweet corn sauce, would do just fine as a Last Meal.

Lapa Lapa (☎ 388-05-99; Malecón Kino & Zaragoza; mains M$110-176; ☉ 10am-10pm Wed-Mon) This thatched-roofed 2nd-floor dining room has a view of the sea and is beautiful at night, lit up by basket luminaries from Guadalajara. A festive bar area and eclectic dishes such as chicken with tamarind sauce ensure its popularity.

Manny's Beach Club (☎ 383-36-05; www.mannysbeachclub.net; Blvd Matamoros, Playa Miramar; ☉ 7am-late) Nobody actually eats here; the star of the show is the mega-popular beachfront location, packed with local riff-raff co-imbibing with tourists of all ilk under a thatched-roofed bar.

RESERVA DE LA BIOSFERA EL PINA-CATE Y GRAN DESIERTO DE ALTAR

Northwest of Rocky Point is the **Reserva de la Biosfera El Pinacate y Gran Desierto de Altar** (Pinacate Biosphere Reserve; ☎ 638-384-90-07; admission M$40; ☻ 8am-5pm), containing extinct volcanic craters, a large lava flow, vast sand dunes and other surreal landscapes. To get there for a hiking adventure, head 45km northeast (in a high-clearance, 4WD vehicle only) on Hwy 8 and register at the sand-toned ranger station at Km 52. From there, you'll really be on your own, as there's no food, water or fuel.

Getting There & Around

Driving south from Arizona, cross at the **Lukeville–Sonoyta border crossing** (☻ 6am-midnight) and follow Hwy 8 to Puerto Peñasco. Though a new international airport is scheduled to open sometime in 2009, the only two commercial flights currently arriving are **Aeroméxico Connect** (☎ in the US 800-237-6639; www.aeromexico.com) from Hermosillo and Los Angeles on Tuesday, Thursday and Sunday. **Kona Shuttle** (☎ in the US 602-956-5696; www.konashuttle.com) offers shuttle-van service from Tucson and Phoenix for US$180 round trip (discounts for groups). You can travel by bus to Puerto Peñasco from Hermosillo via **Albatros** (☎ 662-213-82-40) for about M$180. Also, **ABC** (www.abc.com.mx) makes bus trips throughout the day to all major stops in Baja California from M$350. Take the 6am *ejecutivo* to Tijuana for any semblance of comfort, though.

Once you're in town, it's best to have a car, as there is no usable public transportation and the town is spread out over a wide area. Taxis are cheap and plentiful, though, with most cross-town rides costing no more than M$55.

HERMOSILLO

☎ 662 / pop 641,741 / elevation 238m

Many travelers simply do a fly-by through Hermosillo, a prosperous agricultural center and the capital of Sonora, without so much as rolling down the window (it's too hot out there). That's a shame. It's actually a well-maintained, modern city with a provincial feel that isn't a bad spot to kill a day, get a haircut and nosh on some tasty cuisine.

Don't loiter too long, though – it's a place where commerce and government rule and the heat gets unbearable most afternoons (it's nicknamed 'Sun City' for a reason). But if you're driving through this region, chances are you'll spend at least a night here to break the trip and restock on some serious civilization.

Many of the streets in Hermosillo, founded in 1700 by Juan Bautista Escalante, have names that acknowledge the city's debt to the native revolutionary heroes, including General Álvaro Obregón.

Orientation

Hwy 15 enters Hermosillo from the northeast and becomes Blvd Francisco Eusebio Kino, a wide street lined with orange and laurel trees. Blvd Kino (much of which is known as the Zona Hotelera, or Hotel Zone) continues west through the city, curves southwest and becomes Rodríguez, then Rosales as it passes through the city center, then Vildosola before becoming Hwy 15 again south of the city.

Information

Centro Médico Del Noroeste (☎ 217-45-21; Colosio 23 Ote; ☻ 24hr) Medical services.

Librerías de Cristal (☎ 213-71-97; Serdán 178; ☻ 9am-7:45pm Mon-Sat, 10am-5:45pm Sun) Wide selection of books in Spanish.

Post office (cnr Blvd Rosales & Serdán; ☻ 8am-4pm Mon-Fri, 9am-1pm Sat)

State of Sonora tourist office (☎ 289-58-00, in the US 800-476-6672; www.gotosonora.com; Edificio Sonora Norte, 3rd fl, Comonfort & Paseo del Río; ☻ 8am-9pm Mon-Fri) Grab an excellent map of Hermosillo and Sonora.

Tourist emergency assistance (☎ 800-903-92-00)

Veta Papelería (☎ 212-79-87; Monterrey 86; per hr M$15; ☻ 7am-7:30pm Mon-Fri, 9am-1pm Sun) Internet access.

Sights

PLAZA ZARAGOZA

Not to be confused with the grittier Jardín Juárez, this **plaza** (btwn Blvd Hidalgo & Av Paliza) is shaded by beautiful orange trees, drawing government workers on lunch breaks and creating a peaceful place to hang. Its majestic **Catedral de Nuestra Señora de la Asunción**, also called the Catedral Metropolitana, was constructed between 1877 and 1908 in a mix of neoclassical and baroque styles. The **Palacio de Gobierno** (☎ 213-11-70; ☻ 8am-8pm Mon-Fri, 8am-4pm Sat), completed in 1906, is on the east side of the plaza, and features an airy, neo-Moorish courtyard with colorful, dramatic murals depicting the history of Sonora. At night, the

HERMOSILLO

INFORMATION	
Centro Médico Del Noreste	1 C3
Librerías de Cristal	2 B4
Post Office	3 B4
State of Sonora Tourist Office	4 B6
US Consulate	5 A4
Veta Papelería	6 B4

SIGHTS & ACTIVITIES	
Catedral de Nuestra Señora de la Ascensión	7 A5
Museo de Sonora	8 D5
Palacio de Gobierno	9 A5

SLEEPING	
Colonial Hotel	10 B6
Hotel Washington	11 C3

EATING	
Está Cabral	12 B4
La Galería Café	13 A4
Los Encarbonados	14 A5
Verde Olivo	15 C2

DRINKING	
La Tequilera	16 B4
Siete de Copas	17 B4

TRANSPORT	
Buses to Bahía de Kino	18 D3

0 500 m
0 0.3 miles

To Blvd Kino, La Siesta Motel (3km);
Sonora Steak (3.5km); Fiesta Inn (4km);
Hotel San Martin (5km);
Highway Tourist Office (15km);
Hotels, Nogales (277km)

MEX 15

To Airport (10km);
Bahía de Kino (110km)

Blvd Encinas

Puebla

Blvd Rosales

Jalisco

Niños Héroes

Oaxaca

Blvd Encinas

Universidad de Sonora

Sonora

Jardín Juárez

To Bus Stations (2km)

Blvd Colosio

Noriega

Noriega

Galeana

Monterrey

Pino Suárez

Yañez

García Morales

Carmenia

Guerrero

Matamoros

Juárez

González

Jesús García

Morella

Mercado Municipal

Parque Infantil

Elías Calles

Serdán

Corridor Cultural Hidalgo

Chihuahua

Villegas

Pesqueira

Obregón

No Reelección

Angel Flores

Guadalupe

Blvd Hidalgo

Plaza Zaragoza

Velazco

Av Paliza

Salido

Bravo

Ocampo

Allende

Moreno

Pino Suárez

Bavispe

California

Plaza Tehuantepec

Oposura

Cerro de la Campana

Cucurpe

Cubillas

Comonfort

Michel

Blvd Rosales

MEX 15

Blvd Francisco Serna

Paseo Río Sonora Norte
Paseo Río Sonora Sur

To Jardines de Xochimilco (2km);
Centro Ecológico de Sonora (5km);
Guaymas (136km)

plaza comes alive when vendors hawking Sonoran *tamales* and tasty variations of corn swarm in. A city of over half a million suddenly feels like a small town.

CERRO DE LA CAMPANA

This 'Hill of the Bell' is the most prominent landmark in the area and an easy point of reference night or day. It's named for the legend that striking certain rocks on the hill creates a bell sound. The panoramic view from the top is worth the drive up – though it's a shame about the numerous telecommunication towers.

MUSEO DE SONORA

Hugging the east side of the Cerro de la Campana, this **museum** (☎ 217-27-14; Jesús García s/n; admission M$34, free Sun & holidays; ☼ 9am-5pm Tue-Sat, 9am-4pm Sun) is worth a stroll for its location in a stone-walled, 100-year-old former jail – a museum itself – with interesting exhibits on the history of Sonora housed in former cells.

CENTRO ECOLÓGICO DE SONORA

This **zoo and botanical garden** (☎ 250-67-68; admission M$30; ☼ 8am-5pm) is about 5km south of central Hermosillo. Like a massive park, it features plants and animals of the Desierto Sonorense, as well as an **observatory** (admission M$30) with telescope viewing sessions. To get there by public transit, watch for the 'Luis Orcí' bus at the west side of Jardín Juárez, which departs about every 15 minutes. Ask the driver when to get off, as it's not clearly marked.

Sleeping

Most of Hermosillo's better hotels are in the Zona Hotelera, a convenient 15 minutes from the city center, though budget travelers will need to stick to places downtown.

BUDGET & MIDRANGE

Hotel Washington (☎ 213-11-83; Noriega 68; s/d M$200/220; ❄) Cute colonial Mexican tiles and interesting art line the lobby walls here, along with a free coffee stand and vending machines. The rooms are opium-den musty, but it's a steal at this price. It's on a very busy shopping street about a 15-minute walk from Plaza Zaragoza.

Hotel San Martín (☎ 289-05-50, in the US 877-225-2987; www.hotelsanmartin.net; Blvd Kino 498; s/d M$480/530; P ☒ ☒ ☒ ☝) A complete renovation in 2007 gave this motel a leg up in the hotel zone. There's a great new pool with a Jacuzzi

and slide, a 24-hour restaurant, large TVs and nicely sized rooms with wi-fi and minibars.

La Siesta Motel (☎ 289-19-50; Blvd Kino; r M$550, ste M$700-1000; P ☒ ☒ ☝) Another motel-style option in the hotel zone, popular with Mexican tourists, who enjoy the extra-large rooms and refrigerators. Cleanliness isn't next to godliness here, but it's otherwise comfortable.

TOP END

Colonial Hotel (☎ 259-00-00; www.hotelescolonial.com, Vado del Río 9; r/ste M$1169/1593; P ☒ ☒ ☒ ☒ ☒) The most stylish *motel* you've ever seen, full of modern art and sleek design touches on lush grounds on the road to Guaymas, south of the center. Rates include breakfast.

Fiesta Inn (☎ 289-22-00; www.fiestainn.com; Blvd Kino 375; r M$1989-2147; P ☒ ☒ ☒) A high-end business hotel in tip-top shape with a lovely central courtyard and fantastic canvas Mexican folk art on the walls. All double rooms come with a large living room, giving guests a suite for the price of a double.

Eating & Drinking

Los Encarbonadas (☎ 212-74-74; cnr Av Paliza & Londros; mains M$15-60; ☼ 5pm-midnight) This excellent *asadero* bar serves up Sonora's specialty, *carne asada*, alongside a mouth-watering salsa and condiment cart that flows between tables. The 'order' serves two easily and the *frijoles* might just be Mexico's best. Highly recommended.

La Galería Café (☎ 212-15-16; Blvd Hidalgo 54A; mains M$35-65, desserts M$22-33; ☼ noon-midnight Sun-Fri) A Bohemian hangout steeped in the local art scene. It's a great spot for cappuccinos, bagels and live tunes (on Saturday night).

Verde Olivo (☎ 213-28-81; Niños Héroes 75D; mains M$25-55, buffet M$127; ☼ 7:30am-10pm Mon-Sat, 9am-5pm Sun; Ⓥ) If you have tired of quesadillas and tacos, do not pass go. Do collect M$200. Go straight to Verde Olivo. This gem in the middle of beef country offers excellent grain veggie burgers, fresh juices and smoothies, and PETA-friendly versions of Mexican classics.

Está Cabral (☎ 213-74-74; Velazco 11; mains M$45-60; ☼ 7pm-1am) This large, open-air café occupies the interior of a once-regal building and features Cuban *Nueva Trova* folk music nightly attracting a fun and eclectic crowd.

Sonora Steak (☎ 210-03-13; Blvd Kino 914; mains M$65-187; ☼ noon-1am) Inside this stately colonial home in the hotel zone, Sonora's famed steaks – 28-day aged rib eyes – are weighed tableside (M$60 per 100g), cooked to perfection and served with flour tortillas, grilled onions and jalapeños.

Siete de Copas/La Tequilera (☎ 217-17-71; Serdán 171; ☾ 6pm-2am Wed-Sat) This bar complex features Siete de Copas, a large, somewhat rowdy modern cantina (imagine a contemporary version of the one in Robert Rodriguez' *From Dusk Till Dawn*); and La Tequilera, a two story bar with dueling live music on the open-air roof upstairs and indoors in the bar down below. Both attract the city's young and hip.

Getting There & Away
AIR
The recently renovated airport, about 10km from central Hermosillo on the road to Bahía de Kino, is served by Aerobus, Aero California, Aeroméxico, America West, Aviacsa, Avolar, Azteca, Volaris and Mexicana. Daily direct flights, all with connections to other centers, go to cities including Chihuahua, Ciudad Juárez, Ciudad Obregón, Guadalajara, La Paz, Los Angeles, Los Mochis, Mexicali, Mexico City, Monterrey, Phoenix, Tijuana and Tucson.

BUS
From the **main bus terminal** (☎ 213-44-55; Blvd Encinas), 2km southeast of the city center, 1st-class service is offered by Autobuses Crucero, Elite, Estrella Blanca (EB), Transportes del Pacífico (TP), Transportes y Autobuses del Pacífico (TAP), Transportes Norte de Sonora (TNS) and others. More companies have separate terminals nearby – Transportes Baldomero Corral (TBC) and Albatros is next door. Across the street is Tufesa, about a block west of Blvd Encinas is Estrellas del Pacífico (EP), and TAP has larger offices a few more blocks down. Services to many destinations depart around the clock:

Destination	Fare	Duration
Guaymas	M$60	2hr
Guadalajara	M$848	24hr
Los Angeles	M$996	16hr
Mexico City	M$1295	30hr
Monterrey	M$900	26hr
Nogales	M$140	4hr
Phoenix	M$443	8hr
Puerto Peñasco	M$180	6hr

Second-class buses to Bahía de Kino (M$55, two hours) depart from the AMH and TCH bus terminal in central Hermosillo, on Sonora

between González and Jesús García, 1½ blocks east of Jardín Juárez. They leave hourly from 5:30am to 11:30am and 3:30pm to 6:30pm.

Getting Around
Local buses operate from 5:30am to 10pm daily (M$5). To get to the main bus terminal, take any 'Central,' 'Central Camionera' or 'Ruta 1' bus from Juárez on the east side of Jardín Juárez. A taxi to the airport costs about M$11. Taxis from the main bus station cost M$50 and M$60 for Plaza Zaragoza and the Zona Hotelera, respectively. Count on M$150 from the airport to either.

BAHÍA DE KINO
☎ 740 / pop 5000
Bahía de Kino is the kind of Mexican paradise you see in the movies, but rarely stumble upon in real life. There is a true end-of-the-road feel to the place; it's the most laid-back waterfront town in this region and one that encourages packing it all in and living out your days soaking in the sun and sipping on Sols.

The town was named for Father Eusebio Kino, a Jesuit missionary who established a small mission here for the indigenous Seri people in the late 17th century. It's 110km west of Hermosillo, is flanked by some 10km of beautiful and peaceful Sea of Cortez coastline and, unlike Puerto Peñasco, it hasn't suffered a massive overdose on condominiums at the hands of overzealous developers.

Kino is divided into old and new parts: Kino Viejo, the old quarter, is a dusty, run-down fishing village. Though the town hops with schoolkids and shrimpers during the day, it turns sleepy at dusk and most businesses are closed by 8pm. Kino Nuevo, further west, is where you'll most likely spend most of your time. It's also where you'll find the 'snowbirds' (retired Americans who head south for the winter, when their northern residences turn chilly) who live along this single beachfront road in either spiffy holiday homes or hulking RVs. The main beach is a soft, lengthy, *palapa*-lined piece of paradise and is safe for swimming. High season is November to March; at other times, you may find yourself blissfully alone in any one of the hotels or campgrounds. Go ahead, lose yourself.

Orientation
Route 16 runs west to both parts of town. To get to Viejo, turn left at the Pemex station and

NORTHWEST MEXICO

you'll be heading directly toward the Sea of Cortez, and will be within the small grid that makes up the old portion of town. Bypass the Pemex and keep heading north to venture into Nuevo. You'll soon be able to see the sea from this main road, and will eventually come to the strip of hotels and restaurants.

Information

Centro de Salud Rural (☎ 242-02-97; cnr Blvd Eusebio Kino & Tampico, Kino Viejo) Limited medical services but it beats dying.

Cruz Roja (Red Cross; ☎ 060, 242-00-32) Ambulance and ATM services.

New Space Café (cnr Yavarosa & Topolobampo, Kino Viejo; per hr M$10; ☺ 8:30am-10:30pm) Internet access.

Pemex gas station (cnr Carretera a Kino Viejo & Blvd Eusebio, Kino Viejo) ATM services. There are no banks or exchange services in Bahía de Kino.

Post Office (cnr Blvd Eusebio & Salina Cruz)

Tourism office (cnr Mar de Cortés & Santa Catarina, Kino Nuevo; ☺ 9am-5pm Thu-Tue) This new office is eager to help and has a decent map of the town. It's attached to the bus station.

Sights & Activities

Museo de los Seris (admission M$6; ☺ 8am-3pm Tue-Fri), about halfway along the beachfront road in Kino Nuevo, is a tiny spot that features illuminating exhibits (with all-Spanish texts) about the Seri (see boxed text, opposite). Unfortunately, it was closed indefinitely for remodeling at the time of research.

Punta Chueca is a small village 25km north of Bahía de Kino. It's actually more like a living museum, as it's where most members of the area's Seri tribe live. You'll need a sturdy 4WD with high clearance to make the journey along the dirt road; once you arrive, be prepared to be pounced upon by several Seri women who will want to sell you hand-crafted jewelry, baskets or ironwood carvings. If you're interested in making the boat trip out to **Isla del Tiburón**, a peaceful, uninhabited ecological preserve owned by the Seri tribe through presidential decree, look for Alfredo López, Ernesto Molina or David Morales, all of whom are guides who live in Punta Chueca and can facilitate permits or provide tours (folks at Prescott College's **Kino Bay Center for Cultural and Ecological Studies** can point you in the right direction).

Sleeping

our pick La Playa RV & Hotel (☎ 242-02-73; www.la playarvhotel.com; Blvd Mar de Cortés 101, Kino Nuevo; trailer sites/r M$220/1200; P ⊠ ⚐) This whitewashed beachfront paradise is hands down the best in town – it feels a bit like you're in the Greek Islands. Rooms all boast postcard-perfect sea views and feature stone floors, firm beds, mini kitchen areas with sinks and fridges, large marble bathrooms and private front decks with individual *palapas*. Note: there's a two-night minimum on summer weekends.

Hotel Posada del Mar (☎ 242-01-55; www.hotelposada delmar.com; cnr Blvd Mar de Cortés & Creta; s/d M$440/520, ste M$600-840; P ⊠ ⚐ ⚐) Directly across the street from the beach, this hotel has lovely, shady grounds. The rooms aren't in the best shape but the exposed brick is nice. If you're pinching pesos, ask for a 2nd-floor room for champagne views on a Chevy budget.

Hotel Hacienda (☎ 195-23-90; cnr Blvd Guaymas & Manzanillo, Kino Viejo; r/ste M$600/1200; P ⊠ ⚐) If you prefer the grittier vibe in Kino Viejo, this newcomer is a real gem: a beautiful Mexican hacienda decked out in rust-orange with all rooms surrounding a charming courtyard and pool.

Las Toninas Condominiums (☎ 242-08-92; cnr Blvd Mar de Cortés & Singapur, Kino Nuevo; condos M$850; P ⊠ ⊠ ⚐) These family-friendly rentable condominiums feature full kitchen and sofa beds in the living room, but you'll have to endure the *Brady Bunch*–era decor and facilities.

Eating

La Palapa del Pescador (☎ 242-0210; Blvd Mar de Cortés & Wellinton; mains M$40-300; ☺ 9am-10pm) Whole fried fish or stuffed lobster and various seafood dishes are calling at this seaside joint with an outdoor, *palapa*-covered patio and a jukebox with a mind of its own. It's also popular for a few *cervezes* at night.

Restaurant Dorita (☎ 252-03-49; cnr Blvd Kino & Salina Cruz, Kino Viejo; mains M$45-60; ☺ 7am-8pm Tue-Sun) Dorita and her daughter turned their front room into a restaurant 20 years ago and have been kicking out the best breakfast in either town since. *Omelette ranchero* is all you need to know.

Jorge's Restaurant (☎ 242-00-49; cnr Blvd Mar de Cortés & Alecantres; mains M$45-140; ☺ 8am-10pm) Located on the beach at the end of Kino Nuevo, this spot draws in crowds for its excellent shrimp and fish dishes. It's especially good for taking in Kino's spectacular sunsets.

El Pargo Rojo (☎ 242-02-05; Blvd Mar de Cortés 1426; mains M$50-295; ☺ 7am-10pm) Never mind the

---

THE SERIS

The Seris, or *Com caac* as they call themselves, are the least numerous indigenous people in Sonora – by the 1930s their population had decreased to 300 due to hunger and the introduction of foreign disease. But they are hardy, and have existed in the same region for more than 500 years. Traditionally a nomadic people living by hunting, gathering and fishing – not agriculture, despite the attempts of Christian missionaries to turn them into farmers over the centuries – the Seris roamed along the Sea of Cortez, from roughly El Desemboque in the north to Bahía de Kino in the south, and inland to Hermosillo. Today, an estimated 900 or so are left.

The Seris are one of the few indigenous peoples who do not work for outsiders, preferring to live by fishing, hunting and making handicrafts such as their ubiquitous ironwood carvings (known as *palofierro*) of animals, humans and other figures. These are fading fast, though, as numerous impostors, especially around Hermosillo and Bahía de Kino, are passing themselves off as Seri (some are Oaxacan) and trying to make a quick buck off the ironwood-carving trade. Additionally, since the late 1970s the increased demand for ironwood carvings and charcoal from US markets have devastated local populations of ironwood trees. The end result has been irreparable to the Seri economy and they have moved on to stone as the craft of choice (though you rarely see that either) as well as ecotourism and desert bighorn sheep hunting to make ends meet.

They are no longer strictly nomadic, but still often move from place to place in groups; sometimes you can see numbers camped at Bahía de Kino, or traveling up and down the coast. Most, though, live in villages north of Bahía de Kino, including Punta Chueca (opposite) and the more traditional El Desemboque. It is also important to note there is no substitute for visiting Punta Chueca if you are looking for authentic carvings, necklaces or baskets (hawkers in front of El Pargo Rojo and Jorge's in Kino Nuevo and the post office in Hermosillo are *not* Seri).

---

poorly translated English menu at this festive seafooder, this is the place to enjoy delicious fish dishes and hearty Mexican breakfasts in the midst of Kino Nuevo. The *camarones rellenos* are a real treat.

Getting There & Away

Costa Espresso buses to Hermosillo leave from the new bus depot in Kino Nuevo (attached to the tourism office) roughly every hour from 5am to 7:45pm.

If you're driving, you can make the trip from Hermosillo to Bahía de Kino in a little over an hour. From central Hermosillo, head northwest out of town on Blvd Encinas and just drive until you see the deep-blue Sea of Cortez.

GUAYMAS

☎ 622 / pop 134,153

There's nothing cute about Guaymas, Sonora's main port. Stopping here for any extended length of time had better be due to catastrophic vehicle breakdown or massive coronary. That said, many travelers will transit through here on their way to more interesting destinations to the south, so to make the best of it, you'll need to embrace the town's inextricable link to the sea. It won't

be easy to forget as you stroll the edge of the harbor, watching fishing boats return with the seasonal *camarones gigantes* (massive shrimp), available October to February, that Guaymas is famous for.

This city, founded in 1769 by Spaniards at the site of Yaqui and Guaymenas indigenous villages, later saw its bay become the locus of military campaigns by would-be invaders ranging from the US navy to French pirates.

Today Guaymas is a bustling port and naval-supply center. Currently, the marina is undergoing a multi-year, M$5.7 million transformation that, if it winds up looking anything like the projection photos, will look more Miami than Mexico. Travelers looking for charm will opt to stay in the resort town of San Carlos, 22km northwest.

Orientation

Hwy 15 becomes Blvd García López as it passes along the northern edge of Guaymas. Central Guaymas and the port area are along Av Serdán, the town's main drag, running parallel to and just south of García López; everything you'll need is on or near Av Serdán. García López and Serdán intersect a few blocks west of the Guaymas map's extents.

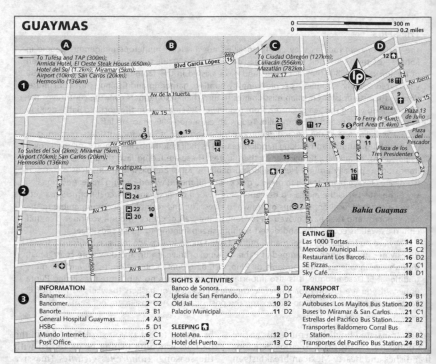

GUAYMAS

EATING 🍴
Las 1000 Tortas	14 B2
Mercado Municipal	15 C2
Restaurant Los Barcos	16 D2
SE Pizzas	17 C1
Sky Café	18 D1

INFORMATION
Banamex	1 C2
Bancomer	2 C2
Banorte	3 B1
General Hospital Guaymas	4 A3
HSBC	5 D1
Mundo Internet	6 C1
Post Office	7 C2

SIGHTS & ACTIVITIES
Banco de Sonora	8 D2
Iglesia de San Fernando	9 D1
Old Jail	10 B2
Palacio Municipal	11 D2

SLEEPING 🛏
Hotel Ana	12 D1
Hotel del Puerto	13 C2

TRANSPORT
Aeroméxico	19 B1
Autobuses Los Mayitos Bus Station	20 B2
Buses to Miramar & San Carlos	21 C1
Estrellas del Pacífico Bus Station	22 B2
Transportes Baldomero Corral Bus Station	23 B2
Transportes del Pacífico Bus Station	24 B2

Information

Banorte, Banamex, Bancomer and HSBC all have ATMs on Av Serdán.

General Hospital Guaymas (☎ 224-01-38; Calle 12)

Mundo Internet (cnr Calle 20 & Av 15; per hr M$10; ⏰ 9am-9pm Mon-Fri, 9am-7pm Sat, 10am-7pm Sun)

Post office (Av 10; ⏰ 8am-4pm Mon-Fri) Between Calles 19 and 20.

Sights & Activities

Everything you will want to check out is in and around the **Plaza de los Tres Presidentes**, which commemorates the three Mexican presidents hailing from Guaymas with an impressive triple-threat monument. Nearby are the 19th-century **Iglesia de San Fernando** and its Plaza 13 de Julio; the **Palacio Municipal** (built in 1899); and the neoclassical **Banco de Sonora**, which someone needs to restore in a hurry. The **old jail** (1900), near the bus station on Calle 15, is also an impressive sight in an otherwise run-down neighborhood. A project is in order to move the now razed **Museo Histórico de Guaymas** here, though not much progress had been made at the time of writing.

Sleeping

Accommodations choices in Guaymas favor budget-minded travelers, but folks looking for atmosphere should continue on to San Carlos.

BUDGET

Hotel Ana (☎ 222-30-48; Calle 25 No 135; d/tr M$250/300; P ❌ 🖥) With its newly tiled floors, bathrooms and walls, this is trailer trash in new shoes. We're digging the retro red-and-white checkered motif in the hallway.

Hotel del Puerto (☎ 224-34-08; Yáñez 92; s/d M$250/350; P ❌ ❌) This might be the best deal in town when all is said and done. Dark but clean rooms, central location and nicely tiled floors and bathrooms.

MIDRANGE & TOP END

Hotel del Sol (☎ 224-94-11; Calz García López 995; r M$480; P ❌ ❌) The newer sister hotel to Suites del Sol, this one is similar – minus the suites but with a more central location (it's walkable from TAP and Tufesa bus stations).

Suites del Sol (☎ 221-29-00; Blvd Benito Juárez Norte 2A; r M$520; P ❌ ❌) On the edge of town, this is a cool and comfortable option, especially if you nab one of the 10 suites with kitchenette and living area – for the same price as a double!

Armida Hotel (☎ 224-30-35; www.hotelarmida .com.mx; Carretera Internacional Salida Norte; r M$570-980; P ✕ ✖) Though it's aged, this option on the northern edge of town has cheery lobby furniture, refrigerators, satellite TV, balconies or terraces, and bathtubs. There's also a café and a popular steak house.

Eating

For goodness' sake, at least eat well while you're here.

Las 1000 Tortas (Av Serdán btwn Calles 17 & 18; tortas M$20-75; ⏰ 8am-11pm) A good snack shop serving *tortas* and hamburgers.

Sky Café (Calle 25, Edificio Guaymense; desserts M$25; ⏰ 7am-10:30pm Mon-Fri, 10am-10:30pm Sat & Sun) Great spot just off the cathedral for cappuccinos and sweet deserts.

SE Pizzas (Av Serdán near Calle 20; buffet from M$35; ⏰ noon-10pm) This all-you-can-eat pizza and salad buffet packs in a vibrant local crowd.

Restaurant Los Barcos (☎ 222-76-50; cnr Malecón & Calle 21; mains M$78-135; ⏰ noon-10pm) This airy, *palapa*-roofed restaurant is the spot to try the town's famous fat shrimp.

El Oeste Steak House (☎ 225-28-00; Hotel Armida; mains M$190-235; ⏰ noon-11pm) This popular steakhouse wins the Innovation In Taxidermy Design award, serving raved-about grilled Sonoran steaks in a saloon-like room decked out in stuffed game.

Like most Mexican towns, Guaymas supports a **Mercado Municipal**, which has stalls where you can sit down to eat cheaply. Popular morning stalls include El Rinconito for *machaca* (rehydrated, spiced beef) and El Vaporcito for *tacos al vapor* (steamed beef) and *birria* (spicy meat stew). Both are in the southwest corner. It's a block south of Av Serdán, on Av Rodríguez between Calles 19 and 20, and opens around 6am.

Getting There & Away

AIR

The airport is about 10km northwest of Guaymas on the highway to San Carlos. **US Airways** (☎ 221-22-66) flies direct from Phoenix once daily all months except September, when it cuts back to Thursday to Sunday. **Aereo Calafia** (☎ 222-55-96) flies to Baja destinations La Paz, Loreto and Los Cabos. **Aéreo Servicio**

> **BEST SONORAN CARNE ASADA**
>
> ■ **Tacos El Grillo** (p323)
> ■ **Asadero Leo's** (boxed text, p322)
> ■ **Los Encarbonadas** (p326)

Guerrero (☎ 221-28-00) heads to Santa Rosalía in Baja. **Aeroméxico** (☎ 222-66-02; Av Serdán 236) has an office in town.

BOAT

Overnight ferries connect Guaymas with Santa Rosalía, Baja California. The passenger/auto ferry *Santa Rosalía*, operated by Operadora Rotuaria del Noroeste, departs at 8pm on Monday, Thursday and Saturday, and arrives around 6am, though strong winter winds may cause delays.

The ticket office is at the **ferry terminal** (☎ 222-02-04; www.ferrysantarosalia.com; Av Serdán; ⏰ 10am-8pm Mon-Fri, 10am-2pm Sat) at the east end of town. Vehicle reservations are accepted by telephone a week in advance. Passenger tickets are sold at the ferry office on the morning of departure, or a few days before. Make reservations at least three days in advance and, even if you have reservations, arrive early at the ticket office. Passenger fares are M$550 for seats and M$750 for cabins. Advance reservations are recommended. See p296 for vehicle fares.

BUS

Guaymas has four small bus stations on Calle 14, about two blocks south of Av Serdán (a ramshackle area, to say the least).

Albatros (cnr Calle 14 & Av 12) Goes to Puerto Peñasco three times a day (9:15am, 5:15pm and 10:15pm).

Autobuses Crucero (Estrellas del Pacífico office, cnr Calle 14 & Av 12) Hourly departures all day and night to locations both north and south.

Autobuses Los Mayitos (Calle 14, btwn Avs 10 & 12) Hourly departures north to Hermosillo and Nogales and south to Navojoa.

Estrellas del Pacífico (cnr Calle 14 & Av 12) Goes to Guadalajara and Tijuana hourly.

Transportes Baldomero Corral (cnr Calle 14 & Av 12) Leaves hourly for Hermosillo, seven times daily for Nogales from 1am, eight daily for Ciudad Obregón from 10:45am and 11 daily for Navojoa from 2:45am. Most notable is its one daily bus (3:45pm) direct to Álamos.

Transportes Chihuahuenses (Estrellas del Pacífico office, cnr Calle 14 & Av 12) Goes to Ciudad Juárez once a day (3:30pm, 12 hours).

Transportes del Pacífico (cnr Calle 14 & Av 12) Also sells tickets for Crucero, Transportes Norte de Sonora and Chihuahuense.

Transportes Norte de Sonora (Estrellas del Pacífico office, cnr Calle 14 & Av 12) Hourly departures to Tijuana and Mexico City.

Transportes y Autobuses del Pacífico (García López) Hourly departures all day and night to locations both north and south.

Tufesa (García López) Heads every few hours to Hermosillo, Nogales, Ciudad Obregón and Navojoa, and once per day to Los Mochis.

Most companies have far-ranging northbound and southbound routes to destinations including the following:

Destination	Fare	Duration
Álamos	M$245	4hr
Guadalajara	M$835	20hr
Hermosillo	M$84	1¾hr
Los Mochis	M$215	5hr
Mexico City	M$780	30hr
Tijuana	M$560	15hr

Getting Around

To get to the airport, catch a bus from Av Serdán heading to Itson or San José, or take a taxi (around M$80). Local buses run along Av Serdán frequently between 6am and 9pm (M$5). Several eastbound buses stop at the ferry terminal; ask for the *transbordador* (ferry).

SAN CARLOS

☎ 622 / pop 4500

Located about 22km northwest of Guaymas, San Carlos has a beautiful desert-and-bay landscape that is presided over by some fairly dramatic mountains – most notably the majestic twin peaks of Cerro Tetakawi – that glow an impressive red-earthed hue as the sun descends upon them towards the end of the day. For a moment, it doesn't even seem like Mexico.

From October to April, the town is overtaken by a massive influx of *norteamericanos*, but at other times you'll find it a quiet, beautiful spot that's a respite from the hot, surrounding desert cities. The town isn't especially known for its beaches, with the exception of Playa Algodones (scenes from the 1970 film *Catch 22* were shot here, hence its nickname, Playa Catch 22), though it does offer a wealth of outdoor activities.

Orientation

San Carlos is based around two marinas: Marina San Carlos, in the heart of town, and the newer Marina Real at Algodones in the northernmost section. Most motels and eateries lie along the strip of Blvd Beltrones, while the larger resorts are toward Algodones.

Information

Banamex (Blvd Manlio Beltrones) Both US dollars and pesos are accepted everywhere. This Banamex, next to the Pemex station on Beltrones, has two ATMs.

Gary's Internet Connection (☎ 226-00-49; www .garysdiveshop.com; Blvd Manlio Beltrones Km 10; per hr M$30; ◷ 8am-6pm Mon-Sat) Located at Gary's Dive Shop.

Guaymas San Carlos Convention & Visitor's Bureau (☎ 226-0202; Blvd Manlio Beltrones Km 9; ◷ 9am-1pm & 2-5pm Mon-Fri, 9am-2pm Sat) Helpful maps and reservation assistance.

Post Office (Blvd Manlio Beltrones near Calle H; ◷ 8am-4pm Mon-Fri)

Activities

San Carlos offers a wealth of beach-related and adventure activities, with sport fishing topping the list.

Catch 22 (☎ 226-21-62; www.catch22mexicofishing .com; Marinaterra 1; ◷ 7am-4pm Tue-Sat) The spot for fishing excursions.

El Mar Diving Center (☎ 226-04-04; www.elmar.com; 263 Creston; ◷ 7am-6pm) Diving, hiking, kayaking and snorkeling.

Gary's Dive Shop (☎ 226-00-49; www.garysdiveshop .com; Blvd Manlio Beltrones Km 10) Diving and fishing.

Ocean Sports (☎ 226-06-96; www.desertdivers.com; Edificio Marina San Carlos; ◷ 8am-5pm Mon, Wed & Thu, 7am-7pm Fri & Sat, 7am-5pm Sun) Sunset cruises, jet-ski rental, whale watching and horseback riding.

Sleeping

Departamentos Adlai (☎ 226-07-70; Calle H; s/d M$450/500; P ⊠ ☀) This small hotel in the residential neighborhood of Las Ranchitas is great value: large, comfortable rooms around an extra-large Jacuzzi. It's popular with hipsters from Ciudad Obregón. To get there, turn right at the first Extra convenience store coming into town and walk 1km; it's the aquagreen building on the left.

Motel Creston (☎ 226-00-20; www.hotelcreston .mx; Blvd Manlio Beltrones Km 10; r M$550; P ⊠ ☀) A good budget option, this somewhat indifferent motor lodge has retro charm and large rooms. The lukewarm showers are an interesting height.

Hotel Fiesta Real San Carlos (☎ 226-13-14; Blvd Manlio Beltrones Km 8.5; s/d M$748/1012; P ✕ ✕ ✉ ✿) This whitewashed, family-run spot has practically everything you'll find at the pricier resorts at a fraction of the cost and with a more down-to-earth vibe. No TVs or telephones.

Marinaterra (☎ 225-20-20; www.marinaterra.com; Gabriel Estrada s/n, Sector La Herradura; r M$1400-2100; P ✕ ✕ ✉ ✿) Overlooking the San Carlos marina, this high-end resort has large rooms with kitchenette, and some with excellent balconies that boast wide hammocks. Ask for a standard with a view toward the dramatic Cerro Tetakawi.

Eating & Drinking

Rosa's Cantina (☎ 226-10-00; Blvd Manlio Beltrones Km 9.5; mains M$32-120; ✆ 6am-9pm) Pink-tinted, Pancho Villa–themed cantina serving up substantial American and Mexican breakfasts and additional favorites throughout the day.

Marina Cantina & Deli (☎ 226-11-22; Edificio Marina San Carlos; sandwiches M$50; ✆ 11am-1am Mon-Fri, 11am-2am Sat & Sun) The town watering hole of choice for gringos and locals alike offers a wide list of sandwiches, salads, mountainous nachos and a worthwhile Happy Hour (4pm to 7pm).

El Bronco (☎ 226-11-30; Blvd Beltrones Km 10; mains M$105-230; ✆ 5-11pm Mon-Thu, 1-11pm Fri & Sat, 1-10pm Sun) A succulent chop house serving perfectly seasoned cuts of Sonora's famed steaks in a great room that looks vaguely mysterious from the outside.

our pick The Hangout/Soggy Peso Bar (☎ 226-17-16; Playa Algodones Km 20; ✆ 11am-sunset) A truly special, hidden gem, this local secret is worth the hike out to Playa Algodones, the most beautiful beach in San Carlos. It's simple: one of the best margaritas in Mexico, on the beach, as the sun goes down. Majestic!

1910 (☎ 226-15-13; cnr Paseo de Los Yaquis & Av de los Seris; cover M$30; ✆ 5pm-3am Wed-Sat) For a serious taste of the hot and wild local crowd that swarms in from Guaymas every weekend, this loud and brash bi-level club is a must. Don't bother showing up before midnight.

Getting There & Around

Buses to San Carlos from Guaymas run west along Av Serdán (starting from between Calles 19 and 20) from 5:30am to 10pm. Return buses leave San Carlos between 6:15am and 11pm. Buses run every 15 minutes (M$10).

ÁLAMOS

☎ 647 / pop 8200 / elevation 432m

As you depart Navojoa on Hwy 13 toward Álamos, the oppressive diesel and dust of the Desierto Sonorense immediately begins yielding to the far more lush, forested foothills of the Sierra Madre Occidental. It's apparent: something special this way comes. The air is cooler, the bus stops are newer and the Pemex stations almost look historical. Álamos lies in wait like a buried treasure, one only half dug up thus far by blue-blood *norteamericanos* and other opportunistic foreigners.

A small and sleepy oasis to land in for several days, Álamos is a place to get lost in provocative history, tales of ghosts and legends, and hushed, cobblestone streets that spark awe and wonder at every turn. You'll notice a Moorish sensibility in much of the architecture, thanks to the influence of 17th-century Andalucian architects, and won't have to wonder why the town was declared both a national historic monument and one of Mexico's 32 Pueblos Mágicos (Magical Towns) – it is currently undergoing a two-year project to remove all telephone poles and bury electricity lines in a bid to become a Unesco World Heritage site.

The town's charms have proven irresistible to a community of American retirees and creative types who, since the '50s, have been snapping up many decaying colonial buildings to renovate and convert to hotels, restaurants and second homes (everyone from the late actor Carroll O'Connor to a Pabst Blue Ribbon heiress has owned homes here). Now, the well-heeled expats – who comprise a small but influential part of the town population (it stood at 400 in 2007, according to one woman who does an annual count) – entertain each other in their enclosed courtyards, remaining largely segregated from their Mexican neighbors. Some have called it a San Miguel de Allende in its infancy.

From mid-October to mid-April, when the air is cool and fresh, *norteamericanos* arrive to take up residence in their winter homes, and the town begins to hum with foreign visitors. Quail- and dove-hunting season, from November to February, also attracts many foreigners. Mexican tourists come in the scorching-hot summer months of July and August, when school is out. At other times you may find scarcely another visitor, though the rainy summer months bring plenty of mosquitoes and no-see-ums to town.

NORTHWEST MEXICO

History

In 1540 this was the campsite of Francisco Vázquez de Coronado, future governor of Nueva Galicia (the colonial name for much of western Mexico), during his wars against the indigenous Mayo and Yaqui (the Yaqui resisted all invaders until 1928). If he had known about the vast amounts of gold and silver that prospectors later found, he would have stayed.

In 1683, silver was discovered at Promontorios, near Álamos, and the Europa mine was opened. Other mines soon followed and Álamos became a boom town of more than 30,000, one of Mexico's principal 18th-century mining centers. Mansions, haciendas, a cathedral, tanneries, metalworks, blacksmiths' shops and later a mint were all built. El Camino Real (The King's Hwy), a well-trodden Spanish mule trail through the foothills, connected Álamos with Culiacán and El Fuerte to the south.

After Mexican independence, Álamos became the capital of the newly formed province of Occidente, a vast area including all of the present states of Sonora and Sinaloa. Don José María Almada, owner of the richest silver mine in Álamos, was appointed as governor.

During the turmoil of the 19th century, and up to the Mexican Revolution, Álamos was attacked repeatedly, both by rebels seeking its vast silver wealth and by the fiercely independent Yaqui. The years of the revolution took a great toll on the town. By the 1920s, most of the population had left and many of the once-beautiful haciendas had fallen into disrepair. Álamos became practically a ghost town.

In 1948 Álamos was reawakened by the arrival of William Levant Alcorn, a Pennsylvania dairy farmer who bought the Almada mansion on Plaza de Armas and restored it as the Hotel Los Portales. Alcorn brought publicity to the town and made a fortune selling Álamos real estate. A number of *norteamericanos* crossed the border, bought crumbling old mansions for good prices and set about the task of lovingly restoring them to their former glory. Many of these people still live in Álamos today.

Today, the copper and silver trade has picked up again (two new mines have opened) and mining is once again big business in the area.

Orientation

The paved road from Navojoa enters Álamos from the west and leads to the green, shady Plaza Alameda, with the market at its east end. The town's other main square, the more uppity Plaza de Armas, is two blocks south of the market. The Arroyo La Aduana (Customs House Stream, which is usually dry) runs along the town's northern edge; the Arroyo Agua Escondida (Hidden Waters Stream, also usually dry) runs along the southern edge. Both converge at the east end of town with the Arroyo La Barranca (Ravine Stream), which runs, dryly, from the northwest.

Information

Álamos Books and Maps (Juárez 8; ☙ 9am-6pm) The best bookshop (and high-end handicraft spot) in town.

Banorte (Madero 37; ☙ 9am-3pm Mon-Fri) ATM and money exchange.

Comps-E (Serdán 4; per hr M$10; ☙ 8am-10pm Mon-Fri, 8am-1pm Sat & Sun) Internet access.

Hospital General de Álamos (☎ 428-02-25; Madero btwn Ramón Ortiz & Cocoteros; ☙ 24hr)

Post office (Palacio de Gobierno, Juárez; ☙ 9am-4pm Mon-Fri)

Tourist office (☎ 428-04-50; Victoria 3; ☙ 9am-6pm Mon-Sat, 8am-2pm Sun) Lots of information about destinations all over Sonora, but oddly short on Álamos info.

Sights

CATEDRAL NUESTRA SEÑORA DE LA CONCEPCIÓN

Known simply as 'the cathedral,' this **church** (Church of the Immaculate Conception; Plaza de Armas; ☙ daily services 8am & 6pm) is the tallest building in Álamos. It was built between 1786 and 1804, as a copy of a Tucson, Arizona church known as the 'White Dove of the Desert.' Inside, the altar rail, lamps, censers and candelabra were fashioned from silver, but were all ordered to be melted down in 1866 by General Ángel Martínez after he booted out French imperialist troops from Álamos. Subterranean passageways (seven or so, it's believed) between the church and several of the mansions – probably built as escape routes for the safety of the rich families in times of attack – were blocked off in the 1950s.

MUSEO COSTUMBRISTA DE SONORA

This well-done **museum** (☎ 428-00-53; Plaza de Armas; admission M$10; ☙ 9am-6pm Wed-Sun), on the east side of the Plaza de Armas, has extensive exhibits (all in Spanish) on the history and traditions of the people of Sonora. Special attention is paid to the influence of mining on Álamos, and the fleeting prosperity it created.

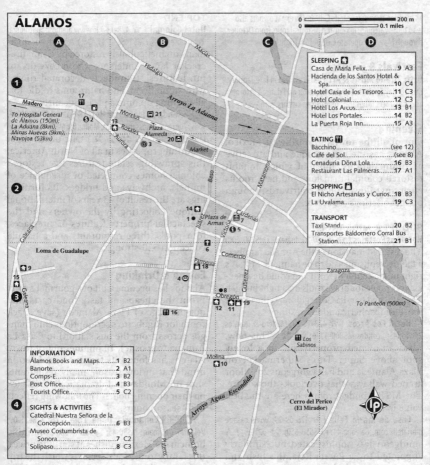

ÁLAMOS

0 ——————— 200 m
0 ——————— 0.1 miles

INFORMATION
Álamos Books and Maps.........**1** B2
Banorte........................**2** A1
Comps-E.......................**3** B2
Post Office....................**4** B3
Tourist Office.................**5** C2

SIGHTS & ACTIVITIES
Catedral Nuestra Señora de la
  Concepción...................**6** B3
Museo Costumbrista de
  Sonora.......................**7** C2
Solipaso.......................**8** C3

SLEEPING
Casa de María Felix.............**9** A3
Hacienda de los Santos Hotel &
  Spa.........................**10** C4
Hotel Casa de los Tesoros.....**11** C3
Hotel Colonial................**12** C3
Hotel Los Arcos...............**13** B1
Hotel Los Portales............**14** B2
La Puerta Roja Inn............**15** A3

EATING
Bacchino.....................(see 12)
Café del Sol..................(see 8)
Cenaduria Dōna Lola...........**16** B3
Restaurant Las Palmeras.......**17** A1

SHOPPING
El Nicho Artesanías y Curios.**18** B3
La Uvalama...................**19** C3

TRANSPORT
Taxi Stand....................**20** B2
Transportes Baldomero Corral Bus
  Station....................**21** B1

EL MIRADOR

This lookout, atop a hill on the southeast edge of town, affords a sweeping view of Álamos and its mountainous surroundings, and is a popular hangout spot at sunset. To get there, take the walking trail that ascends from the Arroyo Agua Escondida next to the now-closed Los Sabinos restaurant. Alternatively, you can walk or drive up the steep, paved road that ascends from its southern approach.

THE PANTEÓN

This deliciously ancient **cemetery** (Álamos Cemetery; cnr Las Delicias & Posada; 6am-6pm) is a fascinating jumble of above-ground tombs, elaborate headstones made of pastel-hued crosses and angel statues, and tall palm trees. It began receiving the dead of wealthy families in 1751, when the practice of burying them inside the church was abolished.

Tours

Tours of Distinction (428-13-68) Lifelong local Emiliano Grajeda offers a variety of walking tours: a History Walk, a Ghosts and Legends Tour and a House and Garden Tour of the most impressive haciendas in town. Tours last two to three hours and cost M$110 per person. He has also added a tour to the nearby former silver-mining town of La Aduana that includes a homemade tortilla-and-cheese lunch at a local home.

Solipaso (428-04-66; www.solipaso.com; Obregón 3; day trips M$100-250) An excellent resource for nature lovers, this ecotour company offers nature excursions, including trips on the Río Mayo and Sea of Cortez, and to La Aduana, all by prior arrangement. Its Californian expat owners also lead bird-watching, hiking and historical tours from October through May, and operate Café del Sol (right).

Festivals & Events

Ortíz Tirado Music & Art Festival Held in late January, this 10-day festival of orchestra, choir and dance performances attracts thousands of Mexican visitors each year.

Sleeping

Out of all the towns in northwest Mexico, Álamos has the most unique and attractive accommodations, most of which inhabit restored colonial mansions and have rooms encircling flower-filled courtyards, though budget offerings are scarce.

BUDGET & MIDRANGE

Hotel Los Portales (☎ 428-02-11; Juárez 6; r M$300-600) The restored mansion of the Almada family is a tad decrepit and said to be haunted. Still, it's right in the center of town and could be a necessary choice for brave souls on a tight budget. The attached bar, La Corregidora, is the town's most atmospheric and interesting.

Hotel Los Arcos (☎ 428-15-28; Madero & Rosales 2; r M$450, condos M$800-1146; ✖ ✖) This new, Mexican-owned property sits in a lovely spot above Super Tito's supermarket on Plaza Alameda and has a gorgeous 2nd-floor arched walkway that overlooks the square. The M$450 budget rooms here are the best value in town.

Casa de María Felix (☎ 428-09-29; www.casademariafelix.com; Galeana 41; r M$550-650; ✖ ✖ ✖) A smidgeon less sophisticated but similarly appointed to La Puerta Roja, this lush and homey property, also a museum, is full of curios, fireplaces, antiques and plenty of dogs and cats.

Hotel Casa de los Tesoros (☎ 428-00-10; www.tesoros-hotel.com; Obregón 10; r M$700-1100; P ✖ ✖ ✖) Formerly an 18th-century convent, this mellow hotel has a breezy, orange tree–shaded courtyard and beautiful archways (though quarters are dim compared to the property at large). The popular cantina here purportedly has the best chips and salsa in town (they are damn good).

La Puerta Roja Inn (☎ 428-01-41; www.lapuertarojainn.com; Galeana 46; r incl breakfast M$990; P ✖) This gorgeous, 150-year-old home combines a Mexican junkyard-chic vibe with eclectic art and furnishings, and has a cheery garden and courtyard.

TOP END

Hotel Colonial (☎ 428-13-71; www.alamoshotelcolonial.com; Obregón 8; r M$1458-1985; ✖) A former silver mansion meticulously restored by Cajun firecracker Janet Anderson, whose cozy dream inn features 10 uniquely decorated rooms with stone floors and bathrooms to die for, all opening up onto a pleasant courtyard.

Hacienda de los Santos Hotel & Spa (☎ 428-02-17; www.haciendadelossantos.com; Molina 8; r M$2940-2970, ste M$3190-15,400; ✖ ✖ ✖ ✖) One of the most beautiful properties in all of North America, this sprawling estate features five restored colonial homes connected by a sequence of tunnels, archways and bridges. Its furnishings are the result of 43 years of international antique collecting by the owners and the spectacular property features 63 fireplaces, four pools, three restaurants and a tequila collection 520-strong.

Eating & Drinking

Álamos has become a bit of a gourmet's hub. From the cheap and tasty food carts that dot the edge of Plaza Alameda (save snack room for Rigoberto's scrumptious chili mangos across from the bus station) to Casa La Aduana (opposite), 10 minutes out of town, Álamos has found its foodie focus. Keep in mind that in low season, many restaurants shut on Monday and dramatically cut back on their opening hours. The following reflects high-season hours.

our pick **Cenaduria Dôna Lola** (☎ 428-11-09; Volantín s/n; mains M$30-45; ☾ 6am-10pm) Stunning homemade Mexican dishes at startling prices, this family-run, locals' secret is worth the trip to Álamos alone (the enchiladas *suizas* are the best in the world). If you hear folks refer to Koky's, they mean here.

Restaurant Las Palmeras (☎ 428-00-65; Madero 48; mains M$35-120; ☾ 6am-10pm Mon-Thu, 6am-2pm Fri-Sun) In a new location just northwest of Plaza Alameda, this town classic still churns out the same excellent *chiles rellenos* (stuffed chilies with cheese or chicken) and memorable homemade tortillas.

Café del Sol (☎ 428-04-66; Obregón 3; meals M$50-70; ☾ 7:30am-6pm Tue-Sat) An airy colonial café ideal for espresso and innovative Nuevo Mexican bites like crepes with *chipotle* cider cream sauce.

Bacchino (☎ 428-13-71; Hotel Colonial; pizzas M$90-120, mains M$70-140; ☾ 11:30am-2:30pm & 5:30-10:30pm; V) This recently opened Italian restaurant with a Louisiana soul (shrimp remoulade, anyone?) churns out wood-fired brick oven pizzas and favorites like six-cheese lasagna in a colorful atmosphere inside Hotel Colonial. There's live romantic Mexican guitar on Wednesday and Saturday nights.

La Puerta Roja Inn (☎ 428-01-41; www.lapuerta rojainn.com; Galeana 46; dinner tasting menu M$200-275; ☟ Wed only) Every Wednesday, guests and nonguests alike are welcome to partake in owner Teri Arnold's delicious meals, made with local produce, fish and fowl (courtesy of her hunter husband). Signature dishes like chocolate-rubbed pork ribs are a major hit with local expats.

Shopping
El Nicho Artesanías y Curios (Juárez 15; ☟ 8:30am-6pm Mon-Sat) Occupying a former silk factory behind the cathedral is this fascinating shop, brimming with antiques, curios, folk art and Mexican handicrafts.

La Uvalama (☎ 428-01-80; cnr Obregon & Gutierrez; ☟ 8am-6pm) It's sparse but the kiln-fired clay pottery is worth taking home. They also do pottery classes in high season (M$40 per person for two hours) and you walk with your own custom-designed pottery.

Getting There & Away
Access to Álamos is via Hwy 13 from Navojoa, 194km from Guaymas. Second-class buses to Álamos depart from Navojoa's **Transportes Baldomero Corral (TBC) station** (cnr Guerrero & No Reelección) sporadically hourly or half-hourly (there are 21 per day) between 6am and 10pm (M$20, one hour). TBC also has 1st-class service for longer trips, including 15 daily buses north to Hermosillo (M$137, five hours), plus several to Tucson (M$465, 11 hours) and Phoenix (M$595, 13 hours).

In Álamos the TBC bus station is on the north side of Plaza Alameda. Buses depart for Navojoa (M$20, one hour) every half-hour from 5:30am to 12:30pm, and then hourly from 1:15pm to 2:15pm, then half-hourly again from 3pm to 6:30pm. A bus to Phoenix (M$549, 12 hours) departs nightly at 9:15pm.

The closest commercial airport is in Ciudad Obregón, about 90 minutes away.

LA ADUANA
There are several small historic villages near Álamos that make interesting day excur-sions, but La Aduana, the mine that once made Álamos rich, is a must, and is often included on guided-tour itineraries. It's a tiny little town with a small main plaza and a rustic feel.

The real star of the place is **Casa La Aduana Restaurant & Hotel** (☎ 647-404-34-73; www.casala duana.com; r with breakfast & dinner for two M$1250; ☟ closed May–mid-Jun). It has basic rooms on the plaza, but the big draw is its lauded restaurant (prix fixe dinner M$180 to M$320), where Italian- and French-trained owner/chef Sam Beardsley turns out lovingly prepared New Sonoran cuisine like shrimp rolled in tomato garlic chili marmalade. The dirt road leading here was being paved during research, so that should make access a little more comfortable.

There is also a budding ecotourism movement happening in La Aduana, led by the **Projecto Ecoturístico La Aduana** (☎ 110-44-79), a woman's cooperative that will take you rappelling down a 35m mine shaft for M$150. There are also over 350 species of birds in the area and spectacular hiking.

If you don't have your own vehicle, a cab from Álamos will cost M$150 to M$200.

NORTHERN SINALOA
With the exception of the lovely El Fuerte (p344), Northern Sinaloa doesn't boast colonial streets or a wealth of activities, though most travelers wind up here for one very compelling reason: it is the western gateway to one of Mexico's most stunning natural attractions, the dramatic Barranca del Cobre (Copper Canyon). Southern Sinaloa, including Mazatlán, is covered in the Central Pacific Coast chapter.

LOS MOCHIS
☎ 668 / pop 231,980
A surprisingly brisk balance of modern urban buzz and small-town friendly energy greets travelers to Los Mochis, 488km south of Hermosillo. Though many travelers now opt to begin or end their Copper Canyon rail journey in more picturesque El Fuerte, rail enthusiasts carry on or begin here in Los Mochis, the western terminus for the scenic railway.

Orientation
The main street through the city, running southwest from Hwy 15D directly into the

center of town, changes names from Calz López Mateos to Leyva as it enters the center. Coming from the ferry terminal at Topolobampo, you will enter the city center on Blvd Castro, another major artery. Some blocks in the center are split by smaller streets (not shown on the Los Mochis map) running parallel to the main streets, and very few streets in the center are two-way.

Information

Centro Médico (☎ 812-08-34; Blvd Castro 130)
Online Café Internet (Obregón; per hr M$12; 🕑 9am-8pm Mon-Sat)
Post office (Ordoñez btwn Zaragoza & Prieto; 🕑 8am-4pm Mon-Fri, 9am-1pm Sat)
Tourist office (☎ 816-20-15; cnr Cuauhtémoc & Allende) There are plans to move to a new location well out of the town center.

Sights & Activities

The whitewashed **Parroquia del Sagrado Corazón de Jesús** (cnr Obregón & Mina), a small church with a graceful tower, stands sentinel near the lovely **Plazuela 27 de Septiembre**, a pleasant, quiet and shady plaza with a classic gazebo, one of the best in northwest Mexico. There is a small museum, the **Museo Regional del Valle del Fuerte** (cnr Blvd Rosales & Obregón; admission M$10, free Sun; 🕑 9am-1pm & 4-8pm Mon-Sat), which has somewhat static exhibits (Spanish language only) on the history and culture of northwest Mexico, with more interesting rotating exhibits by local and international artists. The **Mercado Independencia** (Av Independencia), between Degollado and Zapata, is an energetic marketplace dealing mostly in meat and vegetables, but the outside shops along Av Independencia do offer some choice cowboy wear.

Sleeping

Los Mochis has a good mix of accommodations for all budgets, and if you're heading to the Copper Canyon they can be invaluable for information and logistics.

BUDGET

Hotel Beltran (☎ 812-06-88; cnr Hidalgo & Zaragoza; s/d M$275/320; ❄) You won't send postcards home from here or anything, but budget travelers will find it much more comfortable than other similarly priced options.

Hotel Fénix (☎ 812-26-23; Flores 365 Sur; s/d M$275/326; ❄) Like two hotels in one: the 16 recently renovated rooms are great value for those on a budget; old rooms for the same price are a bit of a ripoff (though some do have improved bathrooms).

Hotel Montecarlo (☎ 812-18-18; Flores 322 Sur; s/d M$290/350; P ❄) A cheerful blue colonial building with rickety rooms around a sunny enclosed courtyard, this place certainly evokes a bygone era. It's worth the M$40 splurge for an upgraded double, but don't expect miracles. It has a lot that allows long-term parking (if you're Copper Canyon bound), but the Fénix is a better deal if that's irrelevant to you.

MIDRANGE & TOP END

Corintios Hotel (☎ 818-22-24; www.hotelcorintios.com; Obregón 580 Pte; s/d M$684/774, ste M$855-1100; P ❄) With its airy courtyard and cozy rooms with marble-tiled bathtubs, the centrally-located Corintios, though deteriorating ('70s minibars, broken coffeemakers), is still a good-value midrange option. The staff members are friendly and guests can park their car here long-term for free (others pay M$80 per day).

Hotel Santa Anita (☎ 818-70-46; www.santaanitahotel.com; cnr Leyva & Hidalgo; s/d M$978/1133; P ⊠ ❄) This is the first link in the Balderrama chain, which owns six hotels in the Copper Canyon region. Two of the four floors have been questionably renovated (pea-colored walls? *No*). The attached travel agency can handle all things Copper Canyon and guests who use their services may leave their car here as well (others pay M$50 per day).

Best Western Los Mochis (☎ 816-30-30; www.bestwestern.com; Obregón 691 Pte; r M$1045; P ⊠ ❄ 💻 🏊 ♿) Though the rooms aren't as high-tech and fancy as the lobby and elevators, this all-amenity chain hotel is the newest, most tastefully decorated and comfortable of all hotels in Mochis. Lower floors are nonsmoking.

Eating & Drinking

You won't go hungry in Los Mochis – its pleasant mix of classic joints and gourmet options allow for a nice gorging before heading into the starved-for-choice canyon.

La Fibra (☎ 812-5674; Hidalgo 540 Pte; sandwiches M$12-17; 🕑 7am-3pm Mon-Sat; V) It's cramped, but the soy burgers and *tortas*, whole wheat quesadillas and array of fresh juices in the middle of cattle country is a welcome change.

La Cabaña de Doña Chayo (☎ 818-54-98; Obregón 99 Pte; mains M$18-32; 🕑 9am-1am) Fabulous quesadil-

LOS MOCHIS

INFORMATION
Centro Médico...............................1 C3
Online Café Internet......................2 B3
Post Office....................................3 B4
Tourist Office.................................4 C4

SIGHTS & ACTIVITIES
Mercado Indepencia......................5 D3
Museo Regional del Valle del Fuerte..6 A2
Parroquia del Sagrado Corazón de
    Jesús.......................................7 B2

SLEEPING
Best Western Los Mochis...............8 B3
Corintios Hotel..............................9 B3
Hotel Beltran...............................10 C3
Hotel Fénix.................................11 B3
Hotel Santa Anita........................12 B3

EATING
El Farallón..................................13 B3
La Cabaña de Doña Chayo............14 B3
La Fibra.....................................15 B2

TRANSPORT
Autotransportes Norte de Sinaloa....16 B4
Azules del Noroeste Bus Station.....17 B3
Bus Terminal...............................18 D4
Buses to Topolobampo..................19 B4
Buses to Train Station....................20 B3
Estrellas del Pacífico Bus Station....21 C2
Taxi Queue.................................22 B3
Transportes del Pacífico Bus Station.23 C2
Transportes y Autobuses Pacífico (TAP) Bus
    Station....................................24 D4
Tufesa Bus Station........................25 D3
Viajes Flamingo......................(see 12)

las and tacos with *carne asada* and *machaca* (spiced shredded dried beef) arrive here in piping-hot, handmade-to-order corn and flour tortillas. A classic.

El Leñador (☎ 812-66-00; Prieto 301 Nte; burgers M$33-38, steaks M$92-169; ☽ noon-11pm) Middle-class Mochis descends on this excellent burger and steak restaurant (try the Mexicana burger!), oddly popular with both families and the young and beautiful. Chips are served with three fantastic salsas.

El Farallón (☎ 812-12-73; cnr Flores & Obregón; mains M$110-130; ☽ 9am-midnight) The upscale atmosphere evokes too much cruise-ship clubhouse, but there's excellent *ceviche*, sushi and endless preparations of shrimp and fish (the *chiletepin* sauce packs a fiery wallop).

Getting There & Away

AIR

The Los Mochis airport is about 14km south of the city off the road to Topolobampo. Daily direct flights (all with connections to other cities) are offered by **Aeroméxico/Aeroméxico Connect** (☎ 812-01-40) to Mexico City, Hermosillo and Guadalajara. **Aero California** (☎ 800-080-90-90) flies to Guadalajara, La Paz, Mexico City and Tijuana. **Alma** (☎ 817-47-67; www.alma.com .mx) flies daily to La Paz, Guadalajara, Tijuana and Puerto Vallarta.

BOAT

Ferries go from Topolobampo, 24km southwest of Los Mochis, to La Paz, Baja California Sur; they leave at 11pm daily. Tickets are sold

NORTHWEST MEXICO

by **Baja Ferries** (www.bajaferries.com.mx) at the ferry terminal in Topolobampo (right). In Los Mochis, **Viajes Flamingo** (☎ 812-818-16-13; www .mexicoscoppercanyon.com; Hotel Santa Anita, cnr Leyva & Hidalgo) sells tickets up to a month in advance. Buses head to Topolobampo consistently throughout the day (M$20).

BUS

In what was surely a bid to win you over with convenience, Los Mochis' numerous bus stations are spread all over town. Elite, Futura and Transportes Chihuahuenses (all 1st-class) share a large **bus terminal** (☎ 812-57-49; cnr Blvd Castro & Constitución) several blocks east of the center. Other 1st-class bus lines have their own terminals, such as **Transportes Norte de Sonora** (☎ 812-17-57; Moreles) and **Transportes del Pacífico** (☎ 812-03-47), who share a small station on Morelos between Zaragoza and Leyva, and **Estrellas del Pacífico** (☎ 818-96-14) next door. These all serve more or less the same major regional destinations. **Tufesa** (☎ 818-22-22; www.tufesa.com.mx), on Zapata between Juárez and Merlos, goes north to Nogales and south to Culiacán on a limited schedule as well as once daily to Los Angeles (12:20pm, 24 hours). **TAP** (☎ 817-59-07; www .tap.com.mx; cnr Blvd Castro & Belizario) is next to the main bus terminal and heads to Mexico City, Guadalajara and Mazatlán among others. **Autotransportes Norte de Sinaloa** (☎ 818-03-57; www.nortedesinaloa.com.mx), at Zaragoza and Ordoñez, has 2nd-class buses to Culiacán and Mazatlán. **Azules del Noroeste** (☎ 812-34-94) goes to El Fuerte and the airport five times a day from a small station on Callejón Juan Escutia.

Destinations served include the following (fares given are 1st-class):

Destination	Fare	Duration
El Fuerte	M$55	2hr
Guadalajara	M$545	12hr
Guaymas	M$180	5hr
Hermosillo	M$250	7hr
Los Angeles	M$1215	24hr
Mazatlán	M$275	6hr
Nogales	M$400	12hr
Topolobampo	M$13	45min

TRAIN

For much more about the train journey between Los Mochis and Chihuahua, see opposite.

The train station is 8km east of the center on Serrano. The ticket window is open from 5am to 7am daily for the morning's departures toward the Copper Canyon and Chihuahua. Tickets are also sold inside the **office** (☎ 824-11-51; ☾ 9am-5:30pm Mon-Fri, 10am-12:30pm Sat, 8-10am Sun).

You can buy *primera express* (1st-class) tickets up to one week in advance of travel. Tickets for *clase económica* (economy-class) trains are sold an hour before the train departs, or the day before. You can also purchase tickets for the same price in *primera express* (if you pay cash) and for an 8% fee in *clase económica* one day in advance through Hotel Santa Anita's in-house travel agency, **Viajes Flamingo** (☎ 818-16-13; www.mexicos coppercanyon.com; cnr Leyva & Hidalgo).

The *primera express* train leaves Los Mochis at 6am, and the *clase económica* at 7am. See the boxed text, p343) for fares and schedules.

Getting Around

Nearly everything of interest to travelers in Los Mochis is within walking distance of the city center. Taxis queue up on Obregón, right in front of the Best Western. A taxi to the airport costs approximately M$140.

'Estación' (or 'Ruta 72') buses to the train station (M$4.50, 20 minutes) depart every 30 minutes between 5am and 8pm from Blvd Castro, between Zaragoza and Prieta. You can take the bus to the station for the *clase económica* train, which departs at 7am, but for the 6am *primera express* departure it's probably safer to fork out M$50 for a taxi.

TOPOLOBAMPO
☎ 668

The second-largest natural deepwater port in the world, 24km southwest of Los Mochis, enjoyed a fleeting glimpse of pop-culture cool when it was the set for a popular Mexican *telenovela* (it was surely picked for its ridiculously awesome name). Unfortunately, there is nothing else terribly awesome about Topolobampo, though it was once the terminus for the Copper Canyon railway train. Now that the train goes no further than Los Mochis, the main importer of visitors here is the ferry that goes between the mainland and La Paz, in Baja.

For lodging, the only game in town is the **Hotel Marina** (☎ 862-01-00; Albert K Owen 33 Pte;

NORTHWEST MEXICO

r M$350; P), an aged inn though the pool and restaurant are nice enough if you're in from La Paz at 9pm. It's easy to find; just follow the signs to the town center.

To make the five-hour excursion over to Baja, you can buy same-day tickets from **Baja Ferries** (862-10-03; www.bajaferries.com; Terminal de Transbordadores; 9am-10:30pm). Passenger fares are M$750 in *salón;* cabins for up to four people cost M$760 extra. Passenger ferries leave at 11:30pm daily, arriving in La Paz at 5am. Returning ferries leave La Paz at 3pm, arriving in Topolobampo at 9pm the same night. See p306 for vehicle fares.

BARRANCA DEL COBRE

Of all the things to see and do in northwest Mexico, none compare in awe and wonder to the dramatic Barranca del Cobre (Copper Canyon). It's a series of more than 20 spectacular canyons that altogether comprise a region that's four times larger than the Grand Canyon in Arizona, and in several parts it's much deeper. Imagine for a moment if a jagged key the size of the Florida panhandle was scraped across a car the size of North Carolina – the resulting damage would be akin to Copper Canyon's stunning chasms.

The best part about the region is that you can travel right up, over and through some of the steepest areas on the Ferrocarril Chihuahua Pacífico (Chihuahua-Pacific Railway, also known as the Copper Canyon Railway), which takes passengers on a scenic journey over 655km of impressively laid rails. The train, which travels between Los Mochis at its western terminus and Chihuahua in the Midwest, is the most popular way to see the canyons. For more, see p343.

The name Copper Canyon, which was misleadingly named by the Spanish (they mistook the greenish-glow of lichen for copper as they traipsed through the area), refers specifically to the stunning Barranca de Urique – which, at an altitude of only 500m (but 1879m deep), is the canyon's deepest point.

The Barranca de Urique has a subtropical climate, while the peaks high above are 2300m above sea level, and are home to conifers and evergreens. The entire region is also home to one of Mexico's largest groups of indigenous people, the Rarámuri (see the boxed text, p346).

Though many people simply ride the train all the way through and then stop overnight before returning, this is an injustice: the best way to truly experience the Barranca del Cobre region is to make a few stops along the way. Creel (p349), approximately eight hours from Los Mochis, is where most people (especially backpackers) choose to break the journey, as it's near plenty of good spots for exploring, and is a town full of traveler amenities. Overnight stays are also possible at Cerocahui, Urique, Posada Barrancas and Divisadero, each allowing you 24 hours before the train passes by again – time enough to get a closer look and explore the canyons.

Many travelers prefer to visit the area in spring or autumn, when the temperatures are not too hot at the bottom of the canyon (as in summer), or too cold at the top (as in winter). A particularly good time to come is late September and October (after the summer rains), when the vegetation is still green. Things dry up from February to June, but you can still glimpse some wildflowers.

FERROCARRIL CHIHUAHUA PACÍFICO

One of the world's most scenic rail journeys, the Ferrocarril Chihuahua Pacífico (Copper Canyon Railway) is also a considerable feat of engineering: it has 37 bridges and 86 tunnels along its 653km of railway line, and connects the mountainous, arid interior of northern Mexico with a town just 24km shy of the Pacific coast. The line, which was opened in 1961 after many decades of building, is now the major link between Chihuahua and the coast, and is used heavily not only by passengers but also for freight. The beauty of the landscape it traverses – sweeping mountain vistas, sheer canyon walls, sparkling lakes and fields of flowers, most of it free of humans and development of any kind – has made it one of Mexico's prime tourist excursions.

The Ferrocarril Chihuahua Pacífico (CHEPE, pronounced *che*-pe) operates two trains: the 1st-class *primera express,* which costs twice as much but makes fewer stops and has a restaurant and bar; and the cheaper and slower *clase económica,* which has a snack bar. Cars on both trains have air-conditioning and heating. The *clase económica* is certainly nice enough for most tourists, so the issue comes down to time – it takes at least 14 hours to make the one-way trip on the *primera*

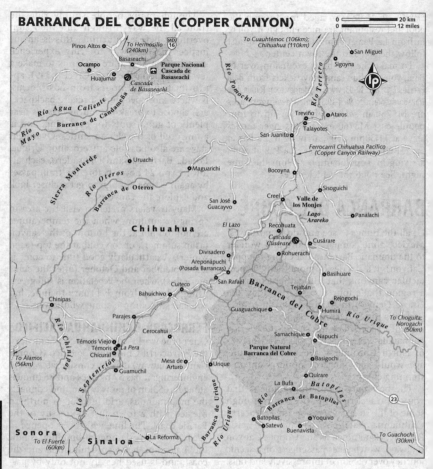

BARRANCA DEL COBRE (COPPER CANYON)

0   20 km
0   12 miles

express, and at least two hours longer on the *clase económica,* which stops frequently along the way.

If you're heading toward Los Mochis from Chihuahua, consider taking the *primera express,* as the *clase económica* runs later and is often behind schedule anyway, and passes much of the best scenery (between Creel and El Fuerte) after dark, especially in winter when the sun sets earlier. Heading in the other direction, you should be able to see the best views on either train, unless the *clase económica* is excessively delayed.

The majority of the good views are on the right side of the carriage heading inland (east), while the left side is best for trips going to the coast (west); if you've got an advance ticket

that's not on the side you were hoping for, just ask the conductor to switch you. Wherever your seat, it's fun to congregate in the vestibules between cars, where the windows open and you can take unobstructed photos and feel the fresh mountain air whoosh past your face.

Between Los Mochis and El Fuerte, the train passes through flat, gray farmland. Shortly after, it begins to climb through fog-shrouded hills speckled with dark pillars of cacti. It passes over the long Río Fuerte bridge and through the first of 87 tunnels about three hours after leaving Los Mochis. Along the way, the train cuts through small canyons (snaking through three ascending loops known as La Pera at Témoris, for its shape like a pear) and hugs the sides of dramatic cliffs as it climbs higher

NORTHWEST MEXICO

and higher through the mountains of the Sierra Tarahumara until the highlight: when the train stops at Divisadero, where you get your first and only glimpse of the actual Barranca del Cobre. The train circles back over itself in a complete loop inside the canyon again at El Lazo before steaming into Creel and Chihuahua.

Tickets

Primera express tickets can be purchased up to one week in advance, while tickets for *clase económica* trains can only be purchased one day in advance. Tickets don't usually require advance purchase, but you definitely shouldn't just walk up during Semana Santa, July or August, or at Christmas.

For a same-day *primera express* ticket, it's prudent to go to the ticket office by 5am, if you're at **Los Mochis station** (☎ 668-824-11-51; ☿ ticket window 5-7am & 9am-5:30pm Mon-Fri, 5-7am & 10am-12:30pm Sat, 5-7am & 8-10am Sun) or **Chihuahua station** (☎ 614-439-72-12; ☿ ticket window 5-7am &

RAILWAY SCHEDULE – FERROCARRIL CHIHUAHUA PACÍFICO

Both the *primera express* and *clase económica* trains run every day. Trains tend to run late, and the times given below comprise just a rough guideline. You will hear people talk about 'normal' times as if they are official due to years of experience with the train. This is worth a listen. Though the train *can* run on time, it has also been known to show up two hours earlier or later than times shown here, so it's best to check with your hotel, at the train stations or with train conductors for the latest schedules. Also, if you are leaving Chihuahua on the *primera express* with hopes of making it to the Baja ferry from Topolobampo that same day, don't count on it. It almost never works out. The *clase económica* train, which is much slower, often arrives at the end of the line around 1:30am. There is no time change between Los Mochis and Chihuahua.

EASTBOUND – LOS MOCHIS TO CHIHUAHUA

	Primera Express Train 75		Clase Económica Train No 75	
Station	Arrives	Fare from Los Mochis	Arrives	Fare from Los Mochis
Los Mochis	6am (departs Los Mochis)	–	7am (departs Los Mochis)	–
El Fuerte	8:30am	M$267	10:15am	M$133
Témoris	11:26am	M$475	1:55pm	M$238
Bahuichivo	12:27pm	M$562	3:10pm	M$281
San Rafael	1:20pm	M$633	4:25pm	M$317
Posada Barrancas	1:40pm	M$655	4:50pm	M$328
Divisadero	1:45pm	M$664	4:55pm	M$332
Creel	3:24pm	M$793	6pm	M$397
Cuauhtémoc	6:23pm	M$1155	10:35pm	M$578
Chihuahua	8:45pm	M$1451	1:30am	M$726

WESTBOUND – CHIHUAHUA TO LOS MOCHIS

	Primera Express Train 74		Clase Económica Train No 76	
Station	Arrives	Fare from Chihuahua	Arrives	Fare from Chihuahua
Chihuahua	6am (departs Chihuahua)	–	7am (departs Chihuahua)	–
Cuauhtémoc	8:15am	M$295	9:55am	M$148
Creel	11:15am	M$660	1:20pm	M$330
Divisadero	12:34pm	M$789	3:25pm	M$399
Posada Barrancas	1pm	M$820	3:30pm	M$399
San Rafael	1:18pm	M$875	4:45pm	M$410
Bahuichivo	2:17pm	M$891	5:10pm	M$446
Témoris	3:15pm	M$978	6:25pm	M$489
El Fuerte	6:10pm	M$1271	10:23pm	M$636
Los Mochis	8:50pm	M$1451	1:30am	M$726

10am-5:30pm Mon- Fri, 5-7am & 9am-12:30pm Sat, 5-7am Sun). Note that advanced sales to the general public are only available in Los Mochis, Creel (*primera express* only, from 11am) and Chihuahua. If you board anywhere else, you have to purchase tickets on the train with cash only, and you do run the risk that they might be sold out by then. Alternatively, any of the many **Balderrama Hotels** (☎ 668-712-16-23, www.mexicoscoppercanyon.com) assist their clients in making reservations for the same cost as the station if you pay cash.

EL FUERTE

☎ 698 / pop 11,920 / elevation 180m

It's not as charming or wealthy as Álamos, but El Fuerte, a sleepy and picturesque little town surrounded by one of Latin America's last standing dry tropical forests, isn't a victim of an expat occupation either. Noted for its colonial ambience, its Spanish architecture and, mostly, for being a good starting or ending point for a trip on the Copper Canyon Railway, El Fuerte has a stuck-in-time feel that probably won't last too much longer.

Founded in 1564 by the Spanish Francisco de Ibarra, El Fuerte – named for its 17th-century fort that Spaniards built to protect settlers from various natives – was an important Spanish settlement throughout the colonial period. For more than three centuries it was a major farming and commercial center, and a trading post on El Camino Real, the Spanish mule trail between Guadalajara and Álamos. In 1824 El Fuerte became the capital of the state of Sinaloa, and remained so for several years.

El Fuerte is usually swarming with bus tours, but independent travelers are starting to find their way here as well. There's not a lot to do in town, but as more indie-minded operators begin to open shop here, the wealth of offerings in the surrounding countryside should begin to see more visitors.

Information

3Amigos Too (☎ 893-50-28; www.amigos3.com; Rosales 104; ☸ 9am-7pm) All of your Copper Canyon needs can be handled by the newly opened El Fuerte offices of this highly regarded Creel operator. They also offer river and hiking tours around El Fuerte and rent kayaks, 4WDs, scooters and bicycles for self-guided tours in the area.

Amigo Trails (☎ 456-00-36; www.amigotrails .com; Rosales 104) The new travel agency, located inside 3Amigos Too and in Creel, books accommodations along

the way, and plans on eventually booking train tickets. It is the only inbound agency within the canyon boundaries. Inquire here about its new boutique hotel as well.

Bancomer (cnr Constitución & Juárez; ☸ 8:30am-4pm Mon-Fri) If you're starting your train journey here, load up on cash. There are no banks between here and Creel and the ATM in Creel is often picky.

Hospital Rural IMSS Solidaridad (☎ 893-07-70; Rebeca Serna s/n)

Police (☎ 893-03-07)

Post Office (Calle 5 de Mayo s/n; ☸ 8am-4pm) Inside the Palacio Municipal.

Uri@s Ciber C@fé (☎ 893-06-15; Juárez 103; per hr M$10; ☸ 8am-8pm Mon-Sat, 9am-3pm Sun) Internet access close to the 3Amigos office.

Sights and Activities

The Palacio Municipal, plaza and church are El Fuerte's most notable features (the Hotel Posada del Hidalgo, though historic, is very underwhelming). You can visit the **Museo de El Fuerte** (☎ 893-15-01; admission M$5; ☸ 9am-8pm), a replica of the original fort, at the top of the town's small *mirador* – called Cerro de las Pilas. This is an excellent vantage point of the town, its surrounding area and the wide Río Fuerte. It's an especially dramatic view at sunset.

Sleeping

El Fuerte as a destination was all but created by packaged group tours, so many hotels are often booked solid. It's best to reserve here on the early side. Most spots will agree to keep an eye on your car – which can be safely parked on the street near the inn – while you're off on the rails.

Hotel Real de Carapoa (☎ 893-17-96; Paseo de la Juventude 102; s/d M$400/450; ☒) A newer, cheaper offering right off the main square. Unfortunately, the sizable rooms here – all with king-size bed – aren't as colorful as the common area, but they are good value when all's said and done. There's free coffee as well.

Río Vista Lodge (☎ 893-04-13; Junto Al Museo Mirador; r M$500; P ☒ ☒) This rustic hotel at the top of the *mirador* does indeed boast lovely views of the river, especially from its peaceful, high-altitude backyard. The owner, an avid birder, has built it room by room from the ground up. Three new rooms offer excellent river views and slate floors and bathrooms. The whole place is a little rural treasure, full of quirky touches like Revolution Winchester rifles and birdfeeders.

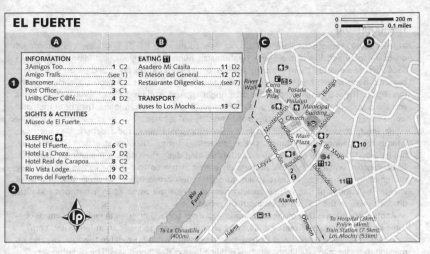

EL FUERTE

0   200 m
0   0.1 miles

INFORMATION
3Amigos Too....................................1 C2
Amigo Trails..............................(see 1)
Bancomer..2 C2
Post Office.....................................3 C1
Uri@s Ciber C@fé.......................4 D2

SIGHTS & ACTIVITIES
Museo de El Fuerte.....................5 C1

SLEEPING
Hotel El Fuerte.............................6 C1
Hotel La Choza.............................7 D2
Hotel Real de Carapoa..............8 C1
Río Vista Lodge............................9 C1
Torres del Fuerte.......................10 D2

EATING
Asadero Mi Casita......................11 D2
El Mesón del General...............12 D2
Restaurante Diligencias.......(see 7)

TRANSPORT
Buses to Los Mochis..................13 C2

Hotel La Choza (☎ 893-12-74; www.hotellachoza.com; Calle 5 de Mayo 101; r M$575-690; P ⊠ ⊠ ⊠) A good midrange option not lacking in style: brick domed ceilings (on the top floors), colorful tile work, moody lighting, brightly sponge-painted walls, cool stone floors and colorful Mexican sinks. The excellent onsite restaurant and private parking lot are also pluses.

Hotel El Fuerte (☎ 893-02-26; Montesclaros 37; r M$750-900; ⊠) The El Fuerte looks like a drunk mariachi swallowed a piñata and threw up all over the place: The clichéd design here is a little over the top. Still, rooms in this 17th-century mansion do have some charm and are set around large, flowering courtyards.

our pick Torres del Fuerte (☎ 893-19-74; www .hotelestorres.com; Robles 102; r M$1000-1500; P ⊠ ⊠) Francisco Torres has turned his family's 400-year-old hacienda into a beautiful boutique hotel. A gorgeous ménage-à-trois of colonial relic, rustic elegance and contemporary art characterizes this new property, from the rescued antique doors to the excavated original columns to the recycled bricks and beams. All 25 rooms are uniquely themed, many with beautiful slate bathrooms and exposed adobe and brick walls. The bar and restaurant are housed within an old foreman's house and ancient Jesuit-built chapel. For the same price, it would be unthinkable not to stay here over Posada del Hidalgo.

Eating

There is a wealth of freshwater on the outskirts of El Fuerte, which produces local specialties you should definitely not leave town without sampling: *cauques* (sweetwater lobster) and *lobina* (black bass).

Asadero Mi Casita (cnr Robles & Zaragoza; mains M$10-55; ⏱ 6pm-1am Wed-Mon) This joint is popular for the house specialty, *papa asada*: grilled beef, loads of gooey cheese, potatoes and butter that you wrap up in tortillas. Legendary!

El Mesón del General (☎ 893-02-60; Juárez 202; mains M$55-198; ⏱ 8am-11pm) The most traditional of El Fuerte's options, this institution serves up several styles of octopus (*polpo*) and offers the best deal on *lobina* and *cauque*: a M$150 combo plate.

La Canastilla (☎ 893-18-64; Juárez 510; mains M$58-185; ⏱ 9am-9pm) The town's main restaurants serve more or less the same dishes, but the food at this riverside spot trumps them all. The stuffed shrimp (*camerónes rellenos*) and flambéed black bass (*flameado*) are both rich and exquisite.

Restaurant Diligencias (☎ 893-12-74; Hotel La Choza, Calle 5 de Mayo 101; mains M$78-178; ⏱ 7am-11pm) Another great spot for *lobina* (try it breaded *zarandeado*-style) and scrumptious *cauques* – expensive but worth it. The breakfast *chilaquiles* are also wonderful.

Getting There & Around

The roads in and out of El Fuerte have seen their share of roadwork in recent years, so if you're driving, the approach from all directions is paved and safe with the exception of the small road from Álamos – you still need a 4WD from there.

NORTHWEST MEXICO

THE RARÁMURI

At least 50,000 indigenous Rarámuri (do not refer to them as the Tarahumara; it is considered politically incorrect) live in the Sierra Tarahumara's numerous canyons, including the Barranca del Cobre. You will see them – mostly women, dressed in colorful skirts and blouses, peddling beautiful hand-woven baskets and carrying infants on their backs – as you travel deeper into this region. The women are known for their bright apparel, while most men wear Western jeans and shirts (except in more remote areas, where you'll still see men in loincloths); both men and women wear sandals hewn from tire-tread and strips of leather.

'Rarámuri' means 'those who run fast' – an appropriate name for a people who are most famous for running long distances swiftly, sometimes up to 20 hours at a time. Traditionally, the Rarámuri hunted by chasing down and exhausting deer, then driving the animals over cliffs to be impaled on wooden sticks strategically placed at the bottom of the canyon. Today, they run grueling footraces of at least 160km through rough canyons, all the while kicking a small wooden ball ahead of them. Their famous runners have also competed in marathons and ultra distance races in the US and throughout the world.

Another tradition is that of the *tesquinada,* a raucous social gathering in which Rarámuris consume copious amounts of *tesquino,* a potent alcoholic beverage made from fermented corn.

Though many are determined to remain isolated within this formidable topography, and do manage to retain many traditions (such as residing in cave dwellings), it will be clear the very first time you see a bargain-happy tourist trying to save M$10 on a basket that the Rarámuri way of life is under serious threat. Between the rapid loss of their language and severe degradation of their environment – by logging, mining, drug cultivation and tourist-based development – the line between the Rarámuri and other Mexicans becomes thinner every day. Because of that, their overwhelming poverty (more than 40% have no income) becomes more and more of an issue. Poor health is also problematic; there are high rates of infant mortality and teenage pregnancy among Rarámuris (it is not uncommon for girls to be taken out of school and married by the age of 14), with some of the only relief coming from Catholic missionaries.

If you want to help, you can purchase Rarámuri wares at Artesanías Misión (p352) in Creel, which donates proceeds to help provide free health care for the Rarámuri; and you can make good use of their ecotourism options outside Creel at Complejo Ecoturístico Arareko (p353). Though donating Western clothes is inappropriate, you can donate 10m of brightly colored cloth so they may continue to make their own garments according to tradition. 3Amigos in Creel (see p350) regularly accepts donations both for the Rarámuri and down-on-their-luck Mexicans as well.

Buses to Los Mochis (M$55, two hours) depart every half-hour between 5am and 7pm from the corner of Juárez and 16 de Septiembre.

The train station is a few kilometers east of town. The departure time for the eastbound *primera express* is 8:30am, though it never arrives before 9am, with the *clase económica* trailing about an hour and a half to two hours behind. You can take a taxi to the station for about M$100.

CEROCAHUI

☎ 635 / pop 1550 / elevation 1600m

Cerocahui is a hub for local travelers and a place where tourists rarely disembark, but those that do are greeted with a tiny pueblo in the middle of a verdant and picturesque valley. Access to Cerocahui is from Bahuichivo station, two stops after El Fuerte and one stop past Témoris. Here and in and around Urique is where you'll get your first glimpse of the Rarámuri (see the boxed text, above), as many live in this area, though they don't come out in droves hawking their beautiful wares until San Rafael.

The town's pretty yellow-domed church, **San Francisco Javier de Cerocahui**, was founded in 1680 by the Jesuit Padre Juan María de Salvatierra. Today, Cerocahui is an *ejido* (communal landholding) dedicated to forestry. It boasts a few good lodging options, a boarding school for Rarámuri girls, a peaceful atmosphere and, best of all, proximity to the surrounding countryside – excellent for bird-watching (over 225 species of birds have been spotted here), hiking and horseback riding.

Any of the hotels here can arrange trips into the canyon, and can pick you up at the train station for the 40-minute, 16km drive into town.

Sleeping & Eating

Cerocahui has a handful of choices for all budgets.

Hotel Paraíso del Oso (☎ in Chihuahua 614-421-33-72, in the US 800-844-3107; www.mexicohorse.com; campsite/dm M$50/100, s/d incl meals & transfers M$1210/1870; P ☒ ☐) Paraíso del Oso occupies a peaceful and picturesque spot just north of Cerocahui village. The down-to-earth vibe here is one that emphasizes ecotourism, bird-watching and equestrian tours. Vegetarian meals are available, as are riverside campsites and five dorm beds. The management can also arrange horseback-riding tours (there are 20 horses on the property) and hiking trips throughout the surrounding area.

Hotel Plaza (☎ 456-52-56; s/d M$200/300) Offers tidy and colorful budget rooms on the main plaza with TV and wood-burning stove.

Cabañas San Isidro (☎ 456-52-57; www.coppercanyonamigos.com; s/d incl all meals & transfers M$900/1300) Perched in the surrounding hillsides 8km from town, this newer, family-run lodge offers charming pine cabins on a rustic working ranch. Rooms have wood-burning stoves, pine furniture, bottle-built stained-glass windows, mural-painted walls and cozy Rarámuri throws. The food is unsophisticated but tasty.

Hotel Misión (☎ in Los Mochis 668-818-70-46; www.hotelmision.com; s/d incl all meals & transfers M$1963.50/2572.50; P ☒) The oldest and best-known hotel in Cerocahui and yet another link in the underwhelming Balderrama chain of Barranca del Cobre hotels, this former hacienda has rustic rooms complete with wood-burning stoves, a bar, a restaurant, gardens and a pool table. Ten new rooms overlook the small vineyard.

Getting There & Away

All the hotels except the Hotel Plaza will pick you up at the Bahuichivo train station, and you can always catch a ride with one of the other hotels' buses, or pick up a lift by thumb. The daily 'school' bus from Bahuichivo to Urique may drop you off in Cerocahui for M$30 if it's not too full.

URIQUE
☎ 635 / pop 1500 / elevation 550m

This starry-skied village, at the bottom of the impressive Barranca de Urique, is also accessed from the Bahuichivo train stop, and is a good base for all kinds of canyon hikes lasting anywhere from one to several days. The three- to four-day hike between Batopilas and Urique is a popular trek. If you organize it on your own, the going rate with a guide is M$1000 per person. For more comfort you may contact **EcoTravel Mexico** (☎ in Chihuahua 614-179-03-92; www.ecotravel-mexico.com; hikes per person from M$1320), which organizes the trip with guides certified by the National Outdoor Leadership School and Leave No Trace.

A mini school bus heads down to Urique from Bahuichivo train station once a day after the last train passes the station (around 4pm, though an earlier bus may be sent if enough people disembark on the *primera express* train). The jarring ride (M$115, three hours) makes a breathtaking 1050m descent on loose gravel and dirt into the Barranca de Urique, the deepest of the canyons. Sit on the right side for all the bare-knuckle views. It departs for the return trip at around 8am (it runs up and down the main street – just flag it down). Alternatively, you may be able to arrange transportation with your hotel in Urique. Hotels in Cerocahui can also arrange for guided trips down into this deep canyon town. Keep in mind, Urique is rural – more Tecates are passed around here than educations – and marijuana fuels the local economy (you thought Rarámuri baskets bought those brand-new Ford trucks?), so be extra wary about town.

Urique has only a few accommodations. **Entre Amigos** (www.amongamigos.com; camp/dm M$50/75, r M$250) is a great option for independent backpackers. Just outside town, it's more peaceful, and the American-run spot has nice stone cabins, dorm rooms, camping sites and a big communal kitchen. Watch out for scorpions!

Hotel Barrancas de Urique (☎ 456-60-76; Principal 201; r M$250-300; ☒) is definitely the nicest and cleanest spot, on the main road at the edge of the river. Bear in mind, though, that the rowdy cantina below can seriously stint your shuteye.

Hotel Estrella del Río (☎ 456-60-03; r M$400; ☒) offers rooms (some with air-con) with commanding views of the Río Urique and surrounding mountains. Inquire at **Restaurant Plaza** (☺ 6am-9pm), across from the plaza, which, incidentally, is the only good and clean spot to eat (the specialty, *aguachile*, is a soupy shrimp cocktail full of onions and tomatoes and spiced up with *chiletepin* peppers, served in a *molcajete*).

POSADA BARRANCAS
☎ 635 / pop 350 / elevation 2220m
About 5km southwest of Divisadero, Posada Barrancas station is next to Areponápuchi, the only village on the train line that is right on the rim of the canyon. Often referred to as Arepo, this village – made up of just a couple of dozen houses, a tiny church and a handful of inns – is where it all comes together for the first time: spectacular views of the canyon dangle precariously under the patios of a few hotels here, making it a don't-miss stopover. Arepo is also a good base for going into the canyon by foot, car or on horseback. Most of the hotels will organize any kind of canyon trip you would like, be it a hike to the rim or a horseback ride down into the deep village Wakajípare, below. If you want to set off on your own, take the trail down to the left of the entrance to Hotel Mirador. Plan on four hours down, six back up (though the Rarámuri do it in three) and carry plenty of food and water as well as layered clothing.

Sleeping & Eating
Cabañas Díaz (☎ 578-30-08; large r with 8 bunks M$100, 1-3-person cabaña with shared/private bathroom M$250/400, 3-5-person cabaña with private bathroom M$600; P) The Díaz family's guest lodge is known for its hospitality, delicious meals (M$70) and tranquil atmosphere. Its various cabins and rooms are basic and cozy, with fireplaces and firm beds, and the family can help arrange custom trips. If no one from here comes to meet the train, just walk down the main road into the village until you see the sign on the right (about 10 minutes).

Cabañas Arepo Barrancas (☎ 578-30-46; s/d incl breakfast M$300/400; P) This is the best budget option – tiled floors, comfy beds – though it's a bit further from the canyon rim. Get one of the six new cabañas here and you've robbed them at these prices. Look for María Dolores at the station – she works the middle food stall – or walk through town five minutes past the sign for Cabañas Diaz. It's on the left. Meals here cost M$35 to M$45.

Hotel Mansión Rarámuri (☎ 800-777-46-68, in Chihuahua 614-415-47-21; incl meals & transfers s M$1210-

1600, d M$1716-2300; P 🐕 ♿) Dubbed 'El Castillo' because it looks like a medieval stone castle, this quirky resort has a variety of cozy, rustic cabins, but the true gems are 17 new rooms on the rim of the canyon with plush beds and wood-beam ceilings. They are more comfortable than the Mirador and boast more or less the same view for M$685 less.

Hotel Posada Mirador (☎ in Los Mochis 668-812-16-13, in the US 888-528-8401; www.mexicoscoppercanyon .com/mirador; s/d incl meals & transfers M$1985/2985; P) One night here costs more than the entire rail journey in 1st class and it's often overrun with tour groups, but this, the only jewel in the Balderrama chain's monopoly, boasts spectacular views from each room's private balcony. Communal meals aren't Michelinworthy but suffice. Since the main attraction here is drinking in the view, the 6pm to 7pm nightly Happy Hour ain't too shabby, either.

Getting There & Away
See the railway schedule on p343 for information on getting to Posada Barrancas by train. Buses between San Rafael and Creel will drop you off in Areponápuchi at the highway entrance (see p353). The bus is much faster and cheaper than the train, but arrange for transportation to the center of town, as there are no taxis.

DIVISADERO
elevation 2240m
If you don't overnight in Posada Barrancas, then Divisidero, definitely a train stop rather than an actual village, will be your first and only chance to see into the miraculous canyon from the train. Luckily, the train stops for 15 minutes, giving you enough time to jump out, gawk and snap some photos at the viewpoint and hop back on. But be prepared to budget your time more carefully, as the place is also a Rarámuri market and spectacular food court. *Gorditas*, tacos and *chiles rellenos*, cooked up in makeshift oil-drum stoves, are worth the stop alone. Just ask for Lucy González. Her food is like edible art. Gobble it all up quickly – the conductors aren't supposed to allow food back onto the train.

If you decide you want to stay longer than 15 minutes, you can check into the **Hotel Divisadero Barrancas** (☎ in the US 888-232-4219, in Chihuahua 614-415-11-99; s/d incl meals Jun-Aug M$1100/1600, Sep-May M$1780/2150), right at the train station, which has 52 beautiful rooms with wood-beam ceilings and views of the canyon. The restaurant-bar, with a spectacular view, is open to the public (overall, this is the most charming option between Posada Barrancas and Divisidero). Get a newer room (numbers 35 to 52) for the best vistas. You can also spend more time here without spending the night if you switch from a *primera express* to *clase económica* train, which is officially three hours behind but often times more like an hour. You will need two separate tickets to do this. Buses also run to Creel six times a day (M$37, one hour), a shorter and slightly cheaper way than continuing on the train. For information on getting to Divisadero by train, see the railway schedule on p343.

CREEL
☎ 635 / pop 5340 / elevation 2338m

Creel, surrounded by pine forests and interesting rock formations, is an unexpected surprise. Oddly, its location and log-fueled architecture feel vaguely reminiscent of an alpine village, albeit a very red, white and green one. Filled with the multi-hued Rarámuri, Creel is (at least for now) a perfect little marriage of travelers and tradition and an excellent base for exploring the surrounding area's numerous natural attractions.

It fully established itself as a traveler's hub in the '90s, and now hotels and guesthouses line the main drags, tour-guide companies are aplenty, and backpackers can be seen stalking up and down the streets in search of bargains several times a day after the train comes through. Unlike many of the towns along the railway, Creel has some fun watering holes and great bargain accommodations and several opportunities for shopping – be it for Rarámuri crafts and Mata Ortiz pottery, or to just stock up on a bit of civilization. There isn't a charming plaza or significant historical relic to explore in town, but from here you can venture out into the rest of the Barranca del Cobre, whether it be down into the canyon village of Batopilas or to nearby Lago Arareko.

Its high elevation means Creel can be very cold in winter, even snowy; and it's none too warm at night in autumn, either. In summer, the cool air and pine-tree aroma from the town's surrounding forests are a welcome relief from the heat of the tropical coastal lowlands and the deserts of northern Mexico. Bring a sweater, even if the rest of Mexico is scorching.

Orientation

Creel is a very small town. Most things you need, including many hotels and restaurants, are on Av López Mateos, the town's main street. This leads south from the town plaza, the site of two churches, the post office, the bank and the Artesanías Misión shop. The train station is one block north of the plaza. Across the tracks are a couple more hotels and restaurants, as well as the bus station.

Av Gran Visión is the highway through town; it heads northeast to Chihuahua and southeast to Guachochi, passing Lago Arareko and Cusárare. There is a paved road that runs southwest from Creel through Divisadero and on to San Rafael. Av López Mateos and Av Gran Visión intersect a couple of kilometers south of the center of town.

Information

Information about local attractions is available from the tour operators and most accommodations. There is fierce competition for tour business, so be sure to compare prices. You can get laundry service at Casa Margarita (p350) for M$50 per load – just don't expect it folded. 3Amigos Canyon Expeditions (p350) is a great source for local info.

Cascada.net (Av López Mateos 49; per hr M$20; �***◌*** 8am-10pm) Internet access.

Clínica Santa Teresa (☎ 456-01-05; ***◌*** 24hr) Behind Casa Margarita.

CompuCenter (Av López Mateos 33; per hr M$20; ***◌*** 9am-10pm Mon-Sat, 9am-5pm Sun) Internet access.

Divisas La Sierra (Av López Mateos 59) Changes US dollars and traveler's checks.

Police station (☎ 060) On the plaza.

Post office (***◌*** 9am-3pm Mon-Fri) On the plaza.

Santander (Av López Mateos 17; ***◌*** 9am-4pm Mon-Fri) ATM.

Sights & Activities

The **Casa de las Artesanías del Estado de Chihuahua y Museo** (☎ 456-00-80; admission M$10; ***◌*** 9am-6pm Mon-Sat, 9am-1pm Sun), overlooking the plaza, is a great spot to delve deeper into Rarámuri culture. There are excellent exhibits with text in English on Rarámuri culture and crafts along with gorgeous woven baskets, traditional clothing, pottery, black-and-white photos and more.

Tours

Most of Creel's hotels offer tours of the surrounding area, with trips to canyons, rivers,

NORTHWEST MEXICO

hot springs, waterfalls and other places. Trips range from a seven-hour tour to the bottom of the Barranca de Urique to an eight-hour excursion to Mennonite settlements in Cuauhtémoc, and overnight excursions to Batopilas, a wonderful canyon village, which descends from an altitude of 2338m at Creel to 495m, via a winding dirt road. This is also prime riding country, and many of Creel's nearby attractions can be enjoyed from horseback; or you can rent a bicycle or scooter and venture out on your own. The whole area is a mountain bike playground and, depending on your skill and fitness level, you could just rent a bike for a few days and take in all the area's attractions without a guide. For those who want just a taste, the most popular mountain biking excursions are to the Valley of the Frogs, Mushrooms and Monks (named for the fat, squashed; thin, big-headed; and tall, slender rock formations that resemble each, respectively), and to the Rarámuri stronghold of Lago Arareko. 3Amigos (below) can give you self-guided maps for the rides.

All tours require a minimum number of people. The easiest place to get a group together is often at Casa Margarita (right); if you're sleeping elsewhere, wander over around 9am. You can also hire your own private guide. Expect to pay around M$300 per person, per day – and much more if you are doing a bigger trip that requires a vehicle and driver; to Batopilas, for example, a private driver with an SUV will run to around M$3000 for one night.

3Amigos Canyon Expeditions (☎ 456-00-36; www .amigos3.com; Av López Mateos 46) Though they now offer guided private tours as well, 3Amigos built their excellent reputation on helping you to 'be your own guide in the Copper Canyon!' by selling self-guided tour packages with Nissan trucks, scooters and mountain bikes. Packages range from M$150 to M$3000 per day, and sometimes include lunch, maps and travel information. This is a great option for independent souls.

El Aventurero (☎ 456-05-57; www.ridemexico.com; Av López Mateos 68; ⊙ 9am-6pm Mon-Fri, 9am-3pm Sat) Enjoy the surrounding countryside on horseback, with an English-speaking guide who will take you on two- to seven-hour adventures that range from M$130 to M$480 per person.

Tarahumara Tours (☎ 456-01-21) With an office on the plaza. Offers all the same tours and guide services as the hotels, often at better prices.

Umarike Expediciones (www.umarike.com.mx; contact@umarike.com.mx) This internet-based outfitter offers guided mountain-bike adventure trips, rock-climbing and canyoning excursions and instruction. It rents out mountain bikes and camping gear, and offers maps and information for do-it-yourself trips. Week-long bike rental costs M$825, an eight-day mountain bike trip to Batopilas costs M$12,650, and a three-day hiking trip within the canyon is M$4620.

Sleeping

Creel offers every kind of lodging experience, from dorm-style bunks to nearly five-star resorts. All spots include breakfast unless otherwise noted.

BUDGET

Casa Margarita (☎ 456-00-45; Av López Mateos 11; dm M$80-100, s/d M$200/300) Margarita's is a bustling backpacker scene, where everyone gathers

---

ALL ABOARD ON THE FERROCARRIL CHIHUAHUA PACÍFICO *Inocencio Reyes Rodríguez*

My favorite part of the train [ride] is El Lazo, because of the work of engineering they did to be able to accomplish it and the vision they had to be able to get through this section of the mines. In order to maintain the required 2.5% rate of ascent, they had to do a loop of 360 degrees inside the canyon.

One of my fondest memories of working on the train was 15 or so years ago, we used to have sleeper cars and observatory cars – we had excellent service back then and it's a special memory for me.

My biggest advice to passengers is to come prepared with their own medicine and prescriptions. If they aren't used to Mexican cuisine, sometimes people get sick and they need their own medicine. It's difficult for us to look after them because we can't give them anything or help them. Not only on the train, but some places in the canyon are very remote and you can't get any medicine.'

Inocencio Reyes Rodríguez has been a porter on the Ferrocarril Chihuahua Pacífico (p341) for 33 years. He lives in Chihuahua.

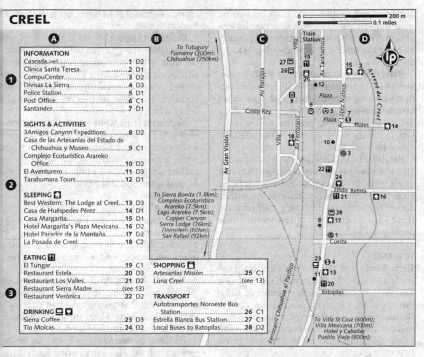

CREEL

INFORMATION
Cascada.net...**1**	D2
Clínica Santa Teresa...........................**2**	D1
CompuCenter..**3**	D2
Divisas La Sierra..................................**4**	D3
Police Station......................................**5**	D1
Post Office...**6**	C1
Santander...**7**	D1

SIGHTS & ACTIVITIES
3Amigos Canyon Expeditions.........**8**	D2
Casa de las Artesanías del Estado de Chihuahua y Museo......................**9**	C1
Complejo Ecoturístico Arareko Office...**10**	D2
El Aventurero.....................................**11**	D3
Tarahumara Tours.............................**12**	D1

SLEEPING
Best Western: The Lodge at Creel....**13**	D3
Casa de Huéspedes Pérez...............**14**	D1
Casa Margarita...................................**15**	D1
Hotel Margarita's Plaza Mexicana...**16**	D2
Hotel Parador de la Montaña..........**17**	D2
La Posada de Creel............................**18**	C2

EATING
El Tungar...**19**	C1
Restaurant Estela..............................**20**	D3
Restaurant Los Valles.......................**21**	D2
Restaurant Sierra Madre...........(see 13)	
Restaurant Verónica.........................**22**	D2

DRINKING
Sierra Coffee.....................................**23**	D3
Tío Molcas...**24**	D2

SHOPPING
Artesanías Misión..............................**25**	C1
Luna Creel...................................(see 13)	

TRANSPORT
Autotransportes Noroeste Bus Station...**26**	C1
Estrella Blanca Bus Station.............**27**	C1
Local Buses to Batopilas..................**28**	D2

Map labels:
To Tutugury; Tsunamy (300km); Chihuahua (250km)
Train Station
Cristo Rey
Plaza
Plaza
Flores
To Sierra Bonita (1.8km); Complejo Ecoturístico Arareko (7.5km); Lago Arareko (7.5km); Copper Canyon Sierra Lodge (26km); Divisadero (50km); San Rafael (92km)
Elfido Batista
Cuesta
Batopilas
Ferrocarril Chihuahua al Pacífico
To Villa St Cruz (600m); Villa Mexicana (700m); Hotel y Cabañas Pueblo Viejo (800m)
0 ___ 200 m
0 ___ 0.1 miles

---

at the table to eat together and swap travel tales, and it's also where you can organize many daily tours (be wary, though: if you don't take a tour, rumor has it you might lose your bed). Rooms are simple but have great water pressure and nice, thick bath towels. Knock off M$50 per day from the prices above if you don't want meals, though one traveler called the full board the best deal they'd seen in all of Mexico.

Casa de Huéspedes Pérez (☎ 456-03-91; Flores 257; dm M$80, r M$250) Roomier and more attractive than Margarita's dorms, this Casa has homey one- to six-person log-walled rooms with wood-stove heating as well as private rooms (some on the 2nd floor overlook Creel). Also on the premises is a communal kitchen and Café Luly, which serves your included breakfast and dinner.

La Posada de Creel (Av Ferrocarril s/n; r with shared bathroom M$150, s/d M$250/400; P) Under new management and slowly being spruced up, this veteran is starting to look like a better deal than Margarita's when you consider the food: each of the basic rooms comes with a voucher for breakfast or dinner at Los Valles

or Veronica's – two of the best – and one beer at Tío Molcas, per day.

MIDRANGE

Villa Mexicana (☎ 456-06-65; www.vmcoppercanyon.com; Prolongación López Mateos s/n; camp sites per person M$75, RV sites with full hookups M$200, 4-person cabins M$1299, 6-person cabins M$1750; P ☆) This well-equipped campground on the south side of Creel has the coziest log cabins in town, as well as communal kitchen, bathrooms, restaurant, bar, small shop, laundry and tours. It's about a 15-minute walk from the center. Breakfast is extra.

Hotel Margarita's Plaza Mexicana (☎ 456-02-45; www.hoteles-margaritas.com; Elfido Batista s/n; s/d M$450/550; P) If you've outgrown the hostel scene but still want a laid-back bargain, head for this comfortable hotel, run by the same family that runs the Casa Margarita. Slightly worn rooms are set around a charming courtyard. Prices include meals, but certainly not peace and quiet or hospitable service.

Villa St Cruz (☎ 456-02-27; www.villastcruz.com; r M$550, cabaña M$600-1200; P ✗) Some of its initial style is wearing thin, but if you don't mind being tucked away on the edge of town, these family-friendly cabañas are huge and come with full kitchens and dining areas. In low season (September to November and January to May) the M$550 double goes for M$150, the best deal in town!

Hotel y Cabañas Pueblo Viejo (☎ 456-05-38; www.puebloviejolodge.com; s/d M$600/700; P) Another option just outside town, this brash spot is set up like an old village backlot – you can sleep in the 'jail,' 'church' or 'pharmacy.' It wins on kitsch, but the service has been occasionally called into question.

Hotel Parador de la Montaña (☎ in Chihuahua 614-415-54-08; www.hotelparadorcreel.com; Av López Mateos 44; s/d M$877/934; P) This alpine-influenced choice is centrally located with comfortable rooms, a decent restaurant and friendly staff (though there's no accounting for taste with those floral-print bedspreads).

TOP END

Sierra Bonita (☎ 456-06-15; www.sierrabonita.com.mx; Gran Visión s/n; r M$1006, cabaña M$3205-3354; P) The furthest place from the center of town but one of the nicest, the Sierra Bonita offers stylish cabañas (save the pink walls) on a dramatic hilltop, a nightclub, bar and restaurant. Rooms 101 to 105 have the best views of town. Breakfast is extra.

Best Western: The Lodge at Creel (☎ 456-00-71, in the US 800-528-1234; www.thelodgeatcreel.com; Av López Mateos 61; r from M$1025; P ⊠) The classiest spot in town, designed to look like a hunting lodge, has well-heeled log cabin–style rooms with gas fireplaces and beautiful wood-beam floors, walls and ceilings. There's also a small fitness center, spa and cozy bar.

Eating

You'll find plenty of budget restaurants, all pretty similar to one another, on Av López Mateos in the few blocks south of the plaza.

El Tungar (meals M$30-60; 🕑 8am-5pm) This don't-miss, next to the tracks just south of the train station, specializes in hangover remedies (hence its nickname, 'Hospital Para Crudos') like *menudo* (tripe stew) and *pozole* (hominy stew). Go on – it's nicer inside than out.

Restaurant Los Valles (Av López Mateos 37; mains M$30-85; 🕑 6:30am-11pm) There are tasty *carne asada,* hamburgers and other Mexican specialties in generous portions at this clean spot on the corner of Batista.

Restaurant Estela (☎ 456-01-88; Av López Mateos s/n; mains M$50; 🕑 7am-6pm) Serves homey *comida corrida* right out of its home kitchen – a good budget option.

Restaurant Verónica (☎ 456-06-31; Av López Mateos 33; mains M$57-110; 🕑 7:30am-10:30pm) The must-try dish at this popular spot for steaks and chicken is *El Norteño,* a cheesy, beefy mess served in a cast-iron skillet that you eat with tortillas. The joint also serves a downright feisty salsa.

Restaurant Sierra Madre (Av López Mateos 61; mains M$68-155) For more upscale dining, try this festive place at the Best Western, with stone walls, exposed wood beams and plenty of taxidermy. It serves a limited dinner menu of steaks, seafood and pasta.

Drinking

Creel's status as a traveler's mecca hasn't yet produced the nightlife you'd expect – Tío Molcas is still the only tried-and-true watering hole – but you can find travelers drinking here and there elsewhere.

Sierra Coffee (☎ 456-07-76; Av López Mateos 60; 🕑 8am-10pm) This humble café serves coffee and espresso that won't make you angry – a rarity in these parts. There are also homemade cookies, pastries and free wi-fi.

Tío Molcas (Av López Mateos 35; 🕑 5pm-1am Sun-Thu, 5pm-2am Fri & Sat) This cozy, wood-heated bar fills up nightly with bedraggled global travelers fresh from the train, itchin' to swap tall travel tales over Dos Equis and *telenovelas*. It's good fun.

Tutugury Tsunamy (cnr Gran Visión & Juárez; 🕑 9pm-2am Thu-Sun) For a serious dose of local color head to this disco-bar, just slightly out of tourist bounds. To get there, head north from the train station and take the first left on Juárez.

Shopping

Many shops in Creel sell Rarámuri handicrafts as well as distinctive Mata Ortiz pottery.

Artesanías Misión (plaza; 🕑 9:30am-1pm & 3-6pm) All of the store's earnings go to support the Catholic mission hospital, which provides free medical care for the Rarámuri. Pick up a pair of *huarache* sandals and you'll blend right in with the indigenous crowd.

Luna Creel (Av López Mateos 61; 🕑 9am-1pm & 3-9pm) A wonderful café/jewelry shop for handmade artisan silver rings and organic soaps by Anna and Luis Pacheco, who studied anthropology and jewelry making near Paquimé. It's attached to the Best Western (left).

Getting There & Around

BICYCLE
Several places rent out bicycles, and the surrounding countryside has many places accessible by pedal power.

3Amigos Canyon Expeditions (☎ 456-00-36; www .amigos3.com; Av López Mateos 46) Half/full day M$90/150.

Casa Margarita (☎ 456-00-45; Av López Mateos 11) Half/full day M$90/150.

Umarike Expediciones (www.umarike.com.mx;) Half/full day M$120/180. Includes map, helmet and tool kit.

BUS
Travel between Creel and Chihuahua, as well as between Creel and Divisadero, may be more convenient via bus than train, as the trips are shorter and the schedules more flexible. The Autotransportes Noroeste bus station, across the tracks from the plaza, runs buses to San Rafael (M$48, 1¼ hours) via Divisadero (M$37, one hour) at 10:30am, 2:30pm and 6:30pm, and buses to Chihuahua (M$190, 4½ hours) at 6:45am, 9am, 11:30am, 1pm and 3pm. This is the nicer of the two companies.

The Estrella Blanca bus station, just north of Autotransportes Noroeste, has nine daily buses to Chihuahua (M$190, 4½ hours), passing through San Juanito (M$25, 45 minutes), La Junta (M$90, 2½ hours) and Cuauhtémoc (M$124, three hours) on the way. Estrella Blanca also has three daily buses to San Rafael (M$47, 1½ hours) via Divisadero (M$4, one hour) and Posada Barrancas (Areponápuchi; M$40, one hour); they depart Creel daily at 10:20am, 2:20pm and 6pm.

The local bus to Batopilas (M$180, five hours) leaves from outside Artesanías El Towi on López Mateos, two blocks south of the plaza, at 7:30am Tuesday, Thursday and Saturday, and at 9:30am Monday, Wednesday and Friday.

CAR & MOTORCYCLE
There's now a paved road all the way from Creel to Divisadero and on to San Rafael. From San Rafael, there's a new road connecting Bahuichivo, Cerocahui, Mesa de Arturo, Piedras Verdes, Tubares (there's a new bridge over the Río San Miguel), Choix, and on to El Fuerte. Note that you will need a 4WD between Mesa Arturo and Tubares (about 70km). Or you could go from San Rafael to Álamos via Bahuichivo, Témoris and Chinipas, crossing the Río Chinipas, though this road is very rough and assaults

have been reported on it, so travel at your own risk.

TRAIN
Creel's train station is half a block from the main plaza. The westbound *primera express* train departs Creel at about 11:15am, and the *clase económica* at about 1:20pm (though it's been known to arrive closer to noon); the eastbound trains depart at about 3:24pm and 6pm. However, times vary greatly and they are usually late. See the schedule on p343 for ticket information.

AROUND CREEL
The area around Creel is rich in natural wonders, offering everything from waterfalls and hot springs to massive speckled boulders and expansive parklands, all of which are only a day's hike, bike ride or drive from town. Local guides offer a variety of guided tours, or, even better, you can venture out on your own on a rented bicycle, scooter or truck.

Sights & Activities
Just 2km outside town is the **Valle de los Monjes**, where vertical rock formations inspired its traditional Rarámuri name, Bisabírachi, meaning the 'Valley of the Erect Penises.' It makes a nice full-day trip on horseback, and takes you past some other animatedly named valleys on the way, including **Valle de las Ranas** and **Valle de los Hongos** – 'frogs' and 'mushrooms,' respectively. The photogenic **San Ignacio Mission** is also in this area.

A popular day trip in the area is to the nearby **Complejo Ecoturístico Arareko**, a Rarámuri *ejido*. It is home to about 400 families who live in caves and small homes among the waterfalls, farmlands, deep canyons, dramatic rock formations and a 200-sq-km forest of thick pine trees, 7.5km south of Creel. A lovely greenish lake, **Lago Arareko**, sits on the *ejido* as well, where it beautifully reflects the surrounding pine trees and rock formations. One tip: the **Rekowata Aguas Termales** (Rekowata Hot Springs) on the *ejido* are really just lukewarm and the springs are more or less a swimming pool. The hike down (beautiful) and up (menacing) is very scenic; just don't be expecting a pristine therapeutic hot spring when you reach the bottom.

The 30m-high **Cascada Cusárare** is a waterfall that's 22km south of Creel, near the Rarámuri village of **Cusárare** (place of eagles). Also in

NORTHWEST MEXICO

Cusárare is the **Loyola Museum** (admission M$15; ☉ 10am-5pm Wed-Mon), dedicated to preserving and displaying its collection of centuries-old paintings that were found wasting away in regional churches and missions.

Even more dramatic than the waterfall in Cusárare is a visit to **Parque Nacional Cascada de Basaseachi**, where you'll find, at 246m, the highest full-time falls in Mexico. Basaseachi is 140km northwest of Creel, and takes a full day to visit, thanks to a bumpy three-hour drive, a one-hour hike to the bottom, two hours to walk back up, and then the return drive. It's a long way to go but if you're up for the challenge, it's worth it. The views of the falls are beautiful from the three viewpoints around its rim, but it's damn near miraculous at the bottom. If you go at midday, the sun creates one stunning rainbow after the other at its base, and you feel close enough to reach out and touch them.

Sleeping & Eating

Once you get out into Creel's natural surroundings for a day trip, you may decide you'd like to spend the night there. The region has several rustic places to choose from – some with campsites, others with cozy bedrooms. Most will feed you, too.

Complejo Ecoturístico Arareko (☎ 635-456-01-26; Av López Mateos, Creel) has an office in Creel, where you can reserve a spot at (and arrange for transportation to) one of the *ejido*'s various options. The *ejido* operates two lodges. **Cabañas de Batosárachi** (r M$100-150) offers three rustic log cabins, which contain either bunk beds or individual rooms, plus hot showers and a communal kitchen, as well as five new individual cabins with small kitchen areas (bring your own camping stove). The more comfortable **Cabaña de Segórachi** (d M$250), a large cabin on the south shore of Lago Arareko, just received a makeover (new carpets, new bathrooms) and includes the use of a rowboat. You can also pitch at tent in either spot, as well as around the lake, for M$15.

Copper Canyon Sierra Lodge (☎ 635-456-00-36, in the US 800-648-8488; www.coppercanyonlodge.com; s/d incl meals M$800/$1600) is an atmospheric mountain lodge with comfy rooms with rustic beamed ceilings, kerosene lamps (there's no electricity), carved pine furniture, fluffy white robes, showers with plenty of hot water, and potbelly stoves (two rooms have working fireplaces). Excellent meals are served in a fine old dining room. The rates above include margaritas (yes, that's *plural*).

BATOPILAS

☎ 649 / pop 1200 / elevation 495m

If you make it alive down the steep, twisting dirt road to Batopilas, a serene 19th-century silver-mining village 140km south of Creel, you can be satisfied that you have made your way deep into canyon country. The journey is a thrilling ride – from an altitude of 2338m, at Creel, to 495m at Batopilas – with dramatic descents and ascents through several canyons, climates and vegetative zones, ending in a warm little village.

The biggest activity once you arrive at Batopilas is enjoying the stuck-in-time feel of the place. Things shut up early here – last call 10pm on weekends – so don't expect any big nights out. However, there's plenty of history to explore (quirky fact: after Mexico City, Batopilas was the second town in Mexico to receive electricity). One of the most popular excursions is to the **Catedral Perdida** (Lost Cathedral) at Satevó, an elaborate cathedral that was discovered in a remote, uninhabited canyon. It's a long 8km hike along the river, or a 20-minute drive. Any hotel can help arrange day trips; the three- to four-day trek to the canyon town of Urique is also a popular – and spectacular – journey.

Like Urique, Batopilas can be a little rough around the edges. The military recently razed the marijuana crops in the surrounding area, effectively bringing the local economy to a grinding halt. As a result, the town has seen an upsurge in robberies and kidnappings. Foreign tourists aren't usually targeted, but do yourself a favor and be vigilant here.

Sleeping

Casa Monse (☎ 456-90-27; Plaza Principal; r M$120) Bare-bones backpackers favor the decaying Hotel Batopilas down the plaza, but these economical rooms are cleaner and come with the homespun character of the house, Monse Alcaraz, who will chat your ear off, fix you Rarámuri cuisine and help with local guides and information.

Hotel Juanita's (☎ 456-90-43; Plaza Principal; s/d M$250/400; ⊠ 😁) These clean and basic rooms come complete with crucifixes, plus a courtyard overlooking the river, a lovely place to gather in the evening. Juanita says if you don't like Jesus, you can go elsewhere.

Real de Minas (☎ 456-90-45; Donato Guerra 1; r M$526.50; P ⊠ ✿) A little Sierra Madre oasis with eight brightly decorated rooms around a lovely courtyard with a fountain as well as an annex just down the road with six airy and immaculate rooms with orange doors and a peaceful vibe. The low doorknobs, however, were surely designed for Oompa-Loompas and Ewoks.

La Hacienda Río Batopilas (☎ in Creel 635-456-02-45; s/d incl meals M$600/1000) If you don't want to deal with the uncertainty of the sometimes open, sometimes closed Riverside Lodge, this is top digs, a 1760 hacienda run by the same folks who own Casa Margarita in Creel. The sizable rooms feature beautiful exposed cobblestone walls, wood-beam ceilings, stained-glass windows and gorgeous tiled bathrooms and bathtubs. An onsite restaurant serves breakfast and dinner. The downside is that it's a good half-hour walk from town.

Eating & Drinking

Eating here is an intimate experience, as most 'restaurants' consist of a few tables on the porch or patio of a private home.

Carolina (Plaza de la Constitución; mains M$40-90; 8am-7:30pm) Good *huevos rancheros* and pancakes for breakfast, and other Mexican specialties throughout the day.

Doña Mica (Plaza de la Constitución; meals M$50-60; 7:30am-9pm) An excellent spot for home-cooked Mexican meals prepared on a wonderful antique stove. There is no menu, just a few choices each day with vegetarian possibilities.

El Puente Colgante (☎ 456-90-23, mains M$50-130; 11am-9pm Sun Wed, 11am-10pm Fri & Sat) Serves a delicious stuffed trout, seasoned steak and savory pitchers of *micheladas*. Its patio is also a good spot for an early nightcap.

Getting There & Away

There's just one road in to town, and it's not for the faint of heart. It slithers down the side of the canyon following the outline of a Christmas tree (with a much longer fall to the floor). The cheapest trip is on the 20-seat public bus from Creel, which is usually crowded and takes at least five hours (M$180, Monday to Saturday). It is not advisable to return to Creel on Tuesday, Thursday or Saturday – on these days, the 'bus' is actually a much more cramped seven-seat Chevy Suburban, and the driver crams as many people in as possible (11 and a baby on our occasion). Though it goes all the way to Chihuahua (M$370, eight hours) on these days, it is extremely uncomfortable and shockingly unsafe. Additionally, passengers to Chihuahua get priority seating over those going to Creel. Both depart from the front of the church at 5am. You can also rent a truck and drive, though it's not recommended as the road is very steep and narrow. Better to join a tour group or hire an experienced driver in Creel.

Central North Mexico

The license plates of Chihuahua, Mexico's largest state, label it Tierra de Encuentro (roughly Land of Discovery), an apt description that also fits its southern neighbor, Durango – the other large, rural state covered in this chapter. Come here to encounter the sometimes surreal natural beauty: carpets of rainy-season wildflowers, spectacular thunderstorms and wide sweeps of cerulean sky. Come here to feel the vibe of *tranquilo* towns, to hear the call of ancient, vanished cultures and to see where many important moments of Mexican history happened.

In the Nahua language Chihuahua means 'dry and sandy zone.' The Desierto Chihuahuense (Chihuahuan Desert) that covers most of the state, and spreads well beyond, is North America's largest. The stark beauty of some of its mountain-lined desertscapes defies description.

For many, the sandy expanses are all they know of the region, but in the west rise the mountains of the Sierra Madre Occidental, cradling fertile valleys and enigmatic archaeological ruins. Chihuahua, Hidalgo del Parral and especially Durango have inviting colonial cores, and history buffs can find museums about revolutionary hero Pancho Villa seemingly everywhere.

Why there are so few visitors here is a mystery. Ciudad Juárez sees some short-term border-hoppers and Chihuahua gets a few foreigners waiting to board the Copper Canyon trains, but most of the central north consists of quiet towns that haven't been spruced up for tourists.

Some folk pass through and wonder what the fuss is about. For others, the first visit becomes the beginning of a whole new journey, an intimate look at a different side of Mexico.

HIGHLIGHTS

- Explore the pre-Hispanic cliffside dwellings in the mountains near Madera, like Cañón de Huápoca's **Cueva Grande** (p367)
- Soak up the colonial charm of **Durango** (p380)
- Shop for pottery in **Mata Ortiz** (p365)
- Get deep into **Mina La Prieta** (p376) in Hidalgo del Parral and **Mina Ojuela** (p380) near Mapimí
- Walk through the mysterious ruins of **Paquimé** (p363)

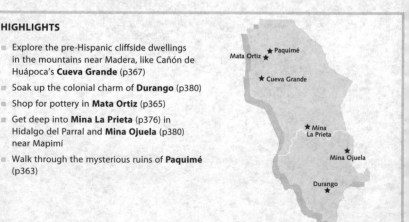

■ CHIHUAHUA JANUARY DAILY HIGH: 18°C | 64°F   ■ CHIHUAHUA JULY DAILY HIGH 32°C | 89°F

History

This region of Mexico was the subject of many fierce battles during the Revolution, giving rise to Pancho Villa's División del Norte, and it will quickly become clear that Villa (see boxed text, p376) remains a revered hero in these parts.

You'll also encounter lingering evidence of the region's early wealth and importance to the power centers further south, whether it be the colonial towns of Chihuahua and Durango, the centuries-old mines around Hidalgo del Parral and Torreón or even the old railway station in Nuevo Casas Grandes. More recently the area was a Hollywood hotspot, its still-pristine vistas making great backdrops for countless classic Westerns.

But the most interesting central north history harks back much further. The ruined city of Paquimé and ancient cliff dwellings like Cueva Grande and Cuarenta Casas are clear reminders that there were flourishing settlements of highly sophisticated peoples living here long before the Spanish arrived.

Climate

This entire region is hot and dry with summer temperatures over 40°C not uncommon. Chihuahua is a bit wetter and warmer than Durango. Snow is fairly common in the mountains in winter, especially around Madera, but it can fall anywhere in the region. Remember, even in the summer, deserts get chilly after dark.

Parks & Reserves

Though the area is very beautiful, there are few large protected places. The most famous is the Reserva de la Biosfera Bolsón de Mapimí (p380), a wild and remote desert. With most visitors bounding off to the Copper Canyon, Parque Nacional Cumbres de Majalco (p372) near Chihuahua is largely overlooked, but its eroded rocks offer good rock-climbing and hiking.

There are also beautiful mountain forests to explore around Madera (p366) and along Hwy 40 (p384) west of Durango.

Getting There & Around

Excellent bus service and good roads make traveling around this region very easy. It's often remote country, so if you're driving, don't set out beyond major highways without a full tank of gas.

WALK IN PANCHO VILLA'S FOOTSTEPS

This region is littered with sites made famous by the revolutionary Pancho Villa. His death is raucously marked each year by Hidalgo del Parral's **Las Jornadas Villistas** (p377). Try the following sites to stand in places where the man made his mark.

- **Quinta Luz** (Museo Histórico de la Revolución Mexicana, p368)
- **Canutillo** (p378)
- **Museo Francisco Villa** (p376)
- **La Casa de los Milagros** (p373)
- **Palacio Alvarado** (p376)

Most people heading into the region from the US cross at Ciudad Juárez (see boxed text, p363, for details). If your plans don't include Juárez you can bypass it (and the long waits) by using the hassle-free Santa Teresa crossing (open 6am to 10pm) in New Mexico, 12 miles northwest of downtown El Paso.

CIUDAD JUÁREZ

☎ 656 / population 1.3 million / elevation 1145m

No doubt about it, Ciudad Juárez is an in-your-face kind of place. But, despite what you may have heard, it's really not all that bad. On the other hand, its modest roster of attractions isn't all that good, and it lacks the charm of many other northern cities. In fact, it lacks any real charm at all. What it does have, however, is energy.

Juárez, the second busiest port of entry on the US–Mexico border, relies heavily on the constant ebb and flow of goods and people from its cross-river mate El Paso, Texas. Trucks full of raw materials and finished goods roll in and out of the city's *maquiladoras* (foreign-owned assembly plants) and Texas daytrippers stream over for bargain shopping and medical care, or under-age drinking at the bustling cantinas and clubs.

Considering all the wonderful places waiting further south, the conventional wisdom – get out of town as quickly as possible – is not without merit, but odds are you'll enjoy a short stay here.

History

In 1598, Conquistador Don Juan de Oñate, known for his cruelty to the indigenous

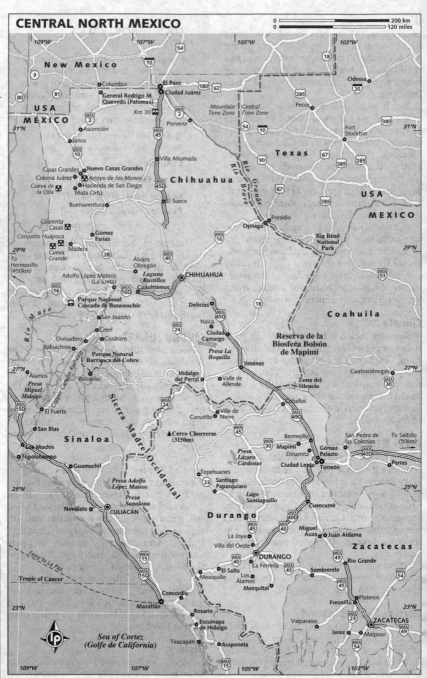

CENTRAL NORTH MEXICO

populations, forded the Río Bravo here during his official expedition to colonize New Mexico. The crossing point he found became a vital stop on the Camino Real de Tierra Adentro (Royal Road of the Interior), a 2560km trade route from Mexico City to Santa Fe, New Mexico.

The Guadalupe Mission was founded in El Paso del Norte (as Juárez was then known) in 1659, and eventually a thriving Wild West town grew up around it. The name was changed in 1888 to honor President Benito Juárez who had fought the French occupation from here in 1865 and 1866.

In May 1911, during the Mexican Revolution, Pancho Villa (see boxed text, p376) stormed the town, forcing the resignation of the dictator Porfirio Díaz. After the 1913 coup against President Francisco Madero, Villa sought refuge in El Paso before crossing the river again with a handful of followers to begin another conquest of Mexico. Within months, he had recruited an army of thousands, known as La División del Norte, and in November he conquered Juárez for a second time.

The Revolution devastated the Mexican economy, but Juárez began its boom years around this time thanks to the USA's Prohibition era (1920–33). Thirsty Americans came from far and wide to enjoy Juárez' lively entertainment, both illicit and classy, and even when beer came back many Americans continued to live it up south of the border.

A second economic boom came after the implementation of the North American Free Trade Agreement (Nafta) in the mid-1990s as US manufacturers took advantage of low-cost labor in Mexico. The new jobs brought thousands of new people from across Mexico to work in the 400 maquiladoras. (Today only 40% of Juárez' residents were born here.) But the success hasn't spread evenly, and there are massive slums on the outskirts.

Juárez' most recent history has been rather inglorious. The city is a key transit point for illicit drugs entering the US, and there has been considerable violence between rival gangs. More disturbing are the deaths and disappearances of hundreds of young local women, many of them raped and tortured, since 1993. Dubbed the 'feminicides,' the murders initially gained little attention from the local authorities or the media, and many critics have denounced both local and national authorities for their indifference and perhaps even culpability. Thankfully, the rate of incidences have declined significantly in recent years. Travelers should simply take the same precautions they would in any town.

Orientation

Ciudad Juárez sprawls south from the Río Bravo, but most places of interest are concentrated in the central area near the twin international bridges that connect Juárez to El Paso. Av Juárez is the main drag through Ciudad Juárez, but the mostly pedestrianized area south of the Plaza de Armas offers much more rewarding shopping and people-watching. East of the center is Zona Pronaf where well-heeled locals and tourists, mostly Mexican Texans, with money to burn come out to play. The main nightlife destinations line Av Lincoln.

Information

All businesses in Juárez accept US dollars, but it's usually better to pay in pesos. There are casas de cambio (exchange bureaus) all across the city, including many on Av Juárez, while banks are clustered along Av 16 de Septiembre. For emergency services, dial ☎ 060.

Comisiones San Luis (☎ 614-20-33; cnr Avs Juárez & 16 de Septiembre) Doesn't have the best rates for cash but it changes traveler's checks (US$50 and US$100 denominations only).

Compu-Rent (per hr M$15) Main branch (cnr Av 16 de Septiembre & Villa) Speedy computers, private booths and a hip young vibe. There's a smaller branch at Av Juárez 243.

El Paso Tourist Information Center (☎ 915-534-0600; Santa Fe St at Main Dr; ⏰ 8am-5pm Mon-Fri, 10am-3pm Sat & Sun)

General Hospital (☎ 613-15-71; Paseo Triunfo de la República 2401) 24-hour emergency department.

Juárez Tourist Information Center (☎ 611-31-74; www.visitajuarez.com; Av de las Américas 2551; ⏰ 9am-9pm Mon-Fri, 10am-6pm Sat & Sun) Bilingual staff; stocks brochures for Juárez and the rest of Mexico.

Post office (cnr Av Lerdo & Peña)

Dangers & Annoyances

Basic street smarts that might apply anywhere apply in Ciudad Juárez, but the city's reputation is worse than its reality. Much of the crime is drug-related; tourists here for legitimate travel will find Juárez welcoming and friendly. The main drag along Av Juárez until it meets Av 16 de Septiembre is well lit and has a regular police presence so walking around is fine until late at night – just don't stray down unlit side streets. East of Av Juárez is a seedy red-light district, which is best avoided. To the south and west many streets get eerily deserted very early in the evening; generally, however, it's safe to walk around them for the first few hours after dark. Don't walk over the Stanton St–Av Lerdo bridge at night.

Never accept 'free' offers (rides, drinks etc), as they're never free and can occasionally be dangerous.

Sights

Juárez' unique **cathedral** (cnr Av 16 de Septiembre & Mariscal; 9am-5pm Mon-Fri, 9am-8pm Sat & Sun), built in 1935 and restored in 1976, is on the central Plaza de Armas. It has gorgeous stained-glass windows and an impressive neoclassical facade. Next door, the **Misión de Guadalupe** (7:30am-7pm, till 3pm Thu), completed in 1668, has an intricately carved wooden ceiling.

The city's grand old customs building now houses the **Museo Histórico de Ciudad Juárez** (Museo Ex-Aduana; 612-4707; cnr Avs Juárez & 16 de Septiembre; admission free; 9am-5pm Tue-Sun) with a few rather flat and unimpressive exhibits (labeled in Spanish) and some fantastic old photographs.

The conical **Museo de Arte** (613-17-08; Av Lincoln s/n; admission free; 10am-6pm Tue-Sun), in the Zona Pronaf, is an architectural curiosity. It's small, but the temporary exhibits can be good.

Sleeping

Be prepared for less than deluxe accommodations in Juárez, and be aware that most of the cheap hotels you pass as you walk around the center have 300% occupancy – that is, guests pay by the hour.

BUDGET

Hotel Correo (615-08-75; Av Lerdo 250 Sur; r from M$130;) The building, near the post office, is crumbling, but the rooms are scrubbed as clean as can be and this little TLC makes Correo one of the best bottom-budget bets in Juárez.

Gardner Hotel (915-532-3661; www.gardnerhotel .com; 311 E Franklin Av, El Paso; dm US$20, r without/with bathroom from US$35/55;) Some people prefer to visit Juárez as a daytrip from Texas before heading south, in which case this El Paso institution is an ideal base. The Gardner,

which opened in 1922 and oozes character and charm, offers both four-bed dorms (at the time of writing some two-bed dorms were planned) and single rooms. The cheapest are rather rough around the edges while others have been thoroughly fixed up: all pass the white glove test and have some original furnishings. Downstairs you'll find a big kitchen and common room with a free pool table. The owner, Joe, has a wealth of knowledge about the area, and leads tours to area attractions like Carlsbad Caverns (in New Mexico).

Hotel Imperial (615-03-23; Vicente Guerrero 206; r M$300;) This funky place, with its big orange wall of windows, isn't fancy, but its cozy rooms (much cheerier than the hallways) are good value for the price.

MIDRANGE

Hotel Monaco (617-17-30; www.hotelmonaco.com .mx; Paseo Triunfo de la República 3335; s/d M$350/400;) This motel-style place with large rooms is a very solid deal, even if you don't factor in its high-class Zona Pronaf locale.

Plaza Continental Hotel (615-00-84; Av Lerdo 112 Sur; s & d M$370, tr M$425;) Decent carpeted rooms are large and clean. An impressive lobby and a funky late-night diner make this place a step up from other similar properties in the area.

Hotel Impala (615-04-31; www.hotel-impala.com; Av Lerdo 670 Nte; s, d & tr M$380, q M$440;) Close to the border, near the Stanton St bridge, this old standby has basic but kind-of-cute rooms and firm beds. There's a restaurant (see p362) and a jolly, plant-filled lobby.

Hotel Suites El Paseo (611-50-00; www.suitesel paseo.com; Paseo Triunfo de la República 4850; r from M$594;) This colorful nouveau colonial-style spot is a top-end hotel with midrange prices. With fountains and statues around the grounds, it has more pizzazz than Juárez' more expensive hotels.

TOP END

Hotel Lucerna (629-99-00; www.lucerna.com.mx; Paseo Triunfo de la República 3976; s/d/ste M$1480/1737/3318;) Catering to business-class travelers (weekend rates usually drop 15%), this luxurious option is a nice though pricey escape with a palm-studded pool area.

Eating & Drinking

For cheap eats, you can't beat the ramshackle roadside stalls where Villa meets Peña. The

CIUDAD JUÁREZ

INFORMATION

Comisiones San Luis	1 B3
Compu-Rent	2 B3
Compu-Rent Av Juárez	3 B3
El Paso Tourist Information Center	4 A1
General Hospital	5 D4
Juárez Tourist Information Center	6 D1
Mexican Consulate	7 B1
Mexican Immigration Office	8 D1
Mexican Immigration Office	9 B3
Post Office	10 B4
US Consulate	11 E2

SIGHTS & ACTIVITIES

Cathedral	12 A4
Misión de Guadalupe	(see 12)
Museo de Arte	13 D3
Museo Histórico de Ciudad Juárez	14 B4

SLEEPING

Gardner Hotel	15 A1
Hotel Correo	16 B4
Hotel Impala	17 B3
Hotel Imperial	18 B4
Hotel Lucerna	19 D4
Hotel Monaco	20 D4
Hotel Suites El Paseo	21 E4
Plaza Continental Hotel	22 B4

EATING

Frida's	23 D4
Restaurant Impala	(see 17)
Villa del Mar	24 B4

DRINKING

Dalí	25 D3
Kentucky Club	26 A3

ENTERTAINMENT

Capital	27 D3
Centro Municipal de las Artes	28 A4
El Cínito	(see 27)

SHOPPING

El Mercado Juárez	29 B3
Mercado Cuauhtémoc	30 A4

TRANSPORT

Amtrak Train Station	31 A2
Buss to Bus Station	32 B4
Buses to Zona Pronaf	33 B4
Greyhound Station	34 A2
Transborde Buses to El Paso	35 B4
Transborde Buses to Juárez	36 A1

0 — 1 km
0 — 0.5 miles

Texas (USA)

Chihuahua (MEXICO)

EL PASO

CIUDAD JUÁREZ

ZONA PRONAF

Rio Grande
Río Bravo del Norte

Bridge of the Americas (Cordova Bridge)

Parque Chamizal

To El Paso International Airport (9km)

Marcos de Niza

Av del Charro

Av Elías Calles

Av Huerta

Av López Mateos

Av de las Américas

Plaza de las Américas

Paseo Triunfo de la República

Vicente Guerrero

Av Lincoln

Av Lerdo

Av Juárez

Av 16 de Septiembre

Av de la Raza

Av de los Insurgentes

Av Reforma

Av 5 de Febrero

To Central Camionera Bus Terminal (4km); Airport (17km)

San Jacinto Plaza
San Francisco Plaza
Civic Center
El Paso Museum of Art

Oregon St
El Paso St
N Campbell St
N Mesa Ave
N Oregon St
N Stanton St
Myrtle Ave
W Texas Ave

S Cotton St
E Delta Dr
Paisano Dr

S Park St
S Tays St
S Hill St
S Vrain St
S Virginia St
S Ochoa St
S Florence St
S Campbell St
S Kansas St
S Stanton St
S Mesa St
S Oregon St
S El Paso St
S Santa Fe St

S Antonio Leon St
S Durango St
San Antonio Ave
Overland Ave
1st St
4th Ave
5th Ave
6th Ave
7th Ave
8th Ave
9th Ave

Border Hwy
Blvd Fronterizo
Av Pérez Serna
Av 5 de Mayo

Constitución
Bolivia
Topeyac
Chapultepec
Tlaxcala
Coyoacán
Villahermosa
Colombia
Costa Rica
Panamá
Ramírez
Monte de Oca

Blvd Norzagaray
Av Turena

Mejía
Ignacio Zaragoza
Braulio de la Peña
Av Borunda
20 de Noviembre

Díaz Ordaz
Av Colegio Militar
José Ma Morelos
Francisco I Madero
De la Paz
Ignacio Mejía
María Martínez
Santiago
Ugarte
Av 16 de Septiembre
Gardenias
Bolívar
Abraham González
Alcalde
Begonias

Mariscal
Cohora
Peña
Caleera
Corona

Lincoln
 Omelas
Mejía

Paso del Norte

fanciest options, as well as nearly all the inter-national flavors (from Japanese to Lebanese) are in and around Zona Pronaf. And if you're just looking to get plastered, close your eyes and walk into the nearest doorway – there's a good chance it will be a bar. Bars open early (often at 8am!) and close at 2am.

Villa del Mar (☎ 612-58-90; Villa 130 Sur; mains M$17-290) If you're downtown and ask a local where you should eat, many will point you to this simple seafood specialist, even if all you want is a taco.

Restaurant Impala (☎ 615-04-31; Av Lerdo 670 Nte; mains M$20-140) The menu, with its cryptic English translations, covers all the usuals, but the massive breakfast platters (M$59) with favorites from both sides of the border set this simple hotel restaurant apart.

Frida's (☎ 639-01-48; Paseo Triunfo de la República 2525; mains M$80-268) Juárez' most beautiful dining room is full of art (including dozens of portraits of its namesake) and red velvet booths. The food, a mix of Mexican and Continental, probably won't wow you as much as the décor, but most people leave satisfied.

Dalí (☎ 611-48-98; Mejía 3118; snacks M$25-80; V) This *tranquilo* café–bar attracts a crowd of intellectuals for coffee, wine, mixed drinks and hookahs. Grab one of the pillow-covered corners and you'll melt right in.

Kentucky Club (☎ 632-61-13; Av Juárez 629; 11am-2am) This polished-wood bar is a fine place to sip a margarita. While the club's claim to have invented that particular cocktail sounds like a publicity ploy, they do make a great one. Classier than most other Av Juárez watering holes.

Entertainment

If you're hoping for fine arts, you'll likely be disappointed. Check the notably slim events calendar in *Juárez Life* magazine.

Students at the **Centro Municipal de las Artes** (CMA; ☎ 615-28-28; Mariscal 105; admission free) behind the cathedral perform folkloric dances every Sunday from 11am to 1pm. Other dance, music and theater performances are held occasionally.

For those who enjoy beer, wine, corndogs and art-house films, try **El Cinito** (The Little Cinema; ☎ 616-04-73; Av Lincoln 445; minimum purchase M$40; 9pm Tue-Sun). At the same address is **Capital** (☎ 616-20-89; Av Lincoln 445; 9pm-2am Thu-Sun), the top spot at the moment for dancing. It hosts live

bands and DJs, the latter sometimes spinning on the outdoor deck.

Shopping

El Mercado Juárez (Av 16 de Septiembre 611; 9:30am-6pm Mon-Sat, 9am-5:30pm Sun) is a souvenir supercenter. It's got endless rows of all the usual (blankets, jewelry, cheese, pottery, wrestling masks), but look long enough and you'll find some quality crafts.

Mexican tourists shop for crafts at the smaller **Mercado Cuauhtémoc** (cnr Guerrero & Mariscal; 9am-6pm).

Getting There & Away

AIR

The best option for international arrivals and departures is **El Paso International Airport** (ELP; ☎ 915-780-4749) where flights from most major US cities cost half of those to Ciudad Juárez.

Ciudad Juárez' **Aeropuerto Internacional Abraham González** (☎ 633-07-34) is just east of Hwy 45, 18km south of the center. Fares to Mexico City and Monterrey are available for as low as M$1700 and M$1400 respectively. You can buy tickets at most hotels.

BUS

In Ciudad Juárez, the **Central Camionera** (☎ 610-70-83; Teófilo Borunda) is 5km southeast of the center. See opposite for information on getting there. Destinations with frequent 1st-class departures include Chihuahua (M$264, five hours), Mexico City's Terminal Norte (M$1319, 24 hours) and Nuevo Casas Grandes (M$161, four hours).

Autobuses Americanos (☎ 610-81-75) has buses direct to US cities (eg Albuquerque, Dallas and Denver) that are priced about the same as Greyhound's walk-up fares from El Paso.

CAR & MOTORCYCLE

If you're driving into the Mexican interior, you must obtain a vehicle permit (see p987). The only place to do so in the Ciudad Juárez area is at the major customs checkpoint at Km 30 on Hwy 45 south.

The highway to Chihuahua is in good condition, but it comes with a M$159 toll. Hwy 2 to Nuevo Casas Grandes branches west at a traffic circle 20km south of town.

TRAIN

El Paso's **Amtrak train station** (☎ 915-545-2247; 700 San Francisco Av, El Paso) serves trains three times a

---

CROSSING THE BORDER

From El Paso you can walk across the Stanton St–Av Lerdo or Santa Fe St–Av Juárez bridges into Mexico (US$0.35), but to return on foot you must use Av Juárez. By car, take Stanton St going south and Av Juárez going north. The vehicle toll is US$2.25.

The easiest way to drive to Juárez is over the toll-free Bridge of the Americas (Cordova Bridge), about 4km east of the Santa Fe St–Av Juárez bridge. Tourist cards are available at the Mexican immigration offices at the ends of the Av Lerdo and Cordova bridges, but not Av Juárez. All three bridges are open 24 hours.

Transborde (US$2; 🕙 7am-7pm Mon-Fri, 8am-6pm Sat, 9am-5pm Sun) buses shuttle between the cities' downtowns every half-hour. In Juárez they stop at the foot of the Av Lerdo bridge and at Av 16 de Septiembre and Villa. In El Paso you they stop by San Jacinto Plaza and along Stanton St. Also, an hourly bus connects the Juárez and El Paso bus stations between 6:30am and 9:30pm for US$6.

A taxi over the border from the El Paso airport costs US$40 to downtown or Zona Pronaf and US$48 to the bus station.

---

week to Los Angeles (US$97, 17 hours) and to New Orleans (US$98, 30 hours). You can also get to Chicago (US$113, 52 hours) if you change trains along the way.

Getting Around

Local buses (M$4.50, 25 minutes) to the Juárez bus station leave from Guerrero, west of Villa; catch any green-and-white 'Permisionarios Unidos' bus or route 1A or 1B. From the bus station to the town center, step out to the highway and take any bus labeled 'Centro.' Inside the station, a booth sells tickets for authorized taxis into town (M$85). You won't save money by walking outside and flagging one down, and you're unlikely to persuade anyone to take you *to* the station for that price.

Catch local buses labeled 'Plaza de las Americas' to Zona Pronaf along Guerrero or Corona; a taxi from Av Juárez will charge around M$70 to M$80.

NUEVO CASAS GRANDES & CASAS GRANDES

☎ 636 / combined pop 54,500 / elevation 1463m

Nuevo Casas Grandes, a four-hour bus trip southwest of Ciudad Juárez, is a sleepy, prosperous country town with wide streets and a vibe similar to dusty small towns in the US west. Its citizenry is a mix of working folk, farming families and Mormon settlers whose presence dates back to the late 19th century.

Although the town itself holds little of interest, the surrounding attractions, particularly the mysterious ruins of Paquimé in the nearby village of Casas Grandes and the world-famous pottery center of Mata Ortiz, are wonderful enough that this ought to be a busy tourist center. As it is, only a slow trickle of visitors passes through, mostly on guided tours.

Information

You'll find banks with ATMs and several *casas de cambio* on Calle 5 de Mayo along both sides of Constitución (the street with railway tracks down the middle). The **post office** (Calle 16 de Septiembre 602) is a short walk southeast and the small **tourist office** (☎ 694-00-50; Av Juárez s/n; 🕙 10am-1pm & 3-6pm Tue-Sat) is inconveniently located 10 blocks north of the main plaza.

For internet access and international phone calls, there's **Copias Y Fax** (cnr Obregón & Calle 5 de Mayo; per hr M$20; 🕙 8am-9pm).

Sights

The ruins of **Paquimé** (☎ 692-41-40; ruins & museum M$43; 🕙 10am-5pm Tue-Sun) are what give Casas Grandes (Big Houses) its name. The maze-like, eroding adobe remnants are from what was the major trading settlement in northern Mexico from around AD 900 until it was invaded, perhaps by Apaches, and sacked in 1340. Excavation and restoration began in the late 1950s, and Unesco declared it a World Heritage Site in 1998, although only a small portion has been unearthed. Large plaques, in Spanish and English, describe the possible uses of some of the structures and discuss Paquimé culture; don't miss the clay parrot cages and the distinctive T-shaped door openings, both of which are still clearly visible. Video use costs M$30.

The affiliated **Museo de las Culturas del Norte**, also with bilingual signage, has displays about many cultures from the greater desert region but mostly, of course, Paquimé. There's a scale model of the site at its prime, an explanation of how the canal system worked (quite an accomplishment here in the desert) and discussions of what is known about daily life in the village.

The Paquimé were great potters and produced pieces from black clay as well as cream-colored earthenware with striking red, brown or black geometric designs; some amazing original examples are on display in the museum. Copying their style has become a huge business in the area, and you can purchase pottery at the museum and many stores around Casas Grandes, as well as Mata Ortiz (opposite), where the revival began.

Sleeping

Alojamientos Fátima (☎ 661-43-54; alley btwn Constitution & Obregón; r M$100) The city's cheapest hotel, in the blue building just north of Calle 5 de Mayo two blocks from the bus station, has run-down, noisy, cell-like rooms without fans, but it's safe and fairly clean. And the plants in the hallway show that the owners care.

Suites Victoria Casa Hotel (alley btwn Constitution & Juárez; r from M$180; 🟦) Although it has also seen better days, this little hotel just south of Calle 5 de Mayo gives you much more for your money than Fátima, including a TV, refrigerator and towel.

Hotel Piñón (☎ 694-06-55; www.hotelpinon.com; Av Juárez 605; s/d M$335/385, tr & q M$400; 🅿 ✕ 🟦 🖥 🛜) On Av Juárez as you enter town from the north, this ultra-friendly lodge features comfy rooms behind a Paquimé-style facade. There's a restaurant offering hearty breakfasts and an outdoor pool. It's not the fanciest lodging in town, but it's only one small step down from the top for about half the price. They'll show you a room full of original Paquimé pottery (M$20 for non-guests) if you ask.

ourpick **Las Guacamayas B&B** (☎ 692-41-44; www.mataortizollas.com; s/d incl breakfast M$535/640; 🅿 ✕ 🟦 🖥) This precious lodge is a stone's throw from the entrance of the Paquimé site. The pink, adobe-style building has 15 charming rooms (sans TVs, though there's TV and wi-fi in the common area) with tiled floors, a lovely garden area with a hammock, and a gallery selling top-notch Mata Ortiz pottery. Breakfast is served in the owner's kitchen. (Note that the establishment uses US dollars.)

You can also spend the night at nearby Mata Ortiz (opposite) and Cueva de la Olla (opposite).

Eating & Drinking

Tortas Chuchy (☎ 694-07-09; Constitución 202; *tortas* M$20; 🕐 8:30am-8pm Mon-Sat) Chuchy's classic lunch counter is the perfect place to enjoy cheap, filling fare, from *tortas* to *licuados*, plus a side of warm chat with Chuchy, the friendly old-timer who has owned the place for nearly three decades.

Constantino (☎ 694-10-05; cnr Juárez & Minerva; mains M$20-110) Located off the corner of the main plaza, the popular Constantino has served fresh, tasty meals since 1954. The *enchiladas verdes* can't be beat.

Dinno's Pizza (☎ 694-02-04; cnr Minerva & Constitución; mains M$25-120; 🕐 8am-9pm) In addition to its good pizzas and super breakfasts, this popular place offers strong coffee that men in cowboy hats are always lingering over.

Restaurante Malmedy (☎ 112-72-46; Av Juárez; mains M$80-115; 🕐 1-9pm Tue-Sun) The biggest surprise in Nuevo Casas Grandes fills an 1896 brick house 3km north of town. The Belgian owner–chef cooks French and Mexican meals, plus a few combinations of the two, such as the beef filet with lime butter.

Chimenea's (☎ 694-06-55; Av Juárez 605) Nuevo Casas Grandes cantinas aren't as rough and tumble as those in the big city, but they're still generally sleazy. The Hotel Piñón's dark and cozy bar is a *tranquilo* exception. Guitarists serenade at weekends.

Getting There & Away

Nuevo Casas Grandes has no bus station; all long-distance services stop on Obregón at Calle 16 de Septiembre. There's frequent service to/from Ciudad Juárez (M$161, four hours), Chihuahua (M$206, four hours) and Tijuana (M$880, 18 hours), plus two a day to Madera ($174, four hours).

If you have a 4WD and a good command of Spanish, you could try heading to Madera on Hwy 11 through the mountains. The route is gorgeous but not well marked, so you'll need to stop often to ask ranchers for directions or reassurance.

Getting Around

Nuevo Casas Grandes is compact enough to walk almost everywhere, though a taxi to the outskirts will cost you only around M$30.

CENTRAL NORTH MEXICO

To reach the ruins, take a 'Casas Grandes' bus (M$6) from Constitución in the center of Nuevo Casas Grandes; they make the 7km run every 45minutes during the day. You'll be let off at Casa Grandes' picturesque main plaza; from there signs direct you to the ruins, a 15-minute walk away. Local taxi drivers chat and play cards at Calle 5 de Mayo and Constitución in Nuevo Casas Grandes. They charge M$100 to Paquimé with a 30-minute wait. For about M$500 you can loop through Paquimé, Mata Ortiz, Hacienda de San Diego and Colonia Juárez.

AROUND NUEVO CASAS GRANDES

Southwest of Nuevo Casas Grandes are interesting little towns, cool forests and a variety of historic sites. You can combine several into a good daytrip.

The ancient petroglyphs along the rugged **Arroyo de los Monos**, 20km to the south, require some effort to reach. The road, Hwy 3, is in good shape up to the village of Colonia Madero, but the final 4km after it calls for 4WD (a car *might* make it). It's another 15 to 20 minutes on foot after that.

Down Hwy 4 past Paquimé is the Mormon village of **Colonia Juárez**, surrounded by apple orchards and with impressive school grounds at its heart, and the **Hacienda de San Diego** (☎ 636-1036004), a dilapidated 1902 mansion once owned by the Terrazas family, who controlled most of pre-revolutionary Chihuahua state. Descendants of a servant of the Terrazas still live there and for a small donation give quick tours. They'll also cook breakfast and lunch if you call ahead.

Mata Ortiz

At the foot of a short string of mountains 27km south of Nuevo Casas Grandes, Mata Ortiz, a tiny town with dusty, unpaved streets, loose chickens and unfinished adobe houses, has become a major pottery center. Artists here use materials, techniques and decorative styles like (or inspired by) those of the ancient Paquimé culture. Their work now attracts shoppers worldwide; the best pieces sell for over US$10,000.

A local potters' association has opened a **store** (🕑 10am-1pm & 3-6pm) in the old train depot at the entrance to town, but you should also stroll through the village where you can see people working. The clay is shaped without a potter's wheel, and the most historically authentic are painted with brushes made from children's hair. Dozens of families have turned their kitchens, living rooms and bedrooms into showrooms, and you might just purchase a pot sitting on someone's stovetop or stereo. Juan Quezada, credited with reviving the pottery tradition, is the most famous of the village's hundreds of potters. His well-marked workshop is a stone's throw from the depot.

Accommodation options include the wonderful **Casa de Marta** (☎ 636-661-71-32; per person incl 3 meals M$375; ⊠), a home-stay in the heart of downtown (no street signs) where you really are made to feel like part of the family. Even the locals will tell you how good Marta's cooking is. US currency is preferred here. A few other hotels are hidden around town.

There's no longer a bus service from Nuevo Casas Grandes. A taxi, including a one-hour wait, will cost you about M$280.

Cueva de la Olla

Tucked away in the mountains west of Mata Ortiz is this unique ruin, named for its shape: a giant pot. Though beautifully preserved, little is known about this place, save that it was clearly connected to the Paquimé culture, as illustrated by the characteristic T-shaped doors. About 30 or 40 people probably once lived here, farming the fertile valley and storing their grain beneath these cliffside overhangs.

Getting here is half the fun. It's a beautiful, though challenging, drive that requires a high-clearance vehicle and rewards with wonderful views of the desert, valley, mountain forests and wildlife. It takes about 2½ hours each way from Nuevo Casas Grandes. **Diana Acosta** (☎ 636-1036004), an enthusiastic college grad who lives at Hacienda de San Diego (see left), has started leading tours here and can also arrange overnight accommodations in some cabins near the cave (US$35 per person including breakfast and dinner).

MADERA

☎ 652 / pop 22,000 / elevation 2092m

The drive to Madera leaves the desert behind, twisting alternately through thick forests on the mountains and fertile plains between the hills. People come to the town for what's around it. The area is lush with mighty pine trees, salmon-colored cliffs, waterfalls and a wealth of archaeological sites. The climate is refreshingly cool, and the town regularly gets winter snow.

There are a few banks and *casas de cambio* around the center. You can get on the internet at **Techno Ciber** (cnr Calle 3 & Morelos; per hr M$10; ☉ 10am-9pm).

Sights

If you've got a little time to kill there are three 'museums' in town. You can see some ancient pottery, some stone tools and a roughly 1000-year-old mummy in the tiny **Museo Real del Bosque** (admission M$5) at the hotel of the same name. Ask at reception for the key. There are a few rocks and old photos at the even smaller **Museo Anasazi** (cnr Calle 3 & Mina; admission free; ☉ 9am-3pm Mon-Fri). Minus the mummy, the most interesting collection of random old stuff is on the walls of **Restaurante/Museo Mariscos La Costa** (☎ 562-09-56; cnr Calle 7 & Independencia; ☉ 8am-10pm).

Madera's **cathedral** (cnr Calle 1 & Ojinaga; ☉ hours vary), built of stone, is also worth a minute of your time.

Sleeping & Eating

If you ask around town, people will put you in touch with the owners of cabins outside town. They tend to be expensive.

Hotel El Prado (☎ 572-04-92; Calle 5 No 2204; r from M$160; **P**) These rooms, at the back of a little restaurant on the south side of town, were probably pretty nice at one time. In its current state, it's still a good budget option, and the women who run it are all smiles.

Hotel Alpino (☎ 572-03-29; cnr Calle 3 & Ojinaga; s/d M$200/250; **※**) From the street, this bright green place looks closed, but once you find your way in you'll see large, good-value rooms.

Hotel Casa Grande Sierra (☎ 572-39-23; cnr Calle 27 & Internacional; s/d/tr M$300/400/450; **P ※ ▣**) In a quiet spot 800m west of the roundabout, Madera's newest hotel is as spic-and-span as you'd expect, and it's the only one with wi-fi.

Hotel Real del Bosque (☎ 572-05-38; s & d/ste M$550/1100; **P ※**) The fanciest place in town, the Real del Bosque is on the highway coming in from Chihuahua. Its rooms are spacious and carpet-free, with simple but effective decorative touches. The restaurant is decent and the bar *tranquilo*.

Cueva del Indio (☎ 572-07-11; cnr Calle 1 & Gonzales; mains M$20-210) This lovely cave-themed spot has a design inspired by the ancient structures around it, T-shaped door and all. Trout, served nine ways, is the specialty of the house, but you ought to consider ordering *vestigios de la cueva* (see boxed text, opposite).

Getting There & Away

Madera's little **bus station** (☎ 572-04-31; cnr Calle 5 & Mina) has services to Chihuahua (M$190, five hours, hourly), Ciudad Juárez (M$360, eight hours, two daily) and Nuevo Casas Grandes (M$174, four hours, two daily).

Take care if driving to Madera during the night; there are some big cliffs and tight turns on the road coming up here.

AROUND MADERA

The following destinations have similar sites and scenery, but if you've got the time, it's well worth hitting both. Bring food and water.

Cuarenta Casas

The existence of cliff dwellings at **Cuarenta Casas** (Forty Houses; ☉ 9am-3pm) was known to the Spaniards as early as the 16th century, when explorer Álvar Núñez Cabeza de Vaca wrote in his chronicles: '…and here by the side of the mountain we forged our way inland more than 50 leagues and found 40 houses.'

Last occupied in the 13th century, Cuarenta Casas was an outlying settlement of Paquimé (p363) and perhaps a garrison for defense of commercial routes to the Pacific. Today about two dozen adobe apartments remain on the west cliffside of a dramatic, highly eroded Arroyo del Garabato. A trail descends into the canyon and climbs the western slopes to the largest group of homes as **La Cueva de las Ventanas** (Cave of the Windows), which is well preserved. The 2km hike isn't easy and takes at least an hour for the round trip. Signs provide historical background along the way, and other homes are visible elsewhere in the canyon.

Cuarenta Casas is 43km north of Madera via a paved road (Hwy 11) through pine forest. From the turnoff, a good dirt road leads 1.5km to the entrance. An 11:30am bus (M$50) from Madera goes by Cuarenta Casas en route to the town of Largo. In the reverse direction, it stops at the site at around 4pm, allowing enough time for a daytrip.

About 4km before the turn-off to Cuarenta Casas, through the gate near the lake (it's OK to open it), is **Cascada El Salto**, which flows mainly during the rainy season (July

EAT LIKE A CAVEMAN

Much is still not known about the ancient people who lived in the mountains around Madera, but one thing is clear: they ate well. Initially hunters and gatherers with no shortage of bounty in the valleys, they adopted agriculture (beans, corn, onions) after the Paquimé colonized them.

Madera's Cueva del Indio restaurant (see opposite) has taken their grotto theme beyond the aesthetics of the dining room and into the kitchen with their *vestigios de la cueva*, a delicious stew similar to food the original cliff dwellers would have eaten. Originally it would have been cooked in a clay pot buried in the ground with hot coals, but the restaurant's modern method uses a stovetop. If you'd like to try it at home, here's how:

- Boil 120g of pinto beans with a bit of onion and a slice of garlic over low heat. The beans are done when the water is thick and the same color as the beans; they should be tender, yet firm. It takes about two hours.
- Melt 100g of pork lard along with a quarter of a medium-sized onion in a frying pan. Continue for a few minutes until the onion gets some color.
- Add two dried red chili peppers and mix well, then stir in a few pinches of flour to thicken the broth.
- Add 150g of natural, salted dried meat (the ancients would have used deer, javalina, lizards, birds or other wild game; at the restaurant they use beef), pounding it until tender.
- Add the beans and mix for a few minutes before serving.
- A dash of paprika gives the dish a little color, but it's optional.

to September). If you have a high-clearance vehicle you can drive down this dirt road. Start listening for the falls after 1½km.

Cañón de Huápoca

This lovely valley west of Madera, thick with flowers August through October and birds year-round, holds more ancient adobe buildings. Head west on the unnamed, unpaved road from Madera's roundabout, taking the northern route at the fork. After 33km you'll come to the **Conjunto Huápoca** (☼ 9am-3pm; admission free), with trails to a triple set of cliff dwellings built about 800 years ago and abandoned 250 years later. You get only distant overlooks of the first two, **Cueva Nido del Águila** and **Cueva Mirador**, but you can enter houses in the **Cueva de la Serpiente**, so named because these restored adobe dwellings cut through to both sides of the cliff. It's down a steep, narrow canyon, and though there are steps it's not an easy walk. It's 2.5km round-trip to see them all.

Keep on down the dusty road and you'll pass **Balneario Huápoca** (admission M$15), a family-friendly, developed set of hot springs at the 40km mark (any guide can lead you to natural hot springs hidden elsewhere around Madera), and then cross the **Puente Colgante** (Suspension Bridge) over the Río Huápoca.

Head up the other side of the canyon and turn off the main road at the sign for **Cueva Grande** (admission free; ☼ 9am-3pm) where three more ancient buildings sit dramatically behind a rainy-season waterfall. It's an easy 600m walk from the parking area.

The road is rough (it would be great fun on a mountain bike), but a car can make it. The last 3km to Cueva Grande are extra bumpy, however. Seek local advice during the rainy and snowy seasons. Camping is allowed, but not campfires. Operating out of Madera, **José Domínguez** (☎ 652-5722211) has been driving tourists around in his van for years and speaks some English. He charges M$300 per person (minimum of two). Taxis, some of which are SUVs, will cost at least M$900.

CHIHUAHUA

☎ 614 / pop 749,000 / elevation 1455m

Peaceful Chihuahua remains unfettered by the trappings of tourism. It has some beautiful parks and plazas, excellent restaurants, and a fine collection of cultural offerings. This capital city of Mexico's largest state has long been a prosperous city, as evidenced by the restored colonial buildings dotting downtown and the remains of the 5.5km-long early-18th-century aqueduct to the southwest. Its modern economic success is best demonstrated by the

CHIHUAHUAS

So what's the connection between Chihuahua and those nervous, yipping little dogs? The puny pups, averaging about 2kg in weight, were discovered in this area of Mexico around 1850. While their exact origins are a mystery, it's widely believed that they first came from Asia or Egypt, and were introduced to Mexico by Spanish settlers. The canines were once thought to be indigenous to Mexico because of similar creatures depicted in ancient Toltec and Aztec art and described by explorers, but there exists no archaeological evidence to support this belief. Those beasts, say experts, must have been rodents that disappeared from Mexico not long after the Spanish conquest in the 16th century.

Chihuahuas are popular pets in their eponymous state. Chihuahua city now features an annual **Dog Parade** with about three dozen fiberglass dogs painted by local artists and put on display along downtown streets from July to September.

flash shopping malls on its outskirts and the proliferation of public art.

The bulk of foreigners use the metropolis only as an overnight stop en route to the Barranca del Cobre railway, so most of the folks you'll encounter will be locals; a pleasing mix of professionals, working-class, students and dapper rancheros decked out in brightly colored cowboy boots. Many Mennonites and colorfully attired Rarámuri come to town too.

History

From the first few Spanish settlers in 1709, Chihuahua grew to become both an administrative center for the surrounding territory and a commercial center for cattle and mining interests. The city had a hand in many of Mexico's defining historical events. In the War of Independence, rebel leader Miguel Hidalgo, after being captured by the Spaniards, was brought here and shot. Chihuahua served as Mexico's capital city from 1864 to 1866 after President Benito Juárez was forced to flee northward by the French troops of Emperor Maximilian.

The Porfirio Díaz regime brought railways to the city and helped consolidate the wealth of the huge cattle fiefdoms that surrounded it. Luis Terrazas, onetime governor, held lands nearly the size of Belgium: 'I am not *from* Chihuahua, Chihuahua is mine,' he once said.

After Pancho Villa's forces took Chihuahua in 1913 during the Mexican Revolution, Villa established his headquarters here. He had schools built and arranged other civic works, contributing to his status as a local hero.

Orientation

Most areas of interest in Chihuahua are within walking distance of the central Plaza de Armas. The Zona Dorada entertainment district, where most of the nightclubs are, is along Av Juárez at Av Colón, just northeast of the center.

Chihuahua uses a grid pattern (though it's very erratic) with Av Independencia serving as a 'zero' point for addresses. Parallel street names spaced by odd numbers (Calle 3, 5, 7, etc) to its north and by even numbers to its south.

Information

Most of the larger banks are around the Plaza de Armas. You'll find many *casas de cambio* on Aldama, southwest of the cathedral. There are many internet cafés in town, but most close fairly early. For late night access, try Mi Café (p373) or Hotel San Juan (p372). Ring ☎ 060 for ambulance, fire and police services.

Clínica del Centro (☎ 439-81-00; Ojinaga 816) Has a 24-hour emergency department.

Post office (Libertad 1700)

Rojo y Casavantes (☎ 439-58-58; www.rojoycasavantes.com; Guerrero 1207) Books bus, train and plane tickets and is an agent for American Express.

State Tourist Office (☎ 429-35-96, 800-508-01-11; www.ah-chihuahua.com; cnr Aldama & Guerrero; ☻ 9am-7pm Mon-Fri, 10am-5pm Sat & Sun) On the ground floor of the Palacio de Gobierno, this information outlet has extraordinarily helpful, English-speaking staff.

Sights

MUSEO HISTÓRICO DE LA REVOLUCIÓN MEXICANA

Housed in Quinta Luz, a 48-room mansion and former headquarters of Pancho Villa, this **museum** (☎ 416-29-58; Calle 10 No 3010; admission M$10; ☻ 9am-1pm & 3-7pm Tue-Sat, 9am-5pm Sun) is a must-see, not only for history buffs but for anyone who appreciates a good made-for-Hollywood story of crime, stakeouts and riches.

After his assassination in 1923, 25 of Villa's 'wives' filed claims for his estate. Government investigations determined that Luz Corral de Villa was the *generalissimo's* legal spouse; the mansion was awarded to her and became known as Quinta Luz. She opened the museum and the army acquired it after her death in 1981. You'll see many of Villa's personal effects plus weapons from his era, but everyone's favorite stop is the back courtyard where the bullet-riddled black Dodge that Villa was driving when he was murdered is on morbid display.

It's a pleasant walk from the center, or take any bus headed down Ocampo.

PLAZA DE ARMAS

Chihuahua's historic heart, with its mass of pigeons, shoe-shine boys and cowboy-hatted men sitting around the ornate iron bandstand (made in Belgium), is a simple but pretty place. Its majestic **cathedral** (10am-2pm & 4-6pm), built between 1725 and 1826, presides over the bustle. Behind its marvelous baroque facade is an altar of Italian marble and the original organ installed in 1796.

On the southeast side is the entrance to the small **Museo de Arte Sacro** (admission M$15; 9am-2pm Mon-Fri), which displays dozens of religious paintings from the big names of the 18th century, including Miguel Cabrera, plus a chair used by Pope John Paul II during his 1990 visit.

CASA CHIHUAHUA

Chihuahua's former Palacio Federal is now a **cultural center** (429-33-00; Libertad 901; adult M$40, child & student M$20, Thu free; 10am-5pm) with several historical galleries and events every Thursday night. The most famous gallery is the **Calabazo de Hidalgo**, where Miguel Hidalgo was held prior to his execution. Then part of a Jesuit convent, the dungeon was incorporated first into the new Mint and later the present structure after each building was razed. The creepy quarters contain replicas of Hidalgo's crucifix and other personal effects, while outside a plaque recalls the verses the revolutionary priest wrote in charcoal on his cell wall in his final hours thanking his captors for their kindness. Upstairs are several rooms full of high-tech displays, from videos of Rarámuri dance to reproductions of an-

cient rock art, about the state of Chihuahua that might inspire you to prolong your travel time in the state.

The sound-and-light show from 7pm to 9:30pm Tuesday to Sunday behind the building at the **Fuentes Danzarinas** (Dancing Fountains) attracts many wide-eyed kids.

PALACIO DE GOBIERNO

The handsome, 19th-century **palace** (429-35-96; cnr Aldama & Guerrero; admission free; 8am-8pm) features fantastic murals by Aaron Piña Mora showing the history of Chihuahua (grab the little guide explaining each of the paintings from the tourist office) surrounding the classic courtyard. On one side of the courtyard is a small room with a flickering 'eternal flame' marking the place where Father Hidalgo (see boxed text, p629) was shot.

In back is a pair of small but good museums. The **Museo de Hidalgo** (admission free; 9am-5pm Tue-Sun) honors its namesake, while the **Galería de Armas** (admission free; 9am-5pm Tue-Sun) has a variety of guns and swords from the Independence era.

PLAZA MAYOR

Fronting the Palacio de Gobierno, this large square has many monuments including the **Ángel de la Libertad** statue representing the freedom of the Mexican people. A laser shoots out of its sword during special events.

The **Templo de San Francisco** (7:30am-1pm & 4:30-8pm), a simple white church at the foot of the square, is the city's oldest. Construction began in 1715. Hidalgo's decapitated body was interred here before being sent to Mexico City in 1827. Another 'eternal flame' marks the spot.

ART MUSEUMS

Manuel Gameros started building the bold, art nouveau **Quinta Gameros** (416-66-84; Paseo Bolívar 401; adult/child & student M$20/10; 11am-2pm & 4-7pm Tue-Sun) in 1907 as a wedding present for his fiancée. By the time it was finished, four years later, she had died, the Revolution had begun and the Gameros family had fled Mexico. Pancho Villa would later use it as offices. As if this story wasn't good enough, some tour guides tell that Gameros' fiancée fell for the architect, Julio Corredor of Colombia, and married him instead. Staff insist there's no truth to this tale. Today the house is gorgeously restored and filled with a mix of period

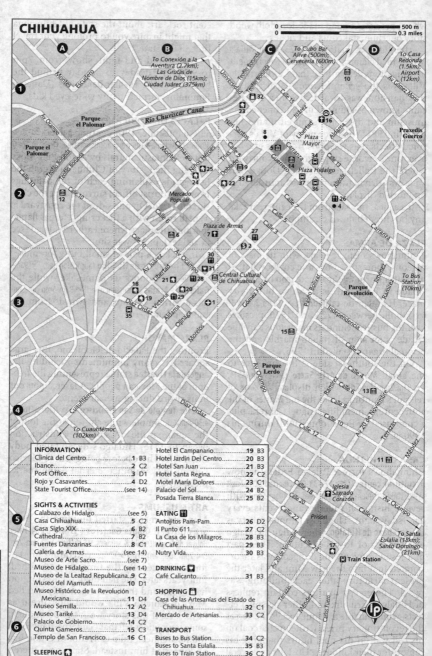

CHIHUAHUA

furnishings and art from the Universidad de Chihuahua's permanent collection.

Filling a former railroad roundhouse, **Casa Redonda** (☎ 414-90-61; Escodero at Colón; admission M$15; ◷ 10am-8pm Tue-Sun, closes 6pm Dec-Jan) now hosts the local museum of contemporary arts, which brings in art from around Mexico (there was a Diego Rivera retrospective last time we visited), and also a few train relics.

The less ambitious **Casa Siglo XIX** (☎ 439-80-80; cnr Calle 6 & Juárez; admission free; ◷ 9am-2pm & 4-7pm), a restored colonial gem of a building, has temporary galleries in the front and small-scale models of the massive metal sculptures by renowned Chihuahuan artist Sebastián, whose work rises in cities around the world, in back. You can see several of the real things around town, including one at the top of Parque el Palomar in the city's northwest.

MUSEO DE LA LEALTAD REPUBLICANA

Casa de Juárez, the home and office of Benito Juárez during the period of French occupation, now houses this **museum** (☎ 410-42-58; Juárez 321; adult/child & student M$10/5; ◷ 9am-6pm Tue-Sun). It maintains an 1860s feel and exhibits its documents signed by the great reformer as well as a replicas of his furniture and horse-drawn carriage.

MUSEO TARIKÉ

This seldom-visited **museum** (☎ 410-28-70; Calle 4 No 2610; adult M$10, child & student M$5; ◷ 9am-6pm Mon-Fri, 10am-4pm Sat & Sun) near Quinta Luz covers the history of the city. The old photos are generally more interesting than the exhibits (labeled in Spanish only), but the rolling toilet used by miners is alone worth the trip.

SCIENCE MUSEUMS

Chihuahua has two science museums that kids will enjoy, even though both have only Spanish signage. The **Museo del Mamuth** (☎ 415-73-78; Juárez 2506; adult M$15, child & student M$10; ◷ 9am-5pm Mon-Sat, 9am-4pm Sun) is a so-so natural history museum with lots of rocks and fossils on display, including an 18,000-year-old mammoth and a giant grey whale skeleton. **Museo Semilla** (☎ 412-39-12; www.museosemilla.com.mx; cnr Calle 10 & Teofilo Burunda; adult/child M$40/35; ◷ 9am-5pm Tue-Fri, noon-7pm Sat & Sun) is an excellent hands-on science center that's often full of school groups.

LAS GRUTAS DE NOMBRE DE DIOS

This cool **cave** (☎ 400-70-59; adult/child M$40/20; ◷ 9am-4pm Tue-Fri, 10am-5pm Sat & Sun) on the north side of town has some impressive stalagmites, stalactites and other rock formations, making the one-hour, 17-room underground journey fun, especially for kids. To get there take either a taxi (M$70) or a 'Nombre de Dios Ojo' bus (M$4.50) from the corner of Calle 4 and Niños Héroes. Ask the driver to tell you when to get off.

SANTA EULALIA & SANTO DOMINGO

Though it's just on the outskirts of Chihuahua, the historic hillside mining village of Santa Eulalia feels worlds away. The area's first silver was dug out of these mountains in the 17th century, and the mines are still going strong. The library (the new orange building) has a little **mining museum** (Av Zaragoza; admission free; ◷ 9am-noon & 3-6pm Mon-Fri) but it's more interesting to look around Chino's **Rock Shop** (Av Juárez) just downhill from the church.

Santo Domingo, 3km uphill from Santa Eulalia, is an interestingly ugly town full of

---

DETOUR: CUEVA DE LOS CRISTALES

Deep under the mountains around the town of Naica, 130km southeast of Chihuahua, Cueva de los Cristales (Crystal Cave) is one of the most incredible, surreal places on earth. Discovered in April 2000 during routine excavations in the Naica-Peñoles silver, zinc and lead mine, the 30m-long cavity is a tangle of translucent beams of selenite (a form of gypsum), some stretching up to 14m long and 3m in diameter – among the largest crystals ever found.

If you want to see it for yourself, plan ahead. Industrias Peñoles has added lighting and leads free tours, but only on Saturdays. Last time we checked the waiting list was three months – you can ask about cancellations but don't count on it.

Not everyone will be up for the visit, since the combination of 50°C temperatures and complete saturation in the cave – emanating from magma down below – can prove fatal after less than 10 minutes. Visitors must be at least 15 years old and have no heart conditions. For reservation or information, call ☎ 621-476-00-56 or ask at the tourist office in Chihuahua (p368).

old mining buildings. Señor Oaxaca, whose father was a miner, leads five-hour **mine tours** (☎ 415-52-60, cell phone 614-1967689; 2 people M$150) and has a big museum at his Bar-Restaurante Oaxaca. He provides hard hats and lanterns. The tourist office in Chihuahua (p368) can make arrangements.

To get to either town, catch a 'Francisco Portillo' bus (M$9, 45 min) across from Hotel El Campanario on Díaz Ordaz in Chihuahua.

Tours

Conexión a la Aventura (☎ 413-79-29; www.conexion alaaventura.com; Miguel Schultz 3701, Colonia Granjas; ☻ 9am-6:30pm Mon-Fri, 10am-2pm Sat) offers numerous outdoor trips all over the region, including rock climbing and rappelling in Parque Nacional Cumbres de Majalco (M$1120 per person, one day), kayaking the Río Conchos (M$2990 per person, two days) and sandboarding at Samalayuca Dunes (M$1380 per person, one day). A nine-day Copper Canyon trip with four days of burro trekking costs US$1135 per person with four people.

Chihuahua's historic-looking **Trolley Turístico** offers a 45-minute narrated (in Spanish) peek at Chihuahua's main historic sights. It departs from Plaza Hidalgo every hour from 9am to noon and 3pm to 7pm, Tuesday to Sunday; buy tickets (adult/child M$30/15) at the tourist office.

Sleeping

Chihuahua's cheapest places may be rougher than you're used to. It pays to look at the rooms before deciding. Most of the lodging west of Juárez and south of Montes is of the by-the-hour variety. All of the midrange and top-end hotels have wi-fi.

BUDGET

Casa de Huéspedes (☎ 410-53-61; Libertad 1209; s/d M$80/100) The rooms at this unnamed place (Casa de Huéspedes simply means guesthouse) are pretty old, but the flower-filled courtyard and no-nonsense *dueña* more than compensate. If you're an early-to-bed kind of person and don't need a TV, this is a steal.

Hotel San Juan (☎ 410-00-35; Victoria 823; s/d/tr/q M$135/145/175/185; ☒ 🖳) This was clearly a primo address back in the day. The decay adds charm to the tile- and arch-filled courtyard, while the rooms are just plain tired. They are, however, good for the price. The bar is

very loud, but you can't hear the music in the back rooms. There is 24-hour internet access (M$10 per hour).

Casa de Chihuahua (☎ 410-08-43; www.casade chihuahua.com; Mendez 2203; dm/d M$140/260; ☒ ☒ 🖳) This new, well-run hostel facing the train station is a budding backpacker base, though a very tranquil one. It's for 'people who like to sleep,' as the Mexican–French couple who own it say, and no alcohol is allowed on the grounds. Features include a large common area with movies, a gym, a book exchange and free wi-fi throughout. Gay couples are requested not to show public affection.

our pick **Hotel Jardín del Centro** (☎ 415-18-32; Victoria 818; r from M$230; P ☒ ☒) Cozy and modern rooms around a plant- and bird-filled courtyard make this one of the best bargains in the city.

Motel María Dolores (☎ 410-47-70; motelmadol@ hotmail.com; Calle 9 No 304; s/d/tr/q M$277/299/377/398; P ☒ 🖳) Just down from Plaza Mayor, this impeccably run motel's basic but modern rooms are a very good deal. They've even got wi-fi.

MIDRANGE

Hotel Santa Regina (☎ 415-38-89; www.hotelessanta regina.com; Calle 3 No 102; r M$310-520; P ☒ 🖳) Small decorative touches cover up the slightly institutional feel of this older but shipshape hotel. The cheapest rooms are a tad dour, but the rest are pretty snazzy. A favorite of Mexican business travelers, it's run like clockwork and has a great downtown location.

Hotel El Campanario (☎ 415-45-45; Díaz Ordaz s/n; s/d M$490/520; ☒ 🖳) Your standard type of spot – lacks style but it's a fine choice with large comfortable rooms and a nice lobby.

Posada Tierra Blanca (☎ 415-00-00; www.posada tierrablanca.com.mx; Niños Héroes 102; s & d M$690, tr/q M$725/760; P ☒ ☒ 🖳 ☒ ☒) Despite the downtown bustle, this large motor lodge–style place with lots of flowers and trees on the grounds makes for a relaxing stay. The rooms are ready for a remodel, but they're large and comfortable. Check out the mural of world cultures in the back, even if you aren't staying here.

TOP END

Palacio del Sol (☎ 412-34-56; www.hotelpalaciodelsol .com; Independencia 116; r from M$1200; P ☒ ☒ 🖳) This white cement high-rise looms over the low-level city. The rooms are positively luxurious, and the doting service is welcome after a long, hot day. There's a small gym and a business center, and the bar has live music in the evenings.

Eating

Antojitos Pam-Pam (☎ 410-51-47; Carranza 1204; mains M$15-83; 8am-10pm Mon-Sat) Nothing fancy, just great home-style cooking, which makes it a favorite with downtown workers at lunchtime. The *chile relleno* burritos are delicious and filling.

Nutry Vida (☎ 410-96-64; Victoria 420; mains M$19-30; 8:30am-8:30pm; V) For vegetarians growing tired of cheese, this little natural-foods café and bakery is a welcome stop. You'll find salads, yogurts, veggie burgers (which aren't very good, frankly), fresh-squeezed juices and a variety of whole-wheat baked goods. Eat in or take out.

Il Punto 611 (Independencia 611; cappuccino M$20; 8am-9pm) The coffees and teas here are very good, and the baked goods are even better.

Mi Café (☎ 410-12-38; Victoria 1000; mains M$25-120;) This American-style greasy-spoon diner caters both to travelers and local cowboys, serving up excellent breakfasts and coffee at big, comfy booths. *Chilaquiles montados con huevos* (corn tortillas with chili and eggs) is great way to start the morning or kick a hangover. Internet access (till 10:30pm) costs M$15 per hour.

our pick **La Casa de los Milagros** (☎ 437-06-93; Victoria 812; mains M$40-98; 5pm-late) Who wouldn't love this place? Legend has it that Pancho Villa and his pals did, and you probably will too. Housed in a beautiful 110-year-old mansion featuring high ceilings, tiled floors and an open-roof courtyard, the food, cocktails list and colonial ambience at this stylish café all merge into a fantastic evening. The light-fare menu features a great selection of coffee drinks, fresh salads and *antojitos* like *quesadillas* filled with *huitlacoche* plus there are some steaks for heartier appetites. There's live music, usually *trova*, on weekends.

Drinking & Entertainment

The dive bar edging the front courtyard of the Hotel San Juan (opposite), open noon till 2am, attracts many Chihuahua hipsters. It has loud rock and metal on the jukebox yet maintains a mellow vibe, and there are usually as many women as men pounding back whiskey and beer.

our pick **Café Calicanto** (☎ 410-44-52; Aldama 411; 4pm-late) Enjoy live jazz and *trova*, luscious cocktails, big sandwiches, light snacks and a very diverse crowd on the tree-lined patio of this intimate café.

Cervecería (cnr Juárez & Pacheco; 11am-midnight) While other Zona Dorada nightspots try to outdo themselves with flash and style, this drive-in, park-like spot guarantees its success with one simple hook: cheap beer. One liter is just 28 pesos. *Norteño* and country bands kick off around 9pm and the earthy crowd makes for great people-watching.

Cubo Bar Alive (☎ 410-68-65; Juárez 3114; cover M$50; 10pm-2am Fri & Sat) Despite the competition elsewhere in the Zona Dorada, Cubo Bat Alive has been the spot to shake your thing for years. Live music gets the crowd crazy: not a chair, table or pole remains un-danced on.

Shopping

Cowboy-boot shoppers should make a beeline to Libertad between Independencía and Díaz Ordaz, where stores jammed with a flashy selection of reasonably priced rawhide, ostrich and lizard boots line the avenue.

Casa de las Artesanías del Estado de Chihuahua (☎ 410-60-73; Niños Héroes 1101; 9am-7pm Mon-Fri, 10am-5pm Sat) This state-run store has a good selection of *chihuahuense* crafts (including Mata Ortiz pottery) and food (pecans, *sotol*, Mennonite cheese), though prices can be high.

Mercado de Artesanías (Aldama 511; 9am-8pm Mon-Sat, 10am-3pm Sun) So overflowing with tacky crap (leather-clad shot glasses, Pancho Villa key chains, Jesus figurines in tequila bottles) you've just got to visit.

Getting There & Away

AIR

Chihuahua's **General Fierro Villalobos Airport** (☎ 446-82-33) has daily flights to Mexico City and major cities in northern Mexico (from around M$1750), as well as Los Angeles, Phoenix, Houston and Dallas in the US.

BUS

Autobuses Americanos (☎ 800-500-0707) services depart daily for Phoenix, Los Angeles, Albuquerque and Denver. Chihuahua's **bus station** (☎ 420-22-86; Av Juan Pablo II), about 10km east from the center of town, is a major center for buses in every direction:

Destination	Fare	Duration	Frequency
Ciudad Juárez	M$264	5hr	every 15min
Creel	M$190	5hr	hourly
Cuauhtémoc	M$64	1½hr	every 30min
Durango	M$421	9hr	frequent
Hidalgo del Parral	M$109	3hr	hourly
Madera	M$190	5hr	hourly
Mexico City (Terminal Norte)	M$1052	18hr	frequent
Monterrey	deluxe M$675	11hr	2 daily
	1st class M$546	11hr	12 daily
Nuevo Casas Grandes	M$206	4hr	11 daily
Zacatecas	M$596	13hr	frequent

CAR & MOTORCYCLE

The easiest way in and out of Chihuahua to/ from the south is along the canal (Av Teofilo Borunda), which has less traffic than Juárez or Aldama. Av Periférico Lombardo Toledano then gets you out to the freeway. Heading out of town to the west, take Cuauhtémoc to Zarco, where you pass many colonial mansions.

TRAIN

Chihuahua is the northeastern terminus of the Barranca del Cobre trains. Tickets are sold at the **station** (☎ 439-72-12; Mendez s/n; ☽ ticket window 5-7am & 10am-5:30pm Mon-Fri, 5-7am & 9am-12:30pm Sat, 5-7am Sun). For more information see p341.

Getting Around

The bus station is a half-hour east of town along Av Pacheco. To get there, catch a 'Circunvalación 2 Sur' or 'Aeropuerto' (which does not go to the airport – no public bus does) bus (M$4.50) on Carranza across the street from Plaza Hidalgo. From the bus stop in front of the station, the 'Aeropuerto' bus goes back to the center.

For the train station, take any bus headed down Ocampo or a 'Cerro de la Cruz' bus on Carranza by Plaza Hidalgo and get off at Iglesia Sagrado Corazón. It's a short walk past the medieval-looking prison. Heading toward the center, catch a 'Circunvalación 2 Sur' bus north on 20 de Noviembre to Plaza Hidalgo.

Taxis charge standard rates from the center to the train station (M$35), bus station (M$60) and airport (M$100). Expect to pay more going from the train station.

CUAUHTÉMOC

☎ 625 / pop 99,000 / elevation 2010m

West of Chihuahua, prosperous Cuauhtémoc is the main center for Mexico's Mennonites

(see boxed text, opposite). The town itself bustles so much that it feels much bigger than it really is; however, once you start searching for things to see and do, its real size quickly reveals itself. Still, some good restaurants make a stopover pleasant, as do the shady town square and a small but stately cathedral.

There are many banks (with ATMs) and *casas de cambio* around the plaza, and the **Módulo de Información Turistica** (☎ 581-34-88; Calle Morelos; ☽ 9am-1pm & 3-5pm Mon-Fri, 9am-noon Sat) is *in* the plaza. To get online, try **IQ Computación** (Av Allende 373; per hr M$10; ☽ 9am-10pm Mon-Fri, 9am-8pm Sat).

Sights

The large **Museo y Centro Cultural Menonita** (☎ 586-18-95; Hwy 5 Km 10; adult/child M$25/15; ☽ 9am-6pm Mon-Sat) holds hundreds of household goods and farm tools. It's remarkable how similar things are to what you'll find in small-town historical museums in the American Midwest. A variety of crafts, cheeses and fruit preserves are sold here. A taxi from downtown will cost you about M$200 with waiting time.

The new **Centro Cultural San Antonio** (☎ 590-4871; cnr Calle 5 & Juárez; admission free; ☽ 9am-3pm & 5-7pm Mon-Fri, 10am-1pm & 3-6pm Sat & Sun) on the other side of the tracks hosts changing art exhibits. So does the **Centro Cultural Cuauhtémoc** (admission free; ☽ 3-6pm Mon-Fri, 9-11am Sat), located in the hilltop **Parque Mirador**.

Sleeping & Eating

Hotel San Francisco (☎ 582-31-52; Calle 3 No 132; s/d/tr/q incl breakfast from M$170/180/250/260; P) Despite what you'd expect at these prices, the modern rooms at this serious bargain, one block off the plaza, sparkle.

Motel Tarahumara Inn (☎ 581-19-19; www.tarahumarainn.com; Av Allende 373; d/tr M$710/760; P ✲ ☐) Rooms are a little more ordinary than you'd expect from seeing what's outside, but still plenty comfy. There are a restaurant, bar and small gym on the premises.

St Cruz Cafe (☎ 582-10-61; Hidalgo 1137; mains M$25-72; ☽ 8am-midnight Mon-Sat, 4pm-midnight Sun) As upscale as Cuauhtémoc gets, this place has enchiladas and crepes with cappuccino, vodka tonics or white zinfandel. There's live music Thursdays to Saturdays from 9pm. A less artsy branch (open 4pm till midnight) is in the Parque Mirador.

Rancho Viejo (☎ 582-43-60; Av Guerrero 333; mains M$44-165) Good ol' Mexican food: choose from shrimp, beef and other traditional options at this homey log cabin. Apple pie finishes off the meal with style.

Getting There & Away

Frequent buses go to Chihuahua (M$64, 1½ hours) and Creel (M$124, 3½ hours). There's no terminal; buses stop at individual company offices. **Estrella Blanca** (☎ 582-10-18; cnr Calle 9 & Allende) is the largest, and all others are nearby.

The train station (see p341 for travel details) can be reached from the end of Calle 3, but the bus is faster and more convenient.

From the town's west end, the Corredor Comercial Álvaro Obregón (Hwy 5) runs north through the principal Mennonite zone, with entrances to the numbered *campos* (villages) along the way.

HIDALGO DEL PARRAL

☎ 627 / pop 101,000 / elevation 1652m

Parral is a pleasantly mellow little town (its courteous drivers even come to complete halts for pedestrians!) with some good museums and unique churches. Its biggest claim to fame is that it's the town where Pancho Villa (see boxed text, p376) was murdered on July 20, 1923, and buried with 30,000 attending his funeral. Soon after his burial, his corpse was beheaded by unknown raiders, and in 1976 his body was moved to Mexico City.

Founded as a mining settlement in 1631, the town took the Hidalgo tag later but is still commonly called just Parral. Throughout the 17th century, enslaved indigenous people mined the rich veins of silver, copper, quartz, lead and other valuable minerals from La Prieta mine, the installations of which still loom above town.

Orientation

Parral doesn't follow the standard grid-plan, which makes wandering the streets confusing but fun. Two main squares, Plaza Principal (home of the Templo de San José) and Plaza Guillermo Baca (fronting the cathedral) are

---

THE MENNONITES

In Cuauhtémoc, Nuevo Casas Grandes and Chihuahua, you'll likely do a double take when you first encounter Mennonite men in baggy overalls and women in American Gothic dresses and black bonnets speaking a dialect of low German to blonde children.

The Mennonite sect, founded by the Dutchman Menno Simons in the 16th century, maintains a code of beliefs that puts it at odds with many governments, particularly an extreme pacifism and refusal to swear oaths of loyalty other than to God. And so, severely persecuted for their beliefs in Europe, many sect members moved to North America, including post-revolutionary Mexico, where thousands settled in the 1920s.

Even today, most Mexican Mennonites lead an isolated existence, speaking little, if any, Spanish, and marrying only among themselves. Unlike the Amish, with whom they are often confused, Mennonites embrace technology, and several factories produce stoves, farm equipment and other goods, while Mennonite cheese and cream are sold across Chihuahua state and beyond.

Mennonite villages are called *campos* and are numbered instead of named. The greatest number (around 150) are clustered around Cuauhtémoc. It feels more like Iowa than Mexico here, with vast cornfields and suburban-type homes.

Most Mennonites remain firmly uninterested in pandering to shutter-clicking tourists. Don't expect cheerful conversations with gregarious Mennonites; most look at outsiders with disinterest or even disdain. But you can tour the *campos*.

Friendly **John Friessen** (☎ 625-5821322; irene@pjtrailers.com), in Cuauhtémoc, has a wealth of information about the local area and is the only person who can arrange a tour in Spanish, English or German. The visits are personalized (so are the prices, but expect a half day trip for two with John driving to cost around M$500) but usually include a visit to a mission church, a small farm, a cheese factory and a restaurant for a meal of Mennonite sausages and baked goods. Friessen's connections to the Mennonites go back generations; his grandfather was excommunicated from the church for choosing to let his children get a different education.

If John is booked out, Cuauhtémoc's Módelo de Información Turística (opposite) or Motel Tarahumara Inn (opposite) can get you a guide. There are never tours on Sundays, and Saturday tours miss out on some things as not all businesses will be open or in full production.

PANCHO VILLA: BANDIT-TURNED-REVOLUTIONARY

Best known as a hero of the Revolution, Francisco 'Pancho' Villa's adulthood was more given to robbing and womanizing than any noble cause, and even his admirers can't deny that for most of his days, he was simply a bad man. Though his life is obscured by contradictory claims, half-truths and outright lies, one thing is certain: Villa detested alcohol. In his *Memorias,* Villa gleefully recalled how he stole a magnificent horse from a man who was preoccupied with getting drunk in a cantina.

After his outlaw years, Pancho Villa had bought a house in Chihuahua. That spring, Chihuahua's revolutionary governor Abraham González began recruiting men to break dictator Porfirio Díaz' grip on Mexico, and among the people he lobbied was Villa. González knew about Villa's past, but he also knew that he needed men like Villa – natural leaders who knew how to fight – if he ever hoped to depose Díaz. Thus, González encouraged Villa to return to marauding, but this time for a noble cause: agrarian reform. The idea appealed to Villa, and he soon joined the Revolution, leading the famous División del Norte.

When rebels under Villa's leadership took Ciudad Juárez in May 1911, Díaz resigned. Francisco Madero, a wealthy liberal from the state of Coahuila, was elected president in November 1911.

But Madero was unable to contain the various factions fighting for control throughout the country, and in early 1913 he was toppled from power by one of his own commanders, General Victoriano Huerta, and executed. Pancho Villa fled across the US border to El Paso, but within a couple of months he was back in Mexico, one of four revolutionary leaders opposed to Huerta. Villa quickly raised an army of thousands, and by the end of 1913 he had taken Ciudad Juárez (again) and Chihuahua with the help of US-supplied guns. His victory at Zacatecas the following year is reckoned to be one of his most brilliant. Huerta was finally defeated and forced to resign in July 1914. With his defeat, the four revolutionary forces split into two camps: the liberal Venustiano Carranza and Álvaro Obregón on one side and the more radical Villa and Emiliano Zapata on the other, though the latter pair never formed a serious alliance. Villa was routed by Obregón in the Battle of Celaya (1915) and never recovered his influence.

---

roughly in a line along the north side of the river, linked by busy Av Mercaderes (also called Herrera). Both of these churches, like most in Parral, are decorated with stone in honor of the city's mining heritage. The bus station at the east end of town is connected to the town center by Av Independencia.

Information

The **Cámara de Comercio** (☎ 522-00-18; Colegio 28; ⏰ 9am-5pm Mon-Fri, 10am-1pm Sat) functions as a tourist office, distributing maps and brochures. For financial needs, there are banks and *casas de cambio* around Plaza Principal, including HSBC, which stays open late. Try **SMAC-Line** (Av Mercaderes; per hr M$10; ⏰ 9am-2pm & 4-7:30pm Mon-Fri, 9:30am-7:30pm Sat), west of Plaza Baca, for internet access.

Sights

Built by a wealthy silver tycoon a block off Plaza Baca, the beautifully restored **Palacio Alvarado** (☎ 522-02-90; Riva Palacio s/n; adult/child M$20/5; ⏰ 10am-5pm) has pressed aluminum ceilings and other artistic flair, plus plenty of original furnishings. Lady Alvarado died

shortly before the house was completed. Her funeral wagon, later used for Pancho Villa, is on display.

The building from which Pancho Villa was shot and killed in 1923, just across the river on the west end of town, now houses the **Museo Francisco Villa** (☎ 525-32-92; cnr Juárez & Barreda; admission M$10; ⏰ 10am-5pm Tue-Sun), with a small collection of photos, guns and memorabilia. Displays are in Spanish only. The best thing to do here is to listen to the often dubious stories the staff tell. The tale about Villa's body being switched with a decoy after the decapitation, and thus not actually being moved to Mexico City, however, may have some credibility. People still lay flowers at his tomb in Parral's cemetery.

Mina La Prieta (☎ 525-44-00; adult/child M$25/15; ⏰ 11am-4:30pm Tue-Sun) was opened in 1629 and closed in 1975, but today you can drop down 100m (you'll be at the same level as the city) in an original elevator and walk through a tunnel cut by hand around 1820. Except for scattered historical displays, which show the difficult and dangerous mining methods used throughout history, the pit still feels like it's being

Villa had expected the US to support his bid to become Mexico's next president, but when US President Wilson recognized Carranza's government, Villa decided to simultaneously discredit Carranza and seek revenge on Wilson by ordering his remaining men to attack Americans. This, he believed, would prompt Wilson to send troops into Mexico. In the early morning hours of March 9, 1916 Villa's men (Villa himself stayed safely several miles behind) sacked Columbus, New Mexico, home to both a US Cavalry garrison and Sam Ravel, who had once cheated Villa on an arms deal. Though around half of Villa's 500 militiamen died that day (there were 18 American deaths) and Ravel wasn't found (he was at the dentist in El Paso), the attack ended up a success for Villa because it did draw the US Army into Mexico in pursuit of the revolutionary. It also further boosted his legend because they never caught him.

In July 1920, after a decade of revolutionary fighting, Villa signed a peace treaty with Adolfo de la Huerta, the man who had been chosen as the provisional president two months earlier. Villa pledged to lay down his arms and retire to an hacienda in Canutillo (p378), 75km south of Hidalgo del Parral, for which the Huerta government paid M$636,000. In addition, Villa was given M$35,926 to cover the wages owed to his troops. He also received money to buy farming tools, pay a security detail of 50 of his former soldiers, and help the widows and orphans of the División del Norte.

For the next three years, Villa led a relatively quiet life. He bought a hotel in Parral and regularly attended cockfights. He installed one of his many 'wives,' Soledad Seañez, in a Parral apartment, and kept another at Canutillo. Then, one day while he was leaving Parral in his big Dodge touring car, a volley of shots rang out. Five of the seven passengers in the car were killed, including the legendary revolutionary. An eight-man assassin team fired the fatal shots, but just who ordered the killings remains a mystery. The light prison sentences the killers received leads many to the conclusion that the command came from President Obregón, though with all the enemies Villa made over the years, there are many suspects.

worked. At the top, some of the old buildings now contain a mining museum (M$10). A taxi up the hill should cost about M$25.

The 1953 **Santuario de Fátima** (Calle Jesús García), located on a hill just below La Prieta, was built from chunks of rock taken out of the mine, and bits of gold, silver, zinc and copper ore sparkle in the thick walls. Rather than pews, the congregation sits on short, pillar-like stools that represent the boundary stones that mark mining lands. The church is usually closed, but if you want to see inside, knock at the grey house on its west side and someone will unlock it for you.

Templo de San Juan de Dios, facing the cathedral across Plaza Baca, has a little **Museo de Arte Sacro** (Sacred Art Museum; ☎ 522-15-22; Mercaderes s/n; adult/child M$5/2; ☻ 10am-1pm & 4-7pm Mon-Sat) with various objects, some made in Parral using Prieta silver.

Festivals
For one debauched week leading up to the anniversary of the death of Pancho Villa (July 20), the city, plus thousands of bikers who show up for the festival, celebrates **Las Jornadas Villistas**. Hundreds of horseback riders make a six-day journey from the north, recalling Villa's famous marathons, and the gun-blazing assassination is re-enacted on the 19th and 20th. Hotels are booked far in advance.

Sleeping & Eating
Hotel Chihuahua (☎ 522-15-13; Colón No 1; r from M$150) This simple but spic-and-span hotel sits between Fátima church and Plaza Baca.

ourpick **Hotel Acosta** (☎ 522-02-21; Barbachano 3; s/d/tr/q M$235/295/365/455; ☐) From the ancient switchboard in the lobby to the original furniture in the rooms, the extremely friendly Acosta is a 1950s time warp. It's just off Plaza Principal and has great views from the roof.

Nueva Vizcaya (☎ 525-56-36; Flores Magón 17; s/d M$350/450; P ☒ ☐) This brand-new hotel north of the river is far from the most expensive in town, but there's none better. All rooms have kitchens and wi-fi, making this a heckuva bargain.

Restaurant La Fuente (☎ 522-30-88; cnr 20 de Noviembre & Colegio; mains M$20-90) Happy yellow walls and big windows add to the warm ambience at this local favorite, where you'll find a good range of dishes including steak, chicken, enchiladas and a fine garlic soup.

Kaleos Café (☎ 523-68-18; Plazuela Independencia 8; mains M$22-48; ☺ 4:30-10pm Tue-Sun) Young and artsy describes both the space and the patrons at this great little place just across the bridge from Plaza Principal. It's got real coffee, good sandwiches and free wi-fi.

For a sweet treat, stop by any *dulcería* for some La Gota de Miel candy, made (usually *without* honey) in Parral since 1932.

Getting There & Around

The bus station, on the southeast outskirts of town, is most easily reached by taxi (M$25 to M$30); it's about 2.5km from the center. Frequent buses run to Chihuahua (M$109, three hours), Torreón (M$212, 4½ hours) and Durango (M$257, six hours).

Hwy 45 to Durango is a long, lonely road. Keep a full tank of gas, and don't drive it at night.

AROUND HIDALGO DEL PARRAL

East of Parral, the village of **Valle de Allende** is lush with trees and offers a lovely look at a simpler life. Much of its early wealth came from walnut orchards. Transportes Ballezanos has hourly 2nd-class buses (M$15, 30 minutes) from Av Flores Magón near 20 de Noviembre north of the river.

The dusty village of **Canutillo**, 75km south of Parral and just over the Durango state border, is where Pancho Villa, a Durango native, spent the last three years of his life. His decaying hacienda, given by the government in exchange for his promise never to take up arms again, is now a **museum** (admission free; ☺ 9am-5pm Tue-Sun). It houses a collection of photos, guns and various personal artifacts and is attached to a 200-year-old church. Any Durango-bound bus from Parral can drop you in Villa Las Nieves (M$50, 75 minutes), from which it's a 6km taxi ride (M$50 round-trip).

TORREÓN

☎ 871 / pop 549,000 / elevation 1150m

Torreón lies midway between Chihuahua and Zacatecas, in the east of Durango state, and that's the best reason to stop here. That, and to use it as a base to visit Mina Ojuela (p380). Despite an attractive Plaza de Armas with several fountains, lots of trees and frequent goings-on, overall this is one ugly city. To be fair, several of its museums are excellent and the people are as pleasant as elsewhere in the north.

The 1911 battle for Torreón was Pancho Villa's División del Norte's first big victory in the Mexican Revolution, giving him control of the railways that radiate from the city. Villa personally led three later battles for Torreón over the next few years. During one, his troops, in their revolutionary zeal, slaughtered some 300 Chinese immigrants.

Orientation

Torreón is located in the state of Coahuila and is contiguous with the cities of Gómez Palacio and Ciudad Lerdo (both in Durango state); all three together are known as La Laguna (though the namesake lagoons around the area fill only in the rainy season). Torreón itself fans out east of the Río Nazas, with the Plaza de Armas at the west end of town. Avs Juárez and Morelos extend east from the plaza, past the main government buildings and several large shaded parks. The Torreón bus station is 7km east of the center on Av Juárez.

Information

You'll find most services you need, including banks with ATMS and internet cafés, on or near Plaza de Armas. Some staff members at **Coahuila Turismo** (☎ 732-22-44; www.ocvlaguna.com; Paseo de la Rosita 308D; ☺ 9am-2pm & 4-7pm Mon-Fri, 9am-2pm Sat), 5km east of the center, speak English.

Dangers & Annoyances

The city center, particularly the Plaza de Armas, can get seedy after dark, so be careful if you're walking around after about 10pm.

Sights

Torreón's shiny new **Museo Arocena** (☎ 712-02-33; www.museoarocena.com; Cepeda 354 Sur; adult M$30, child & student M$10, Sun M$10; ☺ 10am-6pm Tue-Sun, until 8pm Thu), just off the Plaza de Armas, has galleries of Mexican and Spanish art and a small city history exhibit, but the best part is the 4th-floor balcony, which traces the history of Mexico through its art, from Olmec masks to Octavio Paz's poetry. The auditorium shows art-house films (included in the ticket price) on Thursday, Saturday and Sunday (varying times). In front of the museum is an entrance to **Canal de la Perla**, a cool-to-walk-through former aqueduct recently rediscovered by accident.

The **Museo Regional de la Laguna** (☎ 713-95-45; cnr Juárez & Cuauhtémoc; adult/child M$37/free; ☺ 10am-6:30pm Tue-Sun), located inside Torreón's favorite park, known as El Bosque (The Forest), has excellent displays on pre-colonial desert cultures of the north, as well as other cultures from around the nation. The temporary art exhibits are hit or miss.

The key battles for Torreón, including Pancho Villa's escapades, are documented in the **Museo de la Revolución** (☎ 722-69-22; cnr Lerdo de Tejada & Calle 10; admission free; ☺ 10am-6pm Tue-Sun), not far from the Laguna Museum. It's well presented, but you won't get much out of it if you can't read Spanish.

Torreón's municipal cultural office runs three museums. Three blocks off the plaza, the **Museo del Ferrocarril** (☎ 711-34-24; Revolución at Carrillo; adult/child M$10/3 tr-entry ticket M$15, free on Tue; ☺ 10am-5pm Tue-Sun) has half a dozen train cars and related tools in an old railway workshop. Six blocks west is the **Casa del Cerro** (☎ 716-50-72; Calzada Industria; adult/child M$10/3, tr-entry ticket M$15, free on Tue; ☺ 10am-5pm Tue-Sun), the 'House on the Hill.' Of the three museums, this is the one that shouldn't be missed. Built in 1902 by engineer Federico Wulff, the mansion is gorgeous, and so are the original furnishings that fill it. Photos in the bathroom (why not?) show how much work went into restoring it. Surrounded by palm trees and a lush lawn, it's a freakish little oasis in this industrial city. Slip straight through Mercado Alianza and turn left toward the trees to reach the **Museo El Torreón** (☎ 716-36-79; cnr Juárez & Calle 5 de Mayo; adult/child M$10/3, tr-entry ticket M$15, free on Tue; ☺ 10am-5pm Tue-Sun) preserving the facade of an hacienda. It only holds a few historical photos of the city and is home to its builder's grave, under the tower that gave the city its name.

The 20.8m-tall **Cristo de las Noas**, fronting the TV antennas south of the city, is the second-tallest Christ statue in the Americas.

Sleeping & Eating

You'll pass lots of four- and five-star hotels aimed at business travelers on your way into town.

Hotel Galicia (☎ 716-11-19; Cepeda 273 Sur; s/d M$147/160) This 1930s inn is a study in faded elegance, with beautiful tiled halls, stained glass and battered furniture. The owners are very friendly, and the place has genuine character. Toilet seats are missing in most rooms.

Hotel Palacio Real (☎ 716-00-00; Morelos 1280 Pte; r incl breakfast M$380-767; P X ☐) There are several good midrange hotels downtown along Av Morelos, but this 1950s giant is the only one right on the plaza. It's a tad tired these days, but the rooms are large and so are the views.

Del Granero (☎ 712-91-44; Morelos 444 Pte; mains M$20-48; ☺ 8am-9pm; X V) Vegetarians and carnivores alike will love this bright café, which serves delicious meat-free, whole-wheat *gorditas*, burritos and *tortas*. The adjoining bakery also goes the whole-wheat route.

Fu-Hao (☎ 716-55-47; Cepeda 259 Sur; mains M$25-150, buffet adult/child M$78/45; ☺ 11:30am-10:30pm) Besides the ubiquitous buffet found in most Mexican Chinese restaurants, this Chinese-owned place on the plaza has a full menu. And the food is pretty good.

Getting There & Around

There are bus stations in both Torreón and Gómez Palacio, and long-distance buses usually stop at both. Torreón is a major transportation hub, with 1st-class buses departing regularly for the following:

Destination	Fare	Duration
Chihuahua	M$313	6hr
Cuatro Ciénegas	M$137	3½hr
Durango	M$182	3½hr
Mexico City	M$731	13hr
Saltillo	M$192	3½hr
Zacatecas	M$279	6hr

The tolls on the highway to Durango total M$325; most vehicles take the slightly slower free road, unless traffic is really heavy.

Frequent city buses (M$4.50) run up and down Juárez between the Plaza de Armas and the bus station. Buses heading to the center will be marked 'Centro.' To the bus terminal, catch a 'Central,' 'Campo Alianza' or 'División' bus. Taxis, which are metered, will cost about M$30.

AROUND TORREÓN
Mapimí & Ojuela

The deserts north of La Laguna are striking and hold many semiprecious stones for gem hunters. The village of **Mapimí**, founded in 1585, was once the center of an incredibly productive mining area and served the nearby Ojuela Mine between periodic raids by the Cocoyom and Toboso tribes. Benito Juárez passed through Mapimí in 1864 during his flight from French forces. The house where he stayed, near the northwest corner of the plaza, is now the unremarkable **Museo Juárez** (admission free; ⊙ 9am-2pm & 4-6pm). Miguel Hidalgo was imprisoned here in 1811, and locals will be eager to show you that house too. The church tower still has bullet holes from battles during the Revolution.

At the end of the 19th century, the **Mina Ojuela** supported an adjacent town of the same name with a population of over 5000. Today, a cluster of abandoned stone buildings clings to a hillside as a silent reminder of the bonanza years. A precarious 315m-long suspension bridge, the **Puente Colgante de Ojuela** (adult/child M$15/5; ⊙ 9am-6pm), was built over a 100m-deep gorge to carry ore trains from the mine. Today you can walk over it. A site guide (M$15) will lead you into the mine's maze of tunnels with hand-held oil lamps, showing you some mining equipment left behind, including a mummified mule, before taking you out the other side for a good view of the bridge. For an extra M$100 you can return across the gorge on a zip-line.

To reach Mapimí from Torreón, go 40km north on Hwy 49 (stay on Hwy 49 when Hwy 49D splits off) to Bermejillo, then 25km west on Hwy 30. Second-class buses leave Torreón's bus station for Mapimí (M$33, two hours) hourly. The well-signed turn-off for Puente de Ojuela comes 3km before Mapimí. From there a narrow and rough (but easily passable in a car) road winds 7km up to the bridge past a beautiful mountain known as La India. Depending on your bargaining prowess, taxi drivers in Mapimí will want at least M$100 for the round trip with waiting time.

Reserva de la Biosfera Bolsón de Mapimí

Some 170km north of Torreón, where the states of Durango, Chihuahua and Coahuila converge, is a remote desert region known as **Zona del Silencio** (Zone of Silence), so called because of the widespread myth that conditions in the area prevent propagation of radio waves. Some also believe this to be a UFO landing site (thanks in part to a NASA test rocket crashing here in 1970 and the massive, secretive search that followed) while new-agers seek out supposed 'energy' sites. The Zone of Silence is just a small part of this striking biosphere reserve dedicated to the study of arid-region plants and animals,

including the very rare Bolson tortoise (or Mexican giant tortoise). You're very unlikely to spot the tortoise, but you could very well see a horned lizard, coyote or pronghorn antelope. There's no main road through the area, just a series of sandy tracks and, at the time of writing, access was restricted to help protect the preserve. Aventura Pantera (p382) leads tours and can fill you in on what to do if you want to visit on your own.

DURANGO
☎ 618 / pop 464,000 / elevation 1912m

Durango city is a mellow, pleasant cowboy town with a delightful Plaza de Armas, fine colonial architecture and a great selection of hotels and restaurants. It's a fun place to unwind, yet there's also plenty to do.

Founded in 1563 by conquistador Don Francisco de Ibarra, and named after the Spanish city of his birth, Durango is just south of the Cerro del Mercado, one of the world's richest iron-ore deposits. This was the basis for Durango's early importance, along with gold and silver from the Sierra Madre. Other local industries include agriculture and timber, but it's best known for its role in the movie business (see p383). Note that as you cross the border between Chihuahua and Durango states you enter a different time zone; Durango is one hour ahead of Chihuahua.

Orientation

Durango is a good city to walk around, and most interesting places to see and stay are within a few blocks of the two main squares, the Plaza de Armas and Plaza IV Centenario. Av 20 de Noviembre is the main street through town.

Information

Several banks with ATMs, as well as *casas de cambio,* are on the west side of the Plaza de Armas, including **HSBC** (Constitución s/n; ⊙ 8am-7pm Mon-Sat), which cashes traveler's checks.
Boletín Durango Turístico (www.durangoturistico.com) An interesting and helpful Spanish website about Durango state.
Hospital General (☎ 811-91-15; cnr Av 5 de Febrero & Fuentes) For emergencies or walk-in medical care.
Ofinet (Calle Victoria s/n; per hr M$10; ⊙ 9:30am-9pm Mon-Sat) Fast connections and new computers.
Post office (Av 20 de Noviembre Ote 500B; ⊙ 8am-6pm Mon-Fri, 9am-noon Sat)

DURANGO

State Tourism Office (☎ 811-11-07; www.durangoturismo.com; Florida 1006; ☟ 8am-8pm) Has friendly staff, some of whom speak English. They can tell you if the Pancho Villa museum has finally opened.

Sights

The **Plaza de Armas** is one of the loveliest in this region, filled with fountains and flowers, and not a modern-looking building in site. The large band shell (the municipal band plays Thursdays at 6pm) has an *artesanía* shop below the stage. One of the reasons it's so pleasant to while away time in the plaza is the view of the impressive baroque facade of the **Catedral Basílica Menor** (☟ 7:30am-1:15pm & 4-9pm), constructed between 1695 and 1787. The vast Byzantine interior has fine sculptures and ceiling paintings.

Two other noteworthy buildings nearby are the **Palacio de Gobierno** (Av 5 de Febrero 97; ☟ 8am-3pm Mon-Fri), expropriated by the government from a wealthy Spanish mine-owner after the War of Independence and now featuring wonderful murals, and the striking neoclassical **Teatro Ricardo Castro** (☎ 811-46-94; cnr Av 20 de Noviembre & Martínez; ☟ 9am-3pm), featuring decorative carvings in the lobby and bold murals inside.

The not-to-be-missed **Museo de Arte Guillermo Ceniceros** (☎ 825-00-27; Independencia 135 Nte; admission free; ☟ 10am-6pm Tue-Sun) showcases the mysterious landscapes and feminine figures of its Durango-born namesake, who was profoundly influenced by his teacher, the formidable muralist David Alfaro Siqueiros. Temporary exhibitions feature international artists.

Most of the space at the bigger **Museo de Arte Contemporáneo Ángel Zárraga** (☎ 825-55-30; Negrete 301 Pte; admission free; 🕑 9am-6pm Tue-Fri, 11am-5pm Sat & Sun) is given over to temporary exhibitions of young local artists.

The **Museo de Arqueología de Durango Ganot-Peschard** (☎ 813-10-47; Zaragoza 315 Sur; admission M$5; 🕑 10am-6pm Tue-Fri, 11am-6pm Sat & Sun) is an innovative visual feast presenting the archaeological record of the region's indigenous cultures, from prehistoric times to the Spanish conquest, including skulls intentionally deformed through head binding. All descriptions are in Spanish.

Though poorly presented, the displays at the **Museo de las Culturas Populares** (☎ 825-88-27; Juárez 302 Nte; admission M$5; 🕑 Tue-Sun 9am-6pm) offer an interesting look at the former lives of Durango's indigenous cultures. There is a small onsite craft shop.

Other than some Miguel Cabrera paintings, the **Museo Regional de Durango** (☎ 813-10-94; Victoria 100 Sur; admission M$10, Sun free; 🕑 9am-4pm Tue-Sat, 10am-2:45pm Sun) has little you haven't already seen in the archeology and culture museums, but you should take a look at the French-style former mansion that now houses the museum.

The **Museo de Cine** (☎ 837-11-11; Florida 1006; admission M$5; 🕑 9am-6pm, from 10am Sat & Sun) offers a pretty low-budget display, but if you can't make it out to the actual film sets (see opposite), this little museum will have to suffice.

For some greenery and a ton of fun for the little tykes, go to the extensive **Parque Guadiana** just west of the center.

Tours

Aventura Pantera (☎ 813-08-75; www.aventurapantera .com.mx; Pino Suárez 436 Ote; 🕑 10am-3pm Mon-Fri) is run by Walter Bishop, who has been called the 'Dean of Ecotourism in Northern Mexico.' English-speaking guides lead trekking, birdwatching, canyoneering, and mountainbiking trips into the Sierra Madre Occidental mountains and elsewhere. Ask about volunteer opportunities teaching environmentalism or planting trees.

Sleeping

BUDGET

Hotel Buenos Aires (☎ 812-31-28; Constitución 126 Nte; r M$140-220) The Buenos Aires has tidy little rooms, most free of peeling paint, though they can be very loud.

Hotel Durango (☎ 811-55-80; Av 5 de Febrero 103 Ote; s M$199-285, d M$259-350; P ☒ ☒ 🖳) You can't escape the fact that the hallways feel hospital-like (the staff's white uniforms don't help) but the rooms, especially the remodeled ones at the top of the price range, are very cozy and have wi-fi. Some rooms have balconies, but the views are limited.

Hotel Plaza Catedral (☎ 813-24-80; Constitución 216 Sur; s/d M$250/350; P) This cool, 200-year-old castle-like building is a labyrinth of stairways, arches and tile work. With some TLC this could be one of the best hotels in the city; as is, it's easily the best budget option.

MIDRANGE

Hotel Posada Santa Elena (☎ 812-78-18; Negrete 1007 Pte; r from M$420; P) Friendly, small and quiet, this hotel is a find. It features 12 tastefully furnished rooms, some with their own petite courtyard. Beautiful sinks make shaving a luxury.

our pick **Hotel Posada San Agustín** (☎ 837-20-00; www.posadasanagustin.com; Av 20 de Noviembre 906 Pte; s M$440-640, d M$490-690; P ☒ ☒ 🖳) Most of the 14 modern, well-appointed rooms here face a quiet old colonial courtyard where guests are drawn to lounge about.

Hotel Posada San Jorge (☎ 813-32-57; www.hotel posadasanjorge.com.mx; Constitución 102 Sur; s/d M$450/500; P ☒ 🖳) In a handsome 19th-century building with 2nd-floor rooms around a courtyard, the San Jorge has larger rooms than the San Agustín, some with sofas and small balconies, making it one of Durango's finest hotels. The only possible downside is that the courtyard holds a colorful Brazilian restaurant – fine if you want some steak, but the noise can drift into the rooms.

TOP END

Hotel Gobernador (☎ 813-19-19; www.hotelgobernador .com; Av 20 de Noviembre 257 Ote; r M$1350; P ☒ 🖳 ☎) The Gobernador is the best hotel in town featuring lush landscaped grounds and lot of colonial-style design features, including some enormous lamps. Weekend rates drop to M$990.

Eating & Drinking

Durango boasts plenty of good restaurants and will provide a thrill for those craving a bit of variety. Constitución north of the cathedral and Av 20 de Noviembre (which becomes Florida) west of the Plaza de Armas are happy hunting grounds.

Gorditas Gabino (☎ 813-01-21; Constitución 100A Nte; gorditas M$7, mains M$20-80; ☯ 8am-8pm) A cheap-eats haven that bustles with people, all savoring the delicious *gorditas* stuffed with avocados, shredded beef in *salsa verde* and other tasty fillings. Finish things off with the creamy flan.

Cremería Wallander (☎ 813-86-33; Independencia 128 Nte; tortas M$21-48; ☯ 8:30am-8:30pm Mon-Sat, 9am-2:30pm Sun) You'll see trucks and motorcycles zipping all over town delivering these extraordinary *tortas*, made with cold cuts and cheese direct from the Wallander family farm on fresh-baked rolls. It's also a great place to stock up on baked goods, wine, yogurt, honey and granola.

Samadhi (☎ 811-62-27; Negrete 403 Pte; mains M$25-50; ☒ Ⓥ) The food and atmosphere won't knock your socks off, but it offers herbivores a good chance to try foods like *chorizos*.

Restaurant La Gloria (☎ 825-27-77; Martinez 315 Sur; mains M$25-85; ☒) This simple but artsy spot is a nice place to linger. The large menu has good breakfasts, *antojitos*, coffees and salads.

our pick **Fonda de la Tía Chona** (☎ 812-77-48; Nogal 10; mains M$52-135; ☯ 5-11:30pm Mon-Sat, 1-5:30pm Sun) In a city full of classy dining options, none outshine this classic. It fills a gorgeously decorated old building full of nooks and crannies while the menu is dedicated to classic *durangueño* cuisine like the *caldillo* beef stew).

Pizzaly (☎ 812-13-81; Av 20 de Noviembre 1004; medium pizzas from M$95; ☯ 11am-11pm Mon-Sat, noon-10pm Sun) It lacks the romantic vibe of some of the city's other Italian restaurants, but this one gets it right where it counts: the pizza.

Da Vinci Café (Constitución 310 Sur; cappuccino with tequila M$22; ☯ 9:30am-midnight Mon-Sat, 5pm-midnight Sun) A bohemian 2nd-story spot with good coffee and great views of Plaza de Armas. There's an art gallery and free wi-fi.

Au Pied de Chameau (☎ 825-05-50; Florida 1135-; ☯ 2pm-1am, Mon-Sat 1-8pm Sun) You take your chances ordering food – a mix of *nueva cocina Mexicana* and international fusion dishes – but the gorgeous space covered in African and Asian art is great for after-dinner drinks.

Shopping
You can find just about anything in the jumbled maze of stalls at **Mercado Gómez Palacio** (Av 20 de Noviembre; ☯ 8am-8pm), including tacos, pottery, cowboy hats, saddles, dried herbs, flowers and Mennonite cheese.

Getting There & Away
Durango's **Aeropuerto Guadalupe Victoria** (☎ 11-870-12-13), 15km east from the city edge, has six daily flights to Mexico City and less frequent services to Mazatlán, Torreón, Monterrey, Guadalajara and Tijuana, plus US services to Houston, Chicago and Los Angeles.

Good, frequent bus connections are available from Durango to many of the places travelers want to go.

Destination	Fare	Duration
Chihuahua	M$421	9hr
Hidalgo del Parral	M$257	6hr
Mazatlán	deluxe M$385	8hr
	1st-class M$296	8hr
Mexico City	deluxe M$846	12hr
(Terminal Norte)	1st-class M$652	12hr
Torreón	M$182	3½hr
Zacatecas	M$202	5hr

The tolls on the highway to Torreón total M$325; most vehicles take the slightly slower free road, unless traffic is really heavy.

Getting Around
The bus station is on the east side of town; buses (M$5) labeled 'ISSSTE' or 'Centro' departing from the far side of the parking lot will get you to the Plaza de Armas. Taxis, which are metered, cost about M$25 to the center.

To reach the bus station from downtown, catch buses labeled 'Camionera' along Av 20 de Noviembre anywhere near the plaza. Get off before the major intersection with the Pancho Villa monument and walk a short way northeast.

AROUND DURANGO
Movie Locations
From the 1950s to the 1990s, both Hollywood and the Mexican film industry made hundreds of movies in the unspoiled deserts and mountains just outside Durango. John Wayne, Clark Gable and Robert Mitchum spent many hours filming here. More recently, *Revenge* (1990), starring Kevin Costner, and *The Mask of Zorro* (1998), with Antonio Banderas, were shot here. The decline of the Western genre and tax breaks at other locations back in the US have largely ended the city's run as *La Tierra del Cine* (the Land of Cinema). *Bandidas* (2006), starring Salma Hayek and Penélope Cruz, was the last movie made here.

Many of the big-screen cowboys swaggered through **Villa del Oeste** (Hwy 45; admission M$10, Sat & Sun adult/child M$25/15; ☽ noon-6pm Tue-Fri, 11am-7pm Sat & Sun), 12km north of Durango. Today the set is a souvenir-drenched theme park with gunslingers shooting it out at weekends (2:30pm and 4:30pm on Saturdays, 1:30pm, 3:30pm and 5:30pm on Sundays) while the rest of the week it's empty. Either way, it's kind of fun. On weekends, a bus (adult/child M$30/20 including admission) leaves from Durango's Plaza de Armas a half-hour before each show. To get there on weekdays, take any north-bound bus (M$10, every 30 minutes) and remind the driver to drop you there. To get back you'll have to flag down a bus, but many won't stop, so expect to stand in the sun for a while.

Unfazed residents of the small village of **Chupaderos**, 3km north of Villa del Oeste, have moved right into their former set. Big screen–ready cowboys still ride past the saloon here, but they aren't actors.

Another Wild West set, **La Joya**, 44km north of Durango, was once owned by John Wayne. Though it's in a serious state of decay, dedicated Western fans will enjoy it. If you have your own wheels, the tourist office can point you there, or you could take a taxi for around M$375. Buses are not an option.

Durango to Mazatlán

Full of forested peaks and deep canyons, **Hwy 40** west from Durango to the coastal city of Mazatlán is one of Mexico's most scenic drives. Durango's tourist office has a list of mountain cabins for rent along the route and will make reservations for you. High in the mountains, the logging town of **El Salto** is a good place to break the journey. Mountain biking is big around town, and there are many waterfalls in the area. Another 48km west there's a beautiful waterfall, large canyon, odd rock formations and railroad tunnels (built for trains that never came) around **Mexiquillo**. About 165km from Durango is a spectacular stretch of road called **El Espinazo del Diablo** (Devil's Backbone).

You enter a new time zone when you cross the Durango–Sinaloa state border; Sinaloa is one hour behind Durango.

Northeast Mexico

Ignore the know-it-all cynics who tell you the northeast isn't the 'real' Mexico, whatever that's supposed to mean. The fact is, there are many good reasons to visit this region.

A great number of visitors who cross the border here limit their stays to just a break in an overnight journey as they travel further on at full throttle. True, there are no full-fledged beach resorts here (and that's a bad thing?) and the colonial towns and pre-Hispanic remains really are more impressive further south, but the northeast does nature like no other place, and it also has plenty of places of cultural interest to merit diversions off its excellent highways.

Economically, the northeastern states of Nuevo León, Tamaulipas and Coahuila form one of Mexico's most prosperous and business-driven regions. Its biggest city, Monterrey, is a confident, progressive place with iconic modern architecture, terrific museums and some of the best bar-hopping in the country, while up in the mountains, the colonial charm of Saltillo and the atmospheric allure of Parras compete to impress.

Beyond the urban beat you can bird-watch in desert scrub and cloud forest at Reserva de la Biosfera El Cielo, one of Mexico's most biologically diverse corners, and soak away an afternoon in the ethereal waters of Cuatrociénegas, deep in the Chihuahuan desert. The coast has remote beaches, lagoons and wetlands, with a diverse and easily seen marine life.

And, perhaps best of all, those who do take time to explore here can expect a particularly warm welcome from the *norteño* locals, for there's simply no tourist trail in these parts.

HIGHLIGHTS

- Take a 12m leap of faith at **Matacanes** (boxed text, p411) in the mountains around Monterrey
- Snorkel through the sublime desert pools of **Cuatrociénegas** (p389)
- Discover the vibrant artistic scenes in **Monterrey** (p396)
- Hike through the birders' paradise of **Reserva de la Biosfera El Cielo** (p423)
- Feast on fresh fish after swimming in the warm Gulf waters around **Barra del Tordo** (p421)

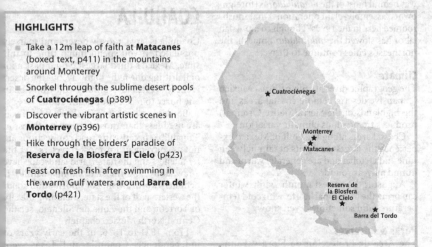

★ Cuatrociénegas

Monterrey ★
★ Matacanes

Reserva de la Biosfera El Cielo ★

★ Barra del Tordo

■ MONTERREY JANUARY DAILY HIGH 23ºC | 67ºF   ■ MONTERREY JULY DAILY HIGH 34ºC | 94ºF

History

It was the crown's search for silver and slaves, and the church's desire to proselytize, that brought the Spanish to this arid region.

The first explorers marched through the northeast as early as 1535, but the harsh conditions and incessant attacks by indigenous Chichimecs and, later, Apaches meant settlement and development came very slowly. Saltillo, the oldest town in northeast Mexico, was founded in 1577, and a few others took root before the end of the century, but widespread settlement didn't come until the early 1800s. Ranching was the main economic activity, and a few large landowners, some commanding private cavalries, dominated affairs here.

Though the northeast played little part in early Mexican history, it was a key area of conflict with the US, and several important battles (all Mexican defeats) of the Mexican-American War (1846–48) were fought here. The Treaty of Guadalupe Hidalgo that ended the war established the Río Bravo del Norte as the frontier between the two nations.

The discovery of petroleum, coal and natural gas and the arrival of the railroad accelerated development, and the region emerged as an industrial leader in the late 19th century.

Today this area is the most Americanized part of the country, with money and resources surging back and forth across the border. The Texas economy is particularly dependent on Mexican workers, while American investment was behind most of the *maquiladoras* (foreign-owned assembly-plant operations) that mushroomed here in the 1990s. Though cheap Asian labor has slowed the *maquiladora* march, the northeast's cities continue to thrive.

Climate

The geographic diversity of northeast Mexico (expansive deserts, remote coastal areas and the highlands of the Sierra Madre Oriental) produces tremendous climatic variation.

Coastal areas along the Gulf of Mexico experience the largest amounts of rain between June and October and are generally warm and humid all year round.

August is the hottest month, while winter can bring the occasional 'norte' with cold temperatures and sometimes even snow.

Parks & Reserves

The Área de Protección de Flora y Fauna Cuatrociénegas (p389) is a desert oasis with a rich aquatic ecosystem. Further south the diverse forests of the Reserva de la Biosfera El Cielo (p423) are particularly rich in birdlife. Biologically speaking, both places are special, and they're very easy to visit.

There's fantastic rock-climbing, canyoneering, hiking, mountain biking and more in the mountains around Monterrey, most of it in Parque Nacional Cumbres de Monterrey (boxed text, p411).

Getting There & Around

The main highways running south from the Texas border are: Hwy 57, bypassing most mountainous areas from Piedras Negras to Saltillo and eventually reaching Mexico City; Hwy 85, also known as the Pan-American Hwy, beginning at Nuevo Laredo and passing through Monterrey and Ciudad Victoria; and Hwy 40, running southwest from Reynosa to Monterrey, Saltillo, Durango and eventually Mazatlán on the Pacific coast. Smaller Hwys 101 and 180 go south from Matamoros down the Gulf coast through Tampico and Veracruz. Hwy 2, the Carretera Ribereña, parallels the Río Bravo between Ciudad Acuña and Matamoros.

Very frequent buses leave the cities on the Mexican side of the border to virtually every town in the region and most major destinations further afield. Numerous international airlines service Monterrey.

COAHUILA

Coahuila is large, mostly desert and sparsely populated. If you spend much time in this state, Mexico's third largest, you'll pass a lot of it drifting down the highway, but the desert scenery is often so stunning you won't be in any hurry to reach your destination.

Border crossings into Coahuila from Texas are used less than those further southeast in Tamaulipas because the road connections are not as convenient for most travelers. Yet the remoteness and the harsh, arid landscape have a raw allure, and the state capital, Saltillo, is definitely worth a visit. For information about the western part of the state, including the city of Torreón and the Zona del Silencio, see the Central North Mexico chapter.

From 1821 to 1836, in the early years of independence, Coahuila and Texas were one state of the new Mexican republic with

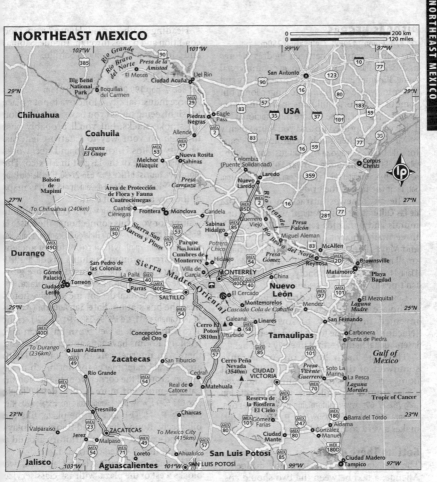

NORTHEAST MEXICO

Monclova and Saltillo each taking a turn as capital. In January 2007 Coahuila became the first state to follow Mexico City's lead and legalize civil unions for gay couples.

CIUDAD ACUÑA

☎ 877 / pop 126,000 / elevation 290m

Ciudad Acuña, a small frontier city just across from Del Rio, Texas, is a fairly busy but hassle-free border crossing, open 24 hours a day. It's a pleasant place and can be fun for an hour or two. The city's main claim to fame is that the movie *El Mariachi* and its big-budget sequel *Desperado* were filmed here.

The main drag, Hidalgo, running west from the border, is chock full of souvenir shops, bars and dentists. There are banks with

ATMs around the plaza, and the **tourist office** (☎ 772-16-00; Lerdo 110 Sur; ☉ 9am-5pm Mon-Fri) is just off Hidalgo.

The rooms at the well-situated **Hotel San Jorge** (☎ 772-54-40; Hidalgo 165; r M$300-350; P ☒) are much cozier than you'd expect from looking at the exterior. Opened in 1923, the lovely dining room at **Crosby's** (☎ 772-20-20; Hidalgo 195; mains US$4-18) is a near-mandatory stop for day-tripping gringos. For local flavors, just step off Hidalgo. The **Corona Club** (Hidalgo 200) is the bar Antonio Banderas shot up in *Desperado*.

The bus station is at Matamoros and Ocampo, just a few minutes' walk from the border. It's a seven-hour bus ride to Saltillo (M$380/322 deluxe/1st-class, one daily/hourly) on good two-lane roads.

PIEDRAS NEGRAS

☎ 878 / pop 142,000 / elevation 250m

The border crossing between Piedras Negras and Eagle Pass, Texas, is a major commercial route. Piedras Negras is not an attractive city and not somewhere you'll want to linger long, but some of the historic buildings around the *plaza principal*, just over the Puente Internacional No 1, have been spruced up and you'll find plenty of Mexican leather goods, ceramics and crafts for sale in the Zaragoza Market just south of the plaza. The **tourist office** (☎ 782-13-54; www.piedras negras.gob.mx; Ocampo s/n; ☯ 9am-5pm Mon-Fri, 9am-1pm Sat) is at the foot of the bridge.

The city's newest attraction is the **Plaza de las Culturas** (Av Fausto Martinez) with sculpture, murals and pyramids representing Mexico's three main ancient cultures: Aztec, Olmec and Maya. The replica Pirámide del Sol has a small **natural history museum** (☯ 9am-9pm Mon-Thu, 11am-11pm Fri-Sun) inside. Sadly, the whole thing isn't nearly as neat as it sounds.

Legend has it that Piedras Negras is the birthplace of the nacho, said to have been invented in 1943 by bar-owner Ignacio (Nacho) Anaya. The town holds its three-day **International Nacho Festival** in early October.

There are many hotels on Av Carranza southwest of the bus station. With bright homey rooms, a good restaurant and even a playground for children, the **California Inn** (☎ 782-77-69; www.californiainn.piedras-negras.com; Carranza 1006; s/d/tr M$430/509/755; P ✖ ☐ ✖ ✖) makes a very comfortable base.

Getting There & Away

The bus station is 1km from the bridge on Allende; a taxi between the two should cost M$20. Autobuses Coahuilenses has a ticket office at the foot of the bridge – buy a ticket here and they'll transport you to the station.

First-class services from Piedras Negras run to many places in Mexico:

Destination	Fare	Duration	Frequency (daily)
Cuatro Ciénegas	M$228	6hr	3
Mexico City	deluxe M$1221	17hr	3
	1st-class M$940	17hr	4
Monterrey	deluxe M$427	5hr	2
	1st class M$350	5hr	7
Saltillo	M$295	7hr	12

Buses also run to towns in Texas, including San Antonio, Austin, Dallas and Houston.

Heading south by road, Hwy 57 is in good condition and passes through Allende, Sabinas and Monclova on its way to Saltillo.

MONCLOVA

☎ 866 / pop 199,000 / elevation 615m

A large industrial city, Monclova is not a place for sightseeing unless you have a predilection for smoke stacks, but you'll probably pass through on your way to Cuatro Ciénegas. The city's Altos Hornos iron and steel works (Ahmsa) is one of the largest in Mexico. The **Monclova tourist office** (☎ 636-27-30; Blvd Harold Pape 455 Nte; ☯ 9am-5pm Mon-Fri, 9am-1pm Sat) has maps of the city and helpful staff.

About the only thing worth your time while waiting for your bus connection is the **Museo El Polvorín** (☎ 633-17-45; cnr Hidalgo & Ocampo; admission free; ☯ 8:30am-7pm), with a room full of ancient objects from around Coahuila inside a 1781 building that the Spanish used to store gunpowder. It's four blocks west of the plaza.

There are several decent, inexpensive hotels near the bus station. **Hotel San Agustin** (☎ 633-11-04; Carranza 311; s/d M$195/238; P ✖ ☐), right across the street, is well worn but clean and friendly. Rooms have fans and cable TV, and there's an internet café in the lobby. There are several cozier places for not much more money around the corner from the station on Cuauhtémoc. For more luxury, **Hotel Olimpia** (☎ 633-62-11; www.hotelolimpia.com.mx; Hidalgo 203 Nte; r M$577; P ✖ ☐), just off the plaza, fills the bill nicely. Rooms have tiled floors and playful hand-carved wooden furniture around a tree- and flower-filled courtyard.

The main bus terminal is on Carranza, two blocks west of the plaza, with 1st-class service to and from the following destinations:

Destination	Fare	Duration	Frequency
Ciudad Acuña	M$228	4½hr	hourly
Monterrey	M$135	3hr	hourly
Nuevo Laredo	M$169	4hr	5 daily
Piedras Negras	M$192	4½hr	hourly
Saltillo	M$140	3hr	hourly
Torreón	M$215	5hr	9 daily

Second-class buses to Cuatro Ciénegas depart hourly until 10:30pm (M$46, two hours). Three luxury (M$875, 12 hours) and six 1st-class (M$673, 14 hours) buses serve Mexico City's Terminal Norte.

Hwy 57 runs south to Saltillo (192km) and north to Piedras Negras (256km). About

25km south of Monclova, Hwy 53 branches southeast to Monterrey (195km). Hwy 30 heads west for 82km to Cuatro Ciénegas, then southwest to Torreón. Gas stations are rare along these routes.

CUATRO CIÉNEGAS
☎ 869 / pop 9500 / elevation 747m

The tranquil town of Cuatro Ciénegas is the perfect base for exploring the Área de Protección de Flora y Fauna Cuatrociénegas. With hundreds of shimmering cerulean *pozas* (pools), some up to 18m deep, and streams in the middle of the Chihuahuan desert, the reserve is special. Fed by a network of over 500 underground springs, it's a desert habitat of both extraordinary beauty and biological diversity. Over 75 endemic species, including three turtles and eleven kinds of fish, thrive in this fragile environment, an 843-sq-km protected reserve.

Within the pellucid waters of these desert aquariums is a wide variety of small fish (who like to nibble on you harmlessly), as well as organisms called *estromatolitos* (stromatolites), found in only two other places on earth, which are similar to the first oxygen-producing life forms. A few of the pools have been set aside as recreational spots and are ideal for swimming and snorkeling (you can buy cheap gear at several stores in town).

The town of Cuatro Ciénegas is an agreeable place with some adobe buildings and a handful of hotels and restaurants. You'll find a bank (with ATM) on the corner of Zaragoza and Escobedo, one block north of the plaza, and an internet café a block and a half to the southeast on Morelos. The tiny **tourist office** (☎ 696-09-02; Carranza 100 Sur; ☼ 9am-3pm Mon-Fri) is in the Presidencia Municipal.

Sights & Activities

A block east of the plaza is the interesting little **Acuario y Herpetario Minckley** (☎ 100-53-52; Morelos 112 Sur; adult/child M$25/15; ☼ 10am-1pm & 4-8pm Tue-Sun), where many of the rare snakes, lizards, toads, turtles, fish, spiders and scorpions endemic to the reserve can be viewed. All the creatures in this education center are well looked after by a knowledgeable biologist.

The **Casa de la Cultura** (☎ 696-05-56; Hidalgo 401 Pte; adult/child & student M$5/3; ☼ 3-7pm Mon, 9am-1pm & 3-7pm Tue-Fri, 10am-6pm Sat & Sun), in the former home of Venustiano Carranza, a revolutionary leader involved in the overthrow of Porfirio Díaz, has a small but excellent display of ancient objects unearthed in the area, including sandals made from the lechuguilla plant and jewelry made from bone. The house Carranza was born in, just north of the plaza, is now the **Museo Casa Carranza** (Carranza 107 Nte; admission free; ☼ 9am-1pm & 3-7pm Tue-Sun) with a hometown-proud display of photos and documents from his life plus a typical early 20th-century kitchen.

You could also visit a winery. **Bodegas Ferriño** (☎ 696-00-33; ☼ 8am-noon & 2-6pm), 1km north of the plaza along Carranza, pressed its first grapes in 1860. Staff at the neighboring **Vinos Vitali** (☎ 696-00-32; ☼ 9am-8pm) will gladly show you around their little operation.

ÁREA DE PROTECCIÓN DE FLORA Y FAUNA CUATROCIÉNEGAS

Most of the reserve's easily accessible sights are signed off Hwy 30 southwest of town. If you're exploring the area on your own, be aware that not all the desert tracks are signposted and they can turn to muck with even just a little rain. Summer temperatures can be extreme, so bring plenty of water and avoid midday excursions. Wearing suntan lotion is prohibited when swimming in the pools. You'll find much more tranquility if you visit on a weekday. Pay the M$20 per person admission fee at the visitor center.

Using the services of a guide is a good idea, and mandatory if you want to see the Dunas de Yeso. Not only are there fascinating tales to tell about this giant oasis, but also most of the *pozas* and other sites left in a natural state are unmarked. English-speaking **Arturo Contreras** (☎ 100-53-52; acuario_minckley@yahoo.com.mx), the biologist who directs the Acuario y Herpetario Minckley, knows the local fauna and environment well, and is highly recommended. He charges M$350 for a four-hour tour, plus another M$300 if he drives. The tourist office and hotels can also connect you with guides and drivers for about the same price.

The **Poza Azul visitor center** (adult/child & student M$15/10; ☼ 10am-5pm Tue-Sun), 8km out of town on Hwy 30, has illustrated displays about the reserve's ecology in Spanish and English. The little **Poza Las Tortugas**, a good spot for spotting turtles, is right behind the center, and 1.5km further back is the aptly named **Poza Azul** (Blue Pond), one of the reserve's most photographed sites.

NORTHEAST MEXICO

Just before the visitor center there's a turnoff on the left for **Río Los Mezquites** (☎ 696-04-08; ☺ 9am-7pm). Follow the rough track for 2km past salt flats (*salinas*) until you see a sublime stretch of slow-flowing blue water. Swimming and snorkeling here with the fish and turtles amid the desert landscape is a surreal, revitalizing experience. There's an overabundance of *palapas* (they ruin many lovely views) for shade, plus toilets and barbecue spots. It's usually deserted during the week but it's popular with families at weekends, when you may be charged M$35 per adult to use the area. **Sertuco** (☎ 696-05-85; www.sertuco.com; Carranza 305 Nte; ☺ 9am-6pm Mon-Fri) rents two-person kayaks (per hour Monday to Friday M$100, Saturday and Sunday M$150) here; it's best to arrange this at their office in town.

Poza La Becerra (☎ 696-05-74; adult/child M$40/20, camping per adult M$40), 7km further on from the visitor center and just off the highway, is the busiest and most developed (bathrooms, showers, snack shop) recreational facility. The water temperature here is a balmy, constant 32°C, but there are cooler areas where springs feed the pools.

Three kilometers past La Becerra is the quieter **Poza del Churince**, also good for snorkeling, where you'll almost certainly have a wonderful, shallow pool to yourself during the week. Entry and camping cost M$5. If the gate is closed, you're allowed to just climb through it.

For something completely different, get up close with the **Dunas de Yeso** (☺ 10am-6pm; per car M$50), also called Las Arenales, where blinding-white gypsum sand dunes contrast superbly with the six mountain ranges that ring the valley. They can be seen from Hwy 30, but to visit properly you must stop by the visitor center first.

Buses to Torreón will drop you off at the entrances to any of these sites, but they usually won't stop to pick people up. Hitching a ride isn't too difficult, but there isn't a whole lot of traffic on this road.

Sleeping & Eating

Camping is permitted at Poza La Becerra, Poza del Churince and Río Los Mezquites. The latter is away from the highway, and thus the best option, but the owner allows only people he likes to spend the night; call ahead or stop by the Acuario y Herpetario Minckley (p389) to arrange permission.

Hotel Ciénegas (☎ 696-06-93; Hidalgo 205 Ote; s/d M$150/200; ℗) The cheapest hotel in town isn't exactly good, but it's good for the price. The rooms lack hot water.

Hotel Ibarra (☎ 696-01-29; Zaragoza 200 Nte; r M$300; ℗ 🛏) The next step up in quality comes at this very ordinary place north of the plaza. It has large clean rooms (with two double beds and cable TV) but could use some TLC.

Hotel Plaza (☎ 696-00-66; www.plazahotel.com.mx; Hidalgo 202 Ote; s/d incl breakfast M$430/615; ℗ 🍴 💻 🛏) This hotel, a well-run and attractive place, a block from the plaza and built in colonial style, is highly recommended. All rooms face a slim, grassy patio and pool and have warm colors, high ceilings, comfy beds and wi-fi. The only negative is that the rooms are small.

Hotel Misión Marielena (☎ 696-11-51; www.hotelmisionmarielena.com.mx; Hidalgo 200 Ote; s/d/tr incl breakfast M$485/615/715, ste incl breakfast M$950-1200; ℗ 🍴 🛏) Directly opposite the Hotel Plaza, this competitor has much larger but less cozy rooms, all with two double beds and wi-fi, set around two rear courtyards.

Los Generales (☎ 696-01-40; Morelos 110 Sur; breakfast M$35, lunch incl drink M$48, dinner M$38; ☺ 7:30am-10pm Mon-Sat, 9am-4:30pm Sun; 🚫) With buffets and set meals, this pleasant little café is a good place to push your pesos.

La Casona (☎ 696-00-73; Zaragoza 109 Sur; mains M$30-120) The Hotel Plaza's restaurant, serving *antojitos*, steaks, salads, pastas, crepes and breakfasts, matches its parent for ambience and quality. It's a good place to start or end your day.

Getting There & Away

The bus terminal occupies the southwest corner of the plaza. Hourly 2nd-class services go to and from Monclova (M$46, two hours). First-class buses run to Torreón (M$137, 3½ hours, six daily), Saltillo (M$167, five hours, one each morning) and Piedras Negras (M$228, six hours, three daily).

SALTILLO

☎ 844 / pop 634,000 / elevation 1600m

Set high in the arid Sierra Madre Oriental, Saltillo is growing fast on the outskirts, but the quiet central area maintains something of a small-town feel. The city also boasts a number of fine colonial buildings, a temperate climate and some good restaurants, while a large student population adds energy. All of this makes it a popular weekend day trip for people from Monterrey. It's also on the main routes between the northeast border and central Mexico, making it an ideal spot to break a journey.

History

The Spanish first settled Saltillo in 1577, making it the northeast's oldest town. In 1591 the Spanish brought native Tlaxcalans from near Mexico City to help stabilize the area, and they set up a colony alongside the Spanish one.

In the late 17th century, Saltillo was the capital of an area that included Coahuila, Nuevo León, Tamaulipas and Texas. The city was occupied by US troops under Zachary Taylor during the Mexican-American War in 1846. The next year, at Buena Vista, south of Saltillo, the 15,000 strong army of General Santa Anna was repulsed by Taylor's 5000-man force in the war's decisive battle for control of the northeast.

During the Porfiriato period, agriculture and ranching prospered in the area, and the coming of the railway brought industry to the city, but Monterrey overtook Saltillo in both size and importance.

Orientation

Saltillo spreads over a large area, but most places of interest are right around the central plazas. The junction of Hidalgo and Juárez, at the southeast corner of Plaza de Armas, serves as a dividing point for Saltillo's street addresses, with those to the south suffixed 'Sur,' those to the east 'Ote' (Oriente), and so on.

The bus station is on the south side of town (a 10-minute bus ride from the center) on Periférico Echeverría Sur, a ring road that lets traffic bypass the inner city.

Information

BOOKSTORES

Libros y Arte (☎ 481-63-51; Instituto Coahuilense de Cultura, Juárez 109) Has a terrific selection of art, history and other Mexico titles.

CULTURAL CENTERS

Alianza Franco-Mexicana (☎ 414-91-05; Hidalgo 140) Shows French films and hosts occasional exhibitions on French culture.

EMERGENCY

Cruz Roja (Red Cross; ☎ 065)

INTERNET ACCESS

Conexión (Zaragoza 229; per hr M$12; ⊙ 9am-8:30pm Mon-Fri, 10:30am-8pm Sat & Sun)
Cyberbase (Padre Flores 159; per hr M$8; ⊙ 8am-10pm Mon-Fri, 10am 10pm Sat)

MEDICAL SERVICES

Hospital Universitario de Saltillo (☎ 412-30-00; Madero 1291)

MONEY

HSBC (Allende 203 Nte; ⊙ 8am-7pm Mon-Sat) Changes traveler's checks.

POST

Post office (Victoria 203 Pte)

TOURIST INFORMATION

Módulo de Información (cnr Juárez & Hidalgo; ⊙ 10am-8pm) This kiosk is conveniently located in the Plaza de Armas.
State tourist office (☎ 416-48-80; Av Universidad 205; www.secturcoahuila.gob.mx; ⊙ 8am-6pm Mon-Fri, 10am-6pm Sat & Sun) Across from Instituto Technológico de Saltillo, the office has brochures for Coahuila and many other states.

TRAVEL AGENCIES

Travel Center (☎ 410-91-25; Aldama 666 Pte; ⊙ 9am-2pm & 4-8pm, 9am-1pm Sat) Plane, bus and hotel reservations.

Sights

CATEDRAL DE SANTIAGO

Built between 1745 and 1800, Saltillo's **cathedral** (⊙ 9am-1pm & 4-7:30pm), arguably the most beautiful in the north, dominates the Plaza de Armas and has one of Mexico's finest Churrigueresque facades, with columns of elaborately carved pale-gray stone. The central dome features carvings of Quetzalcóatl, the Aztec rain god, and the carved wooden doors are also fantastic. Inside, the transepts are full of gilt ornamentation: look for the human figure perched on a ledge at the top of the dome. Ask at the tourist kiosk in Plaza de Armas about climbing the bell tower.

MUSEO DEL DESIERTO

Deserts cover about half of Mexican territory, and this excellent **museum** (☎ 986-90-00; www .museodeldesierto.org; Pérez Treviño 3745; adult/child & student M$65/35; ⊙ 10am-6pm Tue-Sun, last ticket sold 5pm) will teach you a lot about this biome even if you don't speak Spanish. Illuminating exhibits

SALTILLO

INFORMATION
Alianza Franco-Mexicana.................1	C3
Conexción..2	C2
Cyberbase..3	B2
HSBC...4	B2
Libros y Arte.............................(see 12)	
Módulo de Información.....................5	C3
Post Office.......................................6	B2
Travel Center...................................7	A1

SIGHTS & ACTIVITIES
Aventúrate Coahuila..........................8	C3
Casa Purcell.....................................9	C2
Catedral de Santiago.......................10	C3
Centro Cultural Vito Alessio Robles...11	C2
Instituto Coahuilense de Cultura.......12	C3

SLEEPING
Hotel Bristol....................................13	B2
Hotel Colonial Alameda...................14	A2
Hotel Jardin....................................15	B2
Hotel Urdiñola................................16	B2
San Jorge Hotel..............................17	B2

EATING
Dulcería Tres Rojas..........................18	A2
El Rincón Mexicano.........................19	C3
El Sorbito.................................(see 12)	
El Vegetariano Feliz.........................20	B2
Flor y Canela..................................21	C3
Restaurant El Principal.....................22	C1
Restaurant San Antonio...................23	C3

DRINKING
Cerdo de Babel...............................24	B2
Dublin Irish Pub..............................25	B3

ENTERTAINMENT
El Rincón Mexicano...................(see 19)	

SHOPPING
El Sarape de Saltillo.........................26	C3
Mercado Juárez...............................27	C2

TRANSPORT
Local Buses to Airport......................28	B1
Local Buses to Bus Station...............29	C2
Local Buses to Tourist Office & La Canasta.................................(see 11)	

reveal why sea currents can create deserts and how sand dunes are formed. Children will also enjoy the collection of dinosaur fossils. There's also a reptile house with rattlesnakes and lizards, and a botanical garden with over 400 species of cactus. Bus 18, running east down Aldama in the center, will drop you 1km downhill from the entrance.

MUSEO DE LAS AVES DE MÉXICO

Mexico ranks tenth in the world in terms of avian diversity, and this **museum** (Museum of Mexican Birds; ☎ 414-01-67; www.museodelasaves.org; cnr Hidalgo & Bolívar; adult/child & student M$10/5; ⊙ 10am-6pm Tue-Sat, 11am-7pm Sun), a few blocks south of the plaza, displays over 760 stuffed and mounted species (names are given in English), some in convincing dioramas of their natural habitat. There are special sections on feathers, beaks, migration and similar subjects.

ART MUSEUMS

Saltillo's leading cultural center, the beautiful **Instituto Coahuilense de Cultura** (☎ 410-20-33; Juárez 109; admission free; ⊙ 10am-7pm Tue-Sun), on the south side of the plaza, often features good

temporary exhibits by artists from Coahuila and beyond. It also hosts occasional concerts and has a terrific bookstore and café.

Casa Purcell (☎ 414-50-80; Hidalgo 231; admission free; ⊙ 10am-7pm Tue-Sun) is located in a wonderful 19th-century mansion. Built in an English neo-Gothic style with handsome gray stone, many of its rooms have stately fireplaces, stained-glass windows and parquet floors. Besides temporary art exhibits, Casa Purcell hosts semi-regular rock concerts and art-house films.

The book collection of the eponymous historian, now numbering 14,000 volumes from the 17th to 19th centuries, anchors the modest **Centro Cultural Vito Alessio Robles** (☎ 412-84-58; cnr Hidalgo & Aldama; admission free; ⊙ 10am-6pm Tue-Sun). Come to see the striking mural of the city's history splashed across the courtyard, and since you're here take a look at the temporary art exhibits to the right.

Tours

Aventúrate Coahuila (☎ 139-03-32; www.aventura tecoahuila.com; Hidalgo 268 Sur; ⊙ 9am-2pm & 4-7pm) Mónica Silva leads bird-watching tours around Coahuila.

Warthen sparrows and maroon-fronted parrots are two highly sought species.

Ruta Tranvía (adult/child M$30/25; ☻ 10am, 12:30pm, 3pm, 5:30pm) You can take a narrated, 1½-hour tour of the city on this historic-looking trolley, which departs the Plaza de Armas daily. Buy tickets at the tourist kiosk.

Festivals & Events

Aniversario de Saltillo This cultural festival over the second week of July commemorates the city's foundation.

Día del Santo Cristo de la Capilla In honor of Saltillo's patron saint, this festival takes place in the week leading up to August 6. Dance groups from around Coahuila perform in front of the cathedral.

Festival Internacional de las Artes (Coahuila Festival of the Arts) Artistic and musical events in towns and cities throughout the state in October. Saltillo gets most of the high-profile acts.

Sleeping

There are few budget and midrange places in central Saltillo. There are a few more across from the bus station. Several four- and five-star hotels line the highways heading north and east from Saltillo.

BUDGET & MIDRANGE

Hotel Bristol (☎ 154-01-34; Aldama 405 Pte; s/d/tr/q M$150/180/240/260) This old building, surrounding a two-story sky-lit courtyard, has aged fairly gracefully, which makes the rooms a bit of a let-down, especially the rock-hard mattresses. Still, they're pretty clean and have fans and cable TV.

Hotel Jardín (☎ 412-59-16; Padre Flores 211; s/d/tr M$150/200/250) A block over from the Bristol, right on Plaza Acuña, this ugly blue building with garish green rooms lacks the character of the Bristol, but it's quieter and more comfortable.

our pick **Hotel Urdiñola** (☎ 414-09-40; Victoria 251; s/d M$354/387; P ✗ 🖳) Initial impressions are excellent at the Urdiñola, which has a stately lobby with a sweeping marble stairway and a stained-glass window. The rooms are mostly set around a long, narrow courtyard; those on the upper floor enjoy more natural light. The remodeled rooms are the best value in the city, and even the older ones have character.

San Jorge Hotel (☎ 412-22-22; Acuña 240 Nte; s/d/tr M$553/624/683; P ✗ 🖳 🖳) Occupying a large concrete block that must have seemed modern in 1972, this hotel has large carpeted rooms with flowery bedspreads and garish fittings, some with great views. It also boasts a small rooftop pool, a restaurant and a central location.

Hotel Colonial Alameda (☎ 410-00-88; www .hotelcolonialalameda.com; Obregón 222 Nte; s & d/tr/q M$620/679/739; P ✗ 🖳 🖳) The only fancy digs downtown, this fine Spanish colonial-style hotel has a plush lobby and elegant, tastefully presented rooms, each containing a pair of huge beds and smart furnishings plus wi-fi. Ask if weekend discounts are on offer.

TOP END

Quinta Real (☎ 438-84-50; www.quintareal.com; Blvd Sarmiento 1385; ste incl breakfast Mon-Fri from M$2100, Sat & Sun from M$1290; P ✗ 🖳 🖳 🖳) Top of the heap in the top end, this highly impressive colonial-style place is a 15-minute drive north of the plaza off the highway to Monterrey. The spacious accommodations boast lovely furniture and virtually every conceivable amenity, including marble bathrooms with tubs. The hotel's facilities include fitness and business centers and a restaurant.

Eating

Central Saltillo has an excellent selection of cafés and restaurants within a short walk of Plaza de Armas. There are many cheap and popular *taquerías* around Plaza Acuña and some superb *fondas* on Mercado Juárez' 2nd floor.

Dulcería Tres Rojas (☎ 414-52-30; Victoria 701; ☻ 10am-1pm & 3-8pm Mon-Sat) A good place to try *pan de pulque* (M$22), a famous Saltillo food. It's kind of like a beer bread.

El Sorbito (Juárez 109; snacks M$10-32; ☻ 10am-9pm) Tucked away inside the Instituto Coahuilense de Cultura, this civilized little café grinds its own beans for barista-perfect coffee and serves snacks like bagels and cake.

El Rincón Mexicano (☎ 481-51-91; Juárez 314; mains M$15-65; ☻ 3pm-2am Fri, Sat & Mon-Wed, 3-10pm Sun) This likable and informal place specializes in southern Mexican cuisine like *empanadas* and *salbutes yucatecos* (corn tortillas with black beans, pork, cheese, chili and onion). There's live music Thursday and Friday.

El Vegetariano Feliz (☎ 410-08-75; Hidalgo 423 Sur; mains M$35-55; ☻ 9am-8pm Mon-Sat, 11am-4pm Sun; ✗ V) Although it only has three tables, the menu at this restaurant–health food shop–internet café is fairly large.

Flor y Canela (☎ 414-31-43; Juárez 257; mains M$40-50; ☻ 8:30am-9:30pm Mon-Fri, 4:30-9:30pm Sat & Sun) A stylish café ideal for breakfast, a snack, or a fine coffee or tea.

Restaurant San Antonio (☎ 410-81-15; Hidalgo 167 Sur; mains M$50-210; ☉ 8am-11pm Mon-Sat, noon-5pm Sun) Saltillo has many contenders for loveliest restaurant, but we give the nod to this place, with dining in and around a bright-orange, sky-lit courtyard. Service could use a kick in the ass, but the kitchen, turning out a mix of Mexican and international flavors, meets expectations.

our pick **La Canasta** (☎ 415-80-50; Carranza 2485; mains M$65-320; ☉ noon-midnight; ✗) One of Mexico's gastronomic greats, this famous place is decorated with art and antiques and warmed with a roaring fire. The menu is international with lots of meat and seafood selections. The signature dish is *arroz huérfano* (orphan's rice), which is loaded with ham, bacon, pecans, almonds and more.

Restaurant El Principal (☎ 414-33-84; Allende 702 Nte; mains M$85-315) *Cabrito* (kid goat) is the specialty at this family restaurant. It offers assorted cuts of goat like *cabecita* (steamed baby goat's head) and traditional cuts of beef steak. There are two other, less centrally located Principals.

Drinking & Entertainment

our pick **Dublin Irish Pub** (Allende 324 Sur; ☉ 7pm-2am Tue-Sat) Not one of those by-the-numbers Irish pubs you so often find in foreign lands; this is a lovely 1855 house filled with real pub atmosphere. Quaff a pint of Guinness (M$70) or sip something from the long mixed-drinks list. Rock bands rock the house on weekends.

The sociable **Cerdo de Babel** (Ocampo 324; ☉ 7pm-2am Tue-Sat), with jazz and other mellow music on the stereo, is an intimate bar on the pedestrianized part of Ocampo.

El Rincón Mexicano (☎ 481-51-91; Juárez 314; ☉ 3pm-2am Fri, Sat & Mon-Wed, 3-10pm Sun) has live music, mostly *música bohemia* and *trova* Thursday to Saturday nights.

Shopping

Saltillo is so famous for its sarapes that the local baseball team is known as the Saraperos. These days most items are woven in jarring combinations of colors, but some less garish wool ponchos and blankets are usually available.

El Sarape de Saltillo (☎ 414-96-34; Hidalgo 305 Sur; ☉ 9am-1pm & 3-7pm Mon-Sat) Sells fine quality sarapes, rugs, ponchos and tablecloths plus a good choice of *artesanía* from the rest of Mexico. Wool is dyed and woven on treadle looms inside the shop.

Mercado Juárez (☉ 7am-8pm) Next to Plaza Acuña, this market is also worth a look for sarapes, as well as hats, saddles and souvenirs.

Getting There & Away

AIR

Mexicana (☎ 415-03-43) has three daily flights between Mexico City and Saltillo, usually for around M$1700 one way, and **Continental Airlines** (☎ 488-13-14) flies daily to and from Houston, but most people fly from Monterrey. There are buses direct between Saltillo's bus station and Monterrey's airport.

BUS

Saltillo's busy bus station is on the ring road at Libertad, 2.5km south of the center. It has a left-luggage facility (M$5 per hour).

Departures to the following leave at least hourly, except Cuatro Ciénegas, which has just one each evening:

Destination	Fare	Duration
Cuatro Ciénegas	M$167	5hr
Durango	M$346	7hr
Mexico City	deluxe M$748	10hr
(Terminal Norte)	1st-class M$575	10hr
Monclova	M$140	3hr
Monterrey	deluxe M$71	1¾hr
	1st-class M$55	1¾hr
Nuevo Laredo	M$238	5hr
Parras	M$85	2½hr
San Luis Potosí	M$27	5hr
Torreón	M$192	3½hr
Zacatecas	M$240	5hr

Buses also go to Ciudad Acuña, Ciudad Juárez, Guadalajara, Matamoros, Mazatlán, Morelia, Piedras Negras, Puerto Vallarta, Reynosa and Tijuana. **Autobuses Americanos** (☎ 417-04-96) has services to Chicago, Dallas, Houston and San Antonio.

CAR & MOTORCYCLE

Saltillo is a junction of major roads. Hwy 40 going northeast to Monterrey, is a good four-lane road, with no tolls until the Monterrey bypass, though new tolls are planned. Going west to Torreón (262km), Hwy 40D splits of Hwy 40 after 30km, becoming an overpriced toll road. Hwy 40 is free and perfectly good.

The remote Hwy 57 runs north to Monclova (192km) through the dramatic Sierra San Marcos y Pinos while Hwy 54 crosses high dry plains toward Zacatecas (380km).

Getting Around

The airport is 15km northeast of town on Hwy 40; catch a 'Ramos Arizpe' bus (M$8) or a taxi (M$100) along Xicoténcatl. To reach the city center from the bus station, take mini-bus 9 (M$5) from in front of the station. To reach the bus station from the center, catch a No 9 on Aldama, between Zaragoza and Hidalgo. Taxis between the center and the bus station cost about M$30. Buses 5A and 10 run north on Hidalgo to the tourist office and La Canasta.

PARRAS

☎ 842 / pop 33,000 / elevation 1520m

A graceful oasis town located in the heart of the Coahuilan desert some 160km west of Saltillo, Parras is the kind of place that puts a smile on your face. It has a historic center of real colonial character and a delightfully temperate climate, but it's most famous for its wine, and even some no-frills restaurants serve it. Underground streams from the sierra surface here as springs, which have been used to irrigate the *parras* (grapevines) since the late 16th century. Parras is also an important manufacturer of *mezclilla* (denim), which is why jeans are sold in all sorts of strange places like hotels and candy stores.

Orientation & Information

Parras is pretty petite, and you can walk almost everywhere. The bus station is just a few minutes from the center on Arizpe, the principal street through town, and most hotels, restaurants, banks and shops lie on or near this street. Madero, the other significant thoroughfare, is one block south. **Computo y Línea** (Allende 306; per hr M$8; ☼ 9am-9pm) keeps longer hours than most other internet cafés.

The **tourist office** (☎ 422-02-59; www.parrascoahuila com.mx; ☼ 10am-2pm & 4-6pm Mon-Fri, 10am-2pm Sat) is on the road into town, 3km to the north.

Sights

The first winery in the Americas was established at Parras in 1597, a year before the town itself sprang up. Now called **Casa Madero** (☎ 422-01-11; www.madero.com.mx; admission free; ☼ 8am-5:30pm), it's 7km north of the center, in San Lorenzo on the road to the main highway. It's now an industrial-sized operation exporting *vino* all over the world. Free half-hour tours take you past winemaking equipment old and new, including some

wooden fermenting barrels holding over 70,000 liters. You can buy quality wine and brandy on-site too.

El Vesubio (Madero 36; ☼ 9am-1pm & 2-7pm Mon-Fri, 9am-7pm Sat & Sun), founded in 1891, is a much more quaint operation than Casa Madero. You'll find just a few dozen wooden wine barrels and a little shop in front of the family home.

Probably Parras's second most famous attraction after its vineyards, the **Museo de los Monos** (☎ 422-09-38; Madero 37; donations appreciated; ☼ 8am-11pm) is the bizarre dream of José Cruz Hernández, who has created a low-budget wax museum of sorts with not even remotely lifelike statues of his 'amigos,' including Freddy Krueger, Bill Clinton and Favio Alejo, the Univision reporter who came for a look. It's so bad that it's good.

The church perched precariously on the hill on the south edge of town is **Iglesia del Santo Madero** (☼ 10am-6pm Thu-Tue). Locals insist the hill is an extinct volcano: geologists say it isn't. It's a steep climb, but the expansive views are rewarding.

Parras also has stretches of an old **aqueduct**, many colonial buildings, and three **estanques** (large pools where spring water is stored) that are great for swimming.

Festivals & Events

Perhaps it's not very surprising that the **Feria de la Uva** (Grape Fair) is the biggest festival in town. It goes on for much of the month of August, featuring parades, fireworks, horse races, religious celebrations and traditional dances by descendants of the early Tlaxcalan settlers. And, of course, there's lots of wine. The festival moves to Casa Madero on August 9 and 10, the two wildest days.

Sleeping & Eating

Hotel Parras (☎ 422-06-44; Arizpe 105; r M$100) The cheapest lodging in town; with good reason. The price gets you two beds and all-concrete decor. The tree-filled courtyard is a small bonus.

Hotel La Siesta (☎ 422-03-74; Acuña 9; s/d M$250/350) Behind the bus station, this homey little inn is the best budget option in town. Rooms are small, but the host is charming and the lobby and courtyard are inviting.

Hotel Posada Santa Isabel (☎ 422-04-00; Madero 514; r M$500-700; P ☒ ☒) Rooms here are spread out around a tranquil courtyard full of fruit trees (watch out for falling avocados!). It's not quite as atmospheric as Hostal El Faro; however, unlike El Farol (for the moment, anyway), it does have wi-fi. There's a decent restaurant here too.

Hostal El Farol (☎ 422-11-13; www.hostalelfarol .com; Arizpe 301; r M$735-893, ste M$1370; P ✖ ⧉) This excellent colonial-style hotel has spacious rooms with plenty of period character; the best are set off a flower-filled courtyard. Service is top-notch, and so is the restaurant. Rates drop to M$620 Sunday to Thursday.

El Tiburón (Reforma 29 Sur; mains M$20-50) A friendly place for *antojitos* and more.

La Paella (☎ 174-80-22; Madero 102; mains M$25-75; ◷ noon-11pm Fri-Sun & holidays) You can guess the specialty of the house at this colorful place, run by a fun family from Saltillo in their spare time. There are also a few Mexican and Italian dishes.

Restaurant-Bar La Noria (☎ 422-05-47; Hostal El Farol, Arizpe 30l; mains M$45-159) This hospitable hotel restaurant has a courtyard with tables and makes a good choice for breakfast, steaks or seafood. Service is superb.

Parras is packed with *dulcerías,* all selling the region's famous *queso de higo* (fudgy candy made with figs).

Getting There & Away

Only 2nd-class buses serve Parras, but most have 1st-class comfort. There are nine daily to and from Saltillo (M$85, 2½ hours) and five daily to and from Torreón (M$105, three hours). If you want to head to Cuatro Ciénegas without backtracking to Saltillo, you can catch a bus to San Pedro Las Colonias (M$75, 1½ hours, four daily) and then a bus from there to Cuatro Ciénegas (M$119, two hours, nine daily). Parras is easy to reach by car; turn off the highway at La Paila and drive 27km south.

NUEVO LEÓN

With 85% of its 4.2 million residents living in and around the capital city of Monterrey, Nuevo León is one of Mexico's most sparsely populated states. Monterrey's industrial prowess, generating 7.4% of Mexico's GDP, makes the state a pillar of the national economy.

The earliest attempts by the Spanish to settle the area failed due to raids by hostile Chichimecs from the north. In 1596 the founding families of Monterrey finally held on, though periodic attacks continued into the 18th century.

The silver the Spanish sought was never found, but they discovered ranching was viable here. By 1710 Nuevo León still had few human inhabitants, but there were an estimated 1.5 million sheep. Industry arrived with the railroads in the 19th century, and this set the state on its present course.

MONTERREY

☎ 81 / pop 3.6 million (metro area) / elevation 543m

Self-confident Monterrey is Mexico's third-largest city, second-largest industrial center and *numero uno* in per capita income. You may never have heard of it, but 'La Sultana del Norte' is bold enough to have made a bid for the 2016 Olympic Games.

With sprawling suburbs of gargantuan, air-conditioned malls, manicured housing estates and the nation's first new Taco Bells, Monterrey is one of Mexico's most Americanized cities, but those who bypass it in favor of the 'real' Mexico are missing a vital piece of the national puzzle.

Regardless of its station in modern Mexico, Monterrey is well worth a few days of your trip. Its historic heart, where most of the main attractions are clustered, has plenty of metropolitan élan: iconic modern architecture, world-class museums and urbane restaurants. The city is also a good place to party, with a dynamic live-music scene, flashy techno clubs and lovely lounge bars. Jagged mountains, including the distinctive saddle-shaped Cerro de la Silla (1288m), make a dramatic backdrop for the city and provide ample opportunities for outdoor adventures.

History

Though several previous attempts to found a city here failed, in 1596 12 families, led by Diego de Montemayor, settled where the Museo de Historia Mexicana now stands. It wasn't until after Mexican independence, however, that the city began to prosper as its proximity to the US gave it advantages in trade and smuggling.

In 1900 the first heavy industry in Latin America, a vast iron and steel works (now the site of the Parque Fundidora) rose to dominate the cityscape. More mills followed, and Monterrey became known as the 'Pittsburgh of Mexico.' Though many of the smokestacks on the skyline are now idle, Monterrey still produces about 25% of Mexico's raw steel. The city also turns out around 75% of the nation's glass containers, 60% of its cement and half of its beer.

The city is famous for and fiercely proud of its entrepreneurial culture. *Fortune* magazine has rated it 'the best Latin American city to do business,' and over 500 US and Canadian firms base their regional operations here. Economic success and distance from the national power center have given Monterrey's citizens, called *regiomontanos* or *regios*, an independent point of view, and the city resents any 'meddling' in its affairs by the central government. Elsewhere in Mexico, people take umbrage at the city's arrogance, and anyone perceived as *codo* (cheap) is presumed to be from Monterrey.

Monterrey also commands an excellent international reputation for education, with six significant universities, including the Instituto Tecnológico de Monterrey, one of Latin America's best.

Orientation

Central Monterrey focuses on the Zona Rosa, an area of largely pedestrianized streets housing the more expensive hotels, shops and restaurants. The eastern edge of the Zona Rosa brushes the southern end of the Gran Plaza, a series of plazas and gardens studded with monuments. Across the Gran Plaza is the Barrio Antiguo, both the city's historic heart and nightlife nerve-center. San Pedro, 5km southwest of the city center, is Monterrey's most exclusive suburb. These areas are safe to walk around late into the night, as long as you use common sense.

The bus station is about 2.5km northwest of the city center, in a grimy traffic-blighted part of town, and there's cheap lodging around it. This is also a red-light district, though the sleaze largely skips Av Madero and it doesn't extend too far east where many midrange hotels are to be found. While robberies are not unheard of here, it's not a dangerous area overall. Colonia Independencia, around the Basílica de Guadalupe, on the other hand, is somewhere you should not walk through day or night.

Streets in the center follow a grid pattern. The corner of Juárez and Aramberri, roughly halfway between the Zona Rosa and the bus station, is the center of town – the zero point for addresses in both directions.

Information

EMERGENCY
Cruz Roja (Red Cross; ☎ 065)

INTERNET ACCESS
Telephone access is available at these places too.

E Connection (Map pp400-1; Escobedo 831; per hr M$20; ☼ 9am-10pm; Ⓜ Zaragoza)

SendeNet (Map pp400-1; Av Colón; per hr M$20; ☼ 6am-midnight; Ⓜ Cuauhtémoc) In the bus station.

Web Time (Map pp400-1; cnr Morelos & Juárez; per hr M$15; ☼ 10am-8:30pm; Ⓜ Padre Mier) On the 2nd floor of Interplaza Shoptown.

MEDICAL SERVICES
Hospital Muguerza (Map p398; ☎ 8399-3400; Hidalgo 2525 Pte)

Hospital San José (Map p398; ☎ 8347 1010; Av Prieto 3000 Pte)

MONEY
It's not much of an exaggeration to say there are banks and/or ATMs on every block of the Zona Rosa, and there are also many along Av Madero to the north. The most convenient ATMs for the Barrio Antiguo are under the Palacio Municipal. Exchange houses are most common along Ocampo west of Plaza Zaragoza and around the bus station.

POST
Post office (Map pp400-1; Washington 648 Ote)

TOURIST INFORMATION
Infotur (Map pp400-1; ☎ 2020-6789, in the US 866-238-3866; www.turismomonterrey.com; ☼ 9am-6:30pm Mon-Fri, 9am-5pm Sat & Sun) The friendly, English-speaking staff at this info center inside the Antiguo Palacio Federal on Washington have lots of information (much of it published in English and a bit in French) about sights and events across the state of Nuevo León.

Infotur kiosk (cnr Morelos & Zaragoza; ☼ 10am-8pm; Ⓜ Zaragoza) In the Zona Rosa.

TRAVEL AGENCIES
Viajes Santa Rosa (Map pp400-1; ☎ 8344-9202; Galeana 940 Sur; Ⓜ Zaragoza) Reliable for plane tickets.

Sights & Activities

GRAN PLAZA
A monument to Monterrey's ambition, this city-block-wide series of interconnected squares, also known as the **Macroplaza** (Map pp400-1; Ⓜ Zaragoza), was created in the 1980s by

the demolition of a prime chunk of city-center real estate. A controversial, but ultimately successful, piece of redevelopment, its charm has increased over the years as once-naked urban space has been softened by parks, trees, fountains and pools, though it still feels like several parks rather than one. A roster of iconic edifices line the plaza, including many that no doubt seemed cutting-edge back in their day.

At the very southern tip, the **Monumento Homenaje al Sol** is a soaring sculpture designed by Rufino Tamayo on a traffic island. It faces the modern **Palacio Municipal**, a concrete building, which is raised on legs. The municipal band takes the stage underneath it on Sunday (11am to 2pm and 5pm to 9pm) and Thursday (7pm to 9pm), and elderly couples dance away

the day. Just north of this building there's a shady park, **Plaza Zaragoza**, which hosts many concerts and special events. The centerpiece of the plaza is a graceless, 70m-tall orange concrete slab known as the **Faro del Comercio** (Beacon of Commerce). A green laser beams off the top at night.

Facing the southeast corner of Plaza Zaragoza is the terrific **Museo de Arte Contemporáneo** (Marco; ☎ 8262-4500; www.marco.org .mx; cnr Zuazua & Raymundo Jardón; adult/child & student M$50/30, free Wed; ☼ 10am-6pm Tue & Thu-Sun, 10am-8pm Wed), its entrance marked by Juan Soriano's gigantic black dove sculpture. Inside, its idiosyncratic spaces are filled with water and light and major temporary exhibitions. The Sala México, as you probably guessed, has

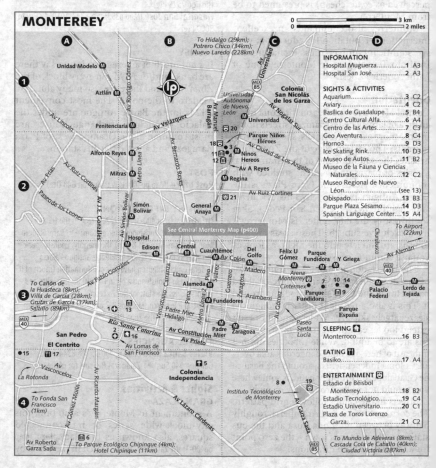

MONTERREY

0 _____ 3 km
0 _____ 2 miles

INFORMATION
Hospital Muguerza..............1 A3
Hospital San José................2 A3

SIGHTS & ACTIVITIES
Aquarium.............................3 C2
Aviary.................................4 C2
Basílica de Guadalupe..........5 B4
Centro Cultural Alfa............6 A4
Centro de las Artes.............7 C3
Geo Aventura.....................8 C4
Horno3...............................9 D3
Ice Skating Rink................10 D3
Museo de Autos................11 B2
Museo de la Fauna y Ciencias
  Naturales.......................12 C2
Museo Regional de Nuevo
  León..........................(see 13)
Obispado..........................13 B3
Parque Plaza Sésamo.........14 D3
Spanish Language Center....15 A4

SLEEPING 🛏
Monterroco.......................16 B3

EATING 🍴
Basiko..............................17 A4

ENTERTAINMENT 🎭
Estadio de Béisbol
  Monterrey.......................18 B2
Estadio Tecnológico...........19 C4
Estadio Universitario..........20 C1
Plaza de Toros Lorenzo
  Garza.............................21 C2

national works, while the other galleries could host just about anything else. Call in advance and you can get a tour in English. Marco also has a fine bookstore and restaurant.

Just north of Marco is the baroque facade of the **cathedral** (🕑 7:30am-8pm Mon-Fri, 9am-8pm Sat, 8am-8pm Sun), built in stages between about 1725 and the 1890s. The neon cross at the top just doesn't seem out of place in Monterrey. Facing the cathedral across the plaza is the 19th-century Palacio Municipal, which now houses the **Museo Metropolitano de Monterrey** (☎ 8344-1971; Zaragoza s/n Sur; admission free; 🕑 10am-6pm Tue-Sun). There's a brief, Spanish-only summary of city history on the ground floor and lovely upstairs galleries featuring the work of contemporary painters and sculptors.

North of Padre Mier is the **Fuente de la Vida** (Fountain of Life) with Neptune riding a chariot and being chased by naked women. Across Zuazua to the east is Monterrey's smallest and, after the cathedral, its oldest church, the adorable 1830 **Capilla de los Dulces Nombres** (Matamoros; 🕑 3-5pm Thu-Sat).

Looming over the church to the north is the bunker-like presence of the concrete **Teatro de la Ciudad**, which sits opposite its brutalist cousin, the lofty **Congreso del Estado**. A concrete leg from the latter drops into a shimmering pool where kids splash about on hot days. Further north again, the **Biblioteca Central** (State Library) and the **Palacio de Justicia** (Courthouse) stand on either side of the **Parque Hundido** (Sunken Park), a favorite spot for courting couples.

North again and down some steps is the **Explanada de los Héroes** (Esplanade of the Heroes) with statues of national heroes in each corner. It's the most formal and traditional of the spaces in the Gran Plaza and has the 1908 neoclassical Palacio de Gobierno on its north side, with the **Museo del Palacio de Gobierno** (☎ 2033-9900; admission free; 🕑 10am-7pm Tue-Fri & 10am-8pm Sat & Sun) filling its ground floor. The displays survey the history of government in Nuevo León, but you'll want to visit just for a look at the building.

Behind the Palacio de Gobierno, little Plaza Cinco de Mayo faces the grand facade of the 1928 **Antiguo Palacio Federal**, now home to the post office and tourist office. The **Templo del Sagrado Corozón** (cnr Zaragoza & Calle 5 de Mayo; 🕑 8am-1pm & 3:30-8pm Mon-Sat, 9am-3pm & 4:30-8pm Sun), completed in 1903, is lovely inside and out, making it popular for weddings.

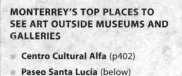

MONTERREY'S TOP PLACES TO SEE ART OUTSIDE MUSEUMS AND GALLERIES

- **Centro Cultural Alfa** (p402)
- **Paseo Santa Lucía** (below)
- **Corredor del Arte** (p408)

PLAZA 400 AÑOS

Yet another wide-open space, this one just east of the Macroplaza, is graced with fountains and pools, and it serves as a grand entrance to the sleek modernist **Museo de Historia Mexicana** (Map pp400–1; ☎ 8345-9898; www.museohistoriamexicana.org.mx; adult/child M$40/free, free Tue; 🕑 10am-7pm Tue-Fri, 10am-8pm Sat & Sun; Ⓜ Zaragoza), which presents an exhaustive but easily manageable chronology of Mexican history. There's also an Earth section full of mounted animals and realistic-looking plants at its heart. All explanations are in Spanish only, but English tours can be arranged by phoning in advance.

Next door, looking like a giant Jenga game, is the impressive **Museo del Noreste**. Technically it's a separate institution, but practically speaking its galleries on the culture and history of Nuevo León, Tamaulipas, Coahuila and Texas, packed with video screens and artifacts, function as a new wing of the history museum with one ticket working for both. Begin on the bottom floor to follow the displays chronologically.

Plaza 400 Años is also the terminus of the **Paseo Santa Lucía**, a waterside promenade lined with fountains, flowers and strolling families stretching 2.4km to Parque Fundidora (p402). **Boat rides** (adult/child round trip M$40/20; 🕑 10am-10pm) down the canal are very popular.

BARRIO ANTIGUO

The most atmospheric part of town, Barrio Antiguo (Map pp400–1) has cobbled streets and fine colonial houses, many of which have been converted into cafés, restaurants and art galleries. Av Constitución to the south and east, Dr Coss to the west and Padre Mier in the north form its historic boundaries (note the old-style street lights and lack of electricity wires), though its vibe extends a few blocks further north. On Thursday, Friday and Saturday nights it becomes a major party zone with an excellent assortment of bars and clubs.

CENTRAL MONTERREY

INFORMATION	
Canadian Consulate	1 E8
E Connection	2 E7
Infotur	3 E6
Infotur Kiosk	4 E7
Post Office	5 E6
SendeNet	(see 71)
US Consulate	6 B7
Viajes Santa Rosa	7 D7
Web Time	(see 46)

SIGHTS & ACTIVITIES	
Antiguo Palacio Federal	(see 3)
Biblioteca Central	8 E7
Capilla de los Dulces Nombres	9 E7
Casa de la Cultura de Nuevo León	10 E3
Casa del Campesino	11 F8
Cathedral	12 E8
Cervecería Cuauhtémoc	13 C1
Congreso del Estado	14 E7
Explanada de los Héroes	15 E6
Faro del Comercio	16 E7
Fuente de la Vida	17 E7
La Casa de los Títeres	18 E8
Monumento Homenaje al Sol	19 E8
Museo de Arte Contemporáneo	20 E8
Museo de Historia Mexicana	21 E6
Museo del Noreste	22 E6
Museo del Palacio de Gobierno	23 E6
Museo del Vidrio	24 E3
Museo Estatal de Culturas Populares	(see 11)
Museo Metropolitano de Monterrey	25 E7
Palacio de Justicia	26 E6
Palacio Municipal	27 E8
Parque Hundido	28 E6
Pinacoteca de Nuevo León	29 D6
Plaza Zaragoza	30 E7
Salón de la Fama	(see 13)
Teatro de la Ciudad	31 E7
Templo del Sagrado Corazón	32 E6

SLEEPING	
Fundador Hotel	33 E7
Hotel Colonial	34 D7
Hotel Del Centro	35 E6
Hotel Mundo	36 C3
Hotel Reforma	37 C3
Hotel Royalty	38 D7
La Casa del Barrio	39 E8
Radisson Plaza Gran Hotel Ancira	40 D7
Santa Rosa Suites	41 D7

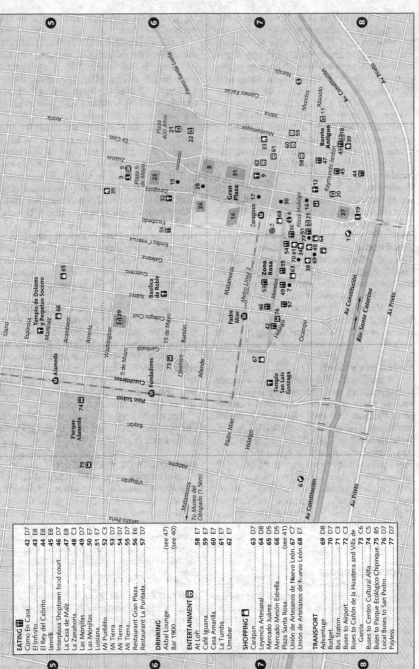

EATING 🍴
Como En Casa............................42 D7
El Infinito..................................43 E8
El Rey del Cabrito......................44 E8
Iannilli.......................................45 E8
Interplaza Shoptown food court...46 D7
La Casa de Maíz.........................47 E8
La Zanahoria...............................48 C3
Las Monjitas...............................49 D7
Las Monjitas...............................50 E7
Luisiana.....................................51 E7
Mi Pueblito...............................52 C3
Mi Tierra....................................53 D7
Mi Tierra....................................54 D7
Mi Tierra....................................55 D7
Restaurant Gran Plaza................56 E6
Restaurant La Puntada...............57 D7

DRINKING 🍷
Akbal Lounge........................(see 47)
Bar 1900...............................(see 40)

ENTERTAINMENT 🎭
At Lof..58 E7
Café Iguana...............................59 E7
Casa Amarilla............................60 E7
La Tumba...................................61 E7
Umabar......................................62 E7

SHOPPING 🛍
Carapan.....................................63 D7
Leyenda Artesanal......................64 D8
Mercado Juárez..........................65 D5
Mercado Mesón Estrella.............66 D5
Plaza Santa Rosa...................(see 41)
Unión de Artesanos de Nuevo León..67 C7
Unión de Artesanos de Nuevo León..68 E7

TRANSPORT
Advantage..................................69 D8
Budget.......................................70 D7
Bus Station.................................71 C3
Buses to Airport.........................72 C3
Buses to Cañón de la Huasteca and Villa de
   García....................................73 C6
Buses to Centro Cultural Alfa......74 C5
Buses to Parque Ecológico Chipinque..75 B5
Local Buses to San Pedro............76 D7
Payless......................................77 D7

Don't miss **La Casa de los Títeres** (Map pp400-1; ☎ 8343-0604; www.baulteatro.com; Raymundo Jardón 910; admission M$20; ☑ 2-6pm Sun-Fri; Ⓜ Zaragoza), which has an extensive collection of antique and modern puppets from all corners of the globe, including European marionettes and Vietnamese water puppets. An excellent puppet show (M$50) is held on Sunday at 4pm.

One of Monterrey's oldest buildings, the 1750 **Casa del Campesino**, built as the governor's residence and later used at various times as a hospital, college and farmers' organization office, now houses the **Museo Estatal de Culturas Populares** (Map pp400-1; ☎ 8344-3030; cnr Abasolo & Mina; admission free; ☑ 11am-7pm Tue-Fri, noon-6pm Sat & Sun; Ⓜ Zaragoza) with various temporary cultural displays and occasional special events. There's a simple but good café.

ZONA ROSA

This upmarket area (Map pp400–1) just west of Plaza Zaragoza contains many of Monterrey's top hotels, and is also a prime shopping district. It extends toward Padre Mier in the north, Zaragoza in the east, Ocampo to the south and Garibaldi to the west. Many of the streets are pedestrianized and usually bustling with life. It's a pleasure to walk around here.

MUSEO DEL VIDRIO

At the back of the Vitro bottle factory (enter from Zaragoza), which has many glass walls so you can watch production, this wonderful **museum** (Map pp400-1; ☎ 8863-1000; www.museodelvidrio .com; Magallanes 517; adult/child & student M$15/10, free Tue; ☑ 9am-6pm Tue-Sun; Ⓜ Del Golfo) focuses on the history, manufacturing and especially the artistic use of glass. The main museum has a bunch of old household objects and a reproduction of a 19th-century stained-glass workshop. The gallery hosts phenomenal temporary exhibitions of glass art in a restored warehouse and has artist workshops attached. You can buy some of the work in the gallery shop. Call ahead to schedule a tour in English.

PARQUE FUNDIDORA

Formerly a vast steel-factory complex, this once-blighted industrial zone has been transformed into a huge **urban park** (Map p398; ☎ 8345-4898; www.parquefundidora.org; ☑ 6am-11pm; Ⓜ Parque Fundidora) that encompasses a variety of attractions, including many that will appeal to children. Cleverly, the park designers retained rusting smoke stacks and other industrial relics, giving a postmodern, apocalyptic feel to parts of the place.

You could easily spend a day here taking in the exhibitions and galleries, enjoying a picnic lunch around the lake and finishing it off by attending a concert. Many special events are held here. A free trolley loops around the park, and there are bike rentals (M$40 per hour) at the north end.

Blast Furnace No 3, which feels like it could start up production again any time, has been converted into **Horno3** (☎ 8126-1100; www.horno3 .org; adult/child & student M$80/50; ☑ 10am-6pm Tue-Fri, 10am-8pm Sat & Sun), a high-tech, hands-on museum of steel and Mexico's steel industry. Don't miss the overly dramatic furnace show. Last tickets are sold one hour before closing.

Three other disemboweled redbrick factories compose the **Centro de las Artes** (☎ 8479-0015; www.cineteca.org.mx; admission free, films M$40; ☑ 10am-9pm Tue-Sun), filled with rotating modern art exhibitions. Centro de las Artes I is known as Cineteca, because it also shows independent and foreign films.

Elsewhere across the park are an **ice skating rink** (pista de hielo; ☎ 8191-8000; incl rental M$70), convention center with adjacent hotels, amphitheater, arena and the **Parque Plaza Sésamo** (Map p398; ☎ 8354-5400; www.parqueplazasesamo.com; admission M$169, young child free; ☑ 3-7pm Wed-Fri, 11am-7pm Sat & Sun), a vast *Sesame Street* theme park with dozens of thrilling rides, a waterpark and shows with the famous characters.

The metro drops you right near the park, but the best way to get here is along Paseo Santa Lucía (p399).

PINACOTECA DE NUEVO LEÓN

This **art museum** (Map pp400-1; ☎ 1340-4358; cnr Washington & Colegio Civil; admission free; ☑ 10am-8pm Wed-Mon; Ⓜ Alameda), in the gorgeous Colegio Civil building, has gathered paintings and sculptures from most of the state's leading contemporary artists, including Julio Galán (1958–2006), once part of Andy Warhol's circle, while the temporary exhibitions come from the rest of Mexico and beyond.

CENTRO CULTURAL ALFA

Usually called **Planetario Alfa** (Map p398; ☎ 8303-0001; www.planetarioalfa.org.mx; Av Roberto Garza Sada 1000; museum & grounds/museum, grounds & theater M$45/80; ☑ 3:30-8pm Tue-Fri, 11:30am-8pm Sat & Sun), the center is 7km south of the city center. Sponsored by the Alfa industrial group, its striking **museum**

MONTERREY FOR KIDS

Monterrey has plenty of attractions that will thrill children. On the east side of **Parque Fundidora** (opposite), **Parque Plaza Sésamo** (opposite) offers kids their *Sesame Street* fix.

Parque Niños Héroes (Map p398; Av Reyes; **M** Niños Héroes), about 5km north of the center, has several family-friendly attractions. Tops is the **Museo de la Fauna y Ciencias Naturales** (☎ 8351-7077; adult/child M$5/free; ⊗ 9am-6:30pm Tue-Fri, 10am-6:30pm Sat & Sun), with stuffed wildlife in dioramas of natural habitats from Saharan Africa to the Arctic. The park also holds a small **aviary** (admission free; ⊗ 9am-4pm), a smaller **aquarium** (admission free; ⊗ 9am-3:30pm) and two buildings full of old cars comprising the **Museo de Autos** (☎ 8331-3890; adult/child M$10/free; ⊗ 10am-7pm Tue-Sun).

Some 10km southwest of Monterrey, **Mundo de Adeveras** (☎ 1160-1160; www.deadeveras.com; Hwy 85 Km 262; admission M$120, young child free; ⊗ hours vary) is a hands-on 'town' where kids can work at various jobs like firefighter and pilot. **Centro Cultural Alfa** (opposite), **Horno3** (opposite) and **La Casa de los Títeres** (opposite) are also guaranteed kid-pleasers.

If you have many mouths to please, consider the **Interplaza Shoptown food court** (cnr Morelos & Juárez; ⊗ 10am-8:30pm) where options include pizza, sushi, Chinese, Cajun and, of course, Mexican.

building looks like a wonky water tank. Most floors are devoted to science and technology exhibits, but there are also superb Mexican antiquities hidden away on the 5th floor. All are labeled in Spanish only. In the center of the building, what was once the planetarium is now an **IMAX cinema**.

Outside are more hands-on science displays plus an aviary, observatory, replica Olmec heads and the striking **Pabellón El Universo**, specially built to showcase a superb stained-glass mural by artist Rufino Tamayo.

Special free buses leave from the southwest corner of Parque Alameda at 3:30pm, 4:30pm, 5:30pm and 6:30pm weekdays and hourly between 11:30am and 7:30pm Saturday and Sunday. The last bus back to central Monterrey departs at 8:45pm.

OBISPADO

The former bishopric palace, on a hill 2.5km west of the Zona Rosa, gives fine views of the city and surrounding mountains, smog permitting. Initiated in 1787 on the orders of the bishop of Linares, the building has an intricate yellow Churrigueresque facade. Now it houses the small **Museo Regional de Nuevo León** (Map p398; ☎ 8346-0404; adult/child M$37/free; ⊗ museum 10am-7pm Tue-Sun, grounds 6am-11pm) which most people will find less intriguing than the views. No buses come here, but bus 4 heading west along Padre Mier turns left at 20 de Noviembre, from where it's a 10- or 15-minute uphill walk – head to the end of the road, up the stairs, turn left then take the first right. It's easier going back; just take any 'Centro' bus down Hidalgo.

CERVECERÍA CUAUHTÉMOC

The **Cuauhtémoc brewery** (Map pp400-1; Alfonso Reyes 2202 Nte; **M** General Anaya), the oldest brewery in Mexico (established in 1890), fills six million bottles of Bohemia, Dos Equis and Tecate and other beers every day. Free **brewery tours** (☎ 8328-5355; ⊗ 9am-5pm Mon-Fri, 9am-2pm Sat) are given more or less hourly. Reservations are recommended (especially if you'd like a tour in English), but you can just show up and see if there's space. Tours start in front of the pleasant outdoor **beer garden** (⊗ 10am-6pm) where they hand out free mugs of Carta Blanca.

Also on-site is the **Salón de la Fama** (☎ 8328-5815; www.salondelafama.com.mx; admission free; ⊗ 9:30am-6pm Mon-Fri, 10:30am-6pm Sat & Sun), a baseball hall of fame for players in the Mexican leagues and a museum about the game itself. You can test your throwing arm and batting skills.

CASA DE LA CULTURA DE NUEVO LEÓN

The lovely 1891 Gulf Line railroad station now houses twin **museums** (Map pp400-1; ☎ 8374-1128; Colón 400 Ote; admission free; **M** Del Golfo) and a stage that regularly hosts dance, theater and arthouse films. The biggest display, appropriately enough, is a so-so **train museum** (⊗ 10am-6pm Tue-Fri, 10am-4pm Sat & Sun) while the small **art museum** (⊗ 10am-6pm Mon-Fri, 10am-4pm Sat & Sun) has temporary displays that are usually good enough to warrant a stop on your way to or from the nearby Museo Del Vidrio.

PARQUE ECOLÓGICO CHIPINQUE

Stretched along a mountainside with a knife-like ridge at the south edge of the city, this **park**

(☎ 8303-0000; www.chipinque.org.mx; pedestrian/cyclist/ vehicle M$20/30/30; ⏱ 6am-8pm) is the most accessible section of the **Parque Nacional Cumbres de Monterrey**, offering urbanites ample opportunities for hiking and mountain biking. The 36km of trail are well maintained, and it doesn't take long to get into some pretty dense pine and oak forest. Butterflies are particularly prolific here, with 174 species represented. Rappelling and 'mini-bungee' jumping are also offered.

Maps, snacks, trail advice and permits for those heading to any of the park's rocky peaks, including **Copete de Águilas** (2200m), the highest, are available at the visitor center near the entrance. A 7km drive further on brings you to La Meseta, where there's a four-star hotel, Hotel Chipinque (opposite) – eat at its restaurant and they'll validate your admission ticket – and several trailheads, including one for **El Empalme**, an easy walk with great views of the city and the mountains.

Free weekend and holiday buses to Chipinque leave from the southeast corner of Parque Alameda at 8am, 10am and noon; be sure to ask when the last bus returns.

Courses
COOKING
Roccatti (off Map p398; ☎ 8335-8478; www.cecroccatti .com; Río Mississippi 116 Ote, Colonia del Valle, San Pedro) A serious culinary school with some three-hour (M$750) and three-day (M$4200) classes available.

SPANISH
Posada El Potrero Chico (p412) Offers language classes along with rock-climbing instruction.
Spanish Language Center (Map p398; ☎ 8335-7546; www.swordvision.net/spanishcenter; Río Potomac 423, Colonia del Valle, San Pedro) Normally does private tutoring, but will try to match you with other students if you prefer small-group study.

Tours
Monterrey's **Paseo Cultural en Tranvía** (M$20; ⏱ 4-10pm Tue-Sun spring-summer, 2-8pm Tue-Sun fall-winter) zips around the Gran Plaza and Zona Rosa in a classic-style trolley. You can join the 45-minute narrated tours at several marked stops, including in front of the Marco art museum and on Padre Mier at Garibaldi.

Festivals & Events
Festival Internacional de Cine en Monterrey
Mexican and international art-house films. Held over two weeks in August.

Aniversario de Independencia Monterrey's biggest celebrations are held on Mexico's Independence Day, September 16, with fireworks, *musica norteña* and a parade.
Nuestra Señora de Guadalupe The second-largest celebration of this Mexican event, on December 12, begins as early as mid-November as thousands of pilgrims head for the Basílica de Guadalupe.

Sleeping
There are just two choices in the Barrio Antiguo, the best neighborhood to lay your head. The Zona Rosa, the next best address, has several midrange and luxury options, including international chain hotels. Most people who stay north of the center around the bus station do so to save money, but others enjoy the bustle. There are many more luxury options south of the center; these are mostly the haunt of business travelers.

See p409 for other options near Monterrey.

BUDGET
Budget hotels fill up fast, especially at weekends. Reservations are an especially good idea at the hostels because if you don't have one, there may be nobody around to check you in.

Monterroco (Map p398; ☎ 1365-4690; www.monterroco.com; Av Lomas de San Francisco 205, Colonia Lomas de San Francisco; dm M$130, r M$340; ✗ ✗ 🖳 🐕) Though it's located far from the action, this hostel is clean and comfy, and hospitable host Mauricio goes out of his way to make sure guests have fun. Facilities include foosball, a swimming pool, barbeques in the garden, a full kitchen and free wi-fi. All the dorm rooms (four, six and eight beds) have lockers. From the bus station, take a Ruta 17 bus heading south on Pino Suárez; a taxi costs about M$30.

Hotel Reforma (Map p400-1; ☎ 8375-3268; Cuauhtémoc 1132 Nte; s/d M$180/220; Ⓜ Cuauhtémoc) These rooms, some of the cheapest to be found in town, aren't fancy, but they're clean. No other place at this price in this area is in the habit of renting rooms for a whole night.

ourpick La Casa del Barrio (Map pp400-1; ☎ 8344-1800; www.lacasadelbarrio.com.mx; Montemayor 1221 Sur; dm M$180, r with shared/private bathroom M$310/415; Ⓜ Zaragoza; ✗ 🖳) This friendly, family-run hostel, ideally located in the heart of the Barrio Antiguo, is a quiet and casual place where guests tend to spend evenings chilling and chatting in the central patio. Dorm rooms range from four to seven beds, and there are nine cozy privates. There's free wi-fi and a kitchen, and everyone is invited to free Sunday afternoon barbeques. Ask about cooking classes.

Hotel Mundo (Map pp400-1; ☎ 8374-6850; Reforma 736 Pte; s/d/tr/q M$340/386/433/457; Ⓜ Cuauhtémoc; ⓅⓍ🖳) A well-maintained and efficiently run place just south of the bus station. The spotless rooms all have simple but attractive decor, reading lights, writing tables and cable TV (but no remote controls) and phones. It offers excellent value for Monterrey.

MIDRANGE

Few of Monterrey's midrange hotels offer good value, unless you head to out-of-the-way locations.

Fundador Hotel (Map pp400-1; ☎ 8343-0121; hotelfundador@prodigy.net.mx; Montemayor 802 Sur; s/d M$351/409; Ⓜ Zaragoza; Ⓟ🖳) This rambling, slightly shabby, historic hotel in the Barrio Antiguo has real ambience with quirky wood-paneled rooms dotted around a warren of stairways and corridors. Room standards and sizes vary a lot so look around before handing over your pesos. Some have refrigerators, microwaves and antique furniture. Those in front can get loud when the Barrio's bars are busy.

Hotel Del Centro (Map pp400-1; ☎ 8340-8754; Zaragoza 208 Sur; r M$450; ⓅⓍ🖳) An antique-filled lobby leads to simple but comfortable rooms that, by Monterrey standards, offer good value. Located just north of the Gran Plaza, it's convenient for sightseeing but not so much for nightlife.

Hotel Colonial (Map pp400-1; ☎ 8380-6800; www.hotelcolonialmty.com; Hidalgo 475 Ote; r incl breakfast M$550-650; Ⓜ Zaragoza; ⓅⓍ🖳) This well-situated place in the heart of the Zona Rosa tries for an air of sophistication, but fails. Still, the rooms aren't bad, especially the pricier remodeled ones, and there's free wi-fi in the lobby.

Hotel Royalty (Map pp400-1; ☎ 8340-2800; www.hotelroyalty.com.mx; Hidalgo 402 Ote; r incl breakfast M$731; Ⓜ Zaragoza; Ⓟ🖳) Fit for a king? Not a chance. But even though the rooms are ready for a remodel, it's a step up from the Colonial down the block. The pool is tiny.

Santa Rosa Suites (Map pp400-1; ☎ 8342-4200; www.santarosa.com.mx; Escobedo 930 Sur; ste incl breakfast from M$819; Ⓜ Zaragoza; ⓅⓍ🖳) Much more intimate than most of Monterrey's pricier hotels, the suites here are plush and quite large, each having a separate living area with sofa bed, DVD player, and a dining area with seating

for four. There's a restaurant and piano bar on the 3rd floor and wi-fi throughout.

TOP END

Radisson Plaza Gran Hotel Ancira (Map pp400-1; ☎ 8150-7000; www.hotel-ancira.com; cnr Hidalgo & Escobedo; r/ste M$1200/1500; Ⓜ Zaragoza; ⓅⓍ🖳) The classiest address in the Zona Rosa, this stylish hotel dates from 1912 and boasts an intricate baroque-style facade and imposing lobby with a sweeping staircase, shops and a grand piano. The ambience sweeps into the restaurant and the accompanying Bar 1900 (p407) but only dusts the rooms, which are standard business class. The gym is large, but the pool is very small. Promotional rates can reduce rates below M$1000 a night.

Hotel Chipinque (off Map p398; ☎ 8173-1777, www.hotelchipinque.com; r M$1250, 6-/8-person cabaña M$2800/3000; ⓅⓍ🖳) Besides a great setting, this hotel high up in Parque Ecológico Chipinque has attractive rooms and *cabañas* with fireplaces, massage service and tennis courts. If only the service could live up to the facilities.

Eating

Monterrey's signature dish is *cabrito al pastor* (roast kid), which, according to various legends, was created here. Supposedly there's none better because of the grass the young goats eat in the area. Another widely held belief among Mexicans is that this is where you'll find Mexico's best *machacado* (pulverized jerky).

A stroll around Barrio Antguo is a good way to find a place to eat, though it pays to book ahead on Friday and Saturday nights. On the other hand, there are surprisingly few good places to eat in the Zona Rosa (except for pricey hotel restaurants), which is thick with international and Mexican fast-food places.

Although the privilege will usually cost you plenty of pesos, you can eat very well in the suburb of San Pedro. The good restaurants are pretty spread out, but El Centrito, a bustling little area just northeast of the traffic circle (La Rotonda), is a good place to poke around. Many international cuisines are represented there, including Japanese, Korean, French and Egyptian.

BUDGET

Las Monjitas (Map pp400-1; ☎ 8344-6713; Escobedo 903 Sur; mains M$25-75; Ⓜ Zaragoza) The waitresses are dressed as nuns and nearly every inch of space is covered in colorful tiles at this bizarre restaurant. The food is only so-so, but it's a fun experience. And, yes; they serve beer. There's another branch at the corner of Morelos and Galeana.

Mi Tierra (Map pp400-1; ☎ 8340-5611; Morelos 350 Ote; mains M$27-62, set lunch M$49; Ⓜ Zaragoza) If you like *mole* you'll love this open-fronted place on the pedestrian mall, or its other locations around the Zona Rosa.

Mi Pueblito (Map pp400-1; ☎ 8375-3756; Madero 830 Pte; mains M$30-75; ⏰ 24hr; Ⓜ Cuauhtémoc) Enjoy filling Mexican standards in this cute little place while using the free wi-fi.

Restaurant La Puntada (Map pp400-1; ☎ 8340-6985; Hidalgo 123 Ote; mains M$30-89; ⏰ 7am-10pm Mon-Sat; Ⓜ Padre Mier) This large, simple place with a long list of Mexican items, plus steaks, at fair prices has had a loyal following since 1955. The food is fantastic.

Como En Casa (Map pp400-1; Hidalgo 137 Ote; complete lunch M$35; ⏰ 12:30-3:30pm; Ⓜ Padre Mier) Popular for the price, of course, but the food isn't bad. You have a choice of eight mains plus soup, salad, beans, rice and a drink. Closing time can depend on when food runs out.

Restaurant Gran Plaza (Map pp400-1; ☎ 8342-0457; Escobedo 480 Sur; mains M$36-95; ⏰ 11am-10:30pm; Ⓜ Zaragoza; ✗) If you get hungry while exploring the Gran Plaza, this popular Chinese-owned Chinese restaurant a block off Explanada de los Héroes will fill you up fast.

ⓄⓊⓇⓅⒾⒸⓀ **La Casa de Maíz** (Map pp400-1; ☎ 8340-4332; Abasolo 870; mains M$40-60; ⏰ 6pm-11:30pm Mon, 6pm-1am Tue-Thu, 2pm-1am Fri & Sat, 1-10:30pm Sun; Ⓜ Zaragoza; Ⓥ) A bohemian place specializing in corn-based comfort food from southern Mexico, including *memelas* (thick tortillas with black beans topped with cheese and more), plus quesadillas and *tostadas*, all served on hand-painted tables.

La Zanahoria (Map pp400-1; ☎ 8372-3258; Rayón 932 Nte; meals M$52-57; ⏰ 8am-6pm; Ⓜ Cuauhtémoc; Ⓥ) Simple little vegetarian place run by yoga fanatics serving food like *beregena gratinada* (eggplant baked with breadcrumbs and tomato and cheese) and mock-meat *milanesa*. All dishes include wholemeal bread, soup, salad and a drink.

MIDRANGE

ⓄⓊⓇⓅⒾⒸⓀ **El Infinito** (Map pp400-1; ☎ 8989-5252; Raymundo Jardón 904; mains M$60-135; ⏰ 9am-1am; Ⓜ Zaragoza; Ⓥ) Highly enjoyable culture café

set inside colonial premises with gorgeous tiled floors, high beamed ceilings and walls adorned with art. Musically, things are kept tranquil with ambient and classical music on the hi-fi and Friday night live jazz on the rooftop terrace. It offers high-priced sandwiches, cheese plates, pizzas, fruit frappés, mango martinis and properly made espresso. There are books to browse and occasional arthouse movies. Ask Pepe, the amiable owner, about his desert tours.

El Rey del Cabrito (Map pp400-1; ☎ 8345-3232; cnr Dr Coss & Av Constitución; mains M$60-185; ⏰ 11am-midnight; Ⓜ Zaragoza) Huge landmark restaurant, complete with a revolving crown on its roof and hunting-lodge-kitsch interior. Your goat arrives at the table still sizzling on a bed of onions, with a large salad and tortillas. Start things off with the *principio de fritada* (fried blood). There's another location to the west of the center on Av Constitución.

TOP END

ⓄⓊⓇⓅⒾⒸⓀ **Fonda San Francisco** (off Map p398; ☎ 8336-6706; Los Aldama 123 Sur, Centro; mains M$60-300; ⏰ 1-11:30pm Mon-Sat; Ⓥ) Like nothing you've tried before, most of the recipes in this cozy little bistro are inspired by pre-Hispanic cooking. English-speaking chef Adrian Herrera will guide you through the menu, which is ripe with delights like *molito de hongos* (mushroom *mole* with chicken) and *pavo en pipian de cacao* (turkey with pumpkin-seed and chocolate sauce). It's located just south of Av Vasconcelos; if you take bus 130 get off by the Super Roma. A sister spot, which will keep the same general philosophy but offer a fancier experience, including proper wine pairings, will be opening down the street in Plaza Express (between De Gollado and Neil Armstrong).

Basiko (Map p398; ☎ 8128-9065; Río Colorado 226, Colonia del Valle; M$180-220; ⏰ 1-11pm Mon-Thu, 1pm-1am Fri & Sat) Another chef-driven place, this one is known for mixing in flavors from the owners' native Ensenada.

Iannilli (Map pp400-1; ☎ 8342-7200; Dr Coss 1221 Sur; mains M$85-198; ⏰ 1-11pm Mon-Sat, 1-10pm Sun; Ⓜ Zaragoza) Seriously elegant and expensive Italian restaurant with intimate dining rooms and formal service. The extensive menu includes risotto with porcini mushroom, gnocchi, shrimp dishes and pizza. The attached Mexican restaurant, Madre Oaxaca, is also very good.

Luisiana (Map pp400-1; ☎ 8343-3753; Hidalgo 530 Ote; mains M$165-412; ☒ noon-midnight Mon-Sat, 5pm-midnight Sun; Ⓜ Zaragoza) Tuxedoed waiters and all the trappings of high-end dining are available at this classic. The meat and seafood menu is a mix of old and new, Mexican and Continental, with choices like *cabrito*, beef stroganoff, Indian curried shrimp and *puto al hono al'orange* (duck à la orange).

Drinking

The best bar action is in the Barrio Antiguo, where stylish places are thick on the ground. El Infinito (opposite) is also a good place to spend some sipping time. Take care if you visit any of the *cantinas* around the bus station; many draw a rough crowd.

our pick Akbal Lounge (Map pp400-1; ☎ 1257-2986; Abasolo 870 Ote; ☒ 9pm-late Tue-Sat; Ⓜ Zaragoza) Enter this opium den–style mélange of red velvet, chandeliers and giant antique mirrors through La Casa de Maíz. Sip a cocktail and lose yourself in the mood music – ambient and lounge sounds during the week, revving up to sexy electro and deep house at weekends – or stargaze on the groovy deck. Sunday night is gay night, but every night is gay-friendly.

Bar 1900 (Map pp400-1; cnr Hidalgo & Escobeda; ☒ noon-1am, noon-2am Fri & Sat; Ⓜ Zaragoza) Elegant and historic bar fronting Zona Rosa's Radisson Plaza Gran Hotel Ancira that, except for the big-screen TV, maintains much of its old-time ambience. Guitarists sing classic *norteño* tunes most nights, and there's a particularly good selection of whiskey.

Entertainment

Monterrey has numerous cinemas and an active cultural life including concerts, theater and art exhibitions. The best sources of what is happening are the daily Gente and Vida sections of *El Norte* newspaper and *Agenda Cultura*, which you can pick up for free at the tourist office and some museums. For the low-down on 'Montegay' scan www.gaymonterrey.net.

LIVE MUSIC & CLUBS

The Barrio Antiguo clubs frequented by Monterrey's affluent younger set are very much the place to get a groove on. Below are a few good places, but the best advice we can give you is to hit the streets and let your ears lead you. El Centrito, in San Pedro, also has a few good dance floors.

Café Iguana (Map pp400-1; ☎ 8343-0822; Montemayor 927 Sur; ☒ 9pm-3:30am Thu-Sat; Ⓜ Zaragoza) The epicenter of alternative Monterrey, where the pierced, multi-tattooed tribe gathers en masse, both inside and on the street out front. The stereo rocks punk and metal bands in front and the same often take the stage; otherwise DJs tone things down a bit back there. Cover charge only for live bands.

Umabar (Map pp400-1; ☎ 8343-9372; Dr Coss 837 Sur; admission M$100; ☒ 10pm-4am Thu-Sat; Ⓜ Zaragoza) Shooting for style rather than fashion, this small, Asian-themed rooftop spot spins a fun mix of music, from Rancid to Maná to the Village People. If you're looking for a more traditional dance floor, head to the east end of Padre Mier.

La Tumba (Map pp400-1; ☎ 8345-6860; Padre Mier 827 Ote; admission Fri & Sat M$25-60; ☒ 7pm-3am Mon-Sat; Ⓜ Zaragoza) This lovely venue, dubbing itself a cultural bar, mostly features live *trova*, blues and singer–songwriters.

Casa Amarilla (Map pp400-1; ☎ 8129-0545; cnr Morelos & Montemayor; ☒ 8pm-2am Wed-Sun; Ⓜ Zaragoza) Monterrey's artistic, wannabe trendsetters fill the various art-filled rooms of this converted house. The music runs from blues on Wednesday to jazz on Sunday with a wide range on the days in between. Cover charge only for the occasional live band.

At Loft (Map pp400-1; ☎ 8342-7031; Morelos 870 Ote; ☒ 8pm-2am Thu-Sat; Ⓜ Zaragoza) The Dali-esque deer head and pulsing lights catch your eye at this uber-chic lounge bar. The weekend begins with a variety of groovy tunes and ends on Saturday with disco downstairs and hip-hop (admission men/women M$80/30) upstairs.

SPORTS

There are professional soccer games on most weekends throughout the year. The Universidad de Nuevo León Tigres play at the **Estadio Universitario** (Map p398; ☎ 8158-6450; Universidad de Nuevo León; Ⓜ Universidad), while the Monterrey Rayados play at the **Estadio Tecnológico** (Map p398; ☎ 8358-2000; Instituto Tecnológico de Monterrey). When the two teams meet, it's a very important event for the city.

Monterrey's Sultanes baseball team plays at **Estadio de Béisbol Monterrey** (Map p398; ☎ 8351-0209; Parque Niños Héroes; Ⓜ Niños Héroes) from March to August.

During the main bullfight season (May to November) *corridas* are held at the **Plaza de Toros Lorenzo Garza** (Map p398; ☎ 8374-0450; www

MEET THE CHEF: ADRIAN HERRERA

What got you started down your unique culinary path? I have been always interested in the roots of things. My country is a mysterious, exotic and enigmatic land. It is comprised of many ethnic groups, a varied geographical environment and an array of indigenous materials that make cuisine our universal cultural heritage. No matter how modern we become, or how strongly foreign cultures influence us, there will always be a basic flowing vein of identity within a society. I seek that essential fluid.

I used to be a sculptor, dealing with petroglyphs, fossils and primitive paintings. I sought our origins through ancient art and biology, but when I became interested in cooking, I changed one laboratory for another, where the materials used could be eaten and processed in a psychological fashion and, at the same time, have a cultural reaction. Cooking is a powerful tool to understand who people are, their identities, origins, the way they see themselves and others, and, in a way, their future. This was a radical idea that mesmerized me.

Where do you get your recipes and ideas from? Directly from the source. I travel to small towns and rustic places. I eat, smell, observe, ask many questions and cook with the people when possible. I also have an interest in home cooking, which is as important as indigenous cooking.

Some recipes I reproduce just as they are, but prepare them with professional techniques. Others I interpret, adding new materials and modern techniques. Some recipes I create freely, based on regional produce, the people I want to portray or a region I desire to understand. I also read a lot. Part of my passion is understanding the conceptual basis of cooking: the relationships between materials, traditions, evolution, etc. I do a lot of research.

A restaurant should not be a culinary museum. Food changes as societies do. Cooking – and eating – are ever-changing phenomena directly associated with culture. But certain basic recipes and principles must be observed, as they are the fundamental elements on which the whole of a society is built.

If you look, it's easy to visualize how the basic recipes that define a country's or region's cultural identity are carried within the newer preparations that, in appearance, seem too modern to have any relationship with rustic food. In essence these new foods carry it, transport it and protect it.

What is the typical reaction of first-time visitors to your restaurant? Customers react with caution, as most of the recipes are unfamiliar for them. But as soon as they taste the food, many of the flavors and aromas they know produce familiar sensations through memories of old recipes and places they've been in the past. For many, the food takes them momentarily away from themselves, on a curious and fulfilling little journey.

Adrian Herrera is the owner and head chef of Fonda San Francisco (p406).

.monumentallorenzogarza.com; Av Reyes 2401 Nte, Colonia del Prado; M$140-1000; (M) General Anaya) at 4pm on Sunday.

Shopping
The **Unión de Artesanos de Nuevo León** (Map pp400–1) mini-malls on both ends of the Zona Rosa (Hidalgo 223 Pte, open 10am to 8pm, and Morelos 547 Ote, open 10am to 8:30pm) have the usual selection of crafts and schlock, as does the **Plaza Santa Rosa** (Map pp400-1; Escobedo 930 Sur; (Y) 10am-8pm; (M) Zaragoza) shopping arcade. **Leyenda Artisanal** (Map pp400-1; (a) 8343-7490; Escobedo 1013 Sur; (Y) 10am-8pm Mon-Sat, 9am-3pm Sun; (M) Zaragoza) has a higher-quality inventory.

ourpick Carápan (Map pp400-1; (a) 8345-4422; www .carapangaleria.com; Hidalgo 305 Ote; (Y) 9am-7pm Mon-Sat; (M) Padre Mier) is in a whole other class, and is Monterrey's best outlet for *artesanía*. The genial owner, who is full of advice about what to see and do in Monterrey, stocks museum-quality work from across Mexico.

Mina St in the Barrio Antiguo becomes the **Corredor del Arte** (Art Corridor; (Y) 10am-6pm), a combination arts-and-crafts and flea market, on Sundays. Bands play too. Also on Sunday, painters also sell their works in the Zona Rosa's Plaza Hidalgo.

Mercado Juárez (Map pp400-1; Av Juárez; (Y) 8am-7pm Mon-Sat, 8am-3pm Sun; (M) Alameda), the main downtown market, sells plenty of everyday items. **Mercado Mesón Estrella** (cnr Martínez & Méndez; (Y) 6am-8pm Mon-Sat, 6am-4:30pm Sun), a block west, is a large food market. Both are fun to browse, and Juárez has many *fondas* with good home cooking.

If you want big malls, small boutiques and trendy brand-name fashions, head to the suburb of San Pedro.

Getting There & Away
AIR
There are direct flights, usually daily, to all major cities in Mexico, plus direct international flights to Houston, Dallas, San Antonio, Los Angeles, Las Vegas, Atlanta, Chicago, Madrid and Barcelona. Most international destinations are best routed via Mexico City, Houston or Dallas.

Airline offices include the following:

Aerobus (☎ 81-8215-0150)
Aero California (☎ 8345-9700)
Aerocaribe (☎ 8356-7201)
Aeroméxico (☎ 8343-5503)
Aeroméxico Connect (☎ 8369-8537)
Air France (☎ 8343-1129)
American Airlines (☎ 8369-0941)
Aviacsa (☎ 8153-4305)
Continental Airlines (☎ 8345-2402)
Delta Airlines (☎ 8335-0912)
Lineas Azteca (☎ 8387-9249)
Mexicana (☎ 8340-5311)
United Airlines (☎ 8335-6117)

BUS
Monterrey's bus station, **Central de Autobuses** (Map pp400-1; Av Colón; M Cuauhtémoc), is a small city unto itself, with restaurants, pharmacies, phones, an internet café and **left-luggage services** (per hr M$5) – the office on the station's west side is open 24 hours. It's busy day and night with departures and arrivals from across Mexico and Texas (see the table on p410).

Getting Around
TO/FROM THE AIRPORT
Monterrey airport is about 30km northeast of the city center, off Hwy 54. A taxi costs around M$200 to M$250, depending on traffic, from downtown. It's standard policy to fix a price rather than use the meter. From the airport you can purchase a ticket for an authorized taxi at a booth in the arrivals area, though you *might* save money if you walk out to the road and wave one down.

No public transportation serves the airport directly; however, if money is tight, Autobuses Amarillos has 2nd-class buses (M$7.5, twice an hour from 5am to 8:45pm) from the bus station that pass about 1½km away, and you can easily flag down a taxi from here.

METRO
The **Metrorrey** (1/5 trips M$4.5/20; ☒ 5am-midnight), Monterrey's modern, efficient metro system, consists of two lines. The elevated Línea 1 runs from the northwest of the city across to the eastern suburbs, passing the Parque Fundidora. Línea 2 begins underground at the Gran Plaza and runs north past Parque Niños Héroes up into the northern suburbs. The two lines cross right by the bus station at Cuauhtémoc station.

BUS
Frequent buses (M$6 to M$9) will get you anywhere you need to go that you can't reach by metro, but often by circuitous routes. One noteworthy bus is Ruta 130, which goes from the corner of Juárez and Hidalgo in Zona Rosa through San Pedro passing La Rotonda (the traffic circle) then heading west along Av Vasconcelos. Other bus information is given in reviews.

TAXI
Taxis (all have meters) are ubiquitous in Monterrey and very reasonably priced. From the Zona Rosa to the bus terminal or Parque Fundidora is usually less than M$30, and it's around M$50 to San Pedro. Call ☎ 8372-8800 or ☎ 8130-0600 for radio taxi service.

CAR & MOTORCYCLE
There are large parking lots, charging M$15 per hour, underneath the Gran Plaza. Another lot, just east of the bus station off Av Colón, costs M$64 for 24 hours.

Local and international car rental agencies cluster around the intersection of Ocampo and Carranza, including the following, which also have desks at the airport:

Advantage (Map pp400-1; ☎ 8345-7334; Ocampo 429 Ote)
Budget (Map pp400-1; ☎ 8369-4100; Hidalgo 433 Ote)
Payless (Map pp400-1; ☎ 8344-6363; Escobedo 1011 Sur)

If you'd rather get a car with a driver, either bargain with a taxi driver or call **Marcelino Hernández** (☎ 1218-3671) who typically charges M$80 per hour in the city and M$100 outside it.

AROUND MONTERREY
Part of what makes Monterrey such a wonderful city is that its boundless energy is countered by the restful villages and awe-inspiring natural attractions just outside it.

BUSES FROM MONTERREY

Destination	Fare	Duration	Frequency (daily)
Chihuahua	deluxe M$675	10hr	2
	1st-class M$546	10hr	12
Ciudad Acuña	deluxe M$445	6½hr	1
	1st-class M$385	6½hr	6
Ciudad Victoria	M$194	4hr	frequent
Dallas	M$550	12hr	8
Durango	deluxe M$516	8hr	5
	1st-class M$419	8hr	15
Houston	M$440	10hr	7
Matamoros	deluxe M$310	5hr	1
	1st-class M$239	5hr	frequent
Mazatlán	deluxe M$857	16hr	1
	1st-class M$659	16hr	2
Mexico City (Terminal Norte)	deluxe M$829	11hr	8
	1st-class M$638	11hr	frequent
Nuevo Laredo	deluxe M$230	3hr	9
	1st-class M$186	3hr	frequent
Piedras Negras	deluxe M$427	5hr	2
	1st-class M$350	5hr	7
Reynosa	deluxe M$218	3hr	3
	1st-class M$178	3hr	frequent
Saltillo	deluxe M$71	1¾hr	10
	1st-class M$55	1¾hr	frequent
San Luis Potosí	deluxe M$438	6½hr	3
	1st -class M$337	6½hr	frequent
Tampico	deluxe M$465	7hr	3
	1st-class M$358	7hr	hourly
Zacatecas	M$293	6½hr	frequent

Cañón de la Huasteca

About 10km west of Monterrey's city center, this large **canyon** (☎ 8191-0664; per vehicle M$10; ☽ 9am-6pm) has some dramatic 300m-tall rock formations and climbing routes reaching grade 5.13c. The picnic area and swimming pool in the middle get very busy at weekends, somewhat reducing its attraction as a wilderness area, but take a short walk and you'll likely have peace and quiet. Though few Huichol people (see the boxed text, p613) live around Monterrey, they believe life began in one corner of the canyon, called Guitarritas (Little Guitars; 15km from picnic area), and they come from all over Mexico during Semana Santa to perform sacred rituals at this spot.

The Huasteca also holds **La Ruta Vértigo**, Mexico's first *via ferrata*, a six-to-eight-hour hour fixed climbing route with zip-lines, overhanging ladders and rappels; no experience necessary. Geo Aventura and Mexplore (see the boxed text, opposite) are two of the companies that guide Vértigo trips.

Reach the mouth of the canyon by taking a Ruta 126 'Santa Catarina' bus (M$7, 45 mintes) from Obelisco in Monterrey.

Cascada Cola de Caballo

Six kilometers uphill from El Cercado, a village 35km south of Monterrey on Hwy 85, you'll find lovely and aptly named **Horsetail Falls** (☎ 8347-1533; adult/child M$30/20; ☽ 9am-7pm May-Oct, 9am-6pm Nov-Apr), which makes a wide, thin 25m-drop. It's most beautiful in August and September, but water flows year-round. You can take a horse (M$30) or a horse-and-buggy ride (M$20) the last 750m to the falls.

Near the entrance to the falls are Mexico's highest (70m) **bungee jump** (☎ 8376-7623; www .bungee.com.mx; M$330; ☽ 3-8pm Fri, 11am-8pm Sat & Sun), a 200-foot **canopy tour** (run by the same company) with four zip-lines and three rappels, and **Hotel Hacienda Cola de Caballo** (☎ 2285-0260; www.coladecaballo.com; r Sun-Wed M$750, Thu-Sat M$1325; ℗ ✖ ☒), a lovely luxury lodge with top-notch facilities.

Autobuses Amarillos runs frequent 2nd-class buses from the Monterrey bus station to El Cercado (M$20, one hour, every 20 minutes) where you can catch microbuses to the falls (M$15, 20 minutes, every 15 minutes) from the plaza.

If you're driving to the falls, consider a small detour to the nearby town of **Santiago**, across Hwy 85 from La Boca reservoir, for a look at its attractive *plaza principal* and some *tacos de cabrito* at **Las Palomas** (☎ 2285-3105; Abasolo 101; mains M$65-215; ☻ 8am-11pm Sun-Thu, 8am-1am Fri & Sat), one of northern Mexico's most renowned restaurants. The adjoining luxury hotel shares the restaurant's owners and its colonial ambience.

Grutas de García

An illuminated, 2.5km route leads through 16 chambers in **García's Caves** (☎ 8347-1533; adult/child M$60/45; ☻ 9am-5pm), located 1100m up in the Sierra El Fraile. The caves, reached by a spectacular ride in a *teleférico* (cable car), are 50 million years old, with lots of stalactites, stalagmites and petrified seashells. Admission includes the cable-car ride and a 50-minute tour.

From Monterrey, city buses 601 from Obelisco near Zona Rosa and 107 from Villagrán next to the bus station run frequently to Villa de García (M$10.5, one hour), 9km from the caves; taxis (M$60) go the rest of the way. The ticket office will call you a cab for the return journey if none are waiting. This is a popular weekend outing so it's easy to join others for the taxi ride on those days. Driving from Monterrey, take Hwy 40 toward Saltillo; at 12km outside the city a sign points the way to the caves, another 25km to the north.

The town of **Villa de García**, which was founded before Monterrey (its historic center was getting a facelift at the time of research), has a pair of intriguing museums showcasing modern *artesanía* using or inspired by traditional styles and techniques. **Museo El Ojo** (☎ 8363-5515; Hidalgo s/n; admission free; ☻ 10am-6pm Tue-Sun) near the plaza has a gorgeously presented collection of pottery, most of it massive and unlike anything you've seen, commissioned from leading artists of Oaxaca, Jalisco, Puebla, Mexico and Michoacán states while **Casa Roja** (☎ 8283-4662; Hidalgo 507; admission free; ☻ 10am-6pm Tue-Sun) displays a more varied collection of styles and media. García has some good budget and midrange hotels if you'd like to soak up more of its spirit.

Potrero Chico

The towering limestone walls of Potrero Chico, 45 minutes northwest of Monterrey and just west of the town of Hidalgo, are an awe-inspiring sight from afar, but most people come here to see them up close; this is one of the world's top rock-climbing spots. The walls of the canyon currently support over 600 routes (most described in *The Whole*

MATACANES & MORE

The mountains around Monterrey, many of which are protected within the **Parque Nacional Cumbres de Monterrey**, are chock full of options for outdoor activities, but the world-class canyoneering is the most popular for the adventurous set. The main destination between April and September, when the rivers run high, is **Matacanes**, a moderately difficult canyon trip (six to eight hours) where you cross two caves, make two rappels and jump off 27 cliffs; the highest being 12m.

The ecotourism agencies listed below have solid reputations, English-speaking guides and regularly scheduled weekend outings (so there's no need to get your own group together to bring down prices) starting at around M$750 per person. Canyoneering destinations that are less demanding than Matacanes are also available, as are rock-climbing, mountain biking and trekking trips. Check the calendars on the websites. Customized trips to these destinations and others are available at any time. The *Aire Libre* booklet, available free at the tourism office, can help you decide on where to go and what to do.

Geo Aventura (Map p398; ☎ 8989-4301; www.geoaventura.com; Río Amazonas 9, Colonia Roma) Has the biggest variety of outings and is the only one offering trips every weekend all year.
Matacanes.Net (☎ 8338-5211; www.matacanes.net)
Mexplore (off Map p398; ☎ 8115-1328; www.mexplore.com.mx; Río Madeira 435, Colonia Del Valle, San Pedro)

Enchilada, a climbing guidebook by Dane Bass) between grades 5.7 and 5.13d. Expert tuition for all levels is available on-site for US$80 per person per day during the high season (October to April); low-season discounts can be substantial.

The area is also great for mountain biking and hiking, including a 2½-hour trek to the summit of El Toro, which overlooks the canyon.

Several places near the canyon rent rooms and tent space, with the modern and comfortable **Posada El Potrero Chico** (☎ 8362-6672; www .elpotrerochico.com.mx; campsites per person M$55, tent rental from M$30, r M$290, cabañas M$620-940; P ⊠ ⊑ ⊜) leading the pack. Facilities include hot-water bathrooms, free wi-fi, kitchen and laundry facilities, and a high-season restaurant. Whether or not you stay here, you can study Spanish (per hour M$107), rent mountain bikes (per hour M$43) and climbing gear, and even join a Nahua sweat lodge ceremony. Prefer US dollars to pesos.

In Monterrey, Autobuses Mina has hourly *directo* service to Hidalgo (M$22, 1½ hours) and from there you'll have to pay a taxi driver the extortionate, fixed price of M$50 to complete the trip. If you're driving, go to the cement factory in the heart of Hidalgo and follow the signs.

TAMAULIPAS

Tamaulipas is a diverse destination. It stretches from the Gulf coast, with several quiet but up-and-coming coastal towns, high into the Sierra Madre mountains, where the bird-watching is world-class, and then runs up the Río Bravo to grab the northeast's major border crossings. It's increasingly popular with Mexican tourists, but it remains off the radar of most foreigners, except for a few in-the-know Texans.

NUEVO LAREDO

☎ 867 / pop 348,000 / elevation 148m

Nuevo Laredo is Mexico's busiest border town (36% of all its international trade passes through here) but it's much more famous as 'Narco' Laredo, a reference to brazen violence between rival drug cartels that has sullied the city's reputation. But it isn't the fear of getting caught in the crossfire that should send you south as fast as you can (Nuevo Laredo is actually quite safe, and there's a heavy police

presence along Guerrero until very late in the evening); it's that the city has little offer other than the usual cheap trinkets, tequila and tricks found in most border towns.

Originally there was only one Laredo, north of the Río Bravo, but in 1848, following the end of the Mexican-American War, the city joined the USA. Over 100 families who didn't give up Mexican citizenship crossed south, bringing all their belongings with them: including, according to legend, the dug-up caskets of their buried relatives. Today 'Los Dos Laredos' remain very close.

Orientation

Two international bridges link the Laredos. You can walk or drive over Puente Internacional No 1, for a toll of M$3 (or US$0.30) for pedestrians and M$30 (or US$3) for vehicles. This bridge leads you to the north end of Av Guerrero, Nuevo Laredo's main thoroughfare. Puente Internacional No 2 (M$24) is vehicles only, and enables drivers to bypass Nuevo Laredo's center by taking Blvd Luis Colosio east around the city. Both bridges have Mexican immigration offices at the southern end.

A third international bridge, Puente Colombia-Solidaridad, crosses the border 32km northwest, enabling motorists to bypass the cities altogether.

Av Guerrero leads seven blocks south to Plaza Hidalgo, a pleasant, well-kept square with a bandstand, clock tower and the Palacio Federal. Most bar-hopping Texans stick to the large clubs on and east of Guerrero; the bars west of Guerrero tend to draw a rough local crowd.

Information

Most services you might need are along Guerrero and Plaza Hidalgo, including *casas de cambio*, banks with ATMs, internet cafés, long-distance call centers, the **post office** (Plaza Hidalgo) and the **tourist office** (☎ 712-73-97; Palacio Federal; www.nuevolaredo.gob.mx; ⊗ 9am-5pm Mon-Fri).

Sights

The colorful, open-air **Mercado Monclovio Herrera** (El Mercado; Av Guerrero; ⊗ 8am-8pm Mon-Fri, 8am-9pm Sat, 9am-7pm Sun), with the usual assortment of T-shirts, silver, sarapes, liquor and leather, is the main tourist magnet.

If you're desperate for something else, you could visit the **Museo Ferrocarril** (☎ 713-7228; López

NUEVO LAREDO

0   500 m
0   0.3 miles

INFORMATION	
Post Office.....................1	C3
Tourist Office................2	C3
SIGHTS & ACTIVITIES	
Mercado Monclovio Herrera.3	C3
SLEEPING	
Motel Romanos................4	C3
EATING	
Restaurante Principal.........5	C3
TRANSPORT	
CIITEV.........................6	D2
Estrella Blanca & Omnibus de	
Mexico Ticket Offices......7	C2
Local Buses to Bus Station....8	C3
Local Buses to Bus Station....9	C2
Mexican Immigration........10	D2
Mexican Immigration........11	C2
US Immigration...............12	C1
US Immigration...............13	D1

de Lara 1106; admission free; 9am-5pm Mon-Fri, 9am-1pm Sat), which has a few railroading relics and a small art gallery in the city's old train station, or see if anything is on stage at the city's shiny new **Centro Cultural** (717-59-59; Blvd Luis Colosio) on the outskirts of town.

Sleeping & Eating

Av Reforma south of Av Guerrero has several overpriced business-class hotels and some good-value midrangers. There are very cheap rooms, especially good for solo travelers, fronting the main bus station.

Motel Romanos (712-23-91; Dr Mier 2420; s & d from M$289; P X) This gaudy Roman-themed hotel has a columned facade and gilded detailing. The 29 well-kept rooms are better, not just better value, than many of the pricier options in the center.

El Nuevo Sol (712-39-20; Obregón 1416; mains M$9-54; 7am-9pm Mon-Sat; X) Take a booth in this bright, happy health-food store–café and you'll feel like you've left Nuevo Laredo. The breakfasts, salads and *antojitos* are made with fresh veggies, *soya* meats and whole-wheat breads. The *comida corrida* costs M$70.

Restaurante Principal (712-13-01; Guerrero 630; mains M$50-140; 10am-11pm) For a crash course in *norteño* food try some cuts of *cabrito* at this well-known restaurant near the plaza; or play it safe and order the grilled chicken.

Getting There & Away

AIR

Nuevo Laredo airport (718-12-70) is off the Monterrey road, 14km south of town. **Mexicana** (719-28-15) has direct flights twice a day to and from Mexico City. The airport at Laredo, Texas, has Continental and American Airlines flights every day to Houston and Dallas.

BUS

Nuevo Laredo's main bus station is about 5km south of Puente Internacional No 1 just off Anáhuac. Ómnibus de México departs from a spot on López de Lara a bit closer to the center. You can also buy tickets for Estrella Blanca and Ómnibus de México routes from offices right at the foot of the bridge: do so, and they'll pay your cab fare to the bus station.

There are daily buses to plus most major cities in northern Mexico, including Ciudad

Victoria, Durango, Guadalajara, Mazatlán, Reynosa, Saltillo and the following:

Destination	Fare	Duration	Frequency
Mexico City (Terminal Norte)	deluxe M$1061	14hr	3 daily
	1st-class M$816	14hr	16 daily
Monclova	M$169	4hr	5 daily
Monterrey	deluxe M$230	3hr	9 daily
	1st-class M$186	3hr	every 20 min
	2nd-class M$151	6hr	13 daily
Tampico	M$518	10hr	5 daily
Zacatecas	M$475	10hr	9 daily

There are also similarly priced direct buses to various cities in Mexico from the **Greyhound bus terminal** (☎ 956-723-4324; 610 Salinas Ave) in Laredo, but because of often very thorough inspections at the border, these take much longer than services from Nuevo Laredo itself.

CAR & MOTORCYCLE

For a vehicle permit, you must go to **CIITEV** (☺ 24hr) between the bridges: follow the blue 'car permits' signs.

The route south via Monterrey is the most direct to central Mexico, the Pacific coast and the Gulf coast. Hwy 85D is a fast, excellent toll road (M$177), while the alternative free road (Hwy 85) is longer and slower.

Getting Around

A good network of city buses (M$5) means getting around Nuevo Laredo is simple enough. Many bus stops have route maps. Frequent buses marked 'Mirador-Reforma' or 'Carretera' leave from the corner of Bravo and Juárez heading down Juárez to the main bus station. Busses labeled 'Puente-Centro' go from directly in front of the station to the Puente Internacional No 1 via the city center. Taxis between the bus station and the center officially cost M$50, though drivers at the foot of the bridge will want much more; try walking a block down to Plaza Juárez.

REYNOSA

☎ 899 / pop 508,000 / elevation 36m

Reynosa, an important commercial border crossing, is one of northeast Mexico's most important industrial towns, with oil refineries, petrochemical plants, cotton mills and *maquiladoras*. It's more attractive and less intimidating than Nuevo Laredo, but not quite as charming as Matamoros. The tourist trade is geared to short-term Texan visitors, many of whom are in town to visit the city's surfeit of dentists, doctors and pharmacists. Across the Río Bravo del Norte is the town of McAllen. There are good road connections into Mexico and Texas.

The city was founded in 1749 as Villa de Nuestra Señora de Guadalupe de Reynosa, 20km from its present location: flooding forced the move in 1802. Reynosa was one of the first towns to rise up in the independence movement of 1810, but little of historical interest remains.

Orientation & Information

Reynosa's central streets are laid out on a grid pattern, between the Río Bravo del Norte and the Canal Anzalduas. The area just below the Puente Internacional is an unfortunate introduction to the city, but things get much nicer very quickly. The Plaza Principal, on a rise a few blocks southwest of the bridge, is the site of the town hall, banks, hotels and a modern cathedral. Extending south of the plaza, Hidalgo is a pedestrianized shopping lane. There are many *casas de cambio* and parking lots, and several internet cafés around the center.

There's a little **tourist office** (☎ 922-51-86, ☺ 8am-5pm Mon-Fri) in the immigration building at the bridge and another hidden on the third floor of the **Presidencia Municipal** (☎ 932-32-73; Morelos 645; ☺ 8am-4pm Mon-Fri).

Between the bridge and the center lies the Zona Rosa, where underage Texans come to party on weekends. The bars here, concentrated on and just off Ocampo, aren't exactly family friendly, but it's not too sleazy a scene. Most of that action (exotic dancing and prostitution) takes place at Reynosa's famous 'Boys' Town' to the west.

Sights

Reynosa's modest little **Museo Histórico** (☎ 922 15-12; cnr Allende & Ortega; admission free; ☺ 9am-2pm & 4-8pm Tue-Fri, 10am-2pm & 4-8pm Sat, 10am-2pm Sun may not offer any flash interactive displays but it does have a curious combination of ancient pottery, old typewriters and historic city photos. In the rear room there's often a temporary exhibition of work by local artists.

REYNOSA

Many of the stores inside **Mercado Zaragoza** (Hidalgo; ☽ 9am-6pm) sell Western wear and *artesanía*.

Sleeping

The city has many good hotels in all price categories, both in the center and on the highways leading into town. The cheap hotels fronting the bus station are fine, but most right by the Puente Internacional aren't meant for overnight guests.

Hotel Nuevo León (☎ 922-13-10; Díaz 580; s & d M$190-240, tr M$215-265, q M$240-290; ✖) This place could sure use a paint job, but rooms are comfy and clean and full of furniture; some might even say they have character. All rooms have cable TV and the more expensive have air-con.

Hotel Isel (☎ 922-10-59; Chapa 1005; s/d/tr/q from M$330/470/580/680; P ✖ ✖ 🖳) The good-sized rooms along the contorted hallways of this spotless, efficiently run hotel have fake plants and cheery pictures. There's a small gym and a 24-hour restaurant.

Hotel La Estancia (☎ 922-99-77; Guerrero 735; s/d/tr M$400/450/600; P ✖) The unassuming but superb value La Estancia doesn't have the

amenities of the big boys, but it's still a great choice for a night. The 12 brightly decorated, cheerful rooms have attractive furniture and modern bathrooms and let you feel like you're sleeping in someone's guest bedroom rather than at a hotel.

Eating

You'll find standard-issue taco and fast-food joints on and around Hidalgo; Mercado Zaragoza in particular has some good ones. Calle Juárez south of Madero seems to be trying to corner the market in seafood restaurants.

Cafetería y Panadería La Superior (☎ 922-96-06; Guerrero 728; mains M$25-60; ☽ 6am-10pm; ✖) No frills, but oodles of charm, from the bullfighter portraits to the locals lingering over mugs of coffee, this classic place draws crowds for *huevos con machacado*, chicken fajitas, quesadillas, and steak sandwiches.

Café Sánchez (☎ 922-57-22; Morelos 575; mains M$25-145; ☽ 7am-8pm) This venerable place with black tie–wearing waiters serves *huevos rancheros* and *enchiladas suizas*, but it's really all about the meat: a two-person *parrillada* with *cabrito* and steak costs M$250.

Capellini (☎ 922-09-00; Ejército Nacional 250; mains M$49-157; ☺ noon-midnight Mon-Sat, noon-9pm Sun) Authentic Italian restaurant using many imported ingredients, it's worth the trip south of the center.

Getting There & Away

AIR

Reynosa's **Aeropuerto General Lucio Blanco** (☎ 958-00-04), is 8km southeast of town, off the Matamoros road. **Aeroméxico** (☎ 922-52-37) has three daily direct flights to and from Mexico City and **Mexicana** (☎ 129 69 89) has two.

BUS

The bus station, just off Colón behind the Gigante supermarket, is walkable from the center. Buses run frequently to the following destinations:

Destination	Fare	Duration
Ciudad Victoria	M$192	4½hr
Mexico City	deluxe M$929	13hr
(Terminal Norte)	1st-class M$715	13hr
Monterrey	deluxe M$218	3hr
	1st-class M$178	3hr
Saltillo	M$207	5hr
Tampico	M$308	8hr
Zacatecas	M$489	10hr

First-class buses also serve Chihuahua, Durango, Matamoros, Nuevo Laredo, San Luis Potosí and Veracruz in Mexico and Houston (US$25), San Antonio (US$25), Austin (US$34) and Dallas (US$46) in Texas.

The nearest Texas transportation center, McAllen, is 9km from the border. **Valley Transit Company** (in McAllen ☎ 956-686-5479) runs frequent buses between the two bus stations (M$30, 5am to 9:45pm). In Reynosa, purchase tickets at the Greyhound counter.

US and Mexican immigration are at their respective ends of the bridge, and there's another Mexican post inside the Reynosa bus station, but it's open only 8am to 4pm Monday to Friday.

CAR & MOTORCYCLE

The vehicle toll at the bridge is US$2.50/M$25. Southeast of the bridge (follow the signs) is the **CIITEV office** (☺ 24hr), which issues car permits. The Pharr Bridge, just east of Reynosa, lets you bypass the city altogether.

Going west to Monterrey (220km), the toll Hwy 40D is excellent, but costs (M$194). The

less direct toll-free Hwy 40 follows roughly the same route and takes 30 minutes to an hour longer. Hwys 97 and 101 south to Tampico are fast and in good shape.

Getting Around

Peseros (as buses are called here) rattle around Reynosa. To get from the bus station to the town center, turn left after exiting the bus station and cross the Gigante parking lot to Colón. Just about all the local buses (M$5) stopping here head to the plaza.

Most taxis have meters: the cost between the bus station and the center is around M$20.

MATAMOROS

☎ 868 / pop 423,000 / elevation 8m

While Matamoros could hardly be described as a cultural mecca, it has the most to offer of all the gritty Mexican border towns that dot the frontier with Texas. With a cluster of historic buildings, a decent contemporary art museum and some stylish restaurants, it makes a relatively easygoing base, though most visitors here are day-trippers from *el otro lado* (the other side).

The city has a shady plaza dotted with a fine blue-tiled Mudéjar bandstand and fountains. Standing on the west side of the square is a Gothic-style cathedral with twin bell towers and a dusky pink facade. Some 150 *maquiladoras* sit west and south of the city.

The area was dubbed Los Esteros Hermosos (The Beautiful Estuaries) by Captain Juan José de Hinojosa, who explored the area in 1706, but it wasn't until 1765 that 13 families settled on the south side of the river. The city was later renamed after Padre Mariano Matamoros, who died during Mexico's battle for independence.

In 1846, Mexican forces in Matamoros attacked the Americans stationed in Fort Texas (later renamed Fort Brown) on the opposite side of the Río Bravo del Norte. In short order General Zachary Taylor's troops routed the Mexican army, took over Matamoros and marched south toward Mexico City.

Orientation

Matamoros lies across the Río Bravo from Brownsville, Texas. The most convenient crossing is the **Puente Nuevo** (International Gateway Bridge; ☺ 24hr) while the **Puente Zaragoza** (Veteran's Bridge; ☺ 6am-midnight), 3km to the east, offers a more direct route south into Mexico. Both have immi-

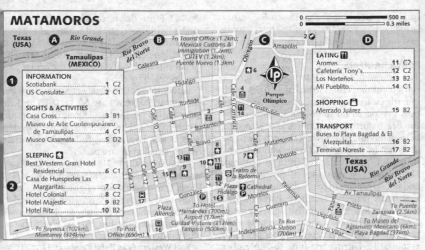

MATAMOROS

INFORMATION
Scotiabank.................................1 C2
US Consulate..............................2 C1

SIGHTS & ACTIVITIES
Casa Cross.................................3 B1
Museo de Arte Contemporáneo
de Tamaulipas.........................4 C1
Museo Casamata.........................5 D2

SLEEPING
Best Western Gran Hotel
Residencial................................6 C1
Casa de Huespedes Las
Margaritas................................7 C2
Hotel Colonial............................8 C2
Hotel Majestic............................9 B2
Hotel Ritz................................10 B2

EATING
Aromas...................................11 C2
Cafetería Tony's........................12 C2
Los Norteños............................13 B2
Mi Pueblito...............................14 C1

SHOPPING
Mercado Juárez.........................15 B2

TRANSPORT
Buses to Playa Bagdad & El
Mezquital................................16 B2
Terminal Noreste........................17 B2

gration offices, open 24 hours and 6am to 10pm respectively. The main bus station also has an immigration office, open 6am to 10pm.

From the southern end of Puente Nuevo, Av Obregón heads down to the town's central grid, 1.5km to the southwest. Abasolo, a pedestrianized shopping street, and Plaza Hidalgo are at the city's heart.

Information

There are lots of internet cafés and banks with ATMs on the blocks around Plaza Hidalgo. **Scotiabank** (cnr Morelos & Calle 6; 9am-5pm Mon-Fri, 10am-3pm Sat) cashes traveler's checks. There are *casas de cambio* all over town. The **post office** (cnr Calle 11 & Río Bravo; 9am-3pm Mon-Fri) is south of the center and the helpful **tourist office** (812-02-12; www.ocvmatamoros.com.mx; Obregón s/n; 9am-5pm Mon-Sat) is just south of Puente Nuevo. Some staff speak English.

Matamoros isn't an especially dangerous destination, but it's not a good idea to walk around the city center once the shops close; away from the Abasolo pedestrian mall and Plaza Hidalgo, that happens pretty early most nights. Plaza Allende gets pretty seedy after dark.

Sights

Matamoros' excellent **Museo de Arte Contemporáneo de Tamaulipas** (MACT; 813-14-99; www.macttamaulipas.com; cnr Calle 5 & Constitución; adult/student M$15/10, free Wed; 9:30am-6pm Tue-Sat, noon-5pm Sun) showcases first-rate exhibitions of photography, sculpture and painting. The building itself is a landmark modernist structure with

a maze-like interior and walls set at oblique angles to the polished concrete floor. Fine local *artesanía* is sold in the foyer.

Filling a remnant of an 1845 fort, all that remains of the original city defenses, plus some newer buildings around it, **Museo Casamata** (813-59-29; cnr Guatemala & Degollado; admission free; 8:30am-4:30pm Tue-Fri, 9am-2pm Sat & Sun) traces the city's history with old photos, artifacts and some English signage.

Casa Cross (812-23-25; cnr Calle 7 & Herrera; admission free; 9am-2pm Mon-Fri), a partly restored brick mansion complete with elaborate verandas and dormer windows that looks straight out of New Orleans, has a fascinating history. Finished in 1885, it was the home of Meliton Cross, whose father had fled South Carolina after his family discovered that he had fallen in love with the black slave who was caring for him during a serious illness. The couple later married and settled in Matamoros. Though it has few furnishings, it's an atmospheric place.

The **Museo del Agrarismo Mexicano** (837-05-27; Hwy Playa Bagdad Km6.5; admission free; 9am-5pm Tue-Fri, 9am-2pm Sat & Sun), a bright-orange building 200m north of the highway, documents the *ejido* movement (a 20th-century campaign that redistributed private farmland into communal holdings) and the history of the Mexican revolution in Tamaulipas. You won't learn any history if you can't read Spanish, but if you like looking at old guns and farm tools, you might enjoy it. Either take one of the Playa Bagdad buses from Plaza Allende

NORTHEAST MEXICO

or a more frequent Technológico-Esperanza (usually abbreviated as 'Tec-Esp') bus heading east on Independencia or Lauro Villar.

PLAYA BAGDAD

The nearest beach to Matamoros is a scruffy settlement that clings to an expansive stretch of fairly clean sand 37km east of town. A large port prospered on the Mexican bank of the Río Bravo north of Matamoros and, according to local folklore, this town was given the name 'Bagdad' by Texans who were astounded by its wealth (mostly derived from smuggling). Hurricanes destroyed the settlement in 1889, and nobody seems to remember anymore how that name traveled over here. Playa Bagdad today consists of a small fishing settlement, a few aging *cabañas* and a seemingly endless row of wind-battered clapboard beach restaurants. During the June-to-September hot season and the Semana Santa holiday the sands are packed with parked cars, while the rest of the year you don't need to walk far from the bus stop to find a peaceful spot on the beach. There's talk of large luxury resorts but these seem more dreams than actual plans. Modern minibuses (M$25, one hour) head here from Calle 10 on the west side of Plaza Allende, leaving hourly most of the year and more often during busy times. The last bus back to Matamoros is usually at 8pm.

Shopping

The 'new market,' **Mercado Juárez** (9am-6pm Mon-Sat, 9am-4pm Sun), has all the usual Mexican crafts and tourist trinkets, but also a few standout craft shops.

Sleeping

Like most border towns in Mexico, accommodation is not great value in Matamoros. Cheap places tend to be very basic, but there are several decent midrange options.

Hotel Majestic (813-36-80; Absalo 131; s/d M$170/240) Clean, if slightly drab, rooms with hot water and cable TV and even a candy dish on the front desk. It's less dispiriting than the Hotel México down the street.

Casa de Huespedes Las Margaritas (813-40-24; Calle 4 No 179; s & d/tr M$200/250;) A well-worn but cheery and friendly place with 10 rooms (with hot water and cable TV) around a colorful, plant-filled courtyard.

Hotel Hernández (812-55-45; www.hotelhernandez .com; cnr Calle 6 & Laguna Madre; s/d from M$395/505;

) Four floors of frumpy but comfy rooms (with wi-fi) stacked around a long narrow courtyard lined by massive palm trees: it almost looks like a Hollywood film set. The location is both convenient to the center and easy to reach by car.

Hotel Ritz (812-11-90; www.ritzhotel.org; Matamoros 612; s/d/tr M$500/600/700;) The Ritz has a garish purple facade, but its rooms are much more sober, with attractive wooden beds, desks, safes and wi-fi. There's a business center, small gym and piano bar.

Hotel Colonial (816-66-06; www.hcolonial.com; Matamoros 603; s/d incl breakfast M$553/598;) From the wrought-iron light fixtures in the lobby to the decorative mirrors and wooden furniture in the cozy guestrooms, Matamoros's most gorgeous hotel has real Old World charm, plus modern conveniences like wi-fi.

Best Western Gran Hotel Residencial (813-94-40; www.bestwestern.com; Obregón 249; s & d/tr incl breakfast M$997/1164;) The 115 fully equipped rooms at this low-rise hotel are cookie-cutter American-chain-hotel boring, but certainly comfortable. They ring a large leafy compound with two pools. There's a popular restaurant and cocktail bar.

Eating & Drinking

Matamoros has a smattering of fashionable restaurants as well as plenty of down-to-earth places where the emphasis is on substance over style. The budget-minded food stalls in Plaza Allende are good places to sample a variety of local fare. Bars kept in business by young Texans are spread out along Obregón.

Cafetería Tony's (Calle 6 No 171; mains M$20-46;) A mixture of good food (breakfasts, *antojitos*, tacos and sandwiches) and low prices keeps this simple place packed much of the day. And that's the only downside; you might have to wait for a seat.

Los Norteños (813-00-37; Matamoros 109; mains M$30-95) A carnivore's delight: head to this simple but classy joint for *cabrito*, steak and chicken cooked over a huge charcoal pit.

Mi Pueblito (816-05-86; cnr Calle 5 & Constitución; mains M$50-125; 7am-midnight, 7am-1am Fri & Sat) Positioned opposite MACT, this gorgeous restaurant is topped by a soaring thatched roof and has colorful textile tablecloths. It offers a menu of Mexican favorites, but its best value is the filling set lunch (M$77, available noon to 4pm), which includes a drink and soup starter. Take your pick from over 200 tequilas.

ourpick Aromas (☎ 812-62-32; Calle 6 No 181; mains M$62-180; ☻ 7am-midnight Sun-Thu, 7am-2am or later Fri & Sat) A second home for some of Matamoros' artists and intellectuals, the city's hippest venue has a ground-floor restaurant featuring avant-garde paintings on exposed brick walls and an intimate garden patio, where you can enjoy breakfasts (M$14 to M$58), filling salads, fruity crepes, and well-executed main dishes including pastas and good seafood. Prices are generally high, but the *comida corrida* (M$49), which includes soup, drink and dessert, is a great deal. The bar area upstairs, with modern booths, is perfect cocktail-quaffing territory and has live *trova* at weekends and jazz and other chill sounds on the stereo weekdays.

Getting There & Away
AIR
Matamoros International Airport (☎ 812-24-67) is 17km out of town on the road to Ciudad Victoria. **Aeroméxico Connect** (☎ 922-52-37) has two daily direct flights to Mexico City. Continental Airlines services the airport in Brownsville through Houston.

BUS
The main **bus station** (Canales) has an immigration office and left-luggage service (per hour M$5). Daily services from Matamoros include the following:

Destination	Fare	Duration	Frequency
Ciudad Victoria	M$197	4	every half-hour
Mexico City (Terminal Norte)	deluxe M$969	13	2 daily
	1st-class M$710	14	14 daily
Monterrey	deluxe M$310	5	1 daily
	1st-class M$239	5	every 20 min
Tampico	deluxe M$486	7	2 daily
	1st-class M$305	7	hourly
Veracruz	deluxe M$986	16	1 daily
	1st-class M$740	18	4 daily
Zacatecas	M$498	12	13 daily

Buses go to many other destinations including Chihuahua, Durango, Guadalajara, Reynosa, Saltillo and San Luis Potosí. Daily buses also head all over the USA including Houston (M$25), Dallas (M$46) and Chicago (M$120). Greyhound, which has an office here, is competitively priced with the Mexican companies.

If you're headed to Monterrey, Reynosa or San Luis Potosí consider using the **Terminal Noreste** (☎ 813-40-50; cnr Abasolo & Calle 12), which has a more convenient downtown location but far fewer departures.

You can also get buses direct to several cities inside Mexico from the **Brownsville bus station** (☎ 956-546-7171; 1134 E St Charles) in Texas, but because of border formalities it's usually quicker to walk across the bridge and take local transportation to the Matamoros bus station.

CAR & MOTORCYCLE
Driving across the bridge to or from Brownsville costs M$24 (or US$2.25). Be sure to get your temporary vehicle permit at the **CIITEV office** (Puente Nuevo ☻ 24hr, Puente Zaragoza ☻ 6am-9pm) on the Mexican side.

The main route into Mexico is Hwy 101 southwest to Ciudad Victoria and into the Bajío region and Hwy 180 branching off south to Tampico. These two-lane roads are both in good condition and free of tolls. Hwy 2D leads west to Reynosa, from where Hwys 40 and 40D continue to Monterrey.

Getting Around
In Matamoros, local buses are called *peseros,* and they cost M$5. Catch a 'Juárez' bus on Louis Aguilar immediately east of the bus station to the center. Back to the station, wave down the same bus heading south on Calle 8. 'Puente' buses head north on Calle 1 from just west of the station to the border; in the opposite direction, take one marked 'Colonia 20 de Noviembre' (usually abbreviated 'Col 20') or 'Central de Autobuses' from behind the tourist office.

City buses marked 'Centro,' also starting behind the tourist office, will get you to or near Plaza Hidalgo, but it's easiest to hop aboard one of the free buses (departing roughly every 15 minutes between 9am and 5pm) that leave from García's crafts shop on Obregón just south of the bridge; these drop you off by Mercado Juárez.

Many taxi drivers ask for a hefty M$100 (or more) from the border or the bus station to the center, though the official price at time of research was M$50.

The city runs a **trolley** (M$40) aimed at day-trippers between the border, Mercado Juárez, Plaza Hidalgo, Museo Casamata and the art museum. There are hourly departures between 9:40am and 4:40pm from the tourist office, and you can hop on and off as you like throughout the day.

NORTHERN GULF COAST

It's 500km from Matamoros to Tampico along Hwys 101 and 180. The route begins through checkerboard-flat cornfields, but eventually the land rises into the foothills of the Sierra Madre Oriental, farming changes to ranching and the scenery turns scenic. The principal towns along the way are **San Fernando** (137km from Matamoros), **Soto La Marina** (267km) and **Aldama** (380km), each with budget and midrange hotels if you need to break your journey here. You may also want to stock up on cash in one of them since none of the coastal towns have banks or ATMs.

From these towns and others, side roads slip east to fishing villages on the coast, most of which consists of lagoons separated from the gulf by narrow sand spits. The largest lagoon is the 225km-long **Laguna Madre**, an ancient outlet of the Río Bravo del Norte. (This lagoon dried up in the mid-20th century, forcing many to leave. When a 1967 hurricane replenished it, the area was resettled by people from Veracruz.) The lagoons, sand dunes and coastal wetlands support a unique ecosystem with many bird species and excellent fishing. If you're lucky, you might spot some leaping whales out to sea.

Hotels in all classes are way overpriced on the coast, but bargaining is usually possible, especially at weekdays. Grills for cooking up the day's catch are a near-standard hotel amenity. Beach camping is generally permitted, but always get local advice before pitching your tent.

El Mezquital

About 20km south of Matamoros, just past the airport, a rough road crosses marshland for 60km before reaching this small fishing village on the long thin spit of land that divides the Laguna Madre from the Gulf. There's a lighthouse and beach, but this is mostly a place to come just to see a different side of Mexico; the wooden shops and houses here almost define ramshackle.

There are several simple places to eat, but the only place to sleep, **Hotel La Isla** (r M$200; P), is very rough and very rarely used nowadays since the attached bar that used to provide most of its customers closed down.

Buses (M$30, 2½ hours) to El Mezquital depart Plaza Allende in Matamoros at 6:30am and 3pm. You can also take a Pereño bus (M$9.5, one hour) departing every six minutes from the same spot to the end of the line and then hop in one of the cars parked in front of the Super T that run shared taxi services (M$50, one hour); they leave when full, and usually fill up quickly.

Carbonera & Punta de Piedra

From San Fernando a pretty good road leads to **Carbonera**, another small fishing village facing the Laguna Madre. The little lighthouse here resembles an Olympic torch. Dolphin sightings are almost guaranteed out by the barrier island from April to October, and fishermen are happy to take you out to see them. The price depends on how far you need to travel (you're mostly paying for the skipper's gas rather than time) but expect to pay around M$400. Between the entrance to town and the not-so-hot La Playita beach are a few simple restaurants and the basic **Hotel Delfín** (r M$350; P), Carbonera's only overnight option.

Sixteen kilometers further on is the ever smaller village of **Punta de Piedra** where **Hotel Playa Bonita** (☎ 841-846-99-49; r M$400; P ☒) faces the lagoon. The eight simple rooms aren't fancy, but they're much newer and nicer than you'd expect from a first look at the exterior. The owners can arrange boats for fishing or dolphin watching and will cook dinner for you which is a bonus since the village's only *comedor* is closed at night. The hotel has no sign; just drive as far south as you can and there it is.

To reach Carbonera and Punta de Piedra from San Fernando, turn left out of the bus station to the stoplight, then left again on Allende for half a block to the little yellow terminal where vans (Carbonera M$30, one hour; Punta de Piedra M$40, 90 minutes) depart about every two hours.

La Pesca

From Soto La Marina, Hwy 52 heads east for 50km to La Pesca, which has made the switch from fishing village to resort town. Families from Ciudad Victoria and Monterrey and even a fair number of Texans cruise in a

SAVING SEA TURTLES

One of the world's most endangered sea turtles, the Kemp's Ridley, known locally as the *tortuga lora* (parrot turtle) because of its beak-like nose, nests on this coastline from March to August. Virtually all that remain in the world lay their eggs between La Pesca and Tampico. Around 6000 nesting females were counted in 2007, up from 283 in 1985. The not-nearly-as-endangered green sea turtle nests here between June and October.

The Tamaulipas state environmental authority has a **turtle conservation center** (admission free; noon-4pm) 1km north of the main beach at La Pesca, and there are five more further south. The center in La Pesca has a little museum with photos and replicas of the Gulf's turtles. Employees at any of the conservation centers will explain the protection efforts and might take you out to see the turtles if they have time. They are often around earlier and later than official opening hours and can let you in.

Volunteers who can give at least a week can help retrieve Ridley eggs and release the hatchlings. Lodging and some food is provided. Contact ☎ 834-318-9474 or ilara_tam@hotmail.com for more information.

weekends for fun in the sun and often some fishing. The Río Soto La Marina and the Laguna Morales have abundant snook, redfish, kingfish and black bass while some of the fish offshore include king mackerel and red snapper. Most hotels can arrange boat rentals with fishing guides for around M$800 a day. Many hotels also feature piers with lights for night casting.

The long, wide, sandy beach, **Playa La Pesca**, 5km east of town, is dotted with *palapa* shades, but you have to walk *very* far before you could call it clean. It's nearly empty much of the year, but packed during Semana Santa and summer months.

Most of La Pesca's lodging is in town or along the river west of town rather than out at the beach. The ordinary **Hotel Titanic** (☎ 835-327-06-04; s & d M$250, tr & q M$300; P ⊠) is typical of the town's cheapies. A room with just a fan costs M$200. Among the fancier choices, the **Rivera del Río** (☎ 835-327-06-58; s/d M$400/800; P ⊠ ⊠ ⅋) makes an excellent base. The 37 rooms are large and rather plain but the well-maintained grounds are lovely, with a swimming pool perched over the river and a good restaurant. Weekday and slow-season discounts are common.

La Pesca's restaurants are mostly unremarkable. For something sort of special, unwind with dishes and seafood under the big thatched roof or out back along the river at **Restaurant Posada** (☎ 835-327-80-00; mains M$30-70; 8am-8pm Sun-Thu, 8am-10pm Fri & Sat), next to the lighthouse at Playa la Pesca.

Transportes Tamaulipecos de la Costa runs 10 2nd-class buses a day between Ciudad Victoria's bus terminal and Playa La Pesca (M$105, three hours). You can catch any of these buses just off Soto La Marina's central plaza, an hour from La Pesca (M$28).

Barra del Tordo

Scenically set on the Río Carrizal, tiny Barra del Tordo, with seemingly more boats than people, is as much of a charmer as you'll find on this stretch of coast. A major golf resort outside town is planned, but it's unlikely to change things much in the village itself.

Walk over the bridge on the east edge of town and in less than 10 minutes you'll be on a wide, clean and probably deserted stretch of sand. Down the shore, Playa No 2 (road access is 4km before town) has *palapas*, a few *comedores* and a turtle conservation center (see the boxed text, above).

The friendly and functional **Hotel La Esperanza** (☎ 833-192-95-29; r M$300-500; P ⊠) will do for a base in town. It has a mix of closet-like bunks and some cozy, large quarters. The restaurant offers 2nd-floor views of a shallow lagoon. Across the street, on the river, **Hotel Jarocho** (☎ 836-274-18-58; r M$350-500; P ⊠) is also fine. Though not cheap, **Villas del Tordo** (☎ 834-314-14-99; www.villasdeltordo.com; s & d/tr & q M$1000/1200; P ⊠ ▯ ⊠ ⅋), on the road into town, is one of the few places on the northern Gulf coast that is reasonably priced for what you get. The modern yellow buildings spread over expansive green grounds along a little lake. It's a good place to relax, or they'll keep you busy with horseback riding, fishing trips, a basketball court and more. Prices are discounted by M$200

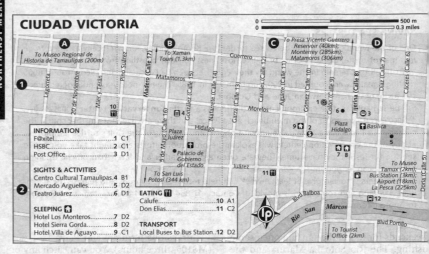

CIUDAD VICTORIA

0 _____ 500 m
0 _____ 0.3 miles

INFORMATION	
F@xitel	1 C1
HSBC	2 C1
Post Office	3 D1

SIGHTS & ACTIVITIES	
Centro Cultural Tamaulipas	4 B1
Mercado Arguelles	5 D2
Teatro Juárez	6 C1

SLEEPING	
Hotel Los Monteros	7 D2
Hotel Sierra Gorda	8 D2
Hotel Villa de Aguayo	9 C1

EATING	
Calufe	10 A1
Don Elias	11 C2

TRANSPORT	
Local Buses to Bus Station	12 D2

weekdays, and kitchenettes are available for M$200 more.

Creaky old vans (M$25, one hour, six daily) connect the village to the city of Aldama, 43km west. In Aldama they depart from in front of Supermercado Wendy's, southwest of the plaza at the corner of Constitución and Matamoros. A taxi from the highway to Wendy's should cost no more than M$30.

CIUDAD VICTORIA

☎ 834 / pop 278,500 / elevation 230m

Despite its status as the state capital, Ciudad Victoria, founded in 1750 and later renamed after Mexico's first president, has a provincial feel. Though it's not exciting, its several historic buildings and tranquil atmosphere make it a pleasant place to wander around.

Orientation

The city center is laid out in a grid pattern. The north–south streets have both numbers (Calle 7, Calle 8 etc) and names (Díaz, Tijerina etc). The main shopping street is Hidalgo between Plaza Hidalgo, the old *plaza de armas*, and Plaza Juárez (aka Plaza de Gobierno and Plaza Hidalgo 15), where the hip kids hang out after school.

Information

F@xitel (Calle 9 No 226; per hr M$7) Fast internet access.

HSBC (cnr Hidalgo & Calle 10; ☎ 8am-7pm Mon-Fri, 9am-3pm Sat) Changes traveler's checks.

Post office (cnr Calle 8 & Morelos; ☎ 8am-3pm Mon-Fri) In the town hall.

Tourist office (☎ 315-60-97; http://turismo.tamaulipas .gob.mx; Hernán Cortes 129; ☎ 8am-9pm Mon-Fri, 9am-3pm Sat & Sun) In the El Peñón building.

Xaman Tours (☎ 316-35-65; www.xaman.com.mx; Calle 14 No 1868; ☎ 9:30am-1:30pm & 4-8pm) Runs regular canyoneering, kayaking and rappelling trips on weekends, and can connect you with guides for anything else in the mountains around town and beyond.

Sights & Activities

The **Museo Tamux** (☎ 315-12-15; www.tamux.go .mx; Blvd Fidel Velázquez; adult/child & student M$30/15 ☎ 10am-6pm Tue-Sat, ticket office closes 5pm) is an excellent interactive natural history museum covering everything from asteroids to cloning to dinosaurs, including some cool replica fossils. The big orange ball is a planetarium, and there's a **botanical garden** (admission free; ☎ 8am-4pm) down below. No buses come here, or even pass nearby.

The **Museo Regional de Historia de Tamaulipas** (☎ 315-14-56; cnr Calle 22 & Allende; admission free ☎ 10am-6pm Tue-Fri, 10am-4pm Sat & Sun), in a lovely yellow building formerly inhabited by nuns and the army, does a good job tracing the state's history. Even if you don't speak Spanish, stop by to see the large collection of Huastec figurines.

The art gallery in the **Centro Cultural Tamaulipas** (☎ 318-83-30; Calle 15; admission free; ☎ 11am-7pm Mon-Sat, 9am-1pm Sun) brings in temporary exhibits from a variety of Mexican artists. Also worth on the art front is the large mural showing the history of Tamaulipas in the lobby of the **Teatro Juárez** (Plaza Hidalgo; ☎ 8am-2pm).

You'll probably want to save your handicraft shopping for another city, but the **Mercado Arguelles** (7am-8pm Mon-Sat, 7am-4pm Sun) is fun to browse.

Sleeping & Eating

Victoria offers good value on the hotel front in all price categories. If you're just passing through there are several good cheapies around the bus station.

Hotel Villa de Aguayo (312-78-18; cnr Calle 10 & Morelos; s/d M$200/240, r air-con M$250-290; P) A hospitable place with plain but scrupulously clean, newly built rooms, all with firm beds and cable TV.

Hotel Los Monteros (312-03-00; Hidalgo 962; s & d M$200-300, tr & q M$350-400; P) The rooms at one of Victoria's oldest hotel are dated, but have the character Villa de Aguaryo lacks, as well as free wi-fi. The tiled lobby and tall courtyard add a charming historic touch.

Hotel Sierra Gorda (312-20-10; Hidalgo 8; s/d/tr M$520/580/640; P   ) The garish (in a good way) neo-colonial decor of the lobby spills into the restaurant and the hallways, but only a little into the rooms, which don't quite have all the extras of the international chain hotels in town but are just as comfortable. There are often discounts.

Calufe (134-09-17; cnr Calle 18 & Hidalgo; coffee & milkshakes M$15-35; 7am-11pm Mon-Sat, 3-11pm Sun;) This stylish place with exposed rock walls and retro vinyl chairs roasts its own coffee on site. There's live music Thursday to Saturday at 8pm.

Don Elias (315-51-56; cnr Calle 11 & Juárez; mains M$35-185; 7am-8pm Mon-Sat) A mix of tasty food, good service and lovely decor (fancy in the front and a fun log-cabin look in back) makes this place popular. The menu is heavy on steak and seafood, but you can eat lighter with the enchiladas *rojas* (enchiladas in red sauce) or salads. A guitar trio plays from 2:30pm to 4:30pm.

Getting There & Away

AIR

Aeropuerto Nacional General Pedro Méndez (316-46 48) is 18km east of town off the Soto La Marina road. There are three daily flights to Mexico City with **Aeromar** (316-96-96) and one with **Click Mexicana** (800-122-54-25).

BUS

The bus station, 3km east of the center, has a left-luggage service (M$5 per hour).

Frequent 1st-class buses run to the following destinations:

Destination	Fare	Duration
Ciudad Mante	M$84	2hr
Matamoros	M$197	4hr
Monterrey	M$194	4hr
Reynosa	M$192	4½hr
San Luis Potosí	M$205	5hr
Tampico	M$150	3½hr

For Mexico City (10 hours) there are eight 1st-class (M$555) and four deluxe (M$719) departures daily. Ten 2nd-class buses go to La Pesca (M$110, three hours). For Reserva de la Biosfera El Cielo, take a Ciudad Mante–bound bus; see p425 for details.

CAR & MOTORCYCLE

Hwys 85 and 101 converge at Ciudad Victoria allowing easy access to and from Tampico, Monterrey and San Luis Potosí; Hwy 101 is an incredibly scenic route up into the mountains. The quickest route to Mexico City is through San Luis Potosí.

Getting Around

To get to the center from the bus station, turn right out the doors and take any bus (M$4.5) labeled 'Centro.' In the other direction, minibuses labeled 'Central' run down Blvd Balboa along the river. Taxis charge M$30 for the same trip, or from the center to the tourist office.

RESERVA DE LA BIOSFERA EL CIELO

An incredibly rich UN-listed biosphere reserve, El Cielo encompasses a 1445-sq-km chunk of steep-sided forested mountains ranging from 200m to 2320m. Marking a transition zone between tropical, temperate and semidesert ecosystems, its diversity is incredible. There are 97 species of reptile and amphibian and 430 bird species (255 resident, 175 migrant) including Tamaulipas pygmy owl and yellow-headed parrot. Though seldom seen, black bear and jaguar live in the reserve. There are also dozens of orchid varieties, mostly within the cloud-forest zone between 800m and 1400m. While it should go without saying, picking wild plants is prohibited: 22 species of orchids have become extinct in Mexico in the last decade.

The main jumping-off point for El Cielo is **Gómez Farías**, a one-road village clinging to a ridge just outside the reserve, 11km up a side road off Hwy 85 between Ciudad Victoria and Ciudad Mante. The village is small and tranquil enough for you to do some decent backyard birding at your hotel. The **tourist office** (☎ 832-236-22-15; ☼ 9am-3:30pm Mon-Fri), just off the plaza, has little to offer.

Twelve kilometers out of Gómez (follow the signs for La Bocatoma) on the road heading back to the highway you can swim in **Poza Azul**, a pond filled with cool blue water. It costs M$30 for a boat across the narrow Río Frío and then it's an easy 500m walk. The restaurant here rents kayaks (M$50 per half hour).

Sights & Activities

While it's possible to make your own way into El Cielo, few trails or natural attractions are labeled, so exploring is best done with a local guide, or at least a driver who knows their way around. If you do go on your own, we recommend you register your plans at the police commander's office behind the tourist office in Gómez Farías. This is remote territory.

The road through the reserve is very rough; it's suitable only for 4WD vehicles with high clearance. Motorcycles are prohibited. Most people visit in the covered, open-sided trucks you'll see parked all over town. These hold up to 10 passengers comfortably and cost between M$1000 and M$1600 per day; prices rise and fall with demand. There's a M$100 fee for trucks from Gómez (just M$20 for private vehicles) to enter or pass through the villages of Alta Cima and San José. Ask if this is included in the price. There's often nobody around to collect the money in San José.

The forest itself is the main attraction. The tall trees are strung with Spanish moss, and from June through November many are bursting with flowers. It teems with birds and butterflies year-round, and bird-watchers are some of El Cielo's principal visitors. The hotels can connect you to guides with ornithological expertise. There are also many caves and rainy season-only waterfalls.

The village of **Alta Cima** (900m) is just 12km from Gómez Farías, but it takes about 90 minutes to reach it, which tells you what you need to know about the condition of the road through the reserve. Behind La Fe restaurant in Alta Cima is a steep interpretive trail up **Cerro de la Cruz** (M$5) where you can see orchids in a patch of cloud forest. A 40-minute walk away is **Cueva del Pino** with some lovely

stalactites, but few people visit because the entry is difficult; guides (M$120) from the village are mandatory.

Six kilometers beyond Alta Cima is a large, vaguely house-shaped rock known as **Casa de Piedra** and about 800m below it is **El Salto**, a 70m waterfall. Camping is allowed here; pay M$25 at La Fe restaurant in Alta Cima.

The best hiking within day-trip distance of Gómez Farías is around **San José** (1470m), another 7km and one hour deeper into the reserve from Alta Cima. **Cerro de Compana**, just before the village, is topped by bizarre rock formations, and a clear trail to the top takes about 30 minutes. The large **Cueva del Agua** with three levels and the very wide **Cascada de Bellas Fuentes**, one of the most beautiful waterfalls in the reserve, are each a 1km walk away. A guide from the village to either destination will probably ask for about M$15 per person to any place. The **Cascada de Caninda**, a smaller but also lovely waterfall, is just before San José, right behind Cabañas Canindo.

Beyond San José there are more waterfalls, caves and villages. Two of the top photo ops are **Piedra del Pollo** (4km away) and **Piedra El Elefante** (8.7km away), rocks shaped like a chicken and an elephant respectively. It's possible to get from Gómez Farías to El Elefante and back in a day, but there won't be much time for stops along the way. Most day-trippers don't travel beyond San José.

Sleeping & Eating

Gómez Farías has just three hotels. None are cheap, but all are good.

Nearly 2km north of the plaza, the casual family-run **Hotel Posada Campestre** (☎ 832-236-22-00; www.posadaenelcielo.com.mx; s & d M$390, each additional person M$100; P ⊠) offers clean, orderly rooms with bunk beds and dim lighting. The leafy garden in back has a few hammocks, space for camping (M$50 per person, including use of showers) and lots of birds.

Just 150m past the plaza, the relaxing **Hostal Casa de Piedra** (☎ 832-236-21-96; s & d/tr incl breakfast M$500/600; P ⊠) has seven beautifully built stone-and-timber rooms (try to reserve 'Magnolia,' which comes with a valley-view balcony) and a little outdoor lounge and restaurant. Air-con costs M$100 extra.

Gómez's newest and fanciest hotel, **Cumbres Inn & Suites** (☎ 832-236-22-18; www.hotelcumbres.com.mx; r/ste from M$780/1229; P ⊠ ▢ ⊠ ♿), at the entrance to town, has stylish rooms (with wi-fi) and a lovely, shady spot on the edge of the valley. Between dips in the two pools you can drop down the rappelling wall or ride the triple zip-line that brings you back to where you started. They also run kayaking trips and have mountain-bike rental (M$50 per hour; daily rates negotiable). Rooms are 15% cheaper on weekdays.

All three hotels serve good food, but the tip of the hat goes to **Cumbres Inn** (mains M$45-120; ☒) for its valley view (Casa de Piedra's view is good too) and broad selection, from salads to *fajitas de pollo a la plancha* (grilled chicken fajitas). There are also several *comedores* around the plaza.

To fully appreciate how isolated and pristine the reserve is, spend a night or two in the mountains. There's nothing nearly as fancy as what's in Gómez, but there are lots of options.

The two-storey **Hotel Alta Cima** (☎ 831-254-84-04; s/d M$250/300, up to 6 people M$600), with simple but agreeable rooms and hot water, is the best choice in the village of the same name. Just across from the hotel, **La Fe** (gorditas & tacos M$4, mains M$25-40; ☽ 9am-5pm), run by the local women's cooperative, has a large menu, but rarely has much of it available. Try the *tortas de napalitos* (cactus sandwiches) if you can. They also sell bird embroidery and fruit preserves.

Just before the village of San José is a pair of rustic wooden lodges facing each other across the road. **Cabañas Canindo 'Hugo Lara'** (☎ 831-254-59-30; per person M$200) on the left as you approach from Alta Cima and **Cabañas Canindo 'Javier Villegas'** (☎ 833-187-00-66; per person M$250). Both have hot water and solar-powered lights; the only real difference is the price. Either bring your own food or let them know in advance you'd like them to cook for you.

Seemingly half the buildings in San José are tourist *cabañas*, some perched on rocky hilltops on the edge of the village; most cost around M$100 per person. There are no restaurants, but some of the cabins have kitchens and all the families will cook dinner for you. The villages of La Gloria (1700m) and Joya de Manantiales (1600m), 3.2km and 10.4km further on from San Jóse, also have simple *cabañas* at similar prices.

Getting There & Away

Six daily LUMX buses link Ciudad Mante to Gómez Farías (M$30, one hour). From Ciudad Victoria, get off your bus at the turnoff for Gómez (called 'La Y de Gómez Farías') on Hwy 85. From here you can catch the bus from Mante or the minivan (M$9) that shuttles people up to town about every two hours. Hitching on the road up to Gómez is easy.

Central Pacific Coast

Those gigantic aquamarine waves keep rolling in, just as they always have along Mexico's central Pacific coast. It's the primal rhythm backing any visit to this land of isolated beaches and giant sunsets. Sit yourself down in the sand for a week or an afternoon and, if you're lucky, spy humpback whales breaching on the horizon, or a pod of dolphins surfacing from the waves. Beyond the beach, experience a natural high in mangrove-fringed lagoons, pristine bays, and ramshackle fishing villages, or mix it up with some good living in a cosmopolitan resort town.

Don't stop there: head deeper inland toward the blue silhouette of the lofty Sierras Madre, where the tourism track becomes a rutted path that sometimes disappears completely. You can take months exploring the coast on the cheap, roaring along the coastal highway in 2nd-class buses, or hanging onto the back of a pickup packed with locals on your way to a fishing village where fishing nets are still strung by hand.

One of the world's top tourist destinations, the coast is also a land of mega-resorts, cruise ships, camera-toting tourists and rowdy spring-breakers on weekend drinking binges. Join in, or ignore them completely. You can snorkel, surf, sail, ride horses, scuba dive, explore lagoons by boat, mountain bike along ocean cliffs and drink yourself silly. Spend a week in a fabulous beachfront guesthouse, where food and drink are prepared fresh daily, or enjoy considerable luxury in a world-class hotel, where you can soak up the sun and read a book before indulging in the best spa treatment or full-body massage of your life. The good life here means finding your own rhythm.

HIGHLIGHTS

- Take the pulse of the new **Old Mazatlán** (p429) in its gorgeously renovated historic center
- Experience the living history of **Mexcaltitán** (p442), thought by some to be the ancestral homeland of the Aztecs
- People-watch and promenade on the beautiful beachfront *malecón* in **Puerto Vallarta** (p453)
- Thrill at the fearless finesse of La Quebrada cliff-divers of **Acapulco** (p503)
- Surf the aggressive barrel swells in **Boca de Pascuales** (p480)

Old Mazatlán ★
Mexcaltitán ★
Puerto Vallarta ★
★ Boca de Pascuales
Acapulco ★

■ PUERTO VALLARTA JANUARY DAILY HIGH: 26°C | 78°F   ■ PUERTO VALLARTA JULY DAILY HIGH: 33°C | 91°F

History

Archaeologists view pre-Hispanic Mexico's Pacific coast as a unified region, defined by its tradition of shaft or chamber tombs (underground burial chambers at the base of a deep shaft). The ceremonial centers around the tombs suggest a fairly developed spiritual and religious life.

The Spanish arrived in Mexico in 1519 and soon traveled to Acapulco, Zihuatanejo, Puerto Vallarta and Manzanillo. In 1564 conquistador Miguel López de Legazpi and Father André de Urdaneta first sailed from Barra de Navidad to the Philippines and soon after claimed it for Spain. Soon after, Acapulco became an established port link in the trade route between Asia and Europe.

It was not until the middle of the 1950s that tourism really hit the coast, starting in Acapulco and Mazatlán, with Puerto Vallarta soon to follow. In recent years more and more foreigners have bought and developed land along the coast, most noticeably around Puerto Vallarta.

Climate

It's hot – very hot – and wet from May and early November. Hurricanes are occasional unwelcome guests in September and October. The high-tourist season understandably coincides with the cooler, dry season from late November to late April.

Dangers & Annoyances

Mexico's central Pacific coast is *tranquilo* (peaceful), with little crime. Major coastal resorts have a large and visible police presence so violent crimes against visitors are rare.

Of the resort cities, Acapulco is the most known for crime, and in recent years several grisly murders have threatened to curb the resort's tourism industry. The violence, however, is primarily related to drug trafficking. Visitors who avoid the town's inland neighborhoods have little to fear. The coastal Hwy 200, which has had an up-and-down safety record, is now mostly safe for travel. The stretch through Michoacán and Guerrero still has a reputation for being unsafe at night, although increased law enforcement has greatly improved the situation. The most likely danger you'll encounter are the powerful undertows that can make swimming deadly. Heed local warnings and swim with caution. Otherwise, kick back – you're on vacation!

Getting There & Away

There are plenty of direct international flights from the US and Canada to Mazatlán, Puerto Vallarta, Zihuatanejo and Acapulco. For those traveling by car, the toll roads between the US border and Tepic make for easy sailing, but they're not cheap. As elsewhere in Mexico, the free roads oscillate between smooth pavement and shock-busting potholes. High quality bus services connects the resort centres to inland Mexico.

Getting Around

Bus travel in this region is easy and surprisingly comfortable. The buses serve nearly every community, large or small, but nicer buses – with air-con, comfortable seats, cleanish bathrooms, TVs and other classy comforts – serve bigger towns.

If you're driving, note that nearly everything on coastal Hwy 200 – service stations, stores, tire shops – closes around sundown.

CULIACÁN

☎ 667 / pop 605,000

Sitting pretty in a fertile river valley, this thriving capital of Sinaloa is first and foremost an administrative and agricultural center. Many travelers pass through en route to other places; the ones that linger come to appreciate the particular rhythms of this typical, primarily middle-class Mexican metropolis. Admire the stately 19th-century cathedral in Culiacán's bustling historic center. Stroll through the atmospheric Plazuela Álvaro Obregón and by the handsome Palacio Municipal. Twilight is sublime on the pretty *malecón* (waterfront street) walkway along the Río Tamazula and Río Humaya. Along the way, you'll pass a good selection of restaurants and well-run hotels.

Frequent buses connect Culiacán with Mazatlán to the south and Los Mochis (p337) to the north – it's about 210km (a three-hour drive) from either place.

MAZATLÁN

☎ 669 / pop 380,000

Having outgrown its image as a chintzy mid-20th century resort town, today's Mazatlán is one of Mexico's most alluring and inviting beach destinations. Over the past decade, the 'Pearl of the Pacific' has breathed new life into its historic center, and the ongoing renewal program continues to bear fruit. The result is something truly unique: a historic city with a

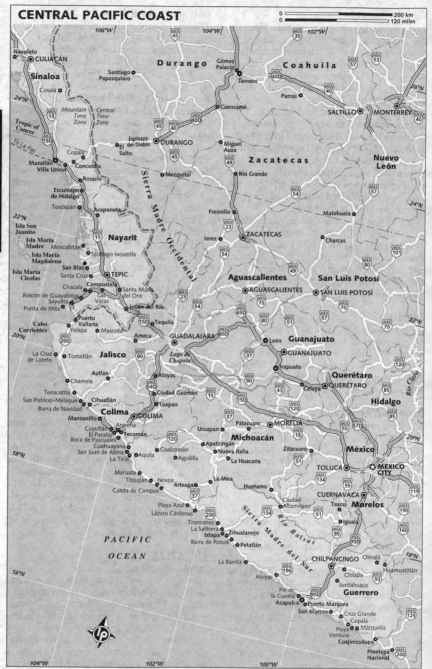

CENTRAL PACIFIC COAST

CENTRAL PACIFIC COAST

resplendent colonial district only a short walk from a 20km-long crescent of sandy beach.

To take the pulse of Mazatlán, don't linger too long in the Zona Dorada (Golden Zone), Mazatlán's traditional tourist playground. There you'll find knick-knack shops, pack-'em-in restaurants and resort hotels lined up like dominoes, but few surprises. Instead head straight for the city's gorgeous *pueblo viejo* (old town). Here, against a backdrop of cobbled streets, crumbling edifices and an ever-increasing number of newly restored gems, you'll find a cultural renaissance under way. Catch a performance at the wonderful refurbished Teatro Ángela Peralta and then a late-night bite at the atmospheric Plazuela Machado. Step into one of Mazatlán's excellent small museums or go treasure hunting in one of the many new small boutiques. One big attraction is free for all – the daily spectacle of rocky islands silhouetted against the tropical sunset, as the fiery red fades into the sea, and another starry night begins.

History
In pre-Hispanic times Mazatlán (which means 'place of deer' in the Náhuatl language) was populated by Totorames, who lived by hunting, gathering, fishing and growing crops. 'Old' Mazatlán, the traditional town center, dates from the 19th century. Tourists started coming in the 1930s, and in the 1950s some hotels appeared along Playa Olas Altas, Mazatlán's first tourist beach. From the 1970s onward, a long strip of hotels and tourist facilities spread north along the coast. More significantly, in the early 1990s restoration efforts began on key downtown buildings, including the theater and other stately edifices facing Plazuela Machado. By 2005 the picturesque plaza had been transformed, and a year later work was concluded on the boardwalk and monuments of Av Olas Altas.

Orientation
Old Mazatlán, the city center, is near the southern end of a peninsula, bounded by the Pacific Ocean on the west and the Bahía Dársena channel on the east. The center of the city is the cathedral, on Plaza Principal, which is surrounded by a rectangular street grid. At the southern tip of the peninsula, El Faro (The Lighthouse) stands on a rocky prominence, overlooking Mazatlán's sportfishing fleet and the La Paz ferry terminal.

The beachside boulevard changes names frequently as it runs along the Pacific side of the peninsula north from Playa Olas Altas. It heads around some rocky outcrops, and around the wide arc of Playa Norte to the Zona Dorada, a concentration of hotels, bars and businesses catering mainly to package tourists. Further north are more hotels, a marina and some time-share condominium developments.

Information
Banamex Old Mazatlán (Map p431; Juarez); Zona Dorada (Map p430; Av Camarón Sábalo) Has branches near Plaza Principal and in the Zona Dorada.
Clínica Balboa (Map p430; ☎ 916-79-33; Av Camarón Sábalo 4480; ☒ 24hr) English is spoken at this well-regarded, walk-in medical clinic.
Coordinación General de Turismo (Map p431; ☎ 981-88-86/87; www.sinaloa-travel.com; Carnaval 1317; ☒ 9am-5pm Mon-Fri) Proffers information about lodging deals and what to see and do in Mazatlán and Sinaloa state.
Cyber Café Mazatlán (Map p430; Av Camarón Sábalo 204; per hr M$35) Pricey but fast and convenient.
Emergency (☎ 060)
Fire (☎ 981-27-69)
Lavandería La Blanca (Map p430; Camarón Sábalo 357; per 3kg M$65)
Main post office (Map p431; Juárez s/n) On the east side of Plaza Principal.
Tourist police (☎ 914-84-44)

Sights
OLD MAZATLÁN
The old town is a forward-thinking place rooted firmly in the past. At its center is the soaring 19th-century **cathedral** (Map p431; cnr Juárez & Calle 21 de Marzo) with its high yellow twin towers and a dramatic interior. Two blocks north, on Juaréz and Valle, is a vibrant local **market** full of clothes, housewares, produce, juice stands and shoppers.

A short southwesterly walk will bring you to the tree-lined **Plazuela Machado** (Map p431; cnr Av Carnaval & Constitución). The plaza and surrounding streets are abuzz with art galleries, cafés and restaurants. The center of attention is the **Teatro Ángela Peralta** (Map p431) half a block south of the plaza. All kinds of cultural events are staged here.

West of the center is **Playa Olas Altas**, a small beach in a small cove. The breezy seafront road, Paseo Olas Altas, strongly evokes 1950s-era Mazatlán, with a couple of faded relic hotels.

MAZATLÁN

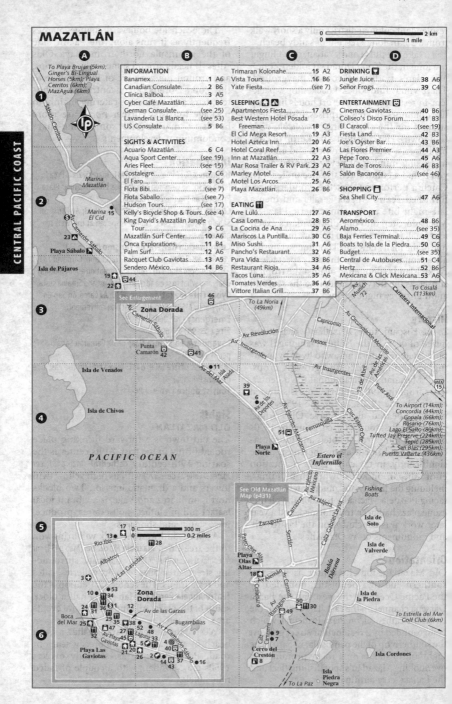

0 ____ 2 km
0 ____ 1 mile

INFORMATION
Banamex...........................1 A6
Canadian Consulate.............2 B6
Clínica Balboa....................3 A5
Cyber Café Mazatlán............4 B6
German Consulate............(see 25)
Lavandería La Blanca.......(see 53)
US Consulate......................5 B6

SIGHTS & ACTIVITIES
Acuario Mazatlán................6 C4
Aqua Sport Center...........(see 19)
Aries Fleet.....................(see 15)
Costalegre.........................7 C6
El Faro..............................8 C6
Flota Bibi........................(see 7)
Flota Saballo...................(see 7)
Hudson Tours..................(see 17)
Kelly's Bicycle Shop & Tours..(see 4)
King David's Mazatlán Jungle
  Tour...............................9 C6
Mazatlán Surf Center........10 B4
Onca Explorations.............11 B4
Palm Surf.........................12 A5
Racquet Club Gaviotas.......13 A5
Sendero México................14 A6

EATING
Arre Lulú.........................27 A6
Casa Loma........................28 B5
La Cocina de Ana..............29 A6
Mariscos La Puntilla..........30 C6
Miso Sushi........................31 A6
Pancho's Restaurant..........32 A6
Pura Vida.........................33 B6
Restaurant Rioja................34 A6
Tacos Luna.......................35 A6
Tomates Verdes.................36 A6
Vittore Italian Grill.............37 B6

Trimaran Kolonahe.............15 A2
Vista Tours.......................16 B6
Yate Fiesta......................(see 7)

SLEEPING
Apartmentos Fiesta............17 A5
Best Western Hotel Posada
  Freeman..........................18 C5
El Cid Mega Resort.............19 A3
Hotel Azteca Inn................20 A6
Hotel Coral Reef.................21 A6
Inn at Mazatlán..................22 A3
Mar Rosa Trailer & RV Park..23 A2
Marley Motel.....................24 A6
Motel Los Arcos.................25 A6
Playa Mazatlán..................26 B6

DRINKING
Jungle Juice......................38 A6
Señor Frogs.......................39 C4

ENTERTAINMENT
Cinemas Gaviotas..............40 B6
Coliseo's Disco Forum.........41 A6
El Caracol......................(see 19)
Fiesta Land.......................42 B3
Joe's Oyster Bar.................43 B6
Las Flores Premier.............44 A3
Pepe Toro........................45 A6
Plaza de Toros...................46 B3
Salón Bacanora...............(see 46)

SHOPPING
Sea Shell City....................47 A6

TRANSPORT
Aeroméxico.......................48 B6
Alamo............................(see 35)
Baja Ferries Terminal..........49 C6
Boats to Isla de la Piedra....50 C6
Budget...........................(see 35)
Central de Autobuses..........51 C4
Hertz...............................52 B6
Mexicana & Click Mexicana..53 A6

OLD MAZATLÁN

0 _____ 400 m
0 _____ 0.2 miles

INFORMATION
Banamex..............................1 C3
Coordinación General de Turismo.2 D4
Main Post Office.....................3 C3

SIGHTS & ACTIVITIES
Casa Machado.......................4 D4
Cathedral............................5 C3
Centro de Idiomas..................6 B4
Clavadistas (Cliff Divers).........7 A3
Fishing pangas......................8 B2
Museo Arqueológico...............9 B4
Museo de Arte.....................10 B4
Saltwater Pool.....................11 B4

SLEEPING 🏠
Hotel Belmar......................12 B4
Hotel del Centro..................13 C3
Hotel del Río......................14 C2
Hotel La Siesta....................15 B4
Hotel Machado....................16 B4
Meson de Cynthia................17 D4
The Melville.......................18 B4

EATING 🍴
Cenaduria El Túnel...............19 D4
Domitila...........................20 D4
La Copa de Leche................21 B4
La Espiga Dorada.................22 B4
La Tramoya........................23 D4
Mariscos El Camichin............24 B2
Mariscos Toño.....................25 B2
Pedro y Lola......................26 D4
Puerto Viejo......................27 B4

DRINKING 🍷
Edgar's Bar........................28 C4
La Tertulia.........................29 D4
Vitrola's Bar.......................30 B3

ENTERTAINMENT 🎭
Teatro Ángela Peralta...........31 D4

SHOPPING 🛍
Casa Etnika........................32 B4
Gallery Michael....................33 B3

Nearby is the platform from which the **clavadistas** (cliff divers; Map p431) cast their bodies into the treacherous ocean swells for your enjoyment. Tip accordingly. You're most likely to see the divers perform around lunchtime on Saturday and Sunday (they won't risk their necks until a crowd has assembled).

At the peninsula's south end, a prominent rocky outcrop is the base for **El Faro** (Map p430), 135m above sea level and said to be the second-highest lighthouse in the world (after the one in Gibraltar). You can climb up there for a spectacular view of the city and coast.

MUSEUMS
The small but absorbing **Museo Arqueológico** (Map p431; ☎ 981-14-55; Sixto Osuna 76; admission M$25;

⏰ 10am-1pm & 4-7pm Tue-Sun) invokes Sinaloan history and culture with changing exhibitions of pre-Hispanic petroglyphs and sculptural objects. There are some wall texts in English. Opposite, the small **Museo de Arte** (Map p431; ☎ 985-35-02; cnr Sixto Osuna & Carranza; admission M$20; ⏰ 10am-2pm & 4-7pm Tue-Sat, 10am-2pm Sun) makes a convincing case for the vitality and innovation of contemporary Mexican art with changing exhibitions of digital works, sculpture, prints and paintings. Wall texts are in Spanish and English.

Also worth a peek is the **Casa Machado** (Map p431; Constitución 79; adult/student M$20/10; ⏰ 10am-6pm), a restored 19th-century house filled with a collection of antique French and Austrian furniture, clothing and other items.

BEACHES & ZONA DORADA

With over 16km of beaches it's easy to find a stretch of sand to call your own. The following beaches are listed in geographic order, from south to north.

In Old Mazatlán, the crescent-shaped **Playa Olas Altas** (Map p431) is where tourism first flourished in the 1950s. The pebbly beach is not ideal for swimming but it's a grand place to soak up some regional history.

Flanked by a broad *malecón* popular with joggers and strollers, the golden sands of **Playa Norte** (Map p431) begin just north of Old Mazatlán. The beach arcs toward **Punta Camarón** (Map p430), a rocky point dominated by the conspicuous castle-like Fiesta Land nightclub complex.

The most luxurious hotels face the fine, uncrowded **Playa Las Gaviotas** (Map p430) and **Playa Sábalo** (Map p430), the latter extending north of the Zona Dorada. Sheltered by picturesque islands, here the waters are generally calm and ideal for swimming and water sports. Further north, past the ever-evolving **Marina Mazatlán** (Map p430), are the serene **Playa Brujas** (Witch Beach, off Map p430) and **Playa Cerritos** (off Map p430). Both have a smattering of excellent seafood restaurants and are surfing destinations. To get to these by bus, catch a 'Cerritos Juárez' bus from the Fiesta Land complex or from along Camarón Sábalo in the Zona Dorada; with a bit of bargaining, transportation by taxi should cost no more than M$100.

ISLANDS

Resembling breaching whales in silhouette, the three photogenic land masses (Map p430) jutting from the sea are Mazatlán's signature islands. With secluded beaches and limpid waters ideal for snorkeling – and great multitudes of seals and marine birds – they provide an ideal day trip destination. On the left is **Isla de Chivos** (Island of Goats); **Isla de Pájaros** (Island of Birds) is on the right. Most visited is the one in the middle, **Isla de Venados** (Deer Island). The islands are part of a wildlife refuge designated to help protect the marine fauna and birds they harbour.

The most popular option for visiting the islands is the five-hour Deer Island Tour (US$42) to Isla de Venados departing at 9:30am Tuesday to Sunday from the marina at El Cid Mega Resort (see p436). The price includes activities and a (frankly, meager) lunch. These trips are often booked to capacity, and at last visit proffered sub-par snorkeling equipment.

If you desire a more reflective, low impact exploration of the island, consider the excellent kayak tour led by Sendero México (p434) for a US$55/30 per adult/child. A short boat ride will drop you off on Isla de Venados, from where you'll spend most of the day kayaking, snorkeling, hiking and sun worshipping. The bilingual guides are pleased to share their wildlife knowledge and sea kayaking expertise.

Isla de la Piedra

Escape artists love Isla de la Piedra (Stone Island, Map p430), located southeast of Old Mazatlán, for its beautiful, long sandy beach bordered by coconut groves. Anyone with an appetite sings the praises of the simple *palapa* (thatched-roof shelter) restaurants. Surfers come for the waves, and on Sunday afternoons and holidays the restaurants draw Mexican families. Most other times you'll have the beach to yourself.

Several companies offer all-inclusive, nohassle excursions to Isla de la Piedra (it's actually a peninsula) including open bar, lunch, and a menu of activities such as water sports and short rides on forlorn, skinny horses. Consider instead **King David's Mazatlán Jungle Tour** (Map p430; ☎ 914-14-44; Calz Joel Montes Camarena s/n; adult/child US$45/30; ☒ Tue-Thu & Sat), which offers a five-hour ecotour into the gorgeous bird-filled mangroves of a protected wildlife refuge. Stops along the way include an enormous coconut plantation, a secluded beach strewn with sand dollars, and a rustic restaurant for a hearty lunch of freshly smoked fish. Offered separately is a five-hour bird-watching tour (adult/child US$50/30), which goes even deeper into Isla de Piedra's protected waterways.

It's a simple matter to get to Isla de Piedra on your own. Take a small water taxi (roundtrip M$10, every 10 minutes from 7am to 6pm) from the Playa Sur *embarcadero* near the Baja Ferries terminal. You'll be dropped off at a jetty just a short walk from the Isla de la Piedra beach. 'Playa Sur' buses leave for the boat dock from the north side of the Plaza Principal (Map p431).

Activities

SURFING

With a season lasting from late March through November, Mazatlán boasts several noteworthy surfing sites and a couple of great surf shops. The longest-established surf shop in town is **Mazatlán Surf Center** (Map p430; ☎ 913-18-21; www.mazatlansurfcenter.com; Av Camarón Sábalo 500-4; board rentals per day/week M$200-250/1000, 2hr lesson M$500; ☯ 10am-9pm Mon-Sat, 1-9pm Sun), known for its popular surfing lessons and infectious passion for the sport. From June to September it conducts improvised one-week surfing expeditions (from US$750) to famous far-flung spots like Patolé, Celestinos and Mármol.

Also consider **Palm Surf** (Map p430; ☎ 914-06-87; palmsurf.com.mx; Av Camarón Sábalo 333; board rentals per day M$250, 2hr lesson M$300-400; ☯ 9:30am-6pm Mon-Sat), with good boards for rent and reputable lessons.

OTHER WATER SPORTS

The **Aqua Sport Center** (Map p430; ☎ 913-33-33; El Cid Mega Resort, Av Camarón Sábalo s/n) is the place to go for other water sports, including scuba diving (one-tank dive M$600), snorkeling rentals (per day M$110), jet skiing (per half-hour M$500), banana-boat rides (M$88), parasailing (M$330), and kayak rentals (M$165 to M$275 per hour). Water sports equipment can also be hired from the beaches of most other large beachfront hotels.

HORSEBACK RIDING

If you love (or would love) to canter beside the sea, your best bet is with **Ginger's Bi-Lingual Horses** (☎ 988-12-54; www.mazinfo.com/gingershorses; Playa Bruja; 1hr tour M$250; ☯ 10am, 11:30am, 1pm & 2:30pm Mon-Sat). The horses are healthy, happy and eager to stretch their legs on the trails leading through coconut plantations and on the bewitching Playa Bruja. Take a 'Cerritos Juárez' bus from Zona Dorada or a taxi to Playa Bruja.

SPORTFISHING

Handily located at the confluence of the Sea of Cortez and the Pacific Ocean, Mazatlán is world famous for its sportfishing – especially for marlin, swordfish, sailfish, tuna and *dorado* (dolphinfish). It can be an expensive activity (US$300 to US$450 per boat for a day in an 11m cruiser with four to six people fishing), though small-game fishing from a 7m *super panga* (fiberglass skiff) is less expensive (US$210 to US$260 per boat with up to six people fishing).

Boats leave from the El Cid Mega Resort marina and Marina Mazatlán, but discounts up to 20% are offered by the operators based on the peninsula on Calz Camarena (Map p430).

If you'd rather negotiate directly with a fisher – while saving a little moolah – confer with the independent operators offering half-day *panga* trips for US$75 to US$125, depending on the season. You'll find them waiting for you on the Playa Norte beach, alongside Paseo Claussen (Map p431).

Aries Fleet (Map p430; ☎ 916-34-68; ariesfleet.elcid .com; Marina El Cid) Supports catch and release practices.

Flota Bibi (Map p430; ☎ 981-36-40; www.bibifleet .com; Calz Camarena s/n) Proudly operates a six-person boat and gives steep discounts in the low season.

Flota Saballo (Map p430; ☎ 981-27-61; Calz Camarena s/n)

GOLF & TENNIS

Mazatlán has two renowned championship golf courses. The most striking is the **Estrella del Mar Golf Club** (off Map p430; ☎ 800-727-4653; www .estrelladelmar.com; Isla de la Piedra; green fees 9/18 holes US$69/110, club rentals US$35-50), just south of the airport along the coast. El Cid Mega Resort (p436) offers a challenging alternative north of the Zona Dorada, with 9/18 holes for US$60/75, but during the high season only guests may be allowed to play.

Play tennis at **Racquet Club Gaviotas** (Map p430; ☎ 913-59-39; Rio Ibis s/n; per hr M$120) in the Zona Dorada, at El Cid Resort and at almost any of the large hotels north of the center.

Courses

Centro de Idiomas (Map p431; ☎ 985-56-06; www .spanishlink.org; Aurora 203; classes per week with/without homestay US$250-285/435-470) offers Spanish courses for three or five hours (Monday to Friday) with a maximum of six students per class. Registration is Saturday morning from 9am to noon. The school also facilitates individual instruction (three/five-hour classes per week US$320/540), volunteer work within the community, and homestays with three meals a day. Prices listed are for the first week of study; discounts are offered for each additional week.

Mazatlán for Children

Kids love this town, if only for the many opportunities to get wet.

Saltwater pool (Map p431; bathroom & changing room M$30; ☯) One of the most economical and enjoyable places to take a dip is at this small, all-natural pool below the Carpe Olivera statue on Paseo Olas Altas. Kids and their adults splash around as waves crash over the pool's seaward edge.

MazAgua (off Map p430; ☎ 988-00-41; Entronque Habal-Cerritos s/n; admission M$120; ☉ 10am-6pm Mar-Dec; ⊛) Splashing around is also the featured activity here, where kids can go hog wild with water toboggans, a wave pool and other amusements. Children under the age of three are free. The 'Cerritos–Juárez' bus takes you there from anywhere along the coastal road.

Acuario Mazatlán (Map p430; ☎ 981-78-15; www .acuariomazatlan.gob.mx; Av de los Deportes 111; adult/child M$60/40; ☉ 9:30am-6pm; ⊛) One of Mexico's largest aquariums with 52 tanks with 250 species of freshwater and saltwater fish and other creatures. Sea lion, diving and bird shows are presented daily at 10:30am, noon and 3pm.

Tours

BICYCLE TOURS

Kelly's Bicycle Shop and Tours (Map p430; ☎ 914-11-87; www.kellys-bikes.com; Av Camarón Sábalo 204; ☉ 10am-2pm & 4:30-8pm Mon-Sat) leads wild and woolly one- to four-hour mountain-bike tours (M$295) into the hills, over scenic paved routes and down challenging single-track trails. Mountain bikes can be rented for M$150 per day.

BOAT TOURS

In addition to Isla de Venados trips (see p432), several boats take three-hour **sightseeing tours** (M$150), most leaving from the marina near El Faro at 11am. Two-hour sunset cruises (sometimes called 'booze cruises') include hors d'oeuvres and alcohol (M$250 to M$350). Check flyers around town, talk to a tour agent or call the operators of boats such as **Costalegre** (Map p430; ☎ 982-31-30; Calz Camarena s/n) and **Yate Fiesta** (Map p430; ☎ 981-71-54; Calz Camarena s/n).

The speedy vessel **Trimaran Kolonahe** (Map p430; ☎ 916-34-68; Marina El Cid) sets sail for Isla de Venados each morning at 9am, and returns to sea again at 2:30pm for a sunset cruise with open bar. Both tours are priced at US$35.

BUS TOURS

Several companies offer a variety of tours in and around Mazatlán. Prices are about the same from company to company for the same tours: a three-hour city tour (US$25); a colonial tour (US$42 to US$50) to the foothill towns of El Quelite, Concordia and Copala; and a tequila factory tour (US$35) that includes the village of La Noria. Hotel pick-ups are standard.

Recommended agencies:

Hudson Tours (Map p430; ☎ 913-17-64; www.hudson tours.com; Apartamentos Fiesta, Ibis 502) Smaller, per-sonalized tours including snorkeling (US$30), city (US$25), spearfishing (US$35), hiking (US$25) and shopping (US$25).

Vista Tours (Map p430; ☎ 986-83-83; www.vistatours .com.mx; Av Camarón Sábalo 51) A variety of tours: El Quelite (US$35), Cosalá (US$75), and the San Ignacio Missions (US$75).

WILDLIFE AND WHALE-WATCHING TOURS

Close to a range of ecosystems – from mangrove-lined estuaries to tropical deciduous and dry thorn forests – Mazatlán offers naturelovers a diverse and enriching experience. For bird-watches, more than 400 species of birds can be seen in and around Mazatlán. With a well-articulated green ethos, **Sendero México** (Map p430; ☎ 940-86-87; www.senderomexico.com; Av Playa Las Gaviotas s/n) offers an impressive array of guided bird-watching tours (US$35 to US$145) including forays by kayak into coastal lagoons and excursions into the foothills east of town.

If being in the wake of cetaceans floats your boat, try **Onca Explorations** (Map p430; ☎ 990-16-32; www.oncaexplorations.com; Av del Mar 1022) and its fourhour whale and dolphin exploration led by biologist Oscar Guzón (US$85, from December to May). During your journey, learn about whale research techniques as the crew collects information on the behavioral ecology of the whales and conducts a photo-identification project. Also offered is a four-hour snorkeling expedition to several islands with an emphasis on marine ecology (US$65, year-round), and a fascinating five-hour tour to the archeological site Las Labradas (US$55), where the only beachside petroglyphs in the Americas exist.

Festivals & Events

Carnaval Mazatlán has Mexico's most flamboyant Carnaval celebrations. For the week leading up to Ash Wednesday (the Wednesday 46 days before Easter), the town goes on a nonstop partying spree. It ends abruptly on the morning of Ash Wednesday, when Roman Catholics go to church to receive ash marks on their foreheads for the first day of Lent. Be sure to reserve a hotel room in advance.

Sinaloa Festival de los Artes Culture vultures should plan to visit in November–December for this art and performance festival centred at the Peralta Theater.

Virgen de Guadalupe The day of the Virgen de Guadalupe is celebrated on December 12 at the cathedral. Children come in colorful costumes.

Sleeping

Befitting an old resort town, Mazatlán has an extensive choice of accommodations for any budget, from luxury resorts to vintage old-style hotels and a growing selection of charming, expat-run B&Bs.

BUDGET

Hotel del Río (Map p431; ☎ 982-44-30; Juárez 2410; d/q M$200/350; ☒) This tidy family-run hotel, close to the beach in a working-class neighborhood, is a long-time traveler favorite. Several rooms are on the dark side; request one of the few bright ones that face seaward. All rooms have cable TV, and the seventh night is free.

Hotel del Centro (Map p431; ☎ 981-26-73; Canizales 717; s/d M$200/300; ☒) Its proximity to both Plaza Principal and the lively public market makes this well-kept cheapie a great choice for budget travelers who favor downtown bustle over the more predictable rhythms of the beach. The 24 rooms are plain and the beds a tad squishy, but they're very clean and otherwise well kept.

Hotel Belmar (Map p431; ☎ 985-11-12/13; Paseo Olas Altas 166 Sur; s/d M$280-330; P ☒ ☒) This totally faded 1950s classic harkens back to Mazatlán's swanky early days as a tourist mecca. The more than 200 rooms run the gamut from threadbare and dingy to perfectly acceptable; ask to see several before making your choice. The best rooms – including the one John Wayne favored – are up a few flights of stairs. These have air-con and sea-view balconies well positioned to benefit from salty breezes and gratifying views over Playa Norte.

Hotel Coral Reef (Map p430; ☎ 913-29-41; Av Playa Gaviotas 4; d M$400-450; ☒ ☒) This old tourist haunt with worn sea- and pool-view rooms clings to life overlooking a nice stretch of sand in the Zona Dorada just north of Hotel Playa Mazatlán.

The trailer parks are near the beaches toward the north end of the town, though most of them are not especially attractive for tent camping. Of these, **Mar Rosa Trailer & RV Park** (Map p430; ☎ 913-61-87; mar_rosarv@mzt.megared.net. mx; Av Camarón Sábalo 702; RV sites M$300-390) gets the thumbs-up for its excellent location overlooking Playa Sábalo, just north of Zona Dorada.

MIDRANGE

Hotel La Siesta (Map p431; ☎ 981-26-40, 800-711-52-29; www.lasiesta.com.mx; Paseo Olas Altas 11 Sur; r with/without view M$450/350; P ☒ ☒ ☒) Sitting pretty above Playa Norte, La Siesta has a lush courtyard and some of the choicest sea-view rooms in

Old Mazatlán. All 51 spacious and tidy rooms have cable TV and a touch of character. The recent addition of an attractive small pool makes this Mazatlán's best value.

Hotel Machado (Map p431; ☎ 982-14-63, 987-22-17; ernestorubio@hotmail.com; Av Sixto Osuno 510; s M$500-600, d M$620-850; ☒ ☒) This new arrival, the only hotel on gorgeous Plazuela Machado, strikes just the right note with its mix of modern conveniences and colonial ambience. Six spacious units with high ceilings and deluxe bathrooms are filled with original art and have fridges and microwaves. A modest breakfast is included. Prices drop on Monday through Wednesday.

Meson de Cynthia (Map p431; ☎ 136-02-84, from the US ☎ 310-633-8739; www.elmesondecynthia.com; Av Sixto Osuno 408; r M$500, ste M$650-700; ☒ ☒) Just a stone's throw from Plazuela Machado is this stylish newcomer with six comfy abodes with cable TV, and a sprawling rooftop terrace with a hot tub.

Apartamentos Fiesta (Map p430; www.mazatlan apartments.com; Rio Ibis 502; 1-/2-bedroom apt M$520/680; P ☒) Features 13 very appealing apartments of different size and layout. All have kitchens and pleasing decor and are peacefully located in or near an ornate, mature tropical garden.

Hotel Azteca Inn (Map p430; ☎ 913-44-77; www .aztecainn.com.mx; Av Playa Gaviotas 307; d M$760; P ☒ ☒ ☒) Situated close to the beach and smack-dab in the middle of the Zona Dorada is this serviceable motor lodge. The 74 rooms lack personality but do have good, firm mattresses and room service from the decent onsite restaurant.

The Melville (Map p431; ☎ 982-84-74, toll-free from the US 866-395-2881; www.themelville.com; Av Constitución 99; 1-bedroom ste M$800-900, 2-bedroom ste M$1000; ☒ ☒) Formerly a telegraph office and later a convent for Carmelite nuns, this lovingly preserved neoclassical building and its large, tranquil courtyard provide the perfect setting for Mazatlán's newest and best boutique hotel. Each distinct suite has a kitchenette and is filled with splendid art, costly antiques, and plenty of period detail.

Marley Motel (Map p430; ☎ 913-55-33; motmarley@ mzt.megared.net.mx; Av Playa Gaviotas 226; 1-bedroom apt M$850-900, 2-bedroom apt M$930-1030; P ☒ ☒) This small Zona Dorada motel offers exceedingly comfortable seafront apartments with well-equipped kitchens and – best of all – privileged beach access.

TOP END

Rooms at Mazatlán's top-end hotels can be reserved quite economically as part of a holiday package – see your travel agent or poke around online.

Motel Los Arcos (Map p430; ☎ 913-50-66; www.motellosarcos.com; Av Playa Gaviotas 214; s/d M$900/1050, ste M$1030-1180; P) Also right on the beach is this attractive hotel featuring bright suites with kitchenettes and dining areas, a small pool and commanding sea views of the offshore islands. They're very comfortable, spacious and clean, and the beach is readily accessible.

Best Western Hotel Posada Freeman (Map p431; ☎ 985-60-60, from the US 866-638-88-06; www.posadafreeman.com; Paseo Olas Altas 79; r incl buffet breakfast M$932-1168, ste M$1534; P) Perched over Old Mazatlán's historic waterfront, this recently reborn hotel offers character, comfort and grand ocean and city views. The well-equipped gym, winning rooftop bar and striking pool make it an exceptional value.

Playa Mazatlán (Map p430; ☎ 989-05-55; www.hotelplaya.net; Av Playa Gaviotas 202; r M$1315-1641, ste M$2198-2632; P) This large resort – the first built in the Zona Dorada – maintains impeccable standards. The 425 rooms – most with ocean views – have satellite TV, private terrace and the thoughtful touches that mark a classy operation. Manicured tropical gardens and a breezy oceanside restaurant make this Mazatlán's best large hotel.

Inn at Mazatlán (Map p430; ☎ 913-55-00; www.innatmaz.com; Camarón Sábalo 6291; r M$1480, ste M$2115-4830; P) This excellent highrise hotel has attentive service and offers 208 bright, cheerful rooms and suites, all with ocean views and private balconies or terraces. It's right on the beach.

El Cid Mega Resort (Map p430; ☎ 913-33-33; www.elcid.com.mx; Av Camarón Sábalo s/n; r M$2124-2360, ste M$4484-6254; P) A behemoth decked out in 1980s-style luxury. This 1068-room, 2.9-sq-km minicity has it all – seven pools, several dive shops, restaurants, travel agencies, kids' areas, gyms and more.

Eating

With all those fishing and shrimping boats heading out to sea every morning, it's no wonder that Mazatlán is famous for fresh seafood. Treat yourself to *pescado zarandeado*, a delicious charcoal-broiled fish stuffed with onion, tomatoes, peppers and spices. A whole kilo, feeding two people well, usually costs around M$100.

The restaurants in the Zona Dorada cater mainly to the tourist trade. For something better, head to Plazuela Machado. It's sublime in the evening when music plays, kids frolic and the plaza is softly lit to create a very romantic atmosphere.

OLD MAZATLÁN

Budget

La Espiga Dorada (Map p431; ☎ 985-18-43; Constitución 217; pastries M$5; 8am-6pm) Doña Betty Pompa has operated this bakery for nearly 50 years from her home in a grand old building built in 1837. Try the fluffy sweet bread called *concheta* or a perfect meringue cookie. There's no sign; just follow your nose.

Mariscos Toño (Map p431; Av 16 de Septiembre s/n; mains M$30-60; noon-8pm) This unassuming old town seafood joint is deservingly popular for its simple seafood cocktails, *ceviches* and tostadas, all served super fresh at tables lining the street. You're unlikely to see too many tourists slurping down the place's *caracol* (sea snail).

Puerto Viejo (Map p430; ☎ 982-18-86; Paseo Olas Altas 25; mains M$30-80; 10am-6pm) A good time crowd of expatriate locals gathers here for drinks at sunset. Many of them will return tomorrow for super fresh seafood sent straight from the port. The well-priced *comida corrida* (prix-fixe menu; M$38) regularly features selections like *mole* and tuna *ceviche*.

Cenaduria El Túnel (Map p431; Av Carnaval 1207; mains M$45-55; noon-midnight) This atmospheric cheapie has been serving local favorites like *pozole* (shredded prok in broth) and smoked marlin enchiladas for over 50 years.

Midrange

Mariscos El Camichín (Map p431; ☎ 985-01-97; Paseo Claussen 97; mains M$50-120; 11am-10pm) Facing Playa Norte, this popular patio restaurant serves delicious seafood under a cool *palapa* roof. Suave elderly mariachis are known to play in the back room.

Pedro y Lola (Map p431; ☎ 982-25-89; Av Carnaval 1303; mains M$50-170; 10am-2am) Named after beloved Mexican singers Pedro Infante and Lola Beltrán, this very popular sidewalk restaurant-bar serves toned-down Mexican favorites and seafood dishes like garlic octopus (M$90) and fish papillote (wrapped in parchment and steamed in white wine, M$110).

La Copa de Leche (Map p431; ☎ 982-57-53; Paseo Olas Altas 122; mains M$60-160; 🕑 8am-7pm) Harkening back to a bygone Mazatlán, this old-timer is prized by the local gentry for its authentic menu. The economical *comida corrida* is served all day long, but for something really delicious you'd do well to try the hearty *sopa de mariscos*, a soup with squid, shrimp, fish and a wedge of lime.

La Tramoya (Map p431; ☎ 985-50-33; Constitución 509; mains M$70-125; 🕑 11am-2am) Hearty Mexican meat dishes are set out on spacious sidewalk tables. Ravenous? Try the *carne azteca* – a steak stuffed with *huitlacoche* (corn fungus) and served on a bed of *nopales* (prickly pear cactus).

Mariscos La Puntilla (Map p430; ☎ 982-88-77; Flota Playa Sur s/n; mains M$75-130; 🕑 8am-7pm) Popular with Mexican families for the weekend breakfast buffet (M$85), this open-air eatery has a relaxed atmosphere and fantastic *pescado zarandeado*. It's near the Isla de la Piedra ferries, on a small point with a view across the water.

Domitila (Map p431; ☎ 136-04-36; Constitución 515; mains M$75-155; 🕑 11am-10pm) This romantic new restaurant is doing its part to raise the ante for gourmet fare on Plazuela Machado. The waiters are quick to replenish your fresh *tamarindo* (tamarind) margarita and the plates are delicious and well presented. Feeling decadent? Try the small squid stuffed with crab meat and salsa with cheese sauce.

ZONA DORADA & AROUND
Budget
Tomates Verdes (Map p430; ☎ 913-21-36; Laguna 42; mains M$35-50; 🕑 9am-5pm Mon-Sat) This cozy and unpretentious lunch spot serves dishes like *pechuga rellena* (stuffed chicken breast) and flavorful soups like *nopales con chipotle* (spicy cactus).

La Cocina de Ana (Map p430; ☎ 916-31-19; Laguna 49; mains M$35-70; 🕑 noon-4pm Mon-Sat) This friendly place offers well-prepared buffet lunch fare such as meatball soup, chili con carne and paella in a small, homey dining area.

Arre Lulú (Map p430; ☎ 916-71-31; Av de las Garzas 18; mains M$55-180; 🕑 7am-11pm) This exuberantly painted little joint starts serving alcohol shortly after sunrise. You may want to stick around for lobster, shrimp or the traditional Mexican dishes. Wash it all down with a refreshing *michelada* (beer mixed with lime juice, chili sauce and a dash of Worcestershire).

Also recommended:

Pura Vida (Map p430; ☎ 916-58-15; cnr Bugambilias & Laguna; juices M$20-35, snacks M$20-60; 🕑 8am-10:30pm) Fresh juices and vegetarian fare.

Tacos Luna (Map p430; Av Camarón Sábalo 400; tacos M$10; 🕑 noon-midnight) Chow down the local way.

Midrange
Miso Sushi (Map p430; ☎ 913-02-99; Av Las Gaviotas 17; sushi rolls M$50-120; 🕑 1pm-11pm) Mazatlán has several sushi restaurants, but none as cosmopolitan as this trendy favorite, recommended for its hipster decor, good music and super-fresh, well-presented fare.

Pancho's Restaurant (Map p430; ☎ 914-09-11; Av Las Gaviotas 408; mains M$86-200; 🕑 7am-11pm) Overlooking Playa Gaviotas, this is a good spot to catch the sunset, slurp a monster margarita, or devour a huge seafood platter including lobster, octopus, a whole red snapper and, for good measure, a pair of frog legs.

Restaurant Rioja (Map p430; ☎ 916-61-80; Av Camarón Sábalo; mains M$100-120; 🕑 7am-11pm) The elderly waiters at this old-fashioned Spanish restaurant dish out authentic paella and a nice selection of well-presented *tapas* and European favorites like coq au vin (chicken stew with wine).

Top End
Vittore Italian Grill (Map p430; ☎ 986-24-24; Av Las Gaviotas 100; mains M$130-250; 🕑 noon-midnight) This elegant spot with romantic patio seating features delicious calorie-rich pasta dishes and memorable seafood and beef dishes (including a delicious beef filet with blackberry sauce, melted Gruyère cheese and wild mushrooms). The service is rather formal.

Casa Loma (Map p430; ☎ 913-53-98; Av Las Gaviotas 104; mains M$150-320; 🕑 1:30-10:30pm; 🕑) Escape the tourist scene and enjoy a sophisticated meal at this genteel dining destination. Enjoy roast duck *à l'orange* or the Mazatlán favorite poached fish *blanca rosa* (M$174) in a swanky dining room or outdoors by the burbling patio fountain.

Drinking
Edgar's Bar (Map p431; ☎ 982-72-18; cnr Serdán & Escobedo; 🕑 9am-midnight) For a taste of Old Mazatlán grab a tequila or two at this crusty old bar, a mainstay since 1949. Friendly old men sing karaoke beneath vintage photographs, and giant shrimp are brought to your table in buckets. According to the sign on the door, women are welcome.

La Tertulia (Map p431; ☎ 983-16-44; Constitución 1406; ☺ Mon-Sat) This lively spot – perfect for top shelf tequila-sipping – is decorated exclusively with bullfighting posters and the stuffed heads of vanquished *toros* (bulls).

Vitrolas's Bar (Map p431; www.vitrolasbar.com; Frias 1608; ☺ 5pm-1am Tue-Sun) This gracious gay bar in a beautifully restored building is romantically lit and, overall, more button-down than mesh muscle-shirt.

Watering holes ideal for heavy partying and youthful exploits:

Jungle Juice (Map p430; ☎ 913-33-15; Av de las Garzas 101) A cantina-style place with exotic fruit drinks and a breezy nook upstairs.

Señor Frogs (Map p430; ☎ 982-19-25; Calz Camarón Sábalo s/n) This brash, ebullient good-time joint gets wild on weekends.

Entertainment

What could be better than a day on a warm beach followed by a night in a town that really knows how to party? Choose from throbbing discos, a couple of thriving gay venues and a much-loved theater. For entertainment listings check *Pacific Pearl* or *Viejo Mazatlán*, available in hotel lobbies around town.

NIGHTCLUBS

Mazatlán has earned its reputation as a nightlife destination with a great selection of high-energy dance clubs. Most charge covers in the M$100 to M$200 range; the price of admission generally includes a free drink. The scene starts percolating around 10pm and boils over after midnight. While some clubs close at 2am, several others remain lively until 5am.

Fiesta Land (Map p430; ☎ 984-16-66; Av del Mar s/n) That ostentatious white castle on Punta Camarón at the south end of the Zona Dorada is home to two of Mazatlán's most popular nightspots. Valentino's draws a mixed crowd to three dance floors throbbing with hip-hop and Latin music. When the DJ offends, you can escape to Bora Bora, popular for its beachside dance floor and lax policy on bar-top dancing. This is the place to go after 2am when other bars begin to close.

Joe's Oyster Bar (Map p430; ☎ 983-53-33; Av Loaiza 100; ☺ 4pm-2am) This popular spot perched over the beach is OK for a sunset drink in the early evening, but it goes ballistic after 11pm when it's packed with college kids dancing on tables, chairs and each other. On a tiny lane that connects Av Playa Gaviotas to the beach.

El Caracol (Map p430; ☎ 913-33-33; El Cid Mega Resort, Av Camarón Sábalo s/n; ☺ Tue-Sat) This after-hours favorite boasts Mazatlán's best light show and a gargantuan two-level dance floor connected by a chute. The smartly dressed crowd stays late for techno, hip-hop, salsa and *cumbia* music.

Coliseo's Disco Forum (Map p430; ☎ 984-16-66; Av del Mar 1223; ☺ 11am-2am) Party like a Roman: the state-of-the-art sound system in this huge club draws talented DJs and a dance-crazed crowd.

Pepe Toro (Map p430; ☎ 914-41-76; www.pepetoro .com; Av de las Garzas 18; ☺ Thu-Sun) This colorful club attracts a fun-loving mostly gay crowd. On Saturday night there's a transvestite strip show at 1am.

THEATER

Teatro Ángela Peralta (Map p431; ☎ 982-44-46; www .teatroangelaperalta.com; Av Carnaval 47) To feel the pulse of Mazatlán's burgeoning culture scene, a night at the Peralta is a must. Built in 1860, the theater was lovingly restored over five years to reopen in 1990. It has an intimate auditorium with three narrow, stacked balconies. Events of all kinds are presented – movies, concerts, opera, theater and more. A kiosk on the walkway out front announces current and upcoming events. The schedule is fullest around the October-November Sinaloa Fiesta de los Artes.

LIVE MUSIC

If you get a chance, try to hear a rousing traditional *banda sinaloense* – a boisterous brass band unique to the state of Sinaloa. Watch for announcements posted around town or broadcasted from slow-moving cars with speakers mounted on top. These and other large music shows are staged at Coliseo's Disco Forum (above) and at the recently opened live music venue **Las Flores Premier** (Map p430; ☎ 990-05-05; Av Camarón Sábalo s/n).

BULLFIGHTS

Tickets for bullfights are available from travel agencies, major hotels and from the **Salón Bacanora** (Map p430; ☎ 986-91-55), beside Plaza de Toros.

Plaza de Toros (Map p430; Av Buelna) Just inland from the Zona Dorada traffic circle, Mazatlán's only bullring hosts *corridas de toros* (bullfights) at 4pm Sunday from mid-December to Easter.

CINEMAS

Cinemas Gaviotas (Map p430; ☎ 983-75-45; Av Camarón Sábalo 218; admission Thu-Tue M$38, Wed M$22) Has six screens showing recent releases, including some in English.

Shopping

The Zona Dorada is replete with stores selling clothes, pottery, jewelry and crafts. One noteworthy stop is **Sea Shell City** (Map p430; ☎ 913-13-01; Av Loaiza 407; 9am-7pm), packed with an unbelievable assortment of you-know-what. For something slightly more rarefied, try the shopping complex at Hotel Playa Mazatlán where several high-end shops sell fine crafts including masks from Guerrero and tinware from Oaxaca.

In Old Mazatlán at the **Centro Mercado** (Central Market; Map p431) you can enjoy a classic Mexican market experience, complete with vegetable stands, spice dealers, food stalls and shops selling bargain-priced crafts.

If you're looking to purchase something special, head to the streets surrounding Plazuela Machado, where a growing selection of galleries and boutiques gives joy to browsers.

Gallery Michael (Map p431; ☎ 69-167-816; Ángel Flores 601) has a broad inventory of high-quality curios, pottery, jewelry and housewares. The family-run **Casa Etnika** (Map p431; ☎ 116-84-71; Av Sixto Osuno 50) offers a small, tasteful inventory of unique objects from Mexico and elsewhere.

Getting There & Away

AIR

Rafael Buelna International Airport (MZT; ☎ 928-04-38) is 27km southeast of the Zona Dorada. Carriers servicing the airport include the following:

Aero California (☎ 985-25-87; Airport) Direct service to Guadalajara, La Paz, Mexico City and Tijuana.

Aeroméxico (Map p430; ☎ 914-11-11; Av Camarón Sábalo 310) Service to Atlanta, Los Angeles, Chicago and San Francisco, via Mexico City. Direct service to San Diego, Phoenix, La Paz, Guadalajara and Mexico City.

Alaska Airlines (☎ 985-27-30; Airport) Direct service to Los Angeles, San Francisco and Seattle.

Continental (☎ 800-900-5000; Airport) Direct service to Houston.

US Airways (☎ 981-11-84; Airport) Direct service to Phoenix.

Mexicana (Map p430; ☎ 913-07-72; Av Camarón Sábalo) Service to Denver, Los Angeles, Los Cabos, via Mexico City. Direct service to Guadalajara and Mexico City.

BOAT

Baja Ferries (Map p430; ☎ 985-04-70; www.bajaferries.com; tickets adult/child M$800/400; ticket office 8am-3pm Mon-Sat, 9am-1pm Sun), with a terminal at the southern end of town, operates ferries between Mazatlán and La Paz in Baja California Sur (actually to the port of Pichilingue, 23km from La Paz). The 17-hour ferry to Pichilingue departs at 3pm (you should be there with ticket in hand at 1pm) on Tuesday, Thursday and Saturday from the terminal. Strong winter winds may cause delays. Tickets are sold from two days in advance until the morning of departure. See p306 for cabin and vehicle prices.

BUS

The full service **Central de Autobuses** (Main Bus Station; Map p430; ☎ 982-83-51; Ferrusquilla s/n) is just off Av Ejército Mexicano, three blocks inland from the northern end of Playa Norte. All bus lines operate from separate halls in the main terminal.

Local buses to small towns nearby (such as Concordia, Copala and Rosario) operate from a smaller terminal, behind the main terminal.

There are several daily long-distance services:

Destination	Fare	Duration	Frequency
Culiacán	M$130	2½hr	24 daily
Durango	M$357	7hr	6 daily
Guadalajara	1st-class M$355	8hr	8 daily
	2nd-class M$310	9hr	12 daily
Manzanillo	M$563	12hr	1 daily
Mexico City (Terminal Norte)	1st-class M$808-950	18hr	6 daily
	2nd-class M$703	20hr	12 daily
Monterrey	M$856	16hr	2 daily
Puerto Vallarta	1st-class M$327	7hr	5 daily
	2nd-class M$280	8hr	2 daily
Tepic	M$170	4½hr	1 daily
Tijuana	1st-class M$900	26hr	3 daily
	2nd-class M$759	28hr	16 daily

Or take a bus to Tepic, where buses leave frequently for Puerto Vallarta.

To get to San Blas, go first to Tepic then get a bus from there – a 2nd-class service from Tepic to San Blas is M$42 and takes one hour.

CAR
Shop around for the best rates, which begin at US$40 per day during the high season. There are several rental agencies in town:

Alamo (Map p430; ☎ 913-10-10; Av Camarón Sábalo 410)

Budget (Map p430; ☎ 913-20-00; Av Camarón Sábalo 402)

Hertz (Map p430; ☎ 913-60-60; Av Camarón Sábalo 314)

Getting Around
TO/FROM THE AIRPORT
Taxi and *colectivo* vans (picking up and dropping off passengers along predetermined routes) operate from the airport to town (27km). Tickets (*colectivo*/taxi M$60/250) can be purchased for both at a transportation booth in the arrival hall. There is no public bus running between Mazatlán and the airport.

BUS
Local buses run from 6am to 10:30pm. Regular white buses cost M$5; air-con green buses cost M$10. Route Sábalo–Centro travels from the Centro Mercado to Playa Norte via Juárez, then north on Av del Mar to the Zona Dorada and further north on Av Camarón Sábalo. Route Playa Sur travels south along Av Ejército Méxicano, near the bus station and through the city center, passing the market, then to the ferry terminal and El Faro.

To get into the center of Mazatlán from the bus terminal, go to Av Ejército Mexicano and catch any bus going south. Alternatively, you can walk 500m from the bus station to the beach and take a Sábalo–Centro bus heading south (left) to the center.

BICYCLE
Kelly's Bicycle Shop and Tours (p434) can provide mountain bikes for M$150 per day.

TAXI
Mazatlán has a special type of taxi called a *pulmonía,* a small open-air vehicle similar to a golf cart. There are also regular red-and-white and green-and-white taxis called 'eco-taxis' that have rates from M$80 to M$100 for trips around town. *Pulmonías* can be slightly cheaper (or much more expensive) depending on your bargaining skills, the time of day and whether or not there is a cruise ship in port.

AROUND MAZATLÁN
Several small, picturesque colonial towns in the Sierra Madre foothills make pleasant day trips from Mazatlán. **Concordia**, founded in 1565, has an 18th-century church with a baroque facade and elaborately decorated columns. The village is known for its manufacture of high-quality pottery and hand-carved furniture. It's about a 45-minute drive east of Mazatlán; head southeast on Hwy 15 for 20km to Villa Unión, turn inland on Hwy 40 (the highway to Durango) and go another 20km.

Also founded in 1565, **Copala**, 40km past Concordia on Hwy 40, was one of Mexico's first mining towns. It still has its colonial church (1748), colonial houses and cobblestoned streets. It's a 1½-hour drive from Mazatlán.

Rosario, 76km southeast of Mazatlán on Hwy 15, is another colonial mining town. It was founded in 1655 and its most famous feature is the towering gold-leaf altar in its church, the Nuestra Señora del Rosario. You can also visit the home of beloved songstress Lola Beltrán, whose long recording career made *ranchera* (Mexico's urban 'country music') popular in the mid-20th century.

In the mountains north of Mazatlán, **Cosalá** is a beautiful colonial mining village that dates from 1550. It has a 17th-century church, a historical and mining museum in a colonial mansion on the plaza, and two simple but clean hotels. To get to Cosalá, go north on Hwy 15 for 113km to the turnoff (opposite the turnoff for La Cruz de Alota on the coast) and then go about 45km up into the mountains.

Buses to Concordia (M$20, one hour, every 15 minutes from 6am to 6pm), Copala (M$30, 1½ hours, three per day) and Cosalá (M$90, three hours, two per day) depart from the small bus terminal at the rear of Mazatlán's main bus station. For Rosario, take an 'Escuinapa' bus or any heading south on Hwy 15 (M$30, 1½ hours, hourly from 6am to 6pm). You can also take tours to any of these towns (see p434).

TEACAPÁN
☎ 695 / pop 3000
Travelers grown weary of the bright lights of the city are increasingly drawn to this small fishing village at the tip of an isolated penin-

CENTRAL PACIFIC COAST

DETOUR: TUFTED JAY PRESERVE

Like some travelers, the tufted jay favors higher elevations, and specifically the cool forested canyons of the Sierra Madre Occidental. This striking bird – white with a long tail, a black bib and wings, and something of a mohawk – attracts bird-watching enthusiasts from afar to the **Tufted Jay Preserve** (☎ 669-940-8687; www.tufted-jay-preserve.org; info@senderomexico.com; cabins M$800-900, 2-/6-person tent M$400/600), a nature resort located high in the mountains southeast of Mazatlán. You don't have to be a birder to be enchanted by this beautiful enclave, an environmental easement created with Pronatura, a Mexican NGO, in 2005 to protect the lush habitat of its endemic namesake. Occupying lands that were until recently selectively logged by the small *ejido* (cooperative) from the nearby community of Palmito, the enterprise has observed the best practices of sustainable community development. With help from the Mexican department of forestry, the *ejido* received money to build accommodations which would be part of a project to promote ecotourism in the area and provide an alternative source of income to the community. Today, nature lovers and escape artists come for hiking, bird watching, horseback riding and simple accommodations, including a pair of appealing two bedroom lantern-lit wooden cabins with kitchenette and hot water (but no electricity or fridge), or in safari tents with wood stoves, flannel sheets and goose down quilts. Hearty meals (M$90 per person) for groups of four or more are prepared by women from the *ejido* in an open-air kitchen, or by you in your cabin. Advance reservations for accommodations and meals are essential.

It's a three-hour journey from Mazatlán by car. From the Villa Unión junction on Hwy 15, drive east on Hwy 40 to the 202km marker, then left on the dirt road for about 20 minutes of bumpy going. Buses (M$82, three hours, five 1st class; or M$70, 3½ hours, four 2nd class) traveling between Mazatlán and Durango stop in Palmito; pre-arranged transportation from town is included as part of your reservation. Single and multi-day bird-watching tours to the Tufted Jay Preserve can also be booked with Sendero México (p434).

sula, 126km south of Mazatlán at the border of Nayarit and Sinaloa. Surrounded by a rich mangrove ecosystem and in close proximity to several pristine beaches, Teacapán is prime territory for escape artists and nature buffs. The surrounding estuaries are replete with egrets, ducks and herons. Boating excursions into the mangrove swamps can be arranged with local fishermen at Boca de Teacapán, the natural marina. Local guides offer overnight trips to Isla de Pájaros, an epic bird-watching spot, and to local archaeological sites.

Villas María Fernanda (☎ 954-53-93; www.villasmaria fernanda.com; r M$450-550, ste M$550, house M$1000-2200; 🏊 🐾) is an attractive small resort offering spacious, comfortable rooms, suites with kitchen and a house for up to 10 people. Kids love the cheerful pool with water slide.

Restaurant & Bungalows Señor Wayne (☎ 954-56-95; r/cabaña M$250/350; 🐾), an immaculate family-run operation, has seven clean rooms and two economical *palapa*-roofed *cabañas*. Also on the premises is Teacapán's best restaurant (mains M$60 to M$120), serving big breakfasts, steaks and seafood.

To get there from Mazatlán's 2nd-class bus terminal, catch one of the frequent buses to Escuinapa (M$20, 2½ hours) and transfer there for a Transportes Esquinapa bus to Teacapán (M$30, one hour). By car, take Hwy 5-23 from Escuinapa on Hwy 15.

SANTIAGO IXCUINTLA
☎ 323 / pop 17,000

Despite its charming plaza and impressive gazebo held aloft by eight busty iron muses, Santiago Ixcuintla is mainly of interest as the jumping-off point for Mexcaltitán. It's not a tourist town but there are a couple of good hotels and an interesting cultural stop. The **Centro Huichol** (☎ 235-11-71; Calle 20 de Noviembre 452; ⏰ 9am-2pm & 4-6pm Mon-Sat) is a handicrafts center where Indigenous Huichol learn skills to create and sell their distinctive arts and crafts as well as market their work and generate sustainable income. You'll find it 10 blocks northeast of the city center on the road to Mexcaltitán.

Hotel Casino Plaza (☎ 235-08-50; Ocampo & Rayón; s/d M$275/320; 🅿 🐾), near the market, is modern and pleasant, with a good **restaurant** (mains M$30-80) featuring a daily breakfast buffet (M$60). The recently opened **Hotel Plaza Los Reyes Santiago** (☎ 235-42-57; 20 Noviembre Ote 89;

s/d/ste M$280/300/300-400; 🐾 🖳) is another good option with its clean, modern rooms.

To get to Santiago by car, turn off Hwy 15 63km northwest of Tepic and travel 7km west. Buses to Santiago Ixcuintla leave frequently from Tepic. From Mazatlán you must take a 2nd-class bus to Penas where frequent local buses go to Ixcuintla.

Combis from Santiago Ixcuintla to La Batanga (M$20, at 7am, 10am, noon and 2pm), the leaving point for boats to Mexcaltitán, go from the Terminal de Taxis Foráneos at 73 Juárez Oriente, one block north of the plaza. Transportes del Pacífico also runs a 2nd-class bus to La Batanga (M$20, one hour, 37km) daily at 7am. A one-way taxi will run to about M$150.

MEXCALTITÁN
☎ 323 / pop 900

This ancient island village, settled some-time around the year AD 500, is believed by some experts to be Aztlán, the ancestral homeland of the Aztec people. Today it's foremost a shrimping town. Men head out into the surrounding wetlands in the early evening in small boats, to return just before dawn with their nets bulging. All day long, shrimp are spread out to dry on any avail-able surface throughout the town, making the prospect of an afternoon stroll a pungent, picturesque proposition.

Tourism has scarcely made a mark here. Mexcaltitán has one hotel, a couple of pleasant waterside restaurants and a small museum, making it a pleasant place to visit for a night.

Sights & Activities
The **Museo Aztlán del Origen** (admission M$5; ☯ 9am-2pm & 4-6:30pm Tue-Sun), on the northern side of the plaza, is small but enchanting. Among the exhibits are many interesting ancient objects and a reproduction of a fascinating long scroll, the *Códice Ruturini*, telling the story of the Aztec peoples' travels, with notes in Spanish.

You can arrange **boat trips** (M$300 per hour) on the lagoon for bird-watching, fishing and sightseeing – every family has one or more boats.

Festivals & Events
Semana Santa Holy Week is celebrated in a big way here. On Good Friday a statue of Christ is put on a cross in the church, then taken down and carried through the streets.

Fiesta de San Pedro Apóstol This raucous festival, cel-ebrating the patron saint of fishing, is on June 29. Statues of St Peter and St Paul are taken out into the lagoon in decorated *lanchas* for the blessing of the waters. Festivities start around June 20, leading up to the big day.

Sleeping & Eating
Hotel Ruta Azteca (☎ 232-02-11, ext 128; Venecia 98; s M$150-300, d M$300-350, tr M$400-450) The town's best, worst, and only hotel. Rooms are simple and marginally clean; ask for one out the back that has a view of the lagoon.

The shrimp *tamales* sold in the morning from a wheelbarrow on the streets are a local culinary highlight. On the east shore, acces-sible by a rickety wooden walkway, **Restaurant Alberca** (mains M$40-60; ☯ 7am-6pm) has a great lagoon view and a menu completely devoted to shrimp. Don't leave town without trying the local specialty of *albóndigas de camarón* (battered and fried shrimp balls served with a savory broth). Or perhaps a rich *jugo de camarón* (shrimp juice) or *paté de camarón*.

Getting There & Away
From Santiago Ixcuintla take a bus, taxi or *colectivo* to La Batanga, a small wharf where *lanchas* depart for Mexcaltitán. The arrival and departure times of the *lanchas* are coordi-nated with the bus schedule. The boat journey takes 15 minutes and costs M$10 per person. If you miss the *lancha* you can hire a private one for M$70 (plus M$15 for each additional person) between 8am and 7pm.

SAN BLAS
☎ 323 / pop 12,000

The tranquil fishing village of San Blas, 70km northwest of Tepic, has been slated by gov-ernment tourism officials to become a big resort town for decades. That's not to say it's changed much. It's still the peaceable, drowsy backwater it's always been, and therein lies its charm. Visitors come to enjoy isolated beaches, fine surfing, abundant bird life, and tropical jungles reached by riverboats, much as they always have. A smattering of enter-taining bars and restaurants and an amiable beach scene add to the mix, making for an enjoyable stay.

San Blas was an important Spanish port from the late 16th century to the 19th cen-tury. The Spanish built a fortress here to pro-tect their trading galleons from marauding British and French pirates. It was also the

---

AZTEC LAUNCHING PAD?

A visit to ancient Mexcaltitán is undeniably evocative of the distant past. But was it really once Aztlán, the mythical ancestral homeland of the Aztecs?

The local version of the town's origin contends that the Aztecs left here around AD 1091 to begin the generations-long migration that led them eventually to Tenochtitlán (modern Mexico City) around 1325. Proponents point to the striking similarities between the cruciform design of Mexcaltitán's streets and the urban layout of early Tenochtitlán. A pre-Hispanic bas-relief in stone found in the area is also provided as evidence – it depicts a heron clutching a snake, an allusion to the sign the Aztecs hoped to find in the promised land. And then there are the chronicles of reports by Aztecs to Spanish missionaries, including one in which it was related that the ancestors lived happily in beautiful Aztlán, where there were all kinds of ducks, herons and other water birds. Indeed, the name Aztlán means 'place of egrets' – and there are certainly plenty of those milling about.

But not everyone is so sure. Competing theories place Aztlán in the Four Corners area of the United States, in Wisconsin and even in Alaska. 'No serious archeological study has ever been done in Mexcaltitán,' says Jesus Jauregui, an expert in western Mexico at the National Institute of Anthropology and History in Mexico City. 'Aztlán is a mythical place, not a historical one.'

Local opinion goes both ways. One fisherman who considered the facts as they're displayed at the town's museum wasn't buying. 'Why would anyone leave?' he asked.

---

port from which Junipero Serra, the 'Father' of the California missions, embarked on his northward peregrination.

Information

Banamex (Av Juárez s/n) Has an ATM.
Caseta Telefónica (☎ 285-41-40; Av Juárez 665; ☼ 7am-10pm)
Cibernet la Web (Canalizo 155; per hr M$10; ☼ 9am-11pm Mon-Sat, noon-11pm Sun) Speedy internet access.
Health Clinic (☎ 285-12-07; cnr Azueta & Campeche; ☼ 24 hrs daily)
Post office (cnr Sonora & Echeverría)
Tourist office (☎ 285-02-21; ☼ 9am-3pm Mon-Fri) This basic tourist office, at Playa El Borrego across from Stoner's Surf Camp, has a few maps and brochures about the area and the state of Nayarit.

Sights & Activities

Although the beaches dominate here, everyone loves the boat tours through the estuaries where birds and wildlife abound.

BOAT TRIPS

A boat trip through the jungle to the freshwater spring of **La Tovara** – a federally protected estuary – is a real San Blas highlight. Small boats go from the *embarcadero*. The three-hour trips go up Estuario San Cristóbal to the spring, passing thick jungle and mangroves. Bring your swimsuit to swim at La Tovara; there's a restaurant there, too. For a few pesos more you can extend the trip from La Tovara

to the **Cocodrilario** (crocodile nursery), where toothy reptiles are reared in captivity for later release in the wild. For a group of up to four people it costs M$360 to go to La Tovara (3½ hours) and M$440 to the Cocodrilario (four hours). Each extra person costs M$90/110 to La Tovara/Cocodrilario.

More boat trips depart from a landing on Estuario El Pozo. They include a trip to **Piedra Blanca** (M$300, two hours) to visit the statue of the Virgin, to **Isla del Rey** (M$10, five minutes) just across from San Blas and to **Playa del Rey**, a 20km beach on the other side of the Isla del Rey peninsula. Here you can also hire boatmen to take you on bird-watching excursions for about M$250 per hour.

You can make an interesting trip further afield to **Isla Isabel**, four hours northwest of San Blas by boat. You really need a couple of days to appreciate this national park and protected ecological preserve. To visit you'll need permission from the port captain. The island is a bird-watcher's paradise, with colonies of many species and a volcanic crater lake. There are no facilities, so be prepared for self-sufficient camping. The official price for transportation of up to five people is M$5000, but deep discounts are possible depending on your negotiation skills. For trips to Isla Isabel, ask at the boat landing on Estuario El Pozo. Alternately, you can make the trip with Diving Beyond Adventures (p445).

INFORMATION		
Banamex	1	B2
Caseta Telefónica	2	B2
Cibernet la Web	3	B1
Health Clinic	4	B3
Post Office	5	B1
Tourist Office	6	B4

SIGHTS & ACTIVITIES		
Boats to Islands	7	A2
Canibal Adventure Tours	(see 22)	
Diving Beyond Adventures	8	A2
Fishing lanchas	9	A2
Jungle Boats to La Tovara	10	D1
La Contaduría Fort	11	C2
Templo de la Virgen del Rosario	12	D1

SLEEPING		
Casa Roxanna Bungalows	13	A2
Hotel Bucanero	14	A2
Hotel Garza Canela	15	B3
Hotel Hacienda Flamingos	16	A2
Hotel Iguana Ranas	17	B2
Hotel Marina San Blas	18	B3
Hotelito Casa del los Cocadas	19	A2
Motel Morelos	20	B2
Stoner's Surf Camp	21	B4

EATING		
Casa del Canibal	22	B2
Mercado	23	B1
Restaurant El Delfin	(see 15)	
Restaurant McDonald	24	B2
Wala Wala	25	A2

DRINKING		
Australia Bar	(see 22)	
El Cocodrillo	26	B2
Mike's Place	(see 24)	
San Blas Social Club	27	B2

TRANSPORT		
Bus Station	28	B1
Local buses to Matanchén, Playa los Cocos & Santa Cruz	29	A2

BEACHES

The beach closest to the town is **Playa El Borrego**, at the end of Azueta. Broad waves roll in with bravado, and swimming can be treacherous in some conditions – beware of rip currents and heed locals' warnings.

The best beaches are southeast of town around Bahía de Matanchén, starting with **Playa Las Islitas**, 7km from San Blas. To get here, take the road toward Hwy 15 and turn off to the right after about 4km. This paved road goes east past the village of Matanchén, where a dirt road goes south to Playa Las Islitas and continues on to follow 8km of wonderfully isolated beach. Further down on the paved road **Playa Los Cocos** and **Playa Miramar**, also popular for surfing, have *palapas*

under which you can lounge and drink fresh coconut milk.

SURFING

With many beach and point breaks, beginner and intermediate surfers choose San Blas as the place to hone their skills. The season starts in May, but the waves are fairly mellow until September and October when the south swell brings amazingly long waves curling into Mantanchén Bay. Surf spots include El Borrego, Second Jetty, La Puntilla, Stoner's, Las Islitas and El Mosco.

At Playa El Borrego, **Stoner's Surf Camp** (☎ 285-04-44; www.stonerssurfcamp.com; surfboard rental per hr/day M$30-50/100-150, lessons per hr M$150) is the nexus of the scene. National longboard champion 'Pompis' Cano gives lessons and holds court under the *palapa*, and you can also stay here.

CERRO DE LA CONTADURÍA
The climb to the top of the Cerro de la Contaduría has a double payoff: a gratifying view and a strong aura of history. Stroll around the ruins of the 18th-century Spanish **La Contaduría Fort**, where colonial riches were once amassed and counted before being shipped off to Mexico City or the Philippines. The place is still guarded by a collection of corroded cannons. Nearby are the gorgeous ruins of the **Templo de la Virgen del Rosario** (admission M$10), built in 1769. You'll find the road up just west of the bridge over Estuario San Cristóbal.

Tours
From December to May, **Diving Beyond Adventures** (☎ 285-12-81; www.divingbeyond.com; Av Juárez 187) leads affordable adventure experiences including diving, kayaking, hiking, bird- and whale-watching. It uses local guides and practices sound low-impact environmental tours. The signature trip is a three-day diving, fishing and camping extravaganza to Isla Isabel (US$300 per person). It also rents kayaks (US$20 for four hours).

Another option is **Canibal Adventure Tours** (☎ 285-14-21; www.casadelcanibal.com; Av Juárez 53), which offers sumptuously catered four- to six-hour personalized tours (US$75 per person) including 'secret beach parties,' waterfall hikes, horseback riding, and mountain zip-line tours.

Sleeping
San Blas has plenty of very reasonably priced hotels and one noteworthy fine hotel. In local parlance, a 'bungalow' sleeps more than two and includes a kitchen.

BUDGET
Stoner's Surf Camp (☎ 285-04-44; campsites M$30, cabins M$100-400) Right on the beach are five rustic cabins with electricity, mosquito nets and fans at this friendly traveler hangout and surf center. There's space to camp, a communal kitchen, lots of hammocks, and a restaurant serving well-prepared fare (including vegetarian meals). Tent rental costs M$20.

Hotel Bucanero (☎ 285-01-01; Av Juárez 75; s/d/tr M$150/250/350; **P**) It's seen better days but still sparkles with old salty character. The dark, rough-around-the-edges rooms face a big leafy courtyard featuring a weathered cannon.

Motel Morelos (☎ 285-13-45; Batallón 108; r M$200) It's stark but homey, with simple fan-cooled rooms around a central courtyard. An old pelican has made the place home for over a decade, ever since the proprietors nursed him back to health after an injury. He's cute but decidedly not cuddly.

Hotel Iguana Ranas (☎ 285-08-95; Batallón 165; d/t M$350/500; **☒**) This friendly hotel with pleasant rooms and new furnishings is the best value in town for an air-conditioned abode. Prepare to get to know the family that runs the place.

MIDRANGE & TOP END
Hotelito Casa de los Cocadas (☎ 285-09-60; Av Juárez 145 Pte; s/d M$500/700; **P** **☒**) With its pleasant location near the estuary, this small family-run hotel in a tastefully renovated building affords a comfortable, carefree stay. The seven rooms are fastidiously kept and include cable TV. Bicycles (M$30 to M$50 per hour) are available to rent.

Casa Roxanna Bungalows (☎ 285-05-73; www.casaroxanna.com; El Rey 1; bungalows M$550-650; **P** **☒** **☒**) This refined haven offers seven capacious bungalows and a long pool on manicured grounds. English is spoken and discounts are offered for longer stays.

Hotel Hacienda Flamingos (☎ 285-09-30; www.sanblas.com.mx; Av Juárez 105; r M$690-850, ste M$800-1060; **P** **☒** **☒**) This superbly restored colonial gem provides the classiest accommodations in town. The spacious rooms and courtyard are evocative of old Mexico without even a whiff of kitsch. There's a classy lounge serving well-crafted cocktails and *botanas* (snacks).

Hotel Marina San Blas (☎ 285-14-37; www.sanblas.com.mx; Cuauhtémoc 197; s/d M$770/960; **P** **☒** **☒**) The 10 bright rooms at this good new hotel all have terraces affording rewarding views across the peaceful estuary to Isla del Rey; Climb into one of the complementary kayaks and paddle across.

Hotel Garza Canela (☎ 285-01-12; www.garzacanela.com; Paredes 106 Sur; s/d M$912/1152, ste M$1344-2357; **P** **☒** **☒**) Modern, professional and comfortable, the Garza Canela is a reliable top-end choice. Standard rooms are spacious and decorated in colonial style; the suites are enormous and contemporary with marble floors. It's also home to the best restaurant, Restaurant El Delfín (p446), and gift shop in town.

Eating

San Blas is a casual town with casual restaurants, all serving fresh seafood. On the beach, *palapa* restaurants are notable for delicious fish cooked in the *campechano* style, with tomatoes, onion, octopus, shrimp and oyster. The cheapest eats can be found at the local *mercado* on the corner of Sonora and Batallón.

Wala Wala (☎ 285-08-63; Av Juárez 183; mains M$45-200; ۞ Mon-Sat) This cheerfully decorated restaurant serves inexpensive, tasty home-style meals. It's mostly basic Mexican and pasta with a few specialties such as lobster (M$200) and *pollo con naranja* (chicken with orange, M$80).

Restaurant McDonald (☎ 285-04-32; Av Juárez 36; mains M$50-100) Recently remodeled after more than 50 years in business, this highly regarded meeting place serves basic *antojitos* (small plates), seafood dishes and beautifully-presented *carne asada* (M$85).

Casa del Canibal (☎ 285-14-12; Av Juárez 53; mains M$75-125; ۞ 5:30-9:30pm Wed-Sat, 9am-noon & 5:30-9:30pm Sun) Beloved among the town's expat population, this friendly eatery does a dynamite shrimp scampi, a rich beef stroganoff and a perfectly cooked steak. The garrulous owner is a true foodie and it shows.

Restaurant El Delfín (☎ 285-01-12; Hotel Garza Canela, Paredes 106 Sur; mains M$70-180) This, the best choice for fine dining, serves an impressive array of rich, gourmet dishes. Desserts are magnificent and the international wines are reasonably priced.

Drinking & Entertainment

The nightlife in San Blas is unexciting but pleasant enough, with a good selection of low-key watering holes from which to choose. Most open up at dusk and close late, which in this town means midnight.

San Blas Social Club (cnr Av Juárez & Canalizo) Jazz records line the wall – you can pick one out and the gentleman bartender will slap it on. There's live music Friday and Saturday, movies on Wednesday and good strong coffee every morning.

Australia House Bar (Av Juárez 34) The long bar of this upstairs pool room, celebrating Down Under chic, is dotted with cool youths and grungy foreigners throwing drinks back. The jukebox is legendary.

Mike's Place (Av Juárez 36) This lively bar primes the dance floor with a good mix of blues and rock. There's live music from Friday to Sunday.

El Cocodrilo (Av Juárez 6) This old favorite still attracts gringos in the evening, using well-priced cocktails as bait.

Getting There & Around

The little **bus station** (cnr Sinaloa & Canalizo) is served by Norte de Sonora and Estrella Blanca 2nd-class buses. For many destinations to the south and east it may be quicker to go to Tepic first. For Mazatlán, transfer in Tepic. Daily departures include the following:

Guadalajara (M$180, 5hr, 1 at 7am)
Puerto Vallarta (M$106, 3½hr, 4 at 7:30am, 10am, 1:30pm & 4:30pm)
Santiago Ixcuintla (M$35, 1hr, 2 at noon and 5pm)
Tepic (M$42, 1hr, hourly 6am-8pm)

Second-class buses also depart from the corner of Sinaloa and Paredes several times a day, serving all the villages and beaches on Bahía de Matanchén.

Taxis will take you around town and to nearby beaches – a good option with two or more people. Rent bicycles from Wala Wala (see left) for M$15/70 per hour/day or Stoner's Surf Camp (see p445) for M$70 per day.

TEPIC

☎ 311 / pop 295,000 / elevation 920m
The capital of Nayarit state, like other Mexican cities of a certain size, can seem dreary in the considerable heat of the afternoon. But at dusk, as the blackbirds cry out from the belfry of the gorgeous cathedral and the historic buildings are transformed by artful lighting, this old town can make even the most jaded traveler swoon.

Founded by the nephew of Hernán Cortés in 1524, today it's a forward-thinking, predominantly middle-class place with a veritable hum of provincial hustle and bustle playing out on its narrow streets. Indigenous Huicholes are often seen here, wearing their colorful traditional clothing, and Huichol artwork is sold on the street and in several shops. Adding interest are an imposing neo-Gothic cathedral and several engrossing museums.

Orientation

Plaza Principal, with the large cathedral at the eastern end, is the heart of the city. Av México, the city's main street, runs south

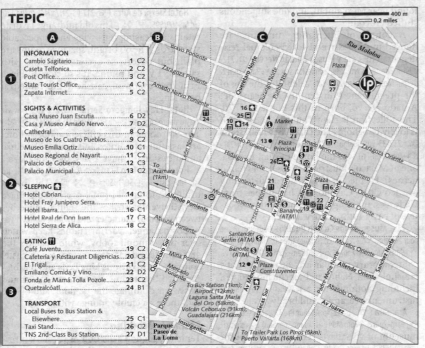

TEPIC

from the cathedral to Plaza Constituyentes, past banks, restaurants, the state museum and other places of interest. The main bus station is on the southeastern side of the city with plenty of buses serving the center.

Information

Banks and *casas de cambio* line Av México Nte between the two plazas. You'll find the post office at the corner of Durango Sur and Morelos.

Cambio Sagitario (Av México Nte 220; ☺ 9am-2pm) Convenient location and so-so rates.

Caseta Telefonica (☎ 212016-74; Lerdo 13 Ote; ☺ 8am-11pm)

State tourist office (☎ 216-56-61, 212-80-36; www .turismonayarit.gob.mx; cnr Puebla Nte & Amado Nervo Pte; ☺ 9am-8pm) A great resource with free maps and extensive information about everything in Tepic and the state of Nayarit.

Zapata Internet (Zapata s/n, per hr M$10) Fast, with good monitors and webcams.

Sights

The ornate **cathedral** on Plaza Principal, dedicated in 1804, casts a regal eye over Plaza

Principal. Take a peek inside to marvel at the over-the-top altar, over which a robed mannequin of the Virgin Mary is hoisted into heaven by a delegation of angels and cherubs. Opposite the cathedral is the **Palacio Municipal** (city hall), where you'll often find Huicholes under the arches selling handicrafts at very reasonable prices. South of the plaza, look inside the **Palacio de Gobierno** (Av México; ☺ 8am-6pm) to see some impressive and colorful murals. Painted by José Luis Soto and finished in 1999, they present a contemporary imagining of the history of Mexico. Soto's frenetic, surreal vision of hell and conflict beneath the cupola is chilling.

MUSEUMS

Residing in a palatial 18th-century neoclassical house with a lovely courtyard, the **Museo Regional de Nayarit** (☎ 212-19-00; Av México Nte 91; admission M$34; ☺ 9am-6pm Mon-Fri, to 3pm Sat) presents changing exhibitions concerned primarily with pre-Hispanic objects, including ancient pottery and tomb artifacts, as well as colonial painting and Huichol culture. Also on hand are an important pre-Hispanic bas-relief found near Mexcaltitán, and one stupendous stuffed crocodile.

A couple of interesting museums are housed in impressive restored colonial residences. The **Casa y Museo Amado Nervo** (☎ 212-29-16; Zacatecas Nte 284; admission free; ☉ 9am-2pm & 4-7pm Mon-Fri, 10am-2pm Sat) celebrates the life of the preeminent 19th century Mexican poet Amado Nervo, born in this house in 1870. The collection is slight, but the house itself is lovely to behold. The **Casa Museo Juan Escutia** (☎ 212-33-90; Hidalgo Ote 71; admission free; ☉ 9am-2pm & 4-7pm Mon-Fri) was the home of Juan Escutia, one of Mexico's illustrious *niños héroes* (child heroes). He died in 1847 at age 17 defending Mexico City's Castillo de Chapultepec from US forces. It's simply furnished and is evocative of early 19th-century Mexico.

The **Museo de los Cuatro Pueblos** (Museum of the Four Peoples; ☎ 212-17-05; Hidalgo Ote 60; admission free; ☉ 9am-2pm & 4-7pm Mon-Fri, 10am-2pm Sat) displays contemporary popular arts of the Nayarit's Huichol, Cora, Nahua and Tepehuano peoples, including clothing, yarn art, weaving, musical instruments, ceramics and beadwork.

Aramara (☎ 216-42-46; Allende Pte 329; admission free; ☉ 9am-2pm & 4-7pm Mon-Sat, 10am-3pm Sun) is a small museum of visual arts. The **Museo Emilia Ortiz** (☎ 212-26-52; Lerdo Pte 192; admission free; ☉ 9am-7pm Mon-Fri, to noon Sat) honors the painter Emilia Ortiz (1917–96) and her work.

Sleeping

In its historic center Tepic rewards travelers with a good selection of comfortable, good-value independent hotels.

Trailer Park Los Pinos (☎ 210-27-28; Blvd Tepic-Xalisco 150; campsites/RV sites M$50/150; ☐) About 5km south of town, this spacious park offers 24 trailer spaces with full hookups and wireless internet. The leafy, grassy grounds make tent camping a pleasure.

Hotel Cibrian (☎ 212-86-98; Amado Nervo Pte 163; s/d M$220/270; P) Budget travelers flock to this squeaky clean central hotel for clean, bright rooms with TV and telephone. The rooms overlooking a busy street can get noisy, but for the price you can't beat it. The economical restaurant downstairs does brisk business.

Hotel Ibarra (☎ 212-32-97; Durango 297 Nte; s/d/t M$330/350/370; P ☒ ☐) The rooms are stark but clean, and the small restaurant serves up good, economical Mexican fare. It's nothing to write home about, but for the money this pragmatic choice offers a decent value.

Hotel Sierra de Alica (☎ 212-03-22; Av México Nte 180; s/d M$460/595; P ☒) This old midrange favorite retains a pleasing retro vibe and impeccable standards. The 60 bright, spacious rooms are plain but otherwise accommodating, with satellite TV and phone. It's so close to Plaza Principal that you can hear the cathedral bells ring.

Hotel Fray Junípero Serra (☎ 212-25-25; www.frayjunipero.com.mx; Lerdo Pte 23; s/d M$849/944; P ☒) The 90 rooms in this efficient modern hotel are tastefully appointed and come with deluxe amenities; many have a view over the plaza.

Hotel Real de Don Juan (☎ /fax 216-18-88; Av México Sur 105; r/ste M$1150/1850; P ☒ ☐) This beautifully done-up old hotel overlooking Plaza Constituyentes strikes the right balance between colonial character and urbane style. Two imposing angel warrior statues keep watch over the tranquil lobby, while upstairs the 48 rooms are decked out in appealing pastel colors, with luxurious king beds and marble-accented bathrooms. A good restaurant and classy bar dominate the 1st floor, and on the roof there's a clubby lounge with a view.

Eating & Drinking

Tepic has a good selection of vegetarian restaurants, but the city's local specialties are shrimp based.

Cafetería y Restaurant Diligencias (☎ 212-15-35; Av México Sur 29; mains M$20-60) There's no better place than this to sit around for hours on end nursing a cup of coffee, nibbling on a buttery biscuit, and poring over a travel guide. Groups of men congregate all day in this vintage dining hall, chatting and ordering snacks and eventually the *comida corrida* (M$60).

Fonda de Mamá Tolla Pozole (☎ 212-41-19; Andador Merida s/n; mains M$30-45; ☉ 8am-5pm Mon-Sat; ☒) The unflappable women who run this exemplary breakfast and lunch nook know a thing or two about hearty Mexican comfort food. A big breakfast will set you back only M$30.

Café Juventu (☎ 216-41-72; Zacatecas 120 Nte; mains M$45-80) A youthful crowd meets here for light meals, drinks and perhaps a game of pool. The street level is set up in an intimate café style; upstairs the vibe is more that of a nightclub.

our pick **Emiliano Comida y Vino** (☎ 216-20-10; Zapata 91 Ote; mains M$97-220) Tepic's cuisine scene gets a lift from this chic restaurant and its intimate bar. They have a nice way of pulling a cork, and stock a selection of the finest wines produced in Mexico. Still, the best reason to show up is the menu, which features artfully crafted dishes from around the country.

Jonesing for soy? Vegetarians rejoice at these two old favorites, both serving economical fare in a pretty courtyard.

El Trigal (☎ 216-40-04; Veracruz Nte 112; M$20-46; Ⓥ) Offerings include wholemeal quesadillas, veggie burgers and an excellent *menú del día* (daily set menu, M$60).

Quetzalcóatl (☎ 212-99-66; León Nte 224; mains under M$40; ☽ 8:30am-5pm Mon-Sat, to 1pm Sun; Ⓥ) The best 15-peso veggie burger in town.

Getting There & Away

AIR
Tepic's **airport** (TPQ; ☎ 214-21-95) is in Pantanal, a 15km drive from Tepic, going toward Guadalajara. There's no public transportation between downtown and the airport; a taxi runs about M$120. **Aero California** (☎ 214-23-20; Airport) offers direct flights to Mexico City and Tijuana, with connections to other centers. **Aeromar** (☎ 800-237-66-27) offers three daily flights to Mexico City.

BUS
The main bus station is on the southeastern outskirts of town; local buses marked 'Estación' make frequent trips between the bus station and the city center, stopping at the corner of Amado Nervo and Durango.

The main bus companies are Elite and Ómnibus de México (both 1st class) and Transportes del Pacífico (1st and 2nd class). Daily departures from Tepic include the following.

Guadalajara (M$194, 3½hr, frequent 1st class; M$169, 3½hr, frequent 2nd class)

Mazatlán (M$170, 4½hr, hourly 1st class; M$147, 4½hr, hourly 2nd class)

Mexico City (M$600, 10hr, hourly 1st class; M$525, 11hr, 6 2nd class)

Puerto Vallarta (M$150, 3½hr, hourly 1st class 3am-9pm; M$115, 3½hr, hourly 2nd class 1am-10pm)

TNS operates a small terminal north of the cathedral near the Río Mololoa, with 2nd-class service to San Blas (M$42, one hour, hourly 2nd class from 5am to 7pm) and Santiago Ixcuintla (M$40, 1½ hours, 30 minutes, hourly 2nd class from 6am to 7pm).

Getting Around
Local buses (M$4) operate from around 6am to 9pm. Combis (M$4) operate along Av México from 6am to midnight. There are also plenty of taxis, and a taxi stand opposite the cathedral.

AROUND TEPIC
Laguna Santa María del Oro
Surrounded by steep, forested mountains, idyllic Laguna Santa María del Oro (elevation 730m) fills a volcanic crater 2km around and is thought to be over 100m deep. The clear, clean water takes on colors ranging from turquoise to slate. It's a pleasure to walk around the lake and in the surrounding mountains, spotting numerous birds (some 250 species) and butterflies along the way. You can also climb to an abandoned gold mine, cycle, swim, row on the lake, kayak or fish for black bass and perch. A growing number of small restaurants serve fresh lake fish and seafood.

Koala Bungalows & RV Park (☎ 311-264-36-98; koala@nayarit.com; camping per child/adult M$25/40, r M$250, bungalow M$450-750) is a peaceful park with a restaurant, campsites and well-maintained bungalows sleeping up to 10 people. Turn left at the terminus of the road which descends to the lake.

For an idyllic upscale experience head to the **Santa María Resort** (☎ 311-214-68-34; www.santamari aresort.com; ste/bungalow M$1521/3325-4171; Ⓟ ☒ ☒). Resembling a stately old hunting lodge with its rustic chic rooms and bungalows and dramatic views, this place has relaxation written all over it. The deluxe amenities, day spa and dramatic pool make for a luxurious stay.

To get here, take the Santa María del Oro turnoff about 40km from Tepic along the Guadalajara road; from the turnoff it's about 10km to Santa María del Oro, then another 8km from the village to the lake. Buses marked 'Laguna' (M$40, one hour) depart from the corner of Amado Nervo and Durango and from in front of the bus station in Tepic periodically during daylight hours.

Volcán Ceboruco
This active volcano consisting of two calderas and three cinder cones last erupted in 1870, so you'll be safe walking the short trails at the top. The 15km cobblestoned road up the volcano passes lava fields and fumaroles (steam vents), with lush vegetation growing on the slopes. The road begins at the village of Jala, 7km off the highway from Tepic to Guadalajara; the turnoff is 76km from Tepic, 12km before you reach Ixtlán del Río. You can also visit as

CENTRAL PACIFIC COAST

part of a tour; several Puerto Vallarta–based companies include a stop at the volcano as part of their 'tequila tour' itineraries.

CHACALA
☎ 327 / pop 300

Like other small towns along this stretch of coast, the tiny coastal fishing village of Chacala is changing fast as its reputation grows as a travelers' destination. For now, it retains its status as a not-quite-so-secret-any-more paradise. Located 96km north of Puerto Vallarta and 10km west of Las Varas on Hwy 200, it sits pretty along a beautiful little cove backed by verdant green slopes and edged by rugged black rock formations at either end. With just one main, sandy thoroughfare and a few cobbled side streets, it's a lovely place to unwind and contemplate the horizon.

There's no ATM; banking and communication services are readily available in Las Varas. Deposito Jorge, on the beach, offers phone and fax service.

Casa Pacífica (☎ 219-40-67; www.casapacificachacala .com; Islas Marias s/n), the de facto town booster office, books a wide range of varied vacation rentals (US$35 to US$100 per night) and operates a popular breakfast café (from 8am to 10am Monday through Saturday).

Activities
Hereabouts, the sea provides most of the action. For small boat excursions ask for Federico, Cundo or Beto at the fishing dock, located at the northern tip of the shoreline. Whale watching and fishing trips cost around M$200 per person, while a surfing expedition to the remote spot La Caleta – where a wicked left breaking point break tries to dump surfers on the rocky beach – runs about M$700 per person. You can also hike to La Caleta; it's a challenging but rewarding two-hour effort each way. Ask at Casa Pacífica (above) for a copy of their hand-drawn map.

Sleeping & Eating
Camping is possible on the beach, and there are several unique accommodations from which to choose.

`our pick` **Techos de Mexico** (☎ 275-02-82; www .playachacala.com/techos.htm; r M$180-400) Travelers interested in befriending the locals should consider arranging their accommodations through this program – a home building project run in partnership with Habitat for

Humanity – which enables residents to help each other build good homes with adjacent guest units with bath. There are currently nine homes, most with room for up to four people. Rooms are separate from the host home and are updated but basic (some come with kitchen). Look for the distinctive Techos signs as you pass through town.

Super-chic and tucked away in the unspoiled jungle overlooking the edge of the cove, **Majahua** (☎ 219-40-54; www.majahua.com; Playa Chacala s/n; r incl breakfast M$1586-2028, ste M$3360) is an earthy eco-lodge. It offers five beautifully designed rooms, an outdoor restaurant and spa services. It's a five-minute walk from the parking area located just up the road from Mar de Jade.

Those who favor the beach head to **Hotel las Brisas** (☎ 219-40-15; www.lasbrisaschacala.com; r M$450; ❌ 🖳), which shares a beachfront locale with Chacala's best seafood restaurant. There are nine clean units upstairs with TV and wireless internet, and downstairs there's shrimp and beer. Sweet.

Run by a young Mexican-American family, **Bungalows Casa Monarca** (☎ 219-4125; Oceano Atlantico s/n; bungalows M$650; 🖳 🖳) offers two fresh and beguilingly appointed bungalows, each with two queen beds. The small pool makes this a good choice for families. It's a short distance up the hill from the fishing dock.

You can grab a meal at any of the dozen-plus *palapa* restaurants on the beach. For super-fresh seafood purchase straight from the fisherman at the pier situated on the northern tip of the shoreline; the daily catch starts coming in at around 7am. Some of the beachside restaurants will cook it up for you for a small fee.

Getting There and Away
For Chacala, get off a Puerto Vallarta–Tepic bus at Las Varas and take a *colectivo* taxi (M$20) from there. If you're driving, the Hwy 200 turnoff is 1km south of Las Varas.

RINCÓN DE GUAYABITOS
☎ 327 / pop 2000

On the coast about 60km north of Puerto Vallarta, 'Guayabitos' is a tailor-made beach-resort town catering to Mexican holidaymakers and to winter visitors from Canada and other cold places. It's nothing fancy and shows its weathered age. Weekends are busy, but the beautiful beach is practically empty during the rest of the week.

Activities include swimming, fishing, horseback riding and hiking up to the cross on the hill for the fine view. Boats take whale-watching trips from November to March.

On the main drag you'll find many economical spots to grab a bite. Most hotels are midrange places offering bungalows with kitchen facilities and accommodations for two, four or more people. Among these, the best are the following:

Hotel Posada la Misión (☎ 274-03-57; posada mision@prodigy.net.mx; Retorno Tabachines 6; d M$400, bungalows M$650-800; ℗ ✗ ⍟) This well-run, colonial-accented hotel offers quaint rooms and bungalows with sea views.

Posada Real (☎ 274-07-07; cnr Av Sol Nuevo & Huanacaxtle; d/q M$650/850, bungalows M$850-1000; ℗ ✗ ⍟) An audaciously painted hotel offering bungalows, a good restaurant and an enormous hot tub.

Villas Buena Vida (☎ 274-02-31; www.villasbuena vida.com; Retorno Laureles s/n; r M$847, ste M$1105-1373; ℗ ✗ ⍟) A luxurious beachfront option with villas and large suite, plus a range of outdoor activities opportunities.

Second-class buses coming from Puerto Vallarta (M$80, 1½ hours) or Tepic (M$60, two hours) may drop you off on the highway at Rincón de Guayabitos, but sometimes they don't stop here. A couple of kilometers toward Tepic, La Peñita is a sure stop. *Colectivo* vans operate frequently between La Peñita and Guayabitos (M$5, 10 minutes) or you can take a taxi (M$30).

AROUND RINCÓN DE GUAYABITOS

There are many pleasant little beach towns south of Rincón de Guayabitos that make good day trips from either Guayabitos or Puerto Vallarta; they all have places to stay and eat. Visit places like **Playa Los Ayala** (Km 96), 3km south of Guayabitos, **Lo del Marco** (Km 108) and **San Francisco** (Km 118). First- and 2nd-class buses traveling along Hwy 200 will drop you off about 1km from the edge of each town.

SAYULITA

☎ 329 / pop 2300

Once upon a time – okay, it was the late 1990s – Sayulita really *was* a tranquil fishing village. Many of the town's *norteamericano* residents still describe it that way, but the truth is that Sayulita, while still low-key, has definitely been 'discovered' and can at times feel like a crowded gringo outpost. The bloom really fell off the rose a few years back when the news got out about Sayulita's growing sewage treatment problem. A new, modern treatment plant, completed in 2006, seems to have solved the problem. Through it all, Sayulita's many admirers have sung the praises of the beautiful sandy beach and amiable surfing scene, the great restaurants and tasteful B&Bs, and of course, those world-famous tacos. Note that there's a time difference between Sayulita, which is in Nayarit state, and Puerto Vallarta, which is in Jalisco (Nayarit is one hour behind Jalisco). Many businesses catering to visitors are closed from May through November.

Information

The nearest full service bank is in Bucerías, 12km to the south on Hwy 200. There are now three ATMs in town, including one on the plaza. There's not a proper tourist office, but most of the vacation rental offices around town are happy to share their maps and brochures.

Galería Internet (Mariscal 43; per hr M$20; 9am-2pm & 5-10pm) Good machines and a speedy connection.

Sayulita Caja de Cambio (☎ 291-30-05; Delfín 44; ⏱ 7am-7pm Mon-Sat) Near the plaza; offers so-so exchange rates.

Sights & Activities

You can arrange bicycle hire, boat trips, horseback riding, trekking or kayaking from operators on the main street. One popular nearby destination is **Playa Los Muertos**, where picnics and boogie-boarding top the action. It's a 15-minute walk south along the coast road. You can also hire a boat to take your group out to the uninhabited **Islas Marietas** – a protected national park – for picnicking, snorkeling and swimming.

Rancho Mi Chaparrita (☎ 291-31-12; www.michapar rita.com; Sánchez 14; ⏱ 9am-4pm) is the best established tour operator, offering horseback rides to Los Muertos and Carrisitos beaches (per person US$25, 1½ hours) and longer rides into the mountains (per person US$85), a zip-line canopy on which thrill seekers can whoosh from tree to tree on 13 lines strung high above the forest floor (adult/child US$75/55) and boat trips to the Islas Marietas (US$180 for up to six people, three to four hours).

SURFING

Sayulita is a classic boarder town, and it's a simple matter to join in the fun. Medium-sized waves pour dependably from both the left and the right, so you can practice your well-honed moves or even take up the sport for the first time.

For rentals or lessons, your best bet is with the well-established **Lunazul** (☎ 291-20-09; Marlin 4; surfboard/body board rentals per day M$300/200, lessons per 90min M$400).

Sleeping

A good selection of private villas can be browsed on the website Sayulita Life (www .sayulitalife.com). The following prices are for the winter high season.

El Camarón Camping (Del Palmar s/n; campsites per person/hut M$40/250) This grassy, kick-back camping spot on the beach north of town is the heart of the scene for young surfers and hippies.

Sayulita Trailer Park & Bungalows (☎ 390-27-50; www.pacificbungalow.com; Miramar s/n; campsites & trailer sites with hookups M$160-240, 1-bedroom bungalow M$550-850, 2-bedroom bungalow M$850) Maintains an attractive, palm-shaded property beside the beach, with a restaurant and snack bar. Discounts are offered to those who stick around for a while.

Hotel Diamante (☎ 291-31-91; www.hoteldiamante sayulita.com; Miramar 40; s/d/q M$375/425/650; ☎ ☒) This well-priced favorite has small, basic but bright rooms and two breezy communal kitchens. The property is well maintained and the service accommodating.

Fiambaláa Hotel (☎ 291-30-86; Las Gaviotas 10; r with shared/private bathroom M$450/700) Above a thriving Argentinean restaurant is this quality basic choice with clean, no-nonsense rooms with ceiling fans and a terrace overlooking the street. There's no proper reception area; present yourself at the restaurant.

our pick **Petit Hotel d'Hafa** (☎ 291-38-06; Revolución 55; www.sayulitalife.com/hafa; r M$550-850) Just steps away from the plaza is this choice newcomer with six fan-cooled rooms with two and three high-quality beds. The charismatic owner, having sailed around the world, brings her considerable creativity and taste to bear in the design and decor, which favors Moorish flourishes, bright colors and welcoming communal spaces. Feeling more like an environment than a small hotel, it's an instant classic.

Bungalows Aurinko (☎ 291-31-50; www.sayu lita-vacations.com; cnr Marlin & Revolución; 1-/2-bedroom bungalows M$889/1389, ste M$1166; ☒) Smooth river-stone floors, open-air kitchens, exposed raw beams and well-appointed decor make this a very memorable place to stay. Huichol art adorns the walls while Oaxacan linen covers the beds. All units have a kitchen and purified water.

Bungalows Los Arbolitos (☎ 291-31-11, in the US 888-453-0501; sayulitabungalow@earthlink.net; Marlin 20; s/d/apt M$950/1250/1960; ☒ ☐) Los Arbolitos harbors nine intimate and luxurious suites, two with kitchens. Craftwork touches, creative design and lush gardens make this a classy night's sleep.

Eating & Drinking

Sayulita has earned its reputation as a foodie paradise. The town has a beguiling selection of small, bistro-style cafés, providing agreeable contrast to the lively, inexpensive *palapas* on the beach.

Sayulita Fish Taco (☎ 291-32-72; José Mariscal 13; tacos from M$20; ☸ noon-3pm & 5:30-9pm Mon-Sat) This place has been doling out real-deal tacos to gringos for years. Some have even rated them as the very best in Mexico. A preposterous claim, perhaps, but it's hard to deny that they're uncommonly good. Ditto for the top-shelf margaritas.

Rollie's (Revolución 58; breakfast M$45-65; ☸ 7am-noon) This is *the* place for breakfast. Rollie and friends lovingly serve Western breakfasts with an occasional Mexican twist, well-pulled espresso and morning cocktails. Choose music from Rollie's collection, or sing along with him.

Sayulita Café (☎ 291-35-11; Revolución 37; mains M$75-135; ☸ 5-11pm) With an atmospheric dining room and candlelit sidewalk tables, this old favorite offers a crash course on traditional dishes from Puebla, Oaxaca, Chiapas and Jalisco. Families with small children are graciously accommodated.

Café Caminito (☎ 291-35-64; Marlín 12; mains M$90-120; ☸ 4:30-10pm Thu-Tue) South American cuisine makes a good showing at this chic spot. Munch on flaky Argentinian empanadas stuffed with fish while taking in the scenery from the 2nd-floor pub overlooking the plaza.

La Bicyclette (☎ 291-36-35; Navarette 9; mains M$170-195; ☸ 6pm-midnight Mon-Fri) An instant success, striking the right balance with its intimate enclosed courtyard and improvisational, ever-changing menu. Think shrimp flambéed in Mexican absinthe and homemade bread and paté. A reggae band sets the tone on Saturday nights.

PUERTO VALLARTA IN FOUR DAYS

Rise and shine! Take a morning dip in the sparkling Bahía de Banderas and a stroll on one of Vallarta's many **beaches** (p454). Stop in at the **Museo del Cuale** (p456) or linger beneath the shady rubber trees on the **Isla Río Cuale River Walk** (p454). Spread out a towel on the beach of your choice and scan the horizon for **whales** (p460). Join the happy throng on the waterfront **malecón** (p454) and enjoy the varied **public sculptures**. Linger over dinner at one of Vallarta's splendid **restaurants** (p462) and then hit one of the sizzling late-night **dance clubs** (p465).

On day two, get up early (yeah, right) and continue indulging in the pleasures of the city with some **shopping** (p466), or take your pick from the many opportunities for **outdoor adventures** (p456): go diving, fishing, or horseback riding.

On your third day, visit the beautiful **Jardines Botánicos de Vallarta** (p456), or hop a boat for the far-flung beaches of **Las Ánimas** (p456), **Quimixto** (p456) or **Yelapa** (p456).

For the fourth day, catch a bus to the kick-back town of **Sayulita** (p451) for a surfing lesson or simply a surf.

Getting There & Around

Sayulita is about 35km north of Puerto Vallarta just west of Hwy 200. Ten buses per day operate between Sayulita and the Puerto Vallarta bus terminal (M$20, one hour), and any 2nd-class bus headed north will drop you at the turnoff. In Puerto Vallarta, you can also catch a bus from the stop fronting Sam's Club. A taxi between Puerto Vallarta and Sayulita costs M$450 to M$600, depending on your negotiation skills.

PUERTO VALLARTA

☎ 322 / pop 151,000

Puerto Vallarta – referred to simply as 'Vallarta' by its many aficionados – is one of Mexico's liveliest and most sophisticated resort destinations. Stretching around the sparkling blue Bahía de Banderas (Bay of Flags) and backed by lush palm-covered mountains, one couldn't ask for a better place to while away a cosmopolitan vacation. Each year millions come to laze on the dazzling sandy beaches, browse in the quaint shops, nosh in the stylish restaurants and wander through the picturesque cobbled streets or along its beautiful *malecón*. If the pretty town beaches aren't enough, you can venture out on cruises, horseback rides, diving trips and day tours – and be back in time for a late dinner and an even later excursion to one of the many sizzling nightspots on offer. Puerto Vallarta is the gay capital of Mexico (see boxed text, p464).

History

Vallarta was just another humble village until 1954, when planes filled with tourists first landed on a dirt airstrip in Emiliano Zapata, an area that is now the center of Vallarta. A decade later John Huston chose the nearby deserted cove of Mismaloya as a location for the film of Tennessee Williams' *The Night of the Iguana*. Hollywood paparazzi descended on the town to report on the tempestuous romance between Richard Burton and Elizabeth Taylor. Vallarta suddenly became world-famous, with an aura of steamy tropical romance. Travelers have been pouring in ever since.

Orientation

The 'old' town center, called Zona Centro, is the area north of Río Cuale, with the small Isla Cuale in the middle of the river. The city's two principal thoroughfares are Morelos and Juárez, which sandwich the Plaza Principal. Many fine houses, quite a few owned by foreigners, are found further up the Río Cuale valley, also known as Gringo Gulch.

South of the river, the Zona Romántica is another tourist district with smaller hotels, restaurants and bars. It has the only two beaches in the city center – Playa Olas Atlas and Playa de los Muertos.

North of the city are a strip of giant luxury hotels called the Zona Hotelera; Marina Vallarta, a large yachting marina (9km from the center); the airport (10km); the bus station (12km); and Nuevo Vallarta, a new resort area of hotel and condominium developments (18km). To the south of the city are a few more large resorts and some of the most beautiful beaches in the area.

For information on getting to the city center from the airport and bus station, see p466.

Information

BOOKSTORES
Libros Libros Books Books (Map pp458-9; ☎ 222-71-05; Calle 31 de Octubre 127) Has a fair selection of magazines and books (including Lonely Planet guides) in English.

EMERGENCY
Ambulance (☎ 222-15-33)
Fire (☎ 223-94-76)
Police (☎ 060, 223-25-00)

INTERNET ACCESS
Aquarius Internet (Map pp458-9; 523 Juárez; per hr M$15; ☾ 24hr) The best, with flat screens, fast connection and plenty of terminals.

LAUNDRY
There are many laundries around town, all of which are closed Sunday and charge about M$40 per load.
Lavandería Blanquita (Map pp458-9; Madero 407A)
Lavandería Elsa (Map pp458-9; Olas Altas 385)

MEDIA
Vallarta Today (www.vallartatoday.com) is a better English-language newspaper than its local competition, the weekly *Vallarta Tribune*. Both papers are free. *Bay Vallarta* is a free monthly guide with useful culture and shopping listings.

MEDICAL SERVICES
San Javier Marina Hospital (Map p455; ☎ 226-10-10; Av Ascencio 2760) Vallarta's best-equipped hospital.

MONEY
Although most businesses in Vallarta accept US dollars as readily as they accept pesos, their exchange rates suck. There are several banks around Plaza Principal; most of them have ATMs.

Vallarta has many *casas de cambio*; their rates differ and are slightly less favorable than the banks. Look for them on Insurgentes, Vallarta and the *malecón*.

POST
Main post office (Map pp458-9; Mina 188)

TELEPHONE & FAX
Pay phones (card only) are plentiful everywhere in town. Many internet cafés offer long-distance service.
Telecomm (Map pp458-9; Hidalgo 582) Offers fax as well as phone service.

TOURIST INFORMATION
Municipal tourist office (Map pp458-9; ☎ 223-25-00, ext 230; Juárez s/n; ☾ 8am-9pm Mon-Fri) Vallarta's busy but competent office, in the municipal building at the northeast corner of Plaza Principal, has free maps, multilingual tourist literature and bilingual staff.

Sights
Puerto Vallarta also has amazing natural scenery and a growing number of cultural attractions. The perfect beaches remain Vallarta's main draw.

The heart of Zona Centro is the **Plaza Principal** (Map pp458–9), also called Plaza de Armas, just near the sea between Morelos and Juárez. On the sea side of the plaza is an outdoor amphitheater backed by **Los Arcos** (Map pp458–9), a row of arches that has become a symbol of the city. The wide **malecón** stretches about 10 blocks north from the amphitheater and is dotted with bars, restaurants, nightclubs and a grand collection of public sculptures. Uphill from the plaza, the crown-topped steeple of the **Templo de Guadalupe** (Map pp458–9) is another Vallarta icon.

A trip to Vallarta wouldn't be complete without lingering on **Isla Río Cuale** (Map pp458–9), where the city's earliest residents built their humble homes. Upstream you'll notice two rickety cable suspension bridges, connecting the island to the Zona Romántica.

BEACHES
The beaches of the Bahía de Banderas strike many personalities. Some are buzzing with cheerful activity, others offer quietude and privacy. Most beaches mentioned here feature on the Puerto Vallarta map (p455).

Only two beaches, **Playa Olas Altas** (pp458–9) and **Playa de los Muertos** (Beach of the Dead; Map pp458–9) are handy to the city center; they're both south of the Río Cuale. On Sundays, join the scores of Mexican families who come to while away their day off. At the southern end of Playa de los Muertos is the stretch of sand called **Blue Chairs**: it's one of Mexico's most famous gay beaches.

North of town, in the Zona Hotelera, are **Playa Camarones**, **Playa Las Glorias**, **Playa Los Tules**, **Playa Las Palmas** and **Playa de Oro**. Nuevo Vallarta also has beaches and there are other, less developed beaches right around the bay to Punta de Mita.

Mismaloya (Map p455), the location for *The Night of the Iguana*, is about 12km south of

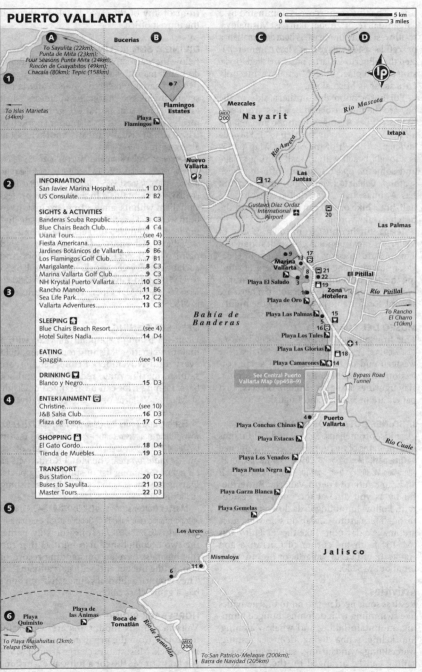

PUERTO VALLARTA

0 —————— 5 km
0 —————— 3 miles

A Bucerías **B** **C** **D**

To Sayulita (22km);
Punta de Mita (23km);
Four Seasons Punta Mita (24km);
Rincón de Guayabitos (49km);
Chacala (80km); Tepic (158km);

To Islas Marietas
(34km)

Flamingos
Estates

Mezcales

Playa
Flamingos

MEX 200

Nayarit

Río Mascota

Ixtapa

Nuevo
Vallarta

Río Ameca

Las
Juntas

Las Palmas

Gustavo Díaz Ordaz
International
Airport

INFORMATION	
San Javier Marina Hospital	1 D3
US Consulate	2 B2

SIGHTS & ACTIVITIES	
Banderas Scuba Republic	3 C3
Blue Chairs Beach Club	4 C4
Diana Tours	(see 4)
Fiesta Americana	5 D3
Jardines Botánicos de Vallarta	6 B6
Los Flamingos Golf Club	7 B1
Marigalante	8 C3
Marina Vallarta Golf Club	9 C3
NH Krystal Puerto Vallarta	10 C3
Rancho Manolo	11 B6
Sea Life Park	12 C2
Vallarta Adventures	13 C3

SLEEPING	
Blue Chairs Beach Resort	(see 4)
Hotel Suites Nadia	14 D4

EATING	
Spaggia	(see 14)

DRINKING	
Blanco y Negro	15 D3

ENTERTAINMENT	
Christine	(see 10)
J&B Salsa Club	16 D3
Plaza de Toros	17 C3

SHOPPING	
El Gato Gordo	18 D4
Tienda de Muebles	19 D3

TRANSPORT	
Bus Station	20 D2
Buses to Sayulita	21 D3
Master Tours	22 D3

Marina
Vallarta

Playa El Salado

Playa de Oro

Playa Las Palmas

El Pitillal

Zona
Hotelera

Río Pitillal

To Rancho
El Charro
(10km)

Bahía de
Banderas

Playa Los Tules

Playa Las Glorias

Playa Camarones

Bypass Road
Tunnel

See Central Puerto
Vallarta Map (pp458–9)

Playa Conchas Chinas

Playa Estacas

Puerto
Vallarta

Río Cuale

Playa Los Venados

Playa Punta Negra

Playa Garza Blanca

Playa Gemelas

Los Arcos

Mismaloya

Jalisco

Playa
Quimixto

Playa de
las Animas

Boca de
Tomatlán

Río de Tomatlán

To Playa Majahuitas (2km);
Yelapa (5km)

MEX 200

To San Patricio-Melaque (200km);
Barra de Navidad (205km)

town. The tiny scenic cove is dominated by a gargantuan resort. About 4km past Mismaloya, southwest along the coast, is **Boca de Tomatlán**, a peaceful seaside village that's less commercialized than Puerto Vallarta. Buses marked 'Boca' stop at both places; the 'Mismaloya' bus only goes as far as Mismaloya.

Further around the southern side of the bay are the more isolated beaches, from east to west, of Las Ánimas, Quimixto and Yelapa, all accessible only by boat (p467). **Playa de las Ánimas** (Beach of the Spirits; Map p455) is a lovely beach with a small fishing village and some *palapa* restaurants offering fresh seafood. **Quimixto** (Map p455), not far from Las Ánimas, has a waterfall accessible by a half-hour hike or you can hire a pony on the beach to take you up.

Yelapa, furthermost from town, is one of Vallarta's most popular cruise destinations. This picturesque cove is crowded with tourists, restaurants and parasailing operators during the day, but empties out when the tourist boats leave in the late afternoon. There are several comfortable places to stay the night.

MUSEO DEL CUALE
This tiny **museum** (Map pp458-9; Paseo Isla Cuale s/n; admission free; ⏱ 10am-3pm & 4-7pm Tue-Sat) near the western end of Isla Cuale has a small collection of beautiful pottery, grinding stones, clay figurines and other ancient objects. Text panels are in Spanish and English.

JARDINES BOTÁNICOS DE VALLARTA
Orchids, bromeliads, agaves and wild palms line the paths of this gorgeous recently opened **nature park** (Map p455; ☎ 205-72-17; Hwy 200, Km 24; admission M$30; ⏱ 9am-6pm Tue-Sun), located half an hour south of Puerto Vallarta. Butterflies flit by as you dine at the open-air restaurant. Follow hummingbirds down paths and through fern grottoes. Slap on some bug juice and make a day of it. Take the 'El Tuito' bus (M$15) from the corner of Carranza and Aguacate in Puerto Vallarta, or hop in a taxi for about M$200.

Activities
Restless souls need not go far to find activities like swimming with dolphins, bungee jumping, mountain biking and whale-watching. Snorkeling, scuba diving, deep-sea fishing, waterskiing, windsurfing, sailing and parasailing can be arranged on the beaches in front of any of the large hotels or through the tourist office.

DIVING & SNORKELING
Below the warm, tranquil waters of the Bahía de Banderas is a world of stingrays, tropical fish and garishly colored corals. Vallarta has several diving and snorkeling operators. Most dives include transportation, gear and light meals. Most dive outfits also offer snorkeling trips, which usually means snorkelers tag along with divers.

Banderas Scuba Republic (Map p455; ☎ 135-78-84; www.bs-republic.com; Av Marina Sur cnr Vela; snorkeling trips US$25, 2-tank dive trips US$85-150, PADI Open Water certification US$350) maintains a high degree of professionalism with its small-group excursions to both well- and lesser-known sites. Private diving tours (from US$400) also are offered.

Vallarta Adventures (see p460) has 'gold palm' (PADI accredited) instructors and acclaimed service. Snorkeling costs US$35 to US$60, two-tank dive trips cost M$80 to M$125, and PADI Open Water certification is M$330.

DEEP-SEA FISHING
Deep-sea fishing is popular all year, with a major international fishing tournament held every mid-November. Prime catches are sailfish, marlin, tuna, red snapper and sea bass. Fishing trips can be arranged dockside at Marina Vallarta or at the cooperative on the *malecón*.

Fishing and Tours PV (Map pp458-9; ☎ 222-12-02; www.fishingandtourspv.com; 1-8 person fishing charters US$200-450; ⏱ 8am-10pm Mon-Sat), with an office on the *malecón* near the Hotel Rosita, acts as an agent for a long list of sportfishing boats. During the low season try your luck at fishing for a discount.

Master Baiter's (Map pp458-9; ☎ 222-40-43; www.mbsportfishing.com; Calle 31 de Octubre 107; 1-8 person fishing charters US$250-900) Despite the silly name, the two accomplished fish hunters that run this business have an outstanding record of connecting their clients with gargantuan fish. They'll return a third of your cash if you don't bag a game-class catch.

HORSEBACK RIDING
Vallarta's jungly mountains are wonderful to explore from the privileged perspective of horseback. Most stables charge around M$15 per hour, or M$100 for a full-day excursion.

CENTRAL PACIFIC COAST

Rancho El Charro (off Map p455; ☎ 224-01-14; www .ranchoelcharro.com; rides US$56-100) is recommended for its healthy horses and scenic three- to eight-hour trots into the Sierra Madres. Several rides have been conceived for kids. Setting it apart from competitors are its multiday tours, including the tempting 'Overnight Lost in the Jungle Ride' (US$350). It provides transportation from Puerto Vallarta hotels.

Rancho Manolo (Map p455; ☎ 228-00-18, 222-36-94; rides US$35) Headquartered in Mismaloya beneath the highway bridge opposite the resort, this cheerful operation keeps 25 horses and ponies fat and happy. Their most popular tour is a three-hour jaunt through jungle landscape to a remote rustic restaurant with a terrific swimming hole.

GOLF & TENNIS

Vallarta's golfing credentials have been burnished in recent years with the opening of four new courses. Most acclaimed is the Jack Nicklaus-designed **Four Seasons Punta Mita** (off Map p455; ☎ 291-60-00; Four Seasons Resort Punta Mita; green fees US$175), where golfers are blissfully distracted from the challenging course by the sweeping ocean vistas. One hole, nicknamed 'Tail of the Whale,' is located on a natural island and requires the use of an amphibious golf cart.

Other courses are listed here:

Los Flamingos Golf Club (Map p455; ☎ 298-06-06; Hwy 200 s/n; green fees US$130) Recently renovated, 13km north of town.

Marina Vallarta Golf Club (Map p455; ☎ 221-05-45; Paseo de la Marina s/n; green fees US$128) An exclusive 18-hole, par-74 course just north of Marina Vallarta.

Most of the resort-style hotels have tennis courts for guests. Hotels welcoming nonguests for tennis include:

NH Krystal Puerto Vallarta (Map p455; ☎ 224-02-02; Av Las Garzas s/n, Zona Hotelera; per hr US$13)

Fiesta Americana (Map p455; ☎ 224-20-10; Paseo de las Palmas s/n, Zona Hotelera; per hr US$18)

CRUISES

A host of daytime, sunset and evening cruises are available in Vallarta. The most popular ones are the cruises to Yelapa and Las Ánimas beaches; others go to the Islas Marietas, further out. Prices are generally negotiable, starting at US$45 for sunset cruises and beach trips; longer trips lasting four to six hours with meals and bottomless cocktails will set you back US$80 to US$100. Leaflets advertising cruises are available throughout town.

On Thursday and Friday **Diana Tours** (☎ 222-15-10) offers an all-day gay and lesbian cruise, with plenty of food, drink and snorkeling (US$75). It leaves from Blue Chairs Beach Resort.

Courses

One-day classes in traditional Mexican cooking (M$850) are held monthly from May through July at El Arrayán Cocina Tradicional (p463). The fee includes breakfast, instruction in the restaurant's kitchen, take-home recipes and a full meal. For more information, call ☎ 222-71-95.

Language courses at **Centro de Estudios Para Extranjeros** (CEPE; Map pp458-9; ☎ 223-20-82; www.cepe .udg.mx; Libertad 105-1) range from US$151 for a week of basic tourist Spanish to US$533 for a month of university credit courses. Private instruction costs US$25 per hour. The center, associated with the Universidad de Guadalajara, arranges homestays with local families for US$437 to US$469 per week.

Puerto Vallarta for Children

If your tot has a pirate fetish, the little lad or lassie won't tolerate missing a cruise on the **Marigalante** (Map p455; ☎ 223-03-09; www.marigalante .com.mx; 🚸), a reproduction Spanish galleon that does pirate-themed daytime cruises (adult/child US$85/42) from 9am to 5pm and an evening cruise from 6pm to 11pm. The latter culminates in a mock pirate attack on the *malecón*. It departs from the Terminal Maritima in Marina Vallarta, off Blvd Francisco Ascencio opposite Sam's Club.

Kids will also get a kick out of **Sea Life Park** (Map p455; ☎ 297-07-24; Carr Tepic Km 155; admission adult/child US$18/14; 🕙 10am-6pm; 🚸), which has 12 waterslides, a lazy river swimming pool and a daily dolphin show.

Tours

Nature and outdoor tours are one of Puerto Vallarta's strongest suits. The following companies tread lightly and follow eco-friendly business practices.

Eco Ride (Map pp458-9; ☎ 222-79-12; www.ecoridemex .com; Miramar 382; tours M$500-1400) Surrounded by the mountains, jungle and sea, Vallarta offers some truly thrilling mountain biking. This outfit offers guided one-day cycling tours suited for beginners and badasses alike.

CENTRAL PACIFIC COAST

CENTRAL PUERTO VALLARTA

INFORMATION	
Aquarius Internet	1 E3
Lavandería Blanquita	2 E6
Lavandería Elsa	3 C7
Libros Libros Books Books	4 E1
Main Post Office	5 D3
Municipal Tourist Office	6 D4
Telecomm	7 E3

SIGHTS & ACTIVITIES	
Centro de Estudios Para Extranjeros	8 D5
Eco Ride	9 E4
EcoTours de México	10 D6
Fishing and Tours PV	11 E1
Los Arcos	12 D4
Master Baiter's	13 E1
Museo del Cuale	14 C5
Templo de Guadalupe	15 D4

SLEEPING	
Abbey Hotel	16 C8
Casa Amorita	17 E4
Casa del Los Cuatro Vientos	18 E3
Casa Dulce Vida	19 E3
Hotel Ana Liz	20 E6
Hotel Azteca	21 F6
Hotel Bernal	22 E6
Hotel Eloísa	23 C6
Hotel Emperador	24 C8
Hotel Posada de Roger	25 D7
Hotel Posada Lily	26 C7
Hotel Rosita	27 E1
Hotel Tropicana	28 C8
Hotel Villa del Mar	29 F6
Hotel Yasmín	30 C7
Terraza Inn	31 C8
Villa David	32 E4
Villa Mercedes Hotel	33 C8

EATING	
Archie's Wok	34 C8
Barrio Sur	35 C8
Café de Olla	36 C7
Café des Artistes	37 E3
Casa de Pancho	38 E3
Cenaduría Doña Raquel	39 E2
Chez Elena	(see 18)
El Arrayán Cocina Tradicional	40 F2
Época	41 C6
Esquina de los Caprichos	42 E4
Guero's Sea Food	43 D6
Joe Jack's Fish Shack	44 C7
La Dolce Vita	45 E2
La Hormiga Feliz	46 D6
La Palapa	47 C8
Las Tres Huastecas	48 C8
Los Xitomates	49 E3
Oscar's Bar & Grill	50 C5
Planeta Vegetariano	51 D4
Restaurant Gilmar	52 E6

DRINKING	
Andale	(see 48)
Café San Angel	53 C8
Frida	54 E6
Kit Kat Klub	55 C8
La Bodeguita del Medio	56 E1
La Noche	57 D6
Memories Café	58 D3
Sama Bar	59 C8

ENTERTAINMENT	
Amphitheater	(see 12)
Anthropology	60 C5
Cine Bahía	61 E6
Club Paco Paco	62 D7
de Santos	63 E2
Hilo	64 D3
Mañana	65 D7
Mariachi Loco	66 D6
Santa Barbara Theater	67 D7
Tequila's	68 D3
Zoo	69 E2

0 — 400 m
0 — 0.2 miles

Parque Hidalgo

To Airport (9km);
Bus Station (11km);
Tepic (176km)

Languria

31 de Octubre

Allende

Zona Centro

Matamoros

Paseo Díaz Ordaz

Morelos

Juárez

Guerrero

Hidalgo

Iturbide

Pino Suárez

Aldama

Corona

Galeana

Miramar

Carranza

Zaragoza

Bahía de Banderas

Malecón

Seahorse Statue

Plaza Principal

Taxi Stand

Banamex

Taxi Stand

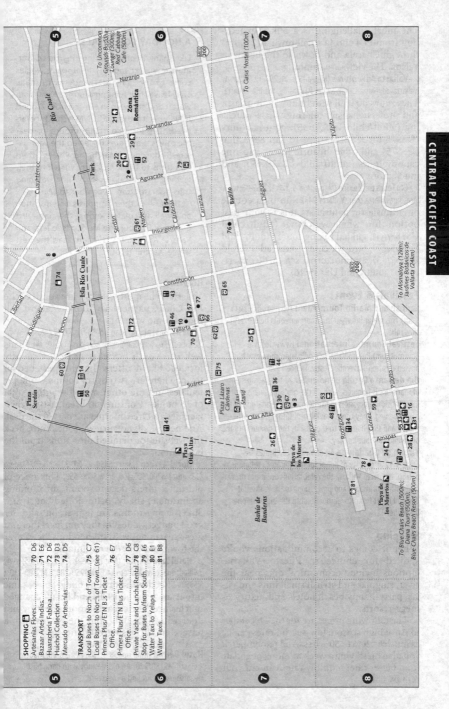

The most challenging is a 50km expedition from El Tuito (a small town at 1100m) through Chacala and down to the beach in Yelapa. The views are stunning.

Vallarta Adventures (Map p455; ☎ 297-12-12; www .vallarta-adventures.com; Av Las Palmas 39, Marina Vallarta) These guys do it all with humor, enthusiasm and professionalism, offering whale-watching (adult/child US$70/35), cultural tours (US$75 to US$210), trips to San Sebastian (US$75) and other historic towns, zip-line canopy tours (adult/child US$79/69), and much more.

EcoTours de México (Map pp458-9; ☎ 222-65-06; www .ecotoursvallarta.com; Vallarta 243) Run by a couple of enthusiastic naturalists, this is your best option for whale-watching (adult/child US$85/65), guided hiking tours (adult/child US$45/57), bird-watching tours (adult/child US$52/73), and nocturnal sea-turtle experiences (adult/child US$35/46).

Festivals & Events

Sailfish and Marlin Tournament (www.fishvallarta .com) This major international tournament is held every November.

Festival Gourmet International (www.festival gourmet.com) Puerto Vallarta's culinary community has hosted this mid-November festival since 1995.

Día de Santa Cecilia On November 22 the patron saint of mariachis is honored, with all the city's mariachis forming a musical procession to the Templo de Guadalupe in the early evening. They come playing and singing, enter the church and sing homage to their saint, then go out into the plaza and continue to play.

Virgen de Guadalupe All of Mexico celebrates December 12 as the day of honor for the country's religious patron. In Puerto Vallarta the celebrations are more drawn out, with pilgrimages and processions to the cathedral day and night from November 30 until the big bash on December 12.

Sleeping

When it comes to accommodations you're spoiled for choice in Puerto Vallarta. Options include economical digs near the river, singular and stylish small inns and villas, party-happy beach hotels and luxurious mega-resorts.

The following prices are for the December to April high season; low-season rates can be as much as 20% to 50% less. And remember, if you plan on staying a week or more, negotiate for a better rate; monthly rates can cut your rent by half.

A HOLIDAY FOR WHALES

Like many people reading this book, during the winter months humpback whales come to the Bahía de Banderas to mate. They leave their feeding grounds in Alaskan waters and show up in Mexico from around November to the end of March. Once arrived, they form courtship groups or bear the calves that were conceived the year before. By the end of March, the whales' attention turns to the long journey back to their feeding grounds up north. Whale-watching trips operate from December to March.

Because of their emphasis on education and well-articulated ethos, the naturalist guides of Ecotours de México (see left) and Vallarta Adventures (see left) lead the best whale-watching tours.

BUDGET

Vallarta's cheapest lodgings are south of the Río Cuale, particularly along Madero. All rooms come with fan.

Oasis Hostel (off Map pp458-9; ☎ 222-26-36; www .oasishostel.com; Libramiento 222; dm M$140; 🖳) This well-run youth hostel is not conveniently located, but it offers the cheapest bed in town. There are two dorm rooms – one for females and the other mixed – with a total of 16 bunks. Continental breakfast, kitchen facilities and free internet are part of the deal. And best of all: no curfew or lockout. Check the website for detailed directions from the bus station.

Hotel Azteca (Map pp458-9; ☎ 222-27-50; Madero 473; s/d/t M$200/300/400, apt M$600-650) This graceful old-timer offers decent rooms surrounding an intimate, shady, palm-potted courtyard. Street-facing rooms are lighter, but all offer good budget value. On the roof level there's a great apartment with tremendous views over the town and into the mountains.

Hotel Villa del Mar (Map pp458-9; ☎ 222-07-85; www .hvilladelmar.com; Madero 440; s M$250-280, d M$300-330, t M$350) This clean, sprawling budget place came into its own in the 1970s and hasn't changed much since. The cheapest rooms are tiny and dour with little light, but the rooms with a terrace are surprisingly terrific.

Also consider these two:

Hotel Bernal (Map pp458-9; ☎ 222-36-05; Madero 423; s/d M$180/220) An old standby with dark, basic cleanish rooms around a courtyard.

Hotel Ana Liz (Map pp458-9; ☎ 222-17-57; Madero 429; s/d/t M$190/250/300) Pleasant, fan-cooled rooms with few frills.

MIDRANGE
Hotel Posada Lily (Map pp458-9; ☎ 222-00-32; hotel-lily@ hotmail.com; Badillo 109; s M$300-350, d M$500-550, with air-con extra M$50; ❄) This amazingly priced option just off the beach offers 18 clean and pleasant rooms with fridge, TV and good natural light. The larger rooms have three beds and small balconies that overlook the street. For air-con, add M$50.

Hotel Yasmín (Map pp458-9; ☎ 222-00-87; Badillo 168; s/d M$433/481; ❄) In spite of the gruff management and typically small rooms, this old budget standby has a terrific location a block from the beach, amidst a dizzying assortment of bars, cafés and restaurants. Hold fast for the brighter and quieter upstairs rooms.

Hotel Eloisa (Map pp458-9; ☎ 222-64-65; www.hotel eloisa.com; Cárdenas 179; s M$602-732, d M$659-789, tr M$745-875, ste M$1193; ❄ 🛋) With a great location near the beach, this recently renovated hotel provides uncommon value. The pleasant standard rooms have rustic furniture, tiled floors and two double beds; some also feature views and furnished balconies. Avoid the darker rooms facing the courtyard.

Casa de Los Cuatro Vientos (Map pp458-9; ☎ 222-01-61; www.cuatrovientos.com; Matamoros 520; r/ste M$725/847; 🛋) The cozy rooms have white brick walls, hand-painted trim and gleaming red-tiled floors. Quality vintage furnishings add style and class. There's also a two-room suite with a large bedroom and two day beds. The rooftop bar is an attraction in itself, affording terrific views of the cathedral and the entire bay. The snazzy candlelit restaurant seals the deal.

Hotel Emperador (Map pp458-9; ☎ 222-17-67; www .hotelemperadorpv.com; Amapas 114; d M$640, ste M$940-2100; ❄ 🖳 🛋) This contemporary beach hotel overlooks an ideal swimming beach. Oceanfront rooms celebrate the sea with large balconies featuring dining tables and kitchenettes – so you can prepare and eat your food alfresco. Each room has a fridge, cable TV, in-room phones, a king-sized bed and a sleeper couch.

Hotel Tropicana (Map pp458-9; ☎ 222-09-12; www .htropicanapv.com; Amapas 214; d M$720-920, ste M$1000-1320; ❄ 🖳 🛋) This venerable 160-room beach hotel is eminently romantic. The standard rooms are appealing with white brick walls, attractive carved headboards, hand-painted woodwork and rustic furniture.

Terraza Inn (Map pp458-9; ☎ 223-54-31; www.terrazainn .com; Amapas 299; r M$900-950) Nestled on terraces opposite Playa de los Muertos, this little gem is the perfect hideaway for couples craving romantic solitude. There are only 10 units – each is unique and attractive, with interesting architectural features like arched doorways, columns and brick ceilings with exposed timbers. Some units have a small kitchen.

Villa Mercedes Hotel (Map pp458-9; ☎ 222-21-48; www.villamercedes.com.mx; Amapas 175; d M$950-1050, ste M$1150-1300, apt M$1300-1600; ❄ 🛋) This small, revitalized hotel in the Los Muertos neighborhood has a fine aesthetic and an aura of tranquility. The 15 units are spotless and accommodating, with kitchenettes or full kitchens. The penthouse apartment sleeps up to six in style, with a terrace and a partial sea view.

Also recommended are the following:
Hotel Rosita (Map pp458-9; ☎ 222-10-33; www .hotelrosita.com; Paseo Díaz Ordaz 901; d/tr M$570-750; ❄ 🛋) A vintage beach hotel with no-nonsense rooms.
Hotel Posada de Roger (Map pp458-9; ☎ 222-08-36; www.posadaroger.com; Badillo 237; s/d/tr/q M$580/660/770/880; ❄) An agreeable, central hotel and travelers' hangout.

TOP END
Puerto Vallarta's top-end options are mostly dominated by large, homogenous resorts. The following are very special, small and stylish places and are a great alternative if you're looking for something intimate.

Casa Dulce Vita (Map pp458-9; ☎ 222-10-08; www.dulce vida.com; Aldama 295; ste M$766-2188; ❄ 🛋) With the look and feel of an Italian villa, this collection of seven spacious suites offers graceful accommodations and delicious privacy. Most have private terraces, high ceilings and plentiful windows, with sunny living areas and extra beds for groups. Even when the place is fully booked it retains a quiet and intimate atmosphere. There's a well-situated pool and manicured tropical gardens.

Hotel Suites Nadia (Map p455; ☎ 222-52-52; www .hotelsuitesnadia.com; Uruguay 127; s M$8/5-1200, d M$1000-1500, t M$1125-1650; ❄ 🖳 🛋) This choice boutique hotel with only 10 units offers seriously classy digs overlooking Playa Camarones. Units are chic and breezy, with flat-screen TVs and large, attractive bathrooms. Furnishings and decor eschew the typical Mexican bric-a-brac in favor of stylish, urbane styling. Up on the roof is a wonderful small pool and hot tub, with rewarding views of bay and beaches.

Casa Amorita (Map pp458-9; ☎ 222-49-26; www .casaamorita.com; Iturbide 309; r M$2190; 🔊) Located on a quiet street above the din of the *malecón*, this romantic getaway with four rooms and a capacity of eight guests offers unique and luxurious accommodations. Some may find it a wee bit precious, but others will swoon. Complimentary breakfasts are fresh, healthy and hearty.

Eating

Foodies are pampered in Puerto Vallarta, and return visitors rate its cuisine scene as a prime attraction. A goodly number of noteworthy chefs from abroad have put down roots, offering competing menus of tremendous breadth and variety. There's also a great selection of economical, family-run eateries serving mouthwatering traditional Mexican fare, and the taco stands lining the streets of the Zona Romántica make for quick, delicious meals.

ISLA RÍO CUALE & SOUTH
Budget

Some of the tastiest and cheapest food in town comes from the taco stands along Madero in the early evening. Women sell delicious *tamales* and *flan* along Insurgentes at dusk.

La Hormiga Feliz (Map pp458-9; cnr Madero & Vallarta; tacos & quesadillas M$5-8; 🕓 8am-5pm & 7pm-1am Mon-Sat) Madero has several open-late taco stands, and every one of them brags about their freshly-made salsa. The salsa here is so good that Miguel – who's been chopping it up and mashing it down since 1998 – just lets it speak for itself. Slather it on an *adobado* (marinated pork) taco and then do it again.

Guero's Sea Food (Map pp458-9; 298 Madero; fish tacos/ tostadas M$10/26; 🕓 noon-7pm Thu-Tue) Come to this unsassuming little hole-in-the-wall for delicious inexpensive crustaceans.

Las Tres Huastecas (Map pp458-9; ☎ 222-30-17; cnr Olas Altas & Rodríguez; mains M$50-95; 🕓 7am-7pm) This is the place for delicious Mexican favorites in a homelike atmosphere, at local prices. The charming owner, a poet calling himself 'El Querreque,' recites verse as readily as he recites the house specialties.

Midrange

Restaurant Gilmar (Map pp458-9; ☎ 222-39-23; Madero 418; breakfast M$25-60, mains M$60-135; 🕓 7am-11pm Mon-Sat) The young owner brings a lot of verve to the table, along with tasty Mexican dishes and seafood at reasonable prices.

Café de Olla (Map pp458-9; ☎ 223-16-26; Badillo 168; mains M$65-210; 🕓 9am-11pm Wed-Mon) This well-loved traditional Mexican restaurant nurtures a lively atmosphere with its sidewalk grill and open kitchen. Mariachis stroll through it all as the owner greets everyone who walks through the door like old family.

Uncommon Grounds Buddha Lounge (off Map pp458-9; ☎ 223-38-34; Cardenas 625; mains M$75-195; 🕓 noon-close Wed-Sun) Part restaurant, part women's social club, this welcoming café is an agreeable place to spend an evening. Beautifully presented dishes with amiable names (anyone for a 'Planet Utopia Salad'?) are trotted out from the kitchen with panache by hosts Lydia and Anne. Vegetarians are well taken care of, as are those in need of a cocktail. You can also get a chair massage and shop in the small boutique.

Época (Map pp458-9; ☎ 222-25-10; Serdán 174; mains M$80-185; 🕓 8am-10:30pm Wed-Mon) A civilized option overlooking Playa Los Muertos, Época has quickly taken its place among Vallarta's top tier beach restaurants. Dine on duck breast tostadas, Oaxacan pork with green *mole*, grilled *nopal* salad, and fried bananas.

Joe Jack's Fish Shack (Map pp458-9; ☎ 222-20-99; Badillo 212; mains M$95-150; 🕓 noon-11pm) Seafood aficionados flock to this joint for fish and chips and dishes like whole sea bass, garlic shrimp and great slabs of mahi mahi. Large groups are graciously accommodated on the pleasant rooftop terrace. The service is jovial and quick, and the music classic rock.

Top End

Red Cabbage Café (off Map pp458-9; ☎ 223-04-11; Rivera del Río 204A; mains M$80-175; 🕓 5-11pm; ✗ 🔊) Though the atmosphere is casual, with fabulous eclectic and bohemian artwork, the food is serious and features old recipes and uncommon indigenous sauces. The soups – including a cream of peanut and a piquant tortilla soup – are to die for. It's a pleasant 10-minute walk from the Zona Romántica; from Cardenas turn right on Rivero del Río where the road crosses the river.

Barrio Sur (Map pp458-9; ☎ 223-03-73; Pulpíto 122; mains M$90-190; 🕓 8am-2pm & 6-11pm Mon-Sat) This spacious alfresco dining retreat is gorgeously lit at night, and the international latin cuisine coupled with the cool world music might make a friendly date turn passionate.

The menu reinvents several standard South American dishes, adding a touch of Euro-Asiatic influences here and there.

Oscar's Bar & Grill (Map pp458-9; ☎ 223-07-89; Isla Rio Cuale 1; mains M$90-225; 🕑 11am-11pm) Inhabiting a beautiful setting on the peaceful seaward tip of Isla Cuale, this restaurant is a fine choice for a romantic meal. Enjoy dishes like fish carpaccio with soy cilantro sauce or Chihuahua cheese fondue.

La Palapa (Map pp458-9; ☎ 222-52-25; Púlpito 103; mains M$110-295; 🕑 8am-11pm) Elegant beach dining at its best. Tables are positioned to take full advantage of the sea views, making it a particularly marvelous spot for breakfast or sunset. Chilean sea bass with blonde miso and pickled ginger is just one of the delicacies on the menu.

Archie's Wok (Map pp458-9; ☎ 222-04-11; Rodríguez 130; mains M$130-210; 🕑 2-11pm Mon-Sat) This elegant, urbane restaurant has long showed Puerto Vallarta a thing or two about good eating. The menu changes but it's always Asian fusion, with savory fish in rich tropical sauces as the highlight. There's live music Thursday through Sunday.

NORTH OF THE RÍO CUALE

Budget

Cenaduría Doña Raquel (Map pp458-9; ☎ 222-30-25; Vicario 131; mains M$30-60; 🕑 6-11:30pm Mon & Wed-Fri, 2-11pm Sat & Sun) You can smell the richness of the traditional Mexican basics served here from a block away. Friendly atmosphere and friendly prices.

Casa de Pancho (Map pp458-9; ☎ 222-00-21; Abasolo 236; mains M$40-50; 🕑 6-11pm) It couldn't be more simple: a few plastic tables set up in a mostly bare room. But the economical *pozole*, enchiladas and other basic dishes are simply splendid. Carlos, the genial waiter/cook/owner, loves to spread the gospel of salsa.

Esquina de los Caprichos (Map pp458-9; ☎ 222-09-11; Miramar 402; tapas M$40-75; 🕑 1-10pm Mon-Sat) A tiny little place with only six tables and a lot of class. Most of the dishes you would expect to find at a tapas bar in Barcelona – delicious garlic-heavy gazpacho, buttery grilled scallops, fava bean stew – are served here on charming handmade plates.

Planeta Vegetariano (Map pp458-9; ☎ 222-30-73; Iturbide 270; tacos & quesadillas M$45-65; 🕑 8am-10pm; Ⓥ) This gem of a place with only 10 tables eschews the cheese for fresh, dairy-free dishes like soy enchiladas, banana lasagna (yes, that's right) and a wide range of creatively conceived salads. The economical buffet and homey atmosphere cause many Vallarta visitors to forget about all that culinary din and return again and again.

Midrange

Los Xitomates (Map pp458-9; ☎ 222-16-95; Morelos 610; mains M$70-180; 🕑 6pm-midnight) This innovative restaurant targets younger diners with its hybrid *alta cocina Mexicana* (gourmet Mexican) cuisine, which takes pre-Hispanic and Mexican recipes and rounds them out with Mediterranean, Asian or Caribbean influences. It can be noisy when busy, but the service is always top notch.

La Dolce Vita (Map pp458-9; ☎ 222-38-52; Paseo Díaz Ordaz 674; mains M$70-105; 🕑 noon-2am) A cheerful, often crowded spot for wood-fired pizzas, well-priced pastas, and people-watching. There's often live jazz music. Request a table upstairs by the window for great views.

Top End

Café des Artistes (Map pp458-9; ☎ 222-32-28; Sánchez 740; mains M$115-240; 🕑 6-11:30pm Mon-Sat) Many consider this to be Vallarta's finest restaurant. Whether or not you're prone to superlatives, you're sure to enjoy its romantic ambience and exquisite French cuisine. The service is formal but unobtrusive, and reservations are recommended.

Chez Elena (Map pp458-9; ☎ 222-01-61; Matamoros 520; mains M$140-210; 🕑 6-11pm) Back in the martini era this small, atmospheric restaurant was a meeting place for the likes of Liz Taylor, Richard Burton, Peter O'Toole and other well-known appetites. Without having ever let down its culinary standards, it's still imbued with gracious allure. Try the savory Mayan pork dish called *cochinita pibil* with achiote chile sauce. And by all means, take in the view from the rooftop lounge.

our pick **El Arrayán Cocina Tradicional** (Map pp458-9; ☎ 222-71-95; Allende 344; mains M$155-230; 🕑 6-11pm Wed-Mon) Owner Carmen Porras takes special pleasure in rescuing old family recipes from obscurity and finding new converts for real traditional Mexican cuisine. Her restaurant, with its open kitchen and romantic courtyard, emphasizes local ingredients: the delicious *panela* cheese comes straight from the small dairy south of Puerto Vallarta and the corn used for the tortillas is locally produced and comes directly from the mill. House specialties include crispy duck *carnitas* with orange sauce

GAY PUERTO VALLARTA

Come on out – the rainbow flag flies high over Puerto Vallarta and its formidable selection of gay bars, nightclubs, restaurants and hotels. With increasing international awareness of Vallarta as a gay destination, the number of annual gay visitors is on the rise. Sadly, most of the nightclubs cater specifically to gay men, but there are several small bars where women congregate. The **Gay Guide Vallarta** (www.gayguidevallarta.com) booklet has tons of information and a helpful map for finding gay-friendly businesses.

Blue Chairs Beach Club (Map p455; Playa de los Muertos) is the most popular, visible gay beach bar, with droves of gay couples enjoying the sun's ubiquitous rays and cool drinks. A great place to start, it's located at the south end of Playa de los Muertos.

Clubs & Nightspots

Most dance clubs stay open until at least 4am and some stay open well past sunrise.

Mañana (Map pp458-9; Carranza 290; cover M$100-200) With both indoor and outdoor spaces, this jubilant new space has taken gay Vallarta by storm.

Club Paco Paco (Map pp458-9; ☎ 222-18-99; Vallarta 278; cover M$50) The new owners have revived the original spirit of this venerable disco-cantina, open until 6am. Simply smashing transvestite reviews are staged Friday through Sunday mornings at 12:30am and 3am.

Anthropology (Map pp458-9; Morelos 101; cover M$50) It's raining men at this sizzling dance mecca with its dark, intimate rooftop patio. Women are unapolgetically disallowed.

The following gay bars are mostly mellow. **Kit Kat Klub** (Map pp458-9; ☎ 223-00-93; Púlpito 120) is an ultra-hip dinner-show spot with wicked martinis. **La Noche** (Map pp458-9; Cárdenas 257; ☒ 4pm-2am)

– scrumptious! – and rib eye steak marinated in Mexican spices with blood orange tequila sauce. Raise a toast to a truly memorable meal with a shot of fiery *raicilla*, a rare agave distillate produced in Jalisco.

Spaggia (Map p455; ☎ 223-94-17; Uruguay 109; mains M$159-275; ☒ 8am-1am) Overlooking Playa Camarones, this cosmopolitan beach restaurant knows how to make an impression. Even in the heat of the afternoon the feeling is breezy and contemporary. You can dine on rack of lamb, seafood *pozole*, tuna sashimi, baked oysters, or pan-fried duck – but be sure to wait at least 20 minutes before taking a dip.

Drinking

Vallarta has many choice spots for sipping a strong coffee or tipping a tipple. It's ridiculously easy to become inebriated here, where two-for-one happy hours are as reliable as the sunset and the margarita glasses look like oversized snifters. Coffee shops open about 7am and close around midnight; most bars keep the lime squeezers occupied until well after that.

La Bodeguita del Medio (Map pp458-9; ☎ 223-15-85; Paseo Díaz Ordaz 858) This graffiti-covered Cuban joint has live music, stiff mojitos and a great beach ambience.

Blanco y Negro (Map p455; ☎ 293-25-56; cnr Lucerna & Niza, Zona Hotelera; ☒ Mon-Sat) Mainly attracting locals, this pleasant bar and café is a great place to make friends and hear *trova* (Latin accoustic pop ballads).

Café San Angel (Map pp458-9; ☎ 223-21-60; Olas Altas 449) Start your day in this artsy, relaxed café that has sidewalk tables filled with gringos sitting pretty, sipping black coffee and nibbling on snacks and sweets.

Other drinking options worth considering include these two:

Memories Café (Map pp458-9; cnr Mina & Juárez; ☒ 7pm-midnight) Conversation is king at this down-to-earth, low-key spot popular with locals and visitors alike.

Andale (Map pp458-9; ☎ 222-10-54; Olas Altas 425) Party hearty with throngs of young vacationers to very loud classic rock.

Entertainment

Vallarta's main forms of nighttime entertainment revolve around dancing, drinking and dining. At night everyone and their brother strolls the *malecón*, choosing from a fantastic selection of restaurants, bars and hot nightspots. Entertainment is often presented in the amphitheater by the sea, opposite Plaza Principal. Softly lit Isla Cuale is a quiet haven for a romantic promenade in the early evening.

is well loved for its convivial atmosphere and buff bartenders. **Sama Bar** (Map pp458-9; ☎ 223-31-82; Olas Altas 510; ◷ 5pm-2am) is a likable small place with big martinis. Women, men, gringos and locals: all make friendly at **Frida** (Map pp458-9; Cárdenas 361), a cozy and sociable cantina featuring enticing drink specials. Ditch the boys at Uncommon Grounds Buddha Lounge (see p462).

Resorts & Inns
Blue Chairs Beach Resort (Map p455; ☎ 222-50-40; www.hotelbluechairs.com; Almendro 4; d/ste M$1082/1950, apt M$1202-1366; ⊠ ⚲) Overlooking one of Mexico's most famous gay beaches, this resort is a good place to let it all hang out (although officially the beach has a 'no nudity' policy). There are bars and restaurants on the beach and a raucous nightspot with live entertainment on the roof. The breezy and attractive rooms have cable TV; apartments have kitchenettes.

Villa David (Map pp458-9; ☎ 223-03-15, toll-free from the US 877-832-3315; www.villadavidpv.com; Galleana 348; r M$1169-1622; ⊠ 🖳 ⚲) Reservations are essential and clothing optional at this swanky gay retreat in a beautiful hacienda-style mansion. It's the only such bed and breakfast in Vallarta's historic district. With gorgeously landscaped grounds and tastefully appointed rooms, this is the perfect choice for a romantic getaway with a special Fred.

Abbey Hotel (Map pp458-9; ☎ 222-44-88; www.abbeyhotelvallarta.com; Púlpito 138; r M$1290-1936, ste M$1740-2450; ⊠ 🖳 ⚲) This mid-sized gay-oriented hotel – well known for its large, sociable hot tub – is smack dab in the middle of the Puerto Vallarta action. The 55 bright units are distinguished by their well-equipped bathrooms with big, luxurious showers and the balconies, many with excellent views.

NIGHTCLUBS & DISCOS
Along the *malecón* are a bunch of places where teen and 20-something tourists get trashed and dance on tables. On a good night, they all stay open until 5am. You can see from the street which one has the most action. Cover charges are normally waived early in the week; on weekends they often include one or two drinks.

de Santos (Map pp458-9; ☎ 223-30-52; Morelos 771; weekend cover M$100; ◷ Wed-Sun) Vallarta's choicest nightspot commands the most artful DJs and an open-air rooftop bar furnished with oversized beds. On the dance floor the music is frenetic, but there's also a mellow chill lounge.

Christine (Map p455; ☎ 224-69-90; Av Las Garzas s/n; cover M$100-200; ◷ Wed-Sun) At the NH Krystal Puerto Vallarta, this flashy dance club is occasionally explosive, with cutting edge sound and lighting systems.

J&B Salsa Club (Map p455; ☎ 224-69-90; Av Ascencio 2043; cover M$100) Vallarta's premier latin dance club (pronounced 'hota-bey') features live bands Thursday through Sunday, with DJs the rest of the week. The salsa lessons (M$20, from 9:30pm to 10:30pm Wednesday to Friday) are a big draw. Also try these places:
Hilo (Map pp458-9; ☎ 223-53-61; Paseo Díaz Ordaz 588; weekend cover M$70-100) With epic statues of revolutionary heroes, it's a cool space well-designed for getting a groove on.

Zoo (Map pp458-9; ☎ 222-49-45; Paseo Díaz Ordaz 638; weekend cover M$100) Good sound system, and cages in which to dance.

THEATERS
Santa Barbara Theater (Map pp458-9; ☎ 223-20-48; Olas Altas 351; admission without dinner M$120-220, with dinner M$250-350; ◷ 8pm Wed-Sat Nov-Apr) This cabaret-style theatre stages musical reviews, concerts, plays and movies. Show up at 6pm for dinner in the breezy upstairs restaurant.

BULLFIGHTS
Bullfights (admission M$250) are held at 5pm on Wednesday from November to April, in the **Plaza de Toros** (Map p455) opposite the marina.

CINEMAS
Cine Bahía (Map pp458-9; ☎ 222-17-17; cnr Insurgentes & Madero; admission adult/child M$38/25) Recent releases are often shown in English with Spanish subtitles.

MARIACHIS
Two places present regular mariachi music. One attracts tourists; the other is mainly for Mexicans.

Tequila's (Map pp458-9; ☎ 222-57-25; Galeana 104) This upstairs restaurant-bar features live mariachi music every night except Monday, between 8pm and 10:30pm. There's no cover, but you'll be expected to tip well if the mariachis serenade your table.

Mariachi Loco (Map pp458-9; ☎ 223-22-05; cnr Cárdenas & Vallarta; cover M$50, dinner M$80-145) Usually attracting a very enthusiastic all-Mexican crowd, this restaurant-bar presents an entertaining (if slightly amateur) show of music, comedy and mariachi every night at 10:30pm Monday and Tuesday and at 11:30pm Wednesday through Saturday. It's a great bit of local color.

Shopping

Vallarta is a haven for shoppers, with many shops and boutiques selling fashionable clothing, beachwear and crafts from all over Mexico. The following places have the good goods, and will pack and ship your purchases.

Mercado de Artesanías (Map pp458-9; ☎ 223-09-25; A Rodríguez 260) Selling everything from Taxco silver, sarapes (blankets with a head opening, worn as a cloak) and huaraches (woven leather sandals), to wool wall-hangings and blown glass.

Tienda de Muebles (Map p455; ☎ 224-08-47; Av Ascensio 2556) With a gargantuan showroom, this is your best bet for best-price Mexican decor, housewares, and furniture.

Bazaar Artes Indias (Map pp458-9; ☎ 222-12-43; Insurgentes 194) Well-stocked store with clothes, jewelry, masks and decor at prices below many similar establishments.

El Gato Gordo (Map p455; ☎ 223-03-00; Av de México 1083) This rather small shop looks harmless enough, but it's chock full of *lucha libre* (Mexican wrestling) masks and Cuban cigars. These two products should not be used simultaneously.

Huaracheria Fabiola (Map pp458-9; ☎ 293-46-57; Vallarta 145) This Vallarta-style cobbler produces custom-made sandals in 24 hours.

Artesanías Flores (Map pp458-9; ☎ 223-07-73; Cardenas 282) and **Huichol Collection** (Map pp458-9; ☎ 223-21-41; Morelos 490) sell Huichol beadwork, thread paintings and jewelry.

Getting There & Away

AIR

Gustavo Díaz Ordaz International Airport (Map p455; PVR; ☎ 221-12-98; Carr Tepic, Km 7.5, Zona Aeropuerto) is 10km north of the city and is served by the following carriers:

Aeroméxico (☎ 221-12-04) Direct service to Acapulco, Los Angeles, León, Mexico City, Monterrey and Tijuana.

Alaska Airlines (☎ 221-13-50) Direct service to Los Angeles, Portland, San Francisco and Seattle.

American Airlines (☎ 221-17-99) Direct service to Chicago, Dallas, Mexico City and St Louis.

Continental (☎ 221-22-12) Direct service to Houston and Newark.

Frontier (☎ from the US 800-432-1359) Direct service to Denver and Kansas City.

Mexicana (☎ 221-18-23) Direct service to Chicago, Los Angeles and Mexico City.

Ted (☎ from the US 800-225-58-33) United's budget carrier offers direct service to Denver and San Francisco.

US Airways/America West (☎ 221-13-33) Direct service to Las Vegas, Los Angeles, Phoenix and San Diego.

BUS

Vallarta's **long-distance bus station** (Map p455) is just off Hwy 200, about 10km north of the city center and 2km northwest of the airport.

Primera Plus and ETN bus lines have offices (Map pp458-9) south of the Río Cuale at Cárdenas 268 and at Insurgentes 276.

See the table opposite for daily departures from the main terminal.

CAR & MOTORCYCLE

Starting at about US$40 to US$50 per day, car rentals are pricey during the high season, but deep discounts are offered at other times. You'll do well to book online. For more information about renting cars in Mexico, see p994.

Car rental agencies at the airport:

Advantage (☎ 221-14-49)**Avis** (☎ 221-11-12)
Budget (☎ 221-17-30)
Dollar (☎ 223-13-54)
Hertz (☎ 221-14-73)
National (☎ 209-03-56)

Master Tours (Map p455; ☎ 209-05-29; Av Ascencio 2740), opposite the Hacienda Hotel & Spa, rents out trail bikes and scooters (M$150 per hour).

Getting Around

TO/FROM THE AIRPORT

The cheapest way to get to/from the airport is on a local bus for M$5. 'Aeropuerto,' 'Juntas' and 'Ixtapa' buses from town all stop right at the airport entrance; 'Centro' and 'Olas Altas' buses go into town from beside the airport entrance. A taxi from the city center costs around M$75. From the airport to the city, taxis ask as much as M$150, but it shouldn't cost more than M$100 to go to most parts of the city.

BICYCLE

For a two-wheeled buzz, check out Eco Ride (p457). It rents out mountain bikes for both guided or self-guided tours, from M$250 per day.

BOAT

Vallarta's water taxis serve the beautiful beaches on the southern side of the bay. These beaches that are accessible only by boat. Departing from the pier at Playa de los Muertos, they head south around the bay, making stops at Playa Las Ánimas (25 minutes), Quimixto (30 minutes) and Yelapa (45 minutes); the round-trip fare is M$220 for any destination. Boats depart at 10am, 11am, 11:30am, 12:30pm, 4pm and 4:30pm, and return mid-afternoon (note that the last two boats from Puerto Vallarta return in the morning).

A water taxi also goes to Yelapa from the beach just south of Hotel Rosita, on the northern end of the *malecón*, departing at 11:30am Monday to Saturday (round-trip M$250, 30 minutes).

Private yachts and *lanchas* can be hired from the southern side of the Playa de los Muertos pier for about US$140 for four hours. They'll take you to any secluded beach around the bay; most have gear aboard for snorkeling and fishing.

BUS

Local buses operate every five minutes from 5am to 11pm on most routes, and cost M$5. Plaza Lázaro Cárdenas at Playa Olas Altas is a major departure hub. Northbound local bus routes also stop in front of the Cine Bahía, on Insurgentes near the corner of Madero.

Northbound buses marked 'Hoteles,' 'Aeropuerto,' 'Ixtapa,' 'Pitillal' and 'Juntas' pass through the city heading north to the airport, the Zona Hotelera and Marina Vallarta; the 'Hoteles,' 'Pitillal' and 'Ixtapa' routes can take you to any of the large hotels north of the city.

Southbound 'Boca de Tomatlán' buses pass along the southern coastal highway through Mismaloya (M$5.50, 20 minutes) to Boca de Tomatlán (M$5.50, 30 minutes). They depart from Carranza near the corner of Aguacate, leaving every 15 minutes from 5:30am to 11pm.

TAXI

Cab prices are regulated by zones; the cost for a ride is determined by how many zones you cross. A typical trip from downtown to the Zona Hotelera costs M$30 to M$80; the fare to Mismaloya is about M$100. Always determine the price of the ride before you get in. Hailing a cab is easy in the city center along the *malecón*. There are several taxi stands,

BUSES FROM PUERTO VALLARTA

Destination	Fare	Duration	Frequency
Barra de Navidad	1st-class M$173	3½hr	4 daily
(can also take any bus to Manzanillo)	2nd-class M$145	3½-4hr	6 daily
Guadalajara	M$250-270	5½hr	frequent
Manzanillo	1st-class M$218	5hr	3 daily
	2nd-class M$184	5hr	5 daily
Mazatlán	1st class M$285	8hr	2 daily, 6pm & 9pm, or take a bus to Tepic for frequent buses depart to Mazatlán.
Mexico City	deluxe M$990	13hr	1
(Terminal Norte)	1st class M$752	14hr	8
Rincón de Guayabitos	1st-class M$70	1½hr	frequent
(buses continute to Tepic)	2nd-class M$55	2½hr	frequent
San Blas	2nd class M$106	3½hr	4 daily, 7am, 10am, noon and 3pm, or take a bus to Tepic for transfer
San Patricio-Melaque	1st-class M$172/140	3½hr	4 daily
	2nd-class M$140	4hr	3 daily
Tepic	M$115	3½hr	frequent
	M$95	4hr	frequent

including one on Paseo Diáz Ordaz at Papila, one on Juárez at Plaza Principal, and one on Carranza at Plaza Lázaro Cárdenas.

COSTALEGRE BEACHES

South of Puerto Vallarta, the stretch of Mexico's Pacific coast from Chamela to Barra de Navidad is blessed with many fine beaches. Tourism promoters and developers refer to this shoreline as the 'Costalegre' (Happy Coast) or the 'Mexican Riviera.'

Following are the beaches from north to south (with kilometer numbers measured from the junction of Hwys 80 and 200 just outside San Patricio-Melaque).

Playa Pérula (Km 76), a sheltered beach at the northern end of tranquil 11km-long Bahía de Chamela, is great for swimming and extended walks. There's a smattering of *palapa* restaurants and cheap accommodations.

At Bahía de Chamela, **Playa Chamela** (Km 72) and **Playa La Negrita** (Km 64) are isolated, relaxing beaches with a couple of restaurants but no hotels. The nine islands in the expansive bay are beautiful to see in silhouette at sunset.

With the help of local activists, endangered hawksbill sea turtles are making a comeback at **Playa Careyes** (Km 52). The only place to stay is the romantic – but pricey – **El Careyes Beach Resort and Spa** (☎ 315-351-00-00; www.elcareyesresort .com; Carretera Barra de Navidad at Km 53.5; d US$365, 1-/2-bedroom, US$420-608, ste US$701-1106; P ⊠ ⊠ ⊡ ⊠).

Escape artists love **Playa Tecuán** (Km 33) for its long deserted white-sand beach and eerie abandoned resort. This is a great option for those wanting to camp. It's a 10km drive off the highway on a rutted gravel road.

On the palm-fringed Bahía Tenacatita, **Playa Tenacatita** (Km 30) has clear snorkeling waters and a large mangrove lagoon with good birdwatching. There are a few enjoyable restaurants and decent 'hotels.' Also on this bay is **Playa Boca de Iguanas** (Km 19) and **Playa La Manzanilla** (Km 13). The surf is mild, the sand is hot and wonderful, and the beach is shallow for a long way out, making it good for a swim. Both villages have restaurants and accommodations.

BAHÍA DE NAVIDAD

The tight arc of the Bahía de Navidad is practically ringed by deep, honey-colored sand with two resort towns at either end, waving amiably at each other. Situated 5km apart, Barra de Navidad and San Patricio-Melaque are siblings with distinct personalities. Barra

is beloved for its attractive cobbled streets and aura of good living while San Patricio-Melaque, the scrappier of the two, draws budget-minded travelers seeking to get back to basics in a place that eschews pretension.

San Patricio-Melaque

☎ 315 / pop 7500

Known by most as Melaque (may-*lah*-kay), this kick-back beach resort hasn't lost its old Mexico charm. Besides being a popular vacation destination for Mexican families and a low-key winter hangout for snowbirds (principally Canadians), the town is famous for its weeklong Fiesta de San Patricio (St Patrick's Day Festival) in March.

INFORMATION

Barra de Navidad's tourist office (see p471) has some basic information on Melaque.

Banamex (Gómez Farías s/n) Has an ATM and will change US and Canadian dollars; traveler's checks are changed from 9am to noon only.

Casa de Cambio Melaque (Gómez Farías s/n, Pasaje Comercial 11) Changes cash and traveler's checks.

Caseta Blanquita (Morelos 52) Offers fax and phone services.

El Navegante (Gómez Farías 48; per hr M$20) Internet access.

Post office (Orozco 13) Located near Corona.

Total Laundry Service (Gómez Farías 26; per kg M$10)

SIGHTS & ACTIVITIES

Simply relax and take it easy. The main activities are swimming, lazing on the beach, watching pelicans fish at sunrise and sunset, climbing to the *mirador* (lookout point) at the bay's west end, prowling the plaza and public market, or walking the beach to Barra de Navidad.

Viajes Fesa (☎ 355-9124; fesaviajes@yahoo.com; Gómez Farías 15C) books one-day tours to Colima (M$300) and Guadalajara (M$305), and sells tickets for boat passage to Tenacatita (M$180) and for ETN buses.

The Only Tours (☎ 355-67-77; raystoursmelaque@ yahoo.com; Las Cabañas 26) runs popular full-day snorkeling tours (M$250) and tours to Colima (M$500). For rent are mountain bikes (M$60/100 per half-/full day), snorkeling gear and body boards (each M$100 per day).

FESTIVALS & EVENTS

Fiesta de San Patricio This festival, honoring the town's patron saint, is Melaque's biggest annual celebration and takes place in March. A week of festivities – in-

SAN PATRICIO–MELAQUE

0 ———— 400 m
0 ———— 0.2 miles

To Hwy. 80 (1km);
Playa La Manzanilla (13km);
Playa Boca de Iguanas (19km);
Playa Tenacatita (30km);
Playa Tecuán (33km);
Playa Careyes (53km);
Playa La Negrita (64km);
Playa Chamela (72km);
Playa Pérula (76km);
Puerto Vallarta (214km);
Guadalajara (296km)

To Plaza de Toros (3km);
Barra de Navidad (5km);
Manzanillo (65km)

To Villa
Obregón
(100m)

To Campground (250m);
Mirador (500m)

Ruins of
Casa Grande
Hotel

Bahía de
Navidad

INFORMATION	
Banamex	1 B2
Casa de Cambio Melaque	2 B2
Caseta Blanquita	3 C1
El Navegante	4 C2
Post Office	5 C2
Total Laundry Service	6 B2

SIGHTS & ACTIVITIES	
The Only Tours	7 C2
Viajes Fesa	8 B2

SLEEPING	
Bungalows Las Hámacas	9 B2
Campground	10 A3
Casa Paula	11 B2
Hotel Bahía	12 A2
Hotel de Legazpi	13 A2
Hotel Las Brisas	14 B2
Las Paloma Oceanfront Retreat	15 D2
Ocean Village	16 D2
Villas Camino del Mar	17 D2

EATING	
Flor Morena	18 C1
Food Stands & Palapa	
Restaurants	19 A2
Kucaramakara Sushi Bar and	
Lounge	20 C2
Mariscos Sinky	21 C1
Restaurant Maya	22 D2

DRINKING	
Surfos & Vagos	23 C1

TRANSPORT	
Buses to Barra de Navidad	24 C1
Primera Plus 2nd-class Bus	
Station	25 B2
Servicios Coordinados Bus	
Station	(see 25)
Taxi Stand	26 C1
Transportes Cihuatlán Bus	
Station	27 B2

cluding all-day parties, rodeos, a carnival, music, dances and nightly fireworks – leads up to St Patrick's Day.

St Patrick's Day Held on March 17, this day is marked with a mass and the blessing of the fishing fleet. Take care when the *borrachos* (drunks) take over after dark.

SLEEPING

Rates vary greatly depending on the season; the following prices are for the high season (November through May). Discounts are common for longer stays.

Budget

Ejidal Campground (campsites per night/month M$30/1000) This beachfront campground at the west end of Av La Primavera has no facilities or hookups, but the setting is undeniably beautiful. At last visit, a shower and bathroom were under construction; in the meantime, the nearby *enramadas* (palapa restaurants) charge a nominal fee for showers and bathroom usage.

Casa Paula (☎ 355-50-93; Vallarta 6; s/d M$150/200) In this simple home there are four basic rooms with concrete floors, TV and fridge around a courtyard. It's very quiet and a pleasant family

atmosphere pervades. Sadly, the mattresses are squishy.

Hotel de Legazpi (☎ 355-53-97; hotel@delegazpi.com; Pino 8; d/tr M$350/400, with kitchen M$550; P 🏊) Right on the beach, the Legazpi has bright, if a bit worn, rooms. It's very popular for its four ocean-view rooms, well-tended pool and a shady circular patio overlooking the beach, perfect for reading, yoga or wave-watching.

Bungalows Las Hámacas (☎ 355-51-13; Gómez Farías 13; d/q/ste M$350/700/900; P 🏊) Ideal for larger groups, the beachfront Las Hamacas has chipping paint and big rooms with full kitchens. Overall, it's well-kept and serene, with lots of quality reading nooks, a peanut-shaped pool, and a good restaurant overlooking the beach. The suite sleeps six comfortably.

Midrange

Hotel Bahía (☎ 355-68-94; Legazpi 5; d/q M$350-450, bungalows M$600; 🏊) Just half a block from the beach, this family-run place is one of Melaque's best deals. It's clean, very well maintained and has a communal open-air kitchen. Four of the 23 units have private kitchen, but several are rather dark.

CENTRAL PACIFIC COAST

Hotel Las Brisas (☎ 355-51-08; Gómez Farías 9; s/d M$350/500, bungalows M$800-1800; ❄ ☒ ☐) The beachfront Las Brisas has one of the nicest pools in the neighborhood, outdoor communal cooking facilities, cheery staff and a small library. All rooms have fridge and TV. The largest bungalow sleeps nine.

Villas Camino del Mar (☎ 355-52-07; www.villas caminodelmar.com.mx; Villa 6; d M$560, ste M$980-1360, penthouse M$1900-2250; ☐P ☒ ☐) Clean and dazzlingly white, this terrific beach hotel has two glorious pools and a wide range of rooms to choose from ranging from small rooms to expansive, luxurious penthouses. It also handles reservations for three other properties in the neighborhood.

Top-End

Ocean Village (☎ 355-52-07; Las Cabañas s/n; villas M$1100-1600; ☐P ☒ ☐) Nine tranquil, beautifully-appointed villas in one- and two-bedroom configurations offer delicious privacy and priveleged beach access via a private stair. Each unit is capacious and brightly decorated with an eye toward color and contrast.

Las Paloma Oceanfront Retreat (☎ 355-53-45; www.lapalomamexico.com; Las Cabañas 13; studios per week M$7400-8800, one-/two-bedroom penthouse per week M$10,440-17,600; ☐P ☒ ☐ ☐) Original art abounds at this unique boutique resort. The 14 singular, comfortable studios have kitchens and terraces with rewarding ocean views. Lush gardens, a 25m beachside swimming pool, a well-stocked library and internet access make an extended stay here extremely tempting. Drawing, painting and mask-making classes are held from November to April. From October to April, units rent by the week; steep discounts and per-night rates are offered during the summer.

EATING & DRINKING

From 6pm to midnight, food stands serve inexpensive Mexican fare a block east of the plaza along Juárez. A row of pleasant *palapa* restaurants stretches along the beach at the west end of town.

Flor Morena (Juárez s/n; mains M$20-40; ⏰6-11pm Wed-Sun) You may have to wait to get a seat in this tiny, all-women-run place, but it's worth it. Everything is made fresh, there are plenty of vegetarian options and even the house specialty, shrimp *pozole*, costs only M$40.

Mariscos Sinky (cnr Hidalgo & Corona; mains M$50-75; ⏰9am-8pm) A simple, time-honored joint with shaded sidewalk tables serving a local sea harvest. The toothsome seafood soup is made to order with a whole fish.

Kucaramakara Sushi Bar and Lounge (☎ 355-50-50; Gómez Farías 47; sushi rolls M$62-72; ⏰1pm-midnight Tue-Sun) On a dusty street, this incongruously hip eatery capitalizes brilliantly on its proximity to the sea, serving super fresh rolls, tempura and sashimi in a contemporary setting.

Restaurant Maya (☎ 102-07-75; www.restaurant maya.com; Obregón 1; mains M$74-150; ⏰6-10:30pm Tue-Sat & 10am-2pm Sun) The menu changes regularly but the quality at this Asian-fusion beachside hotspot is consistently excellent. Dinners include a range of gourmet salads, grilled meats and fish with exotic sauces, and there are appetizers like curried fish cakes and rich salads. Western favorites like eggs Benedict and rich omelettes with Brie rule the brunch menu.

Surfos & Vagos (☎ 355-64-13; Juárez s/n; ⏰8pm-2am Wed-Mon) Rocking to an agreeable beat, this 2nd-floor open *palapa* mixes up margaritas so stiff you can ride a wave on them.

GETTING THERE & AWAY
Air

For information on the nearest airport to Melaque, see p474.

Bus

Melaque has two bus stations. **Transportes Cihuatlán** and **Primera Plus/Servicios Coordinados** are on opposite sides of Carranza at the corner of Gómez Farías. Both have 1st- and 2nd-class buses and ply similar routes for similar fares.

Buses trundling out of these stations include:

Barra de Navidad (M$4, 10min, every 15min 6am-9pm)
Guadalajara (M$242, 5hr, 14 1st class; M$205, 7hr, 20 2nd class)
Manzanillo (M$50, 1-1½hr, 14 1st class; M$40,1-1½hr, 28 2nd class hourly 5am-11:30pm)
Puerto Vallarta (M$170, 4-5hr, 4 1st class; M$90-140, 5hr, 18 2nd class)

Taxi

A taxi between Melaque and Barra should cost no more than M$50; they congregate at the plaza.

Barra de Navidad
☎ 315 / pop 4000

The charming town of Barra de Navidad (usually simply called Barra) is squeezed onto a sandbar between Bahía de Navidad and the Laguna de

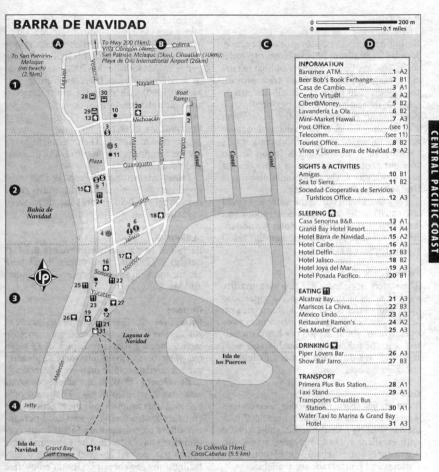

BARRA DE NAVIDAD

INFORMATION	
Banamex ATM	1 A2
Beer Bob's Book Exchange	2 B1
Casa de Cambio	3 A1
Centro Virtu@l	4 A2
Ciber@Money	5 B2
Lavandería La Ola	6 B2
Mini-Market Hawaii	7 A3
Post Office	(see 1)
Telecomm	(see 11)
Tourist Office	8 B2
Vinos y Licores Barra de Navidad	9 A2

SIGHTS & ACTIVITIES	
Amigas	10 B1
Sea to Sierra	11 B2
Sociedad Cooperativa de Servicios Turísticos Office	12 A3

SLEEPING	
Casa Senorina B&B	13 A1
Grand Bay Hotel Resort	14 A4
Hotel Barra de Navidad	15 A2
Hotel Caribe	16 A3
Hotel Delfin	17 B3
Hotel Jalisco	18 B2
Hotel Joya del Mar	19 A3
Hotel Posada Pacífico	20 B1

EATING	
Alcatraz Bay	21 A3
Mariscos La Chiva	22 B3
Mexico Lindo	23 A3
Restaurant Ramon's	24 A2
Sea Master Café	25 A3

DRINKING	
Piper Lovers Bar	26 A3
Show Bar Jarro	27 B3

TRANSPORT	
Primera Plus Bus Station	28 A1
Taxi Stand	29 A1
Transportes Cihuatlán Bus Station	30 A1
Water Taxi to Marina & Grand Bay Hotel	31 A3

Navidad. Barra de Navidad first came to prominence in 1564 when its shipyards produced the galleons used by conquistador Miguel López de Legazpi and Father André de Urdaneta to deliver the Philippines to King Felipe of Spain. By 1600, however, most of the conquests were being conducted from Acapulco, and Barra slipped into sleepy obscurity (a state from which it has yet to fully emerge).

INFORMATION

Banamex (Veracruz s/n) This ATM is air-conditioned.
Ciber@Money (Veracruz 212C; per hr M$25; 9am-3pm Mon-Sat) Has a decent internet connection, and also cashes traveler's checks.
Lavandería La Ola (Jalisco 69, per 3kg M$33) Laundry with same-day pickup.

Post office (Veracruz s/n)
Telecomm (Veracruz 212B; 9am-3pm Mon-Fri) Telephone and fax services.
Tourist office (355-51-00; www.costalegre.com; Jalisco 67; 9am-5pm Mon-Fri, 10am-6pm Sat & Sun) This regional office has information about Barra and the other towns of the Costa Alegre. It also runs an information kiosk on the jetty during the high tourist season.
Vinos y Licores Barra de Navidad (Legazpi s/n; 8:30am-11pm) Money-changing facilities, TelMex cards, and booze.

ACTIVITIES

Barra's steep and narrow beach is lovely to behold, but conditions are sometimes too rough for swimming. The gentlest conditions are generally in the mornings.

CENTRAL PACIFIC COAST

CENTRAL PACIFIC COAST

Boat Trips

Trips into the Laguna de Navidad are a Barra highlight. The boatmen's cooperative, **Sociedad Cooperativa de Servicios Turísticos** (Veracruz 40; 🕙 9am-5pm), books a variety of boat excursions ranging from half-hour trips around the lagoon ($20 per boat) to all-day jungle trips to Tenacatita (M$2500 per boat). One popular tour travels around the lagoon and visits the tiny village of Colimilla, where there are several welcoming seafood restaurants (M$200, three hours). Prices (good for up to eight people) are posted at the open-air lagoonside office. The cooperative also offers fishing, snorkeling and diving trips.

For a short jaunt out on the water you could also catch a water taxi from a nearby dock and head over to the Grand Bay Hotel Wyndham Resort on Isla de Navidad or Colimilla (M$20 round-trip; see p474).

Fishing

The waters near Barra are rife with marlin, swordfish, albacore, dorado, snapper and other more rarefied catches. Fishing trips on *lanchas* can be arranged at the boatman's cooperative for about M$400 per hour, including gear; the fishermen are ready to go most mornings at 6am. Many of the trips include snorkeling stops.

Golf

Grand Bay Golf Course (☎ 337-90-24; Grand Bay Hotel Wyndham Resort, Isla Navidad; green fees 9/18/27 holes US$160/180/200) is a celebrated 27-hole course with excellent vistas and greens carved into ocean dunes against a backdrop of mountains. Caddies and rental clubs are available.

COURSES

Barra's relaxing vibe makes it a good choice for an education vacation. Study Spanish at **Amigas** (☎ 104-1670; www.easyspanish.net; Michoacan 58; lessons per hr private/semi-private US$15/11.50), a friendly small school dedicated to making language instruction fun and instantly applicable. Many of the classes are taught in the town in real life situations, and in addition to the basics of grammar you'll learn a thing or two about Mexican slang.

TOURS

The Mexican-owned **Sea to Sierra** (☎ 355-57-90; www.seatosierra.com; Veracruz 204) offers a wide range of active adventures through remote, gorgeous territory. Choose from mountain bike tours (four/eight-hour tours M$300 to M$700), diving and snorkeling excursions (one/two-tank dives M$850/1200, snorkeling per boat M$1500 to M$2000) and horseback adventure tours (two/seven-hour tour M$500/1200). Ask about the multi-day eco- and cultural-adventure tours.

FESTIVALS & EVENTS

Big-money international fishing tournaments are held annually for marlin, sailfish, tuna and dorado.

Torneo Internacional de Pesca is the most important fishing tournament and is three days long. It's held around the third week in January.

SLEEPING

Barra has fewer beachfront rooms than its neighbor Melaque. The prices listed here are for the high season (between November and May).

Budget

Hotel Caribe (☎ 355-59-52; Sonora 15; s M$150-200, d/t 200/300) For the low price you get a rooftop terrace, hot water and your pick of 18 clean but worn rooms. Downstairs there's a pleasant garden offering respite on a hot afternoon.

Hotel Jalisco (☎ 355-85-05; mariodiaz468@hotmail .com; Jalisco 81; s/d M$150/200; 🖳) The jovial proprietor at this simple hotel enjoys acting as an emissary for his foreign guests, and personally offers complementary Spanish instruction three days a week. The 13 rooms are a mixed bag; several are dark but the street-facing units are cheerful. Guests enjoy free use of bicycles.

Hotel Posada Pacífico (☎ 355-53-59; Mazatlán 136; s/ d M$180/280, bungalow M$400-500; 🅿) This friendly, comfortable posada has 25 large, clean rooms with TV, and an additional four bungalows sleeping up to four people. It's Barra's best budget digs.

Midrange

Hotel Delfín (☎ 355-50-68; www.hoteldelfinmx.com; Morelos 23; d/t/apt M$495/595/1200; 🅿 🖳 🐾) The homey Delfín is one of Barra's best hotels. It has 24 large and pleasant rooms featuring shared balconies, a grassy pool area and an exercise room. Discounts are available for longer stays but repeat customers fill the place in winter.

Hotel Joya del Mar (☎ 355-69-67; hoteljoyadelmar@ yahoo.com.mx; Veracruz 209; s M$450-550, d M$500-600, t M$550-650, ste M$900-950; ☒ ☒ ☒) Right on the main drag, this well-run hotel offers 1st-floor rooms that are blah. Things improve considerably upstairs with comfortably furnished rooms and suites and a pair of breezy suites with commanding views of the lagoon.

our pick Casa Senorina B&B (☎ 355-53-15; www .casasenorina.com; cnr Michoacan & Veracruz; s/d/ste M$600/ 790/1200; ☒ ☒ ☒) Until recently a striking private residence, this property has been reborn as Barra's most stylish accommodations. The eight romantic rooms are uniquely attractive, with Moroccan accents, stained glass, and wood details. Pamper yourself in the splendid pool or with an onsite massage or facial. Classy meals are served on a pleasant terrace by a burbling fountain.

Hotel Barra de Navidad (☎ 355-51-22; www .hotelbarradenavidad.com; Legazpi 250; s/d/tr/bungalows M$820/860/900/1300; ☒ ☒) Providing Barra's best beach access, this glowingly white, modern beachside hotel harbors a shaded intimate courtyard and a small but inviting pool. The best rooms have ocean views and air-con.

Top End

Getting away from it all is a matter of considerable luxury on Isla Navidad, a short water-taxi ride across the lagoon from Barra de Navidad.

Grand Bay Hotel Resort (☎ 355-50-50; www.islanavi dad.com.mx; Rinconada del Capitán s/n, Isla Navidad; d US$500- 560, ste US$593-941; ☒ ☒ ☒) This super-luxury resort with its own marina is magnificent and very large. The same size description applies to the rooms, which have marble floors, hand-carved furniture, and bathrooms big enough to herd sheep in. The numerous amenities include three grass tennis courts, golf packages, a 'kids' club' day-care center and big fluffy bathrobes.

our pick CocoCabañas (☎ cell phone 315-1000441, from the US 281-205-4100; www.ecocabanas.com; Isla de Navidad; d/tr/q M$1000/1150/1300; ☒ ☒) Get off the grid and into a chic beach hut at this off-the-beaten-path resort. With its green wetland water treatment system and impressive solar array which powers the entire inn, you feel good about spending your pesos at this pioneering green lodging outpost – a rarity in Mexico. The four two-storey wood and adobe cabañas – each sleeping two couples comfortably – afford brilliant sea views through the large windows. A good restaurant serving seafood and Mexican dishes also whips up big, fresh breakfasts, which are included in the price. The inn is on Isla de Navidad, 4.5km from the fishing village of Colimilla. To get there, take a water taxi from the lagoon boat dock in Barra (M$10) and place a call from Mary's restaurant for pickup, or negotiate for water taxi service all the way (about M$150). Bicycles are provided for guests for a small fee.

EATING & DRINKING

Several of Barra's many good restaurants are on the beachfront with beautiful sunset views, and others overlook the lagoon. Simple, inexpensive little indoor-outdoor places line Veracruz in the center of town. However, most are open only in the high season.

Mexico Lindo (Legazpi 138; mains M$40-95; ☽ 8:30am- midnight) With simple plastic tables under a corrugated tin roof, this place somehow manages to feel romantic and intimate at night. The menu features regional favorites like savory and sour tortilla soup, quesadillas, garlic fish tacos and shrimp *ceviche*. A good selection of cocktails seals the deal.

Restaurant Ramon's (☎ 355-64-35; Legazpi 260; mains M$45-121; ☽ 7am-11pm) This casual and friendly restaurant is justifiably popular for its excellent fish tacos, *chili rellenos*, and local and gringo favorites like fish and chips. The portions are large and the salsa gratis.

Mariscos La Chiva (Sonora 22; mains M$50-90; ☽ noon- 6pm Wed-Mon) Completely unpretentious, this simple eatery serves super-fresh seafood dishes like *rollo de mar* – a fish fillet stuffed with octopus and crab – and shrimp with poblano chile salsa and cheese. It's a great spot to linger, befriending the local fishermen who lunch here.

Alcatraz Bay (☎ 355-70-41; Veracruz 12; mains M$80- 200; ☽ noon-10pm) This romantic spot overlooking the lagoon is a grand place to while away a hot afternoon watching the *lanchas* come and go while dining on soups, salads or the house specialty, *molcajetes camarón* (shrimp simmering in a cheesy broth), served in a bowl carved from volcanic rock.

Sea Master Café (☎ 355-51-19; Legazpi 146; mains M$85-160; ☽ lunch & dinner) With hip decor, live music and winning sea views, this place scores by taking liberties with seafood, with delicious results. It's also a swanky choice for your sunset happy hour.

Piper Lovers Bar (☎ 355-67-47; www.piperlover.com; Legazpi 154A; ☺ 10am-2am) With its tough motor-cycle-bar look and loud live music Wednesday through Saturday (from 9pm), this is the place to rock.

Show Bar Jarro (Veracruz; ☺ 9pm-4am) A down-to-earth, gay-friendly disco with pool tables and lagoon views, near Yucatán.

GETTING THERE & AROUND
Air
Barra de Navidad and Melaque are served by **Playa de Oro International Airport** (ZLO), 26km southeast of Barra on Hwy 200. The airport also serves Manzanillo. To get to town from the airport, take a taxi (M$300, 30 minutes), or take a bus 15km to Cihuatlán and a cheaper taxi from there. For flight details, see p478.

Boat
Water taxis operate on demand 24 hours a day from the dock at the southern end of Veracruz, offering service to the Grand Bay Hotel Resort, the marina, the golf course and Colimilla. All trips are M$10. Also see p472 for information on boat trips.

Bus
The long-distance buses stopping at San Patricio-Melaque (p470) also stop at Barra de Navidad (15 minutes before or after). Transportes Cihuatlán's station is at Veracruz 228; Primera Plus and ETN operate from small terminals nearby, on the opposite side of Veracruz.

In addition to the long-distance buses, colorful local buses connect Barra and Melaque (M$5, every 15 minutes, 6am to 9pm), stopping in Barra at the long-distance bus stations (buses stopping on the south-bound side of the road loop round Legazpi and back to Melaque).

Taxi
Catch taxis from the official **stand** (cnr Veracruz & Michoacán) to get the best price. A taxi to San Patricio-Melaque shouldn't cost more than M$50.

MANZANILLO
☎ 314 / pop 110,700
Manzanillo has a bit of an identity crisis. On one hand, it is Mexico's busiest commercial seaport, servicing cargo ships, pleasure cruises and naval vessels from around the world. It's also a growing tourist destination, attract-ing beach lovers to its fine golden sands (the famous slow-motion scene of Bo Derek run-ning along the beach in Blake Edwards' *10* was filmed here) and anglers to the self-pro-claimed 'Sailfish Capital of the World.'

The personalities don't always match up. Beaches are often streaked with oil that washes up from the busy harbor. And for every ambi-tious new nightclub or restaurant that opens, another shuts down – a sign that tourism is not keeping up with development. The gov-ernment has poured millions of pesos into renovation projects like the beautiful down-town *malecón*, the seaside *zócalo* and sculp-ture gardens to attract visitors, but tourism remains an afterthought in Manzanillo. Still, it's a fine city to chill out in for a few days or to use as a base for exploring the more charming beaches south of town.

Orientation
Manzanillo extends 16km from northwest to southeast. The resort hotels and finest beaches begin at Playa Azul, across the bay from Playa San Pedrito, the closest beach to the center. Further around the bay is the Península de Santiago, a rocky outcrop holding Brisas Las Hadas resort and Playa La Audiencia. Just west of the peninsula, Bahía de Santiago is lined with excellent beaches.

Central Manzanillo is bound by Bahía de Manzanillo to the north, the Pacific Ocean to the west and Laguna de Cuyutlán to the south. Av Morelos, the main drag, runs along the north edge of the town center, beside the sea. At its east end it meets Av Niños Héroes, which leads to Hwy 200.

For information on getting to the city center from the airport and bus station, see p479.

Information
Several banks with ATMs are scattered around the city center.
Caseta Telefónica (Map p476; Av Morelos 144; ☺ 9am-10pm) Long-distance telephone and fax service. Public telephones are plentiful around the center.
HSBC (Map p476; Av México s/n) Currency exchange.
Lavandería Lavimatic (Map p476; Madero; per kg M$125; ☺ Mon-Sat) Within walking distance of the center, near Domínguez.
Members.com (Map p476; Juárez 116; per hr M$15; ☺ 9am-11:30pm) Offers fast connections in a comfort-able atmosphere.

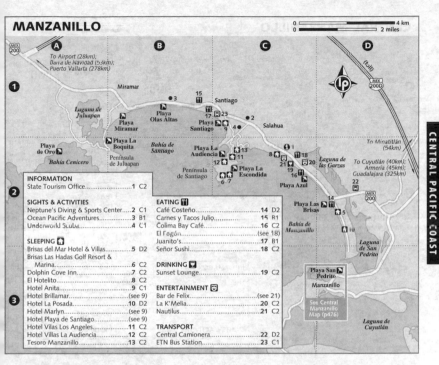

MANZANILLO

INFORMATION	
State Tourism Office..........................1	C2

SIGHTS & ACTIVITIES	
Neptune's Diving & Sports Center...2	C1
Ocean Pacific Adventures...............3	B1
Underworld Scuba............................4	C1

SLEEPING	
Brisas del Mar Hotel & Villas..........5	D2
Brisas Las Hadas Golf Resort &	
Marina..6	C2
Dolphin Cove Inn............................7	C2
El Hotelito......................................8	C2
Hotel Anita.....................................9	C1
Hotel Brillamar.........................(see 9)	
Hotel La Posada..........................10	C2
Hotel Marlyn............................(see 9)	
Hotel Playa de Santiago.............(see 9)	
Hotel Vilas Los Angeles................11	C2
Hotel Villas La Audiencia.............12	C2
Tesoro Manzanillo.......................13	C2

EATING	
Café Costeño...............................14	D2
Carnes y Tacos Julio....................15	B1
Colima Bay Café..........................16	C2
El Fogón..................................(see 18)	
Juanito's......................................17	B1
Señor Sushi.................................18	C2

DRINKING	
Sunset Lounge.............................19	C2

ENTERTAINMENT	
Bar de Felix............................(see 21)	
La K'Melia...................................20	C2
Nautilus......................................21	C2

TRANSPORT	
Central Camionera.......................22	D2
ETN Bus Station...........................23	C1

Post office (Map p476; Galindo 30)

State tourism office (Map p475; ☎ 333-22-64; www .visitacolima.com.mx; Blvd Miguel de la Madrid 4960, Km 8.5; 🕙 9am-3pm & 5-7pm Mon-Thu, 9am-3pm Fri, 10am-2pm Sat) Dispenses information on Manzanillo and the state of Colima.

Tourist police (Map p476; ☎ 332-10-04; cnr Av 21 de Marzo & Madero) Stationed behind the Presidencia Municipal.

Sights & Activities
MUSEO UNIVERSITARIO DE ARQUEOLOGÍA
The University of Colima's **archaeological museum** (Map p476; ☎ 332-22-56; cnr Niños Héroes & Glorieta San Pedrito) presents interesting objects from ancient Colima state and rotating exhibits of contemporary Mexican art. At the time of research, the museum was closed for a long-delayed renovation project, with no end in sight.

BEACHES
Playa San Pedrito (Map p476), 1km northeast of the *zócalo*, is the closest – and dirtiest – beach to town. The next closest stretch of sand, spacious **Playa Las Brisas** (Map p475), caters to a few hotels. **Playa Azul** (Map p475) stretches northwest from Las Brisas and curves around to Las Hadas resort and the best beaches in the area: **La Audiencia**, **Santiago**, **Olas Altas** and **Miramar** (all on Map p475). Miramar and Olas Altas have the best surfing and bodysurfing waves in the area; surfboards can be rented at Miramar. Playa La Audiencia, lining a quiet cove on the west side of the Península de Santiago, has more tranquil water and is popular for waterskiing and other noisy motorized water sports.

Local buses marked 'Santiago,' 'Las Brisas' and 'Miramar' head around the bay to the towns of San Pedrito, Salahua, Santiago, Miramar and beaches along the way. 'Las Hadas' buses take a more circuitous, scenic route down the Península de Santiago. These buses pick up passengers from local bus stops along the length of Av 21 de Marzo, and from the main bus station every 10 minutes from 6am to 11pm.

WATER SPORTS
Snorkeling, windsurfing, sailing, waterskiing and deep-sea fishing are all popular around the bay. The scuba diving in Manzanillo can

CENTRAL PACIFIC COAST

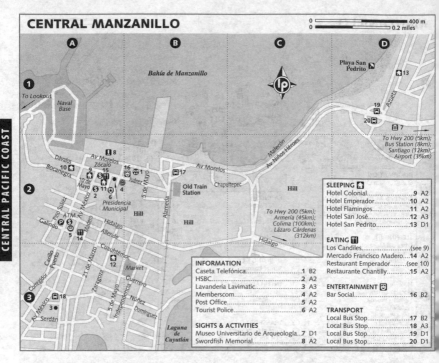

CENTRAL MANZANILLO

INFORMATION
Caseta Telefónica.................................1	B2
HSBC...2	A2
Lavandería Lavimatic............................3	A3
Memberscom.......................................4	A2
Post Office...5	A2
Tourist Police.......................................6	A2

SIGHTS & ACTIVITIES
Museo Universitario de Arqueología..7	D1
Swordfish Memorial..............................8	A2

SLEEPING
Hotel Colonial.......................................9	A2
Hotel Emperador................................10	A2
Hotel Flamingos..................................11	A2
Hotel San José....................................12	A3
Hotel San Pedrito...............................13	D1

EATING
Los Candiles....................................(see 9)	
Mercado Francisco Madero....14	A2
Restaurant Emperador.........(see 10)	
Restaurante Chantilly..........................15	A2

ENTERTAINMENT
Bar Social..16	B2

TRANSPORT
Local Bus Stop....................................17	B2
Local Bus Stop....................................18	A3
Local Bus Stop....................................19	D1
Local Bus Stop....................................20	D1

be spectacular, and there are many sites to explore – either off the beach or out on the bay. Try **Underworld Scuba** (Map p475; ☎ 333-36-78; www.divemanzanillo.com; Hwy 200, Km 15). Its complete PADI dive center charges M$873 for two-tank dives, including equipment, or M$3275 for PADI certification. Another good choice is **Neptune's Diving & Sports Center** (Map p475; ☎ 334-30-01; www.neptunesdiving.com; Hwy 200, Km 14.8), which offers similar dives, costs and services to those of Underworld Scuba. It also takes night dives and snorkeling trips.

FISHING
Sailfish and dorado are found in the waters off Manzanillo during every season of the year, while marlin and tuna are generally in the area from November to March. Supporting Manzanillo's only catch-and-release program (though they also offer standard fishing trips), the well-run **Ocean Pacific Adventures** (Map p475; ☎ 335-06-05; www.gomanzanillo.com/fishing) offers fishing trips on 26ft (M$2730) and 40ft cruisers ($3275); prices are for the whole boat and include gear, drinks and having your fish cooked up for dinner.

Festivals & Events
Fiestas de Mayo These fiestas celebrate the founding of Manzanillo in 1873. Festivities involve sporting competitions and other events over the first 10 days in May.
Sailfish Tournaments Manzanillo's famous international sailfish tournament (pescamanzanillo.com) takes place in early November; a smaller national tournament is held in February.

Sleeping
The cheapest hotels in town are located within a block or two of the *zócalo*. There are more places in the somewhat shabby area a few blocks south of the city center. Prices are naturally higher around the bay and Santiago Peninsula, where the better beaches are located. Prices listed here are for high-season, roughly December 1 to January 10 and Semana Santa (Easter Week). During the low season, prices may drop 20% to 40%.

BUDGET
Hotel San José (Map p476; ☎ 332-51-05; Cuauhtémoc 138; s/d/tr M$150/250/350) This well-kept budget option near the market is a tad more pleasant than the cheapies near the waterfront.

Hotel Emperador (Map p476; ☎ 332-23-74; Dávalos 69; s/d M$150/300) Half a block from the zócalo, this simple but clean refuge has some top-floor rooms that are marginally brighter than the rest. The hotel's restaurant is good and is one of the cheapest in town.

Hotel Flamingos (Map p476; ☎ 332-10-37; Madero 72; s/d M$200/250) On a quiet side street, this old cheapie offers 30 clean, basic rooms. Some can be musty; ask for one with two beds and an outside window.

MIDRANGE

Hotel San Pedrito (Map p476; ☎ 332-05-35; hotel sanpedrito@hotmail.com; Teniente Azueta 3; s/d M$300/400; P ✶ ✷) This hotel sits next to Playa San Pedrito, the beach nearest to downtown. Old tiled rooms are generous in size, but worn and dank – see a few before deciding. From the zócalo, walk 15 leisurely minutes (just over 1km) east along the malecón, or catch a local bus and get off at the archaeology museum.

Hotel Colonial (Map p476; ☎ 332-10-80, 332-06-68; Bocanegra 100; s/d M$320/480; P ✶) This atmospheric old hotel in the heart of downtown retains the character of an hacienda. Big rooms, tiled outdoor hallways and a thick colonial air make it the best deal in town.

Hotel Anita (Map p475; ☎ 333-01-61; s/d M$280/560) This is the cheapest place on Playa Santiago, with endless remodeling efforts and 36 large, faded rooms.

Hotel Villas La Audiencia (Map p475; ☎ 333-08-61; Península de Santiago; r/villas from M$613 P ✶ ✷) Although a bit far from Playa Audiencia (on the Santiago Peninsula), this moderately priced hotel is good value, especially for families. All the villas come with a kitchen and satellite TV.

ourpick Hotel La Posada (Map p475; ☎ 333-18-99; www.hotel-la-posada.info; Cárdenas 201; s/d M$580/780; P ✶ ▯ ✷) This charming, beachside B&B is a Manzanillo gem. Loyal guests return annually to the 'passionate pink' posada for its personalized service and amenities like the open-air dining room and library, big bright rooms decorated in Mexican handicrafts, an honor bar and a small pool overlooking the beach where you can watch ships – and the occasional whale – trawling the harbor.

El Hotelito (Map p475; ☎ 333-61-20; www.manzanillonn-hotelito.com; Blvd Miguel de la Madrid 3181; r incl breakfast M$750 P ✶ ▯ ✷) This cute, intimate inn has high-end amenities at a moderate price like the infinity pool with jacuzzi, bar, wi-fi, TV

and a beachside location that can't be beat. The eight rooms and hotel are tastefully decorated in a Mexican minimalist style.

Brisas del Mar Hotel & Villas (Map p475; ☎ 334-11-97; www.brisasdelmarmanzanillo.com; Playa Las Brisas; d/ste/villa M$800/1700/2400; P ✶ ✷) The beautiful, generous suites and villas at Brisas del Mar are all modern and colorfully decorated. They're beachside and within walking distance of some action. The huge pool is big enough for swimming laps.

Also consider the following hotels.

Hotel Brillamar (Map p475; ☎ 334-11-88; r from M$400, bungalows from M$900; ✶ ✷) All breezy rooms come with TV, and bungalows have a kitchen.

Hotel Marlyn (Map p475; ☎ 333-01-07; d/ste from M$600/650; ✶ ✷) An older property but good value for money, with pleasant rooms with TV and fan. The more expensive rooms have sea views and balconies.

Hotel Playa de Santiago (Map p475; ☎ 333-02-70; hoplasan@prodigy.net.mx; d/tr M$748/871, ste from M$1300) Has a good family rate, with two children under 10 staying free; the private sea-view balconies are amazing.

TOP END

Hotel Villas Los Angeles (Map p475; ☎ 333-17-02; www.villaslosangeles.com; Av La Cima s/n, Península de Santiago; s & d/t M$1000/1500; P ✗ ✶ ✷) A great top-end choice on the Santiago Peninsula, this family-run hotel is located in a secluded forest high above the hustle and bustle of Manzanillo. The rooms are big and comfy (more expensive rooms have kitchenettes), surrounding an immaculate pool and garden.

Dolphin Cove Inn (Map p475; ☎ 333-20-00, 334-15-15; www.dolphincoveinn.com; Av Vista Hermosa s/n, Península de Santiago; s/d M$1270, ste M$1600; P ✗ ✶ ▯ ✷) This cliffside hotel adjacent to Las Hadas and killer views has huge white and blue rooms with large marble bathroom, kitchenette and cable TV.

Tesoro Manzanillo (Map p475; ☎ 333-20-00; Av de la Audiencia 1, Playa Audiencia; d from M$2750; P ✗ ✶ ▯ ✷) A white, sterile hotel above Playa Audiencia. With endless amenities and activities, it mostly caters to tour groups and folks who enjoy spending their holiday in one place.

Brisas Las Hadas Golf Resort & Marina (Map p475; ☎ 331-01-01; www.brisas.com.mx; Av Vistahermosa s/n, Playa Audiencia; r incl breakfast M$3000, ste M$4214; P ✗ ✶ ▯ ✷) Manzanillo's most exclusive hotel sits above the bay like a Moorish seaside kingdom of white marble, spires and domes. The massive complex contains nearly 300 rooms and suites with marble floors, all-white furnishings and plentiful amenities; some have private pools. The Bo Derek flick *10* was shot here.

Eating

Several good down-to-earth options are on the *zócalo*, while chain and chain-like spots line Hwy 200 around the bay.

CENTRAL MANZANILLO

Restaurante Chantilly (Map p476; ☎ 332-01-94; Juárez 44; mains M$18-90) This crowded cafeteria and *nevería* (ice-cream parlor) has reasonably priced meals and snacks, plus a generous *comida corrida*, espresso and good ice cream.

Mercado Francisco Madero (Map p476; cnr Madero & Cuauhtémoc; mains M$20-50; ☑ 7am-6pm) This market has a number of inexpensive food stalls to choose from.

Restaurant Emperador (Map p476; ☎ 332-23-74; Hotel Emperador, Dávalos 69; mains M$20-50) Good, cheap and simple, this intimate ground-floor restaurant is popular with locals and budget travelers. Highlights here are the set breakfasts and the meat-and-seafood *comida corrida*.

Los Candiles (Map p476; ☎ 332-10-80; Hotel Colonial, Bocanegra 100; mains M$40-110) This restaurant opens onto a pleasant patio, has a menu of surf-and-turf fare, and a full bar with sports dominating the satellite TV.

OUTSIDE THE CENTER

Señor Sushi (Map p475; ☎ 334-53-87; Carretera 200, Km. 9.5; sushi from M$10; rolls M$28-60; ☑ noon-midnight) Tired of tacos? This thatched-roof Japanese restaurant serves up great sushi plus tasty teppanyaki and tempura dishes.

Juanito's (Map p475; ☎ 333-94-40/41; www.juanitos .com; Carretera 200, Km 13.5; mains M$20-120; ☑ 8am-11pm) A local tradition since 1976, Juanito's is popular for its American comfort food like pancake breakfasts, hamburgers, BBQ chicken and milkshakes, plus internet access, satellite TV and bookshelf.

Café Costeño (Map p475; ☎ 333-94-60; Lázaro Cárdenas 1613, Playa Las Brisas; breakfasts M$30-M$60; ☑ 9am-10:30pm Mon-Sat, 9am-1pm Sun) A good start to your day: French toast, hotcakes and omelettes are cheerfully served along with espresso and cappuccino. Sit in the shady garden out back.

Carnes y Tacos Julio (Map p475; ☎ 334-00-36; Carretera 200, Km 14.3; mains M$39-55; ☑ 8am-midnight) Savory grilled meat is the specialty at this lively place, but breakfast, pasta and other tourist-friendly fare won't disappoint.

El Fogón (Map p475; ☎ 333-30-94; Carretera 200, Km 9.5; mains M$75-110) This open-air steakhouse is a local favorite – a perfect choice for a romantic dinner. Cow is king here, including prime rib, beef fajitas and the house specialty, *molcajetes* (a hearty dish of meat and veg).

Colima Bay Café (Map p475; ☎ 333-11-50; Carretera 200, Km 6.5, Playa Azul; mains M$98-170; ☑ 2pm-1am) This super-fun Mexican restaurant keeps things lively, with thumping DJ music while guests graze on generous portions.

Drinking

For a perfect sunset with great atmosphere, head to the aptly-named **Sunset Lounge** (Map p475; ☎ 333-68-74 www.sunsetlounge.com.mx; Carretera 200; ☑ dusk to dawn). Happy hour is from 6pm to 8pm. Don't be late!

Behind the doors of the **Bar Social** (Map p476; cnr Av 21 de Marzo & Juárez; ☑ noon-midnight Mon-Sat) is a world frozen in the past; congenial elderly bartenders dote on you as the jukebox plays scratchy decades-old singles.

Entertainment

If you're in town on a Sunday evening, stop by the **zócalo** (Map p476), where multiple generations come out to enjoy ice cream and the warm evening air. On some nights, bands play traditional music from the gazebo. Every night around sunset, in a scene eerily reminiscent of the Hitchcock classic *The Birds*, swallows and blackbirds perch on overhead wires and fil the air with their songs – just make sure you're not standing underneath them for too long.

Manzanillo isn't exacyl known for its nightlife, but there are a few discos to keep club kids happy. The industrial **Nautilus** (Map p475; ☎ 334-33-31; Carretera 200, Km 9.5; admission M$50-150; ☑ Fri & Sat nights), looks like one of the many cargo ships anchored in nearby Manzanillo Bay. A superb sound system, lasers, smoke machines and strong drinks keep the crowds gyrating. Next door, **Bar de Felix** (Map p475; ☎ 333-1875) is a sedate lounge with comfy couches and chill-out Spanish music.

La K'Melia (Map p475; ☎ 333-74-87; Carretera 200 Km 9.5; admission M$20; ☑ noon-midnight) attracts Mexican families to its daily live music and dance shows.

Getting There & Away

AIR

Playa de Oro International Airport lies between a long and secluded white-sand beach and tropical groves of bananas and coconut, 35km northwest of Manzanillo's Zona Hotelera on Hwy 200.

Alaska Airlines (☎ 334-22-11; airport) Direct service to Los Angeles.

America West (☎ from the US 800-235-92-92) Direct service from Phoenix.

Continental (☎ from the US 800-231-08-56) Direct service to Houston.

Providing direct service to Mexico City:

Aeroméxico (☎ from the US 800-237-66-39, airport ☎ 334-12-26)

Mexicana (☎ from the US 800-531-79-21, from Mexico 55-998-5998)

BUS

Manzanillo's airport-like Central Camionera (Map p475) is northeast of the center near Playa Las Brisas, just off Blvd Miguel de la Madrid (Hwy 200). It's an organized place with two tourist offices, phones, eateries and left-luggage facilities. Frequent daily departures:

Destination	Fare	Duration
Armería	M$28	45min
Barra de Navidad	M$50-60	1-1½hr
Colima	M$60	1½-2hr
Guadalajara	M$140-210	4½-8hr
Lázaro Cárdenas	M$170-210	6hr
Mexico City	M$500-620	12hr
Puerto Vallarta	M$180-210	5-6½hr
San Patricio	M$60	1-1½hr
Melaque	M$50	1-1½hr

From its own terminal near Santiago at Carretera 200, Km 13.5, **ETN** (☎ 334-10-50) offers deluxe and 1st-class services to Barra de Navidad (M$60, one to 1½ hours, three daily), Colima (M$80, 1½ to two hours, seven daily) and Guadalajara (M$280, five hours, seven daily). ETN also provides daily service to the airport in Guadalajara (M$280).

Getting Around

There's no bus route to or from the airport, but most resorts have shuttle vans. **Transportes Turísticos Benito Juárez** (☎ 334-15-55) shuttles door-to-door to and from the airport for M$390 per person for private service (one or two people) or M$100 per person when three or more share the ride. A taxi between Manzanillo and the airport costs M$250 to M$350.

Local buses heading around the bay to San Pedrito, Salahua, Santiago, Miramar and beaches along the way depart every 10 minutes from 6am to 11pm from the corner of Madero and Domínguez, the corner of Juárez and Calle 21 de Marzo near the zócalo, and from the main bus station. Fares (pay the driver as you board) are M$5 to M$6, depending on how far you're going.

Taxis are plentiful in Manzanillo. From the bus station, a cab fare is around M$20 to the zócalo or Playa Azul, M$60 to Playa Santiago and M$90 to Playa Miramar. Always agree on a price before you get into the taxi.

CUYUTLÁN & EL PARAÍSO
☎ 313

With their black-sand beaches, gentle waves and laid-back attitudes, the twin resorts of Cuyutlán (population 926) and El Paraíso (population 189) are great places to get away from it all. The quiet little beach towns are popular with Mexican families but see few gringos. Cuyutlán has a better selection of hotels and services, but El Paraíso is less crowded and more tranquil. Bring your flip-flops; the black sand gets very hot!

Orientation & Information
Cuyutlán is at the southeastern end of Laguna de Cuyutlán, 40km southeast of Manzanillo. Sleepy El Paraíso is 6km southeast of Cuyutlán along the coast, but 12km by road. Both resorts have public telephones, mini supers convenience stores and beach supply shops. In Cuyutlán, check your email at **Jacana Ciber Cafe** (☎ 326-40-41; 96A Hidalgo; per hr M$15). For other basic services like banks or a post office, you'll have to visit Armería, a regional market town 12km east of Cuyutlán.

Sights & Activities
Cuyutlán is known for its **ola verde**, a giant green wave which appears offshore at dusk between April and May. It's supposedly caused by little green phosphorescent critters, but it's the subject of much local debate. The **Museo de Sal** (Salt Museum; suggested donation M$10; 9am-6pm), located in an old salt storage barn a block behind the zócalo, traces the region's history of sea salt extraction and economy.

El Tortuguero (☎ 328-86-76; tortugacuyutlan@hotmail.com; admission M$20; 9am-5pm) is a beachside turtle sanctuary located 4km east of Cuyutlán toward Paraíso. Since it opened in 1993, conservationists have released more than 500,000 Green, Black and Leatherback turtle hatchlings into the wild here. The center also has small iguana and crocodile sanctuaries, an education center, swimming pools and a picnic area. Don't miss the Tortuguero's **lagoon trips** on the **Palo Verde Estuary**, a nature preserve that's home to 1007 species of birds, including 257 migratory birds. *Lanchas* sail through mangrove tunnels and past sunbathing crocodiles. Tours cost M$40 for the 45-minute ride. Water conditions permitting, there's also a two-hour round-trip ride to El Paraíso (M$65).

Sleeping & Eating

The area's beachfront accommodations are cheaper than at other coastal resorts, but note that camping on the beaches is no longer permitted. The high seasons here are Christmas and around Semana Santa, when Cuyutlán's hotels are always booked solid. Both beaches are lined by dozens of *enramada* restaurants serving fresh, local seafood. At night, Cuyutlán's *zócalo* comes to life with vendors hawking cheap tacos, hot dogs and other greasy treats.

CUYUTLÁN

Hotel San Miguel (☎ 326-40-62; Hidalgo s/n; s M$140, d without/with breakfast M$280/360; ⌘) The best deal in town, the San Miguel has basic rooms and a rooftop pool and patio overlooking the town.

Hotel Fenix (☎ 326-40-82; www.cuyutlandirectory .com; hotelfenixcuyutlan@yahoo.com; Hidalgo 201; s M$150, d M$300-550 with air-con & TV; ⌘) The friendliest hotel in town is run by American Geoff and his Mexican wife Olivia. Remodeled rooms upstairs have air-con and satellite TV. The Fenix restaurant serves up the best *huevos rancheros* breakfast in town. Olivia, a real estate agent, can also help book extended-rental properties.

Hotel San Rafael (☎ 326-40-15; www.hotelsan rafael.com; Veracruz 46; s/d M$400-600; ⌘) The town's nicest hotel has 28 inviting rooms with sea views, a large pool and a huge outdoor thatched-roof restaurant.

Hotel María Victoria (☎ 326-40-04; Veracruz 10; r M$500-680; P ⌘) With its *Jetsons*-like architecture and beach-front location, Victoria was once Cuyutlán's most exclusive hotel; it has fallen into disrepair and no longer worth the going rates.

EL PARAÍSO

None of the hotels in El Paraíso offer much more than crumbling, grubby cement cells. Your best bet is **Hotel Paraíso** (☎ 322-10-32; M$315-385 with TV & air-con; P ⌘ ⌘), a two-building complex with 60 decent rooms and a nice restaurant. The better rooms are located in the new wing across the street from the beach. The hotel is located to the left of the T-intersection at the entrance to town.

Getting There & Away

Cuyutlán and Paraíso are connected to the world through Armería, a dusty but friendly little service center on Hwy 200, 46km southeast of Manzanillo and 55km southwest of Colima. From Armería a 12km paved road heads west past coconut orchards to Cuyutlán; a similar road runs 8km southwest from Armería to El Paraíso.

To reach either place by bus involves a transfer in Armería. Long-distance buses stop at a small depot on Hwy 200 in downtown Armería. Second-class buses run between Manzanillo to/from Armería every 15 minutes from 6am to midnight (M$25, 45 minutes) and to Colima from Armería every half-hour from 5:45am to 10:30pm (M$25, 45 minutes). Buses also go every 20 minutes to Tecomán (M$70, 15 minutes), where you can connect with buses heading southeast on Hwy 200 to Lázaro Cárdenas and elsewhere. They all stop along the roadside on Hwy 200 in the center of Armería.

Buses to Cuyutlán and El Paraíso depart from Armería's market, two blocks north and one block east of the long-distance bus stop. To Cuyutlán (M$8.50, 20 minutes), they depart every half-hour from 6am to 7:30pm. To El Paraíso (M$60, 15 minutes), they go every 45 minutes.

There are no buses directly between Cuyutlán and El Paraíso; you must return to Armería and change buses again. It's possible to walk along the beach between Cuyutlán and El Paraíso in about two hours; bring plenty of water and only go during daylight. The beach between the Tortuguero and El Paraíso is completely deserted and perfect for skinny-dipping!

BOCA DE PASCUALES

☎ 313 / pop 60

Boca de Pascuales is a legendary surf that attracts the best boarders from around the world. Aggressive barrel swells range from

---

EDGAR ÁLVAREZ

This 30-year-old surfboard shaper and hotel owner lives at Boca de Pascuales.

When did you take up surfing? I learned to surf about 15 years ago and have been doing it ever since. I used to play football (soccer) on the beach and I'd watch the California guys surfing and thought it looked like fun. So I started practicing, little by little, until I could ride the big swells. Boca de Pascuales has some of the best surfing in the world. The waves attract surfers and professionals from as far away as Tasmania.

Can you tell us about your surfboard business? I've been repairing boards for a while and a few years ago I stated making my own boards – Pascuales Surfboards. A new, handmade board costs between M$2500 and M$3000 pesos.

What is it about surfing that attracts you? I think surfing is the greatest sport in the world. You're out there alone, nobody telling you what to do. It's just you and the wave.

2m to 5m in the summer season and storm waves occasionally reach 10m. There's a heavy beach break. Pascuales is strictly for experienced surfers; don't tempt fate if you're not up to speed.

Sleeping & Eating

Hotel Real de Pascuales (☎ 329-4229 or 108-3253; www.pascualessurf.com.mx; tent or hammock per person M$30, r without/with air-con M$250/350) Better known as Edgar's Place, this hotel is the local surfing nexus. Edgar Álvarez welcomes surfers from all over the world and fixes their boards when they get munched. The rooms are spartan to the extreme, but that's the way the dudes seem to like it.

Paco's Hotel (☎ cell phone 200-1247362; magofra_15_38@hotmail.com; r without/with air-con M$350/400) Previously known as Estrella del Surf, Paco's is the nicer of the two hotels in town. Each comfy room has a different flower theme, lovingly painted and decorated by Paco's daughter Lulu. The hotel also has a decent onsite restaurant.

ourpick Las Hamacas del Mayor (☎ 324-0074; www.lashamacasdelmayor.com.mx; mains M$70-180; ☼ 10am-6pm; P ☼) A local tradition since 1953, Las Hamacas is one of the most famous restaurants in Colima state despite its off-the-beaten-path location. The two-level restaurant seats 1000 people and is open every day of the year. Strolling mariachis entertain the crowd. A swimming pool keeps the kids busy. Exquisite seafood specialties include fish fillet stuffed with octopus and shrimp, marinated in garlic sauce. Absolutely divine!

Getting There & Away

To get to Pascuales, travel first to the town of Tecomán, 12km east of Armería. Combis between Tecomán's central bus station and Pascuales run once an hour from 7am to 8pm (M$6, 20 minutes). A taxi in either direction will set you back M$70. If driving, follow the sign from downtown about 10km to the beach.

MICHOACÁN COAST

Highway 200 hugs the shoreline most of the way along the beautiful 250km coast of Michoacán, one of Mexico's most beautiful states. The route passes dozens of untouched beaches – some with wide expanses of golden sand, some tucked into tiny rocky coves, some at river mouths where quiet estuaries harbor multitudes of birds. Several have gentle lapping waves that are good for swimming, while others have big breakers suitable for surfing. Many of the beaches are uninhabited, but some have small communities. Mango, coconut, papaya and banana plantations line the highway, while the green peaks of the Sierra Madre del Sur form a lush backdrop inland. Blue signs or billboards along Highway 200 mark the turnoffs for most beaches.

Boca de Apiza

At the mouth of the Río Coahuayana, which forms the Michoacán–Colima border, Boca de Apiza is a mangrove-lined, hot black-sand beach with a 300m line of competing seafood *enramadas*. On Sunday afternoons it gets quite busy with local kids splashing in the river. To get here, turn off Hwy 200 at the town of Coahuayana (Km 228) and continue about 4km to the beach. On the Michoacán side, Mexican families have built many *palapa* shelters for Sunday picnics. A long beach heads northwards, with a sandy access road going inland 6.5km to meet back with Hwy

200. Kilometer markers begin counting down from Km231 at the state border.

San Juan de Alima

Twenty kilometers south of Boca de Apiza, near where the highway meets the coast, is the cobblestoned town of **San Juan de Alima** (Km 211). It's popular with surfers, with medium-sized waves and creamy breakers just off the coast. There are several beachfront restaurants and modern hotels, *all* of them blue.

Hotel Parador (☎ 327-90-38, 327-90-21; s M$250, d without/with air-con M$400/450; P ❄) A good variety of rooms, some with balconies and views. The hotel also has the most popular restaurant in town.

Hotel San Juan (☎ 327-90-11; r without/with air-con 300/450; P ❄) The light-blue hotel has San Juan's only internet café. Rooms are basic but clean.

Las Brisas

The cliff-hugging road south of San Juan climbs above the coast, offering gorgeous views of desolate sandy beaches below. The tiny white strands of **Las Brisas** (Km 207) is accented by just a few *palapa* restaurants and one hotel, the white stucco **Hotel Paraíso** (☎ 327-90-55; www.paraisolasbrisasmichoacan.com; s/d M$600/800; P ❄). For bird-watchers, there is a nice mangrove lagoon about 1km south of town.

Playa La Ticla

Another renowned surfing destination, **Playa La Ticla** (Km 183) is known for its long, left point break and mostly attracts foreign surfers with their own vehicles. The long beach is divided by a freshwater, swimmable river. There are a few *enramadas* serving fresh seafood; some have basic rooms for rent.

Faro de Bucerías

Faro de Bucerías, or Diver's Lighthouse (Km 173), is a sheltered crescent beach with clear, pale-blue waters and yellow sand that's perfect for snorkeling, swimming or sun worshiping. The local Nahua community operate a long line of *palapa* seafood restaurants offering plentiful, fat lobsters. There are no hotels here, but you can bring your own RV or pitch a tent under a *palapa*.

Playa Maruata

With clear turquoise waters and golden sandy beaches, **Playa Maruata** (Km 150) is the most beautiful beach in Michoacán. The Nahua fishing village has a bit of a hippie reputation, attracting beach bums from all over. It's a tranquil, friendly place to hang out with your sweetie or a large stack of paperbacks.

Maruata actually has three beaches, each with its own unique character. The left (eastern) is the longest, a 3km pristine crescent-shaped beach with creamy yellow sand and calm waves perfect for swimming and snorkeling. The small middle arc is okay for strong swimmers. It's sheltered by climbable rocky heads riddled with caves, tunnels and blow holes, and marked by the unusual **Dedo de Dios** (God's Finger) formation rising from the sea. The far-right (western) beach is known as **Playa de los Muertos** (Beach of the Dead), and for good reason; it has dangerous currents and ferocious waves. During low tide, you can scale the rocks on the far right side of *Muertos* to reach a secluded cove where discreet nude sunbathing is tolerated. But don't get stuck here when the tide comes in. A crucifix on the rocks serves as a stark memorial to the people who have been swallowed by the sea.

Playa Maruata is also the principal Mexican beach where black sea turtles lay their eggs (each night from June to December). Conservationist groups also release hatchlings here.

There's a small grocery store and a restaurant near the town's bleak plaza, but otherwise there are no real concrete structures or hotels. The *enramadas* on the left beach serve delicious fresh seafood and are also your best bet for camping. Most charge M$25 per person to pitch a tent or rent a hammock; some have tents to rent for an extra M$50. Those who need four semi-solid walls can find a few rustic *cabañas* for M$120 to M$250. There are several discreet parking spots for RVs.

Barra de Nexpa

☎ 753 / pop 110

At Km 55.75, just north of Puente Nexpa bridge and 1km from the highway down a rough cobbled road, lies the small community of Nexpa. It's long been a haven for surfers, attracted to the salt-and-pepper sandbar and healthy waves (which build up and curl sharply in the mornings). But word has gotten out, and nonsurfers have now discovered this quaint little village thanks to its welcoming, laid-back atmosphere, lovely empty beach and delicious restaurants.

SLEEPING & EATING

Águilas del Mar (☎ 531-52-55; campsites per person M$25, s/d M$150/180 P) Águilas has several simple rooms with a communal bathroom and shared balconies with hammocks. The restaurant (open Thursday to Tuesday) serves up an amazing *Pulpo al Diablo* – octopus marinated in a sweet and spicy sauce.

Río Nexpa Rooms (☎ 531-52-55; www.surf-mexico .com/sites/nexpa; r M$300; P) This beautifully crafted southeast Asian-style *palapa*, about 200m inland along the river, has four comfortable rooms with three full-sized beds and a loft. There's a shared kitchen, a lagoonside garden area and a tranquil communal sitting room.

Villas Cheyo's (☎ 110-30-93; cheyo_nexpa@hotmail .com; cabañas M$400-800) Originally called Gilberto's, this was the town's first 'hotel,' built by Don Gilberto, the father of Nexpa's surf scene. There's a variety of *cabañas*, some more rustic than others, some with kitchen and most with hammocks. There's also a communal kitchen and shower block for campers/RVs, and Gilberto Jr offers taxi service to Caleta de Campos (M$50). Look for Cheyo's sign on the right side as you enter town.

Mar De Noche (☎ 531-50-37, 118-39-31; www.nex pasurf.com; r & cabañas M$1000, ste M$1500) The most luxurious rooms in town, the two-story *cabañas* have comfy beds, kitchens and private bathrooms. There's also an adjacent six-room hotel with modern amenities. Low-season prices are about a third of the high season ones given. The beachfront restaurant (open 9am to 9pm), decorated with hand-carved wood columns depicting scenes of Mexican life, has a terrific breakfast menu (M$10 to M$35). Dinner costs about M$70 to M$100.

La Isla Restaurant (mains M$25-99) The place where gringos gather in the morning for the serve-yourself coffee.

Restaurant Chicho's (mains M$30-65) Good food, good views and basic *cabañas* for rent (singles/doubles M$150/250,). It's just south of the well-signed and always crowded La Isla Restaurant.

The **Surf Shop** (☎ 106-8553, 🕘 9am-9pm) behind La Isla has a small grocery store, internet café and offers surfboard rentals for M$40 per hour or M$150 per day.

Caleta de Campos
☎ 753 / pop 2000
Caleta (Km 50) is a regional service center that has all the essentials, including a gas sta-

tion, a *caseta*, late-night *taquerías* (taco stalls) and *torta* (sandwich) shops, a pharmacy and several grocery stores. The main part of town is on a bluff overlooking an azure bay. The beach below is not as charming as Nexpa, but it does have a nice selection of seafood *enramadas*, and the protected beach is better for novice surfers. The area's best surf shop, **Surf y Espuma** (☎ 531-52-55; surfboard rental per day M$100), has two locations, one on the main drag near Hotel Yuritzi and a smaller shop on the beach.

Hotel Los Arcos (☎ 531-50-38; s/d M$200/250, s/d with air-con & hot water M$400/500; P 🐾), toward the ocean at the end of the main drag, is a bit run-down, but the owners are friendly and the bird's-eye view of the Bahía de Bufadero's blowhole is stunning.

Hotel Yuritzi (www.hotelyuritzi.com; Corregidora 10; s/d M$350/400, s/d with air-con & TV M$450/550; P 🐾 🛏) is modern, well maintained and comfortable, and is preferred by business travelers and families.

Hourly buses depart Caleta's *zócalo* for Lázaro Cárdenas (M$40, 1½ hours) from 5am to 7pm. A taxi between Caleta de Campos and Barra de Nexpa costs about M$50.

Playa Azul
☎ 753 / pop 3100
The largest, most built-up resort on the Michoacán Coast, Playa Azul is a swimmer's paradise: a wide beach with café con leche–colored sands, clear aqua-green water, gently rolling waves and a sandy shallow bottom – you can walk 100m out to sea and still only be waist-deep. The sounds of strumming mariachis and clinking beer bottles beckon from the many beachside *palapa* restaurants. Unfortunately, Playa Azul's downtown is not as inviting, with litter everywhere, dusty streets covered in potholes and a dilapidated *zócalo* occupied by dodgy-looking folks. A nearby alternative is Laguna Pichi, a freshwater lake 2.5km east of town that's surrounded by palm trees and seafood *enramadas*. Boat trips take visitors to view the flora and fauna that inhabit the surrounding mangrove forest. But don't forget bug spray.

SLEEPING & EATING
Hotel Playa Azul (☎ 536-00 24/91; Carranza s/n; campsites/RV sites M$150/180, r without/with air-con & TV M$550/820; P 🐾 🛏) The upmarket, 73-room Playa Azul has a small trailer park and

enjoyable rooms. Kids will love the huge pool and giant waterslide; adults will love the swim-up bar. The poolside Las Gaviotas restaurant/bar is a good bet for anything from pizza to *pozole*.

Hotel María Isabel (☎ 536-00-16; Madero s/n; s/d M$200/300, s/d with air-con & TV M$250/400; P X R) On the far (east) side of the plaza, this hotel has frugal but clean rooms and friendly staff.

Hotel Andrea (☎ 536-02-51; Emiliano Zapata 879; s/d M$250, tr/q M$550; P) A great budget choice just one block from the beach, this new hotel has modern large rooms and huge bathrooms.

Hotel María Teresa (☎ 536-00-05; Independencia 626; s/d M$250/450, s/d with air-con & TV M$300/550; X R) The 42 large and comfy balconied rooms are fresh and up-to-date. There's also a poolside *palapa* restaurant-bar, an attractive garden patio and a small nightclub. Located two blocks north of the plaza.

There are several *cocina económica* restaurants on Av Aguiles Serdan, around the corner from Hotel Playa Azul. Two good choices are **Restaurant Galdy** and **Cocina Económica Doña Tere**, where you can grab tasty meals for less than M$40.

Colectivo minivans run every 10 minutes from 5am to 9pm between Playa Azul and Lázaro Cárdenas (M$12, 30 minutes, 24km). Taxis between Playa Azul and Lázaro Cárdenas cost around M$100. If you're traveling here by long-distance bus, ask the driver to let you off in La Mira, at the intersection of Hwys 200 and 37. From here, you can catch a *colectivo* to Playa Azul (M$6, 15 minutes).

LÁZARO CÁRDENAS
☎ 753 / pop 74,900

As an industrial port city, Lázaro has nothing of real interest for travelers – but because it's a hub for several bus lines, travelers do pass through. Lázaro is also a regional service center where you will find banks, a post office, pharmacies and a Pemex station.

Sleeping & Eating

There are several cheap hotels and restaurants clustered around the bus terminals.

Hotel Reyna Pio (☎ 532-06-20; Corregidora 78; s/d M$264/319; X) A good, friendly budget hotel with clean, spacious rooms. It's located on the corner of Av 8 de Mayo, a block west of Av Lázaro Cárdenas and near the bus terminals.

Hotel Casablanca (☎ 537-34-81; www.hcasablanca .com.mx; Nicolás Bravo 475; s/d M$480/760; P X 📺 R)

Catering to business travelers, this hotel has 56 modern rooms with balconies and wide windows overlooking the city or mountains. Other features include TVs, pool (with Jacuzzi) and secure parking. Look for this high-rise a block east of Av Lázaro Cárdenas.

NH Krystal Express (☎ 533-290-00; www.nh-hotels .com; Circuito de las Universidades 60; r/ste M$1657/1842; P X R 📺 R) This four-star, corporate hotel has posh rooms with modern amenities including a gym, pool and restaurant. It's located on the Av Lázaro Cárdenas traffic circle about one mile north of the bus terminals.

Getting There & Away

Lázaro has four bus terminals, all within a few blocks of each other. **Galeana** (☎ 532-02-62) and **Parhikuni** (☎ 532-30-06), with services northwest to Manzanillo and inland to Uruapan and Morelia, share a **terminal** (Lázaro Cárdenas 1810). Directly across the street, La Línea, Vía Plus, Sur de Jalisco, Autovías and Ómnibus de Mexico share another **terminal** (☎ 537-18-50; Lázaro Cárdenas 1791) and serve the same destinations as Galeana and Parhikuni, plus Colima, Guadalajara and Mexico City.

The **Estrella Blanca terminal** (☎ 532-11-71; Francisco Villa 65), two blocks west behind the Galeana terminal, is also home base for TuriStar Sur and Elite. From here, buses head southeast to Zihuatanejo, Acapulco and Oaxaca; up the coast to Manzanillo, Mazatlán and Tijuana; and inland to Uruapan, Morelia and Mexico City. The **Estrella de Oro terminal** (☎ 532-02-75; Corregidora 318) is one block north and two blocks west of Estrella Blanca and serves Zihuatanejo, Acapulco and Mexico City.

There are frequent daily buses:

Destination	Fare	Duration
Acapulco	M$144-183	6-7hr
Caleta de Campos	M$44	1½hr
Colima	M$174	4-6½hr
Guadalajara	M$400	9-11hr
Manzanillo	M$175-225	6-7hr
Mexico City	M$450	8-12hr
Morelia	M$300-360	4-8hr
Puerto Vallarta	M$355	12hr
Uruapan	M$160-210	3-6hr
Zihuatanejo	M$61	2-3hr

Combis to Playa Azul via La Mira (M$12, 30 minutes, 24km) trawl Av Lázaro Cárdenas every 10 minutes from 5am to 9pm. A taxi between Lázaro Cárdenas and Playa Azul costs M$100 to M$120.

TRONCONES & MAJAHUA
☎ 755 / pop 600

Not long ago, Troncones was a poor, sleepy fishing and farming village. That all changed in the mid-1990s when wealthy North American colonists arrived and began building luxury beachfront vacation homes and B&Bs. Tourists followed for the unspoiled beaches, relaxing atmosphere and world-class surfing. Development continues and is now spilling over into neighboring Majahua. Despite this, Troncones retains its sleepy village feel; chickens and burros roam wild, the single main street is still unpaved and there is precious little to do aside from relaxing in a hammock and soaking up the sun.

Orientation & Information

Troncones is located about 25km northwest of Ixtapa, at the end of a 3km paved road from Hwy 200. The paved road ends at a T-intersection where it connects to the dusty beachfront road along Troncones.

Troncones is made up of four beach communities: Troncones, Troncones Point, Manzanillo Bay and Majahua. The majority of tourist attractions are to the right (northwest) of the T-intersection, where the dirt road runs 1km past Troncones Point to reach the calmer waters of Manzanillo Bay. The road continues a short way to the small village of Majahua, where another dirt road (rough in the wet season) leads back out to Hwy 200.

Of the four communities, Troncones is the most built up. At the T-intersection you'll find a few small grocery stores, laundry and several cheap food vendors. The surf in Troncones and Troncones Point is rough and more geared to surfers. Manzanillo Bay is a sheltered cove more conducive to swimming and norkeling, either in the bay or in the lovely tide pools that dot the rocky shore. Majahua is a traditional fishing village with a few *enramada* restaurants and a mellow beach layered with fine shells for beachcombers.

Activities

SURFING

Troncones has several world-class surf spots. The beach breaks here can be excellent in summer, but the wave to chase is the left at **Troncones Point**. When it's small, the take-off is right over the rocks (complete with sea urchins), but when it's big, it's beautiful and beefy and rolls halfway across the bay.

The **surf shop** at the Inn at Manzanillo Bay (p486) rents out an excellent selection of short and long boards, as well as boogie boards (M$120 half-day, M$240 full day). It also offers surf lessons (M$500, 90 minutes) and arranges guided boat trips to many of the best local surf spots. **Mexcalli Surf School** (☎ 101-39-04; surfboard rentals M$200 per day), about 100m inland from the T-intersection, offers board lessons, rentals and repairs.

OTHER ACTIVITIES

There's good **snorkeling** and **swimming** in the protected cove off Playa Manzanillo. **Horseback riding** is quite popular; locals stroll the beach with their steeds looking for customers. Other activities include **mountain biking**, **kayaking**, **fishing**, **hiking**, **bird-watching**, **sea-turtle spotting** and **spelunking** through the limestone cave system near Majahua. These and many other activities can be arranged through **Costa Nativa Eco Tours** (☎ cell phone 755-5563616), or through your hotel.

Sleeping & Eating

Reservations are necessary almost everywhere during the high season (November through April); several places also require multiple-night stays. During low season, prices can be 50% lower, but be aware that many lodging facilities close down for the summer.

TRONCONES

Mar y Sol (☎ 553-28-40; r with fan/air-con M$250/300) Above the Miscelánea Jasmín grocery store at the T-intersection, this place has basic rooms, some with a large shared balcony.

our pick Quinta d'Liz (☎ 553-29-14; www.playatroncones.com; d with breakfast M$400) Quinta d'Liz, run by friendly and laid-back owner Luis, is a collection of six colorful, round bungalows just steps from the beach. Each simple room has a private bathroom, fan and a good double bed. There's also a communal kitchen to store your drinks for the nightly gatherings on the patio. It's located southeast (left) of the T.

El Burro Borracho (☎ 553-28-34; www.burroborracho.com; ☉ 11:30am-10pm; mains M$20-M$250) The popular and laid-back Burro Borracho (Drunk Donkey) is owned by Dewey McMillin, the 'father' of modern-day Troncones. House specialties include fresh seafood and US classics. Live folklore dancing is held every Sunday night. Simple bungalows (M$500) are also available.

Casa Ki (☎ 553-28-15; www.casa-ki.com; bungalows M$950-1200, house M$2000) A charming retreat, Ki features a thoughtfully furnished main house sleeping up to six people and four colorful free-standing bungalows with access to a communal kitchen. It's all set on a verdant beachside property.

Present Moment Retreat (☎ 103-00-11; www.present momentretreat.com; s M$2060, d per person M$1215; weekly all-inclusive packages available; restaurant mains M$160-220; P ⚲ V) A stunning 'conscious living' spa resort, Present Moment is a haven for the body and mind, specializing in yoga, meditation and massage. The 10 private, thatched-roof bungalows are minimal but luxurious, all surrounding a beautiful pool and gardens. The organic restaurant is the best (and priciest) in town, with dishes for vegetarians and carnivores alike.

MANZANILLO BAY

Hacienda Edén (☎ 553-28-02; www.edenmex.com; r M$920, bungalows M$920-$1030; ste M$1300; P ⛭) On Playa Manzanillo, 4km north of the T-intersection, this tranquil beachfront gem has lovingly decorated bungalows, hotel rooms and air-conditioned suites. Tropical hardwoods, Talavera tiles, high-beamed ceilings and other touches are used to great advantage. Edén is also home to the gourmet Cocina del Sol restaurant and bar, and the boutique gift shop Fruity Keiko.

Inn at Manzanillo Bay (☎ 553-28-84; www.manzanil lobay.com; Playa Manzanillo; bungalows M$1500; restaurant mains M$80-300; P 🖳 ⚲) This lovely guest house has 10 thatched-roof bungalows with king-sized beds, canopied mosquito netting, traditional Mexican furnishings, ceiling fans and hammocked terraces. There's also a popular restaurant and bar, a surf shop and easy access to the primo break at Troncones Point.

Casa Manzanillo (☎ 553-28-31; www.innmexico .com; r M$1625-2166; P ⛭ ⚲) The whimsical architecture features an open floor plan with a three-story-tall thatched roof, and rooms interconnected by wooden gangways and stairs. Rooms look a bit dated, but are large and comfy. The new infinity pool overlooking the beach is a major plus.

MAJAHUA

The Resort at Majahua Palms (☎ 556-08-51; www .majahuapalms.com; d/q M$1500/2000; apt for 8 M$3000; res-

taurant mains M$65-220; P ⚲) This secluded resort 6km northwest of the T-intersection is a good choice for families, with large, thatched bungalows and pleasant decor. The pool and patio are huge, and the restaurant has an extensive Mexican and American menu.

Getting There & Away

Driving from Ixtapa or Zihuatanejo, head northwest on Hwy 200 toward Lázaro Cárdenas. Just north of Km 30 you'll see the marked turnoff for Troncones; follow this winding paved road 3km west to the beach.

Second-class buses heading northwest toward Lázaro Cárdenas or La Unión from Zihuatanejo's long-distance terminals will drop you at the turnoff for Troncones (M$20, 45 minutes) if you ask. You can also catch La Unión–bound buses from the stop a couple of blocks east of Zihuatanejo's market (M$12).

White *colectivo* vans shuttle between Hwy 200 and Troncones roughly every half-hour (M$6); some continue on to Majahua. In a pinch, hitchhiking is common here.

A taxi from Zihuatanejo airport to Troncones will set you back almost M$700. From Zihuatanejo or Ixtapa, you'll pay about M$350.

IXTAPA
☎ 755 / pop 6400

At first glance, Ixtapa is a model of perfection. The beaches are spotless. The glitzy hotels are modern and luxurious. Not a palm tree or blade of grass out of place. But dig deeper and you'll soon realize it's all a mirage. Ixtapa was a huge coconut plantation until the late 1970s, when Fonatur (the Mexican government's tourism development group) decided that the Pacific coast needed a Cancún-like resort. The result was Ixtapa, a soulless, sterile collection of concrete high-rises and chain restaurants. Locals have attempted to repair that image by opening traditional restaurants and focusing on the area's natural beauty. But Ixtapa remains a Disneyfied resort that will never be able to manufacture the charm or character of its sister city, Zihuatanejo.

Information

Telecomm (🕙 9am-3pm Mon-Fri) Found behind the tourist office.
Tourist office (Sefotur; ☎ 553-19-67; 🕙 8am-8:30pm Mon-Fri, to 3pm Sat) This state-run office is in Plaza Los Patios, across from Señor Frogs. Be aware that the many

IXTAPA & ZIHUATANEJO

unofficial sidewalk kiosks offering 'tourist information' are actually touting time-share schemes.

Tourist police (☎ 553-20-08; Centro Comercial La Puerta) Close to the tourist office.

The *centro commercial* shopping center on Blvd Ixtapa contains banks, ATMs, currency exchange shops, a 24-hour pharmacy, a movie theater, an overpriced Internet café and a grocery store. The nearest post office is in Zihuatanejo.

Sights
BEACHES

Ixtapa's big hotels line **Playa del Palmar**, a long, broad stretch of white sand that's often overrun by parasail and Jet-ski outfits. Be very

careful if you swim here: the large waves crash straight down and there's a powerful undertow. Just getting onto the beach can be a pain if you're not a hotel guest. There are few public access ways to the beach, and the only other option is to cut through a hotel lobby and hope you don't get hassled by snobby doormen.

Playa Escolleras, at the west end of Playa del Palmar near the entrance to the marina, has a strong break and is favored by surfers. Further west past Punta Ixtapa, **Playa Quieta** and **Playa Linda** are popular with locals.

Isla Ixtapa is a beautiful oasis from the concrete jungle of Ixtapa. The turquoise waters are crystal-clear, calm and great for snorkeling (gear rentals cost M$50 per day). Isla Ixtapa has four beaches; **Playa Corales** on the back side of the island is the nicest and quietest, with soft white sand, an offshore coral reef and little tide pools harboring starfish and sea urchins. *Enramada* seafood restaurants and massage providers dot the island. Frequent boats to Isla Ixtapa depart from Playa Linda's pier from 9am to 5pm (M$45 round-trip, five minutes each way).

Playa Linda has a small **Cocodrilario**, or crocodile reserve, that is also home to fat iguanas and several bird species. You can watch the crocs from the safety of the wooden viewing platform located near the bus stop.

Activities

Bicycling is a breeze along a 15km *ciclopista* (bicycle path) that stretches from Playa Linda, north of Ixtapa, practically into Zihuatanejo. Mountain bikes can be rented in Ixtapa from **Fun on Wheels** (☎ 553-02-59; Centro Comercial Los Patios; ☉ 9am-8pm) for M$50/200 per hour/day.

Scuba diving is popular in the warm, clear waters. Both of the Zihuatanejo diving outfits (p491) take trips to several sites in the area.

The **Ixtapa Club de Golf Palma Real** (☎ 553-10-62) and the **Marina Ixtapa Golf Club** (☎ 553-14-10) both have 18-hole courses, tennis courts and swimming pools. The **yacht club** (☎ 553-11-31; Porto Ixtapa) is beside the Ixtapa Marina. **Horseback riding** (M$150 per hour) is available at Playa Linda.

Parque Aventura (☎ 115-17-33; www.parque-aventura.com; ☉ 8:30am-6pm), about 5km north of Ixtapa on Hwy 200, is an outdoor adventure course through the woods with suspension bridges and zip-lines.

Magic World (☎ 553-13-59; admission M$70; ☉ 10:30am-5:30pm) aquatic park has rides, waterslides, toboggans and other amusements. At **Delfiniti** (☎ 553-27-07; www.delfiniti.com; ☉ 10am-4pm), swim with dolphins for a ridiculous M$860 for 20 minutes, or ogle them underwater for free through the side of their glassed aquarium.

Adventours (☎ 553-10-69, 553-19-46; www.ixtapa-adventours.com) offers a variety of guided 'ecological tours' in Ixtapa and Zihuatanejo. Popular packages include a **snorkeling** and **kayaking** tour of Isla Ixtapa, and a **birding** and **crocodile-watching** walking tour.

Sleeping

With the exception of the campground, Ixtapa's resorts are all top-end. Prices listed here are rack rates for high season, which runs from mid-December to mid-January plus Easter week. Prices can drop by 25% or more the rest of the year. Better rates are often available through package deals or from hotel websites.

Trailer Park Ixtapa (☎ 552-02-95; trailerparkixtapa@gmail.com; campsites per person M$70; RV sites M$300) Ixtapa's only budget accommodations is a lovely new beachfront campground located in a coconut grove. The large, gated resort has modern amenities includinf a grocery, showers, clubhouse, restaurant, laundromat and wi-fi. It's located 1.7km north of Playa Linda, where the highway from Ixtapa and the *ciclopista* terminate.

NH Krystal Ixtapa (☎ 553-03-33; www.nh-hotels.com; Blvd Ixtapa s/n; d from M$998; P ⊗ ⊗ ⊛) has some of the best-value rooms on the strip (all with ocean view), an excellent pool, seven restaurants, the popular nightclub Christine and a kids' club.

Holiday Inn Ixtapa (☎ 555-05-00; www.holiday-inn.com; Av Paseo del Palmar 1; rooms M$1302-3363; P ⊗ ⊗ ⊛) A sterile business hotel located two blocks behind the tourist market has comfortable rooms with corporate-style furnishings and sliding glass balcony doors but, oddly, no balconies.

Barceló Ixtapa Beach (☎ 555-20-00; www.barceloixtapa.com; Blvd Ixtapa s/n; per person all-inclusive from M$1515; P ⊗ ⊗ ⊛ ⊛) The Barceló is an all-inclusive resort that caters to families and groups. The hotel has a fine pool and patio area, but the overly loud dance music there is a mood-killer.

Las Brisas Ixtapa Resort (☎ 553-21-21; www.brisas.com.mx; from M$2400; P ⊗ ⊗ ⊔ ⊛ ⊛) An enormous orange wedge rising from the sands, Brisas sits on an isolated stretch of Playa Vista Hermosa south of Ixtapa's main strip. The hotel has recently completed a two-year renovation. The result is a contemporary Mexican interior with lots of color and wood throughout. All 416 rooms have extra-large terraces with 1st-rate ocean views and hammocks. The lobby bar is one of the best in town.

Hotel Presidente Inter-Continental (☎ 553-00-18, in the US 888-424-6835; http://ixtapa.intercontinental.com; Blvd Ixtapa s/n; d incl breakfast M$2560-M$4920; P ⊗ ⊗ ⊔ ⊛ ⊛) One of the most popular beachfront hotels is 1st-class all the way, with a gym, sauna, tennis courts, seven restaurants and a kids' club with Spanish classes for little ones.

Eating

Chili Beans (☎ 553-33-13; www.chilibeansixtapa.com; Ixtapa Plaza; mains M$30-120; ☻ 7:30am-11pm) An excellent choice for good, traditional Mexican food such as *chile rellenos* and chicken *mole*. It's a popular breakfast spot for North American favorites like blueberry pancakes and omelettes as big as your head.

Señor Frog's (☎ 553-22-82; Blvd Ixtapa s/n; mains M$56-215) The Frog serves up zany antics along with familiar Mexican dishes, burgers and iguana.

Frog's Ito (☎ 553-22-82; Blvd Ixtapa s/n; sushi per piece M$15-25, rolls M$25-95) Serves sushi, noodle dishes and Asian salads.

Soleiado (☎ 553-21-01; Blvd Ixtapa; mains M$75-250; ☻ 8am-11pm) Extremely good, moderately priced, always crowded sidewalk café opposite the Park Royal hotel has an extensive international menu ranging from eggs Benedict breakfast to Schezuan chicken or linguini.

Villa de la Selva (☎ 553-03-62; hwww.villadelaselva .com; Paseo de la Roca Lote D; mains M$160-475; ☻ 7pm-late) This elegant contemporary Mediterranean restaurant was once the former home of Mexican president Luis Echeverría. The cliffside villa has superb sunset and ocean views. Offerings include crab tacos, salmon with couscous, duck breast, filet mignon and an extensive wine list. Reservations a must.

Entertainment

All the big hotels have bars and nightclubs. Many also have discos; in the low season most of these charge less and open fewer nights.

Christine (☎ 553-04-56; Blvd Ixtapa s/n; admission women/men M$100/200; ☻ 10:30pm-dawn) Christine has the sizzling sound and light systems you'd expect from one of the most popular discos in town.

El Alebrije (☎ 553-27-10; Paseo de las Garzas s/n; admission M$190) A fog machine, banks of computerized lights, pop, rock, house, salsa and merengue, plus an open bar: what more do you want?

Carlos 'n' Charlie's (☎ 553-00-85; Blvd Ixtapa s/n) Things can get wild on this chain restaurant's dance floor right above the beach; on weekends it fills with hard-partying young tourists and locals.

El Faro (☎ 555-25-00; www.pacifica.com.mx; Ixtapa Marina; ☻ 6pm-11pm). Located at the top of the Pacifica Resort and accessed by a gondola, El Faro has amazing views and live jazz music. Reservations required.

Several of Ixtapa's big hotels including **Dorado Pacífico** (☎ 553-20-25) hold 'Fiesta Mexicana' parties featuring folkloric dancing, mariachis, buffet, open bar, games and sometimes fireworks. Expect to pay between M$320 and M$420. Reservations can be made directly through hotels and are open to non-hotel guests.

Shopping

Tourist market (Paseo Ixtapa s/n; ☻ 9am-10pm) A tacky market packed with everything from T-shirts and shot glasses to silver and pottery. Shopping is much better in Zihuatanejo.

Getting There & Around

For information on getting to Zihuatanejo, the essential stop for getting to Ixtapa, see p497. Private *colectivo* vans provide transportation from the airport to Ixtapa for M$100 per person, but not in the other direction. A taxi to the airport from Ixtapa costs M$120 to M$140.

There is no bus station within Ixtapa itself; the **Central de Autobuses** northwest of Zihuatanejo services both towns. Local buses run frequently between Ixtapa and Zihuatanejo from 5:30am to 11pm (15 minutes, M$7). In Ixtapa, buses stop along the main street in front of all hotels. In Zihuatanejo, buses depart from the corner of Juárez and Morelos. Buses marked 'Zihua–Ixtapa–Playa Linda' continue through Ixtapa to Playa Linda. A bus ride within Ixtapa costs M$4.50.

A taxi between Zihuatanejo and Ixtapa should be around M$50; always agree on a price before getting into a cab.

ZIHUATANEJO

☎ 755 / pop 62,400

The sister cities of Zihuatanejo (see-wah-tah-neh-ho) and Ixtapa could not be more radically different. While Ixtapa is a purpose-built, idyllic version of Mexico, Zihuatanejo is the real deal. Zihuatanejo, or Zihua as it's affectionately called, is a Pacific paradise of beautiful beaches, friendly people and an easygoing lifestyle. Until the 1970s, Zihua was a sleepy fishing village best known as a hideaway for pirates and hippies; Tim Robbins and Morgan Freeman escaped here to live out the simple life in *The Shawshank Redemption*. With the construction of Ixtapa next door, Zihua's population and tourism industry boomed practically overnight.

Parts of the city have become quite touristy, especially when cruise ships are in town. Luxury hotels are slowly replacing old family guesthouses. But for the most part, Zihua has thankfully retained its lovely, historic charm. The downtown narrow cobblestone streets hide wonderful local restaurants, bars, boutique shops and artisan studios. Fishermen still meet every morning on the beach by Paseo del Pescador (Fishermen's Passage) to sell their catch of the day. At night, young lovers and families stroll carefree along the romantic waterfront sidewalk. Zihua is the best of both worlds.

Orientation

Though Zihua's suburbs are slowly spreading beyond the bay and into the hills, the city's center is compressed within a few blocks. It's difficult to get lost; there are only a few streets and they're clearly marked. Ixtapa, 8km northwest, is easily reached by frequent local buses or by taxi. The airport is about 13km southeast of the city, and the long-distance bus terminals are about 2km northeast of town.

Information

EMERGENCY
Emergency (☎ 060; 24hr)
Hospital (☎ 554-36-50; Av Morelos) On Morales and Mar Egeo.
Tourist police (☎ 554-20-40; Alvarez) Next to the basketball court.

INTERNET ACCESS
Zihuatanejo is crawling with Internet cafés.
Infinitum Internet (Bravo 12; per hr M$10) Also has a travel agency.

LAUNDRY
Lavandería del Centro (☎ 554-97-91; Guerrero 17; per 3kg M$15; 8am-8pm Mon-Sat, 10am-4pm Sun) Self-service is also available.

MEDICAL SERVICES
Dr Rogelio Grayeb (☎ 554-33-34, 553-17-11) Provides medical assistance 24/7, speaks English and he makes house calls!

MONEY
Zihuatanejo has many banks and *casas de cambio* where you can change US dollars and traveler's checks. The following banks have ATMs.

Banamex (cnr Ejido & Guerrero)
Bancomer (cnr Juárez & Bravo; 8:30am-4pm Mon-Fri, 10am-2pm Sat)
Banorte (cnr Juárez & Ejido; 9am-4pm Mon-Fri, 10am-2pm Sat)

POST
Post office (☎ 8am-6pm Mon-Fri, 9am-1pm Sat) Located in the same building as Telecomm, behind the big yellow Coppel department store off Morales.

TELEPHONE & FAX
Long-distance telephone and fax services are available at several *casetas*, including two on the corner of Galeana and Ascencio. Telmex card phones are all around town.
Telecomm (8am-6pm Mon-Fri, 9am-1pm Sat) Located within the post office; has fax service.

TOURIST INFORMATION
Tourist kiosk (Álvarez s/n; 9am-8pm high season) Offers free information, maps and brochures in the heart of town.
Tourist office Municipal office (☎ /fax 554-20-01; www .ixtapa-zihuatanejo.com; Zihuatanejo Pte s/n, Colonia La Deportiva; 8am-4pm Mon-Fri); Branch office (off Paseo de la Bahía; 8am-4pm Mon-Fri) The municipal office is found upstairs in the *ayuntamiento* (city hall), 2km northeast of the town center. Local buses between Ixtapa and Zihuatanejo stop out front. The branch office is near the south end of Playa La Ropa.

TRAVEL AGENCIES
Various agencies provide travel services and arrange local tours.
Turismo Internacional del Pacífico (TIP; ☎ 554-75-10/11; cnr Juárez & Álvarez; 9am-2pm & 4-7pm Mon-Sat, 5-7pm Sun)

Dangers & Annoyances

A 2003 study published by Profepa, Mexico's environmental agency, cited 16 of the country's beaches as having unacceptably high levels of bacterial contamination. At the top of the list were Playas La Ropa, Las Gatas and Municipal, all on Bahía Zihuatanejo and caused by insufficiently treated sewage and contaminated runoff. Mexico responded by investing millions of dollars to clean up the bay and modernize sewage systems and fishing boat fleets. Just as things were beginning to look up, in 2007 the government announced plans to build a giant cruise ship terminal smack in the middle of the bay, setting off a heated battle between developers and environmentalists. At the time of writing, no final decision had been made on the controversial project.

Sights

MUSEO ARQUEOLÓGICO DE LA COSTA GRANDE

This small **archeology museum** (☎ 554-75-52; cnr Plaza Olof Palme & Paseo del Pescador; admission M$10; ✆ 10am-6pm Tue-Sun) houses exhibits on the history, archaeology and culture of the Guerrero coast. Most signs are in English and Spanish.

BEACHES

Waves are gentle at all of Bahía de Zihuatanejo's beaches. If you want big ocean waves, head west toward Ixtapa.

Playa Municipal, in front of town, is the least appealing beach on the bay. **Playa Madera** (Wood Beach) is a pleasant five-minute walk east from Playa Municipal along a concrete walkway (popular with young couples in the evening) around the rocky point.

Walk over the hill along the steep Carretera Escénica for another 15 to 20 minutes (less than 1km) from Playa Madera, you'll reach the broad expanse of **Playa La Ropa** (Clothes Beach), named for a Spanish galleon that wrecked and washed its cargo of silks ashore. The beach is bordered by palm trees and seafood restaurants. It's an enjoyable walk, with the road rising up onto cliffs that offer a fine view over the water. One of Zihua's most beautiful beaches, La Ropa is great for swimming, parasailing, waterskiing and sand-soccer. You can also rent sailboards and sailboats.

Isolated **Playa Las Gatas**, or Cat Beach, is named for the whiskered nurse sharks who once inhabited the waters. It's a protected beach, crowded with sunbeds and restaurants. It's good for snorkeling (there's some coral) and as a swimming spot for children, but beware of sea urchins. Beach shacks and restaurants rent out snorkeling gear for around M$50 per day. Boats to Playa Las Gatas depart frequently from the Zihuatanejo pier, from 9am to 5pm. Buy tickets (M$35 round-trip) at the booth at the foot of the pier; one-way tickets can be bought on board.

About 10km south of Zihuatanejo, just before the airport, **Playa Larga** has big waves, beachfront restaurants and horseback riding. Nearby **Playa Manzanillo**, a secluded white-sand beach reachable by boat from Zihuatanejo, offers the best snorkeling in the area. To reach Playa Larga, take a 'Coacoyul' combi (M$6, 10 minutes) from Juárez opposite the market and get off at the turnoff to Playa Larga; another combi will take you from the turnoff to the beach.

Activities

SNORKELING & SCUBA DIVING

Snorkeling is good at Playa Las Gatas and even better at Playa Manzanillo, especially in the dry season, when visibility is best. Marine life is abundant here due to a convergence of currents, and the visibility can be great – up to 35m. Migrating humpback whales pass through from December to February; manta rays can be seen all year, but you're most likely to spot them in summer, when the water is at its most clear, blue and warm. Snorkeling gear can be rented at Playa Las Gatas for around M$50 per day.

Buseo Nautilus Divers (☎ 554-91-91; www.nautilus -divers.com; Álvarez 33; ✆ 8am-4pm Mon-Sat; 1/2 tanks M$542/813) offers a variety of dives and NAUI courses and certification. **Zihua Dive Center**

THE PARTHENON OF ZIHUATANEJO

High on a hilltop above Playa Ropa, partially obscured by the encroaching forest, is a crumbling marble mansion that resembles a certain famous Greek temple. Known locally as 'El Parthenon,' it was built in 1982 by Arturo 'El Negro' Durazo Moreno, Mexico City's former police chief. His official salary was a paltry US$400 per month, but Durazo lived like a king, collecting vintage cars and building gaudy houses across Mexico. He spared no expense on the Parthenon, fitting it with Italian marble, statuary, frescoes, an outdoor disco and a huge pool with priceless views of Zihua Bay. Durazo never got to enjoy his spoils. Shortly after its completion, Durazo came under investigation for extorting millions of dollars from his police officers. He fled the country but after a long manhunt was captured and imprisoned for six years. He died in 2000. As for the Parthenon, it's still there; languishing like an ancient Greek ruin while the government debates its future. *Technically,* it's closed to the public, but if you ask nicely, the guards might let you in for a peek at Mexico's unintended monument to corruption.

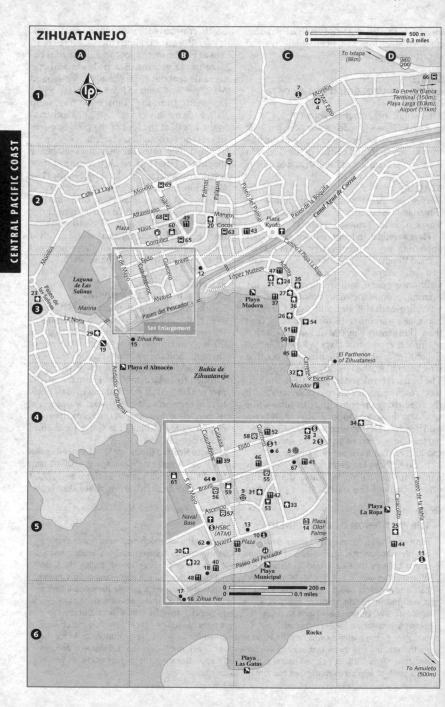

ZIHUATANEJO

(☎ 554-85-54; www.zihuatanejodivecenter.com; Av La Noria 1; M$705/921), offers PADI courses & certification, plus snorkeling, snooba & kayak trips; the staff speak English, Spanish & French.

SPORTFISHING

Sportfishing is popular in Zihuatanejo. Sailfish are caught here year-round; seasonal fish include blue or black marlin (March to May), roosterfish (September to October), wahoo (October), mahi mahi (November to December) and Spanish mackerel (December). Deep-sea fishing trips cost anywhere from M$1950 to M$4335, depending upon the size of the boat. Trips run up to seven hours and usually include equipment.

Two fishing outfits near Zihuatanejo's pier are **Sociedad Cooperativa José Azueta** (☎ 554-20-56; Muelle Municipal) and **Sociedad de Servicios Turísticos** (☎ 554-37-58; Paseo del Pescador 20). English is spoken at **Whisky Water World** (☎ 554-01-47, in the US 800-214-9003; www.ixtapa-sportfishing.com; Paseo del Pescador 38).

Tours

Picante (☎ 554-26-94, 554-82-70; www.picantecruises .com), a 23m catamaran based in Bahía de Zihuatanejo, offers a couple of different excursions. The 'Sail and Snorkel' trip (M$813, from 10am to 2:30pm) sails south of Zihua to the prime snorkeling of Playa Manzanillo's coral reef. The 'Magical Sunset Cruise' (M$542, from 5pm to 7:30pm) heads around the bay and out along the coast of Ixtapa. Prices include open bar, food and transportation to and from your hotel. Reservations required.

Sleeping

Zihuatanejo has a good selection of hotels for all budgets. Prices listed here are rack rates for high season, which generally runs from early December to early January, and Semana Santa. Outside of peak season, prices drop by up to 20%. You can often negotiate for rates, especially during slow periods or for extended days.

BUDGET

our pick **Hostel Rincón del Viajero** (☎ 105-43-98; www.rinconviajerozihua.4t.com; rinconviajerozihua@gmail .com; Paseo las Salinas 50, La Noria; dm per person M$110, d without/with bathroom M$210/280) Part artists' colony, part botanical garden, Rincón del Viajero

CENTRAL PACIFIC COAST

(Traveler's Corner) was once a derelict bodega until owner-artist-surfer Malinalli got her creative hands on it. The colorful, comfy rooms and common areas are decorated with Mali's original artwork and Mexican handicrafts. There's also a communal kitchen, wading pool, rooftop terrace, hammocks, laundry area, bike rentals and a wonderful coffee shop with fruits picked right from the courtyard orchard. Mali speaks Spanish, English, French, Italian and some Portuguese.

Angela's Hotel & Hostel (☎ 112-2191; www.zihua tanejo.com.mx/angelas; Mangos 25; dm/d M$150/250) This friendly hostel with helpful staff has private rooms, dorms, communal kitchen, lockers and luggage storage. It's located behind the municipal market, 15 minutes' walk from the zócalo.

Casa de Huéspedes Elvira (☎ 554-20-61; Álvarez s/n; r without/with air-con M$250/350) A decent cheapie offers eight rooms on two floors surrounding an open courtyard. Upstairs rooms are much better, with more light and privacy.

Posada Citlali (☎ 554-20-43; Guerrero 4; s/d M$300/400) This pleasant older posada has plain but clean rooms around a dark, leafy central courtyard. Keep to the front of the building; the primary school directly behind the hotel might result in an early-morning wake-up screams.

MIDRANGE

Hotel Raúl Tres Marías (☎ 554-21-91; r3marias noria@ yahoo.com; La Noria 4; s/d M$400/580) Across the lagoon footbridge, this economical, popular option comes with clean, spacious rooms. Its best features, however, are the large terraced patios that are dotted with chairs and hammocks and boast great views of the pier.

Hotel Raúl Tres Marías Centro (☎ 554-67-06; www .ixtapa-zihuatanejo.net/r3marias; Álvarez 52; r M$680; P ✕) Rooms at this spot are good and unpretentious, and many come with balcony. There's a popular downstairs restaurant, and in the high season breakfast is included.

Hotel Zihuatanejo Centro (☎ 554-26-69; www .ixtapa-zihuatanejo.net/zihuacenter; Ramírez 2; s/d M$850; P ✕ 💻 🐕) A fantastic choice right in the heart of downtown Zihua, this melon-colored hotel has 74 bright and sunny rooms with amenities normally found at more expensive resorts, including a popular bar and an internet café.

Hotel Palacios (☎ /fax 554-20-55; hotelpalacios@ prodigy.net.mx; Adelita s/n; d M$850-950; P ✕ 🐕) Overlooking the east end of Playa Madera, Hotel Palacios is a family-friendly facility with a small pool and beachfront terrace. Some rooms are small and not all have views, but the renovated rooms all have comfortable beds.

Hotel Irma (☎ 554-84-72; www.hotelirma.com.mx; hotelreserv@prodigy.net.mx; Playa de La Madera s/n; s/d M$924/1041; P ✕ 🐕) Like a reliable relative, Irma attracts regulars back year after year for the family-like atmosphere and service. Located just above Playa Madera, Irma has renovated rooms, some with great views of the bay and the huge pool and terrace below. It's a great moderate choice in low season.

Villas Miramar (☎ 554-2106; www.hotelvillasmiramar .com; r with garden view/ocean view M$950/1050, ste M$1800; P ✕ 🐕) This laid-back complex is divided among two buildings: a tall beachfront hotel right on Playa Madera and a shorter garden-style building across the street. Both are bright orange and have their own pools and large comfortable rooms.

Bungalows Ley (☎ 554-40-87; www.zihua.net /bungalosley; López Mateos s/n; 1-/2-bedroom bungalows M$975/1842; P ✕) Well-kept and spacious, with unbeatable views and beach access. The bungalows are not fancy, but all have thatched terraces with hammocks, room safes and kitchens or kitchenettes (some are outdoors). It's stumbling distance to Playa Madera.

TOP END

Villa Mexicana (☎ 553-36-36; www.hotelvillamexicana .com.mx; Playa La Ropa s/n; s/d from M$1158; P ✕ 💻 🐕) This new hotel in orange and blue hues is one of the few Zihua lodgings located directly on a beach. The large tile and stucco rooms have cable TV, phone and safe. There's a popular pool and beachside bar and restaurant.

Hotel Brisas del Mar (☎ 554-21-42; www.hotelbrisas delmar.com; López Mateos s/n; d from M$1312; ✕ 💻 🐕) A cliff-hugging, red adobe village perched above Playa Madera, Brisas del Mar is perfect for a romantic getaway. The spacious rooms and grounds are decorated in traditional Mexican furnishings, tiles and handicrafts. All have private balconies with exquisite ocean views and a hammock. A steep staircase leads down to the beach and to its Bistro del Mar, one of Zihua's finest restaurants.

Amuleto (☎ 544-6222, in the US 213-280-1037; www .amuleto.net; Escenica 9; from M$3951; P ✕ 💻 🐕) A boutique hotel in the high hills above Playa La Ropa, Amuleto is the newest name in opulence. Each earthy room is decorated in stone, ceramic and woods and the suites have private swimming pools with scrumptious views. Amuleto's resturant is the hottest new thing in Zihua.

La Casa Que Canta (☎ 554-70-30, 800-710-93-45; www.lacasaquecanta.com; Carretera Escénica s/n; r M$5039, ste M$5961-M$9104; **P** **※** **□** **⌨**) Regularly ranked as one of the finest hotels in the world, La Casa Que Canta – The House that Sings – is the epitome of luxury, exclusivity and customer service. Perched on the cliffs between Playas Madera and La Ropa, the thatched-roof hotel contains exquisitely decorated rooms, a restaurant, spa, fitness center and two swimming pools. But perhaps the most valuable amenity may be silence; there are no televisions, and children under 16 are banned.

Eating

Guerrero is famous for its *pozole*, a hearty meat and veg stew that's found on most menus in town (especially on Thursday). *Tiritas* (raw fish slivers marinated with red onion, lemon or lime and chili peppers, and served with soda crackers and spicy sauce) are Zihua's specialty, but you won't find them on many menus – look for them at carts near the bus stations, or request them at any beachfront *enramada*.

PASEO DEL PESCADOR

Seafood here is fresh and delicious; many popular (if touristy) fish restaurants run parallel to Playa Municipal. The following are the best options from west to east.

Café Marina (☎ 554-23-73; Paseo Pescador; mains M$50-125; ☽ 8am-9pm) This tiny place on the west side of the plaza bakes up some good pizzas, along with spaghettis and sandwiches.

Casa Elvira (☎ 554-20-61; Paseo del Pescador 8; mains M$60-160; ☽ 1pm-10:30pm) This old hand turns out some tasty food like oysters Rockefeller, jumbo steamed shrimp and broiled octopus with garlic. Vegetarians will appreciate the soup, salad and spaghetti choices. Order the coconut custard for dessert.

La Sirena Gorda (The Fat Mermaid; ☎ 554-26-87; Paseo del Pescador 90; mains M$60-230; ☽ 8:30am-10:30pm Thu-Tue) Close to the pier, this place is a casual and popular open-air restaurant that's good for garlic shrimp, curry tuna and fish tacos, as well as burgers and traditional Mexican dishes.

CENTRAL ZIHUATANEJO – INLAND

Hearty inexpensive breakfast or lunch is available in the **market** (Juárez; ☽ 7am-6pm), at the corner of Juarez and Gonzalez. Late-night taco stands are ubiquitous around town.

Tamales y Atoles Any (☎ 554-73-73; Guerrero 38; mains M$20-90) This friendly place serves consciously traditional and excellent Mexican cuisine under its big *palapa* roof. For something different, try the *caldo de mi patrón* (my boss's soup), a soup made of chicken liver, heart, feet and gizzard. The real highlights are the to-die-for *tamales* and *atoles*, a flavored sweet hot drink made of corn flower.

Cafetería Nueva Zelanda (☎ 554-23-40; Cuauhtémoc 23-30; mains M$20-60) Step back in time at this spotless diner, where you can order a banana split or chocolate malt with your shrimp taco and chicken fajitas. Everything is available *para llevar* (to go), it's a great place for breakfast, and you can get a decent cappuccino anytime. There are entrances on both Cuauhtémoc and Galeana.

Zihua Pancake House (☎ 554-20-87, 100-59-56; zihuapancake@yahoo.com.mx; cnr Galeana & Ejido; breakfast M$30-50; ☽ 7am-2pm Tue-Sun) The best breakfast spot in town, this popular open-air restaurant with a prime people-watching spot serves American favorites like eggs Benedict, French toast, waffles and, of course, several types of pancakes. It also has a full cocktail bar pouring Mimosas, Bloody Marys and other hair-of-the-dog drinks.

Cenaduría Antelia (☎ 554-30-91; Bravo 14; meals under M$50; ☽ 9am-2:30pm & 6pm-midnight) Antelia's popular and friendly eatery has been dishing out tasty *antojitos mexicanos* and desserts since 1975. Tuck into a *tamal de chile verde* or a bursting bowl of daily *pozole*, and top it off with *calabaza con leche* (squash in milk) for dessert.

Doña Licha (☎ 554-39-33; Cocos 8; mains M$50-85; ☽ 8am-6pm) Licha is well known for its downhome Mexican cooking, casual atmosphere and excellent prices. There are always several *comidas corridas* from which to choose including one delicious specialty, *pollo en cacahuete* (chicken in a peanut sauce); all come with rice, beans and handmade tortillas. Breakfasts are huge.

Il Paccolo (☎ 559-08-38; Bravo 38; mains M$60-110; ☽ 4pm-midnight) Aching for Italian? Il Paccolo has delicious pizzas, pastas, meats and seafood dishes. The atmosphere is dark and low-key, and the bar is friendly.

Coconuts (☎ 554-79-80; Ramírez 1; mains M$90-265; ☽ noon-11pm) For a romantic dinner this upscale place is hard to beat. Fairy lights fill the outdoor courtyard, service is attentive and dishes include garlic snapper, leg of duck, *chiles rellenos*, vegetable tart and herb chicken.

AROUND THE BAY

El Manglar (☎ 554-3752; Playa La Ropa s/n; ◷ noon-9pm Thu-Tue; mains M$45-148) One of several seafood restaurants on Playa La Ropa, El Manglar (the mangrove) is unique for its jungle setting in a protected reserve that's home to crocodiles, iguanas, birds and turtles. The menu features a blackened 27-spice tuna, mahi mahi and filet mignon. Out back, there's also an RV park with showers and bath (M$200 per day).

our pick La Casa Vieja (☎ 557-08-37; www.restaur antcasavieja.com.mx; Josefa Ortiz de Domínguez 7; mains M$45-155 ; ◷ 11am-11pm Mon-Sat, 9am-10pm Sun) A hidden gem located in a residential neighborhood near Playa Madera, Casa Vieja is popular with locals and in-the-know tourists for great, traditional Mexican food and hospitality. Go on Thursday for the two-for-one *pozole* specials and live music.

Puerta del Sol (☎ 554-83-42; Carretera Escénica s/n; mains M$75-200; ◷ 5pm-midnight) This romantic restaurant perched on the cliffs between Playas Madera and La Ropa has spectacular bay and sunset views. And the international menu is on fire, literally. Start with a flambé steak, followed by flambé fruit desert and finish off with flambé coffee. Reservations are a must in high season.

Il Mare (☎ 554-90-67; Escénica a la Ropa 105; www .ilmareristorante.com; mains M$80-225; ◷ noon-10pm) A romantic Italian restaurant in the clouds, Il Mare is well regarded for its Mediterranean specialties like Linguine ai Fruitti di Mare in spicy marinara sauce or bow-tie pasta with smoked salmon.

Bistro del Mar (☎ 554-2142; www.hotelbrisasdelmar .com; Playa Madera s/n; mains M$80-380; ◷ 7am-11pm) This beautiful, beachside bistro – part of the Hotel Brisas del Mar complex – exemplifies contemporary Mexican cuisine by fusing Latin, European and Asian flavors. Rotating specialties include original creations like jumbo shrimp marinated in a sweet and sour sauce, flambéed in tequila, on a bed of sweet-corn cake. With its landmark sail roof over candlelit beachside tables, Bistro del Mar is a romantic treat for the heart, soul and stomach.

Restaurant Kau-Kan (☎ 554-84-46; Carretera Escénica 7; mains M$160-325; ◷ 5pm-midnight) High on the cliffs, this renowned gourmet restaurant enjoys stellar views. Making a selection is exhausting when faced with choices like stingray in black butter sauce, marinated abalone or grilled lamb chops with couscous.

Drinking

Jungle Bar (cnr Ascencio & Ramírez; ◷ 7pm-2am) Bob your head to the kick-back bass pulsing at this streetside bar with fun staff and cheap drinks. It's a good place to meet locals and other travelers. The jungle murals were painted by local artist Malinalli of Hostel Rincón del Viajero fame.

Entertainment

If it's big-time nightlife you're after, head to Ixtapa (see p489); Zihuatanejo is all about being mellow.

our pick Zihuablue (☎ 554-48-44; www.zihuablue .com; Carretera Escénica La Ropa s/n; ◷ 5pm-3am) Opened in late 2006, Zihuablue has quickly become *the* place to see and be seen; it's a hot spot for Mexican celebrities. The huge club is spread over three levels, and includes a hookah bar and an outdoor terrace with canopied beds and comfy couches. The drinks are strong and the views are outstanding. Zihuablue also has an outstanding restaurant run by French chef and Zihua gastronomy pioneer Edmond Benloulou.

Sacbé (cnr Ejido & Guerrero; admission M$50; ◷ 8pm-late Thu-Sun) The only true discothèque in town, Sacbé caters mainly to young Mexican college students and pumps out English and Spanish pop, dance, salsa and *reggaeton*.

Splash (Guerrero s/n; ◷ 7pm-late Mon-Sun) Behind the its sister club, Sacbé, Splash is a karaoke and video dance bar.

Black Bull Rodeo (☎ 554-11-29; cnr Bravo & Guerrero; ◷ from 9pm) This corner country disco claims to have the best *norteño* band in town. There's also *cumbia*, merengue, salsa, electronica and reggae music on offer.

Rick's (☎ 554-2535; Cuauhtémoc 5; ◷ 10am-10pm) A popular hole-in-the-wall in downtown Zihua features live music nightly and cold margaritas.

Cine Paraíso (☎ 554-23-18; Cuauhtémoc; admission M$25) Shows two films nightly, usually in English with Spanish subtitles. It's found near Bravo.

Shopping

Zihua offers abundant Mexican handicrafts, including ceramics, *típica* (characteristic of the region) clothing, leatherwork, Taxco silver, wood carvings and masks from around the state of Guerrero.

El Jumil (☎ 554-61-91; Paseo del Pescador 9; ☯ 9am-2pm & 5-9pm Mon-Sat) This shop specializes in *guerrerense* masks. Guerrero is known for its variety of masks, and El Jumil stocks museum-quality examples. Many of these start at around M$160, but there are also cheaper but delightful coconut-shell masks.

Mercado Turístico La Marina (Calle 5 de Mayo; ☯ 8am-9pm) Has many stalls selling clothes, bags and knickknacks.

Mercado Municipal de las Artesanías (González; ☯ 9am-8pm) Similar to La Marina, but smaller. It's found near Juárez.

A few shops along Cuauhtémoc sell Taxco silver. **Alberto's** (☎ 554-21-61; Cuauhtémoc 12 & 15; ☯ 9am-10pm Mon-Sat, 10am-3pm Sun) and **Pancho's** (☎ 554-52-30; Cuauhtémoc 11; ☯ 9am-9pm Mon-Sat) have the best selection of quality pieces.

Getting There & Away
AIR
The **Ixtapa/Zihuatanejo international airport** (☎ 554-20-70) is 13km southeast of Zihuatanejo, a couple of kilometers off Hwy 200 heading toward Acapulco.

Carriers servicing the airport:

Aeroméxico Airport (☎ 554-22-37, 554-26-34); Zihuatanejo (☎ 554-20-18; Álvarez 34) Service to Mexico City, with many onward connections.

Alaska Airlines (☎ 554-84-57, 001-800-252-75-22; Airport) Service to Los Angeles and San Francisco.

American (☎ 800-904-60-00; Airport) Service to Dallas.

America West (☎ 800-235-92-92; Airport) Service to Phoenix and Las Vegas.

Continental (☎ 554-42-19; Airport) Service to Houston and Minneapolis.

Click Mexicana & Mexicana Airport (☎ 554-22-27); Zihuatanejo (☎ 554-22-08; cnr Bravo & Cuauhtémoc); Ixtapa (☎ 553-22-09; Dorado Pacífico, Blvd Ixtapa) Service to Mexico City.

Northwest (☎ 800-907-47-00; Airport) Service to Houston and Los Angeles.

BUS
Both long-distance bus terminals are on Hwy 200 about 2km northeast of the town center (toward the airport): the **Estrella Blanca terminal** (EB; Map p487; ☎ 554-34-76/77; Central de Autobuses) is a block east of the smaller **Estrella de Oro terminal** (EDO; Map p492; ☎ 554-21-75). The latter also serves several smaller bus lines including Autovías, La Línea, Vía Plus and Parkihuni. See the table below for daily departures.

CAR & MOTORCYCLE
There are several car rental companies in Ixtapa and Zihuatanejo:

Alamo Airport (☎ 554-84-29); Ixtapa (☎ 553-02-06; Centro Comercial Los Patios)

Budget Airport (☎ 554-48-37); Ixtapa (☎ 553-03-97; Centro Comercial Ambiente, Blvd Ixtapa)

Europcar (☎ 553-10-32; Centro Comercial Los Patios, Ixtapa)

Hertz Airport (☎ 554-29-52); Zihuatanejo (☎ 554-22-55; Bravo 29)

BUSES FROM ZIHUATANEJO

Destination	Fare	Duration	Frequency
Acapulco	1st-class M$119	4hr	hourly 5am-7:30pm (EB)
	2nd-class M$86	4hr	hourly (EB)
	1st-class M$119	4hr	5 daily (EDO)
	2nd-class M$99	4hr	18 daily 5:30am-8pm (EDO)
Lázaro Cárdenas	1st-class M$65	1½hr	hourly 5am-7:30pm (EB)
	2nd-class M$54	2hr	hourly 9am-10pm (EB)
	2nd-class M$47	2hr	15 daily (EDO)
Manzanillo (Estrella Blanca)	M$324	8hr	10am, 10:50am, 8pm
Mexico City (Terminal Sur)	premiere M$550	8-9hr	9:15pm (EDO)
	deluxe M$541	8-9hr	10:30pm (EB)
	deluxe M$440	8-9hr	9:55pm, 10pm & 11pm (EDO)
	1st-class M$454	8-9hr	5 daily (EB)
	1st-class M$425	8-9hr	8 daily (EDO)
Morelia	M$328	5hr	3 daily (EDO)
Puerto Escondido	M$260	12hr	7:20pm (EB)

Thrifty Airport (☎ 553-70-20); Ixtapa (☎ 553-30-19; NH Krystal Ixtapa, Blvd Ixtapa)

If you're heading into the Michoacán highlands (to Uruapan or Pátzcuaro, for example) the scenic toll road Hwy 37D will save you hours (and cost you about M$220 in tolls). Gas up before you leave town; there's a long Pemex-less stretch of road before Nueva Italia.

Getting Around
TO/FROM THE AIRPORT
The cheapest way to get to the airport is via a public 'Aeropuerto' *colectivo* (M$70) departing from Juárez near González between 6:20am and 10pm. Private *colectivo* vans provide transportation from the airport to Ixtapa or Zihua (M$100 per person), but they don't offer service to the airport. Taxis from Zihua to the airport cost M$80.

BUS
For details on buses to Ixtapa, see p489.

The 'Correa' route goes to the Central de Autobuses from 5:30am to 9:30pm (M$4, 10 minutes). Catch it on Juárez at the corner of Nava.

'Playa La Ropa' buses go south on Juárez and out to Playa La Ropa every half-hour from 7am to 8pm (M$4).

'Coacoyul' *colectivos* heading toward Playa Larga depart from Juárez near the corner of González, every five minutes from 5am to 10pm (M$7).

TAXI
Cabs are plentiful in Zihuatanejo. Always agree on the fare before getting in. Approximate sample fares (from central Zihua) include: M$50 to Ixtapa, M$25 to Playa La Ropa, M$50 to Playa Larga and M$15 to the Central de Autobuses. Book a taxi in advance by calling **Radio Taxi UTAAZ** (☎ 554-33-11).

SOUTH OF IXTAPA & ZIHUATANEJO
Barra de Potosí
☎ 755 / pop 400
Forty minutes drive south of Zihutanejo is the small fishing village of Barra de Potosí at the end of an endless, palm-fringed sandy-white beach. The calm green-blue water is great for swimming but too cloudy for snorkeling. Several seafood *enramadas* line the beach; **La Condesa** is one of the best. Try their *pescado*

a la talla (broiled fish fillets) or *tiritas*, both local specialties, and don't pass up the savory handmade tortillas.

The south side of the beach empties into **Laguna de Potosí**, a saltwater lagoon about 6.5km long brimming with hundreds of species of birds. **Zoe Kayak Tours** (☎ 553-04-96; www.zoekayaktours.com; M$850) offers guided paddle tours of the lagoon catering to bird-watchers and kayakers. Horseback riding and canoeing are also popular diversions.

SLEEPING
There are a handful of guesthouses along the beachfront. During the low season (May to October), rates at the following places drop by between 20% and 40%.

Casa del Encanto (☎ 104-67-09; www.casadelencanto.com; d incl breakfast M$974-1245) This is a knockout B&B about 300m inland from the beach. Private yet open-air rooms blend interior with exterior to keep things as cool and relaxed as possible, aided by numerous hammocks and fountains.

our pick Bernie's Bed & Breakfast (☎ 556-63-33; www.zihuatanejo.net/playacalli; Playa Calli; d incl breakfast M$1300; ☲) Located about 2km north of the village, Bernie's has four fantastic rooms set in a Spanish-style red-brick home and a welcoming swimming pool. All rooms face the surf and have king-sized beds and ceiling fans. Friendly host Bernie speaks English, German, Spanish and French, and exudes a tranquility over his home.

Solecito (☎ 100-59-76; www.bungalows-solecito.com; M$1245 & M$1732; P ☲) This serene, beachfront retreat features nine contemporary rooms and suites (some with kitchens) in white adobe buildings with Spanish red-tiled roofs. Each oversized room has a terrace overlooking the lush courtyard garden of tall palms and tropical flowers.

GETTING THERE & AWAY
By car from Zihuatanejo, drive southeast on Hwy 200 toward Acapulco. The well-marked turnoff is near Km 225 just south of the Los Achotes River bridge; drive another 9km to Barra de Potosí. By bus, any Petatlán-bound bus will get you here. They depart from both of Zihua's main terminals, and from the stop a couple of blocks east of Zihua's market. Tell the driver to let you off at the Barra de Potosí *crucero*; from there you can catch a *camioneta* (pickup truck) going the rest of the way. The

total trip by bus takes about 90 minutes and costs about M$30. By taxi from Zihua costs M$400/500 one-way/round-trip (negotiable).

Soledad de Maciel
☎ 755 / pop 350

The tiny hamlet of Soledad de Maciel, known locally as 'La Chole,' is a small farming and fishing village that hasn't changed much in 3000 years. The town would be easily dismissed if not for its recently uncovered secret: it's built on top of what may be the largest, most important archeological ruin in the state of Guerrero. La Chole was first discovered in 1930 but remained largely untouched until 2007, when the National Institute of Anthropology and History conducted its first formal excavation of the 10 sq km site. So far, archaeologists have discovered three pyramids – one of which is crowned by five temples – a plaza and a ball court. The area has been continuously occupied for three millennia by different cultures including Tepoztecos, Cuitlatecos and Tomiles.

A few relics are on display in the small **museum** located in a private home in the village center. The most important local artifact is the Chole King, a 1.5m-tall statue depicting deities of life and death; it's on display in the courtyard of the village church. The museum and the archaeological dig depend on donations for their work; please give generously.

Soledad de Maciel is located about 40 minutes' drive south of Zihuatanejo off Hwy 200. The well-marked turnoff is located near Km 214, just south of the town of San Jeronimito. From there, a gravel road leads 8km to the archaeology site and continues another kilometer to the village. Any bus heading south to Petatlán or Acapulco will get you here; ask to be dropped at the intersection for 'La Chole,' where you can hop a *camioneta* (pick-up truck with seats along the sides) into town.

La Barrita
☎ 758 / pop 60

La Barrita (Km 187) is a shell-sized village on an attractive, rocky beach an hour southeast of Zihua (off Hwy 200). Not many tourists stop at this village, but experienced surfers may want to check the beach breaks here and 3km north at **Loma Bonita**. Several restaurants have very basic rooms for rent. Second-class buses heading south from Zihua or north from Acapulco will drop you at La Barrita.

One of the more dramatic stretches of highway in Guerrero starts about 4km south of La Barrita; the road runs along clifftops above beaches and crashing surf. Several roadside restaurants offer opportunities to enjoy the view.

PIE DE LA CUESTA
☎ 744 / pop 200

Just 10km – and 100 years – from Acapulco is the tranquil seaside suburb of Pie de la Cuesta, a rustic beach town occupied by some terrific guesthouses and seafood restaurants. But it's the dramatic sunset views from the wide, west-facing beach that have made Pie de la Cuesta famous. The town sits on a narrow, 2km strip of land bordered by the Pacific Ocean and the Laguna de Coyuca (where Sylvester Stallone filmed *Rambo: First Blood Part II*). The large freshwater lagoon contains several islands including Pájaros, a bird sanctuary. Pie de la Cuesta is much quieter, cheaper and closer to nature than Acapulco, but still close enough for those who want to enjoy the city's attractions and nightlife.

Information

The single main road through town has two names: Av de la Fuerza Aérea Mexicana and Calzada Pie de la Cuesta. The long road runs through Pie de la Cuesta, past an Air Force base, then continues on to Playa Luces. Near the arched intersection of the main road and Hwy 200 is a small tourist office with maps and brochures. Just up the street, **Netxcom** (per hr M$10; ☾ 9am-10pm) offers cheap, fast Internet connections. The town also has a pharmacy, telephones and a few *mini-super* grocery stores; other services are located in Acapulco.

Activities

The surf here can be dangerous due to a riptide and the shape of the waves; the lagoon is better for swimming. **Waterskiing** on the lagoon is one of the most popular pastimes; there are several waterskiing clubs on the lagoon side including **Club de Ski Chuy** (☎ 460-11-04; Calzada Pie de la Cuesta 74; per hr M$600). **Wakeboarding** is another possibility; try **Club Náutico Cadena Ski** (☎ 460-22-83; cadenax@yahoo.com; Calzada Pie de la Cuesta s/n; per hr M$600). Several establishments offer **boat trips** on the lagoon for about M$80 per person including food and drinks; eager captains await your business down by the boat launches along the southeast corner of the lagoon. **Horseback**

riding on the beach costs about M$150 per hour; book from a hotel or directly from the galloping cowboys on the beach.

Sleeping

The room prices listed here can be significantly cheaper outside of peak season, which runs from mid-December to early January and during Easter Week.

BUDGET

Acapulco Trailer Park & Mini-Super (☎ 460-00-10; acatrailerpark@yahoo.com.mx; Calz Pie de la Cuesta s/n; campsites M$216, RV sites M$270; [P] [🏊]) The nicest campground in the Acapulco area has palm-shaded, beachside spaces, clean bathrooms with showers, a pool and a small shop with groceries and camping supplies.

Quinta Karla (☎ 460-12-55; quintakarla@hotmail .com; Calz Pie de la Cuesta 288; r M$250-500; [P] [🏊]) This friendly hotel has 18 clean and comfy rooms; more expensive rooms have a TV and fridge. There's also a good beachfront restaurant with fresh seafood meals for under M$80.

MIDRANGE

Bungalows María Cristina (☎ 460-02-62; Av de la Fuerza Aérea s/n; s/d/bungalows M$300/400/900; [P]) Run by English-speaking Enrique and his friendly family, this is a clean, well-tended, relaxing place with hammocks overlooking the beach. The large, four-to-five-person bungalows have kitchens and ocean-view balconies.

Villa Roxana (☎ 460-32-52; Calz Pie de la Cuesta 302; d without/with terrace M$300/400; [P] [🏊]) This re-cently renovated hotel features 15 comfortable rooms with fan and hot water, all surrounding a lovely courtyard with a relaxing pool and garden.

Villa Nirvana (☎ 460-16-31; www.lavillanirvana.com; Av de la Fuerza Aérea 302; d without/with ocean view M$500/700, q M$900; [P] [🖥] [🏊]) Villa Nirvana's friendly American owners have lovingly landscaped this cheerful property. It has a variety of accommodations, some with ocean views, and all are comfortable and decorated with local crafts.

our pick Quinta Erika (☎ /fax 444-41-31; www.quinta erika.com; Playa Luces s/n; r incl breakfast M$600; [P] [🏊]) For those who just want to get away from it all, Quinta Erika is a hidden, jungle-like retreat located 6km northeast of Pie de la Cuestra in Playa Luces. The estate sits on 1.2 hectares of lagoonside property with more than 200 palm and tropical fruit trees. The six colorful rooms and one bungalow are simple but tastefully decorated with traditional Mexican handicrafts. Stuttgart-born owner Helmut speaks German, Spanish and English and takes great pride in his hideaway.

Villas Ukae Kim (☎ 460-21-87; Av de la Fuerza Aérea 356; r M$600-1000, villa M$1200; [P] [🍴] [🏊]) A small boutique hotel that exudes a friendly, tranquil atmosphere. The sandy-colored complex features lovely rooms, a beachside pool and an open-air bar-restaurant that extends onto a wooden pier over the beach. The pricier rooms , some with air-con, have ocean views; the villa also has Jacuzzi, private terrace and TV.

Hacienda Vayma Beach Club (☎ 460-28-82; www .vayma.com.mx; Calz Pie de La Cuesta 378; r with fan/air-con

M$750/850, ste M$2000; P) This fun yet relaxing Mediterranean-style resort has something for everyone, from the awesome beach with private cabanas and lounge chairs built for two, to the huge pool with islands and swim-up bar. The whitewashed hotel has 25 contemporary, charming rooms, some with canopied beds; splurge for a suite with hot water and Jacuzzi.

Eating & Drinking

Steve's Hideaway/El Escondite (Laguna de Coyuca; mains M$25-90; 9am-midnight) A local favorite since 1968, this hole-in-the-wall sits on stilts over the lagoon with great views over the water. Esteban serves drinks, steaks and fresh catches like red snapper and fish quesadillas. It's located down a dirt road on the southeast side of the lagoon.

Coyuca 2000 (460-56-09; Playa Pie de la Cuesta; mains M$30-130; 8am-10pm) Pull up a chair on the sand, watch the waves and enjoy good fish *al mojo de ajo* (sautéed minced garlic) or in fajitas, plus other tasty seafood and meat dishes. Great mixed drinks enhance the casual atmosphere.

Restaurant and Club de Skis Tres Marías (460-00-11; Fuerza Aérea s/n; breakfast M$40-60, lunch & dinner M$80-120; 8am-7pm;) This popular lagoonside gem is located underneath a huge thatched-covered roof and especially popular for its American-style breakfasts.

our pick **Restaurant Vayma** (460-28-82; www.vayma.com.mx; Calz Pie de La Cuesta 378; mains M$80-180) Located at Hacienda Vayma, this beachfront restaurant has an extensive international menu. Highlights include calamari tacos, Thai shrimp, *mole poblano* chicken and several tasty varieties of pizza. At night, the restaurant and hotel grounds are bathed in the glow of candles and tiki torches; the perfect spot for a romantic sunset dinner.

Getting There & Away

From Acapulco, catch a 'Pie de la Cuesta' bus on La Costera across the street from the Sanborns near the *zócalo*. Buses go every 15 minutes from 6am until around 8pm; the trip costs M$4.50 and takes 30 to 60 minutes, depending on traffic. Buses marked 'Pie de la Cuesta–San Isidro' or 'Pie de la Cuesta–Pedregoso' stop at the fork of Hwy 200 and Pie de la Cuesta's arched entrance; those marked 'Zona Turistica: Pie de la Cuesta–Playa Luces' continue through town and travel 6km further to Playa Luces, terminating just before Quinta Erika.

Colectivo taxis to Pie de la Cuesta operate 24 hours along La Costera and elsewhere in Acapulco's old town, and charge M$15. A taxi from Acapulco costs between M$70 and M$125 one-way, depending on your bartering skills, time of day and point of origin.

ACAPULCO

744 / pop 616,400

Before Cancún and Ixtapa, Acapulco was Mexico's original party town. With stunning yellow beaches and a 24-hour nightlife, it was dubbed the 'Pearl of the Pacific.' During its heyday, Acapulco was the playground for the rich and famous including Frank Sinatra, Elvis Presley, Elizabeth Taylor, Judy Garland; John F. Kennedy and his wife Jacqueline honeymooned here. It was immortalized in films like Elvis's *Fun in Acapulco* and TV's *The Love Boat*.

Acapulco's gorgeous arc of beaches that sweep around Bahía de Acapulco can be a relaxing place to soak up the sun – if you can ignore the pesky beach vendors. But step off the sands and you'll soon be hit by a harsh reality: terrible traffic, crowded sidewalks, smoggy fumes, aggressive touts, poverty, homelessness and a significant crime wave.

Bustling Acapulco does offer pockets of calm: romantic cliffside restaurants, the impressive 17th-century fort, a world-class botanical garden and the old town's charming shady *zócalo*. And when you tire of the crowds, secluded beaches and seaside villages like Pie de la Cuesta and Barra Vieja are just a short drive away.

History

The name Acapulco is derived from ancient Náhuatl words meaning 'place of giant reeds.' Archaeological finds show that when the Spanish discovered the Bahía de Acapulco in 1512, people had already been living in the area for some 2000 years.

The Spanish, eager to find a commercial route to Asia, built a port and shipbuilding facilities in Acapulco, taking advantage of its naturally protected, deepwater harbor. In 1565, Friar Andrés de Urdante discovered Pacific tradewinds that allowed ships to quickly and safely reach the Orient. For more than 250 years, *naos*, or Spanish trading galleons, made the annual voyage from

Acapulco to the Philippines. Gold, silks and spices were unloaded in Acapulco, carried overland to Veracruz, then onto waiting ships for the transatlantic voyage to Spain. Meanwhile, Dutch and English privateers such as Sir Francis Drake were busy looting the ships of their valuable cargo. To protect their investment, the Spanish built the Fuerte de San Diego. But it was the Mexican War of Independence (1810–1822), not pirates, that abruptly killed the trade route.

For the next century, Acapulco declined and remained relatively isolated from the rest of the world until a paved road linked it with Mexico City in 1927. Prosperous Mexicans began vacationing here, Hollywood came calling and by the '50s, Acapulco was becoming a glitzy, jet-set resort. But by the 1970s, over-development and overpopulation had taken their toll, and the bay became polluted with raw sewage. Foreign tourists took their cash to the newer resorts of Cancún and Ixtapa. Once again, Acapulco's heyday was over.

In the late 1990s, the city launched ambitious revitalization programs, pouring millions into cleaning up the bay. The big break came in 2002, when American college students, attracted by cheap rooms and a welcoming hotel industry, began coming to Acapulco in droves, replacing Cancún as Mexico's top Spring Break hot spot. Today, Acapulco is experiencing something of a renaissance, investing in luxury resorts, condos, spas, boutique hotels and restaurants to cater to a more upscale clientele in hopes of reclaiming its title as the 'Pearl of the Pacific.'

Orientation

Acapulco borders the 11km shore of the Bahía de Acapulco ('The Bay'). Street signs are as scarce as safe crosswalks, and building numbers are erratic and often obscured or unused, but inquiring on the street will eventually lead you to your destination. As with most Spanish colonial cities, the cathedral and adjacent *zócalo* dominate the heart of the old central commercial district.

Old Acapulco (sometimes called 'Acapulco Náutico,' meaning Maritime Acapulco) comprises the western part of the city; Acapulco Dorado heads around the bay east from Playa Hornos; and Acapulco Diamante is a newer luxury resort area southeast of Acapulco proper, between the Bahía de Acapulco and the airport.

At the Bahía de Acapulco's west end, the Península de las Playas juts south and east from Old Acapulco. South of the peninsula is Isla de la Roqueta. From Playa Caleta on the south edge of the peninsula, Av López Mateos climbs west and then north to Playa La Angosta and La Quebrada before curling east back toward the city center.

Playa Caleta also marks the beginning of Acapulco's principal bayside avenue, Av Costera Miguel Alemán – often called 'La Costera' or 'Miguel Alemán' – which traverses the peninsula and then hugs the shoreline all the way around the bay to Playa Icacos and the naval base at the bay's eastern end. Most of Acapulco's hotels, restaurants, discos and points of interest are along or near La Costera, especially near 'La Diana' traffic circle. Past the naval base, La Costera becomes Carretera Escénica, which rejoins the main branch of Hwy 200 after 9km, at the turnoff to Puerto Marqués. Hwy 200 then leads southeast past ritzy Playa Revolcadero, the airport and Barra Vieja.

Information

EMERGENCY

Cruz Roja (Red Cross; ☎ 445-59-12) Provides ambulance service.
Locatel (☎ 481-11-00) A 24-hour hotline for all types of emergencies.
Tourist police (☎ 440-70-22)

INTERNET ACCESS

Acapulco has hundreds of cybercafés around town. Competition keeps prices down; most charge about M$10 per hour.
Big M@sternet (Hidalgo 6; ☺ 9am-midnight; ☒) Family-run with air-con.
Internet (Galeana 13; ☺ 10am-11pm) Fifteen computers and loud music.
Vig@net (Hidalgo 8; ☺ 8am-midnight) Keeps more reliable hours than some.

LAUNDRY

Lavandería Azueta (Azueta 14A; per kg M$12; ☺ 9am-7pm Mon-Fri)
Lavandería Lavadín (☎ 482-28-90; cnr La Paz & Iglesias; per kg M$12; ☺ 8am-10pm Mon-Sat) There's a 3kg minimum.

MEDICAL SERVICES

Hospital Magallanes (☎ 485-61-94; Massieu 2) A well-established private hospital with English-speaking doctors and staff, offering a wide range of medical services.

MONEY
Omnipresent banks (many with ATMs) give the best exchange rates, and many will change US-dollar traveler's checks and euro banknotes. *Casas de cambio* pay a slightly lower rate, but are open longer hours and are less busy than banks; shop around, as rates vary. Banks and *casas de cambio* cluster around the *zócalo* and line La Costera. Hotels will also change money, but their rates are usually extortionate.

POST
Main post office (☎ 483-53-63; La Costera 125, Palacio Federal; ☼ 8am-5:30pm Mon-Fri, 9am-1pm Sat)

PUBLICATIONS
English-language books, magazines and newspapers can be found at **Sanborns**, which has several locations along La Costera including near the *zócalo* (☎ 482 61-67, on the corner of Escudero and La Costera) and Playa Condesa (☎ 484-20-44; La Costera 3111).

TELEPHONE & FAX
You can make long-distance calls from the many Telmex card and coin phones throughout the city, or from private *casetas* (with signs saying '*larga distancia*').
Caseta Alameda Telephone and fax services, on the west side of the *zócalo*.
Telecomm (☎ 484-69-76; Main post office, La Costera 125, Palacio Federal) Fax, telephone and limited internet services.

TOURIST INFORMATION
Be aware that many of the kiosks around town offering 'tourist information' are actually time-share schemes.
Municipal tourist kiosk (☼ 8:30am-10pm) On the marina across from the *zócalo*, mostly dispensing brochures.
Casa Consular (☎ /fax 481-25-33; La Costera 4455; ☼ 9am-3pm Mon-Fri) Located at the Centro de Convenciones, provides consular assistance to visitors of all nationalities.
Procuraduría del Turista (☎ /fax 484-45-83; La Costera 4455, Centro de Convenciones; ☼ 8am-11pm) This government office will try to resolve complaints and problems with documents.
State tourist office (Sefotur; ☎ 484-24-23; sefotur@ yahoo.com; La Costera 4455, Centro de Convenciones; ☼ 9am-9pm Mon-Fri)

Dangers & Annoyances
Acapulco has suffered unprecedented levels of violence in recent years, mainly related to the illicit drug trade, and now ranks fifth among Mexican cities for the number of crimes committed per capita, surpassing Mexico City. Rival cartels have been battling for the area's lucrative drug corridor; smugglers use the Guerrero coast as a drop point for Colombian cocaine, which then passes through Acapulco on its way to the United States.

In 2006, things went from bad to worse when the rival Sinaloa and Gulf cartels turned Acapulco into their battleground, carrying out grisly, high-profile murders, including the decapitation of several policemen; one head infamously washed up on Playa Condesa. In 2007 the violence spilled over into the tourist district. Two Canadian visitors were grazed by bullets when they were caught in a crossfire outside their hotel lobby. In Spring 2007, Mexico's new president Felipe Calderón declared war on the drug cartels, deploying more than 7000 soldiers to crime-ridden cities, including Acapulco. For now, the military campaign appears to be working. Violence has subsided, and heavily-armed soldiers and police now regularly patrol the city in Humvees and on foot.

Petty crime is more common. The Casa Consular receives many reports from visitors who have suffered theft from their hotel rooms. Petty thieves trawl the beaches, looking for unattended items. Secure your valuables at all times!

All that said, tourists who avoid Acapulco's inland neighborhoods probably have more to fear from the rough surf at Playa Revolcadero, crazy drivers and crowds. More than one million people now live in the region, and sometimes it can seem as if they are all on the beach at the same time. It's almost impossible to relax on the downtown beaches due to the roar of Jet skis and the endless parade of hawkers selling shells, *tamales*, hair braids and temporary tattoos. A simple 'no, gracias' and smile works wonders.

Sights
There's more to Acapulco than just beaches and all-you-can-drink bars.

LA QUEBRADA CLAVADISTAS
Acapulco's most popular tourist attraction, the famous cliff divers of **La Quebrada** (adult/child M$35/ M$10; ☼ shows 1pm, 7:30pm, 8:30pm, 9:30pm & 10:30pm) have been dazzling audiences since 1934, diving with fearless finesse from heights of 25m

ACAPULCO

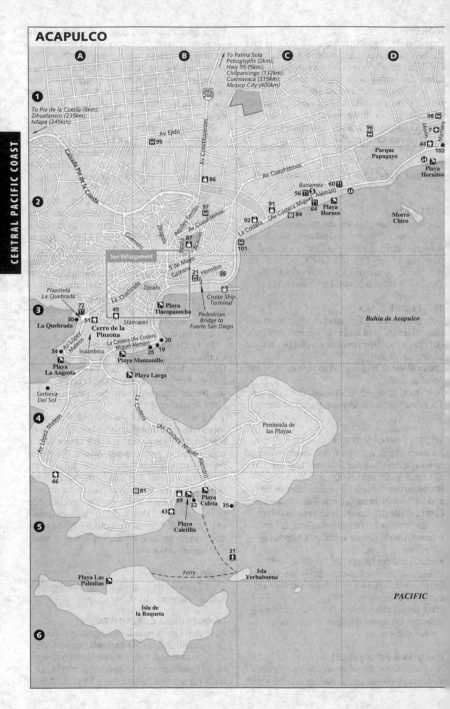

To Palma Sola
Petroglyphs (2km);
Hwy 95 (5km);
Chilpancingo (132km);
Cuernavaca (315km);
Mexico City (400km)

To Pie de la Cuesta (8km);
Zihuatanejo (235km);
Ixtapa (245km)

Av Ejido

95

86

97

Av Cuauhtémoc

92

87

101

Av Cuauhtémoc

91

56

64

Banamex

60

Av Costera Miguel Alemán

84

Playa
Hornos

La Costera

Parque
Papagayo

98

7

44

102

Playa
Hornitos

Morro
Chico

See Enlargement

5 de Mayo

21 Hornitos

26

Galeana

Plazoleta
La Quebrada

72

Zócalo

Playa
Tlacopanocha

Cruise Ship
Terminal

Bahía de Acapulco

30

51

45

La Quebrada

Staircases

Pedestrian
Bridge to
Fuerte San Diego

La Quebrada

Cerro de la
Pinzona

La Costera (Av Costera
Miguel Alemán)

20

34

Av López
Mateos

Inalámbrica

25

19

Playa
La Angosta

Playa Manzanillo

Sinfonia
Del Sol

Playa Larga

La Costera

Av Costera - Miguel Alemán

Península de
las Playas

Av López-Mateos

46

81

89

32

Playa
Caleta

35

43

Playa
Caletilla

31

Ferry

Isla
Yerbabuena

Playa Las
Palmitas

PACIFIC

Isla de
la Roqueta

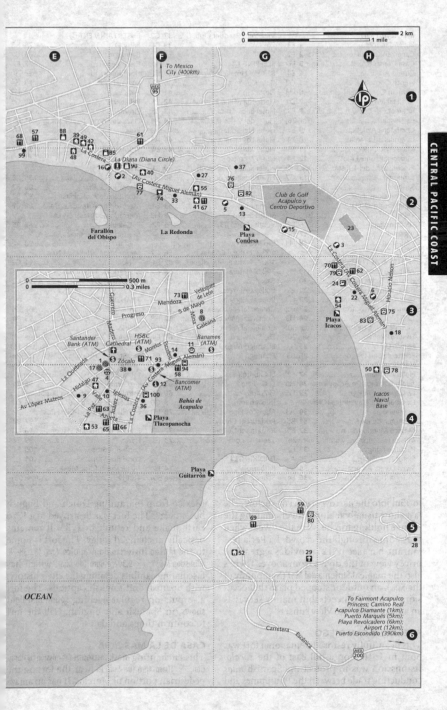

CENTRAL PACIFIC COAST

INFORMATION	
Big M@sternet	1 E3
Canadian Consulate	2 F2
Casa Consular	3 H2
Caseta Alameda	4 E4
French Consulate	5 G2
German Consulate	6 H3
Hospital Magallanes	7 D1
Internet	8 F3
La Tienda	(see 26)
Lavandería Azueta	9 E4
Lavandería Lavadín	10 E4
Main Post Office	11 F3
Municipal Tourist Kiosk	12 F4
Procuraduría del Turista	(see 3)
Sanborns	13 G2
Sanborns	14 F3
Spanish Consulate	15 G2
State Tourist Office	(see 23)
Telecomm	(see 11)
US Consulate	16 E2
Vig@net	17 E4
Wal-Mart	18 H3

SIGHTS & ACTIVITIES	
Acapulco Scuba Center	19 B3
Bonanza Ticket Booth	20 B3
Casa de la Máscara	21 B3
Centro Cultural Acapulco	22 H3
Centro de Convenciones	23 H2
CICI	24 H3
Club de Tenis Hyatt	(see 50)
Fiesta Ticket Booth	(see 20)
Fish-R-Us	25 B3
Fuerte de San Diego	26 B3
Hawaiano Ticket Booth	(see 12)
Hotel Panoramic	27 F2
Jardín Botánico De Acapulco	28 H5
La Capilla de la Paz	29 G5
La Quebrada Clavadistas (Cliff Divers)	30 A3
La Virgen de los Mares	31 B5
Mágico Mundo Marino	32 B5
Museo Histórico de Acapulco	(see 26)
Paradise Bungy	33 F2
Sinfonía del Mar	34 A3
Swiss Divers Association	35 B5
Victoria Ticket Booth	36 F4
Villa Vera Racquet Club	37 G2
Zócalo	38 F4

SLEEPING	
Bali-Hai Hotel	39 E1
Casa Condesa	40 F2
Fiesta Inn	41 F2
Hacíenda Maria Eugenia	42 E1
Hotel Boca Chica	43 B5
Hotel del Valle	44 D1
Hotel Etel Suites	45 A3
Hotel Los Flamingos	46 A5
Hotel Misión	47 E4
Hotel Monaco	48 E2
Hotel Sands Acapulco	49 E1
Hyatt Regency Acapulco	50 H4
La Torre Eiffel	51 A3
Las Brisas	52 G5
Maria Acela	53 E4
Suites Selene	54 H3
Youth Hostel K3	55 F2

EATING	
100% Natural Condesa	56 C2
100% Natural Magallanes	57 E1
100% Natural Zócalo	58 F4
Baikal	59 G5
Bodega Aurrera	60 C2
Bodega Gigante	(see 102)
Comercial Mexicana	61 F1
Comercial Mexicana	62 H3
Comercial Mexicana	(see 92)
Die Bratwurst	63 E4
El Amigo Miguel	64 C2
El Amigo Miguel I	65 E4
El Amigo Miguel II	66 F4
El Cabrito	(see 70)
El Gaucho	67 F2
El Zorrito	68 E1
Kookaburra	69 G5
Mariscos Pipo's	70 H3
Restaurant Charly	71 F3
Restaurant La Perla	72 A3
Taquería Los Pioneros	73 F3

DRINKING	
Barbarroja	74 F2
Señor Frogs	(see 59)

ENTERTAINMENT	
Baby'O	75 H3
Demas	76 G2
Disco Beach	77 F2
Hard Rock Cafe	(see 79)
Los Alebrijes	78 H4
Nina's	79 H3
Palladium	80 G5
Picante	(see 76)
Plaza de Toros	81 B5
Relax	82 G2
Salon Q	83 H3
Tropicana	84 C2

SHOPPING	
Galerías Diana	85 E2
Mercado Central	86 B2
Mercado de Artesanías	87 B2
Mercado de Artesanías Dalia	88 E1
Mercado de Artesanías La Caletilla	89 B5
Mercado de Artesanías La Diana	90 F2
Mercado de Artesanías Noa Noa	91 C2
Mercado de Artesanías Papagayo	92 C2

TRANSPORT	
Aeroméxico	(see 92)
Agencia de Viajes Zócalo	93 F4
Alamo	(see 83)
American Airlines	(see 55)
Budget	(see 16)
Bus Stop for Pie de la Cuesta & Puerto Marqués	94 F3
Estrella Blanca 1st-Class Bus Station (Central Ejido)	95 B1
Estrella Blanca 1st-Class Bus Station (Central Papagayo)	96 D1
Estrella Blanca 2nd-Class Bus Station	97 B2
Estrella de Oro Bus Station	98 D1
Hertz	99 E2
Local Bus Stop	100 F4
Local Bus Stops	101 C2
Mexicana & Click Mexicana	102 D1
Thrifty	(see 99)

to 35m into the narrow ocean cove below. The last show usually features divers making the plunge holding torches. Tip the divers when they come through the crowd. La Perla restaurant-bar (see p512) provides a great but pricey view of the divers from above. There's also the magical **Sinfonía del Mar** (Symphony of the Sea), an outdoor stepped plaza that occasionally hosts concerts, but mainly serves as an amazing place to view sunsets.

FUERTE DE SAN DIEGO

This beautifully restored pentagonal fort was built in 1616 atop a hill east of the *zócalo*. Its mission was to protect the Spanish *naos* conducting trade between the Philippines and

Mexico from marauding Dutch and English buccaneers. The fort was destroyed in a 1776 earthquake and rebuilt in 1783. It remains basically unchanged today. The fort is home to the **Museo Histórico de Acapulco** (☎ 482-38-28; admission M$37; ☺ 9:30am-6pm Tue-Sun), which has fascinating exhibits detailing the city's history, with Spanish and English captions. The fort also puts on regular evening **sound-and-light shows**, in Spanish and English. Call the fort to confirm times and dates.

CASA DE LA MÁSCARA

This enchanting **mask museum** (admission by donation; ☺ 10am-4pm Tue-Sun) is near the fort on the pedestrian portion of Morelos. It has an amazing collection of masks from around Mexico, including some by Afro-Mestizos from the Costa Chica (p515), as well as masks from Cuba, Italy and Africa. A central room displays modern creations. The scant signage is in Spanish.

JARDÍN BOTÁNICO DE ACAPULCO

Located on the campus of Loyola del Pacífico University, the **Jardín Botánico de Acapulco** (☎ 446-52-52; www.acapulcobotanico.org; Av Heroico Colegio Military s/n; suggested donation adult/student M$30/10; ☼ dawn to dusk) houses an impressive collection of flora and fauna. The well-marked footpath climbs from 204m to 411m above sea level through a shaded tropical forest, with plenty of benches to stop and smell the flowers. At the top, there's an education center and an adventure area where visitors can scale borders and explore a virgin forest. Got a green thumb and itching to volunteer? Call ahead and the staff will gladly put you to work.

PALMA SOLA PETROGLYPHS

Located deep in a forest high above Acapulco, the **Palma Sola Archaeological site** (☎ 486-15-14; admission free; ☼ 8am-4pm daily) is one of 12 known petroglyphs sites in the Acapulco area. Palma Sola is the most accessible and contains 18 petroglyphs dating from 200 BC to AD 600. Little is known about the people who created the drawings, which range from simple stick figures to elaborate scenes of ancient life in Acapulco. A steep, sturdy trail winds 400m uphill past the petroglyphs, all marked by Spanish and English signs, and ending at a rewarding view of Acapulco Bay. Bring good hiking shoes and water.

THE ZÓCALO

Every night, Acapulco's old town **zócalo**, or plaza, comes alive with street performers, mariachis, sidewalk cafés and occasional festivals. It's especially popular on Sunday nights with multiple generations of Mexican families. The **Nuestra Señora de la Soledad cathedral**, built in 1930 dominates the square and is unusual for its blue-domed, Byzantine architecture.

LA CAPILLA DE LA PAZ

Perched on a hilltop high above Acapulco, **La Capilla de la Paz** (Vientos Galernos s/n; free admission; ☼ 10am-1pm, 2-6pm daily), or Chapel of Peace, is a beautiful, quiet spot for reflection and

---

ACAPULCO IN...

Two Days

Acapulco may seem like a daunting destination, but you can easy hit the highlights in just a few days if time is an issue.

Start your tour in the heart of Acapulco life and culture, the **zócalo** (above), a good place for a cheap, traditional lunch. From here, walk to the **Fuerte de San Diego** (opposite) for a fantastic view over Acapulco Bay. If time permits, check out the **Casa de la Máscara** (opposite) next door. No trip to Acapulco is complete without watching the cliff divers of **La Quebrada** (p503), especially at night. Consider dining at **Restaurant La Perla** (p512), where you can watch the divers from your table.

Spend the second day exploring the sights and sounds of La Costera. Hit the sands early to beat the crowds at **Playa Condesa** (p508) or **Playa Icacos** (p508), with lunch on the beach. After sunset, take a 2.5km walking tour east from La Diana traffic circle, past the bar area around the bungee tower and finishing for dinner at the landmark **El Cabrito** (p512). Clubbers can keep the party going at one of the famous discos like the **Palladium** (p512).

Four Days

Follow the itinerary for two days, then escape the crowds with a day trip on the third day to **Pie de la Cuesta** (p499) to enjoy the empty beaches, romantic restaurants and unbeatable sunset views from this still-rustic seaside village.

Begin the fourth morning with a visit to **Jardín Botánico de Acapulco** (above), a tropical forest botanical garden. Afterward, head to the opposite end of Acapulco to the beautiful **Isla de la Roqueta** (p508) for a late lunch on the beach. Cap the trip with a sunset dinner and drinks at **Hotel Los Flamingos** (p510).

TOP PLACES TO WATCH THE SUNSET

Acapulco Bay faces south, making it difficult to enjoy a good sunset. But there are a few vantage points in and around town.

- The bar at Hotel Los Flamingos (p510)
- Sinfonía del Mar (p506)
- La Capilla de la Paz (p507)
- Playa La Angosta (below)
- Pie de la Cuesta (p499)

meditation. The minimalist, open-air chapel features cascading water, gardens and benches to savor the beautiful aerial view of Acapulco. The chapel's giant white cross is visible from miles across the bay. Sunset is the best time to visit, when tourists jockey for positions to capture the sun setting within the sculpture of clasped hands. Silence is golden here.

BEACHES
Acapulco's beaches tops the list of must-dos for most visitors. The beaches heading east around the bay from the zócalo – **Playa Hornos**, **Playa Hornitos**, **Playa Condesa** and **Playa Icacos** – are the most popular, though the west end of Hornos sometimes smells of fish. The high-rise hotel district begins on Playa Hornitos, on the east side of Parque Papagayo, and sweeps east. City buses constantly ply La Costera, making it easy to get up and down the long arc of beaches.

Playas Caleta and **Caletilla** are two small, protected beaches blending into each other in a cove on the south side of Península de las Playas. They're both backed by a solid line of seafood palapa restaurants. The area is especially popular with families who have small children, as the water is very calm. All buses marked 'Caleta' heading down La Costera arrive here. The Mágico Mundo Marino aquarium (see opposite) sits on an islet just offshore, forming the imaginary line between the two beaches; boats go regularly from the islet to Isla de la Roqueta.

Playa La Angosta is in a tiny, protected cove on the west side of the peninsula. From the zócalo it takes about 20 minutes to walk here. Or you can take any 'Caleta' bus and get off near Hotel Avenida, on La Costera, just one short block from the beach.

The beaches on **Bahía Puerto Marqués**, about 18km southeast of the zócalo, are very popular, and its calm waters are good for waterskiing and sailing. You get a magnificent view of Bahía de Acapulco as the Carretera Escénica climbs south out of the city. Frequent 'Puerto Marqués' buses run along La Costera every 10 minutes from 5am to 9pm.

Beyond the Puerto Marqués turnoff and before the airport, **Playa Revolcadero** is a long, straight beach that has seen a recent explosion in luxury tourism and residential development. Waves are large and surfing is popular here, especially in summer, but a strong undertow makes swimming dangerous; heed lifeguards' instructions. Horseback riding along the beach is popular.

ISLA DE LA ROQUETA
This island offers a popular (crowded) beach, and snorkeling and diving possibilities. You can rent snorkeling gear, kayaks and other water-sports equipment on the beach. From Playas Caleta and Caletilla, boats make the eight-minute trip (M$40 round-trip) every 20 minutes or so. Alternatively, glass-bottomed boats make a circuitous trip to the island (M$60), departing from the same beaches but traveling via **La Virgen de los Mares** (Virgin of the Seas), a submerged bronze statue of the Virgen de Guadalupe – visibility varies with water conditions. The trip takes about 45 minutes, depending on how many times floating vendors accost your boat.

Activities
As one might expect, Acapulco's activities are largely beach-based. There are nonbeach things to do, but generally everything is in the spirit of mega-vacation with once-in-a-lifetime adventure and/or adrenaline rush promised.

WATER SPORTS
Just about everything that can be done on or below the water is done in Acapulco. On the Bahía de Acapulco, waterskiing, boating, banana-boating and parasailing are all popular activities. To partake in any of these, walk along the Zona Dorada beaches and look for the (usually) orange kiosks. These charge about M$70 for snorkeling gear, M$300 for a five-minute parasailing flight, M$350 for a Jet-ski ride and M$650 for one hour of waterskiing. The smaller Playas Caleta and Caletilla have sailboats, fishing boats, motorboats, pedal boats, canoes, snorkeling gear, inner tubes and water bicycles for rent.

Though Acapulco isn't really a scuba destination, there are some decent dive sites nearby. **Acapulco Scuba Center** (☎ 482-94-74; www .acapulcoscuba.com; Paseo del Pescador 13 & 14) and **Swiss Divers Association** (☎ 482-13-57; www.swissdivers.com; La Costera 100) both charge about M$750 for a two-tank dive.

The best **snorkeling** is off small Playa Las Palmitas on Isla de la Roqueta (opposite). Unless you pony up for an organized snorkeling trip you'll need to scramble over rocks to reach it. You can rent gear on the isla or on Playas Caleta and Caletilla, which also have some decent spots. Both scuba operations above take half-day snorkeling trips for around M$350 per person, including boat, guide, gear, food, drink and hotel transportation.

Sportfishing is very popular. Acapulco Scuba Center (see above) and **Fish-R-Us** (☎ 487-87-87, 482-82-82; www.fish-r-us.com; La Costera 100) offer half-day fishing trips from around M$2700 (for the entire eight-person boat, gear and bait). The captain can often combine individuals into a group large enough to cover the cost of the boat, for M$750 to M$850 per person.

OTHER SPORTS

For golfers, **Club de Golf Acapulco** (☎ 484-07-81; Costera Miguel Alemán s/n; 9/18 holes M$500/800) has a 9-hole course downtown. The **Fairmont Acapulco Princess** and **Fairmont Pierre Marques** share two championship courses (see p511).

For tennis, try **Club de Golf Acapulco** (☎ 484-07-81; Costera Miguel Alemán s/n), **Club de Tenis Hyatt** (☎ 469-12-34; www.acapulco.hyatt.com; La Costera 1), **Villa Vera Racquet Club** (☎ 484-03-34; Lomas del Mar 35) or **Hotel Panoramic** (☎ 481-01-32; Av Condesa 1).

The 50m-high bungee tower at **Paradise Bungy** (☎ 484-75-29; www.paradisebungy.com; La Costera 107; ☺ noon-midnight Mon-Thu, to 2am Fri-Sun) is easy to spot on the Costera, and for M$600 you can throw yourself (bungee included) from its platform while crowds cheer you from the street.

CRUISES

Various boats and yachts offer cruises, most of which depart from around Playa Tlacopanocha or Playa Manzanillo near the zócalo. Cruises – from M$120 for 1½ hours to over M$250 for four hours – are available day and night. They range from glass-bottomed boats to multilevel craft (with blaring salsa music and open bars) to yachts offering quiet sunset cruises around the bay. The **Victoria** (☎ cell phone 744-5162494), **Hawaiano** (☎ 482-21-99),

Fiesta (☎ 482-20-55) and **Bonanza** (☎ 482-20-55) cruise operations are all popular; you can make reservations directly from the eager captains at the marina or through travel agencies and most hotels.

Acapulco for Children

Acapulco is very family friendly, with many fun options designed especially for kids.

PARQUE PAPAGAYO

This large, shaded **children's park** (La Costera; admission free; ☺ 8am-8pm), between Morín and El Cano near Playa Hornitos, is popular with Mexican families. Attractions include a lake with paddleboats, a children's train, a restaurant-bar, an aviary and a small zoo and petting zoo. The 1.2km circuit trail is a good place for a morning jog. Sadly, the neighboring amusement park closed in 2006 and is now a rusting ghost town.

CICI

The family water-sports park, **CICI** (☎ 484-19-60; www.cici.com.mx; La Costera 101; admission adults & children over 3 M$100; ☺ 10am-6pm), is on the east side of Acapulco. Dolphins perform several shows daily, and humans occasionally give diving exhibitions. You can also enjoy an 80m-long water toboggan, a pool with artificial waves and the **Sky Coaster** (M$150 per person) giant swing ride. Any local bus marked 'CICI,' 'Base' or 'Puerto Marqués' will take you there.

MÁGICO MUNDO MARINO

This **aquarium** (☎ 483-12-15; adult/child M$60/30; ☺ 9am-6pm) stands on a small islet off Playas Caleta and Caletilla. Highlights include a sea lion show, swimming pools, water toboggans and crocodile, turtle and piranha feedings.

Festivals & Events

Semana Santa Probably the busiest time of year for tourism in Acapulco. There's lots of action in the discos, on the beaches and all over town.

Festival Francés (French Festival) This festival, which began in 2004, is held in March/April and celebrates French food, cinema, music and literature.

Festivales de Acapulco (Acafest) Held for one week in May, features Mexican and international music stars at venues around town.

Acapulco Fair This annual holiday festival runs from mid-December to early January at the convention center and features carnival rides, games, vendors and festive decorations.

Sleeping

Acapulco has more than 30,000 hotel rooms. Rates vary widely by season; the high season is roughly from mid-December to mid-January, Easter Week and during the July and August school holidays. In low season, you can often bargain for a better rate, especially for extended stays. During Semana Santa or between Christmas and New Year's Day (at which times all bets are off on room prices) it's essential to book ahead. The prices listed here are for high season.

BUDGET

Most of Acapulco's budget hotels are concentrated around the *zócalo* and on La Quebrada.

María Acela (☎ 481-06-61; La Paz 20; r per person M$100) The blue and white hotel is a reliable inn located on a quiet street just three blocks west of the *zócalo*. Rooms are basic and lack hot water, but they are clean and have TV and fan.

Youth Hostel K3 (☎ 481-31-11; www.k3acapulco.com; La Costera 116; dm/r incl continental breakfast M$150/400; 🍴 🖥) It's shared bathrooms only here, and the rooms have almost a Japanese capsule-hotel feel, but there's air-con and the terrace, bar and game room provide ample space for socializing. There's also a shared kitchen. Most importantly, it's right across the highway from the beach.

our pick La Torre Eiffel (☎ 482-16-83; hoteltorreeiffel@hotmail.com; Inalámbrica 110; s M$150, d from M$250; 🅿 🍴 🏊) Perched on a hill above La Quebrada, the popular Eiffel has a small swimming pool, huge shared balconies and spectacular sunset views. It's a bit out of the way, but the friendly helpful staff and comfortable beds make the climb worth it.

Hotel Misión (☎ 482-36-43; hotelmision@hotmail.com; Valle 12; r per person M$250; 🅿) Acapulco's oldest hotel is a charming colonial building with 28 rooms around a leafy, relaxing courtyard. The basic rooms are decorated in colorful tiles, heavy Spanish-style furniture and comfortable beds. Some toilets lack seats.

MIDRANGE

Hotel Etel Suites (☎ 482-22-40/41; etelsuites@terra .com.mx; Av La Pinzona 92; r/ste/apt from M$450/600/900; 🅿 🍴 🏊 🚿) High atop the hill overlooking Old Acapulco, the Etel is renowned for the good value and friendly service. The spotless suites and apartments all sleep at least three

people, and most have expansive terraces with views of La Quebrada and the Pacific to one side and the bay to the other. Amenities include full kitchens, well-manicured gardens, a children's play area and a swimming pool.

Hotel Monaco (☎ 485-64-67; La Costera 137; r M$491; 🅿 🍴 🏊) This great value-for-money motel is located on the beach side of La Costera in the middle of the action. The dated but clean rooms have a TV, air-con, fridge and phone, all surrounding a courtyard pool and patio. The highway and courtyard can get noisy, especially on weekends.

Hotel Sands Acapulco (☎ 484-22-60; www.sands.com .mx; La Costera 178; bungalows/r M$650/875; 🅿 🍴 🏊 🚿) An excellent choice for families, Sands is located across the highway from the beach and has a large children's playground, mini-golf, pools and a water slide. Bungalows are small but cozy; the larger rooms sleep up to four people. All have cable TV, air-con, fridge and safes.

Suites Selene (☎ 484-29-77; suitesselene@hotmail .com; Colón 175; d without kitchen M$702, d/q with kitchen M$819/1287; 🅿 🍴 🏊) Just steps to Playa Icacos, Selene is a great option, especially for long-stay self-caterers. Though a little worn, it has fine firm beds, good air-con (though only fans in the dining room/kitchens), a nice deep pool and cable TV throughout.

Hotel del Valle (☎ 485-83-36/88; cnr Morín & Espinoza; r with fan/air-con M$702/877; 🅿 🍴 🏊) On the east side of Parque Papagayo, near La Costera and popular Playa Hornitos, the del Valle has reasonably comfortable rooms, a small swimming pool and communal kitchens (M$60 surcharge per day).

our pick Hotel Los Flamingos (☎ 482-06-90; www .hotellosflamingos.com; Av López Mateos s/n; r from M$703; 🅿 🍴 🏊) Once owned by John Wayne, Johnny 'Tarzan' Weissmuller and their pals, Los Flamingos is a living museum to Acapulco's heyday. Perched on a cliff 135m above the ocean, this classic boasts one of the finest sunset views in town and a popular bar and restaurant. Images of Hollywood's golden age grace the walls. The rooms are modest and comfortable with great bathrooms.

Bali-Hai Hotel (☎ 485-6622; www.balihai.com.mx; La Costera 186; r from M$800; 🅿 🍴 🏊) A Polynesian themed motel in the heart of Acapulco Bay and across the street from the beach is a good moderate choice, but overpriced during high season. Rooms are decorated with lots of bamboo and marble. The onsite restaurant has a popular breakfast buffet.

Hotel Boca Chica (☎ 483-67-41; www.bocachicahotel .com; Playa Caletilla, r from M$811; P 🏊 🍴) This famous hotel is tucked into the rocks at the end of Playa Caletilla and has a virtually private ocean cove for snorkeling, diving and boating. At the time of research, the Boca Chica was undergoing a major renovation that should be complete by the time you read this.

Fiesta Inn (☎ 435-05-00; www.fiestainn.com; La Costera 2311; r from M$830; P 🏊 💻 🍴 👶) This centrally located, 220-room high-rise has recently-remodeled rooms with contemporary furnishings, flat-screen TV, and private balconies with ocean views. Hotel amenities include a large pool, gym and kids' club.

Hacienda María Eugenia (☎ 511-15-97; www.hacien damariaeugenia.com; La Costera 176; s/d/ste M$850/950/1250; P 🏊 🍴) A modern hotel built in colonial architecture style has 65 spacious, nicely-decorated rooms with kitchenettes, air-con, cable TV and safes. The onsite Maria Bonita restaurant serves traditional Chiapas cuisine, as well as local seafood specialties.

TOP END

The original high-rise zone stretches from the eastern end of Parque Papagayo and curves east around the bay; a new luxury 'strip' is springing up on Playa Revolcadero, east of Puerto Marqués. Prices listed here are the high-season rack rates. Package rates and online bookings can end up providing substantial savings.

Hyatt Regency Acapulco (☎ 469-12-34, in Mexico 800-005-00-00, in the US 800-233-1234; www.acapulco.hyatt .com; La Costera 1; r from M$1894; P 🏊 🍴 💻 🍴 👶) The beachfront Hyatt has 640 plush rooms and suites with marble bathrooms, and most have private balconies. Amenities include two inviting swimming pools, a bevy of bars and restaurants, a fitness center and a new spa. It's also the only kosher hotel in Acapulco, featuring kosher cuisine and an onsite synagogue.

Camino Real Acapulco Diamante (☎ /fax 435-10-10, in the US 800-722-6466; www.caminoreal .com/acapulco; Carretera Escénica, Km 14; r from M$2450; P 🏊 🍴 💻 🍴 👶) This secluded resort sits directly above its own small, rocky stretch of Playa Pichilingüe on the calm bay of Puerto Marqués. Each of the 157 luxuriously appointed rooms have a terrace or balcony looking out over the bay. This well-designed multilevel hotel has a spa, a gym, three shallow swimming pools and several bars and restaurants.

ourpick Las Brisas (☎ 469-69-00, in the US 800-223-6800; www.brisas.com.mx; Carretera Escénica 5255; casitas incl breafast from M$2850; P 🏊 💻 🍴) Romantic, lovely Las Brisas commands amazing views from its vantage point high above the bay. Built in the late 1950s, the place has great bones, including a lot of lovely stonework and tile floors. Each of the 236 casitas has a private terrace or balcony and either a private swimming pool or one shared with, at most, two other casitas. Service gets high ratings (room prices include tips). The hotel's beach club is nestled far below in a rocky cove.

Fairmont Acapulco Princess (☎ 469-10-00, in the US 800-441-1414; www.fairmont.com; Playa Revolcadero s/n; r from M$2900; P 🏊 🏊 💻 🍴 👶) Towering above Playa Revolcadero, this famous hotel was built in 1971 in the shape of a giant Aztec pyramid. The 1017 recently-renovated rooms are divided among three towers; all rooms are spacious and luxurious with marble and contemporary furnishings. The resort sits on 162 acres of lush, landscaped grounds with five freshwater and saltwater swimming pools, waterfalls, a fitness center, a spa, 11 tennis courts, a golf course, seven restaurants, four bars and a nightclub.

Eating

Stock up on groceries, supplies and premade meals at the several megastores along La Costera including Comercial Mexicana, Bodega Aurrera, Bodega Gigante and Wal-Mart.

OLD ACAPULCO

ourpick Taquería Los Pioneros (☎ 482-23-45; cnr Mendoza & Mina; 5 tacos M$20, mains M$35-45; 🕒 9am-3am) The tacos are tiny but their various fillings are tasty, plus you can load up on accompaniments: jalapeños, pickled carrots, onions, cilantro etc.

Restaurant Charly (Carranza s/n; 4 tacos M$20, mains M$35-50) Just steps east of the *zócalo*, on the pedestrian alley of Carranza, economical Charly has shady sidewalk tables and offers up *barbacoa de chivo* (spiced, slow-cooked goat meat surrounded by roasted maguey plants) as both a main dish and in taco form.

El Amigo Miguel (☎ 483-69-81; mains M$40-90) Juárez 16 (🕒 10am-9pm); Juárez 31 (🕒 10am-9pm); La Costera s/n (🕒 11am-8pm) This chain features cheery, busy open-air restaurants with cheap and delicious seafood. Miguel has two restaurants opposite one another, on the same corner, with other branches around town.

Die Bratwurst (☎ 127-15-23; José Azueta 10; mains M$50-75; ⊗ noon-8pm Mon-Sat). When you tire of tacos, head for this traditional German restaurant whose motto is 'real German food made the Mexican way.' Owner Wilde Hilde came from the Bavarian village of Garmisch-Partenkirchen for a vacation 35 years ago and never left. She serves up great sausage with sauerkraut, potatoes, salad, bread and flan, all for M$60.

Restaurant La Perla (☎ 483-11-55; Hotel El Mirador, Plazoleta La Quebrada 74; dinner M$117; ⊗ 7-11pm) First-rate views of the death-defying *clavadistas* almost justify the high price of a meal at this restaurant-bar; candlelit terraces and sea breezes are a bonus. The three-course menu is meat-heavy but includes several fish choices and a couple each of chicken and pasta dishes.

LA COSTERA

El Zorrito (☎ 485-79-14; La Costera s/n; mains M$30-150; ⊗ 24hr) This popular, always-packed restaurant serves up Mexican comfort foods like tasty tacos, *pozole*, shrimp, fish and an extensive dessert menu.

our pick **El Cabrito** (☎ 484-77-11; www.elcabrito -acapulco.com; La Costera 1480; M$60-170; ⊗ 2pm-midnight) A local tradition since 1963, this reader-recommended restaurant has some of the finest traditional Mexican food in town like Oaxaca-style black *mole* made of 32 ingredients. For those who like to eat on a dare, the house specialty is *Cabecita de Cabrito* – broiled head of baby goat. The outdoor tables offer prime people-watching prospects, but avoid sitting too close to the blazing-hot BBQ grill!

El Gaucho (☎ 484-17-00; Hotel Presidente, La Costera 8; mains M$60-200; ⊗ 5pm-midnight) The Gaucho is upscale but not stuffy, and one of the top spots in town for a steak (though you pay dearly for it). All the meat is grilled in true Argentine style, and less carnivorous or extravagant folk can choose from an assortment of pasta dishes. The short but decent wine list includes selections from Mexico, Chile, Spain and Argentina.

our pick **100% Natural** (☎ 485-52-79; www.100 natural.com.mx; mains M$60-275; Ⓥ) zócalo (La Costera s/n); Condesa (La Costera 112); Magallanes (La Costera 200) This health-conscious chain has several branches along La Costera and elsewhere in town, all with a mellow ambience and good, friendly service. The food is consistently good, mostly vegetarian fare, including wholegrain breads

and rolls and a large variety of fruit and veggie juices and shakes. Some locations are open 24 hours.

Mariscos Pipo's (☎ 484-17-00; cnr La Costera & Nao Victoria; mains M$75-205; ⊗ 1-9pm) Pipo's has a varied menu that includes baby shark quesadillas, freshwater bass, grilled crawfish and scallop cocktail, all served in a large dining area with a simple, nautical theme.

Kookaburra (☎ 446-60-20, 446-60-39; Carretera Escénica s/n; mains M$140-315) One of Acapulco's finest and most exclusive restaurants, the thatched Kookaburra has great views and even better food, including such specialties as spaghetti with caviar or filet mignon with *chipotle*. It's a perfect place for a romantic dinner. Reservations required

Baikal (☎ 446-6845; www.baikal.com.mx; Carretera Escénica 22; mains M$200-500) Baikal is not just a restaurant; it's an experience for all five senses. Step down the unusual spiral staircase entrance and you emerge into a cliffside wonderland with stunning views over Acapulco Bay. The cuisine is a fusion of French, Asian and Mediterranean and presented like a masterpiece while live jazz music plays in the background. This is Acapulco's place to see and be seen. Reservations are mandatory.

Entertainment

NIGHTCLUBS

Most clubs open around 10:30pm but don't get rolling until midnight or later. Cover charges vary by the season, night and the doorman's mood. Dress to impress; shorts and sneakers are not permitted.

Palladium (☎ 446-54-90; www.palladium.com.mx; Carretera Escénica s/n; admission incl open bar women/men M$350/450) Hailed by many as the best disco in town, Palladium attracts a 20- to 30-something crowd with its fabulous views from the floor to ceiling windows. DJs pump out hip-hop, house, trance and techno from an ultraluxe sound system. Around 3am, the famous 'Silver Aztec' entertains the screaming crowd with fire and dance. Dress up, and expect to wait in line.

Baby'O (☎ 484-74-74; La Costera 22; admission M$100-400) Very popular with the upscale crowd, the cave-like club has a laser light show and Wednesday theme nights, and spins rock, pop, house and 'everything but electronica.' Drinks are not included in the cover charge.

Los Alebrijes (☎ 484-59-02; La Costera 3308; admission incl open bar women/men M$250/350) This massive club is usually packed with a young Mexican crowd. The music is a middle-of-the-road mix of mostly Latin rock and pop; open bar hours are 1am to 5am.

Disco Beach (☎ 484-82-30; La Costera s/n; admission incl open bar women/men M$250/300; ☽ Wed-Sat) Right in the heart of Playa Condesa, Disco Beach attracts a fairly young crowd. The dress policy and atmosphere are more relaxed than at other clubs. Music is house, disco, techno, hip-hop, '70s and '80s; women get in (and drink) for free on Wednesday; Friday foam parties can be wild. Check out Ibiza Lounge and Thai Bar next door, too.

LIVE MUSIC & BARS

Barbarroja (☎ 484-59-32; La Costera s/n; ☽ noon-5am) Ahoy Matey! From a boat-shaped bar to girls in sexy pirate costumes dancing on tables, this over-the-top, pirate-themed pub is one of several beachfront bars near the bungee tower. But it's the only one where a 30-year-old can walk in and not feel like the oldest person in the world.

Nina's (☎ 484-24-00; La Costera 41; admission incl open bar M$200-250; ☽ 10pm-4am) Nina's is one of the best places in town for live *música tropical* (salsa, *cumbia*, cha-cha, merengue etc); it has a smokin' dance floor, variety acts and impersonators.

Salon Q (☎ 484-32-52, 481-01-14; La Costera 23; admission M$180, with open bar M$240; ☽ 10:30pm-6am) This *'catedral de la salsa'* hosts first-rate salsa singers and bands, celebrity impersonators and a *Carnaval* atmosphere.

Tropicana (La Costera s/n, Playa Hornos; admission M$50; ☽ 10pm-4am) Like Nina's, Tropicana has a full spectrum of live *música tropical*, only without the bells and whistles.

Hotel Los Flamingos (☎ 482-06-90; López Mateos s/n) The one quiet spot in this rowdy bunch, the clifftop bar of Hotel Los Flamingos has the hands-down best sunset-viewing/drinking spot in Acapulco. Not a car or hustler in sight, and you can sip *cocos locos* (cocktails made with rum, tequila, pineapple juice and coconut créme) to your heart's content.

Hard Rock Cafe (☎ 484-00-47; La Costera 37; ☽ noon-2am) It's hard to miss the Hard Rock. Just northwest of CICI, this chain's Acapulco branch has live music from 10pm to 2am.

Señor Frogs (☎ 446-57-34; www.senorfrogs.com; Carretera Escénica 28; ☽ 10am-1am). Yes, it's a chain. Yes, it's cheesy and touristy. But dammit, it's still a lot of fun! The zany antics attract

families by day, and the cheap beer and far-party atmosphere brings in the college kids at night.

GAY VENUES

Acapulco has an active gay scene with several gay bars and clubs, mostly open from 10pm until about 4am.

Demas (☎ 484-13-70; Piedra Picuda 17) is open only to men and has shows on Friday and Saturday; **Picante** (Piedra Picuda 16) is found behind Demas, with a minuscule dance floor, the occasional drag or stripper show, and a mostly male clientele; and **Relax** (☎ 484-04-21; Lomas del Mar 4; ☽ Thu-Sat) welcomes men and women. Acapulco's unofficial **gay beach** is the rocky section of Playa Condesa by the Fiesta Americana hotel. **Casa Condesa** (☎ 484-1616; www .casacondesa.com; Bella Vista 125; r from M$960) is a B&B that caters to gay men.

SPORTS

Bullfights take place at the Plaza de Toros, southeast of La Quebrada and northwest of Playas Caleta and Caletilla, every Sunday at 5:30pm from January to March; for tickets, try your hotel, a travel agency or the **bullring box office** (☎ 482-11-81; Plaza de Toros; ☽ 10am-2pm). The 'Caleta' bus passes near the bullring.

Shopping

Mercado de Artesanías (cnr Parana & Velasquez de Leon) Bargaining is the standard at this 400-stall *mercado*, especially as sellers often find suckers among the many cruise-ship passengers. The market is located between Av Cuauhtémoc and Vicente de León and is Acapulco's main craft market. It's paved and pleasant, and an OK place to get better deals on everything that you see in the hotel shops including hammocks, jewelry, clothing and T-shirts.

Other handicraft markets include the **Mercados de Artesanías Papagayo**, **Noa Noa**, **Dalia** and **La Diana** (all on La Costera), and the **Mercado de Artesanías La Caletilla** at the western end of Playa Caletilla.

Mercado Central (Diego H de Mendoza s/n) This truly local market, a sprawling indoor-outdoor bazaar, has everything from *atole* to *zapatos* (shoes) – not to mention produce, hot food and souvenirs. Any eastbound 'Pie de la Cuesta' or 'Pedregoso' bus will drop you here; get off where the sidewalk turns to tarp-covered stalls.

Galerías Diana (☎ 481-40-21; La Costera 1926; ☽ 7:30am-midnight Sun-Thu, to 2am Fri & Sat) Shop until you drop at this mammoth mall with American and European brand shops such as Zara, Nine West, Puma and, yes, Starbucks. This mall also has a casino, a video arcade and the Cinepolis VIP movie theater featuring bartender service and comfy leather lounge chairs; most flicks are in English with Spanish subtitles.

Getting There & Away

Acapulco is accessible via Hwy 200 from the east and west, and by Hwy 95 and Hwy 95D from the north. It's 400km south of Mexico City and 235km southeast of Zihuatanejo.

AIR

Acapulco's small but busy airport, **Juan Álvarez International Airport** (☎ 466-94-34), has many international flights, most connecting through Mexico City or Guadalajara (both are short hops from Acapulco). All flights mentioned here are direct; some are seasonal.

Aeroméxico (☎ 485-16-25/00; La Costera 286) Service to Guadalajara, Mexico City and Tijuana.

America West (☎ 466-92-75; Airport) Service to Los Angeles and Phoenix.

American Airlines (☎ 481-01-61; La Costera 116, Plaza Condesa, Local 109) Service to Dallas and Chicago.

Aviacsa (☎ 466-92-09; Airport) Service regularly to Oaxaca, Mexico City and Tijuana.

Azteca (☎ 466-90-29; Airport) Service to Ciudad Juárez, Guadalajara and Tijuana.

Continental Airlines (☎ 466-90-46; Airport) Service to Houston, Minneapolis and Newark.

Delta Airlines (☎ 800-902-2100; Airport) Service to Atlanta and Los Angeles.

Mexicana & Click Mexicana (☎ 486-75-70; La Costera 1632, La Gran Plaza) Service to Mexico City and Guadalajara.

Northwest (☎ 800-900-08-00; Airport) Service to Houston.

BUS

There are two major, 1st-class long- distance bus companies in Acapulco: Estrella de Oro and Estrella Blanca. The modern, air-conditioned **Estrella de Oro terminal** (EDO; ☎ 800-900-01-05; Av Cuauhtémoc 1490), just east of Massieu, has free toilets, a Banamex ATM and a ticket machine that accepts bank debit cards (and luggage can also be left for M$2 per hour, per piece). **Estrella Blanca** (EB; ☎ 469-20-80) has two 1st-class terminals: **Central Papagayo** (Av Cuauhtémoc 1605), just north of Parque Papagayo,

and **Central Ejido** (☎ 469-20-28/30; Av Ejido 47). The **Estrella Blanca 2nd-class terminal** (☎ 482-21-84; Av Cuauhtémoc 97) sells tickets for all buses, but only has departures to relatively nearby towns. Estrella Blanca tickets are also sold at a few agencies around town, including **Agencia de Viajes Zócalo** (☎ 482-49-76; La Costera 207, Local 2).

Both companies offer frequent services to Mexico City, with various levels of luxury. See the table opposite for daily services.

CAR & MOTORCYCLE

Many car rental companies rent out 4WDs as well as cars; several have offices at the airport as well as in town, and some offer free delivery to you. Shop around to compare prices.

Rental companies in Acapulco:

Alamo (☎ 484-33-05, 466-94-44; La Costera 2148)

Avis (☎ 462-00-75; Airport)

Budget (☎ 481-24-33, 466-90-03; La Costera 93, Local 2)

Hertz (☎ 485-89-47; La Costera 137)

Thrifty Airport (☎ 466-92-86); La Costera 139 (☎ 486-19-40)

Drivers heading inland on Hwy 95D need to have some cash handy. The tolls to Chilpancingo, about 130km north, total M$279.

Getting Around

TO/FROM THE AIRPORT

Acapulco's airport is 23km southeast of the *zócalo*, beyond the junction for Puerto Marqués. Arriving by air, you can buy a ticket for transportation into town from the *colectivo* desk at the end of the domestic terminal; it's about M$75 per person for a lift to your hotel (a bit more if it's west of the *zócalo*).

Leaving Acapulco, phone **Móvil Aca** (☎ 462-10-95) 24 hours in advance to reserve transportation back to the airport; the cost varies depending on where your pick-up is (from M$150 to M$400 per person or M$300 to M$400 for the whole vehicle holding up to five passengers). Taxis from the center to the airport cost around M$230 to M$330, depending on the amount of luggage.

BUS

Acapulco has a good city bus system (especially good when you get an airbrushed beauty with a bumping sound system). Buses operate from 5am to 11pm and cost M$5.50 with aircon, M$4.50 without. From the *zócalo* area, the bus stop opposite Sanborns department store

DAILY BUSES FROM ACAPULCO

Destination	Fare	Duration	Frequency
Chilpancingo	1st class M$76	1¼hr	several from Central Ejido (EB)
	1st-class M$76	1¾hr	frequent (EDO)
	2nd-class M$59	3hr	every 30 min, 5am-7pm, from 2nd-class terminal (EB)
Cuernavaca	1st-class M$261	4-5hr	3 daily from Central Papagayo (EB)
	1st-class M$220	4-5hr	7 daily
	M$206	5hr	very frequent semi-directo (EDO)
Mexico City (Terminal Norte)	deluxe M$450	6hr	1 daily from Central Papagayo (EB)
	1st-class M$315	6hr	several from Central Papagayo (EB)
	1st-class M$315	6hr	7 daily (EDO0
	1st-class M$272	6hr	2 from Central Ejido (EB)
Mexico City (Terminal Sur)	deluxe M$467	5hr	4 daily from Central Papagayo (EB)
	deluxe M$456	5hr	6 (EDO)
	1st-class M$315	5hr	frequent from Central Papagayo (EB)
	1st-class M$315	5hr	8 daily from Central Ejido (EB)
	1st-class M$315	5hr	frequent (EDO)
Puerto Escondido	1st-class M$239	7hr	5 daily from Central Ejido (EB)
	2nd-class M$195	9½hr	5 daily from Central Ejido (EB)
Taxco	1st-class M$163	4hr	3 daily from Central Ejido (EB)
	1st-class M$163	4hr	2 daily (EDO)
Zihuatanejo	1st-class M$125	4-5hr	10 daily from Central Ejido (EB)
	Primera Plus M$125	4-5hr	13 daily from Central Ejido (EB)
	1st-class M$125	4-5hr	3 daily (EDO)
	2nd-class M$92	4-5hr	12 hourly 5am-5:30pm (EDO)

on La Costera, two blocks east of the *zócalo*, is a good place to catch buses – it's the beginning of several bus routes (including to Pie de la Cuesta) so you can usually get a seat.

Useful city routes include the following:

Base–Caleta From the Icacos naval base at the southeast end of Acapulco, along La Costera, past the *zócalo* to Playa Caleta.

Base–Cine Río–Caleta From the Icacos naval base, cuts inland from La Costera on Av Wilfrido Massieu to Av Cuauhtémoc, heads down Av Cuauhtémoc through the business district, turning back to La Costera just before reaching the *zócalo*, continuing west to Playa Caleta.

Puerto Marqués–Centro From opposite Sanborns, along La Costera to Puerto Marqués.

Zócalo–Playa Pie de la Cuesta From opposite Sanborns, to Pie de la Cuesta.

CAR & MOTORCYCLE

If you can possibly avoid doing any driving in Acapulco, do. The streets are in poor shape and the anarchic traffic is often horridly snarled.

TAXI

Hundreds of zippy blue-and-white VW cabs scurry around Acapulco like cockroaches, maneuvering with an audacity that borders on the comical. Drivers often quote fares higher than the official ones. Local rates are about M$20 to M$50 depending on your destination. Always agree on a price with the driver before getting into the taxi.

BARRA VIEJA

About 40km southeast of central Acapulco lies the small fishing village of Barra Vieja, a rustic beach where the ocean meets Tres Palos lagoon. The beach has a few *enramada* seafood restaurants and a seasonal turtle sanctuary. Other activities include massages, boat rides, horseback riding. The main attraction is the virgin beach, free of Acapulco crowds or pesky vendors.

To get here by car, take the road to the airport and continue 20km further to Barra Vieja. By bus from Acapulco, take a bus to Playa Marques, then change to a *combi* heading to Barra Vieja. A round-trip taxi ride from Acapulco will set you back about M$500.

COSTA CHICA

Guerrero's 'Small Coast,' extending southeast from Acapulco to the Oaxacan border, is much less traveled than its bigger brother to the northwest, but it does have at least one spectacular beach.

Afro-Mestizos (people of mixed African, Indigenous and European descent) make up a large portion of the population. The region was a safe haven for Africans who escaped slavery, some from the interior, others (it's believed) from a slave ship that sank just off the coast.

From Acapulco, Hwy 200 traverses inland past small villages and farmlands. **San Marcos**, about 60km east of Acapulco, **Cruz Grande**, about 40km further east, are the only two towns of significant size before **Cuajinicuilapa** near the Oaxaca border. Both provide basic services including banks, gas stations and simple hotels.

Playa Ventura & Around
☎ 741 / Pop 420

About three hours' drive southeast of Acapulco, **Playa Ventura** (labeled Juan Álvarez on most maps) is a pristine beach with soft white and gold sands and clear, calm water. A town extends inland for about three blocks and features a small village **museum**, simple seafood restaurants and a few beachfront hotels.

The positively pink **Hotel Doña Celsa** (☎ 101-30-69; d/q M$200/350; **P** 🏊) has 20 simple, clean rooms, a nice pool, a seafood restaurant and grocery store.

ourpick La Caracola (☎ 101-30-47; www.playaventura.com; r M$400 & 650; **P** 🏊), 1.5km north (right) of the church, is the nicest place in town. This thatched tree-house-on-stilts has several rooms with basic beds, mosquito netting, hammocks, fans and a communal kitchen. Tiny adobe pyramids on the beach house cheaper rooms.

To get here by car, take Hwy 200 to the village of Copala (Km 124) and follow the signs to Playa Ventura. By bus from Acapulco, take a southeast-bound bus to Copala (M$60, 2½ hours, 120km). From there, camionetas and microbuses depart for Playa Ventura about every half-hour (M$15, 30 minutes, 13km) from just east of the bus stop.

About 13km southeast of Copala on Hwy 200 (Km137) is the market town of **Marquelia**. The town offers access to an immense stretch of beach backed by coco palms – the beach follows the coastline's contours for many kilometers in either direction. From Marquelia's center you can take a camioneta to a section of the beach known as **Playa La Bocana**, where

the Río Marquelia meets the sea and forms a lagoon. La Bocana has some cabañas, as well as comedores (small food stalls) with hammocks where you can spend the night. Another portion of the beach, **Playa Las Peñitas**, is reached by a 5km road heading seaward from the east end of Marquelia. Las Peñitas has two small hotels and some cabañas that also offer camping spaces.

Ometepec
☎ 741 / Pop 20,800

Nestled 600m above sea level in the Sierra Madre mountains, the city of Ometepec is well worth a detour to visit the amazing **Catedral de Santiago Apóstol**. Construction of the imposing blue and white, colonial-style church began in 1981 and continues to this day. Ometepec also has a popular Sunday market where indigenous people come to sell their handmade leather goods. Ometepec is located about 50km northeast of Marquelia, and 175km southeast of Acapulco. From Hwy200, a well-marked turnoff near Km174 winds another 15km to town.

Cuajinicuilapa
☎ 741 / pop 9400

About 200km southeast of Acapulco, Cuajinicuilapa, or Cuaji (kwah-hee), is the nucleus of Afro-Mestizo culture on the Costa Chica. The **Museo de las Culturas Afromestizas** (Museum of Afro-Mestizo Cultures; ☎ 414-03-10; cnr Manuel Zárate & Cuauhtémoc; admission M$10; ☑ 10am-2pm & 4-7pm Tue-Sun) is a tribute to the history of African slaves in Mexico and, specifically, to local Afro-Mestizo culture. Behind the museum are three examples of casas redondas, the round houses typical of West Africa that were built around Cuaji until as late as the 1960s. The museum is a block inland from the Banamex that's just west of the main plaza.

Buses for Cuaji (M$119, five hours) depart Estrella Blanca's Central Ejido station in Acapulco hourly from 5am, and Estrella Blanca has several buses daily from Pinotepa Nacional (M$30, 1½ hours) in Oaxaca state.

Punta Maldonado (also known as El Faro) is the last worthwhile beach before the Oaxaca border. The swimming is good and the surfing, on occasion, is excellent; the break is a reef/point favoring lefts. The village (population 1100) has several seafood restaurants on the beach and one small, unattractive hotel.

To reach Punta Maldonado take a *camioneta* from Cuajinicuilapa (M$20, 45 minutes); they depart half-hourly from just off the main plaza.

CHILPANCINGO

☎ 747 / pop 165,000 / elevation 1360m

Chilpancingo, capital of the state of Guerrero, is a university city and agricultural center. It lies on Hwys 95 and 95D, 130km north of Acapulco and 270km south of Mexico City. It's an administrative center and a rather nondescript place, located between the much more compelling destinations of Taxco and Acapulco.

The former **Palacio Municipal**, on the *zócalo*, has murals showing the city's important place in Mexico's history. In the spring of 1813, rebel leader José María Morelos y Pavón encircled Mexico City with his guerrilla army and demanded a congress in Chilpancingo. The congress issued a Declaration of Independence and began to lay down the principles of a new constitution. But Spanish troops eventually breached the circle around Mexico City, and Morelos was tried for treason and then executed.

Sleeping & Eating

The best eateries and lodgings are around the bus terminal and the *zócalo*.

Hotel El Presidente (☎ 472-97-31; cnr Calle 30 de Agosto & Insurgentes; s M$330-380 d M$400-480; P) A block from the bus station, El Presidente has gaudy grandmotherly decor but is fine in a pinch. The Green Café downstairs serves good breakfast.

Del Parque Hotel (☎ 472-30-12; Colón 5; r M$470) A block from the *zócalo*, the modern Del Parque has clean, spacious, carpeted rooms. Windows are double-glazed to minimize street noise, and the beds and bathrooms are good. The ground floor contains the popular Taco Rock restaurant, where you can get decent pizzas and sandwiches.

Getting There & Away

Chilpancingo bus station is 1.5km away from the *zócalo*. It is served by the bus companies **Estrella Blanca** (☎ 472-06-34) and **Estrella de Oro** (☎ 472-21-30). Among the services offered are frequent buses to Acapulco (M$70, 1½ hours), Mexico City (M$180 to M$230, 3½ hours), and at least two daily buses to Taxco (M$100, three hours).

OLINALÁ

☎ 756 / pop 5200 / elevation 1350m

The cobble-stoned, isolated village of Olinalá is famous throughout Mexico for its beautiful, hand-painted lacquered boxes, chests and other woodcraft. Traditionally, the pieces were made with fragrant linaloe wood that grows here; the scarce tree is now often substituted with pine. Several artisan shops are located along Av Ramon Ibarra behind the *zócalo*; one of the best is Artesanías Ayala. The town's two lovely churches – the **Iglesia de San Francisco de Asís** in the *zócalo* and the magnificent hilltop **Sanatorio de la Virgen Guadalupe** – are both decorated in traditional Olinalá style with lacquered-wood ornamentation and murals. Looking to stay? **Hotel Coral** (☎ 473-06-69; Ramon Ibarra 4; s/d M$150/170) has 35 simple rooms with TV and private bath.

Second-class buses from Chilpancingo to Tlapa will drop you at the crossroads for Olinalá (4½ hours); then catch a 3rd-class bus (one hour) to Olinalá. By car, getting here is half the fun on the winding, rollercoaster road from Chilpancingo (3½ hours). Don't attempt this drive in the dark!

Western Central Highlands

With exquisite colonial architecture, fine food, better tequila, butterfly orgies, lonely indigenous pueblos, bustling cities, battling mariachi bands and volcanic calderas, the western central highlands are your wonderland. This region includes Guadalajara, Colima, Morelia, Pátzcuaro and Uruapan, yet tourists often forego this fascinating land, making it even more appealing. Locals are warm and generous, the streets are perfectly safe, the economy is strong and cultural traditions thrive, especially in the countryside. The climate is superb (sunny, but never too hot, during the days and cool, but seldom too cold, at night) and the natural beauty is diverse and mind-blowing. You'll see layered mountains, expansive lakes, thundering rivers and waterfalls and an endless tapestry of cornfields, avocado groves, agave plantations and cattle ranches. This is Mexico's beating heart.

Guadalajara – capital of Jalisco state – sprawls, but it doesn't overwhelm; it's a great walking city, blessed with handy public transportation. Morelia, Michoacán state's drop-dead gorgeous capital, may be the best city (in the world, not just in Mexico) that you've never heard of. Think stunning colonial architecture, a young population and an emerging hipster scene. Nearby is the Reserva Mariposa Monarca, a forested butterfly sanctuary you'll remember forever. Pátzcuaro, an endearing colonial town and the epicenter of Michoacán's indigenous Purépecha culture, is the place to be during Mexico's Día de Muertos celebration. Uruapan and Colima both have a touch of the subtropical and are near fascinating volcanoes: Paricutín, which rose from the Uruapan countryside almost overnight, the bubbling Volcán de Fuego and the spectacular snowy cones of Volcán Nevado de Colima. Mexico does not get any better than this.

HIGHLIGHTS

- Stroll **Guadalajara** (p520) on a Sunday, when the streets fill with local families, art museums are free, ancient churches buzz with worship and the sidewalk cafés are packed

- Explore spectacular **Morelia** (p556) with its glowing cathedral, rooftop bars and clubs nestled in Spanish relics

- Absorb the beauty of the **Reserva Mariposa Monarca** (Monarch Butterfly Reserve; p563) the winter retreat for millions of butterflies

- Peer into the mystical soul of the Purépecha people in tranquil **Pátzcuaro** (p566)

- Bag two volcanic peaks, the snowy and extinct **Volcán Nevado de Colima** (p555) and young, precocious **Volcán Paricutín** (p581)

★ Guadalajara
★ Volcán Nevado de Colima
★ Pátzcuaro
★ Morelia
★ Volcán Paricutín
★ Reserva Mariposa Monarca

■ GUADALAJARA JANUARY DAILY HIGH: 52°F | 11°C   ■ GUADALAJARA JULY DAILY HIGH: 26°C | 79°F

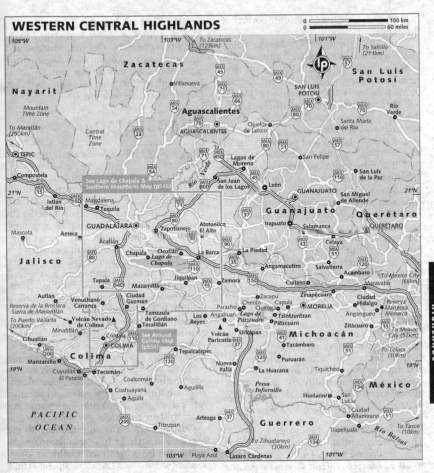

History

The western central highlands were too far from the Maya and Aztecs to fall under their influence, but in the 14th to 16th centuries the Tarascos in northern Michoacán developed a robust pre-Hispanic civilization. When the Aztecs took notice and attacked, the Tarascos were able to hold strong thanks too their copper blades. West of the Tarascos was their rival, Chimalhuacán – u confederation of four indigenous kingdoms that spread through parts of present day Jalisco, Colima and Nayarit states. To the north were the Chichimecs.

Colima, the leading Chimalhuacán kingdom, was conquered by the Spanish in 1523. The whole region, however, was not brought under Spanish control until the notorious campaigns of Nuño de Guzmán. Between 1529 and 1536 he tortured, killed and enslaved indigenous people from Michoacán to Sinaloa. His grizzly victories made him rich and famous and won him governorship of his conquered lands, until news of his war crimes leaked out. He was sent back to Spain and imprisoned for life in 1538.

This fertile ranching and agriculture region developed gradually and Guadalajara (established in 1542 and always one of Mexico's biggest cities) became the 'capital of the west.' The church, with help from the enlightened bishop Vasco de Quiroga, fostered small industries and handicraft traditions around the villages of Lago Pátzcuaro in its effort to ease the continuing poverty of the indigenous people.

In the 1920s the region's two major states, Michoacán and Jalisco, were hotbeds of the Cristero rebellion by Catholics against government antichurch policies. Lázaro Cárdenas of Michoacán, as state governor (1928–32) and then as Mexican president (1934–40), instituted reforms that did much to abate antigovernment sentiments.

Today both Jalisco and Michoacán hold many of Mexico's natural resources – especially timber, mining, livestock and agriculture – and Jalisco has a thriving tech industry. In the past, both states have seen large segments of their population head to the US for work. Michoacán reportedly lost almost half its population to emigrations and money sent home has approached two billion dollars. But with a growing economy and accessible credit, the free flow north has slowed and these days many have decided to return to Mexico and open up businesses on their home soil.

Climate

The climate is pleasantly warm and dry most of the year, with a distinct rainy season from June to September (when rainfall reaches 200mm per month). At lower altitudes, temperature and humidity rise and tropical plants bloom. In higher-altitude towns, such as Pátzcuaro, winter nights are chilly.

Parks & Reserves

The western central highlands has perhaps the most diverse array of wild, green spaces in all of Mexico. Inland Colima's Parque Nacional Volcán Nevado de Colima (p555) is home to two towering volcanoes (3820m and 4240m), the taller one is snow crusted, the other still smolders. On the other end of Inland Colima is the untouched Sierra de Manantlán Biosphere Reserve (p555). Think 1396 sq km of forested limestone mountains with rivers, waterfalls, eight types of forest ecosystems and plenty of adventure options. The unforgettable Reserva Mariposa Monarca (p563) is where you can observe the sublime, harmonic convergence of millions of butterflies who migrate all the way from the Great Lakes and Uruapan's Parque Nacional Barranca del Cupatitzio (p576) is an urban, tropical park par excellence and the source of the magnificent Rio Cupatitzio.

Getting There & Around

All major cities in the western central highlands (Guadalajara, Colima, Morelia and Uruapan) are well connected by regional and national bus lines. Guadalajara and Morelia have regular flights from many other cities in Mexico, as well as from the US.

GUADALAJARA

☎ 33 / pop 4.1 million (metro area) / elevation 1540m

Guadalajara's countless charms are distributed equally and liberally throughout its distinct neighborhoods. The city's Centro Histórico (Historic Center) is dotted with proud colonial relics that house museums, government offices, bars and hotels. There are dozens of leafy plazas with gushing fountains, strolling families and shredding skaters. The Zona Rosa, more modern and spread out, is sprinkled with fashionable restaurants, coffee houses and nightclubs. Mellow suburbs Tlaquepaque (upscale) and Tonalá (grassroots) are the folk-art shoppers' dream destinations; and Zapopan has some interesting colonial sites, but is better known as Guadalajara's Beverly Hills. This is where the beautiful and fabulous live on shady estates accessed by cobblestone streets. Guadalajara residents (nicknamed *tapatíos*, which also refers to anyone Jalisco-born) are warm and eager to share the essence of their city.

Guadalajara's many contributions to the Mexican lifestyle include tequila, mariachi music, the broad-rimmed sombrero, *charreadas* (rodeos) and the Mexican Hat Dance and these days it is also known for its outstanding food. From street-side taco and *torta ahogada* stands to neighborhood cafés to fine dining rooms in restored colonial mansions – you're never far from a great meal in joyful Guadalajara.

HISTORY

Guadalajara weathered some false starts. In 1532 Nuño de Guzmán and a few dozen Spanish families founded the first Guadalajara near Nochistlán, naming it after Guzmán's home city in Spain. Water was scarce, the land was dry and unyielding and the indigenous people were understandably hostile. So, in 1533 the humbled settlers moved to the pre-Hispanic village of Tonalá (today a part

GUADALAJARA

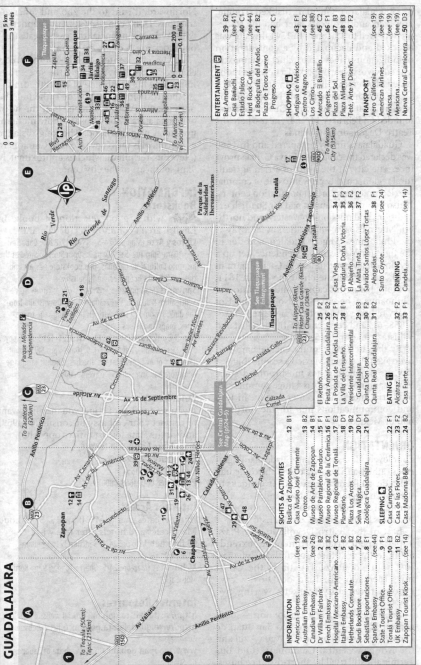

INFORMATION

American Express	(see 19)
Australian Embassy	1 B2
Canadian Embassy	(see 26)
Dr William Fairbank	2 B2
French Embassy	3 B2
Hospital Mexicano Americano	4 C2
Italian Embassy	5 B2
Netherlands Consulate	6 B2
Sandi Bookstore	7 B2
Sebastián Exportaciones	8 E1
Spanish Embassy	9 F1
State Tourist Office	10 E3
Tonalá Tourist Office	11 B2
UK Embassy	11 B2
Zapopan Tourist Kiosk	(see 14)

SIGHTS & ACTIVITIES

Basílica de Zapopan	12 B1
Casa Museo José Clemente Orozco	13 B1
Museo de Arte de Zapopan	14 B1
Museo Pantaleón Panduro	15 F1
Museo Regional de la Cerámica	16 F1
Museo Regional de Tonalá	17 E3
Planetario	18 D1
Plaza Los Arcos	19 B2
Selva Mágica	20 D1
Zoológico Guadalajara	21 D1

SLEEPING

Casa Campos	22 F1
Casa de las Flores	23 B2
Casa Madonna B&B	24 B2
El Retoño	25 F2
Fiesta Americana Guadalajara	26 B2
La Posada de la Media Luna	27 F1
La Villa del Ensueño	28 E1
Presidente Intercontinental Guadalajara	29 B3
Quinta Don José	30 F2
Quinta Real Guadalajara	31 B2

EATING

Alcatraz	32 F1
Casa Fuerte	33 F1
Casa Vieja	34 F1
Cenaduría Doña Victoria	35 F2
El Abajeño	36 F2
La Mata Tinta	37 F2
Salvador Santos López Tortas Ahogadas	38 F1
Santo Coyote	(see 24)

DRINKING

Candela	(see 14)

ENTERTAINMENT

Bar Américas	39 B2
Casa Bañach	(see 41)
Estadio Jalisco	40 C1
Hard Rock Café	(see 44)
La Bodeguita del Medio	41 B2
Plaza de Toros Nuevo Progreso	42 C1

SHOPPING

Antigua ce México	43 F1
Centro Magno	44 B2
Los Cirrios	(see 38)
Mercado El Baratillo	45 C2
Orígenes	46 F1
Plaza del Sol	47 B3
Plaza Milenium	48 B3
Teté, Arte y Diseño	49 F2

TRANSPORT

Aero California	(see 19)
American Airlines	(see 19)
Aviacsa	(see 19)
Mexicana	(see 19)
Nueva Central Camionera	50 D3

of Guadalajara). Guzmán disliked Tonalá, however, and two years later had the settlement moved to Tlacotán. In 1541 this site was attacked and decimated by a confederation of indigenous tribes led by chief Tenamaxtli. The survivors wearily picked a new site in the valley of Atemajac beside San Juan de Dios Creek, which ran where Calz Independencia is today. That's where today's Guadalajara was founded on February 14, 1542, near where the Teatro Degollado now stands.

Guadalajara finally prospered and in 1560 was declared the capital of Nueva Galicia province. The city, at the heart of a rich agricultural region, quickly grew into one of colonial Mexico's most important population centers. It also became the launch pad for Spanish expeditions and missions to western and northern Nueva España – and others as far away as the Philippines. Miguel Hidalgo, a leader in the fight for Mexican independence, set up a revolutionary government in Guadalajara in 1810, but was defeated near the city in 1811, not long before his capture and execution in Chihuahua. The city was also the object of heavy fighting during the War of the Reform (1858–61) and between Constitutionalist and Villista armies in 1915.

By the late 19th century Guadalajara had overtaken Puebla as Mexico's second-biggest city. Its population has mushroomed since WWII and now the city is a huge commercial, industrial and cultural center, and the hi-tech and communications hub for the northern half of Mexico.

ORIENTATION

Four lovely plazas surround Guadalajara's glorious cathedral. The plaza east of the cathedral, Plaza de la Liberación, extends two blocks to the Teatro Degollado, another landmark. This whole area, along with a few surrounding blocks, is known as the Centro Histórico.

East of the Teatro Degollado, the Plaza Tapatía pedestrian promenade extends 500m to the Instituto Cultural de Cabañas. Just south of Plaza Tapatía is the can't-miss Mercado San Juan de Dios, a cavernous, three-story market covering two city blocks.

Calz Independencia is a major north–south central artery. From Mercado San Juan de Dios, it runs south to Parque Agua Azul and the Antigua Central Camionera (Old Bus Terminal), still used by short-distance buses. Northward, it runs to the zoo and other attractions. Don't confuse Calz Independencia with Av Independencia, the east–west street one block north of the cathedral.

In the city center, north–south streets change names at Av Hidalgo, the street running along the north side of the cathedral.

About 20 blocks west of the cathedral, the north–south Av Chapultepec is at the heart of Guadalajara's Zona Rosa, a more modern, upmarket neighborhood. The long-distance bus terminal is the Nueva Central Camionera (New Bus Terminal), which is approximately 9km southeast of the city center.

INFORMATION

Bookstores

Stores with a good selection of books in English aren't common in Guadalajara.

Libros y Arte (Map p524-5; ☎ 3617-8207; Cabañas; ☽ 10am-5pm Tue-Sat, 10am-2:30pm Sun) Located at the Instituto Cultural de Cabañas, this bookstore has art and children's books in Spanish and English.

Sanborns (Map pp524-5; ☎ 3613-6264; cnr Av 16 de Septiembre & Juárez; ☽ 7:30am-1am) Downstairs from the dining room is a rack with English-language magazines, maps and books.

Sandi Bookstore (Map p521; ☎ 3121-4210; Av Tepeyac 718; ☽ 9:30am-7pm Mon-Fri, 9:30am-2pm Sat) About 1km west of Av López Mateos, the best English-language bookstore has an extensive travel section.

Emergency

If you are a victim of crime you may first want to contact your embassy or consulate (p969) and/or the state tourist office (opposite).

Ambulance (☎ 065, 3616-9616)
Emergency (☎ 080)
Fire (☎ 3619-5155)
Police (☎ 060, 3668-0800)

Internet Access

Internet cafés charge M$10 to M$15 per hour. Many cafés and hotels offer free wi-fi.

CB Internet (Map pp524-5; Sanchez 321; ☽ 8am-10:30pm)

XS Internet (Map pp524-5; Guerra 16; ☽ 9am-8pm Mon-Sat)

Internet Resources

http://visita.jalisco.gob.mx Official website of Jalisco.
http://vive.guadalajara.gob.mx Official website of Guadalajara.
www.zapopan.gob.mx Official website of Zapopan (in Spanish).

www.tlaquepaque.gob.mx Official website of Tlaquepaque (in Spanish).
www.tonala.gob.mx Official website of Tonalá (in Spanish).

Laundry

Lavandería Aldama (Map pp524-5; ☎ 3617-6427; Aldama 125; 🕙 9am-8pm Mon-Fri, 9am-7pm Sat) Located just a few blocks from the city center. Four kg of dirty clothes cost M$42 for full service.

Media

There are two Spanish-language papers competing for business around town: the indie *El Informador* and the more prominent *Público*, which offers exhaustive entertainment listings on Friday. The English-language **Guadalajara Reporter** (www.guadalajarareporter.com) caters to local expats.

Medical Services

Dr William Fairbank (Map p521; ☎ 3616-4851; Justo Serra 2515-1; 🕙 9am-2pm Mon-Fri) American doctor located 3km west of the city center.
Farmacia Guadalajara (Map pp524-5; ☎ 3613-7509; Moreno 170; 🕙 7am-10pm) Get your first aid, sundry items and prescribed meds here.
Hospital Mexicano Americano (Map p521; ☎ 3641-3141; Colomos 2110) About 3km northwest of the city center; English-speaking medics available.

Money

Banks are plentiful in Guadalajara and most have ATMs, known as *cajeros*. **HSBC** (Map pp524-5; cnr Av Juarez & Molina; 🕙 8am-7pm Mon-Fri, 8am-3pm Sat) keeps the longest hours.

You can change cash off-hours at one of the eager *casas de cambio* (moneychangers) on López Cotilla, east of Av 16 de Septiembre. Rates are competitive and most will change traveler's checks.

American Express (Map p521; ☎ 3818-2319; Av Vallarta 2440; 🕙 9am-6pm Mon-Fri, 9am-1pm Sat) Located in the Plaza Los Arcos shopping center.

Post

Main post office (Map pp524-5; cnr Carranza & Av Independencia, 🕙 8am-7pm Mon-Fri, 9am-1pm Sat)

Telephone

There aren't many calling offices in Guadalajara. The cheapest way to dial home is to buy a Telmex phone card at an Oxxo store and then find a public phone in as quiet a spot as possible.

Toilets

It's not hard finding a legal place to pee in central Guadalajara. Interestingly enough, it's the free toilets that are nicest; pay public toilets (usually M$3) are pretty nasty. Fast-food outlets, hotels and security at government buildings won't be bothered if you duck in for a leak.

Tourist Information

State tourist office (Map pp524-5; ☎ 3668-1600; Morelos 102 or Paseo Degollado 105; 🕙 9am-8pm Mon-Fri, 10am-2pm Sat & Sun) Enter from either Morelos or Paseo Degollado. English-speaking staff offers information on Guadalajara, the state of Jalisco and the upcoming week's events.
Tourist information booth (Map pp524-5; 🕙 9:30am-2:30pm & 5-7:30pm Mon-Fri, 10am-12.30pm Sat & Sun) In the Palacio de Gobierno, just inside the entrance facing the Plaza de Armas. During cultural events and festivals other information booths pop up around the city center.

SIGHTS
Catedral

Guadalajara's twin-towered **cathedral** (Map pp524-5; Av 16 de Septiembre btwn Morelos & Av Hidalgo; 🕙 8am-8pm, closed during Mass) is the city's most beloved and conspicuous landmark, so you will likely bump shoulders with more tourists than worshippers. Begun in 1558 and consecrated in 1618, it's almost as old as the city itself. And it's magnificent. Time it right and you'll see light filter through stained glass renderings of the Last Supper and hear a working pipe organ rumble sweetly from the rafters. The interior includes Gothic vaults, massive Tuscany-style gold-leaf pillars and 11 richly decorated altars that were given to Guadalajara by King Fernando VII of Spain (1814–33). Its crucifix is one of the most subtle and tasteful in Mexico (Jesus isn't white!). The glass case nearest the north entrance is an extremely popular reliquary, containing the hands and blood of the martyred Santa Inocencia. In the sacristy, which an attendant can open for you on request, is *La Asunción de la Virgen*, painted by Spanish artist Bartolomé Murillo in 1650. Of course, architectural purists may find flaws. Much like the Palacio de Gobierno, the cathedral is a bit of a stylistic hodgepodge including Churrigueresque, baroque and neoclassical influences. And the towers, reconstructed in 1848, are much higher than the originals, which were destroyed in the 1818 earthquake.

CENTRAL GUADALAJARA

WESTERN CENTRAL HIGHLANDS

INFORMATION			
CB Internet	1 F3	Palacio Municipal	22 F2
Farmacia Guadalajara	2 G2	Plaza de los Mariachis	23 H2
German Consulate	3 F3	Rotonda de los Jaliscenses Ilustres	24 F2
HSBC	4 G2	Santuario de Nuestra Señora del	
Lavandería Aldama	5 G3	Carmen	25 E2
Libros y Arte	(see 15)	Templo de Aranzazú	26 F3
Main Post Office	6 G1	Templo de San Francisco	27 F3
Sanborns	7 F2	Templo de Santa María de	
State Tourist Office	8 G2	Gracia	28 G2
Tourist Information Booth	(see 19)	Templo Expiatorio	29 D2
US Consulate	9 B3	Templo Nuestra Señora de la	
XS Internet	10 E2	Mercedes	30 F2
		Templo Santa Eduviges	(see 23)
		Universidad de Guadalajara	31 D2
SIGHTS & ACTIVITIES			
Artes Plásticas	(see 13)	**SLEEPING**	
Casa de las Artesanías de Jalisco	11 F5	Casa Vilasanta	32 D2
Cathedral	12 F2	Don Quixote Hotel	33 F3
CEPE	(see 31)	Hostal de María	34 F3
Galeria Jorge Martinez	13 G1	Hostel Guadalajara	35 F2
IMAC Spanish School	14 E2	Hotel Ana Isabel	36 H2
Instituto Cultural Mexicano-		Hotel Aranzazu	37 F3
Norteamericano de Jalisco	16 E2	Hotel Azteca	38 H2
Libros y Arte	(see 15)	Hotel Cervantes	39 E3
Museo de la Ciudad	17 E1	Hotel Consulado	40 B2
Museo de las Artes	(see 31)	Hotel El Aposento	41 E3
Museo Regional de Guadalajara	18 F2	Hotel Fénix	42 F2
Palacio de Gobierno	19 F2	Hotel Francés	43 F2
Palacio de Justicia	20 G2	Hotel Laffayette	44 A3
Palacio Legislativo	21 F2	Hotel México 70	45 H2
		Hotel Morales	46 F3
		Hotel San Francisco Plaza	47 G3
		La Rotonda	48 F1
		Posada Regis	49 F2
		Posada San Pablo	50 E3
		Santiago de Compostela	51 F3
		Villa Ganz	52 A2
		EATING	
		Alta Fibra	53 F3
		Birriería las Nueve Esquinas	54 F3
		Bisquets Guadalajara	55 B3
		Café Madrid	56 F2
		Chai	57 F2
		Chong Wah	58 E2
		Cocina 88	59 B2
		Danés	60 E3
		El Tió	61 F3
		Karne Garibaldi	62 B1
		Kristy & Edwards	63 G1
		La Antigua	64 F2
		La Chata	65 F2
		La Estación de Lulio	66 B3
		La Fonda de San Miguel	
		Arcángel	67 E2
		LA O	68 A3
		Mercado Corona	69 F2
		Sandy's	70 F2
		Tortas Ahogadas Héroes	71 B4
		Villa Madrid	72 E2

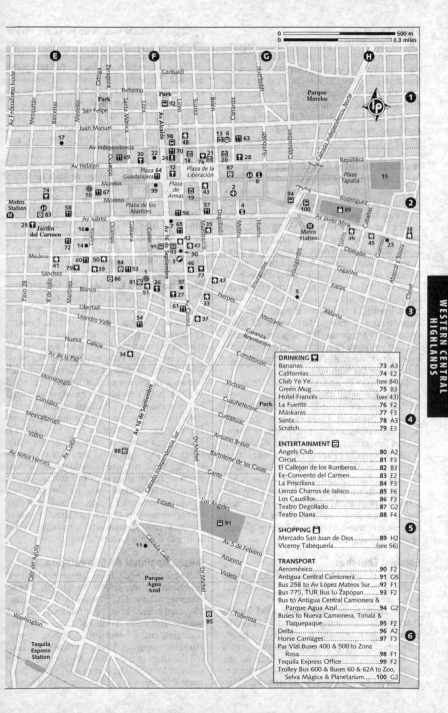

WESTERN CENTRAL HIGHLANDS

DRINKING 🍸
Bananas......................................73 A3
Californias..................................74 E2
Club Ye Ye...........................(see 84)
Green Mug.................................75 B3
Hotel Francés.......................(see 43)
La Fuente...................................76 F2
Máskaras...................................77 F3
Santa..78 A3
Scratch.......................................79 E3

ENTERTAINMENT 🎭
Angels Club................................80 A2
Circus...81 F3
El Callejón de los Rumberos......82 B3
Ex-Convento del Carmen..........83 E2
La Prisciliana.............................84 F3
Lienzo Charros de Jalisco.........85 F6
Los Caudillos.............................86 F3
Teatro Degollado.......................87 G2
Teatro Diana..............................88 F4

SHOPPING 🛍️
Mercado San Juan de Dios........89 H2
Viceroy Tabequería.............(see 56)

TRANSPORT
Aeroméxico................................90 F2
Antigua Central Camionera........91 G5
Bus 258 to Av López Mateos Sur.....92 F1
Bus 275, TUR Bus to Zapopan........93 F2
Bus to Antigua Central Camionera &
   Parque Agua Azul....................94 G2
Buses to Nueva Camionera, Tonalá &
   Tlaquepaque............................95 F2
Delta..96 A2
Horse Carriages........................97 F3
Par Vial Buses 400 & 500 to Zona
   Rosa.......................................98 F1
Tequila Express Office...............99 F2
Trolley Bus 600 & Buses 60 & 62A to Zoo,
   Selva Mágica & Planetarium.....100 G2

Plaza Tapatía

The fabulously wide pedestrian Plaza Tapatía (Map pp524–5) sprawls for more than 500m east from Teatro Degollado. Stroll the plaza on Sundays and you will flow in a sea of locals who shop at low-end crafts markets, snack (from both street vendors and cafés), watch street performers and rest on the short walls of gurgling fountains. The plaza dead-ends beautifully at the Instituto Cultural de Cabañas.

Instituto Cultural de Cabañas

Standing proudly at the east end of the brilliant Plaza Tapatía is another of Guadalajara's architectural gems. Inside its Unesco-certified, neoclassical bones are a school, cultural institute and **museum** (Map pp524-5; ☎ 3818-2800 ext 31014; Cabañas 8; admission M$10, free Sun; ☺ 10am-6pm Tue-Sat, 10am-3pm Sun). Founded by Bishop Don Juan Cruz Ruiz de Cabañas and designed by Spanish architect Manuel Tolsá, it was built between 1805 and 1810 as an orphanage and home for invalids and remained so for 150 years, housing 450 children at once. There are citrus trees and rose gardens in the 23 stone courtyards; temporary photography, painting and sculpture exhibitions; and occasional video installations. But the murals in the main rotunda are the highlight.

Between 1938 and 1939 José Clemente Orozco channeled the archetypal struggle for freedom into these 57 murals, widely regarded as his finest works. They seethe with dark, unnerving and distinctly modern images of fire, armor, broken chains, blood and prayer. Given the issues of Orozco's era, they almost certainly serve as a warning against fascism and any institution that subverts humanity to cultivate power. The museum also features a permanent exhibition of more than 100 Orozco drawings (mostly sketches for his onsite murals). Free tours in English and Spanish are available.

Colonial Churches

Central Guadalajara has dozens of churches in addition to those mentioned previously and some are quite impressive.

The **Santuario de Nuestra Señora del Carmen** (Map pp524–5) – facing the small plaza on the corner of Av Juárez and 8 de Julio – is lovely with lots of gold leaf, old paintings and murals in the dome. Closer to the city center, on the corner of Loza and Av Hidalgo, is the ornate **Templo Nuestra Señora de las Mercedes** (Map

pp524–5), which was built in 1650; inside are several large paintings, crystal chandeliers and more gold leaf. Six blocks further east is the fairly unremarkable **Templo de Santa María de Gracia** (Map pp524–5), which served as the city's first cathedral (1549-1618). The sanctuary at the **Templo Santa Eduviges** (Map pp524–5), built in 1726, is usually packed with worshippers and, during Mass, perfumed with clouds of sandalwood smoke. It's just south of the main market.

On the corner of Av 16 de Septiembre and Blanco, the compact **Templo de Aranzazú** (Map pp524–5) is perhaps the city's most beautiful. Built from 1749 to 1752, it has three ornate Churrigueresque golden altars and lovely ceiling detail. Beside it is the larger but less glamorous **Templo de San Francisco** (Map pp524–5), built two centuries earlier. Come at dusk and see the stained glass glow.

Plaza de Armas & Palacio de Gobierno

The Plaza de Armas (Map pp524–5), on the south side of the cathedral, is a sweet place to rest and absorb the surrounding history. Frequent free concerts take place on the attractive art nouveau bandstand (see p538).

The impressive **Palacio de Gobierno** (Map pp524-5; Av Corona btwn Morelos & Moreno; ☺ 9am-8pm), which houses state government offices, was finished in 1774. It's a neoclassical building accented by more than a few Churrigueresque decorations and an enormous 1937 mural of Miguel Hidalgo looming over an interior stairway. Hidalgo brandishes a torch in one fist while the masses struggle at his feet. José Clemente Orozco, the artist, used this Mexican hero to examine the dueling isms of his day – communism and fascism – and he obviously has a point of view on religion, as well. Another Orozco mural in the ex-Congreso (former Congress Hall) upstairs depicts Hidalgo, Benito Juárez and other historical luminaries.

Museo Regional de Guadalajara

East of the Rotonda de los Jaliscenses Ilustres, this **museum's** (Map pp524-5; ☎ 3614-9957; Liceo 60; admission M$37, free Sun; ☺ 9am-5:30pm Tue-Sat, 9am-4:30pm Sun) eclectic array of antiquated cannons, wagons and worn saddles of grizzled revolutionaries, and a beautiful collection of pre-Hispanic ceramics dating from 600 BC help tell the story of the history and prehistory of western Mexico. The star of the ground-floor natural history wing is a reconstructed woolly

---

GUADALAJARA IN TWO DAYS

Breakfast at **Chai** (p535) then check out the visceral Orozco murals at **Instituto Cultural de Cabañas** (opposite). Stroll through **Mariachi Plaza** (p528) and visit the sandalwood shrouded **Templo Santa Eduviges** (opposite). Explore the stellar **Mercado San Juan de Dios** (p540) and stroll the brilliant **Plaza Tapatía** (opposite) to the **Cathedral** (p523) and **Plaza de Armas** (opposite). Duck into the **Museo Regional de Guadalajara** (opposite) for a taste of Guadalajara's past then get your modern art fix at **Galería Jorge Martínez** (below). By now you'll need a drink, so find **La Fuente** (p537) and enjoy live happy hour music. Dine at the exceptional **Birriería las Nueve Esquinas** (p535) and close the night out with more old Latin tunes at **Hotel Francés** (p537). Hustle up to the roof and take in the view!

Wake up and breakfast at **Café Madrid** (p535), then catch a cab to Tlaquepaque and stroll the suburb's cobblestone streets and fine galleries. Don't miss the **Museo Regional de la Cerámica** (p529) or **El Parián** (p536).

You can't do Tlaquepaque without paying your respects to El Socio. So when it's time for lunch, head to **Mariscos el Social** (p536).

After a siesta, grab a late dinner at **Cocina 88** (p536) then step around the corner to Av Chapultepec and dance all night to live salsa sounds at **El Callejón de Los Rumberos** (p538).

---

mammoth skeleton. The archaeological section houses well-preserved figurines, ceramics and silver and gold artifacts. Upstairs are colonial paintings depicting the Spanish conquest, an ethnography section with displays about indigenous life in Jalisco and a revolutionary wing where the guns, uniforms and desks of Mexico's great rebels are on display. One battlefield rendering features the Mexican rebels taking Guadalajara from the Spanish in 1862.

Universidad de Guadalajara & Templo Expiatorio

West of the city center, where Av Juárez meets Av Federalismo, is shady **Parque Revolución** (Map pp524–5), which has become a haven for pierced skaters. Three blocks further west at Av Juárez 975 is the **Paraninfo** (Theater Hall), one of the main buildings of the **Universidad de Guadalajara** (Map pp524–5). Inside, the stage backdrop and dome feature large, powerful murals by Orozco. In the back of the same building is the **Museo de las Artes** (Map pp524-5; ☎ 3134-1664; admission free; ☉ 10am-6pm Tue-Fri, 10am-4pm Sat & Sun), which houses temporary exhibitions that will scratch your modernist itch once you've overdosed on *antigua*. The **Galería Jorge Martínez** (☎ 3613-2362; Belén 120; admission free; ☉ 9am-6pm) is an interesting modern and conceptual art gallery in the colonial center, adjacent to and benefitting Guadalajara's top art school, Artes Plásticas, operated by UDG.

A block south of Museo de las Artes is the 1897 Gothic **Templo Expiatorio** (Map pp524-5; ☉ 7am-11pm), accented by enormous stone columns, 15m-high mosaic stained-glass windows and a kaleidoscopic steeple. At 9am, noon and 6pm, a door in the clock tower opens and the 12 apostles march right out.

Plaza Guadalajara & Palacio Municipal

Directly west of the cathedral, Plaza Guadalajara (Map pp524–5) is shaded by dozens of laurel trees, has great cathedral views, a few fine cafés and fun people watching. On its north side is the Palacio Municipal (City Hall; Map pp524–5), which was built between 1949 and 1952 but looks ancient. Above its interior stairway is a dark mural by Gabriel Flores depicting the founding of Guadalajara.

Rotonda de los Jaliscenses Ilustres

Welcome to Jalisco's hall of fame. The plaza on the north side of the cathedral is ringed by 20 bronze sculptures of the state's favorite writers, architects, revolutionaries and a composer. Some of them are actually buried beneath the Rotonda de los Jaliscenses (Rotunda of Illustrious Jaliscans; Map pp524–5), the round-pillared monument in the center. Before the macho city establishment added a woman to the mix, the rotunda was 'de los Hombres Ilustres.'

Plaza de la Liberación

East of the cathedral, this plaza (Map pp524–5) was a 1980s urban planner's dream project and two whole blocks of colonial buildings were eviscerated for his concrete slab. But it

WESTERN CENTRAL HIGHLANDS

does gush with fountains and overflow with herds of students, solitary suits on mobiles and love-drunk couples kissing in the sun.

On the north side of the plaza, next to the Museo Regional, is the **Palacio Legislativo** (Map pp524–5). Distinguished by thick stone columns in its interior courtyard, this is where the state congress meets. Across the street to the east is the **Palacio de Justicia** (State Courthouse; Map pp524–5). It was built in 1588 and began life as Guadalajara's first nunnery. Duck inside to the interior stairwell and check out the 1965 mural by Guillermo Chávez depicting legendary Mexican lawmakers, including Benito Juárez.

Teatro Degollado

Construction on the neoclassical **Teatro Degollado** (Map pp524-5; ☎ 3614-4773; Degollado; admission free; ☵ for viewing 12:30-2:30pm Mon-Fri), home of the Guadalajara Philharmonic, was begun in 1856 and completed 30 years later. The five-tiered interior is swathed in red velvet and gold and is crowned by a Gerardo Suárez mural based on the fourth canto of Dante's *Divine Comedy*. Over the columns on its front is a frieze depicting Apollo and the Nine Muses. The Theater was renovated in 2005 and it has a new café.

Plaza de los Mariachis

Tucked behind the Templo Santa Eduviges near the intersection of Av Juarez and Calz Insurgentes, just south of Mercado San Juan de Dios, is the birthplace of mariachi music. By day it's just a narrow walking street, flanked by charming old buildings and dotted with a few plastic tables and chairs and the odd uniformed mariachi man chatting on a cell phone. At night it can get lively, when patrons swill beer and listen to bands play requests for about M$100 per song.

Museo de la Ciudad

This **museum** (Map pp524-5; ☎ 3658-3706; Av Independencia 684; admission M$7.50, free Sun; ☵ 10am-5:30pm Tue-Sat, 10am-2:30pm Sun) has some nice historical details, such as colonial armor, spears and locks, swords and mandolins that tell the history of Guadalajaran laymen.

Casa-Museo José Clemente Orozco

During the 1940s, the great *tapatío* painter and muralist, José Clemente Orozco (1883–1949), lived and worked in this **house** (Map p521; ☎ 3616- 8329; Aurelio Aceves 27; admission free; ☵ 10am-6pm Tue-Sat). There's only one of Orozco's murals on display, but at the time of writing an adjacent Orozco museum was scheduled to open some time in 2008.

Parque Agua Azul

This green oasis, a large, leafy **park** (Map pp524-5; Calz Independencia Sur; adult/child M$4/2; ☵ 10am-6pm Tue-Sun) about 20 blocks south of the city center, is a nice place to rehab from too much urbanity. There are benches and lawns to lounge upon and jogging trails aplenty, so bring a good book or some running shoes. And check out the Orchid House. The orchids look their best in October, November, April and May. Bus 60 (or any marked 'Agua Azul') heading south on Calz Independencia will drop you here from the city center.

The **Casa de las Artesanías de Jalisco** (Map pp524-5; Calz Gallo 20; ☵ 10am-6pm Mon-Fri, 10am-5pm Sat, 10am-3pm Sun) is a large museum-like store selling high-quality Jalisco handicrafts including pottery, glassware, jewelry, textiles and furniture. Prices are reasonable and there's a small, free ceramics museum.

Zoológico Guadalajara, Selva Mágica & Planetario

The zoo, Selva Mágica amusement park and planetarium are near one another on the northern outskirts of the city. Trolleybus R600 and buses 60 and 62A (marked 'Zoológico'), heading north on Calz Independencia, drop you close by.

The **Zoológico Guadalajara** (Map p521; ☎ 3674-4488; www.zooguadalajara.com.mx; Paseo del Zoológico 600; adult/child M$45/25; ☵ 10am-6pm Wed-Sun) is a large, relatively pleasant place with aviaries, a reptile house and a children's petting zoo. Animals include lions, tigers, hippos and flamingos. There's a good view of the Barranca de Oblatos, an impressive 670m-deep canyon, at the north end. Stroller and wheelchair rentals are available.

Beside the zoo, off Calz Independencia Nte, is **Selva Mágica** (Map p521; ☎ 3674-1290; Paseo Zoológica 600; admission M$150; ☵ 10am-8pm). It has four large roller coasters and five live animal (dolphins, seals, birds) shows daily.

Zapopan

The fashionable, upmarket suburb of Zapopan (population 1,022,600) is about 8km from the city center, on the northwestern edge of

Guadalajara. There are some interesting historical sights around the main plaza.

Zapopan's pride and joy, the **Basílica de Zapopan** (Map p521), built in 1730, is home to Nuestra Señora de Zapopan, a petite statue of the Virgin visited by pilgrims year-round. The faithful get extreme during the Fiestas de Octubre, when thousands of kneeling old women crawl behind as the statue is carried here from Guadalajara's central cathedral. The kneeling pilgrims then make the final trek up the basilica's aisle to pray for favors at her altar. The Virgin receives a new car each year for the procession, but the engine is never turned on (thus remaining 'virginal'). It's hauled by men with ropes.

The **Museo de Arte de Zapopan** (MAZ; Map p521; ☎ 3818-2575; www.mazmuseo.com; cnr Paseo Tepitzintli & Andador 23 de Enero; admission M$24; ☺ 10am-6pm Tue-Sun) is one block east of Plaza de las Américas and is Guadalajara's best modern art complex. Permanent exhibitions of some of Mexico's finest including Manuel Álvarez Bravo, Juan Soriano and Luis Barragán are on display; and temporary exhibitions have included works by Diego Rivera, Frida Kahlo and a whimsical showing of Anthony Browne prints that saw the top floor covered with turf, sticks, stones and sand.

Los Arcos is a street with a dozen bars near the plaza, each catering to unique musical tastes, such as electronica or reggae. A **tourist kiosk** (☺ Tue-Sun) can usually be found in front of the Museo de Arte de Zapopan along Paseo Tepitzintli, a pleasant pedestrian street (head straight out the basilica's front door).

Bus 275 Diagonal and the turquoise TUR bus marked 'Zapopan,' heading north on Avs 16 de Septiembre or Alcalde, stop beside the basilica; the trip takes 20 minutes.

Tlaquepaque

Just 7km southeast of downtown Guadalajara is the artisan community of Tlaquepaque (tlah-keh-*pah*-keh; population 510,500), where artisans live behind the pastel colored walls of abandoned old mansions and their goods, such as wood carvings, sculpture, furniture, ceramics, jewelry, leather items and candles, are sold in swank contemporary design boutiques that line the narrow cobblestone streets.

In the 19th century Tlaquepaque was an upper-class suburb of Guadalajara. Now these latter-day homes belong to artisans, restaurateurs and owners of cute garden

B&B's. The plaza is leafy and blooming with flowers and the benches around the fountain are always packed. The eating is very good and the strolling is even better, especially at sunset when the sky behind the gorgeous, white-domed basilica burns orange and families take to the streets, enjoying the last ticks of daylight.

The **tourist office** (Map p521; ☎ 3562-7050 ext 2319; www.tlaquepaque.gob.mx; Morelos 88; ☺ 9am-3pm Mon-Fri) is upstairs in the Casa del Artesano. It offers two- to three-hour **walking tours** (donation) of the area, which include visits to local workshops and museums and can be given in English or Spanish, but you must reserve ahead.

The **Museo Regional de la Cerámica** (Map p521; ☎ 3635-5404; Independencia 237; admission free; ☺ 10am-6pm Tue-Sat, 10am-3pm Sun) is set in a great old adobe building with stone arches and mature trees in the courtyard. It has a nice collection that exhibits the varied styles and clays used in Jalisco and Michoacán. Explanations are in English and Spanish.

More miniature figurines, as well as enormous, lightly fired urns and other ceramic crafts from around Mexico are on display at the **Museo Pantaleón Panduro** (Map p521 ☎ 3639-5646; Sánchez 191; admission free; ☺ 10am-6pm Tue-Sat, 10am-3pm Sun).

To get to Tlaquepaque, take bus 275 Diagonal, 275B or 647 (M$4). The turquoise TUR bus marked 'Tonalá' has air-con and is more comfortable (M$10). All these buses leave central Guadalajara from Av 16 de Septiembre between Cotilla and Madero; the trip takes about 20 minutes. As you near Tlaquepaque, watch for the brick arch and then a traffic circle. Get off at the next stop. Up the street on the left is Independencia, which will take you to the heart of Tlaquepaque.

Tonalá

This dusty, bustling suburb (population 444,500) is about 13km southeast of downtown Guadalajara and home to even more artisans. You can feel this town beginning to take Tlaquepaque's lead with a few airy, inviting showrooms and cafés opening around town, but it remains happily rough around the edges. It's fun to roam through the dark, dusty stores and workshops. Anything you can buy in Tlaquepaque, you can find here for much less, which is what attracts wholesale buyers from all over the world.

WESTERN CENTRAL HIGHLANDS

SHOPPING IN TLAQUEPAQUE

Tlaquepaque has legendary shopping. Large home decor boutiques are stocked with ceramics, exquisite light fixtures and handmade wood furniture. Guadalajara's best interior designers are based here and if you take your time you'll discover some rare and creative pieces.

At **Antigua de México** (Map p521; ☎ 3635-2402; Independencia 255; ⏱ 10am-2pm & 3-7pm Mon-Fri, 10am-6pm Sat) gorgeous furniture showpieces, like benches carved from a single tree, are displayed in expansive, old-world courtyards.

Orígenes (Map p521; ☎ 3563-1041; Independencia 211; ⏱ 10am-7pm Mon-Fri, 11am-7pm Sat, 11am-6pm Sun) is smaller than Antigua de México, but it has a tremendous lighting selection, elegant hammocks in the overstocked courtyard and some funky cowhide sofas.

Teté, Arte y Diseño (Map p521; ☎ 3635-7965; Juárez 173; ⏱ 10am-7:30pm Mon-Sat) has massive chandeliers, reproduction antique hardware and one-of-a-kind woodcarvings.

Los Cirios (☎ 3635-2426; www.loscirios.com.mx; Madero 70; ⏱ 10am-7pm Mon-Sat) is a high-end candle factory and showroom which makes centerpiece candles in all shapes, sizes, colors and scents. Some are nearly 2m tall.

If you need something transported, visit **Sebastián Exportaciones** (Map p521; ☎ 3124-6560; sebastianexp@prodigy.net.mx; Ejército 45; ⏱ 9am-2pm & 4-6pm Mon-Fri), which ships boxes (minimum 1 sq meter) internationally.

On Thursday and Sunday, Tonalá bursts into a huge street market that sprouts on Av Tonaltecas and crawls through dozens of streets and alleys and takes hours to explore. This is where wholesale meets retail. You'll browse stalls that sell masks, glassware, ceramics, furniture, toys, jewelry, handmade soap and DVDs. There are plenty of *torta* and taco stands and there's one *michelada* vendor. You'll have to sift through junk to find great deals and the best pieces are usually found at the workshops and warehouses, not on the street. Still, it's a fun scene.

The **Tonalá tourist office** (Map p521; ☎ 3284-3092; Tonaltecas 140; ⏱ 9am-3pm Mon-Fri), on the main drag in the Casa de Artesanos, gives out maps and information. Ask staff about two- to three-hour **walking tours** (donation) of the area, which include visits to local artisan workshops. They're given in English or Spanish, but need to be reserved a couple of days in advance.

The carved wood and ceramic masks at the **Museo Regional de Tonalá** (Map p521; Ramón Corona 73; admission free; ⏱ 9am-3pm Mon-Fri) are outstanding. Many are decorated with real animal teeth and horsehair.

To reach Tonalá, take bus 275 Diagonal or 275D (both M$4). The turquoise TUR bus marked 'Tonalá' has air-con and is more comfortable (M$10). All these buses leave Guadalajara from Av 16 de Septiembre; the trip takes about 45 minutes. As you enter Tonalá, get off on the corner of Avs Tonalá

and Tonaltecas, then walk three blocks north on Tonaltecas to the tourist office (in the Casa de Artesanos). From the Casa de Artesanos, it's three blocks east and two blocks north to the Plaza Principal.

COURSES

Travelers hell-bent on learning something can choose among a number of language, movement and art at classes available to students of all ages. Prices and curricula vary tremendously.

CEPE (Map pp524-5; ☎ 3616-4399; www.cepe.udg.mx; Universidad de Guadalajara, Apartado Postal 1-2130, Guadalajara, Jalisco 44100) The Universidad de Guadalajara's Centro de Estudios para Extranjeros (Foreign Student Studies Center; CEPE) offers several levels of intensive two- to five-week Spanish-language courses. Day trips and longer excursions to other parts of Mexico are available. It can also arrange homestays.

IMAC Spanish School (Map pp524-5; ☎ 3613-1080; www.spanish-school.com.mx; Guerra 180) The Instituto Mexicano-Americano de Cultura (IMAC) offers one- to 52-week courses. Study from one to four hours per day. Check its website for course fees and homestay options. Music and dance classes are also available.

Artes Plásticas (Map pp524-5; ☎ 3613-2362; www.cuaad.udg.mx/artes; Belén 120) Learn music, dance, photography, design and drama at Guadalajara's best art school, held in a graffiti covered colonial relic in the city center. Exchange students of all ages are welcome, but instruction is in Spanish. Register through the University of Guadalajara.

Yogare (☎ 3170-3912; www.yogare.com; Madero 5850, Zapopan) Yogis can descend to this sweet studio near the

Zapopan plaza. Daily vinyasa yoga classes cost M$100 each, but you can have four for M$240 or an unlimited month's pass for M$480. Instruction is in Spanish.

TOURS

Panoramex (☎ 3810-5057; www.panoramex.com.mx; Federalismo Sur 944) runs tours with English-, French- and Spanish-speaking guides, leaving from the Jardín San Francisco at 9.30am. Tours include visits to Guadalajara's main sights (M$136, five hours, Monday to Saturday), to Chapala and Ajijic (M$174, six hours, Tuesday, Thursday and Sunday); and to the town of Tequila, where you'll roam agave fields and Sauza's tequila distillery before sipping (M$207, 6½ hours, Monday, Wednesday, Friday, Saturday, Sunday).

Spirits of El Panteón de Belén (Belén 684; www.explore-guadalajara.com/panteondebelen.html; M$33 per person; ☺ tours depart 8:30pm, 10pm, midnight Wed-Fri, 1:30am Sat) Check out the haunted, crumbling tombs in one of Guadalajara's oldest cemeteries on this creepy night tour. The later the hour the more spine-tingling the journey. Enjoy the ghosts.

FESTIVALS & EVENTS

Major festivals celebrated in Guadalajara and its suburbs, include:

Feria de Tonalá An annual handicrafts fair in Tonalá, specializing in ceramics, is held the weeks before, during and after Semana Santa (Easter week).

Fiestas de Tlaquepaque Tlaquepaque's annual fiesta and handicrafts fair takes place mid-June to the first week of July.

Fiesta Internacional del Mariachi (www.mariachi -jalisco.com.mx) In late August and early September mariachis come from everywhere to jam, battle and enjoy.

Fiestas de Octubre (www.fiestasdeoctubre.com.mx) Beginning with a parade on the first Sunday in October, these fiestas last all month long and are Guadalajara's principal annual fair. Free entertainment takes place from noon to 10pm daily in the Benito Juárez auditorium at the fairgrounds (5km north of the city center), while elsewhere around the city are livestock shows, art exhibitions and sporting and cultural events. On October 12 there's a procession from the cathedral to Zapopan.

Feria Internacional del Libro (www.fil.com.mx) This is one of the biggest book promotions in Latin America; held during the last week of November and first week of December, headlined by major Spanish language authors, such as Gabriel García Márquez. It closes with a free public concert of a big name band at the convention center.

Guadalajara Winefest (☎ 3812-3614; www.gdlwine fest.com) The inaugural event in November 2007 was held in 20 of Guadalajara's best restaurants. The week was highlighted by courses, conferences and winemaker-sponsored dinners, all accompanied by plenty of bottles of Baja red.

SLEEPING

During holidays (Christmas and Easter) and festivals you *must* reserve ahead. Ask for discounts if you arrive in the low season or will be staying more than a few days.

Central Guadalajara

BUDGET

Hostel Guadalajara (Map pp524-5; ☎ 3562-7520; www .hostelguadalajara.com; Maestranza 147; dm with/without ISIC card M$115/145; ▣) If you like a good party and a better deal then nest at this fine HI hostel, decorated by contemporary paintings and old-world stone columns. The six private and dorm rooms surround one giant loft. Parties are frequent, excursions (think tequila factories, salsa dancing) are a good value, breakfast is free and the crowd is attractive international. The two private rooms are M$300/320 for a single/double.

Hostal de María (Map pp524-5; ☎ 3614-6230; Nueva Galicia 924; dm M$160, r M$320) Less MTV and more old-world Mexico can be found at this sweet hostel tucked into a narrow street near the Nueve Esquinas neighborhood. Breakfast and wireless internet are free. The Puerto Vallarta room on the 2nd floor terrace has the best digs.

Casa Vilasanta (Map pp524-5; ☎ 3124-1277; www.vila santa.com; Rayón 170; s/d M$180/$390) This is the best value in Guadalajara. The bright, pastel-colored rooms are scattered around a cool interior courtyard, decorated with pottery and flowers and a sunny 2nd-story terrace. Singles can feel cramped, but the doubles are large and all rooms have plasma TV, aircon and wireless internet. There's a shared kitchen and plenty of chill space on both floors. But with just 11 rooms and English-speaking management, this place books up. Reserve ahead!

Posada San Pablo (Map pp524-5; ☎ 3614-2811; http://sanpablo1.tripod.com; Madero 429; s/d M$280/350) A pleasant budget choice, complete with grassy garden and sunny terrace. Upstairs rooms with balconies are best.

Southeast of Mercado San Juan de Dios there's a cluster of budget hotels. This part of town is a bit rough, but you can usually find a cheap room here when other places are full.

WESTERN CENTRAL HIGHLANDS

Hotel México 70 (Map pp524–5; ☎ 3617-9978; Av Javier Mina 230; s/d/tw M$170/190/270) Popular among budget-minded Mexican families, which despite the dark, bleak halls means you won't be running into hookers or hourly customers at this hotel (they'll be down the block). Ask for one of the larger, sunnier outside rooms.

Hotel Ana Isabel (Map pp524–5; ☎ 3617-7920; Av Javier Mina 164; s/d M$185/240) This clean and surprisingly quiet budget haunt has soft beds and a lobby perfumed with always brewing (free!) coffee. But the metal doors and dark rooms do have a certain cell-like quality.

Hotel Azteca (Map pp524–5; ☎ 3617-7465; www.hotel azteca.com; Av Javier Mina 311; r from M$350; P) The cleanest hotel in this end of town and even the street-front rooms are remarkably quiet. All have cable TV and fan and the beds are hard (in a good way).

Several cheap accommodation options can be found around the Antigua Central Camionera (Old Bus Terminal) in a busy neighborhood about 10 blocks south of the city center.

MIDRANGE

Posada Regis (Map pp524–5; ☎ 3614-8633; http://posadar egis.tripod.com; Av Corona 171; s/d M$365/430) The rooms at this funky posada are spacious with high, detailed ceilings, but choose wisely: those facing the street are noisy and others are just not clean enough.

Hotel Consulado (Map pp524–5; ☎ 3563-2287, fax 3827-2287; Lopez Cotilla 1405; s/d/tw M$470/540/610; P) At first glance this place feels like your modern Zen oasis. In reality the clean, modern rooms aren't fabulous, but they are the best deal in Zona Rosa so reserve ahead. Amenities include cable TV and wireless internet and it's walking distance to countless cafés, bars and restaurants. Make sure to remind the staff to switch your hot water on before you get in the shower!

Don Quixote Hotel (Map pp524–5; ☎ 3658-1299, fax 3614-2845; Héroes 91; s/d M$490/655; P) Simple, clean, tasteful rooms, even if they are a bit cramped. There's an attached restaurant and the lobby has character. Exhibit A: an antique case displaying a prodigious tequila collection.

Hotel El Aposento (Map pp524–5; ☎ 3614-1612; Madero 545; r from M$500; P) Rooms in this converted 19th-century hospital are large with old-world charm – including lovely tiled bathrooms – but they should be cleaner. Still, they're set around a sunny, open court-

yard filled with plants, a small fountain and tables where you'll enjoy a full American breakfast, gratis.

La Rotonda (Map pp524–5; ☎ 3614-1017; www.hotele selectos.com; Liceo 130; r from M$550; P) Two stories of attractively tiled rooms with hardwood furnishings surround a bright colonial stone courtyard filled with glass tables and potted plants – perfect for your morning coffee. Try to get an upstairs room for more privacy and light.

Hotel San Francisco Plaza (Map pp524–5; ☎ 3613-8954; www.sanfranciscohotel.com.mx; Degollado 267; s/d M$600/650; P) The bright, leafy enclosed courtyard twittering with the sound of parakeets goes along with the beautifully polished exterior. If only the large rooms weren't so dark and the bathrooms so tiny.

Hotel Francés (Map pp524–5; ☎ 3613-1190; www.hotel frances.com, Maestranza 35; r from M$643; P) This living, breathing baroque time capsule has been operating since 1610. You'll feel its age. Rooms are a far cry from luxurious, but they are clean. And if you get one on the 3rd floor, you'll have immediate roof access – and insane views of colonial Guadalajara at your fingertips. Magic!

Hotel Cervantes (Map pp524–5; ☎ 3613-6816; www.hotelcervantes.com.mx; Sánchez 442; s/d M$665/710; P) This modern high-rise with the flashy lobby and sunny rooms is a bit soulless. But it's also comfortable and stocked with amenities, including a swimming pool.

Hotel Laffayette (Map pp524–5; ☎ 3615-0252, fax 3630-1112; www.laffayette.com.mx; Av de la Paz 2055; r from M$755; P) Another 1980s-era high-rise located just off Chapultepec. Rooms are comfortable, not classy, despite the marble baths. But you gotta love the 40in plasma flat screen. Rooms in the upper reaches of this 17-floor tower have spectacular city views.

Santiago de Compostela (Map pp524–5; ☎ 3613-8880, fax 3658-1925; Colón 272; r from M$840; P) The stone facade will draw you in, but like many Guadalajara hotels, the exterior outshines the interior. The location is good, however, and it is a clean and decent three-star hotel, if a touch overpriced.

Hotel Morales (Map pp524–5; ☎ 3658-5232; www.hotel moralescom.mx; Av Corona 243; r from M$850; P) A pretty fountain gurgles and business travelers and families gather in the beautifully tiled lobby. Rooms are a bit dark, but they're reasonably large with firm beds and balconies that overlook sensational city views. Book ahead because this attractive colonial hotel fills up.

Hotel Fénix (Map pp524-5; ☎ 3614-5714; www.fenix guadalajara.com.mx; Av Corona 160; r from M$890; P ⊠ 🐾 ▣) Another modern high-rise. This one has a great central location, English-speaking staff, thin walls and some musty rooms. But the commanding views from those in the upper reaches offer cause to forgive their shortcomings.

TOP END

Hotel Aranzazu (Map pp524-5; ☎ 3942-4042, fax 3942-4035; www.aranzazu.com.mx; r from M$990; P ⊠ 🐾 ▣) Another relatively charm-less executive tower hotel. But it has all the amenities, comfortable rooms with king-sized beds and outstanding 9th floor views.

Casa Madonna B&B (Map p521; ☎ 3615-6554; www.casamadonna.com.mx; Lerdo de Tejada 2308; d/ste M$1200/1400; 🐾 ▣) This intimate boutique hotel offers five cozy rooms in a converted 1920s era Mexican hacienda. Days begin with breakfast on a garden patio and they end around the fireplace with a glass of red. It's a couple of kilometers west of the city center.

Presidente Intercontinental Guadalajara (Map p521; ☎ 3678-1234, fax 3678-1222; www.ichotelsgroup .com; cnr Lopez Mateos Sur & Moctezuma; r from M$1400 P ⊠ 🐾 ▣ 🕽) This is your massive modern glass palace with over 400 rooms, 40 suites, two restaurants and a bar that is generally patronized by suits high on expense accounts. The concierge can arrange tours, rental cars, dinner reservations and a massage at the spa, and rooms are new, carpeted and comfortable. Get one with a balcony and a view (only about M$100 more) as long as you're spending.

Fiesta Americana Guadalajara (Map p521; ☎ 3818-1400; www.fiestamericana.com.mx; Aceves 225; r from M$1443; P ⊠ 🐾 ▣ 🕽) The location – along Av Lopéz Mateos Norte – isn't so magical, but this fine hotel offers 390 rooms on 22 stories and all the services and amenities you could want. Views are stunning from top floors and the glass elevator is a nice touch.

Villa Ganz (Map pp524-5; ☎ 3120 1416; www.villaganz .com; López Cotilla 1739; r from M$2000; P ▣) Without a doubt the best hotel in town. The 10 unique suites in this converted Zona Rosa mansion have sensational features like fireplaces, queen-sized hammocks, oyster shell vanities, brick ceilings, rustic wood furniture and tiled floors throughout. The garden terrace, with

an enormous wood-burning fireplace and too many candles to count, oozes romance.

Quinta Real Guadalajara (Map p521; ☎ 3669-0600; www.quintareal.com; Av México 2727; r from M$2506; P ⊠ 🐾 ▣ 🕽) There is no denying the beauty of this five-star stay, with its exquisite stone and ivy-covered exterior. The lobby and bar are inviting and stylish, the grounds are impeccably manicured and the service is outstanding. But the rooms are a bit cramped and don't live up to the steep price tag.

Tlaquepaque

Just 15 minutes away by bus or taxi from downtown Guadalajara, Tlaquepaque is an excellent option for those who crave small town charm but still want to visit the sights downtown. The shopping is superb, and you won't have to lug your purchases too far.

La Posada de la Media Luna (Map p521; ☎ 3635-6054; http://lamedialuna.tripod.com; Juárez 36; r from M$290) An affordable, basic choice. It's centrally located, the rooms are tidy, not spotless, but the upstairs terrace is sunny and on weekends the sound of countless jamming mariachi drifts in.

El Retoño (Map p521; ☎ 3587-3989; www.lacasadel retono.com; Matamoros 182; s/d M$600/750) Another cute courtyard B&B set on a quiet street. The rooms have arched brick ceilings, exposed stone walls, sweet tiled bathrooms and some have balconies overlooking the backyard. This is an exceptional deal.

Casa Campos (Map p521; ☎ 3838-5296; www.hotel casacampos.com; Miranda 30A; s/d M$850/1000; 🐾 ⊠ ▣) This old converted mansion marries stone columns and wrought iron with sleek wood furnishings, for a stylish blend of old and new. The brilliant courtyard has cages full of rare pygmy monkeys and there's a swank tequila bar.

La Villa del Ensueño (Map p521; ☎ 3635-8792, fax 3659-6152; www.villadelensueno.com; Florida 305; r from M$950; P ⊠ 🐾 ▣ 🕽) Behind its garish purple exterior are 20 modern rooms set around two pools. This place lacks the culture and style of some of the smaller B&Bs in town, but the rooms are quite new and comfortable and it has all the amenities. Breakfast is included.

Quinta Don José (Map p521; ☎ 3635-7522, fax 3838-4641; www.quintadonjose.com; r from M$975; ⊠ ▣ 🕽) You'll enjoy the comfy sunken lobby/lounge and the sunny upstairs rooms with sponged pastel walls. It also has larger and darker rooms accessed from the pool deck. Breakfast is included.

WESTERN CENTRAL
HIGHLANDS

TOP FIVE MEALS IN JALISCO

- Take Jalisco's best fine food distributors, an old, converted Zona Rosa mansion and an ethos to make haute cuisine affordable and you have, **Cocina 88 (opposite)**, Guadalajara's best restaurant. Choose your cut of steak and seafood from the butcher case, pay a small kitchen fee, pluck a bottle of red from the cellar and bring a date!

- If you crave tradition over innovation then step into **Birriería las Nueve Esquinas** (opposite). It serves what could be considered *comida típica*, but it's anything but typical. This attractive, open tiled kitchen prepares the best lamb in the region and it does a mean *birria de chivo* (steamed goat) too. The price is right, the portions are huge and savory and the atmosphere is steeped in old Mexico.

- Ceviche in the highlands, 300km from the sea? Does that sound like a good idea to you? Well, it should. Because the man known mythically as El Socio, proprietor of **Mariscos el Social** (p536), has been dicing and marinating fresh ceviche and crafting huge shrimp and octopus cocktails on a Tlaquepaque street corner for 20 years. He's so popular it's hard to get a seat and he and his staff, who arrive before 7am each day to begin peeling and boiling the shrimp, go through 350kg of seafood each week. It's fresh, absurdly good and you will have a blast. El Socio will make sure of that.

- The spiciest dish we've ever loved can be found at a superb ranch-style restaurant in tequila country. The signature dish at **Real Campestre** (p545) is *aguachile* (a dish where two dozen raw shrimp are cooked in a cold lime juice and chili broth). The shrimp still look raw, but they are tender and full of deliciously tart fire that is immediately addictive. Peruse the menu because everything here is good, especially the bar – which serves 50 varieties of fine highland tequila.

- There's something pure and true about a great taco. It's simple – with only a few ingredients, satisfying to even the most naive and sophisticated palates, but never too filling and no utensils are required, which is always a plus. Rich and poor, old and young, neat and sloppy – everybody loves tacos! And the best taco in Jalisco (which by default puts it on the shortlist for Best Taco Worldwide) is served at **Rica Birria** (p549), a humble stand in a humble mountain town. Go find it!

ourpick Casa de las Flores (Map p521; ☎ 3659-3186; www.casadelasflores.com; Santos Degollado 175; r from M$1030; ✗ ▣) From the outside it looks like just another neighborhood compound, but when you enter this stunning courtyard B&B, you will be hit by a swirl of captivating colors. There's an incredible collection of Mexican folk art, including some very rare pre-Hispanic pieces; a blooming garden and patio patrolled by hummingbirds out back; and a stocked bar and fireplace in the living room. Rooms are all quite large and decorated in the same folksy style as the main building and breakfasts verge on the ultra gourmet – especially when co-owner Stan is on breakfast duty. He trained as a chef at Berkeley's Chez Panisse.

EATING

Guadalajara is a good eating town and if you don't have at least one exceptional meal here – on the street, or in Guadalajara's wide range of restaurants and cafés, then it's either your own fault, or you're a vegetarian. Fact is, this city has phenomenal steak and lamb, superb *carnitas* and *birria*, wonderful roasted chicken dinners, outstanding *ceviche* and too many taquerías and *torta* stands to count. Whether you are downtown, in the Zona Rosa or the suburbs, you will eat well. Everyone does.

Centro Histórico & Around

All fancy hotels sport equally fancy restaurants. The ones at Hotel Francés and Hotel de Mendoza are magnificent old dining rooms. More adventurous stomachs can head to the Mercado San Juan de Dios (Map pp524–5), home to endless savory food stalls serving the cheapest and some of the tastiest eats in town.

El Tío (cnr Corona & Ferrocarril; mains M$3.50-6; ☻ 7:30am-1:30pm) Once the savory, spicy aroma wafts over you, you will not be able to ignore this humble taco stand. All it serves are bean and ground beef tacos with grilled peppers and fiery red salsa. Cue up with the locals and enjoy some exceptional street food.

Danés (☎ 3613-4401; Madero 451; pastries M$5-25; ⏲ 8am-6pm) Dessert lovers flock to this neighborhood bakery that turns out a luscious array of Mexican and European pastries. Dark chocolate oozes from the crust of the *cuerno de chocolate* and its *sorbete de crema* (a custard-stuffed pastry shaped like a cone) are dusted with cinnamon and encrusted with candied pecans.

Kristy & Edwards (Carranza 70; mains from M$21; ⏲ 8am-6pm) This lunch stand with a splash of color is across from the post office and serves burritos, fresh pressed and blended *jugos* (M$10) and burgers.

Alta Fibra (Map pp524-5; ☎ 3424-1510; Sánchez 370B; mains M$25; ⏲ 11am-7pm Mon-Fri, till 6pm Sat; Ⓥ) Not much atmosphere, but a young, conscious crowd descends to snack on shrimp made from carrots, ham crafted from soy and spinach and whole bean tacos. Vegans, rejoice!

La Chata (Map pp524-5; ☎ 3613-0588; Av Corona 126; mains M$31-54) Quality *comida típica*, affordable prices and ample portions keep this family diner packed. The specialty is a *platillo jaliscense* (fried chicken with five sides); it also serves a popular *pozole* (hominy soup).

Café Madrid (Map pp524-5; ☎ 3614-9504; Av Juárez 264; mains M$35-50) What more could you want from a classic diner? The waiters are in white dinner jackets and the cash register, espresso machines and soda fountains are mint condition antiques. Come for breakfast. The *huevos rancheros* and *chilaquiles* have been favorites for 50 years.

Chai (☎ 3613-0001; Juárez 200; mains M$41-65) Chai is your hippie chic café. Booths are actually love seats and sofas and flowers – from fake tulip light boxes to abstract wall paintings – are the general theme. The breakfast menu is superb. Think egg white omelettes and waffles with fresh strawberries.

Chong Wah (Map pp524-5; ☎ 3613-9950; Juárez 558; mains M$45; ⏲ noon-11pm) Overdosed on *comida típica*? Hit Guadalajara's favorite Chinese haunt. All the classics are here – Sichuan shrimp, almond chicken, *lo mein* – and it serves a popular weekend buffet.

Villa Madrid (Map pp524-5; ☎ 3613-4250; López Cotilla 553; mains M$45-70; ⏲ 11:30am-9pm Mon-Sat) Great stop for *licuados*, juices, fruit cocktails and

yoghurt done six different ways. There's live music on Saturday at 7pm.

Sandy's (Map pp524-5; ☎ 3345-4636; Alcalde 130; meals from M$65; ⏲ 1-6pm Mon-Sun; Ⓥ) This bright, 2nd-story lunch spot overlooks the Rotonda de los Jaliscenses Ilustres and the cathedral. It's popular among vegetarians for its salad bar.

La Antigua (Plaza Guadalajara; mains from M$80; ⏲ 11am-9pm) The location and ambience outshine the food at this charming terrace restaurant overlooking the plaza. But it's worth considering for the made-to-order salsa and tortillas and the sizzling *molcajete de arrachera*, a traditional beef and cheese stew simmering in a spicy chili sauce.

La Fonda de San Miguel Arcángel (Map pp524-5; ☎ 3613-0809; Guerra 25; mains M$95; ⏲ 8:30am-midnight Tue-Sat, 8:30am-9pm Sun, 8:30am-6pm Mon) A sweet and funky courtyard retreat from the sun where fountains gurgle, an old piano man tickles the keys and antique sculpture and bird cages are everywhere. Its specialty is a fish *molcajete*. Come at night and dine beneath a magnificent chandelier of wrought iron stars.

Plaza de las Nueve Esquinas

Half a dozen blocks south of the city center is this small and untouristy triangular block where several small streets intersect. It's a little neighborhood popular with eateries specializing in *birria*, meat steamed in its own juices until it is so tender it melts in your mouth.

Birriería las Nueve Esquinas (Map pp524-5; ☎ 3613-6260; Colón 384; mains M$59-79; ⏲ 8:30am-10pm Mon-Sat, 8:30am-7:30pm Sun) This is a can't-miss meal. The open, tiled kitchen, with its in-house tortillería is as beautiful as the tasty and absurdly tender *barbacoa de borrego* (baked lamb) and *birria de chivo* (steamed goat) served in traditional ceramic casseroles. Enjoy them with a stack of fresh tortillas and smaller bowls of guacamole, pickled onions and *salsa verde* swimming with *cilantro* and perfectly ripe chunks of avocado.

Zona Rosa & Around

Guadalajara's Zona Rosa encompasses the few blocks around Av Chapultepec north and south of Av Vallarta. It's home to some of the city's best cuisine. To get here, catch the westbound Par Vial 400 or 500 bus from Avs Independencia and Alcalde. Taxis should cost around M$40.

Tortas Ahogadas Héroes (Map p521; Francia 20; tortas M$25) The menu is simple: there's only *tortas ahogadas*, Guadalajara's beloved and famous hangover cure. Crunchy baguettes are filled with chunks of pork and drenched in a searing chili sauce and a squeeze of lime. Take a bite and your tongue will burn, your stomach unwinds and your head will clear almost instantly.

Bisquets Guadalajara (Map pp524-5; ☎ 3827-1616; Libertad 1985; mains M$35-65) A great breakfast spot, with baskets of fresh pastries – from pan chocolate to pecan rolls to sugary, lemony *astorgas*. It also serves eggs, omelettes, tacos and enchiladas.

La Estación de Lulio (Map pp524-5; Libertad 1982; breakfasts M$55; ⏰ 8am-10pm) It's hard to get a seat for breakfast at this fine café because of the great jazz soundtrack and the complete breakfasts of eggs *al gusto*, spicy beans, *chilaquiles*, coffee and fresh pressed orange, grapefruit or tangerine juice.

Karne Garibaldi (Map p521; ☎ 3826-1286; Garibaldi 1306; mains M$61-90; ⏰ noon-midnight) It has two specialties: *carne en su jugo* (meat cooked in its own broth flavored with beans, bacon and green tomatoes) and fast service (so speedy it landed in the *Guinness Book of Records* in 1996). Neither will disappoint.

our pick Cocina 88 (Map pp524-5; ☎ 3827-5996; Vallarta 1342; mains M$100-200; ⏰ 1:30-7pm, 8:30pm-1am Mon-Sat, 2pm-10pm Sun) By every measure – taste, creativity, service, style and value – this is the best restaurant in Guadalajara. The owners renovated and converted this turn-of-the-century mansion into a restaurant where guests choose their cut of beef or choice of fresh seafood from a butcher case and select their wine from the cellar rather than a list. Here, surf and turf has many meanings – such as perfectly seared scallops and *filet mignon carpaccio*. It's not cheap, but it isn't a total budget buster. Seafood and beef are sold at cost and guests are simply charged a M$58 kitchen fee per person. It only serves two classic cocktails, martinis and margaritas.

Santo Coyote (Map pp524-5; ☎ 3343-2265; Tejada 2379; mains from M$130; ⏰ 1pm-2am) Locals love to send tourists here because of the set piece décor (think massive *palapa* roofs) and Mexican Hat Dance performances (um, not good). But they do make their scintillating three-chili salsa fresh at the tableside and the mostly glass bar is magnificent. Plus, if you sit there you'll avoid the 'entertainment'.

LA O (Map pp524-5; ☎ 3630-2250; www.laorestaurante.com; Zuno 2152; mains M$130; ⏰ 1:30pm-1am Mon-Sat; 2-6pm Sun) Another mansion has been converted by the guys at Cocina 88 into a cool new restaurant. This one serves Spanish, Italian and Mexican tapas and mains come with an endless salad and antipasti bar. Try the tart mango *ceviche* and the crumbly crab cakes sprinkled with *cilantro*.

Tlaquepaque

Just southeast of the main plaza, **El Parián** is a block of dozens of restaurant-bars with patio tables crowding a leafy inner courtyard. This is where you sit, drink and listen to live mariachi music, especially on weekends. Waiters are eager but the food is so-so. Order an appetizer, but when it's time to eat a serious meal find one of these delicious kitchens.

Cenaduria Doña Victoria (Map p521; Degollado 182; mains from M$9; ⏰ 7pm-11pm closed Thu) Victoria serves high quality Mexican soul food. Her street-side skillet overflows with toquitos, tacos, *tortas*, *pozole*, quail, chicken and potatoes. The *pollo dorado* (M$25) is the best seller. It comes with potatoes, salad, tortillas and three kinds of salsa.

Salvador Santos López Tortas Ahogadas; (Map p521; Madero 74; tortas M$18, T-bones M$65; ⏰ 10am-7pm Mon-Sat) A hole in the wall with a street-side grill, where Señor Lopez prepares T-bones and skirt steaks. Steaks are rubbed with olive oil, splashed with soy sauce and served with Greek salad and garlic bread. Don't forget to order a cold beer.

Alcatraz (Map p521; Progreso 124; desserts from M$20; ⏰ 10am-8pm) You'll have to search for the lava stone facade because it has no sign. But it does have the best desserts in town. The light-as-air *jericalla* custard, coffee cakes and blueberry cheesecake have won this family shop a steady stream of local loyalists.

La Mata Tinta (Map p521; ☎ 3659-0207; Juárez 145-13 Plaza de Artesanías; sandwiches M$40; ⏰ 11am-11pm Tue-Sun) This is a wine bar, art gallery and café under one roof – although seating spills into the plaza. It has a prodigious wine list including Mexican vintages and a nice selection of baguettes and paninis. There's live music five nights a week and the walls are covered with rotating exhibitions from local artists. Tuesday night it shows art-house cinema.

our pick Mariscos el Social (off Map p521; ☎ 3838-5754; Calz Delicias 117; ceviche tostadas M$13, cocteles M$52-128; ⏰ 9am-6pm Mon-Sat) The chef, known as 'El

TORTAS AHOGADAS

Last night you drank a few two many tequilas, forgot to chug a liter of water before bed and you're paying for it this morning. Your hair is plastered to your forehead, your eyelids will only open halfway and you have but one choice. It's time to sample Guadalajara's most beloved hangover cure, a *torta ahogada* ('drowned sandwich').

You've no doubt noticed that Guadalajara is home to countless *tortas ahogadas* stands, but no matter where you buy it you'll find three major components. A *birote* baguette is filled with tender chunks of roast pork leg and then smothered with a searing chili sauce (made primarily from a dried chili pepper called *de árbol*, vinegar, garlic and oregano). The crusty, sour *birote* is the key. Similar to San Francisco's famous sourdough, Guadalajara's altitude and climate make its baguettes unique. Crunchy on the outside and soft in the center, their consistency allows the bread to be submerged in sauce without losing its structure. This soggy sandwich has integrity, people! And to bleary-eyed customers, like you, who lost your motor skills at last call, that is a very good thing.

With the sun beating down upon you, desperate for relief you squeeze your soggy beast with lime and crunch. The vinegary chili burns so hot that sweat trickles down your forehead and your eyes water, but it's a welcome irrigation. The tender pork melts in your mouth and the starchy bread instantaneously tames your acidic stomach. Further bites bring a hint of lime, a touch of smooth, creamy avocado and more blessed fire. Within minutes the hangover that furiously gripped your temples relents. Your eyes open fully and completely, your shoulders relax and light floods in. You are finally ready to begin your day.

Socio,' started serving his sensational *ceviche* and delicious shrimp and octopus cocktails from his stainless steel cart on Glendale and Delicias 20 years ago. He still works that corner, but he has a sit-down café down the block that is equally great. Each week El Socio and his crew serve 350kg of shrimp and octopus. So, you know it's fresh. Order a shrimp and octopus plate if you're not into the soupy cocktails.

El Abajeño (Map p521; ☎ 3635-9015; Juárez 231; mains from M$70; ✆ noon-10pm Mon-Sun) *Comida tipica* is dressed up and served to business-types and well-off families on a beautiful brick patio with fountains, chandeliers and roving mariachi. Try the wood grilled lamb (M$92).

Casa Vieja (Map p521; ☎ 3657-6250; Prieto 99; mains M$96-117; ✆ 8am-10:30pm Mon-Thu, 8am-midnight Fri & Sat, 8am-10pm Sun) Dine on tequila-marinated chicken and *arrachera mitla* – tender skirt steak marinated in *achiote* and lime juice, within a chipped and faded pastel courtyard. The food works and the setting is lovely, but the soundtrack is bracing (Gothic classical meets Ryan Seacrest approved pop-rock).

Casa Fuerte (Map p521; ☎ 3639-6481; Independencia 224; mains M$100-200; ✆ 12:30-8pm) This place leans toward fine dining, with an elegant bar, refreshing garden patio and a menu priced like an upscale Mexican restaurant in California. It's one of the more popular spots in town.

DRINKING

La Fuente (Map p524-5; Suárez 78; ✆ 8:30am-11pm Mon-Thu, 8:30am-midnight Fri & Sat) La Fuente, set in the old Edison boiler room, is an institution – and a rather friendly one. It's been open since 1921 and is mostly peopled by regulars – older men who start drinking too early. But they treat newcomers like family and women like queens. A bass, piano, violin trio sets up and jams from sunset until last call.

Scratch (Map pp524-5; ☎ 3614-7433; Guerra 226; ✆ noon-11pm Mon-Thu, noon-midnight Fri & Sat) This new hipster bar in the Centro Historico has elevated the *michelada* (beer and Bloody Mary's lovechild) to fine art and celebrates the days when grunge rock ruled. It also has 12 labels of good tequila.

Hotel Francés (Map pp524-5; ☎ 3613-1190; Maestranza 35; ✆ noon-midnight) The dark marble courtyard bar at this hotel encourages you to relax back into another era, where waiters in bow ties treat you like old friends, happy hour lasts until 8pm and acoustic troubadours strum gorgeous, weepy ballads.

Outside the historic center are some of the city's trendiest watering holes.

Green Mug (Map pp524-5; ☎ 3825-7872; Chapultepec 223A; ✆ 9am-11pm Mon-Fri, 10am-11pm Sat, 6pm-11pm Sun; espresso drinks from M$15) This sleek, indie coffee house is Starbucks' main competition on Chapultepec. There are leather sofas, flat screen TVs and free wi-fi, all enjoyed by a young, hip crowd.

Bananas (Map pp524-5; ☎ 3615-4191; Chapultepec 330; ⏱ 4pm-2am) Beers are cheap, the crowd is young and the music gravitates from hip-hop to global rock and back again. On slow midweek nights this mod-dive always attracts a crowd.

our pick Candela (Map p521; ☎ 3616-9676; Mina 83, Zapopan; ⏱ 1pm-2am Tue-Sun) Drink with Zapopan's young, sexy, moneyed bohemia in this converted home with a courtyard lounge, specialty cocktails and a jazz soundtrack. It serves wood-fired pizzas. Tuesday is the big night.

Santa (Map pp524-5; Luna 2042; ⏱ 8pm-2am) Red carpets and blinking Señora de Guadalupe pictures sum up the eccentric glam interior. It gets crowded on weekends when electronic DJs spin. During the week well-dressed yuppies sip martinis (two for one on Thursday) and listen to lounge music.

ENTERTAINMENT

Guadalajara is a musical place and live performers can be heard any night of the week at one of the city's many venues (including restaurants). Discos and bars are plentiful, but ask around for the newest hot spots.

Peruse the entertainment insert, *Ocio*, in the Friday edition of *Público*. It has the current week's scoop on restaurants, movies, exhibits and the club scene. Spanish-language dailies *Occidental* and *Informador* also have entertainment listings, as does the weekly booklet *Ciento Uno*. Or you can always ask a young and friendly local their thoughts. Guadalajarans love to show off their town.

Several popular venues host a range of drama, dance and music performances. The newest and hippest spot is **Teatro Diana** (Map pp524-5; ☎ 3818-3800 via Ticketmaster; www.teatrodiana.com; Av 16 de Septiembre 710). It stages traveling Broadway shows, concerts with local and international artists and art installations. Other options include the **Teatro Degollado** (Map pp524-5; ☎ 3613-1115) and the **Instituto Cultural de Cabañas** (Map pp524-5; ☎ 3668-1640), both downtown cultural centers, as well as the **Ex-Convento del Carmen** (Map pp524-5; ☎ 3030-1390; Av Juárez 638).

Nightclubs

Guadalajara's hot spots are outside the historic center. You'll be mingling with a young, pretty crowd of well-dressed locals, so ditch the backpacker gear, put on your smell-goods and let

your foreign tongue pacify snarling bouncers. Sometimes the best scene and hottest *chicas*, can be found at the gay clubs (see the boxed text, opposite) – heteros are always welcome.

El Callejón de los Rumberos (Map pp524-5; ☎ 3827-7490; Chapultepec 287; cover charge men/women M$150/30; ⏱ 7pm-1am Wed-Sun) This is the best salsa bar in Guadalajara, where locals dress to the nines and shake their asses on two floors with two bandstands and three bars. Wednesday is the big night.

Bar Américas (Map p521; ☎ 3389-8211; Américas 959; www.baramericas.com; ⏱ 9pm-4am Thu-Sun) Mexican and international DJs spin slamming electronic music for the Jaegermeister swilling masses at this crowded old bunker. There's no sign, so it can be tough to find. You'll hear it before you see it.

Angels Club (Map pp524-5; ☎ 3615-2525; López Cotilla 1495B; ⏱ 9:30pm-5am Wed-Sat, 6am-11am Sun) Welcome to Guadalajara's megaclub. Sure, it's a gay venue, but chicks dig the mod acrylic tables, cool lounge, throwback beanbag room and the three dance floors blasting electronica, hip-hop and progressive rock so heterosexual men should shed their inhibitions and mingle with the party people. Saturday nights get wild. Clubbers often leave for breakfast at around 5am and return for sun-drenched fun after hours.

Mariachis

You can pay your respects to the mariachi tradition in its home city. The Plaza de los Mariachis, just east of the historic center, is an OK place to sit, drink beer and soak in the serenades of passionate Mexican bands.

But you'll be happier at El Parián (p536), a garden complex in Tlaquepaque made up of dozens of small cantinas that all share one plaza occupied by droves of Mariachi. On the weekends the bands battle and jockey for your ears, applause and cash.

Casa Bariachi (Map p521; ☎ 3616-9900; Av Vallarta 2221; ⏱ 1pm-3am Mon-Sat) This bright barn-like restaurant-bar has romantic lighting and leather chairs, along with piñatas and colorful *papel picado* (cutout paper) hanging from the ceiling. This place may fail the hipster test, but the margaritas are bathtub big and mariachi jam from 4pm to 11pm daily. It's about a 10 minute taxi ride west of the city center.

Other Live Music

State and municipal bands present free concerts of typical *música tapatía* in the Plaz

GAY & LESBIAN GUADALAJARA

Guadalajara is one of the gayest cities in the country – some call it the San Francisco of Mexico. It's not nearly as open as SF, however, and discrimination (especially against transgender folks) persists. However, if you know where to go you'll feel comfortable.

Guadalajara's so-called 'gay ghetto' radiates out a few blocks from the corner of Ocampo and Sánchez, in the city center, but Av Chapultepec's Zona Rosa (just west of the city center) is starting to see upscale establishments aimed at a gay clientele.

In June there are gay **pride marches** (www.marchadiversidadgdl.org) and the city even supports a **gay radio** (www.gdlgayradio.com). The best **bar listings**, complete with maps and phone numbers can be found at http://gaybar.com/directory/mexico/guadalajara, www.conciergegdl.com, and www.angelfire.com, which also list hotels, gyms and other gay vortexes in Guadalajara.

La Prisciliana (Map pp524-5; ☎ 3562-0725; Sánchez 394; ⏰ 5pm-1:30am) Laid-back and stylish, with arched windows, burgundy walls, worn tile floors and an antique wood bar in an old colonial building. It can get wild late and there's a drag show from time to time, but usually things stay chill. Downstairs Club Ye Ye is smaller but louder and wilder, with metallic decor and a club soundtrack.

Los Caudillos (Map pp524-5; ☎ 3613-5445; cnr Sánchez 407; ⏰ 5pm-3am Sun & Tue-Thu, 5pm-5am Wed, Fri & Sat) Diagonally across from La Prisciliana, this is a popular two-story disco, with three dance floors and endless lounges and bars. This is a hook-up joint, pure and simple. There's a cover on Fridays and Saturdays.

Circus (Map pp524-5; ☎ 3616-0299; Galeana 277; ⏰ 10pm-4am Mon & Thu, 10pm-5am Wed, 10pm-6am Fri & Sat) Fills up late in the night with hot young hardbodies lounging in heart-shaped chairs and howling at the variety shows. It's also popular with lesbians.

Máskaras (☎ 3614-8103; Maestranza 238; ⏰ 3pm-midnight Mon-Thu, noon-2am Fri-Sun) Enter through the small yellow door on the left and you'll find an upstairs dance floor with a bar and another, more popular bar downstairs where gay men and lesbians mix. It's especially popular in the afternoon.

Californias (Moreno 652; ⏰ 8pm-3am Mon-Sat) This hot spot attracts a diverse and attractive crowd – everything from cowboys to stock brokers. It gets packed around 10pm, and weekend nights are a madhouse, but there's no dancing.

Angels Club (opposite) hosts drag shows on Friday and Saturday at midnight. Cover is M$50.

de Armas at 6:30pm on most Tuesdays, Thursdays and Sundays and on other days as well during holiday seasons (and especially for the Fiestas de Octubre, p531).

La Bodeguita del Medio (Map p521; ☎ 3630-1620; Av Vallarta 2320; ⏰ 1:30pm-2:30am Mon-Sat, 1:30pm-1am Sun) This pseudo-Cuban joint complete with graffiti décor has an upstairs restaurant and a bar downstairs. Live Cuban music plays from 2:30pm to 4:30pm and 9:30pm to 2:30am, Monday to Saturday; no cover. There are Cuban dance lessons on Wednesday and Thursday from 6pm to 9pm.

Hard Rock Café (Map p521; ☎ 3616-4564; Av Vallarta 2425; ⏰ 11am-2am) In the Centro Magno shopping center, this is your typical Hard Rock, with guitars on the walls and Tex-Mex burgers on the menu. Hidden inside, however, is a 1000-seat auditorium that hosts international groups (check with Ticketmaster for bands and showtimes).

Sports

BULLFIGHTS & CHARREADAS

Plaza de Toros Nuevo Progreso (Map p521; ☎ 3637-9982; www.plazanuevoprogreso.com; north end of Calz Independencia; seats M$100-850) There are two bullfighting seasons running from October to November, and February to March. Fights are held on Sundays starting at 4:30pm. A couple of fights usually take place during the October fiestas; the rest of the schedule is sporadic. Check its website or ask for details at the tourist office.

Lienzo Charros de Jalisco (Map pp524-5; ☎ 3619-0515; Dr Michel 572; admission M$30-40) *Charreadas* are held at noon most Sundays in this ring behind Parque Agua Azul. *Charros* (cowboys) come from all over Jalisco and Mexico to wrestle and rope cows. *Escaramuzas* (cowgirls) perform daring side-saddle displays, often showing more riding skill than the *charros*!

SOCCER

Fútbol flows strongly through Guadalajaran blood. The city has three local teams in Mexico's top league, the *primera división*: **Guadalajara** (Las Chivas; www.chivas.com .mx) – the second most popular team in the country – **Atlas** (Los Zorros; www.atlas.com.mx) and **Universidad Autónoma de Guadalajara** (Los Tecos; www.tecos.com.mx). The seasons last from July to December and from January to June and teams play at stadiums around the city. You can get an up-to-date season schedule at www.femexfut.org.mx.

The **Estadio Jalisco** (Map p521; ☎ 3637-0563; Siete Colinas 1772; admission M$35-100), the main venue (seating around 60,000), hosted World Cup matches in 1970 and 1986. Contact the stadium or tourist office for schedule information. Big games will cost you.

Cinemas

Big shopping centers, like **Plaza del Sol** (Map p521; ☎ 3121-5750; Av López Mateos Sur), **Plaza Milenium** (Map p521; ☎ 3634-0509; Av López Mateos Sur) and **Centro Magno** (Map p521; ☎ 3630-1113; Av Vallarta 2425), all have up-to-date multiplexes showing Spanish-language and first-run popcorn pictures from Hollywood. Hollywood movies come dubbed in Spanish or subtitled, so double check which show you're seeing.

SHOPPING

Handicrafts from Jalisco, Michoacán and other Mexican states are available in Guadalajara's many markets. The Casa de las Artesanías de Jalisco (p528), just outside Parque Agua Azul, has the best selection of quality crafts in the city limits.

But Tlaquepaque and Tonalá, two suburbs less than 15km from Guadalajara's center, are both major producers of handicrafts and furniture (see p529 for both). You'll find the best value (read wholesale prices) in Tonalá.

Mercado San Juan de Dios (Map pp524-5; Mercado Libertad; cnr Av Javier Mina & Calz Independencia; ☼ 10am-9pm) This huge market has a whole three floors of stalls offering everything from cowboy boots and DVDs to kitchenware; the salespeople are eager to sell and the food court is outstanding!

Mercado Corona (Map pp524-5; cnr Av Hidalgo & Santa Mónica; ☼ 9am-8pm) Near downtown is this block-long market with cheap electronics, clothes, household items, knick-knacks and food.

Viceroy Tabaquería (Map pp524-5; Corona 72; ☼ 9am-7pm) A central Guadalajara tobacco shop that doubles as downtown's best tequila vendor. It has more than 100 labels of tequila at great prices and even offers tastings.

Guadalajara's richest citizens prefer to browse at the big shopping centers, such as **Centro Magno** (Map p521; Av Vallarta 2425), 2km west of the city center; **Plaza del Sol** (Map p521; Av López Mateos Sur), 7km southwest of the city center; and **Plaza Milenium** (Map p521; Av López Mateos Sur), 7.5km southwest of the city center. All open from approximately 10am to 9pm. To reach them, take bus 258 going west from San Felipe and Av Alcalde, or TUR 707 going west on Av Juárez.

GETTING THERE & AWAY
Air

Guadalajara's **Aeropuerto Internacional Miguel Hidalgo** (☎ 3688-5504) is 17km south of downtown, just off the highway to Chapala. Inside are ATMs, money-exchange, cafés and car-rental booths. There's also a **tourist office** (☼ 8am-6pm).

A multitude of airlines offer direct flights to major cities in Mexico, the US and Canada, including:
Aero California (Map p521; ☎ 800-237-62-25; www .areocalifornia.com)
Aeroméxico (Map pp524-5; ☎ 3658-0799; www .aeromexico.com; Av Corona 196)
American Airlines (Map p521; ☎ 3616-4402, 800-904-60-00; www.aa.com; Av Vallarta 2440, Colonia Arcos Vallarta)
Aviacsa (Map p521; ☎ 800-713-57-44; www.aviacsa .com; Av Vallarta 2440, Colonia Arcos Vallarta)
Delta (Map pp524-5; ☎ 3630-3530; www.delta.com; López Cotilla 1701, Colonia Americana)
Mexicana (Map p521; ☎ 800-502-20-00; www.mexi cana.com; Av Vallarta 2440, Colonia Arcos Vallarta)

Bus

Guadalajara has two bus terminals. The long-distance bus terminal is the **Nueva Central Camionera** (New Bus Terminal; Map p521; ☎ 3600-0495) a large modern V-shaped terminal that is split into seven separate *módulos* (mini-terminals). Each *módulo* has ticket desks for a number of bus lines, plus rest rooms and cafeterias. The Nueva Central Camionera is 9km southeast of Guadalajara city center, past Tlaquepaque.

Buses go to and from just about everywhere in western, central and northern Mexico. Destinations are served by multiple companies, based in the different *módulos*, making price comparisons difficult and time-consuming. The good news is that if you're flexible, you won't have to wait long for a bus.

Destinations include the following (departures are frequent, fares are for 1st-class services):

Destination	Fare	Duration
Barra de Navidad	M$305	5½hr
Colima	M$168	3hr
Guanajuato	M$300	4hr
Manzanillo	M$230	4hr
Mexico City (Terminal Norte)	M$460	7-8hr
Morelia	M$242	4hr
Puerto Vallarta	M$405	5hr
Querétaro	M$345	5½hr
San Juan de los Lagos	M$155	3hr
San Miguel de Allende	M$405	5hr
Tepic	M$195	3hr
Uruapan	M$210	4½hr
Zacatecas	M$345	5hr
Zamora	M$128	2¼hr
Zapotlanejo	M$25	30min

ETN (Módulo 2) offers a deluxe nonstop ride to many of these destinations. You'll pay 20% more, but it's more comfortable, faster and its plush waiting room has wireless internet.

Guadalajara's other bus terminal is the **Antigua Central Camionera** (Old Bus Terminal; Map p524-5; ☎ 3619-3312), about 1.5km south of the cathedral near Parque Agua Azul. From here 2nd-class buses serve destinations within 75km of Guadalajara. There are two sides to it: Sala A is for destinations to the east and northeast; Sala B is for destinations northwest, southwest and south. There's a M$1 charge to enter the terminal, which offers a **left-luggage service** (☯ 7.30am-8pm) in Sala B.

Destination	Fare	Duration	Frequency
Ajijic	M$40	1hr	every 30 min 6am 9pm, Sala A
Chapala	M$37	50min	every 30 min 6am 9pm, Sala A
Ciudad Guzmán	M$100	3hr	hourly, Sala B
San Juan	M$40	1¼hr	every 30 min 6am 9pm, Sala A
Tequila	M$40	1¾hr	every 15 min until 9:15pm, Sala B
Tapalpa	M$75	3hr	hourly, Sala B

Car

Guadalajara is 535km northwest of Mexico City and 344km east of Puerto Vallarta. Highways 15, 15D, 23, 54, 54D, 80, 80D and 90 all converge here, combining temporarily to form the Periférico, a ring road around the city.

Tolls and driving times to main destinations are as follows: Manzanillo ($24, three hours), Puerto Vallarta ($26, 3¾ hours) and Mexico City ($52, 5½ hours).

Guadalajara has many car rental agencies. Several of the large US companies are represented, but you may get a cheaper deal from a local company. Costs average M$600 to M$700 per day. And it will cost you (something like M$3000) to leave the car in any city other than the one you rented it from. Recommended agencies include:

Alamo (☎ 3613-5560)
Budget (☎ 3613-0027, 800-700-17-00)
Dollar (☎ 3826-7959, 3688-5659)
Hertz (☎ 3688-5633, 800-654-30-30)
National (☎ 3614-7994, 800-227-73-68)
Thrifty (☎ 3688-6318)

Train

The only train serving Guadalajara is the *Tequila Express* – a tourist excursion to the nearby town of Amatitán (see p543).

GETTING AROUND
To/From the Airport

The airport is about 17km south of the center of Guadalajara, just off the highway to Chapala. To get into town on public transportation, exit the airport and head to the bus stop in front of the Hotel Casa Grande, about 50m to the right. Take any bus marked 'Zapote' (M$6) or 'Atasa' (M$10) – both run every 15 minutes from about 5am to 10pm and take 40 minutes to the Antigua Central Camionera, where you can hop a bus to the city center.

Taxi prices are M$200 to the city center, M$180 to the Nueva Central Camionera and M$160 to Tlaquepaque. Buy fixed-price tickets inside the airport.

To get to the airport from Guadalajara's center, take bus 174 to the Antigua Central Camionera (the stop is in front of the Gran Hotel Canada) and then get on an 'Aeropuerto' bus (every 20 minutes, 6am to 9pm) from this stop. Metered taxis cost roughly M$180.

WESTERN CENTRAL HIGHLANDS

To/From the Bus Terminals

To reach the city center from the Nueva Central Camionera, take any bus marked 'Centro' (M$5). You can also catch the more comfortable, turquoise-colored TUR bus (M$10). They should be marked 'Zapopan'. Don't take the ones marked 'Tonalá' or you'll be headed away from Guadalajara's center. Taxis to the city center cost around M$180 unless they let the meter tick (some don't use it).

To get to the Nueva Central Camionera from the city center, take any bus marked 'Nueva Central' – these are frequent and leave from the corner of Av 16 de Septiembre and Madero.

To reach the city center from the Antigua Central Camionera, take any bus going north on Calz Independencia. To return to the Antigua Central Camionera from the city center, take bus 174 going south on Calz Independencia. Taxis cost M$40.

Bus 616 (M$5) runs between the two bus terminals.

Bus

Guadalajara has a comprehensive city bus system, but be ready for crowded, rough rides. On major routes, buses run every five minutes or so from 6am to 10pm daily and cost M$5. Many buses pass through the city center, so for a suburban destination you'll have a few stops to choose from. The routes diverge as they get further from the city center and you'll need to know the bus number for the suburb you want. Some bus route numbers are followed by an additional letter indicating which route they take through the suburbs.

The TUR buses, painted a distinctive turquoise color, are a more comfortable alternative. They have air-con and plush seats (M$10). If they roar past without stopping, they're full; this can happen several times in a row during rush hour and may drive you mad.

The tourist office has a list of the complex bus routes in Guadalajara and can help you reach your destination. Following are some common destinations, the buses that go there and a central stop where you can catch them.

Antigua Central Camionera Bus 174 going south on Calz Independencia.

Av López Mateos Sur Bus 258 at San Felipe and Av Alcalde, or TUR 707 going west on Av Juárez.

Nueva Central Camionera Bus 275B, 275 Diagonal or TUR marked 'Tonalá'; catch them all at Av 16 de Septiembre and Madero.

Parque Agua Azul Any bus marked 'Agua Azul' going south on Calz Independencia.

Planetarium, Zoo and Selva Mágica Bus 60 or 62A, or trolleybus R600 going north on Calz Independencia.

Tlaquepaque Bus 275B, 275 Diagonal or TUR marked 'Tlaquepaque' at Av 16 de Septiembre and Madero.

Tonalá Bus 275D, 275 Diagonal or TUR marked 'Tonalá' at Av 16 de Septiembre and Madero.

Zapopan Bus 275 or TUR marked 'Zapopan' going north on Avs 16 de Septiembre or Alcalde.

Zona Rosa Par Vial buses 400 and 500 at Avs (not Calz!) Independencia and Alcalde.

Horse Carriages

If you're a romantic, you can hire a horse carriage for M$150 per half-hour or M$200 per hour. There's a carriage stand right at Jardín San Francisco and another in front of the Museo Regional de Guadalajara.

Metro

The subway system has two lines that cross the city. Stops are marked with a 'T'. But the metro isn't tourist friendly because most stops are far from the sights. Línea 1 stretches north–south for 15km all the way from the Periférico Nte to the Periférico Sur. It runs below Federalismo (seven blocks west of the city center) and Av Colón: catch it at Parque Revolución, on the corner of Av Juárez. Línea 2 runs east–west for 10km below Avs Juárez and Mina.

Taxi

Taxis are everywhere in the city center. They all have meters, but not all drivers use them. Most would rather quote a flat fee for a trip, especially at night. Generally it's cheaper to go by the meter – if you're quoted a flat fee and think it's inflated, feel free to bargain. Note that from 10pm to 6am a 'night meter' is used and fares rise 25%.

AROUND GUADALAJARA

Guadalajara's version of the 21st century is enthralling, but you'd be wise to explore the surrounding countryside, where lonely mountain pueblos and lazy lakeshore towns promise an intoxicating shot of old Mexico. San Juan de los Lagos, 150km northeast of

Guadalajara, is a small, colorful market city and pilgrimage destination for millions. There are two major tequila-producing towns. Tequila, in the lowlands 50km to the northwest, is the obvious tourist's choice. But the good stuff comes from the highlands, around Atotonilco El Alto. Lago de Chapala, just 45km south, offers spectacular lake scenery, traditional working-class towns and bizarre B&B barrios for retired gringos. Further south and west, Jalisco's Zona de Montaña is home to a string of mountain retreats where horses wander free through dusty streets and you may stumble onto the perfect taco.

SAN JUAN DE LOS LAGOS

☎ 395 / pop 47,003 / elevation 1950m

Toward the northeastern finger of Jalisco state lies a town that was built upon a Virgin – the Virgin of San Juan de los Lagos. Legend has it this smallish sculpture of Mary, crafted in the 16th century as one of the Three Sisters of Jalisco, once restored a dead seven-year old girl to life in 1623. Word leaked out, pilgrims began pouring in and they haven't stopped. Hordes arrive around Christmas, Easter, throughout the month of May and during the Fiestas de la Virgen de la Candelaria (January 10 to February 2), Fiestas de la Virgen de la Asunción (August 1 to 15) and Fiestas de la Virgen de la Inmaculada Concepción (December 1 to 8). But odds are you'll see the faithful work their way up the aisle of the gorgeous, rose-washed basilica, on their knees, praying to the *virgencita* no matter when you drop in. Don't forget to wander the endless market stalls huddled on the streets surrounding the basilica where you can haggle for religious trinkets, virgin statuettes, rosaries, jewelry, clothes, blankets and pottery or gorge on sweet coconut candy and *rompope* (a kind of eggnog). Don't capitalism and Catholicism make a lovely couple?

Hotels fill up during holidays and festivals. For information there's a **tourist office** (☎ 785-4479; Segovia 10; ꡩ 9am-5pm Mon-Fri, 10am-1pm Sat & Sun) one block behind the cathedral.

San Juan de los Lagos makes a long day trip from Guadalajara, but you only need a few hours here. Frequent buses leave Guadalajara's Nueva Central Camionera (M$155, three hours). Once you get into town, head left for about three blocks, go over the pedestrian bridge and zigzag around a couple of corners, following the market stalls down to the cathedral.

TEQUILA

☎ 374 / pop 27,600 / elevation 1219m

This valley town 50km northwest of Guadalajara is surrounded by an ocean of blue agave, the gorgeous succulent from which tequila is distilled. The Cuervo family settled here in 1758 to grow agave and distill *mezcal*. In 1795 José Cuervo introduced the first bottle of what we now know as tequila. Tourists come to tour distilleries (yes, samples are given) and troll the cobbled backstreets looking for good deals on, what else, tequila.

If you come by bus, its last stop will probably be on Gorjón. Continue on foot away from the highway for about 10 minutes and you'll eventually arrive at the church; the plaza is beyond it. If you're in town from November 30 to December 12 you'll catch the Feria Nacional de Tequila (Tequila Fair), celebrated with *charreadas*, parades and tequila exhibitions.

The biggest game in town is **Mundo Cuervo** (☎ 742-00-50; cnr Corona & José Cuervo; ꡩ 9am-6pm), which produces more José Cuervo tequila than the world needs. Hourly tours include tastings and a margarita. There are four kinds of tour to choose from, costing between M$100 and M$250. You can't miss the distillery complex located across from the plaza. When it comes time to taste, sip *Tradicional*, Cuervo's saving grace. The makers of *Sauza*, **Perseverancia Distillery** (☎ 742-02-43; Francisco Javier Sauza Mora 80; admission M$35; ꡩ 11am-4pm Mon-Sat, closed Dec 22-Jan 2), located 4½ blocks south, also gives tours.

The **Museo Nacional del Tequila** (Corona 34; adult/child under 11 M$15/8; ꡩ 10am-4pm Tue-Sun) is half a block south from the Cuervo complex. It's very well done, with photos, exhibits, distillation apparatus and good explanations of the mechanics and history of this fairly young industry.

Sleep it off locally at **Hotel Posada del Agave** (☎ 742-07-74; Gorjon 83; s/d M$210/300), which has clean and comfortable budget rooms with TV and fan. For more grace try **Casa Dulce María Hotel** (☎ 742-32-40; hotelcasadulcemaria@yahoo.com.mx; Abasolo 20; s/d M$320/450), a beautiful courtyard hotel with comfortably large rooms.

The most stylish way to travel is via the **Tequila Express** (☎ in Guadalajara 33-3880-9099; www.tequilaexpress.com.mx; adult/child 6-11 M$72/38). It departs Guadalajara's train station, located a couple of blocks south of Parque Agua Azul,

TEQUILA

Mexico's national spirit has a past, but the industry itself is quite young. Spanish conquistadors first cultivated the blue agave plant *(Agave tequilana weber)* as early as the mid-1550s in the state of Jalisco. But tequila, which is only produced in Jalisco, didn't become popular until after the Mexican Revolution when José Cuervo introduced the first bottle to the public.

It all starts in the agave fields. Plants are cultivated for eight to 12 years then the *jimadores* come calling. These tough field hands expertly strip away the spiny foliage until they've found its heart, called a *piña.* The largest weigh up to 150kg, are hauled from the fields by burros, shipped to the distillery by truck and fed into brick or clay ovens where they cook for up to three days. Afterwards the softened pulp is shredded and juiced and the liquid is pumped into fermentation vats where it is usually mixed with yeast. In order to bear the 100% agave label, premium tequilas can legally add nothing else. Lesser tequilas, however, add sugar and sometimes flavoring and/or coloring agents. By law the mixture can contain no less than 51% agave if it is to be called tequila.

There are four varieties of tequila. White or silver (*blanco* or *plata*) tequila is not aged, no colors or flavors are added (though sugar may be) – it has a distinct agave flavor and is best sipped as an aperitif or mixed in a margarita. The similar gold variety *(oro)* also is not aged, but color and flavor, usually caramel, are added. Do yourself a favor and avoid the gold. Most of it is motor oil.

Aged tequila, a fairly recent phenomenon, can be used as a mixer, but it's best sipped neat. Tequila *reposado* (rested) has been aged from two to 11 months in oak barrels and tends to taste sharp and peppery. Tequila *añejo* (aged) is aged at least one year in oak barrels. It's sweet and smooth and works best as an after-dinner drink paired with chocolate.

Don Julio, the progenitor of the fine Don Julio brand, invented aged tequila by accident. He'd kept an oak cask of tequila in his office for years, but only shared it with close friends. After recovering from a major illness in 1988 his family threw him a party, irrigated by the aged tequila. The crowd loved it and offers for the new variety poured in. It took a year to produce the first cask, but in 1989 aged tequila was finally brought to the marketplace for the first time.

In Mexico you can buy a decent bottle of tequila for M$150, though for something special you'll need to spend over M$300. Treat the good stuff like a bottle of single malt and before you sip it, sniff it a few times to prepare your palate for the heat and it won't taste so harsh.

And don't be looking for a 'special' worm *(gusano)* in each bottle. These are placed in bottles of *mezcal* (an agave spirit similar to tequila but distilled outside of Jalisco state) as a marketing ploy – and even if you slurp the critter, you won't get any higher. Blue agave's psychoactive properties will leave you feeling lifted regardless.

at 11am Saturday (occasionally on Sunday). The diesel loco chugs to Amatitán, 39km from Guadalajara where it steams to a halt at the Herradura distillery, easily the best lowland distiller and the only one that harvests and cooks the agave hearts traditionally. You'll get a tour of the distillery, a mariachi show, snacks, lunch and an open bar with *mucho* tequila. Book a few days ahead through **Ticketmaster** (☎ 3818-3800).

For details of bus services from Guadalajara see p540.

ATOTONILCO EL ALTO

☎ 391 / pop 27,276 / elevation 1596m

The soil reddens and the blue agave blooms as the road winds about 150km into the highlands east of Guadalajara. The striking re[d] earth signifies a higher concentration of iro[n] and other nutrients that make agave sweete[r] and the tequila smoother than those distille[d] and bottled in Tequila. Don Julio, the man wh[o] invented aged tequila, is the biggest name, bu[t] 7 Leguas and 50 other producers are scattere[d] through the hills that encircle this quaint colonial town that remains unspoiled by tourism[.] The good side: you'll see a real working tequil[a] town – and Calle Independencia is strun[g] with tequila shops that sell the best bottles i[n] Mexico for a great price. The bad news: tour[s] are hard to come by. **Don Julio** (Díaz 24; 9am-5pm) does have a shop across the street from it[s] distillery where you can get great deals. Pair it[s] *añejo* with is dark chocolate truffles. Divine

Siete Leguas (☎ 917-09-96; www.tequilasieteleguas.com .mx; Independencia 360; ☯ 9am-5pm), another producer of fine tequilas, has a full-functioning visitors centre and rumor has it that it will soon be giving tours.

One more reason to trek out here is to dine at **Real Campestre** (☎ 917-2838; Carretera Atotonilco-Ayotlán Km 3; mains M$90; ☯ noon-8pm). Taste its *aguachile*, a dish in which raw shrimp are cooked in a spicy broth of fresh lemon juice and chili and follow it up with an exquisitely tender and flavorful *arrachera* to absorb that fire. It also has a great tequila bar and soothing mountain views. Too weary to make it home? Check into **Real Cervantes** (☎ 917-4814; Espinoza 26; d/ste M$400/550). This new hotel has Spanish tile, granite staircases and bright, spotless rooms with king sized beds. Excellent value.

Buses depart regularly for Atotonilco El Alto from Guadalajara's Nueva Central Camionera (M$75, two hours).

CHAPALA

☎ 376 / pop 20,700 / elevation 1550m

Lago de Chapala, Mexico's largest natural lake, lies 45km south of Guadalajara. Surrounded by mountains – some of which tumble dramatically to the shore, its beauty is deep and undeniable, but it's not always healthy. Water levels fluctuate due to Guadalajara and Mexico City's water needs and on-again, off-again drought. Commercial fertilizers washed into the lake have nourished water hyacinth, an invasive plant that clogs the lake's surface, blocks sunlight from the depths – leaving the lake dead in some places. But beauty and an addictive climate (always warm during the day and pleasantly cool at night) balance Chapala's eco-sins and continue to lure American and Canadian retirees to the area, which means soaring real estate prices, especially in nearby Ajijic.

The lake's namesake, Chapala, became a well-known resort destination after president Porfirio Díaz vacationed here every year from 1904 to 1909. DH Lawrence wrote most of *The Plumed Serpent* at Zaragoza 307, now a beautiful villa (see Quinta Quetzalcóatl, right). But today Chapala is just a simple working-class Mexican town that gets busy on weekends when Guadalajarans invade. Its best quality is its authenticity and if Ajijic rubs you wrong (you won't be the first), you'll be grateful for this happy, bustling slice of real Mexico.

Information

Chapala has a **tourist office** (☎ 765-31-41; upstairs at Madero 407; ☯ 9am-7pm Mon-Fri, 9am-1pm Sat & Sun) and **Libros de Chapala** (☎ /65 69-90; Madero 230; ☯ 9am-5pm Mon-Sat, 9am-2pm Sun), opposite the plaza, has a few English novels, guidebooks and magazines.

Sights

The **pier** extends from the end of Av Madero, over marshlands and into the sky-blue lake. Relax on one of the white wrought iron benches and catch an afternoon breeze or some morning sun. A ticket booth at the pier's entrance sells boat tickets to **Isla de los Alacranes** (Scorpion Island), 6km from Chapala, which has some restaurants and souvenir stalls but is not very captivating. A round trip, with 30 minutes on the island, costs M$420 per boatload; for one hour it's M$480. A better and pricier option is **Isla de Mezcala**, 15km from Chapala. Here you'll find ruins of a fort where Mexican independence fighters held strong from 1812 to 1816, repulsing several Spanish attacks before finally earning the respect and a full pardon from their enemies. A three-hour round-trip boat ride costs M$1500, for up to eight people.

Near the pier is a small crafts market that spills over a network of lawns running parallel to the *malecón* (waterfront walk).

Sleeping

Rincón de los Sueños (☎ 765-60-00; fax 765-60-01; www .rincondelossuenos.com.mx; Niños Héroes 59; r from M$450; ℗ ⊞) This new, stylish yet understated spot offers 17 modern and sunny upstairs rooms, a comfortable lobby/lounge, a community kitchen and long term discounts.

Lake Chapala Inn (☎ 765-47-86; www.mexonline .com/chapalainn.htm; Paseo Ramon Corona 23; r M$700; ℗ ✕ ⊞ ⊠) Perfectly perched on the lake with views of mountains, swaying palms and bobbing fishing boats is this attractive four-room inn. But book ahead because only two rooms have lake views. Breakfast is included. It has a lap pool.

our pick **Quinta Quetzalcóatl** (☎ 765-36-53; www .accommodationslakechapala.com; Zaragoza 307; r from M$800; ℗ ⊞ ⊠) Behind the regal stone walls are a pool, an acre of lush gardens, a colorfully tiled sun terrace, five unique suites and two houses each with cable TV, a fireplace, private entrance, patio and tap water you can drink. Mexican gourmet breakfasts are included.

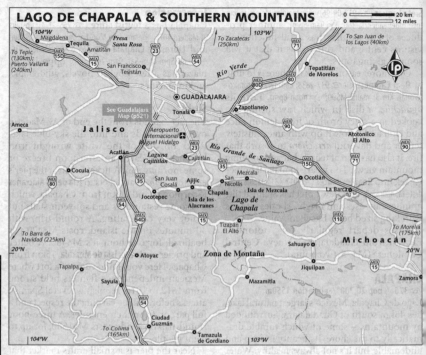

LAGO DE CHAPALA & SOUTHERN MOUNTAINS

This is where DH Lawrence wrote *The Plumed Serpent* in 1923. The Aussie owners tried to read it. 'It's rubbish,' they'll say with a smile. Reserve ahead. Adults only.

Eating

Seafood joints with reasonable prices gather along Paseo Corona. The most popular among expats is Restaurant Cozumel.

Coffee Break (☎ 765-59-31; Madero 413; desserts M$25; ☼ 8am-10:30pm) A young crowd, good tunes, high speed wireless internet and great coffee equals the perfect coffee house.

Café Paris (☎ 765-53-53; Madero 421; mains M$40) This old school diner with groovy bar/counter seating is a Chapala institution. It serves everything from omelettes to tacos to T-bones.

Blue Agave (☎ 765-77-70; Hidalgo 242; burgers M$55, mains from M$95; ☼ 8am-3pm Mon-Sat) Cowboy cuisine with great lake views upstairs at this satisfying, but not sensational, Tex-Mex cantina on the highway to Ajijic. The burgers are good.

Getting There & Away

For details of bus services from Guadalajara see p540. Once you get to Chapala's bus ter-

minal, it's a 10-minute walk down Av Madero to the pier. There are long-distance services to Puerto Vallarta (M$425) and Mexico City ($490), but to anywhere else you'll have to return to Guadalajara.

Buses connect Chapala and Ajijic every 20 minutes (M$8, 15 minutes).

AJIJIC

☎ 376 / pop 14,000 / elevation 1550m

Praise tends to be heaped upon Ajijic (ah-hee-*heek*), the lakeside enclave 7km west of Chapala, and, with its 400 year-old streets and backdrop of sandy peaks, it does have a certain cobblestone charm, but beware the gringo retirees. They've put Ajijic on the map, boosted area real estate and provided a vital market for the town's boutiques, galleries and restaurants, some of which are locally owned, but somehow this place just doesn't feel like Mexico.

Buses will drop you on the highway at the top of Colón, the main street, which leads two blocks down to the main plaza and four more blocks down to the lake. The chapel on the north side of the plaza dates from the 18th century.

Information

Bancomer (8:30am-4pm Mon-Fri) On the plaza, with an ATM.

Ciber café (10am-8:30pm) On the plaza. Offers internet access for M$15 per hour and long-distance calls.

Lavandería (Morelos 24A; per load M$30; 9:30am-2pm & 3-7pm Mon-Sat) Head here for clean clothes; it's off the northwest corner of the plaza.

Sleeping

There is no shortage of B&Bs in Ajijic and a simple Google search will provide a crop to sift through, but remember that many of them feel like grandma's house crowded with ageing in-laws. So if you go that route it may take time to find one that suits you.

Hotel Italo (766-22-21; marianabrandi60@hotmail.com; Guadalupe Victoria 8; s/d M$240/310) Ajijic's cheapest rooms are found at this unfriendly Italian themed joint. But the rooms are clean, the rooftop terrace has a nice view of the lake and apartments are available for longer-term rentals.

Hotel Casablanca (766-44-40; www.casablancaajijic.com; 16 de Septiembre 29; r M$690; P) This comfortable, new Moroccan themed hotel comes with peaked windows, mosaic baths, a roof deck and a Bedouin soundtrack. It also has a great central location, free wi-fi and complimentary breakfasts.

La Nueva Posada (766-14-44; nuevaposada@prodigy.net.mx; Donato Guerra 9; s/d M$900; P) The lobby and restaurant of the Nueva Posada are over decorated, unless you're into multi-hued walls and garish floral prints on the furniture, and the 19 spacious rooms are strangely bland. But be thankful that this is a proper hotel and there will be no obligatory B&B chit-chat at breakfast, which by all accounts is the best in town. The mountain vistas are extraordinary.

Eating & Drinking

Café Grano (766-56-84; Castellanos 15D; coffees from M$19; 9am-9pm) The smell of roasting organic coffee will soothe your soul and your conscience too because only organic free-trade beans from Chiapas are roasted and ground here.

La Tasca (766-52-69; Guerra 22; mains M$100; 4-10:30pm Tue-Sun) Nestled on a sweet lakefront plot is this Flamenco bar and grill. Locals rave about the food, but on most nights you can also simply come for a drink and listen to live Flamenco music.

our pick Ajijic Tango (766-24-58; Morelos 5; mains M$70-105; 12:30-10pm Mon, Wed-Sat, till 6:30pm Sun) You'll dine on exceptional Argentine food at unbelievable prices at Tanjo, Ajijic's most beloved restaurant. The intimately lit indoor–outdoor dining room, with cozy booths and modern art decorating the walls, almost manages the impossible: make Ajijic feel hip. It isn't, but this restaurant rocks, mainly because of the tender cuts of beef that will blow your mind. The wood-fired pizzas look appealing on paper, but don't get distracted: order the steak.

Tom's Bar (766-03-55; Constitución 32; 10am-midnight Sun-Thu, 10am-1am Fri & Sat) If Ajijic has driven you to drink, belly up to this fine knotted wood bar where you can sip, watch movies in the courtyard or ballgames on the big screen. It's Canadian-owned and serves a damn good burger.

Getting There & Around

For details of bus services from Guadalajara see p540. Autotransportes Guadalajara–Chapala buses buses drop you on the highway at Colón. Buses connect Chapala and Ajijic every 20 minutes (M$8, 15 minutes).

Like to bike? Check out **Bicicletas Rayo** (766-53-46; Carretera Ote 11; 10:00am-8pm Mon-Sat). Bike rentals cost M$20 per hour or M$100 per day; you can cruise the 5km bike path that parallels the highway to Chapala, but look out for the ATVs!

SAN JUAN COSALÁ

387 / pop 3000 / elevation 1560m

At San Juan Cosalá, 10km west of Ajijic, there's a popular **thermal spa** (adult/child M$100/50; 8:30am-7pm) on the lake. It has seven steaming pools, plays loud music and attracts Mexican families on weekends. It's located between hotels Balneario San Juan Cosalá and Villa Bordeaux; if you stay at either of these places entry to the spa is free.

Hotel Balneario San Juan Cosalá (761-02-22; www.hotelspacosala.com; La Paz 420; s/d M$708/763; P) has 34 large and somewhat bare tiled rooms; some have lake views. It also offers spa services including hot stone and seaweed massages.

A few kilometers further west in **Jocotepec** you'll see signs for **El Chante Spa Resort** (763-26-08; Ribera del Lago 170; r from M$2574). The concept is a good one – a four-star resort on a nice slice of lakefront – but it hasn't quite pulled it off. However, it has an ample spa menu and a sauna set inside a Disney version of an indigenous sweat lodge.

Autotransportes Guadalajara–Chapala buses depart Sala A every half-hour from 6am to 9pm for San Juan Cosalá (M$40, 1¼ hours). Buses from Ajijic run every 20 minutes (M$8, 15 minutes).

ZONA DE MONTAÑA

South of Lago de Chapala, Jalisco's Zona de Montaña – a seemingly endless range of layered mountains – is an increasingly popular weekend retreat for Guadalajarans who come to enjoy the rangeland, the pines, timeless colonial pueblos, local food and the cooler climes.

Tapalpa

☎ 343 / pop 16,000 / elevation 2100m

A labyrinth of adobe walls, red tiled roofs and cobblestoned streets surround two impressive 16th century churches. It's no wonder that this old mining town just 130km southwest of Guadalajara has become a tourist magnet. Perched on the slopes of the Sierra Tapalpa and ringed by a tapestry of pastureland and pine forests threaded with streams, there is good walking in all directions. Don't miss Las Piedrotas – impressive rock formations in cow pastures 5km north of town. It's an easy walk along a country road to these megaliths, past a funky old paper mill. Taxis cost M$60. El Salto, a jaw-dropping, 105m-high waterfall, is about 13km south of town (taxi M$120).

Don't miss the **Centro de Integración** (CITAC; ☎ 432-05-70; citac96@hotmail.com; Salto de Nogal 100; 9am-2pm & 3-7pm Mon-Thu, 9:30am-4pm Fri), a school for special-needs kids, dedicated to teaching self-confidence along with computer and art skills. Wonderful recycled art is made by the children from *papel malhecho*, a kind of papier-mâché. You can buy these creations at the school, or at its small stall in the Mercado del Artesano on the plaza. Volunteers are welcome. Call the main phone number and ask for Héctor Aguirre if you're interested in helping out. To get to the school, head 200m down Calle Pastores (from Ignacio López) and go right at the fork after about 100m.

There is a Banorte with an ATM on the plaza and dozens of hotels and guesthouses around town, but you should make reservations on weekends and holidays (when Guadalajarans stream in). The basic, musty, but acceptable **Hotel Tapalpa** (Matamoros 35; s/d

M$150/200) is the cheapest and is right on the plaza. **Casa de Maty** (☎ 432-01-89; Matamoros 69; r M$800), almost next door, is the popular choice; rooms border on deluxe, have in-room fireplaces and some open onto verdant gardens. In between, in both value and comfort, **Hostal Posada Las Margaritas** (☎ 432-07-99; 16 de Septiembre 81; s/d M$500/900), uphill from the plaza, with well-decorated, rustic rooms and apartments with kitchenettes.

Local food is tasty in Tapalpa. Munch *tamales de acelga* (chard-filled *tamales*) at the cheap food stalls near the church, and gorge on *borrego al pastor* (grilled lamb) at **El Puente** (☎ 432-04-35; Hidalgo 324; 10am-6pm Thu-Tue; mains M$80), a casual restaurant three blocks down from the church, just after the bridge. Other regional specialties include homemade sweets, *rompope* (eggnog), *ponche* (pomegranate wine) and *Barranca* (a tequila made from wild agave).

Hourly buses to Tapalpa leave from Guadalajara's Antigua Central Camionera (M$75, 3½ hours). There are also buses to/from Ciudad Guzmán (M$50, two hours). Buses in Tapalpa stop at the **Sur de Jalisco bus office** (Ignacio López 10), a block off the plaza.

Mazamitla

☎ 382 / pop 12,500 / elevation 2200m

Mazamitla, a charming whitewashed mountain town south of Lago de Chapala and 132km by road from Guadalajara, is seldom fully awake. Shops close at 5pm, restaurants open at 6pm and *abuelas* (grandmothers) dressed in black wander haphazardly through the hilly cobbled roads, stopping traffic. Mazamitla sports an interesting take on the Swiss alpine theme and you'll see small store fronts selling fruit preserves, cheeses, *rompope* and *cajeta* (milk caramel) around the plaza. There's a small but lively **market** (8am-3pm) on Juárez each Monday. About 5km south of town is the leafy park **Los Cazos** (admission M$10; 9am-5pm), with the 30m waterfall El Salto. You can picnic or ride horses here; a taxi costs M$50.

Mazamitla's **tourist office** (☎ 538-02-30; Portal Degollado 4; 9am-3pm Mon-Fri) is by the church. There's a bank on the plaza. For internet access try **Compuclick** (Galeana 4; 10am-10pm; per hr M$12) across from the food stalls.

There are a few sleeping options in town; prices rise during holidays. Close to the plaza is **Hotel Fiesta Mazamitla** (☎ 538-00-50; Reforma 2 s/d Mon-Thu M$95/150, Fri-Sun M$190/240). The varnished wooden stairwell is enticing and the rooms are large, clean and comfortable, but the hostess can be surly. Unique **Hotel Cabañas Colina de los Ruiseñores** (☎ cell phone 33-34941210, in Guadalajara 33-361-56-45; www.mazamitlahotelcabana.com.mx; Allende 50; r M$300) is a wonderfully rustic place, offering a local spin on the Swiss chalet. There are creative wood accents everywhere. Right on the plaza, **Posada Alpina** (☎ 538-01-04; posada_alpina@yahoo.com.mx; Reforma 8; r M$400) has a leafy interior courtyard, sweet wooden rooms and outstanding views. It also has a smart restaurant that serves the best *molcajete* (M$75) in town.

There are a handful of restaurants in Mazamitla, but if you have time for only one meal you must seek out the greatest taco known to humanity. Tucked into the back corner of a permanent strip of food stalls on the intersection of Galeana and Allende, is the modest **Rica Birria** (tacos M$10; 8am-10pm). Immediately you will notice a different level of cleanliness and care here. You'll also see steaming, tender chunks of beef brisket and, if you come early enough, goat, sizzling on the griddle. Order one and receive a perfectly torched tortilla piled with tender *carne* that melts in the mouth, sprinkled with onions, *cilantro* and splashed with *salsa verde*. It's a simple yet transcendent dish. Call it taco enlightenment. Adjacent stalls serve fresh squeezed juices. **El Rinconcito** (Cárdenas 5; mains M$44-48; 8:30am-8pm) is another good choice. The owner is gracious and charming, and cooks up a mean chicken *mole*.

Frequent buses run daily from Guadalajara's Nueva Central Camionera ($7, three hours); they stop three blocks north of the plaza. From Colima there are seven buses daily (M$105, 2¾ hours); these stop at the market, just a block west of the plaza. Other destinations include Zamora (M$72), Morelia (M$140) and Manzanillo (M$165).

Ciudad Guzmán

☎ 341 / pop 90,300 / elevation 1500m

Busy Ciudad Guzmán (Zapotlán el Grande) is no tourist attraction, but it is the closest city to Volcán Nevado de Colima (p555), a majestic volcano about 25km southwest of Guzmán.

Guzmán's crowded plaza is surrounded by market stalls and shopping arcades set around two churches: the 17th-century **Sagrado Corazón** and a neoclassical **cathedral**. In its center is a stone gazebo with a homage to famous Mexican muralist José Clemente Orozco – called 'Man of Fire' – painted on its ceiling. (the original is in Guadalajara – see Instituto Cultural de Cabañas, p526). Orozco was born here and some of his original carbon illustrations and lithographs are displayed at the small **Museo Regional de las Culturas de Occidente** (Dr Ángel González 21; admission M$25; 9:30am-5:30pm Tue-Sat).

The **tourist office** (☎ 413-53-13 ext 107; Lázaro Cárdenas 80; 8:30am-3pm Mon-Fri) is in the government building, just a few blocks east of the plaza.

There are hotels around the plaza but they tend to be noisy. Try the good-value **Reforma Hotel** (☎ 412-44-54; Reforma 77; s/d M$235/270; P), midway between the bus station and plaza. Another sweet deal is **Tlayolan Hotel** (☎ 412-33 17; Javier Mina 35; s/d M$250/360). It has small, clean and modern rooms a few blocks southeast of the plaza.

The market behind the cathedral has the cheapest eats.

The bus terminal is about four blocks west of the plaza. Destinations include Guadalajara (M$100, two hours), Colima (M$65, one hour), Tapalpa (M$50, two hours) and Mazamitla (M$50, two hours). Buses to El Fresnito, the closest village to Volcán Nevado de Colima, run from the plaza (M$18, 15 minutes).

INLAND COLIMA STATE

The tiny but ecologically rich and diverse state of Colima (5191 sq km) connects lofty volcanoes in the arid northern highlands to idyllic turquoise lagoons near the hot and humid Pacific coast. This section deals with the state's inland area; the narrow coastal plain is covered in the Central Pacific Coast chapter.

Inland Colima should become Mexico's next great adventure hub. The famous volcanoes to the north – the active, constantly steaming but inaccessible Volcán de Fuego (3820m) and the extinct, snowcapped Volcán Nevado de Colima (4240m) – remain the big draw, but the Sierra de Manantlán Biosphere Reserve is a jungle and limestone playground in waiting with single-track mountain biking, exceptional hiking and canyons that see a few canyoneers abseiling, leaping into crystalline streams and bathing in the magical El Salto Falls. Colima is a growing garden city with an exceptional climate and Comala is the perfect place to sip *micheladas* and munch tapas on a lazy Sunday afternoon. Tourism infrastructure hasn't caught up to the area's potential yet, so those who like virgin territory should come now.

History

Pre-Hispanic Colima was remote from the major ancient cultures of Mexico. Seaborne contacts with more distant lands might have been more important: legend says one king of Colima, Ix, had regular treasure-bearing visitors from China. Eventually, northern tribes moved in. The Otomi settled here from about AD 250 to 750, followed by the Toltecs, who flourished between 900 and 1154 and the Chichimecs from 1154 to 1428 .

All of them left behind exceptional pottery, which has been found in over 250 sites, mainly tombs, dating from about 200 BC to AD 800. The pottery includes a variety of comical and expressive figures. The most famous are the plump, hairless dogs, known as xoloitzcuintles.

Two Spanish expeditions were defeated and turned back by the Colimans before Gonzalo de Sandoval, one of Cortés' lieutenants, conquered them in 1523. That year he founded the town of Colima, the third Spanish settlement in Nueva España, after Veracruz and Mexico City. In 1527 the town moved to its present site from its original lowland location near Tecomán.

COLIMA

☎ 312 / pop 129,900 / elevation 550m

Colima is a laid-back city with blooming subtropical gardens, four fine public plazas, a pleasant touch of moisture in the air and the warmest weather in the western central highlands. It would be hard to find a better climate, or a more nurturing city in which to raise children, which is why it's growing so fast. This relatively conservative town is absolutely safe at all hours, but it's not exactly boring. The university attracts intellectuals and a taste of global culture. The one thing it's missing is a steady stream of international tourists, but thanks to the abundant adventure available in the canyons, forests and mountains surrounding Colima, that looks to be changing.

The billowing volcano you see on clear days, Volcán de Fuego – visible 30km to the north – continues to rumble and shake and the city has been hit by several major quakes over the centuries (the last in January 2003). It's no wonder that Colima has few colonial buildings, despite having been the first Spanish city in western Mexico.

Orientation

Colima's Plaza Principal is the heart of the city. Portal Medellín is the row of arches on the north side, with Portal Morelos on the south side. Jardín Quintero lies behind the cathedral, while Jardín Núñez is three blocks further east. Street names change at Plaza Principal (also known as Jardín Libertad). Colima's long-distance bus terminal, the Terminal Foránea, is some 2km east of the city center, on the Guadalajara–Manzanillo road. There's also a local bus terminal, Terminal Rojos, for closer destinations, located 7km west of the city.

Information

You can change money at numerous banks and *casas de cambios* around the city center; most banks have ATMs.

Centro Médico (☎ 312-40-45; Herrera 140; ☽ 24hr)

CI@Internet (Degollado 62; internet per hr M$15; ☽ 9am-9pm)

Lavandería Amana (Domínguez 147-A; per kilo M$14; ☽ 8am-9pm Mon-Sat, 8am-3pm Sun)

Main post office (Madero 247; ☽ 8am-5:30pm Mon-Fri)

State tourist office (☎ 312-43-60; www.visitacolima .com.mx; Palacio de Gobierno; ☽ 8:30am-8pm Mon-Fri, 10am-2pm Sat) Open during holidays.

Sights

AROUND PLAZA PRINCIPAL

Light floods the **cathedral** from the dome windows of this would-be relic on the east side of Plaza Principal (also known as Jardín Libertad). It has been rebuilt several times since the Spanish first erected a cathedral here in 1527, most recently after the 1941 earthquake. So it's too new to offer old-world soul, but it remains a focal point of the community.

Next to the cathedral is the **Palacio de Gobierno**, built between 1884 and 1904. Local artist Jorge Chávez Carrillo painted the stairway murals to celebrate the 200th birthday of independence hero Miguel Hidalgo, who was once parish priest of Colima. The mu-

COLIMA

0   500 m
0   0.3 miles

INFORMATION
Centro Médico...............................1 B2
Ci@Internet...................................2 A3
Lavandería Amana.........................3 B4
Main Post Office.............................4 B3
State Tourist Office.................(see 8)

SIGHTS & ACTIVITIES
Cathedral......................................5 B3
Museo Regional de Historia de
  Colima......................................6 A3
Museo Universitario de Artes
  Populares..................................7 C2
Palacio de Gobierno......................8 B3

Pinacoteca Universitaria Alfonso
  Michel.......................................9 B3
Teatro Hidalgo............................10 A3

SLEEPING
Hospedajes del Rey.....................11 D4
Hotel América.............................12 B4
Hotel Buena Aventura.................13 B4
Hotel Ceballos............................14 B3
Hotel Flamingos..........................15 B4
Hotel Plaza Madero.....................16 B3

EATING
¡Ah Qué Nanishe!.......................17 A2
El Trebol.....................................18 A3
Los Naranjos...............................19 B3
Mercado Constitución..................20 A4
Pichichi Silvon............................21 B3
Pizza Koket.................................22 B2

DRINKING
1800...23 D2
El Subito.....................................24 B3

TRANSPORT
Buses to Terminal Rojos...............25 B3
Super Autos.................................26 B5

*To Villa de Álvarez (3km);
La Campana (5km);
Comala (9km);
Suchitlán (16km)*

*To Terminal
Rojos (7km)*

*To Airport (12km);
Guadalajara (100km)*

*To Terminal Foránea (2km);
Airport (12km);
Manzanillo (100km);
Guadalajara (100km)*

---

als honor freedom fighters, the feminine, the indigenous roots and the beautiful land of Mexico. There's a great collection of pottery in the 1st-floor **museum** (admission free; ☯ 10am-?pm Tue-Sun), including some from 1500 BC, and check out the case 10 ten ceramic frogs estimated by UCLA archaeologists to date from 600AD.

The **Museo Regional de Historia de Colima** (☎ 312-92-28; Portal Morelos 1; admission M$37; ☯ 9am-6pm Tue-Sat, 6-8pm Sun, closed Mondays) once held an extensive ceramic display, but the museum was in transition when we visited. Out was the archaeology and in were oil on canvas meditations on the human form (read male and female full-frontal). There was also a conceptual artist's take on bird nests, next to a mixed media fetus-themed series. OK, then.

The **Teatro Hidalgo** (cnr Degollado & Independencia) was built in neoclassical style between 1871 and 1883 on a site originally donated to the city by Miguel Hidalgo. The theater was destroyed by the earthquakes of 1932 and 1941 and rebuilt once more in 1942. It is only open for special events.

MUSEO UNIVERSITARIO DE ARTES POPULARES

Folk art lovers will be in heaven at this **museum** (University Museum of Popular Arts; ☎ 312-68-69; cnr Barreda & Gallardo; admission M$10, free Sun; ☽ 10am-2pm & 5-8pm Tue-Sat, 10am-1pm Sun). On display is a stellar collection of masks, *mojigangas* (giant puppets that dance in parades), musical instruments, baskets and wood and ceramic sculpture from every state in Mexico.

PINACOTECA UNIVERSITARIA ALFONSO MICHEL

This beautiful **museum** (☎ 312-22-28; cnr Guerrero & Constitución; admission M$10; ☽ 10am-2pm & 5-8pm Tue-Sat, 10am-1pm Sun), in a 19th-century courtyard building, offers four halls filled with surrealist art. Included are a permanent collection of paintings by Colima's Alfonso Michel – a cross between Picasso and Dalí – and works by other Mexican artists, like Alfonso Cabrera and Richard Rocha.

PARKS

The **Parque Regional Metropolitano**, on Degollado a few blocks southwest of the city center, has a depressing zoo, a swimming pool (M$10), snack kiosks and a forest with an artificial lake. Explore the forest paths on quad bikes (M$25 per 30 minutes), or cruise the lake by paddleboat (M$25 per 30 minutes).

East of the city center on Calz Galván, **Parque Piedra Lisa** is named after its mythical Sliding Stone. Legend says that visitors who slide on this stone will some day return to Colima, to marry…or die!

LA CAMPANA

The low, pyramid-like structures at this modest **archaeological site** (☎ 313-49-46; Av Tecnológico s/n; admission M$34; ☽ 9am-5pm Tue-Sun) date from as early as 1500 BC. They have been excavated and restored, along with a small tomb and a ball court (unusual in western Mexico). The structures are oriented due north toward Volcán de Fuego, which makes an impressive backdrop on clear days. It's about 5km north of Colima city and easily accessible by buses 7 and 22; taxis cost M$30.

Festivals & Events

The following festivals take place in or very near Colima city:

Fiestas Charro Taurinas For two weeks in early February this celebration takes place in Villa de Álvarez, 5km north of central Colima. Giant *mojigangas* gather at Colima's cathedral and parade to Villa de Álvarez, where the celebrations continue with food, music, rodeos and bullfights.

Feria de Todos los Santos The Colima state fair (late October and early November) includes agricultural and handicraft exhibitions, cultural events and carnival rides.

Día de la Virgen de Guadalupe From about December 1 to the actual feast day, on December 12, women and children dress in costume to pay homage at the Virgin's altar in the cathedral.

Sleeping

Hotel Flamingos (☎ 312-25-25; Av Rey Colimán 18; s/d/tw M$220/270/300; P) This four-story budget place is family owned, but not friendly, cleanish but not spotless. However, it is popular with Mexican families and does book up.

our pick Hotel Buena Aventura (☎ 136-12-46; Juárez 70; d from M$350; P 🅿 📶) Across from Jardín Núñez, this brand-new hotel is already the best value in town. The large, pastel-colored tiled rooms are sparkling with queen beds A/C and satellite TV. The high-speed internet doesn't disappoint and Angela, the owner will even rent you her truck (just M$300 per day). But, let's be honest, these wheels have seen better days.

Hotel Plaza Madero (☎ 330-28-95; Madero 165; s & d M$400; P 🅿) Some hotels have shopping galleries on the 1st floor. This place has a mall. Rooms could use a bit of the love and charm that were channeled into the attractive reception and lobby area. But it does have satellite TV, wireless internet and excellent people watching. Good value.

Hospedajes del Rey (☎/fax 313-36-83; Av Rey Colimán 125; s/d/tw M$350/450/600; P 🅿 📶) This converted, mod apartment complex looks like something out of Miami Vice. Rooms are basic and clean with wireless internet, cable TV and A/C, but those with two beds are considerably larger. It books up so reserve ahead.

Hotel América (☎ 312-74-88; hamerica@hotel america.com.mx; Morelos 162; s & d from M$702, ste from M$1053; P 🅿 📶 📺) The rooms don't live up to the polished exterior and manicured grounds, but they aren't bad. Interior courtyard rooms are best. Older Executive suites overlook the shady fountain patio, but they are definitely outdated.

Hotel Ceballos (☎ 312-44-44; www.hotelceballos .com; Portal Medellín 12; r from M$950; P ❌ 🖳 🖳) Ignore the Best Western sign and this hotel will make you happy. The large rooms, decorated with antiques, all have high ceilings with crown moldings and some have balconies that overlook Plaza Principal. The halls are decked out with benches, arches and antique folk art, which lends a stately, old-world feel.

Eating & Drinking

Many small restaurants around Plaza Principal offer decent fare and good people-watching on weekends. **Mercado Constitución** (⏱ 7am-6pm Mon-Sat, 7am-2pm Sun), a couple of blocks south of Plaza Principal, has cheap food stalls serving juices, *pozole* and other snacks. **Pichichi Silvon** (churros M$5; ⏱ noon-10pm), operates out of a tiny window on the walking street adjacent to Hotel Ceballos, attracting a stream of customers for its addictive *churros rellenos* – hot, sugar crusted Mexican donuts stuffed with chocolate, caramel or strawberry sauce.

El Subito (☎ 314-70-01; Barreda 4; coffees M$10-12; ⏱ 8am-10pm Mon-Sat) Inexpensive and damn good espresso drinks are served in this cozy, stylish coffee bar decorated with antiquated photos of old Colima. There are no tables, just bar stools.

ourpick El Trebol (☎ 312-29-00; Degollado 59; mains from M$25; ⏱ 8am-10pm Sun-Fri, closed Saturday) Colima's most popular family restaurant also serves the best breakfasts in town. The scent of freshly squeezed orange juice perfumes the dining room and diners devour *huevos a la Mexicana* and scrambles with ham, bacon and chorizo.

Pizza Koket (☎ 314-41-41; cnr Berreda & Matamoros; pizzas M$35-70; ⏱ 11am-10pm) Take an empty gravel lot, install a wood burning oven and a few plastic tables and you've got yourself a pizzeria. It has tons of fresh toppings, serves personal pizzas as well as calzones – and delivers.

Los Naranjos (☎ 312-00-29; Barreda 34; mains M$39-75) The purple-and-burgundy walls lend a laid-back elegance and there's a nice collection of hand blown glass, but come here for the simple and extremely tasty menu with great prices. Get five tacos for just M$39 and make sure to order the *cilantro* heavy guacamole. It

is outstanding and so are the beans. Two for one *micheladas* and great tequila prices too.

¡Ah Qué Nanishe! (☎ 314-21-97; 5 de Mayo 267; mains M$45-75; ⏱ 1pm-midnight Wed-Mon) The name of this restaurant means 'How delicious!' and the rich, chocolaty, but not overwhelming *mole* is superb. Other Oaxacan delicacies like *chile rellenos* (stuffed chili) or *chapulines* (crunchy fried grasshoppers) are also available and on Sunday it serves *barbacoa de borrego* (tender lamb). Half orders of many mains are available which makes this spot a great value.

1800 (5 de Mayo 15; mains from M$60; ⏱ 7pm-2am Mon-Sat) This new, hip restaurant lounge attracts a late coming crowd of uni students for snacks, drinks and, on Thursday nights, an electronic dance party. The menu is all over the place – with pizza, sushi, burritos and more, but you'll be happiest if you duck in for a few late drinks.

Getting There & Around

Colima's airport is near Cuauhtémoc, 12km northeast of the city center off the highway to Guadalajara (taxis M$100). **Aeromar** (☎ 313-55-88) flies to Mexico City daily.

Colima has two bus terminals. The long-distance terminal is Terminal Foránea, 2km east of the city center at the junction of Av Niños Héroes and the city's eastern bypass. There's a **left-luggage facility** (⏱ 6am-10pm). To reach downtown, hop on a Ruta 4 or 5 bus (taxis M$18). For the return trip catch the same buses on 5 de Mayo or Zaragoza. Destinations with frequent departures:

Destination	Fare	Duration
Ciudad Guzmán	M$65	1-2hr
Guadalajara	M$168	3hr
Manzanillo	M$60	2hr
Mexico City (Terminal Norte)	M$610	10hr

Colima's second bus terminal (serving local towns) is Terminal Rojos, about 7km west of Plaza Principal. Ruta 4 or 6 buses run to Colima's center from this terminal (taxis M$20). To get back here, take any bus marked 'Rojos' going north on Morelos. Destinations include Comala (M$7, 15 minutes, every 15 minutes), Manzanillo (M$60, 1¾ hours, every half-hour), Tecomán (M$30, 45 minutes, every 20 minutes) and Armería (M$35, 45 minutes, every half-hour).

Taxi fares within town are M$10 to M$18. For car rentals try **Super Autos** (☎ 312-07-52; Av

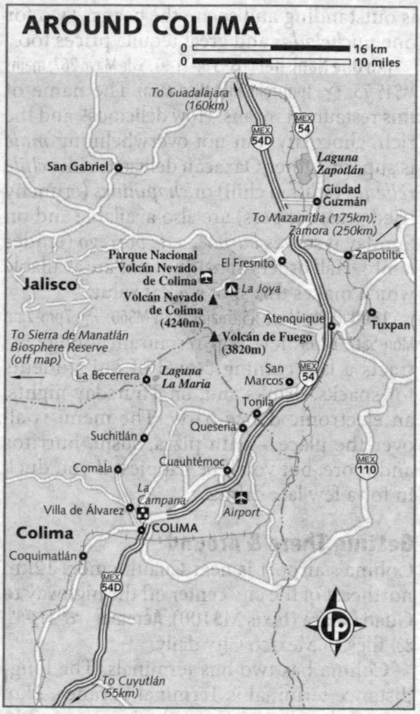
AROUND COLIMA
0 16 km
0 10 miles
To Guadalajara (160km)
MEX 54D
MEX 54
Laguna Zapotlán
San Gabriel
Ciudad Guzmán
To Mazamitla (175km); Zamora (250km)
Parque Nacional Volcán Nevado de Colima
El Fresnito
Zapotiltic
Jalisco
La Joya
Volcán Nevado de Colima (4240m)
Atenquique
Tuxpan
To Sierra de Manatlán Biosphere Reserve (off map)
Volcán de Fuego (3820m)
La Becerrera
Laguna La María
San Marcos
MEX 54
Tonila
Quesería
Suchitlán
Cuauhtémoc
Comala
MEX 110
La Campana
Villa de Álvarez
Airport
COLIMA
Colima
Coquimatlán
MEX 54D
To Cuyutlán (55km)

Rey Colimán 382); its cheapest sedan will cost you around M$600 per day. Hotel Buena Aventura (p552) also rents its uninsured clunker to willing guests. The price is right (just M$300 per day), but she's old and needs work. Proceed at your own risk.

AROUND COLIMA

The outlying villages and countryside around Colima are gorgeous and demand exploration. You can visit most worthy destinations on day trips or by public transportation, but a rental car is liberating.

Comala

☎ 312 / pop 9500 / elevation 600m

There are certainly (much!) worse ways to pass a sleepy afternoon then to sip *micheladas* at *centros botaneros* (tapas bars) and devour free plates of chicken taquitos, guacamole and *ceviche* tostadas in this leafy country town just 9km north of Colima. **Don Camalón** is the most popular patio bar, but **Comala Bar** has better tapas. All the bars are located beneath the arches at the main plaza and are open from noon to 6pm. On clear days you'll see great views of the nearby twin volcanoes, Fuego and Nevado. Sunny weekends fetch Colima locals and the occasional tour bus from Manzanillo full of tourists who love strolling Comala's quiet cobblestone streets.

A 30-minute walk from town is the can't-miss **Museo Alejandro Rangel Hidalgo** (☎ 315-60-28; admission M$25; 🕒 10am-6pm Tue-Sun), in the gorgeous Ex-Hacienda Nogueras. Hidalgo (1923–2000) was a designer, painter and illustrator, whose incredibly detailed work redefines indigenous and religious symbolism and has a captivating magical realism quality. Check out *Angel of Kenya*, his 1962 depiction of a Maasai goddess. There's also a tremendous collection of pre-Hispanic ceramics and a cool sketch of Frida Kahlo. To get here, walk 400m along Calle Degollado (left of the church); turn left at the T-intersection, go 1km, then turn right at the next T-intersection and go another 1km. You can also take a bus (M$5) from behind the church or a taxi (M$20).

Adventure hounds should seek out **Fuego Bike** (☎ 315-54-14; fuegobike@gmail.com; Juárez 25). It rents mountain bikes and runs cycling, kayaking and camping tours throughout the region. Call or email ahead to learn about upcoming tours and prices, and to book your trip.

Comala buses leave from Colima's Terminal Rojos (M$7, 15 minutes, every 15 minutes). Buses back to Colima depart from Comala's plaza.

Suchitlán

☎ 318 / pop 3850 / elevation 1200m

Street chickens own this tiny, hilly pueblo 7km northeast of Comala, known for its animal masks. The masks are carved in home workshops and worn by traditional dancers during the *Danza de los Morenos*, a Semana Santa ritual that commemorates the dancing animals who distracted the Roman guards and enabled the Marys to rescue Christ's body.

There are two places to eat. **Restaurant El Balcón de Don José** (☎ 312-76-75; cnr Galeana & Azucena; mains from M$72; 🕒 8:30am-6:30pm Tue-Sun) on the street into town has a lovely view, but the popular **Restaurant Portales Suchitlán** (☎ 395-44-52; tapas under M$50; 🕒 8:30am-6:30pm Tue-Sun) makes its own tortillas and serves terrific tapas in a beautifully green grove. Colima's day trippers dine here.

Buses to Suchitlán leave half-hourly from Colima's Terminal Rojos (M$12, 45 minutes).

Parque Nacional Volcán Nevado de Colima

This national park, straddling the Colima–Jalisco border, includes two dramatic volcanoes: the still-active Volcán de Fuego and the inactive Volcán Nevado de Colima. Ciudad Guzmán (p549) is the closest city, but Colima is a more pleasant base. **Colima Magic** (☎ 312-310-74-83, www.colimamagic.com) and **Returi** (☎ 312-311-35-26; www.returi.com), the area's two best adventure tour operators, run day trips from Colima to Volcán Nevado de Colima's peak, with English-speaking guides. Tours cost M$818 to M$1308, which includes transportation, food/beverages and entry fees. But you must book in advance. It can be difficult to find a guide on the fly if you only have a few days.

VOLCÁN DE FUEGO

Overlooking Colima, 30km north of the city is steaming Volcán de Fuego (3820m) – Mexico's most active volcano. It has erupted dozens of times in the past four centuries, with a big eruption about every 70 years. A profound belch in 1913 marked the end of one cycle of activity, but another began in the 1960s. Current rumbling started in 1998 and has included pyroclastic flows and the growth of lava domes. In June 2005 a large explosion sent ash 4.8km into the sky, all the way to Colima. Current information about the volcano is posted on the website of the **Universidad de Colima** (www.ucol.mx/volcan).

VOLCÁN NEVADO DE COLIMA

The higher, more northerly peak, Nevado de Colima (4240m) is accessible on foot for most of the year. Patches of pine forest cover Nevado's shoulders, while alpine desert takes over at the highest altitudes. Area wildlife includes deer, wild boar, coyotes and even a few mountain lions.

The best months for climbing are the dry months of December through May. But temperatures from December to February often dip below 0°C and snow does regularly fall on the upper slopes – *nevado* means 'snow covered.' Weather changes fast here and lightning strikes the peak in stormy weather, so make sure you keep an eye on the clouds. The park's winter hours are 7am to 6pm (no cars up after 2pm). The summer rainy season is from July to September, when park hours are longer.

To access the volcano with your own car (rear-wheel drive cars can handle the road during the dry winter) you need to start early. Take highway 54D (the *cuota*, or toll road, M$90) north from Colima, get off at the Tuxpan exit and follow the 'Guadalajara libre' signs. Just before you reach Ciudad Guzmán, turn left onto the El Grullo road. Drive 8.5km and you'll see the gravel road marked 'Nevado de Colima' on the left. Some 20 winding kilometers later you'll reach La Joya/Puerto Las Cruces (3500m), where you can sign in and pay the M$5 entry fee (plus M$10 per car). The *micro-ondas* (radio antennae) are a strenuous 90-minute hike up from the end of the road. If you want to bag the peak, you'll need another 90 minutes and while the peak is easy to see, you shouldn't go alone. There are many trails up and back and it's very easy to get lost or led to areas with hazardous footing. Going with a guide or good maps and GPS (hard to find in Colima) is highly recommended. Bring extra water!

Driving up this volcano on the relatively good dirt road means that you'll be ascending to a high altitude very quickly. If you feel lightheaded or dizzy, you may be suffering from *mal de montaña* (altitude sickness). Descend as quickly as possible, as this condition can be potentially fatal. For more on this health problem, see p1004.

Reserva de la Biosfera Sierra de Manantlán

A 1396-sq-km swath of the jungled limestone mountains northwest of the city of Colima are protected by the UN as critical habitat. It's certainly diverse, ranging in elevation from 400m to 2960m, with eight varieties of forest ecosystem – including tropical, cloud, oak and alpine. This land is rich and alive with nearly 2000 varieties of plants, 160 orchid species, 336 bird species (a third of Mexico's bird species can be found here), 60 types of reptile and the two big cats – puma and jaguar. It's also drop dead gorgeous with spectacular limestone karsts, narrow canyons and powerful waterfalls.

Adventurers will not be bored. There are canyons to explore, 50km of adrenaline-addled downhill single-track for mountain bikers and an abundance of trekking trails. Returi (left) runs canyoneering trips that include abseiling, cliff jumping and conclude at the beautiful **El Salto** (☎ 314-336-00-92; admission

M$10). These massive falls, just outside the reaches of the reserve, gush over granite and tumble 10m into a crystalline pool, which licks a pebble beach. Fuego Bike (p554) and Colima Magic (p555) also run adventure trips to the reserve.

If you choose to go it alone, know that tourist infrastructure is virtually nil. But those who like to break trail will be in heaven. Take the road to Manzanillo out of Colima (Niños Héroes in town) and veer right at the turnoff to El Terero (about 30 minutes). From here it's an hour's drive up a well-maintained dirt road to the reserve's entrance. In the dry season any car can make it. Rangers at the gate will point out trails and good campsites. If you just want to hit El Salto, continue on the road to Manzanillo. Just after the town of Minatitlán you'll see signs for El Salto.

INLAND MICHOACÁN

Michoacán is a treasure chest that holds the best of Mexico's gifts like beautiful secrets. Inside are clouds of rugged butterflies that fly thousands of kilometers to cling, cuddle and shag at the incredible Reserva Mariposa Monarca (Monarch Butterfly Reserve). There are Purépecha pueblos strung through the state's 200km of the impressive 600km-long volcanic mountain range, Cordillera Neovolcánica, home to master craftsmen who create striking masks, pottery and elegant guitars. They also put on the best Day of the Dead celebrations in the country. And there are three great towns – the sweet, dusty colonial town of Pátzcuaro, rich in history and mystical energy; the larger and more Mexican city of Uruapan with the mythic Volcán Paricutín nearby; and spectacular Morelia – with classic, Unesco-certified colonial Spanish architecture, one of Mexico's finest universities, an abundance of festivals and art installations and a young, pretty population that loves to party.

MORELIA

☎ 443 / pop 611,147 / elevation 1920m

Morelia is the coolest place you've never been. The colonial heart of the city is so well preserved that it was declared a Unesco World Heritage site in 1991. The cathedral is not just gorgeous. It's inspirational. Especially on Saturday nights when the stee-ples glow, classical music blares and cannons blast fireworks into a black sky where they explode and drip color on the incandescent bell towers. And that's just an appetizer.

Morelia, founded in 1541, was one of the first Spanish cities in Nueva España. The first viceroy, Antonio de Mendoza, named it Valladolid after the Spanish city and he encouraged Spanish nobility to move here with their families. In 1828, after Nueva España had become the Republic of Mexico, the city was renamed Morelia in honor of local hero José María Morelos y Pavón, a key figure in Mexico's independence.

Sixteenth- and 17th-century stone buildings, baroque facades and archways line the narrow downtown streets, and are home to museums, hotels, restaurants, exquisite bars and rooftop lounges, *chocolaterías*, sidewalk cafés, a popular university and cheap and tasty *taquerías*. Traffic snarls around the cathedral, but Morelia even looks good from inside a traffic jam. There are free public concerts, frequent art installations, and yet so few foreign tourists! Those that do come often extend their stay and enrol in classes to learn how to cook and speak Spanish. Yes, word has started to leak out and more and more internationals are beginning to discover Mexico's best kept secret. So get here soon.

Orientation

The historical center is set on a plateau and newer development snakes down hillsides to the north and south. Morelia's extraordinary cathedral is the soul of the city and a major landmark. East–west streets change their names at the cathedral, while north–south streets change names at Madero.

The elegant row of arched verandas facing the Plaza de Armas is commonly called Portal Hidalgo; the arches on Abasolo facing the west side of the plaza are called Portal Matamoros.

Morelia's bus terminal is about 4km northwest of the city center.

Information

Banks and ATMs are plentiful around the plaza, particularly on and near Av Madero.

La Central Internet (Matamoros 72A; per hr M$8; ☯ 9am-10pm Mon-Sat, noon-10pm Sun)

Lavandería Cósmica (☎ 317-19-38; Tapia 543; 3kg M$30, dry cleaning available; ☯ 8am-8pm Mon-Sat)

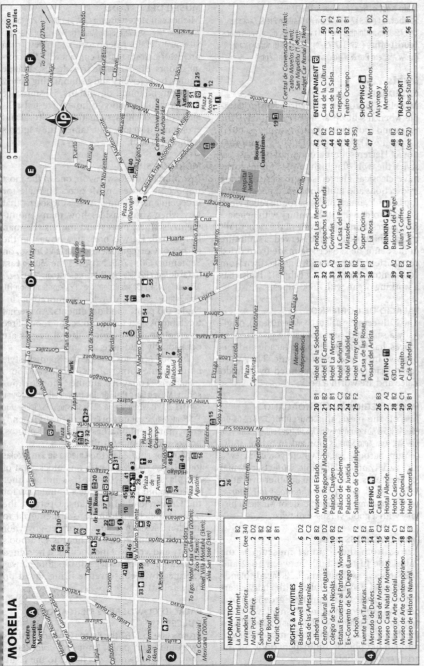

MORELIA

WESTERN CENTRAL HIGHLANDS

0   500 m
0   0.3 miles

INFORMATION
La Central Internet	1 B2
Lavandería Cosmica	(see 34)
Main Post Office	2 D2
Sanborns	3 B2
Tour Booth	4 B2
Tourist Office	5 B1

SIGHTS & ACTIVITIES
Baden-Powell Institute	6 D2
Casa de las Artesanías	7 C2
Cathedral	8 B2
Centro Cultural de Lenguas	9 D2
Colegio de San Nicolás	10 B2
Estatua Ecuestre al Patriota Morelos	11 F2
Ex-Convento de San Diego (Law School)	12 F2
Fuente Las Tarascas	13 E2
Mercado de Dulces	14 B1
Museo Casa de Morelos	15 C2
Museo Casa Natal de Morelos	16 B2
Museo de Arte Colonial	17 C1
Museo de Arte Contemporáneo	18 E2
Museo de Historia Natural	19 E3
Museo del Estado	20 B1
Museo Regional Michoacano	21 B2
Palacio Clavijero	22 B1
Palacio de Gobierno	23 C2
Palacio de Justicia	24 B2
Santuario de Guadalupe	25 F2

SLEEPING
Casa Rosa	26 B3
Hostal Allende	27 A2
Hotel Casino	28 B2
Hotel Colonial	29 C1
Hotel Concordia	30 B1
Hotel de la Soledad	31 B1
Hotel El Carmen	32 C1
Hotel La Merced	33 A2
Hotel Señorial	34 B1
Hotel Valladolid	35 B2
Hotel Virrey de Mendoza	36 B2
La Casa de las Rosas	37 B1
Posada del Artista	38 F2

EATING
630	39 A2
Al Taquito	40 E2
Café Catedral	41 B2
Fonda Las Mercedes	42 A2
Gaspachos La Cerrada	43 B2
Govindas	44 D2
La Casa del Portal	45 B2
Mirasoles	46 B2
Onix	(see 35)
Super Cocina	47 B1
La Rosa	

DRINKING
Balcones del Ángel	48 B2
Lillian's Coffee	49 B2
Velvet Centro	(see 52)

ENTERTAINMENT
Casa de la Cultura	50 C1
Casa de la Salsa	51 F2
C.nepolis	52 B1
Teatro Ocampo	53 B1

SHOPPING
Dulce Morelianos	54 D2
Mayoreo y Menudeo	55 D2

TRANSPORT
Old Bus Station	56 B1

Main post office (Av Madero Ote 369)
Sanborns (☎ 317-84-72; cnr Av Madero Pte & Zaragoza; ☼ 7:30am-midnight) English magazines, novels and maps.
Tourist office (☎ 317-23-71; www.visitmorelia.com; cnr Av Madero Pte & Nigromante; ☼ 9am-7pm)

Sights

CATEDRAL

Morelia's beautiful cathedral (unforgettable when it's lit up at night) dominates the plaza and took more than a century to build (1640–1744), which explains its combination of Herreresque, baroque and neoclassical styles: the twin 70m-high towers, for instance, have classical Herreresque bases, baroque midsections and multicolumned neoclassical tops. Inside, much of the baroque relief work was replaced in the 19th century with neoclassical pieces. Fortunately, one of the cathedral's interior highlights was preserved: a sculpture of the Señor de la Sacristía made from dried corn paste and topped with a gold crown from 16th-century Spanish king Felipe II. It also has a working organ with 4600 pipes.

PALACIO DE GOBIERNO

The 17th-century **palace** (Av Madero Oriente), originally a seminary and now state government offices, has a simple baroque facade and impressive historical murals inside. They were commissioned in 1961, painted by Alfredo Zalce and are worth a peek.

MUSEO REGIONAL MICHOACANO

Just off the plaza, this **museum** (☎ 312-04-07; Allende 305 & Abasolo; admission M$30, free Sun; ☼ 9am-7pm Tue-Sat, 9am-4pm Sun) is housed in a late-18th-century baroque palace where you can view a nice variety of pre-Hispanic artifacts, colonial art and relics. There's also another evocative Alfredo Zalce mural, *Cuauhtémoc y la Historia*, on the stairway. It offers a taste of Mexican history with a good-versus-evil twist.

PALACIO DE JUSTICIA

Across from the regional museum is the Palacio de Justicia, built between 1682 and 1695 to serve as the city hall. Its facade blends French and baroque styles, with stairwell art in the courtyard. An Agustín Cárdenas mural portrays Morelos in action. A small two-room **museum** (admission free; ☼ 10am-2pm & 5-8pm) shares the history of Michoacán's justice system through old photos and papers (look for the grisly cadaver shots).

MUSEO DEL ESTADO

Michoacán **state museum** (☎ 313-06-29; Prieto 176; admission free; ☼ 9am-8pm Mon-Fri, 9am-2pm & 4-7pm Sat & Sun) details Michoacán's journey from prehistoric times to first contact with the conquistadors. Pre-Hispanic arrowheads, ceramic figures, bone jewelry and a shimmering quartz skull can be found downstairs. Upstairs are first-person accounts of how force-fed religion coupled with systematic agricultural and economic development tamed the region's indigenous soul.

MORELOS SITES

José María Morelos y Pavón, one of the most important heroes in Mexico's struggle for independence, is king. At least it seems that way when you consider how many monuments, statues, plazas and murals the man has earned. He was born in a house on the corner of Corregidora and García Obeso, on September 30, 1765. Now it's the **Museo Casa Natal de Morelos** (Morelos Birthplace Museum; ☎ 312-27-93; Corregidora 113; admission free; ☼ 9am-8pm Mon-Fri, 9am-7pm Sat & Sun). Morelos memorabilia includes old photos and documents. An eternal torch burns next to the projection room. Free international films and cultural events are occasionally held here.

In 1801 Morelos bought the Spanish-style house on the corner of Av Morelos and Soto y Saldaña. Today it's another Morelos museum. **Museo Casa de Morelos** (Morelos House Museum; ☎ 313-26-51; Av Morelos Sur 323; admission M$25, free Sun; ☼ 9am-7pm) explains his role in the independence movement and has an array of photos, books and antique furniture.

Morelos studied at the **Colegio de San Nicolás** (cnr Av Madero Pte & Nigromante), one block west of the plaza. Don't worry – it is not another museum, but it has become a foundation for the Universidad Michoacana. Upstairs, the Sala de Melchor Ocampo is a memorial to another Mexican hero, a reformer-governor of Michoacán. Preserved here is Ocampo's library and a copy of the document he signed donating it to the college, just before he was executed by a conservative firing squad on June 3, 1861.

PALACIO CLAVIJERO & MERCADO DE DULCES

From 1660 to 1767 the **Palacio Clavijero**, with its awesome main patio, imposing colonnades and pink stonework, was home to the Jesuit school of St Francis Xavier. After the Jesuits were expelled from Spanish lands, the building became a warehouse, a prison and then in 1970 it was completely renovated, restored and rechristened as state government offices. Who said politics and crime don't mix?

The seductive **Mercado de Dulces** (Sweets Market; 9am-10pm), on the western side of the palace, deals the region's famous sweets (see the boxed text, p562), including spicy chunk chocolate that melts into the perfect hot drink.

MUSEO DE ARTE COLONIAL

Mel Gibson would dig this **museum** (313-92-60; Juárez 240; admission free; 9am-8pm Mon-Fri, 9am-7pm Sat & Sun) south of Plaza del Carmen. There are 100 crucifixes here – many of them quite grizzly and very little else. On the 18th-century canvases Jesus looks healthier – as a baby, a preacher and a healer.

CASA DE LAS ARTESANÍAS

If you don't have time to scour the Purépecha pueblos for the perfect folk art piece, come to the **House of Handicrafts** (312-12-48; Plaza Valladolid; 10am-8pm Mon-Sat, 10am-3pm Sun), a cooperative marketplace launched to benefit indigenous craftspeople. Attached to the renaissance-style Templo de San Francisco, arts and handicrafts from all over Michoacán are displayed and sold here. Prices are high, but so is the quality and all your cash goes directly to the craftspeople. Upstairs, artists demonstrate their craft in small shops that represent specific Michoacán towns. You'll find guitars from Paracho, copper from Santa Clara del Cobre, lacquerware, pottery and much more.

FUENTE LAS TARASCAS & EL ACUEDUCTO

At the east end of Madero Ote, the *fuente* (fountain) erupts from a fruit tray held by three beautiful, topless Tarascan women. The original vanished mysteriously in 1940 and this reproduction was installed in the 1960s.

El Acueducto (Aqueduct) runs for several kilometers along Av Acueducto and bends around Plaza Villalongín. It was built between 1785 and 1788 to meet the city's growing water needs. Its 253 arches are gorgeous when illuminated at night.

PLAZA MORELOS & AROUND

Running east from the Fuente Las Tarascas, the shaded and cobbled Calz Fray Antonio de San Miguel is a wide, romantic pedestrian

promenade framed by exquisite old buildings. It wanders 500m to Plaza Morelos, an irregular, conspicuously vacant plaza surrounding **Estatua Ecuestre al Patriota Morelos**, a majestic statue of – who else – Morelos, on horseback, sculpted by the Italian artist Giuseppe Ingillieri between 1910 and 1913.

On the northeast edge of the plaza, the **Santuario de Guadalupe** feels like the set piece from Willy Wonka's psychedelic spiritual dream. The pink and red walls of this baroque church built from 1708 to 1716 bloom with white flowers and glisten with an abundance of gold leaf. There's so much color, the interior (decorated in 1915) feels like a Hindu temple. It's the kind of place that would inspire Timothy Leary to do up *Virgen de Guadalupe* acid tabs. Beside the church, the much less splashy **Ex-Convento de San Diego** was built in 1761 as a monastery and now houses the law school of the Universidad Michoacana.

The **Bosque Cuauhtémoc** is a large park favored by families because of its shade trees, amusement park and museums. But a city as majestic as Morelia deserves a better maintained, more dynamic green space. Modern art fans will enjoy the **Museo de Arte Contemporáneo** (312-54-04; Acueducto 18; admission free; 10am-8pm Mon-Fri, 10am-6pm Sat & Sun). The 19th-century building hosts temporary exhibitions of contemporary art. The strange, lifeless **Museo de Historia Natural** (312-00-44; Ventura Puente 23; admission free; 9am-6pm), on the east side of the park, displays stuffed, dissected and skeletal animals and human fetuses.

PLANETARIO & ORQUIDARIO

Near the convention center, about 1.5km south of the city center, is a **planetarium** (Parque 150; admission M$40; shows at 7pm Fri & Sat, 6:30pm Sun), with 164 projectors simulating stars on a dome 20m in diameter. There's also a worthwhile **Orchid House** (314-62-29; admission M$5; 9am-6pm Mon-Fri, 10:30am-3pm & 4-6pm Sat & Sun), which exhibits nearly 3000 species of wild and hybrid orchid. The orchids bloom best in April, May and October.

PARQUE ZOOLÓGICO BENITO JUÁREZ

The **zoo** (314-04-88; Calz Juárez s/n; adult/child M$18/10; 10am-5pm Mon-Fri, 10am-6pm Sat & Sun) is 3km south of the Plaza de Armas and surprisingly pleasant, with most critters in decent habitats. Animals include sea lions, giraffes, elephants, lots of birds and reptiles. Gravel paths make it hard for strollers, but kids will love the small train and playground.

The Ruta Guinda and Ruta Rosa combi, or the Santa María bus (white with blue-and-grey stripes), all heading south on Nigromante, will drop you off at the entrance.

Courses

Few foreigners and plenty of culture make Morelia an exceptional place to learn how to cook, dance and speak Spanish. Ask for a discount if taking a course for more than two weeks.

Baden-Powell Institute (☎ 312-40-70; www .baden-powell.com; Antonio Alzate 565; private lessons per hr M$175, group lessons per week M$1908) This small, well-run and affordable school offers courses in Spanish language, as well as Mexican politics, cooking, culture, guitar and salsa dancing. It books homestays (M$262 per day) for students.

Centro Cultural de Lenguas (☎ 312-05-89; www .ccl.com.mx; Av Madero Ote 560; group lessons per week M$1963, private lessons per week M$3053) This school offers Spanish-language classes running from one to four weeks, as well as music, dance and cooking classes. Homestays (from M$218 per day, including meals) are available.

Tours

For tours outside the city ask the tourist office for recommendations.

Leyendas de Morelia (☎ 312-02-34) An interesting 2½ hour night tour (M$70) where guides explain the legends behind the major sites in the city center. Includes a visit to an underground crypt. Tours are in Spanish.

Mex Mich Guías (☎ 390-47-34, 340-46-32; www .mmg.com.mx) Provides personalized tours and transportation to many destinations in the area, including the Santuario Mariposa Monarca (per person M$469).

Festivals & Events

In addition to the usual Mexican celebrations, Morelia's many annual festivals include the following:

Feria de Morelia Morelia's biggest fair, running for three weeks in mid-May, hosts exhibits of handicrafts, agriculture and livestock, plus regional dances, bullfights and fiestas. May 18 is the city's founding date (1541) and is celebrated with a fireworks show.

Cumpleaños de Morelos Morelos' birthday is celebrated on September 30 with a parade and fireworks show.

Festival Internacional de Cine de Morelia (www .moreliafilmfest.com) This major international exhibition for Mexico's vibrant film industry brings a week of parties and star sightings each October.

Día de Muertos Michoacán's outlying villages and smaller cities are the top attraction on the week of November 1, but Morelia hosts free flamenco concerts and stunning art installations in and around Plaza de Armas.

Festival Internacional de Música (www.festival morelia.com) The international classical music festival occurs for two weeks in mid-November with orchestras, choirs and quartets giving concerts in churches, plazas and theaters around town.

Día de la Virgen de Guadalupe The Day of the Virgin of Guadalupe is celebrated on December 12 at the Ex-Convento de San Diego; in the preceding weeks a carnival erupts on Calz Fray Antonio de San Miguel.

Feria Navideña The Christmas Fair, with traditional Christmas items, foods and handicrafts from Michoacán, happens during the month of December.

Sleeping

Rates may rise 20% during the holidays, but in the low season you can negotiate discounts.

BUDGET

Hotel Señorial (Tapia 507; s/d M$55/80) You won't find a cheaper sleep in town. Rooms are basic but spotless, spacious and well located in the heart of downtown. Management is gruff, but you don't pay enough for it to be sweet. Internet and laundry options are located just outside the front door.

Hotel Colonial (☎ 312-18-97; 20 de Noviembre 15; s/d from M$160/250) Colonial courtyard digs with a winding stone staircase leading to 25 clean and basic rooms. Some have high, beamed ceilings. Cable TV costs extra.

Hostal Allende (☎ 312-22-46; Allende 843; s/d M$250/360) Cute, basic rooms, each with its own look, surround a leafy courtyard planted with citrus trees and elephant ear palms. There is roof access with amazing views and wireless internet. The best cheap sleep in town.

Hotel El Carmen (☎ 312-17-25; hotel_elcarmen@ yahoo.com.mx; Ruíz 63; s/d M$275/350; **P**) Centrally located, this tasteful and affordable hotel has exposed stone walls, locally fired tile and a pastel paint job. Rooms can be cramped, but they are clean and comfortable.

MIDRANGE

Hotel La Merced (☎ 312-40-95; reservas_lamerced@hot mail.com; Madero Pte 670; s/d M$351/450; **P**) Rooms are basic but very clean. The staff is warm and friendly and rooms come with cable TV.

Hotel Concordia (☎ 312-30-52; www.hotelcon cordiamorelia.com.mx; Gómez Farías 328; s/d M$450/530; **P** 🖳) A rather soul-less business hotel with decent value rooms in a polished, modern exterior. It'll do, but you can do better.

our pick Casa Rosa (☎ Vonage VoIP +1-773-696-5771; www.casadelarosa.info; Calle Aldama; r M$450; 🖳) This underground posada doesn't publish its address to discourage window shoppers, but you can make an appointment to see the rooms and apartments, which are brushed in pastels and decorated with a lovely array of folk art and framed festival posters. The apartments, especially the Love Shack, are an absolute steal and ideal for long-term rentals.

Hotel Valladolid (☎ 312-00-27; Portal Hidalgo 245; r M$800) A beautiful blend of old bones and new soul are available at Morelia's best midrange hotel. There are exposed stone walls in the halls and the rooms, light boxes built into the hallway floor and everything else, from the doors to the headboards to the flat screens, screams high design.

Hotel Casino (☎ 313-13-28; www.hotelcasino.com.mx; Portal Hidalgo 229; r from M$970; 🅿 🖳) Set front and center on the plaza this Best Western hotel offers the little extras: large rooms with high ceilings and antique wardrobes, a treadmill, free wifi and use of brand new laundry machines, gratis (it provides the soap).

TOP END

Hotel de la Soledad (☎ 312-18-88; www.hsoledad.com; Zaragoza 90; d from M$1000; 🅿) This sweet higher-end hotel is housed in an expansive stone hacienda, accented by a collection of antique carriages (this used to be a carriage house). Rooms aren't fabulous but they are spacious and have lovely stone baths. Some have volcano views.

Posada Del Artista (☎ 317-94-20; www.posadadelartista.com; San Miguel 324; r from M$1500; 🅿 🗙 🖳) Four luxurious rooms, a charming café and art gallery are set around a meticulously tended sculpture garden in the courtyard. It's off the pedestrian plaza, Calzada Fray Antonio de San Miguel, and a real find.

Hotel Virrey de Mendoza (☎ 312-06-33; www.hotelvirrey.com; Av Madero Pte 310; r from M$1900; 🅿 🗙 🖳) The lobby is drop-dead gorgeous with a spectacular stained glass atrium and the rooms have an ageing grace with old wood floors and high ceilings, but they are a little dark, musty and overpriced. Of course, the palatial Virreinal Suite (M$3900), with three rooms and a marvelous stone arched terrace overlooking the cathedral, doesn't suck.

La Casa de las Rosas (☎ 312-45-45; www.lacasadelasrosas.com; Prieto 125; ste M$2180-3200; 🅿 🖳) Long considered the best hotel in town, it offers four gorgeous suites with gauzy curtains around stone bathtubs, gilded mirrors and period furniture. The garden is a little paradise. Breakfast is included.

Hotel Villa Montaña (☎ 314-02-31; www.villamontana.com.mx; Patzimba 201; r from M$2300; 🅿 🗙 🗙 🖳 🖳) Nestled 3km south of the city center is this hacienda like luxury hotel, with huge elegant suites (think antiques, fireplaces and private stone patios) and breathtaking city and mountain views. The verdant grounds include a heated swimming pool, tennis court, business center and spa. If you don't stay here, come have a drink at the bar.

Eating

Al Taquito (Calz Madero Ote 993; tacos M$7; ⏱ 9am-11:30pm) This tiny *taquería*, near the aqueduct and the clandestine make-out promenade – Callejón Romántica – serves up delicious *nopales* (cactus), chorizo, shredded pork and beef tacos and burritos. Its specialty, *alambre,* a diced mixture of onions, sweet peppers, beef and chorizo, covered in cheese and served with griddled tortillas, is a hit with local uni students.

Gazpachos La Cerrada (Hidalgo 67; gazpachos M$22) *Gazpachos* – a salad of diced mango, pineapple and *jicama*, drowned in orange and lime juice and dashed with pepper, chili sauce and cheese (optional) – is a local delicacy served all over town. But according to locals, this place is the best.

Govinda's (☎ 313-13-68; Av Madero Ote 549; mains M$41-52; ⏱ 10:30am-5:15pm; 🅿 Ⓥ) This veggie oasis has volcano and Madero boulevard views, Hindu art on the walls and no meat or dairy in the kitchen. Tasty combo meals include a daily curry, rice and veggies.

Café Catedral (☎ 313-04-06; www.hotelcatedralmorelia.com; Zaragoza 37; mains from M$45; 🅿) Packed from breakfast to the wee hours, this is easily the most popular sidewalk café beneath the arches across from the cathedral. It has great coffee, hot chocolate, tasty breakfasts (make sure to mix that smoked *chipotle* salsa with your eggs) and good pizza.

Super Cocina La Rosa (cnr Tapia & Prieto; mains under M$50; ⏱ 8:30am-4:30pm) Family owned and operated, devour Mexican soul food in this colonial stone relic. Nice!

630 (☎ 313-97-79; Tapia 363; mains M$65-95; ⏱ 2pm-midnight) Ancient architecture and modernism coexist here, sometimes awkwardly, and the menu is likewise off-beat – mingling Italian, Mexican and Thai dishes. But if you order right, you'll leave happy. The octopus carpaccio – with five thin slices of octopus sprinkled with sea salt crystals, parsley and drizzled with flavorful olive oil – is fantastic.

Onix (☎ 317-82-90; Portal Hidalgo 261; mains M$95-150; ⏱ 8am-1pm) This bizarre restaurant has a sleek, seductive décor and exotic menu items like scorpion and steak with star fruit and coconut sauce. The soundtrack is equally schizophrenic, but the food is good. The bar upstairs goes off on Fridays and Saturdays.

Mirasoles (☎ 317-57-75; Av Madero Pte 549; mains from M$105; ⏱ 1-11pm Mon-Sat, 1-6pm Sun) Authentic Michoacán cooking, including traditional bean soup, chicken mole and *chamarro* (pork leg dry rubbed with chili and cooked in a clay pot), is dressed up and served in a gorgeous historic building. It serves over 100 wines.

La Casa del Portal (☎ 317-42-17; Prieto 125; mains M$115-150; ⏱ 8am-11pm Mon-Sun) The setting, a converted three story mansion, has history. Don Juan Villaseñor lived here during the 16th century and Lázaro Cárdenas retreated here when he was President of Mexico from 1934 to 1940. There's a stunning upstairs bar, La Terraza, overlooking the Plaza de Armas, an in-house wine shop, oh and it serves meals. Specialties include a Purépecha trout smothered in red chili sauce and local cheese.

Fonda Las Mercedes (☎ 312-61-13; Guzmán 47; mains M$145-185; ⏱ 1:30pm-midnight Mon-Sat, 1:30-6pm Sun) The bar ceiling at this hip, upscale spot is embedded with 200 clay pots, the intimate courtyard dining room is decorated with old stone columns and spheres and the kitchen serves four cuts of steak 10 different ways.

Villa San José (☎ 324-45-45; Patzimba 77; mains M$145) About 3km south of town is a luxury hotel dining room with world-class views. Grab a table on the terrace and snack on *huitlacoche* quesadillas and marinated, grilled shrimp tacos, as the twinkling city spills out below.

Hotel Virrey de Mendoza (☎ 312-06-33; Av Madero Pte 310; brunch adults/kids M$150/65; ⏱ 9am-2pm) This fancy dining room serves other meals, but brunch is really what it does best. Try an all-encompassing buffet that features fruit, yoghurt, fresh juices, made to order omelettes and scrambles, trays of *chilaquiles*, chorizo,

---

SWEETS IN MORELIA

Dulces morelianos – delicious sweets made with ingredients like fruit, nuts, milk and sugar – are famous throughout the region. They're showcased at Morelia's Mercado de Dulces (p558). Some of the tastiest candies are the cinnamon infused chunk chocolate and *ates* (fruit leathers), which are produced from tamarind, guyaba and mango and have chili, sugar and salt added. Another local specialty – and probably the healthiest – is *gazpachos*, a snack made of chopped *jicama*, mango and pineapple or papaya, with cheese, chili, lime and salt sprinkled on top.

---

tamales and enchiladas, and a dessert table with a fountain of chocolate that gushes over perfectly plump strawberries.

Cheap food stalls with lots of tables can be found under the covered arches at **Plaza San Agustín** (cnr Abasolo & Corregidora; ⏱ 1pm-11pm).

Drinking

OUR PICK Balcones del Ángel (Valladolid; ⏱ 5pm-1am Mon-Sat) A hip and beautiful crowd gathers in this open courtyard lounge on the top floor of a 17th-century building just south of the cathedral. The design is seamless, the music bounces between global pop and electronica and the glowing dome of the cathedral is visible through the open roof. Stunning!

Velvet Centro (cnr Gómez Farías & Tapia; ⏱ 5pm-midnight Tue-Thu, 5pm-1am Fri & Sat) This new spot on the roof of the Cinépolis building is hopelessly hip and extremely white – as in white awnings, white velvet sofas and white light fixtures. Oh and the cathedral views are outstanding. During the film festival producers, directors and stars party here. Saturday night is their big night.

Lillian's Coffee (☎ 312-72-52; Madero Pte 388; www.lillianscoffee.com; coffees from M$12; ⏱ 9am-9:30pm Mon-Sat, 11am-10pm Sun) Students flock here, just a block off the plaza, for morning coffee in this historic building.

Entertainment

Being a university town and the capital of one of Mexico's most interesting states, Morelia has a thriving cultural life. Stop by the tourist office or the **Casa de la Cultura** (☎ 313-12-68; Av Morelos Nte 485) for *Cartelera Cultural*, a free weekly listing of films and cultural events. Daily newspapers *El Sol de Morelia, La Voz de Michoacán* and *El Cambio de Michoacán* also publish current events.

For international films, dance, music and art exhibitions check what's up at the Museo Regional Michoacano (p558), the Museo Casa Natal de Morelos (p558) and the Casa de la Cultura – a hive of creative energy with music and dance classes and a cool coffee house set in an old colonial palace. The cathedral has occasional impressive organ recitals.

For theater experiences visit the **Teatro Ocampo** (☎ 312-37-34; cnr Ocampo & Prieto) or **Teatro Morelos** (☎ 314-62-02; www.ceconexpo.com.mx; cnr Camelinas & Ventura Puente), part of the Centro de Convenciones complex, 1.5km south of the city center. **Cinepolis** (☎ 312-12-88; cnr Gómez Farías & Tapia) screens blockbusters in English with subtitles and dubbed Spanish, so make sure you know which show you're seeing.

Casa de la Salsa (Plaza Morelos 121; admission free ⏰ 7-9pm Mon-Fri, live salsa music & dancing ⏰ 9:30pm-2:30am Wed-Sat) Locals converge to shake their collective ass to a rocking four-piece band on a raised stage in this dark, cavernous club. Don't worry, this is not one of those snooty, show-off salsa clubs, so feel free to get loose. Tequila and beer are priced to move if you need liquid courage.

Ego (☎ 333-48-32; Camiono Jesús del Monte; cover men/women M$100/50; ⏰ 10pm-3am Wed-Sat) On the hillside 3km south of town, Morelia's hottest club thumps, bumps and grinds to house and electronica tunes. Dress code is casual. The crowd is young and pretty and they don't stop dancing til they have to.

Shopping

Dulce Morelianos (Madero Ote 440; sweets from M$5) This old fashioned *chocolatería* is stacked with truffles, preserves, candied nuts and sugary chunks of candied peaches and pumpkin and women in ridiculous starched green uniforms patrol it.

Mayoreo y Menudeo (☎ 312-37-73; Madero Ote 620) Hipster alert! Get Diesel and Furor jeans and accessories for a third of what you'd pay in the US.

Getting There & Around

AIR

The **Francisco J Mújica Airport** (☎ 317-47-11) is 27km north of Morelia, on the Morelia–Zinapécuaro Hwy. There are no public buses,

but taxis to the airport cost M$180. Plenty of flights are available to cities in Mexico and limited flights serve destinations elsewhere in North America.

Airlines servicing Morelia include the following:
Aeromar (☎ 324-67-77; Hotel Fiesta Inn, Pirindas 435)
Mexicana (☎ 313-94-30; Av Acueducto 60, Plaza Rebullones)

BUS & COMBI

Morelia's bus terminal is about 4km north-west of the city center. It's separated into three *módulos*, which correspond to 1st-, 2nd- and 3rd-class buses. To get into town from here take a Roja 1 combi (red) from under the pedestrian bridge, or catch a taxi (M$30). First-class buses depart frequently to the following destinations:

Destination	Fare	Duration
Guadalajara	M$242	4hr
Lázaro Cárdenas	M$310	5hr
Mexico City (Terminal Norte)	M$240	4¾hr
Mexico City (Terminal Poniente)	M$240	4hr
Pátzcuaro	M$35	1hr
Querétaro	M$131	3-4hr
Uruapan	M$100	2hr
Zamora	M$112	2½hr
Zitácuaro	M$89	3hr

Around town, small combis and buses operate from 6am until 10pm daily (M$5). Combi routes are designated by the color of their stripe: Ruta Roja (red), Ruta Amarilla (yellow), Ruta Guinda (pink), Ruta Azul (blue), Ruta Verde (green), Ruta Cafe (brown) and so on. Ask at the tourist office for help with bus and combi routes.

TAXI

Taxis flood the city center and an average ride costs M$30.

CAR & MOTORCYCLE

To rent a car, call **Hertz** (☎ 313-53-28), at the airport, or **Budget** (☎ 315-99-42; Av Camelinas 2315).

RESERVA MARIPOSA MONARCA

In the easternmost corner of Michoacán, straddling the border of México state, lies the incredible 563-sq-km Monarch Butterfly Reserve (admission M$30; ⏰ 9am-6pm mid-Nov–Mar), the site of the butterfly Burning Man. Every autumn, from late October to early November, millions of monarch butterflies flock to these forested Mexican highlands for their winter hibernation, having flown all the way from the Great Lakes region of the US and Canada, some 4500km away. Sometime around the autumnal equinox, they begin their journey alone – flying 12km per hour within 150m of the ground. As they close in on their destination they gather in gentle swarms, crossing highways and fluttering up steep mountainsides where they cling together in clusters that weigh down thick branches of the *oyenal* (fir) trees. When the sun rises and warms the forest, they take to the sky in gold and orange flurries, descending to the humid forest floor for the hottest part of the day. By midafternoon they often carpet the ground brilliantly. The best time to see them is on a warm, sunny afternoon in February (they don't fly as much in cool weather), when the butterflies have already begun their slow descent down the mountain.

In the warm spring temperatures of March the butterflies reach their sexual maturity and the real fun begins. Males fly carrying the females beneath them as they mate – abdomen to abdomen. Each female attracts multiple partners to ensure reproduction and exhausted males don't fall asleep immediately after sex – they die! When the vernal equinox strikes, pregnant females fly north to the southeastern US, where they lay their eggs in milkweed and die fulfilled. Their eggs hatch into caterpillars that feed on the milkweed, then make cocoons and emerge in late May as new butterflies. These young monarchs flutter back to the Great Lakes, where they breed, so that by mid-August yet another generation is ready to start the long trip south. It takes from three to five generations of butterflies (living one to eight months each) to complete the entire round-trip journey from Canada to Mexico and back. This is one of the most complex animal migrations on earth and scientists still have no idea how or why they do it. But they must tune into some kind of *mariposa* collective consciousness hardwired into their dynamic DNA.

Monarch butterflies are not in danger of extinction – there are thriving colonies in other parts of the world. However, the migratory behavior of this particular population is threatened. Milkweed, the plant upon which the monarchs depend, is considered invasive in most of the southeast US and is being sprayed

> ## HIGH IS WHERE IT HAPPENS
> Monarch butterflies like basking at altitude, so getting to them requires hiking (or horseback riding) up to 3000m. Hike slowly, remember to take plenty of breaks (and water) and be aware of the symptoms of altitude sickness (see p1004).

with insecticides. Habitat destruction is also a problem; the area is ecologically significant enough to have been decreed a Reserva de la Biosfera (giving it protected status), but illegal logging still occurs in up to 60% of reserve lands. Local farmers, most strapped for cash, cut down the precious wood, plant corn and allow their livestock into butterfly territory. Some organizations are trying to change these patterns, offering local communities incentives to not only protect their remaining forests, but also to restore habitat via tree planting projects. For more information check out the websites www.michoacanmonarchs.org and www.monarchwatch.org.

Visiting the Reserve

The reserve is divided into five separate areas, four of which are open to visitors from mid-November through March, but exact opening dates depend on weather, temperatures and the butterflies' arrival. El Rosario and Sierra Chincua are the most popular reserve areas. Both are accessible from Angangueo, the closest town to Sierra Chincua (just 8km away) and the best base for this end of the reserve. El Rosario is close to the pueblo of the same name and can be reached from Angangueo via Ocampo. Cerro Pellón is the newest reserve area and has the healthiest habitat. It's best reached from Zitácuaro. At the beginning or end of the season ask for information on butterfly activity at the Morelia or Mexico City tourist offices before heading out here. Some people do day trips or tours from Morelia (see Mex Mich Guías, p560) or Mexico City to see the butterflies, but this means more than eight hours of travel in one day. It's better to take your time and enjoy this unique and beautiful region.

The reserve areas are spread out, so you'll probably only be able to visit one. But the butterflies all look and behave the same in each spot.

El Rosario, which is also the name of a nearby village, is the most popular area and the easiest to reach via public transportation from Anganqueo. But during the height of butterfly voyeurism (February and March) they get as many as 8,000 visitors a day. It is also the most commercial – souvenir stalls abound on the hillside and the habitat has been severely impacted by illegal logging. El Rosario village and the entrance to the El Rosario reserve area are located about 12km up a good gravel road from the small village of Ocampo. Getting to the butterflies requires a steep hike (or horse ride) of 2km to 4km from the reserve's parking lot, depending on the time of year. There are a couple of hotels in Ocampo, but you should stay in the cute village of Anganqueo (just 45 minutes from Ocampo).

Sierra Chincua is 8km beyond Anganqueo, way up in the mountains. This area has also been damaged by logging, but not as badly as El Rosario. It's a less strenuous hike, so this sanctuary is for those who want an easier walk. To get here from Anganqueo take the 'Tlalpujahua' bus ($1) or a taxi ($5).

Cerro Pellón, which is actually located in México state, is the newest reserve area and by far the best choice. The mountains rise high (over 3000m) here, the forest is in great shape and there is barely a trickle of tourism (on its busiest day it may get 80 visitors; when we visited we were all alone on the mountain). Logging has been eliminated and local guides have replanted trees for years to restore habitat. Expect to see huge, cathedral fir trees, moss covered trunks, wildflowers and incredible canyon views. Camping in a natural meadow just below Cerro Pellón peak, only an hour's hike from where the butterflies gather in the early season, is a terrific option. Guides will arrange burros to haul the heavy stuff up the mountain.

This reserve area is about a 40-minute drive southeast of Zitácuaro, Michoacán's third-largest city, where you can buy necessary food, water and supplies. You should bring your own camping gear. There are a couple of access points – Macheros and El Capulín. Both are within 1.5km of each other and can be reached by public transportation from outside Zitácuaro's bus terminal (take a bus marked 'Aputzio,' M$10, which goes as far as the border to México state, then a taxi, M$10 to M$20). A taxi straight from Zitácuaro to either of the reserve areas cost M$180 to M$250. The steep hike from the sanctuary entrances to the butterflies can take

from 90 minutes to over two hours depending upon your condition.

Daily admission for each reserve area costs M$30 and all areas rotate compulsory local guides. Expect to pay around M$150 per horse, if you don't want to hike, plus M$150 for the guide. Note that the length of your hike/horseback ride will be shorter later in the season – as the butterflies work their way down as the weather warms up. Parking is M$20.

ANGANGUEO
☎ 715 / pop 5000 / elevation 2980m

This sweet, drowsy old mining town is the most popular base for butterfly-watchers, because it's close to both the Sierra Chincua and the El Rosario sanctuaries. The town is layered into the hills, knitted with pine forest, grazing land and cornfields. Most services can be found along a single main drag with two names (Nacional and Morelos). Stop at the **tourist office** (☎ 156-00-44; 🕐 8am-8pm Nov-Apr), just downhill from the plaza.

Cheap sleeps include decent and basic **Hotel Real Monarca** (☎ 156-03-24; Nacional 21; r from M$150), with an appealing kitchen; and **Hotel Juárez** (☎ 156-00-23; Nacional 15; r M$320), with basic rooms encircling a gorgeous flower garden. You may have to shout for service. **Albergue Don Bruno** (☎ 156-00-26; Morelos 92; s/d from M$595/865) offers upscale rooms (some with fireplace) and is the class of this tiny town.

Restaurants include **Simon's Restaurant** (Obregón 24; mains M$35) across from the plaza; and **Fonda Villacorzo**, which serves a great chicken and potato dinner in the central market.

Frequent buses from Morelia go first to Zitácuaro (M$89, three hours) where you'll hop another bus to Anganqueo (M$14, 1¼ hours). From Mexico City's Terminal Poniente you can take Autobuses MTZ (M$120, four hours, four daily) direct to Anganqueo; but the majority of buses go through Zitácuaro.

To reach the El Rosario sanctuary from Anganqueo, first take a combi to Ocampo (M$4, 15 minutes, frequent), then another to El Rosario (M$14, 30 minutes, frequent), from the corner of Independencia and Ocampo. In season there are also *camionetas* (open-back trucks) that leave from the *auditorio* (auditorium) in Anganqueo, or from outside hotels; these cost around M$300 for around 10 people and take 45 bumpy minutes (via a back road) to reach the sanctuary.

WESTERN CENTRAL HIGHLANDS

ZITÁCUARO

☎ 715 / pop 79,800/ elevation 1940m

Zitácuaro is Michoacán's third-largest city, but it feels like a provincial working-class town. Known primarily for its baked bread and trout farms, it is also the best base for visiting the butterflies at Cerro Pellón. Other attractions include the **Iglesia de San Pancho** (☺ 9am-2pm & 4-7pm) in the village of San Pancho, just south of Zitácuaro. It's the restored 16th-century church that appeared in the great John Huston–Humphrey Bogart film, *The Treasure of the Sierra Madre* and was visited by Prince Charles in 2002. Come at sunset when light streams through the stained glass. About 16km north of Zitácuaro lie the peaceful Matlazinca ruins, **Pirámides Los Alzati** (☺ 10am-5pm). Veterans of other archaeological sites won't be too impressed by the pyramids, but the views are great and it's a nice picnic spot.

The main drag, Av Revolución, is where you'll find most hotels and restaurants, including the best downtown option, **Hotel America** (☎ 153-11-16; Revolución Sur 8; M$190/250). Their spacious rooms come with a balcony. The modern **Hotel California** (☎ 153-97-98; Revolución Nte 3; s/d M$250/350) has king sized beds and the clean and bright **Hotel Nefer** (☎ 156-79-27; Revolución Nte 4; r from M$260; ℗) is a decent value as well. But the best hotel in the entire butterfly region is just a couple of kilometers south of town. **ourpick Rancho San Cayetano** (☎ 153-19-26; www .ranchosancayetano.com; Carretera a Huetamo Km 2.3; s/d incl service charge from M$900; ℗ 💻 🐕) is owned and run by English- and French-speaking Pablo and Lisette, retirees from Mexico City. Pablo is passionate about the butterflies and offers detailed maps, driving directions and shows background videos to interested guests. He can also arrange transportation to and from the sanctuaries. The grounds are huge with stands of pine and fruit trees and great canyon views. Rooms are rustic chic with exposed stone walls, beamed ceilings and marble baths. And its multi-course, gourmet meals (breakfast/dinner M$150/300; reserve one day in advance) are superb. A taxi here is M$20.

The best downtown restaurant is **La Trucha Alegre** (☎ 153-98-09; Av Revolución Nte 2; mains M$75-90). There are tablecloths and fresh flowers on the table and it cooks up local trout 35 different ways. But it's so fresh it doesn't need mushroom sauce or shrimp stuffing. Get it grilled, give it a squeeze of lime and a douse of *salsa verde*. Divine! Zitácuaro's bus terminal is 1km from the center. There are frequent buses to and from Morelia (M$89, three hours) and Angangueo (M$14, 1¼ hours), among other destinations.

PÁTZCUARO

☎ 434 / pop 49,424 / elevation 2175m

This small, well-preserved colonial town in the Michoacán highlands is also the beating commercial heart of Purépecha country. Indigenous craftspeople from surrounding villages journey here to sell their wares and their presence, as well as Pátzcuaro's dramatic history, infuses the town with a palpable mystical energy.

Its center is defined by impressive old churches – including a hillside basilica – dusty, cobbled streets, tiled adobe buildings brushed white and reddish-brown and by two bustling plazas: Plaza Vasco de Quiroga (known as Plaza Grande) and the smaller Plaza Gertrudis Bocanegra (popularly known as Plaza Chica). At night it is so quiet that you can actually hear the wind (or are they forgotten spirits?) whisper through the narrow back streets.

Just 3km to the north lies scenic Lago de Pátzcuaro, ringed by traditional Purépecha villages and sprinkled with a few islands. Isla Janitzio is Mexico's biggest party magnet during early November's Día de Muertos, when Mexican tourists flock to Pátzcuaro, though plenty also come for Christmas, New Year and Semana Santa. Make advance reservations during holidays and bring warm clothes in winter – you're at altitude here and it gets frigid.

History

Pátzcuaro was the capital of the Tarasco people from about AD 1325 to 1400. After the death of King Tariácuri, the Tarascan state became a three-part league. Comprising Pátzcuaro, Tzintzuntzan and Ihuatzio, the league repulsed repeated Aztec attacks, which may explain why they welcomed the Spanish, who first arrived in 1522. Bad idea. The Spanish returned in 1529 under Nuño de Guzmán, a vicious conquistador.

Guzmán's reign against the indigenous people was brutal, even for those timesThe colonial government recalled Guzmán to Spain, where he was arrested and locked up for life and dispatched Bishop Vasco de

Quiroga, a respected judge and cleric from Mexico City, to clean up his mess. Quiroga was one enlightened dude. When he arrived in 1536, he established village cooperatives based on the humanitarian ideals of Sir Thomas More's Utopia.

To avoid dependence on Spanish mining lords and landowners, Quiroga successfully encouraged education and agricultural self-sufficiency in the Purépecha villages around Lago de Pátzcuaro, with all villagers contributing equally to the community. He also helped each village develop its own craft specialty – from masks to pottery to guitars and violins. The utopian communities declined after his death in 1565, but the crafts traditions continue to this day. Not surprisingly, Tata Vascu, as the Tarascos called Quiroga, has not been forgotten. You'll notice that streets, plazas, restaurants and hotels all over Michoacán are named after him.

Orientation

Life in Central Pátzcuaro revolves around its two plazas. Ahumada heads north out of town toward the old Morelia–Uruapan Hwy (Hwy 14) 2km away. Lago de Pátzcuaro is another 500m further north from the highway.

The bus terminal lies southwest of the city center, about 2km away.

Information

Several banks in the city center will change currency; all have ATMs.

Consultorio Médicos del Centro (☎ 342-45-33; Navarrete 44A; ☽ 9am-2pm & 4-8pm Mon-Fri, 10am-1pm Sat)

Icser Internet (Portal Morelos 64; per hr M$12; ☽ 9am-10pm)

Lavandería San Francisco (☎ 342-39-39; Terán 16; per 3kg M$40; ☽ 9am-9pm Mon-Sat)

Meganet (Mendoza 8; per hr M$12; ☽ 9am-9.30pm)

Municipal tourist office (☎ 342-02-15; Portal Hidalgo 1; ☽ 10am-8pm)

Post office (Obregón 13; ☽ 9am-4pm Mon-Fri, 9am-1pm Sat)

State tourist office (☎ 342-12-14; Calle Buena Vista 7; ☽ 10am-2pm & 5-7pm Mon-Fri, 10am-2pm Sat & Sun)

Sights

PLAZA VASCO DE QUIROGA (PLAZA GRANDE)

Pátzcuaro's leafy **main plaza** is one of Mexico's best hang-out spots. It is framed by the 17th-century facades of old mansions that have

since been converted to hotels, shops and restaurants, and watched over by a serene statue of Vasco de Quiroga which rises from the central fountain. The sides of the plaza are named Portal Hidalgo (west side), Portal Aldama (south side) and Portal Matamoros (east side). The north side is Portal Allende east of Iturbe and Portal Morelos west of Iturbe.

PLAZA GERTRUDIS BOCANEGRA (PLAZA CHICA)

Pátzcuaro's second plaza is named after a local heroine who was shot by firing squad in 1818 for her support of the independence movement. Her statue commands the center of the plaza and she looks like your basic badass.

The local market on the west side of the plaza is where you can find everything from fruit, vegetables and fresh trout to herbal medicines, crafts and clothing – including the region's distinctive striped shawls and sarapes. There's outstanding cheap food, too.

On the north side of the plaza is one of the coolest libraries of all time. The **Biblioteca Gertrudis Bocanegra** (☎ 342-54-41; cnr Padre Lloreda & Titere; ☽ 9am-7pm Mon-Fri, 10am-1pm Sat) occupies the cavernous interior of the 16th-century San Agustín church. There are oyster shell skylights and a massive colorful Juan O'Gorman mural on the rear wall that depicts the history of Michoacán from pre-Hispanic times to the 1910 revolution. It also has high-speed internet for just M$5 per hour.

A tumbledown **Mercado de Artesanías** (☽ 8am-6pm) operates on the side street adjacent to the library. Wooden masks and pastel crucifixes are among the crafts sold here. Quality varies. Prices are low.

On the west side of the library, the **Teatro Emperador Caltzontzin** was a convent until it was converted to a theater in 1936; it hosts occasional films and performances

BASÍLICA DE NUESTRA SEÑORA DE LA SALUD

This gorgeous church, built on the hill atop a pre-Hispanic ceremonial site, was intended to be the centerpiece of Vasco de Quiroga's utopia. The building wasn't completed until the 19th century and only the central nave was faithful to his original design. Quiroga's tomb, the Mausoleo de Don Vasco, is left of the main doors.

Behind the altar at the east end stands a much revered figure of the Virgin, Nuestra

PÁTZCUARO

INFORMATION
CELEP Language School.................1	B4
Consultorio Médicos del Centro.......2	B4
Icser Internet...............................3	C3
Lavandería San Francisco...............4	B4
Meganet....................................5	C3
Municipal Tourist Office.................6	B4
Post Office.................................7	C3
State Tourist Office.......................8	D3

SIGHTS & ACTIVITIES
Basílica de Nuestra Señora de la Salud.9	D3
Biblioteca Gertrudis Bocanegra.......10	C4
Casa de los Once Patios................11	C4
Museo de Artes Populares.............12	C4
Teatro Emperador Caltzontzin........13	C3
Templo de la Compañía................14	C4
Templo del Sagrario.....................15	C4
Templo El Santuario.....................16	B3
Templo San Francisco...................17	B4
Templo San Juan de Dios..............18	B4

SLEEPING
Casa de la Real Aduana.................19	B4
Hostal Santa Fe...........................20	D3
Hotel Concordia.....................(see 25)	
Hotel El Refugio.........................21	C3

Hotel La Parroquia......................22	C3
Hotel Misión San Manuel...............23	C4
Hotel Posada de la Salud...............24	D4
Hotel Posada San Agustín..............25	C3
Hotel Posada San Alejandro............26	D4
Hotel Posada San Rafael................27	C4
Hotel Rincón de Josefa..................28	C3
Hotel Valmen.............................29	C3
La Casa Encantada.......................30	C3
La Mansión de los Sueños..............31	B3
Mesón de San Antonio..................32	D3
Posada de la Basílica....................33	C3
Posada de los Ángeles...................34	C2

EATING
Cenaduría La Pollita Feliz............(see 36)	
Cha Cha Cha.............................35	C3
Food Stalls................................36	C3

La Casa de Arcangeles..............(see 23)	
La Surtidora..............................37	C4
Merza Pack...............................38	C3
Mistonga.................................39	C4
Priscilla's.............................(see 31)	
Restaurante Don Rafa...................40	C3

DRINKING
Akqua....................................41	C3
Campanario Bar.....................(see 23)	
El Refugio.............................(see 21)	

SHOPPING
Mercado de Artesanías.................42	C3

TRANSPORT
Buses to Bus Terminal...................43	C3
Buses to Lake........................(see 43)	

Señora de la Salud (Our Lady of Health), which 16th-century Tarascans crafted the image from a corncob-and-honey paste called *tatzingue*. Soon after, people began to experience miraculous healings and Quiroga had the words 'Salus Infirmorum' (Healer of the Sick) inscribed at the figure's feet. Ever since, pilgrims have come from all over Mexico to pray for miracles. They crawl on their knees across the plaza, into the church and along its nave. Upstairs, behind the image, you'll see many tin impressions of hands, feet and legs that pilgrims have offered the mystical Virgin.

MUSEO DE ARTES POPULARES

This **folk art museum** (☎ 342-10-29; cnr Enseñanza & Alcantarillas; admission M$34; ☯ 9am-7pm Tue-Sat, 9am-

4:30pm Sun) housed in old colonial environs was under renovation during research. In 1540 Quiroga founded the original Colegio de San Nicolás, arguably the Americas' first university, on this site. The building was constructed on pre-Hispanic stone foundations, some of which can be seen behind the museum courtyards.

In the past permanent exhibitions have included impressive collections of ceremonial masks, religious artifacts, gorgeous jewelry and stunning lacquerware. There's also a room set up as a typical Michoacán kitchen (note the large brick oven). Though the museum was closed to the public at the time of writing, it should be up and running, with additional temporary exhibits, during your visit.

OTHER CHURCHES

Built in the 16th century, the **Templo de la Compañía** (cnr Lerín & Alcantarillas) became a Jesuit training college in the 17th century. The church is still in use and houses some Vasco de Quiroga relics. The adjacent college building fell into ruin after the expulsion of the Jesuits. It is now used for community activities and often has free temporary exhibits.

Pátzcuaro has several other old churches of interest, including the creaky **Templo del Sagrario**, **Templo San Juan de Dios**, the pink stone **Templo San Francisco** and **Templo El Santuario**.

CASA DE LOS ONCE PATIOS

This cool, rambling colonial **edifice** (House of the 11 Courtyards; Madrigal de las Altas Torres) was built as a Dominican convent in the 1740s. (Before that, the site held one of Mexico's first hospitals, founded by Vasco de Quiroga.) Today it houses small *artesanías* shops, each specializing in a particular regional craft. Look for copperware from Santa Clara del Cobre and musical instruments from Paracho, as well as lacquerware, hand-painted ceramics and vibrant textiles. You'll likely find privacy on the top floors where you can take in the surrounding natural and architectural beauty.

Most shops are open from 10am to 7pm daily, with a lunch break in the afternoon.

EL ESTRIBO

This hilltop lookout, 3.5km west of the city center and popular with joggers, walkers and couples, has a great view of Lago de Pátzcuaro. It takes about an hour to traverse the cobbled, cypress-lined road up to the viewing pavilion. Take Ponce de León from the southwest corner of Plaza Grande and follow the signs.

Courses

Centro de Lenguas y Ecoturismo de Pátzcuaro (CELEP; ☎ 342-47-64; www.celep.com.mx; Navarrete 50; two-week Spanish language course M$3816; language & culture program M$5888) Courses involve four to six hours of classes Monday to Friday. Cultural programs include seminars in Mexican literature and excursions to the butterfly sanctuary (in season) and local villages. Homestays (including meals) cost M$273 per day.

Tours

Several tour guides operate around the Pátzcuaro area.

Miguel Ángel Núñez (☎ 344-01-08; casadetierra@ hotmail.com) English-speaking Miguel Ángel, an anthro-

pologist, offers insider tours of the Pátzcuaro area and throughout Michoacán. He covers indigenous culture, archaeology, colonial history, art and architecture. Tour prices depend on the destination, but local tours cost M$200 per person; transportation is provided. He can also organize cooking classes and food tours upon request.

Festivals & Events

The villages around Pátzcuaro, most notably Tzintzuntzan and Isla Janitzio, stage the most popular Day of the Dead celebrations in Mexico. Parades, crafts markets, dancing, ceremonies, exhibitions and concerts are held in and around Pátzcuaro on the days before and after Día de Muertos. Cemeteries are packed with observants throughout the festivities.

Other interesting events in Pátzcuaro include:

Pastorelas These dramatizations of the shepherds' journey to see the infant Jesus are staged in Plaza Grande around Christmas. *Pastorelas indígenas*, on the same theme but including mask dances, enact the struggle of angels against the devils that are trying to hinder the shepherds. These *pastorelas* are held in eight villages around Lago de Pátzcuaro, on different days between December 26 and February 2.

Semana Santa Easter week is full of events in Pátzcuaro and the lakeside villages, including Palm Sunday processions; Viacrucis processions on Good Friday morning, enacting Christ's journey to Calvary and the crucifixion; candlelit processions in silence on Good Friday evening; and, on Easter Sunday evening, a ceremonial burning of Judas in Plaza Grande.

Nuestra Señora de la Salud On December 8 a colorful procession to the basilica honors the Virgin of Health. Traditional dances are performed, including Los Reboceros, Los Moros, Los Viejitos and Los Panaderos.

Sleeping

Pátzcuaro has a wide variety of accommodations, but during holidays and festivals, especially Día de Muertos, be sure to secure reservations months ahead (more for the most popular places); or you may be homeless. The best deals can be found near the basilica.

BUDGET

Hotel Valmen (☎ 342-11-61; Padre Lloreda 34; s/d/t M$200/250/300) The leafy interior of this decent budget choice is lit with skylights. The halls are decorated with funky tiles and the rooms are immaculate. Drawbacks include thin mattresses and late night and early morning noise.

DÍA DE MUERTOS WARNING

Pátzcuaro is usually a wonderfully serene little town, but when Día de Muertos rolls around it seems all of Mexico is trying to get in. If you plan on being here around the first two days of November, make sure you've made hotel reservations many months in advance. Be ready for crowds and bring a camera, as the markets and surrounding cemeteries are beautiful.

Isla Janitzio is witness to many colorful festivities, but its small cemetery is ground zero for crushing crowds of young party animals. Instead visit the cemeteries in surrounding villages (try Ihuatzio, Jarácuaro or Capula). Going after 3am is another strategy to avoid crowds (except on Janitzio, which is jam-packed all night long). Tzintzuntzan's cemetery is one of the best, but it's extremely popular and can be crowded. Come early in the day and watch as families decorate the graves.

WESTERN CENTRAL HIGHLANDS

Hotel Estrella (☎ 342-56-99; Lázaro Cárdenas 2; s/d M$220/400) This small, pink, family-run budget spot on the road to the pier is the best among a string of lakeside hotels. The rooms are clean, management speaks English and it helps arrange boat trips to the islands.

Hotel Posada San Agustín (☎ 342-04-42; Portal Juárez 27; s/d M$250/350) Cramped and not nearly clean enough, some rooms have stellar volcano views. It will do for a night or two if you're desperate.

MIDRANGE

Posada de los Ángeles (☎ 342-24-40; posada angeles@hotmail.com; Títere 16; s/d M$300/420) Rooms are spacious, clean and have character (arches and high ceilings). The garden is sunny and warm and the price is right. You won't love the industrial carpeting but it keeps the room warm and it isn't musty.

Hotel Posada San Rafael (☎ 342-07-70; Portal Aldama 13; s/d M$300/420) The lovechild of a colonial mission and a US motel, rooms open onto wide verandas overlooking a driveway and parking area. There are plenty of beautiful details – like columns, beamed ceilings and potted plants. First floor rooms are dark, but upstairs rooms are a great deal. It's located right on Plaza Grande.

Hotel Concordia (☎ 342-00-03; Portal Juárez 31; s/d M$320/450; P) Run by a sweet *abuelita* who will offer same day discounts (to M$280), this is Pátzcuaro's choice budget spot. For a few more bucks you can have a room with a pastel paint job that makes it feel larger than it really is. The showers are not built for basketball players.

Hotel Posada de la Salud (☎ 347-00-58; posadadela salud@hotmail.com; Serrato 9; d/tw M$350/420) A lovely, rambling hotel painted in a pastel yellow that just feels like Mexico. There's cable TV, fairly narrow beds in the simple, clean rooms and plenty of outdoor common space.

Hotel Posada San Alejandro (☎ 342-61-33; Serrato 5A; hpsalejandro@yahoo.com.mx; d from M$480) The simple, tiled rooms are clean, come with soft double beds and cable TV and are set in a quiet end of town. Management is friendly and accommodating.

ourpick Mesón de San Antonio (☎ 342-25-01; www.mesondesanantonio.com; Serrato 33; s/d M$500/600; 💻) This old hacienda-style inn is the best of the midrangers by far. Rooms border a courtyard, the beamed overhangs are held up by ancient timbers and the extremely cozy rooms are decorated with fine Purépecha pottery and have wood burning fireplaces and cable TV.

Hostal Santa Fe (☎ 342-05-12; www.hostaldelvalle.com; Padre Lloreda 27; d/t M$500/700; P) With pottery on the tiled floors and ironwork on the walls, this sunken lobby is as inviting as it is unusual. Some rooms are better than others, but on the whole they are comfortable and spotless. Number 9 has a romantic terrace.

Hotel Rincón de Josefa (☎ 342-11-43; www.hotel rincondejosefa.com.mx; Iturbe 29; s/d M$538/644) Well located between the two plazas is one of the better options in town. The 60 rooms are all unique, some have arced brick ceilings and are furnished with antiques. The lobby vibes with almost 2000 indoor plants. It feels good in here and it's a great deal.

Hotel El Refugio (☎ 342-55-05; hotelcasadelrefugio@hotmail.com; Portal Régules 9; s/d M$750/880) A cozy, stylish choice with spacious rooms that have terra cotta tile floors and high beamed ceilings. Management is warm and gracious. You may want to stay a while.

TOP END

Hotel Misión San Manuel (☎ 342-10-50; www.mision sanmanuel.com; Portal Aldama 12; s/d M$702/1053; P 💻)

The public spaces are endearing at this converted monastery. Think wood columns, a fireplace and exquisite local pottery in the courtyard. But the rooms, though large with high ceilings, are pretty average.

Hotel La Parroquia (☎ 342-25-16; reserva_laparroquia@hotmail.com; Plaza Gertrudis Bocanegra 24; r M$963; P ▣) This palatial three-story hacienda style hotel has been recently renovated, with refinished beams and columns, granite and tile baths and Tempurpedic beds. The Plaza Chica location is excellent.

La Casa Encantada (☎ 342-34-92; www.lacasaencantada.com; Dr Coss 15; r from M$974-1461; P ▣) If you crave affordable luxury, this intimate US-owned B&B offers 10 elegant rooms with local rugs and beautifully tiled baths in a converted 1784 mansion. Amenities include cheap international calls, wireless internet, airport transfers and gourmet breakfasts.

Posada de la Basílica (☎ 342-11-08; www.posadalabasilica.com; Arciga 6; r from M$1350; P ▣) For rustic luxury consider this boutique hotel with terra cotta rooftop and lake views. The 12 huge rooms have wood floors and open fireplaces. The courtyard is plain but the location rocks.

La Mansión de los Sueños (☎ 342-57-08; www.prismas.com.mx; Ibarra 15; r from M$2230) This restored mansion built around three adjacent courtyards offers some of the best digs in town. It has one of the more tasteful collections of folk art and some rooms have fireplaces and lofts. Full breakfast and a welcome cocktail are included and served at Priscilla's, its posh restaurant.

Casa de la Real Aduana (☎ 342-02-65; www.lafoliamx.com; Ponce de León 16; r M$2400-2750) Pátzcuaro's classiest rooms can be snagged at this converted 16th-century colonial house. Think plush linens, fine art on the walls and a stunning historical courtyard that is part-museum, part-garden and hard to leave on a sunny morning. Full breakfast is included; no kids allowed.

Eating

Pátzcuaro has decent, but not great, food. Local specialties include *sopa tarasca,* a rich tomato-based soup with cream, dried chili and bits of crisp tortilla and *corundas – tamales* with a creamy pork and bean filling.

our pick Cenaduria La Pollita Feliz (crnr Obregón & Plaza Chica; mains M$35; ☯ 5-10pm) Enormous skillets sizzle with perfectly crisp and tender chicken, potatoes and carrots and boil with sweet and tangy enchilada sauce at this packed food stall beneath the pink tarp. Its Super Orden (M$140) includes salad, enchiladas, two whole chickens, a pile of steaming *papas* and feeds four. Delicious!

La Surtidora (☎ 342-28-35; Portal Hidalgo 71; mains M$35-120; ☯ 8am-10pm) Waiters are dressed in chef whites, but don't expect fine dining at this old school café, which has been in operation on Plaza Grande since 1916. The beamed interior is perfumed with roasting coffee, it serves all manner of salads and the chicken enchiladas come topped with butternut squash.

La Casa de Arcangeles (☎ 342-10-50; Portal Aldama 12; mains M$50-85; ☯ 8am-10pm) This bright courtyard café attached to Hotel Mision San Manuel serves all the typical Mexican favorites. Pátzcuaro's youngest mariachi band performs on weekends, which is always a good time.

Restaurante Don Rafa (☎ 342-04-98; Mendoza 30; mains from M$60; ☯ 8:30am-9pm) The bow-tied waiters at this narrow, intimate restaurant serve set, three-course menus starring Mexican classics – such as chicken *mole*. There are tablecloths and candles on the tables, but fluorescent lighting spoils the mood. Still, a good deal.

Cha Cha Cha (☎ 342-16-27; www.restaurantchachacha.com; Buena Vista 7; mains M$75-95; ☯ 8:30am-9:30pm) Just off the Plaza Basilica is this funky courtyard café freckled with great Purépecha folk art and photography. Its burgers and fries get rave reviews. The salmon with *chipotle* sauce is tasty and it even has its own organic herb garden.

Mistonga (☎ 342-64-50; Dr Coss 4; mains M$85-115; ☯ 1-10pm Tue-Sun) When you dine Argentine, steak is your best option. This gorgeous enclosed courtyard restaurant serves it in a variety of ways, such as *milanesa* (pounded thin and breaded) and *chimichurri* (marinated in a garlic, parsley and olive oil sauce). It also has a fantastic Argentine wine list.

Priscilla's (☎ 342-57-08; Ibarra 15; mains M$95-150; ☯ 7:30am-10:30pm) Posh and fancy, this fine dining room serves international dishes, like lasagna al prosciutto, fish-filled nopals and cheese fondue. There's courtyard dining on warm days and live music on Saturday nights.

The market on Plaza Chica has inexpensive **food stalls** (☯ 8am-7pm) serving everything from fruit juices to tacos to *tortas.* If you need a supermarket check out **Merza Pack** (Mendoza 24; ☯ 7am-9:45pm).

Drinking

Pátzcuaro seldom parties, but you can toast the saintly Quiroga at the airy sidewalk tables or in the cramped black-lit environs of **Campanario Bar** (Plaza Grande 14; 3-11pm), which offers live bands on occasion. If the Pátzcuaro night has a pulse, this is its heart.

El Refugio (342-55-05; Portal Régules 9; noon-midnight) This elegant hotel bar has two (quite different) points of highlight: the lovely wood burning fireplace that attracts couples and sparks good conversation, and the flat screen TV above the bar that displays global and American football games to an international expat crowd.

Akqua (342-11-11; Plaza Grande 66; 2-10pm) Pátzcuaro's newest bar-lounge attempts to blend modern electronica vibrations into the ancient soul of this quiet town. Brand-new at the time of writing, it wasn't crowded. But the old stone courtyard is a great location and it should find its groove.

Shopping

The Casa de los Once Patios is a good place to seek Michoacán crafts, but you'll get better deals on similar work in the main market and the Mercado de Artesanías, both next to Plaza Chica. On Friday mornings a ceramics market, with pottery from surrounding villages, is held in Plaza San Francisco. There's also a small crafts market in front of the basilica every day.

There are countless villages within a few hours of Pátzcuaro and they all specialize in different crafts. Shoppers will enjoy the hunt.

Getting There & Around

Pátzcuaro's bus terminal is 1.5km southwest of the city center. It has a cafeteria and left-luggage services.

To catch a bus heading to the center, walk outside the terminal, turn right and at the corner take any bus marked 'Centro' (M$5). Taxis cost M$20 (with a small surcharge after 11pm).

Buses back to the terminal (marked 'Central') leave from the northeast corner of Plaza Chica. Buses to the boat pier (marked 'Lago') also leave from here and run from about 6am to 10pm daily.

Common destinations that have frequent services include the following (price quotes are for 1st-class fares):

Destination	Fare	Duration
Erongarícuaro	M$10	35min
Guadalajara	M$200	4½hr
Mexico City (Terminal Poniente)	M$270	5½hr
Mexico City (Terminal Norte)	M$270	5½hr
Morelia	M$35	1hr
Quiroga	M$16	35min
Santa Clara del Cobre	M$8	30min
Tzintzuntzan	M$9	20min
Uruapan	M$37	1hr
Zirahuén	M$14	50min

AROUND PÁTZCUARO

Lago de Pátzcuaro

About 3km north of central Pátzcuaro, you will come over a rise to find a lake so blue that its edge blends seamlessly with the sky. Within it are a few populated islands. It is stream fed, natural and though pollution is a concern, it's still damn beautiful.

To get to the *muelle* (dock), take a bus marked 'Lago' from Pátzcuaro's Plaza Chica. The dock caters to tourists in a profoundly cheesy way – with cheap fish eateries and souvenir shops. The ticket office is about 50m down on the right-hand side.

Isla Janitzio is a popular weekend and holiday destination. It's heavily devoted to tourism, with lots of low-end souvenir stalls, fish restaurants and drunk college kids on holiday. But it is car-less and threaded with foot paths that eventually wind their way to the top, where you'll find a 40m-high **statue** (admission M$6) of independence hero José María Morelos y Pavón. Inside the statue are murals depicting Morelos' life. Want a stellar panoramic view? Climb up to his see-through wrist. The **Hotel Terhunukua** (r M$220;) has small, modest rooms (some with views) and is 50m straight up from the dock.

Round-trip boat rides to Janitzio cost M$40 and take 25 minutes each way; they leave when full (about every 30 minutes, quicker on weekends).

Tiny **Isla Yunuén** is green, tranquil and has a tight-knit Purépecha community. Crash at **Cabañas de Yunuén** (434-342-44-73; cabañas from M$400). These romantic wood *cabañas* sleep up to 16 people; all have TV and kitchenette.

Round-trip boat rides to Yunuén also cost M$40 per person. Boats leave when full, so you may have to wait.

Lakeside Villages

The villages surrounding Lago de Pátzcuaro make perfect day trips and almost all can

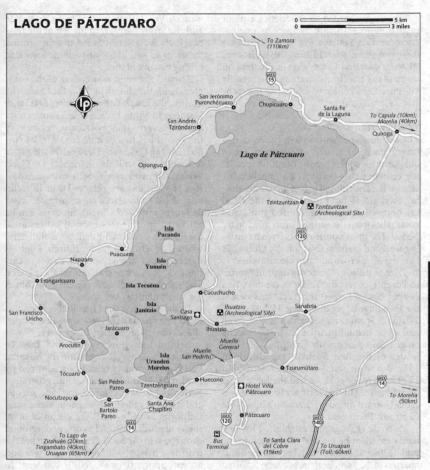

LAGO DE PÁTZCUARO

be reached by local transportation from Pátzcuaro's bus terminal. Or, to avoid backtracking to the bus station, take a 'Lago' bus from Plaza Chica and get off anywhere between the Posada de Don Vasco and Hwy 14; then wait by the roadside for a bus heading to your village. Buses to Ihuatzio run directly from Plaza Chica.

Frequent combis run between the villages, so you can visit several in one day. Transportation between Quiroga and Erongarícuaro is infrequent, however, so travel between the two may be quicker via Pátzcuaro.

IHUATZIO
Ihuatzio, 14km from Pátzcuaro, was capital of the Tarascan league after Pátzcuaro (but

before Tzintzuntzan). Today it's just a slow, dusty village where everyone knows everyone else, until *you* walk into town.

The large and partially restored **Ihuatzio archaeological site** (admission M$25; ☟ 10am-6pm) lies just over 1km up a cobbled road from the village's small plaza. The ruins' best attraction is an open ceremonial space. It is 200m long and features two pyramid-like structures at its west end. Climbing the pyramids is forbidden, but it is possible to walk to the top of the restored wall to their left (south) for good views. Two carved stone coyotes were found at the site; one is in the National Anthropology Museum in Mexico City, the other graces the bell tower of Ihuatzio's church.

If you ever wanted to experience a night or two in an authentic indigenous pueblo, consider **Casa Santiago** (☎ 342-59-62; www.geo cities.com/theothermexico; bed & breakfast M$436, full-board M$545). It's located 1.5km west of Ihuatzio on the road to Cucuchucho and run by a friendly US-Purépecha couple who also run inexpensive shopping tours.

TZINTZUNTZAN

The tiny town of Tzintzuntzan (tseen-*tsoon*-tsahn), about 15km north of Pátzcuaro, has an old nurturing soul. There's a beautiful sprawling cemetery that becomes an unbelievably vibrant floral memorial to lost loved ones during intricate 48-hour-long Day of the Dead celebrations, crumbling Tarasco ruins and some relics from the early Spanish missionary period. The town's pulse comes from its thriving weekend crafts market, saintly Quiroga's beloved olive grove and two old churches.

Tzintzuntzan, or 'Place of Hummingbirds' in Purépecha, was the Tarascan capital when copper blades helped the Tarascans defeat the invading Aztecs in the late 15th century. When the Spanish arrived with a bible in hand and a gun behind their back, the Purépecha chief made peace with Cristóbal de Olid, leader of the first Spanish expedition in 1522. But when Nuño de Guzmán arrived in 1529 hungry for gold, he had the same chief burned alive. This barbaric act is depicted on the O'Gorman mural in Pátzcuaro's Biblioteca Gertrudis Bocanegra.

Vasco de Quiroga also established his first base here when he reached Michoacán in the mid-1530s and Tzintzuntzan became the headquarters of the Franciscan monks who followed him. The town declined in importance after Quiroga shifted his base to Pátzcuaro in 1540.

On the lake side (west) of Av Cárdenas lies the **Ex-Convento de San Francisco**, a religious compound built partly with stones from the Tarascan site up the hill which the Spanish demolished. This is where Franciscan monks began the Spanish missionary effort in Michoacán in the 16th century. The gnarled, shady olive trees in the churchyard came from seedlings planted by Vasco de Quiroga; they're believed to be the oldest olive trees in the Americas. Can you think of a better place to snag an outdoor siesta?

Straight ahead as you walk into the churchyard is the crumbling, but still-functioning **Templo de San Francisco**, built exclusively for the monks. Vegetation sprouts from its facade and the lovely cloister, to the left of the *templo,* includes a set of faded murals around the galleries and Mudejar-patterned wooden ceiling ornamentation.

Toward the right rear corner of the complex stands the church built for the Purépecha masses, the **Templo de Nuestra Señora de la Salud**. Inside is El Santo Entierro de Tzintzuntzan, a much-revered image of Christ. For most of the year it lies in a *caja de cristal* (glass coffin). During Day of the Dead celebrations it is festooned with fruit and marigolds. On Good Friday, following an elaborate costumed passion play, the image is removed from its coffin and nailed to the large cross; being a Cristo de Goznes (hinged Christ), his arms can be extended and his legs crossed. Afterwards, the image is paraded through town until dark, when it is returned to the church. Pilgrims descend from all over, some in chains or carrying crosses, some crawling on their knees. Thousands of candles are placed in the church for an all-night wake.

In the enclosed yard beside this church is the **Capilla Abierta de la Concepción**, an old open chapel that dates to the 16th century.

Behind the church you'll find **Taller De Cerámica**, a converted missionary hospital that is now a rustic ceramics studio run by local artist, Manuel Morales, a fifth generation potter. His work is colorful, intricate, unique and is sold in galleries throughout Mexico and California. Inside you'll see ceramics in all stages of production and a cool, underground showroom in the back. Prices are high but the man is a master. Morales gives classes and accepts apprentices as well. If you want to become a potter, you'd have a hard time finding a more creative learning environment, or a more qualified teacher. But Morales has no phone. You'll just have to show up.

Head out the monastery's front gate, across the highway and up the hill and you'll find the **Tzintzuntzan archeological site** (Las Yácatas; M$34; ⊙ 10am-5pm), an impressive group of five round, reconstructed temples, known as *yácatas*. They are all that remain of the mighty Tarascan empire. The hillside location offers wonderful views of the town, lake and surrounding mountains.

QUIROGA

The bustling market town of Quiroga, named for the man responsible for many of its buildings and handicrafts, is 7km northeast of Tzintzuntzan. Every day there's a busy crafts market and there are hundreds of shops selling brightly painted wooden, ceramic and leather goods, as well as colorful woolen sweaters and sarapes. The town is set at the crossroads of Hwys 15 and 120, so there is seldom a dearth of shoppers.

Traffic also stops for Quiroga's famous *carnitas* (chunks of slow-cooked pork). There are dozens of *carnitas* stands and storefronts to choose from. But the town's best meal can be found at **Taquería Los Compadres**, a hole-in-the-wall on the main road. Despite its name, it specializes in *molcajetes* (M$50 per person) and they could be the best in Mexico. Steak is grilled, sliced into fine ribbons and placed over chunks of onion which are immersed in bubbling salsa in the heated *molcajete* (a volcanic stone grinding bowl). Then chorizo is added along with *carnitas* and the whole pot is slathered with cheese, garnished with grilled nopales and served with griddled tortillas. Extra napkins, please!

On the first Sunday in July the **Fiesta de la Preciosa Sangre de Cristo** (Festival of the Precious Blood of Christ) is celebrated with a long torchlight procession led by a group carrying an image of Christ crafted from a paste made of corncobs and honey.

ERONGARÍCUARO

A pretty 18km trip west from Pátzcuaro, Erongarícuaro (or 'Eronga') is one of the oldest settlements on the lake. French artist André Breton (1896–1966) lived here for a time in the 1950s, visited occasionally by Diego Rivera and Frida Kahlo. Breton made the unusual wrought-iron cross in the forecourt of the church. Peruse the gorgeous gardens behind the old seminary attached to the church and look for the traditional Purépecha *troje* house.

On January 6, the **Fiesta de los Reyes Magos** (Festival of the Magic Kings) is celebrated with music and dance.

TÓCUARO

Some of Mexico's finest mask makers live in this cobblestoned town surrounded by cornfields, 10km west of Pátzcuaro. But there are no traditional shop fronts – just a sign here and there signifying entry into family courtyard compounds with workshops and showrooms.

Tócuaro's best mask maker, Juan Horta, recently passed away, but his son **Orlando Horta** (☎ 443-349-72-31; maskorta@hotline.com; ☽ 10am-6pm) and his brothers carry on. Their gruesome skull, bat and bull masks are decorated with real hair and teeth. Walk up the street (Morelos) from the bus stop; after you pass Hidalgo it is the first house on your left. The town's best wood sculpture can be found at **Taller de Don Salvador Tera e Hijos** (☎ 443-303-37-82; ☽ 9am-6pm) on the highway.

Prepare to spend. It takes a month or more to produce a fine mask, carved from a single piece of wood. The best ones are wonderfully expressive and surreal and thanks to a growing legion of global collectors, can cost hundreds of dollars.

Capula

This small foothill town on Highway 15 between Pátzcuaro and Morelia celebrates the Day of the Dead with more color and flare, and fewer tourists, than anywhere else. The **cemetery** is visible from the highway and open to the public. Graves are covered in moss and marigold crosses, while headstones are wreathed with red roses and purple orchids. There are no raucous, drunken crowds here, just observant families, sitting around graveside fires, staying up all night and keeping tradition alive.

Next to the cemetery is an incredible property owned by another of Mexico's celebrated artists, Juan Torres. Sculpture, dozens of fruit and shade trees and a cactus garden surround Torres' sprawling adobe home and magical chapel, which doubles as an art gallery. Inside a series of large-scale canvases and wood paintings hint at Torres' love of the feminine, the pagan altar is a lone volcanic boulder and before it lies a large terra cotta Christ. The paintings are for sale, but Torres does more business from his showroom, **La Candelaria** (443-320-56-37; juantorrescapula@hotmail .com). This is the type of gallery Jerry Garcia would have loved. Inside are shelf after shelf of *Catrinas* (clay skeletons), smiling, in evening gowns, floral lampshade hats, in Catholic robes and some are knocked up and smoking. It's a colorful, dark and strangely intoxicating space. Don't miss it. In town you can get knock-off *Catrinas,* created by some of Torres' former students, for a third of the price. Look for the **Mercado de Artesanías** on the main road.

URUAPAN

☎ 452 / pop 242,100 / elevation 1620m

All praise the thundering, proud Río Cupatitzio. Because if it weren't for this impressive river that begins life underground and then rises sensationally to the surface – feeding a subtropical garden of palms, orchids and massive shade trees in downtown Uruapan's Parque Nacional Barranca del Cupatitzio, this city would not exist. When the Spanish monk Fray Juan de San Miguel arrived here in 1533 he was so taken with it that he gave the area the Purépecha name, Uruapan (oo-roo-ah-pahn), which roughly translates into 'Eternal Spring.' Fray Juan designed a large market square – still a hit with area families on weekends, built a hospital and chapel and arranged streets into an orderly grid that survives today.

Uruapan quickly grew into a productive agricultural center renowned for high-quality aguacates (avocados) and still holds the title 'Capital Mundial del Aguacate' (see boxed text, opposite). The avocado fair in November underlines that point.

Avocados may pay the bills, but the river is king. The city's nicest neighborhoods kiss the riverside. The national park, a 15-minute walk from the city center, is a rush of waterfalls and trickling streams that wind through thick vegetation; and one of the coolest clubs in Mexico, Bar Rio, is housed in an old underground waterworks, within earshot of the rumbling Cupatitzio.

Uruapan is 500m lower than Pátzcuaro and is much warmer. Don't miss the remarkable volcano Paricutín, 35km to the west.

Orientation

Uruapan's heart is its long, narrow main plaza. Everything you'll need is within walking distance.

Note that street names change often in Uruapan, both at the plaza and at various other points. The portales facing the plaza are named independently of the streets; Portal Degollado is the east side of the plaza, while Portal Carrillo and Portal Matamoros run along the south side. The north portal is Portal Mercado.

Information

Several banks (with ATMs), along with a few cambios, are near the central plaza.

Casa del Turista (☎ 524-06-67; www.uruapan.gob.mx; Carranza 20; ✹ 9am-7:30pm) The municipal tourist office.

Lavandería (☎ 523-26-69; cnr Carranza & Garcia; per kg M$15; ✹ 9am-2pm & 4-8pm Mon-Sat)

Main post office (Jalisco 81; ✹ 9am-3pm Mon-Fri, 9am-1pm Sat)

Mi Cafe JG.Net (Independencia 35; per hr M$5; ✹ 10:30am-10pm, Mon-Sat, 10:30am-4pm Sun)

Secretaría de Turismo (☎ 524-71-99; Ayala 16; ✹ 8:30am-3pm & 4-7pm Mon-Fri, 9am-2pm & 4-7pm Sat, 9am-2pm Sun) The state tourist office.

Sights

MUSEO DE LOS CUATRO PUEBLOS INDIOS

In the Huatápera, an old colonial courtyard building near the northeast corner of the central plaza, is this three-room **museum** (☎ 524-34-34; admission free; ✹ 9:30am-1:30pm & 3:30-6pm Tue-Sun). Built in the 1530s by Vasco de Quiroga, this relic once housed the first hospital in the Americas. The decorations around the doors and windows were carved by Purépecha artisans in a Mudejar style. The museum showcases regional artesanías like ceramics from Capula and lacquerware from Quiroga.

PARQUE NACIONAL BARRANCA DEL CUPATITZIO

This incomparable urban **park** (Independencia; adult/child M$12/5; ✹ 8am-6pm) is just 1km west of the main plaza, but it's another world. Nature is big here. Tropical and subtropical foliage (including burly banana palms) is thick and alive with colorful birds and butterflies. The river boils over boulders, cascades down waterfalls and spreads into wide, crystalline pools. Cobbled paths follow the riverbank from its source at the Rodilla del Diablo pool near the park's north end. There are a few fruit stands and taquerias to choose from and water from hidden springs peels off the surrounding hillsides, before flowing into the great river. There's even a trout farm where you can net your own catch.

FÁBRICA SAN PEDRO

This great old **textile factory** (☎ 524-06-77; telaresuru pan@prodigy.com.mx; Treviño s/n; ✹ tours 9am-6pm Mon-Sat) from the 19th-century is essentially a living museum. Hand-loomed and hand-dyed bedspreads, tablecloths and curtains are made here from pure cotton and wool and are available for sale. The original machines are over 100 years old and are still used. Call ahead for a tour and see the entire weaving process from cotton bale to finished tablecloth.

HOLY GUACAMOLE! THE AMAZING AVOCADO

Avocados are huge in Uruapan. Mexico is the world's largest producer of the fruit and the majority come from gnarled old groves that shade the city's outskirts. All told they produce over one billion kilos of avocados annually, with only about 5% – including the best fruit – being exported. That's a lot of guacamole.

Avocados are native to Mexico, Central America and the Andes range. The word 'avocado' comes from the Spanish 'aguacate,' which came from 'ahuacatl,' the Náhuatl word for testicle. The rich and sensuous fruit do indeed dangle in pairs and the Aztecs even considered the fruit an aphrodisiac. They actually banned young women from strolling outdoors when avocados were being harvested.

Today there are over one hundred avocado varieties. The Hass variety is by far the most popular, accounting for about 80% of worldwide consumption. Commercial trees are produced by grafting (since production is faster and quality superior this way) rather than by seeding and are currently being grown in a wide variety of temperate regions, such as California, South Africa, Spain, Israel, Brazil and, of course, Mexico. Mature avocado trees can produce up to 400 fruit each season and live for over 200 years. The trees around Uruapan produce two crops each year.

The avocado has a diverse fan base. It's blinked into Ecuadorian soups, puréed into Southeast Asian smoothies, mashed into sushi rolls in California and blended into ice-cream in Brazil. You can stuff it, batter it or cream it and spas use it in facials and skin and hair treatments. Its high fiber, cholesterol-lowering abilities and anti-oxidant benefits make this the perfect fruit. Just remember to enjoy it in moderation, as a good-sized avocado can pack over 300 calories! And if you're lucky enough to have access to a tree, keep in mind that those rock-hard avocados don't start ripening until *after* you pick them.

Festivals & Events

Semana Santa Palm Sunday is marked by a procession through the city streets. A major crafts competition takes place on this day and two weeks after Palm Sunday a week-long exhibition of Michoacán handicrafts fills the plaza.

Día de San Francisco St Francis, the patron saint of Uruapan, is honored with colorful festivities on October 4.

Festival del Cristo Rey On the last Sunday of October an evening procession parades an image of Christ along the town's winding streets, which are covered in murals made of flower petals or colored sawdust.

Feria del Aguacate The Avocado Fair erupts for three weeks in November/December and is celebrated with agricultural, industrial and handicraft exhibitions. Previous years have seen record setting attempts for the world's largest guacamole.

Festival de Coros y Danzas A Purépecha dance and choral contest held December 22.

Sleeping

Reserve a room ahead of time for the Día de Muertos (early November) and Semana Santa (March/April) festivities.

BUDGET

Campamento de Área de Montaña (☎ 523-23-09; Lenin s/n; camping per person M$54) Camp within a 182-hectare nature reserve located just 4km west of downtown. Register at Parque Nacional Barranca del Cupatitzio; ask to see the 'Oficina Área de Montaña' to enter the national park without paying admittance. The reserve is best reached by taxi.

Hotel Oseguera (☎ 523-98-56; Portal Degollado 2; s/d M$100/200) The best of the three super-cheapies on the east side of the plaza and that's not necessarily a compliment. Top floors have lovely mountain views.

Hotel del Parque (☎ 524-38-45; Independencia 124; s/d M$190/265; P) Convenient to the national park is this ageing, bargain hotel. Rooms are dark but quite clean – though front rooms funnel traffic noise.

Posada Morelos (☎ 523-23-02; Morelos 30; s/d with private bathroom M$200/300) A brightly painted courtyard hotel, with oddly raised bathroom units and beamed ceilings in the rooms. Grab an interior courtyard room, which are the best in the budget class. Test the beds first. Some share more spring than cushion.

MIDRANGE

Hotel Villa de Flores (☎ 524-28-00; Carranza 15; s/d M$350/480) Street noise and your first impressions fade as you wander deeper into this garden hotel. This place is a find, with pink-washed walls, dark wood headboards, tiled bathrooms and vaulted and beamed ceilings.

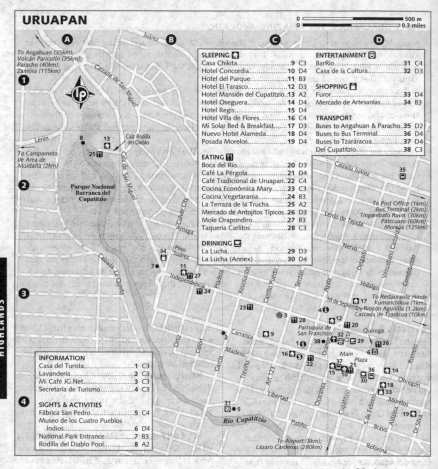

URUAPAN

SLEEPING
Casa Chikita	9 C3
Hotel Concordia	10 D4
Hotel del Parque	11 B3
Hotel El Tarasco	12 D3
Hotel Mansión del Cupatitzio	13 A2
Hotel Oseguera	14 D4
Hotel Regis	15 D4
Hotel Villa de Flores	16 C4
Mi Solar Bed & Breakfast	17 D3
Nuevo Hotel Alameda	18 D4
Posada Morelos	19 D4

EATING
Boca del Rio	20 D3
Café La Pérgola	21 D4
Café Tradicional de Uruapan	22 C4
Cocina Económica Mary	23 C3
Cocina Vegetarania	24 B3
La Terraza de la Trucha	25 A2
Mercado de Antojitos Típicos	26 D3
Mole Orapondiro	27 B3
Taqueria Carlitos	28 C3

DRINKING
La Lucha	29 D3
La Lucha (Annex)	30 D4

ENTERTAINMENT
BarRio	31 C4
Casa de la Cultura	32 D3

SHOPPING
Furor	33 D4
Mercado de Artesanías	34 B3

TRANSPORT
Buses to Angahuan & Paracho	35 D2
Buses to Bus Terminal	36 D4
Buses to Tzaráracua	37 D4
Del Cupatitzio	38 C3

INFORMATION
Casa del Turista	1 C3
Lavandería	2 C3
Mi Café JG.Net	3 C3
Secretaría de Turismo	4 C3

SIGHTS & ACTIVITIES
Fábrica San Pedro	5 C4
Museo de los Cuatro Pueblos Indios	6 D4
National Park Entrance	7 B3
Rodilla del Diablo Pool	8 A2

Nuevo Hotel Alameda (☎ 523-41-00; hotelalameda@vel.com; 5 de Febrero 11; s/d M$360/440; P ⊠ 🖳) Austin Powers would sleep well at this ageing business hotel with a retro switchboard and a funky, mod vibe that defines kitsch. Rooms are bright and clean, top floors have terrific views and it has wireless internet. Groovy, baby!

Hotel Regis (☎ 523-58-44; hotelregis@intermatsa.com.mx; Portal Carrillo 12; s/d M$365/540; P) This is the best value among the plaza hotels. You'll receive a warm reception and will probably enjoy the massive chandelier of dangling stars. The rooms have personality, with hand-painted sinks and headboard murals.

Hotel Concordia (☎ 523-04-00; www.hotelconcordia.com.mx; Portal Carrillo 8; s/d M$365/540) Clean, basic rooms with cable TV and a fabulous location right on the plaza. A nice value.

Casa Chikita (☎ 524-41-74; www.casachikita.com; Carranza 32; s/d M$380/707) This 19th-century house has just five guestrooms set around a garden decorated with local pottery. The rooms won't blow your mind, but they are comfortable and have nice accents – like granite or wooden counters in the bathroom, tiled floors and local art on the walls. Great value!

Hotel El Tarasco (☎ 524-15-00; contacto_hoteltarasco@hotmail.com; Independencia 2; s/d M$755/872; P ⊠ 🖳) Even the switchboard of this ageing hotel on the plaza is from the 1970s. But the creative plasterwork and mosaic bathroom counters in rooms with luscious mountain views keep it feeling youngish.

ourpick **Mi Solar Bed & Breakfast** (☎ 524-09-01; www.hotelmisolaruruapan.com; Delgado 10; r from M$795; P X X 🖳) Recently opened at the time of research, but already the best bed in town. It's a boutique property with 17 spacious rooms on three floors surrounding an atrium bar. Rooms have luscious king beds, high ceilings and wireless internet access. There's a small gym, sauna and it serves a full breakfast.

TOP END

Hotel Mansión del Cupatitzio (☎ 523-21-00; www .mansiondelcupatzio.com; Calz Rodilla del Diablo 20; r from M$1242; P X 🖳 🐾) A beautiful hacienda-style property at the north end of the Parque Nacional Barranca del Cupatitzio. The ageing rooms have a certain 1940s California bungalow charm and the rambling grounds are absolutely gorgeous. If only they would kill that evil elevator music. Discounts are available if you pay cash.

Eating

Hinde Kumanchikua (☎ 524-84-96; Chiapas 4; tacos M$8; 🕑 10am-3am Wed-Mon) After a drunken evening at Bar Rio you'll be eternally grateful for Uruapan's best late night *taqueria*. Munch beef chorizo or tacos *al pastor*, served with three fiery salsas.

Taquería Carlitos (cnr Serdán & Independencia; 6 tacos M$11; 🕑 9:30am-9pm) Locals line up around the block for Carlitos' crunchy, savory rolled tacos filled with beef, potatoes, beans and cheese. An order includes six tacos served in a plastic bag and splashed with red or green salsa. Beef sells out early.

Cocina Vegetarania (Independencia 113; mains M$25-35; 🕑 9am-7pm; V) This hole-in-the-wall vegan café is run by the surliest veggie broker on earth, but she does make pasta with soy chorizo and grills up veggie burgers. It may not be a pleasant meal, but it will be meatless.

Mole Orapondiro (Independencia 112; mains M$30-40, sauce M$40/liter; 🕑 9am-5pm) This sunny café specializes in one thing: a rich, thick and chocolaty *mole* sauce. Local ladies smuggle home bottles of it, so they can pass it off as their own. You can have it ladled over chicken, rice and beans and on *tortas*. Get here early because chicken always sells out.

Café La Pérgola (☎ 523-50-87; Portal Carrillo 4; mains M$30-85) Ambience is old school at this arched, cavernous café that serves everything from enchiladas to sandwiches to salads to cappuccinos. The clientele, mostly old men with backstory etched into their bones, is good fodder for sketch artists and photographers and it has a nice breakfast menu.

Cocina Económica Mary (☎ 519-48-69; Independencia 59; mains M$35; 🕑 8:30am-5.30pm Mon-Sat) This busy family joint just smells delicious. The open, cafeteria-style kitchen serves filling meals with your choice of main (eg, chicken *mole*, pulled pork with squash or *chiles rellenos*), along with soup, rice, beans and freshly made tortillas.

Boca Del Río (☎ 600-00-00; Delgado 2; tostadas M$7, cocteles M$35-60; 🕑 10am-5pm) *Ceviche* tostadas and fresh shrimp and octopus cocktails are the exclusive domain of this café tucked just behind Parroquia San Francisco. It's been here since 1974.

Café Tradicional de Uruapan (☎ 523-56-80; Carranza 5B; snacks & breakfast M$35-65; 🕑 8am-11pm) It's got burgers, hot dogs, quesadillas and subs and all manner of coffees, shakes and cakes. The charming beamed dining room is almost always packed.

ourpick **La Terraza de la Trucha** (☎ 524-86-98; Calz Rodilla del Diablo 13; mains M$70-80; 🕑 9am-6pm; P) Irresistibly nestled at the north entrance of the national park, you'll find a cozy table with shady cascade views and order the trout, of course. Get it grilled, crusted in macadamias or *a la tampiqueña* (with guacamole and beans). It comes with fresh chips and a searing salsa.

Drinking & Entertainment

ourpick **BarRio** (☎ 527-20-90; www.barriodeuruapan .com.mx; Treviño 57; cover M$50; 🕑 8pm-3am Wed-Sun) Located in the basement of an old, abandoned waterworks, this club is the perfect blend of sleek and comfortable and the best night out in Uruapan. There's a large dance floor packed with an exuberant, sexy crowd of 20-somethings, old stone walls that drip with river water, huge exposed pumps, wheels, belts and pipes overhead and a global progressive soundtrack (although musical style and DJs rotate nightly). Service is brilliant. It'll keep you drinking.

La Lucha (☎ 524-03-75; Ortiz 20; coffees M$30; 🕑 9am-9pm Mon-Sat) The dark, arched interior and the black-and-white photos on the wall give the place gravitas and will entice you to sit down with some good coffee.

Casa de la Cultura (☎ 524-76-13; Ortiz 1) This old megalith just north of the plaza has a quiet courtyard, ample public chill space, rotating contemporary art exhibits and it has the word on upcoming concerts and events.

Shopping

Local crafts, such as lacquered trays and boxes, can be found at **Mercado de Artesanías** (☿ 9am-6pm), opposite the entrance to Parque Nacional Barranca del Cupatitzio. The sinuous **Mercado de Antojitos Típicos** (☿ 8am-11pm) is ideal if you're in the market for candy, DVDs, strawberries, bras, cowboy boots, or a taco and it has a few thousand other items on offer. Fábrica San Pedro (p576) is good for textiles. If you want low prices on Italian designer jeans head to **Furor** (☎ 523-85-34; 5 de Febrero 31) two blocks south of the plaza.

Getting There & Around

Uruapan's bus terminal is 2km northeast of central Uruapan on the highway to Pátzcuaro and Morelia. It has a *caseta de teléfono* (public telephone call station), a cafeteria and a **left-luggage facility** (☿ 7am-11pm). Frequent destinations include those on the following table (price quotes are for 1st-class buses when available).

Destination	Fare	Duration	Frequency
Angahuan	M$16	1hr	hourly
Colima	M$252	6-8hr	4 daily
Guadalajara	M$210	4½hr	hourly
Lázaro Cárdenas	M$252	4hr	daily
Mexico City (Terminal Norte)	M$335	7hr	every 2 hrs
Mexico City (Terminal Poniente)	M$335	5½hr	every 2 hrs
Morelia	M$74	2hr	hourly
Paracho	M$16	1hr	hourly
Pátzcuaro	M$37	1hr	hourly
Tingambato	M$10	30min	Same buses as those to Pátzcuaro or Morelia
Zamora	M$65	2hr	hourly

Local buses marked 'Centro' run from just outside the bus terminal to the plaza (M$5). For taxis, buy a ticket inside the bus terminal (M$20). For the return trip catch a 'Central Camionera' bus from the south side of the plaza.

The car-rental agency **Del Cupatitzio** (☎ 523-11-81; autorent@prodigy.net.mx; M$700-850 per day) is located at the Hotel Plaza Uruapan.

AROUND URUAPAN
Cascada de Tzaráracua

Ten kilometers south of downtown Uruapan, the wild Rio Cupatitzio makes its last act count. It pumps hard over the vine covered, 30m-high red rock cliffs and crashes into a misty turquoise pool. This is the Tzaráracua **waterfall** (☎ 106-04-41; www.tzararcua.com.mx; admission M$10, cars extra M$5; ☿ 10am-6pm). On the meandering hike down the 557 slippery steps to the falls you'll see that the raging river has been dammed a few kilometers downstream. The tame lake set against rolling green hills is pretty enough, but it's also a sad fate considering the river's furious beauty. Once you reach the bottom you can forget all that and enjoy the power of the falls by hooking on to the author-tested, 96m **tirolesa** (M$50), a zip line that flies low across the river. Nice!

There's also a 20-minute hike upstream from Tzaráracua to the equally beautiful Tzararacuita, a smaller waterfall. This trail is not as well maintained, so bring waterproof sandals. To get here, follow the steep muddy track beyond the Tzaráracua bridge and after about 10 minutes turn right at the stone outcropping.

If you don't feel like walking down and back from the dusty parking lot, hire one of the lingering horses. They cost M$70 round-trip.

Hourly buses to Tzaráracua depart from in front of the Hotel Regis, on the south side of Uruapan's main plaza (M$5). Taxis cost M$80.

Tingambato

Stroll through luscious avocado groves to the beautiful **ruins** (admission M$34; ☿ 9am-6pm) of this ceremonial site, which predates the Tarascan Empire and thrived from about AD 450 to 900. They are located outside of Tingambato village, about 30km from Uruapan on the road to Pátzcuaro. The ruins, which include two plazas, three altars and a ball court (rare in western Mexico), have a Teotihuacán influence. There's also an 8m-high stepped pyramid and an underground tomb where a skeleton and 32 scattered skulls were found – hinting at beheading or trophy skull rituals.

Buses to Morelia leave from Uruapan' terminal every 20 minutes and stop in Tingambato (M$10, 30 minutes). The ruins are 1.4km downhill on Calle Juárez, the first street on the right as you enter town.

Paracho

☎ 423 / pop 16,100 / elevation 2220m

Paracho, 40km north of Uruapan on Hwy 37, is a small but lovely Purépecha town famous for its high-quality, handmade stringed instruments. If you're looking for a reasonably priced and well-made guitar, violin, cello or traditional Mexican *guitarrón* (Mexican stand-up bass), you've come to the right pueblo. There are dozens of guitar showrooms and workshops scattered around the bustling plaza. You can also attend free guitar concerts by first-rate musicians and watch some of the country's best luthiers at work. The liveliest time to come is during the annual **Feria Nacional de la Guitarra** (National Guitar Fair) in early August; it's a weeklong splurge of music, dance and exhibitions.

About two blocks southeast of the plaza is the **Centro para la Investigación y el Desarrollo de la Guitarra** (CIDEG; ☎ 525-01-90; www.cideg.org; cnr Nicolás Bravo & Hidalgo; admission free; ☾ 9am-1pm & 4-7pm Mon-Fri, 9am-1pm Sat). Among the intricately decorated guitars displayed at this museum – including classical, Flamenco, Hawaiian and steel-string varieties – is one with ample breasts and a woman's mouth for the sound hole. Very Freudian. CIDEG hosts free guitar concerts in its auditorium on the last Friday of every month.

If you're in town for the festival or simply want to stay the night in guitar country, try the new, clean and bright **Hotel Melinda** (☎ 525-00-80; 20 de Noviembre; s/d M$300/360; P). Reserve ahead during festival week. If you're hungry then run to the mercado, opposite the main plaza. Inside you'll find torta and taco stands, gorgeously caramelized rotisserie chickens and the wonderful, **El Pony**, a revelatory *carnitas* and *birria* stand. All it serves is meat. The lamb *birria* is slow cooked and steamed in its own juices. Grab a bar stool, buy it by the kilo (or any fraction thereof) and it will be placed on butcher paper in front of you. Soon an old lady will appear with warm tortillas and you will be crafting a series of unforgettable tacos, which you'll drench with El Pony's delicious *cilantro* heavy tomatillo salsa. Expect to spend less than M$30 for a full, carnivorous meal.

Galeana Ruta Paraíso buses depart Uruapan's bus terminal every 15 minutes (M$16, one hour) and stop along Calz Juárez on their way out of town (so you can avoid backtracking to the bus terminal). There's a stop at the corner of Venustiano Carranza, near the Juárez statue.

Zamora
☎ 351 / pop 125,700 / elevation 1560m
Zamora, a pleasant agricultural town known for its strawberries, is about 115km northwest of Uruapan and 190km southeast of Guadalajara. Pedestrian promenades meander around the lively plaza, which is the hotspot on Sunday nights when live music plays in the bandstand. The high-energy market sells the city's famous and delicious *dulces* (sweets).

For local information head to the **tourist office** (☎ 512-40-15; Morelos Sur 76; ☾ 9am-2pm & 4-7pm Mon-Sat, 10am-2pm Sun). There are plenty of banks with ATMs around the plaza.

Founded in 1574, Zamora has more than its share of churches, including the large, neo-Gothic **Catedral Inconclusa** (5 de Mayo Sur & Cazares Ote), started in 1898 and still not quite finished. Fifteen kilometers southeast of town at Tangancícuaro is the spring-fed and tree-shaded **Laguna de Camécuaro**, a sweet picnic spot

There are a few hotels downtown, which is just a short bus (M$5) or taxi (M$20) ride from the bus terminal. Sleep well at the quiet and good-value **Hotel Ana Isabel** (☎ 515-17-33; hana isabel_01@hotmail.com; Guerrero 108 Pte; s/d M$250/350; P) or the **Hotel Ram Val** (☎ 512-02-28; www.hotel ramval.com.mx; Amado Nervo 40; s/d M$356/616; P ✂). Zamora's ultra-cheapies are fleabags.

The bus terminal has regular connections to Guadalajara (M$128, 2¼ hours), Colima (M$210, five hours), Uruapan (M$105, two hours), Pátzcuaro (M$91, two hours), Morelia (M$112, 2½ hours) and Mexico City (M$392, six hours).

VOLCÁN PARICUTÍN
On February 20, 1943, Dionisio Pulido, a Purépecha farmer, was plowing his cornfield some 35km west of Uruapan when the ground began to quake and spurt steam, sparks and hot ash. The farmer struggled to cover the blast holes, but he quickly realized his futility and ran. Good thing, because like some Hollywood B-movie, a growling volcano began to rise. Within a year it had reached an elevation of 410m above the rolling farmland and its lava had flooded the Purépecha villages of San Salvador Paricutín and San Juan Parangaricutiro. Thankfully, the lava flowed slowly, giving the villagers plenty of time to escape.

The volcano continued to grow until 1952. Today its large black cone whispers warm steam in a few places, but otherwise appears dormant. Near the edge of the 20-sq-km lava field, the top of the ruined **Templo San Juan Parangaricutiro**, San Juan's stone church, protrudes eerily from a sea of black lava. Its tower and altar are the only visible traces of the two buried villages. It's a one-hour walk from where the bus lets you off in nearby Angahuan. Cross the highway and go down the street framed by the wire arch; after 10 minutes turn right at the main plaza, then after 200m go left at the fork. Keep on this road, which eventually leads out of town to the Centro Turístco de Angahuan (right). The easy trail, flanked by cattle fences, starts here. Alternatively, hire horses and a guide (M$250 to M$300 per person). Footing around the church site can be tricky and the black volcanic boulders are sharp, so be careful.

You can visit both the crater and the ruined church during one long, beautiful and bizarre day trip from Uruapan.

Arrive in Angahuan (35km from Uruapan) before 10am if you want to climb Paricutín. Once you step off the bus, guides with horses will offer their services to the ruined church, volcano, or both. Horses and a guide should cost M$400 to M$500 per person per day. Don't be nervous when the man you thought was your guide stops, dismounts and asks his 12-year-old son to lead you. Yes, it's strange and disorienting and it's also normal protocol. The volcano is a 14km round-trip that takes up to eight hours – of which you'll spend nearly six in an evil, unforgiving, wooden saddle – so your legs may cramp, your ass will bruise and your spine will tingle when the horse trots. You'll have to scramble the last few hundred meters up to the summit at 2800m. The view of the massive lava flow is mind-blowing, you'll hear faint announcements from the Angahuan PA system warbling on the wind and feel the steam rising from the earth. It's a rugged hike up, but you'll get to run, jump and slide down the deep volcanic sand on the descent then hit the San Juan church on the way back. The altar is almost always blessed with colorful offerings of candles and flowers and at the entrance you'll see **Maria's Café**. María is a Purépecha woman in traditional braids and colorful dress fixing fresh, blue corn quesadillas on an old, wood burning, oil-can skillet. Bring enough water, wear decent shoes (trainers will suffice) and an bum-pad perhaps and you'll have a good time.

If wooden saddles intimidate you (they should), you can walk to the volcano, but you'll still need a guide (M$300) as the trail through the pine forest can be hard to find. The relaxing hike through avocado groves, agave fields and wildflowers takes about eight hours.

ANGAHUAN
☎ 333 / pop 3000 / elevation 2693m

Angahuan, the nearest town to Volcán Paricutín, is a typical Purépecha town: there are wooden houses, dusty streets, more horses than cars, braided women in ankle-length skirts and colorful shawls and loudspeakers booming announcements in the Purépecha tongue. Greet locals with 'nar erandisti' (good morning) or 'nar chuscu' (good afternoon).

Sights
On the main plaza is the sensational 16th-century **Iglesia de Santiago Apóstol**. Candles and incense burn, fresh flowers crowd the altar and the detailed doorway was carved by a Moorish stonemason who accompanied the early Spanish missionaries here.

Sleeping
Centro Turístico de Angahuan (☎ 203-85-27; in Uruapan 523-39-34; angeles1946@hotmail.com; Camino al Paricutín s/n; campsites per person M$40, cabañas M$600/night; P) This 'tourist' complex feels like an old elementary school or summer camp. There's a cafeteria that shows a video about the eruption and terrific views of the lava field, the protruding San Juan church tower and the volcano itself. The basic, concrete cabañas sleep up to five people but are overpriced.

Cuartos Familiares (☎ 203-85-27; Camino al Paricutín s/n; s/d M$180/250; P) This is the best of the few sleeping options in Angahuan. The rustic cabins have adobe fireplaces and lovely tiled bathrooms and the saloon-like café has a full bar and serves breakfast, lunch and dinner. Look for the orange sign saying 'Cuartos Familiares' on the road to the ruined church, about 1km from the bus stop.

Getting There & Away
Angahuan is 35km from Uruapan. Galeana 2nd-class buses leave the Uruapan bus terminal for Angahuan every 30 minutes from 5am to 7pm (M$16, one hour). Alternatively, flag down a bus marked 'Los Reyes' on Calz Juárez (at Venustiano Carranza, near the Juárez statue) in Uruapan; this will save you backtracking to the bus terminal. Taxis charge M$220 for the same trip.

Buses return to Uruapan every 15 minutes until about 7pm and few cabs are available in town, so unless you've made previous arrangements you may have to hop a bus back.

Northern Central Highlands

Arid deserts to tropical forests, staunchly traditional to 'Americanized' modern, maize to pasta, the region covering the northern central highlands is as varied and colorful as its people, landscapes, food and culture. It was here that former mineral wealth created colonial cities, revolutionary activity left ghost towns in its wake and traditions – festivals, saints' days and celebrations – have survived for centuries.

The region is fondly referred to as the *Cuna de la Independencia* (Cradle of Independence) and it was here that many made their mark in the country's fight for autonomy. The colonial cities have fascinating foci: silver ridden Guanajuato and Zacatecas, plaza-filled San Luis Potosí, arty San Miguel de Allende and former 'activist' hot spots Dolores Hidalgo and Querétaro.

Once you've had your fill of cobbled streets and pretty plazas, cross the deserts and take in the high and dry 'ghost' towns of Pozos and Real de Catorce, national parks such as Parque de Órganos and (the biggest, most unmissable jewel of all) the Sierra Gorda Biosphere Reserve, the eastern arm of Querétaro state. This area boasts over 15 vegetation types and hot off-the-press tourism opportunities, including stunning hikes.

And as for the cuisine…travel a mere few kilometers for yet another take on a trusty tortilla or local dish: each region serves up its own specialties. Culture vultures will be well sated, too. From pre-Hispanic sites to art museums, concerts to nightlife, festivals to *callejoneadas*, this region enjoys pomp and ceremony…and knows how to put on a good (if noisy) party.

HIGHLIGHTS

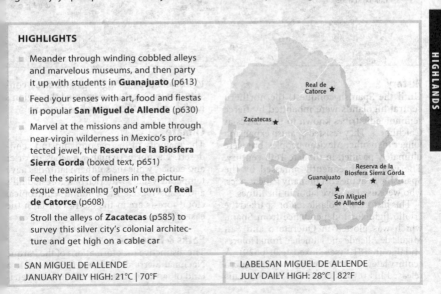

- Meander through winding cobbled alleys and marvelous museums, and then party it up with students in **Guanajuato** (p613)
- Feed your senses with art, food and fiestas in popular **San Miguel de Allende** (p630)
- Marvel at the missions and amble through near-virgin wilderness in Mexico's protected jewel, the **Reserva de la Biosfera Sierra Gorda** (boxed text, p651)
- Feel the spirits of miners in the picturesque reawakening 'ghost' town of **Real de Catorce** (p608)
- Stroll the alleys of **Zacatecas** (p585) to survey this silver city's colonial architecture and get high on a cable car

Real de Catorce ★

Zacatecas ★

Reserva de la Biosfera Sierra Gorda ★
Guanajuato ★
San Miguel de Allende ★

- SAN MIGUEL DE ALLENDE
JANUARY DAILY HIGH: 21°C | 70°F

- LABELSAN MIGUEL DE ALLENDE
JULY DAILY HIGH: 28°C | 82°F

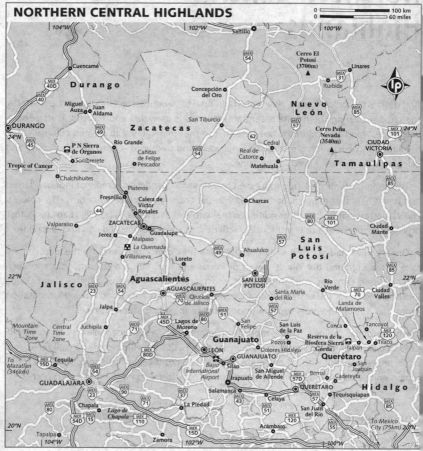

NORTHERN CENTRAL HIGHLANDS

History

Until the Spanish conquest, the northern central highlands were inhabited by fierce seminomadic tribes known to the Aztecs as Chichimecs. They resisted Spanish expansion longer than other Mexican peoples, but were ultimately pacified in the late 16th century. The wealth subsequently amassed by the Spanish was at the cost of many Chichimecs, who were used as slave labor in the mines.

This historically volatile region sparked the criollo fight for independence from Spain, which was plotted in Querétaro and San Miguel de Allende and launched from Dolores Hidalgo in 1810 (see boxed text, p629). A century later revolutionary Francisco Madero released his revolutionary Plan de San Luis

Potosí and the 1917 signing of Mexico's constitution in Querétaro cemented the region's leading role in Mexican political affairs.

Climate

The majority of the region is upland semi-desert. The northern higher reaches are drier and cooler, while the southern latitudes have temperate valleys with rich oak-forested hills and chaparral. The more humid semitropical cloud forests are in the Sierra Gorda in the east of the region.

Parks & Reserves

The distinctive rock formations of the Parque Nacional Sierra de Órganos (p595) create a land of fantastic towering sand castles petrified by time. Replicating organ pipes, among other shapes, this desert national park offers good camping and hidden hikes and has been used by the Hollywood film industry to depict the Wild West.

The diverse ecological zones within the Reserva de la Biosfera Sierra Gorda (p651), in the eastern part of Querétaro states contain little-explored jewels that reward the efforts required to reach them. Tucked into the cloud forests on the leeward side of the Sierra Madre Oriental are waterfalls, caves and excellent hiking opportunities (with new eco-friendly lodges), interspersed with populated mission towns.

Getting There & Around
The Aeropuerto Internacional del Bajío, half way between León and Guanajuato, is the major hub for the region's southern cities. Other airports, all with US flights (some via Mexico City), include Aguascalientes, San Luis Potosí and Zacatecas. Buses constantly ply the toll roads between Mexico City, Guadalajara, Querétaro and San Luis Potosí. These larger hubs, including Zacatecas and Aguascalientes, also host connections to northern Mexico, the US border and beyond. Frequent local buses efficiently connect the major cities and all points in between.

ZACATECAS STATE

The state of Zacatecas (zak-a-tek-as) is a dry, rugged, cactus-strewn expanse on the fringe of Mexico's northern semideserts. The state is best known for the wealthy silver city of the same name. Visitors can enjoy the region's historical and natural monuments: the mysterious ruins of La Quemada are a testament to centuries of cultures and the quirky rock formations of Parque Nacional Sierra de Órganos make a fascinating, if remote, getaway. The state is one of Mexico's largest in area (73,252 sq km) but smallest in population (1.37 million); it is believed that as many people again (1.5 million) from the state currently live in the United States.

ZACATECAS
☎ 492 / pop 123,000 / elevation 2445m
Set amid arid countryside, the most northern of Mexico's fabled silver cities, fascinating Zacatecas – a Unesco World Heritage site – runs along a narrow valley. The large

historic center is jam-packed with opulent colonial buildings, a stupendous cathedral, magnificent museums and steep, winding streets and alleys. Excellent restaurants and fine hotels make it a very comfortable location for any traveler.

The city has a legacy of historical highs and lows: it was here that Pancho Villa defeated a stronghold of soldiers (today he is still much feted by the locals). Here, too, thousands of indigenous slaves were forced by the Spanish to toil in the mines under terrible conditions. Today, travelers can have their own lofty experiences in a teleférico (aerial cable car) to the Cerro de la Bufa, an impressive rock outcrop; the trip affords great views of a collage of church domes and rooftops. Alternatively, you can drop below the surface to tour the infamous Edén mine, or vibrate to the rhythms of its underground disco.

History
Indigenous Zacatecos – one of the Chichimec tribes – mined local mineral deposits for centuries before the Spanish arrived; it's said that the silver rush here was started when a Chichimec gave a piece of the fabled metal to a conquistador. The Spaniards founded a settlement in 1548 and started mining operations that sent caravan after caravan of silver off to Mexico City, creating fabulously wealthy silver barons in Zacatecas.

By the early 18th century, the mines of Zacatecas were producing 20% of Nueva España's silver and the city became an important base for Catholic missionaries.

In the 19th century political instability diminished the flow of silver. Although silver production later improved under Porfirio Díaz, the revolution disrupted it. In 1914 in Zacatecas, Pancho Villa defeated a stronghold of 12,000 soldiers loyal to President Victoriano Huerta. After the revolution, Zacatecas continued to thrive on silver; today, the city's 200-year-old El Bote mine is still productive.

Orientation
The city center is in a valley between Cerro de la Bufa to the northeast and the smaller Cerro del Grillo to the northwest. Most attractions are within walking distance of the center; the cathedral is a good central landmark. The two busiest streets are Av Hidalgo, running roughly north–south, and Av Juárez,

running roughly east–west across the south end of Av Hidalgo. Av Hidalgo becomes Av González Ortega south of its intersection with Av Juárez.

Information

Banks in the center have ATMs and change cash and traveler's checks. Telephone *casetas* are in the bus station and around town, including Callejón de las Cuevas, off Av Hidalgo. Most internet cafés charge M$7 to M$15 per hour for internet access.

Fast Clean Lavandería (Villalpando 203) Wash, dry and delivery M$14 per kg

Hospital Santa Elena (☎ 924-29-28; www.hospital santaelena.com.mx; Guerrero 143)

Lavandería El Indio Triste (Tolosa 826) Wash, dry and fold service M$15 per kg

Post office (☎ 922-01-96; Allende 111; ⏰ 9am-4pm Mon-Fri, 9am-2pm Sat)

Sanborns (cnr Avs Hidalgo & Allende) Best international periodicals and book selection.

State Tourist Office (☎ 924-05-52, 800-712-40-78; www.turismozacatecas.gob.mx; Av Hidalgo 403; ⏰ 8am-8pm Mon-Sat, 10am-7pm Sun) Helpful staff (some speak English); basic maps available.

Vonex (Av Hidalgo 737) Internet access and cheap, internet-based long-distance phone calls.

Sights

This historic city – particularly its Unesco World Heritage-listed central district – has much to detain you for several days, from trips into an old silver mine to excellent museums and a trip to la Bufa by *teleférico*.

CATEDRAL

Built between 1729 and 1752, the pink-stone **cathedral** (admission free) on the south side of the Plaza de Armas is an ultimate expression of Mexican baroque.

The stupendous main facade is a wall of detailed carvings; this has been interpreted as a giant symbol of the tabernacle. A tiny figure of an angel holding a tabernacle is in the middle of the design, the keystone atop the round central window. Above this, in the third tier, is Christ and above Christ is God. The 12 Apostles feature, as does a smaller Virgin figure above the doorway.

The southern facade's central sculpture is of La Virgen de los Zacatecanos, the city's patroness. The north facade shows Christ crucified, attended by the Virgin Mary and St John.

PLAZA DE ARMAS

The plaza is the open space north of the cathedral. The **Palacio de Gobierno** on the plaza's east side was built in the 18th century for a colonial family. In the turret of its main staircase is a mural of the history of Zacatecas state, painted in 1970 by Antonio Rodríguez.

Across the road, the **Palacio de la Mala Noche** was built in the late 18th century for a mine owner and now houses state-government offices.

PLAZUELA FRANCISCO GOITIA

A block south of the cathedral, a broad flight of stairs descends from Av Hidalgo to Tacuba, forming a charming open space. The *plazuela*'s terraces are often used as an informal amphitheater by street performers.

North of the *plazuela*, the **Mercado González Ortega** is an impressive 1880s iron-columned building that used to hold Zacatecas' main market. In the 1980s the upper level was renovated into an upscale shopping center. The lower level was once used as *bodegas* (storage rooms) and now houses several bars and restaurants.

Opposite the *plazuela* on Av Hidalgo, the lovely 1890s **Teatro Calderón** (☎ 922-81-20) dates from the Porfiriato period and is as busy as ever with plays, concerts, films and art exhibitions.

PLAZUELA DE SANTO DOMINGO

A block west of the cathedral, this *plazuela* is dominated by the **Templo de Santo Domingo**. Although the church is done in a more sober baroque style than the cathedral, it has some fine gilded altars and a graceful horseshoe staircase. Built by the Jesuits in the 1740s, the church was taken over by Dominican monks when the Jesuits were expelled in 1767.

Nearby, the extraordinary **Museo Pedro Coronel** (☎ 922-80-21; Plaza de Santo Domingo s/n; admission M$20; ⏰ 10am-5pm Fri-Wed) is housed in a 17th-century former Jesuit college and is one of provincial Mexico's best art museums. Pedro Coronel (1923–85) was an affluent Zacatecan artist who bequeathed his collection of art and artifacts from all over the world, as well as his own works. The collection includes 20th-century works by Picasso, Rouault, Chagall, Kandinsky and Miró; some entertaining Hogarth lithographs; and fine ink drawings by Francisco de Goya. There are pre-Hispanic Mexican ar-

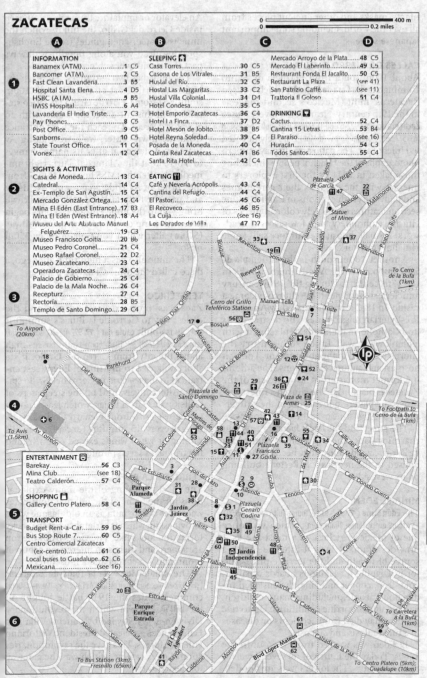

ZACATECAS

0 — 400 m
0 — 0.2 miles

INFORMATION
Banamex (ATM)......................1 C5
Bancomer (ATM)....................2 C5
Fast Clean Lavandería............3 B5
Hospital Santa Elena..............4 D5
HSBC (ATM).........................5 B5
IMSS Hospital........................6 A4
Lavandería El Indio Triste........7 C5
Pay Phones...........................8 C5
Post Office............................9 C5
Sanborns..............................10 C5
State Tourist Office.................11 C4
Vonex..................................12 C4

SIGHTS & ACTIVITIES
Casa de Moneda....................13 C4
Catedral..............................14 C4
Ex-Templo de San Agustín......15 C4
Mercado González Ortega......16 C4
Mina El Edén (East Entrance)...17 B3
Mina El Edén (West Entrance)..18 A4
Museo del Arte Abstracto Manuel
  Felguérez...........................19 C3
Museo Francisco Goitia..........20 B6
Museo Pedro Coronel.............21 C4
Museo Rafael Coronel............22 D2
Museo Zacatecano.................23 C4
Operadora Zacatecas.............24 C4
Palacio de Gobierno...............25 C4
Palacio de la Mala Noche........26 C4
Receptur.............................27 C4
Rectoría..............................28 B5
Templo de Santo Domingo.....29 C4

SLEEPING
Casa Torres..........................30 C5
Casona de Los Vitrales...........31 B5
Hostal del Río.......................32 C5
Hostal Las Margaritas............33 C2
Hostal Villa Colonial..............34 D1
Hotel Condesa......................35 C5
Hotel Emporio Zacatecas........36 C4
Hotel La Finca.......................37 D2
Hotel Mesón de Jobito...........38 B5
Hotel Reyna Soledad.............39 C4
Posada de la Moneda.............40 C4
Quinta Real Zacatecas............41 B6
Santa Rita Hotel....................42 C4

EATING
Café y Nevería Acrópolis.........43 C4
Cantina del Refugio...............44 C4
El Pastor..............................45 C6
El Recoveco.........................46 B5
La Cuija...............................(see 16)
Los Dorados de Villa..............47 D2

Mercado Arroyo de la Plata......48 C5
Mercado El Laberinto.............49 C5
Restaurant Fonda El Jacalito....50 C5
Restaurant La Plaza...............(see 41)
San Patrizio Caffè..................(see 11)
Trattoria Il Goloso.................51 C4

DRINKING
Cactus................................52 C4
Cantina 15 Letras.................53 B4
El Paraíso.............................(see 16)
Huracán..............................54 C3
Todos Santos.......................55 C5

ENTERTAINMENT
Barekay..............................56 C3
Mina Club...........................(see 18)
Teatro Calderón...................57 C4

SHOPPING
Gallery Centro Platero...........58 C4

TRANSPORT
Budget Rent-a-Car................59 D6
Bus Stop Route 7..................60 C5
Centro Comercial Zacatecas
  (ex-centro).........................61 C6
Local buses to Guadalupe........62 C6
Mexicana............................(see 16)

NORTHERN CENTRAL HIGHLANDS

tifacts, masks and other ancient pieces from all over the world, including some important Japanese screens.

CALLES DR HIERRO & AUZA

About 100m south from Plazuela de Santo Domingo is the **Casa de Moneda**, which housed Zacatecas' mint (Mexico's second-biggest) in the 19th century. Nearby, the lovely **Museo Zacatecano** (☎ 922-65-80; Dr Hierro 301; adult/concession M$15/7.50; ☑ 10am-5pm Wed-Mon) is largely devoted to Huichol art. The patio area displays superb photographs of the Huichol people (including those taken in 1934 by the first explorers to interact with the groups), their ceremonies and daily life (with captions in English). One section features exquisitely colorful pieces of Huichol embroidery and a few pieces of bead-work. A small shop at the entrance sells some Huichol craftwork.

Another 100m south is the **Ex-Templo de San Agustín**, built for Augustinian monks in the 17th century. During the 19th-century anticlerical movement, the church became a casino. In 1882 it was purchased by American Presbyterian missionaries who destroyed its 'too Catholic' main facade, replacing it with a blank white wall. In the 20th century the church returned to the government. Today it hosts art and cultural exhibitions. The adjoining former monastery is now the seat of the Zacatecas bishopric. The church's finest feature is the plateresque carving of the conversion of St Augustine over the north doorway.

The street ends at **Jardín Juárez**, a tiny but charming park. The Universidad Autónoma de Zacatecas' administrative headquarters are housed in the neoclassical **Rectoría** building on its west side.

MINA EL EDÉN

The **Edén Mine** (☎ 922-30-02; tours adult/child M$60/30; ☑ tours every 15min 10am-6pm), which was once one of Mexico's richest, is a must-see as it provides dramatic insight into the region's source of wealth and the terrible price paid for it. Digging for fabulous hoards of silver, gold, iron, copper and zinc, the enslaved indigenous people, including many children, worked under horrific conditions. Up to five people a day died from accidents or diseases like tuberculosis and silicosis.

El Edén was worked from 1586 until the 1960s. Today the fourth of its seven levels is open to visitors. The lower levels are flooded.

An elevator or miniature train takes you deep inside Cerro del Grillo, the hill in which the mine is located. Then guides (some English-speaking) lead you along floodlit walkways past shafts and over subterranean pools.

The mine has two entrances. To reach the higher one (the east entrance), walk 100m southwest from Cerro de Grillo *teleférico* station; from this entrance, tours start with an elevator descent. To reach the west entrance from the town center, walk west along Av Juárez and stay on it after its name changes to Torreón at the Alameda. Turn right immediately after the IMSS hospital (bus 7 from the corner of Av Hidalgo goes up Av Juárez and past the hospital) and a short walk will bring you to the mine entrance. Tours begin here with a trip on the narrow-gauge railway (540m) after which you walk another 350m or so.

The mine also has a nighttime alter ego, a disco called the Mina Club (see p592).

TELEFÉRICO

Zacatecas' most exhilarating ride and the easiest way to Cerro de la Bufas's summit is the Swiss-built **cable car** (☎ 922-01-70; adult/child/senior M$24/11/18; ☑ 10am-6pm) that crosses high above the city from Cerro del Grillo. It's a short walk east from Mina El Edén (east entrance) to the *teleférico*'s Cerro del Grillo station. Alternatively, huff up the steep steps of Callejón de García Rojas, which lead straight to the *teleférico* from Genaro Codina. Cars depart every 15 minutes (except when it's raining or when winds exceed 65km/h) and the trip takes seven minutes.

CERRO DE LA BUFA

The most appealing of the many explanations for the name of the hill that dominates Zacatecas is that 'bufa' is an old Basque word for wineskin, which is certainly what the rocky formation looks like. The views from the top are superb and there's an interesting group of monuments, a chapel and a museum.

The small **Museo de la Toma de Zacatecas** (☎ 922-80-66; adult/concession M$12/6; ☑ 10am-4:30pm) commemorates the 1914 battle fought on the hill's slopes in which the revolutionary División del Norte, led by Pancho Villa and Felipe Ángeles, defeated President Victoriano Huerta's forces. This gave the revolutionaries control of Zacatecas, which was the gateway to Mexico City.

La Capilla de la Virgen del Patrocinio, adjacent to the museum, is named after the patron saint of miners. Above the altar of this 18th-century chapel is an image of the Virgin said to be capable of healing the sick. Thousands of pilgrims flock here each year on September 8, when the image is carried to the cathedral.

Facing the chapel stand three imposing equestrian **statues** of the victors of the battle of Zacatecas – Villa, Ángeles and Pánfilo Natera.

From the right of the statues, a paved path along the foot of the rocky hilltop leads to the **Mausoleo de los Hombres Ilustres de Zacatecas**, with the tombs of Zacatecan heroes from 1841 to the present.

An exciting and convenient way to ascend la Bufa (to the church and museum) is by teleférico (see opposite). Alternatively, you can walk up by starting at Calle del Ángel from the cathedral's east end. To reach it by car, take Carretera a la Bufa, which begins at Av López Velarde, a couple of kilometers east of the center. A taxi costs around M$40. You can return to town by the teleférico or by a footpath leading downhill from the statues.

MUSEO DE ARTE ABSTRACTO MANUEL FELGUÉREZ

This **art museum** (☎ 924-37-05; Ex-Seminario de la Purísima Concepción; adult/concession M$20/10; ☺ 10am-5pm Wed-Mon) is worth visiting for the building alone; originally a seminary, it was later used as a prison and has been renovated to create some remarkable exhibition spaces, transforming the former dark, depressing cells and steel walkways into a beautiful site.

It has a stunning and varied collection of abstract art, particularly the work of Zacatecan artist Manuel Felguérez.

MUSEO RAFAEL CORONEL

The extraordinary **Museo Rafael Coronel** (☎ 922-81-16; cnr Abasolo & Matamoros; adult/senior M$20/10; ☺ 10am-5pm Thu-Tue) is not to be missed. Imaginatively housed in the ruins of the lovely 16th-century ex-Convento de San Francisco, it houses Mexican folk art collected by the Zacatecan artist Rafael Coronel, brother of Pedro Coronel and son-in-law of Diego Rivera. The highlight is the astonishing, colorful display of over 3000 masks (the remaining 7,000 are in storage) used in traditional dances and rituals. Also on display are pottery, puppets, instruments, pre-Hispanic objects and sketches by Rivera.

MUSEO FRANCISCO GOITIA

The **Museo Francisco Goitia** (☎ 922-02-11; Estrada 101; adult/concession M$20/10; ☺ 10am-4:45pm Tue-Sun) displays work by several 20th-century Zacatecan artists, including some evocative paintings of indigenous people by Goitia (1882–1960) himself. Other artists represented include Pedro Coronel, Rafael Coronel and Manuel Felguérez. The museum is in a former governor's mansion, above Parque Enrique Estrada and is worth the short walk.

Tours

Agencies run city tours and excursions to nearby places of interest, such as a city tour including the mine and the teleférico (4 hrs, M$220); Guadalupe (four hours, M$200); the archaeological site of La Quemada (six hours, M$250); and Fresnillo/Plateros (four hours, M$200). Agencies recommended for their longevity and professionalism include:

Operadora Zacatecas (☎ 924-00-50; opzac@prodigy .net.mx; Av Hidalgo 630)

Recepturz (☎ 925-24-03; www.recepturz.com; Hidalgo 326-1) English-speaking guides can be arranged.

Festivals & Events

La Morisma Usually held on the last weekend in August. Features a spectacular mock battle commemorating the triumph of the Christians over the Muslims (Moors) in old Spain. Two rival 'armies' – over 2000 participants – parade through the streets in the mornings, then, accompanied by bands of musicians, enact two battle sequences that take place between Lomas de Bracho and Cerro de la Bufa.

Feria de Zacatecas Annual fair during the first three weeks in September. Renowned matadors fight famous local bulls. There are also charreadas (rodeos), concerts, plays, film festivals and agricultural and craft shows. On September 8 the image of La Virgen del Patrocinio is carried to the cathedral from its chapel on Cerro de la Bufa.

Festival Internacional de Teatro de Calle In mid-October, drama takes to the streets in this vibrant week-long celebration of street theater.

Sleeping

Rates for midrange and top-end accommodations in Zacatecas fluctuate considerably throughout the year. They tend to hike their rates during Zacatecas' high seasons – September's festivals, Christmas and Semana Santa.

NORTHERN CENTRAL HIGHLANDS

BUDGET

Hostal Las Margaritas (☎ 925-17-11; lasmargarita shostal@hotmail.com; Calle Segunda de las Margaritas 105; dm/r M$80/110; 🖳) An excellent hostel with a choice of bright dorms and private rooms (all with shared bathroom) and services. There are great places to chill: in a large lounge below or on a massive, sunny rooftop terrace, where there's also a sizeable kitchen. It's in a tranquil part of town behind the Museo el Arte Abstracto Manuel Felguérez.

Hostal Villa Colonial (☎ /fax 922-19-80; hostalvilla colonial@hotmail.com; cnr Calle 1 de Mayo & Callejón Mono Prieto; dm/d M$90/190, d with bathroom M$250-350; 🖳) This lively, HI-affiliate offers a range of accommodations and is *the* rendezvous point for travelers. Dorms have bunks with tiny shared bathrooms; newer double rooms have en-suite bathroom and TV and some more recent and comfortable doubles (plus those with kitchenettes) are located nearby. Amenities include two kitchens, a cable TV/DVD, a lounge, bar, rooftop patio and book exchange. Friendly multilingual owner Ernesto and his staff go out of their way to help guests and also arrange tours to nearby areas.

Hostal del Río (☎ 924-00-35; Av Hidalgo 116; r/tr M$275/400) A realty's advertisement would say that this friendly, rambling and centrally located old place has potential. The spacious, worn rooms upstairs have character, but the downstairs dwellings (former stables) have no windows.

MIDRANGE

All the places reviewed here have in-room phones and TV.

Hotel Condesa (☎ 922-11-60; www.hotelcondesa.com .mx; Av Juárez 102; s/d/tr M$400/490/530) The Condesa's 60 modern rooms, which surround a massive covered courtyard, are pleasant and good value for the price. Most have external facing windows, but few have views. An attached restaurant serves breakfast (M$44 to M$66) and meals.

Posada de la Moneda (☎ 922-08-81; Av Hidalgo 413; s/d/ste M$500/660/950) This imposing old building is a bit like a well-loved sombrero: slightly worn, but comfortable and not tattered enough to discard. The rooms themselves lack old-fashioned charm but the hotel has a perfect location near the cathedral.

Hotel Reyna Soledad (☎ /fax 922-07-90; www.hos talreynasoledad.com.mx; Tacuba 170; r M$820; 🅿) Set in a converted 17th-century convent, the colo-

nial patios of this perfectly located place are tranquil and charming. The rooms are rustic (in a pine-furniture kind of way).

TOP END

Casona de los Vitrales (☎ 92-500-96; www.lacaso nadelosvitrales.com; Callejón del Espejo; s/d/ste M$1170/1520/2106) Travelers report positive experiences in this comfortable – but not over-the-top – hotel. It's in a lovely location overlooking Alameda. Some rooms are small (the suites are better) and have internal-facing windows. Rates listed here are their (highest) Semana Santa rates; they are significantly lower at other times.

Hotel La Finca (☎ 925-03-10; www.lafincadelminero .zac.com.mx; Matamoros s/n; r M$1240) Don't be put off by the price – it halves outside of high season. La Finca's 48 rooms face onto open patios (hurray!) and are simple, but comfortable and light. There's even heating for the cooler winter months.

Hotel Mesón de Jobito (☎ /fax 924-17-22, 800-021-00-40; www.mesondejobito.com; Jardín Juárez 143; r/ste from M$1674/1755; 🅿 🗶 🖳) Guests come here to soak up old-fashioned charm, service and a sense of history. This large place has 53 finely decorated, luxurious rooms, two excellent restaurants, bar and lobby (plus a slanting balcony, a legacy of its construction 200 years ago). Its buffet breakfast is popular with the public.

Quinta Real Zacatecas (☎ 922-91-04, 800-500-40-00; www.quintareal.com; Rayón 434; ste from US$300; 🅿 🗶 🕾) It's worth seeing red (in terms of your bank balance) to experience this luxury treat. Spectacularly situated and around the country's oldest – now retired – bullring and near El Cubo aqueduct, the 49-room hotel is one of Mexico's most contemporary and fetching. The least expensive rooms are spacious, comfortable master suites. An elegant restaurant and bar, La Plaza (see opposite), is in the former holding pens.

Other recommendations:

Casa Torres (☎ 925-32-66; www.hotelcasatorres.com; 1 de Mayo; r M$900, ste from M$1380) A small, new and sleek boutique hotel with original artworks and a top-floor restaurant.

Hotel Emporio Zacatecas (☎ 925-65-00, 01-800-800-61-61; www.hotelesemporio.com; Av Hidalgo 703; s/d/ste M$1930/2050/3276; 🅿 🗶 🕾) Superb location, luxurious rooms and delightful terrace areas.

Santa Rita Hotel (☎ 925-41-41, 800-560-81-15; www.hotelsantarita.com; Av Hidalgo 507A; r M$1751-

2462, ste M$2570; (P X Q) A stylish, contemporary and cosmopolitan choice. Disappointingly, some of the 35 suites have internal facing windows.

Eating

There are some excellent Mexican and international restaurants serving a range of fare. Local specialties feature ingredients like nopal and pumpkin seeds.

In the morning, look around Av Tacuba for *burros* (donkeys) carrying pottery jugs of *aguamiel* (honey water), a nutritional drink derived from the maguey cactus. The two central produce markets are Mercado El Laberinto and Mercado Arroyo de la Plata.

San Patrizio Caffé (☎ 922-43-99; Av Hidalgo 403C; drinks & snacks M$18-60; ☯ 10am-10pm Mon-Sat, 5-10pm Sun) The nicest café in town also does the best cappuccinos. It has relaxing courtyard seating, light snacks, Italian brand coffee and an array of Italian sodas. Plus there's wi-fi.

El Pastor (☎ 922-16-35; Independencia 214; mains M$22-50; ☯ 8am-9pm) You come to this no-nonsense, family-run eatery for the food (not the décor). It dishes out charcoal-roasted chicken and Mexican favorites.

our pick Los Dorados de Villa (☎ 922-57-22; Plazuela de García 1314; mains M$30-65; ☯ 3pm-1am Mon-Sat, 3-11pm Sun) You may have to fight to get into this popular revolutionary-themed restaurant: knock at the door – it's always locked. It's full of atmosphere and relics and serves up a delicious array of everything – except Pancho Villa himself. Don't miss the *enchiladas valentinas* (M$60). Oh and for posterity, a flying visit to the toilet may knock you off your perch! (The toilet alcove is filled with birds – you have to walk through the aviary to get to your cubicle.)

Café y Nevería Acrópolis (☎ 922-12-84; cnr Av Hidalgo & Plazuela Candelario Huizar; mains M$31-100) Near the cathedral, this Greek-owned café is popular with locals and visitors more for its location than its meals – light snacks and coffees.

Restaurant Fonda El Jacalito (☎ 922-07-71; Av Juárez 18; mains M$42-80; ☯ 8am-10:30pm) This bright, airy and very local place offers set breakfasts from M$42, a good *comida corrida* (M$60) and tasty versions of traditional favorites.

Cantina del Refugio (☎ 925-3771; Dr Hierro 409; mains M$45-120; ☯ noon-3am Mon-Sat) This all-out festive Mexican place has hearty servings of reasonably-priced and tasty Mexican fare, grilled meats and draught beer (with all sorts of drinking deals depending on the day).

El Recoveco (☎ 924-20-13; Torreón 513; buffets M$55-65; ☯ 8:30am-7pm) Popular all-you-can-eat breakfast and lunch buffets with Mexican delights, in a friendly, unpretentious, family-run restaurant.

Trattoria Il Goloso (☎ 123-53-99; Dr Hierro 400; mains M$65-120; ☯ 2-9:30pm Tue-Sat, 1-6pm Sun) Trade the tacos for a tasty Italian pasta in this cozy Sicilian-themed place, behind San Patrizio Caffé. Chef Stefano will whip up *squisito* Italian dishes with all the trimmings: cracked pepper, Italian oils and balsamic vinegar.

La Cuija (☎ 922-82-75; Tacuba 5; mains M$100-150; ☯ 1-10pm Mon-Sat) This romantic, special-occasion place, below Mercado González Ortega, has white tablecloths and professional, how-tied waiters.

Restaurant La Plaza (☎ 922-91-04; Quinta Real Zacatecas, Rayón 434; mains M$140-300) The Quinta Real's elegant dining room is especially memorable for its outlook to the aqueduct and bullring, as well as for its refined ambience and superb international cuisine. Charge in for a Sunday brunch (M$180) or an evening cocktail in the former bull-holding pens. Reservations recommended.

Drinking

Zacatecas has a particularly good late-night scene. Things hot up after 9pm in bars and 11pm in clubs.

Cantina 15 Letras (☎ 922-01-78; Martires de Chicago 309; ☯ 2pm-3am Mon-Fri) Stop for a drink at this sometimes smoky and often crowded classic, filled with bohemians, drunks and poets. Photos portray Zacatecas of old; the art showcases some well-known local artists.

El Paraíso (☎ 922-61-64; cnr Hidalgo & Plazuela Goitia; ☯ 2pm-1am Mon-Fri) This smart bar in the southwest corner of the Mercado González Ortega attracts a friendly, varied, mostly 30s clientele; it's busiest on Friday and Saturday.

Todos Santos (☎ 925-46-83; Aguascalientes 235; ☯ 2pm-3am Tue-Sat) A foreigner-friendly, fun bar, with a relaxed atmosphere and long hours. Great place to kick back over a few tequilas and excellent mariachi band.

Huracán (☎ 925-22-11; Genaro Codina 752; ☯ 6pm-3am) This fun bar is a quirky tribute to both kitsch and Huracán, Mexico's favorite champion of *lucha libre* (wrestling). The walls are covered in funky 1960s-style florals superimposed with Huracán's wrestling mask. You can battle your way through a *misil*, a large cylinder filled with 3½ liters of beer (M$90).

Cactus (☎ 922-05-09; Av Hidalgo 634; ☺ 8:30pm-3am Mon-Sat) Loud and happening, the action takes place in a number of rooms to cater for billiards, karaoke, salsa and drinking.

Entertainment

Ask at the tourist office for a copy of the monthly *Agenda Cultural*.

Mina Club (☎ 922-30-02; Dovali s/n; www.minaeleden .com.mx; cover M$100; ☺ 10pm-3am Thu-Sat) Strike it lucky in this unique night club – the tunnel of the Mina El Edén. A mix of electronic music and Spanish pop is the soundtrack to the essential Zacatecas nightlife experience. In the high season dig in by 10pm to avoid missing out.

Teatro Calderón (☎ 922-81-20; Av Hidalgo s/n; ☺ 10am-9pm) This top venue hosts a variety of cultural events including theater, dance and music performances. Check with the tourist office (p586) for current events.

Barekay (☎ 923-80-02; Grillo s/n, bar/disco 10pm-3am Fri & Sat) Mina Club's polar opposite, this happening disco is at the other entrance to the mine, views overlooking the city. Plays a mix of techno and pop.

Shopping

Zacatecas is known for silver and leather products and colorful sarapes. Try along Arroyo de la Plata (and its indoor market) or the upmarket Mercado González Ortega (p586).

The Zacatecas silversmith industry is being revived in a number of workshops at the **Centro Platero** (☎ 899-09-94; ☺ 9am-6pm Mon-Fri, 10am-3pm Sat), a few kilometers east of town at the 18th-century ex-Hacienda de Bernardez on the road to Guadalupe. Tour companies (see p589) can arrange visits, or you can make your own way there by taxi (around M$30 to M$40). Alternatively, shop in its **gallery** (☎ 925-35-50; Villalpando 406; ☺ 10am-7pm) in town.

Getting There & Away

AIR

Zacatecas' airport is 20km north of the city. Mexicana and Click Mexicana fly direct daily

DAILY BUSES FROM ZACATECAS

Destination	Fare	Duration	Frequency
Aguascalientes	1st-class M$91	2hr	frequent (Futura)
	2nd-class M$77-64	3hr	hourly (Estrella Blanca, Transportes de Guadalupe)
Durango	1st-class M$202	4½-6hr	13 daily (Ómnibus de México, Transportes del Norte)
	2nd-class M$170	7hr	6 daily (Estrella Blanca)
Fresnillo	1st-class M$35	1-1½hr	hourly (Transportes del Norte)
	2nd-class M$35	1-1½hr	hourly from main bus station (Estrella Blanca, Camiones de los Altos)
Guadalajara	1st-class M$261	4-5hr	hourly (Ómnibus de México, Chihuahuenses, Transportes del Norte)
	2nd-class M$230	7hr	hourly (Estrella Blanca, Rojo de los Altos)
Guanajuato	–	–	Take a León bus and change there for Guanajuato.
León	M$167	3-4hr	frequent (Ómnibus de México, Futura, Transportes del Norte)
Mexico City (Terminal Norte)	deluxe M$610	8hr	4 daily (ETN)
	1st-class M$459	6-8hr	17 daily (Futura, Chihuahuenses, Ómnibus de México)
Monterrey	1st-class M$293	7hr	9 daily (Transportes del Norte)
	2nd-class M$250	8hr	4 daily (Estrella Blanca, Rojo de los Altos)
Querétaro	1st-class M$303	6hr	hourly (Futura, Chihuahuenses)
San Luis Potosí	1st-class M$120	3hr	hourly (Futura, Ómnibus de México, Chihuahuenses)
	2nd-class M$110	3½hr	5 daily (Estrella Blanca)

Omnibus de México and Estrella Blanca buses also run to Sombrerete.

to/from Mexico City and Tijuana and weekly to/from Chicago and Los Angeles.
Mexicana and **Click Mexicana** (☎ 922-74-29; Av Hidalgo 406-408)

BUS

Zacatecas' main bus station is on the southwest edge of town, around 3km from the center. Many buses are *de paso* (which means they stop here en route between other cities). The station has a luggage checkroom, a pharmacy and telephone *casetas*. The former bus station, Centro Comercial Zacatecas (the 'ex-centro'), is on Blvd López Mateos and has buses for local destinations including Fresnillo and Villanueva (for La Quemada).

See the table opposite for daily departures. There are also frequent buses to Jerez and Torreón and several a day to Chihuahua, Ciudad Juárez, Saltillo and Nuevo Laredo. Durango-bound buses stop in Sombrerete and depart hourly from the central bus station (M$120).

CAR & MOTORCYCLE

Rental prices begin from around M$600 or M$700 per day, with week-long discount packages also available.
Avis (☎ 922-30-03; López Mateos 103)
Budget Rent-a-Car (☎ 922-94-58; Blvd López Mateos 202)

Getting Around

The easiest way to get to/from the airport is by taxi (M$200).

Buses 7 and 8 provide a good tour of the center. Bus 8 from the bus station (M$4) runs directly to the cathedral. Heading out of the center, buses go south on Villalpando. Bus 7 runs from the bus station to the corner of Avs González Ortega and Juárez. Taxis from the bus station to the center cost around M$30 to M$40.

GUADALUPE

☎ 492 / pop 99,572

About 10km east of Zacatecas, Guadalupe boasts a fascinating historic former monastery featuring one of Mexico's best colonial-art collections. The monastery's impressive church attracts pilgrims to honor the country's beloved Virgin. You'll need a couple of hours to wander through the monastery. The quaint plaza, Jardín Juarez, is lined with antique and handicrafts stores.

The **Convento de Guadalupe** was established by Franciscan monks in the early 18th century as an apostolic college. It developed a strong academic tradition and was a base for missionary work in northern Nueva España until the 1850s. The convent now houses the **Museo Virreinal de Guadalupe** (☎ 923-23-86; Jardín Juárez s/n; admission M$37, Sun free; ⌚ 9am-6pm), with the building's original religious paintings by Miguel Cabrera, Juan Correa, Antonio Torres and Cristóbal Villalpando. Wandering through the building is a delight; note the extraordinary perspective of the paintings in the cloisters from where you stand. Visitors can see part of the library and its 9000 original volumes (the oldest dates to 1529 and thousands are in storage), and step into the choir on the church's upper floor, with its fine carved and painted chairs (being renovated and inaccessible at time of research). The beautifully decorated 19th-century **Capilla de Nápoles**, on the church's north side, is open for special occasions only.

Beside the Museo Virreinal, the **Museo Regional de Historia** (☎ 923-20-89; admission free; ⌚ 9am-6pm Tue-Sun) has temporary exhibitions.

The museum hosts a cultural festival at the end of September and the town holds an annual fair during the first two weeks of December, focused on the **Día de la Virgen de Guadalupe** (December 12).

Transportes de Guadalupe buses run between Zacatecas and Guadalupe every few minutes (M$4, 20 minutes); catch one at the bus stop on Blvd López Mateos opposite the old bus station. Disembark at a small plaza in the center of Guadalupe and walk along Madero for 250m to Jardín Juárez, a sizable plaza. The museums are on the plaza's far side.

PLATEROS & FRESNILLO

☎ 493 / Plateros pop 4540; Fresnillo pop 110,892

The village of Plateros, 63km north of Zacatecas, is home to the **Santuario de Plateros**, one of Mexico's most-visited shrines. This is due to miracles attributed to *El Santo Niño de Atocha*, a image of baby Jesus (wearing a colonial pilgrim's feathered hat) that sits on the altar of the 18th-century church. Fresnillo, 5km southwest of Plateros, is a busy but unexciting town, and a transportation hub for pilgrims heading to Plateros. If you're interested in Mexican Catholicism, the shrine is interesting. Otherwise, give both places a miss.

The cloisters of Santuario de Plateros are plastered with thousands of old *retablos* (ex-voto paintings) and more recent paraphernalia, giving thanks to the Santo Niño for responding to prayers ranging from surviving traffic accidents to success in business ventures. The streets around the church are lined with stalls selling gaudy religious artifacts.

The few hotels in Plateros for pilgrims planning to attend 7am Mass aren't very restful; Fresnillo has better hotels.

Hotel Lirmar (☎ 932-45-98; Durango 400, Fresnillo; s/d/tr M$200/250/310; P) Opposite Fresnillo's bus terminal, this reasonably modern place has clean, comfortable rooms.

Hotel Casa Blanca (☎ 932-00-14; García Salinas 503, Fresnillo; s/d/tr M$396/459/522) Three blocks east of Jardín Hidalgo, this place caters to business travelers.

Tour operators in Zacatecas offer organized trips to Plateros (see p589) To get to/from Platero you must go via Fresnillo. Fresnillo's bus station is on Ébano, 1km northeast of the town center on bus 3. For Plateros, buy a ticket at the Parques Industriales counter for an hourly, 2nd-class bus (M$7). Local bus 6 (M$7) also goes to Plateros from Emiliano Zapata, 2½ blocks east of Jardín Madero.

From Fresnillo, regular 1st-class buses serve Durango (M$152, 3½ hours), Torreón (M$234, five hours) and Zacatecas (M$31, one hour); 2nd-class buses are even more frequent.

JEREZ
☎ 494 / pop 38,624
The delightful country town of Jerez, 30km southwest of Zacatecas, is as Mexican as a tortilla. It is a great place to watch the local action, especially on Sunday – market day – when saddle-bound *rancheros* drink outside the saloons. It has some fine 18th- and 19th-century buildings. Jerez holds a lively 10-day Easter fair, featuring, among other activities, *charreadas* and cockfights.

Orientation & Information
Jardín Páez, the pretty main plaza, has an old-fashioned gazebo, trees and benches. The **tourist information office** (☎ 945-51-66; Hospicio 73) also has a **kiosk** (☯ 10am-4pm Mon-Sun) in the plaza. **Compu-Centro** (Bizarra Capital 44; per hr M$10; ☯ 10am-9pm), is a few blocks south of the plaza. Banks (with ATMs) and phones are around the plaza.

Sights
The 18th-century **Parroquia de la Inmaculada Concepción** and the 19th-century **Santuario de la Soledad** have fine stone carvings. Go one block south from Jardín Páez' southeast corner, then one block west for the shrine, or one block east for the church. Just past the shrine, on Jardín Hidalgo's north side, is the beautiful 19th-century **Teatro Hinojosa**.

Sleeping & Eating
Accommodation prices can triple during the Easter Festival.

Hostal del Santuario (☎ 945-61-94; Santuario 27; s/d/tr M$150/200/250) A few blocks south of the plaza, this is the best budget option in town, with fancy swan-themed furniture and cable TV.

Posada Santa Cecilia (☎ 945-24-12; Constitución 4; s/d M$200/250/300) Half a block north of the plaza, this great-value rooms feature décor worthy of Marilyn Monroe: spacious rooms, large pieces of mirrored furniture and cable TV.

Leo Hotel (☎ 945-20-01; Calzada La Suave Patria s/n; r from M$350; P ☯) East of town on the road to Zacatecas, the modern Leo is the fanciest – but blandest – option. Transportation is recommended; buses don't run on Saturday.

Good eating options include **La Cofradía** (☎ 945-42-86; Constitución 19; mains M$78-100; ☯ 9:30am-10:30pm), which keeps long hours and an even longer menu of tasty Mexican dishes; and **Hotel Jardín** (☎ 945-20-26), on the plaza.

Getting There & Around
The Jerez turnoff is near Malpaso, 29km south of Zacatecas on the Zacatecas–Guadalajara road. Zacatecas–Jerez line, Ómnibus de México and Estrella Blanca/Rojo de los Altos have regular services from Zacatecas' bus station to Jerez (M$28). Jerez' bus station is on the east side of town, 1km from the center along Calzada La Suave Patria. 'Centro-Central' buses (M$5) run to/from the center. Several daily services run to/from Fresnillo (M$25).

LA QUEMADA
The impressive **ruins** (admission M$37; ☯ 9am-5:30pm) of La Quemada stand on a hill overlooking a broad valley 45km south of Zacatecas, 2km east of the Zacatecas–Guadalajara road. The remote and scenic setting makes the ruins well worth the day trip from the hustle and bustle of Zacatecas. The area is known to have rattlesnakes; keep an eye – and ear! – out. (No-one has yet fallen victim.)

The exact history and purpose of the site are extremely vague. Many suppositions surround the area – one theory is that it was where the Aztecs halted during their legendary wanderings toward the Valle de México. What is known is that the constructions were destroyed by fire and thus their name, La Quemada.

The modern **site museum** (adult/concession M$8/4; 10am-4pm) has interesting archaeology exhibits and an excellent video (with English subtitles). It's worth heading here first to contextualize the area and view the museum's miniature site model to get your bearings for your wanderings.

La Quemada was inhabited between about AD 300 and 1200, and it is estimated to have peaked between 500 and 900 with as many as 3000 inhabitants. From around 400 it was part of a regional trade network linked to Teotihuacán (see p209), but fortifications suggest that La Quemada later tried to dominate trade in this region.

Of the main structures, the nearest to the site entrance is the **Salón de las Columnas** (Hall of the Columns), probably a ceremonial hall. Slightly further up the hill are a **ball court**, a steep offerings **pyramid** and an equally steep staircase leading toward the site's upper levels. From the upper levels of the main hill, a path leads westward for about 800m to a spur hilltop (the highest point) with the remains of a cluster of buildings called **La Ciudadela** (the Citadel). To return, follow the defensive wall and path back around to the museum. Take water and a hat; it's mighty exposed out there.

Getting There & Away

From Zacatecas' Ex-Central de Autobus ('former' station), board a 2nd-class bus for Villanueva (M$30) and ask beforehand to be let off at *las ruinas;* you'll be deposited at the turnoff, from where it's a 2.5km walk to the site entrance. Returning to Zacatecas, you may have to wait a while for a bus – don't leave the ruins too late. Ómnibus de México and Rojo de los Altos have regular services from Zacatecas' 1st-class bus station to Villanueva and Guadalajara. You can also take an organized tour (M$250) from Zacatecas (see p589).

SOMBRERETE

433 / pop 19,000

Sombrerete is an appealingly archetypical and bustling old Mexican town. Its time-worn co-lonial buildings and traditional streets reflect its history; the first settlements here were in the 1550s and mines began extracting minerals that financed a rich legacy of churches, mansions and public buildings. Locals claim that Thomas Edison was born here. For further information see www.sombrerete.com.mx.

Opposite the cathedral, the **municipal tourist office** (935-14-38; Hidalgo 207) doesn't see many tourists, but the staff can answer questions (in Spanish). Make reservations here if you are interested in guides or transportation in the area, camping or in renting a *cabaña* (with two bedrooms, bathroom and kitchen) in Parque Nacional Sierra de Órganos. Before heading to the park, make sure you visit **La Casa de Usted** (935-01-81; Hidalgo 321) in Sombrerete and speak with enthusiastic Luis Martínez who has explored the Sierra for over 50 years. He named many of the famous formations and still leads trips on the full moon in October. Next door, the small **Museo Municipal** (Hidalgo 207; admission free; 8am-8pm Mon-Fri, 10am-3pm Sat & Sun) has folksy but well-displayed history exhibits.

Hotel Avenida Real (935-02-66; Aldama 345; s/d/ ste 230/260/290) Conveniently located, this hotel has dated but spacious and, on the whole, reasonable rooms. Its restaurant serves breakfasts and meals.

Buses (Omnibus de México and Estrella Blanca) stop outside their individual offices in Sombrerete's town center; if you're driving, the main street is just south of Hwy 45.

PARQUE NACIONAL SIERRA DE ÓRGANOS

High on the western edge of Zacatecas state and declared a national park in 2000, the isolated **Sierra de Órganos** (Organ Range; admission M$10) makes for a fun visit. The region is named for its distinctive rock formations, some of which resemble organ pipes; others are named for their similarity to the likes of ET, Christ and Los Frailes. This archetypal scenery – desert, nopal and rugged rocks – has been an ideal backdrop for hundreds of western movies featuring the likes of John Wayne. Keen campers or hikers may enjoy staying in one of several **campsites** (campsites per person M$20) or contact the municipal tourist office (above) in Sombrerete to rent a **cabaña** (M$500). There are also several picnic areas, but no other facilities and no year-round water source. The park is relatively small (2797 acres) and makes a fascinating visit for a couple of days but beware: there are no maps available, nor designated trails; even experienced hikers require compasses. Be sure to wear a hat and carry food and water.

To get here, turn north off Hwy 45 to San Francisco de los Órganos, 20km west of Sombrerete, then follow the road for 10km to the park entrance (signposted).

AGUASCALIENTES STATE

The state of Aguascalientes (population 1.1 million) is one of Mexico's smallest; its focus is the city of the same name. According to local legend, a kiss planted on the lips of dictator Santa Anna by the wife of a prominent local politician brought about the creation of a separate Aguascalientes state from Zacatecas.

Beyond the museum-rich city formal tourist sites are few, but it's a pleasant enough drive en route to or from Zacatecas, through fertile lands of corn, beans, chilies, fruit and grain. The state's ranches produce beef cattle as well as bulls, which are sacrificed at bullfights countrywide.

AGUASCALIENTES

☎ 449 / pop 663,671 / elevation 1800m

This prosperous industrial city is home to more than half of the state's population. Despite its messy outer, at its heart is a fine plaza and handsome colonial buildings. Museums are its strong point: the Museo de los Muertos well justifies a visit, as do those devoted to José Guadalupe Posada and Saturnino Herrán.

History

Before the Spanish arrived, a labyrinth of catacombs was built here; the first Spaniards called it La Ciudad Perforada (the perforated city). Archaeologists understand little of the tunnels, which are off-limits to visitors.

Conquistador Pedro de Alvarado arrived in 1522 but was driven back by the Chichimecs. A small garrison was founded here in 1575 to protect Zacatecas–Mexico City silver convoys. Eventually, as the Chichimecs were pacified, the region's hot springs sparked the growth of a town; a large tank beside the Ojo Caliente springs helped irrigate local farms that fed hungry mining districts nearby.

Today, the city's industries include textiles, wine, brandy, leather, preserved fruits and car manufacturing.

Orientation

Aguascalientes city is pancake-flat and very easy to get around. The center of town is Plaza de la Patria, surrounded by some lovely pedestrian streets. Av Chávez/Calle 5 de Mayo is the main north–south artery; it passes through a tunnel beneath Plaza de la Patria. Av López Mateos, the main east–west artery, is a couple of blocks south of the plaza. The outer areas are defined by *anillos* (ring roads).

Information
BOOKSTORES
Casa Terán (☎ 994-10-09; Rivero y Gutiérrez 110; 🕑 9am-9pm Mon-Sat) Good bookstore; Mexican cultural center and patio café also within the complex.

INTERNET ACCESS
Most places charge around M$15 per hour.
Internet 3W (Centro Parián; 🕑 9am-9pm Mon-Sat, 11am-6pm Sun)

EMERGENCY
Police (☎ 910-28-81)

LAUNDRY
Lavandería (224 Carranza; per kg M$16; 🕑 10am-2pm & 4-8pm Mon-Fri; 10am-4:30pm Sat)

MEDICAL SERVICES
Several pharmacies in the city center are open 24 hours.
Hospital Hidalgo (☎ 918-50-54, 915-31-42; Galeana 465)

MONEY
Banks with ATMs are common around Plaza de la Patria and Expoplaza. *Casas de cambio* cluster on Hospitalidad, opposite the post office.
Money Tron (Juan de Montoro s/n; 🕑 9am-4pm Mon-Fri) Exchange house half a block east of the plaza with drive-through window.

POST OFFICE & TELEPHONE
Card phones are numerous in the city center.
Post office (☎ 915-21-18; Hospitalidad 108; 🕑 8am-6pm Mon-Fri, 9am-1pm Sat)

TOURIST INFORMATION
State tourist office (☎ 915-95-04, 800-949-49-49; www.aguascalientes.gob.mx; Palacio de Gobierno, Plaza de la Patria; ☎ 9am-8pm Tue-Fri, 10am-6pm Sat & Sun) Free city maps.

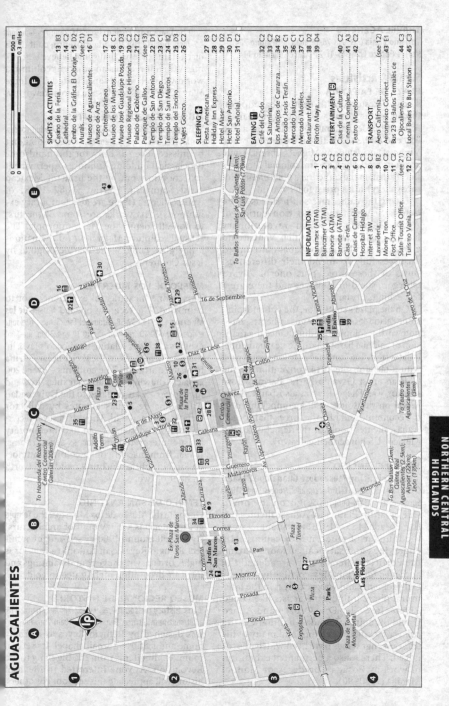

AGUASCALIENTES

0 — 500 m
0 — 0.3 miles

To Baños Thermales de Ojocaliente (3km);
San Luis Potosí (170km)

To Hacienda del Roble (20km);
Centro Comercial Galerias (20km)

To Bus Station (2km);
Quinta Real Aguascalientes (2.5km);
Airport (22km); León (135km)

To Teatro de Aguascalientes (3km)

NORTHERN CENTRAL HIGHLANDS

TRAVEL AGENCIES
Turismo Vania (☎ 918-76-16; Juan de Montoro 204)
Viajes Gomzo (☎ 915-41-24; Juan de Montoro 114)

Sights & Activities
PLAZA DE LA PATRIA
The well-restored 18th-century baroque **cathedral**, on the plaza's west side, is more magnificent inside than out. Over the altar at the east end of the south aisle is a painting of the Virgin of Guadalupe by Miguel Cabrera. There are more works by Cabrera, colonial Mexico's finest artist, in the cathedral's *pinacoteca* (picture gallery); ask a priest to let you in.

Facing the cathedral's south side is **Teatro Morelos**, scene of the 1914 Convention of Aguascalientes, in which revolutionary factions led by Pancho Villa, Venustiano Carranza and Emiliano Zapata attempted unsuccessfully to mend their differences. Busts of these three, plus one of Álvaro Obregón, stand in the foyer and there are a few exhibits upstairs.

On the plaza's south side, the red-and-pink stone **Palacio de Gobierno** is Aguascalientes' most noteworthy colonial building. Once the mansion of colonial baron Marqués de Guadalupe, it dates from 1665 and has a striking courtyard with a **mural** of the 1914 convention by the Chilean artist Osvaldo Barra. Barra, whose mentor was Diego Rivera, also painted the mural on the south wall, a compendium of the economic and historic forces that forged Aguascalientes (look for the depiction of the Mexico–US border being drawn).

JARDÍN EL ENCINO
The fascinating **Museo José Guadalupe Posada** (☎ 915-45-56; Jardín El Encino s/n; adult/concession M$10/5, Sun free; ☽ 11am-6pm Tue-Sun) is on the north side of Jardín El Encino. Aguascalientes native Posada (1852–1913) was in many ways the founder of modern Mexican art. His engravings and satirical cartoons during the Porfiriato dictatorship broadened the audience for art in Mexico, highlighted social problems and was a catalyst in the later mural phase influencing artists like Diego Rivera, José Clemente Orozco and Alfaro David Siqueiros. Posada's hallmark is the *calavera* (skull or skeleton) and many of his *calavera* engravings have been widely reproduced. There's also a permanent exhibition of work by Posada's predecessor Manuel Manilla (1830–90).

The **Templo del Encino** (Jardín El Encino; ☽ 7am-1pm & 5-7pm), beside the Posada museum, contains a black statue of Jesus that some believe is growing. When it reaches an adjacent column, a worldwide calamity is anticipated. The huge *Way of the Cross* murals are also noteworthy.

MUSEO DE AGUASCALIENTES
This **museum** (☎ 915-90-43; Zaragoza 507; adult/concession M$10/5, Sun free; ☽ 11am-6pm Tue-Sun) shouldn't be missed, even if only for the handsome neoclassical building. It houses a permanent collection of work by the brilliant Mexican artist Saturnino Herrán (1887–1918) of Aguascalientes (there are also temporary exhibitions). His works are some of the first to honestly depict the Mexican people. The sensual sculpture *Malgretout* on the patio is a fiberglass copy of the marble original by Jesús Contreras.

MUSEO DE LOS MUERTOS
This is one 'near death' experience not to be missed. The recently-opened **Museo de los Muertos** (☎ 139-32-58; Jardín del Estudiante s/n; adult/concession M$20/10, free Wed; ☽ 10:30am-6:30pm Tue-Sun) exhibits all things relating to Mexico's favorite subject – death – from the skeleton La Catrina to historic artifacts. The contents – over 1200 artifacts, drawings, literature, textiles, toys and miniatures – were donated to the Universidad Autónoma de Aguascalientes by collector Octavio Bajonero Gil. They span several centuries, from Mesoamerican to contemporary artistic interpretations, across seven rooms. It's far from macabre but a colorful, humorous and insightful encounter and well worth an hour or two.

TEMPLO DE SAN ANTONIO
Opposite the Museo de los Muertos, the **Templo de San Antonio** is a crazy quilt of architectural styles built around 1900 by self-taught architect Refugio Reyes. San Antonio's interior is highly ornate, with huge round paintings and intricate decoration highlighted in gold.

MUSEO REGIONAL DE HISTORIA
This **history museum** (☎ 916-52-28; Av Carranza 118; adult/student M$33/free, Sun free; ☽ 10am-7pm Tue-Sun) was designed by Refugio Reyes as a family home and features a small chapel. Its several rooms exhibit items from the Big Bang to the Revolution. Anyone interested in Mexican history will appreciate this section. For others,

the temporary exhibitions can be fascinating; pass by to check what's on.

CONTEMPORARY ART MUSEUMS

The small **Museo de Arte Contemporáneo** (☎ 915-79-53; cnr Morelos & Primo Verdad; adult/concession M$10/5, Sun free; 🕐 11am-5:30pm Tue-Sun), a modern museum displaying the work of Enrique Guzmán (1952–86) as well as temporary exhibitions, is well worth visiting. Nearby, the **Centro de la Gráfica El Obraje** (☎ 994-00-74; Juan de Montoro 222; 🕐 10am-2pm & 4-8pm Mon-Fri), a workshop-studio-gallery for printmakers, hosts free bimonthly exhibitions.

EXPOPLAZA & AROUND

Half a kilometer west of Plaza de la Patria, via Av López Mateos or Nieto, Expoplaza is a modern shopping center. On the mall's south side, the wide and soulless pedestrian promenade comes alive during the annual Feria de San Marcos (see below). At its west end, the mammoth **Plaza de Toros Monumental** is notable for its modern-colonial treatment of traditional bullring architecture.

On Expoplaza's east side the pedestrian street Pani runs two blocks north to the 18th-century **Templo de San Marcos** and the pretty, shady **Jardín de San Marcos**. The **Palenque de Gallos**, in the **Casino de la Feria** building on Pani, is the city's cockfighting arena (only during the *feria*). Near the northeast corner of Jardín de San Marcos the **Ex-Plaza de Toros San Marcos**, the old bullring, is now a school for aspiring matadors.

THERMAL BATHS

Despite the city's name, the only thermal baths near the center are the charming, if slightly shabby **Baños Termales de Ojocaliente** (☎ 970-07-21; Tecnológico 102; private baths from M$120 per hr; 🕐 7am-7pm). The restored 1808 architecture truly turns back the clock; the larger baths are more appealing. Take Bus 23 from Mateos.

Tours

El Tranvía (adult/child M$26/16), an imitation trolley car, offers three different routes through the city (three times daily, Tuesday to Sunday, between 10am and 6pm). Get tickets and information on walking tours from the state tourist office (p596).

Festivals & Events

Mid-April sees Mexico's biggest annual month-long state fair, the **Feria de San Marcos**.

It centers on Expoplaza and attracts a million visitors with exhibitions, bullfights, cockfights, rodeos, concerts and cultural events, including an international film festival. The big parade takes place on the saint's day, April 25.

During the two-week **Festival de las Calaveras** (the dates vary but always encompass November 1 and 2), Aguascalientes celebrates Día de los Muertos (Day of the Dead) with an emphasis on the symbolism of *calavera* skeletons.

Sleeping

Prices skyrocket during the Feria de San Marcos and accommodations are completely booked for the fair's final weekend; residents run a lucrative home-stay service at this time.

BUDGET

Hotel San Antonio (☎ 915-93-41, 916-33-20; Zaragoza 305; s/d/tr M$180/212; **P**) A sign in this great-value and highly recommended place – with 24/7 drive-through service – is strict about not admitting 'couples without luggage.' Management is courteous, rooms are simple and spotless (rooms are cleaned daily and there's cable TV). Ask for a room at the back to avoid the possibility of car engine noise. The central parking area can be noisy; rooms at the back are fine.

Hotel Maser (☎ 915-35-62; fax 915-96-62; Juan de Montoro 303; s/d M$180/250/270; **P**) A friendly, but as basic an option as you can get, with well-worn and time-tried rooms around a covered courtyard. Surprisingly, some have TV (which costs a few extra dollars).

Hotel Señorial (☎ 915-16-30; cnr Colón & Juan de Montoro; s/d M$220/330) The rooms in this friendly, faded place vary greatly – singles are small, dark and depressing while doubles with balconies are light and airy (note for single travelers – it won't negotiate on price if you want the larger option). All come with cable TV, but quality is still a notch down from Hotel San Antonio).

MIDRANGE

Hacienda del Roble (☎ 915-39-94; hotelhaciendadelroble @prodigy.net.mx; 5 de May 540; s/d/tr M$350/450/550) This is by far the pick of the midrange choices, with small but modern carpeted rooms, external-facing windows and reasonable bathrooms. The downside is the noisy location – right on 5 de Mayo – but it's only a 10-minute walk to the plaza.

Holiday Inn Express (☎ 916-16-66, 800-009-99-00; holidayinnags@prodigy.net.mx; Nieto 102; r from US$80; ☒ ☒ ☐) The historic center's most comfortable option has 106 rooms with all the modern conveniences and full facilities for business travelers. Discounts of 25% are available some weekends. Note the establishment quotes prices in US dollars.

TOP END

Fiesta Americana (☎ 918-60-10; www.fiestaamericana.com; Laureles s/n, Colonia Las Flores; r from M$1350; ☐ ☒ ☒ ☐ ☒) This luxury chain hotel is a pleasanft, if predictable, five-star experience; the 192 rooms feature all the amenities and there's a fitness center and inviting pool. Weekend packages for two cost around M$1190 and include buffet breakfast.

Quinta Real Aguascalientes (☎ 978-58-18; www .quintareal.com; Av Aguascalientes Sur 601; ste US$150-250; ☐ ☒ ☒ ☐ ☒) This is the slickest option of the luxurious resort-style hotels near the industrial zone on the outskirts of the city. Another establishment that prefers US dollars.

Eating

Four blocks north of the Plaza de la Patria, fresh produce and cheap eats are available in three markets: Mercado Juárez, Mercado Jesús Terán and Mercado Morelos. Av Carranza west of the plaza has a wonderful array of trendy cafés, offering snacks and drinks in the evenings.

Los Antojos de Carranza (☎ 994-19-77; Carranza 301; mains M$35-109; ⊙ 8:30am-6pm Sun-Tue, 8:30am-11pm Wed-Sat) This colorful and lively place is appealing for its friendly atmosphere, Mexican music (not live) and good-value Mexican cuisine – all the favorites in generous portions. Sunday lunch is popular with locals and half serves are available for children.

Café del Codo (☎ 994-15-87; Callejón del Codo; snacks M$40-80; ⊙ 9am-midnight Mon-Sat, 1-10pm Sun; ☐) The most cosmopolitan café in town, with green brollies and a pretty location under trees. It serves Italian sodas, smoothies plus a range of chais and good baguettes. Has both computers and laptop wi-fi connection.

Restaurant Mitla (☎ 916-61-57; Madero 220; mains M$50-140; ⊙ 7am-10pm) This large, pleasant and popular restaurant is caught in a time warp: 1938, the year it started. There are white-coated waiters, excellent service, plus a grand menu with a choice of Mexican specialties, set breakfasts (M$65) and three-course set lunches (M$70).

Rincón Maya (☎ 916-75-74; Abasolo 113; mains M$56-100; ⊙ 2pm-midnight Mon-Sat, 2-10:30pm Sun) By day, this place has service at La Mestiza Yucatena (open 8am till 2pm), its alter ego next door. Both serve delectable Yucatecan specialties. Don't miss the *sopa de lima* (lime soup; M$41).

La Saturnina (☎ 994-04-49; Carranza 110; mains M$60-65; ⊙ 8:30am-10:30pm) Set in an 18th-century former mansion, this eatery is well known among local diners for its romantic ambience and tasty menu. The name is in honor of the women Saturnino Herrán so beautifully painted; but tales of tragic love and the tormented ghost of the wealthy hacienda-owner's daughter won't ruin your appetite.

Entertainment

Pani, the pedestrian street between the Expoplaza and Jardín de San Marcos, is lively most evenings, with a good selection of bars and restaurants.

The trendy nightspots are out in the suburbs; **Centro Comercial Galerías** (☎ 912-66-12; Independencia 2351) is a shopping mall with several bars and discos, including the popular El Reloj, while the main drag for late-night discos is north of town on Av Colosio.

In a fine 17th-century building, the **Casa de la Cultura** (☎ 910-20-10; Carranza 101) hosts art exhibitions, concerts, theater and dance events. The **Teatro Morelos** (☎ 915-19-41; Nieto 113 Plaza de la Patria) and the **Teatro de Aguascalientes** (☎ 978-54-14; cnr Chávez & Aguascalientes), south of the center, both stage a variety of cultural events.

There's a **cinema complex** (tickets M$45) on Expoplaza.

Getting There & Away

AIR

Aéropuerto Jesús Terán (☎ 915-28-06) is 26km south of Aguascalientes off the road to Mexico City. Aeroméxico Connect has daily direct flights to Guadalajara, Mexico City, Monterrey and Tijuana, plus direct flights to/from Los Angeles and New York. Volaris serves Cancun and Tijuana. Continental has daily flights to Houston and Los Angeles and American flies daily to Dallas.

Airline offices include **Aeroméxico Connect** (☎ 918-21-27; Madero 474).

BUS

The bus station (Central Camionera) is 2km south of the center on Av Convención. It has a post office, card phones, a cafeteria and luggage storage. See the box below for daily departures.

There are also frequent services to Ciudad Juárez, Monterrey, Morelia and Torreón and two buses daily to San Miguel de Allende (M$154).

Getting Around

Most places of interest are within easy walking distance of each other. Regular city buses (M$5) run from 6am to 10:30pm. 'Centro' or '5 de Mayo' buses run from the bus station to the city center. Get off at the first stop after the tunnel under Plaza de la Patria, on 5 de Mayo or Rivero y Gutiérrez. From the city center to the bus station, take any 'Central' bus from the corner Galeana (near Insurgentes).

Taxis charge as per metered fares. Between the bus station and the center the taxi fare is around M$20 to M$25.

SAN LUIS POTOSÍ STATE

The historic state capital city, San Luis Potosí, and the fascinating 'ghost town,' Real de Catorce, are on the high and dry expanses of the state's north and west and are the main reasons visitors come to this region. The pretty tropical, verdant eastern region of Huasteca is popular among local tourists.

The state is steeped in history. Before the Spanish conquest, western San Luis Potosí was inhabited by Guachichiles, warlike hunters. In the 18th century the area gained a reputation for maltreatment of indigenous people, partly because the clergy replaced the more compassionate Franciscans.

Today, mining, agriculture, ranching and industry are the economic mainstays of this fairly prosperous state of 2.4 million.

SAN LUIS POTOSÍ

☎ 444 / pop 685,934 / elevation 1860m

A grand old dame of colonial cities, San Luis Potosí was once a revolutionary hotbed, an important mining town and seat of government. Today she has maintained her poise as the prosperous state capital, orderly industrial center and university seat. A great place to wander through, the city's colonial core is made up of numerous beautiful plazas and manicured parks linked by attractive pedestrian streets. Although not as striking as Zacatecas or Guanajuato, this lively city's cultural elegance is reflected in its delightful colonial buildings, impressive theater and numerous excellent museums.

History

Founded in 1592, 20km west of the silver deposits in Cerro de San Pedro, San Luis

DAILY BUSES FROM AGUASCALIENTES

Destination	Fare	Duration	Frequency
Guadalajara	deluxe M$242	2¾	4 daily (ETN)
	1st-class M$186	2¾	8 daily (Primera Plus)
	1st-class M$172	3	hourly (México & Futura)
Guanajuato	1st-class M$147	3hr	1 daily (Primera Plus; 8pm)
León	1st-class M$104	2hr	every 30 min (Primera Plus)
	2nd-class M$82	3½hr	every 45 min (Flecha Amarilla)
Mexico City (Terminal Norte)	deluxe M$510	6hr	9 daily (ETN)
	1st-class M$333-433	6hr	frequent (Primera Plus, Futura, Ómnibus de México)
	2nd-class M$333	8½hr	2 daily (Flecha Amarilla)
San Luis Potosí	1st-class M$131	3hr	8 daily
	2nd-class M$101	3½hr	hourly (Estrella Blanca)
Zacatecas	deluxe M$130	2hr	8 daily (ETN)
	1st-class M$90	2hr	9 daily (Transporte del Norte)
	1st-class M$91	2hr	hourly (Ómnibus de México & Futura)
	2nd-class M$91	2hr	hourly (Estrella Blanca)

is named Potosí after the immensely rich Bolivian silver town of that name, which the Spanish hoped it would rival.

The mines began to decline in the 1620s, but the city was well enough established as a ranching center to remain the major city of northeastern Mexico until overtaken by Monterrey at the start of the 20th century.

Known in the 19th century for its lavish houses and imported luxury goods, San Luis was twice the seat of President Benito Juárez' government during the 1860s French intervention. In 1910 in San Luis, the dictatorial president Porfirio Díaz jailed Francisco Madero, his liberal opponent, during the presidential campaign. Freed after the election, Madero hatched his Plan de San Luis Potosí (a strategy to depose Díaz), announcing it in San Antonio, Texas, in October 1910; he declared the election illegal, named himself provisional president and designated November 20 as the day for Mexico to rise in revolt – the start of the Mexican Revolution.

Orientation

Central San Luis stretches west from the Alameda park (east) to Calle Independencia (west). This area is made up of neighboring plazas: Plaza del Carmen, Plaza de Armas, Plaza de San Francisco and Plaza de los Fundadores. Some hotels and restaurants are in the center, with cheaper lodgings near the old train station. An upscale commercial strip runs west from Plaza de los Fundadores along Av Carranza.

Information

INTERNET ACCESS
Most places charge around M$10 to M$15 per hour.
Café Cibernetico (Av Carranza 416) Reasonable connections and coffee.
Ciber Café de la Paz (Guerrero 269)

LAUNDRY
Lavandería (5 de Mayo 870)

MEDICAL SERVICES
Red Cross (☎ 815-3635; Calzada de Guadalupe 540)

MONEY
Banks with ATMs are scattered around town, including the Plaza de Armas and Plaza de los Fundadores. Several casas de cambio are along Morelos.

Banamex (cnr Obregón & Allende) Like other banks, changes cash and traveler's checks.

POST OFFICE
Post office (☎ 812-72-86; Universidad 526; ☺ 8am-3pm Mon-Fri)

TELEPHONE
There are many card phones in the center.

TOURIST INFORMATION
Municipal tourist office (☎ 812-27-70; Palacio Municipal, east side of Plaza de Armas; ☎ 8am-8:30pm Mon-Fri, 10am-6pm Sat)
State tourist office (☎ 812-99-39, 800 3433887; www .sanluispotosi.gob.mx; Obregón 520; ☎ 8am-9pm Mon-Fri, 9am-5pm Sat) Has maps and brochures with some off-the-beaten-track attractions in San Luis Potosí state.

TRAVEL & TOUR AGENCIES
Operatour Potosina (☎ 151-22-01; www.operatour potosina.com; Juan Sarabia 120) This friendly and knowledgeable English-speaking outfit offers tours around the city, as well as to haciendas, Real de Catorce and the Huasteca Potosina region. Located in the Hotel Napoles.
2001 Viajes (☎ 812-29-53; Obregón 604)

Sights

The best way to see San Luis Potosí is to plaza-hop on foot. The plazas are within close proximity, and each one offers appealing historical and cultural experiences. Most also have a great selection of culinary options.

PLAZA DE ARMAS & AROUND
Also known as Jardín Hidalgo, this pedestrianized plaza is the city's central square.

The three-nave baroque **cathedral**, built between 1660 and 1730, is on the plaza's east side. Originally it had just one tower; the northern tower was added in the 20th century. The marble apostles on the facade are replicas of statues in Rome's San Juan de Letrán basilica.

Beside the cathedral, the 19th-century **Palacio Municipal** features powerful stone arches. Finished in 1838, it was the home of Bishop Ignacio Montes de Oca from 1892 to 1915. In the rear of the building's patio is a stone fountain carved with the heads of three lions. The city's coat of arms in stained glass overlooks a double staircase.

Behind the cathedral, the **Museo Othoniano** (☎ 812-74-12; Av Othón 225; admission M$5; ☺ 10am-2pm & 4-6pm Tue-Fri, 10am-2pm Sat & Sun) is the birthplace

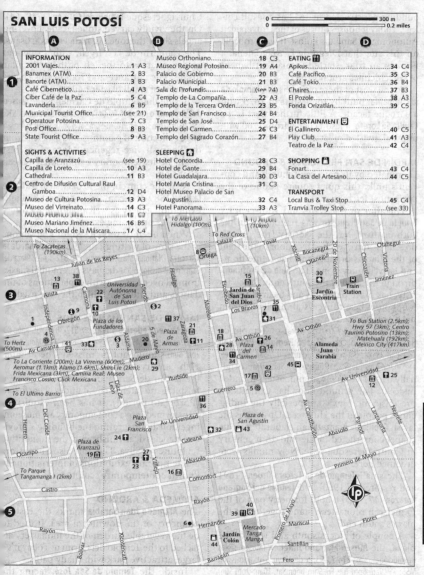

SAN LUIS POTOSÍ

INFORMATION	
2001 Viajes	1 A3
Banamex (ATM)	2 B3
Banorte (ATM)	3 B3
Café Cibernetico	4 A3
Ciber Café de la Paz	5 C4
Lavandería	6 B5
Municipal Tourist Office	(see 21)
Operatour Potosina	7 C3
Post Office	8 B3
State Tourist Office	9 A3

SIGHTS & ACTIVITIES	
Capilla de Aranzazú	(see 19)
Capilla de Loreto	10 A3
Cathedral	11 B3
Centro de Difusión Cultural Raul Gamboa	12 D4
Museo de Cultura Potosina	13 A3
Museo del Virreinato	14 C3
Museo Federico Silva	15 C3
Museo Mariano Jiménez	16 B5
Museo Nacional de la Máscara	17 C4

Museo Orthoniano	18 C3
Museo Regional Potosino	19 A4
Palacio de Gobierno	20 B3
Palacio Municipal	21 B3
5ala de Profundis	(see 24)
Templo de La Compañía	22 A3
Templo de la Tercera Orden	23 B5
Templo de San Francisco	24 B4
Templo de San José	25 D4
Templo del Carmen	26 C3
Templo del Sagrado Corazón	27 B4

SLEEPING	
Hotel Concordia	28 C3
Hotel de Gante	29 B4
Hotel Guadalajara	30 D3
Hotel María Cristina	31 C3
Hotel Museo Palacio de San Augustín	32 C4
Hotel Panorama	33 C3

EATING	
Apikus	34 C4
Café Pacifico	35 C3
Café Tokio	36 B4
Chaires	37 B3
El Pozole	38 A3
Fonda Orizatlán	39 C5

ENTERTAINMENT	
El Gallinero	40 C5
Play Club	41 A3
Teatro de la Paz	42 C4

SHOPPING	
Fonart	43 C4
La Casa del Artesano	44 C5

TRANSPORT	
Local Bus & Taxi Stop	45 C4
Tranvía Trolley Stop	(see 33)

of a much celebrated Mexican poet, Manuel José Othón (1858–1906). The 19th-century home is furnished in period style and exhibits Othón's manuscripts and personal effects.

The neoclassical **Palacio de Gobierno**, built between 1770 and 1816, lines the plaza's west side. Its most illustrious lodger was Benito Juárez – first in 1863 when he was fleeing

from invading French forces, then in 1867 when he confirmed the death sentence on the puppet-emperor Maximilian.

PLAZA DE LOS FUNDADORES & AROUND
The least pretty of the plazas, Plaza de los Fundadores (Founders' Plaza) is where the city was born. On the north side is a large

building constructed in 1653 as a Jesuit college. Today it houses offices of the Universidad Autónoma de San Luis Potosí. It was probably on this site that Diego de la Magdalena, a Franciscan friar, started a small settlement of Guachichiles around 1585.

To the west of these offices is the **Templo de la Compañía**, built by the Jesuits in 1675 with a baroque facade. A little further west is the **Capilla de Loreto**, a Jesuit chapel from 1700 with unusual, twisted pillars.

JARDÍN DE SAN FRANCISCO & AROUND

Dominated by its namesake church and convent's bulk, this quiet square is one of the city's most fetching.

The altar of the 17th- and 18th-century **Templo de San Francisco** was remodeled in the 20th century, but the sacristy (the priest's dressing room), reached by a door to the right of the altar, is original and has a fine dome and carved pink stone. The **Sala de Profundis**, through the arch at the south end of the sacristy, has more paintings and a carved stone fountain. A beautiful crystal ship hangs from the main dome.

Along Galeana to the west of Templo de San Francisco, the **Museo Regional Potosino** (☎ 814-35-72; Galeana 450; admission M$34, Sun free; ☽ 10am-7pm Tue-Sat, 10:30am-7pm Sun) was originally part of a Franciscan monastery founded in 1590. The ground floor has exhibits on pre-Hispanic Mexico, especially the indigenous people of the Huasteca. Upstairs is the lavish **Capilla de Aranzazú**, an elaborate private chapel constructed in the mid-18th century in Churrigueresque style. New monks were ordained here.

The small **Templo de la Tercera Orden** (1694 and restored in 1960) and **Templo del Sagrado Corazón** (1728–31), both formerly part of the Franciscan monastery, stand together at the plaza's south end.

A couple of blocks south and west of the plaza, the **Museo Mariano Jiménez** (Museo de las Revoluciónes; ☎ 814-73-93; 5 de Mayo 610; admission M$5; ☽ 9am-5pm Tue-Fri, 9am-noon Sat, 10am-2pm Sun) covers some of the most dramatic events in Mexican history. It has a rebellion theme and a good account of indigenous resistance to the Spanish conquest.

PLAZA DEL CARMEN

The Plaza del Carmen is dominated by San Luis' most spectacular structure, the Churrigueresque **Templo del Carmen** (1749–64). On the vividly carved stone facade, hovering angels show the touch of indigenous artisans. The Camarín de la Virgen, with a splendid golden altar, is to the left of the main altar inside. The entrance and roof of this chapel are a riot of small plaster figures.

Beside the Templo de Carmen is the **Museo del Virreinato** (☎ 816-09-94; Villerías 155; admission M$10; ☽ 10am-7pm Tue-Fri, 10am-5pm Sat & Sun), which has a large collection of paintings and artifacts from the Spanish vice-regency. More of interest might be its temporary exhibitions – check what's on.

Near the church, the neoclassical **Teatro de la Paz** (1889–94) contains a concert hall and exhibition gallery as well as a theater. Posters announce upcoming events.

When open (it was closed for renovations at the time of writing), the **Museo Nacional de la Máscara** (National Mask Museum; ☎ 812-30-25; Plaza del Carmen; admission M$5) displays ceremonial masks from all over Mexico with explanations of the dances and rituals in which they are used.

JARDÍN DE SAN JUAN DE DIOS

The **Museo Federico Silva** (☎ 812-38-48; Obregón 80 adult/concession M$30/15; ☽ 9am-6pm Wed-Mon, 10am-2pm Sun) should not be missed. The original 17th-century building on the north side of the Jardín de San Juan de Dios was once a hospital and later a school under *el porfiriato* (Porfiriato period). It has been exquisitely transformed into a contemporary art museum, ingeniously integrating the building's previous neoclassical finish with the monolithic sculptures of Silva. There are also a bookstore and temporary exhibitions of internationally known contemporary sculptors.

ALAMEDA & AROUND

The **Alameda Juan Sarabia** marks the eastern boundary of the downtown area. It used to be the vegetable garden of the monastery attached to the Templo del Carmen. Today it's a large, attractive park with shady paths.

Inside the **Templo de San José**, facing the Alameda's south side, lies the image of El Señor de los Trabajos, a Christ figure attracting pilgrims from near and far. Numerous *retablos* around the statue testify to prayers answered in finding jobs, regaining health and passing exams.

The interesting design of **Centro de Difusión Cultural Raul Gamboa** (☎ 816-05-25; cnr Av Universidad

NORTHERN CENTRAL HIGHLANDS

Negrete; galleries (🕙 10am-2pm & 5-8pm Mon-Sat) was inspired by a spiral seashell. Inside, art galleries show changing contemporary exhibitions.

Just over the railway bridge east of the Alameda is the **Centro Taurino Potosino**, comprising the 7000-seat Plaza de Toros (bullring) and a restaurant decorated with matador paraphernalia (open only when bullfights take place).

Tours

The **Tranvía** (☎ 814-22-26; one-hour trip M$50), an imitation of an antique trolley, does a loop around the historic center starting from Hotel Panorama (right). Hours vary seasonally.

Festivals & Events

Semana Santa Holy Week is celebrated with concerts, exhibitions and other activities; on Good Friday at 3pm, Christ's passion is re-enacted in the barrio of San Juan de Guadalupe, followed at 8pm by a silent procession through the city.

Feria Nacional Potosina San Luis' National Fair, normally in the last three weeks of August, includes concerts, bullfights, rodeos, cockfights and agricultural shows.

Día de San Luis Rey de Francia On August 25 the city's patron saint, St Louis IX (King of France) is honored as the highlight of the Feria Nacional. Events include a large parade with floats and *gigantes*.

Festival Internacional de Danza This national festival of contemporary dance is held in the last two weeks of September.

Sleeping

You'll enjoy San Luis more if you choose a hotel in the atmospheric pedestrianized center.

BUDGET

Hotel Guadalajara (☎ 128-64-51; Jiménez 253; s M$300, d M$315-390; P) Around the *zona roja* (red-light district), this might not be to everyone's taste. But it's cheap and 1970s-style modern with small lounge areas and reasonable rooms.

Hotel de Gante (☎ 812-14-92/93; hotel_degante@ hotmail.com; 5 de Mayo 140; s/d/tr M$330/380/450; 🖵) In an unbeatable location, near the corner of Plaza de Armas, Gante has excellent-value, light and spacious rooms with cable TV. The hot water supply can be a bit hit and miss.

MIDRANGE

Hotel María Cristina (☎ 812-94-08, 800-087-07-95; www .mariacristina.com.mx; Sarabia 110; s/d/tr M$515/560/625; P 🖵) The central modern María Cristina caters to business travelers with a restaurant and small but comfortable carpeted rooms with cable TV, fan and phone. Make sure you request windows; some are like peep holes.

Hotel Concordia (☎ 812-06-66, 800-711-13-18; concor dia@prodigy.net.mx; cnr Avs Othón & Morelos; s/d M$561/644; P) The reliable, 1970s-style Concordia occupies an old building and has white and light corridors and 96 carpeted rooms with cable TV and other amenities. Exterior rooms are nicer than interior ones.

Hotel Panorama (☎ 812-17-77, 800-480-01-00; www .hotelpanorama.com.mx; Av Carranza 315; r without/with air-con M$730/860; P 🏊 🖵 🍽) All 126 comfy rooms at this smart hotel opposite the Plaza de los Fundadores have floor-to-ceiling windows. Superior ones on the south side have private balconies overlooking the pool. A marble-clad lobby, restaurant and piano bar make it popular with business travelers.

TOP END

There are several upscale places east of the city fronting the highway near the bus station.

Camina Real (☎ 102-50-00; www.caminoreal.com /sanluis_i/main.php; Carretera a Guadalajara 1100, Fracc. La Loma; r from US$100; P 🖵) This five-star complex is out on a limb in more ways than one. It's on the western edges of town next to La Loma sporting complex and offers a standard five-star chain-hotel experience in plush surroundings. Guests may use the sports club's extensive facilities.

our pick **Hotel Museo Palacio de San Agustín** (☎ 811-77-77; Galeana, esq 5 de Mayo; r US$200-300) 'Warning': this lush and plush experience comes with a snob rating index. This extraordinary place goes beyond a boutique hotel – it is a 'museum.' Formerly part of the San Augustín monastery, it has been restored to its original condition (think hand-painted gold leaf finishes, crystal chandeliers and 700 certified European antiques). Hotel staff in period costume transport you back in time. The *pièce de resistance* has to be the hotel's own replica of the San Agustín facade and *capilla* (we won't spoil the surprise). It's no time for subtleties: this place is for 'appropriate' clientele only and management reserves the right to refuse entry.

Eating

One local specialty is *tacos potosinos* – red, chili-impregnated tacos stuffed with cheese or chicken and topped with chopped potato, carrots, lettuce and loads of *queso blanco* (white cheese). The best, most varied and upscale restaurants are west of the center along Av Carranza ('La Avenida').

Chaires (☎ 811-32-91; Plaza de Armas; snacks M$12-35; ⏰ 8am-10pm) The best ice creamery and café for good quality snacks and surveying the local scene.

Café Pacífico (☎ 812-30-50; Constitución 200; snacks M$15-70) Worth mentioning because of its hours – it's open 24/7 – and serves up snacks and set breakfasts to a loyal clientele. It's light, bright and the nearest thing to a local version of a US diner.

El Pozole (☎ 814-99-00; cnr Carmona & Arista; mains M$25-60; ⏰ noon-3pm) The place to try the local *enchiladas potosinas* – the tortilla dough is red (from mild chili). This place was started by a woman selling antojitos in her home in the 1980s. Demand for her goods was so high she has since opened three restaurants specializing in what she knows best – tacos rojos, pozole, *quesadillas de papa*… Yes, they're that good.

Café Tokio (☎ 814-61-89; cnr Zaragoza & Guerrero; mains M$30-50; ✷) Along the same lines as Pacífico, this bright and sizable café has Japanese owners but Mexican and fast-food standards. Popular for a cheap set lunch.

Fonda Orizatlán (☎ 814-67-86; Hernández 240; mains M$36-90; ⏰ 8:30am-11pm Mon-Sat, 8:30am-7pm Sun) Eight blocks south of the center, the dated but colorful Fonda Orizatlán is locally renowned for its first-class Huasteca-style cuisine. Sunday afternoons from 4pm to 5pm feature folkloric dances. Sunday buffet lunches are M$120.

Frida Mexicana (☎ 811-46-03; www.elmexicodefrida.com; Valentin Gama 646; mains M$45-190; 1pm-midnight Mon-Sat, 1-6pm Sun) Although painted in Kahlo-esque colors, this restaurant is not Frida-kitsch. Rather, the tasteful and tasty menu serves up scrumptious Mexican fare. Try the *chiles ventilla* (M$58), chilies with cheese and the most tantalizing creamy sauces. It's 3km along (and just south of) Carranza.

Shiroi ie (☎ 128-24-44; Av Carranza 1335; mains M$47-70; ⏰ 2pm-1am Mon-Sat, 2-6pm Sun) Unusual name, unusual dishes. Wonderful Japanese fusion creating sushi and sashimi and California rolls with a twist (try the 'matador roll' with beef fillet; M$70). Has a modern, upbeat atmosphere with a red-and-black theme. It's 2km west along Carranza.

Apikus (☎ 128-69-91; Mariana Escobedo 305; mains M$90-185) Sleek and stylish and *a la moda*. Its minimalist setting on the terrace is beautifully offset against the colonial architecture of surrounding buildings. Modern fusion cuisine includes sushi, pasta and meats. Definitely worth the splurge.

La Virreina (☎ 812-37-50; Av Carranza 830; mains M$100-200; ⏰ 1pm-midnight Tue-Sat, 1-6pm Sun) A long-established gourmet favorite, the charmingly old-fashioned Virreina has a classic menu including both international and Mexican dishes, delicious desserts and an excellent reputation. The rumoured-to-be-90-something-year-old owner still presides over quality checks.

Entertainment

San Luis has a reasonably active cultural scene. Ask in the tourist office about what's on and keep your eye out for posters. The free monthly *Guiarte* booklet and posters detail cultural attractions. For a night of dancing, San Luis is steeped in Latin rhythms; if you like salsa, then you are in luck. Other popular discos, bars and music venues are found further west along Av Carranza and Jiménez.

Play Club (☎ 812-56-92; Av Carranza 333; ⏰ 11pm-3am) Within walking distance of the center on Av Carranza, Play Club is all the go.

El Ultimo Barrio (☎ 812-38-73; Jiménez 380A; ⏰ 9pm-3am) Try this one for live rock and pop covers.

Teatro de la Paz (☎ 812-52-09; Villerias 2) This neoclassical, 1500-seat venue presents a variety of local and visiting dance, theater and music ensembles most nights.

Orquestra Sinfónica (☎ 814-36-01; tickets from M$30) Symphony comes to Teatro de la Paz September through November.

A couple of options for dancing to live Caribbean music:

El Gallinero (☎ 812-15-32; Hernández 210; ⏰ 10pm-2am)

La Corriente (Av Carranza 700)

Concerts, theater, exhibitions and cultural events are also presented at places like the **Teatro de la Ciudad**, an open-air theater in Parque Tangamanga I, and the **Museo Francisco Cossio** (☎ 813-22-47; Carranza 1815), 2½km west of Plaza de los Fundadores.

Shopping

The main shopping district is between the Plaza de Armas and the Mercado Hidalgo. A few blocks further northeast is the larger, interesting Mercado República. Look out for the local specialty, milky sweets.

Fonart (☎ 812-39-98; Jardín Guerrero 5) Like other shops in the government-run chain, this outlet has a good selection of quality handicrafts from all over Mexico.

La Casa del Artesano (☎ 814-89-90; Jardín Colon 23) For more local products try this shop full of *potosino* pottery, masks, woodwork and canework.

Getting There & Away

AIR

Aeropuerto Ponciano Arriaga (☎ 822-00-95) is 10km north of the city off Hwy 57. Aeroméxico Connect offers direct service to/from Monterrey with connecting flights to San Antonio, Texas and Mexico City. Aeromar and Mexicana and Click Mexicana serve Mexico City several times daily.

Airline offices:

Aeroméxico Connect (☎ 822-22-29; airport)
Aeromar (☎ 817-50-62; Carranza 1030)
Click Mexicana (☎ 833-04-31; Carranza 1115-1)

BUS

The **Terminal Terrestre Potosina** (TTP; ☎ 816-45-66; Carretera 57), 2½km east of the center, is a busy transportation hub that has deluxe, 1st-class and some 2nd-class bus services passing through. It's available facilities include card phones, 24-hour luggage storage and two cafés.

CAR & MOTORCYCLE

Car-rental prices range from US$50 to US$85 per day. There are also vans and weeklong packages available.

Alamo (☎ 822-83-20; Av Carranza 1415)
Hertz (☎ 812-32-29; Obregón 670)

Getting Around

Taxis charge around M$150 to M$210 for the half-hour trip to/from the airport.

To reach the center from the bus station, take any 'Centro' bus. A convenient place to get off is on the Alameda, outside the train station. A booth in the bus station sells taxi tickets (M$25 to M$35) to the center.

From the center to the bus station, take any 'Central TTP' bus southbound on Av Constitución from the Alameda's west side.

City buses run from 6:30am to 10:30pm (M$5). For places along Av Carranza, catch a 'Morales' or 'Carranza' bus in front of the train station.

DAILY BUSES FROM SAN LUIS POTOSÍ

Destination	Fare	Duration	Frequency
Guadalajara	deluxe M$335	5-6hr	12 daily (ETN)
	1st-class M$257	6hr	hourly (Transportes del Norte)
	2nd-class M$229	6hr	2 daily (Estrella Blanca)
Guanajuato	M$142	5hr	4 daily (Flecha Amarilla)
Matehuala	1st-class M$121	2½hr	hourly (Sendor)
	2nd-class M$105	2½hr	2 daily (Estrella Blanca)
Mexico City (Terminal Norte)	deluxe M$385	5-6hr	12 daily (ETN)
	1st-class M$308	5-6hr	hourly (Primera Plus)
	2nd-class M$265	6½hr	7 daily (Flecha Amarilla)
Monterrey	deluxe M$440	6hr	2 daily (ETN)
	1st-class M$336	7hr	hourly (Transporte del Norte & Futura)
	2nd-class M$336	7hr	3 daily (Estrella Blanca)
Querétaro	deluxe M$290	2½hr	3 daily (ETN)
	1st-class M$154	3½hr	frequent (Primera Plus, Futura & Ómnibus de México)
	2nd-class M$120	4hr	16 daily (Flecha Amarilla)
San Miguel de Allende	M$126	5hr	7 daily (Flecha Amarilla)
Tampico	1st-class M$316	7hr	regular (Oriente Ómnibus de México or Futura)
	2nd-class M$316	7-8hr	14 daily (Vencedor)
Zacatecas	1st-class M$120	3hr	12 daily (Ómnibus de México)
	2nd-class M$120	3hr	hourly (Estrella Blanca)

Daily buses also go to Aguascalientes, Ciudad Juárez, Ciudad Valles, Ciudad Victoria, Chihuahua, Dolores Hidalgo, León, Morelia, Nuevo Laredo, Saltillo and Torreón.

MATEHUALA

☎ 488 / pop 70,150 / elevation 1600m

The only town of any size on Hwy 57 between Saltillo and San Luis Potosí, Matehuala is a pleasant but unremarkable place. It is a compulsory changing point on this route for buses to Real de Catorce.

If you do find yourself stuck here, the bus station is just west of the highway, 2km south of the center. To walk to the center, turn left out of the bus station and continue along Av 5 de Mayo for 1½km, then turn left on Insurgentes for a few blocks to reach the Plaza de Armas. Alternatively, take a microbus marked 'Centro'; microbuses marked 'Central' head in the direction of the terminal (both M$4.50). A taxi costs about M$25.

All essential services (ATMs, phones, internet etc) are around the main plazas – the shady Plaza de Armas and the busy Placita del Rey 300m to its north, which features a neo-Gothic-neoclassical **cathedral**. Cheaper hotels and the town's restaurants are in this area.

Hotel María Esther (☎ 882-07-14; Madero 111; s/d M$250/290; **P**) is a family-run place with rooms facing a plant-filled patio out back behind the restaurant. It's a block north and a block east of Placita del Rey. **Las Palmas Midway Inn** (☎ 882-00-01/02; www.laspalmas.netfirms .com; Carretera 57 Km 617; RV sites M$270, s M$610-816, d M$760-940; **P** ✕ 🖥 🛏 ♿), out by the highway, is a family-oriented place with nice rooms around landscaped gardens. Features a pool, mini-golf and a level trailer park with full hookups. Also has a **tourist office** (☎ 882-50-05) with English-speaking staff.

To appease grumbling stomachs, try the bustling and long-standing local favorite **Restaurant Santa Fe** (☎ 882-07-53; Morelos 709; mains M$32-70) on Plaza de Armas, where bow-tied waiters will serve you a variety of Mexican standards or breakfast deals (M$55 to M$68).

From Matehuala, there are daily bus departures to Mexico City Terminal Norte (M$420, 7½-8 hours, 13 1st-class direct); to Monterrey hourly by 1st-class (M$213, 4½ hours), or two 2nd-class (M$173, five hours); to Saltillo (M$173, 3¼ hours, six 1st-class); to San Luis Potosí hourly 1st-class (M$121, two hours), three 2nd-class (M$105, 2¾ hours); and Querétaro (M$121, seven daily). For bus schedules to/from Real de Catorce see p612.

REAL DE CATORCE

☎ 488 / pop 1105 / elevation 2756m

Energy – in a spiritual sense – is a word commonly ascribed to the alluring village of Real de Catorce. This stark, compact and functioning 'ghost town' sits high on the fringes of the magical Sierra Madre Oriental. It was a wealthy silver-mining town of 40,000 people until early last century. Not long ago, it was nearly deserted, its streets lined with crumbling buildings, its mint a ruin and a few hundred people eking out an existence from the annual influx of pilgrims and old mine tailings.

Over the last few decades Real has experienced a revival; it has attracted several well-to-do Mexicans and foreigners (especially Europeans) who run some of the businesses and hotels in town. Many locals have built dwellings on the town's outskirts. Real is making a gradual comeback, so the 'ghost town' label hardly applies, although doors in abandoned buildings still creak in the breeze, dusty cobblestone streets end abruptly and many buildings are still in ruins.

To soak up its magic and unique atmosphere, you need to stay a night here, longer if you wish to explore the surrounding hills on foot or horseback.

History

Real de Catorce translates as 'Royal of 14': the '14' may have come from 14 Spanish soldiers killed here by indigenous resistance fighters around 1700. The town was founded in the mid-18th century and the church built between 1790 and 1817.

The town reached its peak in the late 19th century, vying to surpass the famed Valenciana mine of Guanajuato. It had opulent houses, a bullring and shops selling European luxury goods.

Just why Real became a ghost town within three decades is a mystery. Some locals claim (as they do in many ghost towns) that during the revolution (1910–20) *bandidos* hid out here and scared off other inhabitants. A more plausible explanation is that the price of silver slumped after 1900.

Orientation

You arrive in Real at the western end of the 2.3km Ogarrio tunnel. From the parking lot follow the road up to the right to Lanzagorta, a dusty, stony street heading west past the

REAL DE CATORCE

INFORMATION	
Café El Quemado...................1 A2	
Card Phone..........................2 B2	
Super la Nueva Sorpresa........3 B3	
Telefone Caseta...................4 B3	
Tourist Office......................5 B3	

SIGHTS & ACTIVITIES	
Galería Vega M57..................6 A2	
Palenque de Gallos...............7 A2	
Plaza de Toros.....................8 A1	
Taller de Platería.................9 B3	
Templo de la Purísima Concepción..................10 B3	

SLEEPING	
El Corral de Conde...............11 B2	
El Corral del Conde II...........12 B3	
Hostal Alcazaba..................13 A1	
Hotel El Ángel y El Corazón....14 B2	
Hotel El Real.....................15 B3	
Hotel El Real II...................16 B3	
Hotel Real de Álamos...........17 B2	
Hotel Shantiniketan.............18 A2	
Mesón de Abundancia..........19 B3	
Mesón de Refugio...............20 C3	
Rincón Magico....................21 A1	

EATING	
Café Azul...........................22 B3	
El Cactus Café....................23 B2	
El Tolentino.......................24 B2	
Eucalipto..........................25 A2	
Malambo...........................26 A3	

SHOPPING	
Artesanía Wixarita Wirikuta...27 B3	

TRANSPORT	
4WDs to Estación de Catorce..........................(see 29)	
Bus Station........................28 C3	
Horses for Hire...................29 A2	
Jeeps to Estación de Catorce..30 A3	

To El Quemado (7km); Estación de Catorce (10km)

Arroyo de la Concepción

To Pueblo Fantasma (4km)

---

church, to the center of town. Real is easy to get around – you can see the town limits from wherever you stand. Streets are in a grid; Lanzagorta and Constitución are the main drags. The municipal buildings are on Constitución and the plaza and Casa de la Moneda are between the two. Libertad heads north out of town to the cemetery and former bullring.

Information

See www.realdecatorce.net for a good overview of the town. Card phones are located around Plaza Hidalgo. There's an ATM in the Municipal building, but on busy weekends it occasionally runs out of money; best to bring cash.

Café El Quemado (Libertad 5; 10am-2pm, 4-6pm Mon-Fri, 2-8pm Sat & Sun; closed Wed) Internet café which shows occasional films (free).

Mesón de la Abundancia (887-50-44; Lanzagorta 11) This hotel changes US dollars, traveler's checks and euros.

Super La Nueva Sorpresa (Lanzagorta 2; 8am-8pm) Changes US dollars if it has pesos on hand.

Telephone caseta (east side Plaza Hidalgo)

Tourist office (887-50-71; Palacio Municipal, Constitución s/n; 9am-8pm) Opening hours are a little flexible; simple flier and good regional map available.

Sights & Activities

The ambience of the desert setting makes up for the lack of actual sights around town. If you're into walking or horseback riding, there's plenty to keep you occupied here for several days.

TEMPLO DE LA PURÍSIMA CONCEPCIÓN

This charming *parroquia* (parish church) is an impressive neoclassical building. The attraction for thousands of Mexican pilgrims is the reputedly miraculous image of St Francis of Assisi on one of the side altars. A cult has grown up around the statue, whose help is sought in solving problems and cleansing sins.

Walk through the door to the left of the altar to find a roomful of *retablos*, small pictures depicting threatening situations from which St Francis has rescued the victim, with a brief description of the incident – car accidents and medical operations, for example –

and some words of gratitude. *Retablos* have become much sought after by collectors and are very occasionally seen in antique shops. Sadly, most of those on sale have been stolen from churches.

Opposite the church's facade, the **Casa de la Moneda** (admission M$10; ☺ 10am-4pm Wed-Sun), the old mint, made coins for a couple of years in the 1860s. This classic monument has been exquisitely restored over the last few years. It now houses a cultural center-cum-gallery with several levels of temporary exhibitions, often on loan from museums in Mexico City. There are plans to incorporate the town's former museum (currently closed) into the site.

Just up the street from the *parroquia* on Juárez there is a local silver workshop, **Taller de Platería**.

GALERÍA VEGA M57

Real's only **art gallery** (Zaragoza 3; ☺ 11am-4pm Sat, until 3pm Sun) hosts exhibitions and installations of contemporary work in a variety of media in a restored colonial building.

PALENQUE DE GALLOS & PLAZA DE TOROS

A block northwest of the plaza lies a monument to the town's heyday – the **Palenque de Gallos** (Xicotencatl s/n; admission free; ☺ 9am-6pm), a cockfighting ring, built like a Roman amphitheater. It was restored in the 1970s and sometimes hosts theater or dance performances. Follow Zaragoza-Libertad north to the edge of the town where there are remains of the former bullring **Plaza de Toros**; the **Capilla de Guadalupe** (☺ 8am-5pm) and *panteón* (cemetery) across the street are free and worth a look.

HIKING

If you prefer to do your own hikes, you can head out from Real in almost any direction. The hike closest to home includes that up the hill to the **Pueblo Fantasmo** (Ghost Town), on the hill behind – and clearly visible from – the town center. Head along Lanzagorta and stay left (avoid the road that veers right to the car park). The track you follow was the former entrance to town before the tunnel existed. Allow at least one hour to get to the top – there is another section around 100m further on behind those ruins visible from the town. Beware that there are two large shafts (about 50m deep) in the ruins.

To extend this hike, head northwest along the ridge to the antennas and to the cross over the town (make sure you note this from the town before you leave as it becomes obscured when on the ridge). Follow the path *behind* the cross before you weave your way down to the cemetery (allow three to four hours).

Another shorter hike is to **Socavón de Purísima**, a large chimney of a former mine. Head down Allende and veer right at its end. You are on the road to Estación de Catorce. Follow this road until you reach the chimney (about 45 minutes one way). The road passes through a cut or split rock, the Cerro Trocado. To enter the mine, speak to the caretaker family (a tip is gratefully received). To return, it's a longer and harder slog back up the hill (one hour one way; on weekends you might be able to grab a lift in a Willys Jeep). Caution: be prepared – tell others where you're headed, take water, a hat and strong footwear; it's dry and unforgiving country.

HORSEBACK RIDING

Ride 'em cowboy! Numerous trails lead out into the dry, stark and fascinating desertscapes – hilly and flat – around Real. The most popular guided trail ride is the three-hour trip to **El Quemado**, the sacred mountain of the Huichol. Here you'll find expansive views of the high-desert plateau and a small shrine to the sun god.

Horse guides now belong to a union, approved by the municipality; if unsure, ask for a guide's credentials. The aim of the union is to standardize prices and safety. Rates are around M$60 per hour. Note that no protective hats are provided; you clomp off at your own risk.

The horses and guides congregate every morning around Plaza Hidalgo. Willys jeep trips can also be arranged to many of the same locations, mainly on weekends. Ask any of the drivers along Lanzagorta or Allende, or at the tourist office. Rates vary according to numbers.

Festivals & Events

Real is quiet during the week and busier on weekends. Semana Santa and Christmas are big events and the **Fiesta de San Francisco** is huge. Between September 25 and October 12, 150,000 pilgrims pay homage to the figure of St Francis of Assisi in the town's church. Many of them just come for the day while thousands stay in the town, filling every rentable room and sleeping rough in the plazas. The streets are lined with stalls selling religious souvenirs and food, while many of the town's more up-market restaurants close for a month. Tourists who desire the more tranquil 'ghost-town experience' should keep well away during this period. The **Festival del Desierto** cultural festival begins the second week in September and features folkloric music and dance performances in towns all around the region.

Sleeping

BUDGET

It can be very cold here in winter in the cheapest digs; bring a sleeping bag or request extra blankets.

Hotel Real de Álamos (Hospedaje Familiar; ☎ 887-50-09; Constitución 21; s/d M$150/250) This place – run by friendly owner Antonia – has small, basic but clean rooms with concrete walls and private bathroom. The terrace provides excellent views of town.

Rincón Mágico (☎ 887-51-13; cnr Libertad & Zaragoza; d without/with bathroom M$400/500). It's almost worth the price just to see the breath-taking and expansive valley views from the patio of this otherwise basic but *simpático* (friendly) place. Its five rooms have a relaxed, slightly disorganized, hippie feel. It's a bit of a dusty walk to get here.

MIDRANGE

Hostal Alcazaba (☎ 887-50-75; Libertad (Zaragoza 33); camping per person M$20, apt M$650-1000; **P**) Opposite the cemetery, this option has four bright, light *casitas*, some with kitchen and all with private bathroom and panoramic views. There's also a house (previously the owners' and great for families). The enormous garden hosts excellent desert flora, but has seen better days.

Hotel El Real (☎ 887-50-58; www.hotelreal.com; Morelos 20; s M$650, d M$750-800; 🖵) This comfortable (if ever-so-slightly tired) restored place has pleasant rooms on three floors crowded around an open courtyard. Some (pricier rooms) have views over the town and the hills. There's a good restaurant. The hotel's second 'branch' – along similar lines but with a bar in front – is on Juaréz and Iturbide.

El Corral del Conde (☎ 887-50-48; Constitución 17; ste from M$650/850) The original 11 spacious stone-walled rooms somehow miss the mark on the boutique hotel front. There's the odd bit of exposed piping and cracked steps, but it's got character. Its second hotel, El Corral

del Conde II – just down the hill on Morelos & Lanzagorta – has another 13 newer rooms.

TOP END

Real has seen a recent surge of restoration of old buildings into inviting upmarket accommodations.

Hotel Shantiniketan (Morada de Paz; ☎ 887-50-98; moradadepaz@realdecatorce.net; cnr Zaragoza & Lerdo; r M$550-1500) There's a definite karma about this recently restored place: the nine rooms are named after Indian spiritual leaders. Each is minimalist and unfussy and surrounds a lovely garden courtyard.

Mesón de Abundancia (☎ 887-50-44; Lanzagorta 11; d M$650-950, tr M$1000, ste M$1000-1200, f M$1500) Re-live the town's bonanza era on the desert plateau in this stone citadel. The 19th century former treasury (*tesorería*) building has been renovated into a hotel and restaurant. All 11 rooms are simply and tastefully decorated with local crafts (minus TV). Rates are cheaper on weekdays (excluding holidays). Ironically, given its cash-oriented past, the hotel accepts some credit cards, except American Express.

Other recommendations:

Hotel El Ángel y El Corazón (☎ 887-50-77; elangel@realdecatorce.net; Iturbide 3; r M$750-1300) In a tranquil location with some stylish, light rooms and two apartments.

Mesón de Refugio (☎ 887-50-68; Ramón Corona s/n; r M$850-1150) More contemporary design than the other renovated options, but some rooms are cramped.

Eating & Drinking

At the entrance to Lanzagorta there are cheap local joints for the ubiquitous Mexican snacks. Several restaurants compete (with each other and with the better hotels) to do the best Italian and Mexican cuisine. Some close during the week if business is slow.

Café Azul (Lanzagorta 27; snacks M$20-50; 🕙 9am-9pm Thu-Tue) Open all day, this Swiss-run scene is perfect for breakfasts and snacks and light meals including excellent crepes and organic salads.

El Cactus Café (☎ 887-50-56; Plaza Hidalgo; mains M$40-90; ✗) This cheery eatery is run by an Italian cook and his Mexican wife. It has a friendly ambience and long wooden bench tables and seats. The menu features homemade bread and pasta (of course), plus there are good Mexican and veggie options.

El Tolentino (☎ 887-50-81; Terán 7; mains M$60-130; 🕙 9am-9:30pm) This Mexican-themed place serves good country specialties and decent breakfasts. The local atmosphere is enhanced during weekends by live music. During the day, head upstairs to the terrace.

Malambo (Lanzagorta 2; mains M$65-140; 2:30pm-9:30pm Mon-Fri, noon-11pm Sat & Sun) With a quaint outdoor setting by a fountain (as well as plainer indoors), this pleasant place serves up a range of delights, including Mexican dishes and Italian pastas. The salads – containing *cabuche* (cactus flower) – are particularly tasty (M$40).

Eucalipto (887-50-51; Cnr Lerdo & Libertad; mains M$80-160; 1-10pm Wed-Sun) Named after the droopy looking eucalyptus gum tree in the courtyard, this pleasant place conjures up a perkier range of pastas and an array of meat dishes (thankfully, not koala) – from rib eye to T-bone – and a selection of wines, from Chile to France. It's one of the priciest in town, but it's excellent quality cuisine.

There are several cozy eating areas at the restaurant in Mesón de Abundancia (p611), one with a bar and fireplace. The hearty (read massive) servings of Italian and Mexican dishes are *muy rico* (delicious). It's open all day, including for breakfast (M$25 to M$50).

Shopping

Dotted around town are numerous *artesanías* shops – jewelry, silverwork and leather products. Many of these are owned by the town's restaurant or hotel proprietors and the selection and quality varies greatly. Worth checking out for Huichol pieces is **Artesanal Wixarita Wirikuta** (Lanzagorta s/n).

Getting There & Away

Sendor runs 1st-class buses from Matehuala's bus station to Real de Catorce (M$47, two hours) at 7:45am, 9:45am, 11:45am, 1:45pm and 5:45pm; the bus can be caught in town 15 minutes later at the Sendor's office on Guerrero, a little east of and across the street from Hotel Álamo on Méndez. Upon arrival in Matehuala, ask if you need to buy a ticket to Real in advance. Return tickets can be purchased in Matehuala only if you are coming back on the same day.

On arrival in Real, buses park at the east entrance of the Ogarrio tunnel. There, in order to pass through the tunnel, you change to a smaller bus which drops off (or picks up if returning to Matehuala) at the western end of the tunnel, in Real. Confirm the return bus schedule upon arrival.

Return buses from Real to Matehuala wer at 7:45am, 11:45am, 1:45pm and 5:45pm (M$47, two hours). Tickets are purchased on board the bus at the tunnel's western entrance in Real.

If driving from Hwy 57 north of Matehuala, turn off toward Cedral, 20km west. After Cedral, you turn south to reach Catorce on what must be one of the world's longest cobblestone roads. It's a slow but spectacula zigzag drive up a steep mountainside. The Ogarrio tunnel (M$20 per vehicle) is only wid enough for one vehicle; workers stationed a each end with telephones control traffic flow between 8am and 11pm. If it's really busy you'll have to leave your car at the eastern tunnel entrance and continue by pick-up or cart If you drive through, you must leave it in the dusty parking area to the left of the market.

Vintage Willys jeeps leave Real around noon (and on demand), downhill from the plaza along Allende, for the rough but spectacular descent to the small hamle of Estación de Catorce (M$30, one hour) From there, buses head to San Tiburcio where there are connections for Saltill and Zacatecas.

GUANAJUATO STATE

The rocky highland state of Guanajuato (population 4.9 million) is full of riche of every kind. In colonial times, mineral resources attracted Spanish prospectors to mine for silver, gold, iron, lead, zinc and tin For two centuries the state produced enor mous wealth, extracting up to 40% of th world's silver. Silver barons in Guanajuato city enjoyed opulent lives at the expense o indigenous people who worked the mines first as slave labor and then as wage slaves Eventually, resenting the dominance o Spanish-born colonists, the well-heeled cri ollo class of the Guanajuato and Querétar states contributed to plans for rebellion (se boxed text, p629).

These days, the state's treasures are th quaint colonial towns of Guanajuato an San Miguel de Allende. The industria town of León is important economically a a center of leather production. Visitors t this region can enjoy its precious legacies stunning colonial architecture, establishe cultural scenes and a stream of never-end

HUICHOL VISIONS

The remote Sierra Madre Occidental, in and around the far north of Jalisco, is the home of the Huichol, one of Mexico's most distinctive and enduring indigenous groups. Fiercely independent people, they were one of the few indigenous groups not subjugated by the Aztecs. Traditionally, they lived by hunting deer and cultivating scattered fields of corn in the high valleys.

The arrival of the Spanish had little immediate effect on the Huichol and it wasn't until the 17th century that the first Catholic missionaries reached the Huichol homelands. Rather than convert to Christianity, the Huichol incorporated various elements of Christian teachings into their traditional animist belief systems. In Huichol mythology, gods become personalized as plants, totem animal species and natural objects, while their supernatural form is explored in religious rituals.

Every year the Huichol leave their isolated homeland and make a pilgrimage of some 400km across Mexico's central plateau to what is now northern San Luis Potosí state. In this harsh desert region, they seek out the *mescal* cactus *(Lophophora williamsii)*, known as peyote cactus. The rounded peyote 'buttons' contain a powerful hallucinogenic drug (whose chief element is mescaline) that is central to the Huichol's rituals and complex spiritual life. Most of the buttons are collected, dried and carried back to the tribal homelands, but a small piece is eaten on the spot, as a gesture to the plant. Small amounts of peyote help to ward off hunger, cold and fatigue, while larger amounts are taken on ritual occasions, such as the return from the annual pilgrimage. In particular, peyote is used by shamans whose visions inform them about when to plant and harvest corn, where to hunt deer or how to treat illnesses.

Peyote is illegal in Mexico. Under Mexican law, Huicholes are permitted to use it for their spiritual purposes. For the Huicholes, it has great cultural and spiritual significance; indiscriminate use is regarded as offensive, even sacrilegious.

Traditionally, the main Huichol art forms were telling stories, making masks and detailed geometric embroidery, or 'yarn pictures.' In the last few decades, the Huichol have been depicting their myths and visions graphically, using brightly colored beads pressed into a beeswax-covered substrate. This exquisite artwork is sold in craft markets, shops and galleries. Prices are usually fixed and the Huichol don't like to haggle. This art may be expensive compared to some (of the tackier) souvenirs, but each takes a long time to produce and each piece is unique. To see the best work, visit one of the specialist museums or shops in Zapopan (Guadalajara), Tepic, Puerto Vallarta or Zacatecas.

ing festivals…not to mention friendly, proud locals and lively university scenes.

GUANAJUATO
☎ 473 / pop 70,798 / elevation 2017m

The extraordinary Unesco World Heritage city of Guanajuato was founded in 1559 due to the region's rich silver and gold deposits. Opulent colonial buildings, stunning tree-filled plazas and brightly-colored houses are crammed onto the steep slopes of a ravine. Excellent museums, handsome theaters and a fine marketplace punctuate the cobblestoned streets. The city's 'main' roads twist around the hillsides and plunge into tunnels, formerly rivers.

The city is best known internationally for its acclaimed annual international arts festival, the Festival Cervantino. Yet this colorful and lively place holds center stage all year long; much of the youthful vibrancy and prolific cultural activ-

ities – *callejoneadas*, films, theater and orchestras – can be attributed to the 20,000 students of the city's own University of Guanajuato.

The city usually boasts fine weather during the day, but beware of cold and windy nights in the winter.

History

One of the hemisphere's richest silver veins was uncovered in 1558 at La Valenciana mine; for 250 years the mine produced 20% of the world's silver. Colonial barons benefiting from this mineral treasure were infuriated when King Carlos III of Spain slashed their share of the wealth in 1765. The king's 1767 decree banishing the Jesuits from Spanish dominions further alienated both the wealthy barons and the poor miners, who held allegiance to the Jesuits.

This anger was focused in the War of Independence. In 1810 rebel leader Miguel

Hidalgo set off the independence movement with his Grito de Independencia (Cry for Independence) in nearby Dolores (see boxed text, p629). Guanajuato citizens joined the independence fighters and defeated the Spanish and loyalists, seizing the city in the rebellion's first military victory. When the Spaniards eventually retook the city they retaliated by conducting the infamous 'lottery of death,' in which names of Guanajuato citizens were drawn at random and the 'winners' were tortured and hanged.

Independence was eventually won, freeing the silver barons to amass further wealth. From this wealth arose many of the mansions, churches and theaters.

In the late 1990s the state prospered under its PAN (National Action Party) governor, Vicente Fox Quesada, with Mexico's lowest unemployment rate and an export rate three times the national average. Fox was chosen as the PAN candidate for the 2000 presidential election and his popularity sealed the victory (he retired in 2006).

Orientation

Guanajuato's center is quite compact, with a few major streets and lots of tiny *callejones*. It's ideal for walking, but tricky to drive around. The main street, running roughly east–west, is called Juárez from the Mercado Hidalgo to the basilica on Plaza de la Paz. East of the basilica, this street continues as a pedestrian street called Obregón to the Jardín de la Unión (the city's main plaza), then continues further east as Sopeña.

Roughly parallel to Juárez/Obregón is another long street, running from the Alhóndiga to the university and bearing the names 28 de Septiembre, Pocitos and Lascuraín de Retana along the way. Hidalgo (aka Cantarranas) parallels Sopeña and is another important street. Once you know these streets you can't get lost – just walk downhill until you find one of them. You can, however, have a great time getting lost among the maze of crooked *callejones* winding up the hills from the center.

Traffic on these main arteries is one-way, traveling east to west. Vehicles (including public buses) going west to east must use the main underground roadway, Subterránea Padre Miguel Hidalgo, a one-way route along the dried-up Río Guanajuato riverbed. (The river was diverted after it flooded the city in 1905.) At least eight other tunnels have been constructed to cope with increasing traffic. The Túnel Noreste Ingeniero Ponciano Aguilar and Túnel Santa Fe, running one-way east to west, enable vehicles to bypass the city center altogether.

Surrounding central Guanajuato is the winding Carretera Panorámica, offering great views of the town and surrounding hills.

Information

INTERNET ACCESS

Several internet places are on Plaza Mexiamora. There are many others around town; most charge M$10 per hour.

Internet Mexiquito (Independencia 6; ☾ 10am–10pm) A chill atmosphere with coffee.

LAUNDRY

Lavandería Automática Internacional (Doblado 28; ☾ 9:30am–8pm Mon-Fri, 10am–5pm Sat) Load of 3kg for M$50.

Lavandería del Centro (Sopeña 26; ☾ 9am–8:30pm Mon-Fri, 9am–4pm Sat) Costs M$30 per 1–3kg or M$50 per 3–5kg.

MEDICAL SERVICES

Hospital General (☎ 733-15-73, 733-15-76; Carretera a Silao, Km 6.5)

MONEY

Banks along Av Juárez change cash and traveler's checks (but some only until 2pm) and have ATMs. Banorte is diagonally opposite the tourist office.

Divisas Dimas (Juárez 33A; ☾ 10am–8pm Mon-Sat) Convenient *casa de cambio*.

Viajes Georama (☎ 732-51-01; Plaza de la Paz 34) American Express agent that books and confirms tickets, but doesn't exchange traveler's checks.

POST OFFICE

Post office (☎ 732-03-85; Ayuntamiento 25)

TELEPHONE & FAX

Card phones are on Pasaje de los Arcos, an alley off the south side of Obregón near the tourist office.

Computel (Ayuntamiento 25) Opposite the post office, with fax and internet.

TOURIST INFORMATION

State tourist office (☎ 732-19-82; www.guanajuato-travel.com, www.guanajuato.gob.mx; Plaza de la Paz 14; ☾ 9am–7pm Mon-Fri, 10am–4pm Sat, 10am–2pm Sun) Friendly staff, with free city maps and brochures (in Spanish & English).

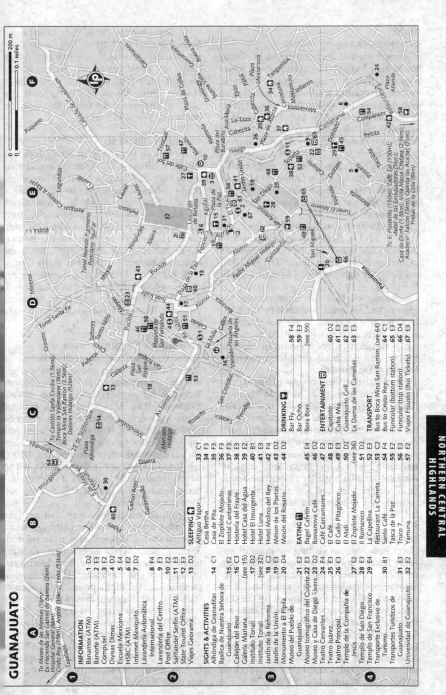

Sights

CENTRAL PLAZAS

A wander around the beautiful main plazas, the bustling hubs of Guanajuato's social life, is a good introduction to Guanajuato's historic center. Pretty **Jardín de la Unión**, surrounded by restaurants and shaded by Indian laurel trees, is the social heart of the city. Here, tourists and well-to-do locals congregate in the late afternoon, along with buskers, shoe shiners and mariachis.

The elegant Teatro Juárez sits on its southeast corner. Walk west on Obregón to **Plaza de la Paz**, the small triangle beside the basilica, surrounded by the former homes of wealthy silver lords.

Meander west and south along the curving Av Juárez to **Plazuela de los Ángeles**, where the steps and ice-cream stands are popular gathering spots for students. The Callejón del Beso (see right) is just a few meters uphill from here.

Continue on Juárez to three picturesque spaces: the handsome **Jardín de la Reforma**, behind the row of classical columns; **Plaza San Roque**, where *entremeses* (theatrical sketches) are performed in the Cervantino festival (p619); and nearby is the pleasant, shady **Plazuela de San Fernando**.

Head further west on Av Juárez to the bustling area in front of Mercado Hidalgo. A block north, **Plaza Alhóndiga** is a usually empty space with wide steps leading up to the Alhóndiga. From there, wander back east along 28 de Septiembre (which changes names several times), past museums and the university, with a few twists and turns, to **Plaza del Baratillo** with its Florentine fountain. A right turn and a short block south from there will bring you back to Jardín de la Unión.

THEATERS

Don't leave without visiting the magnificent **Teatro Juárez** (☎ 732-01-83; Sopeña s/n; adult/concession M$35/15; ⏱ 9am-1:45pm & 5-7:45pm Tue-Sun when no performances are scheduled). It was built between 1873 and 1903 and inaugurated by the dictator Porfirio Díaz, whose lavish tastes are reflected in the plush red and gold interior. The outside is festooned with columns, lamp posts and statues; inside the impression is Moorish, with the bar and lobby gleaming with carved wood, stained glass and precious metals. Video/camera use is M$60/30.

The **Teatro Principal** (☎ 732-15-23; Hidalgo s/n) and **Teatro Cervantes** (☎ 732-11-69; Plaza Allende s/n) are not as spectacular as Teatro Juárez, but they host a full schedule of performances during the Cervantino festival and less-regular shows at other times. Statues of Don Quixote and Sancho Panza grace the small Plaza Allende, in front of Teatro Cervantes.

CALLEJÓN DEL BESO

Narrowest of the many narrow alleys that climb the hills from Guanajuato's main streets is this callejón (the Alley of the Kiss), where the balconies of the houses on either side of the alley practically touch. In a Guanajuato legend, a fine family once lived on this street and their daughter fell in love with a common miner. They were forbidden to see each other, but the miner rented a room opposite and the lovers exchanged furtive *besos* (kisses) from these balconies. Inevitably, the romance was discovered and the couple met a tragic end. From the Plazuela de los Ángeles on Av Juárez, walk about 40m up Callejón del Patrocinio to see the tiny alley on your left.

ALHÓNDIGA DE GRANADITAS

The site of the first major rebel victory in Mexico's War of Independence is now a history and art **museum** (☎ 732-11-12; 28 de Septiembre; admission M$43, Sun free; ⏱ 10am-5:45pm Tue-Sat, 10am-2:45pm Sun). The Alhóndiga was a massive grain-and-seed storehouse built between 1798 and 1808. In 1810 it became a fortress for Spanish troops and loyalist leaders. They barricaded themselves inside when 20,000 rebels led by Miguel Hidalgo attempted to take Guanajuato. It looked as if the outnumbered Spaniards would be able to hold out. Then, on September 28, 1810, a young miner named Juan José de los Reyes Martínez (aka El Pípila), under orders from Hidalgo, tied a stone slab to his back and, thus protected from Spanish bullets, set the gates ablaze. While the Spaniards choked on smoke, the rebels moved in and took the Alhóndiga, killing most of those inside. (El Pípila probably perished in the battle, but some versions of the story have it that he lived to a ripe old age.)

The Alhóndiga was used as a prison for a century, beginning in 1864, but it became a museum in 1967. Don't miss José Chávez Morado's dramatic murals of Guanajuato's history on the staircases. Video or camera use costs M$60.

MUSEO Y CASA DE DIEGO RIVERA

Diego Rivera's birthplace is now an excellent **museum** (☎ 732-11-97; Pocitos 47; adult/student M$15/5; ☑ 10am-6:30pm Tue-Sat, 10am-2:30pm Sun) honoring the painter (the Marxist Rivera was *persona non grata* here for years); it's worth spending an hour or so here, longer if you're a Rivera fan.

Rivera and a twin brother were born in the house in 1886 (his twin died at the age of two) and lived here until the family moved to Mexico City six years later. The museum's ground floor is the Rivera family home, with 19th-century antiques and fine furniture.

The 1st and 2nd floors feature a permanent collection of his original works and preliminary sketches (completed for some of his famous murals in Mexico City), plus there's a nude of Frida Kahlo. The newer renovated upper floors host temporary exhibitions of work by Mexican and international artists. An intimate theater upstairs has occasional films and features B&W photographs of Kahlo and Rivera.

MUSEO ICONOGRÁFICO DEL QUIJOTE

Surprisingly interesting, this **museum** (☎ 732-33-76; Doblado 1; admission M$20; ☑ 10am-6:30pm Tue-Sat, 10am-2:30pm Sun) is worth half an hour of your time. It fronts the tiny plaza in front of the Templo de San Francisco. Every exhibit relates to Don Quixote de la Mancha, the notorious Spanish literary hero, depicted in numerous different media by different artists in different styles. Paintings, statues, tapestries, even chess sets, clocks and postage stamps all feature the quixotic icon and his bumbling companion Sancho Panza.

UNIVERSIDAD DE GUANAJUATO

The main building of this **university** (UGTO; ☎ 732-00-06 ext 8001; www.ugto.mx; Lascuraín de Retana 5), whose ramparts are visible above much of the city, is on Lascuraín de Retana, one block up the hill from the basilica. The distinctive multistory white-and-blue building with the crenelated pediment dates from the 1950s. The design was (and some might say, continues to be) controversial as this dominating structure impedes the characteristic, historic cityscape.

MUSEO DEL PUEBLO DE GUANAJUATO

Located beside the university, this **art museum** (☎ 732-29-90; Pocitos 7; adult/student M$15/5; ☑ 10am-6:30pm Tue-Sat, 10am-3pm Sun) displays a collection of Mexican miniatures, 18th- and 19th-century art and a room featuring works by Guanajuatan painter Hermenegildo Bustos. The museum occupies the former mansion of the Marqueses de San Juan de Rayas, who owned the San Juan de Rayas mine. The private church upstairs in the courtyard contains a powerful mural by José Chávez Morado.

CHURCHES

The **Basílica de Nuestra Señora de Guanajuato** (Plaza de la Paz s/n), a block west of Jardín de la Unión, contains a jewel-covered image of the Virgin, patron of Guanajuato. The wooden statue was supposedly hidden from the Moors in a cave in Spain for 800 years. Felipe II of Spain gave it to Guanajuato in thanks for the wealth it provided to the crown. Next door, the small **Galería Mariana** (Plaza de la Paz s/n; admission M$20 ☑ 10am-6pm Mon & Thu-Sun) is dedicated to images of Mary and other Catholic relics.

Other fine colonial churches include the **Templo de San Diego** (Jardín de la Union s/n), opposite the Jardín de la Unión; the **Templo de San Francisco** (Doblado s/n); and the large **Templo de la Compañía de Jesús** (Lascuraín de Retana s/n), which was completed in 1747 for the Jesuit seminary whose buildings are now occupied by the University of Guanajuato.

FUNICULAR

This **incline railway** (Plaza Constancia s/n; one-way/round-trip M$12/24; ☑ 8am-9:45pm) inches up (and down) the slope behind the Teatro Juárez to a terminal near the El Pípila monument. Heading up is fun, but to descend, save your pennies and walk down (there are two obvious well-paved routes).

MONUMENTO A EL PÍPILA

The monument to El Pípila honors the hero who torched the Alhóndiga gates on September 28, 1810, enabling Hidalgo's forces to win the first victory of the independence movement. The statue shows El Pípila holding his torch high over the city. On the base is the inscription *'Aún hay otras Alhóndigas por incendiar'* ('There are still other Alhóndigas to burn').

Two routes from the center of town go up steep, picturesque lanes. One goes east on Sopeña from Jardín de la Unión, then turns right on Callejón del Calvario (this becomes Pochote; turn right at Subida San Miguel).

Another ascent, unmarked, goes uphill from the small plaza on Alonso. Alternatively, the 'Pípila-ISSSTE' bus heading west on Juárez will let you off right by the statue, or you can ride up in the funicular.

TEMPLO LA VALENCIANA & BOCA MINA SAN RAMÓN

On a hill overlooking Guanajuato, 5km north of the center, is the magnificent **Templo La Valenciana** (Iglesia de San Cayetano). Its facade is spectacular and its interior dazzles with ornate golden altars, filigree carvings and giant paintings. One legend says that the Spaniard who started the nearby San Ramón mine promised San Cayetano that if it made him rich, he would build a church to honor the saint. Another says that the silver baron of La Valenciana, Conde de Rul, tried to atone for exploiting the miners by building the ultimate in Churrigueresque churches. Whatever the motive, ground was broken in 1765 and the church was completed in 1788.

The **Boca Mina San Ramón** (adult/concession M$20/10; 10am-7pm) is part of the famous Valenciana mining district (the best known mine, Boca Mina Valenciana, was closed to visitors at the time of research). Silver was discovered here in 1548. The small visitor's center is worth a quick half-hour. It features some dusty displays and pieces of old mining equipment. More exciting is to descend the steps into a mine shaft to a depth of 60m (note: not for claustrophobics).

To get to Boca Mina San Ramón, take a regular 'Cristo Rey' or 'Valenciana' bus from the bus stop on the corner of Alhóndiga and 28 de Septiembre. Get off at Templo La Valenciana and walk past the church to the mine entrance.

EX-HACIENDA SAN GABRIEL DE BARRERA

To escape Guanajuato's bustling streets, head 2.5km west to this magnificent colonial home which is now a **museum** (732-06-19; Camino Antiguo a Marfil Km 2.5; adult/concession M$22/15; 9am-6pm) with stunning gardens. This tranquil retreat is well worth a couple of hours. Video/camera use costs M$25/20.

Built at the end of the 17th century, this was the grand hacienda of Captain Gabriel de Barrera, whose family was descended from the first Conde de Rul of the famous La Valenciana mine. Opened as a museum in 1979, the hacienda, with its opulent period European furnishings, provides an insight into the lives of the wealthy of the time.

The large, shady grounds, originally devoted to processing ore from La Valenciana, were converted in 1945 to a series of beautiful terraced gardens based on international designs, with pavilions, pools, fountains and footpaths.

Take one of the frequent 'Marfil' buses heading west in the subterranean tunnel under Juárez and ask the driver to drop you at Hotel Misión Guanajuato.

MUSEO DE LAS MOMIAS

This famous **museum** (Museum of the Mummies; 732-06-39; Explanada del Pantéon Municipal s/n; adult/ child M$50/30; 9am-6pm) is one of the most bizarre (some might say grotesque) at the *pantéon*. This popular place is a quintessential example of Mexico's obsession with death; visitors come from all over to see disinterred corpses. A sense of humor may be necessary, not least because some of the descriptions make light of the unfortunate individuals' fates.

While technically these are mummified remains – due to the high levels of lime and clay in the soil which inhibits decomposition – the bodies are not thousands of years old. The first remains were dug up in 1865 to make room for more bodies in the cemeteries. What the authorities uncovered were not skeletons but flesh mummified (many feature grotesque forms and facial expressions). Today the museum displays more than 100 mummies.

The complex is on the western edge of town, a 10-minute ride from Av Juárez on any 'Momias' bus.

CRISTO REY

Cristo Rey (Christ the King) is a 20m bronze statue of Jesus erected in 1950 on the summit of the Cerro de Cubilete, 15km west of Guanajuato. It is said to be the exact geographical center of Mexico. The statue is a popular attraction for Mexican tourists; there is a special significance in having Jesus at the heart of their country.

Tour agencies offer 3½-hour trips to the statue (see opposite), but you can go on your own from the center. Buses marked 'Cubilete' or 'Cristo Rey' depart every hour or so from in front of the Alhóndiga, Calle Alhóndiga (M$15).

Courses

Guanajuato is a university town and has an excellent atmosphere for studying Spanish. Group classes average around US$6.50 per hour and private lessons average US$15 an hour. Schools can arrange homestays with meals for around US$20 per day. Additional costs may include registration and/or placement test fees, excursions and extracurricular activities.

The Universidad de Guanajuato (p617) offers Spanish courses with classes in Mexican and Latin American culture. Summer courses (June and July), semester-long courses (beginning January and August) and monthly courses available.

Academia Falcón (☎ /fax 731-07-45, 731-10-84; www.academiafalcon.com; Paseo de la Presa 80) Well-established language institute, 3km south of the center. Spanish classes have not more than five; private classes also available.

Escuela Mexicana (☎ 732-50-05; www.escuelamexicana.com; Potrero 12) Small school with classes in Spanish (grammar, conversation, literature) and other topics from pre-Hispanic culture to dance and cooking. Homestay and onsite accommodations available. Supports local orphanages and old people's home (visits possible for students).

Instituto Tonali (☎ 732-73-52; Juárez 4) Spanish classes at all levels; homestays organized for around US$20 per day.

Tours

Several agencies offer similar tours of Guanajuato's major sights (usually in Spanish). You can reach all the same places on local buses, but if your time is limited a tour may be useful.

Transporte Exclusivo de Turismo (☎ 732-59-68; cnr Av Juárez & Calle 5 de Mayo), in a kiosk, and **Transportes Turísticos de Guanajuato** (☎ 732-21-34; cnr Obregón & El Truco), below the front courtyard of the basilica, both offer daily Guanajuato colonial tours, which include the mummies, La Valenciana mine and church, the Pípila monument and the Carretera Panorámica. These depart three times daily, last 3½ hours and cost M$100. A three-hour tour heads up to Cristo Rey (M$100; see opposite). The eight-hour 'independence circuit' runs through Dolores Hidalgo and San Miguel de Allende (M$200). Five-hour night tours (M$90) take in Guanajuato's views and nightspots and the street parties called *callejoneadas* (see p624).

Festivals & Events

See disfruteguanajuato.com for forthcoming events under 'Noticias.'

Baile de las Flores The Flower Dance takes place on the Thursday before Semana Santa. The next day, mines are open to the public for sightseeing and celebrations. Miners decorate altars to La Virgen de los Dolores, a manifestation of the Virgin Mary who looks after miners.

Fiestas de San Juan y Presa de la Olla The festivals of San Juan are celebrated at the Presa de la Olla park in late June. The 24th is the big bash for the saint's day itself, with dances, music, fireworks and picnics. Then on the first Monday in July, everyone comes back to the park for another big party celebrating the opening of the dam's floodgates.

Día de la Cueva Cave Day is a country fair held on July 31, when locals walk to a cave in the nearby hills to honor San Ignacio de Loyola and enjoy a festive picnic.

Fiesta de la Virgen de Guanajuato This festival on August 9 commemorates the date when Felipe II gave the people of Guanajuato the jeweled wooden Virgin that now adorns the basilica.

Festival Internacional Cervantino (www.festivalcervantino.gob.mx) In the 1950s the arts festival was merely *entremeses* from Miguel Cervantes' work performed by students. It has grown to become one of Latin America's foremost arts extravaganzas. Music, dance and theater groups arrive from around the world, performing diverse works (mostly non-Cervantes related). The festival lasts two to three weeks starting around the second week of October. Tickets for single events range from US$10 to US$50. Tickets and hotels should be booked in advance. Advance tickets are available through the **Ticketmaster website** (www.ticketmaster.com.mx). In Guanajuato, buy tickets from the ticket office on the southeast side of Teatro Juárez.

Sleeping

The most classy in-town address is Jardín de la Unión, where a couple of 'opulent' colonial-style hotels have rooms, bars and restaurants facing the lively but traffic-free plaza. Many centrally-located budget and midrange options are in converted homes. During the Cervantino Festival in October, prices can go above the normal high-season rates given here, which apply during the Christmas, Semana Santa and summer holiday periods. Prices can be significantly less outside the high seasons.

BUDGET

Casa Bertha (☎ /fax 732-13-16; www.paginasprodigy.com/casabertha; Tamboras 9; r per person without/with private bathroom from M$150/180, apt per person M$200-250) This family-run *casa de huéspedes* is a labyrinth of various sized rooms (a couple have internal-facing windows) and three family-size apartments with cable TV. Travelers praise friendly owner Juan for his hospitality and for

LIVING WITH MOJIGANGAS

Mojigangas (often called *gigantes*, *marmotas*, *monos*, *papa güevos* and – inaccurately – giant puppets) are massive caricature figures 11-13ft high. They were brought to Mexico by the Spanish conquerors around 1600 to represent respected public figures and to cheer along local religious festivities.

According to Guanajuato artists Felipe Olmos, 41, and Japanese-born Mika Matsuishi, 35, the tradition of high-quality *mojigangas*, while heralded in Spain, had languished in Mexico over the years. Felipe was determined to change this. He recalled as a child when *mojigangas* danced during festivals in his village, San Juan de Los Lagos, in Jalisco. In 2002 (by then himself a sculptor and studying at San Miguel de Allende's School of Bellas Artes) Felipe decided to produce and donate 20 *mojigangas* – made with the help of a team of 130 people – to his home town's 2003 Spring parade. 'My project was to bring good quality *mojigangas* back to life.'

Meanwhile, Mika and he romanced over a *mojiganga;* she was studying ceramics alongside Felipe in San Miguel, but was unaware that he was the creator of these beautiful figures that won her heart in one of the town's festivals. 'I saw my first *mojiganga* and thought, *woowww!*' Later, she was invited by Felipe to help design and create *mojigangas* and a professional and personal partnership began. Their creations have received coverage as far away as France, Japan and the US. Creating *mojigangas* is an involved and time-consuming process. Each figure can take up to a month to complete. The artists sketch an idea and then make a plasticine figure. Then they construct a giant bamboo, metal, polyurethane and clay model (up to 200kg of clay can be used), from which a mould is made. This is covered with layers of papier mâché then, when dry, the figure is painted and, finally, dressed.

keeping a homelike and clean place, with great rooftop terrace, town vistas and wireless internet. Head up beside Teatro Principal to Plaza Mexiamora and look for the 'Casa Bertha' sign and arrow painted on a wall. Prices are around M$20 lower out of season.

El Hostelito (☎ 732-54-83; hostalitogto@hotmail .com; Sangre de Cristo 9; dm M$200, r M$250-300;) Just look at the travelers' comments book to see that this centrally located, well-run, HI-affiliated hostel is 'one of the nicest in Mexico.' It has helpful staff, a kitchen, private rooms with bathroom, single-sex dorms, cable TV, breakfast and (dare we admit) even your beds are made for you. Prices are significantly less in low season and there are discounts for HI members and two or more nights.

Casa de Dante (☎ 731-09-09; www.hospedajedante .com; Callejón de Zaragoza 25; dm & s/d incl breakfast M$250/500) 'This house is your house' greets the owner of this ultra-friendly family-run hostel. You can opt for a dormitory or for one of eight well-kept rooms (some with private bathrooms) plus there's a kitchen, DVD movie lounge, an outdoor BBQ on the terrace and hospitality (read frequent farewell parties for longer-term guests who rave about this place). It's a little out of town and up 156 steps, but – phew! – worth the effort. Head up the *callejón* next to Hotel Independencia on Paseo de la Presa.

Casa de Pita (☎ 732-15-32; www.casadepita.com; Cabecita 26; dm M$180, r & apt M$350-450) A literal maze of atmospheric guest rooms in this centrally located converted house. The dormitory has a private bathroom and includes breakfast (M$25 extra for those in rooms). Internet wi-fi connection available.

MIDRANGE
Hotel Molino del Rey (☎ 732-22-23; mach1@avantel .net; cnr Campanero & Belauzaran; s/d/tr M$400/570/730) An easy stroll from the center, the 'King's Mill' is notable for its quiet, convenient location. Its 40 rooms are set around a patio, and some rooms are nicer than others (and some face into the patio). A small ground-floor restaurant serves tasty, inexpensive meals.

Hostal Cantarranas (☎ 732-51-41; www.hostalcantar ranasgtocapital.com; Cantarranas 50; r M$450, with kitchenette M$590) An old building with pleasant rooms (mostly apartments) and a sunny rooftop.

Motel de las Embajadoras (☎ 731-01-05; cnr Embajadoras & Paseo Madero; s/d/tr M$450/750/850;) This reliable motel-style option looks more like an hacienda of the 1970s, around a courtyard of plants, with simple but clean rooms set under a verandah. It's great if you're driving and want to avoid the tunnels and downtown and it's only five minutes from the center on an 'Embajadoras' or 'Presa' bus. The res-

According to Felipe, despite the pre-planning of the figures, they transpire gradually. He says that they only have hearts – and therefore come alive – when they are completely finished. And *mojigangas* never die. 'Although they are very fragile – for example, they can fall in the street and be damaged – they live in the minds of the people who see them or interact with them,' says Felipe.

Included among those who can be said to interact 'intimately' with *mojigangas* are the people who perform inside them. 'Regardless of the character you inhabit – whether Frida Kahlo, Diego Rivera, La Catrina (the skeleton who represents Death in Mexico's Day of the Dead celebrations) – the important thing is that the people inside are having fun. If *they* are having fun, the character is having fun.' Mika says, 'Being anonymous inside the figure gives you much more energy. Men often prefer to be a female character because they are anonymous and can play up their feminine sides.'

Felipe and Mika are proud that *mojigangas* are being recognized as important work and as a form of art, as opposed to simply being a quaint hobby. 'The process is one of sculpture. We transfer it to paper, so that it is functional and so that people can dance, but they are still sculptures.' While they also work in other mediums, including bronze, Felipe and Mika say they like the fact that *mojigangas* seem more alive. 'Bronze statues can't dance – bronze bust sculptures [in public areas] can get shat on by birds. But with *mojigangas* it is different: people can dance and everyone – dancers or viewers – can enjoy themselves. The public speak to the characters (Diego often gets reprimanded for the way he treated Frida!), or they kiss and sympathize with Don Quixote.'

---

restaurant-bar serves inexpensive food. During Cervantino Festival prices are M$100 more and no singles are available.

Hotel El Insurgente (☎ 732-31-92; www.hotelinsurgente.com/; Juárez 226; s/d/tr M$475/620/710) A practical and comfortable option just west of center, this place fills up its 80 rooms fast during holidays and festivals (packages are available for Easter and the Cervantino Festival). It is generally good value though and the upper rooms have fine views of the city.

Mesón del Rosario (☎ /fax 732-32-84; Av Juárez 31; d/tr M$540/630) The knights in shining armor standing in this atmospheric medieval-style entrance (we're not talking bellboys here) promise big things. However, travelers' views differ on this choice. It's centrally located, but some of the 34 rooms are small and dark, while others are more generous in size and light. Check before committing to avoid a duel with the friendly staff.

El Zopilote Mojado (☎ 732-53-11; www.elzopilotemojado.com; Plaza Mexiamora 51 & 53; r/apt M$550/900) The various sleeping options have the feel of a stylish B&B minus the steep prices. Eight tastefully-decorated rooms are located above the Café Zopilote Mojado and in a house nearby. All rooms are cosy and comfortable; those in the house share a delightfully modern and spacious communal kitchen,

lounge/dining area and outdoor terraces. The lion's head mounted above the fireplace is anomalous; that said, this comfortable place is guaranteed to have you purring. Two chic (if dark) apartments and a family house are also near the plaza.

Hostería del Frayle (☎ /fax 732-11-79; www.hosteriadelfrayle.com; Sopeña 3; s/d/tr M$800/1000/1400; [P]) A block from the Jardín, this historic hotel (it was built in 1673 as the Casa de Moneda) has 37 attractive but dark rooms with high wood-beamed or boveda ceilings and satellite TV. The décor is showing a few signs of wear, but the service is friendly and the thick adobe walls keep things quiet.

Mesón de los Poetas (☎ 732-07-05; www.mexonline.com/poetas.htm; Positos 35; d/ste M$950/1500) Built against the hillside, this labyrinth of rooms – each named after a poet – offer, on the whole, comfortable, clean lodgings. You may not wax lyrical about the light (some rooms are dark), but with a kitchenette and bright décor, this option is good value for the price bracket.

TOP END
Some quaint old buildings in various parts of town have been restored as small boutique hotels. The road to La Valenciana has several posh places in lofty locations. Other upmarket places are in Marfil, a 15-minute drive or bus

ride west of town. The following prices can be significantly lower during low season.

Hotel Casa del Agua (☎ 734-19-74; Plaza de la Compañair 4; r from M$1155, ste M$1287-2715; **P**) This remodeled colonial building has been finished with contemporary ambient touches. The floor of the interior courtyard is a quirky glass-covered pool (empty during our visit). The 16 suites are simple, elegant and include all the modern conveniences. Centrally located near the university, this is a good-value option for this range.

Hotel Luna (☎ 732-97-25; www.hotelluna.com.mx; Jardín de la Unión 6; interior r from M$1505, exterior r from M$1820, ste from M$2306) This elegant 100-year-old hotel facing the plaza boasts a stunning foyer. Beyond that, the rooms have an old-style ambience with contemporary facilities, but vary in standard; the internally facing rooms are less appealing. Rates include breakfast; there's a 10% discount if you pay by cash.

our pick **Villa María Cristina** (☎ 731-21-82; www .villamariacristina.com.mx; Paseo de la Presa de La Olla 76; ste M$1850-4100) Recently opened, this stunning converted mansion reeks of expensive perfume. The décor in the spacious rooms features neo-classical French designer furniture, original paintings (by local artist Jesús Gallardo) and beds and bathrooms with all the 'fluffy and puffy' trimmings (there are even Bvlgari toiletries). Outside, various patios and terraces feature everything from fountains and wicker chairs to Jacuzzis plus views of La Bufa. The main patios are covered in the original – and exquisite – tiles. This luxurious option is situated in La Presa, a 15-minute walk from the center.

Antiguo Vapor (☎ 732-32-11; www.hotelavapor .com; Galarza 5; r M$1900) For those with dosh and who want a more personal feel to their accommodations experience, the rooms in this newly-built nest (each room has a bird name) are uniquely decorated in contemporary Mexican with brightly colored bedcovers, tiles and boveda ceilings. Some have much better views than others; some in the rear have high, opaque windows.

Quinta Las Acacias (☎ 731-15-17, in Mexico 800-710-89-38, in USA 888-497-4129; www.quintalasacacias .com.mx; Paseo de la Presa 168; ste with breakfast M$2800-4830; **P** ⓧ ▢ ⓢ) This hideaway combines attentive service and intimate luxury in a former 19th-century French-colonial summer residence. The older style rooms are located in the original house and feature brass bedsteads (and are more or less charming depending on your taste), while the newish master suites located behind the house have hydro-massage tubs. The most peaceful and modern suites (some with LCD TV and all with small patios) have been recently constructed around a stunning protected cactus garden.

Eating

For fresh produce and cheap snacks and lunches, head to the Mercado Hidalgo, a five-minute walk west of the main plaza on Juárez. Another two blocks further down on the right is Central Comercio, with a large supermarket.

JARDÍN DE LA UNIÓN & AROUND

The Jardín de la Unión has good upscale restaurants where you can enjoy the atmosphere of the plaza. But there are other more hidden surprises.

our pick **Truco 7** (☎ 732-83-74; Truco 7; mains M$25-80; ⏲ 8:30am-11:30pm) This intimate, artsy café-restaurant featuring artifacts, paintings and a collection of old radios, is one of the most reliable around – in terms of opening hours and reasonable quality. It attracts everyone from students to travelers and serves Mexican food in a great atmosphere. Set lunches are inexpensive (M$37 to M$42).

Bagel Cafetín (☎ 733-97-33; Potrero 2; bagels M$30; ⏲ 9am-late Mon-Sat) This colorful spot, next to Templo de San Francisco, serves up bagels with a huge choice of fillings, reasonable coffee and wi-fi internet connections (minimum consumption M$20).

Santo Café (Puente de Campanero; mains M$30-40; ⏲ 10am-midnight Mon-Sat, noon-8pm Sun) Stop by this cozy, slightly funky spot on the quaint Venetian-style bridge and check the latest university vibe. It serves good, cheap snacks and drinks overlooking the alley below and there is music of all styles. Musicians sometimes play on weekends.

El Café (☎ 732-25-66; Sopeña 10; mains M$30-80; ⏲ 8am-midnight) This popular hangout is the place to socialize alfresco over cocktails or a light meal. Perfect for people-watching from their tables under umbrellas across the street, alongside Teatro Juárez.

El Gallo Pitagórico (☎ 732-94-89; Constancia 10; mains M$70-140; ⏲ 2-11pm) South of the Jardín, up the path (and then steps) behind Templo San Diego, this romantic restaurant is chock-a-block with folkloric artifacts, friendly atmosphere and fine city views. The Italian cuisine includes assorted antipasti, a range of pastas and great meat dishes. The lengthy wine list can hike the price, but service is good and it's a reliably pleasant experience.

La Capellina (☎ 732-72-24; Sopeña 3; mains M$90-130; ⏰ 1:30-11pm Mon-Thu, 1:30-midnight Fri & Sat, 1:30-7pm Sun) The French chef in this smart 'special occasion' place creates international (mainly French, Italian and Mexican) fusion-cuisine. The menu is à la carte featuring pizzas, pasta and other 'specialties' (all identified by the word 'capellina' in their name).

AV JUÁREZ & AROUND

Restaurant La Carreta (☎ 732-43-58; Av Juárez 96; mains M$25-50; ⏰ 0am-10pm) Follow your nose to La Carreta, an unpretentious café, whose streetfront grill spins out a super-scrumptious *pollo al pastor* (grilled chicken) and *carne asada* (grilled beef), served with large portions of rice and salad.

Tasca de La Paz (☎ 734-22-25; Plaza de la Paz 28; mains M$60-110; ⏰ 8am-10pm) This place opposite the basilica has outdoor tables on picturesque Plaza de la Paz for tapas, paella and other Spanish specialties. It's a bit pricey, but worth it for the authentic flavors and European ambience.

Il Romanico (☎ 732-27-72; Av Juárez 24; mains M$70-160; ⏰ 8am-11pm Mon-Thu, 8am-midnight Fri & Sat, 8am-10pm Sun) A modern Italian-style, all-in-one type place where you can get your morning juice, lunch-time crepes and a gelato snack. In the evening, grab a pizza or pasta and then hit the hip bar, La Juanita, upstairs (open 6pm until late).

PLAZUELA SAN FERNANDO

This little plaza is home to an ever-changing slate of hip hangouts and is a delightful place in the evening for a drink, a snack or a meal.

our pick **El Midi** (Plazuela San Fernando; snacks M$11 per 100g; ⏰ 10:30-6pm Sun-Wed, 10:30am-11:30pm Thu-Fri) This French-run café-restaurant is hard to go past for its fresh delights. *Tartes*, salads and a huge array of daily offerings can be enjoyed on the perfectly pretty plaza under brollies. Morning croissants available; the salad bar starts at 1pm.

Bossanova Café (☎ 732-56-74; Plazuela San Fernando 24; mains M$25-60; ⏰ 10am-11pm) This friendly eatery has a quaint setting on the plaza and intimate interior atmosphere. Be sure to sample

its selection of teas and a huge range of coffees with a house-specialty crepe.

Clave Azul (⏰ 3-10pm) For an authentic experience of Mexican drinking with accompanying *botanas* (tapas-like snacks served free with drinks, in this case between 1pm and 5pm), head to this artifact-filled, atmospheric *cantina* up a small alley to the left of Bossanova Café.

OTHER

Café Tal (☎ 732-62-12; www.cafetal.com.mx; Temezcuitate 4; snacks M$15-30) This slightly grungy, American-owned coffee spot is the wi-fi–enabled study spot for students. It roasts, grinds and serves excellent coffees (*barista* is a word used here!) Don't miss the *beso negro* (black kiss), ultra-concentrated hot chocolate (M$12?)

Café Carcamanes (☎ 732-51-72; Plazuela Carcamanes 8; snacks M$22-30; ⏰ 8am-11pm) Near the uni, this cozy place serves a delicious range of snacks (baguettes, gourmet teas, coffees and breakfasts all recommended). Wi-fi connection makes it popular with students.

El Zopilote Mojado (☎ 732-53-11; Plaza Mexiamora 51; snacks M$30-40; ⏰ 9am-10pm Mon-Sat) A stylish and intimate place with rustic wooden décor, overlooking the tranquil Plaza Mexiamora. Classical music, copies of the *New York Times* and good coffee make it a pleasurable experience.

Yamuna (☎ 732-18-73; Calle del Sol 10; mains M$50-70; ⏰ noon-7pm Mon-Sat; **V**) A great range of quality veg food, most – such as the generous *comida corrida* (M$40-50) – with a very Indian Hindu influence and flavor. Great baguettes for M$35.

Drinking & Entertainment

Every evening, the Jardín de la Unión comes alive with people crowding the outdoor tables, strolling and listening to the street musicians. International films are screened in several locations, including the Teatro Principal, Teatro Cervantes and Museo y Casa de Diego Rivera.

BARS

Bar Ocho (☎ 732-71-79; Constancia 8; ⏰ 3pm-3am) Locals, expats and visitors seem to love this friendly, unpretentious place. It has seating inside and out, good music and snacks and a pool table upstairs.

Bar Fly (Sostenes Rocha 30; ⏰ 7pm-2am; Wed-Sat) A grungy place to go for reggae, ska, rap and electronic grooves and a hippie, trippy vibe.

NORTHERN CENTRAL HIGHLANDS

Bora Bora (Constancia 6; ☽ noon-midnight Mon-Sat) This trendy place attracts young students who love accessibly priced mixed drinks (the 'TNT' is a brain fryer) and *micheladas* (beer, chili salsa and lime juice). It's beside Bar Ocho.

DISCOS & NIGHTCLUBS

Drinking and dancing establishments in Guanajuato generally start late and end in the wee hours.

Cuba Mia (Truco; M$25 on Fri; ☽ 9pm-5am) *The* salsa place in town, where hips, dirty dancing and loud salsa music make the crowds bop 'til they drop.

Guanajuato Grill (☎ 732-02-85; Alonso 4) This rather selective disco and drink spot admits affluent, energetic students who like loud dance music. It's packed after midnight on Friday and Saturday.

Capitolio (Juárez 71; cover M$50; ☽ 10:30pm-3am Wed-Sat) A similar scene to Guanajuato Grill.

La Dama de las Camelias (☎ 732-75-87; Sopeña 32; ☽ 8pm-4am Mon-Sat) For live and recorded Latin sounds and a dose of slinky salsa and merengue moves in an artsy, gay-friendly atmosphere, check out La Dama.

On Friday, Saturday and Sunday evenings at around 8pm (or daily during festivals), the wonderfully fun *callejoneadas* (or *estudiantinas*) depart from in front of San Diego church on the Jardín de la Unión (see boxed text, below).

PERFORMING ARTS

A program of events include theater, music, opera and dance runs from March to December. (It's marketed under 'La Viva La Magia,' but not everybody knows this name.) Ask at Teatro Juáréz if the tourist office doesn't know.

Guanajuato has three fine centrally located theaters, the 100-year-old Teatro Juárez (p616), Teatro Principal (p616) and Teatro Cervantes (p616). Check their posters to see what's on.

Getting There & Away

AIR

Guanajuato is served by the Aeropuerto Internacional del Bajío, which is about 30km west of the city, halfway between Léon and Silao. See p626 for detailed flight information.

BUS

Guanajuato's Central de Autobuses is around 5km southwest of town. It has card phones, a luggage storage (in the café) and a tourist desk. Deluxe and 1st-class bus tickets can be bought in town at **Viajes Frausto** (☎ 732-35-80; Obregón 10). See the box opposite for daily departures.

Getting Around

A taxi to Bajío International Airport will cost about M$300 to M$350. A cheaper option is a frequent bus to Silao (M$20) and a taxi from there (M$150).

Between the bus station and city center, around-the-clock 'Central de Autobuses' buses run constantly. From the center, you can catch them heading west in the tunnels below Juárez (there are several entries: El Jardín, Mercado Hidalgo and Plaza Baratillo). A taxi to the bus station costs around M$30 to M$40.

City buses (M$4) run from 7am to 10pm. Taxis are plentiful in the center and charge about M$25 to M$30 for short trips around town.

CALLEJONEADAS – THE TRADITIONAL WAY TO PARTY, PARTY, PARTY!

The *callejoneada* tradition is said to have come from Spain. A group of professional singers and musicians, dressed in traditional costumes, starts up in a central location such as a plaza, a crowd gathers, then the whole mob winds through the alleyways, streets and plazas playing, dancing and singing heartily. In Guanajuato, they are also called *estudiantinas*. Stories and jokes (in Spanish) are told in between songs often relating to the legends of the alleys. In Zacatecas, there are no stories, but hired bands (in uniform, not traditional dress) lead dancing revelers. On special occasions a burro laden with wine is brought along. Often, strangers are just expected to join the party and the crowd swells. Occasionally, the organizers foot the bill, sometimes you pay a small amount for the wine you drink (or you bring your own!). In Guanajuato, the groups themselves or tour companies sell tickets (around M$90) for the *callejoneadas* and juice (not alcohol) is provided. It's great fun and a traditional way to party hearty!

DAILY BUSES FROM GUANAJUATO

Destination	Fare	Duration	Frequency
Dolores Hidalgo	M$41	1½hr	every 20 min, 5:30am 10:20pm (Flecha Amarilla)
Guadalajara	deluxe M$320	4hr	6 daily (ETN)
	1st-class M$246	4hr	10 daily (Primera Plus)
	2nd-class M$205	4hr	5 daily (Flecha Amarilla)
León	deluxe M$50	1hr	6 daily (ETN)
	1st-class M$36	1hr	9 daily (Primera Plus)
	2nd-class M$30	1¼hr	every 15 min, 5:30am-10pm (Flecha Amarilla or Flecha de Oro)
Mexico City (Terminal Norte)	deluxe M$371	4½hr	9 daily (ETN)
	1st-class M$287	4½hr	11 daily (Primera Plus)
San Luis Potosí	M$142	5hr	2 daily (Flecha Amarilla)
San Miguel de Allende	deluxe M$106	1½hr	3 daily (ETN)
	1st-class M$81	1½hr	7 daily (Primera Plus)
	2nd-class M$61	2hr	8 daily (Flecha Amarilla)

There are also hourly 2nd-class Flecha Amarilla buses to Celaya, plus two to Querétaro. For Morelia, catch an Irapuato-bound bus and change there.

LEÓN

☎ 477 / pop 1.14 million / elevation 1854m

If you are into bargain shopping, then León is a purchaser's paradise. This industrial city, 56km west of Guanajuato, is on the Mexican map for its massive leather industry: shoes, saddles and everything in between. It has a long history of supplying goods: in the 16th century it was the center of Mexico's ranching district, providing meat for the mining towns and processing hides. It has a small but attractive historic center with a lovely plaza.

Orientation & Information

The heart of the city is the wide main Plaza de los Mártires del 2 de Enero (aka Plaza Principal), a well-groomed pedestrian area with the Palacio Municipal on its west side. The adjoining Plaza de los Fundadores and several nearby streets are also pedestrian zones with shops, cafés and restaurants.

If you're walking to the center from the bus station, drop into the **regional tourist office** (☎ 763-44-00/01, 800-716-53-66; www.leon-mexico.com; Lopez Mateo Ote 1511; ◷ 8am-3pm & 5 7pm) for maps and other (shopping-based) information. Otherwise, in the plaza, a **tourist information booth** (◷ 10am-8pm) has a free city map. Other essentials like banks, ATMs and card phones are around the plazas. The tourist office's website (at www.leon-mexico.com) is a useful source.

Sights

Shopping and walking around León's pretty historic heart, where fine architectural buildings abound, are among the main attractions of the city.

The neoclassical **Casa de Cultura** (☎ 714-43-01; www.leon.gob.aix/icl) faces the Plaza de los Fundadores, and the big, twin-towered, baroque **Catedral Basílica** (cnr Obregón & Hidalgo) is a block northeast of the Casa de Cultura. The neoclassical 1869 **Teatro Doblado** (☎ 716-43-01; cnr Aldama & Moreno) still stages concerts, dance and drama. The **Museo de la Ciudad** (☎ 714-50-22; Aldama 134; admission M$2; ◷ 9:30am-2:30pm & 5-7:30pm Tue-Fri, 9:30am-2pm Sat & Sun) exhibits contemporary work by Mexican and international artists.

Festivals & Events

In January and February, the **Guanajuato State Fair** attracts millions of visitors each year with agricultural displays, music, dancing, carnival rides and bullfights. Hundreds of shoemakers display their wares in the **Centro de Exposiciones** (Conexpo; ☎ 771-25-00; cnr López Mateos & Francisco Villa) during the fair.

Like Guanajuato, León also celebrates a Cervantino cultural festival, starting mid-October. If you happen to be in the area, the annual **Festival del Globo** hot-air balloon gathering in November-December is a bit of neck-craning fun.

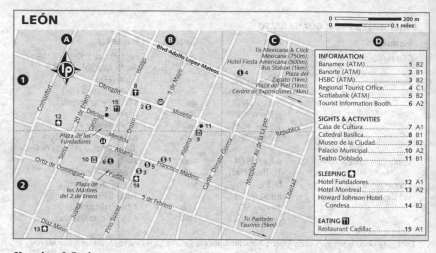

LEÓN

INFORMATION	
Banamex (ATM)	1 B2
Banorte (ATM)	2 B1
HSBC (ATM)	3 B2
Regional Tourist Office	4 C1
Scotiabank (ATM)	5 B2
Tourist Information Booth	6 A2

SIGHTS & ACTIVITIES	
Casa de Cultura	7 A1
Catedral Basílica	8 B1
Museo de la Ciudad	9 B2
Palacio Municipal	10 A1
Teatro Doblado	11 B1

SLEEPING	
Hotel Fundadores	12 A1
Hotel Montreal	13 A2
Howard Johnson Hotel Condesa	14 B2

EATING	
Restaurant Cadillac	15 A1

Sleeping & Eating

Many hotels are located around the bus station, catering to commercial buyers of leather goods attending the fair. The Centro Histórico also has various accommodation options.

Hotel Fundadores (☎ 716-17-27; fax 713-37-01; Ortiz de Domínguez 218; r M$195-290) The two-star Fundadores offers budget rooms with few frills except TV.

Hotel Montreal (☎ 716-37-86; www.hotel-montreal.com.mx Reforma 215; s/d/tr M$400/460/530) Hotel Montreal has 54 clean and modernish (if plain) rooms with cable TV. Suites with air-con cost M$160 extra.

Howard Johnson Hotel Condesa (☎ 788-39-29, 800-710-39-64; www.hjleon.com; Portal Bravo 14; r/ste M$995/1500; P ⌨) On the main plaza, this excellent-value option has comfortable rooms. The restaurant has outdoor tables and a popular buffet lunch (M$100). Frequent 50% discounts are on offer and free airport pick-up if you reserve in advance.

Hotel Fiesta Americana (☎ 719-80-00; www.fiestaamericana.com.mx; López Mateos Ote 1102; r from M$2135; P ✖ ⌨) Leon's luxurious accommodations extravaganza looks more like a shopping mall than a hotel. It's on López Mateos, which runs east from the center and becomes Hwy 45 to the airport.

Restaurant Cadillac (☎ 713-87-30; Hidalgo 107; mains M$35-100; ⏰ 8am-10pm) Movie posters and bright pink chairs feature in this quirky place, located on a pedestrian street north of the plaza. The set meals (M$60 to M$80) of Mexican favorites are good value.

Panteón Taurino (☎ 713-49-69; Calz de los Héroes 408; mains M$70-100). Olé! Charge into this restaurant-bar-museum to eat at the 'crypts' (read homages) of former famous *toreros* (bullfighters). No brave behavior, please – catch a cab at night.

Shopping

Great quality leather buys – shoes and general items – can be found in the main leather district near the bus station, off Blvd Hilario Medina, or further south in the shopping malls of **Plaza del Zapato** and **Plaza Piel** (cnr López Mateos & Hilario Medina).

Getting There & Away

AIR

Aeropuerto Internacional del Bajío is 20km southeast on the Mexico City road. Aeroméxico Connect, Aeroméxico, American, Continental, Mexicana and Click Mexicana offer flights to Acapulco, Guadalajara, Monterrey, Puerto Vallarta and Tijuana, plus a host of cities in the US (often via Mexico City). Magnicharters flies twice a week from Bajío to Cancún.

Mexicana and **Click Mexicana** (☎ 714-95-00; López Mateos 308) have an in-town office, but most other airline offices are at Bajío airport.

BUS

The **Central de Autobuses** (Blvd Hilario Medina s/n), just north of Blvd López Mateos 2½km east of the city center, has a cafeteria, left luggage, money exchange and card phones. There are

NORTHERN CENTRAL HIGHLANDS

regular services to many places in northern and western Mexico.

Daily departures:

Destination	Fare	Duration	Frequency
Guanajuato	deluxe M$45	1hr	6 daily (ETN)
	1st-class M$36	1hr	hourly (Primera Plus)
	2nd-class M$30	1hr	every 15 min (Flecha Amarilla)
Mexico City (Terminal Norte)	deluxe M$375	5hr	15 daily (ETN)
	1st-class	5hr	hourly (Primera Plus), 11 daily (Futura)
	2nd-class M$254	8hr	every 2 hours (Flecha Amarilla)
San Miguel de Allende	deluxe M$145	2¼hr	2 daily (ETN)
	1st-class M$119	2¼hr	6 daily (Primera Plus)

Getting Around

No bus service operates between Bajío airport and central León. Those without too much luggage can opt to walk from the airport to the intersection of the main road and the airport road (10 minutes on foot) and hail a local bus from there (around M$25). A taxi to León from the airport costs about M$250. The closest long-distance-bus station to the airport is in Silao; a taxi there from the airport will cost about M$150.

From the bus station, turn left (south) and walk 150m to López Mateos, where 'Centro' buses (M$4) go west to the city center. To return to the bus station, catch a 'Central' bus east along López Mateos, two blocks north of Plaza Principal. A taxi between the center and the bus station costs M$35.

DOLORES HIDALGO

☎ 418 / pop 57,089 / elevation 1955m

Dolores Hidalgo is a compact town with a pretty plaza, an extremely authentic ambience and an important history. It has acquired pilgrimage status for Mexicans; the Mexican independence movement began in earnest in this small place. At 5am on September 16, 1810, Miguel Hidalgo, the parish priest, rang the bells to summon people to church earlier than usual and issued the Grito de Dolores, also known as the Grito de Independencia. His precise words have been lost to history but their essence was 'Death to bad government and the *gachupines*!' ('*Gachupines*' was a derisive term for the Spanish-born overlords who ruled Mexico.)

Today, Hidalgo is one of Mexico's most revered heroes. Dolores was renamed in his honor in 1824. Mexicans swarm here for Independence Day (September 16), during which time accommodation prices can more than double.

The town's *centro histórico* is worth a day visit from San Miguel de Allende, not only for its interesting independence-themed museums, but also for its colored Talavera ceramics and handmade ice-cream.

Orientation & Information

Most things of interest are within a couple of blocks of the Plaza Principal, known as the *centro histórico,* while the ceramics workshops are several more blocks away and accessible on foot.

The **tourist office** (☎ 182-11-64; ⌚ 10am-4pm) is on the Plaza Principal's north side, in the Presidencia Municipal. The helpful staff provides maps and information.

Cash and traveler's checks can be changed at several banks (with ATMs) around the plaza. There are some *casas de cambio* too. **Ciber Antique** (Mexico 7) has internet connections at M$8 per hour. Card phones are located around the town and at the Flecha Amarilla bus station. The **post office** (☎ 182-08-07; ⌚ 9am-2pm Mon-Sat) is on the corner of Puebla and Veracruz.

Sights

PLAZA PRINCIPAL & AROUND

The **Parroquia de Nuestra Señora de Dolores**, the church where Hidalgo issued the Grito, is on the north side of the plaza. It has a fine 18th-century Churrigueresque facade. Legends surround his 'cry'; some say that Hidalgo uttered his famous words from the pulpit, others claim that he spoke at the church door to the people gathered outside.

Adjacent to the church is the **Presidencia Municipal**, which has two colorful murals on the theme of independence. The plaza contains an **Hidalgo statue** (in Roman garb, on top of a tall column) and also a tree that, according to the plaque beneath it, was a sapling of the tree of the Noche Triste (Sad Night), under which Cortés is said to have wept when his men were driven out of Tenochtitlán in 1520.

The **Casa de Visitas**, on the plaza's west side, was the residence of Don Nicolás Fernández del Rincón and Don Ignacio Díaz de la Cortina, the two representatives of Spanish rule in Dolores. On September 16, 1810, they became the first two prisoners of the independence movement. Today, this is where Mexican presidents and other dignitaries stay when they come to Dolores for ceremonies.

MUSEO DE LA INDEPENDENCIA NACIONAL

This **museum** (National Independence Museum; ☎ 182-77-50 ext 150; Zacatecas 6; adult/concession Mon-Sat M$15/7.50, Sun free; ⏰ 9am-4:45pm) has few relics but plenty of information on the independence movement. The exhibition spans eight rooms and charts the appalling decline in Nueva España's indigenous population between 1519 (an estimated 25 million) and 1605 (1 million) and identifies 23 indigenous rebellions before 1800 as well as several criollo conspiracies in the years leading up to 1810. There are vivid paintings, quotations and details on the heroic last 10 months of Hidalgo's life.

MUSEO CASA DE HIDALGO

Miguel Hidalgo lived in this **house** (☎ 182-01-71; cnr Hidalgo & Morelos; Tue-Sat M$27, Sun free; ⏰ 10am-5:45pm Tue-Sat, 10am-4:45pm Sun) when he was Dolores' parish priest. It was here, in the early hours of September 16, 1810, that Hidalgo, Ignacio Allende and Juan de Aldama conspired to launch the uprising against colonial rule. It is now something of a national shrine.

One large room is devoted to a collection of memorials to Hidalgo. Other rooms contain replicas of Hidalgo's furniture and independence-movement documents, including the order for Hidalgo's excommunication.

Festivals & Events

Dolores is the scene of major **Día de la Independencia** (September 16) celebrations, when the Mexican president may officiate – according to tradition – in his fifth year of office. The dates of the **Fiestas Patrias** festivities change annually, but always run for 10 days that encompass September 16.

Sleeping

Prices can double (even triple) for the independence celebrations in September and at Easter.

Posada Dolores (☎ 182-06-42; Yucatán 8; s/d without bathroom M$60/130, s/d M$130/220) This *casa de huéspedes* has the cheapest sleeps in town. The cell-like and humid downstairs rooms would suit hardy backpackers only; the larger, upstairs rooms with TV are more appealing.

Casa Mia (☎ 182-25-60; www.hotelcasamia.com.mx; San Luis Potosí 9B; s/d M$260/340) The newest hotel on the block, this restored house (with a B&B feel) offers unpretentious, pleasant rooms set around a bougainvillea-courtyard. Excellent value.

Posada Cocomacán (☎ 182-60-86; www.posada cocomacan.com.mx; Plaza Principal 4; s/d/tr M$330/440/550) The centrally located and positively pink Cocomacán is a reliable option. The 36 clean

---

DOLORES HIDALGO

0 — 300 m
0 — 0.2 miles

MIGUEL HIDALGO: ¡VIVA MEXICO!

The balding head of the visionary priest Father Miguel Hidalgo y Costilla is familiar to anyone who's ogled Mexican statues or murals. A genuine rebel idealist, Hidalgo sacrificed his career and risked his life on September 16, 1810, when he launched the independence movement.

Born on May 8, 1753, son of a criollo hacienda manager in Guanajuato, he earned a bachelor's degree and, in 1778, was ordained a priest. He returned to teach at his alma mater in Morelia and eventually became rector. But he was no orthodox cleric: Hidalgo questioned many Catholic traditions, read banned books, gambled, danced and had a mistress.

In 1800 he was brought before the Inquisition. Nothing was proven, but a few years later, in 1804, he found himself transferred as priest to the hick town of Dolores.

Hidalgo's years in Dolores show his growing interest in the economic and cultural welfare of the people. He started several new industries: silk was cultivated, olive groves were planted and vineyards established, all in defiance of the Spanish colonial authorities. Earthenware building products were the foundation of the ceramics industry that today produces fine glazed pots and tiles.

When Hidalgo met Ignacio Allende from San Miguel, they shared a criollo discontent with the Spanish stranglehold on Mexico. Hidalgo's standing among the mestizos and indigenous people of his parish was vital in broadening the base of the rebellion that followed.

Shortly after his Grito de Independencia, Hidalgo was formally excommunicated for 'heresy, apostasy and sedition.' He defended his call for Mexican independence and stated furthermore that the Spanish were not truly Catholic in any religious sense of the word but only for political purposes, specifically to rape, pillage and exploit Mexico. A few days later, on October 19, Hidalgo dictated his first edict calling for the abolition of slavery in Mexico.

Hidalgo led his growing forces from Dolores to San Miguel, Celaya and Guanajuato, north to Zacatecas, south almost to Mexico City and west to Guadalajara. But then, pushed northward, their numbers dwindled and on July 30, 1811, having been captured by the Spanish, Hidalgo was shot by a firing squad in Chihuahua. His head was returned to the city of Guanajuato where it hung in a cage for 10 years on an outer corner of the Alhóndiga de Granaditas, along with the heads of independence leaders Allende, Aldama and Jiménez. Rather than intimidating the people, this lurid display kept the memory, the goal and the example of the heroic martyrs fresh in everyone's mind. After independence the cages were removed and the skulls of the heroes are now in the Monumento a la Independencia in Mexico City.

rooms have TV and phones. Rooms on the upper levels, with windows onto the street, are brighter than those on the ground floor. The restaurant is also recommended.

Hotel Posada Hidalgo (☎ /fax 182-04-77; www.hotelposadahidalgo.com; Hidalgo 15; s/d/tr/ste M$348/398/448/900; P 🖥 🖵) The reception feels a bit like a doctor's surgery, but this super-clean and well managed place offers a comfortable and 'eighties-modern' stay. It's conveniently located between the bus stations and the Plaza Principal. Rates include use of a gym and steam baths downstairs, also open to the public (M$50).

Eating

Don't leave without sampling a hand-turned ice-cream from an **ice-cream** (M$15) vendor on the plaza or around town. You can test your taste-buds on the flavors: *mole, chichar-* *rón* (fried pork skin), avocado, corn, cheese, honey, shrimp, beer, tequila and tropical fruits. The market on the corner of Chihuahua and Michoacan serves up some satisfying corn-based snacks.

FrutiYoghurt (Hidalgo 2; snacks M$12-22; ☒ 8am-10pm) This small café sells good-value and healthy yoghurts, fresh juices and sandwiches.

Café La Taberna (☎ 182-00-55; Plaza Principal 18; mains M$15; ☒ noon-midnight Sun-Fri, 5pm-midnight Sat) The younger crowd may like this super-cheap café and bohemian hangout, where young local artists display their talent.

El Carruaje Restaurant (☎ 182-04-74; Plaza Principal 8; mains M$30-105) This colorful place on the plaza caters to day-tripping families with a M$70 set lunch, live music from Wednesday to Saturday (Thursday to Saturday evenings) and a popular weekend breakfast buffet (M$60) and lunch buffet (M$90).

Restaurant El Delfín (☎ 182-22-99; Veracruz 2; mains M$48-80; ☽ 9am-7pm) This spotless place, one block east of the plaza, dares to be different, serving seafood from the Gulf of Mexico. Get hooked on a selection of tasty fish dishes, *sopa de mariscos* and shrimps.

Restaurant Plaza (☎ 182-02-59; Plaza Principal 17B; mains M$50-140; ☽ 8am-10pm) A central and OK place serving set breakfasts and lunches, as well as meat dishes, pasta and *antojitos*.

Shopping

Talavera ceramics have been the signature handicraft of Dolores ever since Padre Hidalgo founded the town's first ceramics workshop in the early 19th century. On the plaza, **La Casa de las Artesanías** (☎ 182-22-66) sells a selection of items. For better prices and variety, head to the workshops along Av Jimenez, five blocks west of the plaza, or (by car) to Calzada de los Heroes, the exit road to San Miguel de Allende. Some workshops here make 'antique,' colonial-style furniture.

Getting There & Away

Nearly all buses to/from Dolores are 2nd-class. The Primera Plus/Flecha Amarilla station is on Hidalgo, 2½ blocks south of the plaza. The Herradura de Plata/Pegasso Plus station is on Chiapas at Yucatán.

Daily departures include Guanajuato (M$41, 1¼ hours, every 20 minuntes from 5:20am to 9pm, Flecha Amarilla), Mexico City's Terminal Norte (1st-class M$242, five hours, noon, Pegasso Plus; 2nd-class M$200, five to six hours, every 40 minutes, Herradura de Plata or Flecha Amarilla) and San Miguel de Allende (M$26, 45 minutes, frequent, Flecha Amarilla or Herradura de Plata).

There are also regular 2nd-class connections to Querétaro (M$66), León (M$71) and San Luis Potosí (M$96).

SAN MIGUEL DE ALLENDE

☎ 415 / pop 62,034 / elevation 1840m

Many people say that San Miguel is a bit like a Mexican Disneyland for foreign (mainly American) retirees. Indeed, this is a stunning and neat city, with colonial architecture, enchanting cobblestone streets and striking light. Regular festivals, fireworks and parades dominate the local scene.

The town's cosmopolitan panache is reflected in its excellent restaurants and high-class, colonial-style accommodation options.

Numerous galleries are stocked with some of the best of Mexican *artesanías* and cultural activities are on tap for residents and visitors. There are few sights: as a Mexican-declared national monument, San Miguel *is* the sight.

Economically speaking, this is no budget destination and is a far cry from the 1940s, when beatniks and artists shacked up here on a shoestring to pursue their creative ventures. Visitors still flock here to study at the art institutions – Bellas Artes and the Instituto Allende. While the foreign influence is pervasive (more than 10,000 foreigners are believed to live or have houses here), on the whole the population coexists comfortably.

Beneath the smart B&Bs and fancy shops, an authentic (and sometimes poverty-stricken) Mexico exists. You only have to laze in the main plaza, visit the food market or interact with the local people to sense an ambience, color and vibe that is nothing but Mexican.

The climate is agreeable: cool and clear in winter and warm and clear in summer, with occasional thunderstorms and heavy rain.

History

The town, so the story goes, owes its founding to a few over-heated dogs. These hounds were loved by a Franciscan friar, Juan de San Miguel, who started a mission in 1542 near an often-dry river 5km from the present town. One day the dogs wandered off from the mission; they were found reclining at the spring called El Chorro. The mission was moved to this superior site.

San Miguel was then central Mexico's most northern Spanish settlement. Tarascan and Tlaxcalan allies of the Spanish were brought to help pacify the local Otomí and Chichimecs. San Miguel was barely surviving the fierce Chichimec resistance, until in 1555 a Spanish garrison was established to protect the new road from Mexico City to the silver center of Zacatecas. Spanish ranchers settled in the area and it grew into a thriving commercial center and home to some of Guanajuato's wealthy silver barons.

San Miguel's favorite son, Ignacio Allende, was born here in 1779. He became a fervent believer in the need for Mexican independence and was a leader of a Querétaro-based conspiracy that set December 8, 1810, as the date for an armed uprising. When the plan was discovered by the authorities in Querétaro on September 13, a messenger rushed to San Miguel and gave the news to Juan de Aldama, another conspirator. Aldama sped north to Dolores where, in the early hours of September 16, he found Allende at the house of the priest Miguel Hidalgo, also one of the coterie. A few hours later Hidalgo proclaimed rebellion from his church. After initial successes Allende, Hidalgo and other rebel leaders were captured in 1811 in Chihuahua. Allende was executed, but on independence in 1821 he was recognized as a martyr and in 1826 the town was renamed San Miguel de Allende.

The Escuela de Bellas Artes was founded in 1938 and the town started to take on its current character when David Alfaro Siqueiros began mural-painting courses that attracted artists of every persuasion. The Instituto Allende opened in 1951, also attracting foreign students. Many were American veterans (who could settle here under the GI Bill); an influx of artists has continued ever since.

Orientation

The *centro histórico* is compact and straightforward. The Plaza Principal, called El Jardín, is the town's focal point and many places of interest are within easy walking distance of here. The neo-Gothic spires of the *parroquia* beside the Jardín provide the perfect landmark. Most streets change names at the Jardín. Canal/San Francisco on its north side and Umarán/Correo, on the south side, are among the main streets.

Information

BOOKSTORES & LIBRARIES

Biblioteca Pública (☎ 152-02-93; Insurgentes 25; ⏰ 10am-7pm Mon-Fri, 10am-2pm Sat) As well as housing one of the largest collection of books and magazines in English in Latin America, this excellent public library functions as a cultural center. Its financial enterprises (*Atención San Miguel* newspaper, house & garden tours and its onsite café) provide for children's scholarships.

El Colibrí Bookstore (☎ 152-07-51; Diez de Sollano 30; ⏰ 10am-2pm & 4-7pm) Paperbacks, magazines and art books in English and Spanish.

El Tecolote Bookstore (☎ 152-73-95; Jesús 11; ⏰ 10am-6pm Tue-Sat, 10am-4pm Sun) Has titles in English and Spanish.

EMERGENCY

General Emergencies (☎ Ambulance, Fire & Police 152-09-11)

INTERNET ACCESS

Border Crossings (☎ 152-24-97; www.bordercross ingsma com; Mesones 57A; M$15 per hr; ⏰ 9am-6:30pm Mon-Fri, 10am-3pm Sat) Good internet access as well as mail-forwarding and phone-message services.

Internet Café Punto G (☎ 152-16-19; Hidalgo 23; M$20 per hr; ⏰ 9:30am-midnight Mon Sat, 11am midnight Sun) Also known as the Hookah Bar (for its huge hookah pipes). M$65 per pipe-full – internet speed may become irrelevant.

Internet Tranvi_net (cnr Umarán & El Jardín, 1st fl) Good internet services with scanning and printing.

INTERNET RESOURCES

Atención San Miguel (www.atencionsanmiguel.org) Weekly semi-bilingual newspaper that runs an excellent website.

Portal San Miguel (www.portalsanmiguel.com) A commercial website with a good overview of the town.

LAUNDRY

Laundromats charge around M$45 to wash and dry up to 4kg.

Lavandería Arco Iris (☎ 152-53-86; Pasaje Allende, local N; ⏰ 9am-2pm, 4-7pm Mon-Fri; 9am-2pm Sat) Inside arcade off Mesones.

Lavandería El Reloj (☎ 152-38-43; Reloj 34A; ⏰ 8am-8pm Mon-Fri, 8am-5pm Sat)

MEDICAL SERVICES

Hospital de la Fe (☎ 152-22-33; Libramiento a Dolores Hidalgo 43)

MEDIA

Don't contemplate spending time in town without buying the weekly semi-bilingual (English/Spanish) newspaper, **Atención San Miguel** (M$8). Published every Friday, it's chock-a-block with what's on for the coming week including tours, concerts and gallery openings. It also lists yoga, Spanish, art and dance class schedules (plus ads for local businesses, galleries and real estate). You can buy it at the public library and many cafés or from roaming vendors.

MONEY

Most banks have their own ATMs and are located on, or within two blocks east of, the Jardín. There are also *casas de cambio* on Correo.

POST

Post office (cnr Correo & Corregidora) Mexpost express mail next door; DHL is nearby on Correo.

NORTHERN CENTRAL HIGHLANDS

SAN MIGUEL DE ALLENDE

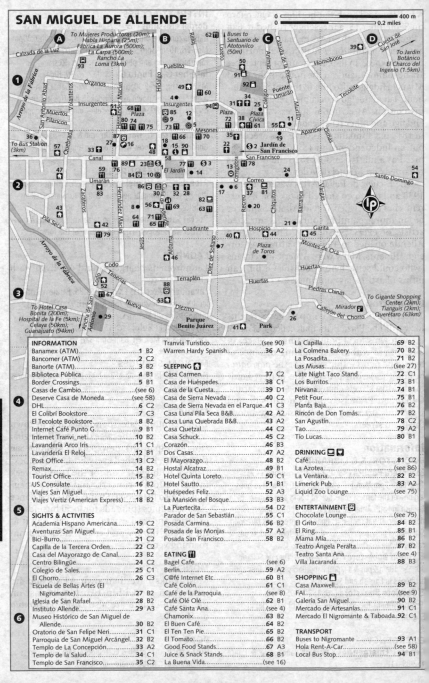

TELEPHONE & FAX

Card phones are plentiful in the center. Faxes can be sent from Border Crossings (p631). Cell phone SIM cards ('chips') can be purchased from any Telcel outlet.

TOURIST INFORMATION

Tourist office (☎ 152-09-00; www.turismosanmiguel .com.mx; Plaza Principal s/n; ⏰ 8:30am-8pm Mon-Fri, 10am-8pm Sat, 10am-5:30pm Sun) On the northern side of El Jardín. Good for maps of the town and promotional pamphlets.

TRAVEL AGENCIES

Viajes San Miguel (☎ 152-25-37; www.viajessan miguel.com; Diez de Sollano 4-Interior 3; ⏰ 9am-7pm Mon-Fri, 10am-2pm Sat) Good deals including airport shuttle service.

Viajes Vertiz (☎ 152-18-56; www.viajesvertiz.com; Hidalgo 1A; ⏰ 9am-2pm & 4-6:30pm Mon-Fri, 10am-2pm Sat) American Express agent (but does not cash traveler's checks); sells domestic and international air tickets.

Sights

PARROQUIA DE SAN MIGUEL ARCÁNGEL

The parish church's pink 'wedding cake' towers dominate the Jardín. These strange pinnacles were designed by indigenous stonemason Zeferino Gutiérrez in the late 19th century. He reputedly based the design on a postcard of a Belgian church and instructed builders by scratching plans in the sand with a stick. The rest of the church dates from the late 17th century. In the chapel to the left of the main altar is the much-revered image of the *Cristo de la Conquista* (Christ of the Conquest), made in Pátzcuaro from cornstalks and orchid bulbs, probably in the 16th century. Irish visitors will be pleased to find a statue of St Patrick, a tribute to the Irish who changed sides to fight alongside the locals in the civil war. The adjacent **Iglesia de San Rafael** was founded in 1742.

MUSEO HISTÓRICO DE SAN MIGUEL DE ALLENDE

Near the *parroquia* is the house where Ignacio Allende was born, now the **history museum** (☎ 152-24-99; Cuna de Allende 1; admission M$34; ⏰ 9am-5pm Tue-Sun). Exhibits relate the interesting history of the San Miguel area, with special displays on Allende and the independence movement. A Latin inscription on the facade reads *Hic natus ubique notus,* which means 'Here born, everywhere known.'.

CASA DEL MAYORAZGO DE CANAL

This historic **house** (cnr Hidalgo & Canal), one of San Miguel's most imposing old residences, now houses Banamex offices. It's a handsome neoclassical structure with some late baroque touches. The original entrance is at Canal 4 and retains beautiful carved wooden doors based on a tapestry design.

TEMPLO DE SAN FRANCISCO

This **church** (cnr San Francisco & Juárez; admission free; ⏰ hours vary) has an elaborate late-18th-century Churrigueresque facade. An image of St Francis of Assisi is at the top.

CAPILLA DE LA TERCERA ORDEN

Built in the early 18th century, this **chapel** (Chapel of the Third Order; cnr San Francisco & Juárez; admission free), like Templo de San Francisco, was part of a Franciscan monastery complex. The main facade shows St Francis and symbols of the Franciscan order.

ORATORIO DE SAN FELIPE NERI

This multi-towered and domed 18th-century **church** (Plaza Cívica) is near the east end of Insurgentes. The pale-pink main facade is baroque with an indigenous influence. A passage to the right of this facade leads to the east wall, where a doorway holds the image of *Nuestra Señora de la Soledad* (Our Lady of Solitude). You can see into the cloister from this side of the church.

Inside the church are 33 oil paintings showing scenes from the life of San Felipe Neri, the 16th-century Florentine who founded the Oratorio Catholic order. In the east transept is a painting of the Virgin of Guadalupe by leading colonial painter Miguel Cabrera. In the west transept is a lavishly decorated 1735 chapel, the **Santa Casa de Loreto**, a replica of a chapel in Loreto, Italy, legendary home of the Virgin Mary. If the chapel doors are open (unfortunately, this is rarely) you can see tiles from Puebla, Valencia and China on the floor and walls and gilded cloth hangings. Behind the altar, the *camerán* (chapel behind the main church) has six elaborately gilded baroque altars. In one is a reclining wax figure of San Columbano; it supposedly contains the saint's bones.

TEMPLO DE LA SALUD

This **church** (Plaza Cívica), with a dome tiled blue and yellow and a big shell carved above its entrance, is just east of San Felipe Neri.

The facade is early Churrigueresque. The church's paintings include one of San Javier by Miguel Cabrera. San Javier (St Francis Xavier, 1506–52) was a founding member of the Jesuits. It was once part of the Colegio de Sales (see below).

COLEGIO DE SALES

Once a college, founded in the mid-18th century by the San Felipe Neri order, **Colegio de Sales** (Plaza Cívica; 8am-2pm, 5-8pm) regained its educational status; it currently houses part of the University of León. Many of the 1810 revolutionaries were educated here. Spaniards were locked up here when the rebels took San Miguel.

TEMPLO DE LA CONCEPCIÓN

This splendid **church** (Church of the Conception; cnr Zacateros & Canal) has a fine altar and several magnificent old oil paintings. Painted on the interior doorway are a number of wise sayings to give pause to those entering the sanctuary. The church was begun in the mid-18th century; its dome, added in the late 19th century by the versatile Zeferino Gutiérrez, was possibly inspired by pictures of *Les Invalides* in Paris.

ESCUELA DE BELLAS ARTES

This **school** (School of Fine Arts; Centro Cultural Nigromante; 152-02-89; Hernández Macías 75; admission free; 9am-7pm) is housed in the beautiful former monastery of La Concepción church, which was converted into a fine-arts school in 1938. It's officially named the Centro Cultural Ignacio Ramírez, after a leading 19th-century liberal thinker. His nickname was El Nigromante (The Sorcerer) and the center is also commonly called by this name.

INSTITUTO ALLENDE

This large 1736 **complex** (Ancha de San Antonio 20 & 22) has recently been divided between a school of higher education and an area focusing on Mexican culture and tourism. Several patios, gardens and an old chapel divide the original home of the Conde Manuel de la Canal. Later it was used as a Carmelite convent, eventually becoming an art and language school in 1951. Above the entrance is a carving of the Virgin of Loreto, patroness of the Canal family.

MIRADOR & PARQUE BENITO JUÁREZ

One of the best views over the town and surrounding country is from the **mirador** (overlook) southeast of town. Take Callejón del Chorro, the track leading directly downhill from here, and turn left at the bottom to reach **El Chorro**, the spring where San Miguel was founded. Today it gushes out of a fountain built in 1960 and there are public washing tubs here. A path – Paseo del Chorro – zigzags down the hill to the shady **Parque Benito Juárez**, a lovely place to relax and meander through.

JARDÍN BOTÁNICO EL CHARCO DEL INGENIO

On the hilltop 1.5km northeast of town is the 220-acre **botanic garden** (154-47-15; www.elcharco.org.mx; off Antiguo Camino Real a Querétaro; admission M$30; dawn-dusk). This wildlife and bird sanctuary, an ongoing project thanks to the efforts of local volunteers, was created to conserve a natural area around the town and to provide a recreational and ceremonial space for the community. Pathways head through magnificent areas of cacti and native plants, through wetlands and above a canyon where lies the namesake freshwater spring, the **Charco del Ingenio**. A map with the pathways and explanations is provided upon entrance. The route incorporates the **Conservatory of Mexican Plants**, which houses a wonderful array of cacti and succulent species, some of which are endangered species. Excellent two-hour tours (in English) depart every Tuesday at 9am (M$50).

Getting to the garden can seem slightly prickly business, thanks to new urban development on the town's outskirts that blocks the original route, but it's worth persevering. Walk uphill from Mercado El Nigromante along Homobono and Cuesta de San José. Fork left up Montitlan past a housing development (known as Los Balcones). Continue for another 15 minutes to the main gate. Be sure to keep the garden boundary fence on your left as much as possible. (Occasionally you may have to head around the new houses on sidewalks, after which you head back to the fence.)

Alternatively, a 2km vehicle track leads north from the Gigante shopping center, 2.5km east of the center on the Querétaro road. Gigante can be reached on 'Gigante' buses from the bus stop on the east side of Jardín de San Francisco. A taxi to the gardens from the center costs around M$25.

Activities

See the Tours section (opposite) for agencies that rent out bicycles and offer other enticing active options.

Posada de la Aldea opens its **swimming pool** (☎ 152-10-22; Ancha de San Antonio 15; admission M$50; ⏰ 9am-6pm) to nonguests most days, but it's more enjoyable to visit the *balnearios* (bathing spots) in the surrounding countryside (see p642).

Rancho La Loma (☎ 152-21-21; rancholaloma@hotmail.com; Carretera Dolores Hidalgo s/n; per hr M$200) rents horses (experience required) and can arrange instruction and guides.

Courses

Several institutions offer Spanish courses, with group or private lessons and optional classes in Mexican culture and history. Most private lessons start around US$15 an hour; group and long-term rates are much lower. There are also many courses in painting, sculpture, ceramics, music and dance. Most courses are available year-round, except December. The Escuela de Bellas Artes has courses in art, dance, crafts and music in Spanish and English, and cost around M$1000 a month, plus materials. Registration is at the beginning of each month. Some classes are not held in July and there are none in August.

Academia Hispano Americana (☎ 152-03-49; www.ahaspeakspanish.com; Mesones 4) This place runs quality courses in the Spanish language and Latin American culture (also taught in elementary Spanish). Private language classes are also available. Homestays with Mexican families – a private room and three meals per day – cost around US$23 per day.

Centro Bilingüe (☎ 152-54-00; www.centrobilingue.com; Correo 46) Offers Spanish instruction; some courses have emphasis on Mexican culture.

Habla Hispana (☎ 152-1535; Calzada de la Luz 25) Offers language classes and can incorporate walking tours and cooking classes.

Instituto Allende (☎ 152-01-90; www.instituto-allende.edu.mx; Ancha de San Antonio 22) Offers courses in fine arts, crafts and Spanish. Arts courses can be joined at any time and usually entail nine hours of attendance a week. Spanish courses for groups begin every four weeks and range from conversational to intensive. Private lessons (total impact) cost US$14 per hour.

Warren Hardy Spanish (☎ 154-40-17; www.warrenhardy.com; San Rafael 6) Offers Spanish instruction using flash cards.

Tours

The tourist office has promotional pamphlets of private English-speaking tour guides.

Aventuras San Miguel (☎ 415 152 6406; aventurasma@yahoo.com; Recreo 9) Offers tours around the region including horseback riding, hiking and camping trips; minimum two people.

Bici-Burro (☎ 152-15-26; www.bici-burro.com; Hospicio 1; trips M$700-1350) Friendly and professional, English-speaking owner Alberto conducts excellent guided mountain-bike tours for groups of two or more. Popular trips include six- or seven-hour excursions to Atotonilco or Pozos. Bike rental also available (M$500 per day).

House and Garden Tour An English-language tour of the loveliest private homes and gardens (mostly of expatriates) in San Miguel begins at noon every Sunday from the Biblioteca Pública (Insurgentes 25). The cost is M$150 for the two-hour tour, with three different houses visited weekly. Proceeds support the library's enterprises.

Centro de Crecimiento (☎ 152-03-18; www.centrodecrecimiento.org) Runs 'Saturday Adventures' every Saturday at 10:30am to ranches, haciendas, vineyards, monasteries and Talavera factories. Tickets are purchased from El Jardín on Fridays 10:30am-12:30pm and Saturdays 9:30am. Proceeds go to the organization, a rehabilitation center for children with disabilities.

Tranvía Turístico (Tourist trolley; Transportadora Turística Imperial; ☎ 154-54-08; www.transtur-imperial.com; Plaza Principal 18, 1st fl; adult/child M$60/40) See the main sights in 1½ hours from the comfort of an original tram. Of the six departures, one is bilingual and departs at 4pm.

Walking Tour This excellent tour takes place every Monday, Wednesday and Friday at 10am, departing from the Jardín (tickets go on sale in the Jardín at 9:45am; M$100). The English-speaking volunteer guides provide a fascinating historical and cultural commentary on the main sights of town. Proceeds go to Patronato Pro Niños (www.patronatoproninos.org), a children's charity.

Festivals & Events

San Miguel is well endowed with churches and patron saints (it has six) and enjoys a multitude of festivals, many imbued with strong spiritual themes. You'll probably learn by firework bursts while you're here. For programs, ask at the tourist office or check the website www.turismosanmiguel.com.mx.

Señor de la Conquista The image of Christ in the *parroquia* is feted on the first Friday in March, with scores of dancers in elaborate pre-Hispanic costumes and plumed headdresses.

Semana Santa A week of religious activities. Two Sundays before Easter, pilgrims carry an image of the Señor de la Columna (Lord of the Column) from Atotonilco, 11km north, to San Miguel's church of San Juan de Dios, departing at midnight on Saturday. During Semana Santa, the many activities include the solemn Procesión del Santo Entierro on Good Friday and the burning or exploding of Judas effigies on Easter Day.

Fiesta de la Santa Cruz This deeply spiritual spring festival has its roots in the 16th century. It happens towards the end of May at Valle del Maíz, 2km from the center of town. Oxen are dressed in lime necklaces and painted tortillas and their yokes festooned with flowers and fruit. A mock battle between 'Indians' and 'Federales' follows. There are *mojigangas* (see boxed text, p620), dancing and musicians, not to mention 96 hours worth of fireworks.

Fiesta de los Locos Part of the Festividad de San Antonio de Padua in mid-June, the festival of the crazies is a colorful Carnavalesque parade through town with floats, blaring music and costumed dancers throwing out candy to (sometimes at!) the crowd.

Expresión en Corto Shared with the city of Guanajuato, this short-film festival in July is internationally recognized.

Chamber Music Festival The Escuela de Bellas Artes sponsors an annual festival of chamber music in the first two weeks of August.

Fiestas Patrias Two months of cultural programs kick off in mid-August, with Independence Day in the middle. Check with the tourist office for a full event schedule.

San Miguel Arcángel Celebrations honoring the town's chief patron saint are held around the weekend nearest September 29. The party is celebrated with an *alborada*, an artificial dawn created by thousands of fireworks around the cathedral and turns into an all-night festivity with extraordinary pre-Hispanic dances.

Festival of Jazz and Blues November sees the recently revived jazz and blues festival with big name acts from the US and jam sessions in restaurants.

San Miguel Music Festival This largely classical music festival toward the end of December presents a daily program with Mexican and international performers in the Teatro Ángela Peralta (see p640).

Sleeping

Accommodations are often full, especially during festivals and high season, so reserve ahead. Many hotels offer discounts to long-term guests. If you decide to stay a while, there are plenty of houses, apartments and rooms to rent (see p638). If you can pull the purse-strings for accommodations, this is the place to do it.

BUDGET

Hostal Alcatraz (☎ 152-85-43; Reloj 54; dm from M$100, r M$280; 🖳) San Miguel's only HI-affiliated hostel is centrally located, with basic dorms and a shared kitchen. Travelers rave about the friendly staff. The owner has recently opened a new associated hostel (Hostel Inn) at Calzada de La Luz 31A charging the same prices.

Casa de Huéspedes (☎ 152-13-78; Mesones 27; s/d M$200/300) This upstairs hostelry has seven sim-

ple rooms, two apartments and a rooftop terrace with good views. If you're a light sleeper, opt for rooms at the back; the street is noisy. Two rooms have basic 'kitchenettes' for the same price.

MIDRANGE

Parador de San Sebastián (☎ 152-70-84; Mesones 7; s/d/tr M$300/400/520; 🅿) The odd globe is missing here and there, but this place has a great atmosphere. The older rooms around the leafy courtyard are more spacious than the newer (darker) ones. You might want to pick your own rather than reserve by phone.

Hotel Sautto (☎ 152-00-52; hotelsautto@yahoo.com.mx; Hernández Maciác 59; s/d/tr M$300/500/600) This delightful former hacienda may be a bit scruffy around the edges, but its lack of pretensions and Mexican feel – a lovely courtyard, garden (complete with bougainvillea and lorikeets) – makes up for any shortcomings for the basic but adequate rooms.

El Mayorazgo (☎ 152-13-09; posadamayorazgo@hotmail.com; Hidalgo 8; r M$400; 🅿) Don't let the unconventional entrance put you off (it resembles an ugly concrete bunker). This centrally located 1980s-style place has plain, but modern(ish) and light rooms. Rates are M$50 cheaper from Monday through Thursday.

Huéspedes Feliz (152-08-54; Codo 30; s/d M$400/500) For those happy to trade a hotel's room service for independence, a street taco for a home-cooked meal and colonial architecture for more modern design, then this is for you a choice of four extremely secure and squeaky clean, (but slightly dark) rooms – each with fully equipped kitchen – set neatly behind the owner's house.

Posada de las Monjas (☎ 152-01-71; www.posadalasmonjas.com; Canal 37; s from M$420, d M$500-600; 🅿) This quirky sprawling monastery-turned-motel remains one of San Miguel's top values. The 65 carpeted rooms are comfortable and simply decorated; rooms in the 'newer' section out back have the edge over the others. Numerous terraces give wonderful views over the valley. Meals are available for an extra cost but readers have warned against the breakfast.

Hotel Quinta Loreto (☎ 152-00-42; www.quintaloreto.com; Loreto 15; s/d/tr M$450/550/650; 🅿 🐾) This motel-style place at the back of the artisans market is spread around large, leafy grounds. Some of the 40 pleasant rooms have a small private patio. TV costs extra and there's a restaurant (open for breakfast and lunch 8am to 11am and 1pm to 5:30pm). Stays of a week or longer net a 10% discount.

La Mansión del Bosque (☎ 152-02-77; www.infosma .com/mansion; Aldama 65; s US$47-65, d US$91-95, tr US$152) Located opposite Parque Benito Juárez and run by the gracefully ageing matriarch Ruth, this long-running guesthouse has 23 unique rooms that still appear c 1968 – and you wouldn't want them to change. Each room has decent, sometimes quirky décor and original art. Rates are higher in winter (December through March), when the breakfast and dinner meal plan (US$20) is mandatory.

Casa Carmen (☎ 152-08-44; www.infosma.com /casacarmen; Correo 31; s/d M$700/950) As the name suggests, this centrally located colonial place is more of a traditional guesthouse than an upmarket B&B. The charming rooms with eclectic Mexican-style décor don't appear to have changed much in decades. There's a pleasant courtyard with a fountain, flowers and orange trees. Rates include breakfast and lunch.

Hotel Casa Bonita (☎ 152-06-46; El Cardo 10; www .casabonitasma.com; d M$850; P ⌨) The six rooms in this Mexican-run B&B-style option are light, airy and bright. The spacious bathrooms, generous breakfast (choice of continental or full American) and quiet location (slightly out of the central district, between Anche de San Antonio and Parque Benito Juárez) are a bonus. Prices are M$50 less per night for week-long stays, or if you pay by cash.

TOP END

Posada Carmina (☎ 152-88-88; www.posadacarmina .com; Cuna de Allende 7; s/d/ste from M$890/1110/1290) This former rambling colonial mansion features 12 newer and 12 older rooms at the back. All have tiled bathroom, phone and TV. It's not luxurious, but attractive and comfortable with olde world charm.

Casa Quetzal (☎ 152-05-01; www.casaquetzalhotel .com; Hospicio 34; d US$175-351) This American-owned boutique hotel is in a compact space, but oozes elegance. It's a good alternative to the B&B scene and offers similar trimmings. Each room is themed (from the ubiquitous Frida suite to the Zihua room) and some have kitchenette with microwave, mini-refrigerator and coffee maker. There's a minimum two-day stay on weekends and extra persons cost US$35.

La Puertecita (☎ 152-50-11; www.lapuertecita.com; Santo Domingo 75; r from US$227; ⌨ ⌨) This secluded property meanders along the forested valley

just above town and *los pocitos* (spring water fountains). The classical rooms – spread along the hillside gardens – range from luxurious 'basic' with fire place and balcony, to suites with full kitchens. The public can indulge in a Sunday buffet breakfast (M$120; 8am to 11am) or lunch (M$165; 1pm to 4pm) in its restaurant overlooking the luxuriant greenery.

Casa de Sierra Nevada (☎ 152-70-40; www.casa desierranevada.com; Hospicio 35; r from M$3175; P ⌨) The most luxurious hotel in town has 32 rooms and suites located in five converted colonial mansions including Casa Parque, on Parque Benito Juárez. It has a heated outdoor pool, two fine restaurants, views over the town, superbly appointed rooms and flawless service.

BOUTIQUE B&BS

San Miguel is the mecca for luxury B&Bs. These plush places reek of modern colonial grandeur with stylish décor and luxuriant gardens or courtyards. The prices match their high style (ie top end) and little distinguishes them in opulence, comfort and service, other than their breakfasts and themed décor such as Asian Zen and stylish folkloric Mexican. Some of those on offer:

Casa Luna (☎ 152-11-11; www.casaluna.com; Pila Seca 11 & Quebrada 117; r US$135-176) This lavish place has more themed décor than a home show. Frida Kahlo has a room devoted to her in this eclectic place, as do stars and saints.

Casa de la Cuesta (☎ 154-43-24; www.casadela cuesta.com; Cuesta de San José 32; r US$145) Perched on the hill just up from the market, no detail was spared in this highly ornate and elegant place and themed rooms. The lavish breakfast is an experience in itself. The owners display their large collection of masks in a nearby museum, 'The Other Face of Mexico' (by appointment only); admission fee goes to charity.

Casa Schuck (☎ /fax 152-06-57; www.casaschuck.com; Garita 3; r from US$169-249) Stylish & slightly opulent rooms with great ambience, ample gardens and fantastic views.

Corazón (☎ 152-01-82; www.posadacorazon.com.mx; Aldama 9; d US$150-170, tr US$170-200) This place is set behind an inconspicuous wall in a delightful plant and sculpture garden. The home's spacious open plan living area, complete with library, can be shared by guests and rooms along a deck are simple and stylish.

Dos Casas (☎ 154-40-73; Quebrada 101; d US$270-390; ⌨) One of the newest and sleekest in town, this option oozes contemporary style – there are lots of cream and black hues, plus Jacuzzis and private terraces.

LONG-TERM ACCOMMODATIONS

A rental house or apartment is a good option for longer-term stays. Rates start at around US$600 a month for a stylish two-bedroom house (much less for a room in a Mexican home). Check the notice boards and fliers around town, scan the free newspapers or contact a local real-estate office. **Remax** (☎ 152-73-63; www.realestate-sma.com; Portal Guadalupe 12) is a good place to make initial enquiries.

Eating

San Miguel's numerous eateries serve a startling variety of quality Mexican and international cuisine. Thrifty travelers enjoy more traditional places catering to loyal crowds of local families. Cafés are the latest trend in San Miguel and many serve good local meals at reasonable prices (M$20 to M$110). Good, inexpensive places are still found in the *centro*.

BUDGET

Los Burritos (Mesones 69A; M$4-25; ☯ 10:30am-6pm Mon-Sat) You definitely don't head here for the décor (although note the carved donkey heads on the chairs), but instead for the vast array of cheap *antojitos* and the mouthwatering, made-to-order *guisados* with a huge selection of delectable fillings from *mole* to *chipotle* and potato.

El Ten Ten Pie (☎ 152-71-89; Cuna de Allende 21; mains M$15-52; ☯ 9am-midnight) This unpretentious hangout is a great choice for home-style Mexican cooking with superb chili sauces – at a less spicy price. Try the inexpensive set lunch (M$80) or the fresh tortillas stuffed to the brim with delicious fillings. Excellent breakfasts and veggie options also.

Café Colón (Mesones 25; set meals M$30-50; ☯ 8am-5pm) This café, run by local character, Irma, is popular with locals for its cheap set breakfasts and lunches.

Café Olé Olé (☎ 152-08-96; Loreto 66; mains M$40-120; ☯ 1-9pm) Charge in to this brightly decorated restaurant – bullfighting posters, matador jackets and a massive bull's head adorn the walls. It's been eternally popular for its special: grilled chicken and beef fajitas.

El Tomato (☎ 154-60-57; Mesones 62; mains M$55-80; ☯ 9am-9pm Mon-Sat; Ⓥ) One of the few wholly vegetarian places, the Tomato serves healthy light meals such as pasta, whole-wheat sandwiches and salads, using fresh and tasty organic ingredients. There are also fresh-squeezed juices and a good-value set lunch (M$80).

MIDRANGE

There are lively places facing the Jardín where you pay a premium for the mariachis and ringside location, but don't be fooled: the best food can be found in hidden locations.

Rincón de Don Tomás (☎ 152-37-80; Portal de Guadalupe 2; mains M$50-130; ☯ 8:30-10pm) An oldie but a goody. This long-standing joint has a solid following and a menu of classic Mexican dishes such as chicken with *moles* and cordites. Given its position on the Jardín, it's not bad value.

La Posadita (☎ 154-88-62; Cuna de Allende 13; M$65-120; ☯ noon-10pm Thu-Tue) This delightful eatery gets five stars for its excellent service, Mexican fare, reasonable prices and location – near the *parroquia*. Head up a steep set of stairs to the restaurant or the wonderful rooftop terrace with great vistas. It serves delicious margaritas, enchiladas and *filete a la tampiqueña*, to name a few.

Tao (☎ 152-29-49; Pila Seca 16; M$70-90; ☯ noon-9pm Tue-Sun) If you need a break from tortillas and tacos, head to this Korean/Japanese eatery for tantalizing tofu, tempura and sushi dishes.

Berlin (☎ 152-94-32; Umarán 19; mains M$60-160; ☯ 1pm-1am) Stop in this cool, artsy spot for a tasty blend of German and Mexican food. The bar is very Euro and if you eavesdrop, you may get the scoop on where to find the next hip art opening.

Planta Baja (☎ 154-65-55; Canal 28; mains M$80-165; ☯ 1pm-midnight) You don't come here to be in Mexico; this contemporary-style place serves eclectic Mexican-Mediterranean fusion fare in funky surroundings by excellent waiters. The experimental dishes (such as caramelized swordfish) are tastier than the more straightforward grilled fish.

TOP END

When money is no object, San Miguel is one of the country's best places to take a break from the lard and savor some fine cuisine.

Bella Italia (☎ 152-49-89; Canal 21; mains M$85-280) Rome meets San Miguel in this smart, slightly old-fashioned place set within an attractive courtyard. Think handmade pasta, mussels in white wine and grilled lamb chops – just as Mama used to make. Excellent musicians perform nightly.

Chamonix (☎ 154-83-63; Diez de Sollano 17; dishes M$90-215; ☯ 1-10pm Tue-Sat) Enter through the pink and orange organza curtains into a pretty garden atmosphere for an unusual but high-quality menu with Mexican with French and Asian flavors. The restaurant also has a pleasant street-side lounge.

Tío Lucas (☎ 152-49-96; Mesones 103; mains M$100-260; ☯ noon-11:30pm) About as Mexican as George W Bush, this stylish place with a silver-star-covered courtyard is known for its beef, especially the fillet steak, and for being 'reliable.' Happy hour runs from 6pm to 8pm on weekdays, and there's live blues or jazz nightly.

Nirvana (☎ 150-00-67; Mesones 101; dishes M$120-180; ☯ 8:30am-11pm Wed-Mon) Artistically prepared international fusion served in one of two settings (one more contemporary than the other). Think venison in black chili seasoning and salmon in mango chutney. The menu indicates a red chili for spicy meals and a heart for low fat dishes.

La Capilla (☎ 152-06-98; Cuna de Allende 10; mains M$150-300; ☯ 1-11pm Wed-Mon) This elegant restaurant's atmosphere and location – in a former chapel of the *parroquia* – is unbeatable. The restaurant's fairy-lighted rooftop terrace affords romantic and spectacular sunset views. The menu, which offers truly international cuisine, doesn't always live up to the location's lofty heights; it gets mixed reviews. Downstairs there's a classy café-bar and counter selling quality chocolates.

CAFÉS

Café de la Parroquia (☎ 152-31-61; Jesús 11; ☯ 8am-4pm Tue-Sat, 8am-2pm Sun) Expats love this place for its tranquil and shaded courtyard setting with fountain and reliable food. In the evening it morphs into La Brasserie (open from 5pm to 10pm, Tuesday to Saturday).

El Buen Café (☎ 152-58-07; Jesús 23; ☯ 9am-4pm Mon-Sat) This simple place does excellent healthy breakfasts, Mexican specialties and sweet home-baked gourmet-style goodies. Think French toast with blackberry sauce (M$60) or thick oatmeal topped with blackberries and crème brûlée.

our pick San Agustín (☎ 154-91-02; San Francisco 21; ☯ 8am-11pm) A 'don't leave San Miguel without…' experience. A sweet tooth's paradise and the best place to go in Mexico for chocolate and churros (M$33).

Petit Four (☎ 154-40-10; Mesones 99-1; ☯ 10am-:30pm Tue-Sun) Another wonderful place to get your sugary hit: French pastries that you can enjoy in a cosy environment. Coffee costs M$15.

Las Musas (Hernández Macías 75; ☯ 9am-6pm Mon-Sat, 10am-2pm Sun) The setting, within the courtyard of Bellas Artes, is among the most beautiful in town, which makes up for the rather average food.

Bagel Cafe (☎ 154-65-24; Correo; ☯ 8am-3pm Mon-Fri, 8am-2pm Sat) An understated place and a fave of expats. It serves cheap bagels (M$10) and egg breakfasts (M$55).

Café Santa Ana (Reloj 50-A; ☯ 8am-8pm Mon-Fri, 8:30am-2pm Sat, 8:30-noon Sun) Another relaxing place popular with culture vultures and in the library annex. Good set breakfasts (M$50); try the *pan árabe*.

C@fe Internet Etc (☎ 154-86-36; Reloj 37; ☯ 9:30am-6pm Mon-Sat) Local expats like this place for its casual atmosphere, good snacks and Juan's extensive music and movie library.

GROCERIES & QUICK EATS

Snack carts on the Jardín offer cheap, tasty Mexican fare like *elutes* (steamed corn ears), hot dogs, fresh fruit salads, *tamales* and hamburgers (locals and expatriates rave about these). Reliable juice stands front the small plaza off Insurgentes.

Downhill toward Instituto Allende, on the corner of Ancha San Antonio and tree-shaded Calle Nueva, several reliable food stands alternate in the mornings and evenings, selling great tasting juice, *gorditas*, burritos and tacos.

Excellent bakeries include **La Buena Vida** (Hernández Macías 72-5; ☯ 8am-5pm Mon-Sat) and **La Colmena Bakery** (Reloj 21; ☯ Mon-Sat).

Mercado El Nigromante (Colegio s/n) Has good produce stands and market eateries. It's centrally located, but light years away from the gringo scene.

Drinking & Entertainment

In San Miguel, drinking and entertainment are often synonymous. Many bars (and restaurants) host live music. Most of the action is on Thursday, Friday and Saturday nights, but some places will have live music nightly.

CAFÉS

Café (154-72-91; Correo 37; cappuccinos M$20; ☯ 8:30am-9pm Mon-Sat) This place is serious about its coffee. Come here for the best coffee in town and wi-fi connection.

La Ventana (Diez de Sollano 11) Stroll up to the window for a take-away coffee (or sit inside) and stock up on your organic roasted beans from Chiapas.

BARS

La Azotea (☎ 152-82-75; Umarán 6) Above the restaurant Pueblo Viejo, this terrace is more of a laid-back lounge and tapas bar, with a smart, gay-friendly crowd and a less-touristy vibe.

Limerick Pub (☎ 154-86-42; Umarán 24) Young Mexicans have some craic in this traditional Irish pub, which has all the paraphernalia to fit the bill: a pool table, darts, 1980s tunes and Guinness. Oh and did you hear the one about the belly dancer? (She sometimes makes an appearance, too.)

Mama Mía (☎ 152-20-63; Umarán 8) This perennially popular place has separate areas to host its weekly schedule of different gigs. Hit Mama's Bar for live rock/funk (Friday and Saturday), or join a more sophisticated crowd in the restaurant patio for live folk music, including South American music (Tuesday to Sunday), salsa (Friday and Saturday) and jazz (Sunday). Up front, Bar Leonardo's shows big-screen sports and La Terrazza, the terrace bar, offers a fine view of the town. Serious nightlife gets going around 11pm.

NIGHTCLUBS

El Ring (☎ 152-19-98; Hidalgo 25; ☉ 10pm-5am Wed, Thu, Fri, Sat, nightly in high season) Young locals come here for a club fix and a blast of Latin, US and European dance music. On Wednesday it's open from 8:30pm to midnight and swings to salsa rhythms for a more refined crowd.

El Grito (☎ 152-00-48; Umarán 15; ☉ 10pm-4am Fri & Sat) An oversized face above the doorway of this upscale disco shouts out 'high prices' to the young, fashionable Mexican crowd queuing outside.

Chocolate Lounge (Mesones 99-1; ☉ 10pm-3am Wed-Sat) The Chocolate Lounge is for disco divas, with all the action happening after 11pm. Upstairs, the separate **Liquid Zoo Lounge** (M$60; ☉ 11pm-5am), with its funky leopard skin seating, caters to a cool hip-hop, martini-loving crowd. Both are gay-friendly establishments.

THEATER & CULTURAL EVENTS

It's one big cultural party in San Miguel; the town seems to host more events than NYC. Check out what's on in *Atención San Miguel*. The Escuela de Bellas Artes (p634) and the Biblioteca (in the Sala Quetzal) host a variety of cultural events, many in English; check their notice boards for schedules.

Teatro Ángela Peralta (☎ 152-63-85; cnr Mesones & Hernández Macías) Built in 1910, this elegant venue often hosts local productions. The ticket office is around the corner in Hernández Macías 62 (8:30am to 4pm Monday to Saturday). Tickets range from gratis to M$200 depending on the production.

La Carpa (☎ 154-69-81; Aurora s/n; ☉ 10am-2pm) This dynamic circus tent sometimes hosts activities such as alternative dance classes, as well as monthly openings including live music, theater, art and circus acts.

CINEMA

Teatro Santa Ana (☎ 152-02-93; Reloj 50A; tickets M$50-150) This small theater inside the Biblioteca Pública plays host to a good selection of independent and international films, as well as local plays.

Villa Jacaranda (☎ 152-10-15; Aldama 53; tickets M$75) Projects recent releases of US and Bollywood movies on a big screen in a ballroom-type setting at 7:30pm daily. Entry includes a drink and popcorn.

Shopping

GALLERIES

Part of the joy of wandering around San Miguel is to stumble upon the many galleries tucked away in streets around town; there are more commercial galleries than cafés (and perhaps, real estate agents) in San Miguel. The largest concentration of contemporary art galleries and design studios (mainly expatriates work) is housed in the trendy **Fábrica La Aurora** (☎ 152-13-12; Aurora s/n; ☉ 10am-6pm), a remodeled raw-cotton factory on the north end of town One of the town's first commercial galleries is **Galería San Miguel** (☎ 152-04-54; Plaza Principal 14 ☉ 9am-2pm & 4-7pm Mon-Sat). Many galleries are promoted in local papers but otherwise, be guided by your whim.

CRAFT SHOPS

San Miguel has a mind-boggling number of craft shops, selling folk art and handicraft from all over the country. Local crafts include tin ware, wrought iron, silver, brass, leather glassware, pottery and textiles. Many shop are along Canal, San Francisco and Zacateros Price and quality can vary widely.

Casa Maxwell (☎ 152-02-47; www.maxwell.freeser ers.com; Canal 14; ☉ 9am-2pm & 4-7pm Mon-Fri, 10am-2pm & 4-8pm Sat, 11am-3pm Sun) This rambling stor (considered an institution in San Miguel) offers a tremendous array of decorative and household goods.

FAI (Save the Children; ☎ 152-36-86; faisavethechildren
.com; Hidalgo 13; ☒ 10:30am-6pm) has a great range
of handicrafts, many of which are made locally. Proceeds from sales go to the charity.

Mujeres Productoras (Female Producers; ☎ 150-
00-25; www.globaljusticecenter.org/mujeres_productoras;
Calzada de la Luz 42) is a rural women's co-opera-
tive from surrounding municipalities which
sells a range of handmade goods, the source of
income (often the only one) for the family.

The **Mercado de Artesanías** (Colegio s/n) is a collection of handicraft stalls of varying quality
in the alleyway between Colegio and Loreto;
prices can be on par with the town's shops
and quality varies. The local market **Mercado
El Nigromante** (Colegio s/n) sells fruit, vegetables
and assorted goods.

Be sure to hit the **Tianguis** (Tuesday market),
the biggest weekly outdoor extravaganza, beside the Gigante shopping center, 2.5km east
of the center on the Querétaro road. Take a
'Gigante' or 'Placita' bus (10 minutes) from
Mesones, near Plaza Civica.

Getting There & Away
AIR
The nearest tarmac is the Aeropuerto
Internacional del Bajío (p626), between León
and Silao, around 1½ hours away by car.

BUS
The small Central de Autobuses is on Canal
(Calzada de la Estación), 3km west of the
center. Tickets can be purchased at the station.
Primera Plus (and Flecha Amarilla) tickets
can be bought at **Transportadora Turística Imperial**
(☎ 154 5408; www.transtur-imperial.com; Plaza Principal 18,
1st fl; ☒ 9am-8pm). Tickets for ETN and Primera
Plus can be purchased from larger hotels.

CAR
If you need a car for more than a few days, it
may be worth organizing one through rental
agencies in Querétaro. The only San Miguel-
based agency is **Hola Rent-a-Car** (☎ 152-01-98;
www.holarentacar.com; Hotel San Francisco; ☒ 9am-2pm
& 4-7pm), inside Posada San Francisco. Prices
start around M$020 per day including insur-
ance. Reserve at least a week ahead, especially
during the high season.

Getting Around
TO/FROM THE AIRPORT
A few agencies provide shuttle transportation
to/from Bajío Airport. These include **Viajes
Vertiz** (☎ 152-18-56), **Viajes San Miguel** (☎ 152-25-
37) and **Transportadora Turística Imperial** (☎ 154-
54-08). Alternatively, take a bus to Silao and get
a taxi from there to the airport. For Mexico

DAILY BUSES FROM SAN MIGUEL DE ALLENDE

Destination	Fare	Duration	Frequency
Celaya	M$42	1¾hr	every 15 min (Flecha Amarilla)
Dolores	M$26	1hr	every 40 min 7am-8pm (Flecha Amarilla Hidalgo or Herradura de Plata)
Guadalajara	deluxe M$405	5¼hr	3 daily (ETN)
	1st-class M$336	5½hr	6 daily (Primera Plus)
Guanajuato	deluxe M$100	1-1¼hr	3 daily (ETN)
	1st-class M$81	1-1½hr	7 daily (Primera Plus)
	1st-class M$78	1-1½hr	1 daily (Ómnibus de México)
	2nd-class M$61	1-1½hr	10 daily (Flecha Amarilla)
León	deluxe M$145	2¼hr	3 daily (ETN)
	1st-class M$119	2¼hr	7 daily (Primera Plus)
Mexico City (Terminal Norte)	deluxe M$260	3½-4hr	4 daily (ETN)
	1st-class M$212	3½hr	2 daily (Primera Plus), 1 daily (Herradura de Plata)
	2nd-class M$173	4¼hr	every 40 min 7am-8pm (Herradura de Plata)
Querétaro	deluxe M$75	1hr	3 daily (ETN)
	2nd-class M$42	1¼hr	every 40 min 7am-8pm (Flecha Amarilla or Herradura de Plata)

Other 1st-class buses serve Aguascalientes, Monterrey and San Luis Potosí. Americanos buses
depart for Texas at 6pm daily (US$70 to US$130).

City airport, get a bus to Querétaro and a bus direct to the airport from there.

No bus service operates between Bajío airport and central León. Those without too much luggage may opt to walk from the airport to the intersection of the main road and the airport road (10 minutes on foot) and hail a local bus from there (around M$25). A taxi to León costs about M$250. For San Miguel, make a bus connection in León.

TO/FROM THE CENTER
Local buses (M$4) run from 7am to 9pm daily. 'Central' buses run regularly between the bus station and the town center. Coming into town these end at the eastern end of Insurgentes after winding through the streets. Heading out of the center, you can pick one up on Canal. A taxi between the center and the bus station costs around M$25, as do most trips around town.

AROUND SAN MIGUEL DE ALLENDE
Hot Springs
The surrounds of San Miguel are blessed with hot mineral springs. Their original spiritual significance, if any, seems to have been lost; they've been developed as commercial *balnearios,* swimming pools. Here, you can soak amid pleasant surroundings, including landscaped gardens and picnic grounds. Most places are crowded with local families on weekends but *muy tranquilo* (very peaceful) during the week.

The *balnearios* are accessed via the highway north of San Miguel and all are clearly signposted. The most convenient, but expensive, transportation is taxis (around M$100 each way; you can ask the driver to return for you at an appointed time). Alternatively, take a Dolores Hidalgo bus from the San Miguel bus station, or a local bus marked 'Santuario' (hourly) from Calzada de la Luz. These buses will stop out front, or at the turnoffs to all the main *balnearios.* To return to town, hail a bus heading along the highway.

Taboada (☎ 152-08-50; admission M$50; ✆ 9am-6pm Wed-Mon), 8km north then 3.25km west is popular for its Olympic-size swimming pool (with very warm water), plus there's a smaller pool for children and a hot thermal spa. A snack kiosk and a bar provide refreshments. Hourly 'Nigromante' minibuses, departing from Calzada de la Luz, will get you within 1.5km of Taboada; alternatively, jump off

where the bus turns to Nigromante and walk the remaining 1.5km to the hot springs.

Nearby, the family-oriented **Balneario Xote** (☎ 155-81-87; www.xoteparqueacuatico.com.mx; adult/child M$70/35; ✆ 9am-6pm) water park is 3.5km off the highway down the same cobblestone road as Taboada.

Two kilometers further on and 1km west up a gravel road **Escondido Place** (☎ 185-20-22; www.escondidoplace.com; admission M$80; ✆ 8am-5:30pm) has seven small outdoor pools and three connected indoor pools, each progressively hotter. The picturesque grounds have plenty of picnicking space and there's a kiosk for drinks and snacks.

Just past Parador del Cortijo at Km 9.5, **La Gruta** (☎ 185-20-99; admission M$6.50; ✆ 8am-5pm) is justifiably a local and tourist favorite; it has three small pools where a thermal spring is channeled. The hottest is in a cave entered through a 27m tunnel, with water gushing from the roof, lit by a single shaft of sunlight.

Santuario de Atotonilco
The hamlet of Atotonilco, 11km north of San Miguel and 3km west off the Dolores Hidalgo highway, is dominated by an extremely important sanctuary, at least in the eyes of Mexicans. The sanctuary was founded in 1740 as a spiritual retreat and Ignacio Allende married here in 1802. Eight years later he returned with Miguel Hidalgo and a band of independence rebels en route from Dolores to San Miguel to take the shrine's banner of the Virgin of Guadalupe as their flag.

A journey to Atotonilco is the goal of pilgrims and penitents from all over Mexico and the starting point of an important and solemn procession two weekends before Easter, in which the image of the Señor de la Columna is carried to the church of San Juan de Dios in San Miguel. Inside, the sanctuary has six chapels and is vibrant with statues, folk murals and paintings. Traditional dances are held here on the third Sunday in July.

From San Miguel, taxis charge around M$100 to M$120 for a one-way trip (some will wait for one hour). Local buses depart from Calzada de La Luz every hour (M$7; 45 minutes).

Pozos
☎ 412 / pop 2261 / elevation 2305m
Less than 100 years ago, Mineral de Pozos was a flourishing silver-mining center of around

70,000 people, but with the 1910 revolution and the flooding of the mines, the population dwindled. Empty houses, a large and unfinished church (note the dome!) and discarded mine workings and shafts were the legacy of abandonment. Today, this tiny place is trying valiantly to win a place on the map. Visitors can explore the crumbling buildings and tour the fascinating surrounds, including several mine ruins, by mountain bike or horse (warning: many mine shafts are unfenced and, at 150m deep, are extremely dangerous). Several expat artists run galleries here.

The town's tourism efforts also includes an 'art walk', a tour of the town's main galleries and craft workshops (some are rudimentary, but support underprivileged community members; maps of the walk are available at hotels and shops). Several workshops make pre-Hispanic musical instruments. For further information on the area, history and lists of festivals and local guides, see www.mineraldepozos.com.

On the plaza, **Casa Mexicana Hotel** (☎ 293-00-14; www.casamexicanahotel.com; Jardín Principal 2; r from M$862; P) is an inviting 100-year-old hacienda with a luxuriant garden. The unique and artistic rooms – some of which feature original Picasso lithographs (the owner was a former art dealer) – are elegant and spacious. One room even has a tree growing inside. In high season, it houses Café des Artistes. Next door, the stunning antique stone building of **Casa Montana** (☎ 293-00-32; www.casamontanahotel.com.mx; Jardín Principal 4A; r/ste M$850/1150) houses a plush and stylish B&B, courtyard and restaurant. Don't miss the *molcajete* (M$120).

The restored 19th-century hacienda, **Posada de las Minas** (☎ 293-02-13; www.posadadelasminas.com; Doblado 1; r/apt M$1100/1300), offers ornate rooms or apartments in a colonial setting. There's a bar, restaurant with a retractable roof (mains M$70 to M$110) and small but impressive cactus garden.

An excellent alternative to the trendy B&B restaurant scene is **Los Famosos de Pozos** (☎ 293-1-12; www.mineraldepozos.com; Hidalgo 10B; mains M$48-18; ☽ 11am-8pm) where you can relax on the terrace and enjoy the view and some good-value Mexican fare.

Pozos is 14km south of San Luis de la Paz, detour east of Hwy 57. To get here by bus from San Miguel, go first to Dolores Hidalgo, then to San Luis de la Paz and then take a third bus to Pozos. By car it's about 45 minutes

from San Miguel. Bici-Burro (see p635) offers bike tours to the town and mines.

QUERÉTARO STATE

Querétaro state (population 1.6 million) is full of surprises. Billed primarily an agricultural and ranching state – with the handsome Querétaro city as its capital – it is packed with diverse geography, quirky sights and historical gems. Natural phenomena, such as the world's third-largest monolith, La Peña de Bernal, plus pre-Hispanic ruins and a jewel of Mexico, the stunning Sierra Gorda Biosphere Reserve, are located in the state's 11,770 sq km. The reserve protects several mission towns, from where the local people run some medium, new community-owned tourism activities, a must for the more intrepid traveler.

QUERÉTARO

☎ 442 / pop 596,450 / elevation 1762m

As far as the silver cities go, Querétaro is sometimes intimated to be the ugly sibling. Indeed, the rather frantic outskirts with their busy freeways can give a misguided first impression. The city's large, historic heart is characterized by charming pedestrian streets, stunning plazas and interesting churches. The city's sophisticated restaurant scene whips up quality cuisine and the museums reflect the city's important role in Mexican history.

History

The Otomí founded a settlement here in the 15th century that was soon absorbed by the Aztecs, then by Spaniards in 1531. Franciscan monks used it as a missionary base not only to Mexico but also to what is now southwestern USA. In the early 19th century, Querétaro became a center of intrigue among disaffected criollos plotting to free Mexico from Spanish rule. Conspirators, including Miguel Hidalgo, met secretly at the house of Doña Josefa Ortiz (La Corregidora), who was the wife of Querétaro's former *corregidor* (district administrator).

When the conspiracy was uncovered, the story goes, Doña Josefa was locked in her house (now the Palacio de Gobierno) but managed to whisper through a keyhole to a co-conspirator, Ignacio Pérez, that their colleagues were in jeopardy, leading

NORTHERN CENTRAL HIGHLANDS

to Padre Hidalgo's call to arms (see boxed text, p629).

In 1917 the Mexican constitution was drawn up by the Constitutionalist faction in Querétaro. The PNR (which later became the PRI, the Institutional Revolutionary Party) was organized in Querétaro in 1929, dominating Mexican politics for the rest of the 20th century.

Orientation

The historic center comprises *andadores* (pedestrian streets) linking a number of lively plazas which make for pleasant strolling. All the plazas are busy hearts: Jardín Zenea, the main plaza, has Av Corregidora, the large downtown street, running along its east side. Plaza de Armas (aka Plaza de la Independencia) is two blocks east and the small Jardín de la Corregidora is a block north. The large and shady Alameda is several blocks south.

Information

There are card phones on Jardín Zenea, Plaza de Armas and elsewhere around the center. Handy no-name internet places are at Libertad 32 and Carranza 9; both charge around M$10 per hour. There are several banks with ATMs around Jardín Zenea. *Casas de cambio* are along Juárez and Colón.

Hospital Luis Martín (☎ 214-25-71; Zaragoza Pte 88)

Lava Express (☎ 212-27-48; Gutiérrez Nájera; M$14 per kg) Tucked in a shopping plaza east of Gutiérrez Nájera, north of Mercado la Cruz.

Librería Cultural del Centro (☎ 224-24-61; cnr 16 de Septiembre & Corregidora; ☽ 9am-8:30pm Mon-Fri, 9:30am-5pm Sat) This central bookstore has a great selection of cultural titles, some of which are in English.

Post office (☎ 212-01-12; Arteaga 5)

Tourist office (☎ 212-12-41, 238-50-67, 800-715-17-42; www.queretaro.travel; Pasteur Nte 4; ☽ 9am-8pm) Has city maps and brochures.

Turismo Beverly (☎ 216-15-00; Tecnológico 118) The American Express agent, which also books airplane tickets.

Sights

TEMPLO DE SAN FRANCISCO

This impressive **church** (cnr Av Corregidora & Andador 5 de Mayo; ☽ 8-10am & 4-9pm) fronts Jardín Zenea. Pretty colored tiles on the dome were brought from Spain in 1540, around the time construction of the church began. Inside are some fine religious paintings from the 17th, 18th and 19th centuries.

MUSEO REGIONAL

This **museum** (☎ 212-20-31; cnr Av Corregidora & Jardín Zenea; admission M$30; ☽ 10am-6pm Tue-Sun) is beside the Templo de San Francisco. The ground floor holds interesting exhibits on pre-Hispanic Mexico, archaeological sites, Spanish occupation and the state's various indigenous groups.

Upstairs exhibits reveal Querétaro's role in the independence movement and post-independence history (plus religious paintings). The table at which the Treaty of Guadalupe Hidalgo was signed in 1848, ending the Mexican-American War, is on display, as is the desk of the tribunal that sentenced Emperor Maximilian to death.

The museum is housed in part of what was once a huge monastery and seminary. Begun in 1540, the seminary became the seat of the Franciscan province of San Pedro y San Pablo de Michoacán by 1567. Building continued until at least 1727. Thanks to its high tower, in the 1860s the monastery was used as a fort both by imperialists supporting Maximilian and by the forces who defeated him in 1867.

MUSEO DE ARTE DE QUERÉTARO

Adjacent to the Templo de San Agustín, Querétaro's **art museum** (☎ 212-23-57; Allende Sur 14; M$30, Tue free; ☽ 10am-6pm Tue-Sun) occupies a splendid baroque monastery built between 1731 and 1748. It is worth visiting to see the building alone: angels, quirky gargoyles, statues and other ornamental details abound, particularly around the stunning courtyard.

The ground-floor display of 16th- and 17th-century European paintings traces influences from Flemish to Spanish to Mexican art. On the same floor you'll find 19th- and 20th-century Mexican paintings. The top floor has works from 16th-century Mannerism to 18th-century baroque. There's a good bookstore-cum-gift-shop.

MUSEO DE LA CIUDAD

Inside the ex-convent and old prison that held Maximilian, the 11-room **Museo de la Ciudad** (☎ 212-47-02; Guerrero Nte 27; admission M$5, students free; ☽ 11am-6:30pm Tue-Sun) has some good alternating contemporary art exhibits. If you can read Spanish or are a real history buff, check out the **Museo de la Restauración de la Republica** (☎ 224-30-04; Guerrero Nte 23; admission free; ☽ 9am-5pm Tue-Sun), next door, which covers Querétaro's role in Mexico's history, particularly the

QUERÉTARO

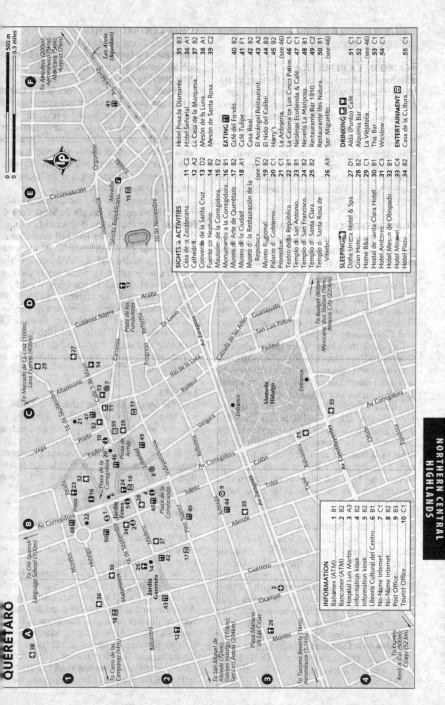

INFORMATION
Banamex (ATM)	1 B1
Bancomer (ATM)	2 B2
Hospital Luis Martín	3 A3
Information kiosk	4 B2
Information kiosk	5 B2
Librería Cultural del Centro	6 B1
No-Name Internet	7 C1
No-Name Internet	8 B2
Post Office	9 B3
Tourist Office	10 C1

SIGHTS & ACTIVITIES
Casa de Zacatecana	11 C2
Cathedral	12 A2
Convento de la Santa Cruz	13 D2
Fuente de Neptuno	14 B2
Mausoleo	15 E2
Monumento a la Corregidora	16 B1
Museo de Arte de Querétaro	17 B2
Museo de la Ciudad	18 A1
Museo de la Restauración de la República	(see 17)
Museo Regional	19 B2
Palacio de Gobierno	20 C1
Promotur	21 C1
Teatro de la República	22 B1
Templo de San Antonio	23 B1
Templo de San Francisco	24 B2
Templo de Santa Clara	25 B2
Templo de Santa Rosa de Viterbo	26 A3

SLEEPING
Doña Urraca Hotel & Spa	27 D1
Gran Hotel	28 B2
Home B&L	29 C1
Hostal de Santa Clara Hotel	30 B1
Hotel Amberes	31 C3
Hotel Mesón de Obispado	32 B2
Hotel Mirabel	33 C4
Hotel Plaza	34 B2
Hotel Posada Diamante	35 B3
Hotel Señorial	36 A1
La Casa de la Marquesa	37 B2
Mesón de la Luna	38 A1
Mesón de Santa Rosa	39 C2

EATING
Café del Fondo	40 B2
Café Tulipe	41 F1
Casa Real	42 B2
El Arcángel Restaurant	43 A2
El Nido del Colibrí	44 B3
Harry's	45 B2
La Antojería	(see 46)
La Casona ce Los Cinco Patios	46 C1
Neblinas Ecotienda & Café	47 C1
Nevería La Mariposa	48 B1
Restaurante Bar 1810	49 C2
Restaurante Ibis Natura	50 B1
San Miguelito	(see 46)

DRINKING
Alda (Punto) Café	51 C1
Alquimia Bar	52 C1
La Viejateca	(see 46)
Tha Bar	53 C1
Wicklow	54 C1

ENTERTAINMENT
Casa de la Cultura	55 C1

To Amadeus (200m); Aerobus (5km); Mexicana (5km); Airport (7km)

Los Arcos (Aqueduct)

500 m
0.3 miles

Circunvalación

To Mercado de La Cruz (100m); Lava Express (400m)

To Old Spanish Language School (700m)

To Cerro de las Campanas (1km)

To San Miguel de Allende (72km); Dolores Hidalgo (204km); San Luis Potosí (204km)

To Turismo Beverly (1km); Aeroméxico (1.1km)

To Budget (800m); Mexicana Bus Station (5km); Mexico City (220km)

To Express Rent-A-Car (500m); To Celaya (52 km)

Alameda Hidalgo

NORTHERN CENTRAL HIGHLANDS

French occupation and the eventual ousting of Emperor Maximilian.

TEATRO DE LA REPÚBLICA

This lovely old and functioning **theater** (☎ 212-03-39; cnr Juárez & Peralta; ☾ 10am-3pm & 5-8pm), complete with impressive chandeliers, was where a tribunal met in 1867 to decide the fate of Emperor Maximilian. Mexico's constitution was also signed here on January 31, 1917. The stage backdrop lists the names of its signatories and the states they represented. In 1929, politicians met in the theater to organize Mexico's ruling party, the PNR (now the PRI).

CONVENTO DE LA SANTA CRUZ

Ten minutes' walk east of the center is one of the city's most interesting sights. The **monastery** (☎ 212-03-35; cnr Acuña & Independencia; donation requested; ☾ 9am-2pm, 4-6pm Tue-Sat, 9am-4:30pm Sun) was built between 1654 and about 1815 on the site of a battle in which a miraculous appearance of Santiago (St James) led the Otomí to surrender to the conquistadors and Christianity. Emperor Maximilian had his headquarters here while under siege in Querétaro from March to May 1867. After his surrender and subsequent death sentence, he was jailed here while awaiting the firing squad. Today it's used as a religious school.

You can visit with a guide – ask at the entrance – although an English tour will need to be arranged beforehand (donation requested). The site's main legend is the growth of the **Árbol de la Cruz**, an ancient tree in the convent's garden whose thorns are in the shape of crosses. This miracle was the result of a walking stick stuck in the earth by a pious friar in 1697.

ACUEDUCTO & MIRADOR

Walk east along Independencia past Convento de la Santa Cruz, then fork right along Ejército Republicano, to the **mirador**. There's a fine view of 'Los Arcos', Querétaro's emblematic 1.28km-long **aqueduct**, with 74 towering sandstone arches built between 1726 and 1738. The aqueduct runs along the center of Av Zaragoza.

Across the street from the mirador is the **Mausoleo de la Corregidora** (Ejercito Republicano s/n; ☾ 9am-6pm), the resting place of Doña Josefa Ortiz and her husband, Miguel Domínguez de Alemán.

OTHER CENTRAL SIGHTS

Plaza de la Corregidora is dominated by the **Monumento a la Corregidora** (cnr Corregidora & Andador 16 de Septiembre), a 1910 statue of Doña Josefa Ortiz bearing the flame of freedom.

A block west of Jardín Zenea is the **Fuente de Neptuno** (Neptune's Fountain; cnr Andador Madero & Allende), designed by noted Mexican neoclassical-architect Eduardo Tresguerras in 1797. Adjacent, the 17th-century **Templo de Santa Clara** (cnr Andador Madero & Allende) has an ornate baroque interior. Two blocks west on Madero is the rather plain 18th-century **cathedral** (cnr Madero & Ocampo).

At the intersection of Arteaga and Monte is the 18th-century **Templo de Santa Rosa de Viterbos**, Querétaro's most splendid baroque church, with its pagoda-like bell tower, unusual exterior paintwork, curling buttresses and lavishly gilded and marbled interior. This church also boasts what some say is the earliest four-sided clock in the New World.

The **Casa de la Zacatecana** (☎ 224-07-58 Independencia 59; admission M$20; ☾ 10am-6pm Tue-Sun) is a finely restored 17th-century home with a fine collection of 18th- and 19th-century furniture and decorations (and its own murder mystery – skeletons were discovered in the basement).

Courses

The **Olé Spanish Language School** (☎ 214-40-2 www.ole.edu.mx; Escobedo 32) offers a range of courses with homestay options and extracurricular programs. Prices start at around US$14 per hour and week-long courses range from moderate group classes for 1 hours from US$142, to intensive 35 one hour private classes for US$365.

Tours

An excellent self-guided audio-walking tour (M$50) of the city is available from the tourist office (p644). You follow a trail along city pavements, marked with gold disks (with the letter 'Q'). The audio-commentary – in several languages including English – provides background on the sites and sight. A credit card is required as security. **Guided tours** of the city center on the Tranvía bus in Spanish (M$70 for one hour, M$80 for two hours), leave from Jardín Zenea, near Plaza Constitución. For details, ask at the tourist office or at the **information kiosk** (☎ 212-34-5 in Plaza Constitución. Also offered are longe trips (M$120 for two hours) to regional attractions. For Spanish speakers, several different companies run fun night tours, **Myths & Legends** (Leyendas & Mitos, or similar names), where actors in period costume dramatically reveal the legends and secrets of their dark lanes and buildings. For details, ask at the tourist office.

Festivals & Events

Querétaro's **Feria Internacional**, one of Mexico's biggest state fairs, happens in the first two weeks of December. It focuses on livestock, but also hosts cultural events.

Sleeping

BUDGET

Mesón de la Luna (☎ 212-14-39; www.hotelelmeson delaluna.com; Escobedo 104; s/d M$310-330/370-400; P) The attractive plant-filled lobby and warm welcome makes up for the odd bit of dodgy wiring in the basic, clean rooms. With cable TV, it's excellent value.

Home B&B (☎ 183-91-39; www.queretarobandb.com; 6 de Septiembre 104; r inc breakfast from M$350 ⊠ 🖳) This friendly Canadian-run place is central and very social. Breakfast is a treat in two respects: it's included in the price and a former owner, a professional chef, prepares morning feasts (eaten communally at 9am). Rooms vary in shape and size, all are light and airy and some have private bathroom. Note: by reservation only.

Other recommendations:

Hostal de Santa Clara Hotel (☎ 212-03-90; Allende 3 Norte; dm M$120, s/d from M$250/450) This hotel-cum-hostal resembles a convent – it's plain but sparkling clean – and has choice of shared or private bathroom.

Hotel Posada Diamante (☎ 212-66-37; Allende Sur 5; s M$260, d M$315-345, tr M$365-415) Simple, clean and respectable and only a short walk to the pedestrian plazas and the Alameda.

Hotel Plaza (☎ 212-11-38; www.travelbymexico.com /quer/hotelplaza; Juárez Nte 23; s/tr from M$320/530, d M$350-80) Hotel Plaza's glory days are over, but its 29 rooms are still tidy, if a little charm-free. For a few more pesos, you can get those facing the jardín, offering French doors and balconies (and plenty of light, air and noise).

MIDRANGE

Hotel Mesón de Obispado (☎ 224-24-64; Andador 16 de Septiembre 13; s/d/tr M$450/570/690) The former bishop of this central old place – located on

a lively pedestrian street – would still feel at home here. The rooms feature a few ceremonial touches, such as a faux Louis XV style bed heads. You might be tempted by the restaurant's brunch buffet; you literally pass through it to access the courtyard and your lodgings.

Hotel Amberes (☎ 212-86-04; hamberes@prodigy.net .mx; Corregidora Sur 188; s/d/tr M$495/620/720; P 🔀 🖳) This remodeled four-star hotel, opposite the Alameda Hidalgo, is a business-traveler favorite. It's got lots of marble, an odor of cleaning agents and carpeted rooms, with air-con, cable TV and phone. Some rooms have park views.

Hotel Señorial (☎ 214-37-00; www.senorial-hotel .com; Guerrero Nte 10A; s M$540-560, d M$585-700; P) It resembles a prison from the outside, but the inside is more appealing, with clean and neat modern rooms, cable TV and extremely friendly staff. It's a US Peace Corps haunt.

Hotel Mirabel (☎ 214-35-35, 800-401-39-00; www .hotelmirabel.com.mx; Av Constituyentes Ote 2; s/d/ste M$645/830/950; P 🔀 🖳) More demanding business travelers prefer the slick Mirabel. The comfy, carpeted standard rooms (some with park views) have air-con and there's room service.

TOP END

La Casa de la Marquesa (☎ 212-00-92; www.lacasa delamarquesa.com; Madero 41; ste from M$2100 P 🔀) For aficionados of fine antiques and history, don't go past this magnificent 1756 baroque-Mudéjar mansion. It is full of legends (of course!), plus lavish period furnishings, carved stonework, tiles and frescoes. The 25 singular suites have names such as Alhambra and Maximiliano y Carlota, with style to match. Rates include continental breakfast and a welcome cocktail.

Doña Urraca Hotel & Spa (☎ 238-54-00, in Mexico 800-021-71-16, in USA 877-278-8018; www.donaurraca .com.mx; Calle 5 de Mayo 117; ste inc breakfast from M$2940; P 🔀 🖳 🛋) Perfect for people who prefer to be pampered. The 23 spacious suites are lavished with all the right 'fluffy features': bath robes and handmade herbal soaps plus sound systems and cable TV. There's a gym, heated pool and outdoor Jacuzzi and the restaurant's wine cellar morphs into a romantic, private dining room for two. Separate luxury packages include holistic spa treatments.

Other recommendations:

Mesón de Santa Rosa (☎ 224-26-23; Pasteur Sur 17; r/ste from US$119/168; P 🖳 🛋) A finely restored

17th-century building built around three patios and located on the Plaza de Armas. Has received mixed traveler reports; our experience is positive. US dollars preferred.

Gran Hotel (☎ 251-80-50; www.granhoteldequeretaro .com.mx; Juárez Sur 5; r/ste from M$1410/2000) Querétaro's newest luxury option; Mexican sleek in a nicely renovated building.

Eating

The central plazas and surrounding pedestrian streets, particularly around Plaza de Armas, are lined with restaurants catering to all tastes and budgets. They have outdoor tables and a vibrant evening atmosphere with live music (sometimes clashing with each other). After 5pm, the cheapest and most genuine eating experiences can be found at the **Mercado de la Cruz** (Gutierrez Nájera).

AROUND PLAZA DE ARMAS

Plaza de Armas has some excellent, more upscale restaurants and cafés with both indoor and outdoor tables.

Restaurante Bar 1810 (☎ 214-33-24; Andador Libertad 62; mains M$85-175; ☺ 8am-11pm Mon-Thu, 8am-midnight Fri & Sat, 8am-10:30pm Sun) Covered with fairy lights, this canopied place overlooking the pretty plaza is *the* eatery for excellent steaks or a variety of pastas and seafood dishes. Live crooners complement (or otherwise) your meal.

our pick La Casona de los Cinco Patios (☎ 224-27-60; www.lacasona.com.mx; Andador 5 de Mayo 39) It's hard to go past trying one of these diverse eating and drinking options, all under the auspice (and location) of a mansion with five patios:

La Antojeria (mains M$25-75) At the entrance to Cinco Patios and at the other end of the pricing scale, this family-friendly, fun and Mexican-themed place serves up every style of *antojito* known in Mexico.

San Miguelito (mains M$100-150; ☺ 1pm-midnight Tue-Sat, 1-6pm Sun) Locals rave about this for its food, old-fashioned service, ambience and décor: each table has different chairs and is decorated with themed hand-painted wooden platters. Popular dishes include *filete de res en salsa de mezquite* (beef fillet with mesquite plant sauce; M$110)

NEAR THE ACUEDUCTO

After the exertions of walking along the aqueduct (and its busy road), take a break at the following:

Café Tulipe (☎ 213-63-91; Calzada de los Arcos 3; M$50-80; ☺ 8am-10pm) This Mexican teashop serves up French-style fare, including quiche, crepes and cheese fondue. There's an excellent afternoon tea deal between 4pm and 7pm – tea or coffee with a huge slab of the cake of your choice (M$37 to M$42).

Amadeus (☎ 213-64-03; Zaragoza 306; mains M$65-110; ☺ 8am-10pm Mon-Fri, 9am-10pm Sun) A temporary refuge from the din of Zaragoza, this German-Mexican café offers local and German treats. It's halfway along the aqueduct.

ELSEWHERE

Nevería La Mariposa (☎ 212-11-66; Ángela Peralta 7; snacks M$17-55; ☺ 8am-9:30pm) Unchanged since 1940 (as the photos will testify), this Querétaro institution is more about the quaint atmosphere than the food. Don't leave without trying the mouthwatering *mantecado* (vanilla ice-cream; M$30).

Restaurante Ibis Natura (☎ 214-22-12; Juárez 47 Nte; mains M$25-50; ☺ 8am-9:30pm; V) Vegetarians and natural-food fans will enjoy wonderfully fresh and reasonably priced veggie food especially the good-value *comida corrida* (M$45) or the soyburgers with mushrooms and cheese.

El Nido del Colibrí (☎ 214-43-36; Arteaga 21-9; mains M$30-45; ☺ 1-5pm Mon-Fri, 10am-5pm Sat & Sun) The bright yellow décor in this happy place provides a good lunching nest ('nido') for a no-nonsense yet filling *comida corrida* (M$35).

Neblinas Ecotienda & Café (☎ 156-90-25; Río de la Loza 1; snacks M$35-55; ☺ from 10am Mon-Sat, 5-10pm Sun; V) This extraordinary shop, café, gallery and cultural center supports communities in the Sierra Gorda. Everything here has an eco-friendly and sustainable message: the café serves delicious snacks (don't miss the hamburgers with the handmade endangered animal shaped rolls or the *penca de nopal*, cactus plate), the neat restaurant-gallery's décor resembles a semi-desert environment and the shop sells organic produce. Cultural performances include live jazz and dance.

Café del Fondo (☎ 212-09-05; Pino Suárez 9; everything under M$40; ☺ 8am-10pm) This relaxed, rambling alternative hangout is popular with newspaper-reading elder statesmen, chess-heads and chatterboxes. Decent set breakfasts go for only M$27. Snacks and a four-course *comida corrida* are also on the menu.

Casa Real (☎ 212-00-92; cnr Madero & Allende; mains M$60-160; ☺ 9am-5pm) Popular among the mature Mexicans, La Casa de la Marquesa's attractive courtyard bistro (up the road from the hotel itself) boasts a gurgling fountain, fine food, superlative service and a good upscale *comida corrida* (M$110).

El Arcángel (☎ 212-65-42; Guerrero Norte 1; mains M$60-115; ☙ 8am-10pm) Join local businessfolk, families and everyone in between at this old-fashioned place. You can enjoy the strains of Mozart over good breakfasts plus a great-value four-course set lunch (weekdays M$89, weekends M$110 to M$119).

Harry's (☎ 214-26-20; Hidalgo 12; Plaza Constitución s/n; mains M$60-250; ☙ 12:30pm-midnight Mon-Fri, 10am-midnight Sat & Sun) Move to the groove at this New Orleans-style café-cum-bar. You can watch the crowds amble by from the patio tables over a jambalaya or a cocktail.

Alda (Punto) Café (☎ 224-40-77; Río de la Loza 4; mains M$75-100; ☙ 2-10:30pm) It seems to have an identity crisis with its name (called Alda by the staff, the signs say Punto), but the modern food here is more grounded. Serves up fabulous focaccias, salads and healthy sandwiches (with hefty prices).

Drinking

There's a thriving bar scene in Querétaro. Bars and clubs are popping up (and sometimes down) in the historic center and beyond. Calle 5 de Mayo is the fashionable drinking strip in the center; trendy barflies hit these places after 10pm. A slew of trendy bars and night clubs can be found further out along Av Constituyentes and Blvd Bernardo Quintana, the city's eastern and western ring roads – take a taxi. Late-night gay bars line Bernardo Quintano.

La Viejateca (La Casona de los Cinco Patios, Andador 5 de Mayo 39) Whatever you do, don't miss your nightly liquid dose at this former pharmacy, now 'barmacy.' It's worth going for the décor alone – apothecary jars, former household paraphernalia and much more – besides which, it's good old-fashioned fun.

Other good options along Calle 5 de Mayo:

Wicklow (☎ 307-60-63; Calle 5 de Mayo 86) This Irish pub is a longstanding favorite.

Thai Bar (☎ 214-61-25; Calle 5 de Mayo 56)

Alquimia Bar (☎ 212-1791; Calle 5 de Mayo 71A) Has some great areas to lounge.

Entertainment

Querétaro is action-packed with cultural activities. For the latest in what's happening around town, look out for posters on bulletin boards, or ask the tourist office. On Sundays, free concerts take place in Plaza de Armas at 1pm and in the evenings in Jardín Zenea.

Casa de la Cultura (☎ 212-56-14; 5 de Mayo 40) Sponsors concerts, dance, theater and art events; stop by during office hours to view the bulletin board. The Teatro Principal has regular symphony concerts most Fridays (M$6 to M$12).

Getting There & Away

AIR

Aeropuerto Internacional (☎ 192-55-00), 8km northeast of the center, is a M$250-to-M$280 taxi-ride away. Primera Plus also runs from the bus terminal to Mexico City airport (M$235; three hours). Aero California runs regular domestic flights to/from Mexico City, Guadalajara and Monterrey while Continental has flights to Los Angeles, San Antonio and Houston in the US.

In-town airline offices include **Aeroméxico Connect** (Av Tecnológico 100, San Ángel) and **Mexicana** and **Click Mexicana** (☎ 215-3907; Av Tecnológico 102, San Ángel).

BUS

Querétaro is a hub for buses in all directions; the modern Central Camionera is 5km southeast of the center. There's one building for deluxe and 1st-class (labeled A), one for 2nd-class (B) and another for local buses (C). Facilities include a café, telephone *casetas*, shops and luggage storage.

See the table on page 650 for daily departures from Querétaro.

CAR & MOTORCYCLE

If you want a car to explore the Sierra Gorda, English-speaking **Express Rent-a-Car** (☎ 242-90-28; Hotel Real de Minas, Av Constituyentes Pte 124) has competitive rates. **Budget** (☎ 213-44-98; Av Constituyentes Ote 73) is also worth checking.

Getting Around

Once you have reached the city center, you can easily visit most sights on foot. City buses (M$5) run from 6am until 9pm or 10pm. They gather in an area at end of the bus terminal; turn right from the 2nd-class terminal, or left from the 1st-class side. Several routes go to the center including buses 8 and 19, both of which go to the Alameda Hidalgo then up Ocampo. For a taxi, get a ticket first from the bus station booth (M$35 for up to four people).

DAILY BUSES FROM QUERÉTARO

Destination	Fare	Duration	Frequency
Guadalajara	deluxe M$345	4½	9 daily (ETN)
	1st-class M$284	5½hr	hourly (Primera Plus)
	2nd-class M$284	5½hr	frequent (Flecha Amarilla), 10 daily (Oriente)
Guanajuato	1st-class M$137	2½-3hr	3 daily (Primera Plus)
	2nd-class M$91	2½-3hr	6 daily (Flecha Amarilla)
Mexico City (Terminal Norte)	deluxe M$210	3hr	every 30 min 5am-10pm (ETN)
	1st-class M$173	3hr	every 20 min 4:45am-11:30pm (Primera Plus)
	1st-class M$160	3½ hr	hourly (Ómnibus de México)
	2nd-class M$138	4½hr	every 40 min (Herradura de Plata)
	2nd-class M$135	3-4hr	(Flecha Amarilla)
Mexico City Airport	$135	3½hr	25 daily (Aeroplus)
Morelia	M$131	3-4hr	hourly (Primera Plus/Servicios Coordinados)
San Luis Potosí	deluxe M$190	2½hr	3 daily (ETN)
	1st-class M$154	2½hr	21 daily (Primera Plus/Servicios Coordinados)
	2nd-class M$154	2¾hr	hourly (Flecha Amarilla)
San Miguel de Allende	deluxe M$75	1hr	4 daily (ETN)
	2nd-class M$42	1½hr	every 40 min 6am-11pm (Herradura de Plata or Flecha Amarilla)
Tequisquiapan	M$34	1hr	every 30 min 6:30am-9pm (Flecha Azul)

To get to the bus station from the center, take city bus 19, 25 or 36 from Zaragoza, or any labeled 'Terminal de Autobuses' heading south on the east side of the Alameda Hidalgo.

AROUND QUERÉTARO
El Cerrito

If you happen to be interested in archaeology, check out **El Cerrito** (Little Hill; admission free; 9am-2:30pm Tue-Sun), a 30m-high pyramid-like structure sitting atop a small hill, located in El Pueblito, 7km from central Querétaro. Archaeologists, who are still excavating the site, believe it was occupied between 600 and 1600 by the Teotihuacán, Toltec, Chichimec, Otomí and Tarasca cultures. Besides the pyramid, there are the remains of a possible ball court and some outlying structures. A later fort-type construction on its top dates from 1876.

Local legend links El Cerrito to the history of the Virgin of El Pueblito, the patron saint of Querétaro.

At the site there are free guides (in Spanish; small tip appreciated) and a small museum. To get there, take a 64 bus (M$5, 25 minutes) from Avenida Constituyentes on the south side of Alameda. It passes through the village and will drop you at the entrance. A taxi costs around M$45.

Bernal
☎ 441/ pop 3750/ elevation 2080

The town of Bernal is quaint, if over-touristy. Its draw card is the 350m-high rock spire, the **Peña de Bernal**, the third-largest monolith in the world and considered mystical by many Mexicans. During the vernal equinox thousands of pilgrims descend on the rock to take in its positive energy. Visitors can climb to the rock's halfway point (allow one hour both ways); only professional rock-climbers can climb to its peak.

Beyond that, you can see Bernal in an hour or so. The town has several **churches** and **El Castillo**, a 16th-century viceregal building. For a more in-depth explanation of the area, the small **tourist office** (☎ 296-41-26; Hidalgo 2; 10am-5pm Thu-Tue) organizes excellent local Spanish-speaking guides. **La Aurora** (Jardín Principal 1; www.bernalmagico.com; 10am-8pm) is an interesting *artesanías* shop; request permission to see the weavers at work at their looms in the workshop behind the shop.

The town comes to life during the weekends; many things are closed on weekdays. If you get stuck here, try the basic and friendly **Posada Peña** (☎ 296-41-49; Iturbide 3; s/d M$250/350).

There are regular Flecha Amarilla buses from/to Querétaro (M$22, one hour). The last return bus to Querétaro departs from the main road at 6pm. For connections to

Tequisquiapan, head to Esquivel Montes (M$12, 30 minutes).

TEQUISQUIAPAN
☎ 414 / pop 26,858 / elevation 1880m
This small town (teh-kees-kee-*ap*-an), 70km southeast of Querétaro, is a quaint weekend retreat from Mexico City or Querétaro. Tequisquiapan used to be known for its thermal springs — Mexican presidents came here to ease their aches and tensions. Today, despite the presence of cool water pools in hotel gardens, it's more known for its pretty, bougainvillea-lined streets, colorful colonial buildings and excellent markets. In March, the town holds the **Feria del Toro de Lidia**, a week of bullfights and activities.

Orientation & Information
The bus terminal is around 2km north from the center in the new part of town. The helpful **tourist office** (☎ 273-02-95; www .tequis.info; east side Plaza Principal; ☯ 9am-7pm) has town maps and information on Querétaro state. On the plaza's southeast side, there's a Bancomer ATM.

Sights & Activities
The wide and attractive Plaza Miguel Hidalgo is surrounded by *portales* (arcades), overlooked by the 19th-century neoclassical **La Parroquia de Santa María de la Asunción** (Plaza Miguel Hidalgo; ☯ 7am-8:30pm) with its pink facade and decorated tower.

Three interesting markets – the **Mercado de Artesanías** (Crafts Market; ☯ 8am-7pm), **Barra y Mumbre** (household items) and the **Guadalupana** (for food) – are all on Carrizal, a block north and northeast of the plaza. The large, verdant **Parque La Pila** is a short distance past the Mercado de Artesanías along Ezequiel Montes.

Many hotels have swimming pools but the popular public pool, **La Vega** (admission M$30; ☯ 9am-6pm; 1.4km northwest of town), has expansive lawns, a large pool and water slides for the kids. To get there, take a micro from the bus shelter in front of the markets on Carrizal.

On weekends head off on guided horse trails into the surrounding countryside (M$100 per hour). Guides and their hacks congregate on Fray Junípero, just north of Parque La Pila.

THE GREEN JEWEL OF CENTRAL MEXICO

Biosphere reserves are a unique conservation strategy seeking to blend sustainable human use with natural area protection (see p116). In the case of the **Reserva de la Biosfera Sierra Gorda**, covering the northeastern third of Querétaro state, over 90% of its 3836 sq km are privately owned and 95,000 people live in its mission towns and scattered mountain villages.

Despite its mixed land use, this rugged arm of the Sierra Madre Oriental encompasses extensive tracts of wilderness, including old- growth cloud forests covered in orchids; semideserts with endemic cactuses and wild oregano; and tropical forests home to jaguars and prolific bird life. With fifteen vegetation types this is the most ecosystem-diverse protected area in Mexico.

Conservation of the Sierra Gorda has always been community-based. Grassroots efforts by local citizens led to the reserve's establishment in 1997 and today numerous communities are engaged in sustainable livelihood activities, including developing a locally-owned and operated ecotourism infrastructure with cabins, camping areas and guides.

Visitors can enjoy hiking to the **Sótano del Barro**, a 410m-deep vertical cave to see resident macaws, camping on the ridge of Cuatro Palos for expansive views, forging the Río Escanela to Puente de Dios waterfall and cavern and experiencing the traditional way of life in rural mountain communities.

Buffy and Ben Lenth

Tours into Reserva de la Biosfera Sierra Gorda

Travelers with time can experience the above activities in this fascinating area departing from Jalpan or other locations (advance notice required for all) with **Sierra Gorda Ecotours** (☎ 441-296-0242; www.sierragorda.net), part of Grupo Ecológico Sierra Gorda, the nonprofit organization which co-manages the reserve. Alternatively, from Querétaro, day trips to the missions plus other longer guided trips can also be arranged through the private tour operator, **Promotur** (☎ 442-212-89-40; www.promoturqueretaro.com.mx; Río de la Loza 21 Norte, Querétaro).

Festivals & Events

Feria del Toro de Lidia (Bullfights) A week of bullfighting activity in March.

Feria Internacional del Queso y del Vino (International Wine and Cheese Fair) From late May to early June; includes tastings and music.

Fiesta de la Asunción Commemorates the town's patron saint on August 15.

Sleeping & Eating

The best budget accommodation options are the posadas along Moctezuma. Demand is low Monday to Thursday, when you may be able to negotiate a discount. Many restaurants around the plaza offer *comida corridas*. The **Mercado Guadalupana** a block east of the plaza has *fondas* (food stalls).

Posada Tequisquiapan (☎ 273-00-10; Moctezuma 6; s/d M$250/500; ☒ P) A good-value place with simple but spacious and clean rooms and cable TV. The sprawling gardens have a grotto-like pool – great for families.

Hotel La Plaza (☎ 273-00-56; www.tequisquiapan .com.mx/la_plaza; Juárez 10; re M$620-928, ste M$1030-1300; P ☒) Facing the plaza, this slightly worn but pleasant hotel has 15 rooms of varying sizes and an upscale restaurant.

Hotel Hacienda Las Delicias (☎ 273-00-17; www.tequis quiapan.com.mx/lasdelicias; 5 de Mayo 1; s/d M$1500/1600; P ☒) A block south of Plaza Principal, the stylish Las Delicias is constructed around a manicured garden with pool. Weekend packages with two meals also available.

K'puchinos (☎ 273-10-46; Morelos 4; mains M$50-90) On the plaza's east side, this active place holds happy hours, salsa nights, live music and good snacks and meals – mainly standard Mexican fare.

Getting There & Around

Tequisquiapan is 20km northeast on Hwy 120 from the larger town of San Juan del Río. Local buses 1, 2 and 5 (M$4) from outside the bus station run to the markets on Carrizal, one block northeast of the Plaza Principal.

Flecha Azul runs half-hourly to/from Querétaro between 6:30am and 8pm (M$34, one hour). Buses also run to Esquivel Montes (change here for Bernal; M$12, 20 minutes). ETN has deluxe buses to/from Mexico City's Terminal Norte (M$165, three hours, eight daily). Flecha Amarilla and Flecha Roja have 2nd-class services to the same destination (M$121, three hours, regular departures).

NORTHEAST QUERÉTARO STATE

Those with a hankering to get off the beaten track – or if you're heading to/from northeast Mexico or to the lush Huasteca (see p657) – shouldn't miss heading to the scenic Sierra Gorda via Hwy 120 northeast from Tequisquiapan. It's possible to get to most places on the way by bus, but it's much easier with your own transportation.

Highway 120

Heading north from Tequisquiapan, you pass the dusty, agricultural town of Ezequiel Montes. More interesting is the next stop, the winery **Cavas de Freixenet** (☎ 441-277-01-47; www .freixenetmexico.com.mx; ☒ tours 11am-3pm), where you can see wine being made by *método champenoise* during free 40-minute tours.

The next big town is Cadereyta, 38km from Tequisquiapan. On the east edge of town, signs point to the **Quinta Fernando Schmoll** (☒ 10am-5pm), a botanic garden with over 4400 varieties of cactus.

Continuing another 38km on Hwy 120, there's a turnoff going east to the quaint town of **San Joaquín**. Follow the good, but very winding, road from the turnoff for 32km through the rugged mountains; stay on that road through San Joaquín and continue a few steeply climbing kilometers to the little-visited archaeological site of **Ranas** (admission M$2.50; ☒ 9am-5pm), with well-built walls and circular steps incorporated into a steep hillside. There are ball courts and a small hilltop pyramid. Dating from as early as the 8th century, the site is appealing for its rugged

---

MEXICAN MORSELS – TOP FIVE AUTHENTIC EATERIES

- **El Pozole** (p606) Get your mouth around some of the best *antojitos* in Mexico

- **Cinco Patios** (p648) Take your pick of fine dining, local *antojitos,* or a quirky bar

- **Los Dorados de Villa** (p591) Enjoy some of the best Mexican enchiladas in the state

- **Clave Azul** (p623) Snack on a genuine *botana* (tapas) experience and a great margarita

- **San Agustín** (p639) Indulge in the sweetest treat of all: churros and chocolate

forest setting. San Joaquín has basic lodgings and eateries.

JALPAN

Within the magnificent Sierra Gorda Biosphere Reserve, Hwy 120 winds up to a height of 2300m at **Pinal de Amoles** and makes dramatic ups and downs (and 860 turns!) before reaching **Jalpan** at 760m. The attractive town centers on the **mission church**, constructed by Franciscan monks and their indigenous converts in the 1750s (see Sierra Gorda Missions, right). The excellent **Museo de la Sierra Gorda** (☎ 441-296-01-65; Fray Junípero Serra 1; adult/child M$10/5; ☑ 10am-3pm & 5-7pm) explores the region's pre-Hispanic cultures and the mission-building period and has superb reduced-size replicas of the mission churches.

On the plaza opposite the church, **Hotel María del Carmen** (☎ 441-296-03-28; Independencia 8; r M$290; P ⌧ ⌧) has clean, comfortable rooms; those with air-con in the new part cost around M$140 more. On the plaza's west side, the attractive **Hotel Misión Jalpan** (☎ 441-296-02-55; www.hotelesmision.com.mx; Fray Junípero Serra s/n; r from M$855; P ⌧ ⌧) has a good restaurant and pleasant rooms, although beware the karaoke bar within the complex – it can get noisy. On the main road, **Restaurante Carretas** (☎ 296-03-68; mains M$40-150; ☑ 8am-10pm) serves up a great feed.

SIERRA GORDA MISSIONS

In the mid-18th century, Franciscans established five beautiful missions in this remote region including Jalpan. These were inscribed as a Unesco World Heritage site in 2003. Founder Fray Junípero Serra went on to found the California mission chain. The restored churches are notable for their extraordinary and colorful facades carved with symbolic figures. East from Jalpan on Hwy 120, there are missions at **Landa de Matamoros** (1760–68); **Tilaco** (1754–62), 10km south of the highway; and **Tancoyol** (1753–60), 20km north of the highway. The mission of **Concá** (1754–58) is 35km north of Jalpan on Hwy 69.

NORTHERN CENTRAL HIGHLANDS

Central Gulf Coast

Set in the crook of Mexico's curve, the central Gulf coast is easily overlooked by tourists searching for the best sun-lounger and a fat piña colada. Yet, decadent opportunities await the adventurer in this tourist-industry wallflower where the locals aren't talking economy when they say, 'We are very rich.'

They are referring to their landscapes: deserted coastline lapping tranquilly, forests Swiss-cheesed with caves, and towering volcanoes propelling rivers and waterfalls. They are talking about their jostling, honking cities, like Xalapa with its anthropology museum and its urbane sensibilities or Veracruz whose atmosphere, thick with marimba, mariachi and *danzón*, and also humidity, enchants you like undulating Latin dance. Their wealth is their architecture: evocative colonial edifices, niched pyramids and even surrealist stairways spiraling skyward. The opulence of this region is their diversity: gorgeous skin shades from Europe, Africa and indigenous communities have melded together in the wake of Cortés' conquest and destruction.

However, the people themselves, both generous and quick to laugh, prove most precious. Don't be surprised to see strangers greet each other or to be offered a ride on the back of a moped. Though you might summit Mexico's highest peak here, your most vivid memories could be of a grandmother you meet in a chaotic market who lets you try her *mole* from a 100-year-old family recipe, or stumbling into a village fiesta during traditionally costumed dances.

Whatever your endeavor, you'll find that the richness of the central Gulf coast is to be encountered, not just served to you over ice with an umbrella…though you'll savor it all the same.

HIGHLIGHTS

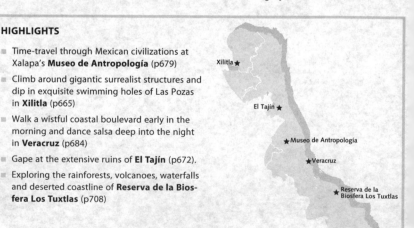

- Time-travel through Mexican civilizations at Xalapa's **Museo de Antropología** (p679)
- Climb around gigantic surrealist structures and dip in exquisite swimming holes of Las Pozas in **Xilitla** (p665)
- Walk a wistful coastal boulevard early in the morning and dance salsa deep into the night in **Veracruz** (p684)
- Gape at the extensive ruins of **El Tajín** (p672).
- Exploring the rainforests, volcanoes, waterfalls and deserted coastline of **Reserva de la Biosfera Los Tuxtlas** (p708)

Xilitla ★

El Tajín ★

★ Museo de Antropología

★ Veracruz

★ Reserva de la Biosfera Los Tuxtlas

■ VERACRUZ JANUARY DAILY HIGH: 25.6°C | 78.1°F   ■ VERACRUZ JULY DAILY HIGH: 30.6°C | 87.1°F

History

The Olmecs, Mesoamerica's earliest known civilization, built their first great center around 1200 BC at San Lorenzo in southern Veracruz state. In 900 BC the city was vio lently destroyed, but Olmec culture lingered for several centuries at Tres Zapotes. During the Classic period (AD 250–900) the Gulf coast developed another distinctive culture, known as the Classic Veracruz civilization. Its most important center was El Tajín, which was at its peak between AD 600 and 900. Classic Veracruz appears to have been particularly obsessed with the ball game (see boxed text, p73), and its hallmark is a style of abstract carving featuring pairs of curved and inter-woven parallel lines. In the Postclassic period the Totonacs established themselves in the region south of Tuxpan. North of Tuxpan, the Huastec civilization flourished from 800 to 1200. During this time, the warlike Toltecs also moved into the Gulf coast area. In the mid-15th century, the Aztecs overtook most of the Totonac and Huastec areas, exacting tributes of goods and sacrificial victims and subduing revolts.

When Cortés arrived in April 1519, he made Zempoala's Totonacs his first allies against the Aztecs by vowing to protect them against re-prisals. Cortés set up his first settlement, Villa Rica de la Vera Cruz (Rich Town of the True Cross), and by 1523 all the Gulf coast was in Spanish hands. Forced slavery, newly intro-duced diseases and the ravages of war severely reduced indigenous populations.

Veracruz harbor became an essential trade and communications link with Spain and was vital for anyone trying to rule Mexico, but the climate, tropical diseases and pirate threats inhibited the growth of Spanish settlements.

Under dictator Porfirio Díaz, Mexico's first railway (1872) linked Veracruz to Mexico City, stimulating industrial development. In 1901 oil was discovered in the Tampico area, and by the 1920s the region was producing a quarter of the world's oil. In the 1980s the Gulf coast still held well over half of Mexico's reserves and refining capacity. Today, the region is not as large a player as it used to be, but is still a significant contributor to Mexico's oil economy.

Climate

The central Gulf coast region is generally warm and humid. It's hotter along the coast and wetter in the foothills – the hottest and wettest of all regions being in the southeast. Two-thirds or more of the rain falls between June and September. Veracruz receives about 1650mm of rain annually. From April to October it features temperatures well over 30°C, falling into the teens at night only from December to February. Tuxpan and Tampico, on the north coast, are a bit drier. In the mountainous region inland it can range from 4°C to 15°C in winter.

Parks & Reserves

The Parque National Pico de Orizaba (p699) protects Mexico's tallest mountain (5611m), a dormant volcano 25km northwest of Orizaba. Just north of here the Parque Nacional Cofre de Perote (p683) encompasses another vol-cano. In the south, the Reserva de la Biosfera Los Tuxtlas (p708) is 155 sq km of pro-tected land that encompasses volcanoes and 11 ecosystems.

Dangers & Annoyances

Crime isn't a huge problem in this region, but travelers should remain wary of petty theft in cheap hotel rooms and pickpocketing in crowded market areas. More ominous is the hurricane potential. Check out the National Hurricane Center's website (www.nhc.noaa .gov) for the latest. Mosquitoes in coastal re-gions carry dengue fever, especially in central and southeastern Veracruz.

Getting There & Around

Veracruz port has a modern international airport, with national flights to Mexico City, Monterrey, Reynosa and Villahermosa, Tampico and Poza Rica. From the US, Continental has direct flights to Tampico and Veracruz from Houston, Texas.

Frequent 1st-class buses go just about everywhere within the region and link the main cities here with Monterrey, Mexico City, Puebla and Oaxaca. The main company serv-ing this area is ADO, with a super-deluxe fleet (UNO) and a deluxe fleet (ADO GL) as well as normal 1st-class buses. Greyhound buses run between the US and Mexico through its Mexican affiliates. Routes include Brownsville, Texas, to Tampico.

The central Gulf coast region's highways are generally in great shape. But don't expect to go speeding through the countryside: the ubiquitous *topes* (speedbumps) will make you smell the roses.

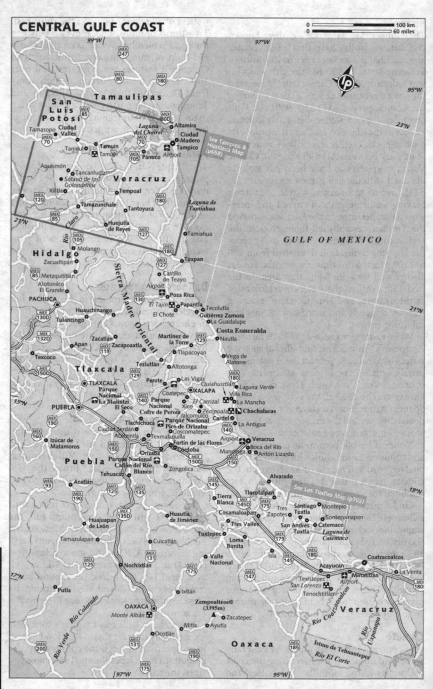

CENTRAL GULF COAST

GULF OF MEXICO

TAMPICO & THE HUASTECA

Industrial, developed Tampico contrasts sharply with the verdant Huasteca inland where the coastal plain meets the fringes of the Sierra Madre Oriental. Spread over the states of southern Tamaulipas, eastern San Luis Potosí, northern Veracruz and small corners of Querétaro and Hidalgo, the Huasteca is named after the indigenous people of the region.

Heading inland from the Huasteca, four steep, winding routes cross the sierra: Hwy 70 from Ciudad Valles to San Luis Potosí; Hwy 120 from Xilitla toward Querétaro; Hwy 85 from Tamazunchale to Ixmiquilpan (near which you can turn off toward Querétaro, Pachuca and Mexico City); and Hwy 105 from Huejutla to Pachuca and on to Mexico City via Hwy 85.

TAMPICO & PLAYA MIRAMAR

☎ 833

At the southern tip of Tamaulipas state, a few kilometers upstream from the Río Pánuco's mouth, Tampico (population 316,000) is Mexico's busiest port. The strengthening presence of US fast food, hotel and commercial chains here is disconcerting in that oh-crap-the-world-is-homogenizing kind of way.

However, the Plaza de la Libertad's newly renovated 19th-century, French-style buildings and the Plaza de Armas' daunting rose-colored kiosk are impressive, even if built recently to bolster tourism. A true jewel of the city is the Metro cultural center. Additionally, you can join the fiesta at Playa Miramar (officially part of Ciudad Madero) over vacations and holidays, but other times you'll have it all to yourself.

History

In the 1530s a mission was established in Tampico to convert the Huastecs. The town was destroyed by pirates in 1684 but refounded in 1823 by families from Altamira. After the 1901 discovery of oil in the area, Tampico suddenly became the world's biggest oil port – rough, tough and booming. Tampico's heyday was in the 1920s, and foreign investors reaped the oil profits until 1938 when the industry was nationalized by President Lázaro Cárdenas. To this day, the Tampico–Ciudad Madero refineries and harbor remain important.

Orientation

Tampico is ringed by extensive marshland, several lakes and numerous estuaries. Going south, the spectacular Puente Tampico (Tampico Bridge) crosses the Río Pánuco into Veracruz state.

PURSUING OUTDOOR ADVENTURES

On the central Gulf coast, don't mistranslate *deportes extremos* as meaning extreme sports, which are commonly associated with images of kayakers plunging down 20m waterfalls or rock climbers tackling an overhang. In this region, the much-advertised *deportes extremos* are basically any activity done in nature with a piece of outdoor equipment. Being lowered by a rappelling device, paddling flat water on blow-up kayaks and biking down a fire road all constitute *deportes extremos*.

This makes sense. The privilege of having time and money to hone an outdoor sport is inaccessible to many people here, and there's also an *extreme* lack of interest. However, the Pico de Orizaba–Cofre de Perote region, the Los Tuxtlas Biosphere Reserve and the Huasteca offer a treasure trove of gorgeous waterfalls, jewel-like swimming holes, lush backroads, craggy mountains, whitewater galore, paragliding spots and hundreds of caves. The majority of these are rarely explored with recreational intention. The DIY possibilities are limited only by your caution.

A helpful resource could be **INEGI** (www.inegi.gob.mx) where you can buy topo maps for every inch of Mexico. Offices are in Veracruz (☎ 935-43-99; Victimas del 5 y 6 de Julio 1045) and Xalapa (☎ 814-64-59; Av Camacho 236). If you have cycling in mind, try www.bicimapas.com.mx, which provides routes with some passable maps and directions. Tourist offices can sometimes point you in an *extreme* direction as well.

Many *deportes extremos* outfits advertise a huge list of activities, including, say, mountain biking because their cousin tried it five years ago. Usually, direct communication will inform you about what's really available.

Downtown Tampico centers on two plazas: the *zócalo* (Plaza de Armas) and the Plaza de la Libertad. South of Plaza de la Libertad are the market, docks, dive bars with their wayward crowds and delicious food court Centro de Gastrónomia. This area is best explored during the day.

Huge hotels and commercial chains dapple the Av Hidalgo strip roaring with traffic running north to south. Eight kilometers northeast of central Tampico is Ciudad Madero, with Playa Miramar another 7km away, on the Gulf of Mexico. The third town in this million-plus industrialized metropolitan area is Altamira, 17km northwest of Tampico.

Information

Numerous banks are scattered around the central plazas, and all have 24-hour ATMs. Public telephones can be found in both plazas, and there are 24-hour lockers at the bus station.

Beneficencia Española, AC (☎ 241-23-63; www .bene.com.mx; Hidalgo 3909) Provides quality medical care.

Canarias Cybercafé (Carranza 214; per hr M$10)

Post office (☎ 212-19-27; Madero 309)

Tourist Office (☎ 217-89-40; www.tampico.gov.mx; Ave Hidalgo 2703; ☿ 9am-5:30pm Mon-Fri) Inconveniently located northwest of the city center near the Holiday Inn Express. The staff doesn't seem to know a lot but provides good city maps.

Tampico Cultural (www.tampicocultural.com.mx) Guide to the cultural happenings in the city.

Sights

The two central squares have some elegant New Orleans–style buildings with intricate wrought-iron balconies. Those on the Plaza de la Libertad seem slightly disjointed with a chaotic market almost spilling in from the south.

The Espacio Cultural Metropolitano, known as **Metro** (☎ 126-08-88; www.metro.tamaulipas.gob.mx; Blvd Adolfo López Mateos s/n; ☿ 10am-6pm), is an extremely well done cultural center. Within this modern, spotless building you'll find couple of art galleries with ongoing exhibits (some with a minor entrance fee). Additionally, there are two theatres, the main one being formal and fit for a symphony and the other one being casual, aimed at experimental theatre and literary readings.

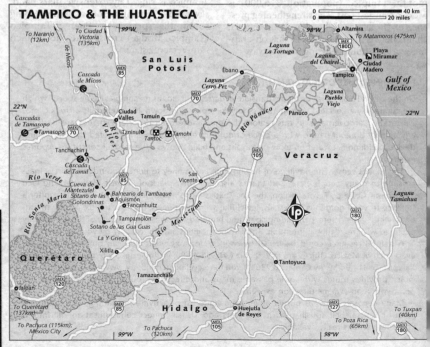

TAMPICO & THE HUASTECA

Metro also houses the **Museo de la Cultura Huasteca** (☎ 210-22-17; admission M$37; ☺ 10am-4:45pm Tue-Sat), which displays well-organized exhibits and artifacts of the Huastec religion and culture and the Mesoamerican fertility cult. It's 2km from Tampico overlooking Lago Carpintero; take a 'Central Camionera' bus from Olmos and get off at the Parque Metropolitano stop. Walk down Topiltzin over a pedestrian bridge. A taxi cost M$30.

Museo Exposición (Edificio de la Aduana; www .tampico1829.org; admission M$10; ☺ 9-12 & 3-6pm) is a concentrated one-room museum that has informative displays and a video telling the history of Tampico's proud victory over the Spaniards in 1829. If the attendant is available, they'll show you around the museum and the **Edificio de la Aduana Tampico**, an old customs building (where the museum is housed) constructed in 1902 at the whim of vicious dictator Porfirio Díaz. Its internationally influenced architecture was built with materials imported from New Orleans, USA, France and England. To walk there from the Plaza de Libertad, follow Aduana toward the river. You'll see it on the left as you cross the railway tracks on the pedestrian bridge.

If you're in town on a Saturday the **Jardín Del Arte** (☎ 229-27-46; Plaza Morelos btwn Obregón & Morelos) is a rich event where painters and sculptors from the city congregate and sell or trade their works.

ACTIVITIES

In the heart of the city is **El Parque Metropolitano** where you can run or walk on paths bordering Lake Carpintero or take a lake tour on a little wooden barge (M$35). If you're lucky, you'll spy one of the park's crocodiles lounging lakeside.

Five kilometers northwest of the city center is **Lago Chairel**, adjoined by pleasant Parque Gray Andrés de Olmos where you can take windsurfing lessons (M$150 for three hours) from Umberto Salinas or wakeboarding lessons from **Safaris Tamesí** (☎ 140-12-04; www .wakecamp.com.mx; Parque Gray Andrés de Olmos), which trains wakeboarders at a competitive level. Tour companies might advertise these activities, but they will charge you much more and probably go through these guys anyway. A taxi costs M$25.

Tampico Adventures (☎ 217-81-02; www.tampico adventures.com) offers guided activities such as water skiing, rafting excursions, spa packages, city tours and fishing trips. Or there's **Interxplora** (☎ 229-35-65; www.interxplora.com; Av Hidalgo 2000), a new shoot-off of a travel agency that offers trips to El Cielo biosphere reserve (p423), rafting on Río Micos outside Ciudad Valles in the Huasteca and Río Filobobos, popularly accessed from Tlapacoyan, and excursions to El Tajín (p672).

Playa Miramar is about 15km from downtown Tampico. The 10km broad sandy beach is pretty clean and the cobalt water is clear, if not crystalline. Beachside restaurants rent shady *palapas* and specialize in *mariscos* (seafood dishes) and margaritas. On holidays and weekends the beach spills over with families and is thick with vendors. At other times there's hardly a soul. From central Tampico, you can take a 'Playa' bus (M$4.50) on Olmos, a *colectivo* (M$4.50) north on Alfaro, or a taxi (M$40).

Festivals & Events

Semana Santa (week preceding Easter Sunday) Activities at Playa Miramar include regattas, fishing and windsurfing competitions, sand-sculpture contests, music, dancing and bonfires. Warning: petty crime rises during this period.
Aniversario de la Repoblación de Tampico (April 12) Features a procession from Altamira that passes Tampico's *zócalo*, celebrating the city's refoundation in 1823.

Sleeping

During holidays downtown places fill up quickly and rates skyrocket, increasing from 10 to 30%. Some hotels pay taxi drivers commission when they deliver customers, so beware (there are some funky hotels in this town).

TOP PLACES TO FIND GREEN IN THE CITY

- **Parque Ecológico Macuiltépetl** (Xalapa, p679) Set on a verdant hill just north of the city, this is a runner's haven and urban retreat with volcano views galore.

- **Lago Chairel** (Tampico, left) Five kilometers from the city center, you can hang out lakeside with a picnic in Gray Andrés Olmos Park.

- **Parque Alameda** (Orizaba, p698) Green and statue-filled, this expansive city park serves as a track, social scene and host to pick-up soccer games.

CENTRAL GULF COAST

BUDGET

Hotel Plaza (☎ 214-17-84; Madero 204 Ote; from M$275; ❄) Its tidy rooms are good for your purse strings. The location is great and there's a pizza place downstairs. Pay parking is available nearby.

Posada del Rey (☎ 214-10-24; www.hotelposada delrey.com.mx; Madero 218; r M$275-470; ❄) Right on the *zócalo*, this hotel is clean, though the un-remodeled rooms are weathered. It offers windowless interior rooms and large rooms with views of the plaza.

MIDRANGE

Best Western Gran Hotel Sevilla (☎ 214-38-33, 800-570-39-11; www.bwgranhotelsevilla.com; Héroes del Cañonero 304 Pte; r M$550-680; ❄ ❄) Staying at a chain can kill the romance, but this hotel has undeniable charm with a curved modern facade and café overlooking the Plaza de la Libertad. Many of its cozy, clean rooms enjoy plaza views and are fairly priced with breakfast included.

Hotel Miramar (☎ 269-00-87; www.hotelmiramarinn .com; Av Álvaro Obregón 202 Nte; r M$500; Ⓟ ❄ 🖳 🖳) A couple of blocks away from Playa Miramar,

this is a doable alternative to the lavish hotels on the beach strip. The establishment is a well-executed affair, though its rooms are unremarkable.

Providencia Express (Emilio Carranza 320-A; s/d M$550/590; Ⓟ ❄) In a town full of dog-eared hotels, the sterile, upright feeling of this very new hotel with modern trimmings is welcome. The rooms on the upper floors have views of the city. It's a good value.

Hotel Marsella (☎ 229-38-14; www.hotelmarsella .com.mx; Altamira 220 Pte; r from M$680; Ⓟ ❄ 🖳) It pulls off European-Renaissance-meets-Mexican-kitsch, surprisingly. The newly remodeled rooms are ample and spotless. Go for a corner room that sports two balconies if you can.

TOP END

Hotel Inglaterra (☎ 230-44-44, 800-715-71-23; www .hotelinglaterra.com.mx; Díaz Mirón 116 Ote; r M$850-1300; Ⓟ ❄ ❄ 🖳 🖳) The newly revamped rooms are upscale and have sleek Asian décor. For a significantly lower price, you can get an un-remodeled room that still has a terrific location on the corner of the *zócalo*, spacious quarters and huge windows. Breakfast is included.

Club Maeva Miramar (☎ 230-02-02, 800-849-19-87; www.maevamiramar.com.mx; Blvd Costero s/n, Playa Miramar; all-inclusive r M$1300-2200; P ☒ ☒ ☐ ☒ ☒) The fanciest option on the beach, this all-inclusive tourist confine creates a separate world of hedonism with its pools, enormous decked-out rooms, live entertainment, private beach access and an armory of activities to entertain any of its bored charges.

Eating

A lot of the higher-end restaurants dot Av Hidalgo, a fume-ridden and traffic-saturated thoroughfare. However, in the center there are some good options. The local specialty is *carne asada a la tampiqueña*, steak marinated in garlic, oil and oregano and usually served with guacamole, strips of chili and corn chips.

El Globito (☎ 212-86-27; Plaza de Armas; mains M$10-30; ☒ 24hrs) In the middle of the plaza; you can drink fresh juices or munch sandwiches all night.

Naturaleza Internacional (☎ 212-49-79; Aduana 107 Nte; mains M$25-55; ☒ 8am-8pm; V ☒) At the rear nook of a 'health food' store, breakfasts and set meals (M$45) are served with whole-wheat rolls. In general, this region hasn't figured out delicious vegetarian, but veggies might want to check it out.

La Troya (☎ 214-10-24; Madero 218; mains M$40-100) This bar–restaurant has breezy balcony seating overlooking the plaza that makes a great place for a cold margarita and savory Mexican food.

Restaurant Elite (☎ 212-03-64; Díaz Mirón 211; mains M$50-110; ☒ 7:30am-11pm) A spacious, popular restaurant with bustling waitresses and a long line-up of Mexican food served in generous portions, including excellent *carne asada a la tampiqueña*.

Centro Gastronomía (between Calles Juárez & Aduana) Join *tampiqueños* as they indulge in fantastic regional seafood such as *cocteles de camarón* (shrimp cocktails) adorned with avocado or a *torta de barda* (named after the protective wall, the *barda*, in the port) which is a sandwich loaded with different meats, cheeses, beans and the (hygenic) kitchen sink. Expect insistent waitstaff to vie for your business, and bring some extra pesos if it's your inclination to give to those who ask. One block south of Plaza de la Libertad in a chaotic arcade of food stands.

Drinking & Entertainment

Coffee shops and bars are scattered throughout the center, and there are some other fun options.

Lohga (☎ 216-86-70; Playa Miramar s/n) A small but fully equipped beachside bar with an ambience more laid-back than hotel bars, but with a debauched, youthful vibe.

Sueños Húmedos (Parque Gray Andrés de Olmos; ☒ 2pm-close) Bar-on-a-barge on Lago Chairel. For M$50 take a spin around the lake while you drink your *cerveza*. They set sail at 6pm for an hour and a half.

Cinemas Plaza (☎ 214-24-39; Colón 100 Sur) Shows recent American films subtitled in Spanish.

Getting There & Away

AIR

Aeropuerto Internacional Francisco Javier Mina is 15km north of downtown. **Mexicana** and **Click Mexicana** (☎ 228-36-62) are among a handful of national airlines that offers daily flights to major Mexican cities. **Continental** (☎ 800-900-50-00) operates regular flights between Tampico and Houston, Texas.

BUS

Tampico's modern bus station (☎ 213-00-47) is 7km north of the center on Rosalio Bustamante. There are stores selling snacks, taco stands, a call center and luggage storage.

First-class buses run to most major towns north of Mexico City and down the Gulf coast.

Destination	Fare	Duration	Frequency
Ciudad Valles	M$10	3hr	6 daily
Matamoros	M$305	7hr	9 daily
Mexico City (Terminal Norte)	M$394	10hr	every 1½ hrs
Monterrey	M$358	7½hr	hourly
Poza Rica	M$106	5hr	½ hourly
San Luis Potosí	M$337	8hr	5 daily
Tuxpan	M$168	4hr	hourly
Veracruz	M$378	9hr	hourly
Xalapa	M$376	10hr	2 daily

Deluxe and 2nd-class services also run to many of these destinations. For Xilitla, the quickest way is to travel to Ciudad Valles and get a connection there.

CAR & MOTORCYCLE

Hwy 180 north of Tampico is a good highway for about 80km, then narrows to a two-lane

northeast to Aldama or northwest on Hwy 81 to Ciudad Victoria. Heading south from Tampico, Hwy 180 crosses Puente Tampico and continues down to Tuxpan, which is an adequate road.

Avis (☎ 228-05-85) and **Budget** (☎ 227-18-80) are some car rental agencies are located at the airport.

Getting Around

Tampico's *colectivo* taxis are large old cars with destinations painted on the doors. They're inexpensive but slower than regular taxis and make frequent stops.

Transporte Terrestre (☎ 228-45-88) runs *colectivo* combis from the airport to anywhere in Tampico–Ciudad Madero for around M$65.

Taxis from the bus station to the city center cost M$30. From the city center to the bus station or Metro take a 'Perimetral' *colectivo* (M$4.50) from Olmos, a block south of the *zócalo*.

CIUDAD VALLES & AROUND

☎ 481 / pop (Ciudad Valles) 110,000 / elevation 71m

Ciudad Valles slumbers on the banks of the huge Río Valles and serves as a good base for trips into the luscious Huasteca. It's also close to the midpoint between Monterrey and Mexico City, at the intersection of Hwy 85 (the Pan-American) and Hwy 70 (running east–west from Tampico to San Luis Potosí). Hence, it's a handy stop for motorists. It also serves as a good base for rafting and trips to caves and waterfalls in the luscious Huasteca.

Orientation & Information

Hwy 85, called Blvd México-Laredo in town, curves north–south through the city. To reach the main plaza, head five blocks west down Av Juárez or Av Hidalgo. Hwy 70 bypasses town on the south side.

The main bus station is located 3km south of the center, off Hwy 85 (Carr Nacional México-Laredo). Just off the Plaza, the staff at the **tourist office** (☎ 381-57-35; www.sanluispotosi .gob.mx; Av Hidalgo 111-113, 2nd fl; ⏲ 8am-9pm Mon-Sat) knows their stuff and will give you lots of helpful information and maps.

Between the plaza and Hwy 85 on Juárez are banks (including a Banamex ATM) and **TOPCOM** (☎ 381-17-81; Juárez 115) with internet access.

Sights & Activities

Valles wouldn't usually be considered a destination point, but at the end of October the town goes all out to celebrate **Xantolo** – the traditional Huasteca variation of Día de Los Muertos – with music, dances and customary food. The modest **Parque Urbano** right off the plaza is perfect for an ice cream–equipped riverside stroll.

Mostly this little town is a great base for adventures (see boxed text, p657) to the Huasteca's azure rivers, lush forests and plunging waterfalls. If you have a car, you can venture out, but make sure you go with the help of the detailed maps you can get from the tourist office.

Alternatively, there are a number of adventure tour companies that run from here. They all tend to offer similar services like rafting, rappelling and zip lines, as well as trips to waterfalls, caves, Tamtoc (below) and Xilitla (p665). A rafting excursion will coast around M$700 per person. Trips are more regular during the busy seasons – other times, you might have the guide to yourself. Often the rule of thumb is the more clients, the cheaper the cost.

Adventure tour companies:

Aventours (☎ 381-04-85; www.aventours.org; Galeana 46) They have a trip to El Cielo Biosphere Reserve (p423).

MS Xpediciones (☎ 381-18-88; www.msxpediciones .com.mx; Blvd México-Laredo 15 Nte) Offers sit-on-top kayaks trips, car rentals with driver/guide included (M$1250 per day) and myriad caving excursions.

Adventura Huasteca (☎ 381-75-16; www.aventura huasteca.net; Blvd México-Laredo 19 Nte) Rafting Río Tampaón and the Río Micos is the specialty of this well-established company.

TAMTOC

The important Huastec ceremonial center of **Tamtoc** (admission M$43; ⏲ 9am-5pm, Sun closed) flourished from AD 700 to 1500. Today it's one of the few maintained Huastec sites. The cleared part of the expansive site is a plaza with platforms made of river stones. Look for a low bench with two conical altars decorated with faded 1000-year-old frescoes believed to represent Quetzalcóatl, the feathered-serpent god.

Southwest of the main site are two unrestored pyramids, and further southwest is Puente de Dios (Bridge of God). At the winter solstice, you can stand on the main platform and watch the sun set into the Puente de Dios, with the pair of pyramids and Río Tampaón perfectly aligned.

On the way to Tamtoc, you'll pass **Tamohi** (also known as El Consuelo), which is another smaller archeological site that also has some other interesting Huastec structures.

To get to the ruins, go to the town of Tamuín, 30km east of Ciudad Valles on Hwy 70. Continue a kilometer east and turn south on the Tamuín–San Vicente road. Around Km 5, you'll see a sign for Tamohi where you turn right. Tamohi is about a kilometer down that road. For Tamtoc, continue straight on the Tamuín–San Vincente road and you'll see a sign for Tamtoc around Km 8 where you take a right and follow a rough road for 10 more kilometers.

There's no public transportation to these sights. A taxi will cost you M$200 from Valles for a round trip. Frequent buses to Tampico go through Tamuín. The Vencedor window in Tamuín sells tickets to San Vincente that will drop you at the turnoffs if you want to walk the rest of the way.

WATERFALLS & SWIMMING SPOTS

Cascadas de Micos is a lovely place to take a dip or rent a canoe near Valles north of Hwy 70. Take the bus to Naranjo from 5 de Mayo near the plaza, and tell the driver to drop you off. The waterfalls are only 200m from the highway.

Southeast of Valles the fantastic **Cascada de Tamul** plunges 105m into the pristine Río Santa María. Take Hwy 70 for 24km, then turn left following signs to the waterfall for another 18km. There's no bus service here, and a round-trip taxi will cost about M$250. You can also arrive from Aquismón. The *lancha* to actually reach the waterfall is M$60 to M$80 per person.

TAMASOPO

Many rivers flow eastward from the slopes of the Sierra Madre Oriental, forming waterfalls and swimming holes. Tamasopo, 5km north of Hwy 70 and 55km west of Ciudad Valles, is set in this luscious area.

Two kilometers from Tamasopo, **Cascadas de Tamasopo** (admission M$20, campsites per person M$50) has gorgeous waterfalls and a beautiful natural arch. **Cosmos Hotel** (☎ 482-387-00-40; Allende 309; s/d M$385/490, with air M$450/575; ✗ P) is the nicest of the smattering of little hotels in small Tamasopo. **Balneario Tamisaqua** (☎ 482-387-03-31; r M$550; P ✗ ⚑ ⚐) is a hotel burrowed in the

forest less than a kilometer past the Casadas de Tamasopo (follow signs) and 2.5km northeast from Tamasopo. It's equipped with a private set of cascades, a pool and a café.

HOTEL TANINUL

On Hwy 70 between Ciudad Valles and Tamuín is the turnoff for Hotel Taninul, a minor hot-springs resort. **Hotel Taninul** (☎ 388-01-43; taninul@avantel.net; Hwy Valles-Tampico, Km 15; from M$660; P ✗ ⚑) is a converted hacienda on extensive grounds in a 700-acre reserve. It has good accommodations, a blissful (slightly sulfurous) hot mineral pool and a fleet of beater bikes on-hand for guests. It offers an array of spa services, including outdoor massage.

Next to the hotel, the small **Museo Lailab** (☎ 382-00-00; admission M$10; ✹ 9am-3pm Tue-Sun) has well-presented exhibits on the Huastec, ancient and contemporary. A taxi from Valles costs around M$120.

Sleeping

Most of the midrange and upmarket places are on Hwy 85.

Hotel Condesa (☎ 382-00-15; Juárez 109; r M$150) Right near the plaza, these low-priced rooms are very simple yet clean, with friendly management. Ask for a room with windows.

ourpick **Hotel Piña** (☎ /fax 382-01-83; www.hotel-pina.com; Av Juárez 210; s/d M$320/420; P ✗) Unlike the hotels on Hwy 85, the Piña doesn't pretend to be upscale, nor does it charge you as such. With its warm-hued decor, pleasant sitting areas and high standards of cleanliness, this well-run hotel is a great deal.

Hotel Aventura Huasteca (☎ 382-01-28; Blvd México-Laredo 19 Nte; s/d M$360/400, with air M$400/450; P ✗ ⚐) This hotel keeps it plain, simple and pretty clean. Adventure Huasteca, a well-established adventure company, conveniently makes its base here.

Hotel San Fernando (☎ 382-22-80; Blvd México-Laredo 17 Nte; s/d M$530/620; P ✗ ⚐) Not unlike a disappointing first date, this hotel presents well upon entrance, but the rooms inside are slightly dilapidated. It's held together by an efficient staff who keep it clean and guests appeased. It's four blocks from the plaza.

Hotel Valles (☎ 382-00-50; www.hotelvalles.com; Blvd México-Laredo 36 Nte; s/d M$910/1130; P ✗ ⚑) Successfully creates a peaceful, verdant getaway right off Hwy 85. The expansive, landscaped grounds have a large pool, and some of

CENTRAL GULF COAST

the spacious, well-kept rooms have stone tubs. There's a casual restaurant and a fancier steak and seafood place on the premises.

Eating

El Cafetto (Central plaza; 8am-9pm; dishes M$10-45;) Smack in the middle of the plaza, this café is as trendy as Valles gets. It serves paninis, refreshing smoothies and coffee drinks.

Todo Light (381-14-93; Morelos cnr Juárez; mains M$25-50; 7am-9pm Mon-Sat, 10am-6pm Sun; V) This eatery on the plaza has whole-wheat goodies, salads, sandwiches and fresh juices. The VIGOR smoothie mixes spinach, orange and pineapple juice.

Torta 'Don Max' (Juarez 227; mains from M$30; 9:30am-11:30pm) A to-the-point sandwich joint and a locals' choice.

La Troje (381-68-44; Av Juárez 210; mains M$30-70;) This popular café connected to Hotel La Piña has friendly service and plentiful, delicious Mexican food.

Getting There & Away

BUS

Just off Hwy 85, 3km south of Juárez, the **bus terminal** (382-39-12) has a left-luggage room and a taxi ticket booth (M$30 to the center). Many buses are *de paso* (therefore often late). First-class buses depart from Ciudad Valles to several destinations:

Destination	Fare	Duration	Frequency
Matamoros	M$360	8hr	11 daily
Mexico City (Terminal Norte)	M$471	10hr	9 daily
Monterrey	M$338	7hr	19 daily
San Luis Potosí	M$238	5hr	frequent
Tampico	M$125	2½hr	hourly

Second-class buses run more frequently and cost about 10% less; local routes go to Pachuca, Ciudad Victoria, Tampico, Tamazunchale, Aquismón and Xilitla.

CAR & MOTORCYCLE

Hwy 70 west of Valles is spectacular. It climbs the Sierra Madre toward San Luis Potosí (262km) on the Altiplano Central (slow trucks will hold you up periodically on this twisting road). East to Tampico, Hwy 70 is straight and fast. Hwy 85 heads south to Tamazunchale and then southwest toward Mexico City. You can also continue east from Tamazunchale to Huejutla, circling the

Huasteca back to Tampico, which is a slower route over rough roads.

AQUISMÓN & AROUND
482 / pop 1900 / elevation 137m

The molasses-paced Huastec village of Aquismón – 45km south of Ciudad Valles and 4km west from Hwy 85 – nestles into dense forest beneath a precipitous limestone ridge. Most people come for the Sotano de las Golondrinas, but few realize that this area is rich in caves, not to mention waterfalls, rivers and forests (see opposite). If you're around on a Saturday, you might want to catch the colorful market. During Semana Santa the city and surrounding areas crawl with Mexican tourists.

On the plaza, the **tourist office** (368-00-22; dirturismo_aquismon@hotmail.com) gives out information enthusiastically. Conveniently, the very eager, for-hire *camionetas* are right outside the office. They quote you a lump price that is split among up to 8 passengers. There is an ATM in the Palacio Municipal on the plaza.

Various tour companies from surrounding cities bring people mostly to the main Sotano. Yet the in-town tourist resources are undeveloped, beyond the *camionetas* for hire, in an area glutted with natural beauty.

A *camioneta* (M$600) will take you to Mexico's second-deepest pit, the astonishing **Sótano de las Golondrinas** (Pit of the Swallows; admission M$10; dawn-dusk), a 376m-deep cave 13km southwest of Aquismón. It's home to thousands of swifts that emerge en masse just after sunrise and return at dusk. Their beating wings sound like river rapids. It takes an hour in each direction on a rough access road suitable for 4WD vehicles only.

A mere 15-minute ride north from Aquismón is **Balneario de Tambaque** where you'll find Río Tanutés crystalline waters cascading and pooling for your dipping pleasure. A *camioneta* there should cost about M$20 per person. Also close to Aquismón are the **Cuevas de Mantezulel** (Mantezulel Caves), which includes a cave with an expansive entrance allowing you to explore a ways without equipment; a *camioneta* costs M$300. There's a back way going north from Aquismón to Cascada de Tamul (p663). A *camioneta* costs M$400.

Aquismón is the center for the lively festivals of **San Miguel Arcángel** (September 28 and 29) and the **Virgen de Guadalupe** (December 12). The Huastec dances performed imitate the

---

DO IT YOURSELF: AQUISMÓN

There's a dog-eared map in the Aquismón tourist office that stores the collective knowledge of foreign spelunkers come and gone, marking the abundant, little known caves. If you're into spelunking, this might be your hog heaven. Possible contact Ateno Genes Pérez lives in the community by the Sótano de las Golondrinas and takes people rappelling into the vast caverns. Go through the tourist office to get in touch with him. **Inegi** (www.inegi.gob.mx) is a good source for detailed topos.

The little-trafficked system of back roads could make for a gorgeous bike tour, especially with all the rural communities, rivers, waterfalls and caves as destination points where camping is usually permitted, with varying fees (free to M$50) and degrees of services. The tourist office offers guided bike trips (M$500 half day) with shoddy rentals. Bringing your own bike and arranging a guide or an SAG vehicle might be the way to go. Or, if you want to roll solo, get info from the friendly tourist office. October, November and March would be prime times to tour because it's uncrowded, cooler and less rainy.

---

movements of wild creatures. Much drinking of *aguardiente* (sugar cane alcohol) accompanies the performances at the festivals.

One of two hotels in town is the very basic **Hotel San Cosme** (☎ 368-00-72; cnr Zaragoza & Av Juárez; s/d M$150; P) just off the plaza. Endure it if you want to save a couple of pesos. Otherwise a short stroll from the plaza, **Hotel La Mansión** (☎ 368-00-04; Carmona 16; s/d M$200/300, air-con M$100 extra; P ❷) is pleasant and contains a restaurant. Its sparse rooms are well attended.

There's a smattering of standard Mexican eateries near the Plaza. In the center of the plaza, **El Kiosko** has sandwiches and fresh fruit drinks made with cinnamon.

Second-class buses from Ciudad Valles or Xilitla drop you at the crossroads of Hwy 85; *colectivo* taxis (M$6-8) take you the last 4km to Aquismón. To get to Xilitla, catch the 'Jalpan' bus (M$22) from the Hwy 85 crossroads.

XILITLA

☎ 489 / pop 5900 / elevation 1151m

Perched on a hilltop, surrounded on all sides by the verdant, sweeping slopes of the Sierra Madre Oriental, Xilitla (he-*leet*-la) is a striking mountain town. Las Pozas is the main tourist draw here, but staying a night or two in Xilitla with its temperate climate and beautiful setting is a laid-back, pleasant experience.

Orientation & Information

The central plaza occupies the highest part of the town, with streets falling away steeply on all sides. Most things are close to this square, including the bus stop (there's no terminal), which is 200m to the southwest. There's a Banorte (with ATM) on the plaza and several internet cafés including **La Nave** (❸ 9am-10pm; per hr M$10), just west of the plaza.

A big festival is the Xilitla coffee fair on August 27, but a few days before and after there are Huapango dances and musical performances – characterized by intricate steps and falsetto singing.

Sights

LAS POZAS

Xilitla's famous attraction is **Las Pozas** (The Pools; admission M$30; ❸ 9am-dusk), a bizarre but beautiful concatenation of concrete temples, pagodas, bridges, pavilions, sculptures and spiral stairways built adjacent to an idyllic series of waterfalls. This surreal creation stands as a monument to the imagination and excessive wealth of Edward James (see boxed text, p666) as well as to the expertise of site manager Plutarco Gastelum and the skill of local workers who cast the elaborate constructions in the 1960s and 1970s. Though the project was never completed – the jungle encroaches on the half-finished structures – this is an amazing place.

The extravagant labyrinth of surreal sculptures and edifices with stairs leading nowhere and random architecture could invigorate anyone's creative inclination. If you're in fairly good shape you could spend the whole day dipping in the lovely swimming holes and climbing around the precarious structures and maze trails within the 36 hectares.

In most places guardrails are nonexistent, which adds to the unreal experience, but could be hazardous. It's a popular picnic spot, but mid-week it can be deserted. The café here is open daily from 10am to 6pm.

EDWARD JAMES

Born into immense wealth in Sussex, England, James (1907–84) rejected aristocratic conventions and sought the company of artists, poets and existentialists. As a generous patron, James became absorbed in surrealist art and amassed the largest private collection in the world.

In 1945 his adventures took him to Xilitla where he met close friend Plutarco Gastelum who helped build Las Pozas. It began with 40 local workers crafting giant, colored, concrete flowers beside an idyllic jungle stream. Then, for 17 years, James and Gastelum created ever larger and stranger structures, many of which were never finished, at an estimated cost of US$5 million.

James died in 1984, making no provision to maintain his creation, which is already decomposing into another Mexican ruin. Currently, there are rumors of its restoration.

Even though Las Pozas is the main shtick here, it's relatively inconvenient to arrive without a car. You can walk there the pleasant back way in about 45 minutes east of Xilitla, or take a *combi* (M$6) to the entrance off the highway and walk the remaining 1km. A taxi is M$60.

MUSEO DE EDWARD JAMES

A tiny **museum** (Ocampo 105; admission M$30; 10am-6pm Tue-Sun) was set up by the Gastelum family who fondly remembers Edward James. It displays the intricate wood molds made by hand that were used to make the incredible structures at Las Pozas. You'll also find some photographs chronicling the construction of Las Pozas and James' life.

CONVENTO DE SAN AGUSTÍN

Brooding over the plaza, the austere former monastery **Convento de San Agustín** was built in 1557. An intriguing feature is the row of tiny windows that line its upper north side, which mark the *celdas* (cells) of the resident monks. The only part of the complex open to the public is the single-naved chapel and small rear patio.

Sleeping

The little town of Xilitla has surprisingly adorable, well-priced places to stay.

Hotel Dolores (365-01-78; www.hoteldoloresxilitla .com; Matamoros 211; s/d M$180/350 with fan, double M$450 with air;) A short walk away from the plaza you'll find this cheery, well-decorated hotel. Most rooms have large windows that provide fantastic views of the mountains. The single room with a fan is a deal.

Hotel Guzmán (365-03-38; Corregidora 208; s/d M$200/350, with air-con M$300/350, suite M$500;) Just off the plaza, this attractive stone hotel run by an eccentric family has three floors of well-kept, clean, comfortable rooms, many

with rich wooden details, rock-embedded floors and mountain views. The top-floor suites are expansive with fantastic views and bathtubs.

Las Pozas (365-03-67; www.laspozas.ya.st; 2/4 people M$300/500;) You can't beat the location of these *cabañas* scattered throughout the lower part of the estate. However, they are bit dated and musty.

Hostel del Café (365-00-18; hostaldelcafe@ hotmail.com; Niños Héroes 116; r M$400-600;) This seven-room, bed-and-breakfast–style hotel is a kilometer or so from town. You'll find the rooms tucked into a luscious hillside with gorgeous details like hand-carved headboards, painted sinks, and showers tiled with river stones. Breakfast is served in the *Cueva*, a colorfully decorated mini-cave looking out onto the communal patio dripping with foliage.

Posada El Castillo (365-00-38; Ocampo 105; www.junglegossip.com; r M$700-1200;) The former Gastelum home where Edward James stayed in Xilitla is now a verdant, Pozas-esque guesthouse run by the family and is the highest end option in town. Its tasteful rooms are decorated with antiques and art, and some claim fantastic views.

Eating

Look out for tasty local *acamaya* (freshwater crayfish) and *enchiladas huastecas*, which are served with *cecina* (thin strips of beef) on the side. Taco and *esquite* (corn-on-the-cob) stands are all around the plaza and seem to win the people's choice award. Also, you're bound to find interesting eats in the Mercado behind the church.

Las Tortugas de Xilitla (365-06-48; Escobedo 218; 12pm-10pm Sun-Fri; sandwiches M$18-28) Plop onto a cushy, red barstool at this popular, cheap sandwich spot and watch the cook whip you up a sandwich with fresh ingredients. The *torta huasteca* (M$22) comes decked with *cecina, chorizo* and shredded cheese.

La Flor de Café (☎ 365-03-76; Hidalgo 215; M$25-40; ☯ 6.30am-9pm) Run by a co-op of Nahua women, this simple place offers local specialties including *zacahuiles* (huge *tamales*) as well as delicious *aguas frescas* (sweetened fruit water).

Restaurant Cayo's (☎ 365-00-44; Alvarado 117; dishes M$40-90; ☯ 9am-10pm) The patio looking onto the Sierra is a gorgeous place to grab a bite. The *sopa de mariscos* is a delightful and impolite adventure with whole, unpeeled crawfish and shrimp.

Getting There & Away

Xilitla has regular connections on comfortable 2nd-class buses to Ciudad Valles (M$54, frequently) that pass Aquismón en route. Buses to Tampico (M$200) also run frequently. There are also buses to San Luis Potosí (M$350). The southeast journey across northern Veracruz state toward Tuxpan is actually quickest traveled via Valles and Tampico.

CAR & MOTORCYCLE

The drive through the Sierras to the market town of Huejutla on Hwy 85 is fantastic. If you pass through Huejutla on a Sunday there's a big market, which many Nahua people in the region attend.

South of Huejutla, Hwy 105 climbs into the lovely Sierra Madre Oriental. It's a tortuous, foggy road to Pachuca. On the way you'll pass old monasteries at Molango and Zacualtipán.

Hwy 120, heading west to Jalpan then southwest toward Querétaro, is an exciting route through the Sierra Gorda. Southeast of Xilitla, Hwy 85 is the most direct route from the Huasteca to Mexico City. It's a steep but scenic route over the Sierra Madre. Start early to avoid fog.

NORTHERN VERACRUZ STATE

The northern half of Veracruz state, between the coast and southern fringes of the Sierra Madre Oriental, mainly consists of lush rolling pastureland. Laguna de Tamiahua claims the region's largest wetland, while the Gulf has some fine isolated (sometimes polluted) sandy beaches. The major archaeological attraction is El Tajín.

At the regular army checkpoints along this coast the soldiers are usually very respectful toward tourists.

TUXPAN

☎ 783 / pop 75,000

Tuxpan (sometimes spelled Túxpam), 300km north of Veracruz and 190km south of Tampico, is a steamy fishing town and minor oil port. If you have some time here, cross the broad Río Tuxpan to visit a little museum devoted to Cuban–Mexican friendship or join vacationing Mexicans on Playa Norte, the beach 12km to the east.

Orientation & Information

The downtown area is on the north bank of the Río Tuxpan, six blocks upstream from the bridge that spans the river. The riverfront road, Blvd Reyes Heroles, passes under the bridge and runs east to Playa Norte. Across the river is the suburb of Santiago de la Peña where the museum is located.

Tuxpan's simple **tourist office** (☎ 834-64-07; turismotuxpam@yahoo.com.mx; Palacio Municipal; ☯ 9am-7pm Mon-Fri, 10am-6pm Sat) has a smattering of maps and tourist brochures. Card phones are in Parque Reforma and banks with ATMs on Juárez. The post office is several blocks away, on Mina, while you'll find internet cafés around the center.

Sights & Activities

On the south side of the river, the **Museo de la Amistad México-Cuba** (Mexican-Cuban Friendship Museum; Obregón s/n; admission free; ☯ 9am-7pm) has a room filled with displays on José Martí and pictures of Che Guevara and Castro as well as other memorabilia. Fidel Castro stayed in this suburban house in 1956 while planning the infiltration of Cuba. On November 26, a private yacht overloaded with 82 revolutionaries set sail from here to Cuba to start the uprising. To get to the museum, take a boat (M$3) across the river, walk several blocks south to Obregón, then turn right – the museum is at the western end of Obregón on the river.

Tuxpan's beach **Playa Norte**, 12km east of town, is a wide strip stretching 20km north from the Río Tuxpan's mouth. At the time of publication, its *palapa* restaurants were

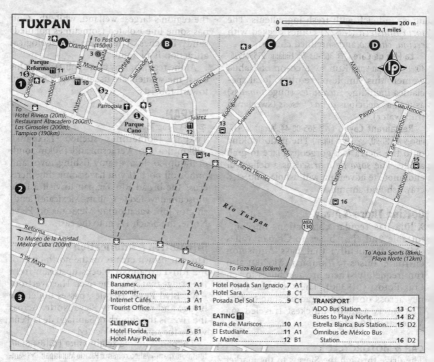

INFORMATION		
Banamex	1	A1
Bancomer	2	A1
Internet Cafés	3	A1
Tourist Office	4	B1

SLEEPING		
Hotel Florida	5	A1
Hotel May Palace	6	A1
Hotel Posada San Ignacio	7	A1
Hotel Sara	8	C1
Posada Del Sol	9	C1

EATING		
Barra de Mariscos	10	A1
El Estudiante	11	A1
Sr Mante	12	B1

TRANSPORT		
ADO Bus Station	13	C1
Buses to Playa Norte	14	B2
Estrella Blanca Bus Station	15	D2
Ómnibus de México Bus Station	16	D2

still recovering from Hurricane Dean and the beach was undergoing a cleaning process, but it's still a chilled-out place to eat cheap seafood and take a break from the city. The hydroelectric plant in the backdrop takes away from the ambience, but the water and sand are fairly clean and – holidays and Sundays apart – it's usually empty. Local buses (M$8, 25 minutes) marked 'Playa' leave regularly from the south side of Blvd Reyes Heroles and drop you at the south end of the beach.

Aqua Sports (☎ 837-02-59; aquasportuxpan@yahoo.com.mx; Hwy Tuxpan–La Bara Km 8.5; 2 dives M$800-1300), around 8km from downtown going toward the beach, is an established scuba-diving operation with quality boats that offers dives on nearby reefs or Isla de Lobos, as well as **fishing trips** (M$1000 per hour). Visibility is best between May and August, and from January to March you can fish for giant tarpon. Camping on the island (with all provisions provided) can be arranged with advanced notice.

Festivals & Events
A big **fishing tournament** brings hundreds of visitors to Tuxpan in late June or early July.

Festivities for the **Assumption** (15 August) continue for a week with folk-dancing contests, bullfights and fireworks.

Sleeping
Hotels fill up quickly during holiday periods, but discounts may be available at other times. Not much of a hot spot on the tourist track, Tuxpan lacks top-end lodgings.

Hotel Posada San Ignacio (☎ 834-29-05; Ocampo 29 s/d M$200/300) This vibrantly decorated, quiet place is a fantastic deal. It's well done up, and the clean rooms surround a courtyard bursting with plants and color.

Posada del Sol (☎ 834-18-59; Guerrero s/n; s/d M$320/420; ✷) Attempts a peaceful hacienda feel but doesn't quite succeed. However, the rooms are clean enough and large with some pleasant details.

Hotel Riviera (☎ 834-53-49; Blvd Reyes Heroles 17; s/d M$420/460; P ✷) This renovated hotel has a good location on the river. Some of the generously sized, well-presented rooms enjoy partial river views. Accommodation in the front of the hotel is more attractive. Street noise can be an issue in some rooms.

CENTRAL GULF COAST

Hotel Florida (☎ 834-02-22; www.hotel-florida .com.mx; Juárez 23; s/d M$470/570; P ⊠ ☎) It's a cheaper, better choice than its neighbor Hotel Reforma. The Florida has friendly staff, spacious rooms with big windows and communal decks that look over bustling Calle Juárez.

Hotel Sara (☎ /fax 834-00-10; www.hotelsaratuxpan ver.com.mx; Garizurieta 44; s/d M$450/650; P ☎ ☎) This hotel is newer and an excellent deal, especially considering it offers discounts for cash. The tidy rooms are large and slick with marble tiling. The awesome rooftop pool with city and river views is a plus.

Hotel May Palace (☎ 834-88-81; Av Juárez 44; s/d M$615/725; P ⊠ ☎ ☎) Locals say this is the best place in town. Some of its immaculate, pleasant rooms have good river as well as zócalo views.

Eating

The zócalo is flanked by good restaurants. Furthermore, the palapas at Playa Norte are ideal for fresh mariscos and cold beers. Additional restaurants include:

El Estudiante (middle of zócalo; juices M$16) You can't get any more central than this. It serves fresh juices and huge fruit salads with granola and honey (M$25), which you can munch under shade umbrellas.

Sr Mante (☎ 834-57-36; Juárez 8; buffet M$80; mains M$45-100; ⏱ 6am-12am) Located on a busy street corner where you can people-watch, this locals' darling has tasty regional food and a buffet that scores for value.

Barra de Mariscos (☎ 834-46-01; Av Juárez 44; seafood M$50-110) An enjoyable, atmospheric place where freshness is valued; try the pulpo con salsa de ajo (octopus in garlic sauce) or camarones a la plancha (grilled shrimp).

Los Girasoles (☎ 834-03-92; cnr Blvd Heroles & Hernández y Hernández; mains M$60-120; ⏱ 12pm-12am) This place has a varied menu including Caesar salads, BBQ and pasta, and its wacky decorations include a cello, water skis and an antique gas pump. Live rock music at weekends.

ourpick Restaurant Atracadero (☎ 834-10-70; Blvd Heroles 35; mains M$60-200) This barge-turned-restaurant docked on the river is a fabulous splurge with its open-air, upscale ambience. Drink red wine while enjoying the house specialty: paella (M$250), which can feed three to four people and is made with all sorts of meat, mariscos and veggies.

Getting There & Around

Most 1st-class buses leaving Tuxpan are de paso (passing through). Booking a seat in advance might be a good idea. There are several bus terminals, but the ADO station (1st-class and deluxe) on Rodríguez is the most convenient from the center. Ómnibus de México (ODM; 1st class) is under the bridge on the north side of the river. The modern Estrella Blanca terminal, two blocks east of the bridge on Alemán, runs mainly 2nd-class services, but also has a few 1st-class buses. First-class departures:

Destination	Fare	Duration	Frequency
Matamoros	M$522	11hr	2 daily
Mexico City	M$380	4hr	1 daily
Mexico City (Terminal Norte)	M$230	6hr	hourly
Papantla	M$50	2hr	1
Poza Rica	M$20	1	hourly
Tampico	M$168	4hr	hourly
Veracruz	M$210	6 hr	hourly
Villahermosa	M$534	14hr	5
Xalapa	M$208	6hr	5

There are also half-hourly 2nd-class services to Poza Rica and Tampico, and several deluxe UNO services to Matamoros. Covered launches (M$3) ferry passengers across the river.

TAMIAHUA

Tamiahua, 43km north of Tuxpan by paved road, is at the southern end of Laguna de Tamiahua. During the local Carnaval the second week in May, Semana Santa and summer vacations, there can be a fair amount of Mexican tourists here. If you visit any other time, you'll be immersed in the warm culture of a small Mexican fishing town. You can rent boats from the docks for **fishing trips** (3 hours; M$400), excursions out to the lagoon's barrier island, or to get to the ocean and pretty **Playa Tamiahua**. Mexican tourists are known to camp on the beach. One of Tamiahua's handful of hotels is **Hotel Barrera** (☎ 768-857-01-64; Hidalgo 7; s/d M$300/400; ☎ P), which is well kept. The town has a few no-frills seafood restaurants, a delightful one being **Restaurant El Veracruzano** (Ruíz Cortines s/n; mains M$20-80; ⏱ breakfast, lunch, dinner) where Ruíz Cortines hits the river. Try the delectable corn empanadas (M$8) stuffed with seafood.

From Tuxpan, take a taxi (M$20) to the Crucero de Tamiahua (Tamiahua crossroads) where frequent 2nd-class buses (M$17) to Tamiahua pass.

POZA RICA
☎ 782 / pop 175,000

The modern industrial oil city of Poza Rica is at the junction of Hwy 180 and Hwy 130, and is a big transportation hub.

If you're stranded overnight, the **Best Western Hotel Poza Rica** (☎ 822-01-12; fax 823-20-32; www .bwpozarica.com; cnr Calles 2 Nte & 10 Ote; s/d M$830/900; P ✕ ⊠) is a good choice with helpful staff, modern amenities and a café–restaurant.

The main Poza Rica bus station, on Puebla east off Blvd Lázaro Cárdenas, has 2nd-class and some 1st-class buses. Second-class Transporte Papantla will take you to coastal towns. Most 1st-class buses leave from the adjoining ADO building, including the following departures:

Destination	Fare	Duration	Frequency
Mexico City (Terminal Norte)	M$192	5hr	hourly
Pachuca	M$128	5hr	at least 2 daily
Papantla	M$16	30min	20 daily
Tampico	M$200	4½hr	25 daily
Tuxpan	M$20	45min	30 daily
Veracruz	M$180	5hr	hourly

For El Tajín take any one of the frequent 2nd-class buses to Coyutla, El Chote, Agua Dulce or San Andrés (M$15) from the main bus station. These pass the turnoff marked 'Desviación El Tajín' and will drop you off. The ruins are 300m from the highway.

The scenic 200km Poza Rica–Pachuca road, Hwy 130, is the direct approach to Mexico City from northern Veracruz. This winding, misty route climbs up to the Sierra Madre, across the semitropical north of Puebla state and into Hidalgo on the way to Pachuca, passing through many Nahua and Totonac towns.

PAPANTLA
☎ 784 / pop 48,000 / elevation 196m

Spread over a hillside, Papantla is a friendly, commerce-oriented town that has a couple of intriguing things for a visitor beyond its traditional role of housing El Tajín–bound tourists. As the center of a vanilla-growing region, markets and shops offer vanilla-based artisan products, and the city also has beautiful murals. Don't be surprised to see Totonacs wearing traditional clothing here – the men in loose white shirts and trousers, women in embroidered blouses and *quechquémitls* (traditional capes).

Orientation & Information
Papantla lies just off Hwy 180, which runs southeast from Poza Rica. The center of town is uphill from the main road. From the *zócalo* downhill is north.

The plaza is 1.5km south of the ADO bus station; turn left out of the terminal, then take the first right into Av Carranza, then left up 20 de Noviembre, past the Transportes Papantla bus terminal and market to the *zócalo*. The ramshackle **tourist office** (☎ 842-38-37; 1st fl, Azueta 101) is just off the northwest corner of the *zócalo*. You'll find two banks with ATMs on Enríquez just east of the *zócalo*, and **Internet** (☎ 842-62-05; 20 de Noviembre 1; ☼ 9am-10pm; per hr M$8) has – big surprise – internet services. The post office is four blocks northwest of the plaza.

Sights
Officially called Parque Téllez, the **zócalo** is terraced into the hillside below the **Iglesia de la Asunción**. Beneath this Franciscan cathedral a 50m-long **mural** (see boxed text, opposite) facing the square depicts Totonac and Veracruz history. A serpent stretches along the mural, bizarrely linking a pre-Hispanic stone carver, El Tajín's Pirámide de los Nichos and an oil rig.

At the top of the hill towers Papantla's **volador monument** (see p673 for information on *voladores* rites). This 1988 statue portrays a musician playing his pipe, preparing for the four fliers to launch. To reach the monument, take the street heading uphill from the southwest corner of the cathedral yard; at the end of the road hang a left.

The **Casa de la Cultura** (16 de Septiembre s/n; ☼ 10am-2pm Mon-Sat) houses art classes and a display of local art work on the top floor. If you're lucky, you'll run into Maestro Teodoro Cano painting. In the workings is the **Museo de la Ciudad Teodoro Cano**, which will have art, Totonac artifacts and an exhibit on Papantla's history. It will replace the recently closed Museo de La Ciudad.

Guide **Gaudencio Simbrón** (☎ 842-01-21; puxko _hermano_mayor@yahoo.com.mx; M$300-400/day) is more commonly known as *el de la ropa típica* (the guy who wears traditional clothes) because he sports Totonac costume. He works through

---

TEODORO CANO: PAPANTLA'S VOICE OF ART

In the late 1940s imagine how enthralled the tiny *pueblo* of Papantla was to have Diego Rivera waltz into the town square. Rivera was in the region visiting El Tajín, the subject of his next mural for the National Palace. A village boy no more than eight years old caught Rivera's attention. Little Teodoro Cano frankly told the famous man that he painted himself. Taken with Cano, Rivera promised the boy that he would help him become a painter. And that he did. When Cano was a teenager he lived in Diego's house in Mexico City for several months cleaning his studio, after which he was sent to Mexico City's famous Academia de San Carlos, where he studied fine arts for five years and was selected 'Best Art Student.'

Subsequently, Cano's life took many paths: he lived as a struggling yet successful artist, painted cars and eventually took the position of Director of Art at the University of Veracruz in Xalapa. Now retired in his hometown of Papantla, he hardly seems retired. Cano gives his time, energy and resources to the Casa de la Cultura where there are exhibitions and art classes. His murals, some of which you can see displayed at El Tajín and near Papantla's plaza, characteristically address Totonac culture and its clash with contemporary society as well as the disconnection between the natural world and modern industry.

Having a modest, contented demeanor, he educates through his art and endears himself to Papantla. It was first a vivacious hotel clerk and then later a young taxi driver who reverently pointed me toward Maestro Cano. He's known to drop what he's doing to explain the history of the region and discuss the dying Totonac culture. Right now he's working on the city's new museum, Museo de la Ciudad Teodoro Cano.

Hotel Tajín and will guide you through El Tajín – where he grew up. He can also show you some of the area's overlooked attractions like the small **nature reserve** at Talpan, a **vanilla plantation** and little-visited **archeological sites**.

Festivals & Events
The fantastic **Feria de Corpus Christi**, in late May and early June, is the big annual event. As well as the bullfights, parades and *charreadas* that are usual in Mexico, Papantla celebrates its Totonac cultural heritage with spectacular indigenous dances. The main procession is on the first Sunday when *voladores* fly two or three times a day.

Papantla's other major celebration is the **Festival de Vainilla** (Vanilla Festival) on June 18, featuring indigenous dancers, gastronomic delights sold in street stalls and vanilla products galore.

Sleeping
Papantla has a fairly limited selection of hotels.

Hotel Pulido (☎ 842-10-79; Enríquez 205; s/d M$180/280, plus M$50 w/air; ⓟ ⌧) A basic but acceptable place 250m east of the *zócalo*. The fan-only rooms are a fair budget deal.

Hotel Familiar La Pasadita (☎ 842-56-73; Obispo de las Casas 102; s/d M$300/400; ⌧ ⓟ) Even though the newish Pasadita has updated furnishings,

fresh tiling and spacious accommodations near the city center, it remains in the shadow of the old-guard, *zócalo* hotel strongholds. Opt for the window rooms and check for smoke factor.

Hotel Totonacapán (☎ 842-12-20; cnr 20 de Noviembre & Olivo; s/d M$350/400; ⌧) About 400m downhill from the *zócalo*, this hotel is pleasant enough and clean enough. Some rooms have balconies, and there's a convenient restaurant downstairs.

Hotel Provincia Express (☎ 842-16-45; hotprovi@ prodigy.net.mx; Enríquez 103; s/d M$370/480; ⌧ ⌨) Shares a prime location with Hotel Tajín and an interior knocking on dilapidation's door, though it can boast fantastic staff and internet access.

Hotel Tajín (☎ 842-01-21; fax 842-10-74; Núñez 104; s/d M$530/620; ⓟ ⌧) It has a prime location on the *zócalo* and a nice communal balcony looking over the city, but the interior is dated.

Eating
You'll find no shortage of the usual delicious Mexican food in Papantla.

Restaurant Totonaca (Hotel Tajín, Núñez 104; ⏱ 8am-10pm; mains M$40-140) This hotel bar–restaurant aims for semi-formal and has an extensive menu. There's also a short wine list (M$80 to M$100), and it serves cocktails made with locally produced vanilla extract.

La Hacienda (☎ 842-06-33; Reforma 100 Altos; mains M$30-100) Offers a slightly cheaper menu and a different perspective of the *zócalo* from its rival, the Pardo. There are the usual Mexican suspects, and good *mariscos*.

Plaza Pardo (☎ 842-00-59; 1st fl, Enríquez 105; M$35-130) Eating enchiladas with a cold beer at a balcony table over the *zócalo* is the best way to enjoy a dying afternoon in Papantla. It has steaks (M$130) for the carnivorously inclined.

Mercado Juárez, at the southwest corner of the plaza opposite the cathedral, has stalls that sell regional food cheap and fresh.

Shopping
As Mexico's leading vanilla-growing center, you'll find quality vanilla extract, vanilla pods and *figuras* (pods woven into the shapes of flowers, insects or crucifixes) in Papantla's Mercado Hidalgo, at the northwest corner of the *zócalo*. Try the regional vanilla liquor or vanilla-infused cigarettes. You'll also encounter traditional Totonac clothing and handmade baskets.

Getting There & Away
Few long-distance buses stop at Papantla's quaint station. Most are *de paso*, but you can make reservations at Ticket Bus just east of the plaza. Or go to Poza Rica to get one of the more frequent buses from there. ADO is the only 1st-class line serving Papantla; 2nd-class Transportes Papantla (TP), which serves the coastal towns to the south, leaves from a separate terminal near the plaza. The following are 1st-class services:

Destination	Fare	Duration	Frequency (daily)
Mexico City (Terminal Norte)	M$280	6hr	6
Poza Rica	M$16	½hr	26
Tampico	M$220	5½hr	6
Tuxpan	M$50	2hr	7
Veracruz	M$150	3½hr	7
Xalapa	M$162	4hr	11

There are also 2nd-class TP services to Poza Rica (every 15 minutes) and Tuxpan (four daily).

EL TAJÍN
Situated on a plain surrounded by low verdant hills 6km west of Papantla, the extensive ruins of El Tajín are the most impressive reminder of Classic Veracruz civilization. The name Tajín is Totonac for 'thunder,' 'lightning' or 'hurricane.'

The years AD 600 to 900 saw its zenith as a town and ceremonial center. Around AD 1200 the site was abandoned, possibly after attacks by Chichimecs, and lay unknown to the Spaniards until about 1785.

Among El Tajín's special features are rows of square niches on the sides of buildings, numerous ball courts, and sculptures depicting human sacrifice connected with the ball game. Archaeologist José García Payón believed that El Tajín's niches and stone mosaics symbolized day and night, light and dark, and life and death in a universe composed of dualities, though many are skeptical of this interpretation.

Orientation & Information
The **El Tajín site** (admission M$45; ☽ 9am-5pm) covers an area of about 10 sq km. To see everything, you'll walk a few kilometers over a couple of hours. There's little shade and it can get blazingly hot, so an early start is recommended. Most buildings and carvings here are labeled in English and Spanish, and some have information panels in German and French as well.

Bordering the parking lot are stalls selling food and handicrafts. The visitor center has a restaurant, left-luggage room, information desk, museum and souvenir shops. Those seeking more information should look for the book *Tajín: Mystery and Beauty*, by Leonardo Zaleta, sometimes available in several languages in the souvenir shops. Guide service is available for M$200 per hour with one to six people.

Sights
PLAZA MENOR
Beyond the Plaza del Arroyo, flanked by pyramids on four sides, is the **Plaza Menor** (Lesser Plaza), part of El Tajín's main ceremonial center and possible marketplace, with a low platform in the middle. All of the structures around this plaza were probably topped by small temples, some decorated with red or blue paint – traces of which remain.

JUEGO DE PELOTA SUR
Some 17 ball courts have been found at El Tajín. The **Juego de Pelota Sur** (Southern Ball

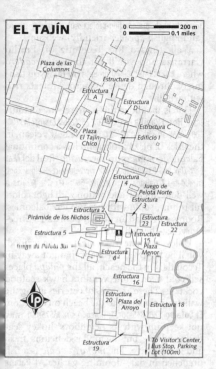

EL TAJÍN

Plaza de las Columnas

Estructura B

Estructura A

Estructura D

Estructura C

Plaza El Tajín Chico

Edificio I

Estructura 4

Juego de Pelota Norte

Estructura 3

Estructura 2

Pirámide de los Nichos

Estructura 23

Estructura 22

Estructura 5

Estructura

Juego de Pelota Sur

Plaza Menor

Estructura 6

Estructura 16

Estructura 20 Plaza del Arroyo

Estructura 18

Estructura 19

To Visitor's Center, Bus Stop, Parking Lot (100m)

Court), which is smaller and older than the southern court and bears fainter carvings on its sides.

Many of the buildings here have geometric stone mosaic patterns known as 'Greco' (Greek). **Edificio I**, probably once a palace, has some terrific carvings. **Estructura C**, on the east side, with three levels and a staircase facing the plaza, was initially painted blue. **Estructura A**, on the plaza's north side, has an arch construction known as a corbeled arch, with two sides jutting closer to each other until they are joined at the top by a single slab, which is typical of Maya architecture. Its presence here is yet another oddity in the jigsaw puzzle of pre-Hispanic cultures.

Northwest of Plaza El Tajín Chico is the unreconstructed **Plaza de las Columnas** (Plaza of the Columns), one of the site's most important structures. It originally housed a large open patio and adjoining buildings stretching over the hillside. Some wonderful carved reassembled columns are displayed in the museum.

VOLADORES PERFORMANCES

The Totonac *voladores* rite (traditionally carried out only once a year, but now performed almost daily for visitors) looks something like a slow-motion bungee jump from the top of a vertiginously tall pole. The rite begins with five men in elaborate ceremonial clothing climbing to the top of the pole. Four of them sit on the edges of a small frame at the top and rotate the frame to twist the ropes around the pole. The fifth man dances on the platform above them while playing a *chirimía*, a small drum with a flute attached. When he stops playing, the others fall backward. Arms outstretched, they revolve gracefully around the pole and descend to the ground, upside down, as their ropes unwind.

One interpretation of the ceremony is that it's a fertility rite and the fliers make invocations to the four corners of the universe. It's also noted that each flier circles the pole 13 times, giving a total of 52 revolutions. The number 52 is not only the number of weeks in the modern year but also was an important number in pre-Hispanic Mexico, which had two calendars, one corresponding to the 365-day solar year, the other to a ritual year of 260 days. The calendars coincided every 52 solar years.

Totonacs carry out the *voladores* rite three times per day beside the visitor center. Before

Court), dates from about 1150 and is the most famous of the courts, owing to the six relief carvings on its walls depicting various aspects of the ball-game ritual.

The panel on the northeast corner is the easiest to make out: in the center, three ballplayers perform a ritual post-game sacrifice with one player ready to plunge a knife into the chest of another, whose arms are held by the third. Death gods and a presiding figure look on. The other panels depict various ceremonial, pulque drinking (p684) scenes.

PIRÁMIDE DE LOS NICHOS

El Tajín's most emblematic structure, the beautifully proportioned Pyramid of the Niches, is just off the Plaza Menor. The six lower levels, each surrounded by rows of small square niches, climb to 18m. Archaeologists believe that there were originally 365 niches, suggesting that the building may have been used as a kind of calendar.

EL TAJÍN CHICO

The path north toward Plaza El Tajín Chico passes the **Juego de Pelota Norte** (Northern Ball

they start, a costumed performer requests donations (M$20) from the audience.

Getting There & Away

Frequent buses come from Poza Rica. From Papantla, buses (M$8) marked 'Pirámides Tajín' leave from opposite the Pemex station at the lower end of 20 de Noviembre. The site is 300m from the highway – buses drop you off near the market, before the entrance to Tajín.

SOUTH OF PAPANTLA

Hwy 180 runs near the coast for most of the 230km from Papantla to Veracruz. Though currents can be strong on this stretch of coast, visiting gives you the chance to check out an awesome turtle conservation project, the sparkling Emerald Coast and Quiahuiztlán, a stunning, out-of-the-way Totonac site. The area is bereft of tourists during the low seasons.

Tecolutla

☎ 766 / pop 3900

This seaside town with pleasant beaches is a popular destination for middle-class Mexican families. The place is dead midweek when it's not a holiday. However, during holiday seasons and Semana Santa, the place is teeming with people and prices can quadruple. There are banks and ATMs on the plaza.

Probably the coolest thing happening here is the **Grupo Ecologista Vida Milenaria** (☎ 846-04-67; www.vidamilenaria.org.mx; donation required; ☉ 9am-dusk). This small turtle conservation center is run by Fernando Manzano Cervantes who is a sweetie-pie of a man, known locally as 'Papá Tortuga.' In addition to educating the public, he has been effectively protecting and releasing green and Kemp's ridley turtles here for over 33 years. Visitors are welcome to look at the hatchlings. If you stop by, think about buying a trinket souvenir because this is a privately funded show. **Volunteers** are especially needed here in April and May, when patrolling the beaches and collecting the turtle eggs is imperative. Camping and the use of kitchen and bathroom facilities are free to volunteers. In late October, you can join hundreds of locals in celebrating the releasing of the baby turtles in the **Festival de Las Tortugas**. A source of information on Tecolutla-based turtle-preservation efforts is the **Tecolutla Turtle Preservation Project** (www

.tecolutla-turtle-preservation-project.org), with a good (and English-speaker-friendly) website.

Walk toward Río Tecolutla on Emilio Carranza and you'll hit the *embarcadero* where **boats** (M$300-400/group) will take you fishing or through dense mangrove forests rich with wildlife.

Hotels abound in this town relying on tourism. **Hotel Vanilla** (☎ 846-02-75; Carranza s/n; r M$200-300 plus M$50 with air; P ✗) is a deal. It's clean, in the thick of plaza action and has a communal balcony looking onto the *zócalo*. **Real del Mar** (☎/fax 846-03-80/846-01-00; www.hotelrealdelmar.com; cnr Aldama & Galeana; from M$580-680; P ✗ ☎) is a well-done, higher-end option with light colorful rooms, some with ocean view balconies. Rooms surround an indoor pool and a three-story, sea-themed mural.

Unless you hate fresh, inexpensive seafood, you'll be happy as the clam that got away in Tecolutla. On the beach, all the *palapa* places sell cold beer, while vendors hawk seafood cocktails. There are tons of eateries along the walk from the plaza to the beach on Obregón. **El Cotarro** (☎ 845-16-71; Obregón s/n; M$25-80) may not keep up with its neighbors' hokey sea-themed décor, but the food is delicious, fresh and inexpensive. The *mojarra al ajo* is a fish drenched in date-dooming garlic. At **Palapa 'El Girosal'** on the beach near the turtle preservation project, you can drink cocktails (M$40) and eat yummy seafood plates (M$80) under *palapas*.

Tecolutla is 41km east of Papantla. There are regular 2nd-class Transportes Papantla buses between Tecolutla and Papantla (M$33). Most 1st-class buses run from Gutiérrez Zamora, but there's an ADO office in Tecolutla a block from the beach, where you can book your ticket in advance. From Tecolutla, ADO offers service to Mexico City's Terminal Norte (M$224), Puebla (M$214) and Pachuca (M$158), as well as frequent service to Poza Rica (M$42) and Papantla (M$35).

Costa Esmeralda

The Emerald Coast's waters – more accurately described as semi-precious – are various shades of azure, though not crystalline, and its waves crash on 20km of grayish-blond beaches. It's a raging summer and holiday spot. The rest of the year, especially midweek, it's tranquilly yours and is a lovely match for the beach-lovers and crowd-haters. You can throw down cash for upscale digs or do it on the cheap. Advertised and unadvertised campgrounds proliferate.

Approaching Casitas from the north, you'll hit Cabo Alto Hotel and Spa, which houses **Spa Xochicalli** (☎ 321-02-59; Hwy 180; massages from M$480). Its good facilities have an extensive list of services if you want some beach hiatus TLC. A bit further south, you'll hit **Hotel Misión del Mar** (☎ 321-08-00; Hwy 180 Km 87, Costa Esmeralda; hotelmisiondelmar@yahoo.com.mx; campsites/s/d M$100/850/1110; P 🌐 🛒 🏊). Just off the beach, its rooms are well equipped and many look onto a courtyard thick with plants. But the *palapa*-ed campgrounds are the deal here, with access to showers, bathrooms, three pools and cafeteria.

At the north end of Casitas is **Hotel Miramar** (☎ 321-03-70; miramarcasitas@yahoo.com.mx; Hwy 100 Km 90 Casitas, s/d M$200/250, plus M$50 w/air), which is good for a budget beach hurrah. The rooms, though unexceptional, are clean and a block from a pleasant beach. Also, the cheap, tasty eats that abound in grubby little Casitas make a better alternative to being stuck at an expensive hotel restaurant away from town.

At the mouth of the Río Filobobos (known as Río Bobos and famous for its rapids), head southwest of Nautla on Hwy 131 and you'll hit **Tlapacoyan** where a handful of rafting companies are based and where the waterfall Cascada de Encanto provides a gorgeous swimming spot. **Aventura Extrema** (☎ 229-178-38-12; www.aventuraextrema.com.mx; rafting packages from M$670) has facilities near Tlapacoyan and offers one- to three-day packages including food, accommodation or camping, and various other adventure activities. A highlight of Bobos rafting is the two riverside archaeological sites, Caujilote and Vega de la Peña, which most companies stop to visit. **Hotel Oliver** (☎ 225-315-07-04; www.hospedajetlapacoyan.tk.com.mx; Cuauhtémoc 400; s/d M$250/380; P 🌐) is an adorable place to stay right off the plaza in Tlapacoyan. Buses (M$42) from Nautla go to Tlapacoyan.

Five kilometers south of Nautla is **Hotel Istirinchá** (☎ 317-42-01; www.hotelistirincha.com; Hwy 180 Km 102; s/d M$800/900; P 🌐 🛒). For a fair price, you can stay in this new hotel's spacious, freshly decorated rooms with ocean-view decks. It arranges kayaking in its lagoon, interpretive walks and horseback riding. The owner is working to restore this once deforested chunk of land to its natural habitat. An on-hand biologist cares for the grounds and its creatures in captivity, such as crocodiles

and toucans. You'll see signs at the entrance on the highway. It's about a 20-minute walk to the hotel from where the bus leaves you.

To get to any coastal location, take a non-direct bus on Hwy 180 and tell the driver where you want to stop.

South of Laguna Verde

Mexico's sole nuclear power station, operating since 1989, is on **Laguna Verde**, about 80km north of Veracruz port on Hwy 180. Government plans for more reactors have been scrapped in the face of public protest. Current reports by Greenpeace (for updates see www.greenpeace.org) and a highly critical 2005 investigation by WANO (the World Association of Nuclear Operators) have highlighted numerous safety concerns, i.e. there's no solid evacuation plan for the local communities.

EcoGuías La Mancha (☎ 296-100-11-63; www.ecoturismolamancha.com; La Mancha–Acotpan; campsites/cabañas M$50/120) is a progressive association of locals who have developed a homespun, grass-roots environment education center. With their facilities a kilometer from the beach, they offer interpretive walks, birding excursions, apiary tours, horseback riding and kayak tours where you can see mangroves and wildlife. Accommodations are rustic, but it's a great off-the-beaten-path choice that supports the local community. From the La Mancha eastbound turnoff on Hwy 180, it's a kilometer down the road. Bring repellent.

Villa Rica, a small fishing village 69km north of Veracruz, is the probable site of the first Spanish settlement in Mexico. You can explore traces of a fort and a church on the Cerro de la Cantera or bask on a lovely beach.

Nearby are the Totonac tombs of **Quiahuiztlán** (🕑 8:30am-5pm; admission M$27). You'd want to be buried here too. This pre-Hispanic cemetery is situated on verdant foothill with a sweeping vista of the coast and is guarded by a towering rocky outcrop, locally known as Cerro los Metates. The site has two pyramids, more than 70 tombs (each resembling a small temple) and some carved monuments. It's a gorgeous, 25-minute walk to the part that overlooks the ocean. Plus, you can experience this sacred Totonac site in solitude and nature, as opposed to other touristed ruins. If you want to arrive by a Hwy 180 bus, have the driver drop you at Quiahuiztlán. From there it's a pretty three-kilometer walk uphill.

CENTRAL GULF COAST

TOP OFF-THE-BEATEN-TRACK ADVENTURES

▪ Caving in **Aquismón** (p664)

▪ Biking the route of Hernán Cortés from Veracruz, where Cortés landed, to Mexico City with **Veracruz en Bicicleta** (p680) – you can just ride sections if you don't want to attempt the whole thing

▪ Climbing **Volcán San Martín** (p704)

▪ Hiking, drinking fabulous coffee and doing yoga at **Ashram Coatepec** (p683) near Coatepec

▪ Rafting and kayaking in **Jalcomulco** (p684)

▪ Contemplating ruins and sweeping views of **Quiahuiztlán** (p675)

CENTRAL VERACRUZ STATE

Curvy Hwy 180 follows the coast past dark-sand beaches (toward Veracruz) to Cardel where Hwy 140 branches west to Xalapa, the state capital. Charming mountain towns sprinkle the inland volcanic ranges laced with dramatic river gorges. From Veracruz, Hwy 150D heads southwest to Córdoba, Fortín de las Flores and Orizaba, on the edge of the Sierra Madre.

CENTRAL COAST

North of the city of Veracruz, the beaches are a popular Mexican vacation spot, and the area also boasts the impressive Zempoala ruins.

Zempoala

☎ 296 / pop 9500

The pre-Hispanic Totonac town of Zempoala (or 'Cempoala') stands 42km north of Veracruz and 4km west of Hwy 180 in modern Zempoala. The turn-off is by a Pemex station 7km north of Cardel. *Voladores* performances are enacted several times daily. Zempoala is most easily reached through Cardel – take a bus marked 'Zempoala' (M$12) from the Cardel bus station, or a taxi (M$70).

HISTORY

Zempoala became a major Totonac center after about AD 1200 and fell to the Aztecs in the mid-15th century. The 30,000-person town boasted defensive walls, underground water and drainage pipes. As Hernán Cortés approached the town, one of his scouts reported that the buildings were made of silver – but it was only white paint shining in the sun.

Zempoala's chief struck an alliance with Cortés for protection against the Aztecs. But his hospitality didn't stop the Spanish from smashing his gods' statues and lecturing his people on the virtues of Christianity. It was at Zempoala in 1520 that Cortés defeated the expedition sent by Cuba's Spanish governor to arrest him.

By the 17th century Zempoala, devastated by disease, was reduced to just eight families. The town was eventually abandoned. The present town dates from 1832.

SIGHTS

The **archaeological site** (admission M$35; ⏲ 9am-5:30pm) is lush with a lovely mountain backdrop. Though not as monumental as El Tajín, it's still astounding. Most of the buildings are faced with smooth, rounded, riverbed stones, but many were originally plastered and painted. A typical feature is battlement-like 'teeth' called *almenas*.

The **Templo Mayor** (Main Temple) is an 11m-high pyramid with a wide staircase ascending to the remains of a shrine. When they first encountered Zempoala, the Cortés and his men lodged in **Las Chimeneas** whose hollow columns were thought to be chimneys – hence the name. There are two main structures on the west side. One is known as the **Templo del Sol** with two stairways climbing its front side in typical Toltec–Aztec style. To its north is the **Templo de la Luna** whose structure is similar to Aztec temples to the wind god Ehecatl.

East of Las Chimeneas is **Las Caritas** (Little Heads), named for niches that once held several small pottery heads. Another large wind-god temple, known as the **Templo Dios del Aire**, is in the town itself – go back south on the site entrance road, cross the main road in town and then go around the corner to the right. The ancient temple, with its characteristic circular shape, is beside an intersection.

The small site **museum** has some interesting clay figurines, polychrome plates and obsidian flints.

Chachalacas

☎ 296 / pop 2000

Ten kilometers northeast of Cardel, this popular, functional beach town has miles of pleasant uncrowded gray sand beaches in either direction. However, Mexican vacation times are chaotic. If you follow the beach to the north for 2km there are some towering sand dunes.

Campgrounds are advertised as you walk the beachside strip where you'll find mostly budget to midrange hotels. The well-run, family-owned **Hotel Quinta Paquita** (☎ 962-60-32; guillermom24@msn.com; Sáenz de la Peña 33; s/d M$300/350; P ✕ ✦) is a clean, bright, economical choice right by the ocean. **Punta Real** (☎ 962-57-98; www.puntareal.com.mx; cnr Sáenz de la Peña & Condor; r from M$1100; P ✕ ✦ ✦) is an upscale option on the less peopled north part of the beach. It has all the amenities you could want plus a spa and deliciously comfy beds.

There is a cluster of seafood *palapas* by the water. Head to **Restaurant Bar Concha Dorada** (☎ 962-59-66; Paseo de las Aves; from M$35) and try its *filete relleno*, a filet of fish stuffed with savory *mariscos*.

Cardel

☎ 296 / pop 18,500

Cardel (or José Cardel) is a lively transit hub. The bus terminal, banks, restaurants and internet cafés are scattered around the plaza. You'll find comfortable accommodations at **Hotel Cardel** (☎ 962-00-14; Emiliano Zapata & Dr J Martínez; s/d M$240/400 with air M$340/450; P ✕).

From the Veracruz bus station, regular 1st-class ADO buses to Cardel cost M$34; frequent 2nd-class AU buses cost M$28. The last bus back to Veracruz from Cardel is at 11:30pm.

La Antigua

☎ 296 / pop 900

Two kilometers east from Hwy 180 and 23km north of Veracruz, this once-busy commercial center is now a dozy little town that rises only from its languor during holidays. However, it's an interesting place to spend an afternoon.

A Spanish settlement was established here in 1525, and it's rumored that this is where conquistador Cortés hid boats from his crew to eliminate thoughts of returning to Spain. The picturesque ruined building you see here is a 16th-century **custom house** (commonly called the 'Casa de Cortés'). The **Ermita del Rosario church**, probably dating from 1523, is one of the oldest in the Americas. The village also boasts an impressively gigantic ceiba tree.

Accommodations are available near the river at **Hotel La Malinche** (s/d M$150/250; P ✕). Along the river there is a cluster of seafood restaurants; at the end of the row is **Restaurant María Felix** (☎ 971-61-09; Emiliano Zapata 1; mains M$35-100) where you can soak up the tranquility at a riverside table and sop up a fish dish with handmade tortillas.

Lancheros will motor you along the pleasant Río Antigua for around M$50 per person. *Colectivo* taxis charge M$6 to M$8 from the village to the highway.

XALAPA

☎ 228 / pop 426,000 / elevation 1427m

In the verdant skirts of stunning Cofre de Perote, this urbane, culturally vibrant state capital possesses trendy, if not cosmopolitan, inclinations. Xalapa – which is sometimes spelled 'Jalapa' but always pronounced 'ha-la-pa' – balances out traffic problems with gorgeous nature parks and well-designed, enjoyable public spaces. The city's superb anthropological museum is definitely a highlight. Xalapa's temperate climate can be refreshing – drizzly, chilly days are common in winter. Take patchouli-lovin' refuge next to university students in the slew of hip bars and coffeehouses. At least a couple of days are needed if you really want to get know the city.

History

Xalapa was part of the Aztec empire when Hernán Cortés and his men passed through in 1519. Because of its appealing climate and location, Spain strategically placed a monastery here to proselytize the indigenous population. By the 17th century it had evolved into a commercial axis and meeting hub. Today Xalapa is still a commercial center for coffee, tobacco and flowers.

Orientation

The city center is on a hillside; uphill is north. The plaza, Parque Juárez, is central and Xalapa's cathedral is on Enríquez, just east of the plaza. Much of the city's action lines traffic-saturated Av Camacho west of

XALAPA

0   400 m
0   0.2 miles

INFORMATION
Banamex	1 C2
Bancomer	2 B2
Banorte	3 A2
El Sarcofago	4 A3
Lavandería 'Las 4 Estaciones'	5 D2
Login	6 C2
Post Office	7 D2
Santander Serfin	8 B2

Telecomm	9 D2
Tourist Information Booth	10 A2

SIGHTS & ACTIVITIES
Cathedral	11 B2
Centro Cultural Los Lagos	12 A4
Escuela para Estudiantes Extranjeros	13 D2
Palacio de Gobierno	14 B2
Palacio Municipal	(see 10)
Pinacoteca Diego Rivera	15 A3
Tranvías	16 B2
Veraventuras	17 D2

SLEEPING
Hostal de la Niebla	18 C2
Hotel Limón	19 B2
Hotel México	20 B2
Maria de San Francisco Posada	21 A1
Posada del Cafeto	22 C3
Posada La Mariquinta	23 C1

EATING
Churrería	(see 21)
Jugos California	24 B2
La Fonda	25 B2
La Hoja Santa	26 C2

DRINKING
Angelo Casa de Té	27 C2
Convivio	28 D2
Italian Coffee Company	29 A3
La Chiva	30 C2

ENTERTAINMENT
El Ágora	31 A3
Tierra Luna	32 D2

SHOPPING
Libélula	(see 32)
Popularte	33 C2

TRANSPORT
Bus to Museo de Antrolpología	(see 3)

the center. CAXA, the bus station, is 2km east of the city center.

Information

BOOKSTORES
Libros y Arte Conaculta (☎ 840-87-43; Museo de Antropología, Av Xalapa s/n; ⏰ 9am-5pm Tue-Sun) Inside the Museo de Antropología, this library offers a wide selection of books about art, architecture and history, including English-language titles

INTERNET ACCESS
El Sarcofugo (Allende 35; per hr M$12) Open late.
Login (Zamora 48; per hr M$10)

INTERNET RESOURCES
Turisteando (www.turisteandoxalapa.com)

Xalapa Tourist Network (www.xalapa.net)

LAUNDRY
Lavandería 'Las 4 Estaciones' (☎ 841-05-99; Pino Suárez 59; M$17 per kg)

MEDIA
Performance Free magazine devoted to the cultural scene.

MEDICAL SERVICES
Centro de Especialidades Médicas (☎ 814-46-24; Ruiz Cortines s/n; ⏰ 8am-6pm) Excellent medical care.

MONEY
There are banks with 24-hour ATMs along Enríquez–Gutiérrez Zamora.

POST
Post office (cnr Gutiérrez Zamora & Diego Leño)

TELEPHONE & FAX
Telecomm (cnr Gutiérrez Zamora & Diego Leño) Next to the post office; it has Western Union services.

TOURIST INFORMATION
Information Booth (☎ 842-12-00, ext 3025; Palacio Municipal; ⏰ 9am-3pm & 4-7pm Mon-Fri) Next to the Palacio Municipal, this booth has some helpful information and maps.

Sights
MUSEO DE ANTROPOLOGÍA
Veracruz University's remarkable **anthropology museum** (☎ 815-09-20; Av Xalapa s/n; M$45; audio-guide M$20; ⏰ 9am-5pm Tue-Sun) is devoted to the archaeology of the state and is one of Mexico's best museums. Its large collection includes seven huge Olmec heads and 29,000 other superb artifacts.

All exhibits are labeled in Spanish, but laminated English information sheets are in many rooms. As there's so much to see, allow yourself a good chunk of time to visit. There's a small café on the upper floor, and an excellent bookstore.

Several spaces concentrate on the Olmec culture from southern Veracruz including the most celebrated piece, **El Señor de Las Limas**. There's also an array of fine work associated with the pre-Hispanic ball game.

The museum is set in spacious gardens on the west side of Av Xalapa, 4km northwest of the city center. To get there take a 'Camcho-Tesorería' (M$5) from Enríquez. To return, take a bus marked 'Centro.' A taxi costs M$20.

CITY CENTER
The centrally located **Parque Juárez** feels like a terrace, with its south side overlooking the valley below and the snowcapped mountains in the distance. Tucked beneath the west side of the plaza, the **Pinacoteca Diego Rivera** (☎ 818-18-19; Herrera 5; admission free; ⏰ 10am-6pm Tue-Sat) houses a modest collection of Rivera's works, as well as pieces from other Mexican artists.

On the plaza's north side is the **Palacio Municipal** and on the east side is the **Palacio de Gobierno**, the seat of Veracruz' state government. The Palacio de Gobierno has a fine mural depicting the history of justice

above the stairway near the eastern entrance on Enríquez.

Facing the Palacio de Gobierno across Enríquez is the unfinished **cathedral** (started in 1772), from where Dr Lucio leads up to the busy market zone and crosses a deep valley via the **Puente Xallitic**, a high, arched bridge with a pretty public space below.

GALERÍA DE ARTE CONTEMPORÁNEO
The town's contemporary art **gallery** (☎ 818-04-12; Xalapeños Ilustres 135; admission free; ⏰ 10am-7pm Tue-Sun) is in a renovated colonial building 1km east of the city center showing worthwhile, sometimes edgy, temporary exhibitions. There's a small movie theatre here that shows artsy films, mostly for free.

MUSEO DEL BOMBERO
Devoted to firefighters and firefighting, this **museum** (☎ 890-22-85; Ortíz 5; admission free; ⏰ 9am-2pm & 4-8pm) exhibits an 1885 English horse-drawn firemen's carriage and plenty of information on the history of firefighting from its origins in ancient Egypt. It's 3km from Parque Juárez.

PARKS
Just south of Parque Juárez is **Parque Paseo de los Lagos** with 3km of delightful lakeside paths (most commonly used for jogging and making out). At its northern end is the **Centro Cultural Los Lagos** (☎ 812-12-99; Paseo los Lagos s/n), a lovely cultural center where you check out the bulletin board to find out about drop-in dance or yoga classes among other cultural event announcements.

Atop a hill north of the city, **Parque Ecológico Macuiltépetl** is actually the heavily wooded cap of an extinct volcano. Spiraling to the top, the park's paths are a treasure for joggers, and provide expansive views of Xalapa and the surrounding area. Waiting at the summit, the small **Museo de la Fauna** (admission M$10; ⏰ 10am-5:30pm Tue-Fri) has some shamefully tethered eagles, snakes and other reptiles. **Parque de los Tecajetes** (Avila Camacho s/n; ⏰ 6am-6pm) is another awesome nature park where you'll forget you're in the city. It's a kilometer from the center on Camacho.

Southwest of the town center the attractive **Jardín Botánico Clavijero** (☎ 842-18-27; Antigua Carr a Coatepec Km 2.5; admission free; ⏰ 9am-5pm) has a nice collection of subtropical and cloud forest plants.

Activities

Veraventuras (☎ 818-95-79, 800-712-65-72; www.vera venturas.com.mx; Santos Degollado 81; trips from M$480) offers rafting excursions and trips to El Carrizal's hot springs (p682).

Local birding guide **Robert Straub** (☎ 818-18-94; tours M$300-750) and member of **COAX** (www .coaxxalapa.org), a conservation-minded birding club. He offers tours in the area. Straub authored a birding guide to Veracruz, *Guía de Sitios*, whose proceeds go to Pronatura, a conservation non-profit.

If you come with your own bike and equipment, **Veracruz en Bicicleta** (☎ 126-10-90; www.veracruzenbicicleta.com) can set you up and guide you on a cyclo-tour (day or half-day, M$500 per day), which is a remarkable way to have a true experience of the countryside and culture.

Courses

The Universidad Veracruzana's **Escuela para Estudiantes Extranjeros** (School for Foreign Students; ☎ 817-86-87; www.uv.mx/eee; Gutiérrez Zamora 25; courses per hr from US$20, for two weeks US$215 plus registration fee) offers short-term, accredited programs in Spanish, Náhuatl languages and Mexican culture – including cooking, dancing, guitar classes and homestays (US$170 per week).

Tours

Green Traveler Online (☎ 818-97-79; www.green traveleronline.com) Offers organized tours of major sites, interesting towns and big cities in Veracruz state.

Tranvías (☎ 817-34-25; Calle de Enriquez Zona Centro; 45-60 minute tour M$40) Historical city tours in an open-air bus that looks like an old-fashioned wooden trolley.

Roy Dudley (☎ 812-05-55; www.xalaparoy.com; M$1800/day) With over 30 years living in Xalapa, this jovial ex-American known as the 'Gringo Xalapeño' has an excellent way of revealing the subtleties of the culture and has extensive knowledge of the area.

Sleeping

BUDGET

Hotel Limón (☎ 817-22-04; fax 817-93-16; Revolución 8; s/d M$140/220) Details like tiling, mosaics and plants make this hotel. It's clean and a good value, though staff is indifferent and the courtyard echoes.

Hostal de la Niebla (☎ 817-21-74; www.delaniebla .com; Gutiérrez Zamora 24; dm/s M$145/220; P ⬜) A modern Scandinavian-style hostel that's extremely well done: it's spotless, organized,

community-oriented and airy with decks and terraces. There's access to lockers and a kitchen.

MIDRANGE

Hotel México (☎ 818-80-00; Lucio 4; s/d M$310/390; ⬚ P) The bright orange-and-blue color scheme works for this fresh, simple, well-priced hotel. Some rooms have balconies with plaza views.

our pick **María de San Francisco Posada** (☎ 817-33-90; Clavijero 17; s/d M$345/420; P) With its old-world feel and calla-lilied courtyard, this well-kept hotel is a great choice. The café below is adorable with women making tortillas in the open.

Posada del Cafeto (☎ /fax 817-00-23; Dr Canovas 8; s/d M$390/460, ste M$850; ⬜) There's a homely atmosphere at this lovely, quiet, secure guesthouse. All the accommodations have real Mexican character, with high ceilings, wooden furniture and decorative local textiles. There's a delightful rear garden and a charming café where your complimentary breakfast is served.

Posada La Mariquinta (☎ 818-11-58; www.lamari quinta.xalapa.net; Alfaro 12; s/d from M$390/490; P) This homey, plant-filled guesthouse is set in an 18th-century colonial residence with rooms arranged around a lovely garden. It rocks to get the M$100 mini-suite upgrade with a balcony.

Hotel Villa Las Margaritas (☎ 840-08-86, 800-719-43-67; www.villamargaritas.com; Dr Lucio 186; s/d M$640/720; P ⬚ ⬜) This most central Margarita hotel has beautiful tile work, wood floors and a sky-lit central area. Décor is slightly reminiscent of your grandmother's lacy pin cushion.

TOP END

There are surprisingly few top-end options near the center, though there are some in outlying areas. The best high-end option nearby is the Posada Coatepec (p683).

Clara Luna Hotel (☎ 167-80-00; Avila Camacho 42; r M$760; P ⬚ ⬜) A short walk from the center, this new upscale hotel welcomes you with a huge mural in lobby of a romanticized Veracruz in the age of Agustín Lara. The comfortable rooms have simple yet elegant and furnishings.

Eating

Stylish cafés and restaurants abound in Xalapa, many offering healthy and vegetarian choices. One local specialty is *chiles rellenos* (stuffed peppers). Of course, jalapeño chilies are from the region too.

Jugos California (☎ 817-22-71; Enríquez 26; juices M$18-30; ☽ 7am-9:30pm; **V**) Besides *antojitos* it serves fantastic volcano-like fruit salads, delicious juice combos, smoothies and even chocolate soy shakes.

Churrería (☎ 817-33-90; Clavijero 17; dishes M$30-70; ☽ 8am-12am) Real Mexican hot chocolate, homemade cinnamon tea and traditional dishes are served with handmade tortillas (you can watch them being made) in this pleasant, airy café.

La Fonda (☎ 818-72-82; Callejón Diamante 1; dishes M$45-100; ☽ 8am-5:30pm Mon-Sat) You can eat in the vibrant, mural festooned interior or grab a cozy two-person, plant-adorned balcony overlooking the street. Try the *mole* here or the *chileatole de pollo* (chicken soup with little floating corns on the cob). The four-course set meal is M$45.

La Hoja Santa (☎ 818-75-08; Xalapeños Illustres 22; dishes M$30-50; **V**) This open vegetarian place has a vividly hand-painted wall and serves breakfasts and a daily set meal (M$33) that is a deal.

Shintai (☎ 820-40-40; Camacho 54; dishes M$45-110; ☽ 1-11pm Mon-Thu, 1pm-1am Fri & Sat, 1-7pm Sun) This newly opened Mexican chain is popular because it delivers satisfying Asian-style food, like sushi rolls and teriyaki, even if it lacks authenticity.

Callejón González Aparicio (btwn Primo Verdad & Mata) This alley is loaded with hip, international eateries and even hipper crowds. Try Cubanias, where you can sip mojitos; La Condesa for salad and sushi; or Shalom to grab falafels.

Mercado de la Rotonda (Revolucíon s/n; ☽ 7am-6pm) At the north end of Revolucíon, this untouristed market with numerous eateries has delicious regional food on the cheap. Ask for *Zarzaparrilla*, a drink made with its namesake root that's used in genuine root beer and known for its medicinal and aphrodisiac qualities.

Drinking

Italian Coffee Company (☎ 812-12-44; Parque Juárez; coffee drinks M$13-25; ☽ 8:30am-10pm) Boasts a wonderful location on the edge of the plaza. The outdoor terrace, with volcano views, is where coffee is meant to be enjoyed.

Angelo Casa de Té (☎ 841-08-39; Primo Verdad 21-A; ☽ 8am-9pm) Linger over a pot of rose tea,

---

> **SOUND RECOMMENDATIONS: MUSIC OF THE CENTRAL GULF COAST**
>
> The region has a passion for a wide variety of music, from local genres to the best Latin America has to offer.
>
> ▪ Mexican rock – Everyone loves **Maná,** a band originally from Mexico
>
> ▪ Trova – Acoustical, romantic **Fernando Delgadillo**
>
> ▪ Reggaetón – Booty-grinding goodness of **Daddy Yankee** for young folk
>
> ▪ Son Jorocho – Harp-filled Afro–indigenous sounds from **Graciana Silva**
>
> ▪ Salsa – **Dark Latin Groove** will inspire your dance skills.

one of many tea choices, while savoring homemade cookies.

Convivio (☎ 818-05-24; Diego Leño 57; ☽ 10am-10:30pm) University professors come here to enjoy wine (M$150 to M$250 per bottle) or foofy espresso drinks (M$12).

La Chiva (Mata 13; ☽ 2pm-2am Tue-Thu, noon-2am Fri & Sat) A tiny boho stronghold very popular for its alternative (electronica, hip-hop and rock) tunes.

Entertainment

El Ágora (☎ 818-57-30; Parque Juárez; ☽ 10am-10pm Tue-Sun, 9am-6pm Mon) is a busy arts center with a cinema, theater, gallery, bookstore and café.

Tierra Luna (☎ 812-13-01; Rayón 18; cafeteatrotierra luna@yahoo.com; ☽ 9am-10pm Mon-Thu, 9am-2am Fri & Sat) Provides poetry readings, music and sanctuary for the artsy fartsy. It serves tasty café fare to boot.

Teatro del Estado Ignacio de la Llave (☎ 818-08-34; cnr Ignacio de la Llave & Avila Camacho; ☽ from 8pm) is the impressive state theatre that hosts performances by both the Orquesta Sinfónica de Xalapa and the Ballet Folklórico of the Universidad Veracruzana.

Blvd (Avila Camacho 97; drinks M$20-30; ☽ 9pm-4am Thu-Sat) One of several discos at the Camacho–Victoria intersection. This video bar specializes in house, electric and pop.

Shopping

An epicenter of Xalapa's alternative culture is **Callejón Diamante**, an alley lined with boutiques and street vendors selling cheap jewelry, incense and paraphernalia.

CENTRAL GULF COAST

Popularte (☎ 841-12-02; Xalapeños Ilustres 3) More spendy, high-quality local handicrafts made by, and supporting, Veracruz' indigenous communities.

Libélula (☎ 106-54-41; Rayón cnr Diego Leño; www .artelibelula.com; ⊗ 11am-10pm Mon-Sat) Artsy trinkets and trendy souvenirs.

Eco-Tienda (☎ 815-41-55; Paseo de las Palmas 23; ⊗ Mon-Sat) Bona fide health-food store, organically yours, with yuppie prices. It boasts awesome sustainable food and body products.

Getting There & Away

Xalapa is a transportation hub with excellent connections throughout the state and beyond.

BUS

Xalapa's modern, well-organized bus station, the **Central de Autobuses de Xalapa** (CAXA; 20 de Noviembre), is 2km east of city center and has an ATM, cafés and telephones. Second-class buses for Xico and Coatepec regularly leave from Los Sauces Mercado, which is a couple of kilometers south of city center on Circuito Presidentes. Deluxe service is offered by UNO, 1st-class service by ADO and good 2nd-class services by AU. Daily services are as follows:

Destination	Fare	Duration	Frequency
Cardel	M$42	1½hr	18 daily
Mexico City (TAPO)	deluxe M$222	5¼hr	6 daily
	1st-class M$206	5¼hr	28 daily
Mexico City (Terminal Norte)	M$206	5¼hr	5 daily
Papantla	M$162	4hr	10 daily
Puebla	M$120	3¼hr	12 daily
Tampico	M$358	10hr	2
Veracruz	M$74	2hr	frequent 5am-11pm
Veracruz airport	M$205	1¾hr	5 daily
Villahermosa	M$380	8½hr	5 daily

Other places served by ADO include Acayucan, Campeche, Cancún, Catemaco, Córdoba, Fortín de las Flores, Mérida, Orizaba, Poza Rica, San Andrés Tuxtla and Santiago Tuxtla.

CAR & MOTORCYCLE

For car rentals, try **Kanguro** (☎ 817-78-78; Avila Camacho 135; from M$545). Hwy 140 to Puebla is narrow and winding until Perote; the Xalapa–Veracruz highway is very fast and smooth. Going to the northern Gulf coast, it's quickest to go to Cardel, then north on Hwy 180; the inland road via Tlapacoyan is scenic but slow.

Getting Around

For buses from CAXA to the city center, follow signs to the taxi stand, then continue downhill to the big road, Av 20 de Noviembre. The bus stop is to the right. Any bus marked 'Centro' will pass within a block or two of Parque Juárez (M$5). For a taxi to the city center, you have to buy a ticket in the bus station (M$30). To return to the bus station, take the 'Camacho–CAXA–SEC' bus from Camacho or Hidalgo. Buses (M$5) that head up Av Camacho, 'Camcho–Tesorería' (M$5), leave from Enriquez.

AROUND XALAPA

The dramatic landscapes around Xalapa, with rivers, gorges and waterfalls, cradle some charming mountain towns and worthwhile places.

Hacienda El Lencero

About 12km southeast from Xalapa on the Veracruz highway, a signposted road branches off to the right for a few kilometers to the impressive **Museo Ex-Hacienda El Lencero** (☎ 228-820-02-70; Hwy Xalapa-Veracruz Km 10; admission M$45; ⊗ 10am-5pm Tue-Sun). Well worth a visit, this grand former estate was one of the first inns between Mexico City and Veracruz. The superbly restored house is furnished with antiques, and the gardens and lake are delightful. Check out the 500-year-old fig tree.

From Xalapa, catch one of the regular 'Miradores' buses (M$10) from the Plaza Cristal shopping center.

El Carrizal

South of the Veracruz road, 44km from Xalapa, the balmy El Carrizal hot springs feed several sulfurous pools. Laze away the day soaking then spend the night in **Hotel el Carrizal** (☎ 228-818-97-79; Hwy Xalapa-Veracruz Km 36; from M$470; [P] [⊠]), which has a good restaurant with fresh seafood.

Coatepec

☎ 228 / pop 48,500 / elevation 1200m
Some 15km south of Xalapa, Coatepec mixes Xalapa urbane sensibilities with small moun-

tain town charm. If you're a coffee lover, you can't miss this café-filled city that literally emits a rich coffee smell. In late September Coatepec vivaciously celebrates its patron saint San Jerónimo. There's a helpful **tourist office** in the Palacio Municipal on the plaza.

Take a walk up **Cerro de Culebra** (Snake Hill) where you'll find cobbled walking paths and magnificent city and mountain views. To get there, walk three blocks west from the plaza on Lerdo then north all the way up Independencia. Also, the impressive **María Cristina orchid garden**, on the main square, is open daily.

For a spiritual retreat, visit **Ashram Coatepec** (☎ 816-10-55; www.ashramcoatepec.org; Javier Mina 100; dm or campsites M$50; P V), on the outskirts of town, for yoga, meditation and walking trails on the lush grounds. The immaculate treatment of the gorgeous meditation and yoga spaces isn't simulated in the dormitories, but it's a manageable place to hang your hat. Only vegetarian food is served here.

Staying at tastefully done-up **San Jeronimo** (☎ 816-54-86; www.posadasanjeronimo.com; 16 de Septiembre 26; s/d M$570/695; P ☼ ☐) is a peaceful experience, and it has a lovely courtyard restaurant. More upscale is the hallmark hotel **Posada de Coatepec** (☎ 816-05-44; www.posadacoatepec.com.mx; Hidalgo 9; r from M$965; P ☼ ☎), a gorgeous place to stay with a fantastic pool and exhibits from local artists.

Coffino (☎ 816-42-36; www.coffino.com.mx; Jiménez del Campillo 17) is a bustling café with rich coffee and superb Mexican food. A short walk from the center is **Café R Opoch** (☎ 816-07-07; 5 de Mayo 66; coffee M$10-20; ☼ 9am-12pm & 4-8pm Mon-Sat, 10-2 Sun) where you can grab a cup of organic joe.

In **La Misión** (☎ 816-41-32; Aldama 6; ☼ 9am-7pm) store you'll find local peace-loving items: organic coffee, essential oils, maguey honey and soymilk.

Regular buses (M$8) arrive from Xalapa's CAXA and Los Sauces terminals, or a taxi is M$85. Near the plaza, buses leave for Xico (M$6). **ADO** (5 de Mayo s/n) serves Puebla and Mexico City.

Xico
☎ 228 / pop 15,000 / elevation 1300m
Eight kilometers south of Coatepec, Xico is a stunning mountain town with cobbled roads and colonial architecture. The same old mansion that houses the small **tourist office** on Hidalgo hosts the **Mercado Ecológica Xicote**,

which sells organic food and regional handcrafts on Sundays.

The famous **Fiesta de Santa Magdalena** takes place here on July 15 to 24. Gigantic floral arches are raised, and streets are artistically decorated with carpets of colored sawdust in preparation for the saint's procession. The Magdalena statue, in the la Parroquia de Santa María Magdalena, located at the end of Av Hidalgo, is clothed in a different elaborate dress each day for 30 days around the fiesta. The **dress museum** (in the Parroquia, Hidalgo & Juárez) displays a rich collection of the saint's past dresses dating from 1910.

Café Gourmet Pepe (☎ 846-74-71; cafepepe@hotmail.com; Xico–Coatepec Km 1; tour M$55) This almost-organic, shade-grown coffee plantation will give you a tour and sell you delicious coffee and liquors. Get off on at the first bus stop in Xico and walk back 150m where you'll see signs on the right.

It's a pleasant, signed 3km walk from Xico past an ex-hacienda to the plunging 80m **Texolo waterfall** and the **Cascada de la Monja** (Waterfall of the Nun) which provides a luxurious place to take a dip.

Just outside Xico, **Coyopolan** (☎ 813-12-66; www.coyopolan.com; Venustiano Carranza Sur s/n; r M$300; P ☼) enjoys an exquisite location right on the river. The economical rooms here are delightful and vibrant, and the restaurant serves superb regional food. Plus **Xico Aventuras**, an outdoor adventure outfit, makes its home here and offers hiking, biking, four-wheeling and rappelling in the fabulous surrounding mountains and canyons.

From Xalapa, take a 'Xico' bus (M$15) from Los Sauces Terminal. From Coatepec, Xico buses (M$6) frequently leave from near the plaza.

Parque Nacional Cofre de Perote
The misty 4274m-high Cofre de Perote volcano is southwest of Xalapa. From the town of Perote, 50km west of Xalapa on Hwy 140, Allende continues southwest to become a dirt road that climbs 1900m in 24km, finishing just below the summit. There's no public transportation here, and it's not recreationist-friendly, having no visitor services. However, the park can be explored via car, mountain bike, or foot. At the entrance to Perote, **Hostería Covadonga** (☎ 282-825-26-42; www.hosteriacovadonga.com; s/d M$265/350) is recommended as a lovely base from which to explore the park.

PULQUE

This alcoholic beverage (depicted being drunk on panels at El Tajín) is made from the fermented *aguamiel* of the maguey plant. The drink was sacred to Mesoamerican civilizations and served to the cultures' honored people (warriors headed for battle, lactating women, etc). It is said to be nutritious and healing, and even to enhance virility. Plus, it's fizzily refreshing and delicious. When cold beer entered the scene, pulque – in its true form – slid toward extinction. However, a few *pulquerías* still survive. In La Vigas, a mountain town outside Xalapa, Pulque y Antojitos Las Vigas serves the drink fresh.

Jalcomulco

Surrounded by lush ravines, this town, just 30km southeast of Xalapa, hugs the Río Antigua (known as the Río Pescados) and is very picturesque. The area is rich with caves and luscious swimming spots, but it's most famous for its rapids, which accommodate beginning white-water enthusiasts and can also satisfy the more advanced. Trips are more regular during the high seasons, but they may be full so it's best to plan in advance. Trips can be more expensive if there are just a few people.

Though Jalcomulco is still relatively under the radar, rafting outfits, both sketchy and experienced, are beginning to migrate to this sleepy town. The tiny **tourist office** in the Palacio Municipal has some info and a small accommodations list.

The well-recommended **Aventuras Sin Límites** (☎ 279-832-35-80; www.raftingsinlimite.com; Zaragoza 58) is a rafting outfit that has high standards. It's also the only outfit here that's run by locals. The basic but clean accommodations are for guests only. Another quality rafting outfit you could try is **México Verde** (☎ 279-832-37-34; www.mexicoverde.com), which has its own resort right on the road coming into town from the northwest. **Ignacio Romero 'Bobillo'** (☎ 279-832-35-80; bobillomx@hot mail.com; 5 de Mayo 14) is a local kayaker who runs courses, rents out real white-water kayaks and provides transportation.

There are buses (M$22) to Jalcomulco from Xalapa at the Azteca bus terminal, as well as buses from Cardel.

VERACRUZ

☎ 229 / pop 569,000

Be careful: Veracruz is intoxicating. Scantily clad, she adorns herself in sea shells, permeates car exhaust and casually testifies her sordid colonial past. She'll gladly share her last taco with you and just as gladly take your last peso. Usually you'll find her swiveling to salsa, boozing, or laughing at her own joke. She gives her inhabitants, the ever-proud and doggedly faithful *jarochos*, a place to fall in love on her sweltering shores saturated with mariachis, seaside cafés, *trova*, and explosive sunsets. And for the broken-hearted, she offers miles of coastline boulevard for solitary rambling – save during her raucous Carnaval, which rocks Mexico. Whatever the case may be, Veracruz, both regal and trashy, could make even the most stoic bloke wax poetic.

History

Hernán Cortés arrived in Veracruz on Good Friday (April 21), 1519, and thus began his siege of Mexico. By 1521, he had crushed the Aztec Empire.

Veracruz provided Mexico's main gateway to the outside world for 400 years. Invaders and pirates, incoming and exiled rulers, settlers, silver and slaves – all came and went, making Veracruz a linchpin in Mexico's history. In 1567, English sailor Francis Drake survived a massive Spanish sea attack. He continued career as a pirate and never ceased to harass the Spanish. In 1683, vicious Frenchman Laurent de Gaff, with 600 men, held the 5000 inhabitants of Veracruz captive, killing escapees, looting, drinking, and raping. Soon after, they left much richer.

In 1838, General Antonio López fled Veracruz in his underwear under bombardment from a French fleet in the Pastry War. But the general managed to respond heroically, expelling the invaders. When Winfield Scott's army attacked Veracruz during the Mexican–American War, more than 1000 Mexicans died before the city surrendered.

In 1861 Benito Juárez announced that Mexico couldn't pay its debts to Spain, France and Britain. The British and Spanish planned only to take over the customhouse, but retreated seeing that Frenchman Napoleon III sought to conquer Mexico. After Napoleon III's five-year intervention ended, Veracruz experienced revitalization. Mexico's first railway was built between Veracruz and Mexico

City in 1872, and foreign investment poured into the city.

In 1914 US troops occupied Veracruz, halting a delivery of German arms to dictator Victoriano Huerta. Later in the Revolution, Veracruz was briefly the capital of the reformist Constitutionalist faction led by Venustiano Carranza.

Today, Veracruz is an important deepwater port, handling exports, manufacturing, and petrochemical industries. Tourism, particularly from the domestic sector, is another large income earner.

Orientation

The cathedral and Palacio Municipal border the *zócalo* to the east. The harbor is 250m east, with the San Juan de Ulúa fort on its far side. Blvd Camacho follows the coast to the south, past anchorages and beaches. About 700m south of the *zócalo* along Av Independencia is the green space of Parque Zamora, with Mercado Hidalgo just to its west. The bus terminal is 2km south of Parque Zamora along Díaz Mirón. 'Boca del Río' signifies both the municipality directly south of the city center and the small city 11km down the coast serving as its municipal head.

Information

BOOKSTORE

Libros y Arte Fototeca (Map p688; ☎ 932-69-43; Callejón El Portal de Miranda 9; ☒ 10am-7:45pm Mon-Sat, Sun from 1pm) Good regional and international selection.

EMERGENCIES

Ambulance, Fire & Police (☎ 066)

INTERNET ACCESS

Internet (Map p688; Lerdo 20A; per hr M$15; ☒ 9am-12am, Sun 10am-11pm).

LAUNDRY

Lavandería Mar y Sol (Map p688; Av Madero 616; wash & dry M$27/load; ☒ 8:30am-9pm Mon-Sat)

LEFT LUGGAGE

There's a 24-hour facility in the 2nd-class bus station.

MEDICAL SERVICES

Beneficencia Española (Map p686; ☎ 932-00-21; Av 16 de Septiembre 955) Hospital offering general medical services.

Hospital Regional (Map p686; ☎ 932-36-90; Av 20 de Noviembre 1074)

MONEY

There's a cluster of banks a block north of the *zócalo* with ATMs.

POST

Post office (Map p688; Plaza de la República 213) A five-minute walk north of the *zócalo*.

TELEPHONE

Card phones proliferate around the *zócalo*.

TOURIST INFORMATION

Tourist office (Map p688; ☎ 922-95-33; www.vera cruzturismo.com.mx; Palacio Municipal; ☒ 10am-6pm Mon-Fri, 10am-6pm Sat & Sun) Has mostly helpful staff and plenty of maps and brochures.

Sights

ZÓCALO

Veracruz' *zócalo* (Map p688) – also called the Plaza de Armas and Plaza Lerdo – is a hub for *jarochos* and visitors alike. It's a handsome public space, framed on three sides by *portales* (arcades), the 17th-century **Palacio Municipal** and an 18th-century **cathedral**. The level of activity accelerates throughout the day until the evening when the *zócalo* becomes thick with music, entertainers, merrymakers and bystanders.

MALECÓN & BOULEVARD

Veracruz' harbor is a busy oil port with rigs off the coast, but that somehow adds to the gritty romanticism of the **waterfront walk** on the *malecón* (harbor boardwalk), starting at the rows of vendor stalls of Plaza de las Artesanías that sell a kaleidoscopic of souvenirs. You'll pass the high-rise **Pemex building** (Map p688), an early example of modern Mexican architecture with some interesting murals.

Heading south the *malecón* becomes a wide pedestrian walkway called the boulevard (pronounced *boo-ley-bar*). Lining the coast, it continues down roughly 8km, passing lighthouse piers, statues of famous government figures, and monuments to the city's defenders and sailors who've died at sea. It makes for a fabulous run. Between Rayón and Víctimas, you'll see what looks like a block-long tarp shelter, but inside you'll find a gritty, bustling **artisans' market** (Map p686) with lower prices, hokiness beyond belief and fantastic finds.

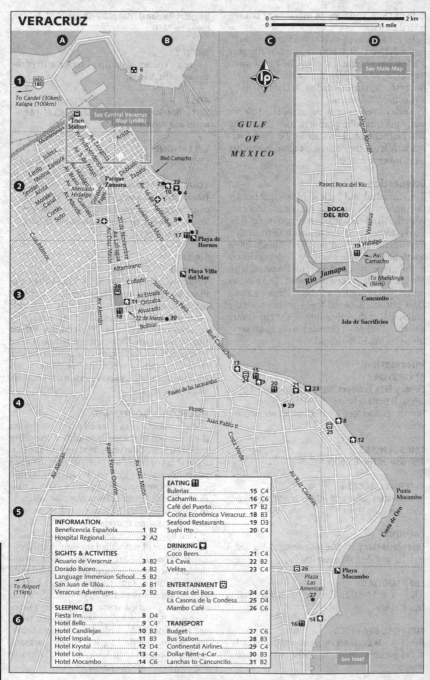

VERACRUZ

To Cardel (30km),
Xalapa (100km)

GULF
OF
MEXICO

See Central Veracruz
Map (p688)

Train
Station

Blvd Camacho

Parque
Zamora

Playa de
Hornos

Playa Villa
del Mar

See Main Map

BOCA
DEL RÍO

Paseo Boca del Río

Río Jamapa

To Mandinga
(8km)

Cancunito

Isla de Sacrificios

Punta
Mocambo

Costa de Oro

Plaza
Las
Américas

Playa
Mocambo

See Inset

To Airport
(11km)

INFORMATION
Beneficencia Española..............1 B2
Hospital Regional....................2 A2

SIGHTS & ACTIVITIES
Acuario de Veracruz.................3 B2
Dorado Buceo..........................4 B2
Language Immersion School....5 B2
San Juan de Ulúa.....................6 B1
Veracruz Adventures...............7 B2

SLEEPING
Fiesta Inn................................8 D4
Hotel Bello..............................9 C4
Hotel Candilejas....................10 B2
Hotel Impala..........................11 B3
Hotel Krystal..........................12 D4
Hotel Lois..............................13 C4
Hotel Mocambo.....................14 C6

EATING
Bulerías.................................15 C4
Cacharrito.............................16 C6
Café del Puerto......................17 B2
Cocina Económica Veracruz..18 B3
Seafood Restaurants..............19 D3
Sushi Itto..............................20 C4

DRINKING
Coco Beers............................21 C4
La Cava.................................22 B2
Velitas...................................23 C4

ENTERTAINMENT
Barricas del Boca...................24 C4
La Casona de la Condesa.......25 D4
Mambo Café 26 C6

TRANSPORT
Budget..................................27 C6
Bus Station............................28 B3
Continental Airlines...............29 C4
Dollar Rent-a-Car..................30 B3
Lanchas to Cancuncito..........31 B2

Two blocks inland from the *malecón* is the 1998 **Altar a la Patria** (Map p688), an obelisk marking the buried the remains of those who defended Veracruz during its numerous conflicts.

FOTOTECA
On the southeast side of the *zócalo* this superb **arts center** (Map p688; ☎ 932-87-67; www.fototecade veracruz.org; Callejón El Portal de Miranda 9; ⊗ 10am-7pm Tue-Sun) has rotating photographic and video exhibitions, from cutting-edge urban images to beautifully composed portraits. It's spread over three floors of a restored colonial building.

FARO CARRANZA
Facing the waterfront on the *malecón*, **Faro Carranza** (Map p688) holds a lighthouse and navy offices guarded by a large statue of Venustiano Carranza. It was here that the 1917 Mexican Constitution was drafted. Every Monday morning the Mexican navy goes through an elaborate parade in front of the building.

SAN JUAN DE ULÚA
This **fortress** (Map p686; ☎ 938-51-51; admission M$37; ⊗ 9am-4:30pm Tue-Sun) protecting Veracruz harbor was originally an island, but it's now connected to the mainland by a causeway. Cortés arrived here in 1519, and the island subsequently became the main entry point for Spanish newcomers to Mexico.

The central part of the fortress was a prison, and a notoriously inhumane one during the Porfirio Díaz regime. Today, San Juan de Ulúa is an empty ruin of passageways, battlements, bridges and stairways. Guided tours are available in Spanish and, sometimes, English. To get there you can take a *lancha* (M$25) from the *malecón* or a taxi (M$50).

BALUARTE DE SANTIAGO
Until 1880 Veracruz was a walled city surrounded by mighty medieval defenses. **Baluarte de Santiago** (Map p688; ☎ 931-10-59; Canal s/n; admission M$33; ⊗ 10am-4pm Tue-Sun), the only surviving fort of nine, was built in 1526 beside what was then the waterfront. A small exhibit of pre-Hispanic gold jewelry is inside. The price covers admission to the fort's interior, but you can walk around the outside battlements for free.

ACUARIO DE VERACRUZ
Veracruz' well-done **aquarium** (Map p686; ☎ 931-10-20; www.acuariodeveracruz.com; Blvd Camacho s/n, adult/child M$60/30, Tiburonería M$300/150; ⊗ 10am-7pm) is a worthwhile visit, located about 2km south of the city center. There's a large donut-shaped tank filled with sharks, rays and turtles that glide around visitors. Other tanks house freshwater and saltwater fish, reptiles and amphibians, river otters and even manatees. But for a really dramatic encounter climb into the Tiburonería – a transparent safety cage that is lowered into a pool of feeding sharks.

MUSEUMS
The displays at the **Museo de la Ciudad de Veracruz** (Veracruz City Museum, Map p688; ☎ 931-63-55; Av Zaragoza 39; admission free; ⊗ 10am-6pm Mon-Sat, Sun till 3pm) do a good job of informing visitors of the city's history from the pre-Hispanic era, but they also give a feel for the essence of this proud and lively city through explanations of its music, its diverse ethnic roots and its politics.

Occupying a former naval academy, the **Museo Histórico Naval** (Map p688; ☎ 931-40-78; Arista 418; admission free; ⊗ 9am-5pm Tue-Sun) covers Mexico's maritime heritage. Get ready for your testosterone to spike: along with rooms full of weapons and model ships, the museum holds well-presented exhibits on the US attacks on Veracruz in 1847 and 1914, and on revolutionary hero Venustiano Carranza.

BEACHES & LAGOONS
Inseparable from the *Jarocho* identity is the beach. You'll find pleasant stretches of them all the way down through Boca del Río. As a rule of thumb, the further from the oil rigs the better, but locales patronize them all.

Alternatively, you can find *lancheros* (M$120) by the aquarium who will bring you to **Cancuncito** (Map p686), a sand bar off the coast touted as the best beach in Veracruz, with light sand and clear water. Another part of the *lanchero* schtick is the **Isla de Sacrificios** (Map p686). It was once an island used for Totonac human sacrifice and later used as a leprosy colony. Now it's a protected nature reserve working on its karma.

Some 11km from the city center, the gritty, off-shoot town of **Boca del Río** (Map p686) has a smattering of brightly colored seafood restaurants looking over the mouth of the river on Blvd Camacho. Also, *lanchas* offering **boat**

CENTRAL VERACRUZ

0   400 m
0   0.2 miles

INFORMATION	
Banamex	1 A2
Bancomer	2 A2
Banorte	3 B2
HSBC	4 A2
Internet	5 B2
Lavanderia Mar y Sol	6 A3
Libros y Arte Fototeca	(see 14)
Post Office	7 B1
Santander Serfin	8 A2
Telecomm	(see 7)
Tourist Office	9 B2

SIGHTS & ACTIVITIES	
Altar a la Patria	10 C2
Amphibian	(see 22)
Artisans' Market	11 D2
Baluarte de Santiago	12 C3
Faro Carranza	13 C1
Fototeca	14 B2
Harbor Tours	15 C1

Museo de la Ciudad de Veracruz..16 B3	
Museo Histórico Naval	17 C2
Palacio Municipal	(see 9)
Pemex Building	18 C1
Transvías Bus	(see 34)

SLEEPING	
Gran Hotel Diligencias	19 A2
Hawaii Hotel	20 B2
Hotel Amparo	21 B2
Hotel Colonial	22 A2
Hotel Concha Dorada	23 B2
Hotel El Faro	24 C2
Hotel Ruiz Milán	25 B2
Hotel Santillana	26 B2
Hotel Sevilla	27 B2
Hotel Veracruz	28 A2

Hotel Villa Rica	29 D3
Mar y Tierra	30 D2
Meson del Mar	31 B2

EATING	
El Portón	32 A2
Gran Café de la Parroquia	33 B2
Gran Café del Portal	34 B2
Nieves de Malecón	35 B2
Sanborns	36 A2

ENTERTAINMENT	
El Rincón de la Trova	37 B2

TRANSPORT	
Buses to Mocambo & Boca del Río..38 B2	
Mexicana	39 A2

tours to mangrove forests leave from here. Over the bridge, the coastal road continues about 8km further down the coast from Boca del Río to **Mandinga**, known for its seafood (especially *langostinos bicolores*), where you can also hire a boat (from the *zona de restaurantes*) to take you around mangrove lagoons rich with wildlife.

Activities

DIVING & SNORKELING

You wouldn't expect good diving right near such a oil-rigged city, but Veracruz has some cool options (including at least one accessible wreck) on the reefs near the offshore islands. Part of the area has been designated an underwater natural park.

Dorado Buceo (Map p688; ☎ 931-43-05; www.dorado buceo.com.mx; Blvd Camacho 865; without/with equipment M$695/945) is a good choice of the various PADI dive schools in the city. It has quality equipment and arranges dive and snorkel excursions from the Veracruz area. Guides speak English.

KAYAKING

The relatively calm waters off the coast invite a day or afternoon of kayaking.

Veracruz Adventures (Map p686; ☎ 931-53-58; www.veracruzadventures.com; Blvd Camacho 681A) will rent you a single or double sit-on-top kayak (prices vary). If you're up for it, you can kayak from here to Cancuncito or Isla de Sacrificios.

ORGANIZED TOURS

Take a city tour, see surrounding sites, or play around in nature while leaving logistics to a tour company.

Amphibian (Map p688; ☎ 931-09-97; www.amphibian .com.mx; Lerdo 117, Hotel Colonial lobby; per person from M$400) is an outfit offering activity-based tours: in addition to diving and snorkeling trips, it also offers rafting trips to nearby rivers, rappelling and sightseeing trips to places like El Tajín and to Roca Partida – a rocky outcrop jutting straight out of the ocean.

Aventura Extrema (☎ 980-84-57; www.aventura extrema.com) offers rappelling, rafting and hiking in the area.

Boats from the *malecón* offer 45-minute **harbor tours** (Map p688; ☎ 935-94-17; www.asdic rnm.mx; per porcon M$75; ⏰ 7am 7pm). They leave when they're full, about every 30 minutes, so be prepared for a wait, particularly in the slow season.

The **Tranvías bus** (p688; ☎ 817-34-25; departs cnr Independencia & Zamora; M$40) is a open air bus with trolley-like wooden trimmings that gives one-hour city tours to the beat of tropical tunes.

Courses

Language Immersion School (p686; ☎ 931-47-16; www.veracruzspanish.com; Alacio Pérez 61; first week US$575 incl homestay) An American-owned school, it offers Spanish courses centered around learning the city, traveling around the state, doing outdoor activities and taking Mexican cooking classes.

Festivals & Events

Carnaval (February or March) Veracruz erupts into a nine-day party before Ash Wednesday each year with flamboyant parades winding through the city daily, beginning with one devoted to the 'burning of bad humor' and ending with the 'funeral of Juan Carnaval.' Chuck in fireworks, dances, salsa and samba music, handicrafts, folklore shows and children's parades, and it adds up to one of Mexico's greatest fiestas. See the tourist office for a program of events.

Festival Internacional Afrocaribeño (last two weeks of July) This festival of Afro-Caribbean culture features academic and business forums and a trade show, but the main attractions are the dance and music performances (many of them free), film screenings and art expositions, with many nations from the Caribbean and Latin America participating.

Sleeping

Hotel prices vary greatly according to demand in Veracruz and can shift from day to day at busy times of the year (mid-July to mid-September, Carnaval, Easter, Semana Santa, Christmas, New Year), during which you should book in advance and know that prices might increase 10% to 40%. Ask about discounts.

It can be entertaining to stay near the *zócalo*, which is music-filled and near museums and the *malecón*. If nightlife is your thing, think about staying on Blvd Camacho. Many higher-end options are on Ruíz Cortínes.

BUDGET

Most budget places are near the bus station or around the fringes of the *zócalo*. Count on

---

VERACRUZ IN TWO DAYS

Day 1

Start with a morning stroll on the **malecón** (p685), stopping at the **Gran Café de la Parroquia** (p691) for breakfast. Find your way to the **Museo de la Ciudad** (p687) to get a feel for the city. Before heading to the **portales** for ice cream and music, swing by **Baluarte de Santiago** (p687), a colonial fortress of yesteryear. After a siesta, spend the rest of the afternoon at soaking up rays at **Cancuncito** (p687) and grab a late dinner and mojito in the acoustical atmosphere of El Rincón de La Trova.

Day 2

Begin the next day by **kayaking** around the harbor which will merit a hearty lunch at a seafood *palapa* on Playa Hornos (p691), right near your next stop, the **aquarium** (p687). Rest up in the afternoon because the night starts with perusing the **artisans' market** (p685) on the Boulevard, then dropping in on an oceanside restaurant where you will fortalize yourself for **Mambo Café** (p692). Whether you end up salsa dancing or people-watching, hopefully an early morning bus ride isn't in store.

hot water, but check for adequate ventilation and working fans.

Hotel Amparo (Map p688; ☎ 932-27-38; www .hotelamparo.com.mx; Serdán 482; s/d M$150/300; P) Compared to other budget hotels, this secure, well-managed place a few blocks south of the *zócalo* is a good deal. It's a simple and central place to collapse at the end of a busy day out and about.

Hotel Santillana (Map p688; ☎ 932-31-16; Landero Y Cos 209; s/d M$200/300) This hotel is weathered with simple, scrubbed accommodations. There's a huge cage of parakeets in the center of the building.

Hotel Villa Rica (Map p688; ☎ 932-48-54; Blvd Camacho 165; s/d M$200/300) A friendly bunch runs this small seaside hotel with bare-bones rooms that are clean and breezy, some with tiny tiled ocean-view balconies.

Hotel Sevilla (Map p688; Zaragoza y Lerdo; from M$250) Just off the *zócalo*, this hotel provides acceptable, cheap shelter and a friendly welcome… but not much else.

Hotel El Faro (Map p688; ☎ 931-65-38; www.hotel elfaro.com.mx; Av 16 de Septiembre 223; s/d M$290/340; ⊠ 💻) A solid economical choice. This quiet hotel has planted sitting areas, a little internet café and rooms that are well maintained.

MIDRANGE

Hotel Impala (Map p686; ☎ 937-01-69; fax 935-12-57; Orizaba 650; s/d M$300/480; P ⊠) Near the bus station, this well-run hotel is a great place to stay before an early morning bus ride. Some, but not all, rooms have sketchy carpet.

Mar y Tierra (Map p688; ☎ 931-38-66, 800-543-41-68; www.hotelmarytierra.com; Sainz de Baranda & Malecón; r M$400/510; P ⊠ 🕿) Some of the rooms are remodeled with bright pop-out windows, and older rooms are cheaper and have balconies. Hang out in the rooftop pool with vistas of the city and sea. The amenities and location are pleasing.

Hotel Concha Dorada (Map p688; ☎ 931-29-96, 800-712-53-42; conchadorada@yahoo.com.mx; Lerdo 77; s/d M$370-520; ⊠) On the fringe of the *zócalo* action, this hotel about equals the quality of its more expensive neighbors who pretend to be fancy. Considering the location, it's a value.

Mesón del Mar (Map p688; ☎ 932-50-43; www.meson delmar.com.mx; Esteban Morales 543; r M$450, ste from M$550; P ⊠ 🕿 🛗) The airy rooms have tall ceilings, and some have cool lofts and balconies. Though not ridiculously clean, the rooms are

very well cared for. The vibrant, trendy café below serves delicious Mexican food.

Hotel Colonial (Map p688; ☎ 932-01-93; www.hcol onial.com.mx; Lerdo 117; r M$450-750; P ⊠ 💻 🕿) The Colonial languidly ages and becomes more and more dated while capitalizing on its fantastic *zócalo* location. The *zócalo*-side accommodations are noisy but a blast. Rooms have a centrally controlled air-conditioning and sound system (so you'd better like 1980s music and love ballads).

our pick **Hotel Candilejas** (Map p688; ☎ 932-58-72; www.travelbymexico.com/vera/candilejas; Juan Barragán 35; s/d M$510/580; P ⊠) This cute hotel modestly flanks the Novo Mar hotel monolith. Many of the rooms have precious balconies with *malécon* views. If you snag a corner room you'll get two balconies. The bare, rooftop patio was made for yoga.

Hotel Ruiz Milán (Map p688; ☎ 932-37-77, 800-221-42-60; www.ruizmilan.com.mx; cnr Malecón & Gómez Farías; from M$580; P ⊠ 🕿) This welcoming hotel has got it together and is located ringside *malécon*. It's worth the price hike to get a view of the harbor.

Hawaii Hotel (Map p688; ☎ 938-00-88; hawaii@infosel .net.mx; Paseo del Malecón 458; s/d M$650/750; P ⊠ 🕿) Who knows why it's called the Hawaii Hotel? The building shape is contemporary with gleaming light-colored marble and white décor inside. Some rooms have marvelous views of the *malécon*.

Hotel Bello (Map p686; ☎ 922-48-28; www.hotelbello .com; Av Ruiz Cortines 258; r M$860; P ⊠ ⊠ 💻 🕿) Both the lobby and the rooms manage to be colorful and cheerful without being cheeseball. Higher-floor double rooms have ample balconies equipped with wooden deck furniture and city or sea views. It's in a bar and restaurant district near the beach, 5km south of the *zócalo*.

Hotel Veracruz (Map p688; ☎ 931-22-33, 800-900-00-00; www.hotelescalinda.com.mx; cnr Av Independencia & Lerdo; r M$950; P ⊠ ⊠ 💻 🕿) With a fine location on the *zócalo*, it provides guests with ample, borderline-stylish rooms and nice amenities plus a pool on the second floor with *zócalo* views.

TOP END

Most upscale options are far from the *zócalo* (except Diligencias) but near restaurants, bars and the beach.

Gran Hotel Diligencias (Map p688; ☎ 923-02-80, 800-505-55-95; www.granhoteldiligencias.com; Av Independencia

1115; r M$1110; (P X X 🖵 ⊠) This fantastically renovated, landmark hotel royally presides over the *zócalo*. The fanciest option on the plaza, the huge rooms manage a business-class elegance but lack personality.

Hotel Mocambo (Map p686; ☎ 922-02-00, 800-290-01-00; www.hotelmocambo.com.mx; Av Ruiz Cortines 4000; r M$910-3000; (P X ⊠) On a hilltop just behind the beach, this aging, Italianate resort retains elegance considering its all-encompassing nautical theme. The rooms are spacious, but simply furnished and with ocean or horizon views. It has three pools and an incredible restaurant.

Hotel Lois (p686; ☎ 937-82-90; www.hotellois.com.mx; Ruiz Cortines 10; M$1350; (P X ⊠) The slick lobby has a chic, feng shui feel. The rooms, though large and well done, don't capture the hipster jive of the lobby. It's very near clubs and bars.

Hotel Krystal (Map p686; ☎ 923-02-32; www.nh-hotels.com; Blvd Camacho, Lote 5 y 6; r M$2000; (P X X 🖵 ⊠) Its slick central lobby, accented with red and natural colors, has plants dripping from the upper floors. Although it's on busy Camacho, the immaculate rooms, pool, and beach access give it a ritzy resort feel.

Fiesta Inn (Map p686; ☎ 923-10-00; www.posadas.com; Blvd Camacho s/n; r M$2450; (P X X 🖵 ⊠) Right on a cute beach, this upscale hotel boasts a great ocean-view pool and all the amenities. Though the rooms won't wow you, the attention to detail is superb.

Eating

If you can tear yourself away from delicious Mexican seafood, international cuisine is available.

ZÓCALO AREA

The cafés under the ever-lively, music-filled *portales* are popular spots for drinks and food. They all offer the same tasty, price-hiked variety. Alternatively, you can join *jarochos* in the mazes of **Mercado Hidalgo** where you can find eatery nooks that serve cheap delectable local favorites like *cocteles de mariscos*, *mondongo* (prepared cow stomach) and delicious moles.

Gran Café del Portal (Map p688; ☎ 931-27-59; cnr Av Independencia & Zamora; mains M$30-100; 7am-midnight) Just off the *zócalo*, you still have a view of the jovial ruckus and get the mariachi overflow. The menu has great variety and regional classics including steak *tampiqueño*.

El Portón (Map p688; Av Independencia s/n; M$45-100; 7am-midnight, open late on weekends) A half a block north of the *zócalo*, El Portón provides refuge from *zócalo* excitement with traditional food and agreeable prices.

Sanborns (Map p688; ☎ 931-00-91; Av Independencia 1069; mains M$50-100) This huge, ever-busy café with a terrace facing the *zócalo* and an extensive international and Mexican menu is a local and tourist staple. Waitresses sport campy indigenous costumes.

HARBOR

our pick **Nieves de Malecón** (Map p688; ☎ 931-70-99; Av Zaragoza 286; dishes M$2.50-8; 11am-7pm) On the way to the *malecón* from the *zócalo*, equip yourself for the stroll by treating yourself to a scrumptious Mexican-style sorbet laden with fruit chunks.

Gran Café de la Parroquia (Map p688; ☎ 932-25-84; Farías 34; mains M$40-120; 6am-midnight) As a Veracruz icon, this busy restaurant–coffeehouse faces the harbor and buzzes from daylight until midnight. The trademark custom is for customers to request refills by clinking spoons on glasses.

DOWN THE COAST

Just south of the aquarium you'll find a smattering of *palapa* seafood restaurants bordering Playa Hornos. You pay for the view and atmosphere via the food's tourist prices (M$150 for a seafood plate) – worth it to some and ridiculous to others.

Café del Puerto (Map p686; ☎ 932-74-47; Blvd Camacho s/n Plaza Acuario; M$40-80 mains; ⊙ 8am-10pm) This air-conditioned café of windows is a terrific waterfront spot for a cappuccino and pastry.

Cocina Económica Veracruz (Map p686; cnr Mirón & Orizaba; mains M$30-90) Right next to the bus station, its enormous fresh fruit juices and delicious *mole* will strengthen your constitution for a long journey.

Bulerías (Map p686; ☎ 202-01-46; www.bulerias .com.mx; Blvd Camacho 9; ⊙ 11am-close; M$50-150) A more upscale tapas bar with seaside ambience, outdoor seating and lovely food. Its huge TV tends to show soccer games, and the patio is good for boulevarde watching.

Cacharrito (Map p686; ☎ 921-60-01; Gaviota 1; M$75-250; ⊙ 1:30pm-11pm, Sun 1:30-6pm) This classy, formal Argentine restaurant near Hotel Mocambo is renowned for its *parrilladas* (barbequed meat) but you'll also find pastas, seafood and salads.

Sushi Itto (Map p686; ☎ 921-76-41; www.sushi-itto .com; Ruíz Cortínes 3501; rolls M$60-100) Wasabi and salsa *chipotle* are equal condiments here. It has some eyebrow-raising Mexican-inspired rolls and 'burgesitas' (M$68) that are hamburger-like creations made with sushi ingredients.

Drinking

The *portales* cafés are drinking strongholds. But head south and you'll find plenty of other choices.

Velitas (Map p686; Blvd Camacho & Militar; drinks M$15-50) This popular little seaside *palapa* could be romantic with its tiki-torch ambience or just a laid-back place to grab a cocktail while checking out the ocean and people strolling past on the boulevard. On weekends there's live music. **Coco Beers** (Map p686; Militar s/n; ⊙ 6pm-close, Wed-Sun) How can one go wrong in a place that serves super-sized beers out of *yardas*: iced, bong-shaped, glass containers? It's loud and popular here, dude.

La Cava (Map p686; Blvd Camacho, btwn Uribe & Barragán; drinks M$15-30; ⊙ 5pm-close) Definitely a neighborhood favorite, this tiny bar illuminated with black lights seems to host lots of laughter and cocktail-induced intimacy.

Entertainment

Of course, there are always marimbas and mariachis on the *zócalo*. And the coastline boulevard is known as *la barra más grande del mundo*, the biggest bar in the world, *barra* referring to both the sandbar and drinks bar. During holiday times, it's an outdoor party with live music and dancing in the streets. Many venues line Blvd Camacho.

El Rincón de la Trova (Map p688; Callejón de la Lagunilla 59; cover M$30; ⊙ 11am-7pm Mon-Wed, 9pm-3am Thu-Sat) Set on a pedestrian side road, this venue has live *trova* as well as *son jarocho* music. You can sip a mojito and eat empanadas while enjoying the show.

La Casona de la Condesa (Map p686; ☎ 130-12-82; www.casonadelacondesa.com; Blvd Camacho 2015; cover M$50 weekends; ⊙ 10pm-5am Tue-Sun) The weird Jesus art is meant to be edgy but feels whacked out. La Casona attracts an older (ie not teenage) crowd and offers solid live music every night it's open.

ᴏᴜʀ ᴘɪᴄᴋ Mambo Café (Map p686; ☎ 927-19-55; www .mambocafe.com.mx; Av Americas 551; ⊙ 10pm-4:30am Wed-Sat; cover women/men M$70/130) The cover is steep in Veracruz terms, but this expansive salsa club with slick fountains and bursting colors is where Latin dancing goes down in this town. Sometimes there are lessons early on weekend nights. Check for ladies' nights specials, too.

Barricas del Boca (Map p686; ☎ 100-37-76; cnr Blvd Camacho & Militar; ⊙ 9pm-3am Wed-Sat) This *Jarocho*-recommended club has *trova*, salsa, pop and rock music. You can hang out at the bar or dance to the DJ.

Getting There & Away

AIR

Frequent flights to Tampico, Villahermosa, Mérida and Mexico City are offered by Aeroméxico and **Mexicana** and **Click Mexicana** (☎ 932-22-42, 800-502-20-00) in addition to a handful of other national airlines. Direct flights from Houston are offered by **Continental Airlines** (☎ 922-60-08; www.continental.com).

BUS

Veracruz is a major hub, with good services up and down the coast and inland along the Córdoba–Puebla–Mexico City corridor. Buses to and from Mexico City can be heavily booked at holiday times.

The bus station is about 3km south of the *zócalo* between Calles Collado and Orizaba on Av Díaz Mirón, and has ATMs. The 1st-class/deluxe area is in the part of the station closest to Orizaba. For more frequent and slightly cheaper and slower 2nd-class services, enter the other side from Av Lafragua. There's a 24-hour luggage room here. Daily 1st-class departures include the following:

Destination	Fare	Duration	Frequency
Acayucan	M$196	3½hr	14 daily
Catemaco	M$100	3½hr	9 daily
Córdoba	M$82	1¾hr	hourly
Mexico City (TAPO)	M$348	5½hr	20 daily
Oaxaca	M$396	7hr	3 daily
Orizaba	M$96	2½hr	28 daily
Papantla	M$150	4½hr	7 daily
Puebla	M$244	3½hr	8 daily
San Andrés	M$94	3hr	10 daily
Santiago	M$94	2½hr	14 daily
Tampico	M$448	9½hr	20 daily
Tuxpan	M$210	6hr	15 daily
Villahermosa	$370	7½hr	13 daily
Xalapa	M$74	2hr	frequent till 11:30pm

Buses leaving Veracruz also go to Campeche, Cancún, Chetumal, Matamoros, Mérida, Nuevo Laredo and Salina Cruz.

CAR & MOTORCYCLE
Many car rental agencies have desks at the Veracruz airport. There are also some larger agencies scattered around town. Rates start at M$600/day.

Budget (Map p686; ☎ 989-05-31; Ruíz Cortínes 3495)
Dollar (Map p686; ☎ 935-88-08; fax 935-88-07; Bolivar 501B)

Getting Around
Veracruz airport (☎ 934-70-00) is 11km southwest of town near Hwy 140. It's small, modern and well organized with a café and several shops. There's no bus service to or from town; taxis cost M$120.

To get into the city center from the 1st-class bus station, take a bus marked 'Díaz Mirón y Madero' (M$5). It will head to Parque Zamora then up Madero. For the *zócalo*, get off on the corner of Madero and Lerdo and turn right. Returning to the bus stations, pick up the same bus going south on Av 5 de Mayo. Booths in the 1st- and 2nd-class stations sell taxi tickets (*zócalo* area, M$30). In the tourist office, you can get a summary sheet of official taxi ride costs that's helpful to guard against tourist price inflation.

Buses marked 'Mocambo–Boca del Río' (M$7 to Boca del Río) leave regularly from the corner of Zaragoza and Serdán, near the *zócalo;* they go via Parque Zamora then down Blvd Camacho to Playa Mocambo (20 minutes) and on to Boca del Río (30 minutes). AU buses also go there from the 2nd-class station.

CÓRDOBA
☎ 271 /pop 135,000 / elevation 924m
Cordobenses are spirited urbanites who are proud of their colonial town where the contract sealing Mexico's independence was signed in 1821. Its historical appeal and agreeably temperate climate might entice you to visit, especially if you're a city-goer. The museum is small but interesting, the cathedral grandiose and the *zócalo* teeming with kids chasing pigeons, grandmothers on benches and shoe shiners hard at work.

Córdoba lies in the foothills of Mexico's central mountains, surrounded by fertile countryside. In 1618 30 Spanish families founded Córdoba in order to inhibit escaped African slaves from attacking travelers between Mexico City and the coast. Today it's a commercial and processing center for sugar cane, tobacco, coffee and fruit.

Orientation
Córdoba's central Plaza de Armas has regal 18th-century *portales* on three sides. Like many towns, streets have numbers rather than names, and avenidas are perpendicular to calles. Even-numbered avenidas are northeast from the plaza and even-numbered calles are northwest, leaving odd numbers southeast and southwest of the plaza, respectively.

Information
Banks around the Plaza de Armas have 24-hour ATMs.
Centro de Lavado (☎ 706-99-44; Calle 2 no 501; Mon-Fri 8am-9pm, Sat 9am-8pm) Laundry at M$9 per kilo.
Cibermania (☎ 712-88-20; Av 2 no 306; per hr M$10) Internet access.
Libros y Regalos (Av 3 no 104 in Plaza Jardín; 10:30am-8:30pm) Just off the *zócalo*.
Post office (Av 3 s/n) Northwest of the plaza.
Sanatorio Covadonga (☎ 714-55-20; www.sanatoriocovadonga.com.mx; Av 7 no 1610; 24hr) Urgent medical care at all hours.
Tourist office (☎ 717-17-00 ext 1778; turismo@mpiocordoba.gob.mx; Palacio Municipal; 8am-7pm Mon-Sat) Helpful staff offers maps and information. Volunteers sometimes give tours of the city.

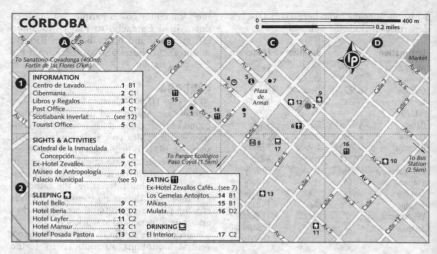

CÓRDOBA

To Sanatorio Covadonga (400m);
Fortín de las Flores (7km)

To Parque Ecológico
Paso Coyol (1.5km)

Plaza de Armas

Market

To Bus
Station
(2.5km)

Sights

The **Ex-Hotel Zevallos**, built in 1687, is former home of the *condes* (counts) of Zevallos. It's on the northeast side of the plaza, behind the *portales*. Plaques in the courtyard record that Juan O'Donojú and Agustín de Iturbide met here on August 24, 1821 and agreed on terms for Mexico's independence. They also concurred that a Mexican, not a European, should be head of state. Iturbide went on to briefly reign as Emperor Agustín I. The building is now notable for its café–restaurants.

At the southeast end of Plaza de Armas is the imposing baroque **Catedral de la Inmaculada Concepción**, which dates from 1688. It has an elaborate facade flanked by twin bell towers. The showy interior is ornate with gold leaf detailing and marble floors. The chapel is flanked with candle-lit statues with altars, such as a gruesome Jesus on the cross and an eerily despairing Virgen de la Soledad. The mixture of glitz and gore is a visual metaphor of a disturbing historical dichotomy: the richness of the conquistadores and the misery that the indigenous people subsequently endured.

Half a block southwest of the plaza, the **Museo de Antropología** (Calle 3 s/n; admission free; 9am-2pm & 4-8pm) has a modest but interesting collection of artifacts. There's a fine Aztec ball-court marker, some Olmec figurines and a replica of the magnificent statue of El Señor de Las Limas that resides in Xalapa's Museo de Antropología. On the 2nd floor there's a lovely overlook to the mountains.

Parque Ecológico Paso Coyol (714-20-84; cnr Calle 6 & Av 19 Bella Vista; admission M$2) is a jewel in the urban rough. The neighborhood joined with the government to turn what was once a 4-hectare abandoned lot overrun by 'delinquents' into a park. Now this eco-conscious park is patronized by *cordobenses* who run and walk its trails snaking around gardens corralled by old tires and plastic bottles. Your meager entrance fee pays for both *campesinos* and biologists alike to maintain the place. Follow Calle 3 south from the plaza for 1.5km. The street changes names, weaves through a suburb and bottoms out at the park.

Festivals & Events

On the evening of **Good Friday**, Córdoba marks Jesus' crucifixion with a procession of silence, in which thousands of residents walk through the streets behind an altar of the Virgin. Everyone holds a lit candle, no one utters a word and the church bells are strangely quiet.

Sleeping

Córdoba's accommodation options are not extensive, but they are well done.

Hotel Iberia (712-13-01; iberiacordoba@prodigy .net.mx; Av 2 no 919; s/d M$165/265, with air-con M$180/280;) A great budget deal, the clean rooms have arched brick windows and there's a courtyard in the center. You can rent a room here for four hours. Wink.

Hotel Posada Pastora (712-88-82; Calle 5 no 517; s/d M$280/300, plus M$50 with air-con;)

There is nothing spectacular about this place, but it's clean and comfortable and solid value for the price. Two rooms have outside-facing windows.

Hotel Mansur (☎ 712-60-00; fax 712-69-89; Av 1 no 301; from M$410; P ✂) This is the most friendly and appealing hotel on the *zócalo*. Its vast balconies with thick wooden chairs are fantastic perches to enjoy cathedral views and people-watching on the lively plaza below. The rooms are simple yet sparkling and have solid wood furnishings.

Hotel Bello (☎ 712-81-22; www.hotelbello.com /cordoba; cnr Av 2 & Calle 5; s/d M$440/520; P ✂ ☐) This modern hotel is spotless and smartly decorated. The rooms are fresh and the staff affable. Go for the top-floor balcony rooms.

Hotel Layfer (☎ 714-05-05; Av 5 no 909; r/d M$550/720, ste add M$200; P ✂ ✂) It's meant to be fancy, but the odd-colored, blockish rooms are more trippy than anything else. The wide array of complimentary body care condiments is strangely pleasing.

Eating & Drinking

our pick Las Gemelas Antojitos (Av 5 no 7; mains M$15-45; ✿ 24hr) At any hour, this colorful eatery serves Mexican food made right in front of you. You can also get the local scoop from chatty ladies behind the counter.

Ex-Hotel Zevallos (☎ 712-18-53; Av 1 No 101; mains M$70-120; ✿ 8am-1am) Multiple fashionable cafés share this colonial building on the plaza, with the more formal choices upstairs. Good food, excellent ambience, higher prices.

Mikasa (☎ 712-76-13; Av 5 no 212; mains M$70-120; ✿ 1-10pm Tue-Sun) Cordoba does sushi. And loves it. You might have to wait for a table at this hole in the wall hotspot.

Mulata (☎ 717-66-63; Av 1 no 721; dishes M$80-140) Named for a legend of a beautiful African slave who escaped from prison through the picture she drew in her cell. Appropriately, there's a gorgeous mural here as well as delectable, internationally influenced food and bakery items.

El Interior (☎ 727-17-17; Av 3 no 318; coffee M$12-25; ✿ 9am-9pm Mon-Sat, 10am-8pm Sun) This café and gift shop has a new-age feel. It sells espresso drinks, unique souvenirs and useful maps.

Getting There & Around

BUS

Córdoba's bus station, which has deluxe, 1st-class and 2nd-class services, is at Av Privada 4, 2.5km southeast of the plaza. To get to the town center from the station, take a local bus marked 'Centro' or buy a taxi ticket (M$20). To Fortín de las Flores and Orizaba, it's more convenient to take a local bus from Av 11 than to go out to the Córdoba bus station.

As always, 2nd-class buses run more often than 1st-class services to closer destinations, take longer and cost 10% less than the corresponding 1st-class service. Deluxe and 1st-class buses from Córdoba include:

Destination	Fare	Duration	Frequency
Mexico City (TAPO)	M$224	5½hr	26 daily
Oaxaca	M$258	6hr	4 daily
Puebla	M$136	3hr	17 daily
Veracruz	M$82	1¾hr	at least 1 hourly
Xalapa	M$120	3hr	11 daily

CAR & MOTORCYCLE

Córdoba, Fortín de las Flores and Orizaba are linked by toll Hwy 150D, the route that most buses take, and by the much slower Hwy 150. A scenic back road goes through the hills from Fortín, via Huatusco, to Xalapa.

ATOYAC

Stop at the town of Atoyac, some 25km from Cordoba, and get messy tearing into the renowned *langostinos* (king prawns) caught in the river. Prepared *al ajillo* (à la garlic), it's scrumptiously served with half a head of fried garlic. Afterwards, cool off at **Playa Bella**, a sandbar where the town's gorgeous river widens and makes for a fantastic swimming spot.

If you have a car or like to walk you can visit the **Cascada de Atoyac**. Continue east through town and turn right onto a dirt road at the deserted railroad station for a couple of kilometers. You'll pass under two hand-hewn tunnels before you see the plunging waterfall next to the picturesque abandoned railroad. Trails of questionable quality drop down to the river.

From Córdoba, buses (M$12) for Atoyac leave from the main bus station.

FORTÍN DE LAS FLORES

☎ 271 / pop 21,000 / elevation 970m

Just west of Córdoba, Fortín de las Flores is a tranquil cut-flower cultivation center, with nurseries and private gardens. It's a peaceful weekend retreat for Mexico City's middle class, though travelers may find this a nice jumping-board town for mountain adventures. It could be preferable to stay in tranquil Fortín – with its cute *zócalo* and lush surroundings – over its industrial neighbors, Córdoba and Orizaba. Fortín's annual **flower festival** runs for a week in late April or early May.

Orientation

Fortín is 7km from central Córdoba, but the towns are starting to grow into each other along Hwy 150. Its attractive, open plaza, the Parque Principal, shelters the Palacio Municipal in the middle and a cathedral on the south side. Streets are arranged like Córdoba's with perpendicular *avenidas* and *calles*.

Information

'El Chat' (☎ 713-31-81; cnr Calle 3 & Av 12; per hr M$10; ☼ 9am-9:30pm)

Post office (Calle 1 btwn Avs 1 & 3) Between El Interior and El Centro de Mariscos through the arcade to the left.

Tourist office (☎ 713-01-02; cnr Calle 5 & Av 1; ☼ 8am-4pm Mon-Fri)

Activities

Take a scenic **walk** from the center west down Av 1, which turns into the Fortín Viejo road. After about 20 minutes you'll come to a point overlooking the old railroad and towering verdant mountains. Continuing down the road for a kilometer or so, you'll pass over the river and turn right for 2km onto a forest dirt road going to **El Corazón** (admission M$10), a basic facility with weathered swimming pools. Past the pools, behind the electric plant, you can climb a huge staircase to get great views. The roads are safest walked during the day.

Xochitl travel agency (☎ 713-29-26; www.groups .msn.com/faraventuras; faraver@hotmail.com; Av 3 Pte no 113; ☼ 10am-12pm & 4-7pm Mon-Fri, 10am-2pm Sat), just a couple of blocks from the plaza, arranges myriad outdoor trips (hiking to waterfalls, rappelling, caving, paragliding) in the phenomenal surrounding areas.

Also, **Cecilia Rábago** (☎ 271-120-20-30; ceci rabago@hotmail.com; M$900-1000/day, 1-4 people) is a well-established, bilingual tour guide in the area and a firecracker of a lady. She's an expert on history and sites in the Fortín–Córdoba–Orizaba area.

Sleeping

Hotel Suites 'Magnolias' (☎ 713-22-98; Av 3 no 105; s/d M$300/500, with Jacuzzi M$700; ⊠ P) Skittles box

meets bad cubism at this quirky little hotel right off the *zócalo*. The bright colors, weird tile schemes and somewhat wacky designs will make for an interesting stay. The sanitary standard isn't rigid.

Hotel Fortín Las Flores (☎ 713-01-08; www .hotelfortindelasflores.com.mx; Av 2 no 210 btwn Calles 5 & 7; s/d M$415/570, ste from M$760) This open-air, plant-filled hotel a short walk from the center is a great value. Rooms over the pool have adorable bay window sitting nooks, and some patios have excellent views of Pico de Orizaba.

Hotel Posada Loma (☎ 713-06-58; www.posadaloma .com; Carretera Córdoba–Fortín Km 333; s/d M$550/650, bungalows per month M$10,000-12,000; P ⊠ ⊠) If you're a garden lover, this is your oasis. Its grounds are a marvel of greenhouses, famous orchid collections, gardens with exotic and local flowers, terraces and a pool. The airy accommodations come with fireplaces for winter nights. The renowned breakfast in its restaurant, with spectacular views of Pico de Orizaba, is unbeatable. Loma is off Hwy 150, about 1km from central Fortín.

Eating and Drinking

Lots of eateries surround the *zócalo*.

El Interior (Calle 1 No 105; snacks M$15-50; ☼ 9am-10:30pm, Sun 10am-10pm) Small-town Mexico goes for trendy…and does alright. This branch café–bookstore is welcoming, bright and known for its *mostachón* (walnut crusted torte filled with cream cheese and fresh strawberries).

ourpick Kiosko Café (Zócalo; mains M$30-70; ☼ 7am-11pm) Smack dab in the middle of the *zócalo*, this café enjoys unmatched real estate. Formerly the library, it now serves coffee, fresh juices and meals. The enchiladas have high acclaim.

El Parián (☎ 713-11-67; Av 1 no 110; mains M$35-80; ☼ 7am-11pm, closed Wed) Just off the center, you'll find hearty plates with good service and pleasant atmosphere. Try *sopa Azteca*, a soup of shredded, fried tortillas and avocado chunks.

Getting There & Away

In Fortín, local bus services arrive and depart from Calle 1 Sur, on the west side of the plaza. The ADO depot on the corner of Av 2 and Calle 6 mainly has long-distance services to Mexico City, Veracruz, Puebla, Orizaba and Xalapa.

Destination	Fare	Duration	Frequency (daily)
Córdoba	M$6	20min	9
Mexico City (TAPO)	M$216	5hr	3
Mexico City (Terminal Norte)	M$216	5hr	1
Orizaba	M$12	25min	12
Veracruz	M$88	2hr	6
Xalapa	M$130	4hr	13

The 2nd-class bus to Orizaba goes through the gorgeous countryside but is more crowded and slower.

COSCOMATEPEC

☎ 272 / pop 13,700 / elevation 1,588

Coscomatepec (referred to as Cosco) is a picturesque mountain town 24km north of Fortín. It is renowned for its intricate hand-made saddles and leather goods, quality cigars and delicious bread.

You can take tours through the famous bakery, cigar factory and saddle shops arranged through the **tourist office** (☎ 737-04-80; turismo cosco@yahoo.com.mx; Amez y Argüelles s/n; ☉ 9am-4pm Mon-Fri) in the Plaza Municipal. Ask for Nacho, who also arranges **outdoor adventure** activities, such as hiking, rappelling, horseback riding, zip-lines and possibly rock climbing in this area rich with caves, rivers, old bridges and waterfalls. There's an ATM in the plaza.

Having one of the only fleets of quality rental mountain bikes in the state is **Aventuras del Nuevo Mundo** (☎ 273-737-07-33; www.coscomatepec .info; nwasoco@hotmail.com) founded and run by a pleasant gringo and his Coscomatepecan wife. It specializes in a bike tour that drives people to the top of a 20km descent and lets them rip. Cross-country bike trips can also be arranged. Note that the DIY biking opportunities here are rich indeed if you have your own bike.

The **Hotel San Antonio** (☎ 737-03-20; Bravo 35; s/d M$180/250) on the plaza has a lovely communal patio and cleanish rooms. Alternatively, the infamous **Posada del Emperador** (☎ 737-15-20; cnr Av Juárez & Domínguez; r M$400-800) is a more upscale option touted as having hosted Maximilian. It's a charming place boasting antique furniture, wood floors, exquisite views and a plant-filled interior.

In between Fortín and Cosco in Monte Salas is **Chula Vista Camping** (☎ 271-732-00-74; Calle 3 no 309; per person M$50). Turn left on Calle 3 off the main road and continue for 3km. Follow signs to the campground. It's by a beautiful turquoise river, with nature trails and caves nearby. Rustic *cabañas* are available.

From Fortín it's an hour bus ride (M$12) or a taxi costs M$60.

ORIZABA

☎ 272 / pop 122,000 / elevation 1219m

More industrial than urbane, Orizaba does a heck of a job making you forget that you're in the middle of gorgeous mountain country. Another strike is that the *zócalo*, Palacio Municipal, and cathedral are scattered about rather than bordering a unifying plaza. Thus, hotels and activity are unfortunately migrating to Av 6 Ote, a thru-way for traffic. But the city does have some worthwhile highlights: the fantastic art museum, interesting architecture, and strolls through Alameda Park and along the river.

The city was founded by the Spanish to guard the Veracruz–Mexico City road. An industrial center in the late 19th century, its factories were early centers of the unrest that led to the unseating of dictator Porfirio Díaz. Today it has a big brewery and is home to cement, textile and chemical industries.

Orientation

The central plaza is Parque Castillo, with the irregularly shaped Parroquia de San Miguel on its north side. The Palacio Municipal is west toward Alameda Park on Av Colón Pte, which is the boundary between the Norte and Sur *calles*. Madero, a busy street bordering the plaza's west side, divides *avenidas* into Ote and Pte. Three blocks south of the plaza is Av Ote 6, the main east–west artery through town.

Information

Banks with ATMs are on Av Ote 2, a block south of the plaza.

Cruz Roja (☎ 725-05-50; Av Colón Ote 253; ☉ 24hr) Provides medical care.

Net-plus (Av Colón Ote s/n, 2nd fl; per hr M$10) Internet access.

Post office (Av Ote 2)

Tourist office (☎ 728-91-36; www.orizaba.gob.mx /turismo.htm; Palacio de Hierro; ☉ 8am-3pm & 4-8pm Mon-Fri, noon-8pm Sat, noon-4pm Sun) Has enthusiastic staff and plenty of brochures, though not much practical information.

Sights

The Parque Castillo has an imposing 17th-century-style, towered parish church, the

ORIZABA

INFORMATION		SIGHTS & ACTIVITIES		DRINKING	
Banamex......................1 B2		Catedral de San Miguel..........8 B2		Forum Café..................12 C2	
Bancomer....................2 B3		Palacio de Hierro...................(see 7)		Gran Café de Orizaba.....13 B2	
Cruz Roja.....................3 C2					
Net-plus......................4 B2		SLEEPING		TRANSPORT	
Post Office...................5 C2		Gran Hotel de France.............9 C3		ADO Bus Station............14 D2	
Santander Serfin.........6 B2		Hotel Arenas....................10 B2			
Tourist Office..............7 B2		Hotel Posada del Viajero.......11 B1			

Catedral de San Miguel. Opposite the church is the **Palacio de Hierro** (Iron Palace), Orizaba's Art Nouveau landmark built entirely from iron and steel. Alexandre Gustave Eiffel, a master of metallurgy who gave his name to the Eiffel Tower and engineered the Statue of Liberty's framework, designed this pavilion, which was built in Paris. Orizaba's mayor, eager to acquire an impressive European-style Palacio Municipal, bought it in 1892. Piece by piece it was shipped, then reassembled in Orizaba.

Orizaba's wonderful **Museo de Arte del Estado** (State Art Museum; ☎ 724-32-00; cnr Av Ote 4 & Calle Sur 25; admission M$10; ⏱ 10am-5pm Tue-Sun) is housed in a gorgeously restored colonial building dating from 1776. The museum is divided into rooms that include one of Mexico's most important permanent Diego Rivera collections; there are also contemporary works by regional artists.

Activities

West of the center, **Parque Alameda** is an expansive, lush city park dotted with statues. It hosts pick-up soccer games, runners and loafers.

The **Cerro del Borrego** looms lusciously over the park and offers brilliant views if you get to the top very early before the mist rolls in. However, avoid it in the evening. The entrance is easy to miss. Walk westbound on Av Pte 3 until it bottoms out, and take a left. Look for a very narrow alleyway entrance on the right, which will lead you past the quirky Ermita de la Virgen de Guadalupe and finally to the trail's stairs.

Also, there's a neat pedestrian **river walk** that weaves nonsensically down the river and tours you under some of city's 13 bridges. You can access it from most of the bridges near the center.

A number of adventure tour operators are based in Orizaba (see boxed text, p657). **Mountain Sports Mexico** (☎ 726-00-18; www.moun tainsmexico.com; elkletus@hotmail.com) arranges various outdoor activities in nearby hills, mountains and canyons, including climbs part way up Pico de Orizaba. **Turismo Aventura Desafío** (☎ 725-06-96; Av Pte 3 No 586) offers similar services. Servimont (p700) in Tlachichuca provides bona fide hiking and biking guides for around the Pico. Highlights of the area include the gorgeous Cañon de la Carbonera near Nogales and the Cascada de Popócatl near Tequila. But, really, exquisite natural places saturate this region. DIY adventures are waiting to be had.

Sleeping

Higher-end options are on the Av Ote 6 traffic strip. Low-end choices are near the center.

Hotel Arenas (☎ /fax 725-23-61; Av Nte 2 no 169; s/d M$120/170) Tucked into a bustling side street, this hotel is a great value. The rooms are well-cared for and look into a central patio sitting area lush with plants and trees.

Hotel Posada del Viajero (☎ 726-33-20; Madero Nte 242; s/d M$100-200; P) The Viajero might look unappealing from the outside, but staying here is a solid value with clean rooms and pleasant staff.

Hotel Ikebana (☎ 725-71-43; Av Pte 3 no 512; hotel_ikebana_ste@hotmail.com; s/d M$240/280; P 🅧) This small, funky Japanese-themed hotel has a restaurant below that strives to offer Asian dishes. The rooms with pop-out windows looking out over the park are fantastic while the windowless internal rooms leave something to be desired.

Gran Hotel de France (☎ 725-23-11; Av Ote 6 no 186; s/d M$350/380; P 🅧) This historic late 19th-century building has a splendid high-ceiling lobby. The rooms are pleasantly simple and the price is right.

Hotel Fiesta Cascada (☎ 724-15-96; fax 724-55-99; www.hotelcascada.com.mx; Hwy Puebla-Córdoba Km 275; s/d M$660/790; P 🅧 🖥 🅡) The Cascada sits above a gorgeous canyon and has a pool, gardens and forest trails, and is near a fantastic waterfall. The spacious rooms come at a terrific price. It's about 2km east of the center.

Eating & Drinking

In sedate Orizaba many restaurants close early. Head to the plaza for tacos and snacks.

La Lechuga (☎ 726-39-81; Av Pte 3 no 542; mains M$25-80 🕒 8:30am-6pm; 🆅) Properly located in front of Alameda Park where the health-conscious population comes to run and walk, this pleasant vegetarian restaurant offers a breakfast buffet and a daily set lunch menu (M$45).

Restaurant Jardín (Av Colón Pte 379; mains M$25-50; 🕒 8am-7pm) You'll almost pass it if you're not careful, but look for an entrance that leads into a plant-filled courtyard. A tranquil spot to lunch on delicious Mexican favorites.

Mariscos Boca del Río (☎ 726-52-99; Av Pte 7 s/n; seafood M$50-100; 🕒 noon-8pm Tue-Sun) Known as the best seafood restaurant in town, its big portions should not leave you hungry.

Gran Café de Orizaba (☎ 724-44-75; cnr Av Pte 2 & Madero) Sitting pretty inside the Palacio de Hierro with its polished wood floors and pictures of old Orizaba, this café has a regal feeling. The patio is a fabulous spot to drink the high-quality tea or coffee.

Forum Café (☎ 725-47-35; Calle Sur 5 No 225; drinks M$10-30; 🕒 10am-10pm Mon-Sat, 5-10pm Sun) It's a fantastic place to enjoy the acoustical delights of *trova* (playing most nights) over a beer or coffee. There's courtyard seating, and the place is adorned with local art.

Getting There & Around

Local buses from Fortín and Córdoba stop four blocks north and six blocks east of the town center, around Ote 9 and Nte 14. The AU 2nd-class bus station is at Zaragoza Pte 425, northwest of the center.

The modern 1st-class bus station is on the corner of Av Ote 6 and Sur 13, and handles all ADO, ADO GL and deluxe UNO services. Daily 1st-class buses are as follows:

Destination	Fare	Duration	Frequency
Córdoba	M$16	40min	every 30 min
Fortín del las Flores	M$12	3½hr	6 daily
Mexico City (TAPO)	M$210	5hr	17 daily
Mexico City (Terminal Norte)	M$210	5hr	7 daily
Oaxaca	M$244	6hr	3 daily
Puebla	M$122	2½hr	16 daily
Veracruz	M$96	2½hr	25 daily
Xalapa	M$130	4hr	10 daily

There are also 1st-class services to Tampico and Villahermosa, as well as slower and slightly cheaper 2nd-class services to Mexico City, Puebla and Veracruz.

Toll Hwy 150D, which bypasses central Orizaba, goes east to Córdoba and west, via a spectacular ascent, to Puebla (160km). Toll-free Hwy 150 runs east to Córdoba and Veracruz (150km) and southwest to Tehuacán, 65km away over the hair-raising Cumbres de Acultzingo.

PICO DE ORIZABA

Mexico's tallest mountain (5611m), called 'Citlaltépetl' (Star Mountain) in the Náhuatl language, is 25km northwest of Orizaba. From the summit of this dormant volcano, one can see the mountains Popocatépetl, Iztaccíhuatl and La Malinche to the west and the Gulf of Mexico to the east. The only higher peaks in North America are Mt McKinley in Alaska and Mt Logan in Canada.

The only recommended local company that guides people to the summit is **Servimont** (☎ 245-451-50-82; www.servimont.com.mx; Ortega 1A, Tlachichuca; packages from US$370), a climber-owned outfit passed down through the Reyes family. As the longest-running operation in the area, it also acts as a Red Cross rescue facility. It's based in the small town of Tlachichuca (2600m), which is a common starting point for expeditions.

Unless you're an experienced climber with mountaineering equipment, you'll need a guide and a good level of fitness. Book your expedition with Servimont two to four months in advance and allow four to seven days to acclimatize, summit and return. Staff will tell you all you need to know about acclimatization, gear, etc.

If you're going to climb unguided, talk to Servimont about the routes; some spots are becoming dangerous due to global warming. Topographical maps can be mail-ordered way ahead of time or bought in person from Inegi offices in Veracruz or Xalapa (see boxed text, p657). Also, *Mexico's Volcanoes*, by RJ Secor, offers some good info. The best climbing period is October to March, with the most popular time being December and January.

Summiting Veracruz' iconic bad boy will prove to be an exhilarating, challenging endeavor as well as a fantastic way to experience the region's spectacular mountainscape. Initially, you hike to a base camp (4200m) where you sleep a touch and begin the final ascent around 2am, reaching the summit around sunrise. The climb is moderately steep and not technically difficult, but you'll still use crampons, ropes and ice axes.

Hostal accommodations at Servimont's base camp (which is a former soap factory adorned with interesting mountaineering antiques) is included in your package. If you want a private room, **Hotel Coyote** (☎ 245-451-54-25; 5 de Mayo s/n; s/d M$150/250; P) is right on the plaza, as is **La Casa Blanca** (mains M$30-80), a restaurant with delightful heating.

From Orizaba, catch a bus from the AU terminal to Ciudad Serdán (M$38, 2 hours), then another to Tlachichuca (M$12, one hour).

SOUTHEAST VERACRUZ STATE

Southeast of Veracruz port you'll find flat, fecund coastal plains crossed by rivers as well as volcano-dappled rainforest with myriad lakes, waterfalls and beaches. As the former heartland of ancient Olmec culture, the area is laden with archaeological sites, both preserved and seldom visited. The far south of the state claims oil metropolises such as Minatitlán and Coatzacoalcos.

TLACOTALPAN
☎ 288 / pop 9000 / elevation 10m

In the 19th century, Tlacotalpan was a major port because of its location on the expansive Río Papaloapan's north bank. Now this is a tranquil little town that's done well to preserve its broad plazas, colorful houses, colonial architecture and cobbled streets, thus receiving Unesco World Heritage status in 1998. Walking around, you're bound to run into an interesting niche museum. Buildings around town have plaques, in both Spanish and English, explaining their respective histories.

Information
There's an ATM on Carranza near the plaza.
Internet Café (Alegre s/n) A block south from the *zócalo*.
Post office (☯ 8am-4pm Mon-Fri) Around the corner from the tourist office.
Tourist office (Palacio Municipal; ☯ 9am-3pm Mon-Fri) Under the green and red *portales* facing Plaza Hidalgo. The office has helpful maps.

Sights & Activities
This little town is rich with interesting mini-museums. The **Museo Salvador Ferrando** (Alegre 6; admission M$20; ☯ 10:30am-5pm Tue-Sun) displays assorted artifacts from the town's colonial history. Move on to the **Casa Museo Agustín Lara** (Beltrán 6; admission M$20; ☯ 10am-5pm Mon-Sat), featuring memorabilia of *tlacotalpeño* Agustín Lara (1900–70), a legendary musician, composer and Casanova. The pink **Casa de la Cultura Agustín Lara** (☎ 884-22-02; Carranza 43; ☯ 9am-5pm) houses art exhibits, folkloric dance rehearsals and *jarocho* music lessons, which are free for visitors to observe; the gallery upstairs may exact an admission fee.

Down the road is the **Mini-Zoológico Museo** (Carranza 25; donation M$10; ☯ 10am-5pm Mon-Sat),

---

AGREEABLE TABLE MANNERS

- Whenever you catch the eye of someone who's eating, stranger or not, you say '*Provecho* ' (Enjoy). Don't avoid this custom. It's good manners and feels nice.

- After finishing a delicious yet messy fish meal, it's not rude to clean your fingers with the rind of the squeezed lime. It's quite practical really.

- When eating outdoors, you may see people stuffing paper napkins in their soda bottlenecks. It keeps the flies away.

---

the home of Don Pío Barrán, who keeps several crocodiles and a range of artifacts, including a locally excavated mastodon tooth and a sword that supposedly belonged to Porfirio Díaz.

If you walk the *malecón* near the restaurants, you're bound to run into a *lanchero* offering to whisk you down the scenic river for a hour-long **boat ride** (M$250 split btwn passengers) to see a nearby lagoon. It's not the Amazon, but it's a lovely way to spend a late afternoon. Or take a stroll by the riverside and down Cházaro, which starts from the Palacio Municipal and has wall-to-wall, whacky colored, colonial-style houses and buildings with high arches and columns and tiles.

Festivals & Events

In late January and early February, Tlacotalpan's lively **Candelaria** festival features bull-running in the streets; and an image of the Virgin is floated down the river followed by a flotilla of small boats.

Sleeping & Eating

Prices triple or quadruple during the Candelaria holiday.

Hotel Reforma (☎ 884-20-22; Av Carranza 2; s/d M$200/250, with air-con M$300/350; P X) It's not squeaky clean, but the rooms are spacious and a good value, especially if you get one with a balcony right over the *zócalo*.

Hotel Blanca (☎ 884-31-20; Beltrán 50; s/d M$260/320; P X) The spick-and-span rooms don't have lots of natural light, but are spacious, comfortable and welcoming with bright linens and colonial-themed decor.

Hotel Tlacotalpan (☎ 884-20-63; hoteltlacotalpan@ tlaco.com.mx; Beltrán 35; s/d M$450/500; P X X) This bright blue-and-yellow building off the main road has fresh rooms that surround a beautifully tiled courtyard. The lobby has an airy, colonial feel with rocking chairs and high ceilings.

Hotel Posada Doña Lala (☎ 884-25-80; Av Carranza 11; s/d M$390/440, with air-con M$440/550; P X X) The huffy staff bank on this hotel's famous reputation, but it has a great location near the river and the *zócalo*.

For good eats, try **Restaurante Tlacotalpan** (☎ 884-34-75; Malecón s/n; M$80-120), one of the numerous terrific open-air eateries on the riverfront that whip up fresh, traditional seafood. They're more expensive than eateries in town, but the ambience is worth it. Also, there are a couple of lovely cafés in the center that face Plaza Hidalgo and the *zócalo*. Alternatively, head to the **market** by ADO for cheap fresh juices and regional favorites.

Getting There & Around

Hwy 175 runs from Tlacotalpan up the Papaloapan valley to Tuxtepec, then twists and turns over the mountains to Oaxaca (320km). ADO offers service to Mexico City, Puebla, Xalapa and Veracruz, while Transportes Los Tuxtlas (TLT) buses cover local routes.

SANTIAGO TUXTLA

☎ 294 / pop 16,000 / elevation 180m

More laid-back and a touch more charming than its rowdy neighbor San Andrés, Santiago (1525) is centered on a lovely, verdant *zócalo* and is surrounded by rolling green foothills of the volcanic Sierra de los Tuxtlas. The plaza is strewn with ladies arm-in-arm, couples lip-to-lip and shoes getting vigorously shined. It's not on the tourist track, per se, but the intriguing little museum, the close proximity (23km) to Tres Zapotes and the possibility of tranquil stay at Mesón de Santiago merit a visit.

All buses arrive and depart near the junction of Morelos and the highway. To get to the center, continue down Morelos, then turn right into Ayuntamiento, which leads to the *zócalo*, a few blocks away. The post office is on the *zócalo*, as are two banks (with sometimes dry ATMs), while a handful of internet places are scattered in close proximity.

The **Olmec head** in the *zócalo* is known as the 'Cobata head,' after the estate where it was found. Thought to be a very late Olmec production, it's the biggest known Olmec head, weighing in at 40 tonnes, and unique in that its eyes are closed.

The **Museo Tuxteco** (☎ 947-10-76; admission M$34; ◷ 9am-6pm Mon-Sat, 9am-4pm Sun), on the plaza, exhibits artifacts such as Olmec stone carvings, including another colossal head, a monkey-faced *hacha* (ax) with obsidian eyes, and a Tres Zapotes altar replica. You can buy books (in Spanish) about the area and pre-Hispanic cultures. The upstairs has local art exhibits.

Santiago celebrates the festivals of **San Juan** (June 24) and **Santiago Apóstol** (St James; July 25) with processions and dances including the Liseres, in which the participants wear jaguar costumes. The week before Christmas is also a time of huge festivity.

Right on the highway, **Hotel Olmeca** (eerras quin@hotmail.com; Carretera Federal; s/d M$190/260, with air M$240/310; P ⌂) is only a few blocks from ADO. Its simple rooms are a bit run-down, but cheap and passable for a night.

ourpick **Hotel Mesón de Santiago** (☎ 947-16-71; 5 de Mayo 202; from M$550; P ⌂ ⌂) is a good choice if you want to linger. With a freshly renovated interior and its external colonial architecture preserved, this fantastic new hotel right on the *zócalo* is a gem. The peaceful, landscaped courtyard has a small pool and is immaculate. Rooms are tastefully decorated with deeply burnished wood furniture and details, fresh white linens and painted tiles. The biggest flaw, really, is that the café sells American-style food, like hot dogs and hamburgers.

Half a block off the *zócalo* is **Jugo La Fuente** (Av Juárez 20; M$20-50) serving deliciously fresh, traditional Mexican fare and squeezed juices, including a mean carrot juice. If there's extra juice from your drink order, it's served up in a colorful bucket on the side. Also on the *zócalo* next to the museum is the **market** where – if you don't mind animal carcasses – you can find a variety of cheap eats.

Getting There & Around

All local and regional buses and *colectivo* taxis to San Andrés Tuxtla are frequent and stop at the junction of Morales and the highway. A private taxi is M$60. Frequent 2nd-class buses also go to Catemaco, Veracruz, Acayucan and Tlacotalpan.

While the TLT and AU stops are just down Morelos, there's a tiny ADO office on the highway itself. Second-class buses are slower, more frequent to closer destinations, and are about 10% less. First-class buses are as follows:

Destination	Fare	Duration	Frequency (daily)
Acayucan	M$66	2½hr	2
Córdoba	M$164	3½hr	1
Mexico City	M$374	8½hr	2
Minatitlan	M$90	3½hr	2
Orizaba	M$152	3½hr	1
Puebla	M$288	5½hr	2
San Andrés	M$12	25min	15
Veracruz	M$90	2½hr	9
Xalapa	M$156	4½hr	3

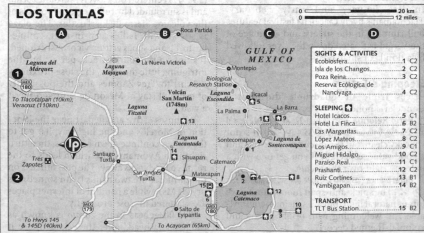

LOS TUXTLAS

0   20 km
0   12 miles

GULF OF MEXICO

To Tlacotalpan (10km); Veracruz (110km)

Laguna del Márquez

Laguna Majagual

Roca Partida

La Nueva Victoria

Montepio

Biological Research Station

Volcán San Martín (1748m)

Laguna Escondida

Jicacal

La Barra

La Palma

Laguna Titzatal

Tres Zapotes

Laguna Encantada

Sihuapan

Sontecomapan

Laguna de Sontecomapan

Santiago Tuxtla

San Andrés Tuxtla

Catemaco

Matacapan

Laguna Catemaco

Salto de Eyipantla

To Hwys 145 & 145D (40km)

To Acayucan (65km)

SIGHTS & ACTIVITIES
Ecobiosfera..................1 C2
Isla de los Changos..................2 C2
Poza Reina..................3 C2
Reserva Ecólogica de Nanciyaga..................4 C2

SLEEPING
Hotel Icacos..................5 C1
Hotel La Finca..................6 B2
Las Margaritas..................7 C2
López Mateos..................8 C2
Los Amigos..................9 C1
Miguel Hidalgo..................10 C2
Paraíso Real..................11 C1
Prashanti..................12 C2
Ruíz Cortines..................13 B1
Yambigapan..................14 B2

TRANSPORT
TLT Bus Station..................15 B2

TEMASCAL

The temascal steam bath ritual of Mesoamerican cultures was considered barbaric and strange by conquering Spaniards, who were notably nonbathing types. These days tourists are eager to hop into the small dome temascal structure (similar idea to the Native American sweat lodge) and to participate in a tradition known to be healing and cleansing both internally and externally. More and more places offer temascal because of its fiscal promise, but the tradition still exists in its truer form in indigenous villages.

TRES ZAPOTES

☎ 294 / pop 3600

The important late-Olmec center of Tres Zapotes is now just a series of mounds in cornfields. However, interesting artifacts are displayed at the museum in the town of Tres Zapotes, 23km west of Santiago Tuxtla. The trip to this tiny town is not convenient, but might be worth it if archaeology floats your boat.

Tres Zapotes was occupied for over 2000 years, from around 1200 BC to AD 1000. It was probably first inhabited while the great Olmec center of La Venta (Tabasco) still flourished. After the destruction of La Venta (about 400 BC), the city carried on in what archaeologists call an 'epi-Olmec' phase – the period during which the Olmec culture dwindled as other civilizations, notably Izapa and the Maya, came to the fore. Most finds are from this later period.

The small **Museo de Tres Zapotes** (admission M$27; �9am-5pm) notably has the 1.5m Tres Zapotes head, an Olmec head dating from about 100 BC. The biggest piece, Stela A, depicts three human figures in the mouth of a jaguar. Other pieces include a sculpture of what may have been a captive with hands tied behind his back and the upturned face of a woman carved into a throne or altar. The museum attendant is happy to answer questions in Spanish or give a tour (tipping is appreciated).

The road to Tres Zapotes goes southwest from Santiago Tuxtla; a 'Zona Arqueológica' sign points the way from Hwy 180. Eight kilometers down this road, you fork right onto a paved stretch for the last 15km to Tres Zapotes. It comes out at a T-junction, from where you go left then left again to reach the museum. From Santiago Tuxtla there are 2nd-class buses (M$20) and taxis (M$20/80 *colectivo*/private). Taxis leave from the Sitio Puente Real, on the far side of the pedestrian bridge at the foot of Zaragoza (the street going downhill beside the Santiago Tuxtla museum).

SAN ANDRÉS TUXTLA

☎ 294 / pop 56,000 / elevation 300m

Surrounded by rolling evergreen landscape and farmland, the bustling town of San Andrés is in the center of Los Tuxtlas and is Mexico's cigar capital. It has a few exciting things going on: cigar factory tours, Yambigapan's cooking classes, or the looming Volcán San Martín (1748m) in the distance begging to be climbed.

Orientation & Information

The main bus station is on Juárez, 1km northwest of the plaza. The cathedral is on the plaza's north side, the Palacio Municipal on the west side with a tiny tourist office, and a Banamex (with ATM) on the south side. The market is three blocks west.

The post office is on Lafragua; head down 20 de Noviembre directly across the plaza from the Palacio Municipal and follow it around to the left. A couple of blocks away from the *zócalo* on Juarez there is a tiny plant-covered shopping center called Plaza Jardín that houses two internet places, **@ctual's** (Av Juarez 106; per hr M$10; �8am-11pm) and **Double Click** (Av Juarez 106; per hr M$10; �8am-11pm).

Sights & Activities

Watch and inhale as the *puros* are speedily rolled by hand at the **Santa Clara cigar factory** (☎ 947-99-00; ventas@tabasa.com; Blvd 5 de Febrero 10; admission free; �7am-10pm Mon-Fri, 10am-10pm Sat), on the highway a block or so from the bus station. Cigars of assorted shapes and sizes, including the monstrous Magnum, are available at factory prices, and the 50 *torcedores* employed here (together rolling 10,000 *puros* a day) are happy to demonstrate their technique.

Twelve kilometers southeast of San Andrés, a 242-step staircase leads down to the impressive **Salto de Eyipantla** (admission M$8), a 50m-high, 40m-wide waterfall. Follow Hwy 180 east for 4km to Sihuapan, then turn right to Eyipantla. Frequent TLT buses (M$10) make the trip, leaving from the corner of Cabada and 5 de Mayo, near the market.

The **Laguna Encantada** (Enchanted Lagoon) occupies a small volcanic crater 3km northeast of San Andrés. A dirt road goes there but no buses do. It's not advisable to walk by the lake alone, as there have been isolated incidences of assault, but guides will take you there from nearby **Yambigapan** (☎ 104-46-39; www.yambigapan.com.mx; campsites/s/d M$50/280/350; P). Three kilometers or so from San Andrés, this family-run campground in the countryside is equipped with two simple *cabañas* with spectacular views. Not to be missed are the **cooking classes** from the doña of the house who will teach you traditional Mexican cooking (in Spanish) and its history in her fantastic kitchen for about M$100 to M$200. There's also swimming in the nearby river and guided hikes to the supposedly magical **Cueva de Diablo** (Devil's Cave) where the *brujos* (see boxed text, p707) do their thing. Taxi (M$35 to M$40) is the easiest way to arrive. Or ask a *pirata* (pickup truck) going to Ruíz Cortines to leave you at the turnoff and follow signs for Yambigapan that eventually lead you up a long dirt driveway. It should cost about M$10.

ourpick **Ruíz Cortines** (☎ 100-50-35; Ejido Ruiz Cortinez; campsites/cabañas M$50/400) Way up in the forest tucked in the base of the volcano, an hour north from Andrés, this little town has installed very rustic *cabañas* and offers horseback riding (M$100 per person) and hikes to caves. Its highlight service is the all-day, breathtaking hike up **Volcán San Martín** (1748m). The little restaurant Comedor Ecoturístico has delicious, pick-out-your-fish fresh food. A taxi from Andrés costs M$90 or a *pirata* is M$25.

Sleeping

San Andrés doesn't have a lot of choices, but you'll be comfortable.

Hotel Colonial (cnr Belisario Domínguez & Pino Suárez; r from M$75) If you feel the need to pinch a penny or two, head north of the *zócalo* and brave the stale, bare-bone rooms here. There's an open, plant-filled sitting area looking over the city.

Hotel Isabel (☎ /fax 942-16-17; Madero 13; s/d M$230/300, with air-con M$310/350; P ❄) With its cheerful, light rooms, this well-kept hotel right off the *zócalo* trumps its more expensive neighboring competition.

Hotel de los Pérez (☎ 942-07-77; Rascón 2; r from M$360; P ❄ ▣) Strives for a business-class feel but ends up being plain.

Hotel Posada San Martín (☎ 942-10-36; Juárez 304; r from M$370; P ❄ ▣) Midway between the bus station and the *zócalo*, this hacienda-style posada is a fabulous deal, with a pool set in a peaceful garden and unique touches, like yellow-and-blue sinks and carved headboards, in the spacious rooms.

Eating

Restaurant Winni's (☎ 942-01-10; Madero 10; dishes M$40) Join the rest of San Andrés here on the corner of the *zócalo* and sip an espresso drink while munching a pastry or a well-priced meal.

ECOTURISMO: WHAT DOES 'ECO' REALLY MEAN?

'Ecotourism' is commonly perceived as tourism based on the ethics of sustainability, with goals of environmental awareness and protection. In the central Gulf coast region, *ecoturismo* signifies any tourist service that doesn't happen to be in the city. A hotel will tag this plug word onto its promotions if it's located outside city bounds, as will a tour company if it offers a 1km hike on a non-paved road.

However, there are small pockets of bona fide, ethics-based ecotourism organizations, many in their infancy. For example, in Los Tuxtlas, some rural communities (see Ruíz Cortines, above; Miguel Hidalgo, p708; and Las Margaritas, p708) have made a collective effort to create economic opportunities for themselves, while protecting their natural environment through the development of ecotourism. Their efforts are somewhat disorganized, and don't offer the reliability of well-established tourist services (eg getting in touch to arrange visits can prove quite difficult). But if you're up for an adventure, hop on a *lancha* or *pirata* to their corners of the rainforest and embark upon a visceral, ideologically sound way to experience the luscious Reserva de la Biosfera Los Tuxtlas.

For further information on budding ecotourism projects in Veracruz, check out Pronatura (www.pronaturaveracruz.org), a conservation organization that is gaining momentum.

Refugio La Casona (☎ 942-07-35; Madero 18; dishes M$40-70; ☽ 7am-2am) Along restaurant-laden Madero, this bar–restaurant serves traditional Mexican fare in its peaceful, leafy rear garden. There's also live bohemian music (from 9pm) most nights.

Caperucita (Av Juárez 108; dishes M$50-80; ☽ 7am-midnight) On the top floor of Plaza Jardin near the zócalo, this open-air restaurant adorned with plants is a great place to hang out on a hot afternoon drinking fresh-squeezed juice and munching antojitos.

Getting There & Around

San Andrés is the transportation center for Los Tuxtlas, with fairly good bus services in every direction, 1st-class with ADO and 2nd-class (meaning no bathroom) with AU. Rickety but regular 2nd-class TLT buses are often the quickest way of getting to local destinations. They leave from a block north of the market and skirt the north side of town on 5 de Febrero (Hwy 180). Regula TLT destinations include Acayucan, Santiago Tuxtla and Veracruz. Frequent colectivo taxis to Catemaco and Santiago also leave from the market – they're speedier than the bus but cost a fraction more. Local taxis abound, and catching one to Catemaco or Santiago Tuxtla will run you M$60.

Destination	Fare	Duration	Frequency
Acayucan	M$50	2hr	9 daily
Catemaco	M$10	25min	10 daily
Cordoba	2nd-class M$155	4hr	1 daily
Mexico City	M$342	8hr	8
Orizaba	2nd-class M$170	5hr	1 daily
Puebla	M$300	6hr	2 daily
Santiago Tuxtla	2nd-class M$12	25min	regular
Veracruz	M$95	3hr	12 daily
Villahermosa	M$300	5hr	5 daily
Xalapa	M$165	5hr	7 daily

CATEMACO

☎ 294 / pop 25,000 / elevation 340m

Nestled among lusciously green hills on the western shore of serene Laguna Catemaco, this small town famous for witchcraft (see boxed text, p707) makes its living from fishing and Mexican tourism. During vacations and holidays, prepare for crowds and fiestas. During the low seasons, when hotels are a third cheaper, Catemaco turns into a charming lakeside town, its precious zócalo trimmed with intricate white wrought iron and scenic malecón festooned with colorful, weather-worn boats. By the water, the lancheros insistently vie for your business, which can be annoying. This is a great place to use a base for visiting beaches, waterfalls and lagoons in the Los Tuxtlas Biosphere Reserve and beyond.

Orientation & Information

Catemaco slopes gently down toward the lake. A **tourist office** (☎ 943-00-16; Municipalidad; ☽ 9am-3pm Mon-Fri) on the north side of the zócalo will impart information, updated or not, about the town and the surrounding region. The **post office** (Cuauhtémoc s/n) is four blocks west of the central plaza. For a very informative website in English, check out www.tuxtlas.com.

Bancomer (Av Boettinger s/n) on the zócalo has an ATM, and there's a Scotiabank ATM a block down. On the west side of the zócalo, @ **ctual's Internet** (Av Boettinger s/n; per hr M$10; ☽ 8am-10pm) is one of numerous central internet places.

Lavandería Sofi (Av Boettinger; 8am-8pm; M$14/kilo) three blocks off the zócalo provides excellent laundry services.

Sights & Activities

Ringed by volcanic hills, **Laguna Catemaco**, which is actually a lake and not a lagoon, is 16km long. East of town are a few modest gray-sand beaches where you can take a dip in cloudy water. Following Av Hidalgo a kilometer east of town, the road tees and you'll hit the less-crowded **Playa Espagoya**. If you take a left on this waterfront road you'll find a sign for **Ecoparque** (☎ 94-304-56; www.ecoparque-lapunta.com; 8 treatments for M$450), a small, jungle-themed rustic spa, offering mud massage and temascal, among other things. The spa also sells arnica soap and other crunchy items.

You can take **boat tours** to several islands within the lake. On the largest, Isla Tenaspi, Olmec sculptures have been discovered. **Isla de los Changos** (Monkey Island; Map p702) shelters red-cheeked monkeys, originally from Thailand. They belong to the University of Veracruz, which acquired them for research. Lancheros, disturbingly, feed the monkeys for the sake of close-up photography. A boat ride costs M$50

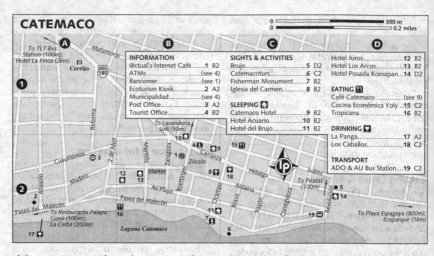

CATEMACO

0   300 m
0   0.2 miles

INFORMATION
@ctual's Internet Café.......1 B2
ATMs.............................(see 4)
Bancomer.....................(see 1)
Ecotourism Kiosk............2 A2
Municipalidad..............(see 4)
Post Office.....................3 A2
Tourist Office.................4 B2

SIGHTS & ACTIVITIES
Brujo...............................5 D2
Catemacoturs..................6 C2
Fisherman Monument.......7 B2
Iglesia del Carmen............8 B2

SLEEPING
Catemaco Hotel...............9 B2
Hotel Acuario.................10 B2
Hotel del Brujo...............11 B2

Hotel Juros....................12 B2
Hotel Los Arcos..............13 B2
Hotel Posada Koniapan....14 D2

EATING
Café Catemaco..............(see 9)
Cocina Económica Yoly...15 C2
Tropicana.......................16 B2

DRINKING
La Panga.......................17 A2
Los Caballos...................18 C2

TRANSPORT
ADO & AU Bus Station....19 C2

Laguna Catemaco

if there is a group of people or M$350 for a private *lancha*.

The town also has a helpful **ecotourism kiosk** (Malecón & Abasolo s/n) that will point you in the direction of rural ecotourism projects in the area (see boxed text, opposite). To support positive use of the rainforest, the kiosk sells goods from local artisans, such as regional botanical remedies and wine holders made from bamboo.

On the *malecón*, **Catemacoturs** (Malecón s/n; www.catemacoturs.com) is a *palapa* hut that rents beat-down adventure gear: low-end mountain bikes, sit-on-top kayaks and pedalboats. It also offers tours to waterfalls and the coast.

If you want to visit a local *brujo*, there's **'El Poder del Tigre' Botánicos y Ciencias Ocultas** ('Power of the Tiger' Botanics & Occult Sciences; ☎ 943-07-46; www .brujogueixpal.com; Av Hidalgo 2). The *brujo* might pull up in his Ford Explorer and tell you to check out his website, or he might be available to see you.

Sleeping
Flexible prices fluctuate dramatically (10 to 35%) according to demand with steep price hikes at high-season weekends, holidays, and the March witch-doctor convention.

BUDGET
La Ceiba Restaurant y Trailer Park (Malecón s/n; campsites or trailer per person M$50) This open-air, tropically decorated, lakeside restaurant has a patch of green grass where you can camp or

hoo up a trailer (water and electricity). There are bathrooms with showers.

Hotel Acuario (☎ 943-04-18; cnr Boettinger & Carranza; s/d M$200/300; P). One of several budget places on the *zócalo*, it's well kept though plain and fan-cooled. Some rooms have views.

Catemaco Hotel (☎ 943-02-03; www.hotelcatemaco .net; Carranza 8; r from M$375; P ⚡ 🐾) On prime *zócalo* real estate, the café below is a popular hub. Its rooms are spotless, though sometimes the showers are cold.

MIDRANGE & TOP-END
Hotel del Brujo (☎ 943-12-05; Malecón s/n; s/d M$350/450; P ⚡) A clean yet simple, secure yet tattered, hotel right on the lakeshore with mostly air-conditioned rooms. Some have magnificent, lake-facing balconies.

Hotel Los Arcos (☎ 943-00-03; www.arcoshotel .com.mx; Madero 7; r from M$500; P ⚡ 🐾 ⚲) The well-managed Los Arcos has helpful staff and a small swimming pool. The light, airy rooms are situated in a way that entices guests to kick back in the breezy, plant-filled sitting areas.

Hotel Juros (☎ 943-00-84; Av Playa 14; s/d M$300/550; P ⚡ 🐾) This hotel runs a tight ship and provides quality rooms. Balcony rooms are fantastic. The roof-top pool has a lounging area with stellar views of the lake.

Hotel Posada Koniapan (☎ 943-00-63; www .hotelposadakoniapan.com.mx; cnr Revolución & Malecón; r incl breakfast from M$550; P ⚡ 🖥 🐾) On the easternmost tip of the *malecón*, the peaceful Posada Koniapan is located a touch outside the hustle and bustle of town. A landscaped swimming pool lies within the gated, ultra-secure grounds. Top floor rooms have fantastic views.

Hotel La Finca (☎ 943-03-22, 800-523-46-22; www.lafinca.com.mx; Hwy 180 Km 47; r from M$750; P X X 🖵 ⚐) Set lakeside in leafy gardens 2km west of town, this resort-like hotel has rooms with large, lakeview balconies and a pool with slides and a hot tub. It's a deal outside peak seasons, if seclusion from town is okay with you. They provide *lancha* and spa services.

Eating

The lake provides the specialties here: *te-gogolo* (a snail, reputed to be an aphrodisiac, eaten with chili, tomato, onion and lime) sold by street vendors and *chipalchole* (shrimp or crab-claw soup). Many tourist-aimed restaurants line the *malecón*. Explore the city's viscera, and you'll find interesting local eateries.

Cocina Económica Yoly (Juárez s/n; dishes M$15-50) Watch Yoly hand-make your fat *memela* (gigantic corn tortilla filled with goodies). Just off the *zócalo*, this local dive has fresh, inexpensive food.

Café Catemaco (☎ 943-02-03; Carranza 8; ☯ 6am-1pm; dishes M$50-100) This common meeting hub and wireless hotspot is patronized by trendy and business-oriented local crowds as well as a tiny international contingent. The food is traditional and tasty.

Restaurante Palapa Gorel (Malecón s/n; dishes M$60-110) On the *malecón* you'll run into this popular, lakeside *palapa*. The hawker trying to entice you inside is annoying, but the seafood is lovely. It has live music on weekends.

Tropicana (☎ 943-12-97; Malecón s/n; dishes M$50-120; ☯ 8am-9pm) Vast waterfront restaurant serving fish, *marsicos* and meat. It does up the iconic colorful Mexican decorations, but still is a cool place to grab a bite.

Drinking

our pick **La Panga** (Paseo de Malecón s/n; ☯ 8am-midnight) This bar–restaurant literally floating on the lake with its own boardwalk is an unbeatable place to lean back, sip *cerveza* and grab a bite to eat while the sun disappears beyond the lake and rolling hills.

Los Caballos (Av Caranza s/n; ☯ 9pm-3am) A block east of the *zócalo*, candle-lit tables, *trova*, and Christmas lights create an ambience soaked with Latin romance. There's live music at weekends.

Getting There & Away

ADO and AU buses operate from a delightful lakeside terminal east of town. Local 2nd-class TLT buses run from a bus stop 700m west of the plaza by the hwy junction. *Colectivo* taxis arrive and depart from El Cerrito, a small hill about 400m to the west of the plaza on Carranza. A taxi to San Andres is M$60.

First-class bus services include the following:

Destination	Fare	Duration	Frequency (daily)
Acayucan	M$48	1½hr	4
Córdoba	M$180	5¼hr	2
Mexico City	M$390	9hr	5
Puebla	M$304	6hr	4
Santiago Tuxtla	M$18	1hr	10
Veracruz	M$100	3½hr	10
Xalapa	M$176	5hr	4

THE WITCHING HOUR

On the first Friday in March each year, hundreds of *brujos* (shamans), witches and healers from all over Mexico descend on Catemaco to perform a mass cleansing ceremony. The event is designed to rid them of the previous year's negative energies, though the whole occasion has become more commercial than supernatural in recent years. Floods of Mexicans also head into town at this time to grab a shamanic consultation or *limpia* (cleansing) and eat, drink and be merry in a bizarre mix of otherworldly fervor and hedonistic indulgence.

Witchcraft traditions in this part of Veracruz go back centuries – mixing ancient indigenous beliefs, Spanish medieval traditions and voodoo practices from West Africa. Many of these *brujos* multitask as medicine men or women (using both traditional herbs and modern pharmaceuticals), shrinks and black magicians (casting evil spells on enemies of their clients). If you're lucky, you could run into a *brujo* on your visit because, really, who couldn't use a little more abracadabra in their life?

To arrive at communities surrounding the lake and toward the coast, take inexpensive *piratas*. They leave from a corner five blocks north of the bus station.

AROUND CATEMACO

In 1998 various nature reserves around Catemaco were conglomerated to make the **Reserva de la Biosfera Los Tuxtlas**, an area containing a splendor of natural beauty. This region, being economically depressed, has little tourism infrastructure. Nevertheless, what it does have is worthwhile. In fact, that which it doesn't have is worthwhile as well.

Laguna Catemaco

On the lake, one-way *lancha* (boat taxi) prices are M$50 *colectivo* or M$350 private.

On the northeast shore of the lake, the well-established **Reserva Ecológica de Nanciyaga** (Map p702; ☎ 294-943-01-99; www.nanciyaga.com; Hwy Catemaco-Coyame; ☼ 9am-2pm & 4-6pm; P) preserves a small tract of rainforest. The grounds are replete with a temascal (see boxed text, p703) ($250 per person), ancient planetarium and Olmec-themed decorations and replicas. Even though it plays up the contrived indigenous theme, this place stands out for its organization and cleanliness. One night's lodging (M$800) in solar-powered cabins includes a mineral mud bath, massage, guided walk and the use of kayaks. Camping is available too. Arrive by *pirata* (M$7), taxi (M$80) or by boat (M$50 per person).

On the east side of the lake, a couple of kilometers past Tebanca, **Prashanti** (Map p702; ☎ 294-107-79-98; www.prashanti.com.mx; Tebanca—Coyame road; r from M$800) is very agreeable (yet overpriced and not immaculate). Rooms are blessed with names like 'Mantra' and 'Genesh,' and you can sacredly rent four-wheelers here as well. It also offers kayak rentals and boat tours. The views of the lake and hills are spectacular from here.

Las Margaritas (Map p702; ☎ 294-945-52-51; www.ecoturismo-lostuxtlas.tx; santos_132j@hotmail.com; campsites M$50, cabaña per person incl meals & two guided trips M$550) No *colectivo* boats go to this little village, spitting distance from the official demarcation of the beginning of the biosphere reserve, so arrive by private *lancha* (M$350) or bumpy *pirata* (M$12). The rural setting by the lake is stunning, but try to give enough notice of your visit for the rustic cabins to be cleaned. Trips are offered to uncharted archaeological sites

and to waterfalls where guides point out birds and medicinal plants. It also rents canoes and kayaks (M$30 per hour).

In the Rainforest

Ecobiosfera (Map p702; ☎ 294-949-73-08; felixaguilar_ecobiosfera@hotmail.com; Carr Catemaco-Dos Amates; campsites M$50, cabañas from M$400) If hidden waterfalls, kayaking, hiking, bird-watching, or beautiful beaches interest you, Ecobiosfera will organize your excursion. Prices vary (about M$400 to M$1000), but the owner, Felix, is a biologist and knows the area very well. He can take you to the deep-green **Poza Reina** (Map p702) swimming hole laden with cascades east of Laguna Catemaco, which is a local favorite and is not signed. For a DIY bike tour, Felix will arrange support vehicles or whatever you need. The *cabañas* at the base camp are charming in a Robinson Crusoe kind of way with a shared bathroom.

Miguel Hidalgo (Map p702; ☎ 294-949-56-03; rcruz90@hotmail.com; campsites/cabañas M$50/450) This little community in the rainforest east of Laguna Catemaco's northeastern shore has rustic lodging. The *cabaña* price includes meals and a short hike. The area's flora, fauna and waterfalls are spectacular. Try to give advance warning of your arrival if you can.

López Mateos (Map p702; ☎ 294-943-11-01; www.ecoturismo-lostuxtlas.tk; elmarinero@tuxtlas.org) East of Laguna Catemaco snuggled up in the rainforest near a beautiful river, this place has a similar thing going but with even less infrastructure. Nothing is guaranteed but an adventure.

Laguna de Sontecomapan

In the town of Sontecomapan, 15km north of Catemaco, there are some lagoon-side restaurants and the idyllic **Pozo de los Enanos** (Well of the Dwarves) swimming hole. You can catch a *lancha* (M$15 to M$25 *colectivo*) from here to any of the following places on the lake.

Family-run **Paraíso Real** (Map p702; ☎ 294-949-59-84; cabañas M$350 & M$600; P), in the tiny town of El Real, has two *cabañas* and a peaceful camping space right on Lake Sonetecomapan.

ourpick Los Amigos (Map p702; ☎ 294-943-01-01; www.losamigos.com.mx; campsites/dm/cabaña M$50/150/350; P) is near where the laguna enters the ocean in the well-run, peaceful retreat. The fantastic *cabañas* tucked into the verdant hillside have lovely hammocked balconies with spectacular views of the bay. There are nature trails to a beautiful lookout, kayak rentals and a restaurant.

The Coast

The small fishing town **La Barra**, with its pleasant beaches and seafood restaurants, can be reached by a *lancha* from Somtecomapan or a side road going east from La Palma, 8km north of Sontcomapan.

North of La Barra is the tiny beach town of **Jicacal**. You can access Jicacal from a rough road that forks east from the main road. Family-run **Hotel Icacos** (r M$300-400) is the only place to stay, with basic rooms, and owns the only restaurant with delectable, fresh-from-the-line seafood. The dirt road to the left right before you hit Jicacal will lead you 10 minutes down a gorgeous wreck of a road to a moldering relic of a hotel. From there, you'll find a path leading to a long set of crumbling stairs going to **Playa Escondida** (Hidden Beach), which earns its name. During the work week in the low season, you'll probably have this gorgeous blond sand beach and its turquoise waters to yourself.

North of the junction to Jicacal, you'll soon hit the **Biological Research Station** (☎ 200-125-54-58; www.ibiologia.unam.mx; museum 🕑 9am-5pm Mon-Fri) where you'll see a handful of camping opportunities, including at Laguna Escondida and Finca Villa Carino. The ornery biologists have a tiny biology museum and limited patience for tourists. They cobbled the roads through their section of the reserve to limit people, speed and traffic.

Farther north is **Montepío**, where there's a picturesque beach at the mouth of the Río Máquina where you can eat seafood on the beach, and **Posada San José** (☎ 294-942-10-10; s/d M$240/270, with air-con M$340/370; P ⊠), a reasonably comfortable place to sleep.

ACAYUCAN

☎ 924 / pop 47,000

Acayucan is an important commercial center and bustles accordingly. It's at the junction of Hwy 180 (between Veracruz and Villahermosa) and Hwy 185. If you're here in transit, you'll find services are good.

The bus station is on the east side of town. To reach the central plaza, walk uphill to Av Hidalgo, turn left and walk six blocks. Several banks alongside the plaza have ATMs. There are internet cafés off the pedestrian alley behind the plaza.

Sleeping & Eating

Hotel Ritz (☎ 245-00-24; Hidalgo 7; s/d M$150/180, M$290/350 with air; P ⊠) Staying at the Ritz is a bargain. This is a colorful, well-kept hotel that is clean and feels separated from the city even though it's on the road connecting the bus station to the *zócalo*.

Hotel Kinaku (☎ /fax 245-04-10; Ocampo Sur 7; s/d M$510/600; P ⊠ ⊠) Acayucan's most expensive hotel, equipped with a formal restaurant, is not a brilliant value for money, but upper-floor rooms have sweeping views.

Cortijo (☎ 245-65-87; Pasaje Bravo btwn Hidalgo & Colonia Centro; mains M$25-60; 🕑 7am-8pm) This locals' choice is off the pedestrian alley behind the plaza (the north side). It has fresh, Mexican fare.

Morenda (mains M$10-50) If you're just passing through town or waiting for a bus, you're in luck, *compadre*. Located between the bus stations is a massive labyrinth of little eateries and merchants selling a myriad of things, including food of all colors, textures and shapes.

Getting There & Away

Local buses (M$5) and taxis (M$15 to M$20) run between the terminal and city center. UNO and ADO GL run a few deluxe services, while ADO is a 1st-class line. You can reserve these ahead of time. Alternatively, AU provides good 2nd-class service. These companies, and more, operate from the same location flanking the market. Direct 1st-class buses are listed below. (There are frequent 2nd-class services to Catemaco and Santiago Tuxtla.)

Destination	Fare	Duration	Frequency (daily)
Catemaco	M$48	1½hr	1
Mexico City (TAPO)	M$469	9hr	3
Santiago Tuxtla	M$54	2¼hr	1
Tuxtla Gutiérrez	M$264	5hr	3
Veracruz	M$140	3½hr	14
Villahermosa	M$144	3hr	12

The toll highway, 145D, passes south of town. Heading east, it's signposted to Minatitlán; heading west, toward Córdoba or Veracruz, it's marked for the town of 'Isla.' The tolls are expensive, costing more than M$300 to get to Córdoba.

SAN LORENZO

Near the small town of Tenochtitlán, 35km southeast of Acayucan, San Lorenzo was the first of the two great Olmec ceremonial centers. It had its heyday from about 1200 to 900 BC.

Ten Olmec heads, stone thrones and numerous smaller artifacts that were found here are now in museums elsewhere. The main structure was gigantic platform, but now it's nothing more than a low hill. The '**museum**' (admission free; ⏰ 8am-5pm) is two tiny rooms of stone artifacts and a large head.

This trip is really worth it only if you geek out on archaeology.

While you're there, **El Azazul**, about 7km past the museum, has some well-carved, kneeling stone figures said to be over 1000 years old.

Arriving by public transportation is a pain in the *nalgas*. A taxi from Acayucan is M$200 and a 90-minute ride. There's no public transportation to the Azazul site, but a taxi driver might be coerced into taking you.

Oaxaca State

The state of Oaxaca (wah-*hah*-kah) has a special magic felt by Mexicans and foreigners alike. Long isolated from other parts of the country by ranks of rugged mountains, it is a redoubt of a traditional, mysterious, strongly indigenous-influenced side to Mexican life that has almost vanished in more accessible regions. Oaxaca has Mexico's most vibrant and creative handicrafts scene, its artists are in the vanguard of Mexican contemporary art, its festivities are among the most colorful and alive in the country, and its uniquely savory, spicy cuisine is starting to combine with outside influences with some spectacular results.

At the center of the state in every way stands beautiful colonial Oaxaca city, a fascinating and hospitable cultural, geographical and political hub. Around the city extend Oaxaca's three Valles Centrales (Central Valleys), always the center of civilization in this part of Mexico and today still full of bustling indigenous markets, spectacular pre-Hispanic ruins and villages full of creative artisans. North of here are the forested highlands of the Sierra Norte, scene of successful community-tourism ventures enabling visitors to hike, bike, climb rocks and ride horses amid some of Mexico's most unusual landscapes. To the south, across yet more mountains, is Oaxaca's fabulous coast, with its endless sandy Pacific beaches, waters full of dolphins, turtles and sport fish, and lagoons teeming with birds. Many of the beaches are completely empty, but there's also a handful of beach towns and villages that will make any traveler happy – Puerto Escondido with its world-class surf; the planned but beautiful and relaxed resort of Bahías de Huatulco; and the sybarite's delights of Puerto Ángel, Zipolite, San Agustinillo and Mazunte.

HIGHLIGHTS

- Indulge in the culture, color and culinary delights of colonial **Oaxaca city** (p713)
- Hike through otherworldly cloud forests between the remote villages of the **Pueblos Mancomunados** (p747)
- Soak up the surf scene of mellow **Puerto Escondido** (p752)
- Chill out for longer than you planned at fabled travelers' hangout **Zipolite** (p768)
- Get a feel for Zapotec village life at the markets and fiestas of the **Valles Centrales** (p736)

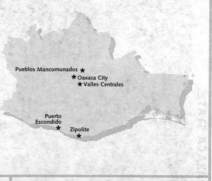

- OAXACA CITY JANUARY DAILY HIGH: 25°C | 77°F
- OAXACA CITY JULY DAILY HIGH: 28°C | 82°F

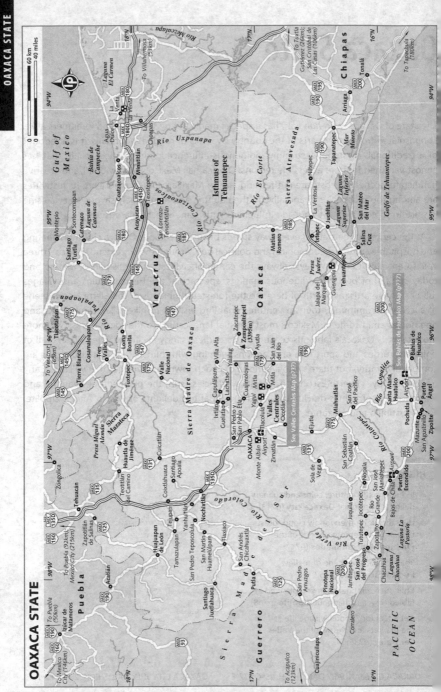

History

Pre-Hispanic cultures in Oaxaca's Valles Centrales (Central Valleys) reached heights rivaling those of central Mexico. The hilltop city of Monte Albán became the center of the Zapotec culture, conquering much of Oaxaca and peaking between AD 300 and 700. Monte Albán then declined suddenly, and from about 1200 the Zapotecs came under the growing dominance of the Mixtecs from Oaxaca's northwest uplands. Mixtecs and Zapotecs alike were conquered by the Aztecs in the 15th and early 16th centuries.

The Spaniards had to send at least four expeditions before they felt safe enough to found the city of Oaxaca in 1529. The indigenous population quickly took a disastrous drop in numbers: the population of the Mixteca in the west is thought to have fallen from 700,000 when the Spanish arrived to about 25,000 by 1700. Unsuccessful indigenous rebellions continued into the 20th century.

Benito Juárez, the great reforming leader of 19th-century Mexico, was a Zapotec from the Oaxaca mountains. He served two terms as Oaxaca's state governor then as president of Mexico from 1861 until his death in 1872 (see p722). Juárez appointed Porfirio Díaz, son of a Oaxaca horse trainer, as Oaxaca state governor in 1862. Díaz rose to control Mexico with an iron fist from 1877 to 1910, bringing the country into the industrial age but also fostering corruption, repression and, eventually, the Revolution in 1910.

After the Revolution about 300 *ejidos* (communal landholdings) were set up in Oaxaca, but land ownership and wealth distribution remain sources of conflict today. Tourism thrives in and around Oaxaca city and in a few places on the coast, but underdevelopment still prevails in the backcountry. The violent confrontations between the authoritarian state government and opposition organizations in Oaxaca in 2006 and 2007 highlighted the gulf between Oaxaca's rich, powerful minority and its poor, disempowered majority.

Climate

The Valles Centrales are warm and dry, with most rain falling between June and September. On the coast and in low-lying areas it's hotter and a bit wetter. The average high in Oaxaca city ranges from 25°C in December and January (when lows average about 8°) to about 30° in March through May.

Parks & Reserves

Combining both dry and damp mountain ranges with low-lying northern, eastern and southern fringes, Oaxaca has greater biological diversity than any other state in Mexico, but little of this is under official protection. Two smallish national parks – 142-sq-km Parque Nacional Lagunas de Chacahua (p763) and 119-sq-km Huatulco (p776) – protect coastal areas. The Reserva de la Biosfera Tehuacán-Cuicatlán spreads over the semiarid tropical ecosystems of northwestern Oaxaca and adjacent southeast Puebla state.

Dangers & Annoyances

Buses and other vehicles traveling isolated stretches of highway, including the coastal Hwy 200 and Hwy 175 from Oaxaca city to Pochutla, have occasionally been stopped and robbed. Though incidents have decreased in recent years, it's still advisable not to travel at night.

Getting There & Around

Continental Airlines flies direct from Houston to Oaxaca and Bahías de Huatulco. There are also flights to both these airports and Puerto Escondido from Mexico City; Oaxaca also has air connections with other Mexican cities. Small planes hop from Oaxaca to Puerto Escondido and Huatulco.

Oaxaca city has good bus links with Mexico City and Puebla to the north and a few daily services to/from Veracruz, Villahermosa, Tuxtla Gutiérrez, San Cristóbal de las Casas and Tapachula. Suburban-type vans provide the most effective service between Oaxaca and Pochutla (the transportation hub for the central Oaxaca coast) and Puerto Escondido, via Hwys 175 and 131 respectively.

Plenty of buses travel along coastal Hwy 200 into Oaxaca from Acapulco and Chiapas.

OAXACA

☎ 951 / pop 268,000 / elevation 1550m

Welcome to one of Mexico's most beautiful and vibrant cities. A colonial city with a lovely, tree-shaded central square, El Zócalo, Oaxaca is the heart of a region whose highly creative populace produces the country's finest range of crafts and some of its most exciting contemporary art. Artists and artisans alike are inspired by the state's deep-rooted

> **TOP THREE THINGS TO DO WITH TIME ON YOUR SIDE IN OAXACA (APART FROM CHILLING AT THE BEACH)**
>
> - Hike from village to village through the forests of the **Sierra Norte** (p747).
>
> - Ride a bike from Oaxaca to Puerto Escondido with **Bicicletas Pedro Martínez** (p723).
>
> - Spend a few days at Teotitlán del Valle's **Casa Sagrada** (p741), riding horses, hiking, watching birds, learning Oaxacan cooking and taking a temascal.

indigenous traditions and by its bright southern light. Oaxaca has top-class museums, lovely architecture, charming inns and hotels and its own flavorsome version of Mexican cuisine. The easygoing southern pace breaks out into frequent lively fiestas, and there's some event going on in the streets or plazas almost every day.

The city is surrounded by fascinating archaeological sites and by colorfully traditional villages and small towns. The dramatic valley and mountain landscapes provide abundant opportunities for hiking, biking, horseback riding and climbing, and good active-tourism operators and successful rural tourism programs make it easy for visitors enjoy these experiences.

Despite its cultural riches, Oaxaca is one of Mexico's poorest states, and the city is the stage on which many of the unresolved tensions between the largely *mestizo* ruling elite and the largely indigenous poor are acted out. The city's fringe settlements of migrant villagers are as impoverished as any in Mexico, and the violent confrontations between the state government and protestors here in 2006 highlighted Oaxaca's deep economic and political divide. The troubles wiped out the city's important tourist industry for more than a year, but by late 2007 calm, and the tourists, had returned.

HISTORY

The Aztec settlement here was called Huaxyácac (meaning 'In the Nose of the Squash'), from which the word 'Oaxaca' is derived. The Spanish laid out a new town around the existing Zócalo in 1529. It quickly became the most important place in southern Mexico.

In the 18th century Oaxaca grew rich from exports of cochineal (a red dye made from tiny insects living on the prickly pear cactus) and from the weaving of textiles. By 1796 it was probably the third-biggest city in Nueva España, with about 20,000 people (including 600 clergy) and 800 cotton looms.

In 1854 an earthquake destroyed much of the city. It was several decades before it began to grow again, but by the 1890s the population passed 30,000. Another earthquake in 1931 left 70% of the city uninhabitable.

Oaxaca's major expansion has come in the past 25 years, with tourism, new businesses and rural poverty all encouraging migration from the countryside. The population of the city proper has almost doubled in this time, and together with formerly separate villages and towns it now forms a conurbation of perhaps 450,000 people.

ORIENTATION

Oaxaca centers on the Zócalo and the adjoining Alameda de León plaza in front of the cathedral. Calle Alcalá, running north from the cathedral to the landmark Iglesia de Santo Domingo, is closed to traffic most of the way.

The main road from Mexico City traverses the northern edge of central Oaxaca as Calz Niños Héroes de Chapultepec then heads on east toward Mitla and the Isthmus of Tehuantepec. The 1st-class bus station is just off this road, 1.75km northeast of the Zócalo. The 2nd-class bus station is almost 1km west of the center, near the main market, the Central de Abastos. Oaxaca airport is 6km south of the city, 500m off Hwy 175. See p735 for details on getting to/from the city center.

The blocks north of the Zócalo are smarter, cleaner and less crowded with traffic and people than those to the south. The commercial area occupies the blocks southwest of the Zócalo.

INFORMATION
Bookstores
Amate (Map pp720-1; ☎ 516-69-60; www.amatebooks .com; Plaza Alcalá, Alcalá 307-2; ☒ 10am-8pm Mon-Sat, 2-7pm Sun) Probably the best English-language bookstore in Mexico, stocking almost every Mexico-related title (in print) in English.
Librería Universitaria (Map pp720-1; ☎ 516-42-43; Guerrero 104; ☒ 10am-3pm & 4:30-8:30pm Mon-Sat)

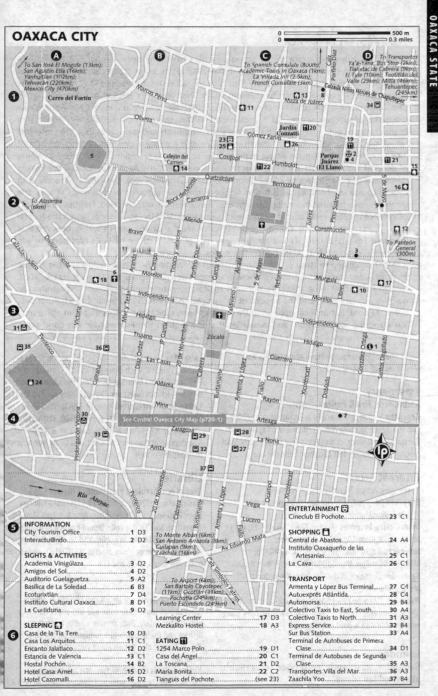

OAXACA CITY

0 ————— 500 m
0 ————— 0.3 miles

INFORMATION
City Tourism Office.....................1 D3
Interactu@ndo............................2 D2

SIGHTS & ACTIVITIES
Academia Vinigúlaza.....................3 D2
Amigos del Sol...........................4 D2
Auditorio Guelaguetza...................5 A2
Basílica de La Soledad..................6 B3
Ecoturixtlán.............................7 D4
Instituto Cultural Oaxaca..............8 D1
La Cutiduría............................9 D2

SLEEPING
Casa de la Tía Tere.....................10 D3
Casa Los Arquitos.......................11 C1
Encanto Jalatlaco.......................12 D2
Estancia de Valencia....................13 D1
Hostal Pochón...........................14 B2
Hotel Casa Arnel........................15 D2
Hotel Cazomalli.........................16 D2
Learning Center.........................17 D3
Mezkalito Hostel........................18 A3

EATING
1254 Marco Polo.........................19 D2
Casa del Ángel..........................20 C1
La Toscana..............................21 D2
María Bonita............................22 C2
Tianguis del Pochote.................(see 23)

ENTERTAINMENT
Cineclub El Pochote.....................23 C1

SHOPPING
Central de Abastos......................24 A4
Instituto Oaxaqueño de las
  Artesanías............................25 C1
La Cava.................................26 C1

TRANSPORT
Armenta y López Bus Terminal............27 C4
Autoexprés Atlántida....................28 C4
Automorsa...............................29 B4
Colectivo Taxis to East, South..........30 A4
Colectivo Taxis to North................31 A3
Express Service.........................32 B4
Sur Bus Station.........................33 A4
Terminal de Autobuses de Primera
  Clase.................................34 D1
Terminal de Autobuses de Segunda
  Clase.................................35 A3
Transportes Villa del Mar...............36 A3
Zaachila Yoo............................37 B4

To San José El Mogote (13km);
San Agustín Etla (16km);
Yanhuitlán (102km);
Tehuacán (220km);
Mexico City (470km)

Cerro del Fortín

To Atzompa (6km)

See Central Oaxaca City Map (p720-1)

To Spanish Consulate (800m);
Academic Tours in Oaxaca (1km);
La Villada Inn (2.5km);
French Consulate (3km)

To Transportes
Ya'a-Yana Bus Stop (2km);
Tlalixtac de Cabrera (9km);
El Tule (10km); Teotitlán del
Valle (29km); Mitla (46km);
Tehuantepec (245km)

To Panteón General (300m)

To Monte Albán (6km);
San Antonio Arrazola (8km);
Cuilapan (9km);
Zaachila (16km)

To Airport (6km);
San Bartolo Coyotepec (11km); Ocotlán (31km);
Pochutla (245km);
Puerto Escondido (249km)

OAXACA STATE

2006: PROTEST IN OAXACA

Small-scale strikes by Oaxaca state's school teachers have long been a ritual part of their annual pay negotiations with the state government. It took an authoritarian and unpopular state governor – Ulises Ruiz, of the PRI party – to turn the 2006 Oaxaca teachers' pay round into the biggest political protest Mexico has seen in years. That year, Ruiz refused to make any significant concessions to the teachers, and the annual strike escalated into a bigger protest that saw thousands of teachers setting up encampments in Oaxaca's city center. On June 14 Ruiz sent in thousands of police to smash the teachers' encampments and barricades, but the protestors retook the Zócalo within hours – and the violence of the police action transformed the protest into a much wider movement whose main goal was to force Ruiz' resignation. A broad grouping of political and social groups came together to form APPO, the Asamblea Popular del Pueblo de Oaxaca (Popular Assembly of the People of Oaxaca), which took over the city center with camps, barricades, bonfires, graffiti and frequent marches hundreds of thousands strong. The summer's main touristic event, the Guelaguetza dance festival, was canceled. Frequent outbreaks of violence resulted in 23 deaths (all protestors or bystanders) by late October, when the federal government sent in heavily armed riot police to retake the city center. It's widely believed that President Fox's refusal to act against Ruiz was part of a deal struck by Fox's PAN party to win the PRI's support for PAN legislation in the national congress.

APPO continued to stage protests and marches demanding Ruiz' resignation and the release of those jailed during the protests. There was more violence before the Guelaguetza in 2007, though the festival went ahead. To outward appearances the city had more or less returned to normality by late 2007, and the important tourism business, which had ground to a halt for over a year, revived. But political opinion in Oaxaca has been radicalized, Ulises Ruiz is in office until 2010, and the social tensions and inequities that the protests highlighted have not gone away.

Sells some English-language books about Oaxaca and Mexico, as well as some maps.

Emergency

Ambulance, Fire & Police (☎ 066)

Ceprotur (Centro de Protección al Turista; Map pp720-1; ☎ 502-12-00; Murguía 206; ☼ 8am-8pm) Ceprotur, at the state tourist office, exists to help tourists with any legal problems, complaints, lost documents and the like.

Internet Access

They're everywhere!

Fray-Net (Map pp720-1; Murguía 309A; per hr M$5; ☼ 9am-9pm Mon-Fri, 9am-4pm Sat)

Inter@ctive Internet (Map pp720-1; Alcalá 503; per hr M$10; ☼ 8:30am-10pm) Good connections.

Interactu@ndo (Map p715; Pino Suárez 804; per hr M$6; ☼ 9am-9pm Mon-Sat) Wi-fi access is free if you have a drink or snack at the café here; if you don't, it's M$10 per hr.

Nred@t (Map pp720-1; Morelos 600; per hr M$10; ☼ 8:30am-8pm Mon-Fri, 8am-4pm Sat) Upstairs place with amiable staff & good connections.

Laundry

Same-day wash-and-dry service is available at several laundries.

Lava-Max (Map pp720-1; ☎ 545-87-46; cnr Bravo & Tinoco y Palacios; wash & dry per kg M$11, minimum 3kg; ☼ 8am-8:30pm Mon-Sat, 8am-1pm Sun) Also has self-service machines (wash per 4kg M$18, dry per 8kg M$12).

Lavandería Antequera (Map pp720-1; ☎ 516-56-94; Murguía 408; wash & dry per kg M$20, 3kg M$50; ☼ 8am-2pm & 4-8pm Mon-Fri, 8am-2pm & 4-7pm Sat) Also does ironing and dry cleaning, and offers free delivery to hotels in the area.

Libraries

Biblioteca Circulante de Oaxaca (Oaxaca Lending Library; Map pp720-1; ☎ 518-70-77; www.oaxlibrary .com; Pino Suárez 519; ☼ 10am-2pm & 4-7pm Mon-Fri, 10am-1pm Sat) Sizable collection of books and magazines on Oaxaca and Mexico in English and Spanish; visitor membership (per one/two months M$100/150) allows you to borrow books, DVDs and CDs.

Media

Go-Oaxaca (www.go-oaxaca.com) Excellent bilingual (English and Spanish) website and free paper normally published monthly. Both contain a lot of interesting articles and useful practical information on the state and city of Oaxaca, plus details about cultural events and small ads.

Notice boards Check these for rental apartments and houses, classes, medical services, English-teaching work and other interesting stuff. There are useful boards in the language schools and the Biblioteca Circulante de Oaxaca (opposite).

Planeta.com (www.planeta.com) This ecotourism website has tons of info on Oaxaca, where its founder lives.

Medical Services

Clínica Hospital Carmen (Map pp/20-1; ☎ 516-00-27; Abasolo 215; ⊗ 24hr) One of the city's best private hospitals, with emergency facilities and English-speaking doctors.

Money

There are plenty of ATMs around the center, and several banks and *casas de cambio* (exchange houses) will change US-dollar cash and traveler's checks.

Banorte (Map pp720-1; García Vigil 103; ⊗ 9am-6pm Mon-Fri, 10am-2pm Sat)

Consultoria Internacional (Map pp720-1; ☎ 514-91-92; Armenta y López 203C; ⊗ 9am-6pm Mon-Fri, 9am-2pm Sat) Also changes cash euros, yen, pounds sterling, Canadian dollars and Swiss francs.

HSBC (Map pp720-1; Guerrero 117; ⊗ 8am-7pm Mon-Sat)

Post

Main post office (Map pp720-1; Alameda de León; ⊗ 8am-10pm Mon-Fri, 10am-5pm Sat)

Telephone & Fax

Telmex card phones are available around the Zócalo and elsewhere. Many call offices are scattered around town.

Ti Yara (Map pp720-1; Calle 20 de Noviembre 402) Cheaper than pay phones for national long-distance calls and calls to Europe; offers fax service as well.

Interactu@ndo (Map p715; Pino Suárez 804; ⊗ 9am-9pm Mon-Sat) Calls cost M$4 per minute to the US, M$8 to the rest of world.

Tourist Information

City Tourism Office (Map p715; Hidalgo 1415) At the time of writing, this was due to open in 2008.

Sectur (Map pp720-1; ☎ 516-01-23; www.oaxaca .travel; Murguía 206; ⊗ 8am-8pm) The Oaxaca state tourism department usually has someone in attendance who can speak English, but workers are often student volunteers with limited knowledge. Also has desks at the Museo de los Pintores Oaxaqueños (p719), the 1st-class bus station and the airport.

DANGERS & ANNOYANCES

It's best not to go up on Cerro del Fortín, the hill with the Guelaguetza auditorium, except for special events such as the Guelaguetza festival. It's a well-known haunt for robbers.

Oaxaca's political disturbances in 2006 scared away tourism until late in 2007, long after the troubles had subsided. Unless there is a revival of confrontation, visitors have nothing to worry about on this score now.

SIGHTS
Zócalo & Alameda

Traffic-free, shaded by tall trees and surrounded by *portales* (arcades) with numerous cafés and restaurants, the Zócalo is the perfect place to soak up the Oaxaca atmosphere. The adjacent Alameda, also traffic-free but without the cafés, is another popular local gathering place.

On the south side of the Zócalo stands the former **Palacio de Gobierno** (State Government Palace; Map pp720-1), now being converted into a museum. Its stairway mural by Arturo García Bustos depicts famous Oaxacans and Oaxaca history, including Benito Juárez and his wife, Margarita Maza, and José María Morelos, Porfirio Díaz, Vicente Guerrero (being shot at Cuilapan) and Juana Inés de la Cruz, a 17th-century nun and love poet.

Oaxaca's **cathedral** (Map pp720-1), begun in 1553 and finished (after several earthquakes) in the 18th century, stands just north of the Zócalo. Its main facade, facing the Alameda, features fine baroque carving.

Around the Zócalo

Fine, carved facades adorn the colonial **Iglesia de La Compañía** (Map pp720-1; cnr Trujano & Flores Magón; ⊗ 7am-12:30pm & 5-8:45pm) and **Iglesia de San Juan de Dios** (Map pp720-1; cnr Aldama & Calle 20 de Noviembre). The latter is a beautiful small 17th-century church, on the site of Oaxaca's first church (which was built in 1526). The 18th-century baroque **Templo de San Felipe Neri** (Map pp720-1; cnr Independencia & JP García) is where Benito Juárez and Margarita Maza were married in 1843; Margarita was the daughter of Antonio Maza, an Italian immigrant merchant who took in the young Benito when he arrived in Oaxaca as a boy.

The **Teatro Macedonio Alcalá** (Map pp720-1; ☎ 516-83-44; Independencia 900; admission free; ⊗ 10am-6pm) was built in 1903 in the elaborate French style that was fashionable under Porfirio Díaz. It has a marble stairway and a five-tier auditorium holding 1300 people.

Calle Alcalá

Pedestrian-only for three blocks, with most of its colonial-era stone buildings cleaned

CHAMPION OF OAXACA'S TREES

More things happened to Francisco Verástegui in his first couple of decades than would happen to most of us in several lifetimes. Francisco was born into a well-to-do Mexico City family in the 1950s, his father an army general and his mother an antiquarian and art restorer. As a child, he was given a paintbrush by the great David Alfaro Siqueiros with the words 'Art is a weapon for attacking social injustice.' When Francisco was in his teens, his parents, his brother and their driver were all killed in a mysterious car crash. Subsequently Francisco gambled away his house in Mexico City's select Condesa neighborhood.

In the 1980s he found refuge among friends in Oaxaca and has lived in the city ever since, developing his own art, which has a strong anarchist dimension (see www.artedeoaxaca.com), and working as a cartoonist and writer for the newspaper *Noticias*.

Fate launched its latest twist to Francisco's story on April 18, 2005, when Oaxaca's city authorities began without public consultation to 'remodel' the Zócalo, the city's beloved central plaza, which is shaded by tall, centenarian Indian laurel trees. As bulldozers moved some of the paving stones, one of the venerable laurels toppled sideways against the Palacio de Gobierno. Francisco was among many who hurried to the Zócalo to see what was happening, and he was one of a handful who decided to stay for a nocturnal vigil. When a team of workers accompanied by police arrived to chop down the leaning tree at about 2am, he took the lead in successfully dissuading them. Thus began a movement of popular protest that saw a 20,000-signature petition raised against cutting the Zócalo trees. The authorities never made their intentions clear, and the Zócalo was fenced around so that no one could see what was happening for five months. When the screens came down, about 10 trees had been removed and the attractive green-stone paving had been replaced with dull gray stone. It seems likely that something much more drastic would have happened if Francisco and others hadn't intervened.

Restless Francisco was inspired to study the history of Oaxaca's trees. He discovered that many were very ancient and had links with famous figures. Ash and fig trees around El Llano park were planted by José María Morelos. A tall 15th-century *ahuehuete* at Oaxaca's train station may have been planted by Aztec invaders. Francisco compiled his findings in a guide-map, *Árboles Históricos y Notables de la Ciudad de Oaxaca* (Historic and Notable Trees of the City of Oaxaca), and in 2007 his work on protecting Oaxaca's trees and raising awareness of the urban environment brought him the Colibri Ecotourism Award, which is presented to 'a leading catalyst working toward responsible travel and ecotourism in Mexico' (see www.planeta.com/colibri.html).

Now there are plans for Oaxaca's historic trees, instead of being demolished, to be marked by official plaques and given protective fences. Francisco leads fascinating historic-tree walks on a private basis, and moves are afoot to train other guides to lead them on a regular public basis – for latest information ask at Oaxaca tourist offices or check www.planeta.com.

up and restored, and strung with interesting shops and galleries, **Calle Alcalá** (Map pp720–1) makes for an obligatory stroll between the Zócalo and the Iglesia de Santo Domingo.

Iglesia de Santo Domingo

Four blocks north of the cathedral, gorgeous **Santo Domingo** (Map pp720-1; cnr Alcalá & Gurrión; ☺ 7am-1pm & 4-8pm except during Mass) is the most splendid of Oaxaca's churches. It was built mainly between 1570 and 1608 as part of the city's Dominican monastery, with the finest artisans from Puebla and elsewhere helping in its construction. Like other big buildings in this earthquake-prone region, Santo Domingo has immensely thick stone walls.

Amid the fine carving on the baroque facade, the figure holding a church is Santo Domingo de Guzmán (1172–1221), the Spanish monk who founded the Dominican order. The Dominicans observed strict vows of poverty, chastity and obedience, and in Mexico they protected the indigenous people from other colonists' excesses.

Nearly every square inch of the church's interior is decorated in 3-D relief: elaborate colored and gilt designs swirl around a profusion of painted figures. An elaborate family tree of Santo Domingo adorns the ceiling immediately inside the main entrance. Most elaborate of all is the decoration in the 18th-century Capilla de la Virgen del Rosario

(Rosary Chapel) on the south side of the nave. The whole church takes on a magically warm glow during candlelit evening Masses.

Museo de las Culturas de Oaxaca

The beautiful monastery buildings adjoining the Iglesia de Santo Domingo house this not-to-be-missed **museum** (Museum of Oaxacan Cultures; Map pp720-1; ☎ 516-29-91; cnr Alcalá & Gurrión; admission M$48; ☑ 10am-7pm Tue-Sun). One of the best regional museums in Mexico, this takes you right through the history and cultures of Oaxaca state up to the present day. Explanatory material is in Spanish, but you can rent good audio guides in English for M$50. Also here is a good book and souvenir shop.

A gorgeous green-stone cloister serves as antechamber to the museum proper. The museum emphasizes the direct lineage between Oaxaca's pre-Hispanic and contemporary indigenous cultures, illustrating continuity in such areas as crafts, medicine, food, drink and music. The greatest highlight is the Mixtec treasure from Tumba 7 at Monte Albán, in Room III. This treasure dates from the 14th century, when Mixtecs reused an old Zapotec tomb to bury one of their kings and their sacrificed servants. With the bodies they placed a hoard of beautifully worked silver, turquoise, coral, jade, amber and pearls, finely carved bone, crystal goblets, a skull covered in turquoise and a lot of gold. The treasure was discovered in 1932 by Alfonso Caso.

The museum's first four rooms are devoted to the pre-Hispanic period, the next four to the colonial period, the following five to Oaxaca in the independence era and after, and the final room (14) to Santo Domingo Monastery itself. At the end of one long corridor, glass doors give a view into the beautifully ornate choir of Santo Domingo Church.

Museo Rufino Tamayo

This top-class **pre-Hispanic art museum** (Map pp720-1; ☎ 516-47-50; Morelos 503; admission M$35; ☑ 10am-2pm & 4-7pm Mon & Wed-Sat, 10am-3pm Sun) was donated to Oaxaca by its most famous artist, the Zapotec Rufino Tamayo (1899–1991). In a fine 17th-century building, the collection focuses on the aesthetic qualities of ancient artifacts and traces artistic developments in preconquest times. It has some truly beautiful pieces and is strong on the Preclassic era and lesser-known civilizations such as those of Veracruz and western Mexico.

Art Museums & Galleries

In the vanguard of Mexican art, Oaxaca attracts artists, dealers and buyers from far and wide.

MUSEO DE LOS PINTORES OAXAQUEÑOS

Housed in a spacious two-story downtown building, the **Museo de los Pintores Oaxaqueños** (Museum of Oaxacan Painters, MUPO; Map pp720-1; ☎ 516-56-45; Independencia 607; admission M$20; ☑ 10am-8pm Tue-Sun), stages changing exhibitions of work by the state's best artists.

MUSEO DE ARTE CONTEMPORÁNEO DE OAXACA

Occupying a handsome colonial house built around 1700, Oaxaca's **contemporary art museum** (MACO; Map pp720-1; ☎ 514-22-28; www.museomaco.com; Alcalá 202; admission M$20; ☑ 10:30am-8pm) exhibits contemporary art from Oaxaca, Mexico and around the world.

INSTITUTO DE ARTES GRÁFICAS DE OAXACA

Almost opposite Santo Domingo, in a beautiful colonial house donated by artist Francisco Toledo, this **institute** (Oaxaca Graphic Arts Institute, IAGO; Map pp720-1; ☎ 516-69-80; Alcalá 507; admission free; ☑ 9:30am-8pm Wed-Mon) offers changing exhibitions of graphic art as well as a superb **arts library** (☑ 9:30am-8pm Mon-Sat).

CENTRO FOTOGRÁFICO ÁLVAREZ BRAVO

This good **photo exhibition center** (Map pp720-1; ☎ 516-98-00; www.cfmab.blogspot.com; Bravo 116; admission free; ☑ 9:30am-8pm Wed-Mon) occupies a space that was very nicely rehabilitated in 2005.

COMMERCIAL GALLERIES

Admission to all these is free:

Arte Contemporáneo Manuel García (Map pp720-1; ☎ 514-10-93; Portal Juárez 110; ☑ 11am-2pm & 4-8pm Mon-Sat) Exhibitions of delightfully avant-garde stuff by Mexican and international artists.

Arte de Oaxaca (Map pp720-1; ☎ 514-15-32; www.artedeoaxaca.com; Murguía 105; ☑ 11am-3pm & 5-8pm Mon-Fri, 11am-6pm Sat) This sophisticated gallery provides a beautiful setting in which to enjoy a wide range of contemporary Oaxacan art. It includes a room devoted to Rodolfo Morales' work.

Bodega Quetzalli (Map pp720-1; ☎ 514-62-68; Murguía 400; ☑ 10am-2pm & 5-8pm Mon-Sat) This

CENTRAL OAXACA CITY

0 _____ 200 m
0 _____ 0.1 miles

EATING
1254 Marco Polo.....................66 D4
Café Alex...............................67 A4
Café Los Cuiles......................68 D2
Casa Crespo........................(see 21)
Casa Maria Lombardo.............69 E3
Casa Oaxaca.........................70 D2
Cenaduría Tlayudas Libres.....71 F3
Comala.................................72 C2
El Asador Vasco....................73 C5
La Biznaga............................74 C1
La Brújula.............................75 C2
La Cafetería..........................76 C4
La Casa del Tasajo................77 C2
La Olla...............................(see 65)
Mercado 20 de Noviembre.....78 B6
Pan & Co............................(see 77)
Pizza Nostrana.....................79 C2
Restaurant Flor de Loto.........80 B3
Restaurante Los Danzantes...81 C2

DRINKING
Bar del Borgo........................82 C3
Café Central..........................83 A4
Café Del Jardín...................(see 73)
Fandango...........................(see 87)
Freebar.................................84 C3
La Casa del Mezcal...............85 C5
La Divina..............................86 D2
La Embajada.........................87 B2
La Pasión..............................88 C3
Tapas & Pisto.....................(see 81)

ENTERTAINMENT
Candela................................89 E3
Casa de Cantera....................90 D3
Hotel Monte Albán................91 B4
La Tentación.........................92 C3

SHOPPING
Artesanías Cocijo..................93 C1
Casa de las Artesanías de
  Oaxaca..............................94 C3
Étnico..................................95 C2
Étnico..................................96 D2
Hecmafer..............................97 C3
La Mano Mágica...................98 C3
MARO..................................99 D3
Mercado de Artesanías.........100 A6
Mercado Juárez...................101 B5
Oro de Monte Albán............102 C2
Oro de Monte Albán............103 C2
Oro de Monte Albán............104 C2
Oro de Monte Albán
  Workshop.........................105 D2

TRANSPORT
Aeroméxico.........................106 B4
Aerotucán........................(see 25)
Aerovega............................107 B4
Alamo.................................108 D3
Autobuses Turísticos (to Monte
  Albán)..............................109 A6
Autotransportes
  Miahuatecas....................110 C6
Aviacsa..............................111 F1
Click Mexicana................(see 115)
es rent a car.......................112 D3
Estacionamiento Trujano......113 B5
Hertz.................................114 D2
Mexicana...........................115 D4
Only Rent-A-Car.................116 C2
Only Rent-A-Car.................117 D3
Ticket Bus..........................118 C4
Ticket Bus..........................119 B4
Transportadora Excelencia...120 A5
Transportes Aeropuerto.......121 B4
Turísticos Marfil...............(see 16)

Parque Juárez
(El Llano)

Cosijoeza

Constitución

Abasolo

Murguía

Morelos

Independencia

OAXACA STATE

CONTEMPORARY ART IN OAXACA

Inspired by diverse influences ranging from the area's contrasting landscapes to indigenous mythology and contemporary globalization, Oaxaca state's talented artists continue to produce some of the country's most vibrant and pioneering art. Many now spend time, exhibit and sell their work in Mexico City, the United States and elsewhere, but Oaxaca city is still by far the best place to get a feel for their great creativity and imagination.

A delight in color and light and a dreamlike feeling are recurring qualities of much Oaxacan art. The Oaxacan artists who laid the basis for today's flowering of art in their homeland were the great muralist and explorer of color and light, Rufino Tamayo (1899–1991), and Francisco Gutiérrez (1906–44). The next generation was led by three artists. The colorful, dreamlike art of Rodolfo Morales (1925–2001) from Ocotlán, with its trademark childlike angel figures, has deep local mythical roots. Rodolfo Nieto (1936–85) populated his work with vividly colorful fantasy animals and dream figures. Francisco Toledo (b 1940), from Juchitán, still a prominent figure in Oaxacan life and tireless worker for the arts, works in many media; his always arresting art often has grotesque or imaginary beasts for its subject matter.

A series of annual workshops for young Oaxacan artists organized by Tamayo in the 1970s encouraged such now highly successful talents as Abelardo López, Arnulfo Mendoza, Ariel Mendoza, Alejandro Santiago and Felipe de Jesús Morales – in part by helping them find markets for their art. Their work is highly varied, but fantasy, landscape, imaginary animals, indigenous roots and that persistent dreamlike quality run consistently through much of it. More or less contemporary are Sergio Hernández, whose limitless imagination melds the figurative with the abstract and the fantastic with the concrete, and Marco Bustamante with his oddly haunting hyper-realist images.

Today, the latest generation of Oaxacan artists seeks to reject the 'folkloric' imagery of its predecessors in a diversity of ways. They may look far beyond Oaxaca to international subjects and themes, and artists such as Demián Flores Cortés and Soid Pastrana often reject representation in favor of almost cartoon-like compositions designed to provoke and make us ponder.

Today any art lover can happily spend days browsing Oaxaca's art museums and quality commercial galleries and, with luck, attending the odd opening, seminar or other art community event at places like La Curtiduría (below) or Café Central (p731).

very large, open space features roughly one artist, usually avant-garde, per month.

Galería Epicentro (Map pp720-1; ☎ 516-80-72; www .marcobustamante.com; Juárez 300; ◷ 10am-2pm & 5-8pm Mon-Sat) Gallery belonging to artist Marco Bustamante displaying his and others' work.

Galería Quetzalli (Map pp720-1; ☎ 514-00-30; Constitución 104; ◷ 10am-2pm & 5-8pm Mon-Sat) Oaxaca's leading serious gallery, handling some of the biggest names such as Francisco Toledo and Sergio Hernández.

La Curtiduría (Map p715; ☎ 951-1199952; lacurti duria@yahoo.com; 5 de Mayo 307, Colonia Jalatlaco; ◷ 10am-2pm Mon-Fri) A diverse cultural center founded in an old tannery by artist Demián Flores Cortés, La Curtiduría stages and facilitates contemporary art exhibits, classes, community projects and assorted events (including films and live music and dance), and runs an artist-in-residence program. Drop by or look for flyers.

Also check out La Mano Mágica (p734). Chiefly a classy crafts store showcasing the weavings of its owner, Arnulfo Mendoza,

the Magic Hand also has some art, including prints by the likes of Tamayo and Toledo.

Jardín Etnobotánico

In former monastic grounds behind the Iglesia de Santo Domingo, this **garden** (Ethnobotanical Garden; Map pp720-1; ☎ 516-79-15; cnr Constitución & Reforma; two-hr tours in English M$100, one-hr tours in Spanish M$50; ◷ English tours 11am Tue & Thu, Spanish tours 10am, noon & 5pm Mon-Sat) features plants from around the state, including a staggering variety of cactuses. Though it has been growing only since the mid-1990s, it's already a fascinating demonstration of Oaxaca's biodiversity. Visits are by guided tour only; for the English-language ones it's a good idea to sign up a day or two beforehand.

Museo Casa de Juárez

One of the few Mexican national heroes with an unsullied reputation, the great reforming president Benito Juárez (1806–72) was born a humble Zapotec villager in Guelatao, 60km northeast of Oaxaca (p748). His parents died when he was three. At the age of 12, young Benito walked to Oaxaca and found work at the house of Antonio Salanueva, a bookbinder. Salanueva saw the boy's potential and decided to help pay for an education he otherwise might not have received. Salanueva's simple house is now the interesting little **museum** (Map pp720-1; ☎ 516-18-60; García Vigil 609; admission M$35, free Sun; ☑ 10am-6pm Tue-Fri, 10am-5pm Sat & Sun). The binding workshop is preserved, along with memorabilia of Benito.

Juárez later started training for the priesthood, but he abandoned this career to work as a lawyer for poor villagers. He rose to become Oaxaca's state governor from 1848 to 1852, during which term he opened schools and cut bureaucracy, and then justice minister in Mexico's new liberal government of 1855. His Ley Juárez (Juárez Law), which transferred the trials of soldiers and priests charged with civil crimes to ordinary civil courts, was the first of the Reform laws, which sought to break the power of the Catholic Church. These laws provoked the War of the Reform of 1858 to 1861, in which the liberals eventually defeated the conservatives.

Juárez was elected Mexico's president in 1861 but had been in office only a few months when France invaded Mexico and forced him into exile. In 1866–67, with US support, Juárez ousted the French and their puppet emperor, Maximilian. One of Juárez' main political achievements was to make primary education free and compulsory. He died in 1872, a year after being elected to his fourth presidential term. Today countless Mexican streets, schools, villages, towns, bus companies and even mountain ranges preserve his name and memory, and his sage maxim 'El respeto al derecho ajeno es la paz' ('Respect for the rights of others is peace') is widely quoted.

Basílica de la Soledad

The image of Oaxaca's patron saint, the Virgen de la Soledad (Virgin of Solitude), resides in the 17th-century **Basílica de la Soledad** (Map p715; Independencia), 3½ blocks west of the Alameda. The church, with a richly carved baroque facade, stands where the image is said to have miraculously appeared in a donkey's pack in 1543. The Virgin was later adorned with enormous worldly riches – but lost her 2kg gold crown, a huge pearl and several hundred diamonds to thieves in the 1990s. The shady plaza **Jardín Sócrates** (Map pp720-1), just east of the basilica, is full of neverías (sorbet stands) and makes a pleasant place in which to relax and observe Oaxacan life.

ACTIVITIES

Oaxaca has become one of Mexico's foremost centers for active tourism. It has several well-established outfits with a sustainability ethic that will take you hiking, biking, climbing, birdwatching or horseback riding amid the spectacular mountains and valleys of Oaxaca state, or welcome your help with the city's impoverished street children.

Bicicletas Pedro Martínez (Map pp720-1; ☎ /fax 514-59-35; www.bicicletaspedromartinez.com; Aldama 418; ☑ 9am-8pm Mon-Sat, 10am 3pm Sun), run by an amiable Mexican Olympic cyclist, offers a variety of unique, mostly off-the-beaten-track bike rides, with van support to cut out the less interesting bits. One-day rides in the Valle de Tlacolula or Sierra Norte cost M$1100 per person for two people or M$900 per person for four. A two-day jaunt runs from Nochixtlán to Santiago Apoala (p750) then across part of the Tehuacán-Cuicatlán biosphere reserve to Cuicatlán on Hwy 135. The four-day Ruta Los Coatlanes, best for intermediate or advanced-level riders, takes you right down to Puerto Escondido on the Pacific coast, crossing the backcountry of the Sierra Madre del Sur. For a minimum of three people, this costs M$5000 (M$4500 with your own bike) including accommodation (one night is camping) and meals.

The **Centro de Esperanza Infantil** (Oaxaca Streetchildren Grassroots; Map pp720-1; ☎ 501-10-69; www .oaxacastreetchildrengrassroots.org; Crespo 308; ☑ 9am-6pm Mon-Fri, 9am-3pm Sat) is a nonpolitical, nonreligious center that sponsors and cares for kids who, without assistance, could not attend school. Many of these children shine shoes or sell gum to help with their families' daily survival. The center has a dining room, library, computers, classrooms and a small kindergarten, and has helped some kids continue education right through to university. The staff does a great job and welcomes donations, sponsors, volunteers and visitors. Volunteers can help with meals, the on-site medical center, admin work and classes such as art, crafts and English, and even a half-day of assistance is helpful.

Expediciones Sierra Norte (Map pp720-1; ☎ 514-82-71; www.sierranorte.org.mx; Bravo 210; ☑ 9am-7pm

Mon-Fri, 9am-2pm Sat) is a well-run and success-ful rural community organization that offers walking, mountain biking, horseback riding and accommodations in the beautiful, moun-tainous Pueblos Mancomunados, northeast of the city. See p747 for more information.

Very well organized **Tierraventura** (Map pp720-1; ☎ 501-13-63; www.tierraventura.com, www.tierraventura .wordpress.com; Abasolo 217; ☒ 10am-2pm & 4-6pm Mon-Fri), run by a multilingual Swiss and German couple, offers a big variety of trips and ac-tivities focused on hiking, nature, meeting locals, traditional indigenous medicine and cooperating with local community tourism projects. Local guides accompany travelers wherever possible. Tierraventura can take the logistical work out of visiting places like the Pueblos Mancomunados (p747) and also offers rare opportunities to learn about tradi-tional medicine through its cooperation with CECIPROC, an NGO working to improve in-digenous health and the traditional medicine center at Capulálpam (p749). On most trips prices range between M$700 and M$1100 per person per day.

Zona Bici (Map pp720-1; ☎ 516-09-53; www.oaxacawebs .org/zonabici; García Vigil 406; ☒ 10:30am-2:30pm & 4:30-8:30pm Mon-Sat) takes easy to moderate four-hour mountain-biking trips in the Valles Centrales for M$400 per person (minimum two people). The Italian owner will set a more strenuous pace if you want.

Based at a ranch west of Monte Albán (Map p737), Mexican- and Italian-run **Rancho Buenavista** (Map pp720-1; ☎ 501-22-82; 951-5696773; www .ranchobuenavista.com.mx; 5 de Mayo 204; ☒ 10am-1pm & 4-8pm Mon-Fri) is perfect for travelers who like to spend their time being as active as possible. The main activities are rock climbing, moun-taineering, hiking and mountain biking, with varied grades of difficulty. Durations are from half a day up, and the guides are professional, friendly, qualified and experienced. Activity locations range from the Valles Centrales to the Sierra Norte, Santiago Apoala and Salina Blanca (a community-run climbing, hiking, swimming and rappelling venue near San José de Gracia on Hwy 190, about 110km south-east of Oaxaca). Buenavista also takes moun-taineering expeditions to Pico de Orizaba, La Malinche and Iztaccíhuatl. There's accommo-dation for 20 people at the Rancho in solar-powered brick cabins with private bathrooms and communal kitchen, costing M$180 per person including continental breakfast. Most

half-day activities cost M$500 to M$600, one-day outings are around M$600 to M$800, and two days' hiking, biking or climbing around Apoala is M$1100 to M$1400.

Ecoturixtlán (Map p715; ☎ 951-514-11-04; Rayón 608; ☒ 8am-2pm & 4-7pm Mon-Fri, 8-11am Sat) is the com-munity tourism organization of the small town of Ixtlán (p748) in Oaxaca's Sierra Norte. The Oaxaca office provides informa-tion and reservations for comfortable forest cabañas, guided hikes and other activities.

Travelers are welcome at the yoga, medi-tation and tai chi classes (up to M$50) at the Casa del Ángel (p730). Yoga classes are given at least three times daily except Saturday; other activities are a few times weekly.

For bird-watching, Oaxaca Birding Tours in Teotitlán del Valle (see p741) is recom-mended. The best riding stable in the area is at Casa Sagrada (p741) in Teotitlán – you can make reservations in Oaxaca at La Mano Mágica (p734).

COURSES

Oaxaca is a very popular place for travelers and visitors to learn some Spanish language or Mexican cooking (see boxed text, p726).

Language Classes

The city has several well-established language schools, and new ones keep popping up. All offer small-group instruction at a variety of levels, and most emphasize the spoken lan-guage. Most also offer extra activities such as dance, weaving or cooking classes, movies, lectures, trips and *intercambios* (meetings with local people for conversation). At most schools you can start any Monday. Most can also provide individual classes and a range of special subjects and packages. Textbooks and other materials are an additional cost at some schools.

Schools generally offer to arrange accom-modations for you in hotels or apartments or with families. Family accommodation normally costs US$16 to US$22 a day with breakfast, US$20 to US$25 with two meals, or US$21 to US$27 with three.

Amigos del Sol (Map p715; ☎ 520-01-18; www.oaxaca news.com/amigosdelsol.htm; Pino Suárez 802; 15hr per week US$105) Good-value school popular with travel-ers. Start any weekday – call the director's cell (☎ 951-1968039) between 2 and 4pm or after 8pm the day before you want to start. No mini-mum duration and no registration charge.

Becari Language School (Map pp720-1; ☎ 514-60-76; www.becari.com.mx; Bravo 210; 15/20/30hr per week US$120/160/240) Medium-sized school where you can start any Monday morning. Walk-ins are forgiven the US$70 registration fee. Optional extras include classes in slang, Zapotec language and woodcarving, and volunteering.

Instituto Cultural Oaxaca (Map p715; ☎ 515-34-04; www.icomexico.com; Juárez 909; main program per 1/2/3/4 weeks US$160/265/365/465) ICO's popular seven-hour-a-day program includes *intercambios* and workshops in arts, crafts and culture; many classes are held in the school's spacious gardens and terraces. US$55 registration fee.

Oaxaca International (Map pp720-1; ☎ 514-73-24; www.oaxacainternational.com; Libres 207; 15/20/30hr per week US$105/140/210) Prices include a wide range of workshops. Classrooms are set round a pleasant patio. The basic course focuses on conversation while the more intensive courses include some literature and more grammar.

Soléxico (Map pp720-1; ☎/fax 516-56-80; www.solexico.com; Abasolo 217; 15/25hr per week M$120/198) Professionally run school with branches in Playa del Carmen and Puerto Vallarta, so students can split time between locations. Can arrange language study combined with local volunteering (mainly with children). Walk-ins are excused the US$80 registration fee.

Also recommended:

Academia Vinigúlaza (Map p715; ☎ 513-27-63; www.vinigulaza.com; Abasolo 503; 15/20hr per week US$105/140)

Español Interactivo (Map pp720-1; ☎ 514-60-62; www.studyspanishinoaxaca.com; Armenta y López 311B; 15/20/30/40hr per week US$120/160/240/320)

Oaxaca Spanish Magic (Map pp720-1; ☎ 516-73-16; www.oaxacaspanishmagic.com; Berriozábal 200; 15/20hr per week US$95/120)

TOURS

If you're short on time, a guided trip can save hassles and be fun. A typical four-hour small-group trip to El Tule, Teotitlán del Valle and Mitla, or to Arrazola, Cuilapan and Zaachila, costs around M$180 per person, as do trips to Monte Albán. Longer trips – for example to El Tule, Teotitlán del Valle, Mitla, Hierve El Agua and a *mezcal* distillery – are around M$280 to M$300. Admission fees and meals are usually extra. You can book these tours at many hotels, or direct with such agencies as **Turismo El Convento** (Map pp720-1; ☎ 516-18-06; www.oaxacaexperts.com; Camino Real Oaxaca, 5 de Mayo 300) and **Continental-Istmo Tours** (Map pp720-1; ☎ 516-96-25; Alcalá 201).

Academic Tours in Oaxaca (Off map p715; ☎ 518-47-28; http://academictoursoaxaca.com; Nieve 208A, Lomas del Crestón) offers recommended customized tours geared to clients' personal interests, with full-day trips for two to four people typically costing US$240 to US$280.

FESTIVALS & EVENTS

All major national festivals are celebrated here, and Oaxaca has some unique fiestas of its own, the biggest and most spectacular being the Guelaguetza (see boxed text, p727).

Día de Muertos (Day of the Dead) November 2 is a big happening here, with events starting several days in advance. These include music and dance at the main cemetery, the Panteón General (off Map p715). Some guesthouses and agencies arrange tours to village events.

Posadas Nine nighttime neighborhood processions symbolizing Mary and Joseph's journey to Bethlehem take place between December 16 and 24.

Día de la Virgen de la Soledad Processions and traditional dances, including the Danza de las Plumas, take place at the Basílica de la Soledad (Map p715) on December 18.

Noche de los Rábanos (Night of the Radishes) On December 23 amazing figures carved from specially grown giant radishes are displayed in the Zócalo.

SLEEPING

Accommodations range from bargain-priced hostels to luxury hotels in historic colonial buildings. There are plenty of charming mid-range hotels and comfy B&Bs. Some places (mostly midrange and top-end) raise rates for four peak seasons: Semana Santa, Guelaguetza, Día de Muertos and Christmas–New Year.

Budget

Oaxaca may have more backpacker hostels than any other city in Mexico. Hostels in the following listings all have, unless stated, shared bathrooms and kitchens where you can cook up your own meals.

Hostal Pochón (Map p715; ☎ 516-13-22; www.hostalpochon.com; Callejón del Carmen 102; dm M$90, d M$230-340, all incl breakfast; ✗ ▯) Popular Pochón provides five small dorms and four private rooms with comfortable beds, a full kitchen, good common areas and no curfew. It also offers self-guided bike tours, cooking classes, luggage storage, cheap phone calls and free internet access.

Mezkalito Hostel (Map p715; ☎ 514-30-01; www.mezkalitohostel.com; Independencia 101; dm M$90, d with/without private bathroom M$300/270, all incl breakfast; ▯) The facilities are good at this relaxed, specially converted, newer hostel. The dorm bunks have thick mattresses, the bathrooms are good and clean, there's a raised back terrace as well as the main courtyard for hanging out in. Luggage storage available too.

La Villada Inn (Off map p715; ☎ 518-62-17; www .lavillada.com; Felipe Ángeles 204, Ejido Guadalupe Victoria; dm M$97, s/d with shared bathroom M$118/238, s/d/tr/q with private bathroom M$238/300/356/475; **P** ☐ ☒) Though set on the far northern edge of the city, La Villada offers superb facilities and friendly, helpful, English-speaking attention in a tranquil location. The public areas include a **restaurant** (⊙ 8am-8pm; dishes M$28-40), a bar with pool table, and an excellent swimming pool. There's no kitchen. Rooms boast art, artisanry, cable TV, and good wooden furniture and private bathrooms. A taxi from the city center should be M$45, but the hostel will pick you up free from the 1st-class bus station between 8am and 8pm. Reservation by internet recommended.

Hotel Posada El Chapulín (Map pp720-1; ☎ 516-16-46; hotelchapulin@hotmail.com; Aldama 317; r M$200-250, tr/q M$280/360; ☐) Small, family-run Chapulín, perennially full of international backpackers, features a graffiti-daubed entrance hall and a roof terrace with a fine view of Monte Albán. The eight rooms are smallish and multicolored, with fan, TV and hot-water bathrooms.

There are plenty of other budget places:

Hostel Luz de Luna Nuyoo (Map pp720-1; ☎ 516-95-76; www.geocities.com/luznuyoo; emayoral71@ hotmail.com; Juárez 101; dm M$70, d with shared/private bathroom M$180/200; ☐) Inexpensive, sociable hostel providing fairly basic facilities, with separate bunk rooms for women, men and couples around a wide patio.

Hostal Santa Isabel (Map pp720-1; ☎ 514-28-65; hostalsantaisabeloax@hotmail.com; Mier y Terán 103; dm M$70, d M$170; ☐) A calm, friendly place with bunk dorms (one for women only) and varied bedrooms around two patios with plants. If you want a private room, go for the airier upstairs ones.

COOKING THE OAXACAN WAY

Oaxaca has its own spicy take on Mexican cuisine, based on its famous seven *moles* (sauces usually served over chicken or pork). Other local specialties include *tasajo* (slices of pounded beef), *tlayudas* (big crisp tortillas with varied toppings, sometimes labeled 'Oaxacan pizza'), *memelas* (thick tortillas topped with cheese, beans, chili sauce and sometimes more), *quesillo* (stringy cheese) and *chapulines* (grasshoppers! – usually fried with chili powder, onion and garlic). Several of Oaxaca's best cooks regularly impart their secrets to visitors, making the city one of the best places in the country to learn Mexican cooking. The following recommended classes are (or can be) held in English, and include market visits to buy ingredients.

Seasons of My Heart (☎ 951-5080469; www.seasonsofmyheart.com; group day class incl transportation per person US$75, longer courses & tours from US$1495) This cooking school at a ranch in the Valle de Etla is run by American chef and Oaxacan food expert Susana Trilling. It offers classes in Mexican and Oaxacan cooking, from one-day group sessions (most Wednesdays) to weeklong courses, plus fascinating culinary tours around Oaxaca state and other Mexican regions.

La Casa de los Sabores (Map pp720-1; ☎ 516-57-04; www.laolla.com.mx; Libres 205; per person US$65) Pilar Cabrera, owner of La Olla restaurant, gives classes from 9:30am to 2pm on Tuesday and Thursday at her guesthouse in central Oaxaca. Participants (minimum four, maximum eight) prepare and eat one of 15 five-course Mexican or Oaxacan menus on offer, usually including some vegetarian dishes.

La Casa de mis Recuerdos (☎ 515-84-83; www.almademitierra.net; Pino Suárez 508; per person US$65) Nora Valencia, from a family of celebrated Oaxacan cooks, conducts four- to five-hour classes for a minimum four people at her family's charming B&B (see p729) or her nearby home; 48 hours' notice is needed. You go to market, prepare a Oaxacan lunch, then sit down to eat it.

Casa Crespo (☎ 514-11-02; www.casacrespo.com; Crespo 415; per person US$60) Amiable Óscar Carrizosa gives classes for small or large groups at his guesthouse (see p728) at 10:30am daily. Options include pre-Hispanic cooking, colonial cooking and festival food. Normally you'll plan a menu with six dishes and two drinks, buy the ingredients at market, then cook and eat your meal – four to five hours total.

Other places you can take cooking classes include the Learning Center (opposite; veg meals), Rancho Buenavista (p724), Hostal Pochón (p725) and Casa Sagrada (p741) in Teotitlán del Valle.

GUELAGUETZAS LARGE AND SMALL

The Guelaguetza is a brilliant feast of Oaxacan folk dance staged on the first two Mondays after July 16. (The only time the dates vary is when July 18, the anniversary of Benito Juárez' death, falls on a Monday. Guelaguetza then happens on July 25 and August 1.) The main event takes place from 10am to 1pm in the open air Auditorio Guelaguetza (Map p715) on Cerro del Fortín: magnificently costumed dancers from the seven regions of Oaxaca state perform a succession of dignified, lively or comical traditional dances, tossing offerings of produce to the crowd as they finish. Excitement climaxes with the incredibly colorful pineapple dance by women of the Papaloapan region; and the stately, prancing Zapotec Danza de las Plumas (Feather Dance), which re-enacts, symbolically, the Spanish conquest. The Guelaguetza period also sees many other colorful events celebrating regional culture in Oaxaca, and many thousands of people flock into the city for the festivities (including visiting pickpockets, so stay alert).

Seats in the amphitheater (which holds about 10,000 people) are divided into four areas called *palcos*. For Palcos A and B, nearest the stage, tickets (around M$400) go on sale from about April from tourist offices in Oaxaca. They're also available through some accommodations and usually **Ticketmaster** (www.ticketmaster.com.mx) and **Go-Oaxaca** (www.go-oaxaca.com). The two bigger rear palcos, C and D, are free and fill up early – if you get in by 8am you'll get a seat, but by 10am you'll be lucky to get even standing room. Wherever you sit, you'll be in the open air, with no shelter, for hours, so equip yourself accordingly.

The Guelaguetza celebrations have their origins in a colonial fusion of indigenous rites with Christian celebrations for the Virgen del Carmen. Reacting to what is seen as pervasive control and exploitation of the official Guelaguetza by the local political powers-that-be, some people now prefer to attend smaller Guelaguetzas in other towns and villages, such as Zaachila, Cuilapan, Tlacochahuaya and Reyes Etla. These are usually held on the same days and also often on hilltops or hillsides, and can make a refreshing change from the hubbub and crowds of Oaxaca.

Banana Magic Hostel (Map pp720-1; ☎ 516-76-67; www.magichostel.com.mx; Murguía 601A; dm M$70, s/d/tr M$170/200/270; 🖵) Another relaxed and social hostel with a comfy sitting area and roof terrace with bar and barbecue. One dorm is women-only.

Hostal Paulina (Map pp720-1; ☎ 516-20-05; www .paulinahostel.com; Trujano 321; dm/s/d/tr/q incl breakfast M$125/280/300/450/600; 🖵) Impeccably clean and efficiently run, this 92-bed hostel provides rooms and dorms for four to 11 people, but no cooking facilities. Get a place away from the very noisy street corner.

Midrange

Oaxaca boasts some delightful hotels and B&Bs, many of them in colonial or colonial-style buildings.

Hotel Posada Catarina (Map pp720-1; ☎ 516-42-70; www.hotelesdeoaxaca.com; Aldama 325; r M$350-450, q M$600; P 🖵) The Catarina is on a busy street southwest of the Zócalo, but inside it's spacious and elegant with small garden patios and a dramatic roof terrace. Rooms are clean and comfortable with telephone, cable TV and old-style wooden furniture. Prices include an hour's internet use.

Hotel Posada del Centro (Map pp720-1; ☎ 516-18-74; www.mexonline.com/posada.htm; Independencia 403; s/d with shared bathroom M$200/300, r with private bathroom M$450; P) Posada del Centro is arranged around two large verdant patios. The 22 rooms are a touch spartan but comfortable enough, with fans and pleasing Oaxacan artisan work. Staff are young, bright and helpful.

Learning Center (Map p715; ☎ 515-01-22; www.learn ingcenteroaxaca.com; Murguía 703; s/d incl breakfast US$35/45, apt per month US$700; 🖵) The Learning Center is a successful, non-profit tutoring center for young villagers who need help in continuing their education or developing careers. What guests pay for the two neat B&B rooms and attractive guest apartment here provides a valuable contribution to running costs. All accommodations have fans, phones, good bathrooms and DSL internet connections.

Hotel Las Mariposas (Map pp720-1; ☎ 515-58-54; www .lasmariposas.com.mx; Pino Suárez 517; s/d M$450/500, apt s/d M$500/550, all incl breakfast; ✗) Las Mariposas offers six studio apartments with small kitchens, and seven rooms. All are large, spotlessly clean and simply but prettily decorated. It's a tranquil, friendly and very secure place. Free wi-fi, a kitchen for guests, luggage storage and a good breakfast are among the extras that make this a good deal.

Casa Los Arquitos (Map p715; ☎ 132-49-75; www
.casalosarquitos.com; Tamayo 818; s M$400-650, d M$500-750,
all incl breakfast; 🖳) A friendly little B&B on a
picturesque lane near the arches of a 400-year-
old aqueduct. Los Arquitos offers four spotless
rooms with good hand-made furnishings and
varied *artesanías*. The 'energetic' breakfast
is made with organically grown ingredients.
Two rooms have small kitchens.

our pick **Hotel Las Golondrinas** (Map pp720-1; ☎
514-21-26; hotellasgolondrinas.com.mx; Tinoco y Palacios
411; s M$480, d M$520-600, tr M$600; ☒ 🖳) Lovingly
tended by friendly owners and staff, this superb small hotel has about 30 rooms around
three beautiful, leafy labyrinthine patios. It's
often full so you should book ahead. None of
the rooms is huge, but all are tastefully decorated and immaculately clean. Good breakfasts (not included in room rates) are served
in one of the patios. A very good value!

our pick **Hotel Azucenas** (Map pp720-1; ☎ 514-79-
18, 800-717-25-40, in the US & Canada 800-882-6089; www
.hotelazucenas.com; Aranda 203; s/d M$500/550; ☒ 🖳)
The Azucenas is a friendly, very well run,
Canadian-owned hotel in a beautifully restored century-old house. The 10 impeccably
clean, cool, tile-floored rooms have ample
bathrooms, and a buffet breakfast (M$44) is
served on the lovely roof terrace.

Hotel Casa Arnel (Map p715; ☎ 515-28-56; www
.casaarnel.com.mx; Aldama 404, Colonia Jalatlaco; s/d
M$165/275, with private bathroom from M$440/550;
🖳) A time-honored travelers' haunt, the
family-run Casa Arnel is five minutes' walk
from the 1st-class bus station. The clean,
smallish, well-kept rooms surround a big,
leafy courtyard, and the upstairs common areas have some great views. Rooms
with private bathroom have recently been
remodeled. Arnel offers many travelers'
services, including breakfast, car rental and
bus-ticket reservations.

Hotel Cazomalli (Map p715; ☎ 513-86-05; www
.hotelcazomalli.com; El Salto 104; s M$470, d M$550-600,
tr/q M$650/720; 🖳) The welcoming Cazomalli,
decked with tasteful Oaxacan artwork including spectacular carved and painted headboards, is five minutes' walk from the 1st-class
bus station, in quiet Colonia Jalatlaco. The
18 rooms all have safe, fan, phone, bottled
drinking water and hair dryer, and the roof
terrace has lovely views. Breakfast is available
from 8 to 10am.

Casa de la Tía Tere (Map p715; ☎ 501-18-45; www
.casadelatiatere.com; Murguía 612; r incl breakfast M$600-700,

q M$850; 🅿 🖳 🖳) Tía Tere is one of the few
midrange accommodations with a swimming pool. Some of the 20 large, mostly bright
rooms have balconies, and all boast good
showers. The four around the rear swimming
pool and lawn have their own kitchens, and
two of them are two-bedroom with sitting-
dining areas. Tere also offers a large, clean
kitchen and dining room, plus free coffee
and internet.

Casa Adobe (☎ 517-72-68; www.casaadobe-bandb
.com; Independencia 11, Tlalixtac de Cabrera; s/d incl breakfast
US$47/57, apt US$65) Eight kilometers east of the
city on a quiet lane in Tlalixtac de Cabrera (see
map p737), this Mexican- and American-run
house is a charming rural retreat. It's 80%
built of adobe bricks and full of lovely art and
artesanías. The three fan-cooled rooms are
set round a beautiful little patio, and there's
a nice roof terrace. The owners will pick you
up on arrival in Oaxaca and offer a free ride
to town on your first day (otherwise a M$70
taxi ride or M$7 in a *colectivo*). There's a mini-
mum stay of two or three days, depending on
when you go.

our pick **Las Bugambilias** (Map pp720-1; ☎/fax
516-11-65, in the US 877-629-2272; www.lasbugambilias
.com; Reforma 402; s US$50-95, d US$65-105, incl breakfast; ☒ ☒ 🖳) This delightful B&B has nine
rooms decorated with inspired combinations
of antiques and folk and contemporary art.
Some have air-con and/or a balcony; all have
tiled bathrooms and fans. A big treat here is
the gourmet two-course Oaxacan breakfast.
Further attractions include high-speed internet, free phone calls to the US and Canada,
and an inviting roof terrace with fantastic
views. There's a 10% discount for cash.

Hotel Parador San Agustín (Map pp720-1; ☎
516-20-22, 800-507-34-09; www.mexonline.com/san
agustin.htm; Armenta y López 215; s/d/tr/q incl breakfast
M$650/750/850/950) A 16th-century mansion with
a beautiful, pillared, green-stone courtyard has
been converted into this attractive 16-room
hotel. Rooms have an appealing Oaxacan atmosphere and are equipped with phone, fan,
cable TV and ample bathrooms.

La Reja (Map pp720-1; ☎ 514-59-39; www.hospederia
lareja.com.mx; Abasolo 103; r incl breakfast M$750-850) A
lovely small hotel with tasteful, comfy rooms
in oranges, yellows and pink tones, around a
tranquil patio with tropical plants.

Casa Crespo (Map pp720-1; ☎ 514-11-02; www.casacrespo
.com; Crespo 415; r incl breakfast US$90) The two large,
luxurious rooms at this welcoming B&B are

done in a mix of classical, Zapotec and Mixtec styles, with some fascinating original art and artifacts. The house has a beautiful courtyard, and you can also take cooking classes and, some nights, dine on Oaxaca's most original food (p731). No kids under 12.

La Casa de mis Recuerdos (Map pp720-1; ☎ 515-56-45; www.misrecuerdos.net; Pino Suárez 508; s US$50-75, d US$90-100, all incl breakfast; ☒ ☒) A marvelous decorative aesthetic prevails throughout this 10-room guesthouse. Old-style tiles, mirrors, masks and all sorts of other Mexican crafts adorn the walls and halls. The best rooms overlook a fragrant central garden; two have air-con and two have a shared bathroom. The large breakfast, a highlight, is served in a beautiful dining room. Host Nora Valencia also offers cultural tours and cooking classes. There's a minimum stay of three nights. The owners also offer B&B with similarly excellent breakfasts in two beautifully decorated smaller houses not much further from the center – **Encanto Jalatlaco** (Map p715; Niños Héroes 115; s/d incl breakfast US$90/120; ☒) and **Estancia de Valencia** (Map p715; Maza de Juárez 207; s/d incl breakfast US$90/120; ☒).

Top End

The best top-end accommodations exude colonial atmosphere.

Hostal CasAntica (Map pp720-1; ☎ 516-26-73; www .hotelcasantica.com; Morelos 601; r M$990-1190; ☒ ☐ ☒) You'll get a friendly welcome at this comfortable hotel, part of which occupies a 200-year-old former convent. The rooms have lots of exposed stone or brick and are furnished in colonial style and equipped with phone, cable TV and wi-fi access. Most have safes. The front courtyard houses a good restaurant and bar, and there's a nice heated pool in the rear courtyard.

Casa de Sierra Azul (Map pp720-1; ☎ 514-84-12; www .hotelcasadesierraazul.com.mx; Hidalgo 1002; r M$1000-1310; p) The Sierra Azul is a 200-year-old house converted into a beautiful small hotel, centered on a broad courtyard with a fountain and stone pillars. The good-sized, tasteful rooms have high ceilings, old-fashioned furnishings, attractive tiled bathrooms and a mix of old prints and modern art.

ourpick **Casa Oaxaca** (Map pp720-1; ☎ 514-41-73; www.casaoaxaca.com.mx; García Vigil 407; s US$177, d US$254-278, ste US$278-354, all incl breakfast; ☒) The seven large rooms and suites in this converted 18th-century house are in stunning contem-porary Oaxacan style with original art and *artesanías*. There's a lovely pool in the rear patio, and a small restaurant (open to non-guests only by reservation) for breakfast and dinner. Children under 12 not admitted.

Camino Real Oaxaca (Map pp720-1; ☎ 501-61-00, 800-9012300, in the US & Canada 800-722-6466; www.caminoreal .com/oaxaca; 5 de Mayo 300; r M$3540, Club r/ste incl breakfast M$4545/5200; ☒ ☒ ☒ ☒) Built in the 16th century as a convent, the Camino Real later served time as a prison, and was converted into a gorgeous hotel in the 1970s. The old chapel is a banquet hall; one of the five attractive courtyards contains an enticing swimming pool; and beautiful thick stone walls help keep the place cool and add to the considerable atmosphere. The 91 rooms are well decorated in colonial styles, and have marble sinks, safes and good bathrooms. Call the hotel or check the website for special rates, which can cut costs by about 40% in some seasons.

EATING

Oaxaca offers an eclectic bunch of restaurants, serving up favorite local dishes as well as other Mexican and international fare. Top of the list for originality are the handful of terrific fusion restaurants.

Around the Zócalo

All the cafés and restaurants beneath the Zócalo arches are great spots for watching Oaxaca life, but quality and service vary.

Mercado 20 de Noviembre (Map pp720-1; btwn Cabrera & Calle 20 de Noviembre; mains M$20-35) Cheap *oaxaqueño* meals can be had in this market south of the Zócalo. Most of the many *comedores* (small eateries) serve up local specialties such as chicken in *mole negro* (cooked in a very dark sauce of chilies, fruits, nuts, spices and chocolate). Pick a *comedor* that's busy. Many stay open until early evening, but the food is freshest early in the day.

La Cafetería (Map pp720-1; ☎ 514-76-16; Portal de Flores 3; dishes M$26-70) La Cafetería has a good position near the northwest corner of the plaza, and serves reliable Oaxacan dishes.

El Asador Vasco (Map pp720-1; ☎ 514-47-55; Portal de Flores 10A; mains M$90-160; ☒ 1:30-11:30pm) Upstairs at the southwest corner of the Zócalo, the Asador Vasco serves up good Oaxacan, Basque and international food. It's strong on meat, seafood and Oaxacan specialties. For a table overlooking the plaza on a warm evening, reserve earlier in the day.

OAXACA STATE

North of the Zócalo
BUDGET

Pan & Co (Map pp720-1; ☎ 501-16-72; Allende 107B; pastries M$10, bread M$25-35; ☑ 9am-9pm Mon-Sat) This European-style bakery turns out delicious baked goods, including multigrain and fruit breads, real croissants and Danish pastries.

La Brújula (Map pp720-1; García Vigil 409D; breakfasts, sandwiches & salads M$15-45; ☑ 8am-9:30pm Mon-Fri, 9am-4pm Sat & Sun) A great stop for good coffee, fruit smoothies, breakfasts (including waffles with fruit), salads, and home-baked bread, cakes and cookies. It's endowed with free wi-fi and is popular among artists and expats.

our pick **Café Los Cuiles** (Map pp720-1; ☎ 514-82-59; Plazuela Labastida 115-1; salads, soups & snacks M$18-45; ☑ 8am-10pm) Los Cuiles is a lovely spot for breakfast and for good light eats (including organic salads) or drinks such as mango lassi or organic coffee at any time of day. Popular with visitors and local students alike, it has a handy central location, free wi-fi and a spacious lounge–gallery feel.

Casa del Ángel (Map p715; ☎ 518-71-67; Dalevuelta 200; sandwiches, salads & burgers M$20-30; ☑ 9am-6pm Mon-Fri, 9am-2pm Sun; V) This small, quiet café adjoins a yoga studio and health-food store near El Llano park. It serves salads, veggie burgers, juices, teas (including Indian chai), good breakfasts and very good whole-wheat sandwiches.

Cenaduría Tlayudas Libres (Map pp720-1; Libres 212; tlayudas around M$30; ☑ 9pm-4:30am) Drivers double-park along the entire block to eat here. The filling, tasty *tlayudas* are large, light, crisp, hot tortillas folded over frijoles, *quesillo* and your choice of salsa. Half the fun is taking in the late-night scene as motherly cooks fan the streetside charcoal grills, raising showers of sparks. Sit on benches around the range or at tables in the adjacent building.

Restaurant Flor de Loto (Map pp720-1; ☎ 514-39-44; Morelos 509; mains M$35-55; V) Flor de Loto takes a pretty good stab at pleasing a range of palates, from vegan to carnivore. The chicken brochette (M$48) is large and tasty, while vegetarian options include spinach burgers, meatless enchiladas and *verduras al gratín* (vegetables with melted cheese).

Comala (Map pp720-1; Allende 109; dishes M$40-60; ☑ 8am-midnight Mon-Sat) This neat and trendy café, with a gently revolutionary theme, serves up tasty and satisfying salads, burgers, sandwiches, egg dishes and Oaxacan specialties including *tlayudas* and *enfrijoladas*, *entomat-* *adas* and *enchiladas* (corn tortillas in bean/to-mato/chili sauce with assorted fillings).

Pizza Nostrana (Map pp720-1; ☎ 514-07-78; Alcalá 501A; mains M$55-100; ☑ 1-11pm) Small, popular Nostrana is always a sound bet for pizzas and pasta. The entrance is actually on Allende, just off Alcalá.

María Bonita (Map p715; ☎ 516-72-33; Alcalá 706B; breakfast M$35-60, mains M$55-110; ☑ 8:30am-9pm Tue-Sat, 8:30am-5pm Sun) Come here for economical and tasty traditional Oaxacan food. Precede your fish, steak or *mole* with a good appetizer or soup, such as the *sopa Xóchitl* (squash, squash blossom and sweet corn). There's a good breakfast range too. The old building is on a noisy corner, but the tasteful art and relaxed service make it all OK.

our pick **La Olla** (Map pp720-1; ☎ 516-66-68; www.laolla.com.mx; Reforma 402; breakfasts M$55-80, mains M$55-120; ☑ 8am-10pm Mon-Sat; V) This excellent little restaurant and café produces marvelous Oaxacan specialties from cactus tacos to *camarones a la diabla* (prawns in a hot chili-and-tomato sauce) and good rye-bread tortas, juices, and salads, all with an emphasis on organic and local ingredients. Breakfasts are excellent.

MIDRANGE
La Casa del Tasajo (Map pp720-1; ☎ 514-98-24; Allende 113; mains M$70-90; ☑ 1-10pm Tue-Sat, 1-8pm Sun) The bright courtyard here is a fine spot to enjoy Oaxaca's beef specialty, *tasajo*. It comes with rice and frijoles in a variety of original ways, including on a spit with onions, green peppers and bacon.

Casa María Lombardo (Map pp720-1; ☎ 516-17-14; Abasolo 314; mains M$70-140; ☑ 1:30-11pm) Thick white walls give a suitable ambience for the well-prepared Mediterranean food here. The wood-oven pizzas and the chicken, steak and salmon grills are all good choices. Sit in the front room to watch the chef tossing the pizza bases for extra elasticity.

our pick **La Biznaga** (Map pp720-1; ☎ 516-18-00; www.labiznaga.com; García Vigil 512; mains M$70-150; ☑ 1-10pm Mon-Thu, 1-11pm Fri & Sun) The work of two brothers from the Distrito Federal, La Biznaga composes terrific fusion dishes – the choices are written up on boards above the spacious courtyard, which is ringed with slick art. You might go for a salad of spinach, grapefruit, bacon and walnut to start, followed by beefsteak with *pasilla* chilies, plums and *mezcal*. There's a good-value set lunch for M$80.

La Toscana (Map p715; ☎ 513-87-42; 5 de Mayo 614, Jalatlaco; mains M$75-150; ⊗ 2-11pm Mon-Sat, 2-6:30pm Sun) Oaxaca meets Tuscany at elegant La Toscana, occupying a beautiful, white-pillared, art-hung courtyard in Colonia Jalatlaco. The delicious dishes on offer run from beef medallions in Gorgonzola sauce to prawns with pineapple purée and a ginger-and-chili sauce.

1254 Marco Polo (Map p715; ☎ 513-43-08; Pino Suárez 806; breakfast M$36-39, mains M$90-155; ⊗ 8am-6pm Wed-Mon) Marco Polo's popular Pino Suárez branch occupies a long, shady, garden patio, with attentive waiters and good-value food. The large breakfasts come with bottomless cups of coffee; from noon until closing, *antojitos* (tortilla-based snacks like tacos), ceviches and oven-baked seafood are the main draws. The downtown branch (Map pp720-1; ☎ 514-43-60; open 8am to 10:30pm Monday to Saturday) at 5 de Mayo 103 has the same excellent menu and good service.

TOP END

Restaurante Los Danzantes (Map pp720-1; ☎ 501-11-84; Alcalá 403; soups, starters & pasta M$50-90, mains M$125-160; ⊗ 2:30-11:30pm) Delicious Mexican fusion food and a spectacular architect-designed setting make Los Danzantes one of Oaxaca's most special dining spots. An old colonial patio now sports high patterned walls of adobe brick and cool pools of water in a highly contemporary configuration, half open to the sky. Welcoming young staff serve up a small but first-class selection of food: try one of the excellent duck dishes. The only gripe is that servings are not on the generous side. Desserts are very good too, and the restaurant has its own brand of *mezcal*.

Casa Oaxaca (Map pp720-1; ☎ 516-88-89; Constitución 104A; mains M$120-230; ⊗ 1pm-10pm Mon-Sat) This restaurant run by the Casa Oaxaca hotel works magic combining Oaxacan and European ingredients and flavors: witness the crispy duck tacos with red *mole*, or the isthmus-style venison *tamales*. Presentation is outstanding, and all is enhanced by the courtyard setting and a good selection of wines.

Casa Crespo (Map pp720-1; ☎ 514-11-02; Crespo 415; dinner M$400; ⊗ 7-10pm) The 'Teatro Culinario' (Culinary Theater) dinner in the lovely patio of this guesthouse – by reservation only – is an incredible experience of approximately seven dishes in which ultra-creative chef José-Luis turns local ingredients into amazing works of art with unique flavors and textures. Drinks are included in the price.

West of the Zócalo

Café Alex (Map pp720-1; ☎ 514-07-15; Díaz Ordaz 218; dishes M$35-50; ⊗ 7am-10pm Mon-Sat, 7am-1pm Sun) Airy, full of people, clean and comfortable, Alex is a great place to fill up on good cheap food. The breakfast combinations (M$38 to M$48) are a good value and so is the M$50 lunchtime *comida corrida* (set menu).

DRINKING

Apart from the more obvious cafés and bars, a good number of arty and bohemian hangouts are scattered around central Oaxaca. If you're into liquors, Oaxaca is *the* place to sip some of that now fashionable spirit, *mezcal*. The world's best *mezcal* is made in Oaxaca state, especially around Santiago Matatlán and the Albarradas group of villages, south and east of Mitla. Just like its cousin tequila, *mezcal* is distilled from agave plants and is usually better when *reposado* or *añejo* (aged). Undiluted white *mezcal* is the most common type, but there are also varieties flavored with herbs or fruit. *Mezcal* bottles may or may not contain a *gusano* (worm) from the agave plant, which some claim is an aphrodisiac.

our pick **Café Central** (Map pp720-1; ☎ 514-20-42; Hidalgo 302; ⊗ approx 9pm-2am Wed-Sat) The social hub of Oaxaca's artsy, bohemian, alternative scene, the Café (or Bar or Colectivo) Central is owned by one of Oaxaca's innovative painters, Guillermo Olguín. It hosts rarely seen live music acts (often on Thursdays), dance and independent films, and uses its wall space as an alternative gallery for celebrated and unheard-of artists. On Friday and Saturday it leans toward a nightclub with an unpredictable, eclectic music mix. There are cover charges for a few events.

Café Del Jardín (Map pp720-1; ☎ 516-20-92; Portal de Flores 10) The Jardín has a peerless position beneath the arches at the southwest corner of the Zócalo. In the evening you're likely to be serenaded by one of the funkiest marimba (wooden xylophone) ensembles in the country.

Freebar (Map pp720-1; Matamoros 100C; ⊗ 9pm-3am Tue-Sun) Freebar hosts a young and vibrant international crowd that doesn't mind being rammed together to soak up beer and the atmosphere. There's space to dance if the crowd isn't too dense.

OAXACA STATE

OAXACA'S FAVORITE HOT DRINK

Chocolate is an ancient Mexican treat and a Oaxacan favorite. A bowl of steaming hot chocolate to drink, with porous sweet bread to dunk, is the perfect warmer when winter sets in 1500m above sea level. The mix, to which hot milk or water is added, typically contains cinnamon, almonds and sugar as well as ground-up cocoa beans. The area around the south end of Oaxaca's Mercado 20 de Noviembre has several shops specializing in this time-honored treat – and not just chocolate for drinking but also chocolate for *moles* (dishes with chili-based sauces). You can sample chocolate with or without cinnamon; light or dark chocolate with varying quantities of sugar; and many other varieties at any of these places. And most of them have vats where you can watch the mixing.

Bar del Borgo (Map pp720-1; Matamoros 100B; 🕙 10am-1am) A very small but neatly arranged space, next door to Freebar, the Borgo offers some unique street views and a jazzy, arty, almost publike atmosphere. Check it out!

La Casa del Mezcal (Map pp720-1; Flores Magón 209; 🕙 10am-1am) Open since 1935, this is one of Oaxaca's most atmospheric bars, 1½ blocks south of the Zócalo. It's a cantina, but a reasonably respectable one. One room has a large stand-up bar and shelves full of *mezcal*; the other room has tables where *botanas* (snacks) are served. Most, but not all, customers are men.

La Embajada (Map pp720-1; Porfirio Díaz 503; 🕙 6pm-1am) One of a trio of interconnecting bars in a corner building known as La Casa de los Perros (House of the Dogs), La Embajada is popular with a student and international crowd for its rock music, magazine-style montage décor and drinks from tea, coffee and chocolate to beer, *mezcal* and wine.

Fandango (Map pp720-1; ☎ 514-95-84; Porfirio Díaz 503; 🕙 8am-2am) Fandango, next door to La Embajada, has a more retro style with a long bar serving cocktails (M$50 to M$60) as well as a small stage for bands.

Tapas & Pisto (Map pp720-1; ☎ 514-40-93; Alcalá 403; 🕙 7pm-2am Tue-Sun) Upstairs from Los Danzantes restaurant and in keeping with its sensuous theme, T&P's main bar is a teens and 1920s haunt with black light and loud music. Its contrasting quiet rooftop **terrace** (🕙 6pm-1am Tue-Sun) offers fabulous views to Santo Domingo Church.

La Pasión (Map pp720-1; ☎ 516-61-13; Alcalá 302; 🕙 8am-2am) This smart contemporary cantina has half a dozen screens for music and sports, and a section of sofas and easy chairs at one side. Live Latin music from 9pm Thursday to Saturday. Enter through the Mayordomo restaurant.

La Divina (Map pp720-1; ☎ 582-05-08, Gurrión 104; 🕙 2pm-1am Tue-Sun) La Divina, facing Santo Domingo Church, has a disco-esque interior and music from salsa to house to trance to reggae. There's live rock a few nights a week and early-evening (6pm) movies on other nights. As the evening progresses the crowd may generate a warm enough atmosphere to spill out into the street.

Comala (p730) and Café Los Cuiles (p730) are two further popular spots for evening drinks.

ENTERTAINMENT

Free **concerts in the Zócalo** are given by the Oaxaca state marimba ensemble, the state band or other groups every evening except Friday, at 6 or 6:30pm, and at noon or 12:30pm on Wednesday, Saturday and Sunday. For further live music, check some of the bars listed under Drinking (p731).

Guelaguetza Shows

If you're not lucky enough to be in Oaxaca for the Guelaguetza itself (see boxed text, p727), it's well worth attending one of the regular imitations. The classy Camino Real hotel (see p729) stages a highly colorful three-hour Guelaguetza show (M$340 including buffet dinner) in what used to be a convent chapel, 7pm on Fridays.

Casa de Cantera (Map pp720-1; ☎ 514-75-85; Murguía 102; admission M$150; 🕙 8:30pm) A lively mini-Guelaguetza is staged here nightly, in colorful costume with live music. To make a reservation, phone or stop by during the afternoon.

Hotel Monte Albán (Map pp720-1; ☎ 516-27-77; Alameda de León 1; admission M$90; 🕙 8:30pm) This hotel presents a 1½-hour version nightly, usually to recorded music.

Dancing

ourpick **Candela** (Map pp720-1; ☎ 514-20-10; Murguía 413; admission M$50; 🕙 from 10pm Thu-Sat) Candela's writhing salsa, *cumbia* and merengue band and beautiful colonial-house setting have kept it at the top of the Oaxaca nightlife lists for years. It's open as a restaurant from 7pm, so arrive fairly early for a good table, and either learn to dance (free classes from 10 to 11pm) or learn to watch.

La Tentación (Map pp720-1; ☎ 514-95-21; Matamoros 101; admission M$40; ☉ 10pm-3am Tue-Sun) Foreigners and residents alike have a great time when this venue gets up a head of steam – best on Friday and Saturday, when you can move to live salsa, merengue and *cumbia*.

Cinemas

Cineclub El Pochote (Map p715; ☎ 514-11-94; www.el pochote.blogspot.com; García Vigil 817; admission free, donations accepted; ☉ screenings usually 6pm & 8pm Tue-Sun) El Pochote shows independent, art-house and classic Mexican and international movies (the latter in their original languages with Spanish subtitles). There's usually a different theme each month. To find it, duck under the old aqueduct into Parque El Pochote.

SHOPPING

The state of Oaxaca has the richest, most inventive folk-art scene in Mexico, and the city is its chief marketplace. You'll find the highest-quality crafts mostly in the smart stores, but prices are lower in the markets. You may not pay more for crafts purchased in the city (rather than in the villages where most of them are made), but a lot of your money may be going to intermediaries. Some artisans have grouped together to market their own products directly (see Craft Shops, right).

Oaxacan artisans' techniques remain pretty traditional – back-strap and pedal looms, hand-turning of pottery – but new products frequently appear in response to the big demand for Oaxacan crafts. The colorful wooden fantasy animals known as *alebrijes* were developed within the last 20 years from toys that Oaxacans had been carving for their children for centuries.

Other special products to look for include the distinctive black pottery from San Bartolo Coyotepec; blankets, rugs and tapestries from Teotitlán del Valle; *huipiles* (women's sleeveless tunics) and other indigenous clothing from anywhere in the state; the creative pottery figures made in Ocotlán and Atzompa; and stamped and colored tin from Oaxaca city

itself. Rugs or blankets with muted colors are less likely to have been made with synthetic dyes than some of the more garish offerings. Jewelry is also made and sold here – you'll find pieces using gold, silver or precious stones. Many shops can mail things home for you.

Just as fascinating as the fancy craft stores, in its own way, is Oaxaca's bustling commercial area stretching over several blocks southwest of the Zócalo. Oaxacans flock here, and to the big Central de Abastos market, for all their everyday needs.

La Cava (Map p715; ☎ 515-23-35; Gómez Farías 212B; ☉ 10am-3pm & 5-8pm Mon-Fri, 10am-3pm Sat) This shop sells particularly high-quality *mezcal* from Santiago Matatlán (up to M$600 a bottle). Several shops southwest of the Zócalo, on streets such as Aldama, JP García and Trujano, also specialize in *mezcal*. Around M$100 will certainly buy you a decent bottle.

Markets

Mercado de Artesanías (Crafts Market; Map pp720-1; cnr JP García & Zaragoza) This indoor crafts market is strong on *alebrijes,* stamped tin ware, embroidered textiles and tablecloths. As you walk through you're likely to see some of the vendors passing the time by plying their crafts, such as weaving or embroidering.

Central de Abastos (Supplies Center; Map p715; Periférico) The enormous main market is a hive of activity every day, with Saturday the biggest day. If you look long enough, you can find almost anything here. Each type of product has a section to itself, and you can easily get lost in the profusion of household goods, CDs and *artesanías* and the overwhelming quantities of fruit, vegetables, sugarcane, maize and other produce that's grown from the coast to the mountaintops.

Mercado Juárez (Map pp720-1; btwn Flores Magón & Calle 20 de Noviembre) This indoor market, a block southwest of the Zócalo, sells a diverse mixture of food, flowers, clothes, hats, sandals and leather belts and bags. Women hawk mounds of grasshoppers on the street outside the Flores Magón entrance.

Craft Shops

MARO (Map pp720-1; ☎ 516-06-70; 5 de Mayo 204; ☉ 9am-8pm) This rabbit warren of a store offers a big range of good work at good prices, all made by the hundreds of members of the MARO women artisans' cooperative around Oaxaca state. Whether you buy a stamped tin mirror or a woven-to-order rug, you know your money is going direct to the makers.

La Mano Mágica (Map pp720-1; ☎ 516-42-75; www .lamanomagica.com; Alcalá 203; ☯ 10:30am-3pm & 4-8pm Mon-Sat) You'll find some wonderfully original and sophisticated craft products at this shop and gallery, including work by one of its owners, the masterly Teotitlán del Valle weaver Arnulfo Mendoza. Some Mendoza pieces go for tens of thousands of dollars, and when you see them you'll understand why.

Instituto Oaxaqueño de las Artesanías (Map p715; ☎ 514-40-30; García Vigil 809; ☯ 9am-8pm Mon-Fri, 10am-5pm Sat, 10am-1pm Sun) Government-run IAO offers a good variety of beautiful craft items, including ceramics, *alebrijes* and some gorgeous textiles.

Casa de las Artesanías de Oaxaca (Map pp720-1; ☎ 516-50-62; www.casadelasartesanias.com.mx; Matamoros 105; ☯ 9am-9pm Mon-Sat, 10am-6pm Sun) This store sells the work of 80 family workshops and craft organizations from around Oaxaca state. Its patio is surrounded by rooms full of rugs, ceramics, tinware, *alebrijes* and other crafts.

Oro de Monte Albán (Map pp720-1; ☎ 516-45-28, www .orodemontealban.com; Gurrión C) This firm's metalsmiths craft beautifully worked jewelry in gold, silver and semiprecious stones, including copies of pre-Hispanic jewelry and pieces inspired by colonial-era designs. The interesting free workshop tour (in Spanish) at the Gurrión branch includes a demonstration of the pre-Hispanic lost-wax casting technique. Other branches are along Alcalá.

These other craft shops (all shown on Map pp720-1) are well worth a look:

Hecmafer (☎ 516-32-58; 5 de Mayo 301) Assorted very high-quality goods.

Étnico (☎ 516-07-34) Allende (Allende 113; ☯ 10am-2pm & 4-8pm Mon-Sat); Gurrión (Gurrión 104; ☯ 10:30am-8pm) Has a very attractive line in patchwork bedspreads and cushions made from pieces of *huipil*.

Artesanías Cocijo (Plazuela del Carmen Alto) A particularly good selection of masks.

GETTING THERE & AWAY
Air
Direct flights to/from Mexico City (one hour) are operated by Mexicana at least five times daily, Click Mexicana and Aeroméxico Connect twice, and Aviacsa once. Continental flies to/from Houston, Texas, four times weekly. Click Mexicana also has a daily flight to Tuxtla Gutiérrez and Mérida. Avolar flies daily

to Cuernavaca and Tijuana; Alma de México flies to Guadalajara and Tuxtla Gutiérrez.

For the spectacular half-hour hop over the Sierra Madre del Sur to Puerto Escondido or Bahías de Huatulco on the Oaxaca coast, Aerotucán flies a 13-seat Cessna daily to/from both destinations, and Aerovega, with its seven-seater (there may be no copilot), flies daily to/from Puerto Escondido and will go via Huatulco if there is a minimum of three passengers going there. One-way fares to Huatulco are around M$1300; to Puerto Escondido it's M$1000 with Aerovega and M$1200 with Aerotucán.

AIRLINE OFFICES
Aeroméxico & Aeroméxico Connect (Map pp720-1; ☎ 516-10-66; Hidalgo 513; ☯ 9am-6pm Mon-Sat)

Aerotucán (Map pp720-1; www.aerotucan.com.mx; ☎ 501-05-30; Interior 204, Alcalá 201; ☯ 7am-8pm Mon-Sat, 10am-2pm Sun)

Aerovega (Map pp720-1; ☎ 516-49-82; www.oaxaca -mio.com/aerovega.htm; Alameda de León 1; ☯ 9am-8pm Mon-Fri, 9am-5pm Sat)

Aviacsa Airport (☎ 511-50-39); Centro (Map pp720-1; ☎ 800-284-22-72; Pino Suárez 604)

Mexicana & Click Mexicana (Map pp720-1; ☎ 516-73-52; Fiallo 102) Also sells Alma de México tickets.

Bus & Van
The **Terminal de Autobuses de Primera Clase** (1st-class bus station; Map p715; ☎ 502-05-60; Calz Niños Héroes de Chapultepec 1036) is 2km northeast of the Zócalo. Also known as the Terminal ADO, it's used by UNO and ADO GL (deluxe service), ADO and OCC (1st class) and Cuenca (2nd class). The **Terminal de Autobuses de Segunda Clase** (2nd-class bus station; Map p715; Las Casas) is 1km west of the Zócalo; the main long-distance companies using it are **Fletes y Pasajes** (Fypsa; ☎ 516-12-18) and **Estrella del Valle/Oaxaca Pacífico** (EV/OP; ☎ 514-07-76). The 2nd-class companies Sur and AU use the **Sur Bus Station** (Map p715; ☎ 514-44-86; Periférico 1014), 500m south of the main 2nd-class terminal. Unless otherwise noted, buses mentioned in this section use one of these three main terminals.

It's advisable to buy your ticket a day or two in advance for some of the less-frequent services, including buses to San Cristóbal de Las Casas. **Ticket Bus** (Map pp720-1) has two branches in the city center: one at Calle 20 de Noviembre 103 (☎ 514-66-55; open 8am to 10pm Monday to Saturday and 8am to 4pm Sunday) and the other at Valdivieso 2 (☎ 516-38-20; open 8am to 10pm Monday to

Saturday, 8am to 9pm Sunday). Both sell tickets for trips with UNO, ADO, ADO GL, OCC, Cuenca, Sur and AU throughout Mexico.

OAXACA COAST

Buses from the 1st-class bus station to the towns on the Oaxaca coast take a long route via Salina Cruz. Unless you're liable to travel sickness on winding mountain roads, it's more convenient to use one of the comfortable van or microbus services that go directly to Puerto Escondido by Hwy 131 and Pochutla by Hwy 175. Both these routes are now well paved.

For Puerto Escondido (M$130, six hours), **Express Service** (Map p715; ☎ 516-40-59; Arista 116) departs nine times daily, 5am to 10pm; and **Transportes Villa del Mar** (Map p715; ☎ 951-1165622; Galeana 322A) goes six times between 6:30am and 5pm.

OTHER DESTINATIONS

Daily bus departures include the following:

Destination	Fare	Duration	Frequency (daily)
Mexico City (mostly TAPO)	M$344-584	6-6½hr	37 from 1st-class terminal
	M$290	6½-7hr	8 from Sur terminal
Puebla	M$256-304	4½hr	9 from 1st-class terminal
	M$224	5¼hr	3 from Sur Terminal
San Cristóbal de Las Casas	M$344-412	11-12hr	3 from 1st-class terminal (7 to 9pm)
Tapachula	M$306	13½hr	1 from 1st-class terminal (7pm)
Tehuantepec	M$152	4½hr	15 from 1st-class terminal
	M$95	5hr	6 from Sur terminal
	M$90-95	5hr	10 Fypsa from 2nd-class terminal
Tuxtla Gutiérrez	M$306-368	10hr	4 from 1st-class terminal (7 to 10:30pm)
	M$196-220	11hr	6 Fypsa from 2nd-class terminal
Veracruz	M$338	6-7hr	3 from 1st-class terminal
Villahermosa	M$434	12hr	4 from 1st-class terminal (5 to 9:30pm)

To Pochutla (M$120, six hours), **Autoexprés Atlántida** (Map p715; ☎ 514-13-46; La Noria 101) runs 14-seat air-conditioned vans nine times daily, 4:30am to 11:30pm; and **Autotransportes Miahuatecas** (Map pp720-1; ☎ 951-1065373; Arteaga 108) goes seven times between 5am and 5:30pm.

A dozen slower 2nd-class EV/OP buses run to Pochutla (M$76 to M$91, six to seven hours) by Hwy 175 from the 2nd-class bus station, and a handful from the **Armenta y López terminal** (Map pp720-1; ☎ 504-18-67; Armenta y López 721), 500m south of the Zócalo. From the 2nd-class bus station **Estrella Roja del Sureste** (☎ 516-06-94) runs seven buses daily to Puerto Escondido (M$110, 6½ to seven hours) by Hwy 131. Also from the 2nd-class bus station, EV/OP runs one bus each to Bahías de Huatulco (M$111, 7½ hours, 10pm) and Puerto Ángel (M$76, seven hours, 11:15pm).

OCC and ADO GL run a total of four buses daily by the longer Salina Cruz route to Bahías de Huatulco (M$216 to M$256, eight hours).

Car & Motorcycle

Hwy 135D branches off the Mexico City–Veracruz highway (150D) to make a spectacular traverse of Oaxaca's northern mountains en route to Oaxaca city. Tolls from Mexico City to Oaxaca on these highways total M$326; the trip takes five to six hours. For some reason the 135D is also numbered 131D in some stretches. Toll-free alternative Hwy 190, via Huajuapan de León, takes several hours longer.

Walk-in car-rental prices in Oaxaca start around M$500 a day with unlimited mileage.
Alamo Airport (☎ 514-85-35; ☯ 8am-8pm Mon-Sat, 8am-7pm Sun); Center (Map pp720-1; ☎ 514-85-34; 5 de Mayo 203; ☯ 8am-8pm Mon-Sat, 9am-7pm Sun)
es rent a car (Map pp720-1; ☎ 514-56-53; 5 de Mayo 315)
Hertz Airport (☎ 511-54-78; ☯ 7am-7pm); Center (Map pp720-1; ☎ 516-24-34; Plazuela Labastida 115; ☯ 8am-8pm Mon-Fri, 9am-7pm Sat, 9am-5pm Sun)
Only Rent-A-Car (Map pp720-1; www.onlyrentacar.com; ☯ 8am-8pm Mon-Sat, 9am-2pm Sun) Alcalá (☎ 516-32-13; Alcalá 401) 5 de Mayo (☎ 514-02-55; 5 de Mayo 215A)

GETTING AROUND
To/From the Airport

The Transportación Terrestre ticket-taxi desk at the south end of the airport terminal charges M$35 per person to anywhere in the city center in a van, or M$148 for a whole cab.

OAXACA STATE

You can book a van seat from the city to the airport a day or more ahead at **Transportes Aeropuerto** (Map pp720-1; ☎ 514-43-50; Alameda de León 1G; ☒ 9am-2pm & 5-8pm Mon-Sat). A taxi from the center to the airport should cost M$120.

Bicycle

Two full-service shops, Bicicletas Pedro Martínez (p723) and Zona Bici (p724), rent out good mountain bikes. Both also offer bike tours besides selling bikes and equipment.

Bus

Most points of importance in the city are within walking distance of each other, but you may want to use city buses (M$3.50) to go to or from the bus stations.

From the 1st-class bus station a westbound 'Juárez' bus will take you down Juárez and Melchor Ocampo, three blocks east of the Zócalo; a 'Tinoco y Palacios' or 'JP García' bus will take you down Tinoco y Palacios, two blocks west of the Zócalo. To return to the bus station, take an 'ADO' bus north up Pino Suárez, four blocks east of the Zócalo, or up Crespo, three blocks west of the Zócalo.

Buses between the 2nd-class bus station and the center crawl along congested streets – it's almost as quick to walk. 'Centro' buses head toward the center along Trujano, then turn north up Crespo.

To the 2nd-class bus station, 'Central' buses go south on Tinoco y Palacios, then west on Las Casas.

Car & Motorcycle

There are several guarded parking lots in the city center.

Estacionamiento Trujano (Map pp720-1; Trujano 219; per hr M$12, overnight M$50; ☒ 6am-11pm)

Taxi

A taxi anywhere within the central area, including the bus stations, costs M$35 to M$40.

VALLES CENTRALES

The countryside, villages and towns around Oaxaca are a big part of the city's appeal. Oaxaca stands at the meeting point of three valleys that have been the regional center of civilization since pre-Hispanic times: the Valle de Tlacolula, stretching 50km east from the city; the Valle de Zimatlán, reaching about 100km south; and the Valle de Etla, stretching about 40km north.

Today these Valles Centrales (Central Valleys), with a population that's mostly indigenous Zapotec, are full of fascinating archaeological sites and traditional villages and small towns that stage bustling weekly markets, produce fine specialty *artesanía* and celebrate their own colorful local fiestas. All these are within easy day-trip distance of Oaxaca city.

Getting There & Away

Many of the Valles Centrales' most interesting places are visited by daily tours run by Oaxaca travel agencies (p725).

There's also plenty of public transportation. Details on bus services are given later in this section. An alternative to traveling by bus, costing about twice as much (but still cheap!) is to take a *colectivo* (shared) taxi. These run

---

MARKET DAYS

Markets in the towns of the Valles Centrales offer all manner of foodstuffs and produce, as well as handicrafts, cookware, recorded music and sundries of all sorts, many of which are cheap imports these days. The scene is not to be missed; markets draw buyers and sellers from near and far, and bombard the senses with colors, sounds and smells.

At markets with plastic tarps set up for shade, taller visitors will find themselves constantly ducking under guy ropes, iron bars and hanging merchandise, but it's a small price to pay to see the continuation of a ritual that has been taking place for many hundreds, if not thousands, of years.

Markets are at their busiest in the morning, and most of them start to wind down in the early afternoon. The region's main markets:

Sunday Tlacolula
Tuesday Atzompa
Wednesday San Pedro y San Pablo Etla
Thursday Zaachila and Ejutla
Friday Ocotlán and San Bartolo Coyotepec
Saturday Mitla

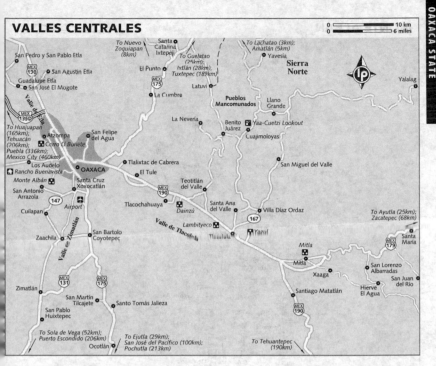

VALLES CENTRALES

to places north of Oaxaca in the Valle de Etla from Trujano on the north side of the 2nd-class bus station; and to places east and south, in the Valles de Tlacolula and Zimatlán, from Prolongación Victoria just southeast of the Central de Abastos market.

They leave when they're full (five or six people).

MONTE ALBÁN
☎ 951

The ancient Zapotec capital of **Monte Albán** (☎ 516-12-15; admission M$48; ⏱ 9am-5pm) stands on a flattened hilltop 400m above the valley floor, just a few kilometers west of Oaxaca. It's one of the most impressive ancient sites in Mexico, with the most spectacular 360-degree views. This strategic position was doubtless one of the reasons why the ancient Zapotecs chose this site for their capital. Its name, Monte Albán, means White Mountain.

At the entrance to the site are a good museum (explanations in Spanish only), a café and a bookstore. Official guides offer their services outside the ticket office for tours in Spanish, English, French and Italian (around M$200 for a small group). Portions of the site are wheelchair-accessible, via a lift and special walkways. Explanatory signs are in Spanish, English and Zapotec.

History
Monte Albán was first occupied around 500 BC, probably by Zapotecs from the start. It likely had early cultural connections with the Olmecs to the northeast.

Archaeologists divide Monte Albán's history into five phases. The years up to about 200 BC (phase Monte Albán I) saw the leveling of the hilltop, the building of temples and probably palaces, and the growth of a town of 10,000 or more people on the hillsides.

Hieroglyphs and dates in a dot-and-bar system carved during this era may mean that the elite of Monte Albán were the first people to use writing, and a written calendar, in Mexico. Between 200 BC and AD 300 (Monte Albán II) the city came to dominate more and more of Oaxaca.

OAXACA STATE

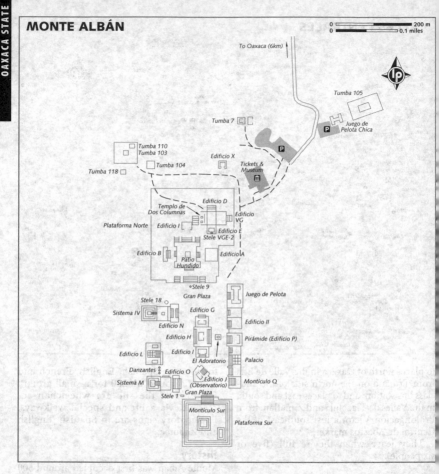

MONTE ALBÁN

The city was at its peak from about 300 to 700 (Monte Albán III), when the main and surrounding hills were terraced for dwellings, and the population reached about 25,000. Most of what we see now dates from this time.

Monte Albán was the center of a highly organized, priest-dominated society, controlling the extensively irrigated Valles Centrales, which held at least 200 other settlements and ceremonial centers.

Many Monte Albán buildings were plastered and painted red, and *talud-tablero* architecture (a stepped building style with alternating vertical and sloping sections) indicates influence from Teotihuacán. Nearly 170 underground tombs from this period have

been found, some of them elaborate and decorated with frescoes.

Between about 700 and 950 (Monte Albán IV), the place was abandoned and fell into ruin. Phase Monte Albán V (950–1521) saw minimal activity, except that Mixtecs arriving from northwestern Oaxaca reused old tombs here to bury their own dignitaries.

Sights

GRAN PLAZA

The **Gran Plaza**, about 300m long and 200m wide, was and is the center of Monte Albán. Some of its structures were temples, others were elite residential quarters. Many of them are now cordoned off to prevent damage by too many visitors' feet.

The stone terraces of the deep, I-shaped **Juego de Pelota** (Ball Court), constructed about 100 BC, were probably part of the playing area, not seats for spectators. It's thought they were covered with a thick coating of lime, meaning the ball would roll down them. The **Pirámide** (Edificio P) was topped by a small pillared temple and was probably an observatory of some sort. Next to it, the **Palacio** (Palace) is topped by a patio surrounded by the remains of typical Monte Albán III residential rooms.

The big **Plataforma Sur** (South Platform), with its wide staircase, is still good for a panorama of the plaza and the surrounding mountains, and has some carvings at the foot of its northeast corner. **Edificio J**, an arrowhead-shaped building constructed about 100 BC and riddled with tunnels and staircases (unfortunately you can't go inside), stands at an angle of 45 degrees to the other Gran Plaza structures and was an observatory. Figures and hieroglyphs carved on its walls record Monte Albán's military conquests of other towns.

Edificio L is an amalgam of the Monte Albán I building that contained the famous Danzante carvings and a later structure built over it. The **Danzantes** (Dancers), some of which are seen around the lower part of the building, are thought to depict leaders of conquered neighboring people.

Carved between 500 and 200 BC, they generally have open mouths (sometimes downturned in Olmec style) and closed eyes. Some have blood flowing from where their genitals have been cut off. Hieroglyphs accompanying them are the earliest known examples of true writing in Mexico.

Sistema IV, the twin to Sistema M at the south end of the plaza, combines typical Monte Albán II construction with overlays from Monte Albán III.

PLATAFORMA NORTE

The **North Platform**, over a rock outcrop, is almost as big as the Gran Plaza, and offers the best views, overall. It was rebuilt several times over the centuries. Chambers on either side of the main staircase contained tombs, and columns at the top of the stairs were part of a roofed hall. On top of the platform is a ceremonial complex built between AD 500 and 800; it includes the **Patio Hundido** (Sunken Patio),

with an altar at its center, **Edificios D**, **VG** and **E** (which were topped with adobe temples) and the **Templo de Dos Columnas**. **Stele VGE-2**, on the southern side of Edificio E, shows members of Monte Albán's ruling class of around AD 800 – four women and a young man represented by a jaguar.

TOMBS

To help preserve them, most of Monte Albán's ancient tombs are usually closed to visitors. But if you're lucky you may be able to peer into one of the following.

Tumba 104

Tomb 104, behind Plataforma Norte, is part of a necropolis in the northwest of the site that dates from AD 500 to 800. Above its underground entrance is an urn in the form of Pitao Cozobi, the Zapotec maize god, wearing a mask of Cocijo, the rain god (whose forked tongue represents lightning). The walls are covered with colorful Teotihuacán-style frescoes. The figure on the left wall is probably the Zapotec god of spring, Xipe Tótec; on the right wall, wearing a big snake-and-feather headdress, is Pitao Cozobi again.

Tumba 7

This tomb, just off the main parking lot, was built around AD 800, beneath a dwelling. In the 14th or 15th century it was reused by Mixtecs to bury a dignitary, two sacrificed servants, and one of the richest ancient treasure hoards in the Americas – the famed Mixtec treasure, now in the Museo de las Culturas de Oaxaca (p719).

Tumba 105

Tomb 105, behind the Juego de Pelota Chica (Small Ball Court), features decaying Teotihuacán-influenced murals of a procession of figures. The figures may represent nine gods of death and their female consorts. It lies beneath one of Monte Albán's biggest palace–residences, built between AD 500 and 800.

Getting There & Away

Autobuses Turísticos (Map pp720-1; ☎ 516-53-27) runs buses to the site from Hotel Rivera del Ángel, at Mina 518 in Oaxaca, six blocks southwest of the Zócalo. The buses leave every hour from 8:30am to 3:30pm, and start back from the site between noon and 5pm (schedule details

PEOPLES OF OAXACA

Much of Oaxaca's special creativity and unique atmosphere owes itself to the indigenous population, who comprise about a third of the state's 3.5 million people. With their deep-rooted, pre-Hispanic–influenced traditions in festivals, handicrafts, cuisine and clothing, Oaxaca's 15 indigenous peoples are the driving force behind the state's fine *artesanías* and unique festivities, and a main inspiration of its booming art scene and its amazing output of creative cuisine.

Each of the 15 groups has its own language, customs and colorful traditional costume (though most of their members also speak Spanish and many wear mainstream clothing). These groups form a strong presence throughout the region.

The people you will probably have most contact with are the Zapotecs, approximately 500,000 strong, who live mainly in and around the Valles Centrales and on the Isthmus of Tehuantepec. About 500,000 Mixtecs are spread around the mountainous borders of Oaxaca, Guerrero and Puebla states, with more than two-thirds of them in Oaxaca. The state's other large indigenous groups include 160,000 or so Mazatecs in the far north, 100,000 Mixes in the mountains northeast of the Valles Centrales, and 100,000 Chinantecs around Valle Nacional in the north.

In Oaxaca city you may well see Triquis, from western Oaxaca; the women wear bright red *huipiles* (sleeveless tunics). The Triquis are only about 15,000 strong and have a long history of violent conflict with mestizos and Mixtecs over land rights.

change from time to time). The M$38 fare includes a return trip at a designated time, giving you about three hours at the site. If you want to leave earlier, you must hope for a spare place on an earlier return bus.

Turísticos Marfil (Map pp720-1; ☎ 516-81-36; www .turisticosmarfil.com; Local 25, Plaza Santo Domingo, Alcala 407) offers an alternative with its Monte Albán Shuttle Service (round-trip M$50) departing five times daily. You'll probably see its flyers around town. It also picks up passengers at Mezkalito Hostel.

VALLE DE TLACOLULA

Most of the following places in the Valle de Tlacolula, east of Oaxaca, are within walking distance of the Oaxaca–Mitla road, Hwy 190. Transportes Oaxaca-Istmo buses to Mitla, running every 15 minutes (6am to 5pm) from Oaxaca's 2nd-class bus station, will drop you anywhere along this road. There are further services to some specific towns and villages.

El Tule
pop 7800 / elevation 1550m
The village of El Tule, 10km east of Oaxaca along Hwy 190, draws crowds of visitors for one very good reason: **El Árbol del Tule** (The Tree of El Tule; admission M$3; ☼ 9am-5pm), which is claimed to be the largest tree in the world. In trunk thickness (it's about 11m in diameter) this claim is probably true. This vast *ahuehuete* (Montezuma cypress), 42m

high, dwarfs the pretty, 17th-century village church in whose churchyard it towers. Its age is equally impressive: the tree is at least 1500 years old, which means it was already growing when the ancient city of Monte Albán was at its peak. A park created in the 1990s stretches out in front of the churchyard.

Long revered by Oaxacans, the Árbol del Tule is under threat from local urban growth and irrigated agriculture that tap its water sources. Local campaigners say some of its aquifers must be restored if it is to survive, and are trying to win Unesco World Heritage status for the tree.

Autotransportes Valle del Norte buses go to El Tule (M$45, every 10 minutes) from the 2nd-class bus station in Oaxaca.

Dainzú
Twenty-one kilometers from Oaxaca along the Mitla road, a track leads 1km south to the small but interesting **ruins of Dainzú** (admission M$29; ☼ 8am-5pm). To the left as you approach is the pyramid-like Edificio A, 50m long and 8m high, built about 300 BC. Along its bottom wall were some 50 bas-reliefs of feline figures, masks and heads, mostly related to the ball game; they're now gathered under a corrugated metal roof. Among the ruins below Edificio A are a partly restored ball court from about AD 1000 and a sunken tomb (inside Edificio B) whose entrance is carved with a representation of a crouching jaguar.

In the scrub on the hilltop behind the site are more rock carvings similar to those of Edificio A, but you'll need a guide to find them (ask the caretaker).

Teotitlán del Valle

☎ 951 / pop 4900 / elevation 1700m

This famous weaving village is 4km north of Hwy 190, about 25km from Oaxaca. The weaving tradition here goes back to pre-Hispanic times: Teotitlán had to pay tributes of cloth to the Aztecs. Quality today is high, and traditional dyes made from cochineal, indigo and moss have been revived. The variety of designs is enormous – from Zapotec gods and Mitla-style geometric patterns to contemporary imitations of paintings by Rivera and Picasso.

Blankets and rugs wave at you from many houses and showrooms along the village streets. From Av Juárez (the street along which you enter Teotitlán from the highway), signs point to the central **Mercado de Artesanías**, where yet more are on sale. Around 150 Teotitlán families specialize in weaving; many of their showrooms are workshops too, and the weavers are usually happy to demonstrate their techniques and their methods of obtaining natural dyes.

Facing the Mercado de Artesanías on the central plaza is the **Museo Comunitario Balaa Xtee Guech Gulal** (☎ 524-44-63; admission M$10; 🕙 10am-6pm Tue-Sun), with local archaeological finds and displays on local crafts and traditions (in English as well as Spanish and Zapotec). Here, with a day's notice, you can organize a guided walk up **Cerro de Picacho**, a sacred hill just outside the village, for M$10 per person. From the plaza, steps rise to a fine broad churchyard with the handsome 17th-century **Templo de la Virgen de la Natividad** (🕙 6am-6pm) in one corner. The church's altar area and transept are adorned with colorful 18th-century frescos. It was built atop a Zapotec ceremonial site, many of whose carved stones can be seen in the church walls; look especially in the inner patio.

English-speaking Roque Antonio Santiago of **Oaxaca Birding Tours** (☎ 524-43-71; www.mexonline.com/oaxacabirdingtours.htm; Cuauhtémoc 5) leads highly recommended bird-watching outings in the Valles Centrales, the nearby Sierra Norte cloud forests and beyond. A surprising number of species can be seen in the environs of Teotitlán alone. A day's outing costs around M$750 per person.

SLEEPING & EATING

Calle 2 de Abril No 12 (☎ 524-41-64; Calle 2 de Abril 12; s/d/tr incl breakfast M$250/350/500), a house belonging to friendly, English-speaking Elena González, has weaving looms in the courtyard and three bright, clean and cool upstairs rooms, each with fan and bathroom with hot water.

our pick **Casa Sagrada** (☎ 516-42-75; www.casasagrada.com; s US$120-150, d US$180-240, all incl breakfast & dinner; P) is the beautiful home and guesthouse of Arnulfo Mendoza, Teotitlán's most celebrated weaver, and his multitalented Canadian wife Mary Jane Gagnier, who also own La Mano Mágica (p734) in Oaxaca. Set on the hill at the top of the village, with panoramic views, this is a great place to stay for a few days and enjoy a combination of relaxation, good food and local activities. The 12 comfortable, tile-floored rooms are decorated with vintage *artesanías*, and most have a patio or terrace with hammocks. Casa Sagrada has a stable of fine horses on which you can take two-hour or half-day rides or treks of several days. Other activities on offer include hiking, bird-watching, cooking classes, temascal sessions, and yoga and writers' retreats. There's a two-night minimum stay, and you should reserve at least one day ahead.

Restaurante Tlamanalli (☎ 524-40-06; Av Juárez 39; mains M$70-180; 🕙 1-4pm Tue-Sun) The traditional Oaxacan dishes here are superbly prepared. Some of them are based on pre-Hispanic recipes, and vegetarian options are offered. Exhibits on weaving add to the interest of lunching here.

GETTING THERE & AWAY

Autotransportes Valle del Norte buses run to Teotitlán (M$10, 50 minutes, hourly 7am to 9pm Monday to Saturday) from Oaxaca's 2nd-class bus station; the last one back to Oaxaca leaves the village about 7pm. Alternatively, get any Mitla-bound bus to the signposted Teotitlán turnoff on Hwy 190, then a *colectivo* taxi (M$5) to the village.

Tlacolula

pop 12,000 / elevation 1650m

Tlacolula, 31km from Oaxaca, holds one of the Valles Centrales' major **markets** every Sunday, with the area around the church becoming a packed throng. Crafts, foods and plenty of everyday goods are on sale. It's a

OAXACA'S COMMUNITY MUSEUMS

Oaxaca state is in the forefront of Mexico's admirable community museums movement. More than 100 villages around the country have set up these small museums to foster their unique cultures and keep their archaeological and cultural treasures 'at home,' and at least 14 are scattered around Oaxaca.

The **Unión de Museos Comunitarios de Oaxaca** (☎ 951-2045690; www.museoscomunitarios oaxaca.org; 5 de Febrero 301A, Colonia Cinco Señores) in Oaxaca city has full information on these small but often fascinating museums. The English-speaking office offers organized trips to various museum villages, including San José El Mogote (p746; per person M$300), Santa Ana del Valle (below; M$360) and San Martín Huamelúlpam (p751; M$670). The prices here are per person for groups of five; they drop significantly for groups of 10. The excursions include traditional local meals and visits to local artisans, healers, archaeological sites and so on. At San Martín Huamelúlpam for example you'll get four meals and a night's lodging, as well as a demonstration of traditional medicine practices and – usually – a temascal. If you're up for an off-the-beaten-track adventure, consider visiting the Museo Comunitario La Mina (p749) at Natividad in the Sierra Norte, with a re-creation of an important old gold and silver mine, or the community museum at San Miguel Tequixtepec (p750) near Coixtlahuaca, with fascinating pre-Hispanic material in the restored 16th-century house of a *cacique* (regional strongman). At most of the museums, local guides can be found to show you other local places of interest, and several villages have cabin accommodation for visitors.

treat for lovers of market atmosphere. Inside the church, the domed 16th-century **Capilla del Santo Cristo** is a riot of golden, indigenous-influenced decoration comparable with the Capilla del Rosario in Oaxaca's Iglesia de Santo Domingo. Among the ceiling ornamentation are plaster martyrs who stand holding their severed heads in their hands.

Transportes Oaxaca-Istmo and Fletes y Pasajes buses run to Tlacolula from Oaxaca's 2nd-class bus station (M$10, one hour, every few minutes).

Santa Ana del Valle

☎ 951 / pop 2000 / elevation 1700m

Santa Ana, 4km north of Tlacolula, has a time-honored textile tradition. Today it produces woolen blankets, sarapes and bags. Natural dyes have been revived and traditional designs – flowers, birds, geometric patterns – are still in use. On the central plaza are the richly decorated 17th-century **Templo de Santa Ana** (☺ hours vary), a small **Mercado de Artesanías**, and the **Museo Comunitario Shan-Dany** (☎ 562-17-05; admission M$10; ☺ 10am-2pm & 3-6pm), a good little community museum with exhibits on local textiles, history, archaeology (it has some fine pre-Hispanic ceramic pieces), and the Zapotec Danza de las Plumas, which is danced in Santa Ana during the Fiesta de Esquipulas (January 12–14), on July 26 and during the fiesta de Santa Ana (11–13 August), usually around

noon. The museum is a good place to ask about textile workshops that you can visit.

English-speaking **Aristeo Gutiérrez Sánchez** leads interesting tours on which you'll visit an old gold mine near the village, learn about the plants from which vegetable dyes and traditional medicines are obtained, and witness a dye-making demonstration. Ask for Aristeo at the museum or the shop opposite. The tours can be done on foot (M$200 per small group), bicycle (add M$30 per bike) or horse (add M$100 per horse).

Buses and minibuses run frequently from Tlacolula to Santa Ana until about 7pm (8pm on Saturday and Sunday).

Yagul

The **Yagul ruins** (admission M$35; ☺ 8am-5pm) are finely sited on a cactus-covered hill, 1.5km north of the Oaxaca–Mitla road. The signposted turnoff is 34km from Oaxaca. Unless you have a vehicle you'll have to walk the 1.5km: lone women shouldn't risk this as we have received a report of a sexual attack on this isolated road.

Yagul was a leading Valles Centrales settlement after the decline of Monte Albán. Most of what's visible was built after AD 750. **Patio 4**, down to the left as you reach the main part of the site, was surrounded by four temples. On its east side is a carved-stone animal, probably a jaguar. Next to the central platform is the entrance to one of several underground **Tumbas Triples** (Triple Tombs).

The beautiful **Juego de Pelota** (Ball Court) is the second-biggest in Mesoamerica (after one at Chichén Itzá – see p938). To its west, on the edge of the hill, is **Patio 1**, with the narrow **Sala de Consejo** (Council Hall) along its north side. The labyrinthine **Palacio de los Seis Patios** (Palace of the Six Patios) was probably the leader's residence. Its walls were plastered and painted red.

It's well worth climbing the **Fortaleza** (Fortress), the huge rock that towers above the ruins. The path passes **Tumba 28**, made of cut stone. Several overgrown ruins perch atop the Fortress – and the views are marvelous.

Mitla
🕾 **051 / pop 7700 / elevation 1700m**
The stone 'mosaics' of ancient Mitla, 46km southeast of Oaxaca, are unique in Mexico. Today they are surrounded by a modern Zapotec town.

ORIENTATION
If you tell the bus conductor from Oaxaca that you're heading for *las ruinas*, you should be dropped at a Y junction (*la cuchilla*). From here it's about 1.5km to the ruins' ticket office: go north along Av Morelos, and continue through the plaza and along Calles 5 de Febrero and Reforma toward the three-domed Iglesia de San Pablo. The ticket office is behind this church.

RUINS
The **ruins** (🕾 568-03-16; admission Grupo de las Columnas & Grupo del Norte M$35; ⏱ 8am-5pm) date mostly from the final two or three centuries before the Spanish conquest. At this time Mitla was probably the most important of the Zapotec religious centers, dominated by high priests who performed heart-wrenching human sacrifices. It's thought that each group of buildings we see at Mitla was reserved for specific occupants – one for the high priest, one for lesser priests, one for the king and so forth.

The **Grupo de las Columnas** (Group of the Columns), the major group of buildings, is just south of the Iglesia de San Pablo. It had two main patios, the Patio Norte and Patio Sur, each lined on three sides by long rooms. Along the north side of the Patio Norte is the **Sala de las Columnas** (Hall of the Columns), 38m

long with six massive columns and unusual, very big one-piece lintels over doorways. At one end of this hall, a passage (still bearing traces of original plaster and red paint) leads into **El Palacio**, which holds some of Mitla's best stonework 'mosaics.' Each little piece of stone was cut to fit the design, then set in mortar on the walls and painted. The 14 different geometric designs at Mitla are thought to symbolize the sky and earth, a feathered serpent and other important beings. Many Mitla buildings were also adorned with painted friezes. The Patio Sur holds two underground tombs.

The **Grupo del Norte** (North Group) is similar to the Grupo de las Columnas but less well preserved. The Spaniards built San Pablo Church over one of its patios in 1590.

The **Grupo del Arroyo** (Stream Group), which you pass on Calle 5 de Febrero, is the most substantial of the other groups of ruins in Mitla. There are the remains of forts, tombs and other structures scattered for many kilometers around.

SLEEPING & EATING
Hotel La Zapoteca (🕾 568-00-26; 5 de Febrero 12; s/d/tr/q M$200/250/350/450; Ⓟ) Between the main plaza and the ruins is this modest, reasonably clean hotel, with a restaurant (and hot water for only a few hours a day).

Hotel Don Cenobio (🕾 568-03-30; www.hoteldon cenobio.com; Av Juárez 3; r M$580-790; Ⓟ 🖾) Set on the central plaza, this is the town's classiest hotel. The 18 themed rooms are spectacularly decorated with multicolored, carved headboards and furniture, from Guadalajara. They're comfortable and fan-cooled, with phone, good bathrooms and in many cases balconies. The hotel has a grassy central garden with pool, with its restaurant and bar just off it.

Restaurant Doña Chica (🕾 568-02-25; Av Morelos 41; mains M$50-60; ⏱ 9am-11pm) Less than 100m from *la cuchilla*, spick-and-span Doña Chica serves straightforward but delicious Oaxacan dishes such as *moles*, enchiladas and *tasajo*. Good soups, *antojitos*, and salads cost M$30 to M$50.

The **restaurant** (mains M$70-120; ⏱ 8am-6:30pm) at Hotel Don Cenobio serves mainly Oaxacan and Mexican fare but gets less favorable reports.

SHOPPING
Mitla's streets are sprinkled with shops selling local *mezcal*. Many of them will invite you to

OAXACA STATE

taste a couple of varieties – as will some of the small-scale *mezcal* distilleries along the road toward Oaxaca. Many other shops, and the large **Mercado de Artesanías** near the ruins, sell local textiles. Some of the tablecloths are attractive buys.

GETTING THERE & AROUND

Transportes Oaxaca-Istmo buses to Mitla (M$15, 1¼ hours, every few minutes from 5am to 7pm) leave from Oaxaca's 2nd-class bus station. The last one back to Oaxaca leaves Mitla at about 9pm. A taxi from *la cuchilla* to the ruins costs M$20.

Hierve El Agua
elevation 1800m

At Hierve El Agua, 13km southeast of Mitla, bubbling **mineral springs** (admission M$15; ☼ 8am-6pm) run into bathing pools with a dramatic cliff-top location and expansive panoramas. Hierve El Agua means 'the Water Boils' but the mineral-laden water is actually cold. Water dribbling over the cliff edge for millennia has created mineral formations that look like huge frozen waterfalls. Altogether the pools here make for a unique bathing experience.

Hierve El Agua is a popular destination for *oaxaqueños* on their days off. Above the pools and cliffs are a number of **comedores** (antojitos M$20-35) and half a dozen **cabañas** (cabins; per person M$70) providing simple rooms with cold-water bathrooms (one bathroom per two rooms).

The area is dotted with maguey fields: villages such as San Lorenzo Albarradas and San Juan del Río produce some of Oaxaca's finest *mezcal*.

Hierve El Agua is on the itinerary of some day tours from Oaxaca. Public transportation is only by *camioneta* (pickup truck) from the street outside Mitla bus station (M$25, one hour). These leave when they have six or seven people, and are infrequent except on Saturday and Sunday. Alternatively, take a taxi from Mitla.

If you're driving, take the 'Hierve El Agua' exit from the highway that bypasses Mitla to the south. This passes through tiny Xaagá, from which an unpaved, very scenic road (steep in parts) leads 11km to the site.

VALLE DE ZIMATLÁN

South from Oaxaca, Hwy 175 goes through San Bartolo Coyotepec, Ocotlán and Ejutla. Hwy 147 goes to Cuilapan and Zaachila.

San Bartolo Coyotepec
☎ 951 / pop 3200 / elevation 1550m

All the polished, black, surprisingly light pottery, called *barro negro*, that you find around Oaxaca (in hundreds of shapes and forms – candlesticks, jugs and vases, decorative animal and bird figures) comes from San Bartolo Coyotepec, 11km south of Oaxaca. To head to the pottery's original source, look for the signs to the **Alfarería Doña Rosa** (☎ 551-00-11; Juárez 24; ☼ 9am-7pm), a short walk east off the highway. It was Rosa Real Mateo (1900–80) who invented the method of burnishing the *barro negro* with quartz stones for the distinctive shine. Her family *alfarería* (potters' workshop) is now the biggest in the village, and demonstrations of the process are given whenever a tour bus rolls in (several times a day). The pieces are hand-molded by an age-old technique that uses two saucers functioning as a rudimentary potters' wheel. They are fired in pit kilns and turn black from smoke and from the iron oxide in the clay.

There are plenty of other blackware shops and workshops around town today, including several on the same street as Alfarería Doña Rosa. The **Plaza Artesanal de Barro Negro**, 300m north off Juárez, has many stalls.

San Bartolo also has an excellent, modern, folk art museum, the **Museo Estatal de Arte Popular de Oaxaca** (☎ 551-00-00; admission M$35; ☼ 10am-7:45pm Tue-Sun), on the south side of the main village plaza, across the highway from the church. It's very nicely done and features folk art from around Oaxaca state, including ceramics, baskets, knives, wood sculptures, rugs, masks, tinwork and more. Changing exhibitions spotlight various towns, and the stuff upstairs is for sale at good fixed prices.

Buses from Oaxaca to San Bartolo (M$5, 20 minutes) leave every few minutes from the terminal at Armenta y López 721, 500m south of the Zócalo.

San Martín Tilcajete & Santo Tomás Jalieza

San Martín Tilcajete (population 1600), 1km west of Hwy 175, 24km south of Oaxaca, is the source of many of the bright copal-wood *alebrijes* (imaginary animal figures) seen in Oaxaca. You can see and buy them in makers' houses, many of which have 'Artesanías de Madera' (Wooden Handicrafts) signs outside.

The women of Santo Tomás Jalieza (population 1000), on the east side of Hwy 175, 2km south of the Tilcajete turnoff, weave high-quality textiles on back-strap looms. A permanent **Mercado de Artesanías** in the village square sells tablecloths, table mats and embroidered dresses as well as more traditional weavings. It opens daily but is busiest on Friday to coincide with the Ocotlán market.

Ocotlán-bound buses from Oaxaca will drop you at the turnoffs to these two villages. *Colectivo* taxis run from Ocotlán itself.

Ocotlán
pop 14,000 / elevation 1500m

Ocotlán, 31km south of Oaxaca, was the hometown of the artist Rodolfo Morales (1925–2001), who turned his international success to the area's benefit by setting up the **Fundación Cultural Rodolfo Morales** (Morelos 108), which is headquartered in his old family home less than a block north of the central plaza. This foundation works to promote the arts, heritage, environment and social welfare locally and has done some marvelous restoration work on village churches – including the handsome 16th-century **Templo de Santo Domingo** just off Ocotlán's main plaza, which now sports beautiful, colorful paintwork inside and out. The foundation also turned the adjoining **Ex-Convento de Santo Domingo** (admission M$15; 9am-6pm), previously a dilapidated jail, into a first-class art museum, including several of Morales' own canvases and a room of folk art dominated by Ocotlán's most renowned artisans, the Aguilar sisters. Morales' ashes are interred here, too. For information on the foundation, see www.artedeoaxaca.com.

The four Aguilar sisters and their families create whimsical, colorful pottery figures of women with all sorts of unusual motifs. Their houses are together on the west side of the highway as you come into Ocotlán from the north – spot them by the pottery women on the wall. Most renowned is the family of **Guillermina Aguilar** (Morelos 430), who turn out, among other things, miniature 3-D re-creations of Frida Kahlo works.

Most visitors come to Ocotlán on Fridays, when its weekly market sprawls around the central plaza. This ancient market is one of the biggest in the Valles Centrales. The covered Mercado Morelos, on the west side of the plaza, is worth a look any day of the week.

Estrella del Valle/Oaxaca Pacífico runs buses to Ocotlán (M$10, 45 minutes, every 15 minutes from 5am to 9:30pm) from the terminal at Armenta y López 721 in Oaxaca. **Automorsa** (514-79-27; cnr Cabrera & Zaragoza) operates a similar service, 6am to 8pm.

San José del Pacífico
951 / pop 500 / elevation 2750m

The small mountain village of San José del Pacífico, 100km south of Ocotlán, is just outside the Valles Centrales on Hwy 175 heading toward the coast. The scenery is spectacular here, and San José is a good base for walks through the cool mountain pine forests to waterfalls. This area is also famed for its magic mushrooms. **Café Express** (internet per hr M$10; 8am-10pm), on the highway in the village, provides internet access, has a good topo map of the area on its wall, and sells warm woolly jumpers, scarves and gloves.

Cabañas y Restaurante Puesta del Sol (951-1008678; www.sanjosedelpacifico.com; r M$300, r/q with fireplace M$400/500; P), beside Hwy 175, 1km north of the village, offers superb views and beautiful rooms in well-built wooden cabins set in spacious hillside grounds. All have hot showers and TV. A decent restaurant serves *antojitos* and omelettes for M$25 to M$30 and meat dishes for M$40 to M$50. Cheaper, more basic rooms are available in the village itself (look for signs).

All Hwy 175 buses between Oaxaca and Pochutla stop at San José, as do Autoexprés Atlántida vans (M$65 from Oaxaca).

San Antonio Arrazola
pop 1000 / elevation 1600m

Below the west side of Monte Albán and 4km off the Cuilapan road, Arrazola produces many of the colorful *alebrijes* that are sold in Oaxaca. You can see and buy *alebrijes* in many artisans' workshops, stores and homes.

Cuilapan
pop 11,000 / elevation 1570m

Cuilapan, 9km southwest of Oaxaca, is one of the few Mixtec towns in the Valles Centrales. It's the site of a beautiful, historic Dominican monastery, the **Ex-Convento Dominicano** (admission to cloister M$27; 9am-6pm), whose pale stone seems almost to grow out of the land.

In 1831 the Mexican independence hero Vicente Guerrero was executed at this monastery by soldiers supporting the rebel conservative Anastasio Bustamante, who had just deposed the liberal Guerrero from the presidency. Guerrero had fled by ship from Acapulco, but the ship's captain put in at Huatulco and betrayed him to the rebels. Guerrero was then transported to Cuilapan to die.

From the monastery entrance you reach a long, low, unfinished church that has stood roofless since work on it stopped in 1560. It has big, stately arches and some detailed stone carving. Beyond is the church that succeeded it, which contains the tomb of Juana Donají (daughter of Cosijoeza, the last Zapotec king of Zaachila) and is open only for Mass (usually 7am to 8am and 5pm to 6pm). Around the church's right-hand end is a two-storey renaissance-style cloister: some rooms here have faded 16th- and 17th-century murals; and a painting of Guerrero hangs in the small room where he was held. Outside a monument marks the spot where he was shot.

From Oaxaca, **Zaachila Yoo** (Bustamante 603) runs buses to Cuilapan (M$5, 20 minutes, every 10 minutes from 6:30am to 9:30pm).

Zaachila

🕿 951 / pop 12,000 / elevation 1520m

This part-Mixtec, part-Zapotec town, about 6km beyond Cuilapan and 4km west of San Bartolo Coyotepec, has a large, busy Thursday market. Zaachila was a Zapotec capital from about AD 1400 until the Spanish conquest. Its last Zapotec king, Cosijoeza, died in the 1520s.

Behind the village church overlooking the main plaza, a sign indicates the entrance to Zaachila's **Zona Arqueológica** (Archaeological Zone; admission M$29; 🕒 8am-5pm), a small assortment of mounds where you can enter two small tombs used by the ancient Mixtecs. Tumba 1 retains sculptures of owls, a turtle-man figure and various long-nosed skull-like masks. Tumba 2 has no decoration but in it was found a Mixtec treasure hoard that's now in the Museo Nacional de Antropología (p153) in Mexico City. When Mexican archaeologists first tried to excavate these tombs in the 1940s and 1950s, they were run off by irate Zaachilans. The tombs were finally excavated under armed guard in 1962. You can see photos of some of the objects that were carted off to Mexico City.

Zaachila Yoo buses to Cuilapan (see above) continue to Zaachila (M$5, 25 minutes from Oaxaca).

VALLE DE ETLA
Atzompa

pop 14,000 / elevation 1600m

The potters of Atzompa, 6km northwest of Oaxaca and now joined to it by urban sprawl, produce very attractive, colorful animal figures, pots, plates, lamps and more. Much work is sold at excellent prices in the **Mercado de Artesanías** (Crafts Market; Av Libertad 303; 🕒 9am-8pm), on the main street that enters Atzompa from Oaxaca. Some of the ceramics bear Atzompa's traditional green glaze; others are in more colorful, innovative styles. Restaurante El Patio at this market is good for a moderately priced snack or lunch.

From the church up in the village center, a 2.5km road (mostly dirt) leads south up **Cerro El Bonete**. The road ends a few minutes' walk before the top of the hill, which is dotted with unrestored pre-Hispanic ruins.

Buses to Atzompa (M$3, 20 minutes) leave Oaxaca's 2nd-class bus station about every 15 minutes. If driving yourself, follow División Oriente northwest out of Oaxaca, go left along Calz Tecnológico (signposted 'Monte Albán') from a big intersection on the fringe of town, then go right at traffic signals after 1.5km.

San José El Mogote

pop 3000 / elevation 1600m

Fourteen kilometers northwest of central Oaxaca on Hwy 190, a westward turnoff (signposted 'Nazareno') leads 1.5km to San José El Mogote. Long ago, before even Monte Albán became important, Mogote was the major settlement in Oaxaca. It was at its peak between 650 and 500 BC, and flourished again between 100 BC and AD 150, with a main plaza that was almost as big as Monte Albán's. The major surviving structures (partly restored) are a ball court and a sizable pyramid mound behind the primary school in the village center.

The **Museo Comunitario Ex-Hacienda El Cacique** (admission M$10; 🕒 10am-6pm) is in the former landowner's hacienda next to the primary school. The museum has interesting material on the villagers' 20th-century struggle for land ownership; an archaeological highlight is 'El Diablo Enchilado', a pre-Hispanic brazier in the form of a bright red grimacing face. If you find the museum closed, ask anyone to point your way to the nearby house of the *encargado* (keeper).

Colectivo taxi (p736) is the simplest way to get to Mogote.

San Agustín Etla

☎ 951 / pop 3100 / elevation 1800m

Pretty San Agustín sits on the eastern slopes of the Valle de Etla, 18km northwest of Oaxaca. Its large, early-20th-century textile mill has been superbly restored as the **Centro de las Artes de San Agustín** (☎ 521-30-43; www.centrodelasartesde sanagustin.com; Independencia s/n; admission free; ☺ 8am-6pm), a spectacular arts center with two long, large halls. The lower hall is used as a gallery for often wonderful craft or art exhibitions; the upper one is a setting for concerts, conferences and other events. The center also hosts courses and workshops in a great variety of arts and crafts. Pools surrounding the building are part of a gravity-powered water system that cools the roof and also supplies a papermaking workshop down the hill.

The turnoff for San Agustín from Hwy 190 is on the east side of the road, signposted 'Vista Hermosa' and 'La Capellania' – 1km past the Nazareno turning on the west side. Head up from the highway for 3km till you arrive by San Agustín's church, which is beside the arts center. You can get here by *colectivo* from Trujano in Oaxaca.

SIERRA NORTE

The mountains separating the Valles Centrales from low-lying far northern Oaxaca are called the Sierra Juárez, and the more southerly parts of this range, closest to Oaxaca, have become known as the Sierra Norte. These beautiful, well-forested highlands are home to some successful community ecotourism ventures that provide comfortable accommodations and a wonderful opportunity to get out on foot, mountain bike or horseback into some of Mexico's loveliest landscapes. The area's natural diversity is amazing: over 400 bird species, 350 butterflies, all six Mexican wild cats and nearly 4000 plants have been recorded in the Sierra Norte. The variety of wildflowers here is astonishing, too. Be prepared for cool temperatures: in the higher, southern villages temperatures sometimes fall below freezing in winter. The rainiest season is from late May to September, but there's little rain from January to April.

Scenic Hwy 175 crosses the *sierras* en route to Tuxtepec (population 97,000), the main town in the far north of the state.

PUEBLOS MANCOMUNADOS

The Pueblos Mancomunados (Commonwealth of Villages) are eight remote Zapotec villages in the thickly forested highlands north of the Valle de Tlacolula. For centuries, in a unique form of cooperation, the villages have pooled the natural resources of their 290-sq-km territory, which include extensive pine and oak forests, sharing the profits from forestry and other enterprises. Today seven of the villages (the exception is Yavesia) also cooperate in an excellent ecotourism program that offers plain but comfortable lodgings and walking, horseback riding and mountain biking along more than 100km of scenic tracks and trails. Elevations range from 2200m to over 3200m, and the landscapes, with their canyons, caves, crags, waterfalls and panoramic lookouts, are spectacular. The villages themselves are mostly simple but picturesque places, and have unique relics of local history or culture to show off.

The ecotourism program's office in Oaxaca is Expediciones Sierra Norte (p723). Several Oaxaca active-tourism agencies (see Activities, p723) offer trips to the Pueblos Mancomunados, from one to several days long, and will provide transportation to the area and take the organizational legwork out of your visit. But you can do it independently, and cheaper, by dealing direct with Expediciones Sierra Norte. The office has English-speaking staff and copious information on trails, villages, accommodations, transportation and how to prepare, and will make reservations. It also sells a very useful guide-map for M$50.

Trained local guides are available for all excursions. They will almost certainly only speak Zapotec and Spanish but are knowledgeable about the plants, wildlife and ecology of these *sierras*. You can head off without a guide, but trail marking is less than perfect. For accommodations and meals, each village has *cabañas* (mostly with hot-water bathrooms and fireplaces), a designated camping ground, and at least one *comedor* serving cheap, good local meals from 8am to 8pm.

Below is a guide to prices for visiting the Pueblos Mancomunados:

- Guide for up to eight people: M$120 to M$200 per day
- Cabaña: M$130 per person (shared); M$450 for up to four people (private)
- Camping: M$40 per person (bring your own tent)

- Meals: M$30 to M$40 each
- Bicycle: M$100/150 per three hours/one day (available in all villages)
- Horse: M$100 per hour (available in some villages)
- *Huentzee* (contribution to maintenance costs): M$50 per person

Routes

You can easily spend several days walking or riding the many scenic tracks and trails. The most common starting villages are Cuajimoloyas, Llano Grande and Benito Juárez, all at the higher, southern end of the Sierra Norte: walks or rides starting here will be more downhill than up.

It's also possible to base yourself in one village and take local walks or rides from there. Each participating village has an information office where you can find out about local routes and organize services.

Some superb lookout points are accessible from the southern villages, such as El Mirador, a 2.5km walk from Benito Juárez, or the 3200m-high Yaa-Cuetzi lookout, 1km from Cuajimoloyas. From Yaa-Cuetzi in clear weather you can see such distant mountains as Pico de Orizaba and Zempoaltépetl. Within a couple of hours' walk of Llano Grande is Piedra Larga, a rocky crag with superb views. From La Nevería additional walking tours have recently been developed, which will take you through the forests to La Cumbre on Hwy 175, or right down to Tlalixtac de Cabrera in the Valle de Tlacolula by an old donkey trail heading for Oaxaca city.

One special highlight walk is the beautiful Latuvi–Lachatao canyon trail, which follows a pre-Hispanic track that connected the Valles Centrales with the Gulf of Mexico and passes through cloud forests festooned with bromeliads and hanging mosses. Lachatao is one of the most atmospheric villages, with a huge 17th-century church (fruit of the riches produced by nearby colonial gold mines); and the food at Magdalena's *comedor* there is particularly good! From Lachatao or nearby Amatlán you can visit the old mines and the remains of a colonial textile mill.

Getting There & Away

Cuajimoloyas and Llano Grande have the area's best bus links with Oaxaca: five or more daily buses (to Cuajimoloyas M$25, two hours; to Llano Grande M$30, 2½ hours) from the 2nd-class bus station with **Flecha del Zempoaltépetl** (☎ 951-516-63-42). **Transportes Ya'a-Yana** (Niño Perdido 306, Colonia Ixcotel, Oaxaca) runs buses to some of the other villages, but these services are occasionally interrupted, so it's worth checking first with Expediciones Sierra Norte. The stop is next to a Pemex gas station on Hwy 190, a couple of kilometers east of Oaxaca's 1st-class bus station. Ya'a-Yana schedules:

Amatlán (M$25, 2¼ hours) Departs Oaxaca 4pm daily; departs Amatlán for Oaxaca 5:15am.

Benito Juárez (M$25, two hours) Departs Oaxaca 4pm (5pm during daylight saving) Tuesday, Friday and Saturday; departs Benito Juárez for Oaxaca 5am Tuesday, Friday and Saturday, and 3pm Sunday.

Lachatao (M$30, 2½ hours) Departs Oaxaca 4pm daily; departs Lachatao for Oaxaca 5am.

Latuvi (M$30, 2½ hours) Departs Oaxaca 4pm Friday; departs Latuvi for Oaxaca 4am Friday.

Another way to reach Benito Juárez is to take a Cuajimoloyas-bound bus to the Benito Juárez turnoff (*desviación de Benito Juárez*), 1¾ hours from Oaxaca, then walk 3.5km west along the unpaved road to the village.

From Ixtlán, *camionetas* leave for Amatlán (M$15, 45 minutes) and Lachatao (M$15, one hour) at 8am, noon and 3pm.

Important: unlike Oaxaca, the Pueblos Mancomunados does not observe daylight saving time (see p978) – so triple-check all bus departure times for your return trip!

GUELATAO

pop 500 / elevation 1900m

On Hwy 175, 60km from Oaxaca, little Guelatao village was the birthplace of national hero Benito Juárez. By the pretty lake at the center of the village are a statue of young Benito as a shepherd and a replica of the adobe house where he lived as a boy. Among the adjacent municipal buildings are two statues of Juárez and a small exhibition, the **Sala Homenaje a Juárez** (admission free; ⏱ 9am-6pm Wed-Sun).

Buses heading to Ixtlán will stop at Guelatao en route.

IXTLÁN

☎ 951 / pop 7200 / elevation 2035m

Ixtlán, 3km beyond Guelatao on Hwy 175, is a friendly and often wet little town with a busy Monday market. Benito Juárez was baptized in Ixtlán's **Templo de Santo Tomás** (⏱ 10am-2pm & 4-7pm). This finely carved 17th-century baroque church stands just above the central plaza. Off the plaza is the office of the enthusiastic local community tourism operation, **Ecoturixtlán** (☎ 553-60-75; www.ecoturixtlan.com; cnr 16 de Septiembre & Revolución; ☑ 9am-8pm). The unusual feature of the Ixtlán area is that elevations range from as low as 1200m to more than 3000m, which makes for much biological diversity. You can traverse seven different ecosystems, from lowland deciduous forest to cloud forest, in one excursion. Guides for three- to five-hour walks cost M$100 to M$200, plus forest admission fees of M$30 to M$60 per person. Vehicle support is available (and can be welcome in this hilly terrain) for up to M$600 per outing. Ecoturixtlán's **cabañas** (d/q M$450/650) are in the forest 5km from town, just off the Capulálpam road (free transportation is provided). They're well built of mud-brick and wood, with tile floors, fireplaces and hot-water bathrooms. You can also camp here (per person M$40; tent rental 1/2 people M$100/150), and at or around the same site are a restaurant (breakfast/lunch/dinner M$40/70/35), zip-line, cave, waterfall, hanging bridge, trout farm, bike trail, and horses (per hour M$100) and mountain bikes (per hour M$30) for rent. It's a little bit like a woodland holiday camp but is still pretty quiet during the week. You can obtain information and make reservations at Ecoturixtlán's Oaxaca office (p724).

Eight daily Cuenca buses depart Oaxaca's 1st-class station for Ixtlán (M$40, 1¾ hours). For M$10 less, the companies **Benito Juárez** (☎ 951-516-57-76) and **Flecha del Zempoaltépetl** (☎ 951-516-63-42) run nine daily buses from Oaxaca's 2nd-class bus station.

CAPULÁLPAM
☎ 951 / pop 1300 / elevation 2000m
The pretty, flower-bright village of Capulálpam is located 9km southeast of Ixtlán, with gorgeous views and a large stone church at its center. It's a tranquil mountain retreat with another community ecotourism program, **Ecoturismo Comunitario Capulálpam** (☎ 539-20-40; www.capulalpam.com.mx; Miguel Méndez 1). Also here is a center for traditional indigenous medicine (based on healing properties of plants and the subject's internal energy balance), where practitioners meet to exchange knowledge and carry out cleansings and healings. You can organize a temascal (M$150) or a *limpia* (cleansing; M$30) through Ecoturismo Comunitario, or come for an indigenous medicine program with Tierraventura (p724).

One kilometer from the village on the Ixtlán road is the turning to Capulálpam's ecotouristic installations, the **Centro Recreativo Los Molinos** (cabañas per person M$150; meals M$50-80; ☑ restaurant 10am-6pm). This offers a zip-line, hanging bridge, bikes for rent, guided trail walks, a restaurant in a verdant riverside site about 1km off the road, and mud-brick *cabañas* on a hilltop about 1.5km from the restaurant. In the village itself, **Posada El Mirador** (☎ 539-20-95; Brasil 1; per person M$100) offers plain, clean rooms with shared bath, plus meals and great views.

A few kilometers beyond Capulálpam, at Natividad, the **Museo Comunitario La Mina** (☑ 10am-2pm Tue-Sun) re-creates the village's important old gold and silver mine.

Benito Juárez (☎ 951-516-57-76) runs five daily buses to Capulálpam (M$35, 2½ hours) from Oaxaca's 2nd-class bus station. There is *colectivo* taxi service from Ixtlán.

WESTERN OAXACA

Western Oaxaca is dramatic, mountainous country with a fairly sparse population and some thick forests as well as overfarmed, eroded and deforested areas. The region offers a chance to get well off the beaten track, enjoy hiking, biking or climbing in remote areas and see some outstanding colonial architecture and little-known pre-Hispanic sites. Guided trips are available from Oaxaca with operators such as Tierraventura, Bicicletas Pedro Martínez and Rancho Buenavista (see Activities, p723) and the Museos Comunitarios (boxed text, p742).

Western Oaxaca (along with adjoining bits of Puebla and Guerrero states) is known as the Mixteca, for its Mixtec indigenous inhabitants. It was from here in about the 12th century that Mixtec dominance began to spread to the Valles Centrales. The Mixtecs were famed workers of gold and precious stones, and it's said that Aztec emperor Moctezuma would eat only off fine Mixteca-Puebla ceramics. In pre-Hispanic times the Mixteca was relatively heavily populated, but today it's one of Oaxaca's poorest regions, with very high emigration rates.

You can visit the Mixteca in a long day trip from Oaxaca, but basic hotels or *casas de huéspedes* are available in places such as Nochixtlán, Coixtlahuaca and San Pedro

Teposcolula, while Tlaxiaco and Huajuapan de León have better lodgings. In Huajuapan, a good inexpensive choice is **Hotel Colón** (☎ 953-532-08-17; Colón 10; r M$250; P), a clean, friendly, motel-style place with two floors of small, fan-cooled rooms around a courtyard.

Getting There & Away

Transportadora Excelencia (Map pp720-1; ☎ 951-516-35-78; Díaz Ordaz 304, Oaxaca) runs comfortable large vans to Teposcolula and Tlaxiaco (M$65, three hours) every half-hour from 6am to 9pm. Other daily departures from Oaxaca city:

Destination	Fare	Duration	Frequency (daily)
Coixtlahuaca	M$61	2hr	10 from 2nd-class terminal (Fypsa)
Huajuapan de León	M$51	3½hr	3 from Sur terminal
Nochixtlán	M$72	1½hr	6 from 1st-class terminal
	M$28	2hr	3 from Sur terminal

Santiago Apoala has a bus connection with Nochixtlán on Wednesday, Saturday and Sunday (normally leaving Apoala at 8am and starting back from Nochixtlán at noon or 1pm). You can also reach Apoala by taxi or *camioneta* from Nochixtlán.

Buses run from Mexico City's TAPO to several Mixteca towns. Several buses a day head south from Tlaxiaco to Pinotepa Nacional.

SANTIAGO APOALA
pop 200 / elevation 2000m

This small village lies in a stunning green valley flanked by cliffs, 40km north of Nochixtlán, and is a great base for hiking, biking and climbing. In traditional Mixtec belief, this valley was the birthplace of humanity. A community tourism scheme provides accommodation, meals and guides. It's easiest to come with an agency from Oaxaca, though you can arrange an independent visit by contacting the village's **Comité de Turismo** (Tourism Committee; ☎ 55-51519154).

The journey from Nochixtlán, via unpaved roads, can take up to two hours. The scenery around Apoala is spectacular, with the 60m waterfall Cascada Cola de la Serpiente and the 400m-deep Cañón Morelos among the highlights. Trips with agencies from Oaxaca are typically of two days, with a three-hour

walk through the canyon to the village on the first day, and a walk to the waterfall (where you can usually swim) the next day.

The tourism committee has a comfortable three-room guesthouse, the **Parador Turístico** (campsites per 4 people M$30, s/d/tr/q M$90/180/250/330, 4-person tent rental M$120, sleeping bags M$20). Meals here cost around M$35 each (you should phone ahead to check availability, and take some supplies in any case); mountain-bike rental is M$100 per day and each group of five people has to pay a M$50 access charge. Guides are M$120 per day for groups of up to six.

YANHUITLÁN, COIXTLAHUACA & SAN PEDRO TEPOSCOLULA

The beautiful 16th-century **Dominican monasteries** in the three Mixteca villages of Yanhuitlán, Coixtlahuaca and San Pedro Teposcolula rank among Mexico's finest architectural treasures. The existence of such large establishments testifies to the size of the indigenous population when the Spanish arrived. The monasteries' restrained stonework fuses medieval, plateresque, renaissance and indigenous styles, and all three have ornate interior decoration, including enormous gilded wooden *retablos* (altarpieces).

Coixtlahuaca, currently undergoing restoration, is perhaps the most interesting of the group. The village is 4km east of the Coixtlahuaca tollbooth on 135D, about 30km north of Nochixtlán. The renaissance-style, white-stone main facade of the church is magnificent, and the graceful, ruined *capilla abierta* (open chapel, used in early Mexican monasteries for preaching to crowds of indigenous people) bears Mixtec religious symbols, most notably serpents and eagles. No admission charge is levied while restoration work proceeds. If you find the church open, you will probably be able to climb to the 2nd floor and roof for views of the rocky landscape. As you approach Coixtlahuaca from Hwy 135D, signs point to **San Miguel Tequixtepec**, 13km away, which has a good community museum with local archaeological finds and crafts in a 16th-century house, and a couple of cheap but quite comfy *cabañas* for visitors.

Yanhuitlán monastery (admission M$29; ✆ 8am-4pm Mon-Sat), built atop an important Mixtec religious site, towers beside Hwy 190, 14km northwest of Nochixtlán. The carving on its north and west facades is beautiful, and inside are valuable works of art. A fine Mudejar ceiling is suspended beneath the choir loft, which has an impressive pipe organ.

About 30km southwest of Yanhuitlán, on Hwy 125, is the relaxed, friendly town of San Pedro Teposcolula, where **Teposcolula monastery** (admission M$29; ☾ 8am-4pm Mon-Sat) has a particularly stately *capilla abierta* with several beautifully carved arches; the adjacent monastic buildings contain a sizable collection of early colonial art. Buildings around the town plaza are painted a lively red and white, and you'll find good accommodation in the clean, tiled rooms of **Hotel Juvi** (☎ 953-518-20-64; 20 de Noviembre 1B; s/d/tr M$180/200/225; **P**), opposite the monastery.

SAN MARTÍN HUAMELÚLPAM

☎ 951 / pop 130 / elevation 2235m

The town off for San Martín is 22km south of San Pedro Teposcolula, and the village itself lies 1km off Hwy 125. The friendly, tranquil community and its piney surrounds are home to practitioners of traditional medicine renowned for their powers. The **Museo Comunitario Hitalulu** (☎ 510-49-49; Plaza Cívica; admission M$10; ☾ 9am-6pm) has one wing focusing on the healers and the plants they use. The other wing holds some excellent artifacts from ancient Huamelúlpam, a Mixtec ceremonial center of about AD 400 to 600 that is spread around the hills to the north and east of the central Plaza Cívica. Explanations are all in Spanish.

The main restored section of ancient Huamelúlpam is 200m east of the plaza, behind a small church. It's built on several levels and includes a ball court, two broad plazas, an altar and a temple whose lower chambers are thought to have been a holding for sacrificial victims. As you pass the church, note the carved figures of skulls that were taken from the site and incorporated into the church's arch and side wall.

TLAXIACO & BEYOND

About 18km south of Huamelúlpam on Hwy 125, lively, friendly Tlaxiaco (population 15,000) is the focus of a large rural region, with a huge Saturday **market** around its main plaza. An enormous colonial church with gothic rib vaulting stands beside a second plaza just 100m away. On the main plaza is **Hotel del Portal** (☎ 953-552-01-54; Plaza de la Constitución 2; r M$210-250; **P**), with clean, quiet rooms out the back and a decent, moderately

priced restaurant in an atmospheric old courtyard in the front.

South of Tlaxiaco, Hwy 125 winds through the remote Sierra Madre del Sur to Pinotepa Nacional, on coastal Hwy 200. The route's major town is Putla, 95km from Tlaxiaco.

OAXACA COAST

Oaxaca's spectacular Pacific coast really has everything any traveler needs for a great time by the ocean. With half a dozen relaxed beach destinations each offering their individual take on the coast's manifold attractions, and the near-empty shoreline between them strung with long, long golden beaches and lagoons full of animal life, it's hard to go wrong. Offshore, you can sail in search of dolphins, turtles and whales, or go diving, snorkeling or sportfishing – not forgetting some of the best surfing swells in North America and plenty of gentler beaches where beginners can learn to surf. In the inland mountains, visit an organic coffee farm, raft white-water rivers or ride horses along jungle trails.

In this tropical climate, the pace of life is never too hectic and the people are welcoming. In the center of the coast sits the small fishing port and beach town of Puerto Ángel. Just to its west are strung three beach villages – Zipolite, San Agustinillo and Mazunte – that are perfect havens for just taking it easy, with a laid-back traveler vibe and plenty of good-value accommodations and food. Further west lies Puerto Escondido, a bigger fishing and market town with a succession of great beaches (including Playa Zicatela, home to the pumping surf of the Mexican Pipeline) and a range of appealing sleeping, eating and nightlife options for all budgets. Toward the eastern end of the coast is Bahías de Huatulco, a modern beach resort along a string of idyllic bays that mostly retains a pleasantly low-key atmosphere.

The spectacular coastline is one of the world's most important sea turtle nesting areas, and the many lagoons behind it are full of birdlife that will delight wildlife lovers. The coastal plain is backed everywhere by dramatic, forested mountains – and the trip down to the coast from Oaxaca city is a spectacular experience in itself, whether you go by bus, car or light plane.

Most of the year's rain here falls between June and September, turning everything green. From October the landscape starts to dry out, and by March many of the trees are leafless. May is the hottest month. A great information website for this coast is the **Pacific Coast of Mexico** (www.tomzap.com).

PUERTO ESCONDIDO
☎ 954 / pop 30,000

The 'Hidden Port' has blossomed into one of the most enjoyable spots on the whole of Mexico's Pacific Coast. Still very much a fishing and market town, Puerto Escondido is famed above all for the legendary surf break known as the Mexican Pipeline. Along with its surf scene, Puerto has several calm beaches good for swimming, tanning and snorkeling. Offshore you can go diving, sportfishing or looking for turtles, dolphins and even whales. There's a great café and restaurant scene, a spot of good nightlife and live music, and plenty of attractive and well-priced accommodations. Within easy day-trip reach are the coastal lagoons of Manialtepec and Chacahua, teeming with birdlife. Best of all is that development here has remained low-key and on a human scale. Puerto's new smattering of imported sophistication has not dented the laid-back charm of the Mexican fishing port and beach town that it has always been. Leave it off your itinerary at your peril!

Orientation

The center of town rises above the small Bahía Principal. Hwy 200, here called the Carretera Costera, runs across the hill, dividing the upper town – where buses arrive and depart and most locals live and work – from the lower, touristic part. The heart of the lower town, referred to as El Adoquín, is the pedestrianized (from 5pm) section of Av Pérez Gasga (*adoquín* is Spanish for paving stone). The west end of Av Pérez Gasga winds up the slope to meet Hwy 200 at an intersection known as El Crucero.

Playa Zicatela, hub of the surf scene, stretches 3km southeast from the east end of Bahía Principal. Most of the action at its northern end, where there are loads of places to stay and eat. Other accommodations and eateries cluster further down the beach in Colonia Brisas de Zicatela, especially at Punta Zicatela, at its south end.

About 1km west of El Crucero, the area above Playa Carrizalillo has a few places to stay, restaurants and services. The airport is

3km west of the center on the north side of Hwy 200.

Information

BOOKSTORES
PJ's Book Bodega (☎ 541-00-36-56; Calle del Morro s/n, Zicatela) A large collection of new and used books in English, Spanish and other languages.

INTERNET ACCESS
The standard rate is M$15 per hour.
Copa Cabana Internet (Av Pérez Gasga 705)
Internet Acuario (Calle del Morro s/n, Zicatela) At the front of the Hotel Acuario building; air-conditioned.

LAUNDRY
Lava-Max (☎ 540-16-17; Av Pérez Gasga 405A; ☺ 8am-8pm Mon-Sat, 8am-4pm Sun) Self-serve costs M$13 per washer load (plus M$8 for detergent and M$14 for dryer); complete wash and dry service costs M$10 per kg.

MEDIA
El Sol de la Costa (www.elsoldelacosta.com) Free monthly paper in Spanish and English, full of information about what's on and what to do.

MEDICAL SERVICES
English-speaking GP **Dr Mario de Alba** (☎ 954-5884018) can normally be contacted through **Farmacia San Antonio** (Av Pérez Gasga s/n).

MONEY
Banks and *casas de cambio* will generally exchange US-dollar traveler's checks and cash US dollars and euros.
Banamex (Av Pérez Gasga s/n; ☺ 9am-4pm Mon-Sat) Currency exchange & ATM.
HSBC (Calle 1 Norte btwn Calles 2 & 3 Pte; ☺ 8am-7pm Mon-Sat) One of several banks offering currency exchange in the upper part of town.
HSBC ATMs Adoquín (Av Pérez Gasga s/n); Zicatela (Calle del Morro s/n)
Money Exchange (Av Pérez Gasga 905; ☺ 10am-3pm & 5:30-9pm Mon-Sat, 10am-3pm Sun) You can exchange cash US or Canadian dollars, euros, pounds sterling, Swiss francs or yen here, plus US- or Canadian-dollar travelers checks.
Money Exchange (Calle del Morro s/n, Zicatela; ☺ 8am-8pm Mon, Tue, Thu-Sat, 8am-6pm Wed, 9am-5pm Sun) At the front of Hotel Acuario, this *casa de cambio* changes euros and Canadian and US dollars in cash or traveler's checks.

TELEPHONE & FAX
You'll find Telmex card phones and a couple of telephone *casetas* on the Adoquín, and

more card phones along Calle del Morro on Zicatela. **Cyberplaya** (Calle del Morro s/n, Zicatela) offers cheap long-distance and international phone calls.

TOURIST INFORMATION
Tourist information kiosk (☎ 582-11-86; ginain puerto@yahoo.com; cnr Av Pérez Gasga & Marina Nacional; ☺ 9am-2pm & 4-6pm Mon-Fri, 10am-2pm Sat) Conveniently placed at the west end of El Adoquín. Gina Machorro, the energetic, multilingual information officer usually found here, happily answers your every question.

TRAVEL AGENCIES
Viajes Dimar (www.viajesdimar.com) Adoquín (☎ 582-02-59; Av Pérez Gasga 905B; ☺ 8am-9:30pm); Zicatela (☎ 582-23-05; Calle del Morro s/n; ☺ 8am-2pm & 6-9pm) You can buy air and bus tickets, rent cars and book excursions here.

Dangers & Annoyances
To minimize any risks, avoid isolated or empty places and stick to well-lit areas at night (or use taxis). Some residents say the greatest danger on the beach at night is the local cops: drinking, peeing or even making out beachside can invite a shakedown.

Beaches
PLAYA ZICATELA
Long, straight Zicatela is Puerto's happening beach, with enticing cafés, restaurants and accommodations as well as the waves of the legendary Mexican Pipeline, which test the mettle of experienced surfers from far and wide.

Nonsurfers beware: the Zicatela waters have a lethal undertow and are definitely not safe for the boardless. Lifeguards rescue several careless people most months (their base, the Cuartel Salvavidas, is in front of Restaurante El Jardín).

BAHÍA PRINCIPAL
The central beach is long enough to accommodate restaurants at its west end, a fishing fleet in its center (Playa Principal) and sun worshipers and young body-boarders at its east end (called Playa Marinero). Pelicans wing in inches above the waves, boats bob on the swell, and a few hawkers wander up and down. The smelly water sometimes entering the bay from inaptly named Laguna Agua Dulce will put you off dipping away from Playa Marinero.

BAHÍA PUERTO ANGELITO
The sheltered bay of Puerto Angelito, about 1km west of Bahía Principal (a 20- to 30-minute walk from El Adoquín), has two smallish beaches. The western one, Playa Angelito, has lots of *comedores* and is very busy with Mexican families at weekends and holidays. Playa Manzanillo, the eastern one, is inaccessible to vehicles but can still get crowded at weekends.

PLAYA CARRIZALILLO
Just west of Puerto Angelito, small Carrizalillo beach is in a rockier cove reached by a stairway of about 170 steps. It's OK for swimming, snorkeling, body-boarding and surfing, and has a bar with a few *palapas* (thatched-roof shelters).

Activities
SURFING
Puerto Escondido has surfable waves most days of the year. The Pipeline near the north end of Playa Zicatela is a world-class beach break, normally at its biggest (it can reach 12m or more) between May and July. Even when the Pipeline is flat, the point break down at Punta Zicatela works almost day in, day out. Playa Carrizalillo has good beginners' waves. Several shops and schools offer surfing lessons (held wherever the waves are suitably small) or rent boards. Some teachers make a 'no stand, no pay' promise. Long- or short-board rental is typically M$100/30 per day/hour; body boards with fins are normally M$50/20 per day/hour.

Oasis Surf Academy (☎ 104-23-30; www.oasissurf factory.com; Blvd Juárez 2; ☺ 9am-6pm Mon-Sat), in the Rinconada area above Playa Carrizalillo, offers classes of 1½ to two hours with experienced and qualified local teachers, for M$300. It's associated with Oasis Surf Factory, run by local pro surfer and board maker Roger Ramírez.

Another good rental and tuition place is **Central Surf** (☎ 582-22-85; www.centralsurfshop.com; Calle del Morro s/n, Zicatela; 2-hr class M$600), where classes are given by brothers René and David Salinas, from a well-known local surfing family.

Further classes for around M$300 to M$350 per hour are offered by **Carrisurf** (☎ 954-1005638; Blvd Juárez 14), near Playa Carrizalillo, and **Delapoint Surf Shop** (☎ 582-26-69, 954-5888058) at Punta Zicatela. Delapoint rents boards too, as do **Surface** (☎ 954-1091405; Bajada de las Brisas s/n; ☺ 11am-6pm Tue-Sun), **Silver Surf** (Calle del Morro s/n)

OAXACA STATE

PUERTO ESCONDIDO

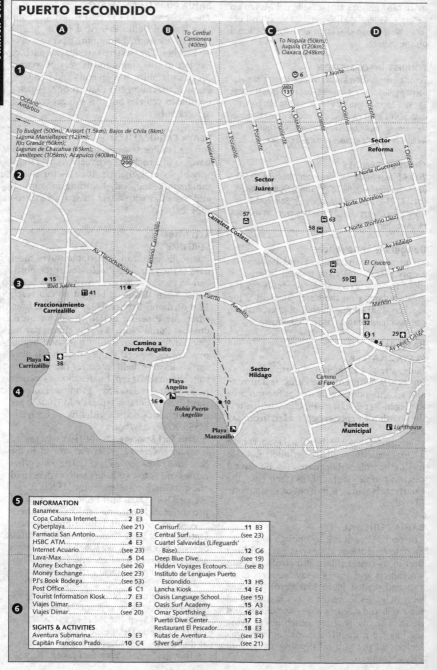

INFORMATION

Banamex	**1** D3
Copa Cabana Internet	**2** E3
Cyberplaya	(see 21)
Farmacia San Antonio	**3** E3
HSBC ATM	**4** E3
Internet Acuario	(see 23)
Lava-Max	**5** D4
Money Exchange	(see 26)
Money Exchange	(see 23)
PJ's Book Bodega	(see 53)
Post Office	**6** C1
Tourist Information Kiosk	**7** E3
Viajes Dimar	**8** E3
Viajes Dimar	(see 20)

SIGHTS & ACTIVITIES

Aventura Submarina	**9** E3
Capitán Francisco Prado	**10** C4

Carrisurf	**11** B3
Central Surf	(see 23)
Cuartel Salvavidas (Lifeguards' Base)	**12** G6
Deep Blue Dive	(see 19)
Hidden Voyages Ecotours	(see 8)
Instituto de Lenguajes Puerto Escondido	**13** H5
Lancha Kiosk	**14** E4
Oasis Language School	(see 15)
Oasis Surf Academy	**15** A3
Omar Sportfishing	**16** B4
Puerto Dive Center	**17** E3
Restaurant El Pescador	**18** E3
Rutas de Aventura	(see 34)
Silver Surf	(see 21)

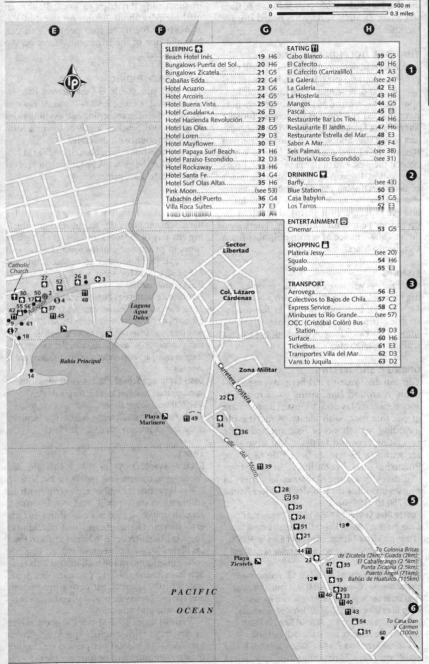

0 _____ 500 m
0 _____ 0.3 miles

SLEEPING

Beach Hotel Inés	19 H6
Bungalows Puerta del Sol	20 H6
Bungalows Zicatela	21 G5
Cabañas Edda	22 G4
Hotel Acuario	23 G6
Hotel Arcoiris	24 G5
Hotel Buena Vista	25 G5
Hotel Casablanca	26 E3
Hotel Hacienda Revolución	27 E3
Hotel Las Olas	28 G5
Hotel Loren	29 D3
Hotel Mayflower	30 E3
Hotel Papaya Surf Beach	31 H6
Hotel Paraíso Escondido	32 D3
Hotel Rockaway	33 H6
Hotel Santa Fe	34 G4
Hotel Surf Olas Altas	35 H6
Pink Moon	(see 53)
Tabachín del Puerto	36 G4
Villa Roca Suites	37 E3
Tito's Cumbine	38 A4

EATING

Cabo Blanco	39 G5
El Cafecito	40 H6
El Cafecito (Carrizalillo)	41 A3
La Galera	(see 24)
La Galería	42 E3
La Hostería	43 H6
Mangos	44 G5
Pascal	45 E3
Restaurante Bar Los Tíos	46 H6
Restaurante El Jardín	47 H6
Restaurante Estrella del Mar	48 E3
Sabor A Mar	49 F4
Seis Palmas	(see 38)
Trattoria Vasco Escondido	(see 31)

DRINKING

Barfly	(see 43)
Blue Station	50 E3
Casa Babylon	51 G5
Los Tarros	52 E3

ENTERTAINMENT

Cinemar	53 G5

SHOPPING

Platería Jessy	(see 20)
Squalo	54 H6
Squalo	55 E3

TRANSPORT

Aerovega	56 E3
Colectivos to Bajos de Chila	57 C2
Express Service	58 C2
Minibuses to Río Grande	(see 57)
OCC (Cristóbal Colón) Bus Station	59 D3
Surface	60 H6
Ticketbus	61 E3
Transportes Villa del Mar	62 D3
Vans to Juquila	63 D2

Catholic Church

Sector Libertad

Col. Lázaro Cárdenas

Laguna Agua Dulce

Bahía Principal

Carretera Costera

Zona Militar

Playa Marinero

Calle del Morro

Playa Zicatela

PACIFIC

OCEAN

To Colonia Brisas de Zicatela (2km); Guada (2km); El Caballerango (2.5km); Punta Zicatela (2.5km); Puerto Ángel (71km); Bahías de Huatulco (115km)

To Casa Dan y Carmen (100m)

and **PJ's Book Bodega** (☎ 541-00-36-56; Calle del Morro s/n), all on Zicatela. Surface has board storage facilities too.

TURTLE- & DOLPHIN-SPOTTING

Lanchas (fast, open, outboard boats) will take groups of four people out for an hour's turtle-spotting (and, in winter, sometimes dolphin-spotting) for around M$300. *Lancha* owners have formed the **Sociedad Cooperativa Turística Nueva Punta Escondido** (☎ 582-16-78; http://tomzap .com/pe-coop.html) and you can contact them at Restaurant El Pescador or the *lancha* kiosk, both at the west end of Bahía Principal. Boats also wait at Playa Angelito. Omar Ramírez of **Omar Sportfishing** (☎ 954-5594406; http://tomzap .com/omar.html; Playa Angelito) specializes in dolphin and even whale-spotting trips, at M$1500 for up to four people for four hours. There's an 80% to 90% chance of seeing dolphins from October to March.

FISHING

Local fishers will take two to four people fishing for marlin and sailfish for three hours for M$900. Contact boat owners as for turtle-spotting trips. The price includes cooking some of the catch for you at one of the town's seafood restaurants.

DIVING & SNORKELING

You can dive year-round here. Average visibility is around 10m, rising to as much as 30m between May and August. The reefs are of volcanic rock, with plenty of marine life including big schools of fish, spotted eagle rays, sting rays and turtles. Most dive sites are within a 15-minute boat ride of town. Puerto has three dive outfits, all offering two-tank dives for around M$650 and a variety of courses including the two-day Discover Scuba (M$750 to M$850):

Puerto Dive Center (☎ 954-1027767; www.puerto divecenter.com; Andador Libertad) American owned, with its shop just off the Adoquín; offers night dives for M$500 and snorkel trips; also conducts a wide range of NAUI and PADI courses.

Aventura Submarina (☎ 582-23-53; asubmarina@ hotmail.com; Av Pérez Gasga 601A) PADI instructor Jorge Pérez Bravo has 30 years' experience in local waters.

Deep Blue Dive (☎ 582-07-92; lorenzo@escondido .com.mx; Calle del Morro s/n, Zicatela) Based in Beach Hotel Inés; the instructor here is also PADI-certified.

Capitán Francisco Prado (☎ 954-5592059) has a booth on Playa Manzanillo and specializes

in snorkeling day trips to Roca Blanca, an offshore islet about 30km northwest of PE, at M$1600 for up to four people. You can lunch at one of the rustic *comedores* on the nearby beach.

HORSEBACK RIDING

The well-run stable **El Caballerango** (☎ 582-34-60; Nayarit 334, Colonia Brisas de Zicatela; 1/2/3hr rides M$200/300/350) offers morning and evening rides to rivers and beaches south of town; a little riding experience is advisable.

For a one-hour sunset beach ride (M$120), just wait for the guys to appear with horses on Playa Zicatela at 5pm.

Courses

Learning Spanish is increasingly popular here. Schools generally accept students starting any day of the week and for any length of time, in private or small-group classes, and offer optional homestay accommodation for M$1250 to M$1500 per week, including at least some meals.

Instituto de Lenguajes Puerto Escondido (☎ 582-20-55; www.puertoschool.com; Carretera Costera, Zicatela; group/private classes per person per hr M$80/120) Offers good language classes taught by native Spanish speakers, with an emphasis on conversation skills, plus a variety of complementary activities, including surfing, cooking and salsa lessons.

Oasis Language School (☎ 104-23-30; www.oasis languageschool.com; Blvd Juárez 2; 2hr private class M$150) Offers a variety of levels, mostly with one-to-one tuition. Playa Carrizalillo is nearby, and Oasis Surf Academy is next door, so you can easily double-task here!

Tours

Rutas de Aventura (☎ 582-01-70, 954-1082074; www .rutasdeaventura.com.mx; Hotel Santa Fe, cnr Blvd Zicatela & Calle del Morro) offers flexible active trips with an emphasis on sustainability and well-informed, English-speaking guides. Possibilities include early morning kayaking and bird-watching at Laguna Manialtepec (p762) and visits to **Finca Las Nieves** (www.fincalasnieves.com.mx), an organic coffee plantation in the lush inland hills near San Juan Lachao, where you can bike, hike, watch birds, learn about coffee production and the local ecosystem, and sleep in comfortable rooms and bungalows.

Viajes Dimar (p753) does a good range of day trips with English-speaking guides for M$300 to M$500 per person (excluding meals; minimum two or four people).

Festivals & Events

Several surf contests are held most years at Playa Zicatela. In recent years the surf event of ESPN's X Games (the 'Olympics' of extreme sports) has happened here in July, and the Association of Professional Towsurfers has staged tow-in events when the Pipeline is at its biggest (12m-plus) between May and July. A longboard contest organized by Puerto's celebrated masked surfer, Ángel Salinas, usually happens in late September or early October – as does a kids' surf festival on Playa Carrizalillo in May or June.

Puerto Blues Some top Canadian and US blues musicians hit Puerto in January and February for this event, usually playing at Club de Playa Belmar on Zicatela with an admission charge of M$60.

Fiestas de Noviembre These last all November with many varied events including concerts by big-name Mexican musical acts, the four-day Festival Costeño de la Danza (a fiesta of Oaxaca coastal dance), an international sailfish contest (www.pescandopuertoescondido.com) and usually the PXM International Surf Tournament, which is Mexico's No 1 regular surf competition. Program information is available at www.elsoldelacosta.com and www .oaxaca.travel.

Sleeping

The two main accommodation zones are the central Av Pérez Gasga area and the surf beach of Playa Zicatela. Zicatela has overall the most appealing surroundings, with great places to eat as well as sleep. The only drawback is that you can't swim there.

Rates given here are those that apply most commonly at each place. Some hotels raise their prices significantly during the Christmas–New Year and Easter holidays (when prices can as much as double) and/or for a few weeks in July and August. Budget places are more likely to stick with the same prices year round.

In the peak seasons the most popular places will often be full, especially on Zicatela. Your best bet, if you haven't reserved ahead, is to ask about 9am or 10am.

BUDGET

Cabañas Edda (☎ 582-23-22; Carretera Costera s/n; camping per person M$30, cabañas s/d M$50/100, with private bathroom M$75/150; P) Though it's not actually a beach place, Edda's extensive grounds and basic lodgings above Zicatela are well kept, and all guests can use the common kitchen and laundry. All rooms have fans and screens or nets. Some units are rather close to the highway.

Hostal Buena Onda (☎ 582-16-63; buenaondazicatela@ hotmail.com; Av Cárdenas 777; camping or hammock per person M$40, dm M$70, r M$130, cabañas M$150) Down in the Punta Zicatela area, the Buena Onda is one of Puerto's most popular hostels. It's set about a palm-shaded central courtyard, with a beachfront *palapa* hangout area. The 10 *cabañas* are equipped with mosquito nets and hammocks, and there are adequate bathrooms and kitchen.

our pick Casa de Dan y Carmen (☎ 582-27-60; www.casadanycarmen.com; Jacaranda 14, Colonia Santa María; r M$200-400; P ⬛ ⬛) This excellent place offers 13 self-contained units of varying size, with fully equipped kitchens, terraces and attractively tiled bathrooms. Everything is set around verdant patios and gardens, and there's a terrific extra-long lap pool as well as a terrace with a perfect view of the Zicatela surf. Dan and Carmen's is up the paved street just south of Hotel Papaya Surf Beach, then right across a small bridge. Weekly and monthly rates are available, and reservations are essential because it's usually full.

our pick Hotel Buena Vista (☎ 582-14-74; www .prodigyweb.net.mx/buenavista101; Calle del Morro s/n; r M$200, with air-con or kitchen M$300, with air-con & kitchen M$350; ⬛) The well-built Buena Vista, set above Playa Zicatela and reached by a steep flight of steps up from Calle del Morro, is an excellent value. Rooms are not fancy but are big and spotlessly clean, all with two beds, mosquito screens or nets, and hot-water bathroom. And many have breezy balconies, some with great views.

Hotel Rockaway (☎ 582-06-68; www.hotelrock away.com; Calle del Morro s/n; s/d cabaña M$120/200, air-con M$300/400; P ⬛ ⬛) A long-time popular surfers' haunt run by the friendly Rock, the Rockaway provides some of Zicatela's most economical lodgings. Its solid wood-and-thatch *cabañas* have fan and bathroom and can hold four people. The air-con rooms, with cable TV, will hold up to six. Everything is set around a spacious courtyard with pool and bar.

Hotel Mayflower (☎ 582-03-67; www.hotel mayflower.net; Andador Libertad s/n; dm/s/d/tr/q M$90/220/300/360/400; ⬛) The popular and friendly Mayflower, beside a flight of steps leading up from El Adoquín, is a sociable hotel-cum-hostel and all kept very clean.

The nine fan-cooled dorms each hold four to seven people (in beds and bunks), and there are 16 attractive private rooms with bathrooms and small balconies. Rates include use of a kitchen with fridge and microwave. There are semi-open sitting areas, a billiard table, lockers and luggage storage facilities. An HI card brings a 10% discount.

Other recommended Zicatela budget places:

Pink Moon (☎ 954-1036341; http://zicatela.org/luna rosa; Calle del Morro s/n; dm M$100, r M$250) Women-only hostel with good terrace areas.

Hotel Papaya Surf Beach (☎ 582-11-68; www.papa yasurf.com; Calle del Morro s/n; s/d with fan M$150/250, air-con M$250/350; 🍴 🖵) Good-value Italian-run spot.

Hotel Las Olas (☎ 582-09-19; www.hotel-lasolas.com; Calle del Morro s/n; d M$250-350; 🍴) Most rooms have balconies overlooking the beach.

MIDRANGE

Hotel Casablanca (☎ 582-01-68; www.ptohcasablanca .com; Av Pérez Gasga 905; s/d/tr/q M$280/400/500/600; 🍴 🖵) The friendly Casablanca is right at the heart of things on the inland side of El Adoquín, and it fills up quickly. It has a small pool and 21 large, clean, tile-floored rooms with fan and cable TV. Some have fridges; the best are streetside with balconies.

Hotel Loren (☎ 582-00-57; fax 582-05-91; Av Pérez Gasga 507; d/tr/q with fan M$400/500/600, with air-con M$500/600/700; P 🍴 🖵) A minute uphill from El Adoquín, this hotel is painted lobster and sky-blue outside, and violet and pink inside (maybe that's what lobsters' insides are like). It's a friendly place with bare, spacious rooms, all equipped with two or three (somewhat springy) double beds, cable TV and balconies; some catch a sea view. There's a nice pool, and it's a fair value.

Hotel Hacienda Revolución (☎ /fax 582-18-18; www.haciendarevolucion.com; Andador Revolución 21; r/casita M$400/500) On a flight of steps leading up from El Adoquín, this Revolution-themed spot has some 15 colorful accommodations facing a garden–courtyard with a central fountain. Most have a patio and hammock.

Bungalows Puerta del Sol (☎ 582-29-22; bunga lowspuertadelsol@hotmail.com; Calle del Morro s/n; d M$300-650; P 🖵) This friendly, very clean Zicatela place has a small pool and a communal kitchen either side of a nice green courtyard; and 16 spacious, solid rooms with balcony, hammock and cheerful art. Weekly and monthly rates available.

OUR PICK Beach Hotel Inés (☎ /fax 582-07-92; www.hotelines.com; Calle del Morro s/n; r M$250-1200; P 🍴 🖵 🖵) German-run Inés has a wide range of bright, cheerful *cabañas*, rooms, apartments and suites. All have safes, good mosquito screens and fans, most have wi-fi, and some come with kitchens or air-con. Lovely art and *artesanías* abound, and other pluses include a sauna, sundeck, spa and a relaxed, shaded pool area with a café serving good food. You can arrange horseback riding and scuba here as well.

Bungalows Zicatela (☎ 582-07-98; www.bungalows zicatela.com.mx; Calle del Morro s/n; s/d M$300/400, r with air-con M$600; 🍴 🖵) Straightforward Zicatela has a good and sociable pool area, and all of its 40-odd accommodations are a good size, solidly built and with good beds and bathrooms and mosquito-netted windows. Most have cable TV.

Hotel Acuario (☎ /fax 582-10-27; www.hotelbungalows acuariozicatela.com.mx; Calle del Morro s/n; s M$300-750, d M$350-800; P 🍴 🖵) The 30 or so accommodations here range from drab rooms to wooden *cabañas* and spacious upstairs suites with terrace and Zicatela beach view. Some have air-con, some have kitchenettes and all share a pleasant central swimming pool. Decor is tired, but it's clean and well located.

Villa Roca Suites (☎ 582-35-25; www.villaroca .mx.vg; Av Pérez Gasga 602; d/tr/q M$600/800/900; 🍴) A pleasing mix of Mexican artifacts and tasteful color-schemes mark out this small hotel with the best rooms on El Adoquín. There are just six rooms, all with air-con, TV and balcony – the two top-floor rooms enjoy good sea views.

Hotel Paraíso Escondido (☎ 582-04-44; www.hotelpe .com; Unión 10; r M$650, ste M$750; 🍴 🖵) Rambling, neocolonial Paraíso is one of Puerto's most original lodgings, decorated with stained glass, pretty *artesanías* and curious stone sculptures. There's an attractive bar–pool area plus 20 rooms with good bathrooms and small terraces – plus five new top-floor suites that enjoy kitchen use and the best bay views.

OUR PICK Tabachín del Puerto (☎ 582-11-79; www.tabachin.com.mx; behind Hotel Santa Fe, Zicatela; d incl breakfast US$65-85, per additional person M$15; P 🍴 🖵) Tabachín's gracious and erudite owner offers six studio-rooms in varying sizes (including enormous) and interesting, tasteful styles (folksy to regency), all of them recently renovated. All have kitchen, TV, air-conditioning, phone, safe, balcony access and views of varying expansiveness. The excellent breakfasts, served from 8am to 11am, include good vegetarian choices and organically grown coffee and fruits from the owner's farm in Nopala. They're open to nonguests as well (dishes M$45 to M$80) and are always lively occasions.

Hotel Arcoiris (☎ /fax 582-04-32; www.oaxaca-mio .com/arcoiris.htm; Calle del Morro s/n; r M$700-900, tr M$750-950, q M$800-1000; P ⬜ ⬚) Attractive, neocolonial Arcoiris is a perennial favorite. Most of its 35 big, clean rooms have balconies or terraces looking straight out to the surf, and there's a large pool plus a good, breezy, upstairs restaurant–bar. Most rooms have two double beds and terraces or balconies, and some have a kitchen.

TOP END
Hotel Santa Fe (☎ /fax 582-01-70, 800-7127057, in the US 888-649-6407; www.hotelsantafe.com.mx; cnr Blvd Zicatela & Calle del Morro; s/d US$110/126, junior ste US$162; P ⬚ ⬜ ⬚) Neocolonial Santa Fe has more than 60 well-designed rooms set around two good pools in palm-shaded garden courtyards. Rooms vary in size and view, but all have air-con, attractive colonial-ranch–style furnishings and safes. It's a well-run hotel with a good, mainly vegetarian restaurant.

Hotel Surf Olas Altas (☎ 582-23-15; ☎ /fax 582-00-94; www.surfolasaltas.com.mx; Calle del Morro 310; r M$1200-1450; P ⬚ ⬚ ⬜ ⬚) This modern, three-storey, 61-room Zicatela hotel has less character than some smaller places, but the rooms are spotless and ample, and set well back from the street. Most have two double beds, coffee-maker, cable TV – and a book of the Buddha's teachings for you to ponder.

Villas Carrizalillo (☎ 582-17-35; www.villascarriza lillo.com; Av Carrizalillo 125, Carrizalillo; apt US$147-230; P ⬚ ⬜ ⬚) Sublimely perched on the cliffs above the Playa Carrizalillo, Villas Carrizalillo has lovely air-conditioned apartments for two to six people, nearly all with fully equipped kitchens and private terraces. A path goes directly down to Playa Carrizalillo, and the hotel has boards, bikes and snorkel gear for rent. Discounts are available if you pay cash. The excellent Seis Palmas restaurant is here too.

Eating
Puerto Escondido has a great selection of eateries, from solidly satisfying Mexican/international places to a handful of enticing new fusion eateries. You'll eat some of the freshest

fish and seafood you've ever had, and most places are at least partly open-air. There is also some good vegetarian fare.

PLAYAS ZICATELA & MARINERO
Hostal A La Casa (☎ 954-5443372; Av Cárdenas; dishes M$30-60) The best meals at Punta Zicatela are found at this hostel right next door to Hostal Buena Onda. The fare is a well-priced Italian-Mexican mix.

our pick El Cafecito (☎ 582-05-16; Calle del Morro s/n; breakfast M$28-40, lunch & dinner dishes M$30-80, cakes & pastries M$12-20; ⏰ 6am-10pm) It sometimes seems as if the whole town is here for breakfast, and with good reason as the combinations (Mexican and international) are tasty and filling, the Zicatela view great and the coffee cups bottomless. The Cafecito also serves up great cinnamon rolls, carrot cake and juices, and tasty lunch and dinner dishes from vegetarian lasagne to Mexican *antojitos*.

Restaurante Bar Los Tíos (☎ 582-28-79; Calle del Morro s/n; dishes M$30-90; ⏰ 9am-10pm Wed-Mon) Right on Zicatela beach, 'the Uncles' serve great *licuados* and fresh juices to go with their tasty egg dishes, *antojitos* and seafood. It's very relaxed and popular with locals.

Restaurante El Jardín (☎ 582-23-15; Calle del Morro s/n; dishes M$45-95; ⏰ 8am-10:30pm; Ⓥ) This *palapa* restaurant serves very good vegetarian dishes, from *gado-gado* (vegetables in peanut sauce) and many salad varieties to tempeh and tofu offerings. The menu also includes plenty of seafood, pizzas and pasta, and a good, long juice list.

Mangos (Calle del Morro s/n; dishes M$45-100; ⏰ 7am-midnight; Ⓥ) Palm-roofed Mangos is good for anything from breakfast combinations (M$25 to M$45) to smoothies to meat or fish meals. Dishes are well prepared and the service friendly.

Trattoria Vasco Escondido (Calle del Morro s/n; mains M$50-120; ⏰ 9am-11pm) Enjoy a friendly welcome and terrific Italian and Mexican fare prepared by your Italian host Vasco at this little spot in front of Hotel Papaya Surf Beach.

La Hostería (☎ 582-00-05; Calle del Morro s/n; mains M$50-150; ⏰ 8am-12:30am; Ⓥ) The Hostería is an Italian labor of love, from its gleaming kitchen (with computerized wood-fired pizza oven) to the Talavera-tiled bathrooms. A broad selection of delicious Italian, Mexican and international dishes – including many veggie selections – is paired with a great wine list, and the espresso is one of the best in town.

La Galera (☎ 582-04-32; Hotel Arcoiris, Calle del Morro s/n; mains M$70-110, menú del día M$60) The breezy upstairs restaurant at Hotel Arcoiris is always a good place to eat, with tasty mixed Mexican and international fare. Main dishes focus on fish and meat, but the three-course *menú del día* has vegetarian options.

Cabo Blanco (☎ 582-03-37; Calle del Morro s/n; mains M$60-170) A great Zicatela spot for prawns, fish steak or *arrachera*, cooked in the open, streetside kitchen – or burgers or *tlayudas* for tighter budgets. It has light and dark beers on tap, too.

our pick Guadua (☎ 954-1079524; www.guadua.com .mx; Tamaulipas s/n, Colonia Brisas de Zicatela; mains M$75-150; ◷ 1-11pm Tue-Sun; **V**) There's nothing quite like Guadua on the Oaxaca coast. A solid wooden deck sits about halfway along Zicatela beach, its thick *palapa* roof supported by bamboo poles. The delicious and attractively presented food is a Pacific–Mediterranean–Asian–Middle Eastern fusion with dishes like shrimp coconut curry, cashew couscous and seared tuna with teriyaki sauce. Guadua is also a hip beach lounge, with a good bar, music from bossa nova to dub to electronica (live Wednesday to Saturday evenings), and quirkily constructed loungers out on the sands in front. And it recycles waste water and trash.

Sabor a Mar (Playa Marinero; mains M$80-130; ◷ 8am-11pm) Tucked under the rocks at the southeast end of Playa Marinero, this little al fresco spot serves probably the best seafood in town.

The airy restaurant at Hotel Santa Fe (p759) looks down on the west end of the Pipeline. Sink into a comfy leather chair and choose from the list of inspired vegetarian and vegan (M$55 to M$95) or seafood (M$100 to M$185) meals. Service is excellent.

AV PÉREZ GASGA

Restaurante Estrella del Mar (mains M$50-110; ◷ 8am-11pm) The pick of the smattering of Mexican restaurants on El Adoquín itself, with good seafood cocktails and *antojitos* as well as seafood main dishes.

La Galería (☎ 582-20-39; mains M$60-120) At the west end of El Adoquín, La Galería is one of Puerto's best Italian spots, with art on the walls and tasty fare on the tables. The pizza and home-made pasta dishes are original and flavorsome, and the jumbo mixed green salad (M$49) is a treat.

our pick Pascal (☎ 954-1030668; Playa Principal; mains M$60-150; ◷ 6pm-midnight) Right under the palms on the Playa Principal sands, Pascal from France prepares original and delicious seafood, meat and home-made pasta dishes with rare flair. You might go for the ravioli with ham, peanuts and ricotta, or the shrimp with orange and tequila. There's a choice of tasty sauces for all pasta dishes, and the seafood is fresh as can be. Your visit might coincide with the occasional live music or trapeze entertainment.

CARRIZALILLO

El Cafecito (☎ 582-34-65; Local 10-11, Blvd Juárez; ◷ 6am-9pm Mon-Sat, 6am-6pm Sun) The Cafecito's Carrizalillo branch has the same great menu as the Zicatela one (p759) even if it can't match the ambience.

Seis Palmas (☎ 582-09-95; Villas Carrizalillo, Av Carrizalillo 125; mains M$70-140; ◷ 8am-11pm Fri-Wed) The fantastic ocean sunsets from this Carrizalillo clifftop perch are the perfect backdrop for the inventive and delicious Californian-Oaxacan dishes arriving at your table. You might start with green-bean tempura with mustard, and follow it with a grilled whole snapper with grilled veggies and caramelized onions.

Drinking

Casa Babylon (Calle del Morro s/n; ◷ 10:30am-2pm & 8pm-late) This cool little Zicatela travelers' bar has a great Mexican mask collection and a big selection of books to exchange. There's live music or a DJ several nights a week. The owner prides herself on her *mojitos* and *caipirinhas*.

Barfly (Calle del Morro s/n; ◷ from 10pm) The rooftop bar above La Hostería restaurant, with video screens, plenty of drink mixes and good music under the stars, draws a lively crowd every night.

Rival drinking dens with loud music on El Adoquín are **Blue Station**, with its upstairs balcony, and **Los Tarros**. They may hold happy hours from 9pm to 10pm, but don't expect much action before 11pm.

Entertainment
LIVE MUSIC

Puerto has a good live music scene combining the talents of locals and expats with sounds ranging from salsa and Mexican folk to jazz, rock and blues. There's usually a band on somewhere several nights a week at bars and restaurants such as Casa Babylon, Pascal, La Galera, Seis Palmas, Guadua and Kahlo at

Punta Zicatela. The scene tends to be busiest from around Christmas to March when visiting musicians from the US, Canada and Europe add their input. Look out especially for gigs by local Latin singer Mayca, who did much of the music in the film *Puerto Escondido*, and the Latin-rock–blues band La Viuda de Romero.

CINEMA

Cinemar (Calle del Morro s/n; admission with popcorn & drink M$50; ⏲ films 7 & 9pm) This air-conditioned minicinema, in the PJ's Book Bodega building, shows films ranging from the best Mexican movies to latest general releases in Spanish and English.

La Hostería (Calle del Morro s/n; admission free; ⏲ 6pm) The Hostería restaurant shows the 1993 Italian travel-and-crime movie *Puerto Escondido* nightly. This film (directed by Gabriele Salvatores) has attracted thousands of Italians and others to Puerto and is worth seeing, even if it makes the town seem more remote than it really is.

Shopping

The Adoquín has a couple of interesting surfwear, jewelry and craft shops among its tacky souvenir stores. On Zicatela, several surf shops sell Brazilian and Mexican surf fashions and a few boards. Mexican company **Squalo** (www.squalo.com) has shops on El Adoquín and Calle del Morro with some funky homegrown Mexican surf designs. **Platería Jessy** (☎ 954-1004606; Calle del Morro s/n) has the best designs in silver.

Getting There & Away

AIR

Aerotucán (☎ 582-34-61; airport) and **Aerovega** (☎ 582-01-51; Av Pérez Gasga 113; ⏲ 9:30am-2pm & 5:30-8pm Mon-Sat) fly to/from Oaxaca – see p734 for details. **Click Mexicana** (☎ 800-112-54-25; www .click.com.mx) flies nonstop to and from Mexico City daily. **Magnicharters** (☎ 800-201-14-04; www .magnicharters.com.mx) flies to/from Mexico City at least twice a week, sometimes via Huatulco.

BUS & VAN

The **OCC bus terminal** (☎ 582-10-73; Carretera Costera btwn Av Oaxaca & 1 Poniente), just west of El Crucero, is used by OCC 1st-class and Sur 2nd-class services. Other long-distance bus lines, including Estrella Blanca (EB) and Turistar, with deluxe and 1st-class services, use the **Central Camionera** (☎ 582-00-86), in the upper part of town between 3 and 4 Poniente, north of 10 Norte. You can buy OCC, Sur, Estrella Blanca and Turistar tickets at **Ticketbus** (☎ 800-702-80-00; www.ticketbus.com.mx; Av Pérez Gasga; ⏲ 10am-2pm & 5-9pm Mon-Fri). Viajes Dimar (p753) sells tickets to Oaxaca and Mexico City.

Keep an eye on your belongings going to or from Acapulco or Oaxaca, and get a ticket for any bags placed in the baggage hold.

Oaxaca

The most convenient way of traveling to Oaxaca is in the comfortable van service via Hwy 131 (M$130, six hours), offered by at least two companies. **Express Service** (☎ 582-08-68; Hotel Luz del Ángel, cnr 1 norte & Av Oaxaca) departs nine times daily, 6am to 10pm; and **Transportes Villa del Mar** (☎ 954-1033134; Av Hidalgo btwn Av Oaxaca & 1 Poniente) goes eight times between 5am and 6:30pm. Second-class La Solteca and Estrella Roja buses (M$110, seven hours) from the Central Camionera take the same route, departing four times between 7 and 10:45am and eight times between 9:30 and 11pm. OCC's 1st-class buses (M$242, 10 hours, three daily) take a long route via Salina Cruz and Hwy 190.

Other Destinations

For Mexico City, the Estrella Blanca and Turistar services via the outskirts of Acapulco are much quicker than OCC, which goes via Salina Cruz. Daily bus departures include the following:

Destination	Fare	Duration	Frequency (daily)
Acapulco	M$238-249	8hr	10 (EB & Turistar)
Bahías de Huatulco	M$82	2½hr	9 (EB & Turistar)
	M$35-76	2½-3hr	34 from OCC terminal
Mexico City (Terminal Sur or Norte)	M$493-667	12hr	5 6:30-8:30pm (EB & Turistar)
	M$604	18hr	2 (OCC)
Pochutla	M$53	1½hr	9 (EB & Turistar)
	M$25-46	1½hr	34 from OCC terminal
San Cristóbal de las Casas	M$396	11½-13hr	at 6:30 & 9:30pm (OCC)
Tehuantepec	M$170	5½hr	4 (OCC)
Tuxtla Gutiérrez	M$344	12hr	at 6:30 & 9:30pm (OCC)

THE OAXACA WETLANDS NETWORK

The **Red de los Humedales de la Costa de Oaxaca** (Oaxaca Coast Wetlands Network; www .humedalesoaxaca.org.mx) is a young grouping of 20 community organizations spread right along the lagoon- and estuary-studded Oaxaca coast that are working to conserve the coastal wetlands and promote sustainable development. The coast has scores of turtle-nesting beaches, is a key bird habitat and is also home to diverse other wildlife including river crocodiles and white-tailed deer. The network's objectives include reforestation, development of crafts and ecological products, protection of turtles and other wildlife, and community tourism. There are opportunities for volunteer work at some of the communities.

The network's membership includes groups in places already frequented by tourists, such as Bahía San Agustín (p778), La Ventanilla (p774), Zapotalito (opposite) and Chacahua (p764), but also organizations that can offer new experiences. **Escobilla** village, between Puerto Escondido and Mazunte, has built comfortable new *cabañas* and is launching a scheme to guide visitors to nearby Playa Escobilla for the mass arrivals of olive ridley turtles there. Around 700,000 olive ridleys come ashore on Playa Escobilla in several massive waves between May and January each year.

For further information ask at the Puerto Escondido tourist information kiosk (p753), or try the Wetlands Network's **office** (☎ /fax 954-582-35-40; 5 Norte 207) in Puerto Escondido.

CAR & MOTORCYCLE

Budget (☎ 582-03-12; Blvd Juárez), opposite the tourist office, charges walk-ins almost M$1000 a day for its cheapest cars, with unlimited kilometers and insurance. You may get better rates reserving by internet. Viajes Dimar (p753) and Hotel Santa Fe (p759) have cars from around M$700 for a day.

Getting Around

Ticket taxis from the airport (M$35 per person) will drop you anywhere in town. You might find a whole cab for a similar price on the main road outside the airport. Taxis from the Central Camionera cost M$20 to El Adoquín or M$22 to Zicatela.

If you don't want to walk between the central Av Pérez Gasga–Bahía Principal area and the outlying beaches, taxis are the only available transportation – they wait at each end of El Adoquín. The standard fare to or from Playa Zicatela is M$25.

There are *colectivo* taxis (M$4) and microbuses (M$3) to Brisas de Zicatela and Punta Zicatela. They are marked 'Zicatela' and run frequently from the Mercado Benito Juárez, down 3 Poniente then east along the Carretera Costera.

Surface (☎ 954-1091405; Bajada de las Brisas s/n; ✆ 11am-6pm Tue-Sun), just off Calle del Morro on Zicatela, rents mountain bikes for M$100 per day and gearless beach cruiser bikes for M$60 per day. It's also an open-air café–lounge with free wi-fi.

WEST OF PUERTO ESCONDIDO

Bajos de Chila

The Mixtec ball game of *pelota mixteca* – a five-a-side team sport descended from the pre-Hispanic ritual ball game – is played every weekend in the village of Bajos de Chila, 10km west of Puerto Escondido along Hwy 200. Games usually begin at 5pm on Saturday or Sunday – check with the tourist information kiosk in Puerto Escondido – and the playing field, called the *patio* or *pasador*, is easy to find in the village (though you'll probably notice a lot more soccer being played than *pelota*). *Colectivos* to Bajos de Chila (M$5, 15 minutes) leave from the corner of Calles 2 Nte and 3 Pte in Puerto Escondido every 30 minutes. For more on the ball game, see the boxed text on p73.

Laguna Manialtepec

This 6km-long lagoon, beginning 14km west of Puerto Escondido along Hwy 200, is a paradise for bird enthusiasts and a fascinating place for anyone interested in nature. Among others, ibises, roseate spoonbills, parrots, pelicans, falcons, ospreys, egrets, herons, kingfishers and several types of hawk and iguana call Manialtepec home for at least part of the year. The best months for observing birds are December to March, and they're best seen in the early morning. The lagoon is mainly surrounded by mangroves, but tropical flowers and palms accent the ocean side, and the channel at the west end winds through mangroves to a pristine sandbar beach.

Several restaurants along the lagoon's north shore (just off Hwy 200) run two-hour trips in shaded boats, costing M$700 for up to seven people. They also offer *colectivo* services (M$80 per person) from about 8am to 5pm during tourism high seasons: these are geared more toward locals who just want to get to the other end of the lagoon than to serious nature observers. Some of the restaurants also rent kayaks and canoes, which are ideal for those with sufficient energy who want to get right in among the lakeside vegetation and side-channels. A rare and magical Manialtepec phenomenon is the appearance of phosphorescent plankton for several days three or four times a year. At these times sunset boat tours are offered, and on the return trip after dark you can swim or trail your hand in the water to activate the strange phosphorescent glow.

To reach the lagoon from Puerto Escondido, take a Río Grande–bound minibus from the corner of 2 Norte and 3 Poniente in the upper part of town, leaving every half-hour from 6am to 7pm (M$9).

Restaurant Isla del Gallo (☎ 954-1009258; www.laisladelgallo.com.mx; seafood M$70-120; 🕑 8am-6pm), about halfway along the lake, offers boat trips that go right through the mangrove channel to the beach, and the boatmen, some of whom speak English, know their birds. One-person kayaks and three-person canoes are for rent at M$50 and M$100 per hour respectively. Good grilled fish and seafood are served at the restaurant.

Restaurante La Puesta del Sol (☎ 954-5883867), toward the west end of the lake, is another recommended embarkation point. It has a bird field guide, and guide Modesto knows the birds' English names. They have two-person kayaks (M$100 per hour) and four-person canoes (M$50) for rent as well. Most dishes in the restaurant here cost M$60 to M$80.

Several early-morning or sunset tours (four to five hours including road time) can be booked from Puerto Escondido. Not all of them include English-speaking guides.

Hidden Voyages Ecotours (www.peleewings.ca; tours for 4-10 people per person M$400-450) offers highly recommended three- to 3½-hour boat trips from about mid-December to mid-March, with binoculars and bird checklists provided. Morning tours (departing Puerto Escondido at 7am Monday, Tuesday, Wednesday, Friday and Saturday) are led by knowledgeable Canadian ornithologist Michael Malone. Book at Viajes Dimar in Puerto Escondido (p753), which also offers year-round trips (per person M$350) with local bird guides who have worked with Hidden Voyages.

Lalo's Ecotours (☎ 954-588-91-64; www.lalo-ecotours.com; Las Negras Manialtepec; tours per person US$35) is run by a lagoon local who has worked for Hidden Voyages and knows his birds. Tours are year-round, with binoculars included. Lalo speaks some English and also leads morning nature hikes, guided kayak and canoe trips, and nighttime boat trips during the periods of phosphorescence. He will arrange transportation from Puerto Escondido, or you can seek him out in the small village of Las Negras, toward the lagoon's western end.

Parque Nacional Lagunas de Chacahua

Heading west from Puerto Escondido toward Acapulco, Hwy 200 wends near a coast studded with lagoons, pristine beaches and prolific bird and plant life. Settlements in this region contain many descendants of African slaves who escaped from the Spanish.

The area around the coastal lagoons of Chacahua and La Pastoría forms the beautiful Parque Nacional Lagunas de Chacahua, which attracts migratory birds from Alaska and Canada in winter. Mangrove-fringed islands harbor roseate spoonbills, ibises, cormorants, wood storks, herons and egrets, as well as mahogany trees, crocodiles and turtles. El Corral, a mangrove-lined waterway filled with countless birds in winter, connects the two lagoons. The boat trip along the lagoons is fabulous, and at its end Chacahua village sits upon a gorgeous beach curving at least 20km eastward, inviting you stop for a meal or a night in rustic *cabañas*.

The starting point for boat trips is the small fishing village of Zapotalito, at the eastern end of Laguna La Pastoría. Two or three boat cooperatives here offer *lancha* service to Chacahua village. There are two basic options, '*terrestre*' and '*por agua*'. *Terrestre* means you go by boat across the lagoon from Zapotalito to meet a *camioneta* that then makes a half-hour trip to Chacahua along the spit of land between lagoons and ocean. *Por agua* means you go all the way to Chacahua by boat, usually with halts at various islands and channels where a Spanish-speaking guide will point out the birds. A four-hour return *por agua* return trip, including two hours at Chacahua village, generally runs around M$800 for up to 10 people. The *terrestre* variation is about M$500. For a one-way trip to Chacahua, expect to pay about M$400 for a boat all the way. When there is sufficient traffic, *colectivo* services are operated for M$50 per person each way *por agua*, or M$30 *terrestre*. Check return times before you settle in at Chacahua for the day!

CHACAHUA

Chacahua village straddles the channel that connects the west end of Chacahua lagoon to the ocean. The ocean side of the village, fronting a wonderful beach, is a perfect place to bliss out. The waves here (a right-hand point break) can be good for surfers, including beginners, but there are some strong currents; check where it's safe to swim. The inland half of the village contains a **crocodile-breeding center** (admission free; ☽ erratic) with a rather sorry collection of creatures kept for protection and reproduction: Chacahua's wild croc population (not humaneating) has been decimated by hunting.

TOURS

Good day trips from Puerto Escondido are offered by **Hidden Voyages Ecotours** (www.peleewings.ca; tours Thu only, approx mid-Dec to mid-Mar, minimum 6 people, per person M$575), which operates with an English-speaking naturalist guide. Book at Viajes Dimar in Puerto Escondido (p753), which also offers its own trips year-round (per person M$450; minimum 4 people) with local guides.

SLEEPING & EATING

Restaurante Siete Mares (☎ 954-540-69-03; cabañas s or d M$100-250, tr or q M$200-250; dishes M$30-90) At the west end of Chacahua beach, Siete Mares prepares excellent fish and seafood meals. It also has some of Chacahua's better *cabañas*, some by the restaurant, some further along the beach and some by the lagoon. The best have two double beds, fans, nets, electric light and clean bathrooms. The señora here will lock up your valuables.

More basic *cabañas* along the beach generally cost M$80 to M$100 for two people. They normally share bathrooms and showers and may have sand floors. Most of these places are attached to *comedores* offering egg, pasta and seafood dishes for around M$25 to M$70. You can usually sleep in a hammock or camp for free if you eat at a particular establishment. Theft is a risk, though.

GETTING THERE & AWAY

To reach Zapotalito from Puerto Escondido you first have to get to the town of Río Grande, 50km west of Puerto on Hwy 200. Río Grande–bound minibuses (M$15, one hour) leave from the corner of 2 Norte and 3 Poniente in Puerto, about every half-hour from 6am to 7pm. Most Acapulco-bound Estrella Blanca buses stop at Río Grande, too. From the minibus stop in Río Grande, cross the dirt road and get a *colectivo* taxi (M$10) to Zapotalito, 13km southwest.

If you're driving, the turning to Zapotalito is marked by a military checkpoint on Hwy 200, 8km west of Río Grande. The 5km approach to Zapoltalito is poorly paved.

Ocho Venado

This **community tourism scheme** (☎ 954-541-02-05; http://ochovenado.wikispaces.com) offers the chance to experience village life in the forested hills behind the Lagunas de Chacahua. This is an opportunity to see a little-visited part of the coastal region, take guided walks, eat home-cooked local food and join in whatever the villagers are doing when you visit. The two main bases, both with comfortable, well-built *cabañas* (per person M$150), are Jocotepec and Tututepec. Jocotepec has deer and wild-boar farms and a hilltop sacred site where locals still go for rain and harvest ceremonies. Tututepec was capital of a coastal Mixtec kingdom that fought off the Aztecs in the 15th century. There are pre-Hispanic carvings in the yard of Tututepec's 17th-century church and a community **archaeological museum** (☎ 954-541-03-10; ☽ 10am-5pm). It's a good bird-watching area, too.

The tourist information kiosk in Puerto Escondido can help you make contact and tell you about transportation.

Pinotepa Nacional

☎ 954 / pop 26,000

This is the biggest town between Puerto Escondido (140km east) and Acapulco (260km west). Pino's shops, commerce and big market (by the main road about 1.5km west of the central plaza) make it the focus for a large area with many indigenous villages, which are famous for crafts such as wooden masks and colorfully embroidered traditional garments.

Hotel Carmona (☎ 543-22-22; Porfirio Díaz 127; s/d M$225/320, with air-con M$330/450; P ✗ ☒), on the main road 500m west of the main plaza, is clean, well run and fairly quiet. Rooms have hot-water bathroom and TV.

The **bus terminal** (☎ 543-31-94) is 1km west of the central plaza. Estrella Blanca and Turistar provide daily buses to Puerto Escondido (M$70 to M$81, three hours) and Acapulco (M$123 to M$140, six hours). First-class OCC buses and 2nd-class Fypsa buses travel north on Hwy 125 through the Mixteca, some reaching Oaxaca (1st-class M$228, 10 hours).

POCHUTLA
☎ 958 / pop 13,000

Bustling, sweaty Pochutla is the market town, banking center and transportation hub for the central part of the Oaxaca coast, which includes the nearby beach spots of Puerto Ángel, Zipolite, San Agustinillo and Mazunte. If you are coming from one of those blissed-out places, welcome back to the real world.

Orientation & Information

Hwy 175 from Oaxaca runs through Pochutla as Av Lázaro Cárdenas, the narrow, traffic-clogged, north–south main street, and meets the coastal Hwy 200 about 1.5km south of town. The bus and van terminals cluster toward the southern, downhill end of Cárdenas. Banks and the better hotels are 300m to 400m north. Street numbers increase as you go downhill.

HSBC (Cárdenas 48; ⏱ 8am-7pm Mon-Fri, 8am-3pm Sat) Changes US-dollar cash and traveler's checks; also has an ATM.

Telnet (Cárdenas 94; internet per hr M$10; ⏱ 8am-10pm Mon-Sat) Opposite the Estrella del Valle/Oaxaca Pacífico bus terminal; has long-distance telephone service too.

Sleeping

Hotel Santa Cruz (☎ 584-01-16; Cárdenas 88; s/d with shared bathroom M$100/120, private bathroom M$120/150, private bathroom & air-con M$250/300; 🞩) The Santa Cruz, about 150m north of the main cluster of bus stations, has simple, adequate, assiduously disinfected rooms. Some private bathrooms are dilapidated, but the air-con is good in those rooms that have it.

Hotel Costa del Sol (☎ /fax 584-03-18; Cárdenas 47; s/d with fan M$200/225, with air-con M$300/350; P 🞩) The best-value central hotel, with a few artistic touches and some greenery. Rooms have good bathrooms, erratic hot water and cable TV.

Getting There & Away

The **OCC bus station** (☎ 584-02-74; Cárdenas 84) is used by OCC (1st-class) and Sur (2nd-class) services. The other main bus terminals are

2nd-class **Estrella del Valle/Oaxaca Pacífico** (☎ 584-03-49), 50m north of OCC on the opposite (east) side of the street, and **Estrella Blanca** (EB; ☎ 584-03-80), 200m south of OCC. Transportes Rápidos de Pochutla runs small buses to Bahías de Huatulco from a terminal 100m north of Estrella del Valle/Oaxaca Pacífico.

OAXACA

Oaxaca is 245km away by the curvy Hwy 175 – 5½ to six hours in the convenient and fairly comfortable air-conditioned van services (M$120) offered by several companies including **Autotransportes Atlántida** (☎ 584-01-16; Hotel Santa Cruz, Cárdenas 88) and **Autotransportes Miahuatecos** (☎ 958-1062103; Cárdenas 94). Both these run about every 1½ to two hours from about 4am to 11pm. With Atlántida you can reserve by phone and pay half an hour before departure. Helpfully, drivers will usually agree to stop when you need a bathroom break, or want to take photos (or vomit, as some people tend to do on this route).

Alternative routes to Oaxaca are the 2nd-class buses of Estrella del Valle/Oaxaca Pacífico (M$75 to M$90, 16 daily, 6½ to seven hours) and OCC's three daily 1st-class buses (M$222, 8½ hours). The OCC buses take a much longer, but less winding, route via Salina Cruz.

OTHER DESTINATIONS
Daily bus departures:

Destination	Fare	Duration	Frequency
Acapulco	M$280-300	8-9hr	8 from EB terminal
Bahías de Huatulco	M$18-30	1hr	36 from OCC terminal
	M$26-30	1hr	9 from EB terminal
	M$16	1hr	Transportes Rápidos de Pochutla every 15 min, 5:30am-8pm
Mexico City	M$520	14-15hr	2 from EB terminal (5 & 5:30pm)
	M$566	15-16hr	2 OCC (4:45 & 7:10pm)
Puerto Escondido	M$53	1½hr	9 from EB terminal
	M$25-46	1½hr	35 from OCC terminal
San Cristóbal de las Casas	M$332	10½-12hr	2 OCC (7:30 & 10:40pm)
Tehuantepec	M$120	4½hr	4 OCC
Tuxtla Gutiérrez	M$284	10hr	2 OCC (7:30 & 10:40pm)

LOCAL TRANSPORTATION

There are three options for travel between Pochutla and the beach towns and villages to its south-west: *camioneta* (pickup trick – a fun way to travel), *colectivo* (shared) taxi and private taxi.

Camionetas and colectivo taxis all start from various Pochutla side streets then travel south down Av Cárdenas picking up passengers as they go. People often wait for them outside Mueblería García, a furniture store about 100m uphill from Hotel Santa Cruz. Fares *(camioneta/colectivo)* are M$5/10 to Puerto Ángel (20 minutes), M$10/15 to Zipolite (30 minutes) and M$8/10 to San Agustinillo (45 minutes) or Mazunte (40 minutes). Vehicles bound for Mazunte do not generally travel through Puerto Ángel but head west along Hwy 200 to San Antonio, then backtrack south-east to Mazunte and continue to San Agustinillo and the west (Roca Blanca) end of Zipolite. Both camionetas and colectivos run about every half-hour from around 7am to 7pm.

Private cabs from Pochutla during the day should cost around M$60 to Puerto Ángel and M$100 to Zipolite, San Agustinillo or Mazunte; at night they charge up to 50% more.

PUERTO ÁNGEL

☎ 958 / pop 2400

Thirteen kilometers south of Pochutla, the small fishing port, naval base and beach town of Puerto Ángel (pwer-toh *ahn*-hel) straggles around a picturesque bay between two rocky headlands. Many travelers prefer to stay out on the beaches a few kilometers west at Zipolite, San Agustinillo or Mazunte, but the marginally more urban Puerto Ángel also offers some good accommodations, along with its own little beaches and activities, and easy transportation to Zipolite.

Orientation

The road from Pochutla emerges at the east end of the small Bahía de Puerto Ángel. The road winds around the back of the bay, over an often-dry *arroyo* (stream) and up a hill. It then forks – right to Zipolite and Mazunte, left down to Playa del Panteón. It's called Blvd Uribe through most of town, though after it crosses the *arroyo* it's also referred to as Carretera a Zipolite.

Information

Banco Azteca (Blvd Uribe; ☉ 9am-9pm) Changes cash US dollars only and may be out of them at weekends; the nearest ATMs are in Pochutla. Several Puerto Ángel accommodations and restaurants will change cash or traveler's checks at their own rates.

Farmacia El Ángel (☎ 584-30-58; Vasconcelos) Dr Constancio Aparicio's practice is here, from 9am to 2pm and 5 to 9pm Monday to Saturday; he also offers 24-hour emergency service.

G@l@p@gos (Blvd Uribe s/n; internet per hr M$12) You can also make phone calls here.

Gel@net (Vasconcelos 3; internet per hr M$12; ☉ 9am-10pm) Has telephone, fax and internet services.

Tourist office (Blvd Uribe; ☉ 9am-2pm & 4-8pm, days variable) In a *palapa*-roofed building at the entrance to the pier; if open, useful for transportation details.

Beaches

Playa del Panteón, on the west side of the bay, is a small, shallow and calm beach, and its waters are cleaner than those near the pier across the bay.

About 500m up the road toward Pochutla, a sign points along a path to **Playa Estacahuite**, 700m away. The three tiny, sandy bays here are good for snorkeling, but watch out for jellyfish. A couple of shack restaurants serve reasonably priced seafood and pasta, and rent snorkels.

The coast northeast of Estacahuite is dotted with more good beaches, none of them very busy. A good one is **Playa La Boquilla**, on a small bay about 5km out, the site of Bahía de la Luna accommodations (p768). You can get here by a 3.5km unpaved road from a turnoff 4km out of Puerto Ángel on the road toward Pochutla (a taxi from Puerto Ángel can cost M$100 each way), but it's fun to go by boat – ask at Puerto Ángel pier or Playa del Panteón. Boats will take a few people for around M$100 to M$150 each, including a return trip at an agreed time.

Activities

Snorkeling and **fishing** are popular, and you can also go **diving**. The drops and canyons out to sea from Puerto Ángel are suitable for very deep dives; there's also a dive to an 1870 shipwreck and lots of fish life.

Several operators on and around Playa del Panteón offer a four-hour, four-beach snorkeling boat trip, including Estacahuite and La Boquilla beaches, with snorkel gear.

included for M$150 per person. En route you should see turtles and, with luck, dolphins and even (from November to May) migrating whales. **Azul Profundo** (☎ 584-34-38; azul_profundomx@hotmail.com) does this trip daily at 9:30am and will pick you up and drop you off at your accommodation in Puerto Ángel or Zipolite; amiable guide Chepe speaks English and German. Other recommended operators (best to make arrangements the day before, and they may require a minimum of four or five people) are **Océanos Tours** (☎ 584-30-83; Restaurant Leyvis y Vicente) and English- and French-speaking **Byron Luna** (☎ 584-31-15), who can be found at his home just behind Playa del Panteón.

The same people will take you sportfishing for marlin, dorado and tuna, for around M$300 per hour (up to three people).

Azul Profundo also offers diving, with one-/two-tank dives costing M$500/800 including equipment and a dive guide.

Sleeping

Places with an elevated location are more likely to catch any breeze.

ourpick **Hotel Puesta del Sol** (☎ /fax 584-30-96; www.puertoangel.net; Blvd Uribe s/n; s/d with shared bathroom M$110/150, d with private bathroom M$250-360; ▢) Trilingual (English, German, Spanish) Puesta del Sol offers sizable, clean rooms with fans and screens. The more expensive ones have their own terraces and hot-water bathroom, and some sleep up to six. A breezy hammock area invites relaxation, breakfast is available, and the touches of art, useful maps, verdant garden, small library and friendly, informative owners make this an excellent choice.

Casa Arnel (☎ /fax 584-30-51; arnelpto.angel@huatulco .net.mx; Azueta s/n; s/d M$150/200; ▢) Up the lane past the market, Arnel has five clean, ample tile-floored rooms with fans, and OK beds and bathrooms. Soft drinks, coffee and tea are available, and there's an upstairs hammock area, a small library and a place to wash and dry clothes.

ourpick **Casa de Huéspedes Gundi y Tomás** (☎ 584-30-68; www.puertoangel-hotel.com; s/d with shared bathroom M$180/250, with private bathroom M$300/350, room for 6 M$700) This relaxed guesthouse above Blvd Uribe has a variety of brightly decorated, basic rooms, all with fans, mosquito nets and/

PUERTO ÁNGEL

0 _____ 200 m
0 _____ 0.1 miles

INFORMATION
Banco Azteca..............................1 C3
Farmacia El Ángel........................2 C2
G@!@p@gos................................3 B2
Gel@net......................................4 C3
Tourist Office...............................5 C3

SIGHTS & ACTIVITIES
Azul Profundo.............................6 A2
Byron Luna.................................7 A3
Océanos Tours......................(see 16)

SLEEPING 🏠
Casa Arnel...................................8 B2
Casa de Huéspedes Gundi y
 Tomás......................................9 B2
El Almendro...............................10 C2
Hotel Cordelia's.........................11 A2
Hotel Puesta del Sol...................12 A2
La Buena Vista..........................13 B1
Villa Serena Florencia.................14 C2

EATING 🍴
Beto's...15 A2
Restaurant Leyvis y Vicente........16 A3
Restaurante Susy........................17 A3

TRANSPORT
Buses to Oaxaca.........................18 C3
Taxi Stand..................................19 C3

To Zipolite (2.5km);
Mazunte (5km);
Puerto Escondido (71km)

To Playa Estacahuite (700m);
Playa La Boquilla;
Bahía de la Luna (7km);
Pochutla (12km)

Panteón
Naval Base
Playa Principal
Beach Restaurants
Playa del Panteón
Blvd Uribe
Azueta
Ya-zconetos
Calle del Tajo
Av Principal

Bahía de Puerto Ángel

La Playita

Pier

or screens, and some offbeat artistic touches. Good food is available, including homemade bread, mainly vegetarian snacks, fruit drinks and a nightly M$75 *menú*. The main dining area has outstanding views. Gundi, the friendly German owner, speaks good English and Spanish and provides a safe for valuables, a book exchange, laundry service, bus reservations, and an exchange service for cash or travelers checks. Her sons Fabián and Bastián rent surfboards and offer surf lessons at Zipolite or San Agustinillo.

El Almendro (☎ 584-30-68; www.puertoangel-hotel .com; s/d M$200/350) In a shady garden up a little lane off Blvd Uribe, El Almendro has five clean, brightly painted, basic rooms with OK beds and bathrooms, plus a bungalow with kitchen for up to six (around M$1500/5000 per week/month).

Villa Serena Florencia (☎ 584-30-44; villaserenaoax@ otmail.com; Blvd Uribe s/n; s/d/tr M$250/350/400, air-con extra M$30) Florencia provides 13 pleasant, colorful, smallish rooms with fans, screens and a dash of art and photos. It also offers a shady sitting area and a good Italian–Mexican restaurant.

Hotel Cordelia's (☎ 584-31-09; Playa del Panteón; r M$350-650; P) Right on Playa del Panteón and run by the same family as Azul Profundo dive shop, Cordelia's has 17 mosquito-screened rooms with nice tiled floors, good wood furniture and some attractive *artesanías*. The best are good big rooms with their own terraces overlooking the bay.

La Buena Vista (☎ /fax 584-31-04; www.labuenavista .com; La Buena Compañía s/n; d M$600-700, per additional person M$70; ☒) The 21 big rooms and six excellent mud-brick bungalows on this verdant property are kept scrupulously clean. Many have breezy balconies with hammocks, some have excellent views, and wood, stone and brick are cleverly used throughout. There's a good restaurant on an expansive terrace and a gorgeous pool area up top. Rates almost halve outside the high seasons of mid-December to early January, Semana Santa and June to August. The only negative is that the staff often seem rather down in the mouth.

Bahía de la Luna (☎ 589-50-20; www.bahiadelaluna .com; Playa La Boquilla; s/d/q incl breakfast US$70/85/140, 6/7-person house from US$220/245; P) This tropical hideaway out at gorgeous Playa La Boquilla (p766) has attractive, bright adobe bungalows with terracotta-tile floors and touches of artisanry, set on a tree-covered hillside overlooking the beach. It also has a good beachside restaurant–

café with moderate prices (dishes M$30 to M$65), and offers guests boat trips and free use of snorkeling gear and sea kayaks.

Eating

La Buena Vista (☎ 584-31-04; La Buena Compañía s/n; breakfast M$2.50-4, dinner mains M$50-80; ☺ 8-11am & 6-10pm Mon-Sat; Ⓥ) On an airy terrace overlooking the bay, La Buena Vista's restaurant offers well-prepared Mexican and American fare, including meatless choices like vegetarian *tamales* or cheese-filled *chiles rellenos* (stuffed chilies).

Villa Serena Florencia (☎ 584-30-44; Blvd Uribe s/n; dishes M$30-90) This reliable Italian–Mexican restaurant turns out good pasta, pizzas, salads and Mexican dishes at very good prices. Breakfasts are a good value.

Beto's (Carretera a Zipolite s/n; dishes M$30-60; ☺ 4pm-midnight) On the uphill stretch of Blvd Uribe, Beto's is a relaxed, economical, friendly and clean little place with a large terrace. Offerings range from fish fillets and ceviches to chicken and beef dishes. Spot it by the string of colored lights leading up the steps.

El Almendro (☎ 584-30-68; off Blvd Uribe; BBQ dinner M$80) From about mid-December to Easter this accommodation holds a 6 to 7pm happy hour followed by a good-value barbecue dinner of marinated meats or fish, salad from the salad bar and baked potatoes.

The restaurants on Playa del Panteón, **Restaurant Cordelia's** (☎ 584-31-09; Hotel Cordelia's), **Restaurante Susy** (☎ 584-30-19) and **Restaurant Leyvis y Vicente** (☎ 584-30-83), all offer fish and seafood for M$50 to M$120, plus cheaper fare such as *entomatadas* (a variation of enchiladas) and eggs. They stay open until 10 or 11pm, and the setting is very pretty after dark. Be careful about the freshness of seafood in the low season.

Getting There & Away

See the boxed text on p766 for details of transportation from Pochutla. An Estrella del Valle/Oaxaca Pacífico bus to Oaxaca (M$76, seven hours) departs at 10pm nightly from near the foot of Vasconcelos. A taxi to or from Zipolite costs M$5 *colectivo* (if you can find one), or M$50 for the whole cab (more after dark).

A taxi to Huatulco airport should cost M$250; to Puerto Escondido airport M$350

ZIPOLITE
☎ 958 / pop 900
The beautiful 1.5km stretch of pale sand called Zipolite, beginning about 2.5km

west of Puerto Ángel, is fabled as southern Mexico's perfect budget chill-out spot. It's a place where you can do as little as you like and enjoy good food and inexpensive accommodation all in wonderfully elemental surroundings of crashing surf, pounding sun, rocky headlands and tree-covered hills. Inexpensive places to stay and eat line the beach, many still reassuringly ramshackle and wooden and with tall thatched roofs that help to create the unique Zipolite landscape. This is one of those magical places where you may find yourself postponing departure more than once.

Zipolite has a certain fame as a nudist beach; in fact total nudity is common only at the western end of the beach and in the small cove called Playa del Amor at the east end.

Orientation

The eastern end of Zipolite (nearest Puerto Ángel) is called Colonia Playa del Amor, the middle part is Centro, and the area toward the western end (divided from Centro by a narrow lagoon and creek) is Colonia Roca Blanca. Av Roca Blanca, a block back from the beach here, is commonly known as El Adoquín, for its paving blocks. The other few streets behind the beach are mostly nameless.

Information

The nearest bank is in Puerto Ángel and the nearest ATM in Pochutla, but some accommodations may exchange or accept payment in US dollars or euros.

Azul Profundo (☎ 584-34-38; Av Roca Blanca; internet per hr M$15, with own laptop M$10; ☺ 8am-10pm) You can phone from here too.

Paty.Net (Av Roca Blanca; same-day laundry service per kg M$14; ☺ 8am-5pm Mon-Sat)

Dangers & Annoyances

Beware: the Zipolite surf is deadly. It's fraught with riptides, changing currents and a strong undertow. Locals don't swim here, and going in deeper than your knees can be risking your life. Local voluntary *salvavidas* (lifeguards) have rescued many, but they don't maintain a permanent watch, and people drown here yearly. The shore break is one only experienced surfers should attempt.

Theft can be a problem, so it's good to stay somewhere where you can lock your valuables in a safe. It's not advisable to

walk alone on the beach, or along the Puerto Ángel–Zipolite road, after dark.

Activities

The essence and glory of Zipolite is that organized activity is very minimal. This is a place for hanging out and doing exactly nothing if that's what you feel like.

Azul Profundo (left) will pick you up and drop you off in Zipolite for its snorkeling, diving and fishing trips from Puerto Ángel (p766).

At **Solstice** (☎ 584-32-35; www.solstice-mexico .com; Colonia Playa del Amor) Brigitte Longueville leads 1½-hour hatha yoga classes (US$7) in a large, inviting upstairs yoga room most days at 9am or 5pm. Five-day retreats and weekend workshops are offered here too. Drop by for a schedule. The meditation hill at Shambhala (p770) is open to all for free.

Piña Palmera (☎ 584-31-47; www.pinapalmera.org; Carretera Zipolite-Mazunte; ☺ 9am-3pm Mon-Sat), an independently run rehabilitation and social integration center for physically and intellectually disabled people from rural communities, does fantastic work with workshops at its beautiful palm-grove site and on village visits. Over 5000 disabled kids, adults and family members have participated in Piña Palmera programs since 1984. Some toys and crafts made here are sold in a shop on the main road. Piña Palmera can use volunteers who speak '40-50%' Spanish and are ready to work 48 hours a week for at least three months.

Sleeping

Many accommodations are right on the beach. Unless otherwise stated, rooms here have shared bathrooms.

A Nice Place on the Beach (☎ 584-31-95; Colonia Roca Blanca; r M$100) A very rustic place right on the beachfront. Rooms have a double bed and mosquito net – no more. Those up the steps and facing the ocean are best, for view and breeze.

Posada Kiko (☎ 584-31-76; Colonia Roca Blanca; d M$80-150) Basic, friendly and right on the beach, Kiko provides simple *cabañas* with mosquito nets but no fans. The best ones are upstairs and face the ocean.

Posada Brisa Marina (☎ 584-31-93; brisamarinaca@ yahoo.com; Colonia Roca Blanca; r with/without bathroom from M$150/100; (P)) At popular, American-owned Brisa, the rooms with bathroom occupy a

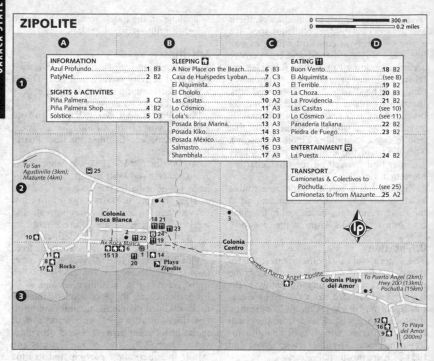

ZIPOLITE

INFORMATION		EATING
Azul Profundo...........................1 B3	SLEEPING	Buon Vento............................18 B2
PatyNet...................................2 B2	A Nice Place on the Beach..........6 B3	El Alquimista ....(see 8)
	Casa de Huéspedes Lyoban........7 C3	El Terrible..............................19 B2
SIGHTS & ACTIVITIES	El Alquimista............................8 A3	La Choza...............................20 B3
Piña Palmera...........................3 C2	El Chololo...............................9 D3	La Providencia........................21 B2
Piña Palmera Shop...................4 B2	Las Casitas.............................10 A2	Las Casitas ....(see 10)
Solstice..................................5 D3	Lo Cósmico............................11 A3	Lo Cósmico ....(see 11)
	Lola's...................................12 D3	Panadería Italiana...................22 B2
	Posada Brisa Marina................13 A3	Piedra de Fuego.....................23 B2
	Posada Kiko...........................14 B3	
	Posada México.......................15 A3	ENTERTAINMENT
	Salmastro.............................16 D3	La Puesta..............................24 B2
	Shambhala............................17 A3	
		TRANSPORT
		Camionetas & Colectivos to
		Pochutla...........................(see 25)
		Camionetas to/from Mazunte...25 A2

three-story concrete building fronting the beach and have safes. Some of them some have balconies and great views. The cheaper rooms are in a rear wooden section. There's also a common safe.

Shambhala (Casa de Gloria; west end Playa Zipolite; http://shambhalavision.tripod.com; hammocks M$35, dm M$80-100, r with private bathroom M$350; P) This ecologically run, long-established guesthouse climbs a hill looking right along the beach, with some great views. In part a spiritual retreat, with its own meditation hill and no alcohol or illegal drugs permitted, it's also a good place for anyone looking for a tranquil and economical place to stay. All the varied accommodations are individually and attractively built, and the shared bathrooms are fine. Shambhala has two **restaurants** (8am-10 or 11pm; V). In the upper one no alcohol or red meat are served and offerings include tabouleh salad and homemade yoghurt; the lower one serves chicken, meat, fish, seafood and vegetarian dishes for M$35 to M$80, plus alcohol. There's a lockup room for valuables. Shambhala hosts a big spiritual festival, embracing all beliefs, every New Year's Eve.

Lo Cósmico (www.locosmico.com; west end Playa Zipolite; cabañas d/tr M$180/250, q with private bathroom M$300) Very relaxed Lo Cósmico has conical-roofed *cabañas* dotted around a tall rock outcrop. Each has a hammock and mosquito net; the cheaper ones are a bit enclosed while the pricier ones have two floors and views. A security box is available, and there's a good onsite restaurant (opposite).

Salmastro (584-31-61; Calle del Amor; hammocks M$50, d M$150-220, q M$350-400; P) At the east end of the beach, Salmastro's eight basic rooms (some upstairs, and some with sea views) have good beds, fans and thatched roofs.

Lola's (584-32-01; Calle del Amor; s/d M$150/200; P) Salmastro's neighbor has rooms with private bath.

our pick Posada México (584-31-94; www.posadamexico.com; Av Roca Blanca; r with shared/private bathroom M$150/250) This joint has the most character among the Roca Blanca beachfront places. The wood-and-palm rooms have safes, good beds with mosquito nets, and their own sandy little sitting-out areas with hammocks. It's friendly and personal, and good breakfasts are served at the beachside café.

Casa de Huéspedes Lyoban (☎ 584-31-77; www .lyoban.com.mx; Centro; hammocks M$70, s/d/tr M$170/210/260, with private bathroom & fan M$250/290/360; 🖳) Relaxed, friendly (and gay-friendly) Lyoban has basic, clean rooms with mosquito nets: the beds are comfy, but the walls don't reach the ceiling in the cheaper, upstairs rooms. Common areas include a sociable bar–restaurant space, small swimming pool, tables for ping-pong, *foosball* and pool, and a breezy upstairs hammock deck. The hammock-sleeping price includes a blanket, a sturdy locker and shower usage. Lyoban has security cameras, too.

El Chololo (☎ 584-31-59; Calle del Amor; r with/without bathroom M$300/200; Ⓟ) With five simple rooms at the far eastern end of the beach, this very friendly place also serves good Mexican and Italian food. The rooms with shared bath, upstairs are basic.

Las Casitas (☎ 958-5878464; www.las-casitas.net; bungalows d M$280-500, tr/q M$350/600) Set back from the west end of Playa Zipolite on a hill, Las Casitas has seven tasteful rooms in semi–open-air, solar-lit *cabañas* of wood, adobe and palm-thatch. Five have private bathrooms and all have kitchen use. Most have good views as well, at least in the dry, leafless season, and some have swinging beds. There's also an excellent restaurant here (right).

El Alquimista (☎ 958-5878961; www.el-alquimista .com; west end Playa Zipolite; bungalows M$600 or M$1200; 🔀) Attached to one of Zipolite's best restaurants (right), this place has 14 fine thatch-roofed beach bungalows, each with homespun textiles, one double bed, fan, net, bathroom and hammocked porch. They're often full. There are also three beautiful superior bungalows for two to three people, in a tower just behind, boasting Sky TV, hot water and (in two cases) air-conditioning.

Eating

Eating and drinking in the open air a few steps from the surf is an inimitable Zipolite experience. Apart from the ubiquitous pizzas, most places serve a mix of Mexican and international fare with a maritime slant.

Panadería Italiana (Av Roca Blanca; items M$15-35; 🕙 11am-2:30pm & 5-8:30pm Mon-Sat) A neat little place to drop into for focaccia and pizza by the slice.

Lo Cósmico (West end Playa Zipolite; dishes M$28-50; 🕙 8am-4pm Tue-Sun; Ⓥ) Mellow out on the rocks above the beach at this open-air restaurant at the accommodations of the same name.

Cósmico provides good food from an impeccably clean kitchen – especially tasty are the crepes (sweet and savory) and salads.

our pick **Piedra de Fuego** (Colonia Roca Blanca; mains M$40-60; 🕙 3-11pm) You'll get a generous serving of fish fillet or prawns, accompanied by rice, salad and tortillas at this superbly simple, family-run place. It's an excellent value and highly popular.

Buon Vento (Colonia Roca Blanca; pasta M$40-65; 🕙 6pm-midnight Thu-Tue) An excellent Italian restaurant with good music, a big video screen and subtle vibes. The huge pasta list includes some delicious baked options, and the wine list is decent for Mexico.

El Terrible (Colonia Roca Blanca; pizzas M$60-85, crepes M$25-55; 🕙 6pm-midnight Tue-Sat) The Francophone couple here make a variety of damn good pizzas, large enough to feed two moderately hungry travelers or one very hungry one. Sweet and savory crepes are also served.

La Choza (☎ 584-31-90; Colonia Roca Blanca; mains M$50-120) La Choza's beachside restaurant provides generous quantities of a wide choice of foods from salads and stuffed avocados to seafood, pasta and whole fish.

Las Casitas (☎ 958-5878464; mains M$80-90; 🕙 8:30-11:30am & 7:30-10:30pm Thu-Mon) There's great homemade pasta (with fish, seafood or vegetable sauces) as well as meat dishes and home-made baked goods at this Italian-run place back from the west end of the beach. For its specialty *pescado al horno de leña* (fish baked in a wood-fired oven; M$120), ask a day before.

our pick **El Alquimista** (☎ 958-5878961; west end Playa Zipolite; mains M$55-120; 🕙 8pm-midnight) The classy Alchemist is delightfully sited in a sandy cove. Its very wide-ranging fare runs from falafel or hummus starters to good meat and seafood dishes and brick-oven pizzas, complemented by a full bar and good espresso.

La Providencia (☎ 958-1009234; Colonia Roca Blanca; mains M$80-130; 🕙 7-11pm Wed-Sun) Zipolite's most suave dining option has an open-air lounge area where you can sip a drink while you peruse the menu and place your order. The flavorsome and well-presented food is a *nuevo mexicano* treat, from cold beetroot and ginger soup to chicken breast in a blue cheese and pumpkin flower sauce.

Drinking & Entertainment

Zipolite's beachfront restaurant–bars have unbeatable locations for drinks from sunset onward. Those toward the west end of the

OAXACA STATE

beach are generally the most popular – especially El Alquimista (p771), which plays cool music and serves cocktails as well as the usual beer, *mezcal* and so forth. The swing seats at the bar can get tricky after you've had a few. Holiday periods and full moons see travelers making merry around bonfires on the beach. The open-air *discoteca* **La Puesta** (☎ 584-31-78; Colonia Roca Blanca; ✆ 9pm-late Tue-Sat) provides slightly more active nightlife, cranking out reggae, funk, techno, hip-hop and Latin tunes into the wee hours, though nothing much happens before midnight.

Getting There & Away
See the boxed text on p766 for details on transportation from Pochutla. The *camionetas* from Pochutla via Mazunte and San Agustinillo terminate at the far west end of Zipolite (about 2km from the east end of the beach). *Colectivo* taxis from Puerto Ángel (M$5), if you can find one, will go to the same spot too, but pass along the length of Zipolite en route, so they are a better bet if you're heading for the east end of the beach.

After dark, a non-*colectivo* taxi is your only option for getting to Puerto Ángel, San Agustinillo or Mazunte (about M$50 until about 10pm, more after that).

SAN AGUSTINILLO
☎ 958 / pop 250
The tiny village of San Agustinillo is centered on a small, curved bay, 4km west of Zipolite by road. The waves here are perfect for body-boarding and often good for body-surfing. The swimming is very good as well, but keep away from the rocks. San Agustinillo has generally higher standards of sanitation than its neighbors Zipolite and Mazunte, and its undeniable charms attract an eclectic bunch of fans, including travelers who are seekinh a less 'sceney' scene than in the neighboring villages. To walk from Zipolite to San Agustinillo, follow footpaths across the headland behind Shambhala at the west end of Zipolite, then continues along the straight and nearly empty Playa Aragón to San Agustinillo.

Until killing sea turtles was banned in Mexico in 1990, San Agustinillo was the site of a slaughterhouse where some 50,000 turtles were killed per year for their meat and shells. Tourism has grown up since then to provide an altogether different local income source.

Hotel Malex (below) provides internet access for M$15 per hour from 8:30am to 9pm Monday to Saturday and from 9am to 8pm on Sunday. Un Secreto (opposite) will do your laundry (M$15 per kg, from 8am to 5pm Monday to Saturday).

Coco Loco Surf Club (www.cocolocosurfclub.com), based at México Lindo (below), rents surfboards for M$50 per hour or M$150 to M$200 per day, and boogie boards or snorkel gear for M$30 per hour. It also offers surfing classes with qualified French instructor David Chouard (two-hour private class for one/two people M$350/500; two-hour group class per person M$200) and three-beach 'discovery trips' combining snorkeling, body boarding and a visit to La Ventanilla (p774) for M$280 per person (minimum four people).

Local fishermen will take up to three people out **sportfishing** for around M$400 per hour, or **marine life–spotting** to look for turtles, dolphins, manta rays and (between November and April) whales, for around M$150 per person (minimum four people) – ask at your accommodation.

Sleeping
Most places are set right on the beach. Rooms have either mosquito-screened windows or mosquito nets.

Palapa Jazmín (☎ 584-32-50; d/q M$200/400) The Jazmín provides economical lodgings toward the west end of the beach. The five good brick-built rooms have fans and clean bathrooms. The three upstairs have sea views; new units are being added.

OUR PICK México Lindo y qué Rico! (faustojasso@gmail.com; r with/without sea view M$350/250; ✆ closed October; **P**) Also near the west end of the beach, México Lindo has friendly, young owners and staff, and its seven large rooms feature slatted windows, fans and some bright touches like tiled bathrooms. Especially good is the breezy upstairs pair of rooms under the tall *palapa* roof. There's excellent food here too (mains M$55 to M$90), including pizzas from a wood-fired brick oven.

Hotel Malex (☎ 589-81-95; malex_hotelweb@hotmail.com; r with/without kitchenette M$350/300, apt M$800) The Malex, at the east end of San Agustinillo, is unprepossessing from outside, but inside, its three upstairs rooms and one spacious apartment are done in cheerful white and blue, each with good bathrooms and beds, and terraces enjoying close-up sea views.

Hotel Paraíso del Pescador (www.paraiso-del-pescador.com; d/q US$35/40, with air-con US$45/50; P) On the inland side of the road in the center of the village, Pescador's six spacious, bright rooms all have tiled floors, good bathrooms and delicious views. The Hungarian–Canadian co-owner specializes in sportfishing trips (four/six hours US$300/450).

Rancho Cerro Largo (ranchocerrolargomx@yahoo.com.mx; Playa Aragón; s M$550-850, d M$700-950, all incl breakfast & dinner; P) With a stunning position above Playa Aragón, Cerro Largo offers excellent accommodations in half a dozen mud-and-wattle *cabañas*. All have ocean views, most have private bathrooms and some have a loft enabling them to accommodate four. The beds and mainly vegetarian meals are top-notch (it makes its own bread, yoghurt and granola), and there's also a nice yoga room with daily 1¾-hour morning sessions (payment by donation). Get there by a drivable track from the Zipolite–San Agustinillo road.

ourpick **Un Sueño** (www.unsueno.com; r M$650, q M$900; P) Sueño, at the east end of Playa San Agustinillo, boasts 12 lovely, good-sized rooms, four in freestanding beachfront *cabañas*, the others in four two-story units behind. All are decorated with art and crafts from different places around the world, and have a semi–open-air feel with bamboo-slat windows. Nearly all have their own terraces with hammocks, and there are nice *palapas* for breakfast and hammock-swinging out front.

ourpick **Punta Placer** (www.puntaplacer.com; r M$800) A creation of the inventive folk from México Lindo (which is a few doors west along the beach), Punta Placer's rooms have a fresh, open-air feel thanks to their breezy terraces and wood-slat windows. The eight beautiful circular rooms have stylish and natural touches like stone-lined showers, and are set around a garden of native plants and stone paving.

Eating & Drinking

Some of the best eateries are attached to accommodations, but there are others too.

Palapa de Evelia (breakfast M$25-35, mains M$70-85; 8am-5pm) Third along from the west end of Playa San Agustinillo, Evelia serves some of the best food on the beach, with well-prepared fish and seafood, and holy guacamole.

Restaurant Alexana (mains M$40-90) The friendly restaurant attached to Hotel Paraíso

del Pescador offers goulash as well as good *carnes, mariscos* and *pescados*.

ourpick **Un Secreto** (mains M$90-120; 8am-11pm) Run by Julien from Un Sueño along the street, Secreto serves up *sabores del Pacífico* with a touch of French flair. The short but sweet seafood-based menu runs from a delicious foil-wrapped fish with mint, to vegetable skewers with *alioli*, and lemon pie to round things off. Excellent breakfasts, *licuados*, light lunches and coffee too!

La Casa Mágica (la_casa_magica@yahoo.ca; 8pm-late Wed-Sun) A favorite with San Ag's amiable little bunch of expats, this welcoming Irish-run bar offers pool, darts, drinks and light food, a couple of hundred meters up the hill opposite Hotel Malex.

Getting There & Away

See the boxed text on p766 for information about transportation from Pochutla. *Colectivo* taxis and *camionetas* for the short trips to or from Zipolite or Mazunte cost M$4 or M$5.

MAZUNTE

958 / pop 700

A kilometer west of San Agustinillo, Mazunte has a fine, curving, sandy beach, an interesting turtle center, and a variety of basic and fancier places to stay and eat. The village is well known as a travelers' hangout and in recent years has seen an increase in foreign residents, attracted either by the area's beauty or, as one put it, the 'old-time hippie vibe.' The economic mainstays here used to be turtle meat and eggs: after the turtle industry was banned in 1990, attempts were made to turn Mazunte into a kind of model ecotouristic village. Some accommodations still maintain an emphasis on sustainability, as do other initiatives launched in the 1990s, such as the natural cosmetics factory and the successful ecotourism scheme at La Ventanilla.

Orientation & Information

The paved road running west from Zipolite to Hwy 200 passes through the middle of Mazunte. Four sandy lanes run about 500m from the road to the beach. The eastern lane, beside the Centro Mexicano de la Tortuga, has no name. The next one, 50m further west, is Calle Principal. Another 200m west is Calle La Barrita, and a further 100m west is the last lane, Camino al Rinconcito, so called because it runs down to the west end of Mazunte beach, which is known as El Rinconcito.

Go online at **Café Internet Dafne** (cnr main road & Calle La Barrita; internet per hr M$10; ⏰ 9am-10pm).

Sights & Activities

The much-visited **Centro Mexicano de la Tortuga** (Mexican Turtle Center; ☎ 584-33-76; cmt@conanp.gob.mx; admission M$20; ⏰ 10am-4:30pm Wed-Sat, 10am-2:30pm Sun) is a turtle aquarium and research center containing specimens of all seven of Mexico's marine turtle species. They're on view in fairly large tanks – it's enthralling to get a close-up view of these creatures, some of which are BIG! Visits are guided (in Spanish) and start every 10 to 15 minutes, although the management is considering introducing non-guided tours. Remodeling work begun in 2008 may mean that parts of the center are closed for some periods.

Cosméticos Naturales (☎ 587-48-60; cosmenat@ hotmail.com; ⏰ 9am-4pm Mon-Sat, 9am-2pm Sun) is beside the main road toward the west end of the village. A small cooperative making and selling shampoo, cosmetics, mosquito repellents, bath gel and soap from natural sources (like maize, coconut, avocado and sesame seeds), it also sells organic coffee and aromatherapy products.

Local fishermen will take three or more people out for three-hour **boat trips** to snorkel, fish if you like, look for turtles, dolphins and whales and check out some of the beaches along the coast. Departure is usually at 8am and the cost M$150 per person, including snorkel equipment. Organize this through your accommodation.

PUNTA COMETA

This rocky cape, jutting out from the west end of Mazunte beach, is the southernmost point in the state of Oaxaca and a fabulous place to be at sunset, with great long-distance views in both directions. You can walk here in 30 minutes, over the rocks from the end of Mazunte beach, or start up the path that leads from the beach to Cabañas Balamjuyuc and Alta Mira but take the first left.

LA VENTANILLA

Some 2.5km along the road west from Mazunte a sign points left to Playa Ventanilla, 1.2km down a dirt track. The small settlement here includes a handful of simple homes, a couple of decent *comedores* (dishes M$25 to

M$80) and the *palapa* of **Servicios Ecoturísticos La Ventanilla** (www.laventanillamx.com; 1½hr lagoon tours adult/child M$50/25, under 6yr free; ⏰ tours 8:30am-5pm). Servicios Ecoturísticos is Ventanilla's successful conservation and ecotourism cooperative. Most popular are its 10-passenger canoe trips on a mangrove-fringed lagoon where you'll see endangered river crocodiles (there are about 1000 of these in the 230,000-sq-meter local protected area) and lots of water birds (most prolific from April to July). For the best wildlife-spotting, go in the early morning. Servicios Ecoturísticos also offers three-hour horseback rides (M$250); specialized birding tours (per person per hr M$50; best at 6am and arranged the day before); and, on certain days, the chance to release turtle hatchlings into the ocean and to join night patrols to see turtles laying and help collect their eggs. There's also accommodation in well-built new *cabañas* with private bathroom (per *cabaña* M$300) and dorms for up to four (per room M$200). Servicios Ecoturísticos' conservation work includes a crocodile nursery, mangrove reforestation and turtle protection. It welcomes volunteers (who pay M$60 per day and are provided with accommodation and kitchen) for work such as reforesting, English-teaching and feeding the deer and young crocs.

Frequent *camionetas* pass the Ventanilla turnoff, leaving you with the 1.2km walk. A taxi from Mazunte should cost M$30.

Sleeping

Most places along Playa Mazunte (including restaurants) have basic rooms or *cabañas*, hammocks to rent and often tent space. Security can be a problem here. There are also a number of more individual and mostly more expensive accommodations set on hills overlooking the beach.

Palapa Omar (☎ 588-32-45; Calle Principal; hammock site & camping per person M$25, rented hammock M$50 s/d M$70/100) Beside the beach end of Calle Principal, Omar provides 13 bare-bones rooms with fans but no mosquito nets in brick and concrete buildings with shared baths.

El Agujón (el_agujon_mazunte@hotmail.com; Camino a Rinconcito; d with shared/private bathroom M$150/250; P) Friendly El Agujón has 13 small, rustic, clean *cabañas* and rooms on the hillside just above its restaurant (opposite).

our pick Cabañas Balamjuyuc (☎ 958-1011808 www.balamjuyuc.com; Camino a Punta Cometa; tents per person

M$70, cabañas s M$180, d M$200-300, tr/q M$350/400; mains M$70-100; (P)) Partly solar-powered Balamjuyuc is perched on a hill above the west end of the beach, with some superb views. The entrance is about 400m up a road that leads uphill off Camino al Rinconcito, and it's also reachable by steps up from the west end of the beach. Balamjuyuc has six *cabaña* rooms, some of which are large and airy; all have mosquito nets, towels and shared showers. The friendly Argentine owners offer harpoon-fishing classes and therapeutic massages, and have their own temascal. The Mexican–Argentine–vegetarian restaurant serves all meals.

our pick Posada del Arquitecto (Camino al Rinconcito; hammocks, camping, dm or estrella M$50, cabañas M$350-400) Built around the natural features of a small hill at the foot of Camino al Rinconcito, this Italian-owned place provides a variety of airy accommodations on several levels, from hilltop open-air hanging beds with mosquito nets, known as *estrellas*, to a dorm with bunks and lockers and assorted attractive *cabañas* built with mostly natural materials (palm leaves, adobe bricks, bamboo and other woods). There's a morning café and a safe for your valuables.

Posada Ziga (s M$150-200, d with private bathroom M$380; (P)) Friendly Ziga sits just above the beach at the end of the lane beside the Centro de la Tortuga. It has an economical restaurant open for breakfast and lunch (dishes M$25 to M$80), a little flower garden and 17 rooms, all with mosquito nets. The doubles are bigger, with tiled private bathrooms and safes, but the best views are from some of the singles above the restaurant.

Posada Arigalan (www.arigalan.com; Cerrada del Museo de la Tortuga; d M$350-450; (P) (X)) Up a steep track from the main road just east of the Turtle Center, Arigalan has commanding views of the coast, nice landscaping, and nine tastefully furnished rooms with air-con and terraces. Breakfast is available in high season.

Alta Mira (☎ 585-51-19; www.altamira-hotel.com; Camino a Punta Cometa; r M$500, bungalows M$600-650; (P)) Next to Cabañas Balamjuyuc and reached by the same road or steps, Alta Mira has 14 solar- and/or candle-powered rooms and bungalows strung beside steps leading down the hillside. Made with much tile, wood and white paint, they're unpretentiously pleasing and very well kept, with good mosquito nets and terraces with hammocks. The upper ones catch the best views and most breeze. The res-taurant serves breakfast and dinner Monday to Saturday, with a mainly Mexican menu (main dishes M$50 to M$80); and there's a safety deposit box.

our pick Casa Pan de Miel (☎ 589-58-44; www.casapandemiel.com; Cerrada del Museo de la Tortuga; r M$1050-1430; (P) (X) (R)) Neighbor to Posada Arigalan and enjoying similarly wonderful views, this is a place designed for real relaxa-tion. The five bright, elegant, air-conditioned rooms are adorned with varied Mexican art, and all have sea views, Sky TV, kitchenette and terraces with hammocks. There's an in-viting large *palapa* area for breakfast (M$50 to M$90) with an infinity pool in front of it, and a variety of massages is available. Kids are not accepted here for safety reasons (the clifftop position).

Eating

La Empanada (sushi M$30-45, rice dishes & baked potatoes M$12-60; ⏱ from 5pm low season, 9am-late high season) Choose from a Mexican–Asian mix of delec-table items including vegetable and fish sushi, all lovingly prepared. La Empanada is on the main road, on the western edge of town.

Estrella Fugaz (Camino al Rinconcito; dishes M$25-50; ⏱ 8am-last customer) This upstairs terrace res-taurant, with a beach view through the palm fronds, has a selection of good Mexican and international dishes, as well as vegetable and fruit drinks, breakfasts and coffees.

El Agujón (Camino al Rinconcito; dishes M$25-70; ⏱ 8am-11pm) Just behind the Estrella Fugaz, this is another good spot with a wide range from big French-bread tortas to crepes, fish and, in the evening, pizzas.

Restaurante Tania (☎ 583-90-13; fish & seafood dishes M$50-100, veg & breakfast dishes M$25-35; ⏱ 9am-11pm; (V)) Tania's scores high for both good-value food and hospitality. It's on the main road, on the west edge of town.

La Dolce Vita (mains M$60-90; ⏱ 4-11pm, closed October) This Italian restaurant, on the main road opposite Camino al Rinconcito, does excellent fish, prawns and spaghetti. For something lighter there are also good salads and crepes.

Entertainment

La Nueva Luna (Calle La Barrita; ⏱ 8pm-2am, closed May-Jun, Sep-Oct) Run by indefatigable Carlos from Argentina, this bar is the nightlife and social center of the Mazunte traveler scene. There's live Latin or reggae from around 10pm to midnight most nights, plus assorted other events such as aerial acrobatics and dance and art classes.

Getting There & Away

See the boxed text on p766 for information about transportation from Pochutla. *Camionetas* run between Mazunte and San Agustinillo (M$4, five minutes) or Zipolite (M$5, 10 minutes).

BAHÍAS DE HUATULCO

☎ 958 / pop 16,000

Mexico's newest planned coastal resort lies along a series of beautiful sandy bays, the Bahías de Huatulco (wah-*tool*-koh), 50km east of Pochutla. This stretch of coast had just one small fishing village until the 1980s. The Mexican government has trodden more gently here than at other resort projects: pockets of development are separated by tracts of unspoiled shoreline, the maximum building height is six stories, and water-processing plants assure no sewage goes into the sea. Lower than expected occupancy rates have slowed development, and, for now, Huatulco is still a relaxed and relatively uncrowded resort, with a succession of scenic beaches lapped by beautiful water and backed by forest. Balancing this, a cruise-ship pier has gone in at Bahía de Santa Cruz, and between October and May an average of two ships a week dock here. Agencies offer all sorts of active pursuits here, from snorkeling and diving to rafting and horseback riding, but Huatulco is not a place to stay long on a very tight budget.

Orientation

The Huatulco bays are strung along the coast about 10km in each direction from the main harbor at Santa Cruz Huatulco. From west to east, the main ones are San Agustín, Chachacual, Cacaluta, Maguey, El Órgano, Santa Cruz, Chahué, Tangolunda and Conejos.

The 'downtown' area is La Crucecita, 1km north of Santa Cruz Huatulco and linked to Hwy 200 by a 5km divided approach road. La Crucecita has nearly all the budget and midrange accommodations and eateries, most shops, the market and the bus stations. Santa Cruz Huatulco has a few plusher hotels as well as the main harbor. The other main developments are at Bahía Chahué, 1km east of Santa Cruz, with mainly midrange hotels and a marina, and Tangolunda, 4km further east with most of the luxury hotels.

The airport is 400m north of Hwy 200, 12km west of the turnoff to La Crucecita.

Information

INTERNET ACCESS

El Telefonito (Map p778; Av Bugambilia 501, La Crucecita; internet per hr M$10; ☉ 9am-11:30pm) Also offers cheap phone calls to Europe.

Terra-Cotta (Gardenia 902, La Crucecita; internet per hr M$10; ☉ 10am-9pm) A nice, clean, air-conditioned facility (see p781).

LAUNDRY

Lavandería Diush (Map p778; ☎ 587-27-37; Av Bugambilia 402, La Crucecita; ☉ 9am-9pm Mon-Sat, 10am-3pm Sun) Washes and dries a minimum 3kg for M$15 per kg, or M$20 for four-hour same-morning service.

MONEY

Banco Azteca (Map p778; Guanacastle 309, La Crucecita; ☉ 9am-9pm) Has an ATM and exchanges cash US dollars.

HSBC (Map p779; Harborside, Santa Cruz; ☉ 8am-7pm Mon-Sat) Currency exchange and ATM.

TOURIST INFORMATION

Tourist information kiosk (Map p778; Plaza Principal, La Crucecita; ☉ 9am-2pm & 4-7pm Mon-Fri, 9am-1pm Sat) Has helpful staff.

Tourist office (Map p778; ☎ 587-18-71; turismohuatulco@hotmail.com; cnr Av Bugambilia & Ceiba, La Crucecita; ☉ 9am-5pm Mon-Fri, 9am-1pm Sat) A municipal office, upstairs in the Casa de la Cultura; some English spoken.

Sights & Activities

La Crucecita's modern church, the **Parroquia de Nuestra Señora de Guadalupe** (Plaza Principal), has an impressively large image of the Virgin painted on its ceiling. The rest of the area's attractions are on the water, at the beaches or in jungle hinterland. You can snorkel, dive, kayak, surf, fish, raft, canoe, walk in the jungle, watch birds, ride horses, cycle, visit a coffee plantation and waterfalls and more. Most outings cost between M$250 and M$400. Hotels, tour kiosks in La Crucecita and travel agencies will book many of these activities.

The **Parque Nacional Huatulco** (Huatulco National Park) protects 119 sq km of land, sea and shoreline west of Santa Cruz Huatulco, including some of Huatulco's most important

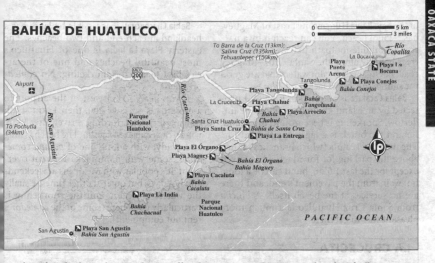

BAHÍAS DE HUATULCO

coral reefs, which in the past have suffered some damage from fishing and touristic activities. Few visitors enter the national park except on guided or escorted trips, and the paying of the M$20 fee for entry to the land zone is normally taken care of by your tour operator: otherwise you can pay it from 9am to noon, Monday to Saturday, at the **national park office** (Map p778; ☎ /fax 587-04-46; cnr Blvd Chahué & Guamuchil, La Crucecita). The M$21 fee for the marine zone is collected at Santa Cruz harbor, along with a M$5 fee to enter the harbor itself. Use of non-biodegradable suntan lotions or sunscreen is prohibited within the national park.

The **Parque Ecológico Rufino Tamayo** (Map p778) on the edge of La Crucecita is a still rather wild city park, composed mainly of natural vegetation, with some paved paths and tile-roofed shelters with benches.

BEACHES

Huatulco's beaches are sandy with clear waters (though boats and jet skis leave an oily film here and there). Like the rest of Mexico, all beaches are under federal control, and anyone can use them – even when hotels appear to treat them as private property. Some have coral offshore and excellent snorkeling, though visibility can be poor in the rainy season.

Lanchas will whisk you out to most of the beaches from Santa Cruz Huatulco harbor (Map p779) any time between 8am and 5pm, and they'll return to collect you by dusk. Taxis can get you to most beaches for less money, but a boat ride is more fun. Round-trip *lancha* rates for up to 10 people from Santa Cruz: Playa La Entrega M$200, Bahía Maguey or Bahía El Órgano M$500, Playa La India M$1000, Bahía San Agustín M$1200.

The small, accessible **Playa Santa Cruz** at Santa Cruz Huatulco is often crowded, and its looks are somewhat marred by the cruise-ship pier. It has several beach restaurants. **Playa La Entrega** lies toward the outer edge of Bahía de Santa Cruz, a five-minute *lancha* trip or 2.5km by paved road from Santa Cruz. This 300m beach, backed by a line of seafood *palapas*, can get crowded, but it has calm water and good snorkeling on a coral plate from which boats are cordoned off – although the coral is in danger of being smothered in silt churned up by the cruise ships entering the bay. 'La Entrega' means 'The Delivery': here in 1831, Mexican independence hero Vicente Guerrero was handed over to his enemies by a Genoese sea captain. Guerrero was taken to Cuilapan near Oaxaca and shot.

Some of the western bays are accessible by road; at times groups of young men congregate in the bays' parking lots, offering to 'watch your car' and touting for the beach restaurants. A 1.5km paved road diverges to **Bahía Maguey** from the road to La Entrega, about half a kilometer out of Santa Cruz. Maguey's fine 400m beach curves around a calm bay between forested headlands. It has a line of seafood *palapas*. There's good snorkeling around the rocks at the left (east) side of the bay. **Bahía El Órgano**, just east of Maguey, has a 250m beach. You can reach it by a narrow 10-minute footpath that heads into the trees halfway along the Santa Cruz–Maguey road. El Órgano has calm waters that are good for snorkeling, but it lacks *comedores*.

Bahía Cacaluta is about 1km long and protected by an island, though there can be undertow. Snorkeling is best around the island. Behind the beach is a lagoon with bird life. The road to Cacaluta (which branches off just above the parking lot for Maguey) is paved except for the last 1.5km, but it can be a long, hot walk from the pavement's end, and there are no services at the beach itself. A *lancha* from Santa Cruz Huatulco is a much more pleasant way to get there.

Bahía Chachacual, inaccessible by land, has a headland at each end and two beaches. The easterly **Playa La India** is one of Huatulco's most beautiful beaches and one of the area's best places for snorkeling. No *comedores* here.

If you head 1.7km west of the airport to a crossroads on Hwy 200, then 13km south down a dirt road, fording a river after 9km, you'll reach **Bahía San Agustín**. The beach is long and sandy, with a long line of *palapa comedores,* some with hammocks for rent overnight. It's popular with Mexicans at weekends and holidays, but quiet at other times. Usually the waters are calm, and the snorkeling is particularly good here (some of the *comedores* rent out equipment).

LA CRUCECITA

0 — 200 m
0 — 0.1 miles

INFORMATION
Banamex (ATM).............................1 B3
Banco Azteca................................2 A3
El Telefonito.................................3 B4
HSBC ATM..........................(see 25)
Lavandería Diush..........................4 B3
Post Office...................................5 C3
Terra-Cotta........................(see 25)
Tourist Information Kiosk.........6 B3
Tourist Office...............................7 B4

SIGHTS & ACTIVITIES
Centro de Buceo Sotavento......8 A4
Park Entrance...............................9 C3
Park Entrance.............................10 B2
Parque Nacional Huatulco
   Office.......................................11 C3
Parroquia de Nuestra Señora
   de Guadalupe..........................12 A3

SLEEPING
Hotel Arenas del Pacífico........13 A4
Hotel Arrecife............................14 A4
Hotel Flamboyant.....................15 A3
Hotel Jaroje...............................16 B4
Hotel María Mixteca.................17 B3
Hotel Posada Leo......................18 B4
Hotel Suites Begonias...............19 B4
Misión de los Arcos..................20 A3

EATING
Comedores................................21 B3
El Patio.....................................22 B3
Iguana Bar.......................(see 24)
Restaurant La Crucecita............23 B4
Restaurante Onix.......................24 B3
Terra-Cotta...............................25 A3

DRINKING
Café Dublín...............................26 B3
La Crema...................................27 A3
Paletería Zamora......................28 B4

ENTERTAINMENT
La Peña....................................29 B3
Tipsy Blowfish..........................30 B4

TRANSPORT
Aerotucán................................31 D4
Colectivo Taxis to Barra de la
   Cruz.......................................32 A1
Europcar...........................(see 31)
OCC Bus Station.......................33 A1
Taxi & Colectivo Taxi Stop.......34 B3
Taxi Stand................................35 B3
Transportes Rápidos de
   Pochutla Bus Stop.................36 A1

To Estrella Blanca Bus Station (600m);
Hwy 200 (5km); Airport (16km);
Pochutla (50km)

Parque Ecológico Rufino Tamayo

Blvd Chahué
Blvd Chahué
Sabalí
Pochote
Gardenia
Jazmín
Palo Verde
Palma Real
Ocotillo
Macuil
Macuhitle
Av Bugambilia
Canizal
Guarumbo
Guanacaste
Priv Tamarindo
Mercado
Guamuchil
Plaza Principal
Flamboyán
Flamboyán
Chacah
Colorín
Canal
Cocotillo
Celba
Acacia
Laurel

Parque Ecológico Rufino Tamayo

Av Oaxaca
Blvd Chahué
Blvd Chahué

To La Bohème (500m)

To Hotel Posada Edén Costa (500m);
Bahía Chahué (1km); Tangolunda (4km)

To Santa Cruz Huatulco (1km)

SANTA CRUZ HUATULCO

0   200 m
0   0.1 miles

INFORMATION	
HSBC	1 C2

SIGHTS & ACTIVITIES	
Hurricane Divers	2 C3
Snorkel Hire	(see 4)

SLEEPING	
Hotel Castillo Huatulco	3 C1

TRANSPORT	
Lancha Tickets & Embarkation	4 C2
Magnicharters	5 C1
Taxi Stand	6 C2

To Chahué Hotels (600m);
Bahía Chahué (600m);
Plaza Chahué (800m);
La Crucecita (1km);
Tangolunda (3km)

Blvd Santa Cruz

Tehuantepec

Mercado de Artesanías

Harbor

Plaza

Monte Albán

Cocijo

Jochutla

Pitin

Huatulco

Mitla

Plaza

Playa Santa Cruz

Bahía de Santa Cruz

Cruise Ship Pier

To Playa La Entrega (2.5km); Bahía Maguey (5km)

A paved road runs to the eastern bays from La Crucecita and Santa Cruz, continuing eventually to Hwy 200. **Bahía Chahué** has a good beach (though the surf can be surprisingly strong) and a marina at its east end. Further east, **Bahía Tangolunda** is the site of the major top-end hotel developments. The sea is sometimes rough here: heed the colored-flag safety system. Three kilometers further east is the long sweep of **Playa Punta Arena**, on Bahía Conejos, an almost virgin beach with sometimes strong surf. Around a headland at the east end of Bahía Conejos is the more sheltered **Playa Conejos**, whose land access is only by a steep path. Two to 3km further east, the road runs down to the coast again at **La Bocana**, at the mouth of the Río Copalita, where you'll find surfable waves and a couple of seafood *comedores*. Another long beach stretches to the east.

SNORKELING & DIVING

You can rent **snorkeling gear**, including a life jacket, at Santa Cruz harbor for M$75 a day. The best snorkeling is generally on the coral plates at Playa La Entrega and Bahías Cacaluta and San Agustín. You can either hire a *lancha*

to take you to snorkel sites or take a tour with outfits such as those listed below.

The Huatulco bays have 13 main dive areas, with a good variety of fish and corals, as well as dolphins and sea turtles. This is a good place to learn to dive, with warm waters, fascinating marine scenery, no serious currents and calm conditions almost year-round. There's a decompression chamber in the local navy hospital. Two companies will take you diving and offer instruction:

Hurricane Divers (☎ 587-11-07; www.hurricanedivers .com) Santa Cruz (Map p779; Playa Santa Cruz; ☷ 9am-6pm Mon-Fri, 9am-4pm Sun); Tangolunda (Plaza Punta Tangolunda; ☷ 9am-3pm Mon-Sat) The very professional international crew here speak English, Spanish, Dutch and German, and offer a variety of courses and dives. This is one of Mexico's few PADI Instructor Development Centers. Options include two-tank dives (US$95), night dives (US$70) and the Discover Scuba beginners' course (US$135 for about six hours over two days). But Hurricane's most popular outing is a full-day excursion for US$120 per person (minimum: two) with snorkeling in at least two bays and a picnic – or US$155 with up to two dives.
Centro de Buceo Sotavento (www.tomzap.com/sota vento.html; scubasota@hotmail.com) La Crucecita

(Map p778; ☎ 587-21-66; Local 18, Plaza Oaxaca Mall, Plaza Principal; ☷ 9am-9pm); Tangolunda (☎ 581-00-51; Local 6, Plaza Las Conchas; ☷ 10am-5pm Mon-Sat) This friendly local company offers a range of options from a four-hour introduction (M$750) to full certification (five days; M$3850) or specialty night dives (M$750). One-/two-tank dives are M$550/850. Sotavento also does four-hour snorkeling trips for M$200 per person (minimum two people).

OTHER ACTIVITIES

The Copalita and Zimatán Rivers near Bahías de Huatulco have waters ranging from Class 1 to Class 5 in rafting terms. They're at their biggest between July and November. The well-established **Rancho Tangolunda** (☎ 587-21-26; www.ranchotangolunda.com; Local 5, Plaza Punta Tangolunda, Blvd Juárez, Tangolunda) not only takes you rafting on the Copalita but also offers river and sea kayaking, horseback riding, climbing, rappelling, a 300m zip-line, walking and bike tours, canyoneering and bird-watching. Most activities cost M$250 to M$400 per person, though the more challenging rafting and kayaking options are M$600 to M$700. The *rancho* is about 1km inland near the Río Copalita at the east end of Bahías area.

Rancho Caballo de Mar (☎ 587-05-30), based at Playa Punta Arena, takes 3½-hour beach and forest rides for around M$350 (reservations are advisable; riding experience isn't necessary). English and French are spoken.

Tangolunda has an 18-hole **golf course** (☎ 581-00-37).

Sleeping

You'll find all the budget and most of the midrange options in La Crucecita, with further midrange possibilities in Santa Cruz and Chahué. The top-end resort hotels are at Tangolunda. Midrange and top-end places tend to raise their rates at peak seasons – a couple of weeks around Christmas–New Year and Easter, and often a month or so in summer, typically mid-July to mid-August.

BUDGET

Hotel Posada Leo (Map p778; ☎ 587-26-01; www .posadaleo.com; Av Bugambilia 302, La Crucecita; s/d with fan M$200/250, air-com M$250/300; ☒) A friendly little budget spot, with half a dozen smallish but neat and well kept rooms, all with hot-water bathrooms.

Hotel Jaroje (Map p778; ☎ 587-27-14; www.hotel huatulco.com.mx; Av Bugambilia 304, La Crucecita; s/d

M$250/300; ☒) Bright, centrally located Jaroje has large, white, clean rooms with mosquito screens, air-con, fans, cable TV and fine bathrooms – a very good value.

Hotel Arrecife (Map p778; ☎ 587-17-07, 800-7177771; www.hotelarrecife.com.mx; Colorín 510, La Crucecita; s from M$200, d with fan/air-con M$350/400; ℗ ☒ ☐ ☒) In a quiet, leafy neighborhood, the Arrecife has a nice little pool with a café. Most of the 24 good, clean rooms are sizable, with pleasing decor, white tile floors, balcony, air-con and cable TV; a few at the side lack air-con but are still attractive, with a king-size and a double bed on two levels.

MIDRANGE

Hotel Arenas del Pacífico (Map p778; ☎ 583-49-89, 800-7177771; www.arenasdelpacifico.com.mx; Colorín 507, La Crucecita; r M$400-450; ℗ ☒ ☐ ☒) Opposite Hotel Arrecife and under the same ownership, the Arenas del Pacífico has a larger pool area with a couple of kids' slides, and all its rooms are air-con, with balconies, writing desk and pleasing blue-tiled bathrooms.

Misión de los Arcos (Map p778; ☎ 587-01-65; www .misiondelosarcos.com; Gardenia 902, La Crucecita; r M$450-500; ☒ ☐) This well-run, welcoming, American-owned hotel is embellished by a touch of colonial style and interior greenery. It has big, bright, comfortable, air-conditioned rooms, most with balcony, and walk-through access to Terra-Cotta restaurant, under the same ownership. There's wi-fi throughout.

Hotel Suites Begonias (Map p778; ☎ 587-03-90; www.hotelbegonias.com; Av Bugambilia 503, La Crucecita; r M$450-500, tr or q M$500-600; ☒) The rooms here are bright and attractive with good wooden furniture, not to mention some highly artistic towel-folding. All are air-conditioned and have cable TV and one double or king-size bed.

Hotel María Mixteca (Map p778; ☎ 587-23-36; www .travelbymexico.com/oaxa/mariamixteca; Guamuchil 204, La Crucecita; s/d/tr M$450/490/530; ℗ ☒) Small and only a few years old, the María Mixteca offers 14 prettily decorated, yellow-and-white rooms on two upper floors, with super-comfy beds, air-conditioning, great bathrooms, cable TV, room safes and wi-fi access.

Hotel Flamboyant (Map p778; ☎ 587-01-13; www .hotelesfarrera.com; Plaza Principal, La Crucecita; r incl breakfast M$550; ℗ ☒ ☒) This yellow downtown hotel has a pleasant courtyard, attractive pool, its own restaurant and 70 good-sized rooms. Decor is Oaxacan folksy. Rates can double, or more, at peak seasons.

Hotel Posada Edén Costa (☎ 587-24-80; www.eden costa.com; Calle Zapoteco s/n, Chahué; r M$600, ste with salon & kitchen M$1000; P 🅿 🖵 🖫) Swiss- and Laotian-owned Edén Costa, a block inland from Bahía Chahué, has quiet and attractive rooms with nice touches including colorful murals. Rooms have two double beds, and most overlook the small central pool. The attached restaurant, L'échalote (right), is a big bonus.

Hotel Castillo Huatulco (Map p779; ☎ 587-01-44, 800-543-90-40; www.hotelcastillohuatulco.com; Blvd Santa Cruz 303, Santa Cruz; r M$932, s/d full board M$1200/1800; P 🅿 🖫) Colonial-style Castillo Huatulco has an attractive pool in its central garden, a restaurant and 113 good-sized, brightly decorated rooms with safes. Transportation to the hotel's beach club on Bahía Chahué is free.

TOP END

Air and lodging packages are your best bet for a good-value holiday in a top-end Huatulco hotel. Another way to save is to look for promotions on hotel websites.

Casa del Mar (☎ 581-02-03, 800-9081142; ventas@ casadelmaroaxaca.com; Balcones de Tangolunda 13, Tangolunda; ste incl breakfast from M$1534; P 🅿 🖵 🖫) Elegant and sensationally sited Casa del Mar, east of Tangolunda's main hotel cluster, has 22 well-appointed suites with great views, and a beautiful pool and restaurant. It often fills up with Mexican families at holiday times.

ourpick Camino Real Zaashila (☎ 583-03-00, 800-9012300; www.caminoreal.com/zaashila; Blvd Juárez 5, Tangolunda; r incl breakfast from M$2200; P 🅿 🖵 🖫 🖫) Toward the east end of Tangolunda, this attractively landscaped, modern-hacienda–style property has a fabulously enormous pool in lovely gardens. There are 148 rooms, most with sea view; 41 come with their own small pool.

Quinta Real (☎ 581-04-28, 800-4005000; www .quintareal.com; Blvd Juárez 2, Tangolunda; ste from US$270; P 🅿 🖵 🖫 🖫) The utterly gorgeous, Moorish-inspired Quinta Real has a hilltop position at the west end of Tangolunda. Its 28 suites all have Jacuzzis, marble bathrooms and ocean views; some have fountain fed private pools that seem to spill down the hillside to the beach and main swimming-pool area.

Eating

LA CRUCECITA

Comedores (Map p778; Mercado, cnr Av Bugambilia & Guanacaste; fish or shrimp platters M$60-80) The very clean *comedores* in La Crucecita's market serve up good, well-priced food, including egg dishes for M$30 and *enfrijoladas* (tortillas smothered in beans, with a sprinkling of cheese) for M$40.

Restaurant La Crucecita (Map p778; ☎ 587-09-06; Av Bugambilia 501; mains M$40-90; 🕑 7:30am-10pm) This inexpensive open-air spot, a block from the plaza, is dependable for fish, chicken and Oaxacan dishes. There's an economical M$40 *menú del día*. Early in the day, watch the chef prepare serious quantities of *salsa roja*.

Iguana Bar (Map p778; ☎ 587-00-70; Plaza Principal; mains M$45-120; 🕑 8am-12:30am) Beneath the classy Restaurante Onix, Iguana is a sound bet for reasonably priced breakfasts and tacos and other Mexican standards.

El Patio (Map p778; ☎ 587-02-11; Flamboyán 214; breakfast M$30-60, mains M$50-130) A appealing garden patio with tables out the back welcomes you here. The breakfasts are good deals; the rest of the day you're offered the usual range of seafood, chicken dishes and Oaxacan specialties, as well as a full selection of alcoholic drinks.

ourpick Terra-Cotta (Map p778; ☎ 587-12-28; Gardenia 902; breakfasts M$40-65, mains M$50-140; 🕑 7:30am-11:30pm) Popular, American-run Terra-Cotta has sidewalk tables as well as a soothing air-con interior. Good service complements the excellent food: breakfasts, shrimp, steaks, *antojitos*, waffles, baguettes and ice cream all go down easy. Breakfast coffee comes with free refills, and there's free wi-fi too.

Restaurante Onix (Map p778; ☎ 587-05-20; Plaza Principal; mains M$75-215; 🕑 2-11pm) Definitely the finest eating in La Crucecita, this airy upstairs locale overlooking the plaza offers very well prepared Mexican and European dishes. Try the mussels with ham and cheese or the *sopa de tortilla*, followed by steak or tuna *al chipotle* (in a fermented-chili sauce).

CHAHUÉ & TANGOLUNDA

ourpick L'échalote (☎ 587-24-80; www.edencosta.com; Hotel Posada Edén Costa, Calle Zapoteco s/n, Chahué; mains M$80-150; 🕑 2-11pm Tue-Sun) The Swiss–French chef prepares very tasty French, southeast Asian, Oaxacan and other dishes. The Thai salad with prawns and bean sprouts is delicious. Main dishes range over fish, steaks and the house-specialty fondues, and the desserts aren't too shabby either.

La Bohème (☎ 587-22-50; Paseo Chahué 5, Sector M; mains M$100-250; ☟ 2-11pm Wed-Mon) La Bohème has some of the highest prices in Huatulco but also some of the best food. The French owner-chef prepares almost exclusively French fare, from snails, mussels or duck foie gras to the rich coq au vin and yummy crepes and profiteroles. Add the elegant setting, friendly welcome and good service, and you'll be glad you found its slightly out-of-the-way location.

Tangolunda's big hotels offer a choice of expensive bars, coffee shops and restaurants. You won't go wrong at the Camino Real Zaashila's **Restaurant Chez-Binni** (☎ 583-03-00; mains M$100-200; ☟ 6-11pm), which specializes in grills and Oaxacan dishes.

BEACHES

There are decent seafood *palapas* at Playas La Entrega, Maguey, San Agustín and La Bocana. A whole grilled *huachinango* (red snapper) costs M$60 to M$100.

Drinking

Paletería Zamora (Map p778; cnr Flamboyán & Av Bugambilia, La Crucecita; drinks M$10-40; ☟ 9am-11pm) Thirst-zapping Zamora blends up a full range of cooling fresh fruit drinks, *licuados* and *aguas frescas* (fruit blended with water and sweetener).

Café Dublin (Map p778; Carrizal 502, La Crucecita; ☟ 6pm-last customer) This popular little Irish bar proffers darts, sports on TV and lots of drinks including Guinness in cans.

La Crema (Map p778; ☎ 587-07-02; Gardenia 311, La Crucecita; ☟ 7pm-2am) Spacious but dark, this quirky, hippie- and rock-themed den, overlooking the Plaza Principal, has a good music mix, the best cocktail list in town, and delicious wood-oven pizza.

Entertainment

La Peña (Map p778; Flamboyán 210, La Crucecita; ☟ from 8pm Tue-Sat) The live Latin bands at this open-to-the-street spot can whip up a good party vibe; the back room has pool tables for quieter moments.

Tipsy Blowfish (Map p778; ☎ 587-28-44; Flamboyán 304, La Crucecita) There's often decent live rock at this friendly Texan-run bar on the Plaza Principal.

La Papaya (☎ 583-94-11; Blvd Juárez, Chahué; admission M$110; ☟ 10pm-5am Thu-Sat, daily in high season) Huatulco's hottest disco attracts mostly an 18-to-25 age group. Dancing on the bar, an aquarium with bikini-clad humans and mud-wrestling help warm up the atmosphere.

Getting There & Away

AIR

Mexicana and its subsidiary Click Mexicana offer three flights daily to/from Mexico City. Magnicharters flies most days to/from Mexico City. Aerotucán and Aerovega fly small planes daily to/from Oaxaca, though Aerovega goes only with a minimum of three passengers.

See p734 for more on these flights. **Continental** (☎ 800-900-50-00) flies direct from Houston, Texas, up to five times a week, and cheap charters from Canada, the US and the UK are sometimes available.

Airline offices:

Aerotucán Airport (☎ 587-60-66); La Crucecita (Map p778; ☎ 587-24-27; Plaza Carmelinas, Blvd Chahué; ☟ 8am-2pm & 4:30-8pm Mon-Sat)

Magnicharters (Map p779; ☎ 581-05-12; Blvd Santa Cruz)

Mexicana and **Click Mexicana** Airport (☎ 581-90-07); Chahué (☎ 587-02-23; Plaza Chahué, Blvd Juárez; ☟ 9am-5:45pm Mon-Sat)

Destination	Fare	Duration	Frequency (daily)
Acapulco	M$307	10hr	8 from EB terminal
Mexico City (Terminal Sur)	M$525-730	14hr	3 from EB terminal
Oaxaca (via Salina Cruz)	M$230-270	7-8½hr	4 from OCC terminal
Pochutla	M$26-30	1hr	9 from EB terminal
	M$18-30	1hr	31 from OCC terminal
	M$16	1hr	Transportes Rápidos de Pochutla every 15 min, 6am-8:30pm
Puerto Escondido	M$69-82	2½hr	9 from EB terminal
	M$35-76	2½hr	31 from OCC terminal 8:30pm
San Cristóbal de Las Casas	M$326	9½-10½hr	OCC, 8:30 & 11:50pm 8:30pm
Tapachula	M$352	12hr	OCC, 7:50pm
Tehuantepec	M$76-100	3½hr	10 from OCC terminal
Tuxtla Gutiérrez	M$276	8-9½hr	OCC, 8:30 & 11:50pm

BUS

Some buses coming to Huatulco are marked 'Santa Cruz Huatulco,' but they still terminate in La Crucecita. Make sure your bus is not headed to Santa María Huatulco, which is a long way inland.

The **OCC bus station** (Map p778; ☎ 587-02-61; Blvd Chahué) is on the north edge of La Crucecita. As well as 1st-class OCC buses, this is the terminal for ADO GL (deluxe) and Sur (2nd class). **Estrella Blanca** (EB; off Map p778; ☎ 587-23-30; Av Carpinteros s/n, Sector V), a further 700m from the center, has further 1st-class and deluxe services. First-class **Turistar** (☎ 587-06-82) also leaves from the EB station.

Transportes Rápidos de Pochutla runs small buses to Pochutla from a stop on Blvd Chahué opposite the north end of Av Bugambilia (Map p778).

CAR

Europcar (www.europcar.com.mx) Airport (☎ 581-90-94; ⏲ 11am-5pm); La Crucecita (Map p778; ☎ 583-47-51; Plaza Carmelinas, Blvd Chahué; ⏲ 8am-1pm & 4-7pm) Recommended for reasonable rates (from M$600 per day) and efficient service.

Hertz (www.hertz.com) Airport (☎ 581-90-92; ⏲ 24hr); Tangolunda (☎ 581-05-88; Crown Pacific Hotel, Blvd Juárez 8; ⏲ 9am-2pm & 4-6pm) Also dependable.

Getting Around

TO/FROM THE AIRPORT

Transportación Terrestre (☎ 581-90-14) provides *colectivo* combis for M$87 per person from the airport to La Crucecita, Santa Cruz or Bahía Chahué and for M$102 to Tangolunda. Get tickets at their airport kiosk. You may be able to pick up a whole cab just outside the airport gate for about M$100 to La Crucecita or Santa Cruz, M$120 to Tangolunda or M$150 to Pochutla. An even cheaper option is to walk 400m down to Hwy 200 and catch a bus for M$7 to La Crucecita or M$15 to Pochutla. Buses heading to La Crucecita may be marked 'Santa Cruz' or 'Bahías Huatulco' or something similar.

TAXI

Taxis provide the only transportation between La Crucecita, Santa Cruz Huatulco and Tangolunda. Rates are posted at the taxi stand on Plaza Principal in La Crucecita, from where you pay M$15 to Santa Cruz, M$25 to Tangolunda and M$45 to Bahía Maguey. By the hour, cabs cost M$150.

Taxis operating on a *colectivo* basis wait outside Plaza Madero mall on Guamuchil in La Crucecita, but they're not very frequent. They charge M$3 per person to Santa Cruz and M$5 to Tangolunda.

BARRA DE LA CRUZ
☎ 958 / pop 750

This well cared-for Chontal village, about 20km east of Huatulco, is famed for its surf but is also a relaxed and friendly place for anyone to chill out for a day or two. The right-hand point break, off the beach 1.5km from the village, gets up to a double overhead and is long and fast. Good swells for experienced surfers are frequent from March to October and generally at their best in June and July. Barra's surf was unknown to the outside world until the mid-1990s, but the word has been well and truly out since the world's top pro surfers assembled here for the Rip Curl Search event in the 2006 Men's World Tour.

A lack of undertow also makes for good swimming. Barra's beach has showers, toilets and a community-run *comedor* with hammocks and shade. The municipality charges M$20 per person to pass along the road to the beach and imposes an 8pm curfew. The fee goes to help maintain the road and keep the beach clean. You can rent surfboards at El Chontal restaurant beside the toll gate for M$100 per day.

Cabañas Pepe (per person M$80), behind El Chontal, has well-built wood-and-palm-thatch cabins with hammocks out front and shared Western-style toilets and showers. Also good is **Barradise** (pablo_rafting@yahoo.com; per person M$80), a couple of hundred meters before El Chontal as you come into Barra, which has four fan-cooled rooms with private bathroom. Barradise is ably run by English-speaking Pablo Narváez, who also gives surf classes (around M$450 for three or four hours) and leads local bird-watching tours. It was Pablo who first brought international surfers to Barra in the 1990s. He sees Barra's surf fame as an opportunity to develop village living standards and social conditions.

El Chontal (mains M$25-50) serves good Mexican standards and is one of several places to eat.

Getting There & Around

Barra de la Cruz is reached via a 2.5km road that heads coastward from Hwy 200 east of the Puente Zimatán bridge. *Colectivo* taxis run to Barra (M$20, 40 minutes) about every half-hour until 7pm from the park just east of the OCC bus station in La Crucecita. A private taxi costs around M$140. Taxis will run you from Barra village to the beach or the highway turnoff for M$30 if you don't want to walk.

ISTHMUS OF TEHUANTEPEC

The southern half of the 200km-wide Isthmus of Tehuantepec (teh-wahn-teh-*pek*), Mexico's narrow waist, forms the eastern end of Oaxaca state. This is hot, flat country and, if you have come down from Oaxaca city, it's a stark reminder that you are well inside the tropics. Indigenous Zapotec culture is strong here, with its own regional twists. In 1496 the isthmus Zapotecs repulsed the Aztecs from the fortress of Guiengola, near Tehuantepec, and the isthmus never became part of the Aztec empire. An independent spirit continues to pervade the region to this day.

If you stay around, you'll encounter a lively, friendly populace, whose open and confident women take leading roles in business and government. Isthmus people let loose their love of music, dancing and partying in numerous annual *velas* (fiestas) lasting several days. If you're here for one of these occasions, you will see women displaying wonderfully worked, highly colorful *huipiles*, gold and silver jewelry, skirts embroidered with fantastic silk flowers, and odd headgear. Many isthmus fiestas feature the *tirada de frutas*, in which women climb on roofs and throw fruit on the men below!

A new toll road, Hwy 185D, bypasses the three main isthmus towns – Salina Cruz, Tehuantepec and Juchitán – and intersects Hwy 190 just west of Tehuantepec. Isthmus culture is stronger in Tehuantepec and Juchitán than in Salina Cruz, which is dominated by its oil refinery. All three towns can be pretty uncomfortable in the heat of the day, but come the evening breezes they take on a more agreeable air. Around La Ventosa, 15km northeast of Juchitán, strong north winds blow, sometimes toppling high vehicles.

TEHUANTEPEC
☎ 971 / pop 37,000
Tehuantepec is a friendly town, 245km from Oaxaca city. June and August are the main months for partying in the fiestas of the 15 *barrios* (neighborhoods), each of which has its own church.

Orientation
Tehuantepec's OCC/ADO bus station, known as La Terminal, is by Hwy 185 on the northern edge of town. To walk to the central plaza from here, head to the left along Av Héroes outside OCC/ADO for 600m until it ends at a T-junction, then turn right along Guerrero. Take the fifth street to the left, Hidalgo, and walk two blocks to the plaza. The Palacio Municipal stands on the south side of the plaza.

Information
Bancomer (⏰ 8:30am-4pm Mon-Fri) and **Banorte** (⏰ 9am-4pm Mon-Fri), both on Calle 5 de Mayo a few steps west of the Palacio Municipal, have ATMs and change cash US dollars.
Cyberweb Grandalf (Romero 64; internet per hr M$10; ⏰ 8am-10pm Mon-Sat, 9am-9pm Sun) Just past Hotel Oasis.
Tourist Information Office (Hwy 185; ⏰ 8am-4pm Mon-Fri, 9am-2pm Sat) Two blocks west from the Palacio Municipal along Calle 5 de Mayo, then 70m south on the highway; they don't see many foreigners here but they are knowledgeable about the area.

Sights
EX-CONVENTO REY COSIJOPÍ
This former Dominican monastery, north of the plaza on a short street off Guerrero, is Tehuantepec's **Casa de la Cultura** (Callejón Rey Cosijopí; admission free; ⏰ 9am-2pm & 5-8pm Mon-Fri, 9am-2pm Sat). It bears traces of old frescos and has modest but interesting exhibits of traditional dress, archaeological finds, historical photos, religious regalia and the like. You may need to ask for some of the rooms to be opened. The last Zapotec king, Cosijopí, provided the funds for its construction in the 16th century, at the urging of Hernán Cortés.

GUIENGOLA
This old hillside **Zapotec stronghold** (admission free; ⏰ 8am-5pm), where King Cosijoeza rebuffed the Aztecs in 1496, is north of Hwy 190 from a turnoff 11km out of Tehuantepec. A sign at

Puente Las Tejas bridge, just past the Km 240 marker, points to 'Ruinas Guiengola.' The unpaved 7km road in is passable in dry weather, though the last kilometer or so (heading uphill) requires a high-clearance vehicle. The road ends at a signed trailhead, and about an hour's sweaty walk uphill through tropical woodland gets you to the remains of two pyramids, a ball court, a 64-room complex and a thick defensive wall. Many more unexposed remains lie overgrown by the surrounding forest. You'll also see interesting limestone formations and some fine views over the isthmus.

Víctor Velázquez Guzmán (☎ 971-1110768 or contact him through Tehuantepec tourist office) guides small groups to Guiengola from Tehuantepec for M$600 per group (M$350 if you have your own vehicle). Víctor will speak Spanish, but he has printed explanatory material in English.

MARKET

Tehuantepec's dim, almost medieval, indoor market is open daily on the west side of the plaza. It spills out into the surrounding streets, where flowers are often for sale.

Sleeping

Hotel Oasis (☎ 715-00-08; h.oasis@hotmail.com; Ocampo 8; s/d/tr with fan M$150/190/270, r with air-con & cable TV M$400; P) The good-value Oasis is a block south of the plaza, and most of its 28 rooms have been recently renovated in attractive yellows and oranges.

Hotel Calli (☎ 715-00-85; www.hotelcalli.com; Carretera Cristóbal Colón Km 790; r M$800, ste M$1300; P) Tehuantepec's best lodgings are beside Hwy 185 about 700m toward Juchitán from La Terminal. The Calli's 100 good-size modern rooms, in pleasing blues and yellows, all boast cable TV, wi-fi access, phone, air-con and small balconies. The ample common areas include a restaurant, a good, partly palm-shaded pool and colorful lobby murals.

Eating

Restaurante Bar Scarú (☎ 715-06-46; Callejón Leona Vicario 4; mains M$50-130; 8am-10:30pm) Two short blocks east and 30m north of Hotel Donají, friendly Scarú occupies an 18th-century house with a courtyard and colorful modern murals of Tehuantepec life. Sit beneath a fan, quaff a *limonada* and sample one of the many varied dishes on offer. At weekends old-timers plunk out marimba tunes.

At night the entire east side of the plaza is lined with tables and chairs beside carts serving cheap tacos and other delights.

Getting There & Away

OCC and ADO (both 1st class) share La Terminal with ADO GL (deluxe) and Sur and AU (both 2nd class). Daily departures (some are *de paso*) include these:

Destination	Fare	Duration	Frequency (daily)
Bahías de Huatulco	1st-class M$100	3½hr	3, 12:10-7:25am
	2nd-class M$76	3½hr	5
Mexico City	deluxe M$684 (TAPO III Terminal Sur)	11hr	3, 6:40-9:30pm
	1st-class M$578	11½hr	4, 7:45-9:55pm
	2nd-class M$512	13hr	3, 5:35-9:05pm
Oaxaca	1st-class M$152	4¼hr	14
Pochutla	1st-class M$128	4½hr	3, 12:10-7:25am
Puerto Escondido	1st-class M$170	6hr	3, 12:10-7:25am
	2nd-class M$132 M$76	6½hr	1 (3pm)
Tapachula	M$250	9hr	1st-class, 11:50pm
Tuxtla Gutiérrez	1st-class M$180	4½- 5½hr	4
Villahermosa	1st-class M$286	7½hr	4

Buses to Juchitán (M$15, 30 minutes) depart across the street from OCC at least every half-hour during daylight.

Getting Around

Taxis between La Terminal and the plaza cost M$15. A unique local transportation option is the *motocarro*, where passengers sit (or stand, to better catch the breeze) on a platform behind the driver. The sight of colorfully garbed women riding tall will linger in your memory.

JUCHITÁN

☎ 971 / pop 69,000

Istmeño culture is strong in this friendly town, which is visited by few gringos. About 30 different neighborhood festivals *(velas)* almost fill the calendar with music, dancing, drinking, eating and fun from mid-April to early September, above all in May. Juchitán is also famed for its *muxes* – the town's openly gay, frequently cross-dressing, men, who are fully accepted in local society and hold their own *vela* in November.

Orientation

Prolongación 16 de Septiembre heads toward the town center from a busy intersection with traffic signals on the north edge of town. The main bus terminal is 100m toward town from this intersection. Past the bus station the street curves left, then right, then divides into 5 de Septiembre (right fork, for southbound traffic) and 16 de Septiembre (left fork, northbound). These two emerge as opposite sides of the central plaza, Jardín Juárez, after seven blocks.

Sights

Jardín Juárez is a lively central square. In the busy two-story market on its east side you'll find locally made hammocks, Isthmus women's costumes, and maybe iguana on the menus of the *comedores*.

Juchitán's **Lidxi Guendabiaani** (Casa de la Cultura; ☎ 711-32-08; Belisario Domínguez; admission free; ☉ 9am-2pm & 4-7pm Mon-Fri, 9am-1pm Sat) is by the San Vicente Ferrer church a block south and west of Jardín Juárez, set around a big patio that buzzes with children. It has a gallery, where there is usually interesting exhibition on, and a small archaeological museum.

Sleeping & Eating

Hotel Don Alex (☎ /fax 711-10-64; 16 de Septiembre No 48; r M$350-400; ⊠) Just 1½ blocks north of Jardín Juárez, the Don Alex has medium-sized rooms, with small touches of art, but they can be a bit airless. All are air-conditioned but only the M$400 ones have hot water or a phone.

Hotel López Lena Palace (☎ 711-13-88; hotellopezlena@hotmail.com; 16 de Septiembre 70; s M$290-384, d/tr/q M$480/600/680; P ⊠ ⌨) Look for the mock Arabic exterior about halfway between the town center and bus station. The Lena's rooms are cheerful with good air-con and cable TV; the best value are the windowless but homey 'minis,' with excellent showers.

Café Jamaica (☎ 712-18-36; 16 de Septiembre s/n; items M$12-40; ☉ 8am-10pm) A bright, clean place for drinks and light meals, from enchiladas to tortas and burgers, with an under-30s vibe and decor dedicated to Bob Marley, the US and the Yucatán Peninsula. It's just a couple of doors off Jardín Juárez.

Casagrande Restaurant (☎ 711-34-60; Jardín Juárez; mains M$65-150; ☉ 8am-10pm) The flashest eatery in town, serving a mix of Oaxacan and international dishes in a pleasant covered courtyard, with ceiling fans and hanging plants. It's on the south side of the plaza; the Casagrande cinema sign makes it easier to find.

Getting There & Away

UNO and ADO GL (deluxe), OCC and ADO (1st class) and Sur, AU and Ecobús (2nd-class) all use the main bus terminal on Prolongación 16 de Septiembre. Some buses here are *de paso*, and many depart between 11pm and 7am.

Destination	Fare	Duration	Frequency (daily)
Bahías de Huatulco	M$91-144	4hr	14
Mexico City (TAPO or Terminal Sur)	M$494-980	10½-12hr	15
Oaxaca	M$100-194	4½-6hr	24
Pochutla	M$122-149	5hr	10
San Cristóbal de Las Casas	M$216	5½-6¾hr	3, 12:15-3:55am
Tapachula	M$252-294	6-8½hr	3
Tehuantepec	M$15-24	30min	56
Tonalá	M$102-126	3-5hr	6
Tuxtla Gutiérrez	M$162-164	4-5½hr	6

Frequent 2nd-class Istmeños buses to Tehuantepec (M$15, 30 minutes) and Salina Cruz (M$25, one hour) stop at the next corner south from the main terminal on Prolongación 16 de Septiembre during daylight.

Getting Around

'Terminal-Centro' buses run between the bus station and Jardín Juárez. A taxi costs about M$15.

Tabasco & Chiapas

Mismatched siblings, the neighboring states of Tabasco and Chiapas are almost a study in contrasts. Smaller Tabasco – between central Mexico and the Yucatán Peninsula – is less diverse than Chiapas, and prone to flooding, as demonstrated by the catastrophic flood of October 2007. A largely flat, steamy, well-watered lowland, it has fewer visitors, but those who do drop in discover a place with fascinating pre-Hispanic heritage from the Olmec and Maya civilizations, a relaxed tropical lifestyle, an entertaining capital city in Villahermosa, and a unique environment of enormous rivers, endless wetlands and good beaches heading out into the Gulf of Mexico.

In Chiapas, pine forest highlands, wildlife-rich rainforest jungles and well-preserved colonial architecture highlight a region of incredible variety. Palenque and Yaxchilán are evocative vestiges of powerful Maya kingdoms, and the presence of modern Maya a constant reminder of the region's rich and uninterrupted history. The colonial hubs of San Cristóbal de Las Casasand Chiapa de Corzo give way to fertile plots of coffee and cacao in the Soconusco, and for outdoor adventurers, excursions to Laguna Miramar and the Cañón del Sumidero are unmissable.

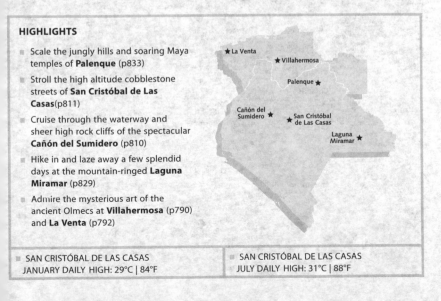

HIGHLIGHTS

- Scale the jungly hills and soaring Maya temples of **Palenque** (p833)
- Stroll the high altitude cobblestone streets of **San Cristóbal de Las Casas**(p811)
- Cruise through the waterway and sheer high rock cliffs of the spectacular **Cañón del Sumidero** (p810)
- Hike in and laze away a few splendid days at the mountain-ringed **Laguna Miramar** (p829)
- Admire the mysterious art of the ancient Olmecs at **Villahermosa** (p790) and **La Venta** (p792)

★ La Venta
★ Villahermosa
Palenque ★
Cañón del Sumidero ★
San Cristóbal ★ de Las Casas
Laguna ★ Miramar

■ SAN CRISTÓBAL DE LAS CASAS JANUARY DAILY HIGH: 29°C | 84°F	■ SAN CRISTÓBAL DE LAS CASAS JULY DAILY HIGH: 31°C | 88°F

TABASCO & CHIAPAS

History

Tabasco and Chiapas have hosted as rich a procession of cultures as anywhere in Mexico. It was at La Venta in western Tabasco that Mesoamerica's 'mother culture,' the Olmec, reached its greatest heights of development between about 800 and 400 BC, after first emerging in San Lorenzo, Veracruz. Olmec religion, art, astronomy and architecture deeply influenced all of Mexico's later civilizations.

Low-lying, jungle-covered eastern Chiapas gave rise to some of the most splendid and powerful city-states of another great civilization, the Maya, during the Classic period (approximately AD 250–900), places such as Palenque, Yaxchilán and Toniná. Dozens of lesser Maya powers – including Bonampak,

Comalcalco and Chinkultic – prospered in eastern Chiapas and Tabasco during this time, as Maya culture reached its peak of artistic and intellectual achievement. The ancestors of many of the distinctive indigenous groups of highland Chiapas today appear to have migrated to that region from the lowlands after the Classic Maya collapse around AD 900.

Pre-Hispanic Tabasco was the prosperous nexus of a far-reaching trade network extending round the Yucatán coast to Honduras, up the rivers to the jungles and mountains of Guatemala, and westward to highland central Mexico. And it was near Frontera, Tabasco, in 1519 that Hernán Cortés and his conquistadors fought their first battle against native Mexicans, afterwards founding a set-

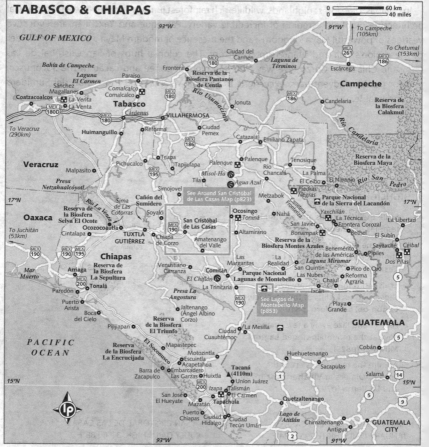

tlement called Santa María de la Victoria. In 1641, Santa María was moved inland to escape pirate attacks, and renamed Villahermosa de San Juan Bautista. However, Tabasco remained an impoverished backwater until recent decades; now the development of its mineral riches, particularly petroleum, has brought widespread prosperity.

Central Chiapas was brought under Spanish control by the 1528 expedition of Diego de Mazariegos, and outlying areas were subdued in the 1530s and '40s, though Spain never gained full control of the Lacandón Jungle. New diseases arrived with the Spaniards, and an epidemic in 1544 killed about half Chiapas' indigenous population. Chiapas was ineffectively administered from Guatemala for most of the colonial era, with little check on the colonists' excesses against its indigenous people, though some church figures, particularly Bartolomé de Las Casas (1474– 1566), the first bishop of Chiapas, did fight for indigenous rights.

In 1822, a newly independent Mexico unsuccessfully attempted to annex Spain's former Central American provinces (including Chiapas), but in 1824 Chiapas opted (by a referendum) to join Mexico, rather than the United Provinces of Central America. From then on, a succession of governors appointed by Mexico City, along with local landowners, maintained an almost feudal control over Chiapas. Periodic uprisings bore witness to bad government, but the world took little notice until January 1, 1994, when Zapatista rebels suddenly and briefly occupied San Cristóbal de Las Casas and nearby towns by military force. The rebel movement, with a firm and committed support base among disenchanted indigenous settlers in eastern Chiapas, quickly retreated to remote jungle bases to campaign for democratic change and indigenous rights. The Zapatistas have failed to win any significant concessions at the national level (see boxed text, p826), although increased government funding steered toward Chiapas did result in noticeable improvements in the state's infrastructure, development of tourist facilities and a growing urban middle class.

Climate

The rainy season is between May and October, with the heaviest rainfall mostly in June, September and early October. During the rainy season the days often start dry and fairly bright, and there's usually a heavy downfall in the afternoon. Tabasco receives particularly heavy rainfall (about 1500mm annually).

Between November and April, warm sunny days are the norm. The hottest months are April and May, when the fields turn a dusty brown before the onset of the rains.

Temperatures in Tabasco and Chiapas don't vary much according to the season – altitude is a much more influential factor. All lowland areas (most of Tabasco, the Lacandón Jungle, Palenque, the Usumacinta area and the Pacific coast) are hot and sticky all year, with punishing humidity and daily highs above 30°C. In the more elevated center of the region, the climate is less enervating.

Parks & Reserves

Several large areas have been declared biosphere reserves in an effort to combine conservation with sustainable human use. Vital wetlands are protected by Tabasco's Reserva de la Biosfera Pantanos de Centla (p802) and the Reserva de la Biosfera La Encrucijada (p856) in Chiapas. The Reserva de la Biosfera Montes Azules (p829) and the Reserva de la Biosfera Lacan-tun (see p844) in eastern Chiapas battle to preserve what's left of the Lacandón Jungle, while the Reserva de la Biosfera El Triunfo (p854) includes rare cloud forests. There are also three national parks here: Cañón del Sumidero (p810), Lagos de Montebello (p852) and Palenque (p833).

Dangers & Annoyances

Drug trafficking and illicit northbound immigration are concerns along the border regions with Guatemala, and military checkpoints are frequent from the Carretera Fronteriza along the Guatemalan border from Palenque to the Lagos de Montebello. These checkpoints generally increase security for travelers, though it's best to be off the Carretera Fronteriza before dark. For similar reasons the border crossings with Guatemala near Tapachula are places you should aim to get through early in the day.

Indigenous villages are often extremely close-knit, and their people can be suspicious of outsiders and particularly sensitive about having their photos taken. In some villages cameras are, at best, tolerated – and sometimes not even that. You may put yourself in physical danger by taking photos without permission. If in any doubt at all, ask first.

There have been no Zapatista-related incidents affecting travelers for some time, though occasional flare-ups occur between Zapatista communities and the army or anti-Zapatista paramilitaries. If you plan to travel off the main roads in the Chiapas highlands, the Ocosingo area and far eastern Chiapas, take local advice about where to avoid going. Unknown outsiders might also be at risk in these areas because of local political or religious conflicts. Travelers to Villahermosa and coastal Tabasco should note the region is subject to seasonal floods. In 2007, catastrophic damage occurred (see boxed text, right) and some areas are still recovering.

Getting There & Around

A toll autopista (expressway) between Coatzacoalcos (Veracruz state) and Ocozocoautla (Chiapas) translates to an average 10-hour driving time from Mexico City to Tuxtla Gutiérrez (the Chiapas state capital), and a new autopista between Ocozocoautla and Arriaga on Chiapas' coastal plain is currently being built.

A fast new toll autopista now flies between Tuxtla Gutiérrez and San Cristóbal de Las Casas, joining the Pan-American Hwy (190) to enter Guatemala at Ciudad Cuauhtémoc/La Mesilla (p854), 84km from Huehuetenango, Guatemala. The other main route to Guatemala is Hwy 200 along Chiapas' coastal plain, leading to two border crossings near the city of Tapachula (p861). It's also possible to cross direct into Guatemala's northern Petén region, using boat services on the Río Usumacinta (Frontera Corozal to Bethel; p845) or Río San Pedro (El Ceibo to El Naranjo; p803).

The airports at Villahermosa (p796), Tuxtla Gutiérrez (p808) and Tapachula (p859) all have direct daily flights to and from Mexico City.

Bus links within the region and to other states are very good; for regional routes, minibuses, combis and colectivo taxis often offer a speedier (though less spacious) alternative.

TABASCO

They say that Tabasco has more water than land, and looking at all the lagoons, rivers and wetlands on the map you can certainly believe that's true – at least during the rainy season. It's always hot and sweaty here, marginally less so when you catch a breeze along the Gulf of Mexico or if you venture into the southern hills. Few travelers linger in Tabasco longer than it takes to see the outstanding Olmec stone sculpture in Villahermosa's Parque-Museo La Venta, but it can be a very rewarding slice of the real Mexico, with few other tourists, some intriguing pre-Hispanic sites (both the Olmecs and the Maya flourished here), a large and lively capital city, a beautiful natural environment and a relaxed populace with an insatiable love for música tropical. Thanks to onshore and offshore oil exploitation by Mexico's state oil company (Pemex), Tabasco has emerged from poverty to become one of Mexico's more prosperous states.

In late October and early November 2007, prolonged heavy rainfall led to major floods here, submerging a whopping 80% of the state. The federal government quickly mobilized food distribution and emergency shelters, and relief donation centers sprouted up nationwide, as people pitched in to head off the humanitarian crisis. Though the floodwaters have receded, full economic recovery is expected to take years. By early 2008, most infrastructure, attractions and travelers' services were already up and running.

VILLAHERMOSA
☎ 993 / pop 673,000
This sprawling, flat, hot and humid city, with over a quarter of Tabasco's population, was never the 'beautiful town' its name implies, but it takes advantage of its position on the winding Río Grijalva, with a welcome river-

---

TABASCO FLOODS OF 2007

Due to the severe flooding that hit the state of Tabasco during the time of this book's research, making all routes nearly impassable, our author could not access the state. Our research for this section consisted of personal contacts by phone and internet, and input from local citizens and fellow travelers. At the time this book went to press, the state was still in recovery. While we've tried our best to ensure the text is current and useful to travelers, some of these listings may be out of date.

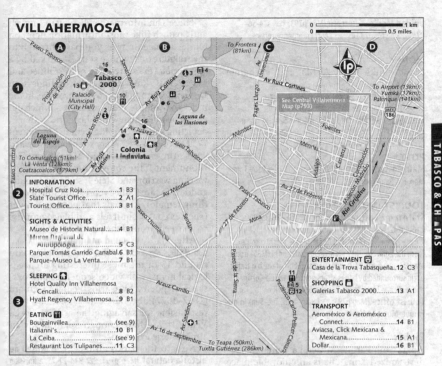

VILLAHERMOSA

0 ———————— 1 km
0 ———————— 0.5 miles

INFORMATION
Hospital Cruz Roja...................1 B3
State Tourist Office..................2 A1
Tourist Office.........................3 B1

SIGHTS & ACTIVITIES
Museo de Historia Natural........4 B1
Museo Regional de
Antropología......................5 C3
Parque Tomás Garrido Canabal.6 B1
Parque-Museo La Venta..........7 B1

SLEEPING
Hotel Quality Inn Villahermosa
Cencali..............................8 B2
Hyatt Regency Villahermosa....9 B1

EATING
Bougainvillea...................(see 9)
Italianni's........................10 B1
La Ceiba..........................(see 9)
Restaurant Los Tulipanes......11 C3

ENTERTAINMENT
Casa de la Trova Tabasqueña..12 C3

SHOPPING
Galerías Tabasco 2000...........13 A1

TRANSPORT
Aeroméxico & Aeroméxico
Connect............................14 B1
Aviacsa, Click Mexicana &
Mexicana..........................15 A1
Dollar..............................16 B1

TABASCO & CHIAPAS

---

side leisure development a couple of blocks from the pedestrianized city center. Still, when the river burst its banks and engulfed the city in 2007, the result looked like New Orleans after Hurricane Katrina.

Villahermosa's main visitor attraction is the open-air Parque-Museo La Venta, a combined Olmec archaeological museum and zoo in an attractive lakeside park. There's also a regional anthropology museum and an improving cultural and entertainment scene that may tempt you to hang around longer than a single day or night.

Oil money has pumped modernity and commerce into some of the outer districts, where you'll find glitzy malls, imposing public buildings and luxury hotels.

Orientation

In this sprawling city you'll find yourself walking some distances in the sticky heat, and occasionally hopping on a minibus (combi) or taking a taxi. The central area, known as the Zona Luz, extends north–south from Parque Juárez to the Plaza de Armas, and east–west from the Río Grijalva to roughly Calle 5 de Mayo. The main bus stations are between 750m and 1km to its north.

Parque-Museo La Venta lies 2km northwest of the Zona Luz, beside Av Ruíz Cortines, the main east–west highway crossing the city. West of Parque-Museo La Venta is the Tabasco 2000 district of modern commercial and government buildings.

Information
INTERNET ACCESS

Cybercafés are plentiful. Rates are M$7 to M$10 per hour.
Milenium (Map p793; Sáenz 130; ⏱ 8am-10pm Mon-Sat, 9am-5pm Sun)
Multiservicios (Map p793; Aldama 621C; ⏱ 8am-9pm Mon-Sat, 9am-5pm Sun)

LAUNDRY
Lavandería Top Klean (Map p793; ☎ 312-28-56; Madero 303A; next-day/same-day service per kg M$18/25; ⏱ 8:30am-8pm Mon-Sat)

MEDICAL SERVICES
Hospital Cruz Roja (Map p791; ☎ 315-55-55; Av Sandino s/n) A short ride southwest of the Zona Luz.

Unidad Médica Guerrero (Map p793; ☎ 314-56-97/98; 5 de Mayo 444; ☼ 24hr) Emergency service.

MONEY
Most banks have ATMs and exchange currency.
Bancomer (Map p793; cnr Zaragoza & Juárez; ☼ 8:30am-4pm Mon-Fri)
Santander Serfin (Map p793; Madero 584; ☼ 9am-4pm Mon-Fri)

POST
Main post office (Map p793; Sáenz 131; ☼ 9am-3pm Mon-Fri, 9am-1pm Sat)

TOURIST INFORMATION
State tourist office (Map p791; ☎ 316-36-33, 800-216-08-42; www.tabasco.gob.mx/turismo; Av de los Ríos s/n; ☼ 8am-5pm Mon-Fri) At the Tabasco 2000 complex. From the Zona Luz, take a 'Fracc Carrizal' combi (M$5) from Madero, just north of Parque Juárez, get off at the big traffic circle surrounded by banks after you cross Av Ruíz Cortines, and walk one block to the left along Av de los Ríos.
Tourist office (Map p791; ☼ 8am-4pm, Tue-Sun) In the Parque-Museo La Venta.

Sights
Apart from Parque-Museo La Venta, the pedestrianized Zona Luz is an enjoyable place to explore, and its busy lanes – full of hawkers' stalls and salsa-blaring clothes stores and dotted with cafés and galleries – buzz with tropical atmosphere.

PARQUE–MUSEO LA VENTA
This fascinating outdoor **park and museum** (Map p791; ☎ 314-16-52; Av Ruíz Cortines; admission M$40; ☼ 8am-5pm, last admission 4pm, zoo closed Mon; ⚹) was created in 1958, when petroleum exploration threatened the highly important ancient Olmec settlement of La Venta in western Tabasco (p799). Archaeologists moved the site's most significant finds, including three colossal stone heads, to Villahermosa.

Plan two to three hours for your visit, and take mosquito repellent (the park is set in humid tropical woodland). Snack stands and a little cafetería provide sustenance. Inside, you come to the **zoo** first. This is devoted to animals from Tabasco and nearby regions: cats include jaguars, ocelots and jaguarundi, and there are white-tailed deer, spider monkeys, crocodiles, boa constrictors, peccaries and plenty of colorful birds, including scarlet macaws and keel-billed toucans.

There's an informative display in English and Spanish (like most information here) on Olmec archaeology as you pass through to the **sculpture trail**, whose start is marked by a giant *ceiba* (the sacred tree of the Olmec and Maya). This 1km walk is lined with finds from La Venta. Among the most impressive, in the order you come to them, are Stele 3, which depicts a bearded man with a headdress; Altar 5, depicting a figure carrying a child; Monument 77, 'El Gobernante,' a very sour-looking seated ruler; the monkey-faced Monument 56; Monument 1, the colossal head of a helmet-wearing warrior; and Stele 1, showing a young goddess (a rare Olmec representation of anything female). Animals that pose no danger (such as coatis, squirrels and black agoutis) roam freely around the park.

After dark, a **sound-and-light show** (admission M$100; ☼ hourly 7-10pm Tue-Sun) takes you around 13 of the most interesting archaeological items, with video sequences and passages of poetry by Carlos Pellicer Cámara (1897–1977), the Tabascan scholar and poet responsible for salvaging the artifacts of La Venta. If you have enough Spanish, it's an atmospheric experience.

Next to the park entrance, the **Museo de Historia Natural** (Map p791; ☎ 314-21-75; admission M$15; ☼ 8am-4pm Tue-Sun) has quite well set-out displays on dinosaurs, space, early humanity and Tabascan ecosystems (all in Spanish).

Parque-Museo La Venta is 3km from the Zona Luz. A 'Fracc Carrizal' combi from Madero, just north of Parque Juárez in the Zona Luz, will drop you on Paseo Tabasco just short of Av Ruíz Cortines; then walk 1km northeast across Parque Tomás Garrido Canabal and along the Malecón de las Ilusiones, a lakeside path, to the entrance.

MUSEO REGIONAL DE ANTROPOLOGÍA
This **regional museum** (Map p791; ☎ 312-63-44; Periférico Carlos Pellicer; admission M$25; ☼ 9am-5pm Tue-Sun) is a little dilapidated and poorly labeled (in Spanish only), but still holds some interesting exhibits. It's best to begin on the upper level, which outlines Mesoamerica's many civilizations with the aid of a pretty good sculpture collection. After you've brushed up on the broad picture, the middle floor concentrates on Olmec and Maya cultures in Tabasco, with second-grade sculptures from La Venta, and Classic Maya urns from Tapijulapa and Tacotalpa. Finally, on the ground floor is one

TABASCO & CHIAPAS

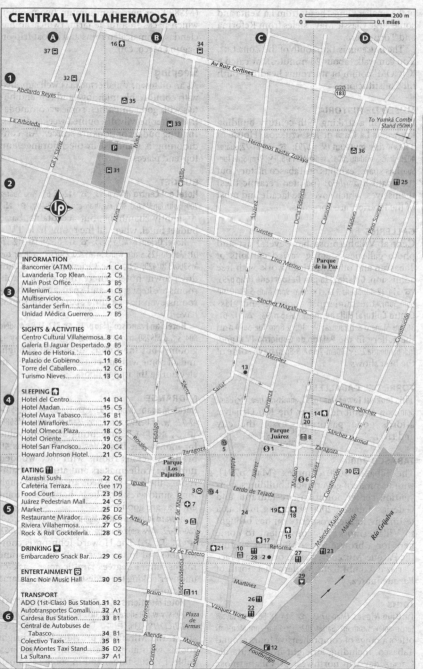

CENTRAL VILLAHERMOSA

0 —————— 200 m
0 —————— 0.1 miles

Av Ruiz Cortines

Abelardo Reyes

La Arboleda

To Yumká Combi
Stand (50m)

Hermanos Bastar Zozaya

Fuentes

Lino Merino

Parque
de la Paz

Sánchez Magallanes

Méndez

Carmen Sánchez

Parque
Juárez

Sánchez Mármol

Zaragoza

Parque
Los
Pajaritos

Iguala

Lerdo de Tejada

27 de Febrero

Reforma

Martínez

Bravo

Vázquez Norte

Plaza
de
Armas

Allende

Macuilla

Footbridge

Río Grijalva

Malecón Madrazo / Malecón

INFORMATION	
Bancomer (ATM)..................**1** C4	
Lavandería Top Klean...........**2** C5	
Main Post Office...................**3** B5	
Milenium.............................**4** C5	
Multiservicios......................**5** C4	
Santander Serfin..................**6** C5	
Unidad Médica Guerrero......**7** B5	

SIGHTS & ACTIVITIES	
Centro Cultural Villahermosa..**8** C4	
Galería El Jaguar Despertado..**9** B5	
Museo de Historia..............**10** C5	
Palacio de Gobierno............**11** B6	
Torre del Caballero.............**12** C6	
Turismo Nieves...................**13** C4	

SLEEPING	
Hotel del Centro................**14** D4	
Hotel Madan.....................**15** C5	
Hotel Maya Tabasco...........**16** B1	
Hotel Miraflores.................**17** C5	
Hotel Olmeca Plaza............**18** C5	
Hotel Oriente....................**19** C5	
Hotel San Francisco............**20** C4	
Howard Johnson Hotel........**21** C5	

EATING	
Atarashi Sushi....................**22** C6	
Cafetería Terraza.............(see 17)	
Food Court........................**23** D5	
Juárez Pedestrian Mall.......**24** C5	
Market.............................**25** D2	
Restaurante Mirador...........**26** C5	
Riviera Villahermosa...........**27** C5	
Rock & Roll Cocktelería......**28** C5	

DRINKING	
Embarcadero Snack Bar......**29** C6	

ENTERTAINMENT	
Blanc Noir Music Hall.........**30** D5	

TRANSPORT	
ADO (1st-Class) Bus Station.**31** B2	
Autotransportes Comalli......**32** A1	
Cardesa Bus Station............**33** B1	
Central de Autobuses de	
Tabasco.........................**34** B1	
Colectivo Taxis..................**35** B1	
Dos Montes Taxi Stand.......**36** D2	
La Sultana........................**37** A1	

of the smaller Olmec heads from La Venta and some large Classic Maya steles from Reforma and Tortuguero.

The museum is 1km south of the Zona Luz. You can walk (about 20 minutes), or catch a 'CICOM' combi or microbus heading south on Constitución.

MUSEO DE HISTORIA

Housed in a striking 19th-century building known as La Casa de los Azulejos (House of Tiles), this **museum** (Map p793; ☎ 314-21-72; Juárez 402; admission adult/child & senior M$15/5; ☼ 9am-5pm Tue-Sun) has sparse exhibits on Tabasco history, but the Spanish *azulejos* (painted ceramic tiles) themselves, which cover the facade and most of the interior, are gorgeous.

GALLERIES

Central Villahermosa has several art and photo galleries, staging varied exhibits of Tabascan and other Mexican work, with free admission. **Galería El Jaguar Despertado** (Map p793; ☎ 314-12-44; Sáenz 117; ☼ 9am-9pm Mon-Sat, 10am-6pm Sun), the modernist concrete-and-glass **Centro Cultural Villahermosa** (Map p793; ☎ 312-61-36; cnr Madero & Zaragoza; ☼ 10am-8pm Tue-Sun) and the gallery in the **Palacio de Gobierno** (Map p793; Independencia 2; ☼ 10am-2pm & 5-8pm) have some of the best shows.

TORRE DEL CABALLERO

This **lookout tower** (Map p793; admission free; ☼ 8am-6pm), on a footbridge over the Río Grijalva, affords good panoramas over the city and river.

TABASCO 2000

The Tabasco 2000 complex (Map p791), with its modern government buildings, convention center, fountains, restaurants and Galerías Tabasco 2000 shopping mall, is a testimony to the prosperity oil has brought to Villahermosa. It's convenient to come here for a browse and a bite after visiting the Parque-Museo La Venta, or take a 'Fracc Carrizal' combi from Madero just north of Parque Juárez.

Tours

Turismo Nieves (Map p793; ☎ 314-18-88; reservaya@turismonieves.com.mx; Sarlat 202; ☼ 8am-7pm Mon-Sat) offers a range of comprehensive tours around Tabasco, including an eight-hour 'Ruta del Cacao' day trip northwest of Villahermosa

(M$890 per person, minimum two people), which packs in a turtle farm, two cacao haciendas, Comalcalco ruins and a boat trip on Laguna Mecoacán.

Sleeping

As an oil town, Villahermosa is well supplied with comfortable midrange and top-end hotels with good amenities; some accommodations offer heavily discounted weekend rates. Inviting budget options are scarcer. Air-conditioning is standard in the midrange and top-end places.

BUDGET

Hotel del Centro (Map p793; ☎ 312-25-65; Pino Suárez 209; r with fan M$200-300, r with air-con M$350-400; P ⊠) A slightly shambolic, but acceptable, basic budget hotel, where all the rooms have TV.

Hotel Oriente (Map p793; ☎ 312-01-21; fax 312-11-01; Madero 425; s/d/tr with fan M$220/250/360, with air-con M$300/330/420; ⊠) The Oriente is a well-run downtown hotel where the comfortable rooms are kept spick-and-span, and the bathrooms even have a little sparkle. All rooms have TV.

Hotel San Francisco (Map p793; ☎ 312-31-98; Madero 604; s & d M$280, tr/q M$360/400; ⊠) The lobby is gloomy, but the rooms are decent enough, and all come with air-con and TV. There's an elevator to the upper floors.

MIDRANGE

Hotel Madan (Map p793; ☎ 314-05-18, 800-543-47-77; www.bestwestern.com; Madero 408; r M$586; P ⊠ ⊠ ⊡) Representing excellent value for money, the Best Western Madan has 40 bright, spacious rooms with nice wooden furniture, coffeemakers and attractive bathrooms; the king-size beds are ample enough for a sumo wrestler. The in-house restaurant and bar are good too.

Howard Johnson Hotel (Map p793; ☎ 314-46-45, 800-780-72-72; www.hojo.com.mx; Aldama 404; s/d M$591/652; P ⊠ ⊡ ⊡) The Howard Johnson is comfortable and in the heart of town, but some rooms suffer a degree of traffic noise – ask for one overlooking the pedestrian streets Aldama or Reforma.

Hotel Miraflores (Map p793; ☎ 358-04-70, 800-234-02-29; www.miraflores.com.mx; Reforma 304; s/d/ste M$617/672/755/838; P ⊠ ⊡) Set on a traffic-free street, the Miraflores provides large, bright rooms with ample bathrooms, telephones, cable TV, tile floors and in some cases balconies. Downstairs is a café, a restaurant and two bars. Not a bad deal.

Hotel Maya Tabasco (Map p793; ☎ 358-11-11, 800-237-77-00; www.bestwestern.com; Av Ruíz Cortines 907; r M$687; P 🅿 🍴 🏊) One kilometer north of the Zona Luz, this business-orientated Best Western hotel has good-sized, well-equipped, modern rooms, most with bathtub. Add the attractive gardens, large pool, good restaurant, two bars with evening entertainment, ATM and free transportation to the airport and Parque-Museo La Venta, and it's a pretty good package.

Hotel Olmeca Plaza (Map p793; ☎ 358-01-02, 800-201-09-09; www.hotelolmecaplaza.com; Madero 418; r M$750, Fri-Sun M$590; P 🚫 🍴 🖥 🏊) The classiest downtown hotel also has an open-air pool and well-equipped gym. Rooms are modern and comfortable, with writing desks and good large bathrooms, and there's a quality onsite restaurant.

Hotel Quality Inn Villahermosa Cencali (Map p791; ☎ 313-66-11, 800-112-50-00; www.qualityinnvillahermosa.com; Av Juárez 105, Colonia Lindavista; r M$874; P 🚫 🍴 🖥 🏊) The Cencali boasts an excellent quiet location not far from Parque-Museo La Venta, and 160 good-size rooms with balconies, bathtubs and, in many cases, views of the Laguna de las Ilusiones. There's a great swimming pool in tropical gardens beside the lake. The rate comes down to M$787 on some weekends.

TOP END

Hyatt Regency Villahermosa (Map p791; ☎ 310-12-34; www.villahermosa.regency.hyatt.com; Av Juárez 106, Colonia Lindavista; r M$1350; P 🚫 🍴 🖥 🏊) Villahermosa's smartest hotel has amenities that include a large swimming pool, a smaller kids' pool, tennis courts, two restaurants, two bars and one restaurant-bar. All 207 bright, luxuriously appointed rooms and suites come with modem connections and glass-walled hydromassage showers. On weekends, breakfast is included in the room rate.

Eating

Villahermosa's eclectic collection of hotel restaurants, chain restaurants and seafood, Tabascan, Japanese and Italian specialists will keep you happy for the duration of your stay.

ZONA LUZ & MALECÓN

Hotel Madan (Map p793; ☎ 314-05-24; Madero 408; breakfast M$30-50, mains M$55-80) It's nothing glam-orous, but this is a very reliable and popular hotel restaurant, with mainly Mexican dishes and efficient, friendly service.

Food Court (Map p793; Malecón Madrazo; mains M$50-100; ⏱ 10am-11pm) This open-air eating and drinking area on the deck beside the river has the greatest location in town. Several of the city's best eateries have branches here.

Rock & Roll Cocktelería (Map p793; ☎ 312-05-93; Reforma 307; seafood cocktails M$65-80; ⏱ 9am-11pm) A maelstrom of heat, swirling fans, a thumping jukebox and garrulous punters. Everyone's here for the *cocteles* (fish or seafood, tomato sauce, lettuce, onions and a lemon squeeze) and the cheap beer.

Restaurante Mirador (Map p793; ☎ 314-34-95; Madero 105; mains M$70-150; ⏱ noon-8pm) A smart, air-conditioned, upstairs restaurant, specializing in fish and seafood.

Riviera Villahermosa (Map p793; ☎ 312-44-68; Constitución 104; mains M$75-160; ⏱ 1pm-2am Mon-Sat, noon-6pm Sun) The Euro-Mex menu is pretty good, and the air-conditioned 4th-floor setting with floor-to-ceiling windows overlooking the river is spectacular. Steaks, seafood and pasta are all good here.

Atarashi Sushi (Map p793; ☎ 314-70-26; Vázquez Norte 203; mains M$90-150; ⏱ noon-midnight Sun-Fri, to 1am Sat) Air-conditioned Atarashi presents a tasty Mexican angle on Japanese food, offering all sorts of tantalizing – and satisfying – seafood, meat, vegetable and sauce combinations.

Also recommended are the following:

Cafetería Terraza (Map p793; ☎ 358-04-70; Hotel Miraflores, Reforma 304; mains M$70-120; ⏱ 7am-11pm) A reliable hotel café-restaurant, with filling portions of well-priced Mexican staples.

Hotel Olmeca Plaza (Map p793; ☎ 358-01-02; Madero 418; mains M$70-125) A quality hotel restaurant with good service.

Juárez pedestrian mall (Map p793) Several cafés have indoor and outdoor tables; good for breakfast or a drink and snacks, though you may be serenaded by a marimba team.

Market (Map p793; Hermanos Bastar Zozaya s/n; ⏱ 5am-7pm) Fresh vegetables, chilies, fish, meat and big dollops of local atmosphere.

OTHER AREAS

Italianni's (Map p791; ☎ 317-72-57; Prolongación Paseo Tabasco 1404; mains M$80-140; ⏱ 1-11pm Mon-Wed, to 1am Thu-Sat, to 10pm Sun) This quality Italian restaurant serves well-prepared pasta, pizzas, salads, chicken and steaks, and plenty of Italian wine, amid classic check tablecloths and even Mediterranean-style window shutters. Don't miss the half-price specials Monday through Thursday after 6pm.

Restaurant Los Tulipanes (Map p791; ☎ 312-92-09; Periférico Carlos Pellicer 511; mains M$80-170; ☼ 8am-9pm) Overlooking the Río Grijalva, near the Museo Regional de Antropología, Los Tulipanes is the best place in town for Tabascan specialties, including seafood-filled corn tortillas, and empanadas of *pejelagarto*, the tasty freshwater 'lizard fish' that is a symbol of Tabasco. It also serves steaks, chicken, *róbalo* (snook) and other fish – and on Sundays a Tabascan buffet (M$180) that's the perfect opportunity to gorge yourself silly.

Hyatt Regency Villahermosa (Map p791; ☎ 310-12-34; Av Juárez 106, Colonia Lindavista) The top hotel in town has two of the best restaurants, both serving a big choice of Mexican and international dishes: the Bougainvillea (mains M$90 to M$140, open 1pm to midnight Monday through Saturday), with live jazz in the evenings, and La Ceiba (sandwiches and salads M$50 to M$70, mains M$130 to M$180, open 6:30am to midnight daily), which also serves some buffet meals.

Drinking

A cluster of bars with and without music is strung along the riverside Malecón Madrazo, and some hotels have good bars too.

For cooling beers, the Malecón's **Food Court** (Map p793; Malecón Madrazo; ☼ 10am-11pm) and **Embarcadero Snack Bar** (Map p793; ☎ 314-46-44; Malecón Madrazo Kiosco 1; snacks M$15-50; ☼ 10am-3am) are fine, breezy, open-air spots. The Embarcadero also provides rock music, big-screen TV and good snacks.

Entertainment

To find out what's on in the way of performances, check the website of **Tabasco's culture department** (http://iec.tabasco.gob.mx).

Blanc Noir Music Hall (Map p793; ☎ 314-51-76; Malecón Madrazo 645; admission M$30; ☼ 8am-3pm Tue-Sat) A two-level club with big windows facing the river, Blanc Noir often has local bands playing after 10pm Thursday to Saturday (the M$30 admission to see bands includes one beer).

Riviera Villahermosa (Map p793; ☎ 312-44-68; Constitución 104; admission free; ☼ 1pm-2am Mon-Sat, noon-8pm Sun) A trendy 5th-floor electro-pop bar with great views.

Casa de la Trova Tabasqueña (Map p791; ☎ 314-21-22; Periférico Carlos Pellicer Cámara s/n; admission free) *Trova* artists play once or twice most weeks, usually at 8pm Wednesday, Thursday or Friday, at this café-style venue next to the Museo Regional de Antropología.

Shopping

You might find something you like among the Tabascan baskets, wickerwork, hats, gourds and pottery at **Artesanías de Tabasco** (☎ 316-28-22) in the **Galerías Tabasco 2000 mall** (Map p791; ☼ 10am-9pm). Galerías Tabasco 2000 also has fashion, jewelry, shoe and music stores, coffee bars and places to eat – all in air-con comfort.

Getting There & Away

AIR

Villahermosa's **Aeropuerto Rovirosa** (☎ 356-01-57) is 13km east of the center, off Hwy 186. Nonstop or one-stop direct flights to/from Villahermosa include the following:

Cancún Click Mexicana, daily.
Houston, Texas Continental, daily.
Mérida Aviacsa and Click Mexicana, both daily.
Mexico City Aeroméxico, Aviacsa and Mexicana; total eight or more daily.
Monterrey Aeroméxico Connect and Aviacsa; both with one daily nonstop.
Oaxaca Click Mexicana, daily.
Tuxtla Gutiérrez Click Mexicana, daily.
Veracruz Aeroméxico Connect, daily.

AIRLINE OFFICES

Aeroméxico & Aeroméxico Connect (Map p791; ☎ 315-27-77; cnr Av Ruíz Cortines & Sagitario)
Aviacsa (Map p791; ☎ 800-284-22-72; Local 8, Plaza D'Atocha Mall, Tabasco 2000)
Continental Airlines (☎ 356-02-67; Aeropuerto Rovirosa)
Mexicana & Click Mexicana (Map p791; ☎ 316-31-33; Locales 5 & 6, Plaza D'Atocha Mall, Tabasco 2000)

BUS & COLECTIVO

Deluxe and 1st-class UNO, ADO and OCC buses run from the **ADO bus station** (Map p793; ☎ 312-84-22; Mina 297), 750m north of the Zona Luz, as do a few 2nd-class services, but many are *de paso* (buses which have started their journeys elsewhere, but are stopping to let off and take on passengers), so buy your onward ticket in advance if possible. It's possible to do this at the Ticket Bus *cajero automático* (ticket machine) on Madero between the Madan and Olmeca Plaza hotels. Departures from the

ADO terminal (most in the evening) include the following:

Destination	Fare	Duration	Frequency (daily)
Campeche	M$278-318	6-7hr	17
Cancún	M$550-960	12-14hr	21
Mérida	M$390-608	8-9hr	19
Mexico City (TAPO)	M$550-998	10-12hr	26
Oaxaca	M$448	12hr	3
Palenque	M$95	2½hr	13
San Cristóbal de Las Casas	M$204	7hr	2
Tenosique	M$130	3-3½hr	13
Tuxtla Gutiérrez	M$200-240	4-8hr	13
Veracruz	M$324-522	6-8hr	24

Transportation to most destinations within Tabasco leaves from other terminals north of the ADO. The 2nd-class **Cardesa bus station** (Map p793; cnr Bastar Zozaya & Castillo) has the following services:

Destination	Fare	Duration	Frequency
Comalcalco	M$25	1½hr	vans every 30 min 5am-9pm
Frontera	M$30	1½hr	hourly buses 5am-9pm
Palenque	M$50	2½hr	8 buses daily
Paraíso	M$30	2hr	18 buses daily

The main 2nd-class bus station is the **Central de Autobuses de Tabasco** (Map p793; ☎ 312-29-77; cnr Av Ruíz Cortines & Castillo) on the north side of Av Ruíz Cortines. Departures include the following:

Destination	Fare	Duration	Frequency
Comalcalco	M$25	1½hr	every 30-60 min 5am-9pm
Frontera	M$27	1½hr	every 30 min 4:30am-9pm
Jonuta	M$50	2½hr	5 daily
La Venta	M$50	2hr	every 30 min 4:30am-11pm
Paraíso	M$30	2hr	every 30-60 min 5am-9pm
Tenosique	M$70	3½hr	11 daily

For Teapa, **La Sultana** (Map p793; ☎ 314-48-82; Av Ruíz Cortines 917) runs comfortable 2nd-class buses (M$30, one hour) every 30 minutes, 5am to 10:30pm. Further vans for Comalcalco (M$25, one hour) are operated by **Autotransportes Somalli** (Map p793; Gil y Sáenz) every 20 minutes, 5:30am to 10pm.

Colectivo taxis to Paraíso (M$45, 1½ hours) and Frontera (M$40, 1¼ hours) go from a yard on Reyes (Map p793), north of the ADO bus station.

CAR & MOTORCYCLE
Most rental companies have desks at the airport.
Dollar (Map p791; ☎ 315-80-88; Torre Empresarial, Paseo Tabasco 1203)

Getting Around
A taxi from the airport to the city costs around M$180 (M$150 from the city to the airport) and takes about 25 minutes. Alternatively, go to the road outside the airport parking lot and pick up a *colectivo* taxi for M$15 per person. These terminate at the **Dos Montes taxi stand** (Map p793; Carranza), about 1km north of the Zona Luz. You can catch them at the same stop to return to the airport.

Any taxi ride within the area between Av Ruíz Cortines, the Río Grijalva and Paseo Usumacinta costs M$15. Combi rides within the same area are M$5. From the ADO bus station to the Zona Luz, it's best to take a taxi, as you have to walk halfway to the Zona Luz to reach a combi route. From the Zona Luz to the ADO, take a 'Chedraui,' 'ADO' or 'Cardesa' combi north on Malecón Madrazo.

YUMKÁ
This Tabascan **safari park** (☎ 356-01-07; www.yumka .org; Ranchería Las Barrancas; over/under-11 M$50/25, lake extra M$20; ◷ 9am-5pm; ⚐), 17km east of Villahermosa (4km past the airport), is hardly a Kenyan game drive, but the space and greenery do offer a break from the city. Yumká is divided into jungle, savanna and lake zones, representing Tabasco's three main ecosystems. Visits take the form of guided tours of the three areas (30 minutes each). In the jungle zone you see regional Mexican species such as howler monkeys, jaguars, scarlet macaws and toucans. The savanna, viewed from a tractor-pulled trolley, has an African section with elephants, giraffes, zebras and hippos, and an Asian section with axis deer, antelope, buffalo and gaur (the largest ox in the world). You tour the lake by boat and should see plenty of birds, including herons and pelicans.

Combis to Yumká (M$9, 40 minutes) go every 15 to 20 minutes from 9am from Amado Nervo, beside Villahermosa market. The last one back leaves Yumká at 5pm.

TABASCO & CHIAPAS

WESTERN TABASCO
Comalcalco
☎ 933 / pop 40,000

Comalcalco, 51km northwest of Villahermosa, is typical of the medium-sized towns of western Tabasco – hot, bustling, quite prosperous and spread around a broad, open central plaza (Parque Juárez).

What makes it especially worth visiting are the impressive ruins of **ancient Comalcalco** (admission M$35; ⏱ 10am-4pm), 3.5km north. This Maya site is unique because many of its buildings are constructed of bricks and/or mortar made from oyster shells. Comalcalco was at its peak between AD 600 and 1000, when ruled by the Chontals. It remained an important center of commerce for several more centuries, trading in a cornucopia of pre-Hispanic luxury goods: cacao, salt, feathers, deer and jaguar skins, wax, honey, turtle shells, tobacco, chilies, manta-ray spines, cotton, polychrome ceramics, copal, jade and greenstone *hachas* (flat, carved-stone objects associated with the ritual ball game).

The museum at the entrance has a fine array of sculptures and engravings of human heads, deities, glyphs and animals such as crocodiles and pelicans.

The buildings within the site have information panels in both Spanish and English. The first building you encounter is the great brick-built, tiered pyramid, **Templo 1**. At its base are the remains of large stucco sculptures, including the feet of a giant winged toad. Further temples line Plaza Norte, in front of Templo I. In the far (southeast) corner of the site rises the **Gran Acrópolis**, with views from its summit over a canopy of palms to the Gulf of Mexico. The Acrópolis is fronted by **Templo V**, a burial pyramid that was once decorated on all sides with stucco sculptures of people, reptiles, birds and aquatic life. At Templo V's western foot is **Templo IX**, with a tomb lined by nine stucco sculptures showing a Comalcalco lord with his priests and courtiers. Above Templo V is the crumbling profile of **El Palacio**, with its parallel 80m-long corbel-arched galleries, probably once Comalcalco's royal residence.

The site is 1km (signposted) off the Comalcalco–Paraíso road. Vans to the turnoff (M$5) stop outside Comalcalco's ADO terminal (see right). A taxi to the site costs around M$20.

Hacienda La Luz (☎ 334-11-29; Blvd Rovirosa; 1hr tour per person M$35; ⏱ 10am-4pm), one of several local plantations making chocolate from home-grown cacao, is just 300m from Comalcalco's central Parque Juárez: walk 250m west along Calle Bosada to its end at Blvd Rovirosa, turn right and you'll see the hacienda's white gateposts across the road. The tour (minimum two people) takes you round the beautiful house, gardens and cacao plantation, and shows traditional methods of turning cacao beans into chocolate.

SLEEPING & EATING
Hotel Santander (☎ 334-44-58; Escobedo 103; s/d M$345/375; [P] [☒]) The Santander, just off the main street (Juárez), offers clean, tile-floored, air-conditioned rooms, free morning coffee and a neat little café.

Hotel Copacabana (☎ 334-19-33, 800-224-77-77; www.hotelcopacabana.com.mx; cnr Juárez & Serdán; s/d M$595/712; [P] [☒]) The best hotel in town, the Copacabana has large, very clean, pink rooms with quality air-conditioning. The staff is professional, and the restaurant (mains M$57 to M$135) here is one of Comalcalco's best, with well-prepared seafood and meat dishes.

Bariloche (☎ 334-63-73; 5 de Mayo 109; mains M$70-130; ⏱ 9am-2am) A fine variety of local and other dishes is on offer at this air-conditioned, art-print-hung restaurant on the plaza, and there's live tropical music from 8pm Wednesday to Saturday. Try the prawns with tequila and *chipotle* (chili) mayonnaise for starters.

GETTING THERE & AWAY
Comalcalco's **ADO terminal** (☎ 334-00-07; cnr López Mateos & Monserrat) by the clock tower (El Reloj) is on the main road, 300m east of the center. It has 1st- and 2nd-class buses to Villahermosa (M$54, 1½ hours, seven daily), Paraíso (M$15, 20 minutes, 25 daily), Frontera (M$66, 2½ hours, three daily) and more distant destinations.

Paraíso & Around
☎ 933 / pop (Paraíso) 25,000

Twenty kilometers north of Comalcalco, Paraíso is doing very nicely from the economic spin-offs of Pemex oil installations on the nearby coast at Dos Bocas, and is something of a recreation center for western Tabasco. Wide, sandy beaches front the warm, clear waters of the Gulf of Mexico north of town: Playa Varadero (7.5km from town), Playa El Paraíso (9km) and Balneario Palmar (10.5km) all have simple beach restaurants but only El Paraíso (where parking costs M$70) normally has midweek service.

At Puerto Ceiba, 6km northeast of Paraíso, the **Parador Turístico Puerto Ceiba** (5 de Febrero s/n; mains M$70-80; ☺ noon-7pm or later) is an enjoyable waterfront restaurant where you can take **boat rides** (up to 14 people M$300; 1¼hr; ☺ 10am-6pm) along the palm-lined Río Seco and into Laguna Mecoacán, with its mangroves and bird life. It's also possible to rent kayaks here. Follow the Puente del Bellote bridge over the lagoon's mouth and you'll reach several more restaurants serving fresh seafood. The first, popular **Restaurant La Posta** (☎ 335-40-93; mains M$55-85; ☺ 9am-8pm), serves seafood on a deck right over Laguna Mecoacán, and offers more boat rides (M$100 for 20 minutes on the *laguna*, or hour-long mangrove trips for M$250, both for up to 10 people). The road continues, through several villages and over many, many *topes* (speed bumps), to Frontera, 75km east.

Westward from Paraíso, a wonderful road makes its way along the **Barra de Tupilco**, a palm-covered sandspit strung between the Gulf of Mexico and a succession of lagoons, all the way to scruffy Sánchez Magallanes, 80km from Paraíso. The spectacular trip passes an endless succession of palm-lined, sandy beaches, with ospreys, pelicans and frigate birds cruising overhead. Where stretches of road have been washed away by the sea, vehicles have to detour through the property of enterprising locals who charge unofficial tolls (adding up to about M$50).

SLEEPING & EATING

Hotel Sabina (☎ 333-24-83; Ocampo 115; r with fan M$250, with air-con M$300-380; ℗ ☒) A cheaper hotel on the plaza; avoid the dank ground-floor singles.

Hotel Solimar (☎ 333-28-72; Ocampo 114; s/d M$532/631; ℗ ☒) Half a block north of Paraíso's plaza, the Solimar has comfortable, pretty, air-conditioned rooms with alpine prints to help you feel cooler, and also one of the best eateries in town, the spick-and-span Restaurant Costa Carey (mains M$50 to M$110).

GETTING THERE & AROUND

Paraíso's **ADO terminal** (☎ 333-02-35; Av Romero Zurita), 1.5km south of the center, has 2nd-class buses to Comalcalco (M$15, 20 minutes, three or four hourly) and Villahermosa (M$68, two hours, every half-hour) and two 1st-class buses to Frontera (M$52, two hours).

A taxi to Puerto Ceiba or any of Paraíso's beaches costs M$20 to M$30. From Paraíso's 2nd class bus station, **Central Camionera** (Serdán s/n), eight blocks north of the central plaza then four blocks east, Transportes Pancho Villa (TPV) runs four daily buses along the Barra de Tupilco to Sánchez Magallanes (M$50, two hours). TPV also runs buses from Sánchez Magallanes to La Venta.

La Venta
☎ 923 / pop 9000

Most of the monuments from La Venta are at Villahermosa's Parque-Museo La Venta (p792), but this ancient Olmec ceremonial center still has the fascination of being the largest and most important 'capital' of Mexico's mother culture. The **site** (admission M$30; ☺ 8am-4pm) is at the small town of La Venta, 128km west of Villahermosa. La Venta flourished between about 800 and 400 BC, on a natural plateau rising about 20m above an area of fertile, seasonally flooded lowlands. Matthew Stirling is credited with discovering, in the early 1940s, four huge Olmec heads sculpted from basalt, the largest more than 2m high. A lot of other fascinating sculpture has been found here too. It's thought that the Olmecs brought the stone for their monuments from hills 100km east and west, using systems of sledges and river rafts.

The museum at the site entrance holds three badly weathered Olmec heads, recovered since the founding of Parque-Museo La Venta in 1958, plus replicas of some of the finest La Venta sculptures that are no longer here. Further replicas are arranged decoratively around the site itself. The heart of the site is the 30m-high Edificio C-1, a rounded pyramid constructed out of clay and sand. Ceremonial areas and more structures stretch to the north and south of this, today mostly defined by low mounds and cleared vegetation. Those to the south stretch far into the jungle area beyond the plaza of Complejo B. At the north end of the site, Complejo A was once an important ceremonial area and many sculptures and rich offerings were found here in the 1940s and '50s – before oil exploitation modified the area.

La Venta town is 4km north of Hwy 180. The **ADO terminal** (☎ 232-03-97; Juárez 37), on the main street, has services to Villahermosa (M$59, two hours) every 30 minutes, 5am to 11pm. The archaeological site is 800m north from the bus station.

Malpasito
pop 360 / elevation 200m

Up in Tabasco's beautiful and mountainous far southwestern corner, tiny Malpasito is the site of mysterious ancient Zoque ruins, and one of several *ejidos* (communal landholdings) in this district with ecotourism activities (promoted under the name Agua Selva). Malpasito is just 1km west of the Caseta Malpasito tollbooth and intersection on the Coatzacoalcos–Ocozocoautla autopista.

Malpasito's **ruins** (admission M$25; ☼ 10am-5pm) are 600m (signposted) above the village. Apart from the beautiful setting, what's remarkable about this little-visited site dating from AD 700–900, is its petroglyphs (rock carvings). Over 100 petroglyphs showing birds, deer, monkeys, people, and temples with stairways are scattered around the Malpasito area, of which about 10 are at the archaeological site.

The site is arranged in a series of stepped platforms on the forested hillside. On the main plaza level is a ball court and a steam bath, which was probably used for pre-game purification rituals. Steps lead up to the Patio Sur, which was the main ceremonial area, dominated by the stepped Structure 13 on its top side. A small path leading half-right from the top of these steps leads to petroglyph groups after 100m and 150m. Past the second group, the path goes through the site's perimeter fence after 30m, and turns sharp right 80m later. After another 200m (downhill), a barely visible side path leads 40m through trees to the large, flat Petroglyph 112, unmarked and partly moss-covered, but with unmistakable temple and stairway carvings. Back on the main path, 100m past the Petroglyph 112 turning, you reach a forest waterfall with an inviting swimming hole at its foot.

More petroglyphs and swimming holes are to be found in Malpasito's **Parque Eco-Arqueológico** (admission M$100; ☼ 8am-5pm), also just above the village, a beautiful slice of jungle, rivers and waterfalls with a rich variety of flora. The admission charge includes a guided walk of about two hours, and you can also

rappel down a waterfall (M$140) or ride a 160m zip-line (M$50).

Malpasito's **Albergue** (☎ in Mexico City 55-5151-5229; cabaña per person M$100; meals M$40-70) provides meals and simple but well looked-after wooden cabins with private cold-water bathroom, concrete floors and tile roofs. Here you can hire guides (M$100 per day) for day walks up some of the dramatic-looking nearby hills.

TRT buses from Villahermosa's 2nd-class bus station (see p796), heading to Tuxtla Gutiérrez by the old Hwy 187, will drop you at the Malpasito turnoff (M$60, three hours, six daily), from which it's 5km west to the village crossing over the autopista en route. Second-class buses from Tuxtla Gutiérrez' OCC terminal (see p808) will drop you at the Caseta Malpasito (M$50, two hours, eight daily), or the autopista just 1km from Malpasito.

SOUTHERN TABASCO
Teapa
☎ 932 / pop 26,000 / elevation 50m

This bustling town, 50km south of Villahermosa, is a good base for exploring southern Tabasco's natural attractions.

At the **Grutas del Coconá** (☎ 322-05-45; admission M$20; ☼ 10am-5pm), 4km northeast of the center, a well-made concrete path leads 500m into a subtly lit cavern, with pools, bats, plenty of stalactites and stalagmites and a small museum contain pre-Hispanic ritual items found in the cave. Combis marked 'Mercado Eureka Coca Florida' (M$5, 10 minutes) will take you there every few minutes from Bastar beside Teapa's central church (and are not part of an international cocaine-trafficking route).

The **Balneario Río Puyacatengo** is a collection of popular riverside restaurants and bathing spots, 3km from town on the Tacotalpa road (M$15 by taxi).

SLEEPING & EATING
Hotel Quintero (☎ 322-00-45; Bastar 108; s/d/t M$300/330/360; ✹) This central hotel provides reasonably sized, clean, air-conditioned rooms, around a rather antiseptic concrete courtyard.

Hacienda Los Azufres (☎ 327-58-06; Carretera Teapa Pichucalco Km 5.5; r M$400, f M$600, with private thermal bath M$700; P ✹ ☎) This hotel-cum-thermal spa is in the countryside, 8km west of central Teapa, on Hwy 195 to Tuxtla Gutiérrez. Public admission to the large, open-air, sulfurous swimming pools is M$30. The rooms are reasonably attractive, with cheery tiling, and some have their own little thermal bathroom open to the sky. Relaxation and exfoliant massages are also available for around M$300.

La Galería (☎ 322-18-37; Méndez 157; 2-person pizzas M$70-80; ☾ 5 11pm) Try juicy pizzas amid a dizzying array of kitsch murals and photographs of local beauty queens. It also serves a good selection of thirst-quenchers.

GETTING THERE & AWAY

The **OCC terminal** (☎ 322-23-11; Méndez 218) is 300m from the plaza, along the main street. Buses leave for Tuxtla Gutiérrez (M$142, six hours) twice daily. **La Sultana** (☎ 322-19-23; Damián Pizá 17), near the market and 600m from the plaza, runs comfortable 2nd-class buses to Villahermosa (M$32, one hour) every 30 minutes, 4am to 9:30pm.

Tapijulapa

☎ 932 / pop 2800 / elevation 200m

This pretty riverside village of red-tile-roof white houses, presided over by a 17th-century church, sits among the lushly forested hills of far southern Tabasco, 36km from Teapa. Several shops sell local wicker and wood crafts.

The beautiful jungle park **Villa Luz** (admission free; ☾ 8am-5pm) is a five-minute boat ride (per person one-way/round-trip M$15/25) along the Río Oxolotán from the village's *embarcadero* (boat landing) – you may have to get local boys to whistle a boat up for you. From the landing, it's a 1km walk to the park's Casa Museo, the former country villa of Tomás Garrido Canabal, the rabidly anticlerical governor of Tabasco in the 1920s and '30s (he demolished Villahermosa's 18th-century baroque cathedral, banned alcohol and gave women the vote). From here other paths lead 600m to the *cascadas* (beautiful waterfalls tumbling into a river, with pools for a refreshing dip) and 900m to the Cueva de las Sardinas Ciegas (Cave of the Blind Sardines), named for the sightless fish that inhabit the sulfurous river inside the cave. You're only permitted to go a few steps down into the cave because of the strong odors. You need about two hours to walk the 5km required to see the waterfalls, house and cave.

Kolem-Jaa' (☎ in Villahermosa 993-314-31-92; www .kolemjaa.com; day package M$270-585, 2-day/1-night package M$1150-1399; ℗ ♿) is a jungle eco-adventure tourism center, adjacent to Villa Luz and 6km by road from Tapijulapa. The excitements include commando trails, zip-lines across a river and through the jungle canopy, and horseback and mountain-bike riding. Accommodations are in comfortable duplex cabins.

On Tapijulapa's central plaza, **Restaurant Mariquito** (Parque Carlos Pellicer; dishes around M$40; ☾ 7am-8:30pm) cooks up local specialties, such as *mone de pollo* (chicken steamed with hierba santa) and *caldo de shote* (a stew made with a type of river mollusk).

To reach Tapijulapa by bus from Teapa, first take a bus to Tacotalpa (M$8, 30 minutes, every 30 minutes 6am to 8pm) from Teapa's OCC terminal. Buses to Tapijulapa (M$0, 45 minutes, hourly until 6pm) leave from Tacotalpa's Mercado Faustino Méndez Jiménez, across the street from the stop where buses from Teapa arrive. The last bus back leaves Tapijulapa at 7pm.

EASTERN TABASCO
Frontera

☎ 913 / pop 29,000

This somewhat rough-and-ready fishing port and oil town sits on the east bank of the vast Río Grijalva, 81km northeast of Villahermosa. The river here, just 8km from its mouth on the Gulf of Mexico, is in fact a combination of the Grijalva and the Usumacinta, Mexico's most voluminous river, whose main branch joins the Grijalva 15km upstream. Between them, these two rivers drain most of Tabasco and Chiapas and about half of Guatemala. Frontera unfortunately fails to make anything of its stunning location, with no public access to the riverfront anywhere near the town center, but you get a great sense of the river's might from the 1km-plus bridge that carries Hwy 180 over it, 4km south of town. In 1519 the Spanish conquistadors under Cortés scored their first military victory near here, defeating the local inhabitants somewhere among the nearby marshes in what's become known as the Battle of Centla. The locals fled in terror from the mounted Spaniards, thinking horse and rider to be one single mighty beast. Afterwards the natives made Cortés a gift of 20 women, one of whom, Doña Marina or La Malinche, became his indispensable interpreter, and lover. In the 20th century, Frontera was probably the setting for Graham Greene's novel *The Power and the Glory*. The main reason to stop here today is to visit the Reserva de la Biosfera Pantanos de Centla (below).

The modernized **Hotel Marmor Plaza** (☎ 332-00-01; Juárez 202; s/d/tr M$375/420/500; P ✕), on Frontera's central plaza, is quite a find: beautiful, good-sized, sparkling-clean rooms come with spot lighting, silent air-conditioning and gleaming bathrooms. **Hospedaje Star** (☎ 332-50-57; Obregón 506; r M$280-330; ✕), just round the corner, is an acceptable alternative, with good big rooms holding up to four.

For eating, the bright, air-conditioned **Café del Puerto** (cnr Madero & Aldama; breakfasts, salads & antojitos M$20-60; ☾ 8:30am-midnight), on the plaza, has the best ambience, and well-prepared food.

From the **ADO terminal** (☎ 332-11-49; Zaragoza 609), six blocks from the plaza, 1st-class buses leave for Villahermosa (M$32, 1½ hours, 25 daily), Paraíso (M$52, two hours, three daily) and Campeche (M$168 to M$204, 4½ hours, three daily).

Reserva de la Biosfera Pantanos de Centla

This 3030-sq-km biosphere reserve protects a good part of the wetlands around the lower reaches of two of Mexico's biggest rivers, the Usumacinta and the Grijalva. These lakes, marshes, rivers, mangroves, savannas and forests are an irreplaceable sanctuary for countless creatures, including the West Indian manatee and Morelet's crocodile (both endangered), six kinds of tortoise, tapir, ocelots, jaguars, howler monkeys, 60 fish species (including the *pejelagarto)*, and 230 bird species – not to mention 15,000 people scattered in 90 small waterside villages.

A paved (and in parts rough) road follows the broad winding Río Usumacinta, right across the reserve from the Grijalva bridge near Frontera, eventually reaching the town of Jonuta (from which other roads lead to the major east–west Hwy 186). Ten kilometers along this road, **Punta Manglar** (☎ 913-403-97-63; Hwy Frontera-Jonuta Km 10; ☾ 9am-4pm Tue-Sun) is an embarkation point for boat-and-foot **excursions** (☎ 913-403-98-42; up to 7 people M$500; ☾ 6am-7pm) into the mangroves, where you should see crocodiles, iguanas, birds and, with luck, howler monkeys.

The reserve's visitors center, the **Centro de Interpretación Uyotot-Ja** (☎ 993-313-93-62; Carretera Frontera-Jonuta Km 12.5; admission M$25; ☾ 9am-4pm Tue-Sun), is a further 2.5km along the road.

Here, a 20m-high observation tower overlooks the awesome confluence of the Grijalva, the Usumacinta and a third large river, the San Pedrito – a spot known as Tres Brazos (Three Arms). Guides lead you round a nature trail and displays on the wetlands, and boat trips (two hours, up to seven people M$500) are available – March to May is the best birding season.

Next door, **El Negro Chon** (mains M$40-80; ☾ 9am-6pm Tue-Sun) serves tasty fish and prawn dishes under a *palapa* (thatched roof) that catches delicious breezes off the river.

Gray combis and *colectivo* taxis from Calle Madero in Frontera (combis half a block south of the plaza, and *colectivos* 1½ blocks south of the plaza) charge M$10 for the 15-minute trip to Punta Manglar or Uyotot-Ja. Some continue to Jonuta (M$50, three hours), where buses leave for Villahermosa, Palenque and other destinations.

Tenosique

☎ 934 / pop 31,500

On the voluminous Río Usumacinta, amid farmland in far southeastern Tabasco, Tenosique is, for travelers, primarily a halt on a route into Guatemala. From the small border town of El Ceibo, 60km southeast of Tenosique, boats head along the Río San Pedro to El Naranjo, Guatemala, where you can catch onward transportation to Flores. A new road between El Ceibo and El Naranjo might be open by the time you get there.

The mighty Usumacinta issues from jungle-clad hills at **Boca del Cerro**, 8km southwest of Tenosique on Hwy 203. *Lancha* (fast, open outboard boat) operators, at the *embarcadero* on the west side of the bridge, charge around M$400 per boat for a 1½-hour trip up the river to the start of the rapids-strewn San José canyon and back.

SLEEPING & EATING

Hotel Hacienda Tabasqueña (☎ 342-27-31; Calle 26 No 512; s/d with fan M$200/222, with air-con M$300/339 ✕) On the main street, this is a large central hotel that is less cared for than nearby La Casona (below) but still acceptable. It has a small, onsite restaurant.

Hotel La Casona (☎ 342-11-51; Calle 27 No 8; r M$300 P ✕) Friendly La Casona, two blocks off the main street (Calle 26, also called Blvd Pino Suárez), has just nine rooms on two floors around a pretty courtyard adorned with lovable ceramic frogs. Rooms have cable TV, air-con, fan and pretty tiled bathrooms.

Restaurant Los Tulipanes (cnr Calles 27 & 22; mains M$40-80; ☺ 7am-5pm) The best place to eat, one block off the main street, spreads under a large palm-thatch roof, with live marimba music from 2pm. A good range of fish, steaks and seafood is served.

GETTING THERE & AROUND

The **ADO bus station** (☎ 342-14-41; Prolongación Calle 20 s/n) is on the southwest edge of town, about 2.5km from the center. Seventeen daily 1st- and 2nd-class services go to Emiliano Zapata (M$25 to M$38, one hour) and Villahermosa (M$70 to M$130, three to 3½ hours). If you're heading for the Yucatán Peninsula, it's usually quicker to get a bus to Emiliano Zapata and change there. Buses (M$5) and *colectivo* taxis (M$15) run from the bus station to the center.

To Guatemala

Buses to the border at El Ceibo (M$30, one hour, hourly 6am to 5pm) leave from the corner of Calles 16 and 45, beside the market two blocks off the main Calle 26. From the border, pickups (M$10 to M$20, 10 minutes) take passengers to the *embarcadero* for frequent *lanchas* up the Río San Pedro to El Naranjo (per person M$30, 30 minutes) until around 5pm. El Naranjo has money-changers, a bank and places to stay, and minibuses and buses (M$35, two to three hours) leave for Flores at least hourly until about 6pm. You can get from Tenosique to Flores in around six hours total.

CHIAPAS

Chilly pine forest highlands, sultry rain-forest jungles and attractive colonial cities exist side by side within Mexico's southernmost state, a region awash with the legacy of Spanish rule and the remnants of the ancient Maya civilization. The state has the second-largest indigenous population in the country, and the modern Maya of Chiapas form a direct link to the past, with a traditional culture that persists to this day. Many indigenous communities rely on subsistence farming and have no running water or electricity, and it was frustration over lack of political power and their historical mistreatment that fueled the Zapatista rebellion, putting a spotlight on the region's distinct inequities.

Chiapas contains swathes of wild green landscape that have nourished its inhabitants for centuries. From the Lacandón Jungle to the reserves of El Triunfo and Selva El Ocote, Chiapas offers incredible opportunities for outdoor adventures. But a rich trove of natural resources also makes it a contentious prize in the struggle for its water, lumber and oil and gas reserves.

TUXTLA GUTIÉRREZ

☎ 961 / pop 490,000 / elevation 530m

In Chiapas, Tuxtla Gutiérrez is as close to the big city as you're going to get. A busy modern metropolis and transportation hub, the state capital doesn't overwhelm with style, though it makes up for it with lots of amenities and nightlife. Most travelers pass through either the shiny new airport or bus station on the way to somewhere else, but it's a comfortable, worthwhile and warm place to spend a day or two.

Orientation

The city center is Plaza Cívica, with the always-busy main east–west street, Av Central, running across its south side. West of the center, Av Central becomes Blvd Dr Belisario Domínguez; many of the Tuxtla's best hotels and restaurants are strung along this road. Eastward, Av Central changes names to Blvd Ángel Albino Corzo.

MAPS

Inegi (☎ 618-72-74; www.inegi.gob.mx; 6a Av Sur Pte 670; ☺ 8:30am-4:30pm Mon-Fri), southwest of the center, sells 1:25,000 and 1:50,000 topographic maps of many parts of Chiapas and other Mexican states.

Information

INTERNET ACCESS

Ciber Center (1a Av Sur Ote 445; per hr M$7; ☺ 9:30am-10:30pm)

El Chi@p@neco (4a Calle Ote Sur 115; per hr M$5; ☺ 8:30am-11pm Mon-Sat, 10am-10pm Sun)

LAUNDRY

Lavandería Zaac (2a Av Nte Pte 440; per 3kg M$30; ☺ 8am-2pm & 4-8pm Mon-Fri, 9am-4pm Sat)

TABASCO & CHIAPAS

TUXTLA GUTIÉRREZ

INFORMATION

Bancomer (ATM)............................1	B3
Ciber Center..................................2	D3
El Chiápy@neco.............................3	D3
HSBC (ATM)...................................4	C3
Inegi...5	B4
Lavandería Zaac...........................6	B2
Municipal Tourist Office...............7	B2
Post Office...................................8	C2
Tourism Information Kiosk............9	A2
Tourism Information Kiosk..........10	C3

SIGHTS & ACTIVITIES

Catedral de San Marcos..............11	C3
Centro de Convivencia	
Infantil.....................................12	F1
Museo Regional de Chiapas.......13	F1
Viajes Kali............................(see 16)	

SLEEPING 🛏

Hotel Casablanca.......................14	C2
Hotel Catedral...........................15	D2
Hotel María Eugenia...................16	D3
Hotel Regional San Marcos.........17	C3
Hotel San Antonio......................18	D3
Hotel Santa María......................19	A2

EATING 🍴

Cafetería del Parque...................20	A2
El Fogón Norteño.......................21	A2
Las Pichanchas..........................22	E3
Naturalíssimo............................23	B2
Naturalíssimo............................24	B2
Restaurante Imperial..................26	C2
Restaurante La Casona...............27	C3

ENTERTAINMENT 🎭

Teatro de la Ciudad....................28	F1

SHOPPING 🛍

La Boutique del Café...................29	A2

TRANSPORT

Aviacsa......................................30	C3
Colectivos to Zoomat..................31	C4
Combis to Chiapa de Corzo.........32	D3
Combis to Oozocoautla (Coita)....33	B3
Corazón de María Van Terminal...34	F3
Monarca Viajes...........................35	A2

MONEY

Many banks exchange currency and have ATMs. An ATM at the airport (departure level) is accessible until 8:30pm.

Bancomer (Av Central Pte 314; 🕑 8:30am-4pm Mon-Fri)

HSBC (Calle Central Nte 137; 🕑 8am-6pm Mon-Sat)

POST

Post office (1a Av Nte Pte; 🕑 9am-4pm Mon-Fri, 8:30am-1pm Sat) In the Palacio Federal.

TOURIST INFORMATION

Airport kiosk (🕑 9am-6pm) In the arrivals level; free city maps.

Information kiosks (🕑 9am-2pm & 4-8pm) At the Jardín de la Marimba and Plaza Cívica.

Municipal Tourist Office (☎ 614-83-83, ext 111; Edificio Valanci, Av Central Pte 554, 4th fl; 🕑 8am-4pm Mon-Fri, until 1pm Sat)

Secretaría de Turismo (☎ 617-05-50, 800-280-35-00; www.turismochiapas.gob.mx; Blvd Belisario Domínguez 950; 🕑 8am-8pm Mon-Sat, 9am-2pm Sun) Chiapas' state tourism department has excellent maps and booklets, and English- and French-speakers are available on its toll-free phone number. The office is in a building marked Secretaría de Desarrollo Económico, 1.6km west of Plaza Cívica.

Sights

The pulse of the city is around the Plaza Cívica, the liveliest area during the daytime, though the main attractions are scattered around the suburbs.

PLAZA CÍVICA

Bustling and broad, Tuxtla's main plaza occupies two blocks flanked by an untidy array of concrete civic and commercial structures. At its southern end, across Av Central, you'll find nice hill views in front of the whitewashed modern **Catedral de San Marcos**. The cathedral's clock tower tinkles out a tune on the hour to accompany a kitsch merry-go-round of apostles' images that emerges from its upper levels.

ZOOLÓGICO MIGUEL ÁLVAREZ DEL TORO

Chiapas, with its huge range of natural environments, has the highest concentration of animal species in North America – including several varieties of big cat, 1200 butterfly species and over 600 birds. About 180 of these species, many of them in danger of extinction, are to be found in relatively spacious enclosures at Tuxtla's excellent **zoo** (☎ 614-47-5; Calz Cerro Hueco s/n; admission M$20, free before 10am &

Tue; 🕑 8:30am-5pm Tue-Sun; 🚻). The Zoológico Miguel Álvarez del Toro (Zoomat) has several innovative features, including a 'museum' about itself with information about the life of its pioneering conservationist founder Dr Miguel Álvarez del Toro. Beasts you'll see here include ocelots, jaguars, pumas, tapirs, red macaws, toucans, three species of crocodile, snakes and spider monkeys. To get to the zoo take a 'Cerro Hueco, Zoológico' *colectivo* (M$4, 25 minutes) from the corner of 1a Calle Ote Sur and 7a Av Sur Ote. A taxi is M$30.

PARQUE MADERO

The **Museo Regional de Chiapas** (☎ 612-04-59; Calz de los Hombres Ilustres s/n; admission M$37; 🕑 9am-6pm Tue-Sun), an imposing modern building, has a sampling of lesser archaeological pieces from Chiapas' many sites, and a slightly more interesting history section, running from the Spanish conquest to the revolution, all in Spanish only. Parque Madero also contains the lush oasis of the **Jardín Botánico** (Botanic Garden; admission free; 🕑 9am-6pm Tue-Sun) – a nice respite from the city heat – and a children's park, the **Centro de Convivencia Infantil** (admission free, rides each M$8-18; 🕑 9am-8pm Tue-Sun; 🚻), with a mini train, carnival games, pony rides and other diversions for the (approximately) under-sevens. A lot of rides don't open weekdays.

Tours

Viajes Kali (☎ 611-31-75; Av Central Ote 507) In the Hotel María Eugenia, organizes trips throughout Chiapas, including day trips to the Sima de Las Cotorras (p810; private tour M$1100, group tour Saturday or Sunday M$120) and the Cañón del Sumidero (M$400 per person).

Sleeping

Budget hotels cluster in the city center, while most midrange and luxury hotels are strung out along Av Central Pte and Blvd Belisario Domínguez, up to 4km west of the center. Cable TV and free parking are standard at these places. The larger hotels have desks at the airport.

BUDGET

our pick **Hotel Casablanca** (☎ 611-0305, 800-560-4422; www.casablancachiapas.com; 2a Av Nte Ote 251; s M$155-215, d/tr M$214-258, d/tr/q with air-con M$401/467/550; 🖳) Funky-fabulous abstract murals in brilliant lime green, hot pink and electric blue give these hotel rooms a dash of unexpected pizzazz. A tranquil open courtyard blooms with palms, and the terrace is a comfy place to survey street life. The upstairs rooms have air-con and more light.

Hotel San Antonio (☎ 612-27-13; 2a Av Sur Ote 540; r M$180, tw & tr M$250; P) Though in a busy part of town, Hotel San Antonio is run by friendly people and has clean, good-value rooms with pretty prints.

Hotel Catedral (☎ 613-08-24; 1a Av Nte Ote 367; s/d/tr M$230/280/330; P) One of the best-value budget options, the well-run Catedral has neat, clean rooms with bathroom, fan and free drinking water. The psychedelic turquoise steps and red velvet sofas in the foyer areas are a nice touch.

Hotel Regional San Marcos (☎ /fax 613-19-40; sanmarcos@chiapas.net; 2a Calle Ote Sur 176; s/d with fan M$249/285, s/d with air-con M$313/359; P ✕) Centrally-located, with very friendly staff, a good restaurant and free wi-fi, the San Marcos has medium-sized rooms with phone just a minute's walk from Plaza Cívica and Av Central.

MIDRANGE

Hotel Santa María (☎ /fax 614-65-77; 8a Calle Pte Nte 160; s/d/tr M$445/550/600; P ✕) Right on the pretty Jardín de la Marimba and near a number of good coffeehouses, this small hotel has rooms with folksy decorations and nice bathrooms with mosaic tiling.

Hotel Bonampak (☎ 602-59-16/21, 800-50-771-77; www.hotelbonampak.com.mx; Blvd Belisario Domínguez 180; s/d/tr/q M$500/572/615/662; P ✕ 🖳 🖵 👶) A comfy middle-class hotel 1.6km west of Plaza Cívica, the Bonampak has good-sized rooms with archaeological prints as well as three excellent restaurants. Avoid the noisier streetside rooms. In the lobby, a vibrant copy of a Bonampak site mural adds a spark to the décor. A small outdoor play structure entertains the kids.

Hotel María Eugenia (☎ 613-37-67; www.mariaeugenia.com.mx; Av Central Ote 507; s/d M$700/800; P ✕ 🖵) This is easily the most comfortable hotel in the center, with a reliable restaurant and good in-house travel agency (see p805) to boot. All 83 airy, bright and spacious rooms have either two double beds or a huge king-size bed, and many have great views. There's also a small garden with pool and free wi-fi.

Hotel Maya Sol (☎ 617-50-60; www.hotelmayasol-chiapas.com; Blvd Belisario Domínguez 1380; r M$800-850, ste M$1300; P ✕ 🖳 🖵) Colorful prints enliven modern, white air-conditioned rooms,

with large mirrors and ample writing desks. A restaurant and small pool fill in the rest of the creature comforts you might need. Located 3km west of Plaza Cívica.

TOP END

Crowne Plaza (☎ 617-22-00, 800-507-79-07; www.crowneplaza.com; Blvd Belisario Domínguez Km 1081; r M$1038, r incl breakfast M$1347-1450; P ✕ 🖳 🖵 🖳) A new luxury hotel ensconced within the already-cushy Holiday Inn, 4km west of the center, its contemporary earth tone rooms have large chairs, easy chairs and lots of executive-oriented amenities. Their website posts significantly lower rates.

Hotel Camino Real (☎ 617-77-77, 800-901-23-00; www.caminoreal.com; Blvd Belisario Domínguez 1195; r M$2106-2457; P ✕ 🖳 🖵 🖳) Lording over all it surveys from a spectacular hillside perch 3km west of Plaza Cívica, the 210-room Camino Real feels more like a feudal castle. A spectacular interior features a pool and waterfall in a large, verdant atrium-courtyard, full of free-flying tropical birds. Corner rooms have especially far-reaching views. Modern rooms trimmed with tasteful Mexican textiles come with green marble bathrooms, and some are fully wheelchair accessible. Other amenities include a spa, tennis courts and a 24-hour restaurant.

Eating

Most upscale and international options are west of the center, along Blvd Belisario Domínguez.

Restaurante Imperial (☎ 612-06-48; Calle Central Nte 263; mains M$24-38, comida corrida M$36; 🕙 8am-6pm) This busy, efficient place beside Plaza Cívica offers a wholesome two-course *comida corrida* (set lunch) with plenty of choice. There's a full breakfast menu too, and good drinking chocolate.

Restaurante La Casona (☎ 612-75-34; 1a Av Sur Pte 134; breakfast M$30-45, mains M$40-60; 🕙 7am-11pm) Beyond stately carved wooden doors, high ceilings, columns and interior arches frame a dramatic tableclothed dining room in a century-old building. Dine on regional dishes like *pollo juchi* (fried chicken with pickled vegetables and potatoes) or *tasajo en salsa de chirmol* (sliced beef in tomato sauce) and listen to marimba performances from 2pm to 6pm.

Naturalíssimo (breakfast M$37-53, antojitos M$27-45, mains M$45-68; V ; 6a Calle Pte Nte 124 ☎ 613-53-43;

7am-10:30pm Mon-Sat, 8am-10:30pm Sun; Av Central Pte 648 ☎ 613-36-16; 7am-10pm; Av Central Ote 523 ☎ 611-12-47; 7am-9pm Mon-Sat) Keeping thankful vegetarians afloat, Naturalíssimo offers healthy breakfasts, whole-wheat bread, *tortas* and veggie *hamburgesas*, as well as thirst-quenching fruit juices and *licuados*, yogurts and ice cream. Their fake meat dishes aren't super-inspiring, but do the trick if you need protein.

Cafetería Bonampak (☎ 602-59-33, ext 127; Hotel Bonampak, Blvd Belisario Domínguez 180; mains M$45-80) For a satisfying meal at any time of day you can't beat this air-conditioned hotel restaurant with bright ambience and good service. The long menu runs from prawn cocktails and *antojitos* (corn- and tortilla-based snacks) to beef, chicken, pasta and some yummy *pasteles* (cakes).

Las Pichanchas (☎ 612-53-51; www.laspichanchas.com.mx; Av Central Ote 837; mains M$45-85; noon-midnight;) This courtyard restaurant specializes in Chiapas food with live marimba music and, from 9pm to 10pm every night, a show of colorful traditional Chiapas dances that whips up quite a party atmosphere. Try the tasty *tamales*, or *pechuga jacuané* (chicken breast stuffed with beans in a hierba santa sauce), and leave room for *chimbos*, a dessert made from egg yolks and cinnamon.

El Fogón Norteño (☎ 612-95-01; cnr 1a Av Nte Pte & 9a Calle Pte Nte; mains M$50-70; 7am-1am) A bustling open air grill house overlooking the Jardín de la Marimba (see right), with well-prepared meat dishes at excellent prices. Most come with tasty *frijoles charros* (beans cooked with bacon or pork).

Cafetería del Parque (☎ 612-6000; 8a Calle Pte Sur 113; antojitos M$40-45, mains M$50-95; 8am-10:30pm) Nice wraparound windows make this one of the better people-watching eateries around the Jardín de la Marimba. With air-conditioning reinforced by an Arctic-blue décor, it's definitely a blissful place to cool off.

Maguey (☎ 602-59-16, ext 224; Hotel Bonampak, Blvd Belisario Domínguez 180; breakfast M$85, mains M$55-150; 7am-5pm) Cacti and floral murals scale a Victorian rotunda of white wainscoting and peach walls, making a cheerful backdrop for a sunny breakfast. Its Sunday brunch (M$90), with live *ranchera* music, is very popular.

Le Chat de la Nuit (☎ 639-63-98; Blvd Belisario Domínguez 2475; mains M$90-245; 2pm-midnight daily, plus 7am-1pm Sun) Fancy French food meets Argentine steakhouse for a culinary collision of *caracoles* (snails) and prime *bistek*. It works delightfully, as does the elegant adjoining bar, with a speakeasy atmosphere and live *trova*, salsa and merengue from 9:30pm till late.

Entertainment

Jardín de la Marimba, a leafy plaza eight blocks west of Plaza Cívica, is fun in the evening, especially at weekends. Popular free marimba concerts are held nightly from 6:30pm to 9:30pm, often with people dancing around the central bandstand. Several places to eat and drink surround the plaza.

Teatro de la Ciudad (☎ 613-13-49; Calz de los Hombres Ilustres, Parque Madero) The City Theater stages everything from opera and folkloric dance to film seasons.

CLUBS

There's no shortage of decent bars and raucous dance spots in the 'Zona Dorada,' 2km to 4km west of the center along Blvd Belisario Domínguez. Most places fill up around 11:30pm on Friday and Saturday (when they generally charge M$25 to M$50), and party till late. Clubs open and close here at a breakneck pace, but most of the following are within walking distance of others.

Baby Rock (☎ 615-91-20; Callejón Emiliano Zapata 207; from 9pm Thu-Sat) Inside a huge faux cave is Tuxtla's headquarters of *grupera* music, or 'Tux-Mex' as they call it here.

Bypass (☎ 616-53-69; Blvd Belisario Domínguez 1849; 9pm-3am Thu-Sat) A retro lounge-bar with a futuristic aura, they play electronica and house music from the '80s and '90s. A well between the two levels lets you spy on everyone shakin' it. Located between the parking garage and Sanborns at the Plaza Cristal mall.

Habana Cafe (☎ 121-49-89; Blvd Las Fuentes 110; 9pm-5am Thu-Sat) *Salseros*, take your places! Tucked next door to the Hotel Camino Real, the city views from this hilltop dance club are as hot as the moves. Stop in from 9pm to 11pm for free salsa classes so you can warm up for the live music starting at midnight.

Live (☎ 149-33-16; Blvd Belisario Domínguez Km 1081; 10pm-5am Thu-Sat) Just west of the Holiday Inn (see Crowne Plaza opposite), you'll find the locals dancing on the seats of this pulsing, packed nightclub. DJs spin a blend of pop, rock and electronica, and there's usually a band playing in the wee margarita-soaked hours. Men cough up a M$120 cover on Fridays and Saturdays.

Santa Diabla (☎ 602-68-62; Blvd Belisario Domínguez 2138; 8pm-4am Wed-Sat) A schizophrenic nightclub: there's an angelic bar lit by tin stars, and a devilish red disco with live rock and salsa starting at 1:30am. Garden of Eden murals round out the ladies' room. It's about 2.5km from Plaza Cívica.

Shopping

Instituto de las Artesanías (☎ 602-65-65; Blvd Belisario Domínguez 2035; ☉ 8am-9pm Mon-Fri, 10am-9pm Sat, 10am-3pm Sun) The Chiapas Crafts Institute, 2km west of Plaza Cívica, sells a great range of the state's *artesanías* (handicrafts), from Amatenango 'tigers' and funky Cintalapa ceramic suns to colorful highland textiles.

La Boutique del Café (☎ 614-78-97; cnr 8a Calle Pte Nte & 1a Av Nte Pte; ☉ 10am-9pm Tue-Fri, 4-9pm Sat-Mon) Selling the aromatic gold of 2000 small-scale *chiapaneco* farmers, this friendly coffee exchange can make a killer cappuccino or send you packing with bags of heady organic ambrosia. Try the Café Mam (M$90 per kilogram), produced by an indigenous cooperative in the remote Motozintla area.

Getting There & Away

AIR

Tuxtla's small and gleaming new **Aeropuerto Ángel Albino Corzo** (☎ 153-60-68) is 35km southeast of the city center and 18km south of Chiapa de Corzo. From Tuxtla, a private taxi will set you back M$150, and **Monarca Viajes** (☎ 132-81-91; 4a Calle Pte Nte 145) has seven daily *colectivos* for M$100. From the airport, pre-pay taxis (for one to three passengers) meet all flights and go to central Tuxtla (M$180, 40 minutes), Chiapa de Corzo (M$200, 30 minutes) and San Cristóbal (M$500, 1½ hours).

Click Mexicana (☎ 800-112-54-25; www.clickmx.com) flies direct to Mexico City six times daily, with connecting flights to Villahermosa, Mérida and Cancún. **Aviacsa** (☎ 800-284-22-72; Av Central Pte 160) has four daily flights to Mexico City and one to Tapachula.

BUS, COLECTIVO & COMBI

A modern new **OCC terminal** (☎ 125-15-80, ext 2433; 5a Av Nte Pte 318) northwest of the Plaza Cívica now houses all the 1st-class buses (including ADO and deluxe UNO) and the 2nd-class Rápidos del Sur line. More 2nd-class buses and combis depart from the **Terminal de Transporte Tuxtla** (cnr 9a Av Sur Ote & 13a Calle Ote Sur), with frequent destinations including San Cristóbal, Ocosingo and Ocozocoautla. Daily departures from the OCC terminal include the following:

Destination	Fare	Duration	Frequency (daily)
Cancún	M$650-806	20hr	1 deluxe, 1 1st-class
Comitán	M$70	3hr	4 deluxe, 10 1st-class
Mérida	M$494-686	14-15hr	2 deluxe, 2 1st-class
Mexico City (most to TAPO)	M$702-834	12hr	3 deluxe, 3 1st-class
Oaxaca	M$306-368	10hr	1 deluxe, 3 1st-class
Palenque	M$150-180	6hr	1 deluxe, 7 1st-class
Puerto Escondido	M$324	11hr	2
San Cristóbal de Las Casas	M$33-36	1-1¼hr	3 deluxe, 21 1st-class
Tapachula	deluxe M$226-416	6-7hr via Tonalá, 8hr via Comitán	6 deluxe, 12 1st-class, 25 2nd-class
Tonalá	M$60-120	3hr	2 deluxe, 13 1st-class, 26 2nd-class
Villahermosa	M$200-240	4-7½hr	2 deluxe, 4 1st-class, 6 2nd-class

Other more frequent options to San Cristóbal de Las Casas (M$35, 1½ hours):

Corazón de María (cnr Av Central Ote & 12a Calle Ote Sur) Combis from 5am to 9pm.

Omnibus de Chiapas (☎ 611-26-56; cnr 15a Calle Ote Sur & 4a Av Sur Ote) Minibuses every 10 minutes from 5am to 10pm.

Combis for Chiapa de Corzo (M$9, 30 minutes) leave every few minutes between 5am and 10:30pm from 1a Av Sur Ote.

CAR & MOTORCYCLE

In addition to companies at the airport, in-town rental agencies include the following:

Alamo (☎ 602-1600; 5a Av Nte Pte 2260) Near the OCC bus station.

Hertz (☎ 615-53-48; Hotel Camino Real, Blvd Belisario Domínguez 1195)

Getting Around

Ruta 1 *colectivos* (M$4) ply Blvd Belisario Domínguez–Av Central–Blvd Albino Corzo running as far as the 'Zona Dorada' clubs to the west, and the Soriana taxi stand to the east.

Stops are marked by blue bus signs, and service ends around 10:30pm. Taxi rides within the city cost M$25 to M$30.

AROUND TUXTLA GUTIÉRREZ

Chiapa de Corzo

☎ 961 / pop 38,000 / elevation 450m

An overlooked jewel set 12km east of Tuxtla Gutiérrez on the way to San Cristóbal, Chiapa de Corzo is a small and attractive colonial town with an easygoing, provincial air. Set on the north bank of the broad Río Grijalva, it's the main starting point for trips into the Cañón del Sumidero (p810).

Chiapa de Corzo has been occupied almost continuously since about 1500 BC. Before the Spaniards arrived, the warlike Chiapa tribe had their capital, Nandalumí, a couple of kilometers downstream, on the opposite bank of the Grijalva. When Diego de Mazariegos invaded the area in 1528, the Chiapa apparently hurled themselves by the hundreds to their death in the canyon rather than surrender.

Mazariegos founded a settlement called Chiapa de Los Indios here, but quickly shifted his base to San Cristóbal de Las Casas, where he found the climate and natives more manageable.

ORIENTATION & INFORMATION

Buses from Tuxtla stop on the north side of central Plaza Ángel Albino Corzo, or just past it on Av 21 de Octubre. The *embarcadero* for Cañón del Sumidero boat trips is two blocks south of the plaza down 5 de Febrero.

BBVA Bancomer (☎ 616-06-53; Plaza Ángel Albino Corzo 5; 🕑 8:30am-4pm Mon-Fri) On the east side of the plaza, it has an ATM.

Tourist office (☎ 616-10-13; Av Domingo Ruíz 1; 🕑 8am-4pm Mon-Fri) Just off the west side of the plaza.

SIGHTS

Impressive arcades frame three sides of the plaza, and a beefy tree called **La Pochota** bucks the sidewalk as it flexes its centuries-old roots. Venerated by the indigenous people who founded the town, it's the oldest ceiba tree along the Río Grijalva. But the focal point of the plaza and the image on all state license plates, **La Pila** (also called the Fuente Colonial) is a handsome brick fountain completed in 1562 in Mudejar-Gothic style. It's said to resemble the Spanish crown.

The large **Templo de Santo Domingo de Guzmán**, one block south of the plaza, was built in the late 16th century by the Dominican order. Its adjoining convent is now the **Centro Cultural** (☎ 616-00-55; Mexicanidad Chiapaneca 10; admission free; 🕑 10am-5pm Tue-Sun), home to an exposition of the wood and lino prints of talented Chiapa-born Franco Lázaro Gómez (1922–49) as well as the **Museo de la Laca**, dedicated to the local craft specialty: lacquered gourds. The museum holds pieces dating back to 1606 and samples of lacquerwork from other centers in Mexico, China, Japan and Thailand.

COURSES

Dunham Institute (☎ 616-14-98; www.dunhaminstitute.com; Zaragoza 23) Has multiweek Spanish classes with homestay available from US$000.

FESTIVALS & EVENTS

The **Fiesta de Enero** (January 9–21) is one of Mexico's liveliest and most extraordinary festivals, including nightly dances involving cross-dressing young men, known as Las Chuntá. Women don the highly colorful, beautifully embroidered *chiapaneca* dress, and blond-wigged, mask-toting *Parachicos* (impersonating conquistadors) parade on January 15, 17 and 20. A canoe battle and fireworks extravaganza follow on the final evening.

SLEEPING

Hotel Los Ángeles (☎ 616-00-48; www.losangeleschiapas.com; Grajales 2; r with fan/air-con M$250/300; P ❄) This hotel at the southeast corner of the plaza has spotless rooms with hot-water bathroom, cable TV and fan. Upstairs rooms lack air-con, but are bigger and catch more breeze.

Hotel La Ceiba (☎ 616-07-73; www.laceibahotel.com; Av Domingo Ruíz 300; s/d/tr/q M$579/643/708/585; P ❄ 🏊) Also a full-service spa, La Ceiba has an inviting pool, a lush garden and 91 simple but well-kept air-conditioned rooms with cable TV. It's two blocks west of the plaza.

EATING

Restaurant Jardines de Chiapa (☎ 616-01-98; Madero 395; mains M$40-80; 🕑 9am-7:30pm summer, 8am-6:30pm fall-spring) Not too far from the plaza, this large place is set around a garden patio with atmospheric brick columns. The long menu includes tasty *cochinito al horno* (oven-baked pork).

Restaurant Los Corredores (☎ 616-07-60; www.loscorredores.com.mx; Madero 35; mains M$50-80; 🕑 9am-7pm) Facing the southwest corner of the plaza,

TABASCO & CHIAPAS

brightly-painted Los Corredores does a bit of everything: good breakfasts, reasonably priced fish plates and a few local specialties including *pepita con tasajo* (beef with a spicy pumpkin-seed sauce). It displays a fascinating collection of historical town photos.

D'Avellino (☎ 616-12-43; Calz Grajales 1103; mains M$50-90, pizza M$85-120; �y 1pm-1am Mon-Sat, to 11pm Sun) A cute Italian restaurant with a rustic old-world dining room and patio seating, it serves fresh pastas and good pizza. It's an easy five- to 10-minute stroll northwest of the plaza, along the main Tuxtla-bound road.

Restaurants on the *embarcadero* have near-identical, and equally overpriced, menus. The river views are nice, though battling marimba players tend to amp up the noise level.

GETTING THERE & AWAY

Combis from Tuxtla Gutiérrez (M$9, 30 minutes), leave from 1a Av Sur Ote (between Calles 5a & 7a Ote Sur), every few minutes from 5am to 10:30pm.

Going from Chiapa de Corzo to San Cristóbal is a bit inconvenient. Option one is to backtrack to Tuxtla and take a bus or combi via the fast new autopista. Option two is to catch a microbus to San Cristóbal (M$25, 1½ hours) from a stop across from the gas station on Hwy 190, on the northeast edge of town. Departures at 6:45am, 10am, 1pm, 3:30pm and 6pm take the slower (and *very* serpentine) old highway. *Colectivos* to this stop (M$4) run from the east side of the plaza; taxis cost M$20.

From San Cristóbal, most people go to Tuxtla Gutiérrez and catch a combi back, but you can also take a Tuxtla-bound van and ask to be let off at the Chiapa de Corzo stop on the highway. From there, it's a M$8 taxi ride to the town center.

Cañón del Sumidero

The Sumidero Canyon is a spectacular fissure in the earth, found east of Tuxtla Gutiérrez. In 1981 the Chicoasén hydroelectric dam was completed at its northern end, damming the Río Grijalva which flows through the canyon, and creating a 25km-long reservoir. Traveling between Tuxtla and Chiapa de Corzo, the road crosses the Grijalva just south of the canyon mouth.

The canyon can be viewed from above at five *miradores* (lookout points); bus tours to these (adult/child M$75/37, 3½ hours) leave

Tuxtla's cathedral at 9am and 1pm daily (except Monday) if a minimum of five people show up. However, the most impressive way to see the canyon is from a **lancha** (return trip M$120; �y 8am-4pm) that speeds between the canyon's towering rock walls. It's about a two-hour return trip, starting at either Chiapa de Corzo or the Embarcadero Cahuaré, 5km north of Chiapa along the road to Tuxtla. You'll rarely have to wait more than half an hour for a boat to fill up. Bring a drink, something to shield you from the sun and, if there's any chance of bad weather, some warm clothing or a waterproof jacket.

It's about 35km from Chiapa de Corzo to the dam. Soon after you pass under Hwy 190, the canyon walls tower an amazing 800m above you. Along the way you'll see a variety of birds – herons, cormorants, vultures, kingfishers – plus probably a crocodile or two. The boat operators will point out a few odd formations of rock and vegetation, including one cliff face covered in thick hanging moss, resembling a giant Christmas tree. *Lanchas* sometimes have to plow through a sheen of floating plastic garbage when wet-season rains wash in trash from Tuxtla Gutiérrez.

Sima de Las Cotorras

Located inside the Reserva de la Biosfera Selva El Ocote, the **Sima de Las Cotorras** (Abyss of the Parrots; admission adult/child over 9 M$20/10) is a dramatic sinkhole punching 160m-wide and 140m-deep into the earth. In the early morning, a green cloud of screeching parrots spirals out for the day, trickling back before dusk. With binoculars you can see a series of red pre-Hispanic rock paintings decorate one side of the cliff face, and you can also hike or rappel down inside this intriguing subterranean hole. **Lodging** (☎ 968-689-02-89; simacotorras@hotmail.com; camping M$100, cabaña M$300-400; P 🖳) is available, as well as a good **restaurant** (breakfast M$15-40, lunch/dinner M$25-50; �y 8am-6pm) serving scrumptious *tamales* and handmade tortillas.

From Tuxtla's Terminal de Transporte Tuxtla, take a combi to Ocozocoautla (also called Coita; M$90, 30 minutes); then call the lodging number to arrange a ride (M$150 per carload) or take a taxi (M$250, 50 minutes). Drivers will need to stop and ask for directions, as the 18km road from Ocozocoautla isn't well signed. Scheduled tours (M$120) from Tuxtla Gutiérrez (see p805) leave Saturday and Sunday mornings, but don't visit during prime parrot-watching hours.

SAN CRISTÓBAL DE LAS CASAS

☎ 967 / pop 142,000 / elevation 2160m

Set in a gorgeous highland valley surrounded by pine forest, the colonial city of San Cristóbal (cris-*toh*-bal) has been a popular travelers' destination for decades. It's a pleasure to explore San Cristóbal's cobbled streets and markets, soaking up the unique ambience and the wonderfully clear highland light. This medium-size city also boasts a comfortable blend of city and countryside, with restored century-old houses giving way to grazing animals and fields of corn.

Surrounded by dozens of traditional Tzotzil and Tzeltal villages, San Cristóbal is at the heart of one of the most deeply rooted indigenous areas in Mexico. A great base for local and regional exploration, it's a place where ancient customs coexist with modern luxuries.

The city is a hotspot for sympathizers (and some opponents) of the Zapatista rebels, and a central location for organizations working with Chiapas' indigenous people. In addition to a solid tourist infrastructure and a dynamic population of artsy and politically progressive foreigners and Mexicans, San Cristóbal also has a great selection of accommodations, and a cosmopolitan array of cafés, bars and restaurants.

History

Diego de Mazariegos founded San Cristóbal as the Spanish regional base in 1528. Its Spanish citizens made fortunes from wheat, while the indigenous people lost their lands and suffered diseases, taxes and forced labor. The church afforded some protection against colonist excesses. Dominican monks reached Chiapas in 1545, and made San Cristóbal their main base. The town is now named after one of them, Bartolomé de Las Casas, who was appointed bishop of Chiapas and became the most prominent Spanish defender of indigenous people in colonial times. In modern times Bishop Samuel Ruiz, who retired in 1999 after a long tenure, followed in Las Casas' footsteps, defending the oppressed indigenous people and earning the hostility of the Chiapas establishment.

San Cristóbal was the Chiapas state capital from 1824 to 1892, but remained relatively isolated until the 1970s, when tourism began to influence its economy. Recent decades have seen an influx of indigenous villagers into the 'Cinturón de Miseria' (Belt of Misery), a series

TABASCO & CHIAPAS

SAN CRISTÓBAL IN...

Two Days

Start the day inhaling the rich aroma of a locally-roasted cup of Chiapan **coffee** (p820) and then limber up with a Posada Ganesha **yoga class** (p816). Put on some comfortable walking shoes and set out to explore the colonial churches of **Templo de Santo Domingo** (p813) and the **cathedral** (p813), and then get lofty, climbing the twin hills of **Cerro de San Cristóbal** and **Cerro de Guadalupe** (p813) to survey the city.

Spend the second day visiting the traditional indigenous villages of Zinacatán and San Juan Chamula by **horseback** (p825) or **bicycle** (p824) and in the evening, drop by a **cinema** (p821) to catch a movie on local history or current events.

Four Days

With more time, build on the itinerary above and refresh your sagging Spanish with a few days of **language classes** (p816). Dig deeper into the local culture with visits to the **Museo de la Medicina Maya** (p816), the ethno-history landmark of **Na Bolom** (p813) and the contemporary **Centro Cultural El Carmen** (p816).

Browse for the best of local *artesanías* at the amazing weaving cooperative of **Sna Jolobil** (p821) and the paper- and book-making workshop of **Taller Leñateros** (p822). Wander the cacophony of sights and smells at the **Mercado Municipal** (p813) and make a date for some hearty **homemade tamales** (p820). Last but not least, dance through the night and bring in the morning, sampling the city's wild **nightlife** (p821).

of impoverished, violence-ridden, makeshift colonies around San Cristóbal's *periférico* (ring road). Many of these people are here because they have been expelled from Chamula and other communities as a result of internal politico-religious conflicts. Most of the craft sellers around Santo Domingo church and the underage hawkers around town come from the Cinturón de Miseria.

San Cristóbal was catapulted into the international limelight on January 1, 1994, when the Zapatista rebels selected it as one of four places in which to launch their revolution, seizing and sacking government offices in the town before being driven out within a few days by the Mexican army. Political and social tensions remain, but San Cristóbal continues to attract travelers, real estate investment and a growing middle class.

Climate

San Cristóbal de Las Casas and Los Altos de Chiapas – the state's central highlands, mostly 2000m to 3000m high – have a very temperate climate. Daytime temperatures are usually warm, but evenings can get incredibly cold between November and February, when you'll want a good jacket to ward off chills.

Orientation

San Cristóbal is very walkable, with straight streets rambling up and down several gentle hills. The Pan-American Hwy (Hwy 190, Blvd Juan Sabines, 'El Bulevar') runs through the southern part of town, and nearly all transportation terminals are on it or nearby. From the OCC bus terminal, it's six blocks north up Insurgentes to the central square, Plaza 31 de Marzo. Calle Real de Guadalupe, heading east from the plaza, has a concentration of places to stay and eat. A long pedestrian mall, the Andador Turístico (or Andador Eclesiástico), runs up Avs Hidalgo and 20 de Noviembre from the Arco de El Carmen in the south to the Templo de Santo Domingo in the north, crossing Plaza 31 de Marzo en route. The Cerro San Cristóbal and Cerro de Guadalupe lord over the town from the west and east, respectively.

Information

BOOKSTORES

La Pared (☎ /fax 678-63-67; lapared9@yahoo.com; Hidalgo 2; ☾ 10am-2pm & 4-8pm Mon-Sat, 3-7:30pm Sun) Stocks a great choice of new and used books in Eng-

lish, including Lonely Planet guides. It's run by a friendly American, who also trades used books.
Librería Chilam Balam (☎ 678-04-86; Utrilla 33; ☾ 9am-8pm)
Libros Soluna (☎ 678-68-05; Real de Guadalupe 13B; ☾ 9:30am-9pm Tue-Sat, 11am-5pm Sun, 9am-1pm & 4-9pm Mon) Selection includes maps and Lonely Planet guides in Spanish.

INTERNET ACCESS

San Cristóbal has dozens of inexpensive cybercafés.
Centro Cultural El Puente (Real de Guadalupe 55; per hr M$6; ☾ closed Sun) Free wi-fi.
Fast-Net Cyber Café (Real de Guadalupe 15D; per hr M$6)

LAUNDRY

Lavandería La Rapidita (☎ 678-80-59; Insurgentes 9; self-service per 5kg M$25, service wash per 3kg M$45; ☾ 9am-8pm Mon-Sat)
Lavandería Las Estrellas (Real de Guadalupe 75; per kg M$10; ☾ 9am-7pm)

MEDICAL SERVICES

Hospital Amigo del Niño y de la Madre (☎ 678-07-70; Insurgentes) General hospital with emergency facilities.
Sanatorio Dr Bonilla (☎ 680-80-50; Juárez 60) Dr Renato Zárate here is an English-speaking doctor.

MONEY

Most banks require a photocopy of your passport if you want to change cash or traveler's checks. There are also handy ATMs at the OCC bus station.
Banamex (Plaza 31 de Marzo; ☾ 9am-4pm Mon-Fri, 10am-2pm Sat) Has an ATM and a dedicated exchange counter.
HSBC (Mazariegos 6; ☾ 8am-7pm Mon-Sat, 10am-2:30pm Sun) Also has an ATM and is open the longest hours.
Lacantún Money Exchange (Real de Guadalupe 12A; ☾ 9am-9pm Mon-Sat, 9am-2pm & 4-9pm Sun) Open outside bank hours but rates are worse.

POST & TELEPHONE

El Locutorio (☎ 631-60-63; Rosas 7C; ☾ 8am-10pm) Offering inexpensive international calls, there are also branches at Belisario Domínguez 6A and Calle 20 de Noviembre 20A.
Main post office (☎ 678-07-65; Allende 3; ☾ 8:30am-7pm Mon-Fri, 8:30am-1pm Sat)

TOURIST INFORMATION

Municipal tourist office (☎ 678-06-65; Palacio Municipal, Plaza 31 de Marzo; ☾ 8am-8pm Mon-Fri, to

TABASCO & CHIAPAS

8pm Sat & Sun) Staff are generally knowledgeable about the San Cristóbal area.

State tourist office (☎ 678-14-67; Hidalgo 1B; 🕑 8am-9pm Mon-Fri, 9am-8pm Sat, 9am-2pm Sun) Has English-speaking staff and plenty of leaflets; one floor up but no signs. It may be moving to the Centro Cultural El Carmen (p816).

Sights

PLAZA 31 DE MARZO

The leafy main plaza is a fine place to take in San Cristóbal's unhurried highland atmosphere. Shoe-shiners, newspaper sellers and *ambulantes* (itinerant vendors) gather around the elaborate iron bandstand.

On the north side of the plaza, the **cathedral** was begun in 1528 but wasn't finally completed till 1815 because of several natural disasters. Sure enough, new earthquakes struck in 1816 and 1847, causing considerable damage, but it was restored again in 1920–22. The gold-leaf interior has five gilded altarpieces featuring 18th-century paintings by Miguel Cabrera.

The Hotel Santa Clara (see p818), on the plaza's southeast corner, was built by Diego de Mazariegos, the Spanish conqueror of Chiapas. His coat of arms is engraved above the main portal. The house is a rare secular example of plateresque style in Mexico.

CERRO DE SAN CRISTÓBAL & CERRO DE GUADALUPE

Want to take in the best views in town? Well, you'll have to work for them, because at this altitude the stairs up these hills can be punishing. Churches crown both lookouts, and the Iglesia de Guadalupe becomes a hotspot for religious devotees around the Día de la Virgen de Guadalupe (December 12).

TEMPLO & EX-CONVENTO DE SANTO DOMINGO

Located just north of the center, the 16th-century **Templo de Santo Domingo** (admission free; 🕑 6:30am-2pm & 4-8pm) is San Cristóbal's most beautiful church, especially when its facade catches the late-afternoon sun. This baroque frontage, with its outstanding filigree stucco work, was added in the 17th century and includes the double-headed Hapsburg eagle, symbol of the Spanish monarchy in those days. The interior is lavishly gilded, especially the ornate pulpit.

Around Santo Domingo and the neighboring **Templo de La Caridad** (built in 1712),

Chamulan women and bohemian types from around Mexico conduct a colorful daily **crafts market** (see p821). The ex-monastery attached to Santo Domingo contains two interesting exhibits: one is the weavers' showroom of **Sna Jolobil** (see p821); the other is the **Centro Cultural de los Altos** (☎ 678-16-09; Calz Lázaro Cárdenas s/n; admission M$33, free Sun & hols; 🕑 10am-5pm Tue-Sun) with a reasonable Spanish-language museum on the history of the San Cristóbal region.

NA BOLOM

An atmospheric **museum–research center** (☎ 678-14-18; www.nabolom.org; Guerrero 33; view house only M$35, 1½hr tour in English or Spanish regular/student M$45/20; 🕑 10am-6pm, Spanish tour 11:30am & English tour 4:30pm, no tours Mon), for many years Na Bolom was the home of Swiss anthropologist and photographer Gertrude Duby-Blom (Trudy Blom; 1901–93) and her Danish archaeologist husband Frans Blom (1893–1963).

They bought the 19th-century house in 1950, and while Frans explored and surveyed ancient Maya sites all over Chiapas (including Palenque, Toniná and Chinkultic), Trudy studied, photographed and fought to protect the scattered Lacandón people of eastern Chiapas and their jungle environment. Since Trudy's death, Na Bolom has continued the thrust of the Bloms' work, with the house operating as a museum and research center for the study and support of Chiapas' indigenous cultures and natural environment, and as a center for community and environmental programs in indigenous areas. The library of more than 9000 books and documents here is a major resource on the Maya.

Na Bolom means 'Jaguar House' in the Tzotzil language (as well as being a play on its former owners' name). It's full of photographs, archaeological and anthropological relics and books. The house tour provides a revealing insight into the lives of the Bloms and the Chiapas of half a century and more ago – though the picture presented of the Lacandones does dwell more on their past than their present.

Na Bolom also offers guest rooms (see p818) and meals made with organic vegetables grown in its garden.

MERCADO MUNICIPAL

For a closer look at local life – and an assault on the senses – visit San Cristóbal's busy municipal **market** (🕑 approx 7am-5pm), eight blocks

SAN CRISTÓBAL DE LAS CASAS

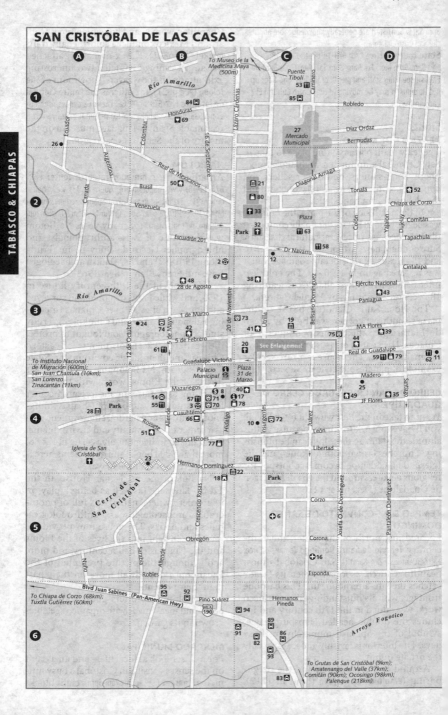

TABASCO & CHIAPAS

INFORMATION

Banamex (ATM)	1 G1
Centro Cultural El Puente	(see 59)
El Locutorio	2 B3
El Locutorio	3 B4
El Locutorio	4 H1
Fast-Net Cyber Café	5 H1
Hospital Amigo del Niño y de la Madre	6 C6
HSBC	7 B4
La Pared	8 B4
Lacantún Money Exchange	9 G1
Lavandería La Rapidita	10 C4
Lavandería Las Estrellas	11 D3
Librería Chilam Balam	12 C2
Libros Soluna	13 H1
Main Post Office	14 B4
Municipal Tourist Office	15 B4
Sanatorio Dr Bonilla	16 C5
State Tourist Office	17 B4

SIGHTS & ACTIVITIES

Arco de El Carmen	18 B5
Café Museo Café	19 C3
Cathedral	20 C3
Centro Cultural de los Altos	21 C2
Centro Cultural El Carmen	22 B4
El Puente Spanish Language School	(see 59)
Escuela de Español Sol Maya	23 B4
Explora	24 B3
Instituto Jovel	25 D4
Latitud 16	(see 31)
Los Pingüinos	26 A1
Mercado Municipal	27 C1
Museo del Ámbar de Chiapas	28 A4
Na Bolom	29 E2
Otisa	30 G1
SendaSur	31 H1
Templo de la Caridad	32 C2
Templo de Santo Domingo	33 C2
Trotamundos	34 H1
Viajes Chincultik	(see 36)
Zapata Tours	(see 60)

SLEEPING

Casa Felipe Flores	35 D4
Casa Margarita	36 H1
Hostal Rincón de los Camellos	37 E3
Hotel Casa Mexicana	38 C3
Hotel Casavieja	39 D3
Hotel Ciudad Real	40 C4
Hotel Diego de Mazariegos	41 C3
Hotel El Paraíso	42 B3
Hotel Posada Jovel	43 D3
Hotel Posada Tepeyac	44 D3
Hotel Santa Clara	45 G1
Le Gite del Sol	46 E4
Parador San Juan de Dios	47 E1
Posada Ganesha	48 B3
Posada México	49 D4
Rossco Backpackers Youth Hostel	50 B2
Villas Casa Azul	51 B4
Villas Casa Morada	52 D2

EATING

Alebrije	53 C1
Cucina Italiana Il Piccolo	54 H1
El Caldero	55 H1
El Gato Gordo	56 G1
Emiliano's Moustache	57 B4
La Casa del Pan	58 C2
La Casa del Pan Papalotl	59 D3
L'Eden	(see 42)
Madre Tierra	60 C4
Mayambé	61 B3
Pierre Restaurant Francés	62 D3
Pizzeria El Punto	63 C2
Restaurante Plaza Real	64 G1
TierrAdentro	65 H1

DRINKING

Café La Selva	66 B4
Cafetería Maya	67 B3
La Viña de Bacco	68 H1
Los Amigos	69 B1

ENTERTAINMENT

Barfly	70 B4
Blue	71 B4
Cinema El Puente	(see 59)
DaDa Club	72 C4
El Zirko	73 C3
Kinoki	74 B3
La Pera	75 D3
Latino's	76 H1

SHOPPING

Instituto de Las Artesanías	77 B4
Lágrimas de la Selva	78 C4
Nemi Zapata	79 D3
Sna Jolobil	80 C2
Taller Leñateros	81 E3

TRANSPORT

AEXA & Ómnibus de Chiapas Bus Station	82 C6
Colectivo Taxis to Grutas de San Cristóbal	83 C6
Combis to San Juan Chamula	84 B1
Combis to Zinacantán	85 C1
Corazon de Maria Suburbans to Tuxtla & Ocosingo	86 C6
Croozy Scooters	87 H1
Mexicana	88 H1
OCC Bus Station	89 C6
Optima	90 A4
Suburbans & Colectivo Taxis to Comitán	91 C6
Suburbans & Colectivo Taxis to Ocosingo	92 B6
Suburbans to Comitán	93 C6
Suburbans to Ocosingo	94 C6
Taxis Jovel (Colectivos to Tuxtla Gutiérrez)	95 B6
Ticket Bus	96 G1

north of the main plaza between Utrilla and Belisario Domínguez. Vendors peer from behind pyramids of tomatoes and mangoes, and you'll find dozens of varieties of chilies, as well as bloody butchers' stalls and fly-plagued dried-shrimp stands.

MUSEO DE LA MEDICINA MAYA

This award-winning **museum** (☎ 678-54-38; www .medicinamaya.org; Av Salomón González Blanco 10; admission M$20; ☽ 10am-6pm Mon-Fri, to 5pm Sat & Sun) introduces the system of traditional medicine used by many indigenous people in the Chiapas highlands. Traditional Maya medicine is a matter of praying to the spirit of the earth, listening to the voice of the blood and expelling bad spirits from the soul, with the aid of candles, bones, pine needles, herbs and the occasional chicken sacrifice. This museum, on the northern edge of town, is run by Organización de Médicos Indígenas del Estado de Chíapas (OMIECH), a group of 600 indigenous healers, midwives, herbalists and prayer specialists. Exhibits include displays of a ritual scene inside a church and a midwife assisting at a birth, and a video about the work of traditional midwives. Information is available in English, Spanish, French and German. Also on the site is a medicinal plant garden, a herbal pharmacy and a *casa de curación*, where treatments are done. It's a 15-minute walk north from Real de Guadalupe or M$18 by taxi.

ARCO, TEMPLO & CENTRO CULTURAL EL CARMEN

The **Arco de El Carmen**, at the southern end of the Andador Turístico on Hidalgo, dates from the late 17th century and was once the city's gateway. The ex-convent just east is a wonderful colonial building, with a large peaceful garden. It's now the **Centro Cultural El Carmen** (Hermanos Domínguez s/n; admission free; ☽ 9am-6pm Tue-Sun), hosting art and photography exhibitions and the occasional musical event.

CAFÉ MUSEO CAFÉ

This combined **café and coffee museum** (☎ 678-78-76; MA Flores 10; admission M$25; ☽ 9am-10pm) is a venture of Coopcafé, a grouping of 17,000 small-scale, mainly indigenous, Chiapas coffee growers. The museum covers the history of coffee and its cultivation in Chiapas, from highly exploitative beginnings to the community-based indigenous coffee production that's increasingly well marketed today. The

information is translated into English and you can taste some of that flavorful organic coffee in the café.

MUSEO DEL ÁMBAR DE CHIAPAS

Chiapas amber – fossilized pine resin, around 30 million years old – is known for its clarity and diverse colors. Most is mined around Simojovel, north of San Cristóbal. The **Museo del Ámber de Chiapas** (Chiapas Amber Museum; www .museodelambar.com.mx; Plazuela de la Merced; admission M$2; ☽ 10am-2pm & 4-7pm Tue-Sun) explains all things amber (with information sheets in English and other languages) and displays and sells some exquisitely carved items and insect-embedded pieces.

Courses

Several good language schools offer instruction in Spanish, with flexibility to meet most level and schedule requirements. Weekly rates given below are for three hours' tuition five days a week, with seven nights' homestay accommodations and three meals a day, but variations are available.

El Puente Spanish Language School (☎ 678-37-23; www.elpuenteweb.com; Real de Guadalupe 55; individual/group per week M$2300/1900) Housed in the Centro Cultural El Puente, which also has a vegetarian café, internet café, cinema, gallery and an alternative therapy center that gives fabulous massages. Classes are offered for any period from one day.

Escuela de Español Sol Maya (☎ 674-67-20; www .solmaya.org; Hermanos Domínguez 25A; individual/group per wk M$2391/2068) A new language school with a number of good community-based volunteer opportunities for students. Classes in Mexican cooking (M$98 to M$163), backstrap loom weaving (M$163), and group salsa lessons (M$54 per hour) are also available.

Instituto Jovel (☎ /fax 678-40-69; www.institutojovel .com; Madero 45; individual/group per wk M$2495/2195, classes-only individual/group per hr M$110/80) Instituto Jovel is professional and friendly, and has a top-class reputation among students. Most tuition is one-to-one, and they have a beautiful new location. Classes in Mexican cooking (US$9 per hour) and jewelry-making with amber and silver (US$22 per hour) are also offered.

Posada Ganesha (☎ 678-02-12; www.ganeshaposada .com; 28 de Agosto 23) Yoga sessions three times daily Monday through Friday (M$30) and twice on Saturdays (M$50); papier mâché classes (M$50) upon request.

Tours

Many agencies in San Cristóbal offer a variety of tours, often with guides who speak

English, French or Italian (for tours of indigenous villages around San Cristóbal, see p824). Following are typical day-trip prices per person (usually with a minimum of four people):

Chiapa de Corzo & Cañón del Sumidero (M$150-250, 6-7hrs)

Lagos de Montebello, Grutas de San Cristóbal, El Chiflón waterfalls (M$200-300, 9-10hrs)

Palenque, Agua Azul, Misol-Ha (M$250-350, 14hrs)

Recommended tour agencies (open approximately 8am to 9pm) include the following:

Otisa (☎ 678-19-33; www.otisatravel.com; Real de Guadalupe 3)

Trotamundos (☎ /fax 678-70-21; Real de Guadalupe 26C)

Viajes Chincultik (☎ 678-09-57; agchincultik@ hotmail.com; Casa Margarita, Real de Guadalupe 34)

Zapata Tours (☎ /fax 674-51-52; www.zapatatours .com; Insurgentes 19) Above Madre Tierra restaurant.

The following agencies specialize in more active trips:

Explora (☎ 678-42-95; www.ecochiapas.com; 1 de Marzo 30; ⏰ 9:30am-2pm & 4-8pm Mon-Fri, 9:30am-2pm Sat) Adventure trips to the Lacandón Jungle (four/five days M$3600/4540, minimum four people) including river kayaking and rafting; also spelunking tours in northwestern Chiapas, and day trips to rappel the Sima de Las Cotorras (p810).

Latitud 16 (☎ 674-69-15; www.latitud16.com; Real de Guadalupe 23)

Los Pingüinos (☎ 678-02-02; Ecuador 4B; www .bikemexico.com/pinguinos; bike hire 4/6/9 hrs M$100/130/150; ⏰ office 10am-2:30pm & 3:30-7pm Mon-Sat) Bicycle tours from half a day to two weeks.

SendaSur (☎ 678-39-09; www.sendasur.com; Real de Guadalupe 23) A partner-based ecotourism network in Chiapas, it can arrange group tours to places like Laguna Miramar (see p829), or help with independent travel.

Festivals & Events
Semana Santa The crucifixion is acted out on Good Friday in the Barrio de Mexicanos in the northwest of town.
Feria de la Primavera y de la Paz (Spring and Peace Fair) Easter Sunday is the start of the week-long town fair, with parades, musical events, bullfights and so on.
Festival Cervantino Barroco In late October and early November, this is a lively cultural program with music, dance and theater.

Sleeping
San Cristóbal has a wealth of budget accommodations, but also a number of appealing and atmospheric midrange hotels, often set in colonial or 19th-century mansions, along with a smattering of top-end luxury. The high seasons here are during Semana Santa and the following week, the months of July and August, plus the Día de Muertos and Christmas–New Year holidays. Most prices dip about 10% outside the high season.

BUDGET
Camping Rancho San Nicolás (☎ 678-00-57; Prolongación León s/n; campsites per person M$50, r with shared bathroom per person M$60, rustic cabaña per person M$60, villa d M$350) Past cornfields and grazing horses, this grassy spot on the edge of town is a tranquil dose of *el campo* in the city. Bring a tent or trailer, or choose from a spectrum of options, including basic rooms and modern apartments with kitchens and fireplaces. Communal kitchen usage is M$10 per day, and bathrooms have hot water.

Hostal Rincón de los Camellos (☎ 116-00-97; los camellos@hotmail.com; Real de Guadalupe 110; dm M$60, s/d/ tr/q with shared bathroom M$140/180/230/270, with private bathroom M$200/220/270/330) 'Camels' Corner' is a clean, tranquil little spot run by welcoming French folk. The brightly-painted rooms are set round two patios, with a grassy little garden out back. A small purple kitchen has free drinking water and coffee, and a shisha café clad in psychedelic fabrics is a pleasant low-key hangout.

Posada México (☎ 678-00-14; www.hostelling mexico.com; Josefa Ortiz de Domínguez 12; dm M$70, r with shared/private bathroom M$180/250, all incl full breakfast; ⊠ 🖳) A large courtyard compound with stunning mountain views, this HI hostel has pretty gardens, good bright rooms and dorms (one for women only), a kitchen and free internet, and tons of comfy terraces, patios and lounges. A 10% discount available for HI card-holders.

Rossco Backpackers Youth Hostel (☎ 674-05-25; www.backpackershostel.com.mx; Real de Mexicanos 16; dm M$85-100, s/d/tr with private bathroom M$200/280/390, all incl breakfast; 🖳) Backpackers is a friendly, sociable and well-run hostel with good dorm rooms (one for women only), a guest kitchen and a grassy garden. Upstairs rooms have nice skylights but not much privacy, as the wall doesn't reach the ceiling. Free wi-fi access and computers are available.

our pick Posada Ganesha (☎ 678-02-12; www .ganeshaposada.com; 28 de Agosto 23; s/d/tr/q with shared bathroom M$100/160/240/320; 🖳) A new incense-infused posada trimmed in Indian fabrics, it's a friendly and vibrant place to rest your head, with yoga and papier mâché classes (see Courses p816) and a guest kitchen. The free-standing *cabaña* room is especially nice.

Hotel Posada Jovel (☎ 678-17-34; www.mundoc hiapas.com/hotelposadajovel; Paniagua 28; posada s/d without bathroom M$150/200, with bathroom M$250/350, 'hotel' s/d/tr/q M$480/500/600/700; P ✗) Most rooms in the original 'posada' building have stripped wooden floors, bedside lights and highland blankets, while those in the 'hotel' section across the street, surrounding a pretty garden, are larger and brightly decorated, with cable TV and a wonderful terrace with views. Check the website for lowest prices.

Hotel Posada Tepeyac (☎ 678-01-18; Real de Guadalupe 40; s/d/tr/q M$200/300/350/400; ☐) A neat small hotel in the heart of the Real de Guadalupe travelers' scene. The 33 clean rooms, around a couple of pretty little patios and a lovely stained-glass foyer, sport zingy color schemes. Number 117 has great views from the balcony.

Le Gite del Sol (☎ 631-60-12; www.legitedelsol .com; Madero 82; s/d/tr/q incl full breakfast M$220/250/ 330/400; P ✗ ☐) Free computer usage and a bountiful breakfast complement simple rooms with floors of radiant sunflower yellow and bathrooms that look a bit like over-sized shower stalls. The friendly owners, a Quebecois-Mexican couple, speak French and English. Guests may use the sunny kitchen and a small roof terrace offers great views. Parking costs M$20.

MIDRANGE

Casa Margarita (☎ 678-09-57; agchincultik@hotmail .com; Real de Guadalupe 34; s/d/tr/q M$350/450/550/650; ☐) This popular and well-run travelers' haunt offers tastefully presented, impeccably clean rooms with reading lights, and a pretty courtyard at the center of things. Rates can go down by M$50 to M$100 off-season. There's free internet, an in-house travel agency and a good restaurant.

Hotel Santa Clara (☎ 678-11-40; www.travelbymex ico.com/chis/santaclara; Insurgentes 1; s/d/tr/q incl breakfast M$450/550/700/800; P ☐ ☒) An atmospheric historic building on the main plaza, the Santa Clara has a number of sizable rooms, though they vary in quality, so ask to look before you check in. Wooden bedsteads, pretty tiling and antique religious art maintain an old-world air. There's a restaurant, a bar-lounge, a court-

yard with caged red macaws and another with a kidney-shaped swimming pool.

Hotel El Paraíso (☎ 678-00-85; www.hotelposada paraiso.com; 5 de Febrero 19; s/d/tr M$450/650/850) Combining colonial style with a boutique hotel feel, El Paraíso has a bright wood-pillared patio and courtyard garden, and loads of character. The high-ceilinged rooms are not huge, and some have limited natural light, but several are bi-level with an extra bed upstairs. The in-house restaurant, L'Eden (p820), is excellent.

Villas Casa Azul (☎ 678-81-81; www.travelbymexico .com/chis/casaazul; Rossete 4; s/d/tr M$520/722/843, per wk 1-4 people M$3500) If you don't mind hoofing up some stairs, these spacious one-bedroom apartments with kitchens have some of the best views in the city. And the higher you climb, the better the payoff.

Na Bolom (☎ 678-14-18; www.nabolom.org; Guerrero 33; s/d/tr/q incl breakfast M$660/880/1045/1100, ste M$1210; P) This famous museum/research institute (p813), about 1km from the plaza, has 16 stylish guest rooms, all loaded with character and all but one with log fires. Meals are served in the house's stately dining room. Room rates include a house tour and wireless internet.

Hotel Diego de Mazariegos (☎ 678-08-33; www.diegodemazariegos.com; 5 de Febrero 1; s/d/tr/q M$730/780/850/920, ste M$1250-1500; P) This classy, long-established hotel occupies two 18th-century mansions built around beautiful, wide courtyards. The 76 rooms are large and decked out with traditional fabrics and fittings, but also have modern comforts including cable TV. Some have fireplaces (M$15 per load of wood), and suites have spa tubs. The hotel has a lively tequila-and-mariachi-theme bar.

Villas Casa Morada (☎ 678-44-40; www.casamo rada.com.mx; Dugelay 45; studio/villa M$750/1200; P) These are tasteful, modern apartments with kitchen, phone, cable TV, fireplaces, daily cleaning and wi-fi access. Rooms face a tranquil fruit tree garden.

Hotel Casa Mexicana (☎ 678-06-98; www.hotel casamexicana.com; 28 de Agosto 1; s/d M$750/850, ste M$1400-1700; P ☐) A gallery as well as charming colonial hotel, the stylish and inviting Casa Mexicana displays modern art alongside traditional fabrics and solid wood pillars and furnishings. The main patio is filled with a lush tropical garden, the 55 attractive rooms are equipped with cable TV, and there's a restaurant, bar and sauna.

Hotel Casavieja (☎ /fax 678-68-68; www.casavieja .com.mx; MA Flores 27; s/d/tr M$800/850/900, ste 950-1000; P 💻) Set in a beautifully renovated 18th-century house with lots of wooden pillars, balustrades and old-world atmosphere, Casavieja also boasts modern comforts. The large comfortable rooms, arranged around flowery courtyards, all have two double beds, heater, cable TV and phone. Service is attentive and friendly, and a neat restaurant serves traditional Mexican dishes.

Hotel Ciudad Real (☎ 678-44-00; www.ciudad real.com.mx; Plaza 31 de Marzo 10; s/d M$900, tr/ste M$1050/1420; P ♿) A modern upscale hotel fashioned from an early 20th century building, it's located right on the main plaza and has 31 clean, if somewhat characterless, rooms arranged around a large courtyard restaurant. Families will enjoy the indoor children's play room.

TOP END

Casa Felipe Flores (☎ 678-39-96; www.felipeflores .com; JF Flores 36; r incl full breakfast US$92-118; ✗) A dreamy colonial guesthouse decorated with outstanding Mexican and Guatemalan art, crafts and furnishings, the 200-year-old building contains five fireplace rooms set off two flowery courtyards. The fireplace lounge is a wonderful place to have a glass of wine and leaf through some of their terrific library. Room 5 is a cozy rooftop hideaway, with a private terrace looking out over tiled rooftops and clusters of bougainvillea.

Parador San Juan de Dios (☎ /fax 678-11-67; www .sanjuandios.com; Calz Roberta 16; ste M$1400-3700; P) A stunning boutique hotel on the northern edge of town, the Parador San Juan de Dios offers voluminous and luxurious suites furnished with fascinating antique and modern art. The hotel occupies the former Rancho Harvard, which dates from the 17th century and has lodged many anthropologists and archaeologists. It has beautiful gardens, vast lawns and a top-class restaurant with an inventive, expensive Chiapas/Mediterranean menu and herbs and vegetables grown in its organic garden.

Eating

The foodie jackpot of Chiapas, San Cristóbal has more tantalizing food options than any other place in the state. If you can verbalize a culinary craving, chances are some restaurant exists here to fulfill it.

Vegetarians are embarrassingly spoiled for choice. ¡Provecho!

REAL DE GUADALUPE AREA

El Gato Gordo (☎ 678-83-13; Real de Guadalupe 20; mains M$25-49; ⏰ 1-11pm Wed-Mon; V) Gato Gordo attracts travelers in droves for its excellent, well-prepared food at terrific prices. There's an unbeatable set lunch (M$28), and excellent pasta, crepes, Mexican snacks and meat dishes, plus a great choice of drinks.

TierrAdentro (☎ 674-67-66; www.tierradentro.org .mx; Real de Guadalupe 24; menús M$30-70; ⏰ 8am-11pm) A popular gathering center for political progressives and coffee-swigging, laptop-toting locals (not that they're mutually exclusive), this large indoor courtyard restaurant and café is a comfortable place to while away the hours. It's run by Zapatista supporters, who hold frequent cultural events and conferences on local issues. A simple *menú compa* (M$30), with rice and beans and handmade tortillas, is hearty and delicious. Also inside are a good (Spanish-only) bookstore and an indigenous women's weaving co-op.

Pierre Restaurant Francés (☎ 678-72-11; Real de Guadalupe 73; mains M$35-165; ⏰ 1:30-10:30pm Wed-Mon, 7-10:30pm Tue) A super French restaurant whose perfectionist owner makes his own pasta, butter, cheese and bread. Favorites include the *cailles en raisin* (quail with raisins) and the *canard aux pêches* (duck with peaches), though there are vegetarian mains as well.

La Casa del Pan Papalotl (☎ 678-72-15; Centro Cultural El Puente, Real de Guadalupe 55; mains M$40-50; ⏰ 8:30am-10:30pm Mon-Sat; V) This excellent courtyard vegetarian restaurant does a particularly filling buffet lunch from 2pm to 5pm (M$65). Fresh bread and locally-grown organic ingredients are staples here.

Restaurante Plaza Real (☎ 678-09-92; Real de Guadalupe 5; mains M$46-100; ⏰ 7am-11pm; V) The well-prepared meat, poultry and vegetarian dishes at this classy eatery have international appeal, but also authentic Mexican flavor. It's set in the tranquil, wood-pillared and warm sunlit courtyard of what was once Chiapas' state congress building, surrounded by upmarket craft and jewelry shops.

Cucina Italiana Il Piccolo (☎ 115-27-26; Real de Guadalupe 13C; mains M$55-95; ⏰ 2-10:30pm Tue-Sun) Originally from Milan, chef Angelo Vinetti makes Italian comfort food that's simple yet downright delectable. Dig into a bowl of house-made tagliatelle, with a big choice of savory sauces, and chase away the San Cris chills with a glass or two of wine. Save room for the heavenly tiramisu.

PLAZA 31 DE MARZO & WEST

El Caldero (Allende 5A; soups M$40; ☼ 10am-10pm Thu-Tue) Simple, friendly little El Caldero specializes in delicious, filling Mexican soups – *pozole* (shredded pork in broth), *mondongo* (tripe), *caldo* (broth) – with avocados, tortillas and various salsas. Great for an authentic and inexpensive local meal.

Mayambé (☎ 674-62-78; 5 de Mayo 10; mains M$45-80; ☼ 9:30am-11pm; **V**) This superb courtyard restaurant boasts a wonderful Asian, Middle Eastern and Mediterranean menu, including plenty of vegetarian options. Tuck into delicious Indian and Thai curries, Greek and Lebanese treats including great hummus and falafel, and to-die-for lassis and juices. There's mellow live music some evenings, and a fireplace to warm things up on those cool highland nights.

L'Eden (☎ 678-00-85; Hotel El Paraíso, 5 de Febrero 19; mains M$45-110; ☼ 7am-noon & 1-11pm) This quality restaurant's tempting European and Mexican menu includes *fondue suiza*, *sopa azteca* and succulent meat dishes. There's a lengthy wine list too, including French and Spanish vintages.

SOUTH OF PLAZA 31 DE MARZO

Emiliano's Moustache (☎ 678-72-46; Rosas 7; breakfasts & snacks M$20-50, mains M$22-60; ☼ 8am-1am) This large, enjoyable place specializes in tacos filled with combinations of meat, vegetable or cheese. The meat *filetes* are also excellent, and vegetarian possibilities exist too (including veggie tacos).

Madre Tierra (☎ 678-42-97; Insurgentes 19; mains M$30-65; ☼ 8am-10pm; **V**) A long-time travelers' favorite, Madre Tierra serves an eclectic and mainly vegetarian menu on a tranquil patio or in an atmospheric dining room. Breakfasts are superb, but perhaps sliding by on its reputation, other meals can be hit-or-miss.

NORTH OF PLAZA 31 DE MARZO

Alebrije (☎ 678-28-56; Caminero 9; mains M$15-25; ☼ 8am-6pm Mon-Sat) A fun, economical and busy *cocina popular* across from the Mercado Municipal, it serves freshly-prepared food like *enfrijoladas con pollo* (tortillas with bean sauce, cheese and chicken), *chilaquiles* and *pollo con verduras* (chicken

and vegetables) to a dedicated local clientele. Vegetarian dishes can be prepared upon request, and the yummy fruit *aguas* are made with purified water.

La Casa del Pan (☎ 678-58-95; Dr Navarro 10; snacks & mains M$32-55; ☼ 8am-10pm Tue-Sun; **V**) This relaxed restaurant-bakery emphasizes local organic ingredients, offering great breakfasts and lots of vegetarian fare through the day: whole-wheat sandwiches, salads, *hojaldres* (vegetable strudels) and pizzas. The three types of empanadas are great for lunch to go.

Pizzería El Punto (☎ 678-79-79; Comitán 13; pizzas M$60-100; ☼ 2-11pm Tue-Sun) Forget the cardboard crap that passes for pizza in some parts, these crispy pies are the best in town, bar none. The brick oven, adorned with a mosaic of change, keeps diners warm on chilly highland nights, though the glass door looking out onto the plaza seems to crack every other week – close it *gently*.

Drinking
COFFEE

The aroma of roasted highland-grown coffee beans wafts through the streets of San Cristóbal, and a strong dose is never far. Along with the Café Museo Café (p816), try any of these courtyard places for the good stuff – organic, indigenous-grown and delicious:

Café La Selva (☎ 678-72-43; Crescencio Rosas 9; ☼ 8:30am-11pm)

Cafetería Maya (☎ 678-91-46; 20 de Noviembre 12C; ☼ 12:30-10:30pm) The patio has a permanent photo exhibition on the Zapatista movement.

TierrAdentro (☎ 674-67-66; Real de Guadalupe 24; ☼ 8am-11pm)

BARS

La Viña de Bacco (☎ 119-19-85; Real de Guadalupe 7; 🕐 1pm-midnight Mon-Sat) San Cristóbal's first wine bar was so successful that it quickly outgrew its first dollhouse-size location. Now located on the main drag, it's still a cozy place to chat, pouring a large selection of Mexican options (among others) starting at a reasonable M$15 per glass.

Los Amigos (Honduras 4; 🕐 10am-8pm) A popular but reasonably unraucous cantina, the two-for-one beers and tasty *botanas* (free snacks) keep it hopping and fun, as do the wander-in mariachi bands.

Entertainment

CLUBS & LIVE MUSIC

Dai fly (☎ 124-32-74, Crescencio Rosas 4, 🕐 8am-3pm Tue-Sat) Stained glass lamps light the bar and a graffiti-style mural splashes across the wall in this dark and funky club. It's a popular space for local musicians, with electronica on Saturdays and reggae, funk and salsa bands at other times.

Blue (☎ 678-22-00; Rosas 2; admission after midnight Thu-Sat M$30; 🕐 9pm-3am Mon-Wed, to 4am Thu-Sat) With tell-tale blue lights outside, Blue features DJs hauling out rock, ska, punk, reggae and electronica grooves in a large dance space. A candle-lit front room is good for chilling out and chatting.

DaDa Club (☎ 631-32-93; www.dadajazz.com; Insurgentes 16A; 🕐 1pm-midnight Mon-Sat) There's never a cover, and live jazz bands wail nightly starting around 9:30pm. Earthy and intimate and dressed up in red, this new club is cozy and inviting.

El Zirko (20 de Noviembre 7; admission Fri & Sat M$20-30; 🕐 8pm-3am) A hip venue that's packed on the weekends. Salsa and Latin rock bands often play the front bar, while a larger back dance floor ringed with red couches opens with a wider range of sounds (including *cumbia* and pop) on Friday and Saturday.

La Pera (☎ 678-12-09; MA Flores 23; 🕐 1-11pm Mon-Sat) An artsy and relaxed café-gallery-bar showing work by local artists, La Pera often stages live music late in the week. It could be blues, jazz, *trova*, hip-hop or tango lessons, but it's always fun.

Latino's (☎ 678-99-27; Madero 23; admission Thu-Sat M$25; 🕐 8pm-3am Mon-Sat) A bright restaurant and dance spot where the city's *salseros* gather to groove. A salsa/merengue/*cumbia* band plays nightly, with the crowds getting thick by 10:30pm or so.

Madre Tierra (☎ 678-42-97; Insurgentes 19; 🕐 8-3pm) A San Cristóbal institution, Madre Tierra's smoky Bar Upstairs presents live reggae and ska bands.

CINEMA

San Cristóbal is a fine place to immerse yourself in Mexican- and Latin American–themed cinema, political documentaries and arthouse movies. The following places show two films a day (usually at 6pm and 8pm), charging M$25 per movie:

Cinema El Puente (☎ 678-37-23; Centro Cultural El Puente, Real de Guadalupe 55) Closed Sunday.

Kinoki (☎ 678-0495; 1 de Marzo 22; 🕐 5:30-11pm) Art space and cooperatively-run café, with two smaller private cinema rooms available as well.

Shopping

Real de Guadalupe and the Andador Turístico have some craft shops, but the busy daily crafts market around Santo Domingo and La Caridad churches are also good places to check out. The outstanding indigenous *artesanías* of the Chiapas highlands are textiles such as *huipiles* (sleeveless tunics), blouses and blankets; Tzotzil weavers are some of the most skilled and inventive in Mexico. Another Chiapas specialty is amber, sold in numerous jewelry shops. When buying amber, beware of plastic imitations: the real thing is never cold and never heavy, and when rubbed should produce static electricity and a resiny smell.

Instituto de Las Artesanías (☎ 678-11-80; cnr Niños Héroes & Hidalgo; 🕐 8am-9pm Mon-Fri, 10am-9pm Sat, 10am-3pm Sun) Sells a good range of Chiapas crafts.

Lágrimas de la Selva (☎ 674-63-48; Hidalgo 1C) A lovely jewelry store where you can watch them work with amber.

Nemi Zapata (☎ 678-74-87; Real de Guadalupe 57A) A fair trade store that sells products made by Zapatista communities – weavings, embroidery, coffee and honey, EZLN cards, posters and books.

Sna Jolobil (☎ 678-26-46; Calz Lázaro Cárdenas s/n; 🕐 9am-2pm & 4-6pm Mon-Sat) Next to Santo Domingo, Sna Jolobil exhibits and sells some of the very best *huipiles*, blouses, skirts, rugs and other woven items, with prices ranging from a few dollars for small items to over M$10,000 for the best *huipiles* (the fruit of many months' work). Sna Jolobil is a cooperative of 800 indigenous women weavers from the Chiapas highlands, founded in the 1970s to foster the important indigenous art of backstrap-loom weaving. It has revived many half-forgotten techniques and designs.

Taller Leñateros (☎ 678-51-74; www.taller lenateros.com; Paniagua 54; 🕑 8:30am-8pm Mon-Fri, 8:30am-2pm Sat) A society of Maya artists, the 'Woodlanders' Workshop' crafts exquisite handmade books, posters and fine art prints from recycled paper infused with local plants, using images inspired by traditional folk art. An open workshop, you can watch their art in progress.

Getting There & Away

Instituto Nacional de Migración (☎ 678-02-92; Diagonal El Centenario 30) is on a corner with the Pan-American Hwy, 1.2km west of the OCC bus station.

From Tuxtla Gutiérrez you'll most likely travel here on the fast new toll *autopista* (M$33 for cars). An increased military and police presence has reduced the number of highway holdups on Hwy 199 between Ocosingo and Palenque, but it' still probably best to travel along this stretch of road during daylight hours.

AIR

San Cristóbal's airport, about 15km from town on the Palenque road, has no regular passenger flights; the main airport serving town is in Tuxtla Gutiérrez. To get there, take a Tuxtla-bound *colectivo* to Soriana (M$35, 1¼ hours) in Tuxtla's eastern suburbs; from the stand at the *colectivo* stop, hire a taxi to the airport (M$150, 30 minutes). A number of tour agencies, including Viajes Chincultik and Otisa (see Tours, p816), run shuttles to the Tuxtla airport for M$150 to M$160 per person, but scheduled service is generally at 9am only. Reserve in advance, especially if you want to leave at another time.

Mexicana (☎ 678-93-09; Belisario Domínguez 2B) sells flights from Tuxtla Gutiérrez.

BUS, COLECTIVO & VAN

There are around a dozen terminals, mostly on or just off the Pan-American Hwy. Most important is the 1st-class **OCC terminal** (☎ 678-02-91; cnr Pan-American Hwy & Insurgentes), also used by ADO and UNO 1st-class and deluxe buses, and 2nd-class Transportes Dr Rodulfo Figueroa (TRF) and Rápidos del Sur. Tickets for all these lines are sold at **Ticket Bus** (☎ 678-85-03; Real de Guadalupe 5A; 🕑 7am-10pm) in the center of town.

First-class **AEXA** (☎ 678-61-78) and 2nd-class Ómnibus de Chiapas share a terminal on the south side of the highway; and various Suburban-type vans and *colectivo* taxi services have depots on the highway in the same area. Daily departures (from the OCC terminal unless otherwise stated) are listed in the box below.

BUSES FROM SAN CRISTÓBAL DE LAS CASAS

Destination	Fare	Duration	Frequency (daily)
Campeche	M$314	11hr	1
Cancún	M$606-724	16-18hr	4
Ciudad Cuauhtémoc (Guatemalan border)	M$100	3½hr	4
Comitán	M$25-30	1¾hr	12 from OCC, vans and *colectivos* leave from the south side of the Pan-American Hwy
Mérida	M$448	13hr	1
Mexico City (TAPO)	M$750-896	13-14hr	8
Oaxaca	M$334-412	11hr	3
Ocosingo	M$30-45	2¼hr	11 from OCC, 4 AEXA, *colectivos* and vans leave every few minutes 3am-9pm from the north side of the Pan-American Hwy
Palenque	M$75-134	5hr	9 from OCC, 3 AEXA
Pochutla	M$332	10-14hr	2
Puerto Escondido	M$372	11-15hr	2
Tuxtla Gutiérrez	M$30-40	1-1¼hr	22 from OCC, 4 AEXA, Ómnibus de Chiapas every 5 min, 5am-10pm, Taxis Jovel *colectivos* operate 24hr and Corazón de María vans leave 5am-11pm
Villahermosa	M$194	7-8hr	2

See Getting There & Away, p810, for connections to Chiapa de Corzo. For Guatemala, most agencies offer daily van service to Quetzaltenango (M$260, eight hours), Panajachel (M$260, 10 hours) and Antigua (M$360, 12 hours) and Flores (via Palenque, M$400).

CAR

Optima (☎ 674-54-09; optimacar1@hotmail.com; Mazariegos 39) rents VW Beetles for M$400 per day and M$2400 per week, including unlimited kilometers, insurance and taxes. Sizeable discounts given for payment in cash.

Getting Around

Combis go up Rosas from the Pan-American Hwy to the town center. Taxis cost M$10 within town.

Friendly Los Pingüinos (p817) rents good-quality mountain bikes with lock and maps and can advise on good and safe routes. You'll need to deposit your passport or credit card.

Under new ownership, **Croozy Scooters** (☎ 631-43-29; www.prodigyweb.net.mx/croozyscooters; Belisario Domínguez 7; scooter hire 1/5/9/24hr M$75/200/250/350;

🕑 9am-7pm) rents well-maintained 80cc scooters. The price includes maps and helmets; passport and deposit required.

AROUND SAN CRISTÓBAL

The inhabitants of the beautiful Chiapas highlands are descended from the ancient Maya and maintain some unique customs, costumes and beliefs (see p824).

Markets and festivals often give the most interesting insight into indigenous life, and there are lots of them. Weekly **markets** at the villages are nearly always on Sunday. Proceedings start as early as dawn, and wind down by lunchtime. Occasions like **Carnaval** (late February/early March), for which Chamula is particularly famous, **Semana Santa**, and **Día de Muertos** (November 2) are celebrated almost everywhere. During Carnaval, groups of minstrels stroll the roads in tall, pointed hats with long, colored tassels, strumming guitars and chanting. Much *pox* (pronounced posh), an alcoholic drink made from sugarcane, is drunk.

It's particularly important to be respectful of local customs in this part of Mexico (see p789). During the day, walking or riding

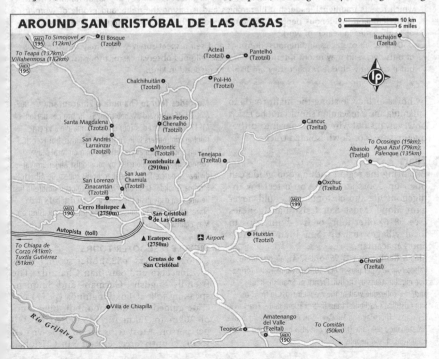

AROUND SAN CRISTÓBAL DE LAS CASAS

INDIGENOUS PEOPLES OF CHIAPAS

Of the 4.2 million people of Chiapas, approximately 1.25 million are indigenous, with language being the key ethnic identifier. Each of the eight principal groups has its own language, beliefs and customs, a cultural variety that makes Chiapas one of the most fascinating states in Mexico.

Travelers to the area around San Cristóbal are most likely to encounter the Tzotziles and the Tzeltales. Their traditional religious life is nominally Catholic, but integrates pre-Hispanic elements. Most people live in the hills outside the villages, which are primarily market and ceremonial centers.

Tzotzil and Tzeltal clothing is among the most varied, colorful and elaborately worked in Mexico. It not only identifies wearers' villages but also continues ancient Maya traditions. Many of the seemingly abstract designs on these costumes are in fact stylized snakes, frogs, butterflies, birds, saints and other beings. Some motifs have religious-magical functions: scorpions, for example, can be a symbolic request for rain, since they are believed to attract lightning.

The Lacandones dwelt deep in the Lacandón Jungle and largely avoided contact with the outside world until the 1950s. They now number 800 or so and live in three main settlements in that same region, with low-key tourism being one of their major means of support. Lacandones are readily recognizable in their white tunics and long black hair cut in a fringe. Most Lacandones have now abandoned their traditional animist religion in favor of Presbyterian or evangelical forms of Christianity.

Traditionally treated as second-class citizens, indigenous groups mostly live on the least productive land in the state, with the least amount of government services or infrastructure. The Zapatista revolution was primarily an uprising against this historical injustice; their rallying cry of *!Ya basta!* (Enough!), a full-throated response to centuries of economic and political discrimination.

Today, long-standing indigenous ways of life are being challenged both by evangelical Christianity – opposed to many traditional animist-Catholic practices – and by the Zapatista movement, which rejects traditional leadership hierarchies and is raising the rights and profile of women. Many highland indigenous people have emigrated to the Lacandón Jungle to clear new land, or to the cities in search of work.

Despite all obstacles, indigenous identities and self-respect survive. They may be suspicious of outsiders, and may resent interference in their religious observances or other aspects of life, but if treated with due respect they are likely to respond in kind.

by horse or bicycle along the main roads to Chamula and Zinacantán should not be risky, however, it's not wise to wander into unfrequented areas or down isolated tracks.

Tours

Exploring the region with a good guide can open up doors and give you a feel for indigenous life and customs you could never gain alone. Most San Cristóbal agencies (see p816) offer four- or five-hour trips to local villages, usually San Juan Chamula and Zinacantán.

Alex & Raúl Tours (☎ 967-678-37-41; alexyraultours@yahoo.com.mx; per person M$150) Enjoyable and informative minibus tours in English, French or Spanish; Raúl and/or a colleague wait at the wooden cross in front of San Cristóbal's cathedral from 8:45-9:30am daily. Trips to Tenejapa (Thursday and Sunday), San Andrés Larráinzar or Amatenango del Valle (M$200) can also be arranged for a minimum of four people.

Mercedes Tour to Chamula & Zinacantán (☎ 967-674-03-76; alexvald@yahoo.com; 5-6hr trip per person M$170) The Mercedes Tour is an informative and entertaining trip (generally in English or Spanish, but French, Italian and German available) dwelling on local Maya cosmology and religion, led by sociologist Alejandro Valdiviezo, a native Tzotzil speaker, or his colleague Alberto Medina. Look for someone twirling a colorful umbrella just before 9am daily near the kiosk in San Cristóbal's main plaza. Also does day tours to Toniná (M$320) focusing on Maya culture.

BICYCLE & SCOOTER TOURS

Croozy Scooters (p823) offer scooter tours to Zinacatán and San Juan Chamula. The friendly English-, German- and Spanish-speaking folk at Los Pingüinos (p817) operate guided half-day mountain-bike tours of 20km to 25km for M$300 to M$330 per person. Most trips are to little-visited scenic country areas east of San Cristóbal, passing through cloud forests. Reserve one day or more ahead; reservations accepted by phone and e-mail on Sundays. Longer tours offered around the Chiapas highlands and beyond.

Marco Antonio Morales (☎ 104-73-09; tonod mar@hotmail.com) offers tailored bike tours of four (M$165) to six (M$200) hours visiting Zinacantán, San Juan Chamula and Rancho Nuevo; speaks English and French.

HORSEBACK RIDING
Almost any travel agency or place to stay in San Cristóbal can arrange a four- or five-hour guided ride to San Juan Chamula for M$100 to M$120. Don't take anything too valuable with you; thefts have occurred in the past.

Getting There & Away
Transportation to most villages goes from points around the Mercado Municipal in San Cristóbal. Combis to San Juan Chamula (M$8) leave from Calle Honduras frequently from 4am to about 6pm; for Zinacantán, combis (M$10) and *colectivo* taxis (M$12) go at least hourly, 5am to 7pm, from a yard off Robledo.

San Juan Chamula
pop 3000 / elevation 2200m
The Chamulans are a fiercely independent Tzotzil group, about 80,000 strong. Their main village, San Juan Chamula, 10km northwest of San Cristóbal, is the center for some unique religious practices – although conflicts between adherents of traditional Chamulan Catholicism and converts to evangelical, Pentecostal and other branches of Christianity have resulted in the expulsion of many thousands of Chamulans from their villages in the past couple of decades. Here, as at other places in Mexico and Central America, rejection of Catholicism was also in part a political rejection of the long-standing supremacy of the Catholic *mestizo* majority. In San Juan Chamula, evangelism is associated with the Zapatista movement. Most of the exiles now inhabit the shantytowns around San Cristóbal.

Chamulan men wear loose homespun tunics of white wool (sometimes, in cool weather, thicker black wool), but *cargo*-holders – those with important religious and ceremonial duties – wear a sleeveless black tunic and a white scarf on the head. Chamulan

women wear fairly plain white or blue blouses and/or shawls and woolen skirts.

Outsiders can visit San Juan Chamula, but a big sign at the entrance to the village strictly forbids photography in the village church or at rituals. Do *not* ignore these restrictions; the community takes them very seriously. Nearby, around the shell of an older church, is the village **graveyard**, with black crosses for people who died old, white for the young, and blue for others.

Sunday is the weekly **market**, when people from the hills stream into the village to shop, trade and visit the main church. A corresponding number of tourist buses also stream in, so you might prefer to come another day (though avoid Wednesday, when the church is often all but deserted due to local superstitions). Local crafts (mainly textiles) are sold every day for the passing tourist trade.

Standing beside the main plaza, Chamula's main church, the **Templo de San Juan**, is a ghostly white, with a vividly painted arch of green and blue. A sign tells visitors to obtain tickets (M$15) at the **tourist office** (☑ 9am-6pm), beside the plaza, before entering the church. Inside the darkened sanctuary, hundreds of flickering candles, clouds of incense, and worshipers kneeling with their faces to the pine-needle-carpeted floor make a powerful impression. Chanting *curanderos* (literally 'curers'; medicine men or women) may be rubbing patients' bodies with eggs or bones. Images of saints are surrounded with mirrors and dressed in holy garments. Chamulans revere San Juan Bautista (St John the Baptist) above Christ, and his image occupies a more important place in the church.

FESTIVALS & EVENTS
Carnaval Festivities also mark the five 'lost' days of the ancient Long Count calendar, which divided time into 20-day periods (18 of these make 360 days, leaving five to complete a year).
Fiesta de San Juan Bautista Up to 20,000 people gather to dance and drink on June 24.
Change of cargo-holders The annual rotation of the honored (but expensive) community leadership positions known as *cargos;* December 30 to January 1.

San Lorenzo Zinacantán
pop 3700 / elevation 2558m
The orderly village of San Lorenzo Zinacantán, about 11km northwest of San Cristóbal, is the main village of the

THE ZAPATISTAS

On January 1, 1994, the day of Nafta's initiation, a previously unknown leftist guerrilla army emerged from the forests to occupy San Cristóbal de Las Casasand other towns in Chiapas. The Ejército Zapatista de Liberación Nacional (EZLN, Zapatista National Liberation Army) linked anti-globalization rhetoric with Mexican revolutionary slogans, declaring that they aimed to overturn the oligarchy's centuries-old hold on land, resources and power and to improve the wretched living standards of Mexico's indigenous people.

The Mexican army evicted the Zapatistas within days, and the rebels retreated to the fringes of the Lacandón Jungle to wage a propaganda war, mainly fought via the internet. The Zapatistas' balaclava-clad, pipe-puffing Subcomandante Marcos (a former university professor named Rafael Guillén) rapidly became a cult figure. High-profile conventions against neoliberalism were held and international supporters flocked to Zapatista headquarters at La Realidad, 80km southeast of Comitán, and Zapatista-aligned peasants took over hundreds of farms and ranches in Chiapas.

In 1996, Zapatista and Mexican government negotiators agreed to a set of accords on indigenous rights and autonomy. However, the governing Institutional Revolutionary Party (PRI) never ratified these agreements, and tension and killings escalated in Chiapas through 1997 and 1998. A PRI-linked paramilitary group massacred 45 people in the village of Acteal, north of San Cristóbal, in 1997. By 1999, an estimated 21,000 villagers had fled their homes after the Mexican army, aided and abetted by paramilitaries, launched a campaign of intimidation.

After Vicente Fox was elected Mexico's president in 2000, two attempts to make the necessary constitutional changes failed. The Zapatistas refused to participate in further talks, concentrating instead on consolidating their revolution and their autonomy in the villages of highland and eastern Chiapas, where they had the most support. In 2003 the Zapatista leadership established five regional 'Juntas de Buen Gobierno' (Committees of Good Government) in villages where they set up schools and clinics. But these frequently-rotating committees, set up to democratize governance and teach leadership skills, have been hampered by a lack of accountability and continuity, and criticized as excessively bureaucratic.

By 2005 Zapatista political influence was slight outside their own enclaves, and many former supporters were disillusioned with the EZLN's intransigence. Then suddenly, after four years of silence, Marcos announced a broad new Zapatista political struggle including all Mexico's exploited and marginalized people, not just the indigenous. He rejected all cooperation or dialog with mainstream political parties, launching instead La Otra Campaña (The Other Campaign), a movement to run parallel to, but distinct from, Mexico's 2006 presidential election campaign. On January 1, 2006, Marcos, now styling himself Subdelegado Zero, set off by motorcycle from the jungle to do a six-month Zapatista tour of all Mexico's states. The aim was to forge a new leftist political front by making contact with other groups around the country, to develop a new methodology of 'liberation from below' and a new civilian, peaceful, anticapitalist approach to politics. However, most observers saw scant momentum resulting from the campaign.

More recently, the Zapatista leadership held three large international gatherings (*Encuentros*) during 2007. Pockets of the Chiapas countryside remain tense, and occasional incidents bubble up over control of land.

It's interesting to note that the Zapatistas have loudly denounced the concept of ecotourism. They see the expansion of government tourism infrastructure as a nonmilitary means to make inroads into autonomous EZLN communities.

Check in on the Zapatistas at www.ezln.org.mx. Further background is available in *The Zapatista Reader*, an anthology of writers from Octavio Paz and Gabriel García Márquez to Marcos himself, and at **Global Exchange** (www.globalexchange.org), **SiPaz** (www.sipaz.org) and **IMC** (chiapas.mediosindependientes .org). Some of Marcos' more recent writings are collected in *The Speed of Dreams*.

Zinacantán municipality (population 45,000). Zinacantán people, like Chamulans, are Tzotzil. The men wear distinctive pink tunics embroidered with flower motifs and may sport flat, round, ribboned palm hats. Women wear pink or purple shawls over richly embroidered blouses.

A small **market** is held on Sundays until noon, and during fiesta times. The most important celebrations are for La Virgen de La

Candelaria (August 7–11) and San Sebastián (January 19–22).

The people of Zinacantán are great flower growers. They have a particular love for the geranium, which – along with pine branches – is offered in rituals for a wide range of benefits.

The huge central **Iglesia de San Lorenzo** (admission M$20) was rebuilt following a fire in 1975. Photography is banned in the church and churchyard. The small thatched-roofed **Museo Jsotz' Levetik** (admission by donation; 9am-5pm), three blocks below the central basketball court, covers local culture and has some fine textiles and musical instruments.

Grutas de San Cristóbal

The entrance to this long **cavern** (admission M$20) 9am-4:30pm) is among pine woods 9km southeast of San Cristóbal, a five-minute walk south of the Pan-American Hwy. The first 350m or so of the cave has a concrete walkway and is lit. The army took control of the land around the caves in 2003, though visitors are still welcome.

To get there take a Teopisca-bound *colectivo* taxi from the Pan-American Hwy, about 150m southeast of the OCC bus station in San Cristóbal, and ask for 'Las Grutas' (M$15).

Amatenango del Valle

pop 4500 / elevation 1869m

The women of this Tzeltal village by the Pan-American Hwy, 37km southeast of San Cristóbal, are renowned potters. Pottery here is still fired by a pre-Hispanic method, building a wood fire around the pieces rather than putting them in a kiln. Amatenango children find a ready tourist market with *animalitos* – little pottery animal figures that are inexpensive but fragile. If you visit the village, expect to be surrounded within minutes by young *animalito* sellers.

From San Cristóbal, take a Comitán-bound bus or combi.

OCOSINGO

919 / pop 35,000 / elevation 900m

A respite from both the steamy lowland jungle and the chilly highlands, the bustling regional market town of Ocosingo sits in a gorgeous and broad temperate valley midway between San Cristóbal and Palenque. The impressive Maya ruins of Toniná are just a few kilometers away.

The market area along Av 2 Sur Ote, three to five blocks east (downhill) from the central plaza, is the busiest part of town. The **Tianguis Campesino** (Peasants' Market; cnr Av 2 Sur Ote & Calle 5 Sur Ote; 6am-5pm) is for the area's small-scale food producers to sell their goods direct; only women are allowed to trade here, and it's a colorful sight, with most of the traders in traditional dress.

The valleys known as Las Cañadas de Ocosingo, between Ocosingo and the Reserva de la Biosfera Montes Azules to the east, form one of the strongest bastions of support for the Zapatistas, and Ocosingo saw the bloodiest fighting during the 1994 uprising, with about 50 rebels killed here by the Mexican army. The town has been calm since, and the Zapatistas have consolidated their support in the region, despite the presence of a large Mexican army garrison near the Toniná ruins.

Orientation & Information

Ocosingo spreads east (downhill) from Hwy 199. Avenida Central runs down from the main road to the broad central plaza, overlooked from its east end by the Templo de San Jacinto. Hotels, restaurants and services are along Calle Central Nte, running off the north side of the plaza, and elsewhere close by.

A **tourism kiosk** (9am-3pm & 6-8pm Mon-Fri) in the plaza has maps and multilingual information on Chiapas, but no city maps. **Santander Serfin** (Central Nte 10; 9am-4pm Mon-Fri, Sat 10am-2pm) and **Banamex** (Av Central; 9am-4pm Mon-Fri) on the plaza both exchange currency and have ATMs. Cybercafés on the plaza and Calle Central Nte charge M$8 per hour.

Sleeping

Hospedaje Esmeralda (/fax 673-00-14; www.rancho esmeralda.net; Central Nte 14; s/d/tr/q with shared bathroom M$140/230/270/340; P) The travelers' haunt of Ocosingo, this small guesthouse has five adequate rooms, all with bright indigenous bedcovers and fans. A welcoming restaurant, bar and terrace area invites lounging and chatting, and the new Mexican owner truly enjoys helping people get to know the area. It also offers horseback-riding excursions (M$200, about two hours) in the countryside outside Ocosingo, and an excellent book exchange. One room, with private bathroom, costs a bit extra.

Hotel La Casona (☎ /fax 673-01-40; cnr 1a Sur & Calle Central; r M$200-350; P ⊠) A modern three-story hotel on the south side of the plaza, it mostly has unexciting rooms, all with TV and air-con. However, the top floor accommodations, with vaulted ceilings and balconies (some with plaza views) are quite nice.

Hotel Margarita (☎ 673-12-15; hotelmargarita@ prodigy.net.mx; Central Nte 19; s/d/tr/q M$220/260/280/350, air-con extra M$50; P ⊠) Next to Hospedaje Esmeralda, the friendly Margarita has clean and comfortable rooms, all with TV, fan, two big double beds and large framed posters of Chiapas attractions.

Eating

Restaurant El Campanario (☎ 673-02-51; Av Central Ote 2; mains M$35-70; ⏱ 7am-10:30pm) Framed by colonial arcades, El Campanario faces the plaza and has bright tablecloths and a tri-lingual menu (Spanish, English, French). It serves a typical Chiapas menu of meat, egg and seafood.

Restaurant Esmeralda (☎ 673-00-14; Hospedaje Esmeralda, Central Nte 14; mains M$50-70) Excellent home-style international and Mexican fare is served here, including healthy buffet breakfasts (M$40) and dinner favorites like goulash, chicken curry and pork fajitas.

Las Delicias (☎ 673-00-24; Av Central 5; mains M$50-85; ⏱ 7am-11pm) On the plaza-facing veranda of the Hotel Central, this reliable restaurant has big portions and good breakfasts (M$30 to M$55).

Fábrica de Quesos Santa Rosa (☎ 673-00-09; 1a Ote Nte 11; ⏱ 8am-2pm & 4-8pm Mon-Sat, 8am-2pm Sun) Ocosingo is known for its *queso amarillo* (yellow cheese). There are six main types, including 'de bola,' which comes in 1kg balls (M$60) with an edible wax coating and a crumbly, whole-fat center.

Getting There & Away

See p840 for a safety note concerning the road to Palenque.

For Laguna Miramar, San Quintín–bound trucks and taxis leave from near the market (see p830). **Servicios Aéreos San Cristóbal** (☎ 673-03-70; 1a Sur Pte 87; www.serviciosaereossancristobal.com) has small-plane flights to San Quintín for M$5000 round-trip (up to four passengers).

Ocosingo's OCC bus terminal (1st-class and deluxe) is on Hwy 199, 600m west of the plaza; AEXA (1st-class) stops at the Restaurante Ave

Fenix across the road. Daily departures are listed in the table. Buses from the OCC terminal also go to Campeche, Cancún, Mérida and Villahermosa.

Destination	Fare	Duration	Frequency (daily)
Palenque	M$40-72	2¼hr	11 from OCC, 3 AEXA & vans leave every 30 min from Hwy 199, 800m north of OCC
San Cristóbal de Las Casas	M$30-40	2¼hr	10 from OCC, 4 AEXA & vans and *colectivo* taxis leave every 20-30 min from a yard just up the road from OCC
Tuxtla Gutiérrez	M$60-98	4hr	10 from OCC, 4 AEXA

TONINÁ

The towering ceremonial core of **Toniná** (☎ 919-108-22-39; admission M$37; ⏱ 8am-5pm), overlooking a pastoral valley 14km east of Ocosingo, comprises one of the Maya world's most imposing temple complexes. This was the city that brought mighty Palenque to its knees.

The year AD 688 saw the inauguration of the Snake Skull–Jaguar Claw dynasty, with ambitious new rulers bent on controlling the region. Palenque was their rival state, and when Toniná captured the Palenque ruler K'an Joy Chitam II in 711, it's likely that he had his head lopped off here.

Toniná became known as the Place of the Celestial Captives, because its chambers held the captured rulers of Palenque and other Maya cities, destined for decapitation or to be ransomed for large sums. A recurring image in Toniná sculpture is of captives before decapitation, thrown to the ground with their hands tied.

To enter the site, follow the road from the entrance and **site museum**, which details Toniná's history (in Spanish) and contains most of the best artifacts. The road turns to a footpath, crosses a stream and climbs to the broad, flat Gran Plaza. At the south end of the Gran Plaza is the **Templo de la Guerra Cósmica** (Temple of Cosmic War), with five altars in front of it. Off one side of the plaza is a **ball court**, inaugurated around AD 780 under the rule of the female regent Smoking Mirror. A decapitation altar stands cheerfully beside it.

To the north rises the ceremonial core of Toniná, a hillside terraced into a number of platforms, rising 80m above the Gran Plaza. At the right-hand end of the steps, rising from the first to the second platform, is the entry to a **ritual labyrinth** of passages.

Higher up on the right-hand side is the **Palacio de las Grecas y de la Guerra** (Palace of the Grecas and War). The *grecas* are a band of geometrical decoration forming a zigzag X-shape, possibly representing Quetzalcóatl. To its right is a rambling series of chambers, passages and stairways, believed to have been Toniná's administrative headquarters.

Higher again is Toniná's most remarkable sculpture, the **Mural de las Cuatro Eras** (Mural of the Four Eras). Created between AD 790 and 840, this stucco relief of four panels – the first, from the left end, has been lost – represents the four suns, or four eras of human history. The people of Toniná believed themselves to be living in the fourth sun – that of winter, mirrors, the direction north and the end of human life. At the center of each panel is the upside-down head of a decapitated prisoner. Blood spurting from the prisoner's neck forms a ring of feathers and, at the same time, a sun. In one panel, a dancing skeleton holds a decapitated head. To the left of the head is a lord of the underworld, resembling an enormous rodent.

Up the next set of steps is the seventh level, with remains of four temples. Behind the second temple from the left, more steps descend into the very narrow **Tumba de Treinta Metros** (Thirty-Meter Tomb), an impossibly slim passageway that's definitely not for the claustrophobic!

Above here is the acropolis, the abode of Toniná's rulers and site of its eight most important temples – four on each of two levels. The right-hand temple on the lower level, the **Templo del Monstruo de la Tierra** (Temple of the Earth Monster), has Toniná's best-preserved roof comb, built around AD 713.

On the topmost level, the tallest temple, the **Templo del Espejo Humeante** (Temple of the Smoking Mirror), was built by Zots-Choj, who took the throne in AD 842. In that era of the fourth sun and the direction north, Zots-Choj had to raise this, Toniná's northernmost temple, highest of all, which necessitated a large, artificial northeast extension of the hill.

Getting There & Away
Combis to Toniná (M$10) leave from opposite the Tianguis Campesino in Ocosingo every 30 minutes from early morning onward. The last one returns around 5pm. A taxi costs M$70.

LAGUNA MIRAMAR
400m
Ringed by rainforest, pristine Laguna Miramar, 140km southeast of Ocosingo in the **Reserva de la Biosfera Montes Azules** (Montes Azules Biosphere Reserve), is one of Mexico's most remote and exquisite lakes. Frequently echoing with the roars of howler monkeys, the 16-sq-km lake is bathtub-warm and virtually unpolluted. Rock ledges extending from small islands make blissful wading spots, and petroglyphs and a sea turtle cave are reachable by canoe.

The lake is accessible thanks to a successful ecotourism project in the Maya community of **Emiliano Zapata**, near its western shore. If you arrive independently, ask for the Presidente de Turismo. Through this representative you must arrange and pay for the services you need – a guide costs M$100 per day, the overnight fee is M$30, and rental of a *cayuco* (traditional canoe for two or three people) for exploring the lake is M$150. Drugs are forbidden in the village; alcohol is permitted for visitors' personal consumption only.

The 7km walk from Emiliano Zapata to the lake, through *milpas* (cornfields) and forest that includes *caoba* (mahogany) and the *matapalo* (strangler fig) trees, takes about 1½ hours and can be very muddy – good closed shoes are highly recommended. At the lake, you may hear jaguars at night. Other wildlife includes spider monkeys, tapirs, macaws and toucans; butterflies are prolific. Locals fish for *mojarra* (perch), and will assure you that the lake's few crocodiles are not dangerous.

Sleeping & Eating
At the lakeshore, you can sling a hammock or **camp** (M$30 per person) under a *palapa* shelter. But if you arrive after noon, you'll need to stay in Emiliano Zapata, as the guides want to make it home before dark. The village has a handful of simple but pretty **cabañas** (M$100 per person) with river views, all with one queen and one twin bed, a fan and shared hot-water bathrooms. A new **comedor** (meals about M$30) right next door was almost ready to debut when we visited. You can also rent a hammock and mosquito

net (M$60) and string it up in a roofed area next to the *cabañas* for M$30.

Getting There & Away

Miramar is not the easiest place to get to. Try to visit outside the late-August to late-October rainy season, when land access can be more difficult and muddy foot trails can resemble quicksand. Some agencies in San Cristóbal de Las Casas run three- or four-day trips to Miramar from San Cristóbal via the river route, with prices starting around M$3500 per person (see p816).

AIR

Servicios Aéreos San Cristóbal has small-plane flights to San Quintín from Comitán (p851) or Ocosingo (p828).

LAND

Hold on tight. From Ocosingo, passenger-carrying trucks called *tres toneladas* (three-tonners) bump along 138km of rough road to reach San Quintín (M$70, about six hours). Departures are at 9am, 10:30am, noon and 2pm from just southeast of Ocosingo's Tianguis Campesino. You can also hire a VW bug *(bocho)* taxi (M$800 to M$1000). The route runs through the area known as Las Cañadas de Ocosingo, a Zapatista stronghold. Your documents may be checked at Mexican army or Zapatista village checkpoints, so keep your passport and tourist card handy.

By land or plane you'll arrive in San Quintín, Emiliano Zapata's neighboring village (which is anti-Zapatista and has a large army garrison). A track opposite a military complex beside San Quintín's airstrip leads to the middle of *ejido* Emiliano Zapata, about a 15- to 20-minute walk. Trucks head back from San Quintín to Ocosingo at 2am, 5am, 8am and noon.

RIVER

From Amatitlán (see p851 for *combi* information), a rough 14km from the Carretera Fronteriza Hwy, you can hire a *lancha* (M$800 one-way, maximum eight passengers, two hours) to Emiliano Zapata via the Río Santo Domingo until about 2pm.

AGUA AZUL & MISOL-HA

These spectacular water attractions – the thundering cascades of Agua Azul and the 35m jungle waterfall of Misol-Ha – are both short detours off the Ocosingo–Palenque road. During the rainy season, they lose part of their beauty as the water gets murky, though the power of the waterfalls is magnified.

Both are most easily visited on an organized day tour from Palenque, though it's possible, but probably not cheaper, to go independently too.

In the past, this area was the scene of repeated robberies and attempted robberies of tourists, though locals say it is safer now. To minimize the risks, don't walk the access roads, and stick to the main paved trail at Agua Azul. Thefts are still common, so don't bring valuables and keep an eye on your belongings.

Agua Azul

Agua Azul is a breathtaking sight, with its powerful and dazzling white waterfalls thundering into turquoise (most of the year) pools surrounded by verdant jungle. On holidays and weekends the place is thronged; at other times you'll have few companions. The temptation to swim is great, but take extreme care, as people do drown here. The current is deceptively fast, the power of the falls obvious, and there are many submerged hazards like rocks and dead trees.

The turnoff for these waterfalls is halfway between Ocosingo and Palenque, some 60km from each. A paved road leads 4.5km down to Agua Azul from Hwy 199, passing through the territory of one *ejido* into a second, whose territory includes the falls. You will probably have to pay M$10 to M$15 per person to enter each *ejido*. A well-made stone and concrete path with steps runs 700m up beside the falls from the parking area, lined by **comedores** (mains M$30-60) and souvenir stalls.

At the time of research, there were reports of paramilitary violence committed against villagers in the adjacent Zapatista community of Bolom Ajaw, allegedly by *ejido* members, and calls for a boycott of the falls.

Misol-Ha

Just 20km south of Palenque, spectacular Misol-Ha cascades 35m into a wonderful wide pool surrounded by lush tropical vegetation. It's a sublime place for a dip when the fall is not excessively pumped up by wet-season rains. A path behind the main fall leads into a cave, which gives a great close-up experience of the power of the fall. **Misol-Ha** (admission

M$10) is 1.5km off Hwy 199 and the turnoff is signposted.

Centro Turístico Ejidal Cascada de Misol-Ha (☎ in Mexico City 55-5329-0995, ext 7006; www.misol-ha.com; d/tr/q M$300/400/520; P) has great wooden cabins among the trees near the fall, with bathrooms and mosquito netting, plus a good open-air restaurant (mains M$50-75; ☑ 7am-6pm).

Getting There & Away

Almost all Palenque travel agencies (see p837) offer daily trips to Misol-Ha and Agua Azul. Trips cost M$120 to M$135 including admission fees, and last six or seven hours, spending 30 to 60 minutes at Misol-Ha and two to three hours at Agua Azul.

To visit the sites independently from Palenque, hire a taxi (around M$500 to Misol-Ha with a one-hour wait, or M$800 to Agua Azul with a two-hour wait); or, for Agua Azul, take a van from 4a or 5a Pte Sur, as far as the Agua Azul *crucero* (turnoff) for M$20. *Camionetas* (pickup trucks) at the turnoff charge M$15 for the run down to Agua Azul.

PALENQUE

☎ 916 / pop 37,000 / elevation 80m

Deservedly one of the top destinations of Chiapas, the soaring jungle-swathed temples of Palenque are a national treasure and one of the best examples of Maya architecture in Mexico. Modern Palenque town, a few kilometers to the east, is a sweaty, humdrum place without much appeal except as a jumping-off point for the ruins. Many prefer to base themselves at one of the forest hideouts along the road between the town and the ruins, including the funky travelers' hangout of El Panchán.

History

The name Palenque (Palisade) is Spanish and has no relation to the city's ancient name, which may have been Lakamha (Big Water). Palenque was first occupied around 100 BC, and flourished from around AD 630 to around 740. The city rose to prominence under the ruler Pakal, who reigned from AD 615 to 683. Archaeologists have determined that Pakal is represented by hieroglyphics of sun and shield, and he is also referred to as Sun Shield (Escudo Solar). He lived to the then-incredible age of 80.

During Pakal's reign, many plazas and buildings, including the superlative Templo de las Inscripciones (Pakal's own mausoleum), were constructed in Palenque. The structures were characterized by mansard roofs and very fine stucco bas-reliefs.

Pakal's son Kan B'alam II (684–702), who is represented in hieroglyphics by the jaguar and the serpent (and also called Jaguar Serpent II), continued Palenque's expansion and artistic development. He presided over the construction of the Grupo de las Cruces temples, placing sizable narrative stone steles within each.

During Kan B'alam II's reign, Palenque extended its zone of control to the Usumacinta river, but was challenged by the rival Maya city of Toniná, 65km south. Kan B'alam's brother and successor, K'an Joy Chitam II (Precious Peccary), was captured by forces from Toniná in 711, and probably executed there. Palenque enjoyed a resurgence between 722 and 736, however, under Ahkal Mo' Nahb' III (Turtle Macaw Lake), who added many substantial buildings.

After AD 900, Palenque was largely abandoned. In an area that receives the heaviest rainfall in Mexico, the ruins were soon overgrown, and the city remained unknown to the Western world until 1746, when Maya hunters revealed the existence of a jungle palace to a Spanish priest named Antonio de Solís. Later explorers claimed Palenque was capital of an Atlantis-like civilization. The eccentric Count de Waldeck, who in his 60s lived atop one of the pyramids for two years (1831–33), even published a book with fanciful neoclassical drawings that made the city resemble a great Mediterranean civilization.

It was not until 1837, when John L Stephens, an amateur archaeology enthusiast from New York, reached Palenque with artist Frederick Catherwood, that the site was insightfully investigated. And another century passed before Alberto Ruz Lhuillier, the tireless Mexican archaeologist, uncovered Pakal's hidden crypt in 1952. Today it continues to yield fascinating and beautiful secrets – most recently, a succession of sculptures and frescoes in the Acrópolis del Sur area, which have vastly expanded our knowledge of Palenque's history.

Frans Blom, the mid-20th-century investigator, remarked: 'The first visit to Palenque is immensely impressive. When one has lived there for some time this ruined city becomes an obsession.' It's not hard to understand why.

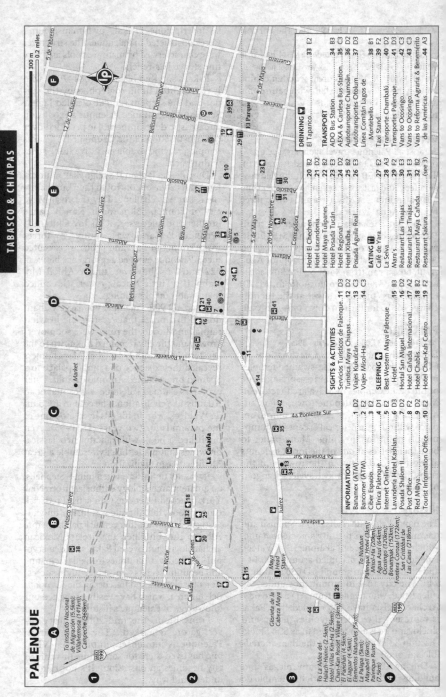

PALENQUE

TABASCO & CHIAPAS

INFORMATION
Banamex (ATM)	1 D2
Bancomer (ATM)	2 E2
Ciber Espacio	3 E2
Clínica Palenque	4 D1
Internet Online	5 E2
Lavandería Hotel Kashlan	6 D3
Posada Shalom II	7 D2
Post Office	8 F2
Red M@ya	9 D2
Tourist Information Office	10 E2

SIGHTS & ACTIVITIES
Servicios Turísticos de Palenque	11 D3
Turística Maya Chiapas	12 D2
Viajes Kukulcán	13 C3
Viajes Misol-Ha	14 C3

SLEEPING
Best Western Maya Palenque Hotel	15 B3
Hostal San Miguel	16 D2
Hotel Cañada Internacional	17 A2
Hotel Chablis	18 B2
Hotel Chan-Kah Centro	19 E2
Hotel El Chechen	20 B2
Hotel Lacandonia	21 D2
Hotel Maya Tulipanes	22 B2
Hotel Posada Tucán	23 E3
Hotel Regional	24 D2
Hotel Xibalba	25 B2
Posada Aguila Real	26 E3

EATING
Café de Yara	27 E2
La Selva	28 A3
Mara's	29 F2
Restaurant Las Tinajas	30 E3
Restaurant Las Tinajas	31 E3
Restaurant Maya Cañada	32 B2
Restaurant Sakura	(see 3)

DRINKING
El Tapanco	33 E2

TRANSPORT
ADO Bus Station	34 B3
AEXA & Cardesa Bus Station	35 C3
Autotransporte Chamoán	36 D2
Autotransportes Otolum	37 D3
Línea Comitán Lagos de Montebello	38 B1
Taxi Stand	39 F2
Transporte Chamballá	40 D2
Transportes Palenque	41 D3
Vans to Ocosingo	42 C3
Vans to Ocosingo	43 C3
Vans to Reforma Agraria & Benemérito de las Américas	44 A3

300 m
0.2 miles

Orientation

Hwy 199 meets Palenque's main street, Av Juárez, at the Glorieta de la Cabeza Maya, an intersection with a large statue of a Maya chieftain's head, at the west end of the town. From here Juárez heads 1km east to the central square, El Parque. The main bus stations are on Juárez just east of the Maya head statue.

A few hundred meters south from the Maya head, the paved road to the Palenque ruins, 7.5km away, diverges west off Hwy 199. This road passes the site museum after about 6.5km, then winds on about 1km further to the main entrance to the ruins.

Accommodations are scattered around the central part of town and along the road to the ruins. The commercial heart of town, where you'll hardly ever see another tourist, is north of the center along Velasco Suárez.

Information

INTERNET ACCESS

There are over a dozen cybercafés; in-town rates range from M$5 to M$15 per hour.

Ciber Espacio (Hidalgo s/n; ☯ 7am-10pm)

El Panchán (Carretera Palenque-Ruinas Km 4.5; per hr M$15; ☯ 10am-10pm)

Internet Online (Juárez s/n; ☯ 7am-10:30pm)

Red M@ya (Juárez 133; ☯ 9am-10pm)

LAUNDRY

Several town-center hotels offer public (often same-day) laundry service.

Posada Shalom II (☎ 345-09-44; Juárez 156; per kg M$15)

Lavandería Hotel Kashlan (5 de Mayo 105; 1-3kg M$50)

MEDICAL SERVICES

Clínica Palenque (☎ 345-02-73; Velasco Suárez 33; ☯ 7am-11pm) Dr Alfonso Martínez speaks English.

MONEY

Outside of banking hours, travel agents will change money. The following banks have ATMs.

Banamex (Juárez 62; ☯ 9am-4pm Mon-Fri)

Bancomer (Juárez 96; ☯ 8:30am-4pm Mon-Fri, 9am-2pm Sat)

POST

Post office (Independencia s/n; ☯ 9am-6pm Mon-Fri, to 1pm Sat)

TOURIST INFORMATION

Tourist information office (cnr Juárez & Abasolo; ☯ 9am-9pm Mon-Sat, 9am-1pm Sun) Has reliable town and transportation information as well as maps.

Sights

PALENQUE RUINS

Ancient **Palenque** (admission M$45; ☯ 8am-5pm, last entry 4:30pm) stands at the precise point where the first hills rise out of the Gulf Coast plain, and the dense jungle covering these hills forms an evocative backdrop to Palenque's exquisite Maya architecture. Hundreds of ruined buildings are spread over 15 sq km, but only a fairly compact central area has been excavated. Everything you see here was built without metal tools, pack animals or the wheel.

As you explore the ruins, try to picture the gray stone edifices as they would have been at the peak of Palenque's power: painted blood-red with elaborate blue and yellow stucco details. The forest around these temples is still home to howler monkeys (whom you might hear or see), toucans and ocelots. The ruins and surrounding forests form a national park, the Parque Nacional Palenque, for which you must pay a separate M$20 admission fee at Km 4.5 on the road to the ruins.

Palenque sees over 1000 visitors on an average day, and visitation spikes in the summer holiday season. Opening time is a good time to visit, when it's cooler and not too crowded, and morning mist may still be wrapping the temples in a picturesque haze. Refreshments, hats and souvenirs are available outside the main entrance, and there are cafés there and at the museum. Vendors carpet many of the paths through the ruins.

Official site **guides** (2hr tour for up to 7 people in English/Spanish/French/Italian M$650/450/700/700) are available by the entrance. A Maya guide association, **Guías e Interpretes Mayas** (☎ 341-76-88), also has a desk here and offers informative two-hour tours in Spanish, English or Italian at the same prices. Fascinating and entertaining in-depth tours of around five hours (usually for groups of five to 10) are given by **Maya Exploration Center** (www.mayaexploration.org), a group of archaeologists who work on Maya sciences such as astronomy and math, and map unexplored ruins. Email them from the website or ask for Alonso Méndez at El Panchán (p836). Their website is packed with interest for Palenque fans – as is another Palenque archaeologists' site, the **Group of the Cross Project** (www.mesoweb.com/palenque).

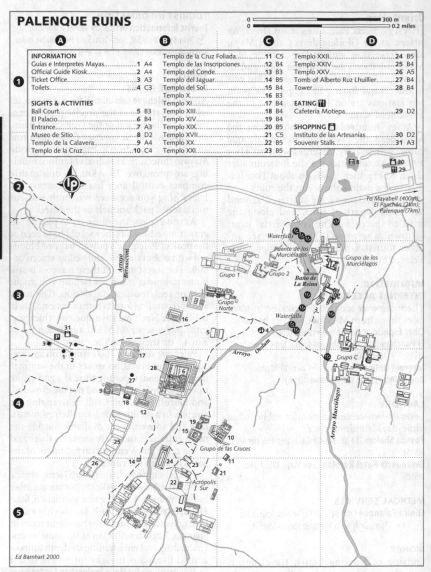

PALENQUE RUINS

0 — 300 m
0 — 0.2 miles

INFORMATION	
Guías e Interpretes Mayas	**1** A4
Official Guide Kiosk	**2** A4
Ticket Office	**3** A3
Toilets	**4** C3

SIGHTS & ACTIVITIES	
Ball Court	**5** B3
El Palacio	**6** B4
Entrance	**7** A3
Museo de Sitio	**8** D2
Templo de la Calavera	**9** A4
Templo de la Cruz	**10** C4

Templo de la Cruz Foliada	**11** C5
Templo de las Inscripciones	**12** B4
Templo del Conde	**13** B3
Templo del Jaguar	**14** B5
Templo del Sol	**15** B4
Templo X	**16** B3
Templo XI	**17** B4
Templo XIII	**18** B4
Templo XIV	**19** B4
Templo XIX	**20** B5
Templo XVII	**21** C5
Templo XX	**22** B5
Templo XXI	**23** B5

Templo XXII	**24** B5
Templo XXIV	**25** B4
Templo XXV	**26** A5
Tomb of Alberto Ruz Lhuillier	**27** B4
Tower	**28** B4

EATING 🍴	
Cafetería Motiepa	**29** D2

SHOPPING 🛍	
Instituto de las Artesanías	**30** D2
Souvenir Stalls	**31** A3

To Mayabell (400m);
El Panchán (2km);
Palenque (7km)

Waterfalls
Puente de los Murciélagos
Grupo 1
Grupo 2
Grupo de los Murciélagos
Baño de La Reina
Grupo Norte
Waterfalls
Arroyo Otolum
Grupo C
Arroyo Murciélagos
Arroyo Berrascorni
Grupo de las Cruces
Acrópolis Sur

Ed Barnhart 2000

Most visitors take a combi or taxi to the ruins' main (upper) entrance, see the major structures and then walk downhill to the museum, visiting minor ruins along the way. Note that it's not permitted to exit the site this way before 9am or after 4pm.

Transportes Chambalú (☎ 345-28-49; Allende s/n) and **Transportes Palenque** (☎ 345-24-30;

cnr Allende & 20 de Noviembre) run combis to the ruins about every 15 minutes from 6am to 7pm daily (M$10 each way). They will pick you up or drop you anywhere along the town-to-ruins road.

Be aware that the mushrooms sold by locals along the road to the ruins from about May to November are the hallucinogenic variety.

Templo de las Inscripciones Group

As you walk in from the entrance, passing to the south of the overgrown Templo XI, the vegetation suddenly peels away to reveal most of Palenque's most magnificent buildings in one sublime vista. A line of temples rises in front of the jungle on your right, culminating in the Templo de las Inscripciones about 100m ahead; El Palacio, with its trademark tower, stands to the left of the Templo de las Inscripciones; and the Grupo de las Cruces rises in the distance beneath a thick jungle backdrop.

The first temple on your right is Templo XII, called the **Templo de La Calavera** (Temple of the Skull) for the relief sculpture of a rabbit or deer skull at the foot of one of its pillars. The second temple has little interest. Third is **Templo XIII**, containing a tomb of a female dignitary, whose remains were found colored red (as a result of treatment with cinnabar) when unearthed in 1994. You can enter this Tumba de la Reina Roja (Tomb of the Red Queen) to see her sarcophagus. With the skeleton were found a malachite mask and about 1000 pieces of jade. Some speculate, from resemblances to Pakal's tomb next door, that the 'queen' buried here was his wife.

The **Templo de las Inscripciones** (Temple of the Inscriptions), perhaps the most celebrated burial monument in the Americas, is the tallest and most stately of Palenque's buildings. Constructed on eight levels, the Templo de las Inscripciones has a central front staircase rising 25m to a series of small rooms. The tall roof comb that once crowned it is long gone, but between the front doorways are stucco panels with reliefs of noble figures. On the interior rear wall are three panels with the long Maya inscription, recounting the history of Palenque and this building, for which Mexican archaeologist Alberto Ruz Lhuillier named the temple. From the top, interior stairs lead down into the tomb of Pakal (now closed to visitors indefinitely, to avoid further damage to its murals from the humidity inevitably exuded by visitors). Pakal's jewel-bedecked skeleton and jade mosaic death mask were removed from the tomb to Mexico City, and the tomb was re-created in the Museo Nacional de Antropología (p153). The priceless death mask was stolen in 1985, but the carved stone sarcophagus lid remains here – you can see a replica in the site museum (see p836).

The tomb of Ruz Lhuillier, who discovered Pakal's tomb in 1952, lies under the trees in front of Templo XIII.

El Palacio

Diagonally opposite the Templo de las Inscripciones is the **Palace**, a large structure divided into four main courtyards, with a maze of corridors and rooms. Built and modified piecemeal over 400 years from the 5th century on, it probably really was the residence of Palenque's rulers. Its tower, built in the 8th century by Ahkal Mo' Nahb' III and restored in 1955, has remnants of fine stucco reliefs on the walls, but you're not allowed to climb up inside it. Archaeologists believe the tower was constructed so that Maya royalty and priests could observe the sun falling directly into the Templo de las Inscripciones during the winter solstice.

The northeastern courtyard, the **Patio de los Cautivos** (Patio of the Captives), contains a collection of relief sculptures that seem disproportionately large for their setting; the theory is that they represent conquered rulers and were brought from elsewhere.

In the southern part of the complex, the extensive subterranean bathrooms included six toilets and a couple of sweat baths.

Grupo de las Cruces

Pakal's son, Kan B'alam II, was a prolific builder, and soon after the death of his father started designing the temples of the Grupo de las Cruces (Group of the Crosses). All three main pyramid-shaped structures surround a plaza southeast of the Templo de las Inscripciones. They were all dedicated in AD 692 as a spiritual focal point for Palenque's triad of patron deities. The 'cross' carvings in some buildings here symbolize the ceiba tree, which in Maya belief held up the universe.

The **Templo del Sol** (Temple of the Sun), on the west side of the plaza, has the best-preserved roof comb at Palenque. Carvings inside, commemorating Kan B'alam's birth in AD 635 and accession in 684, show him facing his father. Some view this beautiful building as sure proof that Palenque's ancient architects were inspired by the local hallucinogenic mushrooms. Make up your own mind!

Steep steps climb to the **Templo de la Cruz** (Temple of the Cross), the largest and most elegantly proportioned in this group. The stone tablet in the central sanctuary shows the lord of the underworld smoking tobacco on the right, and Kan B'alam in full royal attire on the left. Behind is a reproduction of a panel depicting Kan B'alam's accession.

On the **Templo de la Cruz Foliada** (Temple of the Foliated Cross), the corbel arches are fully exposed, revealing how Palenque's architects designed these buildings. A well-preserved inscribed tablet shows a king (probably Pakal) with a sun shield emblazoned on his chest, corn growing from his shoulder blades, and the sacred quetzal bird on his head.

Acrópolis Sur

In the jungle south of the Grupo de las Cruces is the **Southern Acropolis**, where archaeologists have recovered some terrific finds in recent excavations. You may find part of the area roped off. The Acrópolis Sur appears to have been constructed as an extension of the Grupo de las Cruces, with both groups set around what was probably a single long open space.

Templo XVII, between the Cruces group and the Acrópolis Sur, contains a reproduction carved panel depicting Kan B'alam, standing with a spear, with a bound captive kneeling before him (the original is in the site museum).

In 1999, in **Templo XIX**, archaeologists made the most important Palenque find for decades: an 8th-century limestone platform with stunning carvings of seated figures and lengthy hieroglyphic texts that detail Palenque's origins. A reproduction has been placed inside Templo XIX – the central figure on the long south side of the platform is the ruler Ahkal Mo' Nahb' III, who was responsible for several of the buildings of the Acrópolis Sur, just as the Grupo de las Cruces was created by Kan B'alam II. Also on view is a wonderful reproduction of a tall stucco relief of Ahkal Mo' Nahb''s son, U Pakal.

In **Templo XX**, built in 540, a frescoed tomb of an unknown personage was found in 1999. Ahkal Mo' Nahb' undertook a complete remodeling of this pyramid in the 8th century, but his work was never completed.

In **Templo XXI** in 2002, archaeologists discovered a throne with very fine carvings depicting Ahkal Mo' Nahb', his ancestor the great Pakal, and his son U Pakal.

Grupo Norte

North of El Palacio is a **ball court** (*juego de pelota*) and the handsome buildings of the Northern Group. Crazy Count de Waldeck

(see p831) lived in the so-called **Templo del Conde** (Temple of the Count), constructed in AD 647.

Northeastern Groups

East of the Grupo Norte, the main path crosses Arroyo Otolum. Some 70m beyond the stream, a right fork will take you to **Grupo C**, a set of jungle-covered buildings and plazas, thought to have been lived in from about AD 750 to 800.

If you stay on the main path, you'll descend steep steps to a group of low, elongated buildings, probably occupied residentially around AD 770 to 850. The path goes alongside the Arroyo Otolum, which here tumbles down a series of small falls forming natural bathing pools known as the **Baño de la Reina** (Queen's Bath). Unfortunately, one can't bathe here anymore.

The then path continues to another residential quarter, the **Grupo de Los Murciélagos** (Bat Group), and then crosses the **Puente de los Murciélagos**, a footbridge across Arroyo Otolum.

Across the bridge and a bit further downstream, a path goes west to **Grupos 1 and 2**, a short walk uphill. These ruins, only partly uncovered, are in a beautiful jungle setting. The main path continues downriver to the road, where the museum is a short distance along to the right.

Museo de Sitio

Palenque's **museum** (Site Museum; ☎ 348-93-31; Carretera Palenque-Ruinas Km 7; admission free; ☿ 9am-4:30pm Tue-Sun) is worth a wander, displaying finds from the site and interpreting, in English and Spanish, Palenque's history. Highlights include a blissfully air-conditioned room displaying a copy of the lid of Pakal's sarcophagus (depicting his rebirth as the maize god, encircled by serpents, mythical monsters and glyphs recounting his reign), and recent finds from Templo XXI. The Cafetería Motiepa (p839) and **Instituto de las Artesanías** (☎ 348-35-11; ☿ 9am-5pm), a well-stocked handicraft shop, are next door.

EL PANCHÁN

Just off the road to the ruins, **El Panchán** (www .elpanchan.com; Carretera Palenque-Ruinas Km 4.5) is a legendary travelers' hangout, set in a patch of dense rainforest – the epicenter of Palenque's alternative scene and home to a bohemian bunch of Mexican and foreign residents and wanderers, including a number of archaeologists and anthropologists. Once ranchland, the area has been reforested by the remarkable Morales family, some of whom are among the leading archaeological experts on Palenque. El Panchán has several (fairly rustic) places to stay (see p838), a couple of restaurants, a set of sinuous streams rippling their way through every part of the property, nightly entertainment, a meditation temple, a temascal (pre-Hispanic steam bath) and a constant stream of interesting visitors from all over the world. **Maya Exploration Center** (www.mayaexploration.org) provides lectures, slide shows and documentary films at weekends in the main tourism seasons.

Tours
Numerous travel agencies in Palenque offer transportation packages to Agua Azul and Misol-Ha (see p850), to Bonampak, Yaxchilán and Lacanjá, and to Flores, Guatemala (p841). They tend to work together, posting almost identical prices. Agencies include the following, most open from around 8am to 9pm daily:
Servicios Turísticos de Palenque (☎ 345-13-40; www.stpalenque.com; cnr Juárez & 5 de Mayo)
Transportes Chambalú (☎ 345-28-49; Allende s/n)
Turística Maya Chiapas (☎ 345-07-98; www.tmayachiapas.com.mx; Juárez 123)
Viajes Kukulcán (☎ 345-15-06; www.kukulcantravel.com; Juárez 8)
Viajes Misol-Ha (☎ 345-16-14; www.palenquemx.com/viajesmisolha; Juárez 148)

Sleeping
The first choice to make is whether you want to stay in or out of Palenque town. Most out-of-town places, including El Panchán, are along the road to the ruins. Except for leafy La Cañada, Palenque town is not particularly attractive, but if you stay here you'll have plenty of restaurants and services nearby. Budget accommodations predominate both in and out of town, but many of the better budget places are midrange in quality.

Prices given here are for the high season, which is mid-July to mid-August, mid-December to early January, and Semana Santa. Rates drop up to 35% at other times.

IN TOWN
Budget
Hotel Regional (☎ /fax 345-01-83; www.regionalpalenque.com; Juárez 119; s/d/tr/q with fan M$180/230/320/420, tr/

q with air-con M$400/500; ❂) Something slightly different from the run of the Av Juárez mill: bright paintwork and extremely bright murals enliven two floors of rooms around a courtyard with a turtle pond. The bathrooms are tiny.

Posada Shalom II (☎ /fax 345-09 44; www.hotelesshalom.com; Juárez 156; s/d/tr with fan M$250/300/350, s/d with air-con M$350/400; ❂) Airy hallways fringed with potted plants lead to medium-sized rooms with ample bathrooms. Look before unpacking, as some don't have natural light.

Hotel Posada Tucán (☎ 345-18-59; merisuiri@hotmail.com; 5 de Mayo 3; r/tr/q with fan M$250/300/550, r/tr/q with air-con M$300/450/550; ❂) Textured walls in primary colors spice up fair-sized rooms with TV and nicely tiled bathrooms. The 14 breezy rooms, all upstairs, are attractive and clean.

Posada Aguila Real (☎ 345-00-04; 20 de Noviembre s/n; s/d M$350/400, tr M$450-500; ❂ 🖳) Seventeen spotless, well-kept, blue-and-yellow rooms are arranged on three floors around an open-air patio. All have good-quality beds, air-con and TV and courtyard windows. There's a small café-restaurant too.

Other basic options include:
Hostal San Miguel (☎ 345-01-52; Hidalgo 43; dm M$100, r with fan/air-con M$250/450; ❂) Balcony rooms, all with fans and modern bathrooms; dorms are lackluster but economical.
Hotel El Chechen (☎ 345-10-08; hotelelchechen@hotmail.com; Merle Green s/n; s & d M$400, tr/q M$600/700; ▣ ❂ 🖳) The only budget option in forested La Cañada, with free internet and all rooms with air-con.

Midrange
These hotels are in the leafy La Cañada area at the west end of town.
Hotel Lacandonia (☎ 345-00-57; hotel-lacandonia@hotmail.com; Allende s/n; r M$400, tr/q M$550/650; ▣ ❂) A modern hotel with a subtle splash of style. Tasteful, light, airy accommodations all have wrought-iron beds, reading lights and cable TV.
Hotel Chan-Kah Centro (☎ 345-0318; www.chan-kah.com.mx; Juárez 2; s/d/t/q M$468/530/586/650; ❂) In the center and also good, and right on the park, this place has 17 air-conditioned rooms sporting a tropical theme.
Hotel Xibalba (☎ 345-04-11; www.hotelxibalba.com; Merle Green 9; r M$550, tr/q M$600/700; ▣ ❂ 🖳) Preened to perfection by a loving owner, the Xibalba enjoys a tranquil location in two buildings (one in an imitation of the ancient Maya corbel roof style, the other with a full-

size replica of the lid from Pakal's sarcophagus). All rooms have air-con, cable TV and spotless bathrooms, and the bigger ones boast two double beds and bathtubs. The hotel has its own restaurant and travel agency.

Hotel Cañada Internacional (☎ 345-20-94; www .canadainternacional.com.mx; Juárez s/n; r/tr/q M$700/750/800; P ⌗ ⌖) Bright traditional textiles spiff up four stories of large, comfortable rooms, all with air-con and two double beds. Vines creep up a small garden courtyard, and there's a small pool. Rooms in the older section are smaller.

Hotel Chablis (☎ 345-08-70; www.hotelchablis.com; Merle Green 7; r M$720, tr/q M$800/880; P ⌗ 🖳) Opposite the Xibalba, this small hotel offers well-presented, spacious rooms, all with one king or two queen-sized beds, air-con and balcony.

Top End

Best Western Maya Palenque Hotel (☎ 345-07-80, 800-904-75-00; www.bestwestern.com; cnr Juárez & Merle Green; r/ste M$1080/1200; P ⌗ 🖳 ⌖) A comfortable international hotel with good-sized air-conditioned rooms, all with two double beds, cable TV, phone and balcony and plenty of natural light. The big garden pool is a plus.

Hotel Maya Tulipanes (☎ 345-02-01; www.maya tulipanes.com.mx; Cañada 6; r/tr M$1100/1200; P 🖳 ⌖) Popular with tour groups, this plush La Cañada hotel has large, comfortable, air-conditioned rooms with two wrought-iron double beds and a tropical décor. It's designed around a pretty garden with a small pool and restaurant.

OUTSIDE TOWN

Where Palenque town exudes traffic and commerce, the surrounding area, especially between town and the ruins, holds some magical spots, where howler monkeys romp in the tree canopy and unseen animals chirp after dark. The compound of El Panchán is a travelers' favorite, with low-key budget *cabañas* nestled in stream-crossed jungle. Frequent combis between town and the ruins (see p833) will drop you off and pick you up anywhere along this road.

Budget

Mayabell (☎ 341-69-77; www.mayabell.com.mx; Carretera Palenque-Ruinas Km 6; hammock shelter or campsites per person M$40, hammock to rent M$15, small vehicle without hookups M$20, vehicle site with hookups M$150, cabaña with shared bathroom M$250, r with fan M$450, r with air-con M$680; P ⌗ ⌖ 🖳) Once you see the sprawling jungleside pool – frequented by monkeys – you'll long to move in. This spacious grassy campground is just 400m from the site museum and has tons of clean and comfortable sleeping options, plus an enjoyable restaurant (opposite). Rooms with air-con are very homey and comfortable; those with fan are more basic. The temascal is M$80 per person (up to eight people).

Elementos Naturales (enpalenque@yahoo.com.mx; Carretera Palenque-Ruinas Km 5; hammock space/campsites per person M$30, campsites per person incl breakfast M$50, dm incl breakfast M$120, d cabaña incl breakfast M$300; P) It's about 600m on from El Panchán to this calm spot with *cabañas* and *palapa* shelters set around extensive grassy gardens. The *cabañas* (for up to five) and eight-bunk dorms with airy high palapa roofs, all have fans, individual mosquito nets, electric light and their private bathrooms. There's also a restaurant onsite.

Chato's Cabañas (☎ 341-82-09; www.elpanchan.com; El Panchán; cabaña with shared bathroom s/d M$100/120, s/d/tr/q with private bathroom M$150/160/180/220; P) Chato's 40 wood and concrete cabins, dotted around the Panchán jungle, vary a little in design, but all have screened windows and fans, and some have nice little porches. Some are a bit dilapidated, but still waterproof.

Jungle Palace (☎ 341-82-09; www.elpanchan.com; El Panchán; s/d/tr cabaña with shared bathroom M$100/120/180) A more basic option in El Panchán, the Jungle Palace offers rudimentary though well-screened cabins with fans, some of which back onto a stream. The best are freestanding, while others share walls and have less privacy.

El Jaguar (☎ 341-82-09; www.elpanchan.com; Carretera Palenque-Ruinas Km 4.5; cabaña with shared bathroom s/d M$100/120, with private bathroom s/d M$160/200; P) Just across the road from El Panchán, and under the same ownership as Chato's Cabañas, El Jaguar has more open grounds and the same creek running through it. Neat, yellow cabins of wood, plaster and thatch have private bathrooms; simpler ones with mosquito-net windows share clean bathrooms.

Margarita & Ed Cabañas (☎ 348-42-05; El Panchán; cabañas r M$170, r with fan M$250-300, r with air-con M$350, tr & q with air-con M$500; P ⌗ ⌖) Teeming with local information, Margarita has welcomed travelers to her exceptionally homey place in the jungle for more than 10 years. Bright, clean and cheerful rooms have good mosquito netting and the more rustic screened *cabañas* are well kept, too, with reading lights and private bathrooms. There's free drinking water for all.

Midrange

La Aldea del Halach-Huinic (☎ 345-16-93; www .hotel-la-aldea.com.mx; Carretera Palenque-Ruinas Km 2.8; cabaña with shared/private bathroom M$250/350, air-con cabaña M$800; P ⊠ ⌘) Some 3km from town, the Halach-Uinic has over 40 *palapa*-roofed *cubañas* in spacious gardens. The air-conditioned accommodations are large and bright, with their own bathrooms and terraces, and attractive decorations using stone, rock and tree branches. The cheaper *cabañas*, with clean shared bathrooms, are smaller but also fine, with mosquito-screens and nets, indigenous-style blankets and hammocks on a little porch. There's a small pool and a restaurant.

Hotel Villas Kin-Ha (☎ 345-05-33; www.villaskinha .com; Carretera Palenque-Ruinas Km 2.7; r M$660-800, ste M$1320; P ⊠ ⌘) Though it has over 90 rooms and bungalows set around its pretty gardens, the Kin-Ha doesn't seem crowded. Most accommodations are palm-thatched and wood-beamed, and all have air-conditioning. The grounds hold two good pools, an open-sided *palapa* restaurant and a theater.

Nututun Palenque Hotel (☎ 345-01-00; www.nu tutun.com; Carretera Palenque-Ocosingo Km 3.5; campsites per person M$65, r M$800-900, deluxe room M$1000-1200; P ⊠ ⌘) The Nututun, 3.5km south of town on the road toward San Cristóbal, has spacious, comfortable, air-conditioned rooms in large and exuberant tropical gardens. As well as a good pool in the gardens, and a restaurant, there's a wonderful bathing spot (free for guests, M$2 for others) in the Río Chacamax, which flows through the hotel property.

Top End

Chan-Kah Resort Village (☎ 345-11-00; www.chan-kah .com.mx; Carretera Palenque-Ruinas Km 3; r/ste US$120/330; P ⊠ ⌘) Swimmers will go woozy contemplating the Chan-Kah's stupendous 70m stone-lined swimming pool in lush jungle gardens. A quality resort on the road to the ruins, 3km from town, it has handsome well-spaced wood-and-stone cottages with generous bathrooms, ceiling fans, terrace and air-con. There's a good open-air restaurant, bar and games room too. It's rarely busy, except when tour groups block-book the place.

Eating

Palenque is definitely not the gastronomic capital of Mexico, but there's a decent variety of restaurants and prices are fair.

Cafetería Motlepa (Carretera Palenque-Ruinas Km 6; snacks M$20-40; ☉ 8am-3pm) Next to the site museum near the Palenque ruins, this is a good stop for a snack or drink.

Restaurant Sakura (☎ 102-36-56; Hidalgo s/n; mains M$40-85; ☉ 10am-11pm) We can't vouch for the authenticity of the sushi, but the fried rice and other Chinese comfort foods hit the spot. Enjoy the quiet upper terrace with a bird's-eye view of the park.

Restaurant Las Tinajas (☎ 345-49-70; cnr 20 de Noviembre & Abasolo; mains M$50-100; ☉ 7am-11pm) It doesn't take long to figure out why this place is always busy. It slings enormous portions of excellent home-style food, and it's enough to keep you (and possibly another person) fueled up for hours. Of the two branches on either side of the same intersection, the newer and more westerly one is more festive and geared toward tourists, and consequently a tad more pricey than the no-frills original. But both have the same great food. *Pollo a la veracruzana* (chicken in a tomato/olives/onion sauce) and *camarones al guajillo* (shrimp with a not-too-hot type of chili) are both delicious, as is the house salsa.

La Selva (☎ 345-03-63; Hwy 199; mains M$50-160; ☉ 11:30am-11:30pm) Palenque's most upscale restaurant serves up well-prepared steaks, seafood, salads and *antojitos* under an enormous *palapa* roof, with jungle-themed stained-glass panels brightening one wall. The secluded outdoor tables are *muy romántico*.

Mayabell (☎ 341-69-77; Carretera Palenque-Ruinas Km 6; mains M$55-90) The open-sided restaurant at Mayabell serves a good range of *antojitos* and meat and fish dishes. There's live music on some evenings.

Mara's (☎ 345-25-78; Juárez 1; mains M$55-95; ☉ 7am-11pm) On a corner across from the park, this brightly-painted traditional restaurant has a great location. It offers a good range of meat, fish and chicken dishes and patrons can catch an ever-so-welcome tropical breeze.

Don Mucho's (☎ 341-82-09; El Panchán; mains M$55-110) The hotspot of El Panchán, popular Don Mucho's provides great-value meals in a jungly setting, with a candle-lit atmosphere at night. Busy waiters bring pasta, fish, meat, plenty of *antojitos*, and pizzas (cooked in a purpose-built Italian-designed wood-fired oven) that are some of the finest this side of Naples. And there's live music – usually *andina, cumbia* or Cuban – around 8pm or 9pm, plus a rousing fire dancing show most nights.

Café de Yara (☎ 345-02-69; Hidalgo 66; snacks & breakfasts M$40-60, mains M$60-90; ☯ 7am-11pm) A sunny start to the day, this modern and beautiful corner café has great breakfasts and excellent organic Chiapan coffee. In the evening, the lights get intimate, with live salsa and merengue bands serenading diners from Thursday through Saturday.

Restaurant Maya Cañada (☎ 345-02-16; Merle Green s/n; mains M$60-150) This relatively upmarket and professionally run restaurant in the shady La Cañada area serves fine steaks and terrific seafood kebabs. It's open to the air and has a cool upstairs terrace.

Drinking & Entertainment

Palenque doesn't have much of a nightlife scene. In the evenings, you'll often spot more travelers waiting for a night bus than out on the town. A few restaurants – mostly places along the ruins road – have live music.

El Tapanco (☎ 345-04-15; Juárez 65C) At this upstairs 'attic,' look for live rock and *trova* bands on Fridays and Saturdays. Afternoon drinks come with *botanas*, and cooler evenings are a swell time to munch on pizza (M$100) washed down with a *michelada*.

La Palapa (Carretera Palenque-Ruinas Km 5; ☯ until 4am) As freaky-fun as it gets in these parts, this al fresco 'jungle lounge' screens movies (M$10) at 6pm nightly and its DJs spin reggae, salsa and electronica – sometimes punctuated by fire dancing – starting around 11pm. Dance until the wee hours and then dissolve and regroup in sofas under the *palapa* roof.

Getting There & Away

Highway holdups were once weekly occurrences on Hwy 199 between Ocosingo and Palenque, but an increased military and police presence has made this route pretty safe now. Still, most consider daytime travel to be best.

The **Instituto Nacional de Migración** (☎ 103-18-71; ☯ 24hr), 6km north of town on Hwy 199, can be reached by 'Playas' combis that run here from the Autotransportes Otolum terminal on Allende (M$15).

Palenque's airport, 3km north of town along Hwy 199, has been closed to regular passenger flights for several years.

ADO (☎ 345-13-44; Juárez s/n) has the main bus terminal, with deluxe and 1st-class services; it's also used by OCC (1st-class) and TRF (2nd-class). **AEXA** (☎ 345-26-30; Juárez 159), with 1st-class buses, and Cardesa (2nd-class) are 1½ blocks east, with an onsite internet café. Vans to Ocosingo wait on 4 and 5 Pte Sur, near the bus stations, and leave when full. **Transportes Palenque** (☎ 345-24-30; cnr Allende & 20 de Noviembre) runs vans to Tenosique.

It's a good idea to buy your outward bus ticket a day in advance. Daily departures include the following:

Destination	Fare	Duration	Frequency (daily)
Campeche	M$226-230	4½-5½hr	4 from ADO
Cancún	M$498-584	13-14hr	5 from ADO
Mérida	M$316-346	8hr	4 from ADO
Mexico City	M$706	13½hr	2 from ADO
Oaxaca	M$514	14½hr	1 from ADO
Ocosingo	M$40-78	2½hr	11 from ADO, 5 AEXA & vans leave about every 30 min
San Cristóbal de Las Casas	M$75-142	5¼hr	10 from ADO, 5 AEXA
Tenosique	M$50	2hr	Transportes Palenque vans hourly 5am-7pm
Tulum	M$424	11hr	5 from ADO
Tuxtla Gutiérrez	M$105-206	6hr	10 from ADO, 5 AEXA
Villahermosa	M$50-98	2hr	12 from ADO, 11 AEXA

For information on transportation along the Carretera Fronteriza (for Lacanjá Chansayab, Bonampak, Yaxchilán, Guatemala and other destinations), see opposite.

Getting Around

Taxis wait at the northeast corner of El Parque and at the ADO bus station; they charge M$40 to El Panchán or Mayabell, and M$50 to the ruins.

BONAMPAK, YAXCHILÁN & THE CARRETERA FRONTERIZA

The ancient Maya cities of Bonampak and Yaxchilán, southeast of Palenque, are easily accessible thanks to the Carretera Fronteriza, a good paved road running parallel to the Mexico–Guatemala border, all the way from Palenque to the Lagos de Montebello, around the fringe of the Lacandón Jungle. Bonampak,

TABASCO & CHIAPAS

famous for its frescoes, is 148km by road from Palenque; the bigger and more important Yaxchilán, with a peerless jungle setting beside the broad and swift Río Usumacinta, is 173km by road, then about 22km by boat.

The Carretera Fronteriza is the main thoroughfare connecting a number of excellent ecotourism projects including some in the Lacandón village of Lacanjá Chansayab (p843) as well as the excellent Las Guacamayas ecolodge (p847) and the gorgeous watery wonderland at Las Nubes (p848). In addition, it's the main route from Chiapas to Guatemala's northern Petén region (home of several major Maya sites including mighty Tikal), via the town of Frontera Corozal. Phones in this region usually have satellite service or Guatemala-based numbers.

Dangers & Annoyances

Drug trafficking and illegal immigration are facts of life in this border region, and the Carretera Fronteriza more or less encircles the main area of Zapatista rebel activity and support, so expect numerous military checkpoints along the road, and from this area to Palenque and Comitán. You shouldn't have anything to fear from these checks, but don't tempt easy theft by leaving money or valuables unattended during stops. For your own security, it's best to be off the Carretera Fronteriza before dusk – especially the most isolated section in the far southeast, between Benemérito de las Américas and the Chajul turnoff.

This part of Mexico tends to ignore daylight saving time, so double-check all transportation schedules. And don't forget insect repellent.

Tours

There aren't a lot of private cars traveling this area, and though it's perfectly possible to visit here independently and to travel through to Guatemala, there are also tour options. Many Palenque travel agencies (see p837) run day tours to Bonampak and Yaxchilán for around M$500 per person, usually including entry fees, two meals and transportation in an air-conditioned van. There's also a two-day version for around M$800, with an overnight stay at Lacanjá Chansayab (often referred to as the 'Ecological Reserve' in the publicity). Most of the same agencies offer transportation packages from Palenque to Flores, Guatemala – usually via an air-conditioned van to Frontera Corozal, river launch up the Usumacinta to Bethel in Guatemala, and public bus on to Flores – 10 or 11 hours altogether, for around M$300. Two-day packages to Flores, visiting Bonampak and Yaxchilán en route, are around M$800. Always check package inclusions and exclusions, so you can plan your meals and not find yourself digging around to pay for unanticipated park fees.

San Cristóbal–based SendaSur (see p817) and the **Mesoamerican Ecotourism Alliance** (www .travelwithmea.org) organize trips to the region, including the Lacandón villages of Nahá and Metzabok (see below)

Getting There & Away

From Palenque, vans run to Frontera Corozal (M$60, 2½ to three hours, 13 times daily), and to Benemérito (M$60, 3½ hours, every 40 minutes from 4am to 5:30pm).

Línea Comitán Lagos de Montebello (☎ 916-345-12-60; Velasco Suárez s/n), two blocks west of Palenque market, runs vans to Benemérito (M$60) 10 times daily (4am to 2:45pm), with the first five services (4am, 5:30am, 7:15am, 8:45am and 10:15am) continuing round the Carretera Fronteriza to the Lagos de

---

THE BIRDS & THE BUZZ *Manuela Morales Hernández*

I work for two natural protected areas, Nahá and Metzabok, that are both inhabited by the Lacandón community. Nahá means 'house of water' and Metzabok means 'god of thunder.' My job in the reserve is mostly monitoring birds, and we also have a project monitoring mammals. The most common bird we see in the jungle is the toucan.

Right now there is a project growing organic, shade-grown coffee outside of the reserve. Ejido Avendaño has been growing coffee since they first settled the area in the 1970s. They used to practice conventional techniques, and they would clear the jungle and grow coffee without shade. Now they take advantage of the shade and their product is organic and not sprayed with pesticides.

Manuela Morales Hernández works as a biologist for Comisión Nacional de Áreas
Naturales Protegidas (National Commission of Protected Natural Areas)

Montebello (M$160, seven hours to Tziscao) and Comitán (M$170, eight hours).

All these services stop at San Javier (M$45, two hours), the turnoff for Lacanjá Chansayab and Bonampak, 140km from Palenque; and at Crucero Corozal (M$50, 2½ hours), the intersection for Frontera Corozal.

There are no gas stations on the Carretera Fronteriza, but plenty of entrepreneurial locals sell reasonably-priced gasoline from large plastic containers. Look for homemade 'Se vende gasolina' signs.

Bonampak

Bonampak's setting in dense jungle hid it from the outside world until 1946. Stories of how it was revealed are full of mystery and innuendo, but it seems that Charles Frey, a young WWII conscientious objector from the US, and John Bourne, heir to the Singer sewing machine fortune, were the first outsiders to visit the site when Chan Bor, a Lacandón, took them there in February 1946. Later in 1946 an American photographer, Giles Healey, was also led to the site by Chan Bor and found the Templo de las Pinturas, with its famous murals.

The site of **Bonampak** (admission M$37; ☼ 8am-4:45pm) spreads over 2.4 sq km, but all the main ruins stand around the rectangular Gran Plaza. Never a major city, Bonampak spent most of the Classic period under Yaxchilán's sphere of influence. The most impressive surviving monuments were built under Chan Muwan II, a nephew of the Yaxchilán's Itzamnaaj B'alam II, who acceded to Bonampak's throne in AD

BONAMPAK   0 — 50 m

To Site Entrance (500m)

Edificio 15   Edificio 16
Gran Plaza
Stele 1

Edificio 1
(Templo de
las Pinturas)   Edificio 17
Stele 3
Stele 2
Edificio 3

Edificio 2

776. The 6m-high **Stele 1** in the Gran Plaza depicts Chan Muwan holding a ceremonial staff at the height of his reign. He also features in **Stele 2** and **Stele 3** on the Acrópolis, which rises from the south end of the plaza.

However, it's the vivid frescoes inside the modest-looking **Templo de las Pinturas** (Edificio 1) that have given Bonampak its fame – and its name, which means 'Painted Walls' in Yucatecan Maya.

Diagrams outside the temple help interpret these murals, which are the finest known from pre-Hispanic America, but which have weathered badly since their discovery. (Early visitors even chucked kerosene over the walls in an attempt to bring out the colors!) Room 1, on the left as you face the temple, shows the consecration of Chan Muwan II's infant son, who is seen held in arms toward the top of the right end of the room's south wall (facing you as you enter). Witnessing the ceremony are 14 jade-toting noblemen. The central Room 2 shows tumultuous battle scenes on its east and south walls and vault, while on the north wall Chan Muwan II, in jaguar-skin battle dress, presides over the torture (by fingernail removal) and sacrifice of prisoners. A severed head lies below him, beside the foot of a sprawling captive. Room 3 shows a celebratory dance on the Acrópolis steps by lords wearing huge headdresses, and on its east wall three white-robed women puncture their tongues in a ritual bloodletting. The sacrifices, the bloodletting and the dance may all have been part of the ceremonies surrounding the new heir.

In reality, the infant prince probably never got to rule Bonampak; the place was abandoned before the murals were finished, as Classic Maya civilization evaporated.

The Bonampak site abuts the Reserva de la Biosfera Montes Azules, and is rich in wildlife. Drinks and snacks are sold at the entrance to the Monumento Natural Bonampak protected zone, 8km before the ruins, and by the archaeological site entrance.

GETTING THERE & AWAY

Bonampak is 12km from San Javier on the Carretera Fronteriza. The first 3km, to the Lacanjá Chansayab turnoff, is paved, and the rest is good gravel/dirt road through the forest. Taxis will take you from San Javier or the Lacanjá turnoff to the ruins and back for M$70 per person, including waiting time. Private vehicles cannot pass the Monumento Natural Bonampak entrance, 1km past the Lacanjá turnoff, but you can rent bicycles there for M$60 for three hours, or take a combi to the ruins for M$70 round-trip. Free lockers are available at the park entrance.

Lacanjá Chansayab
pop 260 / elevation 320m

Lacanjá Chansayab, the largest Lacandón Maya village, is 6km from San Javier on the Carretera Fronteriza, and 12km from Bonampak. Its family compounds are scattered around a wide area, many of them with creeks or even the Río Lacanjá flowing past their grassy grounds. Nights here are wonderfully quiet, the sky screaming with stars and the ground twinkling with fireflies. Low-key tourism is now an important income-earner and many families run 'campamentos' with rooms, camping and hammock space. As you approach the village you'll cross the Río Lacanjá on a bridge, from which it's about 700m to a central intersection where tracks go left (south), right (north) and straight on (west).

The *campamentos* all offer guided walks through the surrounding forests to the 8m-high, 30m-wide **Cascada Ya Toch Kusam** waterfall, the little-explored ancient Maya **Lacanjá ruins**, and the 2.5km-long **Laguna Lacanjá**. The waterfall can actually be reached by a self-guiding trail, the 2.5km **Sendero Ya Toch Kusam** (admission M$35), which starts 200m west from the central intersection. To continue from the fall to the ruins (a further 2km or so) you do need a guide. A typical three-hour guided walk to the fall and ruins costs M$200 to M$450 per group, plus the admission fee for the trail.

Staying at Lacanjá is an interesting experience, and the Lacandón people are amiable and welcoming, though don't expect to find much evidence of their old way of life: the villagers here are now predominantly Presbyterian and attuned to the modern world, and only some wear the traditional long white Lacandón tunic. Some have developed their traditional crafts into commercial *artesanías*, and you may want to budget some pesos for the pottery, wood carvings, seed necklaces, arrows and drums that they sell.

SLEEPING & EATING
The *campamentos* mentioned here are just a selection from almost a dozen nearby.

Campamento Río Lacanjá (www.ecochiapas .com/lacanja; bunk M$120, d M$290, Ya'ax Can r/tr/q M$480/580/650; P) Two kilometers south of the central intersection, these rustic semi-open-air wood-frame cabins with mosquito nets stand close to the jungle-shrouded Río Lacanjá and open to the sounds and sights of the forest and river. A separate group of large rooms with fans, called Cabañas Ya'ax Can, have two solid wooden double beds, tile floors and hot-water bathroom. There's also a restaurant here serving all meals (M$45 to M$55). As well as guided walks, rafting trips on the Río Lacanjá – which has waterfalls up to 2.5m high but no rapids – are offered for a minimum of two people: a half-day outing including Lacanjá ruins and Cascada Ya Toch Kusam (both reached on foot from the river) costs M$570 per person; an overnight rafting and camping trip also visiting Bonampak ruins is around M$1000 per person. Rafting trips and tours staying at Campamento Río Lacanjá can be reserved through Explora (p817) in San Cristóbal.

Campamento Topche (campamento-topche@hotmail .com; s M$225 d & tr M$325; P) Fronted by mature papaya trees, this comfortable *campamento* about 550m west of the central intersection has three rooms with terracotta tile floors, hot water bathrooms and a vaulted and mosquito-proofed *palapa* roof. There's even internet access, available by satellite, for M$15 per hour. *Topche* is the Lacandón Maya name for a regional wildflower, though the signs to here also say 'Campamento Enrique Paniagua.'

Centro de Alimentos Chankin (mains M$40-50; 8am-8pm) Bordering Enrique Paniagua's *campamento*, this good garden restaurant is run by his daughter. Fragrant walls of flowers attract swarms of hyperactive hummingbirds.

GETTING THERE & AWAY
A taxi to Lacanjá Chansayab from San Javier costs M$50, or M$15 per person *colectivo*.

Frontera Corozal
pop 4000 / elevation 200m

This riverside frontier town (formerly called Frontera Echeverría) is the stepping-stone to the beautiful ruins of Yaxchilán, and is on the main route between Chiapas and Guatemala's Petén region. Inhabited mainly by Chol Maya, who settled here in the 1970s, Frontera Corozal is 16km by paved road from Crucero Corozal junction on

---

THE LACANDÓN JUNGLE

The Selva Lacandona (Lacandón Jungle), in eastern Chiapas, occupies just one-quarter of 1% of Mexico. Yet it contains more than 4300 plant species (about 17% of the Mexican total), 450 types of butterfly (42% of the national total), at least 340 birds (32% of the total) and 163 mammals (30% of the Mexican total). Among these are such emblematic creatures as the jaguar, red macaw, white turtle, tapir and harpy eagle.

This great fund of natural resources and genetic diversity is the southwest end of the Selva Maya, a 30,000-sq-km corridor of tropical rainforest stretching from Chiapas across northern Guatemala into Belize and the southern Yucatán. But the Lacandón Jungle is shrinking fast, under pressure from ranchers, loggers, oil prospectors, and farmers desperate for land. From around 15,000 sq km in the 1950s, an estimated 3000 to 4500 sq km of jungle remains today. Waves of land-hungry settlers deforested the northern third of the Lacandón Jungle by about 1960. Also badly deforested are the far eastern Marqués de Comillas area (settled since the 1970s) and Las Cañadas, between Ocosingo and Montes Azules. Most of what's left is in the Reserva de la Biosfera Montes Azules and the neighboring Reserva de la Biosfera Lacan-tun.

The Mexican government deeded a large section of the land to a small number of Lacandón families in the 1970s, creating tensions with other indigenous communities whose claims were put aside. Land within the region remains incredibly contested. Lacandones and their advocates frame the issue as an environmentally-sensitive indigenous group defending their property against invasive settlers. Other communities within the reserve, who provide some of the Zapatista rebels' strongest support, view it as an obfuscated land grab and pretext for eviction under the guise of environmental protection. Zapatista supporters also argue that the settlers are using the forests in sustainable ways, and claim that the government seeks to exploit the forests for bio-prospecting (patenting) traditional plants.

---

the Carretera Fronteriza. The broad Río Usumacinta, flowing swiftly between jungle-covered banks, forms the Mexico–Guatemala border here.

Long, fast, outboard-powered *lanchas* come and go from the river *embarcadero*. Almost everything you'll need is on the paved street leading back from the river here – including the **immigration office** (8am-6pm), 400m from the *embarcadero*, where you should hand in/obtain a tourist card if you're leaving for/arriving from Guatemala. If it's slow, the officer often closes up early, but anyone in town can tell you where to find him, if need be.

The neat and modern **Museo de la Cuenca del Usumacinta** (Museum of the Usumacinta Basin; admission free; 8am-7pm), opposite the immigration office, has good examples of Chol Maya dress, and some information in Spanish on the area's post-conquest history, but pride of place goes to two fine and intricately carved steles retrieved from the nearby site of Dos Caobas.

SLEEPING & EATING

Escudo Jaguar (502-5353-5637; http://mx.geocities.com/hotel_escudojaguar; campsites per person M$70; cabaña

with shared bathroom d/tr M$200/258, cabaña with 1/2/3 d beds M$380/572/760; P) Professionally run by a local Chol organization, Escudo Jaguar overlooks the river 300m from the *embarcadero*. Its solidly built, pink, thatched *cabañas* are all kept spotless, and come equipped with fan and mosquito net. The best are very spacious and have hot showers and terraces strung with hammocks. Room prices dip by up to 30% outside the high seasons. The restaurant (mains M$70, breakfasts M$40 to M$55, open 7am to 8pm) serves straightforward, well-prepared Mexican dishes.

Tsol K'in Nueva Alianza (502-5353-1395; ctnuevaalianza@hotmail.com; www.ecoturlacandona.com; r per person shared bathroom M$100, f M$600-700; P) Friendly, Chol-run Nueva Alianza, among trees 150m along a side road from the museum, provides well-built family rooms with fan, bathroom and good wooden furniture. The budget rooms are small and plain, with wooden walls that don't reach the ceiling, but are well kept and have cheerful blue cement floors. There's a good onsite restaurant (mains M$35 to M$40, breakfasts M$25 to M$45).

Restaurante Imperio Maya (502-5727-9612; mains M$60-70; 8am-7pm) Attached to the museum, this spacious *palapa*-topped restaurant mostly caters to Yaxchilán-bound tourists, but the locals like it too.

GETTING THERE & AWAY

If you can't get a bus or combi direct to Frontera Corozal, get one to Crucero Corozal, 16km southeast of San Javier on the Carretera Fronteriza, where taxis (M$20 per person *colectivo*, M$70 otherwise) and occasional vans (M$20) run to Frontera Corozal. If you're driving, the *ejido* hits up cars entering town for a M$15 toll.

Autotransporte Chamoán vans run from Frontera Corozal *embarcadero* to Palenque (M$60, 2½ to three hours) around 13 times daily, with the last departure at 6pm.

Lanchas leave for Bethel (40 minutes upstream) on the Guatemalan bank of the Usumacinta, and for La Técnica, directly opposite Frontera Corozal. **Lancha organizations** (boat to Bethel for 3/4/7/10 people M$400/500/600/750) have desks in a thatched building near the *embarcadero*, and all charge the same prices. Information in Frontera Corozal is unreliable on onward buses within Guatemala from Bethel to Flores (Q$60, four hours), but there are normally departures around 11am, 1:30pm, 3pm and 5pm. *Lanchas* to La Técnica go on a *colectivo* basis for M$15 per person. A bus from La Técnica to Flores (US$6, five to six hours) leaves around 8am, stopping for immigration in Bethel.

Yaxchilán

Jungle-shrouded **Yaxchilán** (admission M$45; ☒ 8am-4:30pm, last entry 3:30pm) has a terrific setting above

a horseshoe loop in the Usumacinta. The control this location gave it over river commerce, and a series of successful alliances and conquests, made Yaxchilán one of the most important Classic Maya cities in the Usumacinta region. Archaeologically, Yaxchilán is famed for its ornamented facades and roof combs, and its impressive stone lintels carved with conquest and ceremonial scenes. A flashlight is helpful for exploring some parts of the site.

Howler monkeys inhabit the tall trees here, and are an evocative highlight. You'll almost certainly hear their visceral roars, and you stand a good chance of seeing some. Spider monkeys, and occasionally red macaws, can also be spotted here at times.

Yaxchilán peaked in power and splendor between AD 681 and 800 under the rulers Itzamnaaj B'alam II (Shield Jaguar II, 681–742), Pájaro Jaguar IV (Bird Jaguar IV, 752–68) and Itzamnaaj B'alam III (Shield Jaguar III, 769–800). The city was abandoned around AD 810. Inscriptions here tell more about its 'Jaguar' dynasty than is known of almost any other Maya ruling clan. The shield-and-jaguar symbol appears on many Yaxchilán buildings and steles; Pájaro Jaguar IV's hieroglyph is a small jungle cat with feathers on its back and a bird superimposed on its head.

At the site, *refrescos* (refreshments) are sold at a shack near the river landing. Most of the main monuments have information boards in three languages, including English.

As you walk toward the ruins, a signed path to the right leads up to the **Pequeña Acrópolis**,

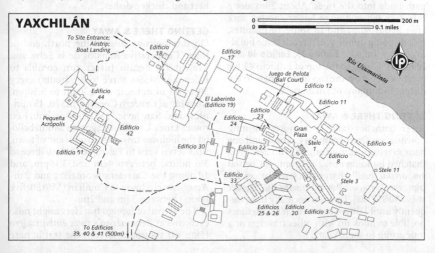

YAXCHILÁN

0   200 m
0   0.1 miles

To Site Entrance;
Airstrip;
Boat Landing

Edificio 18
Edificio 17

Río Usumacinta

Juego de Pelota
(Ball Court)
Edificio 12

Edificio 44
El Laberinto
(Edificio 19)
Edificio 11

Pequeña
Acrópolis
Edificio 42
Edificio 24
Edificio 23

Gran
Plaza
Stele 1
Edificio 5

Edificio 51
Edificio 30
Edificio 22
Edificio 8
Stele 11

Edificio 33
Stele 3

Edificios 25 & 26
Edificio 20
Edificio 3

To Edificios
39, 40 & 41 (500m)

a group of ruins on a small hilltop – you can visit this later. Staying on the main path, you soon reach the mazy passages of **El Laberinto** (Edificio 19), built between AD 742 and 752, during the interregnum between Itzamnaaj B'alam II and Pájaro Jaguar IV. Dozens of bats shelter under the structure's roof today. From this complicated two-level building you emerge at the northwest end of the extensive **Gran Plaza**.

Though it's difficult to imagine anyone here ever wanting to be any hotter than they already were, **Edificio 17** was apparently a sweat house. About halfway along the plaza, **Stele 1**, flanked by weathered sculptures of a crocodile and a jaguar, shows Pájaro Jaguar IV in a ceremony that took place in AD761. **Edificio 20**, from the time of Itzamnaaj B'alam III, was the last significant structure built at Yaxchilán; its lintels are now in Mexico City. **Stele 11**, at the northeast corner of the Gran Plaza, was originally found in front of Edificio 40. The bigger of the two figures visible on it is Pájaro Jaguar IV.

An imposing stairway climbs from Stele 1 to **Edificio 33**, the best-preserved temple at Yaxchilán, with about half of its roof comb intact. The final step in front of the building is carved with ball-game scenes, and splendid relief carvings embellish the undersides of the lintels. Inside is a statue of Pájaro Jaguar IV, minus his head, which he lost to treasure-seeking 19th-century timber cutters.

From the clearing behind Edificio 33, a path leads into the trees. About 20m along this, fork left uphill; go left at another fork after about 80m, and in some 10 minutes, mostly going uphill, you'll reach three buildings on a hilltop: **Edificio 39**, **Edificio 40** and **Edificio 41**. Climb to the top of Edificio 41 for great views across the top of the jungle to the distant mountains of Guatemala.

GETTING THERE & AWAY

River launches take 40 minutes running downstream from Frontera Corozal, and one hour to return. *Lancha* outfits, with desks in a thatched building near the Frontera Corozal *embarcadero,* all charge the same prices for **trips** (return journey with 2½hr at the ruins for 3/4/7/10 people M$650/780/950/1300). *Lanchas* normally leave frequently until 1:30pm or so, and it's sometimes possible to hook up with other travelers or a tour group to share costs.

Benemérito de las Américas
pop 6300 / elevation 200m

South of Frontera Corozal is the far eastern corner of Chiapas known as Marqués de Comillas (for its Spanish former landowner). After oil explorers opened tracks into this jungle region in the 1970s, settlers poured in from all over Mexico. Ranching and logging have made some rich, while others profit from smuggling drugs or immigrants. Note that for your own security, it's best to be off the Carretera Fronteriza before dusk – especially the most isolated section in the far southeast, between Benemérito de las Américas and the Chajul turnoff.

Benemérito de las Américas is the region's main town, but that's not saying much. Situated on the west bank of the Río Salinas, an Usumacinta tributary that forms the Mexico–Guatemala border here, it's a bit forlorn, with no attractions except as a staging post (a possible route into northern Guatemala starts here). The main street is a 1.5km-long stretch of the Carretera Fronteriza, where residents sprinkle pails of water on the streets to tamper down the nonstop dust clouds. The well-signed and brilliant green **Hotel Posada del Sol** (☎ 502-5907-0687; s & d without/with air-con M$150/200, tr & q without/with air-con M$200/250; P 🏠) is a block west in the middle of town, with clean basic rooms and brand new TVs. On the highway and also in the center of town, the **Restaurante Las Cazadores** (☎ 502-5353-1833; mains M$30-75; 🕙 7am-9pm) serves up a myriad of meats like *tepezcuintle* (a type of rodent) and venison, along with the usual beef and chicken dishes.

GETTING THERE & AWAY

On the highway toward the north end of town, Cooperativa Rápidos de la Selva and Transporte Benito Juárez run combis to Palenque (M$60, three to 3½ hours) every 30 or 45 minutes from 4:30am to 5:30pm, stopping at Crucero Corozal (M$20, 45 minutes) and San Javier (M$25, one hour) en route. Línea Comitán Lagos de Montebello, on the highway toward the south end of town, runs seven vans to Palenque (M$60, three to 3½ hours) between 4am and 3:15pm, and 10 along the Carretera Fronteriza and Pan-American Highway to Comitán (M$150, five hours) between 3am and 2pm.

The arrival of foreign travelers might raise eyebrows at Benemérito's river *embarcadero* (1km off the main street); the traffic here

---

TOP PLACES TO HEAR SQUAWKS & SCREAMS

- **Sima de las Cotorras** (p810) A spiraling and shrieking vortex of parrots ascends at dawn.
- **Yaxchilán** (p845) Howler monkeys act like they own the place.
- **Las Guacamayas** (below) This macaw refuge echoes with avian abandon.
- **Las Nubes** (p848) Toucans and howler monkeys duke it out for full-throated dominance.

---

seems to run more toward contraband than tourists. Notwithstanding, you can hire a *lancha* for M$1500 (negotiable) to take you three or four hours up the Río Salinas and Río de la Pasión to Sayaxché (Guatemala), a base for visiting the interesting Maya ruins of Ceibal, Aguateca and Dos Pilas. On the way, you have the opportunity to stop and see more ruins at Pipiles and Altar de los Sacrificios.

An alternative is to take a *lancha* a short distance downriver to Laureles, on the Guatemalan side (*colectivo* M$5, *especial* M$150). Buses leave Laureles at around 3am, 4am and 5am for El Subín (Q$20, 2½ hours), a junction on the Flores–Sayaxché road with plenty of minibuses and buses to both towns.

Benemérito has no immigration post; you must pick up or hand in Mexican tourist cards at Frontera Corozal.

Benemérito de las Américas to Lagos de Montebello

Below Benemérito, the Carretera Fronteriza heads 60km south before turning west. Deforestation gradually gives way to more intact forest, with the road crossing several rivers, but you still pass numerous villages founded in recent decades, some of them settled by Guatemalan refugees. West of Ixcán you climb more than 1000m up to the cooler, pine-forested highlands around the Lagos de Montebello.

LAS GUACAMAYAS

In the small village of **Reforma Agraria**, 49km southwest of Benemérito, the beautiful ecolodge of **Las Guacamayas** (☎ in Mexico City 55-5329-0995, ext 8004; guacamayaescarlata@hotmail.com; www.colegiomexsur.edu.mx/rm_lg.html; Ejido Reforma

Agraria; campsite per person without/with tent & bedding M$50/100, dm M$180, d cabaña M$750-850, tr cabaña M$1000, ste M$950-1100, meals M$60-110; P ☐), is the heart of an impressive community program to protect the local population of scarlet macaws. This spectacular and endangered member of the parrot family once ranged as far north as Veracruz, but its only Mexican home today is far eastern Chiapas. Numbers at Reforma Agraria have increased to more than 100 pairs since 1991, when the 14.5-sq-km macaw reserve was founded. The birds move in and out of the reserve in seasonal pursuit of food; the best months for observing them are December to June, when they are nesting.

The very friendly and welcoming lodge is right on the bank of the broad Río Lacantún, one of the Usumacinta's major tributaries, with the Reserva de la Biosfera Montes Azules on the opposite bank. Large, comfortable, thatch-roofed *cabañas*, with full mosquito screens, verandas and ample bathrooms with hot showers, are spread around the extensive grounds, linked by wooden walkways. There's a good restaurant overlooking the river, serving straightforward but satisfying Mexican meals.

Two-hour guided macaw-spotting walks cost M$300 – they're best in the early morning or at dusk. Boat trips into the Montes Azules reserve cost M$1200/1400 for two/three hours. You should spot crocodiles and howler monkeys, and with luck toucans and white-tailed deer. Villagers in Reforma Agraria also rent out horses for M$100 per hour. Note that all prices drop around 20% in low season.

Getting There & Away

The road to Reforma Agraria turns west off the Carretera Fronteriza 8km south of Benemérito. It's paved as far as Pico de Oro (25km from the highway), then mostly unpaved for 16km. Beyond Reforma Agraria the road continues unpaved for 33km to rejoin the Carretera Fronteriza 5km south of Chajul. It's normally perfectly passable (if very jarring in places) in an ordinary car, but in the rainy season you should ask ahead about its condition.

From a small terminal near the Maya Head statue in Palenque, hourly combis run to Pico de Oro (M$92, four to five hours), leaving from 8am to 4pm. Occasional *camionetas* also run from Benemérito to Pico de Oro (M$25, 40 minutes). *Camionetas* run from Pico de

Oro to Reforma Agraria (M$15, one hour), and vice versa, about hourly from 6am or 7am till early afternoon. A taxi from Benemérito to Reforma Agraria costs around M$200.

From Comitán, around eight vans a day run to Reforma Agraria (M$150, 4½ hours), passing through the Lagos de Montebello en route (see p851 for further details).

LAS NUBES

A bit of a trek but well worth it, **Las Nubes** (☎ 963-100-93-82; ecoturismo_nubes@hotmail.com; cabaña M$550, ste M$800-1000, main dishes M$50-75; **P**) is a heavenly retreat among scores of cascades and rapids on the turquoise Río Santo Domingo. Some of the river pools are great swimming spots, and it's M$10 per person to swim here if you're not staying the night. A swinging bridge straddles a fierce section of water-carved canyon, making an excellent vantage point to swoon over the grandest waterfalls. There's an adrenaline-pumping zip-line (M$50), and you can spelunk and rappel from February through June. A 15-minute hike up to a *mirador* rewards with blue-green jungle views.

Fifteen well-built *cabañas* have hot water and pleasant porches, and an open restaurant serves meals, but no alcohol (though you can bring your own).

Las Nubes is 12km off the Carretera Fronteriza, 55km from Tziscao. From Transportes Tzoyol in Comitán, there are four daily combis (M$45, 3½ to 4 hours) between 8am and 2pm, and four daily returns. From Embarcadero Jerusalén, just east of the Las Nubes highway turnoff (and on the combi route), you can raft to the compound for M$1500 (five to eight passengers).

COMITÁN

☎ 963 / pop 83,000 / elevation 1560m

With a pretty plaza of modern sculpture pieces and mature flat-topped trees where birds flock and chirp in the evening, the colonial town of Comitán has a pleasant artsy atmosphere. Set on a high plain 90km southeast of San Cristóbal, many travelers bypass it on their way to Guatemala, but it's a very agreeable place to spend a few days. It contains some good places to stay and eat, a few interesting little museums, and several natural and archaeological attractions less than an hour away in the surrounding big-sky countryside.

The city's full name is Comitán de Domínguez, in recognition of local doctor Belisario Domínguez (1863–1913), a national senator during the Mexican Revolution. He vigorously protested the political murders of President Victoriano de la Huerta and consequently became a victim himself. The uproar over his assassination led to Huerta's resignation in 1914.

Orientation & Information

Comitán is set on hilly terrain, with a beautiful broad main plaza. Hwy 190 (the Pan-American Hwy), named Blvd Dr Belisario Domínguez here but often just called 'El Bulevar,' passes through the west of town.

Banorte (1a Calle Sur Pte 5; 🕑 9am-4pm Mon-Fri, 10am-2pm Sat) Currency exchange and ATM.

Ciber@dictos (Local 13B, Pasaje Morales; per hr M$5; 🕑 9am-9pm)

Post office (Av Central Sur 45; 🕑 9am-3pm Mon-Fri, 9am-2pm Sat)

Tourist office (☎ 632-40-47; www.visitacomitan.com; Calle Central Ote 6; 🕑 9am-7pm Mon-Fri, to 2pm Sat) On the north side of the plaza, with good maps and helpful English-speaking staff available.

Sights

On the plaza, the **Iglesia de Santo Domingo** (🕑 10am-7pm) dates back to the 16th and 17th centuries, and sports unusual and handsome blind arcading on its tower. Its former monastic buildings next door are now the **Centro Cultural Rosario Castellanos** (admission free; 🕑 9am-8pm Mon-Fri, 10am-5pm Sat & Sun), with a pretty wood-pillared patio featuring a mural on local history.

Just south of the main plaza is the **Casa Museo Dr Belisario Domínguez** (☎ 632-13-00; Av Central Sur 35; admission M$5; 🕑 10am-6:45pm Tue-Sat, 9am-12:45pm Sun), the family home of Comitán's biggest hero and the site of his medical practice. It provides (in Spanish) fascinating insights into the state of medicine and the life of the professional classes in early-20th-century Chiapas (with a reconstruction of the onsite pharmacy), as well as the heroic tale of Domínguez' political career, ending in his assassination.

One block further down this street is a neat little modern art museum, the **Museo de Arte Hermila Domínguez de Castellanos** (☎ 632-20-82; Av Central Sur 51; admission M$5; 🕑 10am-6pm Mon-Sat, to 1pm Sun), with work by prominent Mexican artists, including José Luis Cuevas and Arnulfo Mendoza, as well as good temporary shows.

The **Museo Arqueológico de Comitán** (☎ 632-57-66; 1a Calle Sur Ote; admission free; 🕑 9am-6pm Tue-Sun), just east of the plaza, displays artifacts from the area's many archaeological sites. The misshapen pre-Hispanic skulls on display – deliberately 'beautified' by squeezing infants' heads between boards – make you wonder what kind of thoughts would have taken shape inside such distorted brains.

Festivals & Events

Festival Internacional Rosario Castellanos is a weeklong fiesta in early July, with free admission for many events.

Sleeping

BUDGET

Posada Las Flores (☎ 632-33-34; 1a Av Pte Nte 17; s/d with shared bathroom M$80/130, with private bathroom

M$200/230) Clean rooms with hot water and wood ceilings surround a pretty patio here.

Hospedaje Montebello (☎ 632-35-72; hospedaje montebello@hotmail.com; 1a Calle Nte Pte 10; r with shared bathroom M$120, r with private bathroom M$180-210) A welcoming cheapie with large, tiled and clean rooms around a courtyard with a towering agave as a prickly centerpiece. There's also a small restaurant.

Posada San José (☎ 101-43-03; s/d M$200/250, tr 300-350; P) Has 10 very clean and good-sized rooms, all with private bathriin and exterior windows. There's a tranquil back patio area pepped up with bougainvillea, and the rooms closest to this side are the quietest.

Pensión Delfín (☎ 632-00-13; Av Central Sur 21; s/ d/tr/q M$234/304/409/468; P) The Delfín, on the

COMITÁN

0 — 400 m
0 — 0.2 miles

SIGHTS & ACTIVITIES
Casa Museo Dr Belisario
  Domínguez.....................6 C2
Centro Cultural Rosario
  Castellanos.................(see 18)
Iglesia de Santo Domingo.....7 C1
Museo Arqueológico de
  Comitán.......................8 C1
Museo de Arte Hermila
  Domínguez de
  Castellanos...................9 C2

SLEEPING
Hospedaje Montebello.......10 B1
Hotel del Virrey..............11 B1
Hotel Hacienda de los
  Ángeles......................12 B1
Hotel Internacional..........13 C2
Hotel Posada El Castellano..14 B1
Pensión Delfín...............15 B2
Posada Las Flores...........16 B1
Posada San José.............17 C2

EATING
Café Quiptic..................18 C1
Dante's Pizza.................19 C1
Helen's Enrique Restaurant..20 B2
Juli Moni comedor............21 C1
Matisse.......................22 B1

DRINKING
Jarro Café Bar & Grill.......23 B1

ENTERTAINMENT
Shangri La....................24 B1

TRANSPORT
Autotransportes
  Cuxtepeques................25 A2
Línea Comitán Lagos de
  Montebello.................26 B2
OCC Bus Terminal.............27 B4
Rápidos de los Altos.........28 A3
Transportes Francisco
  Sarabia......................29 B2
Vans to Ciudad
  Cuauhtémoc..................30 A3
Vans to San Cristóbal de Las
  Casas........................31 A3
Vans to San Cristóbal de Las
  Casas........................32 A3

To San Cristóbal de Las Casas (90km);

To Immigration Office (4km);
Servicios Aéreos
San Cristóbal (10km);
Tenam Puente (13km);
Museo Parador
Santa María (39km);
El Chiflón (40km);
Chinkultic (49km);
Parque Nacional Lagunas
de Montebello (54km);
Guatemalan Border (82km)

To Transportes
Tzoyol (3km)

INFORMATION
Banorte.........................1 B2
Ciber@dictos..................2 B1
Guatemalan Consulate.......3 B2
Post Office.....................4 C2
Tourist Office..................5 C1

MEX 190

DRINKS OF CHIAPAS

■ **Comiteco** A unique variant of *mezcal* made with a mix of maguey and *piloncillo* (cooked sugarcane), it's smoother and more syrupy than tequila, with a clear appearance or a greenish tint. Traditionally made in Comitán, it's making a big comeback in popularity.

■ **Tascalate** A cold sweet concoction prepared from ground cacao, pine nuts, toasted corn, cinnamon and *achiote* (annatto). Very interesting and super delicious!

■ **Pox** Inexpensive grain alcohol made from sugarcane, it's pronounced (and sometimes spelled) *posh*. The undisputed choice for those who want to pass out cold on the street, but not so deadly when mixed with lots of fruit juice.

■ **Pozol** A thick heavy mixture of *masa* (corn meal dough) in water, it's often mixed with sugar, and sometimes has chili or chocolate added. It's the indigenous equivalent of an energy drink, and you can see people everywhere carrying it around in re-used plastic liter bottles. Travelers often take a ball of the *masa* and make some up when there's water available.

---

west side of the main plaza with a plant-filled patio, has well-kept, decent-sized rooms, some with wood paneling and all with cable TV.

MIDRANGE & TOP END

Hotel del Virrey (☎ 632-18-11; hotel_delvirrey@hotmail .com; Av Central Nte 13; s M$300-340, d M$420, r 3-6 people M$650; P 🖳) Resident turtles splash in a fountain at the friendly Virrey, a 19th-century house with homey, artfully kitted-out rooms of varying sizes radiating around a flower-draped courtyard. All have cable TV and spotless tiled bathrooms, and some upstairs enjoy a nice view of nearby El Calvario church.

Hotel Posada El Castellano (☎ 632-33-47; www .posadaelcastellano.com.mx; 3a Calle Nte Pte 12; s/d/tr M$360/400/440; P 🖳) This excellent hotel is colonial in style but modern in build and amenities. Comfy rooms, equipped with fan, cable TV and solid wood furniture, are on two floors around wood-pillared patios. The staff is amiable and there's free wi-fi and a nice restaurant.

Hotel Internacional (☎ /fax 632-01-10; Av Central Sur 16; s & d M$420-480, tr M$50-570; P) This downtown hotel is good value considering its comfort levels and stylish décor. All 27 rooms have two double beds, TV and attractive bathrooms. Remodeled ones have newer beige-toned carpets and bedspreads.

Hotel Hacienda de los Ángeles (☎ 632-00-74; www .haciendadelosangeles.com; 2a Calle Nte Pte 6; r M$900, ste M$1200-1500, all incl breakfast; P ✖ 🖳) Comitán's single luxury hotel provides professional service and spacious accommodations with sober, classical-style décor. All rooms have at least two double beds or one king-size bed, air-con,

cable TV, bathtub and quality furnishings, and suites have two levels. There's even a dramatically-lighted pool with its own bar.

Eating

Café Quiptic (☎ 632-06-24; 1a Av Ote Sur s/n; breakfast M$40-70, mains M$55-70; ⏰ 7:30am-1am) A swell spot for coffee on the plaza, the Quiptic is set under an impressive stone colonnade and run by indigenous coffee growers. The menu isn't huge, but it serves tasty and filling breakfasts, plus superb organic coffee, salads, *antojitos*, meat dishes and desserts.

Dante's Pizza (☎ 632-03-09; 1a Av Ote Nte 8; pizzas 1-person M$50-80, 2-person M$80-100; ⏰ 9am-10:30pm; 🚼) A roomy upstairs locale, it serves satisfying pizzas, pasta, empanadas and *quesos fundidos* (melted cheese). Very family friendly, there are plenty of high chairs as well as a kids' playhouse. It's also an internet café (M$10 per hour).

Helen's Enrique Restaurant (☎ 632-17-30; Av Central Sur 19; mains M$60-95; ⏰ 8am-11:30pm) This long-running place, with a terrace overlooking the plaza, is good for chicken and meat dishes, breakfasts and *antojitos* – or just for an evening beer.

Matisse (☎ 632-71-52; 1a Av Pte Nte 16; mains M$70-120; ⏰ 2-11pm Tue-Sat, to 5pm Sun) A step up, the stylish and popular Matisse serves inventive and well-presented dishes in warm, wood-pillared surroundings. Start with a carpaccio or the excellent *fusiole* salad (spinach with nuts, bacon, avocado and balsamic oil), and follow it up with a beef *filete* or a creative pasta dish. There's plenty of wine and cocktails, and a neat patio for alfresco dining when the temperature's right.

For an inexpensive meal or snack, the mercado *comedor* of **Juli Moni** (☂ 6am-5pm) has tasty and filling quesadillas (M$15). The nopales (cactus) and *flor de calabasas* (squash flower) are also a good option for vegetarians.

Drinking & Entertainment

Jarro Café Bar & Grill (☎ 632-21-70; 1a Av Pte Nte 7; ☂ 6pm-2am Tue-Sun) A semi-futuristic space with a burbling fountain, it's a fun all-purpose bar with loud music. Depending on the night, it could be showing *futbol* or patrons might be crooning karaoke tunes.

Shangri La (☎ 110-66-82; 1a Calle Nte Ote 6; ☂ 6pm-3am Tue-Sat) A new indoor/outdoor club, it features live merengue and salsa on Fridays and Saturdays. A stone wall encircles a romantic patio garden lit by lawn lamps, and a stylish interior has four intimate rooms with comfortable seating and fabric-draped ceilings.

Getting There & Around

Comitán's **OCC bus terminal** (☎ 632-09-80; Blvd Dr Belisario Domínguez Sur 43) is on the Pan-American Hwy. Destinations served from here include:

Ciudad Cuauhtémoc (M$52, 1¾ hours, four daily)
San Cristóbal de Las Casas (M$36, 1¾ hours, 15 daily)
Tapachula (M$146, 5½ hours via Motozintla, 6 daily)
Tuxtla Gutiérrez (M$70 to M$84, three hours, 17 daily.)

OCC also serves Oaxaca, Mexico City, Palenque, Villahermosa, Playa del Carmen and Cancún.

'Centro' combis and microbuses, across the road from the OCC terminal, take you to the main plaza for M$4; a taxi is M$18.

You can also reach San Cristóbal by vans (M$30) and *colectivo* taxis (M$35) from **Rápidos de los Altos** (Blvd Dr Belisario Domínguez Sur). Further vans to San Cristóbal leave from two other stops across the road; vans for Ciudad Cuauhtémoc (M$30, every 20 to 30 minutes, 4am to 8pm) leave from a stop just south of Rápidos de los Altos.

Línea Comitán Lagos de Montebello (☎ 632-08-75; 2a Av Pte Sur 23) runs vans to the Lagos de Montebello and along the Carretera Fronteriza, with departures to Laguna Bosque Azul (M$25, one hour) and Tziscao (M$25, 1¼ hours) every 20 to 30 minutes from 3am to 8:30pm; to Reforma Agraria (M$92, 4½ hours) at 3am, 8:55am and

12:20pm; to Benemérito de las Américas (M$150, five hours) 10 times daily, 4am to 2:30pm; and to Palenque (M$175, eight hours) five times daily, 4am to 9:45am.

Transportes Tzoyol (☎ 632-77-39; 4a Av Pte Sur 1039) runs further vans to Reforma Agraria, five times daily, 3am to 12:45pm, as well as to Amatitlán (M$55, three hours), the connection for boats to Laguna Miramar, six times a day between 4am and 2pm.

The local **immigration office** (☎ 632-22-00; Carretera Panamericana; ☂ 8am-3pm Mon-Fri) is on the Pan-American Hwy just past the turnoff for Tzimol, 5km south of the town center.

Servicios Aéreos San Cristóbal (☎ 632-46-62; Carretera Panamericana Km 1262; www.serviciosaereos-sancristobal.com) has four-seater charter flights to San Quintín for Laguna Miramar and day trips to Bonampak and Yaxchilán (M$8000 round-trip).

AROUND COMITÁN
El Chiflón

These mighty waterfalls tumble off the edge of an escarpment 41km southwest of Comitán. For an up-close experience of sheer awesome power, El Chiflón is hard to beat. The local *ejido*, **San Cristobalito La Cascada** (☎ 963-703-65-84; admission M$10; ☂ 7am-5:30pm), has set up a number of attractive amenities on the approach to the falls, including comfortable, well-built **cabañas** (d/q M$300/400), all with river view, bathroom and mosquito nets, and the good open-air **Restaurant La Ceiba** (light meals M$15-35, mains M$50-70; ☂ 8am-6pm). **Camping** (M$26 per person) is permitted as well.

A 1km approach road heads up from Hwy 226 to the parking area, from which a well-made path leads 1.3km up alongside the forest-lined Río San Vicente (which has good swimming spots) to a series of increasingly dramatic and picturesque waterfalls. Finally you reach the 70m Velo de Novia fall: prepare to be drenched by flying spray. You can also fly across the river on a zip-line (M$100).

In the dry season, from roughly February through July, the falls form a foamy line and the blue river water is safe enough to swim in. But during the rainy season, rapid currents turn the river a muddy brown, the falls gush with abandon, and swimming is a death wish.

From Comitán, **Autotransportes Cuxtepeques** (☎ 632-49-22; Blvd Dr Belisario Domínguez Sur), between Calles 1a and 2a Nte Pte, runs vans and buses to the El Chiflón turnoff on Hwy 226 (M$20,

45 minutes), about every 30 minutes, 5am to 4pm. **Mototaxis** (M$5 per person) wait there to ferry passengers up the road. Drivers should take the Tzimol turnoff from the Pan-American Hwy, 5km south of central Comitán.

Tenam Puente

These **Maya ruins** (admission free; ◷ 9am-4pm) feature three ball courts, a 20m tiered pyramid and other structures rising from a terraced, wooded hillside. Like Chinkultic (see below) Tenam Puente was one of a set of fringe Classic Maya settlements in this part of Chiapas that (unlike more famed lowland sites such as Palenque and Yaxchilán) seem to have survived in the Postclassic period, possibly as long as AD 1200. It has a pleasant rural setting and good long-distance views.

A 5km-long paved road leads west to the site from Hwy 190, 9km south of Comitán. **Transportes Francisco Sarabia** (3a Av Pte Sur 8, Comitán) runs combis every 45 minutes, 8am to 6pm, to the site (M$12) or to the village of Francisco Sarabia, 2km before Tenam Puente. The last combi from the ruins returns at 4pm. A taxi costs M$250 to M$300 return (with an hour at the ruins).

Museo Parador Santa María

Evocative of a past era, this beautiful **hotel** (☎ / fax 963-632-51-16; www.paradorsantamaria.com.mx; Carretera La Trinitaria-Lagos de Montebello Km 22; r M$2000; P), 1.5km off the road to the Lagos de Montebello, is the most luxurious and atmospheric place to stay in the Comitán area. The restored 19th-century hacienda is decorated throughout with period furniture and art; some of the eight rooms have tiled bathtubs and fireplaces, and all look over expansive grassy lawns to the countryside beyond. The chapel here is a **religious art museum** (admission M$20; ◷ 9am-5pm) with an interesting array of colonial-era work from Europe and the Philippines as well as Mexico and Guatemala. The excellent **Restaurant Los Geranios** (mains M$110-160; ◷ 8am-8pm) serves Chiapas and international dishes prepared with organic ingredients (including coffee) grown onsite. Look for the 22km marker from La Trinitaria on the Montebello road. Prices drop 50% in the low season, but book lodging two months in advance in high season.

Chinkultic

These dramatically sited **ruins** (admission M$20; ◷ 9am-4pm) lie 2km north of the road to the Lagos de Montebello, 48km from Comitán. The access road is paved.

Chinkultic was a minor Maya power during the late Classic period and, like Tenam Puente, may have survived into Postclassic times. Of 200 mounds scattered over a wide area, only a few have been cleared, but the site is worth a visit.

The ruins are in two groups. From the entrance, first take the path to the left, which curves around to the right below one of Chinkultic's biggest structures, E23, still covered in thick vegetation. The path reaches a grassy plaza with several weathered steles, some carved with human figures, and a long ball court on the right.

Return to the entrance, from which another path heads to the **Plaza Hundida** (Sunken Plaza), crosses a stream, then climbs steeply up to the **Acrópolis**, a partly restored temple atop a rocky escarpment, with remarkable views over the surrounding lakes and forests and down into a cenote 50m below – into which the Maya used to toss offerings of pottery, beads, bones and obsidian knives.

On the highway just over 1km east of the Chinkultic turnoff, **El Pino Feliz** (☎ 963-102-10-89; Carretera La Trinitaria-Lagos de Montebello; r per person M$70; P) has very simple wood cabins with up to three double beds, and hot water in the shared bathrooms. It also provides excellent meals (main dishes M$30).

Lagos de Montebello

The temperate pine and oak forest along the Guatemalan border east of Chinkultic is dotted with over 50 small lakes of varied hues, known as the Lagos (or Lagunas) de Montebello. The area is very picturesque, refreshing and peaceful. The paved road to Montebello turns east off Hwy 190 just north of La Trinitaria, 16km south of Comitán. It passes Chinkultic after 32km, and enters the Parque Nacional Lagunas de Montebello 5km beyond. A further 800m along is a ticket booth, where you must pay a M$20 park admission fee. Here the road forks – north to the Lagunas de Colores (2km to 3km) and east to the village of Tziscao (9km), beyond which it becomes the Carretera Fronteriza, continuing east to Ixcán and ultimately Palenque (see p840).

SIGHTS & ACTIVITIES

From the park ticket booth, the northward road leads to the **Lagunas de Colores**, five lakes

LAGOS DE MONTEBELLO

whose vivid hues range from turquoise to deep green: **Laguna Agua Tinta**, **Laguna Esmeralda**, **Laguna Encantada**, **Laguna Ensueño** and, the biggest, **Laguna Bosque Azul**, on the left where the paved road ends. There's a nice walk from here to the **Grutas San Rafael del Arco**, a group of caves. Follow the track ahead from the parking lot, turn left after 500m at the 'Gruta San Rafael del Arco' sign, then follow the path, mostly downhill, for 500m to come to a 'Grutas' sign. To the left here, a river rushes through a natural rock arch. To the right, the path forks after 60m. The left branch leads 100m to a riverside cave downstream from the rock arch; the right branch leads 40m to a more extensive cave that turns out to be the bottom of a sinkhole.

In the Laguna Bosque Azul parking lot, *camiones* offer shared three- to five-hour lake tours for M$40, or you can do a private tour for M$350. Boys can take you to the caves on horseback for M$80, on a multi-lake excursion that includes **Dos Cenotes** (M$150, two to three hours), a pair of sinkholes in the forest, or to the Laguna de Montebello (about one hour away).

Along the eastward road from the park ticket booth, after 3km a track leads 200m north to the **Laguna de Montebello**, one of the area's larger lakes, with a flat open area along its shore, and more boys offering horseback rides to Dos Cenotes. The local *ejido* charges a M$5 entrance fee to access the lake areas along the Tziscao road; pay once and keep your receipt for the other lakes. Three kilometers further along the Tziscao road, another track leads

left to the **Cinco Lagunas** (Five Lakes). Only four are visible from the road, but the second, **La Cañada**, on the right after about 1.5km is one of the most beautiful Montebello lakes, nearly cut in half by two rocky outcrops.

One kilometer nearer to Tziscao, another track leads 1km north to cobalt-blue **Laguna Pojoj**, with an island in the middle. **Laguna Tziscao**, on the Guatemalan border, comes into view 1km past the Pojoj junction. The turnoff to the Chuj-speaking village of Tziscao, a pretty and spread-out place stretching down to the lakeside, is a little further on. Though deforestation has thinned out their habitat and made them increasingly harder to find, spectacularly-tailed quetzal birds inhabit the border forests here and local guides can suggest places for bird-watching.

SLEEPING & EATING

Cabañas de Doña Josefa (☎ 963-632-59-71; cabaña M$300; P) These rustic, two-story *cabañas* are on the northwest side of Laguna Bosque Azul, 1km along a drivable track from the lake's main parking lot. Two have private bathrooms with hot water, seven others share a toilet and must use the lake for washing. Meals are usually available at weekends and holidays.

Hotel Tziscao (☎ 963-352-40-83; www.tziscao .com; campsites per person M$80, r M$500, 4-person cabaña M$650; restaurant dishes M$30-60; P 💻) By the lake in Tziscao village (2km from the highway turnoff), and run by an *ejido* cooperative, this basic but well-kept place has extensive, grassy grounds that include a sandy beach with terrific views across the lake to the foothills of the Cuchumatanes in Guatemala. You can rent two-person kayaks (M$80 per hour), or bicycles (M$100 per hour, M$300 per day) to go exploring. There are rooms in the main building, but some of the good wooden *cabañas* have an ideal position, almost on the waterside. All accommodations have private bathroom with hot water.

Beside the Laguna Bosque Azul parking lot, several basic **comedores** (dishes M$30-40; ☺ approx 7am-5pm) serve drinks and simple plates of *carne asada* (roasted meat) or quesadillas.

GETTING THERE & AWAY

Public transportation to Chinkultic and the lakes from Comitán is a snap, making it an easy day trip. See p851 for details; vans go to the parking lot at Laguna Bosque Azul and to Tziscao, and will drop you at the turnoffs for Museo Parador Santa María, Chinkultic, and the other lakes mentioned above. The last vehicles back to Comitán leave Tziscao around 5pm, and Laguna Bosque Azul around 5:30pm.

From San Cristóbal de Las Casas, a number of agencies offer tours (p816) that take in the lakes, throw in a visit to El Chiflón, and still get you back by dinnertime.

CIUDAD CUAUHTÉMOC
pop 2900

A blip of a border town that feels like it has more vehicles than people, this is the last and first place in Mexico on the Pan-American Hwy (190). Comitán is 83km north, and the Guatemalan border post is 4km south at La Mesilla. Taxis (M$10 *colectivo*, M$40 private) ferry people between the two sides. There are banks and moneychangers on both sides of the border, which closes to car traffic from 9pm to 6am.

Frequent vans, combis and buses run to and from Comitán (M$30 to M$52, 1¾ hours), about every 20 to 30 minutes, 5am to 5pm. A few OCC buses run to San Cristóbal de Las Casas (M$100, 3½ hours) and beyond between 12:30pm and 9:30pm, but it's usually quicker to get to Comitán and pick up onward transportation there.

From La Mesilla, mototaxis (M$3 or Q$2) can drop you at the depot, where buses leave for Huehuetenango (Q$15, two hours) and Quetzaltenango (Q$30, 3½ hours) at least 20 times a day between 6am and 6pm, and hourly to Guatemala City (Q$72 to Q$110, seven hours) from 6am to 10am.

RESERVA DE LA BIOSFERA EL TRIUNFO

The luxuriant cloud forests, high in the remote El Triunfo Biosphere Reserve in the Sierra Madre de Chiapas, are a bird-lover's paradise and a remarkable world of trees and shrubs festooned with epiphytes, ferns, bromeliads, mosses and vines. The cool cloud forest is formed by moist air rising from the hot, humid lowlands to form clouds and rain on the uplands.

The Sierra Madre de Chiapas is home to over 300 bird species, of which more than 30 are nonexistent or rare elsewhere in Mexico. This is the one place in the country where chances are good of seeing the resplendent quetzal. Also here are the extremely rare horned guan (big as a turkey, but dwelling high in the trees), the azure-rumped tanager, black guan and blue-tailed and wine-throated hummingbirds. Visitors see hundreds of butterfly species and, often, jaguar and tapir tracks.

Visits are controlled. Most visitors go in the driest months, January to May; avoid the wettest months, September and October. Make arrangements about three months in advance by contacting **Claudia Virgen** (☎ 961-125-11-22; eco turismotriunfo@prodigy.net.mx; Calle San Cristóbal 8, Fracc Residencial La Hacienda, Tuxtla Gutiérrez, Chiapas 29030), the visitors program coordinator. A normal visit (US$400 to US$600 per person, minimum four people, maximum 12) starts with one night in a hotel in the nearest town, Jaltenango (also called Ángel Albino Corzo), followed by three or four nights at the basic Campamento El Triunfo, 1850m high in the reserve. The price includes guides who are expert bird-spotters, transportation between Jaltenango and the coffee-growing village of Finca Prusia, and mules to carry your baggage on the 14km hike between Finca Prusia and Campamento El Triunfo (three to four hours uphill on the way in). The **Mesoamerican Ecotourism Alliance** (www .travelwithmea.org) has all-inclusive 10-day trips that also visit La Encrucijada (US$2850).

EL SOCONUSCO

Chiapas' fertile coastal plain, 15km to 35km wide, is called the Soconusco, and is named for the Aztecs' most distant 15th-century province, called Xoconochco. It's hot and humid year-round, with serious rainfall from mid-May to mid-October. The lushly vegetated Sierra Madre de Chiapas, rising steeply from the plain, provides an excellent environment for coffee, bananas and other crops.

Tonalá

☎ 966 / pop 32,000

This sweaty, bustling town on Hwy 200 is the jumping-off point for Puerto Arista. There's a helpful **tourist office** (☎ 663 10 34; Calle 16 de Septiembre 46; ☽ 8am-4pm Mon-Fri) a half-block north of the central plaza. You can check your email back on the corner facing the plaza at **Cyber Cristy** (Av Rayon s/n; per hr M$8; ☽ 8am-10pm) and change money or use the ATM at **Banamex** (Hidalgo 137; ☽ 9am-4pm Mon-Fri, 10am-2pm Sat), a block east of the plaza on the main drag (Hidalgo).

A fine central choice fronting the east side of the plaza, the **Hotel Galilea** (☎ 663-02-39; Hidalgo 138; s/d/tr M$300/400/450; P ✗) has a convenient restaurant and clean medium-sized rooms with dark wooden furniture that give it an Old World feel. **Hotel Grajandra** (☎ 663-01-44; Hidalgo 204; s & d M$450, tr M$750; P ✗) is a friendly place next to the OCC bus terminal, with bright, large rooms with 1970s-era décor and a breezy upstairs restaurant.

The **OCC bus terminal** (☎ 633-05-40; Hidalgo s/n), with deluxe and 1st-class buses, is 600m west of the central plaza. **Rápidos del Sur** (RS; Hidalgo s/n), with 2nd-class buses, is 250m east of the plaza. Daily services include the following:

Tapachula (M$85-164, three to four hours, 34 from OCC, 35 RS)

Tuxtla Gutiérrez (M$60-126, three hours, 16 from OCC, 35 RS)

Most Tapachula buses stop at Escuintla (M$60 to M$95, 2½ hours). OCC also runs buses to Mexico City, Oaxaca and Puerto Escondido. *Colectivo* taxis for Puerto Arista (M$15, 20 minutes) and Boca del Cielo (M$20, 35 minutes) run from the corner of Matamoros and 20 de Marzo, four blocks east of the plaza and one block downhill. Puerto Arista combis (M$12) leave from Juárez, one block further downhill. Taxis and combis run until 7pm. A private taxi to Puerto Arista is M$80 (up to M$100 at night).

Puerto Arista

☎ 994 / pop 900

Most of the time Puerto Arista, 18km southwest of Tonalá, is an ultra-sleepy little fishing and part-time tourist town where the most action you'll see is a piglet breaking into a trot because a dog has gathered the energy to bark at it. You get through a lot of drinks while you watch the waves roll up and down the infinite expanse of gently sloping sands that is Puerto Arista's beach. The torpor is disturbed at weekends, during August and the Christmas–New Year period, and shattered during Semana Santa, when *chiapanecos* roll in from the towns and cities inland. A smattering of international travelers can usually be found hanging out here at most times of year.

PA's single, potholed, street is little more than a scruffy strip of palm-shack restaurants and salt-bitten concrete hotels, but the ultra-relaxed ambience soon starts to grow on you. The endless beach and ocean are wonderfully clean here, and you may never swim in warmer seas, but take care where you go in – riptides (known as *canales*) can quickly sweep you out a long way.

The only real street, called (seemingly interchangeably) Av Matamoros, Blvd Zapotal or Blvd González Blanco, parallels the beach, one block inland. The road from Tonalá hits it at a T-junction by a lighthouse, the midpoint of town. Public transportation terminates here, although *colectivo* taxis will take you to your door for an extra M$15.

A tiny commercial area called the Plaza Puerto Arista (across the street from the Hotel Arista Bugambilias) has an ATM, **satellite internet access** (per hr M$10; ☽ 9am-4pm), and a computer kiosk with tourist information in a closet-sized but wonderfully air-conditioned room.

SIGHTS & ACTIVITIES

During the July-to-October nesting season, the **Campamento Tortuguero** (Turtle Camp; admission free; ☽ 9am-5pm) collects thousands of newly-laid Olive Ridley turtle eggs from 40km of beach. They incubate them and release the hatchlings when they emerge seven weeks later. Located 2.5km northwest along the single street from the lighthouse (taxis charge M$25), visitors are welcome and can help release the hatchlings. At the camp, run by Chiapas' state **ecology institute** (www.ihne.gob.mx), you'll also see injured turtles recuperating in tanks, and caimans bred for release in Reserva de la Biosfera La Encrucijada (p856). There's an annual **Festival de la Tortuga Marina** during the last weekend of October, with events for adults and children and the release of thousands of hatchlings.

About 300m behind the eastern beach, **Estero Prieto** is a treacle-colored mangrove estuary. Rare boat-billed herons and other water birds are common here, and there are small crocodiles, freshwater turtles and a few iguanas. José's (see below) rents canoes.

SLEEPING & EATING

There are plenty of places in both directions from the lighthouse. The more expensive ones drop their prices significantly outside the high seasons of Semana Santa, July-August and Christmas-New Year's. Book at least one month ahead for Semana Santa.

José's Camping Cabañas (☎ 600-90-48; rround ing85@hotmail.com; campsites per person M$35, s/d/tr with shared bathroom M$140/160/190, s/d/tr with private bathroom M$200/225/275; P) Run by a Canadian who's been living here for three decades, this is a welcoming place to stay and relax. It has a small pool and the simple but impeccably kept brick-and-thatch *cabañas* – all with mosquito screens, fan and shaded sitting areas – are dotted about an extensive coconut and citrus grove. José enjoys socializing with his guests and creates good home-cooked meals (M$35 to M$80). Canoe rentals for the bird-rich estuary to the rear are M$100 per day. To find José's, follow the main street southeast from the lighthouse for 800m, then turn left (inland) by Hotel Lucero.

Hotel Arista Bugambilias (☎ /fax 600-90-44; r/ste M$695/1053; P) About 800m northwest of the lighthouse, the Bugambilias has beautiful beachfront grounds, an enticing pool, plus a restaurant and bar. Nice, good-sized rooms all have air-con and TV. Rates are 20% lower during the week.

Hotel Lucero (☎ 600-90-42; Matamoros 800; r M$750, q M$850; P) The Lucero, 800m southeast of the lighthouse and across the street from the beach, has comfortable, pastel-shaded, air-conditioned rooms with up to three double beds, and the upper floors have great ocean views. Its big double pool (M$30 for nonguests) and open-air Restaurant Flamingos (mains M$80 to M$110, open 8am to 5pm, dinner also in high season), front the beach.

There are scores of almost-identical beachfront *palapa* eateries. Those with most customers are likely to be the best.

Fish and shrimp dishes cost M$60 to M$95; eggs, chicken and *bistec* are M$30 to M$70. *Robalo* (snook) is the quality fish here; *huachinango* (snapper), *mojarra* (bass or perch) and *pargo* (sea perch) are pretty good too.

Reserva de la Biosfera La Encrucijada

This large biosphere reserve protects a 1448-sq-km strip of coastal lagoons, sandbars, wetlands, seasonally flooded tropical forest and the country's tallest mangroves (some above 30m). This ecosystem is a vital wintering and breeding ground for migratory birds and harbors one of Mexico's biggest populations of jaguars, plus spider monkeys, turtles, crocodiles, caimans, boa constrictors, fishing eagles and lots of waterfowl – many in danger of extinction.

A ride in a *lancha* through the reserve takes you between towering mangroves and past palm-thatched lagoonside villages. Birding is good any time of year, but best during the November to March nesting season. *Lanchas* also serve Barra de Zacapulco, a small settlement on a sandbar between ocean and lagoon, with a handful of *palapa comedores* and a sea-turtle breeding center nearby.

The nearest town is Acapetahua, 6km southwest of Escuintla. The **Hotel El Carmen** (☎ 918-647-00-62; Av Central s/n, Acapetahua; s/d/tr M$150/220/250; P) has clean, cheerfully painted rooms with bathroom, air-con and TV. At the Barra de Zacapulco *comedores* you can camp or sling a hammock for M$20 per person; some have **cabañas** (r M$150) too. A big plate of seafood costs around M$50.

To get to La Encrucijada, take a bus along Hwy 200 to Escuintla, then a *colectivo* taxi to Acapetahua (M$5, 10 minutes). Beside the abandoned railway in Acapetahua (if you have time, check out the rusting freight trains nearby), get a combi or bus 18km to Embarcadero Las Garzas (M$10, 20 minutes). These run about every 30 minutes till 4pm.

From Embarcadero Las Garzas, a *colectivo lancha* (M$30) to Barra de Zacapulco takes 25 minutes. The last *lancha* back from Barra de Zacapulco may be as early as 3:30pm, and the last combi from Embarcadero Las Garzas to Acapetahua goes about 5pm. Two- to three-hour private *lancha* tours from Embarcadero Las Garzas cost around M$500 for up to four people, but you can try bargaining.

TAPACHULA

☎ 962 / pop 190,000 / elevation 100m

'The Pearl of Soconusco,' Mexico's bustling southernmost city doesn't quite live up to its nickname, though it does have an interesting combination of urban sophistication and tropical tempo. A new cruise ship terminal at nearby Puerto Chiapas has led to an in-

crease in local investment, but trees still grow through crumbling and evocative old houses in the center. The city is an important commercial center, not only for the Soconusco but also for cross-border trade with Guatemala.

When the *cruceros* (cruise ship passengers) stream into town every few weeks, the city sucks in its belly and puts its best

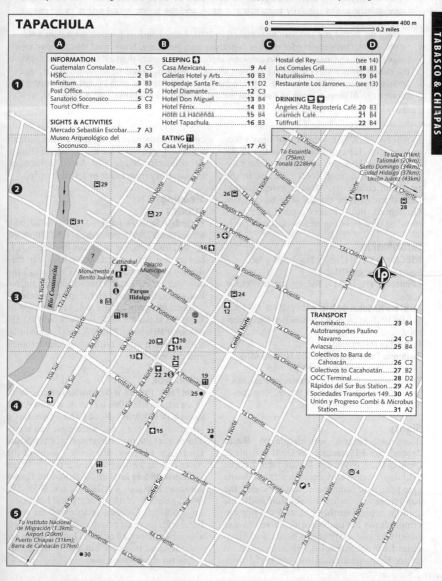

TAPACHULA

INFORMATION	**SLEEPING**	Hostal del Rey.....................(see 14)
Guatemalan Consulate............1 C5	Casa Mexicana.......................9 A4	Los Comales Grill...................18 B3
HSBC.....................................2 B4	Galerías Hotel y Arts.............10 B3	Naturalíssimo........................19 B4
Infinitum................................3 B3	Hospedaje Santa Fe...............11 D2	Restaurante Los Jarrones.....(see 13)
Post Office.............................4 D5	Hotel Diamante.....................12 C3	
Sanatorio Soconusco.............5 C2	Hotel Don Miguel..................13 B4	**DRINKING**
Tourist Office........................6 B3	Hotel Fénix............................14 B3	Ángeles Alta Repostería Café.20 B3
	Hotel La Hacienda.................15 B4	Gramlich Café........................21 B4
SIGHTS & ACTIVITIES	Hotel Tapachula....................16 B3	Tutifruti.................................22 B4
Mercado Sebastián Escobar.....7 A3		
Museo Arqueológico del	**EATING**	
Soconusco..........................8 A3	Casa Viejas............................17 A5	

TRANSPORT	
Aeroméxico.............................23 B4	
Autotransportes Paulino	
Navarro.................................24 C3	
Aviacsa...................................25 B4	
Colectivos to Barra de	
Cahoacán.............................26 C2	
Colectivos to Cacahoatán......27 B2	
OCC Terminal.........................28 D2	
Rápidos del Sur Bus Station....29 A2	
Sociedades Transportes 149...30 A5	
Unión y Progreso Combi & Microbus	
Station...................................31 A2	

DANGER ON THE SOUTHERN BORDER

When immigration and Mexico are heard in the same sentence, most people think of Mexicans heading to the US. However, many Central Americans, driven by even weaker economies in their own countries, cross into Mexico on an epic 2500km-long journey north. While the perils of crossing the US–Mexico border include deadly desert crossings and unscrupulous *coyotes* (people smugglers), the southern border is arguable more dangerous. Immigrants have few rights within Mexico, and are targeted as easy prey by both criminals and the authorities. Opportunistic gangs regularly beat, rob and rape, and the police extort bribes to let people pass without arrest.

Until the last of the southern lines closed in 2007, many migrants jumped the freight trains heading north from the border cities of Tapachula and Tenosique. Nicknamed 'death trains' because fatalities and maimings are so common, many now walk more than 250km north to Arriaga, the closest terminus. For a riveting account of riding Mexican freight trains from Chiapas, read *Enrique's Journey* by Sonia Nazario. For information on volunteering with injured train-hoppers, contact the **Albergue Jesús el Buen Pastor del Pobre y el Migrante** (☎ 962-137-73-43; www .alberguebuenpastor.org.mx; Entronque a Raymundo Enríquez, Tapachula).

foot forward. A hot, humid and busy place year-round, Tapachula's heart is the large, lively Parque Hidalgo, with vistas of the towering 4110m cone of Volcán Tacaná to the north on clear days. Most travelers simply pass through here on the way to or from Guatemala, but it makes a good base for a number of interesting nearby attractions.

Information

HSBC (cnr 2a Nte & 1a Pte; ☒ 8am-7pm Mon-Sat) Money exchange and ATM.

Infinitum (5a Pte 16; per hr M$7; ☒ 9am-8pm) Internet access.

Instituto Nacional de Migración (☎ 128-22-73; Vialidad 435, Fracc Las Vegas; ☒ 8am-3pm) Immigration office.

Post office (1a Ote s/n)

Sanatorio Soconusco (☎ 626-50-74, 4a Nte 68) A clinic with 24-hour emergency service.

Tourist office (☎ 628-77-25; www.turismotapachula .gob.mx; 8a Nte s/n; ☒ 9am-8pm Mon-Fri, 10am-2pm Sat) In the Antiguo Palacio Municipal.

Sights

The modernized, well-displayed **Museo Arqueológico del Soconusco** (☎ 626-41-73; 8a Nte 20; admission M$26; ☒ 9am-6pm Tue-Sun) faces Parque Hidalgo. Steles and ceramics from Izapa (see p860) are prominent – on the steles, the top fringe represents the sky and gods, the middle depicts earthly life, and the bottom fringe shows the underworld. There are also 5000-year-old early stone heads and figurines from the coastal marshes, a collection of pre-Hispanic musical instruments (drums,

conch trumpets, scrapers made from human bones…), and other items displaying Olmec, Teotihuacán, Maya and Aztec influences. Explanatory material is in Spanish only.

Sleeping

BUDGET

Hospedaje Santa Fe (☎ 626-24-28; 1a Nte 107; s/d/tr with fan M$160/220/250, s/d/tr with air-con M$230/260/300; **P** ☒) Just a couple of blocks from the OCC bus station, this budget option has clean medium-sized rooms with cable TV, though the air-con rooms have interior windows only. No hot water, but there's an inexpensive café.

   Hotel Diamante (☎ 628-50-32; 7a Pte 43; s with fan M$196-280, with air-con M$280-364, d with fan M$252-336, with air-con M$364-448; **P** ☒) A good-value hotel with modern air-conditioning, clean rooms and cable TV.

MIDRANGE

Hotel Fénix (☎ 628-96-00; www.fenix.com.mx; 4a Nte 19; s/d with fan M$210/260, with air-con M$360/455, with air-con & TV M$450/560; **P** ☒) The Fénix has a selection of rooms, so look before you sleep. The ones at the rear are generally better. Some fan rooms are good-sized while some of the more expensive ones are smaller.

   Galerías Hotel y Arts (☎ 642-75-90; 4a Nte 21; www .galeriasartshotel.com; s M$380-430, d/tr M$540/650; **P** ☒) Stylish, contemporary and boutique-on-a-budget, Galerías is an excellent small hotel with jazzy art prints and large, comfortable air-conditioned rooms. Double rooms are spacious and two cozy but comfy singles are a deal for those going solo.

our pick **Casa Mexicana** (☎ 626-66-05; www
.casamexicanachiapas.com; 8a Sur 19; s M$575, d M$675-775;
P X ⊠) An exquisite boutique hotel pay-
ing homage to Mexican women in history,
guests can choose from sumptuous rooms
named for heroines such as human rights
lawyer Digna Ochoa or Zapatista Commander
Ramona. Antiques, lush plants and all kinds of
interesting art create a soothing, creative feel.
The 10 rooms on two floors surround a tropical garden-patio that even has a small pool.
With a small bar and a restaurant serving
excellent homemade meals, this is a fabulous
place to stay.

Hotel Tapachula (☎ 626-60-60; www.hoteltapa
chula.com; 9a Pte 17; s/d M$690/790, ste M$890-1040;
P X ⊠) This glass-fronted luxury hotel is
the poshest address in town. Large, stylish,
marble-floored rooms, some with volcano
views, come with either king- or queen-size
beds or two doubles. There's a good restaurant, a small pool and a nifty glass elevator
to take you there.

Also recommended are the following:

Hotel La Hacienda (☎ 626-61-00; fax 625-20-61;
2a Sur 14; s/d/tr M$360/430/540; P X) A modern,
comfortable place; older rooms have more colonial style.

Hotel Don Miguel (☎ 626-11-43; www.hoteldon
miguel.com.mx; 1a Pte 18; s M$504, d M$628-701, ste
M$780-901; P X) Comfy beds in bright, air-condi-
tioned rooms with TV and phone; a good restaurant.

Eating

Naturalíssimo (☎ 625-17-27; cnr Central Nte & 1a Pte;
mains M$25-40; 7am-9:30pm; V) This vegetarian
mainstay is inexpensive, with fresh juices and
a breezy corner location that always hits the
spot on a sweltering afternoon.

Hostal del Rey (☎ 625-07-55; 4a Nte 17; breakfasts
M$40-50, mains M$60-90; 7am-11pm Mon-Sat, 7am-3pm
Sun) Staffed by solicitous bow-tied waiters, the
spacious, air-conditioned Hostal del Rey is
particularly good for leisurely breakfasts.

Los Comales Grill (☎ 626-24-05; 8a Nte 4; mains
M$50-85; 24hr) To feel like you're in the thick
of things, dine in this open-air restaurant with
a prime location in Parque Hidalgo. The menu
includes good *caldo tlalpeño* (hearty chicken,
vegetable and chili soup) and decent steaks.
There's marimba music Thursday, Saturday
and Sunday evenings from 8pm to 11pm.

Restaurante Los Jarrones (☎ 626-11-43; Hotel Don
Miguel, 1a Pte 18; mains M$60-140) Perennially popu-
lar, Los Jarrones provides welcome air-con
and a big choice of Mexican and international

fare. Sit near the windows to escape the painfully hokey live dinner bands.

our pick **Casas Viejas** (☎ 625-27-97; 4a Sur 30; mains
M$75-140 9am-11pm Tue-Sat) Opened in 2007,
this is already one of the finest restaurants in
Chiapas. Set in a gorgeous garden patio of two
'old houses,' chef/owner Matias Klein Kötter
creates a delectable and ever-evolving international menu using regional ingredients. The
pollo al tamarindo (tamarind chicken) and
pasta de salmon (salmon pasta with orange
and tequila) keep the locals in eye-fluttering
rapture, and if it's not too busy, the kitchen
might whip you up a custom dish (including vegetarian options). For dessert, locally-
grown cardamom, chocolate and coffee are
blended together to make scrumptious crepes,
but Kotter won't give up the family secret of
the chocolately *pastel tlacopac*.

A number of clean and popular *comedores*
are hidden upstairs at the **Mercado Sebastián
Escobar** (cnr 5a Pte & 12a Nte; mains M$35-45 6am-5pm),
dishing out mammoth plates of cooked-to-
order Chinese food. Snag a bench seat at the
picnic tables and come hungry!

Drinking

Nestled in the coffee-growing region of the
state, Tapachula has an especially nice coffeehouse culture and lots of evening café life.

Ángeles Alta Repostería Café (☎ 625-6731; 4a Nte
24B; dessert M$12-30, breakfast M$38-45; 7am-11pm)
Bring a book or the newspaper and settle
in for a good read over blood-pumping espresso. Spread out over two levels, this modern air-conditioned café invites lingering over
scrumptious desserts, good breakfasts and
free wi-fi.

Gramlich Café (1a Pte 9; coffees & snacks M$10-35;
8:30am-9:30pm Mon-Fri, 9am-9:30pm Sat, 2-10pm Sun)
Serving up organic coffee grown in the mountains north of town, this popular coffeehouse
has more of an old-fashioned feel.

Tutifruti (☎ 626-67-50; 1a Pte 14A; juices & licuados
M$17; 8am-6pm Mon-Sat) Melt into a freshly-
made fruit juice or a cool *licuado*.

Getting There & Away

AIR

Tapachula's **airport** (☎ 626-41-89; Carretera Tapachula-
Puerto Madero Km 18.5) is 20km southwest of the
city. **Aviacsa** (☎ 625-40-30; Central Nte 18) flies to/
from Mexico City three times daily, and both
Aeroméxico (☎ 626-39-21; Central Ote 4) and Mexicana
have three daily departures.

TABASCO & CHIAPAS

BUS

Deluxe and 1st-class buses go from the **OCC terminal** (☎ 626-28-81; 17a Ote s/n), 1km northeast of Parque Hidalgo. The main 2nd-class services are by **Rápidos del Sur** (RS; ☎ 626-11-61; 9a Pte 62). Daily departures (from OCC unless otherwise stated) include the following:

Destination	Fare	Duration	Frequency (daily)
Comitán	M$154	6hr (via Motozintla)	7
Escuintla	M$20-52	1½hr	12 from OCC, 26 RS
Mexico City	M$830-1200	18hr	12
Oaxaca	M$388	11hr	1
San Cristóbal de Las Casas	M$206	7½hr (via Motozintla)	7
Tonalá	M$85-164	3hr	6 from OCC, 26 RS
Tuxtla Gutiérrez	M$130-434	6hr	10 from OCC, 26 RS

Other buses from the OCC station go to Palenque, Puerto Escondido and Villahermosa. There are also six daily buses from here to Guatemala City (five to six hours): **Trans Galgos Inter** (www.transgalgosinter.com.gt) at 6am, 10am, 11:45am and 2:30pm (M$260 to M$370), **Línea Dorada** (www.tikalmayanworld.com) at 2:30pm (M$150) and **Tica Bus** (www.ticabus.com) at 7am (M$173).

Galgos also runs two daily buses to San Salvador, El Salvador (M$360, nine hours) via Escuintla in Guatemala. The Tica Bus service continues all the way to Panama City, with several long overnight stops en route.

For destinations in western Guatemala, including Quetzaltenango, it's best to get a bus from the border (see opposite).

Getting Around

Sociedades Transportes 149 (☎ 625-12-87; 2a Sur 68) has a booth in the arrivals hall, charging M$65 per person *colectivo* from the airport to the center, or M$150 for a private taxi (up to two people).

Taxis within the central area (including the OCC terminal) cost M$20.

AROUND TAPACHULA
Barra de Cahoacán

Half an hour (37km) southwest of Tapachula, on the coast past the airport and the mammoth Puerto Chiapas cruise terminal, this town has a low-key beach with *palapas* and a pool for rent and a seafood *comedor*. Sea turtles migrate here from July through October, and a project begun in 2007 gathers and releases the eggs. *Colectivos* from Tapachula (M$15) run every 30 minutes; the last departure back leaves at 6:20pm.

Izapa

The pre-Hispanic ruins at Izapa are important to archaeologists, and of real interest to archaeology buffs. Izapa flourished from approximately 200 BC to AD 200, and its carving style (mostly seen on tall slabs known as steles, fronted by round altars) shows descendants of Olmec deities, with their upper lips unnaturally lengthened. Some Maya monuments in Guatemala are similar, and Izapa is considered an important 'bridge' between the Olmecs and the Maya. Izapa had 91 known stele-and-altar pairings, and you can see some well-preserved examples in the Tapachula museum (p858).

Izapa is around 11km east of Tapachula on the Talismán road. There are three groups of **ruins** (admission free, info M$15; ⏰ 10am-5pm Tue-Sun), each looked after by a caretaking family. The northern group is on the left of the road if you're going from Tapachula – watch out for the low pyramid mounds; you'll also see a ball court and several carved steles and altars. For the other groups, go back 700m toward Tapachula and take a signposted dirt road to the left. You'll pass houses with 2000-year-old sculptures lying in their gardens. After 800m you'll reach a fork with signs to Izapa Grupo A and Izapa Grupo B, each about 250m further on. Grupo A has 10 very weathered stele-and-altar pairings around a field. Grupo B is a couple of grass-covered mounds and more stone sculptures, including three curious ball-on-pillar affairs.

To get there from Tapachula take a combi or microbus (M$10) of **Unión y Progreso** (☎ 962-626-33-79; 5a Pte 53).

Santo Domingo, Unión Juárez & Volcán Tacaná
☎ 962

Volcán Tacaná's dormant cone towers over the countryside north of Tapachula. Even if you're not interested in climbing to its summit, two villages on its gorgeously verdant lower slopes make an attractive trip, their cooler climate offering welcome relief from the Tapachula steam bath.

Santo Domingo lies 34km northeast of Tapachula, amid coffee plantations. The imposing three-story wooden 1920s *casa grande* of the German immigrants who formerly owned the coffee plantation here has been restored as the **Centro Turístico Santo Domingo** (☎ 627 00 55; ⏰ 8am-8pm), with a restaurant (mains M$35 to M$80), a small coffee museum (M$10) and a well-tended tropical garden and pool (M$10).

Nine kilometers beyond Santo Domingo, **Unión Juárez** (population 2700, elevation 1300m) is the starting point for ascents of Tacaná and other, less demanding walks. Tapachula folk like to come up here on weekends and holidays to cool off and feast on *parrillada*, a cholesterol-challenging plate of grilled meat and a few vegetables.

The best months to climb Tacaná are late November to March. There are two routes up the mountain from Unión Juárez. Neither requires any technical climbing, but you need to allow two or three days for either, preferably plus time to acclimatize. Be prepared for extreme cold at the top. The less steep route is via Chiquihuites, 12km from Unión Juárez and reachable by vehicle. From there it's a three-hour walk to Papales, where you can sleep in huts for a donation of M$20. From Papales to the summit is about a five-hour ascent. The other route is via Talquián (about two hours' walk from Unión Juárez) and Trigales (five hours from Talquián). It's about a six-hour climb from Trigales to the summit. The two routes meet a couple of hours below the summit, and on both you have access to camping areas.

Combis from Unión Juárez will carry you to the small town of Córdoba, about halfway to Talquián, also passing the turnoff for Chiquihuites (about 1½ hours' walk away). It's a good idea to get a guide for Tacaná in Unión Juárez. Ask for the Valera brothers at **Hotel Colonial Campestre** (☎ 647-20-15), or Humberto Ríos at the **Cafetal de la Montaña** (☎ 647-20-31). Expect to pay about M$500 for an ascent.

Another local place to head for is **Pico del Loro**, a parrot's beak-shaped overhanging rock that offers fine panoramas. The rock is 5km up a drivable track that leaves the Santo Domingo–Unión Juárez road about halfway between the two villages. Or ask directions to **La Ventana** (the Window), a lookout point over the valley of the Río Suchiate (the international border), or the **Cascadas Muxbal**, each about one hour's walk from Unión Juárez.

SLEEPING & EATING
Hotel Aljoad (☎ 647-21-06; s/d M$100/200) Just north of Unión Juárez' plaza, Hotel Aljoad has clean, tidy rooms around a large patio, all with hot-water bathrooms. Inexpensive meals are available.

Hotel Colonial Campestre (☎ 647-20-15; s/d M$200/300; mains M$50-80) This hotel, a couple of blocks below Unión Juárez' plaza, has spacious rooms with bathroom and TV, good views, and a restaurant (parrillada for two M$155).

There are plenty of *comedores* and restaurants around Unión Juárez' plaza.

GETTING THERE & AWAY
From Tapachula, first take a *colectivo* taxi (M$15, 30 minutes) from 10a Norte, between 9a and 11a Pte, to Cacahoatán – 20km north. From where these terminate in Cacahoatán, Transportes Tacaná combis head on to Santo Domingo (M$10, 30 minutes) and Unión Juárez (M$10, 45 minutes).

Coffee Fincas
The hills north of Tapachula are home to numerous coffee *fincas* (ranches), many of them set up by German immigrants over a century ago. These have tours, restaurants and overnight accommodations:

Finca Argovia (☎ 962-692-30-51; www.argovia .com.mx; r per person incl breakfast from M$625)

Finca Hamburgo (☎ 962-626-64-04; www.finca hamburgo.com; d from M$1000)

Finca Irlanda (☎ 962-625-92-03; www.fincairlanda .grupopeters.com; r incl breakfast M$600 per person, 4-person ste incl all meals M$1800)

Border Towns
It's 20km from Tapachula to the international border at Talismán, opposite El Carmen in Guatemala. The border crossing between Ciudad Hidalgo, 37km from Tapachula, opposite Ciudad Tecún Umán in Guatemala, is busier and has more onward connections. Both border points have money-changing facilities and are open 24 hours – though you should get through by early afternoon for greater security and to guarantee onward transportation. Watch out for moneychangers passing counterfeit bills at the Ciudad Hildalgo crossing.

GETTING THERE & AWAY
Combis of **Autotransportes Paulino Navarro** (☎ 962-626-11-52; 7a Pte 5, Tapachula) head to Ciudad

Hidalgo (M$15, 50 minutes) every 10 minutes, 4:30am to 9:30pm.

Combis of **Unión y Progreso** (☎ 962-626-33-79; 5a Pte 53, Tapachula) leave for Talismán every few minutes, between 5am and 10pm (M$10). A taxi from Tapachula to Talismán takes 20 minutes and costs around M$100. You can also catch combis to either border from the street outside the OCC bus station in Tapachula.

Frequent buses leave Ciudad Tecún Umán until about 6pm for Guatemala City (US$8, six hours) by the Pacific slope route, through Retalhuleu and Escuintla. Buses to Quetzaltenango (US$3.50, 3½ hours) depart up to about 2pm.

The majority of bus services from El Carmen, which include around 20 a day to

Guatemala City (US$8.50, seven hours), go via Ciudad Tecún Umán, and then head along the Pacific slope route. For Quetzaltenango, you can either take one of these and change at Coatepeque or Retalhuleu, or alternatively get a *colectivo* taxi to Malacatán, on a more direct road to Quetzaltenango via San Marcos, and then look for onward transportation from there.

If you're heading for Lake Atitlán or Chichicastenango, you need to get to Quetzaltenango first.

Drivers: the processing point for vehicle import permits, whether you're entering or leaving Mexico by these borders, is north of Tapachula on Hwy 200, at Carretera Tapachula-Huixtla Km 8.

Yucatán Peninsula

Caught between the relentless beat of progress and the echoing shouts of tradition, the Yucatán Peninsula stands at a crossroads. On one side you have the brawny mega-resorts with their oft-preposterous pomp and circumstance, on the other are the proud, steadfast traditions of the Maya, the mystery of the ceremonial centers created by their ancestors, and the Old World allure of colonial masterpieces like Mérida and Campeche. And in between, on every peroxide-blonde beach and every patch of jungle still echoing with the roars of howler monkeys, beats the heart of Ixchel, the earth goddess, marveling at her remarkable creation.

Despite overzealous development, the natural beauty of the Yucatán abides. The ethereal coo of the mot-mot still reverberates overhead, while below continue to writhe the creepy-crawlies that keep this scrub-jungle land renewed year after year. Deep below, in the realm of Ah Puch (God of the Underworld), gurgle freshwater rivers that pull their way through massive limestone caverns all the way to the pitch-perfect waters of the Caribbean Sea and Gulf.

From the deep blue rises the Mesoamerican Reef, the world's second-largest barrier reef, making this coast a diving and snorkeling destination par excellence. And several ocean-front lagoons and cenotes (limestone sinkholes) offer spectacular, accessible swimming.

Around here, the past is the present and the present is the past: they intermingle, toil and tangle eternally like two brawling brothers. You'll witness it in the towering temples of the Maya, Toltecs and Itzá, in the cobblestone streets of colonial centers, and in the sagacious smiles of southern Mexico's native sons and daughters, the Maya.

HIGHLIGHTS

- Set out for a morning bird-watching mission from the remote Costa Maya beach town of **Xcalak** (p907), then head out a bit later for a dive at **Banco Chinchorro** (p906)
- Feel the burn as you haul yourself up the massive pyramid of **Calakmul** (p955), heavy-nosed toucans soaring past toward their tree-top jungle hideaways
- Marvel at the colonial architecture or attend a free concert in **Mérida** (p914), the cultural capital of the peninsula
- Find out why they named **Chichén Itzá** (p937) the 'seventh modern wonder of the world,' or why **Ek' Balam** (p945) should have made the list
- Stay out until dawn in one of the happening beachfront clubs in **Playa del Carmen** (p882), before taking the ferry across to **Isla Cozumel** (p886) the next day for a snorkel and swim

- CANCÚN JANUARY DAILY HIGH: 27°C | 80°F
- CANCÚN JULY DAILY HIGH: 31°C | 88°F

History

The Maya – accomplished astronomers and mathematicians, and architects of some of the grandest monuments ever known – created their first settlements in what is now Guatemala as early as 2400 BC. Over the centuries, the expansion of Maya civilization moved steadily northward, and by AD 550 great Maya city-states were established in southern Yucatán. In the 10th century, with the invasion of the bellicose Toltecs from Central Mexico, the great cities of southern Yucatán slowly dissolved, as attention shifted northward to new power centers like Chichén Itzá.

The last of the great Maya capitals, Mayapán (p932), started to collapse around 1440, when the Xiú Maya and the Cocom Maya began a violent and protracted struggle for power. In 1540, Spanish conquistador Francisco de Montejo the Younger (son of legendary conquistador Francisco de Montejo the Elder) utilized the tensions between the still-feuding Maya sects to conquer the area. The Spaniards allied themselves with the Xiú against the Cocom, finally defeating the Cocom and gaining the Xiú as reluctant converts to Christianity.

Francisco de Montejo the Younger, along with his father, Francisco de Montejo the Elder, and cousin (named…you guessed it, Francisco de Montejo) founded Mérida in 1542 and within four years brought most of the Yucatán Peninsula under Spanish rule. The Spaniards divided up the Maya lands into large estates where the natives were put to work as indentured servants.

When Mexico won its independence from Spain in 1821, the new Mexican government used the Yucatecan territory to create huge plantations for the cultivation of tobacco, sugarcane and *henequén* (agave rope fiber). The Maya, though legally free, were enslaved in debt peonage to the rich landowners.

In 1847, after being oppressed for nearly 300 years by the Spanish and their descendants, the Maya rose up in a massive revolt. This was the beginning of the War of the Castes. Finally, in 1901, after more than 50 years of sporadic, but often intense, violence, a tentative peace was reached; however, it would be another 30 years before the territory of Quintana Roo came under official government control. To this day some Maya do not recognize that sovereignty.

The commercial success of Cancún in the early 1970s led to hundreds of kilometers of public beach along the Caribbean coast being sold off to commercial developers, displacing many small fishing communities. While many indigenous people still eke out a living by subsistence agriculture or fishing, large numbers now work in the construction and service industries. Some individuals and communities, often with outside encouragement, are having a go at ecotourism, opening their lands to tourists and/or serving as guides.

Climate

The Yucatán Peninsula is hot and humid. The rainy season is mid-August to mid-October, when there's afternoon showers most days. The best time to visit is during the dryer, slightly cooler months between November and March. Hurricane season runs from June to November.

Parks & Reserves

There are several national parks on the peninsula, some scarcely larger than the ancient Maya cities they contain – Parque Nacional Tulum, home to the Tulum Ruins (p896), is a good example of this. National biosphere reserves covering thousands of hectares of land or sea include Reserva de la Biosfera Ría Lagartos (p946), Reserva de la Biosfera Ría Celestún (p934) and Reserva de la Biosfera Banco Chinchorro (p906). Even more impressive are the vast Reserva de la Biosfera Calakmul (p955) and Reserva de la Biosfera Sian Ka'an (p904).

Dangers & Annoyances

Dangers are few. Violent crime in the Yucatán Peninsula is extremely rare; in fact residents pride themselves on the safety record of their neighborhoods and streets. Theft in big cities like Cancún, Playa del Carmen and Mérida does occasionally occur, usually in very crowded areas, such as busy markets.

Unattended bags and belongings – even that ratty old pair of flip-flops – may be stolen from the beach, and there have been reports of bus travelers having their bags stolen, especially on second-class night buses. One common scheme is to short-change drivers at gas stations: count your pesos carefully.

While these tranquil waters are generally safe for swimming, occasional strong

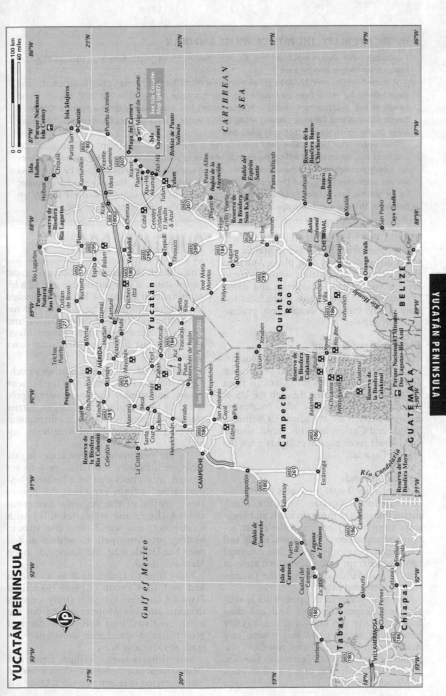

HURRICANE ALLEY: THE PATH OF WILMA AND DEAN

Hurricanes have always walloped the Yucatán, but in recent years it feels as though they are just getting bigger and badder.

It started on October 22, 2005, when Hurricane Wilma hit the Yucatán's northeast coast – and stayed there for more than 30 hours. The 13th hurricane of the turbulent 2005 season – and fourth to reach Category 5 status – Wilma vented her worst forces on Isla Holbox, Cozumel, Puerto Morelos and Cancún, causing M$80 billion in damages. Playa del Carmen and the Riviera Maya to the south were left largely unscathed.

Two years later Dean came into town, leveling the town of Mahahual, displacing 100,000 residents in Chetumal and felling thousands of trees in southern Quintana Roo. While residents are slowly recovering from these hurricanes, the environmental wounds inflicted by Wilma, her wicked stepsister Emily, and Dean could take much longer to heal. Many trees were uprooted by the storms, leaving dead branches that will serve as fuel for fires, adding to those already left behind in the wake of Hurricane Isidore, which ravaged the state of Yucatán in 2002.

---

currents, especially during the *norte* (north wind) season from November to March, can wreck diving and snorkeling plans. And then there are the street hustlers who will try to arrange your sleeps, eats, drugs and dates. It's easiest just to not give these folks the time of day, though a simple, 'no, gracias' normally suffices.

Getting There & Away

The majority of flights into the peninsula arrive at Aeropuerto International de Cancún, and virtually all flights into Cancún pass through the US or Mexico City. The region's other four international airports are at Cozumel, Chetumal, Mérida and Campeche, with only Cozumel and Mérida receiving direct flights from the US and Canada.

Getting Around

Before the late 1960s there was little infrastructure in the Yucatán Peninsula, which means that most of the main roads and highways are relatively new, and the construction and expansion of highways, roads and thoroughfares (mostly to facilitate tourism) continues. Except in the downtown areas of Cancún and Mérida, car travel in the Yucatán is convenient and easy.

The bus system in the peninsula is reliable and inexpensive. First- and 2nd-class buses will carry you safely and comfortably between all major cities and towns, and most sites in between. Buses run from the peninsula's major cities (Campeche, Cancún, Chetumal and Mérida) to most other parts of Mexico as well.

QUINTANA ROO

You'd think that as one of Mexico's most visited states, it'd be impossible to find a bit of solitude in Quintana Roo (pronounced kin-tah-nah *roh*). But beyond the 'hit me baby one more time' clubs of Cancún and 'McMaya' theme parks of the Riviera Maya, you might just find your own quiet sliver of paradise.

There are talcum-powder beaches stretching all the way from Cancún to the Belizean border, unassuming Caribbean islands protected by the world's second-largest barrier reef, and impressive Maya sites throughout this long-arching sliver of limestone, salt and sea.

It's the peninsula's super state, highly developed, heavily touristed, easy to get around, and chock-full of adventure opportunities – from exploring the mysterious depths of the region's numerous cenotes (limestone sinkholes filled with fresh water) and world-class dive sites to beating your own path to seldom visited ruins like Dzinbanché and Kohunlich in the Maya heartland.

Most trips to Quintana Roo will begin and end in Cancún. Chicer-than-thou Playa del Carmen, Cozumel (truly a diver's delight), and Isla Mujeres round out the overly touristed (but still pretty damned good places to spend your vacation) fairylands of Quintana Roo.

Several hurricanes – Wilma, Emily and Dean to name just the biggies – have slammed into the region in recent years. But Quintana

Roo is too big now to be knocked out by mere hurricane winds. It'll take at least a dozen greedy real-estate developers, a ball of twine and a couple million more complacent visitors to signal the death knell.

The high season for Quintana Roo is July and August, mid-December to mid-January and late February to early March (the US spring break). A week on either side of Easter is also high season, but generally coincides with spring break.

CANCÚN

☎ 998 / pop 526,700

Unlike many cities in the world, Cancún just isn't afraid. It's unabashed and unapologetic, and in that lies its high-gloss charm. So send in the Maya dancers, swashbuckling pirates and beer-chugging US Spring Breakers. Cancún can take it. But can you?

Like Las Vegas, Ibiza or Dubai, Cancún is a party city that just won't give up. Top that off with a pretty good beach and you have one of the Western Hemisphere's biggest tourist draws, bringing in as many as 4 million visitors (mostly from the US) each year.

It's hard to believe this little fishing town would become a worldwide phenomenon. In the 1970s Mexico's ambitious planners decided to outdo Acapulco with a brand-new, world-class resort located on the Yucatán Peninsula, and Cancún was born. Although it isn't for everyone – and this type of mass-tourism certainly won't interest all travelers – if you're here, you might as well dig into the kitsch and crap that make this city unique.

Orientation

Cancún is actually made up of two very distinct areas: the downtown area, Ciudad Cancún, and the hotel zone, Zona Hotelera. On the mainland lies Ciudad Cancún. The area of interest to tourists is referred to as *el centro* (downtown). The main north–south thoroughfare is Av Tulum, a 1km-long tree-shaded boulevard lined with banks, shopping centers and restaurants. There are also quite a few nice, small hotels in the downtown area. Though not near the water, the beach is just a taxi or bus ride away from downtown accommodations.

This sandy spit of an island, Isla Cancún, is usually referred to as the Zona Hotelera. Blvd Kukulcán, a four-lane divided avenue,

leaves Ciudad Cancún and goes eastward out on the island for several kilometers, passing condominium developments, several hotels and shopping complexes, to Punta Cancún (Cancún Point) and the Centro de Convenciones (Convention Center).

There aren't many buildings in the Zona Hotelera that have numbered addresses. Instead, because the vast majority of them are on Blvd Kukulcán, their location is described in relation to their distance from Km 0, the boulevard's northern terminus in Ciudad Cancún, identified with a roadside 'Km 0' marker. Each kilometer is similarly marked.

Information

BOOKSTORES
Fama (Map p870; ☎ 884-65-41; Av Tulum 105 SM 22 M4 Lotes 27 & 27A)

EMERGENCY
Cruz Roja (Red Cross; ☎ 884-16-16)
Fire (☎ 060)
Police (Map p869; ☎ 060; Blvd Kukulcán)
Tourist Police (☎ 885-22-77)

INTERNET ACCESS
Internet cafés in Cancún centro are plentiful, speedy and cheap, costing M$15 per hour or less.

LAUNDRY
Lava y Seca (Map p870; ☎ 892-47-89; Crisantemos 20; per kg M$15; ⏰ 9am-6pm Mon-Sat) Downtown.

LEFT LUGGAGE
Pay-in-advance lockers (M$70 per 24 hours) are at the airport, just outside customs at the international arrivals area.

MEDICAL SERVICES
American Medical Care Center (Map p869; ☎ 884-61-33; Plaza Quetzal, Blvd Kukulcán Km 8)

MONEY
There are several banks with ATMs on Av Tulum, between Avs Cobá and Uxmal.

POST
Main post office (Map p870; ☎ 884-14-18; cnr Avs Xel-Há & Sunyaxchén; ⏰ 8am-6pm Mon-Fri, 9am-1pm Sat)

TOURIST INFORMATION
Cancún Convention & Visitors Bureau (Map p870; ☎ 884-65-31; Av Cobá; ☻ 9am-2pm & 4-7pm Mon-Fri)
State Tourist Office (Sedetur; Map p870; ☎ 884-80-73; Pecari 23; ☻ 9am-9pm Mon-Fri)

TRAVEL AGENCIES
Nómadas (Map p870; ☎ 892-23-20; www.nomadas travel.com; Av Cobá 5) Downtown, next to the Soberanis Hostal, Nómadas is a student-oriented agency.

Dangers & Annoyances
Cancún has a reputation for being safe, and the Zona Hotelera is particularly well policed and secure; however, it is always best not to leave valuables unattended in your hotel room or beside your beach towel.

Vehicular traffic on Blvd Kukulcán, particularly as it passes between the malls, bars and discotheques at Punta Cancún, is a serious concern.

A system of colored pennants warns beachgoers of potential dangers:
Blue Normal, safe conditions.
Yellow Use caution; changeable conditions.
Red Unsafe conditions; use a swimming pool instead.

Sights & Activities
MAYA RUINS
There are two sets of Maya ruins in the Zona Hotelera and, though neither is particularly impressive, both are worth a look if time permits. In the **Zona Arqueológica El Rey** (Map p869; admission M$34; ☻ 8am-5pm), on the west side of Blvd Kukulcán between Km 17 and Km 18, there's a small temple and several ceremonial platforms.

The other, smaller site is **Yamil Lu'um** (Map p869; admission free), atop a beachside knoll near the Sheraton Cancún hotel. To reach the site visitors must pass through either of the hotels flanking it or approach it from the beach – there is no direct access from the boulevard. The tiny Maya structure and Chac (Maya rain god) statue on the beautifully kept grounds of the Sheraton Hotel are authentic.

BEACHES
Under Mexican law, you have the right to walk and swim on every beach in the country, except those within military compounds. In practice, it is difficult to approach many stretches of beach without walking through the lobby of a hotel, particularly in the Zona Hotelera. However, unless you look suspicious or like a local (hotels tend to discriminate against locals, particularly the Maya), you'll usually be able to cross the lobby unnoticed and proceed to the beach.

Starting from Ciudad Cancún in the northwest, all of Isla Cancún's beaches are on the left-hand side of the road (the lagoon is on your right; all appear on Map p869). The first beaches are **Playa Las Perlas**, **Playa Juventud**, **Playa Linda**, **Playa Langosta**, **Playa Tortugas** and **Playa Caracol**; after rounding Punta Cancún, the beaches to the south are **Playa Gaviota Azul**, **Playa Chac-Mool**, **Playa Marlin**, the long stretch of **Playa Ballenas** and finally, at Km 17, **Playa Delfines**.

Delfines is about the only beach with a public parking lot; unfortunately, its sand is coarser and darker than the exquisite fine sand of the more northerly beaches.

WATER SPORTS
For decent **snorkeling**, you need to travel to one of the nearby reefs. Resort hotels, travel agencies and various tour operators in the area can book you on day-cruise boats that take snorkelers to the barrier reef, as well as to other good sites within 100km of Cancún. To see the sparse aquatic life off Cancún's beaches, you can rent snorkeling equipment for about M$100 a day from most luxury hotels.

Scuba Cancún (Map p869; ☎ 849-52-26; www .scubacancun.com.mx; Blvd Kukulcán Km 5.2), a family-owned and PADI-certified dive operation with many years of experience, was the first dive shop in Cancún. It offers a Cancún snorkeling tour for M$290 and a variety of dive options (including cenote, night and nitrox dives), as well as fishing trips, at reasonable prices (one-/two-tank M$594/740, equipment rental extra).

Tours
Most hotels and travel agencies work with companies that offer tours to surrounding attractions.

Nómadas Travel (Map p870; ☎ 892-23-20; www.nom adastravel.com; Av Cobá 5) offers a variety of reasonably priced packages to popular destinations.

Sleeping
DOWNTOWN
Budget
The area around Parque Las Palapas has numerous hostels and budget digs as well.

Weary Traveler (Map p870; ☎ 887-01-91; www.weary travelerhostel.com; Palmera 30; dm fan/air-con M$100/110;

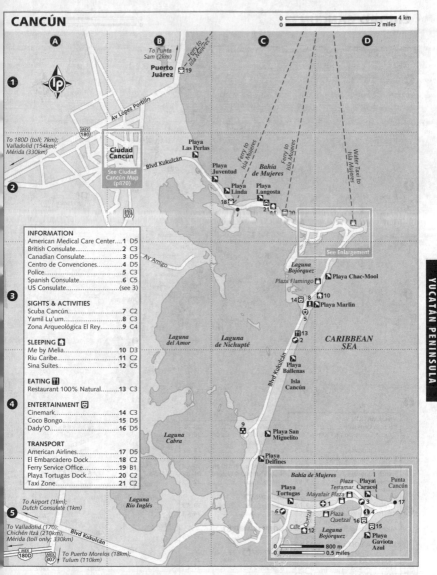

CANCÚN

INFORMATION
American Medical Care Center....1 D5
British Consulate..........................2 C3
Canadian Consulate......................3 C3
Centro de Convenciones..............4 D5
Police..5 D5
Spanish Consulate........................6 C5
US Consulate...........................(see 3)

SIGHTS & ACTIVITIES
Scuba Cancún...............................7 C2
Yamil Lu'um..................................8 C3
Zona Arqueológica El Rey.............9 C4

SLEEPING
Me by Melia................................10 D3
Riu Caribe...................................11 C2
Sina Suites..................................12 C5

EATING
Restaurant 100% Natural.............13 C3

ENTERTAINMENT
Cinemark....................................14 C3
Coco Bongo.................................15 D5
Dady'O..16 D5

TRANSPORT
American Airlines.........................17 D5
El Embarcadero Dock...................18 C2
Ferry Service Office.....................19 B1
Playa Tortugas Dock....................20 C2
Taxi Zone....................................21 C2

YUCATÁN PENINSULA

⊠ ☒ ▣) The cramped shared rooms could use a bit of work, but the Weary Traveler has all the basic ingredients to make a good hostel: a cool rooftop terrace kitchen area for swilling beers and swapping tales, a big breakfast buffet, lots of guests from around the globe and a friendly owner. Ask about private rooms for rent down the street.

Las Palmas Hotel (Map p870; ☎ 884-25-13; Palmera 43; dm/d M$100/300; ☒) A family-run affair, the Palmas has a clean downstairs dorm room with much-appreciated air-con. There's a handful of bright, cheery and affordable rooms upstairs. If you are looking to get away from the backpacker scene for a bit, then stay here. If not, head over to Weary

YUCATÁN PENINSULA

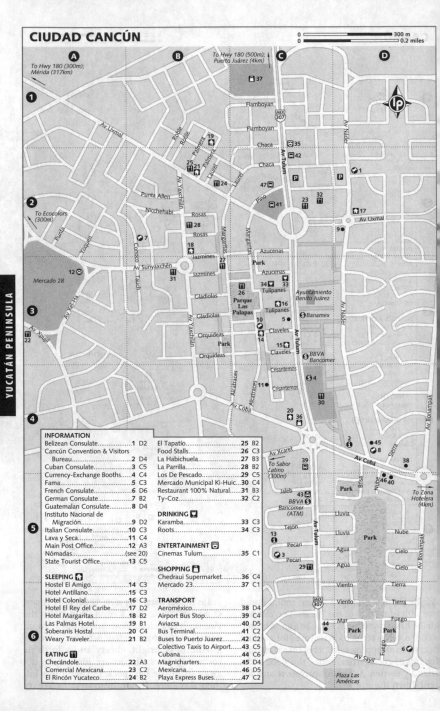

CIUDAD CANCÚN

Traveler-landia or the hostels near Parque Palapas. Continental breakfast includes freshly squeezed orange juice.

Hostel El Amigo (Map p870; ☎ 892-70-56; Alcatraces 29; dm fan/air-con; M$120/140; 🍴 💻) Right on the corner of Parque Las Palapas, this small hostel has shiny new shared rooms, a quiet sitting area for a post-beach *cerveza* and, of course, the requisite computers. The dorms have fewer beds than at other hostels, meaning you won't meet tons of travelers, but will probably get a better night's sleep.

Soberanis Hostal (Map p870; ☎ 884-45-64, 800-101-01-01; www.soberanis.com.mx; Av Cobá 5; dm/d M$120/590; 💻) It's a good value with a nice location, and is a fun place to meet friends. All rooms have very comfortable beds, tiled floors, cable TV and nicely appointed bathrooms. Though primarily a hotel, the Soberanis also has four-bed 'hostel' rooms with the same amenities as the regular rooms, including free continental breakfast. The cafeteria serves decent lunches and dinners, and the hotel also has a bar, internet facilities (per hr M$10), a phone center, a tour agency and also a student-oriented travel agency.

our pick Hotel Colonial (Map p870; ☎ 884-15-35; Tulipanes 22; d fan/air-con M$350/450; 🍴) Perhaps the best buy in its price range, the Colonial has a central courtyard, super-clean rooms with traditional textile bedspreads and a pleasant central courtyard. Get a room toward the back as the street noise in this party district can be a bit much.

Midrange

Hotel Antillano (Map p870; ☎ 884-11-32, 800-288-70-00; fax 884-18-78; www.hotelantillano.com; Claveles 1; d M$500-700; 🍴 🍴) A large beige shoebox with a groovy–groupie–bee-bop feel just off Av Tulum, this is a very pleasant and quiet place with a relaxing lobby, nice pool, good central air-con and cable TV. Rooms on Av Tulum are noisier than those in the back. Rates include a welcome drink, continental breakfast and a Zona Hotelera beach pass.

our pick Hotel El Rey del Caribe (Map p870; ☎ 884-20-28; www.reycaribe.com; cnr Avs Uxmal & Náder; d M$630-820; 🅿 🚫 🍴 🍴 ♿) El Rey is a true eco-tel that composts, employs solar collectors and cisterns, uses gray water on the gardens and even has a few composting toilets. This is a beautiful spot with jungley courtyard, azure swimming pool and small Jacuzzi. Many of the 31 rooms have a fully equipped kitchenette; all

have comfortable beds, hairdryers and safes (you can use your own lock). Two children under 11 can stay for free, and good prices are offered in low season.

Top End

Hotel Margaritas (Map p870; ☎ 884-93-33, 800-537-84-83; www.margaritascancun.com; cnr Avs Yaxchilán & Jazmines; s & d M$1300, tr M$1500; 🍴 🍴) The curvaceous swimming pool is eye-catching. The 100 guestrooms are clean but musty, so check and see if one with a balcony is available. If so, they air out nicely. This place is across the street from the Suites Caribe and also sports six floors. There's a (pricey) restaurant, a decent bar, Jacuzzi and helpful staff.

ZONA HOTELERA
Midrange

Sina Suites (Map p869; ☎ 883-10-17; www.cancunsinasuites.com.mx; Calle Quetzal 33; ste M$800-2000; 🍴 🍴) Right on the lagoon, this is a great deal in low season, when prices drop by as much as 20%. The hotel was completely renovated after Hurricane Wilma, and its 36 spacious suites are still lookin' good: each with two double beds, a separate living room (with a sofa bed) and satellite TV, a kitchen and one and a half bathrooms. Bring some friends to save money. This gleaming white hotel also has a pool and restaurant surrounded by Brady Bunch–inspired Astroturf.

Top End

Me by Meliá (Map p869; ☎ 881-25-00; www.mebymelia.com; Blvd Kukulcán Km 12; d low/high season M$1780/3200; 🅿 🚫 🍴 💻 🍴) 'Enough about you, let's talk about me!' That's the philosophy at this uber-modern, expressionist-inspired hotel. It won't suit everyone, but if you prefer clean lines over your standard Cancún baroque, then Me is the place for you. Only half the rooms have ocean views, and it just ain't worth it to pay this much and not have a view of the Caribbean blue.

Riu Caribe (Map p869; ☎ 848-78-50; www.riu.com; Blvd Kukulcán Km 5.5; s low/high season M$1900/2140, d M$2690/3860; 🅿 🚫 🍴 💻 🍴) Riu rules the Riviera Maya – they're everywhere. This particular Riu has 541 rooms (all with ocean views), including 60 junior suites, and a family-friendly atmosphere – head over to the Riu Palace for romance. All come with private terraces that overlook a dazzling swimming pool and 200m of beach. The gorgeous lobby has pretty tiled floors and stained-glass ceiling, and a nice view of the water. Prices listed are all-inclusive; room-only rates are not available.

Eating

Mercados 23 and 28 have a number of tiny places, and Parque Las Palapas has food stands. These restaurants are all in the downtown area, and there are some good budget places there, too. For groceries, try **Comercial Mexicana** (Map p870; cnr Avs Tulum & Uxmal), a centrally located supermarket close to the bus station.

BUDGET

Los de Pescado (Map p870; Av Tulum 32; ceviche & tacos M$16-75; ⏱ 10am-5:30pm) It's easy to order at this restaurant as there are only two choices: *ceviche* or tacos. Knock either back with a beer or two, and you'll see why this is one of the best budget spots in downtown. With its thatched roof, you can tell the owners take a certain pride in their work – that's why this is always the most crowded restaurant on the block.

Ty-Coz (Map p870; ☎ 884-60-60; Av Tulum; sandwiches M$30-40; ⏱ 9am-11pm Mon-Sat) A bakery–café just north of the Comercial Mexicana supermarket. It has granite tabletops and a pleasing ambience, and serves good coffee, baguettes and croissants, as well as sandwiches made with a variety of meats and cheeses. There's also a spot near Km 7.5 on Blvd Kulkulkán.

El Tapatío (Map p870; ☎ 887-83-17; cnr Avs Uxmal & Palmera; dishes M$40-90; set meals M$35; ⏱ 9-11:30am Sun) Touristy but good – a popular choice for hostel-goers, who suck down the mammoth fruit and veggie juices, shakes and smoothies at any time of day.

El Rincón Yucateco (Map p870; Av Uxmal 24; dishes M$40-100; ⏱ noon-10pm Mon-Sat) A reasonably priced Yucatecan place that's across from Hotel Cotty, serving a nice variety of favorites along with very weak 'American'-style coffee. *Sopa de lima* (chicken soup with lime) is light: a good option for anyone nursing a stomach problem (or a hangover).

MIDRANGE

our pick **Checándole** (Map p870; ☎ 884-71-47; Av Xpujil 6 SM 27; mains M$50-130; ⏱ daily noon-8pm) This is the must-eat-at restaurant in Cancún. It's a bit away from the city center but well worth the trip. Dressed up with a palapa roof, Checándole specializes in Chilango (Mexico City) cuisine. The *menu del día* (fixed three-course meal) is just M$45, and great value.

Restaurant 100% Natural (Map p870; ☎ 884-01-02; Av Sunyaxchén; mains M$40-150; ⏱ 7am-11pm; Ⓥ) Vegetarians and health-food nuts delight in this health food chain near Av Yaxchilán, which serves juice blends (try the 'Crazy Yog' or the 'Vampiro'), a wide selection of yogurt–fruit–vegetable combinations, and brown rice, pasta, fish and chicken dishes. The on-site bakery turns out whole-wheat products, and the entire place is very nicely decorated and landscaped.

La Parrilla (Map p870; ☎ 884-81-93; Av Yaxchilán 51; mains M$70-370; ⏱ noon-2am) Any Cancún eatery founded before the 1980s gets to call itself venerable, and La Parrilla, founded in 1975, should get a capital V. A traditional Mexican restaurant popular with locals and tourists alike, it serves a varied menu from all over Mexico, with Yucatecan specialties thrown in. Try the tasty *calamares al mojo de ajo* (squid in garlic sauce), steaks or sautéed grouper. *Mole* enchiladas and delicious piña coladas both run about M$60.

TOP END

our pick **La Habichuela** (Map p870; ☎ 884-31-58; Margaritas 25; mains M$150-420) An elegant restaurant with a lovely courtyard dining area, just off Parque Las Palapas. The specialty is shrimp and lobster in curry sauce served inside a coconut with tropical fruit, but almost anything on the menu is delicious. The seafood *ceviche* and *tapa al ajillo* (potatoes in garlic) are mouthwatering.

Drinking

Roots (Map p870; ☎ 884-24-37; Tulipanes 26; cover Fri & Sat M$50; ⏱ 6pm-1am Mon-Sat) Pretty much the hippest downtown bar, it features jazz, reggae or rock bands and the occasional flamenco guitarist. It's also a pretty decent restaurant.

Karamba (Map p870; ☎ 884-00-32; cnr Azucenas & Av Tulum; ⏱ 10pm-6am Thu-Sun) Cover ranges from free to M$70. Come here for a varied crowd of gays, lesbians and cross-dressers.

Entertainment

CINEMAS

Cinemark (Map p869; ☎ 883-56-03; La Isla Shopping Village)

NIGHTCLUBS

The Zona Hotelera's main nightlife is loud and booze-oriented. Dance clubs charge around

M$150 cover. Some don't open before 10pm, and most don't close until dawn.

Coco Bongo (Map p869; ☎ 883-50-61; Forum Mall; ☷ 10:30pm-5am) This is often the venue for MTV's coverage of Spring Break, and tends to be a happening venue just about any day of the week.

Dady'O (Map p869; ☎ 800-234-97-97; Blvd Kukulcán Km 9; ☷ 10pm-4:30am) The predominant beats are Latin, house, techno, trance and hip-hop, and the crowd is mainly 20-something.

Sabor Latino (Map p870; ☎ 892-19-16; cnr Avs Xcaret & Tankah; cover men/women M$60/40, Wed free; ☷ 10:30pm-6am, low season closed Sun-Tue) On the 2nd floor of Chinatown Plaza, the live acts feature Dominican salsa and other tropical styles.

Shopping
Mercado Municipal Ki-Huic (Map p870; Av Tulum) This warren of stalls and shops carries a wide variety of souvenirs and handicrafts.

Locals head to either **Mercado 28** (Map p870) or **Mercado 23** (Map p870) for clothes, shoes, inexpensive food stalls, hardware items and so on. Of the two, Mercado 23 is the least frequented by tourists. If you're looking for a place *without* corny T-shirts, this is where to go.

Across Av Tulum is the **Chedraui supermarket** (Map p870), whose upstairs clothing department sometimes has souvenir-grade items at very affordable prices.

Getting There & Away
AIR
About 8km south of the city center, **Aeropuerto International de Cancún** (Cancún International Airport; ☎ 886-00-47) is the busiest in southeast Mexico. The following airlines service Cancún:

Aeroméxico (Map p870; ☎ 287-18-68; Av Cobá 80) Just west of Av Bonampak.

American Airlines (Map p869; ☎ 800-904-60-00; Hotel Fiesta Americana Coral Beach, Blvd Kukulcán Km 8.7) Has an airport counter as well.

Aviacsa (Map p870; ☎ 887-42-14; Av Cobá 39) Also has an airport counter.

Azteca (☎ 886-08-31) Airport counter.

Click (☎ 884-20-00) Airport counter.

Continental (☎ 886-00-06, 800-900-50-00; www.continental.com) Airport counter.

Copa (☎ 886-06-53) Airport counter.

Cubana (Map p870; ☎ 887-72-10; Calle Tulum)

Delta (☎ 800-123-47-10, 886-06-68) Airport counter.

Grupo Taca (☎ 886-00-08; www.taca.com) Airport counter.

Magnicharters (Map p870; ☎ 884-06-00; Av Náder 93)

Mexicana (Map p870; ☎ 881-90-90, 24hr 800-502-20-00; Av Cobá 39)

Northwest (☎ 800-907-47-00) Airport counter.

United Airlines (☎ 800-003-07-77; www.united.com) Airport counter.

US Airways (☎ 800-007-88-00; www.usairways.com) Airport counter.

BOAT
There are several embarkation points to reach Isla Mujeres from Cancún, including Punta Sam (M$15), Puerto Juárez (M$35) and Zona Hotelera (M$70). Head to Chiquilá to get to Holbox. While there are ferries to Cozumel from Cancún, you are better off getting there from Playa del Carmen's dock.

See p878 for details of boats to Isla Mujeres and p881 for boats to Isla Holbox.

BUS
The **bus terminal** (Map p870; cnr Avs Uxmal & Tulum) sits where Avs Uxmal and Tulum meet. Services are available in 1st and 2nd class, and in several luxury options. Across from the bus terminal, a few doors from Av Tulum, is the ticket office and mini-terminal of **Playa Express** (Map p870; Pino). It runs shuttle buses down the Caribbean coast to Tulum about every 30 minutes until early evening, stopping at big towns and points of interest en route. See the box on p874 for major daily routes.

CAR & MOTORCYCLE
Rental-car agencies with facilities at the airport include **Alamo** (☎ 886-01-79), **Avis** (☎ 886-02-22), **Budget** (☎ 884-69-55), **Dollar** (☎ 886-01-79) and **Hertz** (☎ 884-13-26). Hwy 180D, the 238km toll *(cuota)* road running much of the way between Cancún and Mérida, costs M$329 for the distance and has only two exits before the end. The first, at Valladolid, costs M$194 to reach from Cancún, and the second, at Pisté (for Chichén Itzá), is an additional M$48.

Getting Around
TO/FROM THE AIRPORT
White TTC buses to downtown (M$80) leave the airport every 20 minutes or so between 5:30am and 11:30pm, stopping in the domestic and international terminals. In town they travel up Av Tulum and will stop on request.

Going to the airport from downtown, the same TTC airport buses ('Aeropuerto Centro') head south on Av Tulum. You can flag them down anywhere it's feasible, from well north of the bus terminal to well south of Av Cobá.

Colectivos (M$110) depart for the Zona Hotelera and downtown from in front of the international terminal every 15 minutes.

Cheaper ADO shuttles leave from the domestic terminal for downtown (M$35) or Playa del Carmen (M$65). Riviera runs nine express buses to Playa del Carmen between 7am and 7:30pm (M$80, 45 minutes to one hour).

Taxis into town or to the Zona Hotelera cost up to M$450 (up to four people) if you catch them right outside the airport. If you follow the access road out of the airport, however, and past the traffic-monitoring booth (a total of about 300m), you can often flag down an empty taxi leaving the airport that will take you for much less (you can try for M$50).

Colectivos head to the airport from a stand in front of the Hotel Cancún Handall on Av Tulum about a block south of Av Cobá. They charge M$20 per person and leave when full. The official rate for private taxis is M$200.

BUS

To reach the Zona Hotelera from downtown, catch any bus with 'R1,' 'Hoteles' or 'Zona Hotelera' displayed on the windshield as it travels along Av Tulum toward Av Cobá, then eastward on Av Cobá. The one-way fare is M$6.50, but since change is often unavailable this varies between M$6 and M$7. To reach Puerto Juárez

and the Isla Mujeres ferries, catch a Ruta 13 ('Pto Juárez' or 'Punta Sam'; M$4) bus heading north on Av Tulum. Some R1 buses make this trip as well; tickets cost M$6.50.

TAXI

Cancún's taxis don't have meters. Fares are set, but always agree on a price before getting in. From downtown to Punta Cancún is M$80, to Puerto Juárez M$30. Hourly and daily rates should run about M$150 to M$200 and M$700 to M$800 respectively.

ISLA MUJERES
☎ 998 / pop 14,000

If you are going to visit just one of Quintana Roo's islands, then Isla Mujeres (Island of Women) is probably the place for you. It's not as crowded as Cozumel, yet offers more to do and see than chiller-than-thou Holbox. Sure, there are quite a few ticky-tacky tourist shops, but folks still get around by golfcart and the crushed-coral beaches are better than those of Cozumel or Holbox. There's not much here and that's the whole point: come to bask in quiet shallows or stretch out on the sand, to snorkel or scuba dive, or just to put the sunglasses on and open that book you've been dying to finish.

History

The name Isla Mujeres goes at least as far back as Spanish buccaneers, who (legend has

DAILY BUSES FROM CANCÚN

Destination	Fare	Duration	Frequency
Chetumal	M$210	5½–6½hr	frequent
Chichén Itzá	M$140	3–4hr	hourly from 5am to 5pm
Chiquilá (for Isla Holbox)	M$70	3½hr	Mayab buses at 7:50am & 12:40pm, Noreste bus at 1:45pm
Felipe Carrillo Puerto	M$130	3½–4hr	8 daily
Mérida	1st class M$270	4–6hr	15 daily
	2nd-class M$200	4–6hr	hourly (5am–5pm)
Mexico City (TAPO)	M$1100	22–24hr	5 daily
Mexico City (Terminal Norte)	M$1060	24hr	2 daily
Palenque	M$490	12–13hr	4 daily
Playa del Carmen	M$34	1–1¼hr	frequent (see also below)
Puerto Morelos	M$12-17	-	Take Playa del Carmen buses
Ticul	M$190-220	6hr	6 daily
Tizimín	M$85	3–4hr	9 daily
Tulum	M$62	2¼–3hr	frequent
Valladolid	M$110	2–3hr	frequent
Villahermosa	M$540	12hr	11 daily

ISLA MUJERES

Punta Norte

See Isla Mujeres (Town) Map (p876)

CARIBBEAN SEA

Airstrip

Laguna Makax

Bahía de Mujeres

Salina

Tortugranja (Turtle Farm)

Playa Pescador

Playa Lancheros

Arrecife Manchones

Playa Indios

Hotel Garrafón de Castilla

Playa Garrafón

Lighthouse

Punta Sur

Mayan Ruins

Car Ferry to Punta Sam

Ferry to Puerto Juárez

Ferries to Cancún's Zona Hotelera

Car-Sea Esp.

Av Rueda Medina

linked by Av Rueda Medina, a loop road that more or less follows the coast. Between them are a handful of small fishing villages, several saltwater lakes, a string of westward-facing beaches, a large lagoon and a small airstrip.

The eastern shore is washed by the open sea, and the surf there is dangerous. The most popular sand beach (Playa Norte) is at the northern tip of the island.

Information

HSBC Bank (Map p876; Av Rueda Medina)
Internet café (Map p876; cnr Matamoros & Guerrero; per hr M$15; 🕒 9am-10pm Mon-Sat) As yet unnamed; offers access to the web.
Lavandería Automática Tim Pho (Map p876; ☎ 877-05-29; cnr Juarez & Abasolo; 🕒 7am-9pm Mon-Sat, 8am-2pm Sun) Up to 4kg takes two hours and costs M$50.
Mañana (Map p876; ☎ 866-43-47; cnr Matamoros & Guerrero; 🕒 10am-7pm) This café (p878) sells books.
Medical Center (Map p876; Guerrero) Between Madero and Morelos.
Police (☎ 877-00-82)
Post office (Map p876; ☎ 877-00-85; cnr Guerrero & López Mateos; 🕒 9am-4pm Mon-Fri)
Tourist information office (Map p876; ☎ 877-07-67; Av Rueda Medina; 🕒 8am-8pm Mon-Fri, 9am-2pm Sat & Sun)

Sights & Activities
BEACHES & SWIMMING

Once you reach **Playa Norte** (Map p876) the island's main beach, you won't want to leave. Its warm shallow waters are the color of blue-raspberry syrup and the beach is crushed coral. Five kilometers south of town is **Playa Lancheros** (Map p875), the southernmost point served by local buses. The beach is less attractive than Playa Norte, but it sometimes has free musical festivities on Sunday. A taxi ride to Lancheros is M$20. Another 1.5km south of Lancheros is **Playa Garrafón** (Map p875), with translucent waters, colorful fish and no sand. Avoid the overhyped and overpriced Parque Natural (which has constructed a horrendous eyesore of an observation tower that has you praying for a hurricane) and visit instead **Hotel Garrafón de Castilla** (Map p875; ☎ 877-01-07; Carretera Punta Sur Km 6; admission M$20; 🕒 9am-5pm), which provides chairs, umbrellas, showers and baths for the entrance fee. Snorkeling gear is M$60 extra. The hotel rents lockers and towels, and offers snorkeling tours to the offshore reef for M$200. Taxis from town cost M$50.

it) kept their lovers in safe seclusion there while they plundered galleons and pillaged ports on the mainland. An alternate theory suggests that in 1517, when Francisco Hernández de Córdoba sailed from Cuba and arrived here to procure slaves, the expedition discovered a stone temple containing clay figurines of Maya goddesses and may have named the island after the icons.

Today some archaeologists believe that the island was a stopover for the Maya en route to worship their goddess of fertility, Ixchel, on Isla Cozumel. The island may also have figured in the extensive Maya salt trade, which extended for hundreds of miles along the coastline.

Orientation

The island is 8km long, 150m to 800m wide and 11km off the coast. You'll find most of the restaurants and hotels in the town of Isla Mujeres, with the pedestrian mall on Hidalgo serving as the focal point. The ferry arrives in the town proper on the island's northern tip. On the southern tip are the lighthouse and vestiges of the Maya temple. The two are

DIVING & SNORKELING

Many of the diving and snorkeling sites in the Cancún–Isla Mujeres area were affected by Hurricanes Emily and Wilma in 2005. That said, hurricane damage is part of natural reef ecology, and the reefs are now growing anew. Within a short boat ride of the island there's a handful of lovely dives, such as Barracuda, La Bandera, El Jigueo and Manchones. You can expect to see sea turtles, rays and barracuda, along with a wide array of hard and soft corals. A popular nonreef dive is **Ultrafreeze** (or El Frío), where you'll see the intact hull of a 60m-long cargo ship – thought to have been deliberately sunk in 30m of water.

Snorkeling with whale sharks (M$1250) just off Isla Holbox is the latest craze (see boxed text, p880). The season runs from July through September. Folks at the dive shops listed below can arrange your trip.

To protect and preserve the reefs, a M$20 fee is charged for all diving and swimming. At all of the reputable dive centers you need to show your certification card, and you will be expected to have your own gear. Equipment rental adds M$100 to the prices listed here; you'll pay another M$100 if you need a wetsuit.

Sea Hawk Divers (Map p876; ☎ /fax 877-02-96; www .isla-mujeres.net/seahawkdivers; Carlos Lazo) offers dives for M$450 (one tank) to M$600 (two tanks), a resort course for M$850, PADI Open Water certification (M$3200), and snorkeling tours from M$250.

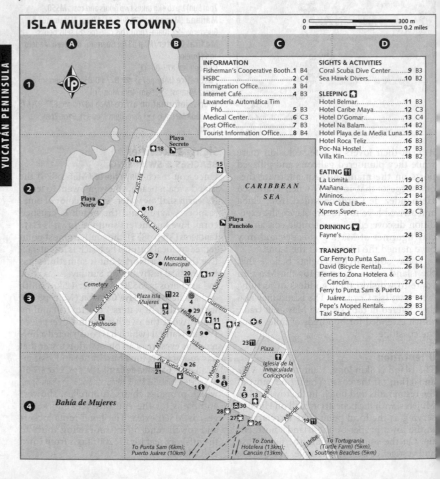

ISLA MUJERES (TOWN)

| 0 | 300 m |
| 0 | 0.2 miles |

INFORMATION
Fisherman's Cooperative Booth..1 B4
HSBC.......................................2 C4
Immigration Office...................3 B4
Internet Café...........................4 B3
Lavandería Automática Tim
   Phó.....................................5 B3
Medical Center.........................6 C3
Post Office...............................7 B3
Tourist Information Office......8 B4

SIGHTS & ACTIVITIES
Coral Scuba Dive Center.........9 B3
Sea Hawk Divers....................10 B2

SLEEPING 🛏
Hotel Belmar.........................11 B3
Hotel Caribe Maya.................12 C3
Hotel D'Gomar.......................13 C4
Hotel Na Balam......................14 B2
Hotel Playa de la Media Luna.15 B2
Hotel Roca Teliz.....................16 B3
Poc-Na Hostel.......................17 B3
Villa Kiin..............................18 B2

EATING 🍴
La Lomita..............................19 C4
Mañana.................................20 B3
Mininos.................................21 B4
Viva Cuba Libre......................22 B3
Xpress Super.........................23 C3

DRINKING 🍸
Fayne's.................................24 B3

TRANSPORT
Car Ferry to Punta Sam..........25 C4
David (Bicycle Rental)............26 B4
Ferries to Zona Hotelera &
   Cancún...............................27 C4
Ferry to Punta Sam & Puerto
   Juárez................................28 B4
Pepe's Moped Rentals...........29 B3
Taxi Stand.............................30 C4

GOING GREEN WITH THE TURTLES

Although they are endangered, sea turtles are still killed throughout Latin America for their eggs and meat, which is considered a delicacy. Three species of sea turtle lay eggs in the sand along the island's calm western shore, and they are now being protected – one *tortuguita* at a time.

In the 1980s, efforts by a local fisherman led to the founding of the **Isla Mujeres Turtle Farm** (Isla Mujeres Tortugranja; Map p875; ☎ 877-05-95; Carretera Sac Bajo Km 5; admission M$30; ⏰ 9am-5pm; ♿), 5km south of town, which protects the turtles' breeding grounds and places wire cages around their eggs to protect against predators.

Hatchlings live in three large pools for up to a year, then are tagged for monitoring and released. Because most turtles in the wild die within their first few months, the practice of guarding them through their first year greatly increases their chances of survival. Moreover, the turtles that leave this protected beach return each year, which means their offspring receive the same protection.

There are several hundred sea turtles on the farm, ranging in weight from 150g to more than 300kg. The farm also has a small but good-quality aquarium, displays on marine life and a gift shop. Tours are conducted in Spanish and English.

If you're driving, biking or walking from the bus stop, bear right at the 'Y' just beyond Hacienda Mundaca's parking lot (the turn is marked by a tiny sign). The facility is easily reached from town by taxi (M$30).

Coral Scuba Dive Center (Map p876; ☎ 877-07-63; www.coralscubadivecenter.com; Hidalgo) offers dives for M$290 to M$590, snorkel trips for M$220 and a variety of courses.

The fisherfolk of Isla Mujeres have formed a cooperative to offer snorkeling tours of various sites from M$200, including the reef off Playa Garrafón, and day trips to Isla Contoy for M$500. You can book through the **Fisherman's Cooperative Booth** (☎ 877-13-63; Av Rueda Medina) in a *palapa* steps away from the dock. Booking here ensures your money goes to locals.

Sleeping
BUDGET

our pick **Poc-Na Hostel** (Map p876; ☎ /fax 877-00-90; www.pocna.com; cnr Matamoros & Carlos Lazo; campsites per person M$65, dm with/without card M$90/110, d M$240-350; ♿ 🖥) Mexico's oldest youth hostel, Poc-Na ranks among the country's best. The large main common area has hammocks to chill in and an excellent sound system putting out tunes until the wee hours. The property extends through 100m of sand and coconut palms to the edge of the Caribbean and the hostel's own beach bar. Though there are no cooking facilities for guests, the kitchen serves good, inexpensive food (and beer and wine).

Hotel Roca Teliz (Map p876; ☎ 877-04-07; jccan opus@hotmail.com; cnr Hidalgo & Abasolo; s low/high season M$100/160, d low/high season M$160/250; ♿) Good

budget digs, especially for solo travelers, the 'Rock' has a cool central courtyard and dark but clean rooms, and is located right on the Hidalgo pedestrian mall. Add M$100 for air-con.

Hotel Caribe Maya (Map p876; ☎ 877-06-84; Madero 9; d with fan/air-con M$250/300; ♿) The old blue tiles need replacing, but this place offers rooms that, though a bit musty, are solid value even in the high season.

MIDRANGE

Hotel D'Gomar (Map p876; ☎ 877-05-41; Av Rueda Medina 150; d with fan M$350, with air-con low/high season M$500/650; ♿) A friendly place facing the ferry dock between Morelos and Bravo, this has four floors of attractive, ample and well-maintained rooms. Most have hammocks, and both coffee and water are free.

Hotel Belmar (Map p876; ☎ 877-04-30; fax 877-04-29; www.rolandi.com; Hidalgo 110; d with air-con low/high season M$350/950, ste with Jacuzzi M$950/1340; ♿) Above the Pizza Rolandi restaurant and run by the same friendly family. All rooms are comfy and well kept, with tiled floors and (some) balconies. Prices span four distinct seasons.

Villa Kiin (Map p876; ☎ 877-10-24; www.villakiin.com; Calle Zazil-Ha s/n; d M$990-1690) This is the best buy in this budget range. Beautiful *cabañas* right by the beach offer something similar to what's in Tulum, while palm-shaded hammocks and a common kitchen make it easy to do nothing all afternoon.

TOP END

Hotel Playa de la Media Luna (Map p876; ☎ 887-07-59; www.playamedialuna.com; Sección Rocas, lotes 9 & 10, Punta Nte; old rooms M$400-600, new rooms M$950-1500; ⌘ ⌨) The budget rooms are a pretty good deal as you get to use the hotel's pool, though the beds are a bit springy. The rooms in the new house are a bit fancier, some with ocean views, all featuring bedspreads that should have left this world when *Three's Company* went off the air. Big spenders should head next door to the Hotel Secreto.

Hotel Na Balam (Map p876; ☎ 877-02-79; fax 877-04-46; www.nabalam.com; Calle Zazil-Ha 118; r low/high season M$1500/2400, ste M$3000/3600; ⌘ ⌨) Butterflies flit around the beautiful hibiscus and palm garden, and many rooms face Playa Norte. All rooms are decorated with simple elegance, and have safes, hammocks, private balconies or patios…and no TVs. The hotel offers yoga and meditation classes as well as massage services, and has a pool and restaurant.

Eating

ourpick Mañana (Map p876; ☎ 877-05-55; cnr Matamoros & Guerrero; dishes M$20-70; ☽ 8am-4pm; ⓥ) A good-vibe place with colorful hand-painted tables, super-friendly service and some excellent veggie options – the hummus and veggie baguette is the restaurant's signature dish – Mañana is perhaps the best lunch spot on the island.

La Lomita (Map p876; Juárez; mains M$40-120; ☽ 9am-10:30pm Mon-Sat) 'The Little Hill' serves good, cheap Mexican food in a small, colorful setting. Seafood and chicken dishes predominate. Try the fantastic bean and avocado soup, or *ceviche*.

Viva Cuba Libre (Map p876; Hidalgo; mains M$60-90; ☽ 5pm-midnight Tue-Sun) It competes for decibel levels with neighboring restaurants, but really, we all like Cuban *son* more than bad disco remixes, don't we? Apart from that, you get a well-deserved break from Mexican fare with *ropa vieja* (slow-cooked shredded beef), Cuban lobster and other Caribbean favorites. Mojitos are two for M$50. Viva Cuba indeed!

Mininos (Map p876; Av Rueda Medina; mains M$60-130; ☽ 11am-9pm) A tiny, colorfully painted shack with a sand floor right on the water, Mininos dishes up cocktails of shrimp, conch and octopus, as well as heaping plates of delicious *ceviche* and seafood soups.

Inside the remodeled **mercado municipal** (town market; Guerrero) are a couple of stalls selling hot

food cheap – a plate of chicken *mole* and rice, or tuna with olives in a tortilla, can go for as little as M$15.

Xpress Super (Map p876), a chain supermarket on the plaza, has a solid selection of groceries, baked goods and snacks.

Drinking & Entertainment

Isla Mujeres' highest concentration of nightlife is along Hidalgo, and hot spots on or near the beach form an arc around the northern edge of town.

Poc-Na Hostel (Map p876; cnr Matamoros & Carlos Lazo; ☽ sunset-sunrise) Has a beachfront joint with bonfires and more hippies than all the magic buses in the world. It's a scene, but it's a chill, cooled-out scene.

Fayne's (Map p876; Hidalgo; ☽ 5pm-midnight) One of the latest disco–bar–restaurants, often featuring live reggae, salsa and other Caribbean sounds.

Getting There & Away

There are several points of embarkation to reach Isla Mujeres. The following description starts from the northernmost port and progresses southeast (see Map p869). To reach Puerto Juárez or Punta Sam from downtown Cancún, catch any bus (M$4) displaying those destinations and/or 'Ruta 13' as it heads north on Av Tulum. Some R1 (Zona Hotelera; M$6.50) buses make the trip as well; ask before boarding.

PUNTA SAM

Car ferries, which also take passengers, depart from Punta Sam, about 8km north of Cancún center, and take about an hour to reach the island. Departure times are 8am, 11am, 2:45pm, 5:30pm and 8:15pm from Punta Sam, and 6:30am, 9:30am, 12:45pm, 4:15pm and 7:15pm from Isla Mujeres. Walk-ons and vehicle passengers pay M$15; drivers are included in the fare for cars (M$190), vans (M$240), motorcycles (M$75) and bicycles (M$60).

PUERTO JUÁREZ

About 4km north of the Cancún city center (15 minutes by bus) is Puerto Juárez. Enclosed, air-con express boats depart from here for Isla Mujeres (M$35 one-way, 25 minutes) every 30 minutes from 6am to 8:30am, then hourly until 12:30am with a final departure at 9pm; they rarely leave on time.

ZONA HOTELERA

Services from the following two spots in the Zona Hotelera change names and schedules frequently; ask your concierge to check for you before heading out to catch boats from any of the following places. All take about 25 minutes to reach Isla Mujeres.

El Embarcadero

Shuttles depart from this dock at Playa Linda four times daily in low season, between 9:30am and 1:30pm, returning from Isla Mujeres at 10:30am, 1:30pm, 3:30pm and 5:15pm. The one-way fare (M$75) includes soft drinks. High season sees up to seven departures each way. El Embarcadero is a beige building between the Gran Costa Real Hotel and the channel, on the mainland side of the bridge (Blvd Kukulcán Km 4).

Playa Tortugas

The **Isla Shuttle** (☎ 883-34-48) leaves from the dock on Playa Tortugas (Blvd Kukulcán Km 6.35) at 9:15am, 11:30am, 1:45pm and 3:45pm, returning from Isla Mujeres at 10:15am, 12:30pm, 3:30pm and 6:30pm. The one-way fare is M$90.

Getting Around

BICYCLE

Cycling is a great way to get around the island. A number of shops rent bikes for about M$20/80 an hour/day. Some places ask for a deposit of about M$100. **David** (Map p876; ☎ 044-998-860-00-75; Av Rueda Medina), near Abasolo, has a decent selection.

BUS & TAXI

Buses depart about every 25 minutes (but don't bank on it) from next to the Centro de Convenciones (near the back of the market) or from the ferry dock, and head along Av Rueda Medina, stopping along the way. You can get to Hacienda Mundaca, within 300m of the Turtle farm, and as far south as Playa Lancheros (1.5km north of Playa Garrafón). Get taxis from the stand or flag one down. Taxi rates are set by the municipal government and posted at the taxi stand just south of the passenger ferry dock. As always, agree on a price before getting in.

MOTORCYCLE & GOLF CART

Inspect the bike carefully before renting. Costs vary, and are sometimes jacked up in high season, but generally start at about M$100 per hour, with a two-hour minimum, M$300 all day (9am to 5pm) and M$350 for 24 hours.

Many people find golf carts a good way to get around the island, and caravans of them can be seen tooling down the roads. They average M$150/450 per hour/day and M$550 for 24 hours. A good, no-nonsense place for both bikes and golf carts is **Pepe's Moped Rentals** (Map p876; ☎ 877-00-19; Hidalgo).

PARQUE NACIONAL ISLA CONTOY

Spectacular Isla Contoy is a bird-lover's delight: a national park and sanctuary that is an easy day trip from Isla Mujeres. About 800m at its widest point and more than 7km long, it has dense foliage that provides ideal shelter for more than 100 species of birds, including brown pelicans, olive cormorants, turkey birds, brown boobies and frigates, as well as being a good place to see red flamingos, snowy egrets and white herons.

Most of the trips stop for snorkeling both en route to and just off Contoy, which sees about 1500 visitors a month. Bring binoculars, mosquito repellent and sunscreen.

For M$100 per person, a park biologist will take you on a tour of Laguna Puerto Viejo, a prime nesting site; funds go toward park upkeep and research projects. Contact the **park headquarters** (☎ 998-877-01-18) on Isla Mujeres. **Amigos de Isla Contoy** (www.islacontoy.org) has an office in downtown Cancún, and their website has good information on the island's ecology.

Getting There & Away

Daily visits to Contoy are offered by the Isla Mujeres **fisherman's cooperative** (Map p876; ☎ 998-877-13-63; Av Rueda Medina). The trip (M$500 per person) lasts from 9am to 5pm and includes a light breakfast, lunch (with fish caught en route), snorkeling (gear provided), park admission, scientific information on the island, and your choice of purified water, soft drinks or beer.

ISLA HOLBOX

☎ 984 / pop 2000

Isn't life great when it's low-fi and low-rise? That's the attitude on friendly Isla Holbox (hol-bosh), with its sand streets, colorful Caribbean buildings and lazing, sun-drunk dogs. The water is not the translucent

A GAME OF DOMINOS – SWIM WITH THE WHALE SHARKS

Between mid-May and mid-September, massive whale sharks congregate around Isla Holbox to feed on plankton. The best time to swim with these gentle giants is in July. A trip will cost you M$800, plus M$20 to visit the marine reserve.

The WWF has been working with the local community since 2003 to develop responsible practices for visiting the whale sharks. Only three swimmers (including your guide) are allowed in the water at a time when swimming with whale sharks. You are not allowed to touch the fish, and are required to wear either a life vest or a wetsuit to ensure you do not dive below them.

Willy's Tours (x875-20-08; holbox@hotmail.com, Av Tiburón Ballena near Mini Súper Besa) offers whale shark (M$800 per person), birding (M$800 to M$1200 per boat), crocodile (M$2270 per boat) and fishing (M$3500 per boat) tours. Boats can accommodate six to 12 people.

turquoise common to Quintana Roo beach sites, because here the Caribbean mingles with the darker Gulf of Mexico.

The island is about 30km long and from 500m to 2km wide, with seemingly endless beaches, tranquil waters and a galaxy of shells in various shapes and colors. Lying within the 1541 sq km Yum Balam reserve, Holbox is home to more than 150 species of bird, including roseate spoonbills, pelicans, herons, ibis and flamingos. In summer, whale sharks congregate relatively nearby in unheard-of quantities.

Orientation & Information

Budget hotels and most of the town's restaurants are clustered around the plaza. A few *cabañas* are further out along the island's northern shore in what locals call the Zona Hotelera. The island has no bank or ATM, and many places to stay and eat do not accept credit cards.

Dial ☎ 066 for police, fire or medical assistance.

Sleeping

Posada La Raza (☎ 875-20-72; Juárez; s with fan/air-con M$250/400, d with fan/air-con M$350/500; ☒) A modest, clean one-story place on the west side of the *parque*. Rooms have one double and one single bed. Fan-cooled rooms have ceiling and pedestal fans, making for good circulation. Guests have use of a small kitchen and hand-laundry facilities, and can hang clothes or sunbathe on the roof.

Posada Los Arcos (☎ 875-20-72; saul954@hotmail .com; Juárez; d with fan M$350, with air-con M$400-550; ☒) Next door to Posada La Raza, this is a touch more upscale. Unfortunately, cracks in the doorframes means tons of mosquitoes can get in (a problem that's easily remedied by buying a mosquito coil and burning it near the door before you go to bed). Its rooms are located around a central courtyard, and all have hot and cold water. Rates rise by 50% in summer.

our pick **Hotel La Palapa** (☎ 875-21-21; www .hotellapalapa.com; d low/high season M$500/700; ☒) Arguably the best midrange option on the island, Palapa is brand-spanking new, and offers cozy beachfront rooms, private patios (complete with hammocks), and a cloistered beach area complete with an outdoor *fogata*. It's 100m east of Juárez along the beach.

Posada Mawimbi (☎ /fax 875-20-03; www.mawimbi .net; d low/high season M$400/600, ste low/high season M$800-1000; ☒) Mosquito nets are a welcome luxury in this pleasant, two-story place just off the beach and about three blocks east of Juárez. Many rooms also have a balcony and hammock, and some have kitchenettes.

Villas Delfines (☎ /fax 875-21-97; www.holbox.com; bungalows M$1200-1500) This eco-tel on the beach about 1km east of town composts waste, catches rainwater and uses solar power. Its large beach bungalows are built on stilts, fully screened and fan-cooled. The hotel rents kayaks and has a restaurant that offers very reasonable meal plans.

Eating

La Isla del Colibrí (breakfast M$35-60, mains M$50-160; ☯ 8am-1pm & 5-10:30pm) A small restaurant in a gaily painted, Caribbean-style wooden house on the southwest corner of the *parque*. It serves huge fruit plates, breakfasts (and coffee), *licuados*, juices and a variety of meat and seafood dishes.

Buena Vista Grill (☎ 875-21-02; mains M$100-200; ☯ 11am-9pm) This casual eatery next to Faro Viejo has plastic chairs, but serves up grilled fish specialties including whole grilled fish or fillets wrapped in banana leaves. The day of the week it is closed varies.

ourpick Los Pelicanos (☎ 998-192-45-75; mains M$60-200; ☺ 5pm-midnight, closed Mon) Half a block south from the plaza's southeast corner, this friendly eatery is lauded by locals as the best restaurant in town. The house specialty is homemade pasta with your choice of sauce. They serve up other Italian favorites and a smattering of seafood dishes, including a pepper-seared tuna and a delicious fish soup.

Getting There & Around

A *barco* (boat) ferries passengers (M$40, 25 minutes) to Holbox from the port village of Chiquilá nine times daily from 5am to 6pm in winter, 6am to 7pm in summer. Buses departing Chiquilá usually wait for the boat to arrive. Smaller, faster and wetter *lanchas* make the crossing whenever anyone's willing to pay M$250 for the entire boat (up to about six people with gear; the fare is higher after dark).

Two Mayab buses leave Cancún daily for Chiquilá (M$70, 3½ hours) at 7:50am and 12:40pm. There's also an Oriente bus from Valladolid (M$70, 2½ hours) at 2:45am. From Mérida, take an overnight Noreste bus to Chiquilá (M$124, 7 hours) at 11:30pm.

Taking a taxi from Cancún is another possibility; you may be able to get a taxi for M$600.

OFF QUINTANA ROO'S BEATEN TRACKS

Many Maya communities are beginning to welcome tourism – it may be the only way to maintain their language and culture as mass migration to boom towns like Cancún draws away the best and brightest, and children ask to study English rather than Yucatec Maya.

Organizations like **Puerta Verde** (www .puertaverde.com.mx) are helping these communities build tourist infrastructure. Two of the program's projects can be found on the road to Chiquilá in the towns of Solferino and San Ángel. You can go kayaking or biking or, learn about medicinal plants in San Ángel. Further north, Solferino has an orchid garden, jungle camping spots and canopy tours.

Buses (all 2nd class) leave Chiquilá for Cancún (M$70) at 7:30am and 1:30pm; Tizimín (M$50) at 7:30am, 1:30pm and 4:30pm; Valladolid (M$70) at 5:30am; and Mérida (M$124) at 5:30am.

If you're driving you can either park your vehicle in the Chiquilá parking lot for M$30 per day (8am to 6pm or any fraction thereof) or take your chances parking it on the pier (which is crowded in high season).

Rentadora El Brother (☎ 875-20-18; cart per hr/day/ 24hr M$100/600/800), on Juárez near the beach rents golf carts.

PUERTO MORELOS

☎ 998 / pop 3000

Halfway between Cancún and Playa del Carmen, Puerto Morelos retains its quiet, small-town feel despite the building boom north and south of town. While the village offers enough restaurants and bars to keep you entertained by night, it's really the shallow Caribbean waters that draw visitors here. Unfortunately, Hurricanes Wilma and Emily knocked down most of the beach's lovely palms – those naughty girls. In their munificence, they did leave behind the sparkling sand beaches. One of the best reasons to come to Puerto Morelos is to hit the artisans' market, one block south of the plaza's west corner.

Two kilometers south of the turnoff for Puerto Morelos is the **Jardín Botánico Yaax Che** (admission M$70; ☺ 9am-5pm Mon-Sat; ♿), a 600,000 sq meter nature reserve with nearly 3km of trails through several native habitats.

For chilling cenote action, check out the 'eco-park' **Boca del Puma** (☎ 577-64-20; www .bocadelpuma.com, 16km west of Puerto Morelos, near the village of Vallarta; ♿) or **Siete Bocas** (☎ 13km west of Puerto Morelos, M$50; ♿), which has seven mouths and some serious tourism development going on.

Orientation & Information

Puerto Morelos' central plaza is 2km east of Hwy 307 nearly at the end of the main road into town (the main dock is the true end of the road). There's an HSBC ATM on the plaza.

Alma Libre Bookstore (☎ 871-07-13; www.alma librebooks.com; ☺ 10am-3pm & 6-9pm Tue-Sat, 4-9pm Sun, closed Jul-Sep)

Dive Puerto Morelos (☎ 206-90-84; www.divepuerto morelos.com; ☺ 8am-7pm)

Goyo's (☎ 221-26-79) On the plaza. Offers jungle tours (adult/child under 12 M$400/200)

Sleeping

Posada Amor (☎ 871-00-33; www.posadaamor.com; s & d from M$380, tr & q M$500) About 100m southwest of the plaza, this posada has been in operation for many years. The simple whitewalled rooms have some creative touches, and ocean-blue bedspreads seem just right.

Posada El Moro (☎ 871-01-59; www.posadaelmoro .com; Av Gomez; s/d M$500/750; 🖳) It has cheery geraniums in the halls and courtyard, and white walls with red trim. Rooms are slightly stuffy, and some have kitchenettes. All have couches that fold out into futons, and there's a small plunge pool. Rates include continental breakfast. Prices drop substantially in low season. All in all, you're probably better off at the Amor.

Hotel Hacienda Morelos (☎ /fax 871-04-48; www .haciendamorelos.com; d M$890; 🖾 🖳) On the waterfront about 150m south of the plaza, the Morelos has 15 very appealing, breezy rooms with sea views, kitchenettes and air-con, as well as a small pool and a good restaurant. This is great value.

Eating

Tío's (mains M$15-30; 🕑 6am-11pm) A modest, friendly place directly across from the lighthouse, just off the northeast corner of the plaza. Serves great fish tacos in the morning (three for M$18!), and good Yucatecan and Mexican dishes.

Le Café d'Amancia (sandwiches M$20-40; 🕑 8am-3pm & 6-10pm; 🛛Ⓥ) This is a spotlessly clean place with pleasing ambience on the southwest corner of the plaza. It serves bagels, sandwiches, pies, coffee and fruit and veggie *licuados*. There's internet machines (FKA computers) upstairs.

Hola Asia (☎ 871-06-79; mains M$70-120; 🕑 1-10pm Wed-Mon) On the south side of the plaza, this Asian restaurant has become a local institution.

John Gray's Kitchen (☎ 871-06-55; Av Niños Héroes L6; mains M$100-200; 🕑 6-10pm Mon-Sat) One block west and two blocks north of the plaza, this 'kitchen' turns out some truly fabulous food. The eclectic menu changes frequently.

Getting There & Away

Most Playa Express and Riviera buses that travel between Cancún and Playa del Carmen drop you on the highway. Some Mayab buses enter town; the Riviera bus running between

Cancún airport and Playa del Carmen will sometimes enter the town on request. The 2nd-class bus fare from Cancún is M$17. *Colectivos* to/from Cancún cost M$4.

Taxis are usually waiting at the turnoff to shuttle people into town (M$20), and there's often a taxi or two near the plaza to shuttle people back to the highway.

PLAYA DEL CARMEN
☎ 984 / pop 100,400

Playa del Carmen, now the third-largest city in Quintana Roo – its population more than doubled over the past five years – is the hippest city in all of the Yucatán Peninsula. Sitting coolly on the lee side of Cozumel, the town's beaches are jammed with superfit Europeans – they let Americans in, too, if they meet the weight requirements! The waters aren't as clear as those of Cancún or Cozumel, and the beach sands aren't quite as champagne-powder-perfect as they are further north, but still Playa (as it's locally known) grows and grows.

With daily cruise ship visitors, Playa is starting to feel like a mass-tourism destination, but it retains its European chic, and one need just head two blocks west of haughty-taughty 5 Av to catch glimpses of real Mexico.

Orientation & Information

Playa is mostly laid out on an easy, one-way grid. Quinta Av (*keen*-ta; 5 Ave) is the most happening street in town, especially along its pedestrian stretch (the Tourist Zone). La Nueva Quinta begins at Calle 22 and stretches north for 10 blocks. The main bus terminal is at the intersection of Quinta Av and Juárez, but there is another one further away on Calle 12.

Banamex (cnr Calle 12 & 10 Av)

Centro de Salud (☎ 873-04-93; cnr 15 Av & Av Juárez)

THOSE MYSTERIOUS ALUXES

Aluxes (a-loosh-es) are Yucatecan forest sprites, and many of the Maya still believe they can bring good or bad luck, even death, to those around them. Therefore, when forests are cleared, whether to make a field or build a house, offerings of food, alcohol and even cigarettes are made to placate them.

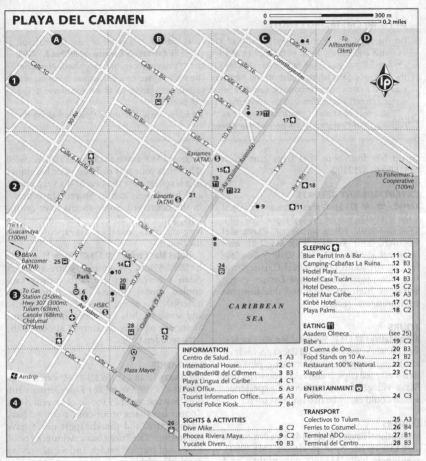

PLAYA DEL CARMEN

YUCATÁN PENINSULA

L@v@nderi@ del C@rmen (Calle 2 No 402; 8am-10pm Mon-Sat) Conveniently has an internet café in front of the *lavandería*.

Post office (cnr 15 Av & Av Juárez; 9am-4pm Mon-Fri)

Tourist information office (873-28-04; cnr Av Juárez & 15 Av; 9am-8:30pm Mon-Fri, to 5pm Sat & Sun)

Tourist police kiosk (873-26-56; 24hr)

Activities

DIVING & SNORKELING

Dive Mike (803-12-28; www.divemike.com; Calle 8) offers snorkeling tours for M$350. To tag along on a dive boat is M$100.

At **Phocea Riviera Maya** (873-12-10; www.phocearivieramaya.com; 1 Av) French, English and Spanish are spoken. **Yucatek Divers** (803-13-63; www.yucatek-divers.com; 15 Av) has German,

French, English, Spanish and Dutch speakers, and offers handicapped/limited-mobility dives.

BEACHES

Beachgoers will agree that it's pretty darn nice here. If crowds aren't your thing, go north of Calle 38, where a few scrawny palms serve for shade. Many go topless in Playa (though it's not a common practice in most of Mexico, and generally frowned upon by locals – except the young bucks, of course). Mamita's Beach, north of Calle 28, is considered the best place to free the girls.

FISHING

Fisherman's Cooperative (984-1309892; kabulyuc@hotmail.com; Beachfront kiosk near Av Constituyentes) This

YUCATÁN PENINSULA

DETOUR: CRISTALINO CENOTE

On the west side of the highway south of Playa del Carmen is a series of cenotes that you can visit and usually swim in for a price. Among these is **Cristalino Cenote** (adult/child M$40/20; ☒ 6am-5:30pm), just south of the Barceló Maya Resort. It's easily accessible, only about 70m from the entrance gate, which is just off the highway. The well-tended cenote has mangrove on one side and a large open section you can dive into by climbing a ladder up to a ledge above it. The water extends about 20m into an overhung, cavelike portion.

Two more sinkholes, Cenote Azul and El Jardín de Edén, are just south of Cristalino along the highway. But Cristalino is the best of the three.

---

co-op has four-hour that trips run from M$1800 to M$2100.

ENTERTAINMENT RESORTS

Xcaret (☎ 984-871-52-00; www.xcaret.com; adult/child 5-12yr M$676/338, with buffet & snorkel gear M$971/481; ☒ 8:30am-9pm), 10km south of Playa del Carmen, and **Xel-Há** (☎ 998-883-32-93; www.xel-ha.com; adult/child 5-11yr M$382/264; ☒ 9am-6pm; ☒), 45km south of Playa del Carmen, are two 'eco-resorts'. Both have Disney-esque activities, high price tags and questionable environmental records.

TOURS

Alltournative (☎ 873-20-36; www.alltournative.com; Av 5 Nte, L3 M200; ☒ 9am-7pm Mon-Sat) Packages include zip-lining, rappelling and kayaking, plus custom-designed trips. It also takes you to nearby Maya villages for an 'authentic' experience, which could easily be had on your own.

Courses

International House (☎ 803-33-88; www.ihrivieramaya .com; Calle 14) has Spanish classes (M$2000), residence hall (M$300 per night) and home stays (M$280 per night). **Playa Lingua del Caribe** (☎ 873-38-76; www.playalingua.com; Calle 20) offers Spanish (M$1850), Maya or cooking classes.

Sleeping

BUDGET

Hostel Playa (☎ 803-32-77; www.hostelplaya.com; Calle 8; dm M$120, d M$300, tr M$450) While it's a bit away from the center, this is Playa's best youth hostel. The best thing about this spirited place is the ambience: it has a huge, central common area and a great kitchen, and both beer and spirits are allowed until 12:30am, when people either head to bed or go out to the clubs.

Camping-Cabañas La Ruina (☎ /fax 873-04-05; laruina@prodigy.net.mx; Calle 2; campsites or hammock spaces per person M$100, d without bathroom M$200, d M$300-550; ☒) Pitch your tent or hang your hammock in a large lot near the beach. It's very casual, and beach gear can be stored (insecurely) in the courtyard. Some rooms have ceiling fans, some have air-con – the cheapest are bare and bleak, and the most expensive front the beach.

Hotel Mar Caribe (☎ 873-02-07; cnr 15 Av & Calle 1; r M$350-550; ☒) A simple, secure and very clean nine-room place with mostly fan-cooled rooms (there's three rooms with air-con). The owners speak French, Spanish and some English. One can almost imagine Steinbeck working on a novel at one of the dark wooden tables.

MIDRANGE

Hotel Casa Tucán (☎ /fax 873-02-83; www.casatucan .de; Calle 4; r M$500-650; ☒ ☒) This German-run hotel is a warren of 29 rooms of several types. Rooms have fans or air-con, a couple have kitchenettes, and the cheapest don't have bathrooms. The Tucán has a swimming pool, a pleasant tropical garden and a café serving good, affordable food.

Playa Palms (☎ 803-39-08; www.playapalms.com; Av 1 Bis, btwn Calles 12 & 14; d low/high season M$720/1330; ☒ ☒) A rip-roaring deal in low season (get the best price online), Playa Palms is right on the beach. The shell-shaped rooms have balconies that look out to the ocean past the curly-whirly dip pool. Go with the cheaper studios to get the best views at the best price. All rooms have kitchenettes.

our pick **Kinbé Hotel** (☎ 873-04-41; www.kinbe.com; Calle 10; d low/high season M$640/830, ste M$1220/1690; ☒) An Italian-owned and operated hotel, it has 29 clean, simple but elegant rooms with lovely aesthetic touches, azure bedspreads, a gorgeous lush courtyard garden and a breezy rooftop terrace with fab views from the 3rd floor.

TOP END

Blue Parrot Inn (☎ 206-33-50, in the US 800-435-0668; Calle 12; r M$2330-5370; 🗶 🖵) Many of the charming units have terraces, sea views and full kitchens. But it's a bit pricey to not be right on the ocean. It also has an immensely popular bar, the Blue Parrot (right).

Hotel Deseo (☎ 879-36-20; www.hoteldeseo.com; 5 Av; d M$1680-2380; 🗶 🖵 🖳) If you can still afford your rock-and-roll lifestyle, then you're going to love the hi-fi lounge atmosphere of Deseo. There's a very chill lounge and plunge pool right in front of your blindingly white room (white is evidently the color of desire).

Eating

Head out of the Tourist Zone to find cheap, quality eats such as great grilled chicken from **Asadero Olmeca** (mains M$30; 🕑 7am-6pm), next to the Tulum-bound *colectivos*. There's a ton of cheap **food stands** on Av 10 between Calles 8 and 10 near the center.

El Cuerna de Oro (cnr Calle 2 & 10 Av; set meals US$3-5; 🕑 7am-10pm) Hearty, home-style set meals are served in this casual eatery near the bus station. You get a giant portion of your selected dish (the three or four options change nightly) plus rice, beans and unlimited refills of the nightly drink, such as hibiscus water or iced tea. The breakfasts are skippable.

La Guacamaya (cnr Calle 1 Sur & Av 30; meal M$60; 🕑 noon-10pm Mon-Sat, to 5pm Sun) Locals love this large open-air restaurant. Veggies beware: if it doesn't have hoofs, it's unlikely to make it onto the menu. Try the *tablazo*, a monstro mixed grill with every cut of meat imaginable for less than M$100.

Babe's (Calle 10; mains M$50-100; 🕑 noon-11:30pm Mon-Sat, 5-11:30pm Sun; 🆅) Babe's serves some excellent Thai food, including a yummy home-style *tom kha gai* (chicken and coconut-milk soup) brimming with veggies. Excellent Vietnamese salad (with shrimp and mango) is another specialty. Most dishes can be done vegetarian, and to mix things up a bit the Swedish cook has some tasty Greek items on the menu as well. There's another Babe's along the Nueva Quinta.

ourpick Restaurant 100% Natural (☎ 873-22-42; cnr Quinta Av & Calle 10 mains M$35-100; 🕑 7am-11pm; 🆅) The trademarks of this quickly establishing chain – vegetable- and fruit-juice blends, salads, various vegetable and chicken dishes and other healthy foods – are delicious and filling.

Xlapak (☎ 879-35-95; Quinta Av; breakfast M$30, lunch & dinner M$70-180; 🕑 8am-11pm) Serves delicious food at unbelievably low prices. Lunch and dinner consists of a starter, a main dish (accompanied by rice, steamed veggies and garlic bread) and a dessert. Try the chicken with *chaya* (a spinachlike green) salsa and wash it down with one of a wide selection of juices and drinks. The restaurant is very nicely done up like a Maya temple, with faithfully rendered reproductions of Maya murals and plants everywhere.

Entertainment

Venues here come and go, so ask around if you're wondering where the party is (or where it isn't).

Blue Parrot Bar (☎ 873-00-83; Calle 12 at beach; 🕑 11am-4am) This is the Blue Parrot Inn's immensely popular open-sided *palapa* beachfront bar with swing chairs, a giant outdoor dance stage, indoor section if the weather's bad…and lots of sand.

ourpick Fusion (Calle 6; 🕑 till late) Groove out beachside under that Playa moon at Fusion. There's live music most nights.

Getting There & Away

BOAT

Ferries to Cozumel (M$110 one-way) leave at 6am, 8am, 9am, 10am, 11am, 1pm, 3pm, 5pm, 6pm, 7pm, 9pm and 11pm. The air-conditioned catamaran takes about half an hour, depending on weather. Buy tickets at the booth on Calle 1 Sur. An open-air boat (same ticket but running less regularly) takes 45 minutes to an hour; it operates mostly in the summer season.

BUS

Playa has two bus terminals; each sells tickets and provides information for at least some of the other's departures. The newer one, **Terminal ADO** (20 Av), just east of Calle 12, is where most 1st-class bus lines arrive and depart. Riviera's buses (which don't entirely deserve the '1st-class' designation anyhow) use the old terminal. A taxi from Terminal ADO to the main plaza will run about M$15.

The old bus station, **Terminal del Centro** (cnr Av Juárez & Quinta Av), gets all the 2nd-class (called 'intermedio' by such lines as Mayab) services. Riviera buses to Cancún and its airport have a separate ticket counter on the Av Juárez side of the terminal.

Destination	Fare	Duration	Frequency
Cancún	M$34	1hr	numerous 4am-midnight
Cancún International Airport	M$80	45min-1hr	frequent 8am-6:15pm
Chetumal	1st-class M$19	5-5½hr	9 daily
	2nd-class M$18	5-5½hr	frequent 1:30am-11:15pm
Chichén Itzá	M$18	3-4hr	1 daily
Cobá	M$68	1-1¾hr	2 daily
Mérida	M$310	5hrs	freqeunt
Palenque	M$540	12-13hr	1 daily
San Cristóba de Las Casas	M$780	16-18hr	1 daily
Tulum	M$22	1hr	frequent
Valladolid	M$77-140	2½-3½hr	2 daily

COLECTIVOS

Colectivos are a great option for cheap travel southward to Tulum (M$25, 45 minutes). They depart from Calle 2 near 20 Av as soon as they fill (about every 10 or 15 minutes) from 5am to 10pm. They will stop anywhere along the highway between Playa and Tulum, charging a minimum of M$10. Luggage space is somewhat limited, but they're great for day trips.

ISLA COZUMEL

☎ 987 / pop 73,200

An immensely popular diving spot since 1961, when Jacques Cousteau, led by local guides, showed its spectacular reefs to the world, Cozumel lies 71km south of Cancún. Measuring 53km by 14km, it is Mexico's largest island. Called Ah-Cuzamil-Peten (Island of Swallows) by its earliest inhabitants, Cozumel has become a world-famous diving and cruise ship destination. Hurricane Wilma did some serious damage to the snorkeling sites around the island, but most of the deep-water reefs missed the brunt of the storm. Sadly, the squadrons of eagle rays have dwindled, due to overfishing of the shellfish stocks – no shellfish, no eagle rays.

While diving and snorkeling are the main draws around here, the tourist zone offers lots of shopping 'deals' (often not very cheap) and a pleasant town square to spend the afternoon. In February there is a festive Carnaval, which brings dancers festooned with feathers out into the streets. There

are also some small Maya ruins and a few eco-themed parks.

History

Maya settlement here dates from AD 300. During the Postclassic period Cozumel flourished as a trade center and, more importantly, a ceremonial site. Every Maya woman living on the Yucatán Peninsula and beyond was expected to make at least one pilgrimage here to pay tribute to Ixchel (the goddess of fertility and the moon) at a temple erected in her honor. Archaeologists believe this temple was at San Gervasio, a bit north of the island's geographical center.

At the time of the first Spanish contact with Cozumel (in 1518, by Juan de Grijalva and his men), there were at least 32 Maya building groups on the island. According to Spanish chronicler Diego de Landa, a year later Cortés sacked one of the Maya centers but left the others intact, apparently satisfied with converting the island's population to Christianity. Smallpox introduced by the Spanish wiped out half the 8000 Maya and, of the survivors, only about 200 escaped genocidal attacks by conquistadors in the late 1540s.

The island remained virtually deserted into the late 17th century, its coves providing sanctuary for several notorious pirates, including Jean Lafitte and Henry Morgan. In 1848 indigenous people fleeing the War of the Castes began to resettle Cozumel. At the beginning of the 20th century the island's (by then mostly *mestizo*) population grew, thanks to the craze for chewing gum. Cozumel was a port of call on the chicle export route, and locals harvested the gum base on the island. After the demise of chicle Cozumel's economy remained strong owing to the construction of a US air base here during WWII.

When the US military departed, the island fell into an economic slump, and many of its people moved away. Those who stayed fished for a living until 1961, when Cousteau's documentary broadcast Cozumel's glorious sea life to the world, after which the tourists began arriving almost overnight.

Orientation & Information

It's easy to make your way on foot around the island's only town, San Miguel de Cozumel. The waterfront boulevard is Av Rafael Melgar; along Melgar south of the main ferry dock

ISLA COZUMEL

0   10 km
0   6 miles

(Muelle Fiscal) is a narrow sand beach. The main plaza is opposite the ferry dock. The airport is 2km northeast. There are ATMs, banks and internet joints on the plaza.

Cozumel Hyperbaric Research (Map p888; ☎ 872-01-03; Calle 6 Nte) In the Médica San Miguel clinic.

Express Lavandería (Map p888; ☎ 872-29-32; Calle Dr Adolfo Rosado Salas; ⏰ 8am-9pm Mon-Sat, 8:30am-4pm Sun) Self-serve washing and drying costs M$50 per load.

Fama (Map p888; ☎ 872-50-20; Av 5 Nte; ⏰ 9am-10pm Mon-Sun) Carries books and periodicals in English and Spanish.

Post office (Map p888; cnr Calle 7 Sur & Av Rafael Melgar; ⏰ 9am-5pm Mon-Fri)

Tourist information booth (Map p888; ☎ tourist information 869-02-11) Operated by the town's tourist information office.

Tourist police (Map p888; cnr Calle 11 Sur & Rafael Melgar; ⏰ 8am-11pm) Patrol the island and staff a kiosk.

Sights & Activities

MUSEO DE LA ISLA DE COZUMEL

Exhibits at this fine **museum** (Map p888; ☎ 872-14-34; Av Rafael Melgar; admission M$30; ⏰ 8am-5pm) present a clear and detailed picture of the island's flora, fauna, geography, geology and ancient Maya history.

DIVING

Despite the massive hit of Hurricane Wilma, Cozumel – and its 65 surrounding reefs – remains one of the most popular diving destinations in the world. It has fantastic year-round visibility (commonly about) and a

SAN MIGUEL DE COZUMEL

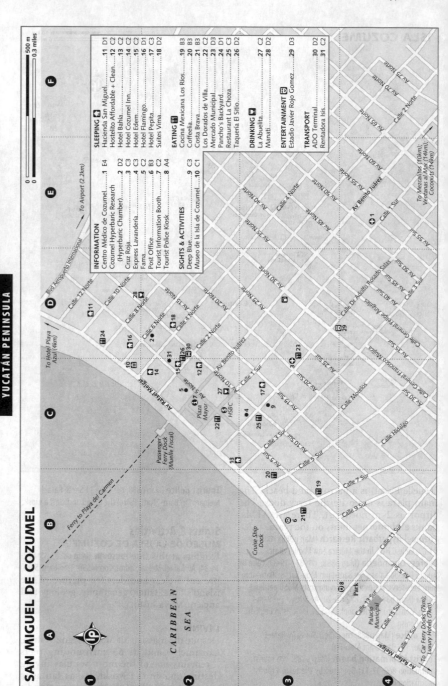

INFORMATION

Centro Médico de Cozumel	1 E4
Cozumel Hyperbaric Research (Hyperbaric Chamber)	2 D2
Cruz Roja	3 C3
Express Lavandería	4 C3
Fama	5 C2
Post Office	6 B3
Tourist Information Booth	7 C2
Tourist Police Kiosk	8 A4

SIGHTS & ACTIVITIES

Deep Blue	9 C3
Museo de la Isla de Cozumel	10 C1

SLEEPING ☐

Hacienda San Miguel	11 D1
Hostelito Affordable + Clean	12 C2
Hotel Bahía	13 C2
Hotel Cozumel Inn	14 C2
Hotel Edem	15 C2
Hotel Flamingo	16 D1
Hotel Pepita	17 C2
Suites Vima	18 D2

EATING ☐

Cocina Mexicana Los Ríos	19 B3
Coffeelia	20 B3
Costa Brava	21 B3
Los Dorados de Villa	22 D3
Mercado Municipal	23 D3
Pancho's Backyard	24 D1
Restaurant La Choza	25 C3
Taquería El Sitio	26 D2

DRINKING ☐

La Abuelita	27 C2
Manatí	28 D2

ENTERTAINMENT ☐

Estadio Javier Rojo Gómez	29 D3

TRANSPORT

ADO Terminal	30 D2
Rentadora Isis	31 C2

RESPONSIBLE DIVING

Please consider the following tips when diving, and help preserve the ecology and beauty of reefs:

■ Never use anchors on the reef, and take care not to ground boats on coral.

■ Avoid touching or standing on living marine organisms, or dragging equipment across the reef. Polyps can be damaged by even the gentlest contact. If you must hold on to the reef, touch only exposed rock or dead coral.

■ Be conscious of your fins. Even without contact, the surge from fin strokes near the reef can damage delicate organisms. Take care not to kick up clouds of sand, which can smother organisms.

■ Practice and maintain proper buoyancy control. Major damage can be done by divers descending too fast and colliding with the reef.

■ Take great care in underwater caves. Spend as little time within them as possible, as your air bubbles may be caught within the roof and thereby leave organisms high and dry. Take turns to inspect the interior of a small cave.

■ Resist the temptation to collect or buy corals or shells, or to loot marine archaeological sites (mainly shipwrecks).

■ Ensure that you take home all your rubbish and any litter you may find as well. Plastics in particular are a serious threat to marine life.

■ Do not feed fish.

■ Minimize your disturbance of marine animals. *Never* ride on the backs of turtles.

For important diver safety information, please refer to the boxed text, p964.

---

jaw-droppingly impressive variety of marine life that includes spotted eagle rays, moray eels, groupers, barracudas, turtles, sharks, brain coral and some huge sponges. The island has strong currents (normally around 3 knots), making drift dives the standard, especially along the many walls. Always keep an eye out (and your ears open) for boat traffic as well. It's best not to snorkel alone away from the beach area.

The top dives in the area include **Santa Rosa Wall**, **Punta Sur Reef**, **Colombia Shallows** and **Palancar Gardens**. Prices vary, but in general expect to pay about M$880 for a two-tank dive (less if you bring your own BCD and regulator), M$650 for an introductory 'resort' course and M$4000 for PADI open-water certification. For more information, pick up a copy of Lonely Planet's *Diving & Snorkeling Cozumel*.

There are scores of dive operators on Cozumel. The following are some reputable ones that come recommended. Some offer snorkeling and deep-sea fishing trips, as well as dives and diving instruction.

Deep Blue (Map p888; ☎ /fax 872-56-53; www.deep

bluecozumel.com; Av 10 Sur) This PADI, NAUI, TDI and IANTD operation has very good gear and fast boats that give you a chance to get more dives out of a day.

Victor Brito Barreiro (☎ /fax 872-32-23; www.angel fire.com/ga/cozumeldiving/MMT.htm) Based south of town. Victor is head of Cozumel's diving instructors association and has many years of experience. Highly recommended.

If you encounter a decompression emergency, head immediately to one of Cozumel's hyperbaric chambers (p887).

SNORKELING

Good snorkeling can be found at Casitas and Dzul-Há. Snorkelers are required to pay M$20 for park admission. The best snorkeling sites are reached by boat. A half-day boat tour will cost from M$350 to US$500. **Ramón Zapata** (☎ 044-987-100-22-56) runs snorkeling trips leaving from Playa Palancar for about M$250 per person, but you'll need to make your own way to the beach.

EXPLORING THE REST OF THE ISLAND

In order to see most of the island you will have to rent a vehicle or take a taxi; cyclists will need to brave the regular strong winds. The following route will take you south from San Miguel, then counterclockwise around the island. There are some places along the way to stop for food and drink, but it's good to bring water all the same.

Several sites along the island's west coast offer horseback riding (although most of the horses look ready to keel over). The asking price is M$160 an hour; bargain hard.

Parque Chankanaab

This **park** (Map p887; admission M$160; ⏰ 7am-6pm; ♿) is a popular snorkeling spot, especially when cruise ships are in port, though there's not a lot to see in the water beyond some brightly colored fish and deliberately sunken artificial objects. The beach is a nice one, though, and 50m inland is a limestone lagoon surrounded by iguanas and inhabited by turtles. You're not allowed to swim or snorkel there, but it's picturesque all the same. The beach is lined with *palapas* and fiberglass lounge chairs, and you can rent snorkel and dive equipment.

Dolphin shows are included in the admission price, as is the use of dressing rooms, lockers and showers. There's a small archaeological park containing replica Olmec heads and Maya artifacts, a small museum featuring objects imported from Chichén Itzá, and a botanical garden with 400 species of tropical plants. Other facilities include a restaurant, a bar and snack shops. A taxi from town costs M$100 one way.

El Cedral

This Maya ruin is the oldest on the island. It's the size of a small house and has no ornamentation, but costs nothing to visit and is easy to reach, unlike San Gervasio and other ruins on Cozumel. It's 3.5km down a signed paved road that heads off to the left (east) a kilometer or two south of Nachi-Cocom's access road, hiding amid a forest of pole structures painted yellow and white and erected as souvenir stalls. El Cedral is thought to have been an important ceremonial site; the small church standing next to the tiny ruin today is evidence that the site still has religious significance for locals.

Playa Palancar

About 17km south of town, Palancar is another great beach. It has a beach club renting hydro bikes, kayaks, snorkel gear and sail-

boats, plus a restaurant and a dive operation. Near the beach, Arrecife Palancar (Palancar Reef) has some very good diving (Palancar Gardens), as well as fine snorkeling (Palancar Shallows), though the shallow spots were marked by Wilma.

Parque Punta Sur

The southern tip of the island has been turned into a rather overpriced 'ecotouristic' **park** (Map p887; ☎ 872-09-14; admission M$100; ⏰ 9am-5pm). Visitors board an open vehicle for the 3km ride to visit picturesque Celarain **lighthouse** and the small nautical museum at its base. Another vehicle carries visitors to **Laguna de Colombia**, part of a three-lagoon system that is the habitat of crocodiles and many resident and migratory waterfowl. Crocs can be seen (when they feel like it) from shore, via a trail through mangrove or a bridge over the lagoon.

East Coast

The eastern shoreline is the wildest part of the island and presents some beautiful seascapes and many small blowholes (there's a bunch around Km 30.5). Swimming is dangerous on most of the east coast because of riptides and undertows. With a bit of care you can sometimes swim at Punta Chiqueros, Playa Chen Río and Punta Morena. As you travel along the coast, consider stopping for lunch or a drink at the Rasta Bar (Km 29.5), El Galeon (Km 43.1) or Coconuts (Km 43.5). El Galeon rents surf and boogie boards for M$200 and M$70 per hour, respectively.

Punta Molas

Beyond where the east coast highway meets the Carretera Transversal, intrepid travelers may take a poorly maintained, infrequently traveled and almost impossible to find track toward Punta Molas, the island's northeast point, accessible only by all-terrain vehicles (ATV) or on foot. About 17km up the road are the Maya ruins known as **El Castillo Real**, and a few kilometers further is **Aguada Grande**. Both sites are quite far gone, their significance lost to time. In the vicinity of Punta Molas are some fairly good beaches and a few more minor ruins.

San Gervasio

This **Maya complex** (Map p887; admission M$60; ⏰ 7am-4pm) is Cozumel's only preserved ruins, and a prime example of the local government's efforts to milk dollars out of cruise-ship passengers. San Gervasio is thought to have been the site of the sanctuary of Ixchel, goddess of fertility, and thus an important pilgrimage site at which Maya women – in particular prospective mothers – worshipped. But its structures are small and crude, and the clay idols of Ixchel were long ago destroyed by the Spaniards.

Sleeping
BUDGET

our pick **Hostelito Affordable + Clean** (Map p888; ☎ 869-81-57; www.hostelito.com; Av 10; dm/d M$120/350) The name says it all: this brand-spanking new Hostelito is affordable *and* clean. There's one shared dorm room downstairs for boys and girls with bamboo privacy screens, giant lockers and amazingly clean showers. Upstairs you'll find a great terrace, kitchen and common area, as well as a six-person group room and two doubles. They have wi-fi and luggage storage.

Hotel Edem (Map p888; ☎ 872-11-66; Calle 2 Nte 124; d with fan/air-con M$180/320; ✷) A great location and saintly rates make the Edem a prime deal. It has a turtle-filled fountain and a friendly Siamese cat, and the no-nonsense señora keeps the doors locked after 9pm. Rooms are clean and simple, with hammock hooks and scalding hot showers. There's a deposit for the threadbare towels (like anyone would run off with them!).

Hotel Cozumel Inn (Map p888; ☎ 872-03-14; fax 872-31-56; Calle 4 Nte; d with fan/air-con M$320/370; ✷ ✸) A green building with 26 well-maintained rooms with good beds and a small (sometimes suspect!) swimming pool, the Cozumel is a good deal, especially in high season. Mustiness airs out quickly.

Hotel Pepita (Map p888; ☎ /fax 872-00-98; Av 15 Sur; d M$400; ✷) The HP's owner, María Teresa, takes pride in her work, and it shows. This is the best economy hotel in the city. It's friendly, with well-maintained rooms grouped around a garden. All have two double beds, refrigerators and air-con (many catch a good breeze), and there's free morning coffee.

MIDRANGE

Suites Vima (Map p888; ☎ /fax 872-51-18; Av 10 Nte; s/d M$400/500; ✷ ✸) Has spotless and spacious modern rooms with tiled floors, Barney Rubble–hard beds, good air-con and bath-

rooms, fridges, tables and chairs. The decor is mint green, highlighted by other pastels. A small swimming pool with a current to swim against lies in a green area in back. No kids aged under 13, please.

Hotel Bahía (Map p888; ☎ 872-90-90, 800-227-26-39; www.suitesbahia.com; cnr Av Rafael Melgar & Calle 3 Sur; d incl breakfast with balcony/ocean view M$660/800; ✷ ▯) Offers some rooms with sea views and balconies. All rooms have cable TV, fridge and air-con. Rates include continental breakfast.

Hotel Flamingo (Map p888; ☎ 872-12-64; www .hotelflamingo.com; Calle 6 Nte 81; r M$850-1600; ✷) The colorful Hotel Flamingo is a nicely decorated place with spacious air-conditioned rooms (some with fridges) sporting direct-dial phones. Common areas include a leafy courtyard where you can eat breakfast, a 2nd-floor pool table, a bar, and a rooftop sundeck with good sea views. Wi-fi access makes it a good choice for laptop-toters. Make reservations via the internet to save a few pesos.

TOP END

Hacienda San Miguel (Map p888; ☎ 872-19-86; www .haciendasanmiguel.com; Calle 10 Nte; r from M$1050; ✷) It's a quiet place built and furnished to resemble an old hacienda, and niceties such as bathrobes and continental breakfast served in your room make this very good value. It offers divers' packages, and long stays can bring rates down by amazing amounts. Check the web for deals.

Presidente Intercontinental Cozumel (Map p887; ☎ 872-95-00; www.intercontinental.com; Carretera a Chankanaab Km 6.5; r from M$2000; ✷ ✸) This is one of the island's oldest luxury hotels. It has a lovely beach and 253 posh guestrooms, many with sea views, set amid tropical gardens and swimming pools. Wild (large!) iguanas roam the grounds. Unlike the all-inclusives further south, the Presidente is sufficiently close to town to allow you several dining options; truth be told, the city has grown south around the hotel.

Hotel Playa Azul (Map p887; ☎ 869-51-60; www .playa-azul.com; Carretera a San Juan Km 4; d/ste from M$2350/2800; ✷ ✸) This is in the sedate area north of town on its own pretty little stretch of beach (it's not deep but it's a gem), and there's good snorkeling (current is sometimes strong). All rooms have a sea view, a balcony or terrace, and one king or two queen beds. The hotel has a bar, restaurant and gorgeous pool, and guests can play golf free at a nearby course. They still get you with a mandatory M$250 cart fee.

Eating
BUDGET

Cheapest of all eating places are the little market *loncherías* (lunch stalls) next to the Mercado Municipal on Calle Dr Adolfo Rosado Salas between Avs 20 and 25 Sur.

Taquería El Sitio (Map p888; Calle 2 Nte; M$15-30; ☺ 7am-1pm) For scrump-diddily-umptious tacos and tortas, head over to El Sitio. They fancied-up the canopy-covered eating area with a mural of a cruise ship and jumping dolphins. It's two doors east of the Hotel Edem.

our pick Coffeelia (Map p888; ☎ 872-74-02; Calle 5 Sur; breakfast M$40-70, set meals M$57; ☺ 7:30am-11pm Mon-Sat, 8am-1pm Sun; Ⓥ) A great way to start or finish the day: head over to Coffeelia for warm smiles and delicious food – and great coffees, including espressos. Coffeelia (rhymes with Ophelia) is a focal point for Cozumel's art community. The menu includes quiche, good salads and vegetarian dishes, and organic Chiapas coffee roasted fresh locally. Thursday is story night in the pleasant garden area.

Cocina Mexicana Los Ríos (Map p888; ☎ 987-800-90-43; cnr Av 5 Sur & Calle 7 Sur; mains M$30-40; ☺ 7am-5pm Mon-Sat) *Ceviches*, chicken and seafood: all simple and good. Red plastic furniture and Bellafonte tunes are part of this cheap, clean café not far from the post office. *Comida corridas* (prix-fixe menus) are M$30 (a smoking deal), and get you a main entrée, a soup, tortillas, soda or other nonalcoholic drinks and dessert.

Costa Brava (Map p888; ☎ 869-00-93; Calle 7 Sur 57; mains M$50-120; ☺ 6:30am-11pm) Painted in bright, preschool primary colors, this casual place with its lovely *Virgencita* shrine has good prices on lobster dishes, chicken and shrimp.

Los Dorados de Villa (Map p888; ☎ 872-01-96; cnr Calle 1 Sur & Av 4 Sur; mains M$50-120; ☺ 8am-midnight) Near the edge of the plaza, it specializes in food from the Distrito Federal (Mexico City and surroundings), but has a wide variety of Mexican dishes including seafood and cuts of meat. The spinach crêpes are great as are the complimentary chips.

Restaurant La Choza (Map p888; ☎ 872-09-58; cnr Dr Adolfo Rosado Salas & Av 10 Sur; mains M$80-170; ☺ 7am-10:30pm) An excellent and popular restaurant specializing in authentic regional cuisine. All mains come with soup. La Choza sometimes offers a *comida corrida* (M$100) in the afternoon.

Pancho's Backyard (Map p888; ☎ 872-21-41; cnr Av Rafael Melgar & Calle 8 Nte; mains M$110-160; ☺ 10am-11pm Mon-Sat, 4-10:30pm Sun) Very atmospheric, set in a beautifully decorated inner courtyard. The food's not bad, either!

Entertainment

Cozumel's nightlife is quiet and subdued. Try the plaza first if you're looking to mingle with the wilder cruise-ship crowd. You are best off asking around, as the clubs change frequently.

La Abuelita (Map p888; cnr Calle 1 Sur & Av 10 Sur) Grab a drink with locals at the 'little grandma.' Turns out granny is quite an enterprising lady: there's an Abuelita Dos *and* Tres in other parts of town.

Manati (Map p888; cnr Calle 8 Nte & Av 10 Nte) Get there early for the *comida corrida* or stay late to listen to live music (Thursday to Saturday) in this cute bistro-bar combo.

Estadio Javier Rojo Gómez (Map p888; cnr Av Dr Adolfo Rosada Salas & Av 30 Sur) hosts rock concerts, *lucha libre* wrestling matches and just about any other event you can think of.

Getting There & Away
AIR

Some airlines fly direct from the USA; European flights are usually routed via the USA or Mexico City. **Continental** (☎ 800-900-50-00, in the US & Canada 800-231-0856; www.continental.com) has direct flights from Newark and Houston. **Delta** (☎ 800-123-47-10, in the US & Canada 800-241-4141; www.delta.com) has a direct flight from Atlanta. **Mexicana** (☎ 800-801-20-10; www.mexicana.com) flies direct to Mexico City, Miami and Dallas. There are currently no direct flights from Cancún to Cozumel; you'll need to fly through Mexico City. In the end, you're better off taking a bus–ferry combo.

BOAT

Passenger ferries run to Cozumel from Playa del Carmen, and vehicle ferries leave the Calica facility (officially known as the Terminal Marítima Punta Venado) south of Playa del Carmen. However, the vehicle ferry does not take rentals. Unless you're driving your own car, use the Playa passenger ferry

(M$110 one-way) instead. There's normally a passenger ferry every hour to and from Cozumel, depending on the season. The ferry runs from 6am to midnight. Schedules are not set in stone, but currently there are six departures from Cozumel for Calica between 4:30am and midnight. Six ferries return from Calica between 2am and 9pm. Sundays have four departures in each direction. Fares are M$500 for cars and M$800 for a van-sized vehicle (both including the driver). You need to line up at least one hour before departure (earlier is better, they say).

BUS

OK, it may sound silly, but you can actually get long-distance bus tickets in advance at the **ADO terminal** (Map p888; ☎ 872-17-06; cnr Av 10 & Calle 2 Nte; ⏲ 6:30am-9pm). Tickets are for services from Playa del Carmen's bus terminal for all over Yucatán and Mexico.

Getting Around

TO/FROM THE AIRPORT

The airport is about 2km northeast of town. You can take a *colectivo* from the airport into town for about M$70 (slightly more to the hotels south of town), but you'll have to take a taxi (M$120 from town to M$200 from southern hotels) to return to the airport.

BICYCLE

A full day's bicycle rental typically costs M$80 to M$150 (depending on season), and can be a great way to get to the northern and southern beaches on the west side of flat Cozumel. The completely separate bicycle/scooter lane on the Chankanaab highway sees a good deal of car traffic from confused tourists and impatient cab drivers, so be careful.

CAR

A car is the best way to get to the island's further reaches, and you'll get plenty of offers to rent one. All rental contracts should automatically include third-party insurance *(daños a terceros)*, which runs about M$100 per day. Check that taxes are included in the price you're quoted – they often are not. Collision insurance is usually about M$150 extra with a M$5000 deductible for the cheapest vehicles. Rates start at around M$450 including third-party insurance (collission is extra and may be covered by your credit card), though you'll pay more during late December and January. There are plenty of agencies around the main plaza, but prices drop about 50% from the dock to the fringes of the tourist zone.

When renting, check with your hotel to see if it has an agreement with any agencies, as you can often get discounts. Note that some agencies will deduct tire damage (repair or replacement) from your deposit, even if tires are old and worn. Be particularly careful about this if you're renting a 4WD for use on unpaved roads; straighten out the details before you sign.

One fairly no-nonsense place, with cars in good shape, is **Rentadora Isis** (Map p888; ☎ 872-33-67; Av 5 Nte btwn Calles 2 & 4 Nte). VW Beetles rent for around M$300 for 24 hours, with little seasonal variation in prices.

If you rent, observe the law on vehicle occupancy. Usually only five people are allowed in a vehicle. If you carry more, the police will fine you. You'll need to return your vehicle with the amount of gas it had when you signed it out or pay a premium. This can be tricky as agencies usually don't rent out cars with full tanks. There's a gas station on Av Benito Juárez five blocks east of the main square.

MOTORCYCLE

Solo touring of the island by motorcycle or scooter is OK provided that you have experience with them and with driving around Mexico. Two people on a bike is asking for trouble, though, as the machines' suspension is barely adequate for one. Many auto drivers speed and pass aggressively on Cozumel, and it has its share of *topes* (speed bumps). Riders are injured in solo crashes nearly every day, and deaths, usually involving other vehicles, are not uncommon. That said, rental opportunities abound, with prices ranging from M$180 to M$400 a day (depending on the agency, the season, volume of business and whether the stars are aligned properly), but you may be able to haggle down to less, with third-party insurance and tax included. Collision insurance is not usually available for motorcycles: you break, you pay.

To rent, you must have a valid driver's license and leave a credit-card slip or put down a deposit (usually M$1000). There is a helmet law, and it is enforced.

Rentadora Isis (see above) rents scooters for M$180 per day – you need to return them before dark.

EXPLORE MORE SOUTH OF PLAYA DEL CARMEN

South of Playa del Carmen are several worthwhile coastal villages. These areas tend toward the upscale, and offer spectacular diving, snorkeling and some amazing beaches. Here are a few of our faves:

- **Rancho Punta Venado** (www.puntavenado.com) Five kilometers south of Xcaret, this is a great spot for horseback riding.
- **Paamul** Eighty-seven kilometers south of Cancún, the secluded beach makes this area popular with visiting RV travelers, sea turtles and divers alike. **Paamul Hotel** (www.paamul.com.mx) offers lodging. **Scuba-Mex** (www.scubamex.com) provides diving services.
- **Xpu-Há** This is a sugary-sweet beach area 95km south of Cancún. Visit www.locogringo.com for lodging information.
- **Tankah** A few kilometers south of the Hwy 307 turnoff for Punta Solimán you'll find this cozy beach community. There's great diving, a series of seven cenotes and some decent midrange hotel options. Visit www.tankah.com for info.

TAXI

As in some other towns in the Yucatán, the taxi syndicate in Cozumel wields a good bit of power. Fares in and around town are M$30 per ride; luggage may cost extra. Carry exact change as it's not uncommon for drivers to claim they are unable to provide it.

AKUMAL
☎ 984

Famous for its beautiful beach and large, swimmable lagoon, Akumal (Place of the Turtles) does indeed see some sea turtles come ashore to lay their eggs in the summer, although fewer and fewer arrive each year, thanks to resort development. Akumal is one of the Yucatán Peninsula's oldest resort areas and consists primarily of pricey hotels, condominiums and residential developments (occupied mostly by Americans and Canadians) on nearly 5km of wide beach bordering four consecutive bays. With the exception of Villa Las Brisas, all sights and facilities are reached by taking the first turnoff, Playa Akumal, as you come south on the highway. It's about 500m from the highway to the entrance.

Activities

Although increasing population is taking its toll on the reefs that parallel Akumal, diving remains the area's primary attraction. Hurricane Dean also reportedly did some minor damage to the area's reef, though we were unable to verify this independently when we passed through town. Ask about conditions before you commit to a trip.

Dive trips and deep-sea fishing excursions are offered by **Akumal Dive Shop** (☎ 875-90-32; www.akumal.com). It also offers snorkeling trips to the reef and beaches unreachable by car for M$250, fishing for M$1500 and diving for M$700.

At the northern end of Akumal, **Laguna Yal-Kú** (adult/child M$75/40; ⏰ 8am-5:30pm; ♿) is a beautiful lagoon 2km from the entrance. The rocky lagoon, without a doubt one of the region's highlights, runs about 500m from its beginning to the sea. It is home to large schools of brightly colored fish and the occasional visiting turtle and manta ray. Cabs from the Playa Akumal entrance charge about M$60 to the lagoon. In an effort to protect the lagoon's fragile environment, sunscreen is prohibited.

You can also simply find a place to park and snorkel or swim on your own, as the shallow waters are pretty and fun. Close to the shore you will not have problems with currents, though at times the surf can be rough.

About 1km south of Xel-Há is the turnoff for **Cenote Dos Ojos**, which provides access to the enormous Dos Ojos cave system. You can take guided snorkel and dive tours of some amazing underwater caverns, floating past illuminated stalactites and stalagmites in an eerie wonderland. With an aggregate length of nearly 57km, it's the third-largest underwater cave system in the world. Ox Bel Ha and Nohoch Nah Chich (about 97km and 61km total length, respectively), are relatively nearby.

Hidden Worlds (☎ 877-85-35; www.hiddenworlds .com.mx) is an American-run outfit offering guided snorkeling tours for M$400 and one- /two-tank dives for M$500/900.

Another way to see part of the system is through the **Dos Ojos** (☼ 8am-4:30pm) operation, a short distance north of Hidden Worlds. It's run by the Maya community who own the land. The entrance fee is M$100 and snorkeling gear is M$70 more. You can dive here as well, if accompanied by a certified cave diver.

Sleeping & Eating

Villa Las Brisas (☎ /fax 876-21-10; www.aventuras -akumal.com; r M$450-2300) On the beach in Aventuras Akumal, this is an attractive, modern place with two hotel-type rooms, some one- and two-bedroom condos and a studio apartment – all under two roofs. The friendly owners Horacio and Kersten speak five Western languages! The turnoff is 2.5km south of the turnoff for Playa Akumal.

Que Onda (☎ 875-91-01; www.queondaakumal.com; r low/high season M$700/900; ▣ ▨) It's set amid an expanse of greenery in a fairly residential area only 50m from Laguna Yal-Ku. The six fan-cooled rooms have white-tiled floors and great beds; some have sofas, and the upstairs ones have terraces. The hotel also offers a gorgeous pool, free internet access, bicycles and snorkeling gear, and half-price admission to the lagoon. The restaurant serves delicious pasta.

Just outside the entrance to Playa Akumal are two minimarkets that stock a good selection of inexpensive food. La Cueva del Pescador restaurant, inside and just north of the entrance, serves three meals a day. Que Onda (see above) has a nice restaurant and serves coffees from 11am to 4pm. Dinner is served from 5pm to 10pm; the bar closes around midnight.

BAHÍAS DE PUNTA SOLIMÁN
☎ 984

These two beautiful, protected bays are separated by a narrow point, 123km south of Cancún and 11km north of Tulum. The area offers good wildlife watching, kayaking, snorkeling and dining opportunities.

A few hundred meters in after the signed turnoff from Hwy 307, you can bear left (north) to reach **Oscar y Lalo's** (☎ 804-69-73; mains M$60-100; campsites per person M$30; ☼ 10am-8pm), a picturesque restaurant that has the entire Bahía Solimán to itself. The kitchen puts out heaping plates of food, including fish fillets and barracuda steaks. Oscar rents **kayaks** (around M$100 an hour); you can paddle out to the reef that shelters the entire mouth of the bay and snorkel or bird-watch. The dense mangrove around the 150m stretch of (somewhat spiky) white beach breeds quite a few mosquitoes and sand flies; you'll want a tent with very good screens if you're camping.

Back on the main access road, heading straight a short distance beyond the turnoff for Oscar's brings you to an intersection. Continuing straight here leads to the end of the point via a road that splits and rejoins itself a few times. The little-traveled track makes a great **nature walk**: you can see both bays, and birding in the perennially dry mangrove area is terrific. Birds of interest here include the Yucatán vireo, Yucatán woodpecker, rose-throated tanager, black catbird and orange oriole.

Turning right (south) at the intersection rather than going straight takes you along the edge of the bay on the other side of the point, also named **Bahía Solimán** (though some call it Bahía de San Francisco). It has terrific coral heads, tons of colorful fish, plenty of grouper and reef sharks, and the occasional sea turtle and even tuna.

A number of **beach houses**, some quite luxurious, line the road along this southern portion of the bay. Most of them rent by the week, at well over M$10,000. A good website for house rentals in the area is www .locogringo.com.

Maya Jardin (☎ 125-88-06; www.mayajardin.com; d M$1250-1900; ▨ ▨) is on the southern end of the bay and offers large rooms, free kayaks and snorkel gear to explore the bay.

The road continues south beyond another point past residential lots, then continues into the Tankah area and loops back northwest to rejoin the highway.

Most people get to Punta Solimán by car, or by taking a bus to Tulum and a taxi from there.

TULUM
☎ 984 / pop 14,800

Tulum's spectacular coastline – with its confectioner sugar sands, jade-green water, balmy breezes and bright sun – make it one of the top beaches in Mexico. Where else can you get all that *and* a dramatically situated Maya ruin?

There are also excellent diving, fun cenotes, great snorkeling, and a variety of lodgings and restaurants to fit every budget.

There is one big drawback. The town center, where the really cheap eats and sleeps are found, sits right on the highway, making it feel more like a truck stop than a tropical paradise. This said, both Cobá to the west and the massive Reserva de la Biosfera Sian Ka'an to the south make doable day trips.

Hurricane Dean brought some minor damage to Tulum's beachfront *cabañas,* but most places should be up and running by the time you read this.

Orientation

Tulum lies some 130km south of Cancún and is spread out over quite a large area. Approaching from the north on Hwy 307 the first thing you reach is Crucero Ruinas, where the old access road (closed to vehicle traffic about 100m in from the highway) heads in a straight line about 800m to the ruins' ticket booth. About 400m further south on Hwy 307 (past the gas station) is the new entrance for vehicles going to the ruins; it leads to a parking lot. Another 1.5km south on the highway brings you to the Cobá junction; turning right (west) takes you to Cobá, and turning east leads about 3km to the north–south road servicing the Zona Hotelera, the string of waterfront lodgings extending for more than 10km south from the ruins. This road eventually enters the Reserva de la Biosfera Sian Ka'an, continuing some 50km past Boca Paila to Punta Allen.

The town center, sometimes referred to as Tulum Pueblo, lies across the highway (called Av Tulum through town) south of the Cobá junction.

Information

Tulum Pueblo has Telmex pay phones, internet cafés, numerous currency-exchange booths (one with an ATM), two **HSBC banks** (☺ 8am-5pm Mon-Sat) and a **post office** (Av Tulum; ☺ 9am-3:30pm Mon-Fri).

Community Tours Sian Ka'an (p904) runs tours to the magnificent Reserva de la Biosfera Sian Ka'an stopping at various ancient Maya sites.

Dangers & Annoyances

If you nod off on the beach, your valuables (and even nonvaluables) may disappear. Bring your own lock if you plan on staying in the cheap no-frills beachfront *cabañas.*

Sights & Activities
TULUM RUINS

The **ruins of Tulum** (admission M$45; ☺ 8am-5pm) preside over a rugged coastline, a strip of brilliant beach and green-and-turquoise waters that will make you want to tear up that return ticket home. It's true the extents and structures are of a modest scale and the late Postclassic design, workmanship and ornamentation are inferior to those of earlier, more grandiose projects – but wow, those Maya occupants must have felt pretty smug each sunrise. Iguanas are everywhere, and many act as if they own the place.

Tulum is a prime destination for large tour groups. To best enjoy the ruins without feeling like part of the herd, you should visit them either early in the morning or late in the afternoon. Parking costs M$40 for cars and M$80 for vans and pickups. A M$20 train takes you to the ticket booth from the entrance, or you could just hoof the 300m. Taxi cabs from town charge M$35 and can drop you off at the old entrance road, about an 800m walk from the ticket booth. There's a less-used foot entrance just north of Cabañas El Mirador.

History

Most archaeologists believe that Tulum was occupied during the late Postclassic period (AD 1200–1521) and that it was an important port town during its heyday. Remember that the Maya sailed up and down this coast, maintaining trading routes all the way down into Belize. When Juan de Grijalva sailed past in 1518, he was amazed by the sight of the walled city, its buildings painted a gleaming red, blue and yellow and a ceremonial fire flaming atop its seaside watchtower.

The ramparts that surround three sides of Tulum (the fourth side being the sea) leave little question as to its strategic function as a fortress. Several meters thick and 3m to 5m high, the walls protected the city during a period of considerable strife between Maya city-states. Not all of Tulum was situated within the walls. The vast majority of the city's residents lived outside them; the civic-ceremonial buildings and palaces likely housed Tulum's ruling class.

The city was abandoned about 75 years after the Spanish conquest. It was one of the

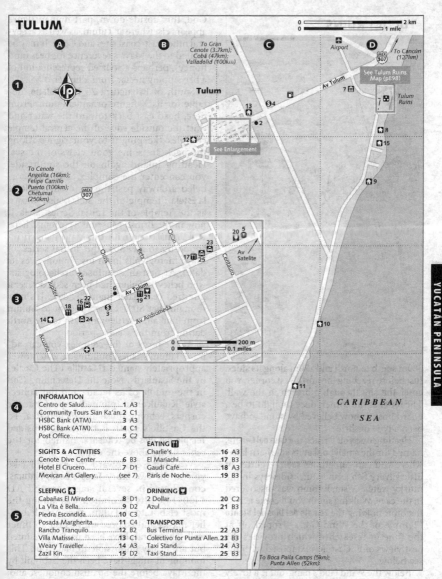

TULUM

last of the ancient cities to be abandoned; most others had been given back to nature long before the arrival of the Spanish. But Maya pilgrims continued to visit over the years, and indigenous refugees from the War of the Castes took shelter here from time to time.

'Tulum' is Maya for 'wall,' though its residents called it Zama (Dawn). The name Tulum was apparently applied by explorers during the early 20th century.

Exploring the Ruins

Visitors are required to follow a prescribed route around the ruins. From the ticket booth, head along nearly half the length of Tulum's enormous **wall**, measuring approximately

TULUM RUINS

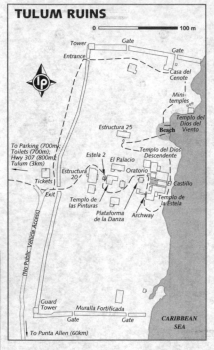

YUCATÁN PENINSULA

380m south to north and 170m along its sides. Just before reaching the northwest corner, you enter the site through a breach in the wall. The **tower** at the corner, once thought to be a guard post, is now believed by some to have been a type of shrine.

Heading east you'll reach the **Casa del Cenote**, named for the small pool at its southern base, where you can sometimes see the glitter of little silvery fish as they turn sideways in the murky water. A small tomb was discovered in the cave. Walking south you'll come across the bluff holding the **Templo del Dios del Viento** (Temple of the Wind God) – roped off at the time of research – which provides the best views of El Castillo juxtaposed with the sea below.

Below the Wind God's hang-out is a lovely little stretch of **beach**. It's quite swimmable when conditions are good, but take note of the lifeguards and the warning flags. After your dip, head west to **Estructura 25**, which has some interesting columns on its raised platform and, above the main doorway (on the south side), a beautiful stucco frieze of the Descending God. Also known as the Diving

God, this upside-down, part-human figure appears elsewhere at Tulum, as well as at several other east-coast sites and Cobá. It may be related to the Maya's reverence for bees (and honey), perhaps a stylized representation of a bee sipping nectar from a flower.

South of Estructura 25 is **El Palacio**, notable for its X-figure ornamentation. From here, head east back toward the water and skirt the outside edge of the central temple complex (keeping it to your right). Along the back are some good views of the sea. Heading inland again on the south side, you can enter the complex through a corbeled archway past the restored **Templo de la Estela** (Temple of the Stela), also known as the Temple of the Initial Series. Stela 1, now in the British Museum, was found here. It was inscribed with the Maya date corresponding to AD 564 (the 'initial series' of Maya hieroglyphs in an inscription gives its date). At first this confused archaeologists, who believed Tulum had been settled several hundred years later than this date. It's now thought that Stela 1 was brought to Tulum from Tankah, a settlement 4km to the north dating from the Classic period.

At the heart of the complex you can admire Tulum's tallest building, a watchtower appropriately named **El Castillo** (The Castle) by the Spaniards. Note the Descending God in the middle of its facade and the Toltec-style 'Kukulcanes' (plumed serpents) at the corners, echoing those at Chichén Itzá. To the Castillo's north is the small, lopsided **Templo del Dios Descendente**, named for the relief figure above the door.

Walking west toward the exit will take you to the two-story **Templo de las Pinturas**, constructed in several stages around AD 1400–1450. Its decoration was among the most elaborate at Tulum and included relief masks and colored murals on an inner wall. The murals have been partially restored but are nearly impossible to make out. This monument might have been the last built by the Maya before the Spanish conquest and, with its columns, carvings and two-story construction, it's probably the most interesting structure at the site.

DIVING & SNORKELING
Cenote Dive Center (☎ 871-22-32; www.cenotedive.com; Av Tulum) is a recommended outfit specializing in guided cave dives, and cenote and cave snor-

keling trips. The staff speak English, Spanish, German and Scandinavian languages.

The dive shop at Zazil-Kin's (right) is a PADI, NACD and TDI operation offering low-cost reef dives and renting snorkel gear for M$100 day.

Snorkeling or swimming right from the beach is possible and fun, but be extra careful of boat traffic (a dive flag is a good idea), as the strip between the beach and reef offshore is traveled both by dive boats and fishermen.

Cenote Angelita

This spectacular cenote is most notable to divers for the unique, curious, even eerie layer of hydrogen sulfide that 'fogs' the water about halfway through the descent. Look up and see the sunlight filtering down through ancient submerged tree branches that are wonderfully creepy, like outstretched witches' arms. The dive is deep and should be done only by experienced divers.

Sleeping

TULUM PUEBLO

You have to use a taxi (or hitchhike) to get to the beach. If you crave sand and surf, consider the Zona Hotelera.

Weary Traveler (☎ 871-23-90; www.wearytraveler.info; Av Tulum; dm M$120; r without/with bath M$300/350; ✗ 🖵) Turn right out of the bus station and walk one block southeast to this fun hostel. A great place to meet friends, the Weary Traveler is known for a full breakfast that includes fruit, eggs, bread, coffee and condiments. There's internet, a shuttle to the beach, and a great central courtyard with hammocks and picnic benches. It even has its own bar. Chilly, pull-style showers and a lack of any shelving for toiletries are the only downsides.

Rancho Tranquilo (☎ 871-27-84; www.ranchotranquilo.com.mx; Av Tulum s/n; dm M$120, r from M$250-480) Another nice option for those looking for hostel-type lodging, Rancho Tranquilo offers a mix of cabañas, dorms and rooms in a low-key, desert-landscaped garden. There's a covered common area and free breakfast. It can get a bit noisy, and for those without wheels it's 300m further southward on Tulum Ave, and pretty dark late at night.

Hotel El Crucero (☎ 871-26-10; www.el-crucero.com; Crucero Ruinas; dm M$85-100; d with fan/air-con M$350/450; ✗ 🖵) You'll feel welcome and well cared for at this friendly hotel. Dorm rooms have

bathrooms and lockers, while air-con rooms are done up in themes, such as the Mexican Mural, Jungle Room and the Lizard Lounge. The hotel has a garden area plus a bar and restaurant, and internet access. You can rent bicycles and store bags as well. It's a 10-minute walk to the ruins, and 15 to the beach. The hotel can arrange low-impact bicycle tours to cenotes. Local artist Enrique Díaz has a gallery here (see p900).

Villa Matisse (☎ 871-26-36; shuvinito@yahoo.com; Av Satélite 19; d low/high season M$400/500) Funky patchwork quilts add a splash of color to the glaringly white clean rooms at the Matisse. Little details like seashell bouquets and fresh plants add an intimacy and closeness. There are even hammocks hanging above the beds in the fan-cooled rooms – a nice touch.

ZONA HOTELERA

The cheapest way to sleep in *cabañas* is to have your own hammock and mosquito net; if you don't, several of the inexpensive places rent them for about M$30 a night. The following picks are ordered north to south.

Cabañas El Mirador (☎ 879-60-19; elfishi@hotmail.com; cabañas with hammock/bed M$130/250) The closest place to the ruins, the Mirador rents tiny 4m x 3m *cabañas* that feel a bit like jail cells – they even stink a little bit. Go for a hammock bungalow as the rooms with beds aren't worth the extra money. There's a decent restaurant with great views sitting up and back from the beach.

Zazil-kin (☎ 984-124-00-82; cabañas without/with bathroom M$400/670) About a 10-minute walk from the ruins, this is a popular place. It has a dive center, a basketball court, a restaurant–bar–disco and a nice stretch of beach. All structures in this little Smurf village are very tidy and nicely painted – Papa Smurf would be proud. The *cabañas*' poles have been filled in with concrete, which makes them more secure (bring your own lock) but hinders ventilation. Be warned that the disco plays music at very high volumes (sometimes until 1am or 2am).

La Vita è Bella (☎ 871-35-01; www.lavitaebella-tulum.com; bungalows low/high season M$1000/2500; s/d without bathroom M$350) Lovely bungalows with tiled floors, big comfy beds, well-screened sliding doors, good bathrooms with colorful basins and wide verandas with hammocks are all on offer here, all overlooking a narrow but nice beach with beach umbrellas and chairs. It's Italian-run (surprise!), so the restaurant serves delicious handmade pastas and thin-crust pizza from its wood-fired oven. Kiteboarding lessons are also offered.

Piedra Escondida (☎ 984-100-38-26; www.piedra escondida.com; r low/high season M$1250/2350) Offers very good service in its large rooms. All have bathrooms and balconies or porches and are nicely decorated; some have excellent views. La Piedra also has a pleasing *palapa*-style restaurant–bar, and shares a small beach with neighboring hotels.

Posada Margherita (☎ 984-100-37-80; www.posada margherita.com; Km 4.5; d low/high season M$1300/2000) Unlike many so-called 'eco-tels,' everything here is totally solar or wind-powered – even the kitchen, which makes amazing food using mainly organic ingredients. All rooms have tiled floors, very good bug screening, 24-hour lights and a terrace or balcony with hammock. The beach here is wide and lovely. The excellent restaurant was being renovated at press time, but should now be up and running. The hotel also has something virtually unheard of in the Yucatán: wheelchair access.

Eating
TULUM PUEBLO
All of the following places are on Av Tulum (Hwy 307). To escape the tourist traffic, you might consider putting the guidebook down for a second, leaving Av Tulum and finding a quiet, friendly *taquería* on a side streets. Most hotels in the Zona Hotelera have surprisingly good restaurants.

Gaudí Café (cnr Av Tulum & Jupiter; mains M$20-60; ☼ 7am-10pm) Just south of the bus station on the same side of the street, Gaudí Café offers great fresh-squeezed juices and good coffee. Spotlessness and relaxing music make it a great way to start the morning.

ourpick El Mariachi (Av Tulum; mains M$65-90; ☼ 7am-3am) They ask you your name when you walk into this tidy little eatery and bar on Tulum, between Orion and Centauro. It seems like a small thing, but it's a barometer for the excellent service and tasty traditional food you are about to enjoy. Popular with locals and tourists alike, this open-air spot delivers yummy slow-cooked pork enchiladas, fresh grilled fish and about every cut of meat you could imagine.

París de Noche (☎ 871-25-32; mains M$70-140; ☼ 11am-11pm Mon-Fri, 7am-11pm Sat & Sun) Serves

some big portions, so bring an appetite or a friend. The French owner won a *Time Out* award at the restaurant he ran in London. He serves a mix of French and Mexican dishes (as well as steaks and seafood) that include escargot, *ceviche* and a delicious green salad with chèvre that's a full meal in itself. There's often two-for-one drink specials and a tasty *comida corrida*.

Charlie's (☎ 871-25-73; mains M$85-140; ☼ 7:30am-11pm Tue-Sun) An old standby with attractive conch-shell decor and a wall made of old glass bottles, it's near the bus station and offers you a choice of indoor or courtyard dining. The food is largely Mexican, with a selection of salads thrown in.

SELF-CATERING
Two small supermarkets provide an alternative to eating out: the Stop 'n' Go, 100m east of Hwy 307 on the road to Cobá, and the Super Mar Caribe, about four blocks north of the bus terminal.

Drinking & Nightlife
Azul (Av Tulum; ☼ 6pm-late) Bathed in white with strips of blue neon, this lounge–disco heats up late.

2 Dollar (Av Tulum) Despite the name, this is a locals' watering hole. It's generally a boys-only club, and there are a few seats outside away from the blaring music.

Shopping
Mexican Art Gallery (☎ 984-745-89-79; inf_art@hotmail .com; ☼ 9am-6pm Mon-Sat) Located at the Hotel El Crucero, it features the brightly colored work of local artist Enrique Diaz, whose motto is to 'paint the colors of Tulum.' His art is vivid and fun, a variety of portraits and landscapes that seem vaguely Picasso-esque.

Getting There & Away
The bus terminal (just a waiting room, really) is toward the southern end of town. When leaving Tulum, you can also wait at Crucero Ruinas (the exit to the ruins) for intercity buses and the *colectivos* to Playa del Carmen.

If you're headed for Valladolid, be sure your bus is traveling the short route through Chemax, not via Cancún. *Colectivos* leave from Av Tulum for Playa del Carmen (M$25, 45 minutes) and Punta Allen (at 2pm), and *colectivos* for Felipe Carrillo Puerto (M$45, one hour) leave from just south of the hostel.

Destination	Fare	Duration	Frequency
Cancún	M$54-67	2hr	numerous
Chetumal	M$107-140	3½-4hr	every 2 hrs
Chichén Itzá	M$101	3½hr	2 daily
Cobá	M$30	45min	about 5 daily
Felipe Carrillo Puerto	M$60	1½hr	numerous, consider taking a *colectivo*
Mahahual	M$122	4hr	1 daily
Mérida	M$172	4hr (2nd-class much longer)	numerous
Playa del Carmen	M$34	1hr	numerous
Valladolid	M$60	2hr	10 daily

Getting Around

Except for the shuttles operated from the youth hostels, there are no *colectivos* out to the beach. You either hitch, ride a taxi, rent a bike or walk. And it's a long walk.

Bicycles can be a good way to get around and usually cost M$150 a day.

Taxi fares are fixed and pretty cheap; from either of the two **taxi stands** (one south of the bus terminal, which has fares posted; the other four blocks north on the opposite side of the street) in Tulum Pueblo to the ruins is M$35. Fares to most *cabañas* mentioned here are M$35 to M$50.

GRAN CENOTE

A little over 3km from Tulum on the road to Cobá is Gran (Grand) Cenote, a worthwhile stop on your way between Tulum and the Cobá ruins, especially if it's a hot day. You can snorkel (M$80) among small fish and see underwater formations in the caverns here if you bring your own gear. A cab from downtown Tulum costs around M$50 one way, or it's an easy bike ride.

COBÁ

☎ 984 / pop 300

Though not as large as some of the more famous ruins, Cobá is 'cool' because you feel like you're in an Indiana Jones flick. It's set deep in the jungle, and many of the ruins have yet to be excavated. Walk along ancient *sacbé* pathways (stone-paved avenues; *sacbeob* is the plural in Maya), climb up vine-covered mounds, and ascend to the top of Nohoch Mul for a spectacular view of the surrounding jungle.

Be careful not to picnic beside the lake, as it has large crocodiles. If you want to snap a picture of a croc, try looking for them near the Club Med in early afternoon from the pier. From a sustainable tourism perspective, it's great to stay the night in small communities like Cobá. The money you spend goes straight to the local economy, encouraging continued rural stewardship and minimizing the mass migration to tourist cities like Cancún. Hiring local guides, buying local crafts and simply stopping here for lunch also helps.

History

Cobá was settled much earlier than nearby Chichén Itzá and Tulum, and construction reached its peak between AD 800 and 1100. Archaeologists believe that this city once covered an area of 50 sq km and held a population of 40,000 Maya.

Cobá's architecture is a curiosity: its towering pyramids and stelae resemble the architecture of Tikal, which is several hundred kilometers away, rather than the much nearer sites of Chichén Itzá and the northern Yucatán Peninsula.

Some archaeologists theorize that an alliance with Tikal was made through marriage, to facilitate trade between the Guatemalan and Yucatecan Maya. Stelae appear to depict female rulers from Tikal holding ceremonial bars and flaunting their power by standing on captives. These Tikal royal females, when married to Cobá's royalty, may have brought architects and artisans with them.

Archaeologists are also baffled by the extensive network of *sacbés* (stone-paved avenues) in this region, with Cobá as the hub. The longest runs nearly 100km, from the base of Cobá's great pyramid Nohoch Mul to the Maya settlement of Yaxuna. In all, some 40 *sacbés* passed through Cobá, parts of the huge astronomical 'time machine' that was evident in every Maya city.

The first excavation was by the Austrian archaeologist Teobert Maler in 1891. There was little subsequent investigation until 1926, when the Carnegie Institute financed the first of two expeditions led by Sir J Eric S Thompson and Harry Pollock. After their 1930 expedition, not much happened until 1973, when the Mexican government began to finance excavation. Archaeologists now estimate that Cobá contains some 6500 structures, of which just a few have been excavated and restored, though work is ongoing.

YUCATÁN PENINSULA

Orientation & Information

The tiny, tranquil village of Cobá, 2.5km west of the Tulum–Chemax road, has a small, cheap hotel, several small, simple and low-cost restaurants and the upscale Villas Arqueológicas Cobá (Club Med) hotel.

The **archaeological site** (admission M$45; ☾ 8am-5pm; ♿) has a parking lot that charges M$15 per car. Be prepared to walk several kilometers on paths, depending on how much you want to see. If you arrive after 11am you'll feel a bit like a sheep in a flock. Bring insect repellent and water; the shop next to the ticket booth sells both at reasonable prices.

A short distance inside, at the Grupo Cobá, is a concession renting bicycles at M$30 per day. Pedi-trikes (two people and driver are M$95 per day) are another popular option for those who are tired or have limited mobility. Guides near the entrance size you up and ask whatever they think you're worth; tours generally run about M$200 to M$400. The Nohoch Mul pyramid is the only structure the public is allowed to climb.

Sights

GRUPO COBÁ

Walking just under 100m along the main path from the entrance and turning right brings you to the **Templo de las Iglesias** (Temple of the Churches), the most prominent structure in the Cobá Group. It's an enormous pyramid, with views from the top taking in the Nohoch Mul pyramid and surrounding lakes, but climbing it is forbidden.

Back on the main path and 30m further along, you pass through the **juego de pelota**, a well-restored ball court.

CONJUNTO DE LAS PINTURAS

Though it's signed to the left at the fork, if you're on foot you can reach the **Conjunto de las Pinturas** (Group of Paintings) by heading toward the Grupo Macanxoc a very short distance and turning left. The temple here bears traces of glyphs and frescoes above its door, and remnants of richly colored plaster inside.

You approach the temple from the southeast. Leave by the trail at the northwest (opposite the temple steps) to see several stelae. The first of these is 20m along, beneath a *palapa*. Here a regal figure stands over two others, one of them kneeling with his hands bound behind him. Sacrificial captives lie beneath

the feet of a ruler at the base. Continue along the path past another badly weathered stela and a small temple to rejoin the Nohoch Mul path and turn right.

GRUPO MACANXOC

About 500m beyond the *juego de pelota*, the path forks. Going straight gets you to the **Grupo Macanxoc**, a group of stelae that bore reliefs of royal women who are thought to have come from Tikal. They are badly eroded, and it's a 1km walk, but the flora along the way is interesting.

NOHOCH MUL

A walk of 800m more brings you to **Nohoch Mul** (Big Mound), also known as the Great Pyramid, built on a natural hill. Along the way is another ball court – at the north end of which lie weathered stelae – and the track then bends between piles of stones (a ruined temple) before passing Templo 10 and Stele 20. The exquisitely carved stela bears a picture of a ruler standing imperiously over two captives. Eighty meters beyond stands the Great Pyramid.

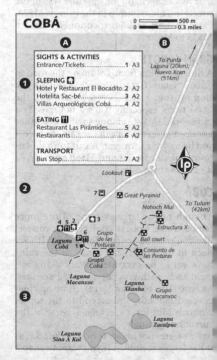

DETOUR: PUNTA LAGUNA

Punta Laguna, 20km northeast of Cobá on the road to Nuevo Xcan, is a fair-sized lake with a small Maya community nearby. The forest around the lake supports populations of spider and howler monkeys, as well as a variety of birds.

A **Tourist Cooperative** (☎ 986-861-40 94) charges M$40 for entrance to the lake area and about M$200 per hour for guided visit. Activities include a zip-line tour (M$125), a cenote rappel (M$200), a shamanic ceremony (M$125) at a 'traditional' altar, and canoeing (M$60 per hour). Intrepid travelers can camp here or reserve a *palapa* for the night.

Public transportation is so sparse as to be nonexistent. In a car, you can reach Punta Laguna by turning southwest off Hwy 180 at Nuevo Xcan and driving 26km, or by heading 18km northeast from the Cobá junction.

At 42m high, the Great Pyramid is the tallest Maya structure on the Yucatán Peninsula. There are two diving gods carved over the doorway of the temple at the top (built in the Postclassic period, AD 1100–1450), similar to the sculptures at Tulum. The view is spectacular!

Sleeping & Eating

There's no organized campsite, but you can try finding a place along the shore of the lake, which is inhabited by crocodiles – local children can show you a safe swimming spot, and you'd do well to heed their advice if you're going near the water.

Hotel y Restaurant El Bocadito (☎ 264-70-70; s/d M$100-150) This place has very basic, fan-cooled rooms all with private bathrooms. Chickens cluck and dogs wander around. The restaurant (mains around M$60) is well run and serves basic food, including an affordable set menu. It will store luggage while you visit the ruins. El Bocadito also serves as Cobá's bus terminal.

Villas Arqueológicas Cobá (☎ 206-70-00; cobc crecol@clubmed.com; s/d/tr M$860/1000/1450; P) A Club Med hotel next to the lake, it was built to resemble an old hacienda, with red-tiled floors and rooms grouped around a large inner courtyard with an expansive swimming pool.

Hotelita Sac-bé (☎ 206-71-40; s/d with fan M$250, with air-con M$400;) Clean and friendly, the Sac-bé is on the opposite side of the street from El Bocadito and about 100m closer to the main road heading out of town. The chickens are a bit noisy in the morning, but it has nice hot showers and comfortable, springy beds.

Restaurant Las Pirámides (mains M$60) A few doors down from the Club Med, it has good lake views and friendly service.

Several small restaurants by the site's parking lot serve inexpensive meals.

Getting There & Away

Most buses serving Cobá swing down in almost to the lake to drop off passengers before turning around. Buses run six to eight times daily between Tulum and Cobá (M$30); six of these also serve Playa del Carmen (M$68, one to 1¾ hours). Buses also run to Valladolid (M$26, 45 minutes) and Chichén Itzá (M$52, 1½ hours).

Day-trippers from Tulum can reach Cobá by forming a group to split the cost of a taxi, which costs about M$500 round-trip, including two hours at the site.

The 31km road from Cobá to Chemax is arrow-straight and in good shape. If you're driving to Valladolid or Chichén Itzá this is the way to go.

TULUM TO PUNTA ALLEN

Punta Allen sits at the end of a narrow spit of land that stretches south nearly 40km from its start below Tulum. There are some charming beaches along the way, with plenty of privacy, and most of the spit is within the protected, wildlife-rich Reserva de la Biosfera Sian Ka'an. Hurricane Dean whipped the region pretty good in late 2007, and the beaches were still littered with debris when we passed through.

The road can be a real muffler-buster between gradings, especially when holes are filled with water from recent rains, making it impossible to gauge their depth. The southern half, south of the bridge at Boca Paila, is the worst stretch – some spots require experienced off-road handling or you'll sink into several feet of sand. It is doable even in a non-4WD vehicle.

There's an entrance gate to the reserve about 10km south of Tulum. Entrance is M$21. At the gate, there's a short nature trail taking you to a rather nondescript cenote (Ben Ha).

This is where DIY adventure really takes off. Bring a couple hammocks, lots of water, a six-pack of *cerveza* and mosquito nets for remote coastal camping. Around 30km from the entrance gate is an excellent camping spot with the lagoon on one side and glorious blue ocean on the other.

At the time of research, one *colectivo* made the three-hour trip daily, leaving Tulum center at 2pm and arriving in Punta Allen about 5pm. Another leaves Punta Allen at 3pm. You may also be able to come on a launch via the mainland, though that is more expensive and less frequent.

Reserva de la Biosfera Sian Ka'an

Over 5000 sq km of tropical jungle, marsh, mangroves and islands on Quintana Roo's coast have been set aside by the Mexican government as a large biosphere reserve. In 1987 the UN classified it as a World Heritage site – an irreplaceable natural treasure.

Sian Ka'an (Where the Sky Begins) is home to howler monkeys, anteaters, foxes, ocelots, pumas, crocodiles, eagles, raccoons, tapirs, peccaries, giant land crabs, jaguars and hundreds of bird species, including *chocolateras* (roseate spoonbills) and some flamingos. There are no hiking trails through the reserve; it's best explored with a professional guide.

Community Tours Sian Ka'an (☎ 984-114-07-50; www.siankaantours.org; Av Tulum) runs tours out of Tulum that include pickup in the Zona Hotelera. They include a guided walk of the interpretive trail at the Muyil archaeological site south of Tulum, and a boat trip or float trip through Lagunas Muyil, Chunyaxché and Boca Paila via an ancient Maya trade route along a natural channel. On the way you can see abundant bird life and visit little-known Maya temples. They also offer snorkeling, birding and fishing trips further into the reserve. Trips cost between M$950 and M$1100. There are discounts for children under 12.

If you can get to Punta Allen, there are three locals with training in English, natural history, interpretation and birding conduct bird-watching, snorkeling and nature tours, mostly by boat, for about M$1000 for five

to six people: **Baltazar Madera** (☎ 984-871-20-01, in Tulum 984-879-82-34), **Marcos Nery** (☎ local phone exchange 984-871-24-24) and **Chary Salazar** (enquire in town at her eponymous restaurant).

Punta Allen

The town of Javier Rojo Gómez is more commonly called by the name of the point 2km south. Hurricane Gilbert nearly destroyed the town in 1988, and there was some damage, and a lot of wind-scrubbed palms, after Hurricane Dean. But Punta Allen is still walking tall. This is truly the end of the road. The 400-some-odd residents mostly work as fishers, and some also work in restaurants that are popular with day-trippers. The village sports a laid-back ambience reminiscent of the Belizean cayes. There's also a healthy reef 400m from shore that offers fishermen, snorkelers and divers wonderful sights.

The area is known primarily for its catch-and-release bonefishing. Tarpon and snook are very popular sport fish as well. The guides listed for Sian Ka'an (left), as well as cooperatives in town (inquire at Galletanes or Vigía Grande), do fishing trips for about M$2000, including lunch. There's also a fishing outfit just north of town called **Pesca Maya** (☎ 998-883-42-04; www.pescamaya.com; ☑ 5am-10pm), which does daily saltwater fly-fishing runs, and it has an onsite restaurant for guests only.

An hour's tour of the lagoon, including turtles, bird-watching and a quick snorkel, costs M$400 to M$500. You'll be offered trips by one of the three co-ops. Encourage your captain not to get so close to birdlife that it is scared away. Though very rare, manatee spottings are possible.

There are no ATMs or internet cafés in town. Electricity generally works between 11am and 2pm, and 4pm to midnight.

SLEEPING & EATING

Posada Sirena (☎ 984-877-85-21; www.casasirena.com; d M$400-600) Offers fully furnished *cabañas* with kitchens and hot-water showers. The rooms are simple and very big; some sport sitting areas and hammocks. There's no maid service, but they can arrange tours.

Cuzán (☎ 983-834-03-53; www.flyfishmx.com; r M$500-900) Just south of the town's center along the main road, Cuzán has ocean-front *cabañas* – one set on the fuselage of an old boat. There's more economic cabins away from the beach. They also offer fishing and snorkeling trips.

Vigía Grande and Galletanes are among several of the town's dining choices, both close to the water and both owned by co ops. They serve Mexican dishes and seafood, naturally including lobster. Neither has a phone, and opening hours vary on the basis of whether any customers are there.

GETTING THERE & AWAY

The best way to reach Punta Allen by public transportation is by *colectivo* out of Tulum: one leaves daily from Tulum center at 2pm and arrives about three hours later. Driving in a rental car is another option, but prepare for 5km/h to 10km/h speeds and more than a few transmission-grinding bumps.

FELIPE CARRILLO PUERTO

☎ 983 / pop 21,500

Now named for a progressive governor of Yucatán, this crossroads town 95km south of Tulum was once known as Chan Santa Cruz, the rebel headquarters during the War of the Castes. Besides its historical and cultural significance, Carrillo Puerto has few attractions other than the only gas station, bank and hotels for some distance around. There's a main square with a clocktower, church and cultural center. Come nighttime, the square fills up as locals take spins around the park in an age-old tradition known as *paseando* (taking a walk). Watching this simple ritual may be enough to keep you occupied for hours – you can even take a couple trips around the plaza yourself.

History

In 1849, when the War of the Castes turned against them, the Maya of the northern Yucatán Peninsula made their way to this town seeking refuge. Regrouping, they were ready to sally forth again in 1850 when a 'miracle' occurred. A wooden cross erected at a cenote on the western edge of the town began to 'talk,' telling the Maya they were the chosen people, exhorting them to continue the struggle against the Spanish and promising victory. The talking was actually done by a ventriloquist who used sound chambers, but the people looked upon it as the authentic voice of their aspirations.

The oracle guided the Maya in battle for more than eight years, until their great victory, conquering the fortress at Bacalar. For the latter part of the 19th century, the Maya in and around Chan Santa Cruz were virtually independent of governments in Mexico City and Mérida.

A military campaign by the Mexican government retook the city and the surrounding area at the beginning of the 20th century, and the talking cross's shrine was desecrated. Many of the Maya fled to small villages in the jungle and kept up the fight into the 1930s; some resisted even into the 1950s.

Carrillo Puerto today remains a center of Maya pride. The talking cross, hidden away in the jungle for many years following the Mexican takeover, has been returned to its shrine, and Maya from around the region still come to visit it, especially on May 3, the day of the Holy Cross.

Sights

The **Santuario de la Cruz Parlante** (Sanctuary of the Talking Cross) is five blocks west of the gas station on Hwy 307. There's no sign at the site, but you can't miss the stone wall with a gate. Some of the town's residents do not like strangers in the sanctuary, and may try to take your camera if they see you using it here.

The **Centro Cultural Chan Santa Cruz** (admission free; 🕙 8am-9:30pm Mon-Fri, 8am-1pm & 6-8pm Sat & Sun), on the plaza, has art exhibitions, workshops, and the occasional exhibit on the War of the Castes.

Sleeping & Eating

Hotel Esquivel (☎ 834-03-44; hotelesquivelfcp@todito .com; Calle 65 No 746; d with fan/air-con M$300/380; 🐱) Around the corner from the plaza and bus terminal, this is the best hotel in town. The air-con rooms are a good deal, with very clean bathrooms and tiled floors, while the fan rooms have good beds and showers, but are dark, windowless and over-perfumed.

Hotel Chan Santa Cruz (☎ 834-00-21; www.hotel chansantacruz.com; cnr Calle 67 & 68; d M$360-400; 🐱) The rooms are just a bit too pink, giving them the feel of Martha Stewart's jail cell, but they are clean, and there's a mighty fine central courtyard complete with gaudy statuary. In the lobby there's an air-hockey table (and we said there was nothing to do in Carrillo Puerto at night)!

Lonchería 25 Horas (Calle 69; sandwhices & tacos M$20; 🕙 24hr) Dirt-cheap without being dirty, this casual eatery sports plastic chairs and fumes of passing trucks, but has a decent selection of eggs, sandwiches, tacos and smoothies. Find it across from the gas station.

Parrilla Galerías (☎ 834-03-13; Calle 65; mains M$40-80) On the plaza, it has the look of a more upscale spot, but serves beer for M$15 and tacos for M$40 for three. The house specialty is a *parrilla* (mixed grill) with lots of accompaniments (M$185 for three people).

Getting There & Away

Most buses serving Carrillo Puerto are *de paso* (they don't originate there).

Colectivos leave for Playa del Carmen (M$110, two hours) and Tulum (M$45, one hour) from Hwy 307 just south of Calle 73.

There are few, if any, gas stations between Carrillo Puertoand Valladolid (Hwy 295), Chetumal (Hwy 307), Tulum (Hwy 307) or José María Morelos (Hwy 184). The one in Mahahual is a 50km detour.

Destination	Fare	Duration	Frequency
Cancún	1st-class M$130	3½-4hr	10 daily
	2nd-class M$100	3½-4hr	hourly to 9pm
Chetumal	1st-class M$94	2-3hr	8 daily
	2nd-class M$54	2-3hr	13 daily
Mérida	1st class M$146	5½hr	1 daily
	2nd-class M$134	5½hr	11 daily
Playa del Carmen	1st-class M$68-76	2½hr	9 daily
	2nd-class M$68-76	2½hr	hourly to 9pm
Ticul	M$100	4½hr	11 daily (change there or at Muna for Uxmal)
Tulum	1st-class M$45	1½hr	9 daily
	2nd-class M$44	1½hr	hourly to 9pm (consider taking a *colectivo*)

THE COSTA MAYA

The Coast south of the Reserva de la Biosfera Sian Ka'an to the small fishing village of Xcalak is often referred to as the Costa Maya. Hurricane Dean did some serious damage to this region, especially the town of Mahahual, but recovery efforts are in place. With amazing beaches and good diving and snorkeling, the region is certain to recover at a quick pace.

Mahahual

Hurricane Dean virtually razed the coastal town of Mahahual, but it is slowly recovering. We passed by just weeks after the hurricane, and the town was still in recovery stage. Rather than eliminate Mahahual from the book entirely, which would only cause further economic hardship for the town's residents, we decided to get a local expert, Kevin Graham, to update the material for us closer to press time.

Now that Mahahual no longer has a cruise ship port – though plans are in place to rebuild it – it may be a bit more welcoming to independent-minded travelers, as it has great beaches, excellent diving nearby, and a fairly laid-back Caribbean appeal. More significantly, Mahahual offers access to **Banco Chinchorro**, the largest coral atoll in the Northern Hemisphere. Chinchorro is some 45km long and up to 14km wide, with its western edge lying about 30km off the coast, and dozens of ships have fallen victim to its barely submerged ring of coral. According to early reports, the Banco Chinchorro may have sustained some serious damage at the hands of Dean. While the reports are splotchy at best – and we were unable to verify the information independently – the mangroves of the above-water portion of the atoll were destroyed, with only the ranger hut left standing.

The atoll and its surrounding waters were made a biosphere reserve (the **Reserva de la Biosfera Banco Chinchorro**) to protect them from depradation. But the reserve lacks the personnel and equipment needed to patrol such a large area, and many abuses go undetected.

There is a ban on wreck dives as many are too shallow (or too looted) for good diving. But there are plenty of other things to see around the bank: coral walls and canyons, rays, turtles, giant sponges, grouper, tangs, eels and, in some spots, reef, tiger and hammerhead sharks. There's good snorkeling as well, including **40 Cannons**, a wooden ship in 5m to 6m of water. Looters have taken all but about 25 of the cannons, and it can be visited only in ideal conditions. The prohibition on wreck dives doesn't apply to snorkelers.

Dreamtime Dive Center (☎ 983-834-58-23; www.dreamtimediving.com; Malecón, 2.7km south of Mahahual) runs trips to stretches of the barrier reef and offers PADI courses.

YUCATÁN PENINSULA

SLEEPING & EATING

Addresses are given as distances from the military checkpoint at the north entrance to town.

Las Cabañas del Doctor (☎ 983-832-21-02; Km 2; cabañas without/with bathroom M$250/350) Across the street from the beach, it offers several fairly simple dwellings. Prices rise by about M$100 in December and Easter week.

Posada Pachamama (☎ 983-834-58-42; www.posada pachamama.net; Km 1; r M$550-750) Located across from the football field, which will become the town plaza on the first street behind the *malecón*, this small comfortable hotel also has a pizzeria.

Doña Marí (mains M$30-50) Septuagenarian Doña Marí is tough as nails. She began digging out the day after the hurricane hit, and eventually moved her operation to the corner of Huchananyu and Calle Hierta Her restaurant still serves tasty fish fillets prepared in various styles, accompanied by beans and tortillas.

GETTING THERE & AROUND

Mahahual is 127km south of Felipe Carrillo Puerto and approximately 100 km northeast of Bacalar. A new ADO bus terminal (a stop, really, operating between 5:30am and 6pm daily) in Mahahual has made getting here easier than ever, though the buses are infrequent. They depart here for Chetumal (M$50, 2½ hours, 6am, 12:30pm and 6pm) and Cancún (M$170, five hours, 8:30am and 6pm), with an additional departure at 3pm on Sundays and Mondays. There's a Pemex gas station if you need to fill your tank.

Xcalak

The rickety wooden houses, beached fishing launches and lazy gliding pelicans make this tiny town plopped in the middle of nowhere a perfect escape. Despite its proximity to Hurricane Dean's Ground Zero in Mahahual, Xcalak (pronounced ish-kah-*lak*) escaped the brunt of the storm. And blessed by virtue of its remoteness and the Chinchorro barrier reef (preventing the creation of a cruise ship port), Xcalak may yet escape the development boom.

After Dean, the inner portions of the coastal reefs near Xcalak are reportedly in better shape than the outer sections, which were hammered by heavy seas (waves reached up to 5m). Ask around before you commit to a tour. Xcalak also offers easy access to the Banco Chinchorro (opposite).

If diving isn't your thing, there's still plenty to do. Come here to walk in dusty streets and sip frozen drinks while frigates soar above translucent green lagoons. Explore a mangrove swamp by kayak, or just doze in a hammock and soak in some sun. Perhaps best of all, you won't hear a single offer for *hamacas* or Cuban cigars. And, though tiny, Xcalak boasts a few nice restaurants and an easygoing mix of foreigners and local fishermen.

The mangrove swamps stretching inland from the coastal road hides some large lagoons and forms tunnels that invite kayakers to explore. It and the drier forest teem with wildlife and, as well as the usual herons, egrets and other waterfowl, you can see agouti, jabiru (storks), iguanas, javelina (peccaries), parakeets, kingfishers, alligators and more. Unfortunately, the mangrove also breeds mosquitoes and some vicious *jejenes* (sand flies). There's a remote Maya ruin on the western side of the lagoon. Your hotelier can tell you how to get there.

Xcalak is actually seeing negative population growth. Specializing in coconuts, it was an important port during the War of the Castes, and the town even had a cinema until a series of hurricanes wiped everything away. Today, there's no signs of getting a bank, grocery store or gas station anytime soon, so stock up before you come.

Aventuras Xcalak to Chinchorro Dive Center (☎ 983-839-88-65; www.xtcdivecenter.com), about 300m north of town on the coastal road, offers dive and snorkel trips (from M$650) to the wondrous barrier reef just offshore, and to Banco Chinchorro (three-tank dive M$1750, not including rental gear). It also rents diving equipment and offers PADI open-water certificate for M$3850, NAUI and SDI instruction, as well as fishing and birding tours.

SLEEPING

The following places are among a handful on the old coastal road leading north from town (mostly run by Americans or Canadians). All have purified drinking water, ceiling fans, 24-hour electricity (from solar or wind with generator backup), bikes and/or sea kayaks for guest use, and private hot-water bathrooms. The first three have docks to swim off, and most arrange fishing excursions.

High season here is mid-December to mid-April (with very slight variations). Most places don't accept credit cards without prior arrangements, and are best contacted through their websites or via email. Addresses here are expressed in kilometers north along the coast from town.

Villas La Guacamaya (☎ 983-839-86-08; www.villa laguacamaya.com; Km 10; d low/high season M$500/1000; 🖳) You'll be greeted by an exuberant parrot at this quiet place 10km north of Xcalak. It has two bright green rooms that face the sea and share use of a fully equipped gourmet kitchen. Each room has a double and a single bed. There's also a separate apartment with kitchen set back from the beach, and a fourth, smallish room with a double bed and a lovely bathroom. It also offers bikes, kayaks and snorkel gear for guest use.

Hotel Tierra Maya (www.tierramaya.net; Km 2; r with ocean view M$800) A modern beachfront hotel featuring six lovely rooms (three quite large), each tastefully appointed and with many architectural details. Each of the rooms has mahogany furniture and a balcony facing the sea – the bigger rooms even have small refrigerators. Mains at the pleasant restaurant are around M$160. Rates include a continental breakfast.

Casa Carolina (www.casacarolina.net; Km 2.5; d low/high season M$750/950) A bright, cheery yellow, the Casa has four guestrooms with large, hammock-equipped balconies facing the sea. Each room has a kitchen with fridge, and the bathrooms try to outdo one another with their beautiful Talavera tile. All levels of scuba instruction (NAUI) are offered here, as well as recreational dives at the barrier reef. Rates include continental breakfast, and the owners offer massage.

Sonrisa (www.playasonrisa.com; Km 7; cabañas from M$950) Sonrisa offers 'clothing optional' European-style sunbathing for couples – and couples only. Come here to lose the tan lines in a low-key, casual setting that includes simple cabañas, a bar–restaurant and friendly owners. Note that the cancellation penalties are steep, so read the website carefully and make sure of your plans. Rates include a continental breakfast.

EATING

Food in Xcalak tends to be tourist-grade seafood or Mexican, though the Leaky Palapa is a delectable exception.

Lonchería Silvia's (mains M$35-90; ☉ 9am-10pm) About three blocks south of the plaza and a block in from the coast, Silvia serves mostly fish fillets and *ceviche*, and keeps pretty regular hours. The long menu doesn't mean that everything is available. You'll likely end up having the fish.

Leaky Palapa (mains M$50-120; ☉ 5-10pm Fri-Mon) Chef and owners Marla and Linda have turned an old standby about three blocks north of the plaza into a new sensation, serving wonderful meals such as lobster in caramel ginger sauce. Opinion is unanimous that this is the best place to go to treat your taste buds.

GETTING THERE & AROUND

Cabs from Limones cost about M$500 (including to the northern hotels). Buses cost M$30, the same as to Mahahual even though they travel an hour longer.

Driving from Limones, turn right (south) after 55km and follow the signs to Xcalak (another 60km). Keep an eye out for the diverse wildlife that frequents the forest and mangrove; a lot of it runs out into the road.

A taxi sporadically works the town, serving the northern hotels for M$100 and available for hire for excursions to further destinations. The route directly from Mahahual to Xcalak, known as the coastal road, was closed at the time of writing and, according to locals, might not re-open.

LAGUNA BACALAR

A large, clear, turquoise freshwater lake with a bottom of gleaming white sand, Laguna Bacalar comes as a surprise in this region of tortured limestone and scrubby jungle.

The small, sleepy town of Bacalar, just east of the highway, 125km south of Felipe Carrillo Puerto, is the only settlement of any size on the lake. It's noted mostly for its old Spanish fortress and its popular *balnearios* (bathing places). Hurricane Dean scrubbed the town clean, felling a number of trees, but things were recovering nicely on our last pass.

The fortress, **Fuerte San Felipe Bacalar** (admission M$20; ☉ 9am-8pm Tue-Sun), was built above the lagoon to protect citizens from raids by pirates and Indians. It served as an important outpost for the whites in the War of the Castes. In 1859 it was seized by Maya rebels, who held the fort until Quintana Roo was finally conquered by Mexican troops in 1901. Today, with formidable cannons still on its ramparts, the fortress remains an imposing sight. It houses a **museum** exhibiting colonial armaments and uniforms from the 17th and 18th centuries.

Just shy of the south end of the *costera* is **Cenote Azul**, a 90m-deep natural pool on the southwest shore of the lake. It's 200m east of Hwy 307, so many buses will drop you nearby. Of the few places to eat right in town, Orizaba's at the northwest corner of the plaza is a good choice.

Sleeping & Eating

Most accommodations and eating spots are found on the *ostera* (also known as Calle 1), which winds south several kilometers along the lakeshore from Bacalar town to Hwy 307 at Cenote Azul. The following places are listed from north to south.

Los Coquitos (campsites per person M$10) A nice camping area on the lakeshore, run by a family who live in a shack on the premises. You can camp in the dense shade of the palm trees, enjoy the view of the lake from the *palapas* and swim from the grassy banks.

Casita Carolina (☎ /fax 983-834-23-34; www.casitacarolina.com; d M$250-450; palapa M$450) This is a delightful place about 1½ blocks south of the fort. It has a large lawn leading down to the lake, five fan rooms and a deluxe *palapa* that sleeps up to four. Guests can explore the lake in the Casita's kayaks. It's best reached by taking a bus into Bacalar and walking or catching a taxi.

Hotel Laguna (☎ 983-834-22-06; www.hotellaguna bacalar.com; d M$420; 🏊) This clean, cool, turquoise place is hospitable. It boasts a small swimming pool, a restaurant, a bar and excellent views of the lake, directly below the hotel. Some rooms are showing their age. It's 2km south of Bacalar town along the *costera* and only 150m east of Hwy 307, so if you're traveling by bus on the highway you can ask the driver to stop at the turnoff.

Amigos B&B Laguna Bacalar (☎ 987-872-38-68; www.bacalar.net; d M$500; 🏊) Brought to you by the same hospitable family who runs Amigos B&B in Cozumel, this ideally located lakefront property (about 500m south of the fort) has five spacious guest rooms and a comfy shared common area. You can save M$100 by skipping the breakfast.

Hostel Ximba Li (☎ 983-834-25-16; cnr Av 3 & Calle 30; dm M$70) This simple new hostel is located a couple of blocks from the lake and a short walk to town. Breakfast included.

Serving consistently good Yucatecan meals, the lake view restaurant at quaintly kitsch Hotel Laguna is popular. The restaurant at Balneario Ejidal serves fresh *ceviche* and good grilled fish.

Getting There & Away

Southbound 2nd-class buses go through Bacalar town on Calle 7, passing a block uphill from the central square *(el parque)*, which is just above the fort and has a taxi stand. Northbound 2nd-class buses run along Calle 5, a block downhill from Calle 7. Most 1st-class buses don't enter town, but many will drop you along Hwy 307 at the turnoffs to Hotel Laguna and Cenote Azul; check before you buy your ticket.

If you're driving from the north and want to reach the town and fort, take the first Bacalar exit and continue several blocks before turning left (east) down the hill. From Chetumal, head west to catch Hwy 307 north; after 25km on the highway you'll reach the signed right turn for Cenote Azul and the *costera*.

CHETUMAL
☎ 983 / pop 136,800

The capital city of Quintana Roo, Chetumal has stylish, friendly people, some decent restaurants, and a lively music scene. Hurricane Dean displaced many of Chetumal's inhabitants, but with a bit of lumber, some tarpaulins, sweat, rummaged nails and a few quick-drying tears, the town is quietly rebuilding. None of the major tourist areas were affected.

The bayside esplanade hosts carnivals and events, and the modern Maya museum is impressive (though a bit short on artifacts). Impressive Maya ruins, amazing jungle and the border to neighboring Belize are all close by. And the Free Zone between the two countries makes for interesting shopping. **Carnaval** (late February or early March) is particularly lively in Chetumal.

Before the Spanish conquest, Chetumal was a Maya port. After the conquest, the town was not actually settled until 1898, when it was founded to put a stop to the illegal trade in arms and lumber carried on by the descendants of the War of the Castes rebels. Dubbed Payo Obispo, the town changed its name to Chetumal in 1936. In 1955, Hurricane Janet virtually obliterated it.

YUCATÁN PENINSULA

The rebuilt city is laid out on a grand plan with a grid of wide boulevards along which traffic speeds (be careful at stop signs).

Orientation & Information

Chetumal is a large city but remains (thanks largely to its network of wide, one-way streets) very driveable (almost unheard of in a state capital). The southern edge is bordered by the water. The main street, Héroes, divides the city into east and west sides, ending at the waterfront. Obregón parallels the bay and leads, heading westward, first to a *glorieta* (traffic circle), then to the airport, then to the turn for Belize.

Most of the hotels and restaurants listed are clustered around the Héroes–Obregón intersection. There are several banks and ATMs around town, including an ATM inside the bus terminal.

Arba Internet (☎ 832-25-81; Efraín Aguilar; per hr M$10; ☼ 8am-1am Mon-Sat, to midnight Sun)

City tourist office (☎ 835-08-00; cnr Blvd Bahía & Av Hidalgo; ☼ 9am-3pm Mon-Sat)

Cruz Roja (☎ 832-05-71; cnr Avs Independencia & Héroes de Chapultepec)

Fire, Medical, Police (☎ 066)

Hospital Morelos (☎ 832-45-95)

HSBC currency exchange counter (San Francisco de Asís supermarket; ☼ 8am-6pm Mon-Sat)

Immigration office (☎ 832-63-53; Av Héroes; ☼ 9am-1pm Mon-Fri)

Post office (☎ 832-22-81; cnr Plutarco Elías Calles & Av 5 de Mayo; ☼ 9am-4pm Mon-Fri)

Telmex (Calle Lázaro Cárdenas; ☼ 8am-6pm Mon-Fri) Between Avs Independencia & Benito Juárez.

Tourist information kiosk (☼ 9am-8pm) In the bus terminal.

Sights

MUSEO DE LA CULTURA MAYA

This **museum** (☎ 832-68-38; Av de los Héroes; admission M$50; ☼ 9am-7pm Sun-Thu, to 8pm Fri & Sat) is the city's claim to cultural fame – a bold showpiece beautifully conceived and executed.

The various exhibits (labeled in Spanish and English) cover all of the Mayab (lands of the Maya), not just Quintana Roo or Mexico, and seek to explain the Maya way of life, thought and belief. The museum's **courtyard**, which you can enter for free, has salons for temporary exhibits of modern artists (such as Rufino Tamayo), paintings reproducing Maya frescoes and a *cinemuseo* giving free film showings.

MUSEO DE LA CIUDAD

The **local history museum** (Héroes de Chapultepec; admission M$10; ☼ 9am-7pm Tue-Sun) is small but neatly done, and worth a 15-minute visit.

Sleeping

Instituto Quintanarroense de la Juventud (☎ 832-05-25; Heróica Escuela Naval btwn Calz Veracruz & Av Cozumel; campsites M$30, dm M$50) Fifty pesos a night is hard to beat, but you're going to be staying in some pretty lo-fi digs. This said, there's a super-friendly staff on hand, and it's relatively clean at this youth center and hostel.

Hotel Ucum (☎ 832-07-11, 832-61-86; Av Mahatma Gandhi 167; d with fan/air-con M$200/$350; P ✦ ✦) This fine motel-like place looks like it may have once been used as a Jackie Chan movie set. And despite the unfortunate name (a town in Campeche), it offers pretty decent rooms, a (slightly milky) swimming pool and a restaurant serving good, inexpensive food.

Hotel Guadalupe (☎ 832-86-49; Calle Ignacio Zaragoza 226; s/d with fan M$250/280, with air-con M$400; P ✦) You could eat dinner off the spotless floors here. Despite the cleanliness, the rooms are slightly stale, although they air out quickly.

ourpick Grand Marlon Hotel (☎ 285-32-79; hotel_grandmarlon@hotmail.com; Av Juárez 88; d M$500; ✦) With modern clean lines, a rather funky pool area (complete with Astroturf and a lukewarm Jacuzzi), the 'Grand' almost achieves 'hip boutique' status, and the simple, stylish rooms are an excellent deal for the price. Or, you could save a few pesos by heading across the street to the plain ol' Marlon.

Hotel Los Cocos (☎ 832-05-44; www.hotelloscocos .com.mx; cnr Av de los Héroes & Calle Héroes de Chapultepec; d with air-con & TV M$750, ste M$1600; ✦ ▢ ✦) Has a great location and a seriously disco-mirrored lobby that gets your inner mojo rising. There's also a nice swimming pool, wireless access, a guarded parking lot and a popular sidewalk restaurant. Rooms have fridges, but are a bit small and musty for the price.

Holiday Inn Chetumal Puerta Maya (☎ 835-04-00; www.holimaya.com.mx; Héroes 171; d M$1300, ste M$1690-3630; ✦ ▢ ✦) The best in town, with comfortable rooms that overlook a small courtyard, a swimming pool set amid tropical gardens, and a restaurant and bar.

Eating & Drinking

Barrios (cnr Avs Othón P Blanco & Independencia; mains M$10-50; ☼ 8am-2pm Mon-Sat) Great little eatery with

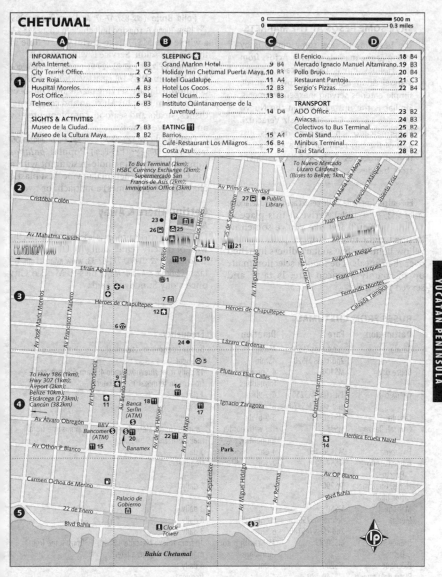

CHETUMAL

0 500 m
0 0.3 miles

INFORMATION	
Arba Internet	1 B3
City Tourist Office	2 C5
Cruz Roja	3 A3
Hospital Morelos	4 B3
Post Office	5 B4
Telmex	6 B3

SIGHTS & ACTIVITIES	
Museo de la Ciudad	7 B3
Museo de la Cultura Maya	8 B2

SLEEPING	
Grand Marlon Hotel	9 B4
Holiday Inn Chetumal Puerta Maya	10 B3
Hotel Guadalupe	11 A4
Hotel Los Cocos	12 B3
Hotel Ucum	13 B3
Instituto Quintanarroense de la Juventud	14 D4

EATING	
Barrios	15 A1
Café-Restaurant Los Milagros	16 B4
Costa Azul	17 B4

El Fenicio	18 B4
Mercado Ignacio Manuel Altamirano	19 B3
Pollo Brujo	20 B4
Restaurant Pantoja	21 C3
Sergio's Pizzas	22 B4

TRANSPORT	
ADO Office	23 B2
Aviacsa	24 B3
Colectivos to Bus Terminal	25 B2
Combi Stand	26 B2
Minibus Terminal	27 C2
Taxi Stand	28 B2

Mexican favorites such as *salbutes* or *quesadillas* and *cebada*, a refreshing barley drink.

Café-Restaurant Los Milagros (☎ 832-44-33; Calle Ignacio Zaragoza; breakfast M$25-70, mains M$40-60; ☼ 7:30am-9pm Mon-Sat, to 1pm Sun) Serves great espresso and food indoors and outdoors. A favorite with Chetumal's student and intellectual set, it's also a place to play chess or domi-

noes, chat, or observe a local radio program being broadcast from one of the tables.

Restaurant Pantoja (☎ 832-39-57; cnr Avs Mahatma Gandhi & 16 de Septiembre; mains M$30-70; ☼ 7am-7pm) A popular, family-run restaurant serving breakfasts, enchiladas and a variety of meat dishes. It offers a M$40 *menu del día*. Fan-cooled, it gets a bit warm in the *tarde*.

SAVE SOME PESOS AT THE MARKETS

The best way to save some dinero is by eating at the markets in town. Across from the Holiday Inn is the Mercado Ignacio Manuel Altamirano and its row of small, simple eateries serving inexpensive meals. Similar is the upstairs area in the Nuevo Mercado Lázaro Cárdenas (Calz Veracruz). Supermercado San Francisco de Asís, just east of the bus terminal, has a wide selection of groceries, and is a full department store besides.

El Fenicio (cnr Av de los Héroes & Calle Ignacio Zaragoza; mains M$35-90; ⊙ 24hr) Arrive at this place at 11pm and you'll feel like you've somehow stepped right into a Hopper painting: the yellow light, the few solitary diners hunched over their meals. The food, a selection made up of mainly Mexican fare, is tasty and served promptly.

Pollo Brujo (☎ 837-47-47; Av Álvaro Obregón 208; ⊙ 10am-10pm) A roasted half chicken costs M$42, a whole one M$77; take it with you or dine in the air-con salon. Service is with a snarl.

Sergio's Pizzas (☎ 832-29-91; cnr Avs Álvaro Obregón & 5 de Mayo; pizza M$45-170, mains M$60-160) A well air-conditioned place serving pizzas and cold beer in frosted mugs, plus Mexican and continental dishes, steaks and seafood, complemented by an extensive wine list.

Costa Azul (☎ 129-20-02; Calle Ignacio Zaragoza 166; mains M$60-120; ⊙ 11:30-8pm) Popular *palapa*-topped airy watering hole–restaurant with a fun Caribbean–Chetumalan vibe. Just plastic chairs and (sometimes) a mariachi or two.

Getting There & Away

AIR

Chetumal's small airport is less than 2km northwest of the city center along Av Obregón.

Aviacsa (☎ 01-800-771-67-33; www.aviacsa.com; cnr Lázaro Cárdenas & Av 5 de Mayo) flies to Mexico City once a day Sunday to Friday.

BUSES FROM CHETUMAL

Destination	Fare	Duration	Frequency
Bacalar	minibuses M$20	45min	hourly from minibus terminal
	2nd-class M$20	45min	frequent
Belize city	M$100	4-5hr with border formalities	18 daily from Nuevo Mercado 4:30am-6:30pm, some from main terminal 15 min later
Campeche	1st-class M$250	6½-9hr	1 daily
	2nd-class M$170	6½-9hr	2 daily
Cancún	M$180-210	5½-6½hr	frequent
Corozal, Belize	M$35	1hr with border formalities	18 from Nuevo Mercado 4:30am-6:30pm, some from main terminal 15 min later
Escárcega	M$120-160	4-6hr	5 daily
Felipe Carrillo Puerto	M$54-90	2-3hr	frequent
Flores, Guatemala (for Tikal)	M$290	8hr	5 daily
Mahahual	M$50	4hr	3 daily
Mérida	deluxe M$250	6-8hr	8 daily
	2nd-class M$180	6-8hr	3 daily
Orange Walk, Belize	M$30-45	3¼hr with border formalities	18 from Nuevo Mercado 4:30am-6:30pm, some from main terminal 15 min later
Palenque	M$280	7-8hr	4 daily
Playa del Carmen	M$140-180	4½-6hr	frequent
Ticul	M$155	6hr	6 daily
Tulum	M$110-144	3½-4hr	frequent
Valladolid	M$140	6hr	6 daily
Veracruz	M$620	16hr	2 daily
Villahermosa	M$330	7-9hr	5 daily
Xcalak	M$66	5hr	3 daily
Xpujil	M$55-78	2-3hr	9 daily

For flights to Belize City (and on to Flores, to reach Tikal) or to Belize's cays, cross the border into Belize then catch a flight from Corozal.

BUS

The main bus terminal is about 2km north of the center, near the intersection of Avs Insurgentes and Belice. Services are provided by Deluxe Omnitur del Caribe, Maya de Oro and Super Expresso (deluxe); ADO and Cristóbal Colón (1st class); and (2nd class) TRT, Sur and Mayab (a cut above), among others. The terminal has lockers (in the store against the east wall, near the pay toilets), a bus information kiosk (open until 3pm), an ATM, a cafeteria and shops.

You can also buy tickets for some lines and get information about most bus services at the **ADO office** (Av Belice; ⏰ 6am-10pm), just west of the Museo de la Cultura Maya.

Many local buses, and those bound for Belize, begin their runs from the **Nuevo Mercado Lázaro Cárdenas** (cnr Calz Veracruz & Confederación Nacional Campesina), about 10 blocks north of Av Primo de Verdad on a corner also called Segundo Circuito by locals. From this market, most 1st-class Belize-bound buses continue to the long-distance terminal and depart from there 15 minutes later; the 2nd-class buses don't. Tickets can be purchased on board the buses for 2nd-class transportation and at the main terminal if you are traveling 1st class or deluxe.

The **minibus terminal** (cnr Avs Primo de Verdad & Miguel Hidalgo) has services to Bacalar and other nearby destinations. Departures listed in the table opposite are from the main terminal unless otherwise noted.

TAXI

Gibson Tours and Transfers (www.gibsontoursandtransfers.com) charges M$250/500 to the border/Corozal.

Getting Around

From anywhere in town taxis charge a flat fare of M$20. From the traffic circle at Av Héroes, you can also get a *combi* (van) for M$3 to the town center via the Santa Maria or Calderitas eastbound busses. To reach the terminal from the center, catch a *combi* from Av Belice behind the Museo de la Cultura Maya. Ask to be left at the *glorieta* (traffic circle) at Av Insurgentes. Head left (west) to reach the terminal. The immigration office is about 800m north of the *glorieta*. (Ask for the *oficina de inmigración*.)

CORREDOR ARQUEOLÓGICO

The Corredor Arqueológico comprises the archaeological sites of **Dzibanché** and **Kohunlich**. At the time of research, Dzibanché was closed due to heavy treefall, after Dean's whirlwind visit. It's open now, but the site is missing many of the trees that made it so great. Kuhunlich also suffered serious treefall, but was open to the public.

Sights

DZIBANCHÉ

Though it's a chore to get to, this **site** (admission M$37) is definitely worth a visit for its secluded, semi-wild nature. Dzibanché ('writing on wood') was a major city extending more than 40 sq km, and on the road in you pass huge mounds covered in trees. There are a number of excavated palaces and pyramids, but the site itself is not completely excavated.

KOHUNLICH

The **archaeological site** (admission M$40, guide M$250) sits on a carpeted green. The ruins, dating from both the late Preclassic (AD 100–200) and the early Classic (AD 300–600) periods, are famous for the great **Templo de los Mascarones** (Temple of the Masks), a pyramidlike structure with a central stairway flanked by huge, 3m-high stucco masks of the sun god.

A few hundred meters southwest of Plaza Merwin are the **27 Escalones** (27 Steps), the remains of an extensive residential area.

The hydraulic engineering used at Kohunlich was a great achievement; 90,000 of the site's 210,000 sq meters were cut to channel rainwater into Kohunlich's once enormous reservoir.

Getting There & Away

The turnoff for Dzibanché from Hwy 186 is about 44km west of Chetumal, on the right just after the Zona Arqueológica sign. From there it's another 24km north and east along a pot-holed road. It's quite passable in a passenger car. Just after the tiny town of Morocoy you'll need to turn right again.

Kohunlich's turnoff is 3km west along Hwy 186 from the Dzibanché turnoff, and the site lies at the end of a paved 8.5km road.

YUCATÁN PENINSULA

There is no public transportation running directly to either of the sites. They're best visited by car, though Kohunlich could conceivably be reached by taking an early bus to the village of Francisco Villa near the turnoff, then either hitchhiking or walking the 8.5km to the site. Flag down a bus from the main highway to get back to Chetumal or Xpujil. Tour operators in Xpujil offer trips to Kohunlich and Dzibanché for M$750.

YUCATÁN STATE

A wild undercurrent, writhing like a liquid goddess, resides beneath the scrub jungle, pyramids and rolling hills of Yucatán state. You feel her tides as you walk beneath the towering Maya pyramids of Chichén Itzá and Uxmal, imagining the rich waves of history, slaughter, deceit, fame and famine that rolled through these mighty power centers. She ebbs and flows in the intact colonial cities of Mérida, Valladolid and Izamal as *huipil*-clad *indígenas* mingle with trendy students, factory workers, tourists and the wealthy elite as they ply the streets of the peninsula's modern-day cultural crossroads. She gurgles and spits and purges and pulls in the bird-clogged estuaries near Celestún and Río Lagartos, and underground in the vast system of caves and cenotes that pock the region. There are a few nice beaches in Celestún and Progreso, but most people come to this area to explore the ancient Maya sites peppered throughout the region, like the Ruta Puuc, which will take you to four or five ruins in just a day.

MÉRIDA
☎ 999 / pop 781,100
Since the Conquest, Mérida has been the cultural capital of the entire peninsula. At times provincial, at others '*muy cosmopolitano*,' it is a town steeped in colonial history, with narrow streets, broad central plazas, and the region's best museums. It's also a perfect hub city to kick off your adventure into the rest of Yucatán State. There are cheap eats, good hostels and hotels, thriving markets, and goings-on just about every night somewhere in the downtown area.

Long popular with European travelers looking to go beyond the hub and bub of Quintana Roo's resort towns, Mérida is not an 'undiscovered Mexican gem' like some of the tourist brochures claim. Simply put, it's a tourist town, but a tourist town too big to feel like a tourist trap. And as the capital of Yucatán state, Mérida is also the cultural crossroads of the region.

History
Francisco de Montejo (the Younger) founded a Spanish colony at Campeche, about 160km to the southwest, in 1540. From this base he took advantage of political dissension among the Maya (see p932), conquering T'ho (now Mérida) in 1542. By decade's end, Yucatán was mostly under Spanish colonial rule.

When Montejo's conquistadors entered T'ho, they found a major Maya settlement of lime-mortared stone that reminded them of the Roman architecture in Mérida, Spain. They promptly renamed the city and proceeded to build it into the regional capital, dismantling the Maya structures and using the materials to construct a cathedral and other stately buildings. Mérida took its colonial orders directly from Spain, not from Mexico City, and Yucatán has had a distinct cultural and political identity ever since.

During the War of the Castes, only Mérida and Campeche were able to hold out against the rebel forces. On the brink of surrender, the ruling class in Mérida was saved by reinforcements sent from central Mexico in exchange for Mérida's agreement to take orders from Mexico City.

Mérida today is the peninsula's center of commerce, a bustling city that has benefited greatly from the *maquiladoras* (assembly plants) that opened in the 1980s and '90s and the tourism industry that picked up during those decades.

Orientation
The Plaza Grande, as *meridanos* call the main square, has been the city's heart since the time of the Maya. Though Mérida now sprawls several kilometers in all directions, most of the services and attractions for visitors are within five blocks of the Plaza Grande. Following the classic colonial plan, the square, holding the cathedral and seats of government, is ringed by several barrios (neighborhoods). Each barrio has its park and church (side by side), usually bearing the same name: for example the Iglesia de Santiago is next to Parque de Santiago in Barrio de Santiago. Locals orient themselves and often give directions referring to the barrios.

Odd-numbered streets run east–west; even-numbered streets run north–south. House numbers may increase very slowly, and addresses are usually given in this form: 'Calle 57 No 481 x 56 y 58' (between streets 56 and 58).

From 8pm Saturday to 11pm Sunday, Calles 60 and 62 are closed to motor vehicles between Plaza Grande and Calle 55.

Information

BOOKSTORES
Librería Dante (☎ 928-36-74; Calle 59; ☽ 8am-9:30pm Mon-Sat, 10am-6pm Sun) Between Calles 60 and 62.

EMERGENCY
Emergency (☎ 066)
Fire (☎ 924-92-42)
Police (☎ 925-20-34)
Red Cross (☎ 924-90-13)
Tourism Police (☎ 925-25-55 ext 260)

INTERNET ACCESS
Most internet places around town charge M$10 per hour. Plans were in the works to make the entire downtown plaza a wi-fi hotspot.

LAUNDRY
Most upmarket hotels offer overnight laundry service.
Lavandería La Fe (☎ 924-45-31; Calle 64; ☽ 8am-6pm Mon-Fri, 8am-2pm Sat) Charges M$40 per 3kg load.

MEDICAL SERVICES
Hospital O'Horán (☎ 924-48-00, 924-11-11; Av de los Itzáes)

MONEY
Banks and ATMs are scattered throughout the city.

POST
Post Office (☎ 928-54-04; Calle 53 No 469; ☽ 9am-4pm Mon-Fri, for stamps only 9am-1pm Sat)

TOURIST INFORMATION
City tourist office (☎ 942-00-00 ext 80119; Calle 62; ☽ 8am-8pm Mon-Sat, 8am-2pm Sun) On Plaza Grande.
State tourist office (☎ 930-31-01; Calle 61; ☽ 8am-9pm) On Plaza Grande.
Tourist Information Center (☎ 924-92-90; cnr Calles 60 & 57A; ☽ 8am-9pm)
Yucatán Today (☎ 927-85-31; www.yucatantoday.com; Calle 39 No 483 int 10) A Spanish-English magazine devoted to tourism in Yucatán.

TRAVEL AGENCIES
Nómadas Travel (☎ 948-11-87; www.nomadastravel.com.mx; Prolongación Paseo de Montejo 370, Colonia Benito Juárez Nte) Books flights and offers services for student travelers.

Dangers & Annoyances
Guard against pickpockets, bag snatchers and bag slashers in the market 70 district and in any crowd. Outright muggings are very rare. Mérida's **Policía Turística** (Tourist Police; ☎ 925-25-55 ext 260) wear brown-and-white uniforms and are your best bet if you've been robbed.

Sights

PLAZA GRANDE
'El Centro' is one of the nicest plazas in Mexico. Huge laurel trees shade the park's benches and wide sidewalks, and it is surrounded by a bustle of pedestrians who shop or sip coffee at the many open-air cafés. It was the religious and social center of ancient T'ho; under the Spanish it was the Plaza de Armas, the parade ground, laid out by Francisco de Montejo the Younger. A ceremony is held daily marking the raising and lowering of the Mexican flag. On Sunday hundreds of *meridanos* take their *paseo* (stroll) here, and there's a cultural exhibit – normally dance or live music – nearly every night.

CATEDRAL DE SAN ILDEFONSO
On the plaza's east side, on the site of a former Maya temple, is Mérida's hulking, severe **cathedral** (☽ 6am-noon & 4-7pm), begun in 1561 and completed in 1598. Some of the stone from the Maya temple was used in its construction. The massive crucifix behind the altar is **Cristo de la Unidad** (Christ of Unity), a symbol of reconciliation between those of Spanish and Maya heritage. To the right over the south door is a painting of Tutul Xiú, *cacique* of the town of Maní, paying his respects to his ally Francisco de Montejo at T'ho (de Montejo and Xiú jointly defeated the Cocomes; Xiú converted to Christianity, and his descendants still live in Mérida).

In the small chapel to the left of the altar is Mérida's most famous religious artifact, a statue called **Cristo de las Ampollas** (Christ of the Blisters). Local legend says the statue was carved from a tree that was hit by lightning and burned for an entire night without charring. It is also said to be the only object to have survived the fiery destruction of the

MÉRIDA

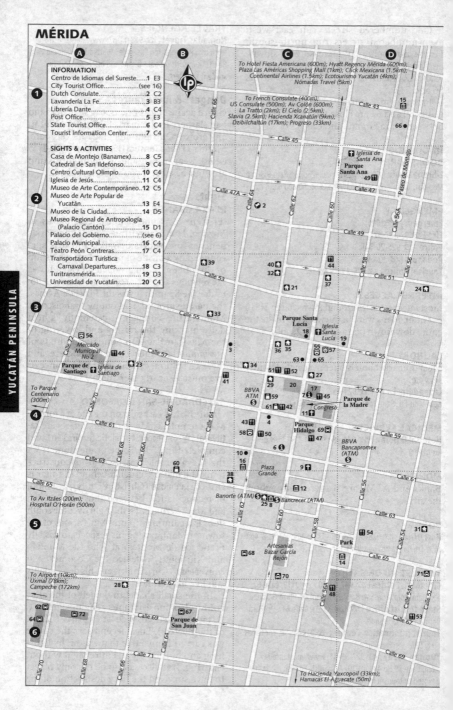

INFORMATION

Centro de Idiomas del Sureste......**1**	E3
City Tourist Office..................(see 16)	
Dutch Consulate......................**2**	C2
Lavandería La Fe.....................**3**	B3
Librería Dante.......................**4**	C4
Post Office..........................**5**	E3
State Tourist Office.................**6**	C4
Tourist Information Center...........**7**	C4

SIGHTS & ACTIVITIES

Casa de Montejo (Banamex)........**8**	C5
Catedral de San Ildefonso.........**9**	C4
Centro Cultural Olimpio...........**10**	C4
Iglesia de Jesús..................**11**	C4
Museo de Arte Contemporáneo...**12**	C5
Museo de Arte Popular de	
Yucatán.......................**13**	E4
Museo de la Ciudad...............**14**	D5
Museo Regional de Antropología	
(Palacio Cantón)..............**15**	D1
Palacio del Gobierno..............(see 6)	
Palacio Municipal................**16**	C4
Teatro Peón Contreras............**17**	C4
Transportadora Turística	
Carnaval Departures...........**18**	C3
Turitransmérida..................**19**	D3
Universidad de Yucatán...........**20**	C4

To Hotel Fiesta Americana (600m); Hyatt Regency Mérida (600m);
Plaza Las Américas Shopping Mall (1km); Click Mexicana (1.5km);
Continental Airlines (1.5km); Ecotourismo Yucatán (4km);
Nómadas Travel (5km)

To French Consulate (400m);
US Consulate (500m); Av Colón (600m);
La Tratto (2km); El Cielo (2.5km);
Slavia (2.5km); Hacienda Xcanatún (9km);
Dzibilchaltún (17km); Progreso (33km)

Iglesia de
Santa Ana

Parque
Santa Ana

Parque Santa
Lucía

Iglesia
Santa
Lucía

Mercado
Municipal
No 2

Parque de
Santiago

Iglesia de
Santiago

To Parque
Centenario
(300m)

BBVA
ATM

Parque de
la Madre

Parque
Hidalgo

To Av Itzáes (200m);
Hospital O'Horán (500m)

Plaza
Grande

Banorte (ATM)

Bancrecer (ATM)

BBVA
Bancapromex
(ATM)

Park

To Airport (10km);
Uxmal (78km);
Campeche (172km)

Artesanías
Bazar García
Rejón

Parque de
San Juan

To Hacienda Yaxcopoil (33km);
Hamacas El Aguacate (50m)

Calle 66
Calle 43
Calle 45
Calle 47A
Calle 47
Calle 49
Calle 51
Calle 53
Calle 55
Calle 57
Calle 59
Calle 61
Calle 63
Calle 65
Calle 67
Calle 69
Calle 71
Calle 62
Calle 60
Calle 58
Calle 56
Calle 56A
Calle 54
Calle 52
Calle 72
Calle 70
Calle 68
Calle 66A
Calle 64
Calle 65
Paseo de Montejo

Congreso

YUCATÁN PENINSULA

```
0                    400 m
0              0.2 miles
```

To Yucatán Today (50m)

SLEEPING
Álvarez Family Guest House	21 C3
Casa Ana B&B	22 E3
Casa Mexilio	23 B4
Hostal del Pelegrino	24 D3
Hostel Zocalo	25 C5
Hotel Aragón	26 E4
Hotel Casa Balam	27 C4
Hotel Casa Becil	28 A6
Hotel Colonial	29 C4
Hotel del Mayab	30 E6
Hotel Dolores Alba	31 D5
Hotel Hacienda Mérida	32 C3
Hotel Medio Mundo	33 B3
Hotel Montejo	34 C4
Hotel Santa Lucía	35 C3
Hotel Trinidad	36 C3
Hotel Trinidad Galería	37 C3
Hotel y Restaurant San José	38 B5
Los Arcos Bed & Breakfast	39 B3
Nómadas Youth Hostel	40 C3

EATING
Alberto's Continental Patio	41 B4
Amaro	42 C4
El Trapiche	43 C4
Fe y Esperanza	44 C3
Il Caffé Italiano	45 C4
La Flor de Santiago	46 A3
Main Street	47 C4
Mercado Municipal Lucas de Gálvez	48 C6
Mercado Santa Ana	49 D2
Pane e Vino	50 C4
Pop Cafetería	51 C4
Restaurante Pórtico del Peregrino	52 C3
Super Bodega	53 D6
Supermarkets	54 D5

ENTERTAINMENT
Caribbean Blue	55 C3
Cines Rex	56 A3
KY60	57 C3
Teatro Mérida	58 C4

SHOPPING
Camisería Canul	59 C4
Casa de las Artesanías	60 B4
Miniaturas	61 C4

TRANSPORT
Airport Bus Stop	62 A6
Avis	(see 65)
Budget	63 C3
CAME Bus Terminal	64 A6
Hertz	65 C4
Mexicana	66 D1
Parque de San Juan Terminus	67 B6
Progreso Bus Terminal	68 C5
Ruta 10 Bus Stop	69 C4
Shared Taxis to Progreso	70 C5
Shared Taxis to Tizimín	71 D5
Terminal de Segunda Clase	72 A6
Terminal Noreste	73 E6

Calle 55

Calle 57

Calle 59

Parque de La Mejorada

Iglesia La Mejorada

To Mayapán (48km);
Chichén Itza (117km);
Valladolid (160km);
Cancún (320km)

church in the town of Ichmul (though it was blackened and blistered from the heat). The statue was moved to the Mérida's cathedral in 1645.

Other than these items, the cathedral's interior is largely plain, its rich decoration having been stripped away by angry peasants at the height of anticlerical fervor of the Mexican Revolution.

AROUND THE CATHEDRAL

South of the cathedral, housed in the former archbishop's palace, is the **Museo de Arte Contemporáneo** (Macay; ☎ 928-32-36; Calle 60; admission free; ☼ 10am-6pm Sun-Thu, to 8pm Fri & Sat). This attractive museum holds permanent exhibits of Yucatán's most famous painters and sculptors, as well as revolving exhibits by local craftspeople.

The **Casa de Montejo** (Palacio de Montejo, Calle 63; ☼ 9am-4pm Mon-Fri, 10am-2pm Sat) is on the south side of the Plaza Grande and dates from 1549. It originally housed soldiers but was soon converted into a mansion that served members of the Montejo family until 1970. These days it houses a bank, and you can enter and look around during bank hours. At other times, content yourself with a close look at the facade, where triumphant conquistadors with halberds hold their feet on the necks of generic barbarians (though they're not Maya, the association is inescapable). Typical of the symbolism in colonial statuary, the vanquished are rendered much smaller than the victors; works on various churches throughout the region feature big priests towering over or in front of little 'Indians.' Also gazing across the plaza from the façade are busts of Montejo the Elder, his wife and his daughter.

Across the square from the cathedral is Mérida's **Palacio Municipal** (City Hall). Originally built in 1542, it was twice refurbished, in the 1730s and the 1850s. Adjoining it is the **Centro Cultural Olimpio** (☎ 924-00-00 ext 80152; cnr Calles 62 & 61), Mérida's municipal cultural center. Attempts to create a modern exterior for the building were halted by government order, to preserve the colonial character of the plaza. The ultramodern interior serves as a venue for music and dance performances (see p922) as well as other exhibitions. Schedules for performances and frequent film showings are posted outside.

On the north side of the plaza, the **Palacio de Gobierno** (admission free; ☼ 8am-10pm) houses the state of Yucatán's executive government offices (and one of its tourist information centers). It was built in 1892 on the site of the palace of the colonial governors. Be sure to have a look inside at the murals painted by local artist Fernando Castro Pacheco. Completed in 1978, they were 25 years in the making and portray a symbolic history of the Maya and their interaction with the Spaniards.

MUSEO DE LA CIUDAD

The **city museum** (☎ 923-68-69; Calle 56; admission free; ⏲ 9am-8pm Tue-Fri, to 2pm Sat & Sun) is housed in the old post office and offers a great reprieve from the hustle, honks and exhaust of this market neighborhood. There are exhibits tracing back the city's history to pre-Conquest days up through the *henequén* belle époque and into the 20th century.

CALLE 60

Rhe 17th-century **Iglesia de Jesús**, also called Iglesia de la Tercera Orden, rises a block north of the Plaza Grande, beyond shady Parque Hidalgo. Built by the Jesuits in 1618, it is the sole surviving edifice from a complex of buildings that once filled the entire city block.

North of the church is the enormous bulk of the **Teatro Peón Contreras** (cnr Calles 60 & 57; ⏲ visitors 9am-6pm Tue-Sat), built between 1900 and 1908, during Mérida's *henequén* heyday. It boasts a main staircase of Carrara marble, a dome with faded frescoes by Italian artists and various paintings and murals throughout the building.

Across Calle 60 from the theater is the main building of the **Universidad de Yucatán**. The modern university was established in the 19th century by Governor Felipe Carrillo Puerto and General Manuel Cepeda Peraza.

A block north of the university is pretty little **Parque Santa Lucía** (cnr Calles 60 & 55), with arcades on the north and west sides. When Mérida was a lot smaller, this was where travelers would get on or off the stagecoaches that linked towns and villages with the provincial capital. The **Bazar de Artesanías**, the local handicrafts market, is held here at 11am on Sunday.

PASEO DE MONTEJO

Paseo de Montejo, which runs parallel to Calles 56 and 58, was an attempt by Mérida's 19th-century city planners to create a wide

boulevard similar to the Paseo de la Reforma in Mexico City or the Champs Élysées in Paris. Though more modest than its predecessors, the Paseo de Montejo is still a beautiful swath of green, relatively open space in an urban conglomeration of stone and concrete. There are rotating sculpture exhibits along the paseo.

Europe's architectural and social influence can be seen along the paseo in the fine mansions built by wealthy families around the end of the 19th century. The greatest concentrations of surviving mansions are north of Calle 37, and on the first block of Av Colón west of Paseo de Montejo.

MUSEO REGIONAL DE ANTROPOLOGÍA

The massive Palacio Cantón houses Yucatán's regional **anthropology museum** (☎ 923-05-57; cnr Paseo de Montejo & Calle 43; admission M$37; ⏲ 8am-8pm Tue-Sat, to 2pm Sun). Construction of the mansion lasted from 1909 to 1911, and its owner, General Francisco Cantón Rosado (1833–1917), lived here for only six years before his death. The *palacio's* splendor and pretension make it a fitting symbol of the grand aspirations of Mérida's elite during the last years of the Porfiriato, the period from 1876 to 1911 when Porfirio Díaz held despotic sway over Mexico.

The museum covers the peninsula's history since the age of mastodons. Exhibits on Maya culture include explanations (many in Spanish only) of such cosmetic practices as forehead-flattening (done to beautify babies), causing eyes to cross and sharpening teeth and implanting them with tiny jewels.

PARQUE CENTENARIO

About 12 blocks west of the Plaza Grande lies this large, verdant **park** (admission free; ⏲ 6am-6pm Tue-Sun), bordered by Av Itzáes, which leads to the airport and becomes the highway to Campeche. The park's **zoo** (admission free; ⏲ 6am-6pm Tue-Sun) features the fauna of Yucatán, as well as some exotic species. To get there, take a bus west along Calle 61 or 65.

MUSEO DE ARTE POPULAR DE YUCATÁN

This **art museum** (Yucatecan Museum of Popular Art; cnr Calle 50A & Calle 57; admission M$30; ⏲ 9:30am-4:30pm Tue-Sat, 9am-2pm Sun) in the Casa Molina is six blocks east of the Plaza Grande in a building built in 1906. There's a small rotating exhibit downstairs that features pop art from around

Mexico, but honestly, you're better off heading to any artisan market in the countryside, where you'll see the same style of work, and it doesn't cost you a single peso, unless you want to buy something. The upstairs exhibits don't have any explanatory signs yet, but they give you an idea of how locals embroider *huipiles* (embroidered tunics), carve ceremonial masks, and weave hammocks.

Across the plaza from the museum is **Iglesia La Mejorada**, a large 17th-century church. The building just north of it was a monastery (el Convento de La Mejorada) until the late 19th century. It now houses an architectural school, but visitors are sometimes allowed to view the grounds.

Tours

CITY TOURS

The **city tourist office** (☎ 942-00-00 ext 80119; Calle 62) on Plaza Grande offers free guided walking tours of the historic center (sometimes in English), focusing on Plaza Grande. Tours depart at 9:30am daily from in front of the Palacio Municipal.

Transportadora Turística Carnaval (☎ 927-61-19) conducts two-hour guided tours of Mérida in English and Spanish on its Paseo Turístico bus (M$75) departing from Parque Santa Lucía (on the corner of Calles 55 and 60) at 10am, 1pm, 4pm and 7pm Monday to Saturday, and 10am and 1pm Sunday. You can buy your tickets ahead of time at nearby Hotel Santa Lucía.

REGIONAL TOURS

Turitransmérida (☎ 928-18-71; www.turitransmerida .com.mx; cnr Calles 55 & 58) is one of the largest of the many agencies offering group tours to sites around Mérida. Prices range from M$300 to M$450.

The owners of reputable **Ecoturismo Yucatán** (☎ 920-27-72; www.ecoyuc.com.mx; Calle 3 No 235) are passionate about both sharing and protecting the state's natural treasures. Trips focus on archaeology, birding, natural history, biking and kayaking. One-day excursions cost around M$1200; eight-day jungle tours M$20,150.

Many hotels will book these tours, as will **Nómadas Youth Hostel** (☎ /fax 924-52-23; www .nomadastravel.com; Calle 62 No 433), which also arranges a variety of other tours, from do-it-yourself trips in your rented car or on public transportation (with written instructions) to nearly all-inclusive (some meals) trips in private buses.

ATS buses conduct a day tour to Uxmal, Kabah, and the Ruta Puuc sites, beginning from the Terminal de Segunda Clase in Mérida at 8am. See Tours, p928, for details.

Courses

You can often find a private tutor through your hostel. **Centro de Idiomas del Sureste (CIS)** (☎ 923-09-54; www.cisyucatan.com.mx; Calle 52 No 455) offers Spanish courses.

Festivals & Events

For most of February the Universidad de Yucatán celebrates its anniversary with free performances by the Ballet Folklórico, concerts of Afro-Cuban music and *son* (Mexican folk music that blends elements of indigenous, Spanish and African musical styles) and other manifestations of Yucatán's cultural roots.

Prior to Lent, in February or March, **Carnaval** features colorful costumes and nonstop festivities. The **Festival de Trova Yucateca** is held in March. For more on *trova* see p83.

Semana Santa (Holy Week) is a major celebration in Mérida. The main feature of the celebrations is the city's Passion Plays.

Between September 22 and October 14, *gremios* (guilds or unions) venerate the Cristo de las Ampollas (Christ of the Blisters) statue in the cathedral with processions.

Another big religious tradition is the **Exposición de Altares de los Muertos** held on the night of November 1. Throughout Mexico families prepare shrines to welcome the spirits of loved ones back to Earth. Many Maya prepare elaborate dinners outside their homes, and Mérida observes the occasion with festivities and displays in the center of town from 11am on November 1 until 11am the next day.

Sleeping

From about December 15 to January 6, and during Semana Santa (Easter week), many midrange and top-end hotels raise their prices by 10% to 20%. These times and July and August (which also see price increases at some places) tend to be the busiest; it's wise to book ahead. Rates quoted in the following listings are for the low season.

BUDGET

Hostel Zócalo (☎ 924-52-23; Calle 63 No 508; dm M$100, s/d M$140/230; 🖳) Great location and a beautiful old colonial building make this hostel unique. Its owners are lovingly restoring it by hand. It has firm beds, and a simple breakfast is included. The hosts are a wealth of information about the area.

our pick Nómadas Youth Hostel (☎ /fax 924-52-23; www.nomadastravel.com; Calle 62 No 433; dm M$85, s or d without/with bathroom M$200/240; P ⛾) This is Mérida's backpacker central, and the best hostel in the city. All rates include breakfast, and guests have use of a fully equipped kitchen with fridge and purified water, 24-hour hot showers, internet and hand-laundry facilities. They even have free salsa classes and are planning on building a pool out back. Bring mosquito repellent and earplugs, as the front rooms can get traffic noise.

Hostal del Peregrino (☎ 924-54-91; www.hostal delperegrino.com; Calle 51 No 488; dm M$130, d M$400) On a quiet street, it's earthy, homey and tasteful. For the price, you are probably better off at Nómadas, but if you're looking to get away from the groovy-groupie backpacker scene, this may be the place for you. Breakfast is included in the price, and they offer low-season discounts and wi-fi.

Álvarez Family Guest House (☎ 924-30-60; casa .alvarez@hotmail.com; Calle 62 No 448; s/d M$350/400, d with air-con M$500; ⛾) Impeccably clean and in a family's home, this 'hostel plus' offers a friendly, one-of-the-family ambience, nice showers, spotless baths and laundry. The guesthouse is full of beautiful antiques, including an old cylinder-style gramophone player, which Enrique, the ever-accommodating owner, may demonstrate on request.

Hotel Casa Becil (☎ 924-67-64; hotelcasabecil@ yahoo.com.mx; Calle 67 No 550C; s/d/tr M$180/220/260, d with air-con M$300-330; ⛾) Almost a hostel but not quite, the Casa Becil's friendly owner calls it a 'BBC,' for breakfast, bed and coffee. The place offers very inexpensive, clean rooms with a fully equipped kitchen downstairs, an intimate courtyard, a sun deck, beautiful tile floors, left-luggage service, book exchange, tours and more. The rooms are breezy, without a hint of stuffiness, and the owner speaks excellent English.

Hotel y Restaurant San José (☎ 928-66-57; san-jose92@latinmail.com; Calle 63; s/d/tr M$140/160/180, with air-con M$260/280/300; ⛾) The walls are crumbling in this fading hotel 30m west of the Plaza Grande, but with a lot of elbow grease and bit of heavy detergent they manage to keep the place spick-and-span. The 30 good-

sized rooms are all set well off the street. This place offers value and is a favorite with visiting Mennonites.

Hotel del Mayab (☎ 928-51-74; Calle 50 No 536A; s/d with fan M$250/270, with air-con M$350/400; P ⛾ ⛾) This place is clean and low-key and offers off-street parking. Streetside rooms can be noisy, but interior rooms are quiet, and the hotel has a large swimming pool.

our pick Casa Ana B&B (☎ 924-00-05; www.casaana .com; Calle 52 No 469; r M$300-450; ⛾ ⛾) Though out of the way, Casa Ana is an intimate escape and the best budget B&B in town. It features a small natural-bottom pool and a cozy overgrown garden complete with Cuban tobacco plants (memories of home for the Cuban owners, no doubt).

Hotel Trinidad Galería (☎ 923-24-63; www .hotelestrinidad.com; Calle 60 No 456; r without/with air-con M$300/400, ste M$450-550; P ⛾ ⛾) It's like walking into the 'General's Labyrinth' or a Salvador Dalí Dream. Odd – at times freakish – artwork and statuary gather dust in every corner of this rambling hotel. You will either love this wacky place or find it disquieting. The rooms vary considerably: some are dark and musty, while others offer well-vented bathrooms with good mosquito screens.

Hotel Dolores Alba (☎ 928-56-50, 800-849-50-60; fax 928-31-63; www.doloresalba.com; Calle 63 btwn Calles 52 & 54; r without air-con M$260; d with air-con M$420-490; ⛾ ⛾ P) Rooms are on three floors (with an elevator) around two large courtyards. Those in the new, modern wing are quite large, have good beds, air-con and TV, and face the lovely pool.

Hotel Trinidad (☎ 923-20-33; www.hotelestrinidad .com; Calle 62 No 464; d M$400; ⛾) Occupies a colonial house and a newer wing, and has a variety of rooms, each with its own unique decor and charm. Some rooms have good kitchenettes, most have air-con, and there's even a rooftop Jacuzzi.

Hotel Santa Lucía (☎ /fax 928-26-72, in the US 1-800-560-2445; hstalucia@prodigy.net.mx; Calle 55 No 508; s/d/tr M$400/450/500; P ⛾ ⛾) Across from the park of the same name, it is clean, secure and popular, and has an attractive lobby. The pool is small but clean, and the rooms have air-con, TV and phones. Rates include breakfast.

MIDRANGE

Hotel Aragón (☎ /fax 924-02-42; www.hotelaragon .com; Calle 57 No 474; s/d M$450/480; P ⛾ ⛾) The common areas of this hotel are great with a large courtyard and a narrow pool along one side. If only they followed the same theme in the modern, rather stagnant rooms. Still, the room rates include a continental breakfast and purified water, making this a solid value.

Hotel Montejo (☎ 928-03-90; fax 924-26-92; www .hotelmontejo.com; Calle 57; s/d/tr with air-con M$440/510/560; ✸) This is an eclectic, one-of-a-kind hotel with a central courtyard loaded with 400-year-old stone columns. Its big, clean rooms with classic colonial doors and tiled bathrooms are distributed around the courtyard on two floors. It's a bit overpriced for what you get.

Hotel Medio Mundo (☎ /fax 924-54-72; www.hotel mediomundo.com; Calle 55 No 533; d with fan M$600, r/ste with air-con M$750; ✸ ✺) This former private residence has been completely remodeled and painted in lovely colors. Its 12 ample, simply furnished rooms have super-comfortable beds, tile floors, beautiful tile sinks, great bathrooms and plenty of natural light.

Casa Mexilio (☎ /fax 928-25-05, in the US ☎ 800-538-6802; www.casamexilio.com; Calle 68 No 495; r M$550-850, ste M$1200; P ✸ ✺) It occupies a well-preserved, historic house with a maze of quiet, beautifully appointed rooms (some with fan, some air-con), a small bar and a postage-stamp–sized pool with Jacuzzi.

Hotel Colonial (☎ 923-64-44; fax 928-39-61; www.hotel colonial.com.mx; Calle 62 No 476; d/tr M$760/850; ✸ ✺) The Colonial features 73 comfortable rooms with air-con in a fairly modern building with a small clover-shaped pool and perhaps Mexico's smallest bar. They've recently renovated a few rooms; ask for a newer room.

our pick **Los Arcos Bed & Breakfast** (☎ 928-02-14; www.losarcosmerida.com; Calle 66; s/d M$850/950; ⬛ ✺) Certainly not for minimalists – there's art on every wall and in every corner – Los Arcos is a lovely, gay-friendly B&B with two guestrooms at the end of a drop-dead-gorgeous garden and pool area. Parrots, chihuahuas, a Jacuzzi and palm trees add to the decor. Rooms have an eclectic assortment of art and antiques, excellent beds and bathrooms, and come stocked with CD players, bathrobes and sarongs.

TOP END
Hotel Casa del Balam (☎ 924-21-50, in the US or Mexico 800-624-8451, fax 924-50-11; www.casabalam.com; Calle 60 No 488; d M$1200; ✸ ✺) This place is centrally located and has a great pool and large, quiet colonial-style rooms with powerful central

air-con. The Balam often offers hefty discounts during quiet times.

Hotel Hacienda Mérida (☎ 924-43-63; www.hotel haciendamerida.com; Calle 62; r M$1500-1750; ✸ ✺) A new entrant in the upscale boutique category, the Hacienda is lovely by night, with illuminated columns leading you past the pool to your classically styled chambers. By day you can see that the hotel still needs a bit of work to qualify for the hefty price tag. This said, it beats staying in a heartless business hotel for most.

Hyatt Regency Mérida (☎ 942-02-02; fax 925-70-02; www.hyatt.com; Av Colón 344; d from M$1700; P ✸ ✺) Not far from the Fiesta Americana (another good high-end bet), the 17-story Hyatt offers some of Mérida's chi-chiest hotel digs, with some 300 rooms, tennis courts, a gym and steam bath, and a great pool with swim-up bar.

Eating
BUDGET
our pick **Mercado Municipal Lucas de Gálvez** (cnr Calles 56A & 67) Mérida's least-expensive eateries are in the Mercado Municipal Lucas de Gálvez.

Mercado Municipal No 2 (Calle 70) Numero Dos is a less crowded, but still cheap and good market on the north side of Parque de Santiago.

Fe y Esperanza (☎ 241-09-95; Calle 60 No 452; tacos & tortas M$8-28; ✹ 7:30am-5:30pm Mon-Sat) This popular hole in the wall offers simple snacks like tacos and tortas. High spenders can go upscale with a set lunch (M$28) with your choice of meat, rice, beans, salad and *agua fresca* fruit juice. The service is super friendly.

La Flor de Santiago (☎ 928-55-91; Calle 70; mains M$30-60; ✹ 7am-11pm) Chiapas coffee is served in incongruous, chipped Willow-ware cups in this cafeteria-style eatery. The guacamole is near perfect, and there is a wide selection of Mexican comfort foods, such as chicken tamales or turkey soup. A Saturday or Sunday breakfast buffet costs M$60. It's all good, and the friendly, no-nonsense waiters are obliging.

El Trapiche (☎ 928-12-31; Calle 62 No 491; mains M$26-50; ✹ 8am-midnight) A great place close to El Centro, El Trapiche has cheap Mexican eats in a casual environment that includes passing visits by just about every peddler around. As you eat, you can stock up on Cuban cigars or Chiapas belts or jewelry. If you don't want to buy anything and just want to eat, choose a table in the back near the fountain. Pitchers of *agua de melón* (cantaloupe blended with water and a touch of sugar) cost only M$45.

A few blocks east of the Plaza Grande are side-by-side **supermarkets** (Calle 56) as well as a branch of **Super Bodega** (cnr Calles 67 & 54A), a market–department store chain.

MIDRANGE

Il Caffé Italiano (☎ 928-00-93; Calle 57A; mains M$75-150; ◷ 8am-midnight Mon-Sat) It's an Italian-style café with nice espressos, good mains and very interesting desserts: the strawberries with balsamic vinegar and ice cream is something completely different.

Pop Cafetería (☎ 928-61-63; Calle 57; breakfast M$28-48, mains M$35-90; ◷ 7am-midnight Mon-Sat, 8am-midnight Sun) There's an Art Deco feel to this little cafeteria-style restaurant, which serves up cheap breakfast combinations and a good variety of Mexican dishes; try the chicken in dark, rich *mole* (M$45).

Main Street (☎ 923-68-50; Calle 60; breakfast M$50-80, mains M$60-140; ◷ 7am-11pm) On the edge of Parque Hidalgo, it serves generous, reasonably priced breakfasts, as well as ample portions of pasta and other dishes, including mediocre pizza. The outdoor tables offer prime people-watching opportunities.

Amaro (☎ 928-24-51; www.restauranteamaro.com; Calle 59; mains M$55-100; ◷ 11am-1am; Ⓥ) The Amaro is a romantic dining spot, especially at night, when there's usually a duo performing ballads. It is set in the courtyard of the house in which Andrés Quintana Roo – poet, statesman and drafter of Mexico's Declaration of Independence – was born in 1787. The service and food are good (but check your bill carefully), and the menu includes Yucatecan dishes and a variety of vegetarian plates, as well as some continental dishes, crepes and pizzas. If it's slow it will close at 11pm.

Pane e Vino (☎ 928-62-28; Calle 62; mains M$70-100; ◷ 6pm-midnight Tue-Sun; Ⓥ) This Italian-run joint serves tasty antipasti and salads (with olive oil and balsamic vinegar if you wish), lasagne, fish, meat and a selection of respectable wines by the glass or bottle. The star attractions are the fresh handmade pastas, which vary daily and usually include gnocchi, ravioli and fettuccine.

TOP END

Restaurante Pórtico del Peregrino (☎ 928-61-63; Calle 57; mains M$70-140; ◷ noon-midnight) There are sev-

eral pleasant, traditional-style dining rooms (some with air-con) surrounding a small courtyard in this upscale eatery. Yucatecan dishes such as *pollo pibil* (chicken flavored with *achiote* sauce and wrapped in banana leaves) are its forte, but you'll find many international dishes and a broad range of seafood and steaks as well. *Mole poblano* (chicken in a chocolate and chili sauce) is a house specialty, as is artery-clogging *queso relleno* (Dutch cheese stuffed with spiced ground beef).

Alberto's Continental Patio (☎ 928-53-67; cnr Calles 64 & 57; mains M$70-170, set dinners M$240-280; ◷ 1pm-11pm Mon-Sat, 6pm-11pm Sun; Ⓥ) Alberto's offers yet more colonial-courtyard (as well as indoor) dining. The setting is extremely atmospheric, chock-a-block with religious artifacts, Maya ceramic figures and greenery. Middle Eastern dishes such as hummus, babaganoush and tabouleh are served with pita bread, and can be a welcome change from Mexican food. The steaks, poultry and seafood are also good, as is the service. Tipplers will appreciate the fine brandy selection.

Entertainment

Mérida offers many folkloric and musical events in parks and historic buildings, put on by local performers of considerable skill. Admission is free except as noted. Check with one of the tourist information offices to confirm schedules and find out about special events; www.yucatantoday.com offers monthly news and often highlights seasonal events. The Centro Cultural Olimpio (see p917) has something on nearly every night, from films to concerts to art installations.

Mérida has several cinemas, most of which show first-run Hollywood fare in English, with Spanish subtitles (ask *'inglés?'* if you need to be sure), as well as other foreign films and Mexican offerings. Cinema tickets cost about M$45 for evening shows, M$25 for matinees. Try **Cines Rex** (Calle 57), between Calles 70 and 72, or **Teatro Mérida** (Calle 62), between Calles 59 and 61.

Take a cab to the Prolongació'n de Montejo, where you'll have your choice of bumping discos and uber-chic lounges. Most charge a cover. **El Cielo** (☎ 944-51-27; Prolongación de Montejo), between Calle 25 and Av Campestre, is a local favorite, as is the nearby **Slavia** (☎ 926-65-87; Prolongación de Montejo s/n).

Caribbean Blue (☎ 923-22-79; Calle 60; M$30 cover; ◷ 10pm-3:30am), between Calles 57 & 55, is one of a cluster of bars on this block that have music and dancing, with a live nine-piece salsa band most nights. The crowd is fairly young, with a mix of locals and visitors.

KY60 (Calle 55 btwn Calles 58 & 60; no cover; 🕙 9pm-3am) is not a gay bar, despite the Village People, men-wearing-construction-outfits vibe. It's got nice pool tables and is popular with guys and gals, gays and straights, locals and tourists, probably because of its reasonably priced beers, which seem to be a universal attraction. It's between Calles 57 and 55.

Shopping

Mérida is a fine place for buying Yucatecan handicrafts. Purchases to consider include hammocks and traditional Maya clothing such as the colorful, embroidered *huipiles*, panama hats and of course the wonderfully comfortable *guayaberas* (thin-fabric shirts with pockets and appliquéd designs worn by Yucatecan men).

During the last days of February or the beginning of March (the dates vary) is **Kihuic**, a market that fills the Plaza Grande with handicraft artisans from all over Mexico.

Mérida's main market, **Mercado Municipal Lucas de Gálvez** (cnr Calles 56A & 67), is a great spot to pick up that perfect piece of kitsch.

HANDICRAFTS

Casa de las Artesanías (☎ 928-66-76; Calle 63; 🕙 9am-8pm Mon-Sat, 9am-2pm Sun) One place to start looking for handicrafts is this government-supported market for local artisans selling just about everything. Prices are fixed and a bit high. It's between Calles 64 and 66.

Artesanías Bazar García Rejón (cnr Calles 65 & 60) Concentrates a wide variety of products into one area of shops.

Miniaturas (☎ 928-65-03; Calle 59; 🕙 10am-8pm) Here you'll find lots of small Día de los Muertos tableaux, tinwork and figurines of every sort, from ceramics to toy soldiers. It's between Calles 60 and 62.

CLOTHING & PANAMA HATS

Camisería Canul (☎ 923-56-61; Calle 62; 🕙 8:30am-9pm Mon-Sat, 10am 1pm Sun) A good place for *guayaberas* and *huipiles*. It has been in business for years, offers fixed prices and does custom tailoring. It's between Calles 57 and 59.

The Campeche town of Bécal is the center of the hat-weaving trade, but you can buy good examples of the hat-makers' art in Mérida.

Getting There & Away

AIR

Mérida's tiny but modern airport is a 10km, 20-minute ride southwest of the Plaza Grande off Hwy 180 (Av de los Itzáes). It has car-rental desks, an ATM and currency-exchange booth and a **tourist office** (🕙 9am-5pm) that helps mainly with hotel reservations.

Most international flights to Mérida are connections through Mexico City or Cancún. Nonstop international services are provided by Aeroméxico (daily from Los Angeles, thrice weekly from Miami), Continental and Northwestern (both from Houston, total eight times weekly). Most domestic flights are operated by small regional airlines, with a few flights by Aeroméxico and Mexicana.

Aeroméxico (☎ at airport 920-12-93, 800-021-40-10; www.aeromexico.com) Flies to Mexico City, Los Angeles and Miami.

Aviacsa (☎ 800-006-22-00, at airport 925-68-90; www .aviacsa.com.mx) Flies to Mexico City.

Click Mexicana (☎ 800-112-54-25, 946-13-66; Paseo de Montejo 500B) Flies between Mérida and Cancún, Veracruz and Villahermosa, with connections to Tuxtla Gutiérrez, Havana and other destinations.

Continental Airlines (☎ 800-900-50-00, 946-18-88; Paseo Montejo 437; www.continental.com) Flies nonstop between Houston and Mérida.

Delta (☎ in the US 1-800-123-4710; www.delta.com) Offers nonstop service from Miami.

Mexicana (☎ 924-66-33, 800-112-54-25; Paseo de Montejo 493) Nonstop flights to Mexico City.

BUS

Mérida is the bus transportation hub of the Yucatán Peninsula. Take care with your gear on night buses and those serving popular tourist destinations (especially 2nd-class buses); we have received many reports of theft on the night runs to Chiapas and of a few daylight thefts on the Chichén Itzá and other routes.

There are a number of bus terminals, and some lines operate out of (and stop at) more than one terminal. Tickets for departure from one terminal can often be bought at another, and destinations overlap greatly among lines. Some lines offer round-trip tickets to nearby towns that bring the fare down quite a bit. Following are some of the terminals, the bus lines operating out of them and areas served.

Hotel Fiesta Americana (☎ 924-08-55; Av Colón) A small 1st-class terminal on the west side of the hotel complex, near Calle 56A, servicing guests of the luxury hotels on Av Colón, north of the center. ADO GL and

Super Expresso services run between here and Cancún, Campeche, Chetumal and Playa del Carmen.

Parque de San Juan (Calle 69) From all around the square and church, vans and *combis* (vans or minibuses) depart for Dzibilchaltún Ruinas, Muna, Oxkutzcab, Tekax, Ticul and other points.

Progreso (Calle 62 No 524 btwn Calles 65 & 67) Progreso has a separate bus terminal for its buses.

CAME Terminal (reservations ☎ 924-83-91; Calle 70 btwn Calles 69 and 71) Sometimes referred to as the 'Terminal de Primera Clase,' Mérida's main terminal has

(mostly 1st-class) buses to points around the Yucatán Peninsula and such places as Mexico City, Palenque, San Cristóbal de Las Casas and Villahermosa. CAME has card phones and an ATM and runs counters for tourist, bus and hotel information. The baggage check is open 6am to midnight daily and charges M$5 for storage from 6am to noon, M$10 for all day.

Terminal de Segunda Clase (Calle 69) Also known as Terminal 69 (Sesenta y Nueve) or simply Terminal de Autobuses, this terminal is located just around the corner from CAME. ADO, Mayab, Oriente, Sur and TRT run mostly

BUSES FROM MÉRIDA

Destination	Fare	Duration	Frequency
Campeche	1st-class M$122 (short route)	2½-3½hr	hourly
	2nd-class M$122	2½-3½hr	every 30min to 7:15pm
Cancún	M$150-260	4-6hr	frequent
Celestún	M$44	2hr	15 daily from Terminal Noreste
Chetumal	deluxe M$170-250	6-8hr	3 daily from Terminal de Segunda Clase
	1st-class M$170-250	6-8hr	2 daily from Terminal CAME
	2nd-class M$170-250	6-8hr	5 daily
Chichén Itzá	deluxe M$80	1¾-hr	3 daily
	2nd-class M$54	2½hr	hourly (Cancún-bound buses stop at Chichén Itzá or nearby Pisté)
Cobá	M$94-106	3½-4hr	1 daily
Escárcega	1st-class M$176	5-5½hr	4 daily
	2nd-class M$150	5-5½hr	frequent
Felipe Carrillo Puerto	1st-class M$134-146	5½-6hr	10 daily
Izamal	M$27	1½hr	frequent from Terminal Noreste
Mayapán Ruinas	M$31	1½hr	15 daily from Terminal Noreste, continuing to Oxkutzcab
Mexico City (Terminal Norte)	M$858-1136	19hr	1 daily (midnight)
Palenque	deluxe M$332	8-9hr	1 daily
	1st-class M$316	8-9hr	4 daily
Playa del Carmen	deluxe M$258-310	4½-8hr	11 daily
	2nd-class M$258-310	4½-8hr	frequent
Progreso	M$12.50	1hr	frequent from the Progreso bus terminal, shared taxis (some with air-con) from a parking lot on Calle 60 between Calles 65 and 67
Río Lagartos	1st-class M$110	3-4hr	3 daily from Terminal Noreste
	2nd-class M$70	3-4hr	3 daily from Terminal Noreste
Ruta Puuc (round-trip)	M$126	8hr	1 daily at 8am (stops 30 min in each site)
Ticul	M$40	1¾hr	frequent; also frequent cheaper and quicker *combis* from Parque de San Juan
Tizimín	M$83	2½-4hr	6 daily Terminal Noreste (for Isla Holbox, connect in Tizimín)
Tulum	deluxe M$172	4hr	3 daily (2nd-class service available but it takes much longer)
Uxmal	M$39	1-1½hr	15 daily; round-trip available
Valladolid	M$66-112	2½-3½hr	hourly, including Super Expresso, 2nd-class Oriente and ATS

YUCATÁN PENINSULA

2nd-class buses to points in the state and around the peninsula. ATS buses run Uxmal and Ruta Puuc from here. The terminal has a luggage checkroom.

Terminal Noreste (Calle 67 btwn Calles 50 and 52) LUS, Occidente and Oriente use this terminal. Destinations served from here include many small towns in the northeast of the peninsula, including Tizimín and Río Lagartos; frequent services to Cancún and points along the way; as well as small towns south and west of Mérida (served by Occidente), Ticul and Oxkutzcab. Some Oriente buses depart from Terminal 69 and stop here; others leave directly from here (eg those to Izamal and Tizimín).

CAR

The most flexible way to tour the many archaeological sites around Mérida is by rental car, especially if you have two or more people to share costs. Assume you will pay a total of M\$550 to M\$650 per day (tax, insurance and gas included) for short-term rental of a cheap car. Getting around Mérida's sprawling tangle of one-way streets and careening buses is better done on foot or on a careening bus.

Several agencies have branches at the airport as well as on Calle 60 between Calles 55 and 57, including **Budget** (☎ 925-19-00; www.budgetcancun.com), **Avis** (☎ 946-15-24; www.avis.com.mx) and **Hertz** (☎ 946-25-54; www.hertz.com.mx). All rent for about M\$350 to M\$500 a day. You'll get the best deal by booking ahead of time over the internet.

See p874 for details of the expensive toll highway between Mérida and Cancún.

Getting Around
TO/FROM THE AIRPORT

Bus 79 (Aviación) travels between the airport and the city center every 15 to 30 minutes until 9pm, with occasional service until 11pm. The half-hour trip (M\$4) is via a roundabout route; the best place to catch the bus to the airport is on Calle 70, south of Calle 69, near the CAME Terminal.

Transporte Terrestre (☎ 946-15-29) provides speedy service between the airport and the center, charging M\$100 per carload (same price for hotel pick-up). A taxi from the center to the airport should cost about M\$80 (but it's hard to get this price *from* the airport, so walk out to the main street and flag one down or else prepare to pay M\$200).

BUS

Most parts of Mérida that you'll want to visit are within five or six blocks of the Plaza Grande and are thus accessible on foot. Given the slow speed of city traffic, particularly in the market areas, travel on foot is also the fastest way to get around.

City buses are cheap at M\$4, but routes can be confusing. Most start in suburban neighborhoods, skirt the city center, and terminate in another distant suburban neighborhood. To travel between the Plaza Grande and the upscale neighborhoods to the north along Paseo de Montejo, catch the Ruta 10 on Calle 57 between Calles 58 and 60, a block north of the Parque Hidalgo, or catch a 'Tecnológico,' 'Hyatt' or 'Montejo' bus on Calle 60 and get out at Av Colón. To return to the city center, catch any bus heading south on Paseo de Montejo displaying the same signs and/or 'Centro.' Many will let you off on Calle 58 north of Calle 61.

TAXI

Taxis in Mérida are not metered. Rates are fixed, with a M\$30 minimum fare, which will get you from the bus terminals to all downtown hotels. Most rides within city limits do not exceed M\$60. Taxi stands can be found at most of the barrio parks, or dial ☎ 982-15-04 or ☎ 982-11-71; service is available 24 hours (dispatch fees are an extra M\$10 to M\$20).

SOUTH OF MÉRIDA

There's a lot to do and see south of Mérida. The major draws are the old *henequen* plantations, some still used for cultivating leaves, and the well-preserved Maya ruins like Uxmal and the lesser known sites along the Ruta Puuc. Beyond these tourist draws you'll find seldom-visited cenotes and caves, and traditional villages where life still moves at an agrarian pace: women still wear *huipiles* and speak Yucatec, and their men still bike out to cut firewood or shoot a pheasant for dinner. The smell of tortillas mixes with the citrus-like scent of the semi-arid plants that call the region home. It's a rough-and-tumble landscape, and one of the few spots on the peninsula where you'll actually find a few hills.

Uxmal

Some visitors rank **Uxmal** (admission M\$95, parking M\$10, guides M\$400; ⏰ 8am-5pm; ♿) (pronounced 'oosh-*mahl*') among the top Maya archaeological sites. It certainly is one of the most harmonious and peaceful. Fascinating, well-preserved structures made of pink-hued limestone cover the wide area. Adding to its appeal is Uxmal's setting in the hilly Puuc region, which lent its name to the architectural patterns in this area. *Puuc* means 'hills,' and these, rising to about 100m, are the only ones in the northwest region of the otherwise flat peninsula.

HISTORY

Uxmal was an important city, and its dominance extended to the nearby towns of Sayil, Kabah, Xlapak and Labná. Although Uxmal means 'Thrice Built' in Maya, it was actually constructed five times.

That a sizable population flourished in this dry area is yet more testimony to the engineering skills of the Maya, who built a series of reservoirs and *chultunes* (cisterns) lined with lime mortar to catch and hold water during the dry season. First settled in about AD 600, Uxmal was influenced by highland Mexico in its architecture, most likely through contact fostered by trade. This influence is reflected in the town's serpent imagery, phallic symbols and columns. The well-proportioned Puuc architecture, with its intricate, geometric mosaics sweeping across the upper parts of elongated facades, was also strongly influenced by the slightly earlier Río Bec and Chenes styles.

The scarcity of water in the region meant that Chac, the rain god or sky serpent, was supreme in importance. His image is ubiquitous at the site, in the form of stucco masks protruding from facades and cornices. There is

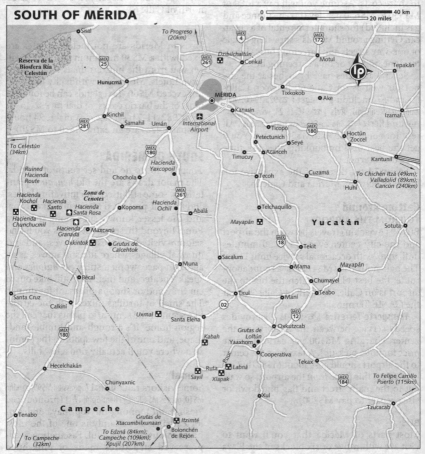

SOUTH OF MÉRIDA

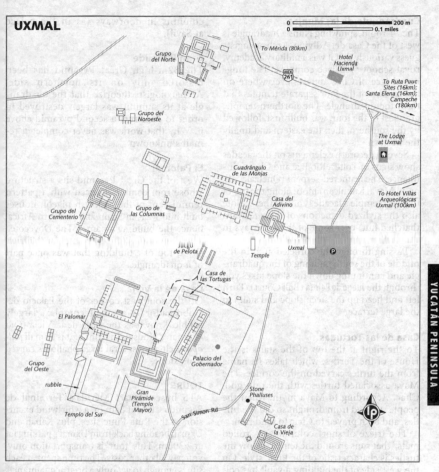

UXMAL

0   200 m
0   0.1 miles

To Mérida (80km)

Hotel Hacienda Uxmal

To Ruta Puuc Sites (16km); Santa Elena (16km); Campeche (180km)

Grupo del Norte

The Lodge at Uxmal

Grupo del Noroeste

Cuadrángulo de las Monjas

To Hotel Villas Arqueológicas Uxmal (100km)

Grupo del Cementerio

Grupo de las Columnas

Casa del Adivino

Uxmal   P

Juego de Pelota

Temple

Casa de las Tortugas

El Palomar

Palacio del Gobernador

Grupo del Oeste

rubble

Stone Phalluses

Gran Pirámide (Templo Mayor)

Templo del Sur

San Simon Rd

Casa de la Vieja

much speculation as to why Uxmal was largely abandoned in about AD 900; drought conditions may have reached such proportions that the inhabitants had to relocate. Later, the Xiu dynasty, which had controlled Uxmal for several hundred years, moved their seat of power to near present-day Maní, launching a rebellion on the kingdom of Mayapán, which had usurped much of the power in the region.

Rediscovered by archaeologists in the 19th century, Uxmal was first excavated in 1929 by Frans Blom. Although much has been restored, much has yet to be discovered.

INFORMATION
The price of admission, if you retain the wristband ticket, includes a 45-minute **sound-and-**

light show (8pm summer, 7pm winter). It's in Spanish, but translation devices are available (M$25). The cost of the show only is M$30, applicable toward the next day's site admission.

SIGHTS
Casa del Adivino
This 39m-high temple (the Magician's House) was built on an oval base. The smoothly sloping sides have been restored, and they date from the temple's fifth incarnation. The four earlier temples were covered in the rebuilding, except for the high doorway on the west side, which remains from the fourth incarnation. Decorated in elaborate Chenes style, the doorway proper forms the mouth of a gigantic Chac mask.

Cuadrángulo de las Monjas

The 74-room, sprawling Nuns' Quadrangle is west of the Casa del Adivino. Archaeologists guess variously that it was a military academy, royal school or palace complex. The long-nosed face of Chac appears everywhere on the facades of the four separate temples that form the quadrangle. The northern temple, grandest of the four, was built first, followed by the southern, then the eastern and finally the western.

Several decorative elements on the facades show signs of Toltec, Río Bec and Chenes influence. The feathered-serpent (Quetzalcóatl, or, in Maya, Kukulcán) motif along the top of the west temple's facade is one of these. Note also the stylized depictions of the *na* (Maya thatched hut) over some of the doorways in the northern and southern buildings.

Passing through the corbeled arch in the middle of the south building of the quadrangle and continuing down the slope takes you through the **Juego de Pelota** (Ball Court). Turn left and head up the steep slope and stairs to the large terrace.

Casa de las Tortugas

To the right at the top of the stairs is the House of the Turtles, which takes its name from the turtles carved on the cornice. The Maya associated turtles with the rain god, Chac. According to Maya myth, when the people suffered from drought so did the turtles, and both prayed to Chac to send rain.

The frieze of short columns, or 'rolled mats,' that runs around the temple below the turtles is characteristic of the Puuc style. On the west side of the building a vault has collapsed, affording a good view of the corbeled arch that supported it.

Palacio del Gobernador

The Governor's Palace has a magnificent facade nearly 100m long, which Mayanist Michael D Coe called 'the finest structure at Uxmal and the culmination of the Puuc style.' Buildings in Puuc style have walls filled with rubble, faced with cement and then covered in a thin veneer of limestone squares; the lower part of the facade is plain, the upper part festooned with stylized Chac faces and geometric designs, often lattice-like or fretted. Other elements of Puuc style are decorated cornices, rows of half-columns (as in the House of the Turtles) and round columns in doorways (as in the palace at Sayil).

Gran Pirámide

The 32m-high Great Pyramid has been restored only on its northern side. Archaeologists theorize that the quadrangle at its summit was largely destroyed in order to construct a second pyramid above it. Why that work was never completed remains unknown.

El Palomar

West of the Great Pyramid sits a structure whose roof comb is latticed with a pattern reminiscent of the Moorish pigeon houses built into walls in Spain and northern Africa, hence the building's name, 'The Dovecote.' The nine honeycombed triangular 'belfries' sit on top of a building that was once part of a quadrangle.

Casa de la Vieja

Off the southeast corner of the Palacio del Gobernador is a small complex, largely rubble, known as the Casa de la Vieja (Old Woman's House). In front of it is a small *palapa* sheltering several large phalluses carved from stone.

TOURS

ATS buses depart Mérida's Terminal de Segunda Clase at 8am on a whirlwind excursion to the Ruta Puuc sites, plus Kabah and Uxmal, heading back from Uxmal's parking lot at 2:30pm. This 'tour' is transportation only; you pay all other costs. The time spent at each site is enough to get only a brief acquaintance, though some say the two hours at Uxmal is sufficient, if barely. The cost is M$126 for the whole deal, or M$78 if you want to be dropped off at Uxmal in the morning and picked up from there in the afternoon.

SLEEPING & EATING

There is no town at Uxmal, only several top-end hotels. Cheaper lodgings can be found in Santa Elena (opposite), 16km away, or in Ticul (see p933), 30km to the east.

Hotel Villas Arqueológicas Uxmal (off Map p927; ☎ / fax 997-974-60-20, in the US 800-514-8244; www.clubmed.com; d/tr M$860/1060; ✷ ♨) This Club Med is a good family spot with a pool, tennis courts and billiards, but the rooms are rather small and the beds are curiously springy.

DIY: EXPLORE THE BACKROADS SOUTH OF MÉRIDA

There are numerous attractions worth seeing as you travel south from Mérida. Here are a few of our favorites:

- **Hacienda Yaxcopoil** A vast estate that grew and processed *henequén*; many of its numerous French Renaissance-style buildings have undergone picturesque restorations.

- **Hacienda Ochil** Provides a fascinating, though basic, look at how *henequén* was grown and processed.

- **Grutas de Calcehtok** These caves are said by some to comprise the longest dry-cave system on the Yucatán Peninsula.

- **Oxkintok** Inscriptions found at the site contain some of the oldest known dates in the Yucatán, and indicate that the city was inhabited from the Preclassic to the Postclassic period (300 BC to AD 1500), reaching its greatest importance between AD 475 to 860.

- **Ruined Hacienda Route** A fascinating alternative return trip if you're driving out of Celestún is to turn south off Hwy 281 where a sign points to Chunchucmil. Here you'll find a series of old haciendas.

- **Ticul to Tihosuco** The route from Ticul to Tihosuco, in Quintana Roo, is seldom traveled by tourists. Part of the route is called the Ruta de los Conventos (Route of the Convents), as each of these tiny villages has a cathedral or church, many in beautiful disrepair.

- **Cuzamá** Three kilometers east of the town of Cuzamá, accessed from the small village of Chunkanan, are the Cenotes de Cuzamá, a series of three amazing limestone sinkholes accessed by horse-drawn railcart in an old *henequén* hacienda.

Hotel Hacienda Uxmal (☎ 997-976-20-12, in the US 800-235-4079; www.mayaland.com; d with air-con M$1480; ✷ ☎) This Mayaland Resort is 500m from the ruins. It housed the archaeologists who explored and restored Uxmal. Wide, tiled verandas, high ceilings, great bathrooms and a beautiful swimming pool make this a very comfortable place to stay.

The Lodge at Uxmal (☎ 997-976-20-10, in the US 800-235-4079; www.mayaland.com; d May-Oct M$2200-2850, Nov-Apr M$3940-4900; ☎ ✷) This Mayaland Resort is Uxmal's newest luxury hotel. The Hacienda's rooms are a bit nicer, but you can't beat the easy access to the ruins. The pool is equally delicious as are the monster basin tubs – some rooms even have Jacuzzis.

GETTING THERE & AWAY

Uxmal is 80km from Mérida. Most buses that take the inland route between Mérida and Campeche will drop you off at Uxmal, Santa Elena, Kabah or the Ruta Puuc turnoff. But be aware that when you want to leave, passing buses may be full (especially on Saturday and Monday).

If you're going from Uxmal to Ticul, first take a northbound bus to Muna (M$5, 20 minutes) then catch one of the frequent buses from there to Ticul (M$8, 30 minutes).

Santa Elena

The nearest town to Uxmal is Santa Elena. It has a small **museum** (admission M$10; ☉ 8am-7pm) dedicated to a gruesome find: 18th-century child mummies found buried beneath the adjoining cathedral, and some *henequén*-related exhibits. Go for a little DIY adventure by heading 4km outside town to the Mulchic pyramid; locals can tell you how to get there.

Bungalows Sacbé (☎ 985-858-12-81 or 997-978-51-58; www.sacbebungalows.com.mx; d M$230-290) There's a nice garden here, and all the rooms have fans, good screens and decent beds. The friendly Mexican and French owners serve a good, cheap breakfast (M$50). To get here, ask the bus driver to drop you off at the *campo de béisbol* (baseball field) *de Santa Elena*. It's about 200m south of the town's southern entrance.

Flycatcher Inn (☎ 997-107-41-26 or 997-102-08-65; www.flycatcherinn.com; d M$400-500, ste or cottage M$600) It features six squeaky-clean rooms, an enormous master suite and a separate cottage. All have great porches, super-comfy imported beds, plus hammocks, excellent screenage and great bathrooms. The inn's driveway is less than 100m north of Santa Elena's southern entrance; there's a bus stop just across the highway from it, near Restaurant El Chac-Mool.

YUCATÁN PENINSULA

Restaurant El Chac-Mool (☎ 999-996-20-25; mains M$40-60; ☺ 8am-9pm) On Hwy 261 at the southern entrance to Santa Elena, this is a friendly place serving Yucatecan food that includes a hearty vegetarian plate of rice, beans and fried bananas. They have a little store here, too.

Santa Elena is 16km southeast of Uxmal and 8km north of Kabah – for details of bus services from Uxmal, see p929; from Ticul see p933.

Kabah

After Uxmal, Kabah (AD 750–950) was the most important city in the region. The **ruins** (admission M$34; ☺ 8am-5pm) straddle Hwy 261. The guard shack-cum-souvenir shop (selling snacks and cold drinks) and the bulk of the restored ruins are on the east side of the highway.

The facade of **El Palacio de los Mascarones** (Palace of Masks) is an amazing sight, covered in nearly 300 masks of Chac, the rain god or sky serpent. Most of their huge curling noses are broken off; the best intact beak is at the building's south end. These curled-up noses may have given the palace its modern Maya name, Codz Poop (Rolled Mat).

Once you're up to your ears in noses, head around back to check out the two restored **atlantes** (an atlas – plural atlantes – is a male figure used as a supporting column). These are especially interesting as they're among the very few 3D human figures you'll see at a Maya site. One is headless and the other wears a jaguar mask atop his head. A third atlas stands by the office near the entrance.

From here be sure to check out **El Palacio** (The Palace), with its groups of decorative *columnillas* (little columns) on the upper part of the facade; these are a distinctive characteristic of Puuc architectural style. A couple of hundred meters through the jungle from here is **Templo de las Columnas**. This building has more rows of impressive decorative columns.

Across the highway from El Palacio, a path leads to the **Gran Pirámide** (Great Pyramid). And from the Great Pyramid the path ends at the impressive, restored **El Arco**. It's said that the *sacbé* (cobbled and elevated ceremonial road) leading all the way from here goes through the jungle all the way to Uxmal, terminating at a smaller arch; in the other direction it goes to Labná. Once, much of the Yucatán Peninsula was con-

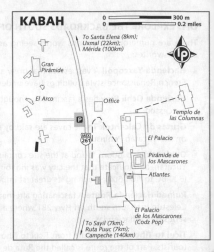

nected by these marvelous 'white roads' of rough limestone.

Kabah is 100km from Mérida, a ride of about two hours (see p929). Buses will usually make flag stops at the entrance to the ruins.

Ruta Puuc

Just 5km south of Kabah on Hwy 261, a road branches off to the east and winds past the ruins of Sayil, Xlapak and Labná, ending at the Grutas de Loltún. This is the Ruta Puuc, and its sites offer some marvelous architectural detail and a deeper acquaintance with the Puuc Maya civilization, which flourished between about AD 750 and 950.

The most convenient way to visit the Ruta Puuc sites is by car; however, there is a reliable bus service that tours the route daily as well (see p933).

SAYIL

The ruins of **Sayil** (admission M$34; ☺ 8am-5pm) are 4.5km from the junction of the Ruta Puuc with Hwy 261.

Sayil is best known for **El Palacio**, the huge three-tiered building with a facade some 85m long, reminiscent of the Minoan palace on Crete. The distinctive columns of Puuc architecture are used here over and over – as supports for the lintels, as decoration between doorways and as a frieze above them – alternating with huge stylized Chac masks and 'descending gods.'

Taking the path south from the palace for about 400m and bearing left, you come to the temple **El Mirador**, whose roosterlike roof comb was once painted bright red. About 100m beyond El Mirador, beneath a protective *palapa,* is a stela bearing the relief of a fertility god with an enormous phallus.

XLAPAK

From the entrance gate at Sayil, it's 6km east to the entrance gate at **Xlapak** (admission free; ☉ 8am-5pm). The name means 'Old Walls' in Maya and was a general term among local people for ancient ruins. The ornate *palacio* at Xlapak (*shla*-pak) is quite a bit smaller than those at Kabah and Sayil, only about 20m in length. It's decorated with the Chac masks, columns and colonnettes, and fretted geometric latticework of the Puuc style. The building is interesting and on a bit of a lean. Plenty of motmots (a colorful bird) brighten up the surrounding forests.

LABNÁ

This is *the* site not to miss. Archaeologists believe that, at one point in the 9th century, some 3000 Maya lived at **Labná** (admission M$34; ☉ 8am-5pm). To support such numbers in these arid hills, water was collected in *chultunes*. At Labná's peak there were some 60 *chultunes* in and around the city; several are still visible.

El Palacio, the first building you come to at Labná, is one of the longest in the Puuc region, and much of its interesting decorative carving is in good shape. On the west corner of the main

structure's facade is a serpent's head with a human face peering out from between its jaws, the symbol of the planet Venus. Toward the hill from this is an impressive Chac mask, and nearby is the lower half of a human figure (possibly a ballplayer) in loincloth and leggings.

The lower level has several more well-preserved Chac masks, and the upper level contains a large *chultún* that still holds water. The view from there, of the site and the hills beyond, is impressive.

From the palace a limestone-paved *sacbé* leads to **El Arco Labná**, which is best known for its magnificent arch, once part of a building that separated two courtyards. The corbeled structure, 3m wide and 6m high, is well preserved, and the reliefs decorating its upper facade are exuberantly Puuc in style.

Standing on the opposite side of the arch and separated from it by the *sacbé* is a pyramid known as **El Mirador**, topped by a temple. The pyramid itself is largely stone rubble. The temple, with its 5m-high roof comb, is well positioned to be a lookout, hence its name.

GRUTAS DE LOLTÚN

Fifteen kilometers northeast of Labná, a sign points out the left turn to the Grutas de Loltún, 5km further northeast. The road passes through lush orchards and some banana and palm groves, a refreshing sight in this dry region.

These **caverns** (admission M$54; ☉ 9am-5pm; 👤) are the largest, most interesting cave system on the Yucatán Peninsula, and a treasure trove of data for archaeologists. Carbon dating of artifacts found here reveals that humans used the caves 2500 years ago. Chest-high murals of hands, faces, animals and geometric motifs were apparent as recently as 20 years ago, but so many people have touched them that barely a trace remains. Now, visitors to the illuminated caves see mostly natural limestone formations, some of which are quite lovely.

To explore the labyrinth, you must take a scheduled guided tour at 9:30am, 11am, 12:30pm, 2pm, 3pm or 4pm. The service of the guides is included in the admission price, but since they receive little of that, an additional tip (M$20 to M$50 per person) is appreciated.

GETTING THERE & AWAY

Renting a car is the best option for reaching the Grutas, and once you're out of Mérida it's easy going on pretty good roads.

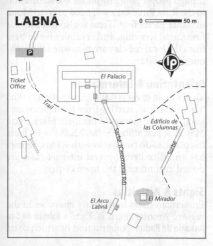

LABNÁ

0 ——— 50 m

P

Ticket Office

Trail

El Palacio

Sacbé (Ceremonial Rd)

Edificio de las Columnas

El Arco Labná

El Mirador

THE RISE OF MAYAPÁN & THE DEATH WARRANT OF MAYA INDEPENDENCE

The rise of Mayapán played an integral role in the ultimate demise of Maya rule in the region. The city was supposedly founded by Kukulcán (Quetzalcóatl) in 1007, shortly after the former ruler of Tula arrived in Yucatán. His dynasty, the Cocom, organized a confederation of city-states that included Uxmal, Chichén Itzá and many other notable cities. Despite their alliance, animosity arose between the Cocomes of Mayapán and the Itzáes of Chichén Itzá during the late 12th century, and the Cocomes stormed Chichén Itzá, forcing the Itzá rulers into exile. The Cocom dynasty emerged supreme in all of northern Yucatán.

Cocom supremacy lasted for almost 250 years, until the ruler of Uxmal, Ah Xupán Xiú, who had moved the capital close to present-day Maní, led a rebellion of the oppressed city-states and overthrew Cocom hegemony. The capital of Mayapán was utterly destroyed and remained uninhabited ever after.

But struggles for power continued in the region until 1542, when Francisco de Montejo the Younger conquered T'ho and established Mérida. At that point the current lord of Maní and ruler of the Xiú people, Ah Kukum Xiú, proposed to Montejo a military alliance against the Cocomes, his ancient rivals. Montejo accepted, and Xiú was baptized as a Christian, taking the name Francisco de Montejo Xiú (original, no?). The Cocomes were defeated and – too late – the Xiú rulers realized that they had signed the death warrant of Maya independence.

There is a bus service to Oxkutzcab (osh-kootz-*kahb*; M$44, 1½ hours), with departures at 8:30am and 12:30pm, from the Centro Bus Station in Mérida. Loltún is 7km southwest of Oxkutzcab, and there is usually some transportation along the road. *Camionetas* (pickups) and *camiones* (trucks) charge about M$10 for a ride

A taxi from Oxkutzcab may cost M$100 or so, one way.

Ruinas de Mayapán

These **ruins** (admission M$27; 🕑 8am-5pm) are some 50km southeast of Mérida, on Hwy 18. Though far less impressive than many Maya sites, Mayapán is historically significant, its main attractions are clustered in a compact core, and visitors usually have the place to themselves.

Among the structures that have been restored is the **Castillo de Kukulcán**, a climbable pyramid with fresco fragments around its base and, at its rear side, friezes depicting decapitated warriors. The reddish color is still faintly visible. The **Templo Redondo** (Round Temple) is vaguely reminiscent of El Caracol at Chichén Itzá. Close by is Itzmal Chen, a cenote that was a major Maya religious sanctuary.

GETTING THERE & AWAY

The Ruinas de Mayapán are just off Hwy 18, a few kilometers southwest of the town of Telchaquillo. LUS runs hourly 2nd-class buses between 5:30am and 8pm from the Noreste

terminal in Mérida (M$14 each way, 1½ hours) that will let you off near the entrance to the ruins and pick you up on your way back. Again, you may want to consider renting a car to get here.

TICUL

☎ 997 / pop 31,100

Ticul, 30km east of Uxmal, is the largest town in this ruin-rich region. It's dusty and quiet, with certainly no nightlife (other than perhaps a watering hole), but it has hotels and restaurants and transportation, and makes an attractive base for day trips to nearby ruins, though people going by public transportation to the Ruta Puuc sites will need to go to Muna or Santa Elena first. Ticul is also a center for fine *huipil* weaving, and ceramics made here from the local red clay are renowned throughout the Yucatán.

Orientation & Information

Ticul's main street is Calle 23, sometimes called 'Calle Principal', starting from the highway and going past the market to the main plaza, Plaza Mayor. A **post office** (🕑 8am-2:30pm Mon-Fri) faces the plaza, as do two banks with ATMs. Telmex has an office here. Several internet cafés are dotted around near the town center.

Sights & Activities

Franciscan friars built many churches in the region. Among them is Ticul's **Iglesia de San Antonio de Padua**, construction of which dates from the late 16th century. Although looted on several occasions, the church has some original touches, among them the stone statues of friars in primitive style flanking the side entrances and a Black Christ altarpiece ringed by crude medallions.

Diaganolly opposite to the Plaza Mayor is the recently built Plaza de la Cultura, which is all cement and stone but nevertheless an agreeable place to take the evening breeze.

Saturday mornings in Ticul are picturesque: Calle 23 near the public market is closed to motorized traffic, and the street fills with three-wheeled cycles transporting shoppers between the market and their homes. **Cine Ideal** (Calle 23), between Calles 26A and 28, shows mostly Spanish-dubbed films.

Sleeping

Hotel San Miguel (Calle 28 No 295D; s/d M$100/130; P) Near the market, the friendly management offers worn, simple rooms (some musty) with fans and bathrooms.

Hotel Sierra Sosa (☎ /fax 972-00-08; Calle 26 No 199A; s M$150, d/tr M$170/190, air-con extra M$60; ✦) The Sierra Sosa is just northwest of the plaza. It's friendly and a bit rundown, but has good beds and OK bathrooms.

Hotel San Antonio (☎ 972-19-83; cnr Calles 25A & 26; s M$260, d/tr M$300/350; P ✦) A clean lobby with TV and shiny tiled floors sets a good impression that is confirmed by decent beds; some rooms have great views of the square. The hotel lacks character, but here in Ticul, that's kind of reassuring.

Hotel Plaza (☎ 972-04-84; www.hotelplazayucatan .com; cnr Calles 23 & 26; d/ste M$360/460; ✦) Spacious rooms with white-tile floors, firm beds, and small but fun balconies make this a nice choice. The old building adds character, though the street-facing rooms are sometimes noisy.

Eating

Restaurant El Colorín (☎ 972-00-94; Calle 26 No 199B; set meal M$35; ✦ 7am-9pm) A cheap restaurant, half a block northwest of the plaza, it offers homemade meals.

Pizzaria La Gondola (☎ 972-01-12; Calle 23 No 208; mains M$40-90; ✦ 8am-1pm, 5pm-11pm) A clean place on the corner that's open late, it has sandwiches and slightly pricey pizzas with the usual plethora of toppings.

Ticul's lively **public market** (Calle 20A), between Calles 21 and 23, provides all the ingredients for picnics and snacks, and offers nice photo ops too. It also has lots of those wonderful eateries where the food is good, the portions generous and the prices low. Stalls at the new **Bazar de Comidas** (Calle 25) serve inexpensive prepared food.

Getting There & Away

BUS, COLECTIVO & TAXI

Ticul's 24-hour **bus terminal** (Calle 24) is behind the massive church. Mayab runs frequent 2nd-class buses between Mérida and Ticul (M$40, 1½ hours) from 4:30am to 9pm. Mayab and ADO run 11 buses to Felipe Carrillo Puerto (M$100, four hours), frequent ones to Oxkutzcab (M$8

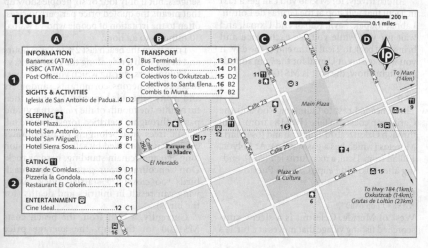

TICUL

0   200 m
0   0.1 miles

INFORMATION
Banamex (ATM).....................1 C1
HSBC (ATM).........................2 D1
Post Office..........................3 C1

SIGHTS & ACTIVITIES
Iglesia de San Antonio de Padua.4 D2

SLEEPING 🏠
Hotel Plaza.........................5 C1
Hotel San Antonio................6 C2
Hotel San Miguel..................7 B1
Hotel Sierra Sosa.................8 C1

EATING 🍴
Bazar de Comidas..................9 D1
Pizzería la Gondola..............10 C1
Restaurant El Colorín...........11 C1

ENTERTAINMENT 🎭
Cine Ideal.........................12 C1

TRANSPORT
Bus Terminal......................13 D1
Colectivos.........................14 D1
Colectivos to Oxkutzcab.......15 D2
Colectivos to Santa Elena....16 B2
Combis to Muna..................17 B2

Parque de la Madre
El Mercado

Main Plaza

Plaza de la Cultura

To Maní (14km)

To Hwy 184 (1km);
Oxkutzcab (14km);
Grutas de Loltún (23km)

to M$12) and five a day to Chetumal (M$150, six hours). There are also eight Mayab buses to Cancún daily (M$210, six hours), three of which also serve Tulum (M$150) and Playa del Carmen (M$170). ADO and Super Expresso have less frequent 2nd- and 1st-class services, respectively, to some of these destinations.

Colectivo vans go direct to Mérida's Parque de San Juan (M$33, 1½ hours) from their shiny new **terminal** (cnr Calles 24 & 25) as soon as they're full between 5am and 7:30pm. *Combis* for Oxkutzcab (M$10, 30 minutes) leave from Calle 25A on the south side of the church between 7am and 8:30pm.

Colectivos to Santa Elena (M$10), between Uxmal and Kabah, depart from Calle 30 between 6:15am and 7:30pm. They take Hwy 02 and drop you in Santa Elena to catch another bus northwest to Uxmal (15km) or south to Kabah (3.5km).

You can take a *combi* or bus to Muna (M$10) from in front of Lonchería Mary on Calle 23 near Calle 28, and then south to Uxmal. Ruta Puuc–bound travelers can catch a 6:30am bus from Ticul to Muna and pick up the ATS tour bus (M$50) for Labná, Sayil, Xlapak, Kabah and Uxmal at 9am on its way from Mérida. It returns to Muna at 3pm. Any of the buses leaving Ticul before 8am for Muna (or Mérida) will get you to Muna in time to catch the ATS Ruta Puuc bus. Another way would be to catch a *colectivo* from Ticul to Santa Elena, then walk a few blocks to Hwy 261, cross it, and wait for the Ruta Puuc bus to come by at about 9:30am.

Alternatively, for M$550 you can get a taxi in Ticul that will stop at the Grutas de Loltún, Labná, Xlapak, Sayil, Kabah and Uxmal, and wait for you while you see each place and bring you back to Ticul at the end of the day. If you wish to stay at Uxmal for the 7pm sound-and-light show, the cost is M$100.

CAR

Those headed east to Quintana Roo and the Caribbean coast can take Hwy 184 from Ticul through Oxkutzcab to Tzucacab and José María Morelos (which has a gas station). At Polyuc, 130km from Ticul, a road turns left (east), ending after 80km in Felipe Carrillo Puerto.

CELESTÚN
☎ 988 / pop 6400

West of Mérida, Celestún is a sleepy sun-scorched fishing village that moves at a turtle's pace – and that's the way locals like it. There's a pretty little square in the center of this town and some nice beaches (though the water is a bit turbid), but the real draw here is the Reserva de la Biosfera Ría Celestún, a wildlife sanctuary abounding in waterfowl, with flamingos as the star attraction.

Orientation & Information

All you need to know is that Calle 11 is the road into town (it comes due west from Mérida), ending at Calle 12, the road paralleling the beach along which lie most of the restaurants and hotels. Don't plan on using high-speed internet here, and bring lots of cash as there are no banks or ATMs.

Sights & Activities
RESERVA DE LA BIOSFERA RÍA CELESTÚN

The 591-sq-km Reserva de la Biosfera Ría Celestún is home to a huge variety of animal and bird life, including a large flamingo colony. The best months to see the flamingos are from March or April to about September, outside the season of the *nortes*. It's best to visit in the morning or late afternoon.

Tours

In Celestún, you can hire a boat for bird-watching either from the bridge on the highway into town (about 1.5km inland) or from the beach itself. Beach departures are from outside Restaurant Celestún, at the foot of Calle 11.

Prices are often quoted assuming eight passengers, but if only four or six people show up that means the quoted price per person rises, often to the irritation of people who've waited 30 minutes to an hour.

Trips from the beach last 2½ to three hours and begin with a ride along the coast for several kilometers, during which you can expect to see egrets, herons, cormorants, sandpipers and many other bird species. The boat then turns into the mouth of the *ría* (estuary) and passes through a 'petrified forest,' where tall coastal trees once belonging to a freshwater ecosystem were killed by saltwater intrusion long ago and remain standing, hard as rock. Don't encourage your captain to approach birds too closely; a startled flock taking wing can result in injuries and deaths (for the birds).

Currently, a boat from the beach costs M$1200 for the trip, the average price with eight people ends up around M$150 per passenger.

Tours from the bridge, where there is a parking lot, ticket booth, and a place to wait for fellow passengers, are slightly cheaper and last about 1½ hours. For M$140 per passenger (maximum six passengers). With either the bridge or beach option, your captain may or may not speak English. An English-speaking guide can be hired at the bridge for about M$200 per hour.

AROUND TOWN

North of town, beyond the small navy post, you'll find more secluded stretches of beach. In the same area, but inland of the road, lies a large section of scrub stretching east to the estuary that also provides good birding opportunities. Flamingos, white pelicans, cormorants, anhingas and many other species frequent the shores and waters of the *ría*. South and east of town is the abandoned Hacienda Real de Salinas, another good area for nature observation.

Sleeping

The following list runs from south to north.

Hotel María del Carmen (☎ /fax 916-21-70; cnr Calles 12 & 15; d with fan/air-con M$250/300; **P** 🖳) This place has 14 clean and pleasant beachfront rooms tucked behind a picturesque maroon-colored false front; rooms on the upper floors have balconies facing the sea. Prices drop when things are slow.

Hostel Ría Celestún (☎ 916-25-97; hostelriacelestun@ hotmail.com; cnr Calles 12 & 13; dm M$60-70, s/d M$100/180; 🖳) It offers a good cheap sleep, with single-sex or mixed fan-cooled dorms (slightly dusty), kitchen and laundry facilities, a courtyard and TV room for common areas, bicycle rentals, and internet access. The staff are great sources of info about the area.

Hotel Sofía (in Mérida ☎ 999-189-89-59; Calle 12; s/d M$150/300; **P**) The rooms smell a bit here, but they are pretty well maintained and a decent value. It also has secure parking, and the owners let guests use the (hand) laundry facilities.

Hotel Los Manglares (☎ 998-916-21-56; www .hotelmanglares.com; Calle 12; d M$850, cabañas M$1600; **P** 🐾 🖳 🖳) While the architecture doesn't perfectly blend with the laid-back feel of town, this is a nice upscale choice. The rooms all have sea views and private balconies. Find it 1km north of Calle 11.

Eating

La Playita (mains M$70-120; ⏰ 10am-7pm) It's right on the (sometimes windy) beach with great views. Cheap seafood and *ceviche* are its main draw.

Restaurante Chivirico (cnr Calles 11 & 12; M$60-120; ⏰ 10am-7:30pm) A large place with wicker chairs and a TV with Spanish soaps as its ambience, the Chivirico has excellent seafood and is well worth a visit. The *ensalada de jaiba* (crab salad, M$60) is delicious.

Restaurant Los Pamponos (Calle 12; ⏰ 11am-7pm) A more-tranquil-than-thou joint on the beach, this is a great spot for afternoon drinks on the sand. Try the octopus *ceviche* or a fish fillet stuffed to the brim with shellfish. It's just north of Calle 11.

Getting There & Away

Buses from Mérida head for Celestún (M$44, two hours) 17 times daily between 5am and 8pm from the terminal on Calle 67, between Calles 50 and 52. The route terminates at Celestún's plaza, a block inland from Calle 12. Returning buses also run from 5am to 8pm.

By car from Mérida, the best route to Celestún is via the new road out of Umán.

DZIBILCHALTÚN

Lying about 17km due north of central Mérida, **Dzibilchaltún** (Place of Inscribed Flat Stones; admission M$63, children under 13 free; ⏰ 8am-5pm) was the longest continuously utilized Maya administrative and ceremonial city, serving the Maya from around 1500 BC until the European conquest in the 1540s. At the height of its greatness, Dzibilchaltún covered 15 sq km. Some 800 structures were mapped by archaeologists in the 1960s; few of these have been excavated and restored.

The **Templo de las Siete Muñecas** (Temple of the Seven Dolls), which got its name from seven grotesque dolls discovered here during excavations, is a 1km walk from the central plaza. It would be most unimpressive but for its precise astronomical orientation: the rising and setting sun of the equinoxes lights up the temple's windows and doors, making them blaze like beacons, signaling the year's important turning points.

The **Cenote Xlacah**, now a public swimming hole, is more than 40m deep. In 1958 a National Geographic Society diving expedition recovered more than 30,000 Maya artifacts, many of ritual significance, from the cenote. The most interesting of these are now on display in the site's museum. South of the cenote is **Estructura 44**, which at 130m is one of the longest Maya structures in existence.

Parking costs M$10. Minibuses and *colectivo* taxis depart frequently from Mérida's **Parque de San Juan** (Calle 69), between Calles 62 and 64, for the village of Dzibilchaltún Ruinas (M$8, 30 minutes), a little over 1km from the museum. Taxis will cost around M$120 round-trip.

PROGRESO
☎ 969 / pop 35,500

If Mérida's heat has you dying for a quick beach fix, or you want to see the longest wharf (7km) in Mexico, head to Progreso (also known as Puerto Progreso). The beach is fine, well groomed and long; however, except for the small *palapas* erected by restaurants it's nearly shadeless and is dominated by the view of the wharf, giving it a rather industrial feel. Winds can hit here full force off the Gulf in the afternoon and can blow well into the night, which should mean good kite-boarding and windsurfing, but currently there's neither, unless you've brought your own. As with other Gulf beaches, the water is murky; visibility even on calm days rarely exceeds 5m. None of this stops *meridanos* from coming in droves on weekends, especially in the summer months.

East of Progreso, you pass **Laguna Rosada**, a good spot for flamingo sighting, on your way to **Telchak Puerto**, a burgeoning tourist town. Along the way, take time to stop at an observation tower in **Uaymitún** and the **Xcambó** Maya ruins.

Even-numbered streets run east–west; odd ones north–south. The **bus terminal** (Calle 29) is west of Calle 82. From the plaza on Calle 80, it is six short blocks to the waterfront *malecón* (Calle 19) and *muelle* (wharf); along the way are two Banamex banks, one with an ATM.

Sleeping & Eating
Hotel Real del Mar (☎ 935-07-98; cnr malecón & Calle 70; s/d M$200/300, seaside r M$550; ❄) There are large balconies offering panoramic ocean views on both floors of this sprawling hotel. The decor is nice, with tiled floors, a small fountain, and

a tropical green-and-yellow paint job, and the satiny sheets are *muy romántico*.

Hotel Tropical Suites (☎ 935-12-63; fax 935-30-93; cnr malecón & Calle 70; d/tw with fan M$250/300, with air-con M$250/350; ❄) Across the street from Hotel Real del Mar, it's a seaside hotel with 21 tidy, non-musty, smallish rooms, some with sea views. The 1st-floor rooms opening on the street don't afford much privacy.

Restaurant Mary Doly (Calle 25; breakfast M$18-30, mains M$30-80; ❤ 7am-9pm) This is a homey place with good, cheap seafood, meat and breakfasts. It's between Calles 74 and 76.

Restaurant El Cordobés (☎ 935-26-21; cnr Calles 80 & 31; mains M$45-90; ❤ 6am-midnight daily) This locals' joint is located on the north side of the plaza in a 100-year-old building. Weak 'American' coffee is served quickly, with a warm smile, and it's a perfect place to relax for a bit, sluice down a *cerveza*, and look out on the main plaza.

Restaurant Los Pelícanos (☎ 935-53-78; cnr Malecón & Calle 70; mains M$55-100, special dishes M$200; ❤ 8am-midnight Mon-Sat, to 8pm Sun) By Hotel Real del Mar, it has a shady terrace, sea views, a good menu and moderate prices, considering its location.

Getting There & Away
Progreso is 33km north of Mérida along a fast four-lane highway that's basically a continuation of the Paseo de Montejo. The bus station (Calle 29, btwn Calles 80 & 82) has numerous Mérida-bound buses from 5:20am to 10pm. For bus information here from Mérida, see p923.

IZAMAL
☎ 988 / pop 15,100

In ancient times, Izamal was a center for the worship of the supreme Maya god, Itzamná, and the sun god, Kinich-Kakmó. A dozen temple pyramids were devoted to these or other gods. It was probably these bold expressions of Maya religiosity that provoked the Spaniards to build the enormous Franciscan monastery that stands today at the heart of this town.

Just under 70km east of Mérida, Izamal is a quiet, colonial gem of a town, nicknamed La Ciudad Amarilla (the Yellow City) for the yellow paint that brightens the walls of practically every building. It is easily explored on foot and makes a great day trip from Mérida.

Sights
When the Spaniards conquered Izamal, they destroyed the major Maya temple,

the Ppapp-Hol-Chac pyramid, and in 1533 began to build from its stones one of the first monasteries in the New World. Work on **Convento de San Antonio de Padua** (admission free; ☼ 6am-8pm) was finished in 1561. Under the monastery's arcades, look for building stones with an unmistakable mazelike design; these were clearly taken from the earlier Maya temple.

The monastery's principal church is the **Santuario de la Virgen de Izamal**. Here the **Atrium**, a huge arcaded courtyard, is where the **fiesta of the Virgin of Izamal** takes place each August 15, and where a dramatic **sound-and-light show** (M$40) is presented at 8:30pm on Tuesday, Thursday and Saturday nights.

Three of the town's original 12 Maya pyramids have been partially restored so far. The largest is the enormous Kinich-Kakmó (free admission; ☼ 8am-5pm), three blocks north of the monastery.

Sleeping & Eating

Posada Flory (☎ 954-05-62; Calle 30 No 267; s/d M$180/250; ☒) There's a nice little center patio in this small, uber-clean budget hotel, probably the best low-end deal in town. You can air-con yourself for a few extra pesos.

our pick Macan Ché (☎ /fax 954-02-87; www .macanche.com; Calle 22 No 305; d M$380-600; ☒ ▢ ☒) It's about three long (yes, long!) blocks east of the monastery (take Calle 31 toward Cancún and turn right on Calle 22) to this very Zen boutique hotel, which has a cluster of cottages and a small cenote pool in a woodsy setting.

El Toro (Calle 31 No 303; mains M$60-90; ☼ 8am-midnight) This small family-run establishment at the southeast cnr of the roundabout in front of the monastary specializes in Yucatecan fare (with a few international favorites thrown in to keep the tourists happy). Try a twist on the traditional with the *pozole con coco* (Maya corn stew with coconut overtones).

Several *loncherías* occupy spaces in the market on the monastery's southwest side.

Getting There & Away

Oriente operates frequent buses between Mérida and Izamal (M$27, 1½ hours) from the 2nd-class terminal. There are buses from Valladolid (M$41, two hours) as well. Coming from Chichén Itzá you must change buses at Hoctún. Izamal's bus terminal is two short blocks west of the monastery.

CHICHÉN ITZÁ

The most famous and best restored of the Yucatán Maya sites, **Chichén Itzá** (Mouth of the Well of the Itzáes; admission M$95, parking M$10, sound-&-light show M$30, guide M$500-600; ☼ 8am-5:30pm winter, to 6pm summer) while tremendously overcrowded – every gawker and their grandmother is trying to check off the new seven wonders of the world – will still impress even the most jaded visitor. Many mysteries of the Maya astronomical calendar are made clear when one understands the design of the 'time temples' here. Other than a few minor passageways, climbing on the structures is not allowed.

At the vernal and autumnal equinoxes (March 20–21 and September 21–22), the morning and afternoon sun produces a light-and-shadow illusion of the serpent ascending or descending the side of El Castillo's staircase. Chichén is mobbed on these dates, however, making it difficult to get close enough to see. The illusion is almost as good in the week preceding and following each equinox, and is re-created nightly in the sound-and-light show year-round.

History

Most archaeologists agree that the first major settlement at Chichén Itzá, during the late Classic period, was pure Maya. In about the 9th century the city was largely abandoned, for reasons unknown. It was resettled around the late 10th century, and Mayanists believe that shortly thereafter it was invaded by the Toltecs, who had migrated from their central highlands capital of Tula, north of Mexico City. Toltec culture was fused with that of the Maya, incorporating the Toltec cult of Quetzalcóatl (Kukulcán, in Maya). Throughout the city, you will see images of both Chac, the Maya rain god, and Quetzalcóatl, the plumed serpent.

The substantial fusion of highland central Mexican and Puuc architectural styles makes Chichén unique among the Yucatán Peninsula's ruins. The fabulous El Castillo and the Plataforma de Venus are outstanding architectural works, built during the height of Toltec cultural input.

The warlike Toltecs contributed more than their architectural skills to the Maya. They elevated human sacrifice to a near obsession, and there are numerous carvings of the bloody ritual in Chichén demonstrating this. After a Maya leader moved his political capital to Mayapán, while keeping Chichén as his religious capital, Chichén Itzá fell into decline. Why it was subsequently abandoned in the 14th century is a mystery, but the once-great city remained the site of Maya pilgrimages for many years.

Orientation

Most of Chichén's lodgings, restaurants and services are ranged along 1km of highway in the village of Pisté, to the western side of the ruins. It's 1.5km from the ruins' main entrance to the first hotel (Pirámide Inn) in Pisté. Highway 180 is known as Calle 15A as it crosses through Pisté.

Information

The western entrance has a large parking lot and a big **visitors center**. As at most sites, filming with a video camera costs M$35 extra, and tripods require a special permit from Mexico City. Hold on to your wristband ticket; it gives you in-and-out privileges and admission to that evening's sound-and-light show. Explanatory plaques around the site are in Spanish, English and Maya.

The 45-minute **sound-and-light show** in Spanish begins at 8pm each evening in summer and 7pm in winter. It costs M$30 if you don't already have a ruins wristband, and it counts toward the admission price the following day. Devices for listening to English, French, German or Italian translations (beamed via infrared) rent for M$25. Specify the language you need or it might not be broadcast.

Sights

EL CASTILLO

As you approach from the visitors center into the site, El Castillo (also called the Pyramid of Kukulcán) rises before you in all its grandeur. The first temple here was pre-Toltec, built around AD 800, but the present 25m-high structure, built over the old one, has the plumed serpent sculpted along the stairways and Toltec warriors represented in the doorway carvings at the top of the temple. You won't get to see these temple-top carvings, as you are not allowed to ascend the pyramid.

The structure is actually a massive Maya calendar formed in stone. Each of El Castillo's nine levels is divided in two by a staircase, making 18 separate terraces that commemorate the 18 20-day months of the Maya Vague Year. The

four stairways have 91 steps each; add the top platform and the total is 365, the number of days in the year. On each façade of the pyramid are 52 flat panels, which are reminders of the 52 years in the Maya Calendar Round. See p48 for more on the Maya calendar.

To top it off, during the spring and autumn equinoxes, light and shadow form a series of triangles on the side of the north staircase that mimic the creep of a serpent (note the carved serpents' heads flanking the bottom of the staircase).

The older pyramid *inside* El Castillo boasts a red jaguar throne with inlaid eyes and spots of jade; also lying behind the screen is a chac-mool figure. The entrance to **El Túnel**, the passage up to the throne, is at the base of El Castillo's north side. You can't go in, though.

GRAN JUEGO DE PELOTA

The great ball court, the largest and most impressive in Mexico, is only one of the city's eight courts, indicative of the importance of the games held here. The court is flanked by temples at either end and bounded by towering parallel walls with stone rings cemented up high.

There is evidence that the ball game may have changed over the years. Some carvings show players with padding on their elbows and knees, and it is thought that they played a soccerlike game with a hard rubber ball, the use of hands forbidden. Other carvings show players wielding bats; it appears that if a player hit the ball through one of the stone hoops, his team was declared the winner. It may be that during the Toltec period the losing captain, and perhaps his teammates as well, were sacrificed. Along the walls of the ball court are stone reliefs, including scenes of players being decapitated.

The court's acoustics are amazing – a conversation at one end can be heard 135m away at the other, and a clap produces multiple loud echoes.

TEMPLO DEL BARBADO & TEMPLO DE LOS JAGUARES Y ESCUDOS

The structure at the northern end of the ball court, called the Temple of the Bearded Man after a carving inside it, has some finely sculpted pillars and reliefs of flowers, birds and trees. The Temple of the Jaguars and Shields, built atop the southeast corner of the ball court's wall, has some columns with carved rattlesnakes and

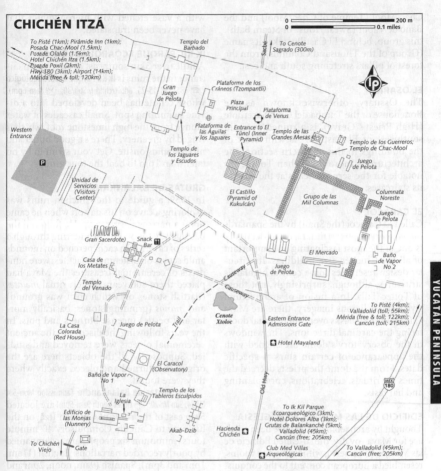

CHICHÉN ITZÁ

To Pisté (1km); Pirámide Inn (1km);
Posada Chac-Mool (1.5km);
Posada Olaldo (1.5km);
Hotel Chichén Itza (1.5km);
Posada Poxil (2km);
Hwy 180 (3km); Airport (14km);
Mérida (free & toll; 120km)

Templo del Barbado

To Cenote Sagrado (300m)

Gran Juego de Pelota

Plataforma de los Cráneos (Tzompantli)

Plaza Principal

Plataforma de Venus

Western Entrance

Plataforma de las Águilas y los Jaguares

Entrance to El Túnel (Inner Pyramid)

Templo de las Grandes Mesas

Templo de los Guerreros; Templo de Chac-Mool

Templo de los Jaguares y Escudos

El Castillo (Pyramid of Kukulcán)

Juego de Pelota

Unidad de Servicios (Visitors Center)

Grupo de las Mil Columnas

Columnata Noreste

Gran Sacerdote

Snack Bar

El Mercado

Juego de Pelota

Baño de Vapor No 2

Casa de los Metates

Templo del Venado

Causeway

Juego de Pelota

Causeway

La Casa Colorada (Red House)

Juego de Pelota

Trail

Cenote Xtoloc

Eastern Entrance Admissions Gate

To Pisté (4km); Valladolid (toll; 55km); Mérida (free & toll; 122km); Cancún (toll; 215km)

Hotel Mayaland

El Caracol (Observatory)

Baño de Vapor No 1

La Iglesia

Templo de los Tableros Esculpidos

Edificio de las Monjas (Nunnery)

Akab-Dzib

To Chichén Viejo *Gate*

To Ik Kil Parque Ecoarqueológico (3km); Hotel Dolores Alba (3km); Grutas de Balankanché (5km); Valladolid (45km); Cancún (free; 205km)

Hacienda Chichén

Club Med Villas Arqueológicas

To Valladolid (45km); Cancún (free; 205km)

0 ———— 200 m
0 ———— 0.1 miles

YUCATÁN PENINSULA

---

tablets with etched jaguars. Inside are faded mural fragments depicting a battle.

PLATAFORMA DE LOS CRÁNEOS

The **Platform of Skulls** (*tzompantli* in Náhuatl) is between the Templo de los Jaguares and El Castillo. You can't mistake it, because the T-shaped platform is festooned with carved skulls and eagles tearing open the chests of men to eat their hearts. In ancient days this platform held the heads of sacrificial victims.

PLATAFORMA DE LAS ÁGUILAS Y LOS JAGUARES

Adjacent to the *tzompantli,* the carvings on the Platform of the Eagles and Jaguars depicts those animals gruesomely grabbing human

hearts in their claws. It is thought that this platform was part of a temple dedicated to the military legions responsible for capturing sacrificial victims.

CENOTE SAGRADO

A 300m rough stone road runs north (a five-minute walk) to the huge sunken well that gave this city its name. The Sacred Cenote is an awesome natural well, some 60m in diameter and 35m deep. The walls between the summit and the water's surface are ensnared in tangled vines and other vegetation.

GRUPO DE LAS MIL COLUMNAS

Comprising the Templo de los Guerreros (Temple of the Warriors), the Templo de

Chac-Mool (Temple of Chac-Mool) and the Baño de Vapor (Sweat House or Steam Bath), this group, behind El Castillo, takes its name (Group of the Thousand Columns) from the forest of pillars stretching south and east.

EL OSARIO

The Ossuary, otherwise known as the Bonehouse or the Tumba del Gran Sacerdote (High Priest's Grave), is a ruined pyramid southwest of El Castillo. As with most of the buildings in this southern section, the architecture is more Puuc than Toltec. It's notable for the serpent heads at the base of its staircases.

EL CARACOL

Called El Caracol (the Snail) by the Spaniards for its interior spiral staircase, this observatory is one of the most fascinating and important of all the Chichén Itzá buildings. Its circular design resembles some central highlands structures, although, surprisingly, not those of Toltec Tula. In a fusion of architectural styles and religious imagery, there are Maya Chac rain-god masks over four external doors facing the cardinal directions. The windows in the observatory's dome are aligned with the appearance of certain stars at specific dates. From the dome the priests decreed the times for rituals, celebrations, corn-planting and harvests.

EDIFICIO DE LAS MONJAS & LA IGLESIA

Thought by archaeologists to have been a palace for Maya royalty, the so-called Edificio de las Monjas (Nunnery), with its myriad rooms, resembled a European convent to the conquistadors, hence their name for the building. The building's dimensions are imposing: its base is 60m long, 30m wide and 20m high. The construction is Maya rather than Toltec, although a Toltec sacrificial stone stands in front of the building. A smaller adjoining building to the east, known as La Iglesia (the Church), is covered almost entirely with carvings.

AKAB-DZIB

On the path east of the Nunnery, the Puuc-style Akab-Dzib is thought by some archaeologists to be the most ancient structure excavated here. The central chambers date from the 2nd century. The name means 'Obscure Writing' in Maya and refers to the south annex door, whose lintel depicts a priest

with a vase etched with hieroglyphics that have never been translated.

IK KIL PARQUE ECOARQUEOLÓGICO

A little over 3km southeast of the eastern entrance to the ruins is **Ik Kil Parque Ecoarqueológico** (☎ 985-858-15-25; adult/child M$60/30; ☽ 8am-6pm), whose cenote has been developed into a divine swimming spot. Small cascades of water plunge from the high limestone roof, which is ringed by greenery. There's a good buffet and nice *cabañas* onsite. Get your swim in by no later than 1pm to beat the tour groups.

GRUTAS DE BALANKANCHÉ

In 1959, a guide to the Chichén ruins was exploring a cave on his day off when he came upon a narrow passageway. He followed the passageway for 300m, meandering through a series of caverns. In each, perched on mounds amid scores of glistening stalactites, were hundreds of ceremonial treasures the Maya had placed there 800 years earlier: ritual *metates* (flattish stones on which corn was ground) and *manos* (grinding stones; basically mortar and pestle) incense burners and pots. In the years following the discovery, the ancient ceremonial objects were removed and studied. Supposedly all the objects here are the originals, returned and placed exactly where they were found.

The **Grutas de Balankanché** (admission Mon-Sat M$54, Sun M$20; ☽ ticket booth 9am-5pm) are located 5km east of the ruins of Chichén Itzá, on the highway to Cancún. Compulsory 40-minute tours (minimum six people) are accompanied by poorly recorded narrations: English (11am, 1pm and 3pm); Spanish (9am, noon, 2pm and 4pm); and French (10am).

Sleeping

Pirámide Inn (☎ 985-851-01-15; www.chichen.com; Calle 15A No 30; hammock or campsites per person M$40, d M$410; ☒ ☒) Apart from the cozy rooms, you can pitch a tent or hang a hammock under a *palapa*, enjoy the inn's pool and watch satellite TV in the lobby.

Posada Olalde (☎ 985-851-00-86; cnr Calles 6 & 17; s/d M$200/250, bungalows M$200) Two blocks south of the highway by Artesanías Guayacán, this is the best of Pisté's several *pensiones*. It has clean, quiet and attractive rooms, a few twiddling parakeets, and four decent-sized bungalows. The friendly manager speaks Spanish and English, as well as some German and Maya.

Posada Poxil (☎ 985-851-01-16; Calle 15A; s/d/tr M$150/200/250) At the western end of Pisté, it has seven bright and cheery rooms with good light, fans and towels that have seen better days. There's also an inexpensive restaurant serving big breakfasts (M$35) and Yucatecan dishes.

Posada Chac-Mool (☎ 985-851-02-70; Calle 15A; s/d with fan M$200/270, with air-con M$350/410; ⊠) Just east of Hotel Chichén Itzá and on the opposite (south) side of the highway in Pisté, it has fairly basic doubles with good screens. Some are available with good air-con to augment the fans.

Hotel Chichén Itzá (☎ 985-851-00-22; fax 985-851-00-23; www.mayaland.com; Calle 15A No 45; r fan only M$300, r M$600-1000; ⊠ ⊠ ⊠) On the west side of Pisté, it has 42 pleasant rooms with tile floors and old-style brick-tile ceilings. Parents may bring two kids under 13 for free.

Hotel Mayaland (☎ 985-851-01-00, in the US 800-235-4079; www.mayaland.com; d/ste/royal ste M$1700/2500/3450; ⊠ ⊠) Less than 100m from the ruins' eastern entrance – from the lobby and front rooms you can look out at El Caracol. The rooms, pools and garden bungalows are very nicely built and well appointed, but when you're at El Caracol you'll wish the management hadn't cut an ugly swath through the unspoiled jungle, just so their patrons could have a nicer view.

Hacienda Chichén (in Mérida ☎ 999-924-21-50; in the US 800-624-8451; www.haciendachichen.com; d M$1700-2200; ⊠ ⊠) About 300m from the ruins' entrance, this is on the grounds of a 16th-century estate. The hacienda's elegant main house and ruined walls make a great setting, and huge ceiba trees offer welcome shade.

Eating

The highway through Pisté is lined with more than 20 eateries, large and small. The cheapest are the market stalls on the main plaza opposite the large tree.

Restaurant Sayil (☎ 985-851-00-33; mains M$35-70; ☼ 7am-9pm) They recently renovated this old standby. There's a pleasant garden, and the regional fare is simple but tasty. It's attached to the new Felix Inn.

Restaurant Hacienda Xaybe'h (☎ 985-851-00-39; buffet lunch & dinner M$110; ☼ 7:30am-6:30pm; ⓥ ⓖ) Set a block back from the highway opposite Hotel Chichén Itzá, this is a large, rather fancy place with nice grounds. It's popular with tours, and the food is a bit overpriced;

the selection of salads makes it a good option for vegetarians. Diners can use the swimming pool free of charge.

Xunan (☎ 985-851-01-31; Calle Principal s/n; mains M$40-90; ☼ 7am to 9pm) Service is a bit slow here, but this colorful eatery (at the front of a souvenir stand) offers good food at reasonable prices and is a nice change from the tourist buffets. Portions are generous.

Getting There & Away

Oriente has ticket offices near the east and west sides of Pisté, and 2nd-class buses passing through town stop almost anywhere along the way. Many 1st-class buses only hit the ruins and the west side of town, close to the toll highway.

When they're running on schedule, Oriente's 2nd-class buses pass through Pisté bound for Mérida (M$52, 2½ hours) hourly between 8:15am and 4:15pm. Hourly Oriente buses to Valladolid (M$36, 50 minutes) and Cancún (M$80, 4½ hours) pass between 7am and 5:30pm. There is a service to Cobá (M$52, 1½ hours) as well.

First-class buses serve Mérida (M$80, 1¾ hours) at 2:25pm and 5pm, Cancún (M$140, 2½ hours) at 4:30pm, Tulum (M$101, 2½ hours) at 8am and 4:30pm, and Playa del Carmen (M$180, four hours).

Shared vans to Valladolid (M$20, 40 minutes) pass through town regularly.

Getting Around

During Chichén Itzá's opening hours 1st- and 2nd-class buses passing through Pisté serve the ruins (hail the bus and check with the driver), and they will take passengers from Pisté for about M$6 when there's room. For a bit more, 2nd-class buses will also take you to the Cenote Ik Kil and the Grutas de Balankanché (be sure to specify your destination when buying your ticket). If you plan to see the ruins and then head directly to another city by 1st-class bus, buy your bus ticket in the visitors center before hitting the ruins, for a better chance of getting a seat.

There is a taxi stand near the west end of town; the price to the ruins is M$25. There are usually cabs at Chichén's parking lot.

VALLADOLID
☎ 985 / pop 45,900
Also known as the Sultaness of the East, Yucatán's third-largest city is known for its

quiet streets and sun-splashed, pastel walls. She certainly is one sultry babe, and it's worth staying here for a few days or even a week, as the provincial town makes a great hub for visits to Río Lagartos, Chichén Itzá, Ek' Balam, and a number of nearby cenotes. The city resides at that magic point where there's plenty to do, yet it still feels small, manageable and affordable.

History

Valladolid has seen its fair share of turmoil and revolt over the years. The city was first founded in 1543 near the Chouac-Ha lagoon some 50km from the coast, but it was too hot and there were way too many mosquitoes for Francisco de Montejo, nephew of Montejo the Elder, and his merry band of conquerors. So they upped and moved the city to the Maya ceremonial center of Zací (sah-kee), where they faced heavy resistance from the local Maya. Eventually the Elder's son, Montejo the Younger, took the town. The Spanish conquerors, in typical fashion, ripped down the town and laid out a new city following the classic colonial plan.

During much of the colonial era, Valladolid's physical isolation from Mérida kept it relatively autonomous from royal rule, and the Maya of the area suffered brutal exploitation, which continued after Mexican independence. Barred from entering many areas of the city, the Maya made Valladolid one of their first points of attack following the 1847 outbreak of the War of the Castes in Tepich, not far south on the border with Quintana Roo. After a two-month siege, the city's defenders were finally overcome.

Orientation & Information

The old highway passes through the center of town, though most signs urge motorists toward the toll road north of town. To follow the old highway eastbound, take Calle 41; westbound, take Calle 39. The main plaza has banks of Telmex card phones in each corner. High-speed internet is available at numerous small cafés in and around the town center for around M$10 per hour.

Hospital Valladolid (☎ 856-28-83; cnr Calles 49 & 52; ☪ 24hr)

Main post office (cnr Calles 40 & 39; ☪ 8:30am-3pm Mon-Fri)

Tourist office (☪ 9am-9pm Mon-Sat, to noon Sun)

Sights

TEMPLO DE SAN BERNARDINO & CONVENTO DE SISAL

The **church** (☪ 8am-noon & 5-9pm) named for San Bernardino de Siena and the Convent of Sisal are about 700m southwest of the plaza. They were constructed between 1552 and 1560 to serve the dual functions of fortress and church.

You may have to knock on the church's left-hand door to gain admittance, or someone may approach and offer you a short tour in exchange for a gratuity. Either way, it's worth peeking inside. Its charming decoration includes beautiful rose-colored walls, arches, some recently uncovered 16th-century frescoes and a small image of the Virgin on the altar. The adjacent **convent** is often closed to the public; your best bets of gaining entrance to it are during the vacation periods of Semana Santa, August and Christmas (December 14 to January 6). It's well worth a visit. The walled grounds hold a cenote with a vaulted dome built over it and a system of channels that once irrigated the large garden.

MUSEO DE SAN ROQUE

This church turned **museum** (Calle 41; admission free; ☪ 9am-9pm), between Calles 38 and 40, has models and exhibits relating the history of the city and the region. Other displays focus on various aspects of traditional Maya life.

CENOTES

Among the region's several underground cenotes is **Cenote Zací** (Calle 36; admission M$25; ☪ 8am-6pm), set in a park that also holds traditional stone-walled thatched houses and a small zoo. People swim in Zací, though being mostly open it has some dust and algae. Enter from Calle 39.

A bit more enticing but less accessible is **Cenote Dzitnup** (Xkekén; admission M$25; ☪ 8am-5pm), 7km west of the plaza. It's artificially lit and very swimmable, and a massive limestone formation dripping with stalactites hangs from its ceiling. Across the road about 100m closer to town is **Cenote Samulá** (admission M$25; ☪ 8am-6pm), a lovely cavern pool with *álamo* roots stretching down many meters from the middle of the ceiling to drink from it. The *ejido* (communal landholding) that maintains both cenotes charges M$35 for use of a video camera in either one.

Pedaling a rented bicycle (see p944) to the cenotes takes about 20 minutes. By bike from

VALLADOLID

0 ———————— 400 m
0 ——————— 0.2 miles

INFORMATION
Hospital Valladolid......................1 A4
Main Post Office.........................2 D2
Tourist Office.............................3 D3

SIGHTS & ACTIVITIES
Cenote Zaci...............................4 D2
Museo de San Roque..................5 D3
Templo de San Bernardino & Convento
de Sisal.................................6 A4

To Ek' Balam (27.5km);
Santa Rita (29.5km);
Tizimín (51km);
Cancún (toll 158km);
Mérida (toll 160km)

Iglesia de
la Candelaria

To Cenote Samulá (6.5km);
Cenote Dzitnup (7km);
Chichén Itzá (40km);
Mérida (160km)

To Mercado
Municipal (200m)

Francisco
Cantón
Rosado

BBVA Bancomer
(ATM)

HSBC
(ATM)

To Cancún
(158km)

Banamex
(ATM)

Catedral de
San Gervasio

To Felipe Carrillo
Puerto (175km)

Park

To Bike Path (1km);
Cenotes (5km)

SLEEPING
Antonio 'Negro' Aguilar..............7 C3
El Mesón del Marqués................8 C2
Hotel María Guadalupe...............9 C3
Hotel San Clemente.................10 C3
Hotel Zaci..............................11 C2

EATING
Bazar Municipal......................12 C2
Hostería del Marqués..........(see 8)
Squimoz................................13 C2

DRINKING
La Chispa de 1910....................14 C3

ENTERTAINMENT
El Atrio..................................15 C3

TRANSPORT
Colectivos to Cancún...............16 C3
Colectivos to Merida................17 C2
Colectivos to Pisté & Chichén Itzá..18 B2
Colectivos to Samulá & Dzitnup...19 C2
Colectivos to Santa Rita (for Ek'
Balam).................................20 C2
Colectivos to Tizimín...............21 D3
Terminal 46............................22 B2
Terminal 54............................23 A2

YUCATÁN PENINSULA

the center of town take Calle 41A (Calz de los Fraies), a street lined entirely with colonial architecture, which leads past the Templo de San Bernardino and the convent. Keep to the right of the park, then turn right on Calle 49. This opens into tree-lined Av de los Fraies and hits the old highway. Turn left onto the *ciclopista* (bike path) paralleling the road to Mérida. Turn left again at the sign for Dzitnup and continue for just under 2km; Samulá will be off this road to the right and Dzitnup a little further on the left.

Shared vans from in front of Hotel María Guadalupe (on Calle 44) go to Dzitnup for M$10. Taxis from Valladolid's main plaza charge M$100 for the round-trip excursion to Dzitnup and Samulá, with an hour's wait.

You also can hop aboard a westbound bus; ask the driver to let you off at the Dzitnup turnoff, then walk the final 2km (20 to 30 minutes) to the site. Dzitnup has a restaurant and drinks stand. Otherwise, bring a picnic.

MERCADO MUNICIPAL
On Calle 32, this is a good, authentic Mexican market where locals come to shop for cheap clothing, homewares, meat, produce and what-have-you, and to eat at inexpensive *taquerías*.

Sleeping
Antonio 'Negro' Aguilar (☎ 856-21-25; Calle 44 btwn Calles 39 & 41; r M$150) This cantankerous old character rents the cheapest separate rooms in

town, and they are actually pretty clean. Stop by his bike rental shop (see right), which is not so clean, for details.

Hotel María Guadalupe (☎ 856-20-68; hotelmaria guadalupe@prodigy.net.mx; Calle 44 No 198A; d/tr M$220/270) This airy, hotel has eight simple and clean fan-cooled rooms, which, though a bit dark, are not musty. The management is friendly and provides purified water. There's a nice common area upstairs to meet fellow travelers or sip something cold after a hot day.

Hotel Zací (☎ /fax 856-21-67; www.hotelzaci.com; Calle 44 No 191; s/d/tr with fan M$240/350/410, with air-con M$340/400/450; 🖭 🖳) Someone here really loves Calla lilies. The 60 rooms with mock-colonial décor are spread around a green courtyard. Some rooms are a bit musty, but they air out.

Hotel San Clemente (☎ /fax 856-22-08; www .hotelsanclemente.com.mx; Calle 42 No 206; s/d/tr with fan M$300/360/410, with air-con M$350/390/470; 🖭 🖳) Offers good value and boasts 64 rooms with optional air-con and decor nearly identical to the Zací's, minus the Calla lilies. The bathrooms are a bit dirty, but it's still a solid deal. There's a pool and central courtyard.

El Mesón del Marqués (☎ 856-20-73; fax 856-22-80; www.mesondelmarques.com; Calle 39 No 203; d standard/ superior M$580/710; 🖭 🖳) It's worth staying in this hotel only if you're willing to anty up for the superior rooms with their crispy-clean bedspreads, quaint blue-and-yellow tilework and firm mattresses. There's also a charming old courtyard with a swimming pool and wi-fi.

Eating

Bazar Municipal (cnr Calles 39 & 40) This place at the plaza's northeast corner is a collection of market-style shops, popular for their big, cheap breakfasts.

Squimoz (☎ 856-41-56; Calle 39 No 219; mains M$20-50; 🕑 7am-10pm Mon-Sat, to 3pm Sun) A delightful little shop just a few doors east of the ADO terminal, Squimoz offers cakes, pastries and good espresso drinks.

Hostería del Marqués (☎ 856-20-73; Calle 39 No 203; mains M$50-130; 🕑 7am-11pm) Probably the best restaurant in town for lunch and dinner, it is in Hotel El Mesón del Marqués. You can dine in the tranquil colonial courtyard with its bubbling fountain or the air-con salon looking onto it. The restaurant also offers some vegetarian choices and steaks priced by weight.

Entertainment

Following a centuries-old tradition, dances are held in the main plaza from 8pm to 9pm Sunday, with music by the municipal band or other local groups.

La Chispa de 1910 (☎ 856-26-68; Calle 41 No 201; 🕑 5pm-1am Mon-Thu, to 2am Fri-Sun) Sparks fly at this bar–restaurant that often features live music.

El Atrio (Calle 42 No 205; drinks M$10-40; 🕑 6pm-midnight) This new café and grill has a very chill atmosphere with comfy sofas in a colonial-era *casona* (large mansion).

Getting There & Away

BUS

Valladolid's main bus station is the convenient **Terminal** 46 (cnr Calles 39 & 46), also called the ADO Terminal. The principal services are Oriente, Mayab and Expresso (2nd class) and ADO and Super Expresso (1st class).

Cancún (M$70-110; 2-3hr) Many buses.

Chetumal (M$140; 6hr; 5 Mayab buses)

Chichén Itzá/Pisté (M$36; 45min) Fourteen Oriente Mérida-bound buses between 7:15am and 5:30pm; stop near ruins during opening hours.

Chiquilá (for Isla Holbox) (M$70; 2½hr) Oriente bus at 2:45am

Cobá (M$26; 45min; 4 buses)

Izamal (M$41; 2hr; 2 buses at 12:45pm & 3:50pm)

Mérida (M$74-110; 2-3hr) Many buses.

Playa del Carmen (M$78-140; 2½-3½hr; 8 buses)

Tizimín (M$20; 1hr; 12 buses)

Tulum (M$47-60; 2hr; 6 buses)

COLECTIVOS

Often faster and more reliable and comfortable than 2nd-class buses, the shared vans leave for various points as soon as their seats are filled. Most operate from 7am or 8am to about 7pm. Direct services to Mérida (from Calle 39, M$60) and Cancún (from the cathedral, M$70) take a little over two hours – confirm they're nonstop, though. *Colectivos* for Pisté and Chichén Itzá (M$20, 40 minutes) leave across the road from the bus terminal, and for Tizimín from the east side of the plaza.

Getting Around

Bicycles are a great way to see the town and get out to the cenotes. **Tres Hermanos** (Calle 44; 🕑 7:30am-8pm Mon-Sat, to 2pm Sun), between Calles 39 and 41, and Antonio 'Negro' Aguila (p943) rent bikes for about M$8 per hour. If you want a motor behind your wheels, taxis charge M$100 per hour.

EK' BALAM

The turnoff for this fascinating **archaeological site** (admission M$27, guide M$250; 8am-5pm) is 17km north of Valladolid. Ek' Balam is another 6km east of this. Vegetation still covers much of the area, but excavations and restoration continue to add to the sights, including an interesting ziggurat-like structure near the entrance, as well as a fine arch and a ball court.

Most impressive is the gargantuan **Acrópolis**, whose well-restored base is 160m long and holds a 'gallery' – actually a series of separate chambers. Built atop the base is Ek' Balam's massive main pyramid, reaching a height of 32m and sporting a huge jaguar mouth with 360-degree dentition. Below the mouth are stucco skulls, while above and to the right sits an amazingly expressive figure. On the right side stand unusual winged human figures (some call them Maya angels).

From the Ek' Balam parking lot you can visit the **X-Canche Cenote** (985-107-47-74; admission M$30, bike rental M$70, bike, rappel & kayak tour M$110; 8am-5pm).

Sleeping & Eating

our pick **Genesis Eco-Retreat** (985-852-79-80; www .genesisretreat.com; d M$400-600;) This is a true eco-tel: gray water is used for landscaping, some rooms are naturally cooled, insects are naturally controlled by a crack squadron of mosquito-hating ducks, and there's even an entire wall made out of plastic bottles. The place is postcard beautiful – there's a chilling dip pool and a temascal steam bath – and the restaurant offers delicious veggie meals. The hotel is sometimes closed between September and early October.

Getting There & Away

It's possible to catch a *colectivo* from Calle 44 between Calles 35 and 37 in Valladolid for Ek' Balam (M$30). A round-trip taxi ride from Valladolid with an hour's wait at the ruins will cost around M$250.

TIZIMÍN

986 / pop 44,200

Tizimín is dusty and 'authentic,' meaning that you won't find much here that's designed with the tourist in mind. Most people find themselves here if they're traveling to Río Lagartos or Holbox. Still, the tree-filled Parque Principal is pleasant, particularly at sundown, and the city fills with people from outlying ranches during its annual fair to celebrate **Día de los Reyes Magos** (Three Kings' Day), which lasts from January 1 to 15.

Two great colonial structures – **Parroquia Los Santos Reyes de Tizimín** (Church of the Three Wise Kings) and its former **Franciscan monastery** (the ex-convento) – are worth looking at while you're waiting to make your bus connection. The church fronts Tizimín's main plaza, the Parque Principal, which has an HSBC with ATM and currency exchange on its southwest side.

Sleeping & Eating

Hotel San Carlos (863-20-94; hsancarlos@hotmail .com; Calle 54 No 407; r with air-con M$290;) Two blocks west of the plaza, this is the nicest hotel in town. All the air-conditioned rooms have private patios looking onto the shared garden area.

The **market** (cnr Calles 47 & 48), half a block west of the Noreste terminal, has the usual cheap eateries.

Getting There & Away

Oriente and Mayab, both offering 2nd-class services, share a **terminal** (Calle 47), between Calles 48 and 46, just east of the market. Noreste's 1st- and 2nd-class terminal is just around the corner on Calle 46.

Cancún (M$85; 3-3½hr) Fifteen Mayab and Noreste buses.

Chiquilá (for Isla Holbox) (M$50, 11½hr) Departures at 7:30am, 1:30pm and 4:30pm.

Izamal (M$55; 2½hr; Oriente bus at 5:30am, 11am and 4pm)

Mérida (M$83; 2½-3½hr) Second-class Noreste buses at 5:30am, 9am, 2:30pm, 4pm and 5pm.

Río Lagartos/San Felipe (M$20-25,1hr) Six Noreste buses between 6am and 4:15pm; some buses continue 12km west to San Felipe (same price); some *colectivos*.

Valladolid (M$20; 1hr) Sixteen Oriente buses between 5:30am and 7:30pm.

A taxi ride to Río Lagartos or San Felipe charge about M$250, and leave from outside both bus terminals. The drivers can be asked to wait for you for M$100 per additional hour.

RÍO LAGARTOS

986 / pop 2100

The largest and most spectacular flamingo colony in Mexico warrants a trip to this fishing village, 103km north of Valladolid, 52km north of Tizimín, lying within the **Reserva** de la Biosfera Ría Lagartos. The mangrove-lined estuary is also home to snowy egrets, red egrets, tiger herons, snowy white ibis, hundreds of other bird species and a small number of the crocodiles that gave the town its name (Alligator River).

The Maya knew the place as Holkobén and used it as a rest stop on their way to the nearby lagoons (Las Coloradas), from which they extracted salt. (Salt continues to be extracted, on a much vaster scale now.) Spanish explorers mistook the inlet for a river and the crocs for alligators, and the rest is history. Intrepid travelers can head east of town past Las Coloradas on a coastal dirt road all the way to the small town of El Cuyo.

Most residents aren't sure of the town's street names, and signs are few. The road into town is the north–south Calle 10, which ends at the waterfront Calle 13. There's no bank or ATM in town, so bring lots of cash.

Flamingo Tours

The brilliant orange-red birds can turn the horizon fiery when they take wing. You can generally get within 100m of flamingos before they walk or fly away. Depending on your luck, you'll see either hundreds or thousands of them.

The four primary haunts, in increasing distance from town, are Punta Garza, Yoluk, Necopal and Nahochín (all flamingo feeding spots named for nearby mangrove patches). Prices vary with boat, group size (maximum five) and destination. The lowest you can expect to pay is around M$500 per boat; a full boat to Nahochín runs to as much as M$700 per boat.

The best tours are given by the licensed guides operating from **Restaurante-Bar Isla Contoy** (☎ 862-00-00; Calle 19) at the waterfront. They offer extensive day tours as well as night excursions. Crocodiles are a common nocturnal sight, and from May through September sea turtles are easily spotted.

Alternatively, you can negotiate with one of the eager men in the waterfront kiosks near the entrance to town. They speak English and will connect you with a captain (who usually doesn't speak English).

Sleeping & Eating

Posada Las Gaviotas (☎ 862-05-07; Calle 12; d M$250) This simple budget option offers clean fan-cooled rooms bathed in avocado green right on the riverfront. There's no toilet seats.

Hotel Villas de Pescadores (☎ 862-00-20; villa_pescadores@prodigy.net.mx; cnr Calle 14 & Calle 9; d fan/air-con M$400/500; ⚡) Near the water's edge, this nice hotel offers nine very clean rooms, each with good cross-ventilation (all face the estuary), two beds and a fan. Upstairs rooms have balconies, and there's a rickety spiral staircase leading up to a rooftop lookout tower.

Restaurante-Bar Isla Contoy (Calle 19; mains M$50-100; ☺ 8am-9pm) A popular eatery at the waterfront, this is a good place to meet other travelers and form groups for the boat tours. Lobster, at market price, is a delicious specialty.

Getting There & Away

Several Noreste buses run daily between Tizimín (M$20 to M$25, one hour), Mérida (M$110, three to four hours) and San Felipe (M$10, 20 minutes) to Río Lagartos. Noreste and Mayab also serve Cancún (M$120, three to four hours) three times daily.

SAN FELIPE

This seldom-visited fishing village, 12km west of Río Lagartos, makes a nice day trip or overnight stay. Birding and the beach are the main attractions, both of which are just across the estuary at Punta Holohit.

Hotel San Felipe de Jesús (☎ 862-20-27; hotelsf@hotmail.com; d M$400-450, with balcony M$490) is a friendly, clean and cleverly constructed hotel at the edge of San Felipe's harbor.

Six buses from Tizimín pass through Río Lagartos and continue to San Felipe (M$20 to M$22, 1½ hours) each way. The bus ride from Río Lagartos (M$10) takes 20 minutes.

CAMPECHE STATE

Campeche state is home to vast stretches of tangled jungle, some of the region's least visited and most imposing Maya ruins, forgotten pastoral villages, bird-choked coastal lagoons and an inspiring colonial-era capital city. It's the least touristed of the Yucatán's states, and in that lies its provincial, lost-land charm.

The backroads of the northern region bring you to forgotten underground wonderworlds, the massive restored Ednzá archaeological site, and a handful of smaller, less-traveled Maya ruins.

This is also the wildest corner of the peninsula, and the Reserva de la Biosfera

Calakmul is Mexico's largest. Beyond the cacophonous roar of the howlers and hic-cupping frogs rise massive Maya ruined cities like Calakmul and Becán. Along the coast, the Laguna de Términos is great for birding expeditions.

The southern coast of Campeche was affected by an oil spill in October 2007, and boomtowns like Ciudad del Carmen are changing the spirit (and environment) of the region. Nevertheless, the age-old grace of the *campechano* people abides.

CAMPECHE
☎ 981 / pop 211,700

Campeche is a colonial fairyland, its walled city center a tight enclave of perfectly restored pastel buildings, narrow cobblestone streets, fortified ramparts and well-preserved mansions. Added to Unesco's list of World Heritage sites in 1999, the state capital has been so painstakingly restored you wonder if it's a real city. Nearly 2000 structures have been renovated. But leave the city's walls and you'll find a real Mexican provincial capital complete with a frenetic market, a quiet waterfront *malecón* (pedestrian walkway) and old fishing docks.

Besides the numerous mansions built by wealthy Spanish families during Campeche's heyday in the 18th and 19th centuries, two segments of the city's famous wall have also survived, as have no fewer than seven of the *baluartes* (bastions or bulwarks) that were built into it.

History
Once a Maya trading village called Ah Kim Pech (Lord Sun Sheep-Tick), Campeche was first briefly approached by the Spaniards in 1517. Resistance by the Maya prevented the Spaniards from fully conquering the region for nearly a quarter-century. Colonial Campeche was founded in 1531, but later abandoned due to Maya hostility. By 1540, however, the conquistadors had gained sufficient control, under the leadership of Francisco de Montejo the Younger, to found a permanent settlement. They named the settlement Villa de San Francisco de Campeche.

The settlement soon flourished as the major port of the Yucatán Peninsula, but this made it subject to pirate attacks. After a particularly appalling attack in 1663 left the city in ruins, the king of Spain ordered construction of Campeche's famous bastions, putting an end to the periodic carnage.

Today the economy of the city is largely driven by fishing and, increasingly, tourism, which to some extent have funded the downtown area's renovation.

Orientation
Though the bastions still stand, the walls have been mostly razed and replaced by Av Circuito Baluartes, which rings the city center as the walls once did. In the classic colonial plan, the center is surrounded by barrios (neighborhoods), each with its own church and square. Particularly charming are San Román, Guadalupe and Santa Ana.

The streets in the central grid follow a numbered sequence: inland-oriented streets have odd numbers and perpendicular ones even.

Information
INTERNET ACCESS
All of the hostels and quite a few hotels provide online services, and 'cibers' abound in the Centro.

LAUNDRY
Kler Lavandería (Calle 16 305; per kilo M$10; ⊠ 8am-6pm Mon-Fri, to 4pm Sat)

MEDICAL SERVICES
Hospital Dr Manuel Campos (☎ 811-17-09; Av Circuito Baluartes Nte) Between Calles 14 and 16.

MONEY
Campeche has numerous banks with ATMs, open 8am to 4pm Monday to Friday, 9am to 2pm Saturday.

POST
Central post office (cnr Av 16 de Septiembre & Calle 53; ⊠ 8:30am-3:30pm Mon-Fri)

TOURIST INFORMATION
Coordinación Municipal de Turismo (☎ 811-39-89; www.ayuntamientodecampeche.gob.mx; Calle 55 No 3; ⊠ 9am-9pm)
Secretaría de Turismo (☎ 816-67-67; Plaza Moch Couoh; ⊠ 9am-9pm)

Sights & Activities
PLAZA PRINCIPAL
Shaded by spreading carob trees, and ringed by tiled benches with broad footpaths radiating from a belle époque kiosk, Campeche's

YUCATÁN PENINSULA

YUCATÁN PENINSULA

CAMPECHE

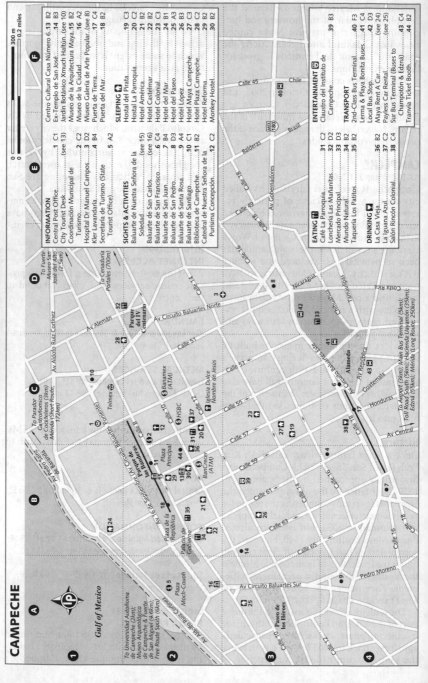

INFORMATION

Central Post Office	1 C1
City Tourist Desk	(see 13)
Coordinación Municipal de Turismo	2 C2
Hospital Dr Manuel Campos	3 D2
Kler Lavandaría	4 B4
Secretaría de Turismo (State Tourist Office)	5 A2

SIGHTS & ACTIVITIES

Baluarte de Nuestra Señora de la Soledad	(see 15)
Baluarte de San Carlos	6 C4
Baluarte de San Francisco	7 B4
Baluarte de San Juan	8 D3
Baluarte de San Pedro	9 A4
Baluarte de Santa Rosa	10 C1
Baluarte de Santiago	11 C3
Biblioteca de Campeche	12 C2
Catedral de Nuestra Señora de la Purísima Concepción	

Centro Cultural Casa Número 6	13 B2
Ex-Templo de San José	14 B3
Jardín Botánico Xmuch Haltún	(see 10)
Museo de la Arquitectura Maya	15 B2
Museo de la Ciudad	16 A2
Museo Galería de Arte Popular	(see 8)
Puerta de Tierra	17 C4
Puerta del Mar	18 B2

SLEEPING

Hostal del Pirata	19 C3
Hostal La Parroquia	20 B2
Hotel América	21 B2
Hotel Castelmar	22 B2
Hotel Colonial	23 C3
Hotel del Mar	24 B1
Hotel del Paseo	25 A3
Hotel López	26 B3
Hotel Maya Campeche	27 C3
Hotel Plaza Campeche	28 C2
Hotel Reforma	29 B2
Monkey Hostel	30 B2

EATING

Café La Parroquia	31 C2
Lonchería Las Mañanitas	32 D2
Mercado Principal	33 D3
Mundo Natural	34 B2
Taquería Los Pattios	35 B2

DRINKING

La Casa Vieja	36 B2
La Iguana Azul	37 C4
Salón Rincón Colonial	38 C4

ENTERTAINMENT

Claustro del Instituto de Campeche	39 B3

TRANSPORT

2nd-Class Bus Terminal	40 F3
Lerma & Playa Bonita Buses	41 C4
Local Bus Stop	42 D3
Maya Rent A Car	(see 24)
Payless Car Rental	(see 25)
Sur Bus Terminal (Buses to Champotón & Edzná)	43 C4
Tranvía Ticket Booth	44 B2

appealingly modest central square started life in 1531 as a military camp. Over the years it became the focus of the town's civic, political and religious activities and remains the core of public life. The plaza is seen at its best on weekend evenings, when it's closed to traffic and concerts are staged (see p952).

The plaza is surrounded by suitably fine buildings. On the northern (seaward) side stands a replica of the old government center, now housing the modern **Biblioteca de Campeche** (State Library; 9am-2:30pm & 3-8:30pm Mon-Fri, to noon Sat). The impressive portico building on the opposite side housed an earlier version of the city hall; it is now occupied by shops and restaurants.

CATEDRAL DE NUESTRA SEÑORA DE LA PURÍSIMA CONCEPCIÓN

Dominating the plaza's east side is the two-towered **cathedral** (admission free; 7am-noon & 4-6pm). The limestone structure has stood on this spot for more than three centuries. Statues of St Peter and St Paul occupy niches in the baroque facade; the sober, single-nave interior is lined with colonial-era paintings.

CENTRO CULTURAL CASA NÚMERO 6

During the pre-revolutionary era, when the mansion was occupied by an upper-class *campechano* family, '**Number Six**' (Calle 57 No 6; admission M$5; 9am-9pm) was a prestigious plaza address. Wandering the premises, you'll get an idea of how the city's high society lived back then.

BALUARTES

After a particularly blistering pirate assault in 1663, the remaining inhabitants of Campeche set about erecting protective walls around their city. Built largely by indigenous labor with limestone extracted from nearby caves, the barrier took more than 50 years to complete. Stretching over 2km around the urban core and rising to a height of 8m, the hexagonal wall was linked by eight bulwarks. The seven that remain display a treasure trove of historical paraphernalia, artifacts and indigenous handicrafts. You can climb atop the bulwarks and stroll sections of the wall for sweeping views of the port.

Two main entrances connected the walled compound with the outside world. The **Puerta del Mar** (Sea Gate; cnr Calles 8 & 59) provided access from the sea, opening onto a wharf where

small craft delivered goods from ships anchored further out. (The shallow waters were later reclaimed so the gate is now several blocks from the waterfront.) The **Puerta de Tierra** (Land Gate; Calle 18; admission free; 9am-9pm), on the eastern side of the town wall, was opened in 1732 as the principal ingress from the suburbs. It is now the venue for a sound-and-light show (p952).

Designed to protect the Puerta del Mar, the **Baluartes de Nuestra Señora de la Soledad** was the largest of the bastions completed in the late 1600s. Appropriately, it was named for the patron saint of sailors. This bulwark contains the fascinating **Museo de la Arquitectura Maya** (admission M$27, free Sun; 8am-7:30pm Tue-Sun), the one must-see museum in Campeche. It provides an excellent overview of the sites around Campeche state and the key architectural styles associated with them. Five halls display stelae taken from various sites, accompanied by graphic representations of their carved inscriptions with brief commentaries in flawless English.

Completed in 1704 – the last of the bulwarks to be built – the **Baluarte de Santiago** (Calle 8 at Calle 49; admission M$10; 9am-9pm) houses the **Jardín Botánico Xmuch Haltún**, a botanical garden with numerous endemic plants. Unless you're really into plants, it's not worth the entrance fee.

Named after Spain's King Carlos II, the **Baluarte de San Carlos** houses the **Museo de la Ciudad** (Calle 8; admission M$27; 8am-7:30pm Tue-Sun) between Calles 63 and 65. This small but worthwhile museum chronologically illustrates the city's tempestuous history via well-displayed objects.

Directly behind San Juan de Dios church, the **Baluarte de San Pedro** (cnr Calle 18 & Av Circuito Baluartes Nte; admission free; 9am-9pm) served a postpiracy defensive function when it repelled a punitive raid from Mérida in 1824. Climb the steep ramp to the roof and look between the battlements to see San Juan's cupola. Downstairs, the **Museo y Galería de Arte Popular** (Museum & Gallery of Folk Art; admission free; 9am-9pm Mon-Sat, to 2pm Sun) displays beautiful indigenous handicrafts.

Once the primary defensive bastion for the adjacent Puerta de la Tierra, the **Baluarte de San Francisco** (Calle 18; admission M$20, incl Baluarte de San Juan; 9am-2pm & 4-7pm Mon-Sat, 9am-2pm Sun), between Calles 55 and 57, houses a small arms museum. Just down the street is the **Baluarte**

de San Juan (Calle 18 btwn Calles 63 & 65; admission free with San Francisco ticket; ☉ 8am-7:30pm Tue-Sun), the smallest of the seven baluartes, containing a permanent exhibition on the history of the bulwarks. And the **Baluarte de Santa Rosa** (cnr Calles 14 & Circuito Baluartes; admission free; ☉ 10am-3pm & 6-9pm), a couple of blocks to the northwest, has Campeche's art gallery.

EX-TEMPLO DE SAN JOSÉ
Faced with flamboyant blue-and-yellow tiles, the former **San José Church** (cnr Calles 10 & 63; admission M$15; ☉ 9am-3pm & 3:45-8:30pm Tue-Sun) is a wonder to behold; note the lighthouse, complete with weather vane, atop the right spire. Built in the early 18th century by Jesuits who ran it as an institute of higher learning until they were booted out of Spanish domains in 1767, it now serves as an exhibition space. It belongs to the Instituto Campechano, the square-block university it's attached to.

MUSEO ARQUEOLÓGICO DE CAMPECHE & FUERTE DE SAN MIGUEL
Campeche's largest colonial fort, facing the Gulf of Mexico some 3.5km southwest of the city center, is now home to the excellent **archaeological museum** (admission M$34; ☉ 9am-7:30pm Tue-Sun). Here you can admire findings from the sites of Calakmul, Edzná and Jaina, an island north of town once used as a burial site for Maya aristocracy.

Buses marked 'Lerma' or 'Playa' depart from the market and travel counterclockwise around the Circuito before heading down the *malecón*. The access road to the fort is 4km southwest of Plaza Moch-Couoh. Hike 700m up the hill (bear left at the fork). Otherwise, take a taxi (M$35) or the *tranvía* (trolley; see right).

FUERTE MUSEO SAN JOSÉ DEL ALTO
San Miguel's northern counterpart, built in the late 18th century, sits atop the Cerro de Bellavista. Cross a drawbridge over a moat to enter the neatly restored fortress. Inside, a **museum** (Av Francisco Morazán; admission M$27, free Sun; ☉ 8am-7pm Tue-Sun) illustrates the port's maritime history through ship models, weaponry and other paraphernalia, including a beautiful ebony rudder carved in the shape of a hound.

To get there, catch a local, green 'Josefa,' 'Bellavista' or 'Morelos' bus from the side of the market.

MALECÓN
A popular path for joggers, cyclists, strolling friends and cooing sweethearts, the **malecón**, Campeche's waterfront promenade, makes a breezy sunrise ramble or sunset bike ride.

Courses
Universidad Autónoma de Campeche Centro de Español y Maya (CEM) (http://etzna.uacam.mx/cem/principal.htm; Av Agustin Melgar), one block east of the *malecón*, offers four- to eight-week summer language courses. Homestays can be arranged. Drop by to sit in on classes or check the notice board for Spanish teachers.

Tours
Monkey Hostel (below), Hostal La Parroquia (opposite) and Hostal del Pirata (below) will all arrange tours and/or shuttle services to the Maya sites. Hostal del Pirata also offers kayaking tours of Isla de Jaina and the Los Petenes Biosphere Reserve (M$300 per person), as well as tarpon-fishing expeditions.

Tranvía de la Ciudad (adult M$80, children under 10 free; ☉ hourly 9am-1pm & 5-9pm) Three different tours by motorized *tranvía* depart from Calle 10 beside the Plaza Principal daily; all last about 45 minutes.

Xtampak Tours (☎ 811-64-73; xtampak_7@yahoo.com.mx; Calle 57 No 14; ☉ 8am-4pm & 5:30-8:30pm) Offers comprehensive city tours at 9am and 4pm daily (four hours, M$250 per person), as well as archaeological tours to Edzná (M$180), the Chenes sites (M$750) and eastern Campeche.

Sleeping
BUDGET
Campeche's three hostels all offer bicycle rentals and tours of archaeological sites.

our pick Monkey Hostel (☎ 811-66-05; www.hostalcampeche.com; cnr Calles 10 & 57; dm M$80, r without bath M$200; ▨) You can't beat the view of the plaza and cathedral from the longest-established and most popular hostel in Campeche. The international social scene is enhanced by cozy common areas with bar, hammocks and well-worn sofas, and a friendly bilingual staff. The beds are firm, but they don't have individual fans, which can make for a hot night.

Hostal del Pirata (☎ 811-17-57; piratehostel@hotmail.com; Calle 59 No 47; dm M$90, r without/with bathroom M$210/230; ▨) A block from the Puerta de Tierra, this HI (Hostelling International) affiliate is ensconced in Campeche's historic center, and the building itself is a 17th-century relic. Though it hasn't attained the Monkey's popularity, the Pirata's neatly kept premises may appeal to more fastidious travelers. Occupying a modern annex, dorms and 'semiprivate' rooms share modest facilities with cramped showers. The beds border on mashed-potato firmness, but you get your own fan.

Hotel La Parroquia (☎ 816-25-30; www.hostalpar roquia.com; Calle 55; dm M$90, d/q without bath M$200/300; 🖵) Half a block from the Plaza Principal, Campeche's newest hostel resides in a magnificent late-16th-century mansion. Rooms with original stone walls and exposed wooden beams flank a grand hallway that opens onto a pleasant patio with small kitchen and adjacent lawn for sunbathing. Of the three hostels, it offers the best complimentary breakfast scheme: fresh fruit, toast and coffee at the café next door. It's between Calles 10 and 12.

Hotel Colonial (☎ 816-22-22; Calle 14 No 122; s M$170, d M$180-200; 🛉) Time stands still within this stubbornly low-tech establishment, a budget travelers' haven for six decades. Indeed, little seems to have changed since it was occupied by king's lieutenant Miguel de Castro in the colonial era. Zealously maintained rooms surround a tranquil tiled courtyard with wicker-backed rockers and a central *aljibe* (rainwater cistern).

Hotel Reforma (☎ 816-44-64; Calle 8 No 257; s M$120-250, d M$300; 🛉) Just off the Plaza Principal, this ancient hotel in a 400-year-old building has all the potential in the world. As is, it's a rather odd, bizarre place. Enormous upstairs rooms have modern tiled bathrooms, high ceilings and great balconies, if you can handle the traffic noise. The threadbare sheets leave something to be desired. Rates vary with inclusion of TV, hot water and/or air-con; the complex scheme is posted over the reception desk.

MIDRANGE

Hotel Maya Campeche (☎ 816-80-53, 800-561-87-30; www.mayacampechehotel.com.mx; Calle 57 No 40; s/d M$380/440; 🖵 🛉) This small, boutique-style hotel in the heart of the walled city has a romantic, pseudo-colonial atmosphere and an at-times taciturn staff. Fifteen rooms with ceiling fans and painted wall motifs face a narrow courtyard.

our pick **Hotel López** (☎ /fax 816-33-44; www.hotel lopezcampeche.com; Calle 12 No 189; d/tr/q M$490/540/590; 🅿 🛉 🐾) This elegant hotel is the best buy in the midrange category, though it lacks the charm of other colonial-styled digs. Comfortably appointed rooms open onto art

deco balconies around oval courtyards and exuberant gardens. There's a lovely new dip pool out back.

Hotel del Paseo (☎ 811-01-00; www.hoteldelpaseo .com; Calle 8 No 215; s/d/tr/q M$500/570/680/770; 🅿 🛉) Named for its proximity to the pleasant *paseo* (promenade) that connects the historic center with the Barrio San Román, this modern option has an interior promenade too, with street lamps, shops and a bar, all beneath your balcony.

Hotel Castelmar (☎ 811-12-04; www.castelmarhotel .com; Calle 61 No 2; s/d/ste M$750/850/1050; 🛉) Once an army barracks, the Castelmar has been operating as a hotel for 100 years now. A recent remodeling job upped the casual refinement of this small hotel. Oversized crucifixes and other colonial-era–inspired ornaments add to the charm, as do the amazingly thick walls. Just try to scream; nobody will hear you.

TOP END

Hotel Plaza Campeche (☎ 811-99-00; www.hotel plazacampeche.com; cnr Calle 10 & Circuito Baluartes; r M$890, junior ste M$2120; 🅿 🛉 🖵 🐾) Just outside the historic center on the lovely Parque IV Centenario, the Plaza caters to business travelers. It aims for Euro-style elegance with faux French furniture, a sumptuous dining room and attentive bellhops. The spacious rooms have soothing color schemes.

Hotel del Mar (☎ 811-91-91; www.delmarhotel.com .mx; Av Ruíz Cortínes 51; r with city/sea view M$950/1320; 🅿 🛉 🖵 🐾) The Miami-style del Mar, on the *malecón*, exudes luxury and a beachy glow. Rooms with sea views have balconies. Lafitte's, the downstairs bar where the waiters have to dress up like pirates, doubles as one of Campeche's more popular nightspots.

Eating

Taquería Los Patitos (Calle 8 No 289; tortas & trancas M$6-14; 🕒 7:30am-3pm) Chow down with the long-shoremen at this friendly hole in the wall, where overseer Doña Hilaria fills *tortas* (sandwiches in rolls) and *trancas* with a variety of scrumptious fillings.

Mundo Natural (cnr Calle 8 & Calle 61; juice M$18, salad M$20; 🕒 7am-4pm Mon-Fri, 8am-1pm Sat; 🅅) This open-air 'natural foods' bar opposite the Palacio de Gobierno prepares fresh juice combos, hefty salads and monstro *sandwichónes*.

Lonchería Las Mañanitas (Calle 49B No 3; snacks & soups M$9-25, mains M$70-120; 🕒 6pm-midnight Thu-Tue)

CHOW DOWN CAMPECHANO-STYLE

On Saturday and Sunday the best place to sample *campechano* cuisine is the Plaza Principal. Before sundown, stalls set up around the plaza to offer an impressive variety of home-cooked fare at reasonable prices.

Though startlingly rustic compared with Campeche's spruced-up center, the main market, **Mercado Principal** (Circuito de Baluartes Este; ☉ 7am-5pm), across the street from the Baluarte de San Pedro, offers some terrific snacks. A number of *cocina economica* (basic eatery) stalls ring the interior rotunda.

our pick **Parador Gastrónomico de Cockteleros** (Av Costera; shrimp cocktails M$40-100, fish M$50-90; ☉ 9am-6:30pm) This complex on the north end of the *malecón*, 2.5km from the Plaza Principal, is the place to sample local seafood.

At the Portales de San Martín, a block north of Av Circuito Baluartes Norte, this place serving regional snacks under the arcades of the plaza is a popular gathering place for families and friends.

Cenaduría Portales (☎ 811-14-91; Calle 10, Portales de San Francisco 86; trancas M$20, soups M$25; ☉ 6pm-midnight) It specializes in regional dishes. On warm evenings, an ice-cold goblet of coconut *horchata* (a rice-based drink) really hits the spot.

Café La Parroquia (☎ 816-25-50; Calle 55 No 8; breakfast combos M$30-40, lunch specials M$35; ☉ 24hr) Any time of day or night, your table awaits at this classic restaurant with a dozen ceiling fans, attentive waiters in white coats and continuous Televisa broadcasts. Not just tourists but also local geezers in *guayaberas* (traditional shirts) hang out here for hours on end.

Drinking

La Casa Vieja (☎ 811-80-16; Calle 10 No 319A; ☉ 8:30am-12:30am) There's no better setting for an evening cocktail than La Casa Vieja's colonnaded balcony overlooking the Plaza Principal.

La Iguana Azul (☎ 816-39-78; Calle 55 No 11; ☉ 6pm-2am Mon-Sat) Toward the weekend this casual restaurant across from Café La Parroquia hosts local cover bands and jazz combos in its colonial courtyard.

Salón Rincon Colonial (☎ 816-83-76; Calle 59 No 60; ☉ noon-8pm) This Cuban-style drinking establishment served as a location for *Original Sin*, a 2001 movie with Antonio Banderas that was set in Havana. The *botanas* (drinking snacks) are exceptionally fine; you get a different selection with each round.

Entertainment

There's invariably someone performing on the Plaza Principal every Saturday and Sunday

evening from around 6:30pm. Also at weekends, tables are set up from 6pm to 10pm in front of the cathedral and library for La Lotería (a Mexican version of Bingo). For Campeche's hottest bars and clubs, head 1km south from the city center along the *malecón* past the Torres del Cristal.

Incidents from Campeche's pirate past are re-enacted several nights a week inside the **Puerta de Tierra** (tickets M$50; ☉ 8pm Tue, Fri & Sat), in a Disney-esque extravaganza with lots of cannon blasts and flashing lights.

The Universidad Autónoma de Campeche (p950) has revolving art exhibits, plays and art-house movies (M$25) at the Cine Teatro Universitario Joaquín Lanz.

Catch a free weekday concert, dance or folklore exhibit at the **Claustro del Instituto de Campeche** (Calle 12 btwn Calles 59 & 61).

Getting There & Away

AIR

The airport is 6km southeast of the center. **Aeroméxico** (☎ 823-40-44, 800-021-40-10) flies to Mexico City at least twice daily.

BUS

Campeche's **main bus terminal** (☎ 816-28-02; Av Patricio Trueba 237), usually called the ADO or 1st-class terminal, is about 2.5km south of Plaza Principal via Av Central. Buses provide 1st-class and deluxe service to Mérida, Cancún, Chetumal (via Xpujil), Palenque, Veracruz and Mexico City, as well as 2nd-class service to Sabancuy, Hecelchakán, Candelaria and points in Tabasco. The **2nd-class terminal** (☎ 816-28-02; Av Gobernadores 289), often referred to as the 'old ADO' station, is 1.5km east of the main market. Second-class buses to Hopelchén, Bolonchén, Xpujil and Bécal depart from here.

To get to the new terminal, catch any 'Las Flores,' 'Solidaridad' or 'Casa de Justicia' bus by the post office. To the 2nd-class terminal, catch a 'Terminal Sur' or 'Ex-ADO' bus from the same point. Another Sur terminal across from the Alameda has rural buses to Champotón and Edzná.

The services in the table are 1st class unless otherwise noted.

Destination	Fare	Duration	Frequency
Bolonchén de Rejón	2nd-class M$50	3hr	5 daily
Cancún	M$340	7hr	7 daily
Chetumal via Xpujil	1st-class M$260	6hr	1 daily (noon)
Ciudad del Carmen	deluxe M$160	3hr	1 daily (noon)
	1st-class M$120	3hr	hourly
Hopelchén	2nd-class M$37	1½hr	hourly till 5pm
Mérida via Bécal	deluxe M$125	2½hr (6:30pm)	1 daily
	1st-class M$105	2½hr	every 30 min
Mérida via Uxmal	2nd-class M$90-140	4½hr	5 daily
Mexico City	deluxe M$1060	17hr	1 daily
	1st-class M$900	17hr	6 daily
Palenque	deluxe M$270	6hr (11:30pm)	1 daily
	1st-class M$220	6hr	4 daily
San Cristóbal de Las Casas	deluxe M$410	9hr (11:30pm)	1 daily
	1st-class M$360	9hr	1 daily
Villahermosa	deluxe M$330	6hr	1 daily (4:30pm)
	1st-class M$230	6hr	multiple
Xpujil	1st-class M$170	5hr	1 daily (noon)
	2nd-class M$130	5hr	5 daily

CAR & MOTORCYCLE

If you're heading for either Edzná, the long route to Mérida or the fast toll road going south, take Av Central and follow signs for the airport and either Edzná or the *cuota* (toll road). For the non-toll route south, just head down the *malecón*. For the short route to Mérida go north on the *malecón*.

Coming to Campeche from the south via the *cuota*, turn left at the roundabout signed for the *universidad*, and follow that road straight to the coast. Turn right up the *malecón* and you will arrive instantly oriented.

In addition to the airport outlets, several car-rental agencies can be found downtown. Rates are generally higher than in Mérida or Cancún.

Maya Rent Car (☎ 811-91-91; Hotel del Mar, Av Ruíz Cortinez 51)

Payless Car Rental (☎ 816-42-14; Hotel del Paseo, Calle 10 No 288, interior 3)

Getting Around

Local buses originate at the market or across the Av Circuito Baluartes from it and go at least partway around the *circuito* before heading to their final destinations. The fare is M$4.50.

Taxis charge a set rate of M$25 (M$35 after dark) for rides within the city; by the hour they're around M$100. Tickets for authorized taxis from the airport to the center (M$80) are sold from a booth in the terminal. To request a taxi, call ☎ 815-55-55 or 816-66-66.

Consider renting a bicycle for a ride along the *malecón* or through the streets of the Centro Histórico. All of Campeche's hostels (p950) rent bicycles at reasonable rates.

Drivers should note that even-numbered streets in the Centro take right-of-way priority, as indicated by the red (stop) or black (go) arrows at every intersection.

AROUND CAMPECHE
Edzná

The closest major ruins to Campeche are about 53km to the southeast. **Edzná** (admission M$37; ☉ 8am-5pm) covered more than 17 sq km and was inhabited from approximately 600 BC to the 15th century AD. Most of the visible carvings date from AD 550–810. Though it's a long way from such Puuc Hills sites as Uxmal and Kabah, some of the architecture here has elements of the Puuc style. What led to Edzná's decline and gradual abandonment remains a mystery.

Beyond the entrance is a *palapa* protecting carvings and stelae from the elements. A path from here leads about 400m through vegetation to the zone's big draw, the **Plaza Principal** (follow the signs for the Gran Acrópolis), which is 160m long, 100m wide and surrounded by temples. On your right as you enter from the north is the **Nohochná** (Big House), a massive, elongated structure that was topped by four long halls likely used for administrative tasks, such as the collection of tributes and the dispensation of justice. The built-in benches facing the main plaza were designed for spectators to view theatrical and ritual events.

Across the plaza is the **Gran Acrópolis**, a raised platform holding several structures, including Edzná's major temple, the 31m-high **Edificio de los Cinco Pisos** (Five-Story Building). It rises five levels from its vast base to the roof comb and contains many vaulted rooms. A great central staircase of 65 steps goes right to the top. Some of the weathered carvings of masks, serpents and jaguars' heads that formerly adorned each level are now in the *palapa* near the ticket office.

The current structure is the last of four remodels, and was done primarily in the Puuc architectural style. Scholars generally agree that this temple is a hybrid of a pyramid and a palace. The impressive roof comb is a clear reference to the sacred buildings at Tikal in Guatemala.

In the Pequeña Acrópolis, to the south of the main plaza, is the *palapa*-protected **Templo de Mascarones** (Temple of Masks), which features carved portrayals of the sun god, Kinich-Ahau. The central motif is the head of a Maya man whose face has been modified to give him the appearance of a jaguar.

GETTING THERE & AWAY

From Campeche, dilapidated buses heading to Champotón and Edzná leave from outside the Sur bus terminal at 7am and 11:15am, They return from the site at 1pm and 4pm (M$20, one hour). Most will drop you 200m from the site entrance, so ask before boarding. It's worth checking the day before you travel, as schedules vary.

The ADO bus company offers a circuit of Edzná and several other destinations. Xtampak Tours (p950) provides an hourly shuttle service from Campeche to Edzná

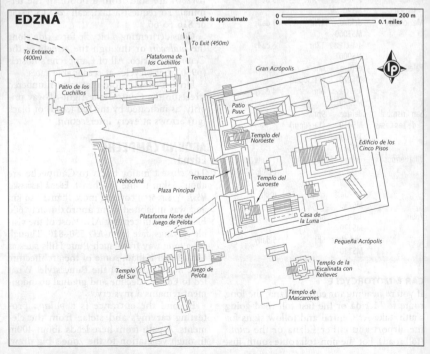

EDZNÁ

Scale is approximate

0 — 200 m
0 — 0.1 miles

To Entrance (400m)

To Exit (450m)

Plataforma de los Cuchillos

Gran Acrópolis

Patio de los Cuchillos

Patio Puuc

Templo del Noroeste

Edificio de los Cinco Pisos

Nohochná

Temazcal

Templo del Suroeste

Plaza Principal

Plataforma Norte del Juego de Pelota

Casa de la Luna

Pequeña Acrópolis

Templo del Sur

Juego de Pelota

Templo de la Escalinata con Relieves

Templo de Mascarones

DIY: EXPLORE MORE OF CAMPECHE

Leave the guidebook behind and head out into the less explored corners of Campeche. Here are some ideas to get you started.

- **Chenes Sites** Northeastern Campeche state is dotted with more than 30 sites in the distinct Chenes style, recognizable by the monster motifs around doorways in the center of long, low buildings of three sections, and temples atop pyramidal bases.
- **Laguna de Términos** The largest lagoon in the Gulf of Mexico area, the Laguna de Términos comprises a network of estuaries, dunes, swamps and ponds that together form a uniquely important coastal habitat.
- **Bécal** While on the surface Bécal may look like a somnolent *campechano* town, underground a multitude is laboring away at the traditional craft of hat making.

(M$180, minimum two passengers) as well as guided tours of the site.

Bolonchén de Rejón & Xtacumbilxunaan

Forty kilometers east of San Antonio Cayal is Hopelchén, where Hwy 261 turns north; there's a Pemex gas station on the west side of town. The next town to appear out of the lush countryside is Bolonchén de Rejón, after 34km. Its local **festival of Santa Cruz** is held each year on May 3.

Bolonchén de Rejón is near the **Grutas de Xtacumbilxunaan** (M$50; ☺ 10am-5pm Tue-Sun; ⚑), pronounced 'Grutas de *shtaa*-koom-beel-shoo-*nahn*,' about 3km south of town. Lighted steps lead down to a barely visible cenote, beyond which a passage leads 100m further. There are few stalactites or stalagmites, but the climb back up to the green forest surrounding the cave is very dramatic.

Hwy 261 continues north into Yucatán state to Uxmal, with a side road leading to the ruins along the Ruta Puuc (p930).

To travel between Xtacumbilxunaan and the city of Campeche by car, follow Hwy 261 south back to the town of San Antonio Cayal where you'll see signs for the clearly marked (though unnumbered) road heading directly west to Campeche (approximately 50km).

ESCÁRCEGA TO XPUJIL

Highway 186 stretches due east across south-ern-central Campeche state, from grubby Escárcega through jungle to Xpujil and on to Chetumal – in Quintana Roo – a 273km ride. It passes several fascinating Maya sites and goes through the ecologically diverse and archaeologically rich **Reserva de la Biosfera Calakmul**. The largest settlement between Escárcega and Chetumal is Xpujil – a great place to stage your exploration of the region – on Hwy 186 about 20km west of the Campeche–Quintana Roo border. The only gas station in the same stretch is about 5km east of Xpujil.

The predominant architectural styles of the region's archaeological sites are Río Bec and Chenes. The former is characterized by long, low buildings that look like they're divided into sections, each with a huge serpent or monster-mouth door. The facades are decorated with smaller masks, geometric designs (with many X forms) and columns. At the corners of the buildings are tall, solid towers with extremely small, steep, nonfunctional steps, topped by small false temples. Many of these towers have roofcombs. The Chenes architectural style shares most of these characteristics, except for the towers.

Balamkú

Discovered in 1990, **Balamkú** (admission M$30; ☺ 8am-5pm) is 60km west of Xpujil (88km east of Escárcega). This small site's attractions are its frescoes and an exquisite, ornate stucco frieze. Amazingly, much original color is still visible on both the frescoes and the frieze. You'll notice toads dominate the designs at Balamkú. These amphibians, not only at home on land and water, were considered to move easily between this world and the next. The toad was a revered spirit guide who helped humans navigate between earth and the underworld.

The frescoes are open to public viewing, but the frieze is housed in a locked building. The caretaker will open the door and even provide a flashlight tour upon request (a tip is appreciated).

Calakmul

First discovered by outsiders in 1931, by US botanist Cyrus Lundell, **Calakmul** (☎ 555-150-20-73; admission M$37, road maintenance fee M$40/car, local tax M$20 per person) means 'Adjacent Mounds.'

Mayanists consider Calakmul to be a site of vital archaeological significance. The site bears comparison in size and historical significance to Tikal in Guatemala, its chief rival for hegemony over the southern lowlands during the Classic era.

From about AD 250 to 695, Calakmul was the leading city in a vast region known as the Kingdom of the Serpent's Head. Its perpetual rival was Tikal, and its decline began with the power struggles and internal conflicts that followed the defeat by Tikal of Calakmul's king Garra de Jaguar (Jaguar Paw).

As at Tikal, there are indications that construction occurred over a period of more than a millennium. Beneath Edificio VII, archaeologists discovered a burial crypt with some 2000 pieces of jade, and tombs continue to yield spectacular jade burial masks; many of these objects are on display in Campeche city's Museo Arqueológico. Calakmul holds at least 120 carved stelae, though many are eroded.

So far, only a fraction of Calakmul's 100-sq-km expanse has been cleared, and few of its 6500 buildings have been consolidated, let alone restored; however, exploration and restoration are ongoing.

Lying at the heart of the vast, untrammeled Reserva de la Biosfera Calakmul, the ruins are surrounded by rainforest, which is best viewed from the top of one of the several pyramids. There are over 250 bird species living in the reserve, and you are likely to see occellated turkeys, parrots and toucans. The menagerie of other wildlife protected by the reserve includes jaguars, spider monkeys, pumas, ocelots and white-lipped peccaries.

SLEEPING & EATING
Rangers allow camping at the **Semarnat post** (☾ from 6am), 20km down the road from the village of Conhuas; they appreciate a donation if you use the shower and toilets.

Campamento Yaax'che (☎ 983-871-60-64; ciitcalak mul@prodigy.net.mx; campsite per person M$50, with tent from M$100) More than just a campground, Yaax'che, 7km along the access road, is the base for tours by Servidores Turísticos Calakmul in Xpujil, a training center for local guides and an experiment in sustainable ecotourism. You can rent a prepitched tent or set up your own under a thatched shelter.

Villas Puerta Calakmul (☎ 988-884-32-78; www .puertacalakmul.com.mx; cabañas M$1200; ☒) This jun-

gle lodge 700m from the highway turnoff is designed for those who want to get into nature without roughing it too much.

GETTING THERE & AWAY
Xtampak Tours (p950) in Campeche and Río Bec Dreams (below) near Chicanná run tours to Calakmul.

By car, the turnoff to Calakmul is 56km west of Xpujil, and the site is 60km south of the highway at the end of a decent paved road. A toll of M$40 per car (more for heavier vehicles) and M$20 per person is levied by the *municipio* (township) of Calakmul at the turnoff from Hwy 186. You'll need to register at the Semarnat post.

Chicanná
Aptly named 'House of the Snake's Jaws,' this Maya **site** (☎ 555-150-20-71; admission M$30; ☾ 8am-5pm) is best known for one remarkably well-preserved doorway with a hideous fanged visage. Located 11km west of Xpujil and 400m south of the highway, Chicanná is a mixture of Chenes and Río Bec architectural styles buried in the jungle. The city attained its peak during the Late Classic period, from AD 550 to 700, as a sort of elite suburb of Becán.

our pick Río Bec Dreams (☎ 983-124-05-01; www .riobecdreams.com; Hwy 186 Km 142; cabañas without/with bathroom M$420/800) provides unquestionably the best accommodation in the area. This Canadian-run jungle lodge has thatched-roofed 'jungalows' sharing a bathhouse and *cabañas* with private bathrooms in the woods. Environmentally sound facilities include composting toilets, rainwater collection devices and solar electricity.

Becán
Eight kilometers west of Xpujil, **Becán** (admission M$30; ☾ 8am-5pm) sits atop a rock outcrop, and a 2km moat snakes its way around the entire city to protect it from attack. Becán (literally 'path of the snake') is also the Maya word for 'canyon' or 'moat.' Seven causeways crossed the moat, providing access to the city. Becán was occupied from 550 BC until AD 1000.

This is among the largest and most elaborate sites in the area. The first thing you'll come to is a plaza. If you walk while keeping it to your left, you'll pass through a rock-walled passageway and beneath a corbeled arch. You will reach a huge twin-towered temple with cylindrical columns at the top of a flight of stairs. This is **Estructura VIII**, dating from about AD 600–730. The view from the top of this temple has become partially obscured by the trees, but on a clear day you can still see structures at the Xpuhil ruins to the east.

Northwest of Estructura VIII is Plaza Central, ringed by 30m-high **Estructura IX** (the tallest building at the site) and the more interesting **Estructura X**. In early 2001, at X's far south side, a stucco mask still bearing some red paint was uncovered. It is enclosed in a wooden shelter with a window for viewing.

In the jungle to the west are more ruins, including the Plaza Oeste, which is surrounded by low buildings and a ball court. Much of this area is still being excavated and restored, so it's open to the public only intermittently.

Loop back east, through the passageway again, to the plaza; cross it diagonally to the right, climbing a stone staircase to the Plaza Sureste. Around this plaza are Estructuras I through IV; a **circular altar** (Estructura IIIA) lies on the east side. **Estructura I** has the two towers typical of the Río Bec style. To exit, you can go around the plaza counterclockwise and descend the stone staircase on the southeast side, or go down the southwest side and head left.

XPUJIL

☎ 983

The hamlet of Xpujil (pronounced 'shpu-*heel*') lies at the junction of east–west Hwy 186 and Campeche Hwy 261, which leads north to Hopelchén and eventually Mérida. A good base from which to explore the area's sites, Xpujil is growing rapidly in the anticipation of a tourist boom. However, it still has no bank or laundry, and the nearest gas station is 5km east of town. Several restaurants, a couple of hotels and a taxi stand are near the bus depot.

From the junction, the Xpuhil ruins are less than 1km west, Becán is 8km west, Chicanná is 12km west, Balamkú is 60km west and the Calakmul ruins are 120km southwest.

Sights

XPUHIL

Within walking distance of the town, **Xpuhil** (admission M$30) boasts a surreal skyscraper that is a striking example of the Río Bec style. The three towers (rather than the usual two) of Estructura I rise above a dozen vaulted rooms. The central tower, soaring 53m, is

the best preserved. With its banded tiers and impractically steep stairways leading up to a temple that displays traces of a zoomorphic mask, it gives a good idea of what the other two must have looked like back in Xpuhil's 8th-century heyday. Go around back to see a fierce jaguar mask embedded in the wall below the temple.

The site's entrance is on the west edge of town on the north side of Hwy 186, at the turnoff for the airport.

Sleeping & Eating

The nicest and most reasonably priced accommodations are in Zoh-Laguna, 10km north of Xpujil. They are all contactable by dialing ☎ 200-125-65-87, the village's central phone booth.

ZOH-LAGUNA

Cabañas Mercedes (s/d M$150/250; **P**) The best-value place in the area has 13 thoughtfully designed bungalows with ceiling fans and large, tiled bathrooms. Good home-cooked meals are served in the thatched-roof dining hall. Don Antonio is both a gracious and well-informed host, who can take you to the major Maya sites.

XPUJIL

Cabañas de Don Jorge (☎ 871-61-28; cabañas M$100) Don Jorge's rustic but perfectly acceptable clapboard cabins sit up on a hill behind his store–eatery, Cocina Económica Xpujil, which is opposite the entrance to the Xpuhil ruins.

Hotel Calakmul (☎ 871-60-29; 2-person cabañas without bathroom M$200, d with air-con M$450; **P** **❖**) About 350m west of the junction, this sterile roadside motel has standard tiled units plus a handful of cramped bungalows out the back. The restaurant, though, comes highly recommended.

Aside from the hotel restaurants, there are various greasy spoons clustered around the bus station and roadside *taquerías* (taco places) toward the Xpuhil ruins. Try **Antojitos Mimi** (⏲ 7am-10pm), opposite Hotel Calakmul, for some pretty fine *salbutes* and an ice-cold *agua de jamaica*.

Getting There & Around

No buses originate in Xpujil, so you must hope to luck into a vacant seat on one passing through. The **bus terminal** (☎ 871-60-27) is just east of the Xpujil junction, on the north side of the highway.

EXPLORE THE RÍO BEC ARCHAEOLOGICAL SITES

'Río Bec' is the designation for an agglomeration of small sites, 70 at last count, in a 100-sq-km area southeast of Xpujil.

Grupo B has some of the best-restored buildings, particularly the magnificent **Estructura I**, dating from around AD 700. This palatial structure features a pair of typical tiered towers crowned by matching temples with cross motifs on their sides. Much of the current restoration work is being done at Grupo A, to the north of Grupo B. Its main structure is a 15m-long **palace** with intact towers and unusual bas-relief glyphs on the lower panels.

Access to the sites is from the collective farm of Ejido 20 de Noviembre. To get there, turn south off Hwy 186, about 10km east of the Xpujil junction, and follow a potholed road 5km to the community and its U'lu'um Chac Yuk Nature Reserve. From there, a very rough road leads 13km further south to the site. It's passable only when dry, and even then you need a high-clearance vehicle. You're best off hiring a guide with a 4WD truck. It's possible to arrange this in Xpujil or at the Ejido; the going rate is M$600 to M$700. A taxi from Xpujil's main junction to the Ejido will charge M$60 for drop-off service; negotiate waiting time. Alternatively, check with Río Bec Dreams (p956) near Chicanná.

For Becán, Hormiguero, Calakmul or other sites you will need to book a tour or hire a cab: Calakmul and Balamkú (M$600), Chicanná and Becán (M$75), Hormiguero M$180). The taxi stand is on the north side of the junction.

AROUND XPUJIL

This southern peninsular region – now bordering modern-day Guatemala – was the earliest established, longest inhabited and most densely populated territory in the Maya world. Here you will find the most ancient and most architecturally elaborate archeological sites on the peninsula.

Ruins

HORMIGUERO

Spanish for 'anthill,' **Hormiguero** (admission M$30; ☻ 8am-5pm) is an old site, with some buildings dating as far back as AD 50; however, the city flourished during the late Classic period. It has one of the most impressive buildings in the region. Entering the site you will see the 50m-long **Estructura II**, which has a giant Chenes-style monster-mouth doorway with much of its decoration in good condition. Also check out **Estructura V**, 60m to the north. Hormiguero is reached by heading 14km south from Xpujil junction, then turning right and heading another 8km west on a shoddily paved road.

Directory

ACCOMMODATIONS

Accommodations in Mexico range from hammocks and huts to hotels of every imaginable standard upwards to super-luxury resorts. This book divides accommodations into three price ranges: budget (where a typical room for two people costs under M$400), midrange (M$400 to M$1000) and top end (above M$1000).

Budget accommodations include camping grounds, hammocks, palm-thatched *cabañas*, backpacker hostels, guesthouses and economical hotels. Recommended accommodations in this range will be simple and without frills but generally clean. Hotel rooms usually have

a private bathroom containing hot shower, WC and washbasin. (In this book, rooms are assumed to have private bathroom unless otherwise stated.)

Midrange accommodations are chiefly hotels, ranging in comfort and atmosphere according to price, though in some areas of Mexico even M$400 can get you a cozy, attractively decorated room in a friendly small hotel. Some midrange hotels have swimming pools, restaurants, in-house travel agencies and other facilities. Many of the country's most appealing and memorable lodgings are in this price bracket – small or medium sized hotels, well designed and cared for, with a friendly atmosphere and personal attention from staff. In some places you'll also find apartments, bungalows and more comfortable *cabañas* in this same price range.

Top-end hotels run from the classier hotels in the cities to deluxe coastal resort hotels and luxurious smaller establishments catering to travelers with a taste for comfort and beautiful design, and the funds to pay for it.

Room prices given in this book, except where stated otherwise, are high-season prices. The exact dates of the high season vary from city to city, and sometimes between different hotels in the same city, but in most of Mexico high season typically means Semana Santa (the week before Easter and a couple of days after it), most of July and August, and the Christmas–New Year holiday period of about two weeks. Outside the high seasons, many midrange and top-end establishments in tourist destinations cut their room prices by 10% to 40%. Budget accommodations are more likely to keep the same rates all year. Through this book we note major deviations from the normal seasonal pattern; in many places on the Pacific coast, for example, high season runs from December right through to Easter. We also note special deals, low weekend rates and other ways you can cut costs.

In this book we use 'single' (abbreviated to 's') to mean a room for one person, and 'double' ('d') to mean a room for two people. Mexicans sometimes use the phrase *cuarto sencillo* (literally, single room) to mean a room with one bed, which may be a *cama matrimonial* (double bed); sometimes one person can occupy such a room for a lower price than two people. A *cuarto doble* often means a room with two beds, which may both be *camas matrimoniales*.

In popular destinations at busy times, it's best to reserve a room in advance or go early in the day to secure a room. Many places take reservations through their websites or by email. Otherwise try by telephone – if the place is not booked out, a simple phone call earlier in the day, saying what time you'll arrive, is usually sufficient. A few places are reluctant to take reservations, but don't worry, you'll always end up with a room somewhere.

Accommodation prices are subject to two taxes: IVA (value-added tax; 15%) and ISH (lodging tax; 2% or 3% depending on the state). Many budget and some midrange establishments only charge these taxes if you require a receipt, and they quote room rates accordingly (ie not including taxes). Generally, though, IVA and ISH are included in quoted prices. In top-end hotels a price may often be given as, say, 'M$1500 *más impuestos*' (M$1500 plus taxes), in which case you must add 17% or 18% to the figure. When in doubt, you can ask, '¿están incluidos los impuestos?' ('are taxes included?'). Prices given in this book are those you are most likely to be charged at each place, with or without the taxes, according to the establishment's policy.

In our accommodations listings the internet icon (🖥) means that the establishment has internet-connected computers for guests to use (this service may or may not be free of charge). A growing number of accommodations also provide wi-fi access for those traveling with their own machines.

The air-con icon (❄) means that the establishment offers at least some rooms with air-conditioning.

Similarly, the nonsmoking icon (🚭) indicates that some rooms, but not necessarily all, are nonsmoking.

Apartments

In many resort areas you can find tourist apartments with fully equipped kitchens. Some are very comfortable and attractive and they can be good value for three or four people, especially if you're staying more than a few days. The internet, local ads and tourist offices are good sources of information on these.

B&Bs

Mexico's growing number of B&Bs, mostly found in tourist destinations, are usually small, comfortable, midrange or top-end guesthouses, often beautifully designed and offering friendly, personal attention from the owners.

Bungalows, Cabañas & Villas

Cabañas are usually huts (of wood, brick, adobe, stone or other materials) with a palm-thatched roof. The most basic have dirt floors and nothing inside but a bed, and you provide the padlock for the door. At the other extreme, some *cabañas* are positively deluxe, with electric light, mosquito nets, large comfy beds, private bathroom, fans, décor, hammock-strung deck and even air-con and kitchen – though they'll usually still have an agreeably rustic, close-to-nature ambience. Prices for simple *cabañas* run from about M$100 to M$200. The most expensive ones are on the Caribbean, where some luxury *cabañas* cost over M$1000.

A bungalow is usually similar to upper-range *cabañas* but more sturdily built and generally forming part of a midrange or top-end hotel. Bungalows are typically free-standing units set in gardens or grounds. Villas, in hotel contexts, tend to be even more sturdy, comfortable and upmarket.

Camping & Trailer Parks

Most organized campgrounds are actually trailer parks set up for RVs (recreational vehicles, camper vans) and trailers (caravans), but are open to tent campers at lower rates. They're most common along the coasts. Some are very basic, others quite luxurious. Expect to pay between M$100 and M$200 to pitch a tent for two, and M$250 to M$300 for two people with a vehicle, using full facilities. Quite a lot of restaurants and guesthouses in beach spots or country areas will let you pitch a tent on their patch for around M$25 to M$40 per person.

Hammocks

You will find hammock space – and often hammocks too – available in many of the more low-key beach spots in the southern half of the country. A hammock can be a very comfortable, not to mention cheap, place to sleep in hot, southern areas (keep mosquito repellent handy). You can rent one and a place to hang it, usually under a palm roof outside a small posada or beach restaurant, for M\$30 or M\$40 in some places, though it can reach M\$100 on the more expensive Caribbean coast. With your own hammock, the cost comes down a bit. It's easy enough to buy hammocks in Mexico, especially in the states of Oaxaca and Chiapas and on the Yucatán Peninsula.

Hostels

There are now hostels suitable for budget travelers in most towns and cities where this kind of traveler congregates. If you follow reasonably well-trodden trails, it's quite easy to stay in nothing but hostels throughout your entire Mexico trip. Hostels provide dormitory accommodation for typically between M\$70 and M\$150 per person, plus communal kitchens, bathrooms, living space and, in many cases, some economical private rooms as well. Some of the best places offer extra enticements such as pools, bars, gardens, sundecks, internet access and even design and charm. Standards of cleanliness and security do vary, but popular hostels are great places for meeting fellow travelers, and word of mouth will often let you know which is the best one in town to head for if you want a party scene/decent sunbathing area/good night's sleep. **Hostelworld** (www .hostelworld.com) and **HostelBookers** (www.hostelbookers.com) provide plentiful listings and offer online reservations.

Fourteen hostels are members of Mexico's HI affiliate, **Hostelling International Mexico** (www .hostellingmexico.com, www.hihostels.com), whose flagship is Hostel Mundo Joven Catedral (p166) in Mexico City. There are small discounts for HI members at these places. **Ciaro Hostels** (www.ciarogroup.com) is a small, independent group with half a dozen hostels in Mexico City and the southeast.

Note that the Spanish word *hostal* actually means 'small hotel' rather than 'hostel', but is now increasingly used for both types of place.

Hotels

Mexico specializes in good midrange hotels, where two people can get a comfortable room with private bathroom, and usually air-con, for about M\$400 to M\$1000. The more you pay within that price range, the more facilities, comfort, style and design the place is likely to have. Many Mexican hotels have modernized and upgraded their facilities in recent years, adding aesthetics and additional comforts to their priorities, often in pleasing combinations of contemporary and traditional, Mexican and internationally influenced taste. Many midrange hotels have a restaurant, bar and internet facilities (often including wi-fi). Quite a lot have swimming pools. Among the most charming lodgings, in both the midrange and the top-end brackets, are the many old mansions, inns, and even monasteries and convents, turned into hotels. These can be wonderfully atmospheric, with fountains gurgling in flower-decked, stone-pillared courtyards or verdant gardens. These are probably the lodgings you will remember most fondly after your trip. Modern hotels are often designed around traditional patio-based plans too.

Every Mexican town also has its cheap hotels. There are clean, friendly, secure ones, and there are dark, dirty, smelly ones where you may not feel your belongings are safe. Adequate rooms with a private hot shower are available for under M\$300 per double in most of the country.

Mexico has plenty of top-end hotels too, particularly in the coastal resort towns and largest cities. They offer the expected levels of luxury – with pools, gyms, bars, restaurants and so on – at prices that are sometimes agreeably modest (and sometimes not!). They range in style from converted haciendas or small, chic boutique hotels to expansive modern resorts, but more often than not the architecture is eye-catching and the facilities and service excellent. Prices at many such establishments are highly flexible, and if you like to stay in luxury but also enjoy saving some money, look for deals on hotel websites or phone them up and ask how to obtain the best price.

Fortunately for families and small groups of travelers, many hotels in all price ranges have rooms for three, four or five people that cost not much more than a double.

PRACTICALITIES

- Mexicans use the metric system for weights and measures.
- Most prerecorded videotapes and DVDs on sale in Mexico (like the rest of the Americas and Japan) use the NTSC image registration system, incompatible with the PAL system common to most of Western Europe and Australia and the Secam system used in France.
- If buying DVDs, look for the numbered globe motif indicating which regions of the world it can be played in. Region 1 is the US and Canada; Europe and Japan are in region 2; and Australia and New Zealand join Mexico in Region 4.
- Electrical current is 110V, 60Hz, and most plugs have two flat prongs, as in the US and Canada.
- Mexico's only English-language daily newspaper is **The News** (www.thenews.com.mx). Distribution is very patchy outside Mexico City. The best and most independent-minded Spanish-language national newspapers include *Reforma* and the left-wing *La Jornada*.

Posadas & Casas de Huéspedes

Posadas are inns, meaning anything from basic budget hotels to tastefully designed, small, midrange places. A *casa de huéspedes* is a guesthouse, a home converted into simple guest lodgings, usually family-run and often with a relaxed, friendly atmosphere.

ACTIVITIES

You can hike, bike, climb, canoe, kayak, raft, ride horses and watch wildlife in some of Mexico's most spectacular areas, and have fun enjoying most imaginable aquatic activities along Mexico's coasts. Active tourism is a fast-growing field in Mexico. The following is a brief introduction to what you can do and where you can do it; for more detail, see the destination sections of this book. Good sources on active tourism in Mexico include **Amtave** (Mexican Association of Adventure Travel & Ecotourism; ☎ 55-5688-3883, 800-654-44-52; www.amtave .com), based in Mexico City with 60 member organizations and companies around the country, and the websites www.planeta.com, www.gorp.com and www.mexonline.com.

Canyoneering, Rappelling & Zip-lining

Matacanes (boxed text, p411) is heaven for canyoneers, with its 27 cliff jumps. Other good bases for this adrenaline-charging activity are Creel (see p349) and Durango (p380). There's exciting rappelling in places like the Sima de las Cotorras (p810) and Coscomatepec (p697), and fun zip-lining at places around Monterrey such as the Cañón de la Huasteca (p410) and Cascada Cola de Caballo (p410), or at Cascada de Tzaráracua (p580), near Uruapan, and Las Nubes (p848) in Chiapas.

Climbing

The Monterrey area is Mexico's mecca for technical climbers, especially the limestone of Potrero Chico (p411), with 600 routes developed. Peaks in Mexico's central volcanic belt, including Pico de Orizaba (p699), Mexico's highest, and Iztaccíhuatl (p231), present fine challenges. A number of good climbing spots, some appropriate for beginners, have been opened up near Oaxaca (p723). You can also climb in the Barranca del Cobre (Copper Canyon) area (p341) and Baja California's Parque Nacional Sierra San Pedro Mártir (p288). Guides are available for all these places. A good book is *Mexico's Volcanoes: A Climbing Guide* by RJ Secor. Conditions at high altitude are best from October to February.

Hiking

Trails in the Barranca del Cobre (Copper Canyon; p341) and Oaxaca's Pueblos Mancomunados (p747) are among the most spectacular, popular and developed. Mountains you can summit without technical climbing include Nevado de Toluca (p269), Volcán Paricutín (p581), Volcán Nevado de Colima (p555), La Malinche (p237), Volcán San Martín (p704) and Volcán Tacaná (p860). There's also good hiking on the lower slopes of Iztaccíhuatl (p231). Other fine hiking areas are the forests of the Reserva de la Biosfera El Cielo (p423), Reserva de la Biosfera Sierra Gorda (boxed text, p651) and Reserva de la Biosfera Calakmul (p955), and the deserts of the Reserva de la Biosfera Sierra de la Laguna (p308). A guide is a very good idea for many routes, as trail marking is generally incipient and walking alone across remote territory can be risky. The best seasons for hiking vary from place to place, but conditions at high altitude are usually best from October to February.

Horseback Riding

Ever more popular among visitors, excellent riding is available at many places, including the Barranca del Cobre (Copper Canyon; p341), Sinaloa's Tufted Jay Preserve (boxed text, p441), Puerto Vallarta (p456), Real de Catorce (p610) and Teotitlán del Valle (p741). And you can canter along the beaches at Mazatlán (p433), Sayulita (p451), Barra de Potosí (p498), Zihuatanejo (p491), Pie de la Cuesta (p499), Puerto Escondido (p756) and many other Pacific resorts.

Mountain Biking

Countless tracks and trails through magnificent country await pedalers. You'll find mountain bikes available for rent or for guided trips of up to several days in places as diverse as Loreto (p300) in Baja California, the mountains around Monterrey (p409), the Barranca del Cobre (Copper Canyon; p341), Coscomatepec (p697), Oaxaca (p723), Puerto Vallarta (p457), around San Cristóbal de Las Casas (p824), and many places on the flat Yucatán Peninsula. See p990 for some tips on cycling in Mexico.

Water Sports

Most coastal resorts rent snorkel gear and can arrange boat and fishing trips. There's great diving along the Caribbean coast, but also some fine spots on the Pacific. Waterskiing, parasailing, jet skiing and 'banana' riding are widespread resort activities. Always cast an eye over the equipment before taking off.

FISHING

Mexico is justly famous for its sportfishing for marlin, swordfish, sailfish and tuna along the Pacific coast and Sea of Cortez. Deep-sea charters are available in all of the major Pacific resorts, many of them now practicing catch-and-release for billfish. The prime locations include Ensenada (p286), San Carlos (p332), Mazatlán (p433), Puerto Vallarta (p456), Barra de Navidad (p472), Manzanillo (p476), Zihuatanejo (p493), Acapulco (p509), Puerto Escondido (p756) and Puerto Ángel (p766). In general the biggest catches occur from April to July and from October to December. Fishing licenses (costing around M$130/250 per day/week) are required for fishing from boats in estuaries and on the ocean; charters usually include them, but you'll need your own if you hire a local fisher to take you out. Most towns have an *oficina de pesca* (fisheries office) that issues licenses.

Elsewhere, there's lake and reservoir fishing inland, and some very good lagoon, river and sea fishing along the Gulf and Caribbean coasts. Fans flock to La Pesca (p420) in the northeast, and Punta Allen (p904) and Xcalak (p907) in the southeast.

KAYAKING, CANOEING & RAFTING

Mexico's many coastal lagoons and sheltered bays make magnificent waters for kayaks and canoes, and there's often interesting wildlife to be seen in the places you'll reach. Rent equipment or take guided trips at prime sites such as Mulegé (p297), La Paz (p303) and Loreto (p300) in Baja California; Mazatlán (p433), Barra de Potosí (p498) and Laguna Manialtepec (p762) on the Pacific coast; Campeche (p950) on the Gulf coast; and on the Caribbean coast at Bahías de Punta Solimán (p895), or Xcalak (p907).

Veracruz state, where rivers fall dramatically from the Sierra Madre Oriental to the coastal plain, is the place for white-water rafting, called *descenso de ríos* in Mexico. The two main centers are Tlapacoyan (p675) and Jalcomulco (p684). You can also raft on some rivers in the Lacandón Jungle in Chiapas (see p817). Always use a reliable company with good equipment and experienced guides.

A Gringo's Guide to Mexican Whitewater by Tom Robey details 56 kayak, canoe and raft runs on 37 different rivers.

SNORKELING & DIVING

The Caribbean is world famous for its wonderful coral reefs and translucent waters full of tropical fish. Great diving locations include Cozumel (p887), Isla Mujeres (p876), Playa del Carmen (p883) and the Banco Chinchorro coral atoll (p906). Most of these are good for snorkeling too. Inland, you can dive some of the Yucatán's famed cenotes (limestone sinkholes) near Akumal (p894) and Tulum (p898) and at Gran Cenote (p901), and there are few more extraordinary experiences than snorkeling amid Mexico's northern deserts in the pellucid pools of Cuatro Ciénegas (p389).

SAFETY GUIDELINES FOR DIVING

Before embarking on a scuba-diving, skin-diving or snorkeling trip, carefully consider the following points to ensure a safe and enjoyable experience:

- Possess a current diving-certification card from a recognized scuba-diving instruction agency (if scuba diving).
- Be sure you are healthy and feel comfortable diving.
- If you don't have your own equipment, ask to see the dive shop's before you commit. And make sure you feel comfortable with your dive master: after all, it's your life.
- Obtain reliable information about physical and environmental conditions at the dive site from a reputable local dive operation, and ask how local trained divers deal with these considerations.
- Be aware of local laws, regulations and etiquette about marine life and the environment.
- Dive only at sites within your level of experience; if available, engage the services of a competent, professionally trained dive instructor or dive master.
- Be aware that underwater conditions vary significantly from one region (or even site) to another. Seasonal changes can significantly alter any site or dive conditions. These differences influence the way divers dress for a dive and what diving techniques they use.
- Know the locations of the nearest decompression chambers and the emergency telephone numbers.
- Avoid diving less than 18 hours before a high-altitude flight.

On the Pacific coast, strap on your tanks at San Blas (p445), Puerto Vallarta (p456), Manzanillo (p475), Zihuatanejo (p491), Puerto Escondido (p756) or Bahías de Huatulco (p779). There's top snorkeling at most of these places too, and elsewhere.

Baja California's top diving and/or snorkeling bases are Mulegé (p297), Loreto (p300), La Paz (p303), La Ventana (p307), Cabo Pulmo (p307) and Cabo San Lucas (p312).

When renting diving equipment, try to make sure that it's up to standard. And beware of dive shops that promise certification after just a few hours' tuition. Make sure the dive shop is certified by **PADI** (www.padi.com), **NAUI** (www.naui.com) or the internationally recognized Mexican diving organization **FMAS** (www.fmas.org.mx), and that its accreditation is up to date.

Coral reefs and other marine ecosystems are particularly fragile environments. For tips on responsible diving, see the boxed text on p889.

SURFING, WINDSURFING & KITEBOARDING

The Pacific coast has awesome surf. Among the very best are the summer breaks at Costa Azul (Zipper's) in Baja California (see p311); the 'world's longest wave' on Bahía de Matanchén (p444), near San Blas; and the barreling 'Mexican Pipeline' at Puerto Escondido (p753). Other fine spots include Ensenada (p284), Todos Santos (p315), Mazatlán (p432), Sayulita (p451), Manzanillo (p475), Boca de Pascuales (p480), Barra de Nexpa (p482), Troncones (p485), Acapulco's Playa Revolcadero (p508) and Barra de la Cruz (p783)…for starters. Most beach breaks receive some sort of surf all year, but wave season is really May to October or November, with June, July and August the biggest months. You can rent surfboards and take classes in many spots. If you're planning to fly to Mexico with your own board, check with the airline first: most of them charge US$50 or more (each way) to carry surfboards, and some won't carry them at all to some destinations or at some times of year.

Los Barriles (p307) is Baja California's windsurfing capital (September to March) and the same winds blow at La Ventana (p307), which is also good for kiteboarding. Further south, Puerto Vallarta (p456) and Manzanillo (p475) can be good too.

Wildlife- & Bird-Watching

Observing Mexico's varied and exotic fauna is an increasingly popular and practicable pastime – see p114 for an introduction to what you can see and where.

BUSINESS HOURS

Stores are typically open from 9am to 8pm, Monday to Saturday. In the south of the country and in small towns, some stores close for a siesta between 2pm and 4pm, then stay open till 9pm. Some don't open on Saturday afternoon.

Offices have similar Monday to Friday hours to stores, with a greater likelihood of the 2pm to 4pm lunch break. Offices with tourist-related business, including airline and car-rental offices, usually open on Saturday too, from at least 9am to 1pm.

Typical restaurant hours are 7am (9am in central Mexico) to midnight. If a restaurant has a closing day, it's usually Sunday, Monday or Tuesday. Cafés typically open from 8am to 10pm daily.

Banks are normally open 9am to 5pm Monday to Friday, and 9am to 1am Saturday. In smaller towns they may close earlier or not open on Saturday. *Casas de cambio* (money-exchange offices) are usually open from 9am to 7pm daily, often with even longer hours in coastal resorts.

Post offices typically open from 8am to 6pm Monday to Friday, and 9am to 1pm Saturday.

In this book we spell out opening hours where they differ from those above.

It's worth remembering that supermarkets and department stores usually open from 9am or 10am to 10pm every day, and stores in malls and coastal resort towns often open on Sunday too.

CHILDREN

Mexicans love children, and will affectionately call any child whose hair is less than jet black *'güero'* (blondie). With a tiny handful of exceptions, children are welcome at all kinds of hotels and in virtually every café and restaurant. In this book you'll find especially child-friendly attractions and places to stay and eat identified with the ⚲ icon.

The sights, sounds and colors of Mexico excite and stimulate most children, but few kids like traveling all the time; they're happier if they can settle into a place for a while and make friends. Try to give them time to get on with some of what they like doing back home. Children are also more easily affected than adults by heat, disrupted sleeping patterns and strange food. They need time to acclimatize and you should take extra care to avoid sunburn. Ensure you replace fluids if a child gets diarrhea (see p1004).

Lonely Planet's *Travel with Children* has lots of practical advice on the subject, drawn from firsthand experience.

Documents for Under-18 Travelers

To conform with regulations aimed at preventing international child abduction, minors (people under 18) traveling to Mexico without one or both of their parents may need to carry a notarized consent form signed by the absent parent or parents, giving permission for the young traveler to make the international journey. Airlines flying to Mexico may refuse to board passengers without it. In the case of divorced parents, a custody document may be required. If one or both parents are dead, or the traveler has only one legal parent, a death certificate or notarized statement of the situation may be required.

Contact a Mexican consulate to find out what you need to do. Required forms for these purposes are usually available from these authorities.

Practicalities

Cots for hotel rooms and high chairs for restaurants are available mainly in midrange and top-end establishments. If you want a rental car with a child safety seat, the major international rental firms are the most reliable providers. You will probably have to pay a few pesos extra per day.

It's usually not hard to find a babysitter if parents want to go out on their own – ask at your hotel. Diapers (nappies) are widely available, but if you depend on some particular cream, lotion, baby food or medicine, bring it with you.

The most family-oriented hotels, with expansive grounds and facilities like pools and playgrounds, tend to be found on the coasts. A few hotels (mostly top-end or upper midrange) offer free accommodation for one or two kids under about 12 if they share a room with their parents. On flights to and within Mexico, children under two generally travel for 10% of the adult fare, as long as they do not occupy a seat, and those aged two to 11 normally pay 67%. Children under 13 pay half price on many Mexican long-distance buses, and if they're small enough to sit on your lap, they will usually go for free.

Sights & Activities

In some places, apart from the obvious beaches and swimming pools, you'll find special kids' attractions such as amusement parks, water parks, zoos, aquariums, safari parks and adventure parks with zip-lines, abseiling and other fun activities. These attractions tend to cluster in and around the cities – such as in Mexico City (p164), Monterrey (boxed text, p403) and Villahermosa (see Parque-Museo La Veta, p792, and Yumká, p797) – and in coastal resorts such as Cancún (p867), Mazatlán (p433) and Acapulco (p509).

Outdoor activity opportunities are growing fast all over Mexico (see p962), and kids don't have to be very old to enjoy snorkeling, watching wildlife, kayaking or riding bicycles or horses. Kids will enjoy some archaeological sites if they're into climbing pyramids and exploring tunnels (few aren't). On the Yucatán Peninsula, away from the beaches and snorkeling, some of the cenotes and caves, such as Boca del Puma (p881), Siete Bocas (p881), Loltún Caverns (p931) and the Grutas de Xtacumbilxunaan (p955), provide a touch of adventure.

CLIMATE CHARTS

June to October are the hottest and wettest months across most of Mexico. For tips on the best seasons to travel, see p31.

COURSES

Taking classes in Mexico is a great way to meet people and get an inside angle on local life as well as study the language, culture or cuisine. The country specializes in short courses in the Spanish language, and as the flavors of Mexican food gain a growing army of fans outside Mexico, cooking classes are becoming ever more popular.

In addition, Mexican universities and colleges often offer tuition to complement college courses you may be taking back home. For long-term study in Mexico you'll need a student visa; contact a Mexican consulate about these.

You'll find helpful links on study possibilities in Mexico on the Lonely Planet website (www .lonelyplanet.com).

Cooking

Oaxaca is Mexico's cooking-school capital (see boxed text, p726). Fans of Mexican food can also learn from experts how to prepare delicious dishes at excellent cooking schools in Monterrey (p404), Puebla (see Restaurant Sacristía, p224), Tlaxcala (p234), Puerto Vallarta (p457) and even little Yambigapan (p704).

Language

Many of Mexico's most attractive and exciting cities are home to Spanish language schools, among them Cuernavaca, Guadalajara, Guanajuato, La Paz, Mérida, Morelia, Oaxaca, Mexico City, Monterrey, Pátzcuaro, Playa del Carmen, Puerto Escondido, Puerto Vallarta, Querétaro, San Cristóbal de Las Casas, San Miguel de Allende, Taxco, Veracruz and Xalapa (see city sections for more details). Many schools are private; some are affiliated to universities.

Depending on the school, you can study for any period from a few hours to a year. In many places you can enroll on the spot and may be able to start the same day. You may be offered accommodations with a local family as part of the deal, which can help your language skills as much as the formal tuition. In a growing number of schools, extra or alternative courses in art, crafts, dance, indigenous languages and in-depth studies of Mexico are also available.

Costs per week, with accommodations and meals included, can range from around M$2000 to over M$5000 depending on the city or town, the school and how intensive the study is.

Useful information is available from the National Registration Center for Study Abroad (www .nrcsa.com), AmeriSpan (www.amerispan.com) and the Council on International Educational Exchange (www.ciee.org).

CUSTOMS

Things that visitors are allowed to bring into Mexico duty-free include items for personal use such as: clothing; two cameras; two mobile phones; a portable computer; a portable radio/CD or DVD player or digital music player; three surfboards or windsurfing boards; one musical instrument; one tent; four fishing rods; medicine for personal use, with prescription in the case of psychotropic drugs; 3L of wine and 3L of other alcoholic drinks (adults only); and 400 cigarettes (adults).

The normal routine when you enter Mexico is to complete a customs declaration form (which lists duty-free allowances), and

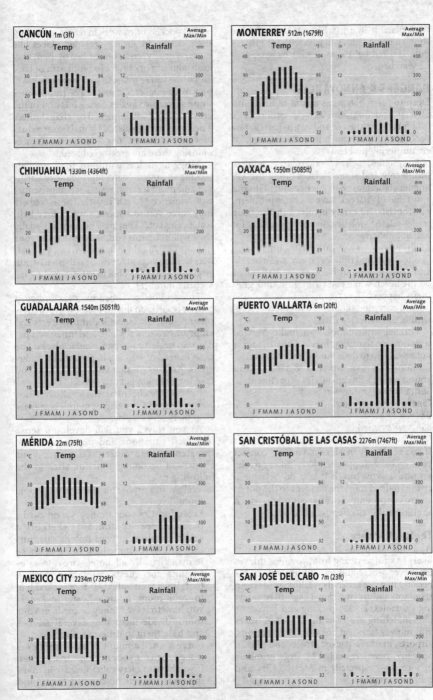

DIRECTORY

then place it in a machine. If the machine shows a green light, you pass without inspection. If a red light shows, your baggage will be searched.

DANGERS & ANNOYANCES

Despite often alarming media reports and official warnings, Mexico is generally a safe place to travel, and with just a few precautions you can minimize the risk of encountering problems.

Some cities, such as Mexico City, Acapulco, Monterrey and several places along the US border (such as Nuevo Laredo, Tijuana and Ciudad Juárez), have a crime problem, but tourists are rarely involved in the drug trade–related violence that brings such a lot of bad publicity.

Enjoy yourself along the coasts, but beware of undertows and riptides on any ocean beach, and don't leave your belongings unattended on the beach while you swim. Run-and-grab thefts happen.

And everyone should be extremely careful with taxis in Mexico City.

Official information can make Mexico sound more alarming than it really is, and is not always up to date, but for a variety of useful information on travel to Mexico consult your country's foreign affairs department:
Australia (www.smartraveller.gov.au)
Canada (www.voyage.gc.ca)
UK (www.fco.gov.uk)
USA (travel.state.gov)

If you're already in Mexico, you can contact your embassy (opposite). Keep an ear to the ground as you travel. If you do become a crime victim, report the incident to the police and to your country's nearest consulate, which should be able to offer useful advice.

Theft & Robbery

As a rule, Mexicans are very honest and unlikely to steal anything from you. But thieves exist everywhere and tourists are vulnerable because they are generally wealthy by Mexican standards and are considered likely to be carrying valuables. Pocket-picking and purse- or bag-snatching are risks on crowded buses and subway trains, at bus stops, bus stations, airports, markets, packed streets and plazas, and anywhere frequented by large numbers of tourists – especially in Mexico City and other large cities.

Pickpockets often work in teams, crowding their victims in already crowded places like markets or city buses: one or two of them may grab your bag or camera (or your arm or leg), and while you're trying to get free another will pick your pocket. Or one may 'drop' something as a crowd jostles onto a bus and in the crush a pocket will be picked or a bag slashed. The objective is to distract you. If your valuables are underneath your clothing, the chances of losing them are greatly reduced.

Mugging is less common than pocket-picking and purse-snatching, but more alarming and more serious: resistance may be met with violence (do *not* resist). These robbers may force you to remove your money belt, watch, rings etc. They may be armed. Usually they will not harm you, they just want your money, fast. But there have been cases of robbers beating victims, or forcing them to drink large amounts of alcohol to extract credit-card security numbers.

To avoid being robbed in cities and even tourist resorts, do not go where there are few other people. This includes empty streets and empty metro cars at night, and little-used pedestrian underpasses and similar places. Use taxis instead of walking in potentially dodgy areas. And, in Mexico City, make sure you take the right kind of cab (see p141).

Isolated stretches of beach can also be risky. Never camp in any lonely spot unless you are absolutely sure it's safe.

As you travel, you will develop a sense of which situations and places are more threatening than others. To reduce your chances of becoming a victim, stick to the following rules:

- Walk with purpose and be alert to people around you.
- Leave most of your money, credit cards, passport, jewelry and air tickets in a sealed envelope in your hotel's safe, unless you have immediate need of these items. Virtually all hotels provide safe-keeping for guests' valuables. Failing that, leave your valuables in a locked bag in your room, or in a hostel locker. If you have to leave money or cards in your room, divide them into several stashes and hide them in different places.
- Carry a small amount of ready money – just enough for your outing – in a pocket. If you have to carry valuables, avoid making your pockets bulge with them, and

preferably keep them in a money belt, shoulder wallet or pouch *underneath* your clothing.

- Don't keep cash, credit cards, purses, bags or cameras in open view any longer than you have to. At ticket counters in bus stations and airports, keep your bag between your feet.
- Do not leave anything valuable looking visible in a parked vehicle.
- Don't accept lifts from strangers.
- Be careful about accepting food or drinks from strangers, especially in resort cities and on buses; there have been cases of drugging followed by robbery and assault, including sexual assault.
- Go easy on alcohol – drunkenness makes you an easier victim.
- Use ATMs only in secure indoor locations, not those open to the street, and try to use them during daylight. Using stand-alone ATMs or booths on the street makes you more vulnerable to theft, and also to card 'cloning' (see p974).
- Cocaine and marijuana are prevalent in Mexico. They are both illegal. The easiest way to avoid problems connected with these drugs is by having nothing to do with them. If you get busted using or transporting illegal drugs, your consulate will not be able to get you out of trouble.

HIGHWAY ROBBERY

Bandits occasionally hold up buses, cars and other vehicles on intercity routes, especially at night, taking luggage or valuables. Sometimes buses are robbed by people who board as passengers. The best ways to avoid highway robbery are to travel by day and to travel on toll highways as much as possible. Deluxe and 1st-class buses use toll highways, where they exist; 2nd-class buses do not. Hwy 200, along the Pacific coast through Michoacán and Guerrero states and as far south as Huatulco in Oaxaca, Hwy 199 between Palenque and Ocosingo in Chiapas, and Hwy 175 between Oaxaca city and Pochutla, have all been the scene of highway robberies over the years.

DISCOUNT CARDS

The ISIC student card, the IYTC card for travelers under 26, and the ITIC card for teachers can help you obtain reduced-price air tickets to or from Mexico at student- and youth-oriented travel agencies. Reduced prices on Mexican buses and at museums and archaeological sites are usually only for those with Mexican education credentials, but the ISIC, IYTC and ITIC will sometimes get you a reduction. The ISIC card is the most widely recognized. It may also get you discounts in a few hostels.

A Hostelling International card will save you M$10 or so in some hostels in Mexico.

EMBASSIES & CONSULATES

If you're having trouble locating your nearest Mexican embassy or consulate, look at the website of Mexico's foreign ministry, the **Secretaría de Relaciones Exteriores** (www.sre.gob.mx), which lists all Mexican diplomatic missions including the more than 30 consulates in US cities. Some Mexican embassy and consulate websites have useful information on visas and similar matters.

Embassies & Consulates in Mexico

Mexico City entries in this list are for embassies or their consular sections; other entries are consulates. Embassy websites are often useful sources of information about Mexico.
Australia Mexico City (Map pp136-7; ☎ 55-1101-2200; www.mexico.embassy.gov.au; Rubén Darío 55, Polanco; Ⓜ Polanco)
Belize Chetumal (☎ 983-832-19-34; Av San Salvador 566, Fraccionamiento Flamboyanes); Mexico City (Map pp136-7; ☎ 55-5520-1274; www.mfa.gov.bz; Bernardo de Gálvez 215, Lomas de Chapultepec; Ⓜ Auditorio)
Canada Acapulco (☎ 744-484-13-05; Local 23, Centro Comercial Marbella); Cancún (☎ 998-883-33-60; Local 330, 3er Piso, Plaza Caracol II, Blvd Kukulcán Km 8.5, Zona Hotelera); Guadalajara (☎ 33-3671-4740; World Trade Center, Piso 8, Torre Pacífico, Av Otero 1249, Colonia Rinconada del Bosque); Mazatlán (☎ 669-913-73-20; Hotel Playa Mazatlán, Av Las Gaviotas 202, Zona Dorada); Mexico City (Map pp136-7; ☎ 55-5724-7900; www.canada.gc.ca; Schiller 529, Polanco; Ⓜ Auditorio); Monterrey (☎ 81-8344-3200; Local 108A, C1 Piso, Edificio Kalos, Zaragoza 1300 Sur); Oaxaca (☎ 951-513-37-77; Local 11B, Pino Suárez 700); Puerto Vallarta (☎ 322-293-00-98; Edificio Obelisco Local 108, Av Francisco Medina Ascencio 1951, Zona Hotelera Las Glorias); San José del Cabo (☎ 624-142-43-33; Local 9, Plaza José Green, Blvd Mijares); Tijuana (☎ 664-684-04-61; Condominio del Parque, Gedovius 10411-101, Zona Río)
Cuba Cancún (☎ 998-884-34-23; Pecari 17, SM 20); Mérida (☎ 999-944-42-15; Calle 1-D No 320, Colonia Campestre); Mexico City (Map pp136-7; ☎ 55-5280-8039; www.embacuba.com.mx; Av Presidente Masaryk 554, Polanco; Ⓜ Polanco)
France Acapulco (☎ 744-484-45-80; Despacho 205, Condominio NIKKO, La Costera 91, Fraccionamiento

Club Deportiva); Cancún (☎ 998-883-98-16; Colegio Británico, Pargo 24, SM 3); Mazatlán (☎ 669-985-12-28; Belisario Domínguez 1008 Sur, Colonia Centro); Mérida (☎ 999-925-28-86; Calle 33B No 528); Mexico City (Map pp136-7; ☎ 55-9171-9700; www.francia.org.mx; Campos Elíseos 339, Polanco; Ⓜ Auditorio); consulate in Mexico City (☎ 55-9171-9840; Lafontaine 32, Polanco); Oaxaca (☎ 951-515-21-84; Planta Baja, 3a Privada de J López Alavez 5, San Felipe del Agua)

Germany Acapulco (☎ 744-484-18-60; Alaminos 26, Casa Tres Fuentes, Colonia Costa Azul); Cancún (☎ 998-884-18-98; Punta Conoco 36, SM24); Guadalajara (☎ 33-3810-2146; Calle 7 No 319, Colonia Ferrocarril); Mazatlán (☎ 669-914-93-10; Av Playa Gaviotas 212, Zona Dorada); Mexico City (Map pp136-7; ☎ 55-5283-2200; www.mexiko.diplo.de; Horacio 1506, Los Morales; Ⓜ Polanco)

Guatemala Ciudad Hidalgo (☎ 962-698-01-84; 9a Calle Ote 11, Colonia San José); Comitán (☎ 963-632-26-69; 1a Calle Sur Pte 35); Mexico City (Map pp136-7; ☎ 55-5540-7520; embaguatemx@minex.gob.gt; Av Explanada 1025, Lomas de Chapultepec; Ⓜ Auditorio); Tapachula (☎ 962-626-12-52; 5A Nte 5)

Ireland (Map pp136-7; ☎ 55-5520-5803; embajada@irlanda.org.mx; Piso 3, Cerrada Blvd Ávila Camacho 76, Lomas de Chapultepec; Ⓜ Auditorio) In Mexico City.

Italy Cancún (☎ 998-884-12-61; Alcatraces 39, SM22); Guadalajara (☎ 33-3616-1700; 1er Piso, Av López Mateos Nte 790, Fraccionamiento Ladrón de Guevara); Mexico City (Map pp126-7; ☎ 55-5596-3655; www.ambcittadelmessic.esteri.it; Paseo de las Palmas 1994, Lomas de Chapultepec)

Japan (Map pp132-3; ☎ 55-5211-0028; www.mx.emb-japan.go.jp; Paseo de la Reforma 395; Ⓜ Sevilla) In Mexico City.

Netherlands Cancún (☎ 998-886-00-70; Martinair, Planta Alta, Terminal 2, Aeropuerto Cancún); Guadalajara (☎ 33-3673-2211; 2 Piso, Av Vallarta 5500, Colonia Lomas Universidad, Zapopan); Mexico City (☎ 55-5258-9921; www.paisesbajos.com.mx; 7th fl, Edificio Calakmul, Av Vasco de Quiroga 3000, Santa Fe)

New Zealand (Map pp136-7; ☎ 55-5283-9460; kiwimexico@prodigy.net.mx; Level 4, Jaime Balmes 8, Los Morales; Ⓜ Polanco) In Mexico City.

Spain Acapulco (☎ 744-484-88-15; La Costera 75); Cancún (☎ 998-848-99-18; Edificio Oásis, cnr Blvd Kukulcán & Cenzontle, Zona Hotelera); Guadalajara (☎ 33-3630-0450; Mezzanine Izquierdo, Torre Sterling, Francisco de Quevedo 117, Sector Juárez); Mexico City (Map pp136-7; ☎ 55-5280-4383; www.mae.es/consulados/mexico; Galileo 114, Polanco; Ⓜ Polanco); Oaxaca (☎ 951-518-00-31; Calzada Porfirio Díaz 341, Colonia Reforma)

UK Cancún (☎ 998- 881-01-00; Royal Sands, Blvd Kukulcán Km 13.5, Zona Hotelera); Guadalajara (☎ 33-3343-2296; Jesús de Rojas 20, Colonia Los Pinos, Zapopan); Mexico City (Map pp132-3; ☎ 55-5242-8500; www.britishembassy .gov.uk/mexico; Río Lerma 71, Colonia Cuauhtémoc; Ⓜ Insurgentes); consulate in Mexico City (☎ 55-5242-8500; Río Usumacinta 26); Tijuana (☎ 664-686-53-20; Blvd Salinas 1500, Fraccionamiento Aviación Tijuana)

USA Acapulco (☎ 744-469-05-56; Hotel Continental Emporio, La Costera 121, Local 14); Cabo San Lucas (☎ 624-143-35-66; Blvd Marina Local C4, Plaza Nautica, Centro); Cancún (☎ 998-883-02-72; 2o Nivel No 320-323, Plaza Caracol Dos, Blvd Kukulcán Km 8.5, Zona Hotelera); Ciudad Juárez (☎ 656-611-30-00; López Mateos 924 Nte); Guadalajara (☎ 33-3268-2100; Progreso 175, Colonia Américas); Hermosillo (☎ 662-289-35-00; Monterrey 141); Ixtapa (☎ 755-553-21-00; Hotel Fontán, Blvd Ixtapa); Matamoros (☎ 868-812-44-02; Calle 1 No 2002); Mazatlán (☎ 669-916-58-89; Hotel Playa Mazatlán, Av Las Gaviotas 202, Zona Dorada); Mérida (☎ 999-942-57-00; Calle 60 No 338K, btwn Calles 29 & 31); Mexico City (Map pp132-3; ☎ 55-5080-2000; www.usembassy-mexico .gov; Paseo de la Reforma 305; Ⓜ Insurgentes); Monterrey (☎ 81-8345-2120; Av Constitución 411 Pte); Nogales (☎ 631-313-81-50; San José s/n, Fraccionamiento Los Álamos); Nuevo Laredo (☎ 867-714-05-12; Allende 3330); Oaxaca (☎ 951-514-30-54; Plaza Santo Domingo, Alcalá 407, Interior 20); Puerto Vallarta (☎ 322-222-00-69; Local 1, Interior 17, Paradise Plaza, Paseo de los Cocoteros 1, Nuevo Vallarta); San Miguel de Allende (☎ 415-152-23-57; Hernández Macías 72); Tijuana (☎ 664-622-74-00; Tapachula 96, Colonia Hipódromo)

FESTIVALS & EVENTS

Mexico's many fiestas are full-blooded, highly colorful affairs, which often go on for several days and provide the chili in the recipe of Mexican life. In addition to the major national festivals listed here, each town has many local saints' days, regional fairs, arts festivals and so on (see destination sections for more information). There's also a national public holiday just about every month (see opposite), often the occasion for yet further partying.

January

Día de los Reyes Magos (Three Kings' Day or Epiphany; January 6) This is the day when Mexican children traditionally receive gifts – rather than at Christmas – although some get two loads of presents!

February/March

Día de la Candelaría (Candlemas; February 2) Commemorates the presentation of Jesus in the temple 40 days after his birth; celebrated with processions, bullfights and dancing in many towns.

Carnaval (late February or early March) A big bash preceding the 40-day penance of Lent, Carnaval takes place during the week or so before Ash Wednesday (which falls

46 days before Easter Sunday). It's celebrated most wildly in Mazatlán, Veracruz and La Paz, with parades and masses of music, food, drink, dancing, fireworks and fun.

March/April
Semana Santa (Holy Week) Starts on Palm Sunday (Domingo de Ramos). Particularly colorful celebrations are held in San Miguel de Allende, Taxco and Pátzcuaro; most of Mexico seems to be on the move at this time.

September
Día de la Independencia (Independence Day; September 16) The anniversary of the start of Mexico's 1810 independence war provokes an upsurge of patriotic feeling: on the evening of the15th, the words of Padre Miguel Hidalgo's famous call to rebellion, the Grito de Dolores, are repeated from the balcony of every town hall in the land, usually followed by fireworks. The biggest celebrations are in Mexico City where the Grito is issued by the national president from the Palacio Nacional.

November
Día de Todos los Santos (All Saints' Day; November 1) and **Día de Muertos** (Day of the Dead; November 2) Every cemetery in the country comes alive as families visit graveyards to commune with their dead on the night of November 1 and the day of November 2, when the souls of the dead are believed to return to earth. The souls of dead children (*angelitos*, little angels) are celebrated on November 1, All Saints' Day (see boxed text, p71).

December
Día de Nuestra Señora de Guadalupe (Day of Our Lady of Guadalupe; December 12) A week or more of festivities throughout Mexico leads up to this celebration in honor of the Virgin who appeared to an indigenous Mexican, Juan Diego, in 1531, and has since become Mexico's religious patron. Children are taken to church dressed as little Juan Diegos or indigenous girls. The biggest festivities are at the Basílica de Guadalupe in Mexico City.
Día de Navidad (December 25) Christmas is traditionally celebrated with a feast in the early hours of December 25, after midnight Mass.

FOOD
Some of the Eating reviews in city sections of this book are divided into budget, midrange and top-end categories. We define a midrange restaurant as one where a main dish at lunch or dinner costs between M$70 and M$130; budget and top-end places charge less than M$70 and over M$130 respectively.

Typical restaurant hours are 7am (9am in central Mexico) to midnight. Restaurant hours are spelt out in this book's Eating sec-

tions if they don't conform to these standard hours. If a restaurant has a closing day, it's usually Sunday, Monday or Tuesday.

For a full introduction to Mexico's fabulously piquant cuisine, see the Food & Drink chapter (p91).

GAY & LESBIAN TRAVELERS
Mexico is more broad-minded about sexuality than you might expect. Gays and lesbians don't generally maintain a high profile, but rarely attract open discrimination or violence. There are large, lively gay communities and/or gay tourism scenes in Mexico City, Puerto Vallarta and Guadalajara (especially), but also in Cancún, Mazatlán, Acapulco, Monterrey and Veracruz. The legalization of gay partnerships in Mexico City has energized the gay scene in the capital. Overall, gay men have a more public profile than lesbians. Discrimination based on sexual orientation has been illegal since 1999, and can be punished with up to three years in prison.

Gay Mexico Network (www.gaymexico.net) offers information plus accommodation and nightlife listings for several cities and has a host of good links. **Gay Mexico** (www.gaymexico.com.mx) has a clickable map linking to gay guides for many cities. **Sergay** (www.sergay.com.mx), a Spanish-language magazine and website, is focused on Mexico City, but with bar, disco and meeting-place listings for the whole country. **Homópolis** (www.homopolis.com.mx) has further listings. Also well worth checking out are **Gay.com** (www.gay.com), with detailed gay travel guides for nine Mexican cities, the **International Gay and Lesbian Travel Association** (www.iglta.org), with worldwide information on travel providers in the gay sector, and **PlanetOut** (www.planetout.com).

San Diego–based **Arco Iris Tours** (www.arcoiris tours.com) specializes in gay travel to Mexico, including group trips to gay festivals in Cancún (May and November), Mexico City's Gay Pride Week (June), and New Year's in Puerto Vallarta.

HOLIDAYS
The chief times when Mexicans take breaks from work are Semana Santa (the week leading up to Easter and a couple of days afterwards), mid-July to mid-August, and the Christmas–New Year period. Transportation and tourist accommodations are heavily booked at these times.

DIRECTORY

The following national holidays see banks, post offices, government offices and many other offices and shops closed throughout Mexico:

Año Nuevo (New Year's Day) January 1
Día de la Constitución (Constitution Day) February 5
Día de Nacimiento de Benito Juárez (anniversary of Benito Juárez' birth) March 21
Día del Trabajo (Labor Day) May 1
Día de la Independencia (Independence Day) September 16
Día de la Revolución (Revolution Day) November 20
Día de Navidad (Christmas Day) December 25

Holidays that fall on Saturday or Sunday are often switched to the nearest Friday or Monday. In addition, many offices and businesses close on the following optional holidays:

Día de la Bandera (Day of the National Flag) February 24
Viernes Santo (Good Friday) Two days before Easter Sunday; April or May
Cinco de Mayo (anniversary of Mexico's victory over the French at Puebla) May 5
Día de la Raza (commemoration of Columbus' discovery of the New World) October 12
Día de Muertos (Day of the Dead) November 2
Día de Nuestra Señora de Guadalupe (Day of Our Lady of Guadalupe) December 12

INSURANCE

A travel-insurance policy to cover theft, loss and medical problems is a good idea. Some policies specifically exclude dangerous activities such as scuba diving, motorcycling and even trekking.

You may prefer a policy that pays doctors or hospitals directly rather than you having to pay on the spot and claim later. If you have to claim later, ensure that you keep all documentation. Check that the policy covers ambulances or an emergency flight home. For further information on medical insurance, see p999.

For information on motor insurance see p994.

Worldwide travel cover is available online at lonelyplanet.com/bookings.

INTERNET ACCESS

Most travelers make constant use of Mexico's thousands of internet cafés (which typically charge M$10 per hour) and free web-based email such as Gmail (mail.google.com), Yahoo (www.yahoo.com) and Hotmail (www.hotmail.com). Many Mexican internet cafés are equipped with CD burners, webcams, head-phones, Skype and so on, but it's a good idea to carry your own or the camera-to-USB cable if you plan on burning photos to CD along the way.

Quite a lot of accommodations have internet-connected computers for guests to use (they receive an 🖳 icon in this book), a service for which they may or may not charge. For travelers with laptops, a growing number of accommodations provide wi-fi *(internet inalámbrico)* access – usually free – as do a few cafés, bars and airports.

For lots of useful stuff on connecting to the web while traveling, visit www.kropla.com. See p35 for some great websites to start your Mexico surfing.

LEGAL MATTERS
Mexican Law

Mexican law is based on the Roman and Napoleonic codes, presuming an accused person is guilty until proven innocent.

The minimum jail sentence for possession of more than a token amount of any narcotic, including marijuana and amphetamines, is 10 months. As in most other countries, the purchase of controlled medication requires a doctor's prescription.

It's against Mexican law to take any firearm or ammunition into the country (even unintentionally) without a permit from a Mexican embassy or consulate.

Road travelers should expect occasional police or military checkpoints. Officials are normally looking for drugs, weapons or illegal migrants. Drivers found with drugs or weapons on board may have their vehicle confiscated and may be detained for months while their cases are investigated.

See p994 for information on the legal aspects of road accidents.

While the legal age for marriage is 12, sex with someone under 18 is illegal if their consent was obtained by deception, such as a false promise of marriage.

Useful warnings on Mexican law are found on the website of the **US Department of State** (www.travel.state.gov).

Getting Legal Help

If arrested, you have the right to contact your embassy or consulate. Consular officials can tell you your rights, provide lists of local lawyers, monitor your case, make sure you are treated humanely, and notify your relatives or friends – but they can't get you out of jail. By Mexican law, the longest a person can be detained by police without a specific accusation is 72 hours.

Tourist offices in Mexico, especially those run by state governments, can often help you with legal problems such as complaints and reporting crimes or lost articles. The national tourism ministry, **Sectur** (☎ 078, 800-987-82-24), has two toll-free numbers offering 24-hour telephone advice.

If you are the victim of a crime, your embassy or consulate, or Sectur or state tourist offices, can give advice. In some cases, you may feel there is little to gain by going to the police, unless you need a statement to present to your insurance company. If you go to the police and your Spanish is poor, take a more fluent speaker. Also take your passport and tourist card, if you still have them. If you just want to report a theft for the purposes of an insurance claim, say you want to *'poner una acta de un robo'* (make a record of a robbery). This should make it clear that you merely want a piece of paper and you should get it without too much trouble.

If Mexican police wrongfully accuse you of an infraction (as they have often been known to do in the hope of obtaining a bribe), you can ask for the officer's identification, to speak to a superior or to be shown documentation about the law you have supposedly broken. You can also note the officer's name, badge number, vehicle number and department (federal, state or municipal). Pay any traffic fines at a police station and get a receipt, then make your complaint at Sectur or a state tourist office.

MAPS

GeoCenter, Nelles, ITM and the AAA (American Automobile Association) all produce good country maps of Mexico, suitable for travel planning, and available internationally for between US$6 and US$15. The GeoCenter map is recommended for its combination of relief (terrain) shading, archaeological sites, national parks, roads (graded by quality) and settlements (graded by size). ITM publishes good 1:1,000,000 (1cm:10km) maps of some Mexican regions (including the Yucatán Peninsula and the Pacific coast). For information on road atlases, see p994.

Tourist offices in Mexico provide free city, town and regional maps of varying quality.

Bookstores and newsstands sell commercially published ones. **Inegi** (Instituto Nacional de Estadística, Geografía e Informática; ☎ 800-490-42-00; www.inegi.gob .mx) publishes two large-scale map series covering all of Mexico at 1:50,000 (1cm:500m) and 1:250,000 (1cm:2.5km), plus state maps at 1:700,000 (1cm:7km). Most of these maps have been updated within the past decade, and they are well worth having if you plan to do any hiking or back-country exploring. Inegi's Centros de Información in every Mexican state capital (listed on the website), and at least three outlets in Mexico City (see p124), sell these maps for M$40 to M$70 each.

A good internet source is **Maps of Mexico** (www.maps-of-mexico.com), with detailed maps of all the states and of 90 cities.

MONEY

Mexico's currency is the peso, usually denoted by the 'M$' sign. Any prices quoted in US dollars will normally be written 'US$5' or '5 USD' to avoid misunderstanding. The peso is divided into 100 centavos. Coins come in denominations of 20 and 50 centavos and one, two, five, 10, 20 and 100 pesos. There are notes of 20, 50, 100, 200, 500 and 1000 pesos.

For exchange rates, see inside the front cover. For information on costs, see p32.

The most convenient form of money in Mexico is a major international credit card or debit card – preferably two if you have them. Visa, MasterCard and American Express cards can be used to obtain cash easily from ATMs in Mexico, and are accepted for payment by most airlines, car-rental companies and travel agents, plus many upper midrange and top-end hotels, and some restaurants and stores. Occasionally there's a surcharge for paying by card, or a discount for paying cash. Making a purchase by credit card normally gives you a more favorable exchange rate than exchanging money at a bank, and isn't subject to commission, but you'll normally have to pay your card issuer a 'foreign exchange' transaction fee of around 2.5%.

As a backup to credit or debit cards, it's a good idea to take a little cash and a few traveler's checks. US dollars are easily the most exchangeable foreign currency in Mexico. In tourist areas and many Mexican cities along the US border, you can often make some purchases in US dollars, though the exchange rate used will probably not be in your favor. Euros, British pounds and Canadian dollars, in cash or as traveler's checks, are accepted by most banks and some *casas de cambio* (exchange houses), but acceptance is less certain if you're away from main cities and tourist centers. Traveler's checks should be a major brand, such as American Express or Visa.

For tips on keeping your money safe while traveling, see p968.

ATMs

ATMs (*caja permanente* or *cajero automático*) are plentiful in Mexico, and are the easiest source of cash. You can use major credit cards and some bank cards, such as those on the Cirrus and Plus systems, to withdraw pesos from ATMs. The exchange rate that banks use for ATM withdrawals is normally better than the 'tourist rate' for currency exchange, though that advantage may be negated by extra handling fees, interest charges and other methods that banks have of taking your money away from you.

To avoid the risk of 'card cloning,' use ATMs only in secure indoor locations, not those in stand-alone booths. Card cloners obtain your card number and PIN by means of hidden cameras, then make a copy of your card and use it to withdraw cash from your account.

Banks & Casas de Cambio

You can exchange cash and traveler's checks in banks or at *casas de cambio*. Banks go through a more time-consuming procedure than *casas de cambio*, and usually have shorter exchange hours (typically 9am to 5pm Monday to Friday and 9am to 1pm Saturday, or shorter hours in some smaller, sleepier towns). *Casas de cambio* are easily found in just about every large or medium-sized town and in many smaller ones. These places are quick and often open evenings or weekends, but some don't accept traveler's checks, whereas banks usually do.

Exchange rates vary a little from one bank or *cambio* to another. There is often a better rate for *efectivo* (cash) than for *documento* (traveler's checks).

If you have trouble finding a place to change money, particularly on a weekend, try a hotel, though the exchange rate won't be the best.

International Transfers

Should you need money wired to you in Mexico, an easy method is the 'Dinero en Minutos' service of **Western Union** (☎ in the US

800-325-6000; www.westernunion.com). It's offered by thousands of bank branches and other businesses around Mexico, identified by black-and-yellow signs proclaiming 'Western Union Dinero en Minutos.' Your sender pays the money online or at a Western Union branch, along with a fee, and gives the details on who is to receive it and where. When you pick it up, take along photo identification. Western Union has offices worldwide.

US post offices (☎ 800-275-8777; www.usps.com) offer reasonably cheap money transfers to branches of Bancomer bank in Mexico. The service is called Dinero Seguro.

Taxes

Mexico's *impuesto de valor agregado* (IVA, value-added tax) is levied at 15%. By law the tax must be included in virtually any price quoted to you, and should not be added afterward. Signs in stores and notices on restaurant menus often state '*IVA incluido*.' Occasionally they state instead that IVA must be added to the quoted prices.

Hotel rooms are also subject to the *impuesto sobre hospedaje* (ISH, lodging tax). Each Mexican state sets its own rate, but in most it's 2%. See p959 for further information on taxes on hotel rooms.

Tipping & Bargaining

In general, workers in small, cheap restaurants don't expect much in the way of tips, while those in expensive resorts expect you to be lavish in your largesse. Workers in the tourism and hospitality industries often depend on tips to supplement miserable basic wages. In resorts frequented by foreigners (such as Cancún, Acapulco and Puerto Vallarta) tipping is up to US levels of 15%; elsewhere 10% is usually plenty. If you stay a few days in one place, you should leave up to 10% of your room costs for the people who have kept your room clean (assuming they have). A porter in a midrange hotel will be happy with M$10 a bag. Taxi drivers don't generally expect tips unless they provide some special service. Car parking attendants expect a tip of M$3 to M$5, and the same is standard for gas-station attendants.

Room rates are pretty firm, though it can be worth asking if any discounts are available, especially if it's low season or you are going to stay a few nights. In markets bargaining is the rule, and you may pay much more than the going rate if you accept the first price quoted. You can also bargain with drivers of unmetered taxis.

POST

An airmail letter or postcard weighing up to 20g costs M$10.50 to the US or Canada, M$13 to Europe or South America, and M$14.50 to the rest of the world. Items between 20g and 50g cost M$18, M$21 and M$23. *Certificado* (registered) service costs an extra M$20. Mark airmail items 'Vía Aérea.' Delivery times (outbound and inbound) are variable. An airmail letter from Mexico to the US or Canada (or vice-versa) should take somewhere between four and 14 days to arrive. Mail to or from Europe takes between one and two weeks.

Post offices *(oficinas de correos)* are typically open from 8am to 6pm Monday to Friday, and 9am to 1pm Saturday. You can receive letters and packages care of a post office if they're addressed to the post office's *lista de correos* (mail list), as follows:

Dolores ABRAM (last name in capitals)
Lista de Correos
Correo Central
Acapulco
Guerrero 00000 (post code)
MEXICO

When the letter reaches the post office, the name of the addressee is placed on an alphabetical list that is updated daily and often pinned up on the wall. To claim your mail, present your passport or other identification. There's no charge, but many post offices only hold *lista* mail for 10 days before returning it to the sender. If you think you might pick mail up more than 10 days after it has arrived, have it sent to Poste Restante, instead of Lista de Correos. Poste Restante may hold mail for up to a month, though no list of what has been received is posted up.

If you're sending a package internationally from Mexico, be prepared to open it for customs inspection at the post office; it's better to take packing materials with you, or not seal it until you get there. For assured and speedy delivery, you can use one of the more expensive international courier services, such as **UPS** (☎ 800-902-92-00; www.ups.com), **Federal Express** (☎ 800-900-11-00; www.fedex.com) or Mexico's **Estafeta** (☎ 800-903-35-00; www.estafeta.com). Packages up to 500g cost up to about M$350 to the US or Canada, or M$450 to Europe.

SHOPPING

Mexico's star buys are the wonderful and amazingly varied regional handicrafts made in all parts of the country, predominantly by indigenous people. You can buy these *artesanías* in the villages where they are produced, or in stores and markets in urban centers. *Artesanías* stores in cities will give you a good overview of what's available and a basis for price comparisons. Places such as Mexico City, Guadalajara, Monterrey, San Miguel de Allende, Puerto Vallarta, Puebla and Oaxaca have stores selling quality handicrafts from all over Mexico. A few cities have special markets devoted to crafts, but ordinary daily or weekly markets always sell crafts too (including everyday pots and baskets as well as more artistic products). The quality and price of market goods may be lower than in stores. Bargaining is expected in markets, whereas stores generally have fixed prices. Traveling to craft-making villages gives you a chance to see artisans at work, and if you buy there you'll know that more of your money is likely to go to the artisans themselves and less to entrepreneurs.

For everyday purchases and consumer goods, middle-class Mexicans like to shop in glitzy suburban malls, supermarkets, hypermarkets and department stores. In city centers you're more likely to find smaller, older shops and markets with more character.

See p88 for an introduction to many Mexican handicrafts: ceramics, masks, woodwork, jewelry, metalwork, lacquerware, indigenous textiles, bark paintings and *retablos* (also called *exvotos*). Following are some other fine products and good buys.

Bags Come in all shapes and sizes, many incorporating indigenous designs. Those made by the Huichol people are among the most authentic and original.

Baskets Handmade baskets of multifarious shapes, sizes and patterns, made of materials like cane, bamboo, wicker, or rush or palm-leaf strips, are common in Mexican markets. They can be useful for carrying other purchases home as well as being appealing in themselves.

Clothes Commercially produced clothing, whether based on traditional designs or with a Mexican take on international fashion trends, can be attractive and good value, including surfwear made by Mexican brands such as Squalo.

Hammocks Usually made of cotton or nylon, hammocks come in a variety of sizes and an infinite number of color patterns – easy to buy in Mérida, Palenque, Acapulco, Puerto Escondido, Zipolite, Mitla and Juchitán.

Leather goods León is Mexico's shoe capital, and has dozens of stores, though every other sizable city has plenty of good ones, too. Finely crafted belts, bags, *huaraches* (sandals), boots, clothes and saddles are available in northern and central ranching towns such as Zacatecas, Chihuahua, Durango, Jerez, Hermosillo, Monterrey, Saltillo and Guadalajara.

Musical Instruments Paracho, Michoacán, is the guitar capital of Mexico, and also produces violins, cellos and other instruments. Elsewhere you'll come across maracas, tambourines, whistles, scrape boards and a variety of drums. Keep an eye open for tongue drums, often-cylindrical hollowed-out pieces of wood attractively carved or decorated, with two central tongues of wood each giving a different note when struck.

SOLO TRAVELERS

A single room normally costs well over half the price of a double room, but budget travelers can cut accommodation costs in many places by staying in hostels. Hostels have the additional advantage of providing ready-made company, full of helpful travel tips, and are often a lot of fun. Lone travelers don't need to remain alone when traveling in Mexico unless they choose to. It's very easy to team up with others as there's a steady stream of people following similar routes around the country. Local tours are a good way to meet people and get more out of a place.

Solo travelers should be especially watchful of their luggage when on the road and should stay in places with good security for their valuables, so they don't have to be burdened with them when out and about. One big drag of traveling alone can be when you want to take a quick dip in the ocean – you're stuck with your possessions and there's no one to watch out for them.

Traveling alone can be a very good way of getting into the local culture and it definitely improves your Spanish skills. You can also get a kick out of doing what you want when you want. Eating by yourself night after night can get a bit tiresome, but you'll only be left alone if you want it that way, as Mexicans are very sociable.

TELEPHONE

Local calls are cheap; international calls can be expensive, but with widely available discount cards they needn't be. Calling from your hotel can be expensive as hotels charge what they like for this service. Following are the most common ways to make calls in Mexico.

Cell Phones

Like other Mexican phone numbers, every Mexican cell phone (*teléfono celular*) has an area code (usually the code of the city it was bought in). The area code and the phone's number total 10 digits. When calling a cell phone from a landline, you dial ☎ 044 before the 10 digits if the cell phone's area code is the same as the area code you are dialing from, or ☎ 045 if the cell phone has a different area code. From cell phone to cell phone, just dial the 10-digit number. To call a Mexican cell phone from another country, dial your international access code, followed by the Mexican country code (☎ 52), then 1, then the 10-digit number.

If you want to use a cell phone in Mexico, the three main operators – **Telcel** (www.telcel .com), **IUSACell** (www.iusacell.com.mx) and **Movistar** (www.movistar.com.mx) – all sell phones for around M$400 to M$800 including a charger and some call credit. For further credit you can buy top-up cards for M$100 or more. Telcel is the most widespread network, with many sales outlets (including one at Mexico City airport) and coverage almost everywhere that has a significant population. Telcel top-up cards are widely available from newsstands and minimarts. Mexican cell phones generally cannot be used in other countries.

Roaming with your own cell phone from home in Mexico is possible if you have a GSM phone but it is generally very expensive. Much cheaper is to buy a local SIM card or 'chip' from a Telcel or Movistar outlet. You can usually top these up online.

A good source for further information on international mobile phone use is www .kropla.com.

Collect Calls

A *llamada por cobrar* (collect call) can cost the receiving party much more than if they call you, so you may prefer to pay for a quick call to the other party to ask them to call you back. If you do need to make a collect call, you can do so from card phones without a card. Call an operator on ☎ 020 for domestic calls, or ☎ 090 for international calls, or use a 'home country direct' service, through which you make an international collect call via an operator in the country you're calling. The Mexican term for 'home country direct' is *país directo*. Mexican international operators may know the access numbers for some countries, but it's best to get this information from your home country before you leave.

Some telephone *casetas* and hotels will make collect calls for you, but they usually charge for the service.

Internet Telephony

For this you need access to high-speed internet, available at most internet cafés and also at hotels, cafés and other places with wi-fi access. You also need an appropriate headset and microphone. Many internet cafés have these; some have telephone service installed and they'll usually advertise this with very low per-minute costs. Travelers who have accounts with internet phone services such as **Skype** (www.skype.com) can use these at internet cafés, and also on their own laptops in places with wi-fi access. Can be the cheapest option if you have an account.

Locutorios & Casetas de Teléfono

These are call offices where an on-the-spot operator connects the call for you. Costs in *casetas* and *locutorios* are often lower than those for Telmex card phones, and their advantages are that they eliminate street noise and you don't need a phone card to use them. They often have a telephone symbol outside, or signs saying 'teléfono,' 'Lada' or 'Larga Distancia.' In Baja California *casetas* are known as *cabinas*.

Long-Distance Discount Cards

Available from kiosks and some minimarts, usually in denominations of M$100, M$200 and M$500, these cards marketed by alternative telephone carriers offer substantial savings on Mexican long-distance calls and international calls when compared with Telmex card phones, *locutorios* and often even private phones. There are many brands – just ask for a *tarjeta para llamadas de larga distancia de descuento* (card for discount long-distance calls). To use them, you call a local or toll-free access number, then dial in the scratch-off code from the card, then dial the number you want in the normal way. You don't put the discount card into the phone and you can use them from hotel-room phones, private phones and Telmex card phones.

Prefixes & Codes

If you're calling a landline number in the town or city you're in, simply dial the local number (eight digits in Mexico City, Guadalajara and Monterrey, seven digits everywhere else).

To call a landline number in another town or city in Mexico, you need to dial the long-distance prefix ☎ 01, followed by the area code (two digits for Mexico City, Guadalajara and Monterrey; three digits for everywhere else) and then the local number. For example, to call from Mexico City to Oaxaca, dial ☎ 01, then the Oaxaca area code ☎ 951, then the seven-digit local number. You'll find area codes listed under city and town headings through this book.

To make an international call, dial the international prefix ☎ 00, followed by the country code, area code and local number. For example, to call New York City from Mexico, dial ☎ 00, then the US country code ☎ 1, then the New York City area code ☎ 212, then the local number.

To call a landline number in Mexico from another country, dial your international access code, then the Mexico country code ☎ 52, then the area code and number.

See opposite for information on prefixes for calls to cell phones.

Public Card Phones

These are common in towns and cities, and you'll usually find some at airports, bus stations and around the main plaza. By far the most common, and most reliable on costs, are those marked with the name of the country's main, almost monopolistic, phone operator, **Telmex** (www.telmex.com). To use a Telmex card phone you need a phone card known as a *tarjeta Ladatel*. These are sold at kiosks and shops everywhere – look for the blue-and-yellow '*Ladatel*' signs. The cards come in denominations of M$30, M$50 and M$100.

Calls from Telmex card phones cost M$1 per minute for local calls; M$4 per minute long-distance within Mexico; M$5 per minute to the US (except Alaska and Hawaii) or Canada; M$10 per minute to Central America; and M$20 to M$25 per minute to the rest of the world. Calls to cell phones are M$3.12 per minute (local) or M$6.12 per minute (long-distance).

Toll-Free & Operator Numbers

Toll-free numbers in Mexico (☎ 800 followed by seven digits) always require the ☎ 01 prefix. You can call most of these numbers, and emergency, numbers from

DIRECTORY

Telmex pay phones without inserting a telephone card.

US and Canadian toll-free numbers are ☎ 800 or ☎ 888 followed by seven digits. Some of these can be reached from Mexico (dial ☎ 001 before the 800), but you may have to pay a charge for the call.

For a domestic operator in Mexico, dial ☎ 020; for an international operator, dial ☎ 090. For Mexican directory information, dial ☎ 040.

TIME

Most of the country is on Hora del Centro, the same as US Central Time (that's GMT minus six hours in winter, and GMT minus five hours during daylight saving). Five northern and western states – Chihuahua, Nayarit, Sinaloa, Sonora and Baja California Sur – are on Hora de las Montañas, the same as US Mountain Time (GMT minus seven hours in winter, GMT minus six hours during daylight saving). Baja California (Norte) observes Hora del Pacífico, the same as US Pacific Time (GMT minus eight hours in winter, GMT minus seven hours during daylight saving).

Daylight saving time ('horario de verano,' summer time) runs from the first Sunday in April to the last Sunday in October. Clocks go forward one hour in April and back one hour in October. The northwestern state of Sonora ignores daylight saving (like its US neighbor Arizona), so remains on GMT minus seven hours all year. Daylight saving is also ignored by a few remote rural zones, such as the Sierra Norte of Oaxaca and the Marqués de Comillas area of eastern Chiapas (to the perdition of bus schedules from nearby towns such as Oaxaca and Palenque).

See the World Map at the back of this book if you need international time zone information.

TOILETS

Public toilets are not common, so take advantage of facilities in places such as hotels, restaurants, bus stations and museums. When out and about, it's a good idea to carry some toilet paper with you, because it may not be provided. If there's a bin beside the toilet, put paper in it because the drains can't cope otherwise.

TOURIST INFORMATION

Just about every town of interest to tourists in Mexico has a state or municipal tourist office. They are generally helpful with maps, brochures and questions, and usually some staff members speak English.

You can call the Mexico City office of the national tourism ministry **Sectur** (☎ 078, 800-987-82-24, in the US 888-401-3880, from Europe 00-52-55-5089-7500; www.visitmexico.com, www.sectur.gob .mx) at any time – 24 hours a day, seven days a week – for information or help in English or Spanish.

Following are the contact details for the head tourism offices of each Mexican state (some websites are in Spanish only).

Aguascalientes (☎ 449-915-95-04; www.aguas calientes.gob.mx/turismo)

Baja California (☎ 078, 664-682-33-67; www.discover bajacalifornia.com)

Baja California Sur (☎ 612-124-01-00; www.bcs .gob.mx)

Campeche (☎ 981-811-92-29, 800-900-22-67; www .campechetravel.com)

Chiapas (☎ 961-617-05-50, 800-280-35-00; www .turismochiapas.gob.mx)

Chihuahua (☎ 614-429-35-96, 800-508-01-11; www .ah-chihuahua.com, www.chihuahua.gob.mx/turismoweb)

Coahuila (☎ 800-718-42-20; www.secturcoahuila .gob.mx)

Colima (☎ 312-316-20-21; www.visitacolima.com.mx)

Durango (☎ 618-811-11-07, 800-624-65-67; www .durangoturismo.com, www.durango.gob.mx)

Guanajuato (☎ 473-732-15-74, 800-714-10-86; www .guanajuato-travel.com)

Guerrero (☎ 747-471-97-00; www. guerrero.gob.mx)

Hidalgo (☎ 771-718-39-37; www.turismo.hidalgo .gob.mx)

Jalisco (☎ 33-3668-1600, 800-363-22-00; www.visita .jalisco.gob.mx)

Mexico City (☎ 800-008-90-90; www.mexicocity.gob.mx)

México State (☎ 722-212-59-98; turismo.edomexico .gob.mx)

Michoacán (☎ 443-317-23-71, 800-450-23-00; www .turismomichoacan.gob.mx)

Morelos (☎ 717-314-39-20; www.morelostravel.com)

Nayarit (☎ 311-214-80-71; www.turnay.gob.mx)

Nuevo León (☎ 81-2020-6789, 800-832-22-00; www .nl.gob.mx)

Oaxaca (☎ 951-516-01-23; www.oaxaca.travel)

Puebla (☎ 800-326-86-56; www.puebla.com.mx)

Querétaro (☎ 442-238-50-67, 800-715-17-42, in the US 888-811-6130; www.venaqueretaro.com)

Quintana Roo (☎ 983-835-08-60; http://sedetur.qroo .gob.mx)

San Luis Potosí (☎ 444-814-14-16, 800-343-38-87; www.descubresanluispotosi.com)

Sinaloa (☎ 669-981-88-86; www.sinaloa-travel.com)

Sonora (☎ 662-289-58-00, in the US 800-476-6672; www.gotosonora.com)

Tabasco (☎ 800-216-08-42, www.visitetabasco.com, www.tabasco.gob.mx/turismo)

Tamaulipas (☎ 834-315-61-36, 800-710-65-32, in the US 888-580-5968; turismo.tamaulipas.gob.mx)

Tlaxcala (☎ 246-465-09-60 ext 1519, 800-509-65-57; www.tlaxcala.gob.mx/turismo)

Veracruz (☎ 800-837-28-87; www.veracruzturismo .com.mx)

Yucatán (☎ 999-930-37-60; www.mayayucatan.com.mx)

Zacatecas (☎ 492-922-67-51, 800-712-40-78; www .turismozacatecas.gob.mx)

TRAVELERS WITH DISABILITIES

Mexico is not yet very disabled-friendly, though some hotels and restaurants (mostly toward the top end of the market) and some public buildings and archaeological sites provide wheelchair access. Very few sidewalks have wheelchair ramps. Mobility is easiest in the major tourist resorts and the more expensive hotels. Bus transportation can be difficult; flying or taking a taxi is easier. The absence of formal facilities is partly compensated by Mexicans' helpful attitudes toward others, and special arrangements are gladly improvised.

Mobility International USA (☎ 541-343-1284; www .miusa.org) advises disabled travelers on mobility issues and runs exchange programs. Its website includes international databases of exchange programs and disability organizations, with several Mexican organizations listed.

In the UK, **Radar** (☎ 020-7250-3222; www.radar .org.uk) is run by and for disabled people. The website has links to good travel and holiday sites.

Three further good sources for disabled travelers are **MossRehab ResourceNet** (www.moss resourcenet.org), **Access-able Travel Source** (www.ac cess-able.com) and **Disability Travel and Recreation Resources** (www.makoa.org/travel.htm).

VISAS

Every tourist must have an easily obtainable Mexican-government tourist card. Some nationalities also need to obtain visas. Because the regulations sometimes change, it's wise to confirm them with a Mexican embassy or consulate before you go. The websites of some Mexican consulates, including the **London consulate** (portal.sre.gob.mx/conreinounido) and the **Los Angeles consulate** (www.sre.gob.mx/losangeles) give useful information on visas and similar matters. The rules are also summarized on the website of Mexico's **Instituto Nacional de Migración** (INM, National Migration Institute; www.inami .gob.mx). The **Lonely Planet website** (www.lonelyplanet .com) has links to updated visa information.

Citizens of the US, Canada, EU countries, Argentina, Australia, Chile, New Zealand, Iceland, Israel, Japan, Norway and Switzerland are among those who do not need visas to enter Mexico as tourists. The list changes sometimes; check well ahead of travel with your local Mexican embassy or consulate. Visa procedures, for those who need them, can take several weeks and you may be required to apply in your country of residence or citizenship.

For information on passport requirements, see p983. Non-US citizens passing (even in transit) through the US on the way to or from Mexico, or visiting Mexico from the US, should also check the passport and visa requirements for the US.

Tourist Card & Tourist Fee

The Mexican tourist card – officially the *forma migratoria para turista* (FMT) – is a brief card document that you must fill out and get stamped by Mexican immigration when you enter Mexico, and keep till you leave. It's available at official border crossings, international airports and ports, and often from airlines, travel agencies and Mexican consulates.

At the US–Mexico border you won't usually be given one automatically – you have to ask for it. And at many crossings here you don't have to get the card stamped at the actual border, as the INM has control points on the highways into the interior where it's also possible to do it. But it's preferable to get it done at the border itself, in case there are complications elsewhere.

One section of the card deals with the length of your stay in Mexico, and this section is filled out by the immigration officer. The maximum possible is 180 days, but immigration officers sometimes put a lower number (as little as 15 or 30 days in some cases) unless you tell them specifically what you need. It's advisable to ask for more days than you think you'll need, in case you are delayed or change your plans.

Though the tourist card itself is free of charge, it brings with it the obligation to pay the tourist fee of US$22, called the *derecho para no inmigrante* (DNI, nonimmigrant fee). The exact amount of the fee in pesos fluctuates with exchange rates. If you enter Mexico by air, the fee is included in your airfare. If you enter by land, you must pay the fee at a bank in Mexico at any time before you reenter the frontier zone on your way out of Mexico (or before you check in at an airport to fly out of Mexico). The frontier zone is the territory between the border itself and the INM's control points on the highways leading into the Mexican interior (usually 20km to 30km from the border). Most Mexican border posts have on-the-spot bank offices where you can pay the DNI fee immediately. When you pay at a bank, your tourist card will be stamped to prove that you have paid.

Look after your tourist card because it may be checked when you leave the country. You can be fined for not having it.

Tourist cards (and fees) are not necessary for visits shorter than 72 hours within the frontier zones along Mexico's northern and southern borders, but be sure to confirm details when you cross the border.

A tourist card only permits you to engage in what are considered to be tourist activities (including sports, health, artistic and cultural activities). If the purpose of your visit is to work (even as a volunteer), report or study, or to participate in humanitarian aid or human-rights observation, you may well need a visa. If you're unsure, check with a Mexican embassy or consulate.

EXTENSIONS & LOST CARDS

If the number of days given on your tourist card is less than the maximum 180 days, its validity may be extended, one or more times, up to the maximum. To get a card extended you have to apply to the INM, which has offices in many towns and cities: they're listed on the **INM website** (www.inm.gob.mx) under 'Servicios Migratorios.' The procedure costs around M$200 and should take between half an hour and three hours, depending on the office. You'll need your passport, tourist card, photocopies of the important pages of these documents and, at some offices, evidence of 'sufficient funds.' A major credit card is usually OK for the latter, or an amount in traveler's checks anywhere from M$100 to M$1000 depending on the office.

Most INM offices will not extend a card until a few days before it is due to expire; don't bother trying earlier.

If you lose your card or need further information, contact your nearest tourist office, or the **Sectur tourist office** (☎ 078, 800-987-82-24) in Mexico City, or your embassy or consulate. Any of these should be able to give you an official note to take to your local INM office, which will issue a replacement for a cost of about M$450.

VOLUNTEERING

A great way to engage with Mexican communities and contribute something other than tourist dollars to the country is to do some volunteer work. Many organizations and projects can use your services for periods from a few hours to a year or more. Work ranges from protecting sea turtles to helping disadvantaged children. Some are looking for people with relevant experience and/or Spanish language skills; others can use almost any willing hand. Longer-term volunteers will often be offered some kind of accommodation. If you arrange volunteer work in Mexico through an organization that specializes in bringing people from other countries, you will often have to pay a significant sum of money for the opportunity. If you can make direct personal contact with a project on the ground in Mexico, your costs are likely to be much lower. You may just be asked to contribute a small amount to the project's running costs.

Many language schools (p966) offer part-time local volunteering opportunities to complement the classes you take.

Volunteer Directories

These sources are good places to start looking for Mexican volunteer opportunities:
Alliance of European Voluntary Service Organisations (www.alliance-network.org)
Coordinating Committee for International Voluntary Service (www.unesco.org/ccivs)
Idealist.org (www.idealist.org)
Transitions Abroad (www.transitionsabroad.com)
Volunteer Abroad (www.volunteerabroad.com)

Mexico-Based Programs

Cuernavaca-based **Por Un Mejor Hoy** (www.hoycommunity.org) is specifically geared to travelers who want to combine volunteer work in varied community projects with cultural immersion and sightseeing. A one-week stay including accommodation and breakfast costs US$300. Oaxaca's Centro de Esperanza Infantil (p723) welcomes volunteers at its center for street kids, and Piña Palmera (p769) at Zipolite on the Oaxaca coast needs volunteers with reasonable Spanish for a minimum three months to help in its work with handicapped kids.

In Chiapas, Na Bolom (p813) accepts volunteers on programs to promote indigenous culture. Tapachula's Albergue Jesús El Buen Pastor (boxed text, p858) can use Spanish speaking volunteers in its work with injured and destitute migrants from Central America. In western Mexico, you can volunteer at the Centro de Integración (p548), a school for special-needs kids in Tapalpa, Jalisco.

Several of the sea-turtle protection projects along Mexico's beaches – including at La Pesca (boxed text, p421), Tecolutla (p674) and Puerto Arista (p855) – use volunteers at least some of the year. **Pronatura** (www.pronatura.org.mx) is a Mexican environmental NGO that seeks volunteers to work at sea-turtle nesting areas in the Yucatán and in other projects.

Other openings for environmental volunteering are with Pulmo Amigos (p308), which helps protect the Cabo Pulmo National Marine Park on the Sea of Cortez, and **Servicios Ecoturísticos La Ventanilla** (p774), conserving crocodiles, mangroves and tropical dry forest on the Oaxaca coast.

Organizations Based Outside Mexico

Adelante Abroad (www.adelanteabroad.com) Combines language-learning with varied volunteer opportunities in Oaxaca. Charges around US$2000/2500/3000 for one/two/three months including accommodation but not flights.

AmeriSpan (www.amerispan.com) Can set you up with a wide range of volunteer placements in Mexico, from orphanages and women's shelters to nature reserves. Volunteering can be combined with language study. Charges fees of at least several hundred dollars.

Amigos de las Américas (www.amigoslink.org) Sends paying volunteers from the US to work on summer health, community and youth projects in Latin America; volunteers receive prior training. Costs around US$4000 including flights.

Council on International Educational Exchange (www.ciee.org) Arranges volunteer trips.

Earthwatch (www.earthwatch.org) With offices in the US, Britain, Australia and Japan, Earthwatch runs environmental projects in Mexico (volunteers usually pay around US$1500 to US$2500 per week, plus flights).

Global Vision International (www.gviusa.com) Work on marine conservation, sustainable tourism and English-teaching in the Yucatán Peninsula. Costs from US$2500 for five weeks or more.

Los Médicos Voladores (www.flyingdocs.org) Based in California and Nevada, LMV runs weekend clinics in northern Mexican areas with poor medical service; needs medical volunteers, translators, pilots and general volunteers.

Sipaz (www.sipaz.org) An international peace group, Sipaz needs Spanish-speaking volunteers to work for a year or more in Chiapas, especially in the fields of information and human rights observation.

WOMEN TRAVELERS

Women usually have a great time in Mexico whether traveling with companions or solo, but it's wise to remember that many Mexicans are still believers in the difference (rather than the equality) between the sexes. Gender equality has come a long way in a few decades, and Mexicans are generally a very polite people, but lone women must expect a few catcalls and attempts to chat them up. Often these men only want to talk to you, but you can discourage unwanted attention by avoiding eye contact (wear sunglasses), dressing modestly, moving confidently and speaking coolly but politely if you are addressed and feel that you must respond. Wearing a wedding ring can prove helpful too. Don't put yourself in peril by doing things that Mexican women would not do, such as challenging a man's masculinity, drinking alone in a cantina, hitchhiking, walking alone through empty streets at night, or going alone to isolated places. Keep a clear head. Excessive alcohol will make you vulnerable. For moral support, and company if you want it, head for accommodations where you're likely to meet other travelers (such as backpacker hostels and popular hotels), and join group excursions and activities.

In beach resorts many Mexican women dress in shorts, skimpy tops or dresses, and swimsuits of all sizes, though others bow to modesty and swim in shorts and a T-shirt. Lone women, and even pairs of women, should be cautious about going to remote beach spots.

On the streets of cities and towns you'll notice that women cover up and don't display too much leg, or even shoulder.

On local transportation it's best to don long or mid-calf-length trousers and a top that meets the top of your pants, with sleeves of some sort. You'll feel most comfortable, and

DIRECTORY

you can also keep your valuables out of sight more easily.

Most of all, appear self-assured.

WORK

Mexicans themselves need jobs, and people who enter Mexico as tourists are not legally allowed to take employment. The many expats working in Mexico have usually been posted there by their companies or organizations with all the necessary papers.

English speakers (and a few German or French speakers) may find teaching jobs in language schools, *preparatorias* (high schools) or universities, or can offer personal tutoring. Mexico City is the best place to get English-teaching work, and Guadalajara is also good. It's possible in other major cities. The pay is low, but you can live on it.

Press ads (especially in local English-language papers and magazines) and telephone yellow pages are sources of job opportunities. Pay rates for personal tutoring are rarely more than M$150 an hour. Positions in high schools or universities are more likely to become available at the beginning of each new term; contact institutions that offer bilingual programs or classes in English. For universities, ask for an appointment with the director of the language department. Language schools tend to offer short courses, so teaching opportunities with them may come up more often.

A foreigner working in Mexico normally needs a permit or government license, but a school will often pay a foreign teacher in the form of a *beca* (scholarship), and thus circumvent the law, or the school's administration will procure the appropriate papers.

It's helpful to know at least a little Spanish, even though only English may be spoken in class.

Apart from teaching, you might find a little bar or restaurant work in tourist areas. It's likely to be part time and short term.

Jobs Abroad (www.jobsabroad.com) posts paid and unpaid job openings in Mexico. The **Lonely Planet website** (www.lonelyplanet.com) has several useful links.

Transportation

CONTENTS

GETTING THERE & AWAY

ENTERING THE COUNTRY

Immigration officers won't generally keep you waiting any longer than it takes them to flick through your passport and enter your length of stay on your tourist card (p979). All you have to do is remain patient and polite, even if procedures are slow. Anyone traveling to Mexico via the US should be sure to check current US visa and passport requirements.

Passport

US and Canadian tourists can enter Mexico without a passport if they have official photo identification, such as a driver's license, plus some proof of their citizenship such as an original birth certificate. But to return to or transit the US by air, a passport or other secure travel document such as a Nexus card is required. To return to or transit the US by land or sea, Americans and Canadians must present either a passport, or other documents proving identity and citizenship (for example driver's license and birth certificate), or the recently introduced US passport card, or a Nexus or other 'trusted traveler' card. Canadians flying back from Mexico to Canada are advised to carry a

passport. Further information is available on the websites of the US State Department (www.travel.state.gov), US Customs & Border Protection (www.cbp.gov), the US Department of Homeland Security (www.dhs.gov) and Canada's Foreign Affairs Ministry (www.voyage.gc.ca).

In any case it's much better to travel to Mexico with a passport because officials of all countries are used to passports and may delay people who have other documents. In Mexico you will often need your passport if you change money and when you check into hotels.

All citizens of countries other than the US and Canada should have a passport that's valid for at least six months after they arrive in Mexico.

Travelers under 18 who are not accompanied by both their parents may need special documentation (see p965).

For information on Mexican visa requirements and the tourist card, see p979.

AIR
Airports & Airlines

The following Mexican airports receive direct international flights. All have flights from the US (some from several US cities, some from only one or two). Only Mexico City and Cancún receive direct scheduled flights from Europe, Canada, Central and South America and Havana, Cuba.

Mexico City, Cancún, Guadalajara and Monterrey have the most international flights.

Acapulco (ACA; ☎ 744-466-94-34; www.oma.bz)

Aguascalientes (AGU; ☎ 449-915-28-06; aguascalientes.aeropuertosgap.com.mx)

Bajío (El Bajío, León; BJX; ☎ 477-713-64-06; guanajuato.aeropuertosgap.com.mx)

Cancún (CUN; ☎ 998-886-00-47; www.cancun-airport.com)

Chihuahua (CUU; ☎ 614-446-82-33; www.oma.bz)

Cozumel (CZM; ☎ 987-872-20-81; www.asur.com.mx)

Durango (DGO; ☎ 618-817-88-98; www.oma.bz)

Guadalajara (GDL; ☎ 33-3688-5504; guadalajara.aeropuertosgap.com.mx)

Guaymas (GYM; ☎ 622-221-05-11; guaymas.asa.gob.mx)

Hermosillo (HMO; ☎ 662-261-00-00; hermosillo.aeropuertosgap.com.mx)

Huatulco (Bahías de Huatulco; HUX; ☎ 958-581-90-04; www.asur.com.mx)

Ixtapa/Zihuatanejo (ZIH; ☎ 755-554-20-70; www.oma.bz)

La Paz (LAP; ☎ 614-124-63-36; lapaz.aeropuertosgap.com.mx)

Loreto (LTO; ☎ 613-135-04-54; loreto.asa.gob.mx)

Los Cabos (SJD; ☎ 624-146-50-13; loscabos.aeropuertosgap.com.mx)

Manzanillo (Playa de Oro; ZLO; ☎ 314-333-11-19; manzanillo.aeropuertosgap.com.mx)

Mazatlán (MZT; ☎ 669-928-04-38; www.oma.bz)

Mérida (MID; ☎ 999-946-15-30; www.asur.com.mx)

Mexico City (MEX; ☎ 55-2482-2424; www.aicm.com.mx)

Monterrey (MTY; ☎ 81-8030-9090; www.adelnorte.com.mx)

Morelia (MLM; ☎ 443-317-14-11; morelia.aeropuertosgap.com.mx)

Oaxaca (OAX; ☎ 951-511-50-88; www.asur.com.mx)

Puebla (PBC; ☎ 222-232-00-32; www.aeropuertopuebla.com)

Puerto Vallarta (PVR; ☎ 322-221-12-98; vallarta.aeropuertosgap.com.mx)

Querétaro (QRO; ☎ 442-192-55-00; www.aiq.com.mx)

San Luis Potosí (SLP; ☎ 444-822-00-95; www.oma.bz)

Tampico (TAM; ☎ 833-224-48-00; www.oma.bz)

Tijuana (TIJ; ☎ 664-683-24-18; tijuana.aeropuertosgap.com.mx)

Toluca (TLC; ☎ 721-213-15-44; www.aeropuertointernacionaldetoluca.com)

Torreón (TRC; ☎ 871-712-82-39; www.oma.bz)

Veracruz (VER; ☎ 229-934-90-08; www.asur.com.mx)

Villahermosa (VSA; ☎ 993-356-01-57; www.asur.com.mx)

Zacatecas (ZCL; ☎ 492-985-02-23; www.oma.bz)

Mexico's two flag airlines are Mexicana and Aeroméxico, both formerly state-controlled. Mexicana was bought by Grupo Posadas, Mexico's biggest hotel company, in 2005, and Aeroméxico was sold to a consortium led by Banamex in 2007. Their safety

CLIMATE CHANGE & TRAVEL

Climate change is a serious threat to the ecosystems that humans rely upon, and air travel is the fastest-growing contributor to the problem. Lonely Planet regards travel, overall, as a global benefit, but believes we all have a responsibility to limit our personal impact on global warming.

Flying & Climate Change

Pretty much every form of motorized travel generates CO_2 (the main cause of human-induced climate change) but planes are far and away the worst offenders, not just because of the sheer distances they allow us to travel, but because they release greenhouse gases high into the atmosphere. The statistics are frightening: two people taking a return flight between Europe and the US will contribute as much to climate change as an average household's gas and electricity consumption over a whole year.

Carbon Offset Schemes

Climatecare.org and other websites use 'carbon calculators' that allow travelers to offset the level of greenhouse gases they are responsible for with financial contributions to sustainable travel schemes that reduce global warming – including projects in India, Honduras, Kazakhstan and Uganda.

Lonely Planet, together with Rough Guides and other concerned partners in the travel industry, support the carbon offset scheme run by climatecare.org. Lonely Planet offsets all of its staff and author travel.

For more information check out our website: www.lonelyplanet.com.

records are comparable to major US and European airlines.

AIRLINES FLYING TO & FROM MEXICO

Aero California (code JR; ☎ 800-237-62-25; www
.aerocalifornia.com; hub Tijuana)

Aerolíneas Argentinas (code AR; ☎ 800 123-85-88;
www.aerolineas.com.ar; hub Buenos Aires)

Aeromar (code VW; ☎ 800-237-66-27; www.aeromar
.com.mx; hub Mexico City)

Aeroméxico (code AM; ☎ 800-021-40-10; www
.aeromexico.com; hub Mexico City)

Air Canada (code AC; ☎ 800-719-28-27; www
.aircanada.ca; hub Toronto)

Air Europa (code UX; ☎ 998-898-22-55; www.air
europa.com; hub Madrid)

Air France (code AF; ☎ 800-123-46-60; www.airfrance
.com; hub Paris)

Alaska (code AS'B, ☎ 800-252-9421, www.alaska.com;
hub Cancún)

Alaska Airlines (code AS; ☎ 800-252-75-22; www
.alaskaair.com; hub Seattle)

American Airlines (code AA; ☎ 800-904-60-00; www
.aa.com; hub Dallas)

America West (code HP; ☎ 800-428-43-22; www
.americawest.com; hub Phoenix)

ATA Airlines (code TZ; ☎ 800-435-92-82; www.ata.com;
hub Chicago)

Aviacsa (code 6A; ☎ 800-284-22-72; www.aviacsa.com;
hub Mexico City)

Avianca (code AV; ☎ 800-123-31-20; www.avianca
.com; hub Bogotá)

British Airways (code BA; ☎ 55-5387-0321; www
.britishairways.com; hub Heathrow Airport, London)

Click Mexicana (code QA; ☎ 800-122-54-25; www
.click.com.mx; hubs Cancún, Mexico City)

Continental Airlines (code CO; ☎ 800-900-50-00;
www.continental.com; hub Houston)

Copa Airlines (code CM; ☎ 800-265-26-72; www
.copaair.com; hub Panama City)

Cubana (code CU; ☎ 52-5250-6355; www.cubana.co.cu;
hub Havana)

Delta Air Lines (code DL; ☎ 800-123-47-10; www
.delta.com; hub Atlanta)

Frontier Airlines (code F9; ☎ in the US 800-432-1359;
www.frontierairlines.com; hub Denver)

Iberia (code IB; ☎ 55-1101-1515; www.iberia.com; hub
Madrid)

Interjet (code 40 ☎ 800-011-23-45; www.interjet.com
.mx; hub Toluca)

Japan Airlines (code JL; ☎ 55-5242-0150; www.ar.jal
.com; hub Tokyo)

KLM (code KL; ☎ 55-5279-5390; www.klm.com; hub
Amsterdam)

Lan Airlines (code LA; ☎ 800-700-67-00; plane.lan
.com; hub Santiago)

LTU (code LT; ☎ 998-887-24-07; www.ltu.de; hub
Dusseldorf)

Lufthansa (code LH; ☎ 55-5230-0000; www.lufthansa
.com; hub Frankfurt)

Mexicana (code MX; ☎ 800-502-20-00; www.mexicana
.com; hub Mexico City)

Northwest Airlines (code NW; ☎ 55-5279-5390; www
.nwa.com; hubs Detroit, Minneapolis/St Paul, Memphis)

Spirit Airlines (code NK; ☎ in the US 800-772-7117;
www.spiritair.com; hub Fort Lauderdale)

Sun Country Airlines (code SY; ☎ in the US 800-800-
6557; www.suncountry.com; hub Minneapolis/St Paul)

TACA Airlines (code TA; ☎ 800-400-8222; www.taca
.com; hub San Salvador)

Ted (code UA; ☎ 800-003-07-77; www.flyted.com; hub
Denver)

United Airlines (code UA; ☎ 800-003-07-77; www
.united.com; hub Los Angeles)

US Airways (code US; ☎ 800-428-43-22; www.usair
ways.com; hub Philadelphia)

Varig (code RG; ☎ 55-5280-9192; www.varig.com.br;
hub São Paulo)

VivaAerobus (code VB; ☎ 81-8215-0150; www
.vivaaerobus.com; hub Monterrey)

Tickets

The cost of flying to Mexico is usually higher around Christmas and New Year, and during July and August. Weekends can be more costly than weekdays. In addition to air-ticket websites and travel agencies, it's often worth checking airlines' own websites for special deals. Newspapers, magazines and websites serving Mexican communities in other countries are also good sources. The **Lonely Planet website** (www.lonelyplanet.com) has good links too.

If Mexico is part of a bigger trip encompassing other countries in Latin America or elsewhere, the best ticket for you may be an open-jaw (where you fly into one place and out of another, covering the intervening distance by land), or a round-the-world ticket (these can cost as little as UK£900 or A$2100), or a Circle Pacific ticket which uses a combination of airlines to travel around the Pacific region. **Airtreks** (www.airtreks.com) is one good source for multistop tickets.

International online booking agencies worth a look include **CheapTickets** (www.cheaptickets.com) and, for students and travelers under the age of 26, **STA Travel** (www.sta travel.com).

Asia

You normally have to make a connection in the US or Canada (often Los Angeles, San Francisco or Vancouver), and maybe one in Asia as well. From more westerly Asian points such as Bangkok, routes via Europe are also an option. For online bookings try www.zuji.com.

Australia & New Zealand

The cheapest routes are usually via the US (normally Los Angeles). You're normally looking at A$2300 or NZ$2300 or more, round-trip (plus several hundred dollars extra at high season).

For online fares try www.travel.com .au or www.zuji.com from Australia, and www.travel.co.nz or www.zuji.co.nz from New Zealand.

Canada

Montreal, Toronto and Vancouver all have direct flights to Mexico, though better deals are often available with a change of flight in the US. Round-trip fares from Toronto start at around C$900 to Mexico City, Cancún or Puerto Vallarta. For online bookings try www.kayak.com, www.expedia.ca and www.travelocity.ca.

Central & South America & the Caribbean

You can fly direct to Mexico City from at least eight cities in South America, and from Panama City, San José (Costa Rica), San Salvador, Guatemala City, Havana (Cuba) and Santo Domingo (Dominican Republic). There are also direct flights to Cancún from São Paulo, Panama City, Havana, Guatemala City and Flores (Guatemala). Round-trip fares to Mexico City start at around US$500 from Guatemala City and US$800 to US$1000 from South America. **Viajo.com** (www.viajo .com) is an online source of air tickets from several countries.

Europe

There are direct flights from Europe to Mexico City, Cancún and Monterrey. Airlines include Aeroméxico, Air France, Air Madrid, British Airways, Iberia, KLM, LTU, Lufthansa and Air Europa. An alternative is to fly with a US or Canadian airline or alliance partner, changing planes in North America.

Round-trip fares to Mexico City or Cancún normally start at around UK£500 to UK£600 from London, or €600 to €700 from Frankfurt, Paris or Madrid. For online bookings throughout Europe, try www .opodo.com or www.ebookers.com.

The USA

You can fly to Mexico without changing planes from around 30 US cities. There are one-stop connecting flights from many others. Continental (from Houston), Aeroméxico and Mexicana all offer large numbers of Mexican destinations.

US budget airlines such as ATA, Spirit Air, America West, Frontier Airlines and Ted all offer flights to Mexico, and economical fares are also available on Mexico's Aero California and Aviacsa. If you're lucky you can get round-trip fares from the US to Mexico for US$250. If you're not lucky, 'budget' operators can cost as much as other airlines. Low-season discounted round-trip fares are typically in the US$350 to US$500 range. In high season you may have to pay US$100 to US$200 more.

For current bargain offers, check **Airfare Watchdog** (www.airfarewatchdog.com). Online tickets are offered by www.cheaptickets .com, www.expedia.com, www.kayak.com, www.lowestfare.com, www.orbitz.com and www.travelocity.com.

LAND
Border Crossings

There are over 40 official crossing points on the US–Mexico border. There are about 10 between Guatemala and Mexico, and two between Belize and Mexico. You'll find more information on the most important crossings in this book's regional chapters. Most Mexican border towns are not places where many travelers have much reason to linger.

Car & Motorcycle

The rules for taking a vehicle into Mexico change from time to time. You can check with a Mexican consulate, **Sanborn's** (☎ 800-222-01-58; www.sanbornsinsurance.com) or, in the US and Canada, the free **Mexican tourist information number** (☎ 800-401-3880).

You may not find gasoline or mechanics available at all Mexico's road borders: before crossing the border, make sure you have enough fuel to get to the next sizable town inside Mexico. For information on driving and motorcycling once you're inside Mexico, see p993.

VEHICLE PERMIT

You will need a *permiso de importación temporal de vehículos* (temporary vehicle import permit) if you want to take a vehicle beyond Baja California, beyond Guaymas in Sonora state, or beyond the border zone that extends 20km to 30km into Mexico along the rest of the US frontier and up to 70km from the Guatemalan and Belize frontiers. Officials at posts of the Instituto Nacional de Migración (INM; National Immigration Institute) in the border zones, and at the ferry terminal at La Paz, Baja California, if you are taking a vehicle across from there to mainland Mexico, will want to see your permit. Permits are not needed to take vehicles into Baja California itself, and the state of Sonora does not require them for travel as far south as Guaymas (see p318 for details of the Sonora regulations).

The permits are issued at offices at border crossings or (in some cases) at posts a few kilometers into Mexico, at Ensenada port and Pichilingue (La Paz) ferry terminal in Baja California, and by the Mexican consulates in Chicago, Houston, Dallas, Austin, Fort Worth, Los Angeles, Sacramento, San Bernardino, Phoenix, Albuquerque and Denver. Details of all these locations are given at www.banjercito.com.mx (click on 'Red de Módulos IITV'). You can also apply for the permit online at www.banjercito.com.mx ('Application for Temporary Import Permit for Vehicles'), in which case it will be delivered to you by courier.

The fee for the permit is the peso equivalent of US$29.70 if obtained at or after the border, US$39.60 from a Mexican consulate, or US$49.50 online. You can also pre-register online which speeds up the process of actually obtaining the permit at a consulate or the border.

The person importing the vehicle will need to carry the original and one or two photocopies of each of the following documents (people at the office may make photocopies for a small fee), which as a rule must all be in his/her own name (except that you can bring in your spouse's, parent's or child's vehicle if you can show a marriage or birth certificate proving your relationship):

- tourist card (FMT): at the border go to *migración* before you process your vehicle permit.
- certificate of title or registration certificate for the vehicle (note that you should have both of these if you plan to drive through Mexico into either Guatemala or Belize).
- a Visa, MasterCard or American Express credit card, issued by a an institution outside of Mexico; if you don't have one you must pay a returnable deposit of between US$200 and US$400 (depending on how old the car is) at the border. Your card details or deposit serve as a guarantee that you'll take the car out of Mexico before your tourist card (FMT) expires. Note: for online and consulate applications, only Visa and MasterCard are accepted.
- proof of citizenship or residency, such as a passport, birth certificate or voter's registration card.
- driver's license.
- if the vehicle is not fully paid for, a credit contract from the financing institution or an invoice letter that is less than three months old.
- for a leased or rented vehicle (though few US rental firms allow their vehicles to be taken into Mexico), the contract, in the name of the person importing the vehicle, and a letter from the rental company authorizing you to take it out of the US.
- for a company car, proof of employment by the company and proof of the company's ownership of the vehicle.

One person cannot bring in two vehicles. If you have a motorcycle attached to your car, you'll need another adult traveling with you to obtain a permit for the motorcycle, and he/she will need to have all the right papers for it.

With the permit you will be given a sticker to be displayed on your windshield.

You have the option to take the vehicle in and out of Mexico for the period shown on your tourist card. Ask for a *tarjetón de internación*, a document which you will exchange for a *comprobante de retorno* each time you leave Mexico; when you return to Mexico, you swap the *comprobante* for another *tarjetón*. When you leave Mexico the last time, you must have the import permit canceled by the Mexican authorities. An official may do this as you enter the border zone, usually 20km to 30km before the border itself. If not, you'll have to find the right official at the border crossing. If you leave Mexico without having the permit canceled, the authorities may assume you've left the vehicle in the country illegally and decide to keep your deposit, charge a fine to your credit card, or deny you permission to bring a vehicle into the country on your next trip.

Only the owner may take the vehicle out of Mexico. If the vehicle is wrecked completely, you must contact your consulate or a Mexican customs office to make arrangements to leave without it.

Belize

Around 18 daily buses run by **Novelo's** (in Belize City ☎ 227-20-25) travel between Belize City and Chetumal, Mexico (US$10, four hours), calling at the Belizean towns of Orange Walk and Corozal en route. See p913 for more details.

Guatemala

The road borders at La Mesilla/Ciudad Cuauhtémoc, Ciudad Tecún Umán/Ciudad Hidalgo and El Carmen/Talismán are all linked to Guatemala City, and nearby cities within Guatemala and Mexico, by plentiful buses and/or combis. A few daily buses are run all the way between Guatemala City and Tapachula, Chiapas (six hours) via Escuintla and Mazatenango by **Trans Galgos Inter** (in Guatemala City ☎ 2232-3661; www.transgalgosinter.com .gt; US$25-35), **Línea Dorada** (in Guatemala City ☎ 2232-5506; www.tikalmayanworld.com; US$15) and **Tica Bus** (in Guatemala City ☎ 2366-4038; www.ticabus.com; US$16).

There are a few daily buses between Flores, Guatemala, and Chetumal (US$28, seven to eight hours), via Belize City, run by **Línea Dorada/Mundo Maya** (in Flores ☎ 7926-0070) and **San Juan Travel** (in Flores ☎ 7926-0041).

For the Río Usumacinta route between Flores and Palenque, Mexico, several daily 2nd-class buses run from Flores to Bethel (US$4, four hours), on the Guatemalan bank of the Usumacinta. The 40-minute boat trip from Bethel to Frontera Corozal, Mexico, costs US$7 to US$13 per person; an alternative is to take a bus from Flores that continues through Bethel to La Técnica (US$6, five to six hours), from which it's only a US$1.50, five-minute river crossing to Frontera Corozal. Vans run from Frontera Corozal to Palenque (US$6, three hours, 13 daily). Travel agencies in Palenque and Flores offer bus-boat-bus packages between the two places from around US$40, but if you're traveling this route it's well worth detouring to the outstanding Maya ruins at Yaxchilán (see p845), near Frontera Corozal.

The USA
BUS
Cross-border bus services, mainly used by Mexicans working in the US, link many US cities with northern Mexican cities. They're not very well publicized: Spanish-language newspapers in the US have the most ads. The major companies include **Autobuses Americanos** (www.autobusesamericanos .com.mx), operating to northeast Mexico, central north Mexico and central Mexico from Los Angeles, Phoenix, Denver, Albuquerque, Chicago and several Texan cities; **Tufesa** (www.tufesa.com.mx), linking Los Angeles, Las Vegas, Phoenix and Tucson with northwest Mexico; **Crucero** (☎ 800-531-5332; www.crucero-usa .com), operating from California, Nevada and Arizona to northwest Mexico; and **Transportes Baldomero Corral** (www.tbcconexionphoenix.com), operating between Arizona and northwest Mexico. **Greyhound** (☎ 800-231-2222; www.grey hound.com) has some cross-border routes: it uses Mexican associate companies to actually carry its passengers on many of them.

Some sample cross-border services:

Route	Fare	Duration
Los Angeles-Hermosillo	US$90	16hr
Los Angeles-Los Mochis	US$110	24hr
Los Angeles-Mexicali	US$35	5hr
Phoenix-Álamos	US$50	12hr
Phoenix-Hermosillo	US$40	8hr
Dallas-Monterrey	US$50	12hr
Dallas-Reynosa	US$46	11hr
Houston-Matamoros	US$25	9hr
Houston-Monterrey	US$40	10hr

You can also, often in little or no extra time, make your way to the border on one bus (or train), cross it on foot or by local bus, and then catch an onward bus on the other side. Greyhound serves many US border cities; to reach others, transfer from Greyhound to a smaller bus line. Greyhound's one-way fares to El Paso, for example, are US$64 from Los Angeles (16 hours), US$129 to US$141 from Chicago (34 hours) and US$128 from New York (52 hours).

CAR & MOTORCYCLE

For information on the procedures for taking a vehicle into Mexico, see p986, and p318 for simpler and cheaper arrangements for much of the state of Sonora.

If you're traveling from Mexico into the US at a busy time of year, have a look at the website of **US Customs & Border Protection** (www .cbp.gov), which posts waiting times at entry points (under 'Travel').

TRAIN

Though there are no regular passenger trains on the Mexican side of the US–Mexico border, it's quite possible to reach the US side of the border by rail. Trains can be quicker and cheaper than buses, or slower and more expensive, depending on the route. **Amtrak** (☎ 800-872-7245; www.amtrak.com) serves four US cities from which access to Mexico is easy: San Diego, California (opposite Tijuana); El Paso, Texas (opposite Ciudad Juárez); Del Rio, Texas (opposite Ciudad Acuña) and San Antonio, Texas, which is linked by bus to Eagle Pass (opposite Piedras Negras) and Laredo (opposite Nuevo Laredo).

SEA

For those who like to combine snatches of Mexico with a life of ease on the high seas, cruises from the US enable you to enjoy activities and attractions on and near Mexico's coasts without having to worry about the logistics of accommodations, eating or transportation. Mexico is the world's most popular cruise destination, with over six million cruise passengers a year arriving at Mexican ports. Caribbean Mexico is the most popular cruise destination, usually in combination with other Caribbean stops and/or Key West, Florida, and Isla Cozumel is the single busiest stop. Mexico's other Caribbean cruise ports are Puerto Morelos and Calica, just south of Playa del Carmen. The Costa Maya terminal at Mahahual was destroyed by Hurricane Dean in 2007 but there are plans to rebuild it.

On the Pacific route (the Mexican Riviera in cruise parlance), the main ports of call are Ensenada, Cabo San Lucas, Mazatlán, Puerto Vallarta and Acapulco; cruises also call at Manzanillo, Zihuatanejo, Bahías de Huatulco and the new Puerto Chiapas, near Tapachula.

A Caribbean cruise from ports in the southeastern US, or a Mexican Riviera cruise from California, can cost well under US$1000 per person for 10 days.

Following are some of the cruise lines visiting Mexico, with US phone numbers:

Carnival Cruise Lines (☎ 888-227-6482; www .carnival.com)

Celebrity Cruises (☎ 800-647-2251; www.celebrity.com)

Crystal Cruises (☎ 888-722-0021; www.crystalcruises .com)

Holland America Line (☎ 877-724-5425; www.holland america.com)

Norwegian Cruise Lines (☎ 800-327-7030; www .ncl.com)

P&O Cruises (☎ 415-382-8900; www.pocruises.com)

Princess Cruises (☎ 800-774-6237; www.princess.com)

Royal Caribbean International (☎ 800-398-9813; www.royalcaribbean.com)

GETTING AROUND

AIR

All large and many smaller cities in Mexico have airports and passenger services. Depending on the fare you get, flying can be good value on longer journeys, especially considering the long bus trip that is probably the alternative. Domestic flights within Mexico are sometimes cheaper if you book them before you go to Mexico, in conjunction with an international roundt-rip ticket.

Airlines in Mexico

Aeroméxico and Mexicana are the country's two major airlines. There are also numerous smaller ones, often cheaper and often flying routes between provincial cities ignored by the bigger two. Several low-cost airlines have started operations in recent years, including Alma de México, with its hub at Guadalajara, Avolar (hub: Tijuana), Interjet (hub: Toluca), VivaAerobus (hub: Monterrey), Volaris (hub: Toluca) and Click Mexicana (Mexicana's no-frills subsidiary). At the time of writing the low-cost Líneas Aéreas Azteca had its

DEPARTURE TAX

A departure tax equivalent to about M$250 is levied on international flights from Mexico. It's usually included in your ticket cost, but if it isn't, you must pay in cash during airport check-in. Ask your travel agent in advance.

TRANSPORTATION

MEXICAN DOMESTIC AIRLINES

Airline	Telephone	Website	Areas served
Aéreo Calafia	☎ 624-143-43-02	www.aereocalafia.com.mx	Baja California & northwest
Aero California	☎ 800-237-62-25	www.aerocalifornia.com	La Paz & 18 other cities around the country
Aeromar	☎ 800-237-66-27	www.aeromar.com.mx	Central Mexico, west, northeast, Gulf coast, southeast
Aeroméxico	☎ 800-021-40-00	www.aeromexico.com	over 50 cities nationwide
Aeroméxico Connect	☎ 800-800-23-76	www.amconnect.com	Central Mexico, Baja California, north, west, Gulf coast
Aladia	☎ 800-252-34-21	www.aladia.com	Mexico City, Monterrey, Guadalajara, Puebla, Acapulco, Cancún
Alma de México	☎ 800-800-25-62	www.alma.com.mx	Guadalajara & 28 other cities around the country
Aviacsa	☎ 800-284-22-72	www.aviacsa.com	Mexico City & 19 other cities around the country
Avolar	☎ 800-212-86-52	www.avolar.com.mx	Tijuana & 18 other cities in the center, west, northwest & southeast
Click Mexicana	☎ 800-122-54-25	www.click.com.mx	Mexico City & 24 other cities around the country
Interjet	☎ 800-011-23-45	www.interjet.com.mx	Toluca & 14 other cities around the country
Magnicharters	☎ 800-201-14-04	www.magnicharters.com.mx	Mexico City, Guadalajara, Monterrey, Bajío, Mérida, coastal resorts
Mexicana	☎ 800-502-20-00	www.mexicana.com	over 50 cities nationwide
VivaAerobus	☎ 81-8215-0150	www.vivaaerobus.com	Monterrey & 18 other cities around the country
Volaris	☎ 800-786-52-74	www.volaris.com.mx	Toluca & 16 other cities around the city

Note: Aeroméxico Connect and Aeromar are affiliates of Aeroméxico and normally share its booking facilities.

operating license suspended by the Mexican authorities because of safety violations.

The US Federal Aviation Administration (FAA) considers Mexico's Civil Aviation Authority to be in compliance with international aviation safety standards.

Fares

Fares can depend on whether you fly at a busy or quiet time of day, week or year, and how far ahead you book and pay. High season generally corresponds to the Mexican holiday seasons (see p971). You'll often save money if you pay for the ticket a few days ahead or if you fly late in the evening. Round-trip fares are usually simply twice the price of one-way tickets, though some cheaper advance-payment deals do exist.

Typical one-way fares from Mexico City with nonbudget airlines to most Mexican cities are between about M$1300 and M$2100 including taxes and charges, depending mainly on distance. Low-cost airlines flying

from Toluca, 50km west of Mexico City, may charge up to 50% less.

BICYCLE

Cycling is not a common way to tour Mexico. The size of the country, reports of highway robbery, poor road surfaces, careless motorists and pedestrians and other road hazards (see p995) are deterrents. However, biking around is certainly possible if you're prepared for the challenges. You should be fit, use the best equipment, and be fully able to handle your own repairs. Take the mountainous topography and hot climate into account when planning your route. Bike lanes are rare.

All cities have bicycle stores: a decent mountain bike suitable for a few weeks' touring costs around M$5000. Don't expect to get much of that back by selling it afterwards unless you have time on your side.

If you're interested in a long Mexican ride, consider the bring-your-own-bike tours of

TRANSPORTATION

the Yucatán Peninsula, Chiapas, Oaxaca, Pacific Mexico and Michoacán, up to a month long, offered by the fun and friendly **!El Tour** (www.bikemexico.com).

BOAT

Vehicle and passenger ferries connecting Baja California with the Mexican mainland sail between Santa Rosalía and Guaymas, La Paz and Mazatlán, and La Paz and Topolobampo. One-way passenger seat fares cost from M$550 to M$800; a car up to 5m in length costs between M$1000 and M$2500. There are also ferries from the Yucatán Peninsula to the islands of Isla Mujeres (p878), Isla Cozumel (p892) and Isla Holbox (p881).

BUS

Mexico has a good road and bus network, and comfortable, frequent, reasonably priced bus services connect all cities. Most cities and towns have one main bus terminal where all long-distance buses arrive and depart. It may be called the Terminal de Autobuses, Central de Autobuses, Central Camionera or simply La Central (not to be confused with *el centro*, the city center!) If there is no single main terminal, different bus companies will have separate terminals scattered around town.

Baggage is safe if stowed in the bus' baggage hold, but get a receipt for it when you hand it over. Keep your most valuable documents (passport, money etc) in the cabin with you, and keep them closely protected.

Highway robbery happens very rarely. The risk is higher at night, on isolated stretches of highway far from cities, and in 2nd-class buses.

Classes
DELUXE
De lujo services, sometimes termed *ejecutivo* (executive), run mainly on the busy routes. They are swift, modern and comfortable, with reclining seats, adequate legroom, aircon, few or no stops, toilets on board (but not necessarily toilet paper), and sometimes drinks or snacks. They usually show movies on video screens.

FIRST CLASS
Primera (1a) clase buses have a comfortable numbered seat for each passenger. All sizable towns have 1st-class bus services. Standards of comfort are adequate at the very least. The buses usually have air-conditioning and a toilet and they stop infrequently. They always show movies (often bad ones) for most of the trip: too bad if you don't want to watch, as all seats face a video screen.

Bring a sweater or jacket to combat overzealous air-conditioning. As with deluxe buses, you buy your ticket in the bus station before boarding.

SECOND CLASS
Segunda (2a) clase buses serve small towns and villages, and provide cheaper, slower travel on some intercity routes. A few are almost as quick, comfortable and direct as 1st-class buses. Others are old, slow and shabby.

Many 2nd-class services have no ticket office; you just pay your fare to the conductor. These buses tend to take slow, nontoll roads in and out of big cities and will stop anywhere to pick up passengers: if you board midroute you might make some of the trip standing. The small amount of money

---

HOW MANY STOPS?

It's useful to understand the difference between the types of bus service on offer:

Sin escalas Nonstop.

Directo Very few stops.

Semi-directo A few more stops than *directo*.

Ordinario Stops wherever passengers want to get on or off the bus; deluxe and 1st-class buses are never *ordinario*.

Express Nonstop on short to medium-length trips; very few stops on long trips.

Local Bus that starts its journey at the bus station you're in and usually leaves on time; *local* service is preferable to *de paso*.

De paso Bus that started its journey somewhere else but is stopping to let off and take on passengers. If the bus company does not have a computer booking system, you may have to wait until the bus arrives before any tickets are sold. If the bus is full, you have to wait for the next one.

Viaje redondo Round-trip.

TRANSPORTATION

MEXICAN BUS COMPANIES

Company	Telephone	Website	Main regions/destinations
ABC	☎ 664-621-24-24	www.abc.com.mx	Baja California
ADO	☎ 800-702-80-00	www.ado.com.mx	Mexico City, Puebla, Gulf coast, Oaxaca, Tabasco, Chiapas, Yucatán Peninsula
ADO GL	☎ 800-702-80-00	www.adogl.com.mx	Mexico City, Puebla, Gulf coast, Tabasco, Oaxaca, Yucatán Peninsula
AU	☎ 800-702-80-00	www.ado.com.mx	Mexico City, Puebla, Gulf coast, Tabasco, Oaxaca, Puebla
Autotransportes Águila	☎ 612-122-78/98	www.abc.com.mx	Southern Baja California
Autovías	☎ 55-5567-4550	N/A	Mexico City, Michoacán, Zihuatanejo
Blancos	☎ 800-507-55-00	www.estrellablanca.com.mx	Mexico City, Gulf coast
Chihuahuenses	☎ 800-507-55-00	www.estrellablanca.com.mx	Mexico City, central Mexico, Pacific coast, central north, northwest
Elite	☎ 800-507-55-00	www.estrellablanca.com.mx	Mexico City, central Mexico, Pacific coast, central north, northwest
Estrella Blanca	☎ 800-507-55-00	www.estrellablanca.com.mx	Mexico City, Gulf coast, Pacific coast
Estrella de Oro	☎ 55-5549-8520 (Mexico City), 800-900-01-05 (other cities)	www.autobus.com.mx/edo	Mexico City, Cuernavaca, Taxco, Pacific coast (Guerrero state)
Estrella Roja	☎ 800-712-22-84	www.estrellaroja.com.mx	Mexico City, Puebla
ETN	☎ 800-800-03-86	www.etn.com.mx	Mexico City, northern & western central highlands, Pacific coast, northeast
Flecha Amarilla	☎ 800-849-90-04	N/A	Mexico City, northern & western central highlands, Manzanillo
Futura	☎ 800-507-55-00	www.estrellablanca.com.mx	Mexico City, central Mexico, Pacific coast, northern Mexico
Gacela	☎ 800-507-55-00	www.estrellablanca.com.mx	Mexico City, Cuernavaca, Pacific coast

you save by traveling 2nd-class is not usually worth the discomfort or extra journey time entailed.

Second-class buses can also be less safe than 1st-class or deluxe buses, for reasons of maintenance or driver standards or because they are more vulnerable to being boarded by bandits on some roads. Out in the remoter areas, however, you'll often find that 2nd-class buses are the only buses available.

Microbuses or 'micros' are small, usually fairly new, 2nd-class buses with around 25 seats, usually running short routes between nearby towns.

Costs

First-class buses typically cost around M$50 to M$70 per hour of travel (70km to 80km). Deluxe buses may cost just 10% or 20% more than 1st class, or about 60% more for super-deluxe services such as ETN, UNO and Turistar Ejecutivo. Second-class buses cost 10% or 20% less than 1st class.

Reservations

For trips of up to four or five hours on busy routes, you can usually just go to the bus terminal, buy a ticket and head out without much delay. For longer trips, or routes with infrequent service, buy a ticket a day or more in advance. Deluxe and 1st-class bus companies have computerized ticket systems that allow you to select your seat when you buy your ticket. Try to avoid the back of the bus, which is where the toilets are and also tends to give a bumpier ride.

Ticketbus (in Mexico City ☎ 55-5133-2424, 800-702-80-00; www.ticketbus.com.mx) provides tickets and reservations for many bus companies, chiefly on routes in the center, south and southeast of Mexico. You can book via the internet or telephone, or at any of its many offices in 44 cities and towns.

If you pay for a bus ticket in cash, cash refunds of 80% to 100% are available from many bus companies if you return your ticket more than an hour or two before the listed departure time.

MEXICAN BUS COMPANIES (CONTINUED)

Company	Telephone	Website	Main regions/destinations
Herradura de Plata	☎ 55-5567-4550	N/A	Mexico City, northern & western central highlands
OCC	☎ 800-702-80-00	www.ado.com.mx	Mexico City, Puebla, Oaxaca, Chiapas (Ómnibus Cristóbal Colón)
Ómnibus de México	☎ 800-765-66-36	www.odm.com.mx	Mexico City, northern central highlands, central north, northeast, Colima, Guadalajara,Tepic
Oriente	☎ 800-507-55-00	www.estrellablanca.com.mx	Mexico City, central Mexico, northeast
Primera Plus	☎ 800-849-90-04	N/A	Mexico City, northern & western central highlands, Pacific coast
Pullman de Morelos	☎ 800-624-03-60	www.pullman.com.mx	Mexico City, Cuernavaca, Cuautla
TAP	☎ 668-812-57-49	N/A	Mexico City, Guadalajara, Puerto Vallarta, northwest
Transportes del Norte	☎ 800-890-90-90	www.gruposenda.com	Mexico City, northeast, San Luis Potosí
Transportes del Pacífico	☎ 55-5587-5310	N/A	Mexico City, Guadalajara, Pacific coast, northwest
Transportes Frontera	☎ 800-507-55-00	www.estrellablanca.com.mx	Mexico City, central Mexico, northeast
Transportes Norte de Sonora	☎ 800-507-55-00	www.estrellablanca.com.mx	Mexico City, Guadalajara, Pacific coast, northwest
Turistar	☎ 800-507-55-00	www.estrellablanca.com.mx	Mexico City, central Mexico, north, Pacific coast
UNO	☎ 800-702-80-00	www.uno.com.mx	Mexico City, Puebla, Gulf coast, Oaxaca, Chiapas, Tabasco, Yucatán Peninsula

Note: many bus lines are part of multiline groups, which may share ticket desks at bus stations. ADO, ADO GL, AU, OCC and UNO are all part of the ADO group. Blancos, Elite, Estrella Blanca, Futura, Gacela, Oriente, Chihuahuenses, Transportes Frontera, Transportes Norte de Sonora and Turistar are all part of Grupo Estrella Blanca.

TRANSPORTATION

CAR & MOTORCYCLE

Driving in Mexico is not as easy as it is north of the border, and rentals are more expensive, but having a vehicle gives you maximum flexibility and freedom.

Bring Your Own Vehicle

Bringing a car to Mexico is most useful for travelers who:

- have plenty of time
- like to get off the beaten track
- have surfboards, diving equipment or other cumbersome luggage
- will be traveling with at least one companion.

Drivers should know at least a little Spanish and have basic mechanical knowledge, reserves of patience and access to extra cash for emergencies. Good makes of car to take to Mexico are Volkswagen, Nissan, Chrysler, General Motors and Ford, which have plants in Mexico and dealers in most big towns. Very big cars are unwieldy on narrow roads and use a lot of gasoline. A sedan with a trunk (boot) provides safer storage than a station wagon or hatchback. Mexican mechanics are resourceful, and most repairs can be done quickly and inexpensively, but it still pays to take as many spare parts as you can manage (spare fuel filters are very useful). Tires (including spare), shock absorbers and suspension should be in good condition. For security, have something to immobilize the steering wheel, and consider getting a kill switch installed.

Motorcycling in Mexico is not for the fainthearted. Roads and traffic can be rough, and parts and mechanics hard to come by. The parts you'll most easily find will be for Kawasaki, Honda and Suzuki bikes.

See p986 for information on the paperwork required for bringing a vehicle into Mexico.

Driver's License

To drive a motor vehicle in Mexico, you need a valid driver's license from your home country.

TRANSPORTATION

Gas (Petrol)

All *gasolina* (gasoline) and diesel fuel in Mexico is sold by the government's monopoly, Pemex (Petróleos Mexicanos). Most towns, even small ones, have a Pemex station, and the stations are pretty common on most major roads. Nevertheless, in remote areas you should fill up whenever you can.

The gasoline on sale is all *sin plomo* (unleaded). There are two varieties: Magna Sin, roughly equivalent to US regular unleaded, and Premium, roughly equivalent to US super unleaded. At the time of research, Magna Sin cost about M$7 per liter (US$2.40 per US gallon), and Premium about M$8.75. Diesel fuel is widely available at around M$6 per liter. Regular Mexican diesel has a higher sulfur content than US diesel, but there is a 'Diesel Sin' with less sulfur. If diesel drivers change their oil and filter about every 3500km, they should have no problems.

Gas stations have pump attendants (who appreciate a tip of M$2 to M$5).

Insurance

It is very foolish to drive in Mexico without Mexican liability insurance. If you are involved in an accident, you can be jailed and have your vehicle impounded while responsibility is assessed. If you are to blame for an accident causing injury or death, you may be detained until you guarantee restitution to the victims and payment of any fines. This could take weeks or months. Adequate Mexican insurance coverage is the only real

protection: it is regarded as a guarantee that restitution will be paid, and will expedite release of the driver.

Mexican law recognizes only Mexican motor insurance *(seguro)*, so a US or Canadian policy, even if it provides coverage, is not acceptable to Mexican officialdom. Sanborn's and the **American Automobile Association** (AAA; www.aaa.com) are worth looking into for Mexico motor insurance. Mexican insurance is also sold in US border towns; as you approach the border from the US you will see billboards advertising offices selling Mexican policies. At the busier border crossings, such as those to Tijuana, Mexicali, Nogales, Agua Prieta, Ciudad Juárez, Nuevo Laredo, Reynosa and Matamoros, there are insurance offices open 24 hours a day. Some deals are better than others.

Short-term insurance is about US$15 a day for full coverage on a car worth under US$10,000; for periods longer than two weeks it's often cheaper to get an annual policy. Liability-only insurance costs around half the full coverage cost.

Insurance is considered invalid if the driver is under the influence of alcohol or drugs.

Maps

Mexican signposting can be poor, and decent road maps are essential. A Mexican road atlas such as Guía Roji's *Por Las Carreteras de México* (M$175) is a worthwhile investment. It's sold at bookstores and some newsstands in Mexico, and is available from internet booksellers for a little more. A new edition is published annually and includes most new highways. Also useful are Quimera publisher's regional road maps.

Rental

Auto rental in Mexico is expensive by US or European standards, but is not hard to organize. You can book by internet, telephone or in person and pick up cars at city offices, airports, many big hotels and sometimes at bus terminals.

Renters must provide a valid driver's license (your home license is OK), passport and major credit card, and are usually required to be at least 21 (sometimes 25, or if you're aged 21 to 24 you may have to pay a surcharge). Read the small print of the rental agreement. In addition to the basic rental rate, you pay tax and insurance costs to the rental

---

THE GREEN ANGELS

The Mexican tourism ministry, Sectur, maintains a network of *Ángeles Verdes* (Green Angels) – bilingual mechanics in green uniforms and green trucks, who patrol 60,000km of major highways throughout the country daily during daylight hours looking for tourists in trouble. They make minor repairs, change tires, provide fuel and oil, and arrange towing and other assistance if necessary. Service is free; parts, gasoline and oil are provided at cost. If you are near a telephone when your car has problems, you can call the **24-hour hotline** (☎ 078). There's a map of the roads they patrol at www.sectur.gob .mx/wb2/sectur/sect_9454_rutas_carreteras.

company. Note: comprehensive insurance can almost double the basic cost quoted in some internet bookings: you'll usually have the option of taking liability-only insurance at a lower rate. Ask exactly what the insurance options cover: theft and damage insurance may only cover a percentage of costs, or the insurance might not be valid for travel on rough country tracks. It's best to have plenty of liability coverage: Mexican law permits the jailing of drivers after an accident until they have met their obligations to third parties. The complimentary car-rental insurance offered with some US credit cards does not usually cover Mexico.

Most agencies offer a choice between a per-kilometer deal or unlimited kilometers. Local firms may or may not be cheaper than the big international ones. In most places the cheapest car available costs M$500 to M$600 a day including unlimited kilometers, insurance and tax. If you rent by the week or month, the per-day cost can come down by 20% to 40%. You can also cut costs by avoiding airport pickups and drop-offs, for which 10% can be added to your total check. The extra charge for drop-off in another city, when available, is usually about M$4 per kilometer.

Here's contact information (with Mexican phone numbers) for some major firms:

Alamo (☎ 800-849-80-01; www.alamo.com)
Avis (☎ 800-288-88-88; www.avis.com.mx)
Budget (☎ 800-700-17-00; www.budget.com.mx)
Dollar (☎ 998-886-02-22; www.dollar.com)
Europcar (☎ 800-201-20-84; www.europcar.com.mx)
Hertz (☎ 800-709-50-00; www.hertz.com)
National (☎ 800-716-66-25; www.nationalcar.com.mx)
Thrifty (☎ 55-5207-1100; www.thrifty.com.mx)

Motorbikes or scooters are available to rent in a few tourist centers. You're usually required to have a driver's license and credit card. It's advisable to look particularly carefully into insurance arrangements here: some renters do not offer any insurance at all. Note that a locally acquired motorcycle license is not valid under some travel insurance policies.

Road Conditions

Many Mexican highways, even some toll highways, are not up to the standards of US, Canadian or European ones. Still, the main roads are serviceable and fairly fast when traffic is not heavy. Mexicans on the whole drive as cautiously and sensibly as people anywhere. Traffic density, poor surfaces and frequent hazards (potholes, speed bumps, animals, bicycles, children) all help to keep speeds down.

Driving on a dark night is best avoided since unlit vehicles, rocks, pedestrians and animals on the roads are common. Hijacks and robberies do occur.

In towns and cities and on rural roads, be especially wary of *Alto* (Stop) signs, *topes* (speed bumps) and holes in the road. They are often not where you'd expect, and missing one can cost you in traffic fines or car damage. Speed bumps are also used to slow traffic on highways that pass through built-up areas. '*Tope*' or '*Vibradores*' signs give you a warning about most speed bumps; the deadly ones are the ones with no warning signs – and if you hit them at any speed, you and your car will get quite a shock.

There is always the chance that you will be pulled over by Mexican traffic police for an imaginary infraction. If this happens, stay calm and polite and don't be in a hurry. You don't have to pay a bribe, and acting dumb and not understanding Spanish may eventually make the cop give up. You can also ask to see documentation about the law you have supposedly broken, ask for the officer's identification, ask to speak to a superior, and/or note the officer's name, badge number, vehicle number and department (federal, state or municipal). Pay any traffic fines at a police station and get a receipt, then if you wish to make a complaint head for a state tourist office.

CITY PARKING

It's not usually a good idea to park on the street overnight. If your hotel doesn't have parking, it's best to find a commercial *estacionamiento* (parking lot). These usually cost around M$50 overnight and M$10 to M$15 per hour during the day.

MOTORCYCLE HAZARDS

Certain aspects of Mexican roads make them particularly hazardous for motorcyclists:

- poor signage of road and lane closures
- lots of dogs on the roads
- debris and deep potholes
- vehicles without taillights
- lack of highway lighting

TRANSPORTATION

HELPFUL (?) SIGNALS

Mexican drivers have a couple of signaling conventions that drivers from other countries may not immediately understand – and need to be treated with caution in any case.

Drivers often warn each other of hazards on the road ahead – a police checkpoint, a tailback, a rock or cow in the road – by a flash of the headlights or hazard-warning lights. Of course you may get round the next few bends and find there's nothing to worry about. Maybe the other driver touched their switch by mistake.

Slow-moving vehicles often flash their left indicators to indicate that the road ahead is clear for a following vehicle to overtake. You should never take their word for it, of course – and remember that they might also be flashing left because they are about to turn left!

TOLL ROADS

Mexico has more than 6000km of autopistas (toll roads), usually four-lane. They are generally in much better condition and a lot quicker than the alternative free roads. *Cuotas* (tolls) average about M$1 per km. Toll information is available at www.sct.gob.mx: click on 'Traza Tu Ruta.'

Road Rules

Drive on the right-hand side of the road.

Speed limits range between 80km and 120km per hour on open highways (less when highways pass through built-up areas), and between 30km and 50km per hour in towns and cities. Seat belts are obligatory for all occupants of a car, and children under five must be strapped into safety seats in the rear. Obeying speed limits, traffic rules and traffic signs will avoid giving police excuses to demand 'fines' payable on the spot.

One-way streets are the rule in cities. Priority at some street intersections is indicated by thin black and red rectangles containing white arrows. A black rectangle facing you means you have priority; a red one means you don't. The white arrows indicate the direction of traffic on the cross street; if the arrow points both ways, it's a two-way street.

Antipollution rules in Mexico City ban most vehicles from the city's roads on one day each week (see p200).

COLECTIVOS & OTHER VEHICLES

In some areas a variety of small vehicles provide alternatives to buses. *Colectivo* (collective) taxis, Volkswagen minibuses (combis) and more comfortable passenger-carrying vans, such as Chevrolet Suburbans, operate shuttle services between some towns, usually leaving whenever they have a full load of passengers. Fares are typically a little less than 1st-class buses. Microbuses or 'micros' are small, usually fairly new, 2nd-class buses with around 25 seats, usually running short routes between nearby towns. More primitive are passenger-carrying *camionetas* (pickups) and *camiones* (trucks) with fares similar to 2nd-class bus fares. Standing in the back of a lurching truck with a couple of dozen *campesinos* (land workers) and their machetes and animals is always an experience to remember!

HITCHHIKING

Hitchhiking is never entirely safe in any country in the world, and is not recommended. Travelers who decide to hitch should understand that they are taking a small but potentially serious risk. People who do choose to hitch will be safer if they travel in pairs and let someone know where they are planning to go. A woman traveling alone certainly should not hitchhike in Mexico, and even two women alone is not advisable.

However, hitching is not an uncommon way of getting to some off-the-beaten-track places poorly served by bus. Always be alert to possible dangers wherever you are. If the driver is another tourist or a private motorist, you may get the ride for free. If it is a work or commercial vehicle, you should offer to pay, something equivalent to the bus fare.

LOCAL TRANSPORTATION
Bicycle

Most Mexican towns and cities are flat enough to make cycling an option. Seek out the less traffic-infested routes and you should enjoy it. Even Mexico City has its biking enthusiasts. You can rent bikes in several towns and cities for M$100 to M$150 per day.

ROAD DISTANCES (km)

	Acapulco	Cancún	Ciudad Juárez	Guadalajara	Guanajuato	Hermosillo	Matamoros	Mazatlán	Mérida	Mexico City	Monterrey	Morelia	Nogales	Oaxaca	Puebla	San Luis Potosí	Tapachula	Tijuana	Tuxtla Gutiérrez	Veracruz	Villahermosa
Cancún	2007																				
Ciudad Juárez	2258	3512																			
Guadalajara	889	2191	1578																		
Guanajuato	760	2014	1570	277																	
Hermosillo	2348	3608	769	1417	1694																
Matamoros	1370	2336	1530	1117	774	1848															
Mazatlán	1431	2891	1347	500	777	917	1250														
Mérida	1690	317	3195	1874	1697	3291	1959	2374													
Mexico City	395	1649	1863	542	365	1959	975	1042	1332												
Monterrey	1328	2363	1202	789	729	1520	328	928	2046	933											
Morelia	697	1951	1705	302	180	1719	954	802	1634	302	913										
Nogales	2625	3885	620	1694	1971	277	2125	1194	3568	2409	2638	1996									
Oaxaca	828	1490	2333	1012	835	2429	1358	1512	1173	470	1056	772	2706								
Puebla	481	1526	1986	665	488	2082	1077	1165	1209	123	425	395	2359	347							
San Luis Potosí	810	2064	1448	340	215	1766	559	809	1747	415	514	395	2043	885	558						
Tapachula	1109	1376	3020	1699	1522	3116	1776	2199	1062	1157	1802	1459	3393	687	834	1572					
Tijuana	3237	4497	1312	2306	2583	889	2737	1806	4180	2848	2409	2608	820	3318	3271	2615	4005				
Tuxtla Gutiérrez	967	1146	2878	1557	1380	2974	1634	2054	829	1015	1661	1317	3251	545	892	1430	412	3863			
Veracruz	760	1373	2265	944	767	2361	963	1444	1056	402	990	704	2638	395	279	817	813	3250	671		
Villahermosa	1126	881	2631	1310	1133	2727	1455	1810	564	768	1482	1070	3004	609	645	1183	636	3616	284	492	
Zacatecas	1000	2254	1258	320	312	1576	797	619	1937	605	469	447	1853	1075	728	190	1762	2425	1620	1007	1373

TRANSPORTATION

Boat

Here and there you may find yourself traveling by boat to an outlying beach, along a river or across a lake or lagoon. The craft are usually fast outboard *lanchas* (launches). Fares vary widely: an average is around M$10 a minute if you have to charter the whole boat (haggle!), or around M$10 for five to 10 minutes if it's a public service.

Bus

Generally known as *camiones,* local buses are often the cheapest way to get around cities and out to nearby towns and villages. They run frequently and are cheap. Fares in cities are rarely more than M$5. In many cities, fleets of small, modern *microbuses* have replaced the noisy, dirty and crowded older buses.

Buses usually halt only at fixed *paradas* (bus stops), though in some places you can hold your hand out to stop one at any street corner.

Colectivo, Combi, Minibus & Pesero

These are all names for vehicles that function as something between a taxi and a bus, running along fixed urban routes usually displayed on the windshield. They're cheaper than taxis and quicker than buses. They will pick you up or drop you off on any corner along their route: to stop one, go to the curb and wave your hand. Tell the driver where you want to go. Usually, you pay at the end of the trip and the fare (a little higher than a bus fare) depends on how far you go. In some northern border towns, 'pesero' is used to mean a city bus.

Metro

Mexico City, Guadalajara and Monterrey all have metro (subway, underground railway) systems. Mexico City's, in particular, is a quick, cheap and useful way of getting around. With 175 stations and used by over four million people every weekday, it's the world's third-busiest subway.

Taxi

Taxis are common in towns and cities, and surprisingly economical. City rides cost around M$10 per kilometer, and in some cities there's a fixed rate for journeys within defined central areas. (See p141 for a warning on taxi crime in Mexico City.) If a taxi has a meter, you can ask the driver if it's working ('*¿Funciona el taxímetro?*'). If it's not, or if the taxi doesn't have a meter, establish the price of the ride before getting in (this may involve a bit of haggling).

Some airports and big bus terminals have a system of authorized ticket-taxis: you buy a fixed-price ticket to your destination from a special *taquilla* (ticket window) and then hand it to the driver instead of paying cash. This saves haggling and major rip-offs, but fares are usually higher than you could get on the street.

In some (usually rural) areas, some taxis operate on a *colectivo* basis, following set routes, often from one town or village to another, and picking up or dropping off passengers anywhere along that route. Fares per person are around one-quarter of the normal cab fare.

Renting a taxi for a day's out-of-town outing generally costs something similar to a cheap rental car – around M$500 or M$600.

TRAIN

The spectacular Ferrocarril Chihuahua al Pacífico that runs between Los Mochis and Chihuahua (p341), known in English as the Copper Canyon Railway, is one of the highlights of traveling in Mexico. But the remainder of Mexico's regular passenger train system effectively ceased to exist after the railroads were privatized in the 1990s. The very few services remaining operate on routes that are of no interest to travelers or are special tourist excursion services. Most prominent among the latter group is the **Tequila Express** (www.tequila express.com.mx) running between Guadalajara and the tequila-distilling town of Amatitán (see p543).

Health Dr David Goldberg

CONTENTS

Travelers to Mexico need to be concerned chiefly about food-borne diseases, though mosquito-borne infections can also be a problem. Most of these illnesses are not life threatening, but they can ruin your trip. Besides getting the proper vaccinations, it's important that you bring along a good insect repellent and exercise great care in what you eat and drink.

BEFORE YOU GO

Bring medications in their original containers, clearly labeled. A signed, dated letter from your physician describing all medical conditions and medications, including generic names, is also a good idea. If carrying syringes or needles, be sure to have a physician's letter documenting their medical necessity.

INSURANCE

Mexican medical treatment is generally inexpensive for common diseases and minor treatment, but if you suffer some serious medical problem, you may want to find a private hospital or fly out for treatment. Travel insurance can typically cover the costs. Some US health-insurance policies stay in effect (at least for a limited time) if you travel abroad, but it's worth checking exactly what you'll be covered for in Mexico. For people whose medical insurance or national health systems don't extend to Mexico – which includes most non-Americans – a travel policy is advisable. US travelers can find links to information on medical evacuation and travel insurance companies on the Mexico page of the **Bureau of Consular Affairs website** (www.travel.state.gov).

You may prefer a policy that pays doctors or hospitals directly, rather than requiring you to pay on the spot and claim later. If you have to claim later, keep all documentation. Some policies ask you to call collect to a center in your home country, where an assessment of your problem is made. Check that the policy covers ambulances or an emergency flight home. Some policies offer different medical-expense options; the higher ones are chiefly for countries such as the USA, which have extremely high medical costs. There is a wide variety of policies available, so check the small print.

RECOMMENDED VACCINATIONS

Since most vaccines don't produce immunity until at least two weeks after they're given, be sure to visit a physician four to eight weeks before departure. Ask your doctor for an international certificate of vaccination (otherwise known as the yellow booklet), which will list all the vaccinations you've received. This is mandatory for countries that require proof of yellow fever vaccination upon entry, but it's a good idea to carry it wherever you travel.

A number of vaccines are recommended; see the table on the next page.

MEDICAL CHECKLIST
- acetaminophen/paracetamol (Tylenol) or aspirin
- adhesive or paper tape
- antibacterial ointment (eg Bactroban) for cuts and abrasions
- antibiotics
- antidiarrheal drugs (eg loperamide)
- anti-inflammatory drugs (eg ibuprofen)
- antihistamines (for hay fever and allergic reactions)
- steroid cream or cortisone (for poison ivy and other allergic rashes)
- bandages, gauze, gauze rolls
- scissors, safety pins, tweezers

Vaccine	Recommended for	Dosage	Side effects
hepatitis A	all travelers	1 dose before trip; booster 6-12 months later	soreness at injection site; headaches; body aches
typhoid	all travelers	4 capsules by mouth, 1 taken every other day	abdominal pain; nausea; rash
hepatitis B	long-term travelers in close contact with the local population	3 doses over 6-month period	soreness at injection site; low-grade fever
rabies	travelers who may have contact with animals and may not have access to medical care	3 doses over 3-4 week period	soreness at injection site; headaches; body aches
tetanus-diphtheria	all travelers who haven't had booster within 10 years	1 dose lasts 10 years	soreness at injection site
measles	travelers born after 1956 who've had only 1 measles vaccination	1 dose	fever; rash; joint pains; allergic reactions
chickenpox	travelers who've never had chickenpox	2 doses, 1 month apart	fever; mild case of chickenpox

- thermometer
- pocket knife
- DEET-containing insect repellent
- permethrin-containing insect spray for clothing, tents and bed nets
- sunblock
- oral rehydration salts
- iodine tablets (for water purification)
- syringes and sterile needles

INTERNET RESOURCES

There is a wealth of travel health advice on the internet. **MD Travel Health** (www.mdtravelhealth.com) provides complete travel health recommendations for every country and is updated daily. The World Health Organization publishes a superb book, **International Travel and Health** (www.who.int/ith/), which is revised annually and is available free online.

It's also a good idea to consult government travel health websites before departure:
Australia www.dfat.gov.au/travel/
Canada http://www.hc-sc.gc.ca
UK www.doh.gov.uk/traveladvice/
United States www.cdc.gov/travel/

FURTHER READING

For further information, see *Healthy Travel Central & South America,* also from Lonely Planet. If you're traveling with children, Lonely Planet's *Travel with Children* may be useful. The *ABC of Healthy Travel,* by E Walker et al, and *Medicine for the Outdoors,* by Paul S Auerbach, are other valuable resources.

IN TRANSIT

DEEP VEIN THROMBOSIS (DVT)

Blood clots may form in the legs (deep vein thrombosis) during plane flights, chiefly because of prolonged immobility. The longer the flight, the greater the risk. Though most blood clots are reabsorbed uneventfully, some may break off and travel through the blood vessels to the lungs, where they could cause life-threatening complications.

The chief symptom of DVT is swelling or pain of the foot, ankle or calf, usually but not always on just one side. When a blood clot travels to the lungs, it may cause chest pain and breathing difficulties. Travelers with any of these symptoms should immediately seek medical attention.

To prevent the development of DVT on long flights you should walk about the cabin, perform isometric compressions of the leg muscles (ie contract the leg muscles while sitting), drink plenty of fluids, and avoid alcohol and tobacco.

JET LAG & MOTION SICKNESS

Jet lag is common when crossing more than five time zones, resulting in insomnia, fatigue, malaise or nausea. To avoid jet lag, try drinking plenty of fluids (nonalcoholic) and eating light meals. Upon arrival, get exposure to natural sunlight and readjust your schedule (for meals, sleep etc) as soon as possible.

Antihistamines such as dimenhydrinate (Dramamine) and meclizine (Antivert, Bonine) are usually the first choice for treating motion sickness. Their main side effect is drowsiness. An herbal alternative is ginger, which works like a charm for some people.

IN MEXICO

AVAILABILITY & COST OF HEALTH CARE

There are a number of first-rate hospitals in Mexico City (p131). In general, private facilities offer better care, though at greater cost, than public hospitals.

Adequate medical care is available in other major cities, but facilities in rural areas may be limited. In many areas, the US consulate provides an online directory to local physicians and hospitals, such as the following:

Ciudad Juarez http://ciudadjuarez.usconsulate.gov/physicians-and-dentists.html

Guadalajara www.usembassy-mexico.gov/guadalajara/GeDoctors.htm

Merida http://merida.usconsulate.gov/merida/doctorlist.html

Nogales http://nogales.usconsulate.gov/doctors.html

Many doctors and hospitals expect payment in cash, regardless of whether you have travel health insurance. If you develop a medical problem that's life threatening, you'll probably want to be evacuated to a country with state-of-the-art medical care. Since this may cost tens of thousands of dollars, be sure you have insurance to cover this before you depart.

Pharmacies are identified by a green cross and a 'Farmacia' sign. Most are well supplied and the pharmacists well trained. Reliable pharmacy chains include Sanborns, Farmacia Guadalajara, Benavides and Farmacia Fenix. Some medications requiring a prescription in the US may be dispensed in Mexico without one. To find an after-hours pharmacy, you can look in the local newspaper, ask your hotel concierge, or check the front door of a local pharmacy, which will often post the name of a nearby pharmacy that is open for the night.

INFECTIOUS DISEASES
Malaria

Malaria occurs in every country in Central America, including parts of Mexico. It's transmitted by mosquito bites, usually between dusk and dawn. The main symptom is high spiking fevers, which may be accompanied by chills, sweats, headache, body aches, weakness, vomiting or diarrhea. Severe cases may involve the central nervous system and lead to seizures, confusion, coma and death.

Taking malaria pills is strongly recommended when visiting rural areas in the states of Oaxaca, Chiapas, Sinaloa, Nayarit, Tabasco and Quintana Roo, and for an area between 24° and 28° north latitude and 106° and 110° west longitude, which includes parts of the states of Sonora, Chihuahua and Durango.

For Mexico, the first-choice malaria pill is chloroquine, taken once weekly in a dosage of 500mg, starting one to two weeks before arrival and continuing through the trip and for four weeks after departure. Chloroquine is safe, inexpensive and highly effective. Side effects are typically mild and may include nausea, abdominal discomfort, headache, dizziness, blurred vision or itching. Severe reactions are uncommon.

Protecting yourself against mosquito bites is just as important as taking malaria pills, since no pills are 100% effective.

If it's possible that you may not have access to medical care while traveling, bring along additional pills for emergency self-treatment, which you should take if you can't reach a doctor and develop symptoms that suggest malaria, such as high spiking fevers. One option is to take four tablets of Malarone once daily for three days. If you start self-medication, you should try to see a doctor at the earliest possible opportunity.

If you develop a fever after returning home, see a physician, as malaria symptoms may not occur for months.

Malaria pills are not recommended for the major resorts along the Pacific and Gulf Coasts.

Dengue Fever

Dengue fever is a viral infection found in most parts of Mexico. An outbreak in 2007 resulted in at least 67,000 cases. Dengue is transmitted by aedes mosquitoes, which usually bite during the day and are usually found close to human habitations, often indoors. They breed primarily in artificial water containers, such as jars, barrels, cans, cisterns, metal drums, plastic containers and discarded tires. As a result, dengue is especially common in densely populated, urban environments.

HEALTH

Dengue usually causes flu-like symptoms including fever, muscle aches, joint pains, headaches, nausea and vomiting, often followed by a rash. The body aches may be quite uncomfortable, but most cases resolve uneventfully in a few days. Severe cases usually occur in children under age 15 who are experiencing their second dengue infection.

There's no treatment for dengue fever except to take analgesics such as acetaminophen/paracetamol (Tylenol) and drink plenty of fluids. Severe cases may require hospitalization for intravenous fluids and supportive care. There is no vaccine. The cornerstone of prevention is insect protection measures (see p1005).

Hepatitis A

Hepatitis A occurs throughout Central America. It's a viral liver infection usually acquired by ingestion of contaminated water, food or ice, though it may also be acquired by direct contact with infected persons. The illness occurs worldwide, but the incidence is higher in developing nations. Symptoms may include fever, malaise, jaundice, nausea, vomiting and abdominal pain. Most cases resolve uneventfully, though it occasionally causes severe liver damage. There is no treatment.

The vaccine for hepatitis A is extremely safe and highly effective. If you get a booster six to 12 months later, it lasts for at least 10 years. You really should get it before you go to Mexico or any other developing nation. Because the safety of hepatitis A vaccine has not been established for pregnant women or children under age two, they should instead be given a gamma-globulin injection.

Hepatitis B

Like hepatitis A, hepatitis B is a liver infection that occurs worldwide but is more common in developing nations. Unlike hepatitis A, the disease is usually acquired by sexual contact or by exposure to infected blood, generally through blood transfusions or contaminated needles. The vaccine is recommended only for long-term travelers (on the road more than six months) who expect to live in rural areas or have close physical contact with the local population. Additionally, the vaccine is recommended for anyone who anticipates sexual contact with the local inhabitants or a possible need for medical, dental or other treatments while abroad, especially if a need for transfusions or injections is expected.

Hepatitis B vaccine is safe and highly effective. However, a total of three injections is necessary to establish full immunity. Several countries added hepatitis B vaccine to the list of routine childhood immunizations in the 1980s, so many young adults are already protected.

Typhoid Fever

Typhoid fever is common throughout Central America. The infection is acquired by ingestion of food or water contaminated by a species of *Salmonella* known as *Salmonella typhi*. Fever occurs in virtually all cases. Other symptoms may include headache, malaise, muscle aches, dizziness, loss of appetite, nausea and abdominal pain. Either diarrhea or constipation may occur. Possible complications include intestinal perforation, intestinal bleeding, confusion, delirium or (rarely) coma.

Unless you expect to take all your meals in major hotels and restaurants, a typhoid vaccine is a good idea. It's usually given orally, but is also available as an injection. Neither vaccine is approved for use in children under age two.

The drug of choice for typhoid fever is usually a quinolone antibiotic such as ciprofloxacin (Cipro) or levofloxacin (Levaquin), which many travelers carry for treatment of travelers' diarrhea. However, if you self-treat for typhoid fever, you may also need to self-treat for malaria, since the symptoms of the two diseases can be indistinguishable.

Rabies

Rabies is a viral infection of the brain and spinal cord that is almost always fatal. The rabies virus is carried in the saliva of infected animals and is typically transmitted through an animal bite, though contamination of any break in the skin with infected saliva may result in rabies. Rabies occurs in all Central American countries. Most cases in Mexico are related to dog bites, but bats and other wild species also remain sources of infection.

Rabies vaccine is safe, but a full series requires three injections and is quite expensive. Those at high risk for rabies, such as animal handlers and spelunkers (cave explorers), should certainly get the vaccine. In addition, those at lower risk for animal bites should consider asking for the vaccine if they are traveling to remote areas and might not have access to appropriate medical care if needed.

The treatment for a possibly rabid bite consists of rabies vaccine with rabies immune globulin. It's effective, but must be given promptly. Most travelers don't need rabies vaccine.

All animal bites and scratches must be promptly and thoroughly cleansed with large amounts of soap and water, and local health authorities should be contacted to determine whether or not further treatment is necessary (see p1006).

Cholera

Cholera is an intestinal infection acquired through ingestion of contaminated food or water. The main symptom is profuse, watery diarrhea, which may be so severe that it causes life-threatening dehydration. The key treatment is drinking oral rehydration solution. Antibiotics are also given, usually tetracycline or doxycycline, though quinolone antibiotics such as ciprofloxacin and levofloxacin are also effective.

Only a handful of cases have been reported in Mexico over the last few years. Cholera vaccine is no longer recommended.

Other Infections

GNATHOSTOMIASIS

Gnathostomiasis is a parasite acquired by eating raw or undercooked freshwater fish, including ceviche, a popular lime-marinated fish salad. Cases have been reported from Acapulco and other parts of Mexico. The chief symptom is intermittent, migratory swellings under the skin, sometimes associated with joint pains, muscle pains or gastrointestinal problems. The symptoms may not begin until many months after exposure.

LEISHMANIASIS

Leishmaniasis occurs in the mountains and jungles of all Central American countries. The infection is transmitted by sand flies, which are about one-third the size of mosquitoes. Leishmaniasis may be limited to the skin, causing slowly-growing ulcers over exposed parts of the body, or (less commonly) may disseminate to the bone marrow, liver and spleen. The disease may be particularly severe in those with HIV. The disseminated form is rare in Mexico and is limited chiefly to the Balsas River basin in the southern states of Guerrero and Puebla. There is no vaccine for leishmaniasis. To protect yourself from sand flies, follow the same precautions as

for mosquitoes (p1005), except that netting must be finer mesh (at least 18 holes to the linear inch).

CHAGAS' DISEASE

Chagas' disease is a parasitic infection transmitted by triatomine insects (reduviid bugs), which inhabit crevices in the walls and roofs of substandard housing in South and Central America. In Mexico, most cases occur in southern and coastal areas. The triatomine insect lays its feces on human skin as it bites, usually at night. A person becomes infected when he or she unknowingly rubs the feces into the bite wound or any other open sore. Chagas' disease is extremely rare in travelers. However, if you sleep in a poorly constructed house, especially one made of mud, adobe or thatch, you should be sure to protect yourself with a bed net and good insecticide.

HISTOPLASMOSIS

Histoplasmosis is caused by a soil-based fungus and is acquired by inhalation, often when soil has been disrupted. Initial symptoms may include fever, chills, dry cough, chest pain and headache, sometimes leading to pneumonia. An outbreak was recently described among visitors to an Acapulco hotel.

COCCIDIOIDOMYCOSIS

Coccidioidomycosis, also known as 'valley fever,' is a fungal infection that is restricted to semiarid areas in the American southwest, nearby areas in northern Mexico, and limited foci in Central and South America. Valley fever is acquired by inhaling dust from contaminated soil. It begins as a lung infection, causing fever, chest pain and coughing, and may spread to other organs, particularly the nervous system, skin and bone. Treatment requires high doses of antibiotics for prolonged periods and is not always curative.

BRUCELLOSIS

Brucellosis is an infection occurring in domestic and wild animals that may be transmitted to humans through direct animal contact, or by consumption of unpasteurized dairy products from infected animals. Symptoms may include fever, malaise, depression, loss of appetite, headache, muscle aches and back pain. Complications can include arthritis, hepatitis, meningitis and endocarditis (heart valve infection).

TICK-BORNE RELAPSING FEVER

Tick-borne relapsing fever, transmitted by either ticks or lice, has been reported from the plateau regions in central Mexico. Relapsing fever is caused by bacteria that are closely related to those that cause Lyme disease and syphilis. The illness is characterized by periods of fever, chills, headaches, body aches, muscle aches and cough, alternating with periods when the fever subsides and the person feels relatively well. To minimize the risk of relapsing fever, follow tick precautions as outlined below and practice good personal hygiene.

TULAREMIA

Tularemia, also known as 'rabbit fever,' is a bacterial infection that primarily affects rodents, rabbits and hares. Humans generally become infected through tick or deerfly bites, or by handling the carcass of an infected animal. Occasional cases are caused by inhalation of an infectious aerosol. In Mexico, most cases occur in the northern rural areas. Tularemia may develop as a flu-like illness, pneumonia or cause skin ulcers with swollen glands, depending upon how the infection is acquired. It usually responds well to antibiotics.

ROCKY MOUNTAIN SPOTTED FEVER

Rocky Mountain spotted fever is a tick-borne infection characterized by fever, headache and muscle aches, followed by a rash. Complications may include pneumonia, meningitis, gangrene and kidney failure, and may be life threatening. Cases have been reported from the central part of the country, the Yucatán Peninsula and Jalisco State.

ONCHOCERCIASIS

Onchocerciasis (river blindness) is caused by a roundworm invading the eye, leading to blindness. The infection is transmitted by black flies, which breed along the banks of rapidly flowing rivers and streams. In Mexico, the disease is reported from highland areas in the states of Oaxaca, Chiapas and Guerrero.

TYPHUS

Typhus may be transmitted by lice in scattered pockets of the country.

HIV/AIDS

HIV/AIDS has been reported from all Central American countries. Be sure to use condoms for all sexual encounters.

TRAVELERS' DIARRHEA

To prevent diarrhea, avoid tap water unless it has been boiled, filtered or chemically disinfected (eg with iodine tablets); only eat fresh fruits or vegetables if cooked or peeled; be wary of dairy products that might contain unpasteurized milk; and be highly selective when eating food from street vendors.

If you develop diarrhea, be sure to drink plenty of fluids, preferably an oral rehydration solution containing lots of salt and sugar. A few loose stools don't require treatment, but if you start having more than four or five stools a day you should start taking an antibiotic (usually a quinolone drug) and an antidiarrheal agent (such as loperamide). If diarrhea is bloody, persists for more than 72 hours or is accompanied by fever, shaking chills or severe abdominal pain you should seek medical attention.

ENVIRONMENTAL HAZARDS & TREATMENT
Altitude Sickness

Altitude sickness may develop in travelers who ascend rapidly to altitudes greater than 2500m. Being physically fit does not lessen your risk of altitude sickness. It seems to be chiefly a matter of genetic predisposition. Those who have experienced altitude sickness in the past are prone to future episodes. The risk increases with faster ascents, higher altitudes and greater exertion. Symptoms may include headaches, nausea, vomiting, dizziness, malaise, insomnia and loss of appetite. Severe cases may be complicated by fluid in the lungs (high-altitude pulmonary edema) or swelling of the brain (high-altitude cerebral edema). Most deaths are caused by high-altitude pulmonary edema.

The standard medication to prevent altitude sickness is a mild diuretic called acetazolamide (Diamox), which should be started 24 hours before ascent and continued for 48 hours after arrival at altitude. Possible side effects include increased urination, numbness, tingling, nausea, drowsiness, nearsightedness and temporary impotence. For those who cannot tolerate acetazolamide, most physicians prescribe dexamethasone, which is a type of steroid. A natural alternative is gingko, which some people find quite helpful. The usual dosage is 100mg twice daily.

To lessen the chance of altitude sickness, you should also be sure to ascend gradually to higher altitudes, avoid overexertion, eat light meals and avoid alcohol.

Symptoms of altitude sickness develop gradually so, with proper care, serious complications can usually be prevented. If you or a companion show any symptoms of altitude sickness, you should not ascend to a higher altitude until the symptoms have cleared. If the symptoms become worse or if someone shows signs of cerebral or pulmonary edema, such as trouble breathing or mental confusion, you must immediately descend to a lower altitude. A descent of 500m to 1000m is generally adequate except in cases of cerebral edema, which may require a greater descent. Supplemental oxygen is helpful if available. Acetazolamide and dexamethasone may be used to treat altitude sickness as well as prevent it.

Travel to high altitudes is generally not recommended for those with a history of heart disease, lung disease, or sickle-cell disease. It is also not recommended for pregnant women.

Mosquito Bites

To prevent mosquito bites, wear long sleeves, long pants, hats and shoes. Bring along a good insect repellent, preferably one containing DEET. Apply it to exposed skin and clothing, but not to eyes, mouth, cuts, wounds or irritated skin. Products containing lower concentrations of DEET are as effective, but for shorter periods of time. In general, adults and children over 12 should use preparations containing 25% to 35% DEET, which usually lasts about six hours. Children between two and 12 years of age should use preparations containing no more than 10% DEET, applied sparingly, which will usually last about three hours. Neurological toxicity has been reported from DEET, especially in children, but appears to be extremely uncommon and generally related to overuse. Don't use DEET-containing compounds on children under two.

Insect repellents containing certain botanical products, including oil of eucalyptus and soybean oil, are effective but last only 1½ to two hours. Where there is a high risk of malaria or yellow fever, use DEET-containing repellents. Products based on citronella are not effective.

For additional protection, apply permethrin to clothing, shoes, tents and bed nets. Permethrin treatments are safe and remain effective for at least two weeks, even when items are laundered. Permethrin should not be applied directly to skin.

Don't sleep with the window open unless there is a screen. If sleeping outdoors or in accommodations that allow entry of mosquitoes, use a bed net treated with permethrin, with edges tucked in under the mattress. The mesh size should be less than 1.5mm. Alternatively, use a mosquito coil, which will fill the room with insecticide through the night. Repellent-impregnated wristbands are not effective.

Tick Bites

To protect yourself from tick bites, follow the same precautions as for mosquitoes, except that boots are preferable to shoes, with pants tucked in. Be sure to perform a thorough tick check at the end of each day. You'll generally need the assistance of a friend or mirror for a full examination. Remove ticks with tweezers, grasping them firmly by the head. Insect repellents based on botanical products, described above, have not been adequately studied for insects other than mosquitoes and cannot be recommended to prevent tick bites.

Water

Tap water in Mexico is generally not safe to drink. Vigorous boiling for one minute is the most effective means of water purification. At altitudes greater than 2000m, boil for three minutes.

Another option is to disinfect water with iodine pills. Instructions are usually enclosed and should be carefully followed. Or you can add 2% tincture of iodine to one quart or liter of water (five drops to clear water, 10 drops to cloudy water) and let stand for 30 minutes. If the water is cold, a longer time may be required. The taste of iodinated water can be improved by adding vitamin C (ascorbic acid). Don't consume iodinated water for more than a few weeks. Pregnant women, those with a history of thyroid disease and those allergic to iodine should not drink iodinated water.

A number of water filters are on the market. Those with smaller pores (reverse osmosis filters) provide the broadest protection, but they are relatively large and are easily plugged by debris. Those with larger pores (microstrainer filters) are ineffective against viruses, although they remove other organisms. Manufacturers' instructions must be carefully followed.

Sun

To protect from excessive sun exposure, stay out of the midday sun, wear sunglasses and a wide-brimmed hat, and apply sunscreen with SPF 15 or higher, providing both UVA and

HEALTH

UVB protection. Sunscreen should be generously applied to all exposed parts of the body approximately 30 minutes before sun exposure and reapplied after swimming or vigorous activity. Drink plenty of fluids and avoid strenuous exercise in high temperatures.

Air Pollution

Air pollution may be a significant problem, especially in Mexico City and Guadalajara. It is typically most severe from December to May. Travelers with respiratory or cardiac conditions and those who are elderly or very young are at greatest risk for complications from air pollution, including coughing, difficulty breathing, wheezing or chest pain. Minimize the risk by staying indoors, avoiding outdoor exercise and drinking plenty of fluids.

Animal Bites

Do not attempt to pet, handle or feed any animal, with the exception of domestic animals known to be free of any infectious disease. Most animal injuries are directly related to a person's attempt to touch or feed the animal.

Any bite or scratch by a mammal, including bats, should be promptly and thoroughly cleansed with large amounts of soap and water, followed by application of an antiseptic such as iodine or alcohol. Contact local health authorities immediately for possible postexposure treatment, whether or not you've been immunized against rabies. It may also be worth starting an antibiotic – wounds caused by animal bites and scratches often become infected. One of the newer quinolones, such as levofloxacin (Levaquin), which many travelers carry in case of diarrhea, would be appropriate.

Snake & Scorpion Bites

Venomous snakes in Central America include the bushmaster, fer-de-lance, coral snake and various species of rattlesnakes. The fer-de-lance is the most lethal. It generally does not attack without provocation, but may bite humans who accidentally come too close as it lies camouflaged on the forest floor. The bushmaster is the world's largest pit viper, measuring up to 4m in length. Like other pit vipers, the bushmaster has a heat-sensing pit between the eye and nostril on each side of its head, which it uses to detect the presence of warm-blooded prey.

Coral snakes are somewhat retiring and tend not to bite humans. North of Mexico

TRADITIONAL MEDICINE	
Problem	Treatment
jet lag	melatonin
motion sickness	ginger
mosquito bite prevention	oil of eucalyptus, soybean oil

City, all coral snakes have a red, yellow, black, yellow, red banding pattern, with red and yellow touching, in contrast to nonvenomous snakes, where the red and yellow bands are separated by black. South of Mexico City, the banding patterns become more complex and this distinction is not useful.

In the event of a venomous snake bite, place the victim at rest, keep the bitten area immobilized, and move the victim immediately to the nearest medical facility. Avoid tourniquets, which are no longer recommended.

Scorpions are a problem in many states. If stung, you should immediately apply ice or cold packs, immobilize the affected body part and go to the nearest emergency room. To prevent scorpion stings, be sure to inspect and shake out clothing, shoes and sleeping bags before use, and wear gloves and protective clothing when working around piles of wood or leaves.

CHILDREN & PREGNANT WOMEN

In general, it's safe for children and pregnant women to go to Mexico. However, as some of the vaccines listed previously are not approved for children or during pregnancy, these travelers should be particularly careful not to drink tap water or consume any questionable food or beverage. Also, when traveling with children, make sure they're up to date on all routine immunizations. It's sometimes appropriate to give children some of their vaccines a little early before visiting a developing nation. You should discuss this with your pediatrician. If pregnant, bear in mind that should a complication such as premature labor develop while abroad, the quality of medical care may not be comparable to that in your home country.

Since yellow-fever vaccine is not recommended for pregnant women or children less than nine months old, if you are arriving from a country with yellow fever, obtain a waiver letter, preferably written on letterhead stationery and bearing the stamp used by official immunization centers to validate the international certificate of vaccination.

Language

CONTENTS

The predominant language of Mexico is Spanish. Mexican Spanish is unlike Castilian Spanish (the language of much of Spain) in two main respects: in Mexico the Castilian lisp has more or less disappeared, and numerous indigenous words have been adopted. About 50 indigenous languages are spoken as a first language by more than seven million people, and about 15% of these don't speak Spanish.

Travelers in cities, towns and larger villages can almost always find someone who speaks at least some English. All the same, it is advantageous and courteous to know at least a few words and phrases in Spanish. Mexicans will generally respond much more positively if you attempt to speak to them in their own language.

It's easy enough to pick up some basic Spanish, and for those who want to learn the language in greater depth, courses are available in several cities in Mexico (see p966). You can also study books, records and tapes before you leave home. These resources are often available free at public libraries. Evening or college courses are also an excellent way to get started.

For a more comprehensive guide to the Spanish of Mexico, get a copy of Lonely Planet's *Mexican Spanish Phrasebook*. For words and phrases that will come in handy when dining, see p100.

PRONUNCIATION

Spanish spelling is phonetically consistent, meaning that there's a clear and consistent relationship between what you see in writing and how it's pronounced. In addition, most Spanish sounds have English equivalents, so English speakers shouldn't have too much trouble being understood.

Vowels

a as in 'father'
e as in 'met'
i as in 'marine'
o as in 'or' (without the 'r' sound)
u as in 'rule'; the 'u' is not pronounced after **q** and in the letter combinations **gue** and **gui**, unless it's marked with a diaeresis (eg *argüir*), in which case it's pronounced as an English 'w'
y at the end of a word or when it stands alone, it's pronounced as the Spanish **i** (eg *ley*); between vowels within a word it's as the 'y' in 'yonder'

Consonants

As a rule, Spanish consonants resemble their English counterparts. The exceptions are listed below.

While the consonants **ch**, **ll** and **ñ** are generally considered distinct letters, **ch** and **ll** are now often listed alphabetically under **c** and **l** respectively. The letter **ñ** is still treated as a separate letter and comes after **n** in dictionaries.

b similar to an English 'b,' but softer; referred to as 'b larga'
c as in 'celery' before **e** and **i**; otherwise as an English 'k'
ch as in 'church'
d as in 'dog,' but between vowels and after **l** or **n**, the sound is closer to the 'th' in 'this'
g as the 'ch' in the Scottish *loch* before **e** and **i** ('kh' in our guides to pronunciation); elsewhere, as in 'go'
h invariably silent. If your name begins with this letter, make sure you listen carefully if you're waiting for public officials to call you.

j	as the 'ch' in Scottish *loch* (written as 'kh' in our guides to pronunciation)
ll	varies between the 'y' in 'yes' and the 'lli' in 'million'
ñ	as the 'ni' in 'onion'
r	a short **r** except at the beginning of a word, and after **l**, **n** or **s**, when it's often rolled
rr	very strongly rolled (not reflected in the pronunciation guides)
v	similar to an English 'b,' but softer; referred to as 'b corta'
x	usually pronounced as **j** above; in some indigenous place names it's pronounced as an 's'; as in 'taxi' in other instances
z	as the 's' in 'sun'

Word Stress

In general, words ending in vowels or the letters **n** or **s** have stress on the next-to-last syllable, while those with other endings have stress on the last syllable. Thus *vaca* (cow) and *caballos* (horses) both carry stress on the next-to-last syllable, while *ciudad* (city) and *infeliz* (unhappy) are both stressed on the last syllable.

Written accents will almost always appear in words that don't follow the rules above, eg *sótano* (basement), *porción* (portion), *América*.

GENDER & PLURALS

In Spanish, nouns are either masculine or feminine, and there are rules to help determine gender (there are of course some exceptions). Feminine nouns generally end with -**a** or with the groups -**ción**, -**sión** or -**dad**. Other endings typically signify a masculine noun. Endings for adjectives also change to agree with the gender of the noun they modify (masculine/feminine -**o**/-**a**). Where both masculine and feminine forms are included in this language guide, they are separated by a slash, with the masculine form first, eg *perdido/a*.

If a noun or adjective ends in a vowel, the plural is formed by adding **s** to the end. If it ends in a consonant, the plural is formed by adding **es** to the end.

ACCOMMODATIONS

I'm looking for ...
Estoy buscando ...   e·*stoy* boos·*kan*·do ...

Where is ...?

¿Dónde hay ...?		*don*·de ai ...
a cabin/cabana		
una cabaña		oo·na ca·*ba*·nya
a camping ground		
un área para acampar		oon *a*·re·a *pa*·ra a·kam·*par*
a guesthouse		
una pensión		oo·na pen·*syon*
a hotel		
un hotel		oon o·*tel*
a lodging house		
una casa de huéspedes		oo·na *ka*·sa de wes·pe·des
a posada		
una posada		oo·na po·*sa*·da
a youth hostel		
un albergue juvenil		oon al·*ber*·ge khoo·ve·*neel*

MAKING A RESERVATION

(for phone or written requests)

To ...	*A ...*
From ...	*De ...*
Date	*Fecha*
I'd like to book ...	*Quisiera reservar ...* (see under 'Accommodations' for bed and room options)
in the name of ...	*en nombre de ...*
for the nights of ...	*para las noches del ...*
credit card ...	*tarjeta de crédito ...*
number	*número*
expiry date	*fecha de vencimiento*
Please confirm ...	*Puede confirmar ...*
availability	*la disponibilidad*
price	*el precio*

Are there any rooms available?
¿Hay habitaciones libres?
ay a·bee·ta·*syon*·es lee·bres

I'd like a ...	*Quisiera una*	kee·*sye*·ra oo·na
room.	*habitación ...*	a·bee·ta·*syon* ...
double	*doble*	*do*·ble
single	*individual*	een·dee·vee·*dwal*
twin	*con dos camas*	kon dos *ka*·mas

How much is it	*¿Cuánto cuesta*	*kwan*·to kwes·ta
per ...?	*por ...?*	por ...
night	*noche*	*no*·che
person	*persona*	per·*so*·na
week	*semana*	se·*ma*·na

full board	*pensión completa*	pen·*syon* kom·*ple*·ta

private/shared	baño privado/	ba·nyo pree·va·do/
bathroom	compartido	kom·par·tee·do
too expensive	demasiado caro	de·ma·sya·do ka·ro
cheaper	más económico	mas e·ko·no·mee·ko
discount	descuento	des·kwen·to

Does it include breakfast?
¿Incluye el desayuno? · een·kloo·ye el de·sa·yoo·no

May I see the room?
¿Puedo ver la · pwe·do ver la
habitación? · a·bee·ta·syon

I don't like it.
No me gusta. · no me goos·ta

It's fine. I'll take it.
Está bien. La tomo. · es·ta byen la to·mo

I'm leaving now.
Me voy ahora. · me voy a·o·ra

CONVERSATION & ESSENTIALS

When approaching a stranger for information you should always extend a greeting, and use only the polite form of address, especially with the police and public officials. Young people may be less likely to expect this, but it's best to stick to the polite form unless you're quite sure you won't offend by using the informal mode. The polite form is used in all cases in this guide; where options are given, the form is indicated by the abbreviations 'pol' and 'inf.'

Saying *por favor* (please) and *gracias* (thank you) are second nature to most Mexicans and a recommended tool in your travel kit.

Hi.	Hola.	o·la (inf)
Hello.	Buen día.	bwe·n dee·a
Good morning.	Buenos días.	bwe·nos dee·as
Good afternoon.	Buenas tardes.	bwe·nas tar·des
Good evening/	Buenas noches.	bwe·nas no·ches
night.		
Goodbye.	Adiós.	a·dyos
See you soon.	Hasta luego.	as·ta lwe·go
Yes.	Sí.	see
No.	No.	no
Please.	Por favor.	por fa·vor
Thank you.	Gracias.	gra·syas
Many thanks.	Muchas gracias.	moo·chas gra·syas
You're welcome.	De nada.	de na·da
Apologies.	Perdón.	per·don
May I?	Permiso.	per·mee·so
Excuse me.	Disculpe.	dees·kool·pe
(used before a request or when apologizing)		

How are things?
¿Qué tal? · ke tal

What's your name?
¿Cómo se llama usted? · ko·mo se ya·ma oo·sted (pol)
¿Cómo te llamas? · ko·mo te ya·mas (inf)

My name is ...
Me llamo ... · me ya·mo ...

It's a pleasure to meet you.
Mucho gusto. · moo·cho goos·to

The pleasure is mine.
El gusto es mío. · el goos·to es mee·o

Where are you from?
¿De dónde es/eres? · de don·de es/er·es (pol/inf)

I'm from ...
Soy de ... · soy de ...

Where are you staying?
¿Dónde está alojado? · don·de es·ta a·lo·kha·do (pol)
¿Dónde estás alojado? · don·de es·tas a·lo·kha·do (inf)

May I take a photo?
¿Puedo sacar una foto? · pwe·do sa·kar oo·na fo·to

DIRECTIONS

How do I get to ...?
¿Cómo llego a ...? · ko·mo ye·go a ...

Is it far?
¿Está lejos? · es·ta le·khos

Go straight ahead.
Siga/Vaya derecho. · see·ga/va·ya de·re·cho

Turn left.
Voltée a la izquierda. · vol·te·e a la ees·kyer·da

Turn right.
Voltée a la derecha. · vol·te·e a la de·re·cha

Can you show me (on the map)?
¿Me lo podría señalar · me lo po·dree·a se·nya·lar
(en el mapa)? · (en el ma·pa)

SIGNS

Entrada	Entrance
Salida	Exit
Información	Information
Abierto	Open
Cerrado	Closed
Prohibido	Prohibited
Comisaria	Police Station
Servicios/Baños	Toilets
Hombres/Varones	Men
Mujeres/Damas	Women

---

north	norte	nor·te
south	sur	soor
east	este	es·te
west	oeste	o·es·te
here	aquí	a·kee
there	ahí	a·ee
block	cuadra	kwa·dra

LANGUAGE

MEXICAN SLANG

Pepper your conversations with a few slang expressions! You'll hear many of these slang words and phrases all around Mexico, but others are particular to Mexico City.

¿Qué onda?
What's up?, What's happening?

¿Qué pasión? (Mexico City)
What's up?, What's going on?

¡Qué padre!
How cool!

fregón
really good at something, way cool, awesome

Este club está fregón.
This club is way cool.

El cantante es un fregón.
The singer is really awesome.

ser muy buena onda
to be really cool, nice

Mi novio es muy buena onda.
My boyfriend is really cool.

Eres muy buena onda.
You're really cool (nice).

pisto (in the north)
booze

alipús
booze

echarse un alipús, echarse un trago
to go get a drink

Echamos un alipús/trago.
Let's go have a drink.

tirar la onda
try to pick someone up, flirt

ligar
to flirt

irse de reventón
go partying

¡Vámonos de reventón!
Let's go party!

reven
a 'rave' (huge party with loud music and wild atmosphere)

un desmadre
a mess

Simón.
Yes.

Nel.
No.

No hay tos.
No problem. (literally 'there's no cough.')

¡Órale! (positive)
Sounds great! (responding to an invitation)

¡Órale! (negative)
What the *#&$!? (taunting exclamation)

¡Caray!
Shit!

¿Te cae?
Are you serious?

Me late.
Sounds really good to me.

Me vale.
I don't care, Whatever.

Sale y vale.
I agree, Sounds good.

¡Paso sin ver!
I can't stand it!, No thank you!

¡Guácatelas! ¡Guácala!
How gross! That's disgusting!

¡Bájale!
Don't exaggerate!, Come on!

¡¿Chale?! (Mexico City)
No way!

¡Te pasas!
That's it! You've gone too far!

¡No manches!
Get outta here!, You must be kidding!

un resto
a lot

lana
money, dough

carnal
brother

cuate, cuaderno
buddy

chavo
guy, dude

chava
girl, gal

jefe
father

jefa
mother

la tira, la julia
the police

la chota (Mexico City)
the police

EMERGENCIES

Help!	*¡Socorro!*	so·ko·ro
Fire!	*¡Fuego!*	fwe·go
I've been robbed.	*Me han robado.*	me an ro·ba·do
Go away!	*¡Déjeme!*	de·khe·me
Get lost!	*¡Váyase!*	va·ya·se
Call ...!	*¡Llame a ...!*	ya·me a
the police	*la policía*	la po·lee·see·a
a doctor	*un médico*	oon me·dee·ko
an ambulance	*una ambulancia*	oo·na am·boo·lan·sya

It's an emergency.
Es una emergencia.   es oo·na e·mer·khen·sya
Could you help me, please?
¿Me puede ayudar,   me pwe·de a·yoo·dar
por favor?   por fo·vor
I'm lost.
Estoy perdido/a.   es·toy per·dee·do/a
Where are the toilets?
¿Dónde están los baños?   don·de stan los ba·nyos

HEALTH

I'm sick.
Estoy enfermo/a.   es·toy en·fer·mo/a
I need a doctor.
Necesito un doctor.   ne·se·see·to oon dok·tor
Where's the hospital?
¿Dónde está el hospital?   don·de es·ta el os·pee·tal
I'm pregnant.
Estoy embarazada.   es·toy em·ba·ra·sa·da
I've been vaccinated.
Estoy vacunado/a.   es·toy va·koo·na·do/a

I have ...	*Tengo ...*	ten·go ...
diarrhea	*diarrea*	dya·re·a
nausea	*náusea*	now·se·a
a headache	*un dolor de cabeza*	oon do·lor de ka·be·sa
a cough	*tos*	tos
I'm allergic to ...	*Soy alérgico/a a ...*	soy a·ler·khee·ko/a a ...
antibiotics	*los antibióticos*	los an·tee·byo·tee·kos
nuts	*las nueces*	las nwe·ses
peanuts	*los cacahuates*	los ka·ka·khwa·tes
I'm ...	*Soy ...*	soy ...
asthmatic	*asmático/a*	as·ma·tee·ko/a
diabetic	*diabético/a*	dya·be·tee·ko/a
epileptic	*epiléptico/a*	e·pee·lep·tee·ko/a

LANGUAGE DIFFICULTIES

Do you speak (English)?
¿Habla/Hablas (inglés)? a·bla/a·blas (een·gles) (pol/inf)
Does anyone here speak English?
¿Hay alguien que hable ai al·gyen ke a·ble
inglés?   een·gles
I (don't) understand.
(No) Entiendo.   (no) en·tyen·do
How do you say ...?
¿Cómo se dice ...?   ko·mo se dee·se ...
What does ...mean?
¿Qué significa ...?   ke seeg·nee·fee·ka ...

Could you please ...?	*¿Puede ..., por favor?*	pwe·de ... por fa·vor
repeat that	*repetirlo*	re·pe·teer·lo
speak more slowly	*hablar más despacio*	a·blar mas des·pa·syo
write it down	*escríbalo*	es·kree·ba·lo

NUMBERS

1	*uno*	oo·no
2	*dos*	dos
3	*tres*	tres
4	*cuatro*	kwa·tro
5	*cinco*	seen·ko
6	*seis*	says
7	*siete*	sye·te
8	*ocho*	o·cho
9	*nueve*	nwe·ve
10	*diez*	dyes
11	*once*	on·se
12	*doce*	do·se
13	*trece*	tre·se
14	*catorce*	ka·tor·se
15	*quince*	keen·se
16	*dieciséis*	dye·see·says
17	*diecisiete*	dye·see·sye·te
18	*dieciocho*	dye·see·o·cho
19	*diecinueve*	dye·see·nwe·ve
20	*veinte*	vayn·te
21	*veintiuno*	vayn·tee·oo·no
30	*treinta*	trayn·ta
31	*treinta y uno*	trayn·ta ee oo·no
40	*cuarenta*	kwa·ren·ta
50	*cincuenta*	seen·kwen·ta
60	*sesenta*	se·sen·ta
70	*setenta*	se·ten·ta
80	*ochenta*	o·chen·ta
90	*noventa*	no·ven·ta
100	*cien*	syen
101	*ciento uno*	syen·to oo·no
200	*doscientos*	do·syen·tos
1000	*mil*	meel
5000	*cinco mil*	seen·ko meel

PAPERWORK

birth certificate	certificado de nacimiento	
border (frontier)	la frontera	
car-owner's title	título de propiedad	
car registration	registración	
customs	aduana	
driver's license	licencia de manejar	
identification	identificación	
immigration	migración	
insurance	seguro	
passport	pasaporte	
temporary vehicle import permit	permiso de importación temporal de vehículo	
tourist card	tarjeta de turista	
visa	visado	

SHOPPING & SERVICES

I'd like to buy ...
Quisiera comprar ...   kee-sye-ra kom-prar ...
I'm just looking.
Sólo estoy mirando.   so-lo es-toy mee-ran-do
May I look at it?
¿Puedo verlo/la?   pwe-do ver-lo/la
How much is it?
¿Cuánto cuesta?   kwan-to kwes-ta
That's too expensive for me.
Es demasiado caro   es de-ma-sya-do ka-ro
   para mí.   pa-ra mee
Could you lower the price?
¿Podría bajar un poco   po-dree-a ba-khar oon po-ko
   el precio?   el pre-syo
I don't like it.
No me gusta.   no me goos-ta
I'll take it.
Lo llevo.   lo ye-vo

Do you accept ...?
¿Aceptan ...?   a-sep-tan ...
   American dollars
   dólares americanos   do-la-res a-me-ree-ka-nos
   credit cards
   tarjetas de crédito   tar-khe-tas de kre-dee-to
   traveler's checks
   cheques de viajero   che-kes de vya-khe-ro

less	menos	me-nos
more	más	mas
large	grande	gran-de
small	pequeño/a	pe-ke-nyo/a

I'm looking for (the) ... Estoy buscando ... es-toy boos-kan-do
   ATM   el cajero   el ka-khe-ro
             automático   ow-to-ma-tee-ko

bank	el banco	el ban-ko
bookstore	la librería	la lee-bre-ree-a
exchange office	la casa de cambio	la ka-sa de kam-byo
general store	la tienda	la tyen-da
laundry	la lavandería	la la-van-de-ree-a
market	el mercado	el mer-ka-do
pharmacy/ chemist	la farmacia	la far-ma-sya
post office	la oficina de correos	la o-fee-see-na de ko-re-os
supermarket	el supermercado	el soo-per-mer-ka-do
tourist office	la oficina de turismo	la o-fee-see-na de too-rees-mo

What time does it open/close?
¿A qué hora abre/cierra?
a ke o-ra a-bre/sye-ra
I want to change some money/traveler's checks.
Quisiera cambiar dinero/cheques de viajero.
kee-sye-ra kam-byar dee-ne-ro/che-kes de vya-khe-ro
What is the exchange rate?
¿Cuál es el tipo de cambio?
kwal es el tee-po de kam-byo
I want to call ...
Quisiera llamar a ...
kee-sye-ra lya-mar a ...

airmail	correo aéreo	ko-re-o a-e-re-o
letter	carta	kar-ta
registered (mail)	certificado	ser-tee-fee-ka-do
stamps	timbres	teem-bres

TIME & DATES

What time is it?
¿Qué hora es?   ke o-ra es
It's one o'clock.
Es la una.   es la oo-na
It's seven o'clock.
Son las siete.   son las sye-te
Half past two.
Dos y media.   dos ee me-dya

midnight	medianoche	me-dya-no-che
noon	mediodía	me-dyo-dee-a
now	ahora	a-o-ra
today	hoy	oy
tonight	esta noche	es-ta no-che
tomorrow	mañana	ma-nya-na
yesterday	ayer	a-yer

Monday	lunes	loo-nes
Tuesday	martes	mar-tes
Wednesday	miércoles	myer-ko-les

Thursday	jueves	khwe·ves
Friday	viernes	vyer·nes
Saturday	sábado	sa·ba·do
Sunday	domingo	do·meen·go

January	enero	e·ne·ro
February	febrero	fe·bre·ro
March	marzo	mar·so
April	abril	a·breel
May	mayo	ma·yo
June	junio	khoo·nyo
July	julio	khoo·lyo
August	agosto	a·gos·to
September	septiembre	sep·tyem·bre
October	octubre	ok·too·bre
November	noviembre	no·vyem·bre
December	diciembre	dee·syem·bre

TRANSPORTATION
Public Transportation

What time does	¿A qué hora ...	a ke o·ra ...
... leave/arrive?	sale/llega?	sa·le/ye·ga
the boat	el barco	el bar·ko
the bus (city)	el camión	el ka·myon
the bus (intercity)	el autobús	el ow·to·boos
the minibus	el pesero	el pe·se·ro
the plane	el avión	el a·vyon

the airport	el aeropuerto	el a·e·ro·pwer·to
the bus station	la estación de autobuses	la es·ta·syon de ow·to·boo·ses
the bus stop	la parada de autobuses	la pa·ra·da de ow·to·boo·ses
a luggage locker	un casillero	oon ka·see·ye·ro
the ticket office	la taquilla	la ta·kee·ya

A ticket to ..., please.
Un boleto a ..., por favor.   oon bo·le·to a ... por fa·vor
What's the fare to ...?
¿Cuánto cuesta hasta ...?   kwan·to kwes·ta a·sta ...

student's	de estudiante	de es·too·dyan·te
1st class	primera clase	pree·me·ra kla·se
2nd class	segunda clase	se·goon·da kla·se
single/one-way	viaje sencillo	vee·a·khe sen·see·yo
round-trip	redondo	re·don·do
taxi	taxi	tak·see

Private Transportation

I'd like to hire a/an ...	Quisiera rentar ...	kee·sye·ra ren·tar ...
4WD	un cuatro por cuatro	oon kwa·tro por kwa·tro
car	un coche	oon ko·che
motorbike	una moto	oo·na mo·to

ROAD SIGNS
Though Mexico mostly uses the familiar international road signs, you should be prepared to encounter these other signs as well:

Acceso	Entrance
Estacionamiento	Parking
Camino en Reparación	Road Repairs
Ceda el Paso	Give Way
Conserve Su Derecha	Keep to the Right
Curva Peligrosa	Dangerous Curve
Derrumbes	Landslides
Despacio	Slow
Desviación	Detour
Dirección Única	One-Way
Escuela (Zona Escolar)	School (zone)
Hombres Trabajando	Men at Work
Mantenga Su Derecha	Keep to the Right
No Adelantar	No Overtaking
No Hay Paso	Road Closed
Pare/Stop	Stop
Peaje	Toll
Peligro	Danger
Prepare Su Cuota	Have Toll Ready
Prohibido Aparcar/ No Estacionar	No Parking
Prohibido el Paso	No Entry
Puente Angosto	Narrow Bridge
Salida de Autopista	Freeway/Highway Exit
Topes/Vibradores	Speed Bumps
Tramo en Reparación	Road Under Repair
Vía Corta	Short Route (often a toll road)
Vía Cuota	Toll Highway

bicycle	bicicleta	bee·see·kle·ta
hitchhike	pedir aventón	pe·deer a·ven·ton
pickup (ute)	pickup	pee·kop
truck	camión	ka·myon

Where's a gas/petrol station?
¿Dónde hay una gasolinera?   don·de ai oo·na ga·so·lee·ne·ra
How much is a liter of gasoline/petrol?
¿Cuánto cuesta el litro de gasolina?   kwan·to kwes·ta el lee·tro de ga·so·lee·na
Please fill it up.
Lleno, por favor.   ye·no por fa·vor
I'd like (100) pesos worth.
Quiero (cien) pesos.   kye·ro (syen) pe·sos

diesel	diesel	dee·sel
gas/petrol	gasolina	ga·so·lee·na
unleaded	gasolina sin plomo	ga·so·lee·na seen plo·mo

oil   *aceite*   a·*say*·te
tire   *llanta*   *yan*·ta
puncture   *agujero*   a·goo·*khe*·ro

Is this the road to (...)?
¿Por aquí se va a (...)?
por a·*kee* se va a (...)

(How long) Can I park here?
¿(Por cuánto tiempo) Puedo estacionarme aquí?
(por *kwan*·to *tyem*·po) *pwe*·do ess·ta·syo·*nar*·me a·*kee*

Where do I pay?
¿Dónde se paga?
don·de se *pa*·ga

I need a mechanic/tow truck.
Necesito un mecánico/remolque.
ne·se·*see*·to oon me·*ka*·nee·ko/re·*mol*·ke

Is there a garage near here?
¿Hay un garaje cerca de aquí?
ai oon ga·*ra*·khe ser·ka de a·*kee*

The car has broken down (in ...).
El coche se se descompuso (en ...).
el *ko*·che se des·kom·*poo*·so (en ...)

The motorbike won't start.
La moto no arranca.
la *mo*·to no a·*ran*·ka

I have a flat tire.
Tengo una llanta ponchada.
ten·go *oo*·na *yan*·ta pon·*cha*·da

I've run out of gas/petrol.
Me quedé sin gasolina.
me ke·*de* seen ga·so·*lee*·na

I've had an accident.
Tuve un accidente.
too·ve oon ak·see·*den*·te

TRAVEL WITH CHILDREN

I need ...
Necesito ...
ne·se·*see*·to ...

Do you have ...?
¿Hay ...?
ai ...

  a car baby seat
  un asiento de seguridad para bebés
  oon a·*syen*·to de se·goo·ree·*dad* pa·ra be·*bes*

  a child-minding service
  un club para niños
  oon kloob pa·*ra* nee·nyos

  a children's menu
  un menú infantil
  oon me·*noo* een·fan·*teel*

  a daycare
  una guardería
  oo·na gwar·de·*ree*·a

  (disposable) diapers/nappies
  pañales (de usar y tirar)
  pa·*nya*·les (de oo·*sar* ee tee·*rar*)

  an (English-speaking) babysitter
  una niñera (que habla inglés)
  oo·na nee·*nye*·ra (ke *a*·bla een·*gles*)

  formula (milk)
  leche en polvo
  le·che en *pol*·vo

  a highchair
  una silla para bebé
  oo·na *see*·ya *pa*·ra be·*be*

  a potty
  una bacinica
  oo·na ba·see·*nee*·ka

  a stroller
  una carreola
  oona ka·re·*o*·la

Do you mind if I breast-feed here?
¿Le molesta que dé el pecho aquí?
le mo·*les*·ta ke de el *pe*·cho a·*kee*

Are children allowed?
¿Se admiten niños?
se ad·*mee*·ten *nee*·nyos

Also available from Lonely Planet:
Mexican Spanish Phrasebook

Glossary

For more food and drink terms, also see the Food & Drink Glossary (p100); for transportation terms, see the Transportation chapter (p983); for general terms, see the Language chapter (p1007).

AC – *antes de Cristo* (before Christ); equivalent to BC

adobe – sun-dried mud brick used for building

aduana – customs

agave – family of plants including the *maguey*

Alameda – name of formal parks in several Mexican cities

albergue de juventud – youth hostel

alebrije – colorful wooden animal figure

alfarería – potters' workshop

alfiz – rectangular frame around a curved arch; an Arabic influence on Spanish and Mexican buildings

Altiplano Central – dry plateau stretching across north central Mexico between the two Sierra Madre ranges

amate – paper made from tree bark

Ángeles Verdes – Green Angels; government-funded mechanics who patrol Mexico's major highways in green vehicles; they help stranded motorists with fuel and spare parts

antro – bar with (often loud) recorded music and usually some space to dance

Apdo – abbreviation for apartado (Box) in addresses; hence Apdo Postal means Post Office Box

arroyo – brook, stream

artesanías – handicrafts, folk arts

atlas, atlantes (pl) – sculpted male figure(s) used instead of a pillar to support a roof or frieze; a *telamon*

atrium – churchyard, usually a big one

autopista – expressway, dual carriageway

azulejo – painted ceramic tile

bahía – bay

balneario – bathing place, often a natural hot spring

baluarte – bulwark, defensive wall

barrio – neighborhood of a town or city, often a poor neighborhood

billete – banknote

boleto – ticket

brujo/a – witch doctor, shaman; similar to *curandero/a*

burro – donkey

caballeros – literally 'horsemen,' but corresponds to 'gentlemen' in English; look for it on toilet doors

cabaña – cabin, simple shelter

cabina – Baja Californian term for a *caseta*

cacique – regional warlord; political strongman

calle – street

callejón – alley

callejoneada – originally a Spanish tradition, still enjoyed in such cities as Guanajuato and Zacatecas; musicians lead a crowd of revelers through the streets, singing and telling stories as they go

calzada – grand boulevard or avenue

calzones – long baggy shorts worn by indigenous men

camarín – chapel beside the main altar in a church; contains ceremonial clothing for images of saints or the Virgin

camión – truck or bus

camioneta – pickup truck

campesino/a – country person, peasant

capilla abierta – open chapel, used in early Mexican monasteries for preaching to large crowds of indigenous people

casa de cambio – exchange house; place where currency is exchanged; faster to use than a bank

casa de huéspedes – cheap and congenial accommodations, often a home converted into simple guest lodgings

caseta de larga distancia, caseta de teléfono, caseta telefónica – public telephone call station

cazuela – clay cooking pot; usually sold in a nested set

cenote – a limestone sinkhole filled with rainwater; often used in Yucatán as a reservoir

central camionera – bus terminal

cerro – hill

Chac – Maya rain god

chac-mool – pre-Hispanic stone sculpture of a hunched-up figure; the stomach may have been used as a sacrificial altar

charreada – Mexican rodeo

charro – Mexican cowboy

chenes – wells (Yucatán Peninsula)

Chilango/a – person from Mexico City

chinampa – Aztec garden built from lake mud and vegetation; versions still exist at Xochimilco, Mexico City

chingar – literally 'to fuck'; it has a wide range of colloquial usages in Mexican Spanish equivalent to those in English

chultún – cement-lined brick cistern found in the *chenes* region in the Puuc hills south of Mérida

Churrigueresque – Spanish late-baroque architectural style; found on many Mexican churches

cigarro – cigarette

clavadistas – cliff divers of Acapulco and Mazatlán

Coatlicue – mother of the Aztec gods

colectivo – minibus or car that picks up and drops off passengers along a predetermined route; can also refer to other types of transportation, such as boats, where passengers share the total fare

coleto/a – citizen of San Cristóbal de Las Casas

colonia – neighborhood of a city, often a wealthy residential area

combi – minibus

comida corrida – set lunch

completo – literally 'full up'; no vacancy; a sign you may see at hotel desks

conde – count (nobleman)

conquistador – early Spanish explorer–conqueror

cordillera – mountain range

correos – post office

coyote – person who smuggles Mexican immigrants into the US

criollo – Mexican-born person of Spanish parentage; in colonial times considered inferior by *peninsulares*

Cristeros – Roman Catholic rebels of the late 1920s

cuota – toll; a *vía cuota* is a toll road

curandero/a – literally 'curer'; a medicine man or woman who uses herbal and/or magical methods and often emphasizes spiritual aspects of disease

damas – ladies; the sign on toilet doors

danzantes – literally 'dancers'; stone carvings at Monte Albán

DC – *después de Cristo* (after Christ); equivalent to AD

degustación – tasting session, especially of wine

de lujo – deluxe; often used with some license

de paso – a bus that began its route somewhere else, but stops to let passengers on or off at various points – often arriving late; a *local* bus is preferable

delegación – a large urban governmental subdivision in Mexico City comprising numerous *colonias*

descompuesto – broken, out of order

DF – Distrito Federal (Federal District); about half of Mexico City lies in the DF

dueño/a – owner

dulcería – candy store

edificio – building

ejido – communal landholding

embarcadero – jetty, boat landing

encomienda – a grant of indigenous labor or tribute to a *conquistador*; in return, the *conquistador* was supposed to protect the indigenous people in question and convert them to Catholicism, but in reality they were usually treated as little more than slaves

enramada – bower or shelter; often refers to a thatch-covered, open-air restaurant

enredo – wraparound skirt

entremeses – hors d'oeuvres; also theatrical sketches like those performed during the Cervantino festival in Guanajuato

escuela – school

esq – abbreviation of *esquina* (corner) in addresses

estación de ferrocarril – train station

estípite – long, narrow, pyramid-shaped, upside-down pilaster; the hallmark of Churrigueresque architecture

ex-convento – former convent or monastery

ex-voto – small painting on wood, tin, cardboard, glass etc; placed in a church to give thanks for miracles, answered prayers etc (see also *retablo*)

excusado – toilet

faja – waist sash used in traditional indigenous costume

feria – fair or carnival, typically occurring during a religious holiday

ferrocarril – railway

ficha – a token or counter; you often need one to operate lockers at bus terminals

fiesta mexicana – touristic show of Mexican folkloristic dance and music, often with dinner and drinks included

fonda – inn

fraccionamiento – subdivision, housing development; similar to a *colonia*, often modern

frontera – a border between political entities

gachupines – derogatory term for the colonial *peninsulares*

giro – money order

gringo/a – US or Canadian (and sometimes European, Australasian etc) visitor to Latin America; can be used derogatorily

grito – literally 'shout'; the Grito de Dolores was the 1810 call to independence by parish priest Miguel Hidalgo, which sparked the struggle for independence from Spain

gruta – cave, grotto

guarache – see *huarache*

guardería de equipaje – room for storing luggage (eg in a bus station)

guayabera – also *guayabarra;* man's shirt with pockets and appliquéd designs up the front, over the shoulders and down the back; worn in place of a jacket and tie in hot regions

güero/a – fair-haired, fair-complexioned person; a more polite alternative to *gringo/a*

hacendado – *hacienda* owner

hacha – flat, carved-stone object from the Classic Vera-cruz civilization; connected with the ritual ball game

hacienda – estate; Hacienda (capitalized) is the Treasury Department

hay – there is, there are; you're also likely to hear *no hay* (there is not, there are not)

henequén – *agave* fiber used to make sisal rope; grown particularly around Mérida

hombres – men; sign on toilet doors

hostal – can mean either a small hotel or a budget hostel

huarache – also *guarache;* woven leather sandal, often with tire tread as the sole

huevos – eggs; also slang for testicles

huipil, huipiles (pl) – indigenous woman's sleeveless tunic, usually highly decorated; can be thigh-length or reach the ankles

Huizilopochtli – Aztec tribal god

iglesia – church

INAH – Instituto Nacional de Antropología e Historia; the body in charge of most ancient sites and some museums

indígena – indigenous, pertaining to the original inhabitants of Latin America; can also refer to the people themselves

INI – Instituto Nacional Indígenista; set up in 1948 to improve the lot of indigenous Mexicans and to integrate them into society; sometimes accused of paternalism and trying to stifle protest

intercambio – interchange; often used to describe meetings with local people for Spanish and English conversation

internet inalámbrico – wireless internet (wi-fi)

ISH – *impuesto sobre hospedaje;* lodging tax on the price of hotel rooms

isla – island

IVA – *impuesto de valor agregado,* or 'ee-bah'; a sales tax added to the price of many items (15% on hotel rooms)

ixtle – *maguey* fiber

jaguar – panther native to southern Mexico and Central and South America; principal symbol of the Olmec civilization

jai alai – the Basque game *pelota,* brought to Mexico by the Spanish; a bit like squash, played on a long court with curved baskets attached to the arm

jardín – garden

jarocho/a – citizen of Veracruz

jefe – boss or leader, especially a political one

jipijapa – Yucatán name for a Panama hat

jorongo – small poncho worn by men

Kukulcán – Maya name for the plumed serpent god *Quetzalcóatl*

lada – short for *larga distancia*

ladino – person of mixed (usually indigenous and Spanish) ancestry

lancha – fast, open, outboard boat

larga distancia – long-distance; usually refers to telephones

latifundio – large landholding; these sprang up after Mexico's independence from Spain

latifundista – powerful landowner who usurped communally owned land to form a *latifundio*

libramiento – road, highway

licenciado – university graduate; abbreviated as Lic and used as an honorific before a person's name; status claimed by many who don't actually possess a degree

lista de correos – literally 'mail list'; list displayed at a post office of people for whom letters are waiting; similar to General Delivery or Poste Restante

lleno full, as with a car's fuel tank

local – can mean premises, such as a numbered shop or an office in a mall or block; or can mean local – a *local* bus is one whose route starts from the bus station you are in

locutorio – same as a *caseta telefónica*

machismo – Mexican masculine bravura

madre – literally 'mother'; the term can also be used colloquially with an astonishing array of meanings

maguey – type of *agave,* with thick pointed leaves growing straight out of the ground; *tequila* and *mezcal* are made from its sap

malecón – waterfront street, boulevard or promenade

mañana – literally 'tomorrow' or 'morning'; in some contexts it may just mean 'sometime in the future'

maquiladora – assembly-plant operation importing equipment, raw materials and parts for assembly or processing in Mexico, then exporting the products

mariachi – small ensemble of street musicians playing traditional ballads on guitars and trumpets

marimba – wooden xylophone-like instrument popular in southeastern Mexico

Mayab – the lands of the Maya

mercado – market; often a building near the center of a town, with shops and open-air stalls in the surrounding streets

Mesoamerica – the region inhabited by the ancient Mexican and Maya cultures

mestizaje – 'mixedness,' Mexico's mixed-blood heritage; officially an object of pride

mestizo – person of mixed (usually indigenous and Spanish) ancestry

metate – shallow stone bowl with legs used for grinding maize and other foods

Mexican Hat Dance – a courtship dance in which a girl and boy dance around the boy's hat

Mexican Revolution – 1910 revolution that ended the *Porfiriato*

milpa – peasant's small cornfield, often cultivated using the slash-and-burn method

mirador, miradores (pl) – lookout point(s)

Montezuma's revenge – Mexican version of Delhi-belly or travelers' diarrhea

mordida – literally 'little bite'; a small bribe to keep the wheels of bureaucracy turning

mota – marijuana

Mudéjar – Moorish architectural style imported to Mexico by the Spanish

mujeres – women; seen on toilet doors

municipio – small local government area; Mexico is divided into 2394 of them

na – Maya thatched hut

Nafta – North American Free Trade Agreement

Náhuatl – language of the Nahua people, descendants of the Aztecs

nao – Spanish trading galleon

norteamericano – North American, someone from north of the US–Mexican border

Nte – abbreviation for *norte* (north), used in street names

Ote – abbreviation for *oriente* (east), used in street names

paceño/a – person from La Paz, Baja California Sur

palacio de gobierno – state capitol, state government headquarters

palacio municipal – town or city hall, headquarters of the municipal corporation

palapa – thatched-roof shelter, usually on a beach

palma – long, paddle-like, carved-stone object from the Classic Veracruz civilization; connected with the ritual ball game

PAN – Partido Acción Nacional (National Action Party); the political party of president Felipe Calderón and his predecessor Vicente Fox

panga – fiberglass skiff for fishing or whale-watching in Baja California

parada – bus stop, usually for city buses

parado – stationary, or standing up, as you often are on 2nd-class buses

parque nacional – national park; an environmentally protected area in which human exploitation is supposed to banned or restricted

parroquia – parish church

paseo – boulevard, walkway or pedestrian street; the tradition of strolling in a circle around the plaza in the evening, men and women moving in opposite directions

Pemex – government-owned petroleum extraction, refining and retailing monopoly

peña – evening of Latin American folk songs, often with a political protest theme

peninsulares – those born in Spain and sent by the Spanish government to rule the colony in Mexico

periférico – ring road

pesero – Mexico City's word for *colectivo;* can mean bus in the northeast

petate – mat, usually made of palm or reed

peyote – a hallucinogenic cactus

pinacoteca – art gallery

piñata – clay pot or papier-mâché mold decorated to resemble an animal, pineapple, star etc filled with sweets and gifts; smashed open at fiestas

pirata – pirate; used to describe passenger-carrying pickup trucks in some parts of Mexico

playa – beach

plaza de toros – bullring

plazuela – small plaza

poblano/a – person from Puebla; something in the style of Puebla

pollero – same as a *coyote*

Porfiriato – reign of Porfirio Díaz as president–dictator of Mexico for 30 years until the Mexican Revolution

portales – arcades

posada – inn

potosino – from the city or state of San Luis Potosí

presidio – fort or fort's garrison

PRI – Partido Revolucionario Institucional (Institutional Revolutionary Party); the political party that ruled Mexico for most of the 20th century

primera – first class

propina – tip; different from a *mordida,* which is closer to a bribe

Pte – abbreviation for *poniente* (west), used in street names

puerto – port

pulque – milky, low-alcohol brew made from the *maguey* plant

quechquémitl – indigenous woman's shoulder cape with an opening for the head; usually colorfully embroidered, often diamond-shaped

quetzal – crested bird with brilliant green, red and white plumage native to southern Mexico, Central America and northern South America; quetzal feathers were highly prized in pre-Hispanic Mexico

Quetzalcóatl – plumed serpent god of pre-Hispanic Mexico

rebozo – long woolen or linen shawl covering the head or shoulders

refugio – a very basic cabin for shelter in the mountains

regiomontano/a – person from Monterrey

reja – wrought-iron window grille

reserva de la biosfera – biosphere reserve; an environmentally protected area where human exploitation is steered toward sustainable activities

retablo – altarpiece; small *ex-voto* painting placed in a church to give thanks for miracles, answered prayers etc

río – river

s/n – *sin número* (without number) used in street addresses

sacbé, sacbeob (pl) – ceremonial avenue(s) between great Maya cities

salvavida – lifeguard

sanatorio – hospital, particularly a small private one

sanitario – literally 'sanitary place'; toilet

sarape – blanket with opening for the head, worn as a cloak

Semana Santa – Holy Week; the week from Palm Sunday to Easter Sunday; Mexico's major holiday period when accommodations and transportation get very busy

servicios – toilets

sierra – mountain range

sitio – taxi stand

stela/stele, stelae/steles (pl) – standing stone monument, usually carved

supermercado – supermarket; anything from a small corner store to a large, US-style supermarket

Sur – south; often seen in street names

taller – shop or workshop; a *taller mecánico* is a mechanic's shop, usually for cars; a *taller de llantas* is a tire-repair shop

talud-tablero – stepped building style typical of Teotihuacán, with alternating vertical *(tablero)* and sloping *(talud)* sections

tapatío/a – person born in the state of Jalisco

taquilla – ticket window

telamon – statue of a male figure, used instead of a pillar to hold up the roof of a temple; an *atlas*

telar de cintura – backstrap loom; the warp (lengthwise) threads are stretched between two horizontal bars, one of which is attached to a post or tree and the other to a strap around the weaver's lower back, and the weft (crosswise) threads are then woven in

teleférico – cable car

teléfono (celular) – (cell/mobile) telephone

temascal – pre-Hispanic–style steam bath, often used for curative purposes; sometimes spelt *temazcal*

templo – church; anything from a chapel to a cathedral

teocalli – Aztec sacred precinct

Tezcatlipoca – multifaceted pre-Hispanic god; lord of life and death and protector of warriors; as a smoking mirror he could see into hearts, as the sun god he needed the blood of sacrificed warriors to ensure he would rise again

tezontle – light red, porous volcanic rock used for buildings by the Aztecs and *conquistadores*

tianguis – indigenous people's market

tienda – store

típico/a – characteristic of a region; particularly used to describe food

Tláloc – pre-Hispanic rain and water god

TLC – Tratado de Libre Comercio; the North American Free Trade Agreement (Nafta)

tope – speed bump; found on the outskirts of many towns and villages, they are only sometimes marked by signs

trapiche – mill; in Baja California usually a sugar mill

tzompantli – rack for the skulls of Aztec sacrificial victims

UNAM – Universidad Nacional Autónoma de México (National Autonomous University of Mexico)

universidad – university

viajero/a – traveler

villa juvenil – youth sports center, often the location of an *albergue de juventud*

voladores – literally 'fliers'; Totonac ritual in which men, suspended by their ankles, whirl around a tall pole

War of Independence – war for Mexican independence from Spain that lasted from 1810 to 1821 and ended three centuries of Spanish rule

War of the Castes – bloody, 19th-century Maya uprising in the Yucatán Peninsula

were-jaguar – half-human, half-jaguar being portrayed in Olmec art

yácata – ceremonial stone structure of the Tarascan civilization

yugo – U-shaped, carved-stone object from the Classic Veracruz civilization; connected with the ritual ball game

zaguán – vestibule or foyer; sometimes a porch

zócalo – literally 'plinth'; used in some Mexican towns to mean the main plaza or square

Zona Rosa – literally 'Pink Zone'; a formerly glitzy, expensive area of shops, hotels, restaurants and entertainment in Mexico City; by extension, a similar glitzy area in another city

The Authors

JOHN NOBLE
Coordinating Author, History, The Culture, The Arts, Environment, Oaxaca State, Directoy, Transportation

John has felt Mexico's pull since reading the story of Cortés and the Aztecs as a teenager in his native England. He first backpacked from Ciudad Juárez to Ciudad Cuauhtémoc, and he has been returning for extended visits ever since. An author on nine editions of this guide (seven as coordinating author), he has explored almost every part of the country. He loves Mexico's art, archaeology, history, music, languages, traditions, food, drinks, beaches, wildlife and stunningly varied landscapes, but most of all its charming people. John now lives in Spain, which provides yet another angle on what makes Mexico tick.

My Favorite Trip

I'll start with a few days in Mexico City (p120) to find out what's making the country tick this year. Then I'll head north to fascinating, beautiful colonial cities Querétaro (p643), Guanajuato (p613), San Miguel de Allende (p630) and the best of the lot, Zacatecas (p585). I'll continue north for a trip on the Copper Canyon Railway (p341) and a bit of hiking in the fantastic Barranca del Cobre (p341). Then, to follow north with south, back to Mexico City and on to gorgeous Oaxaca (p713). A few days there enjoying the artsy scene, the great food, the crafts villages and some hiking in the Sierra Norte (p747) – then it's time for Oaxaca's fabulous Pacific coast. Impossible to decide between Puerto Escondido (p752) and San Agustinillo (p772) so I'll have to go for a week in each (at least).

KATE ARMSTRONG
Northern Central Highlands

An Australian by birth but a Latina (she believes) in a former life, Kate has craved a return to Mexico since her most recent trip several years ago. She thought she'd struck gold when asked to cover the silver cities for this edition. She hiked in the Sierra Gorda, performed as a mojiganga, consumed kilos of quesadillas, and talked and danced her way through the magic of Mexico. At other times, she is a freelance writer, based (occasionally) in Australia. A Spanish speaker, she has contributed to *Bolivia* and *South America on a Shoestring* among other Lonely Planet titles.

LONELY PLANET AUTHORS

Why is our travel information the best in the world? It's simple: our authors are independent, dedicated travellers. They don't research using just the internet or phone, and they don't take freebies, so you can rely on their advice being well researched and impartial. They travel widely, to all the popular spots and off the beaten track. They personally visit thousands of hotels, restaurants, cafés, bars, galleries, palaces, museums and more – and they take pride in getting all the details right, and telling it how it is. Think you can do it? Find out how at lonelyplanet.com.

RAY BARTLETT
Baja California

Ray began travel writing at age 18 by jumping a freight train for 500 miles and selling the story to a local newspaper. Two decades later he is still wandering the world with pen and camera in hand. He has been published in *USA Today*, the *Denver Post*, *Miami Herald* and other newspapers and magazines, and recently appeared on PRI's *The World*. His Lonely Planet titles include *Japan*, *Mexico*, *Yucatán* and *Korea*. More about him can be found at his website, www.kaisora.com. When not traveling, he surfs, writes fiction, drinks way too much coffee and burns way too much midnight oil.

GREG BENCHWICK
Yucatán Peninsula

A former commissioning editor at Lonely Planet, Greg turned down a life of high-walled cubicle insanity to get back to his writing and rambling roots. He's rumbled in the jungles of Peru and Costa Rica, walked across Spain on the Camino de Santiago and challenged the peaks of Alaska and his native Colorado. He specializes in Latin American travel, sustainable travel and new media, and has written more than a dozen guidebooks on travel in Latin America. When he's not on the road, he develops his new-media companies www.monjomedia.com and www.soundtraveler.com. Some day he dreams of being a media magnate or a philosopher warrior poet – whichever comes first.

TIM BEWER
Central North Mexico, Northeast Mexico

While growing up, Tim didn't travel much except for the obligatory pilgrimage to Disney World and an annual summer week at the lake. He's spent most of his adult life making up for this, and has since visited over 50 countries, including many in Latin America. Most of his journeys into Mexico have been in the north, and he is genuinely perplexed at why the region is so often overlooked by travelers. He currently lives in Khon Kaen, Thailand.

BETH KOHN
Tabasco & Chiapas

Someday, Beth is going to make her San Francisco neighbors revolt. Why must she blast those *ranchera* and *norteño* songs while cooking dinner? And is it really necessary for her to sing along? But after spending time in Mexico for more than 20 years, she has a fine appreciation for green jungles with sopping waterfalls and noisy animals, as well as all the soulful songs the combi drivers play. A freelance writer and photographer, she last went south to check in on the world's tallest falls for Lonely Planet's *Venezuela*. You can see more of her work at *www.bethkohn.com*.

THE AUTHORS

TOM MASTERS
Around Mexico City

Tom is a travel writer, journalist and documentary producer based in London. His first experience of Mexico was in the jungles of Chiapas on a two-week filming stint in Palenque. For this edition of *Mexico*, Tom covered the wonderful towns around Mexico City, particularly falling for Malinalco, Valle de Bravo and José Cuervo Black Medallion. You can read more of Tom's work at www.mastersmafia.com.

KEVIN RAUB
Northwest Mexico

Kevin Raub grew up in Atlanta and started his career as a music journalist in New York City, working for *Rolling Stone*. He has traveled extensively throughout Mexico, despite having stared down the barrel of a Federales' automatic weapon on one of his first trips through Northern Baja a few years back. He has previously co-authored Lonely Planet's *Brazil*. He currently lives in Los Angeles and Brazil and travels the world with one goal in mind: membership in the Travelers' Century Club before the age of 40. His country count stands at 56.

MICHAEL READ
Central Pacific Coast

Having never made good on his threat to set up housekeeping south of the border, Michael takes every opportunity to head south from his Oakland, California, home to delve deeper into Mexico's marvelous mysteries. Having done hard time pushing pixels around for LonelyPlanet.com, in 2003 Michael succumbed to a burning case of wanderlust and hit the road as a full-time travel writer. Since then he's contributed nearly half a million words to Lonely Planet guidebooks, including three editions of Mexico and Puerto Vallarta & Pacific Mexico.

JOSEPHINE QUINTERO
Mexico City

Josephine was married for many years to a Mexican–American with a large extended family, leading to a healthy exposure to mariachi music and margaritas. She made frequent trips to Mexico, visiting various Quintero relatives in DF, and continues to be enthralled by the heady mix of vibrant culture, wonderful people, fabulous food and all that history. She currently lives in Andalucía, Spain.

DANIEL C SCHECHTER
Mexico City

Definitely swimming against the tide, native New Yorker Daniel migrated *al otro lado* southward in 1994 to take a peso-salaried teaching post at a university in Mexico City. Shortly afterward, Mexico experienced its worst peso devaluation in decades. Rather than cut and run, Daniel found an even less lucrative job as an editor at Mexico's English-language daily newspaper, launching a midlife career as a writer and translator. After more than a decade in Mexico, Daniel and his wife Myra are back in the US, though the border is a reassuringly quick drive from their adopted city of Austin, Texas.

ADAM SKOLNICK
Western Central Highlands

Adam was diagnosed with travel obsession while working as an environmental activist in the mid-1990s. He has traveled to nearly 40 countries (Indonesia's his favorite) on six continents. He's been lost in the Amazon, scaled Kilimanjaro, backpacked through Mexico and Central America, toured baseball stadiums in Cuba, meditated with Hindu priests in Bali and Buddhist monks in Burma, and hiked through rainforest with devout Muslim farmers in Sumatra. A freelance journalist, he writes about travel, culture, health and the environment for several major American magazines. Between adventures he writes movies. Check out his travel blog at http://blog.myspace.com/adamskolnick.

CÉSAR G SORIANO
Central Pacific Coast

A Mexican–American born to a Guadalajaran father and Chihuahuan mother, César first caught the travel bug at age nine, when his family packed up the minivan for the two-day drive to Disney World. He pursued military and journalism careers, where he got more travel than he ever bargained for. A US Army veteran, he spent six cold months in Bosnia. More recently, César has regularly covered the wars in Afghanistan and Iraq for *USA Today*. He's visited 50 countries and counting, but returns to Mexico as often as possible to fill up on *mole poblano*. César and wife Marsha live in London where – despite what some believe – there is no real Mexican food.

ELLEE THALHEIMER
Central Gulf Coast

Her love of Latin America began during a high school language program in the Dominican Republic where she learned the virtues of trading in baggy corduroy pants and hoodies for tight jeans and big earrings. Since then her fascination with Latin America has deepened and brought her to Costa Rica, Mexico, Belize and Guatemala. Furthermore, she has explored Cuba, Argentina and Chile on her bike, her favorite way to travel. For Ellee, salsa dancing by night and riding by day constitutes the perfect marriage. Hence it pleased her to see that the gracious, sensuous, gorgeous central Gulf coast could uphold this holy matrimony. Ellee calls Portland, Oregon, her home.

CONTRIBUTING AUTHORS

David Goldberg, MD (Health) completed his training in internal medicine and infectious diseases at Columbia-Presbyterian Medical Center in New York City, where he has also served as voluntary faculty. At present, he is an infectious diseases specialist in Scarsdale, New York, and the editor-in-chief of the website MDTravelHealth.com.

Mauricio Velázquez de León (Food & Drink, Regional Cuisines of Mexico) was born in Mexico City, where he was given boiled chicken feet and toasted corn tortillas to sooth his teething pains. Mauricio has worked for a variety of newspapers and magazines, and his food writing has been widely published. He currently works in New York City as an editor, writer and father of twin toddlers, whose teething pains were soothed with toasted corn tortillas.

Behind the Scenes

THIS BOOK

The 11th edition of *Mexico* was coordinated by John Noble, as were the last seven editions. Kate Armstrong, Ray Bartlett, Greg Benchwick, Tim Bewer, Beth Kohn, Tom Masters, Josephine Quintero, Kevin Raub, Michael Read, Daniel Schechter, Adam Skolnick, César Soriano and Ellee Thalheimer were contributing authors. Mauricio Velázquez de León wrote the Food & Drink chapter and the special color section on regional foods. The Health chapter was adapted from text by Dr David Goldberg. Past authors include Sandra Bao, Beth Greenfield, Ben Greensfelder, Andrew Dean Nystrom, Suzanne Plank, Iain Stewart and Alan Tarbell, as well as a few of the current edition's contributors. This guidebook was commissioned in Lonely Planet's Oakland office, and produced by the following:

Commisioning Editor Catherine Craddock-Carrillo
Coordinating Editor Daniel Corbett
Coordinating Cartographer Csanad Csutoros
Coordinating Layout Designer Carlos Solarte
Managing Editor Bruce Evans
Managing Cartographers Mark Griffiths, Alison Lyall
Assisting Editors David Andrew, Cathryn Game, Charlotte Harrison, Kate James, Sally O'Brien, Diana Saad
Assisting Cartographers Alissa Baker, Fatima Basic, Mick Garrett, Malisa Plesa, Andy Rojas, Lyndell Stringer

Assisting Layout Designers Paul Iacono, Indra Kilfoylc, Wibowo Rusli
Cover Designer Pepi Bluck
Project Manager Fabrice Rocher
Language Content Coordinator Quentin Frayne

Thanks to Anita Banh, Owen Eszeki, Pablo Gastar, James Hardy, Aomi Hongo, Laura Jane, Margie Jung, Lisa Knights, Katherine Marsh, Wayne Murphy, Trent Paton, Amanda Sierp, Cara Smith

THANKS
JOHN NOBLE

As always, so many people in Mexico were more than generous with their welcome and their time. Extra special thanks to Ron Mader, Francisco Verástegui, Jorge Velasco and all at Las Golondrinas, Donna Radtke, Mary Jane Gagnier, Gina Machorro, Paul Cleaver, Fausto Jasso, Julien Pardinilla, Mateo Ruiz, Ben Greensfelder, Inés at Puerto Escondido, and Gundi in Puerto Ángel. Also to Cat Craddock-Carrillo and the great author, editing, cartographic and production teams for propelling this book to new heights

KATE ARMSTRONG

So many enthusiastic people have helped me with this update. First and foremost thank you to Giz,

BEHIND THE SCENES

THE LONELY PLANET STORY

Fresh from an epic journey across Europe, Asia and Australia in 1972, Tony and Maureen Wheeler sat at their kitchen table stapling together notes. The first Lonely Planet guidebook, *Across Asia on the Cheap*, was born.

Travelers snapped up the guides. Inspired by their success, the Wheelers began publishing books to Southeast Asia, India and beyond. Demand was prodigious, and the Wheelers expanded the business rapidly to keep up. Over the years, Lonely Planet extended its coverage to every country and into the virtual world via lonelyplanet.com and the Thorn Tree message board.

As Lonely Planet became a globally loved brand, Tony and Maureen received several offers for the company. But it wasn't until 2007 that they found a partner whom they trusted to remain true to the company's principles of traveling widely, treading lightly and giving sustainably. In October of that year, BBC Worldwide acquired a 75% share in the company, pledging to uphold Lonely Planet's commitment to independent travel, trustworthy advice and editorial independence.

Today, Lonely Planet has offices in Melbourne, London and Oakland, with over 500 staff members and 300 authors. Tony and Maureen are still actively involved with Lonely Planet. They're travelling more often than ever, and they're devoting their spare time to charitable projects. And the company is still driven by the philosophy of *Across Asia on the Cheap*: 'All you've got to do is decide to go and the hardest part is over. So go!'

for accompanying me some of the way. *Muchas gracias* to Catherine Craddock-Carrillo and John Noble for their support and efforts, and the *Mexico* team, plus the hoards involved in the production. In Jalpan, a special *gracias* to Dario (guide), Olga (tourist office) and Ben and Buffy Lenth, plus the policeman (cum taxi driver) who assured me a safe and punctual passage; in Bernal, thanks to Ricardo Ramírez for his generous help; in Queretaro, Shelley for her wonderful hospitality, Donna and Tom for their enthusiasm, Thomas Wheaton, and Jonaton and staff at the tourist office; in SLP, three cheers to Lori; in Zacatecas, Ernesto, thanks for everything and more, Rafael Flores Mendoza, *gracias* for opening up the region to me, Manuel the driver extraordinaire, Barry and Barbara for sharing a fun day, and Jimmie in Jerez; in Tequis, José Romero; in Guanajuato, Gerard and Enza, and Carol from Texas for her inspiration; in San Miguel de Allende, many thanks to Suzanne Ludekens, ed and friend extraordinaire, and Gayle St John.

RAY BARTLETT
I was so lucky this time to have friends and family visit me this trip – thanks for putting up with my long hours on the road in what was supposed to be your vacation. Thanks to Cat, John and my fellow authors for being such a great team. I wish I could thank all the people who I met along the way, people who shaped this book and shared their beautiful country with me, but there are just too many. Most of all, a heart-felt thank you to the kind, good-hearted, generous people of Mexico – may you treat each traveler on your precious land the same way you've treated me.

GREG BENCHWICK
My unending love and appreciation goes to my lovely, intelligent and spirited girlfriend, Alejandra Castañeda. Not only was she a great support and travel companion through much of this book's research, she also played a huge role in looking up obscure statistics, correcting my 'gringo-fied' Spanish and keeping things on an even keel. Of course, I'd also like to thank my family – Mom, Dad, George, Cara and Bryan – for all their support over these years. The people of the Yucatán Peninsula are amazing, and I wish to thank each and every person I met along my way. And I especially want to thank Vanessa Trava, Laura Alonzo, Kevin Graham (who runs www.costamayaliving.com and was kind enough to update the Mahahual section months after Hurricane Dean passed through town), and Raul from Nómadas Youth Hostel in Mérida (for being an invaluable source of information). The

editors, cartographers, and everybody that works behind the scenes at Lonely Planet are amazing – especially Catherine Craddock-Carrillo, my ever-patience, ever-incisive commissioning editor. And, a big shout out goes to the great writers that penned the previous editions of this book, and John Noble for bringing all the loose ends together.

TIM BEWER
Muchas, muchas gracias to all the people who answered my endless questions, shared their opinions and showed me the typical *norteño* hospitality. Walter Bishop, Andrea Cárdenas, Bertha Elizondo, Adriana Galván, Lorena Alanis Landa, Lucía Martínez, Patricia Martínez, Idaly Reyes and especially Porfirio Sosa were all especially helpful. Also, to Catherine, John, my fellow authors and the whole Lonely Planet crew, it was a pleasure working with you. Finally, even though she'll surely never read this, special thanks to Paola who got me lost on the way to Santa Eulalia.

BETH KOHN
Abrazos fuertes to Michael Zap and Lulú Castillo for everything I can think of, including the loaner kitty and MB episodes. In Tuxtla Gutiérrez, Abel Ovando of the Chiapas State Tourism Office and Victor Aguilera Osuna helped get me started, and Juan Carlos Castillo Rodas and José Antonio Rodas Alfonso illuminated the finer points of Tapachula and Comitán, respectively. Laila Balderas did some awesome transcribing, and Jen Gorospe and Dillon Dutton get the award for gato-care extraordinaire. *Gracias a* Manuela Morales Hernández, without whom I'd still be stuck shin-deep in mud, and enormous thanks to both Cat Craddock-Carrillo and John Noble.

TOM MASTERS
Big thanks to my Mexico City housemates in the Colonia Roma – Kate, Miranda and Fionn. Thanks also to French Jonny and David Morales Castillo for their help and company and to all the helpful folks I met while travelling, especially the staff at the Casa de la Palma in Puebla. Thanks to Catherine Craddock-Carrillo at Lonely Planet Oakland for sending me to Mexico and to John Noble, the great co-ordinator, for his patience.

KEVIN RAUB
Un beso grande to my wife, Adriana Schmidt, who is actually Brazilian, but we won't hold that against her here. At Lonely Planet, Catherine Craddock-Carrillo, John Noble, and Greg Benchwick. And to all those who helped along the way: Veronica Catalan, Elizabeth Benitez, Tad Pfister, Tim Hinds,

Monica Alejandra Sánchez, Sheila Murphey, Janet Anderson, Monica Moran, Katherine Callingham, Sonny Newman, Francisco Torres, Ivan and Yolando Fernandez, Nausicaa Giavarra, Clotilde Payen, Cécile Alphand, Gregóire Guyot, Marie Mignon, Salvador Garcia and Roberto Morales.

MICHAEL READ
Thanks to the many tourist offices, taxi drivers and random passersby who helped me find the hidden gems and cast out the stones. A heartfelt thank you is gratefully offered to lead author John Noble for his empathy during a time of duress. Thanks also to commissioning editor Catherine Craddock-Carrillo for giving me the nod for this engrossing project, and for her bulletproof author's brief. Most of all, thanks to my wife Irene Constanze Rietschel and our two young daughters Malena and Sylvia for teaching me how to travel without ever leaving the house.

JOSEPHINE QUINTERO
Thanks to fellow author Daniel Schechter for his patience, suggestions and the canal trip in Xochimilco. *Gracias* also to commissioning editor Catherine Craddock-Carrillo for her guidance and email support. I would also like to thank Ruth Alegria who introduced me to *her* Mexico City and invited me to some terrific events. Finally, a wet kiss for my longtime partner and Lonely Planet photographer Robin Chapman for taking care of Marilyn, my cat, during my time in DF.

DANIEL C SCHECHTER
Working on my fourth edition of the Mexico guide, I was able to count on the remarkably enthusiastic assistance of old and new friends. As usual, journalist pals José Fernández Ramos and Jeffrey A Wright offered their invaluable insights on DF issues, Michael K Schuessler and John Rozzo kept me abreast of gay life, and Miriam Martínez translated Chilango slang. *Defeños* and *medio-defeños* Jorge Silva, Monica Campbell, Deborah Bonello, Cynthia Sperry and Michelle Chi Chase, all gamely pitched in with suggestions and on-the-scene assessments. Ruth Alegría, María José Serrano, Rocío González Delgado, Mojdeh Hojjati and Pedro Gellert generously shared their voluminous knowledge of cuisine, *concheros* and Cubans. Myra, *un besote* for setting up the office and lots of other stuff.

ADAM SKOLNICK
First, I'd like to thank the academy, Catherine Craddock-Carrillo, Sandra Bao and all intrepid authors who have walked these streets searching for the truth! I'm also grateful for the following kind souls and friendly faces who educated and entertained me on my blissfully bizarro ride through Mexico: the lovely Aggie, Daphne, Gaby and their Zapopan posse, Teresa, Don Geronimo and their cohorts Nicole and Cameron in Pátzcuaro, Rose and Kate in Morelia, Pablo, Lisette and the beautiful Beatrice in Zitácuaro, Angela at Hotel Buena Aventura in Colima, Stan, José, and their staff at Case de las Flores in Tlaquepaque, Rob and Ozzy in Chapala. Thanks to all the Ajijic people keeping it real, to Alicia and Baby G in Tonala, to Mari in Guadalajara, to Ana who brings a little bit of Kansas City to Tlaquepaque, to sweet Mina of Berlin – may you never again ride a horse with a wooden saddle – to Sister Carrie and the incomparable Emilce Martinez who helped me through my last throws of Deadline Disco, and please, put your hands together, ladies and gentlemen for Ms Jordan Whitley!

CÉSAR G SORIANO
Muchas gracias to all the people who helped me find my way through Mexico, from bus drivers to strangers on the street. A personal shout-out to Edgar and Paco in Boca de Pascuales and Mali in Zihua who clued me in to some amazing, off-the-beaten-path destinations. At Lonely Planet, thanks to Catherine and John for their help and guidance, and especially for putting up with my endless dumb questions. To our loyal readers who sent in valuable tips, suggestions, complaints and compliments: keep those e-mails coming! Finally and foremost, thank you to Marsha, my wife and favorite travel partner, for your enduring patience and support during my physical absence in Mexico, and my emotional absence at home while I was hunkered down in the office writing. *Te amo.*

ELLEE THALHEIMER
Thanks to all the warm people of Veracruz who go out of their way to put me on the right track. *Gracias a* Felix Aguilar for dragging me to the far reaches of the Reserva de la Biosfera Los Tuxtlas and giving me Manás new CD, the soundtrack to my journey. Thanks, Ceci Robago for good conversation, above-and-beyond help, and showing me the beauty of your region. To Roy Dudley for convincing me to go on the Las Vigas bike ride and for your great effort to introduce me *a tu Xalapa*. Rául Reynoso, *eres incredible* and an unbelievable help and inspiration. Thank you to Nimbe in Papantla for your generosity and willingness to share *mate*, to Nacho in the Coscomatepec tourist office, to the fabulous Valles tourist office, and to the Orizaba *chicas* who showed me the way. Romina Contreras,

keep up the great work at METRO and thanks for your generous help. *Gracias por tu corazón abierto*, Emma Viggiano. Close to my heart is Mary Beth Wyne, my tried-and-true voice of reason and fellow English major, who will spend hours talking sentence structure with me. Thanks to Sandra Bao who always throws me a well-needed bone with patience, to Cat Craddock Craddock-Carrillo for checking in and doing a great job, and to Becky Ohlsen for down-to-earth reassurance. I appreciate Jackie Marchand and my beloved Womantours for dealing with my constant change. *Brazos* to my dad who makes sure I don't fall off the face of the planet, to my good friend Alia for enabling my travel habit, to Elliot, Bruce, and Marty at LC for teaching me, to Señor Barreto for starting it all, and to Diane Wilson for raising me with dedication and patience and giving me more than I could ever ask.

OUR READERS

Many thanks to the travellers who used the last edition and wrote to us with helpful hints, useful advice and interesting anecdotes:
A Lionel Aboussouan, Cheryl Adamson, Joerg Affolter, Eva Aguilera, Michele Airoldi, Peter Aldin, Amy Alexander, Graham Alexander, Yves Alexandre, David Allard, Jeff Allen, Horace Andrews, Luan Angel, Oron Anter, Gilles Arfeuille, Ilaria Arienti, Brigitte Auinger, Ana Avitua, Michal Avni **B** Luis Antonio Baeza, Shirley Barrett, Rob Bell, Dominique Berthou, Flavia Bertini, Kourtney Bettinger, Antonio Blanco, Scott Bolton, Julie Booth, Tom Border, Rolf van den Bosch, Bea Bosch van den Knijf, Susy Boyd, Lona Boyte, Meridith Bradshaw, Michael Brakke, Rene Bretschneider, Gerald Brock, Elisa Broseghini, Laura Brown, Zoe Brown, Gustavo Buhacoff, Marc Buholzer, Zuzana Bulirova, Naomi Buneman, Linda Burgett, Ryan Burrow, Kate Burton, Mark Bustard, Miriam Butler **C** Marcela Caballero, Andrea Cardenas, Tania Carrasco, Stuart Carter, Matthias Catón, Sasha Chernenkoff, Christina Cheung, William Clune, Jodie Coles, Michael Coley-Smith, Tracy Collier, Jim Comer, James Condino, R Coney, Michelle Cooper, Paul Cooper, Ted Corrigan, Francesca Costa, Jim Cox, Catherine Coy, Vicki Crawford, Karen Cruz, Javier Cuen **D** Lauren Dall, Eve Davies, David Davis, Dixie Davis, Julia Day, Florentina Debling, Lien Delbecque, Manuela Dessalvi, Arache Djannati-Atai, Cori Donnelly, Irene Doubrawa, Neil Dressell, Margaret Dubois, Roy Dudley, Giorgia Duo, Kate van Dusen **E** Catherine Eggimann, Annet Eggink, David Eidell, Susann Eisert, Ruth Elvin, Katy Eyre **F** Lia Fernandez, Susana Fernandez, Dulcie Few, Nicolas Forget, Samantha Forster, Muriel Foucher, Brad Fox, George Franko, Dario Frigo, Paul Frost, Rick Fuller, John Fusco, Paulina Fusitu'A **G** Vikky Gallagher, Johanne Gauthier, Melati Gaymans, Michael Giffin, Karen Gill, Eliane Godement, Diana Gonzales-Pacheco, Valeria González, Aoife Granville, John Greek, Aaron Groves, Omar Guzman **H** Kristel Haan, James Hampson, Spencer Hamrick, Steve Hansen, Jonny Hardaker, Carl Harris, Sarah Harris, Corinne Hartmann, Alexander Hay, Jane Heinz, David Hellman, Mary Ann Henderson, Valerie Hendrikx, Frank & Kirsten Der van Heyden, Alexa Highfield, Kate Hart Highfield, Simone Hilger, William Hinkle, Vicki Hird, Fred Hoener, Cornelis Hoes, Rick Hogan, Brandon Holland, Jeff Holland, John Holman, Angie Hook, Patricia Hopps, Wiebe Hordijk, Kat Horn, Richard Hough, Bob Hrycan, Brian Hudson **I** Elina Inkeroinen **J** Jill Jefferson, Douglas Jenkins, Jeffrey G Jensen, Dave Jiro, Jaye Johnson, Mary Jones, Christel Jorgenson, Nadine Jung **K** Debby Kajiyama, Susanne Karas, Harriet Katz, Alex Katzman, Eric Kaufman, Waltraud Tale Kaufmann, Andrea De Keijzer, Daniela Keller, Brian Kemsley, Tamil Kendall, Asad Khaja, Kate Kiekhaefer, Marita King, Matt King, Alex Kipp, Wouter Kistemaker, Irina Klapere, Carroll Klein, Hugh Knowles, Zoltan Konder, Theresa Kopecky, Kevin Korell, Karen Kressin, Jody Kriewaldt, Aneta Kubala, Francis Kuipers, Alan Kurczynski, Gwen Kwo **L** Aaron Lambert, Mark Lancaster, Steve Landau, Andrea Langhammer, George Langman, Andreas Lappe, Denis Larsen, Michelle Lavicka, Jeannette Lee, Beatrice Lemucchi, Derek Lerma, Cheryl Lesinski, Eric Lesperance, Anya Letson, Irving Levinson, Laurie Levitan, Nimrod Levy, Ying Li, Doug Liden, Susan Lightfoot, Brook Lillehaugen, Maria Lindgren, Anna Lockyer, Marco Lopez, David Luttig **M** Shannon Macdonald, Helen Macrae, Dee Mahan, Inga Mahle, Elmar Mair, Jim Maloney, Tarne Malor, Dr Bill Mania, Christina Mansi, Yossi Margoninsky, Stephanie Marks, Arturo Martinez, Gordon Maul, Wilfredo Deleon Maximo, Anne Mccarley, Chris Mccart Mccart, Sarah Mcgaughey, Tom Mciver, Stewart Mclean, Sam Meacham, Jesús Mesa, Mila Middelberg, Claire Miller, Curtis Miller, Jesse Miller, Raymond Mizrachi, Derek Monroe, Eliza Monteverde, Eileen Moore, Paula Morton, Laurissa Muehlich, Kirrily Myatt **N** Jet Nauta, Sarah Neustadter, Susan De Nies, Yelac Nillad, Phyllis Noble **O** Mary O'Brien, Gloria O'Byrne, Stephen O'Connell, Dan Öhrling, Luis Orozco, Luz Ariadna Ortiz, Rosario Ortiz, Gina Ossanna, Vincent Otto, Brent Owen **P** Marcia Pace, Abraham Palmer, Elisa Pardini, Frances Partridge, Chinmay Patel, Victor Patenaude, Stacy Pavich, Stuart Pearce, Lasse Pedersem, Alejandro Perez, Nora Peroni, Lisa Persinger, Joseph Pe-

ters, Tom Petersen, Betty Peterson, David Peterson, Bill Phelan, Sarah Phillips, Marta Pacheco Picazo, Grazyna Pilecki, Jan Pilecki, Reinier Pitt, Michael Pohl, Lilach Portnova, Martina Pothmann, Richard Potter, Benjamin Presnell **R** Peter Raeside, Luigi Raffo, Rafael Ramirez, Yolanda Ramirez, Michael Reeves, Georg Reichert, Naomi Reid, Stacey Repas, Marie Anne Ricaud, Ernst Riedwyl, Davide Rimoldi, Marco Roda, Kerry & Ray Rogers, Maribel Rojas, Sherry Ronick, Valeria Rosa, Janna & Rosana, Tom Rothe, Timo Rothhaar, Carmel Rourke, Alma Roussy, Martin Rozendaal, Alec Rubin, Pam & Bill Rumney **S** A S, Elin Sætersdal, Charlotte Sagewood, Paula Sahlman, Andrew Saito, Ricardo Sanchez, Philip Sandberg, Paul Sarfati, Simon Scales, Larry Scheib, Agnes Schmidt, Judith Schwartz, Judith Rodriguez Servin, Krissy Shields, Nick Shirrefs, Judith Shone, Fred & Cindy Shultz, Anni Siesing, Ilyssa Silverman, Pablo Simoes, Mazurelle Simon, Pardeep Singh, Ed Skoch, Uri Skowronski, David Slave, Gary S Smith, Jacqueline Smith, Patricia Snyder, Rob Snyder, Paul Soerensen, Venita De Souza, Mariella Sparv-

ieri, Sharon Speckman, Darin Stanley, Andreas Stavropoulos, Peg Steffensen, Carl Stein, Laurent Steiner, Marsha Stephens, Ronald Stockman, Kenn & Karen Strass, Joan Strouse, Megan Sulok, Anne-Mie Swinnen, Wanda & Barry Syner **T** George Tacik, Mirella Taiariol, Alan Tesler, Matt Thompson, Thomas Toafolia, Isabella Toempe, Daniel Tomanek, Roberto Tonello, Diana Torres, Giuseppe Tozzo, Dina Turkof, James Turner, Martine Twigge **U** Alberto Ugartemendia, Abe Urbina, Brynn Utley **V** Jean Valjean, I van Barron, Monique Veldt, Susan Vincent, Chrissy Vogeley, Andrea Voglino, Valentin Voigt **W** Elizabeth Wadell, Julian Waingortin, Christian Waldau, Richard Walker, Zoe Walker, Charli Rumsey Ben Waller, Cara Waters, Zwika Weinberg, Sophie Westerink, Jack White, Caroline Williams, essa van Williams, Brian Wilson, Mark Wilson, Michael Wong, Sophy Wong **Y** Basil Yokarinis **Z** Tzoda Zarkis, Philipp Zielke, Joseph Zookey, Jim Zosel, Giorgio Zucchetti, Manuele Zunelli, Koos & Pauline Zwaan, Wanda Zyla

ACKNOWLEDGEMENTS

Many thanks to the following for the use of their content:

Globe on title page © Mountain High Maps 1993 Digital Wisdom, Inc.

Thanks to Ed Barnhart 2000 for the use of his map base on the Palenque Ruins map.

Internal photgraphs:

p7 Adrian Sherratt/Alamy; p12 World Pictures/Alamy; p14 Buzz Pictures/Alamy; p15 (#4) Reinhard Dirscherl/Alamy. All other photographs by Lonely Planet Images and p4-5, p6 (#4) Pascale Beroujon; p6 (#1), p16 (#1) Adina Tovy Amsel; p8, p21, p23 (#2) Richard I'Anson; p9 (#1), p10 (#1) p22 (#6) John Neubauer; p9 (#3), p11, p18, p19 (#2), p20-1 John Elk III; p10 (#4), p20 (#5) Witold Skrypczak; p13 Guy Moberly; p15 Ralph Hopkins; p16 (5) Anthony Plummer; p17 Blind Dog Photo Dan Gair; p20 (#1) Julian Bentley; p20 (#4) Jon Davison; p22 (#1) Jeff Greenberg; p23 (#4), p24 David Peevers.

All images are the copyright of the photographers unless otherwise indicated. Many of the images in this guide are available for licensing from Lonely Planet Images: www.lonelyplanetimages.com.

Index

INDEX

INDEX

INDEX

INDEX

INDEX

INDEX

GreenDex

It seems like everyone's going green and eco these days, but how can you know which businesses are really eco-friendly and which are simply jumping on the sustainable bandwagon?

The following listings have all been selected by this book's authors because they demonstrate an active sustainable-tourism policy. Some are involved in conservation or environmental education, and many are owned and operated by local and indigenous operators, thereby helping to support regional identity and culture.

We define sustainable tourism in three ways:

Environment – minimizes negative environmental impacts and, where possible, makes positive contributions.
Socio-cultural – respects culture and traditions and fosters authentic interaction and greater understanding between travelers and hosts.
Economic – has financial benefits for the host community and operates on the principles of fair trade.

We want to keep developing our sustainable-tourism content. If you think we've omitted someone who should be listed here, or if you disagree with our choices, email us at talk2us@lonelyplanet .com.au. For more information about sustainable tourism and Lonely Planet, see www.lonelyplanet .com/responsibletravel.

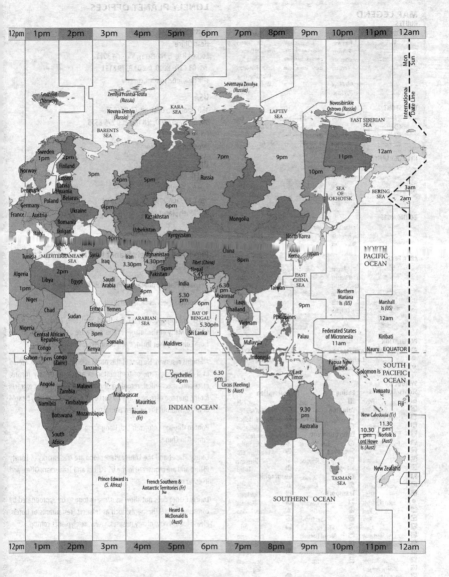

MAP LEGEND

ROUTES

Tollway	Mall/Steps
Freeway	Tunnel
Primary	Pedestrian Overpass
Secondary	Walking Tour
Tertiary	Walking Tour Detour
Lane	Walking Trail
Unsealed Road	Walking Path
One-Way Street	Track

TRANSPORT

Ferry	Rail
Metro	Rail (Underground)
Monorail	Tram
Bus Route	Cable Car, Funicular

HYDROGRAPHY

River, Creek	Canal
Intermittent River	Water
Swamp	Lake (Dry)
Mangrove	Lake (Salt)
Reef	Mudflats

BOUNDARIES

International	Regional, Suburb
State, Provincial	Ancient Wall
Marine Park	Cliff

AREA FEATURES

Airport	Land
Area of Interest	Mall
Beach, Desert	Market
Building	Park
Campus	Reservation
Cemetery, Christian	Rocks
Cemetery, Other	Sports
Forest	Urban

POPULATION

○ CAPITAL (NATIONAL)	◉ CAPITAL (STATE)
● Large City	○ Medium City
● Small City	○ Town, Village

SYMBOLS

Sights/Activities
- Beach
- Bodysurfing
- Canoeing, Kayaking
- Castle, Fortress
- Christian
- Diving, Snorkeling
- Golf
- Islamic
- Jewish
- Monument
- Museum, Gallery
- Music
- Point of Interest
- Pool
- Ruin
- Skiing
- Snorkeling
- Surfing, Surf Beach
- Trail Head
- Windsurfing
- Winery, Vineyard
- Zoo, Bird Sanctuary

Eating
- Eating

Drinking
- Drinking
- Café

Entertainment
- Entertainment

Shopping
- Shopping

Sleeping
- Sleeping
- Camping

Transport
- Airport, Airfield
- Border Crossing
- Bus Station
- Cycling, Bicycle Path
- General Transport
- Parking Area
- Petrol Station
- Taxi Rank

Information
- Bank, ATM
- Embassy/Consulate
- Hospital, Medical
- Information
- Internet Facilities
- Police Station
- Post Office, GPO
- Telephone
- Toilets

Geographic
- Hazard
- Lighthouse
- Lookout
- Mountain, Volcano
- National Park
- Oasis
- Pass, Canyon
- River Flow
- Shelter, Hut
- Spot Height
- Trig Station
- Waterfall

LONELY PLANET OFFICES

Australia
Head Office
Locked Bag 1, Footscray, Victoria 3011
☎ 03 8379 8000, fax 03 8379 8111
talk2us@lonelyplanet.com.au

USA
150 Linden St, Oakland, CA 94607
☎ 510 250 6400, toll free 800 275 8555
fax 510 893 8572
info@lonelyplanet.com

UK
2nd fl, 186 City Rd,
London EC1V 2NT
☎ 020 7106 2100, fax 020 7106 2101
go@lonelyplanet.co.uk

Published by Lonely Planet Publications Pty Ltd
ABN 36 005 607 983

© Lonely Planet Publications Pty Ltd 2008

© photographers as indicated 2008

Cover photograph: Day of the Dead Skeleton, Lindsay Hebberd/ CORBIS. Many of the images in this guide are available for licensing from Lonely Planet Images: www.lonelyplanetimages.com.

Printed through Colorcraft Ltd, Hong Kong.
Printed in China.